Congressional Quarterly's

POLITICS IN AMERICA

1990

The 101st Congress

By CQ's Political Staff
Phil Duncan, Editor

CQ
PRESS
A division of
CONGRESSIONAL QUARTERLY INC.
1414 22nd Street N.W., Washington D.C. 20037

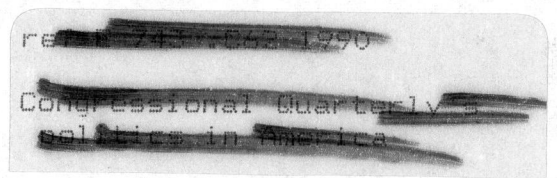

Congressional Quarterly Inc.

Andrew Barnes *Chairman and President*
Wayne P. Kelley *Publisher*
Neil Skene *Executive Editor*
John J. Coyle *General Manager*
Robert E. Cuthriell *Director of Development*

Book Division

David R. Tarr *Editor, Book Department*
Kathryn C. Suárez *Marketing Director, Book Department*

Production

I. D. Fuller *Production Manager*
Michael Emanuel *Assistant Production Manager*
Jhonnie G. Bailey *Assistant to the Production Manager*

Printed in the United States of America

Library of Congress Cataloging in Publication Data

Main entry under title:

Politics in America.

Includes index.

1. United States. Congress — Biography. 2. United States. Congress — Committees. 3. Election districts — United States — Handbooks, manuals, etc. I. Duncan, Phil, 1957- . II. Dessauer, Carin. III. Congressional Quarterly, Inc.
JK1010.P64 1989 328.73'073'025 89-7405
ISBN 0-87187-508-X

Phil Duncan came to Congressional Quarterly in 1979 and joined the politics staff of CQ's *Weekly Report* magazine in 1980. He worked on the four previous editions of "Politics in America" and was associate editor of the fourth edition. In 1987, he became political editor of CQ.

Born in Knoxville, Tenn., Duncan graduated from Davidson College in 1979 and worked for *The Charlotte Observer* and *The Knoxville News-Sentinel* before joining CQ. He lives in Falls Church, Virginia, with his wife Leslie.

POLITICS IN AMERICA

EDITORIAL STAFF

Editor

Phil Duncan

Principal Contributors

Jacqueline Calmes

Bob Benenson
Beth Donovan
Peter Bragdon
Dave Kaplan

Major Contributors

Chuck Alston
Ronald D. Elving
Janet Hook

Other Contributors

Stephen Gettinger

Rhodes Cook
Neil Brown
Andrew Taylor
Carin Dessauer
Betsy Palmer
Paul E. Brown
Stacey Pagel
Sharon M. Page
Robert E. Clayton

PRODUCTION AND RESEARCH STAFF

Associate Editor
Carin Dessauer

Production Coordinator
Dave Kaplan

Research Coordinator
Betsy Palmer

Editorial Assistant
Kerry Capell

Principal Researchers
Mike Barr
Kenneth E. Jaques
Philip Marwill
Sheldon Yett

Other Researchers
Andrew Taylor
Kathleen Walton
Stacey Pagel
Bill Heeley
John Wallin and Lisa Kruger, interns

Copy Editors
Alyson Pytte
Eugene J. Gabler
Karine Roesch
Steve Moyer
Charles Southwell
John Schachter
William Bonn

Cover Design
Bobby Govan

Maps
Barbara Sassa-Daniels
Norieko Bove

Photographers
R. Michael Jenkins
Stan Barouh
Ken Heinen
Karen Ruckman
Teresa Zabala
Lisa Berg
Dave Kaplan
Dennis Brack
Sue Klemens
Marty LaVor
Art Stein
Susan Muniak
Paul Conklin
Paul Robertson
Joseph McCary
Ron Stewart

TABLE OF CONTENTS

Explanation of Statistics

Committees

Standing and select committees and subcommittees are listed for Senate and House members, as are joint committees. Seniority ranking is as of publication date. House seniority rankings include non-voting delegates and the resident commissioner, where applicable.

Elections

House

General-election returns are given for House members for 1986 and 1988. Returns include candidates receiving 5 percent or more of the vote. Primary returns are given for House members for 1988. No primary results are listed if a candidate ran unopposed or was nominated by caucus or convention. Because percentages have been rounded to the nearest whole number, election totals do not always add up to exactly 100 percent.

Senate

Primary and general-election returns are given for each senator's most recent election. No primary results are given if a candidate ran unopposed or was nominated by caucus or convention. For senators with previous service in the House, elections to the House are indicated with a footnote.

Key to Party Abbreviations

AM — American
AMI — American Independent
C — Conservative
CIT — Citizens
CON — Consumer
D — Democratic
I — Independent
IL SOL — Illinois Solidarity
L — Liberal
LIB — Libertarian
LAB F — Labor and Farm
NA — New Alliance
PFP — Peace and Freedom
POP — Populist
PRG SC — Progressive Social
R — Republican
RTL — Right to Life
SOC WORK — Socialist Workers
WL — Workers League

Previous Winning Percentages

Winning election percentages are given for each member's entire congressional career. If no percentage is given, the member either did not run or lost the election that year. Percentages are included for both general elections and special elections.

District Vote for President

The vote presidential candidates received in each congressional district is given for 1976, 1980, 1984 and 1988. The tabulations are for the area within each current district, even though in most cases that area did not constitute a district until 1982.

Data for the district vote for president were compiled by Congressional Quarterly using state and county election agencies' official results. A few county results for 1988 were received from the Republican National Committee; the RNC's figures were taken directly from work sheets compiled by county officials. Results for selected counties in the following states were compiled in this manner: Arizona, Indiana, Mississippi, Missouri and New Jersey.

Some district totals will not correlate with state totals due to variances in tabulating absentee ballots by county election officials.

Vote totals for 1976 and 1980 were not available for Washington state. Vote totals included for independent (I) in 1980 are for John B. Anderson. The independent vote is included only if the candidate received 2 percent or more of the vote in the district. The vote for Anderson was not available for California.

Campaign Finance

Figures are given for all members of Congress and their general-election challengers, if they filed reports with the Federal Election Commission (FEC). If no figures are listed, the candidate either did not file a report (reports are not required if receipts and expenditures are less than $5,000) or the reports listed receipts and expenditures of zero.

For House members, figures are given for the 1986 and 1988 elections. For senators, figures are given for the most recent election.

Campaign finance data cover the receipts and expenditures of each candidate during the two-year election cycle ending on Dec. 31 of the year the election was held. Data for 1986 cover the period Jan. 1, 1985 - Dec. 31, 1986. Data for 1988 cover the period Jan. 1, 1987 - Dec. 31, 1988. The data for 1988 used in "Politics in America" were compiled from Federal Election

Commission reports. Excluded are reports by candidate committees that exist solely to collect money for current or prior campaign debts.

Other candidate transactions, such as contributions to other campaigns, loan repayments, purchase and redemption of certificates of deposit, and debts owed to or by the campaign committees at the end of the election year, were not subtracted from the receipts and expenditures totals.

The figures for political action committee (PAC) receipts are based on the FEC summary report for each candidate.

Key Votes

A series of significant votes has been selected from the roll-call votes taken during the 100th Congress. The following captions give the number of the bill, the major sponsor, a brief description of the bill, a breakdown of the vote, the date the vote was taken and the president's position on the issue, if he took one. The following symbols are used:

Y, voted for (yea)
N, voted against (nay)
#, paired for
+, announced for
X, paired against
-, announced against
P, voted "present"
C, voted "present" to avoid possible conflict of interest
?, did not vote or otherwise make a position known.

SENATE KEY VOTES

1987

HR 2. Omnibus Highway Reauthorization/Veto Override. Passage, over President Reagan's March 27 veto, of the bill to authorize $88 billion for highway and mass transit programs through fiscal 1991. Passed (thus enacted into law) 67-33: R 13-33; D 54-0 (ND 36-0, SD 18-0), April 2, 1987. A two-thirds majority of those present and voting (67 in this case) of both houses is required to override a veto. A "nay" was a vote supporting the president's position.

S 1174. Fiscal 1988-89 Defense Authorization/Missile Tests. Nunn, D-Ga., motion to table (kill) the Warner, R-Va., amendment to strike a provision limiting the development or testing of space-based and other mobile anti-ballistic missile systems. Motion agreed to 58-38: R 8-37; D 50-1 (ND 34-0, SD 16-1), Sept. 17, 1987. A "nay" was a vote supporting the president's position.

S 1174. Fiscal 1988-89 Defense Authorization/Nuclear Testing. Reid, D-Nev., motion to table (kill) the Hatfield, R-Ore., amendment to prohibit in fiscal 1988-89 nuclear test explosions with an explosive power of more than 1 kiloton, subject to certain conditions. Motion agreed to 61-36: R 40-6; D 21-30 (ND 7-27, SD 14-3), Sept. 24, 1987. A "yea" was a vote supporting the president's position.

Bork Nomination. Confirmation of President Reagan's nomination of Robert H. Bork of the District of Columbia to be an associate justice of the Supreme Court. Rejected 42-58: R 40-6; D 2-52 (ND 0-36, SD 2-16), Oct. 23, 1987. A "yea" was a vote supporting the president's position.

1988

S 2. Campaign Finance/Cloture. Byrd, D-W.Va., motion to invoke cloture (thus limiting debate) on the bill to overhaul federal campaign-finance law. The bill would limit campaign spending and the role of political action committees in Senate elections. Motion rejected 53-41: R 3-39; D 50-2 (ND 35-0, SD 15-2), Feb. 26, 1988. A three-fifths majority (60) of the total Senate is required to invoke cloture.

S 557. Civil Rights Restoration Act/Veto Override. Passage, over President Reagan's March 16 veto, of the bill to provide broad coverage of four civil rights laws by making it clear that, if one entity of an institution receives federal funds, the entire institution must abide by the anti-discrimination laws. Passed 73-24: R 21-24; D 52-0 (ND 35-0, SD 17-0), March 22, 1988. A two-thirds majority of those present and voting (65 in this case) of both houses is required to override a veto. A "nay" was a vote supporting the president's position.

HR 3. Omnibus Trade Bill/Veto Override. Passage, over President Reagan's May 24 veto, of the bill to revise statutory procedures for dealing with unfair foreign trade practices and import damage to U.S. industries, to clarify the law against business-related bribes abroad by U.S. businesses, to streamline controls on militarily sensitive exports, to revise agriculture and education programs, to repeal the windfall-profits tax on oil and to require certain employers to provide workers with 60 days' notice of plant closings or layoffs. Rejected 61-37: R 10-35; D 51-2 (ND 33-2, SD 18-0), June 8, 1988. A two-thirds majority of those present and voting (66 in this case) of both houses is required to override a veto. (The House overrode the veto May 24.) A "nay" was a vote supporting the president's position.

S 2455. Death Penalty for Drug-Related Killings. Passage of the bill to allow the death penalty for "drug kingpins" who intentionally kill or who order a killing. The bill would provide a separate hearing before a judge or jury on the issue of punishment, where the judge or jury would have to weigh aggravating and mitigating circumstances before determining whether the death penalty was appropriate. The jury would have to be unanimous in imposing the death penalty. Passed 65-29: R 37-6; D 28-23 (ND 15-19, SD 13-4), June 10, 1988. A "yea" was a vote supporting the president's position.

S 1511. Welfare Reform/'Workfare' Amendment. Moynihan, D-N.Y., motion to table (kill) the Dole, R-Kan., amendment to require that by 1994, states require at least one parent in two-parent families receiving welfare to work a minimum of 16 hours per week in either unpaid community work experience or subsidized jobs. Motion rejected 41-54: R 3-40; D 38-14 (ND 27-7, SD 11-7), June 16, 1988. A "nay" was a vote supporting the president's position.

HOUSE KEY VOTES

1987

H Con Res 77/HR 2. Speed Limit/Omnibus Highway Reauthorization. Adoption of the concurrent resolution to make a correction in the enrollment of the bill, HR 2, to allow states to raise the speed limit to 65 mph on Interstate highways located outside urbanized areas of 50,000 population or more. Adopted 217-206: R 125-50; D 92-156 (ND 45-121, SD 47-35), March 18, 1987.

HR 3. Omnibus Trade Bill/Gephardt Amendment. Gephardt, D-Mo., amendment to require identification of countries with excess trade surpluses with the United States and quantify the extent to which unfair trade practices contribute to that surplus, to mandate negotiations to eliminate those unfair trade practices, and, if negotiations fail or an agreement is not fully implemented, to mandate imposition of tariffs or quotas to yield annual 10 percent reductions in that country's trade surplus. Adopted 218-214: R 17-159; D 201-55 (ND 137-34, SD 64-21), April 29, 1987. A "nay" was a vote supporting the president's position.

HR 1748. Fiscal 1988-89 Defense Authorization/Nuclear Testing. Schroeder, D-Colo., amendment to bar nuclear test explosions larger than one kiloton provided the Soviet Union observes the same limitation. Adopted 234-187: R 26-147; D 208-40 (ND 160-9, SD 48-31), May 19, 1987. A "nay" was a vote supporting the president's position.

HR 2342. Coast Guard Authorization/Re-flagging Kuwaiti Ships. Lowry, D-Wash., amendment to delay until 90 days after enactment the registration under U.S. ownership of any ships owned by Kuwait. Adopted 222-184: R 22-146; D 200-38 (ND 149-12, SD 51-26), July 8, 1987. A "nay" was a vote supporting the president's position.

HR 3545. Fiscal 1988 Budget Reconciliation. Passage of the bill to raise $11.9 billion in revenues and make spending cuts in accordance with the fiscal 1988 budget resolution (H Con Res 93). Passed 206-205: R 1-164; D 205-41 (ND 143-21, SD 62-20), Oct. 29, 1987. A "nay" was a vote supporting the president's position.

1988

H J Res 444. Contra Aid. Passage of the joint resolution to approve President Reagan's request of $36.25 million for continued military and non-military aid to the Nicaraguan contras. Rejected 211-219: R 164-12; D 47-207 (ND 6-166, SD 41-41), Feb. 3, 1988. A "yea" was a vote supporting the president's position.

S 557. Civil Rights Restoration Act/Veto Override. Passage, over President Reagan's March 16 veto, of the bill to provide broad coverage of four civil rights laws by making it clear that, if one entity of an institution receives federal funds, the entire institution must abide by the anti-discrimination laws. Passed (thus enacted into law) 292-133: R 52-123; D 240-10 (ND 167-1, SD 73-9), March 22, 1988. A two-thirds majority of those present and voting (284 in this case) of both houses is required to override a veto. A "nay" was a vote supporting the president's position.

HR 3. Omnibus Trade Bill/Plant Closings. Michel, R-Ill., motion to recommit to the conference committee the conference report on the bill, with instructions to eliminate the requirement to provide workers with 60 days' notice of plant closings or layoffs. (Recommittal of a conference report would permit conferees to reconsider any provision in the legislation.) Motion rejected 167-253: R 144-29; D 23-224 (ND 0-168, SD 23-56), April 21, 1988.

HR 3. Omnibus Trade Bill/Veto Override. Passage, over President Reagan's May 24 veto, of the bill to revise statutory procedures for dealing with unfair foreign trade practices and import damage to U.S. industries, to clarify the law against business-related bribes abroad by U.S. businesses, to streamline controls on militarily sensitive exports, to revise agriculture and education programs, to repeal the windfall-profits tax on oil and to require certain employers to provide workers with 60 days' notice of plant closings or layoffs. Passed 308-113: R 60-112; D 248-1 (ND 167-1, SD 81-0), May 24, 1988. A two-thirds majority of those present and voting (281 in this case) of both houses is required to override a veto. A "nay" was a vote supporting the president's position.

HR 5210. Omnibus Drug Bill/Death Penalty. Gekas, R-Pa., amendment to provide the death penalty for individuals convicted of drug-related murders. Adopted 299-111: R 161-9; D 138-102 (ND 70-93, SD 68-9), Sept. 8, 1988. A "yea" was a vote supporting the president's position.

HR 4783. Fiscal 1989 Labor, Health and Human Services, Education Appropriations/Use of Medicaid Funds for Abortions. Natcher, D-Ky., motion that the House insist on its disagreement to a Senate amendment to allow the use of Medicaid funds for abortions in cases in which pregnancy results from promptly reported cases of rape or incest. The House-passed language permitted use of Medicaid funds for abortion only when the mother's life would be endangered by the pregnancy. Motion agreed to 216-166: R 126-30; D 90-136 (ND 58-98, SD 32-38), Sept. 9, 1988. A "yea" was a vote supporting the president's position.

HR 5210. Omnibus Drug Bill/Waiting Period for Handgun Purchases. McCollum, R-Fla., amendment to strike provisions that sought to establish a seven-day waiting period for handgun purchases and to require the Justice Department to develop and send to Congress a proposal for a system gun dealers could use to identify felons, who are ineligible to own handguns. Adopted 228-182: R 127-45; D 101-137 (ND 45-117, SD 56-20), Sept. 15, 1988.

Voting Studies

Voting studies prepared by Congressional Quarterly for the years since 1981 (97th Congress) indicate members' scores. The scores represent the percentage of the time a member of Congress has supported or opposed a given position. The votes are listed under two columns — S for support, O for opposition. For example, a score of 25 under the S column in the presidential support study would indicate that the member supported the president on 25 percent of the votes that were used in the study.

An explanation of the voting studies follows.

Presidential Support

CQ tries to determine what the president personally, as distinct from other administration officials, does and does not want in the way of legislative action. This is done by analyzing his messages to Congress, press conference remarks and other public statements and documents.

Occasionally, important measures are so extensively amended that it is impossible to characterize final passage as a victory or defeat for the president. These votes have been excluded from the study.

Presidential support is determined by the position of the president at the time of a vote, even though that position may be different from an earlier one or may have been reversed after the vote was taken.

Votes on motions to recommit, to reconsider or to table often are key tests that govern the legislative outcome. Such votes are included in the presidential support tabulations. Failure to vote lowers both support and opposition scores equally. All presidential-issue votes have equal statistical weight in the analysis.

Party Unity

Party unity votes are defined as recorded votes in the Senate and House that split the parties, a majority of voting Democrats opposing a majority of voting Republicans. Votes on which either party divides evenly are excluded.

Party unity scores (S = support) represent the percentage of party unity votes on which a member voted "yea" or "nay" in agreement with a majority of his party. Failure to vote, even if a member announced his stand, lowers his score.

Opposition-to-party scores (O = opposition) represent the percentage of party unity votes on which a member voted "yea" or "nay" in disagreement with a majority of his party. A member's party unity and opposition-to-party scores add up to 100 percent only if he participated on all party unity votes.

Conservative Coalition

As used in this study, the term "conservative coalition" means a voting alliance of Republicans and Southern Democrats against the non-Southern Democrats in Congress. This meaning, rather than any philosophical definition of the "conservative" position, provides the basis for CQ's selection of votes.

A conservative coalition vote is any vote in the Senate or House on which a majority of voting Southern Democrats and a majority of voting Republicans oppose the stand taken by a majority of voting non-Southern Democrats. Votes on which there is an even division within the ranks of voting Northern Democrats, Southern Democrats or Republicans are not included.

The Southern states are defined as Alabama, Arkansas, Florida, Georgia, Kentucky, Louisiana, Mississippi, North Carolina, Oklahoma, South Carolina, Tennessee, Texas and Virginia.

The conservative coalition support score (S = support) represents the percentage of conservative coalition votes on which a member voted "yea" or "nay" in agreement with the position of the conservative coalition. Failure to vote, even if a member announced a stand, lowers the score.

The conservative coalition opposition score (O = opposition) represents the percentage of conservative coalition votes on which a member voted "yea" or "nay" in disagreement with the position of the conservative coalition.

Interest Group Ratings

Ratings of members of Congress by four interest groups are given for the years since 1981 (97th Congress). The groups were chosen to represent liberal, conservative, business and labor viewpoints. Following is a description of each group, along with notes regarding their ratings for particular years.

Americans for Democratic Action (ADA)

Americans for Democratic Action was founded in 1947 by a group of liberal Democrats that included Sen. Hubert H. Humphrey and Eleanor Roosevelt. In 1989 the president was Democratic Rep. Ted Weiss of New York.

American Conservative Union (ACU)

The American Conservative Union was founded in 1964 "to mobilize resources of responsible conservative thought across the country and further the general cause of conservatism." The organization intends to provide education in political activity, "prejudice in the press," foreign and military policy, domestic economic policy, the arts, professions and sciences. In 1989 the chairman was David A. Keene.

American Federation of Labor-Congress of Industrial Organizations (AFL-CIO)

The AFL-CIO was formed when the American Federation of Labor and the Congress of Industrial Organizations merged in 1955. With affiliates claiming more than 13 million members, the AFL-CIO accounts for approximately three-quarters of national union membership. In 1989 the president was Lane Kirkland.

Chamber of Commerce of the United States (CCUS)

The Chamber of Commerce of the United States represents local, regional and state chambers of commerce as well as trade and professional organizations. It was founded in 1912 to be "a voice for organized business." In 1989 the president was Richard L. Lesher.

Statistics and Maps

Each state profile contains figures on the population, area, presidential election vote and composition of the legislature. The U.S. congressional delegations and the membership of the state legislatures are based on 1988 election results and the state legislature numbers do not reflect later changes. Information on the makeup of the state legislatures was obtained from the National Conference of State Legislatures.

The following statistics and demographic data in each state profile section were obtained from the 1980 census:

- Demographic breakdown;
- Work — occupations;
- Money — median family income;
- Education — persons with college degrees.

The 1984 and 1988 voter-turnout rates are based on the number of votes cast in the presidential contests; the 1986 rate is based on the number of votes cast in House races. Figures were computed based on Census Bureau statistics.

The 1988 population estimate was taken from the July 1988 Census Bureau's *Estimates of the Resident Population of the States.* Congressional Quarterly computed the national ranking and the 1980-88 percentage change.

Area and Land Use farm data were based on the 1982 reports of the Departments of Agriculture and Commerce. Forest land figures were taken from the 1987 U.S. Forest Service reports. The percentage of federally owned land is based on *Public Land Statistics 1987* from the Interior Department's Bureau of Land Management. The breakdown of state and local government workers is from the Census Bureau's *Public Employment in 1986.* Tax burden figures reflect 1985 Census Bureau reports. The amount of education spending came from a 1988 Department of Education report; the data is based on 1986 figures, in unadjusted dollars. Violent crime figures are based on the FBI's 1987 report on *Crime in the United States.* The rankings for these categories were computed by Congressional Quarterly.

Ten states were redistricted prior to the beginning of the 99th Congress. Statistics for these states have been recalculated for the new districts, using census data. The 10 states are California, Hawaii, Louisiana, Maine, Mississippi, Montana, New Jersey, New York, Texas and Washington. In 1985 there was some minor redistricting in Ohio. Statistics have been recalculated to reflect the changes.

Each House district description contains statistics about the population, background and age of residents. Statistics are given for white, black and Spanish origin, and for other groups if they equal 1 percent or more of the total district population. Some persons are classified as both black and Hispanic, and some Hispanics are not classified by the Census Bureau as either black or white. All demographic data in the congressional district descriptions are based on the 1980 census; percentages were calculated by Congressional Quarterly.

Maps obtained from the Census Bureau are included for all states. All county names appear in capital letters. City names appear in upper and lower case.

Addenda

Page 55. Biographical Data: Family. Udall has remarried. His wife is Norma Gilbert.

Page 78. Robinson's Party Switch. On July 28, 1989, Democratic Rep. Robinson of Arkansas announced that he was switching to the Republican Party.

Page 430. Biographical Data: Capitol Office. Hyde has moved to Room 2262 in the Rayburn Building.

Page 621. Biographical Data: Capitol Office. Huckaby has moved to Room 2182 in the Rayburn Building.

Page 708. Statistics: Committee. Moakley is also a member of the Rules Subcommittee on Legislative Process.

Page 724. Conyers' Mayoral Bid. Conyers filed petitions July 24, 1989, to run in the Sept. 12, 1989, nonpartisan primary for mayor of Detroit.

Page 740. Biographical Data: Capitol Office. Kildee has moved to Room 2239 in the Rayburn Building.

Page 850. Biographical Data: Family. Buechner is separated.

Page 855. Statistics: Committees. As of press time, Gephardt was still a member of the Ways and Means Committee, where he ranked ninth in seniority. He was expected later in the session to relinquish his seat on Ways and Means and to claim the ranking Democratic position on the Budget Committee that is traditionally held by the majority leader. The listings for the Budget Committee on **page 1684** and for the Ways and Means Committee on **page 1697** reflect Gephardt's expected moves.

Page 1697. Select Aging Committee. Committee Chairman Edward R. Roybal is now chairman of the Subcommittee on Health and Long-Term Care, filling the vacancy left by the death of Claude Pepper. Roybal leaves the chair of the Retirement, Income and Employment Subcommittee. The new Retirement chairman is William J. Hughes of New Jersey.

Introduction

This edition of "Politics in America" was written during a period of extraordinary institutional upheaval in the Congress.

For the first time in history, the Speaker of the House — Texan Jim Wright — was forced from office because of an official inquiry into his professional ethics. Cut down also by the ethics blade was the No. 3 House Democratic leader, Majority Whip Tony Coelho. In rebuilding from this debacle, Democrats chose as their new Speaker Thomas S. Foley of Washington, a man as unlike Wright in style and temperament as night from day.

On the other side of the aisle, House Republicans had their own upheaval, less messy than the Democrats', but no less significant. An unexpected vacancy in the No. 2 GOP leadership job was won by combative conservative Newt Gingrich, instigator of the Wright inquiry and leader of a movement that seeks to transform the House's minority party into a more aggressive force.

Also in the opening months of the 101st Congress, the Senate came under the guiding hand of Majority Leader George J. Mitchell of Maine, the Democrats' first new leader in a dozen years. And there was a notable passing: Seniors champion and Rules Committee Chairman Claude Pepper died at age 88; he was the last member who had served in the 1930s New Deal Congress.

The first six months of 1989 also marked the first time in eight years that Congress had to learn to work with a new president. Here, too, change was considerable, because George Bush set out to deal with Capitol Hill in a manner quite unlike that of Ronald Reagan. Browbeat and brinksmanship were key strategies in Reagan's relationship with Congress. So far, Bush has been more prone to consultation and compromise.

The late spring resignations of Wright and Coelho and the death of Pepper changed the House in many ways great and small. After Foley ascended to the Speaker's chair, there were contests for the four positions below him on the Democratic leadership ladder. Unanticipated committee openings occurred, some of them real plums, such as the Rules vacancy, which went to Louise M. Slaughter of New York. Even office numbers began changing, as members jockeyed for bigger quarters left vacant. Add in Gingrich's March restructuring of the GOP whip apparatus, and it is not hard to see that the House of January and the House of June were very different places.

As a result, completing this fifth edition of "Politics in America" has been a unique challenge. In the profiles of members and in the accompanying reference data, we have done our best to provide the latest information on leadership positions, committee assignments and the like. At press time, however, some of this was still changing.

As difficult as it may be for a Congress to reorganize just a few months after it has first convened, the job of picking new leaders and filling committee vacancies looks simple compared with the task that lies ahead for both the House and the Senate: confronting the growing anger among voters over the fact that money buys influence in the legislative process.

There is nothing new about money and politics walking hand in hand, of course. But President Reagan, by associating with the rich and famous and celebrating the wealth to be gained through free enterprise, helped foster a climate in 1980s Washington that made it quite acceptable for monied interests to enhance their access to congressmen by giving them honoraria, campaign contributions and other remuneration.

It became so acceptable, in fact, that Coelho, as chairman of the Democratic Congressional Campaign Committee, got his party in on the act, too. And he proved such a master at courting business support for Democratic candidates that by 1988, Republicans were complaining that business political action committees (PACs) were shutting out GOP congressional challengers in favor of Democratic incumbents.

In simplest terms, Wright and Coelho were forced from office because it was perceived that wealthy people did them financial favors. It is possible that their downfall marked a turning point in congressional and public attitudes about the proper place of money in politics. That is the fervent hope of those who are now advocating "reforms" to break or weaken the bond between monied interests and lawmakers.

Yet it is also possible that the impetus for reform will fade, as Congress moves on to other issues and away from the preoccupation with self-examination that marked the Wright and Coelho affairs and the early 1989 brouhaha over a proposed 51 percent pay increase.

Unless members are willing to lobby their constituents for at least a modest pay raise, it will be difficult for them to abolish the honoraria that many of them rely on as supplementary income. And while heavy PAC financing of campaigns may not be popular with the public, some of the alternatives could be even less so. The reform proposal for federal financing of congressional elections, for instance, conjures up visions of a massive new central bureaucracy dispensing taxpayer dollars and monitoring their expenditure across the nation — not an appealing notion in these deficit-conscious times.

When Jim Wright came before the House on May 31 to announce his intention to relinquish the speakership, he spent most of the hourlong oration presenting his side of the story on the various ethics charges against him. But toward the end, there was a moment of self-reflection in which he seemed to acknowledge that his leadership style, as much as his ethics problems, had brought about his demise.

"Have I been too partisan?" Wright asked. "Too insistent? Too abrasive? Too determined to have my way? Perhaps. Maybe so."

When George Bush, in his January inaugural address, expressed his hope for "the age of the offered hand" between the executive and legislative branches, the response from seasoned Washington observers was something like a smirk: Pretty words, they said, but ones bound to be discarded in the coming clashes between the Democratic Congress and the Republican White House. This view seemed quickly borne out by the bitter Senate battle over Bush's appointment of John Tower to be defense secretary — one of the few times in early 1989 that action in the Senate stole the spotlight from the House.

Yet within weeks of Tower's rejection, Bush and Congress had rather quietly reached accommodation on a strategy for sustaining the Nicaraguan contras and on an outline for the new federal budget — two issues that nearly always provoked fierce and protracted fighting during the Reagan years.

Certainly, Bush and the Democratic Congress have many tough battles ahead. Throughout the spring and into the summer they were in a standoff over raising the minimum wage and devising a way for parents to meet child-care needs.

But with Foley taking the Speaker's chair from Wright, and with Mitchell leading the Democrats in the Senate, Bush is now working with a Democratic leadership that has enough in common with his outlook on politics and his approach to decision making to make the "offered hand" concept more than wishful rhetoric.

Foley, like Bush, has risen to the top echelon of American politics without displaying the kind of burning ambition usually associated with such success. His guiding philosophy has always been consensus politics. "Heightening tension is just another technique," Foley has said, "and it is not one I find particularly congenial."

Mitchell is a more partisan Democrat than Foley, but he also displayed impressive coalition-building skills in campaigning for the majority leader's job in 1988. Working quietly behind the scenes, he assembled a group of supporters that included all levels of Senate seniority, every region and most of the Senate Democrats' ideological range. And his precise, judicial mien during the 1987 Iran-contra hearings struck a balance between partisanship and patriotism that other Democrats on the panel had failed to find.

When Reagan was president, the Democrats' top congressional leaders — Wright, his predecessor as Speaker, Thomas P. O'Neill Jr., and Senate party leader Robert C. Byrd — were men of strong partisan instincts who entered politics during the 1930s and 1940s. Foley and Mitchell entered politics in the 1960s (as did Bush), and they come from states with centrist political inclinations. With this new Democratic duo leading Congress, there is a chance that the inevitable disputes between a Republican White House and congressional Democrats may not have as hard an edge as they did during much of the Reagan era.

But whatever tone is set at the top, always in Congress there will be plenty of fighting. This book is chock full of stories about headstrong members who never met a clash of wills they didn't like. Without doubt, the highest-profile member of this ilk in the first half of 1989 has been Mr. Gingrich of Georgia. His narrow victory in the GOP whip's race in March represented a lashing-out of frustration by House Republicans desperate to end their 34-year minority status in the chamber.

Gingrich had been fomenting this frustration since the early 1980s, when he and other House conservatives formed a group they called the Conservative Opportunity Society (COS) and began goading "Old Bull" pragmatists in the House GOP leadership to confront the Democratic majority aggressively. In time, another faction that felt its views were not being heard — younger, moderate-to-liberal House Republicans — formed an unholy alliance with the COS, and this united force elected Gingrich to the whip's job over pragmatist Edward Madigan of Illinois, the preferred candidate of Minority Leader Robert H. Michel, an "Old Bull" also of Illinois.

The odds are against the philosophically bifurcate Gingrich coalition presenting a sustained front on the House's legislative agenda. Gingrich himself is known for spinning ideas, not codifying them. Rather, the effectiveness of this "New Guard" will be judged at the polls. The leading faction of the center-left is called the '92 Group, so named because of its goal to elect a Republican House majority in the 1992 elections, a feat that would require capturing 40 or so Democratic seats.

At this point, the New Guard has more ambition than strategy. As effective as Gingrich's ethics crusade against Wright turned out to be, it will be difficult to build a House majority solely on the proposition that Democrats are the party of corruption and Republicans the party of cleanliness. The emerging tale of malfeasance in the Department of Housing and Urban Development during the Reagan administration will help put lie to that notion.

Still, publicity alone sometimes breeds success, and Gingrich and his allies in the House are likely to receive more than their share of media attention in coming months, partly because they are the most interesting sideshow in Congress. The Senate, a pit of partisan fury for most of the 1980s as Democrats and Republicans battled for its majority, is quieter now, with flare-ups such as the Tower fight the exception, not the rule.

This cooling off is partly because the Senate's ranks of staunch GOP conservatives were depleted in the 1986 election; that trend continues with New Right Republicans Gordon J. Humphrey and William L. Armstrong saying they will not seek re-election in 1990. Also, the one-time shouting sentinel of the Democratic left, Edward M. Kennedy, has settled into the quieter work of crafting legislation, his presidential aspirations behind him. And while Minority Leader Bob Dole still shows flashes of his old combativeness, he, too, seems a less-large figure now, in the wake of his unimpressive 1988 presidential campaign. Dole's old Senate floor nemesis, former Democratic leader Byrd, has taken the lower-profile job of chairing the Appropriations Committee, where he busies himself with funneling federal largess to his West Virginia constituents. New leader Mitchell indulges in none of the rhetorical flourish for which Byrd was famous in the media. He seems comfortable in the knowledge that his party heads toward 1990 with a 55-45 advantage in the chamber, with the GOP defending a majority of the 34 Senate seats up for election that November.

As in past editions of "Politics in America," we have made our assessments of senators and representatives by watching them in action, conducting interviews with their peers and researching the public record. Nearly 100 members and key staff people — a cross-section of ideology, region and legislative interest — took the time to talk with us in some depth about Congress. Their observations were taken into account as we wrote our profiles, although no one is quoted directly. Each member of the House and Senate also was asked to provide information about his own work, and most did.

We do not try to decide what members ought to be for or against. Our interest is in explaining how they go about expressing their views, and assessing how effective they are at it. While there is considerable legislative information in these pages, this is primarily a book about people, so legislative detail is often truncated.

We cannot, of course, know all there is to know about each member, but we have tried hard to make our book thorough, balanced and fair. Still, assessing members of Congress is an undeniably subjective process, and we take responsibility for all the judgments contained herein.

I would like to express my heartfelt thanks to the many people at Congressional Quarterly who had a hand in this edition of "Politics in America." A mere listing of names, as appears in the front pages of the book, seems inadequate to communicate just how much effort goes into a project of this size and complexity. Let it suffice to say that whatever credit is due this book should reflect equally on all of the dedicated people who were involved in producing it.

Phil Duncan
June 27, 1989

Alabama

U.S. CONGRESS

SENATE 2 D
HOUSE 5 D, 2 R

LEGISLATURE

Senate 30 D, 5 R
House 89 D, 16 R

ELECTIONS

1988 Presidential Vote

Bush	59%
Dukakis	40%

1984 Presidential Vote

Reagan	61%
Mondale	38%

1980 Presidential Vote

Reagan	49%
Carter	48%
Anderson	1%

Turnout rate in 1984	50%
Turnout rate in 1986	38%
Turnout rate in 1988	46%

(as percentage of voting age population)

POPULATION AND GROWTH

1980 population	3,893,888
1988 population estimate (22nd in the nation)	4,102,000
Percent change 1980-1988	+5%

DEMOGRAPHIC BREAKDOWN

White	74%
Black	26%
(Spanish origin)	1%
Urban	60%
Rural	40%
Born in state	79%
Foreign-born	1%

MAJOR CITIES

Birmingham	277,510
Mobile	203,260
Montgomery	194,290
Huntsville	163,420
Tuscaloosa	73,830

AREA AND LAND USE

Area 50,767 sq. miles (28th)

Farm	31%
Forest	67%
Federally owned	3%

Gov. Guy Hunt (R)
Of Holly Pond — Elected 1986

Born: June 17, 1933, Holly Pond, Ala.
Education: Graduated Holly Pond H.S., 1950.
Military Career: Army, 1954-56.
Occupation: Farmer.
Religion: Baptist.
Political Career: Coleman County probate judge, 1964-76; GOP candidate for Ala. Senate, 1962; GOP nominee for governor, 1978.
Next Election: 1990.

WORK

Occupations

White-collar	47%
Blue-collar	39%
Service workers	12%

Government Workers

Federal	59,445
State	80,191
Local	147,506

MONEY

Median family income	$ 16,347	(46th)
Tax burden per capita	$ 727	(41st)

EDUCATION

Spending per pupil through grade 12	$ 2,565	(46th)
Persons with college degrees	12%	(47th)

CRIME

Violent crime rate 559 per 100,000 (15th)

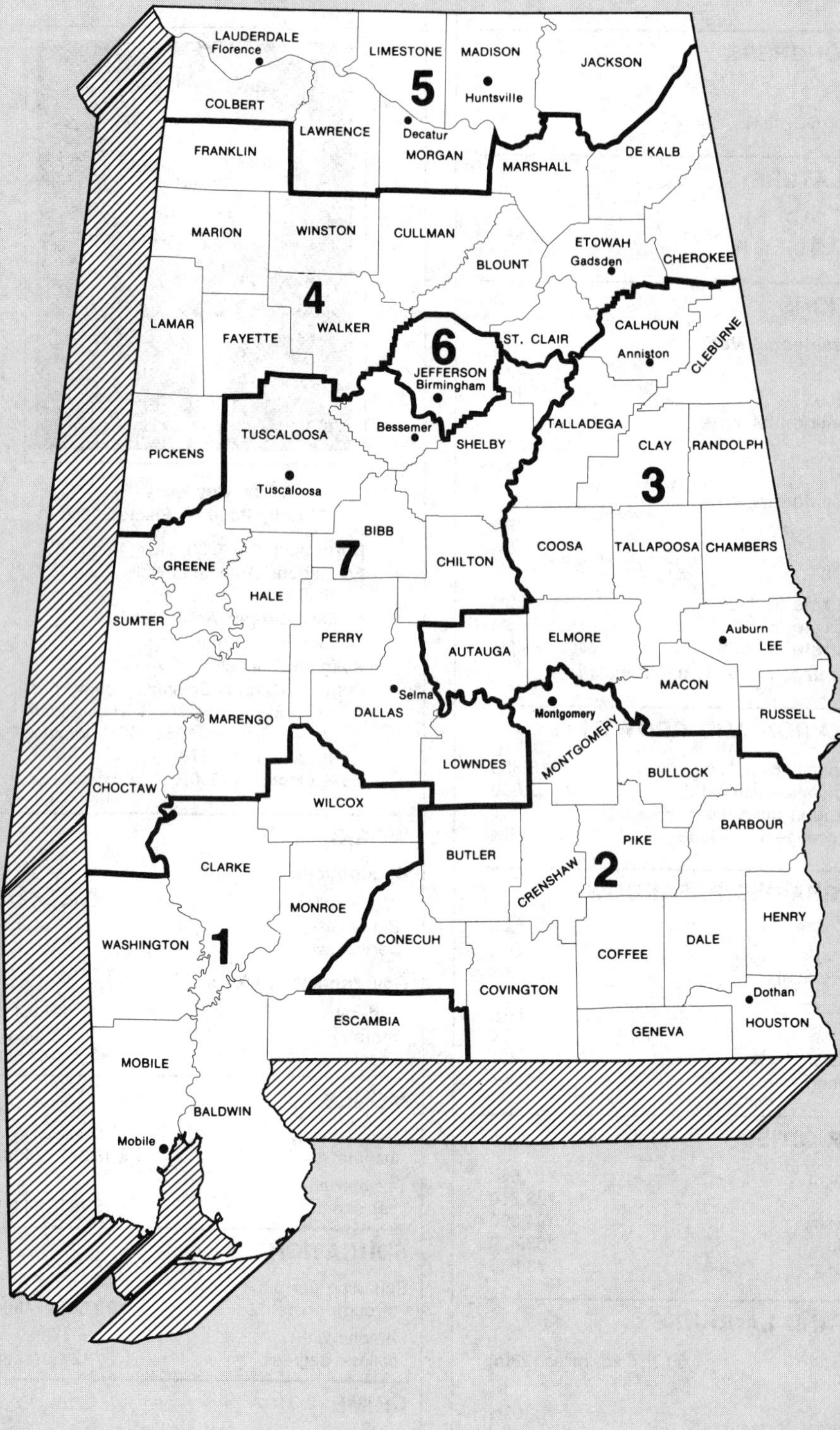
LAUDERDALE
Florence
LIMESTONE
MADISON
Huntsville
JACKSON
5
COLBERT
LAWRENCE
Decatur
MORGAN
FRANKLIN
MARSHALL
DE KALB
MARION
WINSTON
CULLMAN
BLOUNT
ETOWAH
Gadsden
CHEROKEE
4
LAMAR
FAYETTE
WALKER
6
ST. CLAIR
CALHOUN
Anniston
CLEBURNE
JEFFERSON
Birmingham
Bessemer
TUSCALOOSA
Tuscaloosa
SHELBY
TALLADEGA
CLAY
RANDOLPH
PICKENS
3
BIBB
7
GREENE
CHILTON
COOSA
TALLAPOOSA
CHAMBERS
HALE
SUMTER
PERRY
AUTAUGA
ELMORE
Auburn
LEE
Selma
DALLAS
MACON
MARENGO
Montgomery
MONTGOMERY
RUSSELL
LOWNDES
BULLOCK
CHOCTAW
WILCOX
BARBOUR
PIKE
BUTLER
CRENSHAW
2
CLARKE
MONROE
HENRY
WASHINGTON
1
CONECUH
DALE
COFFEE
COVINGTON
Dothan
ESCAMBIA
GENEVA
HOUSTON
MOBILE
BALDWIN
Mobile

Howell Heflin (D)

Of Tuscumbia — Elected 1978

Born: June 19, 1921, Poulan, Ga.
Education: Birmingham Southern College, B.A. 1942; U. of Alabama, J.D. 1948.
Military Career: Marine Corps, 1942-46.
Occupation: Judge; lawyer.
Family: Wife, Elizabeth Ann Carmichael; one child.
Religion: Methodist.
Political Career: Chief justice, Ala. Supreme Court, 1971-77.
Capitol Office: 728 Hart Bldg. 20510; 224-4124.

In Washington: Heflin has a favorite story, one he's told audiences from Alabama to the White House, that goes something like this: A hunter is trapped in a tree with a wildcat, and begs his companion to shoot it. But the friend is afraid he'll hit the hunter instead. "Shoot anyway," the hunter begs. "One of us has got to have some relief!"

As a political metaphor, that treed hunter is Heflin, trapped by one controversy or another and at least halfway wishing that someone would make them go away.

On questions large or commonplace, Heflin typically anguishes over the arguments and resists making decisions. He's known to members, staff and reporters as "the Judge," his preferred title from earlier days as chief justice of the Alabama Supreme Court. In fact, after nearly two terms in the Senate, Heflin continues to see himself that way, not as a senator: "I just try to be the country judge," he said in late 1987. "I don't try to reach an early opinion on something. A judge is supposed to listen to the last argument before he makes up his mind."

But as a result, Heflin's reputation has shifted over time from judicious to indecisive. His nickname has lost some of its original, respectful connotation; it is not uncommon to hear it uttered in sarcasm. Even his jowlish, pear-shaped frame, generously described as imposing, makes him appear in his critics' eyes to be the caricature of an old-time Southern courthouse pol.

The shift in Heflin's image was notable in the 100th Congress, one in which he had unique opportunities for leadership. Due to regard for his probity, Heflin was selected in January 1987 for the special Senate committee investigating the Reagan administration's Iran-contra scandal. Then, as a Southern conservative on the Judiciary Committee, he was poised to be the bellwether vote in the Senate showdown over confirmation of Reagan's Supreme Court nominee, Robert H. Bork. In both controversies, however, many felt that Heflin fell short of the mark expected of a leader.

In Heflin's defense, he is in some ways a victim of others' high expectations. Elected in 1978, he was widely thought to represent the new, more moderate, racially tolerant South. But Heflin is not as moderate as many believed; in Reagan's last two years as president, Heflin supported him more often than any other Senate Democrat. He seems provincial by choice, ducking the lead roles that outsiders expect of him. Moreover, now he is overshadowed by the newer, younger and truly moderate activists elected from his region in the 1980s.

On the Iran-contra committee, Heflin was widely previewed as a potential reprise of Sam Ervin, another self-styled Southern country lawyer and raconteur who drawled his way to national stardom as chairman of the 1974 Senate Watergate Committee. Heflin invited the comparison himself by quoting Ervin in his opening remarks. But throughout the three-month televised hearings, Heflin remained a backbencher and a clumsy interrogator.

In a departure from his characteristic go-slow approach, Heflin opposed committee leaders' bipartisan agreement to postpone the start of hearings several months so an independent counsel could independently develop criminal cases against the key figures, former White House aides Rear Adm. John M. Poindexter and Lt. Col. Oliver L. North.

In this case, "the Judge" turned into a politician, and worried about public reaction to further delay in the investigation of an administration so popular in his region. "The people want to get it behind us," Heflin urged unsuccessfully.

Perhaps his most memorable moment was outside the hearing room, when Heflin told reporters that North's secretary Fawn Hall had smuggled documents from the White House in her brassiere. "She's supposedly got some pretty good capacity to carry the documents," he said. Hall snapped that Heflin was "sexist," but later testified that she did smuggle papers — in her back waistband and boots. At year's end, Heflin signed the committee's final report sharply criticizing the administration, but objected to its conclusion that Reagan deserved some blame for creating an "environment" tolerant of aides skirting the law. That finding, Heflin said, went "too far."

Between the time the Iran-contra hearings ended in August and the committee's report was issued in November, Heflin remained in the spotlight through the Bork confirmation proceedings.

As usual in controversial matters, Judiciary was split along party lines, with three undecided swing voters — Heflin, conservative Democrat Dennis DeConcini of Arizona and liberal Republican Arlen Specter of Pennsylvania — holding both the balance of power and the media's attention. Heflin seemed to relish the attention most, and appeared regularly on the Sunday TV talk shows.

In questioning Bork, Heflin the former judge fretted that he feared Bork would be too willing to overturn court precedents; he said he wished he were a psychiatrist to predict how Bork would behave. Heflin the politician, reflecting some constituents' aversion to Bork's appearance, asked the nominee to explain why he had grown his scraggly beard.

Bork opponents and some commentators suggested Heflin ultimately would lead other Southerners in voting against the conservative judge — out of concern that Bork would seek to reverse landmark civil rights rulings. Instead, Heflin stayed on the fence while a parade of Southern Democrats, including his junior Alabama colleague Richard C. Shelby, went to the Senate floor to state their opposition.

Reagan called Heflin to the White House (where the senator told his "treed hunter" tale) and he emerged still undecided. But already both Heflin and the committee were irrelevant; vote counts showed Bork would lose on the floor. All but ignored, the senator voted against confirmation.

Partly to take the pressure off Heflin and DeConcini, after their anti-Bork votes, congressional leaders decided in 1988 to have the House rather than the Senate act first on the Civil Rights Restoration Act, the so-called *Grove City* bill overturning a Supreme Court decision that had limited enforcement of key civil rights laws. Heflin ultimately joined all other Senate Democrats in voting both to pass the bill and later to override Reagan's veto. "Another nail in my coffin," he was heard to say after the second vote.

The Senate's first major act in the 101st Congress, confirmation of former Texas Sen. John Tower as defense secretary, presented another hard choice. Days before the vote, Heflin became the first Democrat to announce he would support the beleaguered nominee. He said he found the FBI report on allegations of Tower's drinking, womanizing and financial ties to defense contractors "inconclusive," and, after judiciously weighing the evidence for himself, concluded, "I am willing to give him a chance to prove himself." A majority was not, however. Tower was rejected 47-53, with just two other Democrats voting for him.

Heflin was a pivotal swing voter on the Judiciary Committee for the six years the GOP controlled the Senate, before Democrats regained a majority in the 1986 elections. He frequently allied with Chairman Strom Thurmond and other GOP conservatives on major issues. Once, when Thurmond failed to notice Heflin among Democrats during a head count, Sen. Edward M. Kennedy protested, "I believe Mr. Heflin is a Democrat." Said Thurmond: "I always thought he was one of us."

In the 99th Congress, Heflin was the only committee Democrat to back Daniel A. Manion of Indiana for a seat on the 7th U.S. Circuit Court of Appeals. Manion, criticized by Democrats as too rigidly conservative and inexperienced, was confirmed in a bitter, close vote. Heflin also split with his party in backing William H. Rehnquist to be chief justice of the United States, and Edwin Meese III to be attorney general.

After characteristic agonizing, Heflin did remain in the Democratic fold to provide the crucial vote rejecting Reagan's nomination of a fellow Alabamian, U.S. attorney Jefferson B. Sessions III, to be a federal district judge. Critics said Sessions was unqualified and racially insensitive. Before a packed room, Heflin publicly deliberated the pros and cons before finally announcing that, because "I don't know" if Sessions would be a good judge, he would vote against him. Sessions' hometown newspaper in Mobile condemned Heflin as "the Benedict Arnold of Alabama."

Though Judiciary's province includes many of the legal issues Heflin knows best, he has not been a leading participant unless the subject deals with improvement of judicial operations, a favorite of his. Generally, Heflin seems uncomfortable with the legislative pace. Though coy when Republicans floated his name as a potential Supreme Court nominee in 1987, Heflin did express longing for the judiciary's more deliberative, thorough style. He keeps colleagues in suspense as to his position, and occasionally is absent for controversial votes — as he was in 1982 when the panel considered a constitutional amendment to ban abortion.

At times, Heflin's public soul-searching is a self-parody. When the full Senate in 1985 considered a bill naming the rose as the national flower, Heflin wavered between the rose, Alabama's marigold and its state flower, the camellia, in the longest speech of the day. "Roses are red, violets are blue, why must I choose between these two?" he asked. He finally picked the rose.

On the Agriculture Committee, Heflin has less trouble making choices. He is for cotton and whatever else grows in the South. In 1984, he blocked a farm price-support bill to gain concessions for cotton, rice and wheat. So protective is he of the federal peanut subsidy program that Heflin has boasted he's the third senator from Georgia. He espoused a new subsidy program for Southern soybean farmers.

Heflin is an eager player in the committee's commodity-trading approach to legislation, in which members from one region ally with those from other regions to support subsidies for each others' products. During one logrolling session in 1987, with Heflin joking and egging colleagues on, a simple bill for disaster aid to wheat farmers was festooned with provisions benefiting growers of apples, peaches, cotton and hay.

Frequently at odds with environmentalists back home, Heflin in 1988 joined with Republican Jesse Helms to oppose a pesticide regulation bill that was supported by environmentalists and cosponsored by Agriculture Committee Chairman Patrick J. Leahy and ranking Republican Richard G. Lugar. The Heflin-Helms version, backed by farmers and pesticide manufacturers, shifted the burden for paying regulatory costs from manufacturers to taxpayers, and limited farmers' liability. Some of its provisions were incorporated in the much-diluted bill that finally became law.

For the 101st Congress, Heflin joined a third legislative committee, Energy and Natural Resources. Outside his committee assignments, he is a leader in efforts to increase funding for NASA, along with other senators from states with NASA contractors and facilities.

Heflin also is chairman of the Ethics Committee, where the measure of his success has been the panel's near-total secrecy. Typically, Heflin and GOP Vice Chairman Warren B. Rudman handle complaints against colleagues with informal bipartisanship. Because of his background, Heflin was appointed chairman in 1979, making him the first freshman senator to head a committee since 1910.

In 1981, though Heflin had to forfeit the chair when Democrats lost their Senate majority, he was tapped to head the committee's investigation of New Jersey Democrat Harrison A. Williams Jr., who was caught in the FBI's Abscam bribery sting. In early 1982, he took the Senate floor to present the committee's recommendation that Williams be expelled. After Heflin's eloquent denunciation made an expulsion vote all but certain, Williams resigned.

At Home: Heflin spent six years preparing for his 1984 re-election campaign by polishing the reputation he carried when he left Alabama for the Senate. He presented himself as an honest, open, approachable public figure, traveling the dusty Alabama back roads to meet with constituents for "Dutch Treat" breakfasts at which he trotted out his carefully aged stock of country stories.

Republicans never were very enthusiastic about unseating him, but they came up with a credible candidate in former U.S. Rep. Albert Lee Smith, who had lost his Birmingham-based House seat in 1982. Smith had been expected to try a House comeback, but he opted instead for the chance to spread his conservative message before a larger audience.

Known in the House as a zealous promoter of the New Right social agenda, Smith switched gears a little in his Senate campaign, talking more about economics and accusing Heflin of frustrating the Reagan agenda of tax and spending cuts. He also tried to make an issue of Heflin's ties to political action committees, which had given him more money in 1983 than any incumbent senator.

Heflin responded by calling himself an "independent, conservative to moderate" Democrat who backed Ronald Reagan more often than he had backed Jimmy Carter. The Alabama voter, Heflin said, "doesn't want a robot, or a puppet, or some Charlie McCarthy who some president will pop up and vote any way he wants him to."

The incumbent entered the final few weeks with a polling lead so awesome it defied belief. There was talk that Heflin might attract three-quarters of the vote. But presidential coattails eventually allowed Smith to hold Heflin to a slightly more respectable 63 percent. But it was a convincing demonstration of just how effective "folksy judge" politics can be.

Heflin's first campaign for the Senate was not that much more suspenseful than his second. When Democratic Sen. John J. Sparkman announced his retirement in 1978, Gov. George C. Wallace was poised to replace him. But while the governor campaigned unofficially throughout 1977, he never announced, and for good reason. Polls showed Heflin far ahead of him.

One Democrat who did run against Heflin and came to regret it was Walter Flowers, a five-term U.S. House member. In a primary runoff that turned angry and unpleasant, Heflin took all but five counties in the state. Better organized and financed than the congressman, he blasted Flowers for being "part of the Washington crowd." The general election was a formality; the GOP had no candidate.

In his younger days, as a trial attorney in the northern Alabama town of Tuscumbia, Heflin was known as one of the best. He could cajole a jury with down-home stories, cry with them over his client's plight or delight them with an unexpected move. Once he lay down on the counsel's table to show the improbability of an alleged assault victim's story. History does not record whether the table survived.

Heflin's reputation as a lawyer led to his election as chief justice of the Alabama Supreme Court, where he streamlined the state judicial system, which had been hampered by a huge case backlog. To accomplish the task, he needed adoption of a state constitutional amendment, and the voters gave it to him. When political opponents criticized him because the amendment made him eligible for a $30,000 annual pension, Heflin pointed out that he could not receive the money if he served in the Senate or practiced law.

Heflin's uncle, "Cotton Tom" Heflin, served in the Senate from 1920 to 1931. He was an ardent segregationist and anti-Catholic who bolted the Democratic Party when Al Smith was nominated for president in 1928. Fifty-one years later, Howell Heflin made a speech welcoming Pope John Paul II to the United States.

Committees

Select Ethics (Chairman)

Agriculture, Nutrition and Forestry (4th of 10 Democrats)
Rural Development and Rural Electrification (chairman); Agricultural Production and Stabilization of Prices; Conservation and Forestry

Energy and Natural Resources (9th of 10 Democrats)
Energy Research and Development; Mineral Resources Development and Production; Water and Power

Judiciary (6th of 8 Democrats)
Courts and Administrative Practice (chairman); Antitrust, Monopolies and Business Rights; Patents, Copyrights and Trademarks

Elections

1984 General		
Howell Heflin (D)	860,535	(63%)
Albert Lee Smith Jr. (R)	498,508	(36%)
1984 Primary		
Howell Heflin (D)	399,817	(83%)
Charles Borden (D)	47,462	(10%)
Mrs. Frank Ross Stewart (D)	33,114	(7%)

Previous Winning Percentage: 1978 (94%)

Campaign Finance

	Receipts	Receipts from PACs	Expend-itures
1984			
Heflin (D)	$2,247,582	$847,573 (38%)	$1,917,493
Smith (R)	$584,002	$49,629 (8%)	$574,382

Key Votes

1987	
Enact omnibus highway bill over Reagan veto	Y
Limit testing of space-based anti-ballistic missiles	Y
Oppose banning tests of larger nuclear weapons	Y
Confirm Robert H. Bork as Supreme Court justice	N
1988	
Allow vote on campaign-finance overhaul	N
Pass civil rights restoration bill over Reagan veto	Y
Enact omnibus trade bill over Reagan veto	Y
Approve death penalty for drug-related murders	Y
Oppose "workfare" amendment to welfare overhaul bill	N

Voting Studies

	Presidential Support		Party Unity		Conservative Coalition	
Year	**S**	**O**	**S**	**O**	**S**	**O**
1988	73	27	52	47	97	3
1987	54	46	50	50	94	6
1986	76	24	42	57	84	16
1985	54	45	56	43	88	12
1984	75	21	36	59	89	11
1983	42	52	57	41	77†	16†
1982	61	39	57	42	79	17
1981	68	30	64	34	81	15

† Not eligible for all recorded votes.

Interest Group Ratings

Year	ADA	ACU	AFL-CIO	CCUS
1988	30	58	64	50
1987	35	46	80	50
1986	25	65	53	58
1985	25	74	67	45
1984	20	91	45	67
1983	40	72	65	44
1982	25	75	65	75
1981	35	54	58	61

Richard C. Shelby (D)

Of Tuscaloosa — Elected 1986

Born: May 6, 1934, Birmingham, Ala.
Education: U. of Alabama, A.B. 1957; LL.B. 1963.
Occupation: Lawyer.
Family: Wife, Annette Nevin; two children.
Religion: Presbyterian.
Political Career: Ala. Senate, 1971-79; U.S. House, 1979-87.
Capitol Office: 313 Hart Bldg. 20510; 224-5744.

In Washington: Days after his Senate victory in 1986, Shelby said he hoped to join with senior Alabama Sen. Howell Heflin to wield the kind of national influence the state once enjoyed under another Democratic Senate duo, postwar populists John Sparkman and Lister Hill. Instead, in joining Heflin, Shelby completes a conservative pair that fits uneasily in the Democratic-controlled Senate, and plays a more parochial role than the earlier New Deal team.

Shelby's tendency to ally with Senate Republicans was of little surprise to those familiar with his four-term House career and his 1981 flirtation with the GOP. During the 100th Congress, he defected from the Democratic line in several notable partisan showdowns. But he toed that line when the issue was civil rights — reflecting his heightened sensitivity to the black voters who were crucial to his upset of GOP Sen. Jeremiah Denton.

Shelby's independence has had its cost. His bid for the Appropriations Committee in the 101st Congress was squashed in party deliberations. Senate Democratic leaders, while sympathetic to party conservatives' need to break ranks occasionally on issues unpopular back home, nonetheless saw no reason to reward someone who strays so frequently.

Shelby did not endear himself to the new Democratic regime, either, by his stance in the 1988 contest to succeed Majority Leader Robert C. Byrd of West Virginia. Though widely expected to support the conservative Southern candidate, J. Bennett Johnston of Louisiana, Shelby demurred until days before the vote, and then joined the bandwagon for Maine liberal George J. Mitchell. He thereby angered the Johnston camp, gained little in Mitchell's and burnished a reputation for being occasionally indecisive and opportunistic.

Early in the 101st Congress, Shelby redeemed himself a bit with party leaders — at no real political cost to himself in Alabama — by opposing former Sen. John Tower's nomination as defense secretary. Republicans had hoped for Shelby's support, so his surprise early announcement just before voting in the Armed Services Committee presaged Tower's ultimate rejection on the Senate floor. Shelby's decision may not have been all that difficult for him: He was concurring with Sam Nunn of Georgia, the Armed Services chairman he greatly admires, and in Alabama, Bible Belt concern over Tower's alleged drunkenness and womanizing was perceptible.

Shelby's stand with his party in support of civil rights issues marks a break from the pattern of his early congressional career. In 1987, he voted against the confirmation of Robert H. Bork, President Reagan's Supreme Court nominee, whose defeat was a top priority for civil rights groups. In 1988, Shelby joined all Democrats in voting to override Reagan's veto of the Civil Rights Restoration Act, which aimed to overturn a Supreme Court decision limiting enforcement of four key civil rights laws.

Shelby's backing for the Republican president on other issues, however, remained high; during 1987, Shelby was second only to Heflin among Senate Democrats in his frequency of support for Reagan's legislative positions. Like Reagan, Shelby has a political compass that steers a straight anti-communist course in defense and foreign policy, and a pro-business one in domestic affairs.

In the final weeks of the 100th Congress, Shelby allied with Republicans in successful filibusters of two bills central to Democrats' 1988 election agenda. He was one of only three Democrats to oppose a bill raising the minimum wage, and one of eight against Democrats' package of "family" issues — expanded child care subsidies, guaranteed job leave for parents with new or seriously ill children and toughened child-pornography sanctions.

In 1987, when a campaign-finance overhaul bill was before the Senate, only Shelby and Heflin consistently sided with Senate Republicans during their four-month standoff with the Democratic leadership over the legislation. The bill would have capped candidates' spending and introduced limited public financing.

Later that year, Shelby was a leader in the fight to authorize final production of chemical weapons. On his motion, the Senate by a single vote killed a Democratic amendment to deny funds for the controversial Bigeye nerve gas bomb. He was the only one in the Democrats' 11-member Senate class of 1986 to oppose another Democratic arms control amendment — this one successful — mandating U.S. compliance with the missile limits of the unratified SALT II treaty.

So fierce is Shelby's anti-communism that it apparently exceeded even Reagan's. While the president was softening in 1988, in response to overtures from Soviet leader Mikhail S. Gorbachev, Shelby remained suspicious. Even before the two leaders signed the intermediate-range nuclear-forces (INF) treaty, Shelby announced he would oppose it — making him the only Democrat to do so. Along with then-Sen. Dan Quayle, one of the small band of Republicans unhappy with the pact, Shelby worked unsuccessfully to attach conditions that would defer final removal of NATO missiles from Europe until the Soviet bloc reduced its conventional forces there. Still, Shelby ultimately voted for the treaty, both in Armed Services and on the floor, explaining that Senate rejection would send a dangerous signal of NATO disarray.

Even the trade bill offered a vehicle for Shelby's anti-Soviet sentiments. In 1987, he sought a permanent ban on imports from foreign firms that sell advanced technology with military applications to Soviet-bloc nations. His amendment, aimed at Japan's Toshiba Machine Co. and Kongsberg Vaapenfabrikk of Norway, was defeated in favor of a less stringent two-to-five-year ban. Congress ultimately limited the sanctions even further.

On the Banking Committee, Shelby was active mainly in the long-running but inconclusive debate over corporate takeovers. Siding with Republicans, he opposed a Democratic bill aimed at restraining corporate raiders and the securities firms that finance their deals.

Shelby argued the case against the bill in populist terms, saying small shareholders should be free to sell to raiders. Corporate managers, he said, "are not interested in a competitive America, they're interested in perpetuating themselves." When he and other opponents succeeded with floor amendments limiting corporate executives' financial defenses against hostile takeovers, proponents withdrew their bill, killing it for the year.

As a House member, Shelby devoted much of his effort to the Energy and Commerce Committee. House Democratic leaders gave him a seat on the prestigious panel when he arrived in 1979, believing Shelby to be a Southern moderate. They came to regret their decision when he proved to be a reliable vote for the GOP and pro-industry positions on major issues. In 1984, Shelby and a small bloc of Democrats on the Health Subcommittee aligned with Republicans to defeat acid rain provisions in a clean-air bill backed by environmentalists, and to modify the bill to industry specifications.

Shelby's conservative posture on economic and social issues complicated his statewide prospects in 1986, since he had alienated the party's labor and black constituencies. He frequently supported Reagan's initiatives during the early budget battles, and at times seemed receptive to GOP recruitment efforts. "If the Democratic Party continues to go to the left, it will destroy its Southern base," Shelby once warned.

He angered many black voters by opposing both the 1982 extension of the Voting Rights Act on the grounds that it unfairly penalized Southern states, and a national holiday honoring the Rev. Dr. Martin Luther King Jr. Once in the Senate, however, he supported a 1989 measure funding the King holiday commission.

At Home: For most of his 1986 campaign against Denton, Shelby seemed a certain victim of a political mess not of his making: An intraparty rift over the Democratic gubernatorial nomination that overshadowed Shelby's efforts. But with an aggressive closing strategy, he prevailed by just under 7,000 votes.

Denton led in public-opinion surveys throughout the campaign. He had a following among advocates of his staunchly conservative, pro-Reagan politics and those who viewed the former naval officer and longtime Vietnam prisoner of war as a national hero.

But in the Senate, Denton spent much time pursuing goals such as promoting chastity among teenagers — an agenda without strong appeal to the many voters concerned about economic issues. He was frequently ridiculed for being loose with his words (about spousal rape, for instance, he said, "Damn it, when you get married, you kind of expect you're going to get a little sex"). Denton, not skilled at personal politicking, also was criticized for not keeping in touch with his constituency.

But Shelby had problems of his own, caused by his cool relationship with Democratic liberals. The New South Coalition, a black organization headed by Birmingham Mayor Richard Arrington, endorsed Ted McLaughlin, an obscure former federal official, in the Democratic primary. Shelby had another serious primary foe in Jim Allen Jr., a state school board commissioner and son of former Sen. James Allen Sr. Shelby won just 51 percent in the primary, barely avoiding a runoff.

On the same day, Lt. Gov. William J. Baxley and state Atty. Gen. Charles Graddick finished one-two in the Democratic gubernatorial primary, setting up a runoff. After a bitter campaign, the runoff tally showed Graddick winning by 7,000 votes. But Baxley, a moderate, argued that Graddick, a conservative former Republican, had illegally recruited GOP voters to support him in the runoff. After a federal court agreed, a state party committee gave the nomination to Baxley. Eventually, many angry conservative Democrats helped elect Republican Guy Hunt as governor over Baxley.

The schism prompted Shelby to lay low for a while, but when it became clear the storm would not blow over, he started stumping, and made up ground quickly. He ran a TV commercial accusing Denton of voting to cut Social Security, and others portraying Denton as "out of touch and ineffective." Shelby was able to assuage his former foes on the Democratic left, partly because no matter how great their dissatisfaction with Shelby, black and union voters saw Denton as less desirable.

Shelby won with a strong boost from his 7th District base. He took Tuscaloosa County with 64 percent and carried several rural Black Belt counties by 3-to-1 margins. He also did well in traditionally Democratic counties in northwest and south-central Alabama.

Shelby's first election to the House was much less trying. In 1978, his former Tuscaloosa law partner, Democratic Rep. Walter Flowers, gave up the 7th for what turned out to be an unsuccessful Senate primary campaign. Shelby, whose support for such issues as the Equal Rights Amendment had typed him as a progressive Democrat during eight years in the state Legislature, went for Flowers' open seat.

Shelby's strong base in Tuscaloosa, where he had served as a prosecutor, helped him win 48 percent in the primary. In the runoff, he defeated black state Rep. Chris McNair by a 3-to-2 margin, in a campaign free of racial tensions. He easily won that November and never faced significant GOP opposition.

Dissatisfaction with Shelby's conservative House voting record led to one primary challenge from the left, but Shelby beat it back by a margin of nearly 2-to-1.

Committees

Armed Services (10th of 11 Democrats)
Conventional Forces and Alliance Defense; Projection Forces and Regional Defense; Readiness, Sustainability and Support

Banking, Housing and Urban Affairs (8th of 12 Democrats)
International Finance and Monetary Policy; Securities

Special Aging (7th of 10 Democrats)

Elections

1986 General

Richard C. Shelby (D)	609,360	(50%)
Jeremiah Denton (R)	602,537	(50%)

1986 Primary

Richard C. Shelby (D)	420,155	(51%)
Jim Allen Jr. (D)	284,206	(35%)
Ted McLaughlin (D)	70,784	(9%)
Mrs. Frank Ross Stewart (D)	26,723	(3%)
Steve Arnold (D)	16,722	(2%)

Previous Winning Percentages: **1984 *** (97%) **1982 *** (97%) **1980 *** (73%) **1978 *** (94%)

* *House elections.*

Campaign Finance

	Receipts	Receipts from PACs	Expend-itures
1986			
Shelby (D)	$2,400,488	$882,686 (37%)	$2,259,167
Denton (R)	$4,682,587	$673,320 (14%)	$4,617,163

Key Votes

1987

Enact omnibus highway bill over Reagan veto	Y
Limit testing of space-based anti-ballistic missiles	Y
Oppose banning tests of larger nuclear weapons	Y
Confirm Robert H. Bork as Supreme Court justice	N

1988

Allow vote on campaign-finance overhaul	N
Pass civil rights restoration bill over Reagan veto	Y
Enact omnibus trade bill over Reagan veto	Y
Approve death penalty for drug-related murders	Y
Oppose "workfare" amendment to welfare overhaul bill	N

Voting Studies

	Presidential Support		Party Unity		Conservative Coalition	
Year	**S**	**O**	**S**	**O**	**S**	**O**
1988	57	43	56	43	92	5
1987	47	50	61	36	75	16
House Service						
1986	44	49	58	33	84	8
1985	52	41	60	31	85	13
1984	43	45	44	45	78	12
1983	54	44	43	54	76	20
1982	60	40	35	63	86	10
1981	76	21	25	71	93	4

Interest Group Ratings

Year	ADA	ACU	AFL-CIO	CCUS
1988	35	60	71	57
1987	50	43	90	50
House Service				
1986	40	55	93	39
1985	25	67	50	57
1984	15	57	50	46
1983	25	74	53	55
1982	10	73	35	67
1981	0	93	27	89

1 Sonny Callahan (R)

Of Mobile — Elected 1984

Born: Sept. 11, 1932, Mobile, Ala.

Education: Graduated from McGill H.S. (Mobile), 1950.

Military Career: Navy, 1952-54.

Occupation: Moving and storage company executive.

Family: Wife, Karen Reed; six children.

Religion: Roman Catholic.

Political Career: Served as Democrat in Ala. House, 1971-79, and in Ala. Senate, 1979-83; sought Democratic nomination for lieutenant governor, 1982.

Capitol Office: 1232 Longworth Bldg. 20515; 225-4931.

In Washington: Still "Sonny" after all these years, the middle-aged Callahan is a gregarious, good-natured Southerner at ease with the personal give-and-take of the political process. He is the GOP version of a character type abundant in his region — the Democratic courthouse pol. That is not surprising, since Callahan himself was once a Democrat.

As a freshman on Public Works, Callahan cultivated a friendship with Gene Snyder of Kentucky, then the committee's senior Republican. Soon, Callahan was joining Snyder and a few cronies for drinks and cards in the evening, and for hunting on weekends. Callahan's contacts helped him obtain federal money to deepen the Mobile Ship Channel. Ultimately, some $380 million made it through the legislative mill.

By the end of 1986, however, Callahan was aiming higher. He wanted a seat on Energy and Commerce, and ingratiated himself with Minority Whip Trent Lott of Mississippi, who wanted more Southerners in key committee slots. Lott helped Callahan win one of two prize GOP vacancies on that committee for the 100th Congress.

A skeptic of government involvement in the marketplace, Callahan is typical of Energy and Commerce Republicans. He tried unsuccessfully to block a move requiring manufacturers of three-wheeled all-terrain vehicles (ATVs) to offer cash refunds to those who purchased the vehicles before they were banned. Callahan noted that his 31-year-old son made good use of his camouflaged ATV for hunting deer and turkey.

Outside the committee, Callahan's conservatism is also plain to see. In every instance that a majority of Republicans voted with a majority of Southern Democrats in 1988, Callahan was part of that "conservative coalition." And in key 1988 floor votes, Callahan broke from President Reagan's position only once, on a bill to pay Japanese-Americans interned during World War II.

Callahan also has had his share of good fortune. His predecessor, GOP Rep. Jack Edwards, worked for years to get Mobile included in the Navy's "homeporting" force-dispersal strategy. Ground was finally broken for the facility in 1988, giving Callahan a well-timed publicity boost.

At Home: When Edwards announced his retirement in late 1983, his endorsement went to Callahan, and so did the betting money. The only suspense was over which party Callahan would choose. Though he was elected to the Legislature as a Democrat, Callahan's views earned him friends across the aisle. And after losing a 1982 lieutenant governor primary, he moved further right.

Callahan formally joined the GOP in February 1984, and, confident of victory, proceeded to wage a lackadaisical House campaign. Callahan's primary foe, Mobile lawyer Billy Stoudenmire, aggressively criticized him as a Democratic interloper. Callahan brought enough conservative Democrats across party lines to win the primary by a 60-40 margin. But his weakness rekindled hope among Democrats, who nominated Frank McRight, a Mobile trial lawyer.

McRight won his primary by attacking local government corruption. The issue gained salience in the November campaign, when it was reported that Callahan had received an illegal campaign contribution two years earlier from a city official later indicted on other charges.

In October, Callahan finally responded to the challenge. He reminded voters that McRight was twice the Carter-Mondale campaign chairman in Mobile, and he repeatedly asked how McRight would vote for president in 1984. In the end, though, Callahan owed much of his narrow margin to Reagan's smashing triumph in the 1st.

Democrats conceded without a fight in 1986, but recruited John M. Tyson Jr. in 1988. A high-profile member of the state school board and member of a well-known political family, Tyson had the markings of a contender. But he ran a poorly organized, underfunded campaign and never seriously threatened the incumbent.

Alabama 1

Southwest — Mobile

The 1st, in the southwest corner of the state, is dominated by the port city of Mobile, second-largest in the state, with a population of over 200,000. Situated on the state's only coastline, it is isolated from the rest of Alabama, and its Spanish and French heritage and large Catholic population give the city a separate history. Because of the port, Mobile has always had an outward-looking air.

Mobile County has been voting increasingly Republican in recent national elections. It gave Republican Jeremiah Denton more than 60 percent in his 1986 race for U.S. Senate. George Bush carried 61 percent of the Mobile vote in 1988, but in local elections, Democrats still have the edge.

On the eastern side of Mobile Bay is Baldwin County. Though still just one-third the size of Mobile County, Baldwin was the third-fastest growing county in Alabama between 1980 and 1986, when its population increased nearly 20 percent. Bush took 73 percent of the vote there.

The port is the area's largest employer. The 1985 completion of the Tennessee-Tombigbee Waterway, which connects Mobile Bay and the Tennessee River, is expected eventually to help the port of Mobile compete with New Orleans in trade volume, although early volume on the massive waterway has been disappointing.

A continued federal involvement in port development was assured with the 1988 ground-breaking for the Mobile "home-port," part of the Reagan administration's strategy of dispersing U.S. naval forces.

Shipbuilding is a major industry. In addition, the salt domes north of the city have given rise to a chemical industry, and there are oil and gas drilling operations offshore. The other key industry in the 1st is pulp and paper; the raw material for the industry comes from the forests that cover much of the district's rural counties.

The strong GOP vote in Mobile and coastal Baldwin County often outweighs the Democratic strength found in the rural, heavily black counties in the northern part of the district and in Prichard, a suburb of Mobile. Wilcox County, more than two-thirds black, was one of just six Alabama counties to support George McGovern's presidential campaign in 1972, and one of 14 to back Michael S. Dukakis in 1988.

Population: 563,905. White 383,014 (68%), Black 174,657 (31%), Other 4,927(1%). Spanish origin 5,887 (1%). 18 and over 384,289 (68%), 65 and over 60,149 (11%). Median age: 28.

Committee

Energy and Commerce (16th of 17 Republicans)
Energy and Power; Transportation and Hazardous Materials

Elections

1988 General		
Sonny Callahan (R)	115,173	(59%)
John M. Tyson Jr. (D)	77,670	(40%)
1986 General		
Sonny Callahan (R)	96,469	(100%)

Previous Winning Percentage: **1984** (51%)

District Vote For President

	1988		1984		1980		1976	
D	73,312	(37%)	72,298	(35%)	77,758	(41%)	81,012	(48%)
R	121,510	(62%)	134,551	(64%)	107,679	(56%)	83,622	(50%)

Campaign Finance

	Receipts	Receipts from PACs	Expend-itures
1988			
Callahan (R)	$596,631	$253,301 (42%)	$651,127
Tyson (D)	$128,136	$52,400 (41%)	$125,029
1986			
Callahan (R)	$296,605	$114,197 (39%)	$144,314

Key Votes

1987	
Raise speed limit to 65 mph	Y
Approve Gephardt "fair trade" amendment	N
Ban testing of larger nuclear weapons	N
Delay "re-flagging" of Kuwaiti tankers	N
Approve tax-raising deficit-reduction bill	N
1988	
Approve aid to Nicaraguan contras	Y
Enact civil rights restoration bill over Reagan veto	N
Kill 60-day plant-closing notification measure	Y
Pass omnibus trade bill over Reagan veto	N
Approve death penalty for drug-related murders	Y
Bar federal funds for abortions in cases of rape and incest	Y
Oppose seven-day waiting period for purchase of handguns	Y

Voting Studies

	Presidential Support		Party Unity		Conservative Coalition	
Year	**S**	**O**	**S**	**O**	**S**	**O**
1988	63	37	79	17	100	0
1987	68	32	79	16	93	5
1986	73	21	75	21	98	0
1985	74	26	82	16	96	4

Interest Group Ratings

Year	ADA	ACU	AFL-CIO	CCUS
1988	10	96	29	93
1987	4	78	19	87
1986	0	95	29	89
1985	0	86	12	86

2 Bill Dickinson (R)

Of Montgomery — Elected 1964

Born: June 5, 1925, Opelika, Ala.
Education: U. of Alabama Law School, LL.B. 1950.
Military Career: Navy, 1943-46; Air Force Reserve.
Occupation: Lawyer; judge; railroad executive.
Family: Wife, Barbara Edwards; four children.
Religion: Methodist.
Political Career: Opelika city judge, 1951-53; Lee County Court of Common Pleas and Juvenile Court judge, 1953-59; 5th Judicial Circuit judge, 1959-63.
Capitol Office: 2406 Rayburn Bldg. 20515; 225-2901.

In Washington: One of the secondary casualties in the Democrats' 1985 coup against enfeebled Armed Services Committee Chairman Mel Price was Republican Dickinson, who lost much of the influence that he had carved from the leadership void. Since then, however, Dickinson has reached a working accommodation with Chairman Les Aspin that has permitted him a continued, if more limited, role.

In the Bush administration, Dickinson's job as his party's top defense spokesman in the House likely will be further redefined. Much will depend on whether and how President Bush and Defense Secretary Dick Cheney press the Reagan-era fights for higher spending and advanced systems such as the strategic defense initiative (SDI).

Under the ineffectual Price, Dickinson sometimes acted as de facto chairman of Armed Services. He took the lead and credit on many issues; during tours of bases and installations, military officials often thanked Dickinson first for his efforts to procure some new weapon or additional equipment.

But with the 1985 accession of Aspin and his cadre of activist moderates, committee politics became more complicated. The panel's longstanding bipartisan consensus in favor of most Pentagon requests no longer existed; Dickinson had to thread his way among the traditional hawks, liberal arms control proponents and Aspin's aggressive centrists — all of them mutually suspicious in the wake of Price's ouster and the near-successful coup against Aspin two years later.

Deaths and retirements during the 100th Congress considerably depleted the ranks of old Democratic hawks on the committee, while Aspin solidified his control with a broad, middle-of-the-road majority.

Meanwhile, Dickinson's own stance on defense was growing more complex. Once a solid, pro-Pentagon vote, he took an increasingly independent approach during the Reagan administration, as deficits mounted along with evidence of Pentagon procurement fraud. At the outset of the Reagan military buildup in 1981, Dickinson issued a warning about Pentagon spending that seems particularly apt today: "We will only be able to retain public support," he said, "if we can show that the funds are spent wisely."

By the time Reagan's tenure was drawing to a close, Dickinson was often a part of Aspin's broad coalition, anchoring its right flank. That was illustrated during the committee's smooth, businesslike day of drafting the defense authorization bill in 1988. It was Dickinson's amendment that reduced Reagan's request for his top-priority SDI from $4.9 billion to $4.1 billion — "something I can live with" in view of budget constraints, Dickinson said. Over Dickinson's opposition, that amount later was reduced further to $3.5 billion in the full House, which remains much more liberal than Armed Services despite the panel's recent changes.

In late 1986, Dickinson was quick to blast Reagan's still-unreleased fiscal 1988 defense budget. He complained publicly that "it shafts the Army" by slowing production of conventional weapons in order to pay for big-ticket items such as SDI, nuclear-powered naval aircraft carriers and state-of-the-art helicopters. He doggedly, and successfully, fought to restore funds for the M-1 tank, Bradley troop carriers and Apache and Blackhawk helicopters.

When Navy Secretary James H. Webb Jr. resigned to protest Reagan's fiscal 1989 defense budget, which complied with reductions that Reagan had previously negotiated with congressional leaders, Dickinson — a former Navy man himself — led the ho-hum response. "If anybody's living in fat city, it's been the Navy for the past few years," he snapped.

Although supportive of Reagan's requests for military aid to the Nicaraguan contras, Dickinson publicly suggested the administration make more efforts toward diplomacy in the region.

The Aspin-Dickinson axis turns on a general agreement that defense spending must be restrained, while protecting conventional forces

Alabama 2

Southeast — Montgomery; Dothan

Most of the 2nd, which covers the southeast corner of Alabama, is rural territory. But half the population is concentrated in two urban centers at opposite corners of the district.

At the northwest edge is Montgomery County, with more than 200,000 people. The city of Montgomery has long been a national Republican stronghold in Alabama, voting for GOP presidential candidates as far back as 1956.

Montgomery was the first capital of the Confederacy, and to many the city represents the Fort Sumter of the civil rights movement. In 1955, when a black woman named Rosa Parks refused to give up her bus seat to a white man, her arrest resulted in a boycott led by the Rev. Dr. Martin Luther King Jr. and the end of bus segregation.

With the state Capitol crucial to its economy, Montgomery is largely a white-collar town with a government-oriented work force. Nearby Maxwell and Gunter Air Force bases employ nearly 10,000 people.

At the southeastern corner of the district, near the Florida and Georgia borders, is the Houston County seat of Dothan, a city of more than 50,000. Originally a cotton and peanut market town, Dothan has grown and diversified by attracting new industries, including large plants run by Michelin and Sony. Largely non-union, the Dothan plants represent most of the large industry in the 2nd District.

Although Houston County was always fiercely loyal to George C. Wallace, it has been voting regularly for conservative Republicans in other contests over the last decade. In 1986, GOP gubernatorial candidate Guy Hunt won it with 63 percent.

Fort Rucker, where many Army and Air Force helicopter pilots and crews are trained, is northwest of Dothan in Dale County. More than 11,000 military and civilian personnel work at Fort Rucker.

Between these two population centers are the Piney Woods of Alabama and a portion of the state's Black Belt. Sparsely populated, the area grows more peanuts than almost any region in the country, although cotton is still cultivated. As a testament to the success of peanuts, the town of Enterprise in Coffee County erected a monument to the boll weevil, the insect whose destruction of the cotton crop in the early part of the century convinced farmers to switch to peanuts.

Rural Barbour and Bullock counties, George C. Wallace's original home base, have large black populations and are loyally Democratic. But farther south, the black population drops and chances for GOP success increase. The four mostly rural counties around Houston County went Republican in the 1986 Senate and gubernatorial elections as well as in the 1988 presidential race.

Population: 549,505. White 376,259 (69%), Black 168,913 (31%), Other 2,879 (1%). Spanish origin 5,731 (1%). 18 and over 383,150 (70%), 65 and over 64,624 (12%). Median age: 29.

from being cannibalized to pay for expensive new technology. But on several major issues, notably arms control, it regularly breaks down.

In 1987, for instance, the two men agreed that Reagan's $312 billion defense budget was too expensive, but Dickinson resisted Aspin's effort to cut the panel's own $306 billion alternative down to the $289 billion demanded by the Budget Committee. "We are cutting into the bone and sinew of our defense establishment," he complained. During a closed-door committee session, he reportedly grabbed an American flag and marched about the room in protest. Dickinson's viewpoint prevailed on the panel, but the House later made the cuts.

With some success, Dickinson has pushed to fund a rail-mobile launching system for the multi-warhead MX missile. That has put him on the same side as both the White House and the Senate, but against Aspin and a House majority. House Democrats favor the smaller single-warhead Midgetman missile, believing it to be less vulnerable than the huge MX. Also over Aspin's opposition, Dickinson has espoused funding for the anti-satellite missile (ASAT).

For three years running, through 1988, their biggest fights occurred not in committee but on the floor, where arms control advocates prevailed. In 1986, when Aspin acquiesced to his party's liberals and accepted amendments to that year's defense bill calling for a nuclear test ban, chemical weapons ban and continued compliance with the unratified SALT II arms treaty, Dickinson voted against the measure on final passage.

A showdown came in 1988. When the House added the usual arms control amendments to the defense authorization bill, while Reagan was preparing for a meeting with Soviet leader Mikhail S. Gorbachev, Dickinson led conservatives in recommending that the president veto the measure. Reagan did so, despite contrary advice to sign it from Senate GOP leaders and his own defense and national security advisers. The legislative standoff lasted nearly two months, until both sides agreed to a compromise that made minor, face-saving changes.

Just as Aspin faces pressure from his party caucus, so does Dickinson occasionally from the Republican side. He joined with Aspin in 1988 in trying to keep the defense bill free of controversial amendments that would enlist the military in the war on drugs. But ultimately, Dickinson was forced by the House GOP right to carry the most controversial proposal of all by piggybacking it onto one of his own relatively minor amendments for increased Coast Guard equipment. The sweeping new amendment ordered the Pentagon to "substantially halt the unlawful penetration of United States borders by aircraft and vessels carrying narcotics." It passed easily, but later was weakened in the Senate.

Dickinson is not known as a detail man, and he is further handicapped on Armed Services by weak Republicans at the top and restiveness lower in the ranks. But he can be a tough, sarcastic debater; when critics of chemical warfare once tried to argue that world opinion was against it, he remarked, "If the Soviets start to roll and use their chemical agents, we will hit them with an opinion poll. That will stop them in their tracks."

Dickinson has used his position both to see the world and to direct federal defense dollars into his district, home to the Maxwell-Gunter Air Force complex in Montgomery and a helicopter flight-training center at Fort Rucker. Whatever the future of SDI, he is intent on helping his state get its share of work; in a 1987 invitation to local businesses for a how-to briefing on snaring contracts, Dickinson wrote, "Already contractors throughout Huntsville are realizing the boon provided by the new industry of developing a missile defense."

His focus on defense in recent years has overshadowed all else. Dickinson also is the senior Republican in years of service on the House Administration Committee, but he has yielded the "ranking" seat there because party rules allow members to hold the top position on only one panel. Outside his committees, Dickinson tends to the interests of his district's cotton and peanut farmers.

On social issues he is an ardent conservative, although he has moderated from the days since he came into office on Barry Goldwater's coattails, pledging to combat the Great Society and the civil rights movement. While Dickinson voted against Medicare when it was created in 1965, in 1987 he publicly hailed passage of legislation extending coverage to catastrophic illnesses, the biggest expansion of the program since its creation.

His rhetoric of earlier days also has moderated. Though strong words still can obscure his good nature, Dickinson has never again invited the sort of furor that accompanied his 1965 House speech against the civil rights protestors on the Selma-to-Montgomery march. He called the marchers "human flotsam" and "communist dupes" for whom "drunkenness and sex orgies were the order of the day." Lawmakers walked off the floor in protest, some newspapers back home criticized him and Dickinson later conceded he may have erred and had none of the proof he had promised.

At Home: Dickinson has converted his upset victory in the turbulent 1964 Goldwater election into a long-term congressional career. Though it took him 20 years to make the seat secure — he won with 55 percent of the vote or less in five of his first 10 elections — Dickinson has won re-election with increasing ease since 1984.

Dickinson represents a primarily rural, traditionally Democratic area of Alabama. Over the years, his conservative Democratic opponents often received the active support of former Gov. George C. Wallace, whose original home base is Barbour County, at the eastern end of the 2nd.

Dickinson has embellished his conservative credentials with blessings from prominent figures such as the Rev. Jerry Falwell, and he has been able to establish a solid base of support in the population centers of the district, Montgomery and Dothan.

In 1982, however, Dickinson's urban base was barely enough. As Wallace's longtime press secretary and president of the state Public Service Commission, Democratic challenger Billy Joe Camp had excellent name identification. Camp was not an aggressive campaigner and did not have much money. But he benefited from Wallace's presence on the ballot as the gubernatorial nominee. That and a double-digit unemployment rate were nearly enough to send Camp to Congress.

With Camp carrying nine of the district's 13 counties, Dickinson had to run more than 10,000 votes ahead in the Montgomery and Dothan areas to eke out a 1,386-vote victory. It was the smallest margin of his House career.

There was real concern in Republican ranks that Camp would try again in 1984, and that a high black turnout generated by the presidential contest might mean disaster for Dickinson. Those fears turned out to be groundless. Camp, one of a handful of Wallace confidants with wide latitude in running the state, lost interest in coming to Washington. No top-name Democrat stepped forward to replace him. And any increase in the black vote was more than canceled out by the Reagan surge among white voters. Dickinson won with a comfortable 60 percent.

A Democratic circuit judge in Lee County

for four years, Dickinson quit the bench in 1963 to become assistant vice president of the Southern Railroad. But his stay in the business world was brief. He filed for the House just as Goldwater was launching his presidential campaign, and when Goldwater swept Alabama in November 1964, Dickinson easily unseated Democratic Rep. George M. Grant.

Grant had a conservative record, but Dickinson managed to associate him with the national Democratic ticket, which not only was unpopular in the state but also was excluded from an official position at the top of the ballot.

Committees

Armed Services (Ranking)
Research and Development (ranking); Military Installations and Facilities

House Administration (2nd of 8 Republicans)
Office Systems; Personnel and Police

Elections

1988 General

Bill Dickinson (R)	120,408	(94%)
Joel Brooke King (LIB)	7,352	(6%)

1986 General

Bill Dickinson (R)	115,302	(67%)
Mercer Stone (D)	57,568	(33%)

Previous Winning Percentages: **1984** (60%) **1982** (50%) **1980** (61%) **1978** (54%) **1976** (58%) **1974** (66%) **1972** (55%) **1970** (61%) **1968** (55%) **1966** (55%) **1964** (62%)

District Vote For President

	1988	1984	1980	1976
D	71,335 (37%)	73,603 (36%)	83,720 (44%)	88,208 (53%)
R	118,794 (62%)	130,370 (63%)	99,283 (53%)	75,528 (46%)

Campaign Finance

	Receipts	Receipts from PACs	Expend-itures
1988			
Dickinson (R)	$304,708	$168,639 (55%)	$234,923
1986			
Dickinson (R)	$381,367	$180,581 (47%)	$245,555
Stone (D)	$10,542	0	$10,015

Key Votes

1987	
Raise speed limit to 65 mph	Y
Approve Gephardt "fair trade" amendment	N
Ban testing of larger nuclear weapons	N
Delay "re-flagging" of Kuwaiti tankers	N
Approve tax-raising deficit-reduction bill	N
1988	
Approve aid to Nicaraguan contras	Y
Enact civil rights restoration bill over Reagan veto	N
Kill 60-day plant-closing notification measure	Y
Pass omnibus trade bill over Reagan veto	N
Approve death penalty for drug-related murders	Y
Bar federal funds for abortions in cases of rape and incest	N
Oppose seven-day waiting period for purchase of handguns	Y

Voting Studies

	Presidential Support		Party Unity		Conservative Coalition	
Year	S	O	S	O	S	O
1988	63	34	83	9	95	3
1987	64	26	78	13	84	5
1986	71	22	78	14	88	2
1985	63	36	76	17	85	9
1984	64	26	72	18	90	5
1983	78	16	75	17	83	10
1982	75	14	76	11	89	4
1981	72	16	77	14	81	7

Interest Group Ratings

Year	ADA	ACU	AFL-CIO	CCUS
1988	20	92	38	100
1987	16	76	19	86
1986	15	86	38	73
1985	10	65	18	82
1984	10	84	23	60
1983	0	81	6	94
1982	0	100	0	84
1981	5	100	27	100

3 Glen Browder (D)

Of Jacksonville — Elected 1989

Born: Jan. 15, 1943, Sumter, S.C.
Education: Presbyterian College, B.A. 1965; Emory U., M.A. 1971, Ph.D. 1971.
Occupation: College professor; public official.
Family: Wife, Rebecca Moore; one child.
Religion: Methodist.
Political Career: Ala. House, 1983-87; Ala. secretary of state, 1987-89.
Capitol Office: 1630 Longworth Bldg. 20515; 225-3261.

The Path to Washington: Browder is something of an anomaly — a soft-spoken political scientist with a knack for the rough-and-tumble of politics. In seeking the seat of veteran Democratic Rep. Bill Nichols (who died in December 1988), Browder's rivals portrayed him as a labor-backed liberal outside the 3rd's conservative mainstream. But with sharp campaign advertising, Browder put them down.

He made it out of the crowded Democratic primary in February with assistance from an "attack" ad that portrayed his chief conservative rivals as proponents of big tax increases. In the April special election, he overwhelmed his GOP opponent, state Sen. John Rice, with the help of an ad that exploited Rice's nickname of "Hand Grenade."

That Browder beat Rice, a Democrat-turned-Republican, was no surprise. That he beat Rice by a margin of nearly 2-to-1 was. Browder had not been able to get the endorsement of any of his conservative Democratic primary rivals, and Rice pounded away at him as "Professor" Browder, a "Michael Dukakis liberal."

But Browder maintained he was a "conservative Bill Nichols Democrat" — opposed to abortion, in favor of the death penalty — and subtly emphasized that he was a family man by introducing his wife at campaign events (Rice was divorced). Browder's "hand grenade" spots depicted Rice as a radical right-winger.

Outspent by Browder and without much TV advertising, Rice became desperate. He intimated that Browder was a draft dodger during the Vietnam War (Browder said he got a deferment for a congenital back problem), and he charged that Browder was not a true son of the South because he had not supported legislation to keep the Confederate flag flying atop the Alabama Capitol. Rice waved a small Confederate flag during one debate.

In a district that George Bush had won with 60 percent of the vote in 1988, the election was widely viewed as a promising opportunity for Republicans to demonstrate their appeal in Dixie below the presidential level. But seemingly leery of Rice's chances, the national GOP never gave him a public embrace. No leading administration figure appeared in the district.

Meanwhile, nearly all the daily newspapers that made endorsements went for Browder, and he had the support of the AFL-CIO, a potent ally in a district with some 20,000 union members.

Browder came slowly to politics. After graduating from Presbyterian College in South Carolina in 1965, he moved to Atlanta, first working as a sportswriter for the *Atlanta Journal* and then as an investigator for the U.S. Civil Service Commission. But it was not long before Browder returned to college, earning his doctorate in political science at Emory University. With that, he landed a job on the faculty at Jacksonville State University, where he found time to dabble in polling, research and political consulting.

In 1982, Browder ran for an open seat in the Alabama House, emerging victorious from a crowded primary field. He stayed four years, gaining attention for a controversial "career ladder" teacher pay and evaluation plan that he promoted. The measure became law, but drew criticism for being too costly and time-consuming to administer; it was soon repealed.

Browder took a calculated risk in 1986 when he left the Legislature to run for secretary of state against Annie Laurie Gunter, a George Wallace ally and the outgoing state treasurer. Out-organizing his better-known rival, Browder won the pivotal Democratic primary.

Once in office, he successfully lobbied the Legislature for stricter campaign-finance disclosure, which required candidates to make pre-election reports of campaign contributions.

When Nichols died suddenly of a heart attack, Browder was well positioned to go for the 3rd. The lone statewide official in the race, he had high name recognition across the rural, 13-county district. Browder's biggest test was the nine-man Democratic primary; with the help of the ads and labor, he ran first with 25 percent of the vote. After that, Browder had few problems, easily winning a placid runoff against Tuskegee's black mayor, Johnny Ford, and the special election against Rice.

Alabama 3

East — Anniston; Auburn

Taking in the eastern side of the state from the outskirts of Montgomery to the hilly Piedmont Plateau, the 3rd is a conservative rural stronghold.

Textile mills dot the 3rd's landscape, reflecting the traditional prominence of cotton in the area's agricultural economy. Some of the textile workers have been unionized.

There is heavy industry in Anniston, the seat of Calhoun County. With a population of 30,000, Anniston is one of the district's largest cities. It is also home to two huge military facilities, Fort McClellan and the Anniston Army Depot, which repairs small arms and almost all of the Army's tanks and transport vehicles. Several somewhat smaller cities are sprinkled in the southeastern corner of the 3rd, near the Georgia border. The largest is Auburn (Lee County), home of Auburn University. The school has grown from a small land grant agricultural college to become the largest university in the state, with 19,500 students. Its veterinary school and agricultural experimentation station have provided valuable services to local farmers, who raise cotton and cattle. Not far from Auburn is the Lee County seat of Opelika, site of a large Uniroyal rubber factory. And a half-hour's drive from Opelika is Phenix City (Russell County), a suburb of Columbus, Ga.

A notable monument of black culture is located in adjoining Macon County — Tuskegee University, founded in 1881 by Booker T. Washington as one of the nation's first black colleges. In 1968, the city of Tuskegee elected the first black sheriff in the South and the first two black members in the Alabama Legislature. Blacks comprise 84 percent of the population in Macon County, a higher share than any other county in the country, according to the 1980 census. But Macon is the only county in the 3rd with a black majority; districtwide, blacks make up 28 percent of the population.

The towns in the southwestern part of the district, particularly in Elmore County, serve as bedroom communities for the state capital, Montgomery, just across the district line.

Although most voters here consider themselves Democrats and would not think of sending anyone but a Democrat to the state Legislature, statewide Republican candidates can do fairly well — especially in the more urbanized areas, such as Anniston in the north and Auburn and Opelika in the south. Republican Jeremiah Denton carried all three of these communities in his 1980 Senate race, and even in his 1986 loss, he carried more than half of the counties in the 3rd.

Population: 555,321. White 395,332 (71%), Black 156,665 (28%). Spanish origin 5,232 (1%). 18 and over 390,418 (70%), 65 and over 61,108 (11%). Median age: 28.

Committees

Public Works and Transportation (30th of 31 Democrats)
Economic Development; Water Resources

Science, Space and Technology (30th of 30 Democrats)
Science, Research and Technology

Campaign Finance

	Receipts	Receipts from PACs	Expend-itures
1989 Special Election			
Browder (D)	$590,692	$354,100 (60%)	$573,964
Rice (R)	$450,221	$111,250 (25%)	$443,927

Elections

1989 Special Election		
Glen Browder (D)	47,294	(65%)
John Rice (R)	25,142	(35%)
1989 Special Primary Runoff		
Glen Browder (D)	44,647	(63%)
Johnny Ford (D)	26,318	(37%)
1989 Special Primary		
Glen Browder (D)	14,715	(25%)
Johnny Ford (D)	14,440	(24%)
Jim Preuitt (D)	10,184	(17%)
Charles Adams (D)	9,851	(17%)
Gerald Dial (D)	5,882	(10%)
Donald Holmes (D)	3,908	(7%)

District Vote For President

	1988	1984	1980	1976
D	67,936 (38%)	70,024 (37%)	86,753 (50%)	90,034 (58%)
R	106,069 (60%)	113,641 (61%)	80,051 (46%)	62,198 (40%)

4 Tom Bevill (D)

Of Jasper — Elected 1966

Born: March 27, 1921, Townley, Ala.
Education: U. of Alabama, B.S. 1943, LL.B. 1948.
Military Career: Army, 1943-46.
Occupation: Lawyer.
Family: Wife, Lou Betts; three children.
Religion: Baptist.
Political Career: Ala. House, 1959-67; sought Democratic nomination for U.S. House, 1964.
Capitol Office: 2302 Rayburn Bldg. 20515; 225-4876.

In Washington: In the budget-conscious 1980s it has been popular to attack public works projects as wasteful "pork-barrel" spending. But amidst pressures for austerity, Bevill, as chairman of the Energy and Water Development Subcommittee at Appropriations, has regularly produced legislation channeling billions of dollars into those very projects.

Bevill has always treated public works as a personal creed. This is understandable, since much of north Alabama was brought to economic health during the Depression by projects of the Tennessee Valley Authority (TVA). "There is no question," Bevill says, "that water-resources projects have helped develop the nation." He says every dollar invested in flood control has reaped benefits many times over.

When a new national issue seizes the public consciousness, Bevill looks for ways to tie it to the need for water projects. Usually he finds some, as he has recently in the case of trade. He talks about how important waterways and ports are to the nation's trading capacity. "We must consider that investment in modernizing our waterway system is an investment in the future," Bevill says. "Without that, we are more likely to lag behind other nations in the trade arena."

Bevill has encountered some vocal opponents to his appropriations bills, but they are often louder than they are strong. In 1987, the energy and water bill was the first appropriations measure to reach the floor, and as such it was a prime target for budget-cutters. But when they attempted to trim 1.7 percent from every program in the bill, Bevill won 276-143.

Bevill also fended off another in a long series of attacks on the Appalachian Regional Commission (ARC). Only 82 members voted to cut $110 million from highways and projects under ARC, a remnant of the 1960s "War on Poverty" that has long pumped funds into the 4th District.

Bevill's success is not too surprising, given the nature of his legislation, which touches districts all around the country. Bevill is as gentlemanly as anyone in the House, and not the type to make open threats of retaliation against opponents, but more than a few members are aware of the power that he has to deny funds that might otherwise come their way.

In recent years, White Houses, both Democratic and Republican, also have witnessed Bevill's power. Although President Reagan was consistent in his efforts to reduce water-project funding, he was never willing to go to war with Congress over it. That was in part a legacy of Bevill's success in fending off similar efforts by President Carter. In 1977, when the Carter administration tried to cancel 18 projects it said were too expensive and environmentally damaging, Bevill and his committee manned the trenches. They agreed to kill only one project and took the battle to the floor.

The House majority supporting the Bevill forces was not enough to override Carter's threatened veto, and Carter eventually did stop funding for some of the least-popular projects. But in the long run, Bevill was the winner. The fight cost Carter enough political capital to cause any president, even Reagan, to think hard about slashing the public works budget.

There is, however, some evidence of the more restrained budgetary climate in Bevill's water work. In 1988, he had to labor to repress members' desires to build new projects, and produced a bill that provided funding just for ongoing projects. "This has been the most difficult appropriations bill we have put together," Bevill said of the legislation, which was billed as the most austere energy and water bill in memory. With $17.8 billion in funding, it was also the biggest in memory.

Bevill has become inured to the accusations that he is an advocate of "pork-barrel" legislation, but he is sensitive to the criticism. He changed the name of his subcommittee several years ago from "Public Works" to "Energy and Water Development" because the original name had such unpopular connotations.

"Energy was very popular. We thought we could pick up a few votes that way," Bevill said. "It worked. But I still like the term 'public works.' "

Alabama 4

North Central — Gadsden

Stretching across northern Alabama, the 4th is mostly rural, traditionally poor and overwhelmingly white. With a black population of only 7 percent, it has a different character from districts farther south.

The 4th has a long populist Democratic heritage. The "common man" rhetoric of former Gov. James E. Folsom Sr. (who grew up in the 4th's Cullman County) always played well in this region. When the racial tensions of the civil rights era caused Alabama politicians to emphasize segregation over agrarian populism, voters in this area went along, but race-baiting here was never as virulent as in other parts of Alabama because of the small black population.

Bevill's easy elections testify to the continuing dominance of the Democratic Party in the 4th, but recent developments point to some changes in the area's political complexion. During the 1970s, new residents moved into the 4th at a faster pace than into any other Alabama district, and many of the newcomers vote Republican. Two counties on the fringe of metropolitan Birmingham — Blount and St. Clair — supported Republican Jeremiah Denton in both his Senate races; even in his 1986 defeat, five other rural counties also backed Denton. George Bush carried 12 of the district's 14 counties in 1988. Another son of Cullman County now sits in the governor's chair — Republican Guy Hunt.

There is a GOP presence in the district dating to the Civil War. Winston County actually seceded from Alabama when the state seceded from the Union. The so-called "free state of Winston" is the home of Judge Frank M. Johnson Jr., who gained fame during the late 1950s and '60s for landmark decisions on desegregation and mental patients' rights.

The largest concentration of die-hard Democrats is in and around the district's largest city, Gadsden, an industrial center of 45,000 people in Etowah County. Smokestacks from Gulf States Steel and Goodyear Tire belch fumes, and the unionized labor force consistently votes Democratic; Etowah County gave 56 percent to 1986 Democratic gubernatorial nominee Bill Baxley, who lost badly statewide. In 1988, Michael S. Dukakis nearly carried Etowah over George Bush in the presidential contest.

The western part of the 4th contains coal mines, and the United Mine Workers exerts a strong influence for Democratic candidates. Walker County (Jasper) is the state's leading coal producer.

The 1985 completion of the Tennessee-Tombigbee waterway — it cuts through Pickens County, in the district's southwestern corner — provides a new means of transport from the mines to the port of Mobile.

Population: 562,088. White 519,706 (92%), Black 40,660 (7%). Spanish origin 3,200 (1%). 18 and over 397,076 (71%), 65 and over 71,872 (13%). Median age: 31.

Semantics and labeling aside, Bevill has shown as chairman that he is more than a business-as-usual pork-barreler. His panel has become a haven for some new types of pork; Bevill, for instance, takes a strong interest in the high-technology projects that fall under his jurisdiction.

Bevill keeps an eye on his district's public works interests even when his subcommittee does not have jurisdiction. He strongly supported the water-projects bill reported by the Public Works Committee in the 99th Congress. When the bill became law in October 1986, it authorized two of Bevill's pet projects: $225 million for the deepening of Mobile Harbor, and $150 million for lock and dam replacement on Alabama's Black Warrior and Tombigbee rivers.

Each of these projects relates to the one that is dearest to Bevill: the Tennessee-Tombigbee, a massive barge canal that cuts through Alabama on its way to the Gulf of Mexico. Bevill is an emotional defender of the $3 billion waterway, which finally opened in 1985 after years of controversy.

Funding the canal demanded Bevill's eternal vigilance; opponents offered numerous amendments to delete money for the "Tenn-Tom." In 1980, an amendment to cancel funding for the project lost by 20 votes on the House floor; the next year it was 10 votes.

Tennessee-Tombigbee ultimately survived thanks to a trade-off with the embattled Clinch River nuclear breeder reactor in Tennessee, which Bevill long supported. For much of 1982, Bevill and his allies managed to stall floor votes on either project. Late in the year, however, the Bevill side agreed to a vote on Clinch River, and in return environmentalists did not press for one on Tennessee-Tombigbee. The House voted to block funding for Clinch River, and with the 1984 retirement of Tennessee Sen. Howard H. Baker Jr., the breeder reactor lost its most powerful protector.

Tom Bevill, D-Ala.

At Home: It was not a smooth political road that led Bevill to Congress, but he has been on easy street since arriving: Only in his first election in 1966 did he fall below 70 percent of the vote.

Bevill was elected to the Alabama Legislature in 1958, and served as a floor leader for Gov. George C. Wallace. But he lost his first congressional race in 1964, when incumbent Carl Elliott defeated him in the Democratic primary by more than 3-to-2.

Two years later, the district was open. Republican James D. Martin, who had defeated Elliott in November 1964, was running for governor. Elliott did not want to try again.

Bevill entered a four-way Democratic primary that included a popular state representative, Gary Burns, and a former Wallace press secretary, Bill Jones. He led the first round with 36 percent of the vote, and his strength in the western part of the district gave him a runoff victory over Burns with 56 percent.

The general election was much simpler. Bevill beat Republican Wayman Sherrer, the little-known Blount County solicitor, by nearly 2-to-1 — a margin similar to the one by which Martin was losing the governorship to Lurleen B. Wallace.

Since then, Bevill has won every Democratic primary with at least 80 percent of the vote and every general election with at least 70 percent. Generally, his opposition has come from political novices.

His only prominent challenger was Jim Folsom Jr., son of the colorful ex-governor, who made his political debut in 1976 by opposing Bevill for renomination. It was a flop. Bevill drew more than 80 percent.

Committee

Appropriations (8th of 35 Democrats)
Energy and Water Development (chairman); Interior and Related Agencies; Military Construction

Elections

1988 General

Tom Bevill (D)	131,880	(96%)
John Sebastian (LIB)	5,264	(4%)

1986 General

Tom Bevill (D)	132,881	(78%)
Al DeShazo (R)	38,588	(22%)

Previous Winning Percentages: **1984** (100%) **1982** (100%) **1980** (98%) **1978** (100%) **1976** (80%) **1974** (100%) **1972** (70%) **1970** (100%) **1968** (76%) **1966** (64%)

District Vote For President

	1988	1984	1980	1976
D	83,042 (42%)	80,463 (40%)	104,802 (52%)	121,138 (65%)
R	111,528 (57%)	119,562 (59%)	91,768 (46%)	63,181 (34%)

Campaign Finance

	Receipts	Receipts from PACs	Expend-itures
1988			
Bevill (D)	$206,806	$94,850 (46%)	$130,642
1986			
Bevill (D)	$228,724	$107,471 (47%)	$149,263
DeShazo (R)	$9,904	0	$10,287

Key Votes

1987	
Raise speed limit to 65 mph	Y
Approve Gephardt "fair trade" amendment	Y
Ban testing of larger nuclear weapons	N
Delay "re-flagging" of Kuwaiti tankers	?
Approve tax-raising deficit-reduction bill	N
1988	
Approve aid to Nicaraguan contras	Y
Enact civil rights restoration bill over Reagan veto	Y
Kill 60-day plant-closing notification measure	N
Pass omnibus trade bill over Reagan veto	Y
Prohibit District of Columbia from financing abortions	Y
Approve death penalty for drug-related murders	Y
Oppose seven-day waiting period for purchase of handguns	Y

Voting Studies

	Presidential Support		Party Unity		Conservative Coalition	
Year	**S**	**O**	**S**	**O**	**S**	**O**
1988	31	58	71	19	71	11
1987	39	46	71	19	74	16
1986	40	58	67	26	82	18
1985	54	39	66	22	80	15
1984	53	35	55	29	83	7
1983	37	54	62	31	80	17
1982	55	44	70	26	75	19
1981	54	42	54	42	79	11

Interest Group Ratings

Year	ADA	ACU	AFL-CIO	CCUS
1988	45	50	100	46
1987	36	41	75	40
1986	40	50	79	29
1985	25	57	53	35
1984	35	50	58	43
1983	55	43	88	32
1982	20	59	74	47
1981	25	40	71	28

5 Ronnie G. Flippo (D)

Of Florence — Elected 1976

Born: Aug. 15, 1937, Florence, Ala.
Education: U. of North Alabama, B.S. 1965; U. of Alabama, M.A. 1966.
Occupation: Accountant.
Family: Wife, Faye Cooper; six children.
Religion: Church of Christ.
Political Career: Ala. House, 1971-75; Ala. Senate, 1975-77.
Capitol Office: 2334 Rayburn Bldg. 20515; 225-4801.

In Washington: Winning a seat on the House Administration Committee is not always seen as a sign of a legislator's growing influence, but in Flippo's case it was symbolic of the alliance he has formed with one of the most powerful Democrats in the House. Ways and Means Chairman Dan Rostenkowski fought in the Democratic Caucus in late 1988 to place a representative on the panel that oversees committee budgets, and when he got it, he entrusted it to Flippo, who had proven his loyalty during three terms on the tax-writing committee.

As one of the few certified public accountants in the House, Flippo already had an interest in the shape of the tax code when he joined Ways and Means in the 98th Congress. He put that expertise to work when the committee took up tax revision in the 99th Congress, and he cooperated with Rostenkowski to get much of what he wanted in the tax code.

Some of his work flowed from his personal background. Flippo, whose father died after a construction accident and who himself suffered a serious fall when he was an ironworker, has always had an interest in workers' compensation. When there was talk during the tax debate of taxing workers' compensation benefits, Flippo gave an impassioned speech on the subject before the committee and lobbied successfully to have it taken off the table.

Flippo also worked on behalf of his fellow accountants during the tax debate. The committee voted to prevent businesses with gross receipts exceeding $5 million from using cash accounting — a procedure by which income is declared at the time cash is received and deductions taken when an expense is actually paid. Flippo managed to exempt professionals, such as lawyers and accountants.

But Flippo's most conspicuous effort during the tax overhaul came when he departed from his cooperation with Rostenkowski and pushed a provision to give an important tax advantage to banks. The move outraged Rostenkowski and briefly threatened to bring the tax-revision effort to a halt, but ultimately Flippo's effort proved unsuccessful.

Rostenkowski and the Reagan administration wanted to restrict the deductions banks could take for reserves held to cover bad debts, but Flippo initially won a 17-13 vote in committee for a proposal to expand the deduction — at a cost of $4.8 billion more than existing law over a five-year period, and $7.6 billion more than Rostenkowski's plan.

Faced with criticism that his proposal was a blatant special-interest amendment that undermined the effort to produce a revenue-neutral bill, Flippo argued that the provision was needed because taxes on banks would be raised overall.

"This is only one item in a series of items [in the bill] that taken together will raise taxes on the banking industry," he said. "With that kind of impact you have to be concerned about the stability of the banking industry. We see far too many banks going out of business."

Flippo's victory was short-lived. The committee soon reversed its vote, removing the expanded deduction. But the effort underscored the fact that Flippo, despite his labor background, has some fondness for corporate interests. Business lobbyists frequently turn to Flippo when they are unable to get help from some of the committee's more senior members.

Flippo's district is one of the few in the Deep South with a history of moderate representation, and during his House career he has managed to balance an overall tilt to the right with his concern for the views of labor — and an occasional gesture to his party's leadership. His outward appearance seems to reflect his legislative personality. He combines a "good ol' boy" Southern manner with a fondness for conservative three-piece suits and a low-key style in public.

Flippo had labor support in his first campaign, and he has occasionally broken with orthodox Southern Democratic thinking to return the favor, although he has not been as union-oriented as his predecessor. Shortly after he arrived in the House, Flippo opposed the common-site picketing bill that labor badly wanted. In the 100th Congress he voted to kill

Alabama 5

North — Huntsville

The Tennessee River runs through all seven counties of this district at the northern end of the state. Nearly half a century of resource development by the Tennessee Valley Authority (TVA) has contributed to the prosperity of this region, and the federal government remains the largest employer.

With large federal installations in Huntsville and active labor unions in the metals, automobile and chemical plants along the Tennessee River, the 5th has more national Democratic sympathies than other parts of Alabama. Because of the small black population (14 percent), race has rarely been a polarizing issue. In 1980 Jimmy Carter won 54 percent here, his best mark in the state. Even in 1988, as Michael S. Dukakis was being trounced statewide, he managed to carry three of the district's seven counties.

Huntsville, the seat of Madison County, was the only part of the district to side with Reagan against Carter in 1980, and that was by a very slim margin. But the GOP has picked up strength as Madison County's population has grown by nearly 20 percent since then. In 1986, Madison voted solidly Republican in the Senate and gubernatorial elections, and in 1988, the county went for George Bush by better than 2-to-1 over Dukakis.

With more than 160,000 people, Huntsville is the state's fourth-largest city and has a predominantly white-collar work force. It became a boom town during World War II when the Army, largely through the efforts of Sen. John J. Sparkman, a Huntsville native, built the Redstone Arsenal there to produce chemical-warfare material. After the war, the Army used the plant for rocket research under the direction of Wernher von Braun. After the Soviet Union launched Sputnik in October 1957, von Braun headed the Marshall Space Flight Center in Huntsville to perform the principal research for the fledgling National Aeronautics and Space Administration.

Companies that built plants in Huntsville — Boeing, International Business Machines and General Electric among them — stayed and diversified when the high-tech government contracts dwindled. Other industries moved in, including Dunlop and PPG. However, the number of high-technology jobs is below the 1960s' peak.

As one moves downstream along the Tennessee River, blue-collar jobs begin to predominate. Towns such as Decatur and the Quad Cities of Florence, Sheffield, Tuscumbia and Muscle Shoals came into being as a result of the TVA. Muscle Shoals was originally selected as TVA headquarters; the site was later changed to Knoxville, Tenn. The TVA has two huge nuclear complexes in the 5th — Browns Ferry at Decatur and Bellefonte at Scottsboro — but activity at both sites has been stalled by ongoing problems in the agency's nuclear energy program. Browns Ferry generated power from 1973 through 1985, when the reactors were shut down to correct safety deficiencies. One reactor is expected to become operational in 1989. Construction of the Bellefonte reactors has been indefinitely delayed.

Population: 549,844. White 466,851 (85%), Black 78,639 (14%), Other 2,901 (1%). Spanish origin 4,270 (1%). 18 and over 385,388 (70%), 65 and over 51,538 (9%). Median age: 29.

legislation requiring businesses to give workers 60 days' notice before plant shutdowns. But later, he was one of two Alabama Democrats supporting plant-closing-notification provisions.

To get on Ways and Means, Flippo had to give up two other committee assignments — Public Works and Science and Technology. Most members would not hesitate to make that change, but Flippo was a bit apprehensive about leaving Public Works. The Tennessee Valley Authority is a dominant economic interest in northern Alabama, and residents of the 5th District were used to having a strong TVA advocate on Public Works. Flippo's predecessor in the 5th, Democrat Robert Jones, served as Public Works chairman.

But Flippo eased any ill feeling about the committee switch by continuing to pay assiduous attention to TVA. He has been an active member of the TVA caucus and does not hesitate to speak up on issues related to the federal utility. He has pushed steadily for legislation to make the TVA "more responsive" to the areas it serves by expanding the three-member board to include representatives from Alabama and other states. And Flippo has been critical of some TVA actions in recent years. When the board began considering selling off certain assets, he said: "I tell you one thing: TVA is not going to be sold. Let's get that straight right now."

At Home: It was a 55-foot fall that started Flippo on the way to Congress.

The product of a working-class family in the northern Alabama town of Florence, he headed straight for a construction job after high school even though his father had been killed on a construction job when Flippo was 7. "All my people were construction workers," he said years later. "I could climb with any of them and weld with any of them."

Flippo might still be climbing and welding as an ironworker if he had not lost his balance while working on a TVA steam plant one day in 1961. He crashed 30 feet into a steel girder, and then dropped another 25 onto a concrete floor, breaking his arms, legs and pelvic bone. Flippo was confined to bed for the next 18 months.

Barred from any hard labor after that by permanent damage to his knee, Flippo entered college at age 25 on the proceeds of his workmen's compensation, finished first in his class, and went on to a graduate degree in accounting. After three uncomfortable weeks in the New York office of Royal Dutch Shell, he returned home to start his own practice and talk politics at the local café. When the state legislator from Florence retired in 1971, Flippo's café cronies helped him win a seat in the Alabama House.

And when the veteran Jones decided to give up his seat in Congress in 1976, Flippo entered a 10-man race to succeed him. With the backing of organized labor and a strong base in Florence, Muscle Shoals and Sheffield, he ran first in the primary with 25 percent of the vote, then took the runoff by 16,000 votes over John Eyster, a conservative corporate lawyer.

Since then, Flippo has had an easy time. He has faced Republican opposition only three times — in 1982, 1986 and 1988 — and won overwhelmingly each time.

The absence of serious opposition has enabled Flippo to think about higher office. He considered running for the Senate in 1978 and for governor in 1982 before deciding to seek re-election to the House. In July 1989, Flippo formed an exploratory committee to lay the groundwork for a challenge to Republican Gov. Guy Hunt in 1990.

Committees

House Administration (11th of 13 Democrats)
Accounts; Libraries and Memorials; Procurement and Printing

Ways and Means (15th of 23 Democrats)
Oversight; Select Revenue Measures

Elections

1988 General		
Ronnie G. Flippo (D)	120,142	(64%)
Stan McDonald (R)	64,491	(35%)
1986 General		
Ronnie G. Flippo (D)	125,406	(79%)
Herb McCarley (R)	33,528	(21%)

Previous Winning Percentages: **1984** (96%) **1982** (81%) **1980** (94%) **1978** (97%) **1976** (100%)

District Vote For President

	1988	1984	1980	1976
D	77,172 (40%)	80,039 (40%)	96,169 (54%)	106,191 (67%)
R	111,763 (59%)	119,034 (59%)	72,831 (41%)	50,039 (32%)
I			3,746 (2%)	

Campaign Finance

	Receipts	Receipts from PACs	Expend-itures
1988			
Flippo (D)	$711,580	$445,960 (63%)	$504,570
McDonald (R)	$145,297	$14,594 (10%)	$145,327
1986			
Flippo (D)	$438,287	$286,891 (65%)	$172,356

Key Votes

1987	
Raise speed limit to 65 mph	N
Approve Gephardt "fair trade" amendment	Y
Ban testing of larger nuclear weapons	Y
Delay "re-flagging" of Kuwaiti tankers	N
Approve tax-raising deficit-reduction bill	Y
1988	
Approve aid to Nicaraguan contras	Y
Enact civil rights restoration bill over Reagan veto	Y
Kill 60-day plant-closing notification measure	Y
Pass omnibus trade bill over Reagan veto	Y
Approve death penalty for drug-related murders	Y
Bar federal funds for abortions in cases of rape and incest	N
Oppose seven-day waiting period for purchase of handguns	Y

Voting Studies

	Presidential Support		Party Unity		Conservative Coalition	
Year	S	O	S	O	S	O
1988	36	51	65	26	84	8
1987	37	61	67	27	91	7
1986	33	53	64	19	60	16
1985	45	46	69	24	76	13
1984	50	42	61	29	86	10
1983	45	46	57	35	80	13
1982	49	40	66	29	75	19
1981	59	32	53	39	79	11

Interest Group Ratings

Year	ADA	ACU	AFL-CIO	CCUS
1988	45	60	85	71
1987	44	26	63	47
1986	40	33	77	29
1985	35	58	53	43
1984	25	50	64	54
1983	55	41	81	47
1982	20	62	63	55
1981	20	53	73	38

6 Ben Erdreich (D)

Of Birmingham — Elected 1982

Born: Dec. 9, 1938, Birmingham, Ala.
Education: Yale U., B.A. 1960; U. of Alabama, J.D. 1963.
Military Career: Army, 1963-65.
Occupation: Lawyer.
Family: Wife, Ellen Cooper; two children.
Religion: Jewish.
Political Career: Ala. House, 1971-75; Jefferson County Commission, 1975-83; Democratic nominee for U.S. House, 1972.
Capitol Office: 439 Cannon Bldg. 20515; 225-4921.

In Washington: As a junior member of the House, Erdreich followed the unwritten rules of the Alabama delegation: Vote a relatively conservative line, work behind the scenes and wait your turn for a position of influence. But Erdreich wound up with such a position — a Banking subcommittee chairmanship — a bit ahead of schedule.

At the start of the 101st Congress, Erdreich was named acting chairman of the new Policy Research and Insurance Subcommittee, which was created during a Banking Committee reorganization. Two panels dealing with international finance had been merged, but the committee was loath to reduce the total number of subcommittees. The policy research panel was established, with the broad mandate to review problem issues in banking, finance, housing and insurance.

Erdreich was not the senior Democrat on the panel. But Robert Garcia of New York — who had chaired one of the international subcommittees but lost out to a more senior member after the merger — was barred from serving as chairman because of his indictment in the Wedtech bribery case. The next two in line — Bruce A. Morrison of Connecticut and Marcy Kaptur of Ohio — respectively opted to chair another panel's subcommittee and won a seat on the Budget Committee. The chairmanship thus fell to Erdreich.

Erdreich had served on Banking since his arrival in Congress. But his sudden rise to subcommittee chairman is a leap toward prominence for the low-key Democrat. He had mainly stayed in the background during contentious committee debates on such issues as the savings and loan crisis and housing aid.

Erdreich also rarely grabs for headlines back home, and when his name does appear, it is usually connected with a district-oriented issue. During the 100th Congress, Erdreich pushed through funding to plan the Northern Beltline, a highway in suburban Birmingham.

On defense and foreign policy issues, Erdreich voted with President Reagan often enough to maintain the comfort level of the 6th District's conservative majority. However, on domestic issues, Erdreich takes account of his large black constituency and the blue-collar workers in the district's steel industry. During the 100th Congress, he voted for the override of Reagan's veto of the Civil Rights Restoration Act, and for the Gephardt "fair trade" amendment to apply tough trade sanctions against nations that restrict U.S. access to their markets.

This balance is reflected in ratings Erdreich receives from interest groups. His 1988 rating of 50 from the Americans for Democratic Action was the most "liberal" in the Alabama delegation. But he also received a score of 60 from the American Conservative Union.

At Home: Beaten badly in his first House campaign in 1972, Erdreich waited a decade before trying again. But he chose the right moment. His victory over GOP Rep. Albert Lee Smith Jr. gave Democrats the Birmingham House seat for the first time in two decades.

A Birmingham native and a labor lawyer, Erdreich in 1972 challenged entrenched GOP Rep. John H. Buchanan Jr. after only two years in the state House. But Erdreich was frustrated by Buchanan's ability to win over Democrats with his moderate record.

When he launched his second House bid in 1982, Erdreich confronted a GOP incumbent quite unlike Buchanan. The very conservative Smith had ousted Buchanan in a 1980 primary, then barely won the general election. With Birmingham suffering from 15 percent unemployment in the fall of 1982, Erdreich charged that Reagan policies were leading to a depression. With black and labor support, he won by 12,000 votes.

In 1984, GOP leaders persuaded longtime Democratic state legislator J. T. "Jabo" Waggoner to switch parties and run. But Waggoner relied on robotlike Reagan loyalty to cover ineffective local efforts. Erdreich, who had locked up the votes of blacks, labor and the business community, won with enough ease to discourage tough GOP opposition since then.

Alabama 6

Birmingham and Suburbs

The steel industry remains the symbol of Birmingham — atop Red Mountain, overlooking the city, is a statue of the Roman god of fire hammering at a forge. But the symbol is becoming misleading. The city's largest employer is the local branch of the University of Alabama (14,000 students, 1,700 faculty), one of the few college campuses that sprang from a medical school, rather than the other way around. The university has attracted medical and other research facilities, and Birmingham is beginning to depend on its reputation as a health center to move beyond its image as a declining steel town.

By far Alabama's largest city, with more than 275,000 people, Birmingham is 56 percent black. It has an early 20th-century industrial flavor that newer, white-collar Southern cities such as Atlanta lack. It also has problems of urban decay more often associated with the North, and accentuated by the 1980s recession. Birmingham always votes Democratic and has had a black mayor since 1979. But it casts little more than half the 6th District vote; candidates must pull suburban support to win.

The suburbs of the 6th are diverse. South of the Red Mountains, which form the southern edge of the city, are Mountain Brook, Homewood and Hoover, well-to-do bedroom communities that vote Republican. The areas to the north and east, home to conservative, middle-class professionals, are politically volatile — generally Republican, but not to be taken for granted.

Immediately southwest of Birmingham is the Democratic area called the Bessemer Cutoff. The district boundary stops just short of the largely black, labor-oriented steel town of Bessemer, but encloses six other blue-collar Democratic communities.

Population: 554,156. White 360,904 (65%), Black 190,417 (34%). Spanish origin 3,714 (1%). 18 and over 404,782 (73%), 65 and over 67,231 (12%). Median age: 30.

Committees

Banking, Finance and Urban Affairs (16th of 31 Democrats)
Policy Research and Insurance (acting chairman); Consumer Affairs and Coinage; Financial Institutions Supervision, Regulation and Insurance

Government Operations (17th of 24 Democrats)
Legislation and National Security

Select Aging (21st of 39 Democrats)
Health and Long-Term Care.

Elections

1988 General		
Ben Erdreich (D)	138,920	(66%)
Charles Caddis (R)	68,788	(33%)
1986 General		
Ben Erdreich (D)	139,608	(73%)
L. Morgan Williams (R)	51,924	(27%)

Previous Winning Percentages: **1984** (60%) **1982** (53%)

District Vote For President

	1988	1984	1980	1976
D	90,778 (42%)	88,340 (41%)	95,144 (44%)	83,381 (46%)
R	121,663 (57%)	125,716 (59%)	111,373 (51%)	96,737 (53%)

Campaign Finance

	Receipts	Receipts from PACs	Expend-itures
1988			
Erdreich (D)	$251,841	$173,850 (69%)	$159,323
Caddis (R) †	$8,604	0	$8,604
1986			
Erdreich (D)	$342,883	$214,440 (63%)	$216,526
Williams (R)	$6,010	0	$5,534

† Totals based on incomplete data.

Key Votes

1987	
Raise speed limit to 65 mph	Y
Approve Gephardt "fair trade" amendment	Y
Ban testing of larger nuclear weapons	Y
Delay "re-flagging" of Kuwaiti tankers	N
Approve tax-raising deficit-reduction bill	N
1988	
Approve aid to Nicaraguan contras	Y
Enact civil rights restoration bill over Reagan veto	Y
Kill 60-day plant-closing notification measure	Y
Pass omnibus trade bill over Reagan veto	Y
Approve death penalty for drug-related murders	Y
Bar federal funds for abortions in cases of rape and incest	N
Oppose seven-day waiting period for purchase of handguns	Y

Voting Studies

	Presidential Support		Party Unity		Conservative Coalition	
Year	S	O	S	O	S	O
1988	38	62	70	30	84	16
1987	40	60	66	33	91	9
1986	40	59	67	29	82	16
1985	52	48	68	28	76	22
1984	50	45	52	41	81	10
1983	37	63	56	40	78	21

Interest Group Ratings

Year	ADA	ACU	AFL-CIO	CCUS
1988	50	60	79	64
1987	40	30	63	53
1986	55	52	92	50
1985	35	52	59	45
1984	25	57	69	47
1983	50	52	76	40

7 Claude Harris (D)

Of Tuscaloosa — Elected 1986

Born: June 29, 1940, Bessemer, Ala.
Education: U. of Alabama, B.S. 1962, LL.B. 1965.
Military Career: Army National Guard, 1967-present.
Occupation: Judge; lawyer.
Family: Wife, Barbara Cork; two children.
Religion: Baptist.
Political Career: Alabama circuit judge, 6th Circuit, 1977-85.
Capitol Office: 1009 Longworth Bldg. 20515; 225-2665.

In Washington: Harris' freshman term marked the first legislative experience of his political career, but while he carried the title "Judge" with him to Washington, Harris quickly showed he knows how this new game is played. Soon after his swearing-in, Harris sent six dozen Alabama quails to Jack Brooks — a powerful committee chairman and ally of Speaker Jim Wright — for his annual Texas Quail Breakfast.

Sending the quails was a savvy move for an affable newcomer about to buck the leadership on a number of key votes. Early in 1987, Harris was one of just a handful of Democrats to oppose the party's fiscal 1988 budget resolution and to oppose a moratorium on funding for the Nicaraguan contras.

Harris ran for Congress as a business-oriented conservative Democrat. Like his predecessor, Richard C. Shelby, Harris regularly sides with home-state sentiments over the party's national thinking. But while Shelby had stormy relations with blacks and labor, Harris has sought a rapprochement with them.

The omnibus trade bill offered a convenient vehicle to meet labor partway. Backed by unions, the bill also appealed to local steel and textile industries hurting from foreign competition. In a rare floor speech, Harris used a box of candy canes produced in a communist country to illustrate the U.S. trade deficit problem, "Thanks to a controlled labor market, subsidized sugar and subsidized transportation to bring this product to our shores, [it] is being offered at a wholesale price which is below the price of production, and which drives our own products from the American market."

Harris supported the labor-backed Gephardt amendment, which mandated tariffs against countries with unfair trade practices, and he voted to override President Reagan's veto of the trade bill. But on plant-closing notification, a key labor vote, Harris was one of just 23 House Democrats to side with industry.

Harris' record on civil rights issues was similarly mixed. He was one of only 17 Democrats to vote for the GOP substitute to the Civil Rights Restoration Act. But when it failed, he backed the Democratic bill, and he later joined with a vast majority of House members to override Reagan's veto of the measure.

At Home: Harris' efforts to reach out to labor and blacks helped broaden the conservative, business-oriented base established by Shelby. As a result, Harris sailed to a second term.

His initial election was not so easy. Harris began his 1986 race with a strong base in Tuscaloosa, where he had served more than two decades as a county assistant district attorney and then a state circuit judge. But he faced a potent primary rival in Shelby County District Attorney Billy Hill, whose roots were in populous suburban Birmingham.

Hill got a jump on Harris with an early series of TV ads, but he ran low on campaign funds just as Harris was gaining strength. Harris edged Hill in the primary, and his momentum continued to build in the runoff. Harris also was boosted by the endorsement of the New South Coalition, a black organization headed by Birmingham Mayor Richard Arrington. Harris' lopsided advantage in the heavily black counties in the southern part of the 7th helped him win the nomination with 61 percent of the vote.

In the general election — usually a formality for local Democrats — Harris faced Republican Bill McFarland. A real-estate developer and recent party-switcher, he was the GOP's most credible candidate in years. Harris was also threatened by a schism in the state Democratic Party, which had awarded its disputed gubernatorial nomination to populist Lt. Gov. William J. Baxley over state Attorney General Charles Graddick. This spurred a conservative Democratic revolt.

But while the backlash elected Republican Guy Hunt governor, it had little effect on the House contest. Harris was aided by Shelby's presence on the Senate ballot, and he also campaigned ably. He touted his support for the contras, talked about his love for hunting, took time out to meet his National Guard duties and ended up winning by 20 percentage points.

Alabama 7

West Central — Tuscaloosa; Bessemer

The 7th District moves southward from the outskirts of Birmingham, past the small industrial city of Bessemer and the college town of Tuscaloosa into the heart of the Alabama Black Belt, one of the poorest areas in the nation.

While the term "Black Belt" is said to refer not to the racial composition but to the rich, sticky cotton-growing soil, all but one of the eight rural counties in the Black Belt portion of the district have black majorities. These counties, which make up a quarter of the district's population, gave George C. Wallace 73 percent in his 1982 gubernatorial comeback. Even Michael S. Dukakis in 1988 neared 60 percent in many counties here.

Tuscaloosa, with 74,000 people, is the largest city in the 7th District. It has an industrial base that includes manufacturers of chemicals, fertilizer and rubber products, but it is more often identified as the home of the University of Alabama, which has nearly 17,000 students. Tuscaloosa and Tuscaloosa County have become a swing area in Alabama politics.

Shelby and Chilton counties, closer to Birmingham and straddling I-65 on its way south to Montgomery, are growing rapidly and have been voting increasingly Republican.

The Jefferson County part of the 7th, mostly suburban in character, also has been leaning Republican in recent statewide contests. But there is one Democratic enclave — the city of Bessemer, blue-collar, one-half black and weathering hard times due to steel industry layoffs.

Although Republicans run reasonably well through most of the district in national and statewide elections, the area has kept up its tradition of loyalty to conservative Democrats at the congressional level.

Population: 559,069. White 370,555 (66%), Black 186,384 (33%). Spanish origin 5,265 (1%). 18 and over 386,537 (69%), 65 and over 63,493 (11%). Median age: 28.

Committees

Agriculture (20th of 27 Democrats)
Conservation, Credit and Rural Development; Forests, Family Farms and Energy; Livestock, Dairy and Poultry

Veterans' Affairs (11th of 21 Democrats)
Hospitals and Health Care; Housing and Memorial Affairs

Elections

1988 General		
Claude Harris (D)	136,074	(68%)
James E. "Jim" Bacon (R)	63,372	(32%)
1988 Primary		
Claude Harris (D)	70,789	(94%)
Wayne Sowell (D)	4,811	(6%)
1986 General		
Claude Harris (D)	108,126	(60%)
Bill McFarland (R)	72,777	(40%)

District Vote For President

	1988	1984	1980	1976
D	84,638 (41%)	85,248 (40%)	92,384 (48%)	88,502 (55%)
R	123,074 (59%)	124,226 (59%)	91,267 (48%)	70,693 (44%)

Campaign Finance

	Receipts	Receipts from PACs	Expend-itures
1988			
Harris (D)	$405,426	$257,205 (63%)	$328,296
Bacon (R) †	$9,842	0	$8,737
1986			
Harris (D)	$484,220	$182,800 (38%)	$485,560
McFarland (R)	$296,618	$51,967 (18%)	$299,220

† Totals based on incomplete data.

Key Votes

1987	
Raise speed limit to 65 mph	Y
Approve Gephardt "fair trade" amendment	Y
Ban testing of larger nuclear weapons	N
Delay "re-flagging" of Kuwaiti tankers	N
Approve tax-raising deficit-reduction bill	N
1988	
Approve aid to Nicaraguan contras	Y
Enact civil rights restoration bill over Reagan veto	Y
Kill 60-day plant-closing notification measure	Y
Pass omnibus trade bill over Reagan veto	Y
Approve death penalty for drug-related murders	Y
Bar federal funds for abortions in cases of rape and incest	N
Oppose seven-day waiting period for purchase of handguns	Y

Voting Studies

	Presidential Support		Party Unity		Conservative Coalition	
Year	**S**	**O**	**S**	**O**	**S**	**O**
1988	39	60	68	32	87	13
1987	44	54	60	34	86	12

Interest Group Ratings

Year	ADA	ACU	AFL-CIO	CCUS
1988	40	68	79	64
1987	40	45	81	60

Alaska

U.S. CONGRESS

SENATE 2 R
HOUSE 1 R

LEGISLATURE

Senate 8 D, 12 R
House 23 D, 17 R

ELECTIONS

1988 Presidential Vote	
Bush	60%
Dukakis	36%
1984 Presidential Vote	
Reagan	67%
Mondale	30%
1980 Presidential Vote	
Reagan	54%
Carter	26%
Anderson	7%
Turnout rate in 1984	60%
Turnout rate in 1986	48%
Turnout rate in 1988	52%

(as percentage of voting age population)

POPULATION AND GROWTH

1980 population	401,851
1988 population estimate (49th in the nation)	524,000
Percent change 1980-1988	+30%

DEMOGRAPHIC BREAKDOWN

White	77%
Black	3%
Eskimo/Aleut	16%
Other	2%
(Spanish origin)	2%
Urban	64%
Rural	36%
Born in state	32%
Foreign-born	4%

MAJOR CITIES

Anchorage	235,000
Fairbanks	27,610
Juneau	25,000
Sitka	7,700
Ketchikan	7,400

AREA AND LAND USE

Area	570,833 sq. miles (1st)
Farm	0.4%
Forest	36%
Federally owned	87%

Gov. Steve Cowper (D)
Of Fairbanks — Elected 1986

Born: Aug. 21, 1938, Petersburg, Va.
Education: U. of North Carolina, B.A. 1960, LL.B 1963.
Military Career: Army Medical Corps and Army Reserve, 1959-65.
Occupation: Lawyer.
Religion: Episcopalian.
Political Career: Alaska House, 1975-79; sought Democratic nomination for governor, 1982.
Next Election: 1990.

WORK

Occupations	
White-collar	60%
Blue-collar	24%
Service workers	14%
Government Workers	
Federal	14,292
State	23,744
Local	23,732

MONEY

Median family income	$ 28,395	(1st)
Tax burden per capita	$ 3,620	(1st)

EDUCATION

Spending per pupil through grade 12	$ 8,253	(1st)
Persons with college degrees	21%	(2nd)

CRIME

Violent crime rate	455 per 100,000 (22nd)

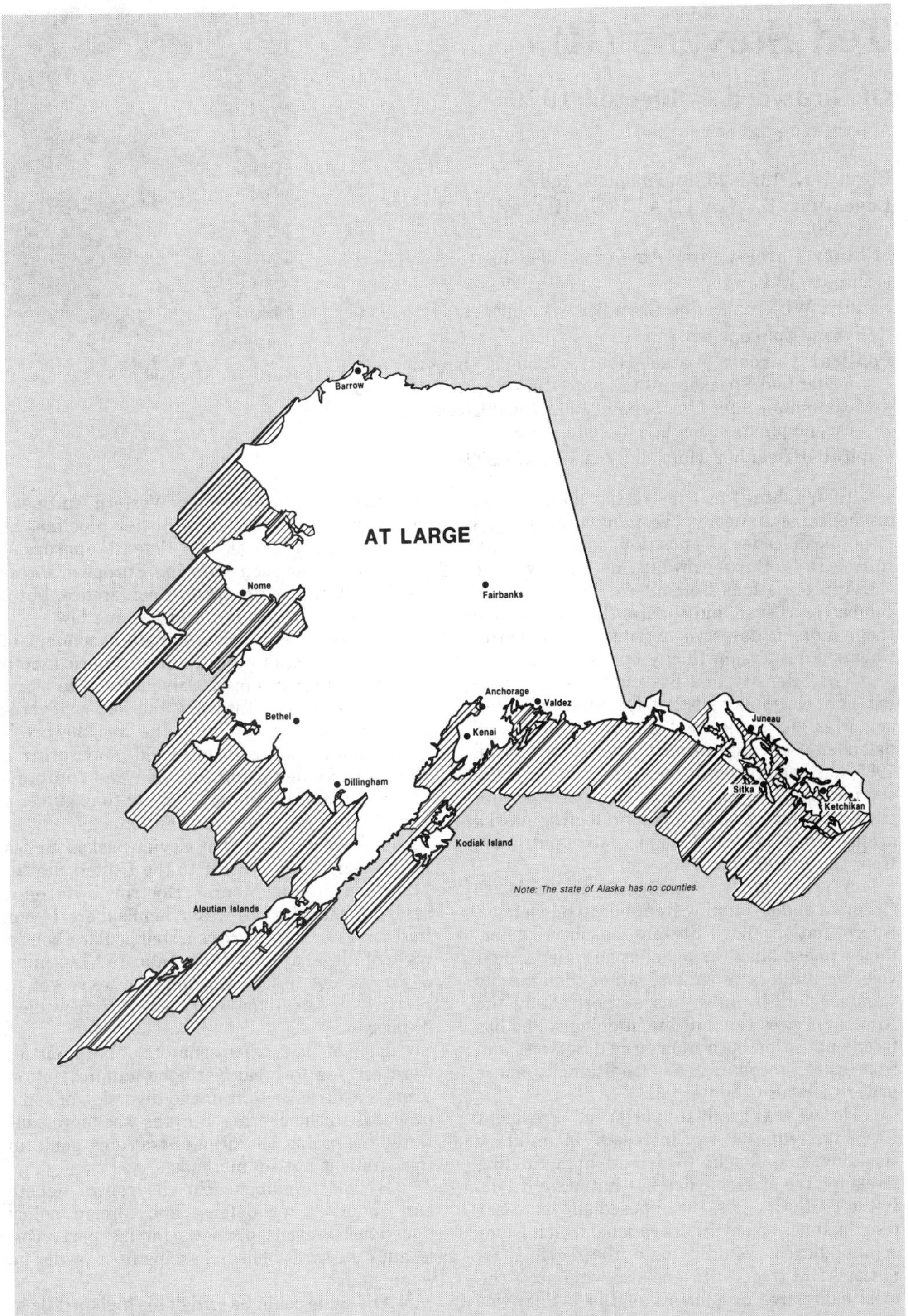
AT LARGE
Barrow
Nome
Fairbanks
Anchorage
Valdez
Juneau
Bethel
Kenai
Dillingham
Sitka
Ketchikan
Kodiak Island
Aleutian Islands
Note: The state of Alaska has no counties.

Ted Stevens (R)

Of Girdwood — Elected 1970

Appointed to the Senate 1968

Born: Nov. 18, 1923, Indianapolis, Ind.
Education: U.C.L.A., B.A. 1947; Harvard U., LL.B. 1950.
Military Career: Army Air Corps, 1943-46.
Occupation: Lawyer.
Family: Wife, Catherine Chandler; six children.
Religion: Episcopalian.
Political Career: Alaska House, 1965-68, majority leader and Speaker pro tempore, 1967-68; Republican nominee for U.S. Senate, 1962; sought Republican nomination for U.S. Senate, 1968.
Capitol Office: 522 Hart Bldg. 20510; 224-3004.

In Washington: Stevens has not given up his hopes of someday becoming the Senate's Republican leader, the position he narrowly lost to Bob Dole. But meanwhile, he toils away on the Appropriations Committee, as cranky and combative as ever, and apparently unpersuaded that a more mellow style might serve him better when the leadership finally opens again.

The intensity that Stevens displayed during eight years as assistant Republican leader, acting as the enforcer of party discipline and defender of congressional perquisites until 1985, has been focused since then on enhancing the power of the Defense Appropriations Subcommittee and, as always, on protecting Alaska against what he views as legislative intruders from the Lower 48.

As subcommittee chairman in the 99th Congress and as ranking Republican on Defense Appropriations now, Stevens has been determined to establish the panel as an independent voice on military programs, rather than merely a bursar for the programs authorized by the Armed Services Committee. In doing so, he has faced opposition both from Armed Services and from the subcommittee's traditionally more powerful House counterpart.

He was a loyal supporter of President Reagan's requests for increases in military spending, and fought to defend high funding levels for the strategic defense initiative (SDI). In the 100th Congress, he opposed efforts to bar tests in space of any SDI weapons, which Democrats alleged would violate the 1972 U.S.-Soviet ABM treaty. Stevens also was one of the most aggressive proponents of the U.S.-Soviet intermediate-range nuclear-force (INF) treaty, helping the administration and Senate Democratic leaders thwart the small band of right-wing opponents.

As budget deficits climbed, Stevens has been a leader in promoting burden-sharing, which would require U.S. allies to pay more of NATO's defense costs. Incensed that Western European countries were financing a Soviet pipeline, he included in the fiscal 1983 defense appropriations bill a provision reducing European forces by 23,000. It was dropped in conference, but a freeze on troop strength did become law.

Stevens was a prime Senate proponent of Reagan's policies toward Central America, both to defeat guerrillas in El Salvador and to assist the contras in overthrowing the leftist government of Nicaragua. In 1987, he was the president's point man on contra aid, sponsoring a $22 million amendment to a year-end appropriations bill and ultimately helping to engineer a compromise for about $15 million.

He is convinced that Soviet-backed forces in the region are a threat to the United States. "I believe in the Monroe Doctrine," he once said. "What goes on in our hemisphere is our business." And he worries in particular about a wave of illegal aliens: "If we indicate a lessening of our resolve in Central America, we've got to prepare ourselves for a wave of 3 to 5 million immigrants."

Late in 1986, when senators of both parties were rushing to break with the administration over its arms sales to Iran and diversion of some proceeds to the contras, Stevens was more cautious, defending the administration's goals in the affair, if not its methods.

By his prominence in the contra debate and on other key defense and foreign policy questions, Stevens previews for his party colleagues the sort of hard-charging floor leader he would make.

The same could be said of his high profile in the 100th Congress during Republicans' successful filibuster of a bill limiting campaign funds and introducing a system of public financing. He derided the bill as an "entitlement program for candidates for the Congress," and said, "I believe that the American taxpayer is not interested in putting up $95 [million] to $100 million to finance the campaigns of senators."

He was one of the most vocal supporters of Attorney General Edwin Meese III, objecting that Meese's financial relationships were being scrutinized unfairly. "I think you've been abused by the process, Mr. Attorney General," Stevens said during a 1987 Governmental Affairs Committee hearing. To reporters covering the Supreme Court nomination of Douglas H. Ginsburg, which collapsed after Ginsburg acknowledged he had smoked marijuana, Stevens snapped, "All you guys have smoked marijuana. Why should we keep him off the court?"

Stevens' near-miss at the majority leadership in December 1984 was one of the biggest surprises in recent Senate politics. Despite his long tenure as chief lieutenant to Majority Leader Howard H. Baker Jr., Stevens was considered by almost everyone as a sure loser in his bid to move up after Baker's retirement. Yet he outpolled three other contenders, losing to Dole on the final ballot by only three votes, 28-25.

That narrow defeat reflected the widespread ambivalence about Stevens. He is easily enraged, confrontational and prone to let legislative differences become personal feuds. Yet many Republicans felt his militance might be needed to restore order to a Senate that had fallen into disarray under Baker's amiable stewardship. Moreover, they could forgive a lot in a man known as "Mr. Perk," who fought so unabashedly and tenaciously for the benefits they wanted but were afraid to pursue openly.

But in the end, Stevens could not overcome the simple fact that too many colleagues consider him a very difficult person to work with. Nevertheless, he seemed to take encouragement from the closeness of the outcome. Early on, he freely acknowledged he would seek the seat again if Dole gave it up to run for president, and even suggested he might not wait for that opening. Despite the rumors of a challenge, though, Stevens joined Republicans in unanimously re-electing Dole in 1986 and 1988.

Stevens is the Senate's angry man. From his first week in the chamber in 1969, when he tangled with Democrats over President Nixon's nomination of Alaska Gov. Walter J. Hickel as interior secretary, colleagues have known that debate with Stevens can quickly degenerate into a shouting match.

Years of battle between Stevens and his opposite number on the Democratic side, equally contentious Ohio liberal Howard M. Metzenbaum, climaxed in the fall of 1982 over a bill to transfer a federal railroad to Alaska. During one particularly nasty fight on the Senate floor, Stevens threatened to go to Ohio to campaign against Metzenbaum.

Stevens does not scrap only with Democrats. During the four years that fellow Republican John Tower chaired Armed Services, Stevens waged several floor battles over his Appropriations subcommittee's right to set defense spending levels. That conflict escalated in 1985, when the Armed Services chair went to Barry Goldwater — bringing two irascible senators head-to-head.

At issue was Appropriations' approval of amounts for various weapons that were above the limits authorized by Armed Services. Stevens insisted the excess funds were essential to negotiating with the House. Otherwise, he said, Senate appropriators constantly would have to bargain down to the normally lower House levels during conferences on spending bills.

The dispute came to a head in 1986, when Appropriations reported a supplemental spending bill that was $5.6 billion over defense authorization limits. Armed Services leaders heatedly objected, and a major floor fight loomed. Negotiating late into the night, Stevens and Goldwater finally compromised.

For all his pugnacity, Stevens generally is not one to simmer and harbor grudges. He and Metzenbaum, for example, have been known to play tennis together. His temper typically flares and just as quickly disappears. A moderate by GOP ideological standards, Stevens can deal effectively with Democrats as well as Republicans. He gets along fine in the collegial, horse-trading culture of Appropriations, where his success can be measured by his catch for Alaska; an Anchorage paper in 1989 called Stevens "the six-billion-dollar man," estimating he has been worth at least that much to the state in federal largess.

Members in both parties appreciate his work for increased congressional salaries and benefits. While most members scurry for cover when the subject of pay raises comes up, Stevens brashly proclaims that Congress is underpaid. "Service in the Senate," he has said, "should not require a sacrifice."

He was a leading cheerleader for a $12,100-a-year raise in early 1987, and two years later for the proposed 51 percent hike to $135,000 a year. But given the Senate's permissive rules, Stevens and Senate leaders were virtually powerless to prevent foes in that chamber from passing resolutions to kill the proposed raises. It was up to House leaders to bury the Senate resolutions, and they succeeded only in 1987.

Over his years as whip, Stevens pushed a variety of schemes to make congressional life more rewarding. The list of measures passed includes pay raises, a tax break for members' Washington, D.C., living expenses, expanded free mailing privileges, an end to limits on senators' outside income and an increased allowance for honoraria.

His unflagging support for federal workers, an important constituency in Alaska, has made Stevens popular with public employee unions. In fact, he is one of the few Senate Republicans to draw sizable campaign help from organized labor. As chairman of the Civil Service, Post Office and General Services Subcommittee at

Governmental Affairs until 1987, he was ideally positioned to look out for federal workers.

He was once a federal employee himself, in the top ranks of the Interior Department in the 1950s, and he fights regularly against caps on federal pay raises, arguing that government workers should not have to suffer from inflation. In early 1989, when it was obvious Congress' own pay raise was doomed, Stevens still championed an increase for bureaucrats.

His relations with federal employee unions were strained during 1982, however, by his advocacy of a proposal to revamp the federal retirement system. Stevens pushed the plan, which involved inclusion of federal workers in the Social Security system, in an unsuccessful effort to hold off attacks on cost-of-living adjustments in the pension systems. Early in 1983, Congress cleared compromise legislation that would bring new federal workers under Social Security.

In the next Congress, Stevens worked with Delaware Republican William V. Roth Jr., then chairman of the Governmental Affairs Committee, to pass legislation establishing a new pension system for federal workers hired after 1983. The bill, enacted into law in 1986 after months of negotiations, was designed to provide new benefits to retired workers at less cost.

On the Commerce Committee, where he has served throughout his Senate career, Stevens mostly gets involved in shipping issues; while Republicans controlled the chamber, he was chairman of the Merchant Marine Subcommittee. He was a key player in the 98th Congress' approval of the first major changes in shipping law in 20 years. The legislation, strongly opposed by consumer groups, expanded the ocean-liner industry's antitrust immunity for setting prices and dividing routes.

The emphasis on perks and defense during recent years marks a contrast with his work of the late 1970s, when one issue — Alaska lands legislation — dominated Stevens' agenda. He fought aggressively to open more state land for development, opposing those who stressed environmental protection and sought new parks.

During those years, Stevens was thoroughly alienated from his fellow Alaskan, Democratic Sen. Mike Gravel. The Stevens-Gravel feud was largely a question of style and tactics. Both wanted to keep the government from barring development in much of Alaska, but they disagreed vehemently on how to do so. Stevens felt the legislation was inevitable and wanted to make it as acceptable to Alaska as he could; Gravel sought to block it through filibusters and similar dilatory tactics, fighting with a showmanship Stevens and many others regarded as pure demagoguery.

"It's hard to do anything about Alaska with Mike Gravel in the Senate," he once complained. In 1980 he took the unusual step of backing Gravel's Democratic primary opponent, who defeated Gravel but then lost that fall to Republican Frank H. Murkowski.

In contrast, Stevens works closely with Murkowski and Republican Don Young, Alaska's only House member. In the 100th Congress, they vigorously joined with the administration to oppose two provisions of the comprehensive trade bill, one limiting exports from Alaska oil refineries and a second, included as a concession to maritime unions, requiring exports to Canada to be shipped from West Coast ports. Both ultimately were stripped from the bill, but mostly to isolate Reagan's only remaining ground for a veto — a provision mandating that workers get advance notice of plant closings; Democrats had made that an election-year priority.

Stevens and his Alaska colleagues have fought for legislation to open the vast Arctic National Wildlife Refuge to the oil industry. However, that uphill fight apparently was shelved, at least for the 101st Congress, in the wake of the oil spill of the tanker *Exxon Valdez* in Prince William Sound in March 1989.

Amid the earlier Alaska lands debate of the 1970s, Stevens was forced to rebuild his personal life after his first wife, mother of their five children, was killed in a 1978 plane crash in which he also was injured. Remarrying in 1980, he bought a town house on the border of Capitol Hill, in a transitional inner-city neighborhood rather than one of the more fashionable suburbs. It was a somewhat surprising choice, given that the city had once been the victim of Stevens' sharp tongue. During a debate on members' tax breaks, he said he knew of "no town that has a worse crime standard, a worse set of schools, a worse circumstance to live and work in than the city of Washington," thus inviting the condemnation of local residents and civic leaders.

At Home: Stevens' careful defense of Alaska interests has made him invulnerable at the polls. Although he has not had his way on every issue, he always seems to have the right political approach — stubborn but pragmatic.

Stevens, who had been majority leader in the Alaska House, got to Washington by appointment when Democratic Sen. E. L. Bartlett died in 1968. He owed his promotion to Walter J. Hickel, the state's GOP governor. Only months before, Stevens had failed to win the Senate GOP primary. Six years earlier, he had been nominated and drew only 41 percent of the vote.

Once in Washington, however, Stevens began digging in politically. In the 1970 contest to fill the final two years of Bartlett's term, he won with almost 60 percent while the GOP was losing the governorship. In that campaign, against liberal Democrat Wendell P. Kay, Stevens favored greater oil and mineral development; Kay was a firm conservationist.

Seeking a full term in 1972, Stevens

crushed Democrat Gene Guess, the state House Speaker, whom he linked to presidential nominee George McGovern. Stevens also appealed to Alaska's hunters by calling Guess pro-gun control.

By 1978 Stevens had been elected to the Senate Republican leadership and no prominent Democrat even considered a serious campaign against him. An electrical contractor and an economics professor fought for the Democratic nomination, and the contractor, who got it, received less than a quarter of the vote.

Though he had little difficulty beating Democrats, Stevens received a rebuke in 1980 from some conservative elements in the Alaska GOP, which by then included a sizable Christian Right contingent. Viewing Stevens as something of a moderate, the conservatives denied him the chairmanship of the Alaska delegation to the 1980 Republican National Convention. However, his strongly pro-Reagan voting record appeared to placate the opposition by 1984, when he was named delegation chairman.

In that same year, Stevens again coasted to re-election. John E. Havelock, a lawyer who served as the state's attorney general in the early 1970s, tried to convince voters that the incumbent was more interested in pursuing his own Senate ambitions than in Alaskan affairs. But Stevens paid his challenger little heed. Armed with a massive campaign treasury, he spent much of the time stumping for other GOP senators in pursuit of his party's Senate leader post. He crushed Havelock with 71 percent of the vote.

Stevens flirted briefly with the idea of returning to state politics in 1985, announcing that he would have been willing to step in if then-Democratic Gov. Bill Sheffield failed to survive impeachment proceedings brought against him over allegations that he had steered a state office lease to a political supporter. But Stevens discarded the notion after it became clear Sheffield would survive long enough to stand for re-election in 1986, and that a number of prominent Republicans were interested in running for governor.

Committees

Rules and Administration (Ranking)

Appropriations (2nd of 13 Republicans)
Defense (ranking); Commerce, Justice, State, the Judiciary and Related Agencies; Interior and Related Agencies; Labor, Health and Human Services, Education and Related Agencies; Military Construction

Commerce, Science and Transportation (4th of 9 Republicans)
National Ocean Policy Study (ranking); Aviation; Communications; Merchant Marine; Science, Technology and Space

Governmental Affairs (2nd of 6 Republicans)
Federal Services, Post Office and Civil Service (ranking); General Services, Federalism and the District of Columbia; Permanent Subcommittee on Investigations

Small Business (9th of 9 Republicans)
Competition and Antitrust Enforcement (ranking); Innovation, Technology and Productivity

Joint Library

Joint Printing

Elections

1984 General		
Ted Stevens (R)	146,919	(71%)
John E. Havelock (D)	58,804	(29%)

Previous Winning Percentages: **1978** (76%) **1972** (77%) **1970 *** (60%)

** Special election. Stevens was appointed in 1968 to fill the vacancy caused by the death of Sen. E. L. Bartlett. The 1970 election was to fill the remainder of Bartlett's term.*

Campaign Finance

	Receipts	Receipts from PACs		Expend-itures
1984				
Stevens (R)	$1,325,135	$637,798	(48%)	$1,195,616
Havelock (D)	$92,982	$6,050	(7%)	$92,001

Key Votes

1987	
Enact omnibus highway bill over Reagan veto	N
Limit testing of space-based anti-ballistic missiles	N
Oppose banning tests of larger nuclear weapons	Y
Confirm Robert H. Bork as Supreme Court justice	Y
1988	
Allow vote on campaign-finance overhaul	?
Pass civil rights restoration bill over Reagan veto	Y
Enact omnibus trade bill over Reagan veto	N
Approve death penalty for drug-related murders	Y
Oppose "workfare" amendment to welfare overhaul bill	N

Voting Studies

	Presidential Support		Party Unity		Conservative Coalition	
Year	**S**	**O**	**S**	**O**	**S**	**O**
1988	67	30	71	27	78	19
1987	65	26	64	27	81	19
1986	83	11	83 †	15 †	88	9
1985	75	16	71	21	90	3
1984	84	12	85	8	94	4
1983	92	5	80	17	77	16
1982	74	18	85	8	90	4
1981	76	14	81	10	79	13

† Not eligible for all recorded votes.

Interest Group Ratings

Year	ADA	ACU	AFL-CIO	CCUS
1988	25	64	36	69
1987	25	65	60	67
1986	15	71	33	74
1985	10	64	25	78
1984	20	67	22	76
1983	15	44	13	74
1982	15	50	35	76
1981	15	53	17	100

Frank H. Murkowski (R)

Of Fairbanks — Elected 1980

Born: March 28, 1933, Seattle, Wash.

Education: Attended U. of Santa Clara, 1951-53; Seattle U., B.A. 1955.

Military Career: Coast Guard, 1955-56.

Occupation: Banker.

Family: Wife, Nancy Gore; six children.

Religion: Roman Catholic.

Political Career: Alaska commissioner of economic development, 1966-70; Republican nominee for U.S. House, 1970.

Capitol Office: 709 Hart Bldg. 20510; 224-6665.

In Washington: Murkowski has used his clout with the Veterans Administration in a way that might surprise politicians in the lower 48: He continually blocks construction of a VA hospital. This is quintessential Alaskan geopolitics, a decision dictated by the state's sprawling size and sparse population. In this case, it is simply easier for veterans to visit their local doctor.

In a Senate career dominated by veterans' issues and home-state concerns, it is the latter that have often proved most difficult for Murkowski to address. Alaskan fishermen, loggers and oil interests tangle among themselves and with outsiders; many in the state chafe that key decisions about tapping or preserving the pristine wilderness — chockablock with natural resources, particularly oil and timber — are made in a capital city five times zones to the east.

Murkowski attends carefully to these local disputes, which sometimes can become major national controversies, as the March 1989 oil spill in Prince William Sound made plain. He also has shown some signs of wanting to broaden his role within the Senate: In late 1988, he mounted a late bid for a leadership post, the largely honorary chair of the GOP Conference, by arguing that its occupant, John H. Chafee of Rhode Island, had opposed President Reagan too frequently.

But on at least one prominent occasion during the 100th Congress, it was Murkowski who crossed the president. He sided with Foreign Relations Committee Democrats on a measure to delay for a year the administration's plan to re-flag Kuwaiti oil tankers in the Persian Gulf as U.S. vessels, thus affording them U.S. military protection.

In later floor action, a Murkowski amendment became an oblique vehicle for protesting the re-flagging policy. The Senate agreed with his "sail America" amendment, a non-binding declaration that the president should consider leasing mothballed U.S. tankers to Kuwait. The policy eventually resulted in at least one laid-up U.S. tanker being pressed back into service.

Expanding Alaskan trade with the Far East is perhaps his chief pursuit as ranking member on the Foreign Relations Subcommittee on East Asian and Pacific Affairs, a panel he once chaired. He regularly leads trade delegations to Pacific Rim countries, encouraging them to buy more Alaskan coal, timber and other products.

That is not an easily attained goal, however, because of obstacles many of those countries have raised against imports. Frustrated with Japan's reluctance to allow increased imports, he sponsored legislation in 1985 to impose a 20 percent surcharge on Japanese goods.

Various such attempts to force reciprocal trade culminated in the 100th Congress with legislation that Murkowski sponsored with House Democrat Jack Brooks of Texas. The Brooks-Murkowski amendment denies foreign participation in all federally funded public works projects when the foreign firm's home market is closed to U.S. construction.

Another barrier to Murkowski's efforts comes from this side of the Pacific: the ban on export of Alaskan crude oil. Murkowski has pushed hard for years to end that export prohibition, but with very limited success. His amendment to end the ban was rejected overwhelmingly by the Senate in 1984, in part because of opposition from U.S. maritime interests who worried that the oil might be transported in foreign ships.

The same interests tried to limit the export of refined oil during the 1988 debate over an omnibus trade bill. Murkowski teamed up with his senior senator, Republican Ted Stevens, to strip the measure.

The Democrats' return to control of the Senate cost Murkowski the chair of the Veterans' Affairs Committee. The panel had provided Murkowski a career milestone that may be denied indefinitely to the other Republicans who came to the Senate in 1980. He was the first of the class to chair a standing committee.

Until some future day when the GOP recaptures control of the chamber, he will be the only one ever to have been a chairman.

Murkowski's elevation to the Veterans' post was not really a mark of special distinction; he got the job because the more senior Republicans on the panel already were busy with more powerful assignments. He had not been a major force on veterans' legislation before taking over the committee in 1985.

Once chairman, Murkowski played a significant role on veterans' issues. In some cases, he worked to protect funding for veterans' programs. He won Senate approval in 1985 of an amendment to the budget resolution, restoring full cost-of-living increases for federal military and civilian retirees. Later that year, he worked with Democrat Alan Cranston, now the committee chairman, to regain $100 million cut by the Appropriations Committee in veterans' health programs.

But Murkowski also has sought to hold down costs of some veterans' programs through cost-saving legislative changes. One measure aimed at cutting health-care spending by encouraging the Veterans Administration to use low-cost alternatives, such as halfway houses and private nursing homes. A former banker, he also wrote legislation to overhaul the veterans' home-loan program in order to bring down high foreclosure rates.

As ranking member, he was active in the efforts to establish the Department of Veterans Affairs.

On Foreign Relations, one of Murkowski's pet projects is reform of the Foreign Military Sales program, which provides loans to other countries to buy U.S. weapons. He argues that the program, a favorite of the administration, only encourages Third World countries to go deeper into debt. During floor debate in 1985, Murkowski wanted to offer an amendment to end a part of the program that allows some countries up to 30 years to repay weapons loans, instead of the customary 12. Although committee Chairman Richard G. Lugar urged Murkowski not to offer the amendment, he went ahead, and lost by a 27-70 margin. However, the final version of the foreign-aid bill that year included a Murkowski-written statement advocating that the loan program be replaced by outright grants.

In 1986, Murkowski split from the administration on legislation related to South Africa and the Middle East. He backed a committee bill providing tough economic measures against South Africa's racial policies, although he voted against several specific sanctions during committee consideration. He was one of four Foreign Relations Republicans to support a bill blocking Reagan's proposed sale of missiles to Saudi Arabia.

At Home: When Murkowski was in his first term, a survey of the Capitol Hill press corps found him to be one of the least visible members of the Senate.

But if Murkowski's low-key approach to politics prompted smirks from the press corps then, it did not leave the Democrats laughing in Alaska. By eschewing the spotlight for a quiet focus on home-state concerns, Murkowski had built a reputation as a formidable political figure back home. As a result, state Democratic leaders had difficulty finding anyone of stature willing to challenge his re-election in 1986.

The candidate who finally did emerge, Alaska Pacific University President Glenn Olds, began his campaign as a political unknown. He had never even been active in Democratic politics in Alaska, let alone run for public office.

Olds did boast a distinguished résumé. A Methodist minister who had taught college philosophy, Olds served in the U.S. delegation at the United Nations from 1969-71, then assumed the presidency of Ohio's Kent State University in the aftermath of the 1970 clash between students and National Guardsmen.

Olds sought to overcome his political anonymity by arguing that Murkowski had done little to stem the slide of Alaska's petroleum-based economy. But if voters were angry over the oil-price slump, most did not vent their frustrations on Murkowski. The incumbent, aided by his connections to the local banking industry, amassed a substantial campaign treasury, touted his efforts to remove a ban on exports of North Slope oil — and emerged with a solid 10-percentage-point victory.

Except for three years in state government and one failed campaign for the House, Murkowski had spent his entire adult life in banking before he announced for the Senate in June 1980.

His status as a relative newcomer to politics hardly seemed an advantage against Democrat Clark S. Gruening, a popular two-term state legislator and grandson of the legendary Ernest Gruening, a former Alaska senator and governor. But Democratic disunity and the Reagan tide brought Murkowski a solid victory.

Throughout much of the early campaign season, Murkowski's effort was obscured by the bitter Democratic primary. To win the Democratic nomination, Gruening had to get past Sen. Mike Gravel, the two-term incumbent. It was a matter of revenge for Gruening; Gravel was the man who had ousted his grandfather from the Senate 12 years before.

Gravel's legislative behavior helped make Gruening's primary victory possible. Battling to prevent the Senate from enacting legislation restricting development of Alaska's lands, Gravel resorted to an obstructionism so strident and obnoxious that he did his cause more harm than good. A few days before the primary, the Senate succeeded in closing debate on a Gravel filibuster against the Alaska bill, lending credence to Gruening's charges that he had lost influence in the chamber. Although forecasters had predicted a tight race, Gruening won by a comfortable margin.

Gruening also outpolled Murkowski by more than 2-to-1 in Alaska's open primary, in which all candidates appear on the same ballot regardless of party affiliation. Although Murkowski took the GOP nomination with ease, the comparison seemed significant — historically, the top vote-getter in the primary has gone on to win the general election.

But Murkowski was able to buck tradition by keeping attention focused on Gruening's record in the Legislature. Accusing him of being too liberal for the state's electorate, Murkowski claimed the Democrat had supported the legalization of marijuana. He also tied Gruening to the environmentalist Sierra Club, anathema to pro-development Alaskans.

Gruening claimed his legislative experience made him more qualified to be a U.S. senator. But most voters did not agree. Buoyed by national Republican help and a treasury exceeding $700,000 — nearly half of which came from political action committees — Murkowski did very well in his Fairbanks base and upset Gruening in the Democrat's hometown of Anchorage, Alaska's largest city.

A Seattle native who moved to Alaska while in high school, Murkowski got his first taste of elective politics in 1970. That year he defeated a member of the John Birch Society in a Republican primary for Alaska's at-large House seat, left vacant when Rep. Howard W. Pollock sought the governorship. He lost the general election to Democratic state Sen. Nick Begich, but the experience whetted his appetite. After serving for nine years as president of the Alaska National Bank of the North, at Fairbanks, he announced for the Senate.

Committees

Veterans' Affairs (Ranking)

Energy and Natural Resources (5th of 9 Republicans)
Mineral Resources Development and Production (ranking); Energy Regulation and Conservation

Foreign Relations (6th of 9 Republicans)
East Asian and Pacific Affairs (ranking); International Economic Policy, Trade, Oceans and Environment; Terrorism, Narcotics and International Operations

Select Indian Affairs (2nd of 3 Republicans)

Select Intelligence (3rd of 7 Republicans)

Elections

1986 General

Frank H. Murkowski (R)	97,674	(54%)
Glenn Olds (D)	79,727	(44%)

Previous Winning Percentage: **1980** (54%)

Campaign Finance

	Receipts	Receipts from PACs	Expenditures
1986			
Murkowski (R)	$1,423,961	$587,608 (41%)	$1,387,756
Olds (D)	$412,857	$150,772 (37%)	$412,074

Key Votes

1987

Enact omnibus highway bill over Reagan veto	N
Limit testing of space-based anti-ballistic missiles	N
Oppose banning tests of larger nuclear weapons	Y
Confirm Robert H. Bork as Supreme Court justice	Y

1988

Allow vote on campaign-finance overhaul	N
Pass civil rights restoration bill over Reagan veto	Y
Enact omnibus trade bill over Reagan veto	N
Approve death penalty for drug-related murders	Y
Oppose "workfare" amendment to welfare overhaul bill	N

Voting Studies

	Presidential Support		Party Unity		Conservative Coalition	
Year	S	O	S	O	S	O
1988	65	18	81	7	89	3
1987	62	35	76	15	84	6
1986	80	17	81	15	88	5
1985	82	11	78	14	90	2
1984	84	12	90	5	94	2
1983	69	14	73	8	80	0
1982	79	11	91	5	89	1
1981	82	11	83	11	85	9

Interest Group Ratings

Year	ADA	ACU	AFL-CIO	CCUS
1988	15	79	23	85
1987	5	76	40	80
1986	20	78	36	65
1985	0	82	26	84
1984	10	86	18	88
1983	0	72	6	75
1982	10	63	24	70
1981	15	79	24	93

AL Don Young (R)

Of Fort Yukon — Elected 1973

Born: June 9, 1933, Meridian, Calif.
Education: Yuba Junior College, A.A. 1952; Chico State College, Calif., B.A. 1958.
Military Career: Army, 1955-57.
Occupation: Elementary school teacher; riverboat captain.
Family: Wife, Lula Fredson; two children.
Religion: Episcopalian.
Political Career: Fort Yukon City Council, 1960-64; mayor of Fort Yukon, 1964-68; Alaska House, 1967-71; Alaska Senate, 1971-73; Republican nominee for U.S. House, 1972.
Capitol Office: 2331 Rayburn Bldg. 20515; 225-5765.

In Washington: Young found himself in rare agreement with Interior Committee Chairman Morris K. Udall of Arizona once in 1988, over Udall's bill to sell a federal tract in Phoenix, and he seized the relatively minor issue to deliver a weighty message: "We should always," Young told the panel, "respect the member's choice regarding his or her district."

The irony, as Young surely intended, is that many of his colleagues have done anything but respect his wishes for his gargantuan district, the state of Alaska. From the time he arrived in 1973 as an advocate of the Trans-Alaska oil pipeline, Young has been making lonely, often losing stands against the "outsiders" from the Lower 48 who want to preserve much of Alaska's unspoiled frontier from the miners, loggers, drillers and developers whose interests Young tenaciously promotes.

A former riverboat captain, Young is a rough-hewn individualist who regularly demands — often in explosive bursts of anger — that Washington stay out of his state's way. Since 1985, he has been well positioned to resist environmentalist legislation as ranking Republican on the Interior Committee. At the same time, the responsibility of the ranking position seems to have prompted the volatile Young to temper some.

Young became the GOP leader on Interior when New Mexico Rep. Manuel Lujan Jr. moved to claim the top Republican spot on another committee. (In 1989, Lujan became President Bush's interior secretary.) Unlike Lujan, Young is aggressively partisan, even though he is a product of Alaska's free-for-all, weak-party politics.

Young was a vocal defender of James G. Watt, Reagan's controversial interior secretary. As a member of the panel that makes House Republicans' committee assignments, Young has been known to grill applicants on party loyalty before supporting them for a seat on Interior. His bluster is often tactical, used to intimidate foes, but Young's combativeness and short fuse can complicate his dealings with fellow members, especially the Democratic majority on Interior.

Nearly a decade later, Young still is seething about passage of a 1980 Alaska lands bill that reserved large portions of the state as federal wilderness. In his three-year fight against that bill, Young succeeded in whittling down its wilderness acreage considerably and winning provisions for development.

But when the bill was passed in the House in 1979, he complained, "People can sit on this floor, and say it is all right to take what is already the people's of Alaska. That is immoral.... None of you has to go home to unemployment created by national legislation," Young added. Then he broke down in tears.

Young's work on that bill crystallized his role in the House as a scrappy underdog, and it still defines his attitude toward others. During committee action on unrelated legislation in 1987, for example, Young turned on Udall, sitting beside him on the dais, and lashed out, "You screwed us in 1980 so royally.... You took land away from us."

The latest Alaska battles are being fought primarily on two fields. One involves a move, which Young supports, to open the Arctic National Wildlife Refuge (ANWR) to oil and gas development along its entire 1.5 million-acre coastal plain. The second effort, which Young opposes, would curb logging in the Tongass National Forest, a temperate-zone rain forest in Alaska's southeast Panhandle.

Advocates of opening the wildlife refuge had strong support from the Reagan administration during the 100th Congress. But opponents, who contend that development would threaten caribou, musk oxen, snow geese and polar bears, were able to prevent bills from reaching the floor in either house. Young's bill

Alaska — At Large

The supertanker *Exxon Valdez* managed to stay afloat in March 1989 after bashing into a reef in Alaska's Prince William Sound. But as 10 million gallons of Alaska crude gushed from the gash in its side, the morale of many Alaskans sank to the bottom.

The oil spill, the worst in U.S. history, was described by environmentalists and state officials alike as an ecological disaster. The pristine waters and shorelines of Prince William Sound, which leads from the oil port of Valdez to the Gulf of Alaska, are tinged with oily ooze. Large numbers of fish, birds and wild animals were killed.

There were immediate economic impacts. The fishing industry, touted by many Alaska boosters as the state's best hope for economic diversification, was disrupted. Although most of the vast state's coastline was unaffected by the spill, many potential tourists canceled plans to visit Alaska. But the most lasting impact from the spill may be the disillusion that many Alaskans feel toward their major industry, energy resource recovery.

Since 1977, when the pipeline carrying crude oil from the Prudhoe Bay fields above the Arctic Circle to Valdez was opened, oil has been Alaska's economic lifeblood. Many Alaskans had been secure in the solid assurances by the oil companies that development could continue without serious environmental consequences; even Democrats with liberal backgrounds, like 1988 House candidate Peter Gruenstein, took the pro-development "pledge." But the overwhelming faith in oil was shattered by the *Exxon Valdez.*

The accident was as untimely as it was devastating. The crash of oil prices in the mid-1980s caused rising unemployment and state budget shortfalls, ending nearly a decade of oil-fueled economic boom (which had enabled the state to build up a $1 billion reserve fund and sparked a wave of emigration that boosted state population by 33 percent between 1980 and 1986). The spill came just as stabilizing oil prices had eased the crisis atmosphere, and just as the state's allies in Congress were readying a push to open Alaska's Arctic National Wildlife Refuge to oil exploration.

With the setbacks to the state's oil industry, state leaders continue to search for ways to diversify the economy, but that is a daunting task. Alaska is distant from mainland markets, and its home population, even after the influx, is still tiny: With just over a half-million people, Alaska barely surpasses Wyoming, the least-populous state.

The nation's largest state in land area, Alaska has its charms, not the least of which is its natural beauty. Warm summers belie Alaska's permafrost image. However, it still takes a hardy type to live this far north during the winter. An arctic front settled over the state for a prolonged period in January 1989, plunging daytime temperatures to 40 below zero and lower.

The pioneer spirit and sheer orneryness required to live here inspire political iconoclasm. The small population also lends itself to a very personal style of politics.

However, the tone of Alaska politics in recent years has been conservative, because of the oil development (which drew many workers from the South), resentment toward "outsiders" who want restraints on development, and anger over the federal control of much of Alaska's land. The GOP holds all three of the state's seats in Congress. In presidential elections, Democrats seldom contest Alaska. It remains to be seen if the oil spill will affect this overriding conservative, pro-growth voting pattern.

Republican strength is considerable in the state's population nexus, Anchorage. The city has 235,000 residents, up 35 percent since 1980. Anchorage and its environs, with nearly three-fifths of the state vote, gave well over 60 percent of their 1988 ballots to Bush.

More than 300 miles north of Anchorage is Fairbanks (population 68,000), the traditional trading center for the villages of inland Alaska. The city's role as the supply center for the Alaska oil pipeline promoted rapid growth and modernization.

Southeast Alaska is separated from the rest of the state by the St. Elias Mountains and the Gulf of Alaska. Juneau, the state capital, is inaccessible by land, and plans to build a road over the mountainous coastal terrain were scrapped.

Alaska's vast "bush" region is dotted with towns that have evocative names but few people. Nome, on Alaska's west coast, has just over 7,000 residents. Native Indians and Eskimos predominate in remote Alaska, which includes the Aleutian Islands.

Population: 401,851. White 309,728 (77%), Black 13,643 (3%), American Indian, Eskimo and Aleut 64,103 (16%), Other 8,054 (2%). Spanish origin 9,507 (2%). 18 and over 271,106 (67%), 65 and over 11,547 (3%). Median age: 26.

was blocked in Interior by Udall, who countered with legislation to make the entire refuge a permanent wilderness.

Young had somewhat better luck in the Merchant Marine Committee, where members are sympathetic to the shippers that would transport any new oil from ANWR. That panel approved a bill by Chairman Walter B. Jones to allow limited drilling, reserve certain areas for caribou calving and earmark 50 percent of tax revenues for conservation. Young unsuccessfully sought to reserve 90 percent of revenues for Alaska, the standard "take" since statehood. Although he disagreed with key aspects of Jones' bill, Young nevertheless supported it.

Proponents began the fight anew in the 101st Congress, only to suspend it indefinitely in response to public furor over the disastrous oil spill of the tanker *Exxon Valdez* off Alaska in early 1989.

The ANWR issue has forced Young and home-state allies to shelve another cause — repealing a ban on exports of Alaskan crude oil. The ban, part of the 1973 pipeline law, was enacted to reduce dependence on foreign oil. A push to export oil undercuts the Alaskans' argument that the refuge needs to be opened in the interest of national energy security.

The Tongass measure got as far as House passage in 1988 — "a cheap environmental vote" at Alaska's expense, Young groused. The bill, from Interior, would have repealed both the timber-harvesting concessions made to that industry in the 1980 Alaska lands law, and the federal subsidies for such costs as forest roads. It also would have required renegotiation of long-term contracts with two troubled pulp mills that get federal timber at below-market prices.

In committee, Young proposed an amendment to retain the timber industry's harvesting allowances and subsidies, but it lost 18-22. "I thought the state of Alaska gave its pound of flesh in 1980," he said. "Don't take another pound."

Young claimed 6,000 jobs were at stake, but opponents said the number was about half that. Moreover, they said, Alaskans in the tourism, recreation and commercial fishing industries opposed the logging companies.

At one subcommittee hearing, Young so berated New York Democrat Robert J. Mrazek, sponsor of the Tongass bill, that acting Chairman Sam Gejdenson of Connecticut recessed the panel and took Young into the hall to cool off. Later, on the House floor, Young erupted at Mrazek again, threatening political retribution while stabbing the air with his ever-present buck knife.

Despite such contentiousness, the Tongass issue actually showed the slightly more temperate side of Young that has emerged in the years since he took Interior's top GOP seat. He made a concerted effort to compromise with Rep. George Miller, a California Democrat, but their effort fell short. In general, Young as ranking member has been less a lone wolf and more of a broker, representing the interests of panel Republicans, who are mostly partisan and pro-development Westerners like himself. He is widely admired for his tenacity.

On Merchant Marine, Young has managed to work with liberal Massachusetts Democrat Gerry E. Studds to protect fishermen's interests and the Coast Guard's budget. In 1988, they cosponsored an amendment to the drug bill limiting the administration's "zero tolerance" policy, under which boats were seized upon finding even minor amounts of illegal narcotics. The new law bars seizures if only personal-use amounts are found, and if the boat owners are not to blame.

In the 99th Congress, Young successfully offered a bill promoting mineral exploration on Alaska's Admiralty Island. He got nowhere, however, with his proposals to tax all imported refined petroleum products, and to provide tax credits for oil and gas companies exploring in frontier areas such as the Arctic.

Young, who claims to be the only trapper in Congress, has fought off repeated attempts to impose a ban on steel-jaw leghold traps, a move sought by animal-rights groups. Once, while testifying before Merchant Marine, he made his point by leaving his hand in a trap until his fingers turned blue.

On broader issues, Young fits the conservative label he claims. But like Ted Stevens, Alaska's senior Republican senator, he knows how to leaven his voting record with support for the construction unions and other labor interests important in state affairs.

At Home: With his at-large House seat providing him a statewide base, Young has often been mentioned as a possible candidate for higher office. With Democratic Gov. Steve Cowper stepping down after the 1990 election, Young is considering a run for governor, and he will decide by fall of 1989.

Born in California, Young moved to Alaska to teach and then went native. He became a licensed riverboat captain and a member of the Dog Mushers Association.

He also went into politics, winning election to the state House in 1966 and the state Senate in 1970. In 1972 he challenged Nick Begich, a popular freshman Democratic representative. Young was in the midst of an uphill campaign when in October a plane carrying Begich and House Majority Leader Hale Boggs from Anchorage to Juneau disappeared without a trace.

Though the missing Begich was re-elected over Young by almost 12,000 votes, his seat was declared vacant in December. A special election was scheduled early in 1973, and Young easily won the GOP nomination. Democrats selected Emil Notti, their former state chairman. Young, who by then had been campaigning for almost a year, pulled out his winning margin in the Anchorage and Fairbanks areas.

In 1974, Young weathered a vigorous challenge from state Sen. William L. Hensley to strengthen his hold on the seat. He won by comfortable margins in the next several elections, taking more than 70 percent of the vote in 1980 and 1982.

In 1984, Young faced Pegge Begich, a former Democratic national committeewoman for Alaska and widow of Nick Begich. Begich's complaints about Young's attendance record failed to stir much voter interest. Bolstered by the top-of-the-ticket presence of Sen. Ted Stevens and President Reagan, Young finished with a comfortable 55 percent.

Begich switched strategies in her 1986 rematch with Young, emphasizing economic diversification. But her new theme sounded a lot like the campaign speeches Young was delivering. He won with 57 percent.

In 1988, Democrats tried a new challenger, former assistant state prosecutor Peter Gruenstein. A New York native, Gruenstein had Washington experience in the 1970s as a House aide and as head of a news service partially funded by consumer advocate Ralph Nader. As a prosecutor, he received accolades across the state for his handling of several well-publicized murder cases.

Like previous challengers, Gruenstein described Young as too abrasive to be effective and assailed his attendance record. But Young trumpeted his tireless work on crusades such as opening ANWR, and, as always, he attributed his slightly lagging attendance to his frequent long-distance trips home. Both he and George Bush won better than 60 percent of the vote.

Committees

Interior and Insular Affairs (Ranking)
Water, Power and Offshore Energy Resources

Merchant Marine and Fisheries (2nd of 17 Republicans)
Fisheries and Wildlife Conservation and the Environment (ranking); Coast Guard and Navigation; Merchant Marine

Post Office and Civil Service (4th of 9 Republicans)
Postal Personnel and Modernization (ranking); Postal Operations and Services

Elections

1988 General		
Don Young (R)	120,595	(62%)
Peter Gruenstein (D)	71,881	(37%)
1988 Primary †		
Don Young (R)	62,803	(55%)
Peter Gruenstein (D)	40,040	(35%)
George Johnston (R)	6,214	(5%)
1986 General		
Don Young (R)	101,799	(57%)
Pegge Begich (D)	74,053	(41%)

† In Alaska's "jungle primary," candidates of all parties are listed on one ballot.

Previous Winning Percentages: **1984** (55%) **1982** (71%) **1980** (74%) **1978** (55%) **1976** (71%) **1974** (54%) **1973 *** (51%)

** Special election.*

District Vote For President

	1988	1984	1980 †	1976
D	72,105 (36%)	62,007 (30%)	41,842 (26%)	44,058 (36%)
R	118,817 (60%)	138,377 (67%)	86,112 (54%)	71,555 (58%)
I	5,459 * (3%)		11,155 (7%)	

** Ron Paul, Libertarian Party*
† In addition, Ed Clark, the Libertarian Party candidate, received 18,389 votes, 12 percent of the total.

Campaign Finance

	Receipts	Receipts from PACs	Expend-itures
1988			
Young (R)	$623,760	$296,950 (48%)	$626,377
Gruenstein (D)	$402,694	$99,084 (25%)	$402,477
1986			
Young (R)	$495,429	$250,133 (51%)	$487,261
Begich (D)	$261,469	$63,647 (24%)	$269,560

Key Votes

1987	
Raise speed limit to 65 mph	Y
Approve Gephardt "fair trade" amendment	N
Ban testing of larger nuclear weapons	N
Delay "re-flagging" of Kuwaiti tankers	?
Approve tax-raising deficit-reduction bill	X
1988	
Approve aid to Nicaraguan contras	Y
Enact civil rights restoration bill over Reagan veto	Y
Kill 60-day plant-closing notification measure	N
Pass omnibus trade bill over Reagan veto	N
Approve death penalty for drug-related murders	Y
Bar federal funds for abortions in cases of rape and incest	Y
Oppose seven-day waiting period for purchase of handguns	Y

Voting Studies

	Presidential Support		Party Unity		Conservative Coalition	
Year	S	O	S	O	S	O
1988	49	42	64	29	71	16
1987	52	37	58	30	81	16
1986	61	33	63	31	90	4
1985	51	46	62	32	82	18
1984	55	43	60	39	88	10
1983	52	34	57	21	78	7
1982	45	26	50	25	66	15
1981	67	17	61	14	89	1

Interest Group Ratings

Year	ADA	ACU	AFL-CIO	CCUS
1988	30	63	64	69
1987	16	63	50	57
1986	20	65	62	56
1985	30	62	53	45
1984	25	57	50	69
1983	20	52	50	56
1982	10	73	25	57
1981	10	92	36	88

Arizona

U.S. CONGRESS

SENATE 1 D, 1 R
HOUSE 1 D, 4 R

LEGISLATURE

Senate 13 D, 17 R
House 26 D, 34 R

ELECTIONS

1988 Presidential Vote	
Bush	60%
Dukakis	39%
1984 Presidential Vote	
Reagan	66%
Mondale	33%
1980 Presidential Vote	
Reagan	61%
Carter	28%
Anderson	9%
Turnout rate in 1984	46%
Turnout rate in 1986	34%
Turnout rate in 1988	45%

(as percentage of voting age population)

POPULATION AND GROWTH

1980 population	2,718,215
1988 population estimate (24th in the nation)	3,489,000
Percent change 1980-1988	+28%

DEMOGRAPHIC BREAKDOWN

White	82%
Black	3%
American Indian	7%
(Spanish origin)	16%
Urban	84%
Rural	16%
Born in state	33%
Foreign-born	6%

MAJOR CITIES

Phoenix	894,070
Tucson	358,850
Mesa	251,430
Tempe	136,480
Glendale	125,820

AREA AND LAND USE

Area	113,508 sq. miles (6th)
Farm	52%
Forest	27%
Federally owned	44%

Gov. Rose Mofford (D)
Of Phoenix — Assumed Office 1988

Born: June 10, 1922, Globe, Ariz.
Education: Graduated from Globe H.S., 1940.
Occupation: Business manager.
Religion: Roman Catholic.
Political Career: Ariz. assistant secretary of state, 1953-75; Ariz. secretary of state, 1977-88 (appointed 1977).
Next Election: 1990.

WORK

Occupations	
White-collar	56%
Blue-collar	28%
Service workers	14%
Government Workers	
Federal	36,132
State	55,710
Local	137,106

MONEY

Median family income	$ 19,017	(30th)
Tax burden per capita	$ 924	(19th)

EDUCATION

Spending per pupil through grade 12	$ 3,093	(39th)
Persons with college degrees	17%	(19th)

CRIME

Violent crime rate	613 per 100,000	(12th)

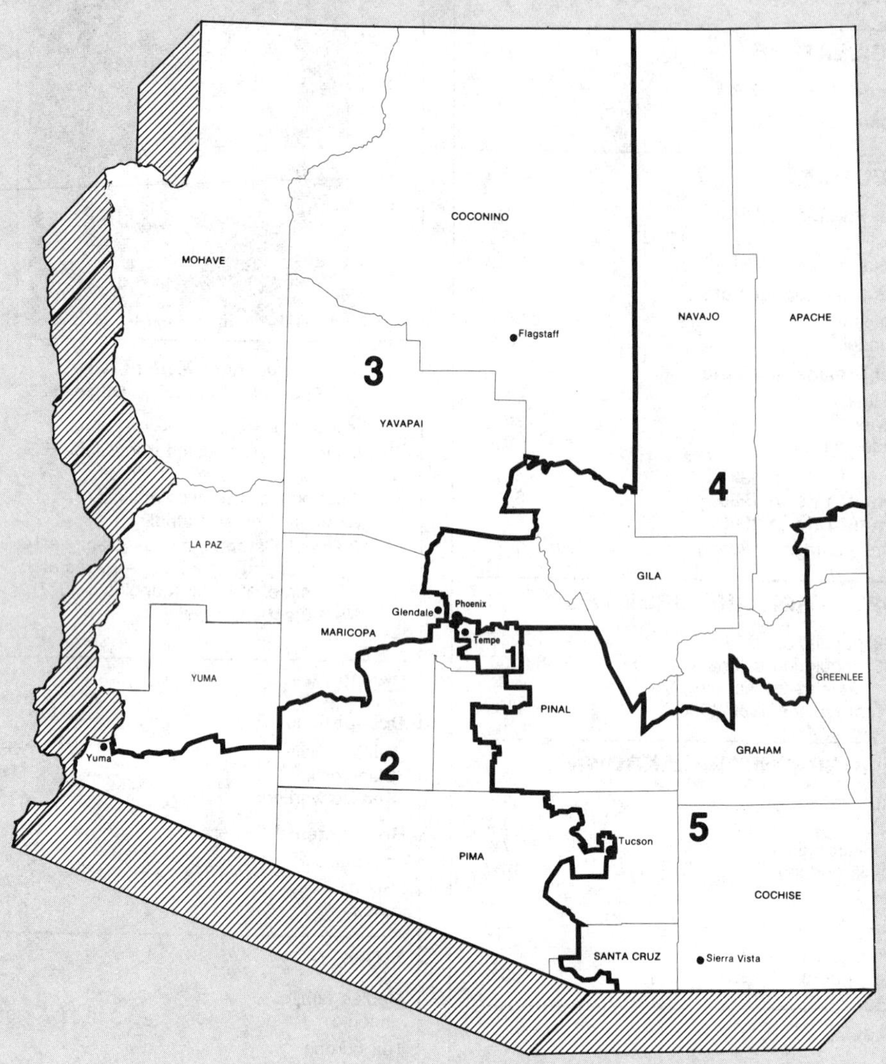
COCONINO
MOHAVE
NAVAJO
APACHE
Flagstaff
3
YAVAPAI
4
LA PAZ
GILA
Glendale
Phoenix
MARICOPA
Tempe
1
YUMA
GREENLEE
PINAL
Yuma
2
GRAHAM
5
Tucson
PIMA
COCHISE
SANTA CRUZ
Sierra Vista

Dennis DeConcini (D)

Of Tucson — Elected 1976

Born: May 8, 1937, Tucson, Ariz.
Education: U. of Arizona, B.A. 1959, LL.B. 1963.
Military Career: Army, 1959-60; Army Reserve, 1960-67.
Occupation: Lawyer.
Family: Wife, Susan Hurley; three children.
Religion: Roman Catholic.
Political Career: Pima County attorney, 1973-76.
Capitol Office: 328 Hart Bldg. 20510; 224-4521.

In Washington: DeConcini came to the Senate as a crime-fighting former prosecutor who wanted to wage a national war against drugs. He rode into his third term as a crime-fighting senator waging an international war against drugs.

His reputation on law-and-order issues is such that two Republican presidents have put him on their short list of nominees for law enforcement posts. President Reagan considered DeConcini for the FBI directorship. President Bush asked the former prosecutor to become the nation's first "drug czar."

Clearly, DeConcini is a Democrat with whom Republicans can work — a reputation that stands him well in conservative Arizona. In the Senate, he is regarded as a solid performer. Though his manner is cautious and his speaking style bland, he has racked up a number of significant legislative accomplishments, and earned some politically helpful headlines, especially on the issue of combating illegal drugs.

DeConcini came to the Senate after serving as the former administrator of the Arizona Drug Control District. He became a frequent critic of the Reagan administration for not doing enough to control the flow of narcotics.

Drug trafficking has become a bigger problem for Arizona, he says, because importers of Latin American narcotics have shifted their primary routes from Florida to the West. He has displayed increasing annoyance with Mexico, which he says has failed to eliminate corruption that encourages the flow of drugs.

To control the influx, he has sought more money for aerial surveillance of his state's vast and isolated border regions. In 1986 the Senate accepted his budget amendment increasing drug-control funds by $200 million; the year before, it had backed his proposal to have Air Force Reserve units hunt for smugglers.

As vice chairman of the Senate Drug Enforcement Caucus, DeConcini was active in the 1986 movement to pressure foreign governments to curb the drug trade at its source. He also got the Senate to repeal a 1975 law that had prohibited U.S. drug agents from participating in drug arrests in other countries.

"The drug problem has not gone away since 1986," he said as he assumed the caucus chair in 1988. With his vice chairman, Alfonse M. D'Amato of New York, he wrote the Senate version of a drug-fighting package that called for $2.4 billion in new spending. This included measures to grant extra funds to state and local police; pay to eradicate drug-producing crops grown abroad; strengthen the interdiction of traffickers at the border; and enhance drug education and treatment programs. The duo also pushed for the death penalty for certain murders related to drug trafficking.

DeConcini's campaign against the drug trade has placed him in potential danger. He once said on national TV that Bolivian government officials were involved in cocaine trafficking; soon after that, he received a telephone death threat and full-time police protection.

As the 101st Congress opened, DeConcini was looking to weaken drug traffickers by banning the sale of nine types of assault weapons. As a member of the Judiciary Committee, he sought to fashion a middle position between gun-control liberals and the gun lobby.

DeConcini's deliberative nature thrust him into the spotlight in 1987 when, as a key swing vote, he was lobbied heavily concerning the nomination of Robert H. Bork to the Supreme Court. In the end, he found Bork's record on racial and sexual discrimination lacking.

DeConcini worried aloud about the political ramifications of the Bork vote, but it proved a savvy political move. He rallied Democrats frustrated by his relatively conservative record, without serious risk of riling the GOP. Bork's strongest supporters in the state were arch-conservatives preoccupied with trying to keep Evan Mecham as governor during the events leading to his impeachment. While Bork campaigned for DeConcini's 1988 opponent, the vote never became a cutting issue.

The movement that provides refuge to Central American immigrants is strong in Arizona, and along with Massachusetts Democratic Rep. Joe Moakley, DeConcini favors legislation to grant Salvadorans and Nicaraguans special immigration status. "Surely this is better than hasty judgments and wasted lives," DeConcini says.

He managed to get the bill through a Judiciary subcommittee in the 99th Congress, but faltered due to opposition from Alan K. Simpson of Wyoming. While Moakley has been able to push the legislation through the House, it was blocked again in the Senate during 1987. The two reintroduced it in early 1989.

When it comes to money, DeConcini's conservative side is more conspicuous. He was the Democratic floor manager for the balanced-budget constitutional amendment the Senate passed in 1982, as well as for the similar measure that came up in 1986. When the amendment failed by one vote to clear the Senate, DeConcini blamed Reagan for not doing enough to help it pass.

He has been an ardent advocate of a "flat-rate" income tax that would replace the tax code with a simple, across-the-board tax rate, without deductions or exemptions. Early in 1985, as the tax reform debate got under way, he introduced a plan, drafted at Stanford's conservative Hoover Institution, to set a flat rate of 19 percent. It went nowhere.

He also was skeptical about some aspects of the Reagan administration's defense buildup. "The time has come to draw the line," he said in opposing the president's 1986 call for giving defense a $10 billion increase over inflation. He said that amount would be sufficient to fund a child immunization program, water projects in Arizona, a toxic-waste cleanup and a host of other programs.

DeConcini has become a severe critic of U.S. missile sales if he thinks the weapons could end up in the hands of terrorists. This has put him at the forefront of efforts to block some arms sales to Arab nations, sometimes even after the pro-Israel lobby has compromised. In 1987, he sought to prevent the sale of shoulder-fired Stinger anti-aircraft missiles to Bahrain. In 1988, he led the Senate forces opposed to the sale of Maverick air-to-ground and air-to-sea missiles. In both cases, he lost, although he did gain restrictions.

He has also worried about the administration's plans to supply Stingers to anti-communist guerrillas in Angola and Afghanistan. He twice offered floor amendments in 1986 to impose strict controls on the missiles to prevent their falling into terrorist hands. Both amendments were rejected, however.

DeConcini has been willing to take on some of the less sexy matters facing the Judiciary Committee. He heads the Patents, Copyrights and Trademarks Subcommittee, for example, and wrote the 1988 legislation that revised a 42-year-old trademark law to make it easier for businesses to gain its protection.

DeConcini is active on the Veterans' Affairs Committee, and there he does not apply his fiscal conservatism so strictly. He nearly always seeks more money for veterans, and opposes cost-cutting in veterans' programs.

As a freshman, DeConcini inadvertently became a major player during the Senate's bruising 1978 debate over the Panama Canal treaties. Just a year into his first term, he wound up playing the pivotal role in ratification of the two pacts. It was through his reservations to the treaties, assuring the United States the right to intervene to keep the canal open in case of trouble, that the leadership finally drew enough support to assure Senate approval.

At Home: The only Democrat to win a Senate election in Arizona in nearly 30 years, DeConcini puts considerable effort into securing himself against a conservative challenge at home. Coupled with a bit of luck — local GOP warfare in 1976 and 1988 and a good Democratic year in 1982 — his efforts have kept him from ever being seriously threatened.

In the two years leading up to his 1988 re-election, DeConcini stockpiled campaign funds and reinforced his well-regarded organization. The GOP, meanwhile, was caught up in a bitter feud sparked by Mecham's election to the governorship. After a stormy 15-month tenure, a messy impeachment fight and a threatened recall election, the GOP-controlled Legislature threw Mecham out of office in April 1988. Just when the GOP might have turned its attention to DeConcini, pro-Mecham forces ousted seven veteran GOP legislators in the September primary, further fracturing the party.

Virtually alone, 39-year-old businessman Keith DeGreen made scant progress against DeConcini, until he raised questions about the incumbent's personal finances; that issue prompted the National Republican Senatorial Committee to fund a $212,000 October TV advertising blitz on DeGreen's behalf.

In 1979, DeConcini — a multi-millionaire with vast real estate holdings — together with his family bought 320 acres of land for $400,000. Before the purchase, the federal Bureau of Reclamation had been publicly considering part of the area as a possible route for a continuation of the Central Arizona Project (CAP), a massive aqueduct. The government chose the site in 1981 and five years later reached a $1.4 million settlement for 136 acres.

DeConcini also made a 1983 investment in a development group that was involved in a similar deal. Land purchased by the partnership for $13,000 per acre was condemned by the federal government in 1984 for construction of the New Waddell Dam, which is part of CAP. In a 1987 settlement, the partnership ceded about half of its original purchase for $20,000 per acre. DeConcini divested his 3.1 percent share of the partnership before the settlement when the U.S. attorney ruled that his involvement in a negotiated water rights settlement would violate a federal law barring contracts between the government and members of Congress. The senator gave his share to his siblings, though the U.S. attorney's decision in the case was subsequently overruled.

DeConcini said he had no privileged knowledge of the government's plans in either deal. He accused DeGreen of dirty campaign tactics and lashed out at GOP Sen. John McCain for tacitly condoning them. The episode added some drama to what was expected to be a walkaway win; some polls in the campaign's final weeks showed considerable volatility in the electorate. But most voters knew too little of DeGreen to switch to him. DeConcini won with a comfortable, if not spectacular, 57 percent.

Had DeConcini not paid such careful attention to his right flank over the years, the flap might have caused him more trouble. But ever since 1978, when enraged conservatives put up billboards across the state condemning his vote for the Panama Canal treaties, the Democrat has rarely strayed far from his moderate base.

In his 1982 campaign, GOP challenger Pete Dunn, a three-term state legislator, used the Panama issue as part of his argument that DeConcini was a labor-backed liberal who "talks like Ronald Reagan in Arizona and votes like Ted Kennedy in Washington."

But by then, DeConcini had compiled a record that made it difficult to brand him a liberal. In 1981, he supported the conservative coalition of Republicans and Southern Democrats 63 percent of the time. He won re-election with 57 percent.

DeConcini campaigned for the Senate as a conservative in 1976, when he defeated GOP Rep. Sam Steiger. Stressing his law enforcement background as Pima County district attorney, he called for a crackdown on organized crime in Arizona. As it happened, neither crime nor any other policy issue had as much to do with the November outcome as a vicious Republican primary between Steiger and fellow Rep. John Conlan, longtime personal enemies.

Supporters of Steiger, a Jew, accused Conlan of pandering to anti-Semitism in a pitch for fundamentalist Christian votes. When Steiger won the primary, Conlan refused to endorse him, and Democrats rallied behind DeConcini in anticipation of a rare statewide victory.

DeConcini has his base in Tucson, the state's second-largest population center. It is where his family made a fortune in real estate. His father was a state Supreme Court justice and his mother a member of the Democratic National Committee. A brother, Dino, is a former Democratic chairman in Tucson.

Committees

Appropriations (8th of 16 Democrats)
Treasury, Postal Service and General Government (chairman); Defense; Energy and Water Development; Foreign Operations; Interior and Related Agencies

Judiciary (4th of 8 Democrats)
Patents, Copyrights and Trademarks (chairman); Antitrust, Monopolies and Business Rights; Constitution

Rules and Administration (5th of 9 Democrats)

Select Indian Affairs (2nd of 5 Democrats)

Select Intelligence (6th of 8 Democrats)

Veterans' Affairs (3rd of 6 Democrats)

Joint Library

Joint Printing

Elections

1988 General

Dennis DeConcini (D)	660,403	(57%)
Keith DeGreen (R)	478,060	(41%)

Previous Winning Percentages: **1982** (57%) **1976** (54%)

Campaign Finance

	Receipts	Receipts from PACs	Expenditures
1988			
DeConcini (D)	$2,818,427	$968,495 (34%)	$2,640,650
DeGreen (R)	$244,971	$20,350 (8%)	$238,369

Key Votes

1987

Enact omnibus highway bill over Reagan veto	Y
Limit testing of space-based anti-ballistic missiles	Y
Oppose banning tests of larger nuclear weapons	N
Confirm Robert H. Bork as Supreme Court justice	N

1988

Allow vote on campaign-finance overhaul	Y
Pass civil rights restoration bill over Reagan veto	Y
Enact omnibus trade bill over Reagan veto	Y
Approve death penalty for drug-related murders	Y
Oppose "workfare" amendment to welfare overhaul bill	N

Voting Studies

	Presidential Support		Party Unity		Conservative Coalition	
Year	**S**	**O**	**S**	**O**	**S**	**O**
1988	52	36	61	30	65	30
1987	46	51	73	26	34	59
1986	43	53	62	35	61	37
1985	45	49	62	31	63	28
1984	42	39	50 †	24 †	45	21
1983	32	47	55	31	52	32
1982	61	34	52	36	74	20
1981	51 †	38 †	59 †	24 †	63 †	24 †

† Not eligible for all recorded votes.

Interest Group Ratings

Year	ADA	ACU	AFL-CIO	CCUS
1988	55	33	92	21
1987	60	27	80	33
1986	45	52	60	35
1985	45	38	62	45
1984	60	38	75	38
1983	45	43	60	41
1982	45	60	82	53
1981	45	57	50	53

John McCain (R)

Of Phoenix — Elected 1986

Born: Aug. 29, 1936, Panama Canal Zone.
Education: U.S. Naval Academy, B.S. 1958; National War College, 1973-74.
Military Career: Navy, 1958-81.
Occupation: Naval officer; beer distributor.
Family: Wife, Cindy Lou Hensley; six children.
Religion: Episcopalian.
Political Career: U.S. House, 1983-87.
Capitol Office: 111 Russell Bldg. 20510; 224-2235.

In Washington: By rising rapidly to the heights of national politics, McCain has compensated as well as anyone could for the nearly six years he lost languishing in North Vietnamese prison camps. Newly arrived in his wife's state less than a decade ago, he already has served Arizona in the House, been elected senator and captured considerable attention among the kingmakers of the Republican Party.

In late 1988, however, McCain's GOP Senate colleagues applied the first brake to his ambitions, rejecting his bid to chair their campaign fund-raising committee. While Don Nickles of Oklahoma won primarily because he was more senior and had a head start on cornering members' commitments, some senators also were sending McCain a message: Slow down.

Despite that glimpse of colleagues' jealousy, McCain remains popular and admired within both parties. He has tried to avoid flaunting his war-hero celebrity and has been helped to that end by his disarming charm and genuine ability. Yet his celebrity means an instant audience whenever McCain speaks out on defense and foreign policy, and he has never shirked from offering his opinion.

Generally, he is a voice of reason from the right, decidedly conservative but pragmatic enough to work with colleagues in both parties. Sometimes, though, an issue can seem to consume him, and on those occasions another McCain takes over — a man tightly wound rather than relaxed, blinded to foes' points of view and more shrill in his argument.

At the start of the 101st Congress, he emerged as the most vocal defender of former Sen. John Tower to be defense secretary, and as one of the most caustic critics of Senate Democrats questioning Tower's conflicts of interest, womanizing and drinking. McCain and Tower had been close since 1977, when McCain began a four-year stint as the Navy's Senate liaison; Tower was senior Republican and then chairman of the Armed Services Committee during that period.

He criticized Armed Services Chairman Sam Nunn for what McCain saw as an open-ended willingness to review charges against Tower. "When allegations about a Russian ballerina will hold up a nomination," he snapped, "we've moved into the twilight zone." Only weeks after McCain had called for renewed bipartisanship in foreign policy, he reacted to Tower's rejection with an angry forecast that "there will be no bipartisanship." He did not alter that assessment after the Senate amicably confirmed President Bush's next choice, Rep. Dick Cheney.

Another issue that has absorbed McCain over a longer period of time is aid to the Nicaraguan contras. Though a new senator in the 100th Congress, he was a leading proponent of President Reagan's policy. Supporters' quest for aid was complicated, however, after the Central American presidents adopted a peace plan in August 1987; though the peace process sputtered on and off, thereafter the only assistance that could pass Congress was "humanitarian," not military.

In early 1988, after the House defeated both Reagan's military aid package and Democratic leaders' humanitarian alternative, temporarily ending all aid, McCain gave $400 to a conservative group's fund for the rebels.

He was enraged by Speaker Jim Wright's intervention in the peace talks; when Wright, an opponent of Reagan's policy, met privately with representatives of the Nicaraguan government, McCain called his activities "at best unseemly and at worst unconstitutional," and said Wright was "taking on the role of mediator for the Sandinista government." Near the end of 1988, Wright agreed to seal a humanitarian aid compromise by promising pro-contra senators that he would not block a House vote if Reagan sought military aid in line with procedures included in the compromise bill. McCain dismissed the pledge as "just mush."

Reagan declined to press for military aid, to McCain's chagrin. The most that he and other conservatives could do was pass a Senate resolution in late 1988 threatening renewal of military aid. It was meaningless enough that the House accepted the language the next day.

Months later, when Bush quickly settled with Democratic leaders for $45 million in humanitarian aid for a year, McCain had "strong misgivings," but added, "A new president deserves an opportunity to get the support of Republicans for a new major foreign policy initiative."

McCain prides himself on being a forceful advocate of a president's constitutional prerogatives in foreign policy, against what he sees as Congress' persistent and dangerous meddling. Yet he was hardly an uncritical, down-the-line supporter of Reagan's policies.

As a House member, he sharply took issue with the Marines' prolonged deployment in Lebanon, which ended in 1983 after the tragic barracks bombing. He criticized Defense Secretary Caspar W. Weinberger for rubber-stamping Pentagon funding requests. Even on the contra issue, McCain repeatedly urged the administration to quit trying to overthrow the Sandinistas and focus on pressing them to respect human rights and hold free elections.

In the Senate, he called Reagan's 1987 decision to provide Navy escorts for Kuwaiti tankers in the Persian Gulf "a dangerous overreaction in perhaps the most violent and unpredictable region of the world." The next year, he criticized Reagan for sending troops to Honduras as a show of force after the Sandinistas crossed the border to disrupt contra camps. While most conservatives applauded the move, McCain said it "harmed the administration's position because it has shifted the focus away from the Sandinista invasion to the issue of, are U.S. troops going to be involved in combat?"

He was openly skeptical when Reagan, heeding GOP political operatives, vetoed a defense bill to dramatize the parties' differences during the 1988 presidential campaign. When Reagan also that year vetoed the *Grove City* civil rights bill, calling instead for a more modest substitute, McCain snapped, "I hate to sound cynical, but where was the substitute when the issue was being debated?"

Despite his criticism of congressional foreign-policy making, in the 100th Congress McCain offered a dramatic initiative of his own over administration objections. With another Vietnam veteran, GOP Rep. Tom Ridge, he proposed a resolution calling for renewed, limited ties with Vietnam. Both men stressed that the proposal stopped short of full relations and was a means to advance U.S. interests.

The resolution picked up support amid a growing feeling that Reagan's hard line was preventing a constructive U.S. role in Asia. But it had powerful foes among both liberals and conservatives, and ultimately McCain abandoned the resolution when Vietnam, citing the administration's "hostile policy," surprisingly suspended an agreement to help search for the remains of U.S. servicemen and to allow emigration of political detainees.

Given his interests, McCain is most active on Armed Services, where he jumped in seniority from ninth to fifth among Republicans as the 101st Congress opened. He champions burden-sharing, a concept that calls on U.S. allies to increase spending for international security, and he favors mandatory national service.

McCain also sits on the Commerce, Science and Transportation Committee, where he pressed successfully in the 100th Congress for a bill requiring that federal agencies' phones be accessible to hearing-impaired callers.

Criticized as a carpetbagger at the outset of his career, McCain also has taken care to be attentive to state affairs. His assignment on the Select Indian Affairs Committee allows him to be active, as he was in the House, on a subject of great concern in Arizona.

In 1989, he co-chaired a special panel to investigate reports of federal mismanagement of Indian programs and corruption on reservations. McCain condemned federal policy as "benign neglect" and charged the Bureau of Indian Affairs with a "clear dereliction of duties."

On another local matter, in the 100th Congress he worked with Arizona Democratic Rep. Morris K. Udall, and against the administration, for a law restricting flights over the Grand Canyon to improve safety and decrease noise.

Meanwhile, McCain has become a national figure; even as a House member he was being touted as a presidential candidate. The roots of this political success story lie in his long ordeal in Vietnam, the years he spent tortured and in solitary confinement in Hanoi-area camps after his plane was shot down in 1967. At the 1988 GOP convention, McCain recounted his experiences for a prime-time national TV audience, further raising his public profile.

At Home: While McCain was ascending Capitol Hill, he also rose to titular head of Arizona's GOP. But sustaining his power may take as much political agility as consolidating it did.

His ascent mirrored the plummet of Republican Gov. Evan Mecham, who was elected in 1986. McCain initially stood by Mecham, but when the governor's impeachment seemed imminent early in 1988, McCain and three of the state's four GOP House members urged him to resign. That was widely viewed as Mecham's death knell.

McCain's abandonment of Mecham infuriated conservatives. Their anger heightened when he gave only lukewarm support to Keith DeGreen, the GOP's 1988 nominee against Democratic Sen. Dennis DeConcini. And yet McCain won no points from DeConcini: He complained that McCain should have blocked a late $212,000 expenditure by the National Republican Senatorial Committee for DeGreen's negative TV ads.

So, while McCain sits high on Arizona's political totem, he will have to watch his left and right with vigilance. His electoral record suggests he is up to the task.

From the time Sen. Barry Goldwater announced plans not to run again in 1986, McCain was widely regarded as his likely successor.

McCain started with a strong pool of political capital. He had impressed GOP activists by winning election to the House in 1982, so soon after his 1981 arrival in the state. Subsequent trips around Arizona as a member of Reagan's 1984 steering committee boosted his visibility. He became such a hot property that potential intraparty rivals backed away.

Democrats, too, were wary of his stature. Gov. Bruce Babbitt decided he would rather risk a run at the presidency than tangle with McCain. After a host of other Democrats also passed up the race, party leaders were relieved when Richard Kimball declared his candidacy.

Kimball had served four years in the state Senate before his election in 1982 to the Corporation Commission, which regulates public utilities and charters corporations doing business with the state. But he never hit stride as a Senate candidate. He spent months holed up to research his stands on issues, which did not enhance his visibility.

McCain's campaign was not without hitches. His plans for a party unity ticket with gubernatorial candidate Burton S. Barr, longtime state House majority leader, faltered when Barr lost to Mecham in the primary. McCain also stumbled by publicly referring to "Leisure World," an enormous senior citizens' center in Arizona, as "Seizure World." In a close race, that kind of gaffe could have proven fatal, but the race was not close. McCain swept all but three small counties.

McCain's initial opening to Congress came in 1982, when House Minority Leader John J. Rhodes decided to give up his 1st District seat. McCain captured the GOP nomination by convincing voters that his experience as Navy liaison to the Senate gave him a knowledge of "how Washington works."

When rivals charged that he was a carpetbagger who would forget Arizona once in Washington, McCain said, "I went to Hanoi and I didn't forget about the United States of America."

There was never much question McCain would be a Navy man; his father commanded U.S. forces in the Pacific during the Vietnam War, and his grandfather was a Pacific aircraft carrier commander in World War II. When he was in a Hanoi prison camp, his captors sarcastically called him the U.S. Navy's "crown prince."

Committees

Select Indian Affairs (Vice Chairman)
Special Committee on Investigations (ranking)

Armed Services (5th of 9 Republicans)
Manpower and Personnel (ranking); Conventional Forces and Alliance Defense; Projection Forces and Regional Defense

Commerce, Science and Transportation (6th of 9 Republicans)
Aviation (ranking); Communications; Consumer

Elections

1986 General		
John McCain (R)	521,850	(61%)
Richard Kimball (D)	340,965	(39%)

Previous Winning Percentages: **1984 *** (78%) **1982 *** (66%)

* *House elections.*

Campaign Finance

	Receipts	Receipts from PACs	Expend-itures
1986			
McCain (R)	$2,510,092	$773,152 (31%)	$2,189,510
Kimball (R)	$550,024	$190,187 (35%)	$531,698

Key Votes

1987	
Enact omnibus highway bill over Reagan veto	N
Limit testing of space-based anti-ballistic missiles	N
Oppose banning tests of larger nuclear weapons	Y
Confirm Robert H. Bork as Supreme Court justice	Y
1988	
Allow vote on campaign-finance overhaul	N
Pass civil rights restoration bill over Reagan veto	Y
Enact omnibus trade bill over Reagan veto	N
Approve death penalty for drug-related murders	Y
Oppose "workfare" amendment to welfare overhaul bill	N

Voting Studies

	Presidential Support		Party Unity		Conservative Coalition	
Year	**S**	**O**	**S**	**O**	**S**	**O**
1988	70	23	84	13	78	16
1987	65	24	84	11	69	25
House Service						
1986	68	29	67	25	76	18
1985	68	25	81	13	84	13
1984	64	27	74 †	13 †	83	8
1983	80	17	83	9	90	7

† *Not eligible for all recorded votes.*

Interest Group Ratings

Year	**ADA**	**ACU**	**AFL-CIO**	**CCUS**
1988	10	80	14	64
1987	15	91	20	100
House Service				
1986	10	73	14	60
1985	5	81	18	91
1984	10	86	31	93
1983	10	96	6	85

1 John J. Rhodes III (R)

Of Mesa — Elected 1986

Born: Sept. 8, 1943, Mesa, Ariz.
Education: Yale U., B.A. 1965; U. of Arizona, J.D. 1968.
Military Career: Army, 1968-70.
Occupation: Lawyer.
Family: Wife, Ann Chase; four children.
Religion: Protestant.
Political Career: Mesa School Board, 1972-76; GOP district chairman, 1973-75; vice president, Central Arizona Water Conservation District, 1983-87.
Capitol Office: 412 Cannon Bldg. 20515; 225-2635.

In Washington: Any representative from Arizona's 1st would face comparison with fast-rising John McCain, who held the seat two terms before jumping to the Senate in 1986. But Rhodes has two tough acts to follow: He is the son of former GOP House leader John J. Rhodes, who represented the district from 1953 to 1983. Compared with his powerful father and the high-profile McCain, Rhodes seems a bit bland, but he is finding a niche for himself in the House.

As a freshman, Rhodes was part of an ad hoc coalition headed by Iowa Republican Tom Tauke and Minnesota Democrat Timothy J. Penny. The group sought modest across-the-board cuts on most appropriations bills, and in 1987, Rhodes carried their amendment calling for a 0.9 percent cut from the military construction budget. "I cannot believe that in any place in this government 1 percent cannot be spared," Rhodes said. He lost 140-281, with just a bare majority of Republicans backing him.

Rhodes' overall voting record reveals his basic conservative instincts, but he has a more cautious nature than some brasher young members on the GOP right. At a Republican retreat in New York City at the start of the 100th Congress, Rhodes took issue with those who talked tough on deficit reduction, but were vague about the consequences. "You talk about farmers wanting to get rid of subsidies," he said, "but [what] we're not saying [is] that when the subsidies are gone, consumers will pay the true cost of agricultural products. I think we ought to tell consumers that in advance."

On home-state issues, Rhodes has found that the political consequences of some budget cuts can loom quite large. When Appropriations' energy and water funding bill came to the full House in 1987, the Tauke-Penny group offered an amendment to cut 1.7 percent from every program in the bill. Amid rumors that the massive Central Arizona Water Project would be threatened if Rhodes and fellow Arizona freshman Jon Kyl supported the reduction, both backed the committee bill instead of the cut.

Rhodes, a member of the Interior Committee, served as chairman of a GOP task force on Indian affairs in the 100th Congress. For the 101st, he is co-chairman of the '92 Group, whose moderate-minded members are looking for ways to gain a GOP majority in the House.

At Home: In his 1986 bid to succeed McCain, Rhodes offered more than just a famous name; he also had a résumé that would have made him formidable on its own. Rhodes had military credentials — a bronze star for service as an intelligence adviser in Vietnam. Active in local GOP affairs, he served stints as district chairman and president of the Mesa Board of Education. In 1982, he was elected to the board of the Central Arizona Project.

But while Rhodes became the early front-runner for the 1st, he proved to be neither entertaining nor inspirational on the stump, and that gave an opening to primary challenger Ray Russell, a Mesa veterinarian who had waged a strong effort against McCain in 1982.

Russell began with a base of support among Mesa's politically active Mormon community. He rented billboards that proclaimed: "Vote for a leader, not a name." But whatever Rhodes' shortcomings as a campaigner, his experience and outlook made him acceptable to mainstream Republicans, who are dominant in the 1st. A lawyer and former president of the Mesa Chamber of Commerce, Rhodes called himself a pragmatic conservative. Rhodes got 44 percent of the primary vote, with Russell 7 points back. That was tantamount to election in this GOP stronghold.

In 1988, Rhodes' father was mentioned as a possible contender in the scheduled recall election of GOP Gov. Evan Mecham. That angered Mecham's conservative backers, and they threatened to field a primary opponent to the younger Rhodes. But Mecham was impeached before the recall, and no one challenged Rhodes in the GOP primary. He won comfortably in November.

Arizona 1

Eastern Phoenix; Tempe; Mesa

Arizona's only truly urban district, the 1st is a collection of Sun Belt cities growing at a breakneck pace. According to one study done in 1984, some 40 percent of the population had lived there less than five years.

The balance of power clearly lies in the suburbs of Phoenix, where the bulk of the area's growth has occurred. Mesa expanded by almost 150 percent during the 1970s and by more than 50 percent between 1980 and 1986. The city now has more than 250,000 residents. Tempe (136,000) and Chandler (68,000) add to the suburban totals.

Electronics and high-technology firms have thrived here in recent years, reinforcing the district's Republican tendencies. Managers and technicians flocking to the 1st have brought their Republican loyalties with them, augmenting those of the retirees who earlier had hastened the area's conservative shift.

Mesa is a reliable source of Republican votes. Founded by Mormons in 1878, it still has a politically active Mormon community and is the site of a large Mormon temple. It also has a McDonnell Douglas plant, and Williams Air Force Base is nearby.

The adjacent community of Tempe was developed around a flour mill built in 1871 and Tempe today has light industries, electronics plants and garment factories. The city usually votes Republican for state and local offices. But Tempe has a significant Democratic presence, thanks in large part to the Arizona State University community, which includes 43,000 students and 2,400 faculty.

The 1st also takes in a politically diverse portion of southeastern Phoenix, a tabletop-flat area of the "Valley of the Sun" that includes upper-middle-class neighborhoods with a distinctly Republican bent as well as the district's only significant populations of blacks and Hispanics. Many of the minority voters live in neighborhoods around Sky Harbor Airport.

Democrats who avoid a liberal label can sometimes win a narrow majority in the 1st in statewide elections. Sen. Dennis DeConcini has done so, as did former Gov. Bruce Babbitt. But in recent congressional and presidential contests, Republicans have had solid margins here.

Population: 543,747. White 474,724 (87%), Black 19,556 (4%), Other 12,582 (2%). Spanish origin 62,119 (11%). 18 and over 399,698 (74%), 65 and over 62,119 (11%). Median age: 29.

Committees

Interior and Insular Affairs (9th of 15 Republicans)
Energy and the Environment; General Oversight and Investigations; National Parks and Public Lands; Water, Power and Offshore Energy Resources

Small Business (11th of 17 Republicans)
Exports, Tax Policy and Special Problems; Procurement, Tourism and Rural Development

Elections

1988 General		
John J. Rhodes III (R)	184,639	(72%)
John M. Fillmore (D)	71,388	(28%)
1986 General		
John J. Rhodes III (R)	127,370	(71%)
Harry Braun III (D)	51,163	(29%)

District Vote For President

	1988		1984		1980		1976	
D	90,383	(34%)	58,492	(27%)	44,473	(25%)	57,839	(37%)
R	171,884	(65%)	154,845	(72%)	113,755	(63%)	93,155	(59%)
I					15,916	(9%)		

Campaign Finance

	Receipts	Receipts from PACs		Expenditures
1988				
Rhodes (R)	$293,044	$135,419	(46%)	$291,961
Fillmore (D)	$13,756	$1,250	(9%)	$11,855
1986				
Rhodes (R)	$498,408	$112,065	(22%)	$493,182
Braun (D)	$32,180	$650	(2%)	$31,528

Key Votes

1987	
Raise speed limit to 65 mph	Y
Approve Gephardt "fair trade" amendment	N
Ban testing of larger nuclear weapons	N
Delay "re-flagging" of Kuwaiti tankers	N
Approve tax-raising deficit-reduction bill	N
1988	
Approve aid to Nicaraguan contras	Y
Enact civil rights restoration bill over Reagan veto	N
Kill 60-day plant-closing notification measure	Y
Pass omnibus trade bill over Reagan veto	N
Approve death penalty for drug-related murders	Y
Bar federal funds for abortions in cases of rape and incest	Y
Oppose seven-day waiting period for purchase of handguns	Y

Voting Studies

	Presidential Support		Party Unity		Conservative Coalition	
Year	S	O	S	O	S	O
1988	70	29	93	5	95	5
1987	71	29	87	11	100	0

Interest Group Ratings

Year	ADA	ACU	AFL-CIO	CCUS
1988	10	96	7	100
1987	4	96	6	93

2 Morris K. Udall (D)

Of Tucson — Elected 1961

Born: June 15, 1922, St. Johns, Ariz.
Education: U. of Arizona, J.D. 1949.
Military Career: Army Air Corps, 1942-46.
Occupation: Lawyer.
Family: Widowed; six children.
Religion: Mormon.
Political Career: Pima County attorney, 1952-54; sought Democratic nomination for president, 1976.
Capitol Office: 235 Cannon Bldg. 20515; 225-4065.

In Washington: Udall's physical health is turning out to be the final and most uncompromising obstacle in a long career marked by unfailing grace, enormous creativity and frequent and disappointing defeat.

Udall long ago gave up his House leadership ambitions, but if he were not suffering from Parkinson's disease, he might now be Speaker. No House Democrat can match Udall's combination of affection and respect among colleagues; a healthy and ambitious Udall would have been the one credible rival to Jim Wright's 1986 accession as Speaker in the wake of the retirement of Thomas P. O'Neill Jr.

While his illness has not impaired his powers of concentration or the output of his Interior Committee, it leaves him in obvious discomfort much of the time, and precludes any broader role in House politics.

There is some irony in Udall's inability to claim the leadership role for which his 14 terms in the House have prepared him. For most of his early career, he had the stamina and ambition to be a leader, but the House did not want to elect him.

In 1969, Udall was the Young Turk challenger to John W. McCormack for Speaker. While Udall never expected to oust McCormack as Speaker, he did expect to become majority leader two years later, and most of his liberal allies expected it as well. But he lost badly to Hale Boggs of Louisiana, a man who had only recently recovered from the effects of a nervous collapse. Boggs offered no threat to the traditional power structure; Udall, a critic of seniority, did.

That defeat marked the turning point in Udall's career. It ended his leadership hopes and drove him deeper into the legislative process, in which he had come to excel.

Udall's legislative career is striking evidence that a member of Congress can find important work to do anywhere in the committee system. For 20 years, Udall never had anything resembling a major assignment — he joined Interior in 1961 to work on Arizona land and mining issues and also went on Post Office at the leadership's request.

He has used his Interior assignment to make himself the chamber's most prolific author of environmental legislation, both before and since he became chairman in 1977. But it has been a difficult and frustrating process. The House passed strip-mine control legislation three times, and twice failed to override President Ford's vetoes, before a bill reasonably close to what Udall wanted became law in 1977. It took four years for Congress to enact legislation dividing Alaska lands between development and wilderness. Two years of struggle ended in deadlock on the last day of the 95th Congress in 1978; a compromise Alaska bill finally passed in 1980.

The 98th Congress saw enactment, after years of bickering, of a bill designating more than 8 million acres of new federal wilderness in 20 states — the first major addition to the wilderness system since 1964. The first wilderness bill to pass was for Arizona.

Other major Udall ideas have run out of steam. His scheme to provide federal aid for local land-use planning as a solution to urban sprawl failed on the House floor amid charges that it smacked of socialism.

As chairman of the Interior Committee, Udall increasingly has delegated responsibility for major bills to other senior members — particularly to his heir apparent, ranking Democrat George Miller of California.

Udall has never been the kind of chairman who exacts retribution from members who cross him. Indeed, he and Miller fought bitterly in 1988 — with no apparent long-term effect on their relationship — over a bill of great interest to the Arizona Democrat. The measure made a controversial land swap that gave a developer some downtown Phoenix real estate in exchange for Florida lands needed for a wildlife refuge. Miller said the deal was a bad bargain for the taxpayer.

Despite Udall's increasing physical frailty, Interior has sent more than its share of bills to the House floor.

The 100th Congress enacted legislation

Arizona 2

Southwest — Western Tucson; Southern Phoenix; Yuma

The 2nd is Arizona's most Hispanic (36 percent) and most Democratic (63 percent) district. It stretches from downtown Phoenix to downtown Tucson and includes much of the classic desert landscape in between, dotted with the large saguaro cactus that is a hallmark of the American Southwest.

The Maricopa County (Phoenix) portion dominates the 2nd politically. Maricopa casts a majority of the district vote, most of it in Hispanic areas. The south side of Phoenix, included in the 2nd, traditionally has been the poorest and most faithfully Democratic part of the city.

The part of Tucson (Pima County) remaining in the district is also Democratic: It contains the Hispanic neighborhoods in the city's western part as well as the University of Arizona, with 33,000 students. Also favorable to Democrats are the copper-mining town of Ajo and the San Xavier and Papago Indian reservations just south of the city.

Tucson, with a population that is one-quarter Hispanic, has a Democratic heritage that an influx of retirees and people attracted by high-tech firms has only lately begun to offset. But change is certain to continue. A 1980 survey found that one in four of the residents in the 2nd had been there four years or less.

The bulk of Pima County's land area lies within the boundaries of the 2nd, although most of the county's residents live in eastern Tucson in the 5th District. North of Pima in the 2nd, Pinal County includes an important Cotton Belt.

The 2nd also takes in the southern tier of Yuma County, in which irrigated farm land grows citrus fruit and vegetables. The city of Yuma is famous for being America's hottest urbanized place.

The 2nd is typically in the Democratic column for state and congressional contests, and is fairly close in presidential balloting. Democrat Bruce Babbitt was extremely strong there in his 1978 and 1982 gubernatorial victories; in 1988, Democratic presidential nominee Michael S. Dukakis swamped George Bush in the 2nd.

Population: 543,187. White: 376,773 (69%), Black 30,548 (6%), American Indian, Eskimo and Aleut 28,327 (5%), Other 5,050 (1%). Spanish origin 192,632 (36%). 18 and over 372,734 (69%), 65 and over 52,322 (10%). Median age: 27.

Udall advocated to raise the limit on liability of commercial nuclear power-plant operators. Some years before that, the 1902 reclamation act was finally rewritten after a drawn-out battle; it increased to 960 acres the size of farms eligible for cheap, federally subsidized water.

Environmentalists have had enough success writing their agenda into law that some of Udall's battles are now won simply by blocking action. For example, in the 100th Congress, he could prevent efforts to open an Alaska wildlife refuge to oil drilling simply by preserving the status quo.

However, the 100th Congress also dealt a blow to another key Udall accomplishment of the early 1980s. After a three-year struggle, Congress in 1982 had approved legislation providing for orderly choice of nuclear-waste disposal sites based on safety and scientific criteria, not politics. That legislation was, in essence, reversed in 1987 when Congress voted to place the nuclear-waste dump in Nevada over the state's vociferous objections. Udall had sought unsuccessfully to delay the decision and to empower a high-level negotiator to find a willing state.

While working on these issues, Udall has been doing what Arizona expects him to do on Interior — protecting the Central Arizona Project, the massive water system for which Udall has struggled throughout his career.

Udall has had what amounted to a second legislative front on the Post Office Committee. A resting place for many of the less ambitious House members, Post Office turned out to be a perfect vehicle for many of Udall's interests. In his first decade there he worked to revise the federal pay system, including the one for Congress, and to make the Postal Service a semi-private corporation. Much later, he won passage of President Carter's civil service reforms, to promote merit pay and more flexibility for managers.

The federal pay legislation sought to end in-house control over congressional salaries, creating a federal commission to deal with the subject. But that idea was left in a shambles in 1989 when, in the face of stormy public opposition, Congress rejected a 51 percent pay raise recommended by the commission. The pay-raise proposal came under fire both because of its size and because it could have taken effect without Congress voting on the matter.

Outside his committees, Udall has spent more than 20 years pushing for changes in the political system, again with mixed results. He was chief sponsor of the 1971 bill that made the first real national rules for campaign finance, limiting expenditures and contributions and providing for voluminous disclosure. But he has failed repeatedly with legislation to establish public financing of congressional campaigns.

Udall's own campaign for the 1976 Democratic presidential nomination, as the leading liberal alternative to Jimmy Carter, left a curious record: He gained wide respect within his party and survived through to the convention in New York without ever winning anything.

Udall finished second in seven primaries and was declared the Wisconsin winner prematurely by two networks, but he never had a first-place finish. He would almost certainly have won in New Hampshire had former Sen. Fred Harris not attracted liberal votes, but by the time Harris withdrew the next month, Carter was too strong to be headed off.

Udall eventually made his peace with Carter and was not one of the more outspoken critics during Carter's presidential term, but he endorsed Edward M. Kennedy's bid for the Democratic nomination in 1980. Eventually he receded into the elder statesman's role that allowed him to give the convention's keynote address. He thought about one more presidential campaign for himself in 1984, but gave the idea up to the realities of declining health.

At Home: By defeating a determined primary challenger in 1986, Udall proved that this seat is his as long as he wants it. No Democrat filed to run against him in 1988, and Udall's Republican opponent did not dent his typically huge general-election margin.

Udall's 1986 primary challenge had its roots in 1982 redistricting, which made his 2nd District Arizona's most heavily Hispanic constituency. State Sen. Luis Gonzales decided it was time the district had Hispanic representation, and because Gonzales had represented a sizable chunk of the 2nd's Hispanic population for eight years in the state Legislature, his candidacy seemed to be more than just an idle threat.

But Gonzales underestimated Udall's political strength. The incumbent was able to draw on the strong support of top Hispanic leaders, many of whom regarded Gonzales' attempt merely as an effort to build name recognition for a future campaign after the incumbent retires. Bolstered further by his backing in the local Anglo community, Udall won going away.

Udall came to politics as a member of one of Arizona's best-known families. His father was a justice of the Arizona Supreme Court; his mother was a local Democratic activist.

A professional basketball player for the old Denver Nuggets despite the handicap of a glass eye, Udall entered law practice with his brother Stewart in 1949 and later was Pima County attorney while Stewart served in Congress. When Stewart Udall resigned from Congress in 1961 to become President Kennedy's interior secretary, Morris ran for the seat in a special election that drew attention as a test of Kennedy's first 100 days in office. Udall backed such Kennedy programs as federal aid to education and medical care for the aged. He won, but with only 51 percent. He was hurt by Stewart Udall's call for evacuation of farmers squatting on federal land along the Colorado River.

For years after that, Udall won easily. But in 1976 he drew less than 60 percent for the first time in a decade. His unsuccessful campaign for the Democratic presidential nomination that year had given high visibility to his liberal views. The presidential publicity generated expensive and bitterly fought House campaigns in 1978 and 1980, with Udall having to fight off heavy GOP spending — which he more than matched — and charges of "socialism" by his Republican challengers. In the 1980 campaign he admitted that he was suffering from Parkinson's disease, but still won by nearly 40,000 votes despite the Reagan presidential victory.

In 1982 Udall was faced with a difficult choice. Arizona's Republican Legislature divided his overpopulated 2nd District in half, with part of his hometown of Tucson in each half. Udall had the option of running either in the redrawn 2nd, which was safely Democratic but extended awkwardly all the way to Phoenix, where he had never run before; or in the 5th, which kept more of his familiar Tucson precincts but included a strong Republican vote.

Udall decided to take legal action. He and his Tucson Democratic allies prepared to take the Legislature to court on the grounds that its district map unfairly splintered the Hispanic vote. The Legislature compromised and placed more of Tucson in the 2nd. Udall ran there, and won easily.

Committees

Interior and Insular Affairs (Chairman)
Energy and the Environment (chairman); Insular and International Affairs; Mining and Natural Resources; Water, Power and Offshore Energy Resources

Foreign Affairs (19th of 28 Democrats)
Arms Control, International Security and Science

Post Office and Civil Service (14th of 15 Democrats)

Elections

1988 General

Morris K. Udall (D)	99,895	(73%)
Joseph D. Sweeney (R)	36,309	(27%)

1986 General

Morris K. Udall (D)	77,239	(73%)
Sheldon Clark (R)	24,522	(23%)

Previous Winning Percentages: **1984** (88%) **1982** (71%) **1980** (58%) **1978** (53%) **1976** (58%) **1974** (62%) **1972** (64%) **1970** (69%) **1968** (70%) **1966** (60%) **1964** (59%) **1962** (58%) **1961** * (51%)

* *Special election.*

District Vote For President

	1988	1984	1980	1976
D	77,470 (56%)	65,829 (48%)	46,830 (43%)	38,769 (41%)
R	60,582 (43%)	70,487 (51%)	48,700 (44%)	51,807 (55%)
I			11,726 (11%)	

Campaign Finance

	Receipts	Receipts from PACs	Expend-itures
1988			
Udall (D)	$119,497	$84,605 (71%)	$99,607
Sweeney (R)	$3,105	0	3,065
1986			
Udall (D)	$403,554	$139,830 (35%)	$447,112

Key Votes

1987

Raise speed limit to 65 mph	Y
Approve Gephardt "fair trade" amendment	Y
Ban testing of larger nuclear weapons	Y
Delay "re-flagging" of Kuwaiti tankers	Y
Approve tax-raising deficit-reduction bill	Y

1988

Approve aid to Nicaraguan contras	N
Enact civil rights restoration bill over Reagan veto	Y
Kill 60-day plant-closing notification measure	N
Pass omnibus trade bill over Reagan veto	Y
Approve death penalty for drug-related murders	Y
Bar federal funds for abortions in cases of rape and incest	N
Oppose seven-day waiting period for purchase of handguns	N

Voting Studies

	Presidential Support		Party Unity		Conservative Coalition	
Year	S	O	S	O	S	O
1988	21	63	78	4	13	74
1987	17	78	90	4	28	70
1986	19	77	89	4	18	76
1985	16	73	84	4	16	75
1984	31	59	85	7	22	69
1983	24	71	86	5	22	69
1982	38	56	86	7	29	62
1981	51	41	76	16	39	59

Interest Group Ratings

Year	ADA	ACU	AFL-CIO	CCUS
1988	75	13	92	29
1987	88	0	93	7
1986	85	5	86	13
1985	80	0	88	20
1984	85	14	92	40
1983	90	0	94	35
1982	85	5	82	25
1981	75	13	87	17

3 Bob Stump (R)

Of Tolleson — Elected 1976

Born: April 4, 1927, Phoenix, Ariz.
Education: Arizona State U., B.S. 1951.
Military Career: Navy, 1943-46.
Occupation: Farmer.
Family: Divorced; three children.
Religion: Seventh-day Adventist.
Political Career: Ariz. House, 1959-67; Ariz. Senate, 1967-77, Senate president, 1975-77.
Capitol Office: 211 Cannon Bldg. 20515; 225-4576.

In Washington: One of the House's most conservative Democrats during his first three terms, Stump found all the comforts of home when he switched to the GOP in 1982. The first of a handful of House Democrats to cross the aisle in the early Reagan years, Stump clearly felt he would be more comfortable — both politically and personally — in the conservative Republican caucus than on the liberal-dominated Democratic side. None would argue with his assessment.

Since the switch, Stump has been a fixture in the GOP's most conservative wing. Though President Reagan's overall support in the House faded during his second term, Stump became even more loyal. He backed Reagan's positions on House legislation more than 80 percent of the time in each of the last four years, a figure that consistently placed him near the top of the list of Reagan loyalists.

Stump's conservative proclivities go beyond his voting record to his relationships with other members. He is friendly with those whom he regards as "right-minded," but he has little time for those with a liberal bent.

The party switch was by far the most public political act of Stump's Washington career. He has introduced few bills for consideration, and he rarely rises to speak on the House floor.

In his most senior committee position, Stump is seldom called upon to man the partisan barricades anyway. He is ranking Republican on the Veterans' Affairs Committee, a panel with a bipartisan consensus in favor of veterans' programs. During the 100th Congress, Stump was a strong supporter of successful efforts to establish the Veterans Administration as a Cabinet-level agency, a measure that had broad backing in both parties.

Stump was even aided by a prominent Democrat in 1986 during one of his few legislative ventures. Then a member of the Select Intelligence Committee, Stump argued for an amendment to an intelligence authorization bill allowing the CIA to continue providing covert military aid to rebels fighting the Marxist government of Angola. When the proposal reached the House floor, Stump was joined by Florida Democrat Claude Pepper, a social-issues liberal but a staunch anti-communist. The amendment passed, 229-186.

Stump maintains his hard-line views about other foreign policy matters as a member of the Armed Services Committee. But while he has risen to the third-ranking Republican position on that committee, he rarely moves beyond his stance as a rock-solid GOP vote. He is not a player in the give-and-take process of shaping broad defense policy.

Stump's party switch in 1982 reflected the political evolution of voters in his 3rd District. Like many of his rural constituents, Stump, a cotton farmer, was raised as a "pinto Democrat," whose conservative philosophy closely matched that of the traditional Democrats of the South. During his early years in the House, Stump described himself as a Democrat who subscribed to "Thomas Jefferson's concept of limited government." But Stump, along with many of his district supporters, became increasingly alienated by the liberal direction of the national Democratic Party.

Though he frequently voted against the policies of Democratic President Jimmy Carter, Stump did not reach the breaking point until 1981, when House Democratic leaders threatened retaliation against those members — especially the conservative, mainly Southern "Boll Weevils" — who had bolted the party to support Reagan's landmark budget- and tax-cutting legislation.

In September of that year, Stump announced that he would run for re-election in 1982 as a Republican. Citing what he described as leadership threats to strip seniority and chairmanships from "renegade" members, Stump said, "No pressure group in or out of Congress is going to dictate to me how I am going to vote on important issues." He also used the occasion to swipe at liberal Democrats, who, he said, had "created a massive, distant, centralized federal government which overtaxes, overspends and overregulates."

Arizona 3

North and West — Glendale; Flagstaff; Part of Phoenix

Once dominated almost entirely by "pinto Democrats" — ranchers and other conservative rural landowners — the 3rd has become prime GOP turf over the years.

Republicans have fared particularly well here in recent presidential elections. In 1984, it was Ronald Reagan's best district in the state; in 1988, the 3rd gave George Bush 64 percent.

The majority of the vote is cast in the Maricopa County suburbs west of Phoenix. Glendale, which produces wide GOP margins, grew by nearly 30 percent between 1980 and 1986. Bush won two-thirds of the vote in the Maricopa portion of the 3rd. In nearby Sun City, an affluent and largely Republican retirement community, political organizations among the retirees contribute to House election turnouts of 90 percent or higher.

Moving west, the 3rd takes in northern Yuma County, a sparsely populated mountainous area whose residents generally have a GOP point of view. Much of this portion of the county is occupied by a national wildlife refuge and an Army proving ground.

Residents of the northernmost portion of Yuma County moved to set up their own local government in June 1982, passing a ballot initiative that transformed northern Yuma into brand-new La Paz County. The La Paz community of Quartzsite swells during the winter, as travelers flock to take advantage of the warm climate and rock and mineral shows.

Mohave County, occupying the northwestern corner of the state, is home to three groups in constant political tension — Indians, pinto Democrats in Kingman and Republican retirees in Lake Havasu City. Though the county has been close in recent statewide elections, Republicans have gained a slight registration advantage over the Democrats; Bush carried Mohave with more than 60 percent of the vote.

To the east lies Coconino County, where partisan sentiments are mixed. The northern end, near the Utah border, includes "the Arizona strip," a heavily Mormon region that bears a staunch affinity for the GOP. Sedona, a city at the county's southern end, also votes Republican.

But old-time Democratic loyalties persist in Flagstaff, the seat of Coconino County and the commercial center of northern Arizona. Among Flagstaff's leading industries are lumber, mining and tourism — which is spurred by the proximity of ski resorts as well as the Grand Canyon to the north and the Oak Creek Canyon to the south.

A drive through Oak Creek Canyon brings one to Yavapai County, a mountainous area that includes ancient Indian ruins and ghost mining towns. The county centers on Prescott, the former territorial capital that hosted the first session of the Arizona Legislature in 1864. Yavapai County has been tough sledding for Democratic Sen. Dennis DeConcini in his last two elections; it was the only county in the state to go against him in 1982, and he just barely carried it in 1988.

Population: 544,870. White 468,924 (86%), Black 8,330 (2%), American Indian, Eskimo and Aleut 27,538 (5%), Other 3,845 (1%). Spanish origin 64,414 (12%). 18 and over 389,150 (71%), 65 and over 79,881 (15%). Median age: 31.

The Republican Party clearly had a welcome mat out for Stump. In 1983, he was appointed to a GOP seat on Armed Services with no loss in seniority. His seniority also was guaranteed on Veterans' Affairs, though he took a leave from that committee to serve on Intelligence, a post he held from 1983 to 1987.

However, Republican hopes that Stump's switch foretold a mass Democratic movement proved ephemeral. During the 97th Congress, only one other Democrat left his party — Eugene V. Atkinson of Pennsylvania — and he lost his seat in the 1982 election. The last Democrat to switch during the Reagan administration, Andy Ireland of Florida, made his move in 1984, and successfully defended his seat; he has since joined Stump on the Armed Services Committee.

At Home: Secure in his northern Arizona seat since his first election in 1976, Stump had plenty of time to mull over his long-contemplated party switch. When he finally filed on the Republican side in 1982, it caused barely a ripple back home.

Stump said his decision would not cost him any significant support in either party. He was right. The middle-class retirees who have flocked to this Sun Belt territory in recent years brought their Republican voting habits along, and the conservative rural Democrats who traditionally have formed the core of Stump's constituency proved willing to move with him. Stump coasted to victory with 63 percent of the vote. Stump's re-elections since then have been uneventful.

Stump served 18 years in the state Legislature and rose to the presidency of the state Senate during the 1975-76 session. When GOP Rep. Sam Steiger tried for the U.S. Senate in 1976, Stump ran for his House seat.

In the 1976 Democratic primary, he defeated a more liberal, free-spending opponent, former state Assistant Attorney General Sid Rosen. Stump drew 31 percent to Rosen's 25 percent, with the rest scattered among three others. In the fall campaign, Stump's GOP opponent was fellow state Sen. Fred Koory, the Senate minority leader. Stump wooed conservative Democrats by criticizing his party's vice presidential nominee, Walter F. Mondale. He was helped in the election by the candidacy of state Sen. Bill McCune, a Republican who ran as an independent and drained GOP votes from Koory.

Committees

Veterans' Affairs (Ranking)
Oversight and Investigations (ranking); Hospitals and Health Care

Armed Services (3rd of 21 Republicans)
Investigations; Research and Development

Elections

1988 General		
Bob Stump (R)	174,453	(69%)
Dave Moss (D)	72,417	(29%)
1986 General		
Bob Stump (R)	146,462	(100%)

Previous Winning Percentages: **1984** (72%) **1982** (63%) **1980 *** (64%) **1978 *** (85%) **1976 *** (48%)

** Stump was elected as a Democrat in 1976-80.*

District Vote For President

	1988	1984	1980	1976
D	89,460 (35%)	61,884 (28%)	48,133 (24%)	63,232 (39%)
R	165,406 (64%)	158,767 (71%)	132,455 (67%)	95,078 (58%)
I			13,103 (7%)	

Campaign Finance

	Receipts	Receipts from PACs	Expend-itures
1988			
Stump (R)	$257,184	$115,046 (45%)	$319,690
Moss (D)	$26,551	0	$26,281
1986			
Stump (R)	$233,689	$97,050 (42%)	$135,636

Key Votes

1987	
Raise speed limit to 65 mph	Y
Approve Gephardt "fair trade" amendment	N
Ban testing of larger nuclear weapons	N
Delay "re-flagging" of Kuwaiti tankers	N
Approve tax-raising deficit-reduction bill	N
1988	
Approve aid to Nicaraguan contras	Y
Enact civil rights restoration bill over Reagan veto	N
Kill 60-day plant-closing notification measure	Y
Pass omnibus trade bill over Reagan veto	N
Approve death penalty for drug-related murders	Y
Bar federal funds for abortions in cases of rape and incest	Y
Oppose seven-day waiting period for purchase of handguns	Y

Voting Studies

	Presidential Support		Party Unity		Conservative Coalition	
Year	S	O	S	O	S	O
1988	84	13	95	3	100	0
1987	81	19	95	3	98	2
1986	88	11	92	6	92	6
1985	84	16	93	6	96	4
1984	67	27	84	7	86	7
1983	77	18	91	6	92	7
1982	82	13	3	93	96	0
1981	74	18	17	81	97	0

Interest Group Ratings

Year	ADA	ACU	AFL-CIO	CCUS
1988	0	100	0	85
1987	4	100	6	100
1986	0	100	8	100
1985	0	100	0	95
1984	5	86	17	79
1983	0	100	6	79
1982	0	100	0	89
1981	0	93	13	95

4 Jon Kyl (R)

Of Phoenix — Elected 1986

Born: April 25, 1942, Oakland, Neb.
Education: U. of Arizona, B.A. 1964; LL.B. 1966.
Occupation: Lawyer.
Family: Wife, Caryll Collins; two children.
Religion: Presbyterian.
Political Career: No previous office.
Capitol Office: 313 Cannon Bldg. 20515; 225-3361.

In Washington: Kyl got a prize committee assignment in his first term — a seat on Armed Services — and he promptly went to work mastering the details of defense, advancing his conservative views on national security policy and mixing it up with Democratic Chairman Les Aspin and committee liberals.

In years past, Armed Services was a panel with a "more is better" pro-defense consensus. But budgets are tighter now, the committee leadership has changed, and there is more attention to setting spending priorities. In that process, the strong-minded Kyl is one of a handful of junior Republicans on the committee who are determined to see that the conservative viewpoint does not get short-shrifted by the savvy Aspin and his Democratic allies.

Some felt that freshman Kyl pushed his views a bit too brashly, but he is not the bystander type; outside Armed Services, his most visible role in the 101st Congress is as chairman of the Conservative Opportunity Society, the group of aggressive younger Republicans whose influence increased with the 1989 election of Georgian Newt Gingrich as GOP whip.

When Armed Services debated the fiscal 1989 military authorization bill, Kyl offered an amendment to restore the Reagan administration's full $4.9 billion request for the strategic defense initiative. Kyl was defeated by voice vote in committee, but tried again on the House floor. There, he lost by a lopsided 105-312, barely carrying a majority of Republicans.

On the South Africa sanctions bill in 1988, Kyl sponsored an administration-sought waiver to allow military cooperation between the U.S. and South African governments. His amendment won Armed Services approval, but was rejected by Rules, which coordinated differences among seven House committees involved in the legislation. When Kyl linked military and intelligence cooperation in an amendment before the full House, he lost 169-214.

Kyl enjoyed his greatest success in his work on smaller-scale parochial matters. He saw two federal land-transfer bills (one involving a school, the other a highway) win passage late in the 100th Congress.

He also demonstrated a willingness to compromise when it came to federal funding for a crucial home-state project. In 1987, when an effort was made to eliminate 1.7 percent from every program in the energy and water appropriations bill, Kyl voted against the reduction. Both he and GOP colleague John J. Rhodes III were under pressure to reject the cut: Senior Appropriations Republicans warned that funding for the Central Arizona Water Project might be axed if an across-the-board reduction passed.

At Home: Launching a House campaign against a well-known former incumbent can be daunting. But for Kyl, the reputation of ex-GOP Rep. John Conlan, his 1986 primary foe, was a blessing. Conlan was the longtime nemesis of Arizona's GOP establishment, which backed Kyl. After dispatching Conlan, Kyl had little trouble thrashing a well-financed Democratic foe in this traditionally GOP district. In 1988, Democrats did not field a candidate.

The 1986 campaign was Kyl's first, but he was no newcomer to politics. The son of former GOP Rep. John H. Kyl of Iowa, he had been active in party affairs and lobbied the state Legislature on behalf of highways, shopping centers and a local water project. A business-oriented attorney and former president of the Phoenix Chamber of Commerce, he won strong support from the corporate establishment.

But Kyl's success also depended on the specter of Conlan. An energetic but abrasive Religious Right activist, Conlan alienated many Republicans in an acrimonious 1976 Senate primary. After losing the primary, Conlan refused to back nominee Sam Steiger, who then lost the general election.

Kyl got endorsements from a string of prominent Republicans who publicly questioned Conlan's abilities and integrity. Conlan sought to exploit Kyl's corporate connections, accusing him of buying the election with special-interest money. But Conlan could not put his troubles to rest, and Kyl trounced him 2-to-1. In November, Kyl easily won the right to succeed retiring GOP Rep. Eldon Rudd.

Arizona 4

Northeast — Northern Phoenix; Scottsdale

The wilds of northeastern Arizona account for most of the territory in the 4th, but the huge majority of the district's vote is cast in the comfortable confines of northern Phoenix. That white-collar area provides ample Republican majorities, as do Scottsdale and other adjoining suburbs in Maricopa County. When the 4th was open in 1986, the part of Maricopa in the 4th cast nearly 80 percent of the district's vote, and GOP nominee Kyl won it with 69 percent.

Scottsdale, an affluent resort community, attracts visitors with its warm, sunny climate, myriad golf courses and fashionable shops. The city grew by more than 35 percent between 1980 and 1989, and is now home to some 120,000 people. Many of its residents are retirees; others commute to work at the management level in Phoenix corporations. The names of suburbs such as Paradise Valley and Carefree symbolize the lifestyle envisioned by their developers and sought by their residents.

The 4th went Republican as soon as it was created in 1972, and rapid population growth has buttressed its conservative nature. The GOP presidential vote has climbed steadily, reaching 71 percent for President Reagan in 1984; George Bush took 65 percent in the 4th in 1988.

Democrats are at parity with the GOP in the region stretching north to the Utah border; its population concentrations are mining towns and Indian reservations. But while the Republican areas prospered, the copper towns of Globe and Miami have not been resuscitated by economic revival. In Navajo and Apache counties, which march side by side down the Arizona border with New Mexico, the Navajo and Hopi Indian tribes make up almost half the population. Of the two, the Navajos show greater Democratic fealty. In Apache County, where the Navajo Indian influence is most dominant, the 1986 Democratic House nominee won by more than a 2-to-1 margin, and in 1988, Democratic presidential nominee Michael S. Dukakis carried the county with 58 percent of the vote.

Population: 543,493. White 442,730 (82%), Black 3,252 (1%), American Indian, Eskimo and Aleut 83,659 (15%), Other 3,264 (1%). Spanish origin 28,557 (5%). 18 and over 375,192 (69%), 65 and over 49,330 (9%). Median age: 30.

Committees

Armed Services (16th of 21 Republicans)
Investigations; Research and Development

Government Operations (7th of 15 Republicans)
Employment and Housing; Legislation and National Security

Elections

1988 General		
Jon Kyl (R)	206,248	(87%)
Gary Sprunk (LIB)	30,430	(13%)
1986 General		
Jon Kyl (R)	121,939	(65%)
Philip R. Davis (D)	66,894	(35%)

District Vote For President

	1988	1984	1980	1976
D	88,773 (34%)	61,600 (28%)	46,274 (24%)	58,837 (36%)
R	167,264 (65%)	155,112 (71%)	130,172 (67%)	99,026 (61%)
I			14,461 (7%)	

Campaign Finance

	Receipts	Receipts from PACs	Expend-itures
1988			
Kyl (R)	$497,313	$178,114 (36%)	$316,476
1986			
Kyl (R)	$1,019,252	$239,561 (24%)	$1,010,199
Davis (D)	$826,080	$46,800 (6%)	$822,030

Key Votes

1987	
Raise speed limit to 65 mph	Y
Approve Gephardt "fair trade" amendment	N
Ban testing of larger nuclear weapons	N
Delay "re-flagging" of Kuwaiti tankers	N
Approve tax-raising deficit-reduction bill	N
1988	
Approve aid to Nicaraguan contras	Y
Enact civil rights restoration bill over Reagan veto	N
Kill 60-day plant-closing notification measure	Y
Pass omnibus trade bill over Reagan veto	N
Approve death penalty for drug-related murders	Y
Bar federal funds for abortions in cases of rape and incest	Y
Oppose seven-day waiting period for purchase of handguns	Y

Voting Studies

	Presidential Support		Party Unity		Conservative Coalition	
Year	S	O	S	O	S	O
1988	78	19	93	3	97	0
1987	76	24	94	3	98	2

Interest Group Ratings

Year	ADA	ACU	AFL-CIO	CCUS
1988	0	100	8	93
1987	0	96	0	93

5 Jim Kolbe (R)

Of Tucson — Elected 1984

Born: June 28, 1942, Evanston, Ill.

Education: Northwestern U., B.A. 1965; Stanford U., M.B.A. 1967.

Military Career: Navy, 1967-69.

Occupation: Real-estate consultant.

Family: Wife, Sarah Dinham.

Religion: Methodist.

Political Career: Ariz. Senate, 1977-83; Republican nominee for U.S. House, 1982.

Capitol Office: 410 Cannon Bldg. 20515; 225-2542.

In Washington: As a member of the Appropriations Committee, Kolbe is well positioned to cut an influential swath in the House. And as an ambitious and aggressive politician, he also seemed eager to cut a swath in Arizona. He gets most excited about issues with a clear Arizona angle, leading some colleagues to regard him as a likely statewide candidate in the future.

That future will not arrive in 1990, however. In early 1989 Kolbe announced he was concentrating on his House career and ended speculation that he would be a gubernatorial candidate.

In the past couple of years, he has become one of Congress' most vocal advocates for the "maquiladora" assembly plant arrangement, by which U.S. companies manufacture components, then ship the items to Mexico, where they are assembled by Mexican workers; under current tariff laws, the assembled products can then be shipped back to the United States at modest cost for final packaging and distribution. Because of Mexico's lower labor costs and the favorable tariff provisions, goods produced under this arrangement can be sold at prices that are competitive with Asian-produced goods, Kolbe says. The maquiladora boom has been an important boost to southern Arizona's economy.

Critics of the "twin plant" method say that it encourages U.S. companies to close their domestic manufacturing plants (often located in the East and Midwest) and transfer manufacturing to cheap-wage Mexico, costing American jobs. The "plant" on the U.S. side of the border, these critics say, is often just a warehouse, providing few jobs.

Another issue that greatly concerns Kolbe is water, always a focal point in Arizona, where some places do not have enough of it, and some have too much. Although he is not on the Energy and Water Subcommittee, Kolbe, the only Arizonan on Appropriations, speaks out for funds aimed at finding a variety of flood control solutions for the state, and for the Central Arizona Project, a massive system that brings water to Phoenix and other areas of the state.

In 1987, when the House debated the Energy and Water appropriations bill, Kolbe offered a successful floor amendment that settled a major controversy over the project. His amendment barred construction of Cliff Dam, which was opposed by a number of environmentalists. And in return, a coalition of environmentalists agreed to drop a lawsuit opposing other parts of the project.

Like other legislators from states along the nation's southern border, Kolbe has concerns about the influx of drugs into the United States. But on the Military Construction Subcommittee he also has raised concerns about the Defense Department budget being raided to fund the war on drugs.

"I have deep reservations about the trend that is being set this year — that of expecting the Department of Defense to pay for other departments' work in the war on drugs," he said in 1988, pointing to funding that was going to boost the Coast Guard and Customs Service.

Kolbe's first term was spent on the Banking Committee, where he unsuccessfully opposed then-chairman Fernand J. St Germain on a number of measures. But Kolbe did have some success with full-court legislative presses on the floor. He won passage of one floor amendment tightening training requirements for military procurement officers, and another cutting off aid to Lebanon until U.S. hostages were released.

At Home: Kolbe's 1984 victory did more than just avenge his narrow loss to Democrat James F. McNulty Jr. in 1982. It proved Kolbe had successfully convinced some rural 5th District residents that he was not as much a city slicker as they had once thought.

Polished, articulate and brimming with nervous energy, Kolbe does not evoke the laid-back image associated with the rural Southwest. He seems a much more comfortable fit with the bustle of high-growth Tucson than with the slower pace of the district's desert and mountain towns.

In the 1982 GOP primary, he devoted almost all his attention to Republican-rich Tuc-

Southeast

Arizona 5

In terms of registered voters, Democrats in the 5th are about on par with Republicans. But that provides Democrats little comfort, because many of the district's Democrats are the rural, conservative, "pinto" variety; they have no qualms about casting GOP ballots. While two-thirds of Tucson is in the 5th, the part of the city most favorable to Democrats — the city's Hispanic neighborhoods — is mostly in the 2nd.

Largely a college town and resort center in the 1950s, Tucson today hosts an impressive number of high-technology firms; an IBM plant on Tucson's southern outskirts is among the most important high-tech employers. White-collar professional communities with firm GOP ties dominate the city's burgeoning east side.

Well-to-do residents of the Santa Catalina foothills and retirees from Davis-Monthan Air Force Base add to the GOP vote. Green Valley, an outlying Pima County town that rivals Sun City among the state's largest retirement communities, also has become a major GOP force. Democrats get some help in the Tucson portion of the 5th from the residential area around the University of Arizona, just across the border in the 2nd. The student body (33,000 in number) has become more conservative, but the faculty and staff retain a Democratic allegiance, and they are more likely than students to vote.

Outside Pima County, the 5th is largely desert. In an area dominated by scrub oaks and cacti, the San Pedro River Valley provides the only relief, irrigating a fertile stretch of land planted in grain and pecans. Greenlee County hosts a copper industry that was flagging earlier in the decade, but has benefited somewhat from a recent upturn in copper prices.

The Old West county of Cochise, anchoring southeastern Arizona, is the home of Tombstone, "the town too tough to die." Notorious for its lawlessness in the late 1800s, Tombstone still mines some silver, but relies mainly on tourism to boost the local economy. Heavily Hispanic Santa Cruz County on the Mexican border is solidly Democratic.

Late in 1988, two large military installations in the district were slated for personnel reductions by the independent commission on base closings: Fort Huachuca Army Base in Sierra Vista and Davis-Monthan Air Force Base in Tucson.

Population: 542,918. White 477,610 (88%), Black 13,291 (2%), Other 10,512 (2%). Spanish origin 92,979 (17%). 18 and over 389,954 (72%), 65 and over 63,710 (12%). Median age: 31.

son and surrounding Pima County to win a tight three-way nomination contest. That effort linked him firmly with the city in the minds of rural residents. Democrat McNulty, a plain-spoken man with a folksy air, pulled enough support in the rural areas for a 2,407-vote edge in November.

In gearing up for the 1984 rematch, Kolbe was determined not to fall into the same trap. Free of any primary opposition, Kolbe canvassed the 5th's desert and mountain counties early in the campaign. He aired television advertisements that showed him traversing the Arizona landscape on a horse. Kolbe took pains to remind voters that he had spent much of his boyhood on a cattle ranch near the town of Sonoita — while McNulty was born and bred in Boston.

Kolbe's strategy paid off. Aided by a marked improvement in his showing in the counties outside Pima, Kolbe ended with a 6,204-vote advantage out of some 228,000 cast.

Kolbe's comeback victory also owed much to a change in the prevailing political conditions in the 5th. In 1982, McNulty had the advantage of running with two popular statewide Democrats at the top of the ticket. In 1984, Reagan's popularity helped Kolbe.

McNulty decided against a 1986 rematch, and local Democrats could not find a nominee of stature. Kolbe won with 65 percent.

In January 1988, Kolbe opened the door to a conservative primary challenge when he became the first Republican in Arizona's congressional delegation to call on embattled GOP Gov. Evan Mecham to resign. Mecham was ultimately removed from office by the GOP-controlled Legislature, but his conservative backers vowed revenge against Kolbe. Two Mecham supporters ran in the 5th District GOP primary; but most of the former governor's activists focused their attention on defeating state legislators — seven veterans were upset. Kolbe easily won both the primary and general election.

The threat from the far right actually may have enhanced Kolbe's position with independents. Their votes would be critical in a statewide race.

During his six years in the Arizona Senate,

Jim Kolbe, R-Ariz.

Kolbe was known as a member of the state GOP's moderate-to-liberal wing and was a source of frustration to some of his more conservative colleagues, with whom he clashed on social service issues.

Kolbe played a key role in passing a state version of the Medicaid program, and was active in a conservation-minded overhaul of the state's groundwater-management plan. He helped establish a system for reviewing foster child-care cases.

Committee

Appropriations (21st of 22 Republicans)
Commerce, Justice and State, the Judiciary and Related Agencies; Military Construction

Elections

1988 General		
Jim Kolbe (R)	164,462	(68%)
Judith E. Belcher (D)	78,115	(32%)
1988 Primary		
Jim Kolbe (R)	38,306	(78%)
Walter Weber (R)	5,875	(12%)
Al Rodriguez (R)	5,094	(10%)
1986 General		
Jim Kolbe (R)	119,647	(65%)
Joel Ireland (D)	64,848	(35%)

Previous Winning Percentage: **1984** (51%)

District Vote For President

	1988	1984	1980	1976
D	107,310 (44%)	86,049 (37%)	60,700 (32%)	76,224 (47%)
R	136,343 (55%)	142,205 (62%)	103,989 (55%)	79,013 (49%)
I			21,697 (11%)	

Campaign Finance

	Receipts	Receipts from PACs	Expend-itures
1988			
Kolbe (R)	$419,090	$158,738 (38%)	$434,665
1986			
Kolbe (R)	$629,076	$183,487 (29%)	$618,796
Ireland (D)	$31,183	$700 (2%)	$31,166

Key Votes

1987	
Raise speed limit to 65 mph	Y
Approve Gephardt "fair trade" amendment	N
Ban testing of larger nuclear weapons	N
Delay "re-flagging" of Kuwaiti tankers	N
Approve tax-raising deficit-reduction bill	N
1988	
Approve aid to Nicaraguan contras	Y
Enact civil rights restoration bill over Reagan veto	Y
Kill 60-day plant-closing notification measure	Y
Pass omnibus trade bill over Reagan veto	N
Approve death penalty for drug-related murders	Y
Bar federal funds for abortions in cases of rape and incest	N
Oppose seven-day waiting period for purchase of handguns	Y

Voting Studies

	Presidential Support		Party Unity		Conservative Coalition	
Year	**S**	**O**	**S**	**O**	**S**	**O**
1988	58	38	88	10	89	3
1987	67	31	84	13	93	7
1986	69	29	84	13	88	8
1985	78	23	86	11	91	9

Interest Group Ratings

Year	ADA	ACU	AFL-CIO	CCUS
1988	20	80	14	93
1987	8	87	6	93
1986	20	73	7	88
1985	0	76	6	95

Arkansas

U.S. CONGRESS

SENATE 2 D
HOUSE 3 D, 1 R

LEGISLATURE

Senate 31 D, 4 R
House 88 D, 11 R, 1 Independent

ELECTIONS

1988 Presidential Vote	
Bush	56%
Dukakis	42%
1984 Presidential Vote	
Reagan	60%
Mondale	38%
1980 Presidential Vote	
Reagan	48%
Carter	48%
Anderson	3%
Turnout rate in 1984	52%
Turnout rate in 1986	39%
Turnout rate in 1988	47%

(as percentage of voting age population)

POPULATION AND GROWTH

1980 population	2,286,435
1988 population estimate (33rd in the nation)	2,395,000
Percent change 1980-1988	+5%

DEMOGRAPHIC BREAKDOWN

White	83%
Black	16%
(Spanish origin)	1%
Urban	52%
Rural	48%
Born in state	69%
Foreign-born	1%

MAJOR CITIES

Little Rock	181,030
Fort Smith	74,320
North Little Rock	63,540
Pine Bluff	61,320
Fayetteville	40,110

AREA AND LAND USE

Area	52,078 sq. miles (27th)
Farm	44%
Forest	51%
Federally owned	10%

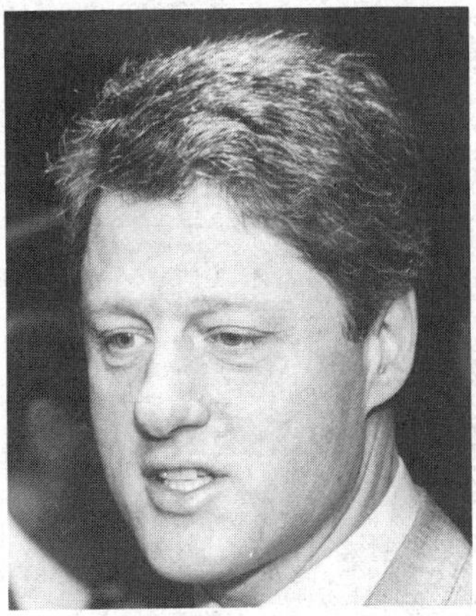

Gov. Bill Clinton (D)
Of Little Rock — Elected 1982
(also served 1979-81)

Born: Aug. 19, 1946, Hope, Ark.
Education: Georgetown U., B.A. 1968; attended Oxford U., England, 1968-70; Yale U., J.D. 1973.
Occupation: Lawyer; law professor.
Religion: Baptist.
Political Career: Ark. attorney general, 1977-79; Democratic nominee for U.S. House, 1974; defeated for re-election as governor, 1980.
Next Election: 1990.

WORK

Occupations	
White-collar	44%
Blue-collar	38%
Service workers	12%
Government Workers	
Federal	18,741
State	44,900
Local	83,063

MONEY

Median family income	$ 14,641	(49th)
Tax burden per capita	$ 740	(38th)

EDUCATION

Spending per pupil through grade 12	$ 2,658	(44th)
Persons with college degrees	11%	(49th)

CRIME

Violent crime rate	412 per 100,000 (28th)

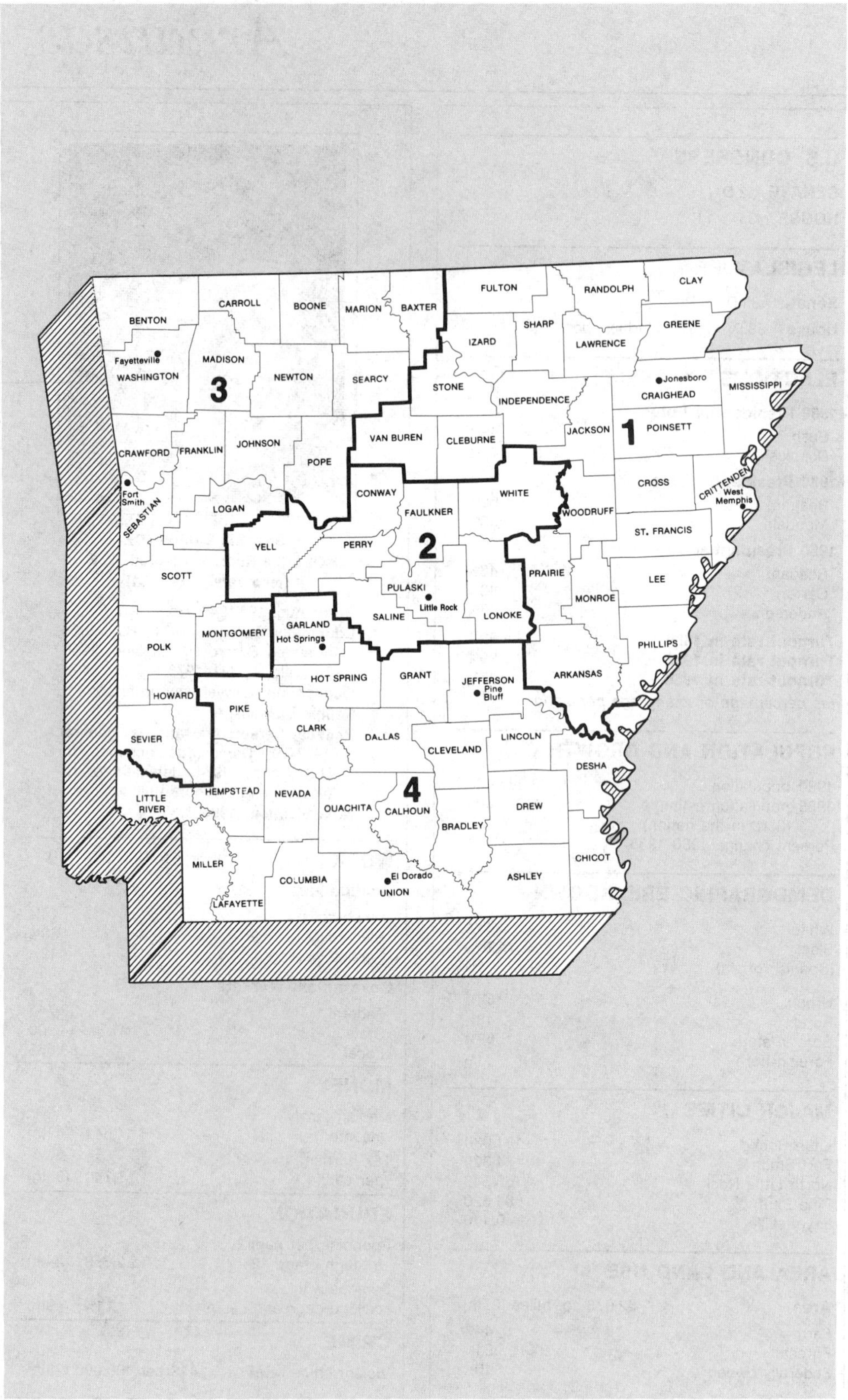

BENTON
CARROLL
BOONE
MARION
BAXTER
FULTON
RANDOLPH
CLAY
Fayetteville
WASHINGTON
MADISON
NEWTON
SEARCY
IZARD
SHARP
LAWRENCE
GREENE
3
STONE
INDEPENDENCE
Jonesboro
CRAIGHEAD
MISSISSIPPI
CRAWFORD
FRANKLIN
JOHNSON
POPE
VAN BUREN
CLEBURNE
JACKSON
1
POINSETT
Fort Smith
SEBASTIAN
LOGAN
CONWAY
FAULKNER
WHITE
WOODRUFF
CROSS
CRITTENDEN
West Memphis
YELL
PERRY
2
ST. FRANCIS
SCOTT
PULASKI
Little Rock
PRAIRIE
LEE
SALINE
LONOKE
MONROE
POLK
MONTGOMERY
GARLAND
Hot Springs
PHILLIPS
HOT SPRING
GRANT
JEFFERSON
Pine Bluff
ARKANSAS
HOWARD
PIKE
CLARK
DALLAS
CLEVELAND
LINCOLN
SEVIER
DESHA
LITTLE RIVER
HEMPSTEAD
NEVADA
4
OUACHITA
CALHOUN
DREW
BRADLEY
MILLER
COLUMBIA
El Dorado
UNION
ASHLEY
CHICOT
LAFAYETTE

Dale Bumpers (D)

Of Charleston — Elected 1974

Born: Aug. 12, 1925, Charleston, Ark.
Education: Attended U. of Arkansas; Northwestern U., LL.B. 1951, J.D. 1965.
Military Career: Marine Corps, 1943-46.
Occupation: Lawyer; farmer; hardware company executive.
Family: Wife, Betty Flanagan; three children.
Religion: Methodist.
Political Career: Ark. governor, 1971-75.
Capitol Office: 229 Dirksen Bldg. 20510; 224-4843.

In Washington: No sooner was Bumpers elected senator in 1974 than speculation about his presidential prospects began, and the talk was fanned when he compiled a progressive record that put him squarely in the national Democratic Party's mainstream. Four times since then he has declined to make the race, citing personal reasons, and now he seems content to finish his career as a senator.

That path would have been made more pleasant had Bumpers gotten his wish for a major chairmanship in the 101st Congress. Louisiana's J. Bennett Johnston lost a bid for majority leader, and returned to the Energy Committee chair that No. 2 Bumpers would have inherited.

And on the Appropriations Committee, South Carolina's Ernest F. Hollings rejected another available subcommittee chairmanship to remain as head of the panel responsible for funding the Commerce, Justice and State departments, the judiciary and various regulatory agencies. Bumpers would have gotten that chair had Hollings left.

Subsequently, Bumpers traded his own chairmanship of Appropriations' Legislative Branch Subcommittee, a housekeeping panel unsuited to a man focused on national and international issues, for the bottom seat at the Defense Subcommittee, where he can better pursue his interests in arms control. He remains chairman of the Small Business Committee, not a major panel but one befitting his populist creed.

The constant in all this is Bumpers' distinctive style, which is appropriate to the Senate, where an individualist can thrive under permissive rules, yet is not always agreeable to fellow senators. He is not quarrelsome, but he takes pleasure in argument. The fewer allies he has, the more likely he is to be on his feet at his back-of-the-chamber desk, extemporaneously weaving facts, figures and anecdotes to explain to absent colleagues why an action they are about to take is senseless.

A natural iconoclast, Bumpers is rarely deterred by an empty chamber. Intellectually brilliant, he delivers orations on topics from nuclear missiles to the rights of satellite dish owners that can be dazzling to hear, if tiresome to those who work with him regularly. Calm, patient and engaging in private, Bumpers can seem downright obstreperous when he gets going in public.

He often votes at odds with others from his region, and in the past was the only Southerner to accept court-ordered busing or oppose mandated prayer in schools. In 1981 he was one of just 11 Senate votes against President Reagan's tax cut.

Perhaps because he does dare to be an outspoken liberal from a conservative region, Bumpers gets vexed that his colleagues take stands he sees as bending to the political winds. In 1988, as the Senate debated an anti-drug bill timed for the campaign season, and adopted various penalties of arguable effect and constitutionality, a scornful Bumpers lectured, "Just to grow hair on your chest here on the Senate floor so you can put out press releases telling everyone back home how tough you are on drugs is no solution."

When North Carolina Republican Jesse Helms offered his amendment to strip federal courts of the power to order busing in the 97th Congress, an indignant Bumpers said he wanted his children and constituents to know "that the beginning of the end of constitutional guarantees in this nation occurred over my strenuous and vehement protest."

Another time, he confronted Alabama Republican Jeremiah Denton during debate over a resolution to establish a "National Peace Day." It was an idea pushed by the organization Peace Links, chaired by the senator's wife, Betty Bumpers. Denton suggested the group had ties to Moscow. Incensed, Bumpers leaped to his feet, warning of a new era of "McCarthyism." "When a resolution like that becomes subversive," he said, "you can kiss everything that had made this country what it is goodbye."

On the Energy Committee, Bumpers'

streak of populism and his environmentalist stance have put him in repeated conflicts with oil and mining interests. He joined other liberals in the late 1970s in fighting deregulation of oil and natural gas prices, and favored a stiff windfall-profits tax on the oil companies.

In the 100th Congress, he finally won an eight-year struggle to reform the system of leasing oil and gas drilling rights on federal lands — a campaign that began when he found that land in Arkansas near hundreds of producing wells was leased for $1 an acre. Arguing that the lottery and over-the-counter lease systems in use were "a scandal . . . outmoded, susceptible to fraud and manipulation, and not designed to provide the government with a fair return," he passed a bill replacing them with a competitive bidding process.

He has been a leading foe of a bill sought by oil companies, Alaska's GOP delegation and Chairman Johnston to open the immense Arctic National Wildlife Refuge to exploration and drilling. In 1988, he proposed banning development for three years pending adoption of a national energy plan, but Johnston's bill prevailed by a single vote in committee. It went no farther, however, and early in the 101st Congress, supporters of exploration had to declare their bill dead, conceding to the public furor aroused by the oil spill of the tanker *Exxon Valdez* off Alaska in March 1989.

He is also a critic of nuclear power, though he has failed in his effort to bar utilities from passing on to consumers the costs of closing nuclear power plants. Bumpers was the most vociferous Senate opponent of the Clinch River breeder reactor in Tennessee. He came within one vote of killing the expensive project in 1982, and finally won in 1984.

In recent years, Bumpers has perhaps been best known as one of the Senate's most outspoken supporters of arms control. With Vermont Democrat Patrick J. Leahy and Republicans John H. Chafee of Rhode Island and John Heinz of Pennsylvania, he has worked at strengthening U.S. support for the unratified SALT II treaty.

They urged the administration not to drop its policy of informally abiding by the treaty's arms limits; such pressure from both Congress and European allies persuaded Reagan to continue compliance in 1984 and 1985. But in 1986, Reagan decided to repudiate the treaty on the grounds of Soviet violations. Bumpers proposed an amendment urging continued compliance, but decided not to offer it when it became clear the Senate would reject the treaty if it came to a vote. In 1987, the Senate adopted Bumpers' amendment 57-41, thanks in part to support from Armed Services Committee Chairman Sam Nunn. Ultimately, a compromise with the administration deleted all references to the SALT treaty and simply mandated that a nuclear-armed submarine be retired, but the effect was the same — keeping the United States within the treaty's numerical missile limits. In 1988 Bumpers tried again with a similar amendment, this time without Nunn's support, and he lost 51-45. Nunn and other critics objected that it would have written into law a U.S. disadvantage in certain missiles.

For Bumpers, who once accused Reagan of not wanting "to spend money on anything that does not explode," the MX missile has been a special target. He offered repeated amendments to kill the MX, which finally was capped at 50 in a 1985 compromise. He also has opposed Reagan's proposed strategic defense initiative.

In the 100th Congress, Bumpers was a leading opponent of Reagan's policy of providing Navy escorts to Kuwaiti tankers in the Persian Gulf. Many members complained that Reagan had not properly consulted Congress before committing U.S. forces, but Bumpers was one of the few favoring legislative action against the policy. That idea met with fierce GOP opposition, however, and even many Democrats were reluctant to challenge an ongoing policy.

On Appropriations, Bumpers has used his various subcommittee posts to espouse health programs for the poor, aid for rural areas and the rice subsidies important to his state. As chairman of the Public Lands Subcommittee, he generally sides with conservationists; an eloquent late-night floor performance in late 1988, for which Bumpers prepped by lunching with Civil War historian James M. McPherson, helped preserve part of the Manassas, Va., battlefield from developers.

As liberal as his work makes Bumpers sound, his iconoclasm makes him difficult to label. In 1978 he was the only senator to vote against popular "sunset" legislation for periodic reviews of all federal agencies. In 1987, as Small Business chairman, he allied with then-Sen. Dan Quayle to oppose Labor Committee Chairman Edward M. Kennedy's bill requiring all employers to provide health insurance.

Then in 1988, he clashed with liberal House members over revamping the scandal-plagued program that reserves federal contracts for minority-owned firms. House negotiators opposed the bill he steered through Small Business and the Senate as too stringent in its requirements that minority firms bid competitively for public jobs and do more private-sector work. Faced with Bumpers' stubbornness, they enlisted GOP Sen. Lowell P. Weicker Jr. to champion the successful effort to relax the Senate standards. Of the compromise that became law, Bumpers said, "There's a real question as to whether we've gone far enough towards cleaning this program up."

At Home: "A smile and a shoeshine" was the phrase Winthrop Rockefeller used to describe the political phenomenon that removed him from the Arkansas governorship in 1970. It was a slur on Bumpers' intellectual substance, but it was not a bad description of the campaign that lifted him from a small-town law practice to the state Capitol in a remarkably short time.

Rockefeller had made Bumpers possible by discrediting and retiring most of the segregationist "old guard" that had dominated the Democratic Party in Arkansas over the previous two decades. After four years of Republican rule under Rockefeller, the state was ready to go Democratic again under a modern leader. Bumpers was so clearly the right man that a smile, a shoeshine and a sophisticated set of TV ads were more than enough to give him a primary victory over the legendary race-baiter Orval E. Faubus in a Democratic runoff and an easy win over Rockefeller in the fall. Issues were beside the point.

Bumpers' gubernatorial campaign was so vague that the state had little reason to know what it was getting when he took office in January 1971. In fact, it was getting a man with a fair degree of liberal Yankee influence, a graduate of Northwestern University law school and a longtime admirer of Adlai E. Stevenson, who was governor of Illinois when Bumpers got his law degree. Bumpers came to the governorship without any political experience beyond the school board in Charleston, Ark., but with a clear sense of where he was going.

Over four years in office, Bumpers presided over a modernization of state government, closing down many of the bureaucratic fiefdoms that old-guard Democrats had controlled for a generation. By early 1974, he was ready for national politics. State Democrats braced themselves for a titanic struggle between the governor and veteran Sen. J. William Fulbright, who had helped raise money for Bumpers in 1970.

As it turned out, the struggle failed to live up to its advance billing. Bumpers decided to run only after political consultant Deloss Walker showed him polls guaranteeing he could not lose. Bumpers defeated Fulbright by nearly 2-to-1 in the Democratic primary without offering a critical word or a divisive issue.

The 1980 election was nothing to worry about either. While other Arkansas Democrats were finally paying the price for a decade of too-easy liberal politics, Bumpers was winning a second term by 150,000 votes.

In 1986, Republicans nominated an aggressive challenger in Asa Hutchinson, who had served as U.S. attorney in Little Rock under the Reagan administration. But Bumpers took nothing for granted, turning up at hundreds of barbecues, fish-fries and other gatherings, reestablishing his roots by using the down-home style that had first vaulted him to success. By September, it was clear Hutchinson was going nowhere; the challenger's Religious Right background had generated more controversy than support. Bumpers improved on his 1980 showing.

Committees

Small Business (Chairman)
Export Expansion; Rural Economy and Family Farming

Appropriations (9th of 16 Democrats)
Agriculture, Rural Development and Related Agencies; Commerce, Justice, State, the Judiciary and Related Agencies; Defense; Interior and Related Agencies; Labor, Health and Human Services, Education and Related Agencies

Energy and Natural Resources (2nd of 10 Democrats)
Public Lands, National Parks and Forests (chairman); Energy Research and Development; Mineral Resources Development and Production

Elections

1986 General

Dale Bumpers (D)	433,092	(62%)
Asa Hutchinson (R)	262,300	(38%)

Previous Winning Percentages: **1980** (59%) **1974** (85%)

Campaign Finance

	Receipts	Receipts from PACs	Expend-itures
1986			
Bumpers (D)	$1,726,383	$507,419 (29%)	$1,672,432
Hutchinson (R)	$916,436	$81,221 (9%)	$910,924

Key Votes

1987

Enact omnibus highway bill over Reagan veto	Y
Limit testing of space-based anti-ballistic missiles	Y
Oppose banning tests of larger nuclear weapons	N
Confirm Robert H. Bork as Supreme Court justice	N

1988

Allow vote on campaign-finance overhaul	Y
Pass civil rights restoration bill over Reagan veto	Y
Enact omnibus trade bill over Reagan veto	Y
Approve death penalty for drug-related murders	Y
Oppose "workfare" amendment to welfare overhaul bill	N

Voting Studies

	Presidential Support		Party Unity		Conservative Coalition	
Year	S	O	S	O	S	O
1988	44	50	84	7	41	57
1987	38	58	89	11	38	59
1986	39	59	77	20	49	47
1985	32	62	79	17	52	45
1984	36	53	76	14	45	51
1983	32	56	85	10	41	45
1982	30	63	86	11	20	74
1981	39	52	81	8	20	69

Interest Group Ratings

Year	ADA	ACU	AFL-CIO	CCUS
1988	80	12	79	33
1987	85	8	70	35
1986	70	22	64	47
1985	70	13	71	45
1984	75	18	60	42
1983	75	17	82	17
1982	85	26	81	21
1981	95	13	84	24

David Pryor (D)

Of Little Rock — Elected 1978

Born: Aug. 29, 1934, Camden, Ark.
Education: U. of Arkansas, B.A. 1957, LL.B. 1964.
Occupation: Lawyer; newspaper publisher.
Family: Wife, Barbara Lunsford; three children.
Religion: Presbyterian.
Political Career: Ark. House, 1961-67; U.S. House, 1967-73; governor, 1975-79; sought Democratic nomination for U.S. Senate, 1972.
Capitol Office: 264 Russell Bldg. 20510; 224-2353.

In Washington: The 101st Congress should be the occasion for the breakthrough Pryor's admirers have long predicted for him. After years of relatively low-profile labors and middling success, 1989 found him in two new positions of power: secretary of the Democratic Conference and chairman of the Special Committee on Aging. Both jobs should magnify his influence on issues of longstanding personal interest and raise his visibility, within the Senate and beyond.

As conference secretary, Pryor is now the third-ranking officer in the Democratic leadership. The position had been occupied by Daniel K. Inouye of Hawaii, who left it to run unsuccessfully for majority leader. Pryor won this post easily in the same closed-door balloting that elected George J. Mitchell of Maine majority leader in November 1988.

Some of Pryor's colleagues indicated that, as the only Southerner on the new leadership team, he had won at least in part for the regional and philosophical balance he lends to Mitchell and Democratic Whip Alan Cranston of California. But Pryor also seemed to have been more personally popular with his colleagues than rival Patrick J. Leahy of Vermont. He seemed especially well regarded by younger members who appreciated his fights against filibusters, dilatory floor tactics, quorum calls and extended roll-call votes.

In his new role, Pryor should have the perfect forum for this crusade. He has long been one of the members most disturbed by the unreasonable demands the Senate schedule often puts on family life. He organized an informal panel of six senators who began pushing for changes aimed at restoring some measure of discipline to the way the Senate conducts its business. In 1985, his efforts helped produce an informal package of time-saving rules, such as limiting most votes to 15 minutes. The group's recommendation that the Senate work three weeks, then take a week off, has become the standard calendar.

The chair of the Aging panel fell to Pryor when predecessor Chairman John Melcher met unexpected defeat in Montana. It is an opportunity for Pryor to re-establish himself as a leader on the issue that helped vault him into prominence. As a young legislator in Little Rock in the 1960s, he showed an inspired knack for attracting public attention to the issue. Later, while serving in the House, Pryor ran a kind of rogue subcommittee on the needs of the elderly, operating out of trailers parked near the House office buildings.

Melcher's upset also raised Pryor to the No. 2 Democratic slot on the Agriculture Committee, behind Leahy. Here he had already proven an effective member, helping create a new loan program for cotton and rice growers in the 1985 farm bill and protecting Southern soybean growers from a price-formula change in 1988. On such matters, Pryor will even reach for some of the procedural tools he generally decries.

When a bill cutting federal farm-price supports came to the Senate floor in 1984, Pryor and Arkansas colleague Dale Bumpers worried that the measure would harm their rice farmers. To delay action on the time-sensitive bill, they began to read their favorite rice recipes into the *Congressional Record.* "I think I know of about 1,000 dishes with rice in them," Pryor said, to the delight of the galleries and the chagrin of the leadership. Pryor has been less active on the Finance Committee, taking a rather hands-off attitude toward most of the tax-reform upheaval of the 99th Congress. But as chairman of the subcommittee on Internal Revenue Service oversight, he has been a critic of the agency's "fearsome" powers and a voice for "taxpayers' rights" legislation.

Perhaps the most interesting test of Pryor's stature in the 101st Congress will come when he takes on other committees' handiwork on the floor. In the past he has pursued difficult, even quixotic, amendments with mixed results. In 1988, he amended the defense appropriations bill to require all consultants hired by the Pentagon to disclose their other clients. Passed by voice vote in the midst of publicity over alleged procurement fraud, Pryor's amendment was Congress' first response to the perceived scandal. But in the fall, House and Senate conferees quietly dropped it.

The military budget had previously attracted Pryor's eye, even before reports that the Pentagon had spent $600 for a toilet seat. But Pryor has had limited success with his efforts to impose stringent controls. One of his prime targets has been "sole source" defense contracts, by which the Pentagon certifies that only one company is qualified to produce a particular weapon. Pryor advocates competitive bidding to award contracts.

In 1983, citing some of the more elaborate examples of Pentagon hardware — such as a $40 million program to build an armored bulldozer to accompany the M-1 tank into battle — Pryor helped push through an amendment establishing an independent agency within the Pentagon to test weapons.

In 1985, Pryor went head-to-head with the Armed Services Committee in an effort to impose strict new procurement rules. He offered a comprehensive amendment to the defense authorization bill requiring that all weapons purchases be arranged through competition involving at least two bidders. In addition, the amendment barred Pentagon procurement officials from taking jobs with defense contractors for three years after they left the government. Preferring a milder alternative offered by the committee, the Senate rejected Pryor's effort, 22-67.

The next year, Pryor found himself defending his weapons-testing office. Armed Services members pushed to include the office under the authority of a new Pentagon procurement "czar" they were creating. Pryor sought to stop them, arguing that the move would undermine the independence of the testing office. He lost on the Senate floor, although the change was dropped in conference.

Pryor's biggest defense target has been the "binary" chemical weapons proposed by the Reagan administration. Although the weapons would be produced in Arkansas, creating jobs in the state, and have had the support of his pro-arms-control colleague, Bumpers, Pryor has been the most vocal opponent of the idea in the Senate. Ironically, Pryor's closest ally in the House on the issue was Rep. Ed Bethune, his 1984 Republican challenger.

Pryor opposes chemical weapons on both moral and economic grounds. Matching Soviet production of the lethal materials would "surrender the high ground as far as world opinion is concerned," he says, arguing also that the weapons would add little to U.S. defense capabilities.

In the 100th Congress, Pryor inserted a provision in the fiscal 1989 defense authorization bill by which the $99 million requested for "Bigeye" binary bombs would be unavailable pending further testing. Conferees later authorized only $15 million, all for bombs to be used in tests.

At Home: Pryor must be considered among the safest of the Democratic senators who face the voters in 1990. In 1984, in a convincing demonstration of the personal popularity he had built up over 21 years in office, Pryor easily defeated the strongest possible GOP challenger even as Arkansas went decisively for President Reagan.

Pryor's 1983 voting record — he opposed Reagan's positions more often than any other senator — encouraged national GOP officials to believe he could be turned out in a Reagan landslide, and they urged Bethune to make the race. Throughout the campaign, Bethune predicted that 1984 would bring a revolutionary change in Arkansas politics as traditional Democrats came to realize that the Democratic Party had been "taken over by the liberals."

But Pryor was well positioned to blunt Bethune's efforts at casting the race in ideological context. In the eyes of most Arkansans, Pryor was not a liberal ogre who had "gone Washington"; he was a personable moderate who kept in touch with a large network of friends he had gained as a state legislator, congressman, governor and senator.

Pryor stressed the more conservative and populist aspects of his record, reminding voters of his support for a balanced-budget constitutional amendment and defense of the Rural Electrification Administration (REA) against Bethune's proposal to abolish the low-rate federal loans the REA grants to utility cooperatives.

Reagan campaigned in Arkansas the weekend before the election, but his presence was no aid to Bethune. Pryor won 58 percent, nearly matching Bumpers' 1980 re-election tally over a much weaker Republican foe.

Pryor has always had a talent for picking issues that bring favorable exposure in Arkansas. He was still in his 20s, struggling outnumbered against the segregationist "Old Guard" in the state Legislature, when he began investigating abuses in nursing homes. That issue helped him win a House seat in 1966, when the 4th District was left vacant with the departure of veteran Democrat Oren Harris. Once settled in Washington, he ran unopposed in 1968 and 1970.

In 1972 Pryor took on a challenge virtually every Democrat in the state told him he could not win — a primary campaign against the venerable senior senator, John L. McClellan. Pryor was determined, and he campaigned intensely all over the state for months, raising the issue of McClellan's age, which was 76. When he held the senator to 44 percent in the initial primary in May, forcing a runoff, Arkansas' startled Democrats assumed he had McClellan cornered. That was the second wrong assumption of the spring. The veteran fought back with surprising vigor in the runoff, seizing on Pryor's labor support to argue that union bosses wanted to get even for past McClellan corruption probes. On runoff night, Pryor found himself beaten by 18,000 votes.

Two years after his defeat, Pryor was elected governor, spoiling a comeback effort by Gov. Orval E. Faubus in that year's runoff. Faubus' once-vaunted political power had faded, along with the race issue that had fueled it, and his allies in the Arkansas business establishment deserted him for Pryor. Faubus called Pryor the "candidate of 52 millionaires" seeking to influence state policy, but the result was not even close. Pryor had no trouble winning the general election that fall, or a second two-year term in 1976.

Late in 1977, McClellan died. Pryor appointed Kaneaster Hodges to fill out the late senator's term. Under state law, Hodges was ineligible to succeed himself, and Pryor moved in on the seat in 1978.

This time he was no longer fighting the Old Guard. His competition in the primary came from two moderate representatives, Jim Guy Tucker of Little Rock and Ray Thornton, Pryor's 4th District successor.

Pryor's pro-labor image had long since faded. As governor, he lost union support by sending in the National Guard to replace striking Pine Bluff firemen. In the two-man runoff, Tucker got the labor endorsement; Pryor made an issue of it.

Pryor won the runoff by a surprising 47,000 votes, picking up much of the southern Arkansas support that had gone at first to Thornton, a close third in the initial primary. The general election against Republican Thomas Kelly was easy; Pryor won by more than 3-to-1.

Committees

Special Aging (Chairman)

Agriculture, Nutrition and Forestry (2nd of 10 Democrats)
Agricultural Production and Stabilization of Prices (chairman); Domestic and Foreign Marketing and Product Promotion; Nutrition and Investigations; Rural Development and Rural Electrification

Finance (8th of 11 Democrats)
Private Retirement Plans and Oversight of the Internal Revenue Service (chairman); Medicare and Long-Term Care; Taxation and Debt Management

Governmental Affairs (5th of 8 Democrats)
Federal Services, Post Office and Civil Service (chairman); Oversight of Government Management; Permanent Subcommittee on Investigations

Select Ethics (2nd of 3 Democrats)

Elections

1984 General

David Pryor (D)	502,341	(57%)
Ed Bethune (R)	373,615	(43%)

Previous Winning Percentages: 1978 (77%) **1970 *** (100%) **1968 *** (100%) **1966 *** (65%)

* *House elections.*

Campaign Finance

	Receipts	Receipts from PACs	Expend-itures
1984			
Pryor (D)	$1,910,676	$711,547 (37%)	$1,761,115
Bethune (R)	$1,076,792	$247,237 (23%)	$1,072,879

Key Votes

1987	
Enact omnibus highway bill over Reagan veto	Y
Limit testing of space-based anti-ballistic missiles	Y
Oppose banning tests of larger nuclear weapons	Y
Confirm Robert H. Bork as Supreme Court justice	N
1988	
Allow vote on campaign-finance overhaul	Y
Pass civil rights restoration bill over Reagan veto	Y
Enact omnibus trade bill over Reagan veto	Y
Approve death penalty for drug-related murders	Y
Oppose "workfare" amendment to welfare overhaul bill	Y

Voting Studies

	Presidential Support		Party Unity		Conservative Coalition	
Year	**S**	**O**	**S**	**O**	**S**	**O**
1988	48	47	85	11	49	43
1987	32	59	87	7	47	41
1986	35	60	70	24	55	38
1985	32	66	79	15	50	42
1984	45	47	60	25	72	23
1983	27	71	78	14	57	34
1982	45	49	73	23	56	35
1981	47	48	80	15	54	42

Interest Group Ratings

Year	ADA	ACU	AFL-CIO	CCUS
1988	75	16	79	43
1987	75	15	67	47
1986	60	33	40	53
1985	80	4	76	41
1984	55	38	60	50
1983	70	28	71	33
1982	70	55	69	45
1981	75	21	47	53

1 Bill Alexander (D)

Of Osceola — Elected 1968

Born: Jan. 16, 1934, Memphis, Tenn.
Education: Southwestern at Memphis, B.A. 1957; Vanderbilt U., LL.B. 1960.
Military Career: Army, 1951-53.
Occupation: Lawyer.
Family: Divorced; one child.
Religion: Episcopalian.
Political Career: No previous office.
Capitol Office: 233 Cannon Bldg. 20515; 225-4076.

In Washington: During his career in the House, Alexander has headed in several different directions — into party leadership circles, toward involvement in foreign policy, and down the pork-barrel politics route. But as he begins his third decade in Congress, Alexander still seems like a man groping for a mission, now that he has fallen from the Democratic leadership ladder, been pounded by bad publicity and survived a stern challenge at the polls.

Alexander's 1986 brush with electoral defeat did help him focus his thoughts on one thing — political survival. During the 100th Congress, he mostly concentrated on issues close to home. His seat on the money-wielding Appropriations Committee put him in a good position to mend fences with his constituents.

But for now at least, Appropriations does not present any immediate avenues for advancement within the House that could return Alexander to a position of broader influence. He is the No. 2 Democrat on two Appropriations subcommittees — Military Construction and Commerce, Justice and State — but neither of the subcommittee chairmen Alexander serves behind seems on the verge of retiring.

Alexander lost his place in the party leadership when, after six years as chief deputy whip, he stumbled badly in his 1986 effort to move up to the No. 3 post of majority whip. Like other candidates for the job, which was being filled by a caucus election for the first time, Alexander was outdistanced early by the aggressive campaigning of Tony Coelho of California.

Although Alexander had gotten his start in the leadership thanks to the man who was about to become Speaker, Jim Wright, that did not translate into a home-field advantage in the whip's race. Alexander was perceived as too much of a loner to be a backslapping natural in leadership circles.

Alexander has a reputation as an unpredictable figure — an image fed by a string of incidents that have showered him with negative publicity.

Early in his career, Alexander drew attention by engaging in a shoving match with a policeman outside National Airport in Washington. In 1985, he gained notoriety from a *Wall Street Journal* report that he waved an African spear and shouted "boogaloo" at a group of lobbyists in his office. Alexander said he actually had shouted a Kenyan greeting, "Jambo, Jambo."

In the summer of 1985, Alexander obtained a military jet to take a "congressional delegation" to Brazil and then turned out to be the only member on the trip. Alexander defended the $50,000 excursion as a useful energy fact-finding mission, but several of his colleagues criticized it as an abuse of congressional privileges.

The 1985 incidents stoked the fires of political opposition at home, giving him a startlingly close Democratic primary in 1986. Chastened, Alexander generally kept a lower profile for the next two years. He played up his public works record, using his seat on Appropriations to get help for the district, such as a $5.3 million appropriation for a harbor project in Helena. He cosponsored a bill to promote the use of ethanol and other alternative fuels — a law he touted as providing a new market for Arkansas farm products.

But Alexander stumbled again in mid-1987 when he opened the way for critics to recycle the portrait of him as a misuser of taxpayer dollars. He inserted into the *Congressional Record* the text of four years of debate on the Boland amendment, a law central to the Iran-contra affair that was then engulfing the Reagan administration. Defenders called it a "must read" but others called it a waste of some $200,000 in printing costs.

Alexander has not abandoned his involvement in the kinds of foreign policy issues that had given fuel to opponents at home. During the Reagan years, Alexander's opposition to military aid for the contras in Nicaragua took considerable political courage in light of his traditional Southern district.

That was not the only issue on which Alexander, while he was Democrats' chief dep-

Arkansas 1

East — Jonesboro

Covering most of the eastern third of the state and some hilly northern counties, the agricultural 1st is the part of Arkansas with the strongest Deep South tradition. Although it is the poorest district in the state, its flat, fertile Mississippi delta has traditionally supported large plantations, some running into tens of thousands of acres. Tied to the cotton trade long before the Civil War, the area now is heavily reliant on rice and soybeans.

Jonesboro, the home of Arkansas State University (8,700 students) and West Memphis, a suburb of Memphis, Tenn., are the district's only major cities.

Despite agriculture's continued domination of the local economy, there is some new industry, and Helena, West Memphis and Osceola, all on the Mississippi River, are developing port cities. Blytheville, a Mississippi River town just south of the Missouri border, has attracted several new companies in recent years.

Forrest City, the seat of St. Francis County, has a Sanyo manufacturing plant that employs roughly 300 people producing color-TV sets. That is a far cry from the early 1980s, when nearly 2,000 people worked at the plant.

Over the past decade, retirees from Northern states have begun to settle in the 1st's hill country, populating retirement communities such as Cherokee Village in Sharp County. Many of these elderly newcomers are accustomed to voting for Republicans, but Alexander has had little trouble attracting their support. George Bush carried the 1st in 1988.

In most elections, the district remains solidly Democratic, especially in the Mississippi delta counties where there is a heavy concentration of blacks. Four of the seven Arkansas counties that the Rev. Jesse Jackson carried in Arkansas' 1988 Democratic presidential primary are in this area. Overall, blacks make up 19 percent of the 1st's population. But as the cotton economy has declined in the delta, the largely black delta counties have steadily lost population.

Population: 573,551. White 462,199 (81%), Black 107,604 (19%), Other 2,607(1%). Spanish origin 4,675 (1%). 18 and over 396,107 (69%), 65 and over 80,097 (14%). Median age: 30.

uty whip, had to balance the demands of his district with those of being part of the national Democratic leadership.

Alexander himself opposed — and lobbied hard against — the Reagan budget in 1981, despite heavy pressure to support the president. His district strongly favored it, and influential Arkansas Democrats urged him to back Reagan to save his political career.

But that would have required breaking with Wright. Alexander worked hard for Wright in the 1976 contest for majority leader, and after the election was over, he was rewarded with Wright's old post in the middle ranks of the Democratic whip structure. In early 1981, when Chief Deputy Whip Dan Rostenkowski of Illinois took the Ways and Means Committee chairmanship, Wright chose Alexander to replace him.

Now a 20-year House veteran at age 55, Alexander shares Wright's enthusiasm for public works spending, especially water projects. He was one of the most outspoken House critics of President Carter's plan to cut back on such spending. "It boils down to a question of who is going to decide water policy," Alexander complained at one point. "Is it going to be the Congress or a few self-appointed people within the administration?"

At Home: Even after the Brazilian-junket controversy, Alexander showed few signs of concern when state Sen. Jim Wood launched a conservative challenge to him for 1986. The veteran Democrat had been challenged from the right before, by well-financed opponents, and had always won handsomely.

The previous challenges, however, were from Republicans, and they failed to ignite much enthusiasm in an old-fashioned Deep South district. Wood was a conservative Democrat, so he had access to a substantial bloc of votes previous challengers could not pry loose.

Wood, an amiable, cherubic state legislator, was not very amiable in his campaign. He called Alexander an "international jet-setter," and ran TV ads accusing him of taking 19 foreign trips at taxpayer expense. He attacked Alexander's support for improved U.S. relations with Cuba and referred darkly to his "affiliation and support for known communists." He said Alexander was too aloof and too arrogant to represent the 1st.

Alexander, slow to respond, spent little time campaigning until the final weeks before the primary. It was a near-fatal strategy. Primary day saw him lose substantial support in his usual strongholds along the Mississippi River, and he lost the white vote districtwide. But for strong backing from the 19 percent black minority in the 1st, Alexander would have lost.

Once past the primary, though, Alexander could afford to relax. Republicans tried to generate interest in their nominee, a 27-year-old radio station manager, but nearly all of Alexander's conservative Democratic critics came back to him in the fall, and he won by a wide margin.

Two years later, Darrell Glascock, the political consultant who had managed Wood's campaign, decided to take on Alexander in the primary. Glascock raised all the same issues as Wood, but having lost the surprise factor, he was no match for Alexander.

Alexander was a young lawyer in the small town of Osceola when he entered the free-for-all 1968 Democratic primary to succeed Rep. Ezekiel "Took" Gathings, who was retiring.

There were nine candidates for the nomination, and Alexander had never held office before. But he was the front-runner from the start. As the son of an old East Arkansas political family, he had instant credentials with the network of large farmers and small-town courthouse Democrats that held great sway over politics in the area.

His main opponent called him "the handpicked man of the big plantation owners and the political bosses." But that rival, Jack Files, a former aide to Sen. J. William Fulbright, ran a distant second to Alexander in the primary. In the runoff, Alexander drew 62 percent.

The resurgent Arkansas Republicans attempted to give Alexander a fight that November. Their candidate was Guy Newcomb, a pharmacist and farmer, also from Osceola. It was the first real general-election contest in the district since Reconstruction, but the Republican came out with only 31 percent of the vote.

Until 1986, the high-water mark for a Republicans challenger in the 1st came in 1982. That year, the GOP candidate was Osceola lawyer Chuck Banks, son of former Mississippi County Judge A. A. "Shug" Banks, a longtime power in northeastern Arkansas Democratic politics. Chuck Banks himself had been a member of the state Democratic Central Committee, and national GOP strategists felt he would appeal to conservative Democratic voters. There had been some local grumbling about Alexander's 1981 opposition to Reagan's economic initiatives, but support for Reaganomics began declining in the 1st long before Election Day. Despite his name and credentials, Banks was dragged down by his party label; he drew just 35 percent of the vote.

Committee

Appropriations (9th of 35 Democrats)
Commerce, Justice and State, the Judiciary and Related Agencies; Military Construction; Treasury, Postal Service and General Government

Elections

1988 General		
Bill Alexander (D)	Unopposed	
1988 Primary		
Bill Alexander (D)	94,978	(67%)
Darrell Glascock (D)	46,974	(33%)
1986 General		
Bill Alexander (D)	105,773	(64%)
Rick H. Albin (R)	58,937	(36%)

Previous Winning Percentages: **1984** (97%) **1982** (65%) **1980** (100%) **1978** (100%) **1976** (69%) **1974** (91%) **1972** (100%) **1970** (100%) **1968** (69%)

District Vote For President

	1988	1984	1980	1976
D	89,812 (48%)	86,743 (43%)	103,906 (52%)	135,001 (70%)
R	95,388 (51%)	114,091 (57%)	88,732 (45%)	57,776 (30%)
I			4,049 (2%)	

Campaign Finance

	Receipts	Receipts from PACs	Expend-itures
1988			
Alexander (D)	$674,287	$321,524 (48%)	$665,445
1986			
Alexander (D)	$630,461	$303,900 (48%)	$703,571
Albin (R)	$55,079	$5,800 (11%)	$52,708

Key Votes

1987	
Raise speed limit to 65 mph	Y
Approve Gephardt "fair trade" amendment	Y
Ban testing of larger nuclear weapons	Y
Delay "re-flagging" of Kuwaiti tankers	Y
Approve tax-raising deficit-reduction bill	Y
1988	
Approve aid to Nicaraguan contras	N
Enact civil rights restoration bill over Reagan veto	Y
Kill 60-day plant-closing notification measure	N
Pass omnibus trade bill over Reagan veto	Y
Approve death penalty for drug-related murders	?
Bar federal funds for abortions in cases of rape and incest	?
Oppose seven-day waiting period for purchase of handguns	Y

Voting Studies

	Presidential Support		Party Unity		Conservative Coalition	
Year	**S**	**O**	**S**	**O**	**S**	**O**
1988	18	69	83	5	26	55
1987	22	68	84	5	42	44
1986	22	67	80	8	58	40
1985	25	68	84	7	36	56
1984	34	44	57	11	42	24
1983	34	52	68	10	39	44
1982	40	49	72	17	60	34
1981	49	42	67	24	60	28

Interest Group Ratings

Year	ADA	ACU	AFL-CIO	CCUS
1988	80	5	100	17
1987	64	0	94	13
1986	75	24	100	29
1985	70	5	82	23
1984	40	20	70	33
1983	65	9	88	39
1982	40	25	79	42
1981	45	20	87	24

2 Tommy F. Robinson (D)

Of Jacksonville — Elected 1984

Born: March 7, 1942, Little Rock, Ark.
Education: U. of Arkansas, Little Rock, B.A. 1976.
Military Career: Navy, 1959-63.
Occupation: Law enforcement officer.
Family: Wife, Carolyn Barber; six children.
Religion: Methodist.
Political Career: Pulaski County (Little Rock) sheriff, 1980-84.
Capitol Office: 1541 Longworth Bldg. 20515; 225-2506.

In Washington: A maverick conservative Democrat and one of the more confrontational personalities in the House, Robinson has the capacity to inspire more controversy in a few weeks than most members do in their whole careers.

One month in early 1989, for instance, Robinson was in the Little Rock newspapers nearly every day: justifying a 1988 campaign commercial he had done for a Republican colleague; vowing to get even with Democrats who stripped him of a committee assignment; and provoking rumors that he might jump to the GOP. He was quoted in a Memphis newspaper describing consumer activist Ralph Nader as a "scum bag" who had exploited the congressional pay raise controversy for his own purposes. And he defended himself against accusations by a condemned Arkansas convict who said that Robinson, while serving as Pulaski County sheriff, had beaten a confession out of him.

Such controversies would send many incumbents scrambling to their consultant for an image remake. Not Robinson. He started talking about running for governor in 1990.

Indeed, such flurries are not new for Robinson, whose swashbuckling demeanor as sheriff made him a villain to some civil libertarians, but a folk hero to law-and-order types in Little Rock and surrounding rural areas. That status frees him from some of the normal protocol of political behavior.

In one 1988 incident, Robinson — a member of the Armed Services Committee and a staunch conservative on defense issues — told a local nuclear-arms control activist who tried to hand him letters opposing the MX missile to "stick 'em where the sun don't shine." Robinson later said he had been provoked by slanderous attacks on his defense record by Arkansas peace activists.

And while many Southern Democrats say their national party is too liberal, Robinson is unusually blunt with his criticism. Shortly after arriving in Congress in 1985, Robinson referred to the Democrats as "a party of homosexuals and weirdos." And in early 1989, he said, "I could care less what the national Democratic Party thinks of me. I don't like their agenda."

That remark came after the House party leadership received a complaint from freshman Democratic Rep. George E. Sangmeister of Illinois that Robinson had taped a campaign commercial for Sangmeister's 1988 opponent, incumbent Republican Jack Davis. The House Democratic Caucus then voted not to renew Robinson's temporary seat on the Education and Labor Committee (though he kept his permanent slots on Armed Services and Veterans' Affairs).

Though Robinson denied authorizing the use of his comments — which praised Davis for his role on a measure Robinson cosponsored to increase the military's role in drug interdiction — neither was he contrite. "If I have a strong Republican on any of my committees, I'm going to work with that person," Robinson said.

He also vowed to even the score with two more moderate House Democrats from Arkansas, Beryl Anthony Jr. (who is chairman of the Democratic Congressional Campaign Committee) and Bill Alexander, who had publicly criticized Robinson. Of Democrats who worked against him, Robinson said, "I'll go right into their district and campaign against them." He then went further, threatening to revive a dormant political action committee that would assist conservative Democratic candidates, including possible challengers to Anthony and Alexander.

The February 1989 defection of Florida Democratic Rep. Bill Grant to the GOP stirred considerable speculation that Robinson, too, would cross the aisle. But at that point, Robinson backed off: He held a peacemaking meeting with Anthony, disavowed plans to recruit challengers to his Democratic colleagues, and told GOP Sen. Phil Gramm of Texas, himself a prominent party-switcher, that he would remain a Democrat.

Robinson's critics say his bluster is just posturing to mask a record of ineffectiveness. "I don't know what he does," Alexander said in

Arkansas 2

Central — Little Rock

The political and industrial capital of Arkansas and home of its only two statewide-circulation newspapers, Little Rock dominates the 2nd District. The city and surrounding Pulaski County have 60 percent of the population, and their political weight is usually enough to determine the outcome of the district's elections.

Once a symbol of the resistance to desegregating public schools in the South, Little Rock today has shed much of its racial tension. One of the first cities in the country to make extensive use of urban renewal funds, the city has turned its attention to rebuilding the downtown and eradicating slum areas.

Little Rock's strong black vote and well-organized labor community, along with the liberal *Arkansas Gazette*, make the city a Democratic stronghold. But the Little Rock suburbs along the Arkansas River bluffs are home to a large managerial and professional community, which makes Pulaski County competitive. In 1984, it went for Republican Judy Petty over Robinson, and in 1988, Pulaski gave George Bush 55 percent of its vote.

Most of the counties that surround Pulaski are more confirmed in their Democratic habits, although in presidential voting, only Conway County went Democratic in 1988. West of Pulaski are Saline County, the nation's sole domestic source of bauxite and home to a politically active union movement in the aluminum industry, and rural Yell and Perry counties, with traditional Southern Democratic loyalties. Lonoke County, just east of Pulaski, is farm country, although some industry has sprung up along Interstate 40, which connects Little Rock with Memphis, Tenn.

White County is a partial exception to the rural Democratic pattern. With one of the strongest GOP organizations in the state and a firmly conservative intellectual direction from the academic community at Harding College, the county tends to be more competitive in state elections than its rural neighbors.

Population: 569,116. White 467,430 (82%), Black 95,739 (17%), Other 3,833 (1%). Spanish origin 4,540 (1%). 18 and over 401,104 (70%), 65 and over 60,593 (11%). Median age: 29.

one exchange. "Just mostly run his mouth."

But Robinson has fought some legislative battles in the House, and has even won a few. Robinson, along with Davis, Republican Duncan Hunter of California and other conservatives, attached provisions to the fiscal 1989 defense authorization bill ordering the Defense Department to provide greater technical assistance to federal agencies involved in the fight against illegal drug smuggling.

The measure was not Robinson's first venture with Hunter: In May 1987, he spoke in favor of Hunter's amendment supporting President Reagan's interpretation of the 1972 antiballistic missile treaty. In answer to opponents who said Reagan's version, which would have allowed space testing of strategic defense initiative (SDI) technology, was provocative to the Soviet Union, Robinson retorted, "I say, 'Screw the Russians.' . . . The simple bottom line is, if you adhere to the narrow interpretation of the ABM treaty, you cannot test or deploy post-1972 SDI technologies." But the Hunter amendment was defeated, 159-262.

Even when treading into broad policy areas, though, Robinson's thoughts do not stray far from home. In January 1989, he told the *Arkansas Gazette* that any decision to run for statewide office would be difficult, because of the benefits of his seat on Armed Services — which he called the "last big pork barrel left" — to Little Rock Air Force Base and other district defense facilities.

Though Robinson is on the right side of his party in the defense realm, he frequently votes with the Democratic majority on federal funding for education and economic development. And ironically, one of his biggest legislative victories was on a labor issue — the minimum wage — handled in Education and Labor, from which he was booted in the Davis ad flap.

In March 1989, a confrontation was brewing between liberals advocating a minimum-wage increase to $4.65 per hour with no subminimum "training wage," and supporters of President Bush, who demanded a $4.25 minimum and a six-month training wage. Robinson, working with Pennsylvanians Austin J. Murphy, a Democrat, and Tom Ridge, a Republican, proposed a compromise calling for $4.55 per hour, with a two-month training wage for first-time employees. The bill passed the House, 248-171.

Robinson's interest in the lowest-paid workers, which enhances his appeal as a populist, also played a role in one of his most paradoxical actions: The hard-bitten critic of Democratic liberalism cast his vote at the 1988 Democratic National Convention for the Rev. Jesse Jackson. Robinson, who grew up poor, later told a mostly black audience, "I voted for Jesse Jackson because I understand what he's trying to do about the disadvantaged."

At Home: Flamboyance and a populist pitch made Robinson one of Arkansas' best-known politicians. Yet restraint and moderation marked his initial House campaign.

The son of a fireman, Robinson served in the Navy after high school, then spent 16 years working his way up in law enforcement. Elected sheriff in 1980 and 1982, by 1984 he was mentioned as a possible gubernatorial candidate. Instead, Robinson entered the 2nd District Democratic primary, surprising Secretary of State Paul Riviere, who had been campaigning for a year. The 2nd was open because of GOP Rep. Ed Bethune's Senate bid.

Robinson borrowed heavily to finance his campaign. He found an issue to seize on when a federal judge ordered consolidation of three public school districts in Pulaski County, and he promised to work in Congress to limit the power of federal judges. Riviere argued that Robinson would be a pawn of his generous campaign donors, but instead of lashing out, Robinson shrugged off the attack, explaining that a common man like himself had to rely on his friends. That understated response was in keeping with Robinson's campaign approach.

Robinson dispatched Riviere in a runoff, then shifted from right to center. Key Democratic groups swung to him, partly because they saw him as a lesser evil than the GOP nominee, state Rep. Judy Petty. She spoke at the GOP National Convention and defended the party's foreign policy platform by saying, "There are some things worse than war." Bumper stickers appeared saying "Judy Petty is worse than war," and Robinson prevailed.

Robinson has subsequently won by huge margins, keeping alive discussion of a future candidacy for higher office. If he runs statewide, he would have no trouble raising money. He is close with many figures in Little Rock's investment community. One of his financial backers is oilman Jerry Jones, who in 1989 bought the Dallas Cowboys football team; his daughter, Charlotte Jones, signed on as Robinson's chief aide shortly after her college graduation.

And name recognition would be no problem for Robinson, who appears frequently on TV in Little Rock, the state's dominant media market. Robinson is well aware that a colorful persona attracts the cameras. "If you don't take stands on controversial issues," he says, "you're not going to be on TV."

Committees

Armed Services (22nd of 31 Democrats)
Military Installations and Facilities; Military Personnel and Compensation; Seapower and Strategic and Critical Materials

Select Aging (28th of 39 Democrats)
Human Services

Veterans' Affairs (9th of 21 Democrats)
Education, Training and Employment; Hospitals and Health Care

Elections

1988 General

Tommy F. Robinson (D)	168,889	(83%)
Warren D. Carpenter (R)	33,475	(17%)

1986 General

Tommy F. Robinson (D)	128,814	(76%)
Keith Hamaker (R)	41,244	(24%)

Previous Winning Percentage: 1984 (47%)

District Vote For President

	1988	1984	1980	1976
D	91,705 (43%)	87,447 (40%)	83,325 (44%)	120,683 (68%)
R	121,130 (56%)	133,093 (60%)	90,488 (48%)	57,936 (32%)
I			6,864 (4%)	

Campaign Finance

	Receipts	Receipts from PACs	Expend-itures
1988			
Robinson (D)	$687,069	$182,980 (27%)	$643,617
Carpenter (R)	$11,299	0	$11,098
1986			
Robinson (D)	$730,648	$296,867 (41%)	$685,296
Hamaker (R)	$81,901	$1,125 (1%)	$81,863

Key Votes

1987	
Raise speed limit to 65 mph	N
Approve Gephardt "fair trade" amendment	N
Ban testing of larger nuclear weapons	N
Delay "re-flagging" of Kuwaiti tankers	N
Approve tax-raising deficit-reduction bill	N
1988	
Approve aid to Nicaraguan contras	Y
Enact civil rights restoration bill over Reagan veto	Y
Kill 60-day plant-closing notification measure	N
Pass omnibus trade bill over Reagan veto	Y
Approve death penalty for drug-related murders	Y
Bar federal funds for abortions in cases of rape and incest	Y
Oppose seven-day waiting period for purchase of handguns	Y

Voting Studies

	Presidential Support		Party Unity		Conservative Coalition	
Year	**S**	**O**	**S**	**O**	**S**	**O**
1988	42	56	71	27	71	29
1987	46	54	56	41	81	19
1986	46	50	54	41	94	6
1985	45	51	66	29	73	25

Interest Group Ratings

Year	ADA	ACU	AFL-CIO	CCUS
1988	55	52	86	50
1987	48	48	81	60
1986	25	68	86	44
1985	40	57	63	45

3 John Paul Hammerschmidt (R)

Of Harrison — Elected 1966

Born: May 4, 1922, Harrison, Ark.
Education: Attended The Citadel, 1938-39; U. of Arkansas, 1940-41; Oklahoma State U., 1945-46.
Military Career: Army, 1942-45; Ark. Army Reserve, 1945-60; D.C. Army Reserve, 1977-81.
Occupation: Lumber company executive.
Family: Wife, Virginia Sharp; one child.
Religion: Presbyterian.
Political Career: Ark. Republican chairman, 1964-66.
Capitol Office: 2110 Rayburn Bldg. 20515; 225-4301.

In Washington: After more than two decades in Congress, Hammerschmidt has the potential power that most House Republicans only dream about. He is the ranking GOP member on the Public Works Committee and an old friend of President Bush, who occasionally comes to meet him in the members' dining room, or at the House gym. Moreover, Hammerschmidt's folksy, genial style makes him popular with his colleagues.

This combination of seniority, access and personality imbues Hammerschmidt with considerable clout, but the Arkansas Republican only rarely wields it publicly.

One of those rare instances came in March 1989, when Hammerschmidt gave a nominating speech on behalf of Georgian Newt Gingrich's bid for GOP whip. Gingrich's two-vote victory margin over Illinois' Edward Madigan was so narrow that it is impossible to isolate a single factor that put him over the top. But in a contest that turned in part on generational and stylistic considerations, it surely did not hurt that "young Turk" Gingrich had the support of Hammerschmidt, the third most-senior House Republican from the South and a man known to prefer collegiality over partisan confrontation.

Partisanship is rarely much of an issue on Hammerschmidt's two committees: Public Works and Veterans' Affairs. By and large, both panels start from a bipartisan assumption that "more is better" — more public works projects, and more benefits for veterans.

The Democratic majority on Public Works knows that Hammerschmidt will rarely be an antagonist as ranking Republican. Though conservative on most issues of broad economic policy, he is strongly supportive of federal spending on public works, and resisted Reagan administration budget-cutting efforts.

At the outset of the 100th Congress, Hammerschmidt was the Republican floor manager for two major pieces of legislation: the Clean Water Act reauthorization and the omnibus highway reauthorization. Both of the widely popular House measures essentially had been drafted in the 99th Congress, when tough and combative GOP Rep. Gene Snyder of Kentucky (then ranking on Public Works) helped hammer out their details in committee. But Snyder did not seek re-election in 1986, so in early 1987, it fell to Hammerschmidt to help guide the override of two presidential vetoes.

The clean-water bill was pocket-vetoed by President Reagan after its passage late in the 99th Congress. In his diplomatic way, Hammerschmidt told the House that Reagan's efforts to reduce federal spending on clean-water programs were commendable. But he added, "The administration's current proposals simply go too far in cutting back ... valuable programs." The bill was again approved in the House and Senate by near-unanimous margins; Reagan's second veto was easily overridden.

The initial highway bill died in conference at the end of the 99th Congress, and at the start of the 100th, the House passed a virtually identical bill and soon reached agreement with the Senate. When Reagan vetoed that bill, Hammerschmidt joined the override effort.

Hammerschmidt has always been careful to look out for his home interests on Public Works. A decorated World War II pilot, he uses his position on the Aviation Subcommittee to preserve federal subsidies that help cushion small airports, including several in his district, against the economic effects of deregulation.

On Veterans' Affairs, where he was ranking Republican in the early 1980s, Hammerschmidt has sometimes frustrated Vietnam veterans because he places such emphasis on providing high benefit levels for World War II veterans. (His district is a mountain retirement mecca with more than 60,000 World War II vets.) But he has backed job-training measures for Vietnam veterans as well as compensation for victims of the chemical Agent Orange.

Hammerschmidt helped push legislation to

Arkansas 3

Northwest — Ozark Plateau; Fort Smith

The hilly 3rd, Arkansas' most reliably Republican constituency, is one of just three Southern districts that has been represented by the same Republican for two decades or longer. The roots of the allegiance go back to the Civil War, a conflict that struck many of the small-scale farmers here as one fought mostly on behalf of wealthy slaveholding plantation owners in the flatter parts of Arkansas. Ronald Reagan won the 3rd by more than 2-to-1 in 1984, and Democratic Gov. Bill Clinton lost nearly half of the district's 20 counties, although he carried every other county in the rest of the state. In 1988, George Bush swept the 3rd.

The district is overwhelmingly white and traditionally has had a poor economy dependent on relatively unproductive farm land. Vast pine forests have provided jobs in sawmills scattered throughout the rural counties.

In recent years, however, the Ozark economy has been boosted by a large influx of new residents. The area's mild climate and natural assets — such as Beaver Lake and Bull Shoals Lake, the Buffalo River and the Ozark and Ouachita national forests — have lured retirees to newly developed planned communities, and service industries, small businesses and tourism have provided work for job-hunting newcomers.

Thousands still work in the Ozark's historic economic underpinnings — poultry, lumber and cattle. Tyson Food Inc., one of the nation's largest poultry-processing companies, has its headquarters in Springdale and numerous plants scattered around the 3rd. In the Ouachita Mountains, timber is a chief source of income, and the large livestock business in the western portion of the district gives the area around Fort Smith, near the Oklahoma border, a distinctly Western flavor.

There are about as many blacks in the northwest corner of Arkansas as in rural parts of Minnesota or Wisconsin. The 1980 census found two 3rd District counties — Searcy and Madison — that had no black residents at all.

The district's two population centers are Fort Smith, the state's second-largest city, and Fayetteville, home of the University of Arkansas. In the past, both have supported Republicans against even popular Democrats. In 1980, Gov. Clinton and President Carter shared the blame for housing Cuban refugees at Fort Chaffee near Fort Smith. The residents of surrounding Sebastian County expressed their opposition to the refugee camps by giving Clinton only 33 percent of the vote and Carter 27 percent. Fort Smith is a manufacturing center, with plants producing furniture and household appliances.

Population: 572,937. White 551,894 (96%), Black 11,794 (2%), Other 7,374 (1%). Spanish origin 4,382 (1%). 18 and over 414,806 (72%), 65 and over 85,231 (15%). Median age: 32.

elevate the Veterans Administration to a Cabinet-level department, a proposal that became law in 1988. Eleven of his colleagues on the Veterans' Affairs Committee wrote President Bush to urge that Hammerschmidt be appointed the first secretary of veterans affairs, but Bush chose former Rep. Edward J. Derwinski.

Hammerschmidt is one of five current Republican members elected to the House with Bush in 1966. During the late 1960s, he and other junior Republicans were frequent guests aboard their Texas colleague's Formula speedboat on the Potomac. The two remained friends after Bush left the House, and in 1980, Hammerschmidt was an early supporter of Bush's first presidential bid.

At Home: Hammerschmidt, the first Republican elected to Congress from Arkansas in the 20th century, is the only consistent success story of the state's modern Republican Party, which established a foothold in 1966 but has performed spottily since then. Other contemporary Arkansas Republicans have flourished briefly — Winthrop Rockefeller and Frank White as governors and Ed Bethune in the House — but Hammerschmidt alone remains in office today.

After returning from service in World War II, Hammerschmidt divided his time between Republican Party work and a lumber firm that had been in his family three generations. From 1964-66 he was the state Republican chairman, helping lay groundwork that ultimately elected Rockefeller to the governorship.

In 1966, Hammerschmidt decided to try for Congress, and the move turned out to be perfectly timed. Two years earlier, the GOP challenger in the 2nd had softened up Democratic Rep. James Trimble, holding him to 55 percent, while Barry Goldwater was drawing a respectable 44 percent of the district's presidential vote. The 1966 election promised national Republican gains, and Hammerschmidt was in the right district to benefit.

Trimble had held the seat since 1944, when he succeeded J. William Fulbright. He was a moderate Democrat, closely identified with Arkansas River and Ozark development projects. Already 72 years old, Trimble had to fight off two strong primary challengers. He never really recovered politically. In November, Hammerschmidt won by almost 10,000 votes.

Since then, only two Democrats have drawn more than a third of the vote against Hammerschmidt. The first was Bill Clinton, who as a 28-year-old law professor in 1974 put on a yearlong campaign that came within 6,300 votes. Only Hammerschmidt's strong showing in Fort Smith, the district's largest city and a center of social and economic conservatism, saved him. Clinton has since won three terms as governor.

Democrats thought the time was right in 1982, and offered banker and one-time Fulbright aide Jim McDougal. An affable and tireless campaigner, he targeted blue-collar voters and tried to tie Hammerschmidt to GOP economic policies, which were unpopular with many senior citizens and military retirees in the 3rd.

But McDougal was unable to dent Hammerschmidt's folksy popularity. Fort Smith and surrounding Sebastian County, even with a high unemployment rate, gave the incumbent a full 79 percent, and Hammerschmidt won two-thirds of the districtwide vote.

In 1988, with Republicans talking openly of the possibility that Hammerschmidt would get a high-level job in the Bush administration, Democrats touted attorney David Stewart. But his challenge did not make an impression on voters; Hammerschmidt won with 75 percent.

Committees

Public Works and Transportation (Ranking)

Veterans' Affairs (2nd of 13 Republicans)
Hospitals and Health Care (ranking)

Select Aging (2nd of 27 Republicans)
Housing and Consumer Interests

Elections

1988 General

John Paul Hammerschmidt (R)	161,623	(75%)
David Stewart (D)	54,767	(25%)

1986 General

John Paul Hammerschmidt (R)	145,113	(80%)
Su Sargent (D)	36,726	(20%)

Previous Winning Percentages: **1984** (100%) **1982** (66%)
1980 (100%) **1978** (78%) **1976** (100%) **1974** (52%)
1972 (77%) **1970** (67%) **1968** (67%) **1966** (53%)

District Vote For President

	1988	1984	1980	1976
D	74,413 (33%)	69,972 (30%)	89,197 (39%)	111,118 (55%)
R	146,498 (66%)	165,217 (70%)	134,908 (58%)	89,063 (44%)
I			7,457 (3%)	

Campaign Finance

	Receipts	Receipts from PACs	Expend-itures
1988			
Hammerschmidt (R)	$330,387	$166,700 (50%)	$159,221
Stewart (D) †	$60,059	$300 (0.5%)	$60,054
1986			
Hammerschmidt (R)	$159,238	$83,950 (53%)	$63,341
Sargent (D)	$11,905	$250 (2%)	$11,904

† Totals based on incomplete data.

Key Votes

1987	
Raise speed limit to 65 mph	N
Approve Gephardt "fair trade" amendment	N
Ban testing of larger nuclear weapons	N
Delay "re-flagging" of Kuwaiti tankers	N
Approve tax-raising deficit-reduction bill	N
1988	
Approve aid to Nicaraguan contras	Y
Enact civil rights restoration bill over Reagan veto	N
Kill 60-day plant-closing notification measure	Y
Pass omnibus trade bill over Reagan veto	N
Approve death penalty for drug-related murders	Y
Bar federal funds for abortions in cases of rape and incest	Y
Oppose seven-day waiting period for purchase of handguns	Y

Voting Studies

	Presidential Support		Party Unity		Conservative Coalition	
Year	S	O	S	O	S	O
1988	64	32	72	25	97	3
1987	57	39	65	30	86	7
1986	69	31	69	29	90	10
1985	64	34	71	27	95	4
1984	58	32	67	22	92	3
1983	66	32	75	21	88	7
1982	65	32	79	20	99	1
1981	79	21	80	20	96	4

Interest Group Ratings

Year	ADA	ACU	AFL-CIO	CCUS
1988	10	96	29	86
1987	12	68	19	87
1986	5	82	14	78
1985	25	81	12	77
1984	15	91	8	60
1983	0	91	13	85
1982	5	73	15	86
1981	5	100	27	89

4 Beryl Anthony Jr. (D)

Of El Dorado — Elected 1978

Born: Feb. 21, 1938, El Dorado, Ark.
Education: U. of Arkansas, B.S., B.A. 1961, J.D. 1963.
Occupation: Lawyer.
Family: Wife, Sheila Foster; two children.
Religion: Episcopalian.
Political Career: Prosecuting attorney, Ark. 13th Judicial District, 1971-77.
Capitol Office: 1117 Longworth Bldg. 20515; 225-3772.

In Washington: Anthony has become a prominent legislator without being responsible for much prominent legislation. Instead, during his career his political instincts have enabled him to promote others' concerns and himself at the same time. But Anthony's best opportunity to put those instincts into play — his chairmanship of the Democratic Congressional Campaign Committee (DCCC) — has turned out to be less satisfying than he might have hoped. Though the DCCC enjoyed some successes in the 100th Congress, Anthony's efforts there did not help him move up the leadership ladder as he had hoped in 1989.

Anthony had a very tough act to follow at the DCCC. California Rep. Tony Coelho had been credited with turning the practically moribund committee into a major-league operation, and it would have been difficult for anyone to shine in the spotlight as much as he did. At the same time, it would have been fairly easy for Coelho's successor to suffer from unfavorable comparisons.

But Anthony proved he could hold his own. He oversaw the committee at a time when Democratic candidates had unprecedented success at wooing financial support from business organizations, and, for the most part, he kept the DCCC from making any news that would harm party candidates. In November, Democrats managed to pick up three House seats. That was a modest gain, but it marked the first time since 1960 that a party has picked up seats while its presidential nominee lost.

Anthony does not get all the credit for the success the DCCC enjoyed, but clearly the organization benefited from some of his strengths. In particular, Anthony is a man with the charm and social graces to market himself and the Democratic Party to a variety of groups. He can please a crowd of rural voters in East Tennessee with homespun wisdom from Arkansas and also mix well with a group of well-heeled donors in West Palm Beach.

Long before taking over the DCCC, Anthony proved he could court business interests as well as anyone in Congress. He has a social background that a number of corporate lobbyists can relate to, and he has never been one to shun the attention he has received from them as a member of the Ways and Means Committee. Even when he did not have a leadership position, Anthony acted as something of a fund-raising entrepreneur for Democrats, arranging hunting and golfing outings at which lobbyists and members could socialize. His success in that informal role no doubt impressed many colleagues, particularly those eager to find a new DCCC chairman who could emulate Coelho's success at raising money from business political action committees.

Anthony's performance at the DCCC was not much of an in-House boost, however. Coelho had successfully used the committee as a springboard to the majority whip position; when he resigned amid controversy in 1989, Anthony campaigned for his leadership spot. But Anthony finished a distant third to Pennsylvania Rep. William H. Gray III, who won the whip position, and Michigan Rep. David E. Bonior. Anthony argued that the leadership needed a Southerner, but he did not corner the Southern vote in his campaign, winning support from only 30 members. Gray, who built up ties across regional and ideological lines as Budget Chairman and in his recent successful campaign to be caucus chairman, finished with 134 votes. Bonior had 97.

Shortly after his loss, Anthony opened himself up for recriminations by publicly accusing Coelho of mismanaging the DCCC's fiscal affairs and saddling the committee with a debt problem. Anthony quickly stepped back from some of his comments, insisting that the DCCC debt of nearly $2 million was the result of many factors. But that did not erase the impression that Anthony was a sour-grapes loser in the whip's race, nor did it endear him to the many allies of Coelho who remain in Congress.

Anthony won a spot on Ways and Means in his second term, helped by party leaders eager to cultivate an ambitious Southern Democrat with moderate political instincts. He has used that position not only to build his ties to business, but also to protect the interests of

Arkansas 4

South — Pine Bluff

When it comes to congressional elections, the voting habits of the 4th are like the flow of water from Hot Springs Mountain — very consistent. The 4th is so firmly Democratic that Republicans have offered a candidate for the House seat only four times in the past 20 years; in no instance did their nominee top 35 percent of the vote.

Stretching across the southern third of Arkansas from the Texas border to the Mississippi River, the 4th is Deep South territory. It has more blacks (28 percent of the population) than any other district in Arkansas, and its white electorate retains a Civil War-era allegiance to the Democratic Party even though the only recent Democratic presidential nominee it has found palatable was Jimmy Carter. George Bush carried the 4th in 1988, Ronald Reagan in 1984, Richard M. Nixon in 1972 and George C. Wallace in 1968.

Much of the district's economy depends on the timber industry. Georgia-Pacific has a paper mill and plant in Crossett that manufactures plywood, paper bags and chemicals. Pine Bluff (population 61,000), the district's largest city, has several pulp and paper mills. With a 49 percent black population, Pine Bluff casts the highest minority vote of any city in Arkansas.

The Pine Bluff Arsenal once produced the nation's entire supply of anti-personnel biological weapons; after an 18-year moratorium on chemical weapons, in December 1987, assembly of binary nerve-gas weapons began at Pine Bluff. The arsenal employs more than 2,000 military and civilian personnel.

The district's second-largest city is Hot Springs (population 37,000), the seat of Garland County and a popular resort for more than a century. The bathhouses and spas of Hot Springs National Park are the center of a tourist economy that includes horse racing and theme parks. Hot Springs is becoming a Republican town, partly because it is acquiring a large population of retirees — a quarter of the city's residents are 65 or older. When redistricting in 1981 moved Garland County from the 3rd District of Republican John Paul Hammerschmidt, Hot Springs citizens tried to block the move in court.

Farther south is the "El Dorado fringe," Arkansas' narrow "oil band" running along the bottom of the state from Texarkana, on the Texas border, through El Dorado, Anthony's hometown and the place where H. L. Hunt got his start. El Dorado and surrounding Union County are the site of several oil refineries and chemical plants; a corps of politically active, conservative oil operators there makes the county a pocket of GOP strength. But Anthony, as a local product, has no trouble.

Population: 570,831. White 408,799 (72%), Black 158,631 (28%). Spanish origin 4,307 (1%). 18 and over 403,044 (71%), 65 and over 86,556 (15%). Median age: 31.

Arkansas timber, agriculture and oil.

During tax-revision efforts in the 99th Congress, Anthony took an interest in a variety of issues, including the taxing of thrift institutions and employee sponsored 401(k) tax-exempt savings plans. Mostly, however, he was interested in timber. He remains on the board of directors of his family business, Anthony Forest Products, and has strongly backed tax language that benefits the industry both directly and indirectly. During tax revision efforts in the 99th Congress, Anthony led an informal group of members in crafting timber provisions adopted by the committee.

Anthony had the support of Ways and Means Chairman Dan Rostenkowski in his bid for DCCC chair, but he will work against the chairman when Arkansas interests are at stake. In the 101st Congress, some of Anthony's attention on Ways and Means went to protecting the interests of Arkansas' poultry industry. In 1987, Rostenkowski proposed raising revenue by changing the accounting requirements for family farms with earnings over $5 million. That change essentially would have required them to treat previously deferred taxes as income. But Anthony pushed an alternative plan in committee that would change the accounting only for farms with incomes over $25 million. Anthony's proposal was approved 11 to 10 by the committee.

Before the tax-revision debate, Anthony helped the securities industry win a major victory on Ways and Means. In 1984, he managed to persuade Rostenkowski to accept a cut in the capital gains withholding period to six months from a year. Part of Anthony's success was timing, since Rostenkowski's hostility toward the idea had cooled over the past few years. But Anthony's careful persistence and hard work played a major role in changing Rostenkowski's mind.

In 1983, Anthony played a part on Ways and Means in the effort to rescue the Social

Security system. To address a deficit expected after the turn of the century, Anthony devised a plan calling for a 5 percent cut in initial benefits and an increase in payroll taxes in the year 2015. The committee accepted it. But the full House opted for saving money in the next century by gradually raising the retirement age.

At Home: Nothing remotely challenging has happened in Anthony's electoral career since he got past his first hurdle in 1978. Most years, all he has to do is file his papers and he is guaranteed another term.

The 4th was open in 1978 because of Rep. Ray Thornton's Senate candidacy, and five major candidates entered the Democratic primary to succeed him. The overwhelming favorite was Arkansas Secretary of State Winston Bryant, an impressive vote-getter who had already been on district ballots several times.

Bryant had a 10,000-vote lead in the initial primary, but he was forced into a runoff against Anthony, then a businessman and prosecuting attorney in El Dorado, who portrayed himself as the "businessman's candidate" and campaigned against Bryant's identification with labor and teachers.

With a family name that was widely recognized and respected in the southern part of the district, Anthony was able to recruit traditional conservative Democrats against Bryant, who had a moderate-to-liberal reputation. Personal wealth from the Anthony family's lumber company and ties with the district's oil and gas producers gave Anthony a strong fund-raising edge over Bryant, and he came from behind to win the runoff by 5,500 votes.

Anthony's only significant general-election contest came in 1982, when Republicans put up Bob Leslie, a Little Rock lawyer and legal counsel to the state GOP who went on to serve as state party chairman.

Leslie contrasted his own upbringing as a sharecropper's son with Anthony's more privileged background and argued that the average voter "needs a congressman who knows what it's like to work for a living." But Anthony was well prepared; on the way to taking 78 percent of the vote in his May primary, he spent weeks touring the district, polishing his down-home style of campaigning. Anthony easily dispatched Leslie. He carried every county in the district.

Committees

Select Children, Youth and Families (7th of 18 Democrats)

Ways and Means (14th of 23 Democrats)
Health; Oversight

Elections

1988 General		
Beryl Anthony Jr. (D)	129,508	(69%)
Roger N. Bell (R)	57,658	(31%)
1986 General		
Beryl Anthony Jr. (D)	115,335	(78%)
Lamar Keels (R)	22,980	(15%)
Stephen A. Bitely (I)	10,604	(7%)

Previous Winning Percentages: **1984** (98%) **1982** (66%) **1980** (100%) **1978** (100%)

District Vote For President

	1988	1984	1980	1976
D	93,307 (46%)	94,484 (44%)	111,613 (54%)	131,802 (68%)
R	103,562 (52%)	122,373 (56%)	89,036 (43%)	63,128 (32%)
I			4,080 (2%)	

Campaign Finance

	Receipts	Receipts from PACs	Expend-itures
1988			
Anthony (D)	$547,244	$353,042 (65%)	$570,155
Bell (R)	$21,709	$880 (4%)	$21,538
1986			
Anthony (D)	$390,697	$276,757 (71%)	$179,169
Keels (R)	$24,760	$500 (2%)	$24,759

Key Votes

1987	
Raise speed limit to 65 mph	N
Approve Gephardt "fair trade" amendment	Y
Ban testing of larger nuclear weapons	Y
Delay "re-flagging" of Kuwaiti tankers	Y
Approve tax-raising deficit-reduction bill	Y
1988	
Approve aid to Nicaraguan contras	N
Enact civil rights restoration bill over Reagan veto	Y
Kill 60-day plant-closing notification measure	N
Pass omnibus trade bill over Reagan veto	Y
Approve death penalty for drug-related murders	Y
Bar federal funds for abortions in cases of rape and incest	N
Oppose seven-day waiting period for purchase of handguns	N

Voting Studies

	Presidential Support		Party Unity		Conservative Coalition	
Year	**S**	**O**	**S**	**O**	**S**	**O**
1988	28	67	81	9	55	39
1987	24	69	85	5	47	37
1986	27	64	78	11	62	36
1985	28	71	81	14	58	36
1984	37	47	58	18	51	32
1983	45	51	69	25	64	36
1982	48	43	63	31	71	21
1981	61	38	61	30	76	15

Interest Group Ratings

Year	ADA	ACU	AFL-CIO	CCUS
1988	80	16	92	46
1987	68	5	88	27
1986	50	30	54	40
1985	55	33	59	32
1984	50	28	27	33
1983	50	24	69	65
1982	40	41	50	56
1981	30	40	73	33

California

U.S. CONGRESS

SENATE 1 D, 1 R

HOUSE 26 D, 18 R, 1 vacancy

LEGISLATURE

Senate 24 D, 15 R, 1 Independent

House 46 D, 33 R, 1 vacancy

ELECTIONS

1988 Presidential Vote	
Bush	51%
Dukakis	48%
1984 Presidential Vote	
Reagan	58%
Mondale	41%
1980 Presidential Vote	
Reagan	53%
Carter	36%
Anderson	9%
Turnout rate in 1984	50%
Turnout rate in 1986	36%
Turnout rate in 1988	47%

(as percentage of voting age population)

POPULATION AND GROWTH

1980 population	23,667,902
1988 population estimate (1st in the nation)	28,314,000
Percent change 1980-1988	+20%

DEMOGRAPHIC BREAKDOWN

White	76%
Black	8%
Other	6%
(Spanish origin)	19%
Urban	91%
Rural	9%
Born in state	45%
Foreign-born	15%

MAJOR CITIES

Los Angeles	3,259,340
San Diego	1,015,190
San Francisco	749,000
San Jose	712,080
Long Beach	396,280

AREA AND LAND USE

Area 156,299 sq. miles (3rd)

Farm	32%
Forest	39%
Federally owned	46%

Gov. George Deukmejian (R)
Of Long Beach — Elected 1982

Born: June 6, 1928, Menands, N.Y.
Education: Siena College, B.A. 1949; St. John's U., J.D. 1952.
Military Career: Army, 1953-55.
Occupation: Lawyer.
Religion: Episcopalian.
Political Career: Calif. Assembly, 1963-67; Calif. Senate, 1967-79, minority leader, 1975-79; Calif. attorney general, 1979-83.
Next Election: 1990.

WORK

Occupations	
White-collar	58%
Blue-collar	27%
Service workers	13%
Government Workers	
Federal	314,020
State	337,324
Local	1,155,504

MONEY

Median family income	$ 21,537	(10th)
Tax burden per capita	$ 1,098	(9th)

EDUCATION

Spending per pupil through grade 12	$ 3,543	(24th)
Persons with college degrees	20%	(8th)

CRIME

Violent crime rate	918 per 100,000 (3rd)

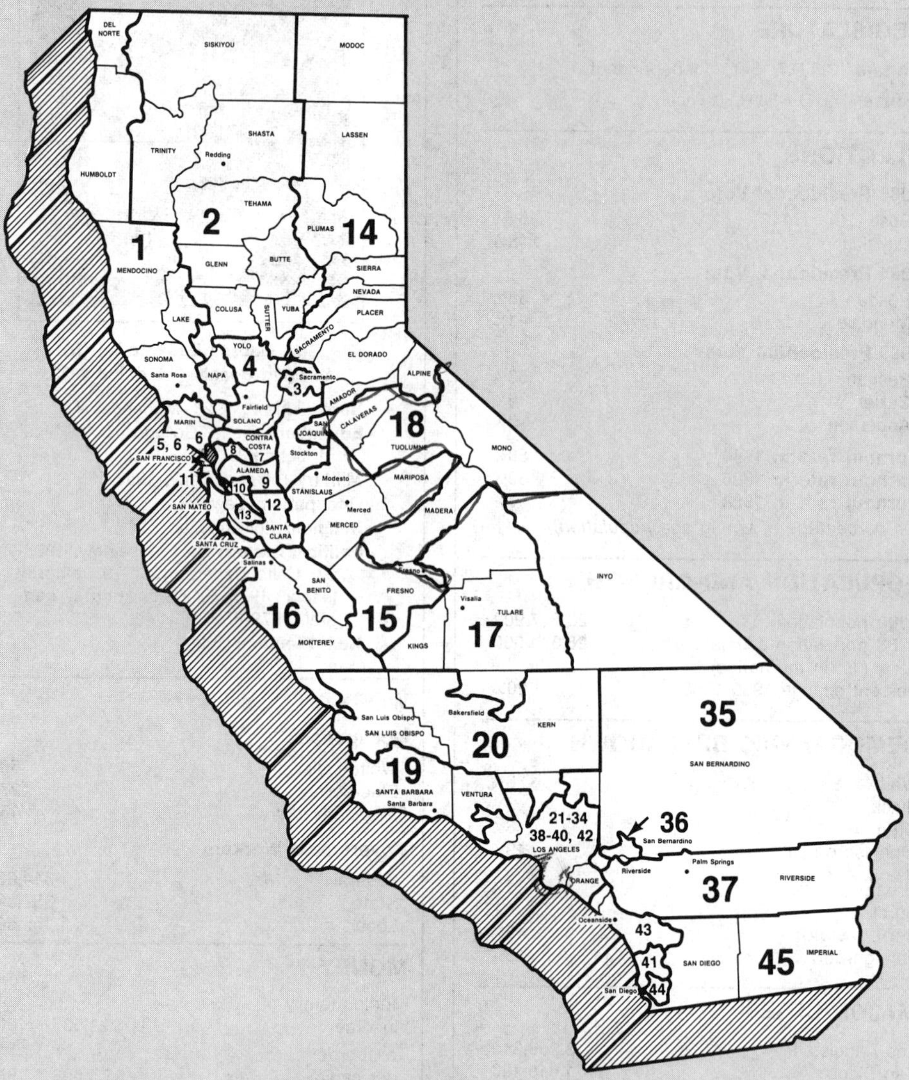
DEL NORTE
SISKIYOU
MODOC
TRINITY
SHASTA
Redding
LASSEN
HUMBOLDT
TEHAMA
2
PLUMAS
14
1
MENDOCINO
GLENN
BUTTE
SIERRA
NEVADA
COLUSA
SUTTER
YUBA
PLACER
LAKE
YOLO
SACRAMENTO
EL DORADO
SONOMA
Santa Rosa
NAPA
4
Sacramento
3
ALPINE
AMADOR
Fairfield
SOLANO
MARIN
CALAVERAS
SAN JOAQUIN
18
5, 6
6
SAN FRANCISCO
8
CONTRA COSTA
7
Stockton
TUOLUMNE
MONO
11
ALAMEDA
9
Modesto
MARIPOSA
10
STANISLAUS
SAN MATEO
12
Merced
MADERA
13
MERCED
SANTA CLARA
SANTA CRUZ
Salinas
SAN BENITO
Fresno
INYO
FRESNO
Visalia
TULARE
16
15
MONTEREY
KINGS
17
35
San Luis Obispo
SAN LUIS OBISPO
Bakersfield
KERN
20
SAN BERNARDINO
19
SANTA BARBARA
Santa Barbara
VENTURA
21-34
38-40, 42
LOS ANGELES
36
San Bernardino
Riverside
Palm Springs
ORANGE
37
RIVERSIDE
Oceanside
43
41
SAN DIEGO
45
IMPERIAL
San Diego
44

Alan Cranston (D)

Of Los Angeles — Elected 1968

Born: June 19, 1914, Palo Alto, Calif.

Education: Attended Pomona College, 1932-33; U. of Mexico, 1933; Stanford U., A.B. 1936.

Military Career: Army, 1944-45.

Occupation: Journalist; real-estate executive; author.

Family: Divorced; one child.

Religion: Protestant.

Political Career: Calif. controller, 1959-67; sought Democratic nomination for U.S. Senate, 1964; sought Democratic nomination for president, 1984.

Capitol Office: 112 Hart Bldg. 20510; 224-3553.

In Washington: Cranston is ambitious enough to have reached for the presidency, but within the Senate, the Democrats' master vote-counter knew better than to try for the chamber's premier post when it opened in 1988. Instead, he kept the No. 2 job of whip, doing the strategizing and nose-counting he relishes so much.

When Majority Leader Robert C. Byrd announced he would step aside after nearly a dozen years, his assistant during all that time, Cranston, was never mentioned among the potential successors — except to be dismissed as too old and too liberal. Moreover, Cranston's image as a consummate Senate insider had been frayed by a dismal 1984 presidential campaign and an all-consuming 1986 re-election. In that time, he was often absent and, when present, distracted.

The two campaigns contributed mightily to Cranston's enigmatic image. He ran for president as an idealistic liberal, so much a crusader for arms control that he came across as a fringe candidate. But when he sought re-election, Cranston was a moderate pragmatist, the mainstream candidate of California business. "When you're effective," Cranston once said, "you don't have any rigid lines."

Cranston's work on behalf of his state's business interests has been a major element of his career, and a cornerstone of his success. That record is best symbolized by his support for the B-1 bomber, built in California, but he has also labored for growers, independent oil, savings and loans, Realtors, aerospace contractors and moviemakers. At the same time, he has been one of the foremost advocates of the liberal causes — civil rights, poverty programs, the environment and arms control — that have large constituencies in the state.

In his 1984 White House bid, for all Cranston's obvious sincerity about arms control, his attempts to compete for attention in the media struck many as incongruous and unbecoming. Questions focused on his age and gaunt visage rather than on issues, prompting Cranston to dye his hair brown and urge reporters to jog with him. Preoccupation with his tough re-election in 1986 made Cranston a marginal figure in the 99th Congress, and those issues in which he was involved — notably, veterans' programs and Israel — were viewed as extensions of his campaign.

Since those times, Cranston has worked to restore his image. And with Democrats back in control of the Senate since 1987, his job as assistant majority leader gives him plenty of opportunity to reassert himself.

Cranston started nose-counting in 1969, his first year in the Senate, when he was given a chance to help manage a Job Corps bill on the floor. He soon started helping round up votes on other measures crucial to his fellow liberals, having discovered a vacuum in the party's leadership of the early 1970s: Majority Leader Mike Mansfield was no arm-twister, and Byrd, then the whip, was no liberal. Cranston was a liberal, one with a skill at building bridges to moderates and conservatives.

His trademark was his tally sheet, a piece of paper covered with scribbled pluses, minuses and question marks. In 1977, when Byrd became majority leader, Cranston easily won election as his deputy. Despite their ideological differences, which narrowed over the years, and Byrd's reluctance to delegate responsibilities, the two worked together with little friction. In 1984 and 1986, when Byrd faced real or threatened challengers, Cranston stuck by him.

In 1988, with the focus on the race to succeed Byrd, Cranston appeared unchallenged for a record seventh term as whip. Then just two months before the Democrats would choose, moderate Wendell H. Ford of Kentucky announced his candidacy. Cranston insisted he had the votes. Indeed, when the tally reached 30-12, Ford moved to stop the count and make Cranston's election unanimous.

Cranston's reputed talent for coalition-building had suffered from the Senate's polarization of the early 1980s, when Ronald Reagan was new in the White House, and then from Cranston's own political preoccupations at mid-decade. But the Californian has never had grandiose notions about his power. "A lot of leadership is just housekeeping now," he said in 1982. "Occasionally you have the opportunity to provide leadership, but not that often. The weapons to keep people in line just aren't there."

Still, back as whip full time in the 100th Congress, Cranston did some important work. He had a lead role in dealing his old California nemesis, Reagan, one of his biggest defeats — rejection of Supreme Court nominee Robert H. Bork — and he helped deliver one of Reagan's major triumphs — ratification of the intermediate-range nuclear-force (INF) treaty.

During the three-month fight over Bork in 1987, Cranston held numerous private meetings, and acted as a liaison between Northern and Southern Democrats. He helped persuade key senators to go public with their opposition to Bork's ideological conservatism, thus creating momentum toward rejection and providing cover for those hesitant to challenge Reagan.

Late in that year, he began strategy meetings for the INF debate, and then led the administration's lobbying for approval. It was a stunning irony. Cranston had been a Reagan antagonist since 1966, when, as state controller, he campaigned against Reagan's election as governor; Reagan, for his part, considered challenging Cranston in the 1974 Senate race. Now the two, in the twilight of their careers, were working for the same end.

The INF treaty alone would minimally reduce the superpowers' arsenals — it was, Cranston said, "a small step away from the nuclear brink." But Cranston felt that if Cold Warrior Reagan concluded an arms-control pact, then conservatives could never again credibly attack the very idea of dealing with the Soviets.

Senate approval of the popular treaty was not in doubt. The fear was that conservatives would add provisions that would force renegotiation with the Soviets, and thus kill the pact. Cranston lined up Democrats to block them. Meanwhile, over vigorous GOP opposition, he also helped Democrats attach a provision of their own — one not subject to renegotiation, but charged with constitutional implications. It barred any president from reinterpreting a treaty. The amendment was aimed not at the INF accord, but at the 1972 ABM treaty, which Reagan had tried to reinterpret to permit space tests of his proposed strategic defense initiative.

The alliance with the administration was not without other bumpy moments. At Foreign Relations, Secretary of State George P. Shultz said the treaty had proved the peace movement wrong, and vindicated the U.S. policy of deploying nuclear arms in Europe to force the Soviets to negotiate cutbacks. Cranston pounced: "The political fact of life is, the concerns about the dangers of nuclear war, expressed by countless Americans and by Europeans, too, have helped focus our government . . . on the task of quelling the arms race."

Cranston's efforts for arms control predate his Senate career, going back to his postwar work in the United World Federalists. On the Foreign Relations Committee since 1981, he has worked not only to reduce the superpowers' arms, but also to block other nations from acquiring them.

In 1984, he and Ohio Democrat John Glenn won Foreign Relations' approval of an amendment halting aid to Pakistan unless the president certified that the nation was not developing nuclear weapons; the panel later weakened it under administration pressure. The next year, he sought unsuccessfully to block Reagan's proposed sale of arms and nuclear-power supplies to China, saying that nation might transfer nuclear technology to Pakistan, its ally. In 1988, he and Glenn failed to kill a 30-year pact providing Japan with uranium supplies for nuclear power, and allowing Japan to process the byproduct plutonium without getting the usual advance U.S. approval for handling the bomb-making material.

Cranston is not particularly active on Foreign Relations except when the subject is arms control or one other — Israel. He repeatedly led efforts to block Reagan's proposed arms sales to Arab nations. A 1981 sale of AWACS radar planes to Saudi Arabia went through, but Cranston mobilized enough opposition to doom arms deals with Jordan in 1985 and with Saudi Arabia in 1987. He also wrote a provision that has had a major impact on U.S. aid to Israel: Since 1984, foreign aid bills have included the so-called Cranston amendment, mandating that Israel get at least as much in economic aid each year as it must repay on past loans.

On the Banking Committee, Cranston has devoted most of his recent efforts to the Housing Subcommittee, which he chairs. In early 1987 he called for a "major reformation" of federal policy. "We cannot return to the costly and confusing programs of the past," Cranston said. "Neither can we abdicate federal responsibility." His first step was a modest but significant one. A yearlong effort in 1987 ended with a last-minute agreement on the first housing authorization bill since 1980.

Cranston had pushed for a "lean" bill, one to freeze existing programs and start small-scale new ones, but in conference he collided with House Democrats who wanted a more expansive bill. Always thinking of advantage over Reagan, he implored them to save their initiatives for 1988, when Democrats could highlight housing problems in an election year while the president was still in office to take the blame. After three months, the two sides finally compromised. The bill passed the House with a single dissent, only to be ambushed in the Senate by conservatives. Efforts to appease them only infuriated House supporters, and Cranston declared the bill dead. That spurred new negotiations, and a deal was approved hours before Congress adjourned for the year.

Since then, Cranston's more ambitious housing plans have floundered on budget concerns and differences with House Banking Committee Chairman Henry B. Gonzalez. Cranston wants dramatically new programs with moderate spending increases, while Gonzalez wants big increases for existing programs.

On financial issues at Banking, Cranston is considered a friend of S&Ls. His state is home to the nation's largest firms, including many of those that fell in the 1980s to mismanagement and fraud, thus draining the Federal Savings and Loan Insurance Corporation (FSLIC). Cranston opposed administration proposals in the 100th and 101st Congresses to bolster the FSLIC by raising S&Ls' premiums and tightening regulations, criticizing the plans as unfair and too costly for healthy firms.

On the question of banking deregulation, he has sided with the securities industry, which wants to keep banks from entering its field. In the debate over hostile corporate takeovers, he has generally opposed restricting the so-called raiders.

Cranston could have become chairman of Banking in 1989, but because that is a major committee, he would have had to forfeit the whip's job. Party rules do allow him to be chairman of the minor Veterans' Affairs Committee, a position he held from 1977-81 and regained in 1987 when Democrats retook the Senate.

The 100th Congress was one of the most generous to veterans in recent years; as chairman, Cranston helped shepherd into law bills expanding health, education and housing benefits. And with House opposition finally dissolved, he won enactment on the fifth try of legislation giving veterans the right to appeal adverse benefits rulings to federal court. Also, the Veterans Administration was given a seat at the Cabinet table.

Even when he was in the minority, Cranston was an important figure on the committee. His close ties with veterans' groups, especially those for Vietnam-era veterans, and his alliance with moderate Republicans allowed him at times to frustrate GOP Chairman Alan K. Simpson's cost-cutting initiatives.

But the two men have had a good relationship, a fact that has significance far beyond Veterans' Affairs, since Simpson likewise is his party's whip. In frequent contact, they have more than once acted as a back channel to unsnarl some partisan Senate knots.

Until he left for Foreign Relations, Cranston was an active member of the then Human Resources Committee. For four years, he chaired its Subcommittee on Child and Human Development. Like Walter F. Mondale, his predecessor, he pressed for expanded child-care support. He also has been an advocate of Head Start, legal aid and bilingual education.

At Home: Cranston is a paradoxical figure in California politics. He is a veteran officeholder representing a constituency fascinated with novelty, a grass-roots politician in the ultimate media state, and a liberal on Ronald Reagan's home turf. Without the benefit of a dynamic personality, he has retained the allegiance of most of California's demanding liberals while also courting audiences in the middle of the spectrum.

He also has become one of California's most enduring politicians without ever laying to rest the notion that he is insecure in his seat. When his fourth term expires in 1992, Cranston will be 78. Older senators have been re-elected, but only from the safest of political sinecures. Cranston, a lifelong sprinter, remains fit. He ran hard in 1988 to keep his job as majority whip. At the same time, he may have contracted a new political difficulty that year by divorcing his wife of 10 years, who is an invalid.

Cranston was blessed in his first three Senate elections with conservative opponents; to win, he just had to appear more moderate than they were. But after each contest, onlookers wondered whether it would be so easy for Cranston if the GOP ever came up with a relatively moderate nominee.

In 1986, that candidate emerged in Rep. Ed Zschau, a one-time high-tech entrepreneur with a moderate record and access to bundles of campaign cash. His relative youth — 46, compared with Cranston's 72 — made him an automatic threat. And Zschau embodied the self-confident, forward-looking entrepreneurship that many Californians have come to consider the hallmark of their state.

But Cranston had ideas of his own about what Zschau could be made to represent. The day after Zschau won the GOP primary, the Cranston campaign began running ads attacking the Republican for "flip-flops" on issues ranging from the MX missile and chemical weapons to child nutrition and apartheid in South Africa.

At the same time, Cranston was running commercials that made the most of one of his greatest potential weaknesses — his longevity in office. Cranston, the ads suggested, had an institutional weight in the Senate that Zschau could not hope to match.

Not until September did Zschau begin to fight back, with salvos accusing Cranston of being soft on drugs and terrorism. As the assaults continued, Zschau began to win over conservatives who had been hostile earlier, and to pick up the support of independents and moderates who liked his free-market beliefs and liberal social outlook. In the end, though, his efforts were not enough. Out of more than 7 million votes, Cranston emerged just 105,000 votes ahead, with 49.3 percent of the vote.

When World War II started, Cranston left his journalism career to become head of the Foreign Language Division of the Office of War Information. After the war, he got involved with the United World Federalists and other peace groups. While working in the family real-estate business in Palo Alto in the late 1940s, Cranston helped form the liberal California Democratic Council (CDC) and served as its first president. The group was vital to launching his political career.

In 1958, Cranston became the first Democrat elected state controller in 72 years. Four years later, he won re-election by a record margin. Thus emboldened, he ran for the Senate in 1964, but narrowly lost the Democratic primary to former White House press secretary Pierre Salinger, who charged that state inheritance tax appraisers had been forced to give to the Cranston campaign. Salinger went on to lose to Republican George Murphy.

The voters dealt Cranston another blow in the Republican year of 1966. They turned him out of his controller's post. But two years later, he tried for the Senate again. He won a five-way primary over a field that included state Sen. Anthony C. Beilenson, now a U.S. House member. That contest was gentle, as the top contenders all were liberals and Vietnam doves.

The general election, however, pitted Cranston against conservative Max Rafferty, the state superintendent of public instruction. Rafferty punched hard, attacking Cranston for ties to "left-wing radical groups" like the CDC and for advocating a Vietnam bombing halt — which he said would endanger U.S. troops.

But the GOP was badly divided, following an angry primary in which Rafferty had unseated moderate incumbent Thomas H. Kuchel, the Senate minority whip. In addition, a newspaper series tarnished Rafferty's super-patriot reputation by alleging that he was a World War II draft-dodger. Cranston won by 350,000 votes.

In 1974 Cranston had an easy time against state Sen. H. L. "Bill" Richardson, an early New Right activist and former John Birch Society field worker. At one point, when the Birch Society announced plans to circulate material linking Cranston to communists, it drew a rebuke from Gov. Reagan.

Cranston was blessed with similarly weak GOP opposition in 1980 from tax-revolt leader Paul Gann, the coauthor of Proposition 13 that cut state property taxes in 1978. But the tax issue had faded in two years, and Gann proved to be hopelessly inarticulate as a candidate.

Committees

Majority Whip

Veterans' Affairs (Chairman)

Banking, Housing and Urban Affairs (2nd of 12 Democrats)
Housing and Urban Affairs (chairman); Securities

Foreign Relations (4th of 10 Democrats)
East Asian and Pacific Affairs (chairman); African Affairs; Western Hemisphere and Peace Corps Affairs

Select Intelligence (5th of 8 Democrats)

Elections

1986 General		
Alan Cranston (D)	3,646,672	(49%)
Ed Zschau (R)	3,541,804	(48%)
1986 Primary		
Alan Cranston (D)	1,807,242	(81%)
Charles Greene (D)	165,594	(7%)
John Hancock Abbott (D)	124,218	(6%)
Robert J. Banuelos (D)	77,286	(3%)
Brian Lantz (D)	64,907	(3%)

Previous Winning Percentages: **1980** (57%) **1974** (61%) **1968** (52%)

Campaign Finance

	Receipts	Receipts from PACs	Expend-itures
1986			
Cranston (D)	$10,851,596	$1,366,173 (13%)	$11,037,707
Zschau (R)	$11,789,533	$1,239,898 (11%)	$11,781,316

Key Votes

1987	
Enact omnibus highway bill over Reagan veto	Y
Limit testing of space-based anti-ballistic missiles	Y
Oppose banning tests of larger nuclear weapons	N
Confirm Robert H. Bork as Supreme Court justice	N
1988	
Allow vote on campaign-finance overhaul	Y
Pass civil rights restoration bill over Reagan veto	Y
Enact omnibus trade bill over Reagan veto	Y
Approve death penalty for drug-related murders	N
Oppose "workfare" amendment to welfare overhaul bill	Y

Voting Studies

	Presidential Support		Party Unity		Conservative Coalition	
Year	**S**	**O**	**S**	**O**	**S**	**O**
1988	33	52	86	6	14	78
1987	36	58	93	4	9	88
1986	20	78	85	9	9	86
1985	25	73	80	16	18	78
1984	19	61	74	7	13	72
1983	28	40	55	7	7	52
1982	26	66	81	10	7	84
1981	38	48	77	10	10	74

Interest Group Ratings

Year	ADA	ACU	AFL-CIO	CCUS
1988	95	0	86	29
1987	75	0	89	33
1986	95	10	87	32
1985	100	4	80	21
1984	95	0	100	20
1983	75	0	100	18
1982	95	5	96	11
1981	85	0	100	13

Pete Wilson (R)

Of San Diego — Elected 1982

Born: Aug. 23, 1933, Lake Forest, Ill.
Education: Yale U., B.A. 1955; U. of California, Berkeley, LL.B. 1962.
Military Career: Marine Corps, 1955-58.
Occupation: Lawyer.
Family: Wife, Gayle Edlund.
Religion: Protestant.
Political Career: Calif. Assembly, 1967-71; San Diego mayor, 1971-83.
Capitol Office: 720 Hart Bldg. 20510; 224-3841.

In Washington: Most of the senators in the 101st Congress will perform with an eye on re-election. Some will also be thinking about running for president. Wilson will be thinking about running for governor of California. But then, many would say this particular senator has always acted as though he was running for governor.

Wilson announced his new political goal in February 1989, just three months after winning a second term in the Senate. In the interim, GOP Gov. George Deukmejian had decided to retire, leaving California Republicans without a clear candidate in 1990. Wilson, the only other Republican who has recently won a statewide office, was all but begged to run by state party leaders.

They called, and Wilson responded, because this particular gubernatorial term will have profound implications for state and even national politics. A Republican governor can check the Democratic Legislature, which would otherwise tinker at will with district lines for legislative and congressional seats after the 1990 U.S. census.

After the 1980 census, a Democratic governor and Legislature approved a redistricting map drawn by Rep. Phillip Burton. That map (with some modifications made in 1983) has enabled Democrats to hold a 3-to-2 advantage in California's House seats. In its drive for parity in the House, the national GOP cannot afford this kind of deficit in California. The new census is expected to award the Golden State five or six new House seats, bringing its total to 50 or 51 — the largest House delegation ever.

California's share of the Electoral College vote thus will also increase. That means Wilson, if he has been elected senator and governor, would become an overwhelming favorite for a future spot on the GOP presidential ticket.

Even without the national imperative, Wilson might have been tempted by the governorship in 1990. If he loses, he can still return to the Senate for at least four more years. And he has been assured the funding he needs and the right to name his Senate successor, should he need one. Besides, some of Wilson's colleagues say, this is the office he has wanted all along. It represents the only office he has sought unsuccessfully; he finished well back in the GOP gubernatorial primary field of 1978.

There is evidence that Wilson has thought in terms of the governorship even as he served in the Senate. All good politicians pay attention to local aspects of a policy question and local opportunities in a program of government spending. But Wilson's obsession with both is usually the foremost characteristic cited when observers and peers review his career.

For example, when he had to choose in the 101st Congress between remaining a member of the Commerce Committee or the Agriculture Committee, he was thought to feel more affinity for the former. But he chose Agriculture after hearing the entreaties of California growers. It was this same constituency that, in the 99th Congress, drove Wilson to perhaps his most memorable performance on domestic legislation to date. Responding to California growers, who have relied heavily on illegal immigrants to pick perishable crops on short notice, Wilson insisted that any overhaul of immigration laws contain a "guest worker" program that would ensure growers easy access to immigrant labor.

In 1985, Wilson clashed with the chief Senate sponsor of immigration reform, Wyoming Republican Alan K. Simpson, who called the growers "greedy" and said Wilson's amendment calling for an open-ended guest worker program was an effort to derail an immigration bill altogether.

Wilson said his proposal was "not a killer amendment. It is a saving amendment. It will save an industry." After losing 50-48, Wilson revised his proposal slightly, led his allies in an intensive lobbying campaign and won on a second vote, 51-44.

But strong feelings on the guest-worker issue persisted, and it took more than a year of off-and-on negotiations between Wilson, Simpson and other senators and House members before a compromise was reached and an immigration bill passed. The compromise protected growers' access to a large seasonal labor pool, but made it fairly easy for those workers to qualify for temporary resident status.

But many interests in California have benefited from Wilson's lobbying. In the 99th Congress, some of his allies in state and local government sought help in easing the impact of a Supreme Court ruling requiring them to pay employees for overtime work. After both chambers passed a bill allowing governments to give employees time off in lieu of overtime pay, Wilson got himself invited to participate in the conference with the House on the measure, even though he was not a Labor Committee member. A persistent Wilson persuaded reluctant conferees to give governments a freer hand to save money by adjusting employee work schedules and job classifications without incurring charges of discrimination.

On the Armed Services Committee, Wilson is one of the most ardent backers of the strategic defense initiative (SDI). Wilson argues strongly that it is a national military necessity; it also would bring in billions in military contracts to California's aerospace and electronics industries. Wilson balked in 1985 when SDI skeptics proposed setting up an advisory council to give senators, especially those not on Armed Services, more data on SDI. The council idea lost.

In the 100th Congress, when calls for restraining SDI funding were growing louder, Wilson was one of several conservative GOP senators telling the administration that it could enhance SDI's appeal by demonstrating that some kind of space defense — even if limited in scope — could be deployed in the next few years.

When the 1989 defense authorization bill cut funding for space-based anti-missile weapons for the 1990s, Wilson helped persuade President Reagan to veto it. He also persuaded George Bush to make the bill — which cut funds for a mobile version of the MX missile and issued orders the White House considered intrusive on its authority — an issue in the 1988 presidential campaign. Wilson called it "one of those happy times when good government and good politics coincide."

At Home: In winning a second term in 1988, Wilson retired a jinx: He was the first incumbent re-elected to this California seat since 1952. Yet, in a sense, the jinx may reassert itself if Wilson wins his race for governor and leaves without serving out that second term.

But if the governor's race has pitfalls, Wilson has already proven himself sure-footed. His ability to avoid giving offense has contributed to the length of his career. He has also seemed content with a minimum profile in the media, going quietly about the business of representing California interests, fostering friends and discouraging rivals.

He also entered the 1988 campaign year with a $3 million cash reserve (the third largest in the Senate). Unopposed in the GOP primary, he opened his campaign on the offensive against the Democrats' nominee, Lt. Gov. Leo T. McCarthy. He maintained the initiative throughout the campaign year, at times blunting McCarthy's next move before it had been made.

Although a liberal from San Francisco, McCarthy had twice been elected lieutenant governor in the midst of Deukmejian's gubernatorial victories. He could not match Wilson's money, but he was able to raise and spend enough ($9 million against Wilson's $15 million) to finance a real race in the state with the nation's most media-driven politics.

McCarthy united the party behind him before the June primary and basked in the midsummer popularity of Democratic presidential nominee Michael S. Dukakis.

McCarthy tried to cast Wilson as both a do-nothing senator who "left no footprints" and as a closet right-winger. But Wilson managed to defend himself on issues such as offshore oil drilling and simultaneously exploit issues that divided McCarthy's base. One was the "homeporting" of the USS *Missouri* in San Francisco, on which McCarthy sided with anti-war groups and against the labor Democrats who saw the homeporting facility creating jobs.

Meanwhile, McCarthy's most memorable moments in the media seemed to highlight his vulnerabilities (such as his condominiums at the posh La Costa resort).

McCarthy managed to cut his deficit in the polls from the teens to single digits, but he never quite pulled even. In time, the state came home to GOP presidential nominee Bush, who won by more than 350,000 votes. Wilson prevailed by more than 850,000.

But both before and after the results were in, some observers argued that a sharper candidate and campaign might have bagged Wilson, who again proved a less-than-inspiring figure on the stump.

"The trouble with campaigning," Wilson once complained, "is it's an exercise in oversimplification." His discomfort showed during the 1982 Senate campaign, in which he often came across as stiff and reserved. He had trouble igniting even Republican audiences in his battle with California's often pyrotechnic Democratic governor, Edmund G. Brown Jr.

But Wilson was anything but uncomfortable as an officeholder. Elected to the state Assembly from San Diego just three years after moving there in 1963, he has held public office since. In the Assembly, he allied himself with moderates (against Ronald Reagan), trying to develop a master environmental plan for California's coastline. That effort failed, but Wilson eventually became chairman of the Assembly's Urban Affairs Committee, and in 1971 he decided to run for mayor of San Diego. Campaigning as an environmentalist pledged to control urban growth, Wilson won in a field of 14 candidates.

Later, Wilson became a vigorous proponent of growth and free enterprise with a reputation for careful fiscal management. His vehement opposition to rent control and his tough stand toward city-employee unions won him accolades from business interests. Liberals and city employees criticized him, but he remained popular, combining long working hours with a lighter side that came out in such endeavors as his singing performance in a local musical revue.

Wilson made one big political misstep — his disastrous 1978 run for governor. He gained notice as the only major GOP hopeful against Proposition 13, the tax-limitation initiative. But Proposition 13 won easily, and Wilson ran fourth in a field of five.

Preparing another gubernatorial campaign for 1982, Wilson saw himself trailing two other GOP candidates in the polls and switched to the Senate contest. Wilson's moderate reputation was an issue: He had supported Gerald R. Ford over Reagan for president in 1976, and had endorsed the Equal Rights Amendment and opposed government restrictions on abortion.

For the primary, however, he played up his conservative credentials, especially his roles as national vice chairman of Reagan's 1980 presidential campaign and chairman of Reagan's transition task force on urban affairs. Most of Northern California's moderate GOP vote went to Rep. Paul N. McCloskey Jr., who campaigned to his left, but the center was broad enough to nominate Wilson with 38 percent.

Wilson began his campaign against Brown as a clear favorite. But his tendency to explore the outer reaches of his thinking almost led to disaster. Wilson suggested that individuals under age 45 be given "greater freedom" to make arrangements for their retirement income than they have currently under the compulsory Social Security plan. Later, he commented that federal judges — including U.S. Supreme Court justices — should be approved periodically by the voters.

Brown charged that Wilson would destroy the Social Security system's fiscal stability, and even some of Wilson's friends criticized his remarks on judicial tenure. Forced into defensive explanations that shifted attention from Brown's record, Wilson saw his lead in the polls vanish by October. Ending his practice of trying to explain where he stood on complex issues, he unleashed a series of broad attacks on Brown's record that stopped the Democrat's advance.

Committees

Agriculture, Nutrition and Forestry (8th of 9 Republicans)
Agricultural Research and General Legislation (ranking); Agricultural Production and Stabilization of Prices; Domestic and Foreign Marketing and Product Promotion

Armed Services (3rd of 9 Republicans)
Conventional Forces and Alliance Defense (ranking); Manpower and Personnel; Strategic Forces and Nuclear Deterrence

Governmental Affairs (6th of 6 Republicans)
Federal Services, Post Office and Civil Service; Oversight of Government Management; Permanent Subcommittee on Investigations

Special Aging (5th of 9 Republicans)

Joint Economic
Economic Goals and Intergovernmental Policy; Education and Health; National Security Economics

Elections

1988 General

Pete Wilson (R)	5,143,409	(53%)
Leo T. McCarthy (D)	4,287,253	(44%)

Previous Winning Percentage: **1982** (52%)

Campaign Finance

	Receipts	Receipts from PACs	Expenditures
1988			
Wilson (R)	$11,384,736	$1,837,925 (16%)	$12,969,294
McCarthy (D)	$6,989,320	$872,988 (12%)	$6,986,342

Key Votes

1987	
Enact omnibus highway bill over Reagan veto	Y
Limit testing of space-based anti-ballistic missiles	N
Oppose banning tests of larger nuclear weapons	Y
Confirm Robert H. Bork as Supreme Court justice	Y
1988	
Allow vote on campaign-finance overhaul	N
Pass civil rights restoration bill over Reagan veto	Y
Enact omnibus trade bill over Reagan veto	N
Approve death penalty for drug-related murders	Y
Oppose "workfare" amendment to welfare overhaul bill	N

Voting Studies

	Presidential Support		Party Unity		Conservative Coalition	
Year	S	O	S	O	S	O
1988	64	34	65	20	68	22
1987	56	32	79	13	66	19
1986	82	18	88 †	12 †	93	7
1985	75	14	74	13	87	10
1984	84	14	93	5	89	6
1983	78	18	90	9	86	7

† Not eligible for all recorded votes.

Interest Group Ratings

Year	ADA	ACU	AFL-CIO	CCUS
1988	15	75	27	77
1987	30	75	40	87
1986	5	83	7	89
1985	10	77	18	93
1984	10	82	0	94
1983	15	60	6	84

1 Douglas H. Bosco (D)

Of Occidental — Elected 1982

Born: July 28, 1946, Brooklyn, N.Y.
Education: Willamette U., B.A. 1968, J.D. 1971.
Occupation: Lawyer.
Family: Wife, Gayle Guynup.
Religion: Roman Catholic.
Political Career: Calif. Assembly, 1979-83; sought Democratic nomination for U.S. House, 1976.
Capitol Office: 225 Cannon Bldg. 20515; 225-3311.

In Washington: During his early years in the House, Bosco operated in the background of the Public Works Committee, devoting himself to the pursuit of funds for federal projects in his district. But of late, Bosco has been moving to broaden his range of interests. In 1988, he claimed a subcommittee chairmanship (albeit a low-profile one) on Public Works; in the 101st Congress, he took a seat on the Foreign Affairs Committee.

On Public Works, Bosco is a steadfast and sometimes brash advocate of federal aid programs. In his defense of "pork-barrel" politics, he appears to be following in the footsteps of another Northern Californian, the late Democratic Rep. Harold T. "Bizz" Johnson, who chaired the Public Works Committee in the 1970s.

During a July 1987 flap over a bill providing federal money for airport-improvement projects, Bosco gave a startlingly frank explanation of why members keep their seats on Public Works. Rep. Joe Kolter, a Pennsylvania Democrat, was catching flak for inviting his Public Works colleagues to submit their pet projects as part of his amendment to the airport bill. Bosco came to Kolter's defense. "As far as I can see, there's only one basic reason to be on the Public Works Committee," the Californian said. "I want to bring home projects for my district. [It is] certainly not for intellectual stimulation."

Later, Bosco said, "As long as the money is going to get apportioned, I'd like to see as much of it get apportioned in my district as possible." He has had a good deal of success at that. Bosco cites funding he obtained under the 1987 highway act for improvements on U.S. 101 in his district as his major legislative accomplishment in the 100th Congress.

A dedicated member of a committee that has a fairly high turnover rate, Bosco has moved quickly into a senior position. In September 1988, Bosco was next in line when the chairman of the Public Works Subcommittee on Public Buildings and Grounds, American Samoa delegate Fofō I. F. Sunia, resigned from Congress. Though Bosco had not been a subcommittee member, he used his overall committee seniority to claim the chair over the more junior members who populate the little-noticed panel.

Bosco's subcommittee colleagues are likely to see a shrewd chairman whose style does not have a sharply partisan edge. Both on Public Works and on Merchant Marine and Fisheries (where he has held a seat since his first term), Bosco has been known for working out compromises in a bipartisan fashion.

His skills as a conciliator have also helped Bosco raise his political stock in the 1st District, where he has solved some sticky local issues. One of his first efforts in Congress was an attempt to balance the interests of the timber companies and environmentalists who were on opposite sides of a dispute over a proposed California wilderness bill.

The measure, putting 2.3 million acres of California's national forest land under wilderness protection, passed the House in 1983. Bosco, then coming off a narrow upset victory over a Republican incumbent, angered environmentalists by siding with Northern California Republicans and the logging, mining and resort industries that opposed the bill.

But after the bill died in the Senate, Bosco quickly moved to mend fences with the pro-wilderness forces, organizing a task force in the 1st — which contained about a third of the affected land — to come up with a compromise. His proposal was very close to the plan pushed through in 1984 by the state's two senators — Democrat Alan Cranston and Republican Pete Wilson.

Bosco also gained some local attention during the 100th Congress for working out a settlement in a complicated and longstanding feud between two Northern California Indian tribes — the Hoopa and the Yurok — over federal timber receipts.

The reservations of the two tribes had been combined by an 1891 federal action. While the Hoopa had a tribal government and maintained a strong community, the Yurok were more loosely organized; many tribe members left the reservation over the years.

California 1

Northern Coast — Santa Rosa; Eureka

With more than 300 miles of Pacific coastline and its majestic stands of redwood trees, the 1st has a bucolic quality. But partisan politics here can be contentious.

In presidential elections, this has become something of a swing district. Californian Ronald Reagan won here in 1984, but not by much. Democrat Michael S. Dukakis took the 1st in 1988 by a wider margin.

For many years this area was the exclusive province of fishermen, lumberjacks, and those who made their livings from the summer tourist trade. But from the 1970s on, these scenic environs drew a new class of immigrants — urban refugees from outside California who are determined to protect the environment at all costs.

The district has also been transformed by the population boom in Sonoma County, the famed wine-making region that reaches down toward the San Francisco metropolis. With housing tracts pressing in on the grapes, the county has grown to 344,000 people. Just under half of the district vote is cast there.

The liberal lean in Sonoma gives Democrats a leg up in carrying the district. Dukakis won 57 percent of the vote there, and Democratic Senate candidate Leo T. McCarthy outran Republican incumbent Pete Wilson by 10,000 votes. However, in the section of neighboring Napa County that is in the district, Republicans are stronger.

Northward in the district, the bulk of the vote is cast in the coastal counties of Humboldt and Mendocino. This is primarily where the liberal transplants have settled, enjoying a serene rural lifestyle epitomized by herbal teas and organic farming. Dukakis carried both counties. Bosco is particularly popular here; he took 67 percent of the vote in Humboldt County in 1988.

Population: 525,986. White 483,984 (92%), Black 4,732 (1%), Other 20,466 (4%). Spanish origin 32,321 (6%). 18 and over 390,186 (74%), 65 and over 69,488 (13%). Median age: 32.

But when the federal government began to pay royalties to the Hoopa tribe in the late 1950s for timber harvested from the reservation, Yurok members flooded the federal courts with lawsuits claiming a share of the proceeds. With the tribes unable to reach a compromise, the federal receipts were placed in an escrow account, where they remained for over 25 years.

Bosco intervened, though, bringing several Yuroks together to meet with representatives of the Hoopa tribe. In April 1988, Bosco submitted a bill to redivide the reservation, provide $22 million out of the escrow account to finance a tribal government for the Yuroks, and take $65 million to pay for any legitimate Yurok claims; any remaining escrow would be divided between the tribes. A companion bill submitted in the Senate by Cranston passed and was signed into law that October.

Despite his ameliorative abilities, there are a few issues on which Bosco shows his combative side. For example, he has nursed a feud with the Texas Air Corp. for years. This argument dates back to Bosco's days in the state Assembly, when he supported legislation the airline wanted in return for what he felt was a promise to maintain its California headquarters. The headquarters was abandoned, and any official of Texas Air who comes to testify at Public Works can still count on an unfriendly reception from Bosco.

In early 1989, when a strike at Texas Air-owned Eastern Airlines brought calls for congressional intervention, Bosco was one of many Democrats portraying Texas Air Chairman Frank Lorenzo as a ruthless buccaneer bent on profiting at the expense of his workers. "A lot of people don't like the tactics of people like Lorenzo," Bosco said.

In his new assignment on Foreign Affairs, Bosco says his priorities are arms control, nuclear non-proliferation, and human-rights violations by foreign recipients of U.S. aid. But he has not neglected to take his constituency's interests with him to Foreign Affairs; he says he will be involved in Pacific Rim trade issues, especially as they affect his district's wine and timber industries.

At Home: Bosco attracted three challengers in the 1988 Democratic primary, an unusual distraction for an established incumbent. But the challenges reflected political factionalism rather than any slippage in Bosco's standing. He easily outpaced the primary field and enjoyed his third-consecutive November with a re-election vote in excess of 60 percent.

Bosco's first winning margin, in 1982, was just 50 percent. But he was the only challenger in California to oust a House member that year, defeating Republican Don H. Clausen to end two decades of Republican tradition in the district.

Unlike previous Clausen opponents, Bosco

was well-known, popular and backed by a unified Democratic Party. During two terms as a state legislator, he had balanced business interests with environmental demands; his timber-industry support was rare for a district Democrat.

Bosco's record cut both ways in his congressional campaign. Though he had worked on a "wild and scenic rivers" bill, his support for timber interests in a herbicide dispute made some environmentalists wary of him. Bosco won back his liberal allies with strong support for a nuclear-weapons freeze, an issue that caused big problems for Clausen.

Clausen had other worries. Over time, former city-dwellers attracted by his district's natural beauty had brought an influx of Democratic votes. Clausen was also weakened by a redistricting plan that had trimmed GOP turf. Helped by the generally Democratic atmosphere in 1982, Bosco won by 5,500 votes.

The 1982 election was Bosco's second bid for Congress. In 1976, as a New York transplant with an obscure law practice in Sonoma County, he ran a shoestring campaign for the Democratic nomination and came in second. In 1978, he won the first of his two legislative terms.

Committees

Foreign Affairs (26th of 28 Democrats)
Arms Control, International Security and Science

Merchant Marine and Fisheries (13th of 26 Democrats)
Fisheries and Wildlife Conservation and the Environment

Public Works and Transportation (10th of 31 Democrats)
Public Buildings and Grounds (chairman); Aviation; Investigations and Oversight

Elections

1988 General		
Douglas H. Bosco (D)	159,815	(63%)
Samuel "Mark" Vanderbilt (R)	72,189	(28%)
Eric Fried (PFP)	22,150	(9%)
1988 Primary		
Douglas H. Bosco (D)	64,653	(68%)
Lionel Gambill (D)	13,598	(14%)
Neil Bethel Sinclair (D)	11,703	(12%)
Darryl Cherney (D)	5,325	(6%)
1986 General		
Douglas H. Bosco (D)	138,174	(67%)
Floyd G. Sampson (R)	54,436	(27%)
Elden McFarland (PFP)	12,149	(6%)

Previous Winning Percentages: **1984** (62%) **1982** (50%)

District Vote For President

	1988	1984	1980	1976
D	145,811 (55%)	119,330 (46%)	77,182 (36%)	80,635 (52%)
R	114,103 (43%)	134,358 (52%)	103,463 (49%)	72,082 (46%)

Campaign Finance

	Receipts	Receipts from PACs	Expend-itures
1988			
Bosco (D)	$256,328	$119,638 (47%)	$251,779
Vanderbilt (R)	$7,795	0	$7,795
Fried (PFP)	$8,022	$300 (4%)	$7,924
1986			
Bosco (D)	$191,849	$97,923 (51%)	$213,608
McFarland (PFP)	$9,615	0	$9,421

Key Votes

1987	
Raise speed limit to 65 mph	N
Approve Gephardt "fair trade" amendment	N
Ban testing of larger nuclear weapons	Y
Delay "re-flagging" of Kuwaiti tankers	Y
Approve tax-raising deficit-reduction bill	Y
1988	
Approve aid to Nicaraguan contras	N
Enact civil rights restoration bill over Reagan veto	Y
Kill 60-day plant-closing notification measure	N
Pass omnibus trade bill over Reagan veto	Y
Approve death penalty for drug-related murders	Y
Bar federal funds for abortions in cases of rape and incest	Y
Oppose seven-day waiting period for purchase of handguns	N

Voting Studies

	Presidential Support		Party Unity		Conservative Coalition	
Year	**S**	**O**	**S**	**O**	**S**	**O**
1988	28	64	87	6	32	63
1987	31	61	75	10	44	49
1986	21	72	78	7	36	50
1985	26	66	74	12	35	56
1984	26	63	71	14	25	63
1983	20	76	78	10	28	61

Interest Group Ratings

Year	ADA	ACU	AFL-CIO	CCUS
1988	80	8	85	36
1987	64	14	77	21
1986	70	15	100	23
1985	65	19	63	33
1984	70	9	62	57
1983	80	13	88	30

2 Wally Herger (R)

Of Rio Oso — Elected 1986

Born: May 20, 1945, Sutter County, Calif.
Education: American River Community College, A.A. 1967; attended California State U., 1968-69.
Occupation: Rancher; gas company president.
Family: Wife, Pamela Sargent; eight children.
Religion: Mormon.
Political Career: Calif. Assembly, 1981-87.
Capitol Office: 1108 Longworth Bldg. 20515; 225-3076.

In Washington: Like Gene Chappie, the Republican he replaced in the House, Herger is a conservative Northern California rancher. But there the similarity ends.

When the colorful Chappie announced his retirement in 1986, he said he needed "to get the hell out of here before they issue me a wheelchair." Herger, a devout Mormon, has never been heard to use language like that. He is a friendly man, but decidedly low-key. His style contributed to the surprising ease with which he first won his seat and then became vice president of his freshman Republican class.

But Herger's personality also contains a strong dose of conservative resolve, as was evident in 1987, when he offered an amendment to the State Department authorization bill aimed at killing $1 million for Ted Turner's 1990 Goodwill Games, to be held in Seattle. Herger said the 1986 games were mainly designed to produce advertising revenue for Turner's cable network, and he argued that Soviet diplomats at the games would be able to scout an area of the country from which they are usually barred. Despite last-minute arm-twisting by the Democratic leadership, Herger's amendment was adopted 203-201.

Democrats promptly vowed to hold a second vote on the amendment, but Herger threatened to stall proceedings if they asked for a revote. When Democratic leaders did call for another vote, Herger employed some of the obstructionist tactics normally associated with conservative GOP "guerrillas" such as Robert S. Walker of Pennsylvania. But after an hour and a half delay, the House killed Herger's amendment, 180-230; some members speculated that the margin might have been closer had Herger not threatened their dinner hours.

On the Agriculture Committee, Herger seeks to protect his district's fruit and nut growers. His interest in averting a trade war with Europe stemmed from the threat of a European retaliatory tariff on U.S. walnuts.

Herger took to the floor several times in his first term to decry alleged human rights abuses committed by the government of India against the Sikh minority in Punjab state. Members of the small Sikh community in Yuba City had told Herger of their concern for their relatives in the Punjab. Herger met with India's ambassador to the United States to discuss the problem.

At Home: At one point in the 1988 campaign, Democratic partisans in California began touting their chances against Herger. But if their champion, rancher Wayne C. Meyer of Sutter, ever had a real chance, it was probably two years earlier, when the seat was open.

The district had belonged to Democrat Harold T. Johnson for 22 years before Republican Gene Chappie ambushed him in 1980. But Chappie decided to retire in 1986 and it was not clear that a Republican would keep the seat. Meyer ran in the 1986 Democratic primary, finishing a close second to Shasta County Supervisor Steve Swendiman. Though Swendiman had been expected to breeze to the nomination, tactical errors in his campaign nearly cost him the primary, and sent him into the general election with no head of steam.

Herger, meanwhile, began his primary from an Assembly district base comprising nearly half the 2nd District. He complemented that asset with superior organizing and fund raising to turn back the mayor of the district's largest city and win the nomination. In the fall, Herger stayed on the offensive. He linked himself to President Reagan and Gov. George Deukmejian and called Swendiman a "tax-and-spend Democrat." When Swendiman portrayed him as a "backbencher" in the Legislature, Herger highlighted his support of popular measures such as workfare and tougher sentencing for criminals.

In the end, Herger beat Swendiman in all 12 counties and took a solid 58 percent. That discouraged most Democrats from tackling Herger in 1988, and Meyer got the nomination unopposed. But it was tough raising money against Herger, who had worked hard to solidify his claim. The incumbent won comfortably.

California 2

North Central — Chico; Redding

The 2nd, in the heart of Northern California, runs from the sparsely populated mountain counties on the Oregon border southward to the Napa Valley.

Its three northern counties — Siskiyou, Trinity and Shasta — make up a huge wilderness area where lumbering is the main occupation. Outdoors-lovers also contribute to the economy; 14,162-foot Mount Shasta and nearby Shasta Lake are tourist magnets.

Democrats have an edge in registration here, but there is more loyalty to the National Rifle Association than to the Democratic label; Ronald Reagan always did well here, as did George Bush in his 1988 race.

Heading south into the Sacramento River basin, the land flattens out and the vast forests give way to agricultural territory. Barley, rice and specialty crops such as olives, kiwi fruit and almonds are the main products. Many of the farmers here are members of families that arrived from the dust bowl during the Depression. They tend to be conservative.

The peach and tomato farmers of Sutter County reside in one of the district's most conservative counties. In 1988, Sutter gave Bush 67 percent of its vote and awarded GOP Sen. Pete Wilson one of his highest county percentages.

Across the low Vaca Mountains are the grape vineyards that cling to terraced hillsides in Napa County. Napa, the second most populous county in the district, is known worldwide for its wineries.

Population: 526,009. White 480,596 (91%), Black 6,235 (1%), Other 17,867 (3%). Spanish origin 34,320 (7%). 18 and over 384,601 (73%), 65 and over 69,055 (13%). Median age: 31.

Committees

Agriculture (15th of 18 Republicans)
Cotton, Rice and Sugar; Domestic Marketing, Consumer Relations and Nutrition; Forests, Family Farms and Energy

Merchant Marine and Fisheries (14th of 17 Republicans)
Fisheries and Wildlife Conservation and the Environment; Oceanography

Select Hunger (8th of 12 Republicans)
Task Force: International

Select Narcotics Abuse and Control (9th of 12 Republicans)

Elections

1988 General		
Wally Herger (R)	139,010	(59%)
Wayne Meyer (D)	91,088	(39%)
1986 General		
Wally Herger (R)	109,758	(58%)
Stephen C. Swendiman (D)	74,602	(40%)

District Vote for President

	1988	1984	1980	1976
D	96,230 (40%)	83,085 (35%)	64,005 (31%)	61,220 (47%)
R	138,756 (58%)	150,641 (63%)	120,259 (58%)	68,548 (52%)

Campaign Finance

	Receipts	Receipts from PACs	Expend-itures
1988			
Herger (R)	$691,969	$258,675 (37%)	$696,748
Meyer (D)	$193,861	$58,900 (30%)	$193,915
1986			
Herger (R)	$646,951	$197,641 (31%)	$628,361
Swendiman (D)	$246,930	$92,669 (38%)	$244,097

Key Votes

1987	
Raise speed limit to 65 mph	Y
Approve Gephardt "fair trade" amendment	N
Ban testing of larger nuclear weapons	N
Delay "re-flagging" of Kuwaiti tankers	N
Approve tax-raising deficit-reduction bill	N
1988	
Approve aid to Nicaraguan contras	Y
Enact civil rights restoration bill over Reagan veto	N
Kill 60-day plant-closing notification measure	Y
Pass omnibus trade bill over Reagan veto	Y
Approve death penalty for drug-related murders	Y
Bar federal funds for abortions in cases of rape and incest	Y
Oppose seven-day waiting period for purchase of handguns	Y

Voting Studies

	Presidential Support		Party Unity		Conservative Coalition	
Year	S	O	S	O	S	O
1988	68	32	91	8	92	5
1987	74	24	89	9	93	7

Interest Group Ratings

Year	ADA	ACU	AFL-CIO	CCUS
1988	0	92	29	93
1987	12	100	13	100

3 Robert T. Matsui (D)

Of Sacramento — Elected 1978

Born: Sept. 17, 1941, Sacramento, Calif.
Education: U. of California, Berkeley, A.B. 1963; Hastings College of Law, J.D. 1966.
Occupation: Lawyer.
Family: Wife, Doris Okada; one child.
Religion: Methodist.
Political Career: Sacramento City Council, 1971-78.
Capitol Office: 2419 Rayburn Bldg. 20515; 225-7163.

In Washington: Now in his fifth term on Ways and Means, Matsui comfortably combines a thoughtful, generally liberal approach to tax policy with an intense interest in serving California business. While liberals can count on his votes on social-policy issues, Matsui has increasingly applied his capacity for hard work to the business side of the committee's ledger.

It is rare for Matsui to pursue a major legislative endeavor outside the purview of Ways and Means, but he did so in the 100th Congress on an issue especially close to his heart. With Rep. Norman Y. Mineta, Matsui was an important force behind passage of legislation to provide federal redress to the surviving Japanese-Americans who were interned during World War II.

In 1942, when he was six months old, Matsui and his family were ousted from their Sacramento home and sent to a detention camp, where they lived more than three years. "Just as the victim of a rape finds her chastity called into question, and finds that she cannot speak out to defend herself, so the Japanese-American community finds its loyalty called into question to such an extent that it could not speak out to protest," Matsui said during deliberations on the compensation bill.

The legislation, passed in 1987, formally apologized to those interned, and established a $1.25 billion fund to give $20,000 to each of the estimated 60,000 surviving victims, half the total number interned. Former detainees who accept the settlement agree to drop further claims against the government.

Ordinarily, Matsui focuses on Ways and Means, where he uses his seat on the Trade Subcommittee to watch out for California industries and to advocate knocking down foreign trade barriers to U.S. high-tech products, many of which are made in California. One trade measure Matsui offered — to mandate retaliation against countries that restrict markets for U.S. telecommunications equipment — was largely folded into the 1988 omnibus trade bill.

When the House took up legislation to carry out the 1988 U.S.-Canada trade pact, Matsui worked to protect not only California's telecommunications industry, but also its motion-picture industry. "Under the guise of protecting its cultural sovereignty, some officials in Canada have threatened to erect barriers against U.S. film companies," he said.

Tax legislation gives Matsui venues for both his business activism and his liberal social concerns. Both political strains were on display as Matsui helped draft the 99th Congress' overhaul of the federal tax code. He watched out for the high-tech industry and other local allies while supporting tax relief for the poor.

Matsui was an active and consistent supporter of the tax-code overhaul, which shifted a sizable share of the revenue burden from individuals to corporations. But while he sometimes bristled at business' resistance to reform, he also championed protection for an important business concern: the tax-exempt bond market. No changes were proposed for municipal bonds used by governments, but the two-thirds of the bonds used to finance private development faced an end to exemptions.

As the pro-bond group gained strength, a personal appeal from Ways and Means Chairman Dan Rostenkowski to Matsui kept the issue from being a stumbling block. "Mr. Chairman, I'm going to help you," Matsui was quoted as saying in "Showdown at Gucci Gulch," a book on the tax bill's passage. "I sure appreciate your asking me." In the end, a handful of bond-related exemptions were allowed, including one for an urban-redevelopment bond popular in California.

Matsui's liberal profile was most prominent on the tax bill when he twice unsuccessfully offered amendments to retain tax credits for political contributions. Matsui and other liberals believed the credits encouraged small contributors and diluted the influence of political action committees.

Matsui earned his reputation as a vigilant spokesman for California business in 1982, when he worked to resolve a tax dispute between the Internal Revenue Service and three California utilities. The IRS alleged the utilities owed $2.2 billion in back taxes because they

California 3

Most of Sacramento; Eastern Suburbs

Though it is the state capital and the metropolis of California's Central Valley, Sacramento typically has been overshadowed by the far larger and more glamorous coastal cities of Los Angeles, San Diego and San Francisco. In recent years, however, Sacramento has been emerging in its own right. A 17 percent increase between 1980 and 1986 boosted the city's population to 324,000; demographers predict that Sacramento will be the state's next boom area.

The southern two-thirds of Sacramento make up the heart of the 3rd District, and provide much of the Democratic base that has made Matsui a dominant district figure. Its 50,000-plus state workers provide a strong pro-government constituency. Blacks and Hispanics make up over a quarter of the city's population. There is a labor segment (Sacramento is a major inland port). The *Sacramento Bee*, the flagship newspaper of the McClatchy chain, takes a generally liberal editorial line.

The city vote has enabled Democrats to maintain their lock on Sacramento's House seat. Democrat John E. Moss represented the city and surrounding areas for 26 years until he retired in 1978; Matsui has been in ever since.

But the balance of the 3rd is mainly suburban territory, with a Republican lean that often sways district results in contests above the House level. In 1988, George Bush carried the district (albeit by less than 1 percentage point); Ronald Reagan won more comfortably in his two presidential contests.

The district's Republican vote has been bolstered over the years by the military presence at Mather Air Force Base, located in Rancho Cordova to the east of Sacramento. However, this presence is soon to be sharply diminished; Mather is targeted for deep personnel cutbacks under the military base-closing plan enacted in April 1989.

Population: 525,774. White 413,400 (79%), Black 43,168 (8%), Asian and Pacific Islander 33,074 (6%), Other 5,290 (1%). Spanish origin 51,010 (10%). 18 and over 390,354 (74%), 65 and over 52,458 (10%). Median age: 30.

had claimed tax breaks without passing them along to their customers. The utilities said the credits were used for investment.

Matsui went to bat for the utilities. Arguing that he was saving jobs and ratepayers' money, he pushed a bill through committee and past the House allowing the tax credits. A filibuster killed the measure on the Senate floor, but it became law as part of the gasoline-tax increase at the end of the year.

Matsui had some success in his first Ways and Means term in 1983, when he sought to ease hospitals into the new Medicare reimbursement plan, which pays a flat fee for treatment based on diagnosis. Matsui's proposal for phasing in the program over four years became law.

More recently, Matsui led a controversial effort to adjust the Medicare reimbursement system to take account of regional variations in non-labor costs, such as energy and malpractice insurance. The 1988 budget-reconciliation bill contains a provision to study the proposal.

Before winning a post on Ways and Means, Matsui had to pay his dues in the House committee system. He spent most of his first term on Judiciary, an assignment he accepted at the behest of House leaders. In 1980, he was rewarded with a spot on the Commerce Committee, where he joined the pro-consumer faction fighting against eased antitrust laws that would allow the American Telephone & Telegraph Co. to enter computer-related fields. Later the issue was largely settled by an out-of-court agreement between the Justice Department and AT&T. Matsui left Commerce for Ways and Means in the 97th Congress.

In 1988, Matsui was the first House member outside the Massachusetts delegation to endorse Michael S. Dukakis for president. This helped Matsui win a spot on the Democratic platform-drafting committee, where he argued against a no-first-use pledge on nuclear weapons.

Matsui is a skilled fund-raiser. He is often near the top of the receipt lists for congressional honoraria and for political action committee contributions.

At Home: Because of his legislative record, his business contacts and his fund-raising ability, Matsui is often mentioned as a potential contender for statewide office. But he has ruled out running for the open governorship in 1990, just as he had withdrawn from the 1988 field of potential challengers to GOP Sen. Pete Wilson.

Matsui's experience in an internment camp helped him establish a strong bond with Sacramento's large Asian community, and he won two elections for the City Council.

In 1972, the year after Matsui began his service on the council, he chaired U.S. Rep. John E. Moss' re-election campaign. Matsui's excellent fund-raising connections made him a perfect choice, and he took the job again in 1974 and 1976 as Moss won easily.

In 1978 Matsui was preparing to run for the county Board of Supervisors when Moss announced his retirement after 26 years. Matsui switched to a congressional campaign, building strong support in the business community and among the Asian voters.

Two other prominent Sacramento Democrats also filed for the House, but Matsui's $225,000 primary campaign budget gave him a clear advantage. He ran television commercials identifying himself as "Citizen Matsui," setting himself apart from his rivals, both of whom had been heavily involved in state politics.

Matsui won the primary and then took the general election comfortably against Republican Sandy Smoley, considered the strongest candidate Sacramento Republicans had run for the House in many years. Moss repeatedly proclaimed his support for Matsui in a series of television commercials.

Republicans have made no similar effort to capture the district since. They have fielded nominees in only two of the decade's elections, and even they were all but invisible most of the year.

Committee

Ways and Means (13th of 23 Democrats)
Human Resources; Trade

Elections

1988 General		
Robert T. Matsui (D)	183,470	(71%)
Lowell Landowski (R)	74,296	(29%)
1986 General		
Robert T. Matsui (D)	158,709	(76%)
Lowell Landowski (R)	50,265	(24%)

Previous Winning Percentages: **1984** (100%) **1982** (90%) **1980** (71%) **1978** (53%)

District Vote For President

	1988	1984	1980	1976
D	130,495 (49%)	112,714 (44%)	86,618 (41%)	96,961 (53%)
R	132,533 (50%)	139,564 (55%)	97,854 (47%)	85,427 (46%)

Campaign Finance

	Receipts	Receipts from PACs	Expend-itures
1988			
Matsui (D)	$916,025	$475,366 (52%)	$638,688
Landowski (R)	$7,695	0	$7,695
1986			
Matsui (D)	$659,793	$300,634 (46%)	$563,150

Key Votes

1987	
Raise speed limit to 65 mph	N
Approve Gephardt "fair trade" amendment	N
Ban testing of larger nuclear weapons	Y
Delay "re-flagging" of Kuwaiti tankers	Y
Approve tax-raising deficit-reduction bill	Y
1988	
Approve aid to Nicaraguan contras	N
Enact civil rights restoration bill over Reagan veto	Y
Kill 60-day plant-closing notification measure	N
Pass omnibus trade bill over Reagan veto	Y
Approve death penalty for drug-related murders	Y
Bar federal funds for abortions in cases of rape and incest	N
Oppose seven-day waiting period for purchase of handguns	N

Voting Studies

	Presidential Support		Party Unity		Conservative Coalition	
Year	**S**	**O**	**S**	**O**	**S**	**O**
1988	20	75	88	2	16	79
1987	20	80	95	2	14	79
1986	20	80	94	3	18	82
1985	20	80	94	2	9	89
1984	32	65	94	3	12	88
1983	32	67	93	6	24	76
1982	40	60	93	5	19	81
1981	45	53	80	17	32	63

Interest Group Ratings

Year	ADA	ACU	AFL-CIO	CCUS
1988	90	4	86	36
1987	92	9	87	20
1986	95	5	79	17
1985	90	5	94	18
1984	80	0	92	38
1983	85	4	94	25
1982	85	5	95	14
1981	70	0	87	17

4 Vic Fazio (D)

Of West Sacramento — Elected 1978

Born: Oct. 11, 1942, Winchester, Mass.
Education: Union College, B.A. 1965.
Occupation: Journalist.
Family: Wife, Judy Kern; four children.
Religion: Episcopalian.
Political Career: Calif. Assembly, 1975-79.
Capitol Office: 2113 Rayburn Bldg. 20515; 225-5716.

In Washington: Fazio operates as well as anybody in the trenches of House politics, and unlike many such operators, he does it without losing sight of the ends that are supposed to justify all the maneuvering. He is a politician in the most creditable sense of that term.

He has learned to negotiate with senior barons on the Appropriations Committee, as the youngest of the 13 subcommittee chairmen known as the "College of Cardinals." He does unpleasant household tasks, such as defending members' mailing privileges and serving on the ethics committee. One California magazine calls him "the Mr. Goodwrench of the Hill." Acknowledging his penchant for getting involved in controversial institutional issues, Fazio once described himself as a "heat-seeking missile." His colleagues finally rewarded him by electing him vice chairman of the Democratic Caucus in mid-1989, when the party leadership was rebuilt after Speaker Wright's resignation.

Fazio was waist-deep in controversial issues — congressional pay, perks and ethics — as the 101st Congress began. He was the leadership's point man defending a controversial 51 percent pay raise for congressmen, a plan shot down by public criticism in early 1989. Fazio was generally admired by his peers for having defended a raise that many members publicly denounced but privately coveted.

Fazio was chief author of an unsuccessful measure to outlaw honoraria — a major restriction on members' outside income that the Democratic leadership hoped, in vain, would make a pay raise more palatable to the public.

In another measure of the leadership's trust in his ability and willingness to take thankless jobs, Fazio was put in charge of a bipartisan task force to review House ethics standards.

But precisely because of Fazio's close ties to the leadership, Republicans viewed with suspicion his role in the House ethics committee's investigation of Speaker Wright. Fazio was ranking Democrat on the ethics committee during that 1988-89 inquiry. Early in the investigation, the GOP passed a resolution calling on Fazio to disqualify himself because he invited Wright to a party fund-raiser held in California after the ethics investigation had begun.

But Fazio had his share of disappointments under the Wright speakership. At the beginning of his first term as Speaker, Wright denied Fazio the leadership post he was angling for: chairmanship of the Democratic Congressional Campaign Committee. This had little to do with Fazio's skills or popularity, however; Tony Coelho of California had already been chosen whip, and members were reluctant to give another top leadership post to someone from the same state. So the job went to Beryl Anthony Jr. of Arkansas.

Much of Congress' institutional dirty work has fallen to Fazio because he is chairman of the Appropriations Subcommittee on the Legislative Branch, which is politically perhaps the least appealing of any of the Appropriations chairs. It handles the money Congress spends on itself, and members are always sensitive to criticism that they waste taxpayers' money by treating themselves too well.

Nevertheless, the subcommittee is Fazio's power base. Because of his work there, members all over the ideological spectrum feel indebted to him.

In addition to giving him leverage over the internal workings of Congress, Fazio's subcommittee chairmanship allows him to leave his mark on a variety of appropriations bills, and he has done so to help the California delegation on issues such as protecting the coastline against offshore oil drilling and pushing for a fund to clean up toxic wastes at military installations, including several in the Sacramento area.

Fazio is also willing to represent the Appropriations panel when it feels its rights are being violated by other committees. In 1985 he sponsored an amendment that successfully prevented Public Works from taking its transportation trust funds out of the budget process, and he helped beat back a similar move in 1986.

As a member of the Budget Committee from 1983-89, he was a frequent mediator in the ongoing squabbles between the two panels. In mid-1987, he joined junior Appropriations members in telling their elders that the committee's bills should adhere to the guidelines set

California 4

Suburban Sacramento to Bay Area

Like a large jaw about to clamp down on the state capital, the 4th District surrounds Sacramento on three sides and takes in the northern part of the city as well. Nearly half the vote is cast in the suburban part of Sacramento County; the rest is split between Solano and Yolo counties to the west.

At the House level, Democrat Fazio has the 4th District firmly in hand. But in statewide contests, the district, though competitive, leans Republican. George Bush carried the 4th with 52 percent of the vote in 1988.

Though the city of Sacramento has a Democratic flavor, the Sacramento County suburbs to the north can be difficult for Democrats. The towns in this area have been growing rapidly — Folsom, with 18,000 residents, grew by over 65 percent between 1980 and 1986 — and their residents have little allegiance to the Sacramento Democratic establishment. The suburban voters also tend to be conservative on crime and other social issues.

Many local residents work in the high-tech industries. Folsom is home to Aerojet, an aerospace firm specializing in space shuttle technology. (The Folsom Prison, made famous by singer Johnny Cash, is just outside the district.)

Solano County, which provides about 30 percent of the 4th's vote, has also boomed, its population growing by over 20 percent in the early 1980s. Fairfield, with 69,000 people, is the dominant city. Democrats tend to have an edge in Solano, but not a huge one: Michael S. Dukakis carried the county with 52 percent of the vote in 1988; Democratic Senate candidate Leo T. McCarthy edged incumbent Pete Wilson there by fewer than 150 votes.

The most liberal territory in the district is Yolo County, one of five counties in the state that went for Walter F. Mondale for president in 1984. Dukakis took 58 percent there in 1988, one of his best showings in California. The city of Davis (41,000 residents) is the county's Democratic bastion; a University of California campus is located there.

Population: 525,764. White 435,421 (83%), Black 30,224 (6%), Other 24,188 (5%). Spanish origin 60,417 (12%). 18 and over 374,278 (71%), 65 and over 41,017 (8%). Median age: 28.

by the annual budget resolution — or else their work would be done for them in budget-cutting amendments on the floor.

Fazio also has tried to help develop compromises on defense issues such as the MX missile and the strategic defense initiative (SDI). He helped cut a deal with the Reagan White House in the 98th Congress that allowed production of some MX missiles, saying he wanted to show "faith in a new bipartisan spirit" that might eventually lead to an arms control agreement. In 1985 he voted for production of 21 MX missiles, but was one of the leaders that year and the next in forcing severe reductions in the president's SDI research program.

The MX issue has hurt Fazio among antinuclear activists back in Sacramento, but he has helped cement his standing at home by working on the Appropriations Committee to win cost-of-living increases for military and federal retirees — both important 4th District constituencies.

At Home: A highly controversial role such as Fazio's defense of the 1988 pay-raise proposal might render some congressmen highly vulnerable in the next election. But in Fazio's case, the burden on a potential challenger is formidable. Fazio ran unopposed in 1988 after averaging 65 percent of the vote in four previous re-elections.

Fazio also had worked hard on behalf of the pay raise members received in 1984. That year, the state GOP leadership considered sinking money into a challenge. But the Republican nomination went to Roger Canfield, who had managed just 36 percent as the nominee in 1982. The party stepped back, and Canfield barely bettered his earlier showing. Fazio spent much of the year coordinating the Democratic delegation's efforts to raise funds in Washington to fight GOP Gov. George Deukmejian's redistricting initiative.

During his years in the California state Capitol — as a journalist, aide to the Assembly Speaker and later an assemblyman himself — Fazio always seemed a few steps ahead of most of the others there. Even while he was a staff aide, he was drafting bills and putting together coalitions.

His skills as a candidate were tested in a 1975 special election to fill an Assembly vacancy. He won by just 472 votes, then set about establishing a strong political base in Sacramento and Yolo counties with an activist approach to energy, consumer and environmental issues. Less than a year later, he won a full term with 74 percent.

That same day, Democratic U.S. Rep. Robert Leggett survived by just 651 votes against Albert Dehr, an obscure railroad worker. Leggett had been accused of taking bribes from South Korean government officials, and had acknowledged going into debt to support a Capitol Hill secretary and their two illegitimate children. It was clear he would draw a more substantial challenge if he tried to run again.

But Leggett kept most Democratic aspirants out of the 1978 primary by insisting for months that he would run again despite the bad publicity. His retirement announcement, made two weeks before the filing deadline, surprised nearly every politician in the 4th except one — Fazio. The assemblyman was the only candidate ready with a campaign, and he coasted to the nomination.

The general election was not particularly close. Republican Rex Hime, a former aide to Ronald Reagan and a state-party staffer, could not match Fazio's fund-raising skills. Fazio lost two agricultural counties in the northern part of the 4th, but carried the rest, most of which he had been representing in the Assembly. He did even better in 1980, winning all five counties against Dehr, making his third try.

Although the 1981 redistricting plan weakened Fazio slightly, no problems showed up in the 1982 election. Republican nominee Canfield was a former reapportionment consultant for the state GOP who went into the contest expecting substantial financial help from the political network of conservative state Sen. H. L. Richardson. But Canfield was never able to raise the money he needed to pose a threat, and Fazio walked off with better than 60 percent in all of the district's counties.

Committees

Appropriations (20th of 35 Democrats)
Legislative Branch (chairman); Energy and Water Development; Military Construction

Select Hunger (4th of 18 Democrats)
Task Force: International

Standards of Official Conduct (2nd of 6 Democrats)

Elections

1988 General		
Vic Fazio (D)	181,184	(99%)
1986 General		
Vic Fazio (D)	128,364	(70%)
Jack D. Hite (R)	54,596	(30%)

Previous Winning Percentages: **1984** (61%) **1982** (64%) **1980** (65%) **1978** (55%)

District Vote For President

	1988	1984	1980	1976
D	121,847 (48%)	96,775 (43%)	73,568 (41%)	77,887 (56%)
R	129,477 (51%)	127,252 (56%)	89,745 (50%)	59,567 (43%)

Campaign Finance

	Receipts	Receipts from PACs	Expend-itures
1988			
Fazio (D)	$752,357	$378,783 (50%)	$659,334
1986			
Fazio (D)	$634,656	$324,157 (51%)	$386,346
Hite (R)	$9,354	0	$9,344

Key Votes

1987	
Raise speed limit to 65 mph	Y
Approve Gephardt "fair trade" amendment	Y
Ban testing of larger nuclear weapons	Y
Delay "re-flagging" of Kuwaiti tankers	Y
Approve tax-raising deficit-reduction bill	#
1988	
Approve aid to Nicaraguan contras	N
Enact civil rights restoration bill over Reagan veto	Y
Kill 60-day plant-closing notification measure	N
Pass omnibus trade bill over Reagan veto	Y
Approve death penalty for drug-related murders	X
Bar federal funds for abortions in cases of rape and incest	N
Oppose seven-day waiting period for purchase of handguns	N

Voting Studies

	Presidential Support		Party Unity		Conservative Coalition	
Year	**S**	**O**	**S**	**O**	**S**	**O**
1988	19	73	92	2	16	74
1987	23	75	92	3	35	63
1986	20	80	93	5	30	64
1985	26	65	90	6	35	65
1984	31	64	88	8	25	68
1983	28	68	91	6	24	72
1982	36	58	92	7	29	67
1981	41	57	81	17	33	64

Interest Group Ratings

Year	ADA	ACU	AFL-CIO	CCUS
1988	85	0	100	29
1987	84	0	94	14
1986	80	9	93	24
1985	75	14	82	32
1984	75	4	85	38
1983	80	9	100	26
1982	80	5	90	14
1981	80	0	87	17

5 Nancy Pelosi (D)

Of San Francisco — Elected 1987

Born: March 26, 1940, Baltimore, Md.
Education: Trinity College, A.B. 1962.
Occupation: Public-relations consultant.
Family: Husband, Paul Pelosi; five children.
Religion: Roman Catholic.
Political Career: No previous office.
Capitol Office: 1005 Longworth Bldg. 20515; 225-4965.

In Washington: Though Pelosi did not hold public office before coming to Congress in 1987, she has the self-assurance one would expect from a woman born into the business. Her father, Thomas J. D'Alesandro Jr., was a New Deal-era House member and then mayor of Baltimore. She has also cut her own path, serving as California Democratic Party chairman and finance chairman of the Democratic Senatorial Campaign Committee.

That background gives her an understanding of the levers of power in Washington that compensates for her lack of legislative experience. On at least one occasion, when she appeared before the Rules Committee to make a request, her wishes were quickly granted because she had already made her case effectively behind the scenes.

Pelosi has been particularly active in promoting legislation to fight AIDS, a serious problem in her district. One successful effort in 1988 involved adding a floor amendment to omnibus AIDS legislation to authorize funds for demonstration projects to provide mental-health services for victims and families who have "serious psychological reactions" after a positive AIDS test is returned.

As the 101st Congress began, Pelosi was involved in a far different fight: She teamed with California Democrat Barbara Boxer to try to reverse a recommendation by a military base-closing commission that the Presidio in San Francisco be shut. The two argued that closing the base, which would then become part of the Golden Gate National Recreation area, would cost millions more per year than keeping it open. They said the commission failed to consider environmental cleanup costs and the expense of closing the base's medical center.

The commission's recommendations were to go into effect unless Congress rejected the entire plan, and the vast majority of the members did not have incentive to reopen the process. Pelosi vowed to try to block appropriators from committing funds for closing the Presidio.

At Home: When she began her first House campaign, Pelosi was more familiar to national Democratic activists than to San Francisco voters. But drawing on financial and political contacts she had developed over years of party service, she narrowly won the Democratic nomination to succeed Rep. Sala Burton, who died Feb. 1, 1987. That victory was tantamount to election in the 5th, one of the country's strongest Democratic districts.

Pelosi entered the contest backed by much of the city and state party establishment. Among those endorsing her were Sen. Alan Cranston, San Francisco Mayor Dianne Feinstein, and Lt. Gov. Leo T. McCarthy. But the most important endorsement was made before the seat became vacant. Burton indicated several days prior to her death that she wanted Pelosi, a longtime friend and political ally, to be her successor.

That backing was crucial because the 5th had long been dominated by the organization loyal to Sala Burton and her late husband, Rep. Phillip Burton. After Sala Burton's death, her closest allies rallied to Pelosi.

But establishment backing did not clear the field for Pelosi. She faced a vigorous challenge from San Francisco Supervisor Harry Britt, the leading homosexual politician in San Francisco. Pointing to his experience as a grass-roots activist, Britt claimed he was the true ideological heir to the Burtons.

In a district where the gay vote is roughly one-fifth of the electorate, Britt started with a large base. And while he said he would be a leading national voice on gay issues — particularly in fighting AIDS — he aimed his campaign at a wider audience. He had worked to win over the large number of renters in the district with his rent-control efforts, and endeared himself to environmentalists with his opposition to new real-estate development.

Pelosi was an energetic candidate, cool under fire, and there was little doubt she had connections. While chairing the state party, she helped attract the 1984 Democratic National Convention to San Francisco. She lost a bid for national party chairman in 1985, but then directed money-raising efforts for the party's successful 1986 effort to retake the Senate. She fell short of 50 percent in the April contest, but took her GOP foe easily in a June runoff.

California 5

Most of San Francisco

San Francisco and the 5th District are liberal Democratic strongholds. The 5th has the highest percentage of registered Democrats — 64 percent — of any district in the state without a black or Hispanic majority.

In 1988, San Francisco County voted by a wide margin against requiring state officials to report the names of those infected with HIV, the AIDS-related virus. Voters there also gave overwhelming majorities to Democratic Senate challenger Leo T. McCarthy, and presidential candidate Michael S. Dukakis.

The 5th contains almost all of San Francisco. It is an ethnic, racial and sexual pastiche. A fifth of its residents are Asian, mostly Japanese and Chinese. Mexican-Americans live in the bustling Mission District. A large homosexual community is centered around Castro and Market streets.

The 5th starts at the northern end of the San Francisco peninsula, just east of the Presidio. Rising to the south is Pacific Heights, home to affluent professionals.

To the east are Nob and Russian hills, equally affluent but with pockets of students and elderly, and North Beach, which is both the city's Italian section and the spiritual home of the Beat Generation. Most of the voters have a socially conscious liberal streak that manifests itself in a solid Democratic vote.

From there, the district passes through Chinatown and the Financial District, into the workaday part of San Francisco south of Market Street. The 5th reaches into the residential neighborhoods south of Market, including depressed Bayshore and Hunters Point, and the Hispanic neighborhoods of the Mission and Potrero Hill. Eventually it passes into the middle- and working-class areas falling away from Twin Peaks and the neat, pastel-painted houses of the Sunset District.

Population: 525,971. White 311,447 (59%), Black 56,892 (11%), Asian and Pacific Islander 113,295 (22%), Other 2,650 (1%). Spanish origin 75,368 (14%). 18 and over 434,190 (83%), 65 and over 83,827 (16%). Median age: 35.

Committees

Banking, Finance and Urban Affairs (28th of 31 Democrats)
Consumer Affairs and Coinage; Financial Institutions Supervision, Regulation and Insurance; Housing and Community Development; International Development, Finance, Trade and Monetary Policy

Government Operations (21st of 24 Democrats)
Human Resources and Intergovernmental Relations

Elections

1988 General		
Nancy Pelosi (D)	133,530	(76%)
Bruce Michael O'Neill (R)	33,692	(19%)
1987 Special Runoff †		
Nancy Pelosi (D)	46,428	(63%)
Harriet Ross (R)	22,478	(31%)
1987 Special Primary †		
Nancy Pelosi (D)	38,927	(36%)
Harry G. Britt (D)	35,008	(32%)
Bill Maher (D)	15,355	(14%)
Doris M. Ward (D)	6,498	(6%)
Harriet Ross (R)	3,016	(3%)

† The special primary was open to candidates of all parties. Because no candidate won 50 percent, a runoff was held among the leading vote-getters from all parties.

District Vote For President

	1988		1984		1980		1976	
D	148,878	(71%)	142,282	(65%)	88,734	(52%)	95,035	(54%)
R	57,846	(28%)	72,437	(33%)	53,398	(32%)	74,062	(42%)

Voting Studies

	Presidential Support		Party Unity		Conservative Coalition	
Year	S	O	S	O	S	O
1988	20	79	95	3	3	97
1987	15 †	84 †	90 †	3 †	0 †	88 †

† Not eligible for all recorded votes.

Key Votes

1987	
Delay "re-flagging" of Kuwaiti tankers	Y
Approve tax-raising deficit-reduction bill	Y
1988	
Approve aid to Nicaraguan contras	N
Enact civil rights restoration bill over Reagan veto	Y
Kill 60-day plant-closing notification measure	N
Pass omnibus trade bill over Reagan veto	Y
Approve death penalty for drug-related murders	N
Bar federal funds for abortions in cases of rape and incest	N
Oppose seven-day waiting period for purchase of handguns	N

Campaign Finance

	Receipts	Receipts from PACs		Expend-itures
1988				
Pelosi (D)	$1,865,268	$548,815	(29%)	$1,799,427
O'Neill (R) †	$19,245	0		$19,245
1987 ‡				
Pelosi (D)	$1,085,819	$215,090	(20%)	$1,033,511
Ross (R)	$25,554	$3,000	(12%)	$14,386

† Totals based on incomplete data.
‡ Totals based on pre-election data.

Interest Group Ratings

Year	ADA	ACU	AFL-CIO	CCUS
1988	100	0	93	21
1987	93	0	100	9

6 Barbara Boxer (D)

Of Greenbrae — Elected 1982

Born: Nov. 11, 1940, Brooklyn, N.Y.
Education: Brooklyn College, B.A. 1962.
Occupation: Stockbroker; journalist.
Family: Husband, Stewart Boxer; two children.
Religion: Jewish.
Political Career: Marin County Board of Supervisors, 1977-83; candidate for Marin County Board of Supervisors, 1972.
Capitol Office: 307 Cannon Bldg. 20515; 225-5161.

In Washington: An outspoken liberal activist, Boxer is often associated with other hard-charging Democrats such as Charles E. Schumer of New York, Marty Russo of Illinois and Vic Fazio of California. But while her peers have edged toward leadership roles, Boxer continues to be viewed largely as a crusader — unyielding in her efforts to cut the defense budget and boost domestic spending, but only modestly successful in bringing her ideas to fruition.

Boxer has not been without impact in her activist role. She is now in her third term on the Budget Committee, a forum in which her criticisms of Reagan and Bush administration fiscal policies have been heard and debated. In the 101st Congress, she heads Budget's Human Resources Task Force, which deals with the health care, child care and education issues close to her heart. A leading critic of Defense Department purchasing practices, she is co-chairman (with Republican Sen. William V. Roth Jr. of Delaware) of the congressional Military Reform Caucus.

But on Armed Services in the 100th Congress, Boxer made more points than she won. Her attacks on the Reagan administration's defense spending proposals marked her as a spokesman for the committee's small group of hard-core liberals. More moderate committee members, however, made the ultimate legislative decisions. Boxer's frequent amendments to eliminate major projects and make deep cuts in the Pentagon budget fell short of passage.

A member of the school that regards gains for the Pentagon as a loss for social programs, Boxer proposed an amendment to a defense authorization bill in May 1988 calling for defense increases to be financed "on a pay-as-you-go basis, without undermining the many domestic programs, such as Social Security and Medicare, which affect the health, safety and welfare of the people." The measure was defeated, 165-220.

Boxer also proposed, along with California Democrat Ronald V. Dellums, to cut funding for the strategic defense initiative (SDI) to $1.3 billion, from the $4.9 billion requested by Reagan and the $4.1 billion approved by Armed Services. The proposal went down by a wide 118-299 margin, in a vote made noteworthy mainly by a breakdown in the House's computerized voting system, which forced a temporary return to the days of the time-consuming roll call.

Boxer's position on Armed Services did enable her to play a more central role in discussions on reforming the Pentagon's procurement policy. It was this issue that first drew attention to Boxer. During her freshman term, she was a caustic critic of Defense Department overpayments for spare parts and other military equipment. In her second term, even before she won a seat on Armed Services, Boxer was appointed to an informal House task force, chaired by Massachusetts Democrat Nicholas Mavroules, to examine the purchasing problems.

After allegations of widespread defense contractor fraud and bribery were publicized in June 1988, Boxer forcefully assailed what she called lax procedures condoned by the Reagan administration. When Robert Costello, the under secretary of defense for acquisition, testified before Armed Services, Boxer rejected his insistence that major procedural changes were unnecessary, and described a Pentagon task force set up to examine procurement problems as "a sham" made up of "the very same people who've brought us this cozy attitude" between government officials and contractors.

Boxer also was a staunch opponent of U.S. aid to the Nicaraguan contras. Her steadfast opposition did not bend even when the congressional leadership arranged a compromise with the Bush administration in early 1989, sustaining non-lethal aid to the contras for a year but increasing Congress' oversight of the policy: She led a group of liberal House advocates of a total aid cutoff who voted against the plan.

Boxer took a leave from Armed Services at the start of the 101st Congress to pursue a seniority position on Government Operations, one of her original panels, where she is next in line for a subcommittee chairmanship. But she

California 6

Northwest San Francisco; Marin County; parts of Sonoma and Solano counties

The 6th is no longer the bizarrely shaped district that earned a place in gerrymandering history in 1981. That version combined four detached pieces of territory connected only by water or a slim segment of railroad yard. But it is still an imaginative display of cartography. There are now three sections of the district, two of them connected by the Golden Gate Bridge and the third by a narrow slip of land.

In land area and population, the largest of the three segments is Marin County. Marin has been stereotyped in fiction and journalism as the home of "mellow" — a uniquely California lifestyle enjoyed by the rich and characterized by a social and cultural permissiveness.

Yet Marin's staunchly liberal voting pattern is of fairly recent vintage: The county went for Gerald R. Ford in 1976 and for Ronald Reagan in 1980. But by 1984, it was one of five California counties that backed Democrat Walter F. Mondale; four years later, Democrat Michael S. Dukakis pushed the 60 percent mark.

Quality-of-life issues such as the environment are important here: In 1988, Marin voters endorsed a water safety and conservation ballot proposition, and they gave a cigarette-tax proposition its highest county vote in the state.

With about half of the district vote cast there, Marin gives Democratic candidates a big jump on capturing the 6th. But it is a slice of liberal San Francisco that cinches the district for the Democrats. The 6th includes Haight-Ashbury, made famous as a colony of hippie "flower children." Today, it is a funky mix of '60s-retro and '80s yuppie.

The third section of the 6th consists of two areas that are geographically and psychologically distant from San Francisco — Solano County (Vallejo) and Sonoma County (Petaluma).

Vallejo is a blue-collar Democratic city that relies on a naval shipyard for its economic support. West of it are Petaluma and other fast-growing Sonoma County suburbs.

Population: 526,020. White 406,963 (77%), Black 51,007 (10%), Asian and Pacific Islander 50,800 (10%), Other 2,685 (1%). Spanish origin 28,187 (5%). 18 and over 409,204 (78%), 65 and over 59,593 (11%). Median age: 32.

will not necessarily have to defer her interest in procurement and other defense issues; she sits on the Government Operations Subcommittee on Legislation and National Security, which has investigative oversight on defense-related issues.

Though she often locks horns with the more conservative members of the House, Boxer manages occasionally to find an issue on which there is common ground. During March 1988 debate on a House budget resolution, she joined with a frequent Budget Committee antagonist, Texas Republican Dick Armey, to propose a $220 million funding increase for Coast Guard drug-interdiction activities. The measure passed the committee easily, with then-Chairman William H. Gray III commenting that the panel could not block the result of such a "historic" alliance.

Boxer also joined with a conservative Armed Services Committee colleague, Virginia Republican Herbert H. Bateman, on an amendment requiring the presidential commission on military base-closing options to consider the environmental and "historic preservation" costs of closing a facility. The provision turned out to be of more benefit to Bateman's district than Boxer's; the commission preserved Virginia's Fort Monroe, but recommended the closure of the scenic Presidio base overlooking downtown San Francisco.

Boxer, along with her Bay-area Democratic colleague Nancy Pelosi, argued against the Presidio's inclusion on the list, stating that the commission had overlooked the high costs of making the site environmentally safe and of transferring it to the Interior Department, as required by law. But despite their arguments, and similar ones from other members faced with local base-closings, the plan was enacted.

Though Boxer clearly is someone with strongly held opinions, her colleagues were still startled by the stridency of her statements in support of the controversial 51 percent congressional pay-raise proposal in early 1989.

During House debate, Boxer warned that if the measure passed, she would hold accountable those "demagogues" who vocally opposed the pay raise but later accepted the money. "I am going to watch who you are and I am going to tell your constituents if you take that pay raise . . . ," Boxer said. "Because to talk against the pay raise and then keep it would be hypocritical and unbecoming a member of Congress."

She took the floor again the next day, just

before the final vote that scuttled the raise, to excoriate critics of the proposal. Then, after all of the strong language, Boxer again surprised her colleagues by joining in the overwhelming House majority voting to kill the raise.

At Home: Boxer was the unintended beneficiary of one of the decade's more creative acts of district line-drawing. The 6th was the keystone of California's 1981 redistricting plan, drawn to shore up Democratic Rep. John Burton after his close 1980 re-election contest. It was a gift from his brother, U.S. Rep. Phillip Burton, who drew the lines himself.

But three days before the filing deadline in 1982, John Burton decided to forgo another term in office. Boxer, then a Marin County supervisor who had worked for Burton in the mid-1970s, stepped up to take his place.

Her opponent in the primary was San Francisco Supervisor Louise Renne, who had the important backing of her city's mayor, Dianne Feinstein. Boxer moved quickly to shore up her Democratic base in Marin, and with Burton's backing, lined up the support of San Francisco's left-liberal activists and politically powerful gay community. That was enough to edge Renne out for the nomination.

In the general election, she ran against Republican Dennis McQuaid, who had made a strong showing against Burton two years before. But Phillip Burton's lines performed for Boxer as well as they would have for John, allowing her to win overwhelmingly in the San Francisco portion of the 6th and take comfortable margins in outlying blue-collar communities, countering a majority for McQuaid in Marin County. In 1984, despite new lines, she easily defeated her Republican opponent, and by 1986 she was up to 74 percent of the vote. She nearly duplicated that showing in 1988.

Committees

Budget (7th of 21 Democrats)
Task Forces: Human Resources (chairman); Urgent Fiscal Issues

Government Operations (12th of 24 Democrats)
Government Activities and Transportation; Legislation and National Security

Select Children, Youth and Families (8th of 18 Democrats)

Elections

1988 General		
Barbara Boxer (D)	176,645	(73%)
William Steinmetz (R)	64,174	(27%)
1986 General		
Barbara Boxer (D)	142,946	(74%)
Franklin "Harry" Ernst III (R)	50,606	(26%)

Previous Winning Percentages: 1984 (68%) **1982** (52%)

District Vote for President

	1988	1984	1980	1976
D	164,296 (64%)	141,884 (56%)	92,724 (44%)	91,399 (50%)
R	89,300 (35%)	106,610 (42%)	83,186 (39%)	85,144 (47%)

Campaign Finance

	Receipts	Receipts from PACs	Expend-itures
1988			
Boxer (D)	$450,306	$185,330 (41%)	$351,687
Steinmetz (R)	$50,955	$6,250 (12%)	$50,532
1986			
Boxer (D)	$358,015	$164,611 (46%)	$279,727
Ernst (R)	$10,175	0	$10,171

Key Votes

1987	
Raise speed limit to 65 mph	N
Approve Gephardt "fair trade" amendment	Y
Ban testing of larger nuclear weapons	Y
Delay "re-flagging" of Kuwaiti tankers	Y
Approve tax-raising deficit-reduction bill	Y
1988	
Approve aid to Nicaraguan contras	N
Enact civil rights restoration bill over Reagan veto	Y
Kill 60-day plant-closing notification measure	N
Pass omnibus trade bill over Reagan veto	Y
Approve death penalty for drug-related murders	Y
Bar federal funds for abortions in cases of rape and incest	N
Oppose seven-day waiting period for purchase of handguns	N

Voting Studies

	Presidential Support		Party Unity		Conservative Coalition	
Year	**S**	**O**	**S**	**O**	**S**	**O**
1988	17	69	86	5	8	87
1987	12	84	88	3	2	93
1986	13	78	84	4	12	82
1985	11	86	88	3	2	93
1984	20	68	86	3	2	92
1983	15	84	94	3	4	92

Interest Group Ratings

Year	ADA	ACU	AFL-CIO	CCUS
1988	80	5	93	27
1987	92	0	93	7
1986	90	5	100	13
1985	95	5	100	19
1984	95	0	92	46
1983	95	0	100	20

7 George Miller (D)

Of Martinez — Elected 1974

Born: May 17, 1945, Richmond, Calif.
Education: San Francisco State College, B.A. 1968; U. of California Law School, J.D. 1972.
Occupation: Lawyer.
Family: Wife, Cynthia Caccavo; two children.
Religion: Roman Catholic.
Political Career: Democratic nominee for Calif. Senate, 1969.
Capitol Office: 2228 Rayburn Bldg. 20515; 225-2095.

In Washington: A partisan who has grazed widely over the landscape of domestic policy, Miller is about to inherit a huge piece of legislative territory all his own: He is the heir presumptive to the Interior Committee chairmanship. Barely into his mid-40s, Miller is apt to have a good long time to imprint environmental legislation with his unusual combination of liberal passion and pay-as-you-go pragmatism.

While Miller waits for the retirement of current Chairman Morris K. Udall, he is honing his brokerage skills as head of the Interior Subcommittee on Water and Power Resources and assuming increasing responsibility for other committee activities. In the 100th Congress, debate over whether to limit logging in Alaska's Tongass National Forest allowed Miller to demonstrate his skill at attaining compromise. He shaved just enough off the conservationists' proposal to soften Alaska Republican Don Young's criticism. This produced a lopsided House victory on the controversial legislation.

Also in the 100th Congress, Udall delegated to Miller responsibility for legislation to permit oil drilling in the Arctic National Wildlife Refuge (ANWR). A massive and controversial bill, ANWR is adamantly opposed by conservationists but supported by such powerful forces as President Bush. When the measure cleared the Merchant Marine Committee in 1988, Miller balked. He kept ANWR on a slow legislative track, arguing for the need for further study. In the wake of the 1989 *Exxon Valdez* oil spill, the bill does not appear viable in the 101st Congress.

A conservationist leading what traditionally had been a pro-development subcommittee, Miller is a vigorous critic of federally financed water projects and is slowly redefining the subcommittee's mission. "In the past, a wink and a nod got you billions of dollars," he once said. "In this day and age, with massive budget deficits, that can no longer be the case. We're trying to get away from measuring success by how much cement we pour."

Reflecting Miller's goals, the 100th Congress enacted legislation to supply water to 400,000 Southern Californians without building any dams and at no cost to the federal government. It does so by authorizing the Metropolitan Water District of Southern California to fund the lining of the earthen parts of the All-American Canal with waterproof material. By eliminating wasteful seepage, the government can settle a water-rights claim by the San Luis Rey River Indians and have enough excess water to make the endeavor profitable for the water district.

While Miller has earned high marks for such efforts, he can still turn purple when legislation fails to mesh with his environmental goals. Long after most conservationists, including Udall, had sanctioned the 1988 Florida-Arizona land exchange, Miller was its loudest critic.

Miller has the luxury of attacking federal water projects because he comes from a water-rich district. This can raise resentments among colleagues from drier parts of the West. Earlier in his career, Miller battled doggedly to change a 1902 reclamation law that allowed agribusiness companies to buy large amounts of cheap, federally subsidized water. After more than two years of angry debate, he agreed to accept modest changes in the law in 1982.

In the 100th Congress, Miller brought his new negotiation talents to the debate and worked out a deal to curb federal subsidies under the 1982 law with fellow Californian Tony Coelho, whose district included many large irrigated farms.

Outside the Interior Committee, Miller has a high-visibility platform for advocating his social services agenda as chairman of the Select Committee on Children, Youth and Families. Though the panel has no legislative jurisdiction, Miller gained a bill-writing forum when he returned to the Education and Labor Committee in the 101st Congress after three terms on the Budget Committee.

Miller thinks hard about his social issues and takes them seriously. He can be quick to express his frustration at those who do not see the urgency of social problems the way he does.

California 7

Most of Contra Costa County; Richmond

Contra Costa County — about 80 percent of which is in the 7th District — is split almost evenly between the urbanized industrial areas along San Pablo Bay and the suburban tracts that have grown like crab grass farther east, behind the San Pablo mountain ridge.

In almost 50 years of unbridled expansion, the county's population has exploded from 100,000 to more than 725,000. The white-collar/blue-collar split in Contra Costa makes it one of California's more politically competitive counties.

Since Ronald Reagan won the county in his first gubernatorial election in 1966, Contra Costa has backed the Democratic candidate for governor only once, in 1978. But in 1984, Reagan ran behind his statewide percentage here, and in 1988, Democratic presidential nominee Michael S. Dukakis carried the county with 52 percent of the vote. Democrat Miller never fails to win his House elections by big margins.

The strongest Democratic area in the 7th is the industrial shoreline from Richmond to Pittsburg, a base for shipping, as well as oil and sugar refining.

The Contra Costa shoreline looks more like northern New Jersey than like placid Marin County, just five miles away across the bay. The blue-collar city of Richmond, nearly 50 percent black, voted overwhelmingly for Walter F. Mondale in 1984 and Dukakis in 1988; the nearby industrial towns are nearly as strong for the Democrats.

The climate — both political and meteorological — is considerably different on the eastern side of the mountains that separate the sunny inland areas of the county from the fogbound coast. Once fertile agricultural area, the inland areas of the district are now largely occupied by housing tracts.

Cities like Concord — the 7th's largest with 106,000 residents — and Walnut Creek are home to thousands of white-collar professionals. A strong showing on this side of the mountains gave Reagan his 7th District win in 1984.

Population: 525,990. White 417,094 (79%), Black 56,929 (11%), Asian and Pacific Islander 23,204 (4%), Other 3,565 (1%). Spanish origin 51,165 (10%). 18 and over 379,409 (72%), 65 and over 49,389 (9%). Median age: 31.

He was outraged at President Reagan's approach to domestic policy and only slightly gentler toward Democrats who showed an interest in compromising with the White House.

But as on Interior, Miller matches his passion with perseverance, and he has seen some of his efforts to protect poor children signed into law. In 1988, the children's committee updated a study of cost-effective child-care programs, and $600 million in new spending was approved for the programs identified. He was also appointed by the leadership to the ad hoc welfare task force that helped propel the legislation.

In 1984, in response to a rash of stories about child abuse in day-care centers, Miller managed to add $25 million to a block grant program for special training for child-care staff and parents. "We have a three-alarm fire going out there," Miller said. "This is the only way in which we can get the money to the states immediately."

During his tenure on the Budget Committee, Miller was one of the strongest union supporters in Congress. He also developed the "pay-as-you-go" budget-freeze concept. As part of his crusade to promote a seemingly conservative budget policy to protect certain liberal social programs, his idea was to freeze virtually all federal spending at current levels and offset new expenditures with tax increases or spending cuts elsewhere. Although the plan was never implemented, he had the satisfaction of seeing the House adopt a version of it in the fiscal 1985 budget blueprint.

During his last term on the committee, Miller was the only Democrat to oppose the fiscal 1988 budget resolution. While he complained that the measure contained too much money for defense, all 11 Republicans on the committee voted with Miller because it contained too little.

Venturing into defense policy, Miller was a ringleader in the effort to oust Les Aspin as Armed Services chairman after the 99th Congress and replace him with Marvin Leath, his own Budget Committee colleague. Miller was part of an aggressive faction of Budget Committee liberals who worked with panel conservatives, including Leath, to draft a consensus budget resolution in 1986.

At Home: Not only is Miller a third-generation resident of his Northern California county — a fact that sets him apart in the state's mobile culture — he is also the third George Miller in his family to earn a living in government.

Miller's grandfather, George Sr., was the

assistant civil engineer in Richmond. His father, George Jr., served 20 years from a state Senate constituency that resembled the current 7th. A football and swimming star in school, George Miller III was a first-year law student in 1969 when his father suddenly died. Only 23, Miller won the Democratic nomination but lost later in the year to Republican John Nejedly.

Miller went to work in the state Capitol anyway, as a legislative aide to state Sen. George Moscone, the Democratic floor leader. In 1974, when Democratic Rep. Jerome Waldie decided to run for governor, Miller ran for Waldie's seat in Congress, challenging a local labor leader and the mayor of Concord, the largest city in the district.

Miller had the family name identification, plus the strong support of Assemblyman John T. Knox, who put his organization to work for him in Richmond, the district's second-largest city. He won the primary with 38 percent.

In the general election, against moderate Republican Gary Fernandez, Miller exploited the Watergate issue, disclosing his campaign finances twice a month and chiding his opponent for not doing likewise. It was a hard-fought election, but Miller won by more than 15,000 votes.

He has not drawn a threatening Republican opponent since and regularly draws two-thirds or more of the vote. In 1988, he registered his highest re-election tally, winning 68 percent.

Committees

Select Children, Youth and Families (Chairman)

Education and Labor (5th of 22 Democrats)
Elementary, Secondary and Vocational Education; Labor-Management Relations; Postsecondary Education

Interior and Insular Affairs (2nd of 26 Democrats)
Water, Power and Offshore Energy Resources (chairman); Energy and the Environment

Elections

1988 General		
George Miller (D)	170,006	(68%)
Jean Last (R)	78,478	(32%)
1986 General		
George Miller (D)	124,174	(67%)
Rosemary Thakar (R)	62,379	(33%)

Previous Winning Percentages: **1984** (67%) **1982** (67%) **1980** (63%) **1978** (63%) **1976** (75%) **1974** (56%)

District Vote for President

	1988	1984	1980	1976
D	136,163 (53%)	114,148 (47%)	84,310 (41%)	91,581 (54%)
R	116,314 (46%)	126,001 (52%)	96,340 (47%)	77,295 (45%)

Campaign Finance

	Receipts	Receipts from PACs	Expend-itures
1988			
Miller (D)	$429,305	$179,984 (42%)	$269,887
Last (R)	$14,818	0	$15,311
1986			
Miller (D)	$391,356	$152,243 (39%)	$312,522
Thakar (R)	$96,662	$2,200 (2%)	$92,496

Key Votes

1987	
Raise speed limit to 65 mph	N
Approve Gephardt "fair trade" amendment	N
Ban testing of larger nuclear weapons	Y
Delay "re-flagging" of Kuwaiti tankers	Y
Approve tax-raising deficit-reduction bill	N
1988	
Approve aid to Nicaraguan contras	N
Enact civil rights restoration bill over Reagan veto	Y
Kill 60-day plant-closing notification measure	N
Pass omnibus trade bill over Reagan veto	Y
Approve death penalty for drug-related murders	N
Bar federal funds for abortions in cases of rape and incest	N
Oppose seven-day waiting period for purchase of handguns	N

Voting Studies

	Presidential Support		Party Unity		Conservative Coalition	
Year	**S**	**O**	**S**	**O**	**S**	**O**
1988	18	69	85	6	5	82
1987	15	81	88	5	5	95
1986	14	80	84	4	8	80
1985	16	76	84	5	9	84
1984	22	69	85	6	7	86
1983	11	78	83	8	13	75
1982	26	71	92	4	7	90
1981	28	70	89	8	0	93

Interest Group Ratings

Year	ADA	ACU	AFL-CIO	CCUS
1988	95	4	93	31
1987	96	13	88	20
1986	90	6	91	15
1985	95	10	80	19
1984	100	4	85	31
1983	90	4	94	16
1982	95	0	95	20
1981	100	0	87	11

8 Ronald V. Dellums (D)

Of Oakland — Elected 1970

Born: Nov. 24, 1935, Oakland, Calif.
Education: San Francisco State College, B.A. 1960; U. of California, Berkeley, M.S.W. 1962.
Military Career: Marine Corps, 1954-56.
Occupation: Psychiatric social worker.
Family: Wife, Leola "Roscoe" Higgs; three children.
Religion: Protestant.
Political Career: Berkeley City Council, 1967-71.
Capitol Office: 2136 Rayburn Bldg. 20515; 225-2661.

In Washington: Dellums has finally achieved enough House seniority and institutional power to join the fringes of the establishment he came to challenge. The passage has been smoother than many expected given his enduring image as a radical, and the constancy of his leftist politics.

For nearly two decades, Dellums has expressed the outrage of the left on the House floor, combining eloquent visions of world peace and angry charges of racism. But in recent years, a new dimension has been added. Dellums speaks from the vantage of a chairman of an Armed Services subcommittee.

In 1983, the conservatives who then led Armed Services had no choice but to give Dellums a subcommittee chair, based on his seniority and the potential embarrassment of refusing a black his rightful seat. All the old guard could do was restrict him to the chair overseeing the non-strategic area of U.S. base construction.

With the 101st Congress, however, pacifist Dellums takes over the Research and Development Subcommittee, with responsibility for the nuclear weaponry he vehemently opposes. It will test his commitment to work through the process, and at a time when Dellums is trying to bury the "personally painful" perception that he is a '60s-style Berkeley bomb-thrower.

His recent record has allayed if not dispelled colleagues' apprehension. As a chairman, Dellums has been courtly even to opponents. He still loses often — as he did when Armed Services approved funds for military construction in Honduras, the site of massive U.S. exercises aimed at intimidating leftist Nicaragua, over his objections. But he has not been obstructionist. Republicans get fair treatment, consistent with his larger commitment to minority rights.

To some extent, Dellums' militancy has been exaggerated from the start, when Vice President Spiro T. Agnew warned he would "bring down the walls." Dellums consistently has urged fellow radicals to work within the system, not to bring it down but to change it. The extremist tactics of his early years — his "unofficial" hearings into charges of U.S. atrocities in Vietnam and racism in the military — were undertaken only when Dellums could not get the pro-Pentagon leaders of Armed Services to act.

Even his impeccable dress is part of his strategy to win acceptance: "I deliberately walked into the House well-groomed," he once said. "If they can relate to me and my clothes, they can relate to my ideas."

As a freshman in 1971, Dellums called for abolishing the seniority system, saying that leadership should not be picked "by how long it sits in one place." Today he is one of the system's strictest proponents, reflecting his own seniority and his recognition that those of minority race and ideology, like himself, might otherwise be denied seats of power.

In 1985, Dellums opposed one-time ally Les Aspin in his successful coup against the enfeebled Armed Services chairman, Pentagon loyalist Melvin Price. After Price's defeat, Dellums still did not back Aspin, but instead voted for the man next in line, Southern conservative Charles E. Bennett.

Two years later, after Aspin had enraged his liberal supporters by backing both the MX missile and military aid to the Nicaraguan contras, Dellums joined the effort to oust him. The Berkeley leftist became one of the most improbable colonels in the unlikely coalition of liberals and hard-liners that supported conservative Texas hawk Marvin Leath.

As Leath said of their unusual friendship: "I told him once, 'Ronnie, I used to think you had to check your grenade at the door.'" Dellums replied, "Well, Marvin, I thought you had to check your hood."

When liberals attacked Leath by circulating his conservative, pro-Pentagon voting record, it was Dellums who countered. "I am against imposing a political litmus test on the chair," he wrote to Democrats. In an emotional nominating speech before the Democratic Caucus, Dellums called Leath "my friend, my brother," and "an honest broker of ideas" who could bring liberals and conservatives together.

California 8

Northern Alameda County — Oakland; Berkeley

The Black Panther Party, the "free-speech movement" and the Symbionese Liberation Army all were born within this district, a mixture of poverty and intellectual ferment. The East Bay cities of Oakland and Berkeley cast about 60 percent of the vote and form the economic, philosophical and political base.

The leftward-leaning constituency in these cities is fodder for Democratic candidates. Large margins there enabled Michael S. Dukakis to carry the 8th with 70 percent of the vote in 1988; Walter F. Mondale did even slightly better four years earlier.

However, even these liberal candidates were well to the right of many of Berkeley's political activists. Since 1977, the city of 104,000 has had self-described socialists as mayors, and their coalition, Berkeley Citizens' Action, has dominated the City Council since 1984.

The University of California's main campus at Berkeley is not the political hotbed it was in the 1960s, when it was a center for anti-war activism and student unrest. But occasionally, the university community appears frozen in time. In 1969, there were bloody confrontations between radical activists and police at "People's Park," a vacant lot on which the university had planned construction.

In May 1989, radicals and activists for the homeless, many of whom were living in the park, held a rally to mark the 20th anniversary and to protest another college building plan; it ended with a siege of vandalism and looting.

To the south is Oakland; with 357,000 residents, it is California's sixth-largest city. The city, which is about one-half black, is also one of the state's poorest. The 8th takes in most of Oakland, including some of its lowest-income black and Hispanic sections, near the Alameda County Coliseum and the Oakland International Airport.

There is a marked contrast between Dellums' constituency in these cities and the mostly white, affluent voters in the Contra Costa County section of the 8th. Dellums' 1988 Republican opponent, John J. Cuddihy Jr., carried the Contra Costa County section by over 12,000 votes in 1988. But Dellums took Alameda County by almost 100,000 votes, winning overall by better than a 2-to-1 margin.

Population: 525,646. White 317,735 (60%), Black 139,730 (27%), Asian and Pacific Islander 43,148 (8%), Other 2,466 (1%). Spanish origin 34,394 (7%). 18 and over 409,168 (78%), 65 and over 63,941 (12%). Median age: 32.

To some observers, the episode marked Dellums' assimilation into the House. Moreover, it came just months after what Dellums called the "highest point of my political life." In 1986, 15 years after he first proposed sanctions against South Africa's apartheid regime, the House finally embraced his call for a trade cutoff and disinvestment by U.S. firms in that country. By voice vote, it chose his tougher substitute over a committee bill providing more modest sanctions. Dellums said it was an "exonerating" experience, adding, "It's been a long journey to this moment."

The victory was something of a fluke. Republicans threw their votes behind Dellums' bill, not because they endorsed it but because they believed it was so radical it would not survive. In fact, however, the GOP strategy probably made the final product stronger.

The House action moved the range of options — and thus the potential middle ground — farther to the left, and made President Reagan's anti-sanctions stand appear more extreme. The Senate reacted by passing a bill significantly stronger than expected, although weaker than the Dellums version. It became law over Reagan's veto.

Early in 1987, as repression in South Africa continued, Dellums renewed the push to break economic relations. Backers hoped for a boost from the political pressure of a presidential election year. In 1988, on the eve of the GOP convention, the House voted roughly along party lines for a slightly milder version of Dellums' bill.

To Republicans' complaints about its political timing, Dellums recounted his 17-year fight. To their argument that sanctions hurt South African blacks, he replied, "Sanctions hurt, but apartheid kills."

He also added a personal note: "Two decades ago, people said, 'Take your anger, your frustration, your pain, your hopes and your dreams and your aspirations inside the political process. . . . Well, in that process you folks taught me humility. I am an activist but you taught me patience. I am a fighter but you taught me discipline."

Both parties gave him a standing ovation. However, in the Senate, the bill lacked the Republican support that sanctions legislation had enjoyed two years earlier, and it died there.

When the 101st Congress opened, Dellums filed his bill to begin the fight anew.

Most of Dellums' initiatives are less successful than the drive for South Africa sanctions. He annually loses by large margins in his bid to slash spending for the strategic defense initiative program. In 1988, he cosponsored an amendment stripping Reagan's $4.9 billion request to $1.3 billion for basic research into antimissile technology. Though his position paralleled that of Democratic presidential candidate Michael S. Dukakis, the House rejected it and approved $3.5 billion.

Year after year, Dellums has tried to cut defense bills, offering his own detailed alternatives with emotional and lengthy speeches. He always puts on an impressive show — and loses overwhelmingly. His budgets reflect his beliefs. He would cancel the MX, cruise, Trident and Pershing nuclear missile programs, based both on his opposition to "first-strike" weapons that go beyond deterrence, and on his insistence that nuclear war is not survivable. He would reduce troop strength intended either for Europe (he says plans for war there are "obsolete") or for intervention in the Third World.

Much of Dellums' anger in recent years stemmed from his distaste for the Reagan administration's foreign policy. He sought a congressional inquiry into the Grenada invasion. He filed a lawsuit to determine whether U.S. support for the Nicaraguan contras violated the Neutrality Act; after a special prosecutor was named in 1986 to investigate the Iran-contra affair, Dellums forwarded his complaints and dropped his own legal action.

Dellums' fierce opposition to the contras led him to break with House leaders in 1988, when they drafted a non-military aid bill. Most liberals grudgingly backed it, realizing that otherwise Reagan's military aid request would pass. Dellums could not: "There are times when you have to vote your conscience and vote your district. This is one of those times."

Voting his conscience another time meant antagonizing some of his San Francisco neighbors. Dellums, an opponent of the Navy's "homeporting" force-dispersal strategy, led an effort in an Armed Services conference committee that resulted in the scuttling of a $22 million Navy plan to base the battleship *Missouri* and a dozen support vessels in San Francisco. "I hold him personally responsible," Mayor Dianne Feinstein said, for thwarting the "largest single economic development" in the city.

Since 1979, Dellums has been a full committee chairman, but of the relatively minor District of Columbia Committee. That panel no longer dominates D.C. affairs as it once did, but it still has some leverage. Dellums favors full autonomy for the majority-black city, but his proposals are no closer to enactment. In fact, pressure from the right in recent years has forced Dellums on the defensive. Over his taunts that Congress is behaving like a mere city council, conservatives have pushed through provisions to reverse D.C. ordinances on such matters as homosexual rights and abortion.

For the 101st Congress, Dellums also has been elected chairman of the Congressional Black Caucus — a post for which he was rejected a decade earlier as too independent and radical.

At Home: Dellums wanted to be a professional baseball pitcher when he grew up, but he has said that encounters with racial prejudice spoiled that dream, leaving him with little ambition after high school. Following two years in the Marines, he went to college with the help of the GI Bill and six years later took a degree in psychiatric social work.

He was a social worker in San Francisco, managing federally assisted poverty programs, when friends persuaded him to pursue his ideas about poverty and discrimination by running for the Berkeley City Council in 1967. He has won every election he has been in since then.

Dellums will never satisfy the conservative elements of his district, but he has always had more than enough of a constituency to get elected without them. He meets with resistance in the upper-income Contra Costa County portion of the district. But in the much larger Alameda County part of the 8th, which includes Berkeley and most of Oakland, he has won well over 60 percent since 1974.

Republicans occasionally take a run at Dellums. But in 1988, facing a 27-year-old health-care worker, he won a 10th term with 67 percent of the vote — his best showing yet.

In 1970, when Dellums launched his primary challenge to six-term Democratic Rep. Jeffery Cohelan, the East Bay region was in a state of turmoil. Student protest over the war in Vietnam was becoming increasingly violent and the Black Panther movement was gaining strength in Oakland's ghettos. Although his credentials as a liberal were solid, Cohelan was considered "old-fashioned" in his approach to politics. Dellums, by contrast, was usually described in the press as "angry and articulate" or "radical and militant."

Dellums put together a coalition of blacks, students and left-leaning intellectuals that has been the core of his support ever since. His major issue was Cohelan's tardiness in opposing the Vietnam War. Dellums registered nearly 15,000 new voters in the district and easily ousted Cohelan with 55 percent.

In the general election, attacks by Vice President Agnew only brought out more support for Dellums among the district's Democrats, and he easily defeated a 25-year-old political neophyte. That victory ushered in a decade of political quiet in the district, in which Dellums rarely encountered more than minor opposition in either party.

After a little-noticed Republican opponent held Dellums to 56 percent in 1980, however, the GOP put more effort into its attacks on him.

In 1982, Claude B. Hutchison Jr., a former bank president and the son of an ex-Berkeley mayor, launched a well-funded effort using former business associates to help finance his campaign and pulling in more than $250,000 from donors eager to see Dellums retired. With support among Republicans virtually guaranteed, Hutchison tried to win over moderate Democrats, minimizing his GOP ties and taking positions similar to Dellums' in favor of funding for public education and against tuition tax credits for private schools.

Dellums fought back. Attacking "the madness of Reagan and Reaganomics," he drew on an impressive array of national left support to swamp Hutchison in raising funds. In the end, the results were like those of previous years — Hutchison easily won the Contra Costa County portion of the 8th, and Dellums just as handily made up the deficit in Oakland and Berkeley.

In 1984, former Black Panther Eldridge Cleaver, now a political conservative, announced that he intended to challenge Dellums as an independent. At the same time, Republicans put up a black banker, Charles Connor. They hoped that Cleaver, despite his ideological metamorphosis, would take enough votes from Dellums to allow Connor to win. But Cleaver dropped out of the contest at the end of the summer. Left on his own, Connor suffered from having to run in one of the few districts in the country where Reagan's coattails would be a liability.

Two years later, it was the turn of Piedmont City Councilman Steve Eigenberg, a young, moderate Republican with close ties to Alameda County Democrats. Republicans hoped he could pick up the backing of moderate blue-collar and middle-class Democrats, but he had little success. He won Contra Costa County by a 2-to-1 margin, but was swamped in Alameda.

Committees

District of Columbia (Chairman)
Fiscal Affairs and Health; Judiciary and Education

Armed Services (4th of 31 Democrats)
Research and Development (chairman); Investigations

Elections

1988 General		
Ronald V. Dellums (D)	163,221	(67%)
John J. Cuddihy Jr. (R)	76,531	(31%)
1986 General		
Ronald V. Dellums (D)	121,790	(60%)
Steven Eigenberg (R)	76,850	(38%)

Previous Winning Percentages: **1984** (60%) **1982** (56%) **1980** (56%) **1978** (57%) **1976** (62%) **1974** (57%) **1972** (56%) **1970** (57%)

District Vote For President

	1988	1984	1980	1976
D	178,864 (70%)	173,055 (65%)	113,944 (51%)	118,408 (59%)
R	74,437 (29%)	88,833 (34%)	73,632 (33%)	78,374 (39%)

Campaign Finance

	Receipts	Receipts from PACs	Expend-itures
1988			
Dellums (D)	$1,153,750	$87,299 (8%)	$1,174,676
Cuddihy (R)	$6,958	$200 (3%)	$7,071
1986			
Dellums (D)	$1,370,820	$93,123 (7%)	$1,223,490
Eigenberg (R)	$76,785	$15,565 (20%)	$74,567

Key Votes

1987	
Raise speed limit to 65 mph	N
Approve Gephardt "fair trade" amendment	Y
Ban testing of larger nuclear weapons	Y
Delay "re-flagging" of Kuwaiti tankers	Y
Approve tax-raising deficit-reduction bill	Y
1988	
Approve aid to Nicaraguan contras	N
Enact civil rights restoration bill over Reagan veto	Y
Kill 60-day plant-closing notification measure	N
Pass omnibus trade bill over Reagan veto	Y
Approve death penalty for drug-related murders	N
Bar federal funds for abortions in cases of rape and incest	N
Oppose seven-day waiting period for purchase of handguns	N

Voting Studies

	Presidential Support		Party Unity		Conservative Coalition	
Year	**S**	**O**	**S**	**O**	**S**	**O**
1988	19	78	88	4	0	95
1987	10	86	91	2	5	95
1986	12	86	89	4	2	92
1985	16	83	91	3	5	91
1984	21	78	89	6	0	100
1983	7	83	82	7	2	91
1982	17	81	90	5	4	96
1981	21	66	83	6	8	87

Interest Group Ratings

Year	ADA	ACU	AFL-CIO	CCUS
1988	100	0	100	23
1987	100	0	100	0
1986	100	0	86	12
1985	95	5	100	19
1984	100	4	85	31
1983	95	5	94	22
1982	85	14	95	18
1981	95	7	80	0

9 Pete Stark (D)

Of Oakland — Elected 1972

Born: Nov. 11, 1931, Milwaukee, Wis.
Education: Massachusetts Institute of Technology, B.S. 1953; U. of California, M.B.A. 1960.
Military Career: Air Force, 1955-57.
Occupation: Banker.
Family: Wife, Carolyn Wente; four children.
Religion: Unitarian.
Political Career: Sought Democratic nomination for Calif. Senate, 1969.
Capitol Office: 1125 Longworth Bldg. 20515; 225-5065.

In Washington: A man of personal sophistication and proven business sense — he made a fortune in banking by the time he was 40 — Stark has become a significant player on the Ways and Means Committee, making his mark on both tax and health policy. His handling of arcane, difficult legislative issues has gone a long way toward dispelling his colleagues' earlier misgivings and transforming his role from liberal maverick to adept insider.

As chairman of the Health Subcommittee, Stark has shown an impressive aptitude for translating liberal goals into pragmatic legislative proposals. Admitting that the battle for national health insurance was lost long ago, Stark has won enactment of incremental measures to improve health services and insurance for those lacking coverage.

In the 100th Congress, he was a key player in the effort to expand Medicare to cover catastrophic health expenses for the elderly. Stark and ranking Health Republican Bill Gradison of Ohio co-authored the measure, which aimed to limit the amount for which beneficiaries could be held liable for Medicare-covered hospital and physician bills.

The goals of the legislation had earlier been endorsed by President Reagan, prompting Stark to comment at the outset of subcommittee consideration, "When you get Gradison and me and [Health and Human Services Secretary Otis R.] Bowen and the president together, you better reserve one of those puppies, because you're not going to get a breeding like that again soon."

Stark and Gradison fended off attempts to derail the bill by a senior citizens' lobbying group and by prescription-drug manufacturers. The elderly lobby objected to the bill because the beneficiaries would finance the added benefits and because it did not address the issue of long-term care. The drug industry sought to kill the House version of a provision covering the cost of prescription drugs. In the end, although the White House balked for a while, the president signed the bill.

From his subcommittee post, Stark is well positioned to reshape a variety of programs as part of the massive, annual reconciliation bill — the omnibus measure that makes spending cuts dictated by the budget. If the budget calls for substantial reductions in Medicare — as it does nearly every year — Stark is a major force in structuring the cuts and can quietly slip in changes in health policy. His strategic position also gives him important leverage with colleagues.

In 1986, when LTV Corp. faced bankruptcy and members wanted laid-off workers to get their health benefits, they saw one clear avenue of legislative relief: They persuaded Stark to include language in a reconciliation bill requiring the company to pay the benefits.

But Stark and other liberal House Democrats, notably Henry A. Waxman of California, chairman of the Health panel on Energy and Commerce, found themselves outgunned on the reconciliation measure passed in late 1987. As part of the budget-summit agreement, Congress cut $2 billion from Medicare in fiscal 1988 and $3.5 billion in 1989. A united Senate and White House overpowered House negotiators to cut nearly half a billion dollars more than was mandated by the budget summit.

House Democrats were furious at the Senate, and particularly Democrats on the Senate Finance Committee. "The Senate sold out to the White House," Stark fumed. He called Senate Democrats "an elitist group of millionaires" and said, "I wouldn't want my mother voting for any of them." While Stark (a millionaire himself) tends to say things for their shock value, several colleagues privately endorsed his basic sentiment.

Stark, with his penchant for impish humor, still seems to relish the confrontational style of the outraged liberal, berating administration witnesses at hearings and flinging epithets at the American Medical Association. But when the time comes for legislative bargaining, he knows how to play a more controlled game.

As chairman of the Health Subcommittee in the 99th Congress and of the Select Revenue

California 9

Suburban Alameda County — Hayward

The 9th is Democratic, but not nearly as liberal as the Democrat it sends to the House. A fast-growing suburban constituency helped Ronald Reagan carry the district in 1980 and 1984. But Michael S. Dukakis returned the 9th to the Democrats in 1988 by a comfortable margin.

Like most of the East Bay districts, the 9th has two separate sections. Working-class Democratic areas lie along the bay; a high-tech, suburban growth area is firmly established on the other side of the hills that form the eastern wall of the San Francisco basin.

The more densely populated bay-side area is dominated by warehouses and older factories that make motor-vehicle parts and office machines. This area includes San Leandro, an old Portuguese enclave that still has a strong blue-collar vote. Reagan's appeal to working-class ethnics enabled him to carry the city, though by just 100 votes in 1984. Dukakis easily prevailed there four years later.

To the north of San Leandro is Oakland. Although the bulk of the city is in the 8th District — the 9th lost much of it in the 1981 remap — Stark still represents about 70,000 residents of the city, most of them either black or Hispanic. Some parts of the city that have been hard-hit by drug-related crime are in the 9th.

Farther south, the district takes in all of Hayward, the district's largest city, with more than 100,000 residents. In the 1970s, Stark represented less than 10 percent of the city, but now he has the entire student population around Hayward's California State University, which works to the advantage of Stark and other Democrats.

The area of greatest concern to Democrats in the 9th is on the eastern side of the San Leandro Hills, where high-tech research industries centered around Livermore and Pleasanton have drawn thousands of affluent suburbanites. In the last 20 years, Livermore has grown by 20 percent, while Pleasanton has increased its population by 40 percent. Stark has overcome some early difficulties here — in 1980, both communities supported his opponent. But at the presidential level, Livermore and Pleasanton still go Republican.

Population: 526,234. White 393,257 (75%), Black 60,908 (12%), Asian and Pacific Islander 34,197 (6%), Other 3,845 (1%). Spanish origin 70,996 (14%). 18 and over 388,528 (74%), 65 and over 52,631 (10%). Median age: 31.

Measures Subcommittee for two terms before that, he showed a persistence that few colleagues expected of him. He has always had one of the more agile minds in the House; as a subcommittee chairman, he learned how to focus his effort on an issue long enough to accomplish his goals.

Stark's experience with one of the most complex areas of tax law — dealing with insurance companies — assured him an influential role as Ways and Means sat down to overhaul the tax code in the 99th Congress. Stark earned Chairman Dan Rostenkowski's gratitude for his work on insurance issues and was a staunch enough loyalist that he became part of the charmed circle of committee members hand-picked to be conferees on the tax-overhaul bill.

Stark was an early supporter of the Treasury Department's initial tax-revision plan because he felt it would roll back many of Reagan's 1981 tax breaks and "get the corporations back into paying their fair share of taxes." When Ways and Means early on voted to expand a big tax break for banks, an obvious retreat from the goal of eliminating special-interest advantages, it was Stark — himself a former banker — who offered an amendment to scale back the break after the committee agreed to reconsider the issue.

The ongoing feud between Stark and the AMA has provided Capitol Hill one of its more entertaining sideshows. It is one in which Stark has usually maintained the upper hand.

At the beginning of the 100th Congress, he easily beat back a last-minute effort by senior member Charles B. Rangel to regain the subcommittee chair Rangel once held. The AMA, which has devoted large sums of money to defeating Stark in the past — its political action committee spent over $250,000 against his 1986 re-election — had wanted J. J. "Jake" Pickle of Texas to challenge him, but he backed off after Stark quickly pocketed the commitments he needed to keep the seat.

Early in 1989, though, Stark and the AMA found themselves on the same side of the battle lines. In wrangling over the organization of a 15-member bipartisan commission to formulate health-care policy, Stark had teamed with Gradison and the six other Republicans to form a bloc on a procedural question. The panel's representative from the AMA, who would have voted with the Stark-GOP faction, was not on hand for the vote, and so Stark lost on a 7-7 tie. "Let it be noted," Stark informed those present, "that this is the first time Pete Stark has ever lost a vote because of the absence of the AMA." The observation broke up the room.

In the 98th Congress, as Select Revenue Measures chairman, Stark sought to turn his once-inactive panel into what he called "a center for tax revision and simplification," instead of "just a subcommittee that deals with miscellaneous 'cats and dogs.'" The panel conducted a major rewrite and simplification of tax laws dealing with insurance corporation profits.

The jurisdictional nature of the Select Revenue panel lent itself to smaller battles, and Stark managed to pick them effectively. When an angry constituent sent him a car dealer's ad showing how a $109,000 Rolls-Royce could create a $66,000 business tax write-off, Stark wrote a bill to deny tax breaks for luxury cars and airplanes; Congress ultimately did impose a limit on such tax write-offs, though not as much as he originally wanted.

However, some of the products of Stark's Select Revenue Measures Subcommittee drew criticism as special-interest legislation. One would have provided tax deductions for business conventions held on U.S.-owned cruise ships. Stark said this would simply treat the ships like hotels on the mainland. One of the four ships holding such conventions operates off the Northern California coast.

Some House members may still remember Stark for his quixotic 1975 effort to join the Black Caucus. Stark argued that although he was white, his constituency and personal sympathies made him eligible. The caucus said it had to "respectfully decline" the request.

Others may recall Stark's participation in an early movement to draft Sen. Edward M. Kennedy to run against President Jimmy Carter in 1980. Stark was one of a group of four House Democrats — led by Richard Nolan of Minnesota and including Edward P. Beard of Rhode Island and Richard L. Ottinger of New York — to press publicly in 1979 for Kennedy's candidacy. Stark was also a leader in the "open convention" drive against Carter after the primaries. One open-convention meeting was held at his home.

At Home: When Stark put an eight-foot-high neon peace symbol atop his bank in conservative Walnut Creek, people knew he was no ordinary banker. Ordinary California bankers did not protest the war in Vietnam or join the consumer movement. But Stark, who left Wisconsin to go to business school in California, relished his role as a maverick banker. And having founded his second bank at age 31, he had the money to play it.

Stark made his first political move in 1969, running for the state Senate. He finished third, losing the nomination to George Miller, now his colleague in the California delegation representing the 7th District.

Three years later, Stark decided to take on another George Miller — the crusty old conservative Democrat who had represented Oakland in Congress for 28 years. Stark spent his money generously and used one of the state's top political consultants to convince the voters that they did not "have to settle for the 81-year-old Congressman George P. Miller anymore," as a campaign brochure put it. Miller's support for the Vietnam War was a major issue. Stark swept him aside easily, winning by 11,000 votes.

Only once since then has Stark had a close call. Lulled by years of easy re-election, he prepared for only a token effort in 1980. But conservative Republican William J. Kennedy, a tireless campaigner, galvanized a host of volunteers to back his challenge. Helped by Ronald Reagan's surprisingly strong showing in the district, Kennedy held Stark to 55 percent.

Kennedy never stopped running after that. He kept his campaign office open, and used his credentials from the 1980 contest to persuade donors and national GOP officials to support him more extensively in 1982.

But Stark was ready this time. He kept a high profile in the district, holding frequent meetings with constituents, and took advantage of the area's rising unemployment to woo back Democrats who had turned out for Reagan two years earlier. After it was discovered that Kennedy had misrepresented his personal background, telling audiences he had voted for a 1978 tax-cutting measure when he had not even been registered to vote, Stark's victory was sealed. He took 61 percent.

Two years later, the only candidate Republicans could find to put up against Stark was an octogenarian former aircraft inspector who had legally changed his name to J. T. Eager Beaver. In 1988, the sacrificial lamb was a 25-year-old tax accountant who managed just 1 percentage point better than Beaver.

Committees

District of Columbia (3rd of 8 Democrats)
Government Operations and Metropolitan Affairs; Judicary and Education

Select Narcotics Abuse and Control (3rd of 18 Democrats)

Ways and Means (5th of 23 Democrats)
Health (chairman); Select Revenue Measures

Joint Economic
Economic Growth, Trade and Taxes; Fiscal and Monetary Policy; Investment, Jobs and Prices

Elections

1988 General

Pete Stark (D)	152,866	(73%)
Howard Hertz (R)	56,656	(27%)

1986 General

Pete Stark (D)	113,490	(70%)
David M. Williams (R)	49,300	(30%)

Previous Winning Percentages: **1984** (70%) **1982** (61%) **1980** (55%) **1978** (65%) **1976** (71%) **1974** (71%) **1972** (53%)

District Vote For President

	1988	1984	1980	1976
D	124,278 (57%)	106,640 (49%)	75,624 (42%)	98,624 (55%)
R	91,519 (42%)	107,925 (50%)	82,449 (46%)	77,320 (44%)

Campaign Finance

	Receipts	Receipts from PACs	Expend-itures
1988			
Stark (D)	$504,708	$325,428 (64%)	$410,540
1986			
Stark (D)	$566,745	$355,263 (63%)	$533,314
Williams (R)	$63,326	$1,099 (2%)	$61,483

Key Votes

1987

Raise speed limit to 65 mph	#
Approve Gephardt "fair trade" amendment	N
Ban testing of larger nuclear weapons	Y
Delay "re-flagging" of Kuwaiti tankers	Y
Approve tax-raising deficit-reduction bill	N

1988

Approve aid to Nicaraguan contras	N
Enact civil rights restoration bill over Reagan veto	Y
Kill 60-day plant-closing notification measure	N
Pass omnibus trade bill over Reagan veto	Y
Approve death penalty for drug-related murders	?
Bar federal funds for abortions in cases of rape and incest	?
Oppose seven-day waiting period for purchase of handguns	?

Voting Studies

	Presidential Support		Party Unity		Conservative Coalition	
Year	**S**	**O**	**S**	**O**	**S**	**O**
1988	15	67	78	5	5	68
1987	12	81	86	4	2	88
1986	18	77	86	4	4	92
1985	18	73	89	3	2	91
1984	25	56	78	4	3	83
1983	21	72	83	7	12	83
1982	23	64	85	4	5	88
1981	29	64	84	8	11	83

Interest Group Ratings

Year	ADA	ACU	AFL-CIO	CCUS
1988	90	0	85	42
1987	96	13	88	20
1986	95	5	77	12
1985	90	11	94	14
1984	90	0	77	25
1983	90	9	93	26
1982	95	0	100	11
1981	95	13	87	11

10 Don Edwards (D)

Of San Jose — Elected 1962

Born: Jan. 6, 1915, San Jose, Calif.

Education: Stanford U., A.B. 1936; graduate work, Stanford Law School, 1936-38.

Military Career: Navy, 1942-45.

Occupation: Title company executive; lawyer; FBI agent.

Family: Wife, Edith Wilkie; five children.

Religion: Unitarian.

Political Career: No previous office.

Capitol Office: 2307 Rayburn Bldg. 20515; 225-3072.

In Washington: The self-doubt that has afflicted many House liberals in recent years has not touched Edwards, who continues to push for social change with the same gentle passion he brought to the House more than a quarter-century ago. With him, there is no hesitation, no retrenchment. "We're absolutely right, you know," he has said.

For Edwards, liberalism means civil rights and civil liberties for everyone, including blacks, Mexican-Americans, women, children and dissenters of all kinds. He is a liberal first and a Democrat second; he has no qualms about opposing his party's leaders on what he considers a moral issue, such as Vietnam or the death penalty. Usually he has fought with restraint and bemused tolerance, although in the Reagan years Edwards was driven to frequent railing against his colleagues' "gutlessness" in the face of conservative initiatives.

For much of his career, Edwards' ardent liberalism left him outside the inner circle of House Democrats, a crusader rather than an operator. But he is not uncompromising. In fact, Edwards likes to play the facilitator, as long as he can remain true to his fundamental principles. In 1988, he shepherded into law two of the most far-reaching civil rights bills since the 1960s, a feat that required key concessions of him and his liberal followers.

Their grudging acceptance of an abortion provision cleared the way for enactment, over President Reagan's veto, of a law that not only overturned the Supreme Court's 1984 *Grove City* decision limiting the scope of four landmark civil rights laws, but also expanded those statutes. The contested abortion language specified that the law did not require hospitals to perform abortions, or colleges to provide health plans covering abortions, just because they receive federal funds.

When the year began, Edwards had declared his bill all but dead, blaming the "pressure of 'right-to-lifers.' " In doing so, however, he put pressure of his own on his allies in abortion rights' groups, forcing them to face the prospect of sacrificing the entire bill, including its protections against sex discrimination, for the third straight Congress. They decided not to stand in the way. By overwhelming margins, the House passed the measure and later overrode Reagan's veto.

Edwards turned next to an even longer-lived stalemate, a 20-year-old fight to put teeth in the 1968 fair-housing law. To appease the housing industry at the time, that law had left federal authorities virtually powerless to be anything more than mediators in discrimination disputes. Edwards wanted new administrative-law judges at the Department of Housing and Urban Development, empowered to levy fines and issue injunctions; Realtors and their Republican allies insisted on the option of a full jury trial.

After intense negotiations, including conference calls between civil rights advocates in Edwards' Capitol office and the Realtors' Chicago headquarters, a compromise was reached incorporating the housing representatives' demand for a trial option. The agreement, which Reagan belatedly endorsed, passed both the House and Senate overwhelmingly.

A third civil rights controversy, this one more than a decade old, also was resolved so that veterans could have "their day in court," as Edwards had long sought. Veterans' Affairs Committee Chairman G. V. "Sonny" Montgomery, who had repeatedly buried legislation to allow veterans to go to federal court to appeal Veterans Administration rulings, finally signaled that he was willing to talk, and the result was a law for a limited right of judicial appeal.

That issue engaged Edwards because it posed a question of constitutional rights. Typically, however, he is not active on Veterans' Affairs, choosing instead to spend his time in the Judiciary Committee, where he is chairman of the Civil and Constitutional Rights Subcommittee. He may not be the committee's intellectual light, but he is perhaps its conscience on the left.

He split with liberal ally Barney Frank of

California 10

Southeast Bay Area — Downtown San Jose; Fremont

Located at the southeastern end of the San Francisco Bay area, the 10th is split between Alameda and Santa Clara counties. It is the most industrial of the East Bay districts.

A large blue-collar Democratic base makes the 10th a safe haven for the pro-labor Edwards. But the district is not nearly as dependable for statewide Democrats. With the votes of conservative, mainly white industrial workers in Fremont, President Reagan narrowly carried the 10th in 1984. However, Michael S. Dukakis won many of those voters back for the Democrats in 1988, enabling him to carry the district by a comfortable margin.

The Alameda County part of the 10th accounts for just over a third of the district's population. It is centered on Fremont, an auto-building city of more than 155,000 that was once known as the Detroit of the West Coast. Today, its manufacturing has an international bent. General Motors Corp. has a joint venture with Toyota in Fremont; the plant turns out GM GEOs and Toyota Corollas.

Reagan's district victory in 1984 was largely the result of his 58 percent showing in Fremont. But in 1988, George Bush bested Dukakis in the city by only 500 votes.

The Santa Clara part of the district revolves around San Jose, which has jousted with San Francisco for the title of California's third-largest city. But the third of San Jose that is in the 10th, including its downtown area, faced a period of decline in the 1970s even as the rest of the city joined in the region's high-tech growth.

There are signs of revival in downtown San Jose, though. Several banks have moved in, and state and federal office buildings have brought more workers, restaurants and shops into the city. The construction of a light-rail system linking downtown with the northern suburbs and high-tech communities on the western edge of the Bay has also stimulated development.

The rest of San Jose in the district has a working-class and ethnic flavor. There is a sizable contingent of Hispanic-Americans, who make up more than a quarter of the 10th's population. Growing communities of Asian-Americans, many of whom have opened up restaurants, groceries and other retail ventures, are having an impact on the city as well.

Population: 525,882. White 355,926 (68%), Black 29,537 (6%), Asian and Pacific Islander 51,517 (10%), Other 4,855 (1%). Spanish origin 147,361 (28%). 18 and over 360,334 (69%), 65 and over 33,111 (6%). Median age: 27.

Massachusetts in the 100th Congress over Frank's ethics bill to limit lobbying by former lawmakers and senior staff, which Reagan ultimately vetoed. One of the few to oppose its passage, Edwards argued during floor debate, "Lobbying Congress and the executive branch is an activity protected by the First Amendment. Getting paid for it doesn't make it any less protected."

When other Judiciary Democrats balked at pushing legislation to repeal insurance companies' antitrust exemption, complaining that too little time remained in the 100th Congress to open such a controversy, Edwards lectured them: "It shows how powerful a monopoly is in this country when it can intimidate Democrats into saying, 'Well, we have to be careful.' We've taken on a Goliath here, and this is what we get paid to do."

The final days of recent Congresses have found Edwards futilely battling election-season tides for punitive anti-drug bills, pleading that various law-enforcement provisions are unconstitutional. He was one of just 30 Democrats to vote against the 1988 drug measure. "Drug legislation plus election-year posturing," he told colleagues, "equals an assault on the Constitution."

The 1988 drug bill marked a victory for death-penalty advocates after a decade-long effort. The best Edwards could do was chip at the provision, winning House approval of amendments to allow juries in capital-punishment cases to consider mitigating circumstances, and to bar executions of some mentally handicapped criminals.

On another occasion, Edwards' liberal call to arms had greater effect. At the start of the 99th Congress in 1985, an unusual coalition of liberals and conservatives ousted Les Aspin from the Armed Services Committee chairmanship, and was poised to elect in his place a popular Boll Weevil Democrat, Marvin Leath of Texas. But days before the second vote, Edwards and fellow liberal Matthew F. McHugh of New York circulated Leath's eight-year voting record, which showed, they wrote, that Leath "has made a career of voting against his party." The stop-Leath tactic worked; Aspin was re-elected by a small margin.

As a senior Democrat on Judiciary, Edwards has been well placed to help House

Democratic leaders bottle up conservatives' measures on volatile social issues, such as abortion, busing and school prayer. Only once, in 1979, did a House majority sign the necessary petition to wrest a measure from his subcommittee, a proposed anti-busing constitutional amendment. Edwards led the successful opposition on the floor. When criticized for being obstructive, he said, "Every member should use the rules any way he can."

Yet Republicans generally respect Edwards as fair and principled. Henry J. Hyde, a frequent GOP foe who is equally devoted to conservatism, has complimentary words about Edwards even after the wars of the Reagan years: "He's a gentleman, he's honorable, he's extremely able. He's courteous, he's bright, he's a pleasure to work with. He's not arrogant or overbearing. He doesn't abuse the power he has."

In the past, Republicans have cooperated with Edwards to move bills they oppose out of his subcommittee, trusting his word that they will have an opportunity to kill or amend the measures in the full committee or on the floor. That was true for the fair-housing bill and for legislation several years ago to extend the 1965 Voting Rights Act.

Passage of the voting rights bill was typical of Edwards' use of the civil rights community to mobilize support for his efforts. The main disputes were over "pre-clearance" — the requirement that Southern states submit election-law changes to the Justice Department — and over those states' demands that they be able to "bail out" of the law's strictures after a period of good behavior.

When Edwards failed to reach agreement with Hyde, the leading GOP spokesman on the issue, he turned to other Republicans, especially Hamilton Fish Jr. of New York. Hyde was annoyed, but more with his fellow Republicans than with Edwards; he ended up supporting the legislation as it cleared the floor easily. It became law in 1983.

Edwards' role as the House's self-appointed guardian of constitutional rights overlaps with another — overseer of the FBI, his one-time employer. He sheds light on the bureau's domestic-surveillance operations when he suspects abuses.

Infuriated that the FBI's Abscam anti-bribery sting may have amounted to entrapment of seven members of Congress, Edwards chaired a lengthy subcommittee investigation of the agency's undercover operations. Its 1984 report found "widespread deviation from avowed standards" resulting in "substantial harm to individuals and public institutions," and recommended advance judicial approval of undercover activities. More recently, he has used his subcommittee to probe both the FBI's two-year surveillance of citizens' groups opposed to U.S. military aid to Central America, and allegations of racism victimizing black and Hispanic agents. Edwards has stopped short of legislative remedies, based on his confidence in FBI Director William S. Sessions' promise of action.

Outside the civil rights arena, Edwards works on behalf of two industries important to California's economy: computers and movies. Also, he is dean of California's 27-member House Democratic delegation, coordinating strategy and information on issues of state interest. He is not the autocrat that the late Phillip Burton was in virtually controlling that large block of votes. Nor could Edwards be, even if he were personally inclined, given the presence in the group of such leaders in their own right as Henry A. Waxman and, up until mid-1989, Tony Coelho. "I want to run [the delegation] as a business," Edwards says.

At Home: Stories about Edwards inevitably emphasize his FBI background, citing it as rather unusual preparation for a career as a civil libertarian. Actually, Edwards was not only an FBI agent as a young man — he also was a Republican. He did not join the Democratic Party until he was 35, and on his way to a fortune as owner of the Valley Title Insurance Company in San Jose.

Wealth only seemed to make Edwards more liberal. He said he gave up on Republicans because they did not seem interested in the international agreements needed to preserve peace.

At the time, Edwards was beginning his long journey into activism. He joined the United World Federalists, the National Association for the Advancement of Colored People, the American Civil Liberties Union and the Americans for Democratic Action (ADA). He was national ADA chairman in 1965 and still speaks at the group's annual meetings.

Most people in Edwards' district seem to care little about the causes that have preoccupied him all his life. What matters to them is that he is a friendly, open man whose staff takes care of their problems. With that combination, Edwards has been able to overcome a long string of challengers, candidates who have questioned his patriotism and warned voters he is too liberal for them.

In 1988, the GOP did not lift a finger against Edwards; his only opponents were a Hispanic challenger in the primary and a Libertarian in the general election.

Edwards had never sought any office before 1962, devoting most of his time to his business. But when a new district was drawn that year to include part of his home city of San Jose, Edwards decided to run.

His two major opponents for the Democratic nomination both had more political experience, but less personal charm. They fought bitterly with each other and Edwards won the Democratic primary by 726 votes, edging Fremont Mayor John Stevenson. It was an overwhelmingly Democratic district, and Edwards easily won in the fall.

Edwards' outspoken support for Eugene J. McCarthy's presidential campaign, and early reports of his possible retirement, gave him a difficult time in 1968. He faced two Santa Clara city councilmen, one in the Democratic primary and one in the general election. But Edwards still won both elections comfortably.

He has had no trouble since then. In 1982 and 1984, Republican candidate Bob Herriott, an airline pilot from his party's conservative wing, received a substantial amount of funding from GOP sources, but was unable to make a dent in Edwards' standing.

Committees

Judiciary (3rd of 21 Democrats)
Civil and Constitutional Rights (chairman); Administrative Law and Governmental Relations; Economic and Commercial Law

Veterans' Affairs (2nd of 21 Democrats)
Oversight and Investigations

Elections

1988 General		
Don Edwards (D)	142,500	(86%)
Kennita Watson (LIB)	22,801	(14%)
1988 Primary		
Don Edwards (D)	48,276	(83%)
Anselmo A. Chavez (D)	9,863	(17%)
1986 General		
Don Edwards (D)	84,240	(71%)
Michael R. La Crone (R)	31,826	(27%)

Previous Winning Percentages: **1984** (62%) **1982** (63%) **1980** (62%) **1978** (67%) **1976** (72%) **1974** (77%) **1972** (72%) **1970** (69%) **1968** (57%) **1966** (63%) **1964** (70%) **1962** (66%)

District Vote For President

	1988	1984	1980	1976
D	101,702 (55%)	83,340 (48%)	57,017 (42%)	72,316 (59%)
R	80,515 (44%)	87,529 (51%)	61,367 (45%)	48,874 (40%)

Campaign Finance

	Receipts	Receipts from PACs	Expend-itures
1988			
Edwards (D)	$166,689	$117,256 (70%)	$173,537
1986			
Edwards (D)	$188,165	$112,625 (60%)	$156,410

Key Votes

1987	
Raise speed limit to 65 mph	N
Approve Gephardt "fair trade" amendment	Y
Ban testing of larger nuclear weapons	Y
Delay "re-flagging" of Kuwaiti tankers	Y
Approve tax-raising deficit-reduction bill	Y
1988	
Approve aid to Nicaraguan contras	N
Enact civil rights restoration bill over Reagan veto	Y
Kill 60-day plant-closing notification measure	N
Pass omnibus trade bill over Reagan veto	Y
Approve death penalty for drug-related murders	N
Bar federal funds for abortions in cases of rape and incest	N
Oppose seven-day waiting period for purchase of handguns	N

Voting Studies

	Presidential Support		Party Unity		Conservative Coalition	
Year	**S**	**O**	**S**	**O**	**S**	**O**
1988	18	80	94	3	5	87
1987	11	85	92	2	2	95
1986	16	84	95	3	4†	94†
1985	20	80	97	2	7	93
1984	24	75	94	5	2	98
1983	15	84	94	3	7	89
1982	27	68	93	7	5	93
1981	29	63	88	3	11	85

† Not eligible for all recorded votes.

Interest Group Ratings

Year	ADA	ACU	AFL-CIO	CCUS
1988	100	0	100	23
1987	100	0	100	0
1986	100	0	93	12
1985	100	0	100	18
1984	100	0	85	31
1983	100	0	100	20
1982	100	0	95	9
1981	95	0	93	12

11 Tom Lantos (D)

Of San Mateo — Elected 1980

Born: Feb. 1, 1928, Budapest, Hungary.
Education: U. of Washington, B.A. 1949, M.A. 1950; U. of California, Berkeley, Ph.D. 1953.
Occupation: Professor of economics.
Family: Wife, Annette Tillemann; two children.
Religion: Jewish.
Political Career: Millbrae Board of Education, 1958-66.
Capitol Office: 1526 Longworth Bldg. 20515; 225-3531.

In Washington: The traits Lantos exhibits in the House have been shaped by a lifetime of varied experience. Born in Hungary, Lantos has the civilized air of a man bred into prewar Central European culture, and the stubborn convictions of a fighter who spent his teenage years in the anti-Nazi resistance in Budapest. He carries himself with the intellectual self-assurance — some say arrogance — of a college professor, which is what he was for a time before running for Congress in 1980.

Lantos can thus provoke very different reactions from those who cross his path. Greeting witnesses in Foreign Affairs hearings with an elaborate Old World courtesy, Lantos can make his more informal colleagues seem crude. But others are annoyed by the condescending air he occasionally conveys, and by his thunderous denunciations of foreign totalitarianism, which can approach the realm of bombast.

Lantos makes no apologies for the boldness of his presentation, nor his certitude that he is right. Few members would be so self-assured as to take being called "ignorant" and "arrogant" as a compliment. But Lantos beamed when his efforts on behalf of Tibetan human rights provoked those insults from Chinese Premier Deng Xiaoping in 1987.

Lantos, co-chairman of the Congressional Human Rights Caucus, had invited Tibet's exiled Dalai Lama to address the group. The Tibetan political and spiritual leader accused the Chinese government of human rights abuses and suppression of Tibetan dissent. Lantos' criticism of harsh Chinese efforts to quell Tibetan rioting later spurred the rebuke from Deng. Undeterred, Lantos visited China in 1988 to press the human rights cause.

Lantos takes a similarly critical line toward the Soviet Union, using human rights as the springboard to assail that nation's totalitarian nature. A strong supporter of the Jewish "refuseniks" seeking to emigrate from the Soviet Union to Israel, Lantos has also taken on the cause of the so-called "captive nations," such as Latvia, which were absorbed by the U.S.S.R. during World War II.

But while Lantos has widely broadcast his distrust of the Soviet Union, he has not joined with those House conservatives who warn against rapprochement. In fact, Lantos for some time has suggested setting up a formal schedule of annual summit meetings between U.S. and Soviet leaders.

During much of 1987, Lantos acted as chairman of Foreign Affairs' Europe and the Middle East Subcommittee because senior Democrat Lee H. Hamilton of Indiana was preoccupied with the Iran-contra investigation. An enthusiastic supporter of Israel and a critic of U.S. overtures to Israel's Arab adversaries, Lantos held hearings at which he criticized the commitment of U.S. naval forces to protect Kuwaiti oil tankers in the Persian Gulf.

During the first Navy-guarded tanker convoy in July 1987, a "re-flagged" Kuwaiti ship was damaged by an Iranian mine. Five days later, Lantos told Assistant Secretary of State Richard W. Murphy that the incident proved the potential for embarrassment to the United States that was inherent in Reagan's policy. "None of us who opposed the re-flagging policy enjoy saying, 'I told you so'...," Lantos told Murphy. "[But] none of us expected to say, 'I told you so,' so soon."

In May 1989, Lantos led House efforts to deter the World Health Organization (WHO) from accepting a petition from the Palestine Liberation Organization (PLO) for admittance. Citing the WHO charter's requirement that members must be sovereign nations, Lantos argued, "Whatever the PLO is, it isn't a sovereign nation-state." His proposal to cut off aid to WHO if it admitted the PLO, which passed the House by a wide margin, contributed to the decision by a WHO assembly to defer action on the PLO request for at least a year.

The California Democrat strongly opposed funding for the Nicaraguan contras, yet he collegially greeted then-Lt. Col. Oliver L. North when he was called before the Foreign Affairs Committee in late 1986. Lantos declared his "respect, affection and admiration" for the staunchly anti-communist North and contrib-

California 11

Most of San Mateo County

The 11th District contains about 85 percent of the San Mateo County vote. But the 11th carefully skirts the most Republican areas of the county (located in the 12th District), which run down the middle of the San Mateo peninsula.

This cartography makes the 11th a Democratic stronghold. Michael S. Dukakis won it by a substantial margin in 1988; Democratic Senate candidate Leo T. McCarthy's strong showing here enabled him to carry San Mateo County as a whole. President Reagan did manage to carry the 11th in 1984, but with barely 50 percent of the vote.

The district reaches south from San Francisco, splitting into two distinct legs that straddle the San Mateo Mountains. Just below San Francisco is Daly City, a largely blue-collar suburb.

To the south are Pacifica, South San Francisco and San Bruno. A coastal, middle-class suburban town, Pacifica has drawn a number of teachers and other education professionals. South San Francisco is the home of Genentech, the gene-splicing firm.

The eastern leg of the 11th is tied together by 30 miles of the Bayshore Freeway. From Millbrae south to San Carlos are upper- and middle-class communities. All of them gave Reagan a majority in 1984, but many switched to Dukakis in 1988. At the southern end are East Palo Alto and the eastern part of Menlo Park, which are poorer.

The western leg is primarily mist, fog and a smattering of small communities tucked into the mountains or perched on bluffs overlooking the sea. Half Moon Bay, at the far western end of the 11th, is a small fishing and agricultural community.

Population: 525,981. White 401,311 (76%), Black 35,104 (7%), Asian and Pacific Islander 53,751 (10%), Other 2,396 (1%). Spanish origin 70,909 (14%). 18 and over 400,549 (76%), 65 and over 53,599 (10%). Median age: 32.

uted $250 to a fund that had been established to defray North's legal expenses.

Though Lantos is preoccupied with foreign policy issues, he also voices his opinions on domestic issues as a member of the Government Operations and Select Aging committees. The chairman of the Government Operations Subcommittee on Employment and Housing, Lantos expressed outrage during May 1989 hearings on the alleged use of the Section 8 housing-rehabilitation program during the Reagan years to benefit consultants and developers, including some former Reagan administration officials, who had strong ties to the Republican establishment.

"A system that allows an outrageously frivolous distribution of hundreds of millions of dollars on the basis of influence-peddling, rather than the desperate need of children and families in dire need of a roof over their heads, cannot and will not be tolerated," Lantos declared.

At Home: It took Lantos two difficult and expensive elections, but he seems to have settled securely into his district.

He was working on Capitol Hill as a consultant to the Senate Foreign Relations Committee when Republican Bill Royer won a 1979 special election to replace Democrat Leo J. Ryan, who had been assassinated the year before in Jonestown, Guyana.

Ryan's assassination brought out a host of Democrats who claimed to be his logical political heir, and by the time the primary was finished, the party was badly splintered. Royer picked his way through the Democratic debris to win the seat for the GOP.

But Lantos, who had been active in local Democratic affairs, left his job right after Royer's victory and began preparing a challenge for 1980. A one-time economics professor at San Francisco State University, he had held elective office only as a school board president in suburban Millbrae. But he had been active in Democratic affairs and had built up name recognition as a foreign affairs commentator for a Bay-area TV station. Since he had held himself apart from the 1979 feuding, he was able to unite his party around him for 1980.

Royer, who had been a city councilman and county supervisor for 23 years before moving on to Congress, went into the contest with a solid political foundation. He had tried to strengthen it over his term in office by taking a highly visible role in the investigation of the events surrounding Ryan's death.

By contrast, Lantos was less well-known, and his funding was limited. But Royer was overconfident, and Lantos was politically astute. In the final weeks, the Democrat filled the airwaves with advertising, while Royer, believing the election was his, yanked his own ads as an economy move. Royer ended up with a budget surplus, but a vote deficit.

It was obvious from the start that Royer would be back two years later, and Lantos began raising money early. With characteristic single-mindedness, he pursued it not only at home, but within Jewish communities in the districts of other members — a habit that led initially to some hard feelings among colleagues who felt they needed the money more than he. At election season he was among the best-funded House candidates in the country.

Royer spent most of his time arguing that Lantos' interest in foreign affairs had come at the district's expense. He compared Lantos' actions unfavorably with the local orientation of his own term in office.

But Lantos was able to counter by stressing his work on local issues such as offshore drilling. He also used more unusual tactics. When Royer adopted the slogan "He's One of Us," a possible reference to Lantos' immigrant background, Lantos aired a five-minute television biography that outlined his early life and resistance work, and stressed his accomplishments since coming to the United States. He won comfortably, and since then has had only nominal GOP opposition.

Committees

Foreign Affairs (10th of 28 Democrats)
Asian and Pacific Affairs; Europe and the Middle East; Human Rights and International Organizations

Government Operations (10th of 24 Democrats)
Employment and Housing (chairman); Government Activities and Transportation

Select Aging (15th of 39 Democrats)
Housing and Consumer Interests; Human Services

Elections

1988 General		
Tom Lantos (D)	145,484	(71%)
G. M. "Bill" Quraishi (R)	50,050	(24%)
1986 General		
Tom Lantos (D)	112,380	(74%)
G. M. "Bill" Quraishi (R)	39,315	(26%)

Previous Winning Percentages: 1984 (70%) **1982** (57%) **1980** (46%)

District Vote For President

	1988	1984	1980	1976
D	126,351 (58%)	109,053 (49%)	74,797 (39%)	84,047 (50%)
R	89,063 (40%)	112,986 (50%)	88,313 (46%)	83,265 (49%)

Campaign Finance

	Receipts	Receipts from PACs	Expend-itures
1988			
Lantos (D)	$386,453	$111,267 (29%)	$269,510
Quraishi (R)	$90,306	$8,100 (9%)	$95,575
1986			
Lantos (D)	$299,231	$58,850 (20%)	$325,435
Quraishi (R)	$69,374	$2,750 (4%)	$63,996

Key Votes

1987	
Raise speed limit to 65 mph	N
Approve Gephardt "fair trade" amendment	Y
Ban testing of larger nuclear weapons	Y
Delay "re-flagging" of Kuwaiti tankers	Y
Approve tax-raising deficit-reduction bill	Y
1988	
Approve aid to Nicaraguan contras	N
Enact civil rights restoration bill over Reagan veto	Y
Kill 60-day plant-closing notification measure	N
Pass omnibus trade bill over Reagan veto	Y
Approve death penalty for drug-related murders	Y
Bar federal funds for abortions in cases of rape and incest	N
Oppose seven-day waiting period for purchase of handguns	N

Voting Studies

	Presidential Support		Party Unity		Conservative Coalition	
Year	**S**	**O**	**S**	**O**	**S**	**O**
1988	27	71	89	6	42	55
1987	21	75	90	5	49	49
1986	23	76	89	5	40	60
1985	19	70	88	4	27	71
1984	27	69	83	4	14	81
1983	21	73	91	5	20	76
1982	31	57	87	4	29	66
1981	46	50	69	14	39	53

Interest Group Ratings

Year	ADA	ACU	AFL-CIO	CCUS
1988	85	8	100	31
1987	84	0	100	20
1986	70	18	100	31
1985	70	5	94	22
1984	85	5	100	43
1983	85	2	100	25
1982	80	10	89	11
1981	70	7	71	24

12 Tom Campbell (R)

Of Stanford — Elected 1988

Born: Aug. 14, 1952, Chicago, Ill.
Education: U. of Chicago, B.A., M.A. 1973, Ph.D. 1980; Harvard U., J.D. 1976.
Occupation: Economist; professor.
Family: Wife, Susanne Martin.
Religion: Roman Catholic.
Political Career: No previous office.
Capitol Office: 1730 Longworth Bldg. 20515; 225-5411.

The Path to Washington: Campbell was one of only seven challengers to defeat a House incumbent in 1988, and the only one to do so in a primary. But then he is an unusual freshman in a number of ways.

More than 40 members of Congress have degrees from Harvard, but Campbell has both a Harvard law degree and a doctorate in economics from the University of Chicago. And he had both before his 28th birthday.

People who spend their 20s in graduate schools rarely go on to Congress — a reflection both of their own sensibilities and those of the voters. But Campbell, who taught at Stanford, was elected in his first try for public office from a district where he had lived for just four years prior to declaring his candidacy. He himself says his career "would have been the most cockamamie way imaginable to get elected to Congress."

The transplanted Midwesterner is the son of a federal judge who had been a prosecutor of organized-crime figures in the Al Capone era. He has spent as much time in Washington as in his new district. As a law clerk for Supreme Court Justice Byron R. White, he met his wife, a District of Columbia native.

In 1980, he was back as a White House fellow, and he then held a series of jobs in the Reagan administration, including director of the Federal Trade Commission's Bureau of Competition.

When Campbell left government to teach at Stanford in 1983, the incumbent in the 12th was Ed Zschau. A high-tech entrepreneur and former business school professor, Zschau was the kind of moderate Republican long favored by the district's disproportionately wealthy and educated electorate.

But Zschau gave up the seat for a Senate campaign in 1986. He was succeeded by conservative Assemblyman Ernie Konnyu, who swept to the nomination after two Republican rivals who fit the district mold made late decisions not to run.

In office, Konnyu was seen as a right-wing firebrand. Campbell said he and others feared this would weaken the district's high-tech, tax and trade agenda. He said he had begun considering a challenge even before stories in *The San Jose Mercury-News* detailed Konnyu's staff turnover and accusations of boorish behavior toward women. Democrats were lining up to tackle Konnyu in 1988.

"I knew that if I didn't stand up and say a few things, I'd regret it the rest of my life," said Campbell, who added that he also wanted to identify the GOP with the enforcement of women's rights.

Campbell attracted far more attention and assistance than most challengers in the GOP. Zschau backed him, as did previous incumbent Paul N. McCloskey Jr., and former Deputy Secretary of Defense David Packard. Although the party officially supported Konnyu, Campbell was able to compete financially.

Konnyu initially ignored his opponent, dismissing him as a closet Democrat. But he later agreed to debate and eventually unleashed a tough negative campaign. With each change of Konnyu's tactics, Campbell seemed stronger — finally prevailing in the June primary with 58 percent.

In the fall, Campbell faced by far the most formidable Democratic nominee the district had seen in a generation. Anna G. Eshoo, a San Mateo County supervisor, had entered the race when Konnyu was the presumed nominee. But she was well organized and spent about $1 million, including $160,000 on a campaign video that was delivered door-to-door.

Campbell's spending exceeded Eshoo's, but he stressed the importance of "town hall" meetings and more than 400 precinct captains in securing his victory.

In the committee-assignment process at the start of the 101st Congress, one of Campbell's aims was to make it onto Science, Space and Technology, a traditional seat for his district. He got that, and a spot on Small Business as well.

California 12

Parts of San Mateo and Santa Clara Counties

Used primarily by Democratic cartographers as a "dumping ground" for Republican votes in the 1980s round of redistricting, the 12th is dominated by a variety of towns with little in common except affluence and Republican inclination. The 12th has the highest median real-estate values in California.

Yet moderate voting tendencies guide many of the district's affluent voters, including a number of young professionals employed in high-tech industries. Though Californian Ronald Reagan won comfortably here, George Bush barely held the district for the Republicans in 1988. And while moderate Ed Zschau was a popular House member in the 12th, his successor, conservative Ernie Konnyu, was not; GOP primary voters dumped him after one term for Campbell, a more centrist figure.

The district begins along the beach in San Mateo County and moves east across the hills to Hillsborough and Woodside, the wealthiest part of the Bay Area. Some residents commute to San Francisco by limousine.

But the heart of the 12th is in Santa Clara County, in the southern portion of the electronics and computer corridor known as Silicon Valley. Towns such as Los Altos, Los Altos Hills, Saratoga and Cupertino are home to such high-tech giants as Apple Computer, Hewlett-Packard and Ford Aerospace.

Palo Alto, the home of Stanford University, is a liberal bastion. The city of 56,000, which casts about 10 percent of the district vote, went for Democrat Michael S. Dukakis in 1988 by a 2-to-1 margin.

The 12th reaches into agricultural territory in southern Santa Clara County. Gilroy, which calls itself the "Garlic Capital of the World," is home to the yearly garlic festival. Morgan Hill has begun to see some housing spillover from Silicon Valley. To the east, the district holds a sliver of Santa Cruz County in the San Lorenzo Valley, taking in a chain of small Republican towns.

Population: 525,731. White 452,459 (86%), Black 9,033 (2%), Asian and Pacific Islander 34,163 (6%), Other 2,448 (1%). Spanish origin 51,848 (10%). 18 and over 397,900 (76%), 65 and over 48,834 (9%). Median age: 32.

Committees

Science, Space and Technology (19th of 19 Republicans)
Science, Research and Technology; Transportation, Aviation and Materials

Small Business (16th of 17 Republicans)
Antitrust, Impact of Deregulation and Privatization; SBA, the General Economy and Minority Enterprise Development

Campaign Finance

	Receipts	Receipts from PACs	Expend-itures
1988			
Campbell (R)	$1,445,770	$239,382 (17%)	$1,440,639
Eshoo (D)	$1,092,766	$422,547 (39%)	$1,089,570

Elections

1988 General		
Tom Campbell (R)	136,384	(52%)
Anna G. Eshoo (D)	121,523	(46%)
1988 Primary		
Tom Campbell (R)	41,867	(58%)
Ernie Konnyu (R)	30,162	(42%)

District Vote For President

	1988	1984	1980	1976
D	132,918 (49%)	108,069 (41%)	69,206 (31%)	76,856 (42%)
R	133,699 (49%)	148,724 (57%)	114,467 (51%)	102,809 (57%)

13 Norman Y. Mineta (D)

Of San Jose — Elected 1974

Born: Nov. 12, 1931, San Jose, Calif.
Education: U. of California, Berkeley, B.S. 1953.
Military Career: Army, 1953-56.
Occupation: Insurance executive.
Family: Separated; two children.
Religion: Methodist.
Political Career: San Jose City Council, 1967-71; mayor of San Jose, 1971-75.
Capitol Office: 2350 Rayburn Bldg. 20515; 225-2631.

In Washington: Mineta began his House career as president of the rebellious 1974 freshman class, and for the next decade he was a key player in House politics who appeared headed for a rung on the leadership ladder. But after he slipped in a weak campaign for majority whip in the 99th Congress, Mineta refocused. He retained his deputy whip's post, but directed more energy toward his legislative base, the Public Works Subcommittee on Aviation.

By the end of the 100th Congress, his transition from the leadership to the legislative ladder was complete. After two years as a high-profile specialist and watchdog of the troubled airline industry, Mineta gave up the chairmanship of Aviation for a more powerful subcommittee — Surface Transportation — in the 101st Congress. Now he has oversight of a far larger budget, and one that more directly serves his district.

Mineta's new post is one known for its locally oriented pork-barrel politics, but on Aviation, he tried to maintain a national perspective, opposing the naming of specific projects in airport bills. In 1987, Mineta steered through the House a $20 billion, five-year airport reauthorization bill that was not adorned with pet-project add-ons. Other House members (including Speaker Jim Wright) had submitted a wish list, but Mineta held fast.

Mineta also brings a keen interest in protecting labor rights to his new subcommittee. In the 100th Congress, he championed a measure requiring airline carriers to pay benefits to workers hurt by mergers. The "labor-protection" provisions (LPPs) cleared the House as part of the transportation appropriations bill, but a veto threat knocked them off the bill in conference.

Mineta advocated a consumer-protection bill that included the LPPs as well as provisions requiring airlines to make extensive public disclosures about flight delays and lost baggage. After both chambers passed legislation in 1987, the Department of Transportation issued rules requiring on-time disclosure. With that accomplished, the bill got bogged down in debate over the LPPs and random drug testing of transportation workers, which Mineta vigorously opposed.

During the 100th Congress, he also pushed legislation to provide protection for aviation "whistleblowers" who call safety violations to the attention of the federal government. While the measure cruised through the House with bipartisan support, it died in the Senate. Some suggested that Mineta's counterpart there, Aviation Subcommittee Chairman Wendell H. Ford of Kentucky, blocked the measure because he felt Mineta was foot-dragging on efforts to make the Federal Aviation Administration an independent agency. Mineta expressed concern that without the backing of the Department of Transportation, the FAA would lack the political clout to promote aviation needs.

Perhaps Mineta's most significant accomplishment during the 100th Congress, however, had nothing to do with aviation. He was a driving force behind passage of legislation to provide compensation for the Japanese-Americans interned by the U.S. government during World War II.

He described the internment as "an act born of racism," and the issue had topped his agenda for more than a decade. In 1978, he won passage of a bill to grant retirement benefits to interned Japanese-American civil servants. "Injustice does not dim with time," he said of the long wait for the 1987 bill.

Some 45 years earlier, Mineta and his family had been sent from their San Jose home to an internment camp in Wyoming, where they lived during the war. "Some say the internment was for our own good," he said. "But even as a boy of 10, I could see that the machine guns and the barbed wire faced inward."

When Congress passed legislation to provide a formal apology and $20,000 to each of the 60,000 surviving victims, Mineta signed the bill on behalf of the House.

Mineta got another high-profile job in the 100th Congress: heading the leadership-appointed task force on legislation requiring employers to grant job-protected leave to new

California 13

Santa Clara County — San Jose; Santa Clara

With its historic image as a working-class town and a market center for surrounding farm country, San Jose lived in the shadow of its more glamorous neighbor to the north, San Francisco. But with its explosive growth over the last four decades, San Jose has become San Francisco's equal in size: The two cities are neck-and-neck for the title of California's third-largest city, behind Los Angeles and San Diego.

San Jose's big burst began after World War II, with the sweep of suburbanization down both sides of San Francisco Bay, and was fueled by the high-tech growth in the "Silicon Valley." State officials estimate that San Jose — 50 miles south of San Francisco in Santa Clara County — has about 730,000 residents.

The 13th, a relatively compact district contained entirely within Santa Clara County, includes just under two-thirds of San Jose (though not the downtown area, which is in the 10th). It takes in the adjoining suburban communities of Santa Clara, Campbell and Los Gatos.

As canneries and fruit-packing firms have given way to high-tech in Silicon Valley, San Jose's white-collar population has grown accordingly. The part of San Jose in the 13th is considerably more Anglo than the heavily Hispanic western side in the 10th.

Most of the voters in the 13th are the type who normally would consider voting Republican. Mineta's personal popularity has made the district comfortably Democratic, but Michael S. Dukakis carried it in 1988 with barely 50 percent of the vote. Ronald Reagan won the 13th easily in 1980 and 1984.

When Democrats do win here, they usually benefit from a Democratic lean in Santa Clara. Many of the city's 89,000 residents work in the high-tech plants in Sunnyvale, located in the neighboring 12th District.

Population: 526,281. White 449,593 (85%), Black 11,881 (2%), Asian and Pacific Islander 33,182 (6%), Other 3,025 (1%). Spanish origin 61,057 (12%). 18 and over 380,270 (72%), 65 and over 35,614 (7%). Median age: 29.

parents and disabled workers. Backed by many leading Democrats and organized labor, the bill was strongly opposed by business interests, and election-year politics blocked its progress in the Senate.

Mineta's toughest legislative job in the 99th Congress involved the transfer of Dulles and National airports in suburban Virginia from federal ownership to control by a regional authority. Although the transfer had been recommended by various experts for more than 30 years, members of Congress balked at losing control of the airports they use to travel to and from their home districts.

To mollify numerous House critics, including some of the most powerful members, Mineta proposed leasing the airports for 50 years, rather than selling them, and creating a federal review board consisting of members of Congress to monitor the regional authority. That allowed a transfer bill to reach the House floor, and eventually to become law.

A member of the House Intelligence Committee from 1977 to 1984, Mineta was outspoken in his criticism of then-CIA Director William J. Casey for not informing Congress about certain agency activities. He was an early supporter of legislation to require advance congressional notice of covert intelligence activities.

Mineta also spent three terms on the Budget Committee, and when he rotated off the panel in 1983, he left behind a significant contribution: the concept of "credit accounting." The procedure created the first formal accounting of the money the federal government spends by guaranteeing private loans.

At Home: San Jose's Japanese-American community was the springboard to Mineta's political career. Running an insurance business with his father in the 1960s, he became active in the city's Japanese American Citizens League. That led him to San Jose's Human Relations Commission, its housing authority and City Council and to the mayoralty in 1971.

The San Jose area was coming out of a decade of unprecedented suburban growth during Mineta's years as mayor, and he allied himself with those calling for limits on further development.

In 1974, the 13th District came open. It had been represented for over two decades by GOP Rep. Charles Gubser, and had voted Republican in every election since World War II. Gubser's retirement gave Democrats an opportunity to take advantage of the demographic changes that had swept the area. Mineta, who had been extremely popular as mayor, had no trouble winning the Democratic primary.

His opponent in the general election was former state Rep. George W. Milias, who had lost an earlier primary for California secretary of state and gone on to work for the Defense

Department in the Nixon administration.

Challenged by more conservative opposition, Milias only squeaked through to the nomination.

Milias was able to pick up campaign funds that had been gathered earlier for Gubser, and worked hard to mend fences with GOP conservatives. But his service in the Nixon administration — despite his attempts to distance himself from Watergate — and his absence from the district in the years before the election hampered his effort. Mineta, by contrast, was immensely strong within San Jose itself, and well recognized in the county surrounding it. He slipped into office by 15,000 votes. Since then, he has never dropped below 58 percent of the vote, although his district no longer has a majority Democratic registration.

Committees

Public Works and Transportation (3rd of 31 Democrats)
Surface Transportation (chairman); Aviation; Investigations and Oversight

Science, Space and Technology (12th of 30 Democrats)
Science, Research and Technology; Space Science and Applications

Elections

1988 General		
Norman Y. Mineta (D)	143,980	(67%)
Luke Sommer (R)	63,959	(30%)
1986 General		
Norman Y. Mineta (D)	107,696	(70%)
Bob Nash (R)	46,754	(30%)

Previous Winning Percentages: **1984** (65%) **1982** (66%) **1980** (59%) **1978** (58%) **1976** (67%) **1974** (53%)

District Vote For President

	1988	1984	1980	1976
D	109,830 (49%)	89,789 (41%)	65,780 (34%)	79,060 (48%)
R	108,817 (49%)	126,585 (58%)	95,437 (50%)	83,744 (51%)

Campaign Finance

	Receipts	Receipts from PACs	Expend-itures
1988			
Mineta (D)	$577,164	$277,450 (48%)	$521,674
Sommer (R)	$26,756	0	$25,511
1986			
Mineta (D)	$546,210	$231,921 (42%)	$443,822
Nash (R)	$34,066	$315 (1%)	$33,297

Key Votes

1987	
Raise speed limit to 65 mph	N
Approve Gephardt "fair trade" amendment	Y
Ban testing of larger nuclear weapons	Y
Delay "re-flagging" of Kuwaiti tankers	Y
Approve tax-raising deficit-reduction bill	Y
1988	
Approve aid to Nicaraguan contras	N
Enact civil rights restoration bill over Reagan veto	Y
Kill 60-day plant-closing notification measure	N
Pass omnibus trade bill over Reagan veto	Y
Approve death penalty for drug-related murders	N
Bar federal funds for abortions in cases of rape and incest	N
Oppose seven-day waiting period for purchase of handguns	N

Voting Studies

	Presidential Support		Party Unity		Conservative Coalition	
Year	**S**	**O**	**S**	**O**	**S**	**O**
1988	20	78	92	2	11	89
1987	13 †	83 †	93 †	4 †	12 †	79 †
1986	22	76	95	5	20	80
1985	21	76	95	3	13	85
1984	26	74	97	1	3	97
1983	16	84	95	4	8	88
1982	40	60	91	8	32	67
1981	50	47	84	13	25	71

† Not eligible for all recorded votes.

Interest Group Ratings

Year	ADA	ACU	AFL-CIO	CCUS
1988	95	4	93	31
1987	92	0	100	7
1986	95	5	79	18
1985	80	5	94	18
1984	90	0	100	38
1983	95	0	100	20
1982	80	0	90	23
1981	80	0	93	32

14 Norman D. Shumway (R)

Of Stockton — Elected 1978

Born: July 28, 1934, Phoenix, Ariz.
Education: Stockton Junior College, A.A. 1954; U. of Utah, B.S. 1960; U. of California Hastings College of Law, J.D. 1963.
Occupation: Lawyer.
Family: Wife, Luana June Schow; six children.
Religion: Mormon.
Political Career: San Joaquin County supervisor, 1975-79.
Capitol Office: 1203 Longworth Bldg. 20515; 225-2511.

In Washington: During his years in the House, the reserved, business-oriented Shumway has often preferred to express himself on national issues in writing rather than in speeches. Conservative journals such as *Human Events, Conservative Digest* and *The Washington Times* have been among those publishing his views.

But this is not to say that Shumway can't get his point across when he chooses to speak.

A primary sponsor of legislation that would make English the official language of the United States, Shumway employed his linguistic skills at a congressional hearing on the measure in the 100th Congress. The California Republican, who speaks fluent Japanese (learned in his days as a Mormon missionary in Japan), began his testimony to the panel in Japanese — hoping to impress upon uncomprehending colleagues the problems faced by immigrants to the United States who do not speak English fluently.

Shumway most often surfaces as a reliable spokesman for business and banking interests on the Banking Subcommittee on Economic Stabilization, where he is the ranking Republican.

This position and a pressing parochial concern have given Shumway a considerable stake in the congressional debate over bailing out the troubled savings and loan industry. The nation's largest thrift — American Savings and Loan — is based in Stockton, Shumway's home. The troubled institution was purchased in 1988 by the wealthy Bass brothers of Texas. During negotiations to save the failing S&L, Stockton's largest employer, Shumway made it clear it was important to him that the institution "remain, intact, in Stockton." It did.

In keeping with his pro-business principles, Shumway has had little sympathy for the recent work place-related initiatives of the House Democratic leadership — dramatically raising the minimum wage, requiring employers to give prior notification of plant closings and instituting mandatory parental-leave policies. He opposed the final version of the welfare reform bill, because in his mind the "workfare" provisions were inadequate. And he has consistently objected to funding for the Legal Services Corporation, claiming that it has "a scandalous record of using tax dollars for advocacy programs."

An outspoken supporter of free trade, Shumway warns that protectionist moves by the United States will provoke retaliation from U.S. trading partners. Shumway's stake in the unimpeded flow of goods is plain: Stockton is California's largest inland shipping port; its ship channel near the San Joaquin and Calaveras rivers gives it access to San Francisco Bay.

The presence of the channel also explains why Shumway, whose district is mainly a heavily forested and farmed area in northeastern California, is the ranking Republican on the Merchant Marine Subcommittee on Oceanography. From that post, Shumway pushed for completion of a project to deepen the ship channel, and he also lobbied for reopening a Coast Guard station at Lake Tahoe that had been closed for lack of funding.

As a member of the Select Committee on Aging, Shumway supported reauthorization of the Older Americans Act in the 100th Congress, and he also has proposed legislation to repeal the outside earnings limitations on Social Security recipients. But he strongly opposed the catastrophic health insurance legislation passed in 1988, calling it "catastrophic taxation and a cruel hoax on the elderly."

Another piece of legislation that brought a similarly strong reaction from Shumway was the Civil Rights Restoration Act of 1988. He called it "runner-up for the worst bill of the Congress after catastrophic coverage" and voted to sustain the president's veto of the measure.

California 14

Northeastern California — Part of San Joaquin County

The 14th is California's most rural district, a long stretch of farm land, mountains, forests and lakes. It reaches 300 miles south from the Oregon border to San Joaquin County in the heart of California's Central Valley.

The district's rural nature gives it a Republican coloration. Ronald Reagan and George Bush swept all the district's counties in the presidential elections of the 1980s. Republican Sen. Pete Wilson similarly dominated the 14th in 1988, as did GOP Gov. George Deukmejian in 1986.

The district is bottom-heavy, with San Joaquin County (part of which is in the 18th) providing a third of its vote. Stockton, an important inland port as well as a marketing center for the surrounding farm country, has been growing: Its population jumped by nearly 23 percent, to 183,000, between 1980 and 1986.

The rich delta lands of San Joaquin County raise asparagus, avocados, walnuts, artichokes, peaches and apricots. Some of this produce is processed and packaged in Lodi, a city of 44,000 that anchors the northern part of the county.

Just to the north are Amador and El Dorado counties, once the core of California's Gold Rush country. It was at Sutter's Sawmill, at what is now Coloma in El Dorado County, that gold was discovered in 1848, sparking the rise of numerous boom towns. Placerville, El Dorado's county seat, at one time rivaled San Francisco and Sacramento.

The boom ended long ago, and the towns faded. But some have recently revived, as refugees from the cities and suburbs, attracted by the Victorian houses and natural setting, moved in. Placerville's population jumped by about 15 percent in the early 1980s. There is also a thriving recreational industry in the Lake Tahoe-Squaw Valley region near the Nevada border. Also in the area is Alpine County which, with 1,300 residents, is by far the state's smallest.

Closer to Oregon, the counties are heavily forested and sparsely populated, given over largely to lumbering. Much of the land is in the national forest system.

Population: 526,030. White 476,228 (91%), Black 6,731 (1%), Other 18,546 (4%). Spanish origin 46,968 (9%). 18 and over 381,713 (73%), 65 and over 58,543 (11%). Median age: 32.

Environmental issues sometimes reveal a streak of moderation in Shumway's record. He voted to override President Reagan's veto of the Clean Water Act and supported efforts to clean up ocean pollution.

Given Shumway's appreciation for the Japanese culture, some were surprised by his opposition in the 100th Congress to a measure that provided compensation to Japanese-Americans detained in U.S. internment camps during World War II. In a *Los Angeles Times* article, Shumway said he opposed the legislation because "it would establish a dangerous precedent in assessing the actions of the past by standards of the present.... Perhaps worst of all, the measure threatens to revive anti-Japanese sentiment."

At Home: Shumway had an aggressive 1988 challenger in Patricia Malberg of Lincoln. But she could only manage to lower his plateau of victory to 63 percent. That was about the level he had enjoyed in his first two re-election campaigns, before climbing over 70 percent in 1984 and 1986.

Shumway's strait-laced style was a major asset in his first campaign for Congress in 1978, when he defeated 11-term Democratic Rep. John J. McFall, the former majority whip.

Less than a month before the general election, the House had voted to reprimand McFall for taking $3,000 from South Korean rice merchant Tongsun Park. Shumway only indirectly mentioned McFall's involvement in "Koreagate," letting the extensive news coverage of the story do most of his work. But by emphasizing his own moral rectitude, Shumway was able to capitalize on McFall's troubles.

Shumway told voters that the 60-year-old McFall had served too long and was not "as alert or energetic as he used to be." Favoring a 12-year limit on House service, Shumway said McFall had overstayed his welcome. When the 101st Congress concludes, Shumway will have served 12 years. He has not indicated whether he will retire.

Shumway became involved in elective politics in 1974, when then-Gov. Ronald Reagan appointed him to the San Joaquin County Board of Supervisors. By 1978, he was chairman of the board and had established enough name recognition to win a seven-candidate GOP congressional primary. More than half the Republican primary vote was cast in his home county, where he won a 5,000-vote margin over his nearest competitor.

After the primary, Shumway received money and help from the national GOP and was able to match McFall dollar for dollar. He invested heavily in television advertising.

Shumway's victory was impressive. McFall carried San Joaquin County, but with only 49 percent of the vote. Two years earlier the veteran Democrat had taken 75 percent there. In the rest of the district, the incumbent received scarcely more than a third of the vote, as Shumway attracted the support of longtime McFall supporters in the agricultural areas.

By 1982, Shumway's style was giving his supporters some concern. Redistricting had given him a huge chunk of unfamiliar territory, most of it in mountain counties where people were comfortable with their previous representative, down-home Republican Gene Chappie.

"The question is, can a good Mormon join the Clampers and win re-election?" one of Shumway's colleagues told the *Sacramento Bee,* referring to a boisterous, hard-drinking crowd, now Shumway's constituents.

Democratic hopes of cashing in on the personality mismatch never bore fruit, however. Their nominee, former Roseville Mayor Baron Reed, pulled in the backing of traditional Democratic interest groups, but made few converts elsewhere. Shumway's free-spending campaign easily prevailed.

In 1984, the Democratic primary produced a somewhat more colorful challenger. Democrat Ruth Carlson, a retired journalist, told reporters FBI agents were tapping her telephone, and announced she was campaigning against "thought control." Then she was arrested on charges of drunken driving in August after leading police on a high-speed chase. The publicity contributed to Shumway's best showing yet. In 1986, he did nearly as well, again surpassing 70 percent of the vote.

Committees

Banking, Finance and Urban Affairs (3rd of 20 Republicans)
Economic Stabilization (ranking); Financial Institutions Supervision, Regulation and Insurance; International Development, Finance, Trade and Monetary Policy

Merchant Marine and Fisheries (4th of 17 Republicans)
Oceanography (ranking); Coast Guard and Navigation; Merchant Marine

Select Aging (4th of 27 Republicans)
Human Services; Retirement Income and Employment

Elections

1988 General		
Norman D. Shumway (R)	173,876	(63%)
Patricia Malberg (D)	103,899	(37%)
1986 General		
Norman D. Shumway (R)	146,906	(72%)
Bill Steele (D)	53,597	(26%)

Previous Winning Percentages: 1984 (73%) **1982** (63%) **1980** (61%) **1978** (53%)

District Vote For President

	1988	1984	1980	1976
D	111,570 (40%)	86,619 (34%)	61,102 (31%)	56,518 (48%)
R	165,850 (59%)	162,239 (64%)	112,499 (58%)	60,700 (51%)

Campaign Finance

	Receipts	Receipts from PACs	Expend-itures
1988			
Shumway (R)	$390,233	$151,635 (39%)	$492,349
Malberg (D)	$112,633	$13,146 (12%)	$103,678
1986			
Shumway (R)	$323,671	$139,565 (43%)	$257,431

Key Votes

1987	
Raise speed limit to 65 mph	Y
Approve Gephardt "fair trade" amendment	N
Ban testing of larger nuclear weapons	N
Delay "re-flagging" of Kuwaiti tankers	N
Approve tax-raising deficit-reduction bill	N
1988	
Approve aid to Nicaraguan contras	Y
Enact civil rights restoration bill over Reagan veto	N
Kill 60-day plant-closing notification measure	Y
Pass omnibus trade bill over Reagan veto	N
Approve death penalty for drug-related murders	Y
Bar federal funds for abortions in cases of rape and incest	Y
Oppose seven-day waiting period for purchase of handguns	Y

Voting Studies

	Presidential Support		Party Unity		Conservative Coalition	
Year	**S**	**O**	**S**	**O**	**S**	**O**
1988	83	14	79	20	92	5
1987	79	21	84	15	88	9
1986	86	14	82	16	90	8
1985	79	18	88	9	91	5
1984	74	25	94	6	90	10
1983	82	11	90	2	90	2
1982	78	16	93	2	89	4
1981	83	16	92	7	95	4

Interest Group Ratings

Year	ADA	ACU	AFL-CIO	CCUS
1988	0	100	0	92
1987	4	96	6	100
1986	0	95	7	94
1985	15	95	12	91
1984	0	100	8	81
1983	0	100	0	85
1982	0	100	0	85
1981	5	100	13	94

15 No Incumbent

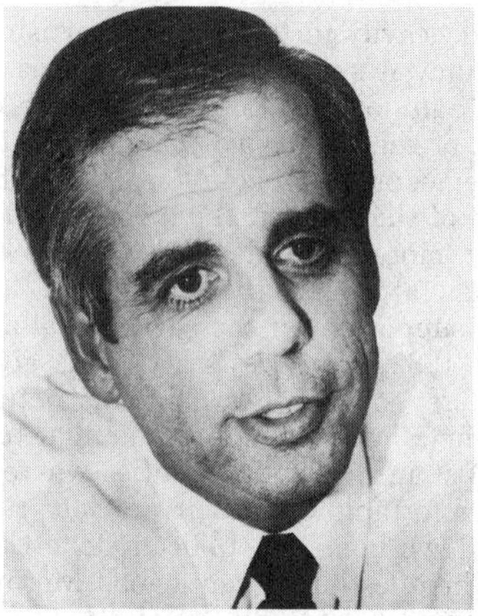

Tony Coelho
House Service: 1979-89

Coelho's spectacular rise from chief party fund-raiser to the No. 3 House Democratic leader after only four terms in Congress was emblematic of a decade in which the pursuit of campaign money became the sine qua non of political strategy.

His fall was just as spectacular. In the face of questions about his personal finances — and amid growing criticism of the world of political money he helped create — Coelho stunned his colleagues in May 1989 by declaring that he would step down as majority whip and resign his House seat the following month, on his 47th birthday, rather than face a protracted ethics investigation.

Reports about a controversial "junk bond" investment of Coelho's had surfaced just as the yearlong controversy over Jim Wright's finances was about to force him from the speakership. Coelho, who had been expected to move up to majority leader in the ensuing leadership shake-up, was clearly in line to be the next target of ethics scrutiny and Republican attack.

"I don't intend to put my party through more turmoil," he said in his resignation statement, given in an exclusive interview with *The New York Times*. "I don't intend to put this institution through more turmoil. And most importantly, I don't intend to put my family through more turmoil."

Coelho insisted he had done no wrong in the junk bond deal, but acknowledged that the transaction was not accurately reported on his financial-disclosure form or on his tax return — an inaccuracy that could have lowered his tax liability.

Coelho had borrowed $100,000 to invest in bonds underwritten by the investment firm of Drexel Burnham Lambert Inc. in 1986. It took weeks for Coelho to arrange the financing; in the meantime, the bonds were bought for Coelho by an executive of the California savings and loan that lent him half the money.

Controversy surrounding the transaction tapped into an uneasiness some Democratic members felt about Coelho — a concern that this man who moved so boldly in the realm of money and political power was sometimes reckless about the means chosen to pursue his ends.

He set fund-raising records as chairman of the Democratic Congressional Campaign Committee, but in the process, he encouraged a coziness between Democrats and monied interests that made some party members uncomfortable. He was one of the Democrats' most brilliant political strategists, but winning elections, not crafting a party philosophy, was his priority.

In mid-1987, it was disclosed Coelho had accepted free use of a yacht owned by a Texas thrift institution for a series of fund-raisers while he was DCCC chairman. That controversy died down after Coelho and the DCCC reimbursed the thrift.

Toward the end of the Wright affair, Coelho drew fire for comments he made in defense of a top Wright aide, John P. Mack, a close friend of Coelho who was forced to resign amid new publicity about a violent crime the aide had committed as a youth.

By the time the junk bond controversy surfaced, it was clear that Coelho's promotion to leader would not go unchallenged.

Coelho's resignation marked an abrupt end to an accomplished 27-month term as majority whip. He had run the whip's organization, like the DCCC, with a determination bordering on religious fervor and a tactical agility reminiscent of the Jesuit order he once hoped to join.

Coelho was a natural for the whip's job: He was a living encyclopedia of information about House members, their districts and their political needs. His strategic skills helped hone the whip's office into a highly centralized organization that controlled votes even in a body of diffuse power.

But to become a working part of the leadership team, Coelho had to overcome some of the suspicion and resentment engendered by his obvious ambition. He himself fueled a sense of rivalry with Thomas S. Foley of Washington, who was elected majority leader when Coelho became whip in late 1986, by telling more than one associate he did not want to wait 10 years to become Speaker.

Despite those tensions, the two men complemented each other well: Coelho, the partisan par excellence, was a good foil for Foley, the consensus-builder.

California 15

Mid-San Joaquin Valley — Modesto

The level, fertile fields of the 15th District connect two major farm centers of the San Joaquin Valley — Modesto in the north and Fresno in the south.

The farmers of the valley have a Democratic heritage spawned in the Oklahoma Dust Bowl era and brought west to California more than a generation ago. In early 1989, voter registration in the 15th stood at 55 percent Democratic, 36 percent Republican.

But even as Coelho won re-election comfortably through the 1980s, the national Democratic Party was not doing so well in the 15th. It voted for Ronald Reagan for president in 1980 and 1984, and George Bush won the district 52-47 percent over Michael S. Dukakis in 1988.

At the northern end of the district are the 133,000 residents of Modesto. The largest city wholly within the district, Modesto is most often remembered for its restless teenagers in the movie "American Graffiti" and for its winery run by the Gallo Brothers. In the 1980s, the city become home for an increasing number of San Francisco Bay-area exurbanites; they helped boost Modesto's population by nearly 25 percent in the early 1980s.

The city has long been a processing and canning center for the crops flowing in from the surrounding fields. Although hard economic times in the early 1980s closed down some of the plants in the city, the opening of two tomato processing plants in nearby Los Banos compensated for much of the loss.

More than 100 miles south along Highway 99 is Fresno. Though the city is almost entirely outside the 15th, it is the major media center for the southern part of the district. The 15th curves around the city from the south and takes in its outskirts on three sides.

Between Fresno and Modesto, the district is sparsely settled. Merced, with 47,000 people, is the only other major city. The influx of Hmong refugees from Laos into the Central Valley has put something of a strain on Merced's services. But with the city's population now about one-fifth Hmong, it has also enjoyed a cultural flowering of Southeast Asian restaurants and craft fairs.

The rest of the 15th's population is scattered throughout the irrigated farm land, where more than 200 different commodities are grown. Besides large concentrations of agribusiness, the district is dotted with smaller dairy farms and vineyards. As in some other parts of the country, successive years of drought have caused problems for farmers. In addition to suffering lower crop yields, the agricultural sector has had to pay higher utility costs because of the need to pump water from increasingly drier wells. Grape growers have also been buffeted by imports of European wines and raisins.

After Coelho's June 15 resignation, Gov. George Deukmejian set a primary to replace him for Sept. 12, with a single ballot listing all candidates. If none exceeds 50 percent of the vote, each major party's top finisher will compete in a Nov. 7 runoff election.

Population: 525,949. White 425,244 (81%), Black 11,779 (2%), Other 16,082 (3%). Spanish origin 127,576 (24%). 18 and over 361,570 (69%), 65 and over 53,130 (10%). Median age: 28.

Coelho was regarded by younger members as their link to the leadership. He won favor with many by working hard, though ultimately without success, to secure for members a 51 percent pay raise in early 1989. Coelho tried to convince members that they could support a pay raise without political risk — particularly if it were linked to a ban on honoraria. But that judgment was not borne out in the vitriolic public reaction that killed the pay increase.

When Coelho was chosen whip in 1986 — the first time Democrats' No. 3 leader was elected and not appointed — almost half the Democratic Caucus still outranked him in seniority.

He easily defeated two rivals in the final balloting — Charles B. Rangel of New York and W. G. "Bill" Hefner of North Carolina. Three other contenders had seen their task as hopeless and dropped out long before the voting took place.

Coelho had anticipated years in advance the series of leadership vacancies generated by Speaker Thomas P. O'Neill Jr.'s retirement and entered the whip's race as the front-runner. He never came close to losing that status.

He sought commitments in an unflagging "eyeball-to-eyeball" campaign that typified his political approach: Touch base with everyone, early and often.

The real foundations of Coelho's support were the political IOUs he collected and wide contacts he established as chairman of the Democratic Congressional Campaign Committee from 1981-86. One-third of the Democrats had been elected during his tenure as DCCC chairman. For many young members, Coelho was among the first House colleagues they met; for all House Democrats, he was the man who signed the campaign checks.

Coelho did not just use the DCCC job to position himself as one of his party's leading political spokesmen; he transformed the committee from an inert cash drawer for incumbents into a state-of-the-art campaign organization that redirected the giving patterns of political action committees (PACs).

He had his work cut out for him when he began. Republicans had picked up 33 House seats in the 1980 Democratic debacle and were confidently predicting at least a 26-seat gain the next time around, enough to give the GOP a House majority. In organizational and financial resources, the two parties were in different leagues entirely. House Republicans had access to millions of dollars and a well-staffed campaign committee; Coelho's DCCC had a handful of staff members and was $300,000 in debt.

Coelho's predecessor, James C. Corman of California, had been too preoccupied with his own re-election (which he lost in 1980) to do much with his post. Coelho turned it into a full-time political position. He targeted weak Democratic incumbents for help and looked hard for vulnerable Republicans. He hired more staff and built a sophisticated radio and television center where candidates could produce ads at discount rates.

Most important, Coelho raised money. In his first two years as campaign chairman, the committee brought in $6 million, far less than the GOP but four times its total in previous election cycles. In the 1983-84 cycle, it raised another $11 million, sinking about a fifth of it directly into campaigns and topping it off with such indirect contributions as polling and mailing lists. By 1985-86, it was up to $15 million.

All of this was greatly appreciated by Democrats, but Coelho did generate some misgivings with his vigorous pursuit of money and support from business groups that normally had concentrated their money on the Republican side.

After the 1982 elections, he got into a well-publicized argument with the U.S. Chamber of Commerce over its down-the-line endorsements of Republican candidates. The fight led the Chamber to reassess its policies; in 1984, it backed more Democrats.

Coelho told other PACs in no uncertain terms that they could not expect warmth and friendliness from incumbent House Democrats if they insisted on investing money in candidates trying to defeat them. As a result, many PACs were less generous to GOP challengers in 1984 and 1986 than they had been in 1980, when 28 incumbent Democrats were defeated.

Some of his party's liberal element were less than happy with Coelho's methods, especially those that resulted in some dependence on independent oil producers and defense contractors. Critics point to the Democrats' 1981 tax-cut proposal — with its breaks for oil and other industries — as proof that Coelho's pursuit of business funds had forced the party too close to corporate interests. Common Cause, the self-styled citizens' lobby, accused Coelho early in 1985 of soliciting campaign contributions from commodity traders in exchange for Democratic backing of legislation protecting their tax status. This drew a sharp denial from the DCCC.

Whatever Democrats thought of Coelho's tactics, they clearly produced results at the polls. In the 1982 elections, Coelho's work combined with recession and Democratic redistricting skill to give the Democrats an additional 26 seats in the House. Two years later, at a time when President Reagan's coattails might have wiped out those gains, Democrats held their losses to 14 seats. By the time Coelho left the DCCC, Republicans were bitterly complaining that business PACs were donating too much to Democrats and giving a cold shoulder to Republican challengers.

In Democratic circles, meanwhile, Coelho took a prominent role in the group of "new ideas" Democrats trying to move the party toward the center. Along with Richard A. Gephardt of Missouri, he spent much of 1984 leading junior House members in private discussions of how to steer the Democratic Party away from liberal and labor pressure groups toward an effective pursuit of middle-class voters. Those discussions caused both men some problems late in the year when it was reported that some of the participants had included replacing O'Neill and Majority Leader Jim Wright as goals for change.

But in Coelho's case, at least, the damage seemed short-term. Neither Wright in his campaign for Speaker in 1987 nor Coelho in his bid for whip had any reason to want to alienate the other.

Coelho's political importance helped him in legislative affairs, if only because fellow Democrats were wary of crossing the man who controlled the purse strings for the campaign committee. But it was hard to find instances of Coelho using his power in an overbearing manner; he preferred a softer touch.

Though he was generally a liberal Democrat in arguments over national politics, Coelho was somewhat different as a member of the Agriculture and Interior committees. He leaned toward the development side and was a strong partisan of the agribusiness interests in his district. He was a member of Agriculture's Dairy Subcommittee and for two years its chairman, overseeing the industry he grew up with. Coelho was raised on his family's dairy farm in the San Joaquin Valley.

Coelho's other major non-political interest also had deep personal meaning: An epileptic, he has spent considerable time and energy raising money and promoting public understanding of the disease that changed the entire course of his life.

Coelho did not learn he had epilepsy, the result of an accident when he was a teenager, until after college, when he was preparing to enter a Jesuit seminary. The disease derailed his seminary plans, since canon law barred epileptics from becoming priests. After a long period of depression, Coelho landed a job in the congressional office of California Rep. B. F. Sisk, the Democrat who became his mentor, and discovered he had a natural talent at politics. Soon he was training to become Sisk's eventual successor.

By the time Sisk was ready to retire in 1978, he knew he wanted his young aide to take over. Coelho had spent so much time in the district as a surrogate for Sisk that he had established his own ties with the district's political leaders. Only one Democrat, Vincent Lavery, dared to challenge the Sisk/Coelho forces in the 1978 primary, and Coelho rolled to nomination with four-fifths of the vote.

Against anyone but Coelho, Republican Chris Patterakis might have stood a chance of winning that November. A former stunt pilot with the Air Force Thunderbird team, Patterakis was a local hero in Modesto, where he was called a "Greek Joe Namath." Modesto was the only town he carried.

Republicans thought they had Coelho in some trouble in 1982, when he was embroiled in controversy over a letter to a local judge in which he asked leniency for the son of a longtime friend and supporter, who was accused of committing a highly publicized murder. They also thought they had the right candidate in retired Sheriff Ed Bates, a law-and-order conservative.

Eager to keep the Democrats' leading congressional fund-raiser penned in at home, the GOP tried to bring in money and Republican celebrities. But Bates was never able to establish himself on any issue other than Coelho's letter, and his impact on that score was softened by Coelho's own energetic campaigning. The result was not even close.

Coelho's three subsequent re-elections were all 2-to-1 victories over the same GOP nominee, Mariposa rancher Carol Harner. In his final re-election, he won 70-28 percent.

District Vote For President

	1988	1984	1980	1976
D	82,799 (47%)	70,069 (40%)	58,104 (41%)	63,302 (52%)
R	92,471 (52%)	101,657 (59%)	69,712 (49%)	55,963 (46%)

16 Leon E. Panetta (D)

Of Carmel Valley — Elected 1976

Born: June 28, 1938, Monterey, Calif.
Education: U. of Santa Clara, B.A. 1960, J.D. 1963.
Military Career: Army, 1963-65.
Occupation: Lawyer.
Family: Wife, Sylvia Marie Varni; three children.
Religion: Roman Catholic.
Political Career: No previous office.
Capitol Office: 339 Cannon Bldg. 20515; 225-2861.

In Washington: With the 101st Congress, Panetta finally assumed the leadership post for which he had been training since arriving in the House a dozen years earlier — chairman of the Budget Committee. Yet well before he had the title, Panetta held unofficial rank as the House's top fiscal authority.

In recent years he had occasionally wondered aloud, with a characteristic boyish laugh, why he would be crazy enough to want the job, given the nation's huge debt and many pressing needs. Yet for all his self-effacement, he knows well that all policy and politics these days spin on the imperative of deficit reduction; the Budget chairmanship puts him at the center of congressional and Democratic Party action, just where he wants to be. "Through the budget," he once said, "you are making a statement about where the nation is at, and where you want it to go."

His knowledge of arcane fiscal details and the bewildering budget-making process are unsurpassed in either house. What information Panetta does not carry in his head is tucked under his arm, within a bulging file that is a constant companion as he stalks the Capitol corridors amid empty-handed colleagues who leave the files and the details to aides.

While Panetta has more expertise than his predecessor, Rep. William H. Gray III of Pennsylvania, the question is whether he has similar political skills. Seeming guileless and unflappable, he has cultivated a reputation as a consensus-builder. But the Budget Committee is inevitably Congress' most partisan panel, where Democrats and Republicans joust for a fiscal plan that most reflects their fundamentally different domestic and defense priorities. With one notable exception, Panetta, a former Republican, is neither known for partisanship nor comfortable with it.

He took the chair just as Democratic congressional leaders were joined at the negotiating table by a new and professedly more conciliatory Republican president. For the 101st Congress, then, Panetta has a lead role in balancing Democrats' interests in reaching accords with Bush against their desires to hold him politically accountable for his campaign pledges of deficit reduction, no new taxes and increased domestic spending.

Panetta began by praising Bush's choice for budget director, Richard G. Darman, as a signal the president was ready to deal. But then he dismissed the first Bush budget, which proposed major cuts without specifying where reductions would come, as "a potential trap" that "left the tough choices to Congress." He insisted that Bush and Darman supply the politically painful details before Democrats would negotiate.

The two sides talked for nine weeks. In April the negotiators arrived at a compromise budget that met the law's $100 billion deficit target — mainly by resorting to accounting gimmicks, rosy economic assumptions and unspecified taxes. The agreement drew much criticism, but most members were not in a mood to fight. With rare speed and bipartisanship, Panetta and Senate Budget Committee Chairman Jim Sasser moved the compromise through both houses and a conference by mid-May.

Moderate-to-liberal generally, on budget questions Panetta is typical of the fiscally conservative Democrats elected since the late 1970s. "The most important question we in government have to face is, do you have resources to address the legitimate needs in society? Our first challenge is to begin to restore the resources," he said just before becoming chairman. "I see the need — people are hurting." But without a lower deficit, he added, "I don't know how to respond to it."

During his first stint on Budget, for six years until 1985, Panetta was a voice for deficit-conscious junior Democrats. That year he was a favorite to win the chairmanship, but his bid snagged on House Democratic rules and leadership politics.

Up against a three-term limit for Budget members, Panetta responded with an ambitious campaign not only to stay on the panel, but also to wrest the chair from conservative James R. Jones of Oklahoma, who also had reached the limit and wanted another term. While most

California 16

Central Coast — Salinas; Monterey

The 16th District follows the scenic highway, state Route 1, for 150 miles along the California coast. Tourism brings in much of the income in the coastal areas. As the district moves inland, agriculture is the major trade.

The 16th takes in San Benito County and part of San Luis Obispo County. But the population is centered in Monterey and Santa Cruz counties, where 80 percent of the district vote is cast.

Panetta has come to dominate through the entire district, easily sweeping all four counties in recent elections. Presidential contests are more competitive. President Reagan carried the district with 53 percent of the vote in 1984. Four years later, George Bush carried three of the four counties included in the district. However, Democrat Michael S. Dukakis' overwhelming margin in liberal Santa Cruz County enabled him to carry the 16th easily.

The county's Democratic tone is set by its namesake city, the site of a University of California campus. The student vote in Santa Cruz (population 46,000) is complemented by the city's long-lived countercultural community, a laid-back throwback to the 1960s.

Santa Cruz is located at the northern end of Monterey Bay. Moving south, the district picks up some more conservative territory, including Castroville — the artichoke capital of the world — and Fort Ord, a major military base that employs a large civilian work force.

Exclusive Monterey Peninsula has drawn liberal Democrats and upper-income Republicans. A little farther south is Big Sur, another gathering spot for the mellow. But life in the 16th District is not all fun and games. The vagaries of the coastal fishing industry were depicted by John Steinbeck in "Cannery Row."

Inland, lettuce fields and almond groves make agriculture king. Salinas, the Monterey County seat and the district's largest city with 97,000 residents, leans Republican for president, but not dramatically so: Bush won the city in 1988 by only 134 votes.

Population: 526,120. White 401,920 (76%), Black 20,897 (4%), Asian and Pacific Islander 26,169 (5%), Other 4,793 (1%). Spanish origin 115,776 (22%). 18 and over 391,002 (74%), 65 and over 58,955 (11%). Median age: 29.1

attention focused on the Jones-Panetta contest and the controversial rules change they proposed, Gray quietly built support for his own ultimately successful candidacy.

Panetta was also foiled by timing. At that moment, he was suspect within the leadership circle because of his close ties to Richard A. Gephardt of Missouri and Tony Coelho of California, who were believed to have considered challenges to Speaker Thomas P. O'Neill Jr., Majority Leader Jim Wright, or both. The coup talk quickly evaporated, but Wright and O'Neill were determined to demonstrate their influence. They joined forces with Gray and the Black Caucus to oppose the rules change. It was defeated, and Panetta's bid with it, by a close vote.

He did not retreat. Over the next four years, he remained prominent in budget debates and did so largely as a sort of institutional minister-without-portfolio for House leaders, indicating that whatever favor he had lost with them had been restored.

In late 1985, he was a key House bargainer with the Senate and President Reagan in negotiating what became the Gramm-Rudman-Hollings budget-balancing law. Two years later, he helped draft the budget-summit agreement between Reagan and Congress that raised taxes and cut spending in both fiscal 1988 and 1989.

By that time, in late 1987, Panetta was the uncontested heir apparent to succeed Gray, although it was more than a year before House Democrats would vote. Two would-be rivals, liberal David R. Obey of Wisconsin and conservative Marvin Leath of Texas, had dropped their own bids after they plumbed and discovered the depth of Panetta's support.

His standing in the House is even more remarkable considering the low-visibility committee assignments he otherwise holds. He is a senior member of the Agriculture Committee, which is important to the farming and processing industries in his district, and of the House Administration Committee, the institution's housekeeping arm.

In the 100th Congress, as chairman of the House Administration Subcommittee on Personnel, Panetta won House approval of rules extending civil rights laws to House employees. The action, limited as it was, is considered a first step toward eventual coverage of all congressional staff under other labor-protection laws governing wages, hours and conditions. "Discrimination is just as wrong inside the Congress as outside," he told the House.

On Agriculture, he helped shape the five-year 1985 farm bill and, in 1986, a landmark immigration law. Representing California growers traditionally dependent on illegal alien workers, Panetta worked arduously with fellow

Californian Howard L. Berman and New Yorker Charles E. Schumer to craft an immigration law providing for a continued flow of unskilled workers while protecting those laborers against abuse. Since then, the sponsors have cooperated to monitor and fine-tune the law's implementation.

Wearing both his Budget and Agriculture hats, Panetta reacted skeptically to Bush's initial budget for fiscal 1990, with its proposed $3.2 billion in agriculture cuts. Throughout the 101st Congress, however, the subsidies on which farmers in California and elsewhere rely are likely to be targeted as members try both to reduce the deficit and to draft a new farm bill.

As former chairman of Agriculture's Subcommittee on Domestic Marketing, Consumer Relations and Nutrition, Panetta was the principal architect of provisions in both the 1985 farm bill and the 1988 welfare-overhaul law expanding eligibility and benefit levels for the food stamp program. He has tried generally to make domestic and foreign food-aid programs less bureaucratic and more responsive to the poor.

His bipartisan work on the nutrition and food stamp provisions of the 1985 farm bill helped Panetta begin restoring his credibility with Republicans, which had been badly damaged during a bitterly partisan dispute over a 1984 Indiana House race.

Democratic leaders, unwilling to seat Republican Richard D. McIntyre despite his apparent victory over Democratic incumbent Frank McCloskey, appointed Panetta to head a recount committee. It was an impossible spot with no chance of bipartisan solution. The panel ruled McCloskey the victor by four votes, contrary to Panetta's expectations. Nevertheless, Republicans aimed their fire at him; a task force member accused him of political "rape" and other Republicans questioned his integrity on the House floor. Perhaps the only consolation for Panetta was that the episode dispelled any lingering doubts among fellow Democrats about his party loyalty.

Panetta has been a Democrat for nearly two decades now, since shortly after he was dismissed from the Nixon administration's Office of Civil Rights for complaining about its slow desegregation efforts. Yet he is not so different from the liberal Republican he once was. His mix of liberal social policy and fiscal conservatism would easily meet the approval of his political hero, California's former Republican governor and later U.S. Chief Justice Earl Warren, whose autographed picture hangs on Panetta's office wall.

He is also active on environmental issues, and during the Reagan years led the fight to protect California's coastal waters from oil and gas drilling. He has long espoused a national youth service and conservation corps. On defense and foreign policy, Panetta's views mesh easily with other House Democrats.

An opponent of the Reagan administration's military aid for the Nicaraguan contras, Panetta sponsored House resolutions in 1986 and 1988 calling for inquiries into how funds were spent. The first probe found millions of dollars unaccounted for; Panetta withdrew the 1988 resolution when federal officials satisfied him that aid was being spent according to law. Three years before, Panetta had been one of the first members of Congress to suggest publicly that White House aide Lt. Col. Oliver L. North was illegally providing aid to the contras — more than a year before the Iran-contra scandal broke.

At Home: Panetta's centrist politics and a healthy degree of attention to his constituents have proved to be a formidable combination. Since he took 53 percent of the vote in ousting Republican incumbent Burt Talcott in 1976, Panetta has made his seat a safe one.

Although Panetta had been close to politics all his adult life — as an aide to GOP Sen. Thomas Kuchel, then with HEW, and later as an adviser to New York City Mayor John V. Lindsay — he had never run for public office until 1976.

By that time, Talcott had been in Washington for 14 years. In the previous two elections a Hispanic candidate, Julian Camacho, had whittled Talcott's margin down to just 2,000 votes, making the incumbent a prime target for Democrats in 1976. Camacho opted against a third try that year, allowing Panetta to battle two other Democrats for the party's nomination.

Panetta was attacked for being a latecomer to the Democratic Party. But his most active primary opponent, John R. Bakalian, had serious problems of his own. He was viewed outside liberal Santa Cruz as being a bit too unconventional for the district's tastes. Bakalian wanted to impeach President Gerald R. Ford for allowing Secretary of State Henry A. Kissinger to threaten an invasion of Cuba.

Although Bakalian carried Santa Cruz County, Panetta won the nomination with a strong showing in Monterey. In the general election, Panetta kept Talcott on the defensive, saying the incumbent had little to show for his years in Congress. Stressing his roots in the Monterey area, Panetta narrowly defeated Talcott there, and beat him more decisively in Santa Cruz and San Luis Obispo counties, running far ahead of the Democratic ticket.

Although by 1982 Panetta was entrenched in his district, his re-election contest that year briefly drew the national spotlight. His opponent was far-right Republican Gary Richard Arnold, who came to the public's attention when he heckled President Reagan at a White House meeting for GOP congressional candidates. In the general election, Panetta won 84 percent.

Since then, against less flamboyant Republican opposition, he has continued to run far ahead of the district's Democratic registration.

Just before the 98th Congress began, Panetta angered colleagues both in California and in Washington by jeopardizing the congressional remap Democrats had drawn up for the 1984 elections. The plan had to pass the state Legislature by the end of a special session in December 1982 if it was to be signed into law by Gov. Edmund G. Brown Jr. before he relinquished control to his Republican replacement.

But Panetta was upset by the removal of the northern section of Santa Cruz County from his district and argued that the county should not be split. He prevailed upon the state senator from the area, Democrat Henry Mello, to try to amend the map; Mello's work in the Senate to accommodate Panetta helped hold up passage of the bill until the 11th hour.

Committees

Budget (Chairman)

Agriculture (6th of 27 Democrats)
Department Operations, Research and Foreign Agriculture; Domestic Marketing, Consumer Relations and Nutrition; Forests, Family Farms and Energy

House Administration (4th of 13 Democrats)
Elections; Personnel and Police

Select Hunger (3rd of 18 Democrats)
Task Force: Domestic

Elections

1988 General		
Leon E. Panetta (D)	177,452	(79%)
Stanley Monteith (R)	48,375	(21%)
1988 Primary		
Leon E. Panetta (D)	76,452	(95%)
Arthur V. Dunn (D)	4,027	(5%)
1986 General		
Leon E. Panetta (D)	128,151	(78%)
Louis Darrigo (R)	31,386	(19%)

Previous Winning Percentages: **1984** (71%) **1982** (84%) **1980** (71%) **1978** (61%) **1976** (53%)

District Vote For President

	1988	1984	1980	1976
D	122,419 (54%)	98,292 (46%)	64,688 (36%)	75,713 (50%)
R	100,293 (44%)	111,375 (53%)	87,820 (49%)	73,818 (49%)

Campaign Finance

	Receipts	Receipts from PACs	Expend-itures
1988			
Panetta (D)	$318,076	$112,600 (35%)	$252,336
Monteith (R)	$71,035	0	$69,563
1986			
Panetta (D)	$166,791	$78,875 (47%)	$115,446
Darrigo (R)	$9,437	$2,156 (23%)	$9,557

Key Votes

1987	
Raise speed limit to 65 mph	Y
Approve Gephardt "fair trade" amendment	Y
Ban testing of larger nuclear weapons	Y
Delay "re-flagging" of Kuwaiti tankers	Y
Approve tax-raising deficit-reduction bill	Y
1988	
Approve aid to Nicaraguan contras	N
Enact civil rights restoration bill over Reagan veto	Y
Kill 60-day plant-closing notification measure	N
Pass omnibus trade bill over Reagan veto	Y
Approve death penalty for drug-related murders	Y
Bar federal funds for abortions in cases of rape and incest	N
Oppose seven-day waiting period for purchase of handguns	N

Voting Studies

	Presidential Support		Party Unity		Conservative Coalition	
Year	**S**	**O**	**S**	**O**	**S**	**O**
1988	22	75	90	6	18	76
1987	16	81	91	4	21	79
1986	20	77	87	9	30	66
1985	20	79	88 †	8 †	25	71
1984	31	66	86	14	25	75
1983	20	79	85 †	10 †	21	78
1982	42	55	86	14	36	63
1981	50	50	78	22	45	55

† Not eligible for all recorded votes.

Interest Group Ratings

Year	ADA	ACU	AFL-CIO	CCUS
1988	90	4	93	33
1987	92	0	87	20
1986	85	11	85	31
1985	75	14	71	32
1984	75	8	54	50
1983	90	9	82	30
1982	75	5	90	18
1981	90	20	80	16

17 Charles "Chip" Pashayan Jr. (R)

Of Fresno — Elected 1978

Born: March 27, 1941, Fresno, Calif.
Education: Pomona College, B.A. 1963; U. of California Hastings Law School, J.D. 1968; Oxford U., England, B.Litt. 1977.
Military Career: Army, 1968-70.
Occupation: Lawyer.
Family: Separated.
Religion: First Congregational Church.
Political Career: No previous office.
Capitol Office: 203 Cannon Bldg. 20515; 225-3341.

In Washington: During a decade on the Interior Committee, Pashayan was a specialist on water policy and a man who argued frequently against anyone trying to threaten the interests of the big agribusiness concerns that are vital to his district's economy. In the 101st Congress, he moves up to a committee he has wanted for some time — Rules — where his lawyerly skills in technical and procedural debate can be fully employed.

But in the early months of 1989, Pashayan was receiving more attention for his role on another committee — Standards of Official Conduct. He played an active role in the investigation of Speaker Jim Wright of Texas, sitting in on more depositions of witnesses than almost any other member of the ethics panel.

Early in the year, a conservative newsletter ran an item that said Pashayan intended to vote with the panel's Democrats, which would give them a one-vote majority and bipartisan exoneration of Wright. Two conservative groups launched an unusual letter-writing campaign pressing the Republican to support strong sanctions against the Speaker.

When these pressure tactics gained media attention, Pashayan circulated a "Dear Colleague" letter in which he said, "I have not and shall not allow political expediency or convenience to affect my judgment." In the end, the unanimous GOP bloc, together with two Democrats, voted in declaring that there was sufficient evidence to charge Wright with numerous violations.

The ethics committee flap occurred just weeks after Pashayan got some unseemly press on a personal matter. Days after the 1988 election, his wife filed for divorce, complaining that Pashayan struck her and once locked her in a room for several hours. Pashayan denied her charges.

Until these episodes, Pashayan had been known primarily for his cigar smoke, his skill at chess and his vigilant protection of his district's needs in debates on water legislation. In the 100th Congress, he was the ranking GOP member of the Interior Committee's Water and Power Resources Subcommittee.

Pashayan's Central Valley district is dominated by large-scale agricultural operations, and he diligently guards their access to cheap water. This at times puts him at odds with the majority of his party. "The genius of our system is that there is some federal involvement in our economy without nationalization," he said in a 1987 newspaper interview. "I am a conservative, not a right-winger. My approach is to see what works and what doesn't."

In the 100th Congress, the Interior Committee struck a deal that satisfied his basic conservative instincts, while still bringing low-cost water to his district. In an effort led by California Democrats George Miller, the ranking Democrat on Interior, and Mel Levine, Pashayan contributed to an innovative agreement to line the earthen portions of the All-American Canal with waterproof material. That step would save enough water to settle a water-rights claim by the San Luis Rey Indians and make the endeavor profitable for the local water district that will finance the lining.

In the past, however, Pashayan's relations with his Democratic colleagues were not always so cooperative. In his first two terms, Democrats on the Interior Committee unsuccessfully sought to place a cap on the number of acres a farmer could own or lease and remain eligible to receive federally subsidized water. Pashayan harshly criticized the effort, calling the 1,600-acre cap "a step backward to feudalism."

Pashayan also frequently clashed with his central California neighbor and Interior Committee colleague, Democrat Tony Coelho. But in the 100th Congress, the two came together on a bill to slow the spread of the Mediterranean fruit fly, a universal California enemy. Pashayan was one of two original cosponsors to Coelho's successful bill to ban interstate mailing of restricted plants.

California 17

Southern San Joaquin Valley

The 17th is the food basket of the nation's most agriculturally productive state. Driving the length of the district from Fresno in the north to Bakersfield in the south, a traveler encounters fields of virtually every kind of fruit and vegetable grown in the Temperate Zone.

Though the district abuts both Fresno and Bakersfield, the majority of the population lives in smaller communities, including farm centers like Tulare and Visalia, with fewer than 65,000 people, and dusty crossroads towns like Pixley and Lemoncove.

The irrigated farm land stretches almost to the eastern border of the district, where the Sierra Nevada Mountains climb steeply into Sequoia National Park. The mountains attract some recreational dollars into the district, but in minuscule amounts compared with the valley's farm income.

Though there is a rural Democratic tradition among some of those whose livelihoods depend on the farm economy, more often than not, they vote Republican. George Bush easily triumphed here in 1988. In Tulare County — which competes with Fresno County for the largest share of the district vote — Bush took 60 percent of the vote.

Bush was only continuing a firmly established pattern in favor of Republican presidential candidates. Ronald Reagan carried the district in both 1980 and 1984, taking 63 percent of the vote in the latter campaign.

The only major statewide Democrat to win the 17th in recent years was Edmund G. Brown Jr. when he was running for governor. As a Senate candidate here in 1982, even Brown was demolished, winning less than 40 percent of the vote.

Population: 526,033. White 392,665 (75%), Black 10,974 (2%), Other 20,245 (4%). Spanish origin 146,304 (28%). 18 and over 356,229 (68%), 65 and over 50,303 (10%). Median age: 28.

Though he was never a strong Reagan loyalist, Pashayan opposed the president more often than he supported him in 1988. On key votes, the Californian broke with Reagan on two important civil rights issues. Pashayan voted to override the president's veto of the Civil Rights Restoration Act and voted to preserve language banning housing discrimination against families with young children. Pashayan also parted with a majority of House Republicans in voting for legislation to provide compensation for Japanese-Americans interned during World War II.

As the only member of Congress of direct Armenian descent and as the representative of a district hosting a significant Armenian population, Pashayan plays a public role in speaking for Armenian-American interests. In the last two Congresses, he worked unsuccessfully to gain official government recognition of the Turkish slaughter of Armenians at the close of World War I. His effort to secure passage in the 99th and 100th Congresses of a resolution commemorating this event failed in the face of lobbying campaigns by the Turkish-American community.

In 1988, soon after the Armenian earthquake, Pashayan's constituent-service operation was able to help two Armenian-American doctors from California get passports and join the first American relief plane.

At Home: Pashayan's sometimes prickly personality and discomfort mixing with ordinary voters are handicaps in one of the few California districts where a politician can still make an impression by campaigning at truck stops, county fairs and small-town coffee shops. But Democrats have had trouble recruiting opponents able to match either Pashayan's money or his access to the agribusiness community.

In 1986, Pashayan faced a relatively significant challenger in John Hartnett, a former aide to neighboring Democratic Rep. Richard H. Lehman. Pashayan was seen as livening his public persona in that race, with considerable help from his wife, 15 years his junior, whom he had married the year before. Pashayan comfortably defeated Hartnett.

Pashayan's original interest in politics grew out of five years in Washington working for the Pentagon and the old Department of Health, Education and Welfare. Having seen how the federal government operated, Pashayan returned to California wanting to curb "the growing threat of an uncontrolled federal bureaucracy" by running for Congress.

At the time, most observers thought Democratic Rep. John Krebs was in good political shape: He had won his second term in 1976 with 66 percent. But Pashayan turned out to be a candidate with good financing and a series of effective issues. Over two terms Krebs had gradually alienated many of his supporters. Some viewed him as self-righteous; others thought he was vindictive. His vote against common-site picketing and his environmental objections to the development of a year-round resort at Mineral King in the Sierras had cost him important allies in organized labor.

By contrast, Pashayan had the valuable help of the district's "mega-farmers" and the loyal backing of the small but influential Armenian community in Fresno, where his family's tire business was already well-known. Outspending Krebs by more than $100,000, Pashayan put on a sophisticated television campaign and won by 13,000 votes.

Although Democrats had hopes of recapturing the seat in 1980, Pashayan quickly put that idea to rest. An easygoing 62-year-old farmer and Fresno County supervisor, Willard "Bill" Johnson, spent a year trying to convince voters Pashayan was a "do-nothing" legislator whose only strength was raising money.

Pashayan's fund-raising talents were beyond question, as he amassed and spent nearly a half-million dollars to Johnson's $75,000. But the other part of Johnson's argument made little impression on the voters, and Pashayan overwhelmed him by more than 75,000 votes.

In 1982, with 54 percent registered as Democrats in his newly altered district, Pashayan had a tougher time. His opponent was Kern County Supervisor Gene Tackett, a well-connected Democrat whose political allies included brother-in-law Ira Reiner, the influential Los Angeles County district attorney.

Unemployment in the area was rising, and Tackett attracted support from labor and portions of the building trades industry angered by Pashayan's vote to sustain President Reagan's veto of a mortgage-subsidy bill. (Pashayan had voted for the bill initially.) But he kept his base among the 17th's influential agribusiness groups, and his spending advantage enabled him to shore up his support in the small farm communities of southern Tulare County, where neither he nor Tackett was known.

Tackett managed a last-minute flurry of advertising that helped him hold Pashayan's margin within 12,000 votes — his smallest ever.

Committees

Rules (4th of 4 Republicans)
Legislative Process; Rules of the House

Standards of Official Conduct (3rd of 6 Republicans)

Elections

1988 General

Charles "Chip" Pashayan Jr. (R)	129,568	(71%)
Vincent Lavery (D)	51,730	(29%)

1986 General

Charles "Chip" Pashayan Jr. (R)	88,787	(60%)
John Hartnett (D)	58,682	(40%)

Previous Winning Percentages: 1984 (72%) **1982** (54%) **1980** (71%) **1978** (55%)

District Vote For President

	1988	1984	1980	1976
D	76,021 (40%)	65,892 (36%)	52,927 (36%)	52,327 (46%)
R	111,250 (59%)	116,975 (63%)	84,025 (57%)	61,548 (54%)

Campaign Finance

	Receipts	Receipts from PACs	Expend-itures
1988			
Pashayan (R)	$216,479	$117,170 (54%)	$206,677
Lavery (D)	$5,867	$1,000 (17%)	$5,227
1986			
Pashayan (R)	$307,169	$105,931 (34%)	$304,194
Hartnett (D)	$233,877	$89,675 (38%)	$228,592

Key Votes

1987	
Raise speed limit to 65 mph	Y
Approve Gephardt "fair trade" amendment	N
Ban testing of larger nuclear weapons	N
Delay "re-flagging" of Kuwaiti tankers	N
Approve tax-raising deficit-reduction bill	N
1988	
Approve aid to Nicaraguan contras	Y
Enact civil rights restoration bill over Reagan veto	Y
Kill 60-day plant-closing notification measure	Y
Pass omnibus trade bill over Reagan veto	N
Approve death penalty for drug-related murders	Y
Bar federal funds for abortions in cases of rape and incest	Y
Oppose seven-day waiting period for purchase of handguns	Y

Voting Studies

	Presidential Support		Party Unity		Conservative Coalition	
Year	S	O	S	O	S	O
1988	46	49	73	25	68	24
1987	56	43	69	27	88	9
1986	58	40	62	33	84	12
1985	59	33	75	18	84	15
1984	57	36	80	12	88	10
1983	73	21	77	9	85	4
1982	71	22	82	14	81	14
1981	68	13	75	13	75	5

Interest Group Ratings

Year	ADA	ACU	AFL-CIO	CCUS
1988	35	64	71	57
1987	24	59	44	73
1986	25	64	77	56
1985	5	80	19	85
1984	10	74	31	88
1983	0	100	6	82
1982	15	77	30	76
1981	5	100	15	94

18 Richard H. Lehman (D)

Of Fresno — Elected 1982

Born: July 20, 1948, Sanger, Calif.

Education: Attended Fresno City College, 1967-68; California State U. (Fresno), 1969; California State U. (Santa Cruz), 1970.

Military Career: Army National Guard, 1970-76.

Occupation: Legislative aide.

Family: Wife, Patricia Ann Kandarian.

Religion: Lutheran.

Political Career: Calif. Assembly, 1977-83.

Capitol Office: 1319 Longworth Bldg. 20515; 225-4540.

In Washington: Lehman knows his district from the ground up, and that is apparent in the way he represents it. He came to Washington after six years in the California Assembly, and he has continued the pursuit of farm and water issues that marked his career in Sacramento.

Now serving his fourth House term, Lehman will be broadening his focus in the 101st Congress: He is taking over a subcommittee chairmanship on the Banking Committee, and he is serving as an at-large whip. The latter position came partly as a reward for his loyalty to the Democratic leadership; he sticks with his party on partisan votes close to 90 percent of the time, and was an ally of Majority Whip Tony Coelho, who represented the neighboring 15th District.

Lehman has used his seat on the Interior Committee to advance legislation protecting his district's huge stretches of farm land and wilderness. He has proven adept at balancing the interests of growers and developers against the concerns of farm workers and environmentalists.

During his first term, he helped write a bill protecting a long stretch of the Tuolumne River under "Wild and Scenic Rivers" legislation. He backed a compromise plan permitting small-scale hydroelectric projects upstream rather than the massive hydro development initially planned.

In his second term, Lehman steered through the Interior Committee and the House a bill requiring congressional approval for any new dam construction in Yosemite National Park. The city of San Francisco had talked about inundating additional parts of Yosemite to provide for future urban water needs. In 1988, Lehman attached an amendment to an unrelated bill to prevent expansion of any existing reservoir within Yosemite without specific congressional approval, effectively blocking expansion of the dam.

Lehman has steered a consumerist course on the Banking Committee. While he has allied himself with activist liberal, mid-tier Banking Democrats such as Charles E. Schumer of New York and Bruce A. Morrison of Connecticut, his own legislative output has not been as prodigious as theirs. In the 101st Congress, though, he is serving as chairman of the Consumer Affairs and Coinage Subcommittee, where he will be able to pursue some of his favorite projects. One, the "Truth in Savings Act," would set tougher standards for the disclosure of interest rates on savings and credit card accounts. He introduced it for the fifth time in 1989.

At Home: Lehman's political rise has been propelled by shrewd instincts worthy of a politician with twice his experience.

His political style has had its detractors. The *California Journal* once commented that he had "learned well the fine points of political one-upmanship, and thrives on its practice."

But in the California Assembly, he showed the same ability to maneuver among competing interests that he has demonstrated in the House. The late Democratic Rep. Phillip Burton, who recast California's congressional map in 1981, drew the 18th with Lehman in mind — not so much because Lehman was a sure liberal ally, but because he would have been hard to stop.

Fueled by funding from local agribusinesses, labor and education interests, and boasting an 80 percent approval rating from the California Farm Bureau, Lehman escaped even minor competition in the 1982 Democratic primary. He won easily that fall and has won reelection by 2-to-1 margins three times since.

Lehman had been working for a Fresno-area state senator in 1975 when he joined with a small group of young political activists to run the successful Fresno City Council campaign of Dan Whitehurst. The following year the area's state Assembly seat opened up. Lehman and his allies set their sights on it, putting together an intense grass-roots campaign that lifted Lehman over Republican Bill Jones, a member of a prominent farm family.

California 18

Central Valley; Fresno

A district of ungainly shape, the 18th's tentacles reach out in all directions for Democratic votes.

Most of the land is in four counties — Mono, Tuolumne, Calaveras and Madera — lightly populated and tilting Republican. The first three are in the southern gold country of the Sierra Nevadas; Madera County mixes timber and cattle raising.

But for Democratic map makers, these counties provide a geographical connection between two cities — Fresno and Stockton — that cast 70 percent of the 18th's vote and are reliably Democratic. The northeast corner of Fresno, in the 17th, tilts Republican.

Fresno, with a population of more than 285,000, is one of the most important agribusiness centers in the nation. Ever since a 1984 study ranked it as the least desirable place to live in America (largely due to its hot climate and high crime rate), civic boosters have been working to buff up the city's image. One characteristic they stress is Fresno's record as a successful ethnic melting pot. Once a magnet for Armenians, Fresno is now absorbing Laotians, Vietnamese, Cambodians and Central Americans.

Stockton, in San Joaquin County, is split between the 18th and 14th districts, but the 18th has by far the larger portion. This city, too, is Democratic, but slightly less so than Fresno. It is the major canning and processing center for local crops.

Because of its odd shape, this is not an easy district in which to campaign. Stockton and Fresno are 115 miles apart and are served by different media markets. Most of the land between them is in the 15th District, not the 18th. But one issue — farm policy — unites the voters at both ends.

Population: 525,990. White 379,833 (72%), Black 38,871 (7%), Other 24,853 (5%). Spanish origin 131,871 (25%). 18 and over 376,078 (71%), 65 and over 62,787 (12%). Median age: 29.

Committees

Banking, Finance and Urban Affairs (13th of 31 Democrats)
Consumer Affairs and Coinage (chairman); Financial Institutions Supervision, Regulation and Insurance; Housing and Community Development

Interior and Insular Affairs (13th of 26 Democrats)
National Parks and Public Lands; Water, Power and Offshore Energy Resources

Elections

1988 General		
Richard H. Lehman (D)	125,715	(70%)
David A. Linn (R)	54,034	(30%)
1986 General		
Richard H. Lehman (D)	101,480	(71%)
David L. Crevelt (R)	40,907	(29%)

Previous Winning Percentages: 1984 (67%) **1982** (60%)

District Vote For President

	1988	1984	1980	1976
D	101,146 (53%)	98,163 (48%)	72,927 (43%)	80,273 (55%)
R	88,016 (46%)	102,593 (51%)	81,436 (48%)	63,568 (44%)

Campaign Finance

	Receipts	Receipts from PACs	Expend-itures
1988			
Lehman (D)	$279,981	$131,276 (47%)	$193,681
Linn (R)	$89,428	$800 (1%)	$89,260
1986			
Lehman (D)	$253,791	$61,770 (24%)	$290,626
Crevelt (R)	$32,548	$1,800 (6%)	$32,503

Key Votes

1987	
Raise speed limit to 65 mph	Y
Approve Gephardt "fair trade" amendment	Y
Ban testing of larger nuclear weapons	Y
Delay "re-flagging" of Kuwaiti tankers	Y
Approve tax-raising deficit-reduction bill	Y
1988	
Approve aid to Nicaraguan contras	N
Enact civil rights restoration bill over Reagan veto	Y
Kill 60-day plant-closing notification measure	N
Pass omnibus trade bill over Reagan veto	Y
Approve death penalty for drug-related murders	Y
Bar federal funds for abortions in cases of rape and incest	N
Oppose seven-day waiting period for purchase of handguns	N

Voting Studies

	Presidential Support		Party Unity		Conservative Coalition	
Year	**S**	**O**	**S**	**O**	**S**	**O**
1988	20	73	89	3	26	63
1987	16	83	91	3	19	79
1986	20	76	87	4	26	68
1985	16	74	83	3	20	71
1984	23	64	81	7	20	71
1983	22	76	91	4	15	79

Interest Group Ratings

Year	ADA	ACU	AFL-CIO	CCUS
1988	85	9	100	25
1987	92	0	94	7
1986	75	10	100	25
1985	80	0	88	15
1984	85	0	77	50
1983	80	0	100	30

19 Robert J. Lagomarsino (R)

Of Ventura — Elected 1974

Born: Sept. 4, 1926, Ventura, Calif.
Education: U. of California, Santa Barbara, B.A. 1950; U. of Santa Clara, LL.B. 1953.
Military Career: Navy, 1944-46.
Occupation: Lawyer.
Family: Wife, Norma Smith; three children.
Religion: Roman Catholic.
Political Career: Ojai City Council, 1958; mayor of Ojai, 1958-61; Calif. Senate, 1961-74.
Capitol Office: 2332 Rayburn Bldg. 20515; 225-3601.

In Washington: During the Reagan years, Lagomarsino enjoyed telling people that the popular president was a resident of his House district. But at times, events in 1988 made it seem that Lagomarsino might follow Reagan into retirement a good deal sooner than he had planned.

In a year marked by minimal competition in House elections, Lagomarsino faced a serious threat to his re-election. In 1988's most expensive House campaign, the GOP incumbent needed to match the $1.5 million spent by his Democratic opponent, state Sen. Gary K. Hart, in order to hold on. He did so, but with barely 50 percent of the vote.

Though he survived this brush with defeat, Lagomarsino was not so fortunate inside the House itself. After serving as secretary of the House Republican Conference — the caucus of GOP House members — during the 100th Congress, Lagomarsino tried to move up to vice chairman. But he was defeated by Bill McCollum of Florida in the December 1988 election.

Generic factors may have contributed to this setback. Some members may have harbored a mild aversion to giving more power to California, since a member of that huge delegation, Jerry Lewis, had been elected Conference chairman, the third-ranking GOP House leader.

But some of it had to do with Lagomarsino. In choosing the younger McCollum, the Republicans opted for his more aggressive manner over Lagomarsino's stolid, low-key style. And though Reagan had few more dependable allies during his two terms, some hard-line conservatives may have been wary of Lagomarsino's reputation as a moderate on environmental issues.

Lying just off Lagomarsino's district is the Santa Barbara Channel, which is protected under the Federal Marine Sanctuaries Act. The Republican opposes offshore oil drilling and often voices his constituents' concerns about water and air pollution as second-ranking Republican member of the Interior Committee. While many Republicans on Interior are frequently at odds with the committee's Democratic majority, Lagomarsino generally tries to cooperate with the liberal chairman, Morris K. Udall of Arizona.

During the 100th Congress, Lagomarsino authored amendments to designate the Santa Barbara Channel on international shipping maps as an "area to be avoided."

Lagomarsino, however, does not always go with the "greens" on Interior. In 1988, committee Democrats said Reagan had packed the National Park Service with political appointees, and pushed a bill to give Congress greater oversight of the agency. Lagomarsino opposed the measure, stating that it amounted to micromanagement of the park system that would be "detrimental and would establish a dangerous precedent."

Positions such as that spurred Lagomarsino's 1988 opponent to claim that the incumbent's environmental credentials were overrated. But while Hart brandished his endorsements from the Sierra Club and the League of Conservation Voters, Lagomarsino could counter with a "Clean Air Champion" medal presented to him by the Sierra Club in 1988. Ever since his days in the California Legislature, Lagomarsino has managed to draw more support from environmentalists than is typical for a Republican.

But if Lagomarsino's environmental record invites interpretation, the Republican leaves no doubt where he stands on U.S. foreign policy. A senior Republican on the Foreign Affairs Committee, Lagomarsino is a staunch conservative voice on the panel, and in the 1988 campaign he did not back off an inch in the face of Democratic charges that he was too far to the right.

One of the most unshakable supporters of Reagan's Central America policy, Lagomarsino frequently called for loosening of human

California 19

South Central Coast — Santa Barbara

The site of the ranch that was President Reagan's home-away-from-home, the 19th has been dependable for Republican presidential candidates. But there are enough Democrats in this district, just beyond the northern fringe of metropolitan Los Angeles, to keep it from being a safely Republican district.

This was proven in the 1988 House election. Lagomarsino defeated his Democratic challenger, state Sen. Gary K. Hart, by less than 2 percentage points. In the same election, however, George Bush carried the district with a healthy 54 percent of the vote. Favorite son Reagan did even better four years earlier, with 62 percent.

The 19th is contained in two counties: Santa Barbara, which accounts for slightly more than 60 percent of the district vote, and Ventura. There are political, economic and social divisions within these areas. The affluent Santa Barbara voters whose hillside homes overlook offshore oil rigs tend to place environmental issues at the top of their priority lists. The oil workers in Oxnard, the ranchers in the foothills of the Coastal Range and the military families near Vandenberg Air Force Base are more interested in economic growth.

Overall, Santa Barbara County gives Republicans little to worry about. But there is a Democratic bloc around Santa Barbara's campus of the University of California. Bush took the county with 54 percent; Lagomarsino secured his narrow re-election with 51 percent in his home base.

Though Ventura County as a whole is a Republican stronghold, most of the county — and its most Republican parts — are in the neighboring 21st District. Bolstered by the Democratic votes in Oxnard's Mexican-American community, Hart edged Lagomarsino by 1,400 votes in the Ventura portion of the 19th.

Population: 526,032. White 405,581 (77%), Black 14,530 (3%), Other 21,409 (4%). Spanish origin 132,623 (25%). 18 and over 384,025 (73%), 65 and over 56,558 (11%). Median age: 29.

rights "conditions" on U.S. aid to El Salvador, and he dependably voted for the administration's proposals to aid the Nicaraguan contras. He had been opposed to the Sandinista government of Nicaragua since its inception; returning from a trip to that nation shortly after the 1979 revolution, he declared it a "Marxist" country and said, "If it looks like a Cuba and walks like a Cuba and quacks like a Cuba . . . it is probably a Cuba."

Outside his committees, Lagomarsino busied himself early in the 101st Congress by fighting the proposal to raise members' pay by 51 percent. Attacking the argument that the raise was justified by a planned ban on honoraria, Lagomarsino said, "We shouldn't be charging fees for doing our job and we certainly can't justify a 50 percent pay increase."

At Home: Lagomarsino had the closest call of any California incumbent in 1988. He probably survived because his position on coastline issues was just good enough to hold off Hart's charge. The Democrat campaigned as the superior environmentalist and as a liberal on issues of foreign and social policy. He benefited from his years of representing four-fifths of the district's population in the Legislature.

But Lagomarsino conceded nothing in the race. He stuck to the conservative guns on which he had relied through most of his three decades in politics. The voters seemed happy enough with the status quo to keep both men in place (Hart's state Senate term expires in 1991).

The incumbent had begun mixing conservatism and environmental values early in his career. In 1965 he was the first recipient of the Legislative Conservationist of the Year award from the California Wildlife Federation. He shared an opposition to offshore oil drilling with veteran Republican Rep. Charles M. Teague.

When Teague died in 1974, Lagomarsino, with his 13 years in the state Senate, was heir apparent. Though the special election that March occurred at the height of the Watergate scandal, Lagomarsino steered the focus of the campaign away from the "mess in Washington" to the mess along the California coast. The district's beaches were still suffering the effects of an offshore oil well blowout, and Lagomarsino called for a ban on oil drilling in the Santa Barbara Channel. He won easily over seven Democratic candidates.

In the 1974 general election, Lagomarsino faced the special election's second-place finisher, Ojai Mayor James Loebl. But Lagomarsino had used his first few months in office to build support at home, and he won a larger percentage than he had in the special election. After one more serious effort to unseat him, in 1976, the Democrats virtually gave Lagomarsino a pass until Hart tired in 1988 of waiting for him to retire.

Committees

Foreign Affairs (3rd of 18 Republicans)
Western Hemisphere Affairs (ranking); Asian and Pacific Affairs

Interior and Insular Affairs (2nd of 15 Republicans)
Insular and International Affairs (ranking); National Parks and Public Lands

Elections

1988 General

Robert J. Lagomarsino (R)	116,026	(50%)
Gary K. Hart (D)	112,033	(49%)

1986 General

Robert J. Lagomarsino (R)	122,578	(72%)
Wayne B. Norris (D)	45,619	(27%)

Previous Winning Percentages: **1984** (67%) **1982** (61%) **1980** (78%) **1978** (72%) **1976** (64%) **1974** (56%) **1974 *** (54%)

** Special election.*

District Vote For President

	1988	1984	1980	1976
D	101,934 (45%)	82,697 (37%)	63,570 (34%)	82,877 (48%)
R	123,145 (54%)	141,327 (62%)	99,908 (53%)	84,905 (50%)

Campaign Finance

	Receipts	Receipts from PACs	Expend-itures
1988			
Lagomarsino (R)	$1,226,229	$338,996 (28%)	$1,470,674
Hart (D)	$1,634,309	$511,277 (31%)	$1,633,020
1986			
Lagomarsino (R)	$341,497	$63,636 (19%)	$333,464
Norris (D)	$16,744	$205 (1%)	$16,041

Key Votes

1987

Raise speed limit to 65 mph	Y
Approve Gephardt "fair trade" amendment	N
Ban testing of larger nuclear weapons	N
Delay "re-flagging" of Kuwaiti tankers	N
Approve tax-raising deficit-reduction bill	N

1988

Approve aid to Nicaraguan contras	Y
Enact civil rights restoration bill over Reagan veto	N
Kill 60-day plant-closing notification measure	Y
Pass omnibus trade bill over Reagan veto	N
Approve death penalty for drug-related murders	Y
Bar federal funds for abortions in cases of rape and incest	Y
Oppose seven-day waiting period for purchase of handguns	N

Voting Studies

	Presidential Support		Party Unity		Conservative Coalition	
Year	S	O	S	O	S	O
1988	63	38	91	9	95	5
1987	71	29	91	9	95	5
1986	80	19	92	7	88	12
1985	80	19	94	5	96	4
1984	68	32	89	11	93	7
1983	85	15	88	12	88	12
1982	83	16	90	10	93	7
1981	82	18	95	5	96	4

Interest Group Ratings

Year	ADA	ACU	AFL-CIO	CCUS
1988	35	80	36	93
1987	8	96	6	100
1986	5	86	7	89
1985	5	90	6	82
1984	5	79	15	94
1983	0	83	12	90
1982	5	86	5	77
1981	5	93	0	100

20 Bill Thomas (R)

Of Bakersfield — Elected 1978

Born: Dec. 6, 1941, Wallace, Idaho.
Education: San Francisco State U., B.A. 1963, M.A. 1965.
Occupation: Political science professor.
Family: Wife, Sharon Lynn Hamilton; two children.
Religion: Baptist.
Political Career: Calif. Assembly, 1975-79.
Capitol Office: 2402 Rayburn Bldg. 20515; 225-2915.

In Washington: Thomas has a combative style that is something of an oddity among Republicans on the Ways and Means Committee. He relishes the role of partisan strategist on a committee that traditionally has been more oriented to bipartisan consensus-building.

From his early weeks in the House, he has been one of the best at watching a floor debate or a committee meeting and taking in all the political implications. In his first term, he plotted strategy for his fellow freshmen in the contest that elected a new GOP leader; since then, he has sought to play a similar role as tactician for the California delegation.

Not all members feel comfortable giving Thomas the pivotal role his ability would seem to command. He can be snide to slower-witted colleagues, and quick to anger when he does not get his way. In the 98th Congress, seeking perhaps the most important California political role of all — representing the state in House GOP committee assignments — he lost out to the more easygoing Jerry Lewis.

There is no doubt that Thomas is positioned to be a significant legislative player. In the 100th Congress he won a spot on Budget. And he is seventh-ranking Republican on Ways and Means, a panel less partisan than most. Thomas has urged Republicans in their private councils to forge a united front, rather than allow themselves to be individually induced to stray from the party line by Chairman Dan Rostenkowski of Illinois.

Thomas' politically combative style has its source in a watershed experience in his other committee assignment, House Administration.

Early in the 99th Congress, Thomas was the lone Republican on the House Administration task force that ruled that Democrat Frank McCloskey was the winner, by four votes, of the bitterly contested 8th District race in Indiana. Thomas furiously opposed the task force report, and referred to the Democrats' seating of McCloskey as a "rape" and "an arrogant use of raw power."

In the legislative arena, Thomas' partisan style can help rally the troops, but it sometimes hampers his ability to exercise influence.

Even though the massive tax-revision bill of the Reagan years was the Republican president's initiative, Thomas seemed to regard it largely as an example of misbehavior on the part of the House majority. Despite Thomas' clear mastery of the subject, his emotional speeches against the bill restricted his chance to alter it.

When the bill reached the floor, Thomas argued unsuccessfully that the committee's 1,379-page bill was "a political vehicle" that would not benefit taxpayers equally and would undermine economic growth. "One reason the bill is so thick," he said, "is that it required a sufficient amount of pork to get it this far."

He had kinder words for the bill that emerged from conference in 1986, but still opposed it, arguing that retroactive provisions were unfair to those who had made financial decisions based on earlier tax law.

Thomas' experience on the tax bill contrasted with his first two years on the committee, when he made his presence known on a variety of issues. Shortly after he took his seat on Ways and Means, he used it to agitate successfully for a higher Social Security retirement age as a way of keeping down future payroll tax increases.

On matters of trade, Thomas has his district's interests to worry about. He has lobbied to protect wine makers (particularly California vintners) and the pistachio growers in his district from imports, and served as spokesman for his state's producers of highly viscous "heavy oil." He supported provisions of the 1987 omnibus trade bill providing import relief for perishable crops. In 1986 he supported an unsuccessful attempt to override Reagan's veto of legislation restricting textile imports that compete with California textiles.

From his seat on House Administration, Thomas has pushed a measure that critics said was designed to help another California constituency — its incumbent members of Congress.

Thomas in 1988 sponsored a bill to bar candidates who solicit contributions for state and local races from using the money to run for

California 20

Bakersfield; San Luis Obispo

Crossing the 20th District from east to west is like riding a roller coaster across Southern California. Beginning in the flat, bare desert lands of Inyo County on the Nevada border, the district rises through the southern end of the Sierra Nevada Mountains, dips down to Bakersfield in the Central Valley, lifts up again across the Coastal Range, then plunges to the Pacific Ocean near Pismo Beach in San Luis Obispo County.

The 20th includes the highest point (Mount Whitney) and the lowest (Death Valley) in the continental United States. Kern County (Bakersfield) is one of the nation's leading agricultural counties.

Politically, however, there is not much variety in the area. It is uniformly conservative. The real power is in the agribusiness community, and the aerospace and defense industries.

The early 1980s boom in the latter contributed to a population jump of nearly 33 percent in Bakersfield. East of the city is the China Lake Weapons Center, which makes Sidewinder missiles.

The core city of the district with 162,000 people, Bakersfield has a Southern flavor, a legacy of the Texans and Oklahomans who arrived in two migrations: first, to escape the "Dust Bowl" poverty of the Great Depression, as depicted in John Steinbeck's "The Grapes of Wrath," then later, in more prosperous times, to work in the region's oil fields. Kern produces more oil than any other U.S. county.

Though Kern County is heavily Republican — it gave 61 percent of its vote to George Bush in 1988 — the most conservative area of the district is at the northern end of Los Angeles County, in the Antelope Valley. Communities like Lancaster and Palmdale have relied economically on the aerospace industry that developed around Edwards Air Force Base. But the once-remote area is being drawn into Los Angeles' sphere, with bedroom suburbs expanding for commuters who do not mind the 50-mile drive across the San Gabriel Mountains.

Population: 525,750. White 440,375 (84%), Black 22,967 (4%), Other 17,043 (3%). Spanish origin 74,169 (14%). 18 and over 371,945 (71%), 65 and over 54,860 (10%). Median age: 30.

federal office — a measure he described as putting challengers without a campaign treasury on equal footing with state and local officeholders. But California incumbents stood to get special comfort from such a bill because a new state campaign-finance law had given state and local candidates a powerful incentive to use their campaign cash to run for federal office.

Despite the intense partisan wrangling on House Administration in early 1985, it also provided a forum for Thomas' more pragmatic side. On the Elections Subcommittee, Thomas worked with Washington Democrat Al Swift on legislation to prevent the TV networks from using election returns from Eastern states to forecast presidential winners before polls closed in the West, as happened in 1980 and 1984. Their bill, which set a uniform poll-closing time for presidential elections, passed the House, but later died in the Senate in the 100th Congress. The bill was revived in the 101st Congress.

The election of conservative firebrand Newt Gingrich as House minority whip early in the 101st Congress forced the Georgian to give up the ranking Republican position on House Administration, clearing the way for Thomas to move up to the top slot.

Although he supported the 1989 election of Gingrich, Thomas has not always embraced his more militant GOP colleagues. He broke ranks with them in 1980, when Michigan Rep. Guy Vander Jagt was trying to build his campaign for Republican leader with support from the most conservative junior members.

Thomas advised his colleagues to remain uncommitted, probably slowing Vander Jagt's momentum against the more moderate Robert H. Michel of Illinois, who eventually won.

At Home: Thomas not only says he is a pragmatic conservative — he has proved it at critical times in his political career.

In 1974, running for the state Assembly in one of the most conservative districts in the state, he responded to support for the death penalty by making it his campaign focus.

Four years later, when three-term GOP Rep. William Ketchum suddenly died after the June primary, Thomas positioned himself as the moderate in a heated nominating convention. Although he was the ranking GOP legislator in the area and the presumed front-runner, it took him seven ballots to defeat two more-conservative but more-obscure opponents.

Thomas' difficulty winning what should have been an easy nomination resulted from differences with GOP leaders in Kern County. He was acknowledged to be a skillful campaigner, but his bluntness sometimes hurt him.

In the fall campaign, Thomas was successful in convincing voters that he would follow Ketchum's philosophy, if not his style, once elected. The two men had had their differences; Thomas backed Gerald R. Ford in the California primary in 1976 and Ketchum supported Ronald Reagan. But Thomas won an endorsement from Ketchum's widow and easily won the general election against Democrat Bob Sogge, a former aide to a popular state senator. Sogge's was one of the strongest campaigns the district had seen by a Democrat in many years, but he came close only in Tulare County, which casts a small fraction of the vote.

Secure in a district that has given him more than 70 percent of the vote in four of his five re-election campaigns, Thomas turned to the battle over congressional redistricting maps drawn up by California Democrats after the 1980 census. The first plan, ready for the 1982 elections, was instrumental in increasing Democratic strength in the state delegation; the second plan, enacted in early 1983, was designed to protect those gains.

In 1981 Thomas was chosen by fellow members of the California Republican delegation to lead their fight against the new maps. He oversaw the successful effort to have the 1982 plan rejected by voters in a ballot referendum; spearheading the drive to have the question placed on the ballot, Thomas enticed President Reagan to become the first registered California voter to sign the petition. The map was turned down decisively; a state court allowed it to remain in effect for 1982 only.

At the end of the year, Democrats in the state Legislature responded to the requirement that they revise the first map with only slight changes. Thomas began to launch a second challenge, but he later quit the GOP task force on reapportionment, frustrated by his colleagues' inability to agree on a course of action. The issue seemed to die down for the decade in 1984, when voters rejected an initiative pushed by GOP Gov. George Deukmejian that would have thrown out the Democrats' map and set up a panel of judges to draw a new one.

Legal challenges to the map continued, but ended when the U.S. Supreme Court refused further review early in 1989.

Committees

House Administration (Ranking)
Elections (ranking); Accounts

Budget (5th of 14 Republicans)
Task Forces: Economic Policy, Projections and Revenues (ranking); Urgent Fiscal Issues

Ways and Means (7th of 13 Republicans)
Trade

Elections

1988 General		
Bill Thomas (R)	162,779	(71%)
Lita Reid (D)	62,037	(27%)
1986 General		
Bill Thomas (R)	129,989	(73%)
Jules H. Moquin (D)	49,027	(27%)

Previous Winning Percentages: **1984** (71%) **1982** (68%) **1980** (71%) **1978** (59%)

District Vote For President

	1988	1984	1980	1976
D	79,866 (34%)	64,244 (30%)	49,807 (29%)	57,159 (44%)
R	150,366 (65%)	151,080 (69%)	106,733 (63%)	72,497 (55%)

Campaign Finance

	Receipts	Receipts from PACs	Expend-itures
1988			
Thomas (R)	$335,586	$215,150 (64%)	$329,354
Reid (D)	$11,879	0	$15,914
1986			
Thomas (R)	$260,680	$165,617 (64%)	$255,261
Moquin (D)	$5,602	$1,000 (18%)	$5,573

Key Votes

1987	
Raise speed limit to 65 mph	Y
Approve Gephardt "fair trade" amendment	N
Ban testing of larger nuclear weapons	N
Delay "re-flagging" of Kuwaiti tankers	N
Approve tax-raising deficit-reduction bill	X
1988	
Approve aid to Nicaraguan contras	Y
Enact civil rights restoration bill over Reagan veto	N
Kill 60-day plant-closing notification measure	Y
Pass omnibus trade bill over Reagan veto	#
Approve death penalty for drug-related murders	Y
Bar federal funds for abortions in cases of rape and incest	N
Oppose seven-day waiting period for purchase of handguns	Y

Voting Studies

	Presidential Support		Party Unity		Conservative Coalition	
Year	**S**	**O**	**S**	**O**	**S**	**O**
1988	60	36	81	15	87	8
1987	64	25	81	8	88	9
1986	76	19	82	10	84	12
1985	61	33	79	15	84	11
1984	64	28	71	17	78	12
1983	74	21	81 †	10 †	84	10
1982	79	10	71	8	84	7
1981	76	14	69	11	75	11

† Not eligible for all recorded votes.

Interest Group Ratings

Year	ADA	ACU	AFL-CIO	CCUS
1988	25	78	43	100
1987	4	70	13	92
1986	10	85	21	93
1985	10	86	13	95
1984	15	64	9	82
1983	15	62	12	89
1982	5	86	0	85
1981	5	83	8	100

21 Elton Gallegly (R)

Of Simi Valley — Elected 1986

Born: March 7, 1944, Huntington Park, Calif.
Education: Attended Los Angeles State College, 1962-63.
Occupation: Real-estate broker.
Family: Wife, Janice Shrader; four children.
Religion: Protestant.
Political Career: Simi Valley City Council, 1979-80; mayor, Simi Valley, 1980-86.
Capitol Office: 107 Cannon Bldg. 20515; 225-5811.

In Washington: While Gallegly does not show the flair and aggressiveness of his predecessor in the 21st, Bobbi Fiedler, he has the same conservative instincts. And like many members from safe seats, he can use unwavering loyalty as a means to gain his leadership's attention.

In the 100th Congress, when Gallegly chaired the freshman caucus, he compiled a near-perfect partisan voting record. In both sessions, he was in the top 10 of Republicans voting most frequently with a majority of their party. On key votes, Gallegly broke with President Reagan only twice — and Reagan lost a majority of House Republicans on those votes anyway.

Gallegly's loyalty was rewarded in the 101st Congress, when he got a seat on Foreign Affairs. In July 1987, Gallegly made a high-profile venture into foreign policy, joining three other House members on the Capitol lawn to bash Toshiba products with sledgehammers. The Japanese firm had acknowledged selling restricted technology to the Soviets.

A member of a GOP task force on drugs, Gallegly talked tough on crime and advocated user accountability. After a Drug Enforcement Agency officer from Simi Valley was killed, Gallegly introduced legislation to reinstate a federal death penalty for anyone convicted of murdering a federal law-enforcement officer.

Gallegly is also a strong believer in the strategic defense initiative. "... If we'd just leave our scientists and engineers alone and give them the resources they need," he said in 1988, "we could help ensure the safety of millions of Americans...."

At Home: Celebrity candidates are common in California, and in 1986 Gallegly had to get past one to reach Congress. Tony Hope, son of comedian Bob Hope, had returned to the district after a 10-year stay in Washington, D.C., and seemed to have access to an unlimited supply of Hollywood money and glitter.

But Hope, concerned he would be viewed as an election-buying carpetbagger, played down his celebrity contacts and did not raise nearly the sum of money he might have. Setting out to prove that he was not just "a pile of money from a distant planet," Hope stressed his policy background, which included work for an accounting firm in Washington and service on the Grace commission on government waste.

Gallegly, meanwhile, was positioned to run even before incumbent Fiedler left the 21st to seek the GOP Senate nomination. Gallegly portrayed Hope as an interloper and cast himself as a mayor with experience solving local problems, promoting balanced growth and providing municipal services. As mayor, he was well-known for having boosted economic development in Simi Valley, once derided in some neighboring areas as "Slimy Valley."

Gallegly also pointed out that Hope had not even registered to vote during his long stay in Washington, and had registered outside the 21st when he returned to California. Hope noted that Gallegly switched his own registration from the GOP to independent in 1974, abandoning the party in the midst of Watergate. But the charge carried little weight; party regulars moved solidly to Gallegly.

Gallegly did have to overcome the issue of his ties to local real-estate developers. His campaign received heavy financial support from developers, some of whose projects needed approval by the City Council on which he sat. Hope wanted to raise questions of propriety, and also tap into the growing anti-development sentiment in the district.

But Hope's campaign never managed to pick up steam. His organization was weaker than Gallegly's, and he neutralized his most important potential asset — money — with his squeamishness about using it. Gallegly, who was relatively unknown outside his Ventura County base when the campaign began, effectively used direct mail to spread his name and message across the populous San Fernando Valley portion of the district, enabling him to win comfortably.

Now ensconced in this Republican-majority district, Gallegly has little cause for concern. He breezed past two GOP primary challengers in 1988 and then crushed his Democratic foe.

California 21

Part of Ventura County; Western San Fernando Valley

The 21st District has shown its conservative Republican colors in presidential elections throughout the 1980s. Ronald Reagan ran roughshod here both times; George Bush took 64 percent of the district vote in 1988.

Ten years earlier, voters in the territory of the 21st supported the property-tax revolt measure, Proposition 13, like those in no other part of the state. Fully 82 percent of the voters in such far-removed Los Angeles suburbs as Thousand Oaks and Simi Valley supported the plan to slash property taxes in half.

The 21st — which begins in Los Angeles County, skirts the San Fernando Valley, then knifes into Ventura County — was drawn to incorporate staunchly Republican areas while leaving out enough Democrats to populate two Democratic districts in between. This is the kind of territory where the Republican candidate with the strongest conservative credentials normally wins.

Though there is a diversified economy here, the aerospace industry is a primary employer. Raytheon, Northrop, Rockwell and Litton have facilities in the San Fernando Valley.

Population: 525,880. White 469,637 (89%), Black 8,866 (2%), Other 20,713 (4%). Spanish origin 54,584 (10%). 18 and over 367,604 (70%), 65 and over 34,644 (7%). Median age: 30.

Committees

Foreign Affairs (16th of 18 Republicans)
Arms Control, International Security and Science; International Operations

Interior and Insular Affairs (10th of 15 Republicans)
Insular and International Affairs; National Parks and Public Lands

Elections

1988 General		
Elton Gallegly (R)	181,413	(69%)
Donald E. Stevens (D)	75,739	(29%)
1988 Primary		
Elton Gallegly (R)	57,568	(82%)
Sang Korman (R)	9,762	(14%)
1986 General		
Elton Gallegly (R)	132,090	(68%)
Gilbert R. Saldana (D)	54,497	(28%)

District Vote For President

	1988	1984	1980	1976
D	95,910 (35%)	65,617 (27%)	48,825 (25%)	51,701 (40%)
R	178,542 (64%)	177,196 (72%)	127,042 (65%)	80,245 (60%)

Campaign Finance

	Receipts	Receipts from PACs	Expenditures
1988			
Gallegly (R)	$506,391	$163,825 (32%)	$465,310
1986			
Gallegly (R)	$631,424	$143,573 (23%)	$591,018
Saldana (D)	$76,114	$4,186 (5%)	$65,501

Key Votes

1987	
Raise speed limit to 65 mph	Y
Approve Gephardt "fair trade" amendment	N
Ban testing of larger nuclear weapons	N
Delay "re-flagging" of Kuwaiti tankers	N
Approve tax-raising deficit-reduction bill	N
1988	
Approve aid to Nicaraguan contras	Y
Enact civil rights restoration bill over Reagan veto	N
Kill 60-day plant-closing notification measure	Y
Pass omnibus trade bill over Reagan veto	N
Approve death penalty for drug-related murders	Y
Bar federal funds for abortions in cases of rape and incest	Y
Oppose seven-day waiting period for purchase of handguns	N

Voting Studies

	Presidential Support		Party Unity		Conservative Coalition	
Year	**S**	**O**	**S**	**O**	**S**	**O**
1988	68	28	94	2	95	3
1987	71	29	94	5	88	12

Interest Group Ratings

Year	ADA	ACU	AFL-CIO	CCUS
1988	15	96	21	100
1987	4	96	6	100

22 Carlos J. Moorhead (R)

Of Glendale — Elected 1972

Born: May 6, 1922, Long Beach, Calif.

Education: U.C.L.A., B.A. 1943; U. of Southern California, J.D. 1949.

Military Career: Army, 1942-45; Army Reserve, 1945-82.

Occupation: Lawyer.

Family: Wife, Valery Joan Tyler; five children.

Religion: Presbyterian.

Political Career: Calif. Assembly, 1967-73.

Capitol Office: 2346 Rayburn Bldg. 20515; 225-4176.

In Washington: Nine terms in the House have not made Moorhead a major presence in the legislative process, although seniority has lifted him to the top tier on two significant committees — Energy and Commerce, where he is the No. 3 Republican, and Judiciary, where he is the GOP's No. 2 man.

But if Moorhead has not used these positions to the extent a more aggressive lawmaker might, he is no work-shirker. A friendly man who has no trouble cooperating with Democrats, he has managed to stake out a few areas of expertise.

During the 100th Congress, Moorhead was most active in his role as ranking Republican on Judiciary's Subcommittee on Courts, Civil Liberties and the Administration of Justice. There, as elsewhere, he consistently supported the agenda of business and the Reagan administration. But despite his conservatism, he worked productively with the panel's liberal chairman, Robert W. Kastenmeier of Wisconsin.

The subcommittee's jurisdiction includes the complex area of patent, trademark and copyright law, and Moorhead sponsored the administration version of legislation to implement the Berne Convention, an international agreement protecting artists' intellectual property rights. Although a Kastenmeier bill was passed in lieu of the measure Moorhead offered, the Republican was credited with playing a constructive role. Moorhead also sponsored legislation extending patent law to cover the importation of products made using U.S.-patented processes; provisions to that end were ultimately included in the omnibus trade bill.

Moorhead played an active role in the subcommittee's markup of an important patent- and trademark-law revision, defending a Senate-passed bill over a less business-oriented measure offered by Kastenmeier.

Moorhead offered a substitute that would have allowed trademark owners to file suit to prevent others from diluting or disparaging their trademarks, or from advertising another's product in a misleading manner. The substitute also excluded Kastenmeier's provision giving consumers the right to sue trademark owners for false advertising. Moorhead's measure failed by party-line votes in the subcommittee and the full committee. Both provisions were ultimately excluded from the conference report on the bill.

In 1986 Moorhead played an important role in the drafting of the Electronic Privacy Act, which was designed to protect new forms of electronic communications, such as electronic mail, against improper interception.

The Justice Department was initially opposed to any changes in wiretap law and was reluctant to participate in talks on the legislation. But Moorhead worked hard to win the administration over, stressing that protection of electronic privacy was important to the business community. The legislation ultimately became law, backed by a broad coalition that included members of both parties, business groups, and the American Civil Liberties Union.

One of Moorhead's long-held goals on Judiciary has been to tighten restrictions on political activies by lawyers in the Legal Services Corporation. In 1985 he argued that the Legal Services authorization bill as written by the committee would turn local aid programs into "political action centers" and "subtly destroy the corporation by dismantling control over local organizations." His amendment failed in subcommittee and full committee. In 1987, Moorhead unsuccessfully sought to eliminate a $19.5 million funding increase for the corporation.

On Energy and Commerce, Moorhead in the 99th Congress was drawn into an active working relationship with Edward J. Markey of Massachusetts, then chairman of the Energy and Power Subcommittee where Moorhead is the ranking Republican. But Markey left to chair another subcommittee in the 100th Congress and was replaced at Energy and Power by

California 22

Glendale; Part of Burbank; Part of Pasadena

This stretch of middle- and upper-middle-class communities flanking the San Gabriel Mountains is one of the most Republican districts in the state. George Bush took 64 percent of the 22nd's vote in 1988, one of his higher district percentages in California. Four years earlier, President Reagan topped 70 percent in the district. Other statewide Republicans, including Gov. George Deukmejian and Sen. Pete Wilson, have thrived here.

The bulk of the district is in two legs on the southern flank of the mountains. With a population of 154,000, Glendale is the largest city located entirely within the district. Formerly a rather homogeneous bedroom community, Glendale has received an influx of Armenian- and Mexican-Americans in recent years. It has been voting overwhelmingly for Moorhead since he began his political career by running for the state Assembly in 1966.

The vote for Republicans is equally enthusiastic in San Marino, named for a tiny European republic surrounded by Italy. The exclusive California community, with a 1985 per capita income of $33,000, is one of the most affluent in the state.

Arcadia and South Pasadena are more modest, but still well-to-do. Temple City and Monrovia, though, have working-class areas that provide some of the district's Democratic votes: Nearly 30 percent of Monrovia's 33,000 residents are black or Hispanic.

The 22nd also includes the more Republican parts of both Burbank and Pasadena. Some of the old mansions of Pasadena — including the Wrigley Mansion, now home office of the Tournament of Roses — are in the district. "Beautiful downtown Burbank" and the middle-class black and Mexican-American areas of Pasadena are not part of the 22nd.

As the district follows the San Gabriels' sweep toward the coast, it picks up the city of Santa Clarita, an incorporation of the developments of Newhall and Valencia, in the area whose ranches provided the backdrop for some of the earliest Hollywood westerns. At its northern end, the 22nd reaches into the "high desert" for half of Palmdale, a city whose defense-related industries add to its conservative tone.

Population: 525,939. White 463,633 (88%), Black 9,710 (2%), Asian and Pacific Islander 23,523 (5%), Other 2,913 (1%). Spanish origin 64,641 (12%). 18 and over 403,471 (77%), 65 and over 74,460 (14%). Median age: 35.

Philip R. Sharp of Indiana; with Markey gone, Moorhead has been less active on the panel.

Markey and Moorhead worked together on legislation setting energy efficiency standards for appliances, a measure that was supported by a broad coalition of more than 40 groups. Though President Reagan pocket-vetoed the measure in the 99th Congress (saying it would interfere with the free market), early in the 100th he signed a nearly identical bill into law. In 1986, Moorhead and Markey won passage of a bill, sought by private utility companies, that disallowed the practice of giving public utilities preferences over private utilities in relicensing of hydroelectric power plants.

In the 100th Congress, Moorhead continued to represent the interests of the power industry; he pushed for renewal of the Price-Anderson nuclear insurance law, which protects nuclear power producers from the financial consequences of serious nuclear disasters, and he sponsored a provision allowing producers to pay their own legal fees from the insurance fund. Moorhead also opposed an unsuccessful effort by liberals to bar the Nuclear Regulatory Commission from relaxing its rules to allow the Shoreham (N.Y.) and Seabrook (N.H.) nuclear plants to open.

Moorhead will never be the most attention-grabbing spokesman for the pro-business philosophy. He rarely speaks in public without reading his material, and he has a tendency to do so with his head nearly touching the paper.

Early in his career, he had an opportunity to be in the spotlight as the Judiciary Committee debated the impeachment of President Nixon in 1974. But he played only a minor role. A staunch defender of the president, he remarked in early 1974 that Nixon "has done a good job considering Congress has spent a million dollars trying to impeach him." When the time came for a vote, Moorhead backed Nixon on every impeachment count, changing his mind only with the release of the "smoking gun" tape.

At Home: Moorhead's electoral career has been a consistent success. His popularity in Glendale and Burbank is hard to shake, and few Democrats have tried.

In 1988, the Democratic nominee, 71-year-old health executive and cleric John Simmons, raised his 1986 showing by 3 percentage points — to 26 percent.

A lifelong Glendale resident, Moorhead was a lawyer in the area for 15 years before entering the state Assembly. When eight-term Republican Rep. H. Allen Smith decided to retire from Congress in 1972, former Nixon adviser Robert H. Finch thought about running. But he opted against it, and nine candidates entered the GOP primary.

The contest quickly narrowed to just two: Moorhead and Dr. Bill McColl, a Covina surgeon who had once played end for the Chicago Bears. Moorhead, who had carried the west side of the district three times in Assembly elections, was the favorite of the local party apparatus over McColl, who had narrowly lost a primary to John H. Rousselot in the neighboring 24th District in 1970. The result was an easy nomination for Moorhead, and an even easier general election.

Moorhead's service on the impeachment panel reduced his vote to 56 percent in 1974, but since then it has been comfortably above 60 percent. In 1980, Democrat Pierce O'Donnell spent nearly as much as all of Moorhead's previous opponents combined. The result, however, was about the same as the one in 1978, when the Democrat hardly campaigned at all.

Moorhead's one moment of political concern came in 1982. After that year's redistricting plan dissolved Rousselot's neighboring district, giving part of it to Moorhead, Rousselot toyed with the idea of challenging Moorhead in a primary. Rousselot was dean of the California GOP delegation, and with a nationwide network of loyal conservative supporters, he would have been a difficult opponent. But Rousselot ran (and eventually lost) in the heavily Democratic 30th. Moorhead was in the clear.

Committees

Energy and Commerce (3rd of 17 Republicans)
Energy and Power (ranking); Telecommunications and Finance

Judiciary (2nd of 14 Republicans)
Courts, Intellectual Property and the Administration of Justice (ranking); Economic and Commercial Law

Elections

1988 General

Carlos J. Moorhead (R)	164,699	(70%)
John G. Simmons (D)	61,555	(26%)

1988 Primary

Carlos J. Moorhead (R)	67,378	(87%)
David Rodger Headrick (R)	10,314	(13%)

1986 General

Carlos J. Moorhead (R)	141,096	(74%)
John G. Simmons (D)	44,036	(23%)

Previous Winning Percentages: **1984** (85%) **1982** (74%) **1980** (64%) **1978** (65%) **1976** (63%) **1974** (56%) **1972** (57%)

District Vote For President

	1988	1984	1980	1976
D	86,732 (35%)	63,874 (26%)	50,770 (23%)	63,493 (31%)
R	158,823 (64%)	175,164 (72%)	147,959 (68%)	137,401 (67%)

Campaign Finance

	Receipts	Receipts from PACs	Expend-itures
1988			
Moorhead (R)	$397,417	$215,165 (54%)	$234,920
Simmons (D)	$18,940	$503 (3%)	$18,046
1986			
Moorhead (R)	$315,365	$154,766 (49%)	$144,132
Simmons (D)	$28,009	0	$26,490

Key Votes

1987	
Raise speed limit to 65 mph	Y
Approve Gephardt "fair trade" amendment	N
Ban testing of larger nuclear weapons	N
Delay "re-flagging" of Kuwaiti tankers	N
Approve tax-raising deficit-reduction bill	N
1988	
Approve aid to Nicaraguan contras	Y
Enact civil rights restoration bill over Reagan veto	N
Kill 60-day plant-closing notification measure	Y
Pass omnibus trade bill over Reagan veto	N
Approve death penalty for drug-related murders	Y
Bar federal funds for abortions in cases of rape and incest	Y
Oppose seven-day waiting period for purchase of handguns	Y

Voting Studies

	Presidential Support		Party Unity		Conservative Coalition	
Year	S	O	S	O	S	O
1988	73	24	98	1	97	0
1987	71	27	91	6	86	12
1986	82	17	92	7	96	4
1985	80	20	96	3	93	5
1984	67	28	91	7	90	7
1983	78	16	92	3	96	2
1982	78	21	92	5	96	3
1981	75	18	91	4	92	4

Interest Group Ratings

Year	ADA	ACU	AFL-CIO	CCUS
1988	10	96	7	100
1987	4	96	0	100
1986	0	95	7	100
1985	5	90	0	95
1984	0	100	15	87
1983	0	100	0	85
1982	0	96	0	90
1981	5	100	0	94

23 Anthony C. Beilenson (D)

Of Los Angeles — Elected 1976

Born: Oct. 26, 1932, New Rochelle, N.Y.
Education: Harvard U., A.B. 1954; Harvard Law School, LL.B. 1957.
Occupation: Lawyer.
Family: Wife, Dolores Martin; three children.
Religion: Jewish.
Political Career: Calif. Assembly, 1963-67; Calif. Senate, 1967-77; sought Democratic nomination for U.S. Senate, 1968.
Capitol Office: 1025 Longworth Bldg. 20515; 225-5911.

In Washington: Beilenson is a thoughtful Democrat with a liberal outlook and a strong distaste for what he sees as wasteful government spending and parochial legislating.

His views lead him to challenge the status quo in ways that earn him some respect and some reproof from colleagues. Though Beilenson holds key positions on important committees — including the No. 4 Democratic spot on Rules — he is too independent-minded to be an insider in the party leadership's power structure.

Critics say it is easy for Beilenson to urge members to put district pressure aside and think nationally; his district is prosperous and solidly Democratic. But that complaint has not deterred Beilenson from continuing to offer his iconoclastic opinions.

In the 101st Congress, Beilenson has two new forums. He is chairman of the Select Intelligence Committee and also holds the Rules Committee seat on Budget, where he will have a chance to speak out on the federal debt.

"What makes the budget problem so frustrating," Beilenson wrote in 1987, "is that unlike other major problems that face us ... the budget deficit can be solved simply by passing the necessary legislation. Our failure to control the deficit is a failure of political will rather than of not knowing what to do or how to do it."

One plan Beilenson has for lowering the deficit is to raise taxes on the wealthy and increase excise taxes on cigarettes, alcohol and gasoline. For the fourth time in as many years, he offered legislation in 1989 to boost the gas tax, this time by 10 cents a year for five years.

He showed similar perseverance when he sought to reform the budget process itself. Beilenson chaired a 1984 House Rules task force on the budget process, but House leaders declined to consider its proposals for procedural reforms and spending controls. Beilenson came up with a bolder plan: a resolution requiring the Budget Committee to produce a plan to balance the budget in three years. That idea, too, was scrapped by the Democratic Caucus. A few months later, however, the Senate and House approved the far more drastic 1985 Gramm-Rudman-Hollings law, imposing a flat requirement of a balanced budget by 1991. While Beilenson was not one of the central players in passage of the bill, some of his original procedural reforms made it into the compromise that was signed into law. (Later in 1986, a Supreme Court decision invalidated the act's automatic spending-cut mechanism.)

During the Gramm-Rudman debate, the blunt-spoken Beilenson accused House leaders of making a bad law inevitable by ignoring his more modest proposal.

On the Rules Committee, he generally votes with his party, but is not an easy man for the leadership to persuade when he wants to go his own way. He is perhaps the panel's most independent Democrat.

Late in 1986, Beilenson clashed with incoming Speaker Jim Wright when he came before Rules to testify for his emergency bill aimed at fighting drugs. Beilenson thought parts of it, especially its capital-punishment provisions and language weakening the prohibition against use of illegally obtained evidence, were a threat to civil liberties, and he told Wright that in no uncertain terms.

That was Beilenson at his independent best, but it was not a very good political move. A television crew was at the committee that day filming Wright's appearance for a later documentary, and the Speaker-to-be was furious that the film might show him being upbraided by one of his own Democratic members.

The episode contributed to Beilenson's near-loss of the Intelligence chairmanship in the 101st Congress. Wright made no secret of his desire to see Oklahoma's Dave McCurdy assume the job. But since Beilenson — the committee's most senior Democrat — had only a year left in his six-year stint on Intelligence,

California 23

Beverly Hills; Part of San Fernando Valley

The 23rd District is divided geographically and culturally by the Santa Monica Mountains. On the southern slope are the lush, well-tended neighborhoods of west Los Angeles, including Bel Air, the post-presidential residence of the Reagans, and Westwood, home of the U.C.L.A. campus.

To the east, at the foot of the mountains, is posh Beverly Hills, and to the south, Century City and Rancho Park. These are, for the most part, the provinces of wealthy, liberal families, many of them Jewish.

The district also holds about two-thirds of West Hollywood, which was incorporated as a separate city in 1984. It has a large homosexual population which is politically well-organized, and a large number of senior citizens.

Farther to the east, the 23rd reaches down to the beaches around Malibu, an ocean-front home for movie stars and a playground for partying surfers. Malibu tends to be somewhat less Democratic than other towns this side of the mountains. But it does have its share of activists, including actor Martin Sheen who, when appointed to the ceremonial post of mayor in 1989, declared Malibu a haven for the homeless.

On the other side of the mountains, where the ocean breezes seldom blow, is a different world. Here are such middle-class San Fernando Valley communities as Reseda, Tarzana, Canoga Park and Woodland Hills — indistinguishable suburbs linked together by commercial strips and shopping centers.

The willingness of many of this area's working-class residents to vote Republican for president counterbalances the liberal voting tendencies west of the mountains; President Reagan carried the district in 1984. But four years later, Michael S. Dukakis carried the 23rd for the Democrats.

Population: 525,936. White 467,002 (89%), Black 16,150 (3%), Other 21,238 (4%). Spanish origin 48,478 (9%). 18 and over 422,708 (80%), 65 and over 64,046 (12%). Median age: 34.

Wright chose not to risk alienating liberals — or the large California delegation — by skipping over him.

When Thomas S. Foley took over as Speaker in mid-1989, he extended Beilenson's term as Intelligence chairman through 1990.

Beilenson rarely worries about casting a lonely vote of opposition. Once he makes up his mind he does not seem to care whether there are four people on his side or 400.

In the 100th Congress, he was one of just 17 members to vote against elevating the Veterans Administration to a Cabinet-level job. "We don't need another federal department," he wrote in *The Wall Street Journal* in 1988. "And we certainly don't need one designed to promote the interests of a special interest group that already is so politically powerful that it gets virtually everything it wants."

Beilenson's go-it-alone style has not made him the best-known member of Congress. Recently his photo appeared in a Capitol Hill newspaper under the headline: "Can You Find the Four Real Congressmen?"

Beilenson brought three special legislative interests with him from California — park land, elephants and family planning. Early in his career, he and Rep. Phillip Burton of California created the Santa Monica Mountains National Recreation Area, and Beilenson doggedly seeks more funding for it.

In the 100th Congress, he succeeded in adding language to the Endangered Species Act that would ban importation of ivory from African countries that do not have effective elephant-conservation programs.

At Home: Beilenson was a 14-year veteran of the state Legislature when Democratic Rep. Thomas M. Rees announced his retirement from Congress in 1976. The district was ideal territory for Beilenson; his record suited him well to voters in some of the most liberal and heavily Jewish parts of Los Angeles.

Beilenson's one major obstacle was cleared away when Howard L. Berman, then the Assembly's majority leader, chose to remain in the Legislature in 1976. Berman had been seen as Rees' likely successor, and he would have had access to an organization difficult for Beilenson to match. But running against five other candidates, none of whom held public office, Beilenson was the clear front-runner.

Wallace Albertson, who headed the state's leading liberal organization, the California Democratic Council, criticized Beilenson for not being active enough in his support for Proposition 15, which would have restricted the development of nuclear power plants in the state. But Proposition 15 fared almost as poorly in the district as it did statewide, drawing 38 percent, and Albertson did even worse, finishing second in the primary with 21 percent to Beilenson's 58 percent.

Beilenson's first worrisome general election came in 1982, and it proved less difficult than had been expected. In order to draw a favorable district for Berman, who now wanted to run for Congress, map makers had removed part of the area near Beverly Hills from the 23rd and added conservative voters in the western San Fernando Valley; Beilenson complained that the change had hurt him badly.

Democrats who drew the district insisted Beilenson was panicking for no reason. "It's a good district for Tony," said Burton, the main architect of California's new congressional map. "He just doesn't know it. He's not a numbers guy." It turned out Burton was right.

Beilenson's Republican opponent was David Armor, a former analyst with the Rand Corporation. Armor had prepared a series of studies on the effects of school busing to achieve integration, and the studies had been used by anti-busing forces during Los Angeles' bitter struggle over the issue at the end of the 1970s. Republicans hoped Armor would do particularly well in the San Fernando section of the district, where anti-busing sentiment had been especially fierce.

With his Beverly Hills base relatively secure, however, Beilenson was able to put most of his effort into the communities new to him. Substantially outspending Armor, he took almost 60 percent, only a slight decline from his previous tallies. In 1986 and 1988, he topped the 60 percent mark, nearly reaching 66 percent in 1986.

Since he moved to the West Coast to practice law at age 25, Beilenson has met with only one political defeat. He was in the middle of his first state Senate term in 1968 when he decided to run for the Senate as a peace candidate, criticizing former state Controller Alan Cranston for what he said was a lukewarm antiwar position. Cranston won the Democratic nomination by more than a million votes.

Committees

Select Intelligence (Chairman)
Program and Budget Authorization (chairman)

Budget (14th of 21 Democrats)
Task Forces: Budget Process, Reconciliation and Enforcement; Economic Policy, Projections and Revenues

Rules (3rd of 9 Democrats)
Rules of the House

Elections

1988 General		
Anthony C. Beilenson (D)	147,858	(64%)
Jim Salomon (R)	77,184	(33%)
1988 Primary		
Anthony C. Beilenson (D)	67,802	(84%)
Val Marmillion (D)	12,755	(16%)
1986 General		
Anthony C. Beilenson (D)	121,468	(66%)
George Woolverton (R)	58,746	(32%)

Previous Winning Percentages: **1984** (62%) **1982** (60%) **1980** (63%) **1978** (66%) **1976** (60%)

District Vote For President

	1988	1984	1980	1976
D	138,264 (56%)	113,020 (46%)	83,218 (38%)	97,602 (50%)
R	106,610 (43%)	129,010 (53%)	109,736 (50%)	92,733 (48%)

Campaign Finance

	Receipts	Receipts from PACs	Expend-itures
1988			
Beilenson (D)	$150,275	0	$140,486
Salomon (R)	$130,438	$6,530 (5%)	$100,956
1986			
Beilenson (D)	$195,166	0	$215,076
Woolverton (R)	$206,646	$20,357 (10%)	$220,313

Key Votes

1987	
Raise speed limit to 65 mph	X
Approve Gephardt "fair trade" amendment	N
Ban testing of larger nuclear weapons	Y
Delay "re-flagging" of Kuwaiti tankers	?
Approve tax-raising deficit-reduction bill	Y
1988	
Approve aid to Nicaraguan contras	N
Enact civil rights restoration bill over Reagan veto	Y
Kill 60-day plant-closing notification measure	N
Pass omnibus trade bill over Reagan veto	Y
Approve death penalty for drug-related murders	N
Bar federal funds for abortions in cases of rape and incest	N
Oppose seven-day waiting period for purchase of handguns	N

Voting Studies

	Presidential Support		Party Unity		Conservative Coalition	
Year	S	O	S	O	S	O
1988	26	65	89	5	11	89
1987	23	72	86	6	5	84
1986	18	81	89	7	20	80
1985	23	69	88	4	11	84
1984	34	65	87	10	12	88
1983	29	66	91	7	16	84
1982	38	53	81	5	11	82
1981	30	64	79	8	8	80

Interest Group Ratings

Year	ADA	ACU	AFL-CIO	CCUS
1988	95	8	77	50
1987	84	13	63	20
1986	80	9	50	18
1985	95	5	88	24
1984	90	9	62	38
1983	85	9	76	40
1982	95	5	84	19
1981	90	0	80	6

24 Henry A. Waxman (D)

Of Los Angeles — Elected 1974

Born: Sept. 12, 1939, Los Angeles, Calif.
Education: U.C.L.A., B.A. 1961, J.D. 1964.
Occupation: Lawyer.
Family: Wife, Janet Kessler; two children.
Religion: Jewish.
Political Career: Calif. Assembly, 1969-75.
Capitol Office: 2418 Rayburn Bldg. 20515; 225-3976.

In Washington: Waxman is one of Congress' master legislators. Like a river forging a new path to the sea, he might take years to wear down the obstacles before him, or to find ways around them, but he nearly always reaches his goal in the end.

"God never meant liberals to be stupid," Waxman once said, and he lives to be proof of that. He sets such ambitious policy aims that colleagues might consider him a pie-in-the-sky fool if they were not by now so familiar with his technique of taking a small slice at a time until years later he is holding the whole pie. Piece by piece, he has helped enact a new national health policy for children, for example, and he did so during the Reagan years of retrenchment for just such programs.

Persistence and patience are his strengths in achieving what initially seems unrealistic. With Democrats back in charge of the Senate as well as the House after the 1986 elections, speculation was widespread that party liberals would embark on a spending spree to address the social demands pent up during the years of GOP White House and Senate control. Waxman knew better. "My time has not yet arrived," he said. Implied, of course, is his certainty that it will.

Waxman did join his frequent partner, Massachusetts Sen. Edward M. Kennedy, in 1987 to unveil grandiose legislation for national health insurance, to be paid by employers and the government for millions of now-uninsured Americans. He unabashedly said what few other politicians would dare: "This will require new taxes. I wouldn't want to fool anybody into thinking we're going to be able to do these things without more money."

Predictably, victory is not his yet. Nor is it likely anytime soon. But Waxman is no prisoner of his rhetoric, and meanwhile he will continue to take what small victories he can in times of huge budget deficits and public skepticism about social welfare spending. Rather than jump from cause to cause with each new session, Waxman reaps the rewards of an uncommonly long legislative attention span.

Over the past decade, he has been instrumental in dramatically expanding Medicaid, mostly — and ironically — by tucking health care provisions for poor women and infants into the massive "reconciliation" bills that have become part of Congress' annual routine to cut the deficit. Such bills — by their size, importance and special protection under congressional rules — offer Waxman's initiatives safety from filibusters, killer amendments and vetoes. "It's become the only place we can make policy changes," Waxman says.

All this is not to suggest Waxman always wins. In late 1987, when he declared that he was not bound by the health spending limits in a budget summit agreement between President Reagan and Congress, House Democratic leaders bridled him into submission. The next month, in a conference negotiating that year's reconciliation bill, Waxman was overwhelmed by White House and Senate Democratic opposition to his costly, far-reaching proposals to stem infant mortality.

The next year, however, Waxman achieved incremental victories on two other fronts. He was a key author of the law providing Medicare coverage to the elderly against catastrophic illnesses. Waxman was largely responsible for major provisions providing first-time coverage for outpatient prescription drugs; preventing impoverishment of those whose spouses are institutionalized so long that Medicaid payments run out; and mandating that Medicaid pay the increased Medicare premiums for elderly beneficiaries who otherwise could not afford the new catastrophic illness coverage.

On the second front, the landmark overhaul of the welfare system, Waxman sponsored a crucial amendment providing continued Medicaid coverage for a year to those who leave the rolls to take jobs. That benefit helped persuade liberals to support the welfare bill despite their disdain for an administration-supported "workfare" provision mandating the first federal work requirement for welfare beneficiaries.

Like his California mentor, the late Phillip Burton, Waxman believes power exists to be used and winning, rather than self-expression, is the ultimate liberal goal. Unlike Burton, he

California 24

Hollywood; Part of San Fernando Valley

More than any other district in the nation, the 24th depends on the entertainment industry for its economic well-being. It includes the symbolic center of the industry — the corner of Hollywood and Vine — as well as Universal Studios, Paramount Pictures, Samuel Goldwyn Studios and the West Coast headquarters of ABC and CBS.

Many of the heavily Jewish "bagel boroughs" of Los Angeles are also within the 24th District. Concentrated near the Wilshire Country Club, the many elderly voters in this area provide a solid core of support for virtually any Democratic candidate. The 24th gave Michael S. Dukakis almost two-thirds of its presidential vote in 1988.

Like the 23rd and 26th districts, the 24th District straddles the Santa Monica Mountains. It reaches into the San Fernando Valley to include the Valley Plaza section. Still, this territory, with its mostly middle-class, blue-collar residents, is not as conservative as the areas of the valley found farther to the west.

One of the few Republican-leaning communities in the 24th is Hancock Park, a favored home of Los Angeles' "old money." During the years preceding World War II, its residents' attitudes forced the newly affluent to look elsewhere for property; Beverly Hills thus became the address of choice for the arriving rich. Hancock Park now includes more modest neighborhoods, including a sizable black community, but its exclusive character still predominates.

The 24th's Democratic lean is reinforced by its Hispanics (who make up about a quarter of the 24th's population); it also has the largest concentration of Asian-American voters in the state outside San Francisco. Many of them are Koreans, concentrated at the southern end of the district, and Vietnamese, who have settled in and around Hollywood. There is a sizable homosexual community in Hollywood and West Hollywood, about a third of which is in the district.

Population: 525,918. White 348,566 (66%), Black 34,301 (7%), Asian and Pacific Islander 61,256 (12%), Other 2,763 (1%). Spanish origin 137,587 (26%). 18 and over 429,288 (82%), 65 and over 80,133 (15%). Median age: 33.

does not have the kind of explosive temper that alienates as many members as can be cultivated through personal favors. Waxman is privately passionate about his issues, and in pursuing them he takes on some of Congress' most formidable and exasperating members, such as GOP Sen. Jesse Helms or House Energy and Commerce Committee Chairman John D. Dingell. Yet publicly, he is all but unflappable.

Waxman's base is Energy and Commerce's Health and Environment Subcommittee, which he has chaired since 1979. It was the bunker from which he fended off Reagan-era attacks on the health budget.

But it has not guaranteed him control on environmental issues. Especially on his main cause, a fight since 1982 to toughen the Clean Air Act against acid rain and urban smog, Waxman is in the minority on his panel; he is outflanked by Dingell, who represents the interests of Detroit's auto industry and of Midwest states with coal-burning industries.

Dingell seemed to solidify control at the outset of the 100th Congress when he filled three Democratic committee vacancies with likely allies from coal-producing districts. Given the continuing impasse, the major action of the Congress came when the House in 1987 had to decide the relatively insignificant question of whether the Clean Air Act's deadlines for cities to meet air-quality standards should be delayed until before the 1988 elections or after. Waxman won that skirmish, as lawmakers rejected Dingell's bid to move the deadline into 1989 so members would not be swayed by pre-election environmentalist pressure.

But in 1988 Waxman encountered the usual vexing hurdles thrown up by Dingell and Edward Madigan, the top Republican on Waxman's panel: lack of quorums, hearings prolonged by dozens of opposition witnesses, lengthy questioning and, at bottom, too few votes. Waxman suspended action at midyear. Meanwhile, the combination of committee members' frustration with stalemate and their sense of voters' growing concern about air pollution gave rise to a bipartisan "group of nine" dedicated to finding a compromise. Neither Waxman nor Dingell embraced its proposals, but the activity seemed to support Waxman's optimism that someday a bill will pass.

If he cannot overcome his foes, Waxman will outlast them — as he did when the Clean Air Act itself was at stake in 1982. With the law up for renewal at that time, Dingell — along with the Reagan administration, utilities and heavy industry — sought to relax emission standards.

But Waxman shrewdly prolonged his panel's work (much as Dingell is now), and he repeated the same stalling tactics after the bill finally reached the full committee. He offered scores of amendments, once wheeling them into the room in a shopping cart, and insisted they be read entirely and voted on. When Waxman actually won some rounds, Dingell abruptly adjourned the meetings, killing his chance to weaken the law.

Most of Waxman's successes in the conservative climate of recent years have been defensive. "The liberal agenda is fighting to keep what we have," he has said. But even when playing defense, Waxman is more interested in results than debating points. He is no fall-on-his-sword liberal. In 1985, he vehemently opposed the Gramm-Rudman budget-balancing law, but did not waste time trying to kill a bill sure to pass. Instead, he worked in a House task force and then in conference with the Senate to win exemptions from the law's threatened cuts for his favorite health programs.

To keep family-planning funding in the budget in 1984, Waxman agreed to package the programs with a former right-wing senator's $15 million proposal for teenagers' instruction in chastity and alternatives to abortion. And in 1986, he crafted a crazy-quilt health bill that combined his measure compensating victims of adverse reactions to childhood vaccines — which Reagan threatened to veto — with minor bills that key senators and the administration wanted; the ploy succeeded and the vaccine bill became law.

In recent years Waxman has led the House effort against AIDS, but it is a fight that taxes his usual legislative patience, given the deadliness of the disease. He is stymied not only by budget pressures but also by the usual resistance that socially divisive issues evoke from the right, in this case from Helms and California Rep. William E. Dannemeyer.

Waxman engineered passage in the 100th Congress of the first comprehensive AIDS bill, authorizing millions of dollars for education, anonymous testing and treatment. But to achieve that, Waxman had to drop two top priorities — confidentiality for AIDS tests and a ban on discrimination against victims, both of which are widely considered essential to encourage potential victims to come forward. Both were endorsed by Reagan's own AIDS commission, but the president's refusal to go along prompted Waxman's retreat. The provisions, he said, were "clearly too controversial for the current political climate. We need the president."

Waxman originally won his subcommittee chairmanship in 1979 with hardball politics that surprised some colleagues. He pioneered a practice that has since become routine in leadership contests, raising money from his wealthy campaign supporters and distributing it to Energy and Commerce Democrats who would choose the subcommittee chairmen. He was accused of attempting to buy the chair, but in any case he prevailed over the highly respected Richardson Preyer of North Carolina, 15-12.

Like Dingell at the full committee level, Waxman has tried to increase his power by broadening his panel's scope. When the Ways and Means Committee proposed a new Medicare payment policy in 1983, Waxman wanted to modify it even though the policy was not under his jurisdiction. But then-Speaker Thomas P. O'Neill Jr. intervened, and Ways and Means amended the plan to Waxman's satisfaction.

With his own re-election campaigns a mere formality every two years, Waxman is free to build his political influence at home and in Congress by helping friends and potential legislative allies win election. In 1982, his homestate organization with Rep. Howard L. Berman aided six of the California House delegation's eight new Democrats.

The one sort of politics Waxman stayed away from for years was the periodic maneuvering for top House leadership posts. The heir to Burton's power base in California's delegation, he has used that role to help allies win key committee assignments. But amid the jockeying for succession in the wake of O'Neill's 1986 retirement, Waxman was quiet as Jim Wright and Thomas S. Foley were promoted to the top two posts and Waxman's sometime-rival, Californian Tony Coelho, was elected majority whip.

Given Coelho's ambitions, geographic considerations made it difficult for Waxman, as another Californian, to seek a top leadership job then. Also, some said he did not want to risk progress on his legislative priorities by getting into a bruising bid for personal power.

Whatever his thinking at that time, it had changed by June 1989, when Wright and Coelho were forced out of the House by ethics controversies. Waxman jumped into the race for Coelho's majority whip post, a vacancy that drew great interest in part because Foley was heir presumptive for Speaker and Missouri's Richard A. Gephardt a strong favorite to succeed him as majority leader. But Waxman soon withdrew his bid for the No. 3 leadership job and went back to his work on Energy and Commerce. There, his creed is still the same as it was in his first congressional campaign in 1974, when he said, "I am a proud, self-confessed, unapologetic liberal."

At Home: One reason Waxman never has any trouble winning in this district is that its heavily Jewish, liberal constituency fits him ideally. The other reason is the so-called "Waxman-Berman machine."

It is not a machine in the sense that it can reward friends with jobs. "A machine traditionally is conservative and corrupt, and tied together by patronage," says Waxman. "We're none of those things." But it is an efficient, smoothly functioning operation that concentrates the vast financial resources of the Los Angeles liberal community, makes extensive use of computer technology and has substantial political power.

The "machine" label was affixed in 1972,

when Waxman, then a two-term assemblyman, teamed with the Berman brothers — Howard and Michael — to win an Assembly seat for Howard Berman. But the Waxman-Berman alliance was originally forged during college days at U.C.L.A., when Waxman and Howard Berman became active in the state's Federation of Young Democrats.

The first visible success for the Waxman-Berman team came in 1968, when Waxman challenged Democratic Assemblyman Lester McMillan in a primary. McMillan had been in office 26 years and was nearing retirement. Rather than waiting until the seat opened up and drew a large field of competitors, Waxman decided to take on the incumbent. With massive volunteer help, much of it recruited from the ranks of the Young Democrats, Waxman beat McMillan with 64 percent of the vote.

That election saw the beginning of what has since become a Waxman-Berman trademark — computerized mailings. Each voter is identified by a variety of socio-political characteristics and given a campaign pitch specifically tailored to his or her interests.

By 1974 the operation was functioning so smoothly that Waxman had little trouble winning a new U.S. House seat created with him in mind. He has had even less trouble retaining it.

In 1984, Waxman had political worries of a different sort. Ever since 1981, California Republicans had been trying to find a way to undo the redistricting plan drawn up by Phil Burton. Their efforts in 1984 centered on a ballot initiative put forward by GOP Gov. George Deukmejian to dissolve the current map before the 1986 elections and place the task of drawing new lines in the hands of a commission of retired judges.

Burton's plan had given Democrats 28 California seats in the U.S. House, and Waxman and his colleagues in the delegation saw the effort as a threat to their political survival. They mobilized to fight it. The actual campaign against the measure was run by Michael Berman and his partner in a political consulting firm, Carl D'Agostino. Responsibility for funding much of it, however, fell to Waxman and other members of the delegation. Waxman and his West Los Angeles allies — Reps. Berman and Mel Levine — tapped their extensive network of sources both in the Los Angeles area and around the country, while other California Democrats approached friends in Washington. In the end, they managed to raise \$3.5 million. The proposition was defeated by 55-45 percent.

The redistricting question continues to fester. In January 1989, the U.S. Supreme Court refused to hear a challenge to the Burton map. But fresh initiatives aimed at limiting legislators' ability to gerrymander will probably be on the state ballot in 1990.

Committees

Energy and Commerce (3rd of 26 Democrats)
Health and the Environment (chairman); Commerce, Consumer Protection and Competitiveness

Government Operations (4th of 24 Democrats)
Commerce, Consumer and Monetary Affairs; Environment, Energy and Natural Resources; Human Resources and Intergovernmental Relations

Select Aging (10th of 39 Democrats)
Health and Long-Term Care

Elections

1988 General		
Henry A. Waxman (D)	112,038	(72%)
John N. Cowles (R)	36,835	(24%)
1986 General		
Henry A. Waxman (D)	103,914	(88%)
George Abrahams (LIB)	8,871	(7%)
James Green (PFP)	5,388	(5%)

Previous Winning Percentages: **1984** (63%) **1982** (65%) **1980** (64%) **1978** (63%) **1976** (68%) **1974** (64%)

District Vote For President

	1988		1984		1980		1976	
D	106,652	(65%)	88,680	(55%)	68,286	(46%)	84,403	(55%)
R	55,756	(34%)	70,370	(44%)	62,782	(42%)	66,304	(43%)

Campaign Finance

	Receipts	Receipts from PACs	Expend-itures
1988			
Waxman (D)	\$345,006	\$257,841 (75%)	\$191,334
Cowles (R)	\$15,835	\$600 (4%)	\$15,449
1986			
Waxman (D)	\$146,746	\$105,900 (72%)	\$136,807

Key Votes

1987	
Raise speed limit to 65 mph	N
Approve Gephardt "fair trade" amendment	N
Ban testing of larger nuclear weapons	Y
Delay "re-flagging" of Kuwaiti tankers	Y
Approve tax-raising deficit-reduction bill	#
1988	
Approve aid to Nicaraguan contras	N
Enact civil rights restoration bill over Reagan veto	Y
Kill 60-day plant-closing notification measure	N
Pass omnibus trade bill over Reagan veto	Y
Approve death penalty for drug-related murders	X
Bar federal funds for abortions in cases of rape and incest	?
Oppose seven-day waiting period for purchase of handguns	X

Voting Studies

	Presidential Support		Party Unity		Conservative Coalition	
Year	**S**	**O**	**S**	**O**	**S**	**O**
1988	21	66	79	4	11	71
1987	18	74	84	3	9	84
1986	12	86	87	4	2	92
1985	28	71	86	3	11	84
1984	25	66	80	5	5	93
1983	22	71	84	3	6	85
1982	36	58	87	7	12	86
1981	25	63	79	5	4	88

Interest Group Ratings

Year	ADA	ACU	AFL-CIO	CCUS
1988	90	0	93	21
1987	92	10	79	17
1986	95	5	92	20
1985	95	16	94	27
1984	100	10	77	42
1983	95	5	94	25
1982	95	5	90	14
1981	85	0	77	11

25 Edward R. Roybal (D)

Of Pasadena — Elected 1962

Born: Feb. 10, 1916, Albuquerque, N.M.

Education: Attended U. of California, Los Angeles, 1935; Southwestern U. School of Law, 1952.

Military Career: Army, 1944-45.

Occupation: Social worker; public health educator.

Family: Wife, Lucille Beserra; three children.

Religion: Roman Catholic.

Political Career: Los Angeles City Council, 1949-62; Democratic candidate for Calif. lieutenant governor, 1954.

Capitol Office: 2211 Rayburn Bldg. 20515; 225-6235.

In Washington: As he nears the end of his third decade in Congress, Roybal holds a prestige position as an Appropriations subcommittee chairman. He also is chairman of the Select Aging Committee, a panel that provides a forum for drawing public attention to issues involving the elderly.

Yet Roybal, a reserved, almost dour figure, rarely makes a splash in these roles. And while he is a prolific generator of legislative proposals, particularly in the areas of health care and the elderly, he lacks zeal for the horse-trading needed to get his plans enacted.

If he possessed a more activist style, Roybal would be a logical successor to the late Rep. Claude Pepper as a national spokesman on elderly issues. But such a role would be a sharp change for Roybal, who was overshadowed by the colorful Florida Democrat, his predecessor as Aging Committee chairman. In 1987, Roybal and Pepper introduced a bill providing funding for long-term health care for the chronically ill. But it was Pepper who led the unsuccessful fight for what came to be known as the "Pepper bill."

Pepper, Roybal and other long-term-care advocates initially tried to attach their plan to a catastrophic health insurance bill, which they said did not cover the devastating costs of caring for victims of such illnesses as Alzheimer's disease or cancer. However, the plan's price tag — $30 billion over five years — sealed its fate at a time when Congress was sweating over how to cut the federal budget deficit. House leaders persuaded Pepper to keep it separate from the catastrophic bill, which passed. Then, in June 1988, the House defeated a rule that would have permitted debate on the long-term bill.

This difficulty in obtaining authorization for large new programs has not forestalled Roybal from proposing them. Roybal is promoting a bill to quadruple funding for Alzheimer's disease research to $500 million by 1992. He says the degenerative disease, which mainly affects the elderly, lags well behind cancer, AIDS and heart disease in its share of federal research money. He has also pursued a program to offset a national nursing shortage by providing funds to recruit and raise the salaries of nurses.

Roybal has also taken on the cause of mental health treatment. In the 100th Congress, he achieved adoption of a pair of amendments, expanding demonstration projects for rural mental health care and establishing a national mental health education program.

The California Democrat works to obtain funds for these programs as a senior member of the Appropriations Committee. As chairman of the Subcommittee on Treasury, Postal Service and General Government, Roybal maintains his usual low profile. But that is fitting: The issues dealt with by the panel, which mainly handles spending by the Treasury Department and the U.S. Postal Service, rarely are subject to heated debate.

A provision in the fiscal 1989 Treasury appropriations bill did lead Roybal into a House skirmish that presaged the 1989 war over a congressional pay raise. The bill contained a 4 percent pay increase for all federal workers. During 1988 floor debate on the bill, conservative Illinois Republican Philip M. Crane proposed an amendment barring the increase for employees who earn over $72,500 a year; though that figure included judges and other senior federal officials, Crane was aiming mostly at members of Congress, who he said should show themselves "capable of fiscal responsibility" before commanding a pay raise. After Roybal's bid to keep the amendment off the floor failed, the House adopted the Crane amendment, 230-170.

Both on Appropriations and off, Roybal takes a particular interest in issues involving his fellow Hispanic-Americans. His ethnic concerns led him into his most public role, as an opponent of the Simpson-Mazzoli immigration bill that was enacted in the 99th Congress.

The bill faced such strong resistance that it had to be brought up in three Congresses before

California 25

Central and East Los Angeles

Hispanics dominate the 25th like no other district in California. Nearly two-thirds of its residents identified themselves as being of Hispanic ancestry in the 1980 census.

The district incorporates the shining glass-and-steel towers of downtown Los Angeles. The area is laced with L.A.'s legendary crowded expressways, all named for suburbs that house the district's daytime, white-collar population: Pasadena, Pomona, Ventura, Glendale, Santa Ana.

But those roads carry commuters past the barrios of Boyle Heights and East Los Angeles, home to many of the Hispanics who form the core of the district's permanent population. These are bustling communities with active businesses and large families seeking to work their way up to the middle class. But poverty and unemployment run high, and Democratic loyalty is virtually unshakable.

The district is actually less Hispanic than it was before the last redistricting. The western side of the district, nearly all Hispanic, was sheared off and replaced by middle-class, racially mixed neighborhoods in western and northern Pasadena. Even with the changes, only a quarter of the population was Anglo and 10 percent black following the remap.

Any group that votes in significant numbers can exert some influence here, because voting participation in the district is the lowest in the state. The 25th is the only constituency in California where fewer than 100,000 people voted for president in 1980 — less than half the statewide average. By 1988, participation was up a bit, to just over 110,000.

Population: 526,013. White 265,979 (51%), Black 50,592 (10%), Asian and Pacific Islander 40,207 (8%), Other 3,156 (1%). Spanish origin 332,862 (63%). 18 and over 358,659 (68%), 65 and over 48,881 (9%). Median age: 27.

its final passage. The measure imposed sanctions on U.S. employers who hired illegal aliens, and national Hispanic organizations felt those sanctions would lead to discrimination against Hispanics falsely suspected of being illegal aliens. As chairman of the Hispanic Caucus in the 97th Congress, Roybal led the opposition the first time the bill was introduced, in 1982.

Because the bill did not come up until the final week of a lame-duck session in December, it was vulnerable to delaying tactics. The Mexican American Legal Defense Fund prepared more than 100 amendments to the bill, and Roybal announced his willingness to offer them and demand a recorded vote on each one. House leaders had no choice but to pull the bill.

He continued to oppose the measure in the 98th and 99th Congresses, on through final passage in 1986. He suggested that Simpson-Mazzoli was a "farm labor" bill, not an immigration reform measure, because its emphasis seemed to be on guaranteeing farmers and growers a continued supply of cheap labor rather than controlling future immigration. He offered an amendment to the House bill authorizing 20,000 additional visas per year from both Mexico and Canada, and he criticized the final conference version because it raised the immigration quota for Europe but not for the Western Hemisphere.

Roybal's record as an ethnic spokesman was a help to him in 1978, when he and two other California colleagues were disciplined by the House in connection with the Korean vote-buying investigation. The ethics committee had recommended reprimands for Charles H. Wilson and John J. McFall, but urged that Roybal be censured, a more serious penalty, for lying to the committee about a $1,000 gift from South Korean lobbyist Tongsun Park.

Many of Roybal's allies considered the distinction a race-related insult. "Two of our white colleagues are brought down here to be slapped on the wrist," complained the black California Democrat, Ronald V. Dellums, "and one of my brown brothers is down here to be totally wiped out in the process."

Roybal called in chits from Hispanic leaders outside Congress, asking them to help reduce the penalty to a reprimand. When the House then agreed, Roybal described the action as "not only a personal victory for me, but for all Hispanics throughout the nation.... [It] shows the potential strength of the Hispanic community when it unifies behind a cause."

He has reciprocated this type of minority-group solidarity over the years. In 1988, he was one of three House members to vote "no" on articles of impeachment against Alcee L. Hastings of Florida, a black federal judge.

At Home: Roybal is a durable man. Despite a style few would call dynamic, he has become a part of the political landscape in the Hispanic neighborhoods of East Los Angeles.

Lately, Roybal has campaigned relatively little. The noisy Pomona Freeway that runs just a few yards from his Los Angeles home does not bother him, an aide once said, "because he is hardly ever there." But while there are younger, more aggressive Hispanic leaders in the East Los Angeles area, none has so far been willing to take on Roybal, who is viewed as a sort of community "elder."

Roybal has not shown any political weaknesses during his long House career. Beginning with his first re-election in 1964, he has never received less than 66 percent in a general election. He has won more than 80 percent the three times he has been challenged in a primary (1970, 1972 and 1976). Even Roybal's reprimand in 1978 had little political impact.

In 1988, the GOP did not even bother to challenge the veteran, who rolled up 85 percent against minor-party opponents.

When Roybal was 4, he moved from New Mexico to the ethnically mixed Boyle Heights section of Los Angeles. Since then, the area has turned almost entirely Hispanic.

During the Depression he worked in the Civilian Conservation Corps, and later he became involved in public health for the California Tuberculosis Association. He was elected to the Los Angeles City Council from a Hispanic East Side district, where he served four terms and then ran for Congress in 1962. In between he made an unsuccessful try for lieutenant governor.

The 1962 campaign was his only challenging contest. The state Legislature had just redrawn the congressional boundaries, pushing the district of nine-term Republican Rep. Gordon L. McDonough far into East Los Angeles. Given the lopsided Democratic registration he looked so vulnerable that five Democrats, including Roybal, entered the 1962 primary.

Roybal had major primary opposition from William Fitzgerald, a Loyola University government professor, and G. Pappy Boyington, a World War II Marine flying ace who had become a hero as the commander of the "Black Sheep Squadron." But with his solid base in the Hispanic community, Roybal won three-fifths of the primary vote and went on to defeat McDonough easily in the general election.

Committees

Select Aging (Chairman)
Retirement, Income and Employment (chairman)

Appropriations (6th of 35 Democrats)
Treasury, Postal Service and General Government (chairman); Labor, Health and Human Services, Education and Related Agencies

Elections

1988 General

Edward R. Roybal (D)	85,378	(85%)
Raul Reyes (PFP)	8,746	(9%)
John C. Thie (LIB)	5,752	(6%)

1986 General

Edward R. Roybal (D)	62,692	(76%)
Gregory L. Hardy (R)	17,558	(21%)

Previous Winning Percentages: **1984** (72%) **1982** (86%) **1980** (66%) **1978** (67%) **1976** (72%) **1974** (100%) **1972** (68%) **1970** (68%) **1968** (67%) **1966** (66%) **1964** (66%) **1962** (57%)

District Vote For President

	1988	1984	1980	1976
D	74,007 (67%)	65,974 (60%)	52,239 (57%)	57,998 (62%)
R	34,925 (32%)	42,375 (39%)	31,338 (34%)	33,920 (36%)

Campaign Finance

	Receipts	Receipts from PACs	Expend-itures
1988			
Roybal (D)	$86,724	$46,800 (54%)	$67,957
1986			
Roybal (D)	$98,919	$40,400 (41%)	$63,996

Key Votes

1987	
Raise speed limit to 65 mph	Y
Approve Gephardt "fair trade" amendment	N
Ban testing of larger nuclear weapons	Y
Delay "re-flagging" of Kuwaiti tankers	Y
Approve tax-raising deficit-reduction bill	Y
1988	
Approve aid to Nicaraguan contras	N
Enact civil rights restoration bill over Reagan veto	Y
Kill 60-day plant-closing notification measure	N
Pass omnibus trade bill over Reagan veto	Y
Approve death penalty for drug-related murders	N
Bar federal funds for abortions in cases of rape and incest	N
Oppose seven-day waiting period for purchase of handguns	N

Voting Studies

	Presidential Support		Party Unity		Conservative Coalition	
Year	**S**	**O**	**S**	**O**	**S**	**O**
1988	20	77	89	3	5	95
1987	11	75	88	2	2	74
1986	16	80	88	5	16	74
1985	16	78	89	3	7	84
1984	24	67	85	4	5	90
1983	15	83	95	3	7	89
1982	23	71	95	2	8	92
1981	34	64	92	7	12	87

Interest Group Ratings

Year	ADA	ACU	AFL-CIO	CCUS
1988	95	0	100	23
1987	88	10	88	7
1986	95	5	85	19
1985	95	5	94	15
1984	100	4	92	38
1983	95	0	88	25
1982	95	9	100	9
1981	95	13	93	5

26 Howard L. Berman (D)

Of Panorama City — Elected 1982

Born: April 15, 1941, Los Angeles, Calif.
Education: U. of California, Los Angeles, B.A. 1962, LL.B. 1965.
Occupation: Lawyer.
Family: Wife, Janis Schwartz; two children.
Religion: Jewish.
Political Career: Calif. Assembly, 1973-83.
Capitol Office: 137 Cannon Bldg. 20515; 225-4695.

In Washington: Berman, now in his fourth term, has finally overcome the burden of the extraordinary expectations that accompanied his arrival in Washington from Sacramento, where he had an impressive career in the California Legislature. In his early House years, Berman was perceived as more adept at politics than legislating. His name was most often mentioned in connection with the "Berman-Waxman" political machine, the powerful Democratic organization in Southern California built by Berman and Rep. Henry A. Waxman.

But Berman appears to have succeeded in a nose-to-the-grindstone effort at gaining respect as a maker of laws. He has studiously carved a niche as a principal on some substantive and reasonably high-profile issues.

Berman was involved in the first major legislative response to the Iran-contra affair. It all started back in 1986 when Berman, as a member of the House Foreign Affairs Committee, enlisted the help of an ideological opposite, Republican Henry J. Hyde of Illinois, in passing an amendment that barred the U.S. government from selling arms to terrorist countries. But the Reagan administration found loopholes in that amendment and went forward with the sale of arms to Iran in what later erupted into the Iran-contra affair.

In the 100th Congress Berman and Hyde tried to plug the loopholes by proposing a requirement that the president tell Congress about any U.S. arms sales to countries — such as Iran — that are believed to support terrorism. Further, the new Berman-Hyde bill prohibited private companies from conducting an arms sale if they have "reason to know" that the weapons will reach a country that supports terrorists.

The bill passed the House, but died in the Senate. Berman and Hyde reintroduced it in the 101st Congress, and the odds for passage seemed more favorable.

As a member of the Judiciary Committee, Berman was one of the key negotiators in producing a new national immigration law in the 99th Congress, after four years of feuding and stalemate. In the 100th Congress he continued to mix it up over U.S. immigration policy.

One of Berman's biggest legislative successes was a law that created a lottery to grant up to 20,000 new immigrants from 162 countries visas to come to the United States. Berman, long an advocate of increasing the geographic diversity of the immigrants to the United States, presided over the first lottery drawing.

Berman also successfully managed passage of a bill on the House floor that would have extended the period in which illegal aliens could seek amnesty, but the measure died in the Senate.

In the 101st Congress, Berman has been out in front in a battle to reform the nation's policy regarding legal immigration. Berman and Democratic Sen. Paul Simon were pitted against Democratic Sen. Edward M. Kennedy and GOP Sen. Alan K. Simpson in that fight.

Kennedy and Simpson have favored a cap on the number of immigrants allowed to enter the United States each year. Their plan would also increase the number of occupation-related visas — at the expense of the number of visas issued to reunite immigrants with their families. Berman and Simon oppose a cap on legal immigration and would increase work visas without reducing family-related visas. Berman was active in trying to craft a compromise.

Berman's desire to emerge as a more significant legislative player was seen in his pursuit of a seat on the House Budget Committee. "I enjoy my committees," he said of Judiciary and Foreign Affairs. "But the one major thing I've not been as involved in as I'd like is the budget process."

Berman spent a year courting the 31-member Democratic Steering and Policy Committee, which makes committee assignments. He was one of 13 Democrats vying for six open seats on the Budget panel. He started by gaining the support from within the California delegation, including the dean of the state's Democrats, Don Edwards. Throughout months of campaigning, he won more members to his side, though he never received a direct commitment

California 26

Santa Monica Mountains; Central San Fernando Valley

Clever Democratic map-making during the last redistricting made Berman's House election a near-certainty. Borrowing liberal territory that was part of Democratic Rep. Anthony C. Beilenson's old 23rd District, they created a solidly Democratic district.

Many of the former Beilenson voters live in the fashionable Mulholland Drive area north of Beverly Hills. Farther west are Sherman Oaks and Studio City, in the San Fernando Valley at the base of the Santa Monica Mountains. Berman represented this area for a decade in the Assembly.

The less favorable part of the district for Democrats is in the heart of the San Fernando Valley — communities such as Van Nuys, Panorama City and Sepulveda. The ranch-style houses that line the endless straight streets here are home to the white-collar professionals and well-paid blue-collar workers who populate the valley.

The aviation and electronics industries are major employers. Lockheed, which came here in 1948, has a huge facility in Burbank. General Motors also has a plant in the Valley that builds Camaros and Firebirds.

Nearly all the areas in the 26th have for years been under Democratic representation in the state Legislature. But the constituency occasionally shows a strong conservative streak on some social and economic issues. In 1988, the area voted for a ballot proposition to require mandatory AIDS testing for certain individuals.

The northernmost end of the district is the most industrialized portion; it has attracted large numbers of Mexican-Americans. Their migration to communities such as San Fernando City and Pacoima has helped boost the overall Hispanic population of the district to 25 percent.

Population: 525,995. White 417,569 (79%), Black 23,218 (4%), Other 21,880 (4%). Spanish origin 131,180 (25%). 18 and over 392,919 (75%), 65 and over 53,364 (10%). Median age: 31.

from House leaders. When the ballots were counted in January 1989, he had 23 votes. It was a strong indication he won the respect of the leadership.

At Home: Together with Waxman, Berman has been a potent force in California Democratic politics since the late 1960s.

The "Berman-Waxman" organization dominates the West Los Angeles political scene. Its detractors label it a "machine," but it is more an informal network of like-minded politicians who pool their resources and back candidates — expected to be future legislative allies — with money, organization, computer technology and the tactical skills of Berman's brother, Michael, a political consultant.

Howard Berman's influence in Democratic politics stretches back to his days at UCLA, where he and Waxman were involved in the Federation of Young Democrats. Their skill at positioning the "YDs" between the party's liberal faction, led by Alan Cranston, and the more traditional wing of Assembly Speaker Jesse Unruh, won them considerable clout at state party conventions through the 1960s. Berman succeeded Waxman in the presidency of the federation in 1967, and helped him win a seat in the state Assembly the following year.

In 1972 Berman was again ready to follow Waxman's lead. Pulling in funds from his by-then extensive contacts and mobilizing Young Democrats and UCLA students, he toppled veteran GOP Assemblyman Charles J. Conrad in a traditionally Republican district that had grown more Democratic with the migration of people from inner-city Los Angeles.

Berman pursued his job in Sacramento with relish, building a strong following in the Legislature and allying himself with Speaker Leo T. McCarthy and Gov. Edmund G. Brown Jr. He was a consummate compromiser and tactician, with a relaxed style that made him approachable even to opponents. In steering through a precedent-setting farm bill, he overrode the objections of the powerful farm lobby by patiently convincing farmers that the bill was the only way to end the nationwide boycott of California grapes and lettuce.

By 1979 McCarthy was letting it be known that he planned a 1982 run for statewide office. Berman was expected to have no trouble following him as Speaker. But rather than wait, he launched a challenge to McCarthy in 1980 that split Assembly Democrats and eventually gave the speakership to Willie L. Brown Jr.

Berman justified his move by contending that McCarthy's statewide ambitions were leading him to raise money for his own efforts, instead of working to elect Democratic candidates to the Legislature. At the end of 1979, Berman won over a majority of the Democratic Caucus. But McCarthy refused to abide by the caucus decision, forcing Berman to muster the votes to depose him in the full Assembly.

By the middle of 1980, the contest had deteriorated into open warfare. Both sides decided to use the 1980 elections to build their own strength; onlookers, referring to the battle between opposing crime families in "The Godfather," sniped that Berman and McCarthy were "going to the mattresses."

As that year's legislative elections approached, both factions funneled money to candidates who could be expected to back them in Sacramento. Once the air had cleared in November, Berman had increased his forces by two members. McCarthy conceded defeat, but his backers, bitterly opposed to a Berman speakership, threw their support to Brown. With the help of Republican members of the Assembly who feared Berman's leadership, Brown was finally elected Speaker.

In the aftermath, with the Democrats sharply divided and the party's leadership forced to work with the GOP, Berman faded from view. Redistricting offered the new Speaker an opportunity to help promote his antagonist out of Sacramento. When Rep. Phillip Burton's remap plan gave Berman a favorable congressional district, Brown was happy to ease its passage.

Still, Berman had to work for it. The GOP nominated wealthy auto dealer Hal Phillips, who had strong financial backing. "This is an opportunity of a lifetime, the chance to retire Howard Berman," wrote Reagan "Kitchen Cabinet" founder Holmes Tuttle in a fund-raising letter.

But Berman was prepared. For the first time since his 1972 Assembly fight, he walked precincts and, with his brother's help, ran an extensive direct-mail campaign. He won with 60 percent of the vote.

In 1984, he could coast to re-election while raising money to fight a redistricting plan pushed by GOP Gov. George Deukmejian. His victory margin actually improved, as it has in each re-election bid since.

Committees

Budget (18th of 21 Democrats)
Task Forces: Budget Process, Reconciliation and Enforcement; Defense, Foreign Policy and Space

Foreign Affairs (14th of 28 Democrats)
Arms Control, International Security and Science; International Operations

Judiciary (16th of 21 Democrats)
Courts, Intellectual Property and the Administration of Justice; Immigration, Refugees and International Law

Elections

1988 General

Howard L. Berman (D)	126,930	(70%)
G. C. "Brodie" Broderson (R)	53,518	(30%)

1986 General

Howard L. Berman (D)	98,091	(65%)
Robert M. Kerns (R)	52,662	(35%)

Previous Winning Percentages: 1984 (63%) **1982** (60%)

District Vote For President

	1988	1984	1980	1976
D	108,660 (55%)	90,429 (45%)	70,242 (38%)	83,316 (52%)
R	85,640 (44%)	108,528 (54%)	93,648 (51%)	74,919 (46%)

Campaign Finance

	Receipts	Receipts from PACs	Expend-itures
1988			
Berman (D)	$528,296	$209,317 (40%)	$409,233
1986			
Berman (D)	$277,688	$118,827 (43%)	$272,956
Kerns (R)	$8,589	0	$10,314

Key Votes

1987	
Raise speed limit to 65 mph	N
Approve Gephardt "fair trade" amendment	Y
Ban testing of larger nuclear weapons	Y
Delay "re-flagging" of Kuwaiti tankers	Y
Approve tax-raising deficit-reduction bill	Y
1988	
Approve aid to Nicaraguan contras	N
Enact civil rights restoration bill over Reagan veto	Y
Kill 60-day plant-closing notification measure	N
Pass omnibus trade bill over Reagan veto	Y
Approve death penalty for drug-related murders	N
Bar federal funds for abortions in cases of rape and incest	N
Oppose seven-day waiting period for purchase of handguns	N

Voting Studies

	Presidential Support		Party Unity		Conservative Coalition	
Year	**S**	**O**	**S**	**O**	**S**	**O**
1988	23	66	90	4	5	84
1987	14	84	89	3	5	93
1986	18	80	89	5	12	82
1985	24	68	91	3	9	85
1984	29	62	84	6	7	88
1983	24	67	85	5	10	88

Interest Group Ratings

Year	ADA	ACU	AFL-CIO	CCUS
1988	95	4	85	36
1987	88	0	88	13
1986	95	5	92	19
1985	100	10	94	24
1984	95	9	77	43
1983	95	0	88	25

27 Mel Levine (D)

Of Pacific Palisades — Elected 1982

Born: June 7, 1943, Los Angeles, Calif.
Education: U. of California, Berkeley, A.B. 1964; Princeton U., M.P.A. 1966; Harvard U., J.D. 1969.
Occupation: Lawyer.
Family: Wife, Jan Greenberg; three children.
Religion: Jewish.
Political Career: Calif. Assembly, 1977-83.
Capitol Office: 132 Cannon Bldg. 20515; 225-6451.

In Washington: During his first few terms in the House, Levine was known primarily as one of those energetic young Democrats with legislative interests in a variety of areas. On the Foreign Affairs Committee, Levine voiced his steadfast support for Israel and his determined opposition to President Reagan's Central America policies. On Interior, he invoked his strong environmentalist tendencies.

But while he shares these stances with dozens of his activist Democratic colleagues, Levine is now emerging with a cutting-edge issue he can call his own. He has become a spokesman for those who believe federal leadership is necessary if the U.S. high-technology industry is to compete successfully with foreign competitors subsidized by their own governments. In 1987, he co-founded Rebuild America, a Washington-based think tank that studies issues related to the nation's high-tech future.

Levine, whose suburban Los Angeles district contains a high-tech sector, says he favors a strategy by which the government promotes consortia of companies, which would research and develop new technologies, by easing antitrust restrictions and, in some cases, providing seed money to get the cooperative arrangements off the ground.

At the start of the 101st Congress, Levine acted on this concept by calling for a government-backed consortium to develop high-definition television (HDTV), an emerging technology that may produce sharper television images. Describing HDTV as the next commercial battlefield in a consumer electronics industry war now dominated by Japan, Levine said that a $1 billion federal investment might be necessary. "Ultimately, the countries that have this industry will find themselves in possession of the most important technologies of the 21st century," Levine said. In early 1989, Levine joined with Pennsylvania Republican Don Ritter, another high-tech-minded member, in a bill to provide $500 million in Commerce Department subsidies to HDTV ventures.

His concern about competitiveness has made Levine wary about availing foreign trading partners of American-invented technology. He was a staunch opponent of the FS-X project, a jet fighter based on the American F-16 to be jointly produced by Japan and the United States. "We cannot ... prevent Japan from becoming a competitor in aerospace, but I do not see why we have to subsidize the development of our own competitors," said Levine, a member of the Foreign Affairs Subcommittee on Trade and co-chairman of the House Export Task Force. The deal, nonetheless, went through.

But while his interest in high-tech issues has spurred his involvement in the trade panels, Levine's main focus on Foreign Affairs continues to be on the Europe and the Middle East Subcommittee. There he is part of the large bloc that fights hard for aid to Israel, and for limits on arms sales to that nation's Middle East adversaries.

In January 1989, Levine joined GOP Sen. Bob Dole of Kansas in calling for U.S. sanctions against foreign companies that sell chemical weapons technology to Iran, Iraq, Libya or Syria. He scored a major, though temporary, triumph in 1986 in his efforts to block U.S. arms sales to Arab nations, when the House voted to disapprove a Reagan administration arms deal with Saudi Arabia. However, the White House later reached a compromise with Congress that allowed the sale to go through.

For such a passionate supporter of Israel, Levine was relatively mellow about the U.S. opening to the Palestine Liberation Organization (PLO) in December 1988; he said at the time he would not "second-guess" the outgoing Reagan administration on the move. But he warned that the United States must make "crystal clear" that its talks with the PLO did not mark any weakening in its commitment to Israel.

Levine's other major role on Foreign Affairs during the Reagan years was as a persistent critic of the administration's Central America policies. To these issues, Levine brought the passion of his days as an angry student activist at Berkeley and Harvard, as he attacked the "gunboat diplomacy" of the Reagan era.

California 27

Pacific Coast — Santa Monica

The 27th hugs the Pacific Coast for 20 miles, from Pacific Palisades in the north down to affluent Redondo Beach. Santa Monica is its political and geographic hub.

A city of 93,000, Santa Monica is a mixture of elderly middle-class residents and young families who like being close to both Los Angeles and the ocean. Political activism runs high here. It is the home base of Assemblyman and former 1960s radical Tom Hayden.

Though Hayden and his wife, activist actress Jane Fonda, separated in early 1989, they have left their mark on the local political scene. Their activities, along with the growth of a tenants' rights movement among its apartment-dwellers, have given Santa Monica a well-earned liberal reputation.

In 1984, the city gave Walter F. Mondale 55 percent of its vote. Michael S. Dukakis took 65 percent in 1988, enabling him to carry the 27th as a whole by a wide margin. That same year, Santa Monica voters gave a majority to a proposition, soundly defeated statewide, to use penalties against violators of housing and restaurant codes to increase funding for the hungry and the homeless.

Just east of Santa Monica is the Brentwood section of Los Angeles, an affluent, heavily Jewish area that has strongly supported Levine over the years. South of it is Venice, an artists' community that has been overrun by young "beach people."

South of Venice, the district runs in a narrow strip past Marina del Rey, taking in the sprawling Los Angeles International Airport and the upper-middle-class communities that run down the coastline to the South Bay area just north of the Palos Verdes Peninsula. There is more of a Republican vote here: The aerospace and defense industries compose the dominant economic force in the South Bay area. Inland, even blue-collar towns like Lawndale have lost some of their Democratic loyalties in recent years.

The only pocket of true Democratic strength in the southern half of the 27th is in Inglewood, a heavily black community added to the district in 1983.

Population: 525,929. White 398,371 (76%), Black 57,636 (11%), Asian and Pacific Islander 29,949 (6%), Other 3,011 (1%). Spanish origin 75,261 (14%). 18 and over 415,975 (79%), 65 and over 50,212 (10%). Median age: 31.

Levine was well ahead of most House members in early 1985, when he called for an investigation into alleged Reagan administration efforts to steer private aid to the Nicaraguan contras to evade a legal prohibition against government support. Nearly two years before the Iran-contra controversy broke, he and Iowa Republican Jim Leach introduced a bill to make any private aid to the contras illegal. In his first year in the House, Levine introduced legislation to restrict the U.S. presence not only in Nicaragua, but in Honduras and El Salvador as well.

Aside from his prevailing interests in futuristic technology and U.S. foreign relations, Levine is best known for the strong environmental views he expresses on Interior. He is a staunch opponent of oil drilling off the California coast. His Interior seat has also enabled him to take on other local ecological issues: In the 100th Congress, he obtained inclusion of Santa Monica Bay in the National Estuaries Program, and pushed for the establishment of a 4.5 million-acre federal wilderness area in the California desert.

Levine's local interests have a bearing on his other assignment, the Select Committee on Narcotics Abuse and Control. He helped engineer the creation of a federal law-enforcement strike force to combat the violent street gangs involved in Los Angeles County's illegal drug trafficking.

And with all the legislative pies he has a finger in, Levine has also grabbed onto a role as a national political operative. Levine, a veteran of the Southern California political machine headed by Democratic House colleagues Henry A. Waxman and Howard L. Berman, is now in his second term as a regional co-chairman of the Democratic Congressional Campaign Committee.

At Home: Levine comes from a wealthy Los Angeles family with ties to both the Republican and Democratic parties, but his own politics have long been ardently liberal.

Eight years out of law school, with a mixed civil and public interest practice, he was tapped by a coalition of Jewish organizations to lobby before the Legislature for legislation prohibiting businesses from complying with the Arab boycott of Israel. He developed a friendship with then-Assemblyman Berman, and in 1977 ran in a special election to replace an assemblyman who wanted to move to the state Senate.

With his wealth, his contacts among West Los Angeles' liberal elite and help from the organization led by Berman and Waxman, Levine had little trouble.

He spent five years in the Assembly, specializing in energy matters. When Republican Rep. Robert K. Dornan decided to give up his coastal Los Angeles seat in 1982 to run for the Senate, Levine was ready to move on. The 27th was redrawn for him in 1981 redistricting, losing its more conservative southern communities. With Waxman-Berman help, Levine was a sure winner from the start. He had no primary opponent, and no Republican of any stature was willing to take him on. In the end, he faced country club owner Bart W. Christensen and won with 60 percent.

Two years later, Levine ran into unexpected opposition. Republican Robert Scribner, a former Los Angeles Rams running back and conservative evangelical, mounted a well-funded effort to unseat him. Levine, perhaps too sure of easy victory, spent most of his time and money fighting a statewide redistricting initiative that would have hurt Democratic House members. He ended up with just 55 percent, enough of a drop to ensure that Scribner would be back for a return engagement.

But the rematch was no contest. Scribner raised even Republican eyebrows by sending out a fund-raising letter to local ministers in 1985, urging them to "agree to link arms with us as we literally 'take territory' for our Lord Jesus Christ." Levine, concentrating on his own campaign this time, easily outraised Scribner and won almost two-thirds of the vote.

Against a minor candidate in 1988, Levine stretched that margin a few percentage points further.

Committees

Foreign Affairs (15th of 28 Democrats)
Europe and the Middle East; International Economic Policy and Trade

Interior and Insular Affairs (18th of 26 Democrats)
General Oversight and Investigations; National Parks and Public Lands; Water, Power and Offshore Energy Resources

Select Narcotics Abuse and Control (11th of 18 Democrats)

Elections

1988 General		
Mel Levine (D)	148,814	(68%)
Dennis Galbraith (R)	65,307	(30%)
1988 Primary		
Mel Levine (D)	66,452	(88%)
Ralph Cole (D)	8,679	(12%)
1986 General		
Mel Levine (D)	110,403	(64%)
Robert Scribner (R)	59,410	(34%)

Previous Winning Percentages: 1984 (55%) **1982** (60%)

District Vote For President

	1988	1984	1980	1976
D	126,695 (55%)	104,031 (46%)	80,285 (40%)	92,212 (49%)
R	102,897 (44%)	117,634 (52%)	92,964 (47%)	91,721 (49%)

Campaign Finance

	Receipts	Receipts from PACs	Expend-itures
1988			
Levine (D)	$893,810	$153,500 (17%)	$398,597
Galbraith (R)	$17,392	$1,240 (7%)	$17,022
1986			
Levine (D)	$711,129	$121,524 (17%)	$498,833
Scribner (R)	$364,728	$10,590 (3%)	$393,860

Key Votes

1987	
Raise speed limit to 65 mph	N
Approve Gephardt "fair trade" amendment	N
Ban testing of larger nuclear weapons	Y
Delay "re-flagging" of Kuwaiti tankers	Y
Approve tax-raising deficit-reduction bill	Y
1988	
Approve aid to Nicaraguan contras	N
Enact civil rights restoration bill over Reagan veto	Y
Kill 60-day plant-closing notification measure	N
Pass omnibus trade bill over Reagan veto	Y
Approve death penalty for drug-related murders	N
Bar federal funds for abortions in cases of rape and incest	N
Oppose seven-day waiting period for purchase of handguns	N

Voting Studies

	Presidential Support		Party Unity		Conservative Coalition	
Year	S	O	S	O	S	O
1988	21	75	92	4	8	84
1987	17	79	96	3	7	91
1986	16	81	92	3	6	86
1985	24	75	94	3	7	91
1984	28	68	88	5	5	88
1983	21	77	86	6	20	76

Interest Group Ratings

Year	ADA	ACU	AFL-CIO	CCUS
1988	95	4	86	36
1987	96	9	88	20
1986	85	5	75	15
1985	100	10	94	27
1984	90	9	92	47
1983	90	0	94	30

28 Julian C. Dixon (D)

Of Culver City — Elected 1978

Born: Aug. 8, 1934, Washington, D.C.
Education: California State U., Los Angeles, B.S. 1962; Southwestern U., LL.B. 1967.
Military Career: Army, 1957-60.
Occupation: Legislative aide; lawyer.
Family: Wife, Betty Lee; one child.
Religion: Episcopalian.
Political Career: Calif. Assembly, 1973-79.
Capitol Office: 2400 Rayburn Bldg. 20515; 225-7084.

In Washington: Dixon has practically made a career of doing thankless jobs for his colleagues. The only question is whether that will help or hurt his political future in the House.

He spent more than four years as chairman of the House ethics committee, a job most lawmakers would run from. While most of his colleagues are grateful to Dixon for handling the sensitive job, he has had to cross some powerful people in the process of doing it.

It fell to Dixon to oversee history in the making: His chairmanship of the ethics committee was capped by the 1988-89 investigation of Jim Wright, which ultimately forced him to resign as Speaker. Dixon's role likely will never be forgotten by hard-core Wright allies who, during the inquiry, threatened retribution against Democrats deemed insufficiently loyal to the Speaker.

The publicity showered on Dixon during the inquiry was unusual for this low-key, pragmatic legislator. Dixon spends most of his time plugging away on the Appropriations Committee seeking funds for programs he supports, rather than publicity for himself or causes. And he has handled one of the most thankless tasks on Appropriations, chairing the subcommittee that handles funding for the District of Columbia.

When ethics opened the Wright inquiry in mid-1988, Dixon's reputation, almost as much as Wright's, was at stake in the case's handling.

Despite initial Republican charges — and Democratic hopes — that the committee under Dixon would safely bury the charges against Wright, no one in the end could accuse the ethics panel of a whitewash.

Dixon defended the work of his committee and the lawyer it hired against criticism by Wright and his defense lawyers and House allies, who portrayed the Speaker as the victim of an overzealous prosecutor who led the committee to misread House rules.

That was not the first time Dixon had to defend his committee's work.

When the ethics panel in 1987 recommended that the House reprimand Pennsylvania Democrat Austin J. Murphy for several rules violations, Murphy won considerable sympathy by portraying himself as a sacrificial lamb being punished in order to quiet critics of the ethics committee. Support for the committee's recommendation ebbed steadily during debate on the House floor — until an angry Dixon got up and delivered an emotional closing speech that turned the vote practically into a referendum on Dixon's integrity. The vote of confidence was solid: The resolution of reprimand passed 324-68.

Dixon was made ethics chairman in part because House leaders believed they could count on him not to be a "hanging judge" when it came to the sensitive task of disciplining wayward colleagues. But Dixon took heat — particularly from conservative Republicans trying to make corruption a political issue — for the committee's track record of frequently finding members guilty of violating House rules but declining to punish them.

Dixon had to defend his committee against those forces on the House floor in mid-1987, when the GOP right wing brought up a resolution to force the committee to reopen an investigation of Fernand J. St Germain of Rhode Island after the panel cleared the House Banking Committee chairman of the most serious charges against him. By a vote of 111-291, the House turned back the GOP effort to force an inquiry into new charges against St Germain.

Dixon's tenure on the ethics committee was extended twice beyond Democrats' traditional two-term limit. By the time the Wright investigation was complete, Dixon was more than ready to quit the job.

After the Wright matter concluded, Dixon's own finances were a target of press scrutiny. News accounts noted his wife's lucrative investment in a duty-free giftshop concession at the Los Angeles International Airport — an investment she made five months after the ethics committee hired an attorney who at the time headed the city's airport commission.

The publicity arose right after Dixon had amended his 1986 financial disclosure report to provide more information on the transaction.

California 28

Southern Los Angeles; Culver City

Located directly south of Beverly Hills and Hollywood and stretching to the edge of downtown Los Angeles, the 28th is a racially mixed collection of neighborhoods, some middle-class and some poor, but nearly all Democratic. It was the second-best California district for Democratic presidential nominee Michael S. Dukakis in 1988, behind the neighboring 29th.

One reason for the Democratic strength is that the 28th has the second-highest percentage of blacks in California, trailing only the 29th. The district has been served by black Democrats — first, Yvonne Brathwaite Burke, then Dixon — since its creation in 1972.

The level of income in the 28th rises as the district moves west, away from central Los Angeles. The portions of the city in the district, centered around the Coliseum area, are largely poor and black.

Windsor Hills and Ladera Heights, west of the city limits, also have many black voters, but they are mainly middle- and upper-middle class. Many neighborhoods in these close-in suburbs have a generous ethnic mix, with whites, blacks, Hispanics and Asians living next to each other in single-family homes.

West of Ladera Heights is middle-class Culver City, a mostly white community of 40,000 that also has drawn well-to-do blacks, including Dixon. The home of MGM, Culver City will occasionally break from the district's Democratic path: In 1984, the city gave Ronald Reagan a majority. But in 1988, Dukakis took 62 percent in Culver City.

Population: 525,993. White 200,378 (38%), Black 202,809 (39%), Asian and Pacific Islander 39,985 (8%), Other 2,724 (1%). Spanish origin 146,604 (28%). 18 and over 395,349 (75%), 65 and over 52,395 (10%). Median age: 30.

Denying any impropriety, Dixon said that he had no involvement in his wife's investment and that there was no connection between the transaction and the lawyer's hiring.

Like his chairmanship of ethics, Dixon's D.C. Appropriations post has little immediate political payoff, but it does have one indirect benefit to Dixon — his presence reassures members of the Black Caucus. By exercising control over the money Congress spends on the largely black nation's capital, Dixon prevents intrusion by a chairman who might be less sympathetic to the city's concerns. Dixon's predecessor in the job, Texan Charles Wilson, was openly hostile to the D.C. government.

Dixon has more impact on District affairs than D.C. Del. Walter E. Fauntroy. The California Democrat has been on the front lines of recurring (and often losing) battles against lawmakers' appetite for dictating policy to the city that is Congress' home.

In 1988, Dixon fought in vain against proposals to overrule a D.C. law on gay rights and to bar the district from using its own local tax dollars to pay for abortions. Although Dixon negotiated a narrower abortion restriction in conference with the Senate, he was rebuffed by a House floor vote; similarly the full House rejected a Dixon proposal to soften the gay-rights language.

But Dixon has never been a soft touch for the city government. When D.C. Mayor Marion S. Barry lobbied to transfer the city's judicial system from federal to local authority, Dixon accused Barry of hoarding power.

Dixon's other interests on Appropriations have shifted from foreign to defense policy. At the beginning of the 101st Congress, he made a concerted effort to win a vacant seat on the Defense Appropriations Subcommittee, giving California its only member on that key panel. But Dixon had to give up his long-held seat on the Foreign Operations Subcommittee to make that move. Dixon also picked up a new seat on the Military Construction Subcommittee.

While on the Foreign Operations panel (which oversees foreign aid), Dixon had been sympathetic to the plight of Third World countries, but asked critical questions about some of the ways they use aid money.

Outraged when the Haitian government spent lavish amounts of government funds on the wedding of the country's president at the time, Jean-Claude Duvalier, Dixon persuaded his subcommittee to reduce U.S. aid to Haiti by 30 percent. Later the House voted to give $1 million of the money back, but through an international development fund.

Dixon can be counted on to argue in favor of higher funding for black Africa, and to use the appropriations process to place pressure on South Africa's apartheid regime.

Dixon has generally been more supportive of Israel than other Black Caucus members, a possible reflection of his close political ties to California Democratic Reps. Henry A. Waxman and Howard L. Berman, both strong Israel loyalists.

During the Reagan administration, Dixon used his post on Appropriations to spotlight dissatisfaction with the president's appointees to the U.S. Civil Rights Commission. Because they consistently supported administration positions — such as opposition to busing and affirmative action — Dixon concluded the commission was no longer fulfilling its statutory obligations.

Dixon was chairman of the Black Caucus in the 98th Congress. His performance there was in character — he moved cautiously, got along with the party leadership and tried to put substance over style.

Risking the ire of his black colleagues, he chose in 1983 to bypass the usual course of presenting a Black Caucus substitute to the leadership budget. Instead, Dixon pronounced the leadership budget acceptable, if slightly higher in its outlays for defense than he would have preferred. But the following year, the caucus did offer its own alternative, which Dixon said had the effect of adding almost $6 billion in jobs and anti-poverty programs to the budget that eventually passed.

At Home: Dixon made his early political career by following in the path of Yvonne Brathwaite Burke. When she left the state Assembly in 1972 to run for the House, Dixon quit his job as an aide to state Sen. (and now U.S. Rep.) Mervyn M. Dymally and captured Burke's Assembly seat. Six years later, when she left Congress to run unsuccessfully for attorney general of California, Dixon beat back eight opponents in the Democratic primary to win her House seat.

The primary turned into a struggle for power among political brokers in Los Angeles' black community. Dixon's closest competitor, state Sen. Nate Holden, was backed by Los Angeles County Supervisor Kenneth Hahn, a white man with considerable popularity in the black South Los Angeles area. Another rival, City Councilman David S. Cunningham, was supported by Mayor Tom Bradley. The strongest power bloc was lined up behind Dixon, the choice of U.S. Rep. Henry A. Waxman and state Assemblyman Howard L. Berman (now a House member). The Waxman-Berman machine brought Dixon a 50-38 percent victory over Holden in the primary. Dixon ran unopposed in November and has had no trouble since.

Committees

Standards of Official Conduct (Chairman)

Appropriations (19th of 35 Democrats)
District of Columbia (chairman); Defense; Military Construction

Elections

1988 General

Julian C. Dixon (D)	109,801	(76%)
George Adams (R)	28,645	(20%)

1986 General

Julian C. Dixon (D)	92,635	(76%)
George Adams (R)	25,858	(21%)

Previous Winning Percentages: 1984 (76%) **1982** (79%) **1980** (79%) **1978** (100%)

District Vote For President

	1988	1984	1980	1976
D	113,133 (73%)	108,287 (67%)	91,978 (64%)	91,936 (66%)
R	40,680 (26%)	51,069 (32%)	41,421 (29%)	44,835 (32%)

Campaign Finance

	Receipts	Receipts from PACs	Expend-itures
1988			
Dixon (D)	$120,740	$70,980 (59%)	$114,523
1986			
Dixon (D)	$148,385	$89,005 (60%)	$103,442
Adams (R)	$40,111	$2,089 (5%)	$39,341

Key Votes

1987	
Raise speed limit to 65 mph	N
Approve Gephardt "fair trade" amendment	Y
Ban testing of larger nuclear weapons	Y
Delay "re-flagging" of Kuwaiti tankers	Y
Approve tax-raising deficit-reduction bill	Y
1988	
Approve aid to Nicaraguan contras	N
Enact civil rights restoration bill over Reagan veto	Y
Kill 60-day plant-closing notification measure	N
Pass omnibus trade bill over Reagan veto	Y
Approve death penalty for drug-related murders	N
Bar federal funds for abortions in cases of rape and incest	N
Oppose seven-day waiting period for purchase of handguns	N

Voting Studies

	Presidential Support		Party Unity		Conservative Coalition	
Year	**S**	**O**	**S**	**O**	**S**	**O**
1988	17	71	85	0	3	92
1987	15	83	81	1	7	79
1986	13	74	80	2	12	70
1985	18	75	84	1	11	67
1984	25	61	79	4	12	75
1983	13	71	81	1	8	80
1982	32	55	79	7	15	73
1981	37	54	85	5	11	71

Interest Group Ratings

Year	ADA	ACU	AFL-CIO	CCUS
1988	85	0	100	25
1987	96	0	100	7
1986	85	0	100	25
1985	80	0	100	15
1984	95	5	83	38
1983	90	0	100	20
1982	85	20	100	32
1981	80	0	100	16

29 Augustus F. Hawkins (D)

Of Los Angeles — Elected 1962

Born: Aug. 31, 1907, Shreveport, La.
Education: U.C.L.A., A.B. 1931; graduate work, U. of Southern California Institute of Government.
Occupation: Real-estate salesman.
Family: Wife, Elsie Taylor; three stepchildren.
Religion: Methodist.
Political Career: Calif. Assembly, 1935-63.
Capitol Office: 2371 Rayburn Bldg. 20515; 225-2201.

In Washington: Gus Hawkins entered politics at the dawn of the New Deal, came to Congress early in the civil rights era and now, in his ninth decade, approaches retirement still true to those times, laboring quietly to leave a legacy of better jobs, education and equal opportunity.

He has been well placed to do so, as chairman since late 1984 of the Education and Labor Committee. The trouble is, these are different times, times of budget austerity. Not only Republican administrations, but also many of Hawkins' younger Democratic colleagues, are hostile to old-style domestic spending programs. As a result, Hawkins has needed to concentrate more on protecting past victories than on adding to them. With his politics out of fashion, both Hawkins and his committee on occasion have been shoved to the sidelines of the legislative process.

Yet it is a measure of the man that Hawkins continues to rack up some successes against the odds. So light-skinned that he is frequently mistaken as white, Hawkins has consistently taken a calm, dispassionate approach that, over the years, has sometimes frustrated fellow blacks and liberals. Even when his own Watts area erupted in riot in the 1960s, he criticized those advocating militancy. "We need clearer thinking and fewer exhibitionists in the civil rights movement," he said.

His pragmatic style, while dedicated to New Deal remedies, invites comparisons with the manner of the younger, more moderate blacks elected to the House in recent years. When Hawkins has been able to get results, he has done so by cutting deals with his opponents in both parties. He resists casting issues in black and white. Although the most senior member of the Black Caucus, he has never been elected its chairman. "Racializing an issue," he once said, "defeats my purpose — which is to get people on my side."

With the times against him, he generally has been content to take the partial loaf, confident that the pendulum will swing his way again. For his accommodation to the era of limits, Hawkins was rewarded in the 100th Congress with the passage of a major $8.3 billion education bill that was named for him and for former GOP Sen. Robert T. Stafford of Vermont. In part, the honor was a recognition that Hawkins might not be around long enough to win the whole loaf.

The bill, which reauthorized federal elementary, secondary and adult education programs and created several small new ones, passed the House nearly unanimously. Hawkins hailed the measure as "the first real increase we've had on a domestic issue in several sessions of Congress." On the floor, his GOP committee allies praised the bill and supported Hawkins in fending off any unwanted amendments.

Hawkins had helped clear the way to House passage, and preserved the carefully nurtured bipartisanship, by forcing a compromise in committee over bilingual education. Most Democrats insisted that federal funds continue to go mainly to programs that teach students English while instructing them in other subjects in their native language. Republicans demanded a larger share for alternative methods, such as "English-only" immersion schools. When committee negotiators stalemated, Hawkins threatened to send the bill to the floor without any provision for bilingual education. His fellow Democrats capitulated.

Also included in the bill was a surprisingly modest proposal to expand "Chapter 1" programs for disadvantaged students, which Hawkins cosponsored with Bill Goodling of Pennsylvania, the senior Republican on the Elementary, Secondary and Vocational Education Subcommittee that Hawkins chairs. Under the provision, remedial education would be available not only to elementary students but also to preschool and high school students. Hawkins said he could not seek more money without losing GOP support. "At least we've protected the program until some better days come along," he said.

California 29

South-Central Los Angeles; Watts; Downey

More than four-fifths of the people in the 29th are either black or Hispanic. The district provides the most overwhelming percentages for Democratic candidates in California.

The 29th's minority communities were once pretty well separated, blacks living in riot-scarred Watts, Hispanics in the adjacent suburbs of Huntington Park, Walnut Park and South Gate to the east. But in recent years, there has been more of a mixing. Only five years ago, the four high schools in Watts were majority-black; today, all are mostly Hispanic.

Watts has seen some improvement since the 1965 riots, with the growth of neighborhood centers and concerted attempts to organize residents around housing and health issues. Despite those efforts and aid from the state and federal governments, poverty, high unemployment, blighted housing and crime persist.

More prosperous Watts residents have moved north as their lot has improved. At the northern end of the district are the Los Angeles Coliseum, site of the 1984 (and 1932) Summer Olympics, and the Los Angeles Sports Arena, home of the L.A. Clippers basketball team and also the place where Democrats nominated John F. Kennedy for president in 1960.

In 1988, presidential nominee Michael S. Dukakis benefited from local blacks' Democratic allegiance, carrying better than 80 percent of the district vote. But the impact of this margin was tempered by the district's poor voter participation. Just over 114,000 29th District residents voted in the presidential contest — the second-lowest total in the state.

District Hispanics are not as staunchly Democratic as its blacks. Huntington Park and South Gate both supported Ronald Reagan for president in 1980 and 1984. But only South Gate went for George Bush in 1988.

South Gate and the portion of Downey in the district also house a number of conservative-minded white working-class voters. South Gate has lost Firestone and General Motors plants, but is still an industrial center.

In the original 1980s redistricting, more of Downey's Republican voters were in the 29th. But in the second round, Maxine Waters, a state assemblywoman from the area and head of the redistricting committee, saw to it that this area, which she called "rednecky," was removed. About three-fourths of the city was transferred from the district, leaving only a small Hispanic portion.

Population: 525,938. White 166,888 (32%), Black 263,190 (50%), Other 7,202 (1%). Spanish origin 192,059 (37%). 18 and over 339,585 (65%), 65 and over 46,391 (9%). Median age: 25.

Also in the 100th Congress, Hawkins shared credit for passing (on a third attempt) a bill overturning the Supreme Court's 1984 *Grove City* decision. The bill, which expanded four landmark civil rights laws barring discrimination based on sex, race, religion or ethnicity by entities receiving federal funds, had foundered on anti-abortion groups' contention that it forced hospitals and educational institutions to support abortions.

The Senate added an anti-abortion amendment. Liberal and women's groups initially dug in to oppose it, but faced with losing the entire bill again, decided not to block the measure in the House. Hawkins' committee and the Judiciary Committee waived further consideration of the bill to expedite House passage.

With the abortion question resolved, debate centered on some Republicans' last-gasp complaint that the measure's anti-bias strictures could burden businesses. The usually taciturn Hawkins was eloquently dismissive: "Those who dip their hands in the public till should not object if a little democracy sticks to their fingers." Approval came easily, 315-98; the bill ultimately was enacted into law over Reagan's veto.

Hawkins' style at Education and Labor stands in contrast to that of the man he succeeded, the late Rep. Carl D. Perkins of Kentucky. Perkins was another New Dealer and a genial, courteous man, but he worried little about procedural niceties in getting where he wanted to go. While the committee remains stacked against Republicans and moderate Democrats, and their frustration thus remains great, Hawkins at least allows minority voices to be heard — even if those voices are rarely heeded. At times, Republicans' amendments have clearly been out of order, yet Hawkins has overruled Democrats' objections so the minority member can proceed — typically to be voted down.

Though Hawkins is more cautious and pragmatic than Perkins was, the committee still risks embarrassing defeats when its liberal majority gets far out of step with the House.

It was widely expected that the 100th Congress would raise the $3.35-an-hour minimum wage, but Hawkins and his pro-labor allies lost that effort in part because they overreached and underestimated the opposition. Early in the Congress, Hawkins and Senate Labor Committee Chairman Edward M. Kennedy introduced legislation setting the level at $4.65 over three years, indexed thereafter to rise with the average private-sector hourly wage. Yet it was a year before an Education and Labor subcommittee took up the bill, only to strip Hawkins' indexing provision on a 7-2 vote.

Even Democrats deserted Hawkins, fearing the provision could be inflationary and would harm the bill's chance of passage. To offset its loss, the full committee approved a $5.05 wage. Democrats also defeated Republicans' bid for a lower "training wage" for teenagers. Ready for floor action, Hawkins vowed he would not compromise, and he would restore the index.

Through spring and summer, however, the bill was repeatedly postponed while Democratic House leaders vainly sought to muster a two-thirds vote — the margin needed to override Reagan's likely veto. Not only Republicans were opposed, but so were many Democrats, under pressure from small businesses. Hawkins was confident of majority support, and refused to weaken the bill to attract a veto-proof, two-thirds vote. "I'd rather wait for a new administration," he said.

Meanwhile, in the Senate, a companion bill died in a Republican filibuster. That left the issue to the 101st Congress and President George Bush, who was willing to consider an increase, but not one so high as the $4.55 wage that both Houses quickly passed.

Also in the 100th Congress, Education and Labor failed to get its stamp on a massive bill overhauling the welfare system, to which a number of House committees contributed. The panel approved education and job-training requirements for welfare recipients that were more generous than those proposed by the more influential Ways and Means Committee. When House leaders later pared the bill's cost so it would have enough support to survive on the floor, most of the Education and Labor provisions were jettisoned.

Hawkins reluctantly voted for the bill on House passage. But after Senate passage, he pronounced it "unacceptable" because senators added a "workfare" provision establishing the first federal work requirement in exchange for welfare benefits. He led the opposition in the conference committee, where the controversy nearly doomed the entire bill. In the end workfare remained in the package. Hawkins voted against the final product, damning workfare as "absurd and unrealistic."

In the 99th Congress, the committee's labor-backed bill to ease the effects of plant closings was rejected by the House even after being drastically watered down. But the 100th Congress did enact legislation requiring advance notice of shutdowns, and over Reagan's veto. Initially, Education and Labor attached the measure to a major trade bill, and insisted it remain there even after Reagan vetoed the entire package. But Hawkins, splitting with one of his committee's senior Democrats, William D. Ford of Michigan, agreed to the leadership's gamble; the plant-closing and trade measures were severed and passed again separately. The ploy succeeded; Reagan relented.

Except for the plant-closing measure and another banning most uses by employers of lie-detector tests, the 100th Congress was not the success for organized labor that some expected when Democrats regained Senate control in 1987. Defeats came not only on the minimum wage, but also on Education and Labor-passed bills requiring companies to provide unpaid job leaves to new parents, subsidize child care and notify workers of job-related health hazards.

Hawkins says the biggest change he has seen in a quarter-century in Congress is the influence of outside forces. A chairman, he said, "has to develop a more dynamic or aggressive attitude toward shaping things. One has to go out and develop a constituency outside Congress." For a reticent man, that requires some adjustment.

Perhaps the most important achievement of Hawkins' career is Title VII of the 1964 Civil Rights Act, which mandated fair employment practices and created the Equal Employment Opportunity Commission (EEOC). However, he remains best known as the lesser-known second half of the 1978 Humphrey-Hawkins full-employment bill, a faint echo of the New Deal.

It originally fixed a goal of 4 percent unemployment by 1983, with the government the employer of last resort to meet that goal. But national opinion was already moving against public jobs, and the bill finally passed essentially as a stripped-down memorial to Hubert H. Humphrey, who had died that year. Gone was the requirement for government employment, and the bill's ambitious unemployment goals were offset with the competing objectives of reducing inflation and balancing the budget.

Before taking over Education and Labor, Hawkins spent four years as chairman of the House Administration Committee, the chamber's housekeeping panel. With deficits spiraling in Reagan's first term, the panel became a center of intense partisan fights between majority Democrats, who wanted more money and staff for House committees, and Republicans, who wanted to cut the legislative budget. Even so, Republicans lauded Hawkins as fair and evenhanded. That caused him some problems with his own leadership, and partly explained why Speaker Thomas P. O'Neill Jr. added three loyalists to the committee in 1983.

At Home: For nearly half a century, Hawkins has been representing black voters in south-central Los Angeles. But during all that time — first in the state Assembly, then in Washington — he has always campaigned on economics rather than race. "Race is just not an issue where I am concerned," Hawkins once told a reporter.

It was not much of a subject for Hawkins even in 1962, when he became California's first black member of Congress. "The Negro votes according to his economic interests," Hawkins maintained after that election.

His style had changed little in the 28 years since he had unseated a veteran Republican member of the Assembly. When Hawkins won his first legislative term, in 1934, he said, "It wasn't I but the times that beat him." Hawkins won 13 more terms, in good times and bad, before his chance at Congress finally came.

Hawkins' father Nyanza had been a "Hoover Republican" until his son was elected. A British-born adventurer, Nyanza Hawkins had explored Africa before coming to the United States at the turn of the century. After a few years in Louisiana, the Hawkins family moved to California, where Augustus spent a few years in the real-estate business, then plunged into Depression-era Democratic politics.

As a member of the Legislature, Hawkins wrote more than 100 pieces of legislation, including a bill to establish child-care centers, which he said was his proudest accomplishment. During his last three years in Sacramento, he was chairman of the Assembly's Rules Committee, a job he was given after he lost the speakership by two votes. By then he was growing tired of state politics and was looking for a way out.

It came in 1962, when a new, mostly black district was created in Los Angeles. Yielding his Assembly seat to Mervyn M. Dymally, then a teacher and now a colleague in Congress, Hawkins easily won both the primary and the general election. He was the first black member of Congress from any Western state, a fact he typically omits from his formal biography.

Although his district has changed its shape four times since then, Hawkins' margins have remained constant. Since he won the 1962 primary by 54-24 percent over his nearest rival, he has had six primary challenges, winning each with more than 80 percent.

Committees

Education and Labor (Chairman)
Elementary, Secondary and Vocational Education (chairman)

Joint Economic
Investment, Jobs and Prices (chairman); Economic Goals and Intergovernmental Policy; Education and Health

Elections

1988 General		
Augustus F. Hawkins (D)	88,169	(83%)
Reuben D. Franco (R)	14,543	(14%)
1988 Primary		
Augustus F. Hawkins (D)	60,656	(90%)
Mervin Evans (D)	6,504	(10%)
1986 General		
Augustus F. Hawkins (D)	78,132	(85%)
John Van de Brooke (R)	13,432	(15%)

Previous Winning Percentages: **1984** (87%) **1982** (80%) **1980** (86%) **1978** (85%) **1976** (85%) **1974** (100%) **1972** (83%) **1970** (95%) **1968** (92%) **1966** (85%) **1964** (90%) **1962** (85%)

District Vote For President

	1988	1984	1980	1976
D	92,086 (80%)	103,221 (77%)	86,730 (76%)	88,163 (77%)
R	22,052 (19%)	29,106 (22%)	23,478 (21%)	23,992 (21%)

Campaign Finance

	Receipts	Receipts from PACs	Expend-itures
1988			
Hawkins (D)	$109,450	$105,550 (96%)	$65,833
Franco (R) †	$5,584	0	$4,629
1986			
Hawkins (D)	$87,403	$80,338 (92%)	$34,061

† Totals based on incomplete data.

Key Votes

1987	
Raise speed limit to 65 mph	N
Approve Gephardt "fair trade" amendment	Y
Ban testing of larger nuclear weapons	Y
Delay "re-flagging" of Kuwaiti tankers	Y
Approve tax-raising deficit-reduction bill	Y
1988	
Approve aid to Nicaraguan contras	N
Enact civil rights restoration bill over Reagan veto	Y
Kill 60-day plant-closing notification measure	N
Pass omnibus trade bill over Reagan veto	Y
Approve death penalty for drug-related murders	N
Bar federal funds for abortions in cases of rape and incest	N
Oppose seven-day waiting period for purchase of handguns	N

Voting Studies

	Presidential Support		Party Unity		Conservative Coalition	
Year	S	O	S	O	S	O
1988	14	64	79	4	3	84
1987	15	73	86	3	12	81
1986	19	73	77	9	6	80
1985	14	73	81	2	4	65
1984	19	58	76	4	3	64
1983	12	76	78	3	11	72
1982	34	60	81	5	16	73
1981	34	59	80	8	8	80

Interest Group Ratings

Year	ADA	ACU	AFL-CIO	CCUS
1988	85	0	100	15
1987	92	0	100	15
1986	85	0	92	15
1985	85	0	100	22
1984	75	5	100	50
1983	85	0	100	16
1982	70	21	100	29
1981	85	0	93	11

30 Matthew G. Martinez (D)

Of Monterey Park — Elected 1982

Born: Feb. 14, 1929, Walsenburg, Colo.
Education: Graduated from Los Angeles Trade-Technical College, 1959.
Military Career: Marine Corps, 1947-50.
Occupation: Upholstery company owner.
Family: Wife, Elvira Yorba; five children.
Religion: Roman Catholic.
Political Career: Monterey Park City Council, 1974-80, mayor, 1974-75; Calif. Assembly, 1981-82.
Capitol Office: 109 Cannon Bldg. 20515; 225-5464.

In Washington: Despite two terms as its chairman, Martinez has yet to leave many fingerprints on legislation handled by his Employment Opportunities Subcommittee. He is still overshadowed by the Education and Labor Committee chairman, California veteran Augustus F. Hawkins, who, in his 14th term, is the guiding hand on employment issues.

Most of the issues that move Martinez tend to involve Hispanics, but even there, his most fervent arguments rarely sway many votes. When a partisan split over bilingual education threatened to derail an education package in 1987, Martinez pleaded with fellow Democrats to resist Republicans' demand to shift funds from traditional native-language instruction to alternative techniques, including English-only immersion. Even other liberals ignored Martinez and compromised in the interest of saving the overall education bill.

In both the 99th and the 100th Congress, Martinez earned some attention by working for legislation supported by labor to prohibit private employers from requiring employees to take lie detector tests as a condition for getting or keeping a job. The measure was enacted into law in 1988.

A reliable pro-labor vote, Martinez has opposed a subminimum training wage, which he calls "a way to get around paying the minimum wage to minorities and those who are at the very bottom of the employment ladder."

At Home: In winning his fourth term, Martinez may have begun building some electoral security — if only by exceeding expectations.

Regarded as something of an underachiever in earlier victories in this majority-Hispanic district, Martinez drew a strong primary challenge in 1988 from Lily Chen, a former Monterey Park mayor. But Martinez surprised his critics, turning back Chen by nearly 3-to-1.

In the fall, Martinez was able to maintain his momentum with 60 percent of the vote over Monterey Park business consultant Ralph Ramirez, a Republican he had struggled to defeat once before.

Martinez is himself a former Republican who got his start on the Monterey Park City Council and served as mayor. He began expanding his horizons in 1980 when then-Assemblyman Howard L. Berman, making a bid for his chamber's speakership, backed him in a primary against veteran Assemblyman Jack R. Fenton.

In 1982, the district's House incumbent retired to take a judgeship. Martinez won a plurality in the special election to fill the vacancy. But he then barely survived a runoff with the GOP's Ramirez, who held him to 51 percent. Later that same year, in seeking a full House term, Martinez was matched against GOP Rep. John H. Rousselot, a canny political infighter whose highly visible brand of conservatism earned him a national following.

Rousselot was running in the 30th because his own district had been dismembered in redistricting. Rather than challenge another GOP incumbent, Rousselot decided to try his luck in the heavily Hispanic 30th, appealing to voters' conservative social instincts and to their ethnicity. He used $1,500 in campaign funds for Spanish lessons for his wife and appeared in a Mexican Independence Day parade. But the demographics proved too much for Rousselot, who stalled at 46 percent.

In 1984, Martinez sank most of his campaign funding into an early primary battle with Gladys C. Danielson, the wife of the Democrat who preceded him in the 30th. While her challenge fell far short, it did soften up Martinez for his GOP opponent, lawyer Richard Gomez, who attacked him for poor constituent service and sought a base in the district's growing Asian-American population. Martinez ended up with less than 52 percent of the vote.

In 1986, however, Gomez decided not to try again. That left Martinez with a non-Hispanic opponent, and he pushed his tally above the 60 percent level for the first time.

California 30

San Gabriel Valley — El Monte; Alhambra

As Los Angeles' Hispanic population spiraled in the 1970s, the Hispanic community moved beyond the inner-city barrios to nearby suburbs such as the ones included in the 30th District. The Hispanic population of the 30th — more than half the district total — is second in the state, behind only the 25th in East Los Angeles.

Once a garden spot of orange, lemon and walnut groves, the area in the 30th has become heavily industrialized. Tract houses and rows of palm trees sit alongside factories devoted to light industry and high-tech.

The district cuts a diagonal swath across the San Gabriel Valley. The heaviest Hispanic concentration — as much as 85 percent in some places — is at the southwestern end, adjoining East Los Angeles. Suburbs such as Maywood, Cudahy and Montebello all have substantial Hispanic majorities.

There is a greater ethnic mix in Martinez' home town of Monterey Park, where Asian-Americans compete with Hispanics and Anglos for power, and in the former citrus-shipping center of Asuza.

El Monte (population 97,000) links the eastern and western parts of the district. It is the largest of the 14 independent municipalities in the 30th. For years, El Monte was a major hog-ranching center.

The only distinctly Republican parts of the district are Alhambra and San Gabriel, represented for years by conservative Republican John H. Rousselot.

Population: 526,018. White 353,519 (67%), Black 5,642 (1%), Asian and Pacific Islander 47,234 (9%), Other 4,800 (1%). Spanish origin 286,251 (54%). 18 and over 360,738 (69%), 65 and over 51,576 (10%). Median age: 27.

Committees

Education and Labor (9th of 22 Democrats)
Employment Opportunities (chairman); Elementary, Secondary and Vocational Education; Select Education

Government Operations (20th of 24 Democrats)
Commerce, Consumer and Monetary Affairs; Employment and Housing

Select Children, Youth and Families (14th of 18 Democrats)

Elections

1988 General		
Matthew G. Martinez (D)	72,253	(60%)
Ralph R. Ramirez (R)	43,833	(36%)
1988 Primary		
Matthew G. Martinez (D)	33,615	(74%)
Lily Chen (D)	12,088	(26%)
1986 General		
Matthew G. Martinez (D)	59,369	(63%)
John W. Almquist (R)	33,705	(36%)

Previous Winning Percentages: **1984** (52%) **1982** (54%) **1982 *** (51%)

* *Special election.*

District Vote for President

	1988	1984	1980	1976
D	66,112 (53%)	56,598 (44%)	50,312 (43%)	58,162 (53%)
R	57,754 (46%)	71,658 (55%)	57,521 (49%)	48,584 (45%)

Campaign Finance

	Receipts	Receipts from PACs	Expend-itures
1988			
Martinez (D)	$437,775	$226,400 (52%)	$460,622
Ramirez (R)	$381,587	$126,421 (33%)	$382,111
1986			
Martinez (D)	$165,641	$119,525 (72%)	$135,854
Almquist (R)	$70,556	$4,300 (6%)	$70,955

Key Votes

1987	
Raise speed limit to 65 mph	N
Approve Gephardt "fair trade" amendment	Y
Ban testing of larger nuclear weapons	Y
Delay "re-flagging" of Kuwaiti tankers	Y
Approve tax-raising deficit-reduction bill	Y
1988	
Approve aid to Nicaraguan contras	N
Enact civil rights restoration bill over Reagan veto	?
Kill 60-day plant-closing notification measure	N
Pass omnibus trade bill over Reagan veto	Y
Approve death penalty for drug-related murders	+
Bar federal funds for abortions in cases of rape and incest	Y
Oppose seven-day waiting period for purchase of handguns	N

Voting Studies

	Presidential Support		Party Unity		Conservative Coalition	
Year	S	O	S	O	S	O
1988	14	72	90	2	13	74
1987	22	72	89	5	33	58
1986	18	76	82	5	16	70
1985	19	75	88	2	15	76
1984	27	71	93	5	10	85
1983	10	59	65	2	7	73
1982	32 †	55 †	82 †	6 †	10 †	73 †

† *Not eligible for all recorded votes.*

Interest Group Ratings

Year	ADA	ACU	AFL-CIO	CCUS
1988	90	0	100	23
1987	80	0	100	8
1986	85	10	100	7
1985	80	5	100	19
1984	95	9	92	38
1983	70	0	100	20
1982	80	19	100	24

31 Mervyn M. Dymally (D)

Of Compton — Elected 1980

Born: May 12, 1926, Cedros, Trinidad.

Education: California State U., Los Angeles, B.A. 1954; California State U., Sacramento, M.A. 1969; U.S. International U., Ph.D. 1978.

Occupation: Special education teacher; data-processing executive.

Family: Wife, Alice M. Gueno; two children.

Religion: Episcopalian.

Political Career: Calif. Assembly, 1963-67; Calif. Senate, 1967-75; Calif. lieutenant governor, 1975-79, defeated for re-election, 1978.

Capitol Office: 1717 Longworth Bldg. 20515; 225-5425.

In Washington: Dymally has devoted himself to human rights and civil rights causes that he believes are too often ignored by the House. His interests range broadly, from the troubles of the Tamil minority in distant Sri Lanka, to the close-at-home issue of working conditions in the cramped House mail-folding room.

The Foreign Affairs Committee has been an important base of operations for Dymally since his freshman term, and his role on the panel was enhanced at the start of the 101st Congress, when he took over the chairmanship of the International Operations Subcommittee. That panel's mandate includes the funding and protection of U.S. embassies and their personnel.

Throughout the 1980s, Dymally has been a liberal voice raised against Republican administration foreign policy. He opposed much of President Reagan's overseas agenda, including aid to the Nicaraguan contras and the 1983 invasion of Grenada.

Dymally is an active supporter of sanctions against South Africa's apartheid government. As he postulates on the inevitability of violence if South Africa does not abolish apartheid, Dymally's soothing Caribbean accent often contrasts with his vivid imagery. "The black people of that country hold their meetings over the coffins of their dead," Dymally said during a 1986 House debate. "But the fighting is not so far away.... Soon the white people will also be meeting over coffins."

During the 100th Congress, he joined other Democrats in attempting to toughen the sanctions signed into law in 1986, adding an amendment in committee to bar U.S. imports of South African diamonds. The bill passed the House in August 1988, but died in the Senate.

Beyond the South Africa situation, Dymally's human rights concerns span the ideological spectrum; he excoriates the Soviet Union, Iran's Islamic-fundamentalist regime, rightist Chile and U.S. ally Israel with equal vigor when he sees human rights at stake.

One issue that has drawn Dymally's attention is the plight of the Jewish "refuseniks" seeking to emigrate from the Soviet Union. He has made a number of statements in support of Jewish emigration; on his own or with groups of House colleagues, he has communicated with Soviet officials on behalf of individual refuseniks. Dymally has also taken up the cause of Ethiopia's small community of Jews, many of whom wish to emigrate to Israel.

Dymally also has been pointed in his criticism of Israel, on issues including its arms trade with South Africa and its efforts to break up the Palestinian protest campaign in the Israeli-occupied West Bank and Gaza Strip. "Like a number of Israelis, I am for self-determination.... I do not understand what is so wrong with that," he says.

In addition, Dymally has interceded on behalf of the Black Hebrews, a group of American blacks who proclaim the right to emigrate to Israel on the grounds that they are descendants of one of the 12 tribes of Israel. Though Israel has described the movement as a fraud and denied its members immigration rights, Dymally has defended the Black Hebrews, and he accuses the Israelis of trying to starve them.

Sensitive to criticism that he is in any way anti-Israel, Dymally points out that he supported the $3 billion earmark for Israel in the foreign aid bill passed in the 100th Congress. In 1988, he distributed a thick booklet, entitled "Dymally, Israel and World Jewry," that compiled his many House speeches, written statements and letters in support of Israeli and Jewish interests.

Dymally's involvement in problems affecting minority-group Americans led him in the 100th Congress to take up the cause of the congressional employees — many of whom are black — in the basement facility where millions of pieces of official House mail are folded for

California 31

Southern Los Angeles County — Compton; Carson

This is a working-class suburban district with more ethnic and racial diversity than is found in almost any district in the state. When the district was shaped in the early 1980s, a third of the residents were black, a quarter were of Spanish origin, and nearly 10 percent were Oriental. Then, as now, most voted Democratic. Michael S. Dukakis carried the 31st in 1988 by close to a 2-to-1 margin.

The district's Democratic vote is anchored in lower-income working-class communities, such as Compton — which is almost all black and Hispanic — and Lynwood. Employment is not what it once was at nearby shipyards and auto plants, causing chronic economic problems.

Bellflower and Paramount, majority-white working-class communities at the district's eastern end, are somewhat better off. Hawthorne is another mostly white suburb at the western end, whose residents work largely in the aerospace industry. All of these communities supported President Reagan in 1984, but only Bellflower went for George Bush in 1988.

Carson, at the southern end, is a town of neat trailer parks and retirement communities. A large community of Samoans draws the attentions of candidates for U.S. delegate from American Samoa. Many of Carson's Samoans are still registered to vote on their native island.

The Asian vote in the district is located primarily in Gardenia, a tidy suburb just off the Harbor Freeway, which bisects the district. Japanese-Americans have been a major part of Gardenia's life and politics for several decades. On occasion, the Japanese-Americans will support Republicans of their own nationality, such as Paul T. Bannai, who represented the area in the state Assembly for eight years through 1980, when his district turned back to the Democrats.

Perhaps the district's most famous resident is the Goodyear blimp *Columbia*, whose permanent mooring is clearly visible from the intersection of the Harbor and San Diego freeways. Those two highways are important to the economy of the 31st District. Twice each day, they are filled with commuters from the 31st going to jobs in the defense and electronics industries. Throughout the rest of the day the highways are clogged with trucks hauling the products of the district: aircraft engines, semiconductors and Mattel toys.

Population: 525,939. White 222,211 (42%), Black 177,923 (34%), Asian and Pacific Islander 41,668 (8%), Other 3,343 (1%). Spanish origin 131,121 (25%). 18 and over 354,360 (67%), 65 and over 37,104 (7%). Median age: 27.

delivery. Dymally publicized the workers' complaints over 70-hour weeks without overtime pay, inadequate ventilation, intimidation by management and other problems. The result was a promise from House officials to remedy the situation.

Dymally also has demonstrated his interest in minority issues as chairman of the Congressional Black Caucus, and as chairman of the House District of Columbia Subcommittee on Judiciary and Education.

In the 100th Congress, Dymally was in the thick of the contentious debate over the supposed "undercount" in the decennial U.S. census. That issue was considered by the Post Office and Civil Service Subcommittee on Census and Population, which Dymally chaired in the 100th Congress prior to obtaining his Foreign Affairs subcommittee chairmanship. Dymally is one of those who believes that a formula should be adopted to adjust the 1990 figures to compensate for the expected undercount of many urban minority-group members.

Dymally's subcommittee appeared poised in September 1988 to report a bill establishing an adjustment process for the 1990 census. However, Indiana Republican Dan Burton attached an amendment barring inclusion of illegal aliens in the census count. Dymally then withdrew his support of the measure, which failed 10-11.

A former teacher, Dymally keeps his hand in educational affairs by serving as chairman of the Institute for Science, Space and Technology at Howard University in Washington, D.C. He has also established a scholarship fund to aid needy students.

At Home: Dymally's smashing primary victory over Democratic Rep. Charles H. Wilson in 1980 resurrected a political career whose future looked bleak after a humiliating statewide loss only two years before.

Dymally had become California's leading black officeholder over a long career that began in 1962, when he won the state Assembly seat vacated by Democrat Augustus F. Hawkins, who moved to Congress.

In 1974, running with Edmund G. Brown Jr., he was elected the state's first black lieutenant governor. But then his political career faltered. Unproven corruption charges, which eventually were investigated and dismissed by the FBI, led Brown to keep him at a distance. In 1978, seeking a second term in a job he himself said was not very enjoyable, Dymally received only 43 percent against Republican Mike Curb.

Heading into 1980, friends urged Dymally to run against Wilson, but he was initially reluctant to take on the nine-term veteran. Then former Democratic Rep. Mark Hannaford moved into the district to challenge Wilson. With two well-known white candidates on the ballot in a district that was more than a third black, Dymally decided he could win the nomination.

He was helped by Wilson's legal problems; less than two months before the primary, the House ethics committee recommended that Wilson be censured on charges that included converting campaign funds to personal use.

Wilson had won renomination to his last term only because of split primary opposition. But in 1980, split opposition did not help him. Dymally had solid backing from blacks and strong support from the liberal political machine run by U.S. Rep. Henry A. Waxman and then-Assemblyman Howard L. Berman. Heavily outspending his opponents, Dymally kept up a constant stream of mailings to district voters and won an impressive 49 percent of the primary vote. He won that November's general election with 64 percent and has since won reelection regularly with more than 70 percent.

Committees

District of Columbia (5th of 8 Democrats)
Judiciary and Education (chairman); Fiscal Affairs and Health

Foreign Affairs (9th of 28 Democrats)
International Operations (chairman); Africa

Post Office and Civil Service (11th of 15 Democrats)
Census and Population

Elections

1988 General		
Mervyn M. Dymally (D)	100,919	(72%)
Arnold C. May (R)	36,017	(26%)
1988 Primary		
Mervyn M. Dymally (D)	58,806	(85%)
Colin Kilpatrick O'Brien (D)	10,037	(15%)
1986 General		
Mervyn M. Dymally (D)	77,126	(70%)
Jack McMurray (R)	30,322	(28%)

Previous Winning Percentages: **1984** (71%) **1982** (72%) **1980** (64%)

District Vote for President

	1988	1984	1980	1976
D	96,554 (64%)	87,740 (58%)	76,696 (59%)	79,682 (67%)
R	51,505 (34%)	61,006 (41%)	45,753 (35%)	37,317 (31%)

Campaign Finance

	Receipts	Receipts from PACs	Expend-itures
1988			
Dymally (D)	$488,149	$156,449 (32%)	$481,799
May (R) †	$10,430	$745 (7%)	$10,169
1986			
Dymally (D)	$386,427	$71,358 (19%)	$385,063
McMurray (R)	$43,486	0	$41,875

† Totals based on incomplete data.

Key Votes

1987	
Raise speed limit to 65 mph	N
Approve Gephardt "fair trade" amendment	Y
Ban testing of larger nuclear weapons	Y
Delay "re-flagging" of Kuwaiti tankers	?
Approve tax-raising deficit-reduction bill	Y
1988	
Approve aid to Nicaraguan contras	N
Enact civil rights restoration bill over Reagan veto	Y
Kill 60-day plant-closing notification measure	?
Pass omnibus trade bill over Reagan veto	Y
Approve death penalty for drug-related murders	N
Bar federal funds for abortions in cases of rape and incest	N
Oppose seven-day waiting period for purchase of handguns	N

Voting Studies

	Presidential Support		Party Unity		Conservative Coalition	
Year	**S**	**O**	**S**	**O**	**S**	**O**
1988	16	69	83	3	0	87
1987	10	75	82	3	7	77
1986	13	83	92	2	8	86
1985	15	78	63	6	9	82
1984	24	55	65	5	10	66
1983	16	77	82	5	11	78
1982	22	56	78	4	11	74
1981	29	43	66	4	11	65

Interest Group Ratings

Year	ADA	ACU	AFL-CIO	CCUS
1988	90	0	100	23
1987	84	0	100	0
1986	100	0	93	19
1985	90	10	87	24
1984	85	6	92	33
1983	85	0	94	18
1982	65	17	100	30
1981	55	0	91	21

32 Glenn M. Anderson (D)

Of San Pedro — Elected 1968

Born: Feb. 21, 1913, Hawthorne, Calif.
Education: U.C.L.A., B.A. 1936.
Military Career: Army, 1943-45.
Occupation: Banker; home builder.
Family: Wife, Lee Dutton; three children.
Religion: Episcopalian.
Political Career: Mayor of Hawthorne, 1941-43; Calif. Assembly, 1943-51; Democratic nominee for Calif. Senate, 1950; lieutenant governor, 1959-67; defeated for re-election, 1966.
Capitol Office: 2329 Rayburn Bldg. 20515; 225-6676.

In Washington: After nearly a half-century in local, state and federal offices, Anderson still leaves many baffled as to how and why he ever got into politics.

This withdrawn, quiet man seems to enjoy neither the camaraderie nor the combat of the political game. Some players rely on personal alliances, while others relish confrontation, but few legislators are like Anderson in their apparent unease with both aspects of the job.

For two decades in Congress, his reserved style and concentration on home-state projects was of little matter to anyone else. But all that has changed now that seniority has made him chairman of the Public Works and Transportation Committee. The 101st Congress will be a test, with committee members watching to see whether Anderson can handle a broader agenda with the mix of aggressiveness and accommodation they want in a chairman.

Anderson told an interviewer in 1972, during his second House term, that he opposed the seniority system because "it discourages leadership." The Speaker should choose chairmen, he said, "on the basis of leadership and ability rather than age." If it were not for that system, however, he might not be chairman today.

He inherited the seat after the sudden death of James J. Howard of New Jersey in March 1988. Months later, Anderson was reelected chairman for the 101st Congress, but only after some committee Democrats determined that the man next in line, Robert A. Roe of New Jersey, was unwilling to be their candidate for a coup.

Anderson's weak position was obvious once the lineup of subcommittee chairmen was announced. Under pressure, he had given up the most coveted chair, of the Surface Transportation Subcommittee that he had headed since 1981, to Norman Y. Mineta of California, and settled instead for the Investigations and Oversight panel. Recent Public Works chairmen have not also held subcommittee chairs; Anderson's move after Howard's death to keep Surface Transportation, which has jurisdiction over all highway and mass-transit projects, antagonized some junior colleagues.

With Howard gone, Anderson not only inherited his chair but also the responsibility for defending the committee's turf. Many battles are against the Appropriations Committee, which routinely earmarks money for projects in its members' districts that Public Works has not authorized. In past years, Anderson deferred to the scrappy Howard in conflicts involving his subcommittee's transportation jurisdiction.

Howard lost as often as not, but colleagues appreciated his doggedness. Now the fear is that Anderson will lose, too, but by forfeit.

An initial skirmish was unpromising. Weeks after becoming chairman, Anderson was disregarded when he went to an Appropriations subcommittee, which was drafting the annual transportation spending bill, and objected to its inclusion of funds for the usual array of unauthorized projects.

The Rules Committee was only slightly more receptive when it set the ground rules for House debate on the transportation measure. Unauthorized projects require waivers from Rules to be included in appropriations bills; Anderson, with surprising vigor, asked that the panel deny waivers for eight road projects. "I believe it is time to stop this deliberate evasion of the proper way to legislate," he said.

But one of his targeted projects was in the district of Rules member David E. Bonior, and missing from the hit list, it was noted, was a provision benefiting Long Beach Transit, included by Appropriations at Anderson's request. Rules denied waivers for just three of the items he opposed.

Months later, however, Appropriations members restored two of them during conference negotiations with the Senate, and they did so in a way that he could not contest. They stipulated that if either project was stripped, Anderson's transit provision also would be de-

California 32

San Pedro; Long Beach

Though Anderson is not a national figure in Congress, his ability to deliver public works funding to his home district has truly put him on the map. Long Beach harbor has been named for Anderson, and he has been known to hand out gift bottles of wine labeled "Long Beach Port."

The shipyards are just part of the 32nd's industrial landscape. Aerospace and automotive plants extend along the flat, brown land, sharing space with fuel tanks and oil wells. In the older homes of Long Beach (population 400,000) are the descendants of the fishermen and sailors of many European nationalities who settled here.

Though there is a working-class Democratic tradition here, blue-collar conservatism often shifts the district to Republican presidential candidates. President Reagan won the 32nd easily in 1984, though George Bush eked out a narrow district victory.

Wilmington, at the district's western end, is the only solidly lower-income area, a home for Hispanics, blacks, Filipinos and other Pacific immigrants. In its snaking path through Long Beach, San Pedro and Lakewood, the 32nd strings together a hodgepodge of communities — quiet, middle-income suburbs, commercial downtown Long Beach, and slightly bedraggled stretches of poorer neighborhoods. Though only the inner harbor of the Port of Los Angeles is left in the district, thousands of its residents are involved in the transportation and shipping industries.

At its northern end, the 32nd sticks a two-block-wide finger past Bellflower to take in the southern two-thirds of Downey, which has a Republican lean. That city's huge Rockwell aerospace plant, where the space shuttle is manufactured, is in the district, as are many of the high-tech workers who are employed there.

Population: 525,922. White 384,734 (73%), Black 46,422 (9%), Asian and Pacific Islander 28,677 (5%), Other 4,527 (1%). Spanish origin 119,563 (23%). 18 and over 383,383 (73%), 65 and over 57,884 (11%). Median age: 30.

leted. "He can't have it both ways," said Democrat William Lehman of Florida, chairman of the Appropriations Subcommittee on Transportation.

On another controversial issue that could resurface in the 101st Congress, drug testing of transportation workers, Anderson in the 100th Congress left observers scratching their heads.

The Senate wanted mandatory random testing of workers in the rail, air, bus and truck industries, approving such requirements in its versions of both a comprehensive anti-drug bill and a consumer-protection measure for air travelers.

Anderson seemed to resist. But the fight against testing was waged mainly by other House Democrats — labor and civil-liberties advocates — who called the tests unreliable and an invasion of workers' privacy.

Then, in an unexpected statement just before Congress adjourned, Anderson seemed to endorse drug testing. But his statement was a bid to break the impasse over the airline consumer bill, which also included a labor provision he wanted protecting workers' jobs in airline mergers. That bill, however, went nowhere, and ultimately, random-testing provisions were not included in the drug bill, either. Anderson subsequently said he strongly favored random testing, but felt legislative action was pointless because the Reagan administration was developing its own regulations.

Anderson has taken a lead in mobilizing opposition to head off any increase in the gasoline tax for deficit reduction. That option is unpopular with the groups that frequent Public Works, including highway builders, asphalt manufacturers, truckers and state highway officials. Anderson objects that the tax is inflationary and regressive. Also, like many in the industry, Anderson believes any gas tax should continue to be dedicated to transportation, not to deficit reduction.

He had been an ally of Howard in the long battle that led in 1982 to enactment of a $70 billion four-year highway and mass-transit program, financed by a gas-tax hike. In 1987, Congress authorized another $88 billion through fiscal 1992, overriding Reagan's veto to do so.

Anderson's personal priority in the bill was completion of the Interstate Highway System. He called it "the principal goal of our committee," rejecting complaints that 97 percent of the system had been built and much of the rest would be in costly, congested urban areas.

His overall priorities to date have reflected the work of the two Public Works subcommittees he has chaired, Aviation and Surface Transportation, and of the Merchant Marine Committee, where he rose to the position of No. 2 Democrat before leaving at the end of the 100th Congress. Both panels address the interests of his coastal district, which is home to shipyards, ports and aerospace plants.

He has been a proponent of airline and intercity bus deregulation, safety regulations for the airline and trucking industries and limitations for safe transport of hazardous materials.

In the 98th Congress, Anderson succeeded in winning enactment of his long-sought legislation to promote the use of child-restraint seats in automobiles. Success resulted after his bill became the vehicle for a larger election-year issue — establishing a national drinking age to combat drunken driving. Once the Senate added language to choke off federal highway funds to states that do not raise their minimum drinking age to 21, the bill coasted through Congress and was signed into law.

In 1979, while still Aviation chairman, he pushed into law a bill limiting airport noise, with some help from "anti-noise" Democrats and President Jimmy Carter. The full Public Works Committee and the Senate approved a milder version of Anderson's subcommittee bill, one that was more to the aviation industry's liking. But pressured by his allies and backed by Carter's promise of a veto, Anderson opposed the diluted House-Senate compromise. Negotiators redrafted a tougher version, which became law.

At Home: In a 1989 interview, Anderson proudly unfurled a navigation map of Los Angeles harbor and said, "In the history of our country, there are but two congressmen after whom ports have been named. Sam Houston of Houston and Glenn Anderson of Los Angeles."

Avidly attentive to the Long Beach harbor and other local matters during his service in the House, Anderson comes across in his district as a quiet, successful businessman more than content to stay out of the limelight. And except for one traumatic moment when he was lieutenant governor, he has stayed out of the limelight successfully throughout his political career.

Anderson entered politics early. At age 27 he was elected mayor of Hawthorne, a Los Angeles suburb which then had 8,000 people. (It now has 56,000.) At that point, Anderson already was a prosperous businessman. After earning his college degree in political science and psychology, he had embarked on a profitable career selling automobiles, running a car-repair shop and operating a service station.

Anderson went from the Hawthorne City Hall to four terms in the state Assembly, where he wrote legislation abolishing segregated schools in California. He was defeated for a state Senate seat in 1950 and spent most of the 1950s expanding his home construction business. He served two years as state Democratic chairman.

In 1958, Anderson returned to public office on the coattails of Edmund G. "Pat" Brown, who was elected governor. For two terms as Brown's lieutenant governor, Anderson quietly and efficiently carried out the thankless tasks Brown gave him to do. He specialized in education and urban problems and was a ceaseless cheerleader for Brown's programs in the Legislature, where he presided benignly over the Senate.

He differed with Brown on only a few issues, one of which was Brown's support of John F. Kennedy for the 1960 Democratic nomination. Anderson was for Adlai E. Stevenson.

Brown frequently traveled outside California, leaving Anderson in charge, a practice that caused no problems until August 1965, when race riots broke out in the Watts area of Los Angeles while Brown was vacationing in Greece. Anderson was not quick to respond, and by the time he sent in the National Guard the situation was out of control with 35 dead, hundreds injured and millions of dollars in property damage. Anderson's hesitancy to act was used against him the next year as he and Brown lost to Republicans Ronald Reagan and Robert H. Finch.

Once again, however, Anderson came back, and this time it took only two years. In 1968 Democrat Cecil R. King retired after serving more than 26 years in the House from the Torrance-San Pedro area.

In both the Democratic primary and the general election, Anderson tried to convince voters he was "a conservative in economic matters and a liberal in human matters." His major primary opponent, Los Angeles City Councilman John S. Gibson Jr., and his Republican opponent, Joseph Blatchford, both sought to persuade voters Anderson was too liberal on all matters.

Anderson won the primary with 35 percent and was helped in the fall by a strong presidential vote in the district for Hubert H. Humphrey. The local Democratic strength allowed Anderson to edge past Blatchford with fewer than 4,000 votes to spare.

By 1970 the exciting days of Anderson's political career seemed to be over. He easily won re-election by lopsided margins throughout the rest of the decade.

In 1982, however, he faced a strong challenge. Previous redistricting had removed Anderson's original political base from his district; under the 1982 plan, Anderson picked up a huge number of voters from Republican Dan Lungren's neighboring Long Beach district and lost several Democratic towns.

Republicans felt they could take advantage of the new lines by nominating Brian Lungren, Dan's younger brother. Just under half the voters in the redrawn 32nd had been in Dan Lungren's old 34th District. Any possible confusion seemed likely to help the challenger.

With little in the way of political experience — he had left his job as a policeman at the end of 1981 to work for a county supervisor — Lungren was forced to rely on his brother's connections in building a political base. The two shared a campaign office, and the younger Lungren tried to tap into Dan's fund-raising network. Taking a leaf from his brother's successful 1978 effort, Brian campaigned door-to-door, stressing his law-and-order stance and branding Anderson as "tax and spend Glenn." He tried to resurrect the issue of Anderson's performance during the Watts riot.

But Anderson was not to be dislodged. He reminded Long Beach residents of his scrupulous attention to the harbor and community economic redevelopment, and lined up vocal support from businessmen, Republicans and Democrats alike. Returning to the district each weekend, he defended his stands against Lungren and reawakened the loyalty of conservative Democrats who had abandoned the party.

In the end, Anderson taught the Republicans a lesson, taking 58 percent of the vote, his lowest score since 1968 but still a comfortable showing for his first competitive election in a decade. In his three subsequent re-election campaigns, Anderson has drawn lesser challengers and regained his greater margins — winning with more than 60 percent. The voters seemed unbothered by his age or by the open-heart surgery he underwent in June 1988. But in 1990, Anderson will turn 77. Beyond that, he must face the possibility that the next re-districting will add as many Republican voters to his district as the last one did.

Committee

Public Works and Transportation (Chairman)
Investigations and Oversight (chairman); Surface Transportation

Elections

1988 General		
Glenn M. Anderson (D)	114,666	(67%)
Sanford W. Kahn (R)	50,710	(30%)
1986 General		
Glenn M. Anderson (D)	90,739	(69%)
Joyce M. Robertson (R)	39,003	(29%)

Previous Winning Percentages: **1984** (61%) **1982** (58%) **1980** (66%) **1978** (71%) **1976** (72%) **1974** (88%) **1972** (75%) **1970** (62%) **1968** (51%)

District Vote for President

	1988	1984	1980	1976
D	87,998 (49%)	71,926 (40%)	61,523 (38%)	77,516 (51%)
R	89,411 (50%)	103,902 (58%)	84,461 (53%)	70,804 (47%)

Campaign Finance

	Receipts	Receipts from PACs	Expend-itures
1988			
Anderson (D)	$493,296	$276,785 (56%)	$457,410
Kahn (R)	$20,634	$400 (2%)	$20,608
1986			
Anderson (D)	$457,477	$218,627 (48%)	$417,066
Robertson (R)	$16,503	$3,651 (22%)	$11,742

Key Votes

1987	
Raise speed limit to 65 mph	N
Approve Gephardt "fair trade" amendment	N
Ban testing of larger nuclear weapons	Y
Delay "re-flagging" of Kuwaiti tankers	Y
Approve tax-raising deficit-reduction bill	Y
1988	
Approve aid to Nicaraguan contras	N
Enact civil rights restoration bill over Reagan veto	Y
Kill 60-day plant-closing notification measure	N
Pass omnibus trade bill over Reagan veto	Y
Approve death penalty for drug-related murders	Y
Bar federal funds for abortions in cases of rape and incest	Y
Oppose seven-day waiting period for purchase of handguns	N

Voting Studies

	Presidential Support		Party Unity		Conservative Coalition	
Year	S	O	S	O	S	O
1988	23	62	84	5	34	61
1987	23	69	84	11	40	53
1986	22	78	84	14	32	68
1985	39	60	84	12	36	62
1984	36	61	74	24	42	58
1983	29	70	76	21	45	54
1982	51	49	66	32	59	41
1981	46	50	77	21	47	51

Interest Group Ratings

Year	ADA	ACU	AFL-CIO	CCUS
1988	70	10	92	0
1987	72	14	69	29
1986	75	23	79	28
1985	70	38	88	19
1984	80	17	92	63
1983	75	26	88	10
1982	55	50	80	64
1981	50	13	80	17

33 David Dreier (R)

Of La Verne — Elected 1980

Born: July 5, 1952, Kansas City, Mo.
Education: Claremont McKenna College, B.A. 1975; Claremont Graduate School, M.A. 1976.
Occupation: Real-estate developer.
Family: Single.
Religion: Christian Scientist.
Political Career: GOP nominee for U.S. House, 1978.
Capitol Office: 411 Cannon Bldg. 20515; 225-2305.

In Washington: Dreier and Ronald Reagan came to Washington in 1981 with the shared mission of sharply scaling back the federal government. Eight years later, Dreier exemplifies the frustration of Reagan's early acolytes. Difficult as it was for Reagan to attain his goals, it has been even more of a struggle for Dreier, as a member of the House minority.

Dreier uses his positions on the Banking and Small Business committees to promote an economic agenda that includes the privatization of government services and elimination of numerous federal agencies. But he has had little success in getting the House to consider his proposals.

Most House members serve on Small Business to obtain help for their constituents from the Small Business Administration; Dreier has used his place there to call for eliminating the SBA, as Reagan sought. But Dreier's bill in the 99th Congress to transfer the SBA's lending functions to the Commerce Department never reached a vote in committee.

Dreier brought his distaste for bureaucracy to the 1988 debate over aid for the homeless, and he was one of the few members to speak against the bill. "We are creating a permanent homeless infrastructure in this country," he said. "What we essentially created is another grass-roots lobby that Congress will be unable to say 'no' to in the future."

On the Banking Committee, Dreier advocates bank industry deregulation, supporting moves to allow banks to sell and underwrite insurance. In the 100th Congress, he co-authored a provision on the housing and community development authorization bill to increase the ceiling on Federal Housing Administration mortgage insurance from $90,000 to $101,250 for home buyers in high-cost areas.

Dreier's conservatism fits reasonably well into the House GOP consensus. But he paid an unusual price for it at the end of the 97th Congress, when a combination of retirements and re-election losses put him in line for the ranking GOP spot on the Banking subcommittee dealing with international lending institutions. The panel's Republicans, who favored an internationalist approach, maneuvered like-minded Nebraska's Doug Bereuter into the job because they feared Dreier would be hostile to the U.S. role in international lending. Retiring senior Republican J. William Stanton of Ohio gave up his subcommittee seat to Bereuter, who then used his overall seniority on Banking to claim the ranking position over Dreier.

At Home: Though Dreier is about as safe as can be (he got 69 percent in 1988), he still acts as if he expects trouble. An extraordinarily ambitious fund-raiser, he showed in his last Federal Election Commission filing in 1988 that he had $1.25 million cash on hand, more than any other House member.

Using the Claremont Colleges as his political base and training ground, Dreier waged a four-year campaign against Democratic Rep. Jim Lloyd and beat him on the second try. From the start, Dreier had the support of the influential Claremont College Republican establishment.

Underfinanced and only 26 years old, Dreier came within 12,000 votes of beating Lloyd in 1978. His 1980 campaign was marked by greater maturity and more effort to discuss issues. Dreier followed much of the national GOP line, supporting the Kemp-Roth tax-cut bill and Reagan's presidential candidacy.

National GOP sources, considering Lloyd the most vulnerable Democratic incumbent in the state that year, helped Dreier out-raise Lloyd by almost 2-to-1 and brought in Reagan to campaign for him. Again there was a 12,000-vote margin, but it was in Dreier's favor.

Dreier ended up in another fight two years later, this time with a fellow Republican. Redistricting had moved his Pomona political base out of the 35th, where he had won in 1980, into the neighboring 33rd District. But the 33rd was also home to GOP Rep. Wayne Grisham.

The resulting primary pitted a sedate, casual Grisham against an aggressive and dynamic Dreier. With voters choosing between different personalities, not different ideologies, Dreier's organization and fund-raising contacts brought him a solid victory.

California 33

Eastern Los Angeles — Pomona; Whittier

Most of the land in this sprawling outer suburban district is given over to uninhabitable mountains and hills. The majority of the people are at the southern end, where a mountain named after cornflakes king W. K. Kellogg separates working-class Covina from the white-collar communities of Pomona and Claremont, home of the Claremont Colleges. Farther west, the La Puente Hills isolate Whittier and La Mirada from the rest of the district.

Pomona, with 116,000 residents, is the largest city in the district. The 30 miles of freeway from Pomona to Los Angeles are packed each day with commuters; a smaller though substantial number of local residents opt for the shorter trips to San Bernardino and Riverside areas to the east.

The district combines two divergent elements of California's suburban culture. Voters south of the La Puente hills tend to be middle-aged homeowners with grown children. To the north, newer developments like Walnut and Diamond Bar, along the L.A. commuter routes, draw younger residents.

Though far from unified geographically or culturally, the district is united in its Republican leanings. George Bush topped 60 percent here in 1988, though he fell short of President Reagan's 70 percent in 1984. The only major GOP candidate to lose the 33rd in recent years was Evelle Younger, who challenged Democratic Gov. Edmund G. Brown Jr. in 1978.

Population: 525,348. White 431,594 (82%), Black 28,402 (5%), Other 25,049 (5%). Spanish origin 100,478 (19%). 18 and over 370,470 (71%), 65 and over 42,959 (8%). Median age: 29.

Committees

Banking, Finance and Urban Affairs (8th of 20 Republicans)
Consumer Affairs and Coinage; Financial Institutions Supervision, Regulation and Insurance; General Oversight and Investigations; Housing and Community Development

Small Business (6th of 17 Republicans)
Antitrust, Impact of Deregulation and Privatization (ranking)

Elections

1988 General		
David Dreier (R)	151,704	(69%)
Nelson Gentry (D)	57,586	(26%)
1986 General		
David Dreier (R)	118,541	(72%)
Monty Hempel (D)	44,312	(27%)

Previous Winning Percentages: 1984 (71%) **1982** (65%) **1980** (52%)

District Vote For President

	1988	1984	1980	1976
D	83,319 (37%)	63,307 (29%)	50,062 (27%)	60,050 (39%)
R	142,335 (62%)	152,606 (70%)	117,761 (64%)	89,237 (59%)

Campaign Finance

	Receipts	Receipts from PACs	Expenditures
1988			
Dreier (R)	$487,407	$101,850 (21%)	$186,183
1986			
Dreier (R)	$491,587	$106,800 (22%)	$148,242
Hempel (D)	$23,124	$4,799 (21%)	$22,733

Key Votes

1987	
Raise speed limit to 65 mph	Y
Approve Gephardt "fair trade" amendment	N
Ban testing of larger nuclear weapons	N
Delay "re-flagging" of Kuwaiti tankers	N
Approve tax-raising deficit-reduction bill	N
1988	
Approve aid to Nicaraguan contras	Y
Enact civil rights restoration bill over Reagan veto	N
Kill 60-day plant-closing notification measure	Y
Pass omnibus trade bill over Reagan veto	N
Approve death penalty for drug-related murders	Y
Bar federal funds for abortions in cases of rape and incest	Y
Oppose seven-day waiting period for purchase of handguns	Y

Voting Studies

	Presidential Support		Party Unity		Conservative Coalition	
Year	**S**	**O**	**S**	**O**	**S**	**O**
1988	76	18	89	4	89	5
1987	80	18	95	5	91	9
1986	83	16	95	4	94	2
1985	84	14	92	4	91	9
1984	73	25	95	4	88	8
1983	85	15	97	2	97	2
1982	78	17	87	2	95	1
1981	78	21	95	5	93	7

Interest Group Ratings

Year	ADA	ACU	AFL-CIO	CCUS
1988	5	100	0	92
1987	4	96	0	100
1986	0	95	0	100
1985	10	90	0	95
1984	5	92	8	81
1983	0	100	0	84
1982	0	100	0	95
1981	5	100	0	95

34 Esteban E. Torres (D)

Of West Covina — Elected 1982

Born: Jan. 27, 1930, Miami, Ariz.

Education: Attended East Los Angeles Community College, 1959-63; California State U., Los Angeles, 1963-64; graduate work, U. of Maryland, 1965, American U., 1966.

Military Career: Army, 1949-53.

Occupation: Autoworker; labor official; international trade executive.

Family: Wife, Arcy Sanchez; five children.

Religion: Roman Catholic.

Political Career: Sought Democratic nomination for U.S. House, 1974.

Capitol Office: 1740 Longworth Bldg. 20515; 225-5256.

In Washington: Torres has the background and the personal passion to be a high-profile leader among Hispanics in Congress. But in all his activities — on the Banking Committee, on Small Business and as chairman of the Congressional Hispanic Caucus in the 100th Congress — he has opted for a quieter role.

Torres is generally comfortable with the legislative agenda of the activist liberal Democrats who call the shots on Banking and Small Business. Where he can, the former ambassador to UNESCO works as a conciliator, smoothing out the rough edges of members' personal and philosophical conflicts to help keep legislation moving.

Torres' diplomatic inclinations came into play late in 1987 when a rift on the Small Business Committee divided its chairman, John J. LaFalce of New York, and some of its black members. Tensions boiled over in a meeting of committee Democrats during discussion of LaFalce's package to revamp the Small Business Administration's scandal-plagued minority set-aside program. LaFalce and Gus Savage, a black Democrat from Chicago and one of the more incendiary members, ended up in a shouting match that centered on questions of LaFalce's commitment to minority businesses. After tempers cooled, Torres voiced support for LaFalce's proposal, which required firms participating in the minority business-development program to meet new competitiveness standards. Torres' backing was seen as important in breaking the impasse and moving the bill to the full committee; it was signed into law in 1988.

During Banking Committee consideration of the fiscal 1988 housing reauthorization bill, Torres won approval for his amendment allowing rental rehabilitation funds to be used to bring subsidized housing units up to local earthquake standards.

Like most Hispanic House members, Torres had reservations about the immigration bill that became law in the 99th Congress. In 1984, he argued against the "guest worker" program for agricultural laborers and voted against the bill itself. But in 1986, Torres overcame his misgivings and voted for the measure.

In 1987, he sharply criticized a proposal by the Immigration and Naturalization Service to charge fees of up to $420 — or $185 for each adult — for undocumented immigrant families seeking legal status.

At Home: Torres, a former laborer, entered public service as UNESCO ambassador and as a Hispanic-affairs adviser to President Jimmy Carter. His 1982 campaign slogan was "Autoworker to Ambassador, the American Dream."

Torres was an assembly-line welder at a Chrysler plant in Los Angeles during the 1950s and became active in the United Auto Workers. In the 1960s, he was tapped by UAW President Walter Reuther to start a community action project in heavily Hispanic East Los Angeles.

In 1968, Torres founded The East Los Angeles Community Union (TELACU), which grew into one of the country's largest anti-poverty agencies. His experience there gave him contacts both in the Los Angeles political community and in national Democratic circles, leading to his selection as ambassador and White House adviser.

Torres ran unsuccessfully for Congress in 1974, but another chance came in 1982, when redistricting created an open 34th District. Torres' most difficult obstacle was an Anglo Democrat, former Rep. Jim Lloyd, who had lost his seat in 1980 but was eager for a comeback and found his home base of West Covina included in the new 34th. But Lloyd had too far to go to catch Torres. With strong financial support from the political organization of Democratic Reps. Henry A. Waxman and Howard L. Berman, Torres won the primary handily. Since then, his re-election margins have been comfortable.

California 34

Los Angeles Suburbs — Norwalk

This elongated slice of blue-collar suburbia twists through parts of Los Angeles County tourists see only if they are driving past on one of the four expressways that keep the area fragmented. The 34th more or less follows the San Gabriel River, a channelized concrete trough, through communities that have little contact with each other.

Torres' political success is stoked by two overlapping constituencies: Hispanics, who make up nearly half the district, and blue-collar workers, drawn to him by his labor background.

But a strong dose of working-class conservatism makes the 34th dicier for Democratic presidential candidates. Ronald Reagan easily carried the district in 1984; Michael S. Dukakis took it for the Democrats in 1988, but by a very narrow margin.

One of the Democrats' problems in the 34th is low voter participation by low-income voters. Turnout here was the sixth-lowest among California districts.

At the two ends of the district are two very different cities. On the southern border is Norwalk, an older working-class suburb with a modestly growing population; it is about 40 percent Hispanic. On the northern border is West Covina, a newer, faster-growing and significantly more affluent town; with about 97,000 residents, it has surpassed Norwalk as the 34th's largest city.

Between are the district's most heavily Hispanic areas, around Pico Rivera and South El Monte. Three-fourths of the residents of these towns are of Hispanic origin. Overall, the 34th has the third-highest concentration of Hispanics among California's House districts.

Population: 526,665. White 392,988 (75%), Black 12,228 (2%), Other 25,863 (5%). Spanish origin 249,778 (47%). 18 and over 348,515 (66%), 65 and over 30,687 (6%). Median age: 26.

Committees

Banking, Finance and Urban Affairs (18th of 31 Democrats)
Financial Institutions Supervision, Regulation and Insurance; Housing and Community Development; International Development, Finance, Trade and Monetary Policy

Small Business (12th of 27 Democrats)
Environment and Labor (chairman); Procurement, Tourism and Rural Development

Elections

1988 General		
Esteban E. Torres (D)	92,087	(63%)
Charles M. House (R)	50,954	(35%)
1986 General		
Esteban E. Torres (D)	66,404	(60%)
Charles M. House (R)	43,659	(40%)

Previous Winning Percentages: 1984 (60%) **1982** (57%)

District Vote for President

	1988	1984	1980	1976
D	76,154 (50%)	60,961 (40%)	52,931 (40%)	69,170 (55%)
R	73,409 (49%)	89,795 (59%)	69,202 (52%)	54,515 (43%)

Campaign Finance

	Receipts	Receipts from PACs	Expend-itures
1988			
Torres (D)	$226,964	$108,280 (48%)	$227,098
House (R)	$167,419	$43,792 (26%)	$149,886
1986			
Torres (D)	$181,729	$93,259 (51%)	$111,685
House (R)	$82,896	$4,000 (5%)	$81,759

Key Votes

1987	
Raise speed limit to 65 mph	N
Approve Gephardt "fair trade" amendment	Y
Ban testing of larger nuclear weapons	Y
Delay "re-flagging" of Kuwaiti tankers	Y
Approve tax-raising deficit-reduction bill	Y
1988	
Approve aid to Nicaraguan contras	N
Enact civil rights restoration bill over Reagan veto	Y
Kill 60-day plant-closing notification measure	N
Pass omnibus trade bill over Reagan veto	Y
Approve death penalty for drug-related murders	#
Bar federal funds for abortions in cases of rape and incest	N
Oppose seven-day waiting period for purchase of handguns	N

Voting Studies

	Presidential Support		Party Unity		Conservative Coalition	
Year	S	O	S	O	S	O
1988	16	76	90	2	11	76
1987	10	79	85	3	12	70
1986	18	80	91	2	10	84
1985	18	75	90	1	11	82
1984	26	73	94	2	5	95
1983	21	77	88	4	12	85

Interest Group Ratings

Year	ADA	ACU	AFL-CIO	CCUS
1988	90	0	100	23
1987	96	0	100	7
1986	90	5	93	18
1985	75	10	94	24
1984	95	0	100	38
1983	90	0	100	30

35 Jerry Lewis (R)

Of Redlands — Elected 1978

Born: Oct. 21, 1934, Seattle, Wash.
Education: U.C.L.A., B.A. 1956.
Occupation: Insurance executive.
Family: Wife, Arlene Willis; four children, three stepchildren.
Religion: Presbyterian.
Political Career: San Bernardino School Board, 1965-68; Calif. Assembly, 1969-79; GOP nominee for Calif. Senate, 1973.
Capitol Office: 2312 Rayburn Bldg. 20515; 225-5861.

In Washington: A genial and well-spoken conservative, Lewis has moved steadily up the Republican leadership ladder. But the ascent has not always been an easy one, so it was not too surprising when Lewis chose not to push his luck by running in the open contest for GOP whip in March 1989.

Lewis is a House insider and legislative player at a time when many Republican members are looking for a different approach to the Democratic majority. Lewis' style has made him something of a power broker and brought him a sizable following, but his two most recent leadership races were very close affairs, with almost as many members opposing him as there were supporting him.

Lewis, who assumed his first formal leadership position in 1983, when he became chairman of the Republican Research Committee, has long been in a good position to endear himself to his colleagues. He has been on the Appropriations Committee since his second term, and he is also California's chief representative in the Republican committee-assignment process. As the primary voice for the single biggest bloc of Republicans in the House, he holds considerable sway. In wielding that power, he undoubtedly has made some enemies, but he also has built up many chits by doing favors for colleagues.

Even within Lewis' home-state delegation, though, there are wide differences of opinion about the proper role of a GOP House leader. When Lewis ran successfully for the chairmanship of the House Republican Policy Committee in 1987, his main opponent was fellow Californian Duncan Hunter. Hunter, who lost out on an 88-82 vote, was known for his involvement with a group of Republican activists bent on confronting Democrats, rather than working with them as Lewis has done.

The next year, when the chairmanship of the GOP Conference opened up, Lewis' main opponent was conference vice chairman Lynn Martin of Illinois. On the first ballot, however, he lost some California support because his delegation colleague William E. Dannemeyer was also in the contest. A hard-charging conservative, Dannemeyer turned out to be only a minor threat.

Lewis' contest with Martin was the most suspenseful leadership race of the year. Martin was very active in George Bush's presidential campaign and had enjoyed a high media profile. At the time of the leadership campaign she was widely rumored to be a potential Bush Cabinet appointee. Lewis, careful and organized, managed to get past her on an 85-82 vote — a showing comparable to his 1987 race.

When GOP Whip Dick Cheney left the House in early 1989 to become defense secretary, Lewis seemed a likely contender for the next rung up on the party's leadership ladder. But Minority Leader Robert H. Michel and others helped convince Lewis that it would minimize party strife if he sat out the contest, which was eventually won by Georgia's Newt Gingrich.

"We would have spent the next two months rearranging the chairs of our leadership and not moving forward on our programs," Lewis explained after announcing he would not seek the whip's post. After the two earlier close races, it may also have been on Lewis' mind that he needed to spend time firming up his base before trying again to advance in the hierarchy, lest he overreach. In the longer run, his ambitions could be aided by the growth of California's House delegation; reapportionment after the next census is expected to give the state upwards of 50 House members (currently it has 45).

Lewis' House career has been a mixture of institutional pragmatism and partisanship, with more evidence of the latter in recent years, as the House minority has become more restive. Upon winning his most recent leadership election, Lewis said his mission was to "keep the majority party honest. And while doing that, prepare ourselves to govern."

His effort to keep others "honest" was evident in a number of pursuits in the 100th Congress, when he was both Policy Committee

California 35

San Bernardino County

The 35th is basically a suburban district — with a huge and very dry backyard. Most of the population is packed into the southwestern corner of the district, surrounding the city of San Bernardino on three sides. But then the 35th ranges east to the Nevada border, taking in the vast and sparsely populated desert lands in between.

The Mojave Desert, Needles (the nation's hottest town), and the oddly named community of Zzyzx are places of Western lore, but they provide few votes. The areas that do, at the edge of the Los Angeles orbit, are well-to-do suburbs that give the 35th its conservative Republican tone. George Bush won nearly two-thirds of the district's vote in 1988.

West of San Bernardino, near the border with Los Angeles County, are communities such as Chino and Upland that have been experiencing exurban growth in recent years; the population in both cities jumped by more than 20 percent in the early 1980s. Republicans are strong here, though a Hispanic population provides some Democratic votes.

The cities of Redlands and Loma Linda, both university towns east of San Bernardino, are located in what was once a citrus-packing area at the edge of the nation's southern Citrus Belt. There are still some orange groves around, but the area today is primarily suburban.

There is a scattering of moderately sized cities outside the suburban hub. Among them is Victorville, whose proximity to George Air Force Base drew a number of military retirees: the city's population jumped by 61 percent, to nearly 23,000, between 1980 and 1986. But the boom may have been brought to a halt in April 1989, when Congress ratified a list of military bases to be closed to save money: George Air Force Base was among the casualties. The closure will cost the Victorville area 5,000 military and civilian jobs.

The George shutdown will not erase the military influence that contributes to the 35th's conservative lean. The district reaches into Los Angeles County's northeast corner, picking up a part of Edwards Air Force Base, where the space shuttle lands, and most of Palmdale, which has a concentration of aerospace and defense plants.

Population: 525,956. White 457,891 (87%), Black 17,057 (3%), Other 15,770 (3%). Spanish origin 72,389 (14%). 18 and over 371,311 (71%), 65 and over 54,588 (10%). Median age: 29.

chairman and co-chairman of the Republican Party's platform-drafting committee. In early 1987, when the House debated a proposal to freeze funding to the Nicaraguan contras until earlier payments could be accounted for, Lewis blasted the idea. "This debate today has ... literally nothing to do with accounting," he said. "It is designed to provide cover for those who are opposed to freedom in Nicaragua, who really want to support but are afraid to support the Sandinistas."

In early 1988, when Democrats pledged greater bipartisanship, Lewis said that Republicans viewed such promises as carefully — and skeptically — as they watched Nicaraguan President Daniel Ortega's promised concessions to political opponents.

Later that year, Lewis was among the Republicans who urged Ronald Reagan to veto a defense bill that reshaped key arms programs and imposed certain arms control policies on the president. A fight, Lewis predicted, would allow the GOP to knock down the "charade" that the Democrats had put on at their presidential nominating convention that summer. "Those people are for less defense," he said, "not more defense."

But the pragmatist has also been evident. Early in the 101st Congress Lewis was visible as one of four members of a bipartisan leadership task force, which came together to craft legislation banning honoraria and to develop tactics for promoting a congressional pay raise. The 51 percent pay raise became extremely controversial, and ultimately Lewis was among the overwhelming majority of members who voted to defeat it.

Lewis has been active in fashioning the GOP position in recent anti-drug crusades. In the 100th Congress, as a co-chairman of the GOP's task force on drugs, he pushed legislation containing harsher penalties for users and dealers than the Democratic plan. The omnibus bill that passed the House late in the 1988 election season had been amended with a number of GOP-sponsored measures, such as one calling for the death penalty for drug-related murders. "This is an entirely different measure than what came out of the committees," Lewis said of the final bill. "This bill now has teeth in it."

As ranking minority member of the Appropriations Subcommittee on the Legislative Branch, Lewis has consistently shown his willingness to work cooperatively with the Democratic majority. The panel's chairman, Vic Fazio, is a California colleague and close friend of Lewis, and they normally forge a united front against efforts to scale back the amount of money Congress spends on itself in the legislative appropriations bill.

Still, some partisanship comes out occasionally during work on the legislative branch appropriations bill. In 1987 Lewis pushed a floor amendment to stop the House television cameras from panning the chamber during special order speeches. The panning practice had been ordered by Speaker Thomas P. O'Neill Jr. in 1984, to show an empty chamber when conservative Republicans were delivering aggressive and unanswered attacks on Democrats. Lewis dubbed his amendment the "Sala Burton/Stewart McKinney Memorial Panning Reform Amendment," because he had been disturbed when the cameras panned during tributes to the deceased members, showing a nearly empty chamber. But despite his arguments that the panning undermined the image of the House, the amendment lost on a party-line vote after some bitter exchanges.

Lewis has made much of his legislative mark on the Appropriations subcommittee that handles foreign aid, and he has made it as an enduring critic of the World Bank and other international development agencies. His rationale is simple enough: "Some of us think it's time we began to seriously look at whether the dollars that are being expended are even beginning to do what they were intended to do." Insisting that he is not dogmatic on the subject, Lewis says he simply wants this lending to be done on sound principles.

His main target has been the International Development Association (IDA), the arm of the World Bank that lends money to the poorest nations. He persuaded the Reagan administration to reduce the budget request for the IDA contribution in 1986. He has worked to limit funding for the World Bank and the International Monetary Fund unless they urge Third World countries to adopt strategies Lewis deems vital to economic growth. Lewis' prescription includes cutting taxes, liberalizing trade and curbing government spending. He also has proposed selling the World Bank and similar institutions to private interests.

Nevertheless, Lewis sees an important role for some kind of international lending in light of the Third World debt crisis. "If just one or two countries default on their loans, that could lead to a ripple effect that in final form would spell disaster," he says. "The countries of the world cannot afford to put their collective heads in the sand and wish this problem away."

In general, however, Lewis wants U.S. aid to be bilateral rather than multilateral, and he wants more of it to be military than economic. In 1986, when his Appropriations subcommittee went into a private session to reaffirm a Democratic package stressing multilateral and economic assistance, he fumed at "prearranged deals made behind closed doors," adding, "To walk in there and know you were going to get rolled, you might have stayed home."

Lewis also is on the VA, HUD and Independent Agencies Subcommittee at Appropriations, where he has the opportunity to help oversee the Environmental Protection Agency. Earlier in his career, he sponsored a resolution with several liberal Democrats reaffirming a congressional commitment to clean air. "Attempts to relax the standards," Lewis said, "could dramatically increase the air-pollution levels throughout the United States."

Closer to home, Lewis has sought to bring water to his desert-dominated district, although he has expressed some qualms about the pork-barrel aspect of water projects. In 1986, President Reagan signed a bill he had introduced, the Lower Colorado Water Supply Act, to improve access to water for small desert communities. Lewis also has a strong interest in earthquake research and has worked on the Appropriations Committee to steer money to the Cajon Pass earthquake research site in California.

At Home: Lewis' political career has followed a steady course from school board to state Legislature to Congress. Each time he has methodically used his existing electoral base to move up the political ladder.

He started a successful insurance business in San Bernardino, entered Republican politics and developed contacts that won him a place on the school board. After three years in that office, he ran for a state Assembly seat in the county and was elected to five Assembly terms with a vote that never fell below 59 percent.

In late 1973, with a major redistricting about to take place, Lewis ran in a special election for the state Senate. He finished first in the special primary, winning with 49 percent. Just 463 more votes would have given Lewis a majority and, by California law, elected him. But he was forced into a runoff with Democrat Ruben S. Ayala, who went on to win the seat with 54 percent.

Lewis was re-elected to the Assembly in 1974 in a redrawn district and, in 1976, even managed to win the Democratic nomination in a write-in campaign, the first Republican assemblyman to do so since state law barred candidates from filing in both parties.

Lewis' new Assembly constituency covered more than half the 37th Congressional District, so he was the obvious successor in 1978 when Republican Rep. Shirley N. Pettis retired. Earlier in his career, Lewis had worked as a field representative for Jerry Pettis, Shirley's husband, who represented the district for eight years before dying in a plane crash in 1975. Declaring himself a candidate in the "Pettis tradition," Lewis won the five-candidate GOP primary with 55 percent of the vote. In the general election, Lewis campaigned virtually as the incumbent, ignoring his Democratic opponent and spending three times as much money to win handily.

In 1982 the Democrats' redistricting plan gave Lewis a choice of two districts in which to run. The chief architect of the remap, Democratic Rep. Phillip Burton, had assumed Lewis would run in the 37th District, which took up most of heavily Republican Riverside County. But Lewis' home had been placed in the neighboring 35th, and he filed there.

His action forced Republican Rep. David Dreier, whose home was also placed in the new 35th, to look elsewhere. Dreier ended up in a nearby district, ousting incumbent GOP Rep. Wayne Grisham in a primary.

The 1983 revision of the redistricting plan again changed Lewis' district, but gave him little to worry about in future elections.

Committee

Appropriations (13th of 22 Republicans)
Legislative Branch (ranking); Foreign Operations; VA, HUD and Independent Agencies

Elections

1988 General		
Jerry Lewis (R)	181,203	(70%)
Paul Sweeney (D)	71,186	(28%)
1986 General		
Jerry Lewis (R)	127,235	(77%)
R. "Sarge" Hall (D)	38,322	(23%)

Previous Winning Percentages: 1984 (85%) **1982** (68%) **1980** (72%) **1978** (61%)

District Vote For President

	1988	1984	1980	1976
D	88,126 (33%)	59,824 (28%)	45,868 (27%)	41,739 (43%)
R	172,872 (65%)	154,583 (71%)	111,606 (65%)	53,027 (55%)

Campaign Finance

	Receipts	Receipts from PACs	Expend-itures
1988			
Lewis (R)	$212,905	$156,400 (73%)	$337,814
1986			
Lewis (R)	$141,143	$105,103 (75%)	$91,355

Key Votes

1987	
Raise speed limit to 65 mph	Y
Approve Gephardt "fair trade" amendment	N
Ban testing of larger nuclear weapons	N
Delay "re-flagging" of Kuwaiti tankers	N
Approve tax-raising deficit-reduction bill	N
1988	
Approve aid to Nicaraguan contras	Y
Enact civil rights restoration bill over Reagan veto	N
Kill 60-day plant-closing notification measure	Y
Pass omnibus trade bill over Reagan veto	N
Approve death penalty for drug-related murders	Y
Bar federal funds for abortions in cases of rape and incest	Y
Oppose seven-day waiting period for purchase of handguns	Y

Voting Studies

	Presidential Support		Party Unity		Conservative Coalition	
Year	**S**	**O**	**S**	**O**	**S**	**O**
1988	44	24	67	12	55	11
1987	68	30	81	12	91	2
1986	63	21	63	14	56	16
1985	65	28	75	18	84	11
1984	71	22	72	18	83	10
1983	70	20	74	17	74	8
1982	81	16	84	13	89	10
1981	72	20	75	15	81	15

Interest Group Ratings

Year	ADA	ACU	AFL-CIO	CCUS
1988	5	90	22	67
1987	8	83	13	93
1986	0	88	15	64
1985	10	76	27	62
1984	10	86	17	81
1983	5	88	13	89
1982	5	91	5	100
1981	5	79	0	100

36 George E. Brown Jr. (D)

Of Riverside — Elected 1962

Did not serve 1971-1973.

Born: March 6, 1920, Holtville, Calif.
Education: Graduated from El Centro Jr. College, 1938; U.C.L.A., B.A. 1946.
Military Career: Army, 1942-46.
Occupation: Physicist; management consultant.
Family: Widowed; four children.
Religion: Methodist.
Political Career: Monterey Park City Council, 1954-55, mayor, 1955-58; Calif. Assembly, 1959-63; sought Democratic nomination for U.S. Senate, 1970.
Capitol Office: 2188 Rayburn Bldg. 20515; 225-6161.

In Washington: Watching Brown today, as he listens patiently to committee testimony on the science budget or shuffles from the House floor to enjoy another cigar in the solitude of the members' lobby, it is hard to recall the spirited anti-war crusader of the 1960s. But he is the same man; Brown has simply mellowed with the times, and perhaps grown weary with the years of political battle.

The impression of a divergence is underscored by fact: Brown has had, in effect, two separate House careers in which to pursue his liberal causes, broken by a one-term absence after his 1970 Senate defeat. Two issues — environmentalism and opposition to nuclear war — are the link between them.

When Brown returned to the House in 1973, the Vietnam War was ending. He settled quietly into the Science and Agriculture committees and followed his issues, thoughtful but detached. Though a senior member of Agriculture now, he only seems engaged when the discussion turns from farm policy to the subject of pesticide regulation. On Science, he is an avid defender of the Environmental Protection Agency, and the leading opponent of military uses of space.

The old peace advocate re-emerges in debates on space-based military programs. Brown has succeeded in at least slowing the development of anti-satellite (ASAT) weapons; for several years before 1988, he sponsored the amendments to annual defense bills that imposed one-year bans on testing ASAT weapons against targets in space, contingent on Soviet abstention.

In 1988, however, he and cosponsor Lawrence Coughlin of Pennsylvania, a Republican moderate, gambled for the kill and lost. They proposed a permanent ban. Though still contingent on mutual Soviet restraint, the proposal caused some members to feel "squeamish," by one's description. It was defeated 197-205.

Brown is one of the more outspoken foes of the strategic defense initiative (SDI). He has supported efforts to cut its funding, and to commit the United States to continued observance of the 1972 anti-ballistic missile treaty — a document he says SDI would violate.

He fights against the Pentagon's growing role in space not only on defense bills, but also on legislation for the National Aeronautics and Space Administration (NASA), over which Science has jurisdiction. A strong believer in civilian exploration, Brown complains about the hefty fraction of NASA's pinched budget that goes for defense-related work. "That's about all NASA is at the present time — an appendage to the Pentagon," he said in 1986.

Brown's anti-military approach to space policy may have cost him a couple of key committee seats. In November 1987 he announced his resignation from the Intelligence Committee, calling it "a protest to the administration's use of the classification system to prevent members of Congress from engaging in vital national debates." However, Brown had come under pressure to resign from conservative Democrats, who agreed with the Reagan administration that Brown had divulged classified information about U.S. military satellite capabilities. He insisted he relied only on published accounts.

Earlier, in 1985 and 1987, the chairmanship of the important Science Subcommittee on Space Science went to a colleague with far less seniority, Bill Nelson of Florida. Nelson's 1985 victory over Brown was explained in part in regional and generational terms: Nelson, whose district includes the Kennedy Space Center, drew support from junior members and the panel's Floridians. But also, Brown's strong opinions about the use of space funds probably

California 36

San Bernardino; Riverside

Of the three districts covering the San Bernardino-Riverside metropolitan area, this is the only one a Democrat can win. Brown has done it in House elections by combining the votes of the blue-collar Anglo residents of San Bernardino and Riverside with those of San Bernardino's large Mexican-American population.

But no liberal candidate can rest comfortably here. This section of Southern California desert country is a conservative area where religious fundamentalism is a crucial factor.

This mixture makes the 36th one of the more competitive California districts in presidential elections. President Reagan carried the 36th with a comfortable 56 percent in 1984, but George Bush prevailed by a more modest margin.

About three-quarters of the district vote is cast in San Bernardino County. The county's "West Valley" area has drawn large numbers of middle-class newcomers pushed out of eastern Los Angeles and Orange counties by high real estate prices.

The city of San Bernardino (population 139,000) was a fruit-packing center in the 1930s. Today, its citrus industry shares space with the many electronics and aerospace firms in the area, as well as Kaiser Steel Corp.'s blast furnace in nearby Fontana.

Though the city has seen years of growth, San Bernardino suffered some blows in early 1989. That April, Congress ratified a military base-closing list that included Norton Air Force Base near the city.

Then, in May, a San Bernardino neighborhood was shattered by a pair of freak accidents. First, a runaway freight train crashed into a group of homes, causing several deaths. Just days later, a gas pipeline nicked by the train wreck erupted in flames, causing more death and destruction.

To the west of San Bernardino is burgeoning Ontario, which supports a major commercial airport and large Lockheed and General Electric plants. With the economy dependent on the local defense plants, Ontario voters have turned increasingly toward Republican candidates.

The 36th then reaches into Riverside County for a portion of the city of Riverside. Though parts of the city are in the 37th, Brown has the more Democratic northern neighborhoods, including blue-collar communities and the area around the University of California at Riverside.

Farther west is Glen Avon, site of the Stringfellow Acid Pits. A cleanup of toxic-contaminated groundwater is under way there.

Population: 525,987. White 402,029 (76%), Black 43,141 (8%), Other 13,913 (3%). Spanish origin 121,631 (23%). 18 and over 362,108 (69%), 65 and over 48,227 (9%). Median age: 27.

alienated some members who believe virtually any space expenditure is a good one. He considered reasserting his seniority claim to the chair again in the 100th Congress, but was dissuaded by a lack of support.

Having lost the Science Subcommittee in 1985, Brown could have retained the chairmanship of the Agriculture Subcommittee on Department Operations and Research that he had held for four years. He chose not to.

That assignment had been frustrating because it involved managing the contentious and unsuccessful legislative effort to renew the Federal Insecticide, Fungicide and Rodenticide Act. The FIFRA debate pitted pesticide manufacturers against environmentalists demanding more industry regulation. Brown was the referee, and not a happy one. "If this ever comes up again while I am on the committee," he said at one point, "I hope you will refer it to another subcommittee."

Nevertheless, in the 100th Congress, Brown not only regained the Agriculture subcommittee (after conceding the Science panel to Nelson), he also took responsibility for the FIFRA bill and helped steer a stripped-down version into law. He and other leaders of the House and Senate Agriculture committees broke the stalemate only by agreeing to drop the bill's most controversial provisions. The final measure required chemical companies to determine the health risks of their products under a mandatory timetable, and charged them fees to help finance EPA reviews of their research. But gone were provisions to allow stronger state laws, excuse farmers from liability and protect groundwater.

On other farm issues, Brown has never been an activist. He ranks third among the 27 Agriculture Democrats, but rarely speaks out and was not a major participant in work on the five-year farm bill in the 99th Congress.

On other issues, Brown casts liberal votes much as he did during the 1960s. Occasionally, however, he has cast pragmatic pro-defense votes he might have denounced two decades ago.

Early in the 101st Congress, he and Republican Jerry Lewis, from the neighboring 35th District, led the futile opposition to a package of proposed military base closures. The package, compiled by a blue-ribbon commission, had widespread support in Congress since most members' home-state bases escaped inclusion. But among the targets was Norton Air Force Base in Brown's district, employer of 4,520 military personnel and 2,133 civilians.

In 1980 he began voting for a California product, the B-1 bomber. "If the B-1 was being built in some other state," he once explained, "and I didn't have two Air Force bases and a lot of retired military people who feel strongly about the B-1, I'd probably have voted the other way."

This is the man, after all, who became a peace advocate as a scientist, and argued his cause from the start of his first term, in 1963. That year, he opposed extension of the draft as it passed the House 388-3. He voted against civil defense money, saying it "created a climate in which nuclear war becomes more credible."

By the spring of 1965, he had already begun speaking out against the Vietnam War, accusing President Johnson of pretending "that the peace of mankind can be won by the slaughter of peasants in Vietnam." For the next five years he kept up such protests, refusing to vote for any military spending while the war continued; in 1966 his was the only House vote against the $58 billion defense bill.

Brown acquired a national reputation for his anti-war work during those years, but even then much of his legislative time was devoted to environmental issues. He supported a ban on offshore oil drilling along the California coast, backed federal land-use planning and proposed to outlaw production of internal combustion engines.

One intriguing legacy from the 1960s is Brown's relationship with President Bush, who served with him in the House late in the decade. Despite his liberalism, Brown was one of a number of Democrats whom Bush befriended. Both had to leave the House after 1970 Senate defeats, and Bush subsequently wrote to his former gym partner that he regretted the loss of "the paddleball earnings that you have made possible for me, my wife and my children."

At Home: Before his 1970 Senate campaign, Brown's political career revolved around the heavily Hispanic community of Monterey Park. His recent phase has focused on middle-class politics in San Bernardino, 50 miles east.

Born in a small town in California's Imperial Valley, Brown attended college in Los Angeles, then settled in Monterey Park after getting his physics degree. While working for the Los Angeles city government, he began dabbling in Monterey Park politics. After four years on the City Council and in the mayor's office, he was elected to the state Assembly, where he focused on housing issues.

In 1962 the new 29th District was created on Brown's home turf. He easily defeated two strong primary opponents and Republican H. L. "Bill" Richardson in the general election.

Once he developed his reputation as an anti-war leader, Brown attracted a series of opponents — Democrats and Republicans — who challenged him on the Vietnam issue. His closest call came in 1966 against Republican Bill Orozco, who capitalized on his Mexican-American heritage. Brown won by 3,000 votes; it was clear he would have tough future races.

Rather than run again for what had become a marginal seat, Brown decided in 1970 to take on GOP Sen. George Murphy. But to do that he had to wage a primary against U.S. Rep. John V. Tunney, son of former boxing champion Gene Tunney. After American troops invaded Cambodia that spring, polls began to show Brown edging in front of Tunney, who had been much less outspoken against the war. Brown called for the impeachment of President Nixon because of the invasion. Tunney then turned his aim on Brown, accusing him of being a radical and advocating student violence. Brown attempted to deflect what he termed Tunney's "dirty" tactics, but failed and lost by a 9-percentage-point margin.

However, Brown exacted a revenge of sorts. His description of Tunney as the "lightweight son of the heavyweight champ" became part of California political folklore and helped end Tunney's career in 1976.

Brown's political resurrection came just two years after his failed Senate bid, in a newly created district in the San Bernardino-Riverside area. There it was middle-class white conservatives, not Mexican-Americans, who caused problems for Brown.

The 1972 Democratic primary in the new district was a fierce battle. Brown was attacked as an extreme liberal, but he prevailed in the eight-candidate field by finishing second in all three parts of the district. While not impressive, his 28 percent of the vote was enough to get him on the fall ballot as the Democratic candidate in a district over 60 percent Democratic in registration. He won comfortably in November.

Brown topped 60 percent in three consecutive elections, even though 1974 redistricting put more of fast-growing and conservative Riverside County into the district, forcing Brown to rely more on San Bernardino County votes to carry him. But in 1980, Brown's tally plunged to 53 percent. He got some help in 1981 from a partisan Democratic remap that patched together the most Democratic district possible for him from portions of Riverside and San Bernardino. Still, changing demographics have brought young, conservative-minded voters into the area, and in recent years Brown has been a focus of GOP attention.

In the 1980 election, Republican John Paul Stark, a conservative whose organization came largely from the Campus Crusade for Christ, held Brown below a majority in Riverside for the first time. Brown survived because of his comfortable margin in San Bernardino County.

Brown increased his margin over Stark in a second campaign in 1982, but the challenger returned in 1984 with what Republicans — and many Democrats — believed would be his strongest effort yet. This time, he had the advantage of President Reagan's name on the top of the GOP ballot. But Brown had prepared carefully for the second rematch. His attention to the Stringfellow Acid Pits, a toxic-waste dump near Riverside, played well among middle-class voters susceptible to Stark's appeal.

In addition, Brown took his campaign onto Stark's home ground. He made the rounds of local churches — mainstream and fundamentalist — delivering his own arguments on the importance of extending "pro-life" views to take in nuclear-weapons issues and humanitarian concerns. He wound up taking 57 percent.

In 1986, Brown faced Bob Henley, a San Bernardino businessman. Henley's more moderate politics gave Republicans hope that he could appeal to a broader coalition than Stark. As it turned out, however, Henley had trouble even getting the business community to warm up to him, and he had great difficulty raising money until late in the campaign. As in 1984, Brown addressed his areas of weakness head-on, using a program of coffees around the district to meet new voters, and working hard to line up endorsements from law enforcement groups and local businessmen. He again took 57 percent.

Stark was back a fourth time in 1988, heartened by the district's declining Democratic registration. He may be right about the demographic trend, but he has yet to broaden his own base. Brown was held to 54 percent, but Stark mustered just 42 percent.

Committees

Agriculture (3rd of 27 Democrats)
Department Operations, Research and Foreign Agriculture (chairman)

Science, Space and Technology (2nd of 30 Democrats)
International Scientific Cooperation; Natural Resources, Agriculture Research and Environment; Science, Research and Technology; Transportation, Aviation and Materials

Elections

1988 General

George E. Brown Jr. (D)	103,493	(54%)
John Paul Stark (R)	81,413	(42%)

1988 Primary

George E. Brown Jr. (D)	48,148	(82%)
James D. Sparks (D)	10,450	(18%)

1986 General

George E. Brown Jr. (D)	78,118	(57%)
Bob Henley (R)	58,660	(43%)

Previous Winning Percentages: **1984** (57%) **1982** (54%) **1980** (53%) **1978** (63%) **1976** (62%) **1974** (63%) **1972** (56%) **1968** (52%) **1966** (51%) **1964** (59%) **1962** (56%)

District Vote For President

	1988	1984	1980	1976
D	92,521 (47%)	80,504 (43%)	58,623 (40%)	66,240 (58%)
R	100,291 (51%)	103,809 (56%)	74,963 (51%)	47,161 (41%)

Campaign Finance

	Receipts	Receipts from PACs	Expend-itures
1988			
Brown (D)	$504,361	$276,543 (55%)	$532,897
Stark (R)	$219,019	$89,155 (41%)	$218,696
1986			
Brown (D)	$547,236	$227,867 (42%)	$511,240
Henley (R)	$212,824	$49,119 (23%)	$210,003

Key Votes

1987

Raise speed limit to 65 mph	Y
Approve Gephardt "fair trade" amendment	N
Ban testing of larger nuclear weapons	Y
Delay "re-flagging" of Kuwaiti tankers	Y
Approve tax-raising deficit-reduction bill	Y

1988

Approve aid to Nicaraguan contras	N
Enact civil rights restoration bill over Reagan veto	Y
Kill 60-day plant-closing notification measure	N
Pass omnibus trade bill over Reagan veto	Y
Approve death penalty for drug-related murders	N
Bar federal funds for abortions in cases of rape and incest	N
Oppose seven-day waiting period for purchase of handguns	?

Voting Studies

	Presidential Support		Party Unity		Conservative Coalition	
Year	S	O	S	O	S	O
1988	13	65	80	3	8	76
1987	18	70	78	5	21	65
1986	18	71	82	3	16	76
1985	20	68	84	5	9	76
1984	27	69	91	5	12	81
1983	16	77	84	5	11	82
1982	32	51	85	5	12	79
1981	38	57	77	10	19	75

Interest Group Ratings

Year	ADA	ACU	AFL-CIO	CCUS
1988	80	5	100	25
1987	76	10	86	7
1986	95	0	92	21
1985	85	6	93	28
1984	95	0	82	33
1983	90	0	100	25
1982	75	5	94	29
1981	85	13	86	12

37 Al McCandless (R)

Of La Quinta — Elected 1982

Born: July 23, 1927, Brawley, Calif.
Education: U.C.L.A., B.A. 1951.
Military Career: Marine Corps, 1945-46, 1950-52.
Occupation: Automobile dealer.
Family: Wife, Gail Walmsley Glass; five children.
Religion: Protestant.
Political Career: Riverside County supervisor, 1970-1982; candidate for Calif. Assembly, 1975.
Capitol Office: 435 Cannon Bldg. 20515; 225-5330.

In Washington: McCandless has spent three terms in the House trying to convey the perspective of a businessman to his colleagues on the Banking Committee and on Government Operations.

Despite his relatively junior status, McCandless is the second-oldest Republican on Banking. Because of his age and his experiences in the automobile sales business, his views on government's proper role in the free enterprise system receive some note.

But McCandless' abiding resentment of federal regulation is so strong that it limits his ability to play a consensus-building role when disputes are being thrashed out. Even some conservative Republicans note that the Californian can be too opinionated to play a significant role in shaping legislation.

One cause McCandless has pursued for much of his House career is reform of the Social Security system. He has proposed legislation to remove Social Security trust funds from the federal budget, and to make the Social Security Administration an independent agency. In the 100th and 101st Congresses, McCandless introduced bills to repeal the limit on Social Security earnings. He calls the limitation "an unnecessary burden on the elderly."

In the 99th Congress, McCandless proposed a "Federal Government Easy Access Act" that would have required federal agencies to include the phone number of a contact person on letters and forms sent to the public. Many of McCandless' speeches on the House floor are broadsides against the federal budget deficit and Congress' ineffectiveness in dealing with it.

McCandless occasionally comes to the defense of a federal program. A member of the Banking Subcommittee on Housing, he favors the mortgage guarantee programs of the Federal Housing Administration. In 1986, the House endorsed his amendment to the Foster Grandparent program. His provision would allow Foster Grandparent services to be provided to mentally retarded individuals over age 21; under existing law, only those adults who received services before age 21 are eligible.

Occasionally, McCandless reaches back into his career in the car business to help him explain points in a policy debate. Arguing once against a nuclear-weapons freeze on the grounds that the United States had inferior weaponry, he complained that "we have Model Ts, and they have Thunderbirds."

At Home: McCandless owes his seat largely to geography. He was hardly known outside his home base around Palm Springs when he decided to run for the House in 1982. The district was open because of redistricting and the decision of GOP Rep. Jerry Lewis to campaign in a constituency to the north.

McCandless was outcampaigned for the nomination by Ken Calvert, a 28-year-old businessman with a base among rank-and-file GOP regulars in the fast-growing Corona area. But Calvert had to contend with seven other candidates from the western side of the district, while McCandless was the only major contender from the desert area around Palm Springs. His reputation as a civic leader brought him heavy local support there, and he edged Calvert by 868 votes.

Because McCandless won the primary with barely a quarter of the vote, some GOP strategists worried that he would have trouble against Democratic nominee Curtis P. "Sam" Cross. The Indio sheriff, Cross had once worked in the Riverside Police Department, and his law-and-order approach seemed to appeal to conservatives of both parties.

But Cross was suspect among liberal Democrats, and he found it difficult to compete with McCandless' social contacts and funding advantage. The Republican had substantial help from the conservative GOP desert elite centered in Rancho Mirage. Frank Sinatra was a contributor, and Bob Hope appeared for him. McCandless also benefited from redistricting, which siphoned off Democrats to protect Democratic Rep. George E. Brown Jr. in an adjoining district. McCandless won with 59 percent of the vote, and in each of the three subsequent elections, he has taken 64 percent.

California 37

Riverside County

This is a solid Republican district, whose tone is set by the affluent neighborhoods of booming Riverside, and by Palm Springs, the desert playground of the wealthy.

Both President Reagan in 1984 and George Bush in 1988 easily carried the 37th. The Republican advantage here is amplified by its booming population. Between 1980 and 1986, the 37th's population increased by 33 percent, the fourth-fastest growth rate among U.S. House districts.

The 37th's population is dispersed over a huge expanse of Riverside County, from the Santa Ana Mountains in the west to the Colorado River at the Arizona border. But much of it is located near Orange County, the suburban L.A. area fabled for its Republican conservatism.

As it has grown, the city of Riverside has been shifted in and out of the Riverside County district. In the 1960s, it was completely included; in the 1970s, it was completely removed. The most recent redistricting split the city, but in a manner beneficial to the already dominant GOP. The more-Democratic northern part of Riverside was placed in the 36th District, while the more upscale southern part went to the 37th.

The GOP edge is bolstered in such fast-growing Riverside suburbs as Norco and Corona. Farther east in the desert are the oasis resorts of Rancho Mirage and Palm Springs, where the leisure class contributes its ample wealth to the local economy. Though former President Gerald R. Ford has made his retirement home in this area, it is better known for its Hollywood set: Singer Sonny Bono is mayor of Palm Springs.

Despite the growth of its suburbs and resorts, farmers continue to play a major role in the 37th's economy and politics. Irrigation ditches knife across Riverside County, and cotton and livestock growers struggle to keep their scarce water resources from being diverted to the urbanized areas. Riverside was originally a trade center for the citrus ranches of the Santa Ana River basin; the first domestic navel orange was grown there in the 1870s.

Population: 525,938. White 439,899 (84%), Black 19,151 (4%), Other 12,338 (2%). Spanish origin 98,238 (19%). 18 and over 383,799 (73%), 65 and over 86,715 (16%). Median age: 33.

Committees

Banking, Finance and Urban Affairs (13th of 20 Republicans)
Financial Institutions Supervision, Regulation and Insurance; General Oversight and Investigations; Housing and Community Development; International Development, Finance, Trade and Monetary Policy

Government Operations (3rd of 15 Republicans)
Government Information, Justice and Agriculture (ranking)

Elections

1988 General		
Al McCandless (R)	174,284	(64%)
Johnny Pearson (D)	89,666	(33%)
1988 Primary		
Al McCandless (R)	58,589	(83%)
Bud Matthewson (R)	11,897	(17%)
1986 General		
Al McCandless (R)	122,416	(64%)
David E. Skinner (D)	69,808	(36%)

Previous Winning Percentages: **1984** (64%) **1982** (59%)

District Vote for President

	1988		1984		1980		1976	
D	108,106	(38%)	80,012	(34%)	55,950	(30%)	65,907	(48%)
R	172,644	(61%)	153,832	(65%)	113,408	(62%)	71,519	(52%)

Campaign Finance

	Receipts	Receipts from PACs	Expend-itures
1988			
McCandless (R)	$129,505	$75,500 (58%)	$122,839
Pearson (D)	$14,204	$8,000 (56%)	$13,767
1986			
McCandless (R)	$151,438	$65,500 (43%)	$127,793
Skinner (D)	$56,185	$1,200 (2%)	$56,185

Key Votes

1987	
Raise speed limit to 65 mph	N
Approve Gephardt "fair trade" amendment	N
Ban testing of larger nuclear weapons	N
Delay "re-flagging" of Kuwaiti tankers	N
Approve tax-raising deficit-reduction bill	N
1988	
Approve aid to Nicaraguan contras	Y
Enact civil rights restoration bill over Reagan veto	N
Kill 60-day plant-closing notification measure	Y
Pass omnibus trade bill over Reagan veto	N
Approve death penalty for drug-related murders	Y
Bar federal funds for abortions in cases of rape and incest	Y
Oppose seven-day waiting period for purchase of handguns	Y

Voting Studies

	Presidential Support		Party Unity		Conservative Coalition	
Year	**S**	**O**	**S**	**O**	**S**	**O**
1988	67	27	84	5	95	3
1987	67	26	83	6	86	9
1986	77	18	84	11	94	6
1985	74	21	89	4	98	0
1984	71	27	90	8	92	8
1983	90	10	86	10	85	11

Interest Group Ratings

Year	ADA	ACU	AFL-CIO	CCUS
1988	10	95	0	92
1987	8	82	7	93
1986	5	95	7	94
1985	5	86	0	91
1984	5	92	0	71
1983	5	87	0	95

38 Robert K. Dornan (R)

Of Garden Grove — Elected 1976

Did not serve 1983-85.

Born: April 3, 1933, New York, N.Y.
Education: Attended Loyola U. (California), 1950-53.
Military Career: Air Force, 1953-58.
Occupation: Broadcast journalist and producer.
Family: Wife, Sallie Hansen; five children.
Religion: Roman Catholic.
Political Career: Candidate for mayor of Los Angeles, 1973; served in U.S. House, 1977-83; sought Republican nomination for U.S. Senate, 1982.
Capitol Office: 301 Cannon Bldg. 20515; 225-2965.

In Washington: Dornan was an actor long before he was a politician, and one way to understand his congressional style is to see it as a form of theater. The incendiary rhetoric and exaggerated political gestures that are Dornan's hallmark sometimes seem more suited to the stage than to a legislative body.

Dornan promotes conservative causes with a flamboyance and lack of inhibition that give him a distinctive place in the House. And outside it, he often has opportunity to speak for those causes, as a frequent guest on nationally televised political talk shows.

As much as Dornan is viewed as a bombastic legislator, he does have some dramatic range. In 1986, when Marine Lt. Col. Oliver L. North appeared before the Foreign Affairs Committee in the Iran-contra affair, Dornan greeted him with his usual flair. He recited part of a Rudyard Kipling poem, with North's name inserted, paying tribute to soldiers who fight for their countries.

But Dornan seems most in his element when he is provoking his opponents. In one notable incident in the 100th Congress, Dornan got so wound up during a floor speech that the acting Speaker had his microphone silenced. The flare-up came during normally routine one-minute speeches that come at the beginning of a day's session. Dornan delivered a stinging response to a speech by then-Majority Whip Tony Coelho, who had blamed Republicans for defeating a Democratic package to aid the Nicaraguan contras.

"In 10 years I have never heard on this floor so obnoxious a statement as I heard from Mr. Coelho, which means 'rabbit' in Portuguese."

Dornan got so worked up that he ignored several warnings from the acting Speaker. Responding to the loud gavel bangs, he shouted at the podium: "Don't get a hernia and break your gavel." The Speaker then directed the sergeant-at-arms to turn off Dornan's microphone, but in an apparent mix-up, only the TV sound-feed was cut off. Other Republicans howled that they were being gagged, and they tried to pass a resolution to prevent the House microphones from being cut off in the future. The next day they did pass without opposition a resolution affirming that House officers could not shut off TV coverage.

Dornan has said his father raised him to be "fearless but not foolhardy." But even some Republicans feel occasionally that he is too fearless for his own good. During one bitter 1985 debate on the House floor, he blasted some Democrats for undermining their own country. "You voted for nothing in your life for defense," he told one Democrat. "You sit up here with your mouth dripping spleen and bile."

During his first three terms in Congress, before he left the House for an unsuccessful 1982 Senate campaign, Dornan proudly carried the nickname "B-1 Bob," for his zealous support of the B-1 bomber and higher military spending. He was also militant on the floor opposing communism and supporting Israel.

Despite his hawkish stance, Dornan sometimes shows up in unexpected alliances. In 1988 he joined with one of the most partisan freshman Democrats, Dave Nagle of Iowa, to add an amendment to a defense bill to stop the development of first-strike missile technology. The two argued for a one-year test ban on so-called depressed trajectory missiles, whose lower trajectory could give them greater potential for sneak-attack use.

Dornan maintained that the amendment should appeal to liberals and conservatives because it would provide a test ban, contingent on Soviet compliance, and protect the B-1 bomber strike force. "We are strangling in its crib a weapons system that is destabilizing in the extreme because its only purpose is a first strike," he said. The amendment passed 262-160, but Dornan later withdrew his support when it was modified.

Dornan will have more opportunity to focus on weapons and defense spending in the

California 38

Northwestern Orange County; Santa Ana; Garden Grove

The 38th ranges from coastal Orange County to the western half of Anaheim, where it takes in Disneyland and Anaheim Stadium, the home of baseball's California Angels. It is an older suburban area that is primarily home to young families.

As redrafted in the 1980s redistricting, the 38th was at first receptive to the genial and moderate Democratic Rep. Jerry M. Patterson. But with many residents with roots in Texas and Oklahoma, the district had a profound conservative tilt that became evident in 1984, when Dornan sought his return to the House. Dornan — whose old 27th District had been dismembered by Democratic mapmakers, prompting his unsuccessful 1982 Senate effort — unseated Patterson with a modest percentage, which he has improved upon in each election since.

Republicans also have a lock on the district at the presidential level. George Bush topped 60 percent there in 1988.

The district's vote is split fairly evenly between the middle-class suburban areas, such as Anaheim and Buena Park, in the northern part of the district, and Garden Grove and Santa Ana, working-class cities in the southern part of the 38th.

Santa Ana (population 237,000), the county seat, is about 45 percent Hispanic. The city is shared with the 39th and 40th districts; but most of the Hispanic neighborhoods are in the 38th, contributing to its Democratic vote.

Garden Grove (135,000 people), best known for the "positive thinking" television ministry of Robert Schuller and his Crystal Cathedral, has traditionally had a much smaller minority population. But in recent years, there has been a heavy influx of Indochinese refugees, spurring a conservative backlash by some of Garden Grove's white, blue-collar voters.

Population: 525,919. White 392,707 (75%), Black 13,438 (3%), Asian and Pacific Islander 36,819 (7%), Other 4,386 (1%). Spanish origin 149,578 (28%). 18 and over 364,684 (69%), 65 and over 36,462 (7%). Median age: 27.

101st Congress, because he has traded his seat on Foreign Affairs for a place on the Armed Services Committee. A former fighter pilot, Dornan said Armed Services needed a member with experience in tactical and strategic air defense. Early in the 101st Congress, he got another new committee assignment, taking a vacancy on the Intelligence Committee.

Dornan has been a persistent and outspoken opponent of abortion throughout his House careers. He has consistently pushed amendments preventing the District of Columbia from using public funds to pay for abortions. Until the 100th Congress he was unable to get such strict language through to the president's desk, but in 1988 he saw a measure enacted into law that prevented the District from using public funds, local or federal, for abortions.

It was not easy. The House initially voted 222-186 for Dornan's amendment, but House conferees resisted the language, accepting a more lenient Senate position that did not place restrictions on use of local funds and allowed more exceptions for federal dollars. Dornan then successfully pushed a motion sending conferees back to deal with the issue. Even after Senate conferees opted for the Dornan language, conferees returned to the full House twice to urge members to support the softer language. Failing in that, and facing a veto threat, conferees agreed to the Dornan language.

Dornan is not the sort of legislator who needs a platform to get noticed, but he does have a formal position that may generate some extra attention, the chairmanship of the Republican Study Committee

At Home: Despite his image as a New Right conservative, Dornan was among the first to endorse the 1988 presidential campaign of Vice President George Bush. Dornan traveled extensively on Bush's behalf during the nominating season and in the fall, but this work did not lead — as some suspected it might — to an executive branch job when Bush took the presidency.

Dornan entered politics after an eclectic career that included five years as an Air Force pilot, various journalism jobs, parts as an extra in TV dramas, and several years as a TV talk show host. He spent much time on the road, registering black voters in Alabama in the 1960s and trying to ban objectionable textbooks in West Virginia in the 1970s. The prisoner-of-war issue also occupied his attention. He boasts of inventing the POW bracelet.

By 1976 Dornan had been off TV for three years and had lost an election for mayor of Los Angeles. But the 27th District of that time provided him an opening: Moderate Republican Rep. Alphonzo Bell was running for the Senate. Former Peace Corps Director Joseph Blatchford and state GOP Treasurer Michael C. Donaldson were the front-runners in the Republican primary, but they split the moderate vote, allowing Dornan to win the nomination on the strength of his conservative support.

The general election between Dornan and Gary Familian, a wealthy Marina del Ray businessman, was an exercise in name calling, the first of a series of vituperative campaigns in which Dornan has been involved. Dornan called Familian a "warmed-over McGovernite." Familian said Dornan was a "paid propagandist" linked to the John Birch Society and the Ku Klux Klan. Dornan won 55 percent of the vote.

In the two elections after that, Dornan's foe was Carey Peck, the son of actor Gregory Peck. Peck was inexperienced and awkward, but he came within 3,500 votes of Dornan in 1978, charging that the incumbent had little to show for all the sound and fury he had generated in Washington. Dornan countered that Peck was simply a rich young man playing at politics.

Dornan was determined to trounce Peck in their 1980 rematch, and he spent nearly $2 million in the effort. Peck improved his campaign style somewhat in the rematch, however, and Dornan barely matched his 1978 vote percentage.

In the 1981 redistricting, Democrats exacted revenge by stripping Dornan's district of its most Republican areas. Dornan declared for the Senate the following year, but wound up running fourth in the GOP primary.

In 1984, he moved from his previous base in Santa Monica to Orange County to make his House comeback. Changing demographics in the 38th had made Democratic Rep. Jerry M. Patterson more vulnerable, and Dornan's national conservative credentials guaranteed him plenty of money.

This, too, was a nasty campaign. Patterson called Dornan "a far-right extremist" and "nearly a lunatic"; Dornan called him a "sneaky little dirtbag." Some Republicans were concerned Dornan would be unable to surmount charges of carpetbagging (he used four different voting addresses at times during the campaign), but it proved more important that he was an articulate conservative in a district unhappy with the national Democratic ticket.

Two years later, Dornan held on against a scrappy attack from state Assemblyman Richard Robinson, who accused him of ignoring Orange County in favor of an obsession with foreign policy. Though Robinson's speeches and direct mail dwelled on that point, the battle was not really joined until Robinson's campaign accused Dornan of having implied that he had served in combat in the Korean War. Dornan angrily denied having falsified his record — he was on active duty after the war ended — and then charged that Robinson had misrepresented his own service as a Marine in Vietnam.

Committees

Armed Services (18th of 21 Republicans)
Military Personnel and Compensation; Readiness; Research and Development

Select Intelligence (7th of 7 Republicans)
Legislation

Select Narcotics Abuse and Control (6th of 12 Republicans)

Elections

1988 General		
Robert K. Dornan (R)	87,690	(60%)
Jerry Yudelson (D)	52,399	(36%)
1986 General		
Robert K. Dornan (R)	66,032	(55%)
Richard Robinson (D)	50,625	(42%)

Previous Winning Percentages: **1984** (53%) **1980** (51%) **1978** (51%) **1976** (55%)

District Vote For President

	1988	1984	1980	1976
D	58,068 (38%)	48,856 (30%)	43,851 (29%)	51,102 (46%)
R	93,697 (61%)	114,786 (69%)	93,281 (62%)	58,138 (53%)

Campaign Finance

	Receipts	Receipts from PACs	Expend-itures
1988			
Dornan (R)	$1,731,883	$83,231 (5%)	$1,755,892
Yudelson (D)	$250,191	$71,971 (29%)	$248,151
1986			
Dornan (R)	$1,190,237	$163,273 (14%)	$1,174,637
Robinson (D)	$592,412	$302,974 (51%)	$581,864

Key Votes

1987	
Raise speed limit to 65 mph	Y
Approve Gephardt "fair trade" amendment	N
Ban testing of larger nuclear weapons	N
Delay "re-flagging" of Kuwaiti tankers	?
Approve tax-raising deficit-reduction bill	N
1988	
Approve aid to Nicaraguan contras	Y
Enact civil rights restoration bill over Reagan veto	N
Kill 60-day plant-closing notification measure	Y
Pass omnibus trade bill over Reagan veto	N
Approve death penalty for drug-related murders	Y
Bar federal funds for abortions in cases of rape and incest	Y
Oppose seven-day waiting period for purchase of handguns	Y

Voting Studies

	Presidential Support		Party Unity		Conservative Coalition	
Year	**S**	**O**	**S**	**O**	**S**	**O**
1988	65	26	84	6	84	5
1987	73	21	82	8	88	9
1986	80	13	82	10	88	12
1985	80	16	79	10	82	13
1982	61	5	68	5	73	4
1981	57	26	67	9	63	8

Interest Group Ratings

Year	ADA	ACU	AFL-CIO	CCUS
1988	0	100	7	91
1987	0	100	7	100
1986	5	95	8	81
1985	10	95	12	81
1982	5	87	0	85
1981	10	93	8	93

39 William E. Dannemeyer (R)

Of Fullerton — Elected 1978

Born: Sept. 22, 1929, Los Angeles, Calif.

Education: Santa Maria Jr. College, 1946-47; Valparaiso U., B.A. 1950; U. of California, Hastings College of Law, J.D. 1952.

Military Career: Army, 1952-54.

Occupation: Lawyer.

Family: Wife, Evelyn Hoemann; three children.

Religion: Lutheran.

Political Career: Calif. Assembly, served as a Democrat, 1963-67, served as a Republican, 1977-79; Democratic nominee for Calif. Senate, 1966; Republican nominee for Calif. Assembly, 1972.

Capitol Office: 2351 Rayburn Bldg. 20515; 225-4111.

In Washington: By the time AIDS became a nationwide concern, Dannemeyer had already made himself the leading conservative House spokesman on controlling the spread of the disease. His unyielding views have won him few legislative victories, but his failures have not weakened his resolve.

Dannemeyer's involvement in the AIDS issue began in earnest during the August 1985 House recess, when four San Francisco nurses complained to him that hospital procedures barred them from wearing protective gowns, masks and gloves. The nurses wanted Dannemeyer to help change the rules. In October, Dannemeyer brought the matter to the House floor, marking the start of his impassioned crusade for "the civil rights of the uninfected."

In many floor speeches since, the bullheaded Californian has freely and forcefully spoken his mind, though critics regularly quarrel with his facts and his suggested solutions. His opponents still cite with amazement the time Dannemeyer declared that restrictions should be placed on AIDS victims because they emit "spores" that can cause birth defects.

Dannemeyer brings to most discussions of AIDS an outspoken criticism of homosexuals. He reminds audiences that God created "Adam and Eve, not Adam and Steve." In 1987, he submitted a vitriolic statement to the *Congressional Record* that complained, "Since the 1960s and the beginning of the sexual revolution, homosexuals have been striving to change American culture. These 'normaphobes' demand that the average American view their aberrant behavior as equal to heterosexuality."

In the 100th Congress, Dannemeyer's primary concern was mandatory AIDS testing and notification of public-health officials. As a member of the powerful Energy and Commerce Committee, he pushed hopeless efforts to test the homeless and marriage-license applicants, and once he complained that he was barred from offering an amendment to test the entire U.S. population for the virus that causes AIDS. He wanted physicians to be required to notify the spouses of anyone who tested positive.

In the Judiciary Committee, Dannemeyer failed in numerous attempts to amend the fair-housing bill to state that those with contagious diseases, namely AIDS, were excluded from the definition of handicapped.

Dannemeyer did, however, win committee approval to require testing of those convicted of prostitution, sexual assault and crimes related to intravenous drug use. The committee also approved a Dannemeyer amendment to make grants to states contingent on a state's certification that intentional transmission of AIDS is punishable as a civil and a criminal offense.

Stopping the spread of AIDS at public bathhouses is of particular concern to Dannemeyer. In the 99th Congress, when he sought to amend the 1986 drug bill to close bathhouses, Democrat Henry A. Waxman became incensed. "This is a really bizarre amendment," said Waxman, pounding the table. "Mr. Dannemeyer is obsessed with bathhouses. Obsessed with them."

In the 100th Congress, a committee bill authorizing funds to combat drug and alcohol abuse included Dannemeyer language to bar states from receiving federal funds under the bill unless they sought to close existing bathhouses.

Dannemeyer has long had tempestuous relations with Waxman, the liberal chairman of the Health Subcommittee. In the 100th Congress, Waxman tried to circumvent Dannemeyer by sending legislation to create a national AIDS advisory commission directly to the full committee. There Waxman scheduled a

California 39

Northern Orange County — Anaheim; Fullerton

The hard-right conservative tradition in affluent Orange County makes the 39th California's most Republican district. President Reagan carried 77 percent of the vote there, and it was the only California district where George Bush topped 70 percent in 1988.

A 1983 redistricting map that took the western part of Anaheim out of the 39th also deprived it of its most famous landmarks, Disneyland and Anaheim Stadium, the home of baseball's California Angels. But the remap left residential neighborhoods that are home to many of Anaheim's middle- and upper-class professionals, who set the district's Republican tone.

Thirty years ago, Anaheim was a sleepy community of 15,000 in the middle of the county's famous orange groves. Today, it is a city of more than 240,000 people (the ninth-largest in California), with thriving electronics and defense-related industries. The 39th has Hughes, Rockwell and Northrop facilities, as well as Chevron and Unical energy research centers.

Population growth in Anaheim slowed somewhat to a modest 10 percent rate between 1980 and 1986. The fastest-growing communities in the 39th are to the east of Anaheim. Yorba Linda (40,000 residents), birthplace of Richard M. Nixon and site of his presidential library, grew by 40 percent in the first part of the 1980s, and has quadrupled in size since 1970.

Fullerton and Orange, both with just over 100,000 people, are the district's other population anchors. Fullerton, Dannemeyer's home base, has a campus of the University of California.

Population: 525,858. White 464,267 (88%), Black 5,472 (1%), Other 23,316 (4%). Spanish origin 70,716 (13%). 18 and over 380,058 (72%), 65 and over 35,906 (7%). Median age: 29.

quick vote just before the full House was to take up the measure under suspension of the rules, a fast-track procedure that bars amendments.

Dannemeyer was furious. He objected to the bill, saying the White House had already established a commission. What was to be a brief hearing turned into a three-hour ordeal as Dannemeyer forced a reading of the bill and demanded roll-call votes. Ultimately, however, the committee and the House approved the bill, though no agreement was reached with the Senate.

When the president's commission released its report in June 1988, Dannemeyer likely regretted his earlier defense of its existence. He condemned the report's proposals to protect AIDS victims from discrimination, saying they were "a rehash of the old line that only the infected have rights."

While Dannemeyer's objections to anti-bias language were consistent with the Reagan administration line, President Bush has said he supports such efforts. A collision seems likely, since Dannemeyer is well-known for berating GOP House leaders for being too conciliatory toward the Democrats.

Ironically, Dannemeyer's rigidity has won him some tactical Democratic favors. When a limited number of floor amendments are allowed on a bill, and some of them have to be offered by Republicans, Democratic leaders often look to Dannemeyer. They can count it as a gesture to the minority, knowing full well that his efforts usually fail. Dannemeyer regularly offers budget alternatives that lose overwhelmingly. In 1987 and 1988, his efforts drew fewer than 50 votes.

In the 100th Congress, Dannemeyer also championed efforts to ban telephone services that allow callers to dial a toll number to hear a pornographic message. After being blocked from moving the bill in Energy and Commerce, Dannemeyer outmaneuvered House leaders and won a vote instructing conferees on the education bill to outlaw "dial-a-porn." When the bill came back with a compromise amendment to deny access to dial-a-porn unless a person subscribed to a service, Dannemeyer and other conservatives blocked a vote on the education bill until the House approved of an outright ban.

Even Dannemeyer's critics concede that he argues from principle and with utter consistency. His amendments rarely have anything to do with a favored industry or part of the country. But Dannemeyer's convictions have not made him widely popular. In a bid late in 1988 to become chairman of the House Republican Conference, Dannemeyer got just seven votes.

Prior to leading the anti-AIDS crusade, Dannemeyer devoted considerable energy to returning the country to the gold standard. Having tracked down nearly every historical reference to back up his argument, he pointed out in a 1987 speech that Dante, in the "Divine Comedy," had a special hell for currency debasers. "Our own attitude is quite different," he complained. "We celebrate our own currency debasers in the Treasury and Federal Reserve. . . ."

A fierce abortion foe, Dannemeyer sparked a heated debate in the 97th Congress by proposing to bar federal funding for research on human fetuses while they are alive. Supporters of the research cited treatments for fetal diseases arising from the findings, but Dannemeyer refused to budge. His amendment passed.

At Home: Dannemeyer has run for office as a Democrat, and he has run as a Republican. But he has never claimed to be anything but a conservative. In 1978, when he won his first House term amid the statewide furor over tax-cutting Proposition 13, he left no doubt where he stood on government spending. And he was on the successful side of the issue.

Even before 1967, when Dannemeyer left the Democratic Party, he was on the political right. He won two Assembly terms as a Democrat in Republican Orange County during the 1960s, but when he tried to move to the state Senate in 1966, he lost to a GOP assemblyman. That was the end of Dannemeyer's Democratic career.

He made his Republican debut in 1972, challenging Assemblyman Ken Cory, one of the few popular Democrats in Orange County. Cory won easily.

But in 1976 Dannemeyer was able to take back the Assembly seat he had won as a Democrat 14 years before, defeating an aide to the Republican who had replaced him. His strong showing convinced Orange County Republicans of Dannemeyer's strength as one of their own.

When Republican Rep. Charles E. Wiggins retired from Congress two years later, nobody tried to challenge Dannemeyer for the GOP nomination. He won the general election easily. The only excitement in Dannemeyer's career since then came in 1986, when he briefly ran for the GOP nomination to oppose Democratic Sen. Alan Cranston. Dannemeyer early on laid claim to the right end of the large Republican field. He attracted some attention but too little money to keep his bid going, and dropped out early in February. That gave him time to file for his House seat, which he again won easily.

In 1988, Dannemeyer concentrated on passing his anti-AIDS proposition on the state ballot. The proposition lost, but Dannemeyer won with ease.

Committees

Energy and Commerce (5th of 17 Republicans)
Commerce, Consumer Protection and Competitiveness; Energy and Power; Health and the Environment

Judiciary (8th of 14 Republicans)
Civil and Constitutional Rights; Economic and Commercial Law

Elections

1988 General		
William E. Dannemeyer (R)	169,360	(74%)
Don E. Marquis (D)	52,162	(23%)
1988 Primary		
William E. Dannemeyer (R)	64,862	(85%)
John M. Gullixson (R)	11,207	(15%)
1986 General		
William E. Dannemeyer (R)	131,603	(75%)
David D. Vest (D)	42,377	(24%)

Previous Winning Percentages: 1984 (76%) **1982** (72%) **1980** (76%) **1978** (64%)

District Vote for President

	1988	1984	1980	1976
D	66,495 (28%)	52,591 (22%)	44,474 (21%)	52,802 (35%)
R	167,142 (71%)	185,491 (77%)	148,010 (70%)	97,978 (64%)

Campaign Finance

	Receipts	Receipts from PACs	Expend-itures
1988			
Dannemeyer (R)	$300,156	$144,472 (48%)	$250,737
Marquis (D)	$1,432	0	$2,892
1986			
Dannemeyer (R)	$264,037	$132,750 (50%)	$260,009
Vest (D)	$7,473	$300 (4%)	$7,473

Key Votes

1987	
Raise speed limit to 65 mph	Y
Approve Gephardt "fair trade" amendment	N
Ban testing of larger nuclear weapons	N
Delay "re-flagging" of Kuwaiti tankers	N
Approve tax-raising deficit-reduction bill	N
1988	
Approve aid to Nicaraguan contras	Y
Enact civil rights restoration bill over Reagan veto	N
Kill 60-day plant-closing notification measure	Y
Pass omnibus trade bill over Reagan veto	N
Approve death penalty for drug-related murders	Y
Bar federal funds for abortions in cases of rape and incest	Y
Oppose seven-day waiting period for purchase of handguns	Y

Voting Studies

	Presidential Support		Party Unity		Conservative Coalition	
Year	**S**	**O**	**S**	**O**	**S**	**O**
1988	69	18	93	2	89	8
1987	74	22	89	4	88	12
1986	81	17	90	5	88	8
1985	78	16	89	3	87	7
1984	77	21	90	6	88	8
1983	77	15	91	4	84	9
1982	81	17	93	5	90	10
1981	74	24	92	5	85	11

Interest Group Ratings

Year	ADA	ACU	AFL-CIO	CCUS
1988	0	100	0	92
1987	12	100	7	100
1986	5	95	0	87
1985	10	90	6	95
1984	0	100	8	71
1983	5	95	0	89
1982	5	100	5	86
1981	10	100	0	100

40 C. Christopher Cox (R)

Of Newport Beach — Elected 1988

Born: Oct. 16, 1952, St. Paul, Minn.
Education: U. of Southern California, B.A. 1973; Harvard U., M.B.A. 1977, J.D. 1977.
Occupation: White House counsel.
Family: Single.
Religion: Roman Catholic.
Political Career: No previous office.
Capitol Office: 510 Cannon Bldg. 20515; 225-5611.

The Path to Washington: Many on Capitol Hill dream of making their move down Pennsylvania Avenue to the White House. Cox spent 1988 making his move the other way — up that street to Congress.

When the year began, he was senior associate counsel to President Reagan. His White House duties had included drafting reform proposals for the current federal budget process. At the time, Cox had little reason to think he would soon be tackling the same budget as a lawmaker.

But before the year was over, Cox would be elected chairman of the House Republicans' freshman caucus for the 101st Congress and named a first-year member of the National Republican Congressional Committee.

Before coming to Washington, Cox taught briefly at Harvard, where he received both his law and graduate business degrees. He had also been a partner in a 350-lawyer firm in Newport Beach, Calif.

Because of his California connections (he also did his undergraduate studies in Southern California and clerked for the U.S. Court of Appeals in San Francisco), Cox took notice when Rep. Robert E. Badham, the veteran congressman from the securely Republican 40th District, announced his retirement in the first week of January 1988.

At first, the coastal-central Orange County district seemed likely to go to one of the well-known state legislators in the area. But when the prime prospects declined to run, Cox took a closer look. On Feb. 1, he resigned from his job at the White House to join a field of Republican primary candidates in the 40th that eventually grew to 14.

Two others in that field were better known and bankrolled. But Cox had friendships to tap from his California years as a student, law clerk and young corporate finance attorney. He soon managed to enlist significant help from members of the Irvine family, still the county's most prominent. By late spring, Cox had pulled even financially. And when the front-runners stumbled politically, Cox was there.

The departing Badham had endorsed another Republican in the primary, Dave Baker, a local college basketball hero and Irvine city councilman. But while Baker was stressing his local backers, Cox's literature pictured him alongside Reagan and Vice President George Bush in the White House. He got endorsements from 18 conservatives in Congress — a positive badge in California's most heavily Republican and deeply conservative district.

Cox also employed his White House contacts and lengthened his conservative suit when he brought in Robert H. Bork, Reagan's unsuccessful nominee to the Supreme Court. Cox said Bork helped him raise $200,000 in one day.

Also appearing for Cox in the late going was retired Marine Lt. Col. Oliver L. North, the key figure in the Iran-contra investigation. But by that time, Cox had pulled ahead in his own polling. Baker suffered from questions raised about his marital fidelity and his handling of money for a non-profit group.

Cox wound up winning 18 of the district's 20 municipalities in the primary. In November, he rolled up 67 percent of the vote against the first of what will probably be a succession of Democratic sacrificial lambs.

Cox may be the first person — and certainly the first Republican — elected to Congress after being a publisher of *Pravda*. While still practicing law in Orange County, Cox, with his retired-publisher father, began producing an independent, English-language version of the official Soviet newspaper.

The project was based in St. Paul, Minn., where Cox grew up and attended a Catholic military academy. The translated Soviet paper was intended to show how the Soviet government propagandizes its own people. After pouring $300,000 of his own into the project, Cox began making arrangements to bring in additional investors. But that effort faltered (and the paper eventually folded) when he turned his attention to running for Congress.

Among the three freshman California Republicans in the 101st Congress, Cox is the link. He was at Harvard with Tom Campbell in the mid-1970s and worked in Reagan's White House with Dana Rohrabacher.

California 40

Coastal and Central Orange County

It is difficult for candidates to be too conservative for the voters of this central and coastal Orange County district. John G. Schmitz, who represented this area for a term in the early 1970s, was later removed from the executive council of the John Birch Society for extremism.

With more mainstream figures like Cox and his predecessor, Robert E. Badham, holding the seat, district voters have not had to think twice about sticking with the Republicans. The same applies in presidential contests. President Reagan won here by a 3-to-1 margin in 1984; George Bush carried the 40th by 2-to-1.

Newport Beach, a wealthy enclave noted for its luxurious housing, is the center of the district. A community of 67,000 people, Newport Beach regularly provides Republican candidates with tremendous margins. Reagan took 78 percent of the vote there in 1984; Bush won 72 percent in 1988.

Many of the residents of the 40th either commute to jobs in Los Angeles or are employed by high-technology companies scattered in gleaming "glass boxes" throughout the district. With the area's population growing and more people streaming onto the highways, traffic congestion has become a major local concern. That fact played a part in Cox's taking a seat on the Public Works Committee, which deals with surface transportation matters.

The University of California's Irvine campus is located in the 40th. But any liberal influence from this academic center is hardly noticed. The only incorporated areas in the district where Democrats have strength are Costa Mesa and Laguna Beach, two very different places.

Trendy Laguna Beach, which saw an influx of counterculture newcomers in the 1960s and 1970s, today is home for many single adults and couples without children. They live in comfortable condominium complexes along the ocean. Costa Mesa, whose airport is named for actor John Wayne, is not so chic. Just north of Newport Beach, it is home for young families in modest suburban homes. Both communities supported Bush by smaller margins than the rest of the district in 1988.

Population: 525,935. White 474,717 (90%), Black 7,078 (1%), Asian and Pacific Islander 23,814 (5%), Other 2,742 (1%). Spanish origin 40,133 (8%). 18 and over 399,759 (76%), 65 and over 54,692 (10%). Median age: 31.

Committees

Government Operations (13th of 15 Republicans)
Commerce, Consumer and Monetary Affairs; Government Activities and Transportation

Public Works and Transportation (19th of 20 Republicans)
Economic Development; Public Buildings and Grounds; Surface Transportation; Water Resources

Campaign Finance

	Receipts	Receipts from PACs	Expend-itures
1988			
Cox (R)	$1,111,321	$198,786 (18%)	$1,110,126
Lenney (D)	$49,834	$2,475 (5%)	$47,746

Elections

1988 General

C. Christopher Cox (R)	181,269	(67%)
Lida Lenney (D)	80,782	(30%)

1988 Primary

C. Christopher Cox (R)	30,713	(31%)
Dave Baker (R)	29,326	(29%)
Nathan Rosenberg (R)	17,647	(18%)
William Yacobozzi Jr. (R)	6,290	(6%)

District Vote For President

	1988	1984	1980	1976
D	87,331 (31%)	63,210 (24%)	47,255 (21%)	53,928 (32%)
R	191,392 (68%)	198,338 (75%)	152,430 (68%)	116,030 (68%)

41 Bill Lowery (R)

Of San Diego — Elected 1980

Born: May 2, 1947, San Diego, Calif.
Education: Attended San Diego State U., 1965-69.
Occupation: Public-relations executive.
Family: Wife, Kathleen Brown; three children.
Religion: Roman Catholic.
Political Career: San Diego City Council, 1977-80; San Diego deputy mayor, 1979-80.
Capitol Office: 438 Cannon Bldg. 20515; 225-3201.

In Washington: A good-natured, outgoing man, Lowery approaches legislation with an attitude of accommodation and an eye on parochialism. He may never lead a great political crusade, but his qualities are a good fit for the Appropriations Committee, where Lowery works well with colleagues both Republican and Democratic.

Lowery pushed at the beginning of his second term for a seat on Appropriations, and easily won the endorsement of the state GOP delegation and the party leadership. But when fellow Californian Bobbi Fiedler decided to run, she split the state vote and the seat went to a third candidate. Many felt that Lowery had gotten a raw deal, and when more Appropriations slots opened up in early 1985, he was an easy choice to fill one.

Local concerns are the focus of Lowery's committee work. As a member of the Interior Subcommittee, he worked with other Californians in the 100th Congress to extend until 1990 the moratorium on oil and gas leasing off the California coast. Like the original moratorium, which he also advocated, the extension was included in the Interior appropriations bill. He also worked with his fellow Californians to secure funding for a new sewage system along the U.S.-Mexican border to clean up sludge flowing over the border from Tijuana into San Diego.

Lowery is also the ranking Republican on Appropriations' Military Construction Subcommittee. In the 99th Congress, he used his influence there to restore nearly $100 million for military construction projects at Camp Pendleton, in his district. Late in the 100th Congress, Lowery turned to his colleagues on another subcommittee to help secure funding to expand the U.S. Customs office at the Mexican border.

Lowery's most visible accomplishment outside his district came in the 99th Congress, when he won passage of an amendment empowering the president to withhold funds from United Nations organizations in proportion to their spending on programs in communist countries. He also promoted language, added to a reconciliation bill, that denies U.S. companies foreign tax credit for taxes paid to countries that practice terrorism.

At Home: Described as a "Republican regular" since the age of 12, Lowery began preparing for a congressional campaign long before GOP Rep. Bob Wilson announced his retirement in early 1980. A friend of President Ford's son, Jack, Lowery lined up $90,000 in commitments early on, and later picked up one of the few primary endorsements given in 1980 by the Republican National Committee.

Although he was the front-runner, Lowery needed the help. His chief primary competitor was Dan McKinnon, wealthy owner of KSON, one of Southern California's strongest AM country music radio stations. Running TV advertisements three months before the primary, McKinnon made a strong bid for San Diego's pro-Reagan vote by positioning himself to Lowery's right; Lowery won by less than 4 percentage points.

In the general election, Lowery's biggest problem was that his opponent had the same name as the retiring incumbent — Bob Wilson. Lowery attacked the conservative Democratic state senator for running on the "good name" of the incumbent. He also formed a committee called "Wilsons for Bill Lowery," made up of other San Diegans named Wilson who supported Lowery, including Pete Wilson, then mayor of San Diego and now California's junior senator. Lowery had been a protégé of the popular mayor since his City Council election.

With national GOP support and a sophisticated media campaign, Lowery pulled out a comfortable 53 to 43 percent win.

His margin climbed to 68 percent in 1982, but two years later there was a spirited challenge from a blind University of San Diego law professor, Robert L. Simmons. With his disability guaranteeing him press attention, Simmons hit Lowery on an issue in which party labels make no difference in coastal California — the environment. He said that Lowery had not dealt enough with environmental concerns. But Simmons was underfunded, and Lowery's credentials were enough for victory. Lowery has had an easy time since.

California 41

North San Diego and Suburbs

The 41st is a predominantly white and affluent northern San Diego district where Republicans have a distinct edge.

The tone is set in strongly Republican Point Loma, on the peninsula guarding San Diego Harbor. From there, the district moves north through Ocean Beach and Banker Hill — mixed communities of students, older people and young professionals. Then come long stretches of middle-class and upper-middle-class neighborhoods such as Scripps Ranch and Rancho Bernardo, where Republican candidates regularly overwhelm their opposition. Pacific Beach and the exclusive La Jolla section are also in the 41st.

There is a Democratic presence at the northern end around Del Mar, contributed by the professors and students of University of California at San Diego. Mission Village, a blue-collar neighborhood farther south, is also amenable to Democratic overtures.

The 41st surrounds the huge Miramar Naval Air Station, the largest such station in the world. Miramar and other naval facilities here give the district a large military constituency. Aerospace and electronics firms associated with the military also are in the area, and employ many of the professionals and executives who live in the district. But some local residents would like to see the base phased out as a military installation and made into a commercial airport serving San Diego.

District population growth has been steady during the 1980s. Most of the newcomers have been young, middle-class types, who lean to the GOP. George Bush won nearly three-fifths of the district vote in 1988; Republicans decisively carried the district in the 1988 Senate and 1986 gubernatorial elections.

Population: 526,043. White 468,089 (89%), Black 12,331 (2%), Asian and Pacific Islander 26,067 (5%), Other 2,564 (1%). Spanish origin 37,897 (7%). 18 and over 412,731 (78%), 65 and over 56,650 (11%). Median age: 31.

Committee

Appropriations (18th of 22 Republicans)
Military Construction (ranking); Interior and Related Agencies; Treasury, Postal Service and General Government

Elections

1988 General		
Bill Lowery (R)	187,380	(66%)
Dan Kripke (D)	88,192	(31%)
1988 Primary		
Bill Lowery (R)	63,485	(89%)
Rick Singer (R)	8,085	(11%)
1986 General		
Bill Lowery (R)	133,566	(68%)
Dan Kripke (D)	59,816	(30%)

Previous Winning Percentages: **1984** (63%) **1982** (69%) **1980** (53%)

District Vote For President

	1988		1984		1980		1976	
D	121,278	(40%)	92,994	(35%)	64,634	(28%)	69,848	(41%)
R	175,588	(58%)	171,535	(64%)	135,569	(58%)	99,696	(58%)

Campaign Finance

	Receipts	Receipts from PACs		Expend-itures
1988				
Lowery (R)	$453,289	$182,415	(40%)	$407,025
Kripke (D)	$50,270	$8,050	(16%)	$45,311
1986				
Lowery (R)	$389,021	$138,149	(36%)	$401,730
Kripke (D)	$155,761	$21,619	(14%)	$153,732

Key Votes

1987	
Raise speed limit to 65 mph	#
Approve Gephardt "fair trade" amendment	N
Ban testing of larger nuclear weapons	N
Delay "re-flagging" of Kuwaiti tankers	N
Approve tax-raising deficit-reduction bill	N
1988	
Approve aid to Nicaraguan contras	Y
Enact civil rights restoration bill over Reagan veto	N
Kill 60-day plant-closing notification measure	Y
Pass omnibus trade bill over Reagan veto	N
Approve death penalty for drug-related murders	Y
Bar federal funds for abortions in cases of rape and incest	Y
Oppose seven-day waiting period for purchase of handguns	N

Voting Studies

	Presidential Support		Party Unity		Conservative Coalition	
Year	**S**	**O**	**S**	**O**	**S**	**O**
1988	62	30	81	9	79	11
1987	63	30	77	16	84	7
1986	76	21	68	22	80	18
1985	71	24	74	16	84	11
1984	69	28	76	16	86	7
1983	79	20	83	13	83	15
1982	78	17	88	10	93	7
1981	74	24	85	11	85	9

Interest Group Ratings

Year	ADA	ACU	AFL-CIO	CCUS
1988	15	92	14	100
1987	4	87	19	73
1986	5	74	8	75
1985	5	81	6	86
1984	5	83	15	80
1983	5	83	0	100
1982	0	91	5	100
1981	5	83	0	100

42 Dana Rohrabacher (R)

Of Palos Verdes Estates — Elected 1988

Born: June 21, 1947, Coronado, Calif.
Education: Attended Los Angeles Harbor College, 1965-67; California State U., Long Beach, B.A. 1969; U. of Southern California, M.A. 1971.
Occupation: Journalist; White House speechwriter.
Family: Single.
Religion: Baptist.
Political Career: No previous office.
Capitol Office: 1017 Longworth Bldg. 20515; 225-2415.

The Path to Washington: Most newly elected members of Congress spent the first weeks after their victories relaxing, converting their campaigns into congressional operations or checking out homes in Washington. Rohrabacher got caught in an artillery duel outside the Afghan city of Jalalabad.

Anti-communist movements in the Third World had been a strong interest for Rohrabacher when he was a speechwriter for President Reagan. So, after rolling up 66 percent of the November vote in the Southern California district vacated by Rep. Dan Lungren's retirement, Rohrabacher took a two-week trip to Burma and Afghanistan.

In Burma, he reported meeting with Burmese dissident students in hiding near the Burmese-Thai border. In Afghanistan, Mujahedeen leaders he had met at the White House arranged for him to spend five days with their forces. At the outskirts of the besieged city of Jalalabad, Rohrabacher said he pitched camp in a ravine while the Mujahedeen fired rockets overhead and artillery responded from within the city.

Rohrabacher's travels were sponsored by the Freedom Research Foundation and by the Christian Anti-Communist Crusade.

Before joining the White House staff as a speechwriter in 1981, Rohrabacher had been assistant press secretary in the Reagan presidential campaigns of 1976 and 1980. Between those campaigns he had been an editorial writer for the *Orange County Register*. Earlier, he worked for the City News Service of Los Angeles, covering such stories as the Patty Hearst kidnapping.

Rohrabacher eventually became senior speechwriter in 1984 and special assistant to the president in 1986. But he had first met Reagan right after the California gubernatorial election in 1966. Active in GOP causes since his mid-teens, the 19-year-old Rohrabacher camped out on Gov.-elect Reagan's front lawn to protest the planned disbanding of "Youth for Reagan." Reagan reportedly came to the door in the midst of shaving and promised to keep the youth group alive.

Rohrabacher arrived in Congress sporting a beard, the only member of the freshman class so adorned. During the campaign, he had rejected advice that he shave. One reason was that he wanted to use his White House photos of himself, bearded, with Reagan.

Lungren had announced his retirement in March, believing the California Supreme Court would uphold his appointment as state treasurer despite a split confirmation vote in the Legislature. The court decision went against Lungren, but by then the race to succeed him was on in earnest.

The 42nd District, once competitive for both parties, had become increasingly Republican during Lungren's five terms. So the key struggle was in the June primary.

At first, Rohrabacher seemed likely to finish no better than third among eight. The early lead was conceded to an Orange County supervisor who had Lungren's blessing. There was also a university president and yet another former staffer from the White House in the field.

But Rohrabacher, who left the White House staff in March, gained steadily in the outside lane. When he discovered that the front-runner did not hold the college degree she had been claiming throughout her political career, he passed that information to a reporter who confirmed and published it.

Later, Rohrabacher brought in retired Marine Lt. Col. Oliver L. North for a fund-raising day that generated more than $100,000. That won Rohrabacher new name recognition among conservatives. It also allowed him to freshen his direct-mail efforts in the campaign's closing days — while the other two leading candidates were training their fire on each other. Rohrabacher wound up winning the primary with 35 percent of the vote, well ahead of his nearest competitor.

In November, Rohrabacher dominated the vote in both the Orange and Los Angeles County portions of his district by nearly 2-to-1.

California 42

Coastal Los Angeles and Orange Counties

The oddly shaped and heavily Republican 42nd was one of the masterworks of the state's Democratic redistricters. Seeking to isolate as many Republicans in as few districts as possible, the map makers crafted the 42nd from parts of the old 27th, then held by GOP Rep. Robert K. Dornan, and the 34th, former Rep. Dan Lungren's previous district.

A strip of land only a few hundred feet wide runs along the Los Angeles and Long Beach waterfronts, joining the two segments. The Long Beach Naval Shipyard, the *Queen Mary* and Howard Hughes' "Spruce Goose" are all located here.

The 42nd is split fairly evenly between the established suburbs of Los Angeles County and the faster-growing environs of Orange County. The two areas are of equally Republican temperament. In his initial House campaign, Rohrabacher took 64 percent of the Los Angeles County vote, and 65 percent in Orange County. George Bush also did well in both areas, en route to carrying the 42nd with nearly two-thirds of the vote.

In Los Angeles County, at the northern and western end of the district, are Torrance and the lush, upper-income Palos Verdes Hills overlooking the Pacific Ocean. The hills contain four exclusive communities — Palos Verdes Estates, Rancho Palos Verdes, Rolling Hills and Rolling Hills Estates — whose voters are overwhelmingly Republican.

The Orange County portion of the 42nd takes in Cypress, Los Alamitos, Seal Beach, Rossmoor, part of Westminster and most of Huntington Beach, a city of 184,000 that forms the southern anchor of the district. A gathering spot for surfers who congregate around the city's pier, Huntington Beach is also a haven for Republican candidates, who can count on a large vote from the white-collar professionals whose split-level houses ring the area's many cul-de-sacs.

Population: 525,909. White 469,685 (89%), Black 6,927 (1%), Asian and Pacific Islander 29,804 (6%), Other 2,952 (1%). Spanish origin 38,446 (7%). 18 and over 400,256 (76%), 65 and over 52,744 (10%). Median age: 33.

Committees

District of Columbia (4th of 4 Republicans)
Government Operations and Metropolitan Affairs; Judiciary and Education

Science, Space and Technology (17th of 19 Republicans)
Space Science and Applications; Transportation, Aviation and Materials

Campaign Finance

	Receipts	Receipts from PACs	Expend-itures
1988			
Rohrabacher (R)	$521,565	$186,427 (36%)	$494,487
Kimbrough (D)	$11,911	$1,750 (15%)	$11,889

Elections

1988 General		
Dana Rohrabacher (R)	153,280	(64%)
Guy C. Kimbrough (D)	78,778	(33%)
1988 Primary		
Dana Rohrabacher (R)	27,507	(35%)
Harriett M. Wieder (R)	17,128	(22%)
Stephen Horn (R)	15,911	(20%)
Andrew J. Littlefair (R)	6,581	(8%)
Bob Welbourn (R)	4,368	(6%)

District Vote For President

	1988	1984	1980	1976
D	86,544 (34%)	67,480 (27%)	56,326 (24%)	66,602 (35%)
R	165,572 (65%)	183,392 (72%)	150,848 (65%)	123,946 (64%)

43 Ron Packard (R)

Of Oceanside — Elected 1982

Born: Jan. 19, 1931, Meridian, Idaho.
Education: Attended Brigham Young U., 1948-50; attended Portland State U., 1952-53; U. of Oregon, D.M.D. 1957.
Military Career: Navy, 1957-59.
Occupation: Dentist.
Family: Wife, Roma Jean Sorenson; seven children.
Religion: Mormon.
Political Career: Carlsbad School Board, 1960-72; Carlsbad City Council, 1976-78; mayor of Carlsbad, 1978-82.
Capitol Office: 316 Cannon Bldg. 20515; 225-3906.

In Washington: Packard came to Congress with the smiling geniality expected of a neighborhood dentist and doggedly held Mormon convictions that inform his sense of right and wrong. But on the Public Works Committee — not much of a forum for moral theorizing — skill at the old-fashioned art of horse-trading is the most valuable personal attribute.

Adjusting to this reality has not always been easy for Packard, but he has made a sincere effort, and begun to reap the rewards. After years of work, he was able to add language to the 1987 omnibus highway bill to provide $15 million in new funding to widen a 12-mile stretch of Highway 78 in his district.

During the 100th Congress, Packard used his seat on the Aviation Subcommittee to help lead the successful effort to require passenger aircraft to install collision-avoidance equipment. While many Republicans worried about airline "re-regulation," Packard expressed support for certain consumer-protection efforts, saying, "The message is loud and clear to elected officials to do something."

In the 99th Congress, Packard ensured that Public Works added an amendment to the 1986 Clean Water Act authorizing filtering systems to defend against sewage seeping across the border from Mexico on the Tijuana River. He also worked to secure authorization for $1.1 billion for Santa Ana River flood control.

During the 1987 debate over legislation to compensate Japanese-Americans interned during World War II, Packard endorsed a federal apology, but opposed compensation. He said that he was one of 17 children raised on an Idaho farm, and when the family was about to lose their property, his father went to work for a government contractor in the South Pacific. Within days of the Japanese attack on Pearl Harbor, his father was taken prisoner, leaving the family destitute during the war. Giving money to the internees, Packard said, "would demean a time when our family learned to work together, pull together and pray together."

At Home: No matter how long Packard serves in Congress, nothing in his electoral career is likely to match the tumult of the contest that first brought him to Congress.

When GOP Rep. Clair W. Burgener announced his retirement in 1982, Packard and 17 other Republicans, some with extensive political backgrounds, filed for the primary. Packard's main worry was recreational-vehicle tycoon Johnnie Crean.

A political neophyte, Crean sank close to $1 million of his fortune into his campaign, which consisted largely of personal attacks on his rivals, some wildly inaccurate. Crean won considerable notoriety and the abiding scorn of many Republicans. He also won the nomination, by 92 votes over Packard.

Afterward, Crean said his campaign's conduct had been the responsibility of his consultants, whom he fired the day after the primary. But many GOP partisans were still unhappy, and they helped persuade Packard to enter the general election as a write-in candidate.

Crean tried to mend fences and reform his image. His supporters argued that Republicans choosing Packard would split the GOP vote, electing the Democratic nominee, government professor Roy Pat Archer. Party officials came out for Crean, and Packard's funding dried up.

But Packard was still strong at the grassroots level. While press coverage kept the Crean controversy fresh, Packard sent out 350,000 pieces of mail proclaiming himself the legitimate GOP alternative. On Election Day, his poll workers handed out pencils with Packard's name, urging their use. Packard edged Archer by 8,000 votes. Crean ran third.

Little in Packard's tranquil political career had prepared him for this. He went from the Carlsbad school board to the City Council and was chosen Carlsbad mayor in 1978. Since his first House victory, Packard has been safe.

California 43

Northern San Diego County; Southern Orange County

The current 43rd District is little different from the one that in 1980 gave its Republican incumbent 299,037 votes — more than any House candidate in U.S. history.

That total was somewhat inflated, coming at the end of a decade of population boom in the suburban/exurban sprawl between Los Angeles and San Diego that the district then covered. But while the last redistricting made the 43rd much more compact, it left the district just as Republican. George Bush received nearly 70 percent of the 1988 vote in the 43rd.

About two-thirds of the district vote is cast in San Diego County, with the rest in Orange County. The two segments are similar. Both are upper-middle-class residential areas, with little industry; Oceanside, Escondido and other fast-growing cities in the district consist mainly of suburban housing tracts.

San Marcos, in San Diego County, has burgeoned; its population (21,500 in 1986) more than tripled in the 1970s and grew by another 25 percent in the early 1980s. Even the town of San Juan Capistrano, famous for the swallows that flock to its ancient Spanish mission each spring, is being transformed. But the town's historic nature remains unscathed; artifacts of California's Mission period were unearthed there recently.

The conservative lean of the area anchored by Oceanside, Carlsbad and San Marcos is influenced by the presence of Camp Pendleton, the Marine Corps base. To the north and east are exclusive Escondido and Rancho Santa Fe, with the citrus and avocado groves of Fallbrook and Valley Center beyond.

The southern end of the district is held down by coastal towns like Cardiff-by-the-Sea and Encinitas. Though these suburbs are filled with commuters, opposition is strong here to the proposed bullet train between Los Angeles and San Diego, which would run past their homes.

Population: 525,956. White 457,997 (87%), Black 13,458 (3%), Other 19,023 (4%). Spanish origin 68,102 (13%). 18 and over 387,050 (74%), 65 and over 61,760 (12%). Median age: 30.

Committees

Public Works and Transportation (8th of 20 Republicans)
Aviation; Surface Transportation; Water Resources

Science, Space and Technology (8th of 19 Republicans)
International Scientific Cooperation (ranking); Space Science and Applications

Select Children, Youth and Families (4th of 12 Republicans)

Elections

1988 General		
Ron Packard (R)	202,478	(72%)
Howard Greenebaum (D)	72,499	(26%)
1986 General		
Ron Packard (R)	137,341	(73%)
Joseph Chirra (D)	45,078	(24%)

Previous Winning Percentages: **1984** (74%) **1982** (37%)

District Vote For President

	1988	1984	1980	1976
D	90,746 (31%)	58,819 (25%)	39,452 (20%)	38,553 (35%)
R	199,744 (68%)	176,550 (74%)	136,966 (70%)	71,659 (64%)

Campaign Finance

	Receipts	Receipts from PACs	Expenditures
1988			
Packard (R)	$215,956	$114,538 (53%)	$160,267
Greenebaum (D)	$75,170	$1,500 (2%)	$74,087
1986			
Packard (R)	$179,593	$87,700 (49%)	$132,967
Chirra (D)	$27,591	$4,525 (16%)	$26,367

Key Votes

1987	
Raise speed limit to 65 mph	N
Approve Gephardt "fair trade" amendment	N
Ban testing of larger nuclear weapons	N
Delay "re-flagging" of Kuwaiti tankers	N
Approve tax-raising deficit-reduction bill	N
1988	
Approve aid to Nicaraguan contras	Y
Enact civil rights restoration bill over Reagan veto	N
Kill 60-day plant-closing notification measure	Y
Pass omnibus trade bill over Reagan veto	N
Approve death penalty for drug-related murders	+
Bar federal funds for abortions in cases of rape and incest	+
Oppose seven-day waiting period for purchase of handguns	Y

Voting Studies

	Presidential Support		Party Unity		Conservative Coalition	
Year	S	O	S	O	S	O
1988	66	26	76	14	87	0
1987	70	27	81	14	88	12
1986	83	16	79	18	88	8
1985	75	24	85	10	91	9
1984	69	28	89	8	95	5
1983	83	16	92 †	5 †	91	2

† Not eligible for all recorded votes.

Interest Group Ratings

Year	ADA	ACU	AFL-CIO	CCUS
1988	5	100	15	92
1987	4	86	6	93
1986	5	91	7	94
1985	10	86	6	95
1984	0	83	8	75
1983	0	96	0	83

44 Jim Bates (D)

Of San Diego — Elected 1982

Born: July 21, 1941, Denver, Colo.
Education: San Diego State U., B.A. 1975.
Military Career: Marine Corps, 1959-63.
Occupation: Marketing analyst.
Family: Wife, Marilyn Brewer; three children.
Religion: Protestant.
Political Career: San Diego City Council, 1971-74; San Diego County Board of Supervisors, 1975-82; sought Democratic nomination for U.S. House, 1980.
Capitol Office: 224 Cannon Bldg. 20515; 225-5452.

In Washington: There is a fine distinction between being independent and merely being erratic. Bates lurched toward the latter in the 100th Congress, seriously marring his public image and making trouble for himself in California and on Capitol Hill.

An orphanage-raised high school dropout who joined the Marines at 18, he got to Washington through sheer determination, without any political establishment paving his way. And he won impressive victories early in his first term. But since then, Bates' habit of marching to his own drummer has limited his ability to operate in the legislative process.

Bates' reputation for unconventional behavior is so widely acknowledged among his colleagues that when *Roll Call*, a Capitol Hill newspaper, ran a story in 1988 detailing allegations of Bates' sexual harassment and verbal abuse of staffers, some members professed no great surprise at the revelations.

Roll Call broke the Bates story less than two months before Election Day, and followed it through the fall. It detailed charges of staff mistreatment spanning Bates' days on the San Diego Board of Supervisors to his tenure in the House. Unnamed current and former staffers recounted numerous occasions on which Bates made unwanted sexual advances and sexually explicit remarks to female staffers; sought embraces from female employees; and once, in full view of his Hill staff, wrapped his legs around a female staffer's leg and began to sway while inquiring about a legislative project.

Bates denies the last incident ever occurred, but acknowledges that he hugged his employees, and that "a couple of things [I did] were out of line." He added that he has sensed some "reservation" among Hill staffers since his return to Washington for the 101st Congress.

Though Bates won re-election, his troubles are far from over. At home, he will have to work to fend off potential competitors who sense he is vulnerable. In Congress, colleagues are watching to see if he behaves responsibly.

In his first term, Bates pulled off a coup by winning a coveted spot on the Energy and Commerce Committee. California was due a Democratic seat, but the delegation could not agree on a choice; Bates convinced colleagues from other parts of the country that he was one Californian who would not take orders from any of the power brokers in his delegation.

Bates began the 101st Congress with a new role — subcommittee chairman — and an added committee. He took over as chairman of the House Administration Subcommittee on Procurement and Printing, and he joined the Government Operations Committee.

Ironically, on House Administration Bates has investigated the pay and working conditions of thousands of skilled and unskilled workers performing service jobs on Capitol Hill.

Bates' new assignment on Government Operations will give him a forum for investigating and auditing government inefficiency, a cause he has pursued for much of his career.

Bates added an amendment to the 1987 defense authorization bill, barring the Navy from accepting from manufacturers any more CH-53E helicopters unless they incorporated several safety improvements the Navy and the contractor had agreed to implement. The modifications were designed to end a string of CH-53E crashes.

In 1989, he led a coalition of conservative Republicans and liberal Democrats to introduce a bill aimed at cutting the cost of the Rural Electrification Administration's loan program.

Many Democratic members of Energy and Commerce blossom into accomplished legislators, taking advantage of the committee's broad jurisdiction to define and pursue a personal agenda. But Bates' priorities have not been clear, and he has been an irregular participant in the panel's deliberations. On important showdowns, he usually sides with the committee's most influential liberal Democrat, Henry A. Waxman of California.

Sometimes he appears distracted and un-

California 44

Central San Diego

As a whole, San Diego County has not voted for a Democratic presidential candidate in four decades; George Bush won there by nearly 200,000 votes in 1988. But the city of San Diego has always had a large enough concentration of Democrats to support one safe Democratic House district.

In the 1970s, that district was the old 42nd, held for 18 years by Lionel Van Deerlin, who was upset in 1980 by Republican Duncan Hunter. (Van Deerlin blamed the loss on President Carter's concession while California polls were still open, and sparked a West Coast movement to bar TV networks from making early evening projections of presidential winners.) San Diego Democrats reclaimed their stake during redistricting, though, drawing a new inner-city district, the 44th, while moving Hunter into the GOP suburbs and rural areas.

The 44th takes in white working-class neighborhoods near the center of town and farther east, the blue-collar suburb of National City to the south, and San Diego's black and Hispanic communities, including the San Ysidro barrio, less than a mile from the Mexican border. The district also extends east into semi-rural Spring Valley, and the middle-income suburb of Chula Vista.

Democratic map makers were careful to exclude San Diego's more Republican precincts, including the downtown business area and a section north of Balboa Park. But the 44th's Democratic tendencies are greatly tempered, at least in presidential contests, by the importance of the military to San Diego's economy. The district, which includes the North Island Naval Air Station and the San Diego Naval Station, went with President Reagan in 1984. In 1988, though, Michael S. Dukakis returned the district to the Democrats by a narrow margin.

Population: 525,868. White 332,075 (63%), Black 73,400 (14%), Asian and Pacific Islander 42,490 (8%), Other 3,773 (1%). Spanish origin 141,823 (27%). 18 and over 379,593 (72%), 65 and over 44,081 (8%). Median age: 26.

willing to concentrate on legislative matters long enough to influence them. In one notable incident, he berated a group of people sitting at the committee's witness table, apparently believing them to be officials of the Federal Communications Commission; in fact, they were employees of the committee itself.

Bates' chief priority in the 100th Congress was his bill to create a new federal grant program to encourage states to develop emergency-care systems for trauma victims. The bill, sponsored in the Senate by California Democrat Alan Cranston, was backed by the American Medical Association but opposed by the American Hospital Association, committee Republicans and the Reagan administration. The committee approved it on a largely party-line vote, and it passed the House by voice vote, but the measure never reached the Senate floor.

Bates reintroduced his trauma-care bill in the 101st Congress. It won approval from Energy and Commerce, but drew opposition from the Bush administration, which said such a program duplicated current state grant services.

Perhaps Bates' biggest legislative mark was made in 1983 on a defense issue: the MX missile. Despite his Marine background, he had long been skeptical of the military — Bates switched parties and became a Democrat in 1968 mainly in protest at the Vietnam War.

When Majority Leader Jim Wright and Whip Thomas S. Foley voted for the MX in spring 1983, helping it survive a key test, Bates persuaded 112 members to sign his petition for a special Democratic caucus to discuss why top party leaders were helping enact Reagan's defense program. The caucus was held in June. The MX narrowly won final approval, but not with help from Foley or Wright, who joined the overwhelming Democratic majority against it.

At Home: The 1988 fall campaign appeared strictly *pro forma* for Bates until *Roll Call* made an issue of his treatment of women on his staff. Bates' opponent splashed the story across purchased pages of the *San Diego Union,* but he lacked the campaign organization to carry the issue much further. Bates controlled the damage, brought out his troops and took 60 percent of the vote. It was his weakest showing in four elections, and that could tempt a stronger challenge in 1990.

Bates carefully cultivated his inner-city San Diego constituency over 11 years in local office. So, when map makers in 1981 crafted a new district based in his political territory, he had enough minority and blue-collar support to become an odds-on favorite.

Still, Bates' 1982 campaign took nothing for granted. He and his volunteers combed the city, walking virtually every precinct in the district. Between the June primary and his easy November contest, Bates wrote more than 10,000 postcards urging people to vote Democratic.

Bates was applying the lessons he had learned in San Diego politics. As chairman of the county Board of Supervisors, he set up two separate citizens' advisory committees, one made up mostly of lower-ranking officeholders and one focused at the grass-roots level.

This attention to constituents brought favorable political returns. It also brought some complaint that Bates, a critic of burgeoning government bureaucracy, had built a bureaucracy of his own.

In two terms as county supervisor, Bates gained notice for his role in developing a county "workfare" ordinance, requiring able-bodied food stamp recipients to earn their benefits in public service jobs. But he also bucked the board's conservative bent at times. He sought federal funding for a local Planned Parenthood operation and was instrumental in promoting affirmative action programs.

Bates was the candidate of the Democratic center in 1980, when he ran for Congress in the old 41st District, covering the white-collar northern section of San Diego. Battling state Sen. Bob Wilson in the Democratic primary for the seat left open by his opponent's namesake, retiring GOP Rep. Bob Wilson, Bates cast the younger Wilson as too conservative for the party's middle ground. Although Bates waged an aggressive campaign, he fell short. The 41st stayed in GOP hands that November.

Bates returned to serve out the remainder of his county board term and was named chairman for the 1981-82 session. But he did not lose sight of his congressional ambitions.

In redistricting, much of San Diego's GOP-leaning territory was moved into a safe Republican district, the new 45th, leaving the inner city to dominate the 44th. After surviving a legal challenge to his petitions for a place on the ballot, Bates rolled up 72 percent of the Democratic primary vote.

Republicans failed to draft a strong candidate; their nominee was Shirley Gissendanner, a bus driver and a former aide to GOP Rep. Duncan Hunter. For the general election, Bates blamed President Reagan's economic policies for contributing to San Diego's unemployment rate (then above 11 percent), but he cautioned against costly solutions of past Democratic administrations. He called himself a social liberal, supporting public financing of abortions for indigents and a bilateral nuclear weapons freeze.

Committees

Energy and Commerce (21st of 26 Democrats)
Energy and Power; Health and the Environment; Transportation and Hazardous Materials

Government Operations (23rd of 24 Democrats)

House Administration (7th of 13 Democrats)
Procurement and Printing (chairman); Elections

Joint Printing

Elections

1988 General		
Jim Bates (D)	90,796	(60%)
Rob Butterfield (R)	55,511	(37%)
1986 General		
Jim Bates (D)	70,557	(64%)
Bill Mitchell (R)	36,359	(33%)

Previous Winning Percentages: 1984 (70%) **1982** (65%)

District Vote For President

	1988	1984	1980	1976
D	80,893 (52%)	71,160 (47%)	52,841 (40%)	54,103 (56%)
R	74,236 (47%)	79,269 (52%)	64,434 (49%)	42,041 (43%)

Campaign Finance

	Receipts	Receipts from PACs	Expend-itures
1988			
Bates (D)	$480,384	$246,105 (51%)	$480,679
Butterfield (R)	$218,593	$47,393 (22%)	$218,388
1986			
Bates (D)	$410,133	$181,291 (44%)	$410,017
Mitchell (R)	$135,640	$18,800 (14%)	$134,980

Key Votes

1987	
Raise speed limit to 65 mph	N
Approve Gephardt "fair trade" amendment	N
Ban testing of larger nuclear weapons	Y
Delay "re-flagging" of Kuwaiti tankers	Y
Approve tax-raising deficit-reduction bill	Y
1988	
Approve aid to Nicaraguan contras	N
Enact civil rights restoration bill over Reagan veto	Y
Kill 60-day plant-closing notification measure	N
Pass omnibus trade bill over Reagan veto	Y
Approve death penalty for drug-related murders	N
Bar federal funds for abortions in cases of rape and incest	N
Oppose seven-day waiting period for purchase of handguns	N

Voting Studies

	Presidential Support		Party Unity		Conservative Coalition	
Year	**S**	**O**	**S**	**O**	**S**	**O**
1988	17	76	86	6	13	79
1987	21	76	77	17	19	77
1986	19	81	83	15	24	76
1985	30	70	79	14	25	73
1984	26	68	84	9	14	78
1983	20	77	86	11	18	78

Interest Group Ratings

Year	ADA	ACU	AFL-CIO	CCUS
1988	95	8	93	46
1987	96	9	73	47
1986	90	0	86	44
1985	80	29	75	41
1984	90	0	82	38
1983	85	9	88	26

45 Duncan Hunter (R)

Of Coronado — Elected 1980

Born: May 31, 1948, Riverside, Calif.
Education: Attended U. of Montana, 1966-67; U. of California, Santa Barbara, 1967-68; Western State U., B.S.L. 1976, J.D. 1976.
Military Career: Army, 1969-71.
Occupation: Lawyer.
Family: Wife, Lynne Layh; two children.
Religion: Baptist.
Political Career: No previous office.
Capitol Office: 133 Cannon Bldg. 20515; 225-5672.

In Washington: Hunter's 1989 ascent into House Republican leadership ranks demonstrates just how much personality and persistence can count for in the realm of internal party politics.

Affable and self-effacing, this class of 1980 conservative is a difficult man not to like. Combined with the younger-generation, right-of-center pedigree that many House Republicans are now looking for in their leaders, Hunter's approachable nature allowed him to overcome qualms about his unfocused enthusiasm and intellectual depth.

His opponent in the race for chairman of the Republican Research Committee was Steve Bartlett of Texas, who was first elected in 1982. Similarly conservative, he is known for his keen mind, but not for being an unselfish team player like Hunter. On the strength of his personal qualities, Hunter won the Research post.

The Californian had worked hard to earn the job. He contributed generously to GOP House incumbents and challengers, and he devoted so much time to campaigning for colleagues that one San Diego newspaper speculated that through late October 1988, he had spent as much time trekking around the country as he had spent in his own district.

In mid-1987, Hunter had come surprisingly close to defeating fellow Californian Jerry Lewis in the race for Policy Committee chairman. That post came open when presidential campaign pressures forced Rep. Jack F. Kemp to give up his leadership berth, touching off a scramble for three positions in the GOP hierarchy.

In many ways, Hunter's 1987 race foreshadowed the later GOP leadership changes of the 101st Congress, which featured the combative Newt Gingrich's elevation to minority whip. The 1987 contest between Hunter and Lewis was cast as a "young Turk" vs. "establishment man" choice. Hunter first gained notice when he chaired the Conservative Opportunity Society (COS), an insurgent faction of young Republicans (including Gingrich) that made its name by eschewing accommodation with the Democratic majority to underscore the differences between the parties.

While Lewis preceded Hunter in the House by just two years, he is a more traditional GOP player who has worked through the system for incremental change, both as a member of the Appropriations Committee and a representative on the Committee on Committees, which makes Republican committee assignments.

Though clearly the underdog, Hunter mounted an energetic campaign; he began working long before anyone knew when or even if Kemp would leave the Policy Committee chairmanship. Even after California Republicans, worried about two of their own fighting for the same post, voted 3-to-1 for Lewis, Hunter stuck with it. In the end, he held the favored Lewis to an 88-82 margin of victory.

Subsequently, Hunter was among those Republicans involved with Gingrich in seeking to spotlight a number of ethical controversies involving House Democrats. In pressing their case, Hunter said the GOP wanted to publicize the Democrats' "double standard" in zealously investigating Reagan administration officials, Wall Street financiers and religious broadcasters, while ignoring their colleagues' alleged sins. Their efforts eventually led to Speaker Jim Wright's downfall in 1989, and helped elevate three former COS chairmen — Gingrich, Hunter and Vin Weber of Minnesota — to GOP leadership positions.

In outlining his goals for the Research Committee, Hunter downplays Democrat-bashing and stresses giving minorities a voice in the party. "I want to make the Research Committee an open house for Hispanic and Asian-American opinion leaders," he said.

While this is a stock Republican line, Hunter can deliver it with some personal conviction: He sees his 1980 election as evidence that GOP views on issues such as communism, defense spending and school prayer can woo minority voters skeptical of what he calls the

California 45

Imperial Valley; Part of San Diego

Crossing the entire southern border of the state from the Colorado River to San Diego's Sunset Cliffs, the 45th has much land that is sparsely populated and many voters who are devoutly Republican.

The 45th was created by redistricting just after Hunter entered the House. The remap gave Hunter a considerable amount of new territory, but he had no complaints. His original district, which he won in a 1980 upset, had large chunks of Democratic turf within the city of San Diego. The 45th, on the other hand, is mainly suburban and rural, and staunchly Republican. Ronald Reagan topped 70 percent here in 1984; George Bush took two-thirds of its vote in 1988.

The 45th has two distinct parts. One is the area around San Diego — the eastern suburbs of the city, such as Chula Vista, El Cajon and Lakeside, as well as the spit of land west of the city — Coronado — that separates the Pacific Ocean from San Diego Bay. Coronado is the home of many retired Navy officers. They give the area a decidedly pro-military, Republican flavor.

The other part of the district lies east of San Diego County — California's Imperial Valley. Below the level of both the Colorado River and the Pacific Ocean, the valley was relatively easy to irrigate at the turn of the century and has become one of the country's most productive farm areas.

As farmers and urban refugees have moved in with their house trailers, the valley has been experiencing its first substantial growth in several decades, with population rising by more than 15 percent in the early 1980s: More than 100,000 people now live there. The voting trend is conservative, but not so much as in the San Diego suburbs: Bush carried Imperial County with 55 percent of the vote.

Population: 525,927. White 447,436 (85%), Black 8,610 (2%), Other 18,518 (4%). Spanish origin 90,291 (17%). 18 and over 373,038 (71%), 65 and over 49,996 (10%). Median age: 29.

Democrats' "special ethnic legislation." In 1980, Hunter's background as an attorney in the San Diego barrio helped him upset a Democratic incumbent in what was then a Democratic district. Redistricting later gave him a safe haven, but it has not dimmed his enthusiasm for the "politics of inclusion" as a way to expand his party's base.

Apart from his leadership endeavors, Hunter was best known during the 1980s for his hard-line defense of Ronald Reagan's military build-up and foreign policy. A staunch supporter of the Nicaraguan contras, Hunter spoke in apocalyptic terms of President Bush's 1989 contra accord with Congress, which did not seek renewal of military aid. "Nicaragua is lost," Hunter said. "The dark curtain of the Sandinista Gestapo has descended on Nicaragua."

From his seat on the Armed Services Committee, the intense Vietnam veteran brings his hawkish agenda to nearly every debate. The size of the federal deficit has not curbed his support for generously funding the strategic defense initiative. "I quarrel with the notion that you give deterrence of nuclear war a cost-of-living increase," he said in 1988.

In the 100th Congress, he was a prime sponsor of legislation to involve the military in drug interdiction. When the House approved a similar Hunter amendment in 1986, it was practically laughed off the Senate floor as Democrat Sam Nunn of Georgia deadpanned an inventory of the large number of men, ships and planes needed to carry out the plan. In 1988, it won approval in both chambers.

Hunter also vigorously defends the interests of his San Diego military bases and shipbuilding facilities. He opposed the Navy's new "homeport" basing strategy because dispersal of ships and ship-repair work to new ports could hurt established ones such as San Diego.

At Home: Hunter has an unusual background for a conservative Republican. For the three years before his initial House campaign, he lived and worked in the Hispanic section of San Diego. Running his own storefront law office, Hunter often gave free legal advice to poor people. When President Reagan called for abolition of the Legal Services Corporation, Hunter was one of the dissenters.

Hunter's work in the usually Democratic inner city was one of the reasons for his 1980 upset victory over Democrat Lionel Van Deerlin, a nine-term House veteran. Running his campaign out of his law office, Hunter attracted volunteers and voters most GOP candidates would have had to write off.

Another reason was Hunter's ceaseless campaigning. He made endless rounds of the compact district, popping up at defense plants and on street corners, shaking 1,000 hands every day while Van Deerlin remained in Washington, assuming he would score a comfortable victory.

Hunter, who won a Bronze Star for participating in 25 helicopter combat assaults in Vietnam, blasted away at what he called Van Deerlin's "anti-defense" voting record. He promised that his own pro-Pentagon stance would keep jobs in the district, where the nation's largest naval base and numerous defense industries are located. "In San Diego," he said, "defense means jobs." The message worked. On Election Day, Hunter stunned the opposition with 53 percent.

In 1982 redistricting, Democrats created a new 44th District in central San Diego, moving Hunter into the solidly Republican 45th outside the city and relieving him of election pressures. He has won two-thirds of the vote or better in every campaign since, topping 70 percent in 1984, 1986, and 1988.

Committees

Armed Services (7th of 21 Republicans)
Research and Development; Seapower and Strategic and Critical Materials

Select Hunger (9th of 12 Republicans)

Elections

1988 General

Duncan Hunter (R)	166,451	(74%)
Pete Lepiscopo (D)	54,012	(24%)

1986 General

Duncan Hunter (R)	118,900	(77%)
Hewitt Fitts Ryan (D)	32,800	(21%)

Previous Winning Percentages: **1984** (75%) **1982** (69%) **1980** (53%)

District Vote For President

	1988	1984	1980	1976
D	76,206 (33%)	58,141 (28%)	45,726 (25%)	53,299 (42%)
R	153,368 (66%)	149,282 (71%)	120,516 (65%)	73,749 (57%)

Campaign Finance

	Receipts	Receipts from PACs	Expenditures
1988			
Hunter (R)	$392,229	$150,718 (38%)	$489,395
Lepiscopo (D)	$8,618	$3,775 (44%)	$8,136
1986			
Hunter (R)	$401,076	$136,710 (34%)	$400,612
Ryan (D)	$22,893	$6,250 (27%)	$21,875

Key Votes

1987	
Raise speed limit to 65 mph	Y
Approve Gephardt "fair trade" amendment	N
Ban testing of larger nuclear weapons	N
Delay "re-flagging" of Kuwaiti tankers	N
Approve tax-raising deficit-reduction bill	N
1988	
Approve aid to Nicaraguan contras	Y
Enact civil rights restoration bill over Reagan veto	N
Kill 60-day plant-closing notification measure	Y
Pass omnibus trade bill over Reagan veto	N
Approve death penalty for drug-related murders	Y
Bar federal funds for abortions in cases of rape and incest	Y
Oppose seven-day waiting period for purchase of handguns	Y

Voting Studies

	Presidential Support		Party Unity		Conservative Coalition	
Year	S	O	S	O	S	O
1988	65	30	89	5	95	3
1987	72	22	86	6	88	7
1986	78	20	85	11	90	8
1985	74	20	75	12	87	11
1984	73	24	80	15	90	8
1983	74	24	88	10	93	7
1982	83	14	84	10	90	5
1981	74	25	89	11	95	5

Interest Group Ratings

Year	ADA	ACU	AFL-CIO	CCUS
1988	0	100	15	77
1987	4	91	13	93
1986	0	82	29	100
1985	10	86	19	76
1984	5	91	42	81
1983	15	91	12	80
1982	5	84	21	82
1981	10	100	27	89

Colorado

U.S. CONGRESS

SENATE 1 D, 1 R

HOUSE 3 D, 3 R

LEGISLATURE

Senate 11 D, 24 R

House 26 D, 39 R

ELECTIONS

1988 Presidential Vote	
Bush	53%
Dukakis	45%
1984 Presidential Vote	
Reagan	63%
Mondale	35%
1980 Presidential Vote	
Reagan	55%
Carter	31%
Anderson	11%
Turnout rate in 1984	55%
Turnout rate in 1986	42%
Turnout rate in 1988	55%

(as percentage of voting age population)

POPULATION AND GROWTH

1980 population	2,889,964
1988 population estimate (26th in the nation)	3,301,000
Percent change 1980-1988	+14%

DEMOGRAPHIC BREAKDOWN

White	89%
Black	4%
Other	2%
(Spanish origin)	12%
Urban	81%
Rural	19%
Born in state	42%
Foreign-born	4%

MAJOR CITIES

Denver	505,000
Colorado Springs	272,660
Aurora	217,990
Lakewood	122,140
Pueblo	101,240

AREA AND LAND USE

Area 103,595 sq. miles (8th)

Farm	51%
Forest	32%
Federally owned	36%

Gov. Roy Romer (D)
Of Denver — Elected 1986

Born: Oct. 31, 1928, Garden City, Kan.
Education: Colorado State U., B.S., 1950; U. of Colorado, LL.B., 1952; graduate work, Yale U., 1954.
Military Career: Air Force legal officer, 1952-53.
Occupation: Lawyer.
Religion: Presbyterian.
Political Career: Colo. House 1959-63; Colo. Senate, 1963-67; assistant minority leader, 1963-67; Colo. treasurer, 1977-87; Democratic nominee for U.S. Senate, 1966.
Next Election: 1990

WORK

Occupations	
White-collar	58%
Blue-collar	27%
Service workers	13%
Government Workers	
Federal	51,948
State	62,468
Local	142,972

MONEY

Median family income	$ 21,279	(12th)
Tax burden per capita	$ 707	(42nd)

EDUCATION

Spending per pupil through grade 12	$ 3,975	(16th)
Persons with college degrees	23%	(1st)

CRIME

Violent crime rate	468 per 100,000 (21st)

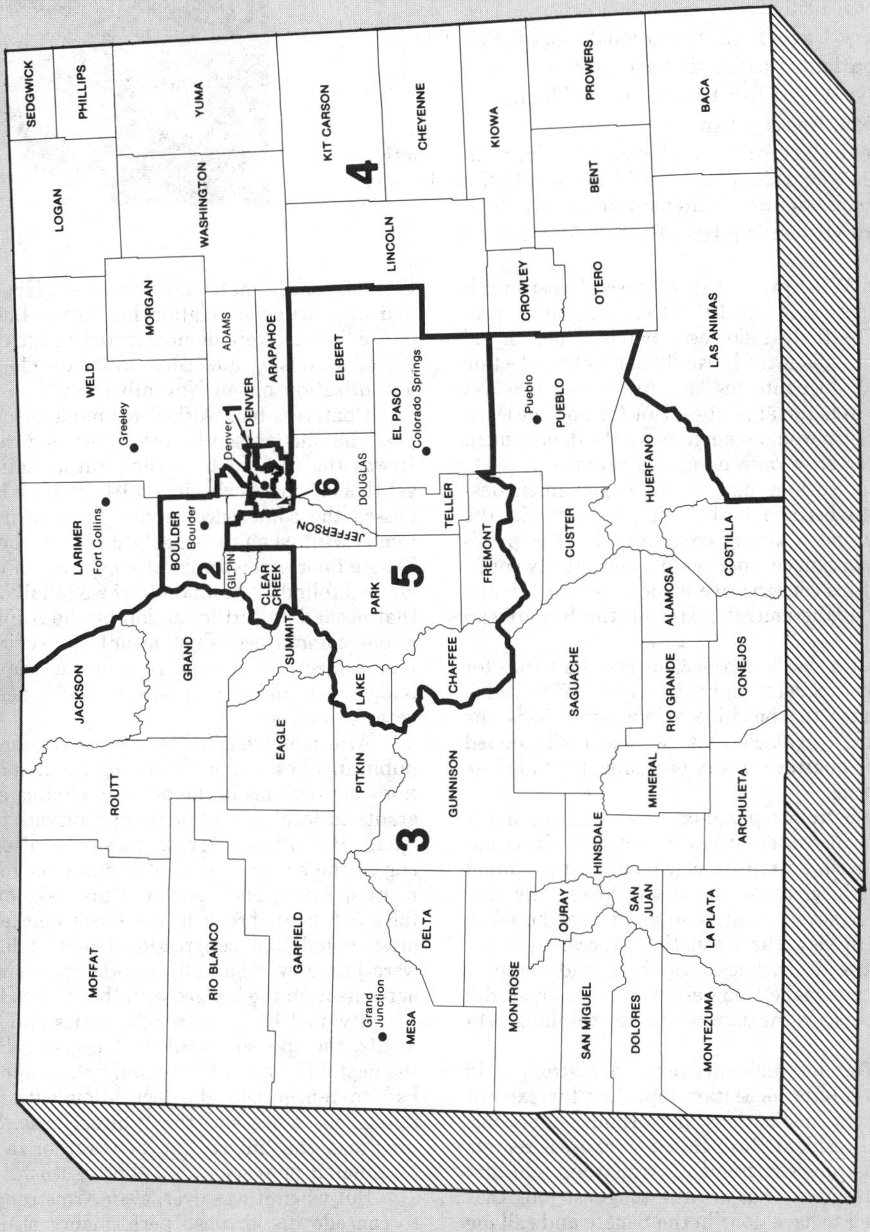
SEDGWICK
PHILLIPS
LOGAN
YUMA
WASHINGTON
KIT CARSON
CHEYENNE
4
KIOWA
PROWERS
BACA
LINCOLN
BENT
CROWLEY
OTERO
LAS ANIMAS
MORGAN
ADAMS
ARAPAHOE
ELBERT
WELD
Greeley
DENVER
1
Denver
EL PASO
Colorado Springs
Pueblo
PUEBLO
LARIMER
Fort Collins
BOULDER
Boulder
6
DOUGLAS
JEFFERSON
TELLER
HUERFANO
2
GILPIN
CLEAR CREEK
5
PARK
FREMONT
CUSTER
COSTILLA
ALAMOSA
SUMMIT
GRAND
JACKSON
CHAFFEE
LAKE
SAGUACHE
RIO GRANDE
CONEJOS
EAGLE
ROUTT
PITKIN
GUNNISON
MINERAL
ARCHULETA
HINSDALE
3
RIO BLANCO
MOFFAT
GARFIELD
DELTA
OURAY
SAN JUAN
LA PLATA
Grand Junction
MESA
MONTROSE
SAN MIGUEL
DOLORES
MONTEZUMA

William L. Armstrong (R)

Of Englewood — Elected 1978

Born: March 16, 1937, Fremont, Neb.
Education: Attended Tulane U., 1954-55; U. of Minnesota, 1955-56.
Military Career: Army National Guard, 1957-63.
Occupation: Broadcasting executive.
Family: Wife, Ellen Eaton; two children.
Religion: Episcopalian.
Political Career: Colo. House, 1963-65; Colo. Senate, 1965-73; U.S. House, 1973-79; sought Republican nomination for lieutenant governor, 1970.
Capitol Office: 528 Hart Bldg. 20510; 224-5941.

In Washington: In a sense, Armstrong is participating in the 101st Congress under protest. The first session was barely a month old when he announced he would not seek re-election in 1990. Just into his 50s, Armstrong may yet return to national politics. But for now, at least, his decision would seem to mark the denouement for a career of once unlimited promise.

Not so long ago, Armstrong seemed destined to become both a major power in the Senate and a strong contender for the presidency. Intelligent, personable and utterly confident of his conservative values, he struck many people as the emerging star on the Republican right.

But a discussion of Congress he wrote for *The Wall Street Journal* early in 1989, which ran under the headline "Congress misses the big jobs," signaled that he was disillusioned with his quarter-century of public life and close to retiring.

Armstrong's paradox has confronted many ideological conservatives in politics. He is engaged in an enterprise of which, in a profound philosophical sense, he disapproves. His distaste for government is so great that he often seems to view the legislative process — especially the deals, back-scratching and compromises that make Congress work — as a sordid affair beneath the dignity of right-thinking people.

After his announcement, Armstrong said he would offer legislation repealing tax-exempt status for institutions performing abortions. When President Bush called to express regrets at Armstrong's retirement, Armstrong told him to "determine what are the toughest jobs that you need to have done in the Senate and call me to do them."

It is possible to see Armstrong in such a role; as chairman of the Republican Policy Committee he is the only clearly defined ideological conservative to hold a GOP Senate leadership post. But it would be a departure from the game he has played best within the Senate, that of consummate obstructionist. His forte, and his particular relationship to the business of the Senate, were demonstrated by his derailing of a housing and community development authorization bill in November 1987.

Conferees had worked for months to compose the bills passed by the House and Senate. It was the first such housing authorization to get this far on its own since 1980, and the House passed the conference product with near unanimity. But when the same product reached the Senate floor, Armstrong raised a point of order. He had found $47 million in the $30 billion bill that needed no further action by the Appropriations committees. That meant the entire bill was subject to special rules from the 1974 budget act and the sponsors would need 60 votes to proceed.

Armstrong, backed by several Western Republican allies, had a list of longstanding objections to programs in the bill — including action grants to local governments and private developers. But while offering these, he also portrayed the key vote as a referendum on government spending and deficits in the wake of that fall's 500-point break in the stock market. He often noted that congressional budget leaders were just down the hall, negotiating a summit agreement on the budget with the White House.

Stymied by Armstrong's tactics and arguments, the sponsors could not proceed. So for the next five weeks, House and Senate sponsors had to renegotiate the legislation with Armstrong, his allies and the White House. Some programs the bill sought to reauthorize were terminated or placed on a shorter leash.

But when it was over, even Armstrong had to concede his virtuoso performance as Horatius at the bridge was only a holding action: "It really says we're going to be back on these issues again later on," he said.

A frequent user of the filibuster as a way of expressing his strong moral stands on the issues, Armstrong faced a dilemma in 1986, when the Senate debated televising its sessions. Armstrong was an outspoken advocate of Senate TV, but he was disturbed by efforts to make the chamber more presentable to viewers by placing restrictions on debate and delaying tactics. He voted for the resolution, but only after amending it to protect the time-honored Senate tradition of allowing amendments whose subject matter is unrelated to the legislation being considered.

Remarkably, however, Armstrong has been able to play an obstructionist role without alienating his colleagues. He has a knack for pushing hard-line conservative positions in a soft-spoken way. While other New Right senators have made themselves unpopular by noisily obstructing business to push their causes, Armstrong has practiced a similar sort of politics in a manner that seemed to threaten few of his opponents.

Not everyone appreciated it, of course, when he kept the Senate up all night to take away a congressional tax benefit, or blocked a vote on a housing-subsidy bill that had majority support. But Armstrong can do those things with less permanent damage to his reputation than most of those who agree with him.

"I find that the way to handle issues is not in an emotional or demagogic way, but in a dispassionate way," he says. "I want to appeal to facts, not to emotions."

Moreover, Armstrong is perceived more often as a fiscal conservative than as a social one. That image is not entirely accurate, since his religious fundamentalism matches that of anybody in Congress. Converted from what he called "a garden-variety institutional Christian" to a born-again evangelical, he has said, "If a person is unable to make a profession of faith, I don't think he's a complete human being."

Armstrong has kept his distance, however, from the political strivings of many on the Christian Right. In a 1986 interview, he criticized those who "try to assume for the church the role of being power brokers.... They should never, never, never give the impression that ... they are somehow speaking with authority of scripture or church or God," he said.

Armstrong came to the Senate as one of the most able spokesmen of the anti-tax, anti-government groundswell of the late 1970s. Some called him the movement's Paul Revere. He sought out the money committees and was placed eventually on three: Budget, Banking and Finance. The first of these provided endless opportunity for addressing the issue of spending, although he may have had more chances to choke it off had he been on Appropriations.

Armstrong was an avid supporter of Reaganomics on the tax side. He was an early and leading advocate of "tax indexing," which prevented inflation-driven wage increases from pushing taxpayers into higher brackets. But he feared the spending cuts of the first Reagan budgets did not go far enough to avoid serious deficits, and even opposed the first Reagan budget in committee on these grounds.

When Finance turned to revising the tax code in 1986, Armstrong was not in the forefront. He opposed, for example, the treatment of capital gains as regular income. But the most significant ramification of the 1986 tax bill for Armstrong was a transition rule he won in committee. The rule allowed eight limited partners in a closely held coal company in Colorado to keep the favorable treatment of their capital gains despite the new law. The *Rocky Mountain News* identified one partner as a conservative publisher and broadcaster with whom Armstrong had business dealings.

Even without evidence of a quid pro quo, the incident created seriously unfavorable publicity for Armstrong both nationally and at home. It did not help that, after the transition rule was dropped from the bill, a printing error restored it. The rule became law and its benefactors used it until a technical-corrections bill expunged it for good in 1988. Armstrong has since spoken of this entire incident as influencing his decision not to seek the GOP presidential nomination in 1988.

If Armstrong will be missed by the Senate GOP, he is all but irreplaceable in his state party. Except for his races, Republicans have not won a single Colorado contest for senator or governor since 1972. That is why, within hours of his announcement, Armstrong was being rumored as a candidate for governor in 1990 or for the Senate in 1992. For now, neither seems likely. Armstrong seems sincere in his plans to pursue his business interests, his involvement in his church and in other religious organizations such as the Campus Crusade for Christ. He retains ample opportunity to be noticed in state politics, should he choose, and on the national stage as well. As a board member of the Free Congress Foundation, he is likely to remain a much-quoted spokesman for "movement conservatives."

At Home: Armstrong's boyish good looks and crisply stated conservatism made him a man of the future among Colorado Republicans from the day he entered the Legislature in 1963 at the age of 25. He was already a successful businessman. At 22, Armstrong had bought a Denver radio station and turned it into a multimillion-dollar operation.

Politically, his life also was charmed. Two years after his only political setback — a loss to John D. Vanderhoof for the GOP nomination for lieutenant governor in 1970 — Armstrong was sent to Congress from a new district in the eastern suburbs of Denver. There was speculation then that he had a hand in creating the district for himself. Whether he did or not, it was perfect for him. Although Democrats and independents outnumbered Republicans there, Armstrong was an easy winner three times.

He angered the party's influential right wing only once — when he backed President Gerald R. Ford over Ronald Reagan for the 1976 GOP presidential nomination. But the Reagan forces forgave him, and the incident faded away when he made his long-planned campaign for the Senate two years later.

Democratic Sen. Floyd Haskell was an obvious Republican target when he came up for re-election in 1978. Haskell had upset three-term Republican Gordon Allott in 1972 with an environmentalist campaign. By 1978, the state was in a far more conservative mood.

There was little doubt that Armstrong would be the Republican nominee. He easily disposed of a primary challenge from astronaut Jack Swigert, who tried to rally the Reagan elements from two years before. Armstrong had mended fences with the party's right wing and drew 73 percent of the primary vote. That set the stage for an ideological debate with Haskell.

Armstrong criticized the incumbent for favoring the Panama Canal treaties and denounced him as ineffective, citing Haskell's inability to dissuade President Jimmy Carter from moving to cancel Colorado water projects. Haskell tried to soften his liberal image by advocating a balanced budget and countered the charges of ineffectiveness by bringing in Carter himself, who called Haskell "a national treasure." But it was no contest; Armstrong won by a margin of nearly 3-to-2.

His re-election victory in 1984 was even more decisive. He was able to capitalize on his personal popularity, an efficient, well-financed organization and strong ticket-mates. Armstrong drew a larger share of the vote than any GOP Senate candidate in Colorado history.

Democrats eased the way for Armstrong by nominating Lt. Gov. Nancy Dick, who was underfinanced and deserted by much of the state party hierarchy. Some of the Democratic leaders were in her corner when she launched her campaign in 1983, but they began to distance themselves after her slow start encouraged opposition from Carlos Lucero, the former head of the state bar association. Although he was not as well-known as Dick, Lucero ran ahead of her at the state party convention before narrowly losing the primary.

The primary proved to be the high-water mark for Dick. She sought to chip away at Armstrong's large lead by depicting him as too conservative. But in a state where Reagan won 63 percent of the vote, Armstrong safely ignored her attacks and went on to an easy win.

Committees

Budget (2nd of 10 Republicans)

Finance (8th of 9 Republicans)
Energy and Agricultural Taxation (ranking); International Debt; International Trade

Elections

1984 General

William L. Armstrong (R)	833,821	(64%)
Nancy Dick (D)	449,327	(35%)

Previous Winning Percentages: **1978** (59%) **1976 *** (66%) **1974 *** (58%) **1972 *** (62%)

* *House elections.*

Campaign Finance

	Receipts	Receipts from PACs	Expend-itures
1984			
Armstrong (R)	$3,105,821	$800,256 (26%)	$2,993,045
Dick (D)	$843,101	$134,157 (16%)	$840,595

Key Votes

1987	
Enact omnibus highway bill over Reagan veto	N
Limit testing of space-based anti-ballistic missiles	N
Oppose banning tests of larger nuclear weapons	Y
Confirm Robert H. Bork as Supreme Court justice	Y
1988	
Allow vote on campaign-finance overhaul	N
Pass civil rights restoration bill over Reagan veto	N
Enact omnibus trade bill over Reagan veto	N
Approve death penalty for drug-related murders	Y
Oppose "workfare" amendment to welfare overhaul bill	N

Voting Studies

	Presidential Support		Party Unity		Conservative Coalition	
Year	**S**	**O**	**S**	**O**	**S**	**O**
1988	83	16	89	9	84	16
1987	81†	14†	96†	3†	94†	6†
1986	94	5	89†	5†	91	5
1985	72	12	87	5	78	5
1984	68	14	84	9	81	4
1983	60	34	83	12	89	5
1982	76	22	91	9	96	4
1981	84	13	88	8	88	7

† *Not eligible for all recorded votes.*

Interest Group Ratings

Year	ADA	ACU	AFL-CIO	CCUS
1988	5	96	7	93
1987	0	100	22	94
1986	0	96	0	100
1985	0	90	0	92
1984	5	86	0	82
1983	10	92	0	84
1982	10	90	4	67
1981	5	93	0	94

Tim Wirth (D)

Of Boulder — Elected 1986

Born: Sept. 22, 1939, Santa Fe, N.M.
Education: Harvard U., A.B. 1961, M.Ed. 1964; Stanford U., Ph.D. 1973.
Military Career: Army Reserve, 1961-67.
Occupation: Education official.
Family: Wife, Wren Winslow; two children.
Religion: Episcopalian.
Political Career: U.S. House, 1975-87.
Capitol Office: 380 Russell Bldg. 20510; 224-5852.

In Washington: Wirth has shown uncommon willingness and ability to grapple with the most nettlesome issues of the day. Yet he does so in a way that leaves people wondering: Is he motivated by results, or by the political points an issue has to offer? And what more might he accomplish if he were better at human relations?

Wirth prides himself on a pragmatic, nonideological legislative style, but once he takes a position, he can be intolerant of dissent. He builds bridges to the other side of the aisle, but then quarrels with liberals and moderates, his natural allies. He is an intellectual standout in both the 1974 House Watergate class and the Democrats' large 1986 Senate crop — two activist groups that continue to change Congress as an institution. Yet he is regarded as a loner, not a member of any coalition.

For all these reasons, Wirth compiled a mixed record in his years as chairman of the House Energy and Commerce Subcommittee on Telecommunications and Finance. His panel's exhaustive investigations and innovative proposals educated the country on telephone, broadcasting and banking deregulation. But when it came to passing bills, Wirth had more than his share of failure.

He has pursued some of the same interests in the Senate, but they take a back seat to a new one Wirth has rapidly staked out as his own — the environmental question of global warming.

Among some of his Democratic colleagues, Wirth's pursuit of environmental issues is seen as the foundation of a future presidential campaign. However, his alliance with environmentalists is occasionally an uneasy one; since his House days, the Coloradan has mixed his pro-environment votes with support for Western water projects and measures benefiting oil and energy industries back home.

Wirth owes his recent prominence on the global warming issue in part to a man hardly considered environmentalists' friend, Energy and Natural Resources Committee Chairman J. Bennett Johnston. The Louisianan has given Wirth free rein on the issue, allowing him to preside over committee hearings and take the lead in drafting legislation to alleviate the "greenhouse effect" on the Earth caused by upper-atmospheric pollutants. In early 1989, Wirth led a delegation of lawmakers and journalists to the Amazon to see the rain forest destruction that is believed to contribute to global climate changes.

In turn, Wirth endorsed Johnston's bid to be majority leader in the 101st Congress, against the Democrat best known as an environmentalist, George J. Mitchell of Maine. For Johnston, Wirth's vote was perhaps his most crucial; it suggested Johnston had support beyond Southerners and conservative Democrats, and it cast doubt on the expectation that Mitchell would sweep the 1986 class. Both implications proved illusory; Mitchell won easily.

On other environmental issues before Senate Energy, Wirth favors strengthening the Clean Air Act and the law regulating interstate transport of hazardous wastes. Before the 1989 *Exxon Valdez* oil spill rendered the debate virtually moot, Wirth opposed efforts to open the vast Arctic National Wildlife Refuge to the oil industry, a stance opposite Johnston's.

Wirth is also an active member of the Banking and Budget committees, to which he brought previous experience from the House Budget Committee and from financial debates in his Energy and Commerce subcommittee. On Budget, he has supported increased funding for education and child care, though liberal activists find that he generally takes a more fiscally conservative line than they do. In late 1987, Wirth joined Republicans and just four other Senate Democrats in blocking floor action on a housing bill that violated budget limits.

Having once pushed a banking deregulation bill through his House subcommittee, Wirth was ready with legislation soon after he joined Senate Banking in 1987. His bill, cosponsored by Florida Democrat Bob Graham, promised more sweeping deregulation than that proposed by Banking Chairman William Proxmire and ranking Republican Jake Garn. It would have allowed banks to engage in a wider range of insurance and securities activities, while strengthening legal barriers against banks' involvement in real estate and commerce. The Senate passed a Proxmire bill but, as usual in the 1980s, the deregulation effort died in a divided House.

As a member of the Armed Services Committee, Wirth has broadened his legislative scope into an area new to him. He has opposed steep funding increases for the strategic defense initiative (SDI), but in defense-minded Colorado, he bases that stance on budgetary concerns, not on outright opposition to an anti-missile system.

In his last few House terms, Wirth spent much of his time promoting deregulation of the communications industry. Because smaller telephone companies and consumer groups feared deregulation would free American Telephone & Telegraph (AT&T) to crush struggling competitors, Wirth drafted legislation allowing AT&T to enter deregulated fields such as data processing only if it set up a separate subsidiary. Telephone rate profits thus could not bankroll the new ventures.

Then early in 1982, the Justice Department reached the antitrust agreement with AT&T under which the company divested itself of its 22 local Bell telephone companies, and concentrated on the long-distance calling, data-processing and computer fields.

Wirth still felt new legislation was needed to clarify AT&T's role. His bill, which his subcommittee approved unanimously, was designed to restructure the company to guard against anti-competitive actions, to prevent unduly high telephone rates and to shore up the newly independent local phone companies. But when it reached full committee, AT&T backers stalled, and Wirth finally had to withdraw the bill.

Wirth and his subcommittee were divided over broadcast deregulation. He was willing to meet some of the TV industry's demands for an end to red tape and periodic license renewals, but he insisted on a minimum guarantee of news, public affairs and educational programs. Meanwhile, committee members secured more than 230 House sponsors for a bipartisan, industry-supported bill. Talks between Wirth and its proponents collapsed in early 1984, with Wirth complaining that his adversaries had shown "bad faith."

He also clashed unsuccessfully with the industry over his proposal to require that TV stations air educational children's shows and limit ads aimed at young viewers — a fight Wirth carried into the Senate. There, Commerce Committee Chairman Ernest F. Hollings gave him wide berth to pursue the issue in the 100th Congress. Meanwhile, his former allies in the House finally passed a compromise bill, only to be frustrated by Wirth when it reached the Senate. He demanded more explicit requirements on broadcasters, but finally relented just as the bill appeared doomed. Reagan vetoed the measure, however, and the drafting effort began anew in the 101st Congress, with Wirth back to pressing his old demands.

Before he took over the Telecommunications Subcommittee, Wirth specialized in energy policy at Commerce, generally voting the environmentalist position but struggling to satisfy his district's energy interests. In the mid-1970s, he favored price controls on oil and natural gas, but changed that view over several years in response to free market arguments and state politics. He helped kill President Jimmy Carter's proposed Energy Mobilization Board, which Western states feared would usurp local water rights.

After Ronald Reagan became president, Wirth contributed in the 97th Congress to an important victory in preserving key portions of the Clean Air Act. He was responsible for environmentalists' first success in the full Energy and Commerce Committee — an amendment to set more stringent deadlines for meeting national air quality standards.

Wirth spent three terms on the House Budget Committee, where he often tried to draft coalition budgets independent of the Democratic and Republican leadership plans. In 1979, he helped lead some junior Democrats into an agreement with Republicans aimed at a balanced budget. The proposal angered some liberals, and fell by the wayside when it proved to be far out of balance. In 1982 he joined some moderate Republicans in offering what they called a coalition budget, increasing funds for high-technology research and other causes Wirth promoted; it received fewer votes than either the Democratic or Republican plan.

Early on, Wirth was viewed as a leader among those young House members variously described as neo-liberals or Atari Democrats. Outside his committee work, he tried to build a coalition for national investment in high technology, arguing that it would make the United States more competitive in international markets.

At Home: Wirth's trek to the Senate proved a more harrowing journey than just about anybody would have predicted when he first announced he wanted to succeed Democrat Gary Hart. At the start of the campaign, even Republicans felt Wirth would probably stroll to victory. He shared the thoughtful, non-ideological manner that brought Hart two terms; it was a style that seemed more suited to Colorado than the ideological belligerence for which Rep. Ken Kramer, the GOP nominee, was known.

As it turned out, Wirth was the reliably smooth candidate he had always been. But Kramer confounded expectations. Though his conservatism was prominent in his campaign — he touted a constitutional amendment to balance the federal budget and backed spending on

SDI — the Republican wild man many Democrats had expected was not in sight. Instead, Kramer was an affable campaigner with a confident manner. And his first major round of ads took a clever jab at Wirth's polished image, telling TV viewers, "I'm not slick. Just good."

Wirth, meanwhile, had more trouble latching onto a clear theme. His attempts to paint Kramer as an extremist were partially undercut by the Republican's moderate manner, and his effort to flesh out his own image for voters did not begin until late in the campaign.

But Wirth had strengths that made up for his diffuse campaign. Adept on the stump, he displayed such ease working crowds that some quipped that his peripheral vision was good enough to read name tags without breaking eye contact. His leadership of the so-called neoliberals in his party gave him a base outside his district. Moreover, Wirth was interested in environmentalism as well as business competition and high-technology development, and willing to blend consumer advocacy with a sympathy for deregulation — stands that appealed to GOP moderates as well as those in his own party.

And Wirth had an organization that ran circles around Kramer's. It responded quickly to thrusts from Kramer or the state GOP and worked adeptly to keep Wirth's name in the news. Its field operations was far superior to Kramer's, especially in their party strongholds.

In the end, it was Wirth's almost 2-to-1 margin in Denver that helped him overcome a deficit elsewhere in the state and take the election by a little over 16,000 votes.

Wirth first rode into Congress in 1974 on a wave of enthusiasm for environmental safeguards and reaction against Watergate.

It was Wirth's political debut. A former White House fellow with a Ph.D. in education from Stanford, he began his campaign early and organized well. He combined an expertise on land, water and energy issues with sharp jabs at GOP Rep. Donald G. Brotzman for supporting President Richard M. Nixon. Building large margins in west Denver and Boulder, Wirth offset Brotzman's lead in Denver's Jefferson County suburbs to win the seat by 7,000 votes.

The district remained difficult for Wirth. Republican candidates criticized him as a big-spending liberal, and they spent a combined total of more than $1 million trying to oust him. Wirth drew over 56 percent only once, in 1982.

In 1984, Wirth's margin was down again, to 53 percent. His Republican challenger was Michael Norton, a former Jefferson County chairman. Norton sought to turn Wirth's national contacts and congressional influence against him. He ran one ad that showed Wirth's face melting into Walter F. Mondale's. He pounded away at the AT&T breakup, charging that Wirth had led the fight for something his constituents did not want and done so at the expense of more pressing district concerns.

The campaign ended on a sour note, with Norton charging that Wirth should be "strung up" for some of his views and Wirth calling Norton the rudest challenger he had ever faced.

Committees

Armed Services (9th of 11 Democrats)
Conventional Forces and Alliance Defense; Defense Industry and Technology; Readiness, Sustainability and Support

Banking, Housing and Urban Affairs (10th of 12 Democrats)
International Finance and Monetary Policy; Securities

Budget (9th of 13 Democrats)

Energy and Natural Resources (7th of 10 Democrats)
Energy Regulation and Conservation; Energy Research and Development; Public Lands, National Parks and Forests

Elections

1986 General

Tim Wirth (D)	529,449	(50%)
Ken Kramer (R)	512,994	(48%)

Previous Winning Percentages: **1984 *** (53%) **1982 *** (62%) **1980 *** (56%) **1978 *** (53%) **1976 *** (51%) **1974 *** (52%)

* *House elections.*

Campaign Finance

	Receipts	Receipts from PACs	Expend-itures
1986			
Wirth (D)	$3,819,308	$845,855 (22%)	$3,787,202
Kramer (R)	$3,829,927	$925,429 (24%)	$3,785,577

Key Votes

1987

Enact omnibus highway bill over Reagan veto	Y
Limit testing of space-based anti-ballistic missiles	Y
Oppose banning tests of larger nuclear weapons	N
Confirm Robert H. Bork as Supreme Court justice	N

1988

Allow vote on campaign-finance overhaul	Y
Pass civil rights restoration bill over Reagan veto	Y
Enact omnibus trade bill over Reagan veto	Y
Approve death penalty for drug-related murders	N
Oppose "workfare" amendment to welfare overhaul bill	Y

Voting Studies

	Presidential Support		Party Unity		Conservative Coalition	
Year	**S**	**O**	**S**	**O**	**S**	**O**
1988	47	52	86	11	27	68
1987	33	60	84	14	44	56
House Service						
1986	27	72	76	15	24	66
1985	21	71	81	10	20	73
1984	27	65	89	7	10	83
1983	18	78	82	7	16	81
1982	34	62	84	9	19	79
1981	38	51	78	14	23	61

Interest Group Ratings

Year	ADA	ACU	AFL-CIO	CCUS
1988	95	0	79	36
1987	85	0	90	41
House Service				
1986	75	14	92	54
1985	70	10	71	38
1984	85	4	92	40
1983	95	0	82	40
1982	95	0	84	14
1981	85	0	71	21

1 Patricia Schroeder (D)

Of Denver — Elected 1972

Born: July 30, 1940, Portland, Ore.
Education: U. of Minnesota, B.A. 1961; Harvard U., J.D. 1964.
Occupation: Lawyer; law instructor.
Family: Husband, James Schroeder; two children.
Religion: United Church of Christ.
Political Career: No previous office.
Capitol Office: 2208 Rayburn Bldg. 20515; 225-4431.

In Washington: Congress has often included a few members who are larger-than-life celebrities outside its halls, but who are cut down to size once back in the Capitol. Schroeder is one of those.

Her status as a political star in liberal, feminist circles led her to consider a presidential campaign in 1988, and later to suggest that 1992 will be her year. She protests, however, that she does not want to be merely a symbol for women. That same complaint echoes throughout her House career, yet after nearly two decades in Congress, Schroeder somehow has fallen short where most other female members have succeeded: in winning acceptance in the male bastion.

When she arrived in 1973 and took a seat on the Armed Services Committee as the Vietnam War ended, it was only natural that the outspoken anti-war activist would meet hostility from the older, sexist Southern hawks who then ran the panel. But she has not developed close relations with the colleagues from her own generation who dominate the House today, thus hampering her effectiveness in an institution that runs largely on collegiality.

In part she suffers from members' jealousy of the media attention she gets. Also, her ideological liberalism puts her in a distinct minority. But Schroeder's style is also a factor.

From the start, she has sent contradictory signals, yearning to fit in while frequently invoking gender to draw distinctions or dramatize a point, such as referring to Pentagon war-planners' male glands. She is invitingly friendly, but the smile and exuberance come off as phony to members who know her as an independent operator. She is as bright as her Harvard law degree would suggest, yet has a reputation as flaky; it was Schroeder who once wore a rabbit suit during an Armed Services trip to China at Eastertime and handed out jelly beans and candy eggs to the startled Chinese. Irreverence and sharp wit enhance her stock on the speaking circuit — it was Schroeder who dubbed Ronald Reagan the "Teflon" president — but those traits annoy some colleagues.

A female House member compared Schroeder's tone to "our mothers' nagging." She is the senior-most of the House's 26 female members, but even among them she does not have particularly warm ties. The tension was noted when New York Rep. Geraldine A. Ferraro was tapped in 1984 to be the first female vice presidential candidate of a major party.

Still, Schroeder is recognized both inside and outside the House as a brainy and articulate voice for women's and family issues, federal employees, military personnel and the anti-nuclear movement. If she remains a gadfly, on one point even critics give her credit: Schroeder has consistently maintained her committed liberalism while others have flagged. She loses much of the time, but resiliently comes back the next year.

She is still in a liberal minority at Armed Services, even though the committee is now headed by her 1970s ally, Les Aspin of Wisconsin; he has built a centrist coalition since turning out the Old Guard in 1985. But in the 101st Congress Schroeder finally claims a leadership position on the panel after past setbacks, assuming the chairmanship of the subcommittee for U.S. military bases. Its jurisdiction does not cover the strategic nuclear weapons she has long opposed.

She and other arms control proponents had some success in reining in Reagan's nuclear arms policies. For each of the last three years of his administration, they won House passage of amendments to the annual defense bills banning all but the smallest nuclear weapons tests, contingent on Soviet abstention. Though the provision was dropped in conference committees with the Senate, the issue contributed to the pressure on the president to negotiate arms control with the Soviets.

Lacking support for a test ban in Armed Services, Schroeder pressed her fight on the more liberal House floor. Initially in 1986, she and her fellow activists, including Edward J. Markey of Massachusetts and Thomas J. Downey of New York, favored a total ban, a goal to which all presidents since Dwight D. Eisen-

Colorado 1

Denver

The 1st District, home to virtually all of Denver's half-million residents, is one of the few Democratic congressional strongholds in the Rocky Mountain region. Hispanics and blacks together make up about one-third of the district's population, and there is a strong liberal white-collar element.

A heavy Democratic vote in Denver often bails out the party's statewide candidates. In 1980 Sen. Gary Hart won the city by 50,000 votes, allowing him to lose the rest of the state by more than 30,000 and still hold his Senate seat.

But with Denver's highly mobile population and the historic absence of a political machine, party roots are not deep and Democratic majorities are not always reliable. In 1988, Michael S. Dukakis became the first Democratic presidential candidate since 1964 to draw more than 51 percent of the Denver vote; he surpassed 60 percent. Ronald Reagan captured the city in 1980, but Walter F. Mondale won it narrowly in 1984.

Denver's population dipped in the 1970s, partly because a number of middle-class families escaped to the sprawling suburbs to avoid the impact of a federal court busing order that applied within the city limits. But population has leveled off in this decade, and Denver is working to secure its place as the Rocky Mountains' business center with its regional energy operations, federal government agencies and half a million takeoffs and landings at Denver Stapleton International Airport.

Despite its scenic locale and casual, attractive lifestyle, Denver has serious problems. It is bedeviled by racial tensions, serious air pollution and an oil-dependent roller-coaster economy currently in a deep slump.

Republican strength is concentrated in the middle- and upper-income neighborhoods of southeast Denver. Farther in that direction are newer subdivisions built in the hills along the Valley Highway (Interstate 25). Republicans also draw some votes downtown, where condominiums have mushroomed in the vicinity of Civil War-era Larimer Square.

Other parts of the city are reliably Democratic. Capitol Hills, perched on the eastern fringe of the downtown area, is home to a mixed population of students, young professionals and senior citizens. To the east and north are heavily black neighborhoods. Westward on the hills beyond the stockyards and the South Platte River live most of the city's Hispanics. The 1st also includes about 6,000 residents who live in Arapahoe County enclaves within the Denver city limits.

Population: 481,672. White 357,775 (74%), Black 59,330 (12%), Other 10,843 (2%). Spanish origin 91,194 (19%). 18 and over 373,579 (78%), 65 and over 61,524 (13%). Median age: 30.

hower had at least paid lip service — until Reagan. However, to address widespread concern about Soviet compliance, they modified their proposal to exclude tests on small weapons that cannot be detected, and conditioned the ban on a U.S.-Soviet agreement for placing monitors on each other's territory.

Forsaking personal visibility in the interest of achieving passage, Schroeder deferred to more moderate Democrats, Aspin and Democratic Caucus Chairman Richard A. Gephardt, to offer the test-ban amendment on the House floor. It was adopted, 234-155. But the test-ban effort lost some steam once Reagan began arms control talks with the Soviets. By 1988, the vote for a test ban was a much closer 214-186. To Schroeder's dismay, the ban provision was scrapped every year by House and Senate negotiators, under pressure from Reagan.

She has often cast a lonely vote against defense authorization bills as they left Armed Services, then continued her budget-cutting efforts on the House floor without much success. Unlike some Democrats, she is not troubled that she will be viewed as "soft" on defense. "We have all become afraid of being called a wimp," she said in 1985, during an unsuccessful attack on the MX missile. "Our constituents are going to think we are the weak ones if we cannot possibly stand on our own two legs and talk back."

Through the years she has led moves to reduce U.S. troop commitments abroad, but her proposals have been too drastic even for some Pentagon critics. In 1986, her amendment to recall half of U.S. ground troops in Europe and one-third of the troops stationed elsewhere over a five-year period failed, 90-322.

Her effort has gained vogue, under the rubric of "burden-sharing," as budget and trade deficits climbed. Proponents argue that prosperous allies such as Japan and West Germany can shoulder more of the military load, and that the United States is subsidizing their defenses while they subsidize their industries that compete with U.S. firms.

Aspin named Schroeder to chair a committee task force on burden-sharing in the 100th

Congress. But even she cooled to the cause in 1988, after Gorbachev signaled that the Soviets would negotiate conventional-forces cuts in Europe. During House debate on the fiscal 1989 defense bill, she opposed two Democrats' amendments calling for troop reductions in Japan and Europe unless the allies raised their defense budgets. Though Democrats were split, GOP opposition was united, and the amendments failed overwhelmingly.

If Aspin has been an important ally for Schroeder over time, she likewise has been a crucial supporter for him. She was one of his colonels in his successful 1985 coup against the enfeebled pro-Pentagon chairman, Melvin Price of Illinois. Two years later she again backed Aspin when disgruntled Democrats, including many liberals, tried to oust him. However, when he lost an initial vote of confidence in the Democratic Caucus, she briefly considered campaigning for the chairmanship herself before rejoining Aspin's cadre to help him win back the job against three challengers.

Amid the turnover at Armed Services, Schroeder suffered for her iconoclastic record. Citing her seniority, in 1985 she sought to claim the Personnel Subcommittee chairmanship that Aspin vacated when he moved up to full committee chairman. But having criticized the seniority system throughout her career, most recently in the Aspin-Price contest, she was hardly in a good position to take advantage of it. Resentful conservative Democrats on the panel threw their support to Beverly B. Byron of Maryland, who came to Congress six years after Schroeder.

To end the showdown, Aspin decided to keep the Personnel chair himself. When he gave it up two years later, Schroeder chose not to compete and instead kept her subcommittee chairmanship on the Post Office and Civil Service Committee.

Having finally won an Armed Services subcommittee in the 101st Congress, she had to give up the Civil Service Subcommittee. There, she had turned what is normally a secondary assignment into one from which she could aggressively pursue both her own interests and those of her many constituents who work for the federal agencies with offices in Denver.

She has worked to increase protection for "whistleblowers" who reveal mismanagement and fraud, calling the existing grievance board for federal employees "a joke." Twice, in the 99th and 100th Congresses, she passed legislation in the House to overhaul the process. The first bill died in the Senate, and the second was vetoed by Reagan. A new version quickly passed in the 101st Congress, and President Bush signed it into law.

From both the Post Office and Armed Services panels she has tried to represent the interests of women and families, targeting her efforts toward those in the military and federal bureaucracy. She has lobbied for better pay, benefits and working conditions for bureaucrats, and, attacking a problem bearing directly on morale in the armed services, worked for better living conditions for military families. For Congress' own staff, she has espoused measures to bring employees under the protection of federal labor laws from which they currently are exempt.

She once promoted a law to liberalize pension rights of foreign service spouses, and later broadened that effort to include divorced spouses of military personnel. Armed Services opposed the change, but she defeated the committee leaders on the floor in 1981. She has prodded the Army not to slack in its recruitment of women.

She is less active on the Judiciary Committee, which she joined in the 97th Congress to help the panel and the House leadership fight anti-abortion bills. When the proposed Equal Rights Amendment died in 1982, she was among the first to reintroduce it, claiming that "a phenomenal, nationwide grass-roots movement will be behind it."

More recently, she has sponsored legislation with Missouri Democrat William L. Clay requiring large employers to grant a limited period of unpaid leave to new parents, disabled workers and those caring for a seriously ill child. For the past two Congresses, the bill has not made it past the committee level in either house, despite numerous compromises and, in the 100th Congress, congressional leaders' designation of the bill as a top Democratic priority.

Its defeat has been a top priority for business groups and Republicans. To their complaints that the legislation would burden U.S. companies and put them at a competitive disadvantage, Schroeder counters, "The countries we're most concerned about competing with already do this."

Also in the 100th Congress, she worked on welfare-overhaul legislation, pushing for more generous treatment of families with children. She protested when House leaders pared the bill to attract conservative Democrats' support. Another disappointment was the failure to enact a child-care bill. "We've got to start kicking the legislation out or we'll lose our credibility," she said at one point, frustrated with Democrats who put deficit reduction and business concerns ahead of social needs. "There's no capital city in the world that talks more about family and does less."

Stymied in Congress, Schroeder has taken to the road. Traveling with a famous pediatrician and a TV producer, in early 1988 she led "The Great American Family Tour" through states with presidential primaries because, she said, none of the candidates "was really addressing these issues." As the 101st Congress began, she was promoting a new book, "Champion of the Great American Family." Speaking engagements generally have made Schroeder one of the House's top earners of honoraria.

The absence of serious challenges at home in 1984 and 1988 enabled Schroeder to become immersed in presidential politics. She served as co-chairman of Gary Hart's two presidential campaigns and, in 1984, was prominently mentioned as a potential vice presidential candidate for nominee Walter F. Mondale. In 1988, after Hart withdrew in the wake of media attention to his philandering, Schroeder publicly expressed bitterness that her longtime associate had lied to her about his activities.

At Home: Schroeder was in the vanguard of the Democratic resurgence in Colorado in the early 1970s, scoring upset victories in the 1972 primary and general election to wrest the Denver House seat from Republican control.

Although she had been a practicing attorney and women's rights activist, Schroeder was a political neophyte at the time. She was encouraged to make the race by her lawyer husband, who had unsuccessfully sought a state House seat in 1970.

Cultivating support from liberals in Denver and feminists and environmentalists at the national level, Schroeder put together an effective grass-roots organization. She drew 55 percent of the vote against state Senate Minority Leader Arch Decker in the primary, and 52 percent in the general election to oust one-term GOP Rep. James "Mike" McKevitt.

The GOP has fielded a variety of candidates against Schroeder since 1972, including an anti-busing leader, a veteran state legislator, a wealthy political newcomer, a woman school board member, a prominent ex-Democrat and a woman stockbroker. The legislator, state Rep. Don Friedman, came the closest, in 1976. He sharply criticized Schroeder's liberal voting record and collected a campaign treasury that exceeded hers. He held her to 53 percent.

Since then, the Republican threat has subsided. Redistricting and population changes have tilted the district toward minority voters, and Schroeder is able to draw on a coalition of liberals, young professionals, blacks and Hispanics.

Committees

Armed Services (5th of 31 Democrats)
Military Installations and Facilities (chairman); Research and Development

Judiciary (8th of 21 Democrats)
Civil and Constitutional Rights; Economic and Commercial Law

Post Office and Civil Service (3rd of 15 Democrats)
Civil Service

Select Children, Youth and Families (3rd of 18 Democrats)

Elections

1988 General		
Patricia Schroeder (D)	133,922	(70%)
Joy Wood (R)	57,587	(30%)
1986 General		
Patricia Schroeder (D)	106,113	(68%)
Joy Wood (R)	49,095	(32%)

Previous Winning Percentages: **1984** (62%) **1982** (60%) **1980** (60%) **1978** (62%) **1976** (53%) **1974** (59%) **1972** (52%)

District Vote For President

	1988	1984	1980	1976
D	124,659 (61%)	108,737 (51%)	81,640 (42%)	101,957 (48%)
R	73,915 (36%)	100,996 (47%)	81,196 (41%)	101,458 (48%)
I			27,128 (14%)	

Campaign Finance

	Receipts	Receipts from PACs	Expend-itures
1988			
Schroeder (D)	$275,795	$131,785 (48%)	$217,503
Wood (R)	$26,529	$920 (3%)	$26,040
1986			
Schroeder (D)	$243,383	$105,815 (43%)	$156,237
Wood (R)	$13,479	$500 (4%)	$13,251

Key Votes

1987	
Raise speed limit to 65 mph	Y
Approve Gephardt "fair trade" amendment	N
Ban testing of larger nuclear weapons	Y
Delay "re-flagging" of Kuwaiti tankers	Y
Approve tax-raising deficit-reduction bill	Y
1988	
Approve aid to Nicaraguan contras	N
Enact civil rights restoration bill over Reagan veto	Y
Kill 60-day plant-closing notification measure	N
Pass omnibus trade bill over Reagan veto	Y
Approve death penalty for drug-related murders	N
Bar federal funds for abortions in cases of rape and incest	-
Oppose seven-day waiting period for purchase of handguns	N

Voting Studies

	Presidential Support		Party Unity		Conservative Coalition	
Year	**S**	**O**	**S**	**O**	**S**	**O**
1988	20	77	70	25	29	68
1987	13	81	68	25	23	70
1986	19	78	66	28	14	82
1985	30	69	58	39	24	76
1984	28	68	73	23	17	81
1983	11	84	81	16	18	78
1982	29	65	75	19	16	82
1981	29	70	76	21	12	85

Interest Group Ratings

Year	ADA	ACU	AFL-CIO	CCUS
1988	95	0	100	31
1987	76	9	64	27
1986	95	5	86	29
1985	80	19	71	55
1984	90	23	62	53
1983	85	17	76	20
1982	90	20	94	25
1981	95	13	80	6

2 David E. Skaggs (D)

Of Boulder — Elected 1986

Born: Feb. 22, 1943, Cincinnati, Ohio.

Education: Wesleyan U., B.A. 1964; attended U. of Virginia Law School, 1964-65; Yale U., LL.B. 1967.

Military Career: Marine Corps, 1968-71; Marine Corps Reserve, 1971-77.

Occupation: Congressional aide; lawyer.

Family: Wife, Laura Driscoll; one child, two stepchildren.

Religion: Congregationalist.

Political Career: Colo. House, 1981-87, minority leader, 1983-85.

Capitol Office: 1709 Longworth Bldg. 20515; 225-2161.

In Washington: A former Marine, Skaggs' demeanor is straightforward and conservative, his approach to legislation orderly and deliberate. His style has gotten him off to a good start in Congress and especially at the polls, where he solidly won his first re-election in a politically marginal district despite his relatively liberal voting record.

Skaggs complemented that voting record in the 100th Congress with assiduous attention to local concerns on his two committees, Science and Public Works. He came to Washington with his sights set on Science, a valuable assignment because of the high-technology industry in his district. He lobbied successfully for the panel, and used it to help secure funds for superconductivity research at the National Bureau of Standards in the 2nd.

On Public Works' Aviation Subcommittee, Skaggs has been the point man in the House for Denver's proposed new airport, which would sit just outside his district. In the 100th Congress, he helped negotiate a deal allowing the city to sell some federally controlled land to help finance the project. In the next five years, city officials want $500 million in federal money for the airport, a sum that will surely test Skaggs' persuasive powers.

While catering to local interests in his politically competitive district, Skaggs showed considerable loyalty to the Democratic leadership. Skaggs toed the leadership line on nearly every key vote in the 100th Congress, including a vote against eliminating a seven-day waiting period for handgun purchases.

At Home: After barely winning his first term, Skaggs was re-elected in 1988 by a wider margin than his predecessor (Democrat Tim Wirth) ever won. Several factors shaped the showing: Skaggs' own political skill, the weakness of the GOP opposition and a possible political settling-in of many voters who for years seemed iffy about sending Democrats to Congress.

Skaggs spent time raising money and improving his organization as the GOP scavenged for a nominee. State Rep. David Bath, a conservative Christian activist and former Democrat, jumped in, but the local GOP sought a moderate. The only one to step up was former Secretary of State Mary Estill Buchanan, who nearly upset Democratic Sen. Gary Hart in 1980. But she was a longtime foe of the right and did not campaign aggressively. Bath won the primary.

Short of cash, Bath was stymied until late in the fall when he drew headlines for demanding the federal government withhold money from Denver's proposed new airport until it lifted a residency requirement on city workers at the facility. Though Skaggs also opposed the rule, he faulted Bath's confrontational style. In the end, the issue helped Skaggs win business-oriented Republicans supporting the airport.

Skaggs got into politics after moving to Colorado in 1971, becoming a precinct committeeman and then Democratic district chairman. That led him to Washington as the chief aide to Wirth after the 1974 election. After a term, he moved back to Colorado, and in 1980, he won a seat in the state House, where he was a leader in the Democratic contingent.

Skaggs' ties to Wirth and high profile in the Boulder area made him a logical candidate for the House when Wirth ran for the Senate in 1986. He won the Democratic nomination handily, but went into the general election against Republican Mike Norton a 20-point underdog. Norton, a former regional administrator with the General Services Administration, had held Wirth to 53 percent of the vote in 1984 and campaigned almost non-stop since.

While quietly building an organization, Skaggs emulated Wirth's centrist approach to issues. In early October, he aired negative TV ads accusing Norton of inconsistency; they gave him enough of a jump in the polls to help him finance his final push.

Colorado 2

Northern Denver Suburbs; Boulder

The Colorado 2nd is rapidly emerging as a Rocky Mountain version of California's Silicon Valley. Nearly three-quarters of the district's voters live in Boulder County and in the populous portion of Adams County added in 1982 redistricting.

Broomfield, which sits on Boulder County's southern border, is bounded on one side by an AT&T research and manufacturing plant and the other by Storage Technology, which makes computer components. Fifteen miles due north is Longmont, a traditional market for sugar beet farmers that now has its fortunes linked to a large Hewlett-Packard plant nearby. Boulder itself, nestled against the Front Range of the Rockies, is the centerpiece of the county. While Boulder's population held steady between 1980 and 1986, Broomfield and Longmont each grew by nearly 20 percent.

An IBM research and manufacturing plant in Louisville, which employs 5,000, is a major employer, along with Ball Aerospace and government research outlets such as the National Oceanic and Atmospheric Administration. In addition, there are smaller, more esoteric businesses that fit in with the relaxed, youth-oriented cultural winds — Boulder is home base for Celestial Seasonings, the herbal-tea producer. The academic community at the University of Colorado (nearly 27,000 students and 1,200 faculty) and the young professional work force create a strong vote in Boulder for liberal candidates, especially if they stress environmentalist values and individual rights.

Southeast of Boulder is suburban Adams County. Arvada is the most affluent of the county's suburbs in the 2nd District. The others, such as Westminster and Northglenn, tend to be blue-collar and have large Hispanic populations. About half of the district's land area — but little of its vote — is in the mountains west of Boulder in Clear Creek and Gilpin counties.

The Rocky Flats nuclear-weapons plant, the state's sixth-largest employer with 6,000 workers, is located in Jefferson County on the 2nd's southern edge.

Population: 481,617. White 450,057 (94%), Black 3,919 (1%), Other 7,718 (2%). Spanish origin 41,944 (9%). 18 and over 339,617 (71%), 65 and over 25,890 (5%). Median age: 27.

Committees

Public Works and Transportation (21st of 31 Democrats)
Aviation; Surface Transportation

Science, Space and Technology (26th of 30 Democrats)
Natural Resources, Agriculture Research and Environment; Science, Research and Technology; Space Science and Applications

Select Children, Youth and Families (17th of 18 Democrats)

Elections

1988 General		
David E. Skaggs (D)	147,437	(63%)
David Bath (R)	87,578	(37%)
1986 General		
David E. Skaggs (D)	91,223	(51%)
Michael J. Norton (R)	86,032	(49%)

District Vote For President

	1988	1984	1980	1976
D	119,132 (50%)	83,357 (38%)	60,570 (33%)	76,702 (45%)
R	112,923 (48%)	130,543 (60%)	93,552 (50%)	84,997 (50%)
I			24,300 (13%)	

Campaign Finance

	Receipts	Receipts from PACs	Expend-itures
1988			
Skaggs (D)	$730,990	$452,772 (62%)	$721,647
Bath (R) †	$93,581	$17,381 (19%)	$85,095
1986			
Skaggs (D)	$513,873	$225,257 (44%)	$512,029
Norton (R)	$497,756	$136,175 (27%)	$491,329

† Totals based on incomplete data.

Key Votes

1987	
Raise speed limit to 65 mph	Y
Approve Gephardt "fair trade" amendment	N
Ban testing of larger nuclear weapons	Y
Delay "re-flagging" of Kuwaiti tankers	Y
Approve tax-raising deficit-reduction bill	Y
1988	
Approve aid to Nicaraguan contras	N
Enact civil rights restoration bill over Reagan veto	Y
Kill 60-day plant-closing notification measure	N
Pass omnibus trade bill over Reagan veto	Y
Approve death penalty for drug-related murders	N
Bar federal funds for abortions in cases of rape and incest	N
Oppose seven-day waiting period for purchase of handguns	N

Voting Studies

	Presidential Support		Party Unity		Conservative Coalition	
Year	S	O	S	O	S	O
1988	29	70	81	61	47	53
1987	24	76	91	9	35	65

Interest Group Ratings

Year	ADA	ACU	AFL-CIO	CCUS
1988	95	16	86	57
1987	84	9	81	33

3 Ben Nighthorse Campbell (D)

Of Ignacio — Elected 1986

Born: April 13, 1933, Auburn, Calif.
Education: San Jose State, B.A. 1957; attended Meiji U., Tokyo, 1960-64.
Military Career: Air Force, 1952-54.
Occupation: Jewelry designer; rancher.
Family: Wife, Linda Price; two children.
Religion: Unspecified.
Political Career: Colo. House, 1983-87.
Capitol Office: 1724 Longworth Bldg. 20515; 225-4761.

In Washington: Campbell is an unconventional politician with a mischievous streak and a tendency to say whatever is on his mind.

A craftsman of contemporary Indian jewelry, Campbell in 1987 donated one gold and 50 silver belt buckles to former Sen. Gary Hart; he was to sell them to raise funds for his 1988 presidential campaign. But Hart dropped out of the race in May 1987 amid reports of his relationship with a Miami model. When Hart restarted his campaign in December 1987, Campbell retreated from offering a similar token of support. "Once around was enough on the belt buckle routine," he said. He declined to say if he would support Hart again, but lauded him as "far and away the most articulate person on foreign affairs — er, let's use the word foreign 'policy.' "

Campbell said in his 1986 House campaign, "People are sick and tired of plastic politicians — professional politicians who have done nothing else with their lives." That is a description no one will ever lay on him. A daily reminder of his nonconformity is his attire: He got special permission in 1988 to wear his trademark bolo tie on the House floor.

His father was Northern Cheyenne, making Campbell the first member of Congress to be half Indian since South Dakota Republican Ben Reifel left in 1971. He was a member of the U.S. judo team at the 1964 Olympics and raises and trains quarter horses on a Western Slope ranch. His talent as a jewelry craftsman makes him one of the few practicing artists in the Congressional Arts Caucus.

Campbell's first term in Washington was nothing spectacular — shoring up his support at home was his top concern. But he did get assignments on Agriculture and Interior, good for the 3rd. His biggest legislative achievement was his bill to implement a settlement of Colorado Ute Indian water rights and pave the way for construction of the Animas-La Plata water project. It passed the House 249-146, and was signed into law.

At Home: A narrow winner in 1986, Campbell made himself something of a folk hero in just two years in Congress. Campbell won re-election with three-fourths of the vote, a record for a Colorado Democratic House member. In early 1989, he was seriously discussed as a candidate for the Senate in 1990, but he declined to run.

Campbell has the kind of individualist streak that often characterizes successful politicians in Colorado, particularly those on the Western Slope. In 1982, he ran for the state House from a conservative district while wearing a ponytail — and won. Two years later, he snipped it off and auctioned the hair to raise money.

In the Legislature, he was a dependable vote for farmers and ranchers on water rights issues and other resource-use proposals. Though he occasionally sided with his party's environmentalists, Campbell's views put him among conservatives in the Democratic Caucus.

That positioned Campbell well for his 1986 challenge to GOP Rep. Mike Strang. To win the 3rd, a Democrat must draw a big vote in blue-collar Pueblo, then hold his own on the conservative Western Slope; Campbell did that.

Strang, who also owned a ranch, had for years suffered financial troubles. As the 1986 elections approached, he faced foreclosure on his ranch because he could not pay a federal loan. Gambling that farmers and ranchers who were struggling to remain solvent would take a dim view of Strang's problems, Campbell ran ads criticizing him for defaulting on his loan. But the ads aroused editorial denunciations, and he took them off the air.

Strang, however, kept the issue alive. Just as foreclosure seemed imminent, he announced a last-minute loan, but compounded the impression that he might have been involved in some questionable dealings by refusing to disclose the source of the loan. By the time he revealed that the money came from his wife's family, it was too late to undo the political damage.

Colorado 3

Western Slope; Pueblo

This huge, mountainous district covers the Republican-oriented western half of the state and two predominantly Democratic areas to the east — populous Pueblo County and the largely Hispanic San Luis Valley.

Most of the votes are on the Western Slope of the Rockies, a booming energy center in the 1970s where growth has tapered off in recent years. The scenic Western Slope still contains the bulk of Colorado's vast mineral wealth. Democrats or independents have a registration advantage in many of the Western Slope counties, but there are more Republicans in the three most populous counties — Mesa, La Plata and Montrose.

As one moves north out of the forested mountains into open Western Slope ranch land, the GOP vote increases, as does the standard of living in good oil years. There are rich oil shale reserves in Colorado's northwest corner, and large coal deposits are located to the east. Grand Junction (population 28,000), the trade center for local energy operations, is the area's largest city.

Democrats are competitive in the 3rd because of the presence of Pueblo, the state's fifth-largest city. Before the last round of redistricting changes in 1982, Pueblo County was the heart of the district. Now it juts like a peninsula out of the southeastern corner. Still, it remains the district's population center, with one-quarter of the vote.

Pueblo, population 101,000, is a steel-producing town and the hub of union activity in Colorado. Both the economy and the population are declining in the Pueblo area, but the area is still a reliable source of Democratic votes.

South of Pueblo is the San Luis Valley, an isolated lettuce- and potato-growing region that is the poorest part of the state. The area favors Democrats; two of the valley counties have Hispanic majorities.

Population: 481,854. White 436,299 (91%), Black 3,198 (1%), Other 6,648 (1%). Spanish origin 82,499 (17%). 18 and over 345,175 (72%), 65 and over 49,403 (10%). Median age: 29.

Committees

Agriculture (21st of 27 Democrats)
Livestock, Dairy and Poultry; Wheat, Soybeans and Feed Grains

Interior and Insular Affairs (22nd of 26 Democrats)
Mining and Natural Resources; National Parks and Public Lands; Water, Power and Offshore Energy Resources

Elections

1988 General		
Ben Nighthorse Campbell (D)	169,284	(78%)
Jim Zartman (R)	47,625	(22%)
1986 General		
Ben Nighthorse Campbell (D)	95,353	(52%)
Mike Strang (R)	88,508	(48%)

District Vote For President

	1988	1984	1980	1976
D	101,242 (46%)	76,712 (36%)	61,341 (33%)	74,039 (43%)
R	113,607 (52%)	132,109 (63%)	106,846 (57%)	92,478 (54%)
I			15,036 (8%)	

Campaign Finance

	Receipts	Receipts from PACs	Expend-itures
1988			
Campbell (D)	$519,957	$302,590 (58%)	$489,534
Zartman (R)	$17,937	0	$17,936
1986			
Campbell (D)	$397,211	$204,968 (52%)	$386,149
Strang (R)	$516,652	$190,090 (37%)	$566,439

Key Votes

1987	
Raise speed limit to 65 mph	Y
Approve Gephardt "fair trade" amendment	Y
Ban testing of larger nuclear weapons	Y
Delay "re-flagging" of Kuwaiti tankers	Y
Approve tax-raising deficit-reduction bill	Y
1988	
Approve aid to Nicaraguan contras	N
Enact civil rights restoration bill over Reagan veto	Y
Kill 60-day plant-closing notification measure	N
Pass omnibus trade bill over Reagan veto	Y
Approve death penalty for drug-related murders	Y
Bar federal funds for abortions in cases of rape and incest	N
Oppose seven-day waiting period for purchase of handguns	Y

Voting Studies

	Presidential Support		Party Unity		Conservative Coalition	
Year	**S**	**O**	**S**	**O**	**S**	**O**
1988	26	65	85	11	47	45
1987	34	66	78	18	65	33

Interest Group Ratings

Year	ADA	ACU	AFL-CIO	CCUS
1988	65	21	92	43
1987	64	9	88	40

4 Hank Brown (R)

Of Greeley — Elected 1980

Born: Feb. 12, 1940, Denver, Colo.
Education: U. of Colorado, B.S. 1961, J.D. 1969; George Washington U., LL.M. 1986.
Military Career: Navy, 1962-66.
Occupation: Tax accountant; meatpacking company executive; lawyer.
Family: Wife, Nan Morrison; three children.
Religion: United Church of Christ.
Political Career: Colo. Senate, 1973-77; Republican nominee for lieutenant governor, 1978.
Capitol Office: 1424 Longworth Bldg. 20515; 225-4676.

In Washington: Brown's overall voting record is that of a conservative Westerner and party loyalist, but his pleasant manner and open-mindedness earn him respect from both parties and both ends of the ideological spectrum.

His personal popularity, maintained despite an iconoclastic streak, could help catapult Brown to the Senate when Colorado voters decide in the 1990 election who will replace retiring Republican William L. Armstrong.

Brown's potential for higher office has been evident almost since the day he came to the House. He backed away from a foray into statewide politics in 1986, after flirting with the idea of running for governor.

But Brown's legislative career has not been conspicuously tailored to position him for a climb up the political ladder. For example, his service on the House ethics committee is more a measure of his standing in the House than of political ambition (although, in this time of increased public attention on congressional ethics, committee service could enhance Brown's image).

In another sign of his colleagues' respect, Brown won a coveted seat on the Ways and Means Committee in 1987. He was thrust immediately into a leadership role as ranking minority member of the Public Assistance Subcommittee just as Congress was gearing up for a major overhaul of the welfare system.

That bill proved to be the most partisan issue before the committee in the 100th Congress, and Republicans' input in House deliberations was therefore limited. But Brown helped his fellow Republicans exert what leverage they could.

He put together a GOP alternative that struck a middle ground between a Democratic-drafted bill they deemed too costly, and a Reagan administration proposal that would have focused not on new federal money and mandates, but on allowing states to experiment with new welfare approaches.

Brown's efforts to mold the bill in committee fell victim to immovable party lines. And the Republican alternative did little better on the House floor, even though the Democratic leadership had a hard time holding onto its conservative flank.

But once the Senate passed a welfare bill with a lower cost and a more stringent work requirement for welfare recipients, Brown had an opening. Republicans won a rare victory when the House approved a Brown motion instructing its conferees to accept the Senate's price tag. Although the cost ultimately exceeded that, Brown's move helped pressure the House negotiators to move closer to the Senate position.

After that one term as top Republican on the least popular of Ways and Means' subcommittees, Brown got a more appealing slot for the 101st Congress, when he became ranking member of the Social Security Subcommittee.

Although he was elected in 1980 with the huge class of Republicans swept into the House on Reagan's coattails, the independent-minded Brown was never a "Reagan robot." He was a solid backer of Reagan's economic policies, but voted against higher funding for the strategic defense initiative (SDI). In 1985, Brown was one of only two Budget Committee Republicans to vote with the Democratic majority on spending for defense. In the 100th Congress' debate on an omnibus trade bill, Brown was one of only 17 Republicans who voted for a controversial "fair trade" amendment sponsored by Missouri Democrat Richard A. Gephardt that critics called protectionist.

Brown's reputation for independent thinking made him a popular choice among conservative Republicans when he was reappointed to the House ethics committee in mid-1988, just as the panel was beginning an investigation of alleged improprieties by Speaker Jim Wright of Texas.

Brown had served on the ethics committee from 1981-84, when he demonstrated a willing-

Colorado 4

North and East — Fort Collins; Greeley

The 4th is Colorado's breadbasket, home of the state's agricultural heartland and its major farm markets.

Most of the voters live near the northern flank of the Front Range in Larimer (Fort Collins) and Weld (Greeley) counties. Both are educational and trade centers for agricultural northern Colorado, an area that was once one of the nation's top suppliers of sugar beets. As beet prices dropped, many farmers switched to corn or beans.

With nearly one-third of the district population, Larimer County is the larger, faster growing and more diverse of the two. Newcomers have been drawn by the spillover of high-tech firms from the Boulder area to Fort Collins and Loveland and the academic community at Colorado State University in Fort Collins (19,000 students).

To the east, on the fringe of the Great Plains, Weld County is more dependent on agriculture. Influenced by German and Russian immigration in the 19th century, it is also home to a large community of Hispanic truck farmers. Hispanics comprise nearly a fifth of the Weld County population.

The University of Northern Colorado (9,500 students) is in Greeley, but ranching is crucial to life in Weld County. Greeley is the home base of Montfort of Colorado, Brown's former employer and one of the largest feed lots and packing plants in the country. Small, family-run competitors dot the county.

The territorial heart of the 4th is the eastern plains, a vast agricultural region that covers one-third of the state but casts barely 30 percent of the district vote. Like neighboring Nebraska and Kansas, this area is conservative and heavily Republican. But it has been a center of agrarian ferment — in the small community of Springfield, in Baca County, the American Agricultural Movement was born in the mid-1970s.

Most of the Democratic votes in the 4th are concentrated in the southern portion of the district. Las Animas County, which straddles the New Mexico border, is nearly half Hispanic, and is the only county that has given Brown any trouble.

Population: 481,512. White 441,718 (92%), Black 2,364 (1%), Other 5,429 (1%). Spanish origin 65,848 (14%). 18 and over 342,745 (71%), 65 and over 49,097 (10%). Median age: 28.

ness to dissent from the committee majority rather than go along with a conclusion he did not buy.

Most notably, Brown in late 1984 filed a dissenting statement when ethics concluded that New York Democratic Rep. Geraldine A. Ferraro violated financial-disclosure requirements, but that the committee should take no further action because she was leaving the House at the end of the year. Brown argued that the decision set up a double standard, noting that Idaho Republican George Hansen had earlier been reprimanded for similar offenses.

Brown has openly criticized what he thinks is inadequate enforcement of ethical standards in the House.

His critique of Congress as an institution goes further, putting him on the opposite side of certain questions from the Democratic leadership. Brown has tried to end Congress' practice of exempting itself from civil rights and other laws it imposes on others. He has made several attempts over the years to cut funding for members' perks such as franked mail, elevator operators and leadership staff.

At Home: Brown has not had much practice at failure. He was student body president at the University of Colorado, a decorated Vietnam War veteran and a successful executive with a Colorado meatpacking firm. His first political campaign brought him election to the state Senate in 1972; two years later he was assistant majority leader.

He actually did lose one election, as the GOP nominee for lieutenant governor in 1978. But even that experience turned out to help more than hurt him. He won high marks for his vigorous campaigning and established solid name identification in the sprawling 4th District. U.S. Rep. Jim Johnson's decision to retire in 1980 set the stage for Brown's promotion.

A former campaign manager for Johnson, Brown was personable, well financed and enough of an orthodox Republican to quiet complaints from district conservatives about his support for the Equal Rights Amendment and resistance toward those seeking to ban abortion. He won the seat easily, routing veteran Democratic Party activist Polly Baca Barragan by more than 2-to-1. In four elections since then, he has never dropped below 70 percent of the vote.

Committee

Ways and Means (9th of 13 Republicans)
Social Security (ranking); Human Resources; Select Revenue Measures

Elections

1988 General

Hank Brown (R)	156,202	(73%)
Charles S. Vigil (D)	57,552	(27%)

1986 General

Hank Brown (R)	117,089	(70%)
David Sprague (D)	50,672	(30%)

Previous Winning Percentages: 1984 (71%) **1982** (70%) **1980** (68%)

District Vote For President

	1988	1984	1980	1976
D	95,025 (44%)	65,303 (31%)	58,221 (29%)	76,026 (42%)
R	119,554 (55%)	139,545 (67%)	115,469 (58%)	99,766 (55%)
I			20,455 (10%)	

Campaign Finance

	Receipts	Receipts from PACs	Expend-itures
1988			
Brown (R)	$287,187	$190,891 (66%)	$109,146
Vigil (D) †	$3,166	0	$3,165
1986			
Brown (R)	$184,809	$64,700 (35%)	$212,172
Sprague (D)	$22,526	$2,600 (12%)	$22,273

† Totals based on incomplete data.

Key Votes

1987

Raise speed limit to 65 mph	Y
Approve Gephardt "fair trade" amendment	Y
Ban testing of larger nuclear weapons	Y
Delay "re-flagging" of Kuwaiti tankers	Y
Approve tax-raising deficit-reduction bill	N

1988

Approve aid to Nicaraguan contras	Y
Enact civil rights restoration bill over Reagan veto	Y
Kill 60-day plant-closing notification measure	Y
Pass omnibus trade bill over Reagan veto	N
Approve death penalty for drug-related murders	Y
Bar federal funds for abortions in cases of rape and incest	N
Oppose seven-day waiting period for purchase of handguns	Y

Voting Studies

	Presidential Support		Party Unity		Conservative Coalition	
Year	**S**	**O**	**S**	**O**	**S**	**O**
1988	68	29	85	12	87	11
1987	58	39	84	11	77	14
1986	67	32	92	7	84	16
1985	70	29	87	11	82	18
1984	65	35	85	15	83	17
1983	67	33	82	18	75	25
1982	68	32	89	11	75	25
1981	66	34	77	23	71	29

Interest Group Ratings

Year	ADA	ACU	AFL-CIO	CCUS
1988	30	72	21	100
1987	16	73	19	85
1986	10	77	0	94
1985	30	67	12	82
1984	10	83	8	75
1983	25	61	12	90
1982	20	86	0	91
1981	20	100	13	89

5 Joel Hefley (R)

Of Colorado Springs — Elected 1986

Born: April 18, 1935, Ardmore, Okla.
Education: Oklahoma Baptist U., B.A. 1957; Oklahoma State U., M.S. 1962.
Occupation: Community planner.
Family: Wife, Lynn Christian; three children.
Religion: Presbyterian.
Political Career: Colo. House, 1977-79; Colo. Senate, 1979-87.
Capitol Office: 222 Cannon Bldg. 20515; 225-4422.

In Washington: A pro-defense Republican from a defense-oriented district, Hefley received some notice as a freshman for his enthusiastic support of the Reagan administration's strategic defense initiative. Hefley has a parochial as well as philosophical interest in SDI: His district, site of the Air Force Academy and Falcon Air Force Station, includes many research facilities for the space-based project.

Hefley's move from the Science Committee to Armed Services in the 101st Congress positions him to play a greater role on defense issues. But he arrives on the committee at a time when President Bush's willingness to limit defense spending puts even Hefley and his pro-defense soulmates under pressure to find savings at the Pentagon. And SDI is a prime budget-cutting candidate, certainly for liberal Democrats, and perhaps even for the Bush administration.

One of Hefley's first House actions, in May 1987, was to propose an amendment to the fiscal 1988 defense authorization bill to raise SDI funding authority to $4 billion from the $3.6 billion level then being discussed. Hefley lost, 129-286. However, he had more success obtaining funds for an SDI-related research facility in the 5th. In 1987, the House eliminated $100 million sought by Reagan for completion of the National Test Facility (NTF) at Falcon Air Force Station. But after lobbying by Hefley and other NTF supporters, $65 million eventually was restored to the project.

Hefley's overall voting record is conservative (he sides with a majority of his GOP colleagues on about nine in 10 votes), and similar to that of his GOP predecessor, Ken Kramer, who left the House for an unsuccessful 1986 Senate campaign. But in personal terms, the men are quite unalike: Kramer could be wearing and abrasive, while Hefley is regarded as genteel and approachable by colleagues in both parties.

On environmental issues, Hefley sometimes veers from the conservative line. His support for strengthening the Clean Air Act and increasing acid-rain controls earned him an award from the environmentalist Sierra Club.

At Home: A business-oriented legislator who lists calf-roping as one of his hobbies, Hefley seems a good fit for the 5th, which combines affluent white-collar suburbs with cattle-ranching areas and mountain communities. But unlike Kramer, Hefley is not known as a "movement conservative," and that caused him some difficulty when he first sought this seat.

Hefley entered the 1986 contest as the front-runner. After 10 years in the Legislature, he was widely known in his Colorado Springs base, site of the Air Force Academy and other underpinnings of the "military-industrial complex." But while his legislative record satisfied his mainly conservative constituency, Hefley generally had avoided lining up with the Legislature's ideological right. His display of what some considered "moderate tendencies" set the stage for a tough primary.

The challenge came from millionaire Harold A. Krause, a Republican national committeeman from the Denver suburbs. Hefley tried to portray himself as the candidate with "proven experience," and Krause as a novice "who's trying to buy his way to the top." But he found his years of experience being used against him. Krause maintained that if legislative experience alone could solve the country's problems, "we'd already have a balanced budget and no trade deficit."

Krause had one tactical advantage: money. It allowed him to wage a serious TV campaign in Colorado Springs, while the high cost of media in the Denver suburbs made it difficult for Hefley to raid Krause's suburban base. In the end, though, money was not enough. Hefley hit pay dirt by appealing to the parochialism of El Paso County voters, reminding them that electing Krause would give the Denver area four House members. In November, Hefley had no trouble with Democratic businessman Bill Story.

In 1988, Kramer threatened a comeback, vaguely complaining that Hefley was not a strong enough advocate of SDI. But he was persuaded to drop his challenge and offered a political appointment in the Department of the Army. Hefley was re-elected handily.

Colorado 5

South Central — Colorado Springs

The solidly Republican 5th revolves around Colorado Springs, the state's second-largest city and the southern anchor of the rapidly growing Front Range. Originally a resort whose sunny climate and proximity to Pikes Peak drew tourists from the East, the Front Range now has a more diversified economy and a fast-growing population that by the mid-1980s had reached 250,000.

Tourism remains the keystone of the local economy. But after World War II, Colorado Springs emerged as a center of military operations in the Rocky Mountains. To the north is the Air Force Academy; east is Peterson Air Force Base; south is Fort Carson; and deep in a mountain to the west is NORAD (the North American Air Defense Command), maintaining a round-the-clock alert for an enemy attack.

To this impressive lineup of military installations, Colorado Springs has added the Air Force's new Space Command at Peterson and the Consolidated Space Operations Complex at the Falcon Air Force Station.

At the same time, electronics firms have been moving to the area in large numbers. Among the major employers are Hewlett-Packard and Digital Corp.

Yet while the economic base has broadened, the politics of Colorado Springs have remained consistently conservative. El Paso County (Colorado Springs) went 3-to-1 for George Bush in 1988.

The large military work force, augmented by a sizable number of military retirees, has made the Colorado Springs area one of the most reliable bastions of conservative Republicanism in the state.

North of El Paso County are suburban Denver communities in southwest Jefferson, southwest Arapahoe and Douglas counties. All have Republican voting habits. Jefferson County's major community within the district is Golden, the site of the Colorado School of Mines, the Adolph Coors brewery and Buffalo Bill's grave.

The rest of the 5th's voters live in Elbert County, a cattle-ranching area inhabited by rock-ribbed Republicans, and in sparsely populated mountain counties between Colorado Springs and the Continental Divide. Ranching, mining and tourism are mainstays of the mountain economy.

Population: 481,627. White: 436,996 (91%), Black 19,829 (4%), Other 8,472 (2%). Spanish origin 32,707 (7%). 18 and over 335,156 (70%), 65 and over 30,725 (6%). Median age: 28.

Committees

Armed Services (19th of 21 Republicans)
Investigations; Military Personnel and Compensation; Readiness

Small Business (12th of 17 Republicans)
Procurement, Tourism and Rural Development; Regulation, Business Opportunity and Energy

Elections

1988 General		
Joel Hefley (R)	181,612	(75%)
John J. Mitchell (D)	60,116	(25%)
1986 General		
Joel Hefley (R)	121,153	(70%)
Bill Story (D)	52,488	(30%)

District Vote For President

	1988		1984		1980		1976	
D	78,785	(31%)	50,683	(24%)	47,248	(25%)	64,460	(39%)
R	168,390	(67%)	155,688	(75%)	121,490	(64%)	94,920	(58%)
I					17,123	(9%)		

Campaign Finance

	Receipts	Receipts from PACs	Expend-itures
1988			
Hefley (R)	$228,896	$112,827 (49%)	$183,229
Mitchell (D) †	$961	0	$930
1986			
Hefley (R)	$298,717	$113,206 (38%)	$283,404
Story (D)	$51,253	$11,250 (22%)	$51,253

† Totals based on incomplete data.

Key Votes

1987	
Raise speed limit to 65 mph	Y
Approve Gephardt "fair trade" amendment	N
Ban testing of larger nuclear weapons	N
Delay "re-flagging" of Kuwaiti tankers	N
Approve tax-raising deficit-reduction bill	N
1988	
Approve aid to Nicaraguan contras	Y
Enact civil rights restoration bill over Reagan veto	N
Kill 60-day plant-closing notification measure	Y
Pass omnibus trade bill over Reagan veto	N
Approve death penalty for drug-related murders	Y
Bar federal funds for abortions in cases of rape and incest	Y
Oppose seven-day waiting period for purchase of handguns	Y

Voting Studies

	Presidential Support		Party Unity		Conservative Coalition	
Year	S	O	S	O	S	O
1988	60	35	91	8	92	3
1987	71	29	85	12	81	14

Interest Group Ratings

Year	ADA	ACU	AFL-CIO	CCUS
1988	5	100	7	100
1987	4	96	6	100

6 Dan Schaefer (R)

Of Lakewood — Elected 1983

Born: Jan. 25, 1936, Gutenberg, Iowa.
Education: Niagara U., B.A. 1961; graduate work at Potsdam State U. (N.Y.), 1961-64.
Military Career: Marine Corps, 1955-57.
Occupation: Public relations consultant.
Family: Wife, Mary Lenney; four children.
Religion: Roman Catholic.
Political Career: Colo. House, 1977-79; Colo. Senate, 1979-83, president pro tempore, 1981-83.
Capitol Office: 1317 Longworth Bldg. 20515; 225-7882.

In Washington: Though Schaefer held an influential position in the Colorado Senate, in Washington he has kept a fairly low profile on a very high-profile committee, Energy and Commerce.

A moderate-to-conservative Republican, Schaefer has a reputation as a party loyalist, if a rather diffident one. In his five full years in the House, he has voted with the Republican majority more than 80 percent of the time; in most years, that has been well above the Republican average.

Home-state politics, however, forced Schaefer to part from Reagan-era GOP rhetoric in 1988 on the Clean Air bill, which was stalemated in Energy and Commerce throughout the 100th Congress. Air quality is a severe problem in the Denver metropolitan area, and in his re-election campaign, Schaefer was confronting a Democratic foe making pointed attacks on his environmental record. Late in 1988 Schaefer gave a rare speech on the House floor urging his colleagues to act on the bill and stressing the "need for a strong federal role in improving the environment."

With the other Denver-area House members, Schaefer also has pushed for continued federal funding for the C-470 beltway being built around Denver, as well as continued operation of the Fitzsimons Army Medical Center.

Colorado is a major source of oil shale, a raw material for synthetic fuel, and as a member of the Fossil and Synthetic Fuels Subcommittee, Schaefer fought in the 99th Congress against abolishing the Synthetic Fuels Corporation. He called the proposal to end the multimillion dollar program "diametrically opposed to our nation's energy security." But in subcommittee, Schaefer's was the only vote against cutting off synfuels funding.

At Home: Schaefer may lack star quality and a long list of legislative accomplishments, but in 1988, he proved decisively that he is a good fit for his suburban district.

The 6th was a brand-new district in 1982, added as a result of reapportionment and carved for a Republican. Schaefer was interested in it, but deferred to Jack Swigert, the popular former Apollo astronaut. Swigert won easily but died of cancer before he was sworn in.

When Schaefer entered the special election to fill the vacancy, his biggest hurdle was securing the GOP nomination at a district convention in January 1983. Aided by a band of national conservative GOP leaders, Schaefer won a fourth-ballot victory and has coasted to re-election ever since.

In 1988, the Democrats recruited a candidate who they thought could wrest the 6th from Schaefer: former Republican state Sen. Martha Ezzard. She had a reputation as a fiscal conservative, but was also an outspoken environmentalist and feminist. This issue agenda appealed to her affluent, well-educated Cherry Hills district, but it caused her big problems with the Legislature's conservative Republican hierarchy, and she quit the party and the Legislature in 1987.

Against Schaefer, Ezzard quickly proved her prowess as a fund-raiser and won headlines dubbing the incumbent "the invisible congressman." Schaefer defended his style as "quietly effective," championed his efforts to secure federal funds for local programs and claimed Ezzard would raise taxes. Ezzard badly underestimated the GOP loyalty of the district's voters and the appeal of Schaefer's parochial focus; she lost by 60,000 votes.

Schaefer came late to politics. The son of a construction worker, he was born in Iowa, raised in North Dakota and educated in New York. After several years as a high school history teacher, he moved to Colorado in his late 20s and opened a public relations firm.

After assisting the campaigns of other local GOP candidates, Schaefer successfully ran for the state House in 1976, and two years later he moved up to the state Senate. Personable and unflappable, he became president pro tem of the Senate in 1981. When he ran for Congress, he was assistant Senate majority leader.

Colorado 6

Denver Suburbs — Aurora; Lakewood

The 6th forms a "U" around Denver on the east, south and west, catching the homes of most white-collar commuters, while missing the working-class suburbs to the north. As electronics and engineering firms have moved to the suburbs, the population has ballooned and Republicans have thrived. In both 1980 and 1984, Reagan ran better in this area than he did statewide, as did George Bush in 1988.

More than half the population of the 6th lives south and east of Denver in Arapahoe County. Another 40 percent lives west of the city in Jefferson County, with the remainder divided between part of Denver itself and a portion of Adams County northeast of the city.

The 6th's largest community is Aurora, which lies east of Denver, straddling the Adams-Arapahoe county line. The smaller Adams County portion of Aurora, one of the 6th's few minority enclaves, is the only part of the district with a Democratic registration advantage. The Arapahoe County portion of Aurora is more affluent and Republican. It has been largely responsible for fueling Aurora's population boom; the city more than doubled in population during the 1970s and continues to grow, climbing toward 220,000. Inexpensive land and an independent water supply have lured developers.

South of Denver are Cherry Hills Village and Greenwood Village, two of the most affluent communities in the state and the backbone of conservative Republicanism in the suburbs. Near Greenwood Village is the Denver Tech Center, a large complex of professional offices and one of the leading destinations of suburban commuters. To the west are the communities of Englewood and Sheridan; both are older, politically marginal suburbs.

The areas west of Denver in Jefferson County are a mix of business executives, government employees and factory workers, most of whom usually vote Republican even though not all are hard-line conservatives. The 6th also includes about 16,500 residents in the southwestern part of Denver, which was a center of anti-busing sentiment in the 1970s.

Population: 481,682. White 448,653 (93%), Black 13,063 (3%), Other 8,874 (2%). Spanish origin 25,525 (5%). 18 and over 344,879 (72%), 65 and over 30,686 (6%). Median age: 29.

Committee

Energy and Commerce (14th of 17 Republicans)
Telecommunications and Finance; Transportation and Hazardous Materials

Elections

1988 General		
Dan Schaefer (R)	136,487	(63%)
Martha M. Ezzard (D)	77,158	(36%)
1986 General		
Dan Schaefer (R)	104,359	(65%)
Chuck Norris (D)	53,834	(34%)

Previous Winning Percentages: **1984** (89%) **1983 *** (63%)

* *Special election.*

District Vote For President

	1988		1984		1980		1976	
D	97,029	(42%)	65,615	(30%)	51,629	(26%)	60,365	(37%)
R	128,649	(56%)	148,388	(68%)	117,916	(60%)	100,216	(61%)
I					23,425	(12%)		

Campaign Finance

	Receipts	Receipts from PACs	Expend-itures
1988			
Schaefer (R)	$618,607	$335,747 (54%)	$636,204
Ezzard (D)	$493,515	$134,339 (27%)	$489,303
1986			
Schaefer (R)	$144,328	$99,833 (69%)	$125,435

Key Votes

1987	
Raise speed limit to 65 mph	Y
Approve Gephardt "fair trade" amendment	N
Ban testing of larger nuclear weapons	N
Delay "re-flagging" of Kuwaiti tankers	N
Approve tax-raising deficit-reduction bill	N
1988	
Approve aid to Nicaraguan contras	Y
Enact civil rights restoration bill over Reagan veto	N
Kill 60-day plant-closing notification measure	N
Pass omnibus trade bill over Reagan veto	Y
Approve death penalty for drug-related murders	Y
Bar federal funds for abortions in cases of rape and incest	Y
Oppose seven-day waiting period for purchase of handguns	Y

Voting Studies

	Presidential Support		Party Unity		Conservative Coalition	
Year	**S**	**O**	**S**	**O**	**S**	**O**
1988	56	41	82	17	87	8
1987	65	27	89	7	79	12
1986	76	21	84	11	90	4
1985	76	20	84	10	91	4
1984	70	30	93	6	95	5
1983	74 †	20 †	93 †	5 †	92 †	7 †

† Not eligible for all recorded votes.

Interest Group Ratings

Year	ADA	ACU	AFL-CIO	CCUS
1988	15	83	50	71
1987	8	87	19	86
1986	0	95	15	88
1985	10	80	13	91
1984	10	92	8	81
1983	0	100	7	76

Connecticut

U.S. CONGRESS

SENATE 2 D
HOUSE 3 D, 3 R

LEGISLATURE

Senate 23 D, 13 R
House 88 D, 63 R

ELECTIONS

1988 Presidential Vote	
Bush	52%
Dukakis	47%
1984 Presidential Vote	
Reagan	61%
Mondale	39%
1980 Presidential Vote	
Reagan	48%
Carter	39%
Anderson	12%
Turnout rate in 1984	61%
Turnout rate in 1986	40%
Turnout rate in 1988	58%

(as percentage of voting age population)

POPULATION AND GROWTH

1980 population	3,107,576
1988 population estimate (28th in the nation)	3,233,000
Percent change 1980-1988	+4%

DEMOGRAPHIC BREAKDOWN

White	90%
Black	7%
Other	1%
(Spanish origin)	4%
Urban	79%
Rural	21%
Born in state	58%
Foreign-born	9%

MAJOR CITIES

Bridgeport	141,860
Hartford	137,980
New Haven	123,450
Waterbury	102,300
Stamford	101,080

AREA AND LAND USE

Area	4,872 sq. miles (48th)
Farm	14%
Forest	59%
Federally owned	0.4%

Gov. William A. O'Neill (D)
Of East Hampton — Elected 1982

Born: Aug. 11, 1930, Hartford, Conn.
Education: Attended New Britain Teachers College, 1948-49; attended U. of Hartford, 1950.
Military Career: Air Force, 1950-53.
Occupation: Restaurateur.
Religion: Roman Catholic.
Political Career: Conn. House, 1967-79, majority leader, 1975-79; lieutenant governor, 1979-80; assumed governorship in 1980.
Next Election: 1990.

WORK

Occupations	
White-collar	58%
Blue-collar	30%
Service workers	11%
Government Workers	
Federal	23,078
State	62,242
Local	107,652

MONEY

Median family income	$ 23,149	(2nd)
Tax burden per capita	$ 1,102	(8th)

EDUCATION

Spending per pupil through grade 12	$ 4,743	(5th)
Persons with college degrees	21%	(3rd)

CRIME

Violent crime rate	419 per 100,000 (26th)

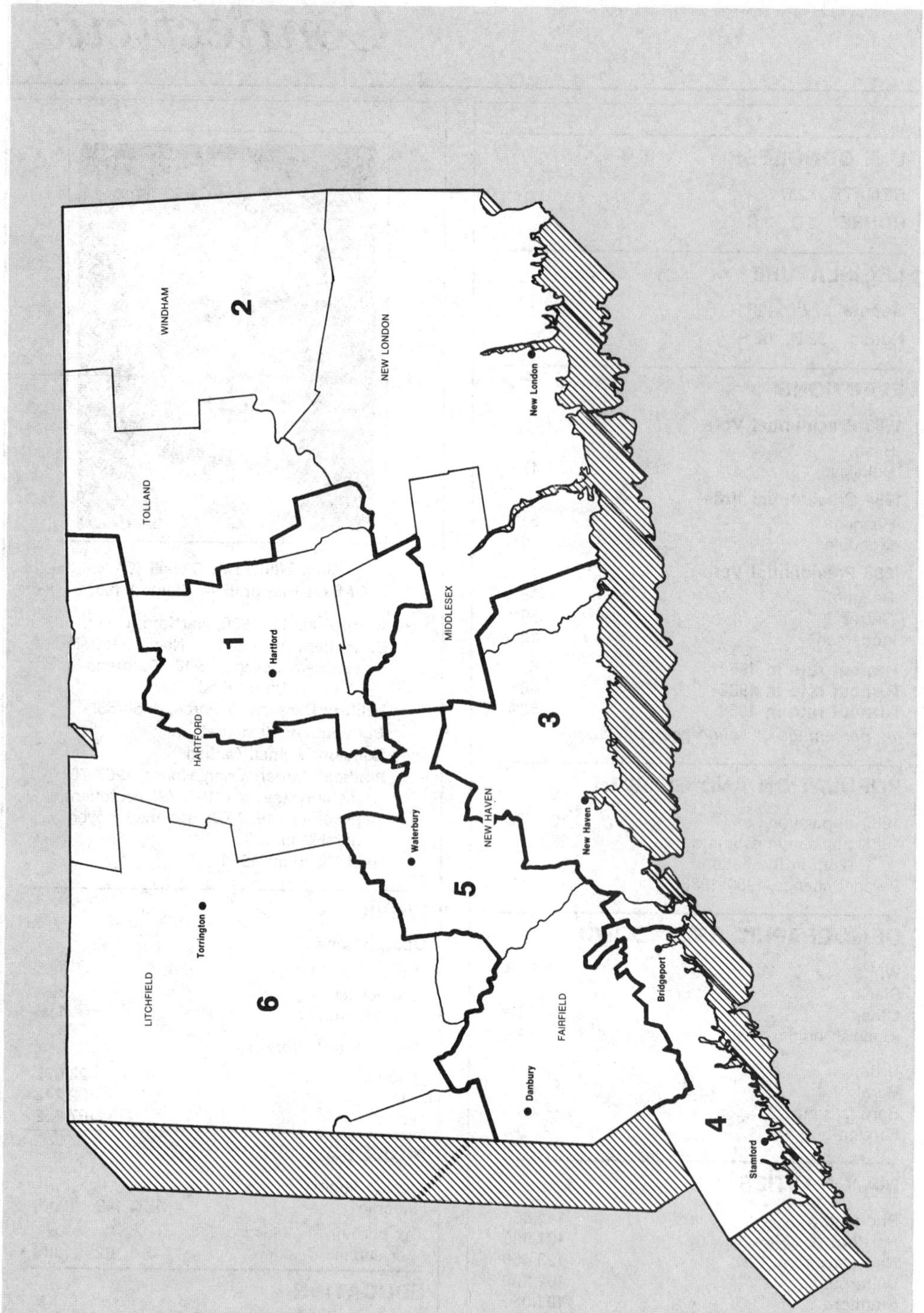
WINDHAM
2
NEW LONDON
TOLLAND
New London
1
Hartford
MIDDLESEX
HARTFORD
3
NEW HAVEN
Waterbury
New Haven
5
Torrington
LITCHFIELD
6
FAIRFIELD
Danbury
Bridgeport
4
Stamford

Christopher J. Dodd (D)

Of East Haddam — Elected 1980

Born: May 27, 1944, Willimantic, Conn.
Education: Providence College, B.A. 1966; U. of Louisville, J.D. 1972.
Military Career: Army Reserve, 1969-75.
Occupation: Lawyer.
Family: Divorced.
Religion: Roman Catholic.
Political Career: U.S. House, 1975-81.
Capitol Office: 444 Russell Bldg. 20510; 224-2823.

In Washington: Dodd's universe has often seemed to begin at the nation's southern border. Arriving in the Senate in 1981, he quickly gained visibility — notoriety at times because of his stridency — as a persistent critic of Reagan administration policy in Central America.

Nonetheless, issues that cut closer to home — indeed, in the home — are just as likely to drive his agenda throughout the 101st Congress. In 1988 he became the chief Senate architect of the Democrats' so-called "family agenda," the party's response to the new demographics of the family and work force.

Dodd's interest in children's issues is longstanding. With Pennsylvania Republican Arlen Specter, he founded the Senate Children's Caucus in 1983. When the Democrats regained control of the Senate after the 1986 elections, Dodd no longer needed this soapbox; he became chairman of the newly created Labor and Human Resources Subcommittee on Children, Family, Drugs and Alcoholism.

Late in the 100th Congress, Dodd and then-Senate Majority Leader Robert C. Byrd of West Virginia stage-managed a Senate floor show designed to highlight the two parties' differences; while the Senate waited on conference reports on other matters, Republicans were forced to block Dodd proposals to expand child care and guarantee unpaid leave for new parents.

A family issue of another sort put Dodd on the spot as the 101st Congress began work. He was one of only three Democrats to vote for the nomination of John Tower as secretary of defense. It did not escape attention that Tower had been one of only five senators to vote in 1967 against censuring Dodd's father, the late Thomas Dodd, for violating Senate rules against converting campaign funds to personal use.

The elder Dodd was a tough talking, two-term senator who was among his party's most virulent anti-communists. When the younger Dodd took his Senate seat in 1981, his siblings gave him his father's pocket watch and chain. He hung a picture of his father in his office. And when he got the chance, he moved into office quarters that include part of his father's old office.

But the younger Dodd, who learned to speak fluent Spanish as a Peace Corps volunteer in the Dominican Republic, reflects the changes a generation has brought to the Democratic view of foreign policy. He is skeptical of adventurism abroad, and has been a leading proponent of using diplomacy, not military force, to gain democracy in Central America.

As chairman of the Western Hemisphere Subcommittee of the Foreign Relations Committee, he is in a position to make his voice heard. In early 1989, he was a key player in the deal struck between the Bush administration and Congress to keep non-military aid flowing to the contras under terms that gave Congress unprecedented say-so over its continuance.

The intensity of Dodd's opposition to Ronald Reagan's policy in Central America has led him to say things that have struck other people as harsh and grating. The best-known example of this came in the spring of 1983, when congressional Democrats needed a spokesman to respond to President Reagan's nationally televised speech on Central America; they turned to Dodd. The senator responded with a blistering attack on Reagan's "formula for failure," accusing the president of condoning Salvadoran security guards who murder people "gangland style — the victim on bended knee, thumbs wired behind the back, a bullet through the brain." The speech angered many Democrats, notably then-House Majority Leader Jim Wright, who thought Dodd had gone far beyond any party consensus on the issue.

The reaction to that speech was an important lesson to Dodd, who concedes that he may have alienated some people with his stridency. "You yourself can become the issue, and I did," he says. He has remained a consistent critic of aid — he considers the contras thugs — but his stridency lessened as he sought to be among those crafting the compromises.

While voicing strong criticisms of the Nicaraguan government, particularly its human rights record, Dodd has worked to maintain ties to the country's Sandinista rulers. He traveled to Nicaragua in December 1986, helping to arrange for the release of captured American flier Eugene Hasenfus, who had been convicted of piloting a CIA plane bearing supplies to the contras.

Dodd works to enforce his views on Central America in a variety of ways. He uses senatorial power to block diplomatic appointees he does not like. Once, he was dressed down by Secretary of State George P. Shultz for intruding in U.S. policy in an untoward manner; Shultz complained after Dodd requested a meeting with a Central American head of state that excluded the U.S. ambassador, a violation of protocol that Shultz said contributed to foreigners' confusion about policy.

Before contra aid became a major issue, Dodd had focused his efforts on limiting U.S. involvement in the civil war in El Salvador. He was chief author of the 1981 law stipulating that the president could not continue aid to El Salvador unless he certified twice a year that the country was making progress in achieving social, economic and political reforms.

On the domestic front, Dodd proved again in the 100th Congress that he knows how to use his Banking Committee seat to look after his political base. During difficult markup sessions on legislation to deregulate the financial services industries — a matter that pitted banks against insurers — Dodd played hardball to protect Connecticut insurance companies. He threatened to force votes on issues on which senators did not want to take stands unless the committee met his demands. After holding the committee up for an intense day and a half, he apologized twice. But he defended his right to protect his state's large insurance industry: "It's like hogs in Iowa," he said.

Dodd can take partial credit for one of the few new domestic spending programs to become law under Reagan. Working with Rep. Charles E. Schumer of New York, he developed a small-scale program aimed at expanding the supply of rental housing for low- and middle-income families; it became law in 1983.

In the House, Dodd was more liberal than most of his colleagues in the Democratic class of 1974, but he reflected his class' general distrust of bureaucracy and its interest in "good government" issues. On the House Judiciary Committee, he supported gun control and lobby disclosure bills. Later he was given a seat on the Rules Committee and was made an at-large whip. Arguing for his energy-poor Northeast constituency, Dodd opposed oil decontrol and tried to increase fuel aid for the poor.

At Home: From the day Democratic Sen. Abraham Ribicoff declared his retirement in 1979, Dodd was viewed as his heir apparent. Dodd was overwhelmingly popular in his 2nd District, and he bore one of the most potent names in Connecticut politics. His father was still revered by many despite his 1967 Senate censure for personal use of campaign funds.

Dodd's only obstacle on the road to the Democratic Senate nomination was his fellow House member, Toby Moffett. When Moffett agreed to wait until 1982 to run for statewide office, Dodd's path was clear; he was nominated by acclamation at the state party convention.

His Republican opponent was former New York Sen. James L. Buckley, who carried the standard of the state GOP's newly resurgent conservative wing. The millionaire brother of columnist William F. Buckley Jr., James Buckley argued that his previous experience and national reputation would make him a significant force for conservatism in the Senate. With a strong constituency in Republican Fairfield County, he hoped to emulate Reagan by making inroads in normally Democratic blue-collar cities and towns to the east.

But Buckley's patrician style did not play well in those areas, and Dodd proved an exuberant campaigner, slipping into crowds with the comfort of a born politician, conversing both in English and fluent Spanish. He attacked Buckley as a conservative ideologue who, as a senator, had neglected the needs of the poor.

Dodd never forced the question of Buckley's carpetbagging; gentle references to it were enough. Dodd quipped that the Constitution mandates two senators for each state, not two states for each senator.

Dodd easily outdistanced Buckley, pulling votes from liberal Democrats on an issue basis and from older ethnic voters on the strength of their traditional Democratic habits. Carrying the major cities by huge margins, he earned a larger plurality than his father did in winning his first Senate term in 1958.

By 1984, Dodd felt politically secure enough at home to endorse the presidential candidacy of Colorado Sen. Gary Hart. The rest of Connecticut's Democratic establishment, including Gov. William A. O'Neill, backed Walter F. Mondale.

Hart won Connecticut's Democratic presidential primary convincingly. Dodd continued to advise and publicly support him even after it became clear that Mondale had enough delegates to win the nomination, and he placed Hart's name in nomination at the national convention in San Francisco. Though Dodd's sustained support for Hart seemed futile, it gave him broad exposure in a party that has begun to reach into his generation for its presidential candidates.

Dodd's reputation as a rising star was enhanced by his landslide 1986 re-election. Initial Republican hopes of threatening Dodd were deflated by the refusal of high-profile personalities to challenge him. The GOP eventually awarded its nomination to 66-year-old Roger W. Eddy, a party national committeeman and former state representative. Though he was popular among party insiders, it turned out that Eddy was little known to voters outside his home area.

Eddy, inventor of the widely used Audubon birdcall, had an image as a "gentleman farmer," but his campaign style turned out to be surprisingly hard-hitting. He attacked Dodd's Central America stands, describing him as "the senator from communist Nicaragua," and implied that Dodd had inherited the Senate seat from his father. In an appeal for labor votes, Eddy made an intemperate attack against Japan. He told a state AFL-CIO meeting that "Japan is sucking us dry," and implied that it is part of the Japanese culture to lie, cheat and steal in order to attain victory.

Eddy's brashness earned him headlines, but did not faze Dodd. He emphasized his support for programs in areas such as housing and higher education, defended his Central America record and brushed off Eddy's attacks as "disappointing." Dodd amassed nearly 65 percent of the vote, the largest Senate vote percentage in state history.

Dodd grew up with Connecticut politics, but he waited until he was 30 to go after public office himself. He was practicing law in New London in 1974 when GOP Rep. Robert H. Steele left his secure 2nd District seat to run for governor. Dodd attached himself to the camp of Democratic gubernatorial candidate Ella T. Grasso early in the spring and began making the rounds of delegates to the 2nd District Democratic convention.

By the time of the convention, he was the clear favorite over John M. Bailey Jr. — son of the state party chairman — and Douglas Bennet, a one-time aide to Ribicoff. Dodd locked up the party's endorsement on the first round of convention balloting, and went on to an easy victory in the general election.

Committees

Banking, Housing and Urban Affairs (4th of 12 Democrats)
Securities (chairman); Housing and Urban Affairs

Budget (12th of 13 Democrats)

Foreign Relations (5th of 10 Democrats)
Western Hemisphere and Peace Corps Affairs (chairman); East Asian and Pacific Affairs; International Economic Policy, Trade, Oceans and Environment

Labor and Human Resources (5th of 9 Democrats)
Children, Family, Drugs and Alcoholism (chairman); Aging; Education, Arts and Humanities

Rules and Administration (8th of 9 Democrats)

Elections

1986 General

Christopher J. Dodd (D)	632,695	(65%)
Roger W. Eddy (R)	340,438	(35%)

Previous Winning Percentages: 1980 (56%) **1978 *** (70%) **1976 *** (65%) **1974 *** (59%)

* *House elections.*

Campaign Finance

	Receipts	Receipts from PACs	Expend-itures
1986			
Dodd (D)	$2,395,798	$624,446 (26%)	$2,276,764
Eddy (R)	$466,915	$35,613 (8%)	$466,894

Key Votes

1987

Enact omnibus highway bill over Reagan veto	Y
Limit testing of space-based anti-ballistic missiles	Y
Oppose banning tests of larger nuclear weapons	N
Confirm Robert H. Bork as Supreme Court justice	N

1988

Allow vote on campaign-finance overhaul	Y
Pass civil rights restoration bill over Reagan veto	Y
Enact omnibus trade bill over Reagan veto	Y
Approve death penalty for drug-related murders	Y
Oppose "workfare" amendment to welfare overhaul bill	Y

Voting Studies

	Presidential Support		Party Unity		Conservative Coalition	
Year	S	O	S	O	S	O
1988	49	40	86	9	38	54
1987	29	56	80	11	28	59
1986	25	73	71	28	29	70
1985	34	64	83	14	27	73
1984	32	61	85	8	6	89
1983	41	53	67	17	14	64
1982	35	61	82	12	5	85
1981	33	59	80	8	3	85

Interest Group Ratings

Year	ADA	ACU	AFL-CIO	CCUS
1988	85	8	86	36
1987	65	0	100	13
1986	85	17	73	44
1985	85	4	95	41
1984	100	10	91	42
1983	80	8	100	24
1982	100	8	96	16
1981	90	7	100	0

Joseph I. Lieberman (D)

Of New Haven — Elected 1988

Born: Feb. 24, 1942, Stamford, Conn.
Education: Yale U., B.A. 1964, LL.B. 1967.
Occupation: Lawyer.
Family: Wife, Hadassah Freilich; four children.
Religion: Jewish.
Political Career: Conn. Senate, 1971-81, majority leader, 1975-81; sought Democratic nomination for U.S. House, 1980; Conn. attorney general, 1983-89.
Capitol Office: 502 Hart Bldg. 20510; 224-4041.

The Path to Washington: Lieberman is not a man to be underestimated. His soft-spoken, judicious manner conveys an ease and warmth that mask his savvy and ambition. And his conservative views on a handful of high-profile issues belie his generally liberal outlook.

Politically, he is battle-tested. In 1988, he was given little chance of ousting 18-year GOP Senate veteran Lowell P. Weicker Jr., but he wound up scoring the only Democratic upset of that year's Senate elections. Earlier in his career, Lieberman gave up a 10-year career in the state Senate (and his job there as majority leader) for a U.S. House bid, only to lose in the primary. But two years later, he bounced back, becoming the top state vote-getter in his election to attorney general.

In 1989, Lieberman entered the Senate in a class of heavyweight Democratic freshmen that includes three former governors, two of whom are Vietnam War veterans already being measured for presidential timber. But if he does not rise to that level of star quality, Lieberman still has managed to draw his share of attention.

Spotlighting the environment, he delivered the Democratic response to President Reagan's final weekly radio address. And in May, he was featured in a "60 Minutes" report on Alar, a chemical used on apples. From his post on the Environment and Public Works Committee, Lieberman raised questions about the Environmental Protection Agency's approval of Alar's use, inquiring into conflicts of interest on the EPA's Scientific Advisory Panel.

Lieberman also earned attention early in 1989 with his maiden speech to the Senate in opposition to John Tower's nomination to be secretary of defense. Courted personally by President Bush, Lieberman was particularly cautious as he waited for a decision from Connecticut's senior Sen. Christopher J. Dodd, whose personal loyalty to Tower eventually persuaded him to support the nomination.

The night before the vote, Lieberman announced his dissent. While his opposition guaranteed Tower's defeat, Lieberman's statement lacked partisan tang. Instead, it was a subdued and methodical review of Senate powers and precedents on confirmation of presidential appointees. A home-state editorial praised the speech as "the product of a good lawyer's gift for stating a case and a good politician's sense of theater."

In his race against Weicker, a series of tough but witty television advertisements met this same standard, and may have been decisive. After months of trailing in opinion polls, Lieberman launched a series of animated ads late in the campaign that portrayed Weicker as a sleeping bear, dozing through important votes but awaking loud and ornery when personally piqued.

All year long, Lieberman had argued that it was a myth that Connecticut benefited from Weicker's maverick reputation. But the electoral appeal of the Republican's go-it-alone style had seemed impenetrable to Lieberman's claim that maverick meant that "you don't even have to make commitments, even to the voters you represent. You just do whatever suits you personally whenever you want to do it. I look at his record and see a pattern of incredible inconsistency."

But the imagery of the bear ads clicked, and their appearance in the closing weeks of a yearlong campaign was perfectly timed. With Lieberman peaking late, Weicker did not have a chance to counterpunch.

Though the support of late-deciding, independent voters was crucial to Lieberman, he had put himself in a good position to catch the wave. He began the campaign well-known from nearly two terms as an activist attorney general. In those years, he won many headlines for his pro-consumer lawsuits against car dealers, grocery stores and public utilities, as well as for his efforts toward stiffer enforcement of hazardous-waste-disposal laws and child support payment requirements.

His visibility on these issues did not endear him to the "Old Guard" in Connecticut's Democratic Party, but his efforts had the liberal lilt needed to woo traditionally Democratic voters, and the party elected to unite behind him in his challenge to Weicker.

Lieberman's profile also enabled him to court crossover voters. His demeanor is far more restrained and serious than Weicker's; where the Republican campaigned with his sleeves rolled up and jacket slung over his shoulder, Lieberman seems reluctant to loosen his tie. He stresses a family-man image, and is known as an Orthodox Jew whose avoidance of Saturday campaigning precluded him from attending even the convention that nominated him.

Lieberman also held the conservative ground on a few select issues. He supported allowing military involvement in drug interdiction, and backed the 1983 invasion of Grenada, both of which Weicker opposed. Striking a sore spot between conservatives and Weicker, Lieberman backed a moment of silence in schools, which may be used for prayer.

This combination won him an endorsement from noted conservative William F. Buckley Jr., who had long disdained Weicker for his social liberalism. While droves of like-minded conservative voters did not turn out for Lieberman, some of them did conclude that a Lieberman victory would be no great catastrophe, so they sat out the Senate race. That deprived Weicker of crucial GOP support.

Lieberman's Democratic base appeared threatened when Weicker landed the AFL-CIO endorsement, but the attorney general moved quickly to gain the advantage on a Democratic touchstone issue, Social Security. He surprised Weicker by coming out swinging at an early summer debate, claiming the incumbent had voted five times to freeze Social Security, breaking a promise never to cut the program.

Weicker cried foul. He protested that they were not cuts but delays of cost-of-living adjustments, that the votes saved the system and were supported by senior citizens' advocate Rep. Claude Pepper of Florida. But Weicker's bluster paled when Lieberman followed with a TV ad that scrolled through each vote.

On Election Day, Lieberman's Democratic base held firm, and he won enough independent votes to eke out a narrow victory. While Democrats were pleased with his success, some liberals felt a twinge of remorse over the departure of Weicker, who so often had championed their causes in the Senate and in the national GOP.

Lieberman may not cut as wide a swath in Senate politics as Weicker did, but the Democrat's quieter, more judicious style could yield a different sort of influence.

Committees

Environment and Public Works (9th of 9 Democrats)
Environmental Protection; Toxic Substances, Environmental Oversight, Research and Development; Water Resources, Transportation and Infrastructure

Governmental Affairs (8th of 8 Democrats)
General Services, Federalism and the District of Columbia; Oversight of Government Management; Permanent Subcommittee on Investigations

Small Business (10th of 10 Democrats)
Competition and Antitrust Enforcement; Export Expansion; Government Contracting and Paperwork Reduction

Election

1988 General

Joseph I. Lieberman (D)	688,499	(50%)
Lowell P. Weicker Jr. (R)	678,454	(49%)

Campaign Finance

	Receipts	Receipts from PACs		Expend-itures
1988				
Lieberman (D)	$2,647,603	$175,566	(7%)	$2,570,779
Weicker (R)	$2,519,961	$947,116	(38%)	$2,609,902

1 Barbara B. Kennelly (D)

Of Hartford — Elected 1982

Born: July 10, 1936, Hartford, Conn.
Education: Trinity College (Washington, D.C.), B.A. 1958; Trinity College (Hartford, Conn.), M.A. 1971.
Occupation: Public official.
Family: Husband, James J. Kennelly; four children.
Religion: Roman Catholic.
Political Career: Hartford Court of Common Council, 1975-79; Conn. secretary of state, 1979-82.
Capitol Office: 204 Cannon Bldg. 20515; 225-2265.

In Washington: Kennelly is equal parts feminist and old pol. She moves easily between those roles, in one breath arguing forcefully for women's issues and in the next breath spinning a tale about "Danny" — Ways and Means Chairman Dan Rostenkowski — in a way that makes it clear the Chicago power broker is someone she likes and understands.

It is not surprising that Kennelly feels at ease around old-fashioned Democrats. She saw plenty of them growing up; her father was John Bailey, the legendary Connecticut party boss and chairman of the Democratic National Committee under Kennedy and Johnson. Kennelly's father also taught her an important skill that has helped her forge relationships with other members — golf. One way to crack any "old boy" network is to mix in socially, and the place Kennelly has mixed with members of Ways and Means is on the fairways and putting greens.

Kennelly's knack for getting along with the male-dominated House leadership has brought her a long way in a short time. She had been in the chamber less than a year when she won a seat on Ways and Means, and in December 1984, then-Speaker Thomas P. O'Neill Jr. appointed her to the Democratic Steering and Policy Committee, which makes committee assignments and helps design legislative and political strategies. In the June 1989 Democratic leadership shake-up that followed Jim Wright's departure as Speaker, Kennelly made a longshot bid for the open post of caucus chairman, but she lost to Steny H. Hoyer of Maryland, who had been the caucus vice chairman.

Insurance is a big industry in Hartford, and is thus a major interest for Kennelly on Ways and Means. At times she seems frustrated about having to focus so much of her attention on one topic, but she can always be counted on to do her homework on the subject.

In working on legislation to overhaul the tax code in the 99th Congress, Kennelly specialized in the complex provisions affecting property- and casualty-insurance companies. In the 100th Congress, as Ways and Means worked on a bill to make technical corrections in the tax code, Kennelly displayed her legislative savvy by winning a surprising victory for the insurance industry over Rostenkowski's strong objections.

Rostenkowski, disturbed that certain types of life insurance were being used to dodge taxation, sought to rewrite the rules to discourage investors from dipping into certain insurance plans for tax-free earnings on premium payments. But Kennelly and New Jersey Democrat Frank J. Guarini felt Rostenkowski's plan was too stringent; they proposed a milder one and persuaded the committee to go along with it at a contentious meeting. An angry Rostenkowski told the committee it was being "rolled" by the insurance industry, and he abruptly called the meeting to a halt. But later, Rostenkowski decided to let the Kennelly-Guarini plan go through. For her part, Kennelly said the insurance industry "is on notice" that it may face harsher penalties if the plan she supported failed to bring about the intended changes.

The insurance industry has had other opportunities to thank Kennelly for her efforts. In the 98th Congress, she had a hand in shaping a major revision of insurance tax laws, lowering the industry's overall tax burden.

Kennelly is a latecomer to feminist issues; she says her three daughters persuaded her to become active. When congressional feminists began pushing their "equity" agenda in 1983, Kennelly said, "Am I going to tell you I am going to change the world of Danny Rostenkowski? No. Am I going to try? Yes."

One of her first accomplishments was winning passage in 1984 of part of the "equity" package — a law to encourage payment of child support. It required states to see that money is withheld from the paychecks of parents who are delinquent in meeting court-ordered child-support payments. Four years later, when Ways and Means produced an overhaul of the welfare system, Kennelly and others pushed for even stricter enforcement requirements, forcing withholding even when payment is not in arrears.

Kennelly also brought the voice of the women's caucus to the tax-law rewrite, fighting

Connecticut 1

Central — Hartford

Hartford, the capital of Connecticut, is a city of contrast. The Travelers, Aetna, CIGNA and other insurance corporations hum with white-collar activity, and state government offers stable employment, yet many of the city's poor blacks and Hispanics stand idle.

The corporate community of Hartford plays a large philanthropic role, paying for housing rehabilitation, job training and other urban-development projects. But the problems are large. After the 1980 census, Hartford was rated the fourth-poorest city in the nation, with one-quarter of its residents living under the poverty line. Some Hartford parents have become so distraught over the condition of the city's schools that they are illegally sending their children to schools in more affluent nearby suburbs; parents have actually been arrested for this offense, called "line-jumping."

In politics, the 1st used to be the fiefdom of state party boss John Bailey, Kennelly's father, who personally determined which Democrat would represent it in Congress every two years. The 1st has sent a Democrat to Congress in every election but one since 1948; in 1981, Hartford, which is one-third black, became the first New England city to elect a black mayor, and it has had one ever since.

Bailey saw to it that all of Hartford's ethnic groups were welcomed under the Democratic banner, and Democratic candidates continue to do well among the city's ethnic and racial groups. In the 1982 House special election, the Italian-American wards in the South End voted for Democrat Kennelly rather than the Italian-American Republican, Ann P. Uccello.

In 1988, support from Hartford's blacks helped Michael S. Dukakis carry the city with 76 percent. Though Hartford's electoral influence is not what it used to be — the city's population dropped by 14 percent in the 1970s, and Hartford now casts less than one-fifth of the total district vote — Dukakis still carried the 1st comfortably. It was the only Connecticut district to back him, and one of three to vote for Democratic Senate nominee Joseph I. Lieberman in 1988.

While Dukakis won the capital city's urbanized neighbors — East Hartford, West Hartford and Manchester — they are not immune to GOP entreaties. Lieberman carried Manchester by just 14 votes and narrowly lost West Hartford to GOP Sen. Lowell P. Weicker Jr. Reagan carried all three of these suburbs in 1984 on his way to winning a majority in the 1st; in 1976 and 1980, Democrat Jimmy Carter carried the district.

United Technologies' Pratt & Whitney headquarters in East Hartford employs 18,000 people — the largest single source of jobs in the district — and most of the employees are involved in skilled, high-technology work. Other aerospace and high-tech firms offering similar jobs have helped build a well-paid work force throughout metropolitan Hartford.

Population: 516,232. White 429,260 (83%), Black 59,723 (12%), Other 4,056 (1%). Spanish origin 32,636 (6%). 18 and over 383,559 (74%), 65 and over 65,558 (13%). Median age: 32.

to preserve the child-care deduction and to expand the standard deduction for single parents.

Starting in the 101st Congress, Kennelly has competition if she is to be the main voice of women — or even of her home state — on Ways and Means. Nancy L. Johnson, Kennelly's Republican colleague from Connecticut, joined the panel in 1989, bringing with her a reputation as an outspoken legislator.

Kennelly wants to liberalize one key restriction from the Tax Reform Act. Reflecting the needs of her urban district, she has backed legislation intended to make a tax credit for investing in low-income housing easier to use. Those efforts did not prove successful in the 100th Congress, but she is pursuing that goal again in the 101st.

At Home: Even though she learned politics at her father's knee, Kennelly took her time getting into the business. She was almost 40, directing two large social-service agencies in Hartford, when she was appointed to fill a vacancy on the City Council in 1975. She easily won a full term soon after.

It took a strikingly independent move to win her next office. Gloria Schaffer, the Democratic secretary of state, decided to step down from her post in 1978. Party protocol called for replacing her with another Jewish woman to balance the ethnic makeup of the statewide ticket. Kennelly ignored precedent. At the state party convention she pieced together an organization that drew comparisons with her father; she finagled the nomination from the party favorites and won easily in November.

Barbara B. Kennelly, D-Conn.

In 1981, two weeks after six-term Democratic Rep. William R. Cotter died of cancer, Kennelly announced her candidacy to replace him. Other Democrats dropped out, and she was nominated by acclamation.

Kennelly had little trouble in the subsequent special election against GOP nominee Ann P. Uccello, a former mayor of Hartford. Although Uccello had been a strong vote-getter when she captured the mayoralty in 1969, her political visibility had faded after a narrowly unsuccessful 1970 campaign against Cotter.

Running in a Democratic stronghold, Kennelly also had a huge financial lead. The national Republican Party wrote off Uccello, and Kennelly won with nearly 60 percent.

Since then, Kennelly has rolled up huge tallies in each of her four re-election campaigns.

Committees

Select Intelligence (8th of 12 Democrats)
Legislation; Oversight and Evaluation

Ways and Means (17th of 23 Democrats)
Human Resources; Select Revenue Measures

Elections

1988 General		
Barabra B. Kennelly (D)	176,463	(77%)
Mario Robles Jr. (R)	51,985	(23%)
1986 General		
Barabra B. Kennelly (D)	128,930	(74%)
Herschel A. Klein (R)	44,122	(25%)

Previous Winning Percentages: 1984 (62%) **1982** (68%) **1982 *** (59%)

* *Special election.*

District Vote For President

	1988	1984	1980	1976
D	133,867 (55%)	115,174 (47%)	109,702 (46%)	125,895 (52%)
R	106,890 (44%)	129,384 (53%)	93,750 (39%)	113,154 (47%)
I			34,942 (15%)	

Campaign Finance

	Receipts	Receipts from PACs	Expend-itures
1988			
Kennelly (D)	$448,010	$269,603 (60%)	$471,530
Robles (R)	$11,522	0	$11,520
1986			
Kennelly (D)	$456,997	$254,783 (56%)	$388,045
Klein (R)	$7,297	$750 (10%)	$6,705

Key Votes

1987	
Raise speed limit to 65 mph	N
Approve Gephardt "fair trade" amendment	Y
Ban testing of larger nuclear weapons	Y
Delay "re-flagging" of Kuwaiti tankers	Y
Approve tax-raising deficit-reduction bill	Y
1988	
Approve aid to Nicaraguan contras	N
Enact civil rights restoration bill over Reagan veto	Y
Kill 60-day plant-closing notification measure	N
Pass omnibus trade bill over Reagan veto	Y
Approve death penalty for drug-related murders	Y
Bar federal funds for abortions in cases of rape and incest	N
Oppose seven-day waiting period for purchase of handguns	N

Voting Studies

	Presidential Support		Party Unity		Conservative Coalition	
Year	**S**	**O**	**S**	**O**	**S**	**O**
1988	28	71	92	6	32	68
1987	22	75	89	5	37	60
1986	20	78	91	4	20	74
1985	23	78	91	5	22	78
1984	31	65	88	7	15	78
1983	16	80	95	3	12	83
1982	34	66	92	8	26	74

Interest Group Ratings

Year	ADA	ACU	AFL-CIO	CCUS
1988	90	8	100	36
1987	84	0	88	21
1986	85	0	93	35
1985	90	10	94	27
1984	85	0	77	38
1983	90	4	94	25
1982	95	0	85	27

2 Sam Gejdenson (D)

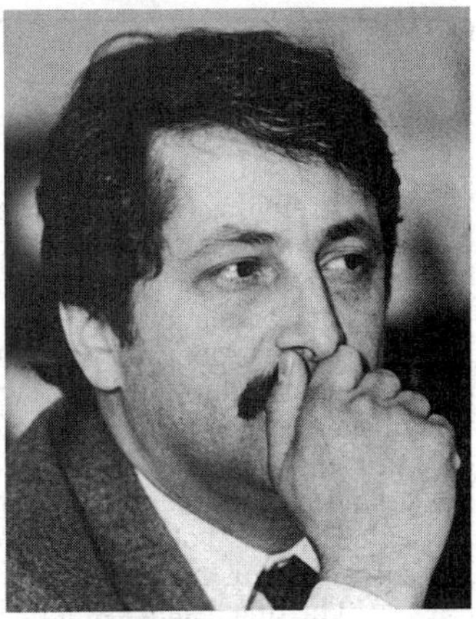

Of Bozrah — Elected 1980

Born: May 20, 1948, Eschwege, Germany.
Education: Mitchell Junior College, A.S. 1968; U. of Connecticut, B.A. 1970.
Occupation: Dairy farmer.
Family: Wife, Karen Fleming; two children.
Religion: Jewish.
Political Career: Conn. House, 1975-79.
Capitol Office: 1410 Longworth Bldg. 20515; 225-2076.

In Washington: During his early years in the House, Gejdenson was best known to many of his colleagues for his irreverent wit. He still can be quick with a quip, but seniority is bringing him greater responsibilities, and he is handling them in a way that marks him as a serious and energetic legislator.

During the 100th Congress, Gejdenson got good marks for his performance as chairman of the Interior Subcommittee on General Oversight and Investigations. In the 101st Congress, he took a higher-profile subcommittee on Foreign Affairs that deals with international economic policy and trade. In noting his move to the new subcommittee, one trade industry publication said that on Interior, Gejdenson had "a reputation for conducting well-researched and focused hearings."

Gejdenson had a chance to prove his leadership mettle in the 100th Congress when he was temporarily chairing the Interior Subcommittee on Energy and the Environment.

The panel was taking testimony on a bill to limit timber harvesting in Alaska's Tongass National Forest. According to custom, the bill's House sponsor, Democrat Robert J. Mrazek, was permitted to testify first, followed by a Senate opponent, Alaska Republican Frank H. Murkowski. However, panel member Don Young, the hot-tempered Alaska Republican and timber-harvest proponent, disrupted the hearing, demanding that Murkowski be allowed to speak first. Gejdenson warned Young to be quiet, but to no avail; he then recessed the hearing and led Young to a hallway, where he cooled him down and explained the order of testimony. The hearing resumed shortly thereafter.

On the Tongass issue and on other environmental matters, Gejdenson is plainly a liberal, but not so dogmatic that he cannot work with opponents. In a 1987 hearing of his oversight subcommittee, Gejdenson criticized the Nuclear Regulatory Commission for being too cozy with the industry it oversees. "I am concerned that the NRC may not be maintaining an arm's-length regulatory posture with the commercial nuclear industry," Gejdenson said. But he is no advocate of extreme nuclear-plant-shutdown proposals; his district has four operating nuclear power plants.

As a member of Foreign Affairs, Gejdenson was a vocal critic of some Reagan administration policies abroad, particularly aid to the Nicaraguan contras. In 1987, he supported a proposal to prohibit the president from soliciting foreign donations to the contras. "We want to make sure that foreign policy is decided here in the Congress and with the president . . . and not with the secretary of state out begging from other nations," Gejdenson said.

He sounded somewhat more conciliatory at the beginning of the Bush administration when expressing approval of Bush's early calls for bipartisanship. "Everybody here is tired of having to look at the other branch of government as some enemy post, where you have to shackle them so they will do what the law says," he said.

Gejdenson will have to rely more on his intellectual abilities than on his partisan skills in his new role as chairman of the Subcommittee on International Economic Policy and Trade. Over the next few years, the panel will be dealing with esoteric, and sometimes tedious, details of such measures as the Export Administration Act, which comes up for renewal in 1990.

Though Gejdenson's overall voting record is steadfastly liberal — he opposed President Reagan's position on House legislation more than 80 percent of the time during the 100th Congress — the issue of defense spending places him in a quandary. His eastern Connecticut district includes Electric Boat Co.'s submarine works and numerous other defense-related installations that are crucial to the region's economy. While Gejdenson was opposed to Reagan's emphasis on defense over domestic spending, he could hardly afford to be as sweeping in his calls for military cutbacks as many of his Democratic colleagues.

Gejdenson defends his support and lobbying on behalf of his district's defense industry, describing the submarine program as "the most proven and effective component of our national

Connecticut 2

East — New London

Stretching from the shores of Long Island Sound to the state's upland hills, the 2nd District covers the least urbanized parts of Connecticut. Its vote varies with its geography. Along the coast, dependably Democratic shipbuilding towns and fishing villages border wealthy WASPish communities that provide Republican majorities. Inland, small manufacturing centers and college towns vote Democratic, while Yankee hill towns maintain the GOP tradition.

The fine balance among the areas helps give the 2nd a volatile voting pattern. When Gejdenson replaced Democrat Christopher J. Dodd in 1980, it marked the first time in nearly 50 years that the district had changed hands without changing parties. Between 1934 and 1950, it switched parties every two years. In close statewide contests, the 2nd is almost always up for grabs. In his successful 1982 Senate campaign and in his losing 1988 re-election effort, Republican Lowell P. Weicker Jr. drew 51 percent here.

Historically a center for seafaring, the southern coast is the home of the Electric Boat shipbuilding installation in Groton. Construction site for the Trident nuclear submarine program, this is the district's largest industrial concern, employing 18,000 people.

Like Connecticut as a whole, the coastal area is heavily dependent on military spending. The Groton maritime complex also features the Naval Underseas Research and Development Center, a Navy submarine port and a submarine training base.

Across the Thames River, in New London, is the U.S. Coast Guard Academy, which coexists peacefully with Connecticut College and several small plastics and hardware plants. To the east is Mystic Seaport, a tourist attraction commemorating the fishing life that once thrived there.

Farther inland, college towns and mill towns are neighbors on the hilly landscape. In Willimantic, Eastern Connecticut State College adjoins needle-and-thread and wire-cable firms. The town of Storrs is dominated by the 24,000 students at its University of Connecticut campus, while Middletown is home to Wesleyan University's 2,700 students.

Population: 518,244. White 493,893 (95%), Black 15,107 (3%), Other 4,710 (1%). Spanish origin 8,931 (2%). 18 and over 378,132 (73%), 65 and over 53,819 (10%). Median age: 30.

security strategy." He also concedes the parochial nature of his defense posture, stating, "National security comes first, but if I don't push for my district no one else will."

Gejdenson, however, has refused to try for a slot on the Armed Services Committee, noting his opposition to most Pentagon priorities. "If you're on a committee and you vote against the committee's major issues constantly, you end up creating real political problems for yourself," he once said. He expresses unhappiness with the degree of influence the defense industry has in Connecticut; in 1987, he helped establish the Southeast Area Technology Development Center (SEATECH), a non-profit corporation aimed at finding ways to diversify his district's economy.

Outside the defense area, Gejdenson has no qualms at all about pushing for district interests. In early 1989, the National Park Service signed off on Gejdenson's proposal to designate a river valley in his district that is dotted with quaint old mill towns as a "National Heritage Corridor." He has also been pushing legislation to set up a national clearinghouse for information on groundwater contamination; many Connecticut residents obtain their drinking water from groundwater wells.

At Home: Gejdenson's district-focused work in Washington is not the only thing that has made him safe in a nominally Republican district. The local media lavish praise on the incumbent for simply being a nice guy. After his 1988 announcement that he was running for re-election, the *New London Day* ran a glowing column about Gejdenson headlined, "Just a Farm Boy Who Spends His Week in Washington."

The story referred to the fact that Gejdenson had grown up on an eastern Connecticut dairy farm still owned by his parents, Lithuanian Jews who survived the World War II Holocaust. Gejdenson himself was born in the displaced persons' camp in Germany from which his family emigrated to America.

Leaving the farm behind to enter politics, Gejdenson served two terms in the state House, and prepared to run for Congress. He got his chance in 1980 when 2nd District Democratic Rep. Christopher J. Dodd vacated the seat to run for the Senate. Though John N. Dempsey Jr., the son of a former governor, won the party endorsement at the Democratic district convention, Gejdenson out-campaigned him in the primary, winning with 62 percent of the vote.

That fall, Gejdenson expected little trouble

from Republican Tony Guglielmo, who won the GOP nomination when the front-runner dropped out. But Guglielmo benefited from the national GOP trend. Reagan carried the 2nd by 18,000 votes, and Gejdenson emerged with just 53 percent.

Guglielmo was back in 1982, aided by groups that traditionally contribute to GOP candidates. But that year's economic downturn put Guglielmo on the defensive, and Gejdenson prevailed with 56 percent.

Gejdenson seemed safe by 1984, when the GOP put up a little-known botany professor, Roberta Koontz. But he was nearly caught off guard. Aided by voters' concerns about Gejdenson's liberalism and by President Reagan's landslide victory in the 2nd, Koontz carried 23 of the district's 57 towns. But Gejdenson held on with 54 percent; his margins in Norwich, New London and Middletown delivered him from an upset.

With three sub-60 percent tallies to Gejdenson's credit, analysts began saying that he would always struggle in November. In 1986, he decisively proved them wrong. Republicans thought they had a strong challenger in Francis M. "Bud" Mullen, a former director of the federal Drug Enforcement Administration and former FBI official. But Gejdenson mauled Mullen, winning two-thirds of the vote.

Trailing badly in fund raising, Mullen resorted to a strategy used by Guglielmo and Koontz: He criticized Gejdenson for not seeking a seat on Armed Services, and for opposing some of Reagan's defense programs. Gejdenson deflected the criticisms by showing that he had helped bring billions of dollars in ship- and submarine-building contracts to the district. With assistance from a strong-running statewide Democratic ticket, Gejdenson carried every district town but one.

Two years later, a grass-roots campaign by political newcomer Glenn Carberry got nowhere against the Democrat.

Committees

Foreign Affairs (8th of 28 Democrats)
International Economic Policy and Trade (chairman); Western Hemisphere Affairs

House Administration (9th of 13 Democrats)
Accounts

Interior and Insular Affairs (11th of 26 Democrats)
Energy and the Environment; General Oversight and Investigations; Water, Power and Offshore Energy

Elections

1988 General		
Sam Gejdenson (D)	143,326	(64%)
Glenn Carberry (R)	81,965	(36%)
1986 General		
Sam Gejdenson (D)	109,229	(67%)
Francis M. "Bud" Mullen (R)	52,869	(33%)

Previous Winning Percentages: 1984 (54%) **1982** (56%) **1980** (53%)

District Vote For President

	1988	1984	1980	1976
D	115,813 (49%)	90,869 (39%)	85,537 (38%)	106,788 (50%)
R	119,947 (50%)	141,593 (61%)	103,603 (46%)	105,737 (50%)
I			31,954 (14%)	

Campaign Finance

	Receipts	Receipts from PACs	Expend-itures
1988			
Gejdenson (D)	$731,513	$208,800 (29%)	$727,919
Carberry (R)	$250,776	$30,354 (12%)	$246,903
1986			
Gejdenson (D)	$975,785	$294,448 (30%)	$987,167
Mullen (R)	$153,407	$12,410 (8%)	$145,336

Key Votes

1987	
Raise speed limit to 65 mph	N
Approve Gephardt "fair trade" amendment	Y
Ban testing of larger nuclear weapons	Y
Delay "re-flagging" of Kuwaiti tankers	Y
Approve tax-raising deficit-reduction bill	Y
1988	
Approve aid to Nicaraguan contras	N
Enact civil rights restoration bill over Reagan veto	Y
Kill 60-day plant-closing notification measure	N
Pass omnibus trade bill over Reagan veto	Y
Approve death penalty for drug-related murders	N
Bar federal funds for abortions in cases of rape and incest	N
Oppose seven-day waiting period for purchase of handguns	N

Voting Studies

	Presidential Support		Party Unity		Conservative Coalition	
Year	S	O	S	O	S	O
1988	19	78	93	3	8	92
1987	15	84	92	4	19	81
1986	13	87	96	3	12	88
1985	23	78	92	4	7	89
1984	27	69	91	7	5	95
1983	20	79	95	3	9	90
1982	36	60	92	4	15	82
1981	22	76	92	7	8	92

Interest Group Ratings

Year	ADA	ACU	AFL-CIO	CCUS
1988	95	0	92	29
1987	92	0	100	20
1986	95	0	100	41
1985	90	10	94	23
1984	95	0	100	50
1983	90	0	100	25
1982	100	0	95	23
1981	95	0	80	5

3 Bruce A. Morrison (D)

Of Hamden — Elected 1982

Born: Oct. 8, 1944, New York, N.Y.
Education: Massachusetts Institute of Technology, B.S. 1965; U. of Illinois, M.S. 1970; Yale U., J.D. 1973.
Occupation: Lawyer.
Family: Wife, Jane Phillips.
Religion: Lutheran.
Political Career: No previous office.
Capitol Office: 330 Cannon Bldg. 20515; 225-3661.

In Washington: The former director of a New Haven legal aid office, Morrison brought a crusading style to Congress. Now in his fourth term, he has had to learn some things about channeling his vigor and intensity in an institution where personal relationships can be as important as passionate arguments.

In the 101st Congress, Morrison's intellectual gifts and his personal style will be on display as he chairs the Judiciary Subcommittee on Immigration, Refugees and International Law. He takes the position under unusual circumstances: In early 1989, the liberals who dominate Judiciary stripped the chairmanship from veteran Democrat Romano L. Mazzoli of Kentucky. Mazzoli was a chief instigator of immigration reform early in the 1980s, but did not nurture close ties with Democrats to his left, so they turned from him to Morrison, one of their ideological soul mates.

Morrison's energy is widely admired, although the breadth of his interests and the intensity of his views set him apart in a chamber where most members specialize and compromise.

"There are two ways to function in the House," Morrison has said. "One is to confine yourself to a couple of narrow things and cast your votes. The other is to try to play a significant role that's more far-reaching."

No one would ever doubt which role Morrison has chosen for himself. He has plunged into a remarkable array of issues — promoting low-income housing programs, fighting President Reagan's deferral of spending ordered by Congress, protecting legal services for the poor, advocating changes in World Bank lending policies to the Third World, opposing bank deregulation legislation and seeking wildlife refuge status for islands off the Connecticut coast, to name a few.

The Judiciary subcommittee chairmanship came at a propitious time for Morrison, because he had encountered trouble in parlaying his ambitious agenda into a more prestigious committee assignment.

When he tried for a seat on the Budget Committee in the 99th Congress, Massachusetts Democrat Chester G. Atkins, a freshman and the choice of Speaker Thomas P. O'Neill Jr., won the slot, even though Morrison had demonstrated an impressive command of the budget and waged a determined campaign.

Late in 1988, Morrison was a candidate for the Appropriations Committee seat vacated by the retirement of Massachusetts Rep. Edward P. Boland. The odds were stacked against him: The Massachusetts delegation — which with 10 members is the driving force in the New England Democratic caucus — claimed the slot, and their only real question was whether Atkins or Joseph P. Kennedy II would get the prize. Morrison lost on the first ballot, unable to draw a single vote from anyone outside Connecticut's three-person Democratic delegation.

A believer in activist government, Morrison arrived in Washington in 1983 annoyed that mounting deficits were chipping away at the federal government's capacity to act. He blamed the red ink not only on the Reagan administration, but also on senior Democrats, who he said "have been excusing deficits all their lives." While a number of members in his Democratic class of 1982 shared Morrison's views about the deficit, some older colleagues thought they heard a more sanctimonious tone in Morrison's voice. "I've never learned to speak casually about billions of dollars," he once said. "I hope I never do."

Time and again in the 99th and 100th Congresses, Morrison offered amendments to appropriations bills that called for across-the-board cuts or spending freezes. Whether the money was for NASA, refugee resettlement, agriculture programs or the Treasury Department, Morrison sought to shave off a little in the name of deficit reduction.

His accomplishments were more symbolic than substantive; even when his spending levels were approved by the House, they were usually raised again in conference with the Senate.

Once in 1985, Morrison got a dose of his own budget medicine on an issue dear to him — public housing. When the House considered the fiscal 1986 Housing and Urban Development (HUD) appropriations bill, Morrison supported

Connecticut 3

South — New Haven

New Haven has slipped from its glory days as Connecticut's largest city and a premier industrial powerhouse of New England, but it is still the political heart of the 3rd; when a big political rally is planned, the New Haven Green is the only site considered.

New Haven was dominated in the 19th century by Yankee Republicans, and in the first half of the 20th, power was divided among the Italian, Polish and Irish communities. House members of Italian extraction held the 3rd from 1953 to 1983, and Italian-Americans still dominate local elections. But Morrison's success signals the emergence of a new type of politics in the district — one in which age, income status and ideology are more important voting determinants than ethnicity.

Today New Haven is almost one-third black, a fact that helps explain why its voting behavior is dramatically different from that of the surrounding communities. In 1988, Democratic presidential nominee Michael S. Dukakis carried New Haven with more than 70 percent of the vote, but narrowly lost the district to George Bush.

Because New Haven casts only about one-fifth of the total district vote, a Democrat cannot succeed in the 3rd unless he makes a respectable showing outside the city. Democratic Senate nominee Joseph I. Lieberman carried the 3rd by winning New Haven with better than 60 percent of the vote, and — like Morrison in his close 1984 election — winning both West Haven and Hamden, the two largest cities in the district outside New Haven.

The district's best-known institution is Yale University, in New Haven. Yale and City Hall have not always enjoyed a model town-gown relationship — there have been disputes over how the city should be compensated for the university's tax-exempt landholdings. But in recent years, Yale has helped the city promote and finance downtown redevelopment projects aimed at keeping shopping and entertainment from fleeing to the suburbs.

Population: 518,677. White 452,956 (87%), Black 53,767 (10%), Other 4,005 (1%). Spanish origin 15,171 (3%). 18 and over 387,740 (75%), 65 and over 64,393 (12%). Median age: 32.

a doubling of the number of public housing units called for. He said that would merely restore earlier levels of funding. Texas Republican Steve Bartlett proposed keeping the number of housing units at the existing level, a move Morrison said was "making a fetish out of a freeze." But Bartlett won, 213-204.

Morrison has been effective at inserting amendments into housing bills that will benefit his district, such as one allowing federal housing funds to be used for rehabilitating existing two- and three-family homes, a boost for the older, multifamily housing stock in New Haven. Early in 1989, HUD approved a request pushed by Morrison to demolish and replace 366 subsidized units at a New Haven high-rise housing project.

In 1988, Morrison teamed with New York Rep. Charles E. Schumer and other liberals critical of certain long-term World Bank loans to developing countries. The Democrats said the loans were not tied to specific development projects, but instead were being used merely to repay loans to U.S. and foreign banks.

When a World Bank funding bill came up in subcommittee, Morrison offered an amendment demanding evidence of demonstrable improvement in the economies and debt burdens of 17 highly indebted countries. After the panel rejected the amendment, Schumer and Morrison opposed sending the bill to the full committee.

On Judiciary, Morrison devoted much energy to fending off Reagan administration assaults on the Legal Services Corporation (LSC), which provides legal help to the poor. He fought proposals to place greater restrictions on LSC lawyers and to give the agency's national board more authority over local LSC offices.

Morrison also has used his Judiciary post to help citizens taking on the Social Security bureaucracy. He has pressured bureaucrats to be more cautious about removing people from the disability rolls, and he has advocated that the government award attorneys' fees to individuals who prevail in administrative hearings on Social Security cases.

At Home: In 1982, Morrison was an idealistic political novice and director of the New Haven office of the Legal Services Corporation; he decided to run for Congress when Reagan proposed abolishing the program. Establishment Democrats reacted with considerable skepticism, but Morrison methodically assembled an energetic grass-roots operation, upset the party favorite in the primary and defeated freshman GOP Rep. Lawrence J. DeNardis. He won an expensive and bitter rematch with DeNardis in 1984, and since then, dispirited Republicans have not posed a serious threat.

The 3rd had been Democratic for more than two decades before 1980, when DeNardis captured it. Though his moderate record seemed likely to spare him from the 1982 anti-Republican tide, New Haven's Democratic Party did not want to miss an opportunity by allowing the nomination to go to a maverick like Morrison. Instead, they backed Stephen Wareck, president of the city's Board of Aldermen.

But Morrison put together a devoted organization of social service workers, community activists and union members. Their enthusiasm stood in marked contrast to the blasé confidence of Wareck's forces. At the district convention, Morrison won enough votes to force a primary. In that contest, Morrison, aided by blacks, Hispanics and organized labor, beat Wareck by 10 percentage points.

Against DeNardis, Morrison played on widespread fear of proposed reductions in Social Security. He also strove for dramatic gestures. In one radio advertisement, a constant "drip, drip, drip" accompanied an announcer intoning that Herbert Hoover had created "trickle-down" economics, Ronald Reagan had continued it and Morrison knew what to do with it. Then came the sound of a toilet flushing.

Though DeNardis was not a Reagan yes-man, he underestimated Morrison and did not aggressively sell himself as an independent voice for the district. The city of New Haven gave Morrison a 14,500-vote advantage, a deficit DeNardis could have overcome with a strong vote from the GOP suburbs. But he lacked his 1980 level of support there.

In the 1984 rematch, DeNardis told voters their choice was his moderation or Morrison's liberal extremism. But the Democrat was well prepared. He had maintained his liberal network and also worked to impress businessmen that he could address their concerns. He also became a master fund-raiser, using a $900,000 treasury to portray himself as a protector of the elderly and poor, and sponsor of measures to rehabilitate housing and prevent beach erosion.

Polls showed Morrison with a 15-point lead, and he was endorsed by the *New Haven Register,* not normally a supporter of liberals. Reagan's coattails helped DeNardis close the gap, but Morrison's huge lead in New Haven overcame DeNardis' advantage in the outlying areas.

Committees

Banking, Finance and Urban Affairs (14th of 31 Democrats)
Housing and Community Development; International Development, Finance, Trade and Monetary Policy; Policy Research and Insurance

District of Columbia (7th of 8 Democrats)

Judiciary (13th of 21 Democrats)
Immigration, Refugees and International Law (chairman); Administrative Law and Governmental Relations

Veterans' Affairs (17th of 21 Democrats)
Hospital and Health Care

Elections

1988 General		
Bruce A. Morrison (D)	147,394	(66%)
Gerard B. Patton (R)	74,275	(34%)
1986 General		
Bruce A. Morrison (D)	114,276	(70%)
Ernest J. Diette Jr. (R)	49,806	(30%)

Previous Winning Percentages: 1984 (53%) **1982** (50%)

District Vote For President

	1988	1984	1980	1976
D	117,432 (49%)	101,877 (41%)	91,123 (39%)	106,441 (46%)
R	119,329 (50%)	146,171 (59%)	118,469 (50%)	122,995 (53%)
I			23,400 (10%)	

Campaign Finance

	Receipts	Receipts from PACs	Expend-itures
1988			
Morrison (D)	$490,274	$224,533 (46%)	$506,799
Patton (R)	$117,237	$4,005 (3%)	$116,117
1986			
Morrison (D)	$598,976	$230,745 (39%)	$567,868
Diette (R)	$14,385	$650 (5%)	$14,307

Key Votes

1987	
Raise speed limit to 65 mph	N
Approve Gephardt "fair trade" amendment	Y
Ban testing of larger nuclear weapons	Y
Delay "re-flagging" of Kuwaiti tankers	Y
Approve tax-raising deficit-reduction bill	Y
1988	
Approve aid to Nicaraguan contras	N
Enact civil rights restoration bill over Reagan veto	Y
Kill 60-day plant-closing notification measure	N
Pass omnibus trade bill over Reagan veto	Y
Approve death penalty for drug-related murders	N
Bar federal funds for abortions in cases of rape and incest	N
Oppose seven-day waiting period for purchase of handguns	N

Voting Studies

	Presidential Support		Party Unity		Conservative Coalition	
Year	**S**	**O**	**S**	**O**	**S**	**O**
1988	20	77	92	5	13	87
1987	15	78	89	5	9	86
1986	16	68	81	4	8	68
1985	28	70	89	4	9	87
1984	25	66	85	8	5	93
1983	16	83	88	4	8	88

Interest Group Ratings

Year	ADA	ACU	AFL-CIO	CCUS
1988	100	4	100	43
1987	92	0	100	7
1986	80	0	93	27
1985	90	5	100	24
1984	90	4	77	40
1983	90	0	94	21

4 Christopher Shays (R)

Of Stamford — Elected 1987

Born: Oct. 18, 1945, Stamford, Conn.
Education: Principia College, B.A. 1968; New York U., M.B.A. 1974, M.P.A. 1978.
Occupation: Real-estate broker.
Family: Wife, Betsi de Raismes; one child.
Religion: Protestant.
Political Career: Conn. House, 1975-87; Republican candidate for mayor of Stamford, 1983.
Capitol Office: 1531 Longworth Bldg. 20515; 225-5541.

In Washington: During his years in state politics, Shays honed an image as a maverick whose liberal views on many issues put him at odds with the state Republican hierarchy. But after he won the 4th District seat in a 1987 special election, Shays was informed by the House GOP leadership that there is such a thing as too much independence.

Shays arrived in town with unusual brio. He said he informed President Reagan at the White House that he could not count on Shays' vote 100 percent of the time.

His next move was the real jaw-dropper: He declined an appointment, made by the House Republican leadership, to the Merchant Marine and Fisheries Committee. Shays told House Minority Leader Robert H. Michel that his district would be better served if he was appointed to Banking, Finance and Urban Affairs (on which his late predecessor, Republican Stewart B. McKinney, had served) and Public Works and Transportation.

The result was that Shays sat without any committee at all for more than two months. When Michel finally handed down Shays' assignments, they were to Government Operations and Science.

Shays took those seats and promoted his district's interests as best he could. With the deaths of 28 Bridgeport construction workers in a building collapse still fresh on members' minds, Shays participated in Government Operations hearings on federal safety regulation of the construction industry. And while he did not get on Public Works, he lobbied for funding of mass-transit projects for his district.

In addition, he busied himself by joining a number of House coalitions. Shays signed up with a task force, headed by Iowa Republican Tom Tauke and Minnesota Democrat Timothy J. Penny, designed to find solutions to the budget morass. But he also joined groups, such as the Congressional Black Caucus, more commonly identified with liberal activism.

In his overall voting behavior, Shays was good to the word he gave Reagan. He voted against the president's position on House legislation more than 60 percent of the time.

At Home: In the 1987 election to succeed McKinney — who died that year during his ninth term — Shays' personable style helped him overcome obstacles on his left and right. Campaigning from the center, Shays was positioned for success in the 4th, long a bastion of moderate Republicanism. As a result, he was virtually unopposed when he sought his first full term in 1988.

Shays stepped up to the House from the state Legislature, where he had a reputation much like that of the state's then-most prominent moderate-to-liberal Republicans. Like McKinney, Shays was an advocate of low-income housing; like former GOP Sen. Lowell P. Weicker Jr., he was known as a stubbornly principled maverick.

In 1985, after criticizing what he said were lax ethical standards in Connecticut's judicial system, Shays attempted to make a courtroom statement criticizing a judge for reducing charges against a lawyer who was accused of tampering with a will. Shays was slapped with a contempt citation and a short jail sentence, but he received plenty of favorable publicity.

Though that episode helped Shays expand his cadre of loyalists, it made many local Republicans wary. At the GOP nominating convention for the special election, Shays initially was denied a line on the ballot, while two conservative businessmen made it. It took a last-minute "fair play" decision by party officials to qualify Shays and a fourth candidate. Nonetheless, with his extensive grass-roots network and tireless personal campaigning, Shays won the primary with a solid 38 percent plurality.

In the general election, Shays' gifts as a campaigner served him well against Democrat Christine M. Niedermeier, who was widely known because she had run a strong 1986 campaign against McKinney. Shays tirelessly sought out voters at supermarkets, train stations and in movie theater queues, and his warm style contrasted favorably with that of Niedermeier. Shays won handily, nearly reaching 60 percent.

Connecticut 4

Southwest — Stamford; Bridgeport

Home to some of the wealthiest communities in the nation, the 4th is the best Republican territory in Connecticut. Towns such as Darien, Westport and New Canaan are symbols of upper-class New York City suburbia. Fairfield County is blanketed by newspapers and broadcasts that report the news of New York, not Connecticut.

Stamford, the largest of the suburban cities, has undergone a great change of character: What once was a small-business center whose outlying areas were dotted with country estates of the wealthy has become a haven for corporate headquarters, many of them fleeing New York's high tax rates. With Pitney-Bowes, GTE, Xerox and numerous others, Stamford by the mid-1980s had become one of the country's largest centers of corporate offices. Demand for more office space has put development pressure on places as far north as Fairfield, prompting distressed residents to organize to fight "commercial creep." Many of those suburbanites settled in the area 20 to 30 years ago.

Moderate Republicanism holds sway in the 4th. George Bush grew up in this area, and the 4th gave him 57 percent of the vote in 1988. This district was slow to embrace Ronald Reagan, though it voted for him over Jimmy Carter. Republican Sen. Lowell P. Weicker Jr.'s ideology was a good match for the 4th. Even in his unsuccessful 1988 re-election bid, it gave him 54 percent, his highest districtwide margin in the state.

Despite the area's reputation as an enclave of white-collar Republican wealth, there are several dependably Democratic areas, including Bridgeport and some working-class areas of Stamford and Norwalk. In the 1988 Senate election, Democrat Joseph I. Lieberman's 7,200-vote margin in Bridgeport was by far his best showing in the 4th. Bridgeport is a workaday industrial city that is very much a part of Connecticut, quite apart from the more chic 4th District suburb-cities farther south, which are part of New York City's cultural orbit.

Now the largest city in Connecticut with 142,000 residents, Bridgeport actually lost 9 percent of its population between 1970 and 1980, but it surpassed Hartford in population because the decline in Hartford was far greater. Since 1980, population in both cities has been relatively stable.

Population: 518,577. White 437,190 (84%), Black 58,253 (11%), Other 4,793 (1%). Spanish origin 39,979 (8%). 18 and over 384,352 (74%), 65 and over 63,553 (12%). Median age: 34.

Committees

Government Operations (8th of 15 Republicans)
Employment and Housing; Legislation and National Security

Science, Space and Technology (16th of 19 Republicans)
Natural Resources, Agriculture Research and Environment; Transportation, Aviation and Materials

Select Narcotics Abuse and Control (10th of 12 Republicans)

Elections

1988 General		
Christopher Shays (R)	147,843	(72%)
Roger Pearson (D)	55,751	(27%)
1987 Special Election		
Christopher Shays (R)	50,518	(57%)
Christine M. Niedermeier (D)	37,293	(42%)
1987 Special Primary		
Christopher Shays (R)	11,142	(38%)
John T. Becker (R)	7,740	(27%)
Frank D. Rich Jr. (R)	7,185	(25%)
John G. Metsopoulos (R)	2,876	(10%)

District Vote For President

	1988		1984		1980		1976	
D	96,177	(42%)	88,941	(36%)	82,004	(35%)	98,250	(41%)
R	128,702	(57%)	154,515	(63%)	124,209	(54%)	139,270	(58%)
I					23,186	(10%)		

Interest Group Ratings

Year	ADA	ACU	AFL-CIO	CCUS
1988	90	24	64	57
1987	89	67	78	40

Key Votes

1987	
Approve tax-raising deficit-reduction bill	N
1988	
Approve aid to Nicaraguan contras	N
Enact civil rights restoration bill over Reagan veto	Y
Kill 60-day plant-closing notification measure	Y
Pass omnibus trade bill over Reagan veto	N
Approve death penalty for drug-related murders	N
Bar federal funds for abortions in cases of rape and incest	N
Oppose seven-day waiting period for purchase of handguns	N

Campaign Finance

	Receipts	Receipts from PACs	Expend-itures
1988			
Shays (R)	$698,441	$151,617 (22%)	$675,079
Pearson (D)	$35,655	0	$46,147
1987 Special Election †			
Shays (R)	$118,504	$13,100 (11%)	$79,404
Niedermeier (D)	$545,044	$163,294 (30%)	$551,033

† Totals based on pre-election data only.

Voting Studies

	Presidential Support		Party Unity		Conservative Coalition	
Year	S	O	S	O	S	O
1988	42	58	59	41	61	39
1987	32 †	68 †	53 †	47 †	25 †	75 †

† Not eligible for all recorded votes.

5 John G. Rowland (R)

Of Waterbury — Elected 1984

Born: May 24, 1957, Waterbury, Conn.
Education: Villanova U., B.S. 1979.
Occupation: Insurance agent.
Family: Wife, Deborah J. Nabhan; three children.
Religion: Roman Catholic.
Political Career: Conn. House, 1981-85.
Capitol Office: 329 Cannon Bldg. 20515; 225-3822.

In Washington: Rowland took a seat on Armed Services at the beginning of the 100th Congress, and he quickly established himself as one of the panel's key young members. He is not as conservative as the junior GOP firebrands on the panel, but he shares some of their desire that the GOP adopt a more aggressive posture toward the committee's Democratic leadership.

Rowland's center-right positioning and popular personality should give him an influential future on Armed Services, unless frustration with the House GOP's seemingly permanent minority status encourages him to make a bid for statewide office. Whatever he decides, he could have a long tenure in politics. At the beginning of his third term in 1989, Rowland was still shy of age 32; he has been Congress' youngest member since arriving in 1985.

Despite its sizable maritime industry and its numerous high-technology companies, Connecticut had not had a member on Armed Services since Democratic Rep. Donald J. Irvin left in 1968. Rowland ended that drought in 1987.

Rowland is more conservative than most of the Republicans that Connecticut and New England have sent to Washington in recent years, but on defense matters he is more moderate than the bulk of his party. This has given him opportunities closed to more ideological colleagues: In 1987 he almost saved face for the Reagan administration's strategic defense initiative (SDI) by proposing a $50 million nick from the $3.6 billion in the pending defense authorization bill, to forestall more serious cuts. Rowland won the votes of 50 Democrats, but he lost 207-213.

In 1988 Rowland thought he had a chance to put arms control advocates in a bind by proposing cancellation of funding for the small, single-warhead Midgetman missile favored by many Democrats, including Armed Services Chairman Les Aspin of Wisconsin. Arms controllers were loath to vote against an amendment that purported to quash a nuclear weapon, but they held their noses and did so because they hated the alternative — the multi-warhead MX missile — even more; Rowland's amendment lost by a 3-to-1 vote.

Rowland's hopes of seducing Democratic votes in the future may have been set back by his attempt to score a publicity coup for his party in the midst of the 1988 presidential contest. As the campaign debate alighted on the issue of Massachusetts Gov. Michael S. Dukakis' vetoing a bill requiring teachers to say the Pledge of Allegiance, Rowland unexpectedly moved to require the House to begin each day with the pledge. The maneuver infuriated the Democratic leadership and was turned aside on a basically party-line vote. But soon afterward, the House took up the practice of saying the pledge at the outset of each day's business.

Rowland is notable more for his witty irreverence than for any ideological preconceptions. Whichever way he plans to vote on a key issue, he usually can be counted on to enliven the debate with a sharp one-liner.

Asked whether intense White House lobbying on a 1985 MX missile vote would influence him, Rowland said, "As soon as the vote is over on Tuesday, they'll be returning my daughter unhurt." When President Reagan called to seek his support for contra aid in March 1986, Rowland said, "I told him right off that I planned to vote no. So I spent 35 minutes trying to get off the phone."

Over the long haul, though, Rowland supports the GOP position more often than not. Three months after opposing Reagan's Nicaragua policy, he supported aid for the contras. As a freshman, Rowland almost always agreed with Reagan on key matters, even on the defense issues that make Northeastern Republicans queasy, such as the MX, chemical weapons and SDI.

But Rowland was among the first members to call for the resignation of Attorney General Edwin Meese III, and he irritated the Pentagon by releasing reports of sightings of Americans still missing in Vietnam. He was one of only a handful of Republicans to cosponsor Rep. Claude Pepper's bill to raise Medicare taxes to pay for long-term care for the elderly and disabled — allying the youngest member of

Connecticut 5

West — Waterbury; Danbury

The rival industrial towns that cast most of the vote here tend to view each other with great wariness. It is said that when a federal grant goes to the Naugatuck Valley, Waterbury residents view the money as foreign aid.

Waterbury, at the northern end, is an old brass-making city where the once-powerful Democratic machine has been crumbling; Waterbury has had a GOP mayor since 1985, and Rowland carried it with 57 percent in 1988. The Naugatuck Valley, below Waterbury, has numerous small factories and conservative-minded working-class voters who are Democratic by registration but often not by practice. The other ingredient in the political mix is the GOP suburban area in New York City's orbit, such as Wilton, Weston and Ridgefield.

Not so very long ago, the 5th was a Democratic stronghold: In 1960, thousands of Waterburians waited long into the night for the arrival of John F. Kennedy, who concluded his campaign there with an election-eve rally. But the zeal of the Democratic faithful has slipped steadily. Hubert H. Humphrey was the last Democratic nominee to carry the 5th, and in 1984, there was another huge presidential campaign rally in Waterbury — for Ronald Reagan.

Blue-collar Democrats continued to defect en masse in 1988 and the southern suburbs delivered their typically huge GOP margins. The 5th was George Bush's best Connecticut district, though GOP Sen. Lowell P. Weicker Jr. barely carried the district in his unsuccessful 1988 re-election bid.

Though Waterbury's population has shrunk a bit over the last 15 years as some factories folded or moved, it remains the district's largest city, with just over 100,000 residents. Nearby Meriden, where business pursuits range from silverware to auto parts, remains more loyally Democratic than Waterbury. The 5th's up-and-coming city is Danbury, where growth has been fueled by the arrival of corporate headquarters and sophisticated industries seeking proximity to New York City. Union Carbide and Boehringer Ingelheim (a pharmaceuticals company) are major employers.

Population: 518,700. White 484,920 (94%), Black 21,582 (4%), Other 3,400 (1%). Spanish origin 17,244 (3%). 18 and over 372,002 (72%), 65 and over 57,224 (11%). Median age: 32.

the 100th Congress with its oldest.

At Home: Many of the issues that Rowland champions in Washington seem carefully chosen to strengthen his hand among blue-collar voters in his Waterbury-based district. Thanks to his success in winning over that traditionally Democratic bloc, Rowland has secured a district that he snatched from Democratic Rep. William R. Ratchford in Ronald Reagan's 1984 sweep.

But some of Rowland's efforts — such as his pushing of the pledge issue in 1988 — have rubbed partisan liberals the wrong way. In 1988, *The New York Times* so objected to what it called Rowland's "grandstanding" that it endorsed his long-shot Democratic opponent, Meriden City Councilman Joseph Marinan Jr. Rowland was the only Connecticut incumbent not endorsed by the Times, but few of his constituents took their voting cue from the paper: Rowland won re-election with 74 percent of the vote.

One thing is clear about Rowland: He carefully calculates the political impact of his moves. When he was in the Connecticut House, he occasionally was lectured by some Republicans for being insufficiently ideological. "Unless you can vote three times," he told them, "I need Democrats and independents to win."

Rowland campaigns as easily in bowling alleys as in board rooms, an essential versatility in the 5th, where registered Republicans are outnumbered. Rowland developed his approach in his native blue-collar Waterbury. In 1980, at age 23, he defeated a four-term Democratic state representative. In 1982, he beat back a concerted Democratic effort to unseat him.

Campaigning for Congress in 1984 against Ratchford, Rowland capitalized on the fact that many working-class voters had come to associate the Democratic Party with excessive taxation and spending, a weak defense and assaults on "traditional values." Rowland talked about his opposition to tax increases and welfare fraud. His slogan — "Fighting for the Future of Connecticut's Families" — highlighted his opposition to abortion. His family-man image was enhanced when his wife gave birth to a daughter in June; local newspapers obliged with flattering Rowland-and-family photos.

Ratchford, who had nearly lost his seat in the 1980 Reagan landslide, did what incumbents in marginal districts are supposed to do: He raised and spent over $500,000, more than twice Rowland's total, and he went into the trenches with his challenger, claiming Rowland would be a right-winger in Congress.

But the Republican dodged the extremist label, endorsing the Equal Rights Amendment and stressing his support in the Legislature for cleaning up hazardous wastes. Reagan's unexpectedly decisive 2-to-1 margin in the 5th helped Rowland run even in Waterbury and hold down his losses in Meriden and Ratchford's hometown of Danbury. The politically moderate suburbs of Wilton, Weston, Easton, Trumbull and Shelton delivered their normal GOP margins, and the blue-collar Naugatuck Valley went for Rowland.

Ratchford decided against a comeback in 1986, and Rowland found himself without strong opposition. Democrat Jim Cohen, a former director of the Sierra Club Legal Defense Fund, had spent much of the previous decade in Washington, moving to the 5th in 1985. Rowland smirked that his 2-year-old daughter had lived in the district longer than Cohen. He won handily.

Two years later, Rowland's win was so easy that talk of a statewide race was heard on election night.

Committees

Armed Services (14th of 21 Republicans)
Procurement and Military Nuclear Systems; Seapower and Strategic and Critical Materials

Select Intelligence (6th of 7 Republicans)

Veterans' Affairs (9th of 13 Republicans)
Hospitals and Health Care; Housing and Memorial Affairs

Elections

1988 General		
John G. Rowland (R)	163,729	(74%)
Joseph Marinan Jr. (D)	58,612	(26%)
1986 General		
John G. Rowland (R)	98,664	(61%)
Jim Cohen (D)	63,371	(39%)

Previous Winning Percentage: **1984** (54%)

District Vote For President

	1988	1984	1980	1976
D	97,553 (40%)	80,816 (33%)	80,411 (35%)	99,444 (45%)
R	141,664 (58%)	163,371 (67%)	123,976 (53%)	117,767 (54%)
I			25,577 (11%)	

Campaign Finance

	Receipts	Receipts from PACs	Expend-itures
1988			
Rowland (R)	$440,111	$148,135 (34%)	$375,660
Marinan (D)	$55,186	$14,000 (25%)	$54,524
1986			
Rowland (R)	$426,052	$183,299 (43%)	$425,611
Cohen (D)	$344,859	$39,962 (12%)	$344,285

Key Votes

1987	
Raise speed limit to 65 mph	N
Approve Gephardt "fair trade" amendment	N
Ban testing of larger nuclear weapons	Y
Delay "re-flagging" of Kuwaiti tankers	Y
Approve tax-raising deficit-reduction bill	N
1988	
Approve aid to Nicaraguan contras	Y
Enact civil rights restoration bill over Reagan veto	Y
Kill 60-day plant-closing notification measure	Y
Pass omnibus trade bill over Reagan veto	N
Approve death penalty for drug-related murders	Y
Bar federal funds for abortions in cases of rape and incest	Y
Oppose seven-day waiting period for purchase of handguns	N

Voting Studies

	Presidential Support		Party Unity		Conservative Coalition	
Year	**S**	**O**	**S**	**O**	**S**	**O**
1988	54	41	72	25	79	18
1987	57	42	68	29	79	19
1986	61	39	59	40	82	18
1985	71	29	76	21	80	18

Interest Group Ratings

Year	ADA	ACU	AFL-CIO	CCUS
1988	45	60	57	54
1987	28	52	50	73
1986	35	64	79	72
1985	10	76	24	86

6 Nancy L. Johnson (R)

Of New Britain — Elected 1982

Born: Jan. 5, 1935, Chicago, Ill.
Education: Attended U. of Chicago, 1951, 1953; Radcliffe College, B.A. 1957; attended U. of London, 1957-58.
Occupation: Civic leader.
Family: Husband, Theodore Johnson; three children.
Religion: Unitarian.
Political Career: Conn. Senate, 1977-83; Republican candidate for New Britain Common Council, 1975.
Capitol Office: 119 Cannon Bldg. 20515; 225-4476.

In Washington: Johnson endured some frustrations in the committee-assignment process during her first several years in Congress, losing bids to get on Armed Services, Energy and Commerce, and Ways and Means. She took a seat on Budget in the 100th Congress, but it was in the 101st Congress that she truly moved up to the big league, winning a place on Ways and Means.

Johnson likes to speak of compassion blended with conservatism, and she has looked for ways to present that mixture. Her record communicates traditional GOP business concerns and liberal social goals.

"Women have always been perceived as more open and more compassionate," she said when first campaigning for Congress. "I'm not sure a man could run as stridently as I have on economics and not be perceived as hard-hearted."

Moving to a committee with wide-ranging jurisdiction will suit Johnson fine, since her legislative agenda is extensive, including concerns as different as trade and child care.

In Connecticut, trade has become an increasingly sensitive issue as heavy industries have been battered by cheaper goods produced abroad. Johnson has been outspoken on a number of trade initiatives, and some of her concerns were incorporated into trade legislation that passed the House in the 100th Congress.

Johnson is co-chairman of the Congressional Bearing Caucus, which looks out for the interests of the ball- and roller-bearing industry, an important employer in Connecticut. One of Johnson's efforts has been to speed governmental review of petitions brought by domestic industries seeking relief from imports on national security grounds. The bearing industry has sought such protections in recent years.

But Johnson is wary of some measures aimed at U.S. competitors. She was opposed to the Gephardt "fair trade" amendment that was intended to force reductions in certain foreign trade surpluses. She warned that such an amendment would spark a trade war and ultimately hurt Connecticut.

"We can prevent our competitors from abusing American markets and consumers, and stealing jobs, without resorting to inflexible retaliation," she said.

Johnson has received some attention for her efforts to craft a comprehensive package of child-care initiatives. In the 100th Congress, one initiative that earned her praise from business groups and a supportive editorial from *The Washington Post* would have established vouchers to pay for child-care fees; revenue needed for the vouchers was to come from cutting back on child-care tax credits for families making over $60,000 per year. But the plan also had its share of opponents, in part because it allowed the vouchers to pay anyone caring for children, rather than just licensed day-care centers.

Johnson is not a predictable vote on the House floor, and on more than one occasion, her case-by-case decision-making approach has made her the target of some fierce lobbying. In 1985 she was pressed by the Reagan administration and the GOP leadership on the question of the MX missile. She had voted against the missile in 1984, but chief U.S. arms negotiator Max M. Kampelman and Defense Secretary Caspar W. Weinberger were among those urging her to change her mind and support spending $1.5 billion to buy 21 missiles. One member said Johnson "got the hell squeezed out of her," but she remained unconvinced, and voted against the funds. "I can honestly say I never considered switching my vote," she said. The House, however, voted 219-213 to approve the missiles.

In 1987 Johnson voted against a defense authorization amendment banning all nuclear test explosions with a force of more than one kiloton, contingent on Soviet compliance, though in 1986 she went against the Reagan administration in supporting such a proposal. She said her change of heart, which was not enough to defeat the amendment, came because the administration was pursuing test-ban nego-

Connecticut 6

Northwest — New Britain

The 6th is diverse both geographically and politically. It includes the family home of William F. Buckley Jr., but it also produced Ralph Nader.

Extending from quiet villages in the pastoral Litchfield Hills to the Hartford-Springfield, Mass., metropolitan area, the 6th is reliably Republican in presidential contests. But in other elections, it is unpredictable.

The "Nutmeggers" of rural Litchfield County, reflecting generations of small-town Yankee control, provide dependable GOP majorities. But that county also has mill towns, such as Torrington and Winsted, that often deliver Democratic margins.

To the southeast, the industrial city of New Britain, with its large Polish population, has been bedrock Democratic territory; Johnson lost it in 1982, but has carried it in her three re-elections. In 1988, Democratic Senate nominee Joseph I. Lieberman carried New Britain with 60 percent of the vote, on his way to a narrow victory in the 6th. Despite population loss in the 1970s, New Britain is the district's largest city, with 72,000 people, and there are still plenty of big job-providers, notably The Stanley Works hardware company and Torrington Company's ball-bearing division.

Nearby Bristol, the second-largest city, has grown slightly in the last two decades and is catching up to New Britain in political clout; it produces a similar array of mechanical and electrical equipment and — except in Johnson's elections — votes heavily Democratic.

The 6th bumps up against the western side of Hartford, taking in strongly Republican upper-crust suburbs such as Farmington, Avon, Canton and Simsbury; even in the 1986 gubernatorial election — a lopsided Democratic victory — those towns voted Republican. Northeast of that area, the 6th includes Windsor Locks and Enfield, centers of large-scale industry along the Connecticut River. Democrats usually roll up their vote totals among Italian-American workers there. The district's largest employer, United Technologies' Hamilton-Standard aerospace division in Windsor Locks, provides 6,500 jobs.

Population: 517,146. White 501,201 (97%), Black 9,001 (2%), Other 2,539 (1%). Spanish origin 10,538 (2%). 18 and over 378,872 (73%), 65 and over 60,317 (12%). Median age: 32.

tiations with Moscow. "Last year there was no progress being made," she said. "Now there is dramatic progress."

As a member of the '92 Group, a coalition of moderate Republicans, and as a member of the GOP platform committee in 1988, Johnson has tried to pull her party toward the political center. She has been particularly active working with '92 Group Republicans on ways to set budget priorities and reduce the deficit. She was a co-chairman of the group in the 100th Congress.

When the Republican Party was writing its national platform in 1988, Johnson joined with moderate Republican Lowell P. Weicker Jr., then the state's senior senator, in challenging the document fashioned by the conservative majority. But the Connecticutans' efforts, including a push to restore GOP support for the Equal Rights Amendment, were mostly unsuccessful.

At Home: Johnson was a rarity in 1982, a victorious Republican in an open district dominated by blue-collar Democrats. For her, that sort of victory was nothing new. In 1977 she became the first Republican in 30 years to represent the industrial city of New Britain in the state Senate, and she was re-elected easily.

Johnson's casual style gives her an appeal across class and party lines. "She can belly up to the toughest bar in town and captivate the customers," a local political reporter once wrote, "just as effectively as she can balance the teacups with totally proper ladies at any church social." That is just the right combination for the 6th, which encompasses lunch-bucket bastions such as New Britain and Bristol, and the Yankee towns of Litchfield County.

Johnson, the wife of an obstetrician, was a longtime activist in New Britain community affairs. When the Republican town chairman asked her in 1976 to run for the state Senate, she agreed, and went on to defeat Democrat Paul S. Amenta by 150 votes.

When Democratic Rep. Toby Moffett announced at the end of 1981 that he was giving up the 6th to challenge incumbent Weicker for the Senate, Johnson moved eagerly to take his place. She quickly captured the backing of the party establishment and influential GOP donors, opening an early lead over her primary opponent, conservative Nicholas Schaus.

Johnson's Democratic opponent in the general election was a colleague from the state Senate, William E. Curry Jr. A liberal in the Moffett tradition, Curry had won a hard-fought primary battle by putting together an impressive grass-roots organization with the support of labor, environmentalists and consumer groups. But he was badly short of funds.

Most of Curry's campaigning was in New Britain, which he managed to carry by 3,000 votes. That effort cost him elsewhere, however; he won the district's other Democratic communities by much smaller margins than Moffett had.

Instead of squabbling over the nomination as they did in 1982, Democrats in 1984 agreed on insurance executive Art House, a candidate knowledgeable in the workings of Washington by virtue of his five years' service as a top aide to former Democratic Sen. Abraham Ribicoff. House accused Johnson of being a wishy-washy politician trying to give something to everyone, but her moderate pitch limited his options for specific attacks. She called Reagan's re-election "crucial," but complained about the administration's defense-spending levels, its cutbacks in education programs and its progress on arms control. House took only 36 percent of the vote.

In 1986, Johnson faced a name from her political past: Amenta, whom she had narrowly beaten in her first state Senate race. This time, Johnson won easily. Two years later, Democrats put scant effort into the 6th, and Johnson won by her biggest margin yet.

Committee

Ways and Means (13th of 13 Republicans)
Health; Human Resources

Elections

1988 General

Nancy L. Johnson (R)	157,020	(66%)
James L. Griffin (D)	78,814	(33%)

1986 General

Nancy L. Johnson (R)	111,304	(64%)
Paul S. Amenta (D)	62,133	(36%)

Previous Winning Percentages: **1984** (64%) **1982** (52%)

District Vote For President

	1988	1984	1980	1976
D	115,742 (46%)	91,920 (37%)	92,955 (39%)	111,077 (48%)
R	133,709 (53%)	155,843 (63%)	113,203 (47%)	120,338 (52%)
I			32,748 (14%)	

Campaign Finance

	Receipts	Receipts from PACs	Expend-itures
1988			
Johnson (R)	$527,164	$135,322 (26%)	$399,370
Griffin (D)	$128,185	$30,175 (24%)	$128,853
1986			
Johnson (R)	$428,767	$135,074 (32%)	$425,553
Amenta (D)	$50,761	$730 (1%)	$41,840

Key Votes

1987	
Raise speed limit to 65 mph	Y
Approve Gephardt "fair trade" amendment	N
Ban testing of larger nuclear weapons	N
Delay "re-flagging" of Kuwaiti tankers	N
Approve tax-raising deficit-reduction bill	N
1988	
Approve aid to Nicaraguan contras	Y
Enact civil rights restoration bill over Reagan veto	Y
Kill 60-day plant-closing notification measure	N
Pass omnibus trade bill over Reagan veto	Y
Approve death penalty for drug-related murders	Y
Bar federal funds for abortions in cases of rape and incest	N
Oppose seven-day waiting period for purchase of handguns	Y

Voting Studies

	Presidential Support		Party Unity		Conservative Coalition	
Year	S	O	S	O	S	O
1988	44	50	52	44	68	24
1987	47	52	53	42	65	28
1986	52	43	38	58	68	32
1985	50	50	45	51	67	33
1984	52	44	48	47	51	42
1983	51	46	43	49	54	46

Interest Group Ratings

Year	ADA	ACU	AFL-CIO	CCUS
1988	50	56	71	69
1987	48	35	50	73
1986	40	55	79	72
1985	40	48	47	64
1984	50	29	38	56
1983	45	26	44	50

Delaware

U.S. CONGRESS

SENATE 1 D, 1 R
HOUSE 1 D

LEGISLATURE

Senate 13 D, 8 R
House 18 D, 23 R

ELECTIONS

1988 Presidential Vote

Bush	56%
Dukakis	44%

1984 Presidential Vote

Reagan	60%
Mondale	40%

1980 Presidential Vote

Reagan	47%
Carter	45%
Anderson	7%

Turnout rate in 1984	56%
Turnout rate in 1986	34%
Turnout rate in 1988	51%

(as percentage of voting age population)

POPULATION AND GROWTH

1980 population	594,338
1988 population estimate (47th in the nation)	660,000
Percent change 1980-1988	+11%

DEMOGRAPHIC BREAKDOWN

White	82%
Black	16%
Other	1%
(Spanish origin)	2%
Urban	71%
Rural	29%
Born in state	52%
Foreign-born	3%

MAJOR CITIES

Wilmington	69,690
Newark	24,180
Dover	22,660
Elsmere	6,330
Milford	5,680

AREA AND LAND USE

Area 1,933 sq. miles (49th)

Farm	53%
Forest	33%
Federally owned	2%

Gov. Michael N. Castle (R)
Of Dover — Elected 1984

Born: July 2, 1939, Wilmington, Del.
Education: Hamilton College, B.A. 1961; Georgetown U., LL.B. 1964.
Occupation: Lawyer.
Religion: Roman Catholic.
Political Career: Del. deputy attorney general, 1965-66; Del. House, 1967-69; Del. Senate, 1969-77, minority leader, 1976-77; lieutenant governor, 1981-85.
Next Election: 1992.

WORK

Occupations

White-collar	55%
Blue-collar	29%
Service workers	13%

Government Workers

Federal	5,323
State	21,553
Local	17,806

MONEY

Median family income	$ 20,817	(17th)
Tax burden per capita	$ 1,312	(3rd)

EDUCATION

Spending per pupil through grade 12	$ 4,610	(7th)
Persons with college degrees	18%	(17th)

CRIME

Violent crime rate	431 per 100,000 (24th)

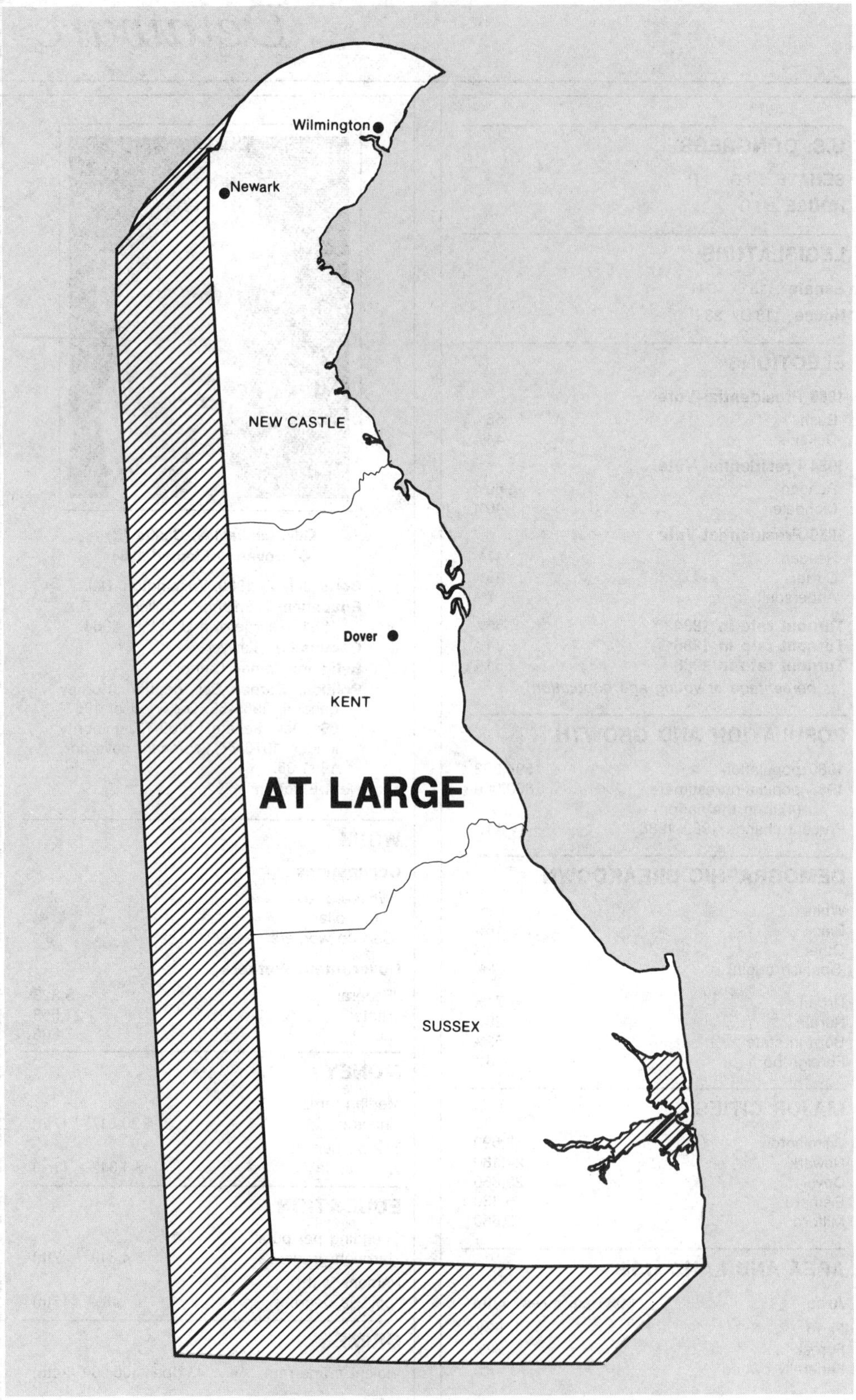
Wilmington
Newark
NEW CASTLE
Dover
KENT
AT LARGE
SUSSEX

William V. Roth Jr. (R)

Of Wilmington — Elected 1970

Born: July 22, 1921, Great Falls, Mont.
Education: U. of Oregon, B.A. 1944; Harvard U., M.B.A. 1947, LL.B. 1949.
Military Career: Army, 1943-46.
Occupation: Lawyer.
Family: Wife, Jane Richards; two children.
Religion: Episcopalian.
Political Career: U.S. House, 1967-71; Republican nominee for Del. lieutenant governor, 1960.
Capitol Office: 104 Hart Bldg. 20510; 224-2441.

In Washington: Roth is a legislator who likes grand ideas — massive tax cuts, huge new savings plans, sweeping revisions of government agencies. He has devoted most of his Senate career to promoting one such idea after another, with one notable success and a string of less-publicized failures. When he is not drumming up support for one of his schemes, he sometimes has trouble making an impact; he is not a senator with an intense interest in the day-to-day chores of legislative life.

Roth did have a season in the national spotlight as an original co-author of President Reagan's 1981 tax cut. He had to settle for second billing, however. While he calls the legislation he sponsored "Roth-Kemp," virtually everyone else in America, at least outside his Senate office, refers to the income-tax cut — 25 percent across the board over three years — as "Kemp-Roth," after the younger and more dynamic co-author, Jack F. Kemp, the Housing and Urban Development secretary and former GOP House member from New York.

Roth has had less success with an idea he has pressed for since 1981, the biennial budget — although its time may be coming. Roth was never able to move budget legislation while he chaired the Governmental Affairs Committee from 1981 through 1987. With the Democrats back in control of the Senate for the 100th Congress, biennial budget legislation that Roth sponsored with Kentucky Democrat Wendell H. Ford passed Governmental Affairs by a 13-0 vote.

The biennial budget idea, now supported by President Bush as well, gained impetus from the budget summit held in late 1987. The Congress budgets on an annual basis, but the summit charted spending for a two-year cycle. The summit was widely credited with speeding up the appropriations process.

Roth has found himself in a defensive legislative posture in the late 1980s — working to preserve the tax exemption for state and local bonds, to protect Individual Retirement Accounts (IRAs) and to guard Delaware's franchise as a haven for corporate charters as the Congress examines the corporate takeover game.

When the Senate Finance Committee was gearing up in 1986 to produce a bill overhauling the federal tax code, Roth liked the Reagan administration's idea that taxes on individuals and corporations should be reduced. But he was concerned that the revenue lost be recouped, and in a way that would preserve incentives for savings and investment. He proposed a "business transfer tax," a kind of value-added tax on gross business receipts, that would have raised somewhere between $70 billion and $115 billion over five years.

Roth wanted to use that revenue to finance lower tax rates and a more generous business depreciation schedule than even Reagan had proposed, and to pay for letting taxpayers establish tax-sheltered "Super Saver Accounts" with none of the withdrawal restrictions that characterize IRAs. The importance of personal savings has been a recurring theme throughout Roth's congressional career.

But the idea was a non-starter. A major new tax lacked appeal, and critics complained that businesses would simply pass the tax along to consumers, hitting low-income people hardest. Roth's idea was not a factor in Finance Committee deliberations.

In fact, after Finance Chairman Bob Packwood pushed a streamlined tax-overhaul bill through his committee in May 1986, Roth had his hands full just trying to save the deductibility of IRA contributions. "I am concerned that we are not doing more to promote savings," Roth said. "We should not be backing off IRAs."

When the tax bill was being considered by the full Senate, Roth attempted to marshal support for several revenue-gaining proposals that would offset the cost of allowing either a tax deduction or a tax credit for IRA contributions. But the Senate heeded Packwood's pleas to keep his committee's bill basically intact, so Roth was reduced to lobbying for passage of a "sense of the Senate" resolution that instructed the chamber's conferees to assign "highest priority to maintaining maximum possible tax benefits for IRAs."

But in the House-Senate conference on the tax bill, neither the resolution nor Roth's pleas carried great weight. Some low- and middle-income taxpayers were allowed to continue deducting IRA contributions, but higher-income individuals and employees with pension plans were not.

As Governmental Affairs chairman, Roth concentrated on instituting a new retirement system for federal employees, looking at new ways to organize federal agencies and reforming federal procurement procedures.

After three years of work in committee and six months of conference negotiations, Congress in 1986 finally approved a new retirement system for all federal employees hired since Jan. 1, 1984. (A separate system covers those hired earlier.) The battle was protracted because the administration was bent on reducing the cost burden of federal retirement benefits, while congressional defenders of federal employees resisted changes that would take money away from workers.

The compromise that was reached tilted to the workers' advantage — it cut the government's costs by 2 percent, whereas the administration had sought a 5 percent cut. But after flirting briefly with a veto threat, Reagan went along. The new system contained one feature with the clear stamp of Roth — an optional tax-deferred savings plan that allowed workers to contribute up to 10 percent of their before-tax salary to a fund, to be matched by a federal contribution of up to 5 percent.

Roth was ultimately unsuccessful in one of his major reorganization efforts at Governmental Affairs — overhauling the structure of the Office of Management and Budget (OMB). Saying, "We're not satisfied with the 'M' " in OMB, Roth in 1986 won unanimous committee approval of a bill creating new positions and lines of authority at OMB with an eye to improving federal accounting, procurement and internal control systems.

But the unanimity of the committee's vote reflected more a consensus for reform than support for the method chosen by Roth. When OMB Director James C. Miller III objected to the plan, and the agency made some policy adjustments to address specific concerns of a few senators, momentum for Roth's overhaul evaporated.

To no greater effect, Roth has long promoted a Department of International Trade and Industry. He argued that creation of the Cabinet-level agency, composed of the Commerce Department, the Office of the U.S. Trade Representative and other federal agencies concerned with international trade, would help the United States to compete better in world markets.

Roth has also been concerned with protecting American interests at home from foreign eyes. In the 100th Congress, he advocated restrictions on the travel of Soviet diplomats as part of a package of espionage legislation that called for the restoration of the death penalty for certain offenses.

At Home: A mild-mannered man, Roth has never been able to generate a great deal of emotion among Delaware voters. But he has been doggedly attentive to state interests, and he has been rewarded for that service with victories in six statewide elections — two for the House and four for the Senate.

Born in Montana and educated at Harvard, Roth came to Delaware to work as a lawyer for a chemical firm and got involved in politics. After narrowly losing a 1960 bid for lieutenant governor, he became state Republican chairman.

Running for Delaware's at-large U.S. House seat in 1966, Roth entered the race against veteran Democrat Harris B. McDowell Jr. as a decided underdog. He talked about Vietnam — backing U.S. efforts there but berating the Johnson administration for not explaining the situation more fully — and about open-housing legislation, saying he was opposed to it but willing to endorse state GOP convention language in favor of it. Riding the coattails of GOP Sen. J. Caleb Boggs and a national Republican wave that brought 47 GOP freshmen to the House in 1966, Roth pulled off an upset.

McDowell tried for a comeback two years later. But he had alienated members of the state Democratic hierarchy by deploring their "old and tired leadership." Buoyed by his first-term record of strong constituent service, Roth pushed his margin of victory to nearly 60 percent of the statewide vote.

With the retirement of GOP Sen. John J. Williams in 1970, Roth became the uncontested choice of his party against the Democratic state House leader, Jacob W. Zimmerman. A Vietnam dove, Zimmerman had little money or statewide name recognition, and the contest was never much in doubt.

In 1976 Roth had a strong Democratic challenger — Wilmington Mayor Thomas C. Maloney. But Roth's efforts against busing had given him an excellent issue to run on, and Maloney was hurt by the coolness of organized labor. Roth's margin was down from 1970, but he was too strong in the suburbs for Maloney to have any chance to beat him.

Running for a third term in 1982, Roth faced his most difficult Senate test. As cosponsor of the supply-side tax cut, he was a visible target for complaints about the economy — and, like other industrial states, Delaware had felt the effects of recession.

David N. Levinson, Roth's hard-charging

Democratic opponent, encouraged voters to link Roth to Reaganomics and the woes he claimed it had produced. Parodying John Steinbeck's novel about the Great Depression, Levinson branded the administration's economic blueprint "The Grapes of Roth."

The incumbent did not shy away from his legislation; billboards advertising his candidacy read, "Bill Roth, the Taxpayer's Best Friend." But he was careful to offer evidence of his concern for Frost Belt economic needs, voting against 1981 reductions in three programs important to Delaware: Conrail, trade adjustment assistance to unemployed workers and energy subsidies for the poor.

Levinson campaigned for the seat for over two years; he got endorsements from labor and most of the other important groups Democrats need to be competitive statewide. But that was not enough. Roth focused on Levinson's out-of-state background, suggesting the Democrat had come into the state just to challenge him. Though he lost Wilmington, Roth more than made up the difference in suburban New Castle County and in the rural territory south of the Chesapeake and Delaware Canal.

In 1988, Roth was aiming to become the first Delaware senator to win a fourth term since Williams was re-elected in 1964. National Democratic officials called him vulnerable, noting that he had never reached the 60 percent mark that denotes electoral security. In preparation for a tough campaign, Roth amassed a huge treasury.

But Democrats' grandest designs were deflated when Rep. Thomas R. Carper declined to challenge Roth. State party leaders scurried to the side of Samuel S. Beard, a wealthy civic activist and party fund-raiser. But maverick Lt. Gov. S. B. Woo spoiled their plans for a smooth nomination. Woo, whose ties to the far-flung Chinese-American community guaranteed him a healthy campaign budget, defeated Beard by 71 votes in a bitter primary battle.

While Woo and Beard were slicing each other up, Roth was stressing his political assets, running a media campaign emphasizing his record of steering federal money to Delaware and his vaunted dedication to constituent service.

Because of Delaware's September primary date, Woo had little time to prepare for the general election. He never really got out of the starting blocks, and Roth surpassed 60 percent for the first time in his long career.

Committees

Governmental Affairs (Ranking)
Permanent Subcommittee on Investigations (ranking)

Banking, Housing and Urban Affairs (7th of 9 Republicans)
International Finance and Monetary Policy

Finance (3rd of 9 Republicans)
Taxation and Debt Management (ranking); Health for Families and the Uninsured; International Trade

Joint Economic
Economic Goals and Intergovernmental Policy; Economic Growth, Trade and Taxes; International Economic Policy

Elections

1988 General

William V. Roth Jr. (R)	151,115	(62%)
S. B. Woo (D)	92,378	(38%)

Previous Winning Percentages: **1982** (55%) **1976** (56%) **1970** (59%) **1968 *** (59%) **1966 *** (56%)

* *House elections.*

Campaign Finance

	Receipts	Receipts from PACs	Expend-itures
1988			
Roth (R)	$1,887,995	$794,191 (42%)	$1,942,119
Woo (D)	$2,409,188	$91,810 (4%)	$2,385,414

Key Votes

1987

Enact omnibus highway bill over Reagan veto	N
Limit testing of space-based anti-ballistic missiles	N
Oppose banning tests of larger nuclear weapons	Y
Confirm Robert H. Bork as Supreme Court justice	Y

1988

Allow vote on campaign-finance overhaul	N
Pass civil rights restoration bill over Reagan veto	Y
Enact omnibus trade bill over Reagan veto	Y
Approve death penalty for drug-related murders	Y
Oppose "workfare" amendment to welfare overhaul bill	N

Voting Studies

	Presidential Support		Party Unity		Conservative Coalition	
Year	S	O	S	O	S	O
1988	72	27	51	47	70	30
1987	65 †	31 †	76 †	20 †	88 †	13 †
1986	83	16	83	13	80	17
1985	84	16	81	19	72	27
1984	74	18	85	10	83	15
1983	76	22	80	18	70	20
1982	77	20	76	22	83	16
1981	75	24	72	26	75	24

† Not eligible for all recorded votes.

Interest Group Ratings

Year	ADA	ACU	AFL-CIO	CCUS
1988	20	60	43	57
1987	20	80	50	94
1986	15	78	13	82
1985	20	70	14	83
1984	10	73	10	83
1983	30	56	13	50
1982	50	47	27	67
1981	20	67	32	78

Joseph R. Biden Jr. (D)

Of Wilmington — Elected 1972

Born: Nov. 20, 1942, Scranton, Pa.
Education: U. of Delaware, B.A. 1965; Syracuse U., J.D. 1968.
Occupation: Lawyer.
Family: Wife, Jill Jacobs; three children.
Religion: Roman Catholic.
Political Career: New Castle County Council, 1970-72.
Capitol Office: 489 Russell Bldg. 20510; 224-5042.

In Washington: He fell as he had risen, fast and recklessly.

Elected to the Senate in an upset at 29, at 45 Biden joined the 1988 presidential race — only to quit in humiliation less than four months later. In a campaign season focused on candidates' character, he fell under the weight of reports that he had plagiarized passages in his speeches and a 1965 law school paper, and finally, that he had exaggerated his résumé in a nasty riposte with a New Hampshire voter.

"There will be other opportunities for me to campaign for president," Biden said as he withdrew in September 1987. Subsequent events, however, called that assertion into question. Still young, and assured of a long-running Senate leadership role as chairman of the Judiciary Committee, Biden arguably could redeem himself politically for another run at the White House. But surgery in 1988 for a near-fatal brain aneurysm cast a shadow over his fitness for the presidency.

The brushes with death, both actual and political, were an extraordinary turn of events for a man who had always seemed destined for big things. From the time Biden arrived in the Senate, he struck observers as having the intelligence and charisma to be an influential Democrat for decades to come. But he was also something of an *enfant terrible* — a brash, impetuous young man whose mouth frequently outran his better judgment, impatient with the tedious details and sustained labors of legislating. And those traits, once dismissed as youthful excesses, remained with Biden as he became a balding, middle-aged senior senator — and perhaps foretold his devastating presidential bid.

Biden's personal development would not command such attention if he did not have so many of the characteristics expected of a leader. Smart and perceptive, he quickly grasps the essence of complex issues. Charming and conciliatory, he has proven adept at legislative negotiations; a 1984 criminal code revision and a 1986 anti-drug measure became law largely due to his talent for compromise. With impassioned eloquence, he can stir audiences around the country.

His oratory is perhaps both his greatest political asset, and his handicap. Among Senate regulars, it has always struck some as overblown or demagogic, as rhetorical posturing. Even Biden, with the self-deprecation that is part of his charm, pokes fun at his long-windedness. He will occasionally think aloud, weighing options, but under the cover of public soul-searching he sometimes appears to be making a calculated political move.

During Judiciary's 1985 debate over the nomination of Edwin Meese III to be attorney general, Biden joined other Democrats in questioning Meese's financial ties to people for whom he had secured federal jobs. After sitting quietly through a long hearing, Biden startled Meese and the audience with a rambling, highly personal speech in which he said the Reagan aide had committed no ethical lapse, but was somehow "beneath the office." The tone, and Biden's suggestion that he really wanted to support Meese, struck many as unctuous, and as an attempt to assault the nominee's character without appearing partisan.

In 1986, foes of the Reagan administration's South Africa policy applauded Biden's long, televised attack on Secretary of State George P. Shultz during a Foreign Relations Committee hearing, but even some of them were uncomfortable with the stridency. "I'm so ashamed at the lack of moral backbone to this policy," Biden thundered.

Once Biden announced that he was a candidate for president in June 1987, his flaws as well as his talents came under an intense spotlight, given that he was a promising new figure largely unknown outside Washington and Delaware. The denouement only amplified the flaws, and by the end of 1988 — recovering from both his political and physical injuries — Biden indicated he was all too aware of the unflattering portrait reporters had drawn. He was on a new path, he said in an interview as the 101st Congress approached, "to demonstrate the staying power and the seriousness a lot of you doubted that I have."

He already had taken the first step, he said, by his stewardship of the Judiciary hearings that led to the Senate's historic October 1987 rejection of Reagan Supreme Court nominee Robert H. Bork. Ironically, those confirmation proceedings had been previewed as a potential showcase for candidate Biden; his fall transformed them into a means for a comeback.

Initially, Biden's handling of Bork's nomination showed the senator at his worst. He had once said he could accept Bork if Reagan nominated the conservative jurist. When Reagan did, Biden said he probably would oppose Bork. Then he announced he definitely would oppose Bork, but he would explain why later. Southern Democrats, who would be crucial to the outcome, wanted to keep their distance from both him and liberal Judiciary colleague Edward M. Kennedy on the politically charged question. Then the plagiarism stories broke, leaving Biden too crippled, it seemed, to attack Bork credibly.

After he withdrew from the presidential race in the second week of hearings, however, Biden returned to his top form. Ultimately, even Republicans and an embittered Bork would concede that Biden had been fair. He set a tone that was serious and respectful, almost obsequious. He ably grilled Bork about the judge's controversial contention that the Constitution was silent about privacy rights, zeroing in for political effect on Bork's criticism of a 1965 case in which the court had cited privacy rights to strike down a state law making it a crime for married couples to use contraceptives.

The hearings were an extraordinary seminar on constitutional law, with Biden and other Democrats probing for evidence that Bork would vote to overturn precedents on civil rights and abortion. "I wanted [the Bork vote] to be a referendum on the past progress of the Supreme Court, and a referendum on the future," Biden said. "I think the American people agree with my view of what the Supreme Court has done. They like where we are."

To Republicans who complained that Democrats had politicized the Senate's constitutional advice-and-consent role, Biden retorted, "Any politicizing has been driven by President Reagan's single-minded pursuit of a judiciary packed with those who are his ideological allies."

Before Bork, liberals and civil rights advocates had felt Biden was too tentative in opposing Reagan's more controversial nominees for the courts and the Justice Department. They complained especially of his hesitance against William Bradford Reynolds, a nominee for associate attorney general who ultimately was rejected in 1985; and against Supreme Court Justice William H. Rehnquist, who in 1986 succeeded in winning promotion to chief justice. "It is never pleasant to oppose an individual," Biden said in late 1988. "Most of us who hold public office do it because we like people."

Once engaged, however, Biden is a formidable fighter, as he was against Bork, Reynolds and, in 1986, against Reagan's nomination of Daniel A. Manion to be a federal judge. Biden nearly ambushed Manion's nomination by surprising majority Republicans with a sudden call for a floor vote, but GOP Leader Bob Dole rallied and prevailed with a disputed parliamentary play.

Still, when Democrats regained the Senate majority in the 1986 elections, some in the civil rights community urged Kennedy to return to the Judiciary chair rather than leave it to Biden. But Kennedy opted to head the Labor Committee.

Biden had a solid record on Judiciary before he became chairman. A swing vote in the 1970s, he was able to form a close working relationship with Chairman Strom Thurmond of South Carolina when Republicans took control of the Senate in 1981. "My Henry Clay," Thurmond liked to call him, in recognition of Biden's skill at bipartisan compromises. Biden, in turn, still calls Thurmond "Boss."

One of Biden's most significant legislative achievements was his role in the 1984 passage of legislation rewriting federal criminal statutes. The culmination of an 11-year effort, the legislation revised sentencing procedures to reduce the disparity in punishments imposed on persons who committed similar crimes, and allowed pretrial detention of some dangerous suspects. He was Democratic floor manager of the bill, and negotiated a deal with House leaders at the close of the 98th Congress.

Two years later, he was a guiding force behind enactment of tough new legislation against illegal drugs. His most important contribution came when the bill was deadlocked in conference, largely over a provision imposing the death penalty for certain drug crimes. Biden helped arrange the informal negotiations that cleared the way for final passage.

The drug bill's passage illustrated the two sides of Biden. In the final episode, he was the talented 11th-hour mediator, riding in to save the day. But as legislation unfolds in all its mind-numbing details, and slowly makes its way through a balky process, Biden often is hardly a presence. He is not a textbook legislator. With his glib tongue, people skills and penchant for quick action, his strength is at the podium and the conference table.

With one major exception, Biden has been a reliable liberal vote on Judiciary. He broke ranks early and memorably over busing. A former participant in sit-ins to desegregate restaurants along U.S. Route 40, he surprised colleagues in 1975 when he won Senate approval of an anti-busing amendment. Suddenly he was allied with Southern conservatives on a wrenching national issue. "It is not a comfortable feeling for me," he said. But it was time, he argued, to admit that "busing does not work."

He has been consistently liberal on foreign policy issues. As a member of the Foreign Relations Committee — and of the Intelligence Committee until 1985 — Biden has pressed for arms control agreements, opposed military intervention in Central America and insisted that Congress be a full partner with the White House in decisions to send U.S. forces to hostile areas.

Sidelined by his brain surgery from taking a lead role in ratifying the intermediate-range nuclear-force (INF) treaty in 1988, Biden nonetheless helped call the big play. Democrats added a version of his resolution binding presidents to the original interpretation of a treaty. The language was aimed not at the INF pact, but at the 1972 ABM treaty, which Reagan had tried to reinterpret to allow space tests for his proposed strategic defense initiative — "a purposeful act of revisionist distortion," Biden called it.

As chairman of an Intelligence subcommittee, he was responsible for a new law against "graymail." The term referred to defendants' threats in espionage cases to disclose classified information in their own defense, which sometimes forced prosecutors to drop charges rather than jeopardize national security. Biden called it legal blackmail. As enacted, his bill allows judges to screen classified information before a trial.

In the mid-1980s, Biden also served a stint on the Budget Committee, where he joined with Republicans Nancy Landon Kassebaum and Charles E. Grassley to propose a budget freeze. The so-called KGB Plan was rejected by the Senate, although it was something of a model for later deficit-reduction efforts.

For all his promise, Biden nearly abandoned his Senate career before it even started. Just weeks after he was elected in 1972, his wife and infant daughter were killed and his two sons injured in an automobile crash. Biden at first said he did not want to take the oath of office, but Majority Leader Mike Mansfield talked him into assuming his seat. He was sworn in at his son's bedside.

However, his first term was mostly spent rebuilding his family in Wilmington rather than laying the foundation for a Senate career in Washington. "The first two years I didn't know where the hell I was and what I was doing. The second two years I was trying to make up for the stupid things I had done, and the third two years I was trying to get re-elected," he said in 1987. "I view the beginning of my Senate career as the day after my second election" in 1978.

At Home: Biden's celebrated brashness pushed him into a 1972 Senate campaign against Republican incumbent J. Caleb Boggs. With service on the New Castle County Council his only electoral credential, Biden seemed a sure loser.

But he ran hard on a dovish Vietnam platform and accused the Republican of being a do-nothing senator. He called for more spending on mass transit and health care services. The Biden campaign was essentially a family operation, without state-of-the-art media management, but it was sophisticated enough to cover a state with an electorate as small as Delaware's. Boggs awoke to the threat too late as his "safe" seat disappeared by 3,162 votes.

Delaware Democratic leaders, certain that a challenge to Boggs was hopeless, had given Biden little support in 1972. And he gave them little attention for most of his first term. At the 1976 Democratic National Convention in New York City, he stayed in one hotel, and the state delegation in another.

By 1978, however, Biden had made up with the party. Of greater political importance, however, was his opposition to busing. As he ran for re-election, a long-disputed busing plan was taking effect in New Castle County, outraging voters in suburban Wilmington.

With this anti-busing position offsetting his liberalism on some other social issues, Biden seemed unbeatable in 1978, and big-name Delaware Republicans refrained from taking him on. The task fell to an obscure southern Delaware poultry farmer, James H. Baxter, who gamely tried to paint the Democrat as too far left for the state. Biden easily beat him.

For a time, it appeared as though Biden might be seriously threatened in 1984. Republican Gov. Pierre S. "Pete" du Pont IV, ineligible to seek a third consecutive term, was pressured to challenge the incumbent by President Reagan and Senate Majority Leader Howard H. Baker Jr. But du Pont chose not to run.

The Republican who eventually emerged was John M. Burris, a businessman and former Republican leader of the Delaware House. While there, Burris was known as an articulate and faithful field general for du Pont.

Burris spent most of his time trying to brand Biden a fiscal profligate, echoing themes from Baxter's 1978 campaign. Burris chastised the incumbent for voting against the president's proposal for a constitutional amendment to balance the budget, and sought to remind voters of his role in helping to enact a state balanced-budget amendment under du Pont.

Burris succeeded in keeping the focus of the campaign on economic issues; Biden dwelt heavily on his "budget freeze" proposal. But that was the Republican's sole consolation. Biden crushed him in New Castle County and carried Delaware's two downstate counties en route to a 60-40 percent win.

Committees

Judiciary (Chairman)

Foreign Relations (2nd of 10 Democrats)
European Affairs (chairman); East Asian and Pacific Affairs

Elections

1984 General

Joseph R. Biden Jr. (D)	147,831	(60%)
John M. Burris (R)	98,101	(40%)

Previous Winning Percentages: **1978** (58%) **1972** (51%)

Campaign Finance

	Receipts	Receipts from PACs	Expend-itures
1984			
Biden (D)	$1,429,164	$404,905 (28%)	$1,439,310
Burris (R)	$817,586	$173,119 (21%)	$816,484

Key Votes

1987

Enact omnibus highway bill over Reagan veto	Y
Limit testing of space-based anti-ballistic missiles	Y
Oppose banning tests of larger nuclear weapons	?
Confirm Robert H. Bork as Supreme Court justice	N

1988

Allow vote on campaign-finance overhaul	?
Pass civil rights restoration bill over Reagan veto	?
Enact omnibus trade bill over Reagan veto	?
Approve death penalty for drug-related murders	?
Oppose "workfare" amendment to welfare overhaul bill	?

Voting Studies

	Presidential Support		Party Unity		Conservative Coalition	
Year	**S**	**O**	**S**	**O**	**S**	**O**
1988	13	3	13	1	3	5
1987	27	41	60	6	6	56
1986	27	67	83	12	25	71
1985	31	64	77	16	18	75
1984	35	65	79	21	28	72
1983	38	60	82	12	23	68
1982	34	61	79	17	28	67
1981	44	54	84	12	24	74

Interest Group Ratings

Year	ADA	ACU	AFL-CIO	CCUS
1988	15	0	80	67
1987	70	0	100	17
1986	80	5	87	38
1985	75	10	81	37
1984	85	18	82	44
1983	85	8	88	22
1982	80	32	84	38
1981	80	20	84	28

AL Thomas R. Carper (D)

Of Wilmington — Elected 1982

Born: Jan. 23, 1947, Beckley, W.Va.
Education: Ohio State U., B.A. 1968; U. of Delaware, M.B.A. 1975.
Military Career: Navy, 1968-73; Naval Reserve, 1973-present.
Occupation: Public official.
Family: Wife, Martha Ann Stacy; one child.
Religion: Presbyterian.
Political Career: Del. treasurer, 1977-83.
Capitol Office: 131 Cannon Bldg. 20515; 225-4165.

In Washington: Carper is a paradox. He is so pleasantly self-effacing and polite he has been known to ask staffers if they could spare him a minute. Yet he will defy even the Speaker of the House to press for what he believes is right.

On a major issue confronting the nation — widespread bankruptcies in the savings and loan industry — Carper took a stand in the 100th Congress that ultimately proved correct. But in his determined effort to push through a package big enough to rescue the industry, he forced an embarrassing defeat on Speaker Jim Wright and Banking Committee Chairman Fernand J. St Germain, advocates of a smaller bailout package.

In another defiant crusade in 1987, Carper went up against Ways and Means Committee Chairman Dan Rostenkowski, tenaciously advocating a less costly welfare-overhaul bill than the chairman and his panel favored.

Such behavior suggests a confident young man who expects either to make his mark regardless of House protocol, or to pursue his political career elsewhere. In Carper's case, it is likely the latter. Having run statewide since 1976, first as state treasurer and then for his at-large House seat, Carper is a popular politician widely expected to reach the Senate someday.

For now, he remains in the House. But to his publicly stated relief, St Germain does not, having been defeated in 1988 after numerous stories of his alleged ethical lapses. Gone, too, is Wright, who resigned in June 1989 amid his own ethics controversy. Carper's relations with Banking's new chairman, Henry B. Gonzalez of Texas, are better. That should give him freer rein in the 101st Congress to continue pushing to remedy the S&L crisis and to deregulate banks along lines favored by Delaware's financial industry.

Off the committee, Carper joins with other fiscal conservatives — particularly those elected with him in the budget-conscious class of 1982 — to agitate for deficit reduction instead of increased social spending. Rather than build support within the more liberal Democratic caucus for a given initiative, Carper and his allies seek backing from conservative Democrats and Republicans. That was true in 1987, when their bipartisan team sought across-the-board cuts in each appropriation bill that came to the floor, with mixed results.

If such tactics do not endear Carper to many Democrats, he at least remains on generally good terms with them because of his pleasant personality. He is respected, if grudgingly, as intelligent and earnest. After hours, he is part of the "gym caucus," joining with other athletic House activists for the basketball games that help make — or mend — legislative relationships.

His confrontation with Wright over the S&L troubles began early in the 100th Congress. Carper won subcommittee approval for a plan (which had Reagan administration support) that called for higher S&L fees to bolster the faltering Federal Savings and Loan Insurance Corporation (FSLIC) by $15 billion over five years.

But Wright personally lobbied the full committee for a smaller package, fearing that a financially strong FSLIC would close the many Texas S&Ls that were all but insolvent due to fraud and the state's economic collapse. The committee then adopted a $5 billion, two-year bailout by a single vote. Asked about Wright's influence, Carper replied, "I'll let today's vote and the broken arms speak for themselves."

But less than a month later, stung by negative publicity, Wright and St Germain reversed field and announced support for the $15 billion plan. Beforehand, Carper had gone to Wright to argue that the S&L problem would only grow, and future bailouts would aggravate the deficit, unless the FSLIC received a large infusion immediately.

Despite Wright's endorsement, the House rejected the larger proposal by an overwhelming 153-258, opting instead for the $5 billion plan favored by the S&L lobby. Ultimately the House and Senate compromised on a $10.8

Delaware — At Large

Delaware is divided by the Chesapeake and Delaware Canal. North of the canal, at the top of the Delmarva (Delaware-Maryland-Virginia) Peninsula, is Wilmington, in New Castle County, the state's only real metropolitan area. Wilmington is dominated economically by the Du Pont Co., far and away its leading source of employment. Recent changes in banking law have brought an influx of new corporations involved in international finance, but to a large extent Wilmington is still a one-company town.

Forty years ago, almost half the state's people resided in Wilmington, but the city itself is down to a population under 70,000 and casts less than 12 percent of the state's vote.

A majority of Wilmington's population is black, but there are Italian, Irish and Polish neighborhoods as well. A Democratic candidate who hopes to win statewide must carry Wilmington by at least 10,000 votes. That means doing well among all the ethnic groups that make up the city's electorate.

While the city has been shrinking, the suburban areas around Wilmington have been growing steadily, so about 70 percent of Delaware's vote is still cast within New Castle County. The Republican voting habits of suburban New Castle are frequently strong enough to overcome the solid Democratic margin turned in by Wilmington.

Below the Chesapeake and Delaware Canal, one notices a change in values, language and attitude similar to those of the border South. Kent and Sussex counties are mostly rural.

Dover, the state capital, has some light industry, but the largest industries in the two southern counties are poultry and tourism. In fact, Sussex is the largest poultry-producing county in the United States. It also has Rehoboth Beach, which attracts thousands of sunbathers every summer; its year-round residents are firmly Republican.

If rural Kent and Sussex have similar cultures, they have slightly different voting habits. Sussex prefers conservative Republicans. It was the only one of the three counties to go for GOP Rep. Thomas B. Evans Jr. against Carper in 1982. Kent, in pure partisan terms, is the most Democratic part of Delaware. But these Democrats are conservative. Along with Sussex voters, they gave Reagan comfortable majorities in 1980 and 1984, and went solidly for George Bush in 1988.

Population: 594,338. White 487,817 (82%), Black 95,845 (16%), Other 5,440 (1%). Spanish origin 9,661 (2%). 18 and over 427,743 (72%), 65 and over 59,179 (10%). Median age: 30.

billion plan. But as Carper predicted, the industry's problems burgeoned.

The issue reclaimed members' attention at the end of the 100th Congress. In Banking's last-minute effort, Carper characteristically offered the middle ground. The panel was at an impasse, with Republicans opposing a provision setting higher capital requirements for newly reconstituted S&Ls as a cushion against any losses, and Democrats pushing for a 2 percent requirement. Carper suggested 1 percent, which was accepted. Despite the flurry of activity in both houses, however, no new legislation emerged, leaving the issue to the 101st Congress and the Bush administration.

Late in 1987, Carper also tried to fashion a bipartisan welfare-overhaul compromise, even though he does not sit on any of the four committees with jurisdiction. Working with Delaware experts, he crafted a full-blown $2.5 billion alternative to the costlier version packaged in Ways and Means, and persuaded Democrats Charles W. Stenholm of Texas, Timothy J. Penny of Minnesota and John M. Spratt Jr. of South Carolina to join with him.

Two days before the scheduled House debate, Carper went to the Rules Committee to get permission to offer his bill, arguing that the Democratic plan was too expensive, while the Republicans' bill passed off too many costs to the states. "I think welfare in this country stinks and needs to be reformed," he said. Rules turned him down and approved Rostenkowski's request for a restrictive rule for debate on Ways and Means' proposal — "a gag rule," Carper called it.

He and his allies then mobilized opposition to the leadership's measure, forcing a delay in floor action. Wright ordered Carper and the bill's sponsor, Thomas J. Downey, to negotiate, but to no avail. Finally, at the leadership's direction, Rules drafted a new rule allowing consideration not of Carper's bill, but of an amendment to shave $500 million from the pending $6.2 billion five-year legislation. He protested at Rules, "We've heard a lot about *glasnost*. We're asking for a little House-nost."

Though Carper opposed the new rule, many of his allies were satisfied, and it was approved narrowly. He then voted for the bill, which passed 230-194. Months later, he was one of 65 Southern and conservative Democrats who helped pass a GOP motion calling on House welfare conferees to adopt the Senate's lower $2.8 billion five-year price tag. The final product cost $3.34 billion.

On Banking, which has been considering deregulation legislation to broaden banks' powers throughout the decade, Carper espouses giving banks wider latitude in the securities field, and he favors letting states such as Delaware maintain their own liberal regulatory policies. Early in 1987, over St Germain's opposition, Carper drew on GOP support to amend the chairman's bill limiting banks' holds on customers' checks so that banks could withhold credit on non-local checks an extra day.

On the Merchant Marine Committee, Carper looks out for Delaware's fishing and tourism industries and backs efforts against coastal pollution. On an issue far beyond his own shores, he tried in the 100th Congress to mediate between environmentalists and the oil industry over the industry's effort to explore the Arctic National Wildlife Refuge. He offered the chief challenge to Chairman Walter B. Jones' industry-backed bill, proposing instead to ban leasing pending a study. His alternative failed 10-16, but Jones' legislation ultimately died.

Despite his reputation as a maverick, Carper has supported the House leadership on about three-quarters of party-line votes. He has been a loyalist on a particularly hot foreign policy issue, opposing military aid to the Nicaraguan contras. In 1986, a conservative group put Carper on its hit list of 33 members targeted for defeat, but he easily hit back: "I never could have imagined when I spent three tours in Southeast Asia as a naval flight officer that an outfit . . . would one day have the temerity to question my commitment to fighting the spread of communism."

At Home: Carper's entrance into politics was so nonchalant as to excuse Delaware Democrats for thinking his career might be brief. But he has been underestimated at home just as he was initially in Washington.

Carper was lying on a beach in 1976 when he heard a radio report that his state's Democratic convention could not find a candidate for state treasurer. He jumped into the race and upset a strongly favored Republican.

In 1982, after Democrats could not find anyone to take on Republican Rep. Thomas B. Evans Jr., Carper stepped into the breach just 90 days before the vote. He won again, returning the state's House seat to Democratic control for the first time since 1966.

Carper's soft-spoken geniality and Delaware's economic problems contributed to his victory. But scandal was the biggest factor. The married Evans was damaged by revelations that he was linked romantically to Paula Parkinson, a lobbyist who had posed nude for *Playboy*.

Carper never raised the Parkinson matter publicly, preferring to focus his fire on Reaganomics and the administration's military buildup. Evans was not as reluctant to discuss Carper's personal difficulties. When the *New York Post* printed a story accusing Carper of wife and child abuse, Evans called on his challenger to answer the "serious allegations." The Wilmington *News-Journal* later reported that some Evans associates first tried to interest the Delaware press in the story, which grew out of a bitter child-custody fight over Carper's two stepchildren.

It all ended up hurting Evans more than Carper. Although heavily outspent, Carper marshaled solid support from organized labor and an effective force of volunteers. He overwhelmed Evans in Wilmington, and clinched victory by carving a narrow edge in its GOP suburbs.

Carper was not able to rest long on his laurels. He was challenged in 1984 by Elise R. W. du Pont, a former official at the Agency for International Development and wife of popular GOP Gov. Pierre S. "Pete" du Pont IV. The match was initially touted as one of the toughest House contests in the country.

Although she had never before sought elective office, Elise du Pont began her first campaign with the kind of assets that would make most neophytes green with envy. Her marriage to Gov. du Pont — as well as her own record as an active participant in public affairs — made her well-known throughout the state. She also had a guaranteed ability to amass enormous sums of money. She used those advantages to try to cast Carper as a big-spending liberal lackey of the national Democratic Party.

But du Pont made some strategic errors that damaged her efforts to get that message across. She abandoned her ambitious pledge to make personal visits to 484 homes throughout the state by Election Day, and waffled on her husband's role in the campaign — seeking to minimize his influence early on, then actively involving him later.

Carper was well positioned to take advantage of du Pont's problems, having carefully cultivated the district via a slew of town hall meetings. Further aided by the top-of-the-ticket presence of Democratic Sen. Joseph R. Biden Jr., he scored a resounding 59-41 percent victory. Carper's unexpectedly decisive margin of victory over du Pont helped discourage top-flight GOP competition in 1986 and 1988.

The Republican candidate who eventually stepped forward in 1986, Wilmington attorney Thomas Neuberger, was a political neophyte. Carper dispatched him by 2-to-1.

In 1988, the suspense among Delaware politicos was not whether Carper would defeat Republican contractor James P. Krapf Sr., but if his victory margin would exceed GOP Gov. Michael N. Castle's re-election mark. Castle's 71 percent tally just surpassed Carper's 68 percent.

Committees

Banking, Finance and Urban Affairs (17th of 31 Democrats)
Financial Institutions Supervision, Regulation and Insurance; Housing and Community Development; International Development, Finance, Trade and Monetary Policy

Merchant Marine and Fisheries (12th of 26 Democrats)
Coast Guard and Navigation; Fisheries and Wildlife Conservation and the Environment

Elections

1988 General		
Thomas R. Carper (D)	158,338	(68%)
James P. Krapf Sr. (R)	76,179	(32%)
1986 General		
Thomas R. Carper (D)	106,351	(66%)
Thomas Stephen Neuberger (R)	53,767	(33%)

Previous Winning Percentages: 1984 (59%) **1982** (52%)

District Vote For President

	1988	1984	1980	1976
D	108,647 (43%)	101,656 (40%)	105,700 (45%)	122,596 (52%)
R	139,639 (56%)	152,190 (60%)	111,185 (47%)	109,831 (47%)
I			16,275 (7%)	

Campaign Finance

	Receipts	Receipts from PACs	Expend-itures
1988			
Carper (D)	$365,432	$161,235 (44%)	$371,747
Krapf (R)	$188,584	$4,675 (2%)	$184,712
1986			
Carper (D)	$326,795	$151,669 (46%)	$307,300
Neuberger (R)	$276,069	$2,585 (1%)	$270,563

Key Votes

1987	
Raise speed limit to 65 mph	N
Approve Gephardt "fair trade" amendment	Y
Ban testing of larger nuclear weapons	Y
Delay "re-flagging" of Kuwaiti tankers	N
Approve tax-raising deficit-reduction bill	N
1988	
Approve aid to Nicaraguan contras	N
Enact civil rights restoration bill over Reagan veto	Y
Kill 60-day plant-closing notification measure	N
Pass omnibus trade bill over Reagan veto	Y
Approve death penalty for drug-related murders	Y
Bar federal funds for abortions in cases of rape and incest	N
Oppose seven-day waiting period for purchase of handguns	N

Voting Studies

	Presidential Support		Party Unity		Conservative Coalition	
Year	S	O	S	O	S	O
1988	30	68	83	13	42	58
1987	31	68	74	22	58	42
1986	30	69	78	21	54	46
1985	43	58	75	22	51	49
1984	41	58	76	24	46	54
1983	33	66	76	23	35	65

Interest Group Ratings

Year	ADA	ACU	AFL-CIO	CCUS
1988	75	24	77	64
1987	72	9	75	53
1986	55	27	86	50
1985	55	24	71	50
1984	65	25	62	38
1983	80	13	59	53

Florida

U.S. CONGRESS

SENATE 1 D, 1 R
HOUSE 8 D, 10 R, 1 vacancy

LEGISLATURE

Senate 23 D, 17 R
House 73 D, 47 R

ELECTIONS

1988 Presidential Vote	
Bush	61%
Dukakis	39%
1984 Presidential Vote	
Reagan	65%
Mondale	35%
1980 Presidential Vote	
Reagan	56%
Carter	39%
Anderson	5%
Turnout rate in 1984	48%
Turnout rate in 1986	24%
Turnout rate in 1988	45%

(as percentage of voting age population)

POPULATION AND GROWTH

1980 population	9,746,324
1988 population estimate (4th in the nation)	12,335,000
Percent change 1980-1988	+27%

DEMOGRAPHIC BREAKDOWN

White	84%
Black	14%
Other	1%
(Spanish origin)	9%
Urban	84%
Rural	16%
Born in state	31%
Foreign-born	11%

MAJOR CITIES

Jacksonville	609,860
Miami	373,940
Tampa	277,580
St. Petersburg	239,410
Hialeah	161,760

AREA AND LAND USE

Area 54,153 sq. miles (26th)

Farm	37%
Forest	48%
Federally owned	12%

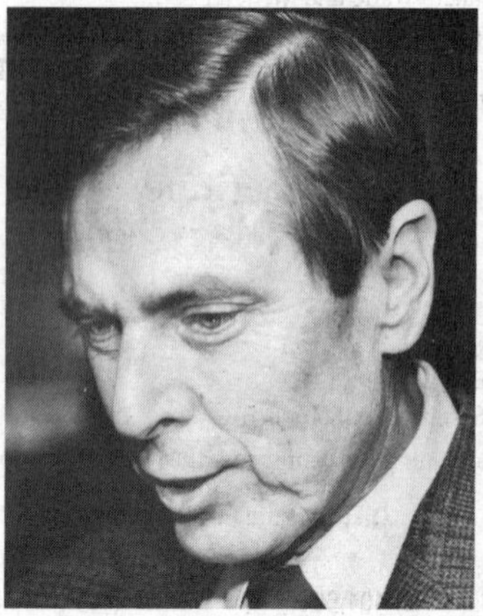

Gov. Bob Martinez (R)
Of Tampa — Elected 1986

Born: Dec. 25, 1934, Tampa, Fla.
Education: U. of Tampa, B.S. 1957; U. of Illinois, M.A. 1964.
Occupation: Teacher.
Religion: Roman Catholic.
Political Career: Mayor of Tampa, 1979-87.
Next Election: 1990.

WORK

Occupations	
White-collar	55%
Blue-collar	27%
Service workers	15%
Government Workers	
Federal	101,071
State	141,520
Local	449,456

MONEY

Median family income	$ 17,280	(39th)
Tax burden per capita	$ 694	(44th)

EDUCATION

Spending per pupil through grade 12	$ 3,529	(26th)
Persons with college degrees	15%	(29th)

CRIME

Violent crime rate 1,024 per 100,000 (1st)

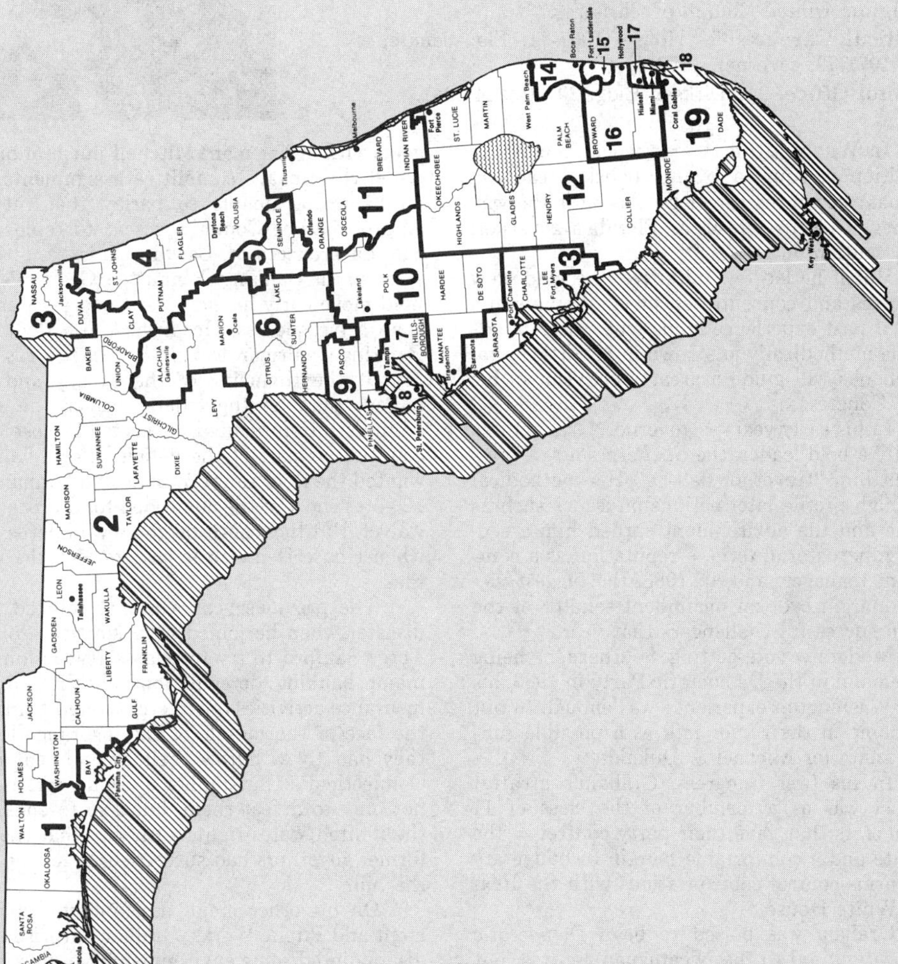
1
2
3
4
5
6
7
8
9
10
11
12
13
14
15
16
17
18
19
ESCAMBIA
SANTA ROSA
OKALOOSA
WALTON
HOLMES
WASHINGTON
BAY
JACKSON
CALHOUN
GULF
GADSDEN
LIBERTY
FRANKLIN
LEON
WAKULLA
JEFFERSON
MADISON
TAYLOR
HAMILTON
SUWANNEE
LAFAYETTE
DIXIE
COLUMBIA
GILCHRIST
LEVY
BAKER
UNION
BRADFORD
ALACHUA
NASSAU
DUVAL
CLAY
ST. JOHNS
PUTNAM
FLAGLER
VOLUSIA
MARION
CITRUS
SUMTER
LAKE
HERNANDO
PASCO
PINELLAS
HILLSBOROUGH
POLK
SEMINOLE
ORANGE
OSCEOLA
BREVARD
INDIAN RIVER
OKEECHOBEE
ST. LUCIE
MARTIN
HIGHLANDS
HARDEE
MANATEE
DE SOTO
SARASOTA
CHARLOTTE
GLADES
PALM BEACH
LEE
HENDRY
COLLIER
BROWARD
MONROE
DADE
Pensacola
Panama City
Tallahassee
Jacksonville
Gainesville
Ocala
Daytona Beach
Titusville
Melbourne
Orlando
Lakeland
Tampa
St. Petersburg
Bradenton
Sarasota
Port Charlotte
Fort Myers
Fort Pierce
West Palm Beach
Boca Raton
Fort Lauderdale
Hollywood
Hialeah
Miami
Coral Gables
Key West

Bob Graham (D)

Of Miami Lakes — Elected 1986

Born: Nov. 9, 1936, Coral Gables, Fla.
Education: U. of Florida, B.A. 1959; Harvard Law School, LL.B. 1962.
Occupation: Developer; cattleman.
Family: Wife, Adele Khoury; four children.
Religion: United Church of Christ.
Political Career: Fla. House, 1967-71; Fla. Senate, 1971-79; governor, 1979-87.
Capitol Office: 241 Dirksen Bldg. 20510; 224-3041.

In Washington: A man whose prodigious ambition is equaled by his political caution, Graham began his career as a senator the way he began his first term as Florida's governor: with caution on top.

But if he led few initiatives, he made few mistakes and concentrated on his home state. And if past experience holds true, the reminders he methodically jots down in his little spiral notebooks will guide a greater activism in his next Congresses.

In his early years as governor, Graham was hardly a bold leader; the *St. Petersburg Times* called him "Governor Jell-O." His methodical but high-profile later actions on issues such as crime and the environment earned him a second gubernatorial term, a reputation as a competent manager, and, in 1986, the biggest victory margin over an incumbent senator of the seven successful challengers that year.

Moderate vote-getting Southerners being in demand in the Democratic Party in 1988, his thin Washington experience was enough to put his name in the rumor mill as a possible running mate for Michael S. Dukakis.

In his first Congress, Graham's greatest impact was as a member of the class of 11 Democrats that gave their party control of the Senate and a comfortable margin in budgetary and arms-control confrontations with the Reagan White House.

Graham was poised to be a Democratic advocate of aid to the Nicaraguan contras, but the roller-coaster peace process in Central America moved faster than Congress could. On the hotly contested nominations of Robert H. Bork for the Supreme Court in 1987 and John Tower for defense secretary in 1989 — nominations on which the votes of Southern Democrats were vigorously courted — Graham came down on the opposition side — but only after others had made the outcome clear.

Similarly, when George J. Mitchell of Maine was wrestling with J. Bennett Johnston of Louisiana for Southern votes in the contest for Senate majority leader, Graham's endorsement of Mitchell came late, doing him little good with either man. Mitchell put him on the panel that makes committee assignments, but Graham was unable to parlay that into an Appropriations Committee seat to replace his Florida predecessor, Lawton Chiles.

On the Banking Committee, Graham's first bold move early in the 101st Congress was less than a big success. He pushed to a floor vote Banking Chairman Donald W. Riegle Jr.'s plan to put the financing of the savings-and-loan bailout plan on the federal books; the Bush administration wanted to keep the cost from counting as part of the deficit. Riegle had not wanted the floor showdown; he and Graham fell 12 votes short of the 60 needed for a procedural waiver. But their position got new impetus later when House Democratic leaders took the same tack.

The previous year, Graham courted floor disaster when he joined with North Carolina's Terry Sanford to try to relax a restriction in a major banking deregulation bill that limited insurance activities of state-chartered banks. In the face of the muscle of the insurance lobby, they had to withdraw their amendment after Connecticut's Christopher J. Dodd threatened not only to defeat them, but also to challenge the limited states-rights authority that the two former governors had succeeded in getting into the bill.

On his other major assignment, Environment and Public Works, Graham surprised and disappointed some environmental groups in his first weeks in office by joining with other freshman Democrats to reverse the committee's position in favor of speeding up removal of billboards along federal highways. A Graham spokesman said he was concerned about "excessive federal regulation"; the vote also showed a keen appreciation of the priorities of the panel's new pro-billboard chairman, Quentin N. Burdick of North Dakota.

On the same bill, a major highway reauthorization, Graham was able to relax a seven-year ban on using federal funds to build toll roads, and to allow Florida to retain tolls on its "Alligator Alley" highway through the Everglades.

One sign that Democratic leaders felt Graham could be helpful in giving cover to Southern Democrats in a floor fight came on the minimum-wage bill in the 101st Congress. Graham was chosen to offer the Democratic amendment drawing the line in the dust with President Bush. In a play for Southern votes, the amendment lopped a dime from the $4.65-an-hour wage backed by labor, and it incorporated a watered-down form of the subminimum "training wage" that labor bitterly fought. The Graham amendment was opposed by only two Southern Democrats and it picked up the votes of eight moderate Republicans. The measure still fell short of a veto-proof margin, however — as it did in the House after Bush vetoed the bill.

Central American politics are a parochial concern for Florida, and Graham has been appropriately active. He joined with Kansas Republican Nancy Landon Kassebaum in 1988 to offer a compromise contra-aid plan in the wake of a Nicaraguan incursion into Honduras, but the plan was wiped out by a cease-fire pact between the Sandinista government and the contras.

Following election irregularities in Haiti, he proposed trade sanctions against the government. In May 1989, after outright election fraud kept Gen. Manuel Antonio Noriega in power, Graham was part of a delegation to visit Panama. Upon returning, he urged continued U.S. pressure, saying, "If we let June slip into July, summer into fall, letting Noriega become more entrenched, democracies of this hemisphere will be making a statement of resigned acceptance."

Graham also has pushed for an extension of the Caribbean Basin Initiative to boost the region's economy through favorable trade terms with the United States.

At Home: In his 1986 challenge to GOP Sen. Paula Hawkins, Graham began the year substantially ahead, and he never lost his lead.

Graham had all the vital advantages. Though Hawkins was highly rated in voter surveys, he ranked higher. The governor maintained an image of vigor by performing muscular tasks as part of his "Workdays" program, while Hawkins had to have surgery during the campaign to relieve her painful back problems.

More important, Graham had an image of competence built on a record of accomplishment on the environmental, economic and social issues facing rapidly growing Florida. Hawkins' popularity, on the other hand, was based on a limited agenda of emotional issues. She acquired a following as an early Senate advocate of action against drug trafficking and child abuse. But Hawkins had not played a visible role on major economic, foreign policy or defense issues. And she had committed several embarrassing and widely reported gaffes. This issue of substance was probably the decisive factor in Graham's comfortable 55-percent victory.

Graham inherited an interest in politics from his father. Ernest "Cap" Graham, a wealthy dairy farmer, was a state senator in the 1930s and 1940s. Bob Graham was born just days after his father's first legislative victory in 1936. The elder Graham ran for governor in 1944, finishing third in the Democratic primary.

After graduating from the University of Florida and Harvard Law School, Graham joined his father in the real-estate business. His projects, including development of the new town of Miami Lakes, helped him amass a fortune.

Graham was eased into politics by his half-brother Phil, the publisher of *The Washington Post*. Before his suicide in 1963, Phil Graham introduced his half-brother to many influential Democrats, including Lyndon B. Johnson, for whom Bob Graham worked at the 1960 Democratic National Convention.

Graham's victory in his 1966 campaign for the state Legislature began his unbroken string of electoral successes. He won a second state House term in 1968, then won the first of two successful state Senate campaigns in 1970.

Though Graham was popular in his own base, he was little known elsewhere when he entered the 1978 contest to succeed Democratic Gov. Reubin Askew. Regarded as rather bland, Graham was thought to have little chance in a field that included state Attorney General Robert L. Shevin, Lt. Gov. Jim Williams, and Secretary of State Bruce Smathers.

But Graham came up with a gimmick that became his trademark. He spent 100 days during the campaign working at average, often menial, jobs in various regions of Florida. These "workdays" (which Graham continued as governor) earned him enormous publicity and gave the wealthy candidate a "common man" appeal. Graham finished a strong second to Shevin in the primary, then raced past him in the runoff, gaining momentum for the general election. He defeated GOP drugstore magnate Jack M. Eckerd with 56 percent.

Graham was not overwhelmingly popular in his early years in office. His support for capital punishment earned him conservative backing, but it also made him a target for anti-death penalty protesters. On other issues, Graham's caution and attention to detail gave rise to the "Governor Jell-O" nickname.

Beginning in 1982, Graham's leadership style changed. He hired staff members who promoted his agenda to the Legislature. He pushed his environmental initiatives, including the Save Our Rivers and Save Our Coasts projects. His high profile helped him sweep to re-election that year over GOP Rep. L. A. "Skip" Bafalis.

Graham's stature grew during his second term. He pushed for a balance between development and land-use planning to preserve the environment. Faced with a crime wave, Graham bolstered state law enforcement efforts and promoted an assault on illegal drug trafficking. He backed several tax increases, each one earmarked for a specific purpose, such as education or transportation.

By 1985, it was evident that Graham would be a formidable challenger to Hawkins. Though she was known as a champion of family-oriented causes, her critics referred to her as a "lightweight." From her early Senate days, when she hosted a sirloin steak luncheon to announce a plan to jail food stamp cheaters, Hawkins had a reputation for eccentricity. Still, she was not considered an easy mark. She had the determined support of the national GOP and, like Graham, had a hefty campaign treasury.

Hawkins' campaign was put on hold for weeks after her April back surgery. When it resumed, the candidates largely ignored each other, running handsome but bland, image-building TV ads produced by Bob Squier (Graham) and Robert Goodman (Hawkins). Goodman presented emotional tales by constituents who had been rescued from serious trouble with the government by Hawkins' intervention, then closed with the line, "Unique and irreplaceable." Graham was pictured riding with state police in a helicopter to spot drug smugglers.

The candidates finally engaged each other directly in October. Though Graham maintained his substantial lead in opinion polls, his advisers feared that Hawkins' emotional ads might gradually earn her a sentimental vote. So he went on the offensive, accusing Hawkins of exaggerating her anti-drug record and of "miniaturizing" the office of senator.

Though Hawkins defended herself and fired back with charges about Graham's record, the Democrat's strategy succeeded. It forced Hawkins to engage in an issues debate that she could not win. By bringing Hawkins out into the open, Graham also increased the likelihood that she would make a misstep. In fact, Hawkins stirred up negative reactions with a pair of comments, one alleging that Graham had communist support, and another, in an appeal for Cuban-American support, that questioned the patriotism of Mexican-Americans.

Graham scored a sweeping victory. He won sizable margins in the populous southeastern counties (Dade, Palm Beach and Broward). On the Gulf coast, he carried Hillsborough County (Tampa) and Pinellas County (St. Petersburg). In north Florida, Graham took Duval County (Jacksonville) as well as Leon (Tallahassee) and Alachua (Gainesville). He won by slimmer margins in central Florida, which included Hawkins' Orange County base.

Hawkins kept the outcome from becoming a rout by carrying the Republican coastal areas in South Florida's 12th and 13th districts. She also swept the conservative western Panhandle.

Committees

Banking, Housing and Urban Affairs (9th of 12 Democrats)
Consumer and Regulatory Affairs; International Finance and Monetary Policy

Environment and Public Works (8th of 9 Democrats)
Environmental Protection; Superfund, Ocean and Water Protection; Water Resources, Transportation and Infrastructure

Special Aging (9th of 10 Democrats)

Veterans' Affairs (6th of 6 Democrats)

Elections

1986 General		
Bob Graham (D)	1,877,543	(55%)
Paula Hawkins (R)	1,552,376	(45%)
1986 Primary		
Bob Graham (D)	851,586	(85%)
Robert P. Kunst (D)	149,797	(15%)

Campaign Finance

	Receipts	Receipts from PACs	Expend-itures
1986			
Graham (D)	$6,215,911	$887,337 (14%)	$6,173,663
Hawkins (R)	$6,566,447	$937,105 (14%)	$6,723,729

Key Votes

1987	
Enact omnibus highway bill over Reagan veto	Y
Limit testing of space-based anti-ballistic missiles	Y
Oppose banning tests of larger nuclear weapons	Y
Confirm Robert H. Bork as Supreme Court justice	N
1988	
Allow vote on campaign-finance overhaul	Y
Pass civil rights restoration bill over Reagan veto	Y
Enact omnibus trade bill over Reagan veto	Y
Approve death penalty for drug-related murders	Y
Oppose "workfare" amendment to welfare overhaul bill	Y

Voting Studies

	Presidential Support		Party Unity		Conservative Coalition	
Year	**S**	**O**	**S**	**O**	**S**	**O**
1988	60	40	83	16	65	35
1987	46	53	82	18	56	44

Interest Group Ratings

Year	ADA	ACU	AFL-CIO	CCUS
1988	55	28	71	38
1987	60	23	100	28

Connie Mack (R)

Of Cape Coral — Elected 1988

Born: Oct. 29, 1940, Philadelphia, Pa.
Education: U. of Florida, B.S. 1966.
Occupation: Banker.
Family: Wife, Priscilla Hobbs; two children.
Religion: Roman Catholic.
Political Career: U.S. House, 1983-89.
Capitol Office: 517 Hart Bldg. 20510; 224-5274.

In Washington: Mack did not leave a long legislative trail on his way to the Senate, but he did leave a mark. In the House he made his reputation as an outspoken member of the Conservative Opportunity Society (COS), a group of Republicans with an aggressive, confrontational approach to the Democratic majority.

Mack showed some ability for maneuvering within his party, launching an intensive and successful lobbying campaign to get on the Budget Committee as a freshman. He was the only member of his class to win a seat on that panel. Two years later, he also joined the Foreign Affairs Committee. A junior member of the House minority needs unusual skills to have any chance at shaping the legislative products of those two committees, and Mack did not stand out in that regard.

Like many younger-generation Republicans, he was far more prone to castigate the Democratic majority than to look for ways to cooperate with it. "In politics, you gain energy from confrontation," Mack once said, capsulizing the COS philosophy.

Narrowly elected to the Senate in 1988, Mack made his way to its Banking and Foreign Relations committees. The former gives him an opportunity to put to use his professional background — he was a bank president at age 35 — and the latter provides him a forum to air his views on the United States' role in world affairs. Though it seemed a settled matter for most of the 1980s, Mack was among those continuing to criticize the Panama Canal treaties, which give Panama control of the canal in 1999. When Panama became engulfed in a political and economic crisis in early 1989, Mack introduced a resolution calling for an abrogation of the treaties. "We should not take one step further towards the transfer of the canal," he said.

On Banking, Mack quickly got involved in the effort to address the crisis in the savings and loan industry. When the Senate in early 1989 passed a bill overhauling the savings and loan regulatory structure, it adopted a Mack amendment requiring national standards for the selection of auditors by thrift institutions and for the conduct of such audits.

In the House, Mack worked hard to identify himself in the 99th Congress with the Gramm-Rudman balanced-budget law. He became its chief GOP sponsor and promoter in the House, and described the measure as "Gramm-Rudman-Mack." He was not noticeably involved in drafting it, however, and did not play a significant role in the process by which members worked out their own language for conference with the Senate.

In 1986, Mack unsuccessfully tried to modify Gramm-Rudman. He introduced legislation to bar cuts in cost-of-living increases for beneficiaries of federal employee retirement programs. A similar protection already existed for Social Security recipients.

At Home: It is no small feat to win a Senate seat in a state as large and diverse as Florida, but if Mack's victory in 1988 had impressive elements, it was still a little surprising that the contest was so close, given the factors working in his favor. Despite a significant head start, a financial advantage, Democratic infighting and an extremely strong GOP tide at the presidential level, Mack's victory was so narrow that the outcome was settled only by the count of absentee ballots.

Mack, a telegenic candidate in a state where media is extremely important, seemed to be charmed for much of the Senate contest. He entered the Senate race as an underdog against Democratic Sen. Lawton Chiles, but Chiles surprised his party by announcing his retirement in late 1987. That boosted Mack, who had already nailed down enough GOP support to ward off a serious primary challenger. But it still did not make him the favorite; popular former Democratic Gov. Reubin Askew decided to make a comeback and was considered a likely winner. But then Askew got skittish and backed out, which helped create a Democratic nomination fight that lasted until a month before the general election. The winner, Democratic Rep. Buddy MacKay, emerged bruised, although with a degree of momentum.

While Mack avoided stiff primary competition, he did suffer some barbs from an aggressive GOP opponent, former U.S. Attorney Robert Merkle, who attacked him as a "packaged product." Merkle ran better than had been expected, and refused to endorse Mack afterwards.

Throughout the campaign — whether he was facing Chiles, Askew or MacKay — Mack framed the voters' choice as one between a conservative and a liberal. He maintained a theme of "less taxing, less spending, less government and more freedom." Even before the October runoff was settled, he ran ads with the tag line: "Hey Buddy, you're liberal."

But even some Republicans considered Mack's message too simplistic and narrow. MacKay was highly regarded among political insiders for his legislative work, both in the House and previously in the state Legislature, and his voting record put him closer to the center of the political spectrum than to the left. Some prominent environmentalists in the GOP said they could not support Mack because he had not addressed environmental issues crucial to fast-growing Florida. In his campaign, MacKay said the choice was "mainstream vs. extreme."

On election night and for a few days following, the race was too close to call, but absentee ballots ultimately put Mack over the top. MacKay considered challenging the results, suggesting that the state's computerized voting system might have failed in some key counties. But he soon abandoned that plan.

Mack may have inherited his desire to serve in Congress. His great-grandfather, John L. Sheppard, was a Democratic House member from Texas; his grandfather, Morris Sheppard, also served in the House, then moved on to a 28-year tenure in the Senate. Mack's step-grandfather, Tom Connally, also served Texas in the Senate, from 1929 to 1953.

But it was another forebear who provided Mack with enviable name recognition when he got into politics: His paternal grandfather was the original Connie Mack, the legendary owner and manager of the Philadephia Athletics baseball team. Like his grandfather, Mack uses the familiar rather than the given version of his name: Cornelius McGillicuddy III.

After GOP Rep. L. A. "Skip" Bafalis decided to run for governor in 1982, Mack's name gave him a winning edge over four GOP primary opponents for the 13th District House seat. Once nominated, he was guaranteed election and re-election in the solid GOP constituency.

Committees

Banking, Housing and Urban Affairs (6th of 9 Republicans)
Housing and Urban Affairs; International Finance and Monetary Policy

Foreign Relations (9th of 9 Republicans)
African Affairs; Western Hemisphere and Peace Corps Affairs

Joint Economic
Economic Growth, Trade and Taxes; International Economic Policy; National Security Economics

Elections

1988 General		
Connie Mack (R)	2,051,071	(50%)
Buddy MacKay (D)	2,016,553	(50%)
1988 Primary		
Connie Mack (R)	405,296	(62%)
Robert W. Merkle (R)	250,730	(38%)

Previous Winning Percentages: **1986 *** (75%) **1984 *** (100%) **1982 *** (65%)

* *House elections.*

Campaign Finance

	Receipts	Receipts from PACs	Expend-itures
1988			
Mack (R)	$5,224,061	$1,018,745 (20%)	$5,181,639
MacKay (D)	$3,622,831	$899,385 (25%)	$3,714,852

Key Votes

House Service	
1987	
Raise speed limit to 65 mph	Y
Approve Gephardt "fair trade" amendment	N
Ban testing of larger nuclear weapons	N
Delay "re-flagging" of Kuwaiti tankers	N
Approve tax-raising deficit-reduction bill	N
1988	
Approve aid to Nicaraguan contras	Y
Enact civil rights restoration bill over Reagan veto	N
Kill 60-day plant-closing notification measure	Y
Pass omnibus trade bill over Reagan veto	N
Approve death penalty for drug-related murders	Y
Bar federal funds for abortions in cases of rape and incest	Y
Oppose seven-day waiting period for purchase of handguns	?

Voting Studies

	Presidential Support		Party Unity		Conservative Coalition	
Year	S	O	S	O	S	O
House Service						
1988	33	11	35	1	37	0
1987	77	19	91	3	91	5
1986	86	12	94	4	98	0
1985	85	15	91	7	91	9
1984	76	21	94	4	92	8
1983	77	20	94	4	92	6

Interest Group Ratings

Year	ADA	ACU	AFL-CIO	CCUS
House Service				
1988	0	100	0	86
1987	0	95	6	93
1986	0	100	7	100
1985	10	95	18	86
1984	5	96	15	94
1983	15	86	6	89

1 Earl Hutto (D)

Of Panama City — Elected 1978

Born: May 12, 1926, Midland City, Ala.
Education: Troy State U., Ala., B.S. 1949; graduate work, Northwestern U., 1951.
Military Career: Navy, 1944-46.
Occupation: High school English teacher; sportscaster; advertising and broadcast executive.
Family: Wife, Nancy Myers; two children.
Religion: Baptist.
Political Career: Fla. House, 1973-79.
Capitol Office: 2435 Rayburn Bldg. 20515; 225-4136.

In Washington: During his early years in the House, Hutto concentrated on maintaining the flow of defense dollars to his military-reliant district. But with his increasing seniority on the Armed Services and Merchant Marine committees, Hutto has also acquired broader responsibilities on defense and related issues.

As chairman of the Merchant Marine Subcommittee on the Coast Guard during the 100th Congress, Hutto worked to expand Coast Guard participation in the war on illegal drug smuggling. His bill, providing $350 million for Coast Guard expenses, personnel and equipment, was attached to the 1988 omnibus drug law.

With the 101st Congress, Hutto moved to the chairmanship of the Armed Services Subcommittee on Readiness. There he will oversee another of his favored subjects: the armed services' counterinsurgency effort. His interest in the Special Operations Force (SOF), such as the Green Berets and Delta Force, also helps him look out for his district, which has SOF operations based at Hurlburt and Duke fields.

Though his role has been adapting with seniority, one aspect of Hutto's record has not changed. He remains a staunchly conservative voice on Armed Services, a member of the thinning ranks of the pro-Pentagon Democratic "Old Guard." During votes on weapons systems and other priority issues, Hutto often sides with his GOP committee colleagues.

With mainly conservative social views to go with his defense posture, Hutto has been one of the Democratic House members most accessible to Republican administrations. He agreed with President Reagan's position on House legislation 53 percent of the time in 1987, the second-highest percentage among Democrats.

This record, and the fact that his Florida Panhandle district has gone Republican for president by huge margins in recent elections, has led GOP officials to let Hutto know he would be welcome in their party. But unlike Bill Grant, his neighbor to the east who made the jump in February 1989, Hutto has declined. To make such a move, Hutto would have to give up the Democratic seniority on Armed Services that means so much to the 1st District.

As a broker of funds for his district, Hutto has followed ably in the footsteps of his predecessor, Robert L. F. Sikes. But he sometimes finds himself in the ironic position, as a subcommittee chairman, of turning down other members' pet projects.

In 1987, Senate Commerce Committee Chairman Ernest F. Hollings of South Carolina set aside $10 million of a Coast Guard reauthorization to build a helicopter base near Charleston, S.C. Hutto initially took a stand against the project, stating the Coast Guard budget was too tight. However, when the bill was returned without Hollings' project, the Senate sat on it for months. Finally, in September 1988, the House relented, approving the Charleston base.

At Home: Before his election to the state Legislature in 1972, Hutto was a television sportscaster in both Panama City and Pensacola, at opposite ends of the 1st. So when he began his 1978 congressional campaign, aiming to succeed the retiring Sikes, his face was already familiar to much of the district.

That was an enormous help to him in the Democratic primary. Rated no higher than third out of four candidates before the voting, Hutto finished a comfortable first in the initial primary, then won easily in the runoff.

With Sikes out of the picture, Republicans were optimistic that their candidate, former Pensacola Mayor Warren Briggs, could take the district in the fall. But Hutto gave Briggs no opening on the right. He promised to protect the 1st's military facilities, and stressed law enforcement and economy in government.

Hutto's involvement in Baptist church affairs was of special help in the district's rural areas, where Briggs' identification with Pensacola business interests was not an advantage. Hutto won 63 percent.

Briggs tried again in 1980, but Hutto was untouchable. Even though Reagan won the district's presidential vote, Briggs barely improved on his 1978 showing. Hutto has won easily since.

Florida 1

Northwest — Pensacola; Panama City

Thanks to Hutto's predecessor, the legendary Robert L. F. Sikes, the 1st is packed with military bases, among them Pensacola's Naval Air Station, Tyndall Air Force Base in Panama City and Eglin Air Force Base, which spans three counties. Their political influence is significant: The bases provide jobs for civilians, and many of the enlisted personnel remain in the area after they leave the service.

This district has found little to love in the recent policies of the national Democratic Party. Escambia County (Pensacola) has voted Republican in the last five presidential elections; Bay County (Panama City) gave Jimmy Carter a slight edge in 1976, then swung decisively back to the GOP in subsequent elections. But like their neighbors in Alabama, many voters here still feel some guilt when they desert Old South traditions of voting Democratic. Hutto's Democratic conservatism just suits them.

In Pensacola, the district's largest city, the military's contribution to the economy is complemented by manufacturing of chemicals, plastics, textiles and paper. Despite its large natural harbor, its potential as a trading port is restricted because close-by Mobile and New Orleans have a lock on most of the gulf trade.

The 100-mile stretch of beach from Pensacola to Panama City, dubbed the "Miracle Strip" by civic boosters, also has been called the "Redneck Riviera" because it attracts many visitors from nearby Georgia, Alabama and other Southeastern states. Along the coastal strip, military retirees have settled in Fort Walton Beach and Destin, both in Okaloosa County just a few miles from Eglin Air Force Base. Okaloosa County gave George Bush about 80 percent in 1988.

Inland, the sparsely settled rural areas are occupied mostly by soybeans, corn, tomatoes, cantaloupes, cattle and pine trees.

Population: 512,821. White 428,075 (83%), Black 71,661 (14%), Other 9,351 (2%). Spanish origin 8,863 (2%). 18 and over 362,491 (71%), 65 and over 43,293 (8%). Median age: 29.

Committees

Armed Services (8th of 31 Democrats)
Readiness (chairman); Military Installations and Facilities; Seapower and Strategic and Critical Materials

Merchant Marine and Fisheries (5th of 26 Democrats)
Coast Guard and Navigation; Fisheries and Wildlife Conservation and the Environment

Elections

1988 General		
Earl Hutto (D)	142,449	(67%)
E. D. Armbruster (R)	70,534	(33%)
1988 Primary		
Earl Hutto (D)	72,508	(72%)
Durell Peaden Jr. (D)	28,883	(28%)
1986 General		
Earl Hutto (D)	97,532	(64%)
Greg Neubeck (R)	55,459	(36%)

Previous Winning Percentages: **1984** (100%) **1982** (74%) **1980** (61%) **1978** (63%)

District Vote For President

	1988		1984		1980		1976	
D	57,822	(27%)	49,401	(24%)	67,301	(35%)	79,481	(48%)
R	156,405	(73%)	155,842	(76%)	117,902	(61%)	85,395	(51%)
I					5,268	(3%)		

Campaign Finance

	Receipts	Receipts from PACs		Expend-itures
1988				
Hutto (D)	$212,973	$109,186	(51%)	$210,940
Armbruster (R)	$23,912	$808	(3%)	$23,912
1986				
Hutto (D)	$85,465	$29,545	(35%)	$134,745
Neubeck (R)	$54,096	$2,600	(5%)	$54,046

Key Votes

1987	
Raise speed limit to 65 mph	Y
Approve Gephardt "fair trade" amendment	N
Ban testing of larger nuclear weapons	N
Delay "re-flagging" of Kuwaiti tankers	N
Approve tax-raising deficit-reduction bill	Y
1988	
Approve aid to Nicaraguan contras	Y
Enact civil rights restoration bill over Reagan veto	N
Kill 60-day plant-closing notification measure	Y
Pass omnibus trade bill over Reagan veto	Y
Approve death penalty for drug-related murders	Y
Bar federal funds for abortions in cases of rape and incest	Y
Oppose seven-day waiting period for purchase of handguns	Y

Voting Studies

	Presidential Support		Party Unity		Conservative Coalition	
Year	**S**	**O**	**S**	**O**	**S**	**O**
1988	41	53	56	41	97	0
1987	53	46	55	40	91	7
1986	57	40	51	45	92	8
1985	56	43	56	40	93	7
1984	57	40	51	46	95	3
1983	61	37	45	51	96	2
1982	62	34	54	43	89	10
1981	74	25	46	53	93	5

Interest Group Ratings

Year	ADA	ACU	AFL-CIO	CCUS
1988	20	76	57	69
1987	24	68	27	64
1986	5	82	29	89
1985	15	76	25	86
1984	20	57	46	46
1983	10	91	24	75
1982	19	71	32	71
1981	10	93	40	78

2 Bill Grant (R)

Of Madison — Elected 1986

Born: Feb. 21, 1943, Lake City, Fla.
Education: Florida State U., B.A. 1963.
Occupation: Banker.
Family: Wife, Janet Kraweic; two children.
Religion: Baptist.
Political Career: Fla. Senate, 1983-87.
Capitol Office: 1330 Longworth Bldg. 20515; 225-5235.

In Washington: Grant, until February 1989 a little-noticed Democratic backbencher, chose his 46th birthday to announce his switch to the GOP. The move, made at a high-profile White House press conference with President Bush, shocked and mystified the House Democratic leadership.

Before his announcement, Democratic leaders had caught no hints that Grant was restive. He had appeared at a presidential rally in Jacksonville with Michael S. Dukakis; at the start of the 101st Congress, he got an entry-level position in the Democratic whip structure.

Unlike fellow Florida Rep. Andy Ireland, whose 1984 switch to the GOP was preceded by clear signals of his unhappiness with the national Democratic Party, Grant in his freshman term had not voted an unusually conservative line: He supported President Reagan's position roughly one-third of the time, about average for a Southern Democrat. And he received a 50 percent rating from the liberal Americans for Democratic Action.

When Democrats made committee assignments for the 101st Congress, Grant had lost out to more senior members in a bid for a place on coveted Energy and Commerce. But junior members often fall short in their first try for that committee. Democratic insiders figured Grant would be a contender for the panel in the future, partly because his pro-business views mesh with those of Chairman John D. Dingell.

Grant said he switched parties to serve his constituents better, and he expressed his intention to seek re-election to the House in 1990. There was, however, a flurry of speculation that the GOP would reward Grant by giving him a place in the near future on the party's ticket for state offices.

House Republicans did give Grant an entry-level place in their whip structure, and they kept him on Public Works, where he had served as a Democrat. Grant also got a new assignment from the GOP: the Agriculture Commitee — politically helpful since the 2nd ranks high nationally in peanut production and in tobacco growing. But on Agriculture as well as on Public Works, Grant is starting over at the bottom, ranking below even those members first elected in 1988.

At Home: Given the Old South Democratic loyalties of the 2nd, Grant would likely have been able to win comfortable re-election margins had he remained a Democrat. Now that he has switched parties, he will still be formidable, because of his incumbency, his well-known name and the growing strength of the GOP in north Florida. In 1988, George Bush won nearly 60 percent of the presidential vote in the 2nd, significantly better than Ronald Reagan had done in 1984.

With a state Senate constituency that included the 2nd's largest city (Tallahassee) and half the district's voters, Grant assumed the favorite's role from the day 12-term Democratic Rep. Don Fuqua announced his 1986 retirement. Grant won a majority of the vote in the Democratic primary, sparing himself a runoff, and he drew no GOP opposition in November.

In the state Senate, Grant had lobbied to improve state marketing efforts for north Florida's agricultural products, and, despite his conservative overall reputation, pleased the Florida State University community in Tallahassee by sponsoring several bills to increase educational funding.

Grant was not a household name in the more rural reaches of the 2nd, but as an officeholder with a background in banking he had fund-raising contacts his opponents could not match.

In several issue areas, Grant hewed closely to Fuqua's conservative line. Like most members of the Florida House delegation, Grant came out in favor of aid to the Nicaraguan contras. But he set himself off from the more conservative faction of Florida Democrats, and from Fuqua, by questioning the need for funds for the B-1 bomber and the MX missile.

Grant was staked to victory by an overwhelming majority in Tallahassee and surrounding Leon County. He padded his margin by taking 72 percent of the vote in two rural counties, Madison and Taylor, that he had represented in the state Senate.

Florida 2

North — Tallahassee

This is the only Florida district where urban interests are secondary to rural concerns in politics. Some 30 percent of the district's people live in Leon County (Tallahassee), but the rest are scattered among 24 counties, none with a town of even 15,000 residents.

Two major Interstate highways intersect in Columbia County: I-75, the route south for most Florida-bound tourists who live in the mid-South, and I-10, connecting Jacksonville with New Orleans and points west. But this is just a passing-through point for most visitors to Florida; the bulk of the 2nd is only beginning to see the changes that have transformed much of the rest of the state.

The "Big Bend" Gulf Coast from Gulf County to Levy County is mostly undeveloped. There are no military installations in the district and no large concentrations of elderly retirees. Pine trees cover endless acres, sustaining companies making paper, pulp and chemicals. Peanuts, tobacco and soybeans are among the important farm products.

Democratic loyalties forged a century ago are still strong in local politics, although the Democratic presidential vote has steadily slid, from 53 percent in 1980 to 40 percent in 1988. Republican voter registration has increased since Grant changed parties in 1989: 500 voters switched immediately after Grant, and more continue to follow his path.

Aiding the Democratic cause are black voters, more numerous here than in all but two other Florida districts. The only Florida county to vote Democratic in the last two presidential elections was black-majority Gadsden County.

Tallahassee, Florida's capital, is economically sustained by state government and two universities, Florida State and Florida A&M. These institutions are diversifying forces, but the city's elegant antebellum homes and flower gardens reveal a persistent Deep South influence, and many Floridians in other parts of the state still view Tallahassee as a sleepy Southern city.

Population: 513,127. White 384,073 (75%), Black 124,421 (24%), Other 2,950 (1%). Spanish origin 6,515 (1%). 18 and over 363,447 (71%), 65 and over 54,766 (11%). Median age: 29.

Committees

Agriculture (18th of 18 Republicans)
Livestock, Dairy and Poultry; Tobacco and Peanuts

Public Works and Transportation (20th of 20 Republicans)
Economic Development; Surface Transportation

Select Narcotics Abuse and Control (12th of 12 Republicans)

Elections

1988 General		
Bill Grant (D) *	134,269	(100%)
1986 General		
Bill Grant (D) *	110,141	(99%)

** Bill Grant was elected as a Democrat in 1986 and 1988. He switched from the Democratic to the Republican Party Feb. 21, 1989.*

District Vote For President

	1988	1984	1980	1976
D	82,000 (40%)	106,997 (47%)	96,530 (53%)	102,936 (60%)
R	120,995 (59%)	121,877 (53%)	79,208 (43%)	63,809 (37%)
I			5,035 (3%)	

Campaign Finance

	Receipts	Receipts from PACs	Expend-itures
1988			
Grant (D)	$264,955	$102,100 (39%)	$223,117
1986			
Grant (D)	$266,597	$113,257 (42%)	$266,068

Key Votes

1987	
Raise speed limit to 65 mph	Y
Approve Gephardt "fair trade" amendment	Y
Ban testing of larger nuclear weapons	N
Delay "re-flagging" of Kuwaiti tankers	Y
Approve tax-raising deficit-reduction bill	Y
1988	
Approve aid to Nicaraguan contras	Y
Enact civil rights restoration bill over Reagan veto	Y
Kill 60-day plant-closing notification measure	N
Pass omnibus trade bill over Reagan veto	Y
Approve death penalty for drug-related murders	Y
Bar federal funds for abortions in cases of rape and incest	Y
Oppose seven-day waiting period for purchase of handguns	Y

Voting Studies

	Presidential Support		Party Unity		Conservative Coalition	
Year	S	O	S	O	S	O
1988	33	64	75	20	82	11
1987	32	63	73	19	81	14

Interest Group Ratings

Year	ADA	ACU	AFL-CIO	CCUS
1988	50	54	79	57
1987	48	25	69	47

3 Charles E. Bennett (D)

Of Jacksonville — Elected 1948

Born: Dec. 2, 1910, Canton, N.Y.
Education: U. of Florida, B.A., J.D. 1934.
Military Career: Army, 1942-47.
Occupation: Lawyer.
Family: Wife, Jean Fay; three children.
Religion: Disciples of Christ.
Political Career: Fla. House, 1941.
Capitol Office: 2107 Rayburn Bldg. 20515; 225-2501.

In Washington: Bennett is a selfless, dedicated man who has lived his long life, including more than four decades in the House, strictly by the rules. But Congress is not the stuff of civics books or morality tales, and Bennett's story is not one that is winding to a happy ending. Although the rules he has so scrupulously observed often were the House's own, his reward from his colleagues has been repeated rejection.

Two decades ago, he helped create the House ethics committee, and then, in what he called "the heaviest rebuke ever given in the Congress," he was denied a seat on the committee for fear he would be too zealous a judge. Years later, having finally won assignment, Bennett rose to chairman only to be replaced in the midst of a major scandal just as the panel was turning to allegations against an ally of then-Speaker Thomas P. O'Neill Jr.

But his greatest disappointment was yet to come. Having waited a generation for the seniority system to give him a turn at chairing the Armed Services Committee, and having climbed to the No. 2 seat, Bennett was spurned for the top job in 1985. When junior Democrats revolted against feeble 80-year-old Chairman Melvin Price, they installed seventh-ranking Les Aspin, then 46, in his place. In a secret ballot after Price's ouster, Aspin defeated the 74-year-old Bennett, 125-103. Two years later, when Aspin's disgruntled allies turned on him, Bennett tried again and ran third in a field of four. Aspin retained the chair.

After his first defeat, a hurt Bennett pointed out to the young rebels that he had waited 36 years for the chairmanship. He missed their point: The rules of seniority had to be broken to free Armed Services of the ineffectual Price; Bennett's unbending loyalty to those rules and to Price meant that he, too, had to be shoved aside.

In that episode, Bennett was a secondary casualty of Congress' recent generational warfare, but from the start of his House career, he has been something of an outsider — well liked and respected, but an outsider all the same. Though he denies being judgmental toward others, his personal ethics code sets him apart from most other politicians.

He accepts no gifts; for years he even returned the fruit baskets that Florida citrus growers sent to the state's congressional delegation. He refuses to cut deals, arguing that legislation should pass on its merits. It was his legislation that made "In God We Trust" the nation's motto. He is so obsessive about answering roll-call votes that his record as he enters his fifth decade is almost perfect. Though crippled from his service in World War II, the result of polio contracted in jungle combat, he has returned hundreds of thousands of dollars' worth of disability checks to the Treasury. He gave back some of his salary, too, and began releasing his financial records in the 1950s, long before disclosure was a political issue. He does not socialize with members, except for a weekly prayer group.

"I don't drink, smoke or run around," he once said. "I'm a pretty simple guy."

Actually, he is quite complex. Though considered self-righteous by some, he is intensely self-deprecating; long ago he called himself "a very egotistical individual. . . . I could make one of the top presidents," but more recently, he has said he does not like himself much for falling short of his ideals. He applied the same ideals to his son, and then blamed himself for his namesake's apparent suicide in 1977. Even before that loss, the former war hero was prone to tears at seemingly inappropriate moments. A genial man, he can turn defensively prickly toward questioners who intend no slight.

To his credit, Bennett has responded to his defeats and tragedy not only with the displays of emotion that so unsettle his colleagues, but also with a renewed determination to make his mark. As he approaches his 80th birthday, he retains a vigor that is unfairly belied by his use of canes and braces.

After a career as a pro-Pentagon hawk, he has become a sort of born-again arms controller, opposing the MX missile on budgetary and strategic grounds, seeking to restrain funding for the strategic defense initiative (SDI), and

Florida 3

Northeast — Jacksonville

The 3rd, which is based in the city of Jacksonville, has grown less rapidly than many of Florida's other House districts. This has not caused much alarm among the business and political leaders of Jacksonville, who seem to prefer steady if unspectacular economic expansion based on the city's traditional economic foundations — shipping, insurance, banking and defense.

One sign that this strategy is working can be seen at the harbor, where hundreds of thousands of imported automobiles are unloaded and prepared for overland shipment. By touting its fine harbor and ready access to rail lines and roads that lead to dealers in the lucrative Southeastern market, Jacksonville has become a leading East Coast port of entry for foreign vehicles. When Japan bowed to U.S. pressure and agreed to curtail shipments of autos to the United States, Jacksonville was not hurt; the Japanese decided to abandon other smaller ports and consolidate their business in Jacksonville, where most of it had already been.

Workers handling cargo and building and repairing ships form a large segment of Jacksonville's blue-collar community. Prudential and Independent Life are among the prominent white-collar employers in the city, which has headquarters or regional offices for two dozen insurance companies. Several of Florida's top 25 financial institutions are based in Jacksonville; only Miami has a larger share. The city's three naval air stations contribute more than $500 million annually to the local economy.

When Jacksonville was developing into a major Atlantic port and land transportation hub earlier this century, its jobs lured farm boys from south Georgia, South Carolina and the Florida Panhandle. People of Deep South origin still dominate the work force and give Jacksonville an ambiance quite different from that of Florida cities that have witnessed large-scale migrations of Northerners or Cubans.

In presidential voting, the 3rd went for Southern Democrat Jimmy Carter in 1976 and 1980, but supported Ronald Reagan in 1984 and gave George Bush more than 60 percent in 1988. The district encompasses most of Jacksonville, including large black communities in the northern and northeastern parts of the city. Blacks account for 27 percent of the district's population, a larger proportion than in any other Florida district.

Population: 512,692. White 364,251 (71%), Black 139,997 (27%), Other 6,241 (1%). Spanish origin 9,195 (2%). 18 and over 362,272 (71%), 65 and over 49,479 (10%). Median age: 29.

lobbying to reform the Pentagon's fraud-scarred purchasing practices. Assisted by a well-regarded staff, he has become a prolific contributor of policy essays to major newspapers and journals.

The 1980s do not mark his first break with the Pentagon. Bennett eventually became a critic of the Vietnam War while other conservatives remained militant. His recent shift reflects the priority he gives to conventional forces over strategic nuclear weapons, particularly as the two areas compete for defense dollars.

On that basis he joined more liberal Democrats in 1982 to oppose the MX missile. Though for several years his name was on the amendments to stop production, he mainly served to lend his conservative credentials to the effort; he was not a leading tactician.

In 1985, months after his Armed Services defeat, Bennett received a standing ovation from the House after his speech against the MX. In part, colleagues were reaching out to him. Some were also sending a message to Aspin, who had betrayed his allies, they felt, by engineering the settlement that preserved MX funds. It was that act that led to Aspin's near-ouster in early 1987.

From 1986 through 1988, it was Bennett's amendments to cut SDI funding that became part of the annual House defense bills. The action in 1988 was typical: Bennett proposed to cut Reagan's $4.9 billion request for fiscal 1989 to $3.5 billion, but lost in Armed Services by a 4-to-1 margin, supported mostly by the panel's few liberals. On the floor, with leadership backing, he won by a 223-195 vote. The Senate as usual approved a higher amount, so in conference Bennett's level served as the lower limit that produced a middle-ground compromise of $4 billion. The result has been a dramatic leveling-off of spending on SDI.

Also in the 100th Congress, Bennett took a hard line against Reagan's decision to provide Navy escorts for Kuwaiti tankers in the Persian Gulf. With Senate Foreign Relations Committee Chairman Claiborne Pell, he sponsored legislation to block the policy, arguing that U.S. forces were being committed to a war zone without congressional authorization. "I do not want to embarrass the president," he said, "but

I read the Constitution." The measure lost, 126-283. Congress, divided over how to respond, in the end did nothing.

Before 1987, Bennett's alliances with more liberal colleagues were interpreted as a sign he had not given up hope of chairing Armed Services, and was positioning himself more in line with the House Democratic mainstream.

But it was Marvin Leath of Texas, a middle-ranking conservative Democrat on Armed Services, who moved first in mid-1986 to exploit the anger against Aspin, and it was his coalition that won a no-confidence vote against Aspin in early 1987. Bennett was aghast. "It would be an absolute affront to me if they twice turned me down," he said, and he forced the issue by announcing his own candidacy to fill the newly vacant chair.

"People have said to me, 'Why do it again? Why put your soul on the chopping block again?' " he said. "I said, 'Well, the reason is, I've never had a fair chance. But I have the seniority. I can eliminate all the wounds on the committee and put it behind us.' " Typically, this man who eschews deals refused to ask members for firm commitments. "I don't want to intrude on their judgment. I'm the most senior and I think I'm qualified," he said.

But even his fellow elders on Armed Services, those who also had been leapfrogged in Aspin's 1985 coup, backed Leath. When the Democratic Caucus chose among four contenders in January 1987, Bennett never got more than 47 votes and was eliminated on the second ballot. Aspin then defeated Leath. Bennett emerged jauntily from the vote, in contrast to his visible shock two years before. "I don't have a morsel of regret, a morsel of sour grapes," he told reporters. But on further questioning, he stared at the group and abruptly walked away.

He remains as head of the Seapower Subcommittee, where he has played an important role in determining long-term naval policy, while on the Merchant Marine Committee he has been able to look after the shipping interests of his Atlantic coast district. He supported the Reagan administration's goal of a 600-ship Navy, and nuclear-powered submarines of the sort advocated by the late Adm. Hyman G. Rickover. Bennett and Rickover developed a close relationship over the years; since Rickover's death, other senior naval officers have continued to influence the panel.

In 1982, Bennett was most visible on the House floor arguing for the Trident II submarine missile. Critics said its speed might provoke the Soviets into a hasty nuclear response, but Bennett countered, "If the Russians are real worried about the Trident II, that is a pretty good indication that perhaps we ought to get it." The opponents lost, 312-89.

In keeping with his concern for ethics, Bennett wants to halt the "revolving door" between the Pentagon and its contractors. Early in the 101st Congress, he expressed almost a sense of betrayal that former Defense Secretary Frank C. Carlucci, whom he had admired, was on the boards of major defense firms only months after leaving office. "If this is true," he said, "I think the spirit of what we are trying to do is just raped."

In the 100th Congress, he was co-chairman of the Military Reform Caucus, an ideologically diverse group pushing for changes at the Pentagon to reduce cost overruns, repairs and fraud. The group's efforts gained momentum when news of a major Pentagon scandal broke in mid-1988, but it was too late for the Congress to take more than limited steps.

Bennett is keeping up his ethics campaign generally, despite the past grief the issue has caused him. He has sponsored legislation to prohibit members in leadership contests from contributing money to their colleagues to curry support, as his rivals in the 1987 Armed Services contest did. "Buying votes is illegal," he says. "So why shouldn't it be prohibited in a leadership race?"

It has been more than 30 years since Bennett drafted the first ethics code for government workers, following scandals in the Eisenhower administration. The code lay dormant for most of that time, and in 1980 he passed legislation requiring that it be posted in all federal offices. Meanwhile, through the years, Bennett introduced dozens of resolutions calling for an ethics committee to police members' behavior; again, scandal provided the necessary boost.

In 1966, Speaker John W. McCormack named a special panel, with Bennett as its head, to investigate New York Democrat Adam Clayton Powell Jr. The committee called for establishing a permanent ethics panel, and the next year the House created the Committee on Standards of Official Conduct.

Bennett, to his sorrow, was not made a member. Eight years later he did get on, at the bottom of a list behind leadership loyalists. But after some retirements and surprise election defeats, he found himself chairman. His tenure coincided with a rash of scandals, including Abscam, and the panel issued recommendations that led to a series of House disciplinary actions, including the first-ever expulsion of a member on corruption charges.

Then, after one term as chairman, Bennett was removed just as the committee began proceedings against the last Abscam figure, John P. Murtha of Pennsylvania, a key lieutenant to Speaker O'Neill. O'Neill replaced Bennett with Ohio Democrat Louis Stokes, a committee member who had been a voice for the accused. The committee ultimately recommended no action against Murtha, provoking its counsel to resign.

The committee's record under Bennett cannot fairly be attributed to any crusading on his part, but rather to the circumstances of the time. In fact, Republicans accused him of being too soft when he recommended censure, not expulsion, for Michigan Democrat Charles C. Diggs Jr., convicted on kickback charges.

Throughout his career, Bennett has typically voted with other Southern conservatives. In the 1960s, he opposed major anti-poverty programs, Medicare and the 1964 Civil Rights Act. But he supported the 1965 Voting Rights Act and the Equal Rights Amendment, and more recently has backed sanctions against South Africa. He has prided himself on winning federal appropriations for ecological projects in the district, but for years incurred environmentalists' wrath for his aggressive support of the Cross-Florida Barge Canal.

At Home: If World War II had not intervened, Bennett might now be serving his 24th term in Congress, rather than his 21st. He launched his first House campaign in late 1941, hoping to build on his political base as a state representative from Jacksonville. But he abandoned the race in 1942 to enlist in the infantry as a private, ignoring the draft deferment granted to legislators.

When he returned home to practice law five years later, he was a war hero, leader of 1,000 guerrillas in the Philippines. But he was also crippled, a victim of polio he contracted during the jungle and mountain fighting.

He was no less determined to run for Congress. In 1948, he challenged Democratic Rep. Emory H. Price, who had been elected instead of him in 1942. Bennett ran on a platform of support for a military draft and opposition to the Truman civil rights program. He won the primary by less than 2,000 votes out of more than 75,000 cast, and took the general election with 91 percent.

Price challenged Bennett in the 1950 primary, but his comeback attempt fell short. That year and throughout the 1950s, Bennett had no general-election opposition.

Republicans fired their best shot in 1964, when prominent Jacksonville businessman William T. Stockton Jr. opposed Bennett. Stockton drew 27 percent of the vote, higher than any GOP percentage before or since, but low enough to convince the party to forget the idea of defeating the veteran Democrat. In the 12 House elections since, Bennett has been unopposed eight times.

Bennett was mentioned twice as a possible Senate candidate. In 1956 there was talk he would oppose first-term Democrat George A. Smathers. When Smathers retired in 1968, he was again considered. Neither rumor lasted long; his sphere has never been statewide.

Committees

Armed Services (2nd of 31 Democrats)
Seapower and Strategic and Critical Materials (chairman); Research and Development

Merchant Marine and Fisheries (16th of 26 Democrats)
Coast Guard and Navigation; Merchant Marine; Oceanography

Elections

1988 General

Charles E. Bennett (D)	Unopposed

1986 General

Charles E. Bennett (D)	Unopposed

Previous Winning Percentages: **1984** (100%) **1982** (84%) **1980** (77%) **1978** (100%) **1976** (100%) **1974** (100%) **1972** (82%) **1970** (100%) **1968** (79%) **1966** (100%) **1964** (73%) **1962** (100%) **1960** (83%) **1958** (100%) **1956** (100%) **1954** (100%) **1952** (100%) **1950** (100%) **1948** (91%)

District Vote For President

	1988	1984	1980	1976
D	65,309 (40%)	70,795 (41%)	69,230 (53%)	80,412 (64%)
R	97,579 (60%)	102,060 (59%)	58,864 (45%)	44,650 (35%)
I			2,655 (2%)	

Campaign Finance

	Receipts	Receipts from PACs	Expend-itures
1988			
Bennett (D)	$104,518	$53,861 (52%)	$19,500
1986			
Bennett (D)	$125,752	$76,441 (61%)	$19,564

Key Votes

1987	
Raise speed limit to 65 mph	N
Approve Gephardt "fair trade" amendment	N
Ban testing of larger nuclear weapons	Y
Delay "re-flagging" of Kuwaiti tankers	Y
Approve tax-raising deficit-reduction bill	Y
1988	
Approve aid to Nicaraguan contras	Y
Enact civil rights restoration bill over Reagan veto	Y
Kill 60-day plant-closing notification measure	N
Pass omnibus trade bill over Reagan veto	Y
Approve death penalty for drug-related murders	Y
Bar federal funds for abortions in cases of rape and incest	N
Oppose seven-day waiting period for purchase of handguns	N

Voting Studies

	Presidential Support		Party Unity		Conservative Coalition	
Year	**S**	**O**	**S**	**O**	**S**	**O**
1988	35	65	82	18	66	34
1987	34	66	79	21	58	42
1986	33	67	82	18	50	50
1985	35	65	82	18	51	49
1984	51	49	59	41	75	25
1983	41	59	61	39	72	28
1982	65	35	55	45	81	19
1981	59	41	48	52	80	20

Interest Group Ratings

Year	ADA	ACU	AFL-CIO	CCUS
1988	65	28	79	43
1987	48	22	50	60
1986	55	27	64	50
1985	70	19	88	32
1984	30	57	46	44
1983	50	57	53	55
1982	40	55	45	64
1981	25	47	40	58

4 Craig T. James (R)

Of DeLand — Elected 1988

Born: May 5, 1941, Augusta, Ga.
Education: Stetson U., B.S. 1963, J.D. 1967.
Military Career: Army National Guard, 1963-65; Army Reserve, 1965-69.
Occupation: Lawyer.
Family: Wife, Katherine Folks.
Religion: Baptist.
Political Career: No previous office.
Capitol Office: 1632 Longworth Bldg. 20515; 225-4035.

The Path to Washington: James, who switched to the Republican Party to run for Congress in 1988, was not a player in elective-office politics before launching his House campaign. But he ended up scoring one of the year's biggest upsets, toppling veteran Democratic Rep. Bill Chappell Jr.

A strongly pro-defense "Boll Weevil" Southern Democrat, Chappell had drawn support from conservatives in both parties in previous elections, and was not perceived as vulnerable at the start of 1988.

But when news broke in the summer about Pentagon procurement irregularities, Chappell was linked in some stories to defense contractors involved in the scandal. News reporters also picked through his financial dealings and raised questions, although Chappell was not accused of any legal wrongdoing.

Local Republican leaders got excited about recruiting a challenger to Chappell, and though James had no background in office, he had been involved in some well-publicized legal cases, earning admirers who saw him as an advocate of taxpayers and critics who felt he was a conservative gadfly. One of James' causes was a successful 1982 court suit to block a $40 million bond issue for building a new jail in Volusia County (Daytona Beach). A less expensive jail was later built.

Still, James was not considered a major threat to Chappell. The incumbent had plenty of money, and when he blew away a primary opponent — albeit a minor one — many took it as a sign he was safe. (Chappell's electoral trouble in the past had come in primaries, because so many liberal Democrats were bothered by his conservatism.) Chappell hailed his primary victory as evidence that local Democrats "know a lie when they hear it." He added: "In November we're going to shoot down that last vulture."

But Chappell's guard was down against James, who made ethics the centerpiece of his campaign. "We need a person who sets a standard of ethics," James said, and he hammered away at the point for the entire campaign, with little response from Chappell.

James did not establish an awesome organization or fund-raising apparatus, but he took every opportunity to make public appearances (unlike Chappell), and he ran enough TV ads to remind voters of the media accounts about Chappell's behavior in office. One James ad stated directly, "He is an embarrassment."

James benefited from a strong GOP year in Florida, and from a general anti-politician sentiment in north Florida that influenced the election outcomes in the neighboring 6th District and in some key state legislative contests as well.

James, who had been to Washington, D.C., only twice before his November election, has shown a streak of independence from the accepted conventions of Congress. He has said that membership in the House "is not supposed to be a professional office," and proposed limiting representatives' careers to eight years. And during the campaign, he said he wanted a seat on the House ethics committee, a panel that is normally composed of more senior members. Instead, when Republicans organized for the 101st Congress, James got Judiciary and Veterans' Affairs.

In ideological terms, James' outlook may not differ all that much from Chappell's. "He espoused many of the conservative views I believe," James said shortly after his narrow victory. That was no comfort to Chappell, though. Refusing to admit defeat, he filed a suit with the Florida Supreme Court questioning the handling of 11,000 ballots. The suit was rejected, and Chappell finally conceded Dec. 16.

When the 1988 class of freshman Republicans first gathered in Washington following the election, most of its members knew little about each other except what they had picked up in the media. That was an advantage for giant-killer James, who put on a full-court press to win election to the position of class president. He won the vote.

James, whose personal financial net worth is substantial, was one of the more vocal freshmen opposing the proposed congressional pay raise that went down to defeat in early 1989.

Florida 4

Northeast — Daytona Beach

Daytona's beach at low tide is as wide as a superhighway, and the clutter sometimes makes it look like one. Ever since Florida's population began to boom in the 1950s, Daytona Beach has been the most popular resort on the state's east coast for vacationers who do not want to bother making a long trip down the peninsula.

Though the winter weather is sometimes cool, the city makes a special push to get winter visitors from Canada, and the Daytona International Speedway schedules its Daytona 500 auto race in February to lure tourists.

Parts of Daytona, however, are less than elegant. The boardwalk and some of the city's motels built in earlier boom days are reaching middle age, and competition from neighboring beaches — and from inland tourist attractions such as Walt Disney World — has stepped up in recent years. Although Daytona's population increased by about 7 percent in the first half of this decade, the rate of growth in Ormond Beach, just to the north, was much more substantial.

And in Flagler County, a few miles farther north, the boom has been even greater, fed by an influx of retirees to the area around Palm Coast. Flagler grew by more than 66 percent from 1980 to 1986.

Because of stiff competition from the nearby metropolitan areas of Jacksonville and Orlando, Daytona's success at attracting new jobs in recent years has been only modest, by Florida standards. Two of the largest employers are General Electric and Associated Coca-Cola Bottling Inc.

Daytona Beach and surrounding Volusia County cast about half the district vote. Although this was reliable Democratic territory for many years, Republicans recently have made significant inroads. In 1988, James ran ahead of Chappell in Volusia, and in the Senate race, Republican Connie Mack and Democrat Buddy MacKay ran almost neck and neck.

Moving north from Volusia, the 4th flanks the St. Johns River as it flows toward Jacksonville and the Atlantic. On the coast, Spanish-founded St. Augustine trades on its tourist-drawing claim of being "the nation's oldest city"; inland, Palatka's economy and air quality bear the stamp of the large Georgia-Pacific paper mill there.

Duval County (Jacksonville) is home to about one-fifth of the district's people. The 4th takes in the southeast corner of Duval, a mostly white-collar, suburban-style area that supplies workers to downtown Jacksonville's offices.

Population: 512,672. White 451,306 (88%), Black 55,840 (11%), Other 3,602 (1%). Spanish origin 8,693 (2%). 18 and over 385,967 (75%), 65 and over 86,302 (17%). Median age: 35.

Committees

Judiciary (14th of 14 Republicans)
Administrative Law and Governmental Relations (ranking); Civil and Constitutional Rights

Veterans' Affairs (11th of 13 Republicans)
Oversight and Investigations

Campaign Finance

	Receipts	Receipts from PACs	Expend-itures
1988			
James (R)	$314,634	$7,295 (2%)	$313,415
Chappell (D)	$955,540	$421,450 (44%)	$1,069,699

Elections

1988 General

Craig T. James (R)	125,608	(50%)
Bill Chappell Jr. (D)	124,817	(50%)

1988 Primary

Craig T. James (R)	19,275	(50%)
Tom Visconti (R)	10,380	(27%)
Ken C. McCarthy (R)	8,694	(23%)

District Vote For President

	1988	1984	1980	1976
D	92,862 (36%)	75,495 (33%)	90,665 (40%)	101,649 (54%)
R	161,656 (63%)	151,283 (67%)	125,277 (56%)	85,485 (45%)
I			7,114 (3%)	

5 Bill McCollum (R)

Of Altamonte Springs — Elected 1980

Born: July 12, 1944, Brooksville, Fla.
Education: U. of Florida, B.A. 1965, J.D. 1968.
Military Career: Navy, 1969-72; Naval Reserve, 1972 to present.
Occupation: Lawyer.
Family: Wife, Ingrid Seebohm; three children.
Religion: Episcopalian.
Political Career: Chairman, Seminole County Republican Executive Committee, 1976-80.
Capitol Office: 1507 Longworth Bldg. 20515; 225-2176.

In Washington: McCollum grabbed a lower rung on the GOP leadership ladder in late 1988, becoming vice chairman of the House Republican Conference. In defeating eight-term California veteran Robert J. Lagomarsino for the post, McCollum publicly demonstrated that he had quietly established a name for himself as one of the more influential junior Republicans.

In the flood of Republican freshmen who came to Washington with President Reagan in 1981, McCollum did not stand out. Neither his political background nor his physical presence was imposing; he was a lawyer who never had held public office, and on first impression he seemed boy-scoutish in appearance and manner.

But McCollum displayed a knack for operating in the institution. He is conservative without being inflexible, persistent without being tiresome.

He started the 100th Congress in the limelight, serving as one of six House Republicans on the committee investigating the Iran-contra affair. Although McCollum was a staunch defender of Reagan's pro-contra policies and questioned the need for the hearings, he was not as unrelenting a defender of the administration as some other GOP members, such as Rep. Henry J. Hyde of Illinois and Sen. Orrin G. Hatch of Utah.

McCollum made news in June 1987 when he said that the testimony of a Justice Department lawyer about a White House meeting showed that three central figures in the affair, William J. Casey, Rear Adm. John M. Poindexter and Lt. Col. Oliver L. North, had engaged in "criminal" behavior and had committed "one of the most treacherous" acts ever against a president. But McCollum did not raise the subject when North and Poindexter testified.

Like many of the Republicans on the panel, McCollum viewed the televised hearings as a chance to plead the case for contra aid before a nationwide audience. "I think many of us want to point out all the facts, but we also want to be sure ... that the public gets the impression of what really did happen and what is at stake in Central America," he said.

Complaining that the hearings had subjected private contra supporters to innuendoes and accusations, he offered an amendment to the State Department authorization bill requiring the State Department to report to Congress the names of U.S. citizens who aid the Sandinista government of Nicaragua. "What is good for the goose is good for the gander," he declared. The House rejected his proposal 103-257.

McCollum has had an impact on two of the more inflammatory issues in modern-day America: gun control and drug abuse. In the 100th Congress, he and Crime Subcommittee Chairman William J. Hughes of New Jersey worked together to draft a bill banning for 10 years the production, importation, sale or delivery of non-detectable firearms — those made mostly of plastic. Reagan signed the bill into law.

The biggest gun-control debate of the 100th Congress was over a proposal to establish a national seven-day waiting period for the purchase of handguns. The waiting period was strongly supported by a coalition of police groups, and vigorously opposed by the National Rifle Association. McCollum drafted a substitute, for which the NRA urged support, to kill the waiting period and replace it with language directing the Justice Department to come up with an identification system to detect felons who try to purchase handguns. The McCollum substitute was adopted, 228-182.

McCollum played an important role in shaping the 100th Congress' $2 billion-plus omnibus anti-drug-abuse bill. The chairman of the House Republican Leadership Task Force on Drugs, McCollum sponsored two legs of what he called his "triad" of user-accountability penalties. The first, adopted 335-67, would bar convicted drug users from receiving federal grants, contracts, loans or public housing. The second, sponsored by Oklahoma Republican Mickey Edwards and adopted 293-115, set a civil penalty of $10,000 per violation for possession of

Florida 5

North Central — Orlando and Northern Suburbs

In a state famous for its coastline, the 5th is the only Florida district without one. But that has been no hindrance to economic development or population growth in and around Orlando. In fact, metropolitan Orlando (encompassing Orange and Seminole counties) has a more diversified economic base than many of Florida's beach meccas, where the economy is skewed toward tourism, condo construction and real-estate speculation.

Orlando has its share of builders and bankers, but it also produces electronic equipment, boats, elevators and pharmaceuticals. It is the base of the Burger King empire and the site of numerous aerospace and defense contractors working on missiles and aircraft-control systems. Tourism is also a major contributor to the economy because the Orlando area is dotted with theme parks. Walt Disney World is across the border in the 11th District, but many of its employees live in the 5th.

When McCollum won the 5th in 1980, it was a much larger district, stretching from the Gulf almost to the Atlantic. But because it had nearly doubled in population during the 1970s, it was divided in redistricting. The part that McCollum kept contains all of downtown Orlando and the city's northern suburbs in Orange and southern Seminole counties.

The affluent Orange County communities of Winter Park and Maitland are home to Orlando's older, established elite, which provides strong support for Republican candidates. Another reliable source of Republican votes is Seminole County, north of Orlando, where many of the upper-level executives new to the area settle. In 1988, George Bush carried almost three-fourths of Seminole's vote. Most of the district's Democratic votes come out of working-class areas within the city of Orlando.

Growth has brought its share of problems to the Orlando area. The city's sewage threatens the health of Lake Tohopekaliga to the south, and paying for capital improvements to control the problem is costly. Demand for water has increased dramatically; lowering of the water table causes occasional sinkholes to open up, swallowing buildings, cars and swimming pools.

Population: 513,005. White 420,215 (82%), Black 84,264 (16%), Other 4,179 (1%). Spanish origin 15,041 (3%). 18 and over 373,987 (73%), 65 and over 61,889 (12%). Median age: 31.

small amounts of illegal drugs. The third amendment would have withheld federal highway funds from states that do not suspend or revoke the driver's licenses of drug offenders. McCollum lost on that count when the House approved a milder amendment to reward states that develop programs to suspend or revoke the licenses of drug offenders.

McCollum combined his assignments on Judiciary and Banking in 1986 and contributed to legislation to bar "money laundering," the practice by which criminals — particularly drug dealers — convert illegal profits into usable cash. McCollum and Hughes co-authored Judiciary's bill, which made a new federal crime of money laundering; it breezed through the House by voice vote during the 99th Congress' drive to enact major anti-drug legislation. The Banking bill addressed federal banking law rather than criminal law. Portions of both bills were included in the $1.7 billion anti-drug package.

The influx of refugees to Florida has led McCollum to take a hard line against illegal aliens, and he played a central role in the long congressional battle over the nation's immigration laws. In 1986, after five years of effort, Congress cleared a bill overhauling those laws. McCollum led the opposition in the 97th, 98th and 99th Congresses to provisions granting legal-resident status to millions of aliens living in the country illegally. His amendment to strike the 1986 bill's amnesty provision was rejected by a close 199-192 vote. McCollum fared better on another immigration issue in the 99th Congress, as Reagan signed into law his bill to tighten restrictions on weddings involving aliens.

On the Banking Committee's Housing Subcommittee, McCollum and Texas Republican Steve Bartlett have led the conservative opposition to the Democratic majority's efforts on behalf of federally subsidized housing.

McCollum's committee assignments do not give him a direct entree to foreign policy issues, but his visit to El Salvador in July 1983 led him to play a more personal role in that nation's affairs than do most congressmen.

Dismayed by the suffering at a Salvadoran refugee camp he visited, McCollum returned home and organized private relief efforts to get medical supplies to people displaced by El Salvador's civil war. McCollum helped accumulate three planeloads' worth of donated supplies, and he persuaded pilots from Rosie O'Grady's Flying Circus in Orlando to volunteer time to fly the planes to El Salvador.

At Home: Spurred by Republican Rep. Richard Kelly's near defeat in 1978, McCollum was already campaigning for the 5th District GOP nomination in 1980 when the FBI snared Kelly in its Abscam investigation.

McCollum, a former Seminole County GOP chairman making his first bid for public office, used his early start to develop a stronger organization than either Kelly or state Sen. Vince Fechtel, who joined the field later. Since there were few issue differences among the men, image rather than substance dominated the campaign. McCollum portrayed himself as a morally upstanding family man qualified to fill a "leadership vacuum."

McCollum got 43 percent of the primary vote, running first in Seminole County and in the Orange County suburbs of Orlando, and also carrying the Gulf Coast GOP strongholds of Pasco and Pinellas counties. Kelly ran a poor third. In the runoff, McCollum again brought his organizational strength to bear against Fechtel, carrying six of the district's eight counties and winning 54 percent.

Democrats chose lawyer David Best, who had polled 49 percent against Kelly in 1978. McCollum, clearly more conservative than Best, caught the district's prevailing mood and was elected with 56 percent.

In 1982 McCollum's Democratic opponent was Dick Batchelor, a popular Orange County state representative who was considered a formidable, although underfunded, campaigner. Fearful of being dragged down by voter discontent with Reaganomics or concern over Social Security, McCollum did not emphasize his party label.

His main theme was repeated from the 1980 campaign — McCollum as the all-American husband and father (compared with the unmarried Batchelor) who had "restored integrity" to the district. With more money to buy media ads, McCollum succeeded in casting Batchelor as a liberal. He won 59 percent of the vote, and local Democrats have not challenged him since.

When Democratic Sen. Lawton Chiles announced his retirement in 1988, McCollum considered running in the GOP primary against fellow Rep. Connie Mack. But Mack had gotten a significant head start securing commitments from state and national Republicans, some of whom publicly urged McCollum to stay in the House. After some thought, that is what he chose to do.

Committees

Banking, Finance and Urban Affairs (5th of 20 Republicans)
Domestic Monetary Policy (ranking); Financial Institutions Supervision, Regulation and Insurance; Housing and Community Development

Judiciary (5th of 14 Republicans)
Crime (ranking); Immigration, Refugees and International Law

Elections

1988 General

Bill McCollum (R)	Unopposed

1986 General

Bill McCollum (R)	Unopposed

Previous Winning Percentages: **1984** (100%) **1982** (59%) **1980** (56%)

District Vote For President

	1988	1984	1980	1976
D	56,030 (31%)	50,693 (29%)	51,295 (34%)	59,891 (46%)
R	123,123 (68%)	125,106 (71%)	93,796 (62%)	68,991 (53%)
I			5,775 (4%)	

Campaign Finance

	Receipts	Receipts from PACs	Expend- itures
1988			
McCollum (R)	$321,887	$117,835 (37%)	$304,853
1986			
McCollum (R)	$165,986	$79,700 (48%)	$121,052

Key Votes

1987	
Raise speed limit to 65 mph	Y
Approve Gephardt "fair trade" amendment	N
Ban testing of larger nuclear weapons	N
Delay "re-flagging" of Kuwaiti tankers	N
Approve tax-raising deficit-reduction bill	N
1988	
Approve aid to Nicaraguan contras	Y
Enact civil rights restoration bill over Reagan veto	N
Kill 60-day plant-closing notification measure	Y
Pass omnibus trade bill over Reagan veto	N
Approve death penalty for drug-related murders	Y
Bar federal funds for abortions in cases of rape and incest	Y
Oppose seven-day waiting period for purchase of handguns	Y

Voting Studies

	Presidential Support		Party Unity		Conservative Coalition	
Year	**S**	**O**	**S**	**O**	**S**	**O**
1988	66	24	82	10	97	0
1987	69	26	82	12	95	2
1986	84	14	81	16	96	4
1985	80	19	82	13	91	9
1984	66	33	85	11	93	7
1983	78	17	89	6	94	3
1982	78	17	91	8	93	7
1981	67	28	83	14	85	12

Interest Group Ratings

Year	ADA	ACU	AFL-CIO	CCUS
1988	0	100	17	75
1987	4	87	0	100
1986	0	82	7	82
1985	5	90	6	90
1984	10	78	8	88
1983	0	100	0	89
1982	10	82	10	82
1981	0	93	13	94

6 Cliff Stearns (R)

Of Ocala — Elected 1988

Born: April 16, 1941, Washington, D.C.
Education: George Washington U., B.S. 1963.
Military Career: Air Force, 1963-67.
Occupation: Motel company executive.
Family: Wife, Joan Moore; three children.
Religion: Presbyterian.
Political Career: No previous office.
Capitol Office: 1723 Longworth Bldg. 20515; 225-5744.

The Path to Washington: Stearns had no political experience when he launched his 1988 campaign for the open 6th District, and he was not considered a major contender by pundits and opponents. But his limited political background gave him a salient populistic theme, and he rode it to a surprising victory in a district that had been in Democratic hands ever since it was created after the 1980 census.

From the outset, Stearns cast the election as a choice not between himself and a particular politician, but between himself and the entire concept of a politician. A heavy underdog to state House Speaker Jon Mills, the Democratic nominee, Stearns stressed that "the time has come for a 'citizen' congressman," and he turned his image of inexperience into a virtue.

For someone who made so much of his novice status, Stearns showed plenty of political savvy in the campaign, putting together a first-rate organizational effort that nicely complemented his rhetoric. And after the election, when the freshman GOP class of 1988 gathered in Washington, Stearns showed his acumen again: He sought and won his class' spot on the influential House GOP panel that parcels out committee assignments to the party's members.

When the 6th came open with Rep. Buddy MacKay's decision to run for the Senate, most eyes turned to Democrat Mills, long pegged as MacKay's successor in the House. Of the six people who filed for the GOP nomination, the two with the most political connections seemed to be Marion County Commissioner Roy Abshier and Jim Cherry, a former state director of the Farmers Home Administration.

But Stearns had developed some contacts of his own in the process of turning an investment in a dilapidated motel into a successful local motel and restaurant management company (called the House of Stearns). He was a director of the local chamber of commerce (where he was active in tourism development), served on the board of a major local hospital and was involved in church and civic groups.

One of Stearns' first moves when the 6th opened up was to send a letter indicating his interest to a few hundred potential supporters. That letter helped Stearns nail down some early commitments for his campaign.

He also had access to a crucial campaign commodity: money. MacKay's announcement came relatively late, leaving little time for candidates to gear up for the primary. Using some of his own money, Stearns started fast, putting up signs and getting his name out.

Stearns finished second to Cherry in the primary, but the results contained signs that he could emerge first in the runoff. Stearns showed his appeal in Marion County (Ocala), his home base, by running ahead of Abshier, who had begun with countywide recognition. In a Republican nomination fight in the 6th, Marion County has more pull than more liberal Alachua County (Gainesville), which was Cherry's home base. That helped spell the difference in the runoff, which Stearns won with votes to spare.

Still, Mills was widely regarded as the all-but-certain November winner. He began with a base of support in Alachua County, had political and fund-raising contacts in Washington and around the state and carried MacKay's endorsement.

But Mills proved somewhat inattentive to the nitty-gritty work of campaigning. Confident of victory, he spent time before the election in Washington making get-acquainted calls on Democratic House leaders. Meanwhile, Stearns campaigned tirelessly in the district and got attention for the primary and runoff elections.

Mills also had a legislative record to defend. He had been an outspoken supporter of a controversial service tax. Though the state's Republican governor had also supported the tax, it proved to be tremendously unpopular. In television ads, Stearns painted Mills as a back-room pol who tried to ram the tax down the throats of Floridians.

Toward the end of the campaign, some of Mills' supporters had an inkling the contest could be closer than anticipated. But none expected the shock they got on Election Day, when Stearns won handily, aided by George Bush's strong showing in the 6th.

Florida 6

North Central — Gainesville; Ocala

The 6th combines a moderate-to-liberal university city with conservative rural areas and a coastal region rapidly attracting Republican retirees. After the 1980 census, it was drawn to give an edge to Democrats in general and Buddy MacKay in particular. MacKay did not have any trouble holding the seat for the first half of the decade, but when he chose to leave, Republicans moved in and took over.

The University of Florida, with more than 34,000 students and 2,800 faculty, puts Gainesville and Alachua County clearly to the left of most of the Florida electorate. Alachua was George McGovern's best county in Florida in 1972. In 1988, Michael S. Dukakis ran 10 percentage points ahead of his 39 percent statewide tally there. Thirty percent of the people in the 6th live in Alachua.

From Alachua County, the district follows the southerly path of Interstate 75 to Ocala in Marion County. Motels, restaurants and gas stations strung along the highway cater to tourists drawn by the region's springs, rivers and lakes. Success in the local restaurant and motel business set Stearns on the path that brought him to Congress.

Some of central Florida's high-technology companies have been expanding operations northward in recent years; Martin Marietta, Microdyne and others moving into Ocala helped boost that city's population by more than 22,000 in the last two decades.

Outside Ocala, Marion County is mostly citrus groves and range land for horse and cattle farms. While the newcomers to Marion County tend to vote Republican, most of its rural people are traditional Southern Democrats. Those two groups were closely matched in 1976, when Jimmy Carter barely carried Marion County over Gerald R. Ford, but in subsequent presidential elections the county has sided with the Republican ticket.

South of Marion, citrus groves continue into Sumter and Lake counties. Watermelons and berries are grown around Leesburg, the geographic center of Florida. Conservative retirees in Lake County make Republican candidates very strong here: George Bush outpolled Dukakis by better than 2-to-1.

The 6th also takes in the Gulf Coast counties of Citrus and Hernando, which have grown by 46 percent and 75 percent, respectively, during this decade. Retirees, responsible for much of the influx, generally help swing the vote to the right.

Population: 512,950. White 434,855 (85%), Black 71,182 (14%), Other 3,386 (1%). Spanish origin 11,761 (2%). 18 and over 394,134 (77%), 65 and over 94,663 (18%). Median age: 34.

Committees

Banking, Finance and Urban Affairs (18th of 20 Republicans)
Financial Institutions Supervision, Regulation and Insurance; Housing and Community Development; International Development, Finance, Trade and Monetary Policy

Select Aging (26th of 27 Republicans)

Veterans' Affairs (12th of 13 Republicans)
Oversight and Investigations

Campaign Finance

	Receipts	Receipts from PACs	Expend-itures
1988			
Stearns (R)	$421,198	$52,270 (12%)	$408,292
Mills (D)	$504,006	$200,800 (40%)	$503,654

Elections

1988 General		
Cliff Stearns (R)	136,415	(53%)
Jon Mills (D)	118,756	(47%)
1988 Primary Runoff		
Cliff Stearns (R)	15,205	(54%)
Jim Cherry (R)	12,882	(46%)
1988 Primary		
Jim Cherry (R)	13,355	(32%)
Cliff Stearns (R)	10,875	(26%)
Roy Abshier (R)	6,459	(16%)
Larry Gallagher (R)	5,984	(15%)
Ken Stepp (R)	2,317	(6%)
Norman F. Cates (R)	2,215	(5%)

District Vote for President

	1988	1984	1980	1976
D	101,003 (39%)	83,273 (35%)	79,547 (42%)	81,083 (55%)
R	157,184 (60%)	152,694 (65%)	101,489 (53%)	65,705 (44%)
I			8,380 (4%)	

7 Sam M. Gibbons (D)

Of Tampa — Elected 1962

Born: Jan. 20, 1920, Tampa, Fla.
Education: U. of Florida, J.D. 1947.
Military Career: Army, 1941-45.
Occupation: Lawyer.
Family: Wife, Martha Hanley; three children.
Religion: Presbyterian.
Political Career: Fla. House, 1953-59; Fla. Senate, 1959-63.
Capitol Office: 2204 Rayburn Bldg. 20515; 225-3376.

In Washington: Gibbons' status as chairman of the Ways and Means Trade Subcommittee has made him an important member of the House, but he has been a man with a difficult role — a longtime free-trader seeking to hold the line in an era of protectionist pressure.

For Gibbons, free trade is not just a political slogan; it is his creed. Raised in the Depression, and battle-scarred by world war, he is convinced that both catastrophes were born of the trade barriers that nations had thrown up. "World War II had a tremendous impact on me," he has said. "I felt one reason it started was people didn't know how to work together. . . . My grand global goal is to make friends through commerce."

His stance is not always conducive to making friends in the House, however. In fact, it led colleagues to snub Gibbons when the subcommittee chairmanship first became available to him more than a decade ago.

And that was before the nation ran up the unprecedented trade deficits of the 1980s, which emboldened Democrats and some Republicans to press harder for import limits and retaliation against nations deemed unfair traders. As his party sought to exploit the trade issue on the campaign front, Gibbons was endorsing President Reagan's anti-protectionist views. "There is nothing through trade policy that Congress could do that will affect our trade deficit," he insisted.

Despite a stubborn streak, Gibbons reluctantly and perhaps unavoidably accepted the need for some congressional effort to get tough with U.S. trading partners. The effort has required the proud and occasionally headstrong Gibbons to balance his own principles against the political desires of his colleagues. Justifying his conciliatory role, he argues that the United States must combat unfair trade practices if it is to convert its partners to free trade. "We are not changing our principles," he said. "We are changing our laws to reflect changed conditions."

Beginning in 1985, he cooperated with Ways and Means Chairman Dan Rostenkowski to help produce what became, three years later, the most far-reaching trade law in years. Yet even as his subcommittee prepared to draft a bill early in the 100th Congress, Gibbons was ever mindful of perhaps the most famous trade law in history, the 1930 Smoot-Hawley Act, which dramatically boosted tariffs and contributed to the ensuing global Depression.

Meeting with reporters in the committee room, he pointed to a portrait of former Ways and Means Chairman Willis C. Hawley and promised them that Smoot's cosponsor would not like whatever emerged from Gibbons' subcommittee. But Gibbons surely did. He fended off a variety of industry-specific protections, and said of his panel's handiwork: "We're on the way to a good trade bill, a really good trade bill, one that has the potential of being historic."

Speaker Jim Wright and other House leaders preferred a tougher measure. They got their wish on the floor, when the House narrowly approved the controversial Gephardt amendment, which would mandate limits on imports from nations such as Japan that maintain big surplus trade balances with the United States. Gibbons admitted that he found the amended bill "a tough one to vote for," but he did anyway, saying, "This is a bicameral organization, and there is hope that we can work out an acceptable bill before we are at the end of all this."

Other than the Gephardt amendment, the House bill contained little that Gibbons found objectionable. With the exception of telecommunications, it did not single out any industries for special treatment. And though it contained some threatening language, it still left the president considerable leeway on most trade matters.

The next step, negotiations with the Senate, proved difficult, in part because of senators' resistance to the Gephardt amendment. Despite his own opposition to it, however, Gibbons joined Rostenkowski in late 1987 in squashing a House Republican motion instructing conferees to drop the provision. Not only

Florida 7

West — Tampa

Ever since a Key West cigar factory moved to Tampa in 1886, this has been a city with a strong blue-collar orientation. Cubans came to work in the cigar business, and they were joined later by Georgians, Alabamans and other Southerners looking for jobs in factories around the harbor.

Tampa still makes cigars, and other traditional industries are strong, among them brewing, commercial fishing, steel-making and ship construction. The city is also a major port, giving it an interest in international markets that coincides with Gibbons' free-trade politics.

The large working-class community makes Tampa the Florida city that most closely approximates industrial cities of the North. The 7th is a Democratic district in most state and national elections, providing a sharp contrast to its neighbor across the bay, the Republican 8th District in St. Petersburg. But Tampa's traditional patterns have been less pronounced in the last two presidential elections; there were not enough Democratic votes in the city to prevent Ronald Reagan or George Bush from carrying surrounding Hillsborough County on a tide of suburban GOP support.

Unlike many Northern industrial cities, however, Tampa has been able to diversify beyond its industrial base to compete for the lucrative tourist trade. Busch Gardens, which started as a simple brewery tour, has been expanded into a 300-acre amusement park that is one of Florida's leading tourist attractions.

The district is 11 percent Hispanic. The influence of the Cuban and Spanish culture is most pronounced in Ybor City, a long-established community in southeast Tampa named after the man who brought his cigar factory here from Key West.

Blacks, who account for 15 percent of the district's population, live mostly in inner-city Tampa. In early 1987, the death of a black man in police custody spurred charges of brutality, and long before that, some black political leaders expressed the view that they had more in common with predominantly black areas of downtown St. Petersburg than with the rest of the 7th District. Early in 1982, the Tampa and St. Petersburg NAACP chapters proposed the creation of a congressional district that would have crossed Tampa Bay, uniting blacks in both cities. Legislators gave the proposal no serious consideration.

Population: 512,905. White 424,343 (83%), Black 76,610 (15%), Other 4,290 (1%). Spanish origin 58,176 (11%). 18 and over 376,478 (73%), 65 and over 62,422 (12%). Median age: 31.

was the amendment a bargaining chip, it also was central to the presidential campaign of its sponsor, Richard A. Gephardt of Missouri, whom both Gibbons and Rostenkowski supported. Months later, Gephardt's faltering showing in the spring presidential primaries freed House negotiators to compromise.

Reagan vetoed the bill because of one non-trade provision requiring advance notice of plant closings. Congress severed the trade and labor bills and passed both a second time, separately; the president signed the trade bill and ultimately let the plant-closing bill become law without his signature.

In the past two Congresses, Gibbons had a more nettlesome role as his panel each time produced a bill he wanted no part of — one limiting textile and apparel imports. Still, he did not use his position to kill it.

The bill had nearly 300 cosponsors in the 99th Congress, indicating enough support to pry it from Gibbons' subcommittee with a discharge petition had he chosen to play the obstructionist. He voluntarily agreed to take it up, but with a promise from the chief sponsor, Georgia Democrat Ed Jenkins, not to support amendments on the floor. That made it tough for Jenkins to broaden the bill's scope and expand his coalition. The measure passed easily, but ultimately fell short of the two-thirds needed to override Reagan's veto.

In the 100th Congress, Gibbons again stood aside as his subcommittee originated a similar bill, once its sponsors agreed not to try to attach their pet to the trade bill. When the House vote for passage fell short of two-thirds, presaging another successful veto, Gibbons declared, "I feel like the [free-trade] cause won."

"No country in the world has ever extended its standard of living by closing its markets," he said. "It hasn't happened in 6,500 years of recorded history."

Gibbons' panel handled one measure in the 100th Congress that he embraced unconditionally — legislation implementing a pact with Canada phasing out tariffs between the two countries. Some members feared the consequences of competition for industries in their states, but Gibbons hoped the treaty would set a pattern. The bill passed overwhelmingly.

For the second Congress, his panel approved legislation from the Foreign Affairs

Committee imposing trade sanctions on the apartheid regime of South Africa; the version in the 100th Congress would have expanded the limited 1986 law to call for a near-total trade ban — "economic warfare," in Gibbons' words. It was not a departure from his free-trade philosophy, Gibbons said: "We're not talking about trade. We're talking about freedom." That bill passed the House, but died in the Senate.

Despite his accommodating approach of late, Gibbons never will go as far toward trade protection as some Democrats would prefer. Consequently, he occasionally must worry about other committees and individuals encroaching on trade matters. In both the 97th and 98th Congresses, the House, over his vigorous opposition, voted for labor-backed bills to protect U.S. automakers by imposing a "domestic content" requirement on automobiles sold domestically. Both bills died in the Senate.

Still, his conciliatory style on the trade bill has brought him closer to the House Democratic mainstream, which is where he would want to be should Rostenkowski decide to retire. Gibbons is next in line to chair Ways and Means, but as recent battles on the Armed Services Committee have shown, seniority does not always assure a member a chairmanship. If he were an unyielding free-trader, Gibbons might face opposition.

Gibbons has some experience with succession struggles. In 1977, his views probably prevented him from becoming chairman of the Trade Subcommittee. The chair was vacant then; he was the panel's senior Democrat and expected to inherit it. But his prospective leadership disturbed many committee Democrats, and Charles Vanik of Ohio, who had not even been on the Trade panel, exercised his full-committee seniority and snatched the chair.

By 1981, though, Gibbons was No. 2 on Ways and Means, and there was nobody to block him when the spot opened again. In fact, he was poised to assume the full-committee chairmanship that year. Retirements and surprise defeats left only Rostenkowski ahead of him, and Rostenkowski was more interested in being majority whip. But Speaker Thomas P. O'Neill Jr., a past rival of Gibbons, urged Rostenkowski to stay at Ways and Means, preferring not to have Gibbons in that pivotal post.

Gibbons' relations with Rostenkowski were strained in the 99th Congress when Gibbons emerged as a vocal critic of the committee's centerpiece legislation, a major revision of the tax code. On one occasion, he presided in the chairman's absence and proceeded to lambaste the bill, prompting staffers to track down their boss, who returned fuming. According to a book on the bill's evolution, "Showdown at Gucci Gulch," one Ways and Means member consoled another who had bemoaned that he was "in a lot of shit" with Rostenkowski by telling him, "If you're in shit, you're standing on Sam Gibbons' shoulders."

In the late 1960s, Gibbons had espoused the very reforms the bill was aimed at — lower rates, fewer loopholes and simplicity. But now he argued that raising business taxes to offset lower individual rates would hurt U.S. firms as they struggled to compete globally. Republicans in his district later would contend that Gibbons was angling for political contributions to build his campaign treasury, since his 1984 election had been the closest of his career.

Despite his objections, he voted for the tax bill. Even so, he did not win a place on the crucial House-Senate conference committee; Rostenkowski ignored seniority and selected the members most likely to support his efforts.

Gibbons is an affable and friendly man, but he can be volatile. During the tax bill deliberations, he would launch into tirades against the Ways and Means staff. That reflected not only his own quick temper, but also a general frustration among panel members with the sway Rostenkowski allows his professional minions.

Like many senior members, Gibbons has modified his early ideas about the House. "Secrecy and seniority," he once said, "are the twin vices of this House." But now, he favors the closed meetings that have become routine at Ways and Means. As a junior Democrat on the Education and Labor Committee in the 1960s, he crusaded to open sessions to the public. He helped draft new rules to restrict unrecorded voting on the House floor and to require confirmation votes on committee chairmen.

In such reformist efforts he was an ally of Arizona Democrat Morris K. Udall. Gibbons managed Udall's unsuccessful bid for majority leader in 1971 against Hale Boggs of Louisiana. Two years later, after Boggs' death, Gibbons launched a brief and futile campaign of his own that would haunt his relations with the House Democratic hierarchy for years. The overwhelming front-runner was O'Neill, who correctly assumed that as majority whip he was the heir apparent. O'Neill and Gibbons had been allies in the past, so Gibbons' challenge was a curious one. He dropped out before the voting and O'Neill won unopposed, but the damage was done.

Before he joined Ways and Means in 1969, Gibbons had attracted national attention as a member of Education and Labor by confronting the flamboyant chairman, Adam Clayton Powell Jr. Gibbons complained that Powell was capricious in hiring and firing people, and that he was often vacationing in the Caribbean while important legislation languished. Gibbons once stalked out of a hearing grumbling, "I'm sick of the whole thing." At his lead, the panel adopted new rules to shift power to the six subcommittee chairmen.

In 1965, during his second term, he successfully served as floor manager for the Johnson administration's anti-poverty program. The White House reckoned it would help to have a white Southerner in charge, and Gibbons' credentials as a national Democrat were solid. He had backed Johnson for president in 1964 and supported most of his policies, including the Vietnam War.

In those early years, Gibbons skirted the line between national Democratic liberalism and conservative Southern sensibilities. He voted against the 1964 and 1968 Civil Rights acts, against school busing and for school prayer. But he voted for poverty programs, the 1965 Voting Rights Act and a 1966 open-housing bill that died in the Senate. Because he hailed from a prominent Tampa family, the establishment there tolerated Gibbons' liberal image.

At Home: Gibbons, now in his 14th House term, is the only representative his Tampa-based district has ever had. He defeated a conservative Democrat to win it in 1962, the year it was created, then in 1968 held off another primary challenge from the right.

In some recent campaigns, Gibbons has been criticized as being aloof from district concerns. But only in the strong Republican year of 1984 did his general-election tally fall below 60 percent, and then just barely. When that spurred talk of a serious challenge in the next election, Gibbons dusted off his campaign machinery, put a new emphasis on fund raising and hired a big-name consultant. He spent hundreds of thousands of dollars, but as it turned out, he was unopposed both in 1986 and 1988.

Before he came to Congress, Gibbons served 10 years in the Legislature, where he drafted his state's first successful urban-renewal measure and supported legislative reapportionment, fighting the north Florida "Pork Chop Gang" that wanted to preserve rural over-representation. Gibbons finished first in the five-way 1962 Democratic congressional primary, but fell far short of a majority. His runoff opponent was retired National Guard Lt. Gen. Sumter L. Lowry, a fervid segregationist and anti-communist.

Lowry was helped by contributions from wealthy conservatives all over the South, but Gibbons picked up the support of the moderate Democratic candidates who had failed to make the runoff. He defeated Lowry and won the general election handily.

Committees

Ways and Means (2nd of 23 Democrats)
Trade (chairman); Social Security

Joint Taxation

Elections

1988 General

Sam Gibbons (D)	Unopposed

1986 General

Sam Gibbons (D)	Unopposed

Previous Winning Percentages: **1984** (59%) **1982** (74%) **1980** (72%) **1978** (100%) **1976** (66%) **1974** (100%) **1972** (68%) **1970** (72%) **1968** (62%) **1966** (100%) **1964** (100%) **1962** (71%)

District Vote For President

	1988	1984	1980	1976
D	76,797 (41%)	70,645 (37%)	73,804 (43%)	79,593 (54%)
R	107,409 (58%)	119,135 (63%)	87,705 (51%)	66,684 (45%)
I			7,679 (5%)	

Campaign Finance

	Receipts	Receipts from PACs	Expend-itures
1988			
Gibbons (D)	$604,570	$345,387 (57%)	$382,889
1986			
Gibbons (D)	$903,485	$560,270 (62%)	$563,509

Key Votes

1987	
Raise speed limit to 65 mph	N
Approve Gephardt "fair trade" amendment	N
Ban testing of larger nuclear weapons	N
Delay "re-flagging" of Kuwaiti tankers	Y
Approve tax-raising deficit-reduction bill	Y
1988	
Approve aid to Nicaraguan contras	Y
Enact civil rights restoration bill over Reagan veto	Y
Kill 60-day plant-closing notification measure	N
Pass omnibus trade bill over Reagan veto	Y
Approve death penalty for drug-related murders	Y
Bar federal funds for abortions in cases of rape and incest	?
Oppose seven-day waiting period for purchase of handguns	N

Voting Studies

	Presidential Support		Party Unity		Conservative Coalition	
Year	**S**	**O**	**S**	**O**	**S**	**O**
1988	35	54	74	20	55	32
1987	29	67	82	12	49	47
1986	33	62	71	19	56	34
1985	50	45	69	20	49	45
1984	45	47	59	24	51	36
1983	45	50	68	23	38	55
1982	65	29	62	35	64	32
1981	62	34	46	45	80	15

Interest Group Ratings

Year	ADA	ACU	AFL-CIO	CCUS
1988	60	35	71	64
1987	56	32	69	33
1986	50	45	31	57
1985	40	38	53	50
1984	35	29	33	25
1983	60	22	53	55
1982	50	41	40	48
1981	30	38	40	50

8 C.W. Bill Young (R)

Of St. Petersburg — Elected 1970

Born: Dec. 16, 1930, Harmarville, Pa.
Education: Attended Pennsylvania public schools.
Military Career: National Guard, 1948-57.
Occupation: Insurance executive.
Family: Wife, Beverly F. Angelo; three children.
Religion: Methodist.
Political Career: Fla. Senate, 1961-71, minority leader, 1967-71.
Capitol Office: 2407 Rayburn Bldg. 20515; 225-5961.

In Washington: Young's blow-dried pompadour hair style sometimes makes him look like a refugee from a country & western band, but he is in reality one of the more serious and effective conservatives in the House.

While Young plays his most substantive role as a GOP stalwart on the Appropriations Subcommittee on Defense, he gained an honorary title of symbolic significance early in the 101st Congress: dean of the majority party in Florida's 19-member House delegation.

When Young was first elected to the state Senate in 1960, he was its only Republican. A decade later, when he won a seat in the U.S. House, he was one of just three Republicans in the 12-member delegation. In the years since, Florida's House contingent and its Republican component have grown, but the GOP did not have a majority of House members until 2nd District Rep. Bill Grant switched parties in February 1989, making the split 10-9 GOP. "I have to admit," Young said, "this is the first time ever in my political career I'm in any kind of majority status."

Whether Young's new status will bring him any additional influence remains to be seen, but he is already known for expanding the purview of the Defense Appropriations Subcommittee where he serves. Young has become the leading congressional advocate of the National Bone Marrow Donor Registry, and he has worked to fund it through the defense budget.

The money initially found its way into a defense funding bill in 1986, when then-Sen. Paul Laxalt of Nevada slipped it in. That same year, Laxalt announced his retirement, and Young came into contact with a 10-year-old girl from his district who was dying of cancer and could not find a bone-marrow donor. Since then, Young has guarded funding for the registry, and in the 100th Congress, he worked to shift it from the Navy (which contracted the registry out to the Red Cross) to the National Institutes of Health.

While he says the registry is his proudest achievement, Young is probably best known for his advocacy of the 1980s defense buildup. Though Young supported nearly all of President Reagan's individual defense initiatives, his seriousness and his willingness to work with Democrats on a number of issues — such as tactical air power and competition in anti-tank weapons — have earned him respect on both sides of the aisle. Young has even suggested that his unyielding stance on some issues is just a strategy to offset the zeal of liberals bent on cutting defense. "I have become one of those who is the counterbalance on the right that makes it possible to compromise in the middle," he once said.

A member of the Intelligence Committee earlier in his House career, Young has continued to pursue national security issues. He is a leading House proponent of expanding random polygraph testing for Defense Department and federal-contractor employees. Two years after approving a polygraph test program in the defense authorization bill, the 100th Congress approved language to permit annual random polygraph tests of up to 20,000 employees of the Defense Department and its contractors.

Young initially faced accusations that his plan was part of a hysterical reaction to spy scandals. But he and other advocates maintained that the plan was simply aimed at improving the government's capacity to discover national security breaches, and he brushed off questions about the reliability of the so-called lie detector. "Give our country the tools to battle the spies and the potential spies, the traitors and the potential traitors," Young said.

While the national security applications of polygraph testing have gained widespread support, Young's enthusiasm for testing in the private sector has never caught on. In 1986 and 1987, the House passed legislation prohibiting most private employers from requiring employees and job applicants to take lie-detector tests. During both debates, Young amendments to permit testing under certain guidelines were defeated.

During his tenure on Intelligence, Young charted an independent course on some matters. He supported efforts to aid anti-commu-

Florida 8

West — St. Petersburg

The modern era of Florida politics began in this district a little over three decades ago, and the 8th is still a good signpost of political change statewide.

In 1954, this district made William C. Cramer the state's first Republican House member of the 20th century. Cramer owed his election to the influence of conservative retirees. In subsequent years, other Republican candidates prospered as the retirees' influence expanded elsewhere in Florida.

Today, the retirees are still crucial in the politics of the 8th, but no candidate can afford to ignore the growing numbers of young people drawn by its steadily diversifying economy. The young newcomers, like their peers flooding into other parts of Florida, are in some ways more conservative, which is good news for the GOP here.

Not too long ago, St. Petersburg was known as almost exclusively a retirement haven. The retirees who settled there — many of them storekeepers, office workers and civil servants from the small-town Midwest — brought their Republican preferences to Florida with them. The economy was mostly service oriented, geared to the needs of elderly residents and tourists. The morning rush hour saw many younger workers from St. Petersburg driving to jobs in Tampa, which provided employment in a greater variety of fields and a faster pace of life than in St. Pete, where the Shuffleboard Hall of Fame is a big attraction.

But during the last decade, St. Petersburg sought to broaden its economic base by stressing that it offers a good climate for business investment. Now, St. Petersburg and Pinellas County firms such as Honeywell, Paradyne, E-Systems and General Electric are busy with research, development, production and marketing of computers, communications equipment and other high-technology items. A number of the major employers and subcontractors are engaged in defense-related work.

The median age of the Pinellas County population has dropped because so many young people attracted to good-paying jobs have moved into the area. Democrats are still competitive in some elections in the 8th, partly because many retirees identify the party as the founder and protector of Social Security. But Republicans and Democrats are at near-parity in the number of registered voters in Pinellas County, and in practice, many of the registered Democrats vote Republican, especially at the national level.

Population: 512,909. White 463,124 (90%), Black 44,983 (9%), Other 3,161 (1%). Spanish origin 7,616 (2%). 18 and over 413,853 (81%), 65 and over 141,405 (28%). Median age: 45.

nist insurgents, including the Nicaraguan contras, and defended the CIA's successful attempt to exempt certain operational files from Freedom of Information Act requests. But he was critical of the agency following disclosures of the CIA role in helping elect Salvadoran President José Napoleón Duarte. "The CIA is not the place to run political campaigns," Young declared. He said he was bothered by the CIA's arrogance in refusing to keep Congress informed.

Young also plays a role in a number of issues closer to home. Together with Florida Democrat William Lehman, Young led the charge in the Appropriations Committee against lifting an existing moratorium on offshore oil drilling in the Gulf of Mexico. When an amendment challenging the drilling ban was offered, the committee turned it back.

Young, who notes that his St. Petersburg-based district contains more Social Security recipients than any other, goes to considerable lengths to help them. Just before the House rejected a rule that would have permitted consideration of the long-term home health-care bill, Young implored his colleagues to vote for the measure. "We talk about the costs, and who will pay for it," he said. "Do not forget these folks who are older Americans today are the very ones who . . . created things in our society, in our economy; they have an outstanding record of service to America." Young was one of just 24 Republicans to vote for the rule on the long-term home health-care bill, which went down to a lopsided defeat.

In 1985, he proposed a bill to prohibit employers from setting any mandatory retirement age; a similar measure became law in 1986. A member of the Appropriations subcommittee that sets spending levels for the Department of Health and Human Services, he has called for more expeditious health-care payments to Medicare recipients, and has proposed legislation guaranteeing that the cost-of-living adjustments for Social Security beneficiaries could not be cut back or eliminated.

At Home: A high-school dropout from a Pennsylvania mining town, Young worked his way to success in the insurance business before going into politics in 1960. Ten years later, he inherited Florida's most dependable Republican seat from Rep. William C. Cramer, who left it when he ran for the U.S. Senate in 1970.

Young had known Cramer a long time. He had met the congressman at a Rotary Club barbecue in 1955, worked in his 1956 campaign and was hired as Cramer's district aide in 1957. In 1960 the Pinellas County GOP organization urged Young to challenge a veteran Democratic state senator. He won, and became the only Republican in the state Senate. By 1967, there were 20 others, and Young was minority leader.

When Cramer announced for the Senate in 1970, there was little question who would replace him. Young won 76 percent of the primary vote and 67 percent in the general election. Since then it has been even easier.

During the 1980s, Young has drawn Democratic opposition only twice. In 1984, he won 80 percent against Democrat Robert Kent, a former Sunshine Skyway toll collector. Kent, a Yugoslavian émigré and frequent congressional candidate from Indiana in the 1960s, changed his name from Ivan Korunek before running against Young, but the strategy failed to broaden his appeal. In 1988, Young got more than 70 percent of the vote against Democrat C. Bette Wimbish, a former St. Petersburg City Council president.

When prominent Republicans were looking for established politicians to challenge Democratic Gov. Bob Graham and Sen. Lawton Chiles in 1982, both Young and Rep. L. A. "Skip" Bafalis were intensively courted. Young pondered a statewide race, then ruled it out, a decision that seemed wise in retrospect. Bafalis took a chance and received a dismal 35 percent against Graham.

Committee

Appropriations (6th of 22 Republicans)
Defense; Labor, Health and Human Services, Education and Related Agencies

Elections

1988 General		
C. W. Bill Young (R)	169,165	(73%)
C. Bette Wimbish (D)	62,539	(27%)
1986 General		
C. W. Bill Young (R)		Unopposed

Previous Winning Percentages: **1984** (80%) **1982** (100%) **1980** (100%) **1978** (79%) **1976** (65%) **1974** (76%) **1972** (76%) **1970** (67%)

District Vote For President

	1988	1984	1980	1976
D	97,452 (45%)	91,393 (37%)	97,234 (41%)	98,426 (49%)
R	120,065 (55%)	153,584 (63%)	124,802 (53%)	100,586 (50%)
I			12,280 (5%)	

Campaign Finance

	Receipts	Receipts from PACs	Expend-itures
1988			
Young (R)	$212,972	$109,600 (51%)	$208,320
Wimbish (D)	$37,501	$14,001 (37%)	$23,655
1986			
Young (R)	$214,687	$91,945 (43%)	$96,142

Key Votes

1987	
Raise speed limit to 65 mph	N
Approve Gephardt "fair trade" amendment	N
Ban testing of larger nuclear weapons	N
Delay "re-flagging" of Kuwaiti tankers	Y
Approve tax-raising deficit-reduction bill	N
1988	
Approve aid to Nicaraguan contras	Y
Enact civil rights restoration bill over Reagan veto	N
Kill 60-day plant-closing notification measure	Y
Pass omnibus trade bill over Reagan veto	Y
Approve death penalty for drug-related murders	Y
Bar federal funds for abortions in cases of rape and incest	Y
Oppose seven-day waiting period for purchase of handguns	N

Voting Studies

	Presidential Support		Party Unity		Conservative Coalition	
Year	**S**	**O**	**S**	**O**	**S**	**O**
1988	59	36	86	8	97	3
1987	59	36	76	17	84	9
1986	72	26	75	18	84	14
1985	74	25	80	14	87	9
1984	54	38	68	24	85	8
1983	74	23	77	18	87	11
1982	74	16	74 †	17 †	84	5
1981	72	24	83	12	88	7

† Not eligible for all recorded votes.

Interest Group Ratings

Year	ADA	ACU	AFL-CIO	CCUS
1988	10	88	36	79
1987	12	87	6	93
1986	5	95	8	67
1985	5	71	24	76
1984	25	58	15	60
1983	5	96	6	75
1982	10	86	5	80
1981	5	100	7	94

9 Michael Bilirakis (R)

Of Palm Harbor — Elected 1982

Born: July 16, 1930, Tarpon Springs, Fla.

Education: U. of Pittsburgh, B.S. 1959; attended George Washington U., 1959-60; U. of Florida, J.D. 1963.

Military Career: Air Force, 1951-55.

Occupation: Lawyer; restaurant owner.

Family: Wife, Evelyn Miaoulis; two children.

Religion: Greek Orthodox.

Political Career: No previous office.

Capitol Office: 1530 Longworth Bldg. 20515; 225-5755.

In Washington: Unfailingly friendly, earnest and diligent, Bilirakis seems content to confine his legislative endeavors to non-controversial issues of concern to his constituents, more than a third of whom are over age 65.

Generally a party loyalist, Bilirakis parts company with the majority of the GOP when his constituency calls. After supporting the Republican alternative to the catastrophic-health insurance bill in the 100th Congress, he was one of 61 House Republicans to ignore the president's veto threat and vote for the Democratic bill. More recently, he joined the chorus of concern about the financial burden the new law's increased premiums place on the elderly.

On the Energy and Commerce Committee, Bilirakis works cooperatively with liberal Health Subcommittee Chairman Henry A. Waxman when it serves his district. In the 99th Congress, the two collaborated to get five Medicare demonstration projects for victims of Alzheimer's disease included in a budget-reconciliation measure.

Bilirakis' attentive concern for the elderly coupled with his geniality helped earn him the chairmanship of the Republican Research Committee's Task Force on the Elderly. He is also a member of the "notch" coalition, which wants Congress to eliminate the Social Security "notch gap" that reduced benefits for those born between 1917 and 1921. He has introduced legislation to that effect in each Congress since he was first elected.

A member of the Veterans' Affairs Committee, Bilirakis has a keen interest in American servicemen missing in action or reported to be still held in Southeast Asia. In the 100th Congress, he authored a successful bill designating "National Women Veterans Recognition Week."

The son of Greek immigrants, Mike Bilirakis takes to the House floor every year on Greek Independence Day to remind his colleagues of the framers' use of ancient Greek sources in writing the U.S. Constitution. In 1988, he also expressed concern about the plight of the Greek minority in Albania.

At Home: When Bilirakis announced plans to make his first political campaign in 1982, local GOP leaders were slightly bemused. But Bilirakis surprised the press, the party hierarchy and nearly everyone else who was supposed to understand Florida politics, turning innocence into a virtue and winning the newly created 9th.

A registered Democrat until 1970, Bilirakis had switched parties to volunteer in L. A. "Skip" Bafalis' bid for governor. Although he was intermittently active in local Republican campaigns during the next decade, he never considered running for office himself until 1982. Asked by a reporter what triggered his candidacy, Bilirakis replied, "I found myself out of challenges."

In the GOP primary, Bilirakis was an underdog to state House Republican leader Curt Kiser. But while Kiser was taking his nomination for granted, Bilirakis was blanketing the district with signs saying that his was "a hard name to spell but an easy one to remember."

Using his own resources and contributions from the Tarpon Springs Greek community, Bilirakis flooded the airwaves with ads stressing his service to the area, as a judge in county and municipal courts and as president of several community organizations. Bilirakis finished well ahead of Kiser and Clearwater Mayor Charles LeCher. In the runoff, Kiser's attempts to make up for his earlier lethargy were in vain; Bilirakis won 54 percent.

Bilirakis emphasized his personality in his general-election campaign against Democratic state Rep. George Sheldon. When he did speak out on issues, he espoused conservative positions — defending President Reagan's economic program and arguing for a constitutional ban on abortions — and he attacked Sheldon's more liberal voting record. Sheldon's tenure in office gave him a strong base of support, but Bilirakis hung on to win by 4,320 votes.

He has quickly become entrenched; in both 1984 and 1986, Bilirakis won more than 70 percent, and in 1988 he was unopposed.

Florida 9

West — Clearwater; Parts of Pasco and Hillsborough Counties

Patching together pieces of three counties in the Tampa-St. Petersburg area, the 9th is a horseshoe-shaped district with a decidedly Republican bent.

About 40 percent of the vote comes from Clearwater and nearby communities in Pinellas County, solidly Republican areas where a Democratic candidate is fortunate to win 45 percent of the vote. Clearwater, traditionally a beach resort, has benefited from the arrival of high-technology industry to metropolitan St. Petersburg. Aerosonic Corp., an aircraft instrument manufacturer, is based in Clearwater.

Republicans also hold the upper hand in Pasco County, which casts about one-third of the vote. But Democrats are more competitive there, since many of the retirees who have settled in the county in recent years come from working-class backgrounds and cling to Democratic voting habits. The eastern part of Pasco County, around Dade City, also has rural Democratic voters among the farm lands and citrus groves. In the 1982 congressional contest, the Democratic nominee against Bilirakis was able to carry Pasco County by 2,700 votes.

Of the three counties in the 9th, Hillsborough County, influenced by Tampa, is the friendliest to Democrats. But Hillsborough has only about one-fourth of the vote, and none of that is inside Tampa itself. In addition, some of the residents of the rural eastern part of the county are conservatives who break party ranks when presented with a Democrat they perceive to be too liberal. To have much hope of winning in the 9th, a Democrat has to carry Hillsborough solidly and neutralize the GOP advantage in Pasco.

Population: 513,191. White 486,066 (95%), Black 21,774 (4%), Other 2,486 (1%). Spanish origin 12,787 (3%). 18 and over 404,361 (79%), 65 and over 123,085 (24%). Median age: 42.

Committees

Energy and Commerce (13th of 17 Republicans)
Energy and Power; Health and the Environment; Oversight and Investigations

Veterans' Affairs (7th of 13 Republicans)
Compensation, Pension and Insurance; Hospitals and Health Care

Elections

1988 General		
Michael Bilirakis (R)	223,925	(100%)
1986 General		
Michael Bilirakis (R)	166,540	(71%)
Gabe Cazares (D)	68,578	(29%)

Previous Winning Percentages: **1984** (79%) **1982** (51%)

District Vote For President

	1988	1984	1980	1976
D	112,844 (39%)	90,475 (33%)	82,783 (39%)	80,804 (51%)
R	172,473 (60%)	187,403 (67%)	119,229 (56%)	76,330 (48%)
I			9,795 (5%)	

Campaign Finance

	Receipts	Receipts from PACs	Expend-itures
1988			
Bilirakis (R)	$399,150	$149,975 (38%)	$193,901
1986			
Bilirakis (R)	$471,612	$151,898 (32%)	$509,321
Cazares (D)	$83,851	$6,575 (8%)	$83,619

Key Votes

1987	
Raise speed limit to 65 mph	Y
Approve Gephardt "fair trade" amendment	N
Ban testing of larger nuclear weapons	N
Delay "re-flagging" of Kuwaiti tankers	N
Approve tax-raising deficit-reduction bill	N
1988	
Approve aid to Nicaraguan contras	Y
Enact civil rights restoration bill over Reagan veto	N
Kill 60-day plant-closing notification measure	Y
Pass omnibus trade bill over Reagan veto	N
Approve death penalty for drug-related murders	Y
Bar federal funds for abortions in cases of rape and incest	Y
Oppose seven-day waiting period for purchase of handguns	N

Voting Studies

	Presidential Support		Party Unity		Conservative Coalition	
Year	**S**	**O**	**S**	**O**	**S**	**O**
1988	67	29	87	8	89	5
1987	66	32	86	10	91	9
1986	77	21	88	9	96	4
1985	75	24	84	10	87	11
1984	63	34	86	14	90	10
1983	79	20	90	9	93	4

Interest Group Ratings

Year	ADA	ACU	AFL-CIO	CCUS
1988	10	96	14	93
1987	16	78	13	87
1986	15	86	29	67
1985	10	71	29	77
1984	10	88	31	80
1983	10	87	18	85

10 Andy Ireland (R)

Of Winter Haven — Elected 1976

Born: Aug. 23, 1930, Cincinnati, Ohio.
Education: Yale U., B.S. 1952; attended Columbia U. School of Business, 1953-54; Louisiana State U. School of Banking, graduated 1959.
Occupation: Banker.
Family: Wife, Nancy Haydock; four children.
Religion: Episcopalian.
Political Career: Winter Haven City Commission, 1966-68; Democratic nominee for Fla. Senate, 1972.
Capitol Office: 2416 Rayburn Bldg. 20515; 225-5015.

In Washington: When President Reagan's policy successes of the early 1980s created the aura of national Republican resurgence, several conservative House Democrats were tempted to switch parties. Ireland was one of the very few who actually made the jump, moving to the GOP in 1984.

Unlike another House Democrat who crossed over to the GOP about the same time — Phil Gramm of Texas — Ireland has never been accused of stealing the show. On his major committee assignment, Armed Services, Ireland has moved mostly in the background, same as he did during four terms as a Democrat on Foreign Affairs.

In the 101st Congress, though, he has shown signs of emerging from the shadows. A strong backer of Reagan's defense spending increases, Ireland has nonetheless been a supporter of efforts to make the military run more efficiently. And in early 1989, he became more outspoken in the cause of Pentagon fiscal responsibility.

That April, Ireland argued that a five-year spending plan presented by Defense Secretary Dick Cheney understated the amount of money actually needed by $45 billion. When Cheney was quoted as saying, "Andy doesn't know what he's talking about," Ireland set out to prove him wrong. Two weeks later, the Florida Republican released a General Accounting Office report he commissioned that appeared to back up his position.

Ireland had gained attention earlier in the year as ranking member of a special Armed Services panel studying ways to get U.S. allies to pick up a larger share of defense costs. The task force, chaired by Colorado Democrat Patricia Schroeder, recommended reducing U.S. troop strength in Europe by 25,000.

Even as he steps out on the Armed Services stage, Ireland remains faithful to his career-long bailiwick — the Small Business Committee. A banker, Ireland describes himself as "a vocal advocate of the interests of American entrepreneurs."

When he switched parties, he lost his seat on Foreign Affairs altogether, and also lost the seniority he had built up on Small Business. But his devotion to the latter committee, which has a high turnover rate, has paid off. Currently, he is the fourth-ranking Republican on Small Business, and the senior member of his party on the Exports, Tax Policy and Special Problems Subcommittee.

When the defense-procurement scandal broke into the news in mid-1988, Ireland used an Armed Services hearing on the issue to promote his favorite cause: "I believe that more involvement by small business in the procurement process would lead us away from a dangerous dependency on a handful of large defense contractors . . . ," Ireland said.

The fate of the Small Business Administration (SBA) was the singular issue on which Ireland clashed with the Reagan administration, even after his partisan conversion. Reagan consistently proposed eliminating the SBA, while Ireland came at the issue from the opposite extreme: At the start of each Congress, he proposed giving the SBA administrator Cabinet-level status.

On the Exports Subcommittee, Ireland involved himself during the 100th Congress in the drafting of the small-business title of the omnibus trade bill — which created a small-business desk in the Office of the U.S. Trade Representative — and he served on the trade bill conference committee. He also was active outside his committee on a trade issue involving his district's citrus industry, joining industry representatives and Florida congressional colleagues in fighting Japanese quotas on American oranges and orange juice.

During his early years in the House, Ireland seemed to be a typical conservative Democrat. He joked and jostled with other Southern Democrats on "Redneck Row" at the back of the House chamber, and came across as a genuine "good ol' boy" — a remarkable feat, considering that he was schooled at Phillips Academy and Yale and had served as treasurer

Florida 10

Central — Lakeland; Winter Haven; Bradenton

All over Florida, land once devoted to agriculture is being eaten away by shopping centers, motels and condominiums. But in Polk County, centerpiece of the 10th District, citrus is still king.

Thousands of area jobs are connected with the growing, picking, packing, processing and loading of oranges, orange concentrate and grapefruit. The biggest companies are well-known — Tropicana and Minute Maid — but there are many lesser growers whose efforts combine to make the 10th the nation's foremost citrus-producing district.

Cold weather here is much more than just an inconvenience; if temperatures drop below freezing, then livelihoods can be threatened as millions of dollars of citrus are lost.

Phosphate rock, the raw material of fertilizer, is another key element of the Polk County economy. Three-fourths of America's phosphate is strip-mined out of Polk, although demand for the product has been uneven in recent years. High interest rates in the late 1970s prevented domestic farmers from buying fertilizer at their usual pace, and then a strong dollar pushed prices higher than foreign buyers would pay.

In addition to work in the citrus and phosphate industries, Polk County's employment offerings include the Piper Aircraft Corp. and the Circus World and Cypress Gardens tourist attractions.

About 60 percent of the people in the 10th live in Polk, with the major concentration in the Lakeland-Winter Haven area. There is a remarkable disparity between party registration figures and election results. Registered Republicans are outnumbered by about 2-to-1 in the county, yet Polk nearly always supports GOP presidential candidates and has given warm approval to Ireland since he left the Democratic Party to run as a Republican.

The 10th has one Gulf Coast county, Manatee, which accounts for about 30 percent of its population. The city of Bradenton there grew 54 percent during the first half of this decade, to a population exceeding 37,000. Manatee County is a popular retirement area for people from Central and Midwestern states where Republican voting was a habit.

Democrats are competitive in local elections in Manatee, but federal elections are a different matter. In the 1984 House contest, Pat Glass, a popular Democratic officeholder in Manatee, challenged Ireland and lost decisively in her own home county.

De Soto and Hardee counties are also included in the 10th. Predominantly agricultural, they have cattle ranches, citrus groves, a scattering of small towns and conservative voters whose ties to the Democratic Party are stronger than in Polk.

Population: 512,890. White 435,256 (85%), Black 66,731 (13%), Other 2,514 (1%). Spanish origin 16,774 (3%). 18 and over 381,628 (74%), 65 and over 92,163 (18%). Median age: 35.

of the Florida Bankers' Association.

But the longer Ireland stayed in Washington, the more ill at ease he felt calling himself a Democrat. "The House Democratic leadership uses the Solid South to sustain itself," he once complained, "but when it comes time for input, they say, 'Go take a hike.' "

Finally, in March 1984, Ireland announced he would join the party he had been voting with all along. Ireland told his supporters that "our views are not heard, not heeded and not wanted" in the Democratic Party.

The Democratic leadership stripped Ireland of his committee assignments when he crossed the aisle, and the GOP could not find a Republican seat for Ireland on Foreign Affairs. That did not stop him from speaking on behalf of the "Reagan doctrine" of providing U.S. aid to anti-communist insurgencies around the world. "If we vote against the side of freedom, we are voting for communist tyranny," Ireland said during debate on aid to the Nicaraguan contras. "There is no middle ground."

At Home: Die-hard Democratic loyalists in the 10th were enraged when Ireland announced his party switch, and they vowed to exact revenge at the polls in 1984. But Ireland easily won a fifth term.

The first sign that Ireland would not have much trouble winning as a Republican in 1984 came July 20, the candidates' filing deadline. There had been talk after Ireland announced his switch that one or more moderate Democratic officeholders from Polk County, the district's largest, would run in the 10th. But none did, leaving the Democratic field to Manatee County Commissioner Patricia M. Glass and two others with no track records.

Glass had been a strong advocate of environmental protection, gaining publicity for fighting to protect the waters of Manatee County from pollution caused by phosphate mining. But she was not well-known in Polk County, and her environmentalist record was not an aid to her there; phosphate mines are an important source of jobs in Polk.

To give herself more time and money to concentrate on Ireland, Glass hoped to win the nomination outright in the September primary. But she was held under 50 percent by Jack Carter, a retired field representative for the Social Security Administration who portrayed himself as more conservative than Glass. She defeated Carter in the October runoff, but by then Ireland was too far ahead.

Though he was campaigning for the first time under the GOP banner, Ireland needed to make few adjustments in his rhetoric. He had always talked about cutting government regulation, providing a strong defense and keeping taxes down. Republican officials in Washington made Ireland's race a priority, and he enjoyed a huge financial advantage over Glass. Aided by Reagan's showing, Ireland swept to an easy victory. By 1986, Democrats seemed resigned that Ireland's conversion had made the 10th a GOP seat. He easily beat his Democratic foe.

Ireland's political career had begun in a 1976 Democratic congressional primary, as he and five others sought to replace retiring Democrat James A. Haley. As a wealthy banker, Ireland had the resources to compensate for his political inexperience. A runoff was expected, but Ireland won the nomination outright with 51 percent. His general-election foe was GOP state Rep. Robert Johnson, in the Legislature for six years but not well-known outside his Sarasota home. Ireland won 58 percent of the vote.

Ireland's voting record was not popular with labor unions, minorities and others who found him too conservative, but the discontent was never widespread enough to cause him trouble in a Democratic primary. Republicans were so satisfied with Ireland that he met only one minor general-election challenge in his three re-election campaigns as a Democrat.

Committees

Armed Services (12th of 21 Republicans)
Investigations; Procurement and Military Nuclear Systems

Small Business (4th of 17 Republicans)
Exports, Tax Policy and Special Problems (ranking)

Elections

1988 General		
Andy Ireland (R)	156,563	(73%)
David B. Higginbottom (D)	56,536	(27%)
1986 General		
Andy Ireland (R)	122,395	(71%)
David B. Higginbottom (D)	49,571	(29%)

Previous Winning Percentages: **1984** (62%) **1982 *** (100%) **1980 *** (69%) **1978 *** (100%) **1976 *** (58%)

** Ireland was elected as a Democrat in 1976-82.*

District Vote For President

	1988	1984	1980	1976
D	69,725 (33%)	60,726 (29%)	71,059 (38%)	77,872 (49%)
R	137,911 (66%)	150,022 (71%)	107,348 (58%)	78,521 (50%)
I			5,857 (3%)	

Campaign Finance

	Receipts	Receipts from PACs	Expend-itures
1988			
Ireland (R)	$405,000	$164,389 (41%)	$460,468
Higginbottom (D)	$33,826	0	$33,823
1986			
Ireland (R)	$463,554	$167,178 (36%)	$402,873
Higginbottom (D)	$12,906	$1,500 (12%)	$12,903

Key Votes

1987	
Raise speed limit to 65 mph	Y
Approve Gephardt "fair trade" amendment	N
Ban testing of larger nuclear weapons	N
Delay "re-flagging" of Kuwaiti tankers	N
Approve tax-raising deficit-reduction bill	N
1988	
Approve aid to Nicaraguan contras	Y
Enact civil rights restoration bill over Reagan veto	N
Kill 60-day plant-closing notification measure	Y
Pass omnibus trade bill over Reagan veto	N
Approve death penalty for drug-related murders	Y
Bar federal funds for abortions in cases of rape and incest	?
Oppose seven-day waiting period for purchase of handguns	Y

Voting Studies

	Presidential Support		Party Unity		Conservative Coalition	
Year	S	O	S	O	S	O
1988	67	27	88	4	87	5
1987	68	28	85	6	91	5
1986	74	18	87	7	86	0
1985	80	19	88	6	89	7
1984	56	35	66 *	32 *	88	7
1983	72	23	31	62	89	7
1982	60	17	22	50	75	5
1981	74	16	29	56	87	7

** Ireland switched from the Democratic to the Republican Party on July 5, 1984. Party Unity scores shown for 1984 are for Republican Party membership. Ireland's scores as a Democrat were 24 percent party support and 62 percent opposition.*

Interest Group Ratings

Year	ADA	ACU	AFL-CIO	CCUS
1988	5	100	14	100
1987	0	96	0	100
1986	0	80	8	100
1985	5	90	6	82
1984	0	61	25	60
1983	10	91	6	89
1982	10	74	6	80
1981	5	87	29	100

11 Bill Nelson (D)

Of Melbourne — Elected 1978

Born: Sept. 29, 1942, Miami, Fla.
Education: Yale U., B.A. 1965; U. of Virginia, J.D. 1968.
Military Career: Army, 1968-70; Reserve, 1965-71.
Occupation: Lawyer.
Family: Wife, Grace Cavert; two children.
Religion: Episcopalian.
Political Career: Fla. House, 1973-79.
Capitol Office: 2404 Rayburn Bldg. 20515; 225-3671.

In Washington: House members considering a run for statewide office in expansive Florida usually face name-recognition deficits outside their districts. But for Nelson, who is nearly certain to run for governor in 1990, this is not as big a problem. He is, after all, the only member to have had the opportunity to wave at all of his potential constituents at once — from outer space.

Nelson, whose 11th District includes the Kennedy Space Center at Cape Canaveral, flew on the space shuttle *Columbia* in January 1986; his flight immediately preceded the *Challenger* disaster. This adventure, more than any specific legislative accomplishment, boosted Nelson into the statewide political arena.

His ongoing interest in space industries, which are important to Florida's economy, continues to inform most of his work in the House. He is chairman of the Science Subcommittee on Space, where he advocates increased federal support for space programs run by the National Aeronautics and Space Administration (NASA) and by private industry.

With his Ivy League diploma and his square-jawed good looks, Nelson was regarded as a member to watch when elected to the House over a decade ago. But in his first few terms, Nelson appeared to flounder a bit. He won a choice seat on the Budget Committee in his first term, but left no footprints in his six-year tenure there.

Having had no major assignment to go back to after leaving Budget, he had to lobby his way onto the Banking Committee in 1985. He got on only after an emotional appeal by Florida Democrat Charles E. Bennett, the state's spokesman in the committee-assignment process.

But Nelson also had his assignment on Science, which enabled him to plug away at the space issues so important to his district. He was thus in a good position when NASA instituted its policy of sending individuals from outside the program into space. He was the second member of Congress — Republican Sen. Jake Garn of Utah was the first — to fly on the shuttle.

He was also the last. Ten days after Nelson and the *Columbia* crew returned to Earth, the *Challenger* lifted off, then exploded seconds later over the Atlantic Ocean. The seven crew members aboard died, including Christa McAuliffe, who was to be the first "teacher in space." NASA then discontinued the policy of sending outsiders up as shuttle passengers.

Though the disaster took some of the luster off Nelson's triumph, it did not diminish his zeal for space. With the space program in disarray, he promised that "we will see what the malfunction is and we'll have it corrected. The American space program will continue."

Nelson had also moved aggressively to ensure himself a major role in perpetuating the program. He beat out a more senior colleague, George E. Brown Jr. of California, for the Space Subcommittee chair. Brown's skepticism about military uses of space made him suspect among conservative committee Democrats, while Nelson's enthusiasm for virtually all types of space exploration was a matter of record.

Science is an authorizing committee for NASA, and most bills dealing with the space program are marked up in Nelson's subcommittee. Nelson therefore has played a leadoff role in promoting NASA requests for increased funds for the renascent shuttle program and for its next major priority, the permanent space station.

One persistent peeve for Nelson is that NASA is lumped into a single appropriations bill with other independent federal agencies and the Department of Housing and Urban Development (HUD). "The worst of all possible worlds is what happened last year, when NASA had to compete for dollars, or against cuts, with the Veterans Administration and with ... HUD," Nelson said in February 1988. "That's not the way it should be." Nelson and other space advocates later fought off efforts by a group of liberal Democrats to take $400 million from NASA and transfer it to housing and environmental programs.

Nelson is also wary of space budget legerdemain in the executive branch. In March

Florida 11

East — Melbourne; Part of Orange County

The 11th fairly staggers with tourist attractions. It includes Walt Disney World, Circus World, Sea World, the Stars Hall of Fame and other diversions that provide low-skill, minimum-wage jobs and take in millions of visitors' dollars every year. Blue-collar support from people in Orange who work in the tourist industry provides Democrats with an electoral cushion against Republican votes elsewhere in the district.

Brevard County, home of the National Aeronautics and Space Administration's Kennedy Space Center, boomed during the era of space flights in the 1960s, then stalled when space exploration slipped from its status as a top-level national priority.

The high-technology industries that had been lured to the area were forced to trim jobs, but a core group of engineers and other skilled workers remained. In the 1980s, the space shuttle program and President Reagan's increased military spending brought new opportunities for aerospace and defense-related work. But the 1986 explosion of the *Challenger* cast an economic and psychological pall over Brevard that only began to lift when shuttle flights resumed in late 1988.

Brevard casts slightly more than half the district vote. Engineers and other professionals make up a significant share of the electorate; they are mostly conservative, satisfied with Nelson but partial to Republicans in presidential elections.

The district also includes nearly all of Osceola and Indian River counties. Most of Osceola's people live in the northern half of the county, which lies on the outskirts of metropolitan Orlando. Southern Osceola has cattle ranches and citrus groves.

Retirees who have settled in Vero Beach and other coastal towns in Indian River County tend to come from North Central states — more Ohioans than New Yorkers. These older people are fairly affluent and accustomed to voting Republican. This area presents a problem for local Democrats, but it has only a small share of the district's population.

Population: 512,691. White 461,407 (90%), Black 40,318 (8%), Other 5,379 (1%). Spanish origin 17,537 (3%). 18 and over 380,011 (74%), 65 and over 59,741 (12%). Median age: 32.

1989, he blasted a Bush administration suggestion that the space station funding be stretched out over a longer period, stating that while the maneuver would create short-term savings, it would inflate long-term costs.

Along with the NASA program, Nelson is also a booster of the fledgling commercial space-launch industry. In the 100th Congress, he wrote a law providing for the federal government to share some of the insurance risk with private industry in case of accident. The measure requires the launch companies to carry $500 million in liability insurance; the government would pick up the tab for any additional damage. Nelson had argued that the infant industry needed the relief in order to compete with foreign companies that received funding from their own governments.

Given his attentions to space issues, Nelson has less time for his assignment on Banking. Though he is on the Financial Institutions Supervision Subcommittee, which is dealing with aspects of the savings and loan problem, Nelson has not been known as a player there.

Nelson is also the chairman of the Congressional Travel and Tourism Caucus. With Disney World, the Kennedy Space Center and miles of beaches within its borders, Nelson's 11th District is a tourist mecca.

At Home: Though Nelson's 1986 flight on the space shuttle was a publicity boon for him, national GOP officials briefly attempted to turn it into a negative, describing it as the "ultimate junket." But the Republican candidate for 1986, 28-year-old computer software analyst Scott Ellis, went nowhere. Nelson won with 73 percent, his biggest-ever percentage. By 1988 Nelson was gearing up a 1990 gubernatorial campaign, and was considered a leading contender for his party's nomination.

Nelson has never had a particularly tough race for his House seat. In 1984, against his most highly touted GOP opponent, Nelson still won with 61 percent.

His opponent that year was Rob Quartel, a 34-year-old consultant who had established connections in Washington by working on Gerald R. Ford's White House staff and in George Bush's 1980 presidential campaign. Quartel argued that Nelson's clean-cut image obscured his lack of substantive legislative accomplishments.

Nelson called Quartel a liar and questioned his challenger's ties to Florida. The Republican grew up in Orlando, but left to attend college and had spent most of his working life in Washington. His business was based in the capital and his wife and child lived there. Quartel did not handle the residency issue very well, saying once that in his business (advising clients on public-policy strategy), "it's more important to have a Washington, D.C., address than a Florida address."

Nelson stressed his support for the space program and reinforced his image as an advocate for local jobs by announcing that a naval training center would locate in the district. He made campaign fund raising less difficult for himself by accepting contributions from political action committees, something he refused to do in his first House campaign. He defeated Quartel by more than 50,000 votes despite Reagan's large margin in the 11th.

Nelson was in his third term as a state representative when the old 9th District came open in 1978, vacated by the gubernatorial campaign of GOP Rep. Louis Frey Jr. Nelson undertook a campaign that had the appearance of an all-American family outing. Nelson's wife, a former college homecoming queen, and his two children accompanied him along the way. He visited nearly every community in the district during an 18-month effort.

The major obstacle he had to overcome was the seat's original occupant, Republican Edward J. Gurney. Gurney had held the district for three terms before going to the Senate in 1968, but he had left politics in 1974 after being indicted on several charges, including bribery. Eventually acquitted of the charges, he attempted a political comeback in 1978.

Gurney's campaign presented him as a conservative, experienced legislator and asked voters to "re-elect" him, as if he had never been away. But Nelson ran exactly the right campaign against a man who, even if wrongly, had been under suspicion for four years. Nelson avoided talking about his opponent's misfortunes but projected a "new politics" image, calling for strict financial-disclosure laws and refusing to accept contributions from business political action committees. Nelson took conservative stands on economic issues and advocated more military spending.

In the end, Gurney's past image and Nelson's personal appeal produced a landslide result. Thought to be narrowly ahead as the election neared, Nelson exceeded 60 percent of the vote.

Committees

Banking, Finance and Urban Affairs (20th of 31 Democrats)
Financial Institutions Supervision, Regulation and Insurance

Science, Space and Technology (9th of 30 Democrats)
Space Science and Applications (chairman); Transportation, Aviation and Materials

Elections

1988 General

Bill Nelson (D)	168,390	(61%)
Bill Tolley (R)	108,373	(39%)

1986 General

Bill Nelson (D)	149,109	(73%)
Scott Ellis (R)	55,952	(27%)

Previous Winning Percentages: 1984 (61%) **1982** (71%) **1980** (70%) **1978** (62%)

District Vote For President

	1988	1984	1980	1976
D	72,912 (29%)	62,999 (26%)	65,216 (33%)	76,194 (47%)
R	178,859 (70%)	180,110 (74%)	120,144 (61%)	82,160 (51%)
I			8,877 (5%)	

Campaign Finance

	Receipts	Receipts from PACs	Expenditures
1988			
Nelson (D)	$550,646	$213,956 (39%)	$659,400
Tolley (R)	$158,326	$7,600 (5%)	$158,208
1986			
Nelson (D)	$280,015	$140,783 (50%)	$235,594
Ellis (R)	$11,896	$295 (2%)	$11,896

Key Votes

1987

Raise speed limit to 65 mph	N
Approve Gephardt "fair trade" amendment	Y
Ban testing of larger nuclear weapons	N
Delay "re-flagging" of Kuwaiti tankers	Y
Approve tax-raising deficit-reduction bill	Y

1988

Approve aid to Nicaraguan contras	Y
Enact civil rights restoration bill over Reagan veto	Y
Kill 60-day plant-closing notification measure	N
Pass omnibus trade bill over Reagan veto	Y
Approve death penalty for drug-related murders	Y
Bar federal funds for abortions in cases of rape and incest	Y
Oppose seven-day waiting period for purchase of handguns	N

Voting Studies

	Presidential Support		Party Unity		Conservative Coalition	
Year	S	O	S	O	S	O
1988	43	51	67	26	76	16
1987	42	58	76	23	72	28
1986	43	56	69	30	94	6
1985	55	19	47	26	60	11
1984	52	44	48	48	83	17
1983	55	40	52	39	84	12
1982	60	36	62	33	78	19
1981	62	25	48	42	75	12

Interest Group Ratings

Year	ADA	ACU	AFL-CIO	CCUS
1988	45	56	71	43
1987	52	35	63	53
1986	15	77	43	61
1985	30	71	47	54
1984	20	59	15	57
1983	40	57	47	55
1982	20	52	40	45
1981	10	71	40	68

12 Tom Lewis (R)

Of North Palm Beach — Elected 1982

Born: Oct. 26, 1924, Philadelphia, Pa.

Education: Attended Palm Beach Junior College, 1956-57; U. of Florida, 1958-59.

Military Career: Air Force, 1943-54.

Occupation: Real-estate broker; aircraft testing specialist.

Family: Wife, Marian Vastine; three children.

Religion: Methodist.

Political Career: Mayor and councilman, North Palm Beach, 1964-71; Fla. House, 1973-81; Fla. Senate, 1981-83.

Capitol Office: 1216 Longworth Bldg. 20515; 225-5792.

In Washington: With seats on Agriculture and on Science, Space and Technology, Lewis has one committee assignment that suits the rural and traditional part of his district, and another that fits his personal expertise as well as the more modern and urbanized elements of his constituency.

Though the best-known parts of the 12th are its affluent bastions on the Atlantic and Gulf coasts, the sprawling expanse in between is mainly farm land that produces vegetables, sugar and livestock.

On Agriculture, Lewis looks out for these interests from his seat on the subcommittees that deal with sugar and livestock issues. He also has joined others in Florida's delegation in efforts to promote state agricultural interests, including a successful protest during the 100th Congress against Japanese quotas on U.S. beef and citrus products.

However, farm issues are not Lewis' forte; his professional background is in aviation, and he was elected to Congress after a successful political career in the wealthy coastal enclave of North Palm Beach. While he has been mostly in the background on the Agriculture Committee, Lewis has made a bigger mark as a member of the Science Committee.

A World War II flyer and a longtime testing specialist for Pratt & Whitney Aircraft, Lewis applies his experience to his duties as ranking Republican on the Science Subcommittee on Transportation, Aviation and Materials. He is also on the subcommittee dealing with a quintessential Florida issue, space science.

Lewis' positions on Science have enabled him to step out front on the currently hot topic of aviation safety. His National Air Safety Act of 1988, which breezed through both houses of Congress, orders the Federal Aviation Administration to spend a minimum of 15 percent of its annual research budget on a variety of safety issues.

Lewis added an amendment to the fiscal 1987 NASA authorization mandating that the name for the space shuttle *Challenger's* replacement be selected from among schoolchildren's suggestions. President Reagan vetoed the bill, but NASA agreed to the idea nonetheless.

At Home: Lewis did not enter politics until he was nearly 40, and he was 58 by the time he came to Congress. But if he was slow to start, he is effective; he has never lost an election.

Lewis' chance for a House seat came when the 12th was created in 1981 redistricting. His two advantages were that his state Senate district encompassed most of the 12th, and that many conservative Democrats were displeased with the Democratic nominee, Brad Culverhouse, a labor-backed lawyer and rancher.

At one point in the campaign, construction workers angered by an ongoing economic downturn disrupted a Lewis rally featuring Vice President George Bush. Though Culverhouse disassociated himself from the protest, public reaction to the incident contributed to his defeat.

Culverhouse's active campaigning did enable him to hold Lewis to 53 percent, but Democrats seem to have given up on testing the incumbent; he has run unopposed since then.

Born in Philadelphia, Lewis was a gunner aboard a B-25 bomber in World War II, flying out of India and China. During the Korean War, he was on the ground directing American war planes to their targets. After leaving the military in 1954, he settled in Florida.

He worked 16 years with Pratt & Whitney as chief of rocket and jet engine testing. During this time, he served on the North Palm Beach City Council, where he was chosen mayor, a post he held throughout his municipal career. When he assumed the more time-consuming duties of the Legislature, he quit Pratt & Whitney and entered the real-estate business. In the Legislature, Lewis' record earned him a 100 percent favorable rating from the American Conservative Union.

Florida 12

South Central — Parts of Palm Beach; West Palm Beach

The huge 12th encompasses much of inland south Florida and runs from the Gulf of Mexico to the Atlantic Ocean, but more than two-thirds of its people live in just three Atlantic Coast counties — Palm Beach, Martin and St. Lucie. The district's base Republican vote in statewide elections is over 55 percent.

The district line runs right through the most populous part of Palm Beach County, placing the northern part of Palm Beach and West Palm Beach in the 12th District, and the rest of each city in the 14th.

In wealthy Palm Beach, the spirit of noblesse oblige creates elaborate charity events but does not interfere with monolithic conservative politics. West Palm Beach, by contrast, is mostly middle-class. Originally a railroad town and home for the Palm Beach servant community, it grew to dwarf the parent city. West Palm Beach today has some poor and minorities in its population and usually votes Democratic. North of West Palm Beach is Riviera Beach, which is two-thirds black.

At one time, Palm Beach was recognized as the northern limit of the densely populated "Gold Coast" region that begins near Miami. But development marches inexorably northward. In north Palm Beach County, Jupiter tripled in size during the 1970s, and grew another 123 percent in the first half of the 1980s. Population in both Martin and St. Lucie counties jumped more than one-third from 1980 to 1986. Martin County is a GOP bastion; Republicans outnumber Democrats among registered voters. St. Lucie County has a Democratic majority by registration and enjoys a liberal Democratic community.

At the other end of the state, on the Gulf Coast, the 12th includes about 39,000 residents of Collier County, a popular retirement area and another county with more registered Republicans than Democrats.

Although the inland areas of the 12th are lightly populated, their agricultural output makes an important contribution to the district's economy.

Population: 513,121. White 397,313 (77%), Black 98,038 (19%), Other 3,362 (1%). Spanish origin 26,625 (5%). 18 and over 384,221 (75%), 65 and over 97,027 (19%). Median age: 36.

Committees

Agriculture (10th of 18 Republicans)
Cotton, Rice and Sugar; Domestic Marketing, Consumer Relations and Nutrition; Livestock, Dairy and Poultry

Science, Space and Technology (5th of 19 Republicans)
Transportation, Aviation and Materials (ranking); Space Science and Applications

Elections

1988 General

Tom Lewis (R) — Unopposed

1986 General

Tom Lewis (R) — 150,244 (99%)

Previous Winning Percentages: **1984** (100%) **1982** (53%)

District Vote For President

	1988		1984		1980		1976	
D	92,423	(35%)	81,535	(33%)	62,153	(34%)	66,662	(48%)
R	167,835	(64%)	168,472	(67%)	110,071	(61%)	70,289	(51%)
I					8,350	(5%)		

Campaign Finance

	Receipts	Receipts from PACs	Expend-itures
1988			
Lewis (R)	$288,963	$64,465 (22%)	$256,081
1986			
Lewis (R)	$309,923	$90,238 (29%)	$285,685

Key Votes

1987

Raise speed limit to 65 mph	Y
Approve Gephardt "fair trade" amendment	N
Ban testing of larger nuclear weapons	N
Delay "re-flagging" of Kuwaiti tankers	N
Approve tax-raising deficit-reduction bill	N

1988

Approve aid to Nicaraguan contras	Y
Enact civil rights restoration bill over Reagan veto	N
Kill 60-day plant-closing notification measure	Y
Pass omnibus trade bill over Reagan veto	N
Approve death penalty for drug-related murders	Y
Bar federal funds for abortions in cases of rape and incest	Y
Oppose seven-day waiting period for purchase of handguns	Y

Voting Studies

	Presidential Support		Party Unity		Conservative Coalition	
Year	S	O	S	O	S	O
1988	69	28	93	5	95	0
1987	63	34	88	8	88	9
1986	71	26	82	14	86	8
1985	66	34	85	12	87	11
1984	58	40	81	16	93	7
1983	67	32	78	18	91	8

Interest Group Ratings

Year	ADA	ACU	AFL-CIO	CCUS
1988	5	100	14	93
1987	8	83	6	93
1986	15	70	21	76
1985	5	81	6	86
1984	20	79	23	88
1983	20	70	18	75

13 Porter J. Goss (R)

Of Sanibel — Elected 1988

Born: Nov. 26, 1938, Waterbury, Conn.
Education: Yale U., B.A. 1960.
Military Career: Army, 1960-62.
Occupation: Investor.
Family: Wife, Mariel Robinson; four children.
Religion: Presbyterian.
Political Career: Sanibel City Council, 1974-80, 1981-82; mayor, 1975-77, 1982; Lee County Commission, 1983-88, chairman, 1985-86.
Capitol Office: 509 Cannon Bldg. 20515; 225-2536.

The Path to Washington: Deep local roots are not an obvious political selling point for a House candidate in fast-growing southwest Florida, where so many residents are new arrivals. But in 1988 Goss made the most of his longtime political service and involvement in local issues, convincing voters in the 13th District that he would do the best job of protecting the environment that lured them to the coast in the first place.

A former employee of the Central Intelligence Agency in Washington, D.C., and abroad, Goss moved to the district in 1971 and was drawn into politics by some of the same "quality-of-life" issues he ended up emphasizing in his House campaign.

When picturesque Sanibel Island was hit by rapid development in the early 1970s, Goss played a major role in pushing for the town to incorporate and forge a consensus on growth-management laws. He became the small city's first mayor in 1974 and helped produce a development model that has been studied in public-policy schools and other localities.

Nearly a decade later, Goss was named to the Lee County Commission by then-Gov. Bob Graham, a Democrat. The appointment caused consternation in some circles, partly because of resentment toward the well-to-do island. Goss, quickly tagged as the commission's environmentalist, got involved in lengthy and controversial debates about managing growth countywide. But he won over most of his critics, and was elected easily to a full term. That put him in a good position to compete for the House seat when Republican Rep. Connie Mack decided to launch a Senate campaign.

Goss had stiff competition for the GOP nomination — the one that counts in this conservative area. In particular, he was threatened by the return of former Rep. L. A. "Skip" Bafalis, who left the House for an unsuccessful gubernatorial bid in 1982. Among the three other GOP contenders was retired Army Brig. Gen. James Dozier, a political novice who nevertheless had some "star" quality because of his well-publicized kidnapping by the Red Brigades in Italy earlier in the 1980s.

Bafalis' earlier service was well remembered in parts of the district, and he used the theme "Re-elect Skip Bafalis." He also worked to label Goss a closet Democrat, telling voters that Goss had contributed to Democratic candidates in the past. That claim played to fears already extant in a few GOP quarters: Even some of Goss' admirers say he is a consensus-builder who could be at ease in either party, and Goss' environmentalist streak made him suspect in certain conservative circles.

But Bafalis found that his political strength had atrophied. After living outside the district for some time, he rented a Sarasota condo shortly before launching his comeback bid. And in the few years he was out of the local spotlight, the district's electorate had changed considerably.

Goss put him on the defensive by contrasting Bafalis' recent absence from the district with his own attention to local issues. And while Bafalis' fund raising failed to meet expectations (and Dozier's bid failed to catch fire), Goss raised enough money to finance heavy use of television and direct mail. Part of the money was used to accuse Bafalis of having cast votes against Social Security — a damning accusation in a district where more than a quarter of the population is 65 or older.

Bafalis had hoped for a boost from his new base in Sarasota County; there is some sense of local rivalry between Sarasota and Goss' Lee County. But in the primary, Goss carried both Sarasota and Lee. Bafalis made it into the October runoff, but his fund-raising and advertising efforts faded. Goss won a lopsided majority in the runoff, and then coasted to the first of what seems likely to be a long string of easy general-election victories.

In the committee-assignment process at the start of the 101st Congress, Goss got seats on Merchant Marine and Foreign Affairs, which should enable him to pursue interests both within and beyond his district.

Florida 13

Southwest — Sarasota; Fort Myers

A glimpse at the 1988 presidential vote from the four counties in the 13th shows just how prohibitive the odds against a Democratic victory are. Michael S. Dukakis did not get more than 36 percent in any of the three counties wholly within the 13th — Lee, Sarasota and Charlotte. Collier County, with about half of its people in the district, gave Dukakis about 25 percent.

The political personality of the 13th is shaped by retirees from the small-town and suburban Midwest. These people changed their addresses but not their party registration, and they are a major contributor to the burgeoning strength of the GOP in Florida. From 1980-86, the 13th was the 10th fastest-growing district in the nation, bulging by more than 30 percent.

Sarasota and Lee counties each have about 40 percent of the district's residents, with the remaining 20 percent divided roughly evenly between Charlotte County and the section of Collier in the 13th.

Sarasota cultivates a refined image with its art museums, theaters and symphony performances, and it draws a wealthier class of retirees than most other west coast communities. It is also the traditional winter home of the Ringling Bros. and Barnum & Bailey Circus, although much of the entourage now spends the winter months a few miles south, at Venice. In Lee County, the city of Cape Coral, incorporated only in 1971, has grown at a rapid clip — to more than 30,000 people by decade's end, and to over 50,000 by 1986.

Fort Myers, also in Lee County, is having some difficulty meeting the demands of its growing population. There are occasional calls for it to adopt a slow-growth policy, following the example of conservationists on the islands of Sanibel and Captiva located just offshore from Fort Myers. These islands enforce stringent restrictions on development in order to protect their natural beauty and animal population.

Naples first won the status of a small city with a 46 percent population explosion during the 1970s, gaining exclusive high-rise condominiums to mark its maturity. By the mid-1980s the population was up to almost 20,000.

Population: 513,048. White 476,818 (93%), Black 29,190 (6%). Spanish origin 11,102 (2%). 18 and over 413,477 (81%), 65 and over (27%). Median age: 47.

Committees

Foreign Affairs (18th of 18 Republicans)
Arms Control, International Security and Science; Western Hemisphere Affairs

Merchant Marine and Fisheries (17th of 17 Republicans)
Coast Guard and Navigation; Oceanography

Campaign Finance

	Receipts	Receipts from PACs	Expend-itures
1988			
Goss (R)	$878,439	$141,976 (16%)	$836,224
Conway (D)	$216,711	$55,150 (25%)	$210,296

Elections

1988 General		
Porter J. Goss (R)	231,170	(71%)
Jack Conway (D)	93,700	(29%)
1988 Primary Runoff		
Porter J. Goss (R)	49,292	(72%)
L. A. "Skip" Bafalis (R)	19,413	(28%)
1988 Primary		
Porter J. Goss (R)	36,875	(38%)
L. A. "Skip" Bafalis (R)	27,958	(29%)
James Dozier (R)	18,048	(19%)
Lee A. Coppuck (R)	6,835	(7%)
Brian Pappas (R)	6,387	(7%)

District Vote for President

	1988	1984	1980	1976
D	106,374 (32%)	73,407 (26%)	68,062 (28%)	72,886 (41%)
R	225,656 (68%)	207,548 (74%)	165,630 (67%)	102,769 (58%)
I			11,406 (5%)	

14 Harry A. Johnston (D)

Of West Palm Beach — Elected 1988

Born: Dec. 2, 1931, West Palm Beach, Fla.
Education: Virginia Military Institute, B.A. 1953; U. of Florida, LL.B. 1958.
Military Career: Army, 1953-55.
Occupation: Lawyer.
Family: Wife, Mary Otley; two children.
Religion: Presbyterian.
Political Career: Fla. Senate, 1975-87, president, 1985-87; sought Democratic nomination for governor, 1986.
Capitol Office: 1517 Longworth Bldg. 20515; 225-3001.

The Path to Washington: A stately, silver-haired attorney, Johnston can project the image of a Southern patrician. But like his rapidly growing district, he is not Old Florida in his politics. As a state legislator, he built a following by taking on the chummy clique of rural legislators who had long ruled the state. As a House candidate in 1988, he combined that experience with a sophisticated campaign effort to win with surprising ease over popular rivals in the primary and general elections.

Johnston portrayed himself as a candidate who could move quickly into the business of congressional legislating. In Tallahassee, he was a well-regarded lawmaker who worked with other influential Democrats, including Gov. (now Sen.) Bob Graham, to replace the rural-oriented leadership with a more urban-flavored coalition committed to "government in the sunshine." Johnston rose quickly to the rank of Senate president and was involved in a variety of initiatives, including a package of strong growth-management laws.

Despite Johnston's reputation as a legislator, there was some doubt about his ability on the campaign trail when he announced for the 14th, which was coming open as Democratic Rep. Daniel A. Mica ran for the Senate. There had been high expectations for Johnston in his last political outing — a 1986 gubernatorial bid. But that effort was surprisingly lackluster; he failed even to reach the runoff. Johnston is not the type of politician who relishes campaigning. He sometimes seems to approach voters as if he is concerned about invading their privacy.

In the Democratic House primary, he faced a foe whose gregariousness he could not hope to match. Dorothy Wilken, an outspoken member of the Palm Beach County Commission, was aggressive on the campaign trail and had built a solid following in the district's largest county. She also nailed down some important union endorsements. She presented herself as the grass-roots candidate and tried to label Johnston the pick of the "good old boy" network.

But Johnston had learned some lessons from his 1986 loss; this time, he moved aggressively to control the campaign debate. A wealthy fifth-generation Floridian and native of West Palm Beach, Johnston used his contacts in the political and business establishment to gain a significant financial edge over Wilken. Thus, he was able to dominate the TV ad debate in the campaign's final weeks. He also gathered endorsements and contributions from influential Democrats around the state.

Johnston's unexpectedly strong primary victory made him a slight favorite over his GOP opponent, Ken Adams. A personable and popular county commissioner, Adams was well positioned to win the 14th, which because of population growth has grown more conservative by the day. Adams aligned himself closely with George Bush and touted a County Commission record that had brought him praise from Democrats and Republicans alike.

Presenting himself as a businessman with a conscience, Adams reminded voters of his efforts to get federal and local funding for public housing in a poor section of the county, and for work to establish a hospice for AIDS victims.

Adams also picked through Johnston's legislative record for evidence that he was "a liberal lawyer legislator." Among other things, he said Johnston had voted to reduce penalties for criminals. But Johnston was in a strong position to sidestep being tagged with the 'L' word. He had long been attentive to local businesses, and he made sure to tout his legislative efforts to balance the state budget and his support for a federal line-item veto.

As in the primary, Johnston kept the rhetorical upper hand. In debate after debate, he read Adams' campaign literature and refuted the charges, calling them "a bucket of crap." And he attacked quickly, arguing that Adams had missed numerous opportunities to vote on the County Commission and in the voting booth. "He is soft on voting," Johnston said. "The man has utter contempt for the democratic system."

Florida 14

Southeast — Parts of Palm Beach and West Palm Beach

The 14th District is centered on West Palm Beach, a town that was developed as the railroad terminus and supply center for the Palm Beach resorts, but today is seven times larger than its wealthy parent. The area's pleasant environment has lured the headquarters of several international corporations, bringing in a cadre of young, well-paid business executives. This migration has changed and broadened the world view of a community that used to be dominated by leisure-minded socialites. Democrats still run well in West Palm Beach, but that is changing. Palm Beach itself is as affluent and Republican as ever.

South of Palm Beach, retirees living in the condominium communities of Boynton Beach and Delray Beach are a potent political force. Some of the people in these complexes are Irish and Italian but most are Jewish, and nearly all come from a Democratic political background in the Northeast. The turnout rate among the condominium residents is very high, thanks in part to "bosses" who have emerged in the turbulent world of condominium politics.

Boca Raton, the next major city down the coast, is an upper-middle-class area that generally votes Republican. It is also home to electronics plants run by Datamedix and International Business Machines. Boynton Beach, Delray Beach and Boca Raton each grew by more than 70 percent during the 1970s, but that seems trifling compared with the incredible population boom in the Broward County parts of the 14th.

In Broward County, the district takes in Coral Springs, Margate, Tamarac, North Lauderdale and parts of Lauderhill and Sunrise, all moderate-to-liberal Democratic areas. Population in each of these communities grew by 300 percent or more during the 1970s. Coral Springs, for example, jumped from 1,489 residents in 1970 to 37,349 10 years later. By 1986, its population was estimated at 60,460, a 62 percent jump from 1980. Overall, the 14th grew by 31.5 percent from 1980-86. It was the ninth-fastest growing congressional district in the country.

After Coral Springs, Sunrise has notched the biggest increase from 1980 to 1986 — its population grew by a third in that time, going over 50,000. Delray Beach, North Lauderdale and Boynton Beach each registered growth rates of over 20 percent in 1980-86, and Boca Raton and Tamarac each grew by more than 15 percent.

Population: 512,803. White 484,198 (94%), Black 20,880 (4%), Other 2,682 (1%). Spanish origin 23,601 (5%). 18 and over 406,873 (79%), 65 and over 124,990 (24%). Median age: 42.

Committees

Foreign Affairs (23rd of 28 Democrats)
International Economic Policy and Trade; Western Hemisphere Affairs

Science, Space and Technology (28th of 30 Democrats)
Science, Research and Technology; Space Science and Applications

Campaign Finance

	Receipts	Receipts from PACs	Expend-itures
1988			
Johnston (D)	$974,743	$296,636 (30%)	$971,883
Adams (R)	$752,874	$67,136 (9%)	$706,832

Elections

1988 General		
Harry A. Johnston (D)	173,292	(55%)
Ken Adams (R)	142,635	(45%)
1988 Primary		
Harry A. Johnston (D)	36,874	(59%)
Dorothy H. Wilken (D)	26,116	(41%)

District Vote for President

	1988	1984	1980	1976
D	140,057 (47%)	110,773 (39%)	82,934 (37%)	85,922 (49%)
R	158,654 (53%)	171,663 (61%)	128,344 (57%)	86,375 (49%)
I			14,294 (6%)	

15 E. Clay Shaw Jr. (R)

Of Fort Lauderdale — Elected 1980

Born: April 19, 1939, Miami, Fla.

Education: Stetson U., B.A. 1961, J.D. 1966; U. of Alabama, M.A. 1963.

Occupation: Nurseryman; lawyer.

Family: Wife, Emilie Costar; four children.

Religion: Roman Catholic.

Political Career: Fort Lauderdale assistant city attorney, 1968; chief city prosecutor, 1968-69; associate municipal judge, 1969-71; city commissioner, 1971-73; vice mayor, 1973-75; mayor, 1975-81.

Capitol Office: 440 Cannon Bldg. 20515; 225-3026.

In Washington: The national outcry over drug abuse in recent years helped Shaw emerge from the GOP backbenches to become a player on drug policy — an issue of pre-eminent concern to his South Florida coastal constituency.

Thanks in part to his dogged, partisan pursuit of the drug issue, Shaw won a coveted assignment in 1988 that will enable him to broaden his legislative focus. The prize: a seat on the Ways and Means Committee.

Shaw unsuccessfully sought Ways and Means at the start of the 100th Congress. Late to announce his intentions, he lost the endorsement of Florida Republicans to colleague Bill McCollum, who later lost his bid for a committee slot. When a committee vacancy occurred late in the Congress, Shaw quickly declared his interest. His perseverance on the drug bill as well as his background as a tax attorney helped him win the state delegation's endorsement over McCollum, and he went on to take the seat.

If Shaw brings to his Ways and Means work the same energy he has applied to drug legislation, he will be a very active player on the powerful committee.

Before moving to Ways and Means, Shaw was a member of the Judiciary Committee and the Select Narcotics Abuse and Control panel. In both the 99th and 100th Congresses, he was appointed to GOP drug task forces set up by Minority Leader Robert H. Michel, and a bill Shaw introduced became the basis of the 1988 Republican anti-drug legislative effort. His measure included several controversial provisions that were dropped two years earlier, but won approval in 1988 — a death penalty for major drug traffickers, a drug "czar" to coordinate federal efforts, and the use of the U.S. military for drug interdiction.

Shaw has met with considerably less success in his battle for widespread drug testing. While the House approved a Shaw amendment instructing conferees on the airline consumer protection bill to include mandatory testing provisions, controversy over the issue contributed to the political stalemate that killed the bill in the 100th Congress. Shaw did win passage of an amendment to a State Department authorization bill requiring drug tests for employees with access to secret information.

In the 99th Congress, Shaw asked his staff to participate in a voluntary drug-testing program, but House rules barred him from paying for the tests with his official allowance. In response, he submitted a bill in 1987 to change the rules. It did not pass.

The Florida Republican's anti-drug crusade began in earnest in the 99th Congress, just a week after then-Speaker Thomas P. O'Neill Jr. announced a major push for drug legislation. Shaw quickly offered a successful amendment to an appropriations bill to prohibit schools from receiving federal education funds unless they have drug-abuse-prevention programs.

As the issue gained national prominence, Shaw responded to accusations that the 1986 drug bill represented an enormous new expense at a time of austerity. He insisted that the cost was outweighed by the urgency of the drug problem. "I think if we can pass a drug bill that's going to have a meaningful effect," he said, "then the price tag is of little consideration."

Issues affecting senior citizens are also of prime importance in Shaw's district, and he pursues them with equal zeal. In the 100th Congress, he drew some criticism for his persistent opposition to an amendment to the Fair Housing Act that barred discrimination against children. Though leading senior citizens' organizations signed off on the provision as workable, Shaw continued to claim that it would put an end to senior-citizen housing. His effort to strike the amendment lost 116-289.

Shaw dabbled in some high-stakes institutional politics during the 100th Congress when the House debated legislation to renew the special-prosecutor law. The Reagan administration opposed the law, saying it was uncon-

Florida 15

Southeast — Fort Lauderdale

Fort Lauderdale, once famous as a "where the boys are" student beach mecca, bills itself now as a stylish "American Venice." But one thing has not changed much — its habit of voting Republican. That habit started more than two decades ago, when conservative retirees from the Midwest started settling in Fort Lauderdale. Those sorts of people nowadays retire mostly to Florida's WASPier West Coast, but Fort Lauderdale still has a conservative flavor — it is less influenced by the liberal attitudes of Northeastern Jewish émigrés than are most other major South Florida cities.

Fort Lauderdale also has a substantial minority population; the blacks and Hispanics who walk some of its faded downtown streets live in a different world from the people who browse through the fashionable stores of Las Olas Boulevard on the waterfront a short distance away.

In recent years, some of Miami's drug traffic has migrated north to Fort Lauderdale, creating new fortunes for a few but causing many residents to fret about "creeping Miamism."

The Republicans' biggest obstacle at election time in the 15th District is the well-organized Democratic political movement based in the district's condominiums. These communities contain the district's heaviest concentration of Northeastern retirees, many of them attracted by advertising campaigns in the New York media. Their lifelong Democratic habits are tough for any Republican to crack.

Fort Lauderdale's manufacturing sector concentrates on production of computer software, electronic circuitry, aerospace components and communications equipment. Its deep-water port makes it a base for cruise ships, drawing a more affluent class of visitor than the Eastertime youth pilgrimage, which is no longer such an important part of Fort Lauderdale's tourism trade.

Population: 512,950. White 415,486 (81%), Black 91,511 (18%), Other 2,615 (1%). Spanish origin 17,532 (3%). 18 and over 411,582 (80%), 65 and over 116,583 (23%). Median age: 39.

stitutional, but a chief point of controversy in the House involved Speaker Jim Wright, whose financial dealings were under investigation. When Shaw proposed an amendment to include members of Congress as potential subjects of independent-counsel investigations, House Democrats withdrew the bill from consideration. Wright subsequently put his financial holdings in a blind trust, and the House rebuffed Shaw's amendment on a largely party-line vote.

Also before his move to Ways and Means, Shaw served on the Public Works Committee, but he was often frustrated there. His pet issue was restricting billboards on federal highways and limiting federal support for billboards. In 1986, Shaw won a modest victory with the adoption of a compromise amendment freezing the total number of billboards allowed on federal highways while continuing to reimburse the billboard industry with federal funds for billboards that are taken down.

At Home: In the early 1980s, Democratic squabbling helped Shaw win and retain the 15th; now he seems to have a lock on it.

In 1980, Democratic primary voters dumped 70-year-old Rep. Edward J. Stack for a younger candidate, former state Rep. Alan Becker. Shaw, who had been mayor of Fort Lauderdale since 1975, was unopposed for the GOP nomination.

Shaw launched a campaign denouncing Becker as a liberal carpetbagger; the Democrat had moved into the 15th in 1979 after four terms in the Legislature representing North Miami. Shaw bragged that real spending in Fort Lauderdale had decreased during his tenure, without cuts in fire or police protection. He claimed credit for broadening the city's economic base and changing its image from that of a beach town to that of a cosmopolitan city.

Shaw picked up support from some conservative Democrats who had liked Stack and were dissatisfied with Becker's liberalism. Becker ran short of money because he had spent heavily from his own pocket to win the primary, and Shaw won the seat with 55 percent.

In 1982 another intraparty fight divided the Democrats. Stack was back, hoping to avenge his 1980 loss, and engaged in a bitter primary battle with a former ally. Stack eked out 51 percent to become the nominee, while Shaw again enjoyed an uncontested primary.

Stack had strong union support and parts of his old condominium organization, but lingering Democratic disunity and his age dragged him down. Shaw, boosted by redrawn district lines that enhanced GOP strength in the 15th, won a second term with 57 percent.

No Democratic heavyweights ran in 1984, and Shaw swamped teacher Bill Humphrey that November. Shaw considered running for governor in 1986, but opted for the safety of his House seat.

Committee

Ways and Means (11th of 13 Republicans)
Human Resources (ranking); Oversight

Elections

1988 General

E. Clay Shaw Jr. (R)	132,090	(66%)
Mike Kuhle (D)	67,746	(34%)

1986 General

E. Clay Shaw Jr. (R)	Unopposed

Previous Winning Percentages: 1984 (66%) **1982** (57%) **1980** (55%)

District Vote For President

	1988	1984	1980	1976
D	83,311 (47%)	93,235 (41%)	77,192 (36%)	82,690 (51%)
R	94,061 (53%)	134,858 (59%)	123,753 (57%)	78,474 (48%)
I			13,190 (6%)	

Campaign Finance

	Receipts	Receipts from PACs	Expend-itures
1988			
Shaw (R)	$348,233	$153,750 (44%)	$455,578
Kuhle (D) †	$48,633	$26,650 (55%)	$36,084
1986			
Shaw (R)	$203,766	$83,075 (41%)	$102,671

† Totals based on incomplete data.

Key Votes

1987	
Raise speed limit to 65 mph	Y
Approve Gephardt "fair trade" amendment	N
Ban testing of larger nuclear weapons	N
Delay "re-flagging" of Kuwaiti tankers	N
Approve tax-raising deficit-reduction bill	N
1988	
Approve aid to Nicaraguan contras	Y
Enact civil rights restoration bill over Reagan veto	N
Kill 60-day plant-closing notification measure	Y
Pass omnibus trade bill over Reagan veto	Y
Approve death penalty for drug-related murders	Y
Bar federal funds for abortions in cases of rape and incest	Y
Oppose seven-day waiting period for purchase of handguns	Y

Voting Studies

	Presidential Support		Party Unity		Conservative Coalition	
Year	**S**	**O**	**S**	**O**	**S**	**O**
1988	65	32	70	23	100	0
1987	70	29	76	20	95	5
1986	79	19	86	10	90	6
1985	70	25	88	8	89	9
1984	61	37	82	14	90	5
1983	78	16	87	8	93	4
1982	77	23	84	16	90	10
1981	78	22	94	6	95	5

Interest Group Ratings

Year	ADA	ACU	AFL-CIO	CCUS
1988	5	96	21	92
1987	4	78	13	93
1986	5	82	7	87
1985	5	81	18	81
1984	5	73	8	86
1983	5	96	0	80
1982	15	77	15	82
1981	10	100	0	89

16 Lawrence J. Smith (D)

Of Hollywood — Elected 1982

Born: April 25, 1941, Brooklyn, N.Y.
Education: Attended New York U., 1958-61; Brooklyn Law School, LL.B. 1964, J.D., 1967.
Occupation: Lawyer.
Family: Wife, Sheila Cohen; two children.
Religion: Jewish.
Political Career: Fla. House, 1979-83.
Capitol Office: 113 Cannon Bldg. 20515; 225-7931.

In Washington: Smith is a good person to have on your side in a House floor fight. A self-confident, street-smart New York transplant, he loves to argue, and he argues with force, if not always with elegance. If he is familiar with the subject under discussion, he lends substance to the case; if not, he can still be counted on to pummel the opposition while his allies figure out their next move.

Smith has concentrated much of his legislative energy on two issues: Israel and the war on drugs. In a district other than the 16th, which has a large Jewish population and includes part of drug-torn Dade County, this could be considered a national focus. But to Smith's constituents, these are important local issues.

Of particular interest to Smith are arms sales to Arab countries. Smith consistently derided Reagan administration initiatives to sell arms to Arab countries as a way of encouraging those countries to negotiate with Israel. "We give them carrots and then beat ourselves over the head with a stick," he has said. "The Arabs take these weapons and then do what they want to do, regardless of what we want or say."

In 1988 Smith helped work out a compromise with the administration to place some restrictions on the sale of weapons — including advanced F-18 aircraft — to Kuwait. Smith opposed the sale altogether and drafted a measure to block it, but it was never put to a vote. His political options were limited, because Kuwait had threatened to turn to Great Britain for similar aircraft.

Smith had better luck in early 1986. As the administration was trying to push through an arms-sale package to Jordan, a State Department official claimed that Jordan was progressing toward direct negotiations with Israel. "Hokum," Smith said. "... A lot of sound and fury signifying nothing." Lee H. Hamilton, chairman of the Foreign Affairs Subcommittee on Europe and the Middle East, complained that "actions which tend to pound on Jordan are counterproductive," but intense lobbying by Israel's allies persuaded Reagan to shelve the arms sale.

Smith is not keen on recent U.S. overtures to the Palestine Liberation Organization (PLO). He believes the Bush administration should not accept PLO leader Yasir Arafat's statement renouncing terrorism. Instead, "They should have drawn a line in the sand, saying [to Arafat]: 'If there are any more terrorist incidents by anybody close to you, we will hold you responsible.' "

Smith has taken a very active interest in combating drug smuggling. In 1988, he sponsored "decertification" resolutions to limit American aid to five countries alleged to be insufficiently cooperative with U.S. drug-control efforts. The Senate voted to decertify Mexico, but Smith backed off after Speaker Jim Wright produced a letter from the Mexican government outlining its campaign against drug trafficking.

In 1989, Smith decided not to press forward with decertification resolutions. "How can I tell other countries that the United States disapproves of their anti-drug efforts when the United States government itself is neglecting to deal with its own failed policies?" Smith said. He favors offering incentives, such as debt forgiveness, to countries that cooperate in the battle against drugs. In May 1989, he supported sending $14 million in economic aid to Peru, Bolivia, Columbia and other drug-producing countries to encourage them to curtail drug production.

Smith helped draft portions of the 1988 omnibus drug bill, including a provision to tighten controls on U.S.-made chemicals that are used abroad to process cocaine and other illegal drugs.

Smith is tough on drugs, but he took a somewhat softer line during the 1988 impeachment hearings against U.S. Judge Alcee L. Hastings, a fellow Floridian and a friend. Smith first persuaded Judiciary Chairman Peter W. Rodino Jr. to delay the committee's impeachment hearing for two weeks to give the panel more time to examine the case against Hastings, which grew out of his 1983 bribery trial. Smith later delivered an emotional speech

Florida 16

Southeast — Hollywood; Part of Dade County

The 16th includes some of the most heavily Jewish precincts in South Florida — those in the condominium communities of Hollywood and other south Broward County cities such as Hallandale, Pembroke Pines and Miramar. Politics is a preoccupation of many of the retirees there; they are responsible for making the 16th a predominantly Democratic district.

This part of Broward County has a larger Jewish community than the neighboring Fort Lauderdale-based 15th, which drew many of its people from Midwestern Protestants and Irish Catholics in the first big postwar migration. The voters in the Broward part of the 16th tend to be Eastern, urban-oriented and liberal.

For years, Hollywood was overshadowed by larger Fort Lauderdale, a situation that had some positive benefits: Hollywood did not attract as much strip development, and it retained more areas of single-family homes that offer a feeling of community.

But in the late 1960s and early 1970s, rapid development of Hollywood's southern beachfront packed it with condominiums. A strain on roads and services induced a wave of anti-development sentiment that led local officials to restrict development of the city's northern beach.

The area that is mainly responsible for making the 16th politically competitive is the Dade County part of the district. It incorporates Westchester and Sweetwater, suburbs lying due west of Miami's S.W. 8th Street, the focal point of Cuban-American culture in South Florida. When upwardly mobile Cubans want to move from Miami to greener spaces, many of them settle in Westchester and Sweetwater, which have come to support Republican candidates by solid margins. But since the Dade County part of the 16th accounts for only about one-third of the district's population, the GOP vote in Dade is offset by Democratic margins in Broward.

Population: 513,365. White 476,065 (93%), Black 25,666 (5%), Other 3,867 (1%). Spanish origin 107,632 (21%). 18 and over 396,409 (77%), 65 and over 91,954 (18%). Median age: 37.

about his friend, but he ultimately voted for impeachment on the House floor.

While Smith votes a generally liberal line on the Foreign Affairs Committee, he occasionally offers rhetoric that appeals to elements of the conservative Cuban community in the 16th.

Mindful of the strong anti-communist sentiment of the Cubans and others in his district, Smith has been touchy about the way his stand on Central American issues is portrayed. He has fumed about being "painted as a communist sympathizer" by Republicans who argue that abandoning the Nicaraguan contras paves the way for the spread of communism in Central America. After opposing aid to the contras in a key 1985 vote, he switched to support contra aid in 1986. In 1988, Smith again voted for contra aid, but the $36 million package was defeated 211-219. In early 1989, he supported the compromise plan worked out between the Bush administration and Congress to provide $49 million in "humanitarian" aid to the contras, subject to congressional restrictions.

As a freshman in the 98th Congress, Smith was actively involved in Judiciary's controversial effort to revise the nation's immigration laws, and he kept up an interest in that legislation in the 99th Congress, although he left Judiciary's Immigration Subcommittee at the start of his second term.

In the 98th Congress, Smith favored a magnanimous legalization program for illegal aliens, but was adamant that the federal government give financial assistance to states such as Florida to defray the increase in social service costs they would incur after illegal aliens were granted legal status. "My state has suffered enough," Smith said, complaining that Florida was not reimbursed for costs resulting from the 1980 Mariel boatlift that brought a flood of Cubans to the state.

At Home: After easily winning a first term in 1982, Smith suffered a slight setback in 1984 when former GOP state Rep. Tom Bush held him to 56 percent. Encouraged, Republicans claimed Smith was too liberal for the 16th and could be toppled by a coalition similar to the one Bush tried to mobilize — elderly conservatives and anti-communist Cuban-Americans.

But Smith's modest tally in 1984 had much more to do with Reagan's strong showing in the district than with any coalition Bush generated on his own. In 1986, GOP recruiting efforts faltered and Smith won with 70 percent; he nearly matched that in 1988, as George Bush carried the 16th for president with 55 percent.

Smith's Brooklyn style sets him apart from Florida's Southern-oriented House members. But his manner is appropriate for the 16th, which is home to hundreds of thousands who moved from the Northeast to Florida in the past two decades. Many transplants grew up in the roisterous world of urban ward politics and are not put off by fast-talking candidates.

Smith moved to Florida in 1968, following his parents, who had become active in local politics. He became known through civic work and his role in founding a temple, and in 1973 he got onto the Broward County Democratic executive committee. He served as chairman of the Hollywood Planning and Zoning Board and in 1978 was elected to the state House.

One of Florida's new House districts after the 1980 census was the 16th, including western Dade County and most of Broward County. It had in it the homes of Smith and former state Rep. Alan Becker, who in 1980 lost to Republican E. Clay Shaw Jr. in the 12th District. Becker and Smith met in a bitterly fought Democratic primary.

Smith, who was supported by the party establishment in Broward and by labor and business leaders, portrayed Becker as a carpetbagger. Becker, who represented condominium tenants in battles with developers, said Smith had sold out to business interests.

Becker enjoyed high name recognition from his 1980 House race and a 1978 campaign for state attorney general. But Smith overcame Becker's advantage by building his own condo network. Burdened by a less-than-obviously Jewish name in a district where the Jewish vote is crucial, Smith distributed pictures of his son's Bar Mitzvah and referred to his wife by her maiden name, Sheila Cohen. Smith lost the Dade portion of the 16th, but easily carried the more populous Broward County section.

Heavily outnumbered among registered voters in the 16th, local Republicans tried to tap the Jewish vote by nominating Maurice Berkowitz. But other districts in Florida offered better potential for Republican victory, so the 16th did not become a priority for the national GOP.

In 1984, Republicans aimed in a new direction with Bush, a native Floridian and fundamentalist Christian. The media played up Bush's efforts to ban abortion and to promote organized prayer and teaching of creationism in the schools. Bush dwelt on pocketbook issues and contended that Smith was too liberal, but fund-raising problems hampered him.

Smith, with plenty of campaign cash, invested heavily in direct mail and media. To temper his liberal image, he stressed his anti-drug and anti-crime efforts.

Committees

Foreign Affairs (13th of 28 Democrats)
Europe and the Middle East; International Operations

Judiciary (15th of 21 Democrats)
Crime; Criminal Justice; Economic and Commercial Law

Select Narcotics Abuse and Control (13th of 18 Democrats)

Elections

1988 General

Lawrence J. Smith (D)	153,032	(69%)
Joseph Smith (R)	67,461	(31%)

1986 General

Lawrence J. Smith (D)	121,219	(70%)
Mary Collins (R)	52,809	(30%)

Previous Winning Percentages: 1984 (56%) **1982** (68%)

District Vote For President

	1988	1984	1980	1976
D	92,263 (45%)	79,174 (39%)	65,583 (35%)	90,882 (55%)
R	113,360 (55%)	124,287 (61%)	107,954 (57%)	72,721 (44%)
I			14,631 (8%)	

Campaign Finance

	Receipts	Receipts from PACs	Expend-itures
1988			
Smith (D)	$700,550	$280,493 (40%)	$606,334
Smith (R)	$15,325	0	$15,325
1986			
Smith (D)	$774,467	$308,283 (40%)	$804,568
Collins (R)	$74,056	$1,131 (2%)	$60,337

Key Votes

1987

Raise speed limit to 65 mph	N
Approve Gephardt "fair trade" amendment	Y
Ban testing of larger nuclear weapons	Y
Delay "re-flagging" of Kuwaiti tankers	Y
Approve tax-raising deficit-reduction bill	Y

1988

Approve aid to Nicaraguan contras	Y
Enact civil rights restoration bill over Reagan veto	Y
Kill 60-day plant-closing notification measure	N
Pass omnibus trade bill over Reagan veto	Y
Approve death penalty for drug-related murders	Y
Bar federal funds for abortions in cases of rape and incest	N
Oppose seven-day waiting period for purchase of handguns	N

Voting Studies

	Presidential Support		Party Unity		Conservative Coalition	
Year	S	O	S	O	S	O
1988	23	72	83	6	21	74
1987	19	74	86	3	33	67
1986	27	73	88	9	38	56
1985	30	61	88	5	27	65
1984	34	59	83	7	25	69
1983	23	74	89	6	26	72

Interest Group Ratings

Year	ADA	ACU	AFL-CIO	CCUS
1988	85	17	100	23
1987	80	9	100	20
1986	65	24	100	27
1985	55	35	94	33
1984	80	14	85	36
1983	85	4	94	25

17 William Lehman (D)

Of Miami — Elected 1972

Born: Oct. 5, 1913, Selma, Ala.
Education: U. of Alabama, B.S. 1934.
Occupation: Automobile dealer; high school English teacher.
Family: Wife, Joan Feibelman; two children.
Religion: Jewish.
Political Career: Dade County School Board, 1966-72, chairman, 1971-72.
Capitol Office: 2347 Rayburn Bldg. 20515; 225-4211.

In Washington: There *is* such a thing as a shy, self-effacing used-car dealer — Lehman proves it. When he gets up to talk on the House floor, smiling meekly and speaking in a soft drawl, it is hard to imagine he once sold Buicks in Miami under the name "Alabama Bill."

But watching him in action as chairman of the Appropriations Subcommittee on Transportation, it becomes clear how he succeeded. Lehman's rather benign style belies a talent for deal-making and power politicking. When he decides he wants something, the odds are good he will get it.

In Congress, Lehman barters on the strength of the personal loyalty members of his subcommittee feel for him. In six years as chairman, he has run the Transportation Subcommittee by consensus. Generally agreeable to earmarking funds for members' home-district projects, Lehman rarely tries to dictate policy decisions.

Lehman's biennial fund-raiser for members of his subcommittee is testament to his style and the rare closeness he enjoys with his subcommittee. Held at his Capitol Hill home each election year, the event attracts even the Republicans who do not benefit from the proceeds.

This loyalty was critical as the 100th Congress pressed to pass all 13 appropriations bills before the end of fiscal year 1988. With the deadline approaching, the transportation bill appeared deadlocked over "labor protection" provisions requiring airlines to pay benefits to workers hurt by mergers. President Reagan threatened to veto a bill that included the provisions, while organized labor and most House conferees on the transportation appropriations bill were demanding them.

Lehman was determined to avoid rolling his carefully crafted bill into a continuing resolution, where increases for air safety and other projects would be threatened. To protect his bill, Lehman set up shop in a small Capitol office. One by one, House conferees filed through a hall lined with labor lobbyists to meet with Chairman Lehman. Telling members, "I really need you this time.... I don't ask you for much," Lehman persuaded the majority to drop the labor provisions.

The source of Lehman's strength — taking care of his members — also tests his skill in institutional wrangling. Lehman's willingness to fund unauthorized local projects directly leads him into perennial turf wars with the Public Works Committee.

Lehman often lost the war of words when Public Works was chaired by the more aggressive James J. Howard. The two had a showdown in the 98th Congress over an appropriations bill in which Lehman earmarked funds for mass transit. Howard called the effort "so egregious" that it threatened "the integrity" of the House. Rather than escalate the feud, Lehman dropped his bill and instead rolled much of what he wanted into an omnibus funding bill.

Now that Public Works is chaired by the more docile Glenn M. Anderson, Lehman still achieves most of his substantive goals, but is no longer overmatched in rhetorical battle. In 1988, after Anderson made a futile attempt to persuade Lehman's subcommittee to stop designating funds for specific projects, he appealed to the Rules Committee. Anderson wanted them to deny Lehman's request to waive House rules banning funding of unauthorized projects. Rules agreed to deny several waivers, thereby knocking them out of the bill. But when House and Senate conferees met, most of the projects were restored — and linked to an initiative Anderson wanted for his district. "He can't have it both ways," said Lehman, as the Public Works chairman dropped the campaign against the appropriations bill.

Nowhere is Lehman's project protection more vigilant than for mass transit and Miami's Metromover. A longtime booster of mass-transit programs, Lehman argues that expressways divide neighborhoods and lead to ecological "disaster." For eight years, he doggedly battled the Reagan administration's efforts to slash funding, and for the most part he prevailed. The last transportation funding bill Reagan signed included more mass-transit funding than

Florida 17

Southeast — North Miami; Part of Hialeah

The 17th is the strongest Democratic district in Dade County, thanks in part to the overwhelming turnout among condominium residents who make this constituency the single most concentrated source of condominium votes in Florida.

All along the Dade County coast, from Golden Beach through North Miami Beach and North Miami down to Miami Shores, entire buildings seem to empty out as condominium residents flock to the polls on Election Day. Some condominiums turn out so many people they become precincts in themselves, with the voting machines placed in lobbies or recreation rooms.

Many of the condominium residents are middle-income retired people from the urban Northeast who maintain lifelong Democratic voting habits. A sizable number of them — about one-quarter of the district's overall population — are Jewish. About 80 percent of the condominium residents in the 17th vote a liberal Democratic line, and their combined tally can give a Democrat a lead of upwards of 30,000 votes in the district.

Also contributing to the Democratic majority in the 17th is the black population, which at 27 percent amounts to the second-largest concentration of blacks in any of the Florida districts. About one-quarter of the electorate is Hispanic, and the district's other "minority" group — WASPs — makes up about one-fifth of the population. In addition to the condominium-filled waterfront area, the district takes in the northern tip of Miami (down to Northwest 62nd Street) and suburban communities such as Carol City, Opa-Locka and most of Hialeah.

In the last redistricting, some Dade County territory in Lehman's old district was moved to the new 16th District, as was a corner of southern Broward County. The changes mean that the 17th is wholly contained within Dade County.

Population: 513,048. White 355,233 (69%), Black 136,887 (27%), Other 3,896 (1%). Spanish origin 126,485 (25%). 18 and over 385,199 (75%), 65 and over 80,913 (16%). Median age: 35.

the president wanted, including a $15.5 million installment for the Miami project.

Lehman takes as good care of his district as he does of his colleagues'. His home-state initiatives range from basic federal grant delivery to humanitarian legislating and daring adventures. In 1988, the $7.4 million federally funded William Lehman Aviation Center opened at Florida Memorial College, a historically black school. Also in the 100th Congress, Lehman pushed a successful amendment to allow federal workers to donate paid leave to co-workers. His effort came about after employees at a local IRS office were barred from giving their leave time to a colleague who was dying of cancer.

Late in 1988, he personally chartered a plane and appealed to Cuban leader Fidel Castro for the release of three longtime political prisoners. Their return to Miami was greeted with triumphant headlines and high praise for Lehman, who has squabbled with local Cuban activists because of his opposition to aid to the Nicaraguan contras.

Lehman's Cuban mission recalled a 1984 episode, when he undertook a suspense-filled mercy mission to aid an ailing Soviet citizen. On an official visit to the U.S.S.R., Lehman smuggled into the country a $2,000 artificial heart valve for a 22-year-old Soviet woman who needed the device for a life-saving heart operation. Lehman and an aide slipped away from their hotel and raced through the streets of Tbilisi to deliver the valve to the woman's family, all the while hoping that their taxi driver was not a KGB agent who would wreck the mission.

Although generally preoccupied with Transportation, Lehman supports generous funding for Israel as a member of the Foreign Operations Subcommittee. He has devoted considerable attention to the plight of Jews in the Soviet Union, and in 1988, he advocated increasing funds for Soviet and other refugee resettlement programs in Israel.

On the House floor, the Miami Democrat generally votes more like his liberal Northern colleagues than his fellow Southerners. He is nearly always a reliable vote to cut defense spending. In 1982, he twice left a New York hospital where he was being treated for cancer of the salivary glands to cast key votes against the MX missile.

Lehman's debut as chairman of the Transportation Subcommittee came in 1982, after the sudden death of Indiana Rep. Adam Benjamin Jr. Lehman had spent years in the shadow of the powerful chairman, and had concentrated almost exclusively on mass transit for South Florida. When he took over the subcommittee, Lehman had just weeks to prepare to manage the $11 billion appropriations bill.

Lehman could not match Benjamin's encyclopedic knowledge of the subject. But after telling the House how difficult it was to take over a bill Benjamin largely had written, he moved it through successfully, fighting off a Republican amendment to cut the bill by $320 million to meet Reagan administration objections. "Appropriations bills should be written in Congress," Lehman said, "not at the Office of Management and Budget."

At Home: Lehman was a surprise winner in 1972, and fellow Democrats gave him no peace for several years after that. His Dade County district, then the 13th, was brand new for the 1972 campaign, and seven Democrats ran there. The favorite was state Sen. Lee Weissenborn, a liberal legislator who had sponsored legislation on handgun control and a state kindergarten system.

Weissenborn finished first in the primary with 27 percent of the vote, but Lehman, who had gone from his successful auto business to the chairmanship of the Dade County School Board, forced a runoff by drawing 20 percent.

Lehman, more centrist by reputation than Weissenborn, said he would work in Congress for higher Social Security benefits and better rapid transit. He surprised many Democrats by winning the runoff easily with 57 percent of the vote. His general-election victory was comfortable, although no runaway.

In 1974 Lehman was thrown into a primary runoff against Dade County Commissioner Joyce Goldberg. But as in 1972, he showed surprising strength in the second round, winning by more than 2-to-1. The 1976 Democratic primary also was crowded, but Lehman won without a runoff and overwhelmed a Republican in the general election.

Since then, threats to Lehman's tenure have faded. In five of his nine general-election contests, including the last four, Lehman has faced no Republican opposition.

In fact, Lehman's only real challenge in recent years has been fending off retirement rumors spurred by his age and occasional health problems. In 1984, Lehman made a major production of announcing his candidacy for re-election, something most secure incumbents do not bother to do. His office had been flooded with calls from people who thought he was retiring, partly because a local state legislator with the same last name had announced his retirement due to poor health. William Lehman, who the year before had had a cancerous tumor removed, wanted all to know that reports of his political demise were false.

Committees

Appropriations (17th of 35 Democrats)
Transportation and Related Agencies (chairman); Foreign Operations

Select Children, Youth and Families (2nd of 18 Democrats)

Elections

1988 General

William Lehman (D)	Unopposed

1986 General

William Lehman (D)	Unopposed

Previous Winning Percentages: **1984** (100%) **1982** (100%) **1980** (75%) **1978** (100%) **1976** (78%) **1974** (100%) **1972** (62%)

District Vote For President

	1988	1984	1980	1976
D	80,126 (59%)	89,283 (54%)	82,646 (51%)	114,887 (66%)
R	54,667 (40%)	76,081 (46%)	66,317 (41%)	57,720 (33%)
I			13,048 (8%)	

Campaign Finance

	Receipts	Receipts from PACs	Expenditures
1988			
Lehman (D)	$324,062	$132,250 (41%)	$257,487
1986			
Lehman (D)	$215,286	$97,700 (45%)	$172,800

Key Votes

1987	
Raise speed limit to 65 mph	N
Approve Gephardt "fair trade" amendment	N
Ban testing of larger nuclear weapons	Y
Delay "re-flagging" of Kuwaiti tankers	Y
Approve tax-raising deficit-reduction bill	Y
1988	
Approve aid to Nicaraguan contras	N
Enact civil rights restoration bill over Reagan veto	Y
Kill 60-day plant-closing notification measure	N
Pass omnibus trade bill over Reagan veto	Y
Approve death penalty for drug-related murders	N
Bar federal funds for abortions in cases of rape and incest	N
Oppose seven-day waiting period for purchase of handguns	N

Voting Studies

	Presidential Support		Party Unity		Conservative Coalition	
Year	S	O	S	O	S	O
1988	22	78	94	5	16	84
1987	14	83	95	2	9	86
1986	20 †	78 †	92	4	18	76
1985	23	78	95	2	11	85
1984	30	59	86	4	10	81
1983	17 †	78 †	85 †	5 †	18 †	77 †
1982	26	56	66 †	3 †	21 †	55 †
1981	39	53	77	8	19	71

† Not eligible for all recorded votes.

Interest Group Ratings

Year	ADA	ACU	AFL-CIO	CCUS
1988	100	8	93	36
1987	92	9	94	21
1986	100	0	83	20
1985	95	5	100	24
1984	85	0	92	42
1983	89	0	93	21
1982	89	6	92	15
1981	85	0	86	18

18 No Incumbent

Claude Pepper
1900-1989

In life, as in politics, Pepper aimed high and had to settle for a little less. He called himself the eyewitness to a century and planned to retire only when it was over. Instead, at age 88 he was felled by cancer.

Pepper's death on May 30, 1989, robbed the Congress and especially the Democratic Party of the last link to the New Deal years; he was a liberal conscience always prodding the country to do more for the poor and the elderly. If younger colleagues in recent years could not understand why Pepper ignored their argument that a nation in debt cannot do more, they lacked a sense of history — the institutional memory that elders like Pepper provide — to know that he had heard it all before.

"I do not believe that from the beginning of history down to the present time there has ever been a social reform proposed ... that there have not been those who raised upon the horizon the red flag of danger that 'It has to be paid for' and 'We can't afford it,' " Pepper said. That was in 1937, in his maiden Senate speech.

The times changed, but Pepper did not. While age drives many politicians to the right and a few to the left, he remained the same crusading liberal that he was as a Senate freshman at age 36, with all the same emotion and intensity. By the end, this homely man with the stooped bearing, ruddy complexion and bulbous nose was a national celebrity as an advocate for the elderly. "The sexiest man in America," Democratic activist Ann Lewis once called him.

The constancy of Pepper's politics would be remarkable in any politician of his longevity, but especially in one who suffered such notable election losses as he did over 60 years. Pepper represented Democratic continuity, and stability — an irony since he would lie in state in the Capitol Rotunda at a time of historic turmoil among House Democrats after the resignations of the Speaker and majority whip.

In his last, unrealized crusade in 1988 — for a multibillion-dollar expansion of Medicare to cover long-term home care for the chronically ill — Pepper had used all his power as Rules Committee chairman, and all the passion that had made him a hero to senior citizens, to press his legislation in the House. His committee drafted a rule that allowed his bill to go straight to the House floor, bypassing two committees with jurisdiction. An emotional Pepper pleaded:

"I ask you, my colleagues, when you go home tonight and you close your eyes and you sleep and you ask, 'What have I done today to lighten the burden upon those who suffer,' at least you could say, 'I helped a little bit today; I voted to help those who needed help.' "

The House gave him a standing ovation, and then voted against him. The defeat left the courtly lawmaker with some bitterness; he felt betrayed by colleagues who had relied on his campaign help in the past. Still, Pepper's efforts put the long-term home care issue on the nation's legislative agenda. A commission, which he had chaired, was to make recommendations by the end of 1989. It seems likely, however, that the crusade will lose momentum without its leader.

"He was out front on long-term care," said Rules colleague Martin Frost of Texas. "At the age of 88, he was still breaking new ground."

Throughout his nearly 41-year career in Congress — more than 14 years in the Senate, almost 27 in the House — Pepper was in on the ground-breaking for the minimum wage, medical research and health aid. On foreign policy, he was an internationalist when many politicians were holding to 19th century isolationism; a colleague in the 1980s professed wonder to learn he was serving with the author of the 1941 Lend-Lease Act, which provided critical military aid to the Allies in World War II.

Foreign policy provided the only major instance in which Pepper broke with liberalism during his career: In the 1980s, to Democrats' chagrin, he was a staunch backer of aid to the Nicaraguan contras. But it was liberalism, not Pepper, that had changed. Vietnam had left liberals suspicious of intervention abroad.

Pepper's fellow Democrats liked to attribute his pro-contra votes to political necessity since he represented many anti-communist Cuban-Americans. Yet that ignored the fact that Pepper did not just vote for contra aid — he also delivered impassioned speeches to close the House debates on President Reagan's periodic aid requests.

Usually, however, Pepper and Reagan were

Florida 18

Southeast — Miami and Miami Beach

Although Pepper won easily in the 18th, the district is not an easy one to represent. With large constituencies of Cubans, blacks and elderly Jews, it is one of the state's more diverse districts. And while it is nominally Democratic, GOP strength has grown considerably in the 1980s, making the district winnable for either party.

Many of the Cubans in Miami came to this country two decades ago, fleeing Castro's takeover. They were well-educated professionals and business people in their homeland, and they have achieved positions of status here. Cubans, Puerto Ricans and Haitians who have arrived recently tend to be unskilled workers, and integrating them into society is more difficult. There are tensions between the middle-class and underclass Cuban communities.

The Cuban-American community for a time was consumed by the desire to overthrow Castro, but in the 1980s attention has turned increasingly toward Miami politics. That has been good news for Republicans. There are some anti-Castro Cubans who have not trusted the Democratic Party since the Bay of Pigs invasion in 1961. The national GOP's more hawkish anti-communist stance has helped to convince most Cuban voters to register Republican.

In the central part of the district is Liberty City, the black neighborhood that erupted in three days of rioting in May 1980, leaving 18 dead. The violence began when a restive black community was infuriated by an all-white jury's decision to acquit four white Miami police officers in the beating death of a black insurance executive. The chamber of commerce has been pushing a program to create jobs for blacks and to promote black business ownership, but progress toward those goals is slow; the grim mood and appearance of Liberty City persist. The area gained national attention once again in 1989, when riots erupted following the shooting of a black motorcyclist by a policeman in Overtown.

Miami Beach is the part of the district that accounts for its high median age — 44 years. Pepper's natural constituency was the lower, less affluent portion of Miami Beach, where there are no luxury hotels and few tourists. Some blacks and Hispanics live there, but the Jewish population is still very large. The Jewish community that gave Miami Beach its New York flavor usually prefers candidates who are moderately liberal on social issues, conservative on defense and strongly supportive of Israel.

Pepper's death in 1989 prompted the first serious political competition the district had seen in decades. Nine Democrats and four Republicans filed for an Aug. 1 special primary. Reflecting the district's diversity, the candidate field included blacks, whites, Cubans and Jews. Prominent Cuban-Americans filed in both parties, boosting hopes in the Cuban community that they would elect a representative to Congress on Aug. 29.

Population: 513,250. White 395,634 (77%), Black 81,137 (16%), Other 3,151 (1%). Spanish origin 260,289 (51%). 18 and over 416,969 (81%), 65 and over 124,773 (24%). Median age: 44.

on opposite sides. When Reagan in 1981 proposed massive cuts in Social Security benefits, Pepper called them "a wholesale assault on the economic security of America's elderly population." From then on, Pepper was his party's standard-bearer against any retrenchment in the popular program — and a media match for the more telegenic Reagan. Referring to the president, Pepper would ask audiences, "How can a man with such a warm smile have such a cold, cold heart?"

Colleagues clamored for Pepper to make campaign visits to their districts. Before the 1982 elections, when House Democrats recovered from their 1980 losses and swept additional seats, he visited 25 states and 70 candidates, often traveling alone and carrying his own bags. "No single person had more of an impact on the 1982 elections," said Rep. Tony Coelho, then chairman of the Democratic Congressional Campaign Committee.

But to the dismay of fiscal conservatives in both parties and of many outside experts, Pepper helped create a political situation in which Social Security was too hot for either party to put on the budget table, precluding any significant deficit reduction for the decade.

Most upset, though, were Republicans, who grumbled that Democrats were demagogues preying on senior citizens, whipping up fears that the Social Security system itself was at stake. The GOP especially objected to a 1982 Democratic mailing to elderly voters, bearing Pepper's signature, that resembled a Social Security notice and warned of a Republican threat to benefits. But Republicans could not attack the messenger — the venerable Pepper — just as Democrats for so long aimed their shots short of Reagan.

In recent years, national GOP officials

tried to boost candidates from among the conservative Cuban-American community in Pepper's district, both to lay a base for the post-Pepper era and to keep the political showman at home more. None of the sacrificial lambs could hold Pepper below 60 percent of the vote.

Pepper achieved his symbolic stature during three terms as the octogenarian chairman of the Select Committee on Aging, until 1983. But he liked to stress that his concern for the elderly predated his own membership in their ranks: His first bill to become law in his one term as a Florida state legislator was a 1930 measure lifting fishing license fees for seniors.

Though Aging had no power to legislate, Pepper made it a well-publicized forum for attacks on Reagan policies, and for promoting his own bills in other committees. Appropriately for a man who began his political comeback as a 62-year-old freshman House member, Pepper was responsible for the 1978 laws raising the mandatory retirement age in the private sector from 65 to 70, and banning mandatory retirement altogether for some federal workers. Eight years later, Congress enacted his bill to bar most private employers from making retirement mandatory.

By the early 1980s, Pepper's standing was such that his endorsement was mandatory for any successful legislation to rescue the troubled Social Security system. Pepper was named to the bipartisan National Commission on Social Security Reform in 1981, and held the line against benefit cuts. The panel struck a balance, recommending benefit delays for current retirees and higher payroll taxes for workers.

Then early in 1983, Pepper succeeded Richard Bolling as Rules chairman, which allowed him to control the terms of House debate when the Social Security bailout was ready for floor action months later. (Pepper gave up Aging, but he retained control of its Health Subcommittee, the platform from which he pushed his top priority in the 100th Congress — insurance against catastrophic illness for the elderly.) Previously, Pepper had played only a modest role on Rules; he was more interested in issues and crusades than in procedure.

He made sure the rule for debate on the Social Security bill allowed a vote on his amendment to raise payroll taxes in the next century rather than raise from 65 to 67 the age at which current retirees receive full benefits, as Republicans on the commission wanted. To Pepper, raising the retirement age was tantamount to cutting benefits. "I have done all I could," he said in debate. "I leave the decision to my colleagues whether you are going to preserve this great institution in its integrity." But the House voted overwhelmingly against him — after a standing ovation.

That loss, like the 1988 defeat on long-term care, showed that Pepper was hardly omnipotent. Yet it was not easy for his colleagues to say no to him, not only because of his clout in the House as Rules chairman, and outside as a man who could sway voters, but also because of their tremendous regard for him.

At Rules, Pepper proved to be a far more collegial and less autocratic chairman than Bolling. Never a great strategist, he was a reliable lieutenant to the House Democratic leaders who pull the strings at Rules. In 1986, when Rules Democrats were divided because then-Majority Leader Jim Wright insisted that Republicans be allowed to offer several controversial amendments to a pending anti-drug bill, including one for the death penalty, Pepper successfully backed Wright.

Pepper also did not hesitate to use his position to benefit his own constituents and causes. In 1985, he buried a bill to allow interstate banking nationwide because Florida banks, part of a Southeast network, did not want competition from outside giants.

This power to kill legislation made most committee chairmen more than happy to appease Pepper by inserting in their bills his special requests. During action on a 1988 tax bill, Ways and Means Chairman Dan Rostenkowski was overheard to say that no member of his committee, himself included, had as many special provisions in the measure as Pepper did — and that Pepper was still making requests when the bill was in conference.

In the 100th Congress, Pepper helped shape the catastrophic illness insurance measure, and especially its provision for Medicare coverage of outpatient prescription drugs — a controversial one because of its cost, but one that relieved senior citizens of a major expense. "He dreams the impossible dream, and we move once a week to accommodate him," Democratic Rep. Pete Stark said at the time.

But to the frustration of the bill's sponsors, Pepper was not satisfied with the limited measure; his insistence on adding home-care coverage threatened to bring the bill down. To dissuade him, Speaker Wright promised a separate vote later on Pepper's proposal. That led to Pepper's subsequent end run around both the Ways and Means and Energy and Commerce committees to expedite the ultimately unsuccessful vote on his measure.

Pepper's attitude was simple. "I would rather live with $200 billion deficits and have more people living, than the reverse," he said in 1983. "And if we don't spend the money fighting cancer and arthritis and poverty and poor housing and all the rest, they'll just spend it on the military or something else."

This was the man who was called a "fighting cock" in his Senate days a half century ago; he first caught President Roosevelt's attention with his maiden speech defending a $1.5 billion bill for New Deal programs, and thereafter castigated those not so staunch as he in backing those programs.

Pepper's Senate career — until his death, many colleagues called him "Senator" — was preceded and concluded by the kind of defeats from which few politicians recover. He was a victim of the two great political forces of his century — racism and anti-communism.

An Alabama farm boy who had worked his way through the state university and Harvard Law School (with government aid he never forgot), Pepper moved to Florida during its 1920s boom and won election to the state House in 1929. But he lost his bid for a second term after voting against a resolution criticizing Mrs. Herbert Hoover for inviting a black congressman's wife to a White House tea.

He lost again in 1934, narrowly missing an upset of Democratic U.S. Sen. Park Trammell. But that campaign helped Pepper win a special election two years later after Sen. Duncan U. Fletcher died. His easy 1938 victory for a full first term was seen as a Southern referendum on the New Deal, and Pepper made the cover of *Time* magazine — as he would again 45 years later.

In the Senate, Pepper cosponsored repeal of the poll tax. In 1937, he was a proponent of the first law for a minimum wage (25 cents an hour), an eight-hour work day and legislation creating the National Cancer Institute, the first of 12 National Institutes of Health (NIH) he helped establish; a dying Pepper's last trip from Walter Reed Army Medical Center was a visit to a new NIH building named for him.

In 1938, he attended a Nazi conference at Nuremberg; alarmed by Hitler's power, Pepper became convinced the United States could not remain isolated. He championed Lend-Lease and the draft. In 1940, outraged mothers hanged Pepper in effigy on the Capitol lawn; he saved the coconut-head dummy, which is on display at Florida State University.

With time, Pepper's unalloyed liberalism on domestic policy became more of a liability, but it was postwar foreign policy controversies that ended his first congressional career. After a 1945 visit to Europe, he called Josef Stalin "a man Americans can trust." He split with President Truman over the Marshall Plan and opposed arms shipments to Greece and Turkey. Doubting Truman's dedication to the New Deal, Pepper tried to draft Dwight D. Eisenhower as Democrats' 1948 nominee. When that failed, he briefly put up his own name.

Truman, in turn, urged Democratic Rep. George A. Smathers to "beat that SOB" in 1950, according to Smathers. McCarthyism was in full swing and the incumbent was dubbed "Red Pepper." Smathers supporters circulated Pepper's remarks about Stalin and photos of the senator with black singer and alleged communist Paul Robeson. Blacks reportedly were hired to shake Pepper's hand, while pictures were snapped for later distribution.

But best remembered in political lore was a speech Smathers reportedly made to some rural voters, in which he called Pepper a "shameless extrovert" who practiced "nepotism" with a relative, had a sister who was a "thespian in wicked New York" and "before his marriage habitually practiced celibacy." Smathers, who won by more than 60,000 votes, always denied making the remarks.

A dejected, indebted Pepper returned to Florida to practice law. In his autobiography, "Pepper: Eyewitness to a Century," he wrote, "I felt like an athlete benched when he was at the peak of his game. I had to watch the players on the field, knowing I could do better than many of them if only I could get back in the game."

Twelve years later, at an age when most people plan to retire, Pepper did make it back to Washington — to the House, representing Miami constituents supportive of his liberalism. He had tried to return to the Senate in 1958, but conservative Sen. Spessard L. Holland won 56 percent of the primary vote. After 1962, Pepper won 13 more terms without difficulty.

Pepper was an ally of Presidents Kennedy and Johnson, supporting the expansion of Social Security, Medicare, education aid and civil rights bills. In 1965 he was a principal sponsor of the Older Americans Act. For a time he was associated with the crime issue, as chairman of a crime committee that he persuaded the House to set up in 1969. The panel held well-publicized hearings and made recommendations on organized crime, drug abuse and prison reform, but several years later it was abolished amid complaints that members used it for self-promotion. In 1977, Pepper took over the Aging panel.

Through his career, Pepper made a priority of government-sponsored medical research. He was motivated by the deaths of his father, who died in 1945 of kidney failure, and of his wife, Mildred, who died of cancer in 1979.

In the final days of his own battle with stomach cancer, Pepper was visited by President Bush, who made him the fourth member of Congress to receive the nation's highest civilian award, the Medal of Freedom. Republican Rep. Silvio O. Conte later told the House that Pepper apologized to Bush for being unable to stand for the honor. "He did not have to stand up," Conte said. "He was a giant."

District Vote For President

	1988	1984	1980	1976
D	47,474 (42%)	57,240 (40%)	58,549 (40%)	78,436 (55%)
R	65,621 (58%)	86,237 (60%)	75,799 (52%)	62,204 (44%)
I			10,006 (7%)	

19 Dante B. Fascell (D)

Of Miami — Elected 1954

Born: March 9, 1917, Bridgehampton, N.Y.
Education: U. of Miami, J.D. 1938.
Military Career: Army, 1941-46.
Profession: Lawyer.
Family: Wife, Jeanne-Marie Pelot; two children.
Religion: Protestant.
Political Career: Fla. House, 1951-54.
Capitol Office: 2354 Rayburn Bldg. 20515; 225-4506.

In Washington: For a man whose domain is diplomacy, Fascell hardly looks the pin-striped part. His squat build and the jowls resting on his collar suggest, instead, a bulldog. He also shares the dog's tenacity, and he has shown it time after time, whether scrapping for his immediate turf — the Foreign Affairs Committee — or for the House, or for the entire Congress in its power struggles with the executive.

Long before he became committee chairman in 1984, Fascell had raised his gravelly voice to insist that the White House recognize Congress' constitutional role in matters of war and peace; in 1973, he was an author of the War Powers Resolution, which remains the lightning rod for executive-legislative relations in foreign policy. Those relations were severely frayed in the Reagan years, but in the 101st Congress they entered a new phase as George Bush took office calling for conciliation.

Fascell was receptive, but with the caution of a man who has heard such pitches from every president since Eisenhower. "A bipartisan foreign policy," Fascell said, "does not mean a unilateral decision by the president, rubber-stamped by the Congress."

While relations with the Republican administration could only get better, those with his Democratic Senate counterparts have been in a bad state. The high hopes for accomplishment after Democrats regained the Senate majority in 1987 were dashed in the 100th Congress as the Senate Foreign Relations Committee repeatedly failed to get major bills to the floor. By the end, Fascell's frustration with his weak Senate counterpart, Chairman Claiborne Pell, had turned to open feuding.

The Senate's inability to move foreign-aid bills complicated Fascell's consuming drive to restore his committee's voice in foreign policy. He had become its chairman after more than a quarter-century of ineffectual leadership, and in 1985 engineered passage of the first foreign-aid law in three years. He continued to push the House to pass his bills in the 100th Congress, even though they were headed toward death in the Senate, because otherwise his committee would be "irrelevant," he said. "We might as well close up shop." Without the foreign-aid authorization bills, power shifts to the Appropriations committees, which then can fund programs as they see fit.

In his fencing with Appropriations, the Senate and the White House, Fascell at least comes from a fairly secure base. Foreign Affairs is as quarrelsome a place as ever, but he holds a tighter rein on the independent-minded subcommittee chairmen, often bringing them together privately to thrash out disputes before public meetings. His predecessor, Clement J. Zablocki, allowed himself to be dominated by the panel's aggressive liberal wing; Fascell bends to it some, but then steers it toward compromise.

In his biggest departure from Zablocki's style, Fascell rejects laid-back deference to the White House, and junior Democrats appreciate that. Fascell is no intellectual with a grand global plan, but he is a shrewd bargainer who yields ground grudgingly.

A patient man, he maps his strategy and leaves little to chance in building a majority. While committee votes frequently follow party lines, he gets along reasonably well with Republicans.

Yet given the committee's — and Congress' — deep philosophical and partisan divisions on the issue of foreign aid, Fascell may never be the force he would wish. Still, it will not be for lack of trying.

In his first year as chairman, Fascell quickly led Foreign Affairs to break its embarrassing pattern of failing to approve foreign-aid authorizations. The 1984 bill passed the House only to die in the Senate, but a year later Fascell helped pilot a revised two-year package into law. In the 1985 bill, he forced Senate conferees to accept House language blocking the CIA or Pentagon from aiding the Nicaraguan contras; though he supported contra aid, he knew the House would not approve the bill without the anti-CIA language. Its passage gave Fascell and his committee new standing.

Then came the disappointing 100th Con-

Florida 19

South — Coral Gables; Key West

Florida's southernmost district once included the whole Miami area. Now it has moved almost entirely out of the city and into the suburbs and rural country extending to the Florida Keys.

Redistricting in 1981 removed liberal areas of Miami as well as Miami Beach, replacing them with more conservative new territory. But there are still plenty of Democratic votes in the 19th.

Florida has taken in tens of thousands of Cuban and Haitian refugees in the 1980s, a frustrating experience for many residents in the 19th. The symbol of the problem is the Krome Avenue detention center, where many of the incoming have been held — often in overcrowded conditions. Federal courts angered a number of local residents by ordering the release of many Haitians earlier in the decade. The Haitian community has also been frustrated by the continued use of the detention center.

As the decade came to a close it was clear that the Latin community was being absorbed into the Miami political community, successfully working to elect Hispanic representatives to the state Legislature.

Much of the land in the district is taken up by the Everglades National Park, which is suffering because there is not an adequate cyclical supply of water. Elected officials hope to cure that by expanding the park.

Coral Gables has liberal academics around the University of Miami, and there are poor and middle-class black neighborhoods, as well as a large Cuban community. The Jewish vote out of Kendall is sizable. Homestead and Florida City are markets for a vegetable and fruit-growing area and the domain of traditional rural Democratic voters.

In the Keys, there is a dispute over development policies. Some who have retired to the area want to discourage growth in order to preserve the islands in their current state. They are opposed by the Conchs, Keys' natives who see tourism and development as their livelihood and want to encourage growth.

Population: 512,886. White 430,795 (84%), Black 61,598 (12%), Other 6,581 (1%). Spanish origin 111,934 (22%). 18 and over 373,329 (73%), 65 and over 45,187 (9%). Median age: 30.

gress. Through both 1987 and 1988, his efforts to craft a foreign-aid bill were bedeviled as usual by disputes with Republicans and the administration over budget constraints and congressional restrictions on the president's flexibility to spend the aid money. But the atmosphere was poisoned further by fallout from the Iran-contra scandal.

Early in 1987, Fascell refereed a fractious Foreign Affairs to draft a bill cutting Reagan's $12 billion request by $1 billion, earmarking more money for economic rather than military aid and limiting the president's freedom to shift money among specific countries, primarily in Central America. When the bill was approved on a party-line vote, Fascell bluntly alerted the administration he would block foreign-aid appropriations unless it helped enact his legislation.

At the same time, he still held out for a bipartisan consensus, inviting Republicans to suggest changes. Months later, more money was authorized and some spending limitations dropped. Ranking committee Republican William S. Broomfield lauded Fascell's good faith, but the compromise was not enough to win GOP or administration backing. Time ran out for Senate action, but Fascell took his bill to the House in December and passed it, in hopes of influencing appropriators then at work.

He was stymied again in 1988. Finally, in a single day just before Congress adjourned, he rushed a package of foreign-aid bills through both his committee and the House. But the effort collapsed in the Senate, under the weight of objections from the administration and senators at each end of the spectrum.

Contributing to the impasse in the 100th Congress was the distraction of the lengthy Iran-contra hearings. Fascell was a member of the special investigating panel, along with other House and Senate foreign policy experts. He had hoped to be chairman of the House team, as a sign of his panel's primacy; wasting no time when news of the scandal broke in late 1986, he had convened hearings in his committee that provided the public's first look at the two central characters, Vice Adm. John M. Poindexter and Lt. Col. Oliver L. North.

However, Speaker Jim Wright instead tapped former Intelligence Committee Chairman Lee H. Hamilton of Indiana. Fascell was named vice chairman. Wright explained that Fascell and other chairmen were busy with their committees. Unspoken factors were Hamilton's greater polish and eloquence — important traits for nationally televised hearings — and his record of opposition to contra aid, which made him more acceptable than Fascell to fellow Democrats.

Despite his hurt, Fascell was an active member. He concluded that "the administration went far astray from the democratic process," and "was so determined to pursue its policy that it ignored the normal checks and balances ... and said, 'We don't care what Congress thinks.'" Of Reagan, Fascell said, "The president knew, or he should have known."

It has sometimes been a problem for Fascell that on key foreign policy issues he tends to be more conservative than many Democrats. In addition to voting for contra aid, he has strongly supported aid to El Salvador, and opposed human rights restrictions on that aid. He has been the committee's senior expert on Latin America, but from the fervid anti-communist vantage of his Miami constituents, many of whom are Cuban exiles. Like them, he has vehemently opposed any suggestion of warming toward the Castro regime. He supported Angola's UNITA rebels against a government buttressed with Cuban and Soviet aid. In 1988 he won House approval of aid for United Nations peace efforts in Angola, contingent on assurances that any settlement would require free elections and departure of all Cuban troops; the aid died in the Senate, blocked by less compromising UNITA supporters.

To a degree, Democrats excuse Fascell's votes on Central American issues as politically required given his district. Moreover, on other important questions, he joins with them. As chairman of the Subcommittee on Arms Control, International Security and Science, he has sided with House arms controllers to support a nuclear test ban and the unratified SALT II treaty, and to oppose chemical weapons, the MX missile and deployment of the proposed strategic defense initiative. Perhaps helped by that record, he successfully blocked a move in the 99th Congress to set up a special arms-control committee, arguing that it would be an unjustified slap at Foreign Affairs.

In 1987, he tried to amend the defense bill to bar final assembly of chemical weapons, but lost, 191-230. That marked the end of a five-year stretch in which arms-control forces blocked production of a new line of such weapons.

Fascell has been most dogged when Congress' foreign policy prerogatives are at stake. He was particularly upset in 1986 when Reagan attacked Libya — not because he disagreed, but because Congress was not consulted. He said administration officials were "waltzing around" the War Powers act, complying with it "only when it suits them." When Reagan said he was defending against terrorism, Fascell said he instead was developing "a new way of going to war, which totally bypasses the Constitution."

In 1987, Fascell criticized Reagan's decision to provide Navy escorts and U.S. flags for Kuwaiti tankers in the Persian Gulf to protect against Iranian attacks. He faulted the administration not only for skirting the War Powers act by committing U.S. forces to war zones without consulting Congress, but also for moving without clear foreign policy goals or adequate military planning. Following 1983 terrorist attacks on U.S. targets in Lebanon, Fascell denounced the administration for cutting an embassy security program.

Fascell protects his turf even when the stakes are smaller. A two-year feud with Republican Senate leader Bob Dole over chairmanship of the "Helsinki commission" human rights panel ended only when Dole relinquished his claim on the position. Then Fascell agreed to a compromise of rotating the chairmanship between House members and senators, but not Dole.

Outside foreign policy, Fascell earlier in his career specialized in reforming House procedures. The Democratic Caucus in 1973 adopted his amendment requiring committee sessions to be open unless members voted in public to close them. Later he moved successfully to open House-Senate conferences. On the Government Operations Committee until 1984, he helped enact the law to open executive agency meetings. Long before it was required, he disclosed his personal finances.

During the late 1960s and early 1970s Fascell used his membership on both Government Operations and Foreign Affairs to oppose what he saw as President Richard M. Nixon's usurpation of power. In addition to the War Powers act, which was enacted over Nixon's veto, he sponsored a bill curbing presidents' claim of executive privilege, and he cast the deciding vote in 1973 to pass legislation making it easier for Congress to force the executive branch to spend appropriated funds.

On domestic issues, Fascell has maintained a moderate-to-liberal record over the years. In 1965 he managed the bill creating the Department of Housing and Urban Development, and he also backed a federal consumer-protection agency and the Department of Education. He opposed the 1964 Civil Rights Act, but voted for later civil rights bills, including the 1965 Voting Rights Act, federal support for school integration and the 1970 Equal Rights Amendment.

Fascell has shown a strong law-and-order streak. He had little sympathy for 1960s protesters, and sponsored legislation setting stiff penalties for inciting a riot. He has favored the death penalty for airline hijackers. In the 1980s, reflecting the concerns of Floridians, his thrust has been against drugs, seeking federal funds for law enforcement and education.

At Home: Like many of the people he represents, Fascell is not a native Southerner. He was brought to Florida from Long Island by his parents when he was eight, and he earned his law degree from the University of Miami before leaving to fight in World War II.

After the war, he used the Dade County Young Democrats and the Italian-American club as an entry into politics, then ran successfully for the state Legislature in 1950.

Four years later, Rep. William Lantaff announced his retirement. With the slogan "Ring the bell for Dante Fascell," the 37-year-old lawyer won a majority in the five-man primary and was unopposed in November.

His first real re-election test was in 1962. Democratic state Rep. David C. Eldredge, a segregationist, criticized Fascell as a consistent supporter of an intrusive federal government and hinted that the incumbent was sympathetic to communism.

When President Kennedy spoke at a Democratic fund-raiser in Miami Beach, he made a point of endorsing Fascell. That hurt Eldredge; he protested Kennedy's intervention, but faded to receive only 35 percent of the primary vote.

Since then, Fascell generally has won well over 60 percent of the vote. Even in the infrequent instances when he has faced vigorous challengers, Fascell has never dropped below 57 percent.

National Republican strategists essentially left Fascell alone until 1982, when they were hopeful that redistricting had made the 19th promising territory for a candidate younger and more conservative than Fascell. In that year's remap, the 19th lost 20,000 solid Democratic votes in south Miami Beach, including poor, elderly people dependent on Social Security.

Fascell's admirers trembled in midsummer 1982, when pollster V. Lance Tarrance released a survey showing the veteran incumbent only 10 percentage points ahead of Republican Glenn Rinker, a TV news anchorman who had not even announced his House candidacy.

Rinker owed his strong showing in the survey to his name recognition, which was remarkably high for a challenger. Prior to his bid, Rinker had appeared regularly for six years on a Miami TV station. Fascell, meanwhile, had been gliding through quiet and easy re-elections; many of the district's residents had moved in after his last serious challenge, in 1972.

Fascell responded to Rinker with a campaign that had both positive and negative sides. He not only reminded voters of the federal largess he had brought the area during his years in the House, but he portrayed Rinker as a shallow ideologue, a tool of the national GOP who would be a Reagan puppet in Congress.

Fascell enjoyed a significant organizational advantage over Rinker, whose campaign started late. The Democrat raised and spent vastly more than he had in any of his previous campaigns — over $450,000. As Fascell's aggressive response became clear, Republican contributors backed out on Rinker, and in the end the challenger was badly outspent. As it turned out, Rinker's strength just about peaked at the time of that midsummer poll. Fascell scored a solid victory, taking 59 percent of the vote.

In both 1984 and 1986, district Republicans were embarrassed when primary voters nominated substitute teacher Bill Flanagan over party organization candidates. Flanagan, known in the media as "Shower Shoes" (a reference to his preferred footwear), was a recluse who made no organized public appearances and tersely, sometimes angrily, refused requests for interviews. Flanagan did not run again in 1988, but the GOP fared even more poorly without him. Fascell, improving on his 1986 tally, won 72 percent of the vote.

Committees

Foreign Affairs (Chairman)
Arms Control, International Security and Science (chairman)

Select Narcotics Abuse and Control (8th of 18 Democrats)

Elections

1988 General

Dante B. Fascell (D)	135,355	(72%)
Ralph Carlos Rocheteau (R)	51,628	(28%)

1988 Primary

Dante B. Fascell (D)	35,630	(85%)
Wes White (D)	6,416	(15%)

1986 General

Dante B. Fascell (D)	99,215	(69%)
Bill Flanagan (R)	44,463	(31%)

Previous Winning Percentages: **1984** (64%) **1982** (59%) **1980** (65%) **1978** (74%) **1976** (70%) **1974** (71%) **1972** (57%) **1970** (72%) **1968** (57%) **1966** (57%) **1964** (64%) **1962** (65%) **1960** (71%) **1958** (100%) **1956** (61%) **1954** (100%)

District Vote For President

	1988	1984	1980	1976
D	74,323 (41%)	65,440 (36%)	56,728 (34%)	84,684 (54%)
R	105,860 (58%)	118,424 (64%)	90,859 (55%)	70,567 (45%)
I			17,626 (11%)	

Campaign Finance

	Receipts	Receipts from PACs	Expend-itures
1988			
Fascell (D)	$490,976	$176,934 (36%)	$337,596
Rocheteau (R)	$4,600	0	$4,907
1986			
Fascell (D)	$473,480	$144,550 (31%)	$293,227

Key Votes

1987

Raise speed limit to 65 mph	N
Approve Gephardt "fair trade" amendment	Y
Ban testing of larger nuclear weapons	Y
Delay "re-flagging" of Kuwaiti tankers	Y
Approve tax-raising deficit-reduction bill	Y

1988

Approve aid to Nicaraguan contras	Y
Enact civil rights restoration bill over Reagan veto	Y
Kill 60-day plant-closing notification measure	N
Pass omnibus trade bill over Reagan veto	Y
Approve death penalty for drug-related murders	Y
Bar federal funds for abortions in cases of rape and incest	N
Oppose seven-day waiting period for purchase of handguns	N

Voting Studies

	Presidential Support		Party Unity		Conservative Coalition	
Year	**S**	**O**	**S**	**O**	**S**	**O**
1988	28	67	88	8	42	55
1987	23	77	94	3	33	67
1986	28	70	88	7	36	60
1985	34	63	88	6	40	58
1984	40	54	84	10	32	66
1983	33	62	86	11	31	66
1982	39	51	71	10	44	49
1981	41	54	83	10	19	73

Interest Group Ratings

Year	ADA	ACU	AFL-CIO	CCUS
1988	75	17	93	36
1987	80	9	100	20
1986	70	23	93	24
1985	60	24	94	11
1984	70	17	85	33
1983	85	9	88	30
1982	75	5	79	25
1981	80	7	87	21

Georgia

U.S. CONGRESS

SENATE 2 D
HOUSE 9 D, 1 R

LEGISLATURE

Senate 45 D, 11 R
House 144 D, 36 R

ELECTIONS

1988 Presidential Vote

Bush	60%
Dukakis	40%

1984 Presidential Vote

Reagan	60%
Mondale	40%

1980 Presidential Vote

Reagan	41%
Carter	56%
Anderson	2%

Turnout rate in 1984	42%
Turnout rate in 1986	24%
Turnout rate in 1988	39%

(as percentage of voting age population)

POPULATION AND GROWTH

1980 population	5,463,105
1988 population estimate (11th in the nation)	6,342,000
Percent change 1980-1988	+16%

DEMOGRAPHIC BREAKDOWN

White	72%
Black	27%
(Spanish origin)	1%
Urban	62%
Rural	38%
Born in state	71%
Foreign-born	2%

MAJOR CITIES

Atlanta	421,910
Columbus	180,180
Savannah	146,800
Macon	118,420
Albany	84,950

AREA AND LAND USE

Area	58,056 sq. miles (21st)
Farm	33%
Forest	65%
Federally owned	6%

Gov. Joe Frank Harris (D)
Of Cartersville — Elected 1982

Born: Feb. 16, 1936, Atco, Ga.
Education: U. of Georgia, B.B.A. 1958.
Military Career: Army and Army Reserve, 1958-64.
Occupation: Industrial development executive.
Religion: Methodist.
Political Career: Ga. House, 1965-83.
Next Election: 1990.

WORK

Occupations

White-collar	50%
Blue-collar	35%
Service workers	12%

Government Workers

Federal	85,848
State	102,500
Local	256,669

MONEY

Median family income	$ 17,414 (37th)
Tax burden per capita	$ 757 (37th)

EDUCATION

Spending per pupil through grade 12	$ 2,966 (43rd)
Persons with college degrees	15% (32nd)

CRIME

Violent crime rate	577 per 100,000 (13th)

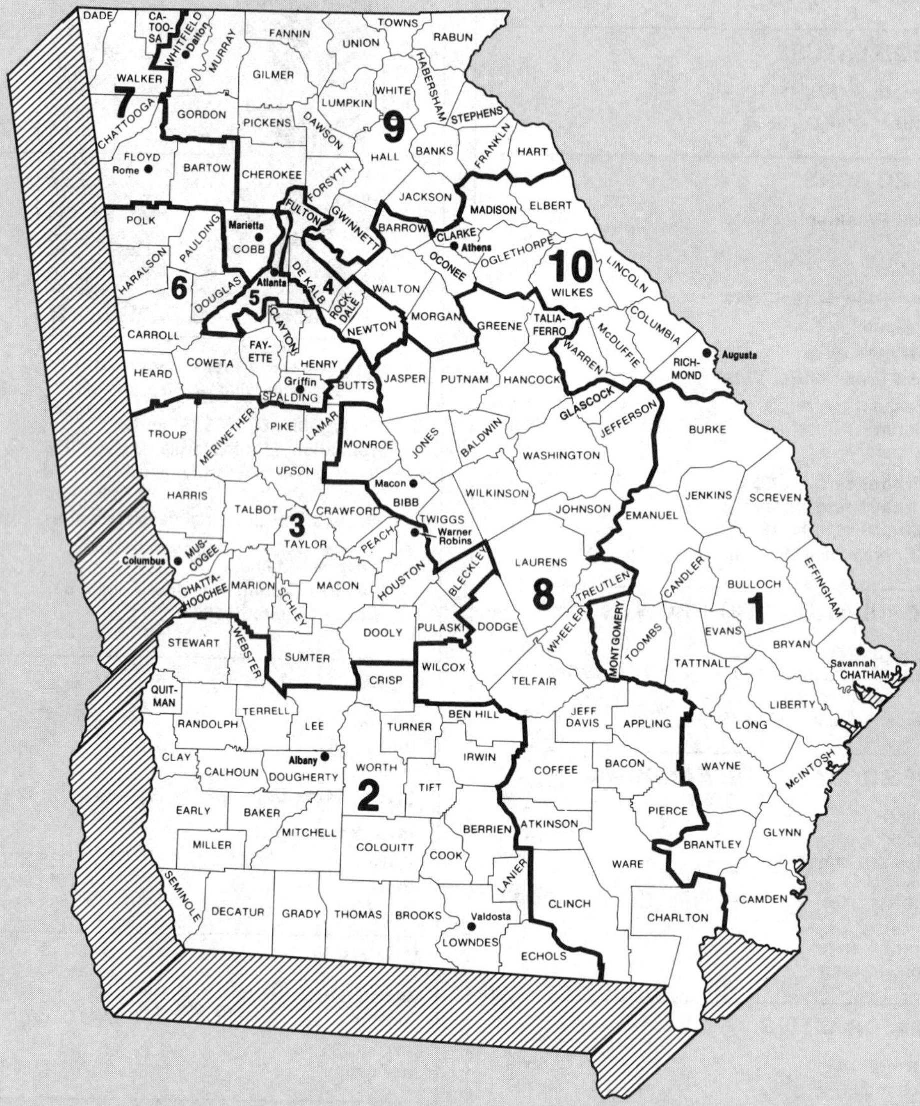
DADE
CA-TOO-SA
WHITFIELD
Dalton
MURRAY
FANNIN
TOWNS
UNION
RABUN
GILMER
HABERSHAM
WHITE
LUMPKIN
WALKER
7
CHATTOOGA
GORDON
PICKENS
DAWSON
9
STEPHENS
FRANKLIN
HART
FLOYD
Rome
BARTOW
CHEROKEE
FORSYTH
HALL
BANKS
JACKSON
MADISON
ELBERT
POLK
PAULDING
Marietta
COBB
FULTON
GWINNETT
BARROW
CLARKE
Athens
OCONEE
OGLETHORPE
10
WILKES
LINCOLN
HARALSON
6
DOUGLAS
Atlanta
5
DE KALB
4
ROCK-DALE
WALTON
MORGAN
NEWTON
GREENE
TALIA-FERRO
COLUMBIA
McDUFFIE
WARREN
RICH-MOND
Augusta
CARROLL
CLAYTON
FAY-ETTE
HENRY
HEARD
COWETA
Griffin
SPALDING
BUTTS
JASPER
PUTNAM
HANCOCK
GLASCOCK
JEFFERSON
TROUP
MERIWETHER
PIKE
LAMAR
MONROE
JONES
BALDWIN
WASHINGTON
BURKE
UPSON
Macon
BIBB
WILKINSON
HARRIS
TALBOT
3
CRAWFORD
TWIGGS
Warner Robins
JOHNSON
EMANUEL
JENKINS
SCREVEN
TAYLOR
PEACH
Columbus
MUS-COGEE
CHATTA-HOOCHEE
MARION
SCHLEY
MACON
HOUSTON
BLECKLEY
LAURENS
8
TREUTLEN
CANDLER
BULLOCH
1
EFFINGHAM
PULASKI
DODGE
WHEELER
MONTGOMERY
TOOMBS
EVANS
BRYAN
DOOLY
STEWART
WEBSTER
SUMTER
WILCOX
TELFAIR
TATTNALL
Savannah
CHATHAM
CRISP
QUIT-MAN
RANDOLPH
TERRELL
LEE
TURNER
BEN HILL
JEFF DAVIS
APPLING
LIBERTY
LONG
CLAY
CALHOUN
Albany
DOUGHERTY
WORTH
IRWIN
COFFEE
BACON
WAYNE
McINTOSH
2
TIFT
EARLY
BAKER
MITCHELL
BERRIEN
ATKINSON
PIERCE
MILLER
COLQUITT
COOK
BRANTLEY
GLYNN
WARE
LANIER
SEMINOLE
DECATUR
GRADY
THOMAS
BROOKS
Valdosta
LOWNDES
CLINCH
CHARLTON
CAMDEN
ECHOLS

Sam Nunn (D)

Of Perry — Elected 1972

Born: Sept. 8, 1938, Perry, Ga.
Education: Attended Georgia Institute of Technology, 1956-59; Emory U., A.B. 1961, LL.B. 1962.
Military Career: Coast Guard, 1959-60; Coast Guard Reserve, 1960-68.
Occupation: Farmer; lawyer.
Family: Wife, Colleen Ann O'Brien; two children.
Religion: Methodist.
Political Career: Ga. House, 1969-72.
Capitol Office: 303 Dirksen Bldg. 20510; 224-3521.

In Washington: The immense power Nunn wields is rooted in his understanding of its limits. His universe of expertise — national security issues — is large, but clearly circumscribed. He reaches his opinions with arduous deliberations and then sticks strongly by them, but recognizes where the doable diverges from his ideal.

His wounding of a GOP presidency not 100 days old over the nomination of John Tower to be secretary of defense heightened Nunn's reputation as the master of his universe. He tested the outer limits of his power, perhaps expanded it, and no doubt enhanced his reputation within the Democratic Party.

But he did so at an uncertain cost to his image as a nonpartisan operator — a key ingredient in his considerable reputation for integrity.

Nunn emerged as Tower's chief opponent in February 1989 in his role as Armed Services chairman. Throughout, Nunn cast the issue as personal, not political — that Tower's manifold problems, including past alcohol abuse and close ties to defense contractors, overrode his record of public service. While he argued that Tower was the wrong man to sit atop the chain of command for nuclear weapons, Republicans, chiefly Minority Leader Bob Dole of Kansas, accused Nunn of gazing longingly across the Potomac at the Pentagon and assailed him for leading Democrats in a naked power grab.

Nunn has often defended the Senate's prerogatives, and he seemed at home guarding its right to advise on and consent to a president's Cabinet nominee. But the Tower defeat was without precedent; never had the Senate denied a president a Cabinet choice at the start of a term. And Nunn looked increasingly uncomfortable as a unique moment in the Republic's history turned into a messy, partisan alley fight. It ended with a vote that broke largely along party lines; with a new and not entirely flattering term, "Nunnpartisanship," introduced into Washington's political lexicon; and with speculation raging about its meaning for Nunn, both in the Senate and in his party.

Nunn's demeanor is a church deacon's: sober, deliberate and stern, his work ethic well worn. But on matters of national defense, he wears the high priest's robes. He retreats into a mountain of facts and emerges with opinions that exert broad influence on defense policy. Becoming chairman of the Armed Services Committee, as Nunn did at the start of the 100th Congress, represented just an incremental increase in the power he already had held in the minority.

While he can maneuver behind the scenes and cultivate useful allies in the Senate, Nunn's importance has always come more from his knowledge and reputation than from his position.

And he has — at least until the Tower affair — positioned himself above the partisan fray. "I can't think of any major problem that can be solved with partisanship," Nunn once said. It was Nunn who advised President Reagan in late 1986 to form a committee of wise men — the Tower commission, as it turned out — to determine what went wrong in the White House during the Iran-contra scandal. He then cautioned Democrats against playing politics with so grave an issue.

Indeed, Nunn has been the Democrat conservative Republicans can love and Democrats cannot do without. A word or two of praise from Chairman Nunn can go a long way toward inoculating a fellow Democrat from a campaign opponent's charge of being soft on national defense.

But if Democrats can't live without him, many would at least like to change their relationship, for in a party far more liberal than he, Nunn faces a paradox. His power stems in part from his cautious use of it; so when he speaks, people listen. To satisfy critics inside his party, Nunn would have to spend his political capital more freely and make bolder moves to moderate the defense agenda, no matter the wishes of the GOP executive branch. As Nunn himself points out: "My critics do me a favor by exaggerating my influence and then criticizing me for not exercising it."

Nunn flirted with a run for the presidency as the 1988 campaign opened. The important role carved out for the South in the nominating contest and the contrast between Nunn's diligence and Reagan's lackadaisical management style worked to focus attention on Nunn as a contender. Interest in him was so strong that even his refusal to campaign for the nomination did not quell interest in his candidacy. He took himself out of consideration in the summer of 1987, citing his responsibilities as chairman, and has said he has no interest in running in 1992.

But even a new-found willingness to fight the party's battles, displayed in the Tower nomination, cannot alter the terms of a second political paradox working against any Nunn bid for the presidency: The very reason he is an attractive candidate — he draws white Southerners and other so-called Reagan Democrats — makes him unlikely ever to win a Democratic nomination.

Nunn is well to the right of the national Democratic Party, even if his differences with the Democratic mainstream have narrowed in recent years. For instance, he voted in 1988 with seven other conservative Democrats to sustain a GOP filibuster against a Democratic package of legislation on day care and parental leave. "I'm still more conservative than most people in the Democratic Party," he says. "But it's not as wide a gap as it used to be, and I like to think that's because they're coming towards the middle."

Nunn derives much of his day-to-day power as chairman from his detailed knowledge of individual weapons programs and his ability to work out a consensus on the hundreds of small decisions that go into each year's defense authorization bill. He has also established himself, however, as an important thinker on more fundamental questions underlying U.S. strategy in a nuclear world.

These attributes coalesced — and put his power clearly on display — in early 1987, when the defense community in Washington was preoccupied with debate over Reagan's efforts to reinterpret the 1972 anti-ballistic-missile treaty. For weeks, Nunn avoided taking a position on whether the treaty allowed, as administration officials argued, tests of a space-based anti-missile system.

Then, one day in March, Nunn began a series of three speeches outlining his views on the issue. He methodically laid out a long, detailed analysis (in printed form, it stretched to 98 heavily footnoted pages) of the history of the negotiation and ratification of the pact. The administration's reinterpretation was "fundamentally flawed," Nunn said, concluding that the intent of the treaty had been to ban the kind of tests Reagan sought.

The speeches ran like electricity through the capital's network of defense experts. Within days, it was clear that the administration would have great difficulty getting its view of the treaty accepted in Congress.

Nunn worked for the remainder of the 100th Congress to ensure his interpretation. Language was added to defense authorization bills to prevent the administration from testing weapons in space without prior congressional approval. He further used the debate over the intermediate-range nuclear-force (INF) treaty in 1988 to add teeth to his interpretation. Nunn also helped force the administration to comply with unratified provisions of the SALT II treaty, negotiated by the Carter administration, concerning the deployment of weapons. In a crucial switch, he decided to drop his opposition to a rider on the 1988 defense authorization bill that tied the administration to the provisions.

An advocate of increased defense spending long before Reagan became president, Nunn generally supported the trillion-dollar defense buildup undertaken by the Reagan administration. But he had sharp criticisms along the way of its management.

Nunn argued that the administration's program lacked strategic coherence. Too much has been spent on nuclear weapons, he feels, and not enough on conventional military strength in Europe and elsewhere, forces necessary to prevent a war from escalating into a nuclear conflict.

A key point of Nunn's critique is that the military spending increases under Reagan were more than matched by an expansion in defense commitments. Typical of that view was his opposition to U.S. military involvement in Lebanon. He was a leading foe of the 1983 War Powers Resolution that permitted Reagan to keep a Marine contingent in Beirut for up to 18 months, arguing that it represented "an unlimited mission . . . with very, very limited military power." Still, he is a consistent backer of the president's right to exercise his powers as commander in chief. In 1987, he worked to maintain support for the president's decision to protect Kuwaiti oil tankers.

Nunn also has argued that defense spending plans have focused too much on complex new weapons systems, and not enough on the spare parts, ammunition and maintenance projects needed to keep the armed forces in day-to-day fighting trim. A serious flaw, Nunn argues, has been the rivalry and lack of coordination among the separate branches of the military. This critique was a key factor in the 1986 passage of legislation reorganizing the military command system. The bill, which was opposed by much of the Pentagon hierarchy, gave added bureaucratic clout to the chairman of the Joint Chiefs of Staff and lessened the independence of the separate services.

NATO nations have been another target of

Nunn's critical scrutiny; he feels that the United States' European allies do not bear enough of the cost of maintaining common defense against the Soviet Union and its Warsaw Pact allies. He sponsored a key amendment in 1984, one that he knew lacked the votes to pass, that would have withdrawn up to 90,000 U.S. troops from Europe unless NATO countries met their longstanding commitment to increase ammunition stockpiles and build certain air-base facilities.

As his stand on the ABM treaty illustrated, Nunn has also become deeply involved in recent years in debate over the strategic defense initiative (SDI). Nunn has not always pleased liberal critics of SDI the way he did in the 1987 treaty reinterpretation debate; he has voted against deep cuts in research funding for SDI.

But Nunn has not been much comfort to staunch SDI supporters, either. His basic position, developed along with ally William S. Cohen, a Maine Republican, was reflected in an Armed Services Committee policy statement on SDI in the 1986 defense authorization bill. An effective anti-missile defense system deserves study, the two argued, but it is probably an impossible goal.

They urged that efforts be directed toward the modest goal of defending U.S. nuclear weapons against a surprise Soviet attack. Nunn further suggested in 1988 that a missile shield might be more useful if its task were limited solely to shooting down missiles fired accidentally.

Nunn has also been at the center of the battle over the MX missile, although he has not been an especially enthusiastic backer, at least since Reagan decided in 1981 to abandon Carter's "race-track" basing mode. He watched in silence as the MX came under increasing attack in 1984, although he did help push a major change in MX policy through the Senate in 1985. He argued that it would be a mistake to deploy more missiles in existing silos, where they could be highly vulnerable to Soviet attack. He negotiated a compromise that gave the president considerably fewer missiles than he wanted while a decision was made on how to base the next generation.

Nunn's concern for manpower needs has made him a forceful and persistent critic of the volunteer Army. As the 101st Congress began, Nunn was pushing legislation to add incentives for military and other forms of national service.

When he took over at Armed Services, Nunn was continuing a Georgia Democratic tradition — he is the grandnephew of Carl Vinson, longtime chairman of the House Armed Services Committee, and he occupies the Senate seat once held by Richard Russell, who chaired Senate Armed Services.

Nunn did not leave the matter of committee assignments to chance when he came to Washington. He teamed up with his great-uncle Vinson, who by then had retired, and visited all the major Senate power brokers, to win the Armed Services assignment.

Nunn inherited some of his great-uncle's skill at bringing defense dollars home to Georgia. He waged a bruising 1982 battle against senior Democratic Sen. Henry M. Jackson of Washington over whether to use some of the money allocated for C-5 transport planes, built in Georgia, to buy Boeing 747s, built in Washington. Jackson's personal lobbying gained an initial victory on the Senate floor, but Nunn won in the end, preserving job-creating contracts for his constituents.

On non-defense issues, Nunn's dominant concern has been in fighting organized crime. As chairman (and formerly ranking Democrat) of the Governmental Affairs Committee's Permanent Subcommittee on Investigations, Nunn has focused on uncovering corruption among union leaders.

At Home: During his rise to dominance in Georgia politics, Nunn was cautiously protective of his conservative image. In 1984, while running for a third Senate term, Nunn joined other state Democratic leaders in distancing himself from the doomed presidential campaign of liberal Democrat Walter F. Mondale.

However, Nunn's overwhelming re-election that year reaffirmed his position as Georgia's pre-eminent Democratic figure, and he has been generous about bestowing his conservative stamp of approval on more liberal Democratic candidates in the years since. In 1988, Nunn endorsed Michael S. Dukakis for president and made a well-publicized speech on his behalf at a rural Georgia rally in the last week of the campaign.

Nunn's assistance was far from enough for Dukakis, whose 40 percent showing in Georgia paralleled his results throughout the South. But two years earlier, Nunn gave a crucial boost to Democratic Rep. Wyche Fowler Jr.'s successful campaign against Republican Sen. Mack Mattingly. Nunn's imprimatur helped Fowler mitigate a liberal reputation, developed during a decade representing Atlanta's majority-black 5th District, as he sought the votes of rural and suburban Georgians.

Nunn had sat out the Democratic Senate primary campaign, during which Fowler's opponents portrayed him as too liberal to win statewide. But once the nomination was decided, Nunn campaigned vigorously, appearing in commercials that portrayed Fowler as an urban representative who looked out for rural voters, especially farmers.

Fowler in turn told audiences that his election could ensure a Democratic Senate majority, which would elevate Nunn's status. "A vote for Wyche Fowler is a vote for Sam Nunn to be chairman of the Armed Services Committee," Fowler said. His frequent dropping of the senior senator's name generated a joke that someone named "Wyche Nunn" was running. Fowler edged Mattingly, Democrats took the Senate and Nunn got his chairmanship.

Nunn was a dark horse himself when he first decided to run for the Senate in 1972, but he turned out to be an ideal candidate against David H. Gambrell, the wealthy and urbane Atlanta lawyer whom Gov. Jimmy Carter named to the Senate after Russell's death.

Nunn also was a lawyer and state legislator, but his central Georgia roots and kinship with Carl Vinson allowed him to run as an old-fashioned rural Democrat. He called Gambrell a "fake conservative" who backed Democratic presidential nominee George McGovern, despite Gambrell's denials of any such link.

Though Gambrell finished first in the primary, he was forced into a runoff with Nunn, who intensified his attacks, all but saying Gambrell's wealthy family had bought the seat by contributing to Carter's gubernatorial campaign. It was enough to sink Gambrell.

The focus shifted in the general election, when Nunn encountered GOP Rep. Fletcher Thompson. This time, it was Thompson who used the McGovern issue. But Nunn countered by obtaining the blessing of Alabama Gov. George C. Wallace, then a conservative icon.

Despite his criticisms of busing and "welfare loafers," Nunn also got the support of black leaders, who claimed Thompson had not spoken to a black audience in four years, even though 40 percent of his Atlanta district was non-white. Further big-name help for Nunn came from Democratic Sen. Herman E. Talmadge, at the time an institution in state politics, whose critical support in rural areas helped Nunn offset his opponent's strength in the Atlanta suburbs. Nunn won by 93,000 votes.

Six years later, Nunn's fiscal conservatism and support for the military put him in such good position that no serious challenger emerged. The luckless Republican candidate, former U.S. Attorney John Stokes, had little money and ran a near-invisible campaign. Nunn's 83 percent was the highest vote any Senate candidate in the country received that fall against a major party opponent. In 1984, a banner year for Republican candidates in Georgia, Nunn took 80 percent of the vote.

Committees

Armed Services (Chairman)

Governmental Affairs (2nd of 8 Democrats)
Permanent Subcommittee on Investigations (chairman); Government Information and Regulation

Select Intelligence (2nd of 8 Democrats)

Small Business (2nd of 10 Democrats)
Rural Economy and Family Farming; Urban and Minority-Owned Business Development

Elections

1984 General		
Sam Nunn (D)	1,344,104	(80%)
Jon Michael Hicks (R)	337,196	(20%)
1984 Primary		
Sam Nunn (D)	801,412	(90%)
Jim Boyd (D)	86,973	(10%)

Previous Winning Percentages: 1978 (83%) **1972** (54%)

Campaign Finance

	Receipts	Receipts from PACs	Expend-itures
1984			
Nunn (D)	$1,292,637	$381,914 (30%)	$729,843

Key Votes

1987	
Enact omnibus highway bill over Reagan veto	Y
Limit testing of space-based anti-ballistic missiles	Y
Oppose banning tests of larger nuclear weapons	Y
Confirm Robert H. Bork as Supreme Court justice	N
1988	
Allow vote on campaign-finance overhaul	Y
Pass civil rights restoration bill over Reagan veto	Y
Enact omnibus trade bill over Reagan veto	Y
Approve death penalty for drug-related murders	Y
Oppose "workfare" amendment to welfare overhaul bill	N

Voting Studies

	Presidential Support		Party Unity		Conservative Coalition	
Year	**S**	**O**	**S**	**O**	**S**	**O**
1988	63	33	68	24	92	5
1987	46	53	77	22	91	6
1986	58	39	50	43	75	16
1985	58	42	57	41	88	10
1984	69	29	44	55	83	17
1983	64	33	49	48	84	11
1982	70	29	57	41	82	16
1981	59	31	59	39	84	15

Interest Group Ratings

Year	ADA	ACU	AFL-CIO	CCUS
1988	40	42	54	50
1987	55	23	100	28
1986	30	55	47	50
1985	30	57	43	59
1984	35	73	45	74
1983	40	28	35	42
1982	45	68	64	67
1981	35	47	32	72

Wyche Fowler Jr. (D)

Of Atlanta — Elected 1986

Born: Oct. 6, 1940, Atlanta, Ga.
Education: Davidson College, A.B. 1962; Emory U., J.D. 1969.
Military Career: Army, 1963-65.
Occupation: Lawyer.
Family: Divorced; one child.
Religion: Presbyterian.
Political Career: Atlanta Board of Aldermen, 1970-74; president, Atlanta City Council, 1974-77; U.S. House, 1977-87; sought Democratic nomination for U.S. House, 1972.
Capitol Office: 204 Russell Bldg. 20510; 224-3643.

In Washington: A big-city politician given to the ponderous, Fowler spent much of his first two years as a senator putting red clay under his fingernails.

To show rural Georgia it had not made a mistake in electing him, he signed up for the Agriculture Committee. He ran a subcommittee important to Georgia's burgeoning forest products industry. He learned to talk tobacco, peanuts and poultry. He worked on the bailout of the Farm Credit System.

But Fowler did more than just court Georgia's farmers in the Senate. A winning manner gained him entry into the chamber's Democratic clubhouse. He built on the respect he had earned in the 1986 election, when he ousted a GOP incumbent despite a liberal-to-moderate House voting record compiled while representing a majority-black district in Atlanta.

Naturally gregarious, Fowler puts colleagues at ease by telling jokes and spinning yarns. He knows the words to more than one hymn. Once at a slack moment in the Senate schedule, while intense negotiations were taking place off the floor, he held forth on the pleasures of baseball.

But his most crucial speech may have been the one he gave to second the nomination of Democrat George J. Mitchell of Maine for majority leader. Fowler was an early supporter of Mitchell, and as a Southerner, a most important one during the 1988 contest.

After his election, Mitchell named Fowler to the Democratic Steering Committee, which makes committee assignments. It was no surprise that Fowler got a leg up on three other Southerners chasing a seat designated for the region on the powerful Appropriations Committee.

Mitchell later named Fowler assistant floor leader, a new post, and one for which the duties appeared most likely to consist of handling routine floor procedures. Still, it put him visibly among the Senate's leaders.

Fowler's voting record has moderated since his House days, but he has been among the most loyal Southerners to his party's line. He has not been afraid to cut against the grain of the South's conservative Democrats. He helped stake out the political turf that made it safe for Southern Democrats to oppose the nomination of Robert H. Bork to the Supreme Court. He withheld judgment at first, chastising those who opposed Bork immediately upon his nomination. Then he advanced the argument that President Reagan had made ideology the issue, and thus it was proper to oppose Bork solely on ideological grounds.

It is not uncommon for Fowler to be on the opposite side of an issue from his conservative colleague, Sam Nunn. Fowler, for instance, often voted with arms control liberals and was one of only four Southern Democrats voting against the death penalty for "drug kingpins."

Fowler left the Energy and Natural Resources Committee to take his place on Appropriations. But he will keep a hand in one of his favorite issues — the conservation and stewardship of resources — by chairing the Conservation and Forestry panel on the Agriculture Committee.

In a career that has reflected an interest in large ideas and discourse, Fowler has displayed an occasional restlessness with the confining details of the legislative process. When he arrived in the House in 1977, he returned an official set of formal law books and lined his shelf with volumes of novels, poetry and bestsellers. When he arrived in the Senate in 1987, he expressed a desire for "a little more time for reading and reflecting before meeting the demand for the day." He has constantly advocated a simpler society, one stripped of technological gadgetry and energy waste. He can work himself into a rage over the decadence of the electric toothbrush.

In the House, Fowler used his position on Ways and Means to promote energy conservation. In 1980 he made a futile, last-minute attempt to amend an oil windfall-profits tax bill with new conservation tax credits. When President Jimmy Carter tried to cut back on Amtrak service, Fowler opposed it as an energy-conservation issue.

His legislative accomplishments were modest in the 100th Congress. He gained Senate approval for legislation to promote federal energy and energy-conservation projects, only to see it dropped before final passage. He amended the Farm Credit System overhaul in committee and on the floor, including a measure to ensure interest-rate relief for farmers.

His conservationist bent showed up in his work on the Arctic National Wildlife Refuge issue, where oil exploration is at issue. He has introduced water-conservation legislation and angled to promote rural development with a revolving-loan program. But Fowler has not neglected his urban constituents. He backed urban development grants in the 100th Congress and sought funds to redevelop the Martin Luther King Historic Site and Preservation District in Atlanta.

Fowler understands clearly how to make Washington work to his advantage back home. As his 1986 Senate campaign approached, he used his Ways and Means seat to delve into the textile trade and farm issues that are of premier importance in outstate Georgia.

His affinity for the abstract had otherwise tempered his influence on Ways and Means. He often seemed detached from the committee's mundane work on the tax code, and had relatively little influence in the crafting of the 1986 tax-revision bill.

Fowler did have a major impact, however, in 1985 deliberations on reauthorizing the "superfund" toxic-waste cleanup program. He proposed an amendment to levy taxes on a range of U.S. industries in order to fund waste-site cleanups. Though the broad-based taxes were opposed by both President Reagan and Ways and Means Chairman Dan Rostenkowski, Fowler's amendment passed Ways and Means by 18-17. A version of his proposal was eventually enacted.

As a House member, Fowler was consistently the leading opponent of Reagan's policies in the Georgia delegation. To insulate himself from charges that he was a liberal, Fowler called himself "moderate in the extreme," and quoted Thomas Jefferson to the effect that government is best when it governs least.

At Home: Sheer political skill enabled Fowler to beat the odds in 1986, when he upset GOP Sen. Mack Mattingly. Widely regarded as too liberal and urban-oriented for Georgia's conservative Democratic yeomanry, Fowler proved a master campaigner with an extraordinary ability to tailor his style to his audience.

Fowler's main campaign asset was his multifaceted political personality. To Atlanta's 5th District, which he represented in the House for nearly 10 years, Fowler was the liberal critic of Reagan's domestic budget-cutting efforts. To voters in suburbs and college towns, the graduate of two of the South's most prestigious educational institutions was a deep-thinking intellectual.

But the persona that was decisive in the Senate contest was that of Good Ol' Wyche. To overcome his liberal image and the antipathy of many Georgians toward Atlanta pols — no Atlantan had ever before won a Senate seat — Fowler put on his best down-home accent and charmed audiences that were expected to be hostile. Though he did not run as well in outstate Georgia as more conservative predecessors, his totals there, combined with his Fulton County base, lifted him past Mattingly.

Many state Democratic officials believed Fowler could not win, and they had tried to recruit more conservative figures, including 9th District Rep. Ed Jenkins and then-University of Georgia football coach Vince Dooley, to seek the Senate nomination.

Fowler did face competition for the nomination, most notably from former Carter White House Chief of Staff Hamilton Jordan, who was coming off successful treatments for cancer. Jordan entered the race as the conservative alternative to Fowler. His earlier celebrity guaranteed him media attention, and he branded Fowler as a liberal in hopes of turning south Georgia voters against him.

But Fowler, a south Georgia native, was able to mitigate his liberal image by peppering his speeches with jokes and folksy stories. And Jordan was burdened by a negative perception of the Carter administration. Winning 82 percent in Fulton County, carrying Atlanta's suburbs and holding down Jordan's rural margins, Fowler took a slim primary majority.

Fowler then turned to Mattingly. Since 1980, Democrats had predicted a short tenure for the Republican, who scored a narrow victory over veteran Democratic Sen. Herman E. Talmadge. The Indiana-born businessman won largely because Talmadge had been tainted by personal scandals, and because metropolitan Atlanta voters had tired of his rural-oriented style.

In the Senate, Mattingly angered few voters, but did little to popularize himself. A backbencher with a wooden speaking style, he was a Reagan loyalist with one pet cause — giving the president line-item veto power.

But Mattingly was well funded for 1986, and he staged a media blitz to undermine Fowler. His main line of attack was on Fowler's House attendance record, which had suffered during his primary campaign: Mattingly ads described Fowler as "Absent for Georgia."

Early polls showed Fowler with a double-digit deficit. But by October, his campaign jelled. Endorsements from previously reluctant

Democrats helped Fowler temper his liberal image. Sam Nunn toured the state to praise Fowler's concern for rural interests.

The decisive factor was Fowler's ability to personalize the campaign. In one TV ad, a puppy enthusiastically licked Fowler's face. He stumped the state with a personal magnetism that mitigated the absenteeism charge.

The voting results differed sharply from 1980, when Mattingly ran up a huge margin in the Atlanta area to offset Talmadge's sweep elsewhere. Fowler carried Fulton County by 2-to-1, and also took suburban De Kalb County, which Mattingly won in 1980. Mattingly's conservatism helped him slice into the usual Democratic majorities in outstate Georgia, but Fowler still won more than half of those counties.

Fowler's countrified campaign was not a complete act; his family has deep roots in Georgia, and as a teenager he appeared as a country singer on an Atlanta talent show.

But basically, Fowler is a white-collar Atlantan. After graduating from Davidson College in 1962, he entered politics as an aide to 5th District Rep. Charles Weltner, a liberal Democrat who retired in 1966 after two terms rather than run on the same ticket with right-wing gubernatorial candidate Lester Maddox.

After graduating from Emory law school, Fowler returned to government in 1970, winning a seat on the Atlanta City Council. He made his initial try for Congress in 1972, badly losing the Democratic primary to civil rights activist Andrew Young. Fowler bounced back the next year, winning the City Council presidency over black activist Hosea L. Williams.

Fowler got another shot at the House in 1977, when Young was appointed to the United Nations by Carter. His main opposition came from another civil rights leader, John Lewis. The vote divided largely along racial lines. Fowler ran ahead in first-round voting and drew a nearly unanimous white vote to win the runoff.

Redistricting increased the black share of the 5th to 65 percent in 1982, but Fowler worked to prevent race-based voting. Quoting the Rev. Dr. Martin Luther King Jr., Fowler told blacks, "I know you're not going to judge me because of the color of my skin, but the content of my character." When Fowler left the 5th in 1986, Lewis won it.

Committees

Agriculture, Nutrition and Forestry (7th of 10 Democrats)
Conservation and Forestry (chairman); Domestic and Foreign Marketing and Product Promotion; Nutrition and Investigations

Appropriations (15th of 16 Democrats)
Agriculture, Rural Development and Related Agencies; District of Columbia; HUD-Independent Agencies; Military Construction

Budget (10th of 13 Democrats)

Elections

1986 General		
Wyche Fowler Jr. (D)	623,707	(51%)
Mack Mattingly (R)	601,241	(49%)
1986 Primary		
Wyche Fowler Jr. (D)	314,787	(50%)
Hamilton Jordan (D)	196,307	(31%)
John D. Russell (D)	100,881	(16%)
Jerry Belsky (D)	14,365	(2%)

Previous Winning Percentages: **1984 *** (100%) **1982 *** (81%) **1980 *** (74%) **1978 *** (76%) **1976 †** (62%)

** House elections.*
† Special House election.

Campaign Finance

	Receipts	Receipts from PACs	Expenditures
1986			
Fowler (D)	$2,912,638	$600,086 (21%)	$2,779,297
Mattingly (R)	$4,856,309	$990,313 (20%)	$5,119,249

Key Votes

1987	
Enact omnibus highway bill over Reagan veto	Y
Limit testing of space-based anti-ballistic missiles	Y
Oppose banning tests of larger nuclear weapons	N
Confirm Robert H. Bork as Supreme Court justice	N
1988	
Allow vote on campaign-finance overhaul	Y
Pass civil rights restoration bill over Reagan veto	Y
Enact omnibus trade bill over Reagan veto	Y
Approve death penalty for drug-related murders	N
Oppose "workfare" amendment to welfare overhaul bill	Y

Voting Studies

	Presidential Support		Party Unity		Conservative Coalition	
Year	**S**	**O**	**S**	**O**	**S**	**O**
1988	51	45	78	18	68	32
1987	35	62	85	13	53	47
House Service						
1986	17	42	30	8	24	16
1985	24	65	73	13	55	38
1984	40	45	66	21	51	42
1983	27	68	83	11	35	62
1982	45	48	70	17	48	44
1981	42	45	60 †	31 †	55	41

† Not eligible for all recorded votes.

Interest Group Ratings

Year	ADA	ACU	AFL-CIO	CCUS
1988	75	8	79	43
1987	90	8	100	22
House Service				
1986	15	44	43	50
1985	50	26	50	50
1984	70	35	69	27
1983	90	13	88	25
1982	65	10	74	35
1981	80	14	64	17

1 Lindsay Thomas (D)

Of Statesboro — Elected 1982

Born: Nov. 20, 1943, Patterson, Ga.
Education: U. of Georgia, B.A. 1965.
Military Career: Ga. Air National Guard, 1966-72.
Occupation: Farmer; investment banker.
Family: Wife, Melinda Ann Fry; three children.
Religion: Methodist.
Political Career: No previous office.
Capitol Office: 431 Cannon Bldg. 20515; 225-5831.

In Washington: For much of his time in Congress, Thomas, an investment banker turned tobacco farmer, has devoted himself to mastering the intricacies of farm issues, and he has emerged as one of the more knowledgeable junior members of the House on agriculture. Midway through the 100th Congress, he carried his command of the nuts and bolts of legislating to a new and prestigious committee assignment — Appropriations.

Thomas got the committee seat of Tennessee Rep. Bill Boner, who resigned in October 1987 to become mayor of Nashville. Other Democrats campaigned for the seat, but they backed off once it became clear that Thomas was the choice of Speaker Jim Wright of Texas. He became the first Georgian on the committee since Thomas' predecessor in the 1st District, Democratic Rep. Bo Ginn (1973-83).

Thomas' profile outside of farm issues has been limited; like most other Georgia Democrats, he prefers a substantive role behind the scenes to prominent displays of oratory or political gamesmanship. In that regard, Thomas and Appropriations are a good match.

With his two Appropriations subcommittees — Energy and Water Development, and Military Construction — Thomas has broadened his focus beyond agriculture. Still, he has used his positions to benefit his home turf: Thomas points to money in the fiscal 1989 military construction appropriations bill for projects at the Kings Bay naval submarine base, near the Florida border, and the Fort Stewart-Hunter Army Airfield complex, near Savannah, as evidence of his clout.

Thomas' district includes all of Georgia's Atlantic coastline, and when he first came to Congress, he headed for the Merchant Marine Committee. From that post, he pushed for funds for harbor widening and other local projects. On Energy and Water at Appropriations, he will be able to direct money toward projects he has supported in the past, such as the expansion of Georgia's deepwater seaports.

When he was on the Agriculture Committee, Thomas' chief expertise was in tobacco, but one of his most significant contributions in the 99th Congress was to the dairy section of the farm bill. Possessing the instincts of an inside dealmaker, Thomas proved to be a key ally of California Democrat Tony Coelho, chairman of the Dairy Subcommittee, in winning passage of what Coelho called a "unity" bill.

Thomas' importance on the dairy provisions owed as much to geography as to his political skills. Coelho wanted to reduce dairy surpluses with a "diversion" program — financed by a fee on all farmers — that would pay some farmers not to produce milk. But farmers in Georgia and other Southeastern states generally opposed paying for the plan because that region did not produce a surplus. To get around that problem, Thomas got Coelho to add "differentials" — geographical bonus payments to farmers in the Southeast that were not available to those in other regions.

The "differentials" did not go over well in many sections of the country, but Thomas' efforts to bring members from the Southeast behind the dairy provisions brought Coelho closer to his "unity" claim and eased passage of the legislation. Conferees later dropped the paid diversion in favor of another House proposal that required the government to reduce surpluses by buying up entire herds of dairy cattle. But the key provision for Southeast farmers, the "differential," remained.

During his tenure on Agriculture, Thomas also worked on behalf of Georgia's sizable egg industry. In particular, he lobbied for a provision outlawing the Egg King, a machine used to crush hundreds of eggs and then separate the liquid from the shells. "It is a hazard to public health," Thomas argued. "Eggs are literally dumped into the machine along with traces of blood, chicken manure, dirt, rot and fragments of paper egg cartons." For egg processors, it was also an issue of economics: The Egg King was providing competition that could eventually put some of them out of business.

The Agriculture Committee agreed with Thomas, but on the floor, California Republican Robert E. Badham, whose district was

Georgia 1

Southeast — Savannah; Brunswick

The 1st is old Georgia, from Savannah and the Golden Isles — the state's only seacoast — to the inland rural counties, where the economy has not changed much in a century and a half.

Savannah, which celebrated its 255th anniversary in 1988, is Georgia's oldest city. Its tidy brick Georgian houses, moss-covered oaks and iron-grilled gateways give it a charm that tourists find irresistible. But the city of 147,000 is also a major Atlantic port, strongly unionized and with a black population approaching 50 percent. Like other cities of the coastal South, it is an ethnic melting pot, home to Irish Catholics, French Huguenots and a substantial Jewish community. The current mayor is of Greek descent.

Savannah provides statewide Democratic candidates with a 1st District base, but the burgeoning suburbs of surrounding Chatham County and neighboring Effingham County usually turn the tide in favor of Republicans. Chatham County as a whole gave 58 percent of its vote to George Bush in 1988; he took Effingham by a 2-to-1 margin. GOP Sen. Mack Mattingly carried both counties in his unsuccessful 1986 reelection bid.

Bordering Chatham County to the south is fast-growing Bryan County, where suburbs are starting to encroach on the soybean, tobacco and peanut fields; the county grew by nearly 30 percent, to 13,000 residents, between 1980 and 1986. Statewide Republicans star here: Bush took 66 percent of the vote; Mattingly won with 60 percent.

The biggest burst of growth in the district has occurred in the southernmost county, Camden. Spurred by a healthy coastal tourist industry and the northward spread of suburban Jacksonville, Fla., Camden's population leaped by 45 percent in the early 1980s, the 25th-highest growth rate in the country. Recent statewide Republican margins have been fairly modest in Camden. But to the north, Glynn County, which contains the city of Brunswick and St. Simons Island, has been a GOP stronghold.

In between the Savannah and Brunswick areas is McIntosh County, a rural-and-coastal region that has maintained its Democratic leanings. Democrat Michael S. Dukakis took 54 percent in the county, the only one in the 1st District that he carried.

The inland 1st is rather sparsely populated farm land and forest country. Large black populations temper the Republican vote in many counties. But there are also some rural Republican bastions; Bush took 79 percent of the vote in Toombs County.

Population: 541,180. White 355,814 (66%), Black 179,817 (33%), Other 3,331 (1%). Spanish origin 6,510 (1%). 18 and over 375,257 (69%), 65 and over 55,349 (10%). Median age: 28.

home to the Egg King inventor, persuaded the House to reject the provision.

Thomas also was active on farm credit issues. As the farm credit crisis heated up in 1984, Thomas joined other committee members in agitating for help for their areas. In a closed-door session with budget director David A. Stockman, he argued vehemently against any cutbacks in credit policies. Early in 1985 he worked on emergency farm credit legislation to aid struggling farmers. That legislation met with a presidential veto.

In his first term, Thomas was actively involved in revising the tobacco program. Farmers in Georgia had been agitating for years to change the allotment system, by which those with quotas to grow tobacco leased them to growers. Many felt this system was geared more to the interests of allotment holders than to the growers themselves. Thomas brought the subcommittee to his district to hold field hearings, then helped rewrite the law to place more leases in the hands of those farmers growing tobacco.

At Home: Thomas' varied career gave him an invaluable edge in bringing the disparate communities of his district together behind him when he first ran for Congress.

After college and training as an investment banker, Thomas spent six years with two Savannah investment-banking firms, becoming an assistant vice president of one of them. In 1973, however, he left the city for a small farming hamlet in Wayne County, deep in rural south Georgia. He began raising tobacco, corn and soybeans, and managing timberland.

A decade later, already active in various public-affairs groups related to agriculture, Thomas joined a crowd of congressional hopefuls when Democratic Rep. Ginn gave up his seat in an unsuccessful 1982 primary bid for governor. The early favorite to win the Democratic nomination was state Sen. Charles H. Wessels of Savannah, heir to a banking and insurance fortune, who had plenty of money to invest in the campaign and support from much of Savannah's black community.

But Thomas had money of his own, and he held several successful fund-raising events, including an auction modeled after the famous Ducks Unlimited hunting auction.

In the crowded field, Thomas' background proved decisive. He drew on the ties to the Savannah business community he had developed during his investment-banking years, combining them with rural support that Wessels could not match. Thomas cited his farming experience to persuade rural voters he was one of them, taking quiet advantage of the antipathy toward urban Savannah interests traditional in the inland southern counties.

Thomas finished first in the primary, then buried Wessels in the runoff. He has had no trouble in any of his four general-election campaigns.

Committee

Appropriations (33rd of 35 Democrats)
Energy and Water Development; Military Construction

Elections

1988 General

Lindsay Thomas (D)	94,531	(67%)
John Christian Meredith (R)	46,552	(33%)

1986 General

Lindsay Thomas (D)	69,440	(100%)

Previous Winning Percentages: **1984** (82%) **1982** (64%)

District Vote For President

	1988	1984	1980	1976
D	62,529 (40%)	69,408 (41%)	82,446 (55%)	92,126 (66%)
R	94,646 (60%)	100,525 (59%)	63,003 (42%)	46,777 (34%)
I			2,363 (2%)	

Campaign Finance

	Receipts	Receipts from PACs	Expend-itures
1988			
Thomas (D)	$339,987	$149,969 (44%)	$337,048
Meredith (R)	$40,511	0	$40,461
1986			
Thomas (D)	$244,400	$132,350 (54%)	$201,603

Key Votes

1987	
Raise speed limit to 65 mph	N
Approve Gephardt "fair trade" amendment	N
Ban testing of larger nuclear weapons	Y
Delay "re-flagging" of Kuwaiti tankers	Y
Approve tax-raising deficit-reduction bill	Y
1988	
Approve aid to Nicaraguan contras	Y
Enact civil rights restoration bill over Reagan veto	Y
Kill 60-day plant-closing notification measure	Y
Pass omnibus trade bill over Reagan veto	Y
Approve death penalty for drug-related murders	Y
Bar federal funds for abortions in cases of rape and incest	N
Oppose seven-day waiting period for purchase of handguns	Y

Voting Studies

	Presidential Support		Party Unity		Conservative Coalition	
Year	**S**	**O**	**S**	**O**	**S**	**O**
1988	38	61	77	23	95	5
1987	42	56	71	23	98	2
1986	47	53	72	28	96	4
1985	50	50	75	25	93	7
1984	54	46	70	29	86	14
1983	49	51	64	36	84	16

Interest Group Ratings

Year	ADA	ACU	AFL-CIO	CCUS
1988	50	48	64	64
1987	40	36	44	60
1986	25	68	43	61
1985	25	67	41	45
1984	45	16	69	50
1983	40	74	35	60

2 Charles Hatcher (D)

Of Newton — Elected 1980

Born: July 1, 1939, Doerun, Ga.
Education: Georgia Southern U., B.S. 1965; U. of Georgia, J.D. 1969.
Military Career: Air Force, 1958-62.
Occupation: Lawyer.
Family: Wife, Ellen Wilson; three children.
Religion: Episcopalian.
Political Career: Ga. House, 1973-81.
Capitol Office: 405 Cannon Bldg. 20515; 225-3631.

In Washington: A quiet Georgian from the kernel of peanut country, Hatcher has risen to an important subcommittee chair without breaking any shells along the way.

His friendly face and polite manner are well-known on the Agriculture Committee, but beyond that arena, Hatcher and his views are indistinct. Now that he has taken over the chairmanship of the Domestic Marketing, Consumer Relations and Nutrition Subcommittee for the 101st Congress, he will be expected to play a bigger role on farm policy in general and on the food-stamp program in particular.

In the 100th Congress, Hatcher led a lower-profile subcommittee, the Small Business Committee's panel on Energy and Agriculture. There, he promoted his bill to expand a Small Business Administration (SBA) loan program in rural areas. The plan was signed into law as part of the SBA reauthorization bill.

On Agriculture, Hatcher has worked, if quietly, for peanuts and tobacco, his district's crucial farm products. When the farm bill came up for renewal in 1985, Hatcher was not a visible presence in the committee's debates. But he made clear his opposition to any new effort to gut existing peanut and tobacco price-support programs.

In 1986, Hatcher backed Agriculture Chairman E. "Kika" de la Garza of Texas to pass emergency farm drought-relief legislation. The bill included $230 million to allow peanut and soybean farmers to receive disaster payments.

At Home: The 1988 Democratic primary put Hatcher in a rematch with former congressional aide Julian Holland, whom Hatcher had narrowly defeated in the 1980 primary that first earned him the seat. This time, though, Hatcher handled Holland with ease, and then went on to dismiss his most determined Republican challenger to date.

Hatcher was assistant floor leader of the Georgia House when he entered the 1980 contest to succeed Democratic Rep. Dawson Mathis, who waged an unsuccessful primary challenge to Democratic Sen. Herman E. Talmadge. Though the experienced Hatcher was regarded as a primary favorite, he failed to win the majority needed to avoid a runoff with Holland, then Mathis' chief legislative aide.

Holland made a strong appeal to rural voters, portraying Hatcher as too liberal and not interested enough in farm issues. But residents of the district's small cities, especially Albany, who had preferred Hatcher in the primary, came through again for him in the runoff. Drawing on his strength in Albany and Valdosta, he won with 53 percent. Hatcher easily dispatched his GOP opponent.

But two years later, Hatcher had primary pressure again, this time from Mathis, who wanted his seat back. Concentrating on the 2nd's rural reaches, Mathis claimed he had done more than Hatcher for the peanut business. A strong campaigner, Mathis swept the district's rural counties, but Hatcher's showing in Albany and Valdosta pulled him through.

Hatcher then coasted until 1988, when Holland, who had spent the intervening years in Washington working mainly as a lobbyist, returned to the 2nd and announced a primary challenge to his old rival.

Holland tried to revive his rural base, blaming Hatcher for failing to block a diesel-fuel tax increase, and stating that Hatcher had voted with the Democratic leadership during procedural votes on issues such as abortion and gun control. He also claimed there was a latent anti-Hatcher mood among businessmen skeptical of the incumbent's ability to boost the district's faltering economy.

But Holland never caught fire. Hatcher denied being a liberal on social issues, and noted his part in the move to roll back the diesel tax. He also cited his efforts to bring businesses, especially in the food-processing industry, to the 2nd. Hatcher won by nearly 2-to-1.

Businessman Ralph T. Hudgens, the vigorous GOP nominee, recycled the liberal characterization, and he tried to paint Hatcher as an elitist because he rode in a Mercedes during Albany's Pecan Festival. But Hatcher won 29 of the district's 30 counties and 62 percent overall.

Georgia 2

Southwest — Albany; Valdosta

There has been a constant refrain in recent years that the Peach State is developing into "two Georgias": booming Atlanta, and rural areas elsewhere that remain dependent on a struggling agricultural economy. The 2nd, in the southwest corner of the state, symbolizes the "other Georgia."

While thousands of new residents have poured into metro Atlanta, the population in the 2nd has remained stagnant. A bloc of rural counties near the Alabama border lost population in the early 1980s. Dougherty County (Albany), the district's largest, grew by 2 percent. The district's biggest city by far, Albany produces beer, soap and thread, and processes the pecans and peanuts grown by local farmers. Still, the area has been nagged by a high unemployment rate.

With its large blue-collar and black contingents, Dougherty County is crucial for statewide Democratic candidates hoping to carry the 2nd. But it has not been particularly dependable for them; George Bush took 51 percent of the county's vote in 1988.

Valdosta (Lowndes County), surrounded by the vast reaches of southern Georgia's piney woods, makes much of its living from the forests; turpentine, planing and paper mills, and sawmills anchor the local economy. Nearby Moody Air Force Base also gives the area a boost. Though Hatcher has maintained his support here, Lowndes tends to favor statewide Republican candidates, including Bush, who took 62 percent of the county's vote in 1988.

The rural counties, many of which have black majorities, continue to provide Democrats with a consistent, though diminishing, support base. Of the 11 counties on the western side of the district that lost population in the 1980s, seven were carried by Democrat Michael S. Dukakis. They were the only counties in the district that he won.

Population: 549,977. White 346,391 (63%), Black 200,556 (37%). Spanish origin 5,869 (1%). 18 and over 369,606 (67%), 65 and over 60,160 (11%). Median age: 28.

Committees

Agriculture (11th of 27 Democrats)
Domestic Marketing, Consumer Relations and Nutrition (chairman); Cotton, Rice and Sugar; Department Operations, Research and Foreign Agriculture; Tobacco and Peanuts

Small Business (7th of 27 Democrats)
Procurement, Tourism and Rural Development

Elections

1988 General		
Charles Hatcher (D)	85,029	(62%)
Ralph T. Hudgens (R)	52,807	(38%)
1988 Primary		
Charles Hatcher (D)	77,789	(67%)
Julian Holland (D)	38,726	(33%)
1986 General		
Charles Hatcher (D)	72,482	(100%)

Previous Winning Percentages: **1984** (100%) **1982** (100%) **1980** (74%)

District Vote For President

	1988	1984	1980	1976
D	57,423 (40%)	62,974 (42%)	82,687 (57%)	93,296 (70%)
R	83,163 (58%)	88,306 (58%)	60,378 (42%)	40,942 (30%)

Campaign Finance

	Receipts	Receipts from PACs	Expenditures
1988			
Hatcher (D)	$348,158	$200,458 (58%)	$368,470
Hudgens (R)	$132,230	$12,740 (10%)	$129,741
1986			
Hatcher (D)	$164,810	$55,950 (34%)	$140,185

Key Votes

1987	
Raise speed limit to 65 mph	Y
Approve Gephardt "fair trade" amendment	N
Ban testing of larger nuclear weapons	Y
Delay "re-flagging" of Kuwaiti tankers	Y
Approve tax-raising deficit-reduction bill	Y
1988	
Approve aid to Nicaraguan contras	Y
Enact civil rights restoration bill over Reagan veto	Y
Kill 60-day plant-closing notification measure	Y
Pass omnibus trade bill over Reagan veto	Y
Approve death penalty for drug-related murders	Y
Bar federal funds for abortions in cases of rape and incest	N
Oppose seven-day waiting period for purchase of handguns	Y

Voting Studies

	Presidential Support		Party Unity		Conservative Coalition	
Year	S	O	S	O	S	O
1988	31	55	72	19	84	5
1987	37	61	70	21	91	7
1986	34	54	67	18	78	16
1985	49	45	73	17	78	13
1984	43	41	58	20	66	10
1983	51	40	62	29	76	12
1982	43	42	53	35	79	8
1981	59	36	50	40	80	13

Interest Group Ratings

Year	ADA	ACU	AFL-CIO	CCUS
1988	50	43	62	64
1987	44	27	44	54
1986	30	56	64	69
1985	35	52	44	42
1984	25	20	67	58
1983	45	43	59	63
1982	25	56	61	65
1981	25	60	57	63

3 Richard Ray (D)

Of Perry — Elected 1982

Born: Feb. 2, 1927, Fort Valley, Ga.
Education: Graduate of Crawford County H.S.
Military Career: Navy, 1944-45.
Occupation: Exterminator; Senate aide.
Family: Wife, Barbara Elizabeth Giles; three children.
Religion: Methodist.
Political Career: Perry City Council, 1962-64; mayor of Perry, 1964-70.
Capitol Office: 425 Cannon Bldg. 20515; 225-5901.

In Washington: It is inevitable that Ray's name would be linked to that of Georgia's senior senator, Democrat Sam Nunn. It was Ray who, as mayor of their hometown of Perry, first coaxed Nunn into public service. When Nunn's own political career took off, Ray followed him to Washington to serve as his senior aide, before winning a House seat of his own.

Even their policy interests mesh. Just as Nunn has established himself as an expert on defense policy, Ray has become a fixture on the House Armed Services Committee. Ray shares Nunn's conservative but questioning attitude on defense issues, and often follows Nunn's lead on such cutting-edge issues as arms control.

But if he is overshadowed by his ally, Ray is certainly not regarded by his colleagues on Armed Services as merely a House proxy for Nunn. With his attention to detail and methodical manner, Ray has earned respect for his expertise on a variety of esoteric defense issues.

At the beginning of the 101st Congress, Ray was named chairman of a special Armed Services panel on environmental problems at U.S. military facilities. This panel will have to deal with the difficult issues of how to dispose of toxic-waste messes at defense installations in a safe and affordable manner.

The appointment to head this panel was a rebound for Ray, who was slowed by health problems during the 100th Congress. He underwent surgery three times, once in May 1987 for a heart condition, and twice in spring 1988 to correct an intestinal inflammation.

But while he missed 28 percent of House votes in 1987 and 30 percent in 1988, Ray managed to play a role in some major defense debates. He has a cordial working relationship with Armed Services Chairman Les Aspin of Wisconsin and other more liberal committee members, and when Ray joined several of those liberals in voting for an unsuccessful 1987 amendment to cut funding for the strategic defense initiative, it was seen as a signal that some conservatives were losing their passion for the space-based anti-missile project.

Ray's interest in defense issues is not without its parochial angle: Defense facilities are major employers for his west Georgia constituents.

Ray also looks out for the 3rd District outside the bounds of his major committee. In 1987, he pushed through legislation designating a National Historic Site in Plains, Ga., hometown of his district's most famous son, former President Jimmy Carter.

At Home: As mayor of Perry in the 1960s, Ray appointed Nunn, a local lawyer, to an advisory panel on race relations. Nunn grew to admire Ray's organizational abilities, and signed him on as his administrative assistant after his Senate election in 1972.

By the time Democratic Rep. Jack Brinkley decided to retire in 1982, Ray had firm ties to local officials throughout the 3rd District. When Ray announced his candidacy, other Democratic aspirants folded their plans to run for the seat.

The Democratic Congressional Campaign Committee passed word to him then that a condition for receiving national money was to be a "loyal" — i.e., non-Boll Weevil — Democrat. Ray publicly denounced such a quid pro quo. The campaign committee ended up giving him just $250, but the publicity was just fine for Ray among his conservative constituents.

Republicans had hopes for their candidate, well-spoken lawyer Tyron Elliott. But Ray's connection to Nunn allowed him to claim the mantle of Pentagon protector that is traditional in the 3rd, where Fort Benning and Robins Air Force Base are important to the local economy. Boosted by Nunn's active campaigning for him, Ray swept every county.

Elections have been even less of a challenge since: Ray has been unopposed in the last two contests. Still, Ray has taken no chances. In his 1988 campaign, he spent upwards of $250,000. His position on the Armed Services Committee facilitates his fund raising: Over half his campaign receipts were from political action committees, many of them defense-related.

Georgia 3

West Central — Columbus

The 3rd District's most prominent citizen is former President Jimmy Carter, whose hometown of Plains is in Sumter County on the district's southern border. Voters here never deserted their favorite son. Even in 1980, when much of Georgia had soured on incumbent Carter, the 3rd gave him 60 percent of its vote.

The district, whose mainly rural expanse is sandwiched between the cities of Columbus and Warner Robins, remains loyal to its ascendant Democrats of the day, Sen. Nunn and Rep. Ray. Their security here is bolstered by a solidly Democratic black population that makes up over one-third of the total.

But at the presidential level, the conservative majority here has shifted to the Republican side. In 1984, President Reagan made a breakthrough by carrying 55 percent of the district vote; George Bush bettered that in 1988, taking 57 percent.

In that election, Bush carried the district's dominant counties, Muscogee (Columbus) and Houston (Warner Robins). Both of these counties have numerous residents who depend on nearby military installations for their economic well-being, and are therefore receptive to national Republican candidates.

Located on the Alabama border, Columbus (population 180,000) enjoys economic benefits from the Army's Fort Benning, a basic-training center that employs about 5,000 civilians.

Warner Robins (population 46,000), on the district's eastern border, is the site of Robins Air Force Base, a major air transport and Air Force supply center.

The dominance of the military economy enabled Bush to carry Houston County with 64 percent of the vote. With more of a blue-collar Democratic base in Muscogee County, the Republican's total was a more modest but solid 55 percent.

Outside the cities are the peanut, peach and pecan farms characteristic of west-central Georgia. Though there are pockets of GOP strength, the rural region, with its substantial black population, has largely remained loyal to the Democrats.

Population: 540,865. White 347,373 (64%), Black 185,763 (34%), Other 4,155 (1%). Spanish origin 8,810 (2%). 18 and over 376,128 (70%), 65 and over 53,146 (10%). Median age: 28.

Committees

Armed Services (17th of 31 Democrats)
Procurement and Military Nuclear Systems; Readiness

Small Business (15th of 27 Democrats)
Exports, Tax Policy and Special Problems

Elections

1988 General		
Richard Ray (D)	97,663	(100%)
1986 General		
Richard Ray (D)	75,850	(100%)

Previous Winning Percentages: **1984** (81%) **1982** (71%)

District Vote For President

	1988		1984		1980		1976	
D	62,028	(42%)	68,149	(45%)	85,268	(60%)	92,186	(70%)
R	84,006	(57%)	83,658	(55%)	52,307	(37%)	39,699	(30%)
I					2,356	(2%)		

Campaign Finance

	Receipts	Receipts from PACs	Expend-itures
1988			
Ray (D)	$281,295	$131,117 (47%)	$256,751
1986			
Ray (D)	$291,691	$120,812 (41%)	$150,796

Key Votes

1987	
Raise speed limit to 65 mph	N
Approve Gephardt "fair trade" amendment	N
Ban testing of larger nuclear weapons	?
Delay "re-flagging" of Kuwaiti tankers	Y
Approve tax-raising deficit-reduction bill	N
1988	
Approve aid to Nicaraguan contras	Y
Enact civil rights restoration bill over Reagan veto	N
Kill 60-day plant-closing notification measure	?
Pass omnibus trade bill over Reagan veto	Y
Approve death penalty for drug-related murders	Y
Bar federal funds for abortions in cases of rape and incest	Y
Oppose seven-day waiting period for purchase of handguns	Y

Voting Studies

	Presidential Support		Party Unity		Conservative Coalition	
Year	S	O	S	O	S	O
1988	22	33	48	21	37	11
1987	32	35	42	27	51	7
1986	56	43	50	48	82	16
1985	56	43	54	44	98	2
1984	52	44	44	53	81	15
1983	66	33	37	62	91	8

Interest Group Ratings

Year	ADA	ACU	AFL-CIO	CCUS
1988	20	53	56	56
1987	28	63	23	73
1986	10	71	21	88
1985	15	71	25	82
1984	20	67	31	47
1983	20	91	24	74

4 Ben Jones (D)

Of Covington — Elected 1988

Born: Aug. 30, 1941, Tarboro, N.C.
Education: Attended U. of North Carolina, 1961-65.
Occupation: Actor.
Family: Wife, Vivian Walker; two children.
Religion: Baptist.
Political Career: Democratic nominee for U.S. House, 1986.
Capitol Office: 514 Cannon Bldg. 20515; 225-4272.

The Path to Washington: During the early 1989 Senate debate over appointing John Tower as secretary of defense, Jones must have felt at least a little sympathy for Tower as he was grilled on his drinking habits and personal conduct.

Jones faced the same kind of scrutiny in his 1986 and 1988 campaigns for Congress. An actor whose folksy humor is part of his appeal, Jones says, "I have more bones in my closet than the Smithsonian Institution." Yet despite a stormy past that is atypical of a successful politician, Jones unseated scandal-plagued GOP Rep. Pat Swindall in his second try.

Swindall — whose alleged involvement in a money-laundering scheme led to an October 1988 indictment on federal perjury charges — tried to save his seat by dragging Jones' "bones" into view: His campaign focused on Jones' behavior prior to his recovery from alcoholism in 1977. But voters judged Swindall's present legal problems as more serious than Jones' past personal woes.

Known mainly for his portrayal of "Cooter," a hayseed auto mechanic on "The Dukes of Hazzard" TV series, Jones had never sought public office prior to his 1986 challenge to Swindall. The conservative Swindall (who upset Democratic Rep. Elliott H. Levitas in 1984) seemed well suited to the affluent district, and Democratic officials that year had no great hopes for Jones.

But Swindall needed a big campaign-spending advantage to win with 53 percent of the vote. Jones called himself a "mainstream Democrat" and scored with his portrayal of Swindall as an ideologue who favored a "chainsaw" approach to federal budget-cutting.

Though Jones spoke freely about his former alcohol abuse, his past was not a major issue in 1986. Neither was the mansion Swindall was building in suburban Stone Mountain. However, these issues would dominate the 1988 campaign.

With costs on his house soaring over $1 million, Swindall sought a loan in September 1987 from Atlanta businessman Charles LeChasney. He did not know LeChasney was the target of a federal sting operation, or that his discussions with LeChasney and an undercover agent posing as a money-launderer were recorded.

In February 1988, Swindall testified before a federal grand jury on his discussions with LeChasney. His re-election hopes were then rocked in June, when the Atlanta *Constitution* published transcripts of the recorded conversations indicating Swindall seriously considered a deal in which laundered money, possibly including illegal drug profits, which would be channeled to him through LeChasney.

Swindall's approval ratings plummeted, but he apologized and fought on. After Jones won the August Democratic primary, Swindall sent him a "congratulatory" telegram which also called on him to release his medical and arrest records.

Jones did release his Georgia arrest record, which included a 1974 simple-battery charge for shoving his second wife. Swindall also unearthed records in North Carolina, where Jones had been arrested for trespassing in a 1967 incident involving his first wife.

But Jones said those incidents only showed that as an alcoholic, he had "suffered from a very serious disease." He pointed to his successful fourth marriage as proof of his recovery.

Describing Swindall's legal dilemma as "the elephant in the room," Jones went easy on attacking the incumbent, instead letting his self-generated bad publicity do him in. Jones' election was cinched in October when Swindall was indicted for perjuring himself during his grand jury testimony.

Swindall demanded an early trial in hopes of pre-election vindication, but the trial judge postponed the case after learning that district residents, including several jurors, received mailings in which Swindall defended his actions. In the worst re-election showing of any incumbent in years, Swindall received just under 40 percent of the vote, even with President Bush running well in the district.

Georgia 4

Atlanta Suburbs — De Kalb County

The removal of several black Atlanta precincts from the 4th in the redistricting of the early 1980s furthered the dominance of the district's affluent De Kalb County suburbs, and reinforced a growing GOP trend. Republican Pat Swindall unseated 4th District Democratic Rep. Elliott H. Levitas in 1984, while President Reagan took 66 percent of the district vote.

However, the growing impression of Republican security in the 4th was shaken in 1988. The scandal-plagued Swindall lost his seat to Democrat Jones in a landslide. George Bush kept the district in the Republican presidential column, but by a narrower margin than Reagan had four years earlier.

As Atlanta blossomed into the South's financial capital during the 1960s and 1970s, De Kalb County — which makes up about two-thirds of the district's population — was in the front lines of the city's suburban growth. With over a half-million people, it is now Georgia's second most-populous county, though the boom has moderated somewhat as development expands farther out: De Kalb grew by about 10 percent between 1980 and 1986, compared with neighboring Gwinnett County's 66 percent growth rate during the same period.

The main image of the 4th District is one of affluence. The well-manicured lawns in Dunwoody and Chamblee are tended by corporate managers and young professionals. Many of these suburbanites were drawn to booming Atlanta from other areas of the country; they came with Yankee accents, and without the Southern Democratic loyalties that traditionally marked the district.

However, Democrats have hardly become a negligible force in De Kalb. The leading political figure there is De Kalb County Commission Chairman Manuel Maloof, head of the county's powerful Democratic organization and owner of an Atlanta tavern that is a famed hangout for state and local politicos.

The Democrats find their base in the central and southern parts of De Kalb, which are demographically mixed. Decatur, the county seat, was a 19th-century commercial center that declined when it lost out as a railroad center to Atlanta. But the city still has some industry, a sizable black population and a Democratic complexion.

The other portions of southern De Kalb also tend to vote Democratic. Emory University and the communities around it, many of them heavily Jewish or black, give local politics a liberal slant.

The two counties to the south continue to sprout subdivisions. Rockdale County, which grew by over 25 percent in the early 1980s, has become solidly Republican. Bush won 74 percent of the vote there in 1988, and Jones held off Swindall by fewer than 50 votes. Newton County, Jones' home base, is more mixed. Bush took 65 percent of the vote there, but Jones carried 57 percent in his House race; Democratic Sen. Wyche Fowler Jr. carried the county in 1986.

The 4th also has a slice of Fulton County, north of Atlanta. This section, mostly white-collar suburbia, contributes about 20 percent of the district vote.

Population: 542,368. White 463,338 (85%), Black 70,048 (13%), Other 6,131 (1%). Spanish origin 8,830 (2%). 18 and over 399,703 (74%), 65 and over 44,801 (8%). Median age: 30.

Committees

Public Works and Transportation (27th of 31 Democrats)
Aviation; Surface Transportation; Water Resources

Veterans' Affairs (20th of 21 Democrats)
Compensation, Pension and Insurance; Housing and Memorial Affairs

Campaign Finance

	Receipts	Receipts from PACs	Expend-itures
1988			
Jones (D)	$522,594	$265,606 (51%)	$516,737
Swindall (R)	$558,724	$193,042 (35%)	$696,301

Elections

1988 General

Ben Jones (D)	148,394	(60%)
Pat Swindall (R)	97,745	(40%)

1988 Primary

Ben Jones (D)	32,982	(62%)
Nick Moraitakis (D)	10,933	(21%)
John Stembler Jr. (D)	8,944	(17%)

District Vote For President

	1988	1984	1980	1976
D	99,212 (41%)	77,481 (34%)	93,881 (51%)	116,288 (59%)
R	142,998 (59%)	148,469 (66%)	79,568 (43%)	79,894 (41%)
I			7,243 (4%)	

5 John Lewis (D)

Of Atlanta — Elected 1986

Born: Feb. 21, 1940, Troy, Ala.
Education: American Baptist Theological Seminary, B.A. 1961; Fisk U., B.A. 1963.
Occupation: Civil rights activist.
Family: Wife, Lillian Miles; one child.
Religion: Baptist.
Political Career: Atlanta City Council, 1982-86; special-election candidate for U.S. House, 1977.
Capitol Office: 501 Cannon Bldg. 20515; 225-3801.

In Washington: Those unfamiliar with Lewis' history are sometimes surprised by the deep respect many colleagues have for this junior legislator, who comes across as a perfectly unexceptional man when he speaks in committee or on the floor.

But many House members vividly recall the picture of a young Lewis being beaten by state troopers as he and other civil rights leaders crossed the Edmund Pettus bridge in Selma, Ala., in 1965. It was a seminal event in the civil rights movement, and Lewis' key role in the front lines of that struggle gives him a special status among his colleagues.

A glimpse of the esteem Lewis commands came in the 1987 debate on imposing sanctions on the apartheid government of South Africa. All seven other Georgia House Democrats made a surprise last-minute decision to vote for the sanctions as a tribute to Lewis, who had let them know that passage of the bill was important to him.

A small gesture, perhaps, but those seven Democrats strayed from the party line on several key votes in the 100th Congress, leaving Lewis the only Georgia House member voting to cut funds from the strategic defense initiative, to preserve plant-closing notification language, and to oppose the death penalty for drug-related murders.

In most ways, Lewis' first term was no different from the typical freshman's. He was a loyal party foot soldier, quietly pursuing issues important to his district. On the Public Works and Transportation Committee, he watches out for Atlanta's rapid transit system, and on Interior and Insular Affairs, he is trying to secure a revolving loan fund to revitalize Atlanta's Auburn Avenue, once a symbol of black economic success. In 1987, Lewis authored a successful amendment to the airport funding bill requiring that 10 percent of all airport construction money go to minority businesses.

At Home: Lewis' 1986 victory in the 5th symbolized the rise of Southern blacks into the halls of political power. But to get to Congress, Lewis had to weather a bitter contest with a longtime ally, state Sen. Julian Bond.

The relationship between the civil rights leaders dated back to the early 1960s. Lewis, son of an Alabama sharecropper, was director of the Student Nonviolent Coordinating Committee (SNCC); Bond, from a middle-class Philadelphia background, was the group's spokesman.

Lewis spoke at the 1963 March on Washington. His fearlessness in the face of arrests and beatings was legendary. But when radical elements took over SNCC, Lewis moved on to head the Atlanta-based Voter Education Project.

Lewis lost his first political bid, a 1977 House primary, to Wyche Fowler Jr. In 1981, he won the first of two terms on the Atlanta City Council; he gained a following among blacks as well as whites in north Atlanta who appreciated his attention to neighborhood matters.

Bond, meanwhile, served 20 years in the Georgia Legislature, where he pushed through a redistricting plan that transformed the 5th District from nearly half white to almost two-thirds black. When Fowler announced his 1986 challenge to Republican Sen. Mack Mattingly, Bond became the favorite to succeed him in the 5th.

Bond did finish ahead in the primary. But Lewis, whose biracial appeal brought him a sizable white vote, held Bond under 50 percent in first-round voting, forcing a runoff.

The campaign became nasty. Bond belittled Lewis' command of issues. But Lewis delivered sharper blows, implying that Bond had held a desk job in the civil rights revolution, and calling on Bond to join him in taking drug tests. Though he never accused Bond outright of using drugs, the implication was there for those who already saw Bond as a jet-setter.

Winning more than 80 percent of the vote in majority-white precincts, and cutting into Bond's margin among blacks, Lewis won nomination with 52 percent. The Democratic rift had little effect on Lewis in the general election; he prevailed by a 3-to-1 margin. By his first reelection, Lewis was a settled incumbent, running without primary opposition and winning with ease in the general election.

Georgia 5

Atlanta

When the delegates poured into downtown Atlanta for the 1988 Democratic National Convention, they were greeted by symbols of prosperity: the steel-and-glass skyscrapers and towering hotels that make Atlanta the commercial center of the Southeast, and the symbolic capital of the New South.

However, in the shadows of those buildings is another Atlanta, a mostly black city struggling with typical urban social problems — unemployment, crime and drugs. While Atlanta's business boom spurred continued suburban sprawl through the early 1980s, the city's population dropped slightly, to just over 420,000.

The 5th takes in most of Atlanta, as well as some suburban territory. Blacks are 65 percent of the population, and they make the district a Democratic bastion. Michael S. Dukakis took better than two-thirds of the vote here in 1988; Democrat Wyche Fowler Jr., who represented the district for 10 years, ran up a crucial 5th District majority in his successful 1986 Senate race.

Lewis' 1986 victory to succeed Fowler returned the 5th to black representation. Fowler was preceded by Andrew Young, Atlanta's departing two-term mayor.

Pockets of Republican strength can be found in the Fulton County suburbs to the north. Roswell used to be a cotton-milling center, but it is now a bedroom community booming with the white-collar, middle-level managers who are flocking to the Atlanta area. The 5th also contains the western half of Sandy Springs, another mostly white suburban community.

South of Atlanta, the district takes in East Point, a lower-middle-class community whose residents work in nearby factories and at Hartsfield Airport. The southwest corner of De Kalb County is also included in the 5th. It is overwhelmingly Democratic: In 1988, Lewis took 76 percent of the vote in the Fulton County part of the 5th, but won 94 percent in De Kalb.

Population: 550,070. White 188,204 (34%), Black 357,303 (65%), Other 2,608 (1%). Spanish origin 6,070 (1%). 18 and over 390,138 (71%), 65 and over 52,426 (10%). Median age: 28.

Committees

Interior and Insular Affairs (21st of 26 Democrats)
Insular and International Affairs; National Parks and Public Lands

Public Works and Transportation (18th of 31 Democrats)
Aviation; Public Buildings and Grounds; Surface Transportation

Elections

1988 General		
John Lewis (D)	135,194	(78%)
J. W. Tibbs Jr. (R)	37,693	(22%)
1986 General		
John Lewis (D)	93,229	(75%)
Portia A. Scott (R)	30,562	(25%)

District Vote For President

	1988	1984	1980	1976
D	113,308 (68%)	124,006 (67%)	111,457 (60%)	104,323 (68%)
R	52,118 (31%)	60,150 (33%)	65,506 (35%)	50,151 (32%)
I			6,768 (4%)	

Campaign Finance

	Receipts	Receipts from PACs	Expend-itures
1988			
Lewis (D)	$193,584	$142,915 (74%)	$101,540
Tibbs (R)	$6,560	$1,000 (15%)	$6,047
1986			
Lewis (D)	$381,754	$157,994 (41%)	$380,314
Scott (R)	$74,767	$1,500 (2%)	$75,862

Key Votes

1987	
Raise speed limit to 65 mph	N
Approve Gephardt "fair trade" amendment	Y
Ban testing of larger nuclear weapons	Y
Delay "re-flagging" of Kuwaiti tankers	Y
Approve tax-raising deficit-reduction bill	Y
1988	
Approve aid to Nicaraguan contras	N
Enact civil rights restoration bill over Reagan veto	Y
Kill 60-day plant-closing notification measure	N
Pass omnibus trade bill over Reagan veto	Y
Approve death penalty for drug-related murders	N
Bar federal funds for abortions in cases of rape and incest	N
Oppose seven-day waiting period for purchase of handguns	N

Voting Studies

	Presidential Support		Party Unity		Conservative Coalition	
Year	S	O	S	O	S	O
1988	13	82	93	3	5	92
1987	13	85	93	4	12	88

Interest Group Ratings

Year	ADA	ACU	AFL-CIO	CCUS
1988	100	0	100	17
1987	96	0	100	20

6 Newt Gingrich (R)

Of Jonesboro — Elected 1978

Born: June 17, 1943, Harrisburg, Pa.
Education: Emory U., B.A. 1965; Tulane U., M.A. 1968, Ph.D. 1971.
Occupation: History professor.
Family: Wife, Marianne Ginther; two children.
Religion: Baptist.
Political Career: Republican nominee for U.S. House, 1974, 1976.
Capitol Office: 2438 Rayburn Bldg. 20515; 225-4501.

In Washington: Not long before Gingrich was elected House Republican whip in 1989, no one would have predicted that this conservative provocateur could mount a credible bid for the leadership, let alone snag its No. 2 post.

But Gingrich rode to power on a wave of restlessness among House Republicans, frustrated by decades of minority status. And he was able to cash in on the new prominence he had gained as instigator of the historic ethics investigation that toppled Speaker Jim Wright.

Gingrich's promotion requires him to channel his boundless intellectual and political energy more carefully, now that he is a spokesman for the party and not just one of its gadflies.

But he remains, at his core, a partisan activist who cares foremost about cutting a sharper profile for his party, and only secondarily about passing legislation and affecting policy.

His success as whip will not be measured in conventional terms. Having been elected to the leadership with a commitment to ending House Republicans' minority status, Gingrich likely will be judged less by his legislative accomplishments than by whether Republicans make substantial gains in the House elections of the early 1990s.

To drive that political realignment, Gingrich is groping for a politically potent idea on par with the Kemp-Roth tax cut that helped propel the Reagan revolution. He hopes to build on the same issue — ethics — that helped him get elected to the leadership. Using the Wright controversy as a springboard, Gingrich seeks to portray Democrats as the party of political corruption and Republicans as the party of reform.

Gingrich's campaign to move into the GOP leadership began within minutes of President Bush's announcement that he was nominating incumbent whip Dick Cheney of Wyoming to be secretary of defense. At that moment, Gingrich had never held a leadership post and was regarded as a long-shot candidate.

His rival for the job, Edward Madigan of Illinois, had the consensus-building, bill-crafting skills traditionally associated with the whip's job. But Gingrich had what many House Republicans were looking for: something different.

Gingrich's victory was a narrow one — a change of two votes would have reversed the outcome — but it was read as a clear mandate for change.

His victory tapped into a growing feeling among Republicans that the Democratic majority was too heavy-handed in its use of power and that incumbent GOP leaders were too compliant. That disaffection ran so deep that some Republican moderates and even a few of the party's "Old Bulls" supported Gingrich.

Gingrich owes his election as much to Jim Wright as to anyone. Wright, in his drive to establish a reputation as a strong Speaker, galvanized all elements of the Republican conference to a more confrontational style.

And Gingrich's ethics crusade against Wright, once it resulted in an investigation of unprecedented breadth, gave him legitimacy he would not otherwise have had.

But Gingrich's crusade began as a lonely one. It was part of a broader effort to highlight the improprieties of powerful Democrats — such as former Banking Committee Chairman Fernand J. St Germain — who had gotten off lightly at the hands of the ethics committee.

When he first called for an ethics investigation into published allegations of impropriety by Wright in 1987, Gingrich was easily dismissed by Democrats. But pressure built in May 1988, when his call was joined by the government-watchdog group Common Cause.

Once the ethics committee began its preliminary inquiry, the matter took on a life of its own and Gingrich kept a comparatively low profile. No jabs from this firebrand could be more devastating than the considered judgment of the bipartisan ethics committee.

In the meantime, however, Democrats responded to Gingrich in kind. They asked the ethics committee to investigate a book-promotion deal of Gingrich's own.

Georgia 6

West Central — Atlanta Suburbs

When the decade began, Democrats hoped that the rural Democratic traditions of the 6th would reassert themselves, enabling them to topple Gingrich. Instead, demographic and political trends worked in the other direction. The booming growth of the suburbs to the south and west of Atlanta, along with growing tolerance for the GOP among rural conservatives, made the 6th a safe haven for Gingrich, and fertile ground for Republican presidential votes.

The biggest growth occurred in the suburbs abutting Atlanta to the south. Clayton County, the district's largest, grew by 13 percent between 1980 and 1986 to over 170,000 residents. The most explosive development was in Fayette County (population 47,000), which grew during that period by over 60 percent.

The population boom was not limited to the close-in communities, though. Of the 11 counties entirely in the district, 10 had population growth rates in the early 1980s of over 10 percent. Only rural Polk County, in the district's northwest corner, lagged, with a modest increase of about 5 percent.

There is no real population center in the 6th. The growth has been divided up between such cities as Griffin, Carrollton, Forest Park, Newnan and College Park, which have populations ranging from 15,000 to 28,000.

These towns are in the shadow of Atlanta and within commuting range of the city. College Park is home to pilots, baggage handlers and others who work at Hartsfield International, the nation's second-busiest airport and the district's largest employer.

The atmosphere changes to the southwest, although Republican habits do not. Newnan's wealth is tied less to Atlanta's recent growth than to the more distant past; spared during the Civil War, Newnan is known as "the City of Homes," for the stately antebellum mansions lining its streets.

The largest source of jobs in Griffin (Spalding County), located in the district's southeast corner, is the cotton mill industry. But the town's special claim is that it is the "pimento capital of the world," and pimento peppers are packed there.

The presidential vote throughout the more developed areas has become staunchly Republican. George Bush took 65 percent of the Clayton County vote, and won 78 percent in Fayette.

Though there has been some spillover growth in Atlanta's western exurbs, the landscape is still dominated by farms where cattle, pecans, peaches and corn are raised. Traditional Democratic tendencies remain fairly firm in some areas: Democrat Wyche Fowler Jr. took three counties in his 1986 Senate race, including Haralson, where Georgia House Speaker Tom Murphy remains the dominant political force. However, the Republican vote for president is as sturdy as elsewhere in the district. Bush carried Douglas and Paulding counties with more than 70 percent of the vote.

Population: 548,959. White 462,791 (84%), Black 81,943 (15%), Other 2,752 (1%). Spanish origin 4,778 (1%). 18 and over 375,209 (68%), 65 and over 44,363 (8%). Median age: 29.

Even as he assumes the mantle of leadership after 10 years in the House, Gingrich still has the freewheeling, undomesticated style of a newcomer. Despite some efforts to smooth his roughest edges, Gingrich has never shed his reputation as a bomb thrower.

That reputation was well deserved in the mid-1980s, when he was the ringleader of a band of junior Republicans who perfected a brash political strategy for coping with their minority status in the House: confronting and harassing the Democrats rather than negotiating with them.

Although the exploits of these Republicans, organized by Gingrich as the Conservative Opportunity Society (COS), were geared largely to conservatives who watch House proceedings on the national cable network C-SPAN, they also helped pressure GOP leaders into adopting a more aggressive, confrontational posture.

Gingrich earned a permanent place in the conservative pantheon in 1984, when he took on the apotheosis of liberalism: then-Speaker Thomas P. O'Neill Jr. of Massachusetts.

Addressing a nearly empty chamber one night in May, Gingrich complained about a letter that 10 House Democrats had written to Nicaraguan leader Daniel Ortega, addressing him as "Dear Commandante" and calling for a settlement between political factions in that country. Gingrich said the letter was undermining U.S. foreign policy and possibly was illegal because it constituted negotiation by private citizens with a foreign power.

A few days later, O'Neill took the floor to charge that Gingrich had "challenged the Americanism of several Democratic members" at a time when they were not present to respond. O'Neill called that "the lowest thing that I have ever seen in my 32 years in Congress."

Republican Whip Trent Lott moved that the Speaker's words be "taken down" — stricken from the record as inappropriate under House rules. Presiding officer Joe Moakley, a Massachusetts Democrat and close friend of O'Neill, had no choice but to accept Lott's motion — the first such embarrassment to a House Speaker since 1797.

Gingrich's record of legislative accomplishment is as sparse as a backbencher's — as befits someone who cares more about big ideas and grand strategies than about passing bills.

But in his campaign as whip, Gingrich said his ability to work with Democrats was abundantly in evidence in his work on two of the most bipartisan committees in Congress: Public Works and House Administration.

Before becoming whip, Gingrich served briefly as ranking Republican on House Administration, which oversees such housekeeping matters as committee staff budgets and office expense allowances. In that brief stint, Gingrich claimed a great triumph when he won for Republicans a larger share of committee staff jobs.

On Public Works, Gingrich could play the legislative game on the Aviation Subcommittee, where he became ranking minority member in 1987. That was a particularly useful spot for Gingrich, because Atlanta's huge Hartsfield International Airport is in his district.

When he became whip, Gingrich gave up both his ranking Republican committee posts and took a leave from the Public Works Committee.

At Home: Gingrich weathered two unsuccessful campaigns before finally capturing the traditionally Democratic 6th in 1978. But aided by the spread of suburban Atlanta into the district and by the growing acceptability of Republican voting among rural conservatives, Gingrich quickly made himself a fixture. In 1982, his closest contest of the decade, Gingrich won with 55 percent of the vote; two years later, he took 69 percent.

The 1988 election provided an example of just how secure Gingrich has become. After presenting a series of very modest challenges, district Democrats hoped they had found a match for the hard-charging incumbent in David Worley, a politically savvy 30-year-old attorney who battered Gingrich with criticism on a wide variety of issues. But Gingrich easily deflected Worley's barrage, winning with 59 percent of the vote.

Worley, a party activist since his teens and a former aide to 4th District Democratic Rep. Elliott H. Levitas, announced his plans to run in mid-1987. He soon drew the attention of national Democrats hoping to inflict some political wounds on one of their chief antagonists. For the next year and a half, Worley found something to criticize in nearly all of Gingrich's actions in Congress.

The main thrust of his campaign was a charge that Gingrich's proposed revamp of the nation's retirement system was actually a plot to destroy Social Security. He accused Gingrich of hypocrisy on ethics (pointing to, among other things, his efforts to have a political associate appointed a federal judge) and berated him for sympathizing with his scandal-plagued Georgia GOP colleague Pat Swindall. He also struck at Gingrich's positions on numerous local issues, especially what he portrayed as Gingrich's waffling on an effort by Hartsfield Airport to build new runways in the northern part of the district.

However, Gingrich proved again that he could give as good as he got. In countering Worley's depiction of his Social Security plan, Gingrich told campaign audiences, "This is a man so despicable and so desperate to be a congressman that he is deliberately scaring 80- and 90-year-old people with what he knows is a lie." He portrayed Worley, a Harvard-educated district native, as a Boston liberal, and frequently portrayed him as a stooge of the ethically tarnished Speaker Wright.

Gingrich ended up carrying all but one of the district's 12 counties; he took populous Clayton County, home base to both candidates, with 58 percent of the vote. Worley won only in the slice of Fulton County (Atlanta) that is in the 6th District.

Like many successful Republican politicians in the South, the Pennsylvania-born Gingrich is not a native. He spent his childhood in various military bases around the world before his family moved to Fort Benning, Ga. After receiving a graduate degree in European history, he taught history and geography at West Georgia College in Carrollton before launching his political career.

Though Gingrich's 1974 campaign was his first political candidacy, he used professional polling and a hired staff, commodities rarely seen before in rural Georgia congressional contests. He surprised veteran Democratic Rep. John J. Flynt Jr., coming within 2,800 votes of victory. Two years later, Gingrich had to contend with a beefed-up Flynt campaign and Georgian Jimmy Carter heading the Democratic ticket. He lost again, but still drew more than 48 percent of the vote.

Flynt retired in 1978, leaving Gingrich as the best-known contender. In previous campaigns, Gingrich had been considered relatively liberal for a Georgia Republican, drawing much of his support from environmentalists. But in 1978 he relied on the tax-cut issue and stressed his opposition to U.S. transfer of the Panama Canal. He swept the northern portion of the district, defeating wealthy Democratic state Sen. Virginia Shapard by 7,600 votes.

After winning easily in 1980, Gingrich

faced some difficulty in 1982 against Jim Wood, a Forest Park newspaper publisher and Democratic state representative who urged voters to pin the blame for harsh economic conditions on the GOP in general — and Gingrich in particular. But the race was overshadowed by other contests around the state, and Wood had trouble getting his message out; Gingrich's ability to outspend him by better than 2-to-1 made the difference.

Gingrich's 1984 opponent, Democratic state Rep. Gerald Johnson, tried to make an issue of the incumbent's growing role in national politics. He accused Gingrich of ignoring the bread-and-butter concerns of his district, and said he lacked effectiveness in the House because of his attacking style. But Gingrich effectively made a virtue of his tactics. "I'm trying to back a national majority that believes the kind of things the people in the 6th District believe," he said en route to an easy victory.

In 1986, Democrats tried to talk up the prospects of Clayton County Administrator Crandle Bray. But Bray, serving in a nonelective post, was not very well-known, and his plodding campaign efforts contrasted poorly with the fiery style of Gingrich, who won with 60 percent.

Committees

Minority Whip

House Administration (3rd of 8 Republicans)
Procurement and Printing

Joint Printing

Elections

1988 General		
Newt Gingrich (R)	110,169	(59%)
David Worley (D)	76,824	(41%)
1986 General		
Newt Gingrich (R)	75,583	(60%)
Crandle Bray (D)	51,352	(40%)

Previous Winning Percentages: **1984** (69%) **1982** (55%) **1980** (59%) **1978** (54%)

District Vote For President

	1988	1984	1980	1976
D	59,118 (33%)	53,929 (31%)	75,853 (52%)	87,232 (68%)
R	121,128 (67%)	117,764 (69%)	65,029 (45%)	41,333 (32%)
I			3,021 (2%)	

Campaign Finance

	Receipts	Receipts from PACs	Expend-itures
1988			
Gingrich (R)	$851,786	$262,976 (31%)	$838,708
Worley (D)	$354,847	$205,252 (58%)	$358,354
1986			
Gingrich (R)	$735,365	$200,726 (27%)	$733,438
Bray (D)	$251,853	$97,945 (39%)	$251,751

Key Votes

1987	
Raise speed limit to 65 mph	Y
Approve Gephardt "fair trade" amendment	N
Ban testing of larger nuclear weapons	N
Delay "re-flagging" of Kuwaiti tankers	N
Approve tax-raising deficit-reduction bill	N
1988	
Approve aid to Nicaraguan contras	Y
Enact civil rights restoration bill over Reagan veto	N
Kill 60-day plant-closing notification measure	Y
Pass omnibus trade bill over Reagan veto	N
Approve death penalty for drug-related murders	Y
Bar federal funds for abortions in cases of rape and incest	Y
Oppose seven-day waiting period for purchase of handguns	Y

Voting Studies

	Presidential Support		Party Unity		Conservative Coalition	
Year	S	O	S	O	S	O
1988	62	32	80	6	92	3
1987	67	28	87	4	93	5
1986	72	23	85	8	80	14
1985	68	30	84	7	89	9
1984	60	29	83	9	86	8
1983	72	24	83	10	87	8
1982	70	26	78	18	75	12
1981	64	24	75	17	76	15

Interest Group Ratings

Year	ADA	ACU	AFL-CIO	CCUS
1988	5	100	15	100
1987	4	96	13	93
1986	0	81	14	94
1985	10	81	12	95
1984	5	78	8	60
1983	10	91	6	79
1982	5	86	10	75
1981	10	92	0	100

7 George "Buddy" Darden (D)

Of Marietta — Elected 1983

Born: Nov. 22, 1943, Hancock Co., Ga.
Education: U. of Georgia, B.A. 1965, J.D. 1967.
Occupation: Lawyer.
Family: Wife, Lillian Budd; two children.
Religion: Methodist.
Political Career: Cobb County district attorney, 1973-77; Ga. House, 1981-83.
Capitol Office: 228 Cannon Bldg. 20515; 225-2931.

In Washington: As a member of the Armed Services Committee, Darden had to choose sides in the 1987 chairmanship fight between the incumbent, Les Aspin of Wisconsin, and his opponent, Marvin Leath of Texas. Representing a northwest Georgia district, it would have been risk-free for Darden to fall in with the conservative Southern challenger. But Darden went with Aspin, whose victory revived his stature as the chairman of the powerful committee.

Signing on to the winning side had benefits for Darden as well. He now has the ear of Aspin, who has been known to include Darden in his informal "kitchen cabinet." And by picking Aspin over Leath, Darden boosted his reputation for initiative and political savvy.

In his first few years in the House, Darden was regarded as a cautious, low-profile member who seemed wary of making too sharp a break from the right-wing record of his predecessor, Democrat Larry McDonald, who died in a Korean airliner downed by the Soviet military in 1983.

In his 1983 special election campaign and again in 1984, Darden's opponents hounded him as a liberal, largely because his views on domestic issues are far more moderate than McDonald's were. As Darden has established himself on Armed Services as a pro-defense Democrat — and an advocate for military programs directed at the huge Lockheed aircraft plant in the 7th District — he has gained confidence and displayed more freedom of movement.

During the 100th Congress, Darden showed he could earn political credits back home, and plaudits on the committee, even in a losing cause.

The Defense Department, as part of its fiscal 1988 authorization request, had committed to replacing the hulking C-5B military cargo plane built at Marietta's Lockheed plant with McDonnell Douglas' C-17, a smaller, more versatile plane to be built in California. After losing in committee, Darden made a last-ditch effort in May 1987 to convince the House that continued production of the C-5B would be more efficient than introducing a new plane.

With the Pentagon pushing hard in the other direction, Darden's amendment to scrap C-17 funding went down, 92-321. But he received praise from other House members for making a reasoned case for the C-5B, while earning the gratitude of his constituents for fighting, albeit fruitlessly, for a project that was a big local job-producer.

At Home: Darden's 1983 victory over McDonald's widow, Kathryn, was the first congressional victory in a decade for the 7th's mainstream Democrats. Larry McDonald, whose outspoken allegiance to the New Right made him a Democrat in name only, had his own bipartisan conservative network.

Elected in 1972 as Cobb County district attorney after five years as an assistant D.A., Darden developed a reputation as a law-and-order prosecutor. But his re-election effort in 1976 failed because he was dogged by charges he had bungled a 1971 murder investigation.

Darden went into private law practice. But in 1980, when one of Cobb County's seats in the state House opened up, he got the support of local Democratic officials and won easily.

After McDonald's death, Darden entered the nonpartisan special election. Calling himself a "responsible conservative," he promised to fight "big spenders in Congress." Though Darden earned a runoff position, he trailed Kathryn McDonald in first-round voting. However, McDonald's roughshod tactics — including an attempt to link Darden to gay rights through his ties to organized labor — alienated voters. Darden swept past her to win with 59 percent.

Again in 1984, Darden defended himself against charges of liberalism, this time from conservative airline pilot William Bronson. In the face of President Reagan's 1984 landslide, Darden won re-election with 55 percent of the vote. In the last two elections, Darden has run up impressive margins, taking about two-thirds of the vote each time.

Georgia 7

Northwest — Rome; Marietta

Though the 7th runs 100 miles through seven counties — from the suburbs of Atlanta to those of Chattanooga, Tenn. — it is bottom-heavy. Cobb County, which borders Atlanta on the northwest, accounts for two-thirds of the district vote.

In recent statewide elections, Cobb has gone heavily Republican. President Reagan took 70 percent of the vote there in 1984; George Bush did even better in 1988, with 73 percent. However, Darden has persevered as a Democratic House candidate in his Cobb base.

Though well within the Atlanta orbit, Marietta (population 43,000) provides Cobb County with its own population center. Darden's home city provides as much of a Democratic coloration as there is in Cobb.

The rest of the county, a collection of middle-income Atlanta suburbs, is largely white-collar. But it also has a military presence, with Dobbins Air Force Base and a large Lockheed aircraft plant, both in Marietta. That Lockheed facility suffered an economic jolt when Congress dropped the C-5B military cargo plane built there. The loss of the contract reduced employment at Lockheed's Marietta plant by about 8,000 jobs. However, Atlanta's economic boom cushioned the blow.

To the north lie three rural counties — Bartow, Floyd and Chattooga — which are dotted with small textile-mill towns. There is more of a Democratic presence here; Democratic Rep. Wyche Fowler Jr. carried all three counties in his 1986 Senate election, though Bush took them with over 60 percent in 1988. Rome, a mill town in Floyd County, was once the district's largest city; but with a population of 30,000, it is now exceeded by Marietta.

The northwestern corner of the district holds three counties that lie within Chattanooga's orbit. GOP tendencies, similar to those in the mountain Republican areas across the Tennessee border, are evident. Bush received 72 percent of the vote in Catoosa County in 1988.

Population: 545,913. White 509,303 (93%), Black 32,641 (6%), Other 2,773 (1%). Spanish origin 4,362 (1%). 18 and over 385,552 (71%), 65 and over 42,933 (8%). Median age: 30.

Committees

Armed Services (21st of 31 Democrats)
Investigations; Research and Development

Interior and Insular Affairs (15th of 26 Democrats)
Energy and the Environment; Insular and International Affairs; National Parks and Public Lands

Elections

1988 General		
George "Buddy" Darden (D)	135,056	(65%)
Robert Lamutt (R)	73,425	(35%)
1986 General		
George "Buddy" Darden (D)	88,636	(66%)
Joe Morecraft (R)	44,891	(34%)

Previous Winning Percentages: 1984 (55%) 1983 * (59%)

* *Special runoff election.*

District Vote For President

	1988		1984		1980		1976	
D	64,396	(29%)	53,882	(27%)	78,101	(47%)	85,939	(61%)
R	155,367	(70%)	144,315	(73%)	81,442	(49%)	55,024	(39%)
I					4,177	(3%)		

Campaign Finance

	Receipts	Receipts from PACs	Expend-itures
1988			
Darden (D)	$448,399	$241,375 (54%)	$382,281
Lamutt (R)	$60,926	0	$61,002
1986			
Darden (D)	$532,328	$252,920 (48%)	$534,239
Morecraft (R)	$249,456	$20,985 (8%)	$246,506

Key Votes

1987	
Raise speed limit to 65 mph	Y
Approve Gephardt "fair trade" amendment	Y
Ban testing of larger nuclear weapons	N
Delay "re-flagging" of Kuwaiti tankers	Y
Approve tax-raising deficit-reduction bill	Y
1988	
Approve aid to Nicaraguan contras	Y
Enact civil rights restoration bill over Reagan veto	Y
Kill 60-day plant-closing notification measure	Y
Pass omnibus trade bill over Reagan veto	Y
Approve death penalty for drug-related murders	Y
Bar federal funds for abortions in cases of rape and incest	Y
Oppose seven-day waiting period for purchase of handguns	Y

Voting Studies

	Presidential Support		Party Unity		Conservative Coalition	
Year	S	O	S	O	S	O
1988	41	58	75	25	92	5
1987	43	57	68	30	91	9
1986	49	48	60	37	80	8
1985	51	46	67	31	87	13
1984	48	51	58	39	86	12
1983	40 †	60 †	48 †	48 †	100 †	0 †

† Not eligible for all recorded votes.

Interest Group Ratings

Year	ADA	ACU	AFL-CIO	CCUS
1988	45	50	64	64
1987	48	39	56	53
1986	10	79	31	82
1985	15	71	44	64
1984	30	54	38	44
1983	—	50	50	—

8 J. Roy Rowland (D)

Of Dublin — Elected 1982

Born: Feb. 3, 1926, Wrightsville, Ga.
Education: Attended Emory U., Oxford, 1943; South Georgia College, 1946-47; U. of Georgia, 1947-48; Medical College of Georgia, M.D. 1952.
Military Career: Army, 1944-46.
Occupation: Physician.
Family: Wife, Luella Price; three children.
Religion: Methodist.
Political Career: Ga. House, 1977-83.
Capitol Office: 423 Cannon Bldg. 20515; 225-6531.

In Washington: Rowland was initially diagnosed as a kindly Georgia physician who would be content with a low-key role in the House, but in the 100th Congress he emerged as an important Southern ally for the Democratic leadership. His work on the AIDS issue and on Nicaraguan contra funding helped win him a place in the hearts of the party hierarchy and a position on one of the most sought-after committees, Energy and Commerce.

Rowland served on leadership task forces dealing with controversial AIDS legislation and with contra aid, and his contribution proved valuable in terms both of substance and of symbolism. As a Southern conservative, Rowland is just the type of Democrat the leadership needs to enhance its credibility across the political spectrum on sensitive issues. And on AIDS in particular, Rowland — then the only physician in the House — brought specific knowledge and even more credibility.

In the 100th Congress, Rowland did not have a seat on the main health-issues panel in the House — Energy and Commerce — but his position on the Veterans' Affairs Committee provided one route to enter the AIDS debate. There, he introduced legislation calling for the creation of a national AIDS advisory commission, to succeed a much-maligned presidential panel.

Although some critics argued that a second commission was not needed, supporters said that, unlike the presidential panel, the new advisory commission would be stocked with experts on the issue. The bill was approved by Veterans' Affairs unanimously, cleared the House 355-68, and later became law.

Rowland was among those in the House who felt the Reagan administration had not done enough to address the deadly disease. When the secretary of health and human services stated in 1987 that it was premature for legislators to push a number of AIDS-related measures, including testing and anti-discrimination provisions, Rowland criticized "a lack of cohesive direction in the fight against AIDS." The administration's statements that much of the effort should be left to the states were "another indication that efforts to develop an effective national policy are in disarray," Rowland said. "The AIDS virus does not stop at state boundary lines. It is a national problem and we need a national strategy."

At the end of 1988, Congress moved closer to mapping that strategy, clearing legislation authorizing $650 million for education, anonymous testing, and home and community-based health care.

Rowland's 1986 vote to give military aid to the Nicaraguan contras came as no surprise to most Democrats, who had come to expect that stand from their Georgia colleagues. But in 1988, Rowland stood apart from all but one of his state's House delegation — John Lewis, of Atlanta — and voted against President Reagan's request for $36 million in military and non-military aid. Later, on a leadership task force, Rowland helped fashion a non-military aid package that became law, altering his image in the eyes of more liberal members.

Rowland's manner does not mark him as an ambitious politician. He has always approached politics on Capitol Hill with the same soft voice and courteous manner that won him the nickname of "Marcus Welby, M.D." in the Georgia Legislature.

But his success at in-House politics was evident in 1988. Before the 100th Congress was over, it was virtually certain that he had a lock on one of two spots on the Energy and Commerce Committee — spots that are not given lightly by the leadership and Chairman John D. Dingell. That was a far cry from two years before, when he tried for the panel and got scant backing.

Involvement in the contra issue was a major departure for Rowland, whose main legislative interests have always flowed out of his medical career.

Rowland takes a special interest in research to reduce infant-mortality rates. A member of the Select Committee on Children, Youth

Georgia 8

South Central — Macon; Waycross

The oddly shaped 8th twists nearly 300 miles from the black-majority counties just south of Athens to the Okefenokee Swamp on the Florida border. Covering 30 counties, it is one of the state's poorest areas; blacks are more than one-third of the population.

Most of this is rural territory, given over to tobacco and corn in the south, dairy farming and cotton farther north. The one large city is Macon, which together with surrounding Bibb County cast about one-third of the district's vote.

An old textile and railroad town, Macon has long been a trading and processing center for the agricultural lands of middle Georgia that surround it. Though Atlanta is little more than an hour up Interstate 75, the boom in the state capital region has not had a great effect on Macon, whose population remained level at 118,000 through the mid-1980s. Macon has undertaken an active redevelopment effort, although a strong preservationist spirit prevails as well; the city has renovated small houses dating from before the Civil War and turned them into low-cost housing.

Outside Macon, the 8th is largely rural, a land of antebellum homes, small country towns and open stretches of crop land. Washington, Wilkinson and Twiggs counties sit with Macon on Georgia's Fall Line between the red foothills of the Piedmont Plateau and the flat coastal plain; they are home to a large kaolin mining industry, which provides the white clay for use in white paint, china and stationery. Dublin and Milledgeville are textile towns.

Democratic traditions are sturdier in the 8th than in most rural districts in Georgia; Democratic presidential candidates remain competitive here. President Bush took 25 of the district's counties in 1988, but carried 60 percent of the vote or better in only five. Bush's margin over Democrat Michael S. Dukakis in Bibb County was a mere 95 votes. Dukakis carried a bloc of three heavily black counties in the northeast section of the 8th, taking Hancock County with 75 percent, by far his best showing in the state.

Population: 541,723. White 348,627 (64%), Black 191,182 (35%). Spanish origin 4,850 (1%). 18 and over 372,727 (69%), 65 and over 62,836 (12%). Median age: 29.

and Families, Rowland has served on the National Commission to Prevent Infant Mortality and on a Congressional Sunbelt Council task force on that subject.

Rowland had been in the House less than a month in 1983 when he introduced legislation to make use of the drug methaqualone (Quaalude) illegal. It had been available as a prescription medicine for insomnia, but Rowland argued that it was being abused. A version of the bill became law in 1984.

Also during his first term, Rowland took the floor to argue for health benefits for the unemployed. He joined with Arkansas Republican John Paul Hammerschmidt to propose legislation compensating veterans exposed to ionizing radiation during atomic-bomb tests; the measure was included in the Agent Orange bill passed by the House early in 1984.

When the House took up a bill allowing doctors to use heroin to relieve pain in terminally ill cancer patients, Rowland said there were medically feasible alternatives. "We do not need to legitimize a drug that we know has been causing a great deal of problems in this country," he said. Rowland's remarks, which had added weight because of his medical background, helped defeat the bill.

At Home: Rowland grew up with politics as the common coin of dinner table conversations — his father was a district attorney and superior court judge, his grandfather and uncle were members of the state Legislature.

But Rowland himself opted for medicine. It was not until 1976, the year he turned 50, that he decided he could leave his practice to run for office. He challenged his local Democratic state representative, putting together a coalition drawn largely from outside the area's political establishment, and won.

Six years later, he scored a similar victory for Congress. Democratic Rep. Billy Lee Evans had drawn embarrassing publicity when the Federal Election Commission fined his campaign for accepting illegal corporate contributions and illegal loans in 1980. The issue did its damage without much help from Rowland, who cited Evans' problems only obliquely; his TV ads urged viewers to "vote for an honest man."

Rowland's reluctance to hit hard served him well. Evans became more and more acerbic as the campaign wore on, and this only succeeded in alienating voters. Evans accused his opponent of performing abortions. Rowland acknowledged that he had and said he had done two such operations to save the mothers' lives.

While Rowland was taking the high road, another challenger, lawyer Edd Wheeler, was attacking Evans directly. He attracted less than 10 percent of the primary vote, but he softened Evans up for Rowland. Still, Wheeler's presence deprived Rowland of an immediate victory in the primary and forced a runoff.

Evans went after the black vote intensively during the runoff campaign. He did well in many black precincts, but it was not enough. Rowland increased his margin of victory the second time, carrying 20 of 30 counties, up from 13 in the primary. He has faced GOP opposition only once, in 1986; he won overwhelmingly.

Committees

Energy and Commerce (25th of 26 Democrats)
Commerce, Consumer Protection and Competitiveness; Health and the Environment

Select Children, Youth and Families (11th of 18 Democrats)

Veterans' Affairs (7th of 21 Democrats)
Hospitals and Health Care; Housing and Memorial Affairs

Elections

1988 General		
J. Roy Rowland (D)	102,696	(100%)
1988 Primary		
J. Roy Rowland (D)	101,845	(86%)
R. Bayne Stone (D)	16,161	(14%)
1986 General		
J. Roy Rowland (D)	82,254	(86%)
Eddie McDowell (R)	12,952	(14%)

Previous Winning Percentages: **1984** (100%) **1982** (100%)

District Vote For President

	1988	1984	1980	1976
D	73,518 (46%)	81,998 (48%)	107,718 (65%)	117,623 (73%)
R	85,540 (54%)	89,777 (52%)	55,844 (34%)	44,388 (27%)

Campaign Finance

	Receipts	Receipts from PACs	Expend-itures
1988			
Rowland (D)	$261,545	$129,637 (50%)	$195,895
1986			
Rowland (D)	$233,269	$90,125 (39%)	$150,139

Key Votes

1987	
Raise speed limit to 65 mph	N
Approve Gephardt "fair trade" amendment	N
Ban testing of larger nuclear weapons	Y
Delay "re-flagging" of Kuwaiti tankers	Y
Approve tax-raising deficit-reduction bill	Y
1988	
Approve aid to Nicaraguan contras	N
Enact civil rights restoration bill over Reagan veto	N
Kill 60-day plant-closing notification measure	Y
Pass omnibus trade bill over Reagan veto	Y
Approve death penalty for drug-related murders	Y
Bar federal funds for abortions in cases of rape and incest	N
Oppose seven-day waiting period for purchase of handguns	Y

Voting Studies

	Presidential Support		Party Unity		Conservative Coalition	
Year	**S**	**O**	**S**	**O**	**S**	**O**
1988	36	62	79	18	82	8
1987	43	57	71	25	93	7
1986	44	56	73	27	88	12
1985	50	50	75	25	96	4
1984	50	48	71	27	78	19
1983	44	55	60	38	88	12

Interest Group Ratings

Year	ADA	ACU	AFL-CIO	CCUS
1988	55	46	57	69
1987	40	30	44	67
1986	40	55	50	56
1985	30	67	41	45
1984	45	42	62	44
1983	40	65	31	55

9 Ed Jenkins (D)

Of Jasper — Elected 1976

Born: Jan. 4, 1933, Young Harris, Ga.
Education: Young Harris College, A.A. 1951; U. of Georgia, LL.B. 1959.
Military Career: Coast Guard, 1952-55.
Occupation: Lawyer.
Family: Wife, Jo Thomasson; two children.
Religion: Baptist.
Political Career: No previous office.
Capitol Office: 2427 Rayburn Bldg. 20515; 225-5211.

In Washington: For much of his career, Jenkins steadily gained influence in the House without appearing to be in pursuit of it. He is a quiet conservative who generally makes his mark behind the scenes, but in doing so, he has impressed colleagues with his shrewdness and built up good will with Democratic leaders. That reputation boosted his bid to become majority leader in 1989, though it was not enough to overcome a more experienced candidate, Richard A. Gephardt.

On the Ways and Means Committee, Jenkins has his share of differences with chairman Dan Rostenkowski, and coming from a conservative Southern district, he does part ways with the Democratic leadership. But Jenkins is personally liked and respected by those powers and by colleagues from his region, and that has helped him serve as a valuable bridge between the leadership and the South. Jenkins often dines with Rostenkowski at Morton's, a Georgetown restaurant where Democratic leadership loyalists tend to gather, and Rostenkowski usually seeks out Jenkins' opinion before making an important move. While Rostenkowski has some allies who speak *for* him, Jenkins is one who speaks *to* him.

In an earlier era, Jenkins' alliances might have been enough to bring him a formal leadership post, but in this era, climbing the ladder requires extensive caucuswide campaigning. Until 1989, Jenkins was always reluctant to launch such an effort, though he was frequently mentioned as a candidate. That earlier reluctance had some cost when the majority leader's post opened up expectedly in mid-1989 after Jim Wright left the speakership. Jenkins, though liked and respected, became an immediate long shot against Gephardt, whose past experience as caucus chairman and presidential candidate had made him a familiar figure to his fellow Democrats. Jenkins claimed the support of Rostenkowski and declared that he was reaching outside the South to win over a number of liberals, but the contest never seemed winnable. Jenkins lost 76-181.

Although Jenkins has not held a leadership position, the leadership has given him visible roles. In the 100th Congress, he was chosen for the select committee investigating the Iran-contra arms scandal. Since he had neither Foreign Affairs nor Intelligence Committee experience, his appointment was surprising. But Jenkins, who has voted in favor of contra aid, supplied ideological and regional balance. His demeanor also provided a balance: His matter-of-fact country lawyer manner helped calm the sometimes-heated hearings.

"Whether one supports [the contras] is not the issue," Jenkins said at one point. "The issue is whether or not we have adherence to the rule of law by the executive branch, not the merits of the issue itself." Jenkins was the first member to question Marine Lt. Col. Oliver L. North after he had undergone intense probing by committee lawyers. The Georgian helped adjust the tone of the debate by calmly and effectively pointing out the pitfalls of North's behavior.

Jenkins also managed to bring the matter home to his Georgia constituents. At several points he chastised the Reagan administration for soliciting aid for the contras from Taiwan during a time when Congress was working on legislation affecting that country — a bill to aid the U.S. textile industry, which has a significant presence in Georgia.

Jenkins has spent much energy trying to protect textile companies and workers from cheap imports. That has brought him attention in Washington and at home, and also some fame in countries whose products he seeks to restrict. When he came to the Philippines in 1986 as part of a Ways and Means delegation, the local press all but ignored other members in favor of Jenkins. "Ed Jenkins Arrives in Manila," one newspaper proclaimed on its front page.

Jenkins greatest visibility on the subject came in the 99th Congress, during a highly publicized crisis in the industry. His efforts brought him up against foreign exporters as well as key players in U.S. trade policy, including President Reagan, Rostenkowski, and Trade Subcommittee Chairman Sam Gibbons. But the bill was extremely popular in many

Georgia 9

Northeast — Gainesville

When it was drawn in the early 1980s, the 9th was oriented mainly toward the farms and factory towns of north Georgia. However, the district takes in a swath of Atlanta's booming outer suburbs, including those in the northern two-thirds of booming Gwinnett County.

The portion of Gwinnett County in the 9th provides far more votes than any of the other 21 counties. Its share of the district's House vote in 1988 was about 25 percent. When growing Cherokee and Forsyth counties are added in, suburban Atlanta supplies about 40 percent of the district vote.

This affluent suburban growth, combined with the native conservatism of the district's rural reaches, helps make the 9th a GOP presidential stronghold. George Bush took 71 percent of the district vote in 1988, but in the House contest, conservative Democrat Jenkins managed to carry every county but Gwinnett.

Locally, Gwinnett, the nation's sixth-fastest growing county between 1980 and 1986, tends to make the most news. But Forsyth County achieved national notoriety in early 1987, when black activists clashed with local whites during a civil rights march. The marchers said blacks had been intimidated in the early part of the century to leave the county, which currently has a black population of less than 1 percent.

Atlanta's spread has had a ripple effect throughout the district: All of its counties experienced population growth in the early 1980s, most by more than 10 percent. But by and large, the region beyond the Atlanta orbit remains rural, with its strong strain of Bible Belt Baptism unaltered.

Though some residents of the central part of the 9th commute to Atlanta, most are employed locally. Textiles and tourism hold key places in the economy, but poultry is king. Chickens are raised and processed in Hall County and throughout the surrounding area. Gainesville (population 16,300), Hall's county seat, calls itself the "broiler capital of the world." In the center of town is the Georgia Poultry Federation's monument to the industry: an obelisk with a chicken statue on top.

Development has begun to change the mountain region of northeast Georgia as urbanites and Floridians with their "Airstream" trailers flock to the unspoiled woods and streams. But the pace of change is slow. Moonshiners still carry on their trade, and the backwoods folkways are alive enough for Rabun County high school students to have chronicled them in the successful series of "Foxfire" books.

The counties in the northwestern corner of the 9th are more industrialized than the rest of the district. Dalton, the seat of Whitfield County and the district's largest city, is one of the country's top carpet-making centers. Despite its blue-collar nature, Whitfield generally favors Republicans in competitive state races: It gave Bush 73 percent in 1988.

Population: 551,782. White 520,435 (94%), Black 28,607 (5%). Spanish origin 3,501 (1%). 18 and over 384,588 (70%), 65 and over 55,248 (10%). Median age: 30.

quarters, and gathered nearly 300 cosponsors.

Rostenkowski and Gibbons had little choice but to allow the legislation to move, because Jenkins probably could have gathered the 218 signatures needed to pry it from committee, or could have tried to attach it to numerous other bills. But Jenkins' foes bargained with him to agree to a closed rule; that made it difficult for him to alter the bill in ways that might give it even broader support.

By the time the textile bill reached the floor in 1985, it was clear it would pass. Members from export-dependent districts said it would prompt a trade war, but many others were eager to send a strong signal to the president. They did that with a 262-159 vote, a sizable margin, but 19 votes shy of the two-thirds majority needed to override a veto. The next year, an election year, Jenkins won on a vote of 276-149, still short in an override attempt.

The issue came up again in the 100th Congress, but it was less explosive politically, partly because members had vented frustration by passing an omnibus trade bill. Jenkins, though always a player, was no longer the primary mover of the textile measure. After Reagan vetoed the bill, the override vote failed 272-152.

Jenkins does not always leave a lot of fingerprints on legislation, but there is rarely any doubt that his hand has helped guide important work. Textiles took priority over tax reform for him in the 99th Congress, but Jenkins did prove helpful to Rostenkowski's efforts to keep the tax bill moving, and he got some key provisions he wanted.

Much of the time, Jenkins concentrated on

narrower provisions that would benefit his district. He pushed to retain depletion allowances for marble, granite and farm-fertilizer materials. He also won tax breaks for small towns that rely on banks to support bond-financed municipal projects.

When Rostenkowski was embroiled in a fight with members from high-tax states over the deduction of state and local taxes, Jenkins' advice was a factor in getting him to retain the provision. He warned that the deduction was favored even in low-tax states such as Georgia.

Jenkins has been a longtime supporter of making a tax change that has been championed by George Bush. Unlike many fellow Democrats, he wants to see capital gains taxes, which were raised during the overhaul, lowered.

At Home: As a former aide to retiring Democratic Rep. Phil Landrum, and as a law partner of the veteran congressman's son, Jenkins had a relatively easy time winning this district when Landrum retired in 1976.

The early favorite in the contest was Lt. Gov. Zell Miller. But Miller decided not to run, and Jenkins' major hurdle was eliminated.

Benefiting from the Landrum connection, the Jasper lawyer finished first in a crowded Democratic primary field with 28 percent. Opponents complained that Jenkins should not have been practicing law and working for Landrum at the same time. But many voters knew Jenkins personally as Landrum's field representative and disregarded the criticism.

Jenkins took the runoff with 55 percent over an older opponent, J. Albert Minish, who had once run a strong primary against Landrum. Jenkins overwhelmed minor GOP opposition in the general election.

In 1978 Jenkins faced a primary challenge launched by a county official from suburban Atlanta, a section of the district far from Jenkins' political base. But drawing on his strength in the rural counties, Jenkins won renomination by a margin of nearly 2-to-1.

Jenkins has not faced a serious challenge since; the 63 percent he got in 1988 was his lowest-ever November tally. Republican Joe Hoffman took 53 percent of the vote in his base, Gwinnett County, whose booming, affluent Atlanta suburbs are becoming increasingly Republican. But Jenkins swept the other 21 counties, most by 2-to-1 or better.

In 1986, Jenkins was lobbied to run against GOP Sen. Mack Mattingly by Democrats who felt that only a conservative could unseat Mattingly. Jenkins declined, and 5th District Rep. Wyche Fowler Jr. of Atlanta overcame his liberal reputation and ousted Mattingly.

Committees

Budget (4th of 21 Democrats)
Task Forces: Community Development and Natural Resources (chairman); Economic Policy, Projections and Revenues

Ways and Means (8th of 23 Democrats)
Trade

Elections

1988 General		
Ed Jenkins (D)	121,800	(63%)
Joe Hoffman (R)	71,905	(37%)
1986 General		
Ed Jenkins (D)	84,303	(100%)

Previous Winning Percentages: **1984** (67%) **1982** (77%) **1980** (68%) **1978** (77%) **1976** (79%)

District Vote For President

	1988		1984		1980		1976	
D	57,200	(29%)	52,706	(31%)	92,811	(57%)	106,905	(73%)
R	140,209	(71%)	118,505	(69%)	64,994	(40%)	38,570	(27%)
I					2,934	(2%)		

Campaign Finance

	Receipts	Receipts from PACs	Expend-itures
1988			
Jenkins (D)	$453,174	$310,897 (69%)	$405,040
Hoffman (R)	$64,419	0	$64,400
1986			
Jenkins (D)	$330,678	$212,473 (64%)	$144,641

Key Votes

1987	
Raise speed limit to 65 mph	N
Approve Gephardt "fair trade" amendment	Y
Ban testing of larger nuclear weapons	Y
Delay "re-flagging" of Kuwaiti tankers	N
Approve tax-raising deficit-reduction bill	Y
1988	
Approve aid to Nicaraguan contras	Y
Enact civil rights restoration bill over Reagan veto	Y
Kill 60-day plant-closing notification measure	Y
Pass omnibus trade bill over Reagan veto	Y
Approve death penalty for drug-related murders	Y
Bar federal funds for abortions in cases of rape and incest	Y
Oppose seven-day waiting period for purchase of handguns	Y

Voting Studies

	Presidential Support		Party Unity		Conservative Coalition	
Year	**S**	**O**	**S**	**O**	**S**	**O**
1988	38	59	68	26	87	11
1987	40	53	66	24	88	5
1986	41	52	65	28	70	16
1985	48	50	69	26	76	22
1984	42	46	57	33	66	19
1983	49	38	47	39	79	12
1982	40	49	47	44	77	15
1981	58	34	42	53	91	4

Interest Group Ratings

Year	ADA	ACU	AFL-CIO	CCUS
1988	45	54	64	71
1987	44	20	56	62
1986	35	58	36	53
1985	25	55	47	50
1984	35	39	54	56
1983	30	89	23	63
1982	30	60	37	57
1981	10	63	40	60

10 Doug Barnard Jr. (D)

Of Augusta — Elected 1976

Born: March 20, 1922, Augusta, Ga.
Education: Mercer U., B.A. 1942, LL.B. 1948.
Military Career: Army, 1943-45.
Occupation: Banker.
Family: Wife, Naomi Elizabeth Holt; three children.
Religion: Baptist.
Political Career: No previous office.
Capitol Office: 2227 Rayburn Bldg. 20515; 225-4101.

In Washington: A banker by profession, Barnard has focused much of his legislative career on making policy to cover the arcane details of his industry — details that many of his colleagues prefer to ignore and most of his constituents fail to understand.

"These are not issues that are really close to the hearts and minds of the 10th District of Georgia," Barnard says, insisting that he is not upset by lack of recognition because "I see the essence of my efforts producing results."

In the House, many regard Barnard as the single most knowledgeable specialist in banking industry matters. In recent years, he has been the only banker on the Financial Institutions Subcommittee, which has worked on a variety of important bills involving the relationship between and solvency of savings and loan institutions and their competitors, the banks.

Much of the time, Barnard acts as the point man for his peers in the banking business. But he has cooperated with other Banking Committee members less favorable to banks to move legislation through the panel.

In 1986, Barnard led the opposition to a bill that would have placed a maximum limit on credit card interest rates, and he also opposed a bill requiring uniform disclosure of credit card interest rates and conditions. Barnard lost in the Banking Committee, but the rate cap and the disclosure requirement died at the end of the 99th Congress.

In 1987, Barnard cosponsored a disclosure-requirement bill with New York Democrat Charles E. Schumer. By changing his ground on that issue, Barnard was able to enlist Schumer's help in staving off pressures to impose an interest-rate cap — an idea being pushed hard by senior Banking Committee Democrat Frank Annunzio of Illinois.

Schumer and Barnard said disclosure was a more effective weapon against exorbitant fees than a cap. "I am strongly opposed to any concept of price controls," said Barnard, "since time and again they've been proven not to work." The cap lost in committee and again on the floor, and the Schumer-Barnard compromise was signed into law in 1988.

Barnard complements his seat on Banking with his chairmanship of the Government Operations Subcommittee on Commerce, Consumer and Monetary Affairs; though it has no legislative authority, Barnard uses the subcommittee as a forum for his views on bank deregulation. He favors curbing many of the prohibitions on bank activities that stem from the 1933 Glass-Steagall Act, the law that erected barriers between banking and securities firms.

In an 80-page treatise issued in 1987 by his Government Operations subcommittee, Barnard said, "The unnecessary and anti-competitive entry barriers in both commercial banking and securities markets should be entirely dismantled so that both banking and securities firms will face completely open competition." He views dismantling barriers as essential to preserving the stability of the banking system.

In 1984, when the Banking Committee was drawing up legislation to restrict banking activity, Barnard favored Senate legislation that would have allowed banks to enter the fields of insurance, real estate and securities. Later that year, the House panel approved a Barnard proposal that preserved the ability of banks to provide discount brokerage services — taking customers' orders to buy stock without giving advice.

In the 100th Congress, Congress worked on legislation to grant banks new authority to affiliate with securities firms. The Senate passed a bill, but the House Banking, Judiciary, and Energy and Commerce committees each approved differing versions of a second bill. Serious jurisdictional disagreements between Banking and the Energy and Commerce Committee scuttled the measures.

During Banking Committee markup of the bank-deregulation measure, Barnard won approval for an amendment to allow bank affiliates to underwrite, or sponsor, mutual funds. The amendment, adopted 35-14, was viewed as the high-water mark for the banks during consideration of the bill.

Barnard's Government Operations subcommittee also cast a negative light on savings

Georgia 10

North Central — Athens; Augusta

The 10th is a rambling swath of eastern Georgia anchored by Augusta on the east and metropolitan Atlanta on the west. In between is a stretch that has been touched by the ripple effect of Atlanta's booming growth, but remains mainly rural; the only population center is Athens, site of the University of Georgia.

Augusta (population 45,000), which sits on the Savannah River just across from South Carolina, has traditionally been the political heart of this district. It is Barnard's home base, and his popularity there provides him with the margins he needs to win re-election easily. In 1988, Barnard carried Augusta and surrounding Richmond County with 78 percent of the vote, and took suburban Columbia County with 64 percent.

But while the city itself has a majority-black population and a blue-collar work force that provides a reliable Democratic vote, the surrounding area has a much more conservative — and Republican — tilt. The area has a sizable military population, and a number of military retirees, associated with nearby Fort Gordon, home of the Army Signal Corps.

The conservative, pro-defense spending attitude is bolstered by the importance to the local economy of the Savannah River federal nuclear facility; located just downriver in Aiken, S.C., the plant processes tritium for use in nuclear weapons, though operations were suspended in late 1988 because of safety and environmental problems.

Military and civilian voters who work at these facilities give the Augusta metropolitan area a Republican cast in elections for high office. George Bush carried Richmond County with 57 percent, and suburban Columbia with an overwhelming 78 percent. Republican Sen. Mack Mattingly took Columbia easily in his unsuccessful 1986 re-election bid, but just edged Democrat Wyche Fowler Jr. in Richmond.

The district rambles 150 miles west, through cotton, soybean, tobacco and corn-growing country that leans Republican for president. When the Republican bastions in suburban Atlanta's Gwinnett County are added in, the 10th becomes a GOP presidential stronghold.

The 10th sticks a finger into southern Gwinnett, close-in to Atlanta and one of the country's fastest-growing areas. Its affluent neighborhoods are filled with newcomers drawn by Atlanta's economic boom and unbound by the region's traditional Democratic ties. Republicans prevail here: Bush won in a landslide, and even Barnard trailed his opponent by a 60-40 percent margin in Gwinnett, the only county he lost in 1988.

Athens, in Clarke County at the center of the district, provides the only base of liberal activists, mainly derived from the university and its 26,000 students. Environmentalists and peace activists are based in Athens; when a nuclear freeze was being debated at the local level in the early 1980s, the Athens City Council endorsed it — the only civic body in the district to do so. Barnard took 71 percent of the Clarke County vote in 1988, and Michael S. Dukakis won the county — by just four votes. Dukakis also carried Warren County, a mostly black rural county west of Augusta.

Population: 550,268. White 404,859 (74%), Black 137,321 (25%), Other 4,999 (1%). Spanish origin 7,680 (1%). 18 and over 388,067 (71%), 65 and over 45,469 (8%). Median age: 27.

and loan institutions in 1986. The panel issued a report that identified fraudulent real-estate appraisal practices at one-fourth of the federally insured savings and loans, and blamed bad appraisals for the fiscal problems faced by many of these institutions. "Go-go lenders, get-rich-quick developers and compliant appraisers are equally to blame for this alarming situation," Barnard said.

Despite his professional ties, Barnard has shown a willingness to oppose the banking industry on occasion. He has disappointed some banking lobbyists who expected him to side with them as a matter of course.

Barnard and the American Bankers Association (ABA) have not always agreed, for example, on Federal Reserve rules. The ABA wanted to maintain the existing voluntary-reserve requirements for national banks; Barnard favored mandatory requirements, the position that eventually won out in the committee.

Barnard's overall voting record places him to the right of the Democratic mainstream. In 1986 and 1987, he supported President Reagan's position on nearly 55 percent of key House votes, one of the highest support scores among House Democrats. In 1984 Barnard was one of a handful of Democrats who called publicly for liberal House Speaker Thomas P. O'Neill Jr. to step down.

At Home: Barnard's 1976 campaign for the House marked his debut in elective politics after an extensive career in state government. As executive secretary to Gov. Carl Sanders (1963-67), Barnard was one of the most influential men in Georgia. He was active in Sanders' comeback attempt in 1970, but Jimmy Carter won the nomination. Barnard then turned to business, serving as executive vice president of the Georgia Railroad Bank in Augusta.

Barnard thus had years' worth of contacts to call upon when Rep. Robert G. Stephens Jr.'s retirement opened the district in 1976. He was not helped in the district's rural counties by his ties to the Atlanta legal and business community, but he was well financed and had a strong base in Augusta.

That foundation gave Barnard the edge he needed to run ahead of a large primary field, taking 27 percent of the vote. In the runoff he was slotted against Mike Padgett, a former aide to Gov. Lester Maddox. Padgett, who had been known as "the man to see" for those seeking favors from Maddox, had rural and conservative support, but had also made enemies during his years of influence. Coming out of Atlanta and Augusta with a 7,000-vote margin, Barnard won the contest by 2,800 votes.

He was unopposed in the general election and in three of his first four re-election campaigns. The blossoming growth of Atlanta's affluent Gwinnett County suburbs has encouraged Republicans to take on Barnard in the last two elections, but neither was close. In 1988, GOP candidate Mark S. Myers, a 32-year-old real-estate agent, carried the Gwinnett County portion of the district by 9,500 votes, but still lost to Barnard by over 50,000 votes districtwide.

Committees

Banking, Finance and Urban Affairs (9th of 31 Democrats)
Consumer Affairs and Coinage; Domestic Monetary Policy; Financial Institutions Supervision, Regulation and Insurance; General Oversight and Investigations

Government Operations (8th of 24 Democrats)
Commerce, Consumer and Monetary Affairs (chairman)

Elections

1988 General

Doug Barnard Jr. (D)	118,156	(64%)
Mark Myers (R)	66,521	(36%)

1986 General

Doug Barnard Jr. (D)	79,548	(67%)
Jim Hill (R)	38,714	(33%)

Previous Winning Percentages: **1984** (100%) **1982** (100%) **1980** (80%) **1978** (100%) **1976** (100%)

District Vote For President

	1988	1984	1980	1976
D	66,060 (35%)	61,545 (35%)	80,511 (53%)	83,491 (64%)
R	122,156 (65%)	114,817 (65%)	66,097 (44%)	46,965 (36%)
I			3,590 (2%)	

Campaign Finance

	Receipts	Receipts from PACs	Expend-itures
1988			
Barnard (D)	$285,060	$148,371 (52%)	$193,123
Myers (R)	$7,375	$500 (7%)	$7,257
1986			
Barnard (D)	$346,980	$183,071 (53%)	$210,274
Hill (R)	$117,315	$100 (0.1%)	$117,315

Key Votes

1987	
Raise speed limit to 65 mph	Y
Approve Gephardt "fair trade" amendment	N
Ban testing of larger nuclear weapons	N
Delay "re-flagging" of Kuwaiti tankers	N
Approve tax-raising deficit-reduction bill	N
1988	
Approve aid to Nicaraguan contras	Y
Enact civil rights restoration bill over Reagan veto	N
Kill 60-day plant-closing notification measure	?
Pass omnibus trade bill over Reagan veto	Y
Approve death penalty for drug-related murders	Y
Bar federal funds for abortions in cases of rape and incest	Y
Oppose seven-day waiting period for purchase of handguns	#

Voting Studies

	Presidential Support		Party Unity		Conservative Coalition	
Year	S	O	S	O	S	O
1988	38	43	56	26	82	0
1987	53	35	50	39	91	2
1986	54	32	52	33	70	4
1985	54	41	53	37	87	5
1984	44	39	48	34	69	8
1983	59	30	41	53	78	12
1982	60	31	46	47	88	5
1981	67	18	26	61	84	1

Interest Group Ratings

Year	ADA	ACU	AFL-CIO	CCUS
1988	25	64	54	67
1987	20	61	33	79
1986	25	72	23	79
1985	15	71	44	50
1984	15	56	50	38
1983	10	82	18	79
1982	10	79	21	63
1981	0	93	20	94

Hawaii

U.S. CONGRESS

SENATE 2 D

HOUSE 1 D, 1 R

LEGISLATURE

Senate 22 D, 3 R

House 45 D, 6 R

ELECTIONS

1988 Presidential Vote	
Bush	45%
Dukakis	54%
1984 Presidential Vote	
Reagan	55%
Mondale	44%
1980 Presidential Vote	
Reagan	43%
Carter	45%
Anderson	11%
Turnout rate in 1984	44%
Turnout rate in 1986	42%
Turnout rate in 1988	43%

(as percentage of voting age population)

POPULATION AND GROWTH

1980 population	964,691
1988 population estimate (39th in the nation)	1,098,000
Percent change 1980-1988	+14%

DEMOGRAPHIC BREAKDOWN

White	33%
Black	2%
Asian and Pacific Islander	61%
(Spanish origin)	7%
Urban	87%
Rural	13%
Born in state	58%
Foreign-born	14%

MAJOR POPULATION CENTERS

Honolulu	372,300
Pearl City	42,575
Kailua	35,812
Hilo	35,269
Aiea	32,879

AREA AND LAND USE

Area 6,425 sq. miles (47th)

Farm	48%
Forest	43%
Federally owned	17%

Gov. John Waihee III (D)
Of Honolulu — Elected 1986

Born: May 19, 1946, Honokaa, Hawaii.
Education: Andrews U., B.A. 1968; Central Michigan U., M.A. 1973; U. of Hawaii, J.D. 1976.
Occupation: Lawyer.
Religion: Christian.
Political Career: Hawaii House, 1981-83; lieutenant governor, 1983-87.
Next Election: 1990.

WORK

Occupations	
White-collar	56%
Blue-collar	23%
Service workers	18%
Government Workers	
Federal	26,577
State	49,068
Local	12,736

MONEY

Median family income	$ 22,750	(5th)
Tax burden per capita	$ 1,293	(4th)

EDUCATION

Spending per pupil through grade 12	$ 3,807	(20th)
Persons with college degrees	20%	(5th)

CRIME

Violent crime rate 263 per 100,000 (38th)

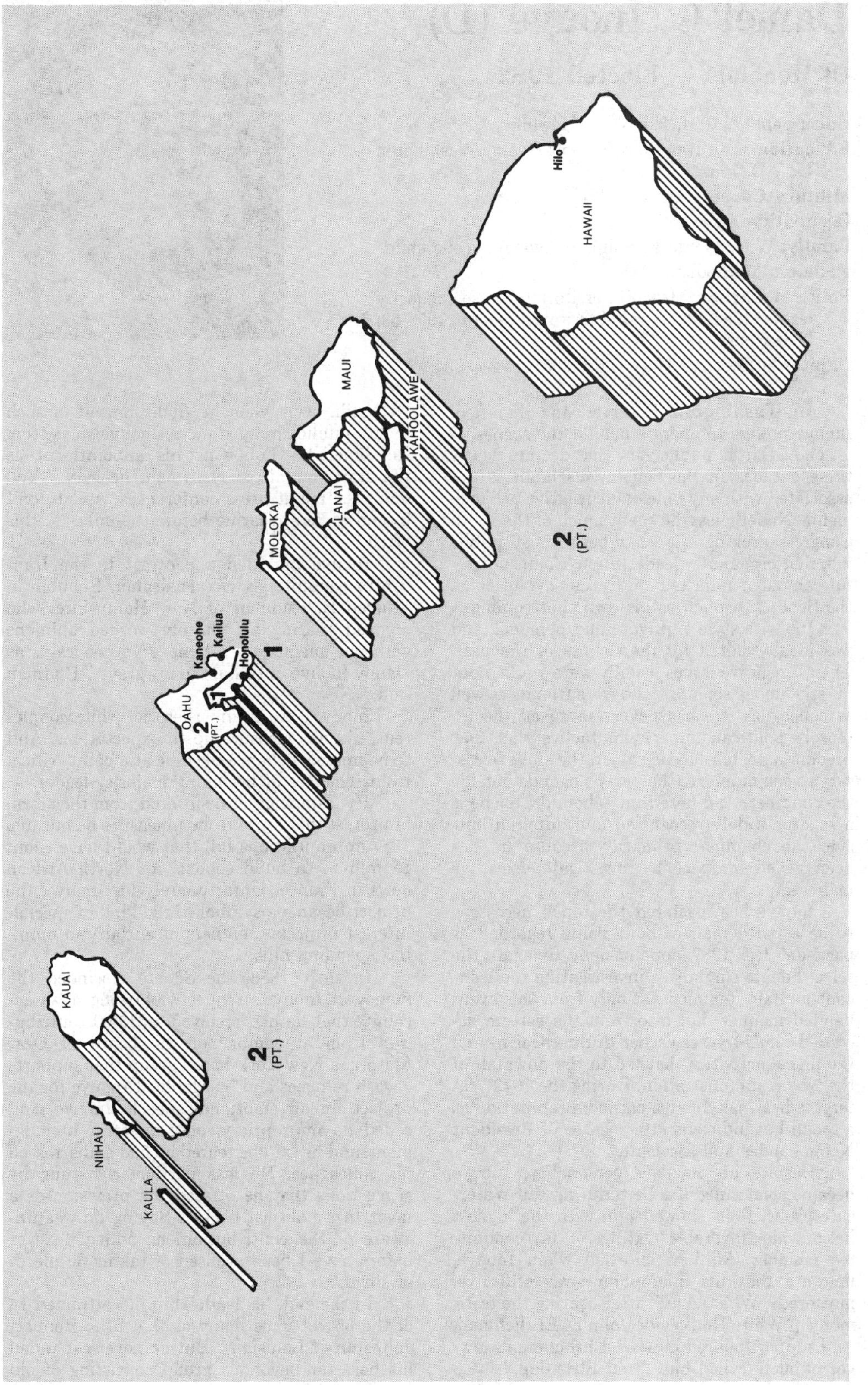
KAUAI
NIIHAU
KAULA
2
(PT.)
OAHU
2
(PT.)
1
Kaneohe
Kailua
Honolulu
1
MOLOKAI
LANAI
MAUI
KAHOOLAWE
2
(PT.)
HAWAII
Hilo

Daniel K. Inouye (D)

Of Honolulu — Elected 1962

Born: Sept. 7, 1924, Honolulu, Hawaii.
Education: U. of Hawaii, A.B. 1950; George Washington U., J.D. 1952.
Military Career: Army, 1943-47.
Occupation: Lawyer.
Family: Wife, Margaret Shinobu Awamura; one child.
Religion: Methodist.
Political Career: Hawaii Territorial House, majority leader, 1954-58; Hawaii Territorial Senate, 1958-59; U.S. House, 1959-63.
Capitol Office: 722 Hart Bldg. 20510; 224-3934.

In Washington: Reserved and dignified, Inouye prefers to operate behind the scenes — far enough from public view that despite nearly three decades in the Senate, his name is not associated with any unusual legislative achievements. Nonetheless, he spent much of the 100th Congress seeking the chamber's most public job, that of majority leader. Inouye's unsuccessful campaign reflected the recent evolution of the Senate as much as his own shortcomings.

Inouye's style is private and personal, and was ideally suited for the Senate of the past, when legislative issues usually were worked out quietly among senators who were friends as well as colleagues. He has never embraced the intensely political, impersonal tactics that now predominate, nor has he valued the skills necessary to communicate the party's agenda outside the chamber. And here irony abounds, for he is a senator widely recognized and admired outside the chamber, primarily because he has been called in twice to investigate executive malfeasance.

Inouye has mastered the touch necessary to be a party man without being regarded as partisan. His 1987 appointment to chair the select Senate committee investigating the Iran-contra affair stemmed not only from this even-handed manner, but also from the esteem accorded him 14 years earlier during hearings on the illegal activities that led to the downfall of the Nixon administration. During the 1973 Watergate hearings, Inouye earned a reputation as a tough but judicious interrogator of President Nixon's aides and associates.

Despite his low-key personality, Inouye became something of a hero during the Watergate probe. Polls showed him with the highest nationwide "favorable" ratings of any committee member. Millions chortled when Inouye, unaware that his microphone was still live, muttered, "What a liar!" after hearing the testimony of White House aide John D. Ehrlichman. And support poured in when Ehrlichman's lawyer publicly called him "that little Jap."

Still, even when he finds himself in such highly public circumstances, Inouye shies from the limelight. Following his appointment as the Iran committee chairman, he said, "You don't see me at press conferences. And I don't intend to be appearing before the mike ... this often."

Inouye provided a contrast to the Iran-contra committee's vice chairman, Republican Warren B. Rudman of New Hampshire, who enjoyed sharing his sharply worded opinions with the media. "I will never be as calm as Danny Inouye until I am in my grave," Rudman said.

Inouye's work and rhetoric, while competent, did not measure up to expectations. And so he missed a chance to shine at a point critical to his chances of becoming majority leader.

His campaign also suffered from the storm of protest that arose from a measure he put in a 1987 appropriations bill that would have spent $8 million to build schools for North African Jews in France. Unfortunately for Inouye, the project became a symbol of the kind of special-interest projects members often bury in omnibus spending bills.

In early 1988, the Senate rescinded the money at Inouye's request, following news accounts that he had received a $1,000 contribution from a member of the board of Ozar Matora, a New York-based group that supports Jewish refugees and had lobbied Inouye for the project. In an emotional speech, Inouye conceded no impropriety, only an error in judgment, and he said he feared he had embarrassed his colleagues. He was particularly stung by suggestions that he offered the provision as a favor to a political backer. Saying he was unaware of the contribution, he added: "Never before have I been accused of taking 30 pieces of silver."

In the end, his leadership bid attracted 14 of the 55 votes, as many as that of J. Bennett Johnston of Louisiana. But he never expanded his base far beyond a group consisting of old hands and colleagues on the Appropriations Committee.

The majority leader bid cost him his post as secretary of the the Senate Democratic Conference, the third-ranking position in the party hierarchy. But the new majority leader, George J. Mitchell of Maine, rewarded Inouye anyway by naming him chairman of the Democratic Steering Committee, the group that hands out committee assignments. His longtime aide, Henry K. Giugni, was also permitted to remain as Senate sergeant-at-arms.

Now in his fifth term, Inouye is the most senior member of his party not to chair a major committee. Still, he has not lacked for important duties outside of the select investigation committees. In 1976-77, for example, he was the first chairman of the Senate Intelligence Committee, where his behind-the-scenes style was welcome.

In the 101st Congress, he has assumed the chair of the Appropriations Subcommittee on Defense, the panel responsible for the largest chunk of the budget. It is a step up from the Foreign Operations Subcommittee he chaired in the 100th Congress, a position he also held before the party lost Senate control in 1981.

Inouye generally won good marks for his role on the Foreign Operations Subcommittee. He conducted a thorough line-by-line review of foreign aid programs before funding them. Subcommittee legislation generally reflected a consensus achieved by giving every party, including the minority and the administration, something to take home.

He was a consistent advocate for increased aid to Israel. During subcommittee hearings on the 1985 foreign aid appropriations bill, Inouye and then-subcommittee chairman Republican Bob Kasten of Wisconsin added $500 million in special military benefits to Israel that the Reagan administration had not requested. When the administration expressed its strong disapproval of the added money, it was deleted by the full committee. Unlike some advocates of Israel in Congress, though, Inouye also works on behalf of foreign aid for Arab countries.

A "Cold War" liberal, his strongly anticommunist views showed in his original backing for the administration's policy of aiding the government of El Salvador against leftist rebels. But in a dramatic 1983 floor speech, he warned, "America is stumbling blindly toward the abyss" of another conflict like the Vietnam War.

With the fading of the El Salvador issue in 1984 following the election of moderate President José Napoleón Duarte, Inouye turned his attention to the CIA's support for the Nicaraguan contras. Arguing as a member of the Intelligence Committee that the agency's involvement was "slowly but surely eroding whatever credibility is left" in the CIA, he helped persuade other Democrats to oppose further assistance to the contras.

On one foreign affairs issue, though, Inouye was well outside the Democratic mainstream. He spoke out in defense of Philippine President Ferdinand E. Marcos, even on the verge of his downfall and exile from the Philippines.

Declaring an affinity for the Philippines, which like Hawaii had long been a territory of the United States, Inouye said that congressional efforts to punish Marcos economically for corruption were hurting the Filipino people. He also said that the hostility toward the Marcos regime was excessive. "If you check the decibel level of criticism, you find that we have never been this critical of any other of our friends and allies," he said.

Earlier in his career, in a very different format, Inouye came to the defense of another beleaguered figure. When Democratic Sen. Harrison A. Williams Jr. was facing Senate expulsion for his role in the Abscam bribery scandal, Inouye came forward to act as his lawyer. Describing the tactics of Abscam investigators as entrapment of a senator by the executive branch, Inouye said, "The integrity of the Senate is challenged by this investigation and the Constitution compels us to reject its advance." But Williams eventually resigned before completion of the expulsion debate.

Although not a man of particular legislative vigor, Inouye has brought energy and passion to the Senate Indian Affairs Committee, where he became chairman in 1987. "This committee has been known as the scrap heap of the Senate," he said. "I'm going to do everything in my power to change that."

He made repeated trips west, particularly to the Northwest, to study Indian matters during the 100th Congress, twice gaining wide notice. He served as intermediary in a proposed $162 million settlement — one of the largest-ever involving an American Indian land claim — between the city of Tacoma and the Puyallup Indian tribe. He also intervened on behalf of Yakima Indians jailed in the so-called "Salmonscam" case, a *cause célèbre* among Northwest Indian tribes that involved violations of federal fishing laws.

Inouye also sits on the Commerce Committee. He chairs its Communications Subcommittee, although he usually lets others take the lead. In general, he has concentrated his Commerce work on helping his island home through shipping and tourism legislation. He consistently promotes shipping interests and has been supported, in return, by both maritime unions and shippers. One of his legislative goals has been to retain shipping laws that bar foreign-flag vessels from plying the U.S. coastal trade. He has sought to expand protections for U.S. shippers by prohibiting foreign vessels from carrying the mail.

Inouye has taken his defense of Hawaii's

interests to the Senate floor. During 1986 debate on a highway bill, he persuaded the Senate to exempt an Interstate road project in Hawaii from a 1984 court injunction issued on environmental grounds. But he failed in a 1985 effort to have proposed import limits in a textile trade bill restricted to finished goods, thus exempting textiles such as the colorful printed cloth that is used to make Hawaii's tropical-style garments.

Inouye's Commerce Committee work also prompted one of his rare references to his service in the legendary Nisei regiment in World War II and the wound that took his right arm. In June 1986, as the committee was on its way to approving a $250,000 cap on certain court awards for pain and suffering, Inouye said, "I guess I can stand it, so I guess we can make [the cap] zilch. But I cannot speak for the rest of those who have lost their limbs."

The room had fallen silent. Support for the cap eroded, and the bill was doomed.

At Home: World War II cost Inouye his right arm, but it made him a hero and built the foundation for a political career of uninterrupted success. Before the war, Inouye had wanted to become a surgeon. After he was wounded, while fighting in Europe with the all Japanese-American 442nd Regiment, he went into law and eventually into politics. He held several party posts, was majority leader in the territorial House of Representatives and then moved to the territorial Senate.

Inouye originally planned to run for the U.S. Senate when Hawaii was granted statehood in 1959. But he withdrew from that race and ran for the House instead, winning with the largest number of votes ever cast in Hawaii up to that time. He explained that he wanted to "give some elder statesman in our party a clear field" for the Senate.

This patience was rewarded. When Democratic Sen. Oren E. Long announced his decision in 1962 not to seek re-election, he endorsed Inouye to succeed him and promised his support. Inouye went on to defeat Republican Benjamin F. Dillingham, a member of one of Hawaii's pioneer families, by a landslide. Since then, he has never fallen below 74 percent.

Committees

Select Indian Affairs (Chairman)

Appropriations (2nd of 16 Democrats)
Defense (chairman); Commerce, Justice, State, the Judiciary and Related Agencies; Foreign Operations; Labor, Health and Human Services, Education and Related Agencies; Military Construction

Commerce, Science and Transportation (2nd of 11 Democrats)
Communications (chairman); Aviation; Merchant Marine; Surface Transportation; National Ocean Policy Study

Rules and Administration (4th of 9 Democrats)

Elections

1986 General

Daniel K. Inouye (D)	241,887	(74%)
Frank Hutchinson (R)	86,910	(26%)

Previous Winning Percentages: 1980 (78%) **1974** (83%) **1968** (83%) **1962** (69%) **1960 *** (74%) **1959 †** (68%)

* *House election.*
† *Special House election.*

Campaign Finance

	Receipts	Receipts from PACs	Expend-itures
1986			
Inouye (D)	$1,173,721	$540,455 (46%)	$1,039,418
Hutchinson (R)	$31,845	$3,450 (11%)	$31,843

Key Votes

1987	
Enact omnibus highway bill over Reagan veto	Y
Limit testing of space-based anti-ballistic missiles	Y
Oppose banning tests of larger nuclear weapons	N
Confirm Robert H. Bork as Supreme Court justice	N
1988	
Allow vote on campaign-finance overhaul	Y
Pass civil rights restoration bill over Reagan veto	Y
Enact omnibus trade bill over Reagan veto	Y
Approve death penalty for drug-related murders	N
Oppose "workfare" amendment to welfare overhaul bill	Y

Voting Studies

	Presidential Support		Party Unity		Conservative Coalition	
Year	S	O	S	O	S	O
1988	42	44	87	7	24	62
1987	33	63	91	5	41	53
1986	17	70	72	16	18	66
1985	20	72	80	7	20	58
1984	39	52	78	14	30	62
1983	33	42	70	9	9	66
1982	28	66	74	14	17	65
1981	47	44	74	13	20	69

Interest Group Ratings

Year	ADA	ACU	AFL-CIO	CCUS
1988	85	4	92	38
1987	95	0	90	29
1986	90	5	100	38
1985	95	5	95	24
1984	85	19	100	29
1983	75	9	93	27
1982	70	24	88	22
1981	70	0	89	44

Spark M. Matsunaga (D)

Of Honolulu — Elected 1976

Born: Oct. 8, 1916, Kukuiula, Kauai, Hawaii.
Education: U. of Hawaii, Ed.B. 1941; Harvard U., J.D. 1951.
Military Career: Army, 1941-45.
Occupation: Lawyer.
Family: Wife, Helene Hatsumi Tokunaga; five children.
Religion: Episcopalian.
Political Career: Hawaii Territorial House, 1954-59, majority leader, 1959; U.S. House, 1963-77.
Capitol Office: 109 Hart Bldg. 20510; 224-6361.

In Washington: While other senators have focused their energies on the floor or in committee hearing rooms, Matsunaga does much of his most important business elsewhere in the Capitol — in the Senate dining room.

Matsunaga spends a good portion of his time entertaining visitors from Hawaii, treating them to lunch and then taking them for a tour of the Senate chamber. Lunch with Matsunaga has become such a popular part of an islander's visit to the capital that the senator divides his time among tables — salad with one group, a main course with another, dessert with a third.

Campaign funds pay the hefty annual tab for these lunches, which Matsunaga calls "a pleasant and effective way" to stay in touch with constituents who have made the long trek to Washington. He asks: "Why should luncheon meetings be restricted to big contributors or corporate executives?"

The lunches are a symbol of the way Matsunaga has operated through two terms in the Senate and 14 years in the House. Although his legislative achievements have been modest, his sunny disposition and generous spirit have made him impossible to dislike, and he has always had the knack for winning a favor from a colleague.

The 100th Congress brought Matsunaga one of his biggest legislative victories — an official government apology and compensation for Japanese-Americans forced into federal internment camps during World War II. Matsunaga, a veteran of the all-Nisei regiment in World War II and a Bronze Star winner wounded twice in the invasion of Italy, fought in Congress to award $20,000 to each of the 60,000 internees still living. During the 1988 floor debate, Matsunaga verged on tears while relating the story of an elderly man killed by machine-gun fire while playing catch with his grandson in a camp. The $1.25 billion measure passed nine years after Matsunaga first introduced it.

For the most part, though, Matsunaga seems content to play the role of Hawaii's goodwill ambassador to the nation's capital. He is frequently photographed wearing a Hawaiian lei and has worn one to Finance Committee meetings. Bowls of macadamia nuts greet office visitors.

At times, those displays of island hospitality give Matsunaga a touching air of innocence. But they have not kept him from being close to the center of power. In the House, he gravitated to the Rules and Administration Committee and rose in the Democratic leadership ranks to be a deputy whip. In the Senate, he was the Democrats' chief deputy whip for 12 years, choosing not to fight when Alan J. Dixon of Illinois sought the elective post in 1988. In 1977, his first year in the Senate, Matsunaga won a place on the Finance Committee; he soon came to call its chairman, Democrat Russell B. Long of Louisiana, his patron.

The affection that senators hold for Matsunaga helped clear the way for enactment of a government institute devoted to the study of peace, a matter of deep conviction for him. In each Congress since his arrival in the House in 1963, Matsunaga had brought up his proposal for waging peace, with little success. But his persistent argument that "peacemaking is as much an art to be learned as war" took hold in 1984. Congress approved the U.S. Institute for Peace as an amendment to defense legislation. Reauthorized for five years in 1988, it distributes grants for the study of ways to resolve conflicts without violence.

His propensity for thinking big also has turned up in his advocacy for development of hydrogen as an alternative fuel and for an International Space Year in 1992. His idealism also was evident in his proposal for a poet laureate for the nation, approved in 1985.

Matsunaga's primary legislative concern, however, has been with measures to aid the Hawaiian economy. During the drafting of energy legislation on Finance, Matsunaga managed to outdo all others in the proposing of "Christmas tree" amendments for matters only tangential to energy. His was a tax credit for an energy-related aspect of the macadamia nut industry. It saw no action.

The Hawaiian economy's heavy dependence on trade with Pacific Rim nations has encouraged Matsunaga to oppose protectionist trade legislation — a stance he continued in the 100th Congress as chairman of the Finance Subcommittee on International Trade. Although the full committee handles markups, the post provides a bully pulpit. He created a stir in Canada, though, when he suggested, to the horror of the government there, that the U.S.-Canada Free Trade Agreement would help blend the cultures, the very argument used against the pact by its opponents.

When island manufacturers needed imported cloth in order to make their distinctive Hawaiian shirts and muumuus, he sought in 1985 to exempt them from textile import restrictions. The amendment was rejected. Equally as true to his character, when Hawaiian interests have been threatened by imports, such as Colombian pineapples, Matsunaga has not hesitated to advocate import measures.

At Home: Matsunaga's election in 1976 gave Hawaii two senators of Japanese ancestry for the first time since statehood. He succeeded Republican Hiram Fong, who retired, and he did it with surprising ease, turning back fellow House member Patsy T. Mink in the Democratic primary and former GOP Gov. William F. Quinn in the general election.

The primary was a popularity contest between Matsunaga and Mink, who differed little on issues. With the support of Democratic Gov. George R. Ariyoshi and the AFL-CIO, Matsunaga won by more than 20,000 votes.

In Quinn, Matsunaga encountered a personable and well-financed campaigner who said the state should have one senator from each party. Quinn ran fairly well in Honolulu and on the island of Hawaii, but Matsunaga still carried both by a bit under 40,000 votes.

Unopposed for renomination to a second term in 1982, Matsunaga buried GOP nominee Clarence J. Brown with 80 percent of the vote. His 1988 contest was similarly unexerting. He dispatched a primary foe, then crushed GOP gadfly Maria M. Hustace. His solid re-election tally came despite Republican rumormongering that he was ill and would resign within two years.

Committees

Finance (2nd of 11 Democrats)
Taxation and Debt Management (chairman); Energy and Agricultural Taxation; International Trade

Labor and Human Resources (4th of 9 Democrats)
Aging (chairman); Education, Arts and Humanities; Labor

Veterans' Affairs (2nd of 6 Democrats)

Joint Taxation

Elections

1988 General		
Spark M. Matsunaga (D)	247,941	(76%)
Maria M. Hustace (R)	66,987	(21%)
1988 Primary		
Spark M. Matsunaga (D)	180,853	(87%)
Bob Zimmerman (D)	27,360	(13%)

Previous Winning Percentages: **1982** (80%) **1976** (54%) **1974** * (59%) **1972** * (55%) **1970** * (73%) **1962-68** †

** House elections.*
† One of two Hawaii House members elected at large.

Campaign Finance

	Receipts	Receipts from PACs	Expend-itures
1988			
Matsunaga (D)	$834,722	$413,325 (50%)	$494,580
Hustace (R)	$58,281	$10,000 (17%)	$47,065

Key Votes

1987	
Enact omnibus highway bill over Reagan veto	Y
Limit testing of space-based anti-ballistic missiles	Y
Oppose banning tests of larger nuclear weapons	N
Confirm Robert H. Bork as Supreme Court justice	N
1988	
Allow vote on campaign-finance overhaul	Y
Pass civil rights restoration bill over Reagan veto	Y
Enact omnibus trade bill over Reagan veto	Y
Approve death penalty for drug-related murders	N
Oppose "workfare" amendment to welfare overhaul bill	Y

Voting Studies

	Presidential Support		Party Unity		Conservative Coalition	
Year	**S**	**O**	**S**	**O**	**S**	**O**
1988	40	49	83	2	14	62
1987	33	62	94	4	25	75
1986	25	71	77	19	28	66
1985	22	77	84	12	32	62
1984	32	60	87	7	17	79
1983	46	53	82	14	27	70
1982	28	66	80	12	14	82
1981	47	49	76	12	17	78

Interest Group Ratings

Year	ADA	ACU	AFL-CIO	CCUS
1988	90	0	92	36
1987	90	0	90	35
1986	85	13	73	39
1985	95	4	85	29
1984	90	5	78	35
1983	95	4	87	37
1982	85	0	88	21
1981	80	0	83	44

1 Patricia Saiki (R)

Of Honolulu — Elected 1986

Born: May 28, 1930, Hilo, Hawaii.
Education: U. of Hawaii, Manoa, B.S. 1952.
Occupation: Legislative aide; teacher.
Family: Husband, Stanley Saiki; five children.
Religion: Episcopalian.
Political Career: Hawaii House, 1969-75; Hawaii Senate, 1975-83; GOP nominee for lieutenant governor, 1982; Hawaii Republican Party chairman, 1983-85.
Capitol Office: 1609 Longworth Bldg. 20515; 225-2726.

In Washington: Saiki's 1986 election was a political landmark. She became the first Republican to serve Hawaii in the House since statehood was granted in 1959.

Perhaps with an eye on winning her first re-election from the nominally Democratic 1st, Saiki moved rather quietly and carefully through her freshman term, tending to constituent needs and compiling a moderate voting record. More often than not on partisan votes in 1988, she opposed her party's position.

Still, on some high-profile partisan issues, she has aligned with the GOP. She voted for President Reagan's request for military aid to the Nicaraguan contras, and she supported the death penalty for those convicted of drug-related murders. However, Saiki also voted to establish a seven-day waiting period for handgun purchases.

In her first term, Saiki cosponsored a bill calling on the government to offer compensation and an apology to the thousands of Japanese-Americans relocated to internment camps during World War II. Though her immediate family was not interned (the U.S. military commander on Hawaii saw no need to intern the thousands of Japanese-Americans there), Saiki had an uncle who was relocated. The bill became law in 1987.

Saiki used her position on Merchant Marine's Fisheries and Wildlife Subcommittee in 1988 to work for a $2.6 million authorization to add land to Hawaii's Kilauea Point National Wildlife Refuge.

At Home: Saiki's 1986 victory was in part a result of her own efforts to rebuild Hawaii's GOP during her state party chairmanship.

She took over a House seat held for nearly five terms by Democrat Cecil Heftel, who resigned in 1986 to run for governor. Saiki's immediate predecessor in the House was Democrat Neil Abercrombie, who won a special election to succeed Heftel. But Abercrombie was doomed to a short tenure when he lost a primary, held at the same time as the special election, for the right to seek a full two-year term in the 1st.

The Democratic schism caused by this result helped Saiki win the seat in November with surprising ease over Mufi Hannemann, the Democrat who defeated Abercrombie in the primary. The fact is, though, that as a respected former legislator and GOP activist of moderate leanings, she would have been competitive without the Democratic infighting.

The general election was expected to be close. It was unclear whether Saiki's Japanese heritage would earn her enough support in the Japanese-American community, the foundation of Democratic dominance in Hawaii. Hannemann's experience as a lobbyist and aide to George Bush enabled him to claim unusual access for a Democrat to business and the White House.

But Saiki's record proved more compelling, and Democrats' disunity debilitating. She won with 59 percent of the vote.

A splintered state GOP gave hope to Democrats in 1988 that they could unseat Saiki. Supporters of GOP presidential candidate Pat Robertson took over the Republican Party, ousting the moderate-to-liberal old guard.

A cordial, three-way Democratic primary produced a resounding win for Mary Bitterman, a former director of the Voice of America with strong ties to the state party. But Bitterman drained her treasury to win the mid-September primary, and could not dent Saiki's popularity. With no primary opposition, Saiki was able to concentrate her efforts entirely on November, and she won comfortably.

Saiki was a teacher before entering state politics in the 1960s as the secretary, then vice chairman, of the state Republican Party.

In 1969 she moved to the Legislature, where she helped set up Hawaii's community college network and the state Emergency Medical Services System. She sponsored the Equal Rights Amendment to the state constitution.

After losing a 1982 bid for lieutenant governor, Saiki served as party chairman from 1983 to 1985. Her recruitment efforts tripled membership, and her business contacts — she was a board member of two Hawaii corporations — helped the GOP raise $800,000.

Hawaii 1

Honolulu

The 1st District is Honolulu, a diverse and cosmopolitan community that serves as a symbol both of Hawaii's natural splendor and of the perils of urban commercialization run amok. Visitors still thrill to the proud profile of Diamond Head and the inviting surf down below. But their enthusiasm is usually tempered by the sight of congested Waikiki Beach, whose skyscrapers and shopping centers make it look like an overdeveloped Pacific cousin to Miami Beach.

Honolulu is an active port city, and it hosts light food industries such as pineapple canning. Its status as the seat of state government also provides jobs. But tourism — hotels, restaurants and travel companies — is the city's economic staple.

The city is an elaborate ethnic patchwork, with substantial populations of Japanese, Chinese, Filipinos, Caucasians and those claiming pure or partial native Hawaiian blood. Neighborhoods such as Waialae-Kahala and the affluent Black Point, near Diamond Head, are largely Caucasian. Northwest of the central part of the city is Kalihi, the city's most impoverished area. It is home to a significant native Hawaiian community, as well as to immigrants from the Philippines, Korea and Southeast Asia.

Though no Republican had ever won Honolulu's House seat before Saiki, there had been some signs that the city's traditional Democratic bias was wavering. In 1984, the city backed President Reagan, reelected a Republican prosecutor and chose as mayor Frank F. Fasi, who had served in that post from 1969-81 as a Democrat. In 1988, Fasi won re-election, but the 1st voted solidly for Michael S. Dukakis for president.

Much of the GOP vote in the district comes from corporate managers, retirees from the mainland, and a group of Republican-voting Mormons connected with the Hawaiian branch of Brigham Young University, which lies in the 2nd. There are also GOP sentiments among members of the military, who are politically significant despite a Hawaii law mandating that anyone who registers to vote must pay state taxes. The entirety of the Pearl Harbor naval base is included within the boundaries of the 1st.

Population: 482,321. White 143,597 (30%), Black 6,996 (2%), Asian and Pacific Islander 311,161 (65%). Spanish origin 27,882 (6%). 18 and over 362,478 (75%), 65 and over 42,643 (9%). Median age: 30.

Committees

Banking, Finance and Urban Affairs (15th of 20 Republicans)
Economic Stabilization; Financial Institutions Supervision, Regulation and Insurance; Housing and Community Development; International Development, Finance, Trade and Monetary Policy

Merchant Marine and Fisheries (13th of 17 Republicans)
Fisheries and Wildlife Conservation and the Environment; Oceanography

Select Aging (23rd of 27 Republicans)
Housing and Consumer Interests; Human Services

Elections

1988 General		
Patricia Saiki (R)	96,848	(55%)
Mary Bitterman (D)	76,394	(43%)
1986 General		
Patricia Saiki (R)	99,683	(59%)
Mufi Hannemann (D)	63,061	(38%)

District Vote For President

	1988		1984		1980		1976	
D	95,347	(54%)	74,912	(44%)	56,298	(43%)	65,216	(49%)
R	79,322	(45%)	93,894	(55%)	58,045	(44%)	67,080	(50%)
I					14,842	(11%)		

Campaign Finance

	Receipts	Receipts from PACs	Expend-itures
1988			
Saiki (R)	$708,391	$261,834 (37%)	$686,165
Bitterman (D)	$682,699	$124,715 (18%)	$638,351
1986			
Saiki (R)	$537,016	$154,550 (29%)	$528,307
Hannemann (D)	$517,083	$103,000 (20%)	$500,716

Key Votes

1987	
Raise speed limit to 65 mph	Y
Approve Gephardt "fair trade" amendment	N
Ban testing of larger nuclear weapons	N
Delay "re-flagging" of Kuwaiti tankers	N
Approve tax-raising deficit-reduction bill	N
1988	
Approve aid to Nicaraguan contras	Y
Enact civil rights restoration bill over Reagan veto	Y
Kill 60-day plant-closing notification measure	Y
Pass omnibus trade bill over Reagan veto	Y
Approve death penalty for drug-related murders	Y
Bar federal funds for abortions in cases of rape and incest	N
Oppose seven-day waiting period for purchase of handguns	N

Voting Studies

	Presidential Support		Party Unity		Conservative Coalition	
Year	**S**	**O**	**S**	**O**	**S**	**O**
1988	41	53	42	51	71	21
1987	55	43	64	33	93	7

Interest Group Ratings

Year	ADA	ACU	AFL-CIO	CCUS
1988	50	39	77	50
1987	28	57	25	73

2 Daniel K. Akaka (D)

Of Honolulu — Elected 1976

Born: Sept. 11, 1924, Honolulu, Hawaii.
Education: U. of Hawaii, B.Ed. 1952, M.Ed. 1966.
Military Career: Army, 1945-47.
Occupation: Elementary school teacher; public official.
Family: Wife, Mary Mildred Chong; five children.
Religion: Congregationalist.
Political Career: Sought Democratic nomination for lieutenant governor, 1974.
Capitol Office: 2301 Rayburn Bldg. 20515; 225-4906.

In Washington: Eight years on the powerful Appropriations Committee have not tempted Akaka to play a broader role in national policy or House politics. He remains a genial and, to many House colleagues, nearly unknown member, whose legislative orientation is entirely focused on his district.

Akaka shrugs off the charge that he is a "do-nothing" by noting his diligence on behalf of Hawaii. In the 100th Congress, his most notable legislative endeavor was a joint effort with Sen. Daniel K. Inouye to improve the health status of native Hawaiians. The bill increased federal support of health care for native Hawaiians by $19.6 million over three years. In the 99th Congress, Akaka backed a successful amendment to a housing bill that extended federal mortgage insurance to native Hawaiians purchasing property on Hawaiian homelands.

Akaka owes his presence on Appropriations to a near-perfect record of loyalty to the Democratic leadership, and he has maintained that record consistently, if not always voluntarily. In 1984, the leadership was one vote short on a crucial roll call as they sought to block President Reagan's request for production of the MX missile. With time running out, Illinois Democrat Marty Russo located Akaka, who had been recorded as a pro-MX vote, lifted him out of a phone booth and carried him into the chamber. Akaka then changed his vote, giving the anti-MX forces a key victory.

From the Appropriations Subcommittee on Agriculture, Akaka looks out for Hawaii commodities such as sugar. In the 100th Congress, when there was talk of changing the federal support program for sugar in a way Akaka opposed, he took to the House floor and said, "I won't let this happen. I wasn't elected to idly stand by and watch as Hawaii's sugar workers get pushed around. . . ." In the end, the basic structure of the sugar program remained intact.

In the 100th Congress, Akaka also sponsored a bill to make "technical and modest" changes to a congressional charter granted to a botanical gardens in his district. To reflect the fact that the facility had received a gift of land in Florida, its name was changed from the "Pacific Tropical Botanical Gardens" to the "National Tropical Botanical Gardens."

Akaka is a member of the Congressional Space Caucus, a group he joined in part because of the presence of a large planetary observatory in his district. A longtime supporter of NASA, he has warned against cutbacks in space science, saying, "We cannot sacrifice the research and development of new technologies on the altar of political expediency."

At Home: Akaka is the only native Hawaiian ever elected to Congress. A close ally of former Democratic Gov. George R. Ariyoshi, he rose through the Honolulu education bureaucracy before entering politics. After serving as a school principal and educational program specialist, he was picked in 1971 to head the state Office of Economic Opportunity.

In 1974 Ariyoshi chose him as his running mate for lieutenant governor in the Democratic primary. Ariyoshi won, but Akaka lost his primary to Nelson Doi. After Ariyoshi became governor, he appointed Akaka as his special assistant for human resources.

In 1976 the 2nd District opened up with the Senate candidacy of its incumbent, Democratic Rep. Patsy Mink. Akaka entered the primary with the backing of Ariyoshi and the state AFL-CIO. He faced formidable primary opposition in state Sen. Joe Kuroda, who had been planning his campaign for months and had the support of a variety of independent labor unions. But Akaka pulled through with a majority of 2,015 votes. In November he won with 80 percent, and he has been re-elected by similarly massive margins since then.

Rumors of Akaka's possible retirement circulated in 1984, when he was mentioned as a candidate for a lucrative open seat on the board of the Bishop Trust, one of Hawaii's largest private estates. But the vacancy ultimately was filled by state House Speaker Henry Peters.

Hawaii 2

Honolulu Suburbs; Outer Islands

The 2nd District encompasses virtually everything in Hawaii but the city of Honolulu. It includes all the islands outside of Oahu, where Honolulu is located, plus suburbs of the city itself. The fast-growing suburbs swelled the population of the 2nd in the 1970s, causing some turf to be transferred to the 1st in 1981 redistricting.

Although the Pearl Harbor naval base lies across district lines in the 1st, the 2nd retains many Oahu military installations, and these, along with wealthy residential neighborhoods in and around Kailua, have generated some respectable Republican showings in national elections, although Democrat Michael S. Dukakis carried the 2nd comfortably in 1988.

In other contests, the Democratic vote elsewhere overwhelms GOP candidates. Since its creation for the 1970 elections, the 2nd always has gone Democratic for the House, unlike the 1st, which switched to the GOP in 1986.

Oahu dominates the district politically. The island of Hawaii, at the chain's southeastern end, is known as "the big island," for it has two-thirds of the state's land area, but it contains only an eighth of Oahu's population. The island's main crop is sugar cane. Cattle, macadamia nuts, coffee beans and orchids also spur the economy.

The other islands of the chain contribute to the state's agricultural wealth but play only a minor part in its politics. The three populated islands of Maui County make up the state's richest pineapple-growing land. Sugar cane and beef cattle are important there and in Kauai County, the lightly populated group of islands at the northernmost end of the archipelago.

Population: 482,370. White 175,173 (36%), Black 10,368 (2%), Asian and Pacific Islander 272,091 (56%). Spanish origin 43,381 (9%). 18 and over 326,630 (68%), 65 and over 33,507 (7%). Median age: 27.

Committees

Appropriations (23rd of 35 Democrats)
Rural Development, Agriculture and Related Agencies; Treasury, Postal Service and General Government

Select Narcotics Abuse and Control (6th of 18 Democrats)

Elections

1988 General		
Daniel K. Akaka (D)	144,802	(89%)
Lloyd Jeffrey Mallan (LIB)	18,006	(11%)
1986 General		
Daniel K. Akaka (D)	123,830	(76%)
Maria M. Hustace (R)	35,371	(22%)

Previous Winning Percentages: **1984** (82%) **1982** (89%) **1980** (90%) **1978** (86%) **1976** (80%)

District Vote For President

	1988	1984	1980	1976
D	97,017 (54%)	72,242 (44%)	79,581 (46%)	81,950 (52%)
R	79,302 (44%)	91,156 (55%)	72,067 (42%)	72,693 (46%)
I			17,179 (10%)	

Campaign Finance

	Receipts	Receipts from PACs	Expend-itures
1988			
Akaka (D)	$255,470	$81,372 (32%)	$153,163
1986			
Akaka (D)	$132,196	$48,735 (37%)	$110,490
Hustace (R)	$37,002	0	$32,339

Key Votes

1987	
Raise speed limit to 65 mph	N
Approve Gephardt "fair trade" amendment	Y
Ban testing of larger nuclear weapons	Y
Delay "re-flagging" of Kuwaiti tankers	?
Approve tax-raising deficit-reduction bill	Y
1988	
Approve aid to Nicaraguan contras	N
Enact civil rights restoration bill over Reagan veto	Y
Kill 60-day plant-closing notification measure	N
Pass omnibus trade bill over Reagan veto	Y
Approve death penalty for drug-related murders	N
Bar federal funds for abortions in cases of rape and incest	N
Oppose seven-day waiting period for purchase of handguns	N

Voting Studies

	Presidential Support		Party Unity		Conservative Coalition	
Year	S	O	S	O	S	O
1988	22	74	88	2	13	82
1987	23	67	87	4	37	58
1986	18	79	89	6	28	68
1985	26	68	86	7	35	58
1984	31	63	85	8	22	75
1983	28	66	86	9	42	56
1982	40	53	81	8	32	58
1981	46	54	81	17	52	48

Interest Group Ratings

Year	ADA	ACU	AFL-CIO	CCUS
1988	85	0	93	23
1987	64	0	88	0
1986	90	9	86	18
1985	65	14	88	22
1984	85	10	92	38
1983	85	4	100	35
1982	65	15	90	21
1981	65	7	100	16

Idaho

U.S. CONGRESS

SENATE 2 R
HOUSE 1 D, 1 R

LEGISLATURE

Senate 19 D, 23 R
House 20 D, 64 R

ELECTIONS

1988 Presidential Vote	
Bush	62%
Dukakis	36%
1984 Presidential Vote	
Reagan	72%
Mondale	26%
1980 Presidential Vote	
Reagan	66%
Carter	25%
Anderson	6%
Turnout rate in 1984	60%
Turnout rate in 1986	53%
Turnout rate in 1988	58%

(as percentage of voting age population)

POPULATION AND GROWTH

1980 population	943,935
1988 population estimate (42nd in the nation)	1,003,000
Percent change 1980-1988	+6%

DEMOGRAPHIC BREAKDOWN

White	96%
Black	0.3%
Other	2%
(Spanish origin)	4%
Urban	54%
Rural	46%
Born in state	49%
Foreign-born	3%

MAJOR CITIES

Boise	108,390
Pocatello	44,420
Idaho Falls	42,830
Nampa	28,250
Twin Falls	27,750

AREA AND LAND USE

Area	82,412 sq. miles (11th)
Farm	26%
Forest	41%
Federally owned	64%

Gov. Cecil D. Andrus (D)
Of Boise — Elected 1986
(also served 1971-77)

Born: Aug. 25, 1931, Hood River, Ore.
Education: Oregon State U., 1948-49.
Military Career: Navy, 1951-55.
Occupation: Lumberjack; sawmill manager; management consultant.
Religion: Lutheran.
Political Career: Idaho Senate, 1961-67, 1969-71; U.S. secretary of the interior, 1977-81; Democratic nominee for governor, 1966.
Next Election: 1990.

WORK

Occupations	
White-collar	50%
Blue-collar	29%
Service workers	13%
Government Workers	
Federal	9,684
State	19,524
Local	42,084

MONEY

Median family income	$ 17,492	(36th)
Tax burden per capita	$ 730	(40th)

EDUCATION

Spending per pupil through grade 12	$ 2,484	(48th)
Persons with college degrees	16%	(25th)

CRIME

Violent crime rate	214 per 100,000 (43rd)

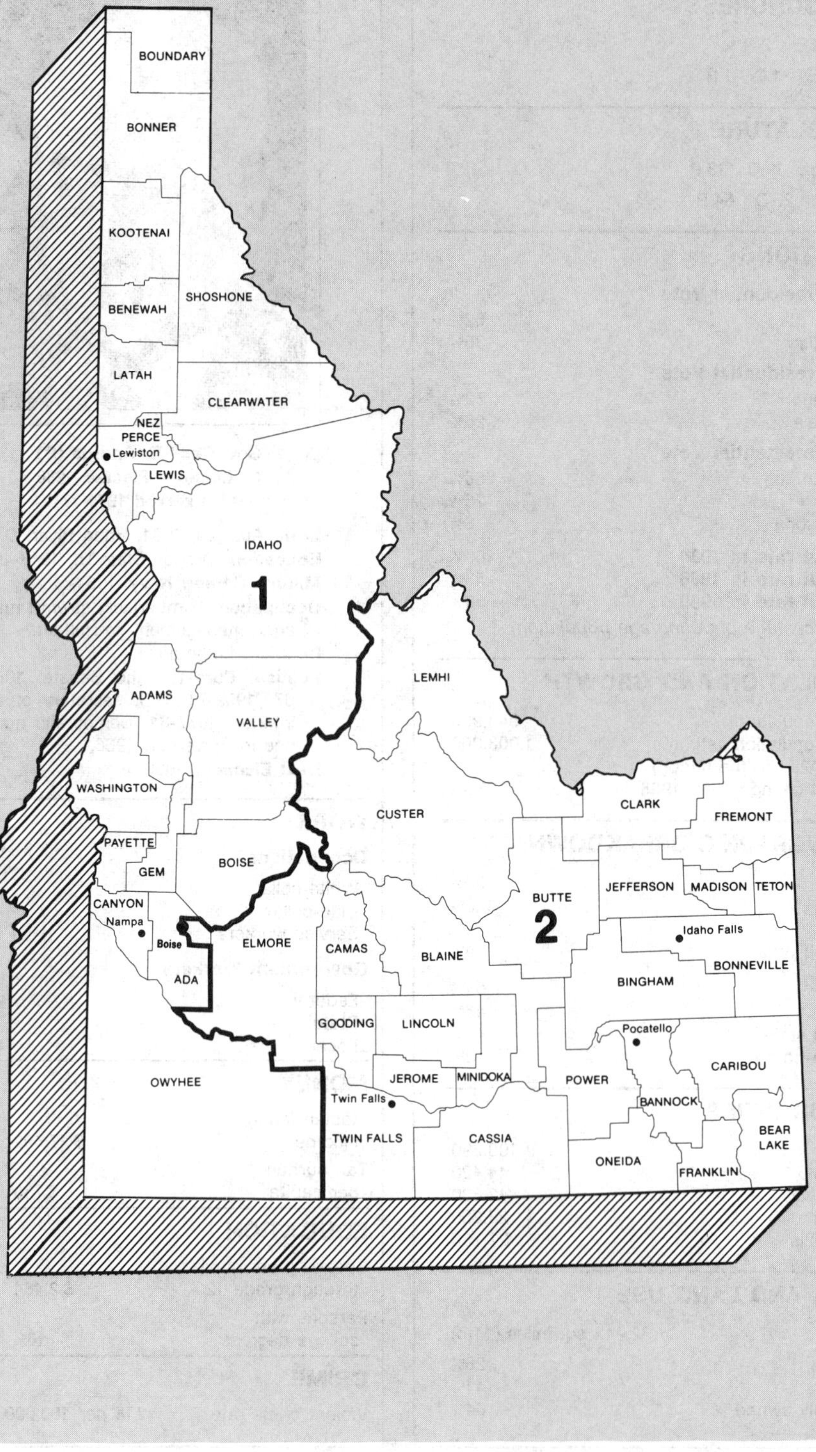
BOUNDARY
BONNER
KOOTENAI
SHOSHONE
BENEWAH
LATAH
CLEARWATER
NEZ PERCE
Lewiston
LEWIS
IDAHO
1
ADAMS
VALLEY
LEMHI
WASHINGTON
CUSTER
CLARK
FREMONT
PAYETTE
BOISE
GEM
JEFFERSON
MADISON
TETON
CANYON
Nampa
Boise
BUTTE
2
Idaho Falls
ELMORE
CAMAS
BLAINE
BONNEVILLE
ADA
BINGHAM
GOODING
LINCOLN
Pocatello
OWYHEE
JEROME
MINIDOKA
POWER
CARIBOU
Twin Falls
BANNOCK
TWIN FALLS
CASSIA
ONEIDA
BEAR LAKE
FRANKLIN

James A. McClure (R)

Of McCall — Elected 1972

Born: Dec. 27, 1924, Payette, Idaho.
Education: U. of Idaho, J.D. 1950.
Military Career: Navy, 1942-45.
Occupation: Lawyer.
Family: Wife, Louise Miller; three children.
Religion: Methodist.
Political Career: Payette County prosecuting attorney, 1951-57; Payette city attorney, 1953-59, 1962-66; Idaho Senate, 1961-67; U.S. House, 1967-73.
Capitol Office: 309 Hart Bldg. 20510; 224-2752.

In Washington: Like most other Senate Republicans, McClure lost a chairmanship with the coming of the Democratic majority in 1987, but the adjustment was less painful for him than for some of his colleagues.

In surrendering the chair of the Energy and Natural Resources Committee, he could take consolation in handing it to J. Bennett Johnston of Louisiana, a Democrat with whom he has long worked closely on many issues.

Besides, through three eventful terms in the Senate, it had been McClure's persistence and his ability to work with conservative Democrats, not his titular power, that made him stand out. And these were the factors behind his achieving two of the signal conservative victories of the mid-1980s.

After years of complaining about Soviet arms control violations, McClure helped persuade President Reagan in 1986 to abandon U.S. observance of the unratified SALT II treaty. And with House Democrat Harold L. Volkmer of Missouri, McClure was the chief sponsor of legislation, enacted in 1986, that substantially weakened federal gun-control laws.

In the 100th Congress, McClure made his presence felt on the intermediate-range nuclear-force (INF) treaty, pressuring the White House for higher standards of verification. At one point, he called the drive to finish the treaty before a U.S.-Soviet summit "stupid" and "terribly wrong." But he was less critical of the White House as a member of the congressional Iran-contra investigating committees. He signed the minority report, which gave Reagan and his administration "a clean bill of legal health" in the affair.

McClure was again in the forefront on gun issues in 1988. When Congress began considering a stringent ban on plastic guns, he cosponsored an alternative with Thomas S. Foley, the House majority leader. Without banning any existing firearms, the McClure-Foley bill aimed to make sure guns with plastic or ceramic frames were still detectable with standard security equipment. Congress eventually cleared a compromise banning guns with less than 3.7 ounces of metal for 10 years but outlawing no weapons currently available.

By contrast, McClure essentially was stymied during his years as Energy chairman. He showed real technical skill as a legislator, and had an important advantage in his simultaneous chairmanship of the Appropriations Subcommittee on Interior, which can spend some of the money the Energy panel authorizes. Nevertheless, he encountered a number of defeats in his attempts to impose a free-market approach in energy policy and reduce federal control over the vast, undeveloped stretches of Idaho and the West.

His difficulties were illustrated by his work on a score of "wilderness" bills, which set aside tracts of federal land to be preserved from various types of development. Coming from a state where the federal government owns two-thirds of the land, he had always been critical of federal land policy and deeply skeptical of the wilderness set-aside concept. The single largest wilderness preserve in the lower 48 states, Idaho's 2.3 million-acre River of No Return Wilderness, was created in 1980 over his loud objections.

Wilderness bills languished during the early years of McClure's chairmanship. The lack of action was due in part to a dispute McClure had with conservationists over the future of pristine areas not designated in legislation as wilderness. Environmentalists wanted to protect such areas from immediate development. McClure, backed by the timber and energy industries, wanted development to go forward.

McClure eventually worked out a compromise with House Democrats that cleared the way for setting aside 8.3 million acres of wilderness. But he did not resolve a deadlock over wilderness areas in Idaho. His original wilderness proposal for the state had angered conservationists, who wanted a much larger area to be protected. The two sides could not reach an agreement, and Idaho wilderness legislation did not pass in the 98th or 99th Congresses.

In the 100th Congress, McClure struck an agreement with new Democratic Gov. Cecil D. Andrus, himself a former secretary of the interior, designating about 1.4 million new acres of wilderness. But by the time the compromise plan was ready at the end of 1987, a queue of other bills had formed in the Senate subcommittee with jurisdiction. The Idaho bill died with adjournment.

Essentially the same plan was reintroduced at the beginning of the 101st Congress, with McClure and Andrus vowing to give the measure more of their time. But environmentalists were skeptical because they felt the bill protected too little, while developers saw its terms as too restrictive.

On energy issues, McClure struggled for years with the twin time bombs of nuclear policy: waste disposal and liability insurance. But it was not until after the Democrats had resumed control of the Senate in 1987 that Johnston and McClure were able to pass legislation making Nevada the prime candidate for a permanent nuclear-waste site. And it took until 1988 to clear a renewal of the 1957 Price-Anderson Act (under which liability in a nuclear accident is limited and insurance is provided) raising the coverage ceiling from $700 million to more than $7 billion.

But McClure's biggest frustration in energy came when he was pushing Reagan's 1983 plan to decontrol the price of natural gas. Lacking a clear majority on the issue within the Energy Committee, he was forced to hold month after month of markup sessions to find a compromise. A bill finally was worked out, but with such weak support that the committee did not even recommend that it be passed. It lost decisively on the floor.

None of McClure's setbacks as Energy chairman was as dramatic as his crushing defeat in the majority leadership race at the start of the 99th Congress. Virtually abandoned by his ideological allies, he was the first of five candidates to be eliminated in the contest.

The poor showing was especially puzzling in light of the substantial advantages that had seemed to make McClure a leading contender for the post. He had been a major voice in setting party policy for four years as chairman of the Senate GOP Conference — the third-ranking post in the party leadership. During that time, he had turned the conference into a sophisticated public-relations machine for his Republican colleagues.

Moreover, McClure worked extremely hard to win the top job. He made clear his desire for it well before the other contenders, and agreed to a number of legislative compromises in 1984 to placate other GOP senators.

Ideology was one reason for McClure's defeat. While his anti-government approach brought him strong support among Senate conservatives, it limited him in building coalitions with the large bloc of moderate Republicans. Also, Western conservatives worried that if McClure became leader, the Energy Committee would be chaired by an Eastern liberal, Lowell P. Weicker Jr. of Connecticut.

Of course, votes in leadership races depend on a complex of personal considerations, including the effect one senator's elevation may have on the standing of others. McClure is generally as genial and unpretentious a man as there is in the chamber, but some members may have wondered how their own priorities and projects would fare in his hands. After the passage of a contentious nuclear-power bill in 1982, some had complained to reporters, although not for attribution, that McClure had taken shortcuts in managing the bill, misrepresenting or altering the actual portent of language that was agreed to on the floor.

At Home: McClure entered the final two years of his third term without indicating whether he would seek a fourth. If he does, he can be expected to overshadow any potential opponent except Andrus, whose term also expires in 1990. Other potential Democratic challengers would be Rep. Richard Stallings and former Gov. John V. Evans, who lost a bid for the Senate in 1986.

But McClure could choose to retire. He would be 66 at the end of 1990; and, with his longtime friend George Bush in the White House, he might well receive an attractive offer to join the administration. Should he take it, McClure could look back on three decades of unbroken electoral success.

He was elected to the Idaho Senate in 1960 and rose to assistant majority leader by 1966. He had been a county prosecutor, and had practiced law with his father in the Snake River town of Payette, specializing in land and irrigation matters.

Redistricting provided his opportunity to come to Congress. Idaho's traditionally Democratic northern district was moved south in 1966 to take in Boise and its surrounding Republican territory. That created an insurmountable problem for two-term House Democrat Compton White Jr., who had nearly lost in 1964 in the old district.

McClure won the Republican House nomination comfortably against Robert B. Purcell, manager of the Lewiston Chamber of Commerce, and then took on White, whom he linked to the Johnson administration's unpopular farm policies.

White focused on McClure's conservative voting record in the Legislature. He condemned McClure for once supporting the so-called Liberty Amendment, which would have abolished the federal graduated income tax. The voters gave McClure a 4,964-vote victory.

After two easy re-elections, McClure found

himself the front-runner in 1972 for the Senate seat of retiring Republican Len B. Jordan. But despite the backing of the state Republican hierarchy, he had a tough four-way primary. His opponents attacked him for congressional absenteeism.

Heading the list of GOP competitors was George Hansen, a former U.S. representative who had given up his seat to run unsuccessfully against Democratic Sen. Frank Church in 1968. Hansen, who later was to return to the House, had a large campaign treasury and a record just as conservative as McClure's.

The other two Republicans had strong campaigns as well. But McClure won the nomination with a little more than a third of the vote, disappointing the second-place Hansen. After the primary, Hansen disappointed McClure. He charged that officials of four Idaho corporations had tried to force him out of the race in 1971 to smooth the way for McClure.

The Democratic nominee, Idaho State University President William E. "Bud" Davis, sought to capitalize on Hansen's allegation. He appeared in newspaper ads next to a map of Idaho with "Not For Sale" stamped on it. In addition, Davis criticized McClure for favoring mining in the Sawtooth recreational area.

Davis, an amiable former football coach, had the advantage of a non-political past. But his inexperience also turned out to be a liability. He endorsed the lettuce boycott then being mounted in behalf of farm workers in California, a seemingly harmless move but one allowing Republicans to claim he would be equally supportive of a potato boycott that might cripple Idaho's economy. His campaign never really recovered from the lettuce-potato controversy. McClure ran nearly 100,000 votes behind President Nixon statewide, but he still defeated Davis by 20,000 votes.

That was McClure's last tough race. The majority of Idahoans like his conservative record, and his adversaries find it difficult to make headway against his agreeable, non-threatening manner.

In 1978 the Democratic Senate nominee was journalist Dwight Jensen, a political novice who had been a Boise television commentator. Although a competent candidate, Jensen attracted little financial support and little attention outside his home base. He blasted McClure for being too close to big corporations and insensitive to the needs of the elderly. But hardly anyone was listening, and McClure won every county in the state.

Six years later, even fewer people listened to Democrat Pete Busch, a Marine Corps veteran and real-estate agent whose campaign against McClure was regarded from the start as a hopeless cause. McClure's winning percentage was the highest in an Idaho Senate election since Republican William E. Borah won his fifth term in 1930 with 72 percent of the vote.

Committees

Energy and Natural Resources (Ranking)

Appropriations (3rd of 13 Republicans)
Interior and Related Agencies (ranking); Agriculture, Rural Development and Related Agencies; Defense; Energy and Water Development; Labor, Health and Human Services, Education and Related Agencies

Rules and Administration (3rd of 7 Republicans)

Elections

1984 General

James A. McClure (R)	293,193	(72%)
Peter M. Busch (D)	105,591	(26%)

Previous Winning Percentages: **1978** (68%) **1972** (52%) **1970 *** (58%) **1968 *** (59%) **1966 *** (52%)

* *House elections.*

Campaign Finance

	Receipts	Receipts from PACs	Expend-itures
1984			
McClure (R)	$1,268,707	$550,496 (43%)	$958,225
Busch (D)	$30,777	$6,500 (21%)	$31,001

Key Votes

1987

Enact omnibus highway bill over Reagan veto	N
Limit testing of space-based anti-ballistic missiles	N
Oppose banning tests of larger nuclear weapons	Y
Confirm Robert H. Bork as Supreme Court justice	Y

1988

Allow vote on campaign-finance overhaul	N
Pass civil rights restoration bill over Reagan veto	N
Enact omnibus trade bill over Reagan veto	N
Approve death penalty for drug-related murders	Y
Oppose "workfare" amendment to welfare overhaul bill	?

Voting Studies

	Presidential Support		Party Unity		Conservative Coalition	
Year	**S**	**O**	**S**	**O**	**S**	**O**
1988	67	23	88	7	92	5
1987	68	22	85	8	100	0
1986	92	6	87	9	93	4
1985	78	20	91	7	93	7
1984	83	10	80	6	83	2
1983	69	31	80	9	82	0
1982	68	24	85	9	88	3
1981	79	15	85	7	89	5

Interest Group Ratings

Year	ADA	ACU	AFL-CIO	CCUS
1988	5	91	0	83
1987	0	96	0	83
1986	0	100	0	95
1985	0	100	5	93
1984	0	100	13	87
1983	0	88	6	78
1982	5	78	8	80
1981	10	93	12	94

Steve Symms (R)

Of Caldwell — Elected 1980

Born: April 23, 1938, Nampa, Idaho.
Education: U. of Idaho, B.S. 1960.
Military Career: Marine Corps, 1960-63.
Occupation: Fruit grower; fitness club owner.
Family: Wife, Frances E. Stockdale; four children.
Religion: Methodist.
Political Career: U.S. House, 1973-81.
Capitol Office: 509 Hart Bldg. 20510; 224-6142.

In Washington: The boyish Symms who appeared in his 1972 TV campaign ads taking a bite from an apple has now turned 50 and spent most of his adult life in Congress. Although as conservative as ever, he must increasingly confront the realization that he is now a part of the Establishment.

Symms came to the Senate from the House in 1981, one of 13 freshmen who had deposed incumbents the previous fall and delivered control of the chamber to the GOP. The ex-Marine was already a veteran of eight years of guerrilla warfare in the House, where he and his allies on the right used demands for roll-call votes, frequent quorum calls and numerous amendments to tie up the Democratic leadership. Symms was not the group leader, but he was one of its most enthusiastic participants, and he never seemed to take the job of legislating very seriously. "I guess I am compromising my principles by even being here," he said at one point.

Throughout his first term, Symms often used his heated rhetoric to make things difficult for the Reagan administration and his party's Senate leadership. Whenever he saw a deviation from the strong conservative values he believed the president stood for personally, Symms did not hesitate to denounce it.

Arms control was a target of many of Symms' attacks. Warning that current trends will lead to "a world ruled by the Soviet Union," Symms argued that arms control negotiations lull the public into a false sense of security about the dangers of communism.

The one foreign policy issue on which Symms did not find Reagan too conciliatory was South Africa. He was one of the few senators to back the president in opposing imposition of sanctions against the white-minority South African regime. "Apartheid for all practical purposes is gone in South Africa," he argued, warning that sanctions could lead to "the same kind of bloodshed in South Africa in 1986 that you had in Virginia and Maryland in 1865."

But in the later years of GOP control in the Senate, he seemed to be moving from gadfly to serious legislator. He won high marks from other senators for his work on federal highway programs as chairman of the Environment Subcommittee on Transportation.

With Republicans no longer in the majority, some wondered whether Symms would resume the guerrilla-warfare approach that marked the earlier part of his career. The answer has been mixed. He has certainly not lost his ideological compass: In 1988 he was the only senator to receive both a perfect score from the American Conservative Union and a zero from both the AFL-CIO and the liberal Americans for Democratic Action.

But Symms has also managed to have a serious impact on selected issues of importance to him or his state. He was, for example, an early advocate of a second production reactor for nuclear materials used in the nation's strategic weapons — a facility that fit his national security philosophy and could be built in Idaho. He was able to pursue the same philosophy in opposing the intermediate-range nuclear-force (INF) treaty with the Soviets. He introduced a series of amendments that would have delayed the treaty's taking effect until the Soviets had complied with a series of earlier treaties.

Symms was also in the front lines of the 100th and 101st Congresses as an opponent of clean-air legislation he and other Westerners viewed as favoring Eastern high-sulfur coal.

Even when he was at his most incendiary on arms control and South Africa, Symms was leading another sort of life as chairman (from 1981-87) of the Transportation Subcommittee. In this role he generally was credited with steadiness and diligence. Although he did not achieve his goal of passing a long-term reauthorization for grants to states from the Highway Trust Fund in the 98th or 99th Congress, Symms was respected for his efforts. And, ironically, when the Democrats took control in 1987, they swiftly passed, over Reagan's veto, the highway bill on which Symms had labored so long.

In earlier Congresses, Symms had tried to push through a highway bill without many of the "demonstration projects" sought by House members for their districts — notably a new highway and tunnel project promoted for Boston by House Speaker Thomas P. O'Neill Jr. Symms compromised to get the bill out of committee and gave a little more to prevail on the Senate floor. But when he balked at demands from the House, his bills died.

In the 99th Congress, Symms managed a one-year emergency bill to fund state highway projects. But a long-term bill remained hostage to demonstration projects and to another Symms issue: the 55 mph speed limit. Westerners had long chafed at the limit on long, lonely stretches of road. But the House would tolerate an increase only if states banned radar detectors and met other conditions the Senate would not accept.

Early in the 100th Congress, with Symms no longer subcommittee chairman and the White House threatening a veto, Congress cleared an $88 billion bill, including $890 million for demonstration projects, and a companion measure that allowed states to raise the speed limit to 65 on rural Interstates. The House easily overrode Reagan's veto. Reagan took the unusual step of coming to the Capitol to plead with GOP senators to sustain his veto, as the Senate prepared for a revote on overriding the president. But all 13 Republicans voting to override the first time — including Symms — refused to switch; the veto was overridden by one vote.

Symms is also a member of the Finance and Budget committees, but he has not been among their most active participants. Throughout much of the 99th Congress, he used his seat on Finance to question Reagan's tax-revision proposal ("a huge gamble with our economy"), although he voted for it in the end. In the 100th Congress, Symms had to leave Finance when its size was reduced.

At Home: Even when he is not on the ballot, Symms' unpredictable nature can generate election-year controversy. In 1988, he told a radio interviewer in Idaho that Kitty Dukakis, wife of the Democratic nominee for president, had been photographed burning an American flag. Challenged, he could produce no evidence. Symms also attracted attention with a fund-raising letter in 1988 that urged help in defeating Idaho Democratic Rep. Richard Stallings before he could become a threat to either of the state's GOP senators.

Both of Symms' Senate elections have been close, but only one was as combative as the figures imply. That was in 1980, when he used his base in the House to launch a campaign against the state's most prestigious and durable liberal, Democrat Frank Church.

National conservative groups had targeted Church for defeat, and heavy negative advertising against him took its toll early in the season. An independent committee labeled ABC (Anybody But Church) ran television ads denouncing the senator's conciliatory stand on U.S. foreign policy issues. Symms charged that the Foreign Relations chairman was weak on national defense, supported too much government spending and hurt the state's economy with his bill to expand Idaho wilderness areas.

Church was a resourceful campaigner, however, and Symms had to deal with a number of side issues that emerged, including rumors that he was a womanizer and charges that he was involved in a conflict of interest through buying silver futures while serving on a House subcommittee overseeing the Commodity Futures Trading Commission. He denied the stories.

The conservative tide carried Symms to a narrow victory, helped along by the concession speech President Jimmy Carter delivered while the polls were still open in parts of the state. Symms' margin was less than 4,300 votes.

In 1986, it was Symms' turn for a challenge. His opponent was Gov. John V. Evans, who was constitutionally required to give up the governorship. At first glance, the contest had all the markings of a classic fight — two of the state's best-known politicians going head-to-head in a year in which control of the Senate was at stake. As it turned out, though, their race lacked the spark that marked other Senate contests that year.

For one thing, both candidates were so well-known that even before the campaign began in earnest, polls were showing most voters had already made up their minds between the two, dividing roughly in half.

But personality factors also made it unlikely from the start that the contest would ignite. Evans, who governed with a low-key, businesslike style, was not the sort to start any flame throwing. And Symms, whose freewheeling manner had been an issue in previous campaigns, seemed intent on projecting an aura of responsibility.

Policy issues had an ambiguous effect. Idaho was suffering through a depressing "triple recession," with mining, timber and agriculture struggling at the same time; Evans, as governor, could not escape some responsibility, and was unable to lay all the blame for economic troubles on national GOP policies.

With Evans maintaining his typical low profile until relatively late in the campaign, Symms barnstormed the state, enthusiastic and affable, drawing crowds at county fairs and rodeos. He tried to counteract his flamboyant reputation with a series of ads offering testimonials from constituents and touting his work for farmers and lumbermen. By the time the election was drawing close, he had clearly strengthened his standing.

The one key uncertainty in the election was the effect of a ballot initiative to undo the state's right-to-work law. Unions, which are still strong in northern Idaho, were organizing fervently on its behalf, and Democrats believed that organized labor's efforts would help Evans.

But Evans never managed to put Symms on the defensive, and the right-to-work initiative provoked a strong turnout of voters who supported the right-to-work law. Evans won many of the counties in the blue-collar belt that runs from the center of the state north through the panhandle. But he could not make enough inroads elsewhere. Voters happy with Symms' ideology were reassured by his efforts to convince them that he was not a flaky maverick, and he carried the bulk of the state's counties on his way to a 52 percent overall tally.

Symms' original campaign for Congress was the climax to a decade of operating around the conservative fringes of Idaho politics, developing a reputation as a genial and appealing man, but also a strident ideologue.

As a Marine in 1962, Symms served at the U.S. military base at Guantanamo during the Cuban missile crisis, and returned lamenting President Kennedy's decision not to launch a full-scale invasion of the island. "It was just a matter of liberating the Cuban people," he said later. Back home in Idaho, he left his Presbyterian church when the parent body contributed to the legal defense of black activist Angela Davis, and became a Methodist instead. Then he began publishing an anti-government newsletter, the *Idaho Compass*, advocating leasing the University of Idaho forestry school to a paper company, and the school of mines to a copper company. He urged the university to permit students to major in capitalism.

By early 1972 Symms was so distressed by the liberal direction of the country — especially the Nixon administration's wage and price controls — that he talked about moving to Australia. But he ran for Congress instead, attracting voters with his enthusiasm and gimmicks such as a commercial in which he chomped on an apple, then asked viewers to elect him and "take a bite out of government."

Committees

Budget (4th of 10 Republicans)

Environment and Public Works (3rd of 7 Republicans)
Water Resources, Transportation and Infrastructure (ranking); Nuclear Regulation; Superfund, Ocean and Water Protection

Finance (9th of 9 Republicans)
Energy and Agricultural Taxation; International Trade; Taxation and Debt Management

Joint Economic
Economic Resources and Competitiveness; Fiscal and Monetary Policy; Investment, Jobs and Prices

Elections

1986 General

Steve Symms (R)	196,958	(52%)
John V. Evans (D)	185,066	(48%)

Previous Winning Percentages: 1980 (50%) **1978 *** (60%) **1976 *** (55%) **1974 *** (58%) **1972 *** (56%)

* *House elections.*

Campaign Finance

	Receipts	Receipts from PACs	Expenditures
1986			
Symms (R)	$3,387,726	$1,366,527 (40%)	$3,229,939
Evans (D)	$2,200,571	$690,398 (31%)	$2,128,223

Key Votes

1987	
Enact omnibus highway bill over Reagan veto	Y
Limit testing of space-based anti-ballistic missiles	N
Oppose banning tests of larger nuclear weapons	Y
Confirm Robert H. Bork as Supreme Court justice	Y
1988	
Allow vote on campaign-finance overhaul	N
Pass civil rights restoration bill over Reagan veto	N
Enact omnibus trade bill over Reagan veto	N
Approve death penalty for drug-related murders	Y
Oppose "workfare" amendment to welfare overhaul bill	N

Voting Studies

	Presidential Support		Party Unity		Conservative Coalition	
Year	**S**	**O**	**S**	**O**	**S**	**O**
1988	70	25	93	1	92	3
1987	74	19	92	4	97	0
1986	86	6	84	6	88	1
1985	81	18	91	7	92	7
1984	81	12	89	3	89	0
1983	62	35	84	12	86	9
1982	79	20	93	6	97	2
1981	80	13	90	7	91	4

Interest Group Ratings

Year	ADA	ACU	AFL-CIO	CCUS
1988	0	100	0	86
1987	0	88	11	94
1986	0	100	0	100
1985	0	100	0	90
1984	0	100	0	88
1983	0	100	0	84
1982	5	79	8	80
1981	0	100	6	100

1 Larry E. Craig (R)

Of Midvale — Elected 1980

Born: July 20, 1945, Council, Idaho.
Education: U. of Idaho, B.A. 1969; graduate work, George Washington U., 1970.
Military Career: National Guard, 1970-72.
Occupation: Farmer; real-estate salesman.
Family: Wife, Suzanne Scott; three stepchildren.
Religion: Methodist.
Political Career: Idaho Senate, 1975-81.
Capitol Office: 1034 Longworth Bldg. 20515; 225-6611.

In Washington: One of 52 House Republicans swept into office in 1980, Craig proudly counted himself a front-ranks leader in the "Reagan Revolution." He shared with the new president roots in the West, a conservative ideology and a confrontational approach to government. But by the end of Reagan's tenure in the White House, Craig was among those Republicans who seemed more ideologically consistent than Reagan himself.

Craig's years in Washington have little dimmed his philosophical certainty or quieted his rabble-rousing on the evils of federal debt. He talks in terms of a "war" against the deficit, and at times sounds dismayed that even after eight years under a president opposed to federal largess, the deficit has multiplied. Unlike many conservatives, however, Craig does not lay the blame squarely on Congress. He sees it as the "mutual responsibility" of the Congress and the president.

Craig is a crusader for a balanced-budget constitutional amendment, and he has carried that mission beyond the halls of Congress. Founder of CLUBB (Congressional Leaders United for a Balanced Budget), Craig urges state legislatures to demand that Congress enact a balanced-budget amendment or call a constitutional convention to draft one.

Craig's ardor for deficit reduction does not keep him from lobbying for home-state projects. But when he delivers, he seems to feel compelled to explain. In the 100th Congress, Craig helped secure the release of $300,000 to conduct a water-quality study in Idaho; he said it was "no pork barrel," but of "great importance" to several Western states. In a letter to constituents, Craig noted that a $1.35 million federal matching grant he helped secure for the Centennial Trail is "not one of the so-called budget-busting measures." The money was already set aside; he just earmarked it for Idaho.

On the House Interior Committee, Craig is a contentious and consistent critic of that panel's conservationist Democratic majority, which has placed millions of acres of federal land in wilderness status, beyond commercial development. Craig has vehemently, and thus far successfully, fought passage of a new Idaho wilderness bill that would increase federal holdings. Also in the 100th Congress, Craig criticized a Democratic plan to reorganize the National Park Service as an effort to create "a new free-wheeling bureacracy."

On one issue before the 100th Congress, however, Craig found himself on the environmental side of a development issue. He pushed a bill to prohibit the building of dams on portions of the Snake and lower Salmon rivers. Before the House unanimously endorsed the bill, which was later enacted, Craig heralded the effort to keep the free-flowing reaches of the rivers available to sportsmen and women.

Craig regularly argues with the government of Canada on behalf of his timber-producing constituents. A member of the Government Operations Committee until 1989, when he switched to Public Works, Craig voted against a bill to carry out the U.S.-Canada free-trade agreement to protest the low fee charged by the Canadians for timber removal from public land, which he says amounts to an unfair subsidy.

In 1985, Craig introduced legislation to restrain U.S. imports of Canadian timber. "I do not expect action from the Canadians," he said, "until we have the two-by-four with which we are preparing to hit them between the eyes squarely in hand." In late 1986, Canada agreed to impose a 15 percent tax on softwood exports.

Craig's district historically has been a major producer of silver, but low prices in recent years have cost many miners their jobs. In the 100th Congress, he backed successful legislation to fund the Mining and Minerals Institute at the University of Idaho. As a freshman, Craig fought a Reagan administration plan to generate revenue by selling silver from the nation's strategic-minerals stockpile. He said this would depress prices.

A strong opponent of gun-control measures, Craig was one of only 21 House members to vote against a 1985 bill banning armor-piercing bullets. He claimed that the bill attempted to curb criminal behavior "by control-

Idaho 1

North and West — Lewiston; Boise

Conservative Republicans are now into their third decade of control in the 1st, which used to be known as "Idaho's Democratic district." From the New Deal until the Great Society years, the 1st nearly always sent Democrats to Congress. It broke that habit for good in 1966, thanks to a redistricting that brought in more Republicans and to the House candidacy of then-state Sen. James A. McClure.

There is still some Democratic strength in the 1st, based on labor influence in the mountainous northern Panhandle, where lumbermen and miners fought to organize unions early in this century. Also prone to go Democratic is a community of relatively liberal voters linked to the 9,000-student University of Idaho at Moscow in Latah County. In the 1980 Senate contest between liberal Democratic Sen. Frank Church and conservative Republican Steve Symms, Idaho's nine northernmost counties sided with Church. Even in 1988, when Michael S. Dukakis was struggling to win 37 percent of the statewide presidential vote, he got 50 percent or better in five of the nine Panhandle counties.

But the Democratic vote in the Panhandle is more than offset by two heavily Republican urbanized areas at the southern end of the district — Canyon County and western Ada County — which together have more than 40 percent of the district's residents.

The state capital, Boise, is in Ada County. Idaho's only city with more than 100,000 residents, Boise has a strong Republican vote cast by white-collar employees of the lumber, paper, food processing, electronics and construction corporations that have their headquarters there. Canyon County has the growing cities of Nampa and Caldwell — agricultural processing centers that usually vote Republican as well. George Bush won Canyon County in 1988 by 2-to-1.

Population: 472,412. White 454,305 (96%), Black 802 (0.2%), Other 7,982 (2%). Spanish origin 15,929 (3%). 18 and over 324,509 (69%), 65 and over 49,720 (11%). Median age: 29.

ling little pieces of metal." He continued, "That approach is what gun control is all about — and this bill, like all other forms of gun control, will fail to achieve its stated objective." Craig strongly supported the 1986 legislation that rolled back some provisions of the Gun Control Act of 1968.

At Home: Craig will be a strong contender for the Senate seat of Republican James A. McClure in 1990 if the three-term incumbent chooses to retire. Enjoying his usual two-thirds of the November vote in his 1st District, Craig had no trouble turning back the 1988 challenge of two-term state legislator Jeanne Givens, a member of the Coeur d'Alene tribe.

An eerie streak of bad fortune had befallen Craig's Democratic opponents in the two previous elections. In 1986, candidate Pete Busch, who two years before had mounted a spirited underdog campaign against McClure, died when the plane he was piloting crashed. Craig took 65 percent against Bill Currie, a former Boundary County commissioner who replaced Busch as the Democratic candidate.

In 1984, the man who initially decided to challenge Craig was killed in a car crash. Craig had won his first two House elections with just 54 percent, but he soared to 69 percent against Bill Hellar, who was named the substitute Democratic nominee after the fatal car crash.

That tally was the highest vote by any 1st District candidate in nearly 50 years. Neither McClure nor Steve Symms, both of whom held the 1st before moving to the Senate, had ever surpassed 60 percent.

In the state Senate, Craig was known as something of a moderate, but in his 1980 House campaign, he tied himself to Symms, then campaigning for the Senate. After winning a tough primary, Craig was rated a solid favorite over underfinanced Democrat Glenn W. Nichols. Still, Nichols gave Craig trouble, drawing attention by walking the length of the 1st, from Canada to Nevada, criticizing Craig's "Sagebrush Rebellion" sympathies.

In 1982, Democrats nominated Larry LaRocco, who had worked as a field representative for former Democratic Sen. Frank Church. LaRocco said Craig favored wholesale privatization of federal lands. Craig complained he was the victim of "falsehoods, misrepresentations and misreporting." Strong support for LaRocco from the economically depressed northern part of the 1st did not derail Craig.

Committees

Interior and Insular Affairs (4th of 15 Republicans)
Mining and Natural Resources (ranking); National Parks and Public Lands; Water, Power and Offshore Energy Resources

Public Works and Transportation (16th of 20 Republicans)
Economic Development; Surface Transportation; Water Resources

Standards of Official Conduct (5th of 6 Republicans)

Elections

1988 General

Larry E. Craig (R)	135,221	(66%)
Jeanne Givens (D)	70,328	(34%)

1986 General

Larry E. Craig (R)	120,553	(65%)
Bill Currie (D)	59,723	(32%)

Previous Winning Percentages: 1984 (69%) **1982** (54%) **1980** (54%)

District Vote For President

	1988	1984	1980	1976
D	80,657 (39%)	62,588 (30%)	47,191 (31%)	65,243 (39%)
R	121,632 (59%)	141,459 (68%)	90,676 (59%)	96,377 (58%)
I			10,164 (7%)	

Campaign Finance

	Receipts	Receipts from PACs	Expenditures
1988			
Craig (R)	$356,033	$159,060 (45%)	$361,113
Givens (D)	$117,516	$64,378 (55%)	$116,109
1986			
Craig (R)	$318,428	$115,056 (36%)	$310,471
Currie (D)	$12,697	$800 (6%)	$12,507

Key Votes

1987	
Raise speed limit to 65 mph	Y
Approve Gephardt "fair trade" amendment	N
Ban testing of larger nuclear weapons	N
Delay "re-flagging" of Kuwaiti tankers	Y
Approve tax-raising deficit-reduction bill	N
1988	
Approve aid to Nicaraguan contras	Y
Enact civil rights restoration bill over Reagan veto	N
Kill 60-day plant-closing notification measure	Y
Pass omnibus trade bill over Reagan veto	N
Approve death penalty for drug-related murders	Y
Bar federal funds for abortions in cases of rape and incest	Y
Oppose seven-day waiting period for purchase of handguns	Y

Voting Studies

	Presidential Support		Party Unity		Conservative Coalition	
Year	**S**	**O**	**S**	**O**	**S**	**O**
1988	66	23	87	5	76	5
1987	65 †	28 †	83 †	8 †	93 †	5 †
1986	79	21	85	9	92	6
1985	75	24	91	5	96	2
1984	73	22	86	4	93	5
1983	73	16	86	4	93	3
1982	75	23	85	7	86	8
1981	72	24	91	5	91	4

† Not eligible for all recorded votes.

Interest Group Ratings

Year	ADA	ACU	AFL-CIO	CCUS
1988	5	100	7	92
1987	8	86	13	93
1986	5	86	21	100
1985	0	90	0	91
1984	5	91	15	87
1983	0	100	0	84
1982	5	95	5	90
1981	0	100	13	95

2 Richard Stallings (D)

Of Rexburg — Elected 1984

Born: Oct. 7, 1940, Ogden, Utah.
Education: Weber State College, B.S. 1965; Utah State U., M.A. 1968.
Occupation: History professor.
Family: Wife, Ranae Garner; three children.
Religion: Mormon.
Political Career: Democratic nominee for Idaho House, 1974, 1978; Democratic nominee for U.S. House, 1982.
Capitol Office: 1221 Longworth Bldg. 20515; 225-5531.

In Washington: Stallings left his career as a history professor to come to Congress, but every day he teaches Republicans a lesson about the task they face in building a House majority. As long as Democrats such as Stallings routinely win election in places as conservative as eastern Idaho, a GOP majority is almost certainly a distant dream.

Representing a district that gave George Bush 65 percent of its vote in 1988, Stallings does not have the freedom to venture much outside issues that have a direct impact on his constituents. Yet he often seems to feel freer to vote his conscience than some members from safe districts.

When Stallings began his House career in the 99th Congress, Democratic leaders plotting strategy on key votes would worry about how to win him over, expecting that he would be a tough sell because of his constituency. But the leadership soon discovered that, often as not, Stallings did not need any lobbying: He already had decided to vote with them. He voted to delay President Reagan's plan to provide naval escorts for Kuwaiti oil tankers in the Persian Gulf, and against the president's requests on the MX missile and funding for the Nicaraguan contras.

"If I can't stick my neck out for something that is right," Stallings said after defying Reagan on the contras in 1986, "perhaps the office isn't worth it."

Coming from most congressmen, that statement would sound like grandstanding. But it is believable in Stallings, a polite, workaday academician who, when asked by a colleague to cite the most memorable event of his young congressional career, mentioned a tour he took of the battlefield at Gettysburg.

But if Stallings sides with his party more often than many expected — 71 percent of the time in 1988 — his critics at home have had trouble painting him as being out of step with Idaho. His middle-of-the-road record includes votes against a ban on the testing of larger nuclear weapons and for the death penalty for drug-related murders; he is no different from his GOP colleagues serving Idaho when it comes to gun control or raising the speed limit to 65 mph. His opposition to abortion is well enough known that three anti-abortion activists at the 1988 Democratic National Convention voted to nominate Stallings, not Michael S. Dukakis, as the party's standard-bearer.

Stallings has said of the leadership: "I think they recognize ... that I can give them 100 percent of the votes for two years, but that would be the end of it." He is correct. The leadership has gone out of its way to help Stallings hold his district. He got the committee assignments he wanted — Agriculture and Science — and two influential Westerners, Majority Whip Tony Coelho of California and Majority Leader Thomas S. Foley of Washington, saw to it that Stallings got every chance to shine when the farm bill was produced in the 99th Congress.

When perfecting amendments to the legislation were needed, Stallings often was assigned the public task of offering them. He spoke up frequently on behalf of Idahoans who raise potatoes, dry edible beans and sugar beets, and he succeeded with his amendment to require the federal government to control its range lands for crop-eating grasshoppers.

In his second term on Agriculture, Stallings took special interest in efforts to save the ailing farm credit system, and he was among those insisting that the government do more than provide a multibillion-dollar bailout. He said a rescue plan should include a new policy for restructuring loans and subsidizing interest rates on outstanding loans.

Stallings was particularly active in pushing a successful plan establishing a secondary market for agricultural real estate. The plan, known as "Farmer Mac," was intended to enable private lenders to diversify their risk by pooling different types of loans and selling them to others. Stallings and other proponents maintained that the secondary market would allow small banks and insurance companies to make

Idaho 2

East — Pocatello; Idaho Falls

Mormons migrating north from Utah first settled southeastern Idaho in the mid-1800s, and today their influence is pervasive in the area. Almost two-thirds of the people in southeastern Idaho are Mormon, and like their co-religionists elsewhere, they support conservative candidates and causes.

Bonneville County (Idaho Falls) is the largest county in the 2nd, and also the most conservative. Republican presidential candidates typically average well above 60 percent of the vote in Bonneville. George Bush won 75 percent there in 1988, well above his 63 percent statewide tally.

Idaho Falls processes potatoes grown in the surrounding upper Snake River Valley. It is 30 miles from the test site that pioneered commercial nuclear power in the 1950s, and nuclear energy retains considerable support. Bonneville and a handful of upper Snake River area counties on the eastern edge of the 2nd backed GOP Rep. George Hansen loyally throughout his career, voting strongly for him even in 1984.

On the western side of the district, the Republican voters are conservative, but less fervently so. Twin Falls County gave Bush 64 percent in 1988; it also was the base of an anti-Hansen group of Republicans who were crucial to Stallings in 1984. With their help, he carried the county by 698 votes.

Twin Falls is in the center of the Magic Valley farming area, so named because the sandy soils in this region, when irrigated with Snake River water, produce remarkable yields of potatoes, sugar beets and other cash crops.

The largest pocket of Democratic strength, which springs from a heavy labor vote and a sizable student vote from Idaho State University, is in Bannock County. The city of Pocatello there is a railroad and chemical center specializing in phosphate fertilizers.

Two other centers of Democratic support in the 2nd are Blaine County, home of the Sun Valley resorts, and the eastern section of Boise, around Boise State University.

Population: 471,523. White 447,336 (95%), Black 1,914 (0.4%), Other 8,487 (2%). Spanish origin 20,686 (4%). 18 and over 312,761 (66%), 65 and over 43,960 (9%). Median age: 26.

more farm real-estate loans, stabilizing the market and bringing lower interest rates.

Stallings manages to blend his congressional business and academic interests frequently in Washington. Assiduous attention to his constituents often means accompanying groups from Idaho on tours of the Capitol and the White House.

At Home: Stallings probably can look forward to the devoted attentions of Republican strategists for as long as he is in office. He won election in 1984 because his opponent was a convicted felon; however successful he is at holding his seat in years to come, the 2nd is likely to remain one of the most conservative and Republican in the country.

But if the GOP is to unseat Stallings, it will have to do better than its last two efforts. In 1988, the party nominated former state Sen. Dane Watkins, an also-ran from the 1986 primary. Watkins' only rival for the 1988 nomination was a political neophyte who listed her occupation as poet and yet received more than 40 percent of the primary vote.

In the general election, Watkins tried to paint Stallings as a liberal national Democrat. But the Mormon incumbent's locally popular stands on a balanced budget, gun control and the 65 mph speed limit were widely known.

Watkins also mishandled the issue of a plutonium-refining project sought for the Idaho National Engineering Laboratory. He prematurely portrayed the project as dead, and the state's GOP senators weighed in on Stallings' side of the story. In the end, Stallings pushed his victory tally to a stunning 63 percent, even as the district's presidential vote broke just as decisively for the GOP.

In 1986, the Republican champion was Idaho Falls sports announcer Mel Richardson, who won the nomination by defeating four others.

Richardson seemed, at first glance, an ideal candidate. Three decades in broadcasting had given him enormous recognition in the Idaho Falls area, and he had an easygoing, friendly manner that his backers hoped would help him expand his base of support.

But he never made much progress. High-profile Senate and gubernatorial contests soaked up much of Idaho's available funding.

In the few direct encounters between the two, Stallings made the most of Richardson's legislative inexperience, accusing him of misunderstanding complex farm and government spending issues. For most of the campaign, however, he tried to firm up the base he had built since his 1984 election. He paid close attention to the Boise area, where voters are more moderate than those farther east, and to farmers in the Magic Valley, around Twin Falls.

On Election Day, Stallings took 54 percent, carrying 15 of the district's 26 counties and losing only in the conservative upper Snake River Valley and heavily Mormon southeast.

Stallings' 1984 success came after several disappointments. He lost two state legislative campaigns and also managed the 1976 House campaign of Democrat Stan Kress, who narrowly lost to GOP Rep. George Hansen. In 1982, Stallings was the Democratic nominee against Hansen. A late start hampered him, but he still got 48 percent.

For his second campaign against Hansen, Stallings started early, built a sizable organization and attracted ample funding. The accumulated weight of Hansen's legal and financial problems boosted Stallings' stock. Hansen, who had been convicted in federal court of filing false financial disclosure reports, barely survived a primary challenge. In June, he was sentenced to a five- to 15-month prison term and fined $40,000.

Stallings told voters he could put the district's needs first instead of being preoccupied with defending his personal integrity. He claimed that midyear polling data showed him leading by roughly 2-to-1.

But his luck began to sour in July, when Democratic vice presidential nominee Geraldine A. Ferraro became embroiled in controversy over her financial-disclosure reports. Hansen expertly turned the issue to his advantage. When Democrats played down Ferraro's problems, Hansen railed at the double standard that he said excused a liberal Eastern Democrat while a conservative Western Republican was persecuted.

Stallings spent much of the fall on the defensive. At one point, he expressed reservations about voting for Mondale and Ferraro. Complaints from Democrats prompted him to pledge to support the ticket, but later, he voiced doubts about Ferraro's qualifications. In the end, Stallings finished on top by just 170 votes.

Now, with two successful re-election campaigns behind him, Stallings must be considered a potential candidate for statewide office. He has already prevailed in the half of the state that votes most heavily Republican. Opportunity could arise as soon as 1990, when the terms of both GOP Sen. James A. McClure and Democratic Gov. Cecil D. Andrus expire.

Committees

Agriculture (16th of 27 Democrats)
Conservation, Credit and Rural Development; Cotton, Rice and Sugar; Forests, Family Farms and Energy

Science, Space and Technology (17th of 30 Democrats)
Energy Research and Development; Space Science and Applications

Select Aging (29th of 39 Democrats)
Retirement, Income and Employment

Elections

1988 General		
Richard Stallings (D)	127,956	(63%)
Dane Watkins (R)	68,226	(34%)
1986 General		
Richard Stallings (D)	103,035	(54%)
Mel Richardson (R)	86,528	(46%)

Previous Winning Percentage: **1984** (50%)

District Vote For President

	1988	1984	1980	1976
D	66,615 (33%)	45,922 (23%)	63,001 (22%)	61,306 (35%)
R	132,249 (65%)	156,064 (77%)	200,023 (71%)	107,774 (62%)
I	5,313 *(3%)		16,894 (6%)	

* *Ron Paul, Libertarian*

Campaign Finance

	Receipts	Receipts from PACs	Expend-itures
1988			
Stallings (D)	$498,997	$266,739 (53%)	$502,083
Watkins (R)	$205,847	$26,450 (13%)	$206,960
1986			
Stallings (D)	$474,949	$271,815 (57%)	$470,363
Richardson (R)	$326,827	$87,157 (27%)	$325,004

Key Votes

1987	
Raise speed limit to 65 mph	Y
Approve Gephardt "fair trade" amendment	N
Ban testing of larger nuclear weapons	Y
Delay "re-flagging" of Kuwaiti tankers	Y
Approve tax-raising deficit-reduction bill	N
1988	
Approve aid to Nicaraguan contras	N
Enact civil rights restoration bill over Reagan veto	Y
Kill 60-day plant-closing notification measure	N
Pass omnibus trade bill over Reagan veto	Y
Approve death penalty for drug-related murders	Y
Bar federal funds for abortions in cases of rape and incest	Y
Oppose seven-day waiting period for purchase of handguns	Y

Voting Studies

	Presidential Support		Party Unity		Conservative Coalition	
Year	S	O	S	O	S	O
1988	35	58	71	24	79	11
1987	41	56	71	25	74	26
1986	42	58	62	34	72	26
1985	41	58	69	24	58	36

Interest Group Ratings

Year	ADA	ACU	AFL-CIO	CCUS
1988	55	48	71	71
1987	52	27	56	67
1986	45	32	57	71
1985	35	40	44	55

Illinois

U.S. CONGRESS

SENATE 2 D

HOUSE 14 D, 8 R

LEGISLATURE

Senate 31 D, 28 R

House 67 D, 51 R

ELECTIONS

1988 Presidential Vote	
Bush	51%
Dukakis	49%
1984 Presidential Vote	
Reagan	56%
Mondale	43%
1980 Presidential Vote	
Reagan	50%
Carter	42%
Anderson	7%
Turnout rate in 1984	57%
Turnout rate in 1986	36%
Turnout rate in 1988	53%

(as percentage of voting age population)

POPULATION AND GROWTH

1980 population	11,426,518
1988 population estimate (6th in the nation)	11,614,000
Percent change 1980-1988	+2%

DEMOGRAPHIC BREAKDOWN

White	81%
Black	15%
Other	1%
(Spanish origin)	6%
Urban	83%
Rural	17%
Born in state	69%
Foreign-born	7%

MAJOR CITIES

Chicago	3,009,530
Rockford	135,760
Peoria	110,290
Springfield	100,290
Decatur	90,360

AREA AND LAND USE

Area 55,645 sq. miles (24th)

Farm	81%
Forest	12%
Federally owned	1%

Gov. James R. Thompson (R)
Of Chicago — Elected 1976

Born: May 8, 1936, Chicago, Ill.

Education: Attended U. of Illinois, Chicago, 1953-55; Washington U., St. Louis, 1955-56; Northwestern U., J.D. 1959.

Occupation: Lawyer.

Religion: Presbyterian.

Political Career: U.S. attorney for the Northern District of Illinois, 1971-75.

Next Election: 1990.

WORK

Occupations	
White-collar	54%
Blue-collar	31%
Service workers	13%
Government Workers	
Federal	103,787
State	158,458
Local	475,748

MONEY

Median family income	$ 22,746	(6th)
Tax burden per capita	$ 800	(32nd)

EDUCATION

Spending per pupil through grade 12	$ 3,781	(21st)
Persons with college degrees	16%	(24th)

CRIME

Violent crime rate 796 per 100,000 (4th)

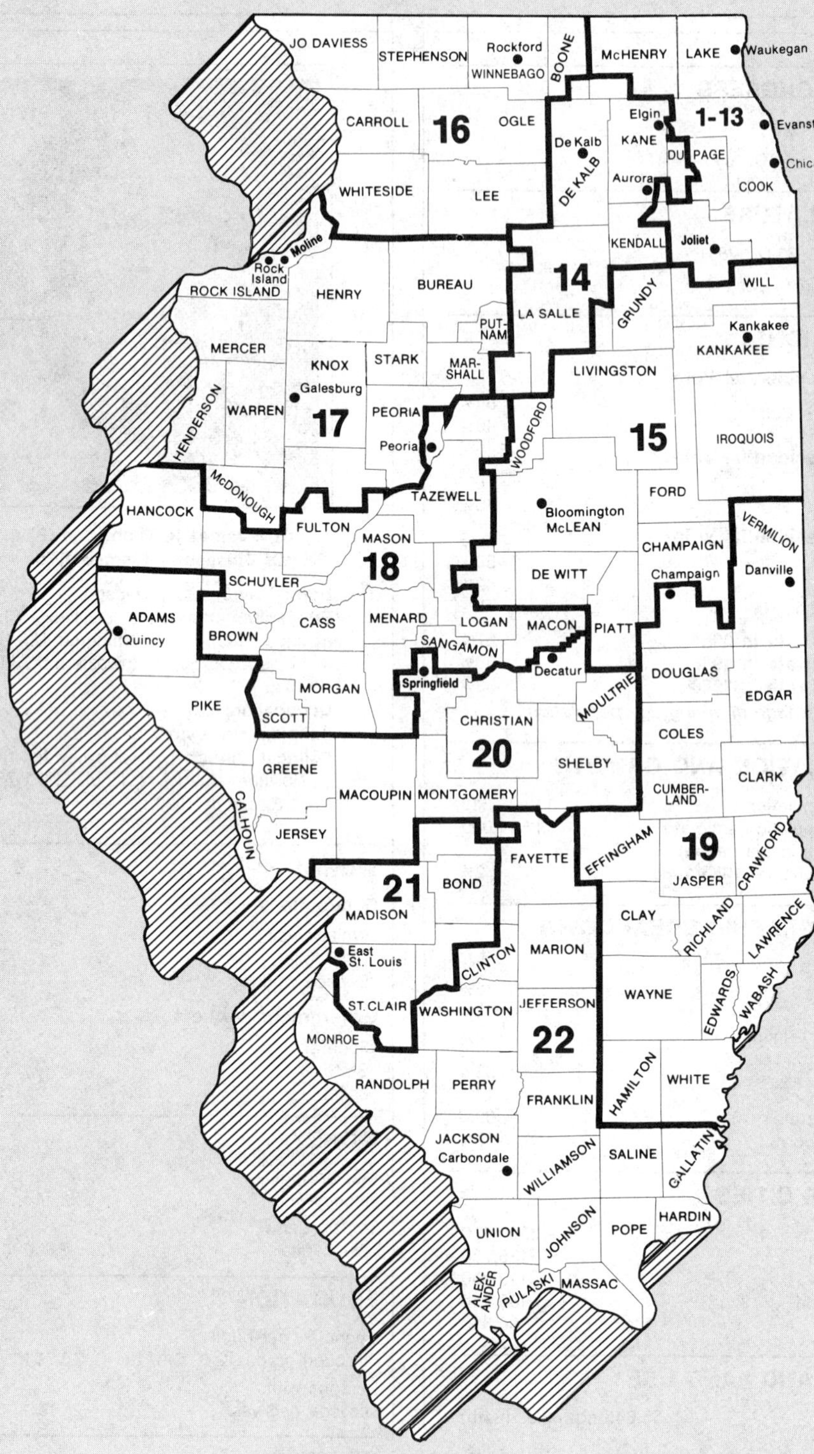
JO DAVIESS
STEPHENSON
Rockford
WINNEBAGO
BOONE
McHENRY
LAKE
Waukegan
CARROLL
16
OGLE
De Kalb
DE KALB
Elgin
KANE
1-13
Evanston
DU PAGE
Chicago
Aurora
COOK
WHITESIDE
LEE
KENDALL
Joliet
Moline
Rock Island
ROCK ISLAND
HENRY
BUREAU
14
WILL
PUT-NAM
LA SALLE
GRUNDY
Kankakee
KANKAKEE
MERCER
KNOX
STARK
MAR-SHALL
LIVINGSTON
HENDERSON
Galesburg
WARREN
17
PEORIA
Peoria
WOODFORD
15
IROQUOIS
McDONOUGH
TAZEWELL
FORD
HANCOCK
FULTON
Bloomington
McLEAN
VERMILION
MASON
18
CHAMPAIGN
SCHUYLER
DE WITT
Champaign
Danville
ADAMS
Quincy
BROWN
CASS
MENARD
LOGAN
MACON
PIATT
SANGAMON
Decatur
Springfield
DOUGLAS
MORGAN
MOULTRIE
EDGAR
PIKE
SCOTT
CHRISTIAN
COLES
20
SHELBY
GREENE
CLARK
CUMBER-LAND
MACOUPIN
MONTGOMERY
CALHOUN
JERSEY
FAYETTE
EFFINGHAM
19
CRAWFORD
JASPER
21
BOND
MADISON
CLAY
RICHLAND
LAWRENCE
East St. Louis
CLINTON
MARION
WAYNE
EDWARDS
WABASH
ST. CLAIR
WASHINGTON
JEFFERSON
MONROE
22
HAMILTON
WHITE
RANDOLPH
PERRY
FRANKLIN
JACKSON
Carbondale
WILLIAMSON
SALINE
GALLATIN
UNION
JOHNSON
POPE
HARDIN
ALEX-ANDER
PULASKI
MASSAC

Alan J. Dixon (D)

Of Belleville — Elected 1980

Born: July 7, 1927, Belleville, Ill.

Education: U. of Illinois, B.S. 1949; Washington U., St. Louis, LL.B. 1949.

Military Career: Naval Air Cadet, 1945-46.

Occupation: Lawyer.

Family: Wife, Joan Louise Fox; three children.

Religion: Presbyterian.

Political Career: Ill. House 1951-63; Ill. Senate, 1963-71; Ill. treasurer, 1971-77; Ill. secretary of state, 1977-81.

Capitol Office: 331 Hart Bldg. 20510; 224-2854.

In Washington: Dixon's steady rise in Illinois politics was based on tried-and-true maxims of electoral success: Cultivate your base, avoid divisive issues and show voters they are getting their share of government largess. His nickname — "Al the Pal" — came to summarize both his genial personality and his ability to deliver roads, sewers, jobs or government checks for constituents.

He has followed the same path in the Senate. His intellect is not dazzling, and only occasionally does he champion a broad policy initiative. But he has mastered the small devices of political life in the Senate as thoroughly as he did in Springfield. While he may appear less often on television talk shows than some other senators, he has few peers in the art of cutting deals, giving and demanding favors and even, when the occasion requires it, bringing business to a halt in order to get what he wants.

One of the more informal and accessible senators, he spends much of his time in Washington meeting with a steady stream of Illinois visitors, from auto dealers and insurance agents to sheriffs and sanitation officials. His former Senate colleague, Charles H. Percy, once called him "wonderfully parochial," an observation Dixon repeats with pride.

But in the 101st Congress, Dixon's agenda could broaden — and in the nuts-and-bolts fashion he best understands. As the chief deputy whip, Dixon's task will be to build party coalitions. Until he began campaigning for the post, it was appointive. He persuaded each candidate running for majority leader to leave the decision to the Democratic Conference and then won the one-man election.

The position was mostly honorific under Dixon's predecessor, but the majority's new leadership structure has broadened its duties. Moreover, Dixon should complement the whip, Alan Cranston of California, a shrewd vote-counter whose other premier talent is fund raising, not coalition building.

Dixon showed a knack for the whip's job during the maneuvering preceding the Senate's rewrite of the Glass-Steagall Act, the legal wall built around commercial banks in 1933. Dixon played the go-between role on the Banking Committee, cheerleading, cajoling and encouraging a consensus among the disparate forces. At one point, he coaxed the key players into a room and told them to come out in an hour with a deal. They did.

Dixon's caution and ideology — specifically, his abundance of the former and lack of the latter — could help him bridge even broader party factions. On issues without an Illinois angle, his position often is unclear until late in the game. "Put Dixon down as a man who votes for every one separately and makes up his mind on that one," Dixon once told a reporter after voting uncharacteristically against a contra-aid proposal in 1988.

Although he votes with liberal Democrats on some issues — particularly if they involve backing for government spending programs — he seems most comfortable in the political center, both from personal conviction and from the belief that that is where the action is. "I happen to think that those of us who are moderates, who are centrists, most often make the difference," he says. This independence, a reflection in part of being one of only two Democrats elected to the Senate in 1980, has translated into a voting record not always in line with his party — a luxury that could end with his move into the leadership.

Dixon acts with abandon when Illinois is the issue, even in minor ways. In 1987, he asked the majority leader to hold open the confirmation vote for Transportation Secretary Jim Burnley until he returned to Washington; he wanted to go on record in favor of Burnley, who had promised to help solve some Illinois problems. In 1988, he worked against legislation to set in motion military base closings without congressional approval. He won a modification that allowed the Congress to reject *in toto* the recommendations of a special base-closing commission. He correctly foresaw that Illinois would lose thousands of jobs. And when the 101st Congress opened, the mayor of Rantoul, Ill., looked on as Dixon in a hearing called the town's loss of a base and jobs nothing less than "an American tragedy."

Illinois interests were also apparent in Dixon's vigorous defense of the futures industry following the stock market crash of 1987. Chicago is home to the world's largest futures markets.

Beyond the local realm, Dixon has constantly championed line-item veto power for the president and, of late, a series of regional presidential primaries.

Dixon lobbied hard in 1983 to win a vacant seat on the Armed Services Committee. His efforts paid off, bringing him the first Illinois place on the committee in years. He now chairs the subcommittee that authorizes the largest portion of the defense budget, and he makes vigorous use of that position to obtain more defense spending for Illinois. Defense contractors who seek his aid are firmly reminded about the great capacities of his state's subcontractors.

Dixon's interest in the mechanics of defense spending extends beyond the narrow scope of Illinois' interests, however. He played an active role pushing proposals in 1986 to impose tighter controls on the Pentagon's system for buying weapons, notably by establishing a "procurement czar" to oversee all aspects of weapons purchasing. In the 100th Congress, he tried to give the position line authority over procurement chiefs in the services.

Dixon also has done some personal weapons testing. He wedged himself into the tight confines of an M-48 tank one day to try out the controversial DIVAD anti-aircraft gun. It was not a happy moment for the project's promoters, however: One gun jammed and Dixon could not bring down the target with the other, despite repeated tries. "This is not the gun," Dixon said, and soon after that, the Defense Department killed it.

Dixon had even sharper things to say about the Pentagon in 1985, when Defense Secretary Caspar W. Weinberger announced that the department had an extra $4 billion in its accounts left over from inflation adjustments given them in previous years. Outraged by the apparent deception, Dixon denounced defense officials. "They treat us like the adversary," he complained. The Senate quickly adopted Dixon's amendment requiring the department to report regularly to Congress on any accumulated excess funds.

But nothing makes him madder than an attempt to cut Illinois out of some federal benefits. When a highway bill arrived on the Senate floor in 1984 with a provision that would have cost Illinois $30 million in federal funds, Dixon staged a filibuster that left other senators sputtering in frustration over the threat to their own states' highway money. The filibuster was easily quashed, but at the price of a compromise retaining the Illinois money.

In the long run, Dixon wants to protect the interests of Illinois and other Frost Belt states through passage of legislation guaranteeing that each state receive at least 90 cents in federal spending for every dollar paid by its citizens in federal taxes.

In 1986, Dixon found himself at loggerheads with most of the Senate over Illinois' share of the agricultural export market. Shipping and farm interests were trying to overcome their longstanding conflict over federal "cargo preference" laws requiring export of commodities in U.S.-flag vessels. Their compromise amendment to the farm bill stirred up the wrath of Dixon, who feared that it would result in reductions in shipping through the Great Lakes. Working with Minnesota Republican Rudy Boschwitz, Dixon sought to block proceedings by offering a long series of amendments. Their efforts resulted in a face-saving compromise encouraging continuation of existing Great Lakes shipping levels.

At Home: Dixon's election to the Senate in 1980 lifted him out of a 30-year concentration on the nuts and bolts of Illinois politics into the broader forum he coveted but waited patiently to seek.

His background was something of a liability in his Senate contest, since he started out unfamiliar with major national issues. But by studying, holding press conferences and agreeing to debate his GOP opponent, Dixon erased the notion that he was a lightweight.

Democratic Sen. Adlai E. Stevenson III had chosen not to run for re-election in 1980, and Democrats turned to Dixon for one reason: He was a champion vote-getter. In his two races for the secretary of state's office, he led the state ticket, winning a phenomenal 74 percent in 1978. In his 1980 Senate primary, Dixon swamped Alex Seith, who had given GOP Sen. Charles H. Percy a strong challenge in 1978.

The favorite for the GOP nomination had been state Attorney General William J. Scott, but he became entangled in a long trial on income-tax evasion charges. So the GOP chose Lt. Gov. David E. O'Neal.

Although he was the No. 2 official in Illinois, O'Neal labored in the obscurity that usually accompanies the office of lieutenant governor. To shore up his name identity, he began running commercials in late summer introducing himself to the voters. But Dixon's higher name recognition, his personal popularity and his efforts to show himself as a substantive candidate kept him in the lead.

Dixon's victory came in part because he has always managed to stay on good terms with the Chicago Democratic organization without being seen as a creature of it. This mixture of cooperation and independence earned him support from a broad spectrum of Illinois voters and brought him few enemies. It served him well in 1980, when bitter fighting broke out in the Chicago organization between Mayor Jane Byrne and Richard M. Daley, son of the late mayor. Both factions supported Dixon.

As 1986 drew near, Illinois Republicans went through a long public search for a candidate to oppose Dixon. The list of possibilities who bowed out included several House members, former Secretary of Defense Donald Rumsfeld and popular Illinois Secretary of State Jim Edgar. Former Rep. Tom Corcoran ran briefly and then — when he did not get the party's unified backing — dropped out.

In the end, the GOP nominated state Rep. Judy Koehler, a downstate conservative with a gadfly's role in the Legislature. She adopted the same posture during the campaign. She started off by running an ad labeling Dixon a "wimp" for remaining on the Democratic ticket with two statewide candidates allied with Lyndon H. LaRouche Jr. who had won their nominations in a fluke. Then she made an issue of an article Dixon had written for *Playboy* magazine on terrorism. "The women of Illinois," she said, "have been insulted and disgraced."

But Koehler made little headway. The establishment wing of the GOP was clearly uncomfortable with her, and though Republicans had once hoped to take advantage of disarray in Democratic ranks caused by the LaRouche imbroglio, the party never gave Koehler its wholehearted support. Dixon took advantage of the disunity to make direct appeals to moderate Republicans, and he wound up winning 90 of the state's 102 counties.

Committees

Armed Services (6th of 11 Democrats)
Readiness, Sustainability and Support (chairman); Conventional Forces and Alliance Defense; Projection Forces and Regional Defense

Banking, Housing and Urban Affairs (5th of 12 Democrats)
Consumer and Regulatory Affairs (chairman); International Finance and Monetary Policy

Small Business (5th of 10 Democrats)
Government Contracting and Paperwork Reduction (chairman); Rural Economy and Family Farming

Elections

1986 General		
Alan J. Dixon (D)	2,033,926	(65%)
Judy Koehler (R)	1,053,793	(34%)
1986 Primary		
Alan J. Dixon (D)	720,571	(85%)
Sheila Jones (D)	129,474	(15%)

Previous Winning Percentage: **1980** (56%)

Campaign Finance

	Receipts	Receipts from PACs	Expenditures
1986			
Dixon (D)	$2,219,982	$984,408 (44%)	$1,928,750
Koehler (R)	$871,586	$74,178 (9%)	$851,305

Key Votes

1987	
Enact omnibus highway bill over Reagan veto	Y
Limit testing of space-based anti-ballistic missiles	Y
Oppose banning tests of larger nuclear weapons	Y
Confirm Robert H. Bork as Supreme Court justice	N
1988	
Allow vote on campaign-finance overhaul	Y
Pass civil rights restoration bill over Reagan veto	Y
Enact omnibus trade bill over Reagan veto	Y
Approve death penalty for drug-related murders	Y
Oppose "workfare" amendment to welfare overhaul bill	N

Voting Studies

	Presidential Support		Party Unity		Conservative Coalition	
Year	**S**	**O**	**S**	**O**	**S**	**O**
1988	56	32	60	30	89	11
1987	41	55	75	23	84	16
1986	51	46	62	36	59	38
1985	46	50	69	29	50	47
1984	42	45	56	35	49	38
1983	54	41	70	26	55	43
1982	45	50	76	20	39	54
1981	57	41	73	26	57	38

Interest Group Ratings

Year	ADA	ACU	AFL-CIO	CCUS
1988	45	44	69	57
1987	60	20	80	41
1986	65	43	80	58
1985	60	41	81	43
1984	70	27	64	58
1983	60	29	76	32
1982	80	39	88	33
1981	65	20	61	61

Paul Simon (D)

Of Makanda — Elected 1984

Born: Nov. 29, 1928, Eugene, Ore.
Education: Attended U. of Oregon, 1945-46; Dana College, 1946-48.
Military Career: Army, 1951-53.
Occupation: Author; newspaper publisher.
Family: Wife, Jeanne Hurley; two children.
Religion: Lutheran.
Political Career: Ill. House, 1955-63; Ill. Senate, 1963-69; Ill. lieutenant governor, 1969-73; U.S. House, 1975-85; sought Democratic nomination for governor, 1972; sought Democratic nomination for president, 1988.
Capitol Office: 462 Dirksen Bldg. 20510; 224-2152.

In Washington: Simon spent his first year in the Senate getting established, his second raising the banner of New Deal liberalism. His third and fourth years were dominated by his campaign for president. Now the question is whether, by sticking to his knitting in 1989 and 1990, he can persuade Illinois voters to give him a second term.

If they do, Simon now tells interviewers, he is "very unlikely" to run for president again in 1992 — even though he says most of the rest of the 1988 Democratic field will try again.

Simon's 1988 bid sputtered out after he received just 5 percent of the Democratic primary vote in Wisconsin. The highlight had been his home state's primary, which he won despite having to share favorite-son status with the Rev. Jesse Jackson.

Simon's close-second finish in the Iowa precinct caucuses that began the nomination process suggested he might have gone much further than he did. He returns to this point repeatedly in his most recent book, "Winners and Losers," a personal account of the 1988 campaign. In the end, though, Simon looked rather quixotic in his quest. He garnered about 1 million votes and 170.5 delegates (by The Associated Press' count), but most of both came from Illinois. He never raised the money the multi-state Super Tuesday primaries required. And his unreconstructed traditional approach, apparently pitched to lunch-bucket voters, ironically showed more appeal among liberals in affluent suburbs and academic communities.

Simon was the candidate most willing to embrace his party and its history ("I am a not a neo-anything; I am a Democrat"), but his promises of a balanced budget struck many as lacking the detail to be credible. The man who seemed in many ways the editorial writer's ideal was hampered by the quick-hit nature of a national campaign, which made some of his own prescriptions seem facile.

Still, Simon can look to the record and the rectitude that sustained him through three decades of state politics, culminating in his Senate victory in 1984. And he has shown every sign of paying all the back-home attention one state can stand during the 101st Congress.

Serving on four committees helped Simon get back in the flow once he folded his presidential tent. Weighing in on issues as disparate as abortion rules, minimum wage, long-term health care, postal improvements and sanctions against Panama and South Africa, Simon exploited the full range of a senator's opportunities. Just as important, he was attending to impending military base closings in Illinois and chronicling it all in the weekly columns he produces for local newspapers.

Simon's predominant interest during his House career was federal aid to education, and he remains active in that area from his seat on the Labor and Human Resources Committee.

When the committee debated a bill to reauthorize the Higher Education Act in the 99th Congress, Simon promoted a number of causes, including aid to historically black colleges and a new limited program of federal support for graduate students — having more success with the former than the latter.

When Democrat Edward M. Kennedy took the Labor and Human Resources chair in 1987 and held hearings to explore policy initiatives, Simon voiced the harshest criticisms of Education Secretary William J. Bennett. Comparing Bennett unfavorably with his predecessor, Terrel H. Bell, Simon said, "He fought for every dollar he could get for education.... You're leading the retreat instead of the charge."

Simon's positions on a wide range of other issues reveal his belief that government should be active in social services at home and restrained in military activities abroad. He has advocated an expanded federal role in overseeing the insurance industry, hoping to discourage price-fixing that gouges consumers; he called for tighter accounting of U.S. aid to the Nicaraguan contras well before the Iran-contra arms scandal surfaced.

Many liberals were surprised when Simon in 1986 joined the fight for a constitutional amendment to balance the budget. But Simon was acting in character. He has an aversion to red ink that you might expect from someone who got his start in business, running a small-town southern Illinois newspaper. Doing nothing in the face of mounting deficits, he once wrote, is "a policy of folly," similar to 1920s policies that led to the Great Depression.

Before throwing in with the conservatives on the balanced-budget amendment, Simon got them to include language specifying that a tax increase to erase the deficit could be approved by a simple majority vote in each chamber. And he later added a provision requiring the president to submit a balanced budget to Congress, something President Reagan had failed to do. Those "sweeteners" persuaded a number of skeptical Democrats to support the amendment, which fell one vote short of the two-thirds majority required for Senate approval.

Despite his self-identification as a forthright liberal, former journalist Simon sometimes goes out of his way to see both sides of a story. This trait, added to his natural politeness, has sometimes prompted exasperated colleagues to express dissatisfaction with his leadership skills.

In 1986, Simon was chastised by liberals for supporting Reagan's nomination of Sidney A. Fitzwater to be a federal district judge, even though Fitzwater once had posted signs in black-majority wards warning voters that they could be prosecuted for election fraud. Liberals saw Fitzwater as insensitive to minorities, and they expected help from Simon, who had been designated by Judiciary Committee Democrats as the point man for monitoring the fitness of judicial nominees.

Simon would later help lead the opposition to Robert H. Bork's nomination to the Supreme Court. But while he called Fitzwater's sign-posting a mistake, he said he saw no "pattern of racism." After that, many squeamish moderates felt they could go along. Fitzwater was approved, 52-42.

At Home: Other senators who have run for president have suffered for making their states feel neglected. During the campaign months of 1987 and 1988, Simon was singed in headlines as "Senator No-Show" when his attendance for votes deteriorated. His ratings from some interest groups, such as the Americans for Democratic Action, fell off because he missed the votes they counted.

Among the candidates often mentioned as a 1990 challenger to Simon is Rep. Lynn Martin of Rockford, who has found the House GOP leadership ladder crowded above her.

Because Simon had been a popular figure in Illinois politics for many years, his 1984 campaign against GOP Sen. Charles H. Percy was a battle of political equals, not a challenge by an upstart House member.

Despite three terms in the Senate, Percy had never won an intensely loyal following. His image as an aloof and somewhat aristocratic business executive did not sit well with many voters; only his moderate GOP politics allowed him to outflank the more conservative Chicago Democrats who twice challenged him.

By the beginning of 1984, however, Percy was under fire from all sides — conservatives thought him too liberal, liberals disliked his support of the Reagan administration, and rank-and-file voters thought he ignored their state in favor of his role as Senate Foreign Relations chairman.

Simon was the best known of the four Democrats who wanted to run against Percy in 1984. As lieutenant governor in the late 1960s and early 1970s, he had built a favorable reformist image that voters still remembered with affection. Simon had strong support from organized labor, especially in the downstate counties, and that helped him pull in a majority of the vote there. Together with solid backing in Chicago's liberal lakefront wards and suburban areas, he took the nomination with 36 percent.

Percy had staved off a conservative primary challenge with an ad campaign stressing that he was "the Illinois advantage" in Washington, and he carried that theme into the general election. Breaking with his history of centrist re-election politics, he also cast himself as a conservative defender of the Reagan administration and painted Simon as "ultraliberal."

Percy needed to keep intact the unwieldy coalition that had elected him three times before — blacks, suburbanites, independents in general, and the hard-core conservative GOP vote downstate. It was not possible, even in a year when Reagan won Illinois comfortably.

Percy carried the suburbs and most downstate counties, but by margins far smaller than Reagan's. Meanwhile, Simon benefited from a heavy vote in both the black and white ethnic wards of Chicago. Combining that strength with a more than respectable showing downstate, Simon edged Percy.

Illinois was also good to Simon in 1988, giving him a temporary lift after his dismal showings in the early presidential primaries failed to establish him as a contender. He won Illinois' primary with 43 percent, outrunning Jackson, who had 31 percent, and dealing a setback to eventual nominee Michael S. Dukakis, who finished a distant third. Under Illinois' modified winner-take-all system, Simon earned nearly 80 percent of the state's delegates to the Democratic National Convention.

However, Simon's campaign quickly fell back to Earth, and even his Illinois win had fallout with long-term implications. When it became obvious that Simon would have to quit the presidential campaign, Jackson supporters urged him to withdraw before the June state Democratic convention so that Jackson, the primary runner-up, could lay claim to his Illinois delegates. But Simon chose merely to suspend his campaign, enabling his home-state loyalists to cinch their trips to Atlanta.

Simon assured black leaders that his actions were intended simply to guarantee his own supporters of delegate slots, but some black leaders accused him of being a stalking horse for Dukakis (whom most of the Simon delegates eventually backed) and of being part of a stop-Jackson movement. Though the conflicting parties publicly buried the hatchet by the time of the Democratic convention, Simon may have to go to some lengths to reignite the enthusiasm of Chicago's black leadership in 1990.

Simon first made a name for himself as editor of the *Troy Tribune* in southern Illinois in the early 1950s, crusading against vice and political corruption in Madison and St. Clair counties. In 1954, at the age of 25, he decided to take advantage of the standing he had earned and run for the Illinois House himself. With an intensive door-to-door campaign, he drew more votes than two organization-backed incumbents in the Democratic primary. Eight years later he went on to the state Senate, where he established impeccable reform credentials.

In 1968, Democratic leaders picked him as their candidate for lieutenant governor, hoping that his reform reputation would help a state ticket struggling against reported scandal and an expected Republican tide. The gubernatorial and Senate candidates lost, but Simon won, and immediately became the premier Democratic officeholder in the state and heir apparent to the 1972 gubernatorial nomination.

Things did not work out as planned. A wealthy corporate lawyer challenged him with a populist campaign, convincing voters that Simon was a tool of Mayor Richard J. Daley's Chicago Democrats — even though the Daley machine was clinging to Simon, rather than the other way around. Simon lost, and taught political science for two years at a Springfield college.

In 1974, however, the southern 24th District was made available by retirement. Simon ran, and although the district was south of his old home base, was favored from the start. He won easily, and was re-elected routinely in every year except 1980, when Reagan's popularity boosted Simon's opponent.

Committees

Budget (7th of 13 Democrats)

Foreign Relations (7th of 10 Democrats)
African Affairs (chairman); European Affairs

Judiciary (7th of 8 Democrats)
Constitution (chairman); Antitrust, Monopolies and Business Rights; Immigration and Refugee Affairs

Labor and Human Resources (6th of 9 Democrats)
Employment and Productivity (chairman); Education, Arts and Humanities; Handicapped

Elections

1984 General		
Paul Simon (D)	2,397,303	(50%)
Charles H. Percy (R)	2,308,039	(48%)
1984 Primary		
Paul Simon (D)	556,757	(36%)
Roland W. Burris (D)	360,182	(23%)
Alex Seith (D)	327,125	(21%)
Philip J. Rock (D)	303,397	(19%)
Gerald M. Rose (D)	17,985	(1%)

Previous Winning Percentages: **1982 *** (66%) **1980 *** (49%) **1978 *** (66%) **1976 *** (67%) **1974 *** (60%)

* *House elections.*

Campaign Finance

	Receipts	Receipts from PACs	Expend-itures
1984			
Simon (D)	$4,586,036	$907,762 (20%)	$4,578,703
Percy (R)	$5,331,736	$1,090,872 (20%)	$5,296,561

Key Votes

1987	
Enact omnibus highway bill over Reagan veto	Y
Limit testing of space-based anti-ballistic missiles	?
Oppose banning tests of larger nuclear weapons	-
Confirm Robert H. Bork as Supreme Court justice	N
1988	
Allow vote on campaign-finance overhaul	Y
Pass civil rights restoration bill over Reagan veto	Y
Enact omnibus trade bill over Reagan veto	Y
Approve death penalty for drug-related murders	N
Oppose "workfare" amendment to welfare overhaul bill	Y

Voting Studies

	Presidential Support		Party Unity		Conservative Coalition	
Year	**S**	**O**	**S**	**O**	**S**	**O**
1988	31	42	70	1	0	54
1987	6	32	49	2	6	22
1986	19	78	89	11	13	86
1985	25	67	89	4	10	78
House Service						
1984	12	31	42	3	7	44
1983	15	59	74	4	17	56
1982	31	56	81	4	16	73
1981	36	59	76	11	28	64

Interest Group Ratings

Year	ADA	ACU	AFL-CIO	CCUS
1988	85	0	91	42
1987	35	0	100	13
1986	80	9	80	32
1985	85	5	95	34
House Service				
1984	45	13	100	67
1983	70	0	100	18
1982	75	6	95	15
1981	75	0	79	12

1 Charles A. Hayes (D)

Of Chicago — Elected 1983

Born: Feb. 17, 1918, Cairo, Ill.
Education: High school graduate.
Occupation: Labor official; packinghouse worker.
Family: Wife, Edna J. Miller; two children, two stepchildren.
Religion: Baptist.
Political Career: No previous office.
Capitol Office: 1028 Longworth Bldg. 20515; 225-4372.

In Washington: Hayes spent nearly 50 years on the front lines of the labor movement in Illinois, and it shows. A burly, blunt-spoken man, he approaches his House work with the moral certainty that characterized most of his fellow Depression-era union organizers. "I do not have a problem of delineating justice from injustice or right from wrong," he once said on the House floor.

Early in the 101st Congress, Hayes felt he was the victim of injustice when he lost to a less-senior Democrat in his bid for a seat on the Post Office and Civil Service Committee. Democrat Paul E. Kanjorski, the candidate of Pennsylvania colleague and power broker John P. Murtha, won the post. It was the second time Hayes had lost a Post Office bid to a member with less seniority: In 1987, Ohio freshman Thomas C. Sawyer beat him out.

Hayes, who said in 1989 that he had enough votes "until they got behind closed doors," says race was a factor in his defeat. "You have to be part of the 'in' crowd, and I feel that there was a little racism involved," he said. "When you meet all of the other requirements, what else could it be?"

The activist fervor Hayes developed while organizing packinghouse workers in Chicago did not mellow when he began his second career as a House member at age 65. An outspoken opponent of South Africa's apartheid policies, Hayes was one of the first members of Congress arrested for picketing that country's embassy in Washington. He was 40 years older than most of those with him on the picket line.

Hayes boasts proudly of his 100 percent lifetime House vote rating from the AFL-CIO. He devotes much time to Education and Labor, pumping for federal aid to the poor.

In the 99th Congress, Hayes proposed a bill to provide state and local governments with $50 million over three years for projects aimed at reducing school dropout rates. The bill stalled in the Senate, but in the 100th Congress, he added it to the omnibus education bill during Elementary Education Subcommittee consideration. It was later signed into law.

One of Hayes' pet proposals is his Income and Jobs Action bill. The measure, which aims to revive the goals of the Employment Act of 1946 and the Humphrey-Hawkins full-employment act of 1978, affirms that "every American citizen is entitled to a job at decent wages." But a provision to transfer 1 percent of the defense budget to programs aimed at full employment has kept the bill from going very far. "What our country needs today," Hayes said in 1987, "is a sufficient equivalent to our military spending" to alleviate unemployment.

In 1989, Hayes was one of 48 members to vote to keep the 51 percent congressional pay raise.

At Home: Hayes' election in mid-1983 provided one of the first signs of strain within the coalition that elected Democrat Harold Washington — Hayes' predecessor in the 1st District — as Chicago's first black mayor.

An international vice president of the United Food and Commercial Workers Union, Hayes was a longtime friend of Washington and helped organize the strong union backing that was crucial to Washington's victory.

Two other prominent supporters of Washington also wanted to replace him in the House — Lu Palmer, a radio commentator and community activist, and Al Raby, a veteran civil rights leader. Palmer was Hayes' chief threat; his 12 years of broadcast exposure were tough to match. Palmer's constituency was among the poorest in the 1st — those in public-housing projects. His organizing in the projects was as much responsible for Washington's mayoral triumph as Hayes' work with the unions.

While Washington's endorsement gave Hayes crucial backing from South Side Democratic wards, the turnout of Palmer's supporters was poor. Hayes won 45 percent in the 14-way primary and has been easily re-elected since.

Hayes' involvement with unions began in the late 1930s. A machine operator in Cairo, Ill., he helped organize a carpenters' local and was elected its president. Later, he organized the 3,500 workers in a Chicago meatpacking plant into a United Packinghouse Workers local, which forced elimination of worker segregation and discriminatory employment practices.

Illinois 1

Chicago — South Side

The 1st contains the heart of Chicago's black South Side — an area that has been important in local politics since the 1920s, before most Northern cities even had substantial black populations. It took on added significance in the early 1980s, as the political base for black political leader Harold Washington. After winning two elections as 1st District House member, Washington was elected in 1983 as Chicago's first black mayor. He died shortly after his re-election in 1987.

Although the 1st is a very poor area, with the decaying buildings common to inner cities everywhere, it also has had a stable black middle class. In the 1960s, when blacks on the more transient West Side rioted, this area was quiet.

Before World War II, most of the city's black population was concentrated here, just west of the wealthy residential areas on the Lake Michigan shore. But in recent years, as racial barriers fell in other parts of the city and its southern suburbs, many have left the South Side. The 1st lost 20 percent of its people in the 1970s.

The 1st is overwhelmingly Democratic. More than 90 percent of its residents are black, and its small white population, centered around the University of Chicago, is nearly as Democratic as the black majority.

Some of the district's middle-class professionals live around the Michael Reese Hospital complex on the district's northern border. Others live in Chatham, which established itself as a prosperous black residential neighborhood in the 1950s. Blue-collar workers profited for years from good-paying jobs at the steel mills of South Chicago; that industry's decline has caused economic hardship.

Many of the district's poorer black residents live in public-housing projects, buildings seen as enlightened urban renewal when built in the 1950s but now derided as "vertical ghettos." One, the Robert Taylor Homes, is the country's largest such project.

Population: 519,045. White 33,477 (6%), Black 477,790 (92%), Other 4,077 (1%). Spanish origin 5,467 (1%). 18 and over 358,925 (69%), 65 and over 53,927 (10%). Median age: 28.

Committees

Education and Labor (11th of 22 Democrats)
Elementary, Secondary and Vocational Education; Labor-Management Relations; Labor Standards; Postsecondary Education

Small Business (16th of 27 Democrats)
SBA, the General Economy and Minority Enterprise Development

Elections

1988 General		
Charles A. Hayes (D)	164,125	(96%)
Stephen J. Evans (R)	6,753	(4%)
1988 Primary		
Charles A. Hayes (D)	97,168	(87%)
Inez M. Gardner (D)	13,930	(13%)
1986 General		
Charles A. Hayes (D)	122,376	(96%)
Joseph C. Faulkner (R)	4,572	(4%)

Previous Winning Percentages: **1984** (96%) **1983 *** (94%)

* *Special election.*

District Vote For President

	1988		1984		1980		1976	
D	174,793	(95%)	196,351	(94%)	177,491	(91%)	188,194	(90%)
R	7,168	(4%)	10,153	(5%)	10,912	(6%)	20,620	(10%)
I					3,991	(2%)		

Campaign Finance

	Receipts	Receipts from PACs	Expend-itures
1988			
Hayes (D)	$161,960	$115,634 (71%)	$156,905
1986			
Hayes (D)	$147,286	$83,475 (57%)	$113,459

Key Votes

1987	
Raise speed limit to 65 mph	N
Approve Gephardt "fair trade" amendment	Y
Ban testing of larger nuclear weapons	Y
Delay "re-flagging" of Kuwaiti tankers	Y
Approve tax-raising deficit-reduction bill	Y
1988	
Approve aid to Nicaraguan contras	N
Enact civil rights restoration bill over Reagan veto	Y
Kill 60-day plant-closing notification measure	N
Pass omnibus trade bill over Reagan veto	Y
Approve death penalty for drug-related murders	N
Bar federal funds for abortions in cases of rape and incest	N
Oppose seven-day waiting period for purchase of handguns	N

Voting Studies

	Presidential Support		Party Unity		Conservative Coalition	
Year	S	O	S	O	S	O
1988	14	80	91	3	3	95
1987	10	90	95	2	2	98
1986	13	84	89	5	4	92
1985	15	84	93	1	4	93
1984	19	80	93	4	2	97
1983	7†	86†	87†	7†	9†	85†

† *Not eligible for all recorded votes.*

Interest Group Ratings

Year	ADA	ACU	AFL-CIO	CCUS
1988	95	0	100	14
1987	100	0	100	7
1986	95	0	100	6
1985	100	0	100	14
1984	100	4	100	38
1983	—	0	100	22

2 Gus Savage (D)

Of Chicago — Elected 1980

Born: Oct. 30, 1925, Detroit, Mich.
Education: Roosevelt U., B.A. 1951; graduate work in political science, 1952; attended Chicago-Kent College of Law, 1952-53.
Military Career: Army, 1943-46.
Occupation: Newspaper publisher.
Family: Widowed; two children.
Religion: Baptist.
Political Career: Sought Democratic nomination for U.S. House, 1968 and 1970.
Capitol Office: 1121 Longworth Bldg. 20515; 225-0773.

In Washington: A subcommittee chairman on Public Works, Savage is now positioned to be an influential member of an establishment he viscerally distrusts. But his growing seniority has not significantly tempered his style. "It is plumb foolish," Savage once said, "to depend on legislation from a white Congress to provide for black liberation."

Heading toward his 10th year in Congress, Savage still tries to advance his civil rights agenda mainly through angry denunciations of racial inequities. Most questions of his style or agenda are turned back as "racist," and he seems to disdain blacks pursuing more traditional paths to power.

When Democratic Party Chairman Ron Brown, who is black, said in 1989 that he would appear in Chicago with white Democratic mayoral candidate Richard M. Daley, who faced a black third-party foe, Savage attacked Brown: "When Ron Brown brings his Oreo you-know-what into Chicago, I'll guarantee I'm going to help organize a reception party for him at the airport and follow him all the way to some white hotel to denounce his coming in."

Savage's fiery rhetoric ensures him plenty of headlines. At the 1988 Democratic convention, he led a protest march against the vice presidential nomination of Lloyd Bentsen, whom Savage labeled a "reactionary Reaganite warhawk." Giving the keynote address at a Nation of Islam convention in 1985, he likened controversial Black Muslim leader Louis Farrakhan to the Rev. Dr. Martin Luther King Jr. and described black liberation in the 1980s as "not integration ... but getting our rock — not small, individual pieces of their rock."

Although his weekly column, which appears in many black newspapers, gives Savage a large audience, his effectiveness inside the House is restricted by his temperament and rhetoric. In the 99th Congress, Savage did win House approval of an amendment to reserve 10 percent of the military procurement budget for minority contractors, but it was not an amendment House conferees were willing to fight for. The result was a non-binding goal of 5 percent.

Considering Savage's penchant for getting attention, the Public Works Economic Development Subcommittee that he chairs has been notably quiet. He took over the panel at the start of the 100th Congress, and is credited with having a staff strong enough to script most proceedings. One of the few bills the subcommittee steered to House approval in the 100th Congress was a minor economic-development package. The House had approved similar measures in each of the previous three Congresses, knowing Senate action was unlikely.

A real measure of Savage's goals — and congressional tolerance of his style — could come if his seniority on Public Works would enable him to assume a more powerful chairmanship. There was some concern that he could take the Aviation Subcommittee at the start of the 101st Congress, but the more senior James L. Oberstar of Minnesota opted for the chairmanship.

On his other committee, Small Business, Savage tested his welcome when he provoked a shouting match with Chairman John J. LaFalce over legislation to revamp a federal program to foster minority business development.

At a 1987 meeting of Procurement Subcommittee Democrats to negotiate the final details of the overhaul, Savage angrily called the LaFalce plan a disaster. LaFalce, in turn, accused Savage of sending people to his Buffalo district to campaign against him, to which Savage replied that he did not need to send anyone — he would gladly campaign against LaFalce himself. As the dispute escalated, the committee's two black freshmen, Floyd H. Flake of New York and Kweisi Mfume of Maryland, sought to calm Savage. A deal that met with unanimous approval was ultimately worked out.

Late in 1988, Savage got some unwelcome publicity when allegations arose that his son Thomas was on the payroll of Washington, D.C., Del. Walter E. Fauntroy while the younger

Illinois 2

South Side Chicago; Harvey

The 2nd does not have the rich political history of its neighboring South Side district, which elected the nation's first black congressman of this century more than 50 years ago. Created only in 1971, the 2nd was represented by a white Democrat for eight years, even after its population was majority-black. Savage's election in 1980 marked its emergence as a black constituency.

Roughly U-shaped, the 2nd takes in Chicago's Far South Side and several of the southern Cook County suburbs. Blacks, both urban and suburban, make up more than two-thirds of the population. Harvey, an older industrial city, and Dixmoor, a suburb, are about two-thirds black. Phoenix, a village of about 3,000, has been nearly all-black for the past 60 years.

The traditional economic base of the district is the vast industrial area around the Calumet River, where the sky, trees and grass long have been blackened with soot, but where factory workers could count on steady work and decent pay. These days the grass is still gray, but the mills are hulking shadows of their former selves.

The 2nd does have some middle-class black neighborhoods, toward its southern end and along its western fork, around Morgan Park. Unable to shake Savage's hold on lower-income voters, his primary challengers tend to focus their efforts here.

The Chicago portion of the district contains the 2nd's most politically significant white presence, although "white flight" has lowered it since the early 1970s. Chicago's 10th Ward, an ethnic blue-collar bastion near Lake Calumet, is the political base for Edward R. Vrdolyak, the former Cook County Democratic chairman who made a celebrated switch to the Republican Party. His efforts to galvanize an ethnic white surge to the GOP, of no great success citywide, have had no effect whatsoever on the black Democratic dominance in the 2nd; Savage's worries cease at the end of his Democratic primary campaigns.

The district's white suburban territory includes Riverdale and parts of Dolton and Calumet City, all blue-collar and less than 10 percent black in 1980. Many of the people here moved out from the Far South Side of the city in the past two decades.

Population: 518,931. White 131,211 (25%), Black 364,584 (70%). Spanish origin 38,249 (7%). 18 and over 340,827 (66%), 65 and over 35,955 (7%). Median age: 26.

Savage was living in Chicago, a violation of House rules.

In July 1989, Savage again appeared in news headlines — this time for allegedly sexually assaulting a Peace Corps volunteer during an official visit to Zaire in March. Three House Democrats asked the ethics committee to look into the allegations, which Savage denied.

At Home: Savage has faced fierce primary opposition in each of his five House campaigns from opponents who described him as an ineffective bully. But Savage has persevered in the mainly black 2nd District, with the support of a sizable core of voters who view him as a civil rights hero and a voice for the dispossessed.

Savage entered politics with a base derived from decades in the front lines of the civil rights movement. In the late 1940s he organized sit-ins protesting discrimination against blacks in the hiring of department store clerks. Two decades later, he helped organize a wildcat strike of black bus drivers aimed at ending union discrimination.

Turning his attention to politics, Savage fought the Democratic machine that ruled Chicago until the death of Mayor Richard J. Daley in 1976. Savage was active in the Chicago League of Negro Voters, the first organization of black "independents" that held itself apart from the regular Democratic organization. Savage concentrated on the South Side, whose growing black middle class sparked a political movement. In 1967, Savage and two other independent activists ran for alderman. The others won; Savage, who split the vote with another independent, did not. In 1968 and 1970 he tried for the House, losing to machine-backed candidates both times.

Several years later, Savage was in the forefront of efforts to persuade Democratic Rep. Harold Washington of Chicago to embark on a 1977 mayoral bid that foreshadowed his 1983 election as the city's first black mayor.

In 1980, Savage got his own opportunity, when Democratic Rep. Morgan F. Murphy retired. The machine had held the 2nd easily with Murphy, who was white, even though the district became majority-black in the 1970s. With Murphy's departure, the machine agreed to support a black successor, Reginald Brown. But many blacks resented having white party leaders handpick a candidate. As publisher of a chain of community newspapers and a longtime organization opponent, Savage had enough credibility to ride resentment over Brown's anointment to a primary victory, taking 45 percent of the vote.

In 1982 the machine challenged Savage with another black, Eugene M. Barnes, a former state legislator and Chicago Transit Authority chairman. Barnes said he could achieve more by working within the system than Savage did with his brash manner. A third candidate, state Rep. Monica Faith Stewart, was even harsher, stating that Savage had embarrassed the 2nd District by behaving like a "clown."

The organization failed to unite behind Barnes, partly because some precinct captains were unhappy with his delivery of patronage jobs as transit chairman. Stewart drew some anti-organization and anti-Savage voters, but Savage won renomination with 39 percent.

In 1984, Leon Davis, an executive with the People's Gas Company, ran a woefully unorganized campaign. But Savage's modest 44 percent victory convinced his critics that he remained vulnerable.

Two years later, Savage faced telephone company executive Raymond Arias, who drew Hispanic support, and the Rev. Al Sampson, a founder of the Chicago Council of Black Churches. But neither Arias nor Sampson could move beyond their bases of support, and Savage took just under 50 percent.

Finally, in 1988, Savage won a primary with a majority of the vote. He did so despite opposition from state Sen. Emil Jones and Mel Reynolds, a political consultant running on his own for the first time.

Jones had a sizable constituent base to draw on. But with his longtime ties to the Chicago Democratic organization, he was also vulnerable to Savage's portrayal of him as a "machine" candidate. Reynolds campaigned aggressively, touting his educational credentials — he was a Rhodes scholar — and winning endorsements from Chicago's two main daily papers. But Reynolds was not known by most district voters, and Jones' effort was lacking. Savage took 52 percent of the vote, besting Jones by better than 2-to-1 and Reynolds by nearly 4-to-1.

Committees

Public Works and Transportation (9th of 31 Democrats)
Economic Development (chairman); Public Buildings and Grounds; Surface Transportation; Water Resources

Small Business (10th of 27 Democrats)
SBA, the General Economy and Minority Enterprise Development

Elections

1988 General		
Gus Savage (D)	138,256	(83%)
William T. Hespel (R)	28,831	(17%)
1988 Primary		
Gus Savage (D)	56,405	(52%)
Emil Jones Jr. (D)	26,797	(25%)
Mel Reynolds (D)	14,641	(14%)
Niles Sherman (D)	5,688	(5%)
1986 General		
Gus Savage (D)	99,268	(84%)
Ron Taylor (R)	19,149	(16%)

Previous Winning Percentages: **1984** (83%) **1982** (87%) **1980** (88%)

District Vote For President

	1988	1984	1980	1976
D	150,387 (85%)	168,174 (83%)	151,227 (73%)	120,666 (73%)
R	25,896 (15%)	32,693 (16%)	47,347 (23%)	45,713 (27%)
I			4,853 (2%)	

Campaign Finance

	Receipts	Receipts from PACs	Expend- itures
1988			
Savage (D)	$240,244	$116,218 (48%)	$242,487
Hespel (R) †	$6,167	$220 (4%)	$6,392
1986			
Savage (D)	$153,332	$81,500 (53%)	$150,979

† Totals based on incomplete data.

Key Votes

1987	
Raise speed limit to 65 mph	N
Approve Gephardt "fair trade" amendment	Y
Ban testing of larger nuclear weapons	Y
Delay "re-flagging" of Kuwaiti tankers	Y
Approve tax-raising deficit-reduction bill	Y
1988	
Approve aid to Nicaraguan contras	N
Enact civil rights restoration bill over Reagan veto	Y
Kill 60-day plant-closing notification measure	N
Pass omnibus trade bill over Reagan veto	Y
Approve death penalty for drug-related murders	N
Bar federal funds for abortions in cases of rape and incest	N
Oppose seven-day waiting period for purchase of handguns	N

Voting Studies

	Presidential Support		Party Unity		Conservative Coalition	
Year	S	O	S	O	S	O
1988	18	72	82	4	5	92
1987	10	88	87	3	5	88
1986	14	80	79	4	2	90
1985	13	84	85	3	2	87
1984	15	70	76	5	0	85
1983	7	87	88	4	4	84
1982	17	62	63	7	8	77
1981	14	49	57	5	5	49

Interest Group Ratings

Year	ADA	ACU	AFL-CIO	CCUS
1988	100	0	100	23
1987	100	0	100	0
1986	95	0	100	7
1985	100	5	100	18
1984	95	5	91	36
1983	95	0	100	16
1982	75	12	94	26
1981	65	7	100	0

3 Marty Russo (D)

Of South Holland — Elected 1974

Born: Jan. 23, 1944, Chicago, Ill.
Education: DePaul U., B.A. 1965, J.D. 1967.
Occupation: Lawyer.
Family: Wife, Karen Jorgenson; two children.
Religion: Roman Catholic.
Political Career: Assistant Cook County state's attorney, 1971-73.
Capitol Office: 2233 Rayburn Bldg. 20515; 225-5736.

In Washington: Russo's boisterous and sometimes crude style has made it difficult for him to fight the perception that he is simply a political hack who speaks for his mentor, Ways and Means Chairman Dan Rostenkowski, and for a combination of Chicago business and labor interests. But if he seems to treat the House as an oversized college fraternity, he is nonetheless a serious legislator capable of thinking and acting on his own.

He paid an additional price for being cast as Rostenkowski's man when the House came to be run by Jim Wright of Texas, who viewed the Ways and Means chairman as one of his few potential rivals for the speakership.

Though Russo holds the post of deputy whip, leadership loyalists regard him with some suspicion. He is not always a reliable leadership ally: On some pivotal votes in the 100th Congress, Russo conspicuously strayed from the party line.

In the waning hours of the 1987 session, he voted against a governmentwide appropriations bill backed by the leadership, complaining that it went too far to accommodate the White House.

Then, after voting in early March 1988 for a bill overturning the Supreme Court's *Grove City* decision, which narrowed the scope of several civil rights laws, Russo three weeks later voted to sustain President Reagan's veto of the bill. He cited complaints from religious groups in his district.

And many members were irritated in late 1987 over Russo's handling of a controversial budget bill that linked spending cuts, tax increases and a welfare-reform bill. Russo headed the leadership task force rounding up votes to bring the package to the floor. When the House blocked the bill on a procedural vote, the leadership dropped the welfare provisions and brought it back to the floor. It passed by a one-vote margin — with Russo voting against it.

Russo said he felt undercut by the leadership's change in strategy and called the final product a "totally different animal" from the bill he had agreed to round up votes for. But it galled some Democrats who had been whipped into voting the party line — despite personal reservations and political risks — to see Russo voting against it because it didn't suit him.

Some members said that episode would hurt Russo in future efforts to round up votes. But he retains many of the attributes that have made him one of the most effective whips in the House. He has both persistence and a seat on Ways and Means, which gives him leverage with members looking for favors. Standing well over six feet, Russo also can be physically intimidating.

He cemented his reputation as a whip who takes his job seriously — some would say literally — one day in 1984 when the leadership was struggling to win approval of an amendment delaying MX-missile production. As the final seconds of the roll call ticked away, party strategists gathered around a computer terminal indicating defeat by one vote. Russo raced into the Democratic cloakroom, where he found Daniel K. Akaka of Hawaii, a usual leadership loyalist who had been recorded on the pro-MX side. Russo lifted Akaka out of a telephone booth and carried him onto the House floor, where he arrived at the rostrum and reversed himself just as the presiding officer was banging down the gavel. The amendment carried by one vote.

As would be expected of a Rostenkowski protégé on Ways and Means, Russo was very active in the effort to overhaul the tax code in the 99th Congress. But he was not just a follower. Early in 1985, before drafting began on the basic tax-revision bill, Russo joined with New York Democrat Charles E. Schumer in pushing a new 25 percent minimum tax on corporations and on wealthy individuals making over $100,000 per year. They argued that preventing the affluent from escaping taxation would reduce the deficit and make the tax code fairer. Initially, Russo seemed to feel that a minimum tax might be the only reform needed.

After Rostenkowski committed himself to a full rewrite of the code, however, Russo worked successfully to get the minimum tax included in the bill produced by Ways and

Illinois 3

Southwest Chicago and Suburbs

The line between the 2nd and 3rd districts is also the line between black and white Chicago. Russo's district, concentrated on the west side of Western Avenue and in the suburbs just beyond the city, was 92 percent white when it was drawn in the early 1980s.

The city portions of the 3rd are dominated by blue-collar ethnics, many of Polish and Lithuanian origin. But Beverly, traditional home for Chicago's well-to-do Irish Catholics, is also included.

Most of the ethnics here retain fond memories of Mayor Richard J. Daley's Democratic Party in Chicago. With Daley's death in 1976 and the election of a black mayor in 1983, the party began to lose strength: Ronald Reagan carried the Chicago portion of the district in 1984 and Bush did well there in 1988. However, the 1989 election of Cook County State's Attorney Richard M. Daley to fill the mayor's chair long owned by his late father may breathe new life into the remnants of the old Democratic organization.

The suburbs in the 3rd include Blue Island, developed for Illinois Central railroad workers, and Oak Lawn, a 19th-century suburb that now has a large Greek-American population. Midlothian and Oak Forest, built up in the 1960s, have drawn blue-collar workers from South Chicago. Most of the district's small black population is in Robbins, which has been majority-black for a generation, and Markham, which lost many of its white residents in the 1970s and is now about two-thirds black.

Russo lives in South Holland, which has a significant Dutch population but has also attracted Italians, Poles and others from Chicago's South Side. In many ways he is typical of the district. He grew up in an Italian neighborhood in the city and then lived in an apartment in Calumet Park before buying his South Holland home.

Many of the suburban ethnics became prosperous in the 1960s, when they left the city and began to vote Republican in some contests. The recessions of the 1970s shocked many of these people, threatening their fragile middle-class status. In 1974 the old 3rd District turned out Republican Rep. Robert Hanrahan for Russo, who has firmly established himself. But these communities have swung back and forth between the parties in state elections, while solidly favoring Republicans for president.

Population: 519,040. White 477,098 (92%), Black 29,518 (6%), Other 3,999 (1%). Spanish origin 18,049 (4%). 18 and over 379,396 (73%), 65 and over 65,329 (13%). Median age: 32.

Means, and then worked hard to get the entire package through the House.

Russo did differ with Rostenkowski on some provisions in the bill, but there was little doubt that his support could be counted on when needed. That loyalty enabled him to get a coveted spot on the House-Senate conference committee. It also gave Rostenkowski an ally who, if not the subtlest of legislators, is good at putting together coalitions when necessary.

There is no question that much of the work Russo does has a Chicago connection. During Ways and Means' efforts to cut Medicare costs in 1987, he was lead sponsor of an amendment backed by Illinois hospitals that would channel more money to industrial states. He said the change was needed to reflect regional variations in costs, but critics derided it as "pure pork."

But in addition to sponsoring limited-interest provisions aimed at helping important local allies, Russo also has been an activist on such issues as defense and gun control — subjects on which the only reason to participate is a genuine concern about national policy.

Russo has now reached the top ranks of the Budget Committee, where he is part of an aggressive bloc of young activist Democrats that includes Schumer. Those two have personal as well as political ties, sharing a house together in Washington along with California Democrats Leon E. Panetta, chairman of the Budget Committee, and George Miller, former member of the panel.

Russo is interested in arms control, and was highly critical of the defense buildup during the Reagan years. Those concerns led him to take a central role in the effort to oust Wisconsin Democrat Les Aspin as Armed Services chairman in the 100th Congress.

Angered by Aspin's support for the MX missile and the Nicaraguan contras, Russo, Miller and other activists worked to build a broad coalition behind Marvin Leath, a conservative Texas Democrat who had built up considerable good will on the Budget Committee.

The effort produced one startling but short-lived triumph. Early in January, the Democratic Caucus decided against Aspin in an up-or-down vote on his chairmanship, but the following week, when it came to a showdown between Aspin and Leath, the outcome was reversed and Aspin won a comfortable victory.

At Home: When Russo launched his House candidacy in 1974 in a district drawn to favor a Republican, his credentials seemed modest. He had served as president of the Young Democrats of Calumet Park, and was an assistant Cook County state's attorney from 1971 to 1973. Chosen by the Daley organization and unopposed for the nomination, he was looked upon as a long-shot candidate against freshman Republican Rep. Robert Hanrahan.

But he pulled off one of the sleeper upsets of 1974, coming from far behind in the closing weeks to surprise an overly confident incumbent who did little campaigning until mid-October. Russo had strong support from organized labor and the Cook County Democratic machine, and the advantage of the Watergate scandal, which contributed to a low Republican turnout.

With constituent service and good campaign skills, Russo has steadily boosted his margins since then. He won 64 percent in 1984 and 62 percent in 1988 despite the district's heavy vote for the Republican presidential candidates in those years.

Russo's career was briefly threatened in 1982 by redistricting and his cool relations with then-Chicago Mayor Jane M. Byrne. The 1981 remap shifted the balance of power in his district's Democratic organization to ward and township leaders allied with Byrne.

When party slatemakers met in early 1982 to endorse a candidate for the primary, Russo lost out to state Sen. Frank Savickas, a Byrne ally. Russo vowed to challenge Savickas in the primary, but he was spared the trouble. Byrne had a change of heart, and persuaded Savickas to drop out.

Committees

Budget (3rd of 21 Democrats)
Task Forces: Budget Process, Reconciliation and Enforcement (chairman); Defense, Foreign Policy and Space

Ways and Means (11th of 23 Democrats)
Trade

Elections

1988 General		
Marty Russo (D)	132,111	(62%)
Joseph J. McCarthy (R)	80,181	(38%)
1988 Primary		
Marty Russo (D)	76,930	(91%)
Maurice E. Johnson (D)	7,793	(9%)
1986 General		
Marty Russo (D)	102,949	(66%)
James J. Tierney (R)	52,618	(34%)

Previous Winning Percentages: **1984** (64%) **1982** (74%) **1980** (69%) **1978** (65%) **1976** (59%) **1974** (53%)

District Vote For President

	1988	1984	1980	1976
D	92,108 (41%)	84,752 (35%)	95,274 (44%)	79,792 (43%)
R	103,606 (59%)	158,281 (65%)	105,358 (49%)	104,166 (56%)
I			12,786 (6%)	

Campaign Finance

	Receipts	Receipts from PACs	Expend-itures
1988			
Russo (D)	$558,458	$357,996 (64%)	$558,273
McCarthy (R)	$83,234	$25 (0%)	$81,325
1986			
Russo (D)	$478,353	$281,755 (59%)	$483,102
Tierney (R)	$43,178	0	$42,977

Key Votes

1987	
Raise speed limit to 65 mph	Y
Approve Gephardt "fair trade" amendment	Y
Ban testing of larger nuclear weapons	Y
Delay "re-flagging" of Kuwaiti tankers	Y
Approve tax-raising deficit-reduction bill	N
1988	
Approve aid to Nicaraguan contras	N
Enact civil rights restoration bill over Reagan veto	N
Kill 60-day plant-closing notification measure	N
Pass omnibus trade bill over Reagan veto	Y
Approve death penalty for drug-related murders	Y
Bar federal funds for abortions in cases of rape and incest	Y
Oppose seven-day waiting period for purchase of handguns	N

Voting Studies

	Presidential Support		Party Unity		Conservative Coalition	
Year	S	O	S	O	S	O
1988	29	63	78	15	39	58
1987	24	75	79	12	21	74
1986	18	79	81	13	26	64
1985	23	78	82	11	24	75
1984	27	63	74	18	22	69
1983	16	74	76†	13†	26	72
1982	30	62	81	15	32	68
1981	38	54	64	25	39	57

† Not eligible for all recorded votes.

Interest Group Ratings

Year	ADA	ACU	AFL-CIO	CCUS
1988	80	28	93	46
1987	84	17	93	33
1986	65	9	86	38
1985	70	14	82	36
1984	85	8	85	31
1983	75	30	69	20
1982	80	10	85	27
1981	55	14	73	25

4 George E. Sangmeister (D)

Of Mokena — Elected 1988

Born: Feb. 16, 1931, Joliet, Ill.
Education: Elmhurst College, B.A. 1957; John Marshall Law School, J.D. 1960.
Military Career: Army, 1951-53.
Occupation: Lawyer.
Family: Wife, Doris M. Hinspeter; two children.
Religion: Lutheran.
Political Career: Ill. House, 1973-76; Ill. Senate, 1976-87; sought Democratic nomination for lieutenant governor, 1986.
Capitol Office: 1607 Longworth Bldg., 20515; 225-3635.

The Path to Washington: The town hall in the 4th District village of Frankfort dates back almost 50 years, but the dedication plaque at its front door has a very familiar political name engraved on it: George Sangmeister.

That Sangmeister, who was mayor of Frankfort for 32 years, is the father of the man who was elected to represent the 4th in the 101st Congress. The deep roots of the Sangmeister family and the Democrat's attention to local organizing in 1988 were instrumental in tipping a hard-fought contest away from first-term Republican Jack Davis.

For Sangmeister, the House race was a back-to-basics battle to erase the memory of a 1986 defeat so terrifically embarrassing that it threatened to make a footnote of everything he had accomplished in a long career as lawyer and politician.

After 14 years' service in the state Legislature, Sangmeister was slated by party leaders as their choice for lieutenant governor in the 1986 Democratic primary. But the party organization's complacency during the campaign yielded a shocking and embarrassing result: Sangmeister and the party-slated candidate for secretary of state both lost to disciples of fringe political figure Lyndon H. LaRouche Jr.

Even in the final weeks of the 1988 House campaign, Sangmeister was still trying to live down the defeat. At one public forum, a citizen asked how he could be trusted to look out for them in Washington if he did not have the sense to see the LaRouche fiasco developing.

But Sangmeister is a precise man, not one to make the same mistake twice, and he left little to chance in his bid for the House, putting together a campaign that impressively out-researched, out-organized and outspent incumbent Davis.

It was a nasty duel, with Sangmeister's operation repeatedly offering up stories that portrayed Davis or one of his local GOP allies as a shady pol. Davis gamely returned the rhetorical fire, saying in one debate that Sangmeister "speaks with a forked tongue" and that he had an "arrogant, chauvinistic attitude" toward women. Befitting such a heated campaign, the election-night tally did not settle the matter. In fact, Davis did not concede until Nov. 30; the margin was just 1,039 votes.

Sangmeister built his career close to home. Born in Joliet, the 4th's biggest city, he earned his college and law degrees in nearby Chicago. By age 30, Sangmeister was on the officeholding track. He served as circuit court magistrate and then state's attorney in Will County before moving to the state House in 1972.

He ousted a Republican state senator in 1976, and went on to chair the Judiciary Committee and earn high marks for working to improve Illinois' probation system and to enact stricter juvenile-crime laws.

When Sangmeister entered the House, he was just a month shy of age 58, making him the oldest member of the freshman Democratic class of 1988. For a man who wielded considerable influence in Springfield, it may not be easy to adjust to life as a House freshman. But at least he is operating on somewhat familiar turf: When Democrats passed out committee assignments, they gave Sangmeister a seat on the Judiciary Committee.

When he got to Washington, Sangmeister wasted no time registering a complaint with party leaders over the actions of Arkansas Democrat Tommy F. Robinson. Sangmeister charged that Robinson had taped a campaign ad for Davis, with whom he had served on the Armed Services Committee. Though Robinson denied authorizing the use of his comments, he did not sound convincingly contrite; the House Democratic Caucus voted to punish Robinson by not renewing his temporary seat on the Education and Labor Committee.

Illinois 4

Southern Chicago Suburbs; Joliet; Aurora

The 4th is a transitional district, one where metropolitan Chicago peters out into less heavily settled northern Illinois. In most maps of "Chicago and vicinity," the 4th's two largest cities, Aurora and Joliet, are just barely included.

About 90 percent of the district's voting population is evenly divided between the northern part of Will County, centered on Joliet, and the southern suburbs of Cook County, including Chicago Heights. The 4th also takes in corners of Kane County, including part of the city of Aurora, and Kendall County.

The Will County part of the district has tended Republican over the years, especially at the presidential level. However, there is a base Democratic vote in the economically depressed Joliet area. Sangmeister, like his father, has proven that Democrats can be successful in Will County; his 7,500-vote margin there was crucial to his 1988 victory over Republican Rep. Jack Davis.

Joliet, a largely blue-collar city of about 76,000, has suffered from a decline in its heavy-industry base, including the 1979 shutdown of a U.S. Steel plant. During his brief tenure, Davis tried to expand his support in Joliet by working to target federal contracts to defense projects at the Joliet Arsenal. He also devoted much of his efforts toward the planning of a proposed third Chicago-area airport south of Chicago; though it would likely be located outside the 4th if it is ever built, it would provide jobs and other economic benefits for district residents.

The Republican vote is more dependable in Bloom Township, which includes the blue-collar Cook County communities around the old industrial city of Chicago Heights. That city's mayor, Charles Panici, founded an efficient Republican organization in the once-heavily Italian-American area, which now has a sizable black population. Davis' success in the Cook County suburbs won him the House seat in 1986, and nearly saved him in 1988.

Nestled in the district's northwest corner are Aurora, about 60 percent of which is in the 4th, and a section of Kendall County around the small town of Oswego. Aurora is a 19th-century industrial city on the Fox River that still has a heavy-equipment industry.

Much of the 4th District portion of the city is somewhat run-down; Aurora's development is taking place in its northern and eastern sections. It is trying to draw high-tech firms taking advantage of the proximity to the Fermi National Accelerator Laboratory, which is located just outside the 4th.

Population: 519,049. White 439,484 (85%), Black 57,912 (11%), Other 4,529 (1%). Spanish origin 35,659 (7%). 18 and over 356,524 (69%), 65 and over 43,743 (8%). Median age: 28.

Committees

Judiciary (21st of 21 Democrats)
Courts, Intellectual Property and the Administration of Justice; Criminal Justice

Veterans' Affairs (18th of 21 Democrats)
Compensation, Pension and Insurance; Education, Training and Employment

Campaign Finance

	Receipts	Receipts from PACs	Expend-itures
1988			
Sangmeister (D)	$378,294	$144,294 (38%)	$359,942
Davis (R)	$388,118	$266,768 (69%)	$348,339

Elections

1988 General		
George E. Sangmeister (D)	91,282	(50%)
Jack Davis (R)	90,243	(50%)
1988 Primary		
George E. Sangmeister (D)	27,064	(78%)
George M. Lawrence (D)	7,537	(22%)

District Vote For President

	1988	1984	1980	1976
D	82,661 (44%)	77,291 (39%)	71,355 (36%)	111,214 (48%)
R	103,720 (56%)	120,290 (61%)	109,523 (56%)	118,762 (51%)
I			13,844 (7%)	

5 William O. Lipinski (D)

Of Chicago — Elected 1982

Born: Dec. 22, 1937, Chicago, Ill.
Education: Attended Loras College, 1957-58.
Military Career: Army Reserve, 1961-67.
Occupation: Parks supervisor.
Family: Wife, Rose Marie Lapinski; two children.
Religion: Roman Catholic.
Political Career: Chicago city alderman, 1975-83.
Capitol Office: 1032 Longworth Bldg. 20515; 225-5701.

In Washington: Representing South Chicago and some of its close-in suburbs, Lipinski is very nearly the definition of the Northern urban voter his party has been unable to win in recent presidential elections. Of Polish descent, he is a friend of organized labor and supports many New Deal-type programs. But he also is a persistent and sometimes emotional spokesman for conservative ethnic values he thinks Democrats have discarded in recent years.

The label "white ethnic," however, angers Lipinski. "These same political types who have made the term fashionable," he complains, "have at the same time tried to make it unfashionable to exhibit many of [the] beliefs real ethnics hold, implying that it's immoral to oppose all abortions, racist to support capital punishment. . . ."

In the 100th Congress, Lipinski was able to find common ground with his party on family issues. He criticized conservatives who, he says, base answers to current family problems on "an image of the family that no longer squares with the facts. . . ." He wants Congress to enact legislation to establish IRA-type accounts for post-secondary education and for first-time home buyers, and he supports a day-care tax credit.

Lipinski comes from the old school of Chicago politics. This training came into play in 1986 when he got an unexpected call from Ronald Reagan. The president wanted to know where Lipinski stood on aid to the Nicaraguan contras. Lipinski said there was "a need to stop communism" and he would be voting with the administration. Reagan then said to let the White House know if he could use any favors, a request that no politician who grew up in Mayor Richard J. Daley's machine could ever ignore.

"Have you ever heard of the Southwest Rapid Transit Line?" Lipinski asked. Reagan had not heard of it, but before the conversation was over he had promised to find out why money for it was delayed. Four months later, a federal contract for $496 million to start work on the line, which will run from downtown to Midway Airport, won approval.

Lipinski spends much of his time on the Public Works Committee lobbying for local projects, and outside the committee, he tries to be a watchdog for ethnic rights on a variety of fronts. In 1985, he complained that European ethnics were not mentioned in a bill to end discrimination in the federal civil service, and language was added including them. Lipinski is also co-chairman of the Democratic National Committee's Council on Ethnic Americans.

At Home: When Cook County State's Attorney Richard M. Daley began his campaign for mayor of Chicago in 1989, Lipinski was one Democratic House member he knew he could count on for support. Lipinski owes his political career to Daley's late father.

In fact, Lipinski made it to Congress in 1982 as the result of an early skirmish in the younger Daley's unsuccessful first bid for mayor in 1983. Lipinski's House primary battle against Democratic Rep. John Fary was a bitter match that tested the remnants of Chicago's legendary political machine.

At the time of the 1982 House primary, the chief mayoral rivals were Daley and incumbent Jane M. Byrne (Harold Washington, the Democratic House member who would ride a wave of minority support to become Chicago's first black mayor, entered later). Fary, a longtime state legislator who had been tapped for Congress in 1975 as a reward for his devoted service to Mayor Daley, was being pressured to step down as early as 1980 by a group of South Side Democrats allied with Daley's son. Fary did not depart that year, however; he reportedly asked for one more term to shore up his retirement benefits, and the Daley forces obliged him.

As that "last" term came to a close, the 70-year-old Fary insisted on running again, denying he had made any commitment to retire. This time, the Daley organization officially endorsed Lipinski.

A lifelong Chicago resident and party loyalist, Lipinski had climbed through the ranks in the city Parks Department over 17 years. He began as a weekend athletic instructor and, thanks to his Daley machine contacts, rose to the position of area administrator, from which

Illinois 5

South Central Chicago and Suburbs

The 5th begins about a mile from Lake Michigan and, following the Adlai Stevenson Expressway, extends west to the split-levels of suburban Willow Springs.

It includes the home of the late Mayor Richard J. Daley and the political organization he dominated. Daley lived his entire life in Bridgeport, an almost exclusively Irish neighborhood, but Eastern Europeans, especially Poles, dominate the broader territory within the congressional district.

In local politics, the district has held to its traditions. The Daley machine stayed intact here even as it decayed elsewhere in Chicago, and local Democratic officials rejoiced when Richard M. Daley brought the legendary family name back to the mayor's office in 1989. But the bitter political battles between Chicago's black and white ethnic communities, stemming from Harold Washington's 1983 election as the city's first black mayor, have had their effect at the polls.

President Reagan made a breakthrough for the Republicans in 1984, winning 58 percent of the vote in the 5th, which had even stood by Jimmy Carter in 1980. The 1988 presidential contest was more competitive, but George Bush prevailed with 52 percent.

There are some longtime Republican pockets in the 5th. The Czech and Bohemian enclaves of Cicero and Berwyn have been voting Republican in most recent contests, and the white-collar suburbs of Bridgeview and Hickory Hills lean to the GOP. But the inner suburban communities of McCook, Countryside, Hodgkins and Summit, all industrial, generally have echoed the Democratic tendencies of the Chicago part of the 5th.

At the district's eastern end, on Chicago's South Side, is the Union Stockyards, a few blocks from the Daley home. Largely abandoned in the 1950s by the meatpacking industry, the huge stockyards area has in recent years become an industrial park, with warehouses and light industrial operations.

Population: 518,971. White 413,301 (80%), Black 17,899 (3%), Other 9,358 (2%). Spanish origin 135,062 (26%). 18 and over 377,195 (73%), 65 and over 61,278 (12%). Median age: 30.

he managed personnel and programs at several local parks. He was elected to the City Council in 1975.

The 1982 primary was exceptionally tense even though there was little substantive difference between the two candidates on most issues. Lipinski challenged Fary's ability to be an effective legislator at age 70, insisting that he would be a more vigorous representative. Fary accused his opponent of being a puppet for Richard M. Daley.

As the campaign drew to a close, Fary asked federal officials to monitor the polls on Election Day, saying he did not trust Daley to guard against voting irregularities — part of Daley's duties as state's attorney. In a joint appearance with Daley, Lipinski charged that Byrne had broken her vow of neutrality and was secretly working to help Fary, in hopes of embarrassing Daley.

The outcome was not even close. Although Fary drew support from Polish ethnic organizations and from some old-guard machine backers still loyal to Byrne, the mayor was unable to pull much weight in southwest Chicago's 23rd Ward, where Daley and Lipinski (the Democratic ward committeeman) turned out a huge vote. Lipinski drew over 60 percent of the vote to take the nomination, which was tantamount to election in the solidly Democratic 5th.

The election was the culmination of an increasingly bitter relationship between Lipinski and Byrne. When Byrne won control of City Hall in 1979, Lipinski became one of her earliest backers on the City Council, and many saw him as a likely point man for the mayor's legislative proposals. But it soon became clear that she would not grant Lipinski the clout he sought. The alderman became openly critical of Byrne and moved to align himself with Richard M. Daley's forces. Lipinski cemented the allegiance in 1980, when he worked in Daley's campaign for state's attorney against a Byrne-backed candidate.

Lipinski exasperated Byrne from his post as chairman of the newly created Education Committee, a body Lipinski had fought to establish. When Byrne sought to re-staff the Chicago Board of Education with her own appointees, Lipinski voted against virtually every Byrne nominee; he later pushed to make the school board an elective body. He also sponsored a number of bills prohibiting mandatory busing.

Although liberal Democrats deplored his votes against some black and Hispanic school board nominees, Lipinski was praised for conducting fair and open committee hearings on the matter. During his seven years on the council, he gained a reputation for accessibility, straight talk and service to his home territory. Lipinski made a pet project of lobbying for the establishment of the Southwest Rapid Transit Line for the only part of the city that was without such service.

Though his mainly white, ethnic constituency became openly skeptical of the Democratic Party and hostile to the city administrations of Washington and his black successor, Eugene Sawyer, Lipinski never suffered at the polls. And with Richard M. Daley finally winning the mayoral office in 1989, Lipinski's constituents should feel much closer to the "new" Democratic machine in City Hall.

Committees

Merchant Marine and Fisheries (10th of 26 Democrats)
Merchant Marine; Panama Canal/Outer Continental Shelf

Public Works and Transportation (15th of 31 Democrats)
Aviation; Investigations and Oversight; Surface Transportation

Elections

1988 General		
William O. Lipinski (D)	93,567	(61%)
John J. Holowinski (R)	59,128	(39%)
1986 General		
William O. Lipinski (D)	82,466	(70%)
Daniel John Sobieski (R)	34,738	(30%)

Previous Winning Percentages: 1984 (64%) **1982** (75%)

District Vote For President

	1988	1984	1980	1976
D	77,783 (48%)	76,570 (42%)	103,702 (52%)	99,925 (53%)
R	83,892 (52%)	107,199 (58%)	83,448 (42%)	87,259 (47%)
I			10,315 (5%)	

Campaign Finance

	Receipts	Receipts from PACs	Expend-itures
1988			
Lipinski (D)	$154,568	$96,464 (62%)	$165,144
Holowinski (R)	$55,457	$500 (1%)	$55,187
1986			
Lipinski (D)	$150,297	$64,925 (43%)	$152,573
Sobieski (R)	$11,396	$1,950 (17%)	$11,303

Key Votes

1987	
Raise speed limit to 65 mph	N
Approve Gephardt "fair trade" amendment	Y
Ban testing of larger nuclear weapons	N
Delay "re-flagging" of Kuwaiti tankers	N
Approve tax-raising deficit-reduction bill	?
1988	
Approve aid to Nicaraguan contras	Y
Enact civil rights restoration bill over Reagan veto	Y
Kill 60-day plant-closing notification measure	N
Pass omnibus trade bill over Reagan veto	Y
Approve death penalty for drug-related murders	Y
Bar federal funds for abortions in cases of rape and incest	?
Oppose seven-day waiting period for purchase of handguns	N

Voting Studies

	Presidential Support		Party Unity		Conservative Coalition	
Year	S	O	S	O	S	O
1988	33	56	68	20	47	42
1987	35	56	69	16	53	40
1986	42	54	74	18	52	42
1985	36	59	78	12	45	49
1984	45	46	71	14	46	41
1983	40	55	66	24	55	42

Interest Group Ratings

Year	ADA	ACU	AFL-CIO	CCUS
1988	55	35	100	45
1987	52	16	93	46
1986	45	45	92	27
1985	55	33	100	14
1984	60	35	92	33
1983	50	61	76	40

6 Henry J. Hyde (R)

Of Bensenville — Elected 1974

Born: April 18, 1924, Chicago, Ill.
Education: Attended Duke U., 1943-44; Georgetown U., B.S. 1947; Loyola U., J.D. 1949.
Military Career: Navy, 1944-46; Navy Reserve, 1942-44, 1946-68.
Occupation: Lawyer.
Family: Wife, Jeanne Simpson; four children.
Religion: Roman Catholic.
Political Career: Ill. House, 1967-75, majority leader, 1971-72; Republican nominee for U.S. House, 1962.
Capitol Office: 2104 Rayburn Bldg. 20515; 225-4561.

In Washington: It is increasingly hard to recall that Hyde once was typecast as a fringe conservative interested in one issue, abortion. He has since become so indispensable to Republicans as a point man on defense and foreign policy that it is not far-fetched to speculate he might be their leader one day.

Hyde would be a prominent presence even if he were not a hulk of a man with a luminous white mane. He may be the best debater in the House. No matter who is the nominal sponsor of a conservative initiative, Hyde is likely to be its most impressive spokesman, waiting for flawed liberal arguments and then pouncing with all the wit and sarcasm he once used as a Chicago trial lawyer. If there is one criticism, it is that Hyde has more zest for argument than he does for the less glamorous task of legislating.

But Hyde's style is consistent with his view of a minority member's role: "If you come to understand your role is to be a gadfly, a conscience factor, and try to work some influence in committee ... if that's enough and you don't need to be chairman of a subcommittee or see your name on a bill, this can be very rewarding."

He recognizes the risk of overexposure. "The more you speak on a variety of subjects, the less credence you're given," he says. "You have to husband your pearls before you cast them profligately about the chamber." At the same time, Hyde is a man who takes pleasure in argument for its own sake. In his opinion, "Conflict and disputation are the heart and soul of drama, the heart and soul of literature and the heart and soul of the legislative process — if we're not all to die of boredom."

That spirit is a contrast with the palpable frustration felt by so many House Republicans after years in the minority. So it was little surprise that Hyde's name surfaced for the No. 2 GOP job, minority whip, when Dick Cheney left early in the 101st Congress to become defense secretary.

The contenders were two conservatives with opposite styles, pragmatist Edward Madigan and ideologue Newt Gingrich. Then New York's Gerald B. H. Solomon launched a draft-Hyde boomlet, reflecting some members' desire for a conservative who would be as combative as Gingrich while retaining enough respect among Democrats to be productive. Hyde quashed the move, recognizing that many potential supporters were committed, and hesitating to challenge Illinoisans Madigan and Minority Leader Robert H. Michel, a Madigan backer.

But Hyde made it clear he would be a willing leadership candidate in the future; a former Illinois House majority leader, he lost a 1979 bid for House GOP Conference chairman by just three votes, in a race in which he was the militant young conservatives' choice against the candidate of old-line Republicans. Speculation that Hyde could be minority leader someday occurs even though he is just a year younger than Michel — a reflection of Hyde's greater vigor and dynamism and the widespread sentiment that Michel but not Hyde will retire before long.

Once the leader of the conservative forces on the Judiciary Committee, in recent years Hyde has focused on the Foreign Affairs and Intelligence committees; he is the ranking Republican on the latter. In the 100th Congress, he was President Reagan's biggest defender on the special Iran-contra investigating committee.

Initially Hyde criticized Reagan for not informing Congress about arms sales to Iran; he is the author with California Democrat Howard L. Berman of a 1986 law requiring administration notice of arms sales to terrorist nations. And he lamented after the reports of illegal aid to the contras that he was "in a considerable quandary, because I think saving the contras ... is a transcendent task. [But] the law is important, too."

Nevertheless, throughout the hearings Hyde derided the law against aiding the contras as "murky." And while he agreed the administration should not have lied to Congress, he

Illinois 6

Far West Chicago Suburbs — Wheaton

The 6th is a white-collar suburban district in which any Republican could feel at home. Taking in parts of Cook and Du Page counties, it follows the route of two commuter rail lines that drew Chicagoans westward as early as the 1930s.

The southern part of the district is made up of such established suburbs as Elmhurst, Villa Park, Lombard, Glen Ellyn and Wheaton. It is the northern part, straddling the Du Page and Cook lines, that has enjoyed a big burst of suburban growth. Schaumburg, still rural in 1960, has seen its population soar to over 60,000, as condominiums and apartment complexes filled in around the enormous Woodfield shopping center. Roselle (population 20,000) has more than doubled in size since 1970. Itasca still has a modest population, but has seen a boom in commercial development because of its location near Interstate 290 in the O'Hare Airport corridor.

In between the boom towns in the north and the affluent older cities in the south are some more modest suburban areas, where most of whatever Democratic vote the district has can be found. Glendale Heights and Addison have some light industry and a blue-collar population. An industrial park is located near Elk Grove Village, another fast-growing suburb to the north. Bensenville, which years ago attracted migrant workers drawn by the farms of the area, still has a small Hispanic community.

On its northeastern border, the 6th hooks over to take in the older, prosperous suburbs of Des Plaines and Park Ridge. Des Plaines adjoins O'Hare, which is still the world's busiest airport, and is home to many airline employees.

Population: 519,015. White 494,144 (95%), Black 4,321 (1%), Other 14,812 (3%). Spanish origin 15,155 (3%). 18 and over 367,916 (71%), 65 and over 38,548 (7%). Median age: 30.

implied Congress asked for it because of past leaks.

Hyde also orchestrated House Republicans' strategy of using the hearings to promote Reagan's contra policy. He rarely questioned witnesses, instead favoring one-liners and long speeches. Hyde once asked a question, then told the witness, "I'd rather answer it myself," and did so. He helped draft a minority report that exonerated the president.

Hyde has been noted for his grace toward opponents and his appreciation of a worthy adversary. But at times in recent years, his intense feelings on foreign policy, especially contra aid, have made him less charitable toward those who disagree with him. He even has had harsh words for fellow Catholics who oppose U.S. policies in Central America, denouncing the "liberal clergy, the trendy vicars, the networking nuns."

At Hyde's urging, during a 1987 House debate, Republicans closed their arguments for contra aid with the same refrain — saying they opposed "handing Central America over to the Soviet Union." In 1988 he led the party's successful call for a House investigation after Speaker Jim Wright told reporters the CIA was fomenting unrest in Nicaragua. Hyde and other Republicans accused Wright of leaking classified information, while denying such information existed. "He accepts the Sandinistas' version of everything," Hyde snapped.

Hyde also defended the mining of Nicaraguan harbors, saying, "Why legitimize the Sandinistas? They came into power on a lie, on fraud ... and they stay in power through repression." In 1989, when President Bush quickly compromised with Democrats on a contra package limited to non-military aid, a disappointed Hyde said backing the plan was like chemotherapy: "It makes you sick to take it, but it just might save your life."

Hyde's quick and memorable ripostes can make for some effective sloganeering. He led the opposition in the early 1980s to a nuclear-weapons freeze, deriding it as "government by bumper sticker." The House passed a weakened freeze resolution in 1983, but Hyde was among those who turned a potent Democratic rallying point into a resolution without significance.

To foes of the MX missile, he warned, "Peace is not served by a horse and buggy defense." In opposing a nuclear test-ban resolution in 1986, Hyde said, "If this is in our interest, I can't figure out why Gorbachev wants it." And in the 100th Congress, he twice helped lead the unsuccessful fight against efforts to mandate compliance with a strict reading of the 1972 ABM treaty in order to prevent space tests of the strategic defense initiative; in 1988 Hyde said the amendment illustrated Democrats' "nuclear masochism.... The Soviets have violated the ABM treaty, so how do we penalize them? Put shackles on our negotiators."

Hyde's rhetoric can get him into trouble. In the 98th Congress, after the House passed an amendment barring use of U.S. troops in El Salvador and Nicaragua unless Congress approved or U.S. personnel were clearly threatened, Hyde blistered his colleagues for "a blatantly cowardly and political amendment." That enraged Dan Daniel, a Democratic hawk then on the Armed Services Committee. When he tried to have Hyde ruled out of order for insulting the patriotism and bravery of committee members who originally approved the provision, Hyde withdrew his comments.

Despite his high profile on foreign policy matters in recent years, Hyde still is best known for the Hyde amendment against federal funding of abortions, which he passed as a freshman in 1976. Hyde's anti-abortion crusading brought him attention beyond the reach of most of his colleagues. But it also gave him a reputation for fanaticism that clearly troubled him. "When an issue develops," Hyde once said, "you either evade it or you grapple with it. I grappled with it, and now it's grappling back."

That first famous amendment became Hyde's by legislative fluke; he was enlisted as sponsor by Maryland Republican Robert E. Bauman, who reckoned that the unknown freshman would draw less fire than a known conservative agitator like himself. The House passed the amendment, though the Senate modified it to allow payment for abortions to save the life of the mother. At that time, the government was paying for up to 300,000 abortions a year, mostly for poor Medicaid recipients; within a few years, the number had declined to about 2,000 annually.

By 1981 the Hyde amendment was firmly in place, upheld by the Supreme Court, and subsequently it became an all-but-routine part of the annual health appropriations bills. But in 1988, controversy flared again. The Senate overwhelmingly voted to allow abortion funding for rape and incest victims, but the House objected and a conference deadlocked. The House then voted to stand fast against the change, after an emotional debate in which Hyde thundered, "While rape is a terrible thing, abortion is worse." The Senate backed down.

Hyde also has introduced legislation to identify conception as the beginning of life, but he has made no real attempt to pass it. "We don't have the votes," he admits.

For all the intensity of his conservatism, Hyde is not always ideologically predictable. And when he does take a surprising stand, he can be quite influential. Such was the case in the 97th Congress, when his conversion on the Voting Rights Act helped guarantee that the House would pass a strong revision of the law.

When Judiciary began debating extension of the 1965 act, Hyde argued for easing the law's restrictions on Southern states. Those states have to clear any election law changes with the federal government, and Hyde said they should be able to "bail out" for good behavior. "A handful of Southern states have been in the penalty box for nearly 17 years," he said. He also talked of writing a new law applicable to all regions. But testimony on the issue changed his mind, and Hyde admitted it with the candor that is part of his appeal. "I have learned from the hearings," he said, "that there are still enormous difficulties with people getting the right to vote in the South."

Still, Hyde disagreed with the Democrats' version of the bill, and he tangled with Democrat Don Edwards of California, chairman of the subcommittee that wrote it. During floor debate over final passage of the conference report, Hyde and Edwards got into a procedural dispute that provoked Hyde to storm from the chamber. He resigned from Edwards' subcommittee soon after, although since then he has had warm words for his liberal adversary.

Hyde has surprised his colleagues on other occasions. He fought against a proposal to bar strikes by Legal Services Corporation lawyers, arguing that they had a constitutional right to strike. He also opposed a bill against child pornography, contending that it might be unconstitutional. He often forms odd-couple alliances with liberal House Democrats; for example, Hyde has cosponsored measures with Henry A. Waxman to expand Medicaid coverage to more poor women and children.

Prominent in Hyde's office are both a bust and a portrait of St. Thomas More, the 16th-century English lord chancellor and Catholic martyr. By way of explaining, Hyde notes that More is the patron saint of lawyers, and a man who gave his life for his principles. More's career also reflected a mix of the secular and the religious that marks Hyde's own.

While Hyde believes it is appropriate to debate the morality of a public-policy decision, whether abortion or arms control, he resists judging the morality of individuals.

In 1983 he opposed conservatives' motion to expel Illinois Republican Daniel B. Crane for sexual misconduct with a House page. "The Judeo-Christian tradition says, 'Hate the sin, love the sinner,' " Hyde said. "We are on record as hating the sin, some more ostentatiously than others. I think it is time to love the sinner." He also tried to help Bauman when his old ally in the abortion debate was defeated in 1980 after admitting to alcoholism and homosexuality; Hyde called numerous House Republicans, asking them to help find work for a fellow conservative who had suffered enough.

At Home: Hyde grew up as an Irish Catholic Democrat in Chicago, but began having doubts about the Democratic Party in the late 1940s. By 1952, he had switched parties and backed Dwight D. Eisenhower for president.

After practicing law in the Chicago area for more than 10 years, and serving as a GOP precinct committeeman, Hyde was chosen by the party organization in 1962 to challenge Democratic Rep. Roman Pucinski in a northwest Chicago House district. A Republican had represented the heavily ethnic district before Pucinski won it in 1958, and Hyde came within 10,000 votes of taking it back for the GOP.

Elected to the Illinois House in 1966, he was one of its most outspoken and articulate debaters. In 1971 Hyde became majority leader; he unsuccessfully ran for Speaker in 1973.

In 1974, longtime GOP Rep. Harold Collier retired from the suburban 6th District just west of Chicago. Much of the 6th was unfamiliar to Hyde, but he dominated the six-man GOP primary anyway. Calling on his political contacts for help, he won with 49 percent.

The general election was tougher. Hyde's Democratic opponent was Edward V. Hanrahan, a former Cook County state's attorney attempting a political comeback. Hanrahan had made a controversial name for himself five years earlier, when Chicago policemen attached to his office raided Black Panther Party headquarters, killing two Panther leaders. Hanrahan was indicted for attempting to obstruct the ensuing federal investigation. He was acquitted, but he was beaten for re-election in 1972.

Nonetheless, Hyde went into his contest at a disadvantage. Hanrahan's past exploits had given him wide name recognition and made him a sort of folk hero among local blue-collar ethnics. Moreover, with Republicans deserting their party in droves in that Watergate year, the district's nominally GOP nature was not expected to hurt Hanrahan.

But Hanrahan could not keep pace with Hyde in fund raising, organizing or personal campaigning. The Democrat used his record of antagonism to the Daley machine to tout his independence, but traditional sources of party funding were dry for him.

On Election Day, Hyde's superior resources won out. Using telephone banks and an army of precinct workers, his staff turned out enough voters to give him an 8,000-vote plurality over Hanrahan while GOP districts nationwide were falling to Democrats.

Since then, Hyde has been invincible. The 1981 redistricting gave him an almost all-new constituency and an aggressive primary rival from the new area might have made Hyde work to hold the redrawn district. But no Republican bothered to challenge Hyde in 1982, and by 1984 no one dared.

Committees

Select Intelligence (Ranking)
Program and Budget Authorization (ranking)

Foreign Affairs (7th of 18 Republicans)
Arms Control, International Security and Science; Western Hemisphere Affairs

Judiciary (3rd of 14 Republicans)
Courts, Intellectual Property and the Administration of Justice; Economic and Commercial Law

Elections

1988 General

Henry J. Hyde (R)	153,425	(74%)
William J. Andrle (D)	54,804	(26%)

1986 General

Henry J. Hyde (R)	98,196	(75%)
Robert H. Renshaw (D)	32,064	(25%)

Previous Winning Percentages: **1984** (75%) **1982** (68%) **1980** (67%) **1978** (66%) **1976** (61%) **1974** (53%)

District Vote For President

	1988		1984		1980		1976	
D	67,356	(31%)	52,170	(24%)	51,049	(25%)	72,192	(33%)
R	147,387	(69%)	166,170	(76%)	126,318	(63%)	142,229	(65%)
I					21,069	(11%)		

Campaign Finance

	Receipts	Receipts from PACs	Expend-itures
1988			
Hyde (R)	$303,395	$121,453 (40%)	$281,229
Andrle (D)	$27,274	$10,600 (39%)	$26,555
1986			
Hyde (R)	$241,958	$93,337 (39%)	$229,898
Renshaw (D)	$6,378	0	$6,378

Key Votes

1987

Raise speed limit to 65 mph	Y
Approve Gephardt "fair trade" amendment	N
Ban testing of larger nuclear weapons	N
Delay "re-flagging" of Kuwaiti tankers	N
Approve tax-raising deficit-reduction bill	N

1988

Approve aid to Nicaraguan contras	Y
Enact civil rights restoration bill over Reagan veto	N
Kill 60-day plant-closing notification measure	Y
Pass omnibus trade bill over Reagan veto	N
Approve death penalty for drug-related murders	Y
Bar federal funds for abortions in cases of rape and incest	Y
Oppose seven-day waiting period for purchase of handguns	N

Voting Studies

	Presidential Support		Party Unity		Conservative Coalition	
Year	S	O	S	O	S	O
1988	70	28	84	10	92	8
1987	65	32	76	18	86	9
1986	76	21	75	18	80	20
1985	71	19	75	17	85	9
1984	71	25	79	15	88	7
1983	89	10	83	15	88	12
1982	75	17	79 †	19 †	86	8
1981	79	20	77	19	81	16

† Not eligible for all recorded votes.

Interest Group Ratings

Year	ADA	ACU	AFL-CIO	CCUS
1988	15	92	14	100
1987	12	96	6	100
1986	5	90	7	75
1985	15	81	21	74
1984	10	88	8	87
1983	5	86	0	95
1982	15	85	11	81
1981	10	93	7	94

7 Cardiss Collins (D)

Of Chicago — Elected 1973

Born: Sept. 24, 1931, St. Louis, Mo.
Education: Attended Northwestern U., 1949-50.
Occupation: Auditor.
Family: Widow of Rep. George W. Collins; one child.
Religion: Baptist.
Political Career: No previous office.
Capitol Office: 2264 Rayburn Bldg. 20515; 225-5006.

In Washington: When they were in the House, Shirley Chisholm of New York and Barbara Jordan of Texas earned considerable attention as black women who were involved in debates on issues of national policy. Collins, now in her eighth full term, has more House seniority than either Chisholm or Jordan accumulated, but unlike them, she has never drawn the spotlight for her quiet work on a handful of issues.

On the powerful Energy and Commerce Committee, the low-profile Collins is generally — though not automatically — a liberal vote. On clean-air legislation, she is reluctant to vote for stringent controls on acid rain because of the potential cost those controls might impose on heavy industry in her district. She likes to point out that her first priority has to be keeping her constituents employed. Also, when regulatory legislation aimed at the securities markets is discussed, Collins is wary of any threat to the Chicago futures markets.

On the Health Subcommittee in the 100th Congress, Collins sought to encourage the use of cancer-screening tests. She successfully offered an amendment to the catastrophic health insurance bill that allows costs for certain screening tests to be counted when determining whether an individual has reached the limit on out-of-pocket expenses. The subcommittee also approved a Collins amendment to the health services block grant reauthorization to allow states to use the funds to pay for screening of breast and uterine cancer.

From her post on the Telecommunications Subcommittee, Collins has criticized the Federal Communications Commission for not working to encourage minorities and women to enter the broadcasting industry. For the past several Congresses, she has introduced legislation to preserve preferences for minority and female applicants seeking broadcasting licenses from the FCC.

Collins is somewhat more conspicuous on Government Operations, where she has risen to the position of No. 2 Democrat, just behind committee Chairman John Conyers Jr. of Michigan. Collins is chairman of the Subcommittee on Government Activities and Transportation, and while that panel has a fairly limited legislative mandate, she was part of the air-safety debate during the 100th Congress. Collins held oversight hearings on the Federal Aviation Administration's performance and criticized the FAA for failing "to rebuild the air-traffic controller work force, particularly at Chicago's O'Hare Airport," and for not doing enough to recruit minority and female controllers.

When the full House debated the airport authorization bill in 1987, Collins offered an amendment requiring that at least 10 percent of revenues from airport concessions go to small businesses owned by minorities or women. The amendment was unanimously approved.

Shortly after the bombing of Pan Am Flight 103 over Lockerbie, Scotland, it was Collins who made public the FAA security bulletins that had warned U.S. embassy personnel of a potential terrorist threat. She criticized the bulletins as being ineffective and "dangerously inaccurate."

In her first few years chairing the Government Activities Subcommittee, Collins used it as a platform to criticize the Reagan administration for its civil rights policies. She was particularly peeved by the refusal of three federal agencies, including the Justice Department, to comply with a directive of the Equal Employment Opportunity Commission that all agencies set goals for hiring women and minorities. Administration officials said the EEOC had exceeded its authority; Collins said the executive branch inaction was "a disgrace."

In the 98th Congress, Collins and Conyers temporarily blocked a bill by Jack Brooks of Texas (then Government Operations chairman) to increase competition in the bidding for federal contracts. The measure was opposed by small and minority-owned businesses, which feared it would allow conglomerates to take over their contracts. Protections for small businesses ultimately were included in the legislation.

Collins was a novice at politics in 1973, when the Chicago organization placed her in the House as successor to her husband, George

Illinois 7

Chicago — Downtown; West Side

Only a few blocks west of Chicago's lakefront, with its elegant high-rises and nearby shops, the rank poverty of the West Side begins, with burned-out buildings and abandoned factories that stretch for miles. The West Side has traditionally been a port of entry for migrants to the city, Jews and Italians early in this century and blacks in the past generation. Roosevelt Road, the district's main artery running west from downtown out to the city limits, was the urban riot corridor in the 1960s. The 7th as a whole is nearly 70 percent black.

Once contained almost entirely within Chicago, the 7th now stretches from Lake Michigan more than a dozen miles west to suburban Bellwood. It mixes residential areas with industrial zones. The University of Illinois at Chicago is in the district, as is the West Side medical center complex.

But the heart of the 7th lies in the miles of low-income housing on the West Side. The picture is not one of unmitigated gloom; there are carefully tended houses sitting cheek-by-jowl with dusty lots and boarded-up buildings. But the West Side's poverty made it an early target for the national civil rights movement as far back as the mid-1960s.

In national politics, the Chicago portion of the district is uniformly Democratic and liberal. On questions of Chicago politics, however, it is more complicated. The Daley machine held sway on the West Side longer than it did on the South Side, chiefly because the transient character of the West Side neighborhoods made organizing against the machine difficult. But the independent movement has made inroads over the last decade; Collins' roots in the traditional Democratic organization have caused her occasional problems with the independents.

Toward the western edge of the city, the 7th includes Austin, traditionally Eastern European in ethnic makeup but increasingly black. Farther west, it takes in some white-collar suburban territory, including generally liberal Oak Park, one of the city's oldest suburbs, and Republican River Forest. The suburbs of Maywood and Bellwood (one of the few district areas to see growth in the early 1980s, with the population up by nearly 10 percent) are predominantly black and vote Democratic.

Population: 519,034. White 150,445 (29%), Black 347,007 (67%), Other 7,409 (1%). Spanish origin 24,273 (5%). 18 and over 343,964 (66%), 65 and over 44,535 (9%). Median age: 26.

W. Collins, who was killed in an airplane crash. She soon became an active participant in the Congressional Black Caucus, and by 1979 she was in line for the chairmanship. She took the post at a time of increasing black disillusionment with Jimmy Carter's administration, and she became a widely quoted voice of that discontent. When the House refused to make the Rev. Dr. Martin Luther King Jr.'s birthday a legal holiday, Collins charged that "racism had a part in it" and blamed the Carter administration, which had endorsed the idea, for not working enough to round up votes. It was not until 1983 that Congress finally approved a national holiday to honor King.

At Home: The movement that elected Harold Washington as the first black mayor of Chicago in 1983 put Collins in a difficult position. Caught in the cross-fire between Washington's allies and remnants of the Daley political machine that had promoted her, Collins had to face serious primary challenges in 1984 and 1986.

Collins' husband, George, was a loyal lieutenant of the late Mayor Richard J. Daley, for which he was awarded a City Council seat and then a seat in Congress in 1970. A month after his 1972 re-election, however, he was killed when his Washington-to-Chicago flight crashed near Chicago's Midway Airport. The organization that had sponsored him picked his widow as successor. She won 93 percent in the special election.

Through the ensuing years, Collins kept her distance from the city's black independent movement. For a time, that created no problems for her. But after Daley's death in 1976, machine loyalties began unraveling in the black community; the independent movement, which had scored scattered successes earlier, began to pick up steam.

When Jane M. Byrne became mayor in 1979 and showed little apparent concern for black interests, a wave of independent activism began gathering force on the West Side, much of which Collins represents. Collins not only avoided the activists, she supported Byrne for renomination against Washington in 1983.

That gave the independents the basis for a challenge a year later. Alderman Danny K. Davis, a strong Washington supporter, launched a primary bid against Collins. By withholding her support from Washington, he said, she "ignored the hue and cry of the people and turned her back on those who were looking to her and to her office for leadership."

A one-time community health administrator, Davis tapped into the network of West Side ministers and grass-roots organizers who had supported Washington in the mayoral race. Taking his campaign into storefront churches and community meetings, Davis tried to tie himself to the flood of "self-empowerment" sentiment that had supported Washington.

But the fervor that had built up with the mayoral election had died down, and Davis' financially strapped campaign had trouble stoking it up again. While several members of Washington's staff took prominent roles in Davis' effort, the mayor himself did not endorse Davis until a few days before the election.

Collins, meanwhile, had help not only from old-line black machine Democrats but from labor unions and white liberals in Oak Park and lakefront Chicago who liked her environmentalist and feminist credentials. Collins finally took 49 percent to Davis' 38 percent.

Davis tried again in 1986, but got no further. Though he was somewhat better organized than in his first try, the non-presidential year ballot offered no other primaries to spark voters' interest. Turnout was low in the black community, and Collins ended up with 60 percent.

Though Collins endorsed Washington in his 1987 re-election campaign against the comeback-minded Byrne, Davis again hinted at a challenge in the 1988 House primary. However, he was distracted by the political turmoil that ensued in late 1987 after Washington's death and the controversial City Council choice of black Alderman Eugene Sawyer as his interim replacement. He eschewed the House race and announced plans to run in the 1989 special mayoral election before throwing his support to Washington ally Timothy Evans. Davis' preoccupation freed Collins for an easy re-election campaign.

Collins never had been involved directly in politics before 1973, although she had political contacts through her husband, a Democratic precinct captain and patronage employee in the Chicago and Cook County governments for years. She worked as an auditor in the Illinois Revenue Department before her election to Congress.

Committees

Energy and Commerce (11th of 26 Democrats)
Health and the Environment; Oversight and Investigations; Telecommunications and Finance

Government Operations (2nd of 24 Democrats)
Government Activities and Transportation (chairman)

Select Narcotics Abuse and Control (5th of 18 Democrats)

Elections

1988 General		
Cardiss Collins (D)	135,331	(100%)
1988 Primary		
Cardiss Collins (D)	69,624	(89%)
Keith A. Klopfenstein (D)	8,408	(11%)
1986 General		
Cardiss Collins (D)	90,761	(80%)
Caroline K. Kallas (R)	21,055	(19%)

Previous Winning Percentages: **1984** (78%) **1982** (86%) **1980** (85%) **1978** (86%) **1976** (85%) **1974** (88%) **1973 *** (93%)

* *Special election.*

District Vote For President

	1988		1984		1980		1976	
D	132,656	(77%)	141,185	(74%)	124,826	(70%)	117,450	(68%)
R	38,432	(22%)	47,301	(25%)	40,421	(23%)	53,344	(31%)
I					9,431	(5%)		

Campaign Finance

	Receipts	Receipts from PACs		Expend-itures
1988				
Collins (D)	$235,058	$199,043	(85%)	$127,487
1986				
Collins (D)	$304,742	$230,570	(76%)	$233,583
Kallas (R)	$9,962	$300	(3%)	$9,302

Key Votes

1987	
Raise speed limit to 65 mph	?
Approve Gephardt "fair trade" amendment	Y
Ban testing of larger nuclear weapons	Y
Delay "re-flagging" of Kuwaiti tankers	Y
Approve tax-raising deficit-reduction bill	Y
1988	
Approve aid to Nicaraguan contras	N
Enact civil rights restoration bill over Reagan veto	Y
Kill 60-day plant-closing notification measure	N
Pass omnibus trade bill over Reagan veto	Y
Approve death penalty for drug-related murders	N
Bar federal funds for abortions in cases of rape and incest	X
Oppose seven-day waiting period for purchase of handguns	?

Voting Studies

	Presidential Support		Party Unity		Conservative Coalition	
Year	**S**	**O**	**S**	**O**	**S**	**O**
1988	16	70	87	2	3	84
1987	8	85	85	2	0	86
1986	12	71	78	3	6	84
1985	16	76	87	1	2	89
1984	21	65	82	5	5	83
1983	5	80	85	3	7	88
1982	25	65	86	6	7	85
1981	28	70	83	7	4	85

Interest Group Ratings

Year	ADA	ACU	AFL-CIO	CCUS
1988	90	0	100	21
1987	92	0	100	0
1986	95	0	100	13
1985	95	5	100	10
1984	95	4	92	36
1983	90	0	100	15
1982	90	0	100	33
1981	85	0	87	6

8 Dan Rostenkowski (D)

Of Chicago — Elected 1958

Born: Jan. 2, 1928, Chicago, Ill.
Education: Attended Loyola U., 1948-51.
Military Career: Army, 1946-48.
Occupation: Insurance executive.
Family: Wife, LaVerne Pirkins; four children.
Religion: Roman Catholic.
Political Career: Ill. House, 1953-55; Ill. Senate, 1955-59.
Capitol Office: 2111 Rayburn Bldg. 20515; 225-4061.

In Washington: Rostenkowski discovered late in life that government can be just as much fun as politics. After nearly three decades in the House accumulating political power as if it were an end in itself, he has begun taking conspicuous pride in applying himself to larger legislative purposes, such as overhauling U.S. trade law and the welfare system.

He has a reputation both in Chicago and Washington as a rather unsubtle ward politician. But it has become increasingly clear that Rostenkowski, now in his fifth term as chairman of the Ways and Means Committee, wants to be known by the end of his career for something beyond the hoarding of influence.

It seems likely that Rostenkowski's chief legacy will be his remarkable achievement of the 99th Congress, when he maneuvered a new federal tax code through a reluctant House and on into law. Many others played key roles in that drama, but none did quite what he did.

"I've had a reputation as a gut politician, a total political animal from the city of Chicago," he said early in 1985. "But I'm also trying . . . to do the responsible thing."

Still, Rostenkowski has a pride in his raw political skills that is rare in an institution coming to be dominated by new-breed Democrats who are more inclined to distance themselves from their party and the institution.

Both Rostenkowski's pride and his irritation with his colleagues were on display in early 1989, when he chastised the House for lacking the self-respect to accept a pay raise.

"In my hometown of Chicago they call politics a blood sport," he said. "I have been pretty successful at it. I don't apologize for getting in the arena and I'll be damned if I'll apologize for winning."

The frustration evident in that speech raised questions about Rostenkowski's long-term political plans. It is not clear what big legislative challenge lies ahead for a man whose chairmanship has produced landmark laws in virtually every area of his committee's jurisdiction: taxes, Social Security, trade and Medicare.

The key to Rostenkowski's legislative success has been the horse-trading skills he learned under Chicago Mayor Richard J. Daley. Indeed, Rostenkowski has managed to turn the Ways and Means Committee into a well-oiled political machine of its own. He has treated his committee like a big-city ward, where personal loyalty counts for more than ideology. He has built members' allegiance the old-fashioned way, by doing favors, keeping his word, and taking down the names of those who do not go along.

Rostenkowski has maximized his strength by recruiting for Ways and Means as many party loyalists as he could find to fill the Democratic slots. In 1985, for example, the chairman threw all his political weight behind an effort to win a Ways and Means seat for William J. Coyne of Pennsylvania, a quiet organization Democrat known mainly for voting the leadership line. The more such Democrats there are on the committee, the more Rostenkowski is in control.

Despite his background in Democratic machine politics, Rostenkowski's preferred mode of legislating is bipartisan. He is willing to deal with Republicans as well as Democrats in his patented way of building coalitions within the committee: Give everyone an opportunity to participate in the decision-making process, but exact a stiff price for participation.

On any important bill, Rostenkowski's subcommittee chairmen are given a relatively free hand at preparing provisions under their jurisdiction. Rostenkowski backs them in full committee, on the floor and in conference. They are expected to pledge loyalty to the entire bill and maintain it until the legislation is signed. The only question about Rostenkowski's power over the committee is whether his troops may someday turn restless.

His grip on the committee and its products has not always been so strong. His chairmanship was badly tarnished in the early years of the Reagan administration when House Democrats were either ignored or ambushed on important tax matters.

Illinois 8

Chicago — North and Northwest Sides

The 8th District is exactly the right kind of constituency for Rostenkowski. It stretches out along Milwaukee Avenue, Chicago's traditional "Polish corridor," taking in such symbolic places as St. Hyacinth Parish, still a first stop for Polish immigrants and a spot where a question asked in Polish may draw a ready response. The lines of the 8th essentially chart the movement of Rostenkowski's lifelong political allies as they have made their way northwest from the inner city, out Milwaukee Avenue. Even Rostenkowski's suburban constituents, in communities such as River Grove and Elmwood Park, are largely ethnic and transplanted from the city.

Nearly any statewide Democratic candidate can still carry the 8th comfortably. However, there have been changes wrought by the political tensions between white ethnics and blacks, stemming from the 1983 election of black Mayor Harold Washington. Ronald Reagan also provided an unusual appeal to 8th District ethnics; he narrowly won there in 1984, after getting just 34 percent four years earlier. But in 1988, Rostenkowski helped bring the district back to the Democratic fold; Michael S. Dukakis took the 8th with 59 percent of the vote.

The strength of Democratic loyalty appears inversely proportional to distance from the heart of the city. The three wards farthest from downtown voted for Reagan in 1984, with the heaviest GOP vote in the Italian 36th Ward at the western edge. Closer to downtown, political loyalties are still decidedly Democratic. Rostenkowski's own ward, the 32nd, gave just 34 percent of its vote to Reagan in 1984.

The 8th's Hispanic population, somewhat more than 30 percent of the total, lives mainly along lower Milwaukee Avenue, and generally provides a Democratic cushion. The 31st and 26th wards in particular have strong Hispanic political organizations.

Population: 519,034. White 392,337 (76%), Black 22,464 (4%), Other 13,318 (3%). Spanish origin 164,164 (32%). 18 and over 375,186 (72%), 65 and over 64,532 (12%). Median age: 30.

In 1981, his first year as Ways and Means chairman, Rostenkowski suffered an acutely embarrassing defeat when he laced a tax bill with special-interest provisions so he could beat Reagan on the House floor, and ended up losing. "If we accept the president's substitute," he said on the floor, "we accept his dominance of the House in the months ahead." The House accepted the Reagan substitute by a vote of 238-195.

In his second year as chairman, Rostenkowski had to stand by helplessly as his committee's Democrats refused even to write a tax bill, thus giving up Ways and Means' traditional leverage in negotiating with the Senate in revenue matters.

In the Congress after that, Rostenkowski won some notable legislative victories — his committee moved through a bill keeping the Social Security system solvent for the foreseeable future — but he seemed most concerned with achieving control over his committee. He gradually restored the power of the Ways and Means chair, which had ebbed under the tenure of his predecessor, the well-informed but ineffectual Al Ullman of Oregon.

Rostenkowski's power-building efforts paid off handsomely when Reagan made overhauling the tax code the top domestic priority of his second term.

At first, Rostenkowski saw political danger for Democrats if they stood in the way of a popular president who wanted to see the tax code rewritten. But most of the pressures turned out to be in the opposite direction. There never was much grass-roots support for tax revision; what there was in great quantities was resistance from economic interests that stood to lose through its enactment. And throughout the process, liberal House Democrats continued to insist that some of the revenues generated by eliminating tax subsidies be used to reduce the federal deficit — a sure-fire way to lose Reagan's crucial support.

In drafting the tax-overhaul bill, Rostenkowski asked members of both parties what it would take to win their support for the massive project. He agreed to consider meeting those demands only if the member, in return, would give an ironclad commitment to support the final product. If not, he saw no reason to deal. "You might as well kick a guy's brains out if he's not for you," he said at one point.

Before going to conference with the Senate on the tax-overhaul bill, Rostenkowski did a thorough loyalty check of his troops. Only tested and reliable allies were named to the conference committee. The basic role of House conferees was to keep quiet and support the chairman. Indeed, Rostenkowski negotiated many of the most difficult provisions of the final bill himself, head-to-head with Senate

Finance Committee Chairman Bob Packwood.

The new federal revenue code that became law on Jan. 1, 1987, reduced the top individual tax rate to 28 percent — far below the 38 percent recommended in the House bill. But in many ways, it represented a triumph for Rostenkowski and the House position. The bill written by Rostenkowski's committee recouped an estimated $140 billion over five years through the cancellation of business-tax subsidies enacted over a long period of time. The final bill incorporated the vast majority of those changes.

Ironically, Rostenkowski's very success in overhauling the tax code made his job tougher in subsequent years. The growing deficit and the new presumption against adding new tax breaks left Rostenkowski with less of the currency of influence he had used to round up votes in the past: special tax breaks.

He ran into trouble even when he doled out such favors on a smaller scale, as he struggled to put together a 1987 tax bill that Republicans refused to support. When the year's major budget decisions were made — in a high-level summit called in the wake of the October 1987 stock market crash — tax goodies were thrown out, infuriating Rostenkowski.

The odds are now overwhelming that Rostenkowski will close his House career in the job he now holds, maneuvering over economic policy and focusing most of his politics on the committee he chairs. There is some irony in that. Rostenkowski never planned to be a tax specialist. For more than 20 years he played pure House politics, trading votes and committee assignments and angling for a top leadership position.

The success of Rostenkowski's tax-revision crusade rekindled speculation that he might mount a campaign for Speaker in 1987 against Jim Wright, whom he helped make majority leader in 1976, but who had not been his closest ally in more recent times. Rostenkowski, however, never made the move.

Wright had actively courted the junior members who cast most of the votes in leadership contests. Rostenkowski, on the other hand, no longer had close ties to many of the younger members, with the exception of those on Ways and Means. And the ethnic machine Democrats, his natural constituency in any leadership contest, are a diminishing breed in the House Democratic Caucus.

When Rostenkowski decided in 1981 to take the Ways and Means chairmanship, he did not believe he might be putting the top rung of the leadership out of his reach.

At the time, he was also in line to become Democratic whip, the third-ranking position in the leadership and steppingstone for the last two Speakers. For weeks, Rostenkowski agonized, consulted friends and then took Ways and Means.

His close friend Thomas P. O'Neill Jr. and business lobbyists were equally happy at the decision: Rostenkowski was sure to be a more predictable ally for both than Sam M. Gibbons of Florida, an independent-minded free-trader who was next in line.

Becoming Ways and Means chairman meant a major change in the tempo of Rostenkowski's life. Until then, he had showed little interest in haggling over the details of the revenue code. And for most of the late 1970s, he was not one of the hardest workers in the House. He had joined Ways and Means in 1965 mainly because it then made the committee assignments for all House Democrats; it offered virtually unlimited opportunities for politicking. When Ways and Means lost that function in 1975, he lost much of his interest. He chaired its Health Subcommittee for four years, but gave it up in 1979 to take a minor panel, Select Revenue Measures.

The 1970s were not as successful for Rostenkowski as he had reason to hope they would be. The echoes of a miscalculation he had made in 1968 blocked what seemed to be a steady rise in the party leadership. But for a slight political lapse then, he might be Speaker today.

Rostenkowski stepped in at the command of President Johnson to restore order at the tumultuous 1968 Democratic National Convention in Chicago. He physically took the gavel from House Majority Leader Carl Albert, who had lost control of the situation. Later Rostenkowski talked openly about having done it, and Albert was insulted. In 1971 Albert moved up from majority leader to Speaker of the House. Rostenkowski threw his influence behind Hale Boggs of Louisiana for majority leader, in exchange for a Boggs promise to appoint Rostenkowski as Democratic whip. Boggs was elected leader.

But Albert was still angry over the convention squabble, and his attitude did not improve when Rostenkowski took his time endorsing him for Speaker. Albert vetoed Rostenkowski as whip. The man chosen instead was O'Neill.

In all the maneuvering that year, Rostenkowski also forgot to protect the position he already held as Democratic Caucus chairman. Texans quietly rounded up the votes to elect their candidate, Olin E. "Tiger" Teague. Some Northern liberals cooperated with them, feeling Rostenkowski had banged his gavel a little too quickly on anti-war speakers while presiding over the House. It took six years for Rostenkowski to make it back into the leadership. By that time, O'Neill was the newly elected Speaker. Rostenkowski had endorsed dark horse Jim Wright of Texas for majority leader, and Wright and O'Neill agreed that a place should be found for Rostenkowski. They made him chief deputy whip.

At Home: If Rostenkowski's role as

"Mayor Daley's man in Congress" helped make him a force in House politics, it also stamped him as a leader among Chicago Democrats at an unusually early age. He was barely 30 when the city's politicians began talking about him as a successor to Daley in City Hall — someday. That day never came. By the time the office opened up in 1977, Rostenkowski was a comfortable and influential 18-year House veteran.

Still, Rostenkowski's political life was focused to an extraordinary degree on Chicago. Until he became Ways and Means chairman in 1981, he spent much of his time in the city, working on strategy with the regular Democratic faction that opposed Mayor Jane Byrne.

Rostenkowski worked hard to defeat Byrne in 1983 and replace her with Richard M. Daley, son of the late mayor. He got half his wish: Byrne was beaten, but by Harold Washington, a black House member to whom neither Rostenkowski nor anyone else in the Daley machine had ever been close.

After more than a decade in eclipse, Rostenkowski's longtime allies from the Daley days surged back in the 1989 special mayoral election that came as a result of Washington's death. In the primary, the younger Daley defeated controversial interim Chicago Mayor Eugene Sawyer. But Rostenkowski's responsibilities in Washington kept him from playing as strong a role in that mayor's race as he would have in the past.

It must have been difficult for Rostenkowski to keep from being distracted by the turmoil back home. He has spent his entire adult life in the thick of Chicago politics. At 24, he became the youngest member of the Illinois House. At 26, he was the youngest in the Illinois Senate. And at 30, he was a member of Congress. When Rostenkowski went to the Legislature, the elder Daley was Cook County clerk, and they developed the relationship that proved fruitful for both for a quarter-century.

It was not just youth and talent that brought Rostenkowski so far so fast; it was family. The Rostenkowskis were a sort of political elite on the city's Polish Northwest Side. The congressman's father, Joseph, was a Chicago alderman and ward committeeman for 20 years and later U.S. collector of customs.

Joe Rostenkowski was influential in launching his son's political career and dissuading him from professional baseball. At one point, the younger Rostenkowski turned down an offer from Connie Mack, owner of the Philadelphia Athletics.

In 1958, Democratic Rep. Thomas Gordon of Chicago, chairman of the House Foreign Affairs Committee, decided to retire. Daley was mayor by then and it was his task to pick a successor. He anointed Rostenkowski. At that point, the average age of the Chicago Democratic delegation in the House was 72. Daley felt some youth was needed.

Rostenkowski remained a committed loyalist, even when he was chastised, as he was by a Chicago judge in 1963, for paying constituents' traffic tickets out of Democratic Party funds.

In 1966, a year of high racial tension and strong white backlash in Chicago, Rostenkowski ran his only "scared" race. His opponent was John Leszynski, a cab driver who openly appealed to the backlash against open-housing demonstrations. Rostenkowski was re-elected, but his percentage fell below 60 percent for the only time in his career.

Since then, his position has been impregnable. Even the drift of many of his district's white ethnics away from their traditional Democratic moorings in the 1980s has done him little harm: In each of his last three elections, he has topped 70 percent of the vote.

Every two years, however, Rostenkowski raises money as if he were in the fight of his life. In 1988, he raised over \$850,000, boosting his campaign reserve to over \$1 million.

Even before he took over the Ways and Means chairmanship, his presence on the tax-writing committee guaranteed him ample financing from interests with a stake in the way taxes were written. In 1982 he held his first Washington, D.C., fund-raiser, and by election time had taken in more than \$500,000.

Unnecessary as this money was, Rostenkowski found ways to spend it. In the spring of 1982, some \$300 was donated to a private group buying bulletproof vests for the Chicago police; \$1,639 went to entertain friends of the chairman at six Chicago restaurants. "There's a political machine alive in Chicago," a Rostenkowski aide said, "and you reach it with personal noodling over dinner."

Committees

Ways and Means (Chairman)
Trade

Joint Taxation (Chairman)

Elections

1988 General

Dan Rostenkowski (D)	107,728	(75%)
V. Stephen Vetter (R)	34,659	(24%)

1986 General

Dan Rostenkowski (D)	82,873	(79%)
Thomas J. DeFazio (R)	22,383	(21%)

Previous Winning Percentages: **1984** (71%) **1982** (83%)
1980 (85%) **1978** (86%) **1976** (81%) **1974** (87%)
1972 (74%) **1970** (74%) **1968** (63%) **1966** (60%)
1964 (66%) **1962** (61%) **1960** (67%) **1958** (75%)

District Vote For President

	1988	1984	1980	1976
D	92,135 (59%)	85,928 (48%)	111,965 (59%)	122,652 (60%)
R	63,885 (41%)	90,875 (51%)	65,215 (34%)	80,327 (39%)
I			10,043 (5%)	

Campaign Finance

	Receipts	Receipts from PACs	Expend-itures
1988			
Rostenkowski (D)	$866,341	$444,698 (51%)	$428,607
1986			
Rostenkowski (D)	$243,976	$199,124 (82%)	$240,208

Key Votes

1987

Raise speed limit to 65 mph	Y
Approve Gephardt "fair trade" amendment	N
Ban testing of larger nuclear weapons	Y
Delay "re-flagging" of Kuwaiti tankers	?
Approve tax-raising deficit-reduction bill	Y

1988

Approve aid to Nicaraguan contras	N
Enact civil rights restoration bill over Reagan veto	Y
Kill 60-day plant-closing notification measure	N
Pass omnibus trade bill over Reagan veto	Y
Approve death penalty for drug-related murders	Y
Bar federal funds for abortions in cases of rape and incest	Y
Oppose seven-day waiting period for purchase of handguns	X

Voting Studies

	Presidential Support		Party Unity		Conservative Coalition	
Year	**S**	**O**	**S**	**O**	**S**	**O**
1988	29	58	80	9	32	58
1987	20	66	73	5	37	47
1986	19	66	84	5	36	58
1985	28	61	82	6	18	73
1984	39	42	68	11	34	46
1983	41	52	77	12	33	64
1982	44	44	80	14	42	56
1981	50	49	77	18	44	52

Interest Group Ratings

Year	ADA	ACU	AFL-CIO	CCUS
1988	65	19	85	50
1987	68	18	77	22
1986	65	15	86	35
1985	75	20	81	36
1984	65	10	83	36
1983	65	9	81	39
1982	85	10	85	35
1981	55	14	73	26

9 Sidney R. Yates (D)

Of Chicago — Elected 1948
Did not serve 1963-65.

Born: Aug. 27, 1909, Chicago, Ill.
Education: U. of Chicago, Ph.B. 1931, J.D. 1933.
Military Career: Navy, 1944-46.
Occupation: Lawyer.
Family: Wife, Adeline Holleb; one child.
Religion: Jewish.
Political Career: Democratic nominee for U.S. Senate, 1962.
Capitol Office: 2234 Rayburn Bldg. 20515; 225-2111.

In Washington: Though he has served four decades on the powerful Appropriations Committee, Yates is unlikely ever to be its chairman. If that bothers him, he characteristically does not show it. Instead, as a member of the panel's "College of Cardinals," heading one of its 13 subcommittees, he contentedly has carved his own sphere of influence as a defender of the environment and the arts.

Even as he approached his 80th birthday, Yates waged his fights against Reagan-era budget cuts with all the vigor he brought to past crusades for public housing in the 1950s and against the SST in the 1970s. Generally Yates works behind the scenes as chairman of the Interior Subcommittee, but he was often provoked into the spotlight during the Reagan years — from 1981, when he blocked a proposed 50 percent funding reduction for the National Endowment for the Arts, to 1988, when he engineered a far-reaching moratorium against administration plans to lease offshore lands for oil drilling. During the Bush administration, Yates is likely to be a leader as congressional Democrats hold the new president to his pro-environment campaign rhetoric.

Yates has a reputation as one of Appropriations' toughest subcommittee chairmen. His hearings are among the most detailed in the House; he does much of his own research on issues and always seems familiar with each budget item. He employs the probing style of a crafty lawyer to corner administration witnesses, and to nudge his own colleagues — from Chairman Jamie L. Whitten on down — toward his position. But he is also personable and witty, and respected both for the grace of his argument and the quality of his work.

Within the House, Yates is one of the committee's most loyal advocates in protesting the limitations imposed on it by the 1985 Gramm-Rudman-Hollings law; he detests what he sees as the phoniness of the law's budget-balancing targets and the arbitrariness of its threatened cuts. He is equally outspoken within the committee, and has concurred with junior colleagues who chafe at the panel's traditional stricture against offering amendments.

He stakes out the liberal ground, at times too liberal in some fellow Democrats' view. On the floor, however, he occasionally seems to lose his taste for a good fight. In 1985, he went more than halfway to accommodate conservative Republicans who proposed a 10 percent cut in an arts budget because they said the agency supported authors of sexually explicit poems. Rather than try to defeat the amendment outright, Yates agreed to a smaller reduction.

But his 1981 skirmish over arts spending was more typical. His subcommittee simply ignored Reagan's requested cuts. The president finally signed the measure, and never again sought such major bites from arts funding.

Yates is fourth-ranking on Appropriations, but nowhere near so close to the chair as his proximity would suggest. He is older than all three men ahead of him, including Whitten, who in any case is expected to remain a few more years. So Yates' fiefdom probably will remain limited to his subcommittee, which itself holds broad sway over the budgets for the Interior Department, national parks, mines, Indian affairs, the national endowments for the arts and humanities and the Smithsonian Institution.

He is a dedicated environmentalist, and his subcommittee is one of the few on Appropriations that regularly grapples with controversial policy issues, not just budget numbers. He played a key role in blocking some of the Reagan administration's more controversial resource-development policies, including leasing of federal lands for coal mining and offshore oil and gas drilling. Annually, over administration objections, Yates' panel would include more funding for energy conservation, park land acquisition and Indian health programs.

He had indicated in 1984 that he would not seek extension of a four-year moratorium on California offshore oil leases because of improvements at Interior. But after a tentative agreement between California lawmakers and Interior officials fell apart in 1985, Yates tried

Illinois 9

Chicago — North Side Lakefront; Northern Suburbs

Narrow at its base along Lake Michigan, the 9th District widens and turns westward once it reaches Chicago's northern limits, ending in a hook around the suburbs of Glenview and Northbrook. The purpose of the elaborate cartography, performed in the 1981 redistricting, was to make a secure district for Yates by including liberal areas within the city and heavily Jewish suburban communities.

The 9th is anchored on the North Side of Chicago, but it runs north along the lake all the way to Evanston, and its western portion takes in Skokie, Wilmette, Morton Grove and a chunk of Northfield township.

The city portion of the 9th includes a mixture of neighborhoods from the opulent lakefront high-rises to the two- and three-story walk-ups just a few blocks west. These apartments house many of the prosperous singles and couples who work in professional jobs in downtown Chicago. There is an urban-restoration contingent living in older homes in the area. The city portion of the 9th also contains some of Chicago's few Republican wards.

The large Jewish population in the urban lakefront part of the district is predominantly middle-aged, well-to-do and politically active. While most white voters in Chicago rejected black Democratic mayoral candidate Harold Washington, many liberal Jewish voters from this area went with him and provided him with margins crucial to his victories in 1983 and 1987.

The two wards west of the more prosperous neighborhoods are made up mostly of Hispanics, who comprise about 10 percent of the overall population of the district. The 9th is also about 10 percent black.

The parts of the 9th that lie beyond Chicago are not typically suburban in their political outlook. Evanston, once a bastion of conservative Republicanism, has a large liberal community around Northwestern University; it has also attracted young married professionals from Chicago, who tend to vote Democratic. Aiding the Democrats in Evanston is the racial makeup — the city of about 72,000 is over 20 percent black.

West of Evanston are Morton Grove and Skokie, two heavily Jewish towns that made headlines in recent years. Morton Grove was in the news for passing a stringent gun-control law. Skokie gained attention because of efforts by its Jewish population, including some survivors of World War II concentration camps, to prevent American Nazis from rallying in their town.

Population 519,120. White 407,592 (79%), Black 50,716 (10%), Asian and Pacific Islander 30,708 (6%). Spanish origin 49,558 (10%). 18 and over 422,900 (81%), 65 and over 70,023 (13%). Median age: 32.

to extend the ban one more year. He lost by one vote in Appropriations. Moratorium supporters, not sure they could win the issue on the floor either, agreed to a compromise with Interior officials that was later approved by the House.

By 1988, Californians and Interior had another shaky truce, and the administration agreed to postpone lease sales until 1989 — after the 1988 presidential election. Then-candidate Bush promised a further delay if elected. Yates decided to take no chances and seize the initiative. This time, he successfully amended the Interior appropriations bill to include a one-year ban on leases not only off California's coast but also on the Georges Bank off Massachusetts and off Florida's Gulf Coast.

As part of that bill, he included reduced appropriations for the nation's largest national forest, Tongass in Alaska; the annual payments are controversial because they support development related to logging operations there. Also in the 100th Congress, Yates raised a procedural challenge that helped obstruct a bill to open Alaska's vast Arctic National Wildlife Refuge for oil and gas exploration.

In 1988, his subcommittee's bill became the vehicle for a junior member's amendment that split the disciplined, collegial culture of Appropriations. But Yates allied with the younger member, Robert J. Mrazek of New York, illustrating not only his own scorn for Appropriations' no-amendments tradition, but also his interest in the arts.

The amendment would have limited "colorization" of classic black-and-white films, and it pitted those on the movie industry's creative side — writers, directors and actors — against film owners and producers. Though Mrazek was not a member of Yates' subcommittee, Yates included his anti-colorization provision in the Interior bill. In full committee, a move to delete it failed, 20-25. On the floor, however, Yates and Mrazek had to compromise; otherwise, the proposal might have fallen to a point of order against legislating in an appropriations bill.

Yates has been a jealous guardian of congressional spending prerogatives. In the 99th Congress, he led a drive to revoke the president's authority to defer appropriations by Congress — a power he felt Reagan had abused.

Although Congress did not enact Yates' amendment, subsequent federal court rulings circumscribed the president's deferral authority.

Yates' low-key style masks a stubbornness that allows him to stick with an issue for years, if necessary, to get what he wants. That was true in the long debate over the supersonic transport plane, which was first proposed in 1963 at an estimated cost of $1.5 billion, but was sidelined until President Richard M. Nixon came into office in 1969.

Yates had opposed the idea from the beginning, complaining that it was an "incredible distortion of our national priorities" to spend that much public money for a private purpose. Throughout the 1960s, his amendments to eliminate SST funds had been defeated regularly, always on non-recorded votes. Millions of dollars already had been spent on preliminary planning when, in 1971, the House finally confronted the issue directly.

Newly adopted rules forced an on-the-record vote for the first time, and Yates was ready with stacks of facts and figures. Backing him was a well-organized environmental lobby and a carefully orchestrated publicity campaign. Yates, who had never called a press conference (and has not to this day), suddenly was quite willing to answer reporters' questions. The pending confrontation was widely publicized. In the roll-call vote, he won, 217-203.

Yates was just a freshman when he won a place on Appropriations in 1949. An energetic urban liberal in the 1950s, he became a leading advocate for the government's efforts to provide aid to older cities like Chicago.

When the GOP-controlled House sought to kill the public housing program in 1953, Yates fought back. "We need a program that will satisfy the housing needs of all Americans, of every economic level," he said, "not just those who can afford to buy their own houses." In the end, a compromise authorized 20,000 new housing units (compared with the 75,000 President Harry S Truman sought before leaving office). Yates also advocated legislation in those days to make mortgage credit money more easily available.

In his second term, he took up a different kind of campaign, to convince the Navy it should promote Hyman G. Rickover to admiral. The renowned advocate of nuclear submarines had been bypassed and was about to leave the service. Yates thought that was wrong and said so, repeatedly. The resulting congressional hearings and public attention brought the desired result. Rickover was promoted, and remained on active duty until 1982.

Yates was out of Congress for two years in the 1960s, after an unsuccessful Senate campaign. When he came back to the House in 1965, he returned to Appropriations. This time he was placed on the Transportation Subcommittee, where he was drawn into the SST fight. Later Yates switched to the Interior Subcommittee; he became its chairman in 1975.

He also serves on Appropriations' Foreign Operations Subcommittee, where he is a strong supporter of aid to Israel. Otherwise, he does not invest much time or attention on the panel. At the full committee, Yates has fought the MX missile and the B-1 bomber, recalling his marathon crusade in the 1960s against the old antiballistic missile system. His amendment to block funding for the B-1 failed in committee in 1982, 22-27.

He is no more fond of small weapons than of large ones. One of the most resolute House supporters of gun control, he espouses legislation to ban the sale, manufacture and distribution of all handguns.

Perhaps nothing better reflects Yates' priorities in the twilight of his career than his compact legislative portfolio for the 100th Congress. It included, of course, the fiscal 1988 and 1989 Interior appropriations bills, and also a handgun control bill, a resolution designating "National Humanities Week" and a second resolution involving a ceremony to honor Holocaust victims.

At Home: Only one member of the current House — Mississippi's Whitten — entered it before Yates did in January 1949. But despite his many years in Congress, Yates has not received the full benefits of his seniority because he made one wrong move: He left the House in 1962 to run for the Senate against GOP leader Everett M. Dirksen. When Yates came back to the House two years later, he was at the bottom again.

Yates' Senate campaign had the backing of Chicago Mayor Richard J. Daley and the Democratic organization, and he made a respectable showing with 47 percent, more than any Democrat ever received against Dirksen.

There was a bit of intraparty controversy over that election. Some Democrats contended that President John F. Kennedy secretly favored Dirksen, considering him the friendliest Republican Senate leader he was likely to get, and withheld backing for Yates. The Cuban missile crisis took place in the final month of the campaign, and Dirksen was consulted often and openly by the White House.

Yates said at the time he was satisfied with Kennedy's conduct, and he has expressed no grievances since then. In 1963, Kennedy appointed him U.S. representative to the United Nations Trusteeship Council, a post he held for more than a year.

In the fall of 1964, the Chicago Democratic organization suddenly found a judgeship for Rep. Edward Finnegan, whom it had chosen to replace Yates in the House. Since Finnegan had already been renominated, the local party had the right to designate a candidate for the vacancy, and to no one's surprise, Yates was the choice. He had been spared the trouble of a primary, and four months later he was back in the House. He has held the seat without too much difficulty ever since, cordial but not subservient to organization regulars.

Yates originally won his seat as a last-minute organization choice in a much different situation. In 1948, recently returned to his Chicago law practice after World War II, he had been drafted to run against Republican Rep. Robert J. Twyman, who was expected to win re-election easily in a national Dewey landslide. But the Democratic ticket swept Illinois that year, and Yates came in with an 18,000-vote majority. He kept his seat narrowly in 1950 and 1952, and thereafter he was safe.

In 1982, Yates easily overcame district Republicans' only real effort to challenge him. The GOP ran an articulate moderate, 32-year-old Catherine Bertini, and launched a vigorous "time for a change" campaign. Bertini argued that Yates, then 73, could not identify with his constituents because he first went to Washington before many of them were born.

Considerable attention and funding came Bertini's way. She was well connected to the national party (she was director of youth programs for the Republican National Committee in 1975-76), and her job at Container Corporation of America brought her into contact with directors of corporate political action committees.

But Bertini's challenge was uphill from the outset, since the 9th was carefully redrawn in 1981 to help Yates. The veteran incumbent took the challenge seriously; though his wife's illness limited his campaign time, he strove to introduce himself to the thousands of new constituents redistricting had given him.

They found his House record suitable and saw no reason to trade his experience for Bertini's promise of fresh leadership. Yates won re-election with 67 percent. In his last three campaigns, Yates has bested Republican doctor-lawyer Herbert Sohn by 2-to-1 or better.

Committee

Appropriations (4th of 35 Democrats)
Interior and Related Agencies (chairman); Foreign Operations; Legislative Branch

Elections

1988 General		
Sidney R. Yates (D)	135,583	(66%)
Herbert Sohn (R)	67,604	(33%)
1986 General		
Sidney R. Yates (D)	92,738	(72%)
Herbert Sohn (R)	36,715	(28%)

Previous Winning Percentages: **1984** (68%) **1982** (67%) **1980** (73%) **1978** (75%) **1976** (72%) **1974** (100%) **1972** (68%) **1970** (76%) **1968** (64%) **1966** (60%) **1964** (64%) **1960** (60%) **1958** (67%) **1956** (54%) **1954** (60%) **1952** (52%) **1950** (52%) **1948** (55%)

District Vote For President

	1988	1984	1980	1976
D	137,259 (61%)	129,644 (55%)	110,744 (49%)	129,098 (51%)
R	85,855 (38%)	106,151 (45%)	83,961 (37%)	121,293 (48%)
I			28,537 (13%)	

Campaign Finance

	Receipts	Receipts from PACs	Expend-itures
1988			
Yates (D)	$126,705	$25,250 (20%)	$122,900
Sohn (R)	$41,986	0	$36,837
1986			
Yates (D)	$149,145	$16,401 (11%)	$97,479
Sohn (R)	$36,585	$12,250 (33%)	$38,385

Key Votes

1987	
Raise speed limit to 65 mph	N
Approve Gephardt "fair trade" amendment	N
Ban testing of larger nuclear weapons	Y
Delay "re-flagging" of Kuwaiti tankers	Y
Approve tax-raising deficit-reduction bill	Y
1988	
Approve aid to Nicaraguan contras	N
Enact civil rights restoration bill over Reagan veto	Y
Kill 60-day plant-closing notification measure	N
Pass omnibus trade bill over Reagan veto	Y
Approve death penalty for drug-related murders	N
Bar federal funds for abortions in cases of rape and incest	N
Oppose seven-day waiting period for purchase of handguns	N

Voting Studies

	Presidential Support		Party Unity		Conservative Coalition	
Year	**S**	**O**	**S**	**O**	**S**	**O**
1988	17	66	81	5	8	71
1987	12	86	95	2	2	95
1986	18	77	88	3	2	86
1985	31	68	93	4	7	91
1984	28	71	91	8	5	93
1983	17	77	95	4	7	87
1982	19	53	75	4	4	70
1981	26	71	90	9	5	95

Interest Group Ratings

Year	ADA	ACU	AFL-CIO	CCUS
1988	80	5	100	36
1987	96	9	87	7
1986	90	0	85	12
1985	100	10	88	20
1984	95	0	92	31
1983	95	4	100	10
1982	75	0	100	13
1981	100	0	80	11

10 John Porter (R)

Of Wilmette — Elected 1980

Born: June 1, 1935, Evanston, Ill.

Education: Attended Massachusetts Institute of Technology, 1953-54; Northwestern U., B.S., B.A. 1957; U. of Michigan, J.D. 1961.

Military Career: Army Reserve, 1958-64.

Occupation: Lawyer.

Family: Wife, Kathryn Cameron; five children.

Religion: Presbyterian.

Political Career: Ill. House, 1973-79; Republican nominee for U.S. House, 1978; Republican nominee for Cook County circuit court judge, 1970.

Capitol Office: 1501 Longworth Bldg. 20515; 225-4835.

In Washington: He is silver-haired and rather reserved, and his overall voting record places him near the middle of the political spectrum, but Porter should not be mistaken for a middle-of-the-roader. He converges on the center from both sides. When he fights the Republicans on population control or chemical weapons, he lines up with the most liberal House members. When he takes Democrats to task for wasting federal money on useless programs, he sounds like a spokesman for the U.S. Chamber of Commerce.

Porter has also been known to take iconoclastic stands that pit him against the left and the right simultaneously. In the 100th Congress, he was one of only 17 House members to vote against elevating the Veterans Administration (VA) to a Cabinet-level bureaucracy. "At a time when deficits have reached crisis proportions and courage to make the tough decision is needed more than ever before," Porter scolded, "the Congress ... is obviously still gripped in the craven fear of special interests."

While Porter's independence earns him praise — his views on the VA prompted a *Washington Post* editorial praising the "truth fairy" perched on his shoulder — he is in an unusually comfortable political position, one that gives him leeway to speak his mind. He represents a firmly Republican and relatively affluent district north of Chicago; most of his constituents do not have a pressing need for federal goods and services.

Porter's approach to the federal budget deficit is pure conservative. In each year of the last two Congresses, he has co-authored alternative budgets that would freeze most spending, including cost-of-living adjustments in entitlement programs. Porter decries Congress' failure to meet the targets in the Gramm-Rudman-Hollings deficit-reduction law, and he regularly blasts the overall budget process as undisciplined.

Porter refers to the effect of the federal debt on future generations as "fiscal child abuse." This is somewhat tamer rhetoric than he used earlier in his career, when he gave a floor speech chastising Democrats: "Ladies and gentlemen of the far left, you are the problem. ... The stagnation and unemployment we are suffering you have caused. Not President Reagan. Not supply-side economics. Not tax cuts. You."

But on select issues, Porter stands shoulder-to-shoulder with liberals. On 1988 legislation to require a seven-day waiting period for handgun purchases, he implored his colleagues to show "the courage to do something to stop the handgun carnage in America." The measure was soundly defeated. A few months before the vote, a woman had opened fire on a classroom in Porter's district, killing one child and wounding five others.

On chemical weapons, no such direct district concern enters the equation. A harsh critic of the Pentagon's contention that chemical weapons could be quickly deployed in Europe in the event of armed confrontation with the Soviet Union, Porter fought to ban the controversial weapons in the 99th Congress. In 1985, proponents succeeded in authorizing $124 million for chemical-weapons production, but when the issue came before Appropriations, Porter successfully pushed an amendment to block the funding. A year later, Porter contributed to another effort to ban chemical weapon production; it passed by a bare 210-209 vote.

Meanwhile, as a member of the Appropriations Subcommittee on Foreign Operations, Porter has taken on social conservatives by fighting to preserve U.S. funding for international population-control efforts. He is a leading member of the Congressional Coalition on Population and Development, and an advocate of increased U.S. assistance for international efforts to fight AIDS.

But conservatives unnerved by Porter's stands on these issues have little reason to find

Illinois 10

North and Northwest Chicago Suburbs — Waukegan

Though Porter's roots are in Evanston, he has no political complaints about the redistricting of the early 1980s that removed that mainly Democratic city from his district. The 10th begins in the affluent northern Chicago suburbs in Cook County, crosses into Lake County and extends all the way to the Wisconsin border. It is firmly Republican.

The district's closest-in towns — Kenilworth, Winnetka, Glencoe — are Illinois' wealthiest. These communities along Lake Michigan are among Chicago's oldest suburbs. They are solidly Republican: Porter took 76 percent of the Cook County vote in 1988.

Lake County, most of which votes in the 10th, is a GOP stronghold. George Bush carried it with 63 percent in 1988, and in the last two gubernatorial elections, Republican Gov. James R. Thompson won Lake with well over 60 percent of the vote.

The only major Democratic enclave in the county — or in the district — is the old port city of Waukegan. Now a manufacturing center producing pharmaceuticals, hospital supplies and outboard motors, Waukegan has a population that is about 15 percent Hispanic.

Though the traditional commuting pattern from the district is to downtown Chicago, corporate outposts have sprung up among the bedroom communities in recent years. Allstate and Kemper Insurance, Walgreen's and Household Finance are major employers in the district. Also in the 10th is the Great Lakes Naval Training Center, on the lake near North Chicago. The largest such operation in the country, it employs well over 20,000 people.

Population: 519,660. White 469,474 (90%), Black 29,339 (6%), Other 10,315 (2%). Spanish origin 22,202 (4%). 18 and over 368,611 (71%), 65 and over 40,566 (8%). Median age: 30.

fault with him on most other defense and foreign policy questions. He has supported funding for the strategic defense initiative and for the Nicaraguan contras. And notwithstanding his population control and AIDS efforts, he is skeptical of most other forms of humanitarian foreign aid.

As a result of Porter's conservative position on most budget questions, some of his colleagues bristle when he lobbies the Appropriations Committee to provide funds for projects in his district. But so far, little revenge seems to have been exacted. In October 1988, he was on hand for the dedication of a new air-traffic-control tower at Waukegan Regional Airport in his district. Porter was credited with winning federal funding for it.

Porter also defends federal spending for favored programs from his position on the Appropriations subcommittee that funds the Departments of Labor, Health and Human Services, and Education. He has worked for higher funding for the National Eye Institute, and tried to establish centers around the country to educate and ease resettlement of refugees.

Like many members of Congress, Porter occassionally sees a future president in the mirror in the morning. "I realize how difficult it is to achieve," he once admitted to a local reporter. "Still, I'm aiming for the office. I'd like nothing better than to continue my programs for human rights, conservation and debt reduction, among others, from the White House. Meanwhile, I'll continue my work at the lower level."

At Home: The son of a well-known judge in Evanston, Porter returned to the affluent Cook County suburbs north of Chicago from Washington after a stint with the Kennedy Justice Department in the early 1960s. He set up a law practice, and worked to build a political base. Porter's first goal was to follow in his father's footsteps to a judgeship. The path he chose, though — work in the Young Republicans organization — was not necessarily the best for an ambitious young lawyer in an area dominated at a countywide level by Chicago Democrats. In 1970, he tried unsuccessfully to win election as Cook County circuit court judge as part of a GOP slate dubbed "the suicide squad."

But the bid helped build his credentials within GOP circles. Immersed in Evanston Republican affairs, Porter had no trouble winning a state House seat in 1972, and in winning re-election twice.

His first run for Congress came in 1978. Democratic Rep. Abner J. Mikva, one of the most liberal Democrats in the House, had won the old 10th by scanty margins in both 1974 and 1976. Porter was one of seven Republicans who wanted to take him on again.

During his six years in the state Legislature, Porter had been viewed as a moderate, at least on social issues, and had received high ratings from the liberal Independent Voters of Illinois. His chief opponent in the 1978 primary, Daniel Hales, had support from national New Right organizations. The crucial asset for Porter was the backing of the local GOP apparatus, including the two key Republican township organizations in the district. He won the primary comfortably.

His contest with Mikva proved rougher. Porter raised more money from political action committees than any other House candidate in the country that year, and spent it freely. But Mikva, no mean fund-raiser himself, had a slight edge in organization, and nudged Porter out by 650 votes.

Mikva was appointed to a federal judgeship only a few months later, and both parties realized that the seat probably would not remain Democratic without him. This time, Porter had no trouble winning nomination. In his 1980 special election against Democrat Robert Weinberger, a former Commerce Department aide, he had a massive spending advantage and emerged with 54 percent. Seeking a full term in November 1980, he was returned to office by a convincing margin of nearly 50,000 votes.

It seemed at first that he would have no chance to rest. In the 1981 remap, Porter's Evanston home was placed in the heavily Democratic 9th District. Porter announced he would move north to challenge GOP Rep. Robert McClory in the newly drawn 10th, where Republican loyalties were solid. But the showdown between the Republican incumbents never took place. The 74-year-old McClory, after filing and announcing for an 11th term, decided in January 1982 that he would step down for his younger colleague.

Though only one-fifth of the people in the new 10th came from Porter's old district, no one challenged him in the primary, and he won comfortably in November against an experienced Democratic state legislator, Eugenia S. Chapman. His elections since have been routine.

Committees

Appropriations (14th of 22 Republicans)
Foreign Operations; Labor, Health and Human Services, Education and Related Agencies; Legislative Branch

Select Aging (24th of 27 Republicans)

Elections

1988 General		
John Porter (R)	158,519	(72%)
Eugene F. Friedman (D)	60,187	(28%)
1986 General		
John Porter (R)	87,530	(75%)
Robert A. Cleland (D)	28,990	(25%)

Previous Winning Percentages: 1984 (73%) **1982** (59%) **1980** (61%) **1980** * (54%)

* *Special election.*

District Vote For President

	1988	1984	1980	1976
D	86,280 (38%)	70,881 (31%)	60,308 (28%)	70,251 (33%)
R	143,022 (62%)	154,106 (68%)	129,386 (59%)	139,680 (65%)
I			25,273 (12%)	

Campaign Finance

	Receipts	Receipts from PACs	Expend-itures
1988			
Porter (R)	$245,366	$115,321 (47%)	$212,630
Friedman (D)	$62,786	$21,800 (35%)	$62,560
1986			
Porter (R)	$188,340	$77,041 (41%)	$176,228
Cleland (D)	$104,263	$100 (0.1%)	$103,817

Key Votes

1987	
Raise speed limit to 65 mph	Y
Approve Gephardt "fair trade" amendment	N
Ban testing of larger nuclear weapons	Y
Delay "re-flagging" of Kuwaiti tankers	N
Approve tax-raising deficit-reduction bill	N
1988	
Approve aid to Nicaraguan contras	Y
Enact civil rights restoration bill over Reagan veto	Y
Kill 60-day plant-closing notification measure	Y
Pass omnibus trade bill over Reagan veto	N
Approve death penalty for drug-related murders	Y
Bar federal funds for abortions in cases of rape and incest	Y
Oppose seven-day waiting period for purchase of handguns	N

Voting Studies

	Presidential Support		Party Unity		Conservative Coalition	
Year	**S**	**O**	**S**	**O**	**S**	**O**
1988	57	42	71	22	82	18
1987	54	41	69	25	81	19
1986	59	39	68	28	68	32
1985	68	30	71	25	73	25
1984	58	40	65	31	80	19
1983	73	22	69	29	67	30
1982	60	32	66	28	62	32
1981	68	32	65	33	61	36

Interest Group Ratings

Year	ADA	ACU	AFL-CIO	CCUS
1988	30	68	15	100
1987	20	62	6	100
1986	15	64	7	94
1985	20	71	24	82
1984	40	42	23	81
1983	25	52	6	95
1982	35	67	17	81
1981	30	67	7	89

11 Frank Annunzio (D)

Of Chicago — Elected 1964

Born: Jan. 12, 1915, Chicago, Ill.
Education: De Paul U., B.S. 1940, M.A. 1942.
Occupation: Teacher; labor official.
Family: Wife, Angeline Alesia; three children.
Religion: Roman Catholic.
Political Career: Illinois labor director, 1949-52.
Capitol Office: 2303 Rayburn Bldg. 20515; 225-6661.

In Washington: Numismatists wept with Annunzio's 1989 decision to leave the chair of the Subcommittee on Consumer Affairs and Coinage. For 14 years, he watched over the nation's pocket change and folding money and sought to celebrate historical events — and even reduce the deficit — with the minting and selling of commemorative coins.

But the coin collectors' loss was the savings and loan industry's gain. The re-election loss of Banking Chairman Fernand J. St Germain opened up the chair of the Financial Institutions Subcommittee, a panel positioned to play a key role in the 101st Congress' efforts to bail out the bankrupt thrift deposit insurance fund. Annunzio moved over from Consumer Affairs and Coinage.

True to his past, Annunzio pressed the S&Ls' cause in the debate's early goings. He has been their consistent champion. In his world, S&Ls befriend the little guy while banks protect big business and profits. He has been closely identified with the U.S. League of Savings Institutions, formerly headquartered in Chicago. He also has looked out for the interests of another venerable Chicago institution, Sears, Roebuck and Co., the retailer that expanded aggressively into financial services as the industry was deregulated in the 1980s.

But position alone is not power, and although Annunzio has devoted most of his attention to the Banking Committee, it would be out of character for him to emerge as a major player in the twilight of his legislative career. He relies increasingly on a subcommittee staff whose relations within the House do not always well serve him.

A product of former Chicago Mayor Richard J. Daley's Democratic organization, Annunzio stands somewhere between the pure patronage politics of his Chicago generation and the politics of his younger colleagues. He takes himself and his issues seriously, and he has never been an easy man for the House leadership or the Chicago organization to control, even in Mayor Daley's heyday. Intensely proud, he is a difficult vote to change on sensitive matters.

In addition to his Banking subcommittee, he chairs the House Administration Committee and thus holds sway over important housekeeping matters, including the House purse. Still, Annunzio has never reached the first rank of senior legislators. When he wins, it is normally on the basis of sheer stubbornness, not legislative wizardry.

He has argued for truth-in-lending legislation, and denounced unscrupulous debt collectors, high interest rates and credit card abuses. But while he fancies himself as the populist protector of the common man, the results are thin. He failed again in the 100th Congress to make the case against one of his favorite issues, cost of credit card interest. Annunzio railed against "plastic loan sharking," but his colleagues beyond the subcommittee turned a deaf ear on his efforts to cap interest rates. The cap was stripped by Banking and defeated by a 56-356 vote on the floor.

The credit card battle reflected his stubbornness and his unwillingness to compromise. Even consumer groups backed off the cap to avoid losing measures to help consumers wade through the financial fine print of credit. Still, the defeat represented a slight measure of progress for Annunzio, who in the 99th Congress could not even get the cap out of subcommittee. "I feel like I'm being left out," Annunzio complained then. "I feel like I'm being punished by not even being consulted."

While Annunzio's mind is not the subtlest in the House, his other qualities — he is stubborn and strong-willed — have stood him in good stead.

It was stubbornness that gave Annunzio a satisfying victory on the issue of minting coins to commemorate the 1984 Olympics in Los Angeles. Annunzio was determined that the Olympic coins be minted and sold by the U.S. Treasury, not privately, and he had to fight not only the Senate, which passed a bill providing for private production of the coins, but also St Germain, who never saw the reason for Annunzio's concern.

He insisted on fighting, and fought with his usual intensity. He even organized a grass-roots "living room" lobby whose members vowed to

Illinois 11

Northwest Chicago and Suburbs

Despite a Republican trend in statewide elections, the 11th has remained secure home turf for Annunzio. His appeal is not hard to explain. Many of his constituents moved out during the 1970s from the old West Side 7th; like other Chicago Democrats, Annunzio simply followed them to the suburbs. "These are my people," he once said. "Lincolnwood? My daughter lives in Lincolnwood. Stone Park? There's a seminary there for Italian priests, and an Italian-American cultural center. Northlake? That's where we have an Italian old folks' home."

But these suburbs are not so kind to other Democrats. Stretching north to Niles and west to O'Hare Airport, the district takes in a collection of middle-class suburban developments built in the 1950s and early 1960s. Most of the residents of this area are ethnic in background, but they have moved beyond their blue-collar roots; many of them have voted for Republican candidates in statewide elections regularly during the past decade. President Reagan easily carried the 11th in 1984 with 61 percent of the vote; George Bush won with a more modest 54 percent four years later. Republican Sen. Charles H. Percy put in a strong showing there as well in his losing 1984 bid for re-election.

The city part of Annunzio's district is not all that different politically. Middle-class ethnic wards such as the 41st and 45th, in the northwest corner of the city, went heavily for Reagan and Percy in 1984. A Republican candidate dwelling on law and order and fiscal conservatism could expect to do well there in any battle following Annunzio's retirement.

A somewhat more liberal vote comes out of the 50th Ward, at the northeast end of the city, which has a substantial Jewish presence around Rogers Park.

The 39th Ward, which is generally conservative and ethnic, also has a Jewish vote that tempers its Republican nature; Reagan carried the 39th in 1984, but Democrat Paul Simon edged out Percy in the Senate contest there.

The district is overwhelmingly white. About 6 percent of the population is Hispanic; less than 1 percent is black. The Chicago Jewish communities are reinforced by a large Jewish population in Skokie, which is split between the 11th and the 9th.

Population: 518,995. White 475,460 (92%), Black 2,010 (0.4%), Asian and Pacific Islander 24,400 (5%). Spanish origin 31,425 (6%). 18 and over 409,539 (79%), 65 and over 86,119 (17%). Median age: 37.

buy $1 government coins. When the issue reached the House floor, Annunzio won a 302-84 victory that seemed to surprise even him.

House Administration's chief role is to set committee budgets — a once-routine task that in recent years has become a bitterly partisan battle, as Republicans have tried to limit the extra staff, equipment and perquisites Democrats wanted to add.

But it is the committee's capacity as overseer of election legislation that could prove interesting in the 101st Congress. Voter registration and uniform poll-closing legislation are at the top of the committee's agenda. A campaign-finance reform movement has re-emerged, and Annunzio has joined in efforts to control campaign costs. Most of his previous efforts in this field went into his unsuccessful effort to print political action committee finances in the *Congressional Record.*

At Home: The labor movement was Annunzio's route to elective office in Chicago. More than 20 years before he was given the party's endorsement for Congress, he was a familiar figure in city politics as a strategist for the United Steelworkers of America. By 1948 Annunzio was secretary-treasurer of the CIO's Illinois Political Action Committee. The next year, he was appointed director of labor for the state of Illinois.

In 1952, Gov. Adlai E. Stevenson, who had appointed Annunzio to that position, asked him to resign. Annunzio had formed his own insurance company, and suspicions arose that he might be using his state position to help his private business. Annunzio sharply denied the charges, but he gave up his state job.

His political career was only beginning. Annunzio was personally close to a fellow member of Stevenson's state Cabinet, Revenue Director Richard J. Daley. He remained active in ward politics in the 1950s, while running a personnel agency, and eventually an opportunity opened up for him.

By 1964 there were so many rumors about Democratic Rep. Roland Libonati's Mafia connections that the Cook County organization found him an embarrassment. Libonati gave up his 7th District House seat voluntarily, and Daley's organization turned to Annunzio to replace him. There was no primary and Annunzio was never threatened for re-election in his eight years representing the 7th District, on the city's old Near West Side.

But redistricting in 1971 caused him serious problems. Republicans wrote the plan in the Illinois Legislature, and it threw Annunzio and black Rep. George Collins into the same district. At first, Annunzio insisted he would oppose Collins in what promised to be a bloody primary. But Rep. Roman Pucinski of the 11th District had decided to run for the U.S. Senate, leaving that seat open. Daley and Democratic organization leaders persuaded Annunzio to accept nomination in the 11th District, in the northwest corner of the city.

This was a harder district for a Democrat than Annunzio's old 7th. There were more Republicans in the 11th, and many of its Democrats were disaffected by their party's liberalism and the presidential candidacy of George McGovern. Republicans nominated well-known Chicago Alderman John Hoellen, and Annunzio held on with only 53 percent of the vote. That was his closest brush with defeat.

The 1981 redistricting caused Annunzio no problems, even though it extended his territory beyond Chicago's city limits for the first time. He rolled to a 10th term in 1982 with 73 percent of the vote. Even in 1984, when white ethnic voters in northwest Chicago were voting heavily for Ronald Reagan, Annunzio emerged with 63 percent.

Annunzio's advancing age and the 11th's continued GOP trend may sustain Republicans' hopes of someday taking the district, but their designs will probably remain on hold until Annunzio departs. In 1986 and 1988, Republicans promoted the law-and-order image of their candidate, Chicago police detective George S. Gottlieb, in appeals to Annunzio's ethnic supporters. But the incumbent won easily.

Committees

House Administration (Chairman)

Banking, Finance and Urban Affairs (2nd of 31 Democrats)
Financial Institutions Supervision, Regulations and Insurance (chairman); Domestic Monetary Policy; General Oversight and Investigations

Joint Library (Chairman)

Joint Printing (Vice Chairman)

Elections

1988 General

Frank Annunzio (D)	131,753	(65%)
George S. Gottlieb (R)	72,489	(35%)

1986 General

Frank Annunzio (D)	106,970	(71%)
George S. Gottlieb (R)	44,341	(29%)

Previous Winning Percentages: **1984** (63%) **1982** (73%) **1980** (70%) **1978** (74%) **1976** (67%) **1974** (72%) **1972** (53%) **1970** (87%) **1968** (83%) **1966** (81%) **1964** (86%)

District Vote For President

	1988	1984	1980	1976
D	101,346 (46%)	93,584 (38%)	111,641 (45%)	123,612 (48%)
R	117,883 (54%)	149,521 (61%)	114,691 (46%)	135,612 (52%)
I			19,979 (8%)	

Campaign Finance

	Receipts	Receipts from PACs	Expend-itures
1988			
Annunzio (D)	$260,514	$158,200 (61%)	$239,158
Gottlieb (R)	$39,882	$1,730 (4%)	$41,259
1986			
Annunzio (D)	$225,627	$130,832 (58%)	$171,298
Gottlieb (R)	$31,254	$5,155 (16%)	$29,870

Key Votes

1987

Raise speed limit to 65 mph	N
Approve Gephardt "fair trade" amendment	?
Ban testing of larger nuclear weapons	?
Delay "re-flagging" of Kuwaiti tankers	Y
Approve tax-raising deficit-reduction bill	Y

1988

Approve aid to Nicaraguan contras	N
Enact civil rights restoration bill over Reagan veto	Y
Kill 60-day plant-closing notification measure	N
Pass omnibus trade bill over Reagan veto	Y
Approve death penalty for drug-related murders	Y
Bar federal funds for abortions in cases of rape and incest	Y
Oppose seven-day waiting period for purchase of handguns	N

Voting Studies

	Presidential Support		Party Unity		Conservative Coalition	
Year	**S**	**O**	**S**	**O**	**S**	**O**
1988	27	69	90	8	50	47
1987	14	42	66	3	28	30
1986	23	73	90	5	32	66
1985	29	71	89	7	33	62
1984	42	57	86	12	39	58
1983	29	62	83	12	38	56
1982	51	43	85	11	47	52
1981	55	45	77	22	59	41

Interest Group Ratings

Year	ADA	ACU	AFL-CIO	CCUS
1988	75	17	100	25
1987	48	9	93	20
1986	70	5	93	39
1985	75	5	100	23
1984	70	25	92	31
1983	70	14	94	21
1982	65	19	95	24
1981	45	0	80	21

12 Philip M. Crane (R)

Of Mount Prospect — Elected 1969

Born: Nov. 3, 1930, Chicago, Ill.
Education: Attended DePauw U., 1948-50; Hillsdale College, B.A. 1952; attended U. of Michigan, 1952-54; U. of Vienna, 1953-56; Indiana U., M.A. 1961, Ph.D. 1963.
Military Career: Army, 1954-56.
Occupation: Author; history professor.
Family: Wife, Arlene Catherine Johnson; eight children.
Religion: Protestant.
Political Career: Sought GOP nomination for president, 1980.
Capitol Office: 1035 Longworth Bldg. 20515; 225-3711.

In Washington: A dozen years ago, Crane was well positioned to take the conservative torch that he was sure would pass from an aging Ronald Reagan to a generation of younger Republicans. But Crane found in 1980 that he had jumped the gun; his presidential bid went nowhere.

Now, Reagan is gone and the right *is* looking for a new, high-profile hero. But in the House, instead of to Crane, the torch is being passed to an even younger generation of Republicans — the combative House conservatives who elected Newt Gingrich as minority whip early in the 101st Congress. The Georgian is 13 years younger than Crane, and 10 years his junior in the House.

As the conservative movement adjusts to the post-Reagan era, Crane is beginning his third decade of House service. If that tenure has not brought him the national visibility he wanted, it has at least brought him seniority on the powerful Ways and Means Committee, a forum he could use to enhance his profile.

But while few question Crane's intellectual abilities or his oratorical skills, he has never quite had the mindset needed for the give and take of legislating. Even Crane describes some of his rigidly conservative legislative endeavors as "spitting in the wind."

In the 100th Congress, there were 11 floor votes in which only one Republican in the entire House voted "no." On six occasions, Crane was that lone dissenter. He twice cast the solo vote against an education bill, and once was the only holdout on a housing bill.

Of all the solitary votes in his career, the one Crane says he remembers best is his 1984 vote against legislation to ease a Reagan administration policy that had purged thousands of disabled Social Security beneficiaries from government roles.

Crane was a fairly low-profile member of Ways and Means for a number of years, but in the 99th Congress, he assumed the ranking position on the Trade Subcommittee. He has emerged as a vocal opponent of efforts to protect domestic industries from imports.

Many other members share his concern about protectionist attempts to reduce the U.S. trade deficit, but few feel as strongly as Crane. Early in 1987, he was one of only two Ways and Means members to vote against reporting an omnibus trade bill to the floor. Although others complained about various parts of the legislation, Crane was virtually alone in questioning the need for any bill at all.

More than once in his career, Crane's opinions on tax policy have been ahead of the curve of debate on the subject. But when the ideas he was espousing began working their way through the legislative process, Crane was not known for fighting in the trenches for their passage.

He was one of the earliest congressional supporters of tax indexing, introducing legislation as far back as 1974. But while he could claim victory with its passage in 1981, he was not prominent in the key negotiations on the issue.

Well before tax-code revision became a major issue, Crane proposed a flat-rate tax of 10 percent on income, with no deductions or credits, and a $2,000 personal exemption. But in 1985, when Ways and Means produced a tax-revision bill incorporating some of his ideas, he described the bill — which had White House backing — as "poorly and thoughtlessly crafted" and burdensome on business. Unlike President Reagan and most House members, Crane did not want a revenue-neutral bill. He wanted one that would substantially lower the tax burden.

The elimination of preferential treatment for capital gains was a key reason Crane opposed the tax-overhaul bill, and he still wants to see it restored. With the backing of President Bush, the idea could become an issue in the 101st Congress, and a new test of Crane's legislative role.

Illinois 12

Far Northwest Cook County Suburbs — Palatine

When Crane won his first term in 1969, his district came in all the way to the Chicago city limits. Not an inch of that original territory remains within the 12th District boundaries today.

Crane still has a chunk of the suburban territory that he represented during the 1970s. But the 12th is now a demographic hodgepodge, dominated by the affluent and rapidly growing outer Cook County suburbs, yet taking in a mix of blue-collar towns and rural areas as well.

The one thing the various district constituencies share is their Republican orientation; this is rock-solid GOP territory. President Reagan won the 12th by a 3-to-1 margin in 1984; George Bush also topped 70 percent four years later.

The population center of the district is in the suburban towns of northwest Cook County. These communities, populated largely by younger professionals, have grown dramatically in the past 20 years. Arlington Heights, the largest, now has over 70,000 residents. Hoffman Estates has more than 40,000. Inverness is still an affluent village, though its population — 5,400 in 1986 — was up over 33 percent in the early part of the decade.

Just below, in the southwest corner of Crane's Cook County territory, are blue-collar suburbs, settled by people who work in Chicago or in small industrial cities such as Elgin. There are pockets of Democratic votes here, but they rarely have an impact on the district vote for statewide office.

Crane's constituency also extends beyond metropolitan Chicago, taking in most of semi-rural McHenry County and part of Lake County.

Southern Lake County, like northern Cook County, is populated by professionals and wealthy executives who commute to Chicago or to the offices springing up in the suburbs to the south. But as its name suggests, the county has several large recreational lakes; in the summer, its population explodes as Chicagoans and suburbanites converge on it to go fishing or boating or spend their time in summer homes.

Heavily Republican McHenry County has about a third of the voters in the 12th. McHenry has seen some development spillover from Lake, but is still mainly dairy farms and small market towns. Its largest city, Woodstock, has about 12,500 residents. Harvard, in western McHenry, bills itself as the "Milk Capital of the World."

Population: 519,181. White 500,456 (96%), Black 4,078 (1%), Other 7,779 (2%). Spanish origin 15,651 (3%). 18 and over 356,939 (69%), 65 and over 35,082 (7%). Median age: 29.

On the expenditures side of the federal ledger, Crane is a sure vote to cut spending for domestic programs. Neither education, housing, mail service nor a variety of other programs are mandatory federal functions, according to his philosophy.

In the 100th Congress, he offered an amendment to cut almost 5 percent from the Commerce, Justice and State departments. By immunizing the Drug Enforcement Agency from cuts, the Crane amendment got a majority of the GOP vote, but Democrats handed him a lopsided defeat. He also tried to cut the funding bill for the Department of Housing and Urban Development and independent agencies (exempting the Veterans Administration and NASA), but that, too, failed.

Crane did score two legislative successes in the 100th Congress. In 1988, he successfully offered an amendment on the floor to bar federal employees earning more than $72,500 — which includes members of Congress — from receiving a 4 percent cost-of-living raise. He also succeeded in amending the McKinney homeless-aid bill to allow certain transitional housing facilities to pay residents to maintain the structures or to transport residents to other jobs.

Matters of broad fiscal impact do not occupy all of Crane's time. In the 99th Congress he led the effort to try to make it easier for members of Congress to find parking spaces at Washington's National Airport. Crane, with 37 other members, asked the Federal Aviation Administration to prohibit Supreme Court justices and diplomats from using the airport's free "officials" parking lot. There were not enough spaces in the lot, he argued, and members of Congress were forced to cope with "irregular and unpredictable time constraints." The FAA refused.

Throughout his years in the House, Crane has kept up a busy speaking schedule outside the institution, pitching free enterprise and the need for a strong national defense to groups across the country. His efforts generally place him on the high end of House honoraria-earners.

Crane launched his 1980 presidential campaign from his base as chairman of the American Conservative Union. After a year of trying to organize support for the New Hampshire primary, Crane drew a hostile reception from William Loeb, then the acerbic Manchester *Union Leader* publisher and political baron. The newspaper ran articles accusing Crane of heavy drinking and womanizing. By the time New Hampshire voted, Crane was a minor candidate and received just 1.8 percent of the vote. He eventually won five convention delegates, but withdrew from the contest and endorsed Reagan.

At Home: Crane's conservative political philosophy was formed early, and the principal catalyst was his father, Dr. George Washington Crane III, a psychologist and writer. The senior Crane imbued Philip with a philosophy that emphasized self-reliance, free enterprise and the wisdom of the Founding Fathers.

George Crane may not have launched a political dynasty, but he generated a long series of congressional campaigns by his sons. Philip's younger brother, Daniel B. Crane, a dentist, was elected to the U.S. House from the 22nd District of Illinois in 1978, and served three terms before being unseated in 1984. David Crane, a psychiatrist and lawyer, lost three House races in Indiana's old 6th District.

The Cranes lived in modest circumstances in a working-class neighborhood on the South Side of Chicago. They were strict Methodists. After his older brother's death in an airplane crash, Philip Crane abandoned his early career in advertising and went back to school. In 1967, he became director of Westminster Academy, a private, conservative-oriented school north of Chicago.

In 1969 Crane entered the GOP House primary in a special election held after Donald Rumsfeld resigned from Congress to become head of the Office of Economic Opportunity in the Nixon administration. Crane's meticulous organization of conservative activists brought him 22 percent of the vote, and in a field of seven Republican candidates, that was enough.

Crane's Democratic opponent, Edward A. Warman, turned the election into a referendum on the Vietnam War. Soft-spoken and articulate, Crane managed to rebuff Warman's attempt to paint him as an extremist. He won with 58 percent and has had no trouble in 10 elections since.

Committee

Ways and Means (3rd of 13 Republicans)
Trade (ranking); Health

Elections

1988 General		
Philip M. Crane (R)	165,913	(75%)
John A. Leonardi (D)	54,769	(25%)
1986 General		
Philip M. Crane (R)	89,044	(78%)
John A. Leonardi (D)	25,536	(22%)

Previous Winning Percentages: **1984** (78%) **1982** (66%) **1980** (74%) **1978** (80%) **1976** (73%) **1974** (61%) **1972** (74%) **1970** (58%) **1969** * (58%)

* *Special election.*

District Vote For President

	1988	1984	1980	1976
D	66,474 (29%)	49,605 (23%)	50,189 (24%)	66,018 (31%)
R	161,488 (71%)	163,832 (76%)	131,495 (64%)	146,331 (68%)
I			20,394 (10%)	

Campaign Finance

	Receipts	Receipts from PACs	Expend-itures
1988			
Crane (R)	$466,894	0	$480,460
Leonardi (D)	$11,798	$7,150 (61%)	$11,955
1986			
Crane (R)	$338,802	$1,000 (0.3%)	$365,682
Leonardi (D)	$8,017	$4,000 (50%)	$7,879

Key Votes

1987	
Raise speed limit to 65 mph	Y
Approve Gephardt "fair trade" amendment	N
Ban testing of larger nuclear weapons	N
Delay "re-flagging" of Kuwaiti tankers	N
Approve tax-raising deficit-reduction bill	N
1988	
Approve aid to Nicaraguan contras	Y
Enact civil rights restoration bill over Reagan veto	N
Kill 60-day plant-closing notification measure	Y
Pass omnibus trade bill over Reagan veto	N
Approve death penalty for drug-related murders	Y
Bar federal funds for abortions in cases of rape and incest	Y
Oppose seven-day waiting period for purchase of handguns	Y

Voting Studies

	Presidential Support		Party Unity		Conservative Coalition	
Year	**S**	**O**	**S**	**O**	**S**	**O**
1988	79	15	91	2	92	3
1987	71	16	83	2	72	9
1986	82	16	87	4	90	4
1985	80	11	79	5	76	9
1984	73	21	86	7	85	10
1983	76	16	92	4	92	6
1982	79	18	81	5	89	7
1981	64	28	81	9	80	13

Interest Group Ratings

Year	ADA	ACU	AFL-CIO	CCUS
1988	0	100	0	93
1987	4	100	0	92
1986	0	100	0	93
1985	5	95	6	82
1984	0	100	15	93
1983	5	100	6	85
1982	0	100	0	85
1981	10	100	0	89

13 Harris W. Fawell (R)

Of Naperville — Elected 1984

Born: March 25, 1929, West Chicago, Ill.
Education: Attended North Central College, 1947-49; Chicago-Kent College of Law, J.D. 1952.
Occupation: Lawyer.
Family: Wife, Ruth Johnson; three children.
Religion: Methodist.
Political Career: Ill. Senate, 1963-77; candidate for Ill. Supreme Court, 1976.
Capitol Office: 318 Cannon Bldg. 20515; 225-3515.

In Washington: Fawell brings to his legislative work the same attention to detail that made him a successful attorney. By the time a bill comes before one of his committees, Fawell not only has read it line by line, he is likely to have underlined and highlighted the document and scribbled notes in the margins about questions he wants to raise.

This precision makes Fawell something of a bug on esoteric funding issues that most House members overlook. But a couple of these matters turned into unexpected victories for the Illinois Republican during the 100th Congress.

In early 1988, Fawell led the effort to overturn an $8 million appropriation to build schools in Paris for Jewish refugees from North Africa. The funding had been a pet project of Democratic Sen. Daniel K. Inouye of Hawaii, who attached it to a 1987 catchall appropriations bill at the behest of a U.S. refugee-assistance group. But Fawell, who regarded the measure as a boondoggle, submitted a bill to rescind the money, and organized more than two dozen House members to protest it. After the issue attracted media attention, a chastened Inouye asked that the funding be dropped.

That August, Fawell also opposed a bill to allow Boston College to write off $12 million on a loan it obtained to build a library named after former House Speaker Thomas P. O'Neill Jr. Fawell said the write-off would constitute an inappropriate grant for a private college's general-purpose library, since the facility was not dedicated to O'Neill's House career. Though Fawell was one of only two members to speak against the bill on the House floor, it was defeated, 158-239.

On the broader issues that come before Education and Labor, his major committee assignment, Fawell reflects the conservative business orientation of his suburban district. He is averse to any federal mandate that would raise the cost of doing business.

An opponent of measures to require business owners to provide health insurance to employees, Fawell says, "Many small business firms simply cannot pay the $1,800 to $3,600 per-employee, per-year cost." In 1988, he described a proposed minimum-wage increase as a "maximum job-loss bill."

But while Fawell supported most Reagan administration economic and defense policies, his voting record did not place him in the ranks of House hard-liners: He opposed Reagan's position on just over a third of House legislation in the 100th Congress. Most notably, Fawell advocated strengthening the Clean Air Act, a stand that earned him a "Clean Air Champion" award from the environmentalist Sierra Club.

At Home: Fawell can afford to talk about the need to assess issues from a "businessman's point of view." The political mainstream in the 13th ranges from the moderate to far right within the Republican Party. Fawell's only electoral worries would arise within his own party, and those are unlikely; he has rolled over his Democratic opponents.

As the campaign treasurer for his longtime friend, veteran Rep. John N. Erlenborn, Fawell was perfectly positioned in 1984 when Erlenborn announced his surprise resignation after 20 years of service. He picked up most of Erlenborn's old political network, and Erlenborn's veteran chief aide became his campaign manager.

That help proved invaluable in winning the GOP primary. Fawell, who as a state legislator had promoted measures to aid the handicapped, faced two conservative opponents — state Sen. George Ray Hudson and former state Sen. Mark Rhoads — who tried to portray him as a liberal. But Hudson and Rhoads were waging their own dogfight, complete with name-calling over who was the more genuine ideologue.

With backing from the formal Du Page and Cook County GOP organizations as well as conservative contacts, Hudson seemed at least an even bet to defeat Fawell as the campaign entered the last few weeks. But he lost some support because of his age (64), and he was further weakened when he fell off a stage and broke his leg during the campaign. Fawell took the nomination over Hudson by more than 3,000 votes, and coasted through November.

Illinois 13

Southwest Chicago Suburbs — Downers Grove

The affluent, suburban 13th is one of the most Republican constituencies in the country. Once concentrated almost entirely within Du Page County, the 13th was redrawn in the early 1980s to include the southwest Cook County suburbs of Chicago, which account for more than 40 percent of the population.

The section of Du Page in the district casts a little over half the 13th's vote. Rapid growth there in Naperville has boosted the city's population to 67,000 — an increase of 57 percent between 1980 and 1986. Naperville (part of which is in the neighboring 14th District) is strategically located on the East-West Tollway to the north and near Interstate 55 in the south.

Closer to Chicago are the more established suburbs clustered along the Burlington Northern railroad tracks that extend from the Cook County towns of Riverside and Western Springs to Hinsdale, Clarendon and Downers Grove in Du Page. The cul-de-sacs of Riverside, one of the area's first planned suburban developments, were copied again and again as suburbia crept along the railroad line out from Cook County into Du Page.

The only blue-collar territory in the 13th is in prewar industrial suburbs such as Broadview. But even Lisle, a traditional working-class town, saw its per capita income double in the early 1980s. Any Democratic votes here are canceled out by those of the affluent communities surrounding them.

In the geographic center of the district is the Argonne National Laboratory, a federal energy research center. South of it, at the southern end of Cook County, the district opens up to rolling countryside that has pockets of newer residential developments. Several forest preserves and lakes in the Cook County park system are located in this area. The district also includes a corner of Will County, located between Joliet and Chicago. Seven percent of the vote is cast in Will County.

Population: 519,441. White 494,504 (95%), Black 7,925 (2%), Other 13,078 (3%). Spanish origin 9,184 (2%). 18 and over 370,153 (71%), 65 and over 44,505 (9%). Median age: 31.

Committees

Education and Labor (9th of 13 Republicans)
Elementary, Secondary and Vocational Education; Labor-Management Relations; Labor Standards

Science, Space and Technology (11th of 19 Republicans)
Energy Research and Development; International Scientific Cooperation

Select Aging (15th of 27 Republicans)
Retirement, Income and Employment

Elections

1988 General		
Harris W. Fawell (R)	174,992	(70%)
Evelyn E. Craig (D)	74,424	(30%)
1988 Primary		
Harris W. Fawell (R)	36,233	(77%)
George T. Hamilton (R)	10,806	(23%)
1986 General		
Harris W. Fawell (R)	107,227	(73%)
Dominick J. Jeffrey (D)	38,874	(27%)

Previous Winning Percentage: 1984 (67%)

District Vote For President

	1988		1984		1980		1976	
D	81,899	(31%)	62,647	(25%)	68,726	(26%)	69,653	(29%)
R	179,221	(69%)	184,195	(74%)	164,990	(62%)	164,699	(69%)
I					25,915	(10%)		

Campaign Finance

	Receipts	Receipts from PACs	Expenditures
1988			
Fawell (R)	$292,896	$98,171 (34%)	$289,190
Craig (D)	$45,825	$18,700 (41%)	$45,760
1986			
Fawell (R)	$194,887	$71,028 (36%)	$193,882

Key Votes

1987	
Raise speed limit to 65 mph	N
Approve Gephardt "fair trade" amendment	N
Ban testing of larger nuclear weapons	Y
Delay "re-flagging" of Kuwaiti tankers	N
Approve tax-raising deficit-reduction bill	N
1988	
Approve aid to Nicaraguan contras	Y
Enact civil rights restoration bill over Reagan veto	N
Kill 60-day plant-closing notification measure	Y
Pass omnibus trade bill over Reagan veto	N
Approve death penalty for drug-related murders	Y
Bar federal funds for abortions in cases of rape and incest	N
Oppose seven-day waiting period for purchase of handguns	N

Voting Studies

	Presidential Support		Party Unity		Conservative Coalition	
Year	S	O	S	O	S	O
1988	61	36	80	18	92	8
1987	64	34	74	23	84	16
1986	69	30	83	17	78	22
1985	85	15	79	18	78	22

Interest Group Ratings

Year	ADA	ACU	AFL-CIO	CCUS
1988	40	64	14	92
1987	24	70	0	100
1986	20	73	14	89
1985	15	81	6	95

14 Dennis Hastert (R)

Of Yorkville — Elected 1986

Born: Jan. 2, 1942, Aurora, Ill.
Education: Wheaton College, B.A. 1964; Northern Illinois U., M.S. 1967.
Occupation: Teacher; restaurateur.
Family: Wife, Jean Kahl; two children.
Religion: Protestant.
Political Career: Ill. House, 1981-87.
Capitol Office: 515 Cannon Bldg. 20515; 225-2976.

In Washington: Hastert is a beefy former wrestling coach who once headed the National Wrestling Congress, but he is not a stereotypical jock. He is a serious and rather reticent legislator who came to Washington to serve as ombudsman for his constituents, just as he had done in the Illinois Legislature.

Among the issues of direct concern to his constituents is the cleanup of low-level nuclear waste. West Chicago is home to many of Hastert's constituents and also to a site where a now-defunct plant once buried low-level nuclear waste. One of Hastert's efforts in his first term was to try to pass an amendment blocking the Nuclear Regulatory Commission (NRC) from designating a permanent waste site in the district until other alternatives had been studied.

"Certainly small communities should not be asked to gamble with the lives of their residents if better and safer solutions exist," Hastert said when he pushed for an amendment to the NRC authorization bill on the House floor. The amendment was accepted, but was not adopted by the Senate.

Hastert was also active in other areas, trying to focus some federal attention on problems of local concern, ranging from reducing radium levels in water to intervening with the Immigration and Naturalization Service to reunite members of a Vietnamese family.

Hastert's own attention is focused primarily on the Public Works Committee, but he also has an important role outside that panel: He has a place on the GOP's Committee on Committees, the panel that makes Republican committee assignments, and has impressed some of his senior colleagues with his political sensibilities.

At Home: Hastert went a long way in politics without breaking a sweat. Appointed to the Illinois House in 1981 to fill a vacancy, Hastert was selected in 1986 as the 14th District nominee by a Republican convention after GOP Rep. John E. Grotberg was forced to retire because of a terminal illness.

But in the general election that year, Hastert had to struggle to maintain the Republican hold on the district. His Democratic opponent, Kane County coroner Mary Lou Kearns, enjoyed some advantages that made the election close.

Whereas Kearns was an official in the district's largest county, Hastert came from the southeast corner of the 14th, away from its population centers. And while Kearns had begun to campaign in summer 1985, Hastert was not nominated until June 1986, leaving him just a little more than four months to summon the district's normal GOP loyalties.

Hastert was hindered in that effort by the bruised feelings left over from the convention that nominated him. The backers of two other candidates — West Chicago lawyer Tom Johnson and Elgin Mayor Richard Verbic — complained the convention was stacked in Hastert's favor.

Kearns added to Hastert's troubles, attacking him for supporting a utility measure in the Legislature that she claimed would result in rate increases. In the final weeks, amid widespread GOP concern that a safe seat might be slipping out of reach, Hastert's sluggish effort finally came together. He promoted his experience in Springfield, where he was GOP spokesman on the state House Appropriations Committee. He gave his campaign an organizational boost by bringing in a consultant who had helped elect Grotberg in 1984. He also went after Kearns, reminding district Republicans that she was a presidential convention delegate in 1984 for Walter F. Mondale. Hastert still faced the resentment of some Republicans over the convention outcome, but one of his rivals, Johnson, finally offered public backing late in the campaign.

Hastert went on to win by about 7,000 votes, edging Kearns in her home base of Kane County. Kearns considered a rematch in 1988, but decided against it. Hastert then coasted to re-election with 74 percent of the vote against auto dealer Stephen Youhanaie.

An evangelical Christian, Hastert has a reputation as a conservative, but not an ideologue. He was respected for his knowledge of budget matters during his tenure in the state House, where he was an ally of GOP Gov. James R. Thompson.

Illinois 14

North Central — De Kalb; Elgin

The 14th stretches from Naperville, whose commuters hop the train for Chicago, south to Wenona, a crossroads farm town that serves the surrounding agricultural community in Marshall County. In between, in the valleys of the Illinois and Fox rivers, are a host of light industrial plants in such LaSalle County towns as Ottawa and Streator.

The semi-industrial character of the district does not interfere with its Republican loyalties. Hastert's struggle in 1986 had more to do with his late start and his opponent's aggressive efforts than any latent Democratic sympathies. By 1988, he had established himself and won easily.

Solid Republican majorities are recorded in most of the nine counties that are all or part in the district. The only Democratic bloc of any size is in LaSalle, where George Bush lost to Michael S. Dukakis in 1988 by 105 votes. That outcome was erased many times over by the Republican's strong showing in Kane County, which provides nearly 40 percent of the district's vote: Bush won there by almost 30,000 votes.

The Kane County population is largely in Elgin (part of which is in the 12th District) and Aurora (which is shared with the 4th). Located on the Fox River in the northern part of Kane, Elgin is a longtime industrial center; its name is on much of the country's street-sweeping equipment. In recent years, it has also become a suburban outpost for white-collar Chicagoans who have settled on its east side, near the Cook County line. The city's population rose by 13 percent from 1980-86, to over 72,000. The 14th also takes in the portion of industrial Aurora in southern Kane County, including the city's white-collar residential section.

Outside Kane County, the 14th begins to move the Illinois congressional map out of the Chicago metropolitan area. Corn and soybeans remain important to the economy in De Kalb and La Salle counties, where the farm land is among the richest in the country.

The largest city in the 14th's more rural reaches is De Kalb, in De Kalb County. An agricultural research center, it is the site of Northern Illinois University, which has about 25,000 students. Independent candidate John B. Anderson's strong showing hindered Ronald Reagan' 1980 effort in De Kalb, but Reagan won by 2-to-1 in 1984. Bush's 1988 tally was 58 percent.

Population: 521,909. White 496,962 (95%), Black 9,991 (2%), Other 5,150 (1%). Spanish origin 20,362 (4%). 18 and over 367,441 (70%), 65 and over 49,852 (10%). Median age: 29.

Committees

Government Operations (6th of 15 Republicans)
Commerce, Consumer and Monetary Affairs (ranking)

Public Works and Transportation (11th of 20 Republicans)
Economic Development; Investigations and Oversight; Surface Transportation; Water Resources

Select Children, Youth and Families (5th of 12 Republicans)

Elections

1988 General

Dennis Hastert (R)	161,146	(74%)
Stephen Youhanaie (D)	57,482	(26%)

1986 General

Dennis Hastert (R)	77,288	(52%)
Mary Lou Kearns (D)	70,293	(48%)

District Vote For President

	1988		1984		1980		1976	
D	81,320	(36%)	69,139	(31%)	61,516	(28%)	76,024	(38%)
R	144,966	(64%)	153,315	(69%)	136,573	(61%)	118,335	(60%)
I					21,114	(10%)		

Campaign Finance

	Receipts	Receipts from PACs	Expend-itures
1988			
Hastert (R)	$373,879	$148,608 (40%)	$346,785
1986			
Hastert (R)	$342,005	$138,737 (41%)	$327,219
Kearns (D)	$329,065	$183,554 (56%)	$322,625

Key Votes

1987	
Raise speed limit to 65 mph	N
Approve Gephardt "fair trade" amendment	N
Ban testing of larger nuclear weapons	N
Delay "re-flagging" of Kuwaiti tankers	N
Approve tax-raising deficit-reduction bill	N
1988	
Approve aid to Nicaraguan contras	Y
Enact civil rights restoration bill over Reagan veto	N
Kill 60-day plant-closing notification measure	Y
Pass omnibus trade bill over Reagan veto	N
Approve death penalty for drug-related murders	Y
Bar federal funds for abortions in cases of rape and incest	Y
Oppose seven-day waiting period for purchase of handguns	Y

Voting Studies

	Presidential Support		Party Unity		Conservative Coalition	
Year	S	O	S	O	S	O
1988	62	34	92	6	95	3
1987	66	33	90	7	91	9

Interest Group Ratings

Year	ADA	ACU	AFL-CIO	CCUS
1988	10	92	21	86
1987	8	87	13	87

15 Edward Madigan (R)

Of Lincoln — Elected 1972

Born: Jan. 13, 1936, Lincoln, Ill.
Education: Lincoln College, A.A. 1956.
Occupation: Automobile leasing executive.
Family: Wife, Evelyn M. George; three children.
Religion: Roman Catholic.
Political Career: Ill. House, 1967-73.
Capitol Office: 2109 Rayburn Bldg. 20515; 225-2371.

In Washington: A legislative craftsman and savvy inside player, Madigan seems made to order for the job of House Republican whip. Unfortunately for Madigan, his best chance for that No. 2 leadership post came at a time when many House Republicans' impatience with his brand of pragmatic politics had peaked. Early in the 101st Congress, their frustration propelled the election of a man whose style could not be more different from Madigan's — Newt Gingrich of Georgia.

Madigan's defeat sent him back to doing what he does best: Getting as much out of legislative deals as Republicans probably can hope for in a chamber where Democrats vastly outnumber them.

Madigan is a reserved man, even cryptic and aloof at times. But as a senior Republican on the Agriculture and Energy and Commerce committees, he has had as much impact on public policy over the last decade as all but a few senior Democrats. His key role has required of him a willingness to compromise — a trait that more ideological GOP colleagues regard with suspicion. They see him as more concerned about being part of the bargain than about resisting Democratic efforts to broaden the scope of the federal government.

In his campaign to succeed Dick Cheney as whip after the Wyoming Republican became President Bush's secretary of defense in March 1989, Madigan could note his experience since 1987 in the job of chief deputy whip, an appointive position. And he had the backing of Minority Leader Robert H. Michel, a fellow Illinoisan who had no desire to see the combative Gingrich ascend to the top rungs of the leadership.

But Madigan's link to Michel hurt as much as it helped: Many members did not want to have two top leaders from the same state, and others wanted a whip who complemented rather than duplicated Michel's strengths.

Madigan was portrayed as the candidate of the "Old Bulls" and the status quo — a bad rap at a time when House Republicans were seething in frustration after more than three decades as the minority party in the House. Gingrich's call for radical change found many receptive ears in the GOP caucus.

Although a change of two votes would have reversed the outcome of Gingrich's 87-85 victory, Madigan's defeat was perceived as a message to legislators of his generation that younger members wanted a more aggressive, confrontational leadership.

It is not surprising that Madigan would find it hard to sympathize with the complaints of junior Republicans who feel shut out. In his legislative work, Madigan is a walking rejoinder to Republicans who argue that their minority status compels them to confrontation with a Democratic majority that has robbed them of influence.

As ranking Republican on the Agriculture Committee and also on Energy and Commerce's Subcommittee on Health and the Environment, Madigan has found a way around the partisan imbalance that frustrates many of his GOP colleagues. While his detractors portray him as a conciliator, his legislative adversaries know Madigan as a tough customer.

In 1987, when initial efforts to work out a bipartisan compromise on a bailout of the farm credit system failed, Madigan threw up procedural roadblocks to prevent the Agriculture Committee from meeting, rather than letting the Democratic chairman push ahead with a bill he wrote on his own.

Madigan does not often have to resort to such obstructionist tactics, because usually he has a well-placed seat at the bargaining table. Especially on issues before his committees, he knows there are plenty of issues on which Democrats are divided, giving Republicans the opportunity to be players if they are willing to enter the game.

Madigan seized such an opportunity and left a huge imprint on the 1985 farm bill, winning approval of an amendment that in effect determined the measure's main thrust. His amendment killed a proposal to allow farmers to vote on whether the government should impose production controls to raise grain prices.

In fighting against the production-control concept, Madigan went head to head with Dem-

Illinois 15

Central — Bloomington; Kankakee

The spacious 15th ranges from Kankakee, just beyond the fringe of metropolitan Chicago, south to the outskirts of Champaign, then west to Madigan's hometown of Lincoln, squarely in the center of Illinois. In between is a great expanse of black-soil farm land, fertile territory for corn, soybeans — and Republicans.

Rural Republicanism is the chief political thread in the 15th; Democrats rarely make a pretense about competing here. Corn and soybean counties such as Iroquois and Ford are among the most Republican in the state. Both gave President Reagan about three-fourths of their 1984 vote; George Bush, who entered the 1988 contest without a natural base in farm country, took better than two-thirds in each county.

The district's largest urban region is the Bloomington-Normal area in the west. Bloomington, with over 46,000 residents, is the national headquarters of State Farm Insurance, the largest auto insurer in the world.

Normal (population 37,000) is best known as the site of Illinois State University, which has 22,000 students; the city's name refers to the school's origins as a teachers' college, or "normal" school.

In the eastern sections of the district, the economic picture is mixed. Although neither Champaign nor Urbana is in the district, some of their northern suburban areas that are in the 15th have benefited from the growth of the University of Illinois and the high-tech industry that is blooming around it. However, the shutdown of Chanute Air Force Base at nearby Rantoul, under the base-closure plan enacted in April 1989, could cost the area over 3,000 military and civilian jobs.

Hard times came several years ago to the district's other urban locale, Kankakee, whose population declined by nearly 10 percent to just over 27,000 between 1980 and 1986. The city is struggling to replace the blue-collar jobs lost when Roper Appliance, A. O. Smith and other industrial firms closed down factories. Many local officials have lined up behind efforts to build a third Chicago-area airport south of the city — preferably in Kankakee County — in hopes that it will provide jobs and spur economic development.

Though still mainly farm land, parts of Will County at the northern edge of the 15th are being drawn into the Chicago exurbs. For instance, the farm community of Peotone has sprouted single-family subdivisions that have boosted its population to nearly 3,000.

Population: 518,995. White 482,975 (93%), Black 29,524 (6%), Other 2,925 (1%). Spanish origin 6,364 (1%). 18 and over 370,509 (71%), 65 and over 56,330 (11%). Median age: 29.

ocratic leaders — who saw political advantage in backing a "populist" program vehemently opposed by the Reagan administration — and won. In the end, 82 Democrats deserted the leadership and voted for the Madigan amendment; he held on to all but 10 Republicans.

As the Agriculture Committee's ranking Republican, Madigan dutifully performed the chore of introducing the Reagan administration's "market oriented" farm bill in 1985, but he kept it at arm's length. With the farm economy ailing, Madigan feared election-year fallout if Republicans were associated with the administration's bare-bones farm program. When the White House sought a meeting with him the night before a critical House vote on the farm bill, he declined. In a typical display of Madiganesque subtlety, he said he was otherwise engaged, having the turn signal fixed on his car.

Madigan's other sphere of influence is the Health Subcommittee, where he and Chairman Henry A. Waxman of California seem to operate in a climate of mutual respect. Although they consistently differ on key environmental questions and on spending levels for social programs, Madigan and Waxman have managed to find common ground on a variety of health issues.

Madigan has not been shy about joining Waxman in opposing a Republican president, particularly during the Reagan years when the White House ventured far from mainstream health-policy thinking in Congress. Madigan helped draft an alternative to Reagan's early proposal to fold nine major health programs into a block grant to states. And he worked with Waxman in 1985 to override Reagan's veto of a National Institutes of Health authorization, which included a pet Madigan proposal to set up a new research institute on nursing.

During committee debates, Madigan sometimes assumes the role of mediator between Waxman's liberal views and the staunch conservatism of William E. Dannemeyer of California on such politically sensitive questions as federal

AIDS policy.

On the other side of the subcommittee's jurisdiction, Madigan has been at odds with Waxman over the most controversial environmental issue of recent years — legislation to control acid rain. Environmentalists claim that sulfur dioxide from coal-burning utilities in Illinois and other Midwestern states has been causing the poisonous rain in parts of the Northeast. Madigan takes the side of the utilities in arguing that the case against them is not proved and that they should not be stuck with the new restrictions.

Madigan has been known to resort to delaying tactics to block Waxman's efforts to advance acid-rain legislation. In the 99th Congress, he once bogged down the subcommittee for the better part of a week by introducing a 51-page substitute and insisting that the entire text be read aloud.

He has had a powerful ally in his opposition to the strict acid-rain restrictions Waxman has proposed: Energy and Commerce Chairman John D. Dingell of Michigan. Together, they have been able to stall action. Their grip on the issue might be broken by a group of moderate Democrats dubbed the "group of nine" that began a search for a compromise in the 100th Congress.

While Madigan has left his greatest mark in the legislative arena, his whip campaign was not his first foray into leadership politics.

He had been chairman of the Republican Research Committee in 1981-82, and stepped off the leadership ladder to take the ranking Agriculture seat as a favor to Michel. A combination of retirement and defeat had placed liberal Republican James M. Jeffords of Vermont in line to be the party's ranking member on Agriculture. Jeffords had cast the only vote from his side against President Reagan's 1981 tax cut and conservatives were determined that he not be given an important committee position. Madigan had not even been on Agriculture in the previous Congress, but he had served eight years there before and had the right to reclaim his seniority and take the ranking job. He agreed to do it.

At Home: Madigan was in the right place in 1972, when Republican Rep. William Springer retired. He was chairman of the state House Reapportionment Committee, charged with drawing the new Illinois congressional map. The new plan had to go through a federal court, but it ultimately preserved the Republican leanings of Springer's old 17th District, in which Madigan's hometown was located. Shortly after it was approved in court, Madigan filed for Congress.

He easily won the primary, but his first general election was not quite as simple as had been expected. Democrats nominated Champaign County District Attorney Lawrence Johnson, one of their strongest candidates in years. Johnson was a proven vote-getter in a Republican county and was popular with the large bloc of newly enfranchised student voters in the district.

Madigan made it, but his 55 percent of the vote was not impressive at a time when President Nixon and Republican Sen. Charles H. Percy were sweeping to victory. However, Madigan quickly consolidated his position and has settled into the habit of easy re-election victories, winning each time with over 65 percent of the vote. In 1986 — a year in which Republican House members from the Midwest fretted about the political effects of a slumping farm economy — Madigan, the ranking Republican on Agriculture, ran unopposed.

Committees

Agriculture (Ranking)

Energy and Commerce (2nd of 17 Republicans)
Health and the Environment (ranking); Telecommunications and Finance

Elections

1988 General

Edward R. Madigan (R)	140,171	(72%)
Thomas J. "Tom" Curl (D)	55,260	(28%)

1986 General

Edward R. Madigan (R)	115,284	(100%)

Previous Winning Percentages: **1984** (73%) **1982** (66%) **1980** (68%) **1978** (78%) **1976** (75%) **1974** (66%) **1972** (55%)

District Vote For President

	1988	1984	1980	1976
D	74,315 (37%)	66,325 (32%)	60,415 (29%)	81,858 (39%)
R	124,923 (63%)	140,964 (68%)	134,660 (64%)	123,957 (59%)
I			13,070 (6%)	

Campaign Finance

	Receipts	Receipts from PACs	Expend-itures
1988			
Madigan (R)	$500,508	$334,315 (67%)	$374,760
Curl (D)	$40,856	$7,345 (18%)	$37,785
1986			
Madigan (R)	$334,872	$194,796 (58%)	$209,409

Key Votes

1987	
Raise speed limit to 65 mph	Y
Approve Gephardt "fair trade" amendment	N
Ban testing of larger nuclear weapons	N
Delay "re-flagging" of Kuwaiti tankers	N
Approve tax-raising deficit-reduction bill	?
1988	
Approve aid to Nicaraguan contras	Y
Enact civil rights restoration bill over Reagan veto	?
Kill 60-day plant-closing notification measure	Y
Pass omnibus trade bill over Reagan veto	N
Approve death penalty for drug-related murders	Y
Bar federal funds for abortions in cases of rape and incest	?
Oppose seven-day waiting period for purchase of handguns	Y

Voting Studies

	Presidential Support		Party Unity		Conservative Coalition	
Year	**S**	**O**	**S**	**O**	**S**	**O**
1988	59	35	81	11	89	11
1987	69	27	78	17	91	5
1986	67	23	70	18	82	10
1985	60	35	71	19	84	16
1984	63	33	69	24	88	10
1983	74	20	73	22	75	18
1982	68	27	65	26	70	21
1981	68	20	70	12	71	12

Interest Group Ratings

Year	ADA	ACU	AFL-CIO	CCUS
1988	15	77	27	85
1987	8	76	25	92
1986	0	76	25	79
1985	30	71	29	71
1984	15	58	25	64
1983	15	61	29	80
1982	20	67	30	68
1981	5	92	14	100

16 Lynn Martin (R)

Of Loves Park — Elected 1980

Born: Dec. 26, 1939, Chicago, Ill.
Education: U. of Illinois, B.A. 1960.
Occupation: English teacher.
Family: Husband, Harry D. Leinenweber; two children, five stepchildren.
Religion: Roman Catholic.
Political Career: Winnebago County Board, 1972-76; Ill. House, 1977-79; Ill. Senate, 1979-81.
Capitol Office: 1214 Longworth Bldg. 20515; 225-5676.

In Washington: Martin's failed effort for a spot in the GOP House leadership at the start of the 101st Congress hardly marred her image as a rising Republican star. First, she was seriously considered for a Bush administration Cabinet post. Then, in June 1989, at the urging of Illinois GOP Gov. James R. Thompson, she announced that she will challenge Democratic Sen. Paul Simon in 1990. As she prepares for the Senate race, Martin will benefit from her recent appointment to the high-profile Rules Committee.

Now in her fifth House term, Martin has risen quickly in the House partly from her gender and her connection to the House Republican leader, Illinois colleague Robert H. Michel. After two terms, Martin was elected vice chairman of the Republican Conference with the sponsorship of Michel, who was looking to counter the Democrats' nomination of Geraldine A. Ferraro for vice president.

But if Martin had some inherent advantages that helped her onto the leadership stage, she performed well once she got there. Her good-natured, raspy-voiced candor, combined with partisanship and a sarcastic sense of humor, earned her attention from the media as she tried to put Democrats on the defensive.

Those qualities helped make Martin a strong candidate for the full chairmanship of the conference in late 1988. She fell just a few votes shy of California Rep. Jerry Lewis, who had built up years of chits on the Appropriations Committee and on the committee that makes GOP committee assignments, and who represents the state with the largest single block of Republicans in the House. Martin said afterwards that she had been hurt to some extent by absences on the day of the voting. She also lost some votes not otherwise solid for Lewis because her record on social issues was not sufficiently conservative.

Martin, however, did win another prize for the 101st Congress that gives her an opportunity to make her presence felt in the House. Backed by Michel, she took a spot on the Rules Committee. On that panel, where four Republicans are outnumbered by nine Democrats, Martin could be an important voice for the minority party. The member who had served as the high-profile GOP spokesman on Rules, Mississippi's Trent Lott, was elected to the Senate in 1988.

Early in the 101st Congress, Martin displayed her ability for cutting but jocular rhetoric when she led the GOP floor attack on a restricted rule for legislation directing the president to establish a board to investigate the Eastern Airlines controversy.

"The soothsayer told us to 'Beware of the ides of March.' And sure enough, it is March 15, and the Rules Committee is sticking it to us once again with one of its restrictive rules," Martin said. She was complaining of the bill's so-called "modified open rule," which placed limits on debate and amendments. "This is modified open about as much as the 'Incredible Hulk' is a modified ballerina."

Sometimes Martin's humor is forced, as if she feels she has to be outrageous to preserve the image that has taken her so far in a short time. The *Chicago Tribune* once called her "the political version of Joan Rivers."

In her tenure on the Budget Committee (which ended in 1986), Martin showed a blend of legislative skills. Her oratorical abilities made her an effective spokesman for her party, and her personality helped open bipartisan lines of communication, something the committee had long been lacking. ("She comes off as everybody's sister," one Democrat said.)

In early 1986, when Ohio's Delbert L. Latta, the ranking GOP member, was out for several months following heart surgery, Martin took over leadership of her outnumbered forces on the panel and, many members felt, outshone Latta. She worked to establish a friendly relationship with Democrat William H. Gray III, then chairman.

Her most significant achievement on Budget, however, involved the fiscal 1986 "reconciliation" bill, a package of deficit-cutting measures that was batted back and forth between the Senate and House an unprecedented nine times in late 1985 and early 1986. Martin held firm against Democratic leadership attempts to

Illinois 16

Northwest — Rockford

Though the 16th, nestled snugly in the northwest corner of Illinois, has a mainly rural feel, the presence of blue-collar Rockford in the district has made it a temptation for Democrats. Their hopes have been illusory, though; the district remains immovably Republican, as it has been throughout the century.

Rockford — the state's second-largest city, with 135,000 residents — and surrounding Winnebago County account for some 50 percent of the district's vote. From its early days as a sawmill town, the city has been an industrial center, making farm implements, machine tools, furniture, automotive parts and aviation equipment.

Recent recessions hit the city hard, with unemployment soaring to the 20 percent level in the early 1980s. Yet the city's park system and other amenities have kept it more livable than factory towns, helping prevent a steep decline: Rockford's 3 percent population loss from 1980 to 1986 was minimal compared with that of many Midwestern cities.

Despite the economic instability, voters also held fast to their Republican tendencies. Martin has always done well in Winnebago County, winning there with 63 percent of the vote in 1988. George Bush took 55 percent of the county vote in 1988.

Other nearby cities, such as Belvidere (Boone County) to the east and Freeport (Stephenson County) to the west, also have a heavy-manufacturing base. There, also, Republicans tend to hold the upper hand.

The rest of the district is largely rural, settled by Germans, Swedes and Yankees transplanted from New England. Their labors help make the 16th the state's leading district for dairy farming.

The northwest corner of the 16th is a vacation area, with antique stores and state parks scattered throughout hilly Jo Daviess County. The home of President Ulysses S. Grant is a historical site in Galena; Ronald Reagan's boyhood homes are also in the district, at Dixon and Tampico.

Population: 519,035. White 484,432 (93%), Black 24,906 (5%), Other 2,728 (1%). Spanish origin 13,405 (3%). 18 and over 364,824 (70%), 65 and over 58,988 (11%). Median age: 30.

include provisions that would increase spending, and was finally able to reach agreement with a group of Democrats who were eager to preserve provisions helpful to tobacco growers and oil-producing coastal states. With 84 Democrats joining Martin and the Republican majority and bucking their own leadership, the House finally accepted an administration-backed Senate version of the legislation.

Martin loves to use House debate to bring male egos back to earth with a sarcastic image of domestic life. When the 1985 session was stumbling to a close in a stormy late-night session, Martin said, "It's never wise to keep the House in after 11. It's like managing a nursery school without a nap."

When Democrats on the Budget Committee, under pressure from urban mayors, voted to leave the door open for revival of a costly revenue-sharing program they had previously agreed to phase out, Martin blurted, "Maybe girls learn to say 'no' easier than boys."

For several years, Martin managed to mix partisanship and women's rights issues as a member of the House Administration Committee, where she challenged Democratic chairmen of other committees to tell her how many women employees they had, and how much they were being paid. A survey she conducted showed that women employees were concentrated at the low end of the salary spectrum, while men held most of the high-paying jobs.

Although Martin left House Administration in 1985, she has been a leader in the effort to see that Congress does not exempt itself from anti-discrimination laws that apply to private enterprise. When a Capitol Hill staffer committed suicide in 1988 after newspaper reports of his involvement in bizarre employment practices in one House office, Martin complained that the tragedy "might not have happened if those people had a route to complain rather than going to the front page of the newspapers."

The House overwhelmingly passed a resolution providing new complaint procedures for House employees and applicants who feel discriminated against, but Martin has pushed more far-reaching legislation.

At Home: For someone who professes a dislike for elections — "I hate that someone has to lose," she says — Martin is remarkably adept at winning them. She began the 1970s teaching in the Rockford public schools. She began the next decade with a seat in Congress.

Martin launched her political career in 1972, when she decided that the Winnebago County Board, which was dominated by Rockford Democrats, was "out of touch." She won a seat on it, and became the Republicans' spokesman. In 1976 she entered the Illinois House after a refreshingly unprofessional campaign in which junior-high-school classmates of one of her children stumped for her door-to-door.

In the Legislature, Martin's plain-spoken fiscal conservatism cemented her popularity in the Rockford area. Several weeks after she announced for the state Senate against a Democratic incumbent in 1978, the Democrat decided to retire. Martin moved on up.

She did not have to wait long for a chance at Congress. In 1980 Republican Rep. John B. Anderson announced his White House candidacy. Martin and four other Republicans announced for the seat. Her toughest competition came from the Rev. Don Lyon, who had used help from national conservative organizations to win 42 percent in a 1978 primary challenge to Anderson. Martin's asset was name recognition in Winnebago County.

The Illinois presidential primary and Martin's congressional primary were on the same day. Many Democrats and independents crossed over to help Anderson, and in the House primary they generally preferred Martin to her more conservative GOP opponents.

Martin proved her political resiliency in her first re-election contest. Though Ronald Reagan's roots are in the 16th District, he could do nothing as president to prevent the recession of 1982 from laying waste to the local industrial economy; Rockford was hit harder than almost any other U.S. city. But Martin still won 57 percent of the vote against Democratic farmer Carl R. Schwerdtfeger.

After beating Schwerdtfeger again in 1984, Martin coasted in her next two elections. Her strong home base and growing prominence in national Republican politics spawned early speculation — which she later fulfilled — that she would challenge Simon, who is expected to seek a second term in 1990.

Committee

Rules (3rd of 4 Republicans)
Legislative Process (ranking)

Elections

1988 General		
Lynn Martin (R)	128,365	(64%)
Steven E. Mahan (D)	72,431	(36%)
1986 General		
Lynn Martin (R)	92,982	(67%)
Kenneth F. Bohnsack (D)	46,087	(33%)

Previous Winning Percentages: 1984 (58%) **1982** (57%) **1980** (67%)

District Vote For President

	1988	1984	1980	1976
D	85,552 (42%)	80,648 (37%)	60,910 (28%)	84,993 (42%)
R	116,627 (58%)	138,250 (63%)	117,600 (55%)	115,618 (57%)
I			33,015 (15%)	

Campaign Finance

	Receipts	Receipts from PACs	Expend-itures
1988			
Martin (R)	$456,255	$186,532 (41%)	$329,598
Mahan (D)	$25,426	$7,650 (30%)	$25,424
1986			
Martin (R)	$359,953	$153,261 (43%)	$239,059
Bohnsack (D)	$44,817	$1,000 (2%)	$44,369

Key Votes

1987	
Raise speed limit to 65 mph	N
Approve Gephardt "fair trade" amendment	N
Ban testing of larger nuclear weapons	N
Delay "re-flagging" of Kuwaiti tankers	N
Approve tax-raising deficit-reduction bill	N
1988	
Approve aid to Nicaraguan contras	Y
Enact civil rights restoration bill over Reagan veto	Y
Kill 60-day plant-closing notification measure	N
Pass omnibus trade bill over Reagan veto	N
Approve death penalty for drug-related murders	#
Bar federal funds for abortions in cases of rape and incest	#
Oppose seven-day waiting period for purchase of handguns	Y

Voting Studies

	Presidential Support		Party Unity		Conservative Coalition	
Year	**S**	**O**	**S**	**O**	**S**	**O**
1988	56	38	83	8	82	5
1987	66	29	87	8	88	12
1986	74	24	81	16	80	18
1985	61	35	84	11	84	16
1984	53	43	73	23	73	22
1983	61	35	74	22	66	31
1982	49	48	65	31	58	41
1981	57	41	67	27	72	24

Interest Group Ratings

Year	ADA	ACU	AFL-CIO	CCUS
1988	30	76	46	69
1987	20	74	19	73
1986	15	68	38	94
1985	20	67	18	81
1984	30	52	23	69
1983	35	61	29	68
1982	30	57	40	59
1981	30	86	29	88

17 Lane Evans (D)

Of Rock Island — Elected 1982

Born: Aug. 4, 1951, Rock Island, Ill.
Education: Augustana College (Ill.), A.B. 1974; Georgetown U., J.D. 1978.
Military Career: Marine Corps, 1969-71.
Occupation: Lawyer.
Family: Single.
Religion: Roman Catholic.
Political Career: No previous office.
Capitol Office: 328 Cannon Bldg. 20515; 225-5905.

In Washington: At first glance, it may seem odd that the 17th, a historically Republican district, sends to the House a Democrat whose voting record is as liberal as any member's.

But a closer look reveals that historical vote patterns don't count for much anymore in this economically struggling part of Illinois. And even if they did, Evans has the energy and personality to overcome them.

A self-described populist, Evans pays assiduous attention to his constituents' needs, spending much of his time lobbying for the hard-pressed factory laborers and farmers in his district. He is not a strident speaker or an aggressive participant in committee or on the House floor. He is, in short, a very hard person to dislike — even for his conservative critics.

The 1980s exodus of industrial jobs from the Quad Cities and other areas of the 17th has prompted Evans to focus on winning funding for job-training programs, and he is always on the lookout for ways to help local businesses win government contracts. He describes himself as a "card-carrying capitalist," but argues that the economy should be organized with the interests of the little man and the small business in mind. "We're always consulted by corporations when they want something," he once complained. "When they want to leave town, they do it overnight."

As chairman of the caucus of Vietnam-era veterans in Congress and as a member of the Veterans' Affairs Committee, he has been a strong proponent of funding for counseling centers that help Vietnam veterans battle war-related emotional problems. In the 101st Congress, he took over as chairman of Veterans' Oversight and Investigations Subcommittee.

In 1988, Evans was involved in pushing legislation to grant judicial review for veterans who think they have been unfairly denied government benefits — a right that veterans had been seeking for a decade. The measure created a federal court to handle appeals cases. In addition, Evans sought to win committee approval to allow veterans to appeal adverse rulings from the new court to a higher federal court, a provision supported by Vietnam Veterans of America.

He lost on that count, but still worked for passage of the overall package. He and other Democrats who are Vietnam-era veterans, including Chief Deputy Whip David E. Bonior of Michigan, urged Speaker Jim Wright to press Veterans' Affairs Chairman G. V. "Sonny" Montgomery to find a compromise between House and Senate versions of the bill. Montgomery had battled every previous attempt to pass judicial-review legislation.

Judicial-review proponents threatened to hold hostage one of Montgomery's pet projects — a bill upgrading the Veterans Administration to Cabinet status — until progress was seen on the judicial-review bill. The pressure on Montgomery yielded success: A compromise bill cleared Congress and was signed into law.

In May 1988, with the backing of state colleagues Dan Rostenkowski and Marty Russo (two Illinois Democrats on the Steering and Policy Committee), Evans won a permanent assignment to the Armed Services Committee. He filled the vacancy left by the death of Illinois Rep. Melvin Price.

In joining Armed Services, Evans had to give up his seat on the Agriculture Committee. There, he had supported an ambitious and so far unsuccessful plan to increase prices through mandatory production controls on major crops. He was not particularly active in drafting the 1985 farm bill, however.

Evans seems confident that he can compile as liberal a voting record as he likes and defend it successfully at home. He was always among the leaders in the House in casting votes against President Reagan. In 1986, he was one of five House Democrats cosponsoring a conference held by the "National Liberal Coalition," a group chaired by socialist writer Michael Harrington. Evans was the only cosponsor from the House who did not represent an inner-city black district or an enclave of white liberalism.

At Home: Though his capture of the traditionally Republican seat in 1982 was a surprise,

Illinois 17

West — Rock Island; Moline; Galesburg

Cradled between the Mississippi and Illinois rivers, the 17th is prime farm land where most corn and soybean growers can survive even bad years. But it is also a troubled region of small industrial cities.

Its urban center is at the northwestern edge in Rock Island County, where Rock Island and Moline join with Iowa's Davenport and Bettendorf to make up the "Quad Cities." Moline and Rock Island, of nearly equal size, have a combined total of about 90,000 residents.

However, the population has dropped somewhat in recent years, a result of a decline in the region's heavy industrial base. Though it has one of the country's most intensive concentrations of farm equipment manufacturing — the John Deere company is headquartered at Moline — the region's economy was injured when several International Harvester factories were closed down in 1983 following a corporate buyout.

That move and other problems — such as layoffs at the Caterpillar plant across the river in Davenport — had devastating effects on the area's economy. Though the situation has eased somewhat, double-digit unemployment was a fact of life in the Illinois portion of the Quad Cities, in rural Rock Island County and in the city of Galesburg through much of the 1980s.

Hard times have provided an opening to Democratic candidates that is unavailable to them in most downstate locations. Though Republicans continue to insist the 17th should be their district, the 1988 results may have finally disillusioned them: Michael S. Dukakis took the district with 53 percent of the vote — winning 59 percent in Rock Island County — and Evans ran up a personal-best percentage.

Traditionally, rural areas such as Bureau and Henry counties — the self-proclaimed "Hog Capital of the World" — were able to outvote the cities of Rock Island, Moline and Galesburg in congressional elections. However, Evans has even converted many of his district's rural voters: he swept all 14 counties in the district his last time out.

Population: 519,333. White 496,650 (96%), Black 14,261 (3%), Other 2,566 (1%). Spanish origin 11,662 (2%). 18 and over 372,502 (72%), 65 and over 66,095 (13%). Median age: 30.

---

the hard-working and personable Evans quickly became a fixture. In his first two re-election campaigns, district Republicans tried, but failed, to convince voters that Evans was an undesirable liberal extremist. By 1988, a less aggressive GOP watched in frustration as Evans ran up 65 percent of the vote.

Evans wins in part because he works tirelessly at home — conducting meetings to study the district's economic problems, popping up at every county fair and small-town celebration, making himself available to the local media, and putting in countless hours helping constituents.

In 1982, Evans emerged from his community legal clinic in Rock Island to make his first run for public office. It was an effort that seemed futile until primary day in March of that year, when former state Sen. Kenneth G. McMillan, a New Right stalwart, defeated Rep. Tom Railsback, a moderate eight-term Republican who always enjoyed broad bipartisan support.

Railsback's defeat set up a clear ideological choice for the voters. McMillan, who had castigated Railsback for not giving Reagan enough support, asked that the administration's program be given more time to prove itself.

Evans, who had worked in the presidential campaign of Sen. Edward M. Kennedy in 1980, managed to deflect the "Kennedy liberal" label and focus the contest on McMillan and Reagan. He urged voters to use his candidacy as a way to "send Reagan a message," and forced McMillan to vow, somewhat defensively, that he would not vote to cut farm subsidies.

By Election Day, Evans had successfully painted his foe into a right-wing corner. With crucial help from the United Auto Workers in Rock Island and Moline, he won decisively there, offsetting McMillan's rural strength.

The 1984 election brought a rematch. McMillan moderated his rhetoric, trying to appeal both to conservative voters in the rural, southern counties of the district and to blue-collar voters in the industrial cities to the north. But Evans carried nine of the district's 14 counties.

In 1986, the GOP offered Rock Island lawyer Sam McHard, who had strengths where McMillan was weak. McHard came out of the party's moderate wing and had been an active supporter of Railsback in 1982. Railsback's support gave McHard the unified backing of the district's GOP establishment, and greater credibility in the Rock Island area, which is crucial to any Republican hoping to cut into Evans' base.

Like McMillan before him, McHard tried

to paint Evans as ideologically unfit. But he was unable to dent Evans' personal popularity — he cut slightly into Evans' margin in Rock Island County, but not enough to pose much of a threat. Evans carried the same nine counties he had carried two years before.

With no big-name candidates offering to challenge Evans in 1988, the Republicans put up William E. Stewart, a low-key attorney from the small Henry County city of Kewanee. Evans, never seriously threatened, outdid himself. He swept all of the district's counties, running away in Rock Island County with 70 percent of the vote.

Committees

Armed Services (28th of 31 Democrats)
Investigations; Procurement and Military Nuclear Systems

Select Children, Youth and Families (15th of 18 Democrats)

Veterans' Affairs (4th of 21 Democrats)
Oversight and Investigations (chairman); Compensation, Pension and Insurance; Education, Training and Employment

Elections

1988 General		
Lane Evans (D)	132,130	(65%)
William E. Stewart (R)	71,560	(35%)
1986 General		
Lane Evans (D)	85,442	(56%)
Sam McHard (R)	68,101	(44%)

Previous Winning Percentages: **1984** (57%) **1982** (53%)

District Vote For President

	1988	1984	1980	1976
D	107,639 (53%)	103,510 (46%)	80,889 (36%)	100,760 (45%)
R	95,672 (47%)	123,117 (54%)	125,591 (56%)	119,970 (54%)
I			15,447 (7%)	

Campaign Finance

	Receipts	Receipts from PACs	Expend-itures
1988			
Evans (D)	$461,211	$211,218 (46%)	$471,233
Stewart (R)	$125,065	$14,951 (12%)	$124,133
1986			
Evans (D)	$632,359	$334,136 (53%)	$620,183
McHard (R)	$313,050	$76,616 (24%)	$312,698

Key Votes

1987	
Raise speed limit to 65 mph	N
Approve Gephardt "fair trade" amendment	Y
Ban testing of larger nuclear weapons	Y
Delay "re-flagging" of Kuwaiti tankers	Y
Approve tax-raising deficit-reduction bill	Y
1988	
Approve aid to Nicaraguan contras	N
Enact civil rights restoration bill over Reagan veto	Y
Kill 60-day plant-closing notification measure	N
Pass omnibus trade bill over Reagan veto	Y
Approve death penalty for drug-related murders	N
Bar federal funds for abortions in cases of rape and incest	N
Oppose seven-day waiting period for purchase of handguns	N

Voting Studies

	Presidential Support		Party Unity		Conservative Coalition	
Year	S	O	S	O	S	O
1988	17	83	97	2	8	92
1987	11	87	94	3	2	93
1986	13	86	95	4	6	92
1985	14	86	96	1	5	93
1984	24	73	94	6	7	92
1983	9	90	91	6	13	84

Interest Group Ratings

Year	ADA	ACU	AFL-CIO	CCUS
1988	100	0	100	14
1987	100	0	94	0
1986	100	0	93	11
1985	100	5	100	18
1984	90	0	85	38
1983	95	4	94	10

18 Robert H. Michel (R)

Of Peoria — Elected 1956

Born: March 2, 1923, Peoria, Ill.
Education: Bradley U., B.S. 1948.
Military Career: Army, 1942-46.
Occupation: Congressional aide.
Family: Wife, Corinne Woodruff; four children.
Religion: Apostolic Christian.
Political Career: No previous office.
Capitol Office: 2112 Rayburn Bldg. 20515; 225-6201.

In Washington: To borrow from Michelese, the House Republican leader is one doggone decent son of a gun. And that sentiment goes a long way toward explaining how this amiable son of Peoria has survived as leader and maintained unity during nearly a decade in which his ranks have been as restless and rebellious as at any time in memory.

Like many House leaders before him, Michel patiently waited years to reach the top, only to be accused once there of being wrong for the times. He is one of the "Old Bulls," a traditional Republican from the small-town chamber of commerce set. He is a conservative, to be sure, but also a pragmatist, a man who can tangle with a Democrat but then cut a deal with him and go out for a bipartisan round of golf. Yet by the time he came to power in 1981, Michel faced a new generation of ideologically conservative and combative young Republicans, and a strong-minded new president in Ronald Reagan. The rest of the decade would be as different from his previous quarter-century in Congress as could be.

Michel has tried to keep pace with the times. As he said in early 1989, after the latest and most serious challenge to his style of leadership, "From time to time you have to go with the flow. I think that part of my success has been the fact that I have been able to accommodate some of the vicissitudes of life that come up."

Indeed, Michel has been eminently adaptable, though sometimes at the expense of a forceful image and clear direction. In recent years, he has been torn not only by the right and the left of the House GOP, but also by political pressures at home, by an increasingly assertive Democratic majority and by both a Republican administration and, until 1987, a GOP Senate that alternately dominated and disregarded the House minority.

But his adaptability, together with members' affection for him and Michel's own instinct for House politics, have combined to carry him into a fifth term as leader. Among many Republicans — fellow bulls and devoted moderates — Michel is secure; the young Turks on the right, meanwhile, have chosen to battle for lower leadership jobs, partly from a sense that Michel will retire from his post before long.

Michel is hardly one of the House's best orators, and he has no particular policy expertise. His parliamentary skills are good, but not unusual. He is neither charismatic nor intimidating. But more often than he has been given credit for, he steered his party to victories it had no numerical reason to win. Some certainly were due in part to Reagan's popularity, but Michel knew how to work the Reagan factor for every vote it could produce. "You can't treat two alike," he once explained. "I know what I can get and what I can't, when to back off and when to push harder. It's not a matter of twisting arms. It's bringing them along by gentle persuasion."

Increasingly, Michel complains about life in the seemingly permanent minority. "I haven't chaired a subcommittee or full committee in my 30 years in Congress," he laments. "It's a pretty doggone discouraging and debilitating thing." Ambitious Republicans have begun looking to 1992, speculating that Michel will retire rather than fight the Illinois Legislature to protect his district from being dismembered or redrawn in reapportionment.

Meanwhile, for better or worse, developments early in the 101st Congress dramatically altered the landscape for Michel. The succession of George Bush to the presidency in January, and of Washington's Thomas S. Foley to the Speaker's chair in June 1989, augured a more conciliatory brand of politics. That could ease Michel's job as White House legislative salesman, but it also could make it harder for him to lead conservatives who believe Reagan-style confrontation is the route to a GOP House majority.

The most significant development for Michel personally was an unexpected GOP leadership duel in March that indirectly aimed at him. The race to succeed Defense Secretary Dick Cheney in the No. 2 job of minority whip became a referendum on party tactics — a showdown between conservative guerrilla Newt

Illinois 18

Central — Peoria

The 18th zigs and zags from Peoria south to the outskirts of Decatur and Springfield and west to Hancock County on the Mississippi. A mostly rural area, it is linked by the broad Illinois River basin, ideal for growing corn.

The district's troubled industrial base, centered in Peoria, is the 18th's dominant economic issue, however. The region has staged a modest comeback since the depths of the recession in the early 1980s. But many of the high-paying blue-collar jobs lost then have not returned.

Massive layoffs in the early 1980s by the Caterpillar Tractor Co., which has its international headquarters in Peoria and has several large plants in the district, caused severe economic dislocation. Michel had to fight to keep his seat during the 1982 recession.

His opponent that year, Democrat G. Douglas Stephens, staked a 1988 comeback attempt on the long-term effects of the industrial decline: Peoria's population had dropped 11 percent, to 110,000, between 1980 and 1986. But Michel effectively presented his own sets of numbers, showing a slippage in unemployment and increased hiring by Caterpillar. There has also been an upswing in agricultural research, funded by federal money channeled to the district by Michel.

Michel's 1988 victory over Stephens, as well as Ronald Reagan's and George Bush's success in the district, indicate that hard times have not had a lasting effect on the district's Republican tendencies. Bolstered by the GOP base in the district's more rural areas, Reagan captured 60 percent in the 18th in 1984; Bush took 55 percent four years later.

Peoria is the constant in a district whose lines have changed often during Michel's long tenure. In the 1960s Peoria anchored the southern end of the district; in the '70s it was in the center. For the '80s it is perched at the northern tip. Peoria and Tazewell (Pekin) counties are the only territories remaining from the district that elected Michel in 1970. The 18th now is a particularly fragmented constituency. Michel once represented eight counties and most of a ninth; now he is responsible not only for eight complete counties but also parts of eight more.

Population: 519,026. White 490,556 (95%), Black 23,919 (5%), Other 2,764 (1%). Spanish origin 3,728 (1%). 18 and over 368,659 (71%), 65 and over 62,341 (12%). Median age: 30.

Gingrich of Georgia and Edward Madigan, Michel's Illinois ally and fellow pragmatist.

Michel was publicly neutral but privately for Madigan. Meanwhile, Gingrich got support not only from conservatives but also from some moderates, who agreed that Michel's low-key leadership needed a complement to infuse it with energy and ideas. When Gingrich narrowly won, an obviously pained Michel appeared with him before reporters and candidly interpreted the result: "What that says to me is that they want us to be more activated and more visible and more aggressive, and that we can't be content with business as usual."

For a man of Michel's laid-back nature, it is hard to imagine how he could top the 100th Congress for partisan confrontation. Michel, who remained close to Speaker Thomas P. O'Neill Jr. even at the height of conservatives' attacks on the Democratic leader, had no such personal ties to Speaker Jim Wright. Their relationship only deteriorated after Wright took over as Speaker in 1987.

That fall, Michel was enraged when Wright forced passage of a deficit-cutting bill, which called for taxes that Republicans opposed, by holding the vote open an extra 10 minutes so a Texas ally could change his vote — making the result 206-205. Republicans saved the episode on videotape to stoke their anger. "You play and replay that tape; it's devastating," Michel said. "You can't forgive that."

In 1988, Michel charged that Wright broke a promise to allow a vote on the Republicans' bill for military aid to the Nicaraguan contras, a substitute for Democrats' "humanitarian" aid package. "In over 30 years as a member of this institution, I have kept my word," Michel said afterward. "I expect others to do the same."

All this time, however, Michel remained aloof from Gingrich's crusade for the ethics inquiry that ultimately brought Wright down. "I've told Newt to be careful," Michel said in early 1988. "I have tried to help as much as I can, but I still have to keep day-to-day contact with the Speaker." In May, he was the only GOP leader not to sign the petition that helped launch the House ethics committee's probe. But in September, Michel led the call for an investigation of whether Wright disclosed classified information when he told reporters that the CIA was fomenting unrest in Nicaragua.

At year's end, Michel was unusually strident in his acceptance speech to Republicans after his re-election as leader. He called House Democrats' ethics enforcement a "national disgrace," and said he would support a credible "coalition candidate" to run against Wright for Speaker. Yet as Wright's leadership crumbled in the opening months of the 101st Congress, Michel was mostly quiet.

For all the debate among House Republicans about the level of combat with Democrats, at times the greater frustration for Michel and his minions was with fellow Republicans in the administration and Senate — especially during the six years the GOP held the Senate. Time after time, he would object that House Republicans had not been consulted, but were expected to fall docilely in line.

In 1981, the White House had depended on Michel for a sense of strategy and timing in passing its budget and tax bills through the Democratic House; the virtual unanimity of the GOP vote, a combined 568-3 on the trio of measures, was partly a tribute to his skills. But Michel's job got harder as the Republicans' numbers declined with succeeding elections and as Democrats reunited; he no longer had the working majority of Republicans and Boll Weevil Democrats he enjoyed in his first term as leader. Also complicating Michel's work was Reagan's waning influence in the face of recession, flagging legislative ingenuity and finally the Iran-contra scandal.

Of the revelations of secret arms sales to Iran and diversion of profits to the contras, Michel said, "I am personally offended that I was left out of the loop for so long." But he continued to represent the lame-duck president loyally, though for Michel and Republicans generally there were notable breaks.

At the opening of the 100th Congress, he refused to back Reagan's veto of a highway bill, although the White House portrayed the vote as a test of Reagan's strength amid the scandal. Michel, like many Republicans, had a project for his district in the bill, and he was not swayed by a rare visit from Reagan. Michel also participated in the push for a trade bill, reflecting a sensitivity to his ailing district and his own political standing there that many fellow Republicans shared.

While Michel still backed Reagan's contra policy, he kept urging the president to emphasize negotiations over military aid. "I can't be unrealistic when I see votes slipping away," he said. But, illustrating the ongoing tension between Michel's pragmatism and hard-liners' combativeness, the latter refused to quit pressing for military aid. "We're not going to give up on Central America," said Michel's deputy, Cheney. But Michel was right; Congress has not voted for military aid since 1986.

Left groping for a role to play on major issues, Michel and House Republicans at times adopted strategies that looked like desperation tactics — minority psychology run amok.

In 1985, they orchestrated a vote to block House action on a bill to overhaul the tax code — Reagan's No. 1 domestic priority. While some Republicans opposed the bill itself, at bottom, the move was their awkward protest about having been frozen out of the legislative process while Reagan made common cause with Ways and Means Committee Democrats.

The next year, Republicans threw their votes behind passage of the more radical of two bills to impose sanctions against racist South Africa. They believed that such an extreme measure would doom the Democrats' sanctions campaign. Instead, it moved the debate to the left, and ultimately pressured the GOP Senate to approve stronger sanctions than expected. The Senate bill became law over Reagan's veto.

Also in 1986, Michel resorted to a high-risk strategy to abort the Democrats' proposal giving Reagan some of the contra aid he wanted, but with strings attached. Republicans voted with liberals for an amendment to withhold aid, effectively blocking consideration of the Democratic leaders' compromise and forcing them to halt action. "There was no way around it except simply to throw a monkey wrench into the machinery and try to upset the apple cart for the moment," Michel said — in one of the most memorable examples of his folksy speaking style and tendency toward mixed metaphors.

Democrats claimed Republicans won attention and nothing more. But the tactic did open the way for a clear-cut Reagan victory on contra aid, albeit several months later.

The current image of Michel, as a moderate coming to terms with militant conservatism, would surprise anyone familiar with the House in the 1960s, when he was clearly on the GOP right, an orthodox Midwestern Republican decrying wasteful government.

Back then, the GOP was split between conservatives of his stripe and Northeastern moderates. Since that time, the moderates have declined while a Sun Belt-based power bloc emerged, committed to a New Right social agenda and supply-side economics. Michel votes with this group on social issues, though he does not stress them. To carry out Reagan's economic program, he had to shelve his traditional conservative view that reducing deficits is a higher priority than reducing taxes. But as Michel's district hit hard times, some of the Reaganomics votes popular among Southern and Western Republicans did not play well in Peoria, as Michel's near-loss in 1982 proved.

Michel's ties to the moderate wing of the GOP brought him their support when he ran for party leader in 1981, and they reluctantly backed Reagan's first budget partly as a favor to him. Late that year, he dissuaded some conservatives from forming a pro-Reagan group to counter the moderate Gypsy Moths, saying of them, "They're too good as people to dismiss. I love those guys, even if we've been voting on opposite sides for years."

Most Reaganites had backed Guy Vander Jagt of Michigan for leader. But Michel won the 103-87 decision on the same qualities that until recent years had traditionally won House GOP leadership races — cloakroom companionship, homespun Midwestern conservatism, aptitude for legislative detail and a grasp of the rules.

Like his immediate predecessors, John J. Rhodes and Gerald R. Ford, Michel is a product of the collegial Appropriations Committee. He spent a quarter-century there focused on details rather than broad policy, but became a top-flight negotiator in the process. On its Labor-Health, Education and Welfare Subcommittee, for years he opposed a working majority of liberals and Republicans; annually, he took the floor to complain that the subcommittee's bill cost too much.

The Michel-Vander Jagt race began in December 1979, when Rhodes announced his impending retirement. Michel had an advantage among senior members and moderates, but Vander Jagt, as chairman of the campaign committee that donated money to GOP candidates, had the edge among those recently elected.

The sparring extended to the 1980 GOP convention. When Vander Jagt was selected as keynote speaker, Michel's forces complained and their man was made Reagan's floor manager. The election brought 52 new Republicans, more than even Vander Jagt had imagined. But by giving Republicans control of the White House and Senate, the election actually helped Michel; he argued successfully that Reagan needed a legislative tactician in the House, not a fiery speaker. Vander Jagt got most of the newcomers, but Michel got the leadership job.

Though Michel has since gone unchallenged for re-election as leader, his half-a-loaf politics have never satisfied the junior firebrands, who by the mid-1980s had won national media attention under the banner of the Conservative Opportunity Society. COS leaders Gingrich and Vin Weber of Minnesota argued that Republicans should turn the House floor into a theater for partisan warfare, televised live on cable TV. "I'm hard-pressed to see where compromise has advanced the Republican agenda," Weber once said.

Michel's initial advice to the militants was to calm down. "It's one thing to be out there on the stump, flapping your gums," he said, "and it is another thing to put something together. Some of the greatest talkers around here can't legislate their way out of a paper bag." In 1984, when Gingrich lambasted 10 Democrats for advocating talks with Nicaragua, and O'Neill responded with an outburst that brought a rebuke from the presiding officer, many Republicans gave Gingrich a standing ovation. Michel kept his seat.

While he has grown more inclined to strike a confrontational pose, Michel will always be a reluctant convert to militancy. Like every Republican, he was outraged in 1985 by Democrats' refusal to seat Richard D. McIntyre, an Indiana Republican who had been declared the winner in his district. Initially hesitant, Michel joined the GOP protest by trying to force McIntyre's seating on a day when no legislative business was expected — an ambush that sparked a rare reproach from O'Neill.

But a few weeks later, when the Democrats prevailed in seating Democrat Frank McCloskey, Michel walked over and shook McCloskey's hand after his swearing in, something other Republicans pointedly did not do.

At Home: Michel's position at the top of the Republican leadership has earned him the respect, but not the awe, of the constituents in his central Illinois district. Centered on Peoria, the 18th struggled against economic vagaries in its industrial and farm sectors through much of the 1980s. During this period, Michel was often called to task for supporting administration policies that many voters believed were hurtful, or at least less than helpful, to the district.

The contests of 1982 and 1988 caused Michel the greatest difficulties of his House career. In both years, he faced labor attorney G. Douglas Stephens, who blamed the district's economic problems on the incumbent.

Running an anti-Reagan campaign at the height of the 1982 recession, Stephens held Michel to 52 percent, his closest call ever. But while Stephens was equally relentless, and better funded, in 1988, the stabilized local economy and an attentive campaign brought Michel a more comfortable, if still modest, 55 percent.

Stephens' 1982 surge caught Michel by surprise. The Democrat, then 31, was making his first bid for elective office. But Stephens told voters that Michel's role as chief mover of Reagan programs in the House put him at odds with the district's factory workers, farmers, small-business people, poor and elderly, all of whom Stephens said had been adversely affected.

The Democrat criticized Michel particularly for failing to persuade Reagan to lift U.S. sanctions on selling natural gas pipeline equipment to the Soviet Union. Those sanctions cost Caterpillar Tractor Co. and other Illinois heavy-equipment companies lucrative contracts, exacerbating already high unemployment. The Democratic Party did not give Stephens a great deal of financial help, but it did focus attention on the campaign, hoping for an upset that would be seen as a resounding rejection of Reaganomics from the heartland.

Michel's task was complicated by redistricting, which had given him a territory where some 45 percent of the people were new to him. Initially slow to counterattack, Michel began to cast Stephens as a puppet of organized labor and a negativist foe with a limited record of community involvement. Michel proved capable at blending modern media appeals with traditional personal campaigning.

Shortly before the election, Reagan appeared in the district on Michel's behalf and hinted at the forthcoming removal of sanctions on the pipeline equipment sales.

In the two most populous counties of the district — Peoria and Tazewell — Stephens held Michel to 51 percent, and he finished first in four other counties. But Michel's slim margins in the 10 remaining counties pulled him to victory by 6,125 votes.

By 1984, circumstances had shifted in Michel's favor. Though the national economic recovery had not enveloped the 18th, the worst of the recession was over, and Reagan was more popular. Michel changed his political style, setting up a campaign organization early and dropping his long-held aversion to trumpeting federal projects he had attained for the district. With Stephens bypassing the contest, Michel went over 60 percent, and stayed there in 1986.

Hoping that the end of the Reagan era would portend a Democratic year, Stephens tried again in 1988. Updating his 1982 theme, he said declining unemployment figures masked the decline of the region's industries and exodus of their blue-collar workers from the area.

But Michel was ready for Stephens' challenge. He presented statistics showing how the district economy had improved, and pointed to Caterpillar's modest rehiring. He also boasted of the public works and agricultural research projects he had obtained. Michel's win in Peoria County was marginal (just over 50 percent) and he lost Tazewell County, but he swept nearly all the remaining counties.

Michel was born in Peoria, the son of a French immigrant factory worker. Shortly after graduating from Bradley University in Peoria, he went to work for the district's new representative, Republican Harold Velde.

Velde became chairman of the old House Un-American Activities Committee during the Republican-dominated 83rd Congress (1953-55) and received much publicity for his hunt for communist subversives. Michel rose to become Velde's administrative assistant.

In 1956 Velde retired and Michel ran for the seat. Not very well-known in the district, Michel still had the support of many county organizations, for whom he had been a political contact in Washington. He won the primary with 48 percent against four opponents.

Minority Leader

Elections

1988 General		
Robert H. Michel (R)	114,458	(55%)
G. Douglas Stephens (D)	94,763	(45%)
1988 Primary		
Robert H. Michel (R)	45,228	(86%)
James E. Unsicker (R)	7,496	(14%)
1986 General		
Robert H. Michel (R)	94,308	(63%)
Jim Dawson (D)	56,331	(37%)

Previous Winning Percentages:

				1984	(61%)	**1982**	(52%)
1980	(62%)	**1978**	(66%)	**1976**	(58%)	**1974**	(55%)
1972	(65%)	**1970**	(66%)	**1968**	(61%)	**1966**	(58%)
1964	(54%)	**1962**	(61%)	**1960**	(59%)	**1958**	(60%)
1956	(59%)						

District Vote For President

	1988		1984		1980		1976	
D	94,732	(45%)	89,490	(40%)	71,861	(32%)	92,613	(44%)
R	114,841	(55%)	135,170	(60%)	137,198	(61%)	114,120	(55%)
I					12,710	(6%)		

Campaign Finance

	Receipts	Receipts from PACs	Expend-itures
1988			
Michel (R)	$874,026	$555,417 (64%)	$861,969
Stephens (D) †	$242,764	$80,600 (33%)	$231,511
1986			
Michel (R)	$689,849	$456,371 (66%)	$639,765
Dawson (D)	$12,208	$2,358 (19%)	$11,949

† Totals based on incomplete data.

Key Votes

1987	
Raise speed limit to 65 mph	Y
Approve Gephardt "fair trade" amendment	N
Ban testing of larger nuclear weapons	N
Delay "re-flagging" of Kuwaiti tankers	N
Approve tax-raising deficit-reduction bill	N
1988	
Approve aid to Nicaraguan contras	Y
Enact civil rights restoration bill over Reagan veto	N
Kill 60-day plant-closing notification measure	Y
Pass omnibus trade bill over Reagan veto	N
Approve death penalty for drug-related murders	Y
Bar federal funds for abortions in cases of rape and incest	#
Oppose seven-day waiting period for purchase of handguns	Y

Voting Studies

	Presidential Support		Party Unity		Conservative Coalition	
Year	**S**	**O**	**S**	**O**	**S**	**O**
1988	64	30	76	14	82	8
1987	77 †	17 †	85 †	9 †	93 †	2 †
1986	74	18	73	20	76	18
1985	85	11	78 †	15 †	91	7
1984	75	20	80	11	90	3
1983	84	7	71 †	20 †	81	15
1982	83	12	81	16	89	10
1981	80	17	82 †	11 †	83	13

† Not eligible for all recorded votes.

Interest Group Ratings

Year	ADA	ACU	AFL-CIO	CCUS
1988	10	92	31	85
1987	0	86	6	86
1986	5	86	8	88
1985	5	86	6	81
1984	5	82	8	81
1983	5	81	12	100
1982	5	82	10	80
1981	10	86	0	100

19 Terry L. Bruce (D)

Of Olney — Elected 1984

Born: March 25, 1944, Olney, Ill.
Education: U. of Illinois, B.S. 1966, J.D. 1969.
Occupation: Lawyer; farmer.
Family: Wife, Charlotte Roberts; two children.
Religion: Methodist.
Political Career: Ill. Senate, 1971-85; Democratic nominee for U.S. House, 1978.
Capitol Office: 419 Cannon Bldg. 20515; 225-5001.

In Washington: Though he only arrived in Congress in 1985, Bruce acts more like a seasoned legislative veteran than many members who are years his senior. In fact, he *is* a seasoned veteran. In his mid-20s he began learning the art of legislative politics as a member of the Illinois Senate; the knowledge he gained in 14 years there is now applied to pulling the levers of power in the House.

During his freshman term, Bruce set his sights on winning a coveted spot on the Energy and Commerce Committee. He got it by pursuing committee Chairman John D. Dingell of Michigan. Bruce made it clear he was the sort of member Dingell wanted — a liberal team player on most issues, but not a down-the-line environmentalist who would fight the chairman over controversial clean-air legislation.

While Bruce represents a sizable liberal academic community at the University of Illinois at Champaign-Urbana, he must balance their concerns against those of constituents who work in the coal and auto industries and could be hurt by tough environmental legislation.

Bruce got a fast start on the committee in the 100th Congress, hooking up with an ad hoc caucus of key moderate-to-conservative Democrats who worked behind the scenes to try to break a six-year deadlock on reauthorizing the Clean Air Act. On the full Energy and Commerce Committee, Dingell and more industry-oriented members had been at odds with California Democrat Henry A. Waxman and an environmentalist faction for years over anti-smog and anti-acid rain measures. The so-called "group of nine," to which Bruce belonged, hoped to find some acceptable compromise.

As the only member of the group to sit on Waxman's Health Subcommittee — where much of the work on clean air originates — Bruce was viewed as a key figure. Because the politics of his district make the clean-air issue so sensitive, Bruce was a cautious, but active, participant as the group worked privately to hammer out a proposal for the smog section of the legislation.

The detailed "group of nine" plan generally extended the timetable for cities to meet clean-air standards and imposed somewhat less stringent controls. The 100th Congress eventually ran out of time to move any legislation, but the plan was seen as a step forward that would lay some groundwork for the 101st Congress.

On another front, Bruce was active in an effort to place limits on the advertising that can be shown on children's television, and to encourage broadcasters to provide educational programming for children.

The Federal Communications Commission had abolished limits in 1984, and Bruce, along with Democrats John Bryant of Texas and Edward J. Markey of Massachusetts, felt a bill was needed to prevent the airwaves from polluting children's minds. They came close to succeeding. Congress passed legislation that was somewhat softer than Bruce had pushed, but President Reagan, citing concerns about freedom of speech, killed it with a pocket veto.

At Home: Bruce evened an old political account when he unseated GOP Rep. Daniel B. Crane in 1984. Crane had defeated Bruce in an open-seat House race in 1978, taking the 19th District out of Democratic hands for the first time in two decades.

Crane won re-election twice, but in 1983 he was censured by the House for an affair with a female congressional page several years earlier. For a conservative "family advocate" like Crane, that episode had devastating potential; for Bruce, it was a golden opportunity.

Despite the censure, Crane's defeat was no foregone conclusion. He spent the summer campaigning, and he went on TV early with hard-hitting ads attacking Bruce for "flip-flopping" on issues such as the Equal Rights Amendment, which Bruce belatedly had come to support.

When Bruce's ads hit the airwaves, however, they made their point. Crane's 1982 foe had aggressively attacked the incumbent as ineffective, and Bruce pursued the same issue. He scored Crane for never having passed a bill, for missing committee hearings, for his mention in the *Washington Monthly* as one of the House's worst members, and for the censure.

Illinois 19

Southeast — Danville; Champaign-Urbana

The Republican tradition in the Corn Belt counties that make up much of the 19th has not changed. However, the addition of the university town of Champaign in the redistricting of the 1980s made Democratic candidates for national office somewhat more competitive, and has helped make Democrat Bruce a dominant figure in the district.

Before the last redistricting, the largest city in the 19th was Danville (population 37,000). But the remap brought in three-quarters of Champaign County, including the University of Illinois. Champaign and its twin city of Urbana together have about 95,000 people, and the university influence leads them into the Democratic column in many statewide contests. When he toppled GOP incumbent Crane in 1984, Democrat Bruce took almost two-thirds of Champaign County. But in 1988, George Bush carried the county (part of which is in the 15th District) with 53 percent of the vote.

Danville, in Vermillion County, has deep Republican roots: It sent autocratic Republican Speaker Joseph G. Cannon to Congress for 30 years, around the beginning of this century. But it is also an aging industrial center whose blue-collar population provides a Democratic tinge. Democrat Michael S. Dukakis took Vermillion County with 52 percent in 1988.

Dukakis fell just short in the southernmost counties, where oil and coal are the major industries. Hamilton and White counties are laced with stripper oil wells. White has been the major oil-producing county in the state, with Hamilton not far behind. Bush carried Hamilton County by just four votes, and won White County with 51 percent.

However, the Republican built his winning edge in the 19th by sweeping through the farm counties in between. He carried Effingham, one of the larger rural counties, with 65 percent.

Population: 518,350. White 491,245 (95%), Black 20,051 (4%), Other 4,403 (1%). Spanish origin 4,254 (1%). 18 and over 386,732 (75%), 65 and over 68,713 (13%). Median age: 29.

Crane had tried hard to minimize the impact of the scandal, tearfully apologizing to his colleagues and making the rounds of the 19th to plead for his constituents' forgiveness. For a time, the issue seemed to die down. But Bruce's ads reawakened it and tied it to the matter of Crane's general performance in the House. With the help of organized labor and liberal activists, Bruce swamped Crane in Champaign, easily offsetting his deficit elsewhere in the district; he won with 52 percent.

In both 1986 and 1988, the GOP mounted only token challenges. Bruce was thus easily able to embellish his record of political success — marred only by his 1978 loss to Crane — that dates to 1970, when he won a state Senate seat.

Committees

Energy and Commerce (24th of 26 Democrats)
Energy and Power; Health and the Environment

Science, Space and Technology (16th of 30 Democrats)
Energy Research and Development; Science, Research and Technology

Elections

1988 General		
Terry L. Bruce (D)	132,889	(64%)
Robert F. Kerans (R)	73,981	(36%)
1986 General		
Terry L. Bruce (D)	111,105	(66%)
Al Salvi (R)	56,186	(34%)

Previous Winning Percentage: **1984** (52%)

District Vote For President

	1988	1984	1980	1976
D	95,599 (45%)	86,323 (38%)	78,359 (34%)	101,969 (46%)
R	114,212 (54%)	141,611 (62%)	131,504 (57%)	117,017 (53%)
I			16,801 (7%)	

Campaign Finance

	Receipts	Receipts from PACs	Expend-itures
1988			
Bruce (D)	$457,955	$276,182 (60%)	$193,205
Kerans (R)	$16,445	$1,250 (8%)	$16,241
1986			
Bruce (D)	$371,735	$221,790 (60%)	$278,421
Salvi (R)	$37,573	$4,250 (11%)	$37,570

Key Votes

1987	
Raise speed limit to 65 mph	N
Approve Gephardt "fair trade" amendment	Y
Ban testing of larger nuclear weapons	+
Delay "re-flagging" of Kuwaiti tankers	Y
Approve tax-raising deficit-reduction bill	Y
1988	
Approve aid to Nicaraguan contras	N
Enact civil rights restoration bill over Reagan veto	Y
Kill 60-day plant-closing notification measure	N
Pass omnibus trade bill over Reagan veto	Y
Approve death penalty for drug-related murders	Y
Bar federal funds for abortions in cases of rape and incest	Y
Oppose seven-day waiting period for purchase of handguns	Y

Voting Studies

	Presidential Support		Party Unity		Conservative Coalition	
Year	**S**	**O**	**S**	**O**	**S**	**O**
1988	23	77	89	9	39	61
1987	14	79	88	5	23	67
1986	20	80	88	12	34	66
1985	29	71	89	10	25	75

Interest Group Ratings

Year	ADA	ACU	AFL-CIO	CCUS
1988	75	24	100	36
1987	80	9	94	13
1986	80	9	100	33
1985	70	19	76	36

20 Richard J. Durbin (D)

Of Springfield — Elected 1982

Born: Nov. 21, 1944, East St. Louis, Ill.
Education: Georgetown U., B.S. (Foreign Service) 1966, J.D. 1969.
Occupation: Lawyer.
Family: Wife, Loretta Schaefer; three children.
Religion: Roman Catholic.
Political Career: Democratic nominee for Ill. Senate, 1976; Democratic nominee for lieutenant governor, 1978.
Capitol Office: 129 Cannon Bldg. 20515; 225-5271.

In Washington: Durbin came to Congress with an understanding of its rules and a knack for playing its internal politics — a combination that has given him the savvy and self-assurance to act the parts of both insider and insurgent.

An amiable man with the face of an aging choir boy, he is well acquainted with legislative procedure, having been a parliamentarian of the Illinois Senate; from the start, House leaders tapped him to preside over the chamber even during controversial debates. Like a number of Democrats first elected in the 1982 recession, he is a budget-conscious liberal trying to rebuild his party's fiscal credibility. He quickly emerged as a popular figure among younger House members, while forging ties with current leaders that got him a prize seat on Appropriations in his second term.

At the same time, Durbin has challenged Appropriations' hierarchy, bucking its stricture against controversial amendments and otherwise opposing the powerful "College of Cardinals" subcommittee chairmen. A strong-willed activist, he abhors deferential inaction more than he fears his elders' revenge. He has attacked congressional pay raises and other perquisites; many members regard that as demagogic, even disloyal. Some probably were pleased to see him run last in a four-way race for Democratic Caucus vice chairman in June 1989. Durbin escapes harsher judgment from his opponents because of his geniality, articulate argument and sense of fair play.

That is not to say Durbin has not made enemies of some powerful people. He will be long remembered for his successful advocacy in 1987 of a smoking ban on most airline flights; it was the first time Congress had proscribed smoking for health reasons. Two in particular who will never forget his victory are Appropriations "Cardinals" William H. Natcher and W. G. "Bill" Hefner, from the tobacco states of Kentucky and North Carolina, respectively.

Durbin, whose chain-smoking father died of lung cancer when Durbin was 14, was aroused to action after taking a Phoenix-to-Chicago flight on which he had to sit between two smokers. He proposed banning smoking on all flights, but his amendment to the fiscal 1988 transportation funding bill was easily defeated, first in the Transportation Subcommittee and later in the full committee.

He had come armed with scientific evidence of the dangers of "passive smoke" to nonsmokers. And when the tobacco-state lawmakers countered with a procedural argument that Durbin was violating a House rule against adding legislation to a spending bill, the rules expert shot back with an opinion from the House parliamentarian that the amendment was proper since it would achieve its purpose indirectly through appropriations; it would bar federal grants to airports providing landing rights to airlines that permit smoking.

Beaten in committee, Durbin carried the battle to the House floor, a rare step for an Appropriations member, one akin to airing family laundry. Durbin had modified his provision to gain support, limiting it to flights of two hours or less, or about 80 percent of all trips. After an emotional debate, the House passed it, 198-193, surprising even Durbin. With support from New Jersey Sen. Frank R. Lautenberg, chairman of the Senate's Transportation Appropriations Subcommittee, a similar measure passed in the Senate. The compromise that became law banned smoking on flights of two hours or less for a two-year trial period. At the opening of the 101st Congress, Durbin was ready with legislation for a permanent ban.

Also in the 100th Congress, Durbin and several colleagues opposed Transportation Subcommittee Chairman William Lehman of Florida and pushed a pro-labor provision benefiting workers whose jobs are threatened in airline mergers. Lehman wanted to drop the item, fearing it would provoke Reagan to veto the entire fiscal 1989 transportation funding bill. Durbin said it was "painful" to oppose the chairman, but he did. With Speaker Jim Wright's intervention, however, the provision was dropped.

Illinois 20

Central — Springfield; Decatur; Quincy

The 20th District sweeps across Illinois at mid-state, starting in traditionally Democratic counties and working its way west to Republican territory along the Missouri border. Redistricting in 1981 took away the suburbs of Springfield and other good GOP areas, boosting the prospects of statewide Democratic candidates in the 20th, and providing a cushion for Durbin once he established himself as the district's Democratic House member.

But while Democrat Michael S. Dukakis was quite competitive in the 20th, George Bush kept it in the Republican presidential column with 51 percent of the vote. In 1984, President Reagan carried the district with 58 percent.

The 20th has the Mississippi River port of Quincy and the inner-city section of Springfield, with the state Capitol and a substantial bloc of white-collar workers in state government. Springfield and surrounding Sangamon County cast more than 30 percent of the district vote.

Agriculture remains the economic base of the district, thanks to the rich bottom lands of the Illinois and Mississippi rivers. Hogs, corn and soybeans are important; the soybean market in Decatur sets prices for a large area of the Midwest. But coal took on greater importance in the 20th than it once did, with the addition in 1981 of the mining counties of Christian, Shelby and Moultrie. The third-largest coal mine in the world is in Macoupin County.

The Southern Democratic traditions of these southern Illinois counties have shifted somewhat. Reagan carried all three counties easily both in 1980 and 1984, and Bush carried Shelby and Moultrie. However, Democrat Paul Simon, whose base was the nearby 22nd District, won the counties in his 1984 Senate contest.

The industrial city of Decatur (population 90,000), can be counted on to vote Democratic in most elections. For more than half a century, Decatur's leading employer has been the Staley company, a soybean processing firm; the Decatur Staleys were one of the original teams in the National Football League.

Population: 519,015. White 489,038 (94%), Black 26,679 (5%). Spanish origin 2,666 (1%). 18 and over 375,764 (72%), 65 and over 75,365 (15%). Median age: 32.

Durbin also challenged Edward P. Boland, chairman of the Appropriations subcommittee with jurisdiction ranging from housing to space. More than once in 1988, liberals sought to shift money from space programs to worldly needs; Durbin took his shot in Appropriations, proposing that $35 million earmarked for NASA in Boland's budget go instead to asbestos removal in schools. Durbin lost overwhelmingly, 2-32. A month later, however, the committee added $25 million for the asbestos program, and it became law.

While some Appropriations members focus their attention almost entirely on the committee, Durbin has also made a mark elsewhere in the House. In the 100th Congress, he joined the Budget Committee, taking one of the slots reserved for an Appropriations representative.

Appropriations Chairman Jamie L. Whitten reminded Durbin that he was an Appropriations member on Budget, and not the other way around. Still, Durbin joined with other junior Appropriations members to coax Whitten to comply with the non-binding budget resolution or else face threats of across-the-board cuts on the floor. Whitten reluctantly did so.

Durbin is well placed on Appropriations to look after his district, which includes both farm land and urban areas such as Springfield. As a member of the Agriculture Subcommittee in the 99th Congress, he secured funds for an agricultural research facility at the nearby University of Illinois, and staved off Reagan administration attempts to cut funds for the Foreign Agricultural Service, which seeks new agricultural markets abroad. On the Transportation Subcommittee, Durbin has fought to protect funding for rail service in his district.

Convinced that Illinois benefits from bipartisan cooperation, he also has extended a hand to the GOP side of the aisle. "I made it clear from the start I was not going to be antagonistic to people like Bob Michel and Ed Madigan," he said in 1986, referring to senior Illinois Republicans. In the 99th Congress, he helped GOP leader Michel win funding for an agricultural lab in Peoria, his hometown.

In 1986, Durbin played an important role in another sort of money fight outside Appropriations. He led a successful revolt of junior members to reverse a vote, engineered by House leaders without most members' knowledge, that raised the limit on lawmakers' earnings from speeches and professional fees. Younger members, who are not in such demand for appearances anyway, were concerned about the political implications of that change at a time of budget cutbacks.

Such anti-perk crusades rile senior members, but Durbin is more interested in cultivating his peers in the younger, issue-oriented and increasingly influential group of Democrats who are trying to adapt traditional party doctrine to modern realities. In his first term, he allied with Missouri's Richard A. Gephardt and California's Tony Coelho, meeting with them regularly to discuss policy and strategy. In his second term, alarmed at Reagan's strong 1984 showing among college-age voters, he organized a short-lived outreach program that took House Democrats to campuses; the reaction was mixed, but the program made Durbin a more visible player in national Democratic politics.

At Home: Just as he has quickly become a key player in the House, Durbin became ensconced in his district in a short time, a remarkable feat considering that much of its territory had been loyally Republican for four decades. In 1982, Durbin unseated 11-term GOP Rep. Paul N. Findley by 1,410 votes; two years later, Durbin was already over 60 percent.

Durbin was helped the first time by redistricting. The Democratic-oriented map in effect for 1982 transformed the 20th from about 53 percent Republican to about 53 percent Democratic, and gave Findley more than 175,000 new and unfamiliar constituents.

That was only one of several factors favoring Durbin. The district's agricultural economy was dismal in 1982, and the blue-collar work force was burdened with layoffs in the slumping farm-implement industry. And Durbin was generously financed by pro-Israel groups offended by Findley's close ties to the Palestine Liberation Organization.

Though Durbin barely edged the veteran incumbent, within two years he was clearly in charge. Republican Richard Austin, chairman of the Sangamon County (Springfield) Board, tried his hand at Durbin in 1984, but was hopelessly overmatched. Durbin's visible efforts to funnel redevelopment funds to depressed communities and his attempts to obtain a major coal gasification project for the district paid political dividends. He carried every county, and by 1986 the GOP appeared to have given up.

Durbin's political mentor was Democrat Paul Simon, now Illinois' junior senator. When Simon became lieutenant governor in 1969, he hired Durbin as an adviser. Following Simon's loss in the 1972 gubernatorial primary, Durbin became chief Democratic staff aide on the Illinois Senate Judiciary Committee, and then Senate parliamentarian. He was the Democratic nominee for lieutenant governor in 1978.

Committees

Appropriations (30th of 35 Democrats)
Rural Development, Agriculture and Related Agencies; Transportation and Related Agencies

Budget (11th of 21 Democrats)
Task Forces: Economic Policy, Projections and Revenues; Human Resources

Select Children, Youth and Family (16th of 18 Democrats)

Elections

1988 General		
Richard J. Durbin (D)	153,341	(69%)
Paul E. Jurgens (R)	69,303	(31%)
1986 General		
Richard J. Durbin (D)	126,556	(68%)
Kevin B. McCarthy (R)	59,291	(32%)

Previous Winning Percentages: **1984** (61%) **1982** (50%)

District Vote For President

	1988	1984	1980	1976
D	109,922 (49%)	99,163 (42%)	89,095 (38%)	114,032 (48%)
R	113,401 (51%)	135,523 (58%)	132,407 (57%)	119,329 (51%)
I			11,303 (5%)	

Campaign Finance

	Receipts	Receipts from PACs	Expend-itures
1988			
Durbin (D)	$367,468	$220,605 (60%)	$251,634
Jurgens (R)	$58,532	$8,300 (14%)	$57,708
1986			
Durbin (D)	$343,599	$168,774 (49%)	$289,085
McCarthy (R)	$107,837	$25,487 (24%)	$108,129

Key Votes

1987	
Raise speed limit to 65 mph	Y
Approve Gephardt "fair trade" amendment	Y
Ban testing of larger nuclear weapons	Y
Delay "re-flagging" of Kuwaiti tankers	Y
Approve tax-raising deficit-reduction bill	Y
1988	
Approve aid to Nicaraguan contras	N
Enact civil rights restoration bill over Reagan veto	Y
Kill 60-day plant-closing notification measure	N
Pass omnibus trade bill over Reagan veto	Y
Approve death penalty for drug-related murders	Y
Bar federal funds for abortions in cases of rape and incest	Y
Oppose seven-day waiting period for purchase of handguns	N

Voting Studies

	Presidential Support		Party Unity		Conservative Coalition	
Year	S	O	S	O	S	O
1988	24	76	88	9	18	82
1987	13	84	91	5	19	77
1986	17	82	90	9	22	78
1985	28	73	79	19	20	78
1984	32	66	82	18	29	69
1983	13	85	77	17	31	69

Interest Group Ratings

Year	ADA	ACU	AFL-CIO	CCUS
1988	90	16	100	36
1987	92	4	94	0
1986	85	14	93	22
1985	65	19	82	36
1984	70	13	85	31
1983	85	13	76	20

21 Jerry F. Costello (D)

Of Belleville — Elected 1988

Born: Sept. 25, 1949, East St. Louis, Ill.
Education: Belleville Area College, A.A. 1970; Maryville College of the Sacred Heart, B.A. 1972.
Occupation: Law enforcement administrator.
Family: Wife, Georgia Cockrum; three children.
Religion: Roman Catholic.
Political Career: St. Clair County Board chairman, 1980-88.
Capitol Office: 1529 Longworth Bldg. 20515; 225-5661.

In Washington: Costello was long regarded as heir apparent to Democratic Rep. Melvin Price. The executive officer of a county suffering from industrial decline, Costello had made himself a familiar figure in Springfield — and even to some in Washington — through his efforts to obtain development money. Costello also exhibited prodigious fund-raising ability, amassing nearly $1 million within weeks of Price's December 1987 retirement announcement. (Price died in April 1988.)

But while Costello was well prepared, his House bid still encountered fierce opposition. Though Costello insisted that St. Clair County's unsavory history of machine politics was a thing of the past, opponents in both parties portrayed him as an iron-fisted boss of a shady machine. Costello survived his party's primary with just a plurality, and he only narrowly won an August 1988 special election to succeed the late Price.

Though there was little time remaining in the 100th Congress when Costello took his seat, he got a politically helpful committee assignment: Public Works. His office then issued a stream of news releases on grants for the 21st, many of which had been in the pipeline during Price's tenure. Maintaining his visibility, Costello won the November general election by a larger, though still modest, margin.

Now able to distance himself from the roughhouse of St. Clair politics, Costello can turn his full attention to using his Public Works position to pursue local projects, including a light-rail system linking his district to the job market on the St. Louis side of the Mississippi. In the 101st Congress, Costello also got seats on the Science and Select Aging committees.

At Home: Costello was born into politics. His father, the late Dan E. Costello, served in the Illinois Legislature and as sheriff and later treasurer of St. Clair County. After serving as a state circuit court probation director for four years, the younger Costello was elected County Commission chairman in 1980.

He emerged as one of the dominant political figures in his heavily Democratic region. As chairman of the metropolitan St. Louis Council of Governments, Costello drew the attention of GOP Gov. James R. Thompson, who appointed him to lead a study of the conversion of Scott Air Force Base to joint military-civilian use.

In 1984, Costello threatened to challenge Price, whose waning abilities were then on the verge of costing him the chairmanship of the Armed Services Committee. But loyalties to Price, who served more than four decades in the House, were strong, and Costello backed off.

Costello also sat out the 1986 contest. But Price's near-defeat that year at the hands of Republican Robert H. Gaffner (who was making his third try for the seat) predestined Price's retirement. Costello was already raising money and lining up endorsements from the district Democratic leadership when Price announced that he would step down.

Costello's primary foes — particularly Madison County Auditor Pete Fields, who had challenged Price in the 1986 primary — accused him of carrying on the hardball tradition of a county Democratic machine that guaranteed its success by dominating heavily black and economically distressed East St. Louis. Costello won the primary, but with only a 46 percent plurality.

It was expected that Costello would have an easier time against Gaffner, a college official whose 1986 performance against Price was widely laid on the incumbent's frailty. But the campaign was complicated by the special election necessitated by Price's death. Gaffner copied the line of attack used by Costello's Democratic opponents: The Republican ran ads suggesting that voters call Costello and quiz him about a list of ethics questions.

Costello won the special election with 51.5 percent. He attributed his showing to weak turnout for the midsummer contest, and promised to do better in his November rematch with Gaffner.

Though Gaffner continued to belabor the ethics issue to some effect, Costello again held on, winning just under 53 percent of the vote. But he trailed the Democratic presidential ticket in the 21st, and barely carried St. Clair.

Illinois 21

Southwest — East St. Louis; Alton

The southwestern Illinois region covered by the 21st has long been identified by the grimy industrial cities across the Mississippi River from St. Louis. But while the grime remains, much of the industry has left; the district's steel, petroleum-refining and glass industries have suffered a serious long-term decline.

East St. Louis, formerly the district's dominant city, has suffered the most. A national meatpacking center as recently as the late 1960s, the city has been abandoned by manufacturing firms, and has also lost much of its retail base.

A population decline of 21 percent in the 1970s, and another 10 percent drop between 1980 and 1986, have left East St. Louis with just under 50,000 residents, 95 percent of whom are black. Unemployment rates linger near the 20 percent level. The lack of a revenue base has pushed the city government close to insolvency on several occasions in recent years.

Though the economic problems carry over to neighboring Belleville (population 43,000), the St. Clair County seat has weathered the vagaries somewhat better. The city includes a number of St. Louis commuters and a much smaller proportion of minority poor.

With its blue-collar and minority populations (and an active coal-mining industry in its southern reaches), St. Clair remains one of the most dependable Democratic bastions south of Chicago. It is the home base of Democratic Sen. Alan J. Dixon; Democratic presidential candidate Michael S. Dukakis took 57 percent of its vote in 1988.

However, with East St. Louis' decline and stagnant population growth elsewhere, St. Clair does not carry the weight it once did. Madison County to the north, which includes such industrial cities as Alton and Granite City, provides slightly more votes than St. Clair in most statewide elections. But Madison usually bolsters St. Clair's partisan direction: Dukakis won the county with 55 percent.

Three mainly rural counties — Bond, Montgomery and Clinton — fill out the balance of the district, and provide it with a Republican counterweight. Bond, the only one of the three entirely within the 21st, gave a slight edge to George Bush in 1988.

Population: 521,036. White 439,188 (84%), Black 76,733 (15%), Other 2,821 (1%). Spanish origin 5,779 (1%). 18 and over 367,291 (71%), 65 and over 62,217 (12%). Median age: 30.

Committees

Public Works and Transportation (25th of 31 Democrats)
Aviation; Surface Transportation; Water Resources

Science, Space and Technology (27th of 30 Democrats)
Energy Research and Development; Science, Research and Technology

Select Aging (35th of 39 Democrats)
Retirement, Income and Employment

Elections

1988 General		
Jerry F. Costello (D)	105,836	(53%)
Robert H. Gaffner (R)	95,385	(47%)
1988 Primary		
Jerry F. Costello (D)	35,279	(46%)
Pete Fields (D)	20,500	(27%)
Mike Mansfield (D)	19,223	(25%)
1988 Special Election		
Jerry F. Costello (D)	33,144	(51%)
Robert H. Gaffner (R)	31,257	(49%)
1988 Special Primary		
Jerry F. Costello (D)	18,259	(90%)
Clarence Ellis Sr. (D)	2,062	(10%)

District Vote For President

	1988	1984	1980	1976
D	110,653 (54%)	100,109 (46%)	93,309 (45%)	120,941 (56%)
R	92,956 (46%)	114,839 (53%)	104,414 (50%)	92,047 (43%)
I			8,437 (4%)	

Campaign Finance

	Receipts	Receipts from PACs	Expend-itures
1988			
Costello (D)	$1,106,495	$329,661 (30%)	$1,106,233
Gaffner (R) †	$159,271	$33,798 (21%)	$157,171
1988 Special Election †			
Costello (D)	$266,795	$85,775 (32%)	$374,496
Gaffner (R)	$66,501	$6,200 (11%)	$34,934

† Totals based on incomplete data.

Key Votes

1988	
Approve death penalty for drug-related murders	Y
Bar federal funds for abortions in cases of rape and incest	Y
Oppose seven-day waiting period for purchase of handguns	Y

Voting Studies

	Presidential Support		Party Unity		Conservative Coalition	
Year	S	O	S	O	S	O
1988	24 †	76 †	86 †	11 †	67 †	33 †

† Not eligible for all recorded votes.

Interest Group Ratings

Year	ADA	ACU	AFL-CIO	CCUS
1988	—	57	100	—

22 Glenn Poshard (D)

Of Carterville — Elected 1988

Born: Oct. 30, 1945, Herald, Ill.
Education: Southern Illinois U., B.S. 1970, M.S. 1974, Ph.D. 1984.
Military Career: Army, 1962-65.
Occupation: Educator.
Family: Wife, Jo Roetzel; two children.
Religion: Baptist.
Political Career: Ill. Senate, 1984-89; sought Democratic nomination for Ill. Senate, 1982.
Capitol Office: 1229 Longworth Bldg. 20515; 225-5201.

The Path to Washington: An intellectual with working-class roots, Poshard was widely regarded by Democrats as the logical successor to Democratic Rep. Kenneth J. Gray, who decided not to seek re-election in 1988. Poshard fulfilled the party's expectations of his electoral appeal, winning the general election by nearly a 2-to-1 margin.

In terms of background, the contrast between Poshard and his predecessor is striking. Gray, a showman known for his flashy clothes and boisterous personality, never attended college, and worked as a car dealer and auctioneer prior to entering politics. Poshard has a doctorate in educational administration from Southern Illinois University (SIU) in Carbondale, and he headed a regional program for gifted students. Though Poshard is an engaging campaigner, he is not nearly as flamboyant as Gray.

However, Gray and Poshard share at least one thing: a populist style that has appeal in southern Illinois' coal-mining communities and Ohio River towns, where Southern Democratic voting tendencies remain strong.

Poshard, whose state Senate district included a number of economically hard-pressed counties in the southern and eastern parts of the 22nd, expresses his concern for his blue-collar constituents with a rhetorical flair that first brought him to the attention of the local and state Democratic leadership.

Though he had been involved in local politics during his career as an educator, Poshard first made his presence felt in 1982, waging an unsuccessful primary challenge to a veteran Democratic state senator. The campaign was not rancorous, and Poshard impressed party officials with his political skills.

When the senator died in mid-1984, county Democratic leaders unanimously nominated Poshard for appointment to the vacancy. Within months, Poshard successfully defended the seat in a tough campaign against a Republican state House member. He coasted to re-election in 1986.

Poshard quickly became a prolific legislator in Springfield. He used his expertise to establish a record on education issues, worked on the overhaul of the state workmen's compensation law and tended to local interests such as rural health care and "clean coal" technology.

Though some colleagues complained that Poshard was too much a young man in a hurry, he caught the eye of the Democratic leadership. He was named keynote speaker for the 1986 state party convention, and was appointed chairman of the state Senate Labor and Commerce Committee, a traditional province of Chicago-area Democrats.

These credentials enhanced Poshard's already strong position in the House contest. Formidable in his own jurisdiction, Poshard also had personal ties to Carbondale, the district's largest city.

Poshard's Republican opponent, Patrick Kelley, a law professor at SIU, articulately spelled out an agenda that hewed to the national GOP platform on most issues. But he was not well-known outside Carbondale, where he had served two terms on the City Council. And his effort to frame the election as an ideological contest fell short against Poshard, who is a social-issues conservative opposed to abortion and supportive of school prayer.

Poshard carried 19 of the district's 21 counties, winning 70 percent of the vote or better in five counties in his state Senate district. He did nearly as well in most other areas, taking Jackson County (Carbondale) with 63 percent. Only in the northern part of the district, where Kelley carried two counties, was the election competitive.

Poshard's background made him a natural for a spot on the Education and Labor Committee. He was one of four freshmen named to that committee for the 101st Congress, and he also took a seat on Small Business.

Illinois 22

South — Carbondale

In the southern part of Illinois the prairies give way to hilly countryside, and coal mining replaces large-scale farming as a dominant economic activity. About 15,000 miners work in the Illinois Basin, a coal vein that runs under Franklin, Williamson, Saline, Perry and Jefferson counties.

The people here are descendants of 19th-century settlers from places like Kentucky and Tennessee. And like their peers farther south, the voters here have slipped from their conservative Democratic traditions: President Reagan won the 22nd with 56 percent of the vote in 1984.

However, continued hard economic times in the coal country and in the fading Ohio River port towns have stemmed the Republican tide somewhat. In 1988, Democrat Michael S. Dukakis carried the 22nd with 52 percent.

Carbondale (population 24,000) is the largest of the small cities that lie along the Main Street of the district: state Route 13. Carbondale is dominated by Southern Illinois University, with 24,000 students.

At the southern tip of the district is Alexander County, in the region called "Little Egypt." The depressed river town of Cairo, the Alexander County seat, has as bitter a history of racial confrontation as almost any community in the Deep South. Cairo is now majority black, and its vote helped Dukakis carry Alexander County with nearly 58 percent of its vote. Overall, Dukakis carried 10 district counties, including eight in a broad swath across the center of the district.

The Republican vote is most consistent in the farm territory toward the northern end of the district. In 1984, Washington County gave Reagan nearly 70 percent of its vote, and awarded more than 55 percent to Republican Sen. Charles H. Percy against successful Democratic challenger Paul Simon, who was then representing the 22nd District in the House. George Bush took 61 percent in 1988.

Population: 521,303. White 483,298 (93%), Black 33,771 (7%). Spanish origin 3,284 (1%). 18 and over 381,684 (73%), 65 and over 77,842 (15%). Median age: 31.

Committees

Education and Labor (16th of 22 Democrats)
Elementary, Secondary and Vocational Education; Human Resources; Postsecondary Education

Small Business (26th of 27 Democrats)
Environment and Labor; Procurement, Tourism and Rural Development

Campaign Finance

	Receipts	Receipts from PACs	Expend-itures
1988			
Poshard (D)	$430,240	$248,970 (58%)	$392,791
Kelley (R)	$81,763	$15,872 (19%)	$80,675

Elections

1988 General

Glenn Poshard (D)	139,392	(65%)
Patrick J. Kelley (R)	75,462	(35%)

District Vote For President

	1988	1984	1980	1976
D	113,071 (52%)	103,010 (43%)	95,562 (42%)	127,388 (54%)
R	104,886 (48%)	133,547 (56%)	125,032 (54%)	103,843 (44%)
I			8,427 (4%)	

Indiana

U.S. CONGRESS

SENATE 2 R

HOUSE 7 D, 3 R

LEGISLATURE

Senate 24 D, 26 R

House 50 D, 50 R

ELECTIONS

1988 Presidential Vote	
Bush	60%
Dukakis	40%
1984 Presidential Vote	
Reagan	62%
Mondale	38%
1980 Presidential Vote	
Reagan	56%
Carter	38%
Anderson	5%
Turnout rate in 1984	56%
Turnout rate in 1986	39%
Turnout rate in 1988	53%

(as percentage of voting age population)

POPULATION AND GROWTH

1980 population	5,490,224
1988 population estimate (14th in the nation)	5,556,000
Percent change 1980-1988	+1%

DEMOGRAPHIC BREAKDOWN

White	91%
Black	8%
(Spanish origin)	2%
Urban	64%
Rural	36%
Born in state	71%
Foreign-born	2%

MAJOR CITIES

Indianapolis	719,820
Fort Wayne	172,900
Gary	136,790
Evansville	129,480
South Bend	107,190

AREA AND LAND USE

Area 35,932 sq. miles (38th)

Farm	71%
Forest	19%
Federally owned	2%

Gov. Evan Bayh (D)
Of Indianapolis — Elected 1988

Born: Dec. 26, 1955, Terre Haute, Ind.
Education: Indiana U., B.S. 1978; U. of Virginia, J.D. 1981.
Occupation: Lawyer.
Religion: Christian.
Political Career: Ind. secretary of state, 1986-89.
Next Election: 1992.

WORK

Occupations	
White-collar	47%
Blue-collar	38%
Service workers	13%
Government Workers	
Federal	41,109
State	96,132
Local	220,047

MONEY

Median family income	$ 20,535	(18th)
Tax burden per capita	$ 789	(33rd)

EDUCATION

Spending per pupil through grade 12	$ 3,275	(34th)
Persons with college degrees	13%	(45th)

CRIME

Violent crime rate 329 per 100,000 (33rd)

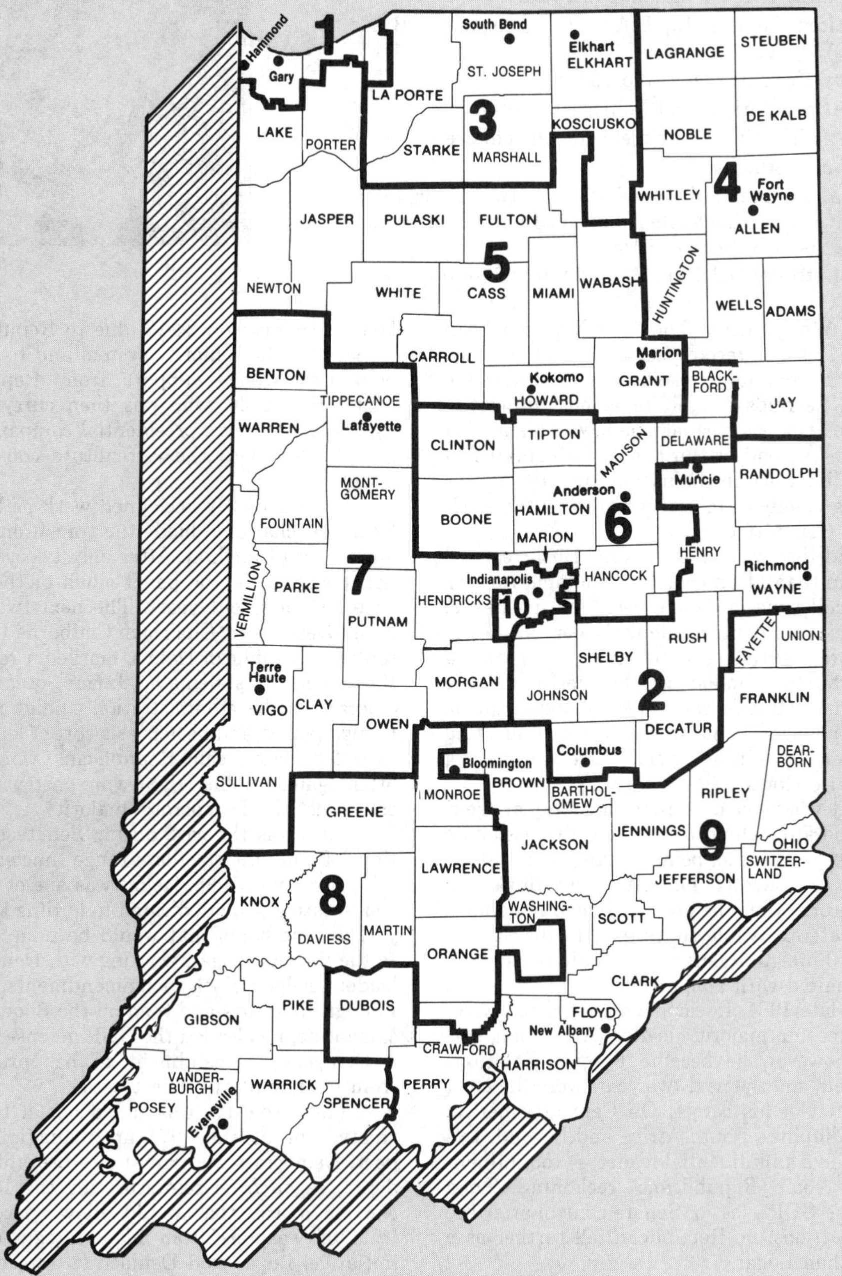
1
Hammond
Gary
LAKE
PORTER
LA PORTE
South Bend
ST. JOSEPH
Elkhart
ELKHART
LAGRANGE
STEUBEN
3
STARKE
MARSHALL
KOSCIUSKO
NOBLE
DE KALB
4
WHITLEY
Fort Wayne
ALLEN
JASPER
PULASKI
FULTON
5
NEWTON
WHITE
CASS
MIAMI
WABASH
HUNTINGTON
WELLS
ADAMS
BENTON
CARROLL
Marion
GRANT
BLACK-FORD
JAY
Kokomo
HOWARD
TIPPECANOE
Lafayette
WARREN
CLINTON
TIPTON
MADISON
DELAWARE
Muncie
RANDOLPH
MONT-GOMERY
Anderson
FOUNTAIN
BOONE
HAMILTON
6
MARION
HENRY
7
VERMILLION
PARKE
Indianapolis
HANCOCK
Richmond
WAYNE
HENDRICKS
10
PUTNAM
RUSH
FAYETTE
UNION
Terre Haute
SHELBY
2
VIGO
CLAY
MORGAN
JOHNSON
FRANKLIN
OWEN
DECATUR
Columbus
Bloomington
DEAR-BORN
SULLIVAN
MONROE
BROWN
BARTHOL-OMEW
RIPLEY
GREENE
JENNINGS
9
JACKSON
OHIO
LAWRENCE
SWITZER-LAND
JEFFERSON
KNOX
8
WASHING-TON
SCOTT
DAVIESS
MARTIN
ORANGE
CLARK
GIBSON
PIKE
DUBOIS
FLOYD
New Albany
CRAWFORD
HARRISON
VANDER-BURGH
WARRICK
PERRY
POSEY
Evansville
SPENCER

Richard G. Lugar (R)

Of Indianapolis — Elected 1976

Born: April, 4, 1932, Indianapolis, Ind.
Education: Denison U., B.A. 1954; Oxford U., B.A., M.A. 1956.
Military Career: Navy, 1957-60.
Occupation: Agricultural industries executive.
Family: Wife, Charlene Smeltzer; four children.
Religion: Methodist.
Political Career: Indianapolis School Board, 1964-67; mayor of Indianapolis, 1968-75; Republican nominee for U.S. Senate, 1974.
Capitol Office: 306 Hart Bldg. 20510; 224-4814.

In Washington: The fates have not been kind to Lugar in recent years. Through no fault of his own, and quite in spite of his considerable talents, he finds himself in a most unworthy position. Once a virtual shadow secretary of state, the second or third most influential foreign policy voice in the nation, by 1987 he was laboring chiefly as minority leader on the Agriculture Committee.

And that was before George Bush reached over him to tap Dan Quayle of Indiana, Lugar's junior colleague in Senate years and influence, to be vice president. Suddenly Lugar, one of the most presidential senators in either party, a man who first announced his desire for the presidency while he was mayor of Indianapolis, had a younger home-state rival complicating whatever hopes he still held of one day seeking the White House.

Yet whatever disappointment Lugar feels, he harbors it behind a reserved, dispassionate bearing. Meanwhile, being nothing if not dutiful, he has devoted himself to his duties on Agriculture, where he previously had not shown much interest, while continuing to play a role on the Foreign Relations Committee that he once chaired with aplomb.

In late 1984, Lugar placed third in a five-man race for majority leader. After that setback, however, he became Foreign Relations chairman, and the next two years were the most celebrated of his career. On Central America, the Philippines, South Africa and beyond, Lugar became an influential leader — too influential by some Republicans' reckoning. Then came the GOP's loss of Senate control after the 1986 elections; no Republican fell further as a result than Lugar.

He not only lost his chairmanship, but also the top Republican seat. The more senior Jesse Helms, who previously had opted to chair Agriculture, reasserted his right to lead Republicans on Foreign Relations. That sparked a bruising ideological battle between the pragmatic conservative Lugar and doctrinaire conservative Helms. Helms won 24-17, due to Republicans' respect for the seniority system and to Helms' behind-the-scenes support from Republican leader Bob Dole, who was then currying the right's favor for his presidential campaign. Lugar was left with the Agriculture consolation prize.

Lugar's widely acclaimed work as Foreign Relations chairman made the transition all the more painful for him. After only two years, he had regained for the panel much of the influence lost in recent years. The next two years, under Democratic Chairman Claiborne Pell and ranking Republican Helms, marked a return to the days of stalemate. Lugar occasionally emerges as the administration's point man on foreign policy, and he acts as a sort of leader-in-exile for mainstream Republicans, working as often against Helms' right-wing obstructionism as against the Democratic majority.

That was the case during Senate ratification of the intermediate-range nuclear-force (INF) treaty in 1988. Helms was one of a small conservative band dedicated to larding the pact with amendments that would be unacceptable to the Soviets. Lugar, working with Democratic leaders, helped block such amendments, first in Foreign Relations and then on the floor. At the same time, he also led the GOP defense against a Democratic amendment to bar presidents from later reinterpreting treaties.

That provision was aimed not at the INF treaty, but at the 1972 anti-ballistic missile pact; Democrats were aiming to prevent President Reagan from reinterpreting the 1972 accord in a way that would allow space-based tests of weapons from his strategic defense initiative. Lugar said Democrats were engaged in "a deliberate attempt to embarrass the president." Finally, however, he helped negotiate a compromise amendment, recognizing that Democrats would delay the treaty's ratification unless the issue was resolved.

The reputation for forceful, effective stewardship that Lugar had earned as chairman of

Foreign Relations is ironic considering that, in the 1984 GOP leadership race, the one private misgiving senators had was that he was too nice and accommodating to be a strong leader. Even those colleagues who agreed with Lugar that "to ask people to follow in lock step is not going to work," questioned whether he would exercise the kind of discipline many craved after the parliamentary chaos under the easygoing regime of Majority Leader Howard H. Baker Jr., Lugar's mentor. Lugar trailed two more aggressive rivals, Ted Stevens and the eventual winner, Dole.

But once installed as chairman of Foreign Relations, Lugar showed clear leadership, establishing consensus on a deeply divided panel and brokering between Reagan and a Congress often hostile to the president. He reined in the autonomous subcommittees, taking from one the responsibility for the divisive topic of arms control. Though one of Congress' most conservative members, he showed a knack for building coalitions and a willingness to listen to opposing points of view.

The consensus policy quickly bore fruit; in 1985 Congress approved a two-year foreign aid bill, the first since 1981. Lugar worked out a compromise on funding with committee Democrats, and steered the bill through the Senate with ease after persuading members not to offer controversial amendments. In contrast, after Lugar's departure from the chair in the 100th Congress, House-passed foreign aid bills died in the Senate in both 1987 and 1988.

In 1986, the genocide treaty that had languished for years finally was approved after Lugar resolved conservatives' objections. With delicate negotiations and a bit of hardball, he steered through the Senate a controversial extradition agreement with Great Britain. The treaty, which eased the British government's ability to capture Irish Republican Army terrorists who had fled to the United States, faced opposition from liberal and conservative senators. At one point, Lugar held up action on a House bill for aid to Northern Ireland until he got a deal.

But Lugar's most difficult and controversial accomplishments were in mediating between Senate majorities and Reagan. He several times helped save the president from embarrassing defeats. In 1985, for example, he persuaded Reagan to withdraw a proposal to sell arms to Jordan, thereby avoiding certain rejection. The next year, Lugar was instrumental both in winning Senate approval by a one-vote margin for Reagan's proposed missile sale to Saudi Arabia, and in guiding his request for $100 million in contra aid through Congress.

Though his overall record consistently ranked him as one of Reagan's most loyal supporters, Lugar became best known for his rare and personally painful splits with the administration. Some Republicans' resentment about those episodes, and their jealousy about the media attention Lugar drew as a result, were secondary factors in his ultimate defeat by Helms for the Foreign Relations seat.

Early in 1986, Reagan asked Lugar to head a U.S. delegation monitoring the Philippines presidential election between Ferdinand E. Marcos and challenger Corazon Aquino. Lugar quickly concluded that Marcos was stealing the election. Privately he implored Reagan to denounce Marcos, but Reagan argued instead that there had been fraud on both sides.

Lugar persisted. Eventually the administration pressured Marcos to leave office peacefully, in what came to be regarded as one of Reagan's chief foreign policy achievements. But in 1989, Aquino gave the credit to Lugar. "Without him," she said, "there would be no Philippine-U.S. relations to speak of by now."

Lugar's relations with Reagan over the issue of sanctions against South Africa followed a similar pattern, but ended radically different. Throughout 1985, Lugar pressed the administration to accommodate the overwhelming sentiment in Congress against South Africa's racist policies by imposing economic penalties. Finally, with Congress on the verge of clearing its own bill, Reagan responded with mild penalties and thus blunted the measure's momentum. Then Lugar and Dole took the unusual — and, for Lugar, highly uncharacteristic — step of preventing action on the bill by locking it in the Foreign Relations safe.

But as South Africa's repression increased, the drive for sanctions resumed with greater force the next year. Once again Lugar pleaded with Reagan to respond positively, but Reagan was adamant against further steps. Faced with losing control of the issue to Democrats, Lugar pushed his own sanctions bill. He crafted a compromise with broad support in Foreign Relations, and held off stringent Democratic amendments on the floor. Then he got House leaders to accept the Senate bill unchanged to avoid a conservative filibuster against the conference report.

Reagan's veto set the stage for Lugar's confrontation with the president he had served so faithfully. Meanwhile, his long-running fights with Helms exploded into open antipathy. Helms arranged for the South African foreign minister to lobby two farm-state senators, to warn of retaliation against U.S. farm products if sanctions were enacted. Outraged, Lugar denounced the attempts as "despicable," and condemned Helms' move as "an affront to the decency of the American people."

In the end, Lugar won easily, dealing Reagan one of the most serious congressional defeats of his presidency. The victory was deeply distressing for Lugar, who seemed to blame himself: Reagan "didn't take my advice the first, second, third or even fourth time," he said wearily. "I simply wish we had been more effective in persuading the president."

In 1988, no longer chairman, Lugar helped avert another showdown on the issue. He opposed Democrats' push for a near-total trade embargo, saying Congress "would be reckless" to remove all U.S. presence in South Africa before the next administration could take office. Without support from him and from other GOP centrists, a House-passed bill died in the Senate.

On Agriculture, Lugar has transferred his consensus-building skills to a different set of issues. His new leadership role there required some adjustment, not only because the committee's work has not been his top priority, but also because he has been one of the panel's few skeptics about farm subsidy programs.

Lugar's free-market philosophy often had made him Reagan's most reliable ally in seeking to reduce farm spending. In early 1981, he pressured the committee to make many of the cuts Reagan had proposed in his maiden budget. During action on the 1985 farm bill, he carried an administration proposal to cut farm income subsidies; it lost, 48-51, but made way for a modified version. His biggest test will come as the committee works on the 1990 farm bill.

In 1987, his first year as ranking member, Lugar blunted Democrats' effort to limit the administration's ability to reduce price support rates for various commodities. The 1985 farm law permitted the president to lower income subsidies up to 5 percent a year; Democrats wanted a 2 percent limit. In a conference with the House, he engineered an agreement limiting reductions for 1988 crop price supports to 3 percent while raising the cap to 7 percent for 1989.

Lugar often worked closely in the 100th Congress with liberal Democratic Chairman Patrick J. Leahy. Together they shepherded a major drought aid bill through the Senate, fending off attempts to broaden its provisions. They cosponsored a pesticide regulation bill that had some environmentalists' support though not that of manufacturers and farm groups; a stripped-down compromise became law, breaking years of deadlock.

The two men could not agree in 1987 on a bill to overhaul the troubled Farm Credit System, and Lugar finally proposed his own with other Agriculture Republicans. Near the end of committee action on a compromise, he scoffed at some members' complaints that it would benefit lenders more than farmers. Referring to farmers, he said, "There is no group in society that has been so benefited by any act of Congress."

Lugar's activity with Agriculture recalls the concentration on domestic issues that marked his first term. For all his commitment to conservative free-market principles, his most notable accomplishments during that period were in espousing emergency federal help for two ailing institutions.

In 1979, he played a key role in bailing out the Chrysler Corporation, which employed thousands of his constituents. Lugar also was responsible for a provision of the bailout bill requiring Chrysler's unions to make a pay concession. His support for aid to New York City in 1978 had no such political benefits at home, but it reflected his experience as mayor of Indianapolis. Lugar worked on a compromise aid bill because, he said, he "understood the problems of New York City finance."

At Home: If Lugar has been denied some of the distinction many feel he deserves in the Senate, his status at home is unassailable.

He overcame a popular House Democrat in winning re-election in 1982. Six years later, with Hoosier Democrats on the march (they captured the governorship and gained parity in the Legislature), Lugar essentially drew a pass.

The only Democrat who filed to oppose him was Jack Wickes, an Indianapolis lawyer who had never run for office. Personable and energetic as Wickes was, his principal credential was that he had run Gary Hart's successful presidential primary campaign in Indiana in 1984. Wickes never raised nearly enough money to make a serious race against Lugar. He was not even able to run television advertisements. Lugar got more votes (1.43 million) and a wider victory margin (761,747 votes) than any previous candidate in Indiana history. His vote share (68 percent) easily eclipsed the previous record for a Senate race in the state.

Lugar's success is doubly remarkable given his modest gifts as a campaigner. He meets crowds woodenly and his style borders on lecturing. But he has always managed to impress the Indiana electorate as a man of substance.

Even in 1974, running for the Senate in a Watergate-dominated year with a reputation as "Richard Nixon's favorite mayor," he came within a respectable 75,000 votes against Democrat Birch Bayh. Two years later, against a much weaker Democrat, Sen. Vance Hartke, he won handily. In his 1982 re-election bid, Lugar's personal popularity — and massive campaign treasury — put him out of reach of his Democratic challenger, Rep. Floyd Fithian.

If Lugar's record as mayor of Indianapolis was no help to him in 1974, it still stands as the basis of his political career. His conservative, efficiency-minded administration won him favorable notices all over Indiana, and he attracted national attention by defeating John V. Lindsay of New York City for vice president of the National League of Cities in 1970.

A Rhodes scholar, Lugar served in the Navy as a briefing officer at the Pentagon before returning home to run the family tool business. He won his first election in 1964, to the Indianapolis School Board.

Three years later, he saw an opportunity to

take over the mayor's office. The Democrats were divided, and with the help of powerful Marion County GOP Chairman Keith Bulen, he beat incumbent Democrat John Barton.

Lugar's foremost accomplishment as Indianapolis mayor was creation of Uni-Gov, the consolidation of the city and its suburbs, which he lobbied through the state Legislature.

Lugar's election over Lindsay was national news because he won it in an electorate of big-city mayors, most of whom were Democrats. He was a spokesman for Nixon administration policies, and from that time on the president began to take an interest in him.

He came to regret those ties in 1974, when he was saddled with the Nixon connection. In an attempt to deal with it, he declared that the Oval Office tape transcripts "revealed a moral tragedy" in the White House. But this alienated segments of the Republican right in Indiana and made his campaign against Bayh even more difficult.

Still, he came close enough to be the logical contender in 1976 against Hartke. Hartke had nearly been beaten six years earlier and was severely damaged by a primary challenger who charged him with foreign junketing and slavish loyalty to the communications industry. Lugar coasted to an easy win.

Working to ensure the same result in 1982, Lugar began preparing two years in advance. By the time the election drew near, he had organizations in every county. By contrast, Democrat Fithian got off to a slow start. After his old 2nd District was dismembered in redistricting, Fithian initially announced plans to run for Indiana secretary of state, then switched to the Senate contest — angering other Democrats already in the race and prompting some observers to brand him "Flip-Flop Floyd."

Seeking to make up lost ground, Fithian attacked Lugar's record on Social Security, charging that the incumbent voted 16 times to reduce minimum benefits. He tied Lugar to Reagan policies Fithian claimed were responsible for Indiana's economic woes. Lugar acknowledged the troubled economic climate — billing himself as a "good man for tough times" — but put the blame on previous Democratic administrations. Lugar did not go to great lengths to identify himself with the White House, however. He criticized the president for vetoing the supplemental appropriation that included his own emergency housing legislation.

Fithian did manage to shore up support in predominantly Democratic southern Indiana, taking 14 counties in this region. In most areas, though, Lugar was a comfortable winner, and he finished with 54 percent statewide.

Committees

Agriculture, Nutrition and Forestry (Ranking)

Foreign Relations (2nd of 9 Republicans)
Western Hemisphere and Peace Corps Affairs (ranking); East Asian and Pacific Affairs; International Economic Policy, Trade, Oceans and Environment

Elections

1988 General

Richard G. Lugar (R)	1,430,525	(68%)
Jack Wickes (D)	668,778	(32%)

Previous Winning Percentages: **1982** (54%) **1976** (59%)

Campaign Finance

	Receipts	Receipts from PACs	Expend-itures
1988			
Lugar (R)	$3,029,708	$775,836 (26%)	$3,022,597
Wickes (D)	$338,465	$119,150 (35%)	$314,233

Key Votes

1987

Enact omnibus highway bill over Reagan veto	N
Limit testing of space-based anti-ballistic missiles	N
Oppose banning tests of larger nuclear weapons	Y
Confirm Robert H. Bork as Supreme Court justice	Y

1988

Allow vote on campaign-finance overhaul	N
Pass civil rights restoration bill over Reagan veto	N
Enact omnibus trade bill over Reagan veto	N
Approve death penalty for drug-related murders	Y
Oppose "workfare" amendment to welfare overhaul bill	N

Voting Studies

	Presidential Support		Party Unity		Conservative Coalition	
Year	**S**	**O**	**S**	**O**	**S**	**O**
1988	86	13	76	19	86	14
1987	76	21	77	20	78	13
1986	88	11	89	10	88	9
1985	89	10	92	8	88	12
1984	92	8	94	6	87	13
1983	95	5	92	8	95	5
1982	83	15	85	14	84	16
1981	90	9	93	7	90	10

Interest Group Ratings

Year	ADA	ACU	AFL-CIO	CCUS
1988	10	88	21	92
1987	5	72	20	88
1986	10	78	0	89
1985	5	74	10	90
1984	10	82	18	79
1983	15	44	12	68
1982	15	63	28	70
1981	5	100	0	94

Daniel R. Coats (R)

Of Fort Wayne — Appointed 1988

Born: May 16, 1943, Jackson, Mich.
Education: Wheaton College, B.A. 1965; Indiana U., J.D. 1971.
Military Career: Army Corps of Engineers, 1966-68.
Occupation: Lawyer.
Family: Wife, Marcia Anne Crawford; three children.
Religion: Baptist.
Political Career: U.S. House, 1981-89.
Capitol Office: 411 Russell Bldg. 20510; 224-5623.

In Washington: It is not unusual for one politician to be carried some distance by the career successes of another, but few have come as far this way as Coats.

Starting as a staff aide to Dan Quayle when Quayle represented northeast Indiana in the House, Coats has moved up behind his boss. When Quayle went to the Senate in 1980, Coats ran for and won his House seat. And after Quayle was elected vice president in 1988, Indiana's retiring GOP Gov. Robert D. Orr appointed Coats to succeed Quayle in the Senate.

There is, of course, nothing wrong with being appointed to the Senate in place of one's political mentor. That was how Senate Majority Leader George J. Mitchell of Maine first arrived in 1980. The key is how one proceeds from there.

Like his former boss, Coats now confronts a political challenge that has broadened as much as his horizon. Just as Quayle must prove himself on a national and international stage, his protégé must make himself at home in the Senate and compete statewide in less than two years.

Coats' appointment only lasts through the 101st Congress; it must be ratified by the voters in November 1990. If he wins then, he must defend the seat in its regular re-election cycle in 1992 (Quayle was re-elected in 1986). So Coats will be acquainting himself not only with unfamiliar committee territory (his assignments are Quayle's old ones, including Armed Services) but with unfamiliar voters, as well.

That may require a kind of energy and focus beyond what Coats has had to muster thus far. On the other hand, Coats has been one of the class of 1980 who not only survived electorally but established a kind of détente with the government he opposed in getting elected. Many of his classmates who had ridden Ronald Reagan's 1980 coattails came a cropper in the recession of 1982; Coats actually ran stronger that year than in either of Reagan's landslides.

He did it, in part, by watching out for the district's economic interests. In 1982 he voted less frequently with the conservative coalition of Republicans and Southern Democrats than he had the year before. His ratings by ideological interest groups also moderated that year.

On issues, Coats has become well-known primarily as a serious social conservative given to pondering the implications of his Christian-based, "pro-family" politics. He argues for the need to move beyond such issues as school prayer and abortion to a concern for the material welfare of children and the poor. But his role is limited by his reluctance to depart from the conservative orthodoxy and suspicion of government he brought with him to Congress.

In the House, Coats spent much of his time at the Select Committee on Children, Youth and Families, where he was ranking Republican. He defended programs for underprivileged families that some conservatives assail as too expensive. In 1985, Coats argued for eight controversial education and health programs for the poor. "These strands of the social safety net — from the Head Start program to prenatal care to education for the handicapped — are working as intended," Coats said.

In 1988, worrying that government decisions had "aggravated trends" by which families across the economic spectrum were "losing ground," Coats backed a spending plan on education, nutrition and health that he called "a coming together of conservatives who want to be cost-conscious and liberals who want to be compassionate."

During the 1988 presidential campaign, he and California GOP Rep. Jerry Lewis proposed a $1.9 billion "American Family Act," which included tax credits for low-income families with children younger than 6.

Easing the family's tax burden has been a longstanding interest for Coats. In 1985, he began talking about a "Tax Fairness to Families" bill, which would raise the personal exemption from $1,040 to $2,000. The tax-revision bill that became law in 1986 does exactly that, increasing the exemption on a gradual basis. Coats was not a major player in the tax debate, but his early efforts helped frame the issue.

But when new programs involving direct governmental service are proposed, he tends to be against them. He characterizes himself as reluctant to support federal involvement in child-care services, for example.

Coats had a prize committee assignment at Energy and Commerce. Over his years there, he allied with moderates and liberals seeking to protect consumers from price increases during natural-gas deregulation, and with conservatives in behalf of cuts in the Amtrak rail system.

During his early years in the House, Coats was identified most with the issue of school prayer. In 1984, he attempted to attach an amendment to an omnibus education bill that would have cut off federal aid to schools and states banning voluntary school prayer. Coats' amendment was defeated on the floor.

At Home: When Orr named Coats to replace Quayle in the Senate a month after the 1988 presidential election, he was formalizing what many Indiana observers had considered a fait accompli. Coats was presumed to be Quayle's choice, just as he had been when Quayle left the House eight years earlier.

As Quayle's district representative from 1978 through 1980, Coats cultivated the role of surrogate congressman. He handled constituents' problems personally, and sometimes stepped in for Quayle to give a "government is too big" speech. When Quayle ran for the Senate in 1980, Coats had a spot on the ballot just below him and shared the highly effective organization both had helped build. Coats actually ran ahead of Quayle that November in the 4th.

By tradition, appointed senators have not fared well in defending their windfall before the voters. And the timing of Coats' ascent might have been better. Among the more reliably GOP states in recent years, Indiana has shown signs of restiveness of late. In 1988 it elected its first Democratic governor in two decades and gave Democrats a share of control in the Legislature.

More disturbing yet, when Coats vacated his and Quayle's old House seat in the 4th District, their chosen successor failed to hold it in a special election. The new occupant, Jill Long, had been beaten by Coats in 1988 and by Quayle two years earlier. Her upset win gave Democrats seven of the state's 10 House seats.

Coats, however, should be stronger than most. He has a base in his old district and he can expect to run with no serious opposition for the GOP nomination. He will also enjoy the obvious backing of the vice president; and the president, too, can be expected to take a special interest in holding this seat.

When he first ran for Congress in 1980, Coats was still a relative newcomer to the district. He had to get past a bitter GOP primary against two candidates with much stronger local roots. But he easily surmounted that problem, winning the primary by carrying every county. In November, Coats smashed Democrat John D. Walda in Walda's second try. Four re-election campaigns produced no surprises.

Committees

Armed Services (9th of 9 Republicans)
Conventional Forces and Alliance Defense; Defense Industry and Technology; Readiness, Sustainability and Support

Labor and Human Resources (4th of 7 Republicans)
Children, Family, Drugs and Alcoholism (ranking); Aging

Elections

1988 General *		
Daniel R. Coats (R)	132,843	(62%)
Jill Long (D)	80,915	(38%)

Previous Winning Percentages: **1986 *** (70%) **1984 *** (61%) **1982 *** (64%) **1980 *** (61%)

* *House elections.*

Campaign Finance

	Receipts	Receipts from PACs	Expend-itures
1988			
Coats (R)	$351,827	$190,152 (54%)	$266,016
Long (D)	$115,103	$42,690 (37%)	$114,454

Key Votes

House Service

1987	
Raise speed limit to 65 mph	Y
Approve Gephardt "fair trade" amendment	N
Ban testing of larger nuclear weapons	N
Delay "re-flagging" of Kuwaiti tankers	N
Approve tax-raising deficit-reduction bill	N
1988	
Approve aid to Nicaraguan contras	Y
Enact civil rights restoration bill over Reagan veto	N
Kill 60-day plant-closing notification measure	N
Pass omnibus trade bill over Reagan veto	N
Approve death penalty for drug-related murders	Y
Bar federal funds for abortions in cases of rape and incest	Y
Oppose seven-day waiting period for purchase of handguns	Y

Voting Studies

	Presidential Support		Party Unity		Conservative Coalition	
Year	**S**	**O**	**S**	**O**	**S**	**O**
House Service						
1988	59	38	77	20	84	11
1987	64	36	83	16	86	12
1986	70	29	84	15	84	16
1985	74	26	81	17	80	20
1984	67	30	92	8	90	10
1983	78	21	88 †	12 †	84	16
1982	71	29	84	13	82	18
1981	74	26	86	14	91	9

† Not eligible for all recorded votes.

Interest Group Ratings

Year	ADA	ACU	AFL-CIO	CCUS
House Service				
1988	10	92	29	93
1987	8	91	0	100
1986	10	82	14	94
1985	20	86	18	86
1984	5	92	0	69
1983	10	87	6	85
1982	30	73	15	73
1981	10	93	20	100

1 Peter J. Visclosky (D)

Of Merrillville — Elected 1984

Born: Aug. 13, 1949, Gary, Ind.
Education: Indiana U., B.S. 1970; Notre Dame U., J.D. 1973; Georgetown U., LL.M. 1982.
Occupation: Lawyer.
Family: Wife, Ann Marie O'Keefe; one child.
Religion: Roman Catholic.
Political Career: No previous office.
Capitol Office: 420 Cannon Bldg. 20515; 225-2461.

In Washington: Visclosky came to Congress with a bold ambition: to accede to the influential role that his predecessor and mentor Adam Benjamin held on the Appropriations Committee, that of numbers specialist.

Now in his third term, Visclosky is still waiting for a spot on Appropriations. But he is waiting patiently, taking care to avoid brash comments or a headline-grabbing style that would be inconsistent with that committee's method of doing business. Carefully honing a reputation as a thoughtful and loyal Democrat, he has been rewarded with two terms as an at-large whip. He remains optimistic that a seat on the money committee will eventually come.

In the meantime, Visclosky tends to the home front. His floor statements honoring veterans, Lithuanians and the Rev. Dr. Martin Luther King Jr. reflect the roots and concerns of his solidly Democratic, but diverse district. Steel is the common ground for many Visclosky constituents, and he serves the industry and its workers from his committee posts on Education and Labor as well as Public Works.

Indiana's 1st produces more steel than any other district, and it has suffered devastating economic losses in the last two decades. Visclosky rarely misses an opportunity to speak out for American steel. When the omnibus highway bill was debated on the floor, Visclosky reminded his colleagues how important highway projects are for the steel industry.

A member of the executive committee of the Congressional Steel Caucus, Visclosky advocated provisions in the 1988 trade bill to increase the U.S. trade representative's enforcement authority. The new law clarifies that foreign countries' voluntary steel import restrictions cannot be circumvented by processing the steel in a third country. At the start of the 101st Congress, Visclosky held a hearing in Gary to discuss legislation to extend the Voluntary Restraint Agreements on steel imports, which are due to expire in late 1989.

Visclosky also serves on the Interior Committee, where, in the 99th Congress, he successfully promoted legislation enlarging the Indiana Dunes National Lakeshore, a longtime *cause célèbre* for Midwest environmentalists and one of the few tourist attractions in northwest Indiana.

At Home: After finishing law school in 1973, Visclosky linked his fortunes to Benjamin, then a state senator and rising star. Visclosky coordinated Benjamin's successful campaign for Congress in 1976 and worked with him in Washington for the next six years.

When Benjamin died in September 1982, Gary's longtime black mayor, Richard G. Hatcher, was the 1st District Democratic chairman, and thus had the legal right to choose the Democratic nominee. He picked Katie Hall, a black state senator and loyal ally. She survived the general election and sought renomination in 1984. Visclosky and Jack Crawford, the Lake County prosecutor, challenged her, and at first, Crawford seemed the more formidable of the two white candidates.

In the end, though, Visclosky had greater appeal. To contrast his modestly funded bid with Crawford's high-budget operation, Visclosky put on dozens of "dog-and-bean" fund-raisers — $2 dinners aimed at attracting the young, the elderly and the unemployed. His Eastern European background also helped him (he called himself "the Slovak Kid"), and older voters responded favorably because they remembered his father, John, who had served as Gary's comptroller and mayor.

Visclosky won over late-deciding white voters whose first priority was defeating Hall. She finished second, Crawford a close third. Visclosky swamped Republican Joseph B. Grenchik, the mayor of Whiting, in November.

In 1986, Hall tried a comeback. She retained her support in the black community, where Visclosky had alienated some voters by failing to close his congressional office on the Martin Luther King Jr. holiday in 1985.

But with Hall as his only serious foe in this white-majority district, Visclosky's renomination was all but assured. She drew about one-third of the vote, the same as in 1984, and Visclosky got 57 percent. He faced only minor opposition in the primary and general elections in 1988.

Indiana 1

Industrial Belt — Gary; Hammond

The 1st stretches from the Illinois line at Hammond through Gary all the way to Michigan City, 40 miles to the east, covering almost the entire Indiana shoreline along Lake Michigan. It extends inland only slightly beyond the congested, polluted lakefront industrial area.

Crossing through the heart of the 1st on the Indiana Toll Road, one sees the maze of refineries and steel plants that form the district's economic base. A generation ago, Gary was dominated by Eastern European ethnic factory workers; today it is 70 percent black. Indiana's third-largest city with a population of about 137,000, it remains heavily unionized and was the political base for former Mayor Richard G. Hatcher, whose two decades of service made him one of the nation's most durable black officeholders. He was defeated for renomination in 1987.

Gary, nearby industrial Hammond and the surrounding northern half of Lake County provide the bulk of Democratic strength in the 1st. More than four-fifths of the vote is cast in the district's Lake County portion.

The remaining fifth of the voters live in LaPorte and Porter counties. This side of the district is neither as Democratic nor as industrial as Lake County. There are pockets of Democratic strength, however, in northern Porter County and in Michigan City, located in agricultural LaPorte County. Michigan City, once a larger lake port than Chicago, is now a depressed industrial town. Porter County contains the state's only active shipping port, at Burns Harbor, and there are several steel mills and a large state prison in the area. The suburban tracts of Porter County are populated by many Eastern European ethnic steelworkers and oil refinery workers who moved out of the depressed inner-city areas of Gary and Hammond.

Population: 547,100. White 390,290 (71%), Black 132,650 (24%), Other 2,945 (1%). Spanish origin 44,985 (8%). 18 and over 375,863 (69%), 65 and over 47,696 (9%). Median age: 28.

Committees

Education and Labor (20th of 22 Democrats)
Labor-Management Relations

Interior and Insular Affairs (16th of 26 Democrats)
National Parks and Public Lands

Public Works and Transportation (16th of 31 Democrats)
Aviation; Investigations and Oversight; Surface Transportation

Elections

1988 General		
Peter J. Visclosky (D)	138,251	(77%)
Owen W. Crumpacker (R)	41,076	(23%)
1988 Primary		
Peter J. Visclosky (D)	75,785	(84%)
Sandra Kay Smith (D)	14,527	(16%)
1986 General		
Peter J. Visclosky (D)	86,983	(73%)
William Costas (R)	30,395	(26%)

Previous Winning Percentage: 1984 (71%)

District Vote For President

	1988	1984	1980	1976
D	112,133 (59%)	125,803 (56%)	106,716 (50%)	127,309 (57%)
R	78,440 (41%)	95,657 (43%)	95,848 (45%)	94,741 (42%)
I			8,712 (4%)	

Campaign Finance

	Receipts	Receipts from PACs	Expend-itures
1988			
Visclosky (D)	$222,620	$157,250 (71%)	$141,855
1986			
Visclosky (D)	$158,528	$97,067 (61%)	$163,283
Costas (R)	$63,575	$19 (0%)	$63,460

Key Votes

1987	
Raise speed limit to 65 mph	N
Approve Gephardt "fair trade" amendment	Y
Ban testing of larger nuclear weapons	Y
Delay "re-flagging" of Kuwaiti tankers	Y
Approve tax-raising deficit-reduction bill	Y
1988	
Approve aid to Nicaraguan contras	N
Enact civil rights restoration bill over Reagan veto	Y
Kill 60-day plant-closing notification measure	N
Pass omnibus trade bill over Reagan veto	Y
Approve death penalty for drug-related murders	N
Bar federal funds for abortions in cases of rape and incest	Y
Oppose seven-day waiting period for purchase of handguns	N

Voting Studies

	Presidential Support		Party Unity		Conservative Coalition	
Year	S	O	S	O	S	O
1988	22	78	91	9	18	82
1987	19	81	94	6	28	72
1986	19	81	93	7	20	80
1985	30	70	90	9	33	67

Interest Group Ratings

Year	ADA	ACU	AFL-CIO	CCUS
1988	100	0	100	36
1987	92	0	94	13
1986	90	0	93	33
1985	80	5	71	36

2 Philip R. Sharp (D)

Of Muncie — Elected 1974

Born: July 15, 1942, Baltimore, Md.

Education: Georgetown U., B.S. 1964; graduate work, Oxford U., 1966; Georgetown U., Ph.D. 1974.

Occupation: Political science professor.

Family: Wife, Marilyn Augburn; two children.

Religion: Methodist.

Political Career: Democratic nominee for U.S. House, 1970 and 1972.

Capitol Office: 2217 Rayburn Bldg. 20515; 225-3021.

In Washington: Sharp is a survivor. Elected from a Republican district in the Democratic Party's Watergate-year sweep, he is one of the few House members who always has to fight hard to stay in office. Seven times he has won re-election, but at a cost he probably never could have imagined when he arrived in Congress as an idealistic young professor: upwards of $1 million raised from lobby groups, and unknown numbers of cautious and compromised votes.

In the large Democratic class of 1974, Sharp stood out among its activists: hard-working, sober and intellectually curious. By his second term he was tapped for a role in shepherding President Jimmy Carter's energy package into law, and he developed a reputation for expertise in that field that he holds to this day. Now he has the title, too: chairman of the Energy and Power Subcommittee.

In recent years, however, Sharp has had a more peripheral role in overall House affairs. One explanation is that his issue, energy, is no longer at the top of the congressional agenda. Also, he was distracted by a family illness in the 100th Congress. He is by nature cautious and slow to step out front, and his insecure electoral standing serves to amplify that trait, making him worry about offending voters or financial contributors, or both. "It does shape your attitude on the House floor," he once said, describing the care with which he approaches each vote.

Sharp's overall record is moderate to liberal, despite some concessions to his more conservative constituency, such as his votes against gun control. As a subcommittee chairman, Sharp is judicious, committed to finding consensus but reluctant to pressure wavering Democrats. Reflecting his academic bent, he conducts hearings like seminars and explores all sides of an issue. A personable and approachable man, he is liked and admired by colleagues of both parties. Yet some Democrats are restive; there are complaints that he lacks aggressiveness and that his subcommittee is all but dormant.

The subcommittee provides a wide legislative field within the Energy and Commerce Committee; in the 100th Congress, it was formed by consolidating the old Fossil Fuels panel, which Sharp had chaired since 1981, and another subcommittee responsible for nuclear power and conservation. Sharp's influence over such issues is enhanced by the fact that he also is a senior member of the Interior Committee's Energy Subcommittee.

On Interior, Sharp generally takes an environmentalist view, but his record and style are conciliatory enough that he sometimes serves as a bridge between liberal Chairman Morris K. Udall of Arizona and more conservative Democrats.

His pragmatic drive for solutions was evident in the 100th Congress' effort to overhaul the 1957 Price-Anderson Act, which limited utilities' liability for nuclear-reactor accidents. With Udall, Sharp cosponsored a bill to raise utilities' joint liability tenfold, to $7 billion — still far below estimates of what a major accident would cost.

The original bill also would have barred the compensation fund from being used to pay utility and insurance company lawyers. But when that prohibition threatened to sink the legislation — due to the companies' fierce opposition — Sharp was ready to jettison it, while more junior Democrats pressed the fight. After Interior approved partial recovery of legal fees, Sharp's subcommittee at Energy and Commerce upped it to 100 percent.

Amid intense lobbying, the full Energy and Commerce Committee reversed Sharp's panel, voting that all funds be reserved for victims. Then, it reversed itself — with Sharp's support. He argued that providing for legal fees would encourage industry to defend itself vigorously, thus discouraging frivolous claims. Also, he said he did not want to jeopardize his entire bill.

He helped Udall manage the bill on the House floor, calling it "a bargain" providing greater certainty of victims' compensation. Foes disagreed. One called the bill "a K-Mart blue-light special for the nuclear power industry."

Indiana 2

East Central — Muncie; Richmond

Shaped like the letter "J," this district runs through a collection of areas with little in common — Indianapolis suburbs, lightly populated farm lands and three widely dispersed industrial cities.

Two-thirds of the vote is cast in the vicinities of Indianapolis, Muncie, Richmond and Columbus. Voters in those cities read different newspapers and watch different television stations. The only economic thread common to the cities is a dependence on the automobile industry.

Muncie, the model for "Middletown," the sociological study of small-town American life in the 1920s, is the largest city in the district, with a population of about 73,000. It was settled largely by Southerners and tends to be more Democratic than the other cities in the district.

In addition to auto-parts factories, the Ball Corporation (of canning jar fame) is a major employer, although the jars are now made elsewhere. Muncie and surrounding Delaware County strongly support Democrat Sharp; even in close House contests it has not been unusual for him to approach the 70 percent level in Delaware County. In 1988, when Sharp was held to 53 percent districtwide, he still won the county by 2-to-1.

Wayne County (Richmond) and Bartholomew County (Columbus) both went for George Bush in 1988, but Wayne County voted Democratic for governor and for the House, while Bartholomew went Republican in those elections. The city of Columbus is the home of the Cummins Engine Company, manufacturers of diesel engines.

The portions of metropolitan Indianapolis (Marion County) in the 2nd are primarily conservative, middle-income suburban areas. The suburban part of the 2nd also extends south of Indianapolis into Johnson County, which is almost as conservative. Those counties were added to the 2nd in 1981 redistricting in order to give Sharp trouble, and they have. In 1988, Republican House nominee Mike Pence won handily in Marion County and also carried Johnson County. Two years earlier, Marion was the only county in the 2nd that was carried by the GOP nominee.

The corn and hog farmers of the district usually prefer Republicans; all the smaller counties in the 2nd went Republican in the 1988 presidential and Senate races, but they voted for Sharp and successful Democratic gubernatorial candidate Evan Bayh by smaller margins.

Population: 553,510. White 535,065 (97%), Black 14,576 (3%). Spanish origin 3,225 (1%). 18 and over 390,981 (71%), 65 and over 58,462 (11%). Median age: 30.

Backed by environmental, consumer and taxpayer groups, opponents tried in vain to increase utilities' liability and to strike the legal-fees language. In the end, the bill passed the House overwhelmingly; the Senate approved its version the next year, and a compromise was signed into law.

On a non-energy issue in 1988, legislation for a federal product-liability law, Sharp was one of the few Energy and Commerce Democrats to support a GOP amendment limiting manufacturers' liability in cases where consumers alter or misuse a product. He also voted for the bill, to the dismay of consumer groups and trial lawyers. But the measure went no further.

Following Udall's lead, Sharp worked to revive the search for a high-level nuclear-waste disposal site, finally compromising in 1987 on a Senate plan that ensured Nevada's selection. In 1988, he helped block a deal between the administration and several Republican senators to bail out the uranium industry.

Sharp has not been as active in efforts to strengthen the Clean Air Act and attack acid rain as his senior position would suggest, although he was a member of the moderate-to-conservative "group of nine" that sought a solution at Energy and Commerce. The home-state pressures Sharp faces on the clean air issue are great: The auto industry is important in Indiana, the state ranks high in emissions of sulfur dioxide (an ingredient in acid rain), and state utilities rely on high-sulfur coal.

Generally, Sharp has supported relaxing auto-emission standards, though not by as much as industry would like. In the 1982 debate on renewal of the Clean Air Act, Energy and Commerce approved his compromise amendment splitting the difference between an industry proposal and the emission levels in existing law. The revision died in committee.

In the 100th Congress, Sharp guided into law two conservation bills that reflected both his and Congress' more modest aims, in contrast to the expansive energy and environmental initiatives Sharp pushed in the 1970s.

A bill to set energy efficiency standards for large appliances, which President Reagan had vetoed the Congress before, was enacted after a minor change.

The second measure established pilot projects and other inducements for automakers, service stations, federal agencies and consumers to move toward vehicles that burn gasoline alternatives, methanol and ethanol. Sharp said he wanted to see if incentives rather than federal mandates would work. He called the legislation "the single most important step we can take" to reduce oil imports and air pollution.

During his years as Fossil Fuels chairman, Sharp was at the center of debate over natural gas prices. When prices shot up in late 1982, House members began feeling constituent pressure for relief. In the 98th Congress, liberal Democrats and some Midwestern Republicans started agitating for tighter controls. President Reagan proposed eliminating all existing controls over a three-year period, arguing that this would lead to an increased supply and lower prices.

Maneuvering between pro-producer and pro-consumer factions on his subcommittee, Sharp steered through a bill that forced producers to lower their prices in some contracts in exchange for eased regulations. Neither side was happy; the producer side derisively called it "re-regulation" and Democrats split along regional lines. The bill cleared Energy and Commerce, but it died in the Rules Committee, which deadlocked 6-6 on whether to send it to the floor.

Still, Sharp could point to some success from the effort. He demonstrated his political skill simply by getting the bill through committee, given the lack of cooperation between consumer and producer groups and the opposition of Chairman John D. Dingell. And gas producers began exercising some voluntary price restraint. By 1989, after several years of low and stable gas prices, Sharp easily won House approval of legislation ending all price controls.

In the 97th Congress, over Reagan's objections, Sharp pushed through a measure giving the president standby authority to allocate oil in a time of severe shortage. But Reagan vetoed the bill, and the Republican-controlled Senate sustained the veto.

By the 99th Congress, the sparse energy agenda consisted largely of dismantling policies of Sharp's first years, as the 1970s energy crisis gave way to the economic crisis in the oil states.

The House in 1986 passed a bill drafted by Sharp's subcommittee repealing a 1978 law aimed at encouraging industries and utilities to burn coal instead of oil or gas. It died in the Senate, but Sharp revived the bill early in the 100th Congress, and both chambers quickly passed it. He also backed the drive to kill the Synthetic Fuels Corporation, established in 1980 to develop petroleum substitutes. Sharp had reassessed his past support in light of the budget deficit, declining oil prices and the corporation's management problems.

Sharp had not been in the House long before he conceded that his experiences had deeply affected his attitude toward government. "In many cases we've gone toward excessive regulation," he said in late 1979. "I have a greater appreciation for the market than I did when I first ran."

At times, his tilt toward business has led to conflict with the United Auto Workers (UAW), the strongest labor presence in Sharp's district. But he and the union were together in 1979 on bills to provide loan guarantees for the Chrysler Corporation, and to impose a "domestic content" requirement on imported cars. He has pleased both the UAW and auto manufacturers by his work to relax auto-emission standards.

At Home: When Sharp began his initial campaign for Congress in 1970, he was a 28-year-old political science professor with little campaign experience and limited contacts in the district. Doggedly determined, he out-organized most of his six rivals to win the Democratic nomination with 22 percent of the vote, edging former Rep. John R. Walsh by 424 votes. In November, with recession worrying people in the industrial cities of central Indiana, Sharp came within 2,500 votes against Republican David W. Dennis.

His second campaign was a disappointment. Sharp was better known and even better prepared in 1972, but President Richard M. Nixon won Indiana by 2-to-1, helping Dennis boost his share of the vote to 57 percent.

On his third try, Sharp had all the name recognition he needed, and it was the right year. Even in Indiana, Republicans were on the run in 1974, and Dennis hurt himself by defending Nixon during the House Judiciary Committee's impeachment investigation. Sharp won with 54 percent of the vote.

In the next three elections, Sharp faced the same opponent — farmer William G. Frazier. A gregarious campaigner with a devoted core of rural followers, Frazier was unable to broaden his base for general elections. Sharp helped himself by assuming a high personal profile and by tending to the needs of constituents regardless of their partisan affiliation.

In the 1981 redistricting, Indiana's Republican Legislature stripped Sharp of over half his old constituency, placing him in a redrawn district with clear Republican leanings. The GOP thought it had a good candidate in Ralph Van Natta, a former Shelbyville mayor who had gained further visibility as head of the state Bureau of Motor Vehicles under popular GOP Gov. Otis R. Bowen. But Van Natta did not live up to expectations.

Economic troubles were causing many to fear for their jobs, and Van Natta was encumbered by publicity about investigations of the state's patronage-controlled motor vehicle bureaus, which he oversaw in Bowen's administration. Sharp outspent Van Natta by nearly

$100,000, carried his Democratic base of Muncie by 2-to-1, and won easily.

Kenneth MacKenzie, the 1984 GOP nominee, was different from Frazier and Van Natta. He was able to compete with Sharp in debating ability and fund raising. A former congressional aide on leave from his job as public affairs director for Muncie's Ball Corp., MacKenzie stressed his support for Reagan's efforts to give free enterprise a larger role in the economy.

Sharp accused MacKenzie of placing his loyalty to Reagan above the district; he called MacKenzie one of the few Midwest Republicans favoring full decontrol of natural-gas prices. But Sharp's constituent service did far more for him than any of the issues he stressed. "The reason for my success is my service," he said as returns gave him a comfortable win on election night. "A lot of people who consider themselves Republicans voted for me."

The 1986 campaign provided an entirely new experience for Sharp, and a welcome one. In the aftermath of MacKenzie's costly failure, no prominent Republican in the 2nd District wanted to bother challenging the incumbent. Donald Lynch, a 31-year-old Nazarene minister with no political experience, mobilized an army of evangelical Christians and won the GOP nomination after a campaign he suggested was divinely inspired.

Lynch raised little money for the fall campaign, and his religious agenda alienated much of the traditional middle-class Republican electorate. For the first time in his political career, Sharp broke 60 percent of the vote in November.

But the security was short-lived. In 1988, with neighbor Dan Quayle on the national GOP ticket, Sharp had to contend with another six-figure outpouring of Republican votes in the 2nd. His hope was that his underfinanced opponent, Mike Pence, would not be strong enough to ride the tide all the way home.

But Pence, a 29-year-old attorney from the Indianapolis area, turned his weakness to advantage. He not only ran his own campaign without any political action committee (PAC) money, he succeeded in making PACs the central issue of the local campaign by taking the incumbent to task for his heavy PAC reliance.

For this Pence received favorable press both locally and nationally. He still came up short (47 percent), but he reversed Sharp's trend. And he did well enough to convince himself he should run again in 1990. He declared his candidacy shortly after the new cycle began.

Committees

Energy and Commerce (4th of 26 Democrats)
Energy and Power (chairman); Commerce, Consumer Protection and Competitiveness

Interior and Insular Affairs (3rd of 26 Democrats)
Energy and the Environment; Water, Power and Offshore Energy Resources

Elections

1988 General		
Philip R. Sharp (D)	116,915	(53%)
Mike Pence (R)	102,846	(47%)
1986 General		
Philip R. Sharp (D)	102,456	(62%)
Donald J. Lynch (R)	62,013	(37%)

Previous Winning Percentages: **1984** (53%) **1982** (56%) **1980** (53%) **1978** (56%) **1976** (60%) **1974** (54%)

District Vote For President

	1988	1984	1980	1976
D	83,849 (38%)	72,085 (32%)	76,120 (34%)	92,744 (42%)
R	137,236 (62%)	151,136 (67%)	138,118 (61%)	126,543 (57%)
I			10,143 (5%)	

Campaign Finance

	Receipts	Receipts from PACs	Expend-itures
1988			
Sharp (D)	$465,414	$311,581 (67%)	$444,422
Pence (R)	$380,667	0	$332,880
1986			
Sharp (D)	$403,720	$264,410 (65%)	$384,009
Lynch (R)	$117,819	$9,050 (8%)	$117,598

Key Votes

1987	
Raise speed limit to 65 mph	Y
Approve Gephardt "fair trade" amendment	Y
Ban testing of larger nuclear weapons	Y
Delay "re-flagging" of Kuwaiti tankers	Y
Approve tax-raising deficit-reduction bill	Y
1988	
Approve aid to Nicaraguan contras	N
Enact civil rights restoration bill over Reagan veto	Y
Kill 60-day plant-closing notification measure	N
Pass omnibus trade bill over Reagan veto	Y
Approve death penalty for drug-related murders	N
Bar federal funds for abortions in cases of rape and incest	N
Oppose seven-day waiting period for purchase of handguns	Y

Voting Studies

	Presidential Support		Party Unity		Conservative Coalition	
Year	**S**	**O**	**S**	**O**	**S**	**O**
1988	31	64	79	19	61	39
1987	25	73	81	14	47	51
1986	24	73	81	16	42	56
1985	43	56	76	21	36	62
1984	38	50	63	31	47	36
1983	22	77	79	20	35	64
1982	42	57	69	28	36	64
1981	43	57	70	27	52	47

Interest Group Ratings

Year	ADA	ACU	AFL-CIO	CCUS
1988	75	20	100	50
1987	72	4	93	38
1986	65	10	86	41
1985	65	38	71	50
1984	50	43	54	14
1983	80	18	88	25
1982	80	14	95	41
1981	65	20	57	21

3 John Hiler (R)

Of La Porte — Elected 1980

Born: April 24, 1953, Chicago, Ill.
Education: Williams College, B.A. 1975; U. of Chicago, M.B.A. 1977.
Occupation: Foundry executive.
Family: Wife, Catherine Sands; two children.
Religion: Roman Catholic.
Political Career: Republican nominee for Ind. House, 1978.
Capitol Office: 407 Cannon Bldg. 20515; 225-3915.

In Washington: A survivor of four hard-fought re-elections since he came to Congress in 1981, Hiler has struggled to accommodate his strong conservative instincts with the demands of his politically marginal district — one that is happy to accept the sort of federal economic assistance that Hiler campaigned against in 1980.

Hiler acknowledges that he has altered his approach to government since winning his first election. "It's a change in tone," he told the *South Bend Tribune* in 1988, "[but not] a change in philosophy. I think it's a maturation of philosophy and a better appreciation for the positive force that government can be. . . ."

Though his overall voting record remains one of the more conservative in the House, Hiler now calls attention to his ability to secure funding for the 3rd from the very federal programs he shunned and sought to slash in his early House years.

As a freshman in Ronald Reagan's first Congress, Hiler was so committed to cutting government spending that he tried to wean his district from it, something few first-termers dare. "My solution," he once said, "is to cut down on the tax money flowing from South Bend to Washington, rather than to increase the grant money flowing from Washington to South Bend."

When South Bend civic leaders asked him to help secure a federal loan guarantee for an ethanol plant, a project that had been supported by his Democratic predecessor, Hiler backed off. "I have very serious questions about the government getting in the ethanol business," he said. Only after it became clear that ethanol loans would be handed out anyway did he support the South Bend project.

Following his near-defeat in 1982, Hiler seemed to alter course in his second term. He boasted unabashedly of his role when South Bend received urban development action grants (UDAGs) and local manufacturers won contracts to build postal vehicles. But vestiges of Hiler's deep skepticism of government continued to surface well into his House career.

In 1986, he offered an amendment on the House floor to kill UDAGs altogether. His proposal was defeated, 93-289. On the Small Business Committee, he waged a battle to reduce drastically the loan authority of the Small Business Administration. In 1985, Hiler's proposal to cut SBA direct-loan authority almost in half passed the House 257-158, although somewhat more generous funding was incorporated in the bill's final version. In 1986, Hiler proposed eliminating all funding for the SBA loan program, except for $54 million for minority businesses and handicapped assistance. That idea lost, 118-243.

In the 100th Congress, Hiler's efforts on the Banking Committee revealed something of the "maturation" he says he has undergone as a legislator. As ranking member of the Subcommittee on Consumer Affairs and Coinage, Hiler worked with Democratic Chairman Frank Annunzio to craft legislation to clarify credit-card terms. Hiler supported a bill placing new disclosure requirements on banks, department stores and other firms issuing credit cards, though he opposed Annunzio's unsuccessful efforts to impose a federally mandated floating cap on credit-card interest rates. In 1988, Hiler was one of only three Republicans on the Banking Committee to back the panel's bank-deregulation package.

Hiler also spent a good deal of time in the 100th Congress working on an omnibus housing authorization package. On the floor, he tried to make across-the-board cuts in its authorization levels, but was blocked by Housing Subcommittee Chairman Henry B. Gonzalez. Hiler voted against the bill's passage, but then worked on the House-Senate conference and ultimately supported the final bill.

When the housing measure was in subcommittee, Hiler fought to strike a section that required mobile homes to meet minimum heating-efficiency standards; he warned that extra manufacturing expense required in doing that would price mobile homes beyond the reach of many low-income families. Proponents of the requirement said any higher purchase cost

Indiana 3

North Central — South Bend

Anchored by the industrial cities of South Bend and Elkhart, the 3rd is a swing district. Hiler has never won more than 55 percent in his five elections, and his Democratic predecessor, Rep. John Brademas, held the seat for 11 terms, but reached 60 percent only twice.

South Bend, besides being the home of the University of Notre Dame, has several Bendix facilities that make automobile and airplane parts, and an AM General plant that once claimed to be the largest military truck-assembly facility outside of the Soviet Union. South Bend's population of 107,000 is a mixture of blue-collar workers and university-related professionals.

St. Joseph County, which includes South Bend, often supports Democrats at the state and local levels: Hiler's opponents typically carry it, and in the 1988 presidential contest, Democratic presidential nominee Michael S. Dukakis received 49 percent of the county's vote, far above his 40 percent statewide tally.

The city of Elkhart's economy is less closely tied to the auto industry, and therefore healthier than South Bend's. It depends more on the manufactured housing and recreational-vehicle industries, which are responsible for over 50,000 jobs in the 3rd.

Elkhart is also headquarters for Miles Laboratories and is the band instrument capital of the United States. At one time nearly 60 percent of the world's band instruments came from there.

The more prosperous voters of Elkhart — combined with a Mennonite community based in Goshen, the seat of Elkhart County — give the county a GOP flavor. Republicans routinely draw more than 60 percent of the Elkhart County vote in local and statewide elections.

Elkhart County casts about a fifth of the district's vote; St. Joseph County contributes a little less than half. But the large GOP pluralities from Elkhart frequently offset the smaller Democratic margins from St. Joseph, particularly when combined with the GOP strength of the district's farmers.

About a third of the vote comes from four rural counties to the south and west of South Bend and Elkhart. The cattle and dairy farmers of Kosciusko, Marshall and LaPorte counties traditionally vote a strong Republican ticket. In Starke County, where potatoes are a major crop, the voters sometimes side with the Democrats. Hiler lost Starke in 1988.

Population: 558,100. White 521,400 (93%), Black 29,558 (5%), Other 3,139 (1%). Spanish origin 7,746 (1%). 18 and over 395,121 (71%), 65 and over 62,682 (11%). Median age: 30.

would be offset by savings from lower heating bills. Hiler's point prevailed in subcommittee, but in the full committee, Kentucky Democrat Carroll Hubbard Jr. persuaded a majority to put the energy requirement back into the bill.

Hiler also failed in committee and on the floor to get the UDAG program to give priority to rehabilitating vacant industrial buildings. The amendment would have applied to an abandoned Studebaker plant in the 3rd.

At Home: Hiler started his congressional career impressively at age 27, defeating House Majority Whip John Brademas in one of 1980's biggest upsets. But since then, Hiler has yet to match the 55 percent vote share he won in his first time out.

His last two campaigns were against Thomas W. Ward, a lawyer from rural Starke County who began his 1986 bid as a politically inexperienced dark horse challenger and nearly knocked an unsuspecting Hiler from his perch. Only after a formal recount and two months of legal haggling did Hiler prevail — by 47 votes.

Ward had begun with little more than a mimeograph machine, but he hammered away at Hiler, accusing him of not obtaining defense contracts and opposing a trade bill that might have saved industrial jobs for the district.

After his near-miss, Ward scarcely stopped campaigning, and national Democratic campaign officials made him one of 1988's best-financed challengers. Moreover, with Evan Bayh on his way to becoming Indiana's first Democratic governor in 20 years, Ward had a chance to survive the heavy Republican vote Indiana delivers in presidential-election years.

The odds got longer in August, when Sen. Dan Quayle became the GOP nominee for vice president. But the biggest stumbling block for Ward was the fact that Hiler was not about to be caught napping twice. More visible in the district than ever before, Hiler also was more attentive in Washington to local needs. He also easily broke the district record for campaign spending that he had set in 1984.

Hiler's campaign mixed anti-tax absolutism with more flexible attitudes on issues such as the environment. This dovetailed well with national GOP themes; Hiler got 54 percent.

Hiler's political career began in 1978. Then

just out of graduate school, he was working in his father's foundry when party leaders picked him to fill a last-minute vacancy in a state Legislature election. He came within 500 votes of winning, impressing party leaders.

Hiler moved on to Washington in 1980 by blaming Congress, and specifically incumbent Brademas, for most of the nation's ills. The immediate problem he cited was unemployment, over 15 percent in parts of the district. Brademas had sensed a rightward swing in the electorate, so he started early playing up the federal grants he brought into the district and painting Hiler as inexperienced and simplistic. But Hiler convinced voters that the 22-year House veteran was a major architect of failed Democratic economic policies.

Some credited Hiler's 1980 victory to presidential coattails, but he ran ahead of Reagan in two counties and matched Reagan's 49 percent in St. Joseph. Rolling up 55 percent districtwide, Hiler became the second-youngest member of the 97th Congress.

In 1982, the tables were turned; Hiler faced charges that Reagan's economic program was the real problem in his recession-wracked industrial district. Democrats nominated state Rep. Richard C. Bodine, a veteran legislator with a proven capacity for drawing votes from both parties. But the underfinanced Bodine organization did not really move until September. Bodine carried St. Joseph County easily, but Hiler survived by 3,912 votes.

In 1984, Democrats offered a strong candidate in Michael P. Barnes, who twice had been elected county prosecutor in St. Joseph County (South Bend), which casts nearly half the district's vote. Barnes called Hiler a "rigid and inflexible" Reaganite who voted with an administration that favored the Sun Belt over the Midwest. Hiler concentrated on coming across as pleasant and reasonable in order to squelch his reputation as a conservative zealot. Once again, St. Joseph County went heavily Democratic, but Hiler was saved by voters in smaller cities and rural areas.

Committees

Banking, Finance and Urban Affairs (9th of 20 Republicans)
Consumer Affairs and Coinage (ranking); Financial Institutions Supervision, Regulation and Insurance; Housing and Community Development

House Administration (7th of 8 Republicans)
Accounts; Elections

Small Business (5th of 17 Republicans)
Environment and Labor (ranking)

Elections

1988 General		
John Hiler (R)	116,309	(54%)
Thomas W. Ward (D)	97,934	(46%)
1986 General		
John Hiler (R)	75,979	(50%)
Thomas W. Ward (D)	75,932	(50%)

Previous Winning Percentages: 1984 (52%) **1982** (51%) **1980** (55%)

District Vote For President

	1988	1984	1980	1976
D	87,080 (40%)	82,107 (38%)	81,627 (37%)	95,289 (44%)
R	128,039 (59%)	135,263 (62%)	124,750 (56%)	118,782 (55%)
I			13,777 (6%)	

Campaign Finance

	Receipts	Receipts from PACs	Expend-itures
1988			
Hiler (R)	$971,929	$346,741 (36%)	$1,085,140
Ward (D)	$592,580	$386,413 (65%)	$579,413
1986			
Hiler (R)	$400,335	$135,101 (34%)	$336,768
Ward (D)	$190,264	$96,750 (51%)	$189,509

Key Votes

1987	
Raise speed limit to 65 mph	Y
Approve Gephardt "fair trade" amendment	N
Ban testing of larger nuclear weapons	N
Delay "re-flagging" of Kuwaiti tankers	N
Approve tax-raising deficit-reduction bill	N
1988	
Approve aid to Nicaraguan contras	Y
Enact civil rights restoration bill over Reagan veto	N
Kill 60-day plant-closing notification measure	Y
Pass omnibus trade bill over Reagan veto	N
Approve death penalty for drug-related murders	Y
Bar federal funds for abortions in cases of rape and incest	Y
Oppose seven-day waiting period for purchase of handguns	Y

Voting Studies

	Presidential Support		Party Unity		Conservative Coalition	
Year	**S**	**O**	**S**	**O**	**S**	**O**
1988	63	31	89	6	89	3
1987	74	26	90	6	100	0
1986	78	21	89	9	88	8
1985	80	18	95	3	91	9
1984	66	31	91	5	88	8
1983	83	17	94	4	92	8
1982	86	14	92	5	93	5
1981	78	21	87	13	85	15

Interest Group Ratings

Year	ADA	ACU	AFL-CIO	CCUS
1988	5	100	14	100
1987	0	87	6	93
1986	0	86	0	94
1985	5	90	12	91
1984	10	83	0	69
1983	10	91	0	85
1982	5	96	5	86
1981	25	93	13	95

4 Jill Long (D)

Of Larwill — Elected 1989

Born: July 15, 1952, Warsaw, Ind.
Education: Valparaiso U., B.S. 1974; Indiana U., M.B.A. 1978, Ph.D. 1984.
Occupation: College professor.
Family: Single.
Religion: Methodist.
Political Career: Valparaiso City Council, 1983-86; Democratic nominee for U.S. Senate, 1986; Democratic nominee for U.S. House, 1988.
Capitol Office: 1632 Longworth Bldg. 20515; 225-4436.

The Path to Washington: In winning the 4th District in a March 1989 special election, Long finally found a "Dan" she could beat. She had been routed by Dan Quayle in a 1986 Senate bid and by Dan Coats in a 1988 House race. But those campaigns gave her high name recognition and a volunteer network — crucial ingredients in her narrow victory over Fort Wayne lawyer and city administrator Dan Heath.

Heath was making his first run for elective office. Long's own government experience was limited to three years on the Valparaiso City Council when she was teaching in northwest Indiana in the mid-1980s.

But she did learn some valuable lessons from her earlier campaigns. In her 1986 Senate race, she laid out a liberal agenda that included support for legalized abortion and a nuclear test-ban treaty, as well as opposition to public prayer in schools and deployment of the strategic defense initiative. Against Heath, she did her best to avoid ideological typecasting. She called on Democrats with more moderate reputations to campaign for her, such as Tennessee Sen. Al Gore and Indiana's new governor, Evan Bayh.

And after campaigning in a generally gracious, low-key manner against Quayle and Coats, she ran more aggressively against Heath. While Heath sought to dismiss her as a tax-and-spend liberal, she was able to keep the focus on his connection to controversial efforts of the Fort Wayne city government to impose a local income tax and to annex some suburban neighborhoods. She was endorsed by both Fort Wayne newspapers and ended up carrying Allen County (Fort Wayne) by a margin just large enough to offset Heath's edge in the rural counties.

Her victory was an embarrassment to the Republican Party. The seat had been held by both Quayle and Coats, whose appointment to Quayle's Senate seat in December 1988 created the need for the special election.

Heath tied himself as closely as he could to popular big-name Republicans. Quayle and Coats campaigned for him. So did first lady Barbara Bush, who worked the phones at Heath headquarters for a while on St. Patrick's Day. On election eve, Heath ran TV ads featuring endorsements from Quayle and President Bush.

The outcome was also a blow to the GOP's new leadership team in Washington, featuring Lee Atwater at the Republican National Committee and Edward J. Rollins at the National Republican Congressional Committee. The contest in the 4th was the first of three special House elections in the spring of 1989, and it was the one Republicans were considered most likely to win. In defeat, Atwater said he was "ashamed."

But while Democrats in Washington were chortling, Long was careful not to draw any national ramifications from her victory: "This was just a race between two individuals in northeast Indiana," she said.

Although the last three years of Long's life have featured non-stop campaigning, politics has been an avocation for her rather than a career. Most of her paychecks have come from college teaching. Long has a doctorate in business from Indiana University and had to balance her campaign schedule in 1989 with two business courses at Indiana University/Purdue University-Fort Wayne. Even on Election Day, she had to break away from greeting voters to teach a noontime class.

After teaching and politics, the third facet of Long's background is farming. She grew up on a farm, and before her election to Congress, she lived on an 80-acre farm in Whitley County, and helped her parents run their farm nearby. One of Long's ads featured shots of her driving a tractor, and her agrarian roots were no doubt a help in holding down her deficit in normally Republican rural areas of the district.

But this seat will not be an easy one for her to hold. Former Rep. J. Edward Roush, who left the House a dozen years ago, was the last Democrat to represent the 4th; in eight victories, he never took more than 56 percent of the vote.

Indiana 4

Northeast — Fort Wayne

Planted in the northeastern corner of the state, the 4th is dominated politically and economically by Fort Wayne, Indiana's second-largest city. Allen County, which includes Fort Wayne, has more than half of the district's population. With about 173,000 people, Fort Wayne is where voters in the surrounding nine counties look for news and commercial needs.

Located where the St. Mary's and St. Joseph rivers meet to form the Maumee, Fort Wayne has been a transportation and manufacturing center since the first half of the 19th century. General Electric, General Motors and Magnavox are currently among its major employers.

With a large German ethnic population, Fort Wayne is a strongly Republican town. Only once in the last 40 years — in 1964 — has Allen County failed to support the GOP presidential nominee. George Bush won the county by nearly 2-to-1 in 1988. The surrounding farm counties usually vote as consistently for the GOP as Fort Wayne does. The small town of Huntington, about 25 miles southwest of Fort Wayne, is the home of Vice President Dan Quayle.

Yet while Republican voting habits in the district may be strong, they are not cast in stone. In winning the Indiana governorship in 1988, Democrat Evan Bayh carried six of the district's 10 counties. In winning the open House seat in March 1989, Long won five.

Long not only took Allen County, but also broke the expected grip of her GOP opponent on the rural vote by winning four smaller counties. Long effectively promoted her agrarian roots — she owns a farm in Whitley County — and benefited from some antipathy to her GOP opponent, Fort Wayne lawyer Dan Heath. One of his prime challengers for the Republican nomination had come from De Kalb County, a GOP stronghold that Long ultimately carried.

Population: 553,698. White 520,079 (94%), Black 26,628 (5%), Other 2,670 (1%). Spanish origin 7,128 (1%). 18 and over 382,150 (69%), 65 and over 58,015 (10%). Median age: 29.

Committees

Agriculture (24th of 27 Democrats)
Conservation, Credit and Rural Development; Livestock, Dairy and Poultry; Wheat, Soybeans and Feed Grains

Veterans' Affairs (21st of 21 Democrats)
Education, Training and Employment; Oversight and Investigations

Campaign Finance

	Receipts	Receipts from PACs	Expend-itures
1989 Special Election			
Long (D)	$326,025	$182,763 (56%)	$313,724
Heath (R)	$393,716	$131,200 (33%)	$378,441

Election

1989 Special Election

Jill Long (D)	65,272	(51%)
Dan Heath (R)	63,494	(49%)

District Vote For President

	1988	1984	1980	1976
D	71,156 (33%)	70,300 (33%)	73,699 (33%)	88,170 (40%)
R	143,461 (66%)	144,009 (67%)	128,189 (58%)	127,446 (58%)
I			16,699 (8%)	

5 Jim Jontz (D)

Of Monticello — Elected 1986

Born: Dec. 18, 1951, Indianapolis, Ind.
Education: Indiana U., B.S. 1973.
Occupation: Public official.
Family: Single.
Religion: Methodist.
Political Career: Ind. House, 1975-85; Ind. Senate, 1985-87.
Capitol Office: 1039 Longworth Bldg. 20515; 225-5037.

In Washington: Jontz is the kind of extraordinary politician who can live happily in one party and appeal to voters in the other. In 1987 and 1988, Jontz received ratings of 100 and 95 from the liberal Americans for Democratic Action. Yet he was endorsed for reelection by the Farm Bureau, the Veterans of Foreign Wars and the National Rifle Association — all groups generally considered conservative.

Such breadth of support obviously requires more than the typical freshman's frenzy of service to constituents. It requires a careful balancing of interests.

While he reached for such traditional pork barrel as construction-project money for Grissom Air Force Base, Jontz also refused the 1987 pay raise and used the funds to sponsor scholarships in his district. While returning home each weekend and holding nearly 200 town meetings (by staff count), Jontz was also a visible player on the Agriculture Committee. And he was principal sponsor of five bills that passed the House.

His measures got through as attachments to larger bills becoming laws. One expanded veterans benefits, another allowed communities to repay federal loans at a lower rate of interest, and another lowered loan rates for small agriculture cooperatives hurt by drought.

So the Farm Bureau was apparently pleased with Jontz' work and vote on the drought-relief bill. The NRA endorsement stemmed largely from Jontz' vote against the 1988 legislation requiring a seven-day waiting period for gun buyers. And the VFW may well have noticed his support for Congress authorizing a Service Medal for any prisoner of war held from World War I on (or their next of kin).

Jontz is able to pay such persuasive attention to a given group that it will overlook some of his votes and regard him as acceptable.

This has been a key to Jontz' career from its inception. He has run and won in basically Republican territory through a mix of energy, attentiveness and political footwork. Some thought it an incredible gaffe when Jontz told *USA Today* in 1988 that his hero was Eugene Debs, the Indiana-born union organizer who was five times the Socialist candidate for president. Yet in the same election cycle, Jontz was a cosponsor of the resolution calling for a balanced-budget amendment to the Constitution. And he was eighth among House members in political action committee (PAC) receipts. And when courting voters directly, he concentrates on the ones who would consider Debs a dangerous radical. He rarely wastes time on Democrats he knows will support him if he can find a group of Republicans who, someday, just might.

At Home: In the spring of 1989, having just begun his second term in the House, Jontz was seriously considering a 1990 challenge to appointive GOP Sen. Daniel R. Coats. Jontz had urged the race on Rep. Lee H. Hamilton, the state's senior Democrat and one of the most respected men in the House. When Hamilton said no, Jontz quickly emerged as the party's next choice.

In May, however, Jontz opted out, saying he wanted a chance to establish himself in the House. Had he chosen to run, he might also have needed more time to become known beyond his district, which is located between the metropolitan areas of Chicago and Indianapolis. A tireless campaigner, his dedication to the game has been legendary in Indiana for years. When he first ran for Congress, his stated goal was to knock on every door in his district. But even he acknowledges one cannot rely on such tactics statewide.

Jontz' remarkable rise began when, at the age of 22, he challenged the Republican leader of the Indiana House and unseated him by two votes. A decade later, he ran for the state Senate in the midst of the Reagan presidential tide, and took a seat out of GOP hands.

Despite that track record, many Republicans in the 5th District seemed to pass the entire 1986 campaign unaware of what was awaiting them. For months after Republican Rep. Elwood Hillis announced his retirement plans, the 5th was not prominent on the national party's roster of districts to worry about. As late as two weeks before Election Day,

Indiana 5

North — Kokomo

The 5th travels northwest from Kokomo, a small industrial center, to the suburbs of Chicago in Lake County. In between is mile upon mile of flat farmland. There once was a time when these three distinct political worlds shared one common element — they voted Republican. But that was before Jim Jontz. In 1988, he carried all but one of the 14 counties included in whole or part in the 5th District. Also in 1988, the collapse of normal GOP margins in the farming counties spread to the governor's contest, helping seal the statewide defeat of GOP nominee John Mutz.

Traditionally, the part of the district friendliest to Republicans has been the southeast corner, in and around Kokomo (Howard County) and Marion (Grant County), another industrial city. Both have numerous small factories and a few very large ones, most of them related to the automobile industry. They also serve as major distribution points for the area's agricultural output. About 30 percent of the district's vote comes from these two counties.

The downturn in the auto industry during the last recession had as serious an effect on these communities as on any in the nation, with unemployment exceeding 15 percent in several places. In 1986, frustration over continuing industrial malaise helped Jontz overcome the straight-ticket GOP voting habits that usually prevail in Howard County and Grant County. By 1988, the employment picture in most factories was better, if not rosy, and George Bush took more than 60 percent in both Howard and Grant. That did not, however, deter Jontz from winning the counties with 53 and 54 percent, respectively.

Ninety miles to the northwest are the residents of southern Lake and Porter counties. These fast-growing suburban areas are attracting some employees from the steel mills along Lake Michigan, as well as former Chicago residents who are escaping to what they hope will be a slower-paced life. More than one-fourth of the district vote comes out of Lake and Porter counties, which are separated from the rest of the district psychologically as well as geographically. Voters there watch Chicago television stations and read newspapers from Chicago and Gary. Jontz carried both with 55 percent in 1988.

Linking the small industrial cities and the burgeoning outer suburban fringe are expanses of corn and soybeans. All 10 of the predominantly rural counties voted for Bush in 1988, but nearly every one also went for Jontz, and sometimes by tallies exceeding 60 percent of the vote.

Population: 548,257. White 530,879 (97%), Black 11,875 (2%), Other 2,820 (1%). Spanish origin 6,106 (1%). 18 and over 380,248 (69%), 65 and over 55,952 (10%). Median age: 29.

strategists for the Republican nominee boasted to reporters that they had a 20-point lead. Only on election night, as county after county failed to turn out the vote they expected, did it become clear that they had been had.

Jontz is not only good, he is lucky. His 1974 upset victory was made possible by the Watergate malaise that hurt Republicans all over the country. His election to Congress 12 years later was in part the result of an angry primary that pitted the district's entrenched GOP establishment against an energetic group of conservative Christian activists.

The winner of that primary was James Butcher, a Kokomo lawyer, state Senate colleague of Jontz, and favorite of the evangelical Christians. After dispatching his primary opponent, state Treasurer Julian Ridlen, Butcher was careful to move to the political center, stressing his effectiveness as a legislator and insisting he was no religious zealot.

But while Butcher was repositioning himself for the general election, Jontz was pressing on quietly with the campaign he had begun in the fall of 1985, shortly after Hillis made his retirement announcement. That was a full-time person-to-person effort in all 14 of the district's counties, augmented by a fund-raising drive that brought in a surprising amount of money for a Democratic challenger in a district that had not elected a Democrat in decades. By the beginning of October, Jontz had a treasury approaching $400,000 and a paid staff of eight full-time field coordinators.

Meanwhile, Jontz was given some unexpected ammunition in May when Hillis bucked his party's majority and voted for the Democratic trade bill aimed at restricting foreign industrial competition. Butcher opposed the bill, and for months Jontz missed no opportunity to tell voters that he and the popular Hillis were on the side of protecting jobs, and Butcher and President Reagan were on the other side. That was good politics: There have been times in recent years when it was not safe to drive a foreign car through the streets of some of the district's small industrial cities.

Butcher had plenty of ammunition of his own. Jontz styles himself a populist, but with a 12-year legislative record of close ties to unions, environmental activists and peace groups, it was easy to make a credible case that Jontz was an unswerving liberal trying to camouflage his true ideology. The United Auto Workers and other liberal labor groups financed a large portion of his campaign.

Butcher liked to remind voters that the Democrat was a bachelor and had spent his entire adult life in public office. "He's a man who talks about jobs," said Butcher, "but he's never had a full-time job. He talks about family values, but he's never had a family."

But the Republican never managed to make those charges stick. His media efforts were hampered in part by the nature of the district. Spread over several commercial media markets, the 5th is not a good district for a television campaign; it is better suited to the sort of grass-roots organizing Jontz decided to focus on. Butcher was no slouch at grass-roots politics himself — his network of Christian volunteers had been crucial to his nomination over Ridlen — but in the fall, with Butcher playing down religious issues, the evangelical network simply did not perform for him. Jontz prevailed by 5,000 votes.

Some viewed this as a fluke victory. Yet few Republicans lined up to prove the point in 1988. The party found itself nominating Patricia Williams, who was then running the Kokomo Board of Realtors after having worked in Hillis' office for 16 years. Williams' strategy relied on a big turnout for the presidential ticket, in part because running-mate Quayle hailed from a county that borders the district. The turnout was large, but enough GOP voters split their tickets to re-elect Jontz with more than 56 percent.

During the campaign, Speaker Jim Wright came to a Jontz fund-raiser in the district. Williams tried to make an issue of his case before the House ethics committee. Serious as that case turned out to be, it failed to ignite as an issue in Indiana that fall. Williams could not convince enough voters that Jontz belonged to Wright more than he belonged to them.

Committees

Agriculture (18th of 27 Democrats)
Conservation, Credit and Rural Development; Department Operations, Research and Foreign Agriculture; Forests, Family Farms and Energy; Wheat, Soybeans and Feed Grains

Education and Labor (21st of 22 Democrats)
Select Education

Select Aging (34th of 39 Democrats)
Retirement, Income and Employment

Veterans' Affairs (15th of 21 Democrats)
Education, Training and Employment; Hospitals and Health Care

Elections

1988 General		
Jim Jontz (D)	116,240	(56%)
Patricia L. Williams (R)	90,163	(44%)
1988 Primary		
Jim Jontz (D)	44,788	(92%)
S. Gopal Raju (D)	3,752	(8%)
1986 General		
Jim Jontz (D)	80,772	(51%)
James R. Butcher (R)	75,507	(48%)

District Vote For President

	1988	1984	1980	1976
D	73,065 (35%)	67,224 (31%)	68,760 (31%)	81,118 (41%)
R	136,223 (65%)	150,354 (69%)	140,368 (63%)	114,774 (58%)
I			9,677 (4%)	

Campaign Finance

	Receipts	Receipts from PACs	Expenditures
1988			
Jontz (D)	$721,637	$471,725 (65%)	$689,086
Williams (R)	$247,010	$90,262 (37%)	$244,985
1986			
Jontz (D)	$463,733	$292,749 (63%)	$462,970
Butcher (R)	$421,693	$161,638 (38%)	$422,689

Key Votes

1987	
Raise speed limit to 65 mph	Y
Approve Gephardt "fair trade" amendment	Y
Ban testing of larger nuclear weapons	Y
Delay "re-flagging" of Kuwaiti tankers	Y
Approve tax-raising deficit-reduction bill	Y
1988	
Approve aid to Nicaraguan contras	N
Enact civil rights restoration bill over Reagan veto	Y
Kill 60-day plant-closing notification measure	N
Pass omnibus trade bill over Reagan veto	Y
Approve death penalty for drug-related murders	N
Bar federal funds for abortions in cases of rape and incest	N
Oppose seven-day waiting period for purchase of handguns	Y

Voting Studies

	Presidential Support		Party Unity		Conservative Coalition	
Year	S	O	S	O	S	O
1988	16	84	91	8	26	74
1987	11	89	93	7	12	88

Interest Group Ratings

Year	ADA	ACU	AFL-CIO	CCUS
1988	95	4	100	21
1987	100	0	94	20

6 Dan Burton (R)

Of Indianapolis — Elected 1982

Born: June 21, 1938, Indianapolis, Ind.
Education: Attended Indiana U., 1958-59; Cincinnati Bible Seminary, 1959-60.
Military Career: Army, 1956-57; Army Reserve, 1957-62.
Occupation: Insurance and real-estate agent.
Family: Wife, Barbara Logan; three children.
Religion: Protestant.
Political Career: Ind. Senate, 1969-71, 1981-83; Ind. House, 1967-69, 1977-81; Republican nominee for U.S. House, 1970; sought Republican nomination for U.S. House, 1972.
Capitol Office: 120 Cannon Bldg. 20515; 225-2276.

In Washington: There are no shades of gray in Burton's world view. One of the most conservative members of the Foreign Affairs Committee, he regards communist governments and movements with unstinting hostility. And he is not much kinder to fellow House members who do not see things his way.

Burton unloosed one of his harshest attacks during a 1987 debate over U.S. aid to the contras. "My colleagues on the left," Burton said, "need to admit forthrightly that they support the communist government of Nicaragua and quit this charade that they try to put forth on the American people."

Burton's targets are usually his liberal Democratic antagonists on Foreign Affairs. But he has also gone after GOP officials who support policies he regards as insufficiently hardline. During the 100th Congress, he blasted Reagan administration overtures toward Mozambique, whose leftist government was battling anti-communist rebels. Though careful not to blame President Reagan, Burton assailed the "State Department bureaucracy, which has a policy of appeasement" toward Marxism.

His pyrotechnic outbursts on foreign policy have led Burton's critics to dismiss him as a right-wing demagogue. But he occasionally shows a willingness to take a more subtle approach.

In 1988, Burton presented what he cleverly packaged as a "black empowerment" alternative to a bill to impose stiff sanctions against the apartheid government of South Africa. His amendment promised U.S. aid for black businesses in South Africa, and provided tax benefits for American companies that followed non-discriminatory practices in South Africa.

Burton said his measure would enable blacks to gain economic and political power, while sanctions would create an economic crisis "that will lead to an escalating spiral of violence and repression." But while Burton got some credit for shaping his anti-sanctions position into a politically palatable form, the House defeated the proposal by a wide margin.

Though Burton's position as ranking Republican on the Africa Subcommittee means he spends a lot of time on Foreign Affairs work, he does not ignore domestic issues. One of his priorities has been to prevent inclusion of illegal aliens in the decennial census. Burton claims their inclusion cost Indiana (which has few such immigrants) a House seat after the 1980 census. "I won't let this happen again," he said during a 1988 Post Office and Civil Service Committee debate on a bill aimed at adjusting the 1990 census to offset an expected "undercount" of minorities. "Illegal aliens are not citizens, so they should not be counted." Burton won passage of an amendment barring the counting of illegal aliens, leading committee Democrats to scuttle the whole bill.

At Home: Burton settled an old intra-party score by winning his 1982 primary.

A decade earlier he had lost to William Hudnut by 81 votes for the nomination in a nearby district; Hudnut served a term in the House and later became mayor of Indianapolis. When the new 6th was created in 1981, Mayor Hudnut hoped to secure the nomination for his GOP ally, state party Chairman Bruce Melchert. Against Melchert, however, Burton won.

Burton and Melchert agreed on most issues, and the competition was mostly amiable. But the Burton-Hudnut feud surfaced at one point, when Burton suggested that the mayor had engineered the last-minute candidacy of political unknown Ricky Bartl to deprive Burton of first position on the alphabetical ballot.

Burton won the primary by 5,260 votes of over 72,000 cast, and in November he began what seems sure to be a long streak of decisive general-election victories by taking 65 percent.

Burton served 10 years in the state Legislature, his tenure interrupted by two congressional campaigns — the losing 1972 primary against Hudnut, and an unsuccessful 1970 bid against Democratic Rep. Andrew Jacobs Jr.

Indiana 6

Northern Indianapolis; Anderson

No Democrat need apply in the 6th, a "lifetime appointment" for any GOP incumbent who stays clear of primary trouble.

One-fourth of the vote is cast in the affluent Washington Township area of Indianapolis, some of Indiana's most Republican turf. A Democratic candidate does well to top 25 percent here.

Hamilton County, north of Indianapolis, outdoes even Washington Township in its partisan loyalty. It is the single most Republican county in Indiana, as well as the fastest-growing in recent years. Even in 1982, a down year for the GOP, both Burton and GOP Sen. Richard G. Lugar received 79 percent here.

After Indianapolis, the only other sizable city is Anderson, with about 61,000 people. It and surrounding Madison County contribute another quarter of the district's vote. General Motors has been crucial to Anderson's economy since the 1920s; the city has a large group of United Auto Workers and a hard-core Democratic vote. During economic downturns, Anderson's vote is almost enough to tip Madison County away from the GOP. In 1982, with record-high unemployment in Anderson, Burton barely won Madison County. Usually, though, Republican votes outside Anderson keep the county in the GOP column. Since 1948, the county has voted Democratic for president only once, in 1964.

The remaining third of the district is primarily rural. Farmers in the counties north and east of Indianapolis are not thrilled to be part of a mostly urban and suburban district, but conservative farmers and conservative suburbanites have enough in common to make for a relatively homogeneous district politics.

Population: 540,939. White 520,429 (96%), Black 16,369 (3%), Other 2,849 (1%). Spanish origin 3,445 (1%). 18 and over 381,833 (71%), 65 and over 54,972 (10%). Median age: 31.

Committees

Foreign Affairs (11th of 18 Republicans)
Africa (ranking); Western Hemisphere Affairs

Post Office and Civil Service (5th of 9 Republicans)
Human Resources (ranking)

Veterans' Affairs (6th of 13 Republicans)
Housing and Memorial Affairs (ranking); Hospitals and Health Care

Elections

1988 General		
Dan Burton (R)	192,064	(73%)
George Thomas Holland (D)	71,447	(27%)
1986 General		
Dan Burton (R)	118,363	(68%)
Thomas F. McKenna (D)	53,431	(31%)

Previous Winning Percentages: **1984** (73%) **1982** (65%)

District Vote For President

	1988	1984	1980	1976
D	81,466 (31%)	80,918 (33%)	73,070 (29%)	86,898 (38%)
R	183,075 (69%)	160,491 (66%)	161,358 (65%)	139,352 (61%)
I			12,404 (5%)	

Campaign Finance

	Receipts	Receipts from PACs	Expend-itures
1988			
Burton (R)	$383,170	$141,170 (37%)	$333,723
Holland (D)	$12,319	$5,000 (41%)	$11,743
1986			
Burton (R)	$325,163	$143,292 (44%)	$215,790
McKenna (D)	$50,043	$6,500 (13%)	$48,045

Key Votes

1987	
Raise speed limit to 65 mph	Y
Approve Gephardt "fair trade" amendment	N
Ban testing of larger nuclear weapons	N
Delay "re-flagging" of Kuwaiti tankers	N
Approve tax-raising deficit-reduction bill	N
1988	
Approve aid to Nicaraguan contras	Y
Enact civil rights restoration bill over Reagan veto	N
Kill 60-day plant-closing notification measure	Y
Pass omnibus trade bill over Reagan veto	N
Approve death penalty for drug-related murders	Y
Bar federal funds for abortions in cases of rape and incest	Y
Oppose seven-day waiting period for purchase of handguns	Y

Voting Studies

	Presidential Support		Party Unity		Conservative Coalition	
Year	S	O	S	O	S	O
1988	84	16	96	2	95	0
1987	76	19	93	3	93	7
1986	81	18	94	4	96	4
1985	80	16	94	2	100	0
1984	73	20	93	3	90	5
1983	83	16	92	4	93	6

Interest Group Ratings

Year	ADA	ACU	AFL-CIO	CCUS
1988	0	100	0	93
1987	8	100	0	93
1986	5	100	21	89
1985	5	100	0	86
1984	0	83	23	86
1983	10	91	13	80

7 John T. Myers (R)

Of Covington — Elected 1966

Born: Feb. 8, 1927, Covington, Ind.
Education: Indiana State U., B.S. 1951.
Military Career: Army, 1945-46.
Occupation: Banker; farmer.
Family: Wife, Carol Carruthers; two children.
Religion: Episcopalian.
Political Career: No previous office.
Capitol Office: 2372 Rayburn Bldg. 20515; 225-5805.

In Washington: Myers is the kind of old-fashioned, middle-American moderate Republican that is practically becoming an endangered species in the House GOP Conference.

A banker, a Mason, an Elk and a Lion, and a former head of the Congressional Prayer Group, Myers has been schooled in the ways of bipartisanship by years of service on the House Appropriations Committee. In 1988, he voted with the GOP majority on a modest 60 percent of key legislative votes.

He has taken on a raft of assignments concerning matters that hit members closest to home: He is a member of the subcommittee that handles Congress' own budget. He sits on the Post Office Committee, which oversees members' pay and perquisites. He is even a member of the committee that supervises the House gym.

Myers is, in short, a member's member, as few of the GOP's young partisans ever will be.

He increasingly comes into conflict with these younger conservatives, who think Myers and other senior GOP appropriators are more loyal to their committees' products than to party principles of fiscal conservatism.

Myers applies his most determined efforts to protecting the spending prerogatives of the Appropriations Subcommittee on Energy and Water Development, where he is ranking Republican. He likes to describe the panel's spending measure as "an All-American bill" that would "touch every congressional district in our country directly."

He once said the provisions of the bill would help assure the supply of the electricity Americans use when they "plug the toaster in and turn on the electric stove and use our electric razors or the curling irons for the ladies," and the water "we drew this morning for our showers, that we use daily in our consumption, not only in our homes, but also in industry."

It is the subcommittee's control over the water projects that many members covet for their districts — and conservatives deride as "pork" — that makes the panel an important power base for Myers.

Though he can be a genial jokester in the Republican cloakroom, Myers is noted for playing hardball on bills he had a hand in, and he keeps close track of those members who vote with and against him. Once in a private meeting with Republicans, Myers pulled just such a list of names from his suit pocket and brandished it for all to see.

Myers can be sharp toward Republicans who try to implement their fiscal conservatism by moving to cut the energy and water bill. In mid-1987, he told some members they would lose pet projects if they supported efforts to cut the bill on the House floor. Saying it would be hard in a House-Senate conference to defend projects of members who did not support the whole bill, Myers later explained, "It's not a threat. It's a fact of life."

Although Myers is viewed suspiciously by activist conservative Republicans, he does have the minority leader's confidence. One sign of that trust was his appointment to be ranking Republican on the House ethics committee in mid-1988, just as the panel was beginning its investigation of Speaker Jim Wright.

Myers moved up to succeed South Carolina Republican Floyd D. Spence, who resigned from the ethics committee for health reasons, and he played a central role in the Wright inquiry. Some matters — such as the selection of the outside attorney to head the probe — were delegated almost entirely to Myers and ethics Chairman Julian C. Dixon of California. Myers came under heavy pressure from conservatives who feared Myers would go too easy on Wright.

But those concerns proved unjustified. Wright was toppled by the controversy unleashed by the ethics committee report based on the devastating findings of the investigator hired by Myers and Dixon.

At Home: Myers began his winning ways in 1966, when redistricting produced a 7th District without an incumbent. His 29 percent was enough to give him the GOP nomination over five opponents, one of whom, Daniel B. Crane, later served in the House from Illinois.

Indiana 7

West Central — Terre Haute; Lafayette

The 7th is the district of the Wabash River, a broad tributary of the Ohio that Hoosier chauvinists still rhapsodize about when they sing "My Indiana Home." The Wabash flows through six of the 14 counties in the district. It is the state's longest river and was responsible for the rapid development of the area in the early 19th century, when newcomers arrived in western Indiana via flatboats and steamers.

The Wabash crosses some of the richest glaciated farm land in the Midwest, land used primarily for grain and livestock farming. The voters here are the kind of solid Republican farmers whose opinions have determined the course of state politics over most of this century.

The 7th is Indiana's second-largest district in area, with only two real population centers — Terre Haute and Lafayette — at opposite ends of the district. Vigo County (Terre Haute) and Tippecanoe County (Lafayette) each account for about a fifth of the district's population.

Terre Haute, once part of a small coal-mining region that has since turned to light industry and food processing, has Democratic roots. Many of its citizens came originally from Indiana's southern hill country, rather than from the more prosperous Republican farm land to the north. Flanking Vigo County on the north and south are Vermillion and Sullivan counties, also supporting Democrats.

Lafayette, with its smaller twin, West Lafayette, rests comfortably in the Republican heartland, 85 miles north of Terre Haute. Tippecanoe County voters rarely swing to the Democratic Party. With its emphasis on agriculture and engineering, Purdue University, the economic mainstay of West Lafayette, has spawned a conservative, GOP-leaning academic community. The economy of the area is diversifying; a Subaru-Isuzu plant is being built in Lafayette. Due for completion at the end of 1989, it could eventually employ more than 3,000 people.

The most Republican counties in the 7th District, however, are Hendricks and Morgan, near Indianapolis. Here almost any GOP candidate can expect to receive at least twice as many votes as any Democrat. And as conservative homeowners move out of Indianapolis to outlying suburbs and small towns in these counties, the GOP margins continue to grow.

Population: 555,192. White 540,436 (97%), Black 9,381 (2%), Other 3,507 (1%). Spanish origin 3,483 (1%). 18 and over 403,139 (73%), 65 and over 62,715 (11%). Median age: 29.

As a small-town banker and farmer, Myers long had been active in the Republican Party, mostly on the local level in Covington. He also worked in Young Republican ranks.

For years, Democrats helped Myers by nominating candidates of limited appeal. In 1966 he defeated Elden C. Tipton, a former naval officer and farmer who had already been beaten twice before. Tipton tried two more campaigns against Myers but never came close. His son, J. Elden Tipton, ran a similarly weak campaign against Myers in 1976.

By 1978, many Democrats in the 7th were saying that Myers' only real strength was his ability to draw the Tiptons as his opposition. That year, Democrat Charlotte Zietlow, a former Bloomington City Council president, ran a spirited race against Myers, basing her campaign on the claim that consumers were being ripped off by utility-rate increases. But Myers' rural support canceled out Democratic strength in Bloomington, and he enjoyed a comfortable win.

Redistricting in 1981 significantly altered Myers' constituency, but not to his detriment. Democratic Bloomington was moved from the 7th and the more conservative city of Lafayette was added, as well as GOP turf near Indianapolis. Running in the reshaped district in 1982, Myers faced a credible but underfinanced foe, Stephen S. Bonney, a former Purdue University professor. Myers got 62 percent.

Democrats had a vigorous challenger in 1984 in Art Smith, a 29-year-old former congressional aide, but he lost badly. That scared away significant opposition in 1986 and made Democratic leaders pessimistic about their prospects in 1988. Their nominee, 27-year-old attorney Mark R. Waterfill, wound up running the strongest Democratic campaign of the 1980s. Even so, he failed to reach 40 percent.

Committees

Standards of Official Conduct (Ranking)

Appropriations (3rd of 22 Republicans)
Energy and Water Development (ranking); Legislative Branch; Rural Development, Agriculture and Related Agencies

Post Office and Civil Service (3rd of 9 Republicans)
Compensation and Employee Benefits (ranking); Postal Personnel and Modernization

Elections

1988 General

John T. Myers (R)	130,578	(62%)
Mark R. Waterfill (D)	80,738	(38%)

1986 General

John T. Myers (R)	104,965	(67%)
L. Eugene Smith (D)	49,675	(32%)

Previous Winning Percentages: **1984** (67%) **1982** (62%) **1980** (66%) **1978** (56%) **1976** (63%) **1974** (57%) **1972** (62%) **1970** (57%) **1968** (60%) **1966** (54%)

District Vote For President

	1988	1984	1980	1976
D	79,244 (37%)	73,751 (33%)	77,802 (34%)	98,966 (44%)
R	136,233 (63%)	147,763 (66%)	136,445 (59%)	126,314 (56%)
I			12,080 (5%)	

Campaign Finance

	Receipts	Receipts from PACs	Expend-itures
1988			
Myers (R)	$171,287	$96,500 (56%)	$163,280
Waterfill (D)	$67,889	$34,800 (51%)	$67,591
1986			
Myers (R)	$178,884	$79,000 (44%)	$161,277
Smith (D)	$27,140	$500 (2%)	$27,139

Key Votes

1987	
Raise speed limit to 65 mph	Y
Approve Gephardt "fair trade" amendment	N
Ban testing of larger nuclear weapons	N
Delay "re-flagging" of Kuwaiti tankers	?
Approve tax-raising deficit-reduction bill	N
1988	
Approve aid to Nicaraguan contras	Y
Enact civil rights restoration bill over Reagan veto	N
Kill 60-day plant-closing notification measure	Y
Pass omnibus trade bill over Reagan veto	N
Approve death penalty for drug-related murders	Y
Bar federal funds for abortions in cases of rape and incest	Y
Oppose seven-day waiting period for purchase of handguns	Y

Voting Studies

	Presidential Support		Party Unity		Conservative Coalition	
Year	**S**	**O**	**S**	**O**	**S**	**O**
1988	57	33	60	34	82	13
1987	65	29	59	36	88	7
1986	67	31	54	45	82	18
1985	69	28	58	39	91	9
1984	59	40	69	26	93	7
1983	68	27	72	25	88	8
1982	70	27	84	16	89	11
1981	75	25	77	21	91	9

Interest Group Ratings

Year	ADA	ACU	AFL-CIO	CCUS
1988	15	83	15	92
1987	8	87	19	60
1986	20	91	36	50
1985	20	71	18	73
1984	15	74	15	50
1983	10	83	0	90
1982	5	85	15	86
1981	0	93	29	83

8 Frank McCloskey (D)

Of Bloomington — Elected 1982

Born: June 12, 1939, Philadelphia, Pa.
Education: Indiana U., A.B. 1968, J.D. 1971.
Military Career: Air Force, 1957-61.
Occupation: Lawyer; journalist.
Family: Wife, Roberta Ann Barker; two children.
Religion: Roman Catholic.
Political Career: Democratic nominee for Ind. House, 1970; mayor of Bloomington, 1972-83.
Capitol Office: 127 Cannon Bldg. 20515; 225-4636.

In Washington: For many House Republicans, McCloskey's presence in Congress symbolizes what they regard as the highhanded arrogance of the chamber's Democratic leadership. The majority's decision to seat McCloskey in 1985 — after his hotly disputed four-vote election margin — sowed seeds of discontent on the GOP side that ultimately strengthened the hand of confrontational conservatives such as Georgia's Newt Gingrich, the newly elected Republican whip.

For his part, McCloskey has worked very hard since the 1985 controversy to become known as something other than the "four-vote wonder." He has applied himself to the work of his Armed Services and Post Office committees, and now he also has a seat on Foreign Affairs.

McCloskey's highest-profile legislative ventures involved President Reagan's strategic defense initiative (SDI). A member of the Armed Services Subcommittee on Research and Development in the 100th Congress, McCloskey was not unalterably opposed to SDI research: The $3.85 billion he proposed in a 1987 amendment was higher than the $3.2 billion approved by his subcommittee. But like many Democrats, McCloskey is skeptical of SDI's value and worried about its effect on arms control negotiations.

He particularly opposes early deployment of SDI. This sentiment moved McCloskey to attempt to block development of the "space-based kinetic kill vehicle," a heat-seeking rocket designed to destroy Soviet missiles. It could be the linchpin for any near-term SDI deployment.

When the Research and Development panel considered the defense authorization bill in 1987, McCloskey attached an amendment to bar development and testing of the rocket. After the full committee dropped the provision, McCloskey, joined by South Carolina Democrat John M. Spratt Jr., presented a similar amendment during House deliberations; it was defeated on a 203-216 vote.

McCloskey also has been engaged in some lower-profile defense issues. In his position on Armed Services' Investigations Subcommittee, McCloskey launched a probe of military flight accidents linked to the use of "night vision goggles." His interest was spurred by a 1988 nighttime collision between two Army helicopters at Fort Campbell, Ky., which killed 18 servicemen.

Safety issues also mark McCloskey's work on Post Office and Civil Service, where he chairs the Postal Personnel and Modernization Subcommittee. During the 100th Congress, McCloskey held a hearing on whether toxic biological agents, such as anthrax, should be banned from U.S. mail shipment. However, after contacting laboratories, McCloskey determined that a ban could be damaging to medical research, and called instead for strict enforcement of existing regulations.

McCloskey's overall record put him on the liberal side of the Democratic spectrum: In both 1987 and 1988, he voted nearly 80 percent of the time against Reagan's position on House legislation. But since his near-defeat in 1984, McCloskey's work for local interests has placated some of his conservative critics. In 1988, both Evansville daily newspapers noted their continued discomfort with McCloskey's liberalism, but strongly endorsed him based on his efforts to bring highway funding, mine reclamation projects and other federal monies to the 8th District.

That McCloskey would ever engender broad support at home seemed difficult to imagine in the aftermath of his 1984 election war with GOP challenger Richard D. McIntyre. Attacking McCloskey as much too liberal for the southern Indiana district, and riding Reagan's long coattails, McIntyre had McCloskey on the run.

In fact, McIntyre was certified the winner of the contest at one point. Though the election night canvass showed McCloskey leading by 72 votes, a full recount by state officials showed McIntyre with a 418-vote lead; more than 4,800 ballots were discarded for technical reasons.

But before the formal swearing-in, Democrats asked McIntyre to step aside. They

Indiana 8

Southwest — Evansville

The Democrats have now held the 8th in four straight elections, and McCloskey's solid victory in 1988 marked the first time since 1972 that a candidate for the 8th has received more than 60 percent of the vote. The Democrat seems to be bringing electoral stability to a district that was once among the nation's most politically marginal. It was Republican until 1974, Democratic for the next four years, and then Republican for four years before switching back to the Democrats in 1982.

Evansville, with 129,000 people, is the economic center of southern Indiana. The state's fourth-largest city, it has a diversified industrial base and a largely middle-class population. From the time when former U.S. Sen. Vance Hartke was mayor in the 1950s, the city has tried to entice new industry to replace major corporations that pulled out after World War II. In recent years, Evansville has taken an interest in its history as an important Ohio River port; commercial and cultural offerings are envisioned in a redeveloped riverbank sector.

Evansville's political influence extends over the southern half of the 8th. More than half the district's voters watch Evansville television stations, and the city provides jobs for a large area along the Ohio River. The Democratic heritage of the river counties, which dates back to their original settlement 150 years ago, remains strong. McCloskey carried Vanderburgh County (Evansville) with 68 percent in 1988, and all the counties around Vanderburgh also backed him.

Before 1966, the district stretched nearly the entire width of the state along the Ohio River. A series of redistricting changes diminished the clout of the southern river counties somewhat, and at the same time moved the 8th north into more prosperous, Republican farm areas.

The 8th now stretches north all the way to Bloomington, taking in the southern, most prosperous third of the city and most of the surrounding Monroe County suburbs. This area normally votes Republican, although it does include some students and faculty from Indiana University. In the last round of redistricting, the GOP-controlled Legislature deliberately placed most of the university community in the neighboring 9th, an unsuccessful effort to help keep the district Republican in 1982.

Population: 546,744. White 528,659 (97%), Black 14,832 (3%). Spanish origin 2,461 (1%). 18 and over 395,151 (72%), 65 and over 70,673 (13%). Median age: 31.

---

claimed that the election results from the 8th were such a tangle that the real winner was not yet known, and they proposed holding the seat vacant pending an investigation by the House. That proposal passed on a party-line vote.

The House Administration Committee appointed a task force of two Democrats and one Republican to oversee another recount; auditors from the U.S. General Accounting Office did the counting. The task force directed the auditors to ignore many of the technicalities that had prompted Indiana officials to throw out ballots, and when the final count was announced April 22, McCloskey led by four votes.

California's Bill Thomas, the GOP representative on the task force, said the Democratic-directed recount was "nothing short of a rape." Many Republicans threatened retribution; some proposed physically blocking McCloskey from taking the oath of office. Such threats hardened the Democrats' resolve to seat McCloskey, although many agreed that one seat was not worth the rancor that resulted.

Republican leaders realized that sustained disruption of House proceedings could delay Reagan's legislative initiatives. So in the end, the GOP settled for a momentary walkout when McCloskey was sworn in May 1.

At Home: As soon as McCloskey took his seat after the recount dispute in 1985, Republicans vowed revenge at the polls. National GOP strategists felt that 8th District voters were sufficiently convinced of Democratic misconduct to make McIntyre a likely rematch winner, but McIntyre was not so sure; he delayed announcing a second House campaign and toyed with running instead for statewide office. Eventually, though, he agreed to take on McCloskey.

In retrospect, it is easy to see why McIntyre hesitated. He did not have the Reagan coattails that boosted him in 1984, and he still had the disadvantage of coming from small Lawrence County, in the 8th's northeast corner. McCloskey won in 1984 largely because of his support in populous Evansville, and there was little reason to believe he would be much weaker there, or McIntyre much stronger, in 1986.

And as it turned out, the recount issue was not much on voters' minds when they went to the polls in November, a full 18 months after McCloskey's disputed seating. McIntyre himself admitted that people were weary of the dispute. He looked for another issue, but never found a good one.

McIntyre chose to play hardball, reaching back into the Democrat's record as Bloomington mayor in the 1970s to argue that McCloskey had been irresponsible in his denunciations of the Vietnam War and soft in dealing with drug offenses. But he probably went too far in charging that McCloskey had smoked opium; no convincing evidence was ever found.

McCloskey, meanwhile, had played effective incumbent politics, talking up his work for the Crane Naval Weapons Center and bringing Armed Services Chairman Les Aspin to promise that the center would not be closed. McCloskey also reaped valuable publicity investigating possible PCB contamination from a Union Carbide plant on the district border.

McIntyre-McCloskey II was not another cliffhanger. The incumbent won Evansville overwhelmingly, carried nine of 16 counties, and scored a comfortable 13,000-vote victory.

In 1988, the Republican nominee was John L. Myers, a newspaper publisher whose strongest asset may have been his name's similarity to that of the incumbent GOP congressman in the neighboring 7th District, John T. Myers. For the first time, McCloskey had an easy time.

Were it not for an auto accident, McCloskey might never have made it to the House. The Indiana Legislature redrew the 8th in 1981 to make it secure for GOP Rep. Joel Deckard, and at the outset of his 1982 campaign, he was favored over challenger McCloskey. But Deckard drove his car into a tree in early October and admitted afterward that he had been drinking. That incident, combined with Depression-level unemployment in parts of the 8th, boosted McCloskey to a 51 percent win.

A former newspaper reporter, McCloskey was first elected Bloomington's mayor in 1971, the year he finished law school. He won that race with the help of students at Indiana University, who were attracted by his liberal politics. But after his 1975 re-election campaign, which he won by a narrower margin against a weaker opponent, he modified some of his more liberal positions and led a successful drive to promote economic development and neighborhood restoration in Bloomington. Those efforts broadened his base beyond the academic community, and he was re-elected in 1979.

Committees

Armed Services (19th of 31 Democrats)
Investigations; Procurement and Military Nuclear Systems

Foreign Affairs (27th of 28 Democrats)
Africa

Post Office and Civil Service (9th of 15 Democrats)
Postal Personnel and Modernization (chairman); Civil Service

Elections

1988 General		
Frank McCloskey (D)	141,355	(62%)
John L. Myers (R)	87,321	(38%)
1988 Primary		
Frank McCloskey (D)	62,944	(89%)
John W. Taylor (D)	8,101	(11%)
1986 General		
Frank McCloskey (D)	106,662	(53%)
Richard D. McIntyre (R)	93,586	(47%)

Previous Winning Percentages: 1984 (50%) **1982** (51%)

District Vote For President

	1988	1984	1980	1976
D	97,530 (42%)	88,851 (38%)	95,833 (40%)	115,188 (49%)
R	133,017 (57%)	143,526 (61%)	127,427 (54%)	118,212 (50%)
I			10,846 (5%)	

Campaign Finance

	Receipts	Receipts from PACs	Expend-itures
1988			
McCloskey (D)	$549,096	$342,058 (62%)	$551,484
Myers (R)	$132,638	$19,665 (15%)	$130,243
1986			
McCloskey (D)	$622,667	$337,686 (54%)	$625,188
McIntyre (R)	$574,060	$251,557 (44%)	$581,786

Key Votes

1987	
Raise speed limit to 65 mph	Y
Approve Gephardt "fair trade" amendment	Y
Ban testing of larger nuclear weapons	Y
Delay "re-flagging" of Kuwaiti tankers	Y
Approve tax-raising deficit-reduction bill	Y
1988	
Approve aid to Nicaraguan contras	N
Enact civil rights restoration bill over Reagan veto	Y
Kill 60-day plant-closing notification measure	N
Pass omnibus trade bill over Reagan veto	Y
Approve death penalty for drug-related murders	Y
Bar federal funds for abortions in cases of rape and incest	N
Oppose seven-day waiting period for purchase of handguns	Y

Voting Studies

	Presidential Support		Party Unity		Conservative Coalition	
Year	**S**	**O**	**S**	**O**	**S**	**O**
1988	20	78	91	7	29	71
1987	20	79	90	5	28	72
1986	24	76	84	13	52	48
1985	29 †	71 †	89 †	10 †	27 †	73 †
1984	37	59	84	9	25	69
1983	17	82	89	10	29	69

† Not eligible for all recorded votes.

Interest Group Ratings

Year	ADA	ACU	AFL-CIO	CCUS
1988	75	16	100	21
1987	80	4	94	14
1986	55	18	86	50
1985	68	28	76	30
1984	75	13	85	31
1983	85	22	94	20

9 Lee H. Hamilton (D)

Of Nashville — Elected 1964

Born: April 20, 1931, Daytona Beach, Fla.
Education: DePauw U., B.A. 1952; attended Goethe U., Frankfurt, West Germany, 1952-53; Indiana U., J.D. 1956.
Occupation: Lawyer.
Family: Wife, Nancy Nelson; three children.
Religion: Methodist.
Political Career: No previous office.
Capitol Office: 2187 Rayburn Bldg. 20515; 225-5315.

In Washington: For House Democrats, Hamilton's is the quiet voice that resounds. During a quarter-century in Congress, the professorial Hoosier has built a reservoir of respect few members can match, thanks to his intellectual power and his unquestioned personal integrity.

Colleagues' one complaint is that he so rarely taps that reservoir, that he shies from the bold steps that might antagonize one faction or another. Judicious caution, the key to Hamilton's influence and credibility, can also be his handicap. Never was that more clear than in the evolution of the Iran-contra scandal.

In the 100th Congress, Hamilton did a much-commended job as House chairman of the special committee that investigated the Reagan administration's 1985-86 arms sales to Iran and the diversion of profits to the Nicaraguan rebels in violation of a ban on contra aid. Yet the facts of the affair might have emerged sooner if Hamilton, as Intelligence Committee chairman in 1985 and 1986, had not held back from probing early reports of illegal White House activity in his reluctance to engage in partisan warfare.

Hamilton's hesitation was all the more crucial since he is one of Congress' most respected foreign policy voices, a longtime member of the Foreign Affairs Committee besides being a former Intelligence chairman. "One of the emerging lessons from these events," Hamilton said as the scandal unfolded, "is that we did not have sufficient oversight." The committees involved, he added, including his own, "did not do as good a job as we should have done."

But, as he was to ask over and over, what can Congress do — what can he do — if questions are met with administration lies? The initial lie was told to Hamilton directly. In September 1985, he had called then-national security adviser Robert C. McFarlane before Intelligence; McFarlane assured Hamilton that National Security Council aide Lt. Col. Oliver L. North had not "in any way been involved with funds for the contras." "I for one am willing to take you at your word," Hamilton replied, and the matter was dropped.

That incident, and the subsequent revelations during the Iran-contra hearings, seemed to leave this minister's son with both a sense of betrayal and a penitence about his own role. How that might affect his lawyerly style is unclear, particularly given the change of administrations and President Bush's pledge to cooperate with Congress. But when the affair followed Hamilton into the 101st Congress, he was quick to respond.

Documents disclosed in North's 1989 criminal trial provided new evidence to contradict Reagan's and then-Vice President Bush's denials of their involvement, and raised questions about why the Iran-contra committee did not get the documents. Hamilton in April asked Bush for explanations and urged Intelligence, of which he is no longer a member, to investigate.

House Democratic leaders' selection of Hamilton to chair the Iran-contra hearings — jointly with a Senate team, as it turned out — was a reflection of their confidence that the Indianan, with his straight, crew-cut appearance and low-key, articulate style, would set a fair and non-prosecutorial tone for a national television audience. He asked few questions through the summer hearings, but gave lengthy summations following key figures' testimony that laid calm emphasis on their evidence of lies and subversion of foreign policy.

That occasionally irritated House Republican members of the panel; one accused Hamilton of "pontificating," of sounding "like a judge passing judgment on a witness." Generally, however, Republicans gave Hamilton high marks for his fairness in conducting the proceedings.

To State Department aide Elliott Abrams, who testified that his past responses to Congress had been misleading but literally correct, Hamilton replied, "The object here is not to avoid a perjury indictment.... The object is to make the Constitution of the United States work. Congress is a partner, not an adversary." In impassioned remarks to North, Hamilton said, "I don't have any doubt at all, Colonel

Indiana 9

Southeast — Bloomington; New Albany

This is the largest and least urbanized district in the state. The hilly forests and farm lands are more akin to Kentucky and parts of southern Ohio and Illinois than to the flat Hoosier farm lands farther north. Many of those who settled here came from the South and brought with them their Democratic allegiances.

Poultry and cattle are the major agricultural commodities of the area, which is also the center of some of the nation's finest and most abundant limestone quarries. Stone cutters, like those portrayed in the movie "Breaking Away," regularly excavate rock that is used for building material throughout the country.

The Indiana suburbs of Louisville, Ky., along the Ohio River, make up the district's largest concentration of voters. The focal point of this mostly middle-income area is New Albany, which lies just across the Ohio River from Louisville and is the district's largest city, with 37,000 people.

In the days of the steamboats, when Indiana's economy depended upon the cargoes that came up the Ohio River, New Albany was the state's largest city. Although the river's contribution to the local livelihood has dropped off considerably in the last hundred years, the 9th still depends upon river traffic and industries located along the river bank for many jobs.

In its northwest corner, the 9th takes in most of the Democratic parts of Bloomington, the home of Indiana University (enrollment 33,000). The district boundary runs along 3rd Street in Bloomington, placing the northern two-thirds of the city's 53,000 residents in the 9th. Included in that area is all of Indiana University's campus as well as most of the off-campus housing and faculty neighborhoods.

Population: 544,873. White 530,291 (97%), Black 10,205 (2%). Spanish origin 3,180 (1%). 18 and over 383,018 (70%), 65 and over 56,470 (10%). Median age: 28.

North, that you are a patriot. . . . But there is another form of patriotism that is unique to democracy. It resides in those who have a deep respect for the rule of law and faith in America's democratic traditions."

Hamilton accepted the testimony of Vice Adm. John M. Poindexter, McFarlane's successor as national security adviser, that he did not inform Reagan about the diversion of funds to the contras; Hamilton's co-chairman, Sen. Daniel K. Inouye, was more skeptical. Ultimately, the committee's majority concluded that Reagan was responsible for the mistakes and illegalities of his "cabal of zealots." But Hamilton had to admit again that Congress did not get to the bottom of the affair.

Hamilton's two years heading Intelligence in the 99th Congress marked perhaps the first time in his career that did not evoke universal praise. But overall, he handled the panel's work with his customary fairness and grace, maintaining the independent approach to the CIA that had established the committee's reputation.

His style and policy views have formed during his long service on Foreign Affairs, which he joined as a freshman in 1965. He is chairman of its Europe and Middle East Subcommittee, and one of a handful of members who have made the once-passive Foreign Affairs equal in stature to its traditionally dominant Senate counterpart. He is now the committee's No. 2 Democrat, and is 14 years younger than current Chairman Dante B. Fascell of Florida.

Despite his evenhandedness, Hamilton does have strongly held views. He was a leader of the opposition to Reagan's contra-aid policy from the time it was disclosed in the early 1980s; he said diplomacy involving Central American leaders would have a better chance of success than trying to force Nicaragua to negotiate democratic changes "with a gun to its head."

He drafted a compromise proposal in 1985 designed to aid Nicaraguan refugees and promote a regional peace treaty — "tough-minded diplomacy" he called it. But the House voted for contra aid, which Hamilton opposed even though it was limited to "humanitarian" assistance. A year later, he again was on the losing side as the House gave the contras an additional $100 million, mostly military aid.

Behind Hamilton's stance is a basic discomfort with an American military presence in Central America. "The problems there are fundamentally economic and social, and we're responding with military might," he once said. However, in 1988 the pragmatic Hamilton broke ranks with Democratic anti-contra purists to support a humanitarian aid proposal that House Democratic leaders put forward to block Reagan's military aid request. And in 1989 Hamilton voted for a humanitarian aid compromise drafted by congressional leaders and Secretary of State James A. Baker III.

Hamilton believes emphatically that Congress should be consulted as an equal partner in foreign policy. In 1986, he unsuccessfully opposed Reagan's covert aid to guerrillas in Angola, saying it amounted to a major policy shift that should be publicly debated. The president, he said, "cannot expect sustained support for foreign policy initiatives, including covert action operations, that are generally unpopular or where a covert action mechanism can be viewed as having been chosen to avoid public debate or a congressional vote on the matter."

Lawmakers' suspicion of the Reagan administration's failure to inform them, or to carry out Congress' mandates, only led them to add more such strings to foreign aid bills. Against his instincts, Hamilton was a leader in the effort. With Central America in mind, in 1987 he sponsored provisions limiting the president's flexibility to decide which countries get aid, how much and what type. With the end of the Reagan administration, however, Hamilton headed a bipartisan Foreign Affairs task force that in early 1989 recommended dropping many such limitations in return for the administration's cooperation.

On his subcommittee, Hamilton has sought to steer a middle course between the panel's dominant pro-Israel faction and those who want to strike some balance toward friendly Arab states. Unlike many in Congress, he is not reflexively opposed to arms sales to Arab nations, but instead considers requests case by case. It is the kind of controversial issue Hamilton likes to avoid, yet his position makes that impossible. Underlying his approach is a sense that U.S. arms do not much advance Mideast peace, but that realpolitik requires the United States to accommodate moderate Arab states and to help secure them against their radical neighbors — as long as any military aid is not a direct threat to Israel.

Hamilton does maintain good relations with the formidable Israel lobby; to do otherwise would threaten his standing and influence among his colleagues. But he sharply criticized Israeli raids on Palestinian camps in Lebanon and, in the 98th Congress, was one of only four committee members who voted against a House resolution seeking to move the U.S. Embassy in Israel from Tel Aviv to Jerusalem — a high priority for many supporters of Israel. In 1988 he was one of 37 signatories to a letter protesting Israel's deportation of a Palestinian-American advocate of non-violent resistance in the occupied territories.

From the start of his House career, Hamilton has enjoyed his colleagues' high regard. He was president of the huge freshman Democratic class elected in 1964. In 1965, he received widespread attention with a letter to President Johnson saying it was "time to pause" in action on Great Society social programs.

In 1972, Hamilton sponsored the first measure that Foreign Affairs adopted to stop the Vietnam War. The proposal, which called for a U.S. withdrawal contingent on release of all prisoners of war and on a cease-fire plan with North Vietnam, later was killed on the House floor, but it helped set the stage for later congressional actions to end the war.

In the post-Watergate period of public concern for government integrity, Hamilton was one of the members to whom the House turned for guidance on ethics issues. In 1977 he chaired a task force that recommended new House rules limiting members' outside income and honoraria. In 1979-80, amid a rash of scandals, Hamilton was the dominant Democrat on the House ethics committee rather than its mercurial chairman, Charles E. Bennett of Florida.

He worked on the committee's recommendation of censure for Michigan Democrat Charles C. Diggs Jr., convicted in a kickback scheme, and on the Abscam bribery investigations. On Abscam, Hamilton broke with the committee when it recommended that Pennsylvania Democrat Michael "Ozzie" Myers be expelled following his bribery conviction. The matter came to the floor the day the House was to recess for the 1980 elections, and Hamilton said the rushed atmosphere denied Myers due process. But the House voted to expel Myers, making him the first member in history ousted for corruption.

In 1988, Hamilton was among those considered as a running mate for Democratic presidential nominee Michael S. Dukakis. By the next year, the ethics spotlight was on the House again, with the resignations under fire of Speaker Jim Wright and Democratic Whip Tony Coelho. Hamilton was briefly discussed — privately among House Democrats and publicly in the press — as a potential leadership draftee who could help restore the image of the party and the House. But even his admirers predicted Hamilton's caution would dissuade him. "I really had a large number of contacts suggesting that I do [run]," he said. "But I am not pursuing them."

At Home: In the early months of 1989, Hamilton was contemplating an unexpected and momentous question in Indiana. Party leaders were urging him to challenge junior GOP Sen. Daniel R. Coats in the 1990 special election to fill the remainder of Vice President Dan Quayle's Senate term.

Despite the limits of his base in the state's rural southeast, Indiana political observers considered him the party's most promising candidate against Coats. So great was the respect for Hamilton in both the state and national party structures that the nomination was almost literally his to refuse.

But refuse it he did. The special Senate election will coincide with the regular congressional election, so Hamilton would have been forced to sacrifice his seat and 13 terms of House seniority to take on Coats. Even if he won, he would have faced another campaign just two years later, when the Quayle term expired. For a cautious man like Hamilton, that was a venture worth walking away from.

The son and brother of ministers, Hamilton has a devotion to work that comes out of his traditional Methodist family. From his days in Evansville High School in 1948, when he helped propel the basketball team to the state finals, to his race for Congress in 1964, he displayed a quiet, consistent determination.

When he graduated from DePauw University in 1952, he received an award as the outstanding senior. He accepted a scholarship to Goethe University in Germany for further study.

Hamilton practiced law for a while in Chicago, but soon decided to settle in Columbus, Ind., where his interest in politics led him into the local Democratic Party. In 1960 he was chairman of the Bartholomew County (Columbus) Citizens for Kennedy. Two years later he managed Birch Bayh's Senate campaign in Columbus.

He was the consensus choice of the local Democratic organization for the 9th District House nomination in 1964, and won the primary with 46 percent of the vote in a field of five candidates. He went on to defeat longtime Republican Rep. Earl Wilson, a crusty fiscal watchdog who had represented the district for almost a quarter of a century.

Hamilton has been re-elected easily ever since. After a few years, Republicans gave up on defeating him and added Democrats to his district to give GOP candidates a better chance elsewhere in the state. In 1976, for the first time in the history of the district, the Republicans put up no candidate at all. In 1980 and 1984, Reagan's popularity in Indiana caused Hamilton no trouble.

Conceding that Hamilton was unbeatable, the GOP Legislature made no effort to weaken him in 1981 redistricting, although they removed Hamilton's hometown of Columbus from the district. He moved to the next county, was re-elected with 67 percent and has won since by similar margins.

Committees

Foreign Affairs (2nd of 28 Democrats)
Europe and the Middle East (chairman)

Science, Space and Technology (19th of 30 Democrats)
International Scientific Cooperation; Science, Research and Technology

Joint Economic (Chairman)
Economic Goals and Intergovernmental Policy (chairman); Economic Growth, Trade and Taxes; International Economic Policy

Elections

1988 General		
Lee H. Hamilton (D)	147,193	(71%)
Floyd Eugene Coats (R)	60,946	(29%)
1986 General		
Lee H. Hamilton (D)	120,586	(72%)
Robert Walter Kilroy (R)	46,398	(28%)

Previous Winning Percentages: **1984** (65%) **1982** (67%) **1980** (64%) **1978** (66%) **1976** (100%) **1974** (71%) **1972** (63%) **1970** (63%) **1968** (54%) **1966** (54%) **1964** (54%)

District Vote For President

	1988	1984	1980	1976
D	89,744 (42%)	93,283 (40%)	92,931 (43%)	109,023 (52%)
R	123,198 (58%)	139,901 (60%)	112,568 (52%)	98,908 (47%)
I			8,747 (4%)	

Campaign Finance

	Receipts	Receipts from PACs	Expenditures
1988			
Hamilton (D)	$369,547	$152,066 (41%)	$333,957
1986			
Hamilton (D)	$286,915	$124,400 (43%)	$306,485
Kilroy (R)	$17,276	$100 (1%)	$16,610

Key Votes

1987	
Raise speed limit to 65 mph	Y
Approve Gephardt "fair trade" amendment	Y
Ban testing of larger nuclear weapons	Y
Delay "re-flagging" of Kuwaiti tankers	N
Approve tax-raising deficit-reduction bill	N
1988	
Approve aid to Nicaraguan contras	N
Enact civil rights restoration bill over Reagan veto	Y
Kill 60-day plant-closing notification measure	N
Pass omnibus trade bill over Reagan veto	Y
Approve death penalty for drug-related murders	N
Bar federal funds for abortions in cases of rape and incest	Y
Oppose seven-day waiting period for purchase of handguns	Y

Voting Studies

	Presidential Support		Party Unity		Conservative Coalition	
Year	S	O	S	O	S	O
1988	25	74	88	12	47	50
1987	26	74	84	16	51	49
1986	33	67	83	17	48	52
1985	38	63	82	18	42	56
1984	49	51	71	29	54	46
1983	35	65	82	17	42	58
1982	47	52	66	33	58	42
1981	47	51	71	27	56	44

Interest Group Ratings

Year	ADA	ACU	AFL-CIO	CCUS
1988	85	8	100	36
1987	72	9	69	47
1986	55	23	57	56
1985	60	33	69	57
1984	55	42	54	38
1983	75	17	71	45
1982	70	18	80	45
1981	65	20	67	28

10 Andrew Jacobs Jr. (D)

Of Indianapolis — Elected 1964

Did not serve 1973-75.

Born: Feb. 24, 1932, Indianapolis, Ind.
Education: Indiana U., B.S. 1954, LL.B. 1958.
Military Career: Marine Corps, 1950-52.
Occupation: Lawyer.
Family: Wife, Kimberly Hood.
Religion: Roman Catholic.
Political Career: Ind. House, 1959-61; Democratic nominee for U.S. House, 1962; defeated for re-election to U.S. House, 1972; re-elected, 1974.
Capitol Office: 2313 Rayburn Bldg. 20515; 225-4011.

In Washington: Jacobs marches to drummers even Thoreau might not hear, but his eccentricity is so appealing back home that he has become an exception within Congress in yet another regard: Despite one long-ago defeat that would have shocked most members into hoarding a massive campaign treasury, Jacobs refuses lobbyists' money, spends little and still scores solid re-election victories.

Democrats and Republicans alike in Indianapolis seem attracted by the very traits that make Jacobs an outsider in House politics after nearly a quarter-century in Congress. He is outspoken to the point of showmanship in his fiscal conservatism and attention to federal waste. He opposes lawmakers' pay raises, perks and what he views as payoffs from special-interest groups. While he is liberal on social questions and dovish on defense, he is best known as independent and unpredictable.

He is a self-styled and sharp-tongued government skinflint, congressional moralist and political maverick. Those are roles Jacobs seems to relish, though he does so at some cost to his effectiveness within a collegial body. "I am not the best go-alonger in the House," he once acknowledged. "Frankly, sometimes I do not get along very well." He then complained of waiting 19 hours to offer an amendment but being "constantly bumped."

Jacobs' manner is perhaps least suited to the tightly disciplined Ways and Means Committee. But he is senior enough there that he cannot be ignored. And he has not been; the American Medical Association, seeking revenge for Jacobs' actions as chairman of the Health Subcommittee, spent over $300,000 in a futile bid to defeat him in 1986. Since the 100th Congress, Jacobs has headed the Social Security Subcommittee, where he aggressively monitored the program's operation for the final two years of the Reagan administration.

As chairman, Jacobs has proposed making the Social Security Administration an independent agency, to prevent the Treasury from dipping into its reserves as was done during the Reagan administration. Such action is unlikely, however, because as long as the program is included within the federal budget, its surplus makes the deficit look smaller.

During the 99th Congress, Jacobs chose not to chair a subcommittee. Democrat James R. Jones of Oklahoma had returned to an active role at Ways and Means after his term as Budget Committee chairman expired, and his claim to head a subcommittee triggered a musical chairs process that unseated one existing chairman. California Democrat Pete Stark claimed the Health Subcommittee that was Jacobs' in the previous two Congresses.

Jacobs' response was unusual for the House, but typical of him. He had the seniority to claim the Public Assistance panel, but declined, saying he did not want to displace its chairman, Harold E. Ford of Tennessee, because Ford had the expertise for the job.

Jacobs had never seemed particularly enthusiastic about chairing the Health Subcommittee. On taking over in 1981, he said he did so "without excitement," and only because "it was what was left."

Perhaps surprisingly, given his nonchalance, the subcommittee did some important work while Jacobs chaired it. He won a crucial victory in 1983 in cutting the Medicare budget, although much of the impetus came from the Reagan administration. When the Social Security reform bill reached Ways and Means, Jacobs added a Medicare payment plan setting fixed costs for inpatient treatment of various diseases. For the first time, prices paid were to be linked to services delivered.

Jacobs also took a tough approach toward Medicare payments to doctors, which ultimately provoked their lobby's costly effort to eliminate him politically. He pushed to freeze those payments, and to prevent physicians from charging patients extra fees beyond those Medicare paid. "Vote for the canes, not for the stethoscopes," he said.

Indiana 10

Indianapolis

Indianapolis has a larger population than Boston or Washington, D.C., but it has retained a small-city flavor. It does not have the ethnic mixture of other areas in the industrial Midwest; most of its white residents are Protestants with small-town roots in Indiana or neighboring states, and they still reflect those roots after a generation or more of urban life.

The city's diversified economy ranges from pharmaceuticals (Eli Lilly) and grocery store chains (Kroger) to automotive plants (Ford, General Motors and Chrysler). Also contributing to the local economy are state government and the Fort Benjamin Harrison Army base.

The 10th includes about 70 percent of Indianapolis' population, leaving out the heavily Republican section in northern Washington Township. The major Democratic strength in the district lies in Center Township, which is about 40 percent black and contributes more than a third of the district's vote. Center Township is large enough to tilt the 10th Democratic even though Indianapolis' white population is more conservative than in most cities of comparable size. In 1988, the 10th was one of just two districts in Dan Quayle's Indiana to vote for the Democratic White House ticket.

North of the downtown area, behind the old mansions that line Meridian Street, are middle-income, integrated neighborhoods with large trees and broad streets. This area, in the southern part of Washington Township, has been loyal to Democratic House candidates, particularly Jacobs, who grew up here.

The western side of the district features the nationally famous town of Speedway and its Memorial Day classic, the Indianapolis 500. When not overrun with race-car enthusiasts, this is a white-collar, middle-income area that often votes Republican.

Population: 541,811. White 386,866 (71%), Black 148,711 (27%), Other 3,428 (1%). Spanish origin 5,288 (1%). 18 and over 384,402 (71%), 65 and over 57,747 (11%). Median age: 28.

But in the 100th Congress, Jacobs shelved his concern for the pocketbooks of the elderly and taxpayers when a corporate constituent's interests were at stake. When Ways and Means drafted a bill expanding Medicare to cover catastrophic illness and outpatient prescription drugs, Jacobs succeeded in deleting a provision encouraging use of generic drugs rather than the more expensive name-brand versions. The provision would save the government $400 million, it was estimated, but it would cost drug manufacturers like Indianapolis-based Eli Lilly. When another committee restored the generic drug requirement, Jacobs tried again to strike it but the House rejected his move, 161-265, despite drug companies' intense lobbying.

In the 99th Congress, Jacobs dealt himself out of the major action at the committee, opposing its efforts to revise the tax code. When the administration first introduced its tax proposal, he called it "the emperor's new cut" to reduce taxes on the wealthy. He was not much kinder to Congress' version, which sought to eliminate deductions and raise business taxes while phasing in lower individual tax rates. "The mother lode on this bill," he said in late 1986, "is to give people with over $200,000 in income a year a walloping tax cut." Meanwhile, he complained, it would result in an immediate tax increase for many at the lower end of the spectrum, and hurt charitable organizations dependent on deductible donations.

In his other work on Ways and Means, Jacobs generally has acted as a conventional liberal. He is one of the committee's strongest defenders of public employees, sponsoring a move in 1983 to keep them out of the Social Security system. He lost on a voice vote. In 1982 he led his subcommittee in defeating a plan to make federal employees subject to the hospital benefits portion of the Social Security tax; the full committee overruled him.

Ways and Means provides Jacobs with a platform to rail about the dangers of smoking. He was a sponsor of the law that established separate smoking sections on commercial airliners, and he advocates doubling the cigarette tax and earmarking extra revenues for the Social Security hospital insurance trust fund. In 1985, when Ways and Means agreed to a compromise that extended the 16-cents-per-pack tax while earmarking 1 cent for tobacco subsidies, Jacobs pushed to earmark 1 cent for the Medicare hospital trust fund. His proposal was rejected on a tie vote.

To many members, Jacobs is known for his longstanding war on the perquisites of congressional office. Over the years he has returned tens of thousands of dollars to the Treasury from his own salary, veterans' disability payments, mileage reimbursements and office allowances. That has earned Jacobs big political points among voters, but none with his colleagues, who often resent such actions as self-righteous grandstanding.

But what is worse, in their minds, are actions aimed at their benefits as well as his. Earlier in his career, Jacobs protested House leaders' use of chauffeured limousines. He was instrumental in a 1977 effort to block a pay raise for House members, and opposed the proposed 51 percent hike that divided the 101st Congress before it was finally defeated.

His ethics portfolio includes proposals to close a loophole that allows members elected before 1980, including himself, to pocket left-over campaign funds when they retire; to prohibit members from earning outside income, and to limit them to $100 worth of postage stamps for their own use. Another resolution, drafted in Jacobs' typically irreverent, tell-it-like-it-is style, would require the House to take recorded votes on any measures affecting their salaries or "freebies."

He stopped taking money from political action committees (PACs) in 1976 because, he said, a lobbyist complained about a vote. "Now when I go down to the Ways and Means Committee and look at the sea of $1,500 suits, I know that none of those lobbyists can blow cigar smoke in my face and tell me not only what his organization did for me but also what it won't do for me in the next election," Jacobs said in 1984. "It's a great feeling of liberation."

One incident during the committee's drafting of the tax-reform bill illustrated both Jacobs' anti-PAC stance and his zaniness. According to a book on the bill's passage, "Showdown at Gucci Gulch," when Chairman Dan Rostenkowski kept members late into the final night to seal the package, Jacobs distributed disposable urinals so that his colleagues could avoid the lavatories where lobbyists would trail them.

He is even more opposed to the honoraria that members routinely accept from lobby groups. "Imagine if a federal judge, during the recess of a trial, went across the street and made a little talk to the litigant's organization and got $2,000, and walked back to court. It would be, 'Good morning, Judge,' 'Good afternoon, Sheriff,' and 'Good evening, Warden,'" Jacobs once said. "The only reason it is not bribery is because Congress gets to say what bribery is."

One time Jacobs nearly was penalized for his independence. He voted with Republicans against Democratic leaders' package of House rules at the start of the 97th Congress in 1981. The leaders threatened to oust him from Ways and Means, where he had just become the Health Subcommittee chairman. Nothing was done, but Jacobs' reputation as a misfit was reinforced.

He once told a reporter that "a man can be a liberal without being a spendthrift," and Jacobs' efforts as fiscal watchdog truly have made him hard to label. He usually votes against spending both for defense and public-works projects. Like the most conservative Republicans, he supports a constitutional amendment requiring a balanced budget. When Reagan reiterated his call for such an amendment in 1982, after approving large deficits, Jacobs retorted, "None is so chaste as those who have just sinned."

He perennially sponsors legislation — "The Former Presidents Enough Is Enough and Taxpayers Relief Act" — limiting ex-presidents' benefits to 10 times the official poverty level for a family of four. In the 99th Congress the House did vote to scale back presidents' expense accounts — a "slush fund," Jacobs calls it — but rejected his proposal to eliminate them entirely. In the 100th, the House endorsed a $200,000 cut in the $1.3 million appropriation for presidents' pensions and allowances as an alternative to Jacobs' proposed $1 million cut.

He is prolific in drafting bills if not in passing them. His portfolio has included animal-rights measures, a resolution aimed at providing meatless federal school lunches (he is a vegetarian) and a proposed anti-abortion constitutional amendment.

Early in his career, he was best known as a critic of the Vietnam War. In recent years, he vocally opposed Reagan's policy of militarily aiding the contras fighting Nicaragua's leftist rulers, insisting that either side would rule as dictators, resulting in a flood of illegal immigrants to the United States.

At Home: Jacobs entered politics with an old score to settle. His father, Andrew Jacobs Sr., was elected to Congress from Indianapolis in 1948 but was turned out of office after one term. The younger Jacobs began moving early toward the congressional career his father never got to carry out.

In 1958, at the age of 26, Jacobs won a seat in the state House. Four years later he tried for Congress but was defeated by GOP Rep. Donald Bruce. In 1964 Bruce retired, and Jacobs ran again. With the help of the national Democratic landslide, he edged into office by 3,000 votes out of 295,000 cast.

It would have been difficult for Jacobs to win re-election in 1966 within the same district boundaries. But under court mandate the lines were redrawn, and, with Democrats controlling that process, Jacobs got a more favorable district. He was re-elected regularly until 1972, when Republican redistricting, combined with Richard M. Nixon's presidential landslide, cost him his seat. He lost to Republican William Hudnut, a Presbyterian minister.

Jacobs did not give up, and he was able to come back to office in the 1974 Democratic Watergate surge, winning by about 7,000 votes over Hudnut, who was later elected mayor of Indianapolis. Throughout the rest of the decade, Jacobs carried his district by convincing, though not overwhelming, margins.

But redistricting following the 1980 census

brought Jacobs new headaches. With Republicans again in control of the process, the remap eliminated Democrat David W. Evans' old 6th District. Rather than run in one of several heavily Republican constituencies or launch a statewide campaign in 1982, Evans took the risk of a primary challenge to Jacobs, his fellow Democrat and personal friend.

Jacobs began with a geographic advantage: He had represented just over half the redrawn district. But Evans' tenuous political career — comprising four narrow House elections — had taught him how to fight. A near-fanatic on the campaign trail, Evans went after voters with everything from computerized direct mail to doorbell-ringing. By contrast, Jacobs maintained a low campaign profile.

Emerging from the Democratic slating process with the party's endorsement and financial help, Jacobs went into the primary with a slight edge. But few anticipated the ease with which he won the seat. Popular among black voters, Jacobs outpolled Evans by as much as 4-to-1 in some black precincts, won the primary with 60 percent and had no trouble in November.

In 1986, Republicans gave a convincing demonstration of just how much money it is possible to spend against Jacobs and accomplish nothing in return. Jim Eynon, a 40-year-old Indianapolis real-estate manager, mounted an enthusiastic fund-raising effort that netted $533,000. The American Medical Association, upset at Jacobs' support for freezing physicians' fees, ran its own independent barrage of ads against the incumbent.

Eynon talked in glowing terms about a new Indianapolis that had emerged in recent years, spurred on by such downtown renewal projects as a domed sports stadium and a rebuilt railroad station/shopping center. He complained that Jacobs, who had opposed both projects, was an unconstructive naysayer.

But if many people were listening, the results on election night did not seem to show it. Jacobs, running with his usual low-budget ($40,000) nonchalance, took 58 percent of the vote, roughly what he had received in 1984 against a Republican who had spent barely one-fifth as much as Eynon.

In 1988, the GOP was back to its less ambitious program against Jacobs, who skated to a 61 percent share of the vote over a former official of the Department of Housing and Urban Development.

Committee

Ways and Means (6th of 23 Democrats)
Social Security (chairman); Oversight

Elections

1988 General		
Andrew Jacobs Jr. (D)	105,846	(61%)
James C. Cummings (R)	68,978	(39%)
1988 Primary		
Andrew Jacobs Jr. (D)	40,116	(92%)
Joe L. Turner (D)	3,393	(8%)
1986 General		
Andrew Jacobs Jr. (D)	68,817	(58%)
Jim Eynon (R)	49,064	(41%)

Previous Winning Percentages: **1984** (59%) **1982** (67%)
1980 (57%) **1978** (57%) **1976** (60%) **1974** (53%)
1970 (58%) **1968** (53%) **1966** (56%) **1964** (51%)

District Vote For President

	1988		1984		1980		1976	
D	91,726	(51%)	87,159	(44%)	97,427	(49%)	120,009	(50%)
R	85,967	(48%)	109,130	(55%)	90,132	(45%)	118,886	(49%)
I					8,493	(4%)		

Campaign Finance

	Receipts	Receipts from PACs		Expend-itures
1988				
Jacobs (D)	$35,731	0		$35,786
Cummings (R)	$45,743	$2,800	(6%)	$42,857
1986				
Jacobs (D)	$52,005	0		$40,577
Eynon (R)	$533,222	$46,521	(9%)	$531,148

Key Votes

1987	
Raise speed limit to 65 mph	N
Approve Gephardt "fair trade" amendment	Y
Ban testing of larger nuclear weapons	Y
Delay "re-flagging" of Kuwaiti tankers	Y
Approve tax-raising deficit-reduction bill	Y
1988	
Approve aid to Nicaraguan contras	N
Enact civil rights restoration bill over Reagan veto	Y
Kill 60-day plant-closing notification measure	N
Pass omnibus trade bill over Reagan veto	Y
Approve death penalty for drug-related murders	N
Bar federal funds for abortions in cases of rape and incest	N
Oppose seven-day waiting period for purchase of handguns	N

Voting Studies

	Presidential Support		Party Unity		Conservative Coalition	
Year	**S**	**O**	**S**	**O**	**S**	**O**
1988	26 †	68 †	58 †	35 †	26 †	68 †
1987	18	82	61	36	19	81
1986	17	80	61	38	26	74
1985	35	65	53	44	27	71
1984	27	68	65	29	15	80
1983	23	68	61	31	31	64
1982	39	60	62	29	26	74
1981	34	64	73	24	25	75

† Not eligible for all recorded votes.

Interest Group Ratings

Year	ADA	ACU	AFL-CIO	CCUS
1988	95	12	100	42
1987	96	4	94	33
1986	85	0	79	50
1985	80	24	65	59
1984	80	25	69	44
1983	75	19	87	29
1982	85	32	90	41
1981	90	36	67	16

Iowa

U.S. CONGRESS

SENATE 1 D, 1 R
HOUSE 2 D, 4 R

LEGISLATURE

Senate 30 D, 20 R
House 61 D, 39 R

ELECTIONS

1988 Presidential Vote

Bush	45%
Dukakis	55%

1984 Presidential Vote

Reagan	53%
Mondale	46%

1980 Presidential Vote

Reagan	51%
Carter	39%
Anderson	9%

Turnout rate in 1984	62%
Turnout rate in 1986	42%
Turnout rate in 1988	59%

(as percentage of voting age population)

POPULATION AND GROWTH

1980 population	2,913,808
1988 population estimate (29th in the nation)	2,834,000
Percent change 1980-1988	−3%

DEMOGRAPHIC BREAKDOWN

White	97%
Black	1%
(Spanish origin)	1%
Urban	59%
Rural	41%
Born in state	78%
Foreign-born	2%

MAJOR CITIES

Des Moines	192,060
Cedar Rapids	108,370
Davenport	98,750
Sioux City	79,590
Waterloo	70,010

AREA AND LAND USE

Area 55,966 sq. miles (23rd)

Farm	91%
Forest	4%
Federally owned	0.4%

Gov. Terry E. Branstad (R)
Of Des Moines — Elected 1982

Born: Nov. 17, 1946, Leland, Iowa.
Education: U. of Iowa, B.A. 1969; Drake U., J.D. 1974.
Military Career: Army, 1969-71.
Occupation: Lawyer; farmer.
Religion: Roman Catholic.
Political Career: Iowa House, 1973-79; lieutenant governor, 1979-83.
Next Election: 1990.

WORK

Occupations

White-collar	47%
Blue-collar	30%
Service workers	14%

Government Workers

Federal	18,248
State	58,665
Local	129,747

MONEY

Median family income	$ 20,052	(20th)
Tax burden per capita	$ 800	(31st)

EDUCATION

Spending per pupil through grade 12	$ 3,619	(23rd)
Persons with college degrees	14%	(37th)

CRIME

Violent crime rate 231 per 100,000 (41st)

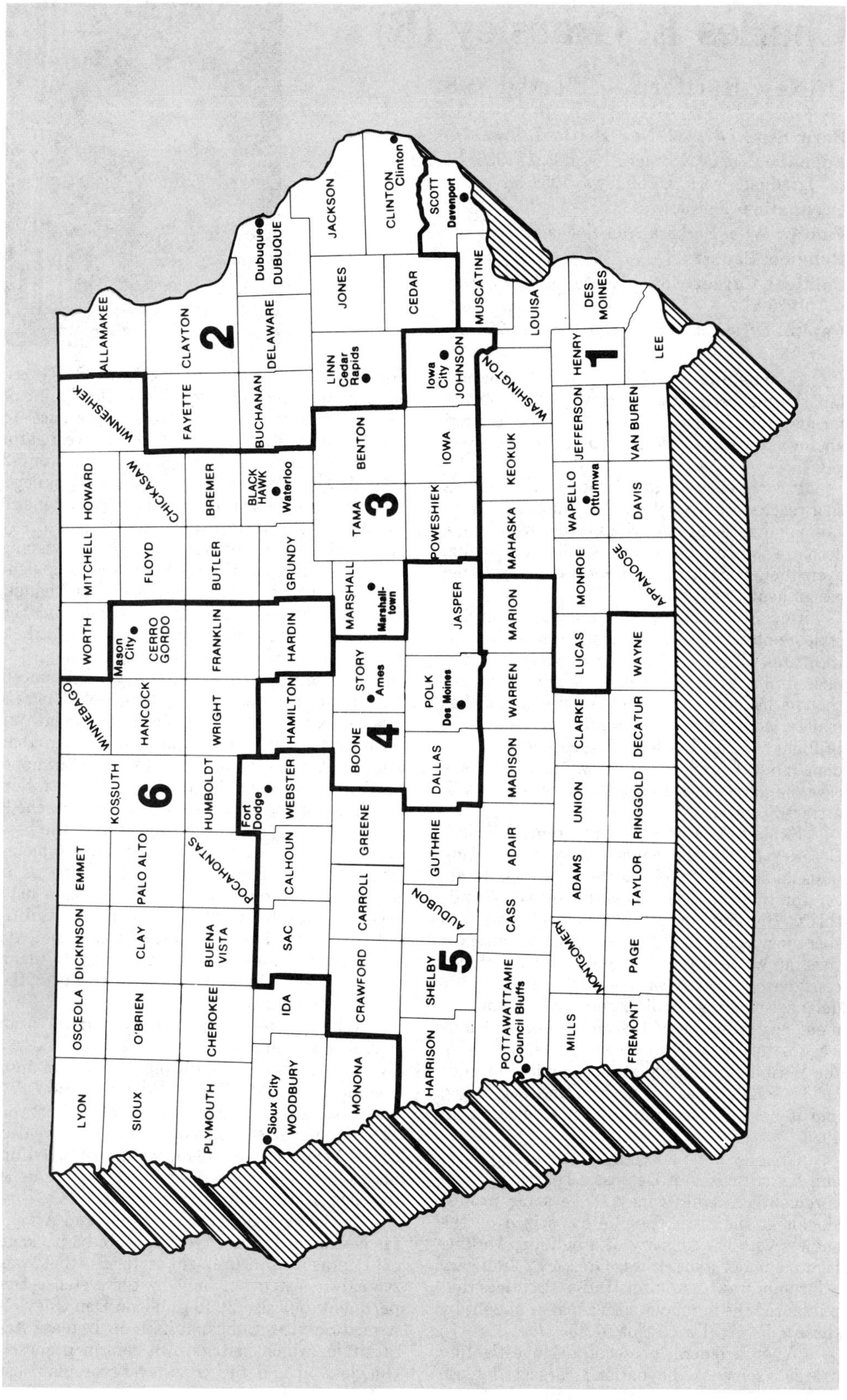
1
2
3
4
5
6
ALLAMAKEE
WINNESHIEK
HOWARD
MITCHELL
WORTH
WINNEBAGO
KOSSUTH
EMMET
DICKINSON
OSCEOLA
LYON
CLAYTON
FAYETTE
CHICKASAW
FLOYD
Mason City
CERRO GORDO
HANCOCK
PALO ALTO
CLAY
O'BRIEN
SIOUX
BREMER
BUTLER
FRANKLIN
WRIGHT
HUMBOLDT
POCAHONTAS
BUENA VISTA
CHEROKEE
PLYMOUTH
Dubuque
DUBUQUE
DELAWARE
BUCHANAN
BLACK HAWK
Waterloo
GRUNDY
HARDIN
HAMILTON
WEBSTER
Fort Dodge
CALHOUN
SAC
IDA
Sioux City
WOODBURY
JACKSON
JONES
LINN
Cedar Rapids
BENTON
TAMA
MARSHALL
Marshall-town
STORY
Ames
BOONE
GREENE
CARROLL
CRAWFORD
MONONA
CLINTON
Clinton
CEDAR
Iowa City
JOHNSON
IOWA
POWESHIEK
JASPER
POLK
Des Moines
DALLAS
GUTHRIE
AUDUBON
SHELBY
HARRISON
SCOTT
Davenport
MUSCATINE
LOUISA
WASHINGTON
KEOKUK
MAHASKA
MARION
WARREN
MADISON
ADAIR
CASS
POTTAWATTAMIE
Council Bluffs
DES MOINES
HENRY
JEFFERSON
WAPELLO
Ottumwa
MONROE
LUCAS
CLARKE
UNION
ADAMS
MONTGOMERY
MILLS
LEE
VAN BUREN
DAVIS
APPANOOSE
WAYNE
DECATUR
RINGGOLD
TAYLOR
PAGE
FREMONT

Charles E. Grassley (R)

Of New Hartford — Elected 1980

Born: Sept. 17, 1933, New Hartford, Iowa.
Education: U. of Northern Iowa, B.A. 1955, M.A. 1956; graduate work, U. of Iowa, 1957-58.
Occupation: Farmer.
Family: Wife, Barbara Ann Speicher; five children.
Religion: Baptist.
Political Career: Iowa House, 1959-75; U.S. House, 1975-81.
Capitol Office: 135 Hart Bldg. 20510; 224-3744.

In Washington: Nobody does the bumpkin routine better than Grassley. "I'm just a farmer from Butler County," he once assured an Iowa audience. "What you see is what you get."

It is not entirely an act. Grassley's intellectual reach does have its limits. And aside from campaigning against obvious evils, his Senate accomplishments have not been broad-ranging, even though he has had important committee assignments.

But if Grassley's slow-talking, farm-boy style reinforces all the Eastern stereotypes of the rural Midwest, the liberals who once dismissed him as a right-wing rube now recognize that he has a keen instinct for the issues that make a political career. Grassley may not be a brilliant theorist, but he is dogged and independent-minded, and when he wants to make a case, he knows how to do it in a way that will attract attention.

Exhibit A is defense procurement fraud. Grassley got to the Senate by demonstrating unusual skill at exploiting the widespread perception that the federal government is a spendthrift. His chief target has not been welfare spending, as one might expect from a conservative, but waste at the Pentagon — a good choice considering most Iowans' skepticism of heavy defense spending. While Pentagon mismanagement has been one of the most popular bandwagons in Congress in recent years, achieving the Washington sobriquet of "scandal" in mid-1988, Grassley was on it from the beginning, and it helped carry him to easy re-election in 1986.

Grassley is no specialist in defense policy, and his criticisms of Defense Department procurement procedures may strike some professionals as simplistic. But he has seized on the subject with the tenacity of a bulldog, working it into a major issue. It was Grassley's Judiciary Subcommittee on Administrative Practices that publicized the infamous coffee maker bought by the Air Force at a cost of $7,600.

When a federal prosecutor's investigation dragged some of the nation's largest defense contractors onto the front pages in 1988, Grassley's picture accompanied the critics' point of view. Grassley called a press conference to release the testimony of a federal investigator who, three years previously, had been prevented from detailing fraudulent practices to Grassley's subcommittee when a deputy attorney general grabbed the investigator's microphone to say that such revelations would inhibit an ongoing court case. Even as George Bush was campaigning to keep the administration in GOP hands, Grassley charged that the Pentagon and the Justice Department had for years "turned their backs" on evidence of defense corruption.

At one point in 1984, Grassley announced his intention to seek a contempt-of-Congress citation against the Justice Department for refusing to turn over documents, a plan that angered Judiciary Chairman Strom Thurmond of South Carolina as well as administration officials. An accommodation was later reached.

Grassley sums up his approach to the procurement issue with the kind of homey metaphor that endears him to Iowans even as it leads Washingtonians to regard him as a hayseed. "To teach an old dog new tricks is difficult," he says, "but starve the dog, get him to do tricks for food, and you'll get him to do them. That's what we're going to have to do to the Defense Department."

While Grassley's stance won praise from liberals pleasantly surprised to find a conservative taking on the Pentagon, it got him into arguments with the Reagan administration. After resisting the president's pleas to support the MX missile in a 1985 vote, Grassley revealed that a White House operative had summed up his feelings for the senator by saying, "I hope that son-of-a-bitchin' Grassley dies."

In the 99th Congress, Grassley and Arkansas Democrat David Pryor promoted a package of Pentagon procurement reforms that was strongly resisted not only by the Defense Department, but also by Republican Dan Quayle's Armed Services Subcommittee on Defense Acquisition, which had its own reform proposal. Quayle won and the Grassley-Pryor plan lost

22-67 in 1985; Grassley was its only GOP supporter.

But Grassley succeeded in a 1986 attack on dishonest military contractors. He won passage of a bill updating the penalties and enforcement procedures of the federal False Claims Act, a law passed during the Civil War to crack down on suppliers who bilked the Union Army. In 1988, Grassley and Ohio Democrat Howard M. Metzenbaum succeeded in creating a new crime statute to deal specificially with fraud in government contracts, with possible penalties of 10 years' imprisonment and fines up to $5 million.

Grassley's concern with defense fraud made him a major sponsor of legislation to protect workers who blow the whistle on abuse of tax dollars. After Reagan issued a surprise veto of the bill near the end of his term, Grassley said the administration "hasn't exactly a sterling record where whistleblowers are concerned." Grassley helped smooth out compromises the next year that let President Bush sign a basically similar measure.

Another of Grassley's protect-the-taxpayers crusades that eventually ripened concerned congressional pay. In 1987 and 1988 he sponsored a provision to require roll-call votes in both chambers for a pay raise to take effect, a reaction to a hands-off procedure that brought a 16 percent raise in early 1987. The Senate backed Grassley's proposal several times, but each time House leaders jettisoned it. Grassley had the last laugh in early 1989, when public outrage over a proposed 51 percent pay increase forced floor votes that killed it.

Grassley has been talking about the curse of federal deficits ever since his first days in the House in 1975. In recent years, he has favored an overall budget freeze to bring the swelling deficit under control — even if that meant scrimping on Reagan's priority, defense. Along with fellow Budget Committee members Nancy Landon Kassebaum and Joseph R. Biden Jr., he cosponsored a 1984 plan that called for holding funds for federal agencies, including Defense, at the previous year's level. The plan drew significant support in the Budget panel, but was defeated handily on the floor in 1984, and again in 1985.

When Reagan issued a 1986 budget seeking more for defense and less for domestic programs, Grassley balked. "People are finding it difficult to justify a big increase in defense when we're cutting Social Security," he said.

Grassley supported a budget offered by Senate GOP leaders that paired an elimination of Social Security cost-of-living increases with a hold-the-line approach to defense spending. When Reagan later struck a deal with House Democrats to get more defense money in exchange for restoring COLAs, a bitter Grassley said, "If the president can't support us, he ought to keep his mouth shut."

While not a front-line player in budget battles, Grassley has learned how little these tussles can have to do with real-world dollars. In 1987 he regaled a near-empty Senate chamber with an imaginary consultation with philosophers of past centuries, in which he concluded that "realities like God, immortality, and the true size of the deficit, transcend our ability to know with certainty."

A belief in fiscal restraint was by no means Grassley's only motive for slowing defense spending; he wanted some of that money to go instead to farmers, especially those facing foreclosure. In early 1985, he was incensed when Reagan vetoed an emergency farm credit relief bill that he and seven other GOP farm-state senators supported. Grassley harped on the issue during the 1985 farm bill debate, and when the Senate finally passed the farm bill, Grassley voted against it — even though the efforts of Majority Leader Bob Dole had significantly watered down the price-support provisions Reagan sought. Given the unpopularity of federal farm policies in the 1986 elections, it was smart politics.

In 1987 Grassley teamed with Dole to try to speed up some income payments to corn farmers, but the attempt failed. The corn connection held in the 1988 presidential nominating race, as Grassley helped Dole win the Iowa caucuses.

Looking out for Iowa interests was Grassley's chief role during the Finance Committee's 1986 debate on tax-code revision. He won a tax break for farmers who are forced into bankruptcy, and another benefiting a Des Moines trucking firm run by one of his campaign contributors. But he was not a significant player in the broader debate over tax policy.

Earlier on Finance, Grassley was active in the 1982 passage of "revenue-enhancing" legislation. He helped develop provisions aimed at raising more money by increasing penalties for tax evasion and strengthening enforcement powers of the Internal Revenue Service. In the committee shuffle following the Democrats' 1987 Senate takeover, Grassley lost his seats on Finance and on Labor, but he won assignment to Appropriations and its Agriculture Subcommittee.

On the major Judiciary issue of the 100th Congress, Grassley stuck with Robert H. Bork for the Supreme Court, charging that his victorious detractors "spent millions to willfully smear an American citizen." Some of his bitterest comments were directed at Reagan, however, for vacationing when the Bork battle was joined. "Reagan almost blew the mandate he won in the 1980 and 1984 elections," he said.

Grassley did help the Reagan administration achieve one of its few successes in eliminating social programs. Fed up with the way Urban Development Action Grants were used to funnel tax dollars to the Northeast, Grassley succeeded in 1987 — after four years of effort — in revising the formula under which they were distributed. In 1988, with UDAG's geographic base weakened by the Grassley formula, the program was killed by appropriators with only token resistance.

At Home: Grassley plays to the Iowa audience with understated artistry, blending shrewd political positioning with the homespun simplicity of the farm country he grew up in. This skill has made him unstoppable since he entered politics at the age of 25.

Grassley joined the Iowa House in 1959, rose to become chairman of its Appropriations Committee and developed a reputation for personal integrity and suspicion of government.

When veteran GOP Rep. H. R. Gross announced his retirement from Congress in 1974, Grassley organized the 3rd District's most conservative elements and won the GOP nomination with 42 percent of the vote against four opponents. In November, he eked out 51 percent against an aggressive young Democrat in a Democratic year.

After conservative Republicans helped Roger W. Jepsen to victory over liberal Democratic Sen. Dick Clark in 1978, attention focused on Grassley as a 1980 challenger to Clark's liberal Senate colleague, John C. Culver.

Grassley's announcement of his Senate candidacy mobilized conservatives, who built a strong grass-roots organization across Iowa. Against a well-financed, moderate GOP primary opponent who was endorsed by popular Gov. Robert Ray, Grassley won 90 of the state's 99 counties.

Then Grassley ran head-on into Culver, who conducted an insistent and impassioned defense of his liberal Senate voting record and characterized Grassley's legislative accomplishments as mediocre. Targeted for defeat by the Moral Majority and the National Conservative Political Action Committee, Culver lashed out at Grassley's New Right supporters, calling them a "poison in the political bloodstream."

But Grassley, an earnest, easygoing farmer, did not fit the part of a fanatic. He disassociated himself from New Right tactics without losing conservative support, and he turned voters' attention to pocketbook issues by charging that Democratic economic policies brought high inflation. Outpolling Reagan in Iowa, Grassley won 54 percent of the vote. (Reagan carried Iowa with 51 percent.)

By 1986, Grassley's crusades against federal waste had built him a constituency that was unaffected by Iowa's massive farm discontent and anti-Reagan feelings. No prominent Democrat wanted to run against him, and the candidate who did, Des Moines lawyer John Roehrick, was never really in the contest. Grassley won a second Senate term with two-thirds of the vote.

Committees

Appropriations (11th of 13 Republicans)
Military Construction (ranking); Agriculture, Rural Development and Related Agencies; HUD-Independent Agencies; Transportation and Related Agencies

Budget (5th of 10 Republicans)

Judiciary (4th of 6 Republicans)
Courts and Administrative Practice (ranking); Patents, Copyrights and Trademarks

Small Business (6th of 9 Republicans)
Government Contracting and Paperwork Reduction (ranking); Rural Economy and Family Farming

Special Aging (4th of 9 Republicans)

Elections

1986 General		
Charles E. Grassley (R)	588,880	(66%)
John P. Roehrick (D)	299,406	(34%)

Previous Winning Percentages: **1980** (54%) **1978 *** (75%) **1976 *** (57%) **1974 *** (51%)

** House elections.*

Campaign Finance

	Receipts	Receipts from PACs	Expend-itures
1986			
Grassley (R)	$2,749,564	$971,730 (35%)	$2,513,319
Roehrick (D)	$256,057	$88,672 (35%)	$255,673

Key Votes

1987	
Enact omnibus highway bill over Reagan veto	N
Limit testing of space-based anti-ballistic missiles	N
Oppose banning tests of larger nuclear weapons	Y
Confirm Robert H. Bork as Supreme Court justice	Y
1988	
Allow vote on campaign-finance overhaul	N
Pass civil rights restoration bill over Reagan veto	N
Enact omnibus trade bill over Reagan veto	N
Approve death penalty for drug-related murders	Y
Oppose "workfare" amendment to welfare overhaul bill	N

Voting Studies

	Presidential Support		Party Unity		Conservative Coalition	
Year	S	O	S	O	S	O
1988	78	20	87	13	86	14
1987	58	40	77	22	69	31
1986	67	31	72	28	82	18
1985	66	34	64	35	78	22
1984	74	25	79	18	89	11
1983	74	26	81	19	77	23
1982	84	16	82	17	86	12
1981	81	16	84	15	91	7

Interest Group Ratings

Year	ADA	ACU	AFL-CIO	CCUS
1988	5	88	21	93
1987	25	81	30	83
1986	30	70	27	74
1985	10	57	33	69
1984	15	73	9	79
1983	15	64	12	58
1982	30	60	19	62
1981	5	87	6	94

Tom Harkin (D)

Of Cumming — Elected 1984

Born: Nov. 19, 1939, Cumming, Iowa.

Education: Iowa State U., B.S. 1962; Catholic U. Law School, J.D. 1972.

Military Career: Navy, 1962-67; Naval Reserve, 1968-74.

Occupation: Lawyer.

Family: Wife, Ruth Raduenz; two children.

Religion: Roman Catholic.

Political Career: Democratic nominee for U.S. House, 1972; U.S. House, 1975-85.

Capitol Office: 316 Hart Bldg. 20510; 224-3254.

In Washington: No Iowa Democrat has ever served a full elected term in the Senate and then been re-elected. But if Iowa has sent Democrats to the Senate primarily as a temporary protest, Harkin has been a harsher, tougher breed of protester. And his re-election campaign may be one of the more interesting tests of the political currents in 1990.

Harkin has striven to create the political bonds and debts back home that help extend one term into another. But he has not played it safe in Washington. He has built a reputation for taking positions and promoting ideas distinctive enough to divide people — sometimes in a style that riles them, as well.

He has applied his notable energy to four committees — including Agriculture and Appropriations, where he sits on the Foreign Operations Subcommittee. This suggests the poles of his legislative interests, a balance between his practical interest in the farm and his more ideological fascination with the foreign.

And while he has not sought a place in his party's leadership, he has devoted considerable time to being chairman of Independent Action, a political action committee that funnels money to candidates.

Most of Independent Action's beneficiaries call themselves progressives. Others may call them liberals — a term Harkin will hear often in the campaign year of 1990. Harkin usually scores around 100 with the Americans for Democratic Action, the foremost liberal rating group. But the term he likes most may be populist.

Harkin views himself as a defender of the interests of the common folk against the rich and powerful. He can be blunt in his language. "In a free economic system," he once said, "there come times when too few people have too much wealth and too much power, and too many people have neither of both. It's the primary purpose of government to redress that imbalance."

So the appeal of Harkin's legislative ideas tends to be to farmers and others who have little personal clout and distrust those who have. Some of these ideas appall those with a different view of the corporate or international economy, and Harkin has had little success in advancing his economic theories since the farm crisis began to ease in late 1987.

The prime example is the "Save the Family Farm Act," a radically different approach to farm programs that Harkin introduced in 1985 and then reintroduced in 1987 with Rep. Richard A. Gephardt of Missouri. Gephardt was running for the Democratic nomination for president at the time and focusing closely on the Iowa caucuses.

In essence, the plan would replace existing farm-subsidy programs with stringent federal controls on production and marketing of farm products. The aim would be to reduce supplies enough to cause much higher prices, perhaps as much as doubling them. Production controls would be implemented if approved by referendum among farmers.

Harkin has made some progress on this issue, but opposition from traditional farm lobby groups and worries about the effect on consumer food costs make it unlikely to be enacted soon. He was defeated, 36-56, when he offered the plan as an amendment to the 1985 farm bill. He did manage to get the government to hold a non-binding referendum on the topic in 1986, though, and that poll showed a majority of farmers responding in favor of it.

As a House member, Harkin gained a fair share of influence even as he spurned the cautious approach of most of his 1974 Democratic classmates. While they were portraying themselves as budget-balancers, Harkin was complaining about militarism and taking a purist stand on human rights.

In the Senate, though, the manner that helped set Harkin apart in the House became a stumbling block. The belligerence of his crusade for farmers and against the Nicaraguan contras has jarred the nerves even of colleagues who agree with him, and alienated those who do not.

It did not help that, shortly after arriving in the Senate, he began lecturing his colleagues on farm problems in a way that implied they had scarcely heard of the issue before. Although he later toned down his rhetoric, he continued to clash with the leadership of both parties — especially GOP leader Bob Dole, whose distaste for his farm-state neighbor has been evident on more than one occasion. Several times, Harkin has entered into confrontations with the leadership, only to discover that he had just a handful of allies backing him up.

For example, Harkin's tactics on the 1985 farm bill did not help his legislative position. He and his allies were seeking to protect farmers from future cuts in target prices by suggesting a four-year freeze on current levels, in place of the one-year freeze backed by Dole and the Reagan administration. During complicated floor maneuvering, Harkin offered an amendment calling for a four-year freeze.

The 55-42 rejection of the amendment played into Dole's hands, by forcing the Senate to go on record against the idea, and thus strengthening its stand in bargaining with the House. Harkin tried to pull a fast one, Dole chortled, and ended up hurting his own cause. Ultimately, however, Harkin did manage to win some concessions on the issue from Dole.

Harkin's work on agriculture competes for attention with his outspoken record on foreign policy, especially Central America, and the human-rights records of other countries.

Harkin's interest in human rights came out of an experience in 1970, when, as an investigator for a House committee, he traveled to Vietnam and discovered the "tiger cages" in which prisoners of war were being kept. He has never served on the Foreign Affairs or Foreign Relations committees, but his has been one of the loudest foreign policy voices on the floor.

In his first House term, Harkin introduced a successful amendment that became a national issue during the Carter administration. It barred U.S. aid to any country engaging in a consistent pattern of violations of human rights. In 1976 Harkin also induced the House to approve an amendment prohibiting Inter-American Development Bank loans to countries violating "internationally recognized" human rights.

That approach was exactly the one Jimmy Carter took in his 1976 campaign, but not the one he recommended as president. Three months after Carter took office, he criticized Harkin's amendment as "a mistake" and said it gave him no bargaining room. But the House refused to give in.

Harkin has built his successful political career on a willingness to flout conventional wisdom. His ability to win re-election repeatedly from a conservative House district and to score a solid Senate victory in a Republican year offered proof of his unorthodox belief that Iowa voters would accept even the most liberal ideological record if explained with conviction.

That belief will be tested in 1990, when Harkin can be expected to hear about his defense of gay rights and of public funding for abortions in the District of Columbia — not to mention his obsessive opposition to the Reagan administration's campaign against the Sandinista government in Nicaragua.

On the other hand, some of Harkin's crusading is easily explained. He has a brother who is deaf, and in 1988 he was the Senate sponsor of legislation creating a National Deafness Institute. His vigorous opposition to military involvement in Central America stems in part from his experiences as a Vietnam veteran (and reflects a common sentiment in Iowa). And he can point to other positions closer to the social mainstream of his state. He has, for example, sponsored a bill to crack down on marijuana growers in national forests.

At Home: Harkin opened his 1990 re-election battle by announcing his county-by-county campaign chairmen early in 1989.

It was a pre-emptive strike, designed in part to dissuade potential challengers. In that sense it failed. Rep. Tom Tauke, perhaps the strongest candidate the Republicans could nominate other than GOP Gov. Terry Branstad, entered the race soon thereafter. But Harkin's list was also a measure of the seriousness with which this freshman contemplates winning a second term.

Harkin's 1984 campaign against Republican Sen. Roger W. Jepsen was one of the year's heavyweight bouts, but it bore more resemblance to a mud-wrestling match than to an encounter fought by Marquess of Queensberry rules.

Six years earlier, Jepsen had stunned Iowa Democrats by unseating Sen. Dick Clark. There never was much doubt that he would be vulnerable in 1984, and Harkin, as a strong campaigner who had proven his popularity by securing a Republican district, was the logical challenger. By early 1983, having pre-empted much of the party establishment's support, he was the acknowledged Democratic candidate.

Jepsen had a serious problem — most of the events by which he had distinguished himself in office reflected badly on him. He had cited constitutional immunity in 1983 to escape paying a traffic ticket while driving to work; later that year it was disclosed that a Marine Corps officer paid by the military was working for him in his Senate office. In the summer of 1984 two Iowa radio stations reported that Jepsen in 1977 had applied for membership in a Des Moines "health spa" that was later closed for prostitution.

Those incidents kept Jepsen trailing in the polls as the campaign got under way. But with national conservative organizations flocking to his defense, Jepsen had the money he needed for a barrage of television and radio ads skewering Harkin for opposing a balanced-budget constitutional amendment and favoring higher taxes. As fiscally conservative voters — especially in the rural counties — began to respond, Jepsen's standing in the polls rose.

Harkin answered with a news conference, complete with charts and graphs, claiming that Jepsen was freer with tax dollars than any other recent Iowa senator. He dubbed the Republican "Red Ink Roger," a nickname Harkin supporters gleefully latched onto.

As the campaign wore on, the candidates traded charges, quarreling over who had a combat record in the military and whose views on nuclear arms were more dangerous.

Polls showed a close race, but Harkin easily outdistanced Jepsen in the cities and carried much of the countryside, winning just over 55 percent. He won 72 of the state's 99 counties — including 55 that voted for Reagan at the top of the ticket.

Republicans saw little cause for worry when Harkin first announced for Congress in 1972 against a well-entrenched GOP incumbent in a solidly conservative district. But they soon found themselves up against one of the more resourceful Democrats in recent Iowa politics.

Harkin projected his concern for agriculture in rural west Iowa and drew publicity with his gimmick of "work days," spending a day at a time as a truck driver, as a gas station attendant and in other blue-collar work to convince voters of his empathy with their concerns. Republican Rep. William Scherle defeated him, but by the lowest percentage of his House career.

Harkin launched his 1974 bid early, built a stronger organization and raised more money. Scherle, activated by his unimpressive 1972 showing, made more appearances and tried to distance himself from the unpopular Republican administration.

Most people assumed this would be enough to rekindle the district's Republican voting habits. But Harkin won on the strength of his showing in Story County (Ames), which he took by 6,195 votes.

Committees

Agriculture, Nutrition and Forestry (5th of 10 Democrats)
Nutrition and Investigations (chairman); Agricultural Production and Stabilization of Prices; Domestic and Foreign Marketing and Product Promotion

Appropriations (11th of 16 Democrats)
Labor, Health and Human Services, Education and Related Agencies (chairman); Agriculture, Rural Development and Related Agencies; Defense; Foreign Operations; Transportation and Related Agencies

Labor and Human Resources (7th of 9 Democrats)
Handicapped (chairman); Children, Family, Drugs and Alcoholism; Employment and Productivity; Labor

Small Business (7th of 10 Democrats)
Competition and Antitrust Enforcement (chairman); Export Expansion

Elections

1984 General

Tom Harkin (D)	716,883	(56%)
Roger W. Jepsen (R)	564,381	(44%)

Previous Winning Percentages: **1982** * (59%) **1980** * (60%) **1978** * (59%) **1976** * (65%) **1974** * (51%)

* *House elections.*

Campaign Finance

	Receipts	Receipts from PACs	Expend-itures
1984			
Harkin (D)	$2,848,763	$800,827 (28%)	$2,843,695
Jepsen (R)	$2,661,443	$865,442 (33%)	$2,883,465

Key Votes

1987	
Enact omnibus highway bill over Reagan veto	Y
Limit testing of space-based anti-ballistic missiles	Y
Oppose banning tests of larger nuclear weapons	N
Confirm Robert H. Bork as Supreme Court justice	N
1988	
Allow vote on campaign-finance overhaul	Y
Pass civil rights restoration bill over Reagan veto	Y
Enact omnibus trade bill over Reagan veto	Y
Approve death penalty for drug-related murders	N
Oppose "workfare" amendment to welfare overhaul bill	Y

Voting Studies

	Presidential Support		Party Unity		Conservative Coalition	
Year	**S**	**O**	**S**	**O**	**S**	**O**
1988	42	57	89	6	8	86
1987	31	65	87	8	16	81
1986	19	78	91	5	5	91
1985	22	77	90	8	17	82
House Service						
1984	29	66	79	14	17	80
1983	7	85	82	10	16	81
1982	26	69	83	12	12	86
1981	25	70	81	14	21	73

Interest Group Ratings

Year	ADA	ACU	AFL-CIO	CCUS
1988	95	0	92	36
1987	95	4	90	44
1986	90	14	93	28
1985	100	5	90	24
House Service				
1984	75	21	46	33
1983	90	5	88	20
1982	95	0	95	24
1981	85	7	73	5

1 Jim Leach (R)

Of Davenport — Elected 1976

Born: Oct. 15, 1942, Davenport, Iowa.

Education: Princeton U., B.A. 1964; Johns Hopkins U., M.A. 1966; graduate work, London School of Economics, 1966-68.

Occupation: Foreign service officer; propane gas company executive.

Family: Wife, Elisabeth Ann "Deba" Foxley; two children.

Religion: Episcopalian.

Political Career: Republican nominee for U.S. House, 1974.

Capitol Office: 1514 Longworth Bldg. 20515; 225-6576.

In Washington: The 1988 elections transformed Jim Leach from a heretic bucking GOP atavism on the Foreign Affairs Committee to the champion of a new president among the warring fiefdoms of the Banking Committee.

Leach has changed neither his outlook nor his assignments, but the splintering of the Banking Committee following the defeat of its longtime warlord and the ascendancy of his friend George Bush have given him new authority.

Leach's association with Bush dates to the early 1970s, when Bush was United Nations ambassador and Leach was a young foreign service officer there. In 1980, Leach helped Bush win the Iowa caucuses — a turning point in Bush's ascension to Ronald Reagan's running mate and successor.

Despite his professorial demeanor, Leach's outspoken foreign policy views have made him something of a pariah to his party's dominant right wing. It does not seem to bother Leach, who often relishes the chance to demonstrate his iconoclasm and prove that policy is more important to him than party.

Not that Leach is uninterested in being a party man. He simply wants the party to come to him. He has tried to use organizations such as the Ripon Society, which he chaired, and the Republican Mainstream Committee, which he founded, to raise a moderate voice in GOP politics.

The Bush presidency should make Leach feel less isolated, and his need to confront the right wing has diminished. At the 1988 Republican National Convention, for instance, he kept mum as his party's conservatives shoved the platform toward the right. This was a sharp contrast to the 1984 convention in Dallas, when he was part of an embattled minority waging a futile crusade against the conservative tide, reaping political and personal abuse for his trouble.

Despite his vigorous denunciations of Reagan foreign policies, Leach can legitimately claim that reports of his liberalism are exaggerated. There is nothing particularly liberal about his domestic policy voting record — he rarely draws even a mediocre rating, for example, from the AFL-CIO.

Leach's independence has found room to operate on the Banking Committee following the surprise 1988 defeat of its chairman, Fernand J. St Germain of Rhode Island. St Germain's secretive autocracy has been replaced by the more tenuous grip of Henry B. Gonzalez of Texas, and policy is set by shifting alliances that transcend seniority and party. Leach often outshines the uninventive senior Republican, Chalmers P. Wylie of Ohio, and forms common cause with the emerging center of power at the committee's middle level on both sides of the dais.

What remains to be seen is whether Leach will begin to consult with his GOP colleagues, or continue to free-lance. In the past, he has shown a preference for going down in flames on causes he considers right.

For years, Leach's cause has been to require financial institutions to keep more capital on hand and to make safer investments. He was among the first to warn of an impending crisis in the nation's savings-and-loan industry, and when it finally burst into public view, he cast blame widely on Congress, the Reagan administration, the industry and state regulators.

Eventually, the House came around to Leach's views. In 1987, a Leach amendment to restrict speculative investments by thrifts was defeated on the floor 17-391. That did not deter Leach. In 1988, he tried a slightly different tack, suggesting that regulators use the same rules on risky investments for thrifts as for banks; that lost 20-29 in committee. But in the 1989 thrift bailout, he won as a leading proponent of the administration's plan to toughen up on the industry: The committee adopted 28-23 his amendment to apply federal restrictions on

Iowa 1

Southeast — Davenport

The 1st stretches west from a string of manufacturing cities along the Mississippi River — Bettendorf, Davenport, Muscatine and Burlington — across almost half of southern Iowa. It takes in 16 southeastern Iowa counties. But more than half of the vote is cast in its urban areas.

Both parts of the district have been hurting. Like most industrialized areas, the 16th suffered badly in the economic slump of the early 1980s, when unemployment districtwide hovered around 15 percent. The jobless rate in Wapello County (Ottumwa) is still well above 10 percent, but unemployment has decreased in most of the district's other industrial counties, partly because the jobless have left, and partly due to the revival of some industries.

The depression and drought that have hit the farm economy have left their mark on the cities; Davenport lost its Caterpillar facility, and Iowans who worked at International Harvester across the river in Illinois lost their jobs when the farm implement division was closed down.

With a population of 157,000, Scott County (Davenport) is by far the 1st District's largest population center. Despite the loss of Caterpillar, Davenport remains a heavy-industry town: Alcoa's aluminum plant there is one of the largest in the world.

While it has a large blue-collar vote, however, Scott County can be agreeable territory for Republicans. In the last three House elections, Leach has taken no less than 62 percent of the county's vote. Scott also voted for Republican Charles E. Grassley in his 1980 and 1986 Senate races. But in 1988 presidential voting, Michael S. Dukakis edged George Bush in Scott County by 3,390 votes.

Down-river from Davenport are Muscatine (Muscatine County) and Burlington (Des Moines County). Muscatine is consistently Republican (it supported Republican Sen. Roger W. Jepsen in his weak re-election campaign in 1984), but Democrats running statewide often win Burlington. Dukakis carried it by nearly 3,000 votes in 1988. Leach has no trouble in either place.

The northern rural portions of the district have shown steady allegiance to the GOP. But in the southern tier of rural counties along the Missouri border, the soil is poorer, crop land gives way to grazing land, and Democratic loyalties are stronger. Partly because the GOP establishment in this area is weaker, presidential hopeful Pat Robertson ran well here in the 1988 GOP caucuses; he won six of the 16 counties in the 1st.

Though there are signs that economic conditions are stabilizing, the farm crisis has had an effect on politics throughout the district, boosting the visibility of groups with a liberal outlook, such as the Iowa Farm Unity Coalition, Rural America and the American Agriculture Movement.

Population: 485,961. White 469,441 (97%), Black 9,732 (2%), Other 2,408 (1%). Spanish origin 7,886 (2%). 18 and over 345,540 (71%), 65 and over 64,556 (13%). Median age: 30.

direct investments to all thrifts, even if they are state-chartered.

Leach cast one of two votes against the bailout bill in committee, saying it was not tough enough. But he supported it on the floor after winning a surprise victory with a 412-7 stampede for his proposal to strike a list of special-interest provisions.

Leach also would apply stricter standards and stiffer regulation to banks. When the panel in 1988 considered legislation that would let banks enter into the securities business, Leach sought to persuade the House to increase capital requirements for banks wanting to do so, a stance that would protect smaller institutions in Iowa against domination by high-rolling New York banks with extensive Third World loans. An amendment to that effect was adopted 29-21 in committee; the legislation never made it to the floor.

Leach's background at the London School of Economics and his assignment on Foreign Affairs has made him one of the few members active on international debt issues, in contrast with the Main Street focus of most in Congress. In past years, he has tried to preserve funding for the Export-Import Bank, a tool he says is under-used in helping American industry sell its products abroad. When Reagan tried to cut bank funding as part of a budget-reduction package, Leach offered a compromise that combined continued funding of the bank, which makes direct loans, with a subsidy of interest rates to encourage commercial banks to offer more loans to foreign customers of U.S. exports.

The thrift crisis drew Leach from the cul-de-sac of Foreign Affairs, where the growing conservatism of the Republican contingent had left him isolated. Conservative Republicans have often resented the aura of bipartisanship he sometimes lends to Democrats by cosponsoring their bills or joining their initiatives, such as a trip to Cuba in 1984 with Rep. Bill Alexander of Arkansas. He sometimes lectures his GOP colleagues on the value of a more conciliatory U.S. approach toward its role in the world.

In Reagan's second term, Leach was often the leading Republican critic of Reagan's policies on issues such as Central America, arms control and South Africa. In supporting sanctions against the apartheid regime in South Africa, he said, "All we ask of this Republican president is that he advance a foreign policy consistent with the views of the first Republican president, Abraham Lincoln."

Leach has been a consistent opponent of U.S. aid to the Nicaraguan contras. He was an early critic of U.S. involvement in Central America, drafting in 1982 a letter to the president urging him to allow Mexico's president to mediate the Salvadoran conflict.

When the Iran-contra affair began to unfold, Leach was harsh in his assessment. "The administration trusted its secrets with an anarchist in Tehran and not with legislators in Washington," he said. But he was equally critical of Congress, saying that by watering down restrictions on covert involvement in 1985, it invited mischief. Democrats, he said, had buried their heads in the sand when reports of that mischief began to surface, out of fear that they would be blamed for "losing Central America" to communism. "The issue is backbone, not oversight," he said.

Occasionally Leach finds himself criticizing even the Democrats on Foreign Affairs as practicing too blatant an interventionism — as when he opposed the first proposals to give aid to rebels fighting the communist regime in Cambodia.

The normally mild-mannered Leach lost his temper near the end of the 100th Congress when he castigated senators and the Interior Committee for stalling a bill that would have granted independence to the tiny Pacific island chain of Palau.

Early in his career, Leach often sounded more conservative than he does now. As a freshman, for example, he amended the 1978 Civil Service Act to place a ceiling on the number of federal workers. It was an idea that struck a popular anti-bureaucratic theme, and it sailed through the House on a 251-96 vote. It gave President Carter a year to shrink the work force to 1977 levels — a reduction of 68,000 employees — and made Leach a target of criticism from the bureaucracy for years.

His restiveness with the domination of conservatives came to flower in 1981, when he was installed as president of the Ripon Society, a moderate GOP group that had fallen into quiescence during the 1970s. Leach all but declared war on the party's conservative social-issue activists. Leach said he had no intention of being "lashed to the guillotine of the New Right's social and security agenda." He declared a "moderate manifesto" touting the need for arms control and the Equal Rights Amendment.

In 1984, Leach formed the Republican Mainstream Committee, a loose coalition of moderates, to fight on the GOP platform.

Leach recognizes that moderates have been outflanked in fund raising and publicity. "The temper and tone of [moderates'] position-taking is not best suited to the harsh appeals of direct mail or best suited to get the attention of the media," he said. In the future, he says, moderates "must cease being moderate if they are going to recapture public leadership."

At Home: Since Leach took the 1st District out of Democratic hands in 1976, his moderate House voting record and high visibility at home have enabled him to choke off challenges with ease. He carried every county in the district in 1978 and 1980; in 1986, with a devastated farm economy cutting into Republican strength, he still carried all but one. The 1st District registered distinct disenchantment with the GOP national ticket in 1988, but Leach still carried 14 out of 16 counties.

Leach brought a varied background to his first campaign, in 1974, against first-term Democrat Edward Mezvinsky. Leach had studied at Princeton and at the London School of Economics, worked in the Office of Economic Opportunity and in the Foreign Service, was assigned to the Arms Control and Disarmament Agency, then returned to Iowa to run the propane gas manufacturing firm owned by his family.

He lost to Mezvinsky in 1974 by 12,147 votes, but that was a good showing for a Republican newcomer in a Democratic year. During the next two years, he spoke regularly in the district, held his organization together and built a $200,000 campaign fund.

In 1976 Leach stressed his ties to Robert Ray, Iowa's moderate Republican governor. He described himself as a "Bob Ray Republican" and called Mezvinsky "a Bella Abzug Democrat." Leach won by carrying his home base of Scott County (Davenport), which Mezvinsky had taken in 1974. The Democrat carried Iowa City, Burlington and Keokuk, but they were not enough.

In 1978 Leach's courting of the voters in the areas where he had run poorly two years earlier paid off. He drew 64 percent, the first time in 16 years that any House candidate in the 1st had won more than 55 percent.

The only Democrat who has given Leach any trouble since he won the seat was the 1982 nominee, former Scott County Supervisor William E. Gluba, a forceful campaigner with a populist flair and over 10 years of political involvement in the 1st's most populous county.

But Gluba was so little known outside his

home county that he gave up 37 percent of the Democratic primary vote to a candidate who had spent several years in prison for a variety of offenses, including burglary and armed robbery.

That embarrassment made it difficult for Gluba to convince potential contributors he could win, and he never obtained the resources necessary to match Leach's organization. Also, Gluba was unsuccessful at tying Leach to Reaganomics. Leach could point to his role as a leading Republican critic of Reagan's priorities for defense, education and social services. Gluba ended up with two counties.

Gluba was back in 1988, winning the nomination after former gubernatorial nominee Lowell Junkins had passed on it. But Gluba was even more woefully underfunded than in 1982. He again carried just two counties, and his share of the districtwide vote slipped below 40 percent.

Committees

Banking, Finance and Urban Affairs (2nd of 20 Republicans)
International Development, Finance, Trade and Monetary Policy (ranking); Domestic Monetary Policy; Financial Institutions Supervision, Regulation and Insurance

Foreign Affairs (4th of 18 Republicans)
Asian and Pacific Affairs (ranking); Europe and the Middle East

Elections

1988 General		
Jim Leach (R)	112,746	(61%)
Bill Gluba (D)	71,280	(38%)
1986 General		
Jim Leach (R)	86,834	(66%)
John R. Whitaker (D)	43,985	(34%)

Previous Winning Percentages: **1984** (67%) **1982** (59%) **1980** (64%) **1978** (64%) **1976** (52%)

District Vote For President

	1988	1984	1980	1976
D	106,756 (55%)	99,112 (47%)	85,545 (41%)	100,738 (50%)
R	86,724 (44%)	110,057 (52%)	104,062 (50%)	99,128 (49%)
I			14,763 (7%)	

Campaign Finance

	Receipts	Receipts from PACs	Expend-itures
1988			
Leach (R)	$206,618	0	$218,707
Gluba (D)	$62,395	$36,151 (58%)	$59,204
1986			
Leach (R)	$229,607	0	$231,937
Whitaker (D)	$23,532	$2,850 (12%)	$23,526

Key Votes

1987	
Raise speed limit to 65 mph	N
Approve Gephardt "fair trade" amendment	N
Ban testing of larger nuclear weapons	Y
Delay "re-flagging" of Kuwaiti tankers	Y
Approve tax-raising deficit-reduction bill	N
1988	
Approve aid to Nicaraguan contras	N
Enact civil rights restoration bill over Reagan veto	Y
Kill 60-day plant-closing notification measure	N
Pass omnibus trade bill over Reagan veto	Y
Approve death penalty for drug-related murders	N
Bar federal funds for abortions in cases of rape and incest	N
Oppose seven-day waiting period for purchase of handguns	Y

Voting Studies

	Presidential Support		Party Unity		Conservative Coalition	
Year	**S**	**O**	**S**	**O**	**S**	**O**
1988	35	65	62	35	61	39
1987	38	59	58	32	42	58
1986	47	52	58	39	37 †	63 †
1985	34	64	53	40	22	78
1984	42	53	51	42	36	58
1983	39	55	40	51	28	71
1982	45	52	43	54	36	62
1981	58	42	54	45	48	51

† Not eligible for all recorded votes.

Interest Group Ratings

Year	ADA	ACU	AFL-CIO	CCUS
1988	75	32	79	64
1987	52	38	31	79
1986	55	32	21	61
1985	60	33	53	50
1984	50	30	8	67
1983	50	18	33	65
1982	65	23	45	45
1981	55	73	20	79

2 Tom Tauke (R)

Of Dubuque — Elected 1978

Born: Oct. 11, 1950, Dubuque, Iowa.
Education: Loras College, B.A. 1972; U. of Iowa, J.D. 1974.
Occupation: Lawyer.
Family: Wife, Beverly Hubble; one child.
Religion: Roman Catholic.
Political Career: Iowa House, 1975-79.
Capitol Office: 2244 Rayburn Bldg. 20515; 225-2911.

In Washington: House members listen to Tauke, even if they sometimes do not care very much for what he has to say.

During a decade in the House, this serious and reserved moderate Republican has deftly managed to earn a reputation as a thoughtful legislator even as he has pursued some issues that are clearly unpopular with his colleagues.

Tauke started off the 101st Congress by leading an effort to see to it that congressmen did not receive a 51 percent pay raise scheduled to go into effect if Congress did not act to stop it. He argued that the large increase was unseemly at a time of tight budgets, and that it was wrong for an increase to be automatic. It was not a new position for Tauke. Since coming to Congress, Tauke has tried to pass legislation that would require Congress to vote on any pay raise and would prevent a raise from taking effect until members had stood for re-election.

Political heat generated by Tauke and others helped put members on the defensive over the pay increase and ultimately forced a vote that killed it. Many of those who sided with Tauke in the end did not take kindly to his efforts, but few held it against him personally. Unlike some pay-raise foes whose rhetoric crossed the line into hot-headed demagoguery, the cool Tauke employed a more subtle argument, portraying the pay raise and the automatic mechanism for getting it as beneath the dignity of the institution. "The American people believe Congress is incapable of dealing with congressional salaries in anything other than a chaotic and complicated manner," he said.

Even if Tauke's pay-raise activism strained some of his relationships in the House, that is unlikely to matter much to him, because he is already aiming for a 1990 Senate contest against Democratic incumbent Tom Harkin.

An ambitious legislator, Tauke manages to keep many balls in the air at one time while avoiding a common pitfall — the appearance of being spread too thin. Serving on the Education and Labor Committee and on Energy and Commerce, he is well positioned to pursue a variety of legislative interests.

Many of his efforts on Energy and Commerce revolve around health care. He has co-chaired a rural health care coalition, which has pushed to correct changes in the Medicare system that many rural lawmakers feel are detrimental to health care in their districts. During the budget reconciliation process in 1987, the coalition succeeded in passing a number of measures, including a special payment increase to rural hospitals and the creation of an Office of Rural Health Policy in the Department of Health and Human Services. Tauke is also concerned about infant mortality and in the 100th Congress served on a national commission to study the problem and make recommendations.

Serving on the Telecommunications Subcommittee, Tauke has worked with Washington Democrat Al Swift in pushing a bill to allow seven regional Bell Telephone companies to compete in new business areas, including manufacturing and information services, that have been declared off-limits by the courts.

Meanwhile, Tauke is an active participant in debates on Education and Labor. As ranking Republican on the Human Resources Subcommittee, and as chairman of a Republican task force on child care in the 100th Congress, Tauke was very involved in crafting a GOP alternative to the Democratic child care agenda.

While Democrats put together legislation that involved establishing and expanding child-care facilities, subsidizing family payments and imposing new federal regulations, Tauke pushed a plan that relied more heavily on tax credits for parents and funding for states to address quality and availability. A child-care bill did not pass Congress, and Tauke continued to pursue the issue in the 101st Congress.

Also in the 100th Congress, when Education and Labor reauthorized the popular Older Americans Act, which authorizes grants to the states to provide a variety of services to the elderly, the only partisan rancor was sparked by Tauke amendments. In one effort he argued against a planned across-the-board increase because some programs were already nearing their authorized ceilings, but his amendment to re-

Iowa 2

Northeast — Cedar Rapids

The Iowa 2nd remains what it has been for decades: a triangle of interdependent industrial cities surrounded by corn, livestock and dairy farms. The points of the triangle — and the district's population centers — are the cities of Cedar Rapids, Dubuque and Clinton.

Cedar Rapids is the second-largest city in Iowa and one of the country's leading manufacturers of goods for export. It is a center for meatpacking, grain processing and production of pumps, valves and electronic and telecommunication equipment. Once firmly Republican, it swung to the Democratic side in statewide contests during the 1970s. Since then, it has shifted again. Linn County, the home of Cedar Rapids, gave Republican Roger W. Jepsen a slight edge in his 1978 Senate contest, but turned against him when he ran unsuccessfully for re-election in 1984. The same year, Ronald Reagan took just over 51 percent in Linn County. In 1988, Michael S. Dukakis won the county by nearly 10,000 votes.

Dubuque, which sits on the west bank of the Mississippi River, is largely Catholic and historically friendlier to Democrats than Cedar Rapids. The city's Democratic leanings made Dubuque County one of only four Iowa counties carried by Jimmy Carter in 1980; Dukakis won it comfortably in 1988.

Dubuque grew up as a processing center for the dairy and meat industries; it also builds tractors and heavy industrial machinery. The area was hit particularly hard by unemployment in the early 1980s. The local economy has improved some since then, but it rides in part with the agricultural economy, and so remains volatile.

Clinton, about half the size of Dubuque, is another manufacturing center on the west bank of the Mississippi. Democratic strength in Clinton County has dropped dramatically during the past decade, though Dukakis managed a 2,000-vote victory there in 1988.

Population: 485,708. White 478,593 (99%), Black 3,734 (1%). Spanish origin 2,755 (1%). 18 and over 338,272 (70%), 65 and over 58,801 (12%). Median age: 29.

distribute the increase lost in committee on a 13-21 party-line vote, and by 95-297 on the floor.

Tauke also insisted it was necessary to test some cost-sharing provisions for services because of a "need for expansion of services at a time of budgetary restraint." But there was strong feeling that would discourage the elderly from seeking services. By voice vote the panel rejected his amendment to test cost-sharing for some services in 10 states.

Outside his committees, Tauke played a leading role in the 100th Congress in a bipartisan group of moderates pushing for across-the-board cuts in appropriations bills to reduce the deficit. "Where we have the chance, we have to hold the line," he implored in one debate. Most of the floor amendments failed, but the group was clearly a force. Sensing the growing strength of the budget-cutting activists, Appropriations leaders had little choice but to restrain some of their spending.

At Home: Tauke was barely out of college in 1972 when he became chairman of the Dubuque County GOP, and he won election to the state Legislature shortly after graduating from law school in 1974.

He considered a 1976 congressional bid, but decided that, at age 25, he could afford to serve another term in the Iowa House before aiming for Washington. That was a wise decision. By 1978, the national GOP was ready to invest substantially in a campaign against Democratic Rep. Michael T. Blouin, who had won twice by unimpressive margins. Tauke was able to outspend Blouin by $100,000.

Tauke had built a following as a state legislator among anti-abortion Democrats in Dubuque. But Blouin also opposed abortion, and he did not expect many defections on that issue. In 1976 the Democrat had won 62 percent in Dubuque County. He was counting on a similar vote for 1978. Blouin also was depending on his labor allies in the district's two other population centers, Cedar Rapids (Linn County) and Clinton. Tauke did not enter the campaign with much name recognition in either place.

But Tauke's monetary advantage and a surprisingly low Democratic turnout combined to produce an upset. In Dubuque County, Blouin got a mediocre 54 percent, and Tauke carried Linn and Clinton counties. The Republican padded his margin with a combined 57 percent in eight generally Republican rural counties.

Democrats felt they had a strong 1980 challenger in former state Sen. Steve Sovern, a native of the Cedar Rapids area. His strategy was to win convincingly in his home county, increase the Democratic percentage in Dubuque and cut his losses in Clinton and the rural areas.

But Tauke's voting record had generated no widespread dissatisfaction, and his campaign receipts exceeded $300,000, more than twice what Sovern had. Tauke, again running very well in the rural areas of the district, won re-election with 54 percent overall.

Since then, Iowa Democrats have come to realize that unseating Tauke is a long-shot proposition, even in good years for their party. The past three Democratic nominees have all been respectable candidates, but not one of them has reached 45 percent of the vote.

The 1986 campaign seemed to offer some hopes of a competitive contest, given the intensity of farm discontent and resentment against Reagan administration agricultural policy in eastern Iowa. Democrats nominated an articulate young challenger in Eric Tabor, who not only came from a well-established farm family but had studied law at Harvard and Soviet affairs at the University of Leningrad. Tabor performed reasonably well at fund raising, and positioned himself to take advantage of any farm revolt that might manifest itself at the polls on Election Day. Tauke, meanwhile, insisted there would be no such revolt; he said his constituents were ready to look on the bright side of things after months of wallowing in economic depression. "Iowa farmers," he said, "are sick and tired of being sick and tired."

As it turned out, Tauke was right. Tabor failed to crack 40 percent. He came back for more in 1988 and managed to reach 43 percent in a year when Iowa's electoral votes were making an unusual appearance in the Democratic column. But Tauke's demonstrated ability to hold off all comers in traditionally Democratic Dubuque has established him as a strong contender for a statewide office. In February 1989 he formed an exploratory committee, a preliminary step toward challenging Sen. Harkin in 1990.

Committees

Education and Labor (7th of 13 Republicans)
Human Resources (ranking); Postsecondary Education

Energy and Commerce (7th of 17 Republicans)
Health and the Environment; Telecommunications and Finance; Transportation and Hazardous Materials

Select Aging (6th of 27 Republicans)
Retirement, Income and Employment (ranking)

Elections

1988 General		
Tom Tauke (R)	113,543	(57%)
Eric Tabor (D)	86,438	(43%)
1986 General		
Tom Tauke (R)	88,708	(61%)
Eric Tabor (D)	55,903	(39%)

Previous Winning Percentages: **1984** (64%) **1982** (59%) **1980** (54%) **1978** (52%)

District Vote For President

	1988	1984	1980	1976
D	113,993 (56%)	100,647 (47%)	86,085 (40%)	101,630 (49%)
R	86,874 (43%)	113,814 (53%)	106,157 (49%)	103,412 (49%)
I			19,774 (9%)	

Campaign Finance

	Receipts	Receipts from PACs	Expend-itures
1988			
Tauke (R)	$601,558	$290,210 (48%)	$581,514
Tabor (D)	$259,207	$151,975 (59%)	$258,106
1986			
Tauke (R)	$392,207	$181,394 (46%)	$387,840
Tabor (D)	$170,929	$97,357 (57%)	$170,816

Key Votes

1987	
Raise speed limit to 65 mph	Y
Approve Gephardt "fair trade" amendment	N
Ban testing of larger nuclear weapons	Y
Delay "re-flagging" of Kuwaiti tankers	N
Approve tax-raising deficit-reduction bill	N
1988	
Approve aid to Nicaraguan contras	N
Enact civil rights restoration bill over Reagan veto	N
Kill 60-day plant-closing notification measure	Y
Pass omnibus trade bill over Reagan veto	N
Approve death penalty for drug-related murders	N
Bar federal funds for abortions in cases of rape and incest	Y
Oppose seven-day waiting period for purchase of handguns	Y

Voting Studies

	Presidential Support		Party Unity		Conservative Coalition	
Year	S	O	S	O	S	O
1988	54	42	80	17	87	13
1987	60	39	75	21	72	26
1986	53	43	71	25	58	38
1985	52	46	77	21	64	36
1984	54	42	65	31	56	39
1983	59	38	65	32	42	53
1982	49	47	51	41	53	44
1981	62	38	65	30	67	29

Interest Group Ratings

Year	ADA	ACU	AFL-CIO	CCUS
1988	45	67	23	85
1987	36	50	25	80
1986	30	43	21	88
1985	35	57	24	82
1984	40	55	0	67
1983	25	65	12	95
1982	60	30	25	70
1981	45	73	14	83

3 Dave Nagle (D)

Of Cedar Falls — Elected 1986

Born: April 15, 1943, Grinnell, Iowa.
Education: Attended U. of Northern Iowa, 1961-1965; U. of Iowa, LL.B. 1968.
Occupation: Lawyer.
Family: Wife, Diane Lewis; one child.
Religion: Roman Catholic.
Political Career: Black Hawk County Democratic chairman, 1978-82; Iowa Democratic chairman, 1982-85.
Capitol Office: 214 Cannon Bldg. 20515; 225-3301.

In Washington: "A lot of us wonder why the hell we're here in Congress," Nagle lamented several months into the 101st Congress.

That blunt expression of gloom came as Nagle found himself caught up in the historic fall of the Speaker of the House in the spring of 1989. Nagle had been enlisted by Jim Wright's forces to control political damage done to Wright as revelations of his questionable business dealings emerged in the press almost daily.

After one particularly damaging spate of news reports on Wright, Nagle called a meeting of about a dozen influential Democrats to discuss the Speaker's strategy. The members fell into bickering about what Wright should do. One widely respected Democrat, 20-year House veteran David R. Obey of Wisconsin, suggested for the first time that Wright should quit.

The meeting was regarded as a critical downturn in Wright's political fortunes. When *The New York Times* reported details of the meeting on its front page the next day, it noted that Nagle had organized the gathering. "Any time you get your name on the front page, short of receiving the medal of honor, it's generally not a good omen," Nagle said as he read the story while riding the subway to work.

The ethics furor on the Hill and the eventual fall of Wright made it tough times to be a House Democrat, but at least for Nagle it was a chance to do two things: increase his visibility and prove again to the leadership that he is a politician who can be counted on.

The operative word is politician. Nagle, a former state Democratic Party chairman, is given more to politics than to legislating. He is well regarded in leadership circles as an ambitious trooper for the party, eager to help the whip organization and interested in a place for himself in the power structure. Nagle's taste for politics made him one of the most likely of the junior Democrats to be called on in the Wright affair. He also owed Wright a debt: The Texan had campaigned for Nagle in Iowa in 1986, and later delivered on his pledge to get Nagle onto the Agriculture Committee.

After Wright's departure, Nagle was quick to display his loyalty to the new leadership. When the Republican National Committee (RNC) circulated a memorandum viewed as an attempt to smear new Speaker Thomas S. Foley of Washington, Nagle began soliciting signatures from House Democrats for a letter to President Bush calling for the resignation of RNC Chairman Lee Atwater. Foley, who had called for an end to the enmity in the House, called on Nagle to abandon the idea. "While I may disagree with the Speaker's assessment, I recognize that it is his judgment to make," Nagle said, withdrawing the letter.

In his drive for influence in the House, Nagle faces the challenge of matching his love of politics with substantive legislative accomplishments.

On the Science Committee's Space Science and Applications Subcommittee, Nagle is known as the "pit bull" because of his inclination to quarrel with Republicans. As one of the most vocal critics of a plan to help a private company, Space Industries Inc., send a space station into orbit, Nagle said Congress should be suspicious of the firm because it has business ties to members of both the Reagan and Bush administrations.

The subcommittee agreed to prohibit NASA from doing anything on the project other than accept bids, and Nagle succeeded in pushing an amendment that raised from two to three the number of firms that must submit bids.

On the full committee, Nagle has done battle with the panel's senior Republican, Pennsylvanian Robert S. Walker, who championed the cause of a drug-free work place.

Nagle frequently gave Walker fits, often with sarcastic remarks, by trying to thwart his controversial amendment prohibiting the spending of federal money in any work place if there is proof that illegal drugs were ever used there. Nagle called Walker's idea ridiculous and said the Republican was trying to create a "police state" at federally funded laboratories.

While other foes of Walker's proposal

Iowa 3

North Central — Waterloo; Iowa City

The votes of liberal Johnson County (Iowa City) helped swing the 3rd into Democratic hands in 1986 and keep it there in 1988. Home to the University of Iowa (29,000 students, 1,600 faculty), Johnson County went for Nagle by 2-to-1 in both those elections. The county's left-of-center tendencies were obvious throughout the 1980s: Ronald Reagan won only 32 percent of the Johnson vote in 1980; eight years later, George Bush got 35 percent there.

Johnson County was added to the 3rd after the 1980 census, changing what had been a secure GOP constituency into a battleground. But Nagle would not have prevailed in 1986 had he not won also in Black Hawk County, which casts the district's largest single bloc of votes, nearly 30 percent.

With two major towns — Waterloo (population 70,000) and Cedar Falls (population 33,000) — Black Hawk is Iowa's fourth-largest metropolitan area. Meatpacking and the farm-implement industry are crucial, and labor unions have demonstrated political strength here, although there has been a long Republican tradition in House voting. Until the 100th Congress, Waterloo was the only major city in Iowa that had not been represented by a Democrat since World War II. But as is the case all across Iowa, Democrats have been more successful in Black Hawk County in recent years: Nagle has won it twice, and Michael S. Dukakis carried it in 1988 presidential voting.

The 3rd stretches from Johnson County all the way north to the Minnesota border, and much of it is made up of rural counties that have a long Republican tradition. The land in most of the 3rd is flatter and richer than it is farther south, and until recently, farmers were comparatively well off. But hard times in agriculture during the 1980s have loosened GOP allegiances; Nagle in 1988 carried every county in the district but one, and Dukakis won all but three.

Population: 485,529. White 469,367 (97%), Black 10,319 (2%), Other 3,838 (1%). Spanish origin 2,783 (1%). 18 and over 352,455 (73%), 65 and over 60,717 (13%). Median age: 29.

worked to fashion some kind of compromise, Nagle dug in. The ultimate result, however, was that Nagle found himself on the sidelines. Walker got his drug-free work place amendment through Congress, and Democrats more pragmatic than Nagle succeeded in loading the amendment with enough language to render it fairly innocuous.

On the Agriculture Committee, Nagle was active in the 100th Congress' work on overhauling the ailing Farm Credit System, though his success was mixed. He helped draft an initial compromise that kept competing farm interests at the table. But he lost on two amendments tinkering with the management powers of the Farm Credit System.

Nagle, generally a liberal, scored a legislative victory when he teamed with a staunchly conservative Republican, Robert K. Dornan of California. The two cosponsored an amendment to the 1989 defense authorization bill that would prohibit for one year testing of so-called depressed trajectory missiles, as long as the Soviet Union also observes the ban. The amendment was adopted 262-160, but Dornan later withdrew his support when it was modified.

At Home: Prior to 1986, Republicans had won 26 consecutive elections here, in good GOP years and bad. Whenever a competitive situation developed, Democrats squandered it by running an urban liberal with no appeal to the district's rural majority. By those standards of history, Nagle was the wrong man to nominate when GOP Rep. Cooper Evans retired in 1986.

But Nagle proved to be the kind of politician who sees opportunity and makes thorough use of it. A tough, serious, intense Waterloo lawyer, he came out of a background in party organization, and his closest ties were to labor and the liberal activists who now play a crucial role in Iowa's Democratic ranks.

These assets were of dubious value in the rural venues of the 3rd. But then two accidents befell the Republicans. First, the candidate with the strongest ties to Evans, attorney Donald Redfern, failed to file his nomination papers on time. That gave the GOP nomination to former state Rep. John McIntee, whose claim on rural votes was weaker than Nagle's.

McIntee, a real-estate developer, began his fall campaign with a howling blunder. He wrote President Reagan a letter in which he suggested that farmers might relieve the shortage of storage space by keeping their crop in the ground all winter. Knowledgeable farm spokesmen laughed at this (the Iowa Corn Growers said most of the crop would rot in the fields).

Nagle told audiences that unlike McIntee, he not only knew how to plant corn, but also when to take it out of the ground. McIntee admitted his error, but never recovered his momentum.

It would be a mistake, though, to attribute Nagle's victory solely to McIntee's inept remarks. Despite his urban image and Type-A style, the Democrat began with a solid network of contacts in all the district's counties, including the rural ones, built during three hard-working years as state party chairman.

Nagle took pains to note that he was raised in a community of fewer than 3,000 people, and that he owned a 100-acre wildlife preserve on the Wapsipinicon River in Chickasaw County.

Equally important, the 3rd had been changed significantly by redistricting in 1981. Map makers that year added Johnson County, home to a liberally oriented population centered around the University of Iowa in Iowa City. Nagle courted this vote by decrying the Reagan administration's cutbacks in aid to education, and he also played up his opposition to U.S. aid to the Nicaraguan contras.

Two years later, Nagle had to prove his claim to the district against Redfern, who came back to stake his own. Redfern, a former chairman of the party in Black Hawk County, seemed ideal to retake what was once the province of the legendary anti-government champion H. R. Gross (1949-75). Redfern cast Nagle as another profligate, high-spending national Democrat out of touch with the home folks. After House Speaker Wright came to the district on Nagle's behalf, Redfern campaigned against Wright's ethical conduct.

But Nagle had been making the most of his opportunity since 1986. He had worked the small towns and farmlands of his district well, and made sure his contributions to bills such as the farm credit legislation of 1987 were widely known. So well had Nagle insulated himself against Redfern's attacks that he pushed his winning tally well over 60 percent, outpolling Redfern by more than 50,000 votes.

Nagle entered Democratic politics as a young lawyer in Waterloo in the early 1970s, spent four years as county chairman there, and then took over the state Democratic Party in 1982.

The state post was an important one for Nagle, because his tenure coincided with the caucuses that launched the Democrats' national nominating process in 1984. As state chairman, Nagle had the responsibility for running those caucuses, and the publicity they received guaranteed him name recognition unusual for a non-elected state party official.

Committees

Agriculture (17th of 27 Democrats)
Conservation, Credit and Rural Development; Livestock, Dairy and Poultry; Wheat, Soybeans and Feed Grains

Science, Space and Technology (24th of 30 Democrats)
Investigations and Oversight; Science, Research and Technology; Space Science and Applications

Elections

1988 General		
Dave Nagle (D)	129,204	(63%)
Donald B. Redfern (R)	74,682	(37%)
1988 Primary		
Dave Nagle (D)	15,803	(92%)
James R. Cox (D)	1,396	(8%)
1986 General		
Dave Nagle (D)	83,504	(55%)
John McIntee (R)	69,386	(45%)

District Vote For President

	1988	1984	1980	1976
D	118,602 (57%)	108,563 (47%)	91,217 (40%)	105,877 (48%)
R	89,365 (43%)	118,411 (52%)	111,226 (49%)	108,818 (49%)
I			23,484 (10%)	

Campaign Finance

	Receipts	Receipts from PACs	Expenditures
1988			
Nagle (D)	$608,264	$406,018 (67%)	$596,950
Redfern (R)	$262,188	$39,753 (15%)	$261,911
1986			
Nagle (D)	$291,713	$171,017 (59%)	$294,811
McIntee (R)	$418,995	$178,280 (43%)	$418,486

Key Votes

1987	
Raise speed limit to 65 mph	Y
Approve Gephardt "fair trade" amendment	Y
Ban testing of larger nuclear weapons	Y
Delay "re-flagging" of Kuwaiti tankers	N
Approve tax-raising deficit-reduction bill	Y
1988	
Approve aid to Nicaraguan contras	N
Enact civil rights restoration bill over Reagan veto	Y
Kill 60-day plant-closing notification measure	N
Pass omnibus trade bill over Reagan veto	Y
Approve death penalty for drug-related murders	N
Bar federal funds for abortions in cases of rape and incest	N
Oppose seven-day waiting period for purchase of handguns	Y

Voting Studies

	Presidential Support		Party Unity		Conservative Coalition	
Year	S	O	S	O	S	O
1988	21	76	86	8	45	55
1987	22	77	89	5	26	74

Interest Group Ratings

Year	ADA	ACU	AFL-CIO	CCUS
1988	80	8	100	36
1987	88	0	94	7

4 Neal Smith (D)

Of Altoona — Elected 1958

Born: March 23, 1920, Hedrick, Iowa.
Education: Attended U. of Missouri, 1945-46; Syracuse U., 1946-47; Drake U., LL.B. 1950.
Military Career: Army Air Corps, 1942-45.
Occupation: Farmer; lawyer.
Family: Wife, Beatrix Havens; two children.
Religion: Methodist.
Political Career: Sought Democratic nomination for U.S. House, 1956.
Capitol Office: 2373 Rayburn Bldg. 20515; 225-4426.

In Washington: Smith's long House career is one of contrasts. His name would not appear on any short list of activists in Congress, yet he has seized a few issues with the determination of a crusader. He is an institutionalist, as befits his seniority, yet he has occasionally tilted at the House system and its leaders with the rebelliousness of a maverick.

Generally, Smith has spent recent years outside the spotlight, tending to his chairmanship of the Appropriations Subcommittee on Commerce, Justice, State and the Judiciary, tenaciously defending programs under his jurisdiction against White House budget assaults, and tinkering with crop subsidies, dam construction and other Appropriations business that affects his district.

Meanwhile, as third in line at Appropriations behind two near-octogenarians, he thinks about running the full committee someday, although he will turn 70 in the 101st Congress. "I can't help it," he said in 1986. "Everyone keeps telling me I'll be chairman."

If lawmakers occasionally find Chairman Jamie L. Whitten intractable, Smith could pose an even greater problem. Though he is a fair and honest broker as subcommittee chairman, he can be bullheaded about pressing his causes, most recently for anti-drug funding. Perhaps more than any other subcommittee chairman in Appropriations' "College of Cardinals," Smith resists the strictures imposed on appropriations bills by recent budget laws and by free-lance attacks from junior budget-cutters on the House floor. Typically quiet and understated — "bland and boring," a GOP foe once said — he can turn fierce when his subcommittee's annual bill is challenged.

He is intimately familiar with its wide-ranging details, which fund three disparate Cabinet departments, the federal courts and 23 agencies, including the Federal Trade, Communications and Securities and Exchange commissions and the Small Business Administration. A man of liberal instincts rooted in Depression-era Iowa, he cannot understand how other members, particularly Democrats, can put deficit reduction ahead of addressing society's needs.

Throughout the Reagan years, he successfully battled administration efforts to kill such programs as the Legal Services Corporation, the Economic Development Administration, juvenile delinquency grants and drug-abuse funding. On spending bills other than his own, Smith has been a dogged fighter for programs subsidizing assistance to senior citizens, nurses' training and education grants to poor communities.

In recent years, Smith's more formidable foes often have been his colleagues. In both 1987 and 1988, he so opposed the House-passed budget resolution that he devised a way for his subcommittee to ignore the budget's limits when drafting his panel's annual appropriations bill. His subcommittee omitted funding for some programs that either had not been authorized, or were so popular that members would surely cough up more money for his panel to allocate.

Smith was protesting what he sees as some colleagues' politically opportunistic attempts to have it both ways — voting to authorize expensive new initiatives but later opposing appropriations for them in the name of deficit reduction. "Some members that talk big about wanting to control deficits, they also want all these things — drug abuse, homeless money," he groused in mid-1987.

Within his subcommittee, he operated as usual by consensus, keeping debate going until agreement was reached without resorting to votes. Then, both years, he took his bill to the full committee and acted as both its manager and chief critic.

In 1987 he told Appropriations his fiscal 1988 measure was "woefully inadequate" because of the "crazy accounting" of Congress' budget process; in the end, he did get relief to fund the FBI, the Drug Enforcement Administration and the United States Information Agency. In 1988, he presented his fiscal 1989 measure, saying, "Everyone should oppose this

Iowa 4

Central — Des Moines; Ames

More than 60 percent of the 4th District's voters are in Polk County, and most of them are in Des Moines. Surrounding farm counties and smaller industrial towns in the 4th look to Des Moines as the region's commercial, financial and governmental center.

Predominantly white, Protestant and middle class, Des Moines has little of the ethnic flavor of other Midwestern industrial cities such as Chicago or Omaha. More than 50 insurance companies have their headquarters there, making it the nation's second-largest insurance city. A sizable group of government workers live in and around the capital city, adding to its white-collar work force. The city also depends on grain marketing, publishing and the manufacture of farm equipment.

With about 4,000 members and a regional office in Des Moines, the United Auto Workers is a significant political presence. Workers in the farm equipment business are UAW members, and have been hard hit by the farm depression. The UAW has been important to past Democratic successes in the Des Moines area.

In 1980 presidential voting, a growing preference for the GOP was evident in the suburbs of Des Moines. That enabled Ronald Reagan to win Polk County by a slim margin over Jimmy Carter. But over the course of the Reagan administration, many more of Polk's voters turned away from the GOP than toward it. Walter F. Mondale narrowly carried the county in 1984, and Michael S. Dukakis decisively defeated George Bush there in 1988. The 4th, in fact, was Dukakis' best district in Iowa, giving him nearly 60 percent of its vote.

North of Polk, in Story County, is Ames (population 44,000), the home of Iowa State University's 26,000 students. In the 1980 presidential election, Story gave independent John B. Anderson more than 19 percent, his fifth-best county showing in the nation. Four years later, it was narrowly in Reagan's corner, but Story voted for Dukakis in 1988.

Population: 485,480. White 461,514 (95%), Black 14,645 (3%), Other 4,601 (1%). Spanish origin 5,722 (1%). 18 and over 356,227 (73%), 65 and over 53,382 (11%). Median age: 29.

bill on its merits. There just isn't enough money."

On the floor in 1987, Smith was powerless to block an attack by Republicans and some conservative Democrats that reduced his bill by 2.45 percent. Smith said the bill merely funded programs like those in the 1986 drug bill that Congress had previously authorized. "If you didn't want the drug bill," he snapped at his adversaries, "why'd you vote for it?"

In 1989, Smith was more successful. Arguing that it was time to pay for the ballyhooed $2.8 billion anti-drug bill of 1988 (for which just $500 million had been appropriated), he stubbornly and successfully insisted that the House include $822 million more in the year's supplemental appropriations bill. Smith had the advantages of a politically potent argument and his own proven willpower; after a standoff of more than a month, he prevailed over both the White House and Democratic leaders concerned about meeting deficit limits.

Outside Appropriations, Smith has been active in the late 1980s in fighting for tougher meat-inspection laws, a drive that recalls a crusade of two decades ago that resulted in perhaps his single most notable achievement.

That effort began in 1961, characteristically low-key, and it ended with passage of the 1967 Wholesome Meat Act and the 1968 Wholesome Poultry Products Act. The legislation marked the first major overhaul of the law regulating the meatpacking industry since its passage during the Theodore Roosevelt administration, in the wake of the exposé "The Jungle." Similarly, Smith's long-sought success in the 1960s followed reports of scandalous conditions in meatpacking houses, this time by the *Des Moines Register,* which won a Pulitzer Prize.

Though his quiet persistence had been largely responsible for forcing the issue, the 1967 law did not go nearly as far as Smith wanted. He tried to amend it to impose federal standards on the industry, but failed in the House by six votes. Congress eventually cleared a bill simply providing funds for states to upgrade their facilities.

In the past couple of Congresses, Smith has rejoined the battle to improve poultry processing. He has helped block an industry push for more lenient federal supervision, and took the offensive by proposing increased inspections in response to reports of growing incidents of poultry contamination. Again his home-state newspaper has boosted the cause with investigative reporting. Though he is not on the Agriculture Committee, which has jurisdiction, Smith testifies there as a sort of expert witness.

He does play a role in farm policy as a

member of Appropriations' Agriculture Subcommittee. In 1986, Smith worked with Republican Silvio O. Conte of Massachusetts on an amendment to limit federal subsidies to $250,000 per individual producer after news reports that some large cotton and rice producers had received as much as $20 million under the 1985 farm law.

Meanwhile, from his place on the Small Business Committee, Smith pursues his personal war against monopolies, including those in agriculture-related industries. In 1980, his last year as Small Business chairman, Smith introduced a bill to prevent any meatpacker from slaughtering more than 25 percent of the national production of cattle and hogs, and to bar the larger companies from operating retail food outlets. He claimed consumers lost $98.5 billion through concentration in the food industry between 1973 and 1978.

Smith's reformist approach to agriculture has been a consistent theme in his career. He was instrumental in creating the Commodity Futures Trading Commission to avoid grain trading abuses, and in setting up strict federal procedures for grain inspection. He spent much time in recent years fighting Reagan administration efforts to turn grain inspection back to private enterprise. "They cheated before," he has said of private grain interests, "and there's no indication they wouldn't cheat again."

His most famous reform, however, had nothing to do with agriculture. It was a rule against nepotism on congressional payrolls. As of the late 1960s, more than 50 members had hired relatives as aides. Smith's measure prevented that, although it "grandfathered" those already employed.

To get his rule past the House, Smith had to offer it as an amendment to a related bill, and he found a vehicle in legislation increasing federal salaries. Before most members knew what had happened, the House had passed it.

That bit of parliamentary gamesmanship demonstrated the fascination Smith always has had with House procedure. He has proposed a variety of rules changes over the years, including the one in 1973 that reduced the dominance of the seniority system by making all committee chairmen subject to a Democratic Caucus vote at the start of each Congress.

Despite his parliamentary skill and the wide respect he enjoys, Smith never has excelled at internal politics. Along the way, he acquired a reputation in some quarters as arrogant and self-centered.

In 1975, he tried to become House Budget Committee chairman, but lost to Brock Adams of Washington, 148-119. In 1979 and 1980, circumstances allowed Smith temporarily to be chairman of both Small Business and his Appropriations subcommittee, though members expected him to give one up. Instead, he kept both until the next Congress chose its leaders, arguing that he needed the extra boost the dual posts would give him for his 1980 re-election. His move angered both Bill Alexander of Arkansas, who was waiting to inherit the Appropriations panel, and members of the Black Caucus, who felt the Small Business chair should have gone immediately to Parren J. Mitchell of Maryland, the veteran black Democrat who was next in line there. Mitchell took over in 1981, when Smith kept his Appropriations job.

Smith's headstrong pursuit of his aims periodically tests his relations with House leaders. In the 99th Congress, he mounted a quixotic challenge to a member of the Democratic Steering and Policy Committee, even though no incumbent on that leadership panel had ever been defeated that way. Eventually Smith gave up.

In August 1985, with the House trying to pass a budget resolution one day before the summer recess, Smith blocked the leadership's bid to waive a House rule that requires a three-day waiting period so members can study a document. The tactic was his way of lodging his annual protest of the Budget Committee's work. But the leadership circumvented Smith's objection by ordering the Rules Committee to draft a waiver. It passed the House, as did the budget, and the recess started on time.

At Home: Smith's even-tempered, unaffected manner has always brought him votes beyond the normal Democratic constituency in Iowa. His long run of easy re-elections was interrupted by a poor showing in 1980, but he rebounded convincingly two years later, and has had no problems since.

Until 1980, Smith had not seen tough elections since the early years of his political career. After serving as national president of the Young Democrats of America, he first ran for Congress in 1956, losing the Democratic primary to state Rep. William Denman, who nearly unseated GOP Rep. Paul Cunningham in the general election.

In 1958 Smith finished first in a five-man Democratic primary field. But he fell short of winning the 35 percent plurality required by state party rules, so the party's district convention was left to choose the nominee. Although Smith had to overcome some opposition from Des Moines labor unions, he won the nomination easily at the convention.

Cunningham's narrow 1956 victory marked him as vulnerable in 1958, but Democratic unity had been damaged by the bitter nomination fight. Smith had to struggle to win with 52 percent, aided by a national Democratic tide that took three Iowa congressional seats from Republican control.

In 1960 Smith was the sole survivor among the state's three first-term Democrats. His Republican opponent, Des Moines physician Floyd Burgeson, was a forceful speaker but an inexperienced politician. Smith prevailed with

53 percent and won easily during the next decade.

Redistricting after the 1970 census threw Smith into the same district with Republican Rep. John Kyl. The national Democratic Party and labor groups gave Smith extra support, and he easily overcame Kyl (whose son Jon now serves in the House from Arizona). Smith coasted through subsequent elections until he met Republican Don Young in 1980.

Smith's close call against Young capped a year of unusual activity among 4th District Republicans. A Des Moines physician, Young used financial and organizational help from the national GOP to build a respectable campaign organization and raise about $250,000. He called the congressman an entrenched fixture of a Democratic Congress that had weakened the nation's economy and defense.

Disquieted by polls showing a sharp drop in his popularity, Smith fought back with radio, television and billboard advertisements in the closing weeks of the campaign. He won just over 55 percent in Polk County (Des Moines) and Wapello County (Ottumwa), but lost two rural, small-town counties and was held to a bare majority in six others. Young's 46 percent tally marked the first time in 20 years that Smith had been held below 60 percent.

The strong showing by Young generated considerable optimism among Republicans that Smith could be toppled in 1982. The optimism faded, however, when Young announced in late 1981 that he would forgo a rematch and concentrate on running his medical clinic.

Des Moines state Sen. Dave Readinger stepped in to take the GOP nomination. He blanketed the district with billboards to increase his name recognition and tried to portray Smith as having spent too much time in Washington to be attuned to Iowa concerns.

But the conservative mood that aided Young in 1980 had passed. Smith won 67 percent in Polk County and carried every other county in the district. Since then, Republicans have forgone heavily investing in the 4th.

Committees

Appropriations (3rd of 35 Democrats)
Commerce, Justice and State, the Judiciary and Related Agencies (chairman); Labor, Health and Human Services, Education and Related Agencies; Rural Development, Agriculture and Related Agencies

Small Business (2nd of 27 Democrats)
SBA, the General Economy and Minority Enterprise Development

Elections

1988 General		
Neal Smith (D)	157,065	(72%)
Paul Lunde (R)	62,056	(28%)
1988 Primary		
Neal Smith (D)	12,101	(90%)
Maurice W. Stoutenberg (D)	1,293	(10%)
1986 General		
Neal Smith (D)	107,271	(68%)
Bob Lockard (R)	49,641	(32%)

Previous Winning Percentages: **1984** (61%) **1982** (66%) **1980** (54%) **1978** (65%) **1976** (69%) **1974** (64%) **1972** (60%) **1970** (65%) **1968** (62%) **1966** (60%) **1964** (70%) **1962** (63%) **1960** (53%) **1958** (52%)

District Vote For President

	1988	1984	1980	1976
D	131,356 (59%)	118,092 (50%)	95,948 (42%)	113,687 (51%)
R	90,855 (41%)	115,898 (49%)	105,044 (45%)	103,091 (46%)
I			27,252 (12%)	

Campaign Finance

	Receipts	Receipts from PACs	Expend-itures
1988			
Smith (D)	$205,035	$162,585 (79%)	$83,474
1986			
Smith (D)	$153,681	$109,400 (71%)	$100,675
Lockard (R)	$65,232	$13,500 (21%)	$65,866

Key Votes

1987	
Raise speed limit to 65 mph	Y
Approve Gephardt "fair trade" amendment	N
Ban testing of larger nuclear weapons	Y
Delay "re-flagging" of Kuwaiti tankers	?
Approve tax-raising deficit-reduction bill	Y
1988	
Approve aid to Nicaraguan contras	N
Enact civil rights restoration bill over Reagan veto	Y
Kill 60-day plant-closing notification measure	N
Pass omnibus trade bill over Reagan veto	Y
Approve death penalty for drug-related murders	N
Bar federal funds for abortions in cases of rape and incest	?
Oppose seven-day waiting period for purchase of handguns	Y

Voting Studies

	Presidential Support		Party Unity		Conservative Coalition	
Year	S	O	S	O	S	O
1988	30	63	79	12	37	53
1987	27	69	87	8	47	49
1986	22	70	80	13	44	52
1985	30	66	85	11	35	62
1984	38	55	71	17	42	47
1983	30	68	84	13	29	66
1982	40	56	83	17	30	67
1981	42	55	76	20	40	55

Interest Group Ratings

Year	ADA	ACU	AFL-CIO	CCUS
1988	80	16	86	46
1987	76	9	81	14
1986	70	14	83	22
1985	75	10	75	24
1984	70	21	62	53
1983	70	17	76	61
1982	80	19	70	45
1981	55	20	64	18

5 Jim Ross Lightfoot (R)

Of Shenandoah — Elected 1984

Born: Sept. 27, 1938, Sioux City, Iowa.
Education: Attended U. of Iowa; U. of Tulsa.
Military Career: Army, 1955-56; Army Reserve, 1956-63.
Occupation: Radio broadcaster; store owner; police officer.
Family: Wife, Nancy Harrison; four children.
Religion: Roman Catholic.
Political Career: Corsicana, Texas, City Commission, 1974-76.
Capitol Office: 1222 Longworth Bldg. 20515; 225-3806.

In Washington: Critics say Lightfoot is stronger on anecdotes than on evidence, but he has won two convincing re-elections in his agriculture-dependent district at a time when many have criticized the GOP for turning breadbasket Iowa into an economic basket case.

An easygoing radio broadcaster with a homespun wit and an instinct for small-town values, Lightfoot is prone to defend his conservative record with a story, not a stack of documents.

Facing criticism in 1986 that he and the GOP had ignored the plight of hard-pressed farmers, Lightfoot said he was sure the farm recession had bottomed out, because business was better at the two women's apparel stores he and his wife own in the 5th District.

"I think the people in the communities realistically took a look at the situation and said, 'Hey, Uncle Sam and the state aren't going to fix it,' and they decided to do something about it," he explained. "And I think our role in government is not to get in their way."

In 1987, he disputed the bleak picture of rural America painted by witnesses at Senate Agriculture Committee hearings held in the Midwest. He went to the House floor to point out "a few of the positive signs cropping up in rural America.... Cautiously but steadily, people are stepping away from the gloom-and-doom view of American agriculture and recognizing that we have made substantial progress from the troubling days of the early and mid-'80s."

In a state where GOP House members such as Tom Tauke and Jim Leach carved out niches well to the left of the Reagan administration, Lightfoot has usually followed a conservative line, not only on agricultural issues, where he stresses reliance on the free market, but also on many of the defense and foreign policy questions that excite Iowa's dovish, quasi-isolationist instincts. His first major vote in the 99th Congress was for the MX missile; no other Iowan in the House or Senate supported it. He also has voted for the strategic defense initiative, chemical weapons and aid to anti-communist rebels in Angola. In each of his four years in Washington, he supported President Reagan's position on House floor votes more often than any other Iowa House member.

But Lightfoot did register a conspicuous difference with the administration in 1986 by opposing aid to the Nicaraguan contras.

Lightfoot's views on agricultural policy are well received by those farmers in the 5th who are not battling bankruptcy and who remain suspicious of the federal role in agriculture even as they benefit from some programs.

He projects his minimalist view of government's role in agriculture as chairman of the House Rural Communities Task Force. "I believe we owe it to our rural communities to help them help themselves," he has said.

In 1985, Lightfoot voted against permitting a farmers' referendum on establishing production controls on wheat and feed grains and against an export-subsidy program, a move that angered liberal farm activists.

After being turned away from the Agriculture Committee upon arriving in Washington — with two Iowans on the panel, the state was thought to have its share of seats — Lightfoot took a seat on Public Works. When a seat on Agriculture opened up two years later, he said he would rather keep Public Works, "because it's where the money is. There's no money in the Agriculture Committee." On Public Works, he lobbied for a flood-control project as well as for a federal buy-out of farmers' land flooded by a lake in the district. He has also pushed for local bridge improvements, airport projects and a highway demonstration project.

A former pilot, Lightfoot devotes a good deal of attention to aviation matters from the Aviation Subcommittee at Public Works. At a 1989 hearing on airport and airline safety following the December 1988 terrorist bombing of an airliner over Scotland, Lightfoot noted that he had a special perspective on the tragedy,

Iowa 5

Southwest — Council Bluffs; Fort Dodge

The 5th is farm country, a sprawling patch of southwest Iowa whose health is measured in dollars-per-bushel and debt-to-asset ratios. Its small towns, some little more than a main street lined by worn, wood-planked sidewalks and faded storefronts, live off the agricultural economy. Only one other district in the country has a higher percentage of its population living on farms.

The rural counties of the 5th are divided by a line that roughly follows Interstate 80 between Council Bluffs and Des Moines. To the north, the land is flatter, the soil richer, and the farms — until recently — more prosperous. The land to the south is rocky and pocked with gullies, more suitable for raising livestock than for growing crops. The counties along the Missouri border have historically been among the poorest in the state; the farm-debt crisis and three years of drought followed by 1984 flooding devastated many farms in the area.

Even so, the southwest corner of the district is staunchly Republican. Pottawattamie County and those counties to the south, east and northwest of it voted solidly Republican in 1984 and in 1988.

There are only two cities of any size, Council Bluffs and Fort Dodge. Council Bluffs, the seat of Pottawattamie County, is the larger, with about 57,000 people. An old trading settlement built against the Missouri River bluffs across from Omaha, it makes its living from meatpacking, railroads and light manufacturing. Council Bluffs has a good-sized union population, but it also has a middle class, almost suburban character that has made it resistant to major Democratic inroads.

At the northern end of the district, Fort Dodge (population 27,000), the Webster County seat, is much more reliable Democratic territory. An industrial center near large gypsum deposits, the city is in the heart of a region settled by Irish Catholics. Webster County and its heavily Catholic neighbor, Greene County, were two of the three counties in the 5th that voted Democratic for president in 1984. In 1988, Democratic Party fortunes soared in the 5th, with Michael S. Dukakis carrying 19 of the district's 27 counties.

At its eastern end, the district holds southern suburbs of Des Moines in Warren County. This county was the state's fastest growing in the 1970s, but the growth has leveled off in recent years.

Population: 485,639. White 480,799 (99%), Black 1,649 (0.3%). Spanish origin 3,071 (1%). 18 and over 346,800 (71%), 65 and over 75,869 (16%). Median age: 32.

since he had worked as a policeman and charter plane operator as well as a pilot.

One of Lightfoot's goals has been to create a National Park Service site to commemorate the westward expansion in the 19th century along a system of trails. His bill, cosponsored by Utah Republican Howard C. Nielson, would establish the Western Historic Trails Center in Council Bluffs, Iowa, presenting historic documents and educational and cultural programs to recount exploration along such paths as the Lewis and Clark, Mormon and Oregon trails.

Lightfoot will be better situated to promote his proposal in the 101st Congress with his new assignment on the Interior Committee; there, he has a spot on the National Parks and Public Lands Subcommittee.

The 100th Congress was a rough time for Lightfoot. In late 1987, he broke two toes rushing down some stairs. Later quizzed on the open shoe he wore, he explained, "I went to the Gerald Ford School of Walking, where you have to fall down and break something to graduate." Lightfoot missed work in the first three months of 1988 recovering from double-bypass heart surgery.

At Home: Affable and unassuming, Lightfoot fits his district like a comfortable pair of dungarees. "I've been involved in agriculture for many years," he has said, "and involved in a business on Main Street. I was a blue-collar worker.... That's what this district is made of — small business, blue-collar workers and farms." In 1984, he brought the GOP its first victory in the 5th in a decade.

When Democrat Tom Harkin left the 5th to run for the Senate, Lightfoot was an obvious contender for the Republican nomination. For 16 years, off and on, he had been a farm editor and announcer for KMA, the major farm station in southwest Iowa. With his highly personal delivery of market and weather reports, farm news and comments on local and national affairs a daily feature of life for farm families, he had developed a big following. His appearances at hog roasts, county fairs, rodeos and charity events cemented his celebrity status.

In addition, after years of farm reporting and quiet support for various Republican causes, Lightfoot had ready access to county-by-county networks of pork producers and cattlemen, and to GOP regulars. When he was urged to run for Congress after returning from a well-publicized trip to the Far East with President Reagan in 1983, Lightfoot agreed. He proved his potency in a primary against four Republicans.

The general election proved much tougher. Lightfoot was no longer selling himself just to the faithful. Southern Iowa's farm economy was in wretched shape, and voters were in no mood to accept generic GOP assurances.

Moreover, Democrat Jerry Fitzgerald was no average candidate himself. A former state House majority leader, he had run twice for governor, in 1978 and 1982. Well-known in the district's northern counties, he had extensive ties to Democratic activists and the added strength of Harkin on the Senate ballot to pull him along.

Lightfoot's campaign cultivated an image of neighbors getting together to help a friend — on the back of the campaign cards he handed out was a recipe for "Florence Falk's sour cream apple pie." Fitzgerald, more cerebral and reserved, could not compete on the level of personality, but he came across as the more substantive of the two. He attacked Lightfoot as ill-informed about federal policy.

Fitzgerald's tactics paid off where neither candidate was known, especially in the southeastern counties outside of KMA's listening radius. But Lightfoot built up huge margins in his home territory, and he won by just over 3,000 votes districtwide.

Democrats were optimistic they could unseat Lightfoot in 1986 amid the deepening farm discontent, but they never quite came together on how to do it. The preferred candidate of many of the Harkin Democrats was state Sen. Leonard Boswell, a farmer and former military officer. But Boswell ran sluggishly and lost the nomination to Scott Hughes, a little-known Council Bluffs lawyer.

Hughes had some credibility with farmers from his work in fighting foreclosures, and he tried to paint Lightfoot as insensitive to the rural crisis. He accused Lightfoot, who had voted for the 1985 farm bill, of placing his Reagan loyalties ahead of agricultural needs.

But Lightfoot's years of contact with the farm community made that case difficult to sell. As depressed as conditions were in southwest Iowa, voters seemed unwilling to blame Lightfoot. He won every county for a victory margin exceeding 25,000 votes. He nearly doubled that margin in 1988.

Committees

Interior and Insular Affairs (13th of 15 Republicans)
Energy and the Environment; National Parks and Public Lands

Public Works and Transportation (10th of 20 Republicans)
Aviation; Public Buildings and Grounds; Water Resources

Select Aging (14th of 27 Republicans)
Health and Long-Term Care

Elections

1988 General		
Jim Ross Lightfoot (R)	117,761	(64%)
Gene Freund (D)	66,599	(36%)
1986 General		
Jim Ross Lightfoot (R)	85,025	(59%)
Scott Hughes (D)	58,552	(41%)

Previous Winning Percentage: **1984** (51%)

District Vote For President

	1988	1984	1980	1976
D	100,734 (52%)	88,949 (42%)	74,675 (35%)	101,119 (49%)
R	92,323 (47%)	123,243 (58%)	123,622 (58%)	103,428 (50%)
I			14,128 (7%)	

Campaign Finance

	Receipts	Receipts from PACs	Expend-itures
1988			
Lightfoot (R)	$478,842	$166,077 (35%)	$420,730
Freund (D)	$133,183	$68,275 (51%)	$131,599
1986			
Lightfoot (R)	$464,116	$207,047 (45%)	$474,179
Hughes (D)	$250,405	$106,097 (42%)	$250,384

Key Votes

1987	
Raise speed limit to 65 mph	Y
Approve Gephardt "fair trade" amendment	N
Ban testing of larger nuclear weapons	N
Delay "re-flagging" of Kuwaiti tankers	N
Approve tax-raising deficit-reduction bill	N
1988	
Approve aid to Nicaraguan contras	?
Enact civil rights restoration bill over Reagan veto	?
Kill 60-day plant-closing notification measure	Y
Pass omnibus trade bill over Reagan veto	N
Approve death penalty for drug-related murders	Y
Bar federal funds for abortions in cases of rape and incest	Y
Oppose seven-day waiting period for purchase of handguns	Y

Voting Studies

	Presidential Support		Party Unity		Conservative Coalition	
Year	S	O	S	O	S	O
1988	63	26	76	8	92	3
1987	65	34	89	10	88	12
1986	70	30	83	16	84	16
1985	63	38	85	14	84	16

Interest Group Ratings

Year	ADA	ACU	AFL-CIO	CCUS
1988	10	90	15	85
1987	8	74	6	87
1986	10	64	14	94
1985	10	81	24	82

6 Fred Grandy (R)

Of Sioux City — Elected 1986

Born: June 29, 1948, Sioux City, Iowa.
Education: Harvard U., B.A. 1970.
Occupation: Actor.
Family: Wife, Catherine Mann; three children.
Religion: Episcopalian.
Political Career: No previous office.
Capitol Office: 1711 Longworth Bldg. 20515; 225-5476.

In Washington: Since leaving Harvard, Grandy has made his fortune by handling three roles well. The first was "Gopher Smith," the bumbling and likable ship's purser on the "Love Boat" television series, which made Grandy famous. The second was the role of prodigal son returned, which he played well enough to be elected to Congress by the residents of Sioux City, his boyhood home.

The third is the role of successful congressman, and Grandy is good enough in this part that he may someday find himself appearing on the statewide political stage.

The latter chance is not likely to occur in 1990. Republican Gov. Terry Branstad wants to run for a third term and veteran GOP Rep. Tom Tauke is taking on Democratic Sen. Tom Harkin. But Grandy may have too much career momentum to be satisfied with a long stretch in the House minority. And redistricting may create further uncertainty in the not too distant future.

The 1990 census will cost Iowa one of its six House seats, and it is possible the state's two western districts will be combined. That could mean a do-or-die primary battle with neighboring GOP Rep. Jim Ross Lightfoot, who seems at least as entrenched as Grandy. The outcome of a Grandy-Lightfoot duel could depend on who gets more of his current constituents into the new, combined district.

Grandy left college divided between ambitions in government and theater. At first, he chose the former, becoming a legislative aide and speechwriter to Rep. Wiley Mayne, then the GOP representative for northwest Iowa. But show business beckoned. Grandy was soon appearing in off-Broadway productions and films, and in 1975 his run with "Love Boat" began.

As that commercial success wound down, Grandy turned his attention again to Washington. And the road to Washington lay through Sioux City, where luck gave him a shot at an open seat in 1986. Grandy won by about 3,000 votes, a margin that left him keenly aware that his re-election battle was already under way. District matters, especially farm policy, would dominate his agenda and dictate his style in Washington.

Grandy did receive some notice on his Education and Labor subcommittee by casting one of two votes against a bill restricting private employers' use of lie-detector tests (he later voted for the bill on the floor in its final form), and for his objections to portions of the Act for Better Child Care Services.

But primarily, Grandy focused on the Agriculture Committee, where he has earned a reputation for intelligence, incisiveness and homework. "He asks good questions," says one Democratic colleague. "Too good." He was named to the House-Senate conference committee on the 1987 farm-credit bill, the most important agriculture legislation of the 100th Congress. He was also one of the GOP floor managers for the groundwater-protection bill that passed Congress in 1987, and a co-author of the Drought Assistance Act of 1988.

Grandy does not react to farm issues reflexively. When Congress was extending the authority of the Federal Grain Inspection Service in 1988, Grandy wanted to amend the bill to require tougher inspection to ensure export grains would not rot en route. Although tougher standards might create problems for grain producers and shippers, Grandy argued that grain arriving in poor condition would spoil market opportunities in the long run.

Another salient feature of Grandy's first term was his struggle with the issue of aid to the Nicaraguan contras. In 1987, he voted with the president and the House majority in renewing direct military aid. But by early 1988, he was acknowledging the mounting unpopularity of that aid among his constituents. His staff said his mail was running 70 percent against the president's package of $36 million in military and non-military aid.

But Grandy made a visit to the White House and wound up standing by the president in his losing cause (the aid was denied by a vote of 211-219). He was the only member of the Iowa delegation to do so. (Lightfoot, usually the most conservative Iowan, was absent because of health problems.)

At Home: When Grandy first started run-

Iowa 6

Northwest — Sioux City

Northwestern Iowa's flat, rich soil makes it one of the most agriculturally productive areas of the nation, with consistently impressive yields for both corn and soybeans. But as farming has become a more costly, technologically more complex business, many small-scale farmers have sold their land to agribusiness operations, eliminating jobs and causing migration from the district. Of the 23 counties in the 6th, all but seven have lost population in the last two decades.

Some of the more industrialized pockets of the district were hit hard by the 1982 recession and have yet to recover; Emmet County, in the north-central part, saw its unemployment soar to 16 percent that year, the result of meatpacking plant closings.

There are troubles in the rural counties as well. In the western part of the district, where farmers expanded considerably in the 1970s, some counties have seen scores of farms go on the market with no purchasers.

Sioux City, western Iowa's largest city (population 80,000), is the political core of the 6th District. An old meatpacking town on the Missouri River, Sioux City has grown into an urban center with a massive downtown urban renewal project that includes a regional shopping center. The city ran into troubles a bit earlier than its neighbors, due to the closing of a large Zenith electronics plant in 1978. Since then, its condition has stabilized with the influx of some small industries.

The city and surrounding Woodbury County have about a fifth of the district's population and generally vote Republican. Despite the flap over his comments on Sioux City, Grandy narrowly won Woodbury County in 1986, and he carried it easily two years later.

Notwithstanding Grandy's cruise to reelection in 1988, his district is becoming somewhat less enamored of the national Republican Party. Democratic nominee Michael S. Dukakis won 15 of the district's 23 counties, but still lost the district by a tenth of a percentage point. Four years earlier, Ronald Reagan carried the district comfortably, but even he lost Cerro Gordo County, the second most populous in the 6th. Mason City, the county seat, is a producer of ice machines and building materials and a processor of meat and dairy products. It is also the town that inspired Meredith Willson, a native son, to write "The Music Man."

Population: 485,491. White 479,511 (99%), Black 1,621 (0.3%), Other 2,510 (1%). Spanish origin 3,319 (1%). 18 and over 348,641 (72%), 65 and over 74,259 (15%). Median age: 32.

ning for Congress in 1985, his bid was viewed as just a curiosity. An actor from California who had left Iowa as a young teenager, he returned to an area where he had never even voted to wage a campaign against popular six-term incumbent Rep. Berkley Bedell (who had defeated Mayne, Grandy's former boss, in 1974). But the laughter stopped abruptly when Bedell, early in 1986, decided not to run.

Left in the lurch, 6th District Democrats nominated Clayton Hodgson, who had been Bedell's chief agricultural aide in northwest Iowa for a decade. Despite his late start and low name recognition, Hodgson had strengths that Grandy lacked: a solid agricultural background, both as a Bedell aide and as a farmer himself; lifelong residency in the state; and strong support from Bedell. Grandy, more colorful and stylish than the low-key Democrat, seemed to fit the rural district about as well as a three-piece business suit.

But Grandy proved surprisingly successful at deflecting jokes about his show business career and charges that he was a carpetbagger. An articulate graduate of Exeter and Harvard, Grandy set out early to, as he put it, "make people understand that there is a long-pants version of Fred Grandy, not just Gopher Smith in short pants." He worked hard to master issues of importance to Iowa, and was equally successful at building a large campaign treasury.

While Hodgson stressed that he was an Iowan and Grandy was not, Grandy pointed out that his father's name still graced an insurance company in Sioux City, the district's largest population center. He criticized his former home state of California as a "superficial environment." Grandy praised Iowa's sense of community and thanked residents for welcoming him back so warmly.

During the summer, the contest between Hodgson and Grandy provided one of the strangest political controversies of the year, as Democrats accused the former actor of having made derogatory remarks about Iowa on the "Tonight Show." Grandy initially refused demands that he release copies of the tapes, which seemed to make the situation worse. But when he later agreed to show the tapes to the media, they produced no "smoking gun." Grandy did poke fun at his hometown of Sioux City, comparing the annual river festival there to a "big testimonial to ringworm," but the controversy died down long before Election Day.

Ideological differences between the candidates were largely overshadowed by questions of background and style, but they did exist. Grandy tried to have the best of both worlds, appearing with President Reagan at the signing of the 1985 farm bill, but taking care not to defend the administration's agricultural policies. To troubled farmers he stressed the need to expand exports, with federal subsidies if necessary. Hodgson called Grandy's farm proposals "a welfare check for farmers" and pushed for production controls that Bedell had advocated.

Grandy's victory was far from overwhelming. He carried only 11 of 23 counties in the district. But those who expected him to fall when first challenged were soon surprised by both the job he did in Washington and his ability back home. In his first term, Grandy held four town meetings in each of the 23 counties. He opened three district offices.

Democrats had thought Grandy vulnerable for his vote on contra aid and for the time he had spent campaigning for other GOP candidates or visiting back in California. But the party was unable to field a candidate who could make that sort of ammunition count.

Their nominee was 30-year-old lawyer David O'Brien of Sioux Falls. Although he had excellent political contacts in the district, O'Brien could raise and spend less than a third as much as Grandy. His attacks on Grandy for being less attuned to the district than Bedell did not persuade people to change horses again. Grandy easily carried every county.

Committees

Agriculture (14th of 18 Republicans)
Conservation, Credit and Rural Development; Department Operations, Research and Foreign Agriculture; Wheat, Soybeans and Feed Grains

Education and Labor (11th of 13 Republicans)
Elementary, Secondary and Vocational Education; Human Resources; Labor-Management Relations

Select Children, Youth and Families (7th of 12 Republicans)

Standards of Official Conduct (6th of 6 Republicans)

Elections

1988 General		
Fred Grandy (R)	125,859	(64%)
Dave O'Brien (D)	69,614	(36%)
1986 General		
Fred Grandy (R)	81,861	(51%)
Clayton Hodgson (D)	78,807	(49%)

District Vote For President

	1988	1984	1980	1976
D	99,116 (50%)	90,257 (42%)	75,202 (34%)	96,880 (45%)
R	99,214 (50%)	121,665 (57%)	125,915 (57%)	114,986 (53%)
I			16,232 (7%)	

Campaign Finance

	Receipts	Receipts from PACs	Expend-itures
1988			
Grandy (R)	$527,487	$294,944 (56%)	$523,108
O'Brien (D)	$174,475	$74,825 (43%)	$175,951
1986			
Grandy (R)	$680,193	$231,472 (34%)	$677,082
Hodgson (D)	$407,661	$220,990 (54%)	$407,916

Key Votes

1987	
Raise speed limit to 65 mph	Y
Approve Gephardt "fair trade" amendment	N
Ban testing of larger nuclear weapons	Y
Delay "re-flagging" of Kuwaiti tankers	N
Approve tax-raising deficit-reduction bill	N
1988	
Approve aid to Nicaraguan contras	Y
Enact civil rights restoration bill over Reagan veto	N
Kill 60-day plant-closing notification measure	N
Pass omnibus trade bill over Reagan veto	Y
Approve death penalty for drug-related murders	Y
Bar federal funds for abortions in cases of rape and incest	Y
Oppose seven-day waiting period for purchase of handguns	Y

Voting Studies

	Presidential Support		Party Unity		Conservative Coalition	
Year	**S**	**O**	**S**	**O**	**S**	**O**
1988	52	43	70	27	87	11
1987	63	37	77	20	86	14

Interest Group Ratings

Year	ADA	ACU	AFL-CIO	CCUS
1988	40	64	57	86
1987	20	57	19	80

Kansas

U.S. CONGRESS

SENATE 2 R

HOUSE 2 D, 3 R

LEGISLATURE

Senate 18 D, 22 R

House 58 D, 67 R

ELECTIONS

1988 Presidential Vote

Bush	56%
Dukakis	43%

1984 Presidential Vote

Reagan	66%
Mondale	33%

1980 Presidential Vote

Reagan	58%
Carter	33%
Anderson	7%

Turnout rate in 1984	57%
Turnout rate in 1986	44%
Turnout rate in 1988	54%

(as percentage of voting age population)

POPULATION AND GROWTH

1980 population	2,363,679
1988 population estimate (32nd in the nation)	2,495,000
Percent change 1980-1988	+6%

DEMOGRAPHIC BREAKDOWN

White	92%
Black	5%
Other	2%
(Spanish origin)	3%
Urban	67%
Rural	33%
Born in state	63%
Foreign-born	2%

MAJOR CITIES

Wichita	288,870
Kansas City	162,070
Topeka	118,580
Overland Park	96,510
Lawrence	56,490

AREA AND LAND USE

Area 81,778 sq. miles (13th)

Farm	90%
Forest	3%
Federally owned	1%

Gov. Mike Hayden (R)
Of Atwood — Elected 1986

Born: March 16, 1944, Colby, Kan.
Education: Kansas State U., B.S. 1966; Fort Hays State U., M.S. 1974.
Military Career: Army, 1967-70.
Occupation: Insurance agent.
Religion: United Methodist.
Political Career: Kan. House, 1972-87, Speaker, 1983-87.
Next Election: 1990.

WORK

Occupations

White-collar	51%
Blue-collar	30%
Service workers	13%

Government Workers

Federal	24,255
State	54,026
Local	120,130

MONEY

Median family income	$ 19,707 (26th)
Tax burden per capita	$ 782 (35th)

EDUCATION

Spending per pupil through grade 12	$ 3,829 (19th)
Persons with college degrees	17% (22nd)

CRIME

Violent crime rate 361 per 100,000 (30th)

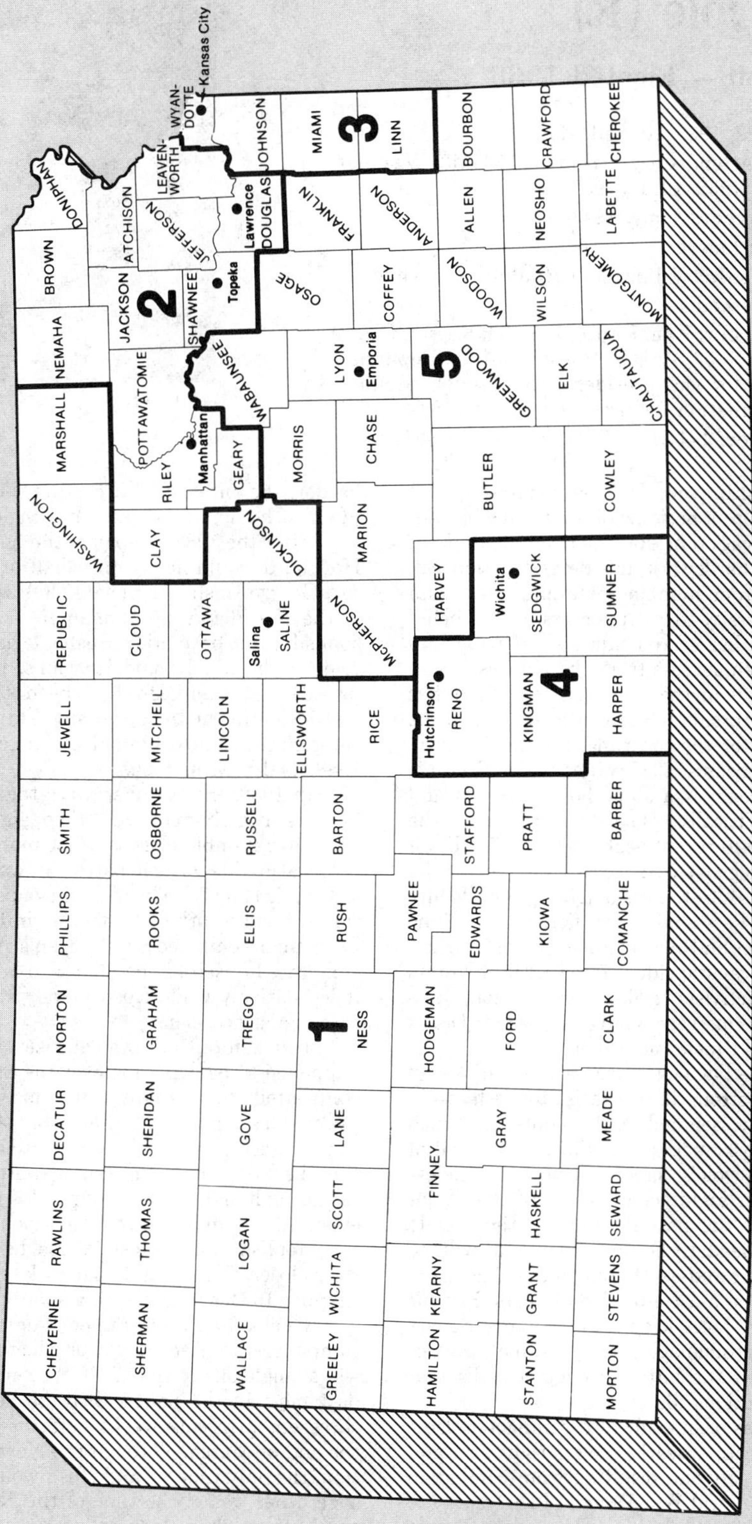
Kansas City
WYAN-
DOTTE
JOHNSON
MIAMI
3
LINN
BOURBON
CRAWFORD
CHEROKEE
DONIPHAN
LEAVEN-
WORTH
ATCHISON
JEFFERSON
Lawrence
DOUGLAS
FRANKLIN
ANDERSON
ALLEN
NEOSHO
LABETTE
BROWN
JACKSON
2
SHAWNEE
Topeka
OSAGE
COFFEY
WOODSON
WILSON
MONTGOMERY
NEMAHA
POTTAWATOMIE
WABAUNSEE
LYON
Emporia
5
GREENWOOD
ELK
CHAUTAUQUA
MARSHALL
RILEY
Manhattan
GEARY
MORRIS
CHASE
BUTLER
COWLEY
WASHINGTON
CLAY
DICKINSON
MARION
HARVEY
Wichita
SEDGWICK
SUMNER
REPUBLIC
CLOUD
OTTAWA
Salina
SALINE
McPHERSON
Hutchinson
RENO
KINGMAN
4
HARPER
JEWELL
MITCHELL
LINCOLN
ELLSWORTH
RICE
SMITH
OSBORNE
RUSSELL
BARTON
STAFFORD
PRATT
BARBER
PHILLIPS
ROOKS
ELLIS
RUSH
PAWNEE
EDWARDS
KIOWA
COMANCHE
NORTON
GRAHAM
TREGO
1
NESS
HODGEMAN
FORD
CLARK
DECATUR
SHERIDAN
GOVE
LANE
FINNEY
GRAY
MEADE
RAWLINS
THOMAS
LOGAN
SCOTT
HASKELL
SEWARD
CHEYENNE
SHERMAN
WALLACE
WICHITA
KEARNY
GRANT
STEVENS
GREELEY
HAMILTON
STANTON
MORTON

Bob Dole (R)

Of Russell — Elected 1968

Born: July 22, 1923, Russell, Kan.
Education: Attended U. of Kansas, 1941-43; Washburn U., A.B. 1952, LL.B. 1952.
Military Career: Army, 1943-48.
Occupation: Lawyer.
Family: Wife, Mary Elizabeth Hanford; one child.
Religion: Methodist.
Political Career: Kan. House, 1951-53; Russell County attorney, 1953-61; U.S. House, 1961-69; Republican nominee for vice president, 1976; sought Republican nomination for president, 1980, 1988.
Capitol Office: 141 Hart Bldg. 20510; 224-6521.

In Washington: Dole sees himself, and had hoped voters nationwide would see him, as the personification of the American ideal, proof certain that hard work and determination can lift a man from humble roots and carry him through adversity to great success. Dole's belief in that ethic has served him well, driving him with unbroken success from the Kansas House to the top job in the U.S. Senate. But it has proved heartbreakingly insufficient when he has reached for the top rung, the presidency.

The Kansan's 1988 effort to realize his American dream is a story both personal and political. Politically, Dole's experience is the best example in recent years of the difficulty of translating legislative success, and the traits that account for it, into a triumphant White House bid. Personally, his fierce go-it-alone determination and new evidence of his darker, occasionally caustic side offered little to voters and party activists seeking inspiration, intimacy and a message conveying what Dole's election would mean for them.

But Dole has never been a visionary or an idealist. His strength as a legislator is his skill as a pragmatic dealmaker; if, to outsiders, such backroom work suggests shadiness or a lack of convictions, Dole's labors have nonetheless made him an architect of much of the major legislation of the past decade. As the Senate Republican leader, he has shown a will to exercise power and exert control that has made him one of the most effective in years. But his insistence on both keeping his taxing Senate post and micromanaging his presidential campaign doomed the latter, leaving it a disorganized, contentious disaster.

Much has been made of the impact on Dole of his handicap, a nearly useless right arm and an impaired left one resulting from combat in Italy late in World War II, and of the years the once-athletic farm boy spent recovering. Clearly his character was indelibly marked. He is intensely competitive and self-sufficient. "I do try harder," he once said. "If I didn't, I'd be sitting in a rest home, in a rocker, drawing disability."

After the 1988 campaign, the question was, How hard would he try on behalf of his former foe, George Bush? As Senate GOP leader, Dole is the president's point man in Congress, responsible for promoting Bush's legislative program as he did Ronald Reagan's. Dole's 1980 presidential campaign had been too fleeting and insignificant to spawn any bad blood with Reagan; the same could not be said of his bitter 1988 rivalry with Bush.

In 1988, the two men were the main combatants in a six-man GOP field, fighting what came to resemble class conflict more than any political or ideological battle. It was Dole the self-made son of the heartland against Bush the son of Eastern privilege, at least in Dole's eyes. Both men competed for Reagan's mantle, but Dole cast himself as the man who helped shape it legislatively while Bush merely stood by for ceremonial occasions.

Just before the Iowa caucuses, when Bush happened to be presiding over the Senate, Dole confronted him audibly for his "lowdown, nasty, mean politics." Dole won that pivotal first contest, proving his farm-state appeal. But then he went on to New Hampshire, where he set up such high expectations of his victory and eventual nomination that he looked all the more foolish when he lost. Worse, he looked like a sore loser; that night on network television, he snapped to Bush, "Stop lying about my record."

Weeks later, on Super Tuesday, Dole's campaign was effectively over when he failed to win a single one of the 17 GOP events held that day, most in the South. Still, he persisted for three embarrassing weeks before conceding at the end of March. Through the November election, the only time he and Bush would speak to each other was at the time of the New Orleans convention, when Bush called to say that Dole was not his choice for vice president. Despite their feuding, Dole had plainly wanted the job.

Finally, weeks after the election, they met and pledged cooperation. "We've both been in politics for quite a while," Dole said. "We understand that when the election is over, it's over." Later, Bush named Dole's wife, Elizabeth, to be labor secretary.

That did not still the questions about Dole's willingness to wage Bush's wars on Capitol Hill. But however deep Dole's resentments, he is also a staunch Republican partisan, and a fighter who fights to win; many times he took up Reagan's cause reluctantly, only to become totally committed once he did so.

In the first test of Bush's presidency, the Senate rejected his nomination of former Sen. John Tower to be defense secretary, after months of allegations about Tower's womanizing, drunkenness and financial conflicts. Tower was not popular among senators, but his defeat — and, more important, Bush's — was not for lack of a fight from Dole; the GOP leader turned in a vintage performance.

He vigorously argued that a president has the benefit of the doubt in choosing aides. But on a lower plane, Dole also got personal, exchanging hostilities on the floor with outspoken Democratic Sen. Ernest F. Hollings, and accusing Armed Services Committee Chairman Sam Nunn of a power grab in leading the opposition to Tower. Finally, with Tower's defeat looming, Dole proposed an extraordinary tactic typical of his no-holds-barred drive to win. He suggested Tower be approved for a probationary six months, after which time the Texan would be judged again. Democrats dismissed the idea as "a desperation move."

Now in his third term as Republican leader, Dole is a somewhat less formidable figure than he was as majority leader in his first term, which covered the last two years of Republicans' Senate control. In the minority, he responds to the Democrats' program, rather than initiating his own. Still, his brief stint as majority leader will long be remembered, for it proved a point that badly needed proving: The Senate could be led.

"You have to produce and you have to prove leadership," he said shortly after Republicans elected him over four contenders in late 1984. Dole did both, even if he failed to achieve a number of his most important goals.

Beyond the major bills that passed with his help — tax revision, a new immigration law, a five-year farm bill and aid to the Nicaraguan contras, among others — Dole's chief accomplishment was to undermine the ability of small groups of senators to bring the chamber regularly to a standstill. His success rested on the palpable sense of his will to use power. "I did not become majority leader to lose," he once said.

Dole's style contrasted with that of his predecessor, the amiable Howard H. Baker Jr. of Tennessee, who tended to let his colleagues fight it out in hopes that eventually, exhausted, they would agree to something. "I don't wait for the consensus," Dole said. "I try to help build it."

His aggressive use of power occasionally embittered colleagues, mostly Democrats. During consideration of South Africa sanctions in 1985, Dole had the official legislation locked in a safe, preventing further action on it. In 1986, Dole averted defeat on a vote to confirm a bitterly contested judicial nominee, Daniel A. Manion, by persuading two opponents to withhold their votes as a traditional courtesy to two Republican supporters who were absent. When it was learned that the absent Republicans had not made up their minds, Democrats and some Republicans complained they had been misled.

At one point in 1986, Dole got into an unusually angry confrontation with Democratic leader Robert C. Byrd, who accused him of trying to suppress senators' rights. Dole was typically defiant: "I don't intend to be intimidated by anyone in the Senate."

Despite the call to arms that his election as leader had represented, Dole got off to a slow start in 1985, failing to block a Democratic farm-credit bill or to resolve deep divisions among Republicans over the budget. Forced to bring a budget plan to the floor without a clear majority, Dole seemed on the verge of defeat. But he pushed Reagan to accept a smaller defense increase while cajoling his GOP colleagues to support a Social Security freeze and elimination of several domestic programs. At the climactic moment, Dole had an ashen Pete Wilson of California brought from a hospital in the middle of the night, just 24 hours after appendicitis surgery, to cast the tying vote. Bush, called back from a trip West, broke the tie to pass the budget.

Dole still hails that budget, with its estimated $50 billion in deficit reduction, as one of his proudest achievements. It reflected his old-line Republican fealty to balanced budgets, a goal for which Dole was willing to raise taxes until the 1988 presidential campaign made him a subscriber to anti-tax rhetoric. To Dole, it also reflected leadership and political courage, given the cuts in programs such as Social Security. But to his lasting chagrin, Reagan later disowned the budget and, a year later, it was blamed for contributing to the party's 1986 losses that returned the Senate to the Democrats' control. Ultimately, Dole made only modest progress against the deficit.

His bitterness about the episode lingered like a grudge once Democrats were in charge. He expressed contempt for Democrats' claims in 1987 that deficit targets could not be met. Recalling Republicans' 1985 effort, he said, "We did not look at the monstrous deficit — larger than it is today — and say, 'It's too hard. It's too big.' " When Reagan weighed Democrats' invitation for budget negotiations, Dole said he advised the president, "You never would sit down when we were in charge. Why sit down when they are in charge?"

Unlike most recent Senate leaders, who have tended to withdraw from committee work to focus on floor duties, Dole also plays a significant role on major bills before his committees.

He was virtually chairman of the Agriculture Committee during work on the 1985 farm bill, since titular Chairman Jesse Helms of North Carolina was politically isolated, and preoccupied with foreign policy controversies. On the floor, Dole's leadership was severely tested when differences over price supports for farmers threatened to kill the bill, but he put together a compromise with enough sweeteners for different commodities to secure a majority.

In the 101st Congress, Dole has been prominent in the early work to draft the 1990 farm bill. He also is one of Congress' leading champions of ethanol, espousing tax breaks, subsidies and import controls for the infant industry. That stance benefits not only Kansas corn farmers but also Illinois-based Archer Daniels Midland Co., the agribusiness giant that has more than half the U.S. ethanol market and is headed by longtime Dole supporter Dwayne Andreas.

Dole's work on the landmark 1986 tax bill was not so obvious, especially compared with his dominant role in enacting three major tax bills as Finance Committee chairman in Reagan's first term. But by quietly indicating support for the dramatic tax-code overhaul proposed by Finance Chairman Bob Packwood of Oregon, Dole helped solidify the necessary Republican support.

In 1988, after Packwood had given up and left, Dole emerged as the chief Senate Republican negotiator for a package of tax corrections, increases and deductions and helped pass a compromise in the 100th Congress' final hours. He also sponsored the key amendment on the Senate floor that cleared the way for Finance's major welfare-overhaul bill that year.

Dole's sponsorship of that proposal, mandating the first federal work requirement for welfare recipients, was indicative of his nonideological pragmatism. While cosponsor William L. Armstrong of Colorado offered the conservative arguments for "workfare," Dole made clear he just wanted Reagan's signature. "It is not a major program," he said, "but it will have a major impact on the people listening at 1600 Pennsylvania Avenue."

Throughout his leadership, Dole has walked fine lines between loyalty to the White House, dedication to his party colleagues' political interests and attention to his own. Although he worked hard to protect Republicans in the 1986 elections, Dole proved unexpectedly loyal to the administration at crucial moments. On issues such as farm aid and South Africa sanctions, he stuck by Reagan despite warnings of the potential cost to his Senate allies.

The 100th Congress was particularly trying, since Reagan was a lame duck further wounded by the Iran-contra scandal and Dole was gearing up for his own presidential campaign.

On occasion, he continued to be loyal even when many Republicans might have preferred otherwise. Dole publicly backed Reagan's vetoes of clean-water and highway bills in early 1987, though both had passed Congress overwhelmingly and contained many projects for Republicans' districts. "Now we can get down to the nitty-gritty of loyalty and support for the president," he said, appealing for votes to support the highway bill veto. But despite a Capitol visit from Reagan, no Republicans switched their votes. Later that year, Dole tried to round up opposition to a popular trade bill Reagan opposed, but he had little luck.

He struggled without success to win confirmation of Robert H. Bork, Reagan's controversial conservative nominee to the Supreme Court. His repeated accusations that Judiciary Committee Chairman Joseph R. Biden Jr. was stalling provoked the Delaware Democrat to snap that "Dole was being his typical, partisan, cheap-shot self." When Bork's rejection became obvious, Dole proposed that Reagan put the judge on the court as a recess appointee, which would allow Bork to serve without confirmation through the 100th Congress; even Judiciary's senior Republican, Strom Thurmond, disavowed that idea.

If it was crucial to Dole's nomination hopes to appear to be Reagan's good soldier, sometimes he found it essential to oppose the administration. The Iran-contra scandal, Dole said early in 1987, "does indicate that blunders were made of colossal proportions." Long a supporter of civil rights bills, Dole said that "the president made a mistake" in vetoing the 1988 Civil Rights Restoration Act, and Dole did not work to sustain the veto.

With drugs a major issue among voters in 1988, Dole actually spearheaded the opposition to the administration after reports it was considering dropping U.S. drug charges against Panamanian strongman Manuel Antonio Noriega if he would agree to exile. Dole won the Senate's 86-10 approval of a resolution against any such deal, saying, "Sending Noriega off into retirement with a legal golden parachute, by dropping these indictments, would have been the wrong step at the wrong time."

Sometimes Dole was less certain of the proper course. At a time when he was seeking favor with the GOP right wing, Dole joined Helms in opposing the administration's rapprochement with socialist Mozambique, and helped to block Reagan's nominee for ambassador; he finally backed off amid reports that the rebels he supported were guilty of widespread atrocities. Dole initially criticized Reagan's 1987 decision to provide Navy escorts for Kuwaiti tankers in the Persian Gulf, and worked with Democrats on a bipartisan response; when that failed, he jumped squarely to Reagan's side, condemning the Democrats' final measure as "an effort to embarrass the Reagan administration, pure and simple."

But the issue that got the most attention in the early days of his contest against Bush was the 1987 U.S.-Soviet intermediate-range nuclear-force (INF) treaty. At first, Dole withheld his endorsement, saying he needed to study the details, and he belittled Bush's immediate, unequivocal support. But within a week, as polls in pro-arms control Iowa showed Bush gaining as a result, Dole became a treaty cheerleader. During the Senate's ratification debate in 1988, he helped block amendments from conservatives that might have doomed the pact.

Dole's partisanship, and his loyal support for Republican presidents, is consistent with the man who first arrived in the Senate two decades ago. If anything, leadership has tempered him. He was President Richard M. Nixon's most strident Senate backer, defending in often abrasive terms his Vietnam policies, his Supreme Court nominations of Clement F. Haynsworth Jr. and G. Harrold Carswell, his ABM program and almost every other move Nixon made.

The Kansan's performance did not sit well with some Senate colleagues; in 1971, Ohio Republican William B. Saxbe said Dole was a "hatchet man" who "couldn't sell beer on a troopship." But Nixon rewarded Dole in 1971 by naming him national party chairman. Dole never got along with the White House staff, however, and was pushed from the party leadership in January 1973 — a stroke of good fortune, since he escaped the subsequent Watergate scandal. Although he had been GOP chairman when the June 1972 burglary occurred, Dole never knew what was going on at the Nixon re-election committee. "Watergate happened on my night off," he later said.

He re-emerged as Gerald R. Ford's vice presidential running mate in 1976, but his subsequent denunciation of the 20th century's "Democrat wars" gave national circulation to the hatchet-man label that haunts Dole still. Only after days of controversy did Dole grudgingly back away from the remark.

That campaign may have been a turning point. While Dole never accepted the notion that his negative style cost Ford the presidency, he has rarely sounded so strident since. Some attribute this to the influence of his wife, whom he married in 1975 when she was a federal trade commissioner. When she appeared before a Senate committee prior to her confirmation as Reagan's transportation secretary in 1983, Dole said, "I regret that I have but one wife to give for my country's infrastructure."

Dole is often as funny as that, but most of the time there is more bite to his humor. Early in 1982, he told listeners he had good news and bad news. "The good news," he said, "is that a bus full of supply-siders went off a cliff. The bad news is that two seats were empty."

That joke symbolized Dole's doubts about the philosophy behind Reagan's 1981 tax cut. Dole wanted targeted tax incentives aimed at boosting savings, investment and productivity, rather than across-the-board reduction. But as Finance chairman he loyally shepherded the Reagan plan through the Senate, though he did persuade Reagan to scale back the cut from 30 percent to 25 percent over three years.

The next year, as deficits climbed, Dole moved quickly to change the law. First he had to persuade a reluctant Reagan to accept the need for added revenues. He did so by painting his proposal as tax reform, rather than a rejection of Reaganomics. "We are not making a U-turn; we are merely adjusting the route to keep from going off the road," he said. It took all of Dole's skill to maneuver that three-year, $100 billion tax bill into law.

On Finance, Dole was also at the center of debate on Social Security. As a member of a special national commission, he played a key role in the compromise that led to the commission's recommendations on saving the system, which Congress used as the basis for its 1983 rescue bill.

As a member of Agriculture, and of Judiciary until 1985, Dole has built a supportive record on two issues — civil rights and food stamps — that stands out from his otherwise consistent conservatism. He has also been a crusader for federal aid to the handicapped.

In 1982, Dole formulated a compromise (over administration opposition) that allowed the bill extending the Voting Rights Act to emerge from Judiciary with provisions making it easier to prove voting rights violations.

He routinely has broken conservative ranks to protect and enlarge the food stamp program, popular among Kansas farmers as well as the poor. In the 1970s, Dole's advocacy regularly brought him into alliance with liberal South Dakota Democrat George McGovern, whom he roundly criticized in the 1972 presidential campaign. In 1981, he worked with Democrat Patrick J. Leahy of Vermont and against Helms to soften the administration's proposed drastic reductions.

At Home: Kansas voters have been good to Dole in the 1980s, giving him two decisive re-election victories that established him as the state's foremost political figure and encouraged his national ambitions.

But the road to political security was a bit rough. Another 982 votes in his 1960 House primary would have sent another man to Washington. A swing of 2,600 would have unseated him four years later. One percentage point would have defeated him in his 1974 Senate race.

Dole emerged from his World War II ordeal with ambition and an ample share of discipline. Before completing his law degree, he won a term in the Kansas House. Two years later, he became Russell County prosecutor.

Eight years later, he was a candidate for the U.S. House, running for the GOP nomination against Keith G. Sebelius, a Republican from nearby Norton County. Dole defeated him by 982 votes, forcing Sebelius to wait eight years for a House vacancy. In the fall, Dole was an easy winner, keeping the old 6th District in its traditionally Republican hands.

In 1962 the state's two western districts were combined, and Dole had to run against a Democratic incumbent, J. Floyd Breeding. He beat him by more than 20,000 votes.

But he had a difficult time in 1964 coping with the national Democratic landslide and with Bill Bork, a farmers' co-op official. Democrat Bork said he would be a better friend of agriculture than Dole, who he pointed out was a small-town lawyer, not a farmer. Dole won by 5,126 votes.

In 1968, Republican Frank Carlson announced his retirement from the Senate, and Dole competed with former Gov. William H. Avery for the GOP nomination to succeed him. Avery had been ousted from the governorship two years earlier by Democrat Robert Docking, and he seemed preoccupied during much of the primary campaign with Docking rather than Dole. The result was a Dole victory by a remarkable plurality of more than 100,000 votes.

That fall, Dole also had an easy time against Democrat William I. Robinson, a Wichita attorney who criticized him for opposing federal aid to schools. Dole talked about the social unrest of that year and blamed much of it on the Johnson administration.

The 1974 campaign was different. Dole was burdened by his earlier Nixon connections, which were played up, probably to an unwise degree, by Democratic challenger William Roy, a two-term House member. Roy continued to refer to Nixon and Watergate though he had built a comfortable lead against Dole. This enabled Dole to strike back with an ad in which a mud-splattered poster of himself was gradually wiped clean as he insisted on his honesty. Dole came from behind in the final weeks to win.

Since then, he has had nothing to worry about. He met only weak opposition for a third term in 1980. In 1986, as the defeats of several Senate GOP colleagues cost him the job of majority leader, Dole coasted.

Committees

Minority Leader

Agriculture, Nutrition and Forestry (2nd of 9 Republicans)
Agricultural Production and Stabilization of Prices; Nutrition and Investigations

Finance (2nd of 9 Republicans)
International Debt (ranking); Social Security and Family Policy (ranking); Medicare and Long-Term Care

Rules and Administration (5th of 7 Republicans)

Joint Taxation

Elections

1986 General		
Bob Dole (R)	576,902	(70%)
Guy MacDonald (D)	246,664	(30%)
1986 Primary		
Bob Dole (R)	228,301	(84%)
Shirley J. Ashley Landis (R)	42,237	(16%)

Previous Winning Percentages: **1980** (64%) **1974** (51%) **1968** (60%) **1966 *** (69%) **1964 *** (51%) **1962 *** (56%) **1960 *** (59%)

* *House elections.*

Campaign Finance

	Receipts	Receipts from PACs	Expend-itures
1986			
Dole (R)	$2,640,050	$1,034,324 (39%)	$1,517,585

Key Votes

1987

Enact omnibus highway bill over Reagan veto	N
Limit testing of space-based anti-ballistic missiles	N
Oppose banning tests of larger nuclear weapons	Y
Confirm Robert H. Bork as Supreme Court justice	Y

1988

Allow vote on campaign-finance overhaul	?
Pass civil rights restoration bill over Reagan veto	?
Enact omnibus trade bill over Reagan veto	N
Approve death penalty for drug-related murders	Y
Oppose "workfare" amendment to welfare overhaul bill	N

Voting Studies

	Presidential Support		Party Unity		Conservative Coalition	
Year	**S**	**O**	**S**	**O**	**S**	**O**
1988	68	19	70	12	86	5
1987	71	24	85	10	81	6
1986	92	8	92	7	95	4
1985	92	7	92	6	92	5
1984	90	9	90	8	96	2
1983	78	21	88	8	89	7
1982	86	13	91	8	85	10
1981	85	7	94	5	92	5

Interest Group Ratings

Year	ADA	ACU	AFL-CIO	CCUS
1988	15	91	33	91
1987	5	77	20	83
1986	0	91	0	89
1985	0	91	10	90
1984	10	86	0	83
1983	5	64	19	56
1982	15	80	20	62
1981	5	76	11	100

Nancy Landon Kassebaum (R)

Of Burdick — Elected 1978

Born: July 29, 1932, Topeka, Kan.
Education: U. of Kansas, B.A. 1954; U. of Michigan, M.A. 1956.
Occupation: Broadcasting executive.
Family: Divorced; four children.
Religion: Episcopalian.
Political Career: Maize School Board, 1973-75.
Capitol Office: 302 Russell Bldg. 20510; 224-4774.

In Washington: It is usually easy to be cynical about candidates who campaign for the Senate pledging to serve just two terms, and then run for a third. Not so with Kassebaum.

Her decision to seek re-election in 1990 just confirmed what had long been clear: This former housewife is at home in the Senate. Her announcement cheered Republicans, who had sported "Run, Nancy, Run" buttons, knowing they risked losing the Kansas seat to a Democrat if she bowed out. But probably some Democrats were not unhappy, either, since they occasionally can count on Kassebaum to break GOP ranks and bestow on their position a semblance of bipartisanship. Party loyalties aside, she is widely regarded as a quiet, positive force within the institution.

Most others who come to Congress promising to be short-term "citizen legislators" soon become just as concerned about partisan advantage as the professional politicians they once reviled. But more than a decade in the Senate has not worked that change on Kassebaum. Perhaps more than anyone else there, she still has the plain-spoken honesty and common sense she had when she arrived in 1979 as an almost complete political neophyte.

In the best sense, she remains an amateur — an intelligent homemaker and businesswoman brought out of obscurity to make decisions on national policy. Kassebaum is a conservative, but not in an ideological way. She seems to be able to cast individual votes on merit without fitting them into some larger scheme.

In early 1989, admirers and critics alike found ammunition in her vote against President Bush's nominee for defense secretary, former Republican Sen. John Tower. While the Senate was roiled for weeks by bitter partisan debate over reports of Tower's drinking, womanizing and financial conflicts of interest, Kassebaum was typically quiet. She told few except Bush about her qualms, so it was a surprise to many when she cast the only Republican "no" vote. Fans praised Kassebaum for once again showing the courage of her convictions. But skeptics saw the opposite in her statement afterward that she had told Bush she would support Tower had her vote been needed for confirmation.

Kassebaum's style has not changed much over the years. She still appears on occasion to be a shy woman uneasy in a public role. "Someday I'm going to hit someone over the head for calling me diminutive and soft-spoken," she once said. "But I am." She chafes at comparisons to Dorothy in "The Wizard of Oz," yet Kassebaum has enough humor about her image that her staff felt free to include representations of the film in a patchwork quilt they made her.

At times, Kassebaum's lack of guile can cause problems for her. During the Senate's bitter 1986 debate over the nomination of Daniel A. Manion to be a federal judge, she extended a common Senate courtesy by "pairing" her vote with the absent Barry Goldwater. Assured by Manion strategist Sen. Dan Quayle that Goldwater intended to vote for the nomination, Kassebaum in effect withdrew her own negative vote, thus providing the margin needed for the nomination to go through. But Goldwater actually was undecided, she later discovered. Ruefully she said she had been "misled," but characteristically she added that she did not think the misleading had been intentional.

Kassebaum has a tough side as well, one that has emerged in the budget and foreign policy battles of recent years. She does not like to be used as a symbol, even though she is one of only two women in the Senate. When officials of the 1984 GOP convention sought to have her appear on the podium with other prominent Republican women, she pointedly declined. "I'd be happy to speak on substantive issues," she said, "but to be treated as a bauble on a tree is not particularly constructive." She expressed the same skepticism toward suggestions she might be the GOP vice presidential candidate in 1988.

On the Foreign Relations Committee, Kassebaum has played an important role on issues involving Central America and South Africa. She sought to steer an independent course between President Reagan and his congressional critics, though that proved a tortuous journey during the years of contention over Reagan's pro-contra policy. While Kassebaum voted for military aid, she grew increasingly critical of both the rebels and the president.

In 1986, she joined other Republican centrists to extract concessions from the president. Kassebaum was a principal architect of a resulting $100 million military aid package that included Reagan's promises to push contra leaders to curb human rights abuses and to end their own internal disunity. But she was dismayed by administration lobbying tactics, and lambasted supporters for portraying the issue as "a disagreement between Republicans in white hats and Democrats in red banners."

A year later, she singled out the president himself in expressing regrets about the 1986 package. It had been intended as leverage to force Nicaragua into peace talks, Kassebaum said. But, she added, "I am not confident that the president has taken to heart the message — that without a sustained diplomatic policy, military aid to the contras makes no sense." After all the years, she lamented, his policy remained confused: "Are we seeking the ouster of [Nicaraguan President Daniel] Ortega, or his containment with the Soviet influence removed? What do we want to achieve?" Even so, in 1988 she supported Reagan's bid for $36 million in military and non-military aid. When that failed, she allied with a bipartisan centrist group to pass $48 million in "humanitarian" aid.

Earlier, when attention focused on El Salvador, she sponsored a successful amendment in committee in 1983 reducing military aid to that regime amid widespread reports of human rights violations, and calling for unconditional talks between the government and leftist rebels. The measure declared support for the Salvadoran government, she said, but did not "write a blank check to escalate fighting and impose a military solution."

From her position on the Africa Subcommittee, which she chaired when Republicans controlled the Senate, Kassebaum has influenced the debate on sanctions against South Africa.

She was initially skeptical about the value of sanctions, warning they could do much harm to oppressed blacks. But by 1986, South Africa's stepped-up repression helped allay Kassebaum's doubts. She prodded Reagan to take action. When he did not, she backed sanctions and opposed his veto in order to "send a decisive message" of U.S. condemnation. So did full committee Chairman Richard G. Lugar, and it was his break with Reagan that was the focus of attention.

But in 1988, the two Republicans opposed a new House bill for a near-total trade embargo. "If I felt this legislation would bring an end to apartheid . . . I would support it," she said, but "I never thought it was wise to bring South Africa to its knees." Lacking such key GOP support, the bill died in the Senate.

Kassebaum formerly was a leading critic of the United Nations, while taking pains to distance herself from ideological U.N.-bashers in the GOP right wing. In 1983 and 1985 she offered amendments that cut U.S. contributions contingent on the U.N. reforming its bureaucracy. "The U.N. can no longer be a sacred cow," she said. In 1987, satisfied by the body's performance, she sponsored the provision to resume full payments.

Kassebaum has been among the most pro-arms control Republicans. In 1986 she supported a Democratic amendment cutting Reagan's funding request for the strategic defense initiative. But the next year, she opposed a similar effort, saying the Senate should approve a higher amount to bargain up the House's much lower figure. Also in 1987, she was one of only three Republicans opposing a GOP filibuster against a defense bill barring the administration from conducting space tests of SDI.

Kassebaum's pragmatic independence on defense and foreign policy questions has been even more notable since she not infrequently has been at odds with Kansas' senior senator, GOP leader Bob Dole, whose job it is to shepherd Republicans behind administration positions. Her stands, and the expertise she brings to them, have helped to remove Kassebaum from Dole's shadow.

Kassebaum likewise has charted her own course on economic issues. As a member of the Budget Committee, in 1984 and 1985 she promoted a bipartisan budget-freeze proposal with Republican Charles E. Grassley and Democrat Joseph R. Biden Jr. With estimated savings of $250 billion over three years, the so-called KGB plan almost won Budget's approval in 1984, but it was defeated 2-to-1 in the Senate after GOP leaders argued it would weaken defense. It met a similar fate in 1985.

Disdainful of what she considers empty gestures, Kassebaum opposed Senate passage of the 1985 Gramm-Rudman-Hollings budget-balancing law after sponsors exempted Social Security and other programs from its strictures. It could not work, she said, if Congress singled out sacred cows for special protection. Similarly, in late 1987, she objected to a budget pact between Reagan and Congress because, by ruling out significant tax increases or Social Security cutbacks, it had minimal impact against the deficit. She again proposed a KGB-like freeze with some taxes, but lost 71-25.

That budget effort was a sort of desperation tactic. Kassebaum had become so frustrated by the ongoing deficit impasse and the low-yield work on Budget that she not only considered leaving the committee but also proposed to dissolve it altogether. She had stayed on Budget only at the urging of GOP leaders, who did not want to open a spot for maverick Texas Republican Phil Gramm. Finally, however, she had had enough; for the 101st Congress, Kassebaum left Budget and Gramm took her seat.

She also left the Commerce Committee, and instead joined the Labor and Banking panels. On Commerce, where she once was chairman of the Aviation Subcommittee, Kassebaum helped enact a complex airport development and tax bill in 1982. She was less successful with legislation to limit small plane manufacturers' accident liability (Kansas is home to Cessna and Beech), and in working to channel federal airport funds to states through block grants rather than specific "pork-barrel" appropriations.

At Home: Kassebaum can trace much of her success to her middle name — it links her to her father, Alfred M. Landon, the ex-governor of Kansas and 1936 GOP presidential nominee. (He died in 1987, just after his 100th birthday.)

Before 1978, Kassebaum's political activity had been confined to the school board in a town of 785 people and one year as an aide to GOP Sen. James B. Pearson. Most of her adult life had been spent raising four children and managing a Wichita radio station. But when Pearson in 1978 announced plans to retire, she joined a large field of aspirants.

Most of the contestants, including eight other Republicans in the August primary, found it difficult to attract much attention in the crowd. Kassebaum had instant name recognition, however, and she built upon it with a series of TV ads featuring her father, then 91 years old. The result was a clear victory.

That fall, she faced a well-known Democrat, former Rep. Bill Roy, who had nearly ousted Sen. Dole in 1974. Roy, however, turned out to be weaker than expected. The Watergate resentment that had helped him against Dole had faded, and the farm discontent aimed at a GOP administration in 1974 now focused on President Carter. Kassebaum, meanwhile, had no record for Roy to aim at, and her gentle style made attacks on her inexperience seem unmannerly. She beat Roy more comfortably than Dole had.

Kassebaum's moderate record has satisfied nearly everyone in Kansas except dyed-in-the-wool Democrats and the Right to Life lobby, which has picketed her appearances to protest her support for legalized abortion.

Any 1984 re-election worries she had ended in March 1983, when Democratic Rep. Dan Glickman decided not to risk running against her. The Democratic nomination went by default to investment executive Jim Maher, who lost two earlier Senate bids. Kassebaum obliterated him.

Committees

Banking, Housing and Urban Affairs (8th of 9 Republicans)
Housing and Urban Affairs; Securities

Foreign Relations (3rd of 9 Republicans)
African Affairs (ranking); Near Eastern and South Asian Affairs; Western Hemisphere and Peace Corps Affairs

Labor and Human Resources (2nd of 7 Republicans)
Education, Arts and Humanities (ranking); Children, Family, Drugs and Alcoholism; Employment and Productivity

Special Aging (9th of 9 Republicans)

Elections

1984 General

Nancy Landon Kassebaum (R)	757,402	(76%)
James R. Maher (D)	211,664	(21%)

Previous Winning Percentage: **1978** (54%)

Campaign Finance

	Receipts	Receipts from PACs	Expend-itures
1984			
Kassebaum (R)	$576,455	$234,595 (41%)	$360,964
Maher (D)	$32,909	$2,450 (7%)	$30,444

Key Votes

1987

Enact omnibus highway bill over Reagan veto	N
Limit testing of space-based anti-ballistic missiles	Y
Oppose banning tests of larger nuclear weapons	Y
Confirm Robert H. Bork as Supreme Court justice	Y

1988

Allow vote on campaign-finance overhaul	Y
Pass civil rights restoration bill over Reagan veto	Y
Enact omnibus trade bill over Reagan veto	N
Approve death penalty for drug-related murders	Y
Oppose "workfare" amendment to welfare overhaul bill	N

Voting Studies

	Presidential Support		Party Unity		Conservative Coalition	
Year	S	O	S	O	S	O
1988	69	28	61	32	81	8
1987	59	28	65	22	72	22
1986	70	24	77	21	80	13
1985	76	19	79	17	75	22
1984	79	19	75	24	81	17
1983	78	20	71	25	59	36
1982	78	19	74	24	77	21
1981	82	17	77	20	80	18

Interest Group Ratings

Year	ADA	ACU	AFL-CIO	CCUS
1988	30	61	23	71
1987	30	60	20	71
1986	45	41	21	58
1985	35	48	10	69
1984	45	55	45	61
1983	35	36	24	42
1982	50	42	29	53
1981	35	60	5	88

1 Pat Roberts (R)

Of Dodge City — Elected 1980

Born: April 20, 1936, Topeka, Kan.
Education: Kansas State U., B.A. 1958.
Military Career: Marine Corps, 1958-62.
Occupation: Journalist; congressional aide.
Family: Wife, Franki Fann; three children.
Religion: Methodist.
Political Career: No previous office.
Capitol Office: 1323 Longworth Bldg. 20515; 225-2715.

In Washington: Roberts' enormous district requires him to pay attention to the concerns of constituents in the western two-thirds of Kansas, a territory larger than a good many states. But the job is less complicated than it might appear. The economy of the rural district is tied to the dominant crop, wheat, and Roberts spends much of his time as the wheat-growers' spokesman in Washington.

And he does speak out. He has been an active player on the Agriculture Committee, where he is viewed not only as an advocate for Kansas farmers, but also as the resident wit. Pleasantly irascible, Roberts has a sarcastic sense of humor similar to that of Kansas' senior senator, Republican Bob Dole, who represented the 1st in the 1960s. Sometimes, deliberately or not, he even projects inflections and mannerisms similar to Dole's.

Colleagues also compare Roberts to Dole in another way. He is widely viewed as a man with both the interest and ability to serve in the other chamber of Congress in the event Dole or GOP Sen. Nancy Landon Kassebaum moves on.

Roberts is ranking member on the Agriculture Subcommittee on Department Operations, Research and Foreign Agriculture, and that has involved him in efforts to write pesticide laws. Much of that activity centered on an overhaul of the Federal Insecticide, Fungicide and Rodenticide Act (FIFRA).

In 1986, after a long delay in reaching some consensus on FIFRA legislation, Roberts worked to help craft a bill that won support from farmers, farm chemical manufacturers, environmentalists, public-health groups and labor unions. The bill would have accelerated health testing and registration of pesticides and required manufacturers to help pay for it.

There was considerable disagreement over one provision that Roberts pushed passionately. On the House floor he won a fight over an amendment to set uniform national limits on the amount of pesticide residue allowed in foods. He said that differing standards around the country would make it more difficult for farmers to market their products.

The FIFRA bill did not emerge from the 99th Congress because of objections in the Senate, and in the 100th Congress Roberts carried on his fight, insisting that uniform standards were needed to avoid marketing chaos. "Aunt Jemima was OK in Oklahoma," he said, "but not in Texas; Betty Crocker could be marketed in the state of Massachusetts, perhaps, but not in the state of Maine."

But Roberts' strong desire for uniform standards was surpassed by pragmatism. "We have those who will prefer an issue," he said in 1987, "and we have those who will prefer a bill. It is time we had a FIFRA bill." By the end of the 100th Congress that was what they had. The bill, dubbed "FIFRA Lite" by some, dropped many controversial issues, including the question of uniform limits nationwide.

Roberts' outlook is nearly always a reflection more of his rural district than of his partisan label. During the debate over the farm bill in the 99th Congress he freely attacked the unpopular Reagan farm policy — which he described as a "so-called" policy. Expressing farmers' frustration, he once warned that Air Force One would get a "pitchfork in the belly" if it flew too low over Kansas.

Working on the wheat section of the 1985 farm bill, Roberts supported what he called a "market oriented" approach that would make U.S. commodities more competitive in the world market by cutting prices. The approach included a new program of price supports called "marketing loans." Unlike existing commodity loans, which allow farmers to default and simply turn over their crops, marketing loans would have to be repaid by the farmers, but only at the relatively low price the crops brought at the market. The proposal passed the Wheat Subcommittee, but the panel later reversed itself, stripping the plan's substance.

In general, Roberts did not look favorably on efforts by liberal Democrats to raise farm prices a different way — by imposing mandatory controls on the amount farmers could produce. But when the production control issue came to a close decision in committee, Roberts clearly was nervous about casting the deciding

Kansas 1

West — Salina; Dodge City

The farm lands of western Kansas used to be populous enough to support two congressional districts. By the 1960s, however, the exodus of farmers from the land had cost the region a seat. And as population continued its fall with each census, the lines of the remaining district — the 1st — moved farther to the east. The "Big First" now stretches across 58 counties and two-thirds of the state's land area.

Though the population continues to slip in many of the grain-growing areas — more than half the district's counties had a net loss in the first half of the 1980s — the 1st continues to produce the huge harvests of winter wheat that help make Kansas the nation's leading wheat-producing state. And industrial expansions by several of southwest Kansas' major meatpackers have actually brought a flush of fresh growth to such cities as Garden City and Dodge City.

The district has a solidly rural character and a conservative political outlook. The farmers and ranchers are traditionally suspicious of federal involvement in agriculture, and Republican registrants far outnumber Democrats.

An occasional wave of prairie populism will sweep through the 1st, as in 1976, when a protest against President Gerald R. Ford's farm policies limited the Republican to 52 percent of the district vote. But in 1984, in the midst of a supposed "farm crisis," President Reagan took 74 percent in the 1st. George Bush won in 1988 with a somewhat more modest 60 percent.

For years, the district's only sizable city was Salina, near the eastern edge of the 1st. Once the place where farmers flocked for Saturday marketing and entertainment, Salina evolved into a source of jobs for some of those who gave up full-time farming. The city's population jumped by about 11 percent in the 1970s, thanks to plant expansion by such companies as Westinghouse and Beech Aircraft. But growth has been fairly flat through the 1980s.

It is not a great distance from Salina to Russell County, home base of senior Sen. Bob Dole. But just to the west is Ellis County (Hays), home of Fort Hays State University, which helps give it a Democratic flavor unusual for western Kansas. Ellis was one of three Kansas counties to go for Democrat Michael S. Dukakis in 1988.

Moving west, the ranches grow larger and the population more sparse. But the endless horizons are broken by that handful of industrial towns whose growth has been a bright spot for the 1st.

Lying about 50 miles apart along the Arkansas River, Garden City and Dodge City were rivals in the late 19th century; Garden City was founded as a center for farming, while Dodge City was a stopover for cowboys driving cattle that needed to eat the grass the farmers were plowing up.

Today, the two towns compete for the title of southwest Kansas' biggest city. Garden City has the lead with about 23,000 people. Dodge City, best known for its re-creation of the "Old West" Front Street, is pushing 20,000.

The only other southwest city of any size is Liberal, in Seward County near the Oklahoma border. The city's name has little to do with its politics, which are generally as GOP as the surrounding country; Seward gave 71 percent of its 1988 vote to Bush.

Population: 472,139. White 456,427 (97%), Black 4,280 (1%), Other 2,611 (1%). Spanish origin 14,643 (3%). 18 and over 342,439 (73%), 65 and over 75,593 (16%). Median age: 32.

vote against it. As Agriculture began voting on a production control amendment, Roberts left the room. Later, when it was clear it would pass, he returned and voted against it, after exchanging a glance with the amendment's sponsor, Iowa Democrat Berkley Bedell.

Meanwhile, Roberts was involved in a dispute with members representing the maritime industry over a federal law requiring half of government-backed grain exports to be loaded on expensive U.S.-flag ships. Roberts and other farm-state representatives charged that cargo rules undercut exports by making the price of the sale too high. Although he managed to add an amendment in Agriculture exempting government-backed farm exports from the preference requirements, the Merchant Marine Committee insisted that the nation's dwindling merchant fleet needed the subsidies to survive. That panel included new language to the bill to protect the status quo and persuaded the Rules Committee to go along.

Roberts' district, while dominated by wheat, has been changing over time, with some new crops moving in. That will no doubt be reflected in his activity when the next farm bill rolls around.

Roberts has other rural interests outside the Agriculture Committee. In the 100th Congress he was a member of the bipartisan Rural

Health Care Coalition, a group that worked to make changes in the Medicare system, which many legislators consider unfair and harmful to rural health services.

The group was successful in pushing a number of measures, including the creation of an office of rural health policy within the Department of Health and Human Services and a special payment increase to rural hospitals.

At Home: Roberts understudied the role of U.S. representative for 12 years as top aide to Republican Rep. Keith G. Sebelius. When Sebelius retired in 1980, Roberts was ready.

His GOP primary opponent tried to paint Roberts as a carpetbagger, noting that the Topeka native had established residence in the 1st only that year. But most GOP county chairmen backed Roberts, and he won with 56 percent.

Roberts' victory in November was scarcely in doubt in his strongly Republican district in a Republican year. Capitalizing on the popularity of Sebelius, who had remained neutral in the primary but endorsed him warmly in the fall, Roberts referred to "our record" so frequently that he sounded like an incumbent. Democrat Phil Martin said his five years in the Legislature better prepared him for Congress, but voters gave Roberts a resounding 62 percent. In 1982, running against another Democratic state legislator, Roberts improved to 68 percent.

Hard times on the farm generated some loud opposition in 1984. Democrat Darrell Ringer, facing foreclosure of his farm, ran in the 1st because he believed the government would neglect the nation's agriculture problems unless more farmers won congressional seats. But most voters concluded that Ringer, an activist in the American Agricultural Movement, would be more strident than successful; Roberts won by 3-to-1. After a similar Roberts performance in 1986, Democrats lost hope of seriously challenging the popular incumbent, who ran unopposed in 1988.

Roberts grew up with Kansas GOP politics. His father, C. Wesley Roberts, was a longtime Republican Party stalwart and, in the late 1940s, a successful state GOP chairman. Early in 1953, C. Wesley Roberts was chosen to be chairman of the Republican National Committee. But the Kansas City *Star* soon after accused him of having improperly used his influence as a state party leader to affect an appropriation by the state Legislature. Nine weeks after taking his GOP post, he resigned.

Committees

Agriculture (6th of 18 Republicans)
Department Operations, Research and Foreign Agriculture (ranking); Wheat, Soybeans and Feed Grains

House Administration (5th of 8 Republicans)
Personnel and Police (ranking); Procurement and Printing (ranking); Elections

Joint Printing

Elections

1988 General		
Pat Roberts (R)	168,700	(100%)
1986 General		
Pat Roberts (R)	141,297	(77%)
Dale Lyon (D)	43,359	(23%)

Previous Winning Percentages: **1984** (76%) **1982** (68%) **1980** (62%)

District Vote For President

	1988	1984	1980	1976
D	74,713 (38%)	54,565 (25%)	56,219 (26%)	96,421 (45%)
R	120,325 (60%)	161,439 (74%)	140,375 (66%)	111,433 (52%)
I			12,501 (6%)	

Campaign Finance

	Receipts	Receipts from PACs	Expend-itures
1988			
Roberts (R)	$191,584	$99,600 (52%)	$81,140
1986			
Roberts (R)	$181,783	$101,606 (56%)	$87,221
Lyon (D)	$10,242	$500 (5%)	$8,637

Key Votes

1987	
Raise speed limit to 65 mph	Y
Approve Gephardt "fair trade" amendment	N
Ban testing of larger nuclear weapons	N
Delay "re-flagging" of Kuwaiti tankers	?
Approve tax-raising deficit-reduction bill	N
1988	
Approve aid to Nicaraguan contras	Y
Enact civil rights restoration bill over Reagan veto	N
Kill 60-day plant-closing notification measure	Y
Pass omnibus trade bill over Reagan veto	Y
Approve death penalty for drug-related murders	Y
Bar federal funds for abortions in cases of rape and incest	Y
Oppose seven-day waiting period for purchase of handguns	Y

Voting Studies

	Presidential Support		Party Unity		Conservative Coalition	
Year	S	O	S	O	S	O
1988	62	33	86	10	95	3
1987	63	31	83	10	81	9
1986	69	31	87	11	90	8
1985	63	38	83	10	80	16
1984	63	35	84	8	85	10
1983	73	27	87	11	85	13
1982	62	36	86	11	84	14
1981	67	30	86	11	91	5

Interest Group Ratings

Year	ADA	ACU	AFL-CIO	CCUS
1988	10	79	25	100
1987	4	86	0	100
1986	0	82	7	94
1985	15	71	12	95
1984	5	96	8	80
1983	10	91	6	90
1982	15	82	0	90
1981	10	100	0	84

2 Jim Slattery (D)

Of Topeka — Elected 1982

Born: Aug. 4, 1948, Good Intent, Kan.
Education: Attended Netherlands School of International Economics and Business, 1969-70; Washburn U., B.S. 1970, J.D. 1974.
Military Career: Army National Guard, 1970-75.
Occupation: Realtor.
Family: Wife, Linda Smith; two children.
Religion: Roman Catholic.
Political Career: Kan. House, 1973-79.
Capitol Office: 1440 Longworth Bldg. 20515; 225-6601.

In Washington: Like several other Democrats first elected to Congress in 1982, Slattery spends much of his time brooding about the red ink on the federal budget ledger. When he discusses the deficit, which he has called "the political equivalent of the Vietnam War," his engaging manner turns cold.

But if the deficit seems a constant concern, it is not Slattery's only priority. He is respected for his work on the Energy and Commerce Committee, an influential panel that allows him to pursue a variety of interests, most of them important to his home state, where he is considered a possible gubernatorial candidate.

Since he came to Congress, Slattery has been at the core of a House budget group trying to form a new center of gravity on budget issues within the Democratic Party. In that role, he has shown a willingness to face the pain of getting the federal ledger under control, even when that means bucking the Democratic leadership. He sees his party's challenge as "reconciling the political priorities of the '60s and '70s with the economic realities of the '80s and '90s." And he concedes that "it isn't a pleasant process."

Sometimes Slattery sounds like the fiscal conscience of his party when spending is being considered. When a number of Democrats began talking up new spending for child care and other "family" programs to boost the party's image during the 1988 election year, Slattery was among those voicing budget concerns. "There are too many [Democratic voters] that are still overtaxed. We have the compassion to care; the question is, do we have the toughness to govern and make tough choices."

When Energy and Commerce passed legislation to protect Medicare beneficiaries from catastrophic medical costs, Slattery, with a number of Republicans, expressed concerns that the bill tried to do too much. "Here we're talking about expanding Medicare at a time when this country can't pay its bills," he said, adding that benefits might have to be stripped to get "back more to the realm of reality."

Slattery was one of three moderate-to-conservative Democrats appointed to the Budget Committee in 1985 when Speaker Thomas P. O'Neill Jr. was under pressure to change its liberal tilt. In 1985 the group proposed a budget that called for a freeze on most federal programs, domestic as well as military, and included Social Security among those eligible to be frozen. It lost on the floor by a vote of 56-372. "There was an obvious coalition there," said one supporter. "We just didn't hit them at the peak of their courage."

The Budget Committee has helped to give Slattery some boost at home. Field hearings have been held in Atchison, and in the 101st Congress Slattery chairs a Budget Committee task force looking into rural health care and economic development. Also, by speaking up for Energy and Commerce issues on Budget — even those he did not necessarily support — Slattery has built up good will on the Energy panel.

As a freshman, Slattery was able to get a choice spot on Energy and Commerce because he had something to offer nearly all the factions in his party. Liberals could look at his pro-consumer record in the Kansas Legislature; energy interests could reasonably assume that, as a member from an oil-and-gas state, he would listen to them on issues they cared about.

Slattery does have a middle-of-the-road view on many issues before the committee. He is considered close to business, but supports measures pushed by environmental groups a little more often than he opposes them. In the 100th Congress, Slattery was part of an informal caucus of moderate-to-conservative Democrats, the so-called "group of nine," who banded together to try to break a six-year deadlock on reauthorizing the Clean Air Act. No legislation ever emerged from the committee, which has long been caught in a shootout between industry-oriented legislators and an environmentalist faction, but the group of nine did move the ball forward with a detailed proposal addressing the problem of urban smog.

Kansas 2

Topeka; Lawrence

Slattery has gained firm control of the 2nd since taking it from the GOP in 1982. But the district still trends Republican in statewide contests. George Bush's 53 percent in 1988 was well off President Reagan's 63 percent four years earlier, and he won two counties with less than 50 percent of the total vote. But he did manage to carry all 13 of the district's counties.

Topeka, Kansas' capital and third-largest city (about 120,000), is the heart of the 2nd. In addition to state government's crucial role in Topeka and surrounding Shawnee County, there is a substantial manufacturing base as well. One of several large health-care facilities in Topeka is the prominent Menninger Foundation, which specializes in psychiatric care.

There is more Democratic strength in Shawnee County than in less-urbanized parts of the state. The county has voted Democratic in the last three gubernatorial contests, giving 1986 Democratic nominee Tom Docking 52 percent in his loss to Republican Mike Hayden. But Bush edged Democrat Michael S. Dukakis with 51 percent of the vote, and Reagan won Shawnee easily.

Dukakis did slightly better in Douglas County (Lawrence), site of the University of Kansas and its 30,000 students; Bush won there by under 400 votes. Douglas has been a source of strength for Slattery, whose House prospects were boosted by the addition of the county to the 2nd in the last redistricting. Docking won the county decisively in his gubernatorial bid.

The district's other major academic center, Riley County (Manhattan), is a counterweight to the liberal influence of Douglas County. Manhattan is home to Kansas State University, an agriculture-oriented school with 17,000 students that has a more conservative atmosphere than the University of Kansas. Riley County went solidly for Bush in 1988 and Hayden in 1986. Clay County, at the district's western edge, is an even stronger GOP bastion; Bush took 72 percent there.

Federal installations are a considerable presence in the 2nd. In Leavenworth, along with the federal prison, the Army maintains the Command and General Staff College at Fort Leavenworth, the military's largest tactical training center. Junction City has Fort Riley, an Army base.

Population: 472,988. White 418,516 (88%), Black 34,559 (7%), Other 10,392 (2%). Spanish origin 14,179 (3%). 18 and over 348,994 (74%), 65 and over 51,790 (11%). Median age: 28.

In the 99th Congress, Slattery sided with Michigan's John D. Dingell, Energy and Commerce's powerful chairman, in a confrontation with environmentalists over renewal of the chemical-waste "superfund." Slattery and Dingell backed a somewhat less stringent plan than the one the environmental faction wanted.

In the last two Congresses Slattery has tried to help mediate the dispute in his party over aid to the Nicaraguan contras, which he had previously opposed. As a key swing vote on the issue, Slattery worked with other moderates to try to push the White House to use diplomacy rather than force in Nicaragua; at the same time, he was a supporter of sending non-military aid to the contras. "We are not abandoning the contras," he said of Democratic efforts to end military aid. "We are simply giving them a rest." When the House Democratic leadership's first non-military aid package was defeated in 1988, some Democrats were bitter about opposition from Republicans. Not Slattery. "I'm prepared to work with anybody and everybody who is willing to shape a policy consistent with the peace process without abandoning the contras," he said. Later in the year the House passed an aid package.

At Home: Slattery is a natural at politics. His profile earns him comparisons to Robert F. Kennedy, and his discourse is easygoing and articulate. Even the name of the farming community in which he grew up — Good Intent — is a fortunate happenstance most politicians would love to inherit.

The good fortune Slattery has enjoyed in his House campaigns has earned him a place on the short list of likely statewide Democratic candidates. He is seen as a possible challenger to Republican Gov. Mike Hayden in 1990.

Slattery has never been coy about his political ambitions. He was 24 and still in law school when he defeated an incumbent Republican state representative from Topeka. As part of a Democratic clique that included John Carlin, later the governor, Slattery pushed through the first major revision of the state's income-tax code in 30 years, and led a drive to make workers' compensation laws more to labor's liking.

In 1978 Slattery left the Legislature to develop his Topeka real-estate business and prepare a run for Congress. Democrats had lost the 2nd to Republican Jim Jeffries in 1978, but by 1982, Jeffries' reputation as a blustery, tactless ideologue had eroded his support. Slattery launched his campaign before Jeffries had decided whether to run again. An unfavorable remap helped persuade Jeffries to retire.

In his place, the GOP chose former legislator and state party Chairman Morris Kay. He tied himself closely to President Reagan and called Slattery "another Boston liberal." Slattery's retort was an effective one: "This isn't a race between Tip O'Neill and Ronald Reagan," he said. "It's between Jim Slattery and Morris Kay."

Slattery appealed to Republicans by stressing his farm background and his ties to the Topeka business community. He carried all but two of the district's 13 counties. Despite continued Republican efforts to profile him as a liberal, Slattery easily won in 1984 and 1986.

With speculation already rife about Slattery's 1990 plans, the GOP hoped to slow him down by running a high-profile candidate in 1988. They even tried to recruit David Eisenhower, son-in-law of former President Richard M. Nixon and grandson of the late President Dwight D. Eisenhower, a Kansas native.

When Eisenhower demurred, the Republicans settled on Phil Meinhardt, a recently retired Air Force lieutenant colonel who originally hailed from Kansas. Meinhardt tried to portray Slattery as a "tax-and-spend" liberal, badgering him to sign a "no tax increase" pledge. But Meinhardt, who returned to his home state in 1988 after a military career of more than three decades, lacked the name identification or financial backing to make a serious run at Slattery, who won by his biggest margin yet.

Committees

Budget (8th of 21 Democrats)
Task Forces: Economic Policy, Projections and Revenues (chairman); Urgent Fiscal Issues

Energy and Commerce (18th of 26 Democrats)
Commerce, Consumer Protection and Competitiveness; Telecommunications and Finance; Transportation and Hazardous Materials

Elections

1988 General

Jim Slattery (D)	135,694	(73%)
Phil Meinhardt (R)	49,498	(27%)

1986 General

Jim Slattery (D)	110,737	(71%)
Phill Kline (R)	46,029	(29%)

Previous Winning Percentages: 1984 (60%) **1982** (57%)

District Vote For President

	1988	1984	1980	1976
D	85,689 (46%)	66,539 (36%)	61,150 (34%)	76,297 (43%)
R	99,411 (53%)	117,971 (63%)	100,343 (56%)	97,716 (55%)
I			16,303 (9%)	

Campaign Finance

	Receipts	Receipts from PACs	Expend-itures
1988			
Slattery (D)	$453,832	$266,122 (59%)	$388,866
Meinhardt (R)	$86,328	$7,577 (9%)	$86,273
1986			
Slattery (D)	$378,797	$240,455 (63%)	$359,251
Kline (R)	$32,884	$11,200 (34%)	$20,414

Key Votes

1987	
Raise speed limit to 65 mph	Y
Approve Gephardt "fair trade" amendment	Y
Ban testing of larger nuclear weapons	Y
Delay "re-flagging" of Kuwaiti tankers	N
Approve tax-raising deficit-reduction bill	Y
1988	
Approve aid to Nicaraguan contras	N
Enact civil rights restoration bill over Reagan veto	Y
Kill 60-day plant-closing notification measure	N
Pass omnibus trade bill over Reagan veto	Y
Approve death penalty for drug-related murders	Y
Bar federal funds for abortions in cases of rape and incest	Y
Oppose seven-day waiting period for purchase of handguns	Y

Voting Studies

	Presidential Support		Party Unity		Conservative Coalition	
Year	**S**	**O**	**S**	**O**	**S**	**O**
1988	32	61	78	19	61	29
1987	38	60	73	24	63	33
1986	34	66	68	30	62	38
1985	43	58	71	27	65	35
1984	39	61	60	39	49	51
1983	39	61	57	38	58	38

Interest Group Ratings

Year	ADA	ACU	AFL-CIO	CCUS
1988	55	33	85	38
1987	68	4	69	47
1986	45	27	57	56
1985	55	33	53	36
1984	50	38	38	44
1983	55	36	71	55

3 Jan Meyers (R)

Of Overland Park — Elected 1984

Born: July 20, 1928, Lincoln, Neb.
Education: William Woods College, A.F.A. 1948; U. of Nebraska, B.A. 1951.
Occupation: Homemaker; public official.
Family: Husband, Louis "Dutch" Meyers; two children.
Religion: Methodist.
Political Career: Overland Park City Council, 1967-72; Kan. Senate, 1973-85; sought Republican nomination for U.S. Senate, 1978.
Capitol Office: 315 Cannon Bldg. 20515; 225-2865.

In Washington: In her search for an influential role in Congress, Meyers took the traditional route of gaining favor with House Republican leader Robert H. Michel, with whom she shares a capacity for legislative compromise. During her first term, she served on a party task force aimed at preventing recount disputes, such as the one that embroiled the 1984 contest in Indiana's 8th District. In 1988, she took on the chore of chairing a panel that revised the rules of the House Republican Conference.

However, when Meyers ventured at the start of the 101st Congress for a leadership position of her own — that of conference secretary — she learned that being an insider is not enough anymore.

Even before the election of Georgia's Newt Gingrich as minority whip, the Republican caucus was showing signs of a tilt toward the more assertive, highly partisan tactics perfected by Gingrich's Conservative Opportunity Society. In the contest for secretary, Meyers, who did little campaigning, was swept aside by Vin Weber of Minnesota, who was later Gingrich's key lieutenant in the whip race.

Meyers' setback, mild though it was, mirrored her struggle to gain a footing in the House committee process. Though she came in brimming with hopes for a seat on a high-profile panel, such as Ways and Means or Appropriations, she had to settle for Science and Small Business.

After two terms, she did get on Foreign Affairs. However, with her conciliatory nature, she rarely played a visible role in the heated foreign policy debates between the committee's very liberal Democrats and very conservative Republicans. Her strongest efforts came in discussions on international drug trafficking; she urged that Foreign Affairs pay greater attention to the issue, which she described as a major impediment to improved relations between the United States and Latin America.

Meyers has made the issue of drug abuse a central focus of her career. She insists that attacking the "demand" side of the drug trade is vital in defeating the problem. "We must make the user's life so difficult, and the use of drugs so socially unacceptable, that people will not start drug use," Meyers said during a 1988 floor speech. She proposed a bill to increase criminal penalties for operators of common carriers involved in accidents that cause death and injury while under the influence of drugs or alcohol; provisions of that measure were attached to the 1988 omnibus drug act.

At Home: Though Meyers has built no legislative empires in Washington, she is well-known and well liked at home. Meyers was one of several members of the Kansas delegation mentioned as possible candidates if Republican Sen. Nancy Landon Kassebaum had decided to retire in 1990; in May 1989, Kassebaum announced she would run for a third term.

Meyers has made one attempt for statewide office, but it was not a success. She ran in the 1978 GOP Senate primary, won by Kassebaum, and finished fourth with just under 10 percent of the vote.

However, she did much better in 1984, when Republican Larry Winn Jr.'s retirement opened the 3rd District seat. Meyers' 17 years as a city and state officeholder made her the front-runner over four GOP challengers. She had established a moderate reputation in the state Senate, where she was involved in issues such as care for the elderly, prevention of child abuse and drunken driving. To assert her conservative credentials, Meyers stressed that her efforts cost the state little, since they relied as much as possible on local funding.

After easily winning the primary, Meyers took on Kansas City's Democratic mayor, Jack Reardon. While Reardon was a colorful campaigner, Meyers scored by emphasizing her political experience and covering Johnson County with signs reading "Jan Can." With Kassebaum and President Reagan on the ticket, a strong Republican turnout boosted Meyers to victory. Meyers quickly solidified her position, running without opposition in 1986 and defeating a Democratic opponent by 3-to-1 in 1988.

Kansas 3

East — Kansas City

When Rodgers and Hammerstein wrote "Everything's up-to-date in Kansas City," they meant Kansas City, Mo. Kansas City, Kan., on the western bank of the Missouri River, lives on in the shadow of its larger, more bustling namesake. The 3rd, centered around blue-collar Kansas City, Kan., and the Johnson County suburbs to the south, remains within the orbit of Missouri's economy, though it is developing an economic identity all its own.

Booming Johnson County boasts over 60 percent of the district's population; the county grew by more than 15 percent in the first half of the 1980s alone. One of the nation's top counties in per-capita income, Johnson County is reliably Republican. George Bush took 63 percent of the county vote in 1988, running up a 40,000-vote margin on Democrat Michael S. Dukakis.

Though the dominant image of Johnson County is one of stately homes and manicured lawns, there are more modest, older suburban towns, such as Lenexa, many of them settled by immigrants who worked in the various industries of the two Kansas Citys. Sprawling south and farther west is the county's boom corridor, reaching to Olathe and beyond — a mix of farm land and new office buildings and shopping centers.

There is little in common between suburban Johnson County and urban, industrial Wyandotte County (Kansas City) to the north. Kansas City, once one of the Great Plains' major stockyard centers, suffered from years of decline. But efforts to diversify the economy have stemmed the city's population shrinkage.

The city maintains the Democratic tradition dating back to the halcyon days of its ethnic-oriented political machine. The city's large black population — 25 percent of the total — is dependably Democratic. Wyandotte County gave Dukakis 66 percent of its vote in 1988, and was one of three Kansas counties won by the Democrat.

Population: 472,456. White 416,244 (88%), Black 45,319 (10%), Other 4,490 (1%). Spanish origin 12,360 (3%). 18 and over 334,153 (71%), 65 and over 45,786 (10%). Median age: 30.

Committees

Foreign Affairs (12th of 18 Republicans)
Europe and the Middle East; Human Rights and International Organizations

Select Aging (16th of 27 Republicans)
Health and Long-Term Care; Human Services

Small Business (8th of 17 Republicans)
Exports, Tax Policy and Special Problems; SBA, the General Economy and Minority Business Development

Elections

1988 General		
Jan Meyers (R)	150,223	(74%)
Lionel Kunst (D)	53,959	(26%)
1988 Primary		
Jan Meyers (R)	25,993	(85%)
Charles B. Masterson (R)	4,570	(15%)
1986 General		
Jan Meyers (R)	109,266	(100%)

Previous Winning Percentage: 1984 (55%)

District Vote For President

	1988		1984		1980		1976	
D	99,785	(45%)	78,289	(36%)	70,201	(36%)	78,764	(42%)
R	121,658	(54%)	138,118	(63%)	108,207	(55%)	104,811	(56%)
I					14,436	(7%)		

Campaign Finance

	Receipts	Receipts from PACs	Expend-itures
1988			
Meyers (R)	$201,229	$110,395 (55%)	$234,583
Kunst (D) †	$13,483	0	$13,483
1986			
Meyers (R)	$172,359	$108,612 (63%)	$139,791

† Totals based on incomplete data.

Key Votes

1987	
Raise speed limit to 65 mph	Y
Approve Gephardt "fair trade" amendment	N
Ban testing of larger nuclear weapons	Y
Delay "re-flagging" of Kuwaiti tankers	N
Approve tax-raising deficit-reduction bill	N
1988	
Approve aid to Nicaraguan contras	Y
Enact civil rights restoration bill over Reagan veto	Y
Kill 60-day plant-closing notification measure	Y
Pass omnibus trade bill over Reagan veto	N
Approve death penalty for drug-related murders	Y
Bar federal funds for abortions in cases of rape and incest	N
Oppose seven-day waiting period for purchase of handguns	N

Voting Studies

	Presidential Support		Party Unity		Conservative Coalition	
Year	S	O	S	O	S	O
1988	52	45	71	24	87	13
1987	59	41	71	26	77	21
1986	59	39	73	27	70	30
1985	68	31	68	26	78	18

Interest Group Ratings

Year	ADA	ACU	AFL-CIO	CCUS
1988	35	58	23	85
1987	12	61	6	93
1986	25	55	14	78
1985	15	71	19	86

4 Dan Glickman (D)

Of Wichita — Elected 1976

Born: Nov. 24, 1944, Wichita, Kan.
Education: U. of Michigan, B.A. 1966; George Washington U., J.D. 1969.
Occupation: Lawyer.
Family: Wife, Rhoda Yura; two children.
Religion: Jewish.
Political Career: Wichita Board of Education, 1973-76, president, 1975-76.
Capitol Office: 1212 Longworth Bldg. 20515; 225-6216.

In Washington: Unfettered by the House's tendency to specialize, Glickman has extended his legislative tentacles from farm policy to aeronautics research to product-liability law. Whether or not he ever reaches the Senate — his well-known ambition — his legislative résumé already is as broad as those of many senators.

The Kansas Democrat serves on four committees, and manages to be a serious player on each — Agriculture, Judiciary, Science, and Intelligence. He seems to have an amendment for nearly every major bill those committees bring to the floor, and every subcommittee he chairs becomes a legislative factory. This industry has helped Glickman move beyond his early reputation as merely a media-seeking maverick.

At the start of the 100th Congress, he inherited a powerful new position, the chairmanship of the Agriculture Subcommittee on Wheat, Soybeans and Feed Grains. When he took over the panel, Democrats were deeply divided over the future of federal agriculture programs and the ailing farm economy. Though the divisions have not narrowed much, Glickman succeeded in steering several important measures to passage in the 100th Congress.

When urban Democrats began agitating to reduce the Agriculture budget by cutting federal farm payments to corporations, Glickman recognized action was inevitable and moved to pass legislation that farm-state voters could accept. The 1987 budget-reconciliation bill capped farm-income support payments at $100,000, thereby limiting the payments to corporate farmers. The bill also allowed wheat and feed grain producers to enroll in a program for 1988 and 1989 that would give them 92 percent of projected income subsidies on land taken out of production.

On the 1988 drought-relief bill, Glickman backed language to give farmers more flexibility. The new law guarantees farmers their base payments while allowing them to shift 10 to 25 percent of their land to soybeans or sunflowers, which were in high demand. It was also a Glickman amendment to the trade bill that increased the agricultural Export Enhancement Program.

Glickman navigates potentially rough waters in working with Agriculture Chairman E. "Kika" de la Garza of Texas. In 1980, Glickman helped lead a group of dissident committee Democrats who tried to deny de la Garza the chairmanship. While they are now cordial, the tension has not entirely vanished.

A central player on the 1985 farm bill, Glickman was one of a group of younger House Democrats who wanted Congress to try new approaches for federal price-support programs. After several were rejected — which he attributed to "institutional conservatism" — Glickman was one of 96 members who voted against the final farm bill.

Though considered an expert on commodity futures, Glickman has not endeared himself to some of his colleagues by going up against the powerful financial interests in the futures markets, an important source of honoraria for Agriculture Committee members. But with recent federal investigations into trading fraud in the two largest markets, Glickman is likely to reassert himself. In 1982 debate over commodity futures regulation, Glickman wanted federal regulators to have greater power to protect consumers, and he wanted consumers to have the right to sue commodity-law violators. Both ideas became law.

Earlier in his career, Glickman was chairman of the Science Subcommittee on Aviation. He managed to win more money for aeronautics research than the Reagan administration requested, and kept a close watch over Federal Aviation Administration plans to modernize the air-traffic control system. In the 100th Congress, he was active in the Science Committee's work on successful legislation to tighten security over government computers.

Glickman also once chaired the Judiciary Subcommittee on Administrative Law, a seemingly dry jurisdiction that he transformed into one of the most active Judiciary subcommittees. Glickman cranked out legislation to improve

Kansas 4

Central — Wichita

Aircraft workers with Southern roots give a blue-collar Democratic presence to Wichita and surrounding Sedgwick County, where more than three of every four votes in the 4th are cast. Wichita was the base of unsuccessful 1986 Democratic gubernatorial nominee Tom Docking, and in the governor's race of 1982, Democratic incumbent John Carlin won Sedgwick County's vote even though his opponent came from Wichita. Sedgwick's working-class voters have been the backbone of Glickman's strength, although Glickman also runs well among the county's suburban and rural voters as well.

This Democratic cast has become less and less evident at the presidential level, though. In 1976, President Ford edged Democrat Jimmy Carter in Sedgwick. In 1984, President Reagan won the county with 63 percent. George Bush continued the pattern in 1988, with a comfortable 55 percent victory over Democrat Michael S. Dukakis.

The Republican lean at the national level is partly due to the beneficial local effect of the increased defense spending levels of the Reagan years. Boeing's military aviation works in Wichita enjoyed a boom during the period, cushioning the region's economy even from the recession of the early 1980s. McConnell Air Force Base, outside Wichita, which has facilities for basing B-1 bombers, also provides economic benefits for the district.

Civilian aviation is the other economic mainstay of Wichita, a city of more than 280,000 people that includes some of the state's largest minority communities outside Kansas City. Thousands are employed on the assembly lines of Boeing's commercial divisions, Cessna, Beech and Gates-Learjet, and by their subcontractors. However, the commercial-aviation business tends to be more cyclical and more subject to foreign competition than the military aircraft industry.

In addition to the aviation industry, Wichita retains an identity as a corporate base for Kansas' oil industry, which played an important role in the city's early development. But the oil bust took a considerable toll in Kansas, costing jobs from the executive suites to the oil fields.

Outside of Wichita, farming remains the mainstay of the five-county district. The only other city of size in the 4th is Hutchinson (Reno County), with about 41,500 people.

Population: 473,180. White 421,885 (89%), Black 33,405 (7%), Other 8,356 (2%). Spanish origin 14,288 (3%). 18 and over 341,718 (72%), 65 and over 51,611 (11%). Median age: 29.

federal debt collection, combat medical malpractice in the military and crack down on fraud, particularly by defense contractors.

In the 100th Congress, his seat on Judiciary gave him the forum he needed to pass two bills; one made crimes motivated by religious bias federal offenses; another stiffened criminal penalties for airlines that do not comply with federal aviation standards.

In keeping with his past criticism of congressional perquisites, Glickman during the 100th Congress was a leading advocate of including members of Congress under a governmentwide ethics bill, which was ultimately vetoed by President Reagan. But that was a tame endeavor compared with the "reform" crusades that Glickman waged early in his House career — crusades that had much to do with him getting a "media hot dog" image.

Glickman once proposed denying members a hand-bound set of the *Congressional Record* for personal use, and sought to restrict insertions in the Record to items "relevant to government matters" so as to save taxpayers' money. He also proposed taking elevator operators — patronage employees — off most of the automatic elevators in the Capitol.

At Home: Bolstered politically by his senior positions on committees dealing with district interests, Glickman amplifies his visibility by making himself accessible, on an almost daily basis, to the Wichita media. "I am never too busy to talk to local TV, period, exclamation point," Glickman has said.

In 1976, Glickman became the first Democrat to win this Wichita-based district in 36 years. He has been returned to office so easily that he perennially leads the list of possible Democratic contenders for statewide office.

Though Glickman has been urged to run in three Senate races — in 1980 and 1986 against Republican Bob Dole, and in 1984 against junior GOP Sen. Nancy Landon Kassebaum — so far he has opted for the safety of his House seat. Democratic speculation over the 1990 Senate race centered again on Glickman, but he opted not to challenge Kassebaum.

A member of a wealthy and prominent Wichita family, Glickman was elected to the Wichita school board in 1973, at age 28, and became president two years later. In 1974 he was a regional coordinator for William Roy's Democratic Senate campaign against Dole.

While Glickman was working for Roy in 1974, he was keeping an eye on the politics of the 4th District, where veteran Republican Garner E. Shriver was winning re-election by a surprisingly small margin. Glickman decided on a House campaign of his own for 1976. As school board president, he kept his name visible in the Wichita media by pushing for open board meetings and a school ombudsman.

In 1976, campaigning as a fiscal conservative and a moderate on other issues, he worked vigorously to paint Shriver as a tired, inactive House member. "You've had 16 years of a professional politician. Now is the time for a citizen congressman," Glickman's campaign literature urged; Glickman himself called for six-term limits on House tenure. The 64-year-old Shriver, quiet and complacent, was slow to respond. Glickman won by 3,235 votes.

After this narrow upset, Glickman's work on behalf of district interests quickly made him a popular figure. From 1978 through 1984, he regularly won with over 70 percent. In 1986, he got 65 percent against Republican Bob Knight, a Wichita city councilman and former mayor. Like previous challengers, Knight was a conservative who failed to persuade voters that Glickman was too liberal for the 4th.

In 1988, Republicans tried a different tack, nominating attorney Lee Thompson, a moderate with political ties to Kassebaum. He centered his campaign on the "six terms and out" idea Glickman advocated in 1976; he reminded voters that Glickman was seeking a seventh term.

But Glickman easily deflected this thrust, noting that he had tried with no success as a House freshman to push his limited-tenure plan, and reminding voters that his departure would weaken their voice when the House draws up the 1990 farm bill. He won with 64 percent.

Committees

Agriculture (8th of 27 Democrats)
Wheat, Soybeans and Feed Grains (chairman); Department Operations, Research and Foreign Agriculture; Domestic Marketing, Consumer Relations and Nutrition

Judiciary (9th of 21 Democrats)
Administrative Law and Governmental Relations; Economic and Commercial Law

Science, Space and Technology (6th of 30 Democrats)
Transportation, Aviation and Materials

Select Intelligence (9th of 12 Democrats)
Legislation; Program and Budget Authority

Elections

1988 General		
Dan Glickman (D)	122,777	(64%)
Lee Thompson (R)	69,165	(36%)
1986 General		
Dan Glickman (D)	111,164	(65%)
Bob Knight (R)	61,178	(35%)

Previous Winning Percentages: **1984** (74%) **1982** (74%) **1980** (69%) **1978** (70%) **1976** (50%)

District Vote For President

	1988	1984	1980	1976
D	84,235 (43%)	70,140 (36%)	70,871 (37%)	87,817 (48%)
R	108,417 (55%)	124,731 (63%)	100,757 (53%)	89,301 (49%)
I			13,477 (8%)	

Campaign Finance

	Receipts	Receipts from PACs	Expend-itures
1988			
Glickman (D)	$562,266	$280,540 (50%)	$545,755
Thompson (R)	$149,704	$8,400 (6%)	$149,035
1986			
Glickman (D)	$456,405	$180,225 (39%)	$523,533
Knight (R)	$231,000	$18,170 (8%)	$227,587

Key Votes

1987	
Raise speed limit to 65 mph	Y
Approve Gephardt "fair trade" amendment	N
Ban testing of larger nuclear weapons	Y
Delay "re-flagging" of Kuwaiti tankers	Y
Approve tax-raising deficit-reduction bill	Y
1988	
Approve aid to Nicaraguan contras	N
Enact civil rights restoration bill over Reagan veto	Y
Kill 60-day plant-closing notification measure	N
Pass omnibus trade bill over Reagan veto	Y
Approve death penalty for drug-related murders	Y
Bar federal funds for abortions in cases of rape and incest	N
Oppose seven-day waiting period for purchase of handguns	N

Voting Studies

	Presidential Support		Party Unity		Conservative Coalition	
Year	S	O	S	O	S	O
1988	32	65	75	20	61	39
1987	26	74	80	17	58	42
1986	28	70	76	21	60	40
1985	36	63	76	22	53	45
1984	40	59	69	29	44	53
1983	43	57	73	23	46	53
1982	47	53	74	26	45	53
1981	47	53	70	30	48	51

Interest Group Ratings

Year	ADA	ACU	AFL-CIO	CCUS
1988	80	16	86	43
1987	80	9	75	47
1986	55	32	64	50
1985	55	35	59	41
1984	60	29	62	38
1983	70	22	63	55
1982	70	18	80	24
1981	75	27	60	26

5 Bob Whittaker (R)

Of Augusta — Elected 1978

Born: Sept. 18, 1939, Eureka, Kan.
Education: Attended U. of Kansas, 1957-59; Emporia State U., 1959; Illinois College of Optometry, B.S., O.D. 1962.
Occupation: Optometrist.
Family: Wife, Marlene Faye Arnold; three children.
Religion: Christian Church.
Political Career: Kan. House, 1975-77.
Capitol Office: 2436 Rayburn Bldg. 20515; 225-3911.

In Washington: A clean-cut, private man, Whittaker has spent much of his House career quietly tending to constituent needs from his post on the Energy and Commerce Committee. He is generally a GOP loyalist on the committee, but on some issues finds enough common ground with Democrats to work with them.

In the 100th Congress, Whittaker stepped up from the GOP backbenches to become the ranking member of the Transportation Subcommittee. Together with subcommittee Chairman Thomas A. Luken of Ohio, Whittaker offered legislation mandating random drug testing for employees involved in rail-safety jobs. Committee Democrats, including Luken, were skittish about the issue and insisted on language to ensure that workers who tested positive would not be fired but allowed to enter rehabilitation programs instead. Whittaker concurred, and the bill eventually won House approval. But the administration and Senate Republicans were adamantly opposed to the modified language. Despite Whittaker's pleas that accepting it was preferable to doing nothing, the stalemate killed the bill in the 100th Congress.

Whittaker occasionally strays from his basic conservative instincts when the issue is health. During Health Subcommittee debate on the catastrophic health insurance bill, Whittaker was the only Republican to vote to allow "respite care" for homebound, frail elderly. Whittaker also joined the debate in favor of increasing federal regulation of cigarettes and other tobacco products and spoke out in favor of the Smoke-Free Hospitals Act.

Representing a predominantly rural district, Whittaker is particularly attentive to rural health issues. In the 101st Congress, he offered legislation to create another high-level bureaucratic post: deputy under secretary for rural health. In the previous Congress, he introduced successful legislation to expand the number of hospitals eligible for Medicare's "swing bed" program. The new law allows hospitals with fewer than 100 beds — up from 50 beds — to use empty beds to care for patients who qualify for care in a skilled-nursing facility.

When environmentalists clash with pro-industry forces on Energy and Commerce, Whittaker is nearly always on the industry side. He backed efforts to relax the strictures of the Clean Air Act in the early 1980s, and also backed natural-gas producers in their efforts to avoid any new forms of regulation.

In the past, Whittaker had shown an interest in energy policy when there was an obvious Kansas connection. In 1982, after more than two years of trying, he persuaded the Energy Department to locate a $4.6 million solar energy development project in Osage City, Kan.

At Home: Like most of his Kansas House colleagues, Whittaker is considered a possible future candidate for statewide office. He briefly considered running for governor in 1986, but opted for his safe House seat when a crowded gubernatorial primary field developed.

Whittaker won the House seat in a highly competitive primary to succeed retiring Republican Rep. Joe Skubitz in 1978. A little-known, two-term state representative, he resigned his legislative seat in May 1977 and began a long, meticulous campaign for the seat. He campaigned door-to-door and held "work days" as a nursing home attendant, garbage collector and grain elevator worker.

His strategy paid off when he won the Republican nomination with 39 percent of the vote in a five-man field, defeating manufacturer Don Johnston by nearly 3,000 votes. In the general election, Whittaker comfortably defeated Democratic state Sen. Don Allegrucci following a campaign in which he criticized Allegrucci's opposition to capital punishment and support for liquor-by-the-drink in local restaurants.

Whittaker has never had any trouble winning re-election. In 1988, he repeated his 1984 landslide victory over Democrat John A. Barnes, an industrial engineer.

An optometrist by profession, Whittaker was a regional coordinator in 1974 for Sen. Bob Dole's re-election campaign. In the same year, he won the first of his two elections to the state House.

Kansas 5

Southeast — Emporia; Pittsburg

Economic slumps in two of southeast Kansas' leading industries — agriculture and energy resource production — brought hard times to wide areas of the 5th District in the 1980s. Of the district's 25 counties, 19 lost population from 1980-86, with seven incurring losses of 5 percent or more.

The problems in the local economy have not shaken district voters from their conservative tendencies, however. George Bush took 56 percent of the district vote in 1988, his second-highest figure in the state, and carried all but one county.

Though no Democrat has held the 5th since 1960, the region used to have some amenability to Democrats. Numerous Southerners moved north to work in the wheat and oil fields of southeast Kansas, and so many Eastern Europeans migrated to work in the coal mines of the area that it took on the name of "the Balkans." That name is also a reference to the region's hilly landscape, which belies the image of Kansas as a flat, arid expanse of wheat.

Lingering Democratic sympathies are most evident in Crawford County, site of the industrial city of Pittsburg. The city has a population of just over 18,000, including a sizable blue-collar work force. In 1988, Democrat Michael S. Dukakis took 52 percent of the vote in Crawford County, one of three counties in all of Kansas that he won.

The Republican tilt in Lyon County — which includes Emporia, the district's largest city with about 24,600 residents — is much more standard for the district. Located at the center of the Flint Hills, which run the length of eastern Kansas, Emporia is the 5th's major commercial hub. Some of Emporia's large population of Welsh extraction still celebrate St. David's Day, honoring the patron saint of Wales.

The region once boasted booming ore mines. Now the 5th's economy depends on agriculture, primarily soybeans and wheat.

Population: 472,916. White 455,149 (96%), Black 8,564 (2%), Other 4,602 (1%). Spanish origin 7,869 (2%). 18 and over 347,340 (74%), 65 and over 81,483 (17%). Median age: 33.

Committee

Energy and Commerce (6th of 17 Republicans)
Transportation and Hazardous Materials (ranking); Health and the Environment

Elections

1988 General

Bob Whittaker (R)	127,722	(70%)
John A. Barnes (D)	54,327	(30%)

1986 General

Bob Whittaker (R)	116,800	(71%)
Kym E. Myers (D)	47,540	(29%)

Previous Winning Percentages: **1984** (74%) **1982** (68%) **1980** (74%) **1978** (57%)

District Vote For President

	1988		1984		1980		1976	
D	78,214	(42%)	63,616	(32%)	67,709	(34%)	91,122	(47%)
R	104,238	(56%)	135,037	(67%)	117,130	(59%)	99,491	(51%)
I					11,514	(6%)		

Campaign Finance

	Receipts	Receipts from PACs	Expend-itures
1988			
Whittaker (R)	$222,261	$155,056 (70%)	$117,312
1986			
Whittaker (R)	$210,029	$116,795 (56%)	$97,850

Key Votes

1987	
Raise speed limit to 65 mph	Y
Approve Gephardt "fair trade" amendment	N
Ban testing of larger nuclear weapons	X
Delay "re-flagging" of Kuwaiti tankers	N
Approve tax-raising deficit-reduction bill	N
1988	
Approve aid to Nicaraguan contras	Y
Enact civil rights restoration bill over Reagan veto	N
Kill 60-day plant-closing notification measure	Y
Pass omnibus trade bill over Reagan veto	Y
Approve death penalty for drug-related murders	Y
Bar federal funds for abortions in cases of rape and incest	N
Oppose seven-day waiting period for purchase of handguns	Y

Voting Studies

	Presidential Support		Party Unity		Conservative Coalition	
Year	**S**	**O**	**S**	**O**	**S**	**O**
1988	61	38	84	11	89	3
1987	66 †	31 †	81 †	15 †	86 †	12 †
1986	67	31	83	15	90	10
1985	58	40	79	13	84	13
1984	67	31	83	14	85	10
1983	68	30	84	14	92	8
1982	65	35	84	12	82	16
1981	70	30	84	14	91	9

† Not eligible for all recorded votes.

Interest Group Ratings

Year	ADA	ACU	AFL-CIO	CCUS
1988	10	88	29	100
1987	8	73	13	87
1986	10	91	15	94
1985	10	81	12	86
1984	10	82	0	73
1983	15	74	6	80
1982	15	86	5	90
1981	15	100	7	89

Kentucky

U.S. CONGRESS

SENATE 1 D, 1 R

HOUSE 4 D, 3 R

LEGISLATURE

Senate 30 D, 8 R

House 72 D, 28 R

ELECTIONS

1988 Presidential Vote

Bush	56%
Dukakis	44%

1984 Presidential Vote

Reagan	60%
Mondale	39%

1980 Presidential Vote

Reagan	49%
Carter	48%
Anderson	2%

Turnout rate in 1984	51%
Turnout rate in 1986	23%
Turnout rate in 1988	48%

(as percentage of voting age population)

POPULATION AND GROWTH

1980 population	3,660,777
1988 population estimate (23rd in the nation)	3,727,000
Percent change 1980-1988	+2%

DEMOGRAPHIC BREAKDOWN

White	92%
Black	7%
(Spanish origin)	1%
Urban	51%
Rural	49%
Born in state	79%
Foreign-born	1%

MAJOR CITIES

Louisville	286,470
Lexington-Fayette	212,900
Owensboro	56,280
Covington	45,670
Bowling Green	41,300

AREA AND LAND USE

Area 39,669 sq. miles (37th)

Farm	56%
Forest	48%
Federally owned	5%

Gov. Wallace G. Wilkinson (D)
Of Lexington — Elected 1987

Born: Dec. 12, 1941, Liberty, Ky.
Education: Attended U. of Kentucky, 1961.
Occupation: Businessman.
Religion: Christian.
Political Career: No previous office.
Next Election: 1991.

WORK

Occupations

White-collar	46%
Blue-collar	37%
Service workers	13%

Government Workers

Federal	32,826
State	72,459
Local	116,890

MONEY

Median family income	$ 16,444 (45th)
Tax burden per capita	$ 809 (28th)

EDUCATION

Spending per pupil through grade 12	$ 2,486 (47th)
Persons with college degrees	11% (48th)

CRIME

Violent crime rate	338 per 100,000 (32nd)

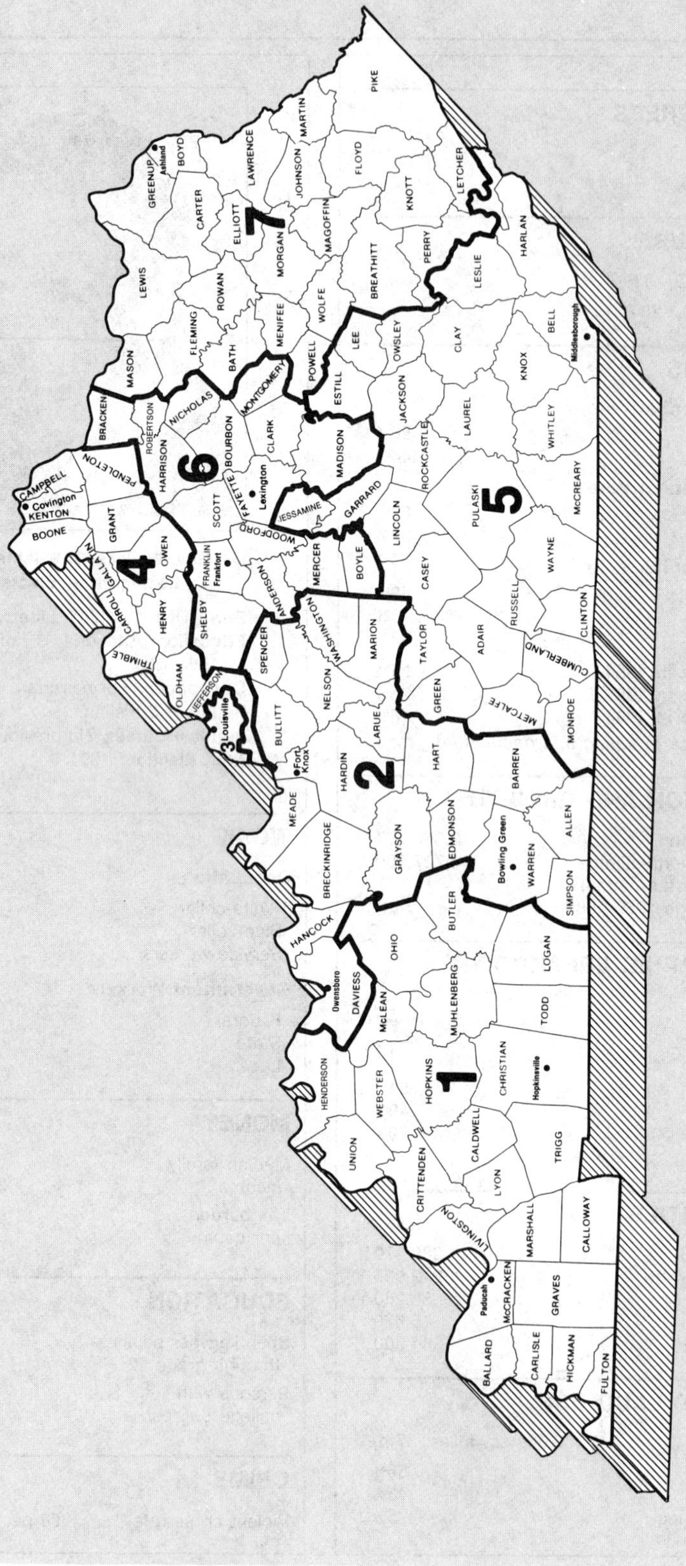
1
2
3
4
5
6
7
PIKE
MARTIN
LAWRENCE
BOYD
Ashland
GREENUP
CARTER
ELLIOTT
JOHNSON
FLOYD
KNOTT
LETCHER
HARLAN
LESLIE
PERRY
BREATHITT
MAGOFFIN
MORGAN
ROWAN
LEWIS
FLEMING
MASON
BRACKEN
ROBERTSON
NICHOLAS
BATH
MENIFEE
WOLFE
MONTGOMERY
POWELL
LEE
OWSLEY
CLAY
BELL
Middlesborough
KNOX
LAUREL
JACKSON
ESTILL
CLARK
BOURBON
HARRISON
PENDLETON
CAMPBELL
Covington
KENTON
BOONE
GRANT
OWEN
GALLATIN
CARROLL
TRIMBLE
HENRY
OLDHAM
SCOTT
FAYETTE
Lexington
MADISON
JESSAMINE
GARRARD
ROCKCASTLE
WHITLEY
McCREARY
PULASKI
LINCOLN
WOODFORD
FRANKLIN
Frankfort
SHELBY
ANDERSON
MERCER
BOYLE
CASEY
WAYNE
RUSSELL
CLINTON
ADAIR
TAYLOR
MARION
WASHINGTON
SPENCER
JEFFERSON
Louisville
BULLITT
NELSON
LARUE
GREEN
CUMBERLAND
METCALFE
MONROE
HART
BARREN
ALLEN
HARDIN
Fort Knox
MEADE
BRECKINRIDGE
GRAYSON
EDMONSON
WARREN
Bowling Green
SIMPSON
BUTLER
LOGAN
HANCOCK
OHIO
DAVIESS
Owensboro
McLEAN
MUHLENBERG
TODD
CHRISTIAN
Hopkinsville
HOPKINS
HENDERSON
WEBSTER
UNION
CRITTENDEN
CALDWELL
LYON
TRIGG
LIVINGSTON
MARSHALL
CALLOWAY
McCRACKEN
Paducah
GRAVES
BALLARD
CARLISLE
HICKMAN
FULTON

Wendell H. Ford (D)

Of Owensboro — Elected 1974

Born: Sept. 8, 1924, Daviess County, Ky.
Education: Attended U. of Kentucky, 1942-43.
Military Career: Army, 1944-46; National Guard, 1949-62.
Occupation: Insurance executive.
Family: Wife, Jean Neel; two children.
Religion: Baptist.
Political Career: Ky. Senate, 1965-67; lieutenant governor, 1967-71; governor, 1971-74.
Capitol Office: 173A Russell Bldg. 20510; 224-4343.

In Washington: Ford is one of the few senators for whom the idea of the Senate as a club is no myth. He is one of the most avid and wily practitioners of the chamber's peculiar rules, with a gambler's style befitting a man from a state that takes its horse racing, poker and politics equally seriously.

It is the game that fascinates Ford more than the abstractions of public policy. He has called himself "a dumb country boy with dirt between his toes," but colleagues do not for a moment doubt his shrewdness. He sizes up a rival or a situation with the sharp eye of a horse-trader. He does not get all he wants, but he almost always comes away with something.

Usually, Ford comes away from a back room, which is smoke-filled by the time this tobacco champion leaves it. He seldom seeks the spotlight, preferring to work through private negotiations in committee, at the conference table or in the cloakroom. "Why make a speech when you can sit down with your colleagues and work something out?" he once asked.

Ford's politics are nothing if not negotiable. He is a deal-maker, usually for business interests and particularly for those in Kentucky — tobacco, liquor and coal. That puts him in frequent alliance with Republicans. Yet he can be as partisan as any "yellow-dog" Southern Democrat, and he votes frequently enough for labor, anti-poverty programs and party positions on defense and foreign policy to rank as a loyal Democrat.

As a consummate Senate insider, Ford had long been expected to seek a leadership post. But when he finally announced late in 1988 that he would challenge the No. 2 Democrat, longtime Democratic Whip Alan Cranston, Ford's gamble proved so uncharacteristically clumsy, his defeat so humiliating and his reaction so ungracious that colleagues accustomed to an astute and engaging Ford were left baffled.

Cranston had appeared headed to uncontested re-election, and attention was fixed on a three-way race to succeed Majority Leader Robert C. Byrd, when Ford unexpectedly announced his candidacy just two months before the November caucus vote. He vaguely said he would try "to improve the efficiency of the Senate," as he had as Rules Committee chairman, and suggested that Cranston was no longer up to the job.

Most Democrats felt otherwise. The vote was 30-12 for Cranston when Ford moved to stop the count and declare Cranston's election unanimous. Then he made a less-than-magnanimous concession that amounted to a declaration of his candidacy for whip two years hence. Worse, back in Kentucky that week, he said the team of Cranston and new Majority Leader George J. Mitchell put "two extreme liberals" in charge of the Senate. Ford later amended that to "fairly liberal," but the damage was done.

As a result, much of Ford's time in the 101st Congress might well be spent quietly repairing relations with fellow members — especially if he intends another leadership bid. The Rules chairmanship could be of some use. Ford controls many aspects of internal housekeeping, from postage-stamp accounts to parking spaces; they are of little consequence to the public, but of great importance to his colleagues.

He is most active on two other committees — Commerce, Science and Transportation; and Energy and Natural Resources — where his close ties to business have made him one of the Senate's top fund-raisers. In recognition of his money-raising prowess, Ford's colleagues chose him to head the Democratic Senatorial Campaign Committee from 1976 through 1982.

In 1987, Ford became chairman of Commerce's Aviation Subcommittee. There, he works to steer grants to small airports, such as those common in Kentucky, and to base awards not only on an airport's passenger traffic but also on cargo: Louisville is home to United Parcel Service's air-freight business. In his first year, Ford helped enact a $20 billion authorization for airport expansions and air-traffic control improvements, aided by intense public concern about both safety and flight delays.

Like the airline industry, Ford favors removing the Federal Aviation Administration from the Transportation Department. Supporters say that would free the FAA of department politicking, but foes complain that the agency is too close to the industry. Prospects for an independent FAA improved in the 101st Congress, however, when proponent James L. Oberstar replaced foe Norman Y. Mineta as Ford's counterpart on the House Aviation panel.

On Commerce, Ford also has been a critic of federal business regulation; he sponsored the legislation enacted in 1980 to trim the authority of the Federal Trade Commission. He also opposes efforts to restrict billboards, a position that allies Ford not only with the wealthy billboard lobby but also with his home-state liquor and cigarette interests, which rely on outdoor advertising.

Insurance is the business Ford is closest to — so close, in fact, that opponents have lodged conflict-of-interest complaints against him. Ford owned two Kentucky insurance companies during most of his first decade in the Senate, and recused himself when insurance issues came before Commerce. He completed the sale of his interests to family members in 1985.

Once those ties were cut, Ford began working openly on the industry's behalf. In 1986, he fought to weaken a provision requiring insurance companies to report certain information to the federal government, and opposed a bill making it easier for other businesses to form their own liability insurance pools. "I want you to know that I'm one of the family," he once told a group of insurance executives. "I belong to you."

Ford is also one of the tobacco family, and he fits the part with his ever-present cigarette, a ruddily handsome face with skin like smoked-leather and a raspy drawl. In 1984 he temporarily blocked a bill mandating new health warnings on cigarettes; the bill eventually moved, but only after Ford secured an agreement to drop some language critical of tobacco.

The next year, along with North Carolina Republican Jesse Helms, he helped engineer a complex deal establishing a new tobacco price-support program in return for tobacco interests' agreement to a permanent extension of the 16-cents-a-pack cigarette tax. Ford lobbied Democrats on the Finance Committee to attach the compromise to a deficit-reduction bill, thus easing the controversial tobacco program's way past floor opposition. The package became law early in 1986.

During 1987 debate on a proposal to restrict tobacco exports, Ford angrily threatened to target for defeat any legislation beneficial to Republican sponsor John H. Chafee's home state of Rhode Island. Chafee called Ford's remarks "vindictive" and "just foolishness."

Having long helped bury legislation requiring warning labels on liquor, Ford joined in Commerce's unanimous approval of a labeling bill in 1988. The industry publicly objected, but privately it favored the federal warning as a potential defense against liability lawsuits and as a uniform standard to prevent a proliferation of state-passed requirements.

On Energy, Ford is in a good position to defend Kentucky's coal producers. He has repeatedly sought repeal of tough federal strip-mining regulations, and in 1986 killed a provision imposing penalties on states that failed to enforce federal requirements for the restoration of strip-mined land. In 1987, he agreed to a repeal of the 1978 law requiring utilities to use coal rather than oil and gas, which was enacted during an oil shortage, but he did add language stipulating that new power plants must not be unadaptable to coal use.

Ford has fought Western coal producers' efforts for a coal-slurry pipeline, which would transport their coal more cheaply, thus making it competitive with Appalachian coal in Eastern and Southern markets.

A booster of the troubled uranium industry, in 1988 Ford won easy Senate approval for a bailout proposal, but it died in the House. He has cosponsored legislation to end remaining controls on natural gas prices, and opposes environmentalist Democrats' efforts on Energy to raise autos' fuel-efficiency standards.

At the outset of his Rules chairmanship, Ford made it clear he would not let Republicans forget they had lost the prerogatives of the majority they held from 1981-87. Early in 1987, Ford brought a committee funding resolution to the floor that was the target of a Republican attempt to cut spending. Ford said the effort was just pique at losing control. "I did not hear much noise last year about reducing the committees' budgets," he said.

House members also have to be wary of the Kentucky horse-trader. In 1986, Ford proposed a 50-50 split of franked mailing funds between the two chambers. Considering that the larger House traditionally spends much more than the Senate, that amounted to a sizable potential reduction for House members. The provision was killed in conference.

Perhaps because of his preference for working behind the scenes, Ford initially was a leading opponent of televising Senate debates. In an emotional 1982 speech at a Democratic caucus, he contrasted the expense of a broadcast system with cuts in child-nutrition programs. That speech probably turned the tide against Majority Leader Howard H. Baker Jr.'s TV proposal. Baker made a last bid before retiring in 1984, but Ford helped kill that one, too.

All along he favored less expensive radio broadcasts, and when the estimated costs for TV were reduced, Ford switched to support the idea. As ranking member on Rules, he helped guide a television plan for live, gavel-to-gavel coverage through the Senate in 1986.

At Home: Ford plays Kentucky politics to win, and he plays it just about full time. Faced with the likelihood of weak opposition in his first Senate re-election (in 1980), Ford still amassed a huge campaign treasury just in case a serious challenger came along. None did, but he conducted an exhausting campaign anyway and crushed long-shot Republican Mary Louise Foust.

In 1986, he actually had a reason to be cautious. Two years before, his Democratic colleague, Walter D. Huddleston, had been ousted in a surprise GOP victory, and Republicans hoped for a repeat performance.

But in the wake of Huddleston's defeat, Ford commissioned a series of polls to test where in the state he might be in danger. He then set about shoring up his support there. He again began raising money early, and by the end of 1985 had more than enough to give any prospective GOP candidate pause. As it turned out, Ford's opponent was a Louisville lawyer named Jackson M. Andrews, an unknown who asked voters not to confuse him with "a dead president." Ford won 74 percent of the vote.

While building his insurance business, Ford started in politics as a protégé of Democratic Gov. Bert Combs, for whom he worked as an aide from 1959-63. But that relationship turned sour. By 1971, after a term in the state Senate and one as lieutenant governor, Ford was ready for the governorship. Combs, however, decided on a comeback the same year.

Their contest for the Democratic nomination was rough. Ford said Combs was the candidate of the "fat cats and the courthouse crowd." Combs said Ford was a "punchless promiser with both hands tied behind him by special interests." Combs had his traditional base in eastern Kentucky, but Ford did better in Louisville and the counties to the west and defeated his old mentor soundly. He had little trouble beating Republican Tom Emberton that fall.

As governor, Ford earned popularity by cutting taxes imposed under his Republican predecessor, Louie B. Nunn. This left him in good stead when he ran for the Senate in 1974 against one-term GOP incumbent Marlow W. Cook. The Ford-Cook race was no more pleasant than the earlier gubernatorial contest. Cook accused Ford of using state contracts as governor to reward his political allies. Ford labeled Cook "marvelous Marlow, the wonderful wobbler." Cook was hurt by his earlier defense of Richard M. Nixon. In a Democratic year, Ford won comfortably.

After deciding not to run for governor in 1983, Ford conducted the race vicariously by helping an ally, Lt. Gov. Martha Layne Collins, win. In 1984, he was notably less successful. He volunteered to chair the state campaign for Democratic presidential nominee Walter F. Mondale, hoping to hold down Reagan's margin and thereby protect Huddleston. Mondale lost badly, and Huddleston fell with him.

Committees

Rules and Administration (Chairman)

Commerce, Science and Transportation (3rd of 11 Democrats)
Aviation (chairman); Communications; Consumer; National Ocean Policy Study

Energy and Natural Resources (3rd of 10 Democrats)
Energy Research and Development (chairman); Mineral Resources Development and Production; Water and Power

Joint Printing (Chairman)

Elections

1986 General

Wendell H. Ford (D)	503,775	(74%)
Jackson M. Andrews (R)	173,330	(26%)

Previous Winning Percentages: **1980** (65%) **1974** (54%)

Campaign Finance

	Receipts	Receipts from PACs	Expend-itures
1986			
Ford (D)	$1,519,672	$843,282 (55%)	$1,201,624
Andrews (R)	$58,616	$3,500 (6%)	$58,572

Key Votes

1987	
Enact omnibus highway bill over Reagan veto	Y
Limit testing of space-based anti-ballistic missiles	Y
Oppose banning tests of larger nuclear weapons	Y
Confirm Robert H. Bork as Supreme Court justice	N
1988	
Allow vote on campaign-finance overhaul	Y
Pass civil rights restoration bill over Reagan veto	Y
Enact omnibus trade bill over Reagan veto	Y
Approve death penalty for drug-related murders	Y
Oppose "workfare" amendment to welfare overhaul bill	Y

Voting Studies

	Presidential Support		Party Unity		Conservative Coalition	
Year	**S**	**O**	**S**	**O**	**S**	**O**
1988	64	33	70	29	78	22
1987	35	64	85	13	66	34
1986	34	66	74	25	47	53
1985	39	60	76	23	68	28
1984	45	51	76 †	22 †	55	38
1983	40	56	81	17	52	43
1982	32	60	75	24	66	33
1981	56	44	84	14	58	41

† Not eligible for all recorded votes.

Interest Group Ratings

Year	ADA	ACU	AFL-CIO	CCUS
1988	65	24	93	21
1987	75	19	100	22
1986	55	35	67	53
1985	50	43	81	48
1984	80	23	82	39
1983	70	20	88	32
1982	70	55	81	55
1981	70	13	63	50

Mitch McConnell (R)

Of Louisville — Elected 1984

Born: Feb. 20, 1942, Sheffield, Ala.
Education: U. of Louisville, B.A. 1964; U. of Kentucky, J.D. 1967.
Occupation: Lawyer.
Family: Divorced; three children.
Religion: Baptist.
Political Career: Jefferson County judge/executive, 1978-85.
Capitol Office: 120 Russell Bldg. 20510; 224-2541.

In Washington: McConnell got into the Senate by ambushing a veteran Democrat whom he dubbed a "shadow senator." But he has proven to be no dynamo himself, in part by calculation. He has approached the job in a studied fashion, searching for a few issues on which he can learn and lead.

He has worked with his Kentucky colleague, Democrat Wendell H. Ford, on behalf of tobacco farmers, for example. But he does not pretend to be an expert on overall U.S. farm policy — a sensible move, since his prior officeholding experience in a metropolitan county government did little to prepare him for the Agriculture Committee's complex subject matter.

McConnell found a chance to move down the learning curve with one of the most divisive issues to come before the Senate in the 100th Congress. He helped lead the Republican filibuster against Democratic legislation to overhaul congressional campaign finance. The Democrats tried, and failed, to shut off debate a record eight times.

McConnell's stance has become the GOP line in the Senate, and as the ethics of public office became a hot political issue in early 1989, his role seemed ready to widen further. Late in the 100th Congress, the Senate Republican leader, Bob Dole of Kansas, named McConnell to head a GOP task force on campaign finance law.

McConnell proposes smaller political action committee (PAC) contributions and larger individual contributions for candidates, and he seeks to enhance the role of party committees by letting them spend more on campaigns. In essence, the finance system he envisions plays to the strengths of the GOP, which has a large individual donor base and a sophisticated party operation, but a worsening record of collecting PAC money. McConnell's opposition to Democratic plans stems first from their attempt to limit campaign spending, and second from their reliance on various public financing schemes to induce adherence to the spending limit.

On Agriculture, McConnell's guiding philosophy has been, in his own words: "When it comes to tobacco, I'm prepared to wheel and deal." He did just that in 1985, helping Democrats get a farm bill out of the Agriculture Committee in exchange for Democratic backing of a revamped tobacco price-support system that was being considered in Finance.

Democratic Sens. David Pryor of Arkansas and David L. Boren of Oklahoma — both members of Agriculture as well as Finance — agreed to support tobacco in the Finance Committee if McConnell would back their farm bill in Agriculture. The Republican agreed, even though during three previous months of farm bill markups he had voted faithfully with GOP farm proposals pushed by Jesse Helms and Dole.

"My only interest is in the 150,000 people in Kentucky who grow tobacco," McConnell said after the September 1985 committee vote, although he added that his commitment to the Democratic measure was only temporary. "I have cooperated in getting the farm bill out on the floor. I'm not bound by that vote on the floor." Later, McConnell voted with nearly every other GOP senator for a Dole-drafted compromise farm bill that passed the Senate.

But on U.S. policy toward South Africa, McConnell quickly made it clear he was not comfortable with the party line. "I think the administration is not in touch with reality on this issue," he said in June 1985. "We don't want young people in this country to think that only liberal senators are interested in doing something about a 17th-century society."

McConnell joined with Delaware Republican William V. Roth Jr. to offer a package of sanctions against South Africa that struck a middle ground between the White House position and stiffer penalties sought by Sens. Edward M. Kennedy and Lowell P. Weicker Jr. This bill served as a starting point for the Foreign Relations Committee as it went on to write the sanctions bill that eventually became law over President Reagan's veto.

The venture seemed to whet McConnell's appetite for the foreign policy realm; at the beginning of the 100th Congress, he left his seats on the Judiciary and Intelligence committees and took a spot on Foreign Relations. On a committee where a rigid ideological predisposition often determines a senator's position, McConnell has shown himself open-minded and amenable to argument.

For the 101st Congress, McConnell joined the Rules and Administration Committee, where Sen. Ford is chairman and the jurisdiction includes campaign-finance law.

At Home: Three things brought McConnell to Congress: bloodhounds, Ronald Reagan and dogged persistence in the face of daunting odds.

For much of 1984, few people believed McConnell had much chance of defeating two-term Democratic Sen. Walter D. Huddleston. Even some GOP leaders complained that McConnell had a "citified" image that would not play well in most parts of Kentucky; his base was metropolitan Louisville, where he had twice been elected Jefferson County judge, the county's top administrative post.

McConnell's campaign struggled for quite a long time; he even lost the endorsement of Marlow Cook, the last Republican to win a Senate election in Kentucky and McConnell's boss when he was a Senate aide in the 1960s. At times, it seemed that McConnell's bid was surviving on little more than the candidate's fierce ambition to be a senator, a goal he admitted having harbored for two decades.

Then the challenger hit upon a clever, homey gimmick to get across his claim that Huddleston was a senator of limited influence who was often absent from committee meetings. McConnell aired TV ads showing bloodhounds sniffing frantically around Washington in search of the incumbent.

The hound dog gimmick got people talking about a race they had ignored, and many concluded McConnell had a point — they were not exactly sure what Huddleston had been doing since he went to Congress in 1973. The incumbent, an easygoing mainstream Democrat, had worked behind the scenes on Kentucky issues, such as tobacco and coal, never causing much controversy and never earning much publicity.

Huddleston's overconfident campaign failed to devise an imaginative counter to McConnell's ads, and with Reagan crushing Walter F. Mondale by more than 280,000 votes statewide, McConnell had long coattails to latch onto. He won by four-tenths of a percentage point.

A lifelong political overachiever, McConnell was student body president in high school and college, and president of the student bar association at law school. After earning his law degree in 1967, he worked for Cook and then served as deputy assistant U.S. attorney general in the Gerald R. Ford administration. In his 1977 campaign for Jefferson County judge, McConnell defeated a Democratic incumbent; four years later, he won re-election by a narrow margin and started laying the groundwork for a statewide campaign.

Committees

Agriculture, Nutrition and Forestry (6th of 9 Republicans)
Rural Development and Rural Electrification (ranking); Agricultural Production and Stabilization of Prices; Domestic and Foreign Marketing and Product Promotion

Energy and Natural Resources (9th of 9 Republicans)
Energy Research and Development; Mineral Resources Development and Production

Foreign Relations (7th of 9 Republicans)
Terrorism, Narcotics and International Operations (ranking); East Asian and Pacific Affairs; Western Hemisphere and Peace Corps Affairs

Rules and Administration (7th of 7 Republicans)

Elections

1984 General		
Mitch McConnell (R)	644,990	(50%)
Walter D. Huddleston (D)	639,721	(50%)
1984 Primary		
Mitch McConnell (R)	39,465	(79%)
C. Roger Harker (R)	3,798	(8%)
Tommy Klein (R)	3,352	(7%)
Thurman J. Hamlin (R)	3,202	(6%)

Campaign Finance

	Receipts	Receipts from PACs	Expend-itures
1984			
McConnell (R)	$1,591,303	$284,496 (18%)	$1,776,128
Huddleston (D)	$2,189,001	$809,279 (37%)	$2,380,239

Key Votes

1987	
Enact omnibus highway bill over Reagan veto	Y
Limit testing of space-based anti-ballistic missiles	N
Oppose banning tests of larger nuclear weapons	Y
Confirm Robert H. Bork as Supreme Court justice	Y
1988	
Allow vote on campaign-finance overhaul	N
Pass civil rights restoration bill over Reagan veto	N
Enact omnibus trade bill over Reagan veto	N
Approve death penalty for drug-related murders	Y
Oppose "workfare" amendment to welfare overhaul bill	N

Voting Studies

	Presidential Support		Party Unity		Conservative Coalition	
Year	S	O	S	O	S	O
1988	85	15	80	18	92	8
1987	65	32	85	13	91	6
1986	87	13	90	10	92	8
1985	85	14	82	16	90	8

Interest Group Ratings

Year	ADA	ACU	AFL-CIO	CCUS
1988	5	92	29	93
1987	10	80	33	89
1986	0	83	7	89
1985	5	78	10	79

1 Carroll Hubbard Jr. (D)

Of Mayfield — Elected 1974

Born: July 7, 1937, Murray, Ky.
Education: Georgetown College, B.S. 1959; U. of Louisville, J.D. 1962.
Military Career: Ky. Air National Guard, 1962-67; Ky. Army National Guard, 1968-70.
Occupation: Lawyer.
Family: Wife, Carol Brown; two children, three stepchildren.
Religion: Baptist.
Political Career: Ky. Senate, 1968-75; sought Democratic gubernatorial nomination, 1979.
Capitol Office: 2267 Rayburn Bldg. 20515; 225-3115.

In Washington: Though seniority has failed to make Hubbard a force of note in House politics, he was duly compensated for his labors on behalf of Jim Wright during the Texas Democrat's rise to and tenure as House Speaker.

At Wright's behest, Hubbard served as an at-large party whip for five consecutive terms. In the 101st Congress, he started a second term as a regional whip, responsible for lining up Democrats in his state and four others.

In return, Hubbard went to some lengths in his support of Wright. Several years ago, he acceded to the then-majority leader's request and removed his name from a petition favoring a vote on a constitutional amendment to balance the federal budget. In 1986, Hubbard sharply rebuked former Rep. Richard Bolling of Missouri, the retired Rules Committee chairman, who had written sourly in *The Washington Post* of Wright's campaign for Speaker.

And in April 1989, one day after the House ethics committee announced that it found "reason to believe" Wright had violated House rules in 69 instances over 10 years, Hubbard took the House floor to praise the embattled Speaker. He recalled several energy and water projects Wright helped secure for Kentucky's 1st District, concluding, "As a congressman from western Kentucky, I stand here today and say, thank you, Jim Wright, for what you have done for our country and what you have done for the 1st Congressional District."

In the early 1980s, Hubbard found it easier to find a place as a party insider in the Wright regime than to establish a position of legislative influence.

In 1983, Hubbard was in line for a Banking subcommittee chairmanship when the important Economic Stabilization panel came open. However, John J. LaFalce of New York, who was one place behind Hubbard in seniority on Banking, got that chairmanship instead.

At the time, there was talk Hubbard had been asked to stand aside by colleagues who viewed LaFalce as better equipped intellectually for the post. Hubbard insists he never was interested in the job and never pursued it. Hubbard did not go after the Economic Stabilization chairmanship at the start of the 100th Congress, when LaFalce moved on to become chairman of the Small Business Committee.

Instead, Hubbard kept his chairmanship of the Banking Subcommittee on General Oversight and Investigations, which he had assumed at the start of the 99th Congress. His panel held hearings on several issues related to the savings and loan crisis in the 100th Congress.

During Banking Committee consideration in the 100th Congress of an authorization bill for housing programs, Hubbard restored a section of the bill that required mobile homes to meet minimum heating-efficiency standards. Hubbard's amendment reversed the vote of the Housing Subcommittee, which had agreed to an amendment by Indiana Republican John Hiler striking the requirement. Hubbard, who had voted with Hiler in subcommittee, said he reversed his position because of complaints about high heating bills from many mobile-home residents in his district and from national consumer groups.

Hubbard has always put great stock in the prevailing public opinion in his district. He publicizes the results of his "Hubbard poll," a yearly questionnaire on issues that he sends to his constituents.

Most of Hubbard's legislative activities have a district orientation. In the 100th Congress, he was in the forefront of tobacco-state members arguing vigorously against a measure banning smoking on most domestic airline flights. "This amendment is another direct attack upon the tobacco farmers and the tobacco industry, which gives an income to hundreds of thousands of Americans and in turn provides multimillions of ... tax dollars to our federal and state governments," he said. Despite the

Kentucky 1

West — Paducah

The birthplace of Jefferson Davis, Kentucky's 1st District has a stronger Deep South flavor than any other part of the state.

In contests for governor and for the U.S. Senate, the 1st usually turns in solid Democratic majorities. Democratic Sen. Walter D. Huddleston carried the 1st by 20,000 votes in his 1984 statewide loss to Republican Mitch McConnell. Jimmy Carter won the district in 1976 and 1980, and even Massachusetts Democrat Michael S. Dukakis nearly won it in 1988. Year in and year out, the only district in the state as faithfully Democratic as the 1st is eastern Kentucky's 7th District, which also is influenced by the United Mine Workers.

The 1st is the only part of Kentucky where cotton is grown. The western lowlands near the Mississippi River — known as the Jackson Purchase — were once slaveholding territory. Today, the 1st does not have a massive black population; only one of the 24 counties in the district is over 20 percent black. But the heritage of the 1st and its relative poverty made it fertile ground for the rural populism of George C. Wallace. Four of the five Kentucky counties Wallace carried in his 1968 presidential campaign are in the 1st.

Like Wallace's success in 1968, the presidential victories by Ronald Reagan and George Bush in the 1st indicated that voters there are not so bound by tradition that they will accept any Democratic presidential nominee.

No city in the 1st has more than 30,000 people. Most of the area is closely tied to agriculture; soybeans and dark-fired (or smokeless) tobacco are major crops. Coal fields provide employment in the northeastern part of the district. Relatively small factories producing textiles and chemicals are prominent in cities such as Paducah and Hopkinsville.

The Ohio River port of Paducah (McCracken County) long has been the population center and political capital of western Kentucky. It was the home of Alben W. Barkley, longtime Democratic senator and vice president under Harry S Truman. Barkley helped provide an economic shot in the arm to Paducah by steering an Atomic Energy Commission plant to the area. The Energy Department's gaseous-diffusion plant in Paducah is still operating, but the city has lost population since 1950.

Southeast of Paducah is Hopkinsville (Christian County), an agricultural market and trade center for the nearby Fort Campbell military base. With its mobile population, the Hopkinsville area has more independent voting habits than the rest of the 1st. Christian County voted GOP in the 1984 Senate race.

Population: 525,844. White 475,701 (90%), Black 46,405 (9%). Spanish origin 4,662 (1%). 18 and over 379,011 (72%), 65 and over 72,755 (14%). Median age: 31.

heated opposition, the amendment was adopted and became law.

In 1986, the Banking subcommittee he chairs held a hearing in his hometown of Mayfield on farm credit problems. On the full committee, Hubbard supports small banks in their battles with larger financial institutions.

With the large Fort Campbell military base in his district, Hubbard generally takes a hawkish stand on defense issues. He also joined in sponsoring a bill calling for increased death benefits for the families of the 248 members of the 101st Airborne Division, based at Fort Campbell, who were killed in the December 1985 crash of a chartered jet in Newfoundland.

Hubbard has worked to secure projects for the Department of Energy's gaseous diffusion plant, operated by Martin Marietta in West Paducah. Early in the Bush administration, he met with Energy Secretary James D. Watkins to lobby for assigning new uranium-enrichment technology to the Paducah plant. He also introduced a bill in 1989 to establish a government-owned U.S. Enrichment Corporation to get DOE out of the uranium-enrichment business.

In 1987, Hubbard alleged that western Kentucky was a major distribution center for cocaine and marijuana, and that smugglers were bringing illegal drugs into the country from Colombia and Mexico through airfields in the 1st. Hubbard testified before a grand jury about his allegations.

In 1986, Hubbard spoke out on behalf of his district's satellite television dish owners, who were upset by signal-scrambling that had been instituted by some TV program providers. "Today the No. 1 issue here in Washington is aid to the contras in Nicaragua," Hubbard told the Energy and Commerce Subcommittee on Telecommunications. "But in portions of western Kentucky, aid to satellite-dish owners is also important."

At Home: Hubbard's political enemies hoped his political career had come full circle in 1988. His aggressive primary challenger attacked him as a generally lethargic legislator and a chronic absentee from congressional committee meetings — a line of assault that Hubbard had generally followed in ousting veteran Democratic Rep. Frank Stubblefield in 1974. But on primary night, the only similarity with that earlier campaign was that Hubbard had won.

Challenger Lacey T. Smith had the resources to defeat Hubbard in 1988. A wealthy lawyer, businessman and former state senator, Smith pumped roughly $500,000 of his own money into a high-profile campaign portraying the incumbent as a "pen pal" more effective at sending calendars and congratulatory letters to his constituents than at promoting the district's economic development.

But Smith was stung by media accounts of his controversial past, which included an indictment for influence-peddling while an aide to Louisville Mayor Harvey Sloane in the mid-1970s (he was later acquitted) and a reputation for high living when he resided in south Florida in the mid-1980s.

Meanwhile, Hubbard ran effective advertising that twitted Smith as a well-to-do carpetbagger whose interest in economically beleaguered western Kentucky was limited to its House seat. The final result was not even close: Hubbard swept all 24 counties in the district and outpolled Smith by a margin of nearly 3-to-1.

In the staunchly Democratic 1st, Hubbard's only serious contests have come in the 1974 and 1988 primaries. And organized labor, led by the United Mine Workers, was in his corner both times. In 1974, labor backing helped Hubbard overcome Stubblefield's support from farmers and the official courthouse organizations to win by 629 votes out of nearly 60,000 cast.

In contrast to Hubbard's firm grip on his House seat, his one attempt to broaden his appeal statewide — a 1979 gubernatorial bid — ended in defeat. His campaign, based on his brand of personal politics, got lost in the confusion of a nine-candidate field, forcing him to try to use his House office to gain publicity. Without large-scale funding or the support of any significant party bloc, he was never really a factor. He finished a distant fourth with only 12 percent of the vote, carrying his home district but little else.

Committees

Banking, Finance and Urban Affairs (5th of 31 Democrats)
General Oversight and Investigations (chairman); Consumer Affairs and Coinage; Financial Institutions Supervision, Regulation and Insurance; Housing and Community Development

Merchant Marine and Fisheries (3rd of 26 Democrats)
Merchant Marine

Elections

1988 General		
Carroll Hubbard Jr. (D)	117,288	(95%)
Charles K. Hatchett (I)	6,106	(5%)
1988 Primary		
Carroll Hubbard Jr. (D)	63,136	(73%)
Lacey T. Smith (D)	23,153	(27%)
1986 General		
Carroll Hubbard Jr. (D)	64,315	(100%)

Previous Winning Percentages: **1984** (100%) **1982** (100%) **1980** (100%) **1978** (100%) **1976** (82%) **1974** (78%)

District Vote For President

	1988	1984	1980	1976
D	92,391 (49%)	87,339 (45%)	102,503 (54%)	114,194 (65%)
R	96,150 (51%)	104,613 (54%)	83,296 (44%)	59,226 (34%)

Campaign Finance

	Receipts	Receipts from PACs	Expend-itures
1988			
Hubbard (D)	$518,338	$356,663 (69%)	$546,908
1986			
Hubbard (D)	$288,918	$196,775 (68%)	$237,748

Key Votes

1987	
Raise speed limit to 65 mph	Y
Approve Gephardt "fair trade" amendment	Y
Ban testing of larger nuclear weapons	N
Delay "re-flagging" of Kuwaiti tankers	N
Approve tax-raising deficit-reduction bill	N
1988	
Approve aid to Nicaraguan contras	Y
Enact civil rights restoration bill over Reagan veto	N
Kill 60-day plant-closing notification measure	N
Pass omnibus trade bill over Reagan veto	#
Approve death penalty for drug-related murders	Y
Bar federal funds for abortions in cases of rape and incest	Y
Oppose seven-day waiting period for purchase of handguns	Y

Voting Studies

	Presidential Support		Party Unity		Conservative Coalition	
Year	**S**	**O**	**S**	**O**	**S**	**O**
1988	39	58	67	30	68	24
1987	36	53	57	33	74	12
1986	52	48	49	49	94	6
1985	59	36	48	44	76	15
1984	46	43	37	52	73	20
1983	46	35	44	46	70	25
1982	55	42	43	47	86	11
1981	58	41	49	48	87	13

Interest Group Ratings

Year	ADA	ACU	AFL-CIO	CCUS
1988	50	54	86	50
1987	52	19	81	53
1986	35	59	86	50
1985	20	63	63	68
1984	30	67	82	55
1983	50	55	82	42
1982	25	64	50	71
1981	25	40	71	37

2 William H. Natcher (D)

Of Bowling Green — Elected 1953

Born: Sept. 11, 1909, Bowling Green, Ky.
Education: Western Kentucky State College, A.B. 1930; Ohio State U., LL.B. 1933.
Military Career: Navy, 1942-45.
Occupation: Lawyer.
Family: Wife, Virginia Reardon; two children.
Religion: Baptist.
Political Career: Warren County attorney, 1937-49; commonwealth attorney of Allen and Warren counties, 1951-53.
Capitol Office: 2333 Rayburn Bldg. 20515; 225-3501.

In Washington: Natcher is a one-of-a-kind congressman, a vestige of another era. He eschews publicity, maintains a tiny staff and never misses a vote on the House floor. Ever since he won his first House race in 1953, he has been running for re-election the old-fashioned way: He accepts no campaign contributions, does no television advertising, and keeps in touch with constituents by roaming his district without entourage.

His gentlemanly manner and commitment to the House as an institution has earned him respect even from the most partisan Republicans.

"He reminds you of the world that once was, in which politics happens in your district and governing happens in Washington," Republican firebrand Newt Gingrich of Georgia once said.

Natcher is a man of great precision. He dresses carefully, votes carefully and keeps a detailed diary of his everyday life. He is called on to preside over the House's most contentious floor debates because of his evenhanded, controlled judgment in the Speaker's chair.

Members of Congress who are that respected and exacting often find their way to the Appropriations Committee, and Natcher has served there since his second year in the House. Three decades and a half later, he now is next in line to be chairman of that powerful committee. But it is not clear when, if ever, the gavel will be relinquished to Natcher by Jamie L. Whitten of Mississippi, who shows no sign of retiring.

In the meantime, Natcher already has more power than most full committee chairmen. Whitten trusts Natcher implicitly and often defers to his judgment. And the Appropriations Subcommittee on Labor, Health and Human Services, and Education, which Natcher chairs, has more expansive jurisdiction than any other subcommittee but Defense.

Even in the budget-cutting Reagan era, Natcher has been in the enviable position of watching his share of the budget pie grow. While overall budget constraints have grown tighter, House Democrats still have wanted to add first to the social programs under Natcher's purview.

Further, Natcher "is so highly regarded that people feel hesitant to vote against his bill or even to change the bill," said one of his adversaries on spending questions, Minnesota Democrat Timothy J. Penny.

At a time when Penny and other self-appointed budget-cutters were having some success imposing across-the-board reductions on the bills reported by Appropriations in 1987, Natcher and his subcommittee's ranking Republican, Silvio O. Conte of Massachusetts, turned back four amendments to scale down their bill.

Natcher is not a man to be stampeded, either by the Senate or by his more aggressive House colleagues. When he wants to, Natcher can sit in meetings for day after day waiting for others to meet his terms. But sometimes Natcher seems to care more about getting his bill signed into law than about the details of what it contains.

It is hard to imagine what could offend Natcher's sense of order more than the way Congress handled appropriations for much of the Reagan era: in omnibus bills, known as continuing resolutions, that lumped all or most of the 13 regular spending bills into one.

When the entire government was financed in a single bill for the second year in a row in 1987, Natcher said, "Just because we've done it for two years doesn't mean we've done it right. When you put all 13 together, it's not the proper manner to do it."

Despite Natcher's diligence, Congress has not passed a separate Labor-HHS bill for seven of the 10 years he has been subcommittee chairman. More often than not, the bill bogged down in disputes over social issues such as abortion and school prayer. In several cases, Natcher has suggested the formula that has

Kentucky 2

West Central — Owensboro

Perched between the staunchly Democratic 1st and the reliably Republican 5th, the 2nd is a swing district in state and national elections.

Republicans are consistent winners in only three small counties — Allen, Edmonson and Grayson, hotbeds of Union support during the Civil War. But in good Republican years, statewide GOP candidates also have a chance to carry the three major population centers — Daviess County (Owensboro), Hardin County (Elizabethtown) and Warren County (Bowling Green), which together cast nearly half the district's vote. In 1984, successful GOP Senate candidate Mitch McConnell won Daviess and Warren.

The district includes parts of three distinct areas: the Bluegrass region in the east, the Louisville suburbs in the north and the rolling hill country of the Pennyrile in the southwest. The geographic heart of the 2nd is the Knobs area, a region of sinkholes and caves that includes the Mammoth Cave National Park. Although primarily agricultural, the district has some light industry in Owensboro and Bowling Green.

Warren County (Bowling Green) grew 24 percent in the 1970s, marking the largest increase in any of the district's major population centers, and it showed an even faster growth rate in the first half of the 1980s. Bowling Green is the home of Western Kentucky University, with more than 10,000 students, the largest college in the state west of Louisville.

Outside the population centers, the fastest growth has been in Bullitt County, a part of the Louisville suburbs. A busing plan in metropolitan Louisville helped fuel a 66 percent growth rate in neighboring Bullitt during the 1970s, although the growth rate has slowed markedly during the more placid 1980s. With a sizable blue-collar element that frequently bolts the Democratic ticket, Bullitt was the only Kentucky county outside the 1st to vote for George C. Wallace for president in 1968. Both Reagan and McConnell won it in 1984. In the 1988 presidential contest, George Bush clobbered Democratic nominee Michael S. Dukakis.

Along the Ohio River in the northwest corner of the district is Owensboro, the largest city in the 2nd and the third-largest in the state. Nearby oil and coal fields and a large General Electric plant provide an industrial base.

Between Owensboro and Louisville is Hardin County, the home of Fort Knox. The rest of the district is rural. Tobacco and livestock are mainstays of the economy. Republicans are strongest in the poorer farm counties in the center of the district; Democrats run best in the outer Bluegrass counties to the northeast.

Population: 520,634. White 483,696 (93%), Black 31,693 (6%), Other 2,752 (1%). Spanish origin 5,441 (1%). 18 and over 361,229 (69%), 65 and over 52,022 (10%). Median age: 27.

allowed both sides to claim a measure of victory.

But he infuriated abortion-rights advocates in 1987, during the final stages of drafting the Labor-HHS bill, when he opposed a Senate provision to allow federally funded family-planning clinics to make abortion referrals. Although he was outnumbered among House-Senate conferees, he stood fast in opposition to the provision, which he said was sure to prompt a presidential veto.

During House floor debate on that bill in 1987, he managed to forestall controversy by setting a time limit on debate that prevented Republicans from offering amendments on such nettlesome social issues as federal AIDS policy.

All the while he is overseeing a huge slice of the federal budget, Natcher makes sure his predominantly rural Kentucky district gets its share. He has secured local funding for programs from flood control to education of the disadvantaged.

But despite a tooth-and-nail fight, even the respected Natcher could not prevent a major defeat for his district's powerful tobacco interests in 1987, when Congress passed an amendment banning smoking on airplane flights of at least two hours' duration.

In a rare departure from his perfect-gentleman demeanor, Natcher was uncharacteristically blunt in his opposition to the amendment, sponsored by Illinois Democrat Richard J. Durbin. It was blocked in subcommittee and full committee, but passed on the House floor. Natcher is unlikely to forgive and forget.

Natcher knew when he arrived in the House that he wanted to be on Appropriations, but had to wait a year to serve there. He had to be even more patient before he got his Labor-HHS Subcommittee chair, which he inherited in 1979 from Daniel J. Flood.

In his first year as Labor-HHS chairman,

Natcher attracted attention by announcing that he wanted to close the subcommittee's markup session, and then presided over an 8-4 vote that closed it for the first time in several years. Health and labor lobbyists swarmed outside the committee room, and Natcher said it would be difficult to produce a fiscally responsible bill had they been allowed to record how the members voted. Natcher has kept his subcommittee markups closed ever since.

Before that, he spent 18 years as chairman of one of the least politically appealing Appropriations subcommittees, on the District of Columbia. Natcher clashed often with Washington city officials — particularly over the subway system then on the drawing boards. Three years in a row he delayed the D.C. budget for months while he pressured local officials to finish their highway projects before demanding subway money. Natcher got much of what he wanted.

Natcher was known in Washington by his local press clippings, which were generally unfavorable. Some of the city's liberals and black leaders called him a racist. When he first took over the D.C. Subcommittee, he said his two main concerns were the city's crime rate and its number of illegitimate births. He said the district "should not be turned into a haven for those who roost on welfare payments."

Natcher did vote against most of the early civil rights laws, but he supported the Voting Rights Act of 1965 and most of the anti-poverty programs of the Johnson administration.

Natcher's response to press criticism is to ignore it. He seldom grants interviews. He refuses to allow reporters to accompany him on campaign trips. He transcribes his daily activities onto book-sized pages that are then bound by the Government Printing Office (at Natcher's expense). There are now 50 volumes.

Natcher does issue one press release a year. It announces the new record he has set for attendance at roll calls on the House floor. He has not missed one since the day he was sworn in, Jan. 6, 1954 — an all-time record. By the end of the 100th Congress he had cast 11,748 consecutive votes, quorum calls not included.

At Home: Nearly as important to Natcher as his perfect voting record is his persistent refusal to accept campaign contributions. The small political bills he incurs, seldom more than $5,000 per election, he pays himself. "Some people are spending $1 million on House races," Natcher once lamented. "That's wrong. It's morally wrong. I don't believe they can really represent their people if they are taking money from these groups [political action committees]."

It was no great burden for Natcher to pay his own campaign expenses; he usually escaped serious opposition. But in 1982 and 1984, Natcher faced primary fights that would have induced most other incumbents to collect and spend bundles of cash. Natcher stuck to his old ways; he spent only about $21,000 in both years combined, all from his own pocket.

In 1982, three major challengers felt Natcher was aging and might be ripe for an upset. They contended he was too eccentric and too liberal for the rural 2nd. His personal frugality, they said, masked a liberal big spender who voted for all major appropriations bills. Altogether, Natcher's foes spent over $400,000 on the campaign, not including thousands of dollars that the National Conservative Political Action Committee pumped into an independent anti-Natcher ad campaign.

To Natcher's advantage, his primary rivals came from the three corners of the far-flung district; none was well-known outside his home area. With a low turnout and a regional split in the anti-Natcher vote, the incumbent carried all but one of the district's 18 counties, winning renomination with 60 percent.

In 1984, Natcher was challenged by Democratic state Sen. Frank Miller, who as chairman of the Senate Banking and Insurance Committee had access to ample funding. Miller, copying the 1982 attempt to portray Natcher as penny-wise but pound-foolish, complained that he had not used his leadership position on Appropriations to curb the federal deficit. But Natcher won with 70 percent of the vote.

Yet it is clear there is also a substantial minority of voters in the 2nd District who are ready for Natcher to retire. His Democratic primary challenger in 1988 bought just one yard sign and won nearly 25 percent of the vote. His under-financed GOP opponent that fall drew nearly 40 percent.

The Republican, retired Army Maj. Martin Tori, was a political novice but had a knack for attracting media ink. He brought in retired Air Force Maj. Gen. Richard V. Secord, a key figure in the Iran-contra arms deal, to complain about Natcher's votes against contra aid. And Tori lambasted Natcher for not doing more to attract and protect jobs in the district. "We don't need nice old guys" in Congress, he said. "You need a mean, nasty guy — me."

No matter who challenges him, Natcher campaigns in his same old-fashioned manner. He shuns "media events," reporters and other campaign entourage, preferring to drive through the district unaccompanied and stop to chat with people in courthouses and Main Street stores, delivering a simple message: "I'm Bill Natcher, up there in Washington trying to do a good job for you."

Though Natcher does not command a formidable political machine — many of those who helped him secure the district in the 1950s are no longer politically active — he still keeps in touch with a few influential people in most towns, people who have backed him for many years. And most average voters know about his refusal to accept campaign contributions, about his attendance record, and about the millions of dollars in federal money he has brought the district. Also, the accumulated weight of nearly four decades of constituent service means that Natcher's work has touched just about every family in the 2nd.

Natcher had congressional ambitions even as a teenager. After serving in several local political offices in Warren County (Bowling Green) and as president of the Kentucky Young Democrats, he got his chance in 1953, when Democratic Rep. Garrett L. Withers died. Party leaders united behind him, and he won without opposition in a special election.

Since then, the success of GOP presidential and statewide candidates in the 2nd has occasionally encouraged the party to make bids to unseat Natcher. But Republicans came close to beating him only once, in 1956, when Dwight D. Eisenhower's coattails pulled the GOP candidate to within 3,000 votes of victory.

Committee

Appropriations (2nd of 35 Democrats)
Labor, Health and Human Services, Education and Related Agencies (chairman); District of Columbia; Rural Development, Agriculture and Related Agencies

Elections

1988 General		
William H. Natcher (D)	92,184	(61%)
Martin A. Tori (R)	59,907	(39%)
1988 Primary		
William H. Natcher (D)	26,918	(76%)
Bob Evans (D)	8,324	(24%)
1986 General		
William H. Natcher (D)	57,644	(100%)

Previous Winning Percentages: **1984** (62%) **1982** (74%) **1980** (66%) **1978** (100%) **1976** (60%) **1974** (73%) **1972** (62%) **1970** (100%) **1968** (56%) **1966** (59%) **1964** (68%) **1962** (100%) **1960** (100%) **1958** (76%) **1956** (51%) **1954** (100%) **1953** * (100%)

* *Special election.*

District Vote For President

	1988	1984	1980	1976
D	72,768 (41%)	64,163 (36%)	78,356 (47%)	75,633 (55%)
R	102,721 (58%)	112,019 (63%)	83,861 (50%)	60,030 (44%)
I			3,009 (2%)	

Campaign Finance

	Receipts	Receipts from PACs	Expend-itures
1988			
Natcher (D)	$8,397	0	$8,397
Tori (R) †	$84,270	$1,950 (2%)	$84,102
1986			
Natcher (D)	$5,717	0	$5,714

† *Totals based on incomplete data.*

Key Votes

1987	
Raise speed limit to 65 mph	N
Approve Gephardt "fair trade" amendment	Y
Ban testing of larger nuclear weapons	N
Delay "re-flagging" of Kuwaiti tankers	Y
Approve tax-raising deficit-reduction bill	Y
1988	
Approve aid to Nicaraguan contras	N
Enact civil rights restoration bill over Reagan veto	Y
Kill 60-day plant-closing notification measure	N
Pass omnibus trade bill over Reagan veto	Y
Approve death penalty for drug-related murders	Y
Bar federal funds for abortions in cases of rape and incest	Y
Oppose seven-day waiting period for purchase of handguns	Y

Voting Studies

	Presidential Support		Party Unity		Conservative Coalition	
Year	**S**	**O**	**S**	**O**	**S**	**O**
1988	26	74	94	6	42	58
1987	34	66	91	9	65	35
1986	29	71	89	11	58	42
1985	30	70	87	13	56	44
1984	34	66	85	15	46	54
1983	32	68	83	17	53	47
1982	48	52	74	26	63	37
1981	54	46	69	31	75	25

Interest Group Ratings

Year	ADA	ACU	AFL-CIO	CCUS
1988	75	16	100	21
1987	76	13	94	13
1986	65	23	93	28
1985	60	24	76	23
1984	60	29	69	44
1983	65	26	82	25
1982	55	41	80	55
1981	35	20	80	26

3 Romano L. Mazzoli (D)

Of Louisville — Elected 1970

Born: Nov. 2, 1932, Louisville, Ky.
Education: Notre Dame U., B.S. 1954; U. of Louisville, J.D. 1960.
Military Career: Army, 1954-56.
Occupation: Lawyer; law professor.
Family: Wife, Helen Dillon; two children.
Religion: Roman Catholic.
Political Career: Ky. Senate, 1968-70; sought Democratic nomination for mayor of Louisville, 1969.
Capitol Office: 2246 Rayburn Bldg. 20515; 225-5401.

In Washington: Unfortunately for Mazzoli, the six-year roller coaster ride to passage of his landmark immigration bill did not end at the exhilarating top, when the historic Simpson-Mazzoli bill became law in 1986. The final fall came in early 1989, when Democratic colleagues on the Judiciary Committee ousted him from the chairmanship of the Immigration Subcommittee.

The fact that the thankless immigration issue had provided Mazzoli with both the greatest triumph and humiliation of his two-decade House career was even more remarkable considering that the subject holds little interest to Mazzoli's Louisville constituents, and thus no political gain for him. After negotiations on the legislation concluded in 1986, Mazzoli made a comment that proved prescient: "This bill has remarkable durability and life," he said, "but it also has the capacity to rise up and strike its handlers."

The seeds of his ultimate rejection had been sown during the long, stormy legislative battle, when Mazzoli was alternately contentious and withdrawn. He became even more isolated and stolid in the two years after final passage. But at bottom, Mazzoli lost his chairmanship for being a maverick and a Republican sympathizer on a committee dominated by activist liberal Democrats.

Days before Judiciary Democrats met to ratify their leaders at the outset of the 101st Congress, Mazzoli got word of the impending coup and tried to head it off. But it was too late; the committee voted 16-5 to strip him of the job he had held for eight years. Mazzoli conceded in an interview afterward, "The subcommittee did kind of get a little bit sloppy, a little directionless." Because of his preoccupation with a tough 1988 primary race, Mazzoli said, "I was a bit of an absentee landlord." But he was bitter nonetheless, so much so that there was some speculation he would defect to the GOP.

A party switch would be in keeping with Mazzoli's reputation for capriciousness, but not with his overall voting record. Though he is best known for the times he broke ranks — routinely on Judiciary, on President Reagan's 1981 budget and tax-cut bills, and, most memorably, on the party-line 1985 vote to seat Democratic incumbent Frank McCloskey rather than his GOP rival in a disputed Indiana election — Mazzoli has been a moderate Democrat, voting with his party leadership more than three-quarters of the time.

He was considered a liberal when first elected in 1970 as an anti-war candidate, and more recently has opposed the MX missile, contra aid and chemical weapons, and supported South Africa sanctions and a waiting period for handgun purchases. But Mazzoli has sided with conservatives on many economic issues and on abortion, and alienated Democrats with what they see as a pattern of disloyalty — voting against the party in the Indiana matter, calling on Speaker Thomas P. O'Neill Jr. to step down in 1981 for being too liberal for the times, and demanding from the House floor in 1976 that Ohio Democrat Wayne Hays resign for putting his mistress on the payroll.

Actually, such headline-making stands are uncharacteristic of Mazzoli. He is hard-working and lawyerlike, a legislator who quietly tends to details and leaves the posturing to others. He has spent long hours on the floor discussing Judiciary matters many find too technical to bother with, such as bankruptcy law and changes in the antitrust act.

Mazzoli steps out of his technician's role on Judiciary for one issue — abortion. On that he is vocal and militant; a leader of the congressional Pro-Life Caucus, he helped draft legislation to redefine the word "person" to include the unborn, possibly allowing states to declare abortion murder. He also serves on the Small Business Committee and, until the 101st Congress, on the District of Columbia Committee, a chore that most members avoid and one that, like immigration, could not possibly do him any political good.

"We have a lot of wonderful orators here," he once said. "A lot of bright, overwhelmingly

Kentucky 3

Louisville and Suburbs

To many rural and small-town Kentuckians, Louisville is something strange, an influence to be guarded against. In a state where blacks make up just 7 percent of the population, Louisville is almost 30 percent black. It also has an exceptionally large Catholic population, a legacy of massive German immigration in the mid-19th century. And Louisville's *Courier-Journal* newspaper is a leading liberal voice in a state that generally prefers moderate-to-conservative politicians.

Louisville's reputation in the hinterlands seems a bit undeserved, since, in its social history, the city has faced South. Its public places were not fully desegregated until well after World War II. In recent years court-ordered busing has been a major problem, particularly in blue-collar neighborhoods in the South End and in neighboring Shively. The anti-abortion movement is strong within the conservative Catholic constituency.

Louisville's South End is predominantly white, blue-collar and Democratic. Most blacks live near downtown in the West End, an area that regularly turns in heavy Democratic majorities. The affluent, Republican East End includes mansions on the bluffs overlooking the Ohio River.

Louisville Republicans elected two mayors in a row in the 1960s, partly by appealing to black voters against a decayed Democratic organization. But Democrats swept back into City Hall in 1969 and have held it since then. One recent mayor, Harvey Sloane, twice felt the sting of the state's anti-Louisville sentiment; he was runner-up in both the 1979 and 1983 Democratic gubernatorial primaries.

The Louisvillian most recently elected to statewide office was not a liberal Democrat, but a conservative Republican — Mitch McConnell, who moved from his job as Jefferson County executive to the U.S. Senate in 1984. In 1990, he might face a challenge from Sloane, who is now Jefferson County executive.

Prior to 1982 redistricting, the 3rd took in Louisville and only a few of the city's inner suburbs, a combination that made the district reliably Democratic. As redrawn to compensate for Louisville's population loss in the 1970s, the 3rd is less Democratic, though Louisville still casts a majority of the district vote.

Most of the voters added in the remap live south and southeast of the city in such blue-collar communities as Buechel, Fern Creek and Jeffersontown. Many work in suburban Louisville's General Electric, Ford and International Harvester plants. While a large share are registered Democrats, they are swing voters. Their support for Republican candidates frequently puts metropolitan Jefferson County in the GOP column.

Population: 522,252. White 413,605 (79%), Black 104,573 (20%), Other 2,493 (1%). Spanish origin 3,265 (1%). 18 and over 381,792 (73%), 65 and over 63,347 (12%). Median age: 30.

intelligent people. But sometimes the modern Demosthenes doesn't carry the day.... Sometimes those gray drudges can carry the day."

Mazzoli's day was Oct. 17, 1986, when Congress finally cleared the Simpson-Mazzoli immigration bill. The law penalizes employers who knowingly hire illegal aliens, and offered amnesty to illegal aliens who could prove that they had been in the United States before 1982.

By the time of final passage, however, Mazzoli had relinquished the leadership role he had played for most of the process. Emotionally spent from polarizing fights in the two past Congresses, he contented himself with working behind the scenes, lending technical expertise to the debate while others stepped into the spotlight. "The fight's gone out of the dog," one House Democrat said of Mazzoli.

Picking up the mantle of leadership that Mazzoli had let fall were three younger House Democrats: Judiciary's Charles E. Schumer of New York and Howard L. Berman of California, and Californian Leon E. Panetta of the Agriculture Committee. In 1989, Schumer and Berman would be among the leaders of the successful move to unseat Mazzoli, and to install in the Immigration chair a liberal colleague, Bruce A. Morrison of Connecticut.

If Mazzoli sometimes seemed like the forgotten man in the final stages of the immigration bill, GOP Sen. Alan K. Simpson of Wyoming and others who conducted the concluding negotiations left no doubt that Mazzoli had helped make it all possible. Moreover, the Kentucky Democrat had emerged in the end to deal with one of the bill's most controversial aspects — the proposal to establish a permanent "guest worker" program for growers who rely on foreign labor. He helped draft a compromise between growers, who said they needed the help, and organized labor, which insisted the program was exploitive, just when the dispute threatened to sink the entire bill for the third consecutive time.

The first time, during the 97th Congress, the immigration bill had passed the Senate, but did not reach the House floor until the closing days in 1982. At that point, Hispanic Caucus Chairman Edward R. Roybal of California killed it by threatening to demand roll-call votes on more than 100 amendments. When Mazzoli reluctantly pulled the bill, his colleagues gave him a standing ovation for his efforts.

Early in the 98th Congress, the Senate again passed an immigration bill, but Speaker O'Neill refused to bring the issue to the House floor in 1983. The next year, stung by criticism that he was stifling a needed reform for political purposes, O'Neill relented. Mazzoli orchestrated a week of debate on dozens of amendments; he went out of his way to lavish praise on virtually everyone who addressed the subject, even opponents, for making a constructive contribution.

The House narrowly passed the bill, 216-211, after the balance had seesawed until the last seconds. "I begged those guys," Mazzoli said later. "I said, 'For God's sake, don't let us come up empty-handed.' " But as he suspected even then, it was to prove impossible to reach agreement with the Senate. Also, immigration had become an issue in the Democratic Party's presidential campaign, with nominee Walter F. Mondale and the national party leadership joining Hispanics in opposing the bill. Victory would have to wait for the 99th Congress.

Once the bill was law, in the 100th Congress immigration experts monitored its implementation. By the first anniversary in late 1987, Mazzoli would proudly say, "Even the most implacable foes of the bill have had to eat some crow."

Meanwhile, his Judiciary colleagues were restless to do more than savor past successes. In 1987, Mazzoli was the only Democrat on his subcommittee and the full committee to join Republicans in opposing a bill to allow extended stays in the United States for refugees of El Salvador and Nicaragua until conditions at home improve. Then Mazzoli proposed an alternative safe-haven bill for refugees of armed conflict or environmental disaster, but it died in the Senate.

His subcommittee Democrats also wanted to extend the 1986 immigration law's amnesty period for another year, to ensure that all eligible aliens took advantage of the opening. And having successfully tackled illegal immigration, they wanted to begin work on revising the legal-immigration system, with its country-by-country quotas and eligibility standards that are widely considered outdated. Mazzoli wanted to undertake neither effort.

Pressed by a majority of his panel, however, Mazzoli finally agreed to a vote on the proposed amnesty extension just weeks before the law's May 1988 deadline. He proposed a six-month extension as a compromise; the full committee, acting within an hour of the subcommittee, settled on seven months. The measure narrowly was passed by the House, but died in a Senate filibuster. The amnesty deadline passed, leaving committee Democrats resentful that Mazzoli had waited until it was too late for action.

Meanwhile, that year the Senate passed a bill overhauling the legal-immigration system, but Mazzoli remained uninterested. Finally, under pressure again from subcommittee Democrats, he committed to take up the issue in the 101st Congress. However, his subsequent ouster rendered that promise moot, leaving it to Morrison to lead the effort.

At Home: Whether in Washington or Louisville, Mazzoli seems to encounter as much opposition from fellow Democrats as he does Republicans. It has been years since the GOP has seriously tested Mazzoli at the polls, but on three occasions since 1976 he has drawn significant primary opposition.

A furor over school busing provided the ammunition for the 1976 challenge. Mazzoli at first accepted busing as a means of desegregating the Louisville schools, then switched to an anti-busing position after the city's turmoil began. But the shift in positions came too late and was too mild for vocal busing foes. He was held to 56 percent of the primary vote.

The second primary challenge came in 1982, fueled by lingering resentment over the busing crisis and an unfavorable 1982 remap that extended his district deep into the Republican suburbs of Louisville. His opponent, state Rep. Mark O'Brien, sought to tie the busing issue to a controversial school-tax referendum, saying that if there were no busing, the proposed county surtax on the state income tax would be unnecessary. But because O'Brien's campaign was underfinanced and late-starting, it turned out to be more smoke than fire; Mazzoli comfortably surpassed the 60 percent mark.

The third primary challenge came in 1988, from Jeffrey Hutter, administrative director of the Humana Heart Institute and a former Louisville TV reporter. He was not especially well financed either, but made up for it with brashness. He accused Mazzoli of ignoring Louisville and voting against its interests. The incumbent "isn't dopey," Hutter said, "but he has been voting like Sleepy."

Hutter had support from the 80,000-member Greater Louisville Central Labor Council, which was upset with Mazzoli for his support of a smoking ban on domestic airplane flights of two hours or less (a vote labor saw as a threat to jobs in the state's lucrative tobacco industry) and his opposition to the Gephardt "fair trade" amendment.

Yet while Hutter carried blue-collar precincts, he could not crack the base that Mazzoli had constructed over nine terms among the district's many Catholic and elderly voters. Mazzoli got 61 percent of the vote.

Mazzoli's base has shifted a bit since he first ran for the House in 1970. Then, he was an opponent of the Vietnam War, with a strong base among blacks, young liberals and blue-collar Catholics. But the decisive factor in his House victory that year was the bitter intraparty feud between GOP incumbent William O. Cowger and Republican Gov. Louie B. Nunn over local patronage.

Cowger had challenged the governor to run a candidate for Congress against him in the primary. Nunn responded by saying Cowger was in need of a "psychiatric examination." The breach never healed and Mazzoli took advantage of it to win a 211-vote victory.

Since then, Republicans have held Mazzoli below 60 percent only once, in 1976 when Louisville was at the height of the busing furor. The GOP was optimistic about unseating him after the state's 1982 remap expanded the 3rd further into Jefferson County.

However, the GOP challenge was short-circuited by Mazzoli's aggressive efforts to court his new constituents. By a margin of 2-to-1, he overwhelmed GOP nominee Carl Brown, a Jefferson County commissioner, who had trouble raising money and building an organization.

Committees

Judiciary (5th of 21 Democrats)
Crime; Economic and Commercial Law; Immigration, Refugees and International Law

Small Business (5th of 27 Democrats)
Exports, Tax Policy and Special Problems; SBA, the General Economy and Minority Enterprise Development

Elections

1988 General		
Romano L. Mazzoli (D)	131,981	(70%)
Philip Dunnagan (R)	57,387	(30%)
1988 Primary		
Romano L. Mazzoli (D)	31,288	(61%)
Jeffrey Hutter (D)	20,207	(39%)
1986 General		
Romano L. Mazzoli (D)	81,943	(73%)
Lee Holmes (R)	29,348	(26%)

Previous Winning Percentages: **1984** (68%) **1982** (65%) **1980** (64%) **1978** (66%) **1976** (57%) **1974** (70%) **1972** (62%) **1970** (49%)

District Vote For President

	1988	1984	1980	1976
D	102,383 (53%)	99,200 (48%)	101,315 (52%)	106,071 (54%)
R	90,291 (47%)	109,042 (52%)	83,848 (43%)	83,972 (43%)
I			6,699 (4%)	

Campaign Finance

	Receipts	Receipts from PACs	Expend-itures
1988			
Mazzoli (D)	$378,438	$196,650 (52%)	$371,431
Dunnagan (R)	$6,916	0	$4,931
1986			
Mazzoli (D)	$146,795	$79,700 (54%)	$125,577
Holmes (R)	$5,670	0	$169

Key Votes

1987	
Raise speed limit to 65 mph	N
Approve Gephardt "fair trade" amendment	N
Ban testing of larger nuclear weapons	Y
Delay "re-flagging" of Kuwaiti tankers	Y
Approve tax-raising deficit-reduction bill	N
1988	
Approve aid to Nicaraguan contras	N
Enact civil rights restoration bill over Reagan veto	Y
Kill 60-day plant-closing notification measure	N
Pass omnibus trade bill over Reagan veto	Y
Approve death penalty for drug-related murders	Y
Bar federal funds for abortions in cases of rape and incest	Y
Oppose seven-day waiting period for purchase of handguns	N

Voting Studies

	Presidential Support		Party Unity		Conservative Coalition	
Year	**S**	**O**	**S**	**O**	**S**	**O**
1988	33	62	84	14	42	50
1987	42	57	84	15	74	26
1986	40	58	78	20	62	38
1985	48	52	74	25	62	36
1984	40	57	79	20	47	53
1983	40	59	78	20	51	48
1982	44	53	75	22	49	49
1981	47	43	62	29	49	36

Interest Group Ratings

Year	ADA	ACU	AFL-CIO	CCUS
1988	75	21	77	54
1987	52	30	56	33
1986	50	32	64	24
1985	55	33	47	50
1984	65	38	38	38
1983	65	35	53	55
1982	70	27	90	41
1981	60	36	64	44

4 Jim Bunning (R)

Of Fort Thomas — Elected 1986

Born: Oct. 23, 1931, Campbell County, Ky.
Education: Xavier U., B.S. 1953.
Occupation: Professional baseball player; investment broker.
Family: Wife, Mary Catherine Theis; nine children.
Religion: Roman Catholic.
Political Career: Fort Thomas City Council, 1977-79; Ky. Senate, 1979-83; Republican nominee for governor, 1983.
Capitol Office: 116 Cannon Bldg. 20515; 225-3465.

In Washington: People who watched Bunning as an athlete generally described him as a tough, stubborn competitor who hated to lose and never liked to yield an inch to an opposing batter. Those who have watched him in politics have found some of the same characteristics. Democrats sometimes describe him as obstinate and unyielding in the legislative process. Republicans prefer to stress his diligence at mastering the details of the job.

As a freshman, Bunning was elected by his classmates to be their representative on the GOP Committee on Committees, which determines committee assignments. Bunning made some useful contacts there with more senior Republicans, although he fell short in the 101st Congress when he tried for a vacancy on the highly coveted Ways and Means Committee.

Bunning took an aggressive, partisan stance in his first term. A vociferous defender of President Reagan and his conservative agenda, Bunning took to the floor to speak for administration causes such as the contras and Supreme Court nominee Robert H. Bork.

Less than a month after being sworn in, Bunning inveighed against a proposed pay raise for Congress, arguing that since members had not balanced the budget, "we haven't earned our keep, much less a raise."

In his first term on the Banking Committee, Bunning followed a firm conservative line. When the International Development Institutions Subcommittee was considering a bill in 1988 to authorize payments to the World Bank, he tried to tie the authorization directly to the bank's willingness to listen to U.S. complaints about loans. His plan was rejected by voice vote.

Bunning's presence offers House Republicans a chance for guaranteed supremacy in one of the few areas of partisan competition they have dominated in recent years — the congressional baseball game. Not since 1975 has there been a major league player in the House, and there has never been one like Bunning, who pitched two no-hitters and won 224 games over a 15-year big-league career. In 1987, he narrowly missed election to the Baseball Hall of Fame.

At Home: After retiring as an active player in 1971, Bunning tried minor league managing for a while, then returned to his native Kentucky, where he set up as an investment broker and agent to professional athletes.

He also got involved in civic activities that led him to a seat on the Fort Thomas City Council, where in 1977 he began his rapid political rise. After just two years, Bunning unseated a longtime Democratic state senator. He quickly became the minority leader for the small group of Senate Republicans.

In 1983, Kentucky Republicans, searching for a viable gubernatorial candidate, recruited Bunning. In his uphill campaign against Democrat Martha Layne Collins, he claimed the state's economy had stagnated during a long period of Democratic rule. He also took a "tough man" approach that seemed designed for voters uncomfortable with the idea of a woman governor. Bunning got a respectable 44 percent.

He initially had planned on another try for the governorship in 1987. But GOP Rep. Gene Snyder announced his retirement in 1986, and though his 4th District seat had been Republican for 20 years, GOP officials were worried about holding it. They needed a strong candidate, and enlisted Bunning.

His opponent was Democratic state Rep. Terry Mann, who had lost to Snyder by only 12,000 votes in 1982 and had considerable strength in Bunning's Campbell County political base, just across the Ohio River from Cincinnati.

Mann contrasted his 14 years in the Legislature to Bunning's four. But Mann drew negative press in March, when it was reported that he had rigged his state House voting lever with a rubber band so he would be recorded as present while he was absent from a session.

That episode, coupled with Bunning's image as a conservative in Snyder's mold and a big GOP financial edge, helped Bunning build a winning margin in the Cincinnati-area counties of Kenton and Boone and in the populous Louisville suburbs of Jefferson County.

Kentucky 4

Louisville Suburbs; Covington; Newport

A full 80 percent of the 4th's vote is cast either in the suburbs of Louisville, at the western end of the district, or in those of Cincinnati, at the eastern end. Both areas lean Republican and have made the district the state's best GOP territory outside the mountainous 5th. Along the Ohio River between the two population centers are four predominantly rural Democratic counties.

Redistricting in 1982 shifted the focus of the district more toward the eastern end of the district. Roughly half of the population now lives in Boone, Campbell (Newport) and Kenton (Covington) counties near Cincinnati. This suburban territory is largely blue-collar, but it has never had strong Democratic ties. The Cincinnati commuters and factory workers who live here regularly turn in Republican majorities.

Covington and Newport are old factory towns directly across the Ohio River from Cincinnati. Like the Louisville area, they have a large Catholic population of German extraction. Anti-abortion candidate Ellen McCormack ran a close second to Jimmy Carter there in the 1976 Democratic presidential primary.

The major population growth in the Kentucky suburbs of Cincinnati has been in Boone County. Attracting spillover from Campbell and Kenton counties, its population grew more than 50 percent from 1970-86.

The suburban Louisville portion of the district is diverse. Communities at the southern end of Jefferson County are largely blue-collar. But in the northeastern sector are some of the wealthiest suburbs in the country, and it is here that most of the county's GOP loyalists live. Their support helped Bunning carry Jefferson with 63 percent of the vote in 1986.

Oldham County, just north of Jefferson, is taking in more and more people seeking to escape the crowding closer to Louisville. Oldham's population boomed by 91 percent in the 1970s, the largest growth rate in the state. The influx has slowed since then, but it is still one of Kentucky's fastest-growing counties. Like Jefferson, Oldham has voted solidly for Bunning.

The other seven counties in the 4th are rural and predominantly Democratic. Unsuccessful Democratic presidential candidate Michael S. Dukakis carried all but two of them in 1988.

Population: 523,090. White 507,366 (97%), Black 12,547 (2%). Spanish origin 2,885 (1%). 18 and over 363,075 (69%), 65 and over 50,877 (10%). Median age: 30.

Committees

Banking, Finance and Urban Affairs (16th of 20 Republicans)
Domestic Monetary Policy; Financial Institutions Supervision, Regulation and Insurance; Housing and Community Development; International Development, Finance, Trade and Monetary Policy

Merchant Marine and Fisheries (15th of 17 Republicans)
Coast Guard and Navigation; Merchant Marine

Elections

1988 General		
Jim Bunning (R)	145,609	(74%)
Richard V. Beliles (D)	50,575	(26%)
1986 General		
Jim Bunning (R)	67,626	(55%)
Terry L. Mann (D)	53,906	(44%)

District Vote For President

	1988		1984		1980		1976	
D	71,505	(35%)	62,253	(30%)	77,599	(40%)	71,300	(41%)
R	133,660	(65%)	143,262	(69%)	108,825	(56%)	99,199	(58%)
I					6,657	(3%)		

Campaign Finance

	Receipts	Receipts from PACs	Expend-itures
1988			
Bunning (R)	$593,585	$236,184 (40%)	$468,870
Beliles (D)	$23,752	$16,425 (69%)	$23,636
1986			
Bunning (R)	$898,648	$250,865 (28%)	$895,709
Mann (D)	$333,809	$121,010 (36%)	$332,845

Key Votes

1987	
Raise speed limit to 65 mph	Y
Approve Gephardt "fair trade" amendment	N
Ban testing of larger nuclear weapons	N
Delay "re-flagging" of Kuwaiti tankers	N
Approve tax-raising deficit-reduction bill	N
1988	
Approve aid to Nicaraguan contras	Y
Enact civil rights restoration bill over Reagan veto	N
Kill 60-day plant-closing notification measure	Y
Pass omnibus trade bill over Reagan veto	N
Approve death penalty for drug-related murders	Y
Bar federal funds for abortions in cases of rape and incest	Y
Oppose seven-day waiting period for purchase of handguns	Y

Voting Studies

Year	Presidential Support S	Presidential Support O	Party Unity S	Party Unity O	Conservative Coalition S	Conservative Coalition O
1988	65	29	92	3	97	0
1987	74	24	95	4	95	5

Interest Group Ratings

Year	ADA	ACU	AFL-CIO	CCUS
1988	0	100	8	100
1987	4	87	6	93

5 Harold Rogers (R)

Of Somerset — Elected 1980

Born: Dec. 31, 1937, Barrier, Ky.
Education: Attended Western Kentucky U., 1956-57; U. of Kentucky, B.A. 1962, LL.B. 1964.
Military Career: Army National Guard, 1956-64.
Occupation: Lawyer.
Family: Wife, Shirley McDowell; three children.
Religion: Baptist.
Political Career: Commonwealth attorney, Pulaski and Rockcastle counties, 1969-79; GOP nominee for lieutenant governor, 1979.
Capitol Office: 434 Cannon Bldg. 20515; 225-4601.

In Washington: Taking the House floor one day to talk about an appropriation bill he had helped draft, Rogers managed not only to express his legislative views but also to reveal his style of operating in Congress. He said he had tried to knock some funds out of the bill, and had gotten nowhere. But he would vote for it anyway. "They are included," he said, "and so be it, that is the way this system works."

Rogers likes to operate within the system, and he operates effectively, although with a restricted agenda. He seldom attracts much publicity, but he has learned to thread his way through the politics of the institution, finding the appropriate levers to press to land the right seat on the right committee at the right time. Some of Rogers' colleagues in the GOP class of 1980 are just now getting good committee assignments; Rogers has already worked his way up to Appropriations and Budget.

So far his focus has been principally parochial, mostly on water projects and tobacco. But in the 100th Congress he broadened his horizons as he moved up to become ranking Republican on the Commerce, Justice and State Appropriations Subcommittee. In 1987, he successfully argued for an uptick in funds for federal prosecutors and agents fighting illegal immigration and drugs. He also helped the Reagan administration by fighting against a determined effort to reimpose rules requiring broadcasters to air all sides of controversial issues (the "fairness doctrine").

While such subjects offer only tangential benefits to his district, the top spot on the subcommittee puts Rogers in a position to influence other spending bills.

Rogers' behind-the-scenes skills are well suited to Appropriations, where Democrats and Republicans usually work together closely to draft money bills that all panel members can support. It is a good outpost for advancing projects in the 5th, such as flood control on the Upper Cumberland River and a major tunnel at the Cumberland Gap.

Tobacco is the one subject that seems to get the easygoing Rogers excited: He views the "right to smoke" as an issue of personal liberty. That is good politics, since tobacco sustains the 5th District's rural economy. There are 40,000 allotments in the district, most of them held by small-scale farmers.

In 1985, perturbed by administration proposals to phase out parts of the tobacco price-support system, Rogers "took a walk" during a high-profile Appropriations Committee vote on the MX missile. His refusal to vote on the issue had the intended effect — it attracted attention at the White House. Quickly, a meeting was arranged for Rogers with Chief of Staff Donald T. Regan. The Kentucky Republican fully vented his tobacco concerns before agreeing to back President Reagan on the MX.

Fighting to protect tobacco, however, has increasingly been a rear-guard action. In 1987, Rogers helped snuff out in subcommittee a plan by Illinois Democrat Richard J. Durbin to ban smoking on airplane flights — only to have Durbin win on the House floor and in conference. The trend is not lost on Rogers, who has been seeking funds for aquaculture and crop diversification to broaden his district's economic base. He also sponsored a task force to entice vacationers to southeastern Kentucky's parks and lakes.

Rogers got to Appropriations by fast maneuvering. When he arrived as a freshman in 1981, he asked to be selected as freshman GOP representative on the party panel that handed out committee seats. That gave him leverage over his own assignment, and he made it onto one of the most powerful committees, Energy and Commerce. Two years later he decided Appropriations was an even juicier plum, and he became the only one-term member among the committee's 21 Republicans.

In the 100th Congress, Rogers added to his collection by taking a seat on Budget. While that assignment gives him a broad overview of federal spending, his fiscally conservative in-

Kentucky 5

Southeast — Middlesboro

Eastern Kentucky's mountain counties have been voting Republican since the 1860s, when their small-scale farmers were hostile to the slaveholding secessionist Democrats elsewhere in the state. Republican Alfred M. Landon carried the 5th against Franklin D. Roosevelt in 1936; Barry Goldwater won it in 1964.

The only significant sources of Democratic votes here are in the coal-producing southeast corner of the district. Harlan and Letcher (the southern portion of which is in the 5th) counties were the only ones in the district to back Michael S. Dukakis in 1988. Both also backed Walter F. Mondale and Sen. Walter D. Huddleston in 1984, while nearly everyplace else in the 5th was going heavily for Reagan and GOP Senate candidate Mitch McConnell. Rogers campaigned actively for McConnell in the 5th, and the effort paid off: McConnell's 37,000-vote margin there was crucial in his narrow statewide victory.

In spite of some of the richest coal deposits in the nation along the district's eastern border, the 5th is the poorest district in Kentucky and one of the poorest in the nation. In 1970 nearly one-quarter of the residents lacked a sixth-grade education. Coal mining can be a good provider, but the boom-and-bust cycle of the industry leaves many without a reliable source of income. None of the counties in the 5th has a per capita income that approaches the statewide level.

Tobacco, apples, poultry and livestock are mainstays of the farm economy in the rolling hill country in the central and western parts of the district. Poor transportation and the absence of major population centers have hampered industrial development; textile mills are the biggest employers. The 5th is the only district in the state — and may turn out to be the only one in the country in the 1980s — without a city of 15,000 people. Its largest community, Nicholasville, has just over 14,000 residents.

Population: 523,664. White 511,632 (98%), Black 10,751 (2%). Spanish origin 4,275 (1%). 18 and over 359,513 (69%), 65 and over 63,341 (12%). Median age: 29.

stincts have been offended by much that he sees. And considering his normally low-key manner, Rogers has been rather forward with his criticisms.

After President Bush and congressional leaders announced a bipartisan budget accord in April 1989, Rogers balked at the pact's underlying economic assumptions and its accounting maneuvers aimed at achieving short-term savings. When the House Budget Committee considered the accord, Rogers joined with New Jersey Democrat Frank J. Guarini to propose an amendment adding $1 billion to drug treatment and education programs, to be offset with an across-the-board cut in all discretionary spending, including defense and foreign aid. With committee leaders from both parties arguing against any change in the basic agreement with the White House, that amendment and several others were rejected in committee by margins of 2-to-1. Later, Rogers was one of 61 Republicans voting against the budget resolution when it passed the full House.

At Home: Rogers, a protégé of GOP Rep. Tim Lee Carter, who retired in 1980, is generally identified as a moderate on the Kentucky GOP spectrum. In 1976, when most of the state party backed Reagan, Rogers ran Gerald R. Ford's primary campaign.

Rogers made his name locally in the 1960s as a civic activist promoting industrial development in Somerset. He took over as the commonwealth's attorney in 1969 and continued to play a conspicuous role in politics as the prosecutor for Pulaski and Rockcastle counties.

He was unsuccessful as the GOP nominee for lieutenant governor in 1979, but the race helped him build name recognition, and that paid off in the House campaign. Carter's retirement touched off a scramble, but Rogers quickly moved to the front of the 11-candidate GOP field. The primary revolved around personalities, geography and political alliances, not issues. Although Carter remained neutral, Rogers capitalized on their past association. He chaired Carter's re-election committee in 1978.

Rogers drew barely one-fifth of the vote, but carried 11 of the district's 28 counties, most of them around his home base in the center of the 5th. Fall elections are Rogers' runaways in the Republican 5th; Democrats did not even field a candidate against him in 1986 or 1988.

Committees

Appropriations (15th of 22 Republicans)
Commerce, Justice and State, the Judiciary and Related Agencies (ranking)

Budget (6th of 14 Republicans)
Task Forces: Community Development and Natural Resources (ranking); Economic Policy, Projections and Revenues

Elections

1988 General

Harold Rogers (R)	104,467	(100%)

1986 General

Harold Rogers (R)	56,760	(100%)

Previous Winning Percentages: 1984 (76%) **1982** (65%) **1980** (68%)

District Vote For President

	1988	1984	1980	1976
D	59,941 (33%)	58,788 (30%)	69,640 (37%)	67,794 (42%)
R	121,651 (67%)	134,073 (69%)	116,015 (61%)	92,134 (57%)

Campaign Finance

	Receipts	Receipts from PACs	Expend-itures
1988			
Rogers (R)	$177,242	$69,566 (39%)	$119,720
1986			
Rogers (R)	$253,110	$63,962 (25%)	$172,875

Key Votes

1987	
Raise speed limit to 65 mph	N
Approve Gephardt "fair trade" amendment	N
Ban testing of larger nuclear weapons	N
Delay "re-flagging" of Kuwaiti tankers	?
Approve tax-raising deficit-reduction bill	N
1988	
Approve aid to Nicaraguan contras	Y
Enact civil rights restoration bill over Reagan veto	N
Kill 60-day plant-closing notification measure	Y
Pass omnibus trade bill over Reagan veto	N
Approve death penalty for drug-related murders	Y
Bar federal funds for abortions in cases of rape and incest	Y
Oppose seven-day waiting period for purchase of handguns	Y

Voting Studies

	Presidential Support		Party Unity		Conservative Coalition	
Year	S	O	S	O	S	O
1988	62	38	85	11	87	11
1987	62	34	77	18	91	5
1986	70	29	76	23	92	8
1985	64	34	75	21	89	9
1984	54	41	66	28	92	7
1983	70	29	80	19	89	10
1982	70	29	73	20	86	12
1981	72	28	81	18	88	9

Interest Group Ratings

Year	ADA	ACU	AFL-CIO	CCUS
1988	5	96	21	100
1987	4	78	13	80
1986	10	86	43	67
1985	10	76	18	76
1984	25	71	38	73
1983	5	87	12	74
1982	15	76	30	77
1981	10	93	40	84

6 Larry J. Hopkins (R)

Of Lexington — Elected 1978

Born: Oct. 25, 1933, Detroit, Mich.
Education: Attended Murray State U., 1952-54.
Military Career: Marine Corps, 1954-56.
Occupation: Stockbroker.
Family: Wife, Carolyn Pennebaker; three children.
Religion: Methodist.
Political Career: Ky. House, 1972-78; Ky. Senate, 1978-79; Republican nominee for Fayette County Commission, 1970.
Capitol Office: 2437 Rayburn Bldg. 20515; 225-4706.

In Washington: With seats on the Agriculture and Armed Services committees, Hopkins is in a good position to tend to the needs of his district, and he does so. But he is not just a predictable parochialist. He has also ventured into debates on broader topics such as the War Powers act and the organization of the Joint Chiefs of Staff.

Hopkins was generally supportive of the Reagan-era military buildup, but occasionally he has spoken out against major weapons programs. When Armed Services voted on a 1987 amendment boosting the Pentagon's share of strategic defense initiative funding from $3.2 billion to $3.5 billion, Hopkins voted "no." At times in his career, he has opposed both the MX missile and nerve gas production.

Nerve gas is an especially tough issue for Hopkins because of the presence in his district of the Lexington Bluegrass Army Depot, with massive stockpiles of older chemical weapons. Hopkins' solution has been to vote for the production of new weapons, but to offer his own amendment requiring the dismantling of one of the old ones for each new one built. That meant phasing out the Lexington stockpile and replacing it with a different one, presumably in someone else's district.

His success, however, has raised another tough issue: how to dispose of the weapons, which are stored at the Bluegrass section of the Depot, in Madison County. The Army plans to incinerate the weapons where they are now stored, and more than a few of Hopkins' constituents want the nerve gas destroyed elsewhere. He has worked to see that the Army demonstrates the environmental soundness of incineration on an island in the Pacific.

In late 1988, a commission assessing U.S. military bases gave Hopkins a new concern: It recommended closing the Lexington portion of the depot. Hopkins argued strenuously that the commission, which recommended nearly 100 base closings, had not presented any conclusive evidence that shutting down Lexington would save the government money. But in early 1989, the House voted not to reject the commission's list; Hopkins' was one of just 43 votes in favor of rejection.

Hopkins' support for military spending coexists with the skepticism of an old Marine Corps private about the Pentagon bureaucracy. One of his major policy-making efforts was helping to push through Armed Services a sweeping reorganization of the U.S. military during the 99th Congress.

Both the House and Senate approved bills shifting bureaucratic power within the Defense Department from the separate armed services to the senior officials intended to coordinate the services — the chairman of the Joint Chiefs and the commanders in chief of the field combat forces. Studies in recent years had concluded that the services' competing viewpoints had led to poor and self-serving advice to the president on budgetary and tactical matters.

Legislation cleared Congress despite vigorous opposition from the top leadership of the services — what Hopkins described as "a sustained frontal assault orchestrated by opponents at the Pentagon who are determined to maintain the status quo."

Hopkins has strongly criticized the War Powers act, the law designed to force consultation between the president and Congress when troops are engaged abroad. Saying that presidents ignore the law and Congress fails to demand compliance, he has introduced legislation intended to expedite the process of authorizing troop activity or calling for disengagement.

Hopkins is a genial and good-humored man, but he can be haughty and harsh at times in committee hearings. He was a militant critic of the U.S. Marine presence in Lebanon in 1983, and even predicted its tragic fate, telling military leaders bluntly a few weeks before the Beirut bombing, "You guys are going to be in the green bag business again." He later supported a committee report blasting military commanders for not being better prepared for the bomb attack, which killed more than 240

Kentucky 6

North Central — Lexington; Frankfort

The 6th is Kentucky as the rest of the nation pictures it. Horses, tobacco and whiskey are the mainstays of its culture and economy. Its centerpiece is Lexington (Fayette County), de facto capital of the Bluegrass even though the 6th also contains the state capital of Frankfort.

Lexington is best known for its thoroughbred horse farms that regularly produce Kentucky Derby champions, but the University of Kentucky (enrollment 22,000) and the city's pleasant setting have attracted high-technology industry there, and Lexington's rapid growth has generated employment in engineering and other white-collar jobs.

The boom has swung Lexington into the Republican column. In his competitive early elections, Hopkins depended on Fayette to offset the Democratic vote in the district's farm counties. In 1984, Fayette gave GOP Senate candidate Mitch McConnell 54 percent; in 1988, George Bush took it by a margin of 3-to-2.

There also has been significant population and manufacturing growth in rural Bluegrass counties within commuting distance of Lexington. The largest of the adjoining counties is Madison (Richmond). Madison County, although nominally more Democratic than Fayette County, voted just like its larger neighbor — for Reagan and McConnell in 1984; for Bush in 1988. The northern portion of Madison County is dotted with bedroom communities whose residents work in Lexington. The southern portion revolves around Richmond, a tobacco market and site of Eastern Kentucky University (12,500 students). Ten percent of the district population lives in Madison, making it the second most populous county in the 6th.

Frankfort (Franklin County) is the district's other major population center. Chosen as the state capital in a 1792 compromise between competing Lexington and Louisville, it has never grown into a metropolis and today remains a small city of 26,000 people with picturesque old buildings. The long heritage of Democratic governors has produced a loyal pool of state workers who help keep Franklin County in the Democratic column. It voted solidly for Democratic incumbent Walter D. Huddleston in the close 1984 Senate contest.

Population: 519,009. White 467,159 (90%), Black 48,249 (9%). Spanish origin 3,325 (1%). 18 and over 377,249 (73%), 65 and over 53,093 (10%). Median age: 29.

Americans.

Meanwhile, as ranking Republican on the Tobacco Subcommittee at Agriculture, Hopkins champions one important Kentucky cause. It not only has to be tobacco to interest him — it pretty much has to be burley. The problems of those who grow other types of tobacco in North Carolina or Virginia do not keep him awake at night. Still, in his ranking position, he has had to serve as a voice for a broader tobacco-growing coalition.

That is a difficult responsibility during an era in which smoking is under ceaseless attack. Hopkins, a non-smoker, says he does not promote the practice, but that he is put in the position of defending it. Asked on one television program if smoking caused cancer, he responded: "How would I know that? I'm not a physician or a scientist. I can't actually say — I don't think it's good for you."

In the 99th Congress, anti-tobacco members were determined to cut tobacco price supports, and Hopkins figured prominently in the program's preservation. North Carolina's Jesse Helms, the Republican chairman of the Senate Agriculture Committee, balked at dealing with Democrat Charlie Rose, the chairman of the Tobacco Subcommittee in the House and a home-state Helms rival. Hopkins became the key House negotiator.

Helms and Rose offered separate subsidy plans. Helms wanted to allow cigarette manufacturers to buy surplus tobacco from the government, in many cases at 90 percent discounts. Rose wanted to earmark 1 cent of the 16-cent-per-pack cigarette tax to finance tobacco price supports. Helms' plan, which Hopkins supported, prevailed in a House-Senate conference.

At Home: The surprising defeat of Rep. John B. Breckinridge in the 1978 Democratic primary gave Republicans and Hopkins an opportunity they had not expected. Hopkins capitalized on that opportunity, becoming the first Republican in 50 years to win the 6th. Since then, prodigious fund raising and an ability to draw Democratic votes have helped Hopkins dig in. By outdistancing active Democratic opponents in 1980 and 1982, he discouraged future challengers and has scored over 70 percent against weak opposition.

Going into 1978, Breckinridge was considered unbeatable, so neither Hopkins nor any other formidable Republican candidates entered the GOP primary. But when Breckinridge lost to a more liberal Democrat, Republican leaders met and substituted Hopkins for the GOP's token candidate, a 68-year-old former state auditor. Hopkins, a popular state senator from Lexington, the district's largest city, was able to mount an expensive television campaign to make up for his late start.

Over the previous decade, he had built a strong electoral base in his hometown. After running unsuccessfully for the county commission, he was appointed county clerk of courts and then elected to the Legislature.

Hopkins' well-organized congressional campaign aimed its appeal at conservative farmers and blue-collar workers. He portrayed his opponent, maverick state Sen. Tom Easterly, as a pawn of the unions. In return, Easterly labeled the shuffling that put Hopkins in the contest a Watergate-style maneuver.

But the Democrat was unable to heal the party divisions that resulted from his campaign against Breckinridge, and Hopkins outspent him by more than 2-to-1. Winning Fayette County (Lexington) by nearly 12,000 votes, Hopkins captured the seat with 51 percent.

Easterly tried again in 1980, but the rematch with Hopkins was anticlimactic. Easterly had offended some of his 1978 supporters by attempting to mute his liberal image, and Hopkins had solidified his base by developing a good constituent-service operation. The incumbent won re-election by nearly 3-to-2.

In 1982 Democrats counted on favorable redistricting and the recession to give Hopkins a scare. They nominated Democrat Don Mills, a former editor of the Lexington *Herald*, who shared Hopkins' home base. A one-time press secretary to Gov. Edward T. Breathitt and an aide to Gov. John Y. Brown, Mills drew the primary-eve endorsement of three former Kentucky governors to win the Democratic nomination easily. But his general election campaign was woefully underfinanced.

While Mills ran almost even with Hopkins in the rural counties of the Bluegrass, the incumbent swamped him by 16,000 votes in the Lexington area.

Hopkins' string of victories in the politically marginal 6th has increased his attractiveness to GOP leaders as a potential statewide candidate. Hopkins considered party overtures to run for the GOP gubernatorial nomination in 1983 and again in 1987, but each time he decided to remain in Congress.

Committees

Agriculture (4th of 18 Republicans)
Tobacco and Peanuts (ranking); Livestock, Dairy and Poultry

Armed Services (5th of 21 Republicans)
Investigations (ranking); Procurement and Military Nuclear Systems

Elections

1988 General

Larry J. Hopkins (R)	128,898	(74%)
Milton Patton (D)	45,339	(26%)

1986 General

Larry J. Hopkins (R)	75,906	(74%)
Jerry Hammond (D)	26,315	(26%)

Previous Winning Percentages: **1984** (71%) **1982** (57%) **1980** (59%) **1978** (51%)

District Vote For President

	1988	1984	1980	1976
D	82,755 (42%)	72,942 (37%)	90,271 (49%)	83,835 (52%)
R	112,162 (57%)	123,859 (62%)	83,127 (45%)	74,110 (46%)
I			8,031 (4%)	

Campaign Finance

	Receipts	Receipts from PACs	Expend-itures
1988			
Hopkins (R)	$356,281	$134,335 (38%)	$295,333
Patton (D)	$41,638	$10,000 (24%)	$41,610
1986			
Hopkins (R)	$409,277	$129,428 (32%)	$160,669
Hammond (D)	$10,039	0	$10,141

Key Votes

1987	
Raise speed limit to 65 mph	Y
Approve Gephardt "fair trade" amendment	N
Ban testing of larger nuclear weapons	N
Delay "re-flagging" of Kuwaiti tankers	N
Approve tax-raising deficit-reduction bill	N
1988	
Approve aid to Nicaraguan contras	Y
Enact civil rights restoration bill over Reagan veto	Y
Kill 60-day plant-closing notification measure	Y
Pass omnibus trade bill over Reagan veto	N
Approve death penalty for drug-related murders	Y
Bar federal funds for abortions in cases of rape and incest	Y
Oppose seven-day waiting period for purchase of handguns	Y

Voting Studies

	Presidential Support		Party Unity		Conservative Coalition	
Year	S	O	S	O	S	O
1988	63	37	80	20	92	8
1987	70	29	91	6	98	2
1986	72	27	82	16	96	4
1985	61	38	71	25	84	15
1984	60	39	77	22	80	20
1983	65	34	84	14	85	12
1982	58	39	77	22	78	21
1981	68	29	79	20	80	16

Interest Group Ratings

Year	ADA	ACU	AFL-CIO	CCUS
1988	20	76	36	93
1987	0	77	13	93
1986	10	73	21	94
1985	10	71	24	81
1984	20	75	31	69
1983	20	74	12	80
1982	20	67	40	68
1981	20	93	40	76

7 Carl C. Perkins (D)

Of Hindman — Elected 1984

Born: Aug. 6, 1954, Washington, D.C.
Education: Davidson College, B.A. 1976; U. of Louisville, J.D. 1979.
Occupation: Lawyer.
Family: Wife, Janet Neville; two children.
Religion: Baptist.
Political Career: Ky. House, 1982-84.
Capitol Office: 1004 Longworth Bldg. 20515; 225-4935.

In Washington: First impressions can be deceiving, and a bad first impression can fade over time. But young Chris Perkins has a long, long way to go to achieve the respect and prominence enjoyed by his late father, veteran Rep. Carl D. Perkins.

Succeeding the most famous hillbilly in Congress was no easy job. Carl Perkins represented the 7th District for 35 years until his death in 1984. A New Deal liberal, he was devoted to federal anti-poverty programs as chairman of the Education and Labor Committee, and fondly called "Uncle Carl" by many.

Son Chris has the capacity to reprise or revise his father's style of representation. He does a convincing hillbilly routine, and could use that to draw attention to the concerns of his poor and rural district. Or he could employ his establishment education and suburban Washington upbringing to become an inside player in House politics and policy.

Instead, Perkins has largely become known as a member struggling to adapt to the demands and pressures of congressional life. He was divorced, remarried and had a son in the space of three months in 1987. On the 1988 Democratic Caucus retreat to Greenbrier, W.Va., Perkins and his new wife were involved in an early-morning commotion at a bar. Talk of the incident and of his drinking prompted two senior Democrats to sit Chris down for some fatherly advice.

In 1988, Perkins' Republican opponent exploited these matters, holding the incumbent under 60 percent of the vote — a noteworthy feat given the 7th District's steadfast Democratic tradition. (Michael S. Dukakis carried it easily for president.)

On the occasions that Perkins does find his legislative voice, he is outspoken in his belief that government should help the poor. A passionate critic of the Reagan administration, he claimed it was insensitive to "a lost class of people that is out there begging for some sort of assistance."

In House votes, Perkins clearly reflects his constituents' Democratic values. He is a near-certain supporter of the Democratic leadership line, which has helped him secure three committee assignments: Education and Labor, Science, and Public Works. (Public Works, which he relinquished early in the 101st Congress, was a temporary seat, since Democrats are allowed only two permanent committee assignments.)

On Education and Labor, he tries to ensure that aid is equitably distributed between rural and urban areas. In 1988, that committee approved a Perkins amendment to the minimum-wage bill that would have added a fourth-year raise to $5.05 an hour. Though strongly supported by organized labor, the proposal did not factor in 1989 discussions on raising the minimum wage.

At Home: Perkins took over the 7th after his father's death in 1984, but he did not face a stern test at the polls until 1988.

Perkins defeated minor GOP foes in 1984 and 1986, but in 1988 Republicans presented a challenger, Will Scott, with money and a strong résumé. A paratrooper in the Vietnam War who served four years as a state circuit court judge, Scott raised more than $400,000.

Despite the Democratic tradition of the poverty-stricken 7th, Scott believed the incumbent was vulnerable. He spoke glowingly of the elder Perkins, but dismissed his Washington-raised son as a stranger in his own district. Scott's slogan — "Winning Respect in Washington" — questioned the younger Perkins' effectiveness in Congress and implicitly recalled controversies in his personal life.

Perkins focused much of his fire on Scott's GOP label, charging that Reagan administration cutbacks had stymied badly needed highway and bridge construction in Appalachia. And though outspent, Perkins had the backing of the politically potent United Mine Workers.

But his biggest asset was his name. Although he is widely known as Chris, he invites voters to recall his father by listing himself on congressional ballots as Carl C. Perkins. The family name and the Democratic label were enough to put down the Republican challenge. But whether his 29,000-vote win was big enough to discourage further opposition is an open question.

Kentucky 7

East — Ashland

Coal booms come and go, but the Appalachian 7th remains one of the nation's poorest districts. The 1970s were a boom time here; a coal revival and the decline of industry in the urban Midwest brought many former residents back to their hometowns in the hills and hollows. But demand for coal has slackened, and the 1980s have been grim. "What I see ... in some places in my district [is that] 20, 30, 35, 40 percent unemployment exists," Perkins said on the House floor in 1986. "You say that is unbelievable, but it is true."

With the United Mine Workers (UMW) a major force in politics, the 7th is a Democratic bastion. It has supported the party's presidential nominee in seven of the last eight elections, failing only in 1972. Even Walter F. Mondale won the 7th in 1984, albeit narrowly, and Michael S. Dukakis carried it easily in 1988.

Democratic strength is greatest in the southern two-thirds of the district, a rugged area that is one of the nation's leading producers of bituminous coal. Since the New Deal and the UMW transformed politics here, the coal counties have turned in some of the highest Democratic percentages in the state.

The northern portion of the 7th, stretching from the West Virginia boundary northwestward into the Ohio River Valley, is primarily agricultural. Major products include tobacco, cattle and fruit. But compared with Kentucky's fertile Bluegrass region farther west, it is mediocre land dominated by small-scale and subsistence farming.

The urbanized exception in the north is the area around Ashland, the Ohio River city that is headquarters for the Ashland Oil Co. In good times and bad, strong unions help keep the Ashland area — industrialized Boyd and Greenup counties — in the Democratic column.

Population: 526,284. White 519,847 (99%), Black 5,259 (1%). Spanish origin 3,553 (1%). 18 and over 356,178 (68%), 65 and over 54,393 (10%). Median age: 28.

Committees

Education and Labor (12th of 22 Democrats)
Elementary, Secondary and Vocational Education; Labor Standards; Postsecondary Education

Science, Space and Technology (21st of 30 Democrats)
Science, Research and Technology; Space Science and Applications

Elections

1988 General

Carl C. Perkins (D)	96,946	(59%)
William T. "Will" Scott (R)	68,165	(41%)

1986 General

Carl C. Perkins (D)	90,619	(80%)
James T. Polley (R)	23,209	(20%)

Previous Winning Percentage: **1984** † (74%)

† Elected to a full term and to fill a vacancy at the same time.

District Vote For President

	1988		1984		1980		1976	
D	98,314	(56%)	91,955	(51%)	97,733	(55%)	97,090	(60%)
R	77,474	(44%)	88,477	(49%)	76,302	(43%)	62,781	(39%)

Campaign Finance

	Receipts	Receipts from PACs	Expend-itures
1988			
Perkins (D)	$418,749	$264,300 (63%)	$411,699
Scott (R)	$435,370	$37,330 (9%)	$432,403
1986			
Perkins (D)	$217,949	$144,200 (66%)	$240,757
Polley (R)	$57,908	$200 (0.3%)	$57,712

Key Votes

1987	
Raise speed limit to 65 mph	N
Approve Gephardt "fair trade" amendment	Y
Ban testing of larger nuclear weapons	Y
Delay "re-flagging" of Kuwaiti tankers	Y
Approve tax-raising deficit-reduction bill	Y
1988	
Approve aid to Nicaraguan contras	N
Enact civil rights restoration bill over Reagan veto	Y
Kill 60-day plant-closing notification measure	N
Pass omnibus trade bill over Reagan veto	Y
Approve death penalty for drug-related murders	Y
Bar federal funds for abortions in cases of rape and incest	Y
Oppose seven-day waiting period for purchase of handguns	Y

Voting Studies

	Presidential Support		Party Unity		Conservative Coalition	
Year	**S**	**O**	**S**	**O**	**S**	**O**
1988	20	80	95	5	26	74
1987	19	81	95	5	19	81
1986	22	78	89	10	40	60
1985	20	80	94	6	27	73

Interest Group Ratings

Year	ADA	ACU	AFL-CIO	CCUS
1988	85	12	100	14
1987	84	4	100	7
1986	80	9	93	17
1985	85	10	88	23

Louisiana

U.S. CONGRESS

SENATE 2 D

HOUSE 4 D, 4 R

LEGISLATURE

Senate 34 D, 5 R

House 86 D, 18 R, 1 Vacancy

ELECTIONS

1988 Presidential Vote

Bush	54%
Dukakis	44%

1984 Presidential Vote

Reagan	61%
Mondale	38%

1980 Presidential Vote

Reagan	51%
Carter	46%
Anderson	2%

Turnout rate in 1984	55%
Turnout rate in 1986	12%
Turnout rate in 1988	51%

(as percentage of voting age population)

POPULATION AND GROWTH

1980 population	4,205,900
1988 population estimate (20th in the nation)	4,408,000
Percent change 1980-1988	+5%

DEMOGRAPHIC BREAKDOWN

White	69%
Black	29%
Other	1%
(Spanish origin)	3%
Urban	69%
Rural	31%
Born in state	78%
Foreign-born	2%

MAJOR CITIES

New Orleans	554,500
Baton Rouge	241,130
Shreveport	220,380
Lafayette	89,830
Kenner	75,710

AREA AND LAND USE

Area 44,522 sq. miles (33rd)

Farm	31%
Forest	49%
Federally owned	4%

Gov. Buddy Roemer (D)
Of Bossier City — Elected 1987

Born: Oct. 4, 1943, Shreveport, La.
Education: Harvard U., B.A. 1964, M.B.A., 1967.
Occupation: Banker; political consultant; data processing executive.
Religion: Methodist.
Political Career: U.S. House, 1981-88; Democratic nominee for U.S. House, 1978.
Next Election: 1991.

WORK

Occupations

White-collar	50%
Blue-collar	34%
Service workers	13%

Government Workers

Federal	33,116
State	100,334
Local	166,532

MONEY

Median family income	$ 18,088	(33rd)
Tax burden per capita	$ 860	(23rd)

EDUCATION

Spending per pupil through grade 12	$ 3,187	(37th)
Persons with college degrees	14%	(38th)

CRIME

Violent crime rate	693 per 100,000 (8th)

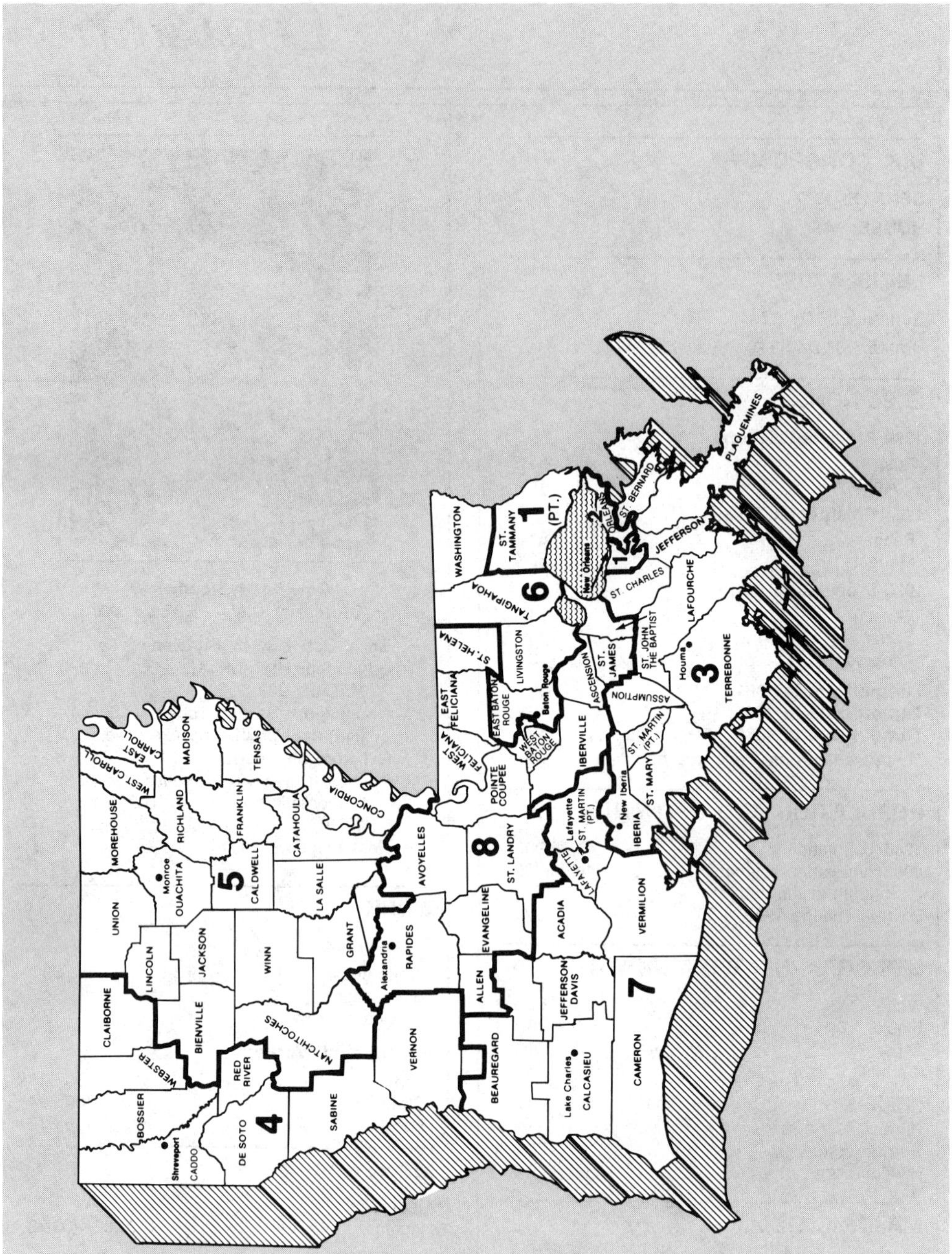
1
(PT.)
2
3
4
5
6
7
8
CADDO
Shreveport
BOSSIER
WEBSTER
CLAIBORNE
LINCOLN
UNION
MOREHOUSE
WEST CARROLL
EAST CARROLL
MADISON
RICHLAND
OUACHITA
Monroe
JACKSON
BIENVILLE
RED RIVER
DE SOTO
SABINE
NATCHITOCHES
WINN
CALDWELL
FRANKLIN
TENSAS
CATAHOULA
CONCORDIA
LA SALLE
GRANT
RAPIDES
Alexandria
VERNON
BEAUREGARD
ALLEN
EVANGELINE
AVOYELLES
ST. LANDRY
POINTE COUPEE
WEST FELICIANA
EAST FELICIANA
ST. HELENA
TANGIPAHOA
WASHINGTON
ST. TAMMANY
LIVINGSTON
EAST BATON ROUGE
Baton Rouge
WEST BATON ROUGE
IBERVILLE
ASCENSION
ST. JAMES
ST. JOHN THE BAPTIST
ST. CHARLES
New Orleans
ORLEANS
ST. BERNARD
PLAQUEMINES
JEFFERSON
LAFOURCHE
TERREBONNE
Houma
ASSUMPTION
ST. MARTIN (PT.)
ST. MARY
IBERIA
New Iberia
LAFAYETTE
Lafayette
ACADIA
VERMILION
JEFFERSON DAVIS
CALCASIEU
Lake Charles
CAMERON

J. Bennett Johnston (D)

Of Shreveport — Elected 1972

Born: June 10, 1932, Shreveport, La.

Education: Attended Washington and Lee U., 1950-51, 1952-53; attended U.S. Military Academy, 1951-52; Louisiana State U., LL.B. 1956.

Military Career: Army, 1956-59.

Occupation: Lawyer.

Family: Wife, Mary Gunn; four children.

Religion: Baptist.

Political Career: La. House, 1964-68; La. Senate, 1968-72; sought Democratic nomination for governor, 1971.

Capitol Office: 136 Hart Bldg. 20510; 224-5824.

In Washington: A master of the poker-faced political bluff, Johnston brought that game to his 1988 bid for Senate majority leader, working hard to create a perception in the media and in Democratic ranks that his success was assured. Bringing his bravado public, however, only highlighted Johnston's reputation as the chamber's consummate wheeler-dealer. As it turned out, that was not the image Senate Democrats wanted in their new leader; the job went easily to George J. Mitchell of Maine, whose campaign for the post was as low-key as Johnston's was brash.

The defeat — Johnston's second failed attempt for the position — may well have marked his last chance for a leadership post. Johnston's influence also slipped a notch on the Appropriations Committee, where ailing Chairman John C. Stennis of Mississippi once routinely tapped him to manage important legislation. Stennis retired after the 100th Congress, and former Majority Leader Robert C. Byrd of West Virginia took over Appropriations in 1989, determined to assert his authority.

Of course, Johnston is not without considerable clout. He chairs the Energy and Natural Resources Committee as well as the Appropriations Subcommittee on Energy and Water, giving him leviathan power on issues important to his economically troubled oil-patch state. But his political climb has clearly been braked. Now fourth in line for the Appropriations chairmanship, Johnston will have to wait his turn for advancement, and waiting is not an activity Johnston enjoys.

When Johnston gets involved in an issue, he tends to take charge. Whether working in a closed conference or managing a bill on the floor, he absorbs the legislative fine points and then bargains with aplomb. A master crafter of the pragmatic coalition, he can cut a deal that gives something to everyone — or at least to everyone who stays alert.

Some find Johnston's horse-trading unsavory, but he gladly acts the part. Waiting for other senators to bring amendments to the floor, he will open his arms and let a big grin happen as he says: "We're open for business here."

For those unwilling to do business, Johnston has sharp elbows and no qualms about bruising his way past a foe. This method makes him a legislator who gets things done, but it does not facilitate formation of the kind of personal relationships that are paramount in leadership races.

Johnston's first bid for Senate Democratic leader essentially ended on election night 1986, when voters returned a Democratic majority to the Senate. Six months earlier, he had announced his challenge to then-Minority Leader Byrd hoping to transform inchoate dissatisfaction with his leadership into an insurgency. But when Democratic Senate candidates emerged victorious that November, Byrd was widely interviewed in post-election analysis as the new majority leader, with nary a mention of his challenger.

Days later, Johnston quit the race, saying he could not dissolve Byrd's "aura of electability" and privately concluding that he lost because he failed to control the media "spin."

Johnston's second try began when Stennis announced his retirement late in 1987. Rumors flourished that Byrd would step down as majority leader to take over Appropriations. Johnston immediately set up a political action committee, Pelican PAC, to raise money for colleagues facing re-election in 1988, and to offset the reputed fund-raising prowess of anticipated rivals Mitchell and Daniel K. Inouye of Hawaii.

A critical issue in the race, particularly for younger members, was the frustration with the Senate's procedures and its unpredictable, delay-ridden schedule. Throughout the 100th Congress, Johnston regularly demonstrated his definition of a more efficient Senate with hard-nosed legislating.

In early 1988, on the third day of debate on the Price-Anderson nuclear-insurance law, the Senate took up an amendment by Ohio Democrat John Glenn to increase safety supervision of nuclear power plants. It was a Friday, so senators had airplane tickets in their pockets, ready to jet home for the weekend.

Long a supporter of energy development in all its forms, Johnston opposed Glenn's amendment, and after two hours of debate, he rolled out the heavy artillery. Citing the array of committee leaders on his side, Johnston pronounced Glenn's defeat inevitable. It was patented Johnston strategy: Achieve victory by declaring victory.

When Glenn refused to pin down a time certain for a vote, Johnston moved to kill his amendment by tabling it, in effect unilaterally cutting off debate. He narrowly succeeded, and the bill passed shortly thereafter — at 3 p.m., in plenty of time for senators to get to the airport.

Divide and conquer is another well-known Johnston legislative device. He employed this tactic in 1987, when he almost single-handedly rammed a nuclear-waste plan through Congress. Johnston's initial plan was to abandon a search for an Eastern disposal site and put all waste in one of three Western states. He assembled a Senate majority by uniting states with just one thing in common: None wanted to host the nation's permanent radioactive-waste dump.

The House had drawn up a vastly different plan that called for the Department of Energy (DOE) to suspend a waste-siting decision and seek a voluntary agreement. When Johnston got his bill attached to the 1987 budget-reconciliation package, a showdown was set.

In tense negotiations on a variety of details, Johnston engineered a plan to put all the waste in Nevada, a state that had no representatives on the conference committee. One conferee condemned the plan as "a goddamned outrage," and angry Nevadans cried foul. But it passed, and Johnston calmly noted, "If I were a Nevadan living in the real world, I would be happy with this bill. I would bet that in a very few years, Nevada will deem this one of their most treasured industries."

Johnston was not unaware of the potential backlash his style might have in the leadership contest, but he proceeded without apology. "Anytime you put together a coalition, you're putting together deals in effect," he once said. "If somebody is not part of the deal they can feel like it's tricky. It's not being tricky. It's just being successful."

Energy Appropriations is Johnston's most important legislative showcase, and one where he will boldly flex his muscle. Also a member of the Budget Committee — now its third-ranking Democrat — Johnston dropped out of active participation in the panel's work in 1988 when it recommended less spending for energy programs than he wanted.

To counterattack, he spearheaded meetings of Appropriations' subcommittee chairmen to draft their own spending blueprint. The Appropriations Committee eventually approved the controversial plan. Liberals complained that the allocation scheme was too stingy with education programs, and forced an unusual Democratic caucus vote instructing Appropriations to remedy the problem. Johnston took the matter back to committee, but his original plan was upheld.

Complementing these demonstrations of legislative strength, Johnston gradually stepped toward the political center in his leadership bid. While his conservative Southern instincts and background were an essential ingredient of his candidacy, he could not afford to be fighting openly with environmentalists and other liberals.

In 1985, Johnston emerged as a leading Senate critic of the strategic defense initiative (SDI). In pursuit of limiting the program, he struck some unusual alliances, but characteristically, he proved to be a powerful player. In the 99th Congress, Johnston organized a group of 48 senators who wrote to President Reagan urging him to cut his SDI request. Soon thereafter, he offered a floor amendment that came within one vote, 49-50, of cutting SDI funding below the amount recommended by the Armed Services Committee.

In 1987, Johnston was a leader in opposing Reagan's nomination of Robert H. Bork to the Supreme Court. At one late-night meeting in the Senate dining room, Johnston held court with a group of Southern freshmen to talk about the impending vote. "This nomination is going to go down," he told them, "because people like you are going to vote against it. And you want to know why? You're going to vote against it because you're not going to turn your back on the 91 percent of black voters ... who got you here."

In the end, there was a nearly solid Southern vote against Bork, and the wily Louisianan was credited with helping get it all started.

Johnston's role surprised those who remembered him as a young lawyer defending segregation. As late as 1981, when a controversy raged over busing to achieve integration in Baton Rouge schools, he took the lead on a Senate proposal to bar the courts from ordering busing except in limited cases. After a protracted floor struggle, he managed to get the measure through the Senate, though the House balked.

But in 1987, the year of the Bork vote, Johnston received a career-high rating of 70 from the liberal Americans for Democratic Action. His ADA rating had taken a sudden turn upward in 1984, the year he won his third Senate term.

Seeking the majority leader job in the fall of 1988, Johnston exuded confidence that he was headed for victory. When he landed the vote of Colorado's Tim Wirth, exemplar of the new-breed Democratic liberal, Johnston and his operatives spread the word that his candidacy was surging, hoping to stampede fence-sitters into his camp.

For a time, the strategy appeared to be working. He was asked to appear on TV news talk shows, and some pundits called him the front-runner. But when the votes were counted Nov. 29, he had just 14 supporters, and narrowly missed finishing last. With Mitchell just one vote shy of a majority in the three-way balloting, Johnston and Inouye moved to make the vote unanimous.

Johnston's power as Energy Committee chairman is considerable, but for a man who reached for the Senate's top job, the chair must seem a bit old hat. He essentially served as the committee's leader early in his career: In the late 1970s, with the encouragement of then-Chairman Henry M. Jackson of Washington, who was preoccupied with defense issues, Johnston ran the committee. Though he had to step aside when Republican James A. McClure of Idaho chaired the panel in the years of GOP Senate control, he still managed to retain a fair portion of influence, partly because his market-oriented approach to energy policy meshed well with GOP ideas.

Johnston predictably looks out for the oil and gas industries vital to Louisiana. One particularly notable accomplishment occurred in 1986, when he brokered a complex deal dividing up some $6.4 billion in offshore oil drilling revenues between the federal government and the coastal states. Tacked onto the deficit-reduction bill, the compromise gave Louisiana a lump sum payment of $635 million.

At Home: Another 5,000 votes would have made Johnston governor of Louisiana in 1972. Rather than slowing him down, however, Johnston's near-miss in the Democratic runoff against Edwin W. Edwards brought him the public attention he needed for a successful Senate campaign a few months later.

Still, it took an unexpected turn of events to bring Johnston to Washington. After losing the governor's race, he decided on a primary challenge to veteran Sen. Allen J. Ellender, who was running for a seventh full term at 81. Ellender's age did not at first seem like a winning issue for Johnston; Ellender was a man of remarkable vigor, almost a symbol of perpetual youth. He was also chairman of the Senate Appropriations Committee and a master at providing federal money for Louisiana. But on July 27, three weeks before the Democratic primary, Ellender died suddenly of a heart attack. Johnston had a clear path to election.

Before his 1971 campaign for governor, Johnston had been just a moderately visible conservative state legislator from northern Louisiana and a lawyer practicing with his father in Shreveport. In the Legislature, his major issue was completion of an Interstate highway linking his home city with New Orleans.

Campaigning against each other in the Democratic runoff, Johnston and Edwards differed politically, regionally and personally. Edwards, a Catholic from Cajun southern Louisiana, had moderate social views and a flamboyant manner. Johnston called for racial moderation, but he was more aloof in style, and, as a Baptist from the Protestant north, he was universally perceived as being to Edwards' right.

Johnston attacked Edwards for absenteeism during his six and a half years in the U.S. House, and painted him as a pawn of organized labor. Edwards blasted back at Johnston for voting to pass a series of state tax increases.

There was little Edwards or anyone else could do to stop Johnston in 1972 once Ellender died. Former Gov. John J. McKeithen tried a last-minute move to reopen filing for the August primary, but the state Democratic committee turned him down. Johnston then won the nomination by more than 6-to-1 against a little-known cotton farmer.

In the fall, McKeithen ran as an independent, making a bid for the votes of blacks and low-income whites by characterizing Johnston as the candidate of the wealthy. "He lives three strokes from the country club," he said.

The former governor had a problem, however, in the well-publicized indictments of key members of his administration. McKeithen himself was never accused of wrongdoing, but Johnston was able to campaign on the need for a return to honest government.

The Republican nominee was Ben C. Toledano, who had run unsuccessfully for mayor of New Orleans in 1970. Toledano sought to link Johnston to the Democratic presidential nominee, George McGovern, but Johnston used his conservative voting record in the Legislature to refute any connection. Rather than hurting Johnston, Toledano and McKeithen offset each other. Johnston won his first Senate term with more than 55 percent of the vote.

By 1978, Johnston had some problems at home. He had a reputation among some local Democrats as being aloof and Washington-oriented, and among others as insufficiently conservative. He drew a serious challenge from Democratic state Rep. Louis "Woody" Jenkins, who had worked for George C. Wallace in national politics.

Jenkins labeled the senator a devotee of high taxes and spending, and seemed for much of the summer to be making inroads on Johnston's popularity. But after a slow start, Johnston put on an aggressive drive for renomination. He had taken away Jenkins' best issue earlier in the year by voting against ratification of the Panama Canal treaties. Johnston won 59 percent of the primary vote, assuring him re-election under Louisiana law.

Johnston's re-election contest in 1984 made the 1978 campaign seem like a cliff-hanger. Once former GOP Gov. David C. Treen dropped his brief bid to oppose him, Johnston had clear sailing. He swamped two little-known Republican candidates with 86 percent; his nearest challenger managed only 9 percent.

Committees

Energy and Natural Resources (Chairman)

Appropriations (4th of 16 Democrats)
Energy and Water Development (chairman); Defense; Foreign Operations; HUD-Independent Agencies; Interior and Related Agencies

Budget (3rd of 13 Democrats)

Special Aging (5th of 10 Democrats)

Elections

1984 Primary †

J. Bennett Johnston (D)	838,181	(86%)
Robert M. Ross (R)	86,546	(9%)
Larry N. Cooper (R)	52,746	(5%)

† In Louisiana the primary is open to candidates of all parties. If a candidate wins 50 percent or more of the vote in the primary, no general election is held.

Previous Winning Percentages: 1978 (59%) **1972** (55%)

Campaign Finance

	Receipts	Receipts from PACs	Expend-itures
1984			
Johnston (D)	$1,484,557	$553,085 (37%)	$1,179,239
Cooper (R)	$5,050	0	$10,489

Key Votes

1987	
Enact omnibus highway bill over Reagan veto	Y
Limit testing of space-based anti-ballistic missiles	Y
Oppose banning tests of larger nuclear weapons	Y
Confirm Robert H. Bork as Supreme Court justice	N
1988	
Allow vote on campaign-finance overhaul	Y
Pass civil rights restoration bill over Reagan veto	Y
Enact omnibus trade bill over Reagan veto	Y
Approve death penalty for drug-related murders	Y
Oppose "workfare" amendment to welfare overhaul bill	Y

Voting Studies

	Presidential Support		Party Unity		Conservative Coalition	
Year	**S**	**O**	**S**	**O**	**S**	**O**
1988	63	35	77	20	86	11
1987	44	54	82	17	88	13
1986	58	42	61	37	67	30
1985	45	53	63	33	68	27
1984	61	30	51	44	83	11
1983	55	44	54	40	82	5
1982	61	37	47	48	93	6
1981	68	26	49	45	93	3

Interest Group Ratings

Year	ADA	ACU	AFL-CIO	CCUS
1988	55	36	86	50
1987	70	20	90	33
1986	50	35	67	44
1985	60	45	80	28
1984	55	59	56	47
1983	20	56	43	67
1982	35	63	50	67
1981	25	27	35	82

John B. Breaux (D)

Of Crowley — Elected 1986

Born: March 1, 1944, Crowley, La.
Education: U. of Southwestern Louisiana, B.A. 1964; Louisiana State U., J.D. 1967.
Occupation: Lawyer.
Family: Wife, Lois Daigle; four children.
Religion: Roman Catholic.
Political Career: U.S. House, 1972-87.
Capitol Office: 516 Hart Bldg. 20510; 224-4623.

In Washington: Surrounded by colleagues who see future presidents when they look in a mirror, Breaux sees a senator ambitious to rise to power within the chamber. He has as much talent and brains as any of the others, and a record that puts him just inside the Democratic Party mainstream. But as the unapologetic protégé of discredited former Gov. Edwin W. Edwards and a roguish charmer in his own right, from a state whose politics and oil industry already are suspect on the outside, Breaux would have some formidable barriers to leap to win national office.

He already has begun his ascent in the Senate. With more congressional experience after seven House terms than any of the 13 freshman senators who arrived in 1987, Breaux had the rare privilege of immediately becoming chairman of two subcommittees. Then late in 1988, newly elected Majority Leader George J. Mitchell picked Breaux for the position that Mitchell himself had parlayed into his leadership victory: chairman of the fund-raising Democratic Senatorial Campaign Committee.

Breaux was chosen even though he had been campaign manager for Mitchell's rival for majority leader, senior Louisiana Sen. J. Bennett Johnston. The choice appeared to be an olive branch from Mitchell, but the fact was, no one was better for the job than Breaux. He cannot get enough of politics, whether fund raising, strategizing or legislating. And, true to the Cajun let-the-good-times-roll tradition, he makes it look like great fun.

As one who simply loves the game for its own sake, Breaux does not bring ideology or great policy aims to the table. However, like other moderate-to-conservative Southerners, he has called for the party to move rightward. He opposed the selection of a black, Ronald H. Brown, as national party chairman in early 1989, frankly arguing that Democrats need to court white males who have left the party. Breaux's objections sparked some controversy, given his new status as a party campaign spokesman and the fact that he owed his 1986 election to overwhelming black support.

Breaux is similarly unabashed about courting business. His shrewd pragmatism is almost shameless, endearingly so, as illustrated by his now-legendary remark in 1981 explaining that he would support President Reagan's proposed social spending cuts in return for concessions on natural gas policy and sugar subsidies. Breaux quipped that while his vote could not be bought, "it can be rented."

In 1987 he waged the banking lobby's partly successful Senate fight against a bill that would continue to bar banks from the real estate, securities and insurance fields. Breaux, who does not sit on the Banking Committee, admitted, "I don't know much about the subject.... I was approached by the banks and they made a good point about equity."

More often, Breaux is an advocate for Louisiana's interests, especially energy and commercial fishing. His committee assignments reflect his priorities just as they did in the House. On Environment and Public Works, he chairs the Nuclear Regulation Subcommittee; on Commerce, Science and Transportation, he heads the Merchant Marine panel.

On Nuclear Regulation, Breaux has worked closely with ranking Republican Alan K. Simpson of Wyoming. They had a lead role in the effort that renewed the Price-Anderson law on nuclear accident insurance, cosponsoring legislation to raise utilities' liability tenfold to about $7 billion. Unlike other proposals that were vague on the question, their bill specified that any victims' claims beyond the limit would be paid from the Treasury. That drew opposition from taxpayer and environmental groups, who insisted utilities should bear all costs. The committee approved the bill unanimously in 1987, but jurisdictional tiffs with Johnston's Energy Committee prevented final action until the next year, when the Senate acted on a House-passed bill.

Breaux also scrapped with Johnston in 1987, unsuccessfully, over Johnston's proposal making Nevada the nation's first high-level nuclear waste disposal site. Johnston, also chairman of the Appropriations Subcommittee on Energy, attached his plan to his panel's annual appropriations bill. Breaux, and others on Congress' authorizing committees for energy, favored a delay in the site-selection process to give the government time to bargain with a willing state. But the Senate rejected Breaux's amendment opposing Johnston's plan, 34-61.

Despite his dedication to nuclear power and the petrochemical industry, Breaux also has to balance the safety and environmental concerns of Louisianans, especially those involved in fishing. He generally has represented industry viewpoints during Environment's debate on strengthening the Clean Air Act, but early in 1989 he cosponsored legislation against toxic emissions, a health hazard in Louisiana. He has proposed a bill to restore eroding wetlands, like his state's shrimp-rich coast, by using a share of federal oil-leasing revenues.

Breaux has been critical of the Nuclear Regulatory Commission (NRC) for being too close to the industry and too lax about safety lapses at power plants. He has proposed legislation to replace the NRC with a single administrator as the industry wants, but also to create an independent safety board that industry adamantly opposes. His plan passed the Senate in the 100th Congress, but died in the House.

Given his long House experience, Breaux hit the Senate running. First elected at 28, he became a power broker while most of his contemporaries were still learning the process. He might have risen higher, if not for his 1981 defection to Reaganomics. In 1983, House leaders dispensed prize committee seats as rewards for party loyalty, and denied Breaux a Budget Committee spot he wanted.

He built his House career in part by filling a power vacuum. Finding that most members of the Merchant Marine and Fisheries Committee paid little attention to it, he chose to concentrate there, not only for his district's fishing interests but also for the panel's potential role in energy and environmental policy. As chairman of the Subcommittee on Fisheries and Wildlife Conservation and the Environment, Breaux helped force the committee's way into a number of important legislative battles.

In the late 1970s, he was at the center of the controversy over development on the Outer Continental Shelf. As it turned out, Breaux and the oil industry fought a Merchant Marine bill that would have increased regulation of smaller companies' exploration, but the House rejected his substitute. Over the next few days of debate, however, Breaux amended most of the substitute to the bill, allowing him to claim victory in the end.

Later, he stepped in to resolve some coastal states' longstanding fight with the federal government for a larger share of the revenues from offshore drilling leases. Since 1978, a huge sum had built up in escrow and Louisiana stood to gain enormously. By late 1985, the political maneuvering over the treasure grew as intense as the legislative fight. Breaux and GOP Rep. W. Henson Moore were heading into a 1986 Senate face-off, and both wanted to claim credit for a lucrative settlement.

The Reagan administration did its best to give Moore credit. He was invited to the White House to receive the president's approval of the eventual compromise, and emerged to announce to waiting TV crews that he had "saved" the settlement money for Louisiana. In fact, much of the work had been done by Breaux and other Louisiana Democrats.

In 1985, they had added to a budget bill a provision giving the affected states 27 percent of the revenues, a compromise between the states' initial bid for 37 percent and the administration's 16 percent offer. Though the underlying bill was derailed, in 1986 Breaux revived the plan and negotiated with the Senate for the compromise that finally cleared.

Breaux has long been active on the side of energy companies in debates on the "superfund" toxic-waste cleanup program. During the drafting of the 1980 law, he drew up a compromise guaranteeing that those companies would be paying strictly for the cleanup of oil spills, rather than chemical spills as well. When the 98th Congress renewed the superfund, Breaux worked to limit the fund's size, and thus the assessments on the oil industry.

As he has in the Senate, in the House Breaux tempered his pro-business approach with an occasional tilt toward environmental causes. In the 97th Congress, he managed a bill to extend the Endangered Species Act for three years, generally pleasing environmentalists and disappointing business interests that wanted fewer limits on energy development. He again resisted industry-supported changes when the act came up for renewal in the 99th Congress; after passing the House, however, the measure died in the Senate.

At Home: Breaux learned his trade from one of Louisiana's masters — Edwards, the state's three-term governor and a former U.S. representative. Breaux was Edwards' junior law partner and served for four years as one of his top congressional aides.

When Edwards first won the governorship in February 1972, he pushed for Breaux to be his successor in the House. With Edwards' organization, Breaux easily paced the field of six Democratic primary candidates, then won the September runoff with 55 percent of the vote over TV newscaster Gary Tyler, the same man Edwards had defeated to win his first congressional term seven years earlier.

Breaux does not, however, owe his ascent to the Senate to Edwards' influence. If anything, his one-time mentor made his 1986 bid to replace retiring Democratic Sen. Russell B. Long more difficult.

During Edwards' third term, Louisiana's

oil industry had foundered, and by the time of the 1986 Senate contest the state's economy was reeling. Many voters were in a mood to blame the Democrats. Moreover, Edwards' image had suffered even more during two trials on corruption charges, even though he was eventually acquitted.

Those circumstances gave the Republicans one of their best openings in years. Early in 1986, Republican Moore began airing ads designed to exploit voters' restlessness. "The party is over," they said. "It's time to go back to work." Democrats, he charged, had squandered the state's resources and prostituted the political system to their own advantage. Republicans, Moore argued, were the party of reform. He quickly moved into the lead.

If Moore had continued on the same tack, he might have won. But as the nonpartisan September primary approached, he pushed to win more than 50 percent of the vote and avoid a runoff. He shifted his emphasis, beginning a wave of ads and mailings that attacked Breaux directly. "The politician's politician, always putting himself first," one mailer called the Democrat. At the same time, the national GOP mounted a program to purge ineligible voters from the rolls in black precincts.

None of those tactics sat well with Louisiana's basically Democratic electorate. Moore seemed mean-spirited, especially in contrast with Breaux's roguish Cajun charm. And the "ballot security" program infuriated black voters — a boost for Breaux, since many blacks had considered him too conservative.

The primary was a turning point. Moore came in first, but he did not run as strongly as many had expected. Over the next month, Breaux worked to take the high ground Moore had squandered, arguing that the state's problems stemmed not from the state government, but from a Republican administration in Washington that had followed misguided trade and farm policies. Moore's first allegiance, he charged, was to his party and to Reagan, not to Louisiana. Moore tried to recoup, softening his message, but Breaux carried 42 of 64 parishes.

Committees

Commerce, Science and Transportation (9th of 11 Democrats)
Merchant Marine (chairman); Communications; Surface Transportation; National Ocean Policy Study

Environment and Public Works (6th of 9 Democrats)
Nuclear Regulation (chairman); Environmental Protection; Water Resources, Transportation and Infrastructure

Special Aging (6th of 10 Democrats)

Elections

1986 General		
John B. Breaux (D)	723,586	(53%)
W. Henson Moore (R)	646,311	(47%)
1986 Primary †		
W. Henson Moore (R)	529,433	(44%)
John B. Breaux (D)	447,328	(37%)
Samuel B. Nunez (D)	73,505	(6%)
J. E. Jumonville Jr. (D)	53,394	(5%)
Sherman A. Bernard (D)	52,479	(4%)
Others	41,102	(3%)

† In Louisiana the primary is open to candidates of all parties. If a candidate wins 50 percent or more of the vote in the primary, no general election is held.

Previous Winning Percentages: **1984 *** (86%) **1982 *** (79%) **1980 *** (100%) **1978 *** (60%) **1976 *** (83%) **1974 *** (89%) **1972 †** (100%)

** House elections.*
† Special House election.

Campaign Finance

	Receipts	Receipts from PACs	Expend-itures
1986			
Breaux (D)	$2,990,614	$898,173 (30%)	$2,948,313
Moore (R)	$6,002,459	$1,204,936 (20%)	$5,986,460

Key Votes

1987	
Enact omnibus highway bill over Reagan veto	Y
Limit testing of space-based anti-ballistic missiles	Y
Oppose banning tests of larger nuclear weapons	Y
Confirm Robert H. Bork as Supreme Court justice	N
1988	
Allow vote on campaign-finance overhaul	Y
Pass civil rights restoration bill over Reagan veto	Y
Enact omnibus trade bill over Reagan veto	Y
Approve death penalty for drug-related murders	Y
Oppose "workfare" amendment to welfare overhaul bill	Y

Voting Studies

	Presidential Support		Party Unity		Conservative Coalition	
Year	**S**	**O**	**S**	**O**	**S**	**O**
1988	61	36	73	25	92	5
1987	42	58	84	15	81	19
House Service						
1986	21	28	24	11	32	0
1985	49	44	53	36	89	5
1984	50	38	49	36	80	8
1983	52	40	41	50	85	9
1982	58	27	44	42	64	14
1981	61	24	35	42	63	7

Interest Group Ratings

Year	ADA	ACU	AFL-CIO	CCUS
1988	50	44	85	43
1987	70	19	90	28
House Service				
1986	30	63	100	25
1985	35	62	53	62
1984	15	52	25	40
1983	20	70	31	65
1982	15	71	22	67
1981	0	69	20	84

1 Bob Livingston (R)

Of Metairie — Elected 1977

Born: April 30, 1943, Colorado Springs, Colo.
Education: Tulane U., B.A. 1967, J.D. 1968.
Military Career: Navy, 1961-63; Navy Reserve, 1963-67.
Occupation: Lawyer.
Family: Wife, Bonnie Robichaux; four children.
Religion: Episcopalian.
Political Career: Republican nominee for U.S. House, 1976; Republican candidate for governor, 1987.
Capitol Office: 2412 Rayburn Bldg. 20515; 225-3015.

In Washington: A former federal prosecutor, Livingston brings an adversarial style to the normally collaborative House Appropriations Committee. While his conservative fervor seems out of place there, the committee has given Livingston a forum for supporting the Nicaraguan contras, and for his more parochial mission of delivering defense dollars to his economically struggling state.

For the first year of the 100th Congress, Livingston was trying to get out of Washington; he was running for governor of Louisiana. With his solid 1st District base and early support within the GOP, he stood a good chance of making the 1987 runoff. But his candidacy floundered badly, and the Metairie Republican wound up back in the House fighting old foes.

During the Reagan-era battles over contra aid, Livingston seemed to view each vote on the issue as a test of patriotism; Democrats usually failed the test by advancing what he saw as a policy of appeasement toward leftists in Latin America. At one point in 1986, Livingston said Congress had to provide contra aid "or else we have to admit that we are conceding Central America to the Soviet Union." A vote against that aid, he said, "will be a triumph for those who are insensitive to the cause of freedom. . . ."

After the House narrowly defeated a "humanitarian" contra-aid package in 1988, Livingston took to the House well to warn, "We might ultimately have to send our boys to some Central America front before very long because we have given peace a chance."

Livingston was also a player when the customary bipartisanship of the Intelligence Committee collapsed in the 100th Congress. The feud centered on a Democratic proposal to require that Congress be notified of all covert activities within 48 hours. In the wake of the Iran-contra scandal, Livingston sought to divert heat from the administration by focusing attention on congressional "leaks" of sensitive information. Livingston offered an amendment to the intelligence oversight bill that imposed criminal penalties on anyone who knowingly disclosed classified information.

Though his amendment lost in committee on a tie vote, several Democrats indicated they might reconsider when it came before the full House. But days before that was slated to occur, the administration accused Speaker Jim Wright of leaking classified information about events in Central America. The Rules Committee stonewalled Livingston's attempt to bring his amendment to the floor, and the subsequent flap helped derail the 48-hour notification bill.

When not battling liberals on matters of foreign policy, Livingston spends his time looking for ways to bring defense dollars home. Livingston's biography includes a list of items included in the fiscal 1989 defense appropriation that will help Louisiana: a new cargo plane for the state's Air National Guard, continued funds for Air Force reconnaissance of hurricanes, and numerous weapons systems that will be at least partially built in the state.

In the 1987 supplemental appropriations bill, Livingston championed protection for the Pelican State's shrimpers. He attached an amendment telling the federal government to back off regulations requiring shrimpers to equip their nets with "turtle-excluder devices" (TEDs). The controversial TEDs are 50-pound metal frames, each equipped with a trapdoor that opens when a netted turtle presses against it. Fine in clear-water areas, TEDs get jammed with sticks and mud in Louisiana's less pristine waters, and shrimpers lose much of their catch. After a battle with the Rules Committee — where the chairman of the fisheries committee complained that the issue was far more complex than Livingston presented — a delay in the regulation was approved.

When neither Louisiana nor the contras are involved, Livingston hews to a cost-cutting approach to appropriating. Of his willingness to cut social programs and boost defense spending, he once said: "I happen to think that none of our social programs will function too well under the red boot."

In 1988, he submitted a statement to the

Louisiana 1

Southeast — Jefferson Parish

The 1st is a largely suburban and decidedly conservative constituency. The only part of New Orleans in the district is the wealthy Lakeview section of the city.

The heart of the 1st is the heavily populated northern half of Jefferson Parish. Known for decades as the "Free State of Jefferson" because of its tolerance for casinos, slot machines and cockfights, the parish has undergone a whitewashing in the public mind as suburbanization has cleaned it up. Gambling in recent years has been restricted to horse races.

The populous east bank of Jefferson Parish is more white-collar, affluent and Republican than the areas on the west bank of the Mississippi. Elegant homes are concentrated near the shore of Lake Pontchartrain, in communities like Metairie, New Orleans' original suburb. Metairie's politics received national attention in early 1989 when Republican David Duke, a former leader of the Ku Klux Klan, was elected to the Louisiana Legislature. National Republican leaders blasted Duke as a bigot, but that did not prevent his narrow runoff victory over John Treen, brother of former GOP Gov. David C. Treen.

The west bank tends to be blue-collar, although its voters like Livingston's conservative orientation on defense and foreign policy issues. Shipbuilding and offshore oil supply companies line the Harvey Canal on the west bank. At Avondale is one of the largest shipyards in the country, the district's largest employer. Hard times in the maritime industry have forced it to rely heavily on Navy contracts for survival. Many ship workers live in nearby Gretna and Westwego, the most populous towns on the west bank. Both began as railheads; neither has shown much growth in recent years.

From Jefferson Parish, the 1st jumps some 25 miles across Lake Pontchartrain to take in St. Tammany Parish — which Livingston considered so important to his political survival that he threatened to run for the U.S. Senate in 1984 if the Legislature removed it from the 1st. Once an isolated vacation area for residents escaping the heat and humidity of New Orleans, St. Tammany Parish now is a booming suburban haven.

St. Tammany has been the fastest growing parish in the state in the last two decades. In the 1970s it had a 74 percent increase; in the 1980s it has grown more than 30 percent. Many of the newcomers are transplants from the East and Midwest who have maintained Republican voting habits. St. Tammany gave George Bush roughly 70 percent of its vote in 1988.

Population: 525,883. White 457,630 (87%), Black 58,073 (11%), Other 6,215 (1%). Spanish origin 22,817 (4%). 18 and over 367,724 (70%), 65 and over 43,197 (8%). Median age: 29.

Congressional Record about the difficulty a constituent was having filling a $5-an-hour doughnut-making job, despite the state's high unemployment. "We in Congress are always professing our concern for the less fortunate through the passage of new programs," he opined. "Perhaps it is time to start making the ones we have on the books work."

Earlier in his career, Livingston was a congressional ethics specialist, spending much of his time on business before the Committee on Standards of Official Conduct. He was one of the hard-line members of the committee, arguing strongly for the expulsion of Pennsylvania Democrat Michael "Ozzie" Myers in an Abscam bribery case and for censure of Charles H. Wilson, a California Democrat accused of several kickback charges.

At Home: The 1st District did not come close to electing a Republican to the House for a century after Reconstruction, but now that it has one, it seems quite satisfied. Livingston has had no difficulty holding the seat he won in a 1977 special election.

But Livingston has shown some restlessness in Congress. Late in 1986 he told the Baton Rouge magazine *Gris Gris*, "I've been here 10 years and I'm 43 years old. In all likelihood, in 10 years I'll be 53 years old and still broke and the only thing I can say then is that I've been here 20 years."

That led in part to his decision to run for governor in 1987. Livingston's visibility among Republicans in the New Orleans area put him in a strong position to finish near the top of a field of five major candidates, which included colorful and scandal-tainted Democratic Gov. Edwin W. Edwards, and Democratic Reps. W. J. "Billy" Tauzin and Buddy Roemer. All candidates appear on the same primary ballot in Louisiana, and as the only major Republican, Livingston had an inside track to the runoff. Many felt he could win the governorship if his runoff foe was the troubled incumbent, Edwards.

But Roemer, the eventual winner, was a

dynamic candidate who successfully appealed to many conservatives who might have voted Republican. Meanwhile, Livingston proved to be a somewhat plodding candidate; during one televised debate he lost his train of thought and fell silent during a statement on education. Livingston finished third, behind both Roemer and Edwards.

A prosperous New Orleans lawyer, former assistant U.S. attorney and veteran party worker, Livingston made his first bid for Congress in 1976, when Democrat F. Edward Hebert retired. He lost narrowly to a labor-backed Democrat, state Rep. Richard A. Tonry.

Livingston did not have to wait long, however, for a second try. Tonry's 1976 primary opponent succeeded in pressing a vote-fraud case against him, and Tonry resigned from the House in May 1977. He sought vindication in a second Democratic primary that June, but lost to state Rep. Ron Faucheux. Tonry later pleaded guilty to violations of federal campaign finance law and went to prison.

Livingston was ready to run as soon as Tonry resigned. He mounted a well-financed campaign against Faucheux that drew significant blue-collar support as well as backing from more traditional GOP voters in white-collar areas. Spending over $500,000, Livingston launched an ad blitz that showed him in his earlier job as a welder, and as a devoted family man (in contrast to Faucheux, a young bachelor). With organized labor refusing to support Faucheux, Livingston won easily, and he has met no formidable Democratic challenger since.

The only threat to his House career was posed in 1981 by the Democratic Legislature, which passed a redistricting bill that would have forced Livingston to run in a new district heavily weighted with blue-collar sections of Jefferson Parish. When Republican Gov. David C. Treen threatened a veto, the Legislature backed off.

Court-ordered redistricting in 1983 further strengthened Livingston's position, when the Legislature shifted most of New Orleans out of the 1st in exchange for the affluent "east bank" of Jefferson Parish.

Committees

Appropriations (11th of 22 Republicans)
Defense

Select Intelligence (2nd of 7 Republicans)
Legislation (ranking); Program and Budget Authorization

Elections

1988 Primary †		
Bob Livingston (R)	67,679	(78%)
George Mustakas (D)	13,091	(15%)
Eric Honig (D)	5,457	(6%)
1986 Primary ‡		
Bob Livingston (R)		Unopposed

† In Louisiana the primary is open to candidates of all parties. If a candidate wins 50 percent or more of the vote in the primary, no general election is held.

‡ In Louisiana a candidate unopposed in the primary and general elections is declared elected. His name does not appear on the ballot in either election.

Previous Winning Percentages: **1984** (88%) **1982** (86%) **1980** (88%) **1978** (86%) **1977 *** (51%)

* *Special election.*

District Vote For President

	1988	1984	1980	1976
D	61,017 (29%)	45,633 (22%)	59,716 (30%)	63,032 (39%)
R	147,346 (70%)	157,865 (77%)	130,452 (66%)	94,430 (59%)
I			4,726 (2%)	

Campaign Finance

	Receipts	Receipts from PACs	Expend-itures
1988			
Livingston (R)	$262,408	$127,834 (49%)	$555,058
Mustakas (D) †	$102,880	0	$99,065
Honig (D)	$27,006	$854 (3%)	$26,106
1986			
Livingston (R)	$236,023	$46,995 (20%)	$151,033

† Totals based on incomplete data.

Key Votes

1987	
Raise speed limit to 65 mph	Y
Approve Gephardt "fair trade" amendment	N
Ban testing of larger nuclear weapons	N
Delay "re-flagging" of Kuwaiti tankers	Y
Approve tax-raising deficit-reduction bill	N
1988	
Approve aid to Nicaraguan contras	Y
Enact civil rights restoration bill over Reagan veto	N
Kill 60-day plant-closing notification measure	Y
Pass omnibus trade bill over Reagan veto	N
Approve death penalty for drug-related murders	Y
Bar federal funds for abortions in cases of rape and incest	Y
Oppose seven-day waiting period for purchase of handguns	Y

Voting Studies

	Presidential Support		Party Unity		Conservative Coalition	
Year	S	O	S	O	S	O
1988	63	26	78	11	95	3
1987	43	22	41	16	70	2
1986	76	19	71	21	92	6
1985	74	24	81	15	96	4
1984	75	24	86	12	95	5
1983	77	18	76	17	85	12
1982	79	14	76	20	84	11
1981	76	21	71	20	76	17

Interest Group Ratings

Year	ADA	ACU	AFL-CIO	CCUS
1988	5	100	8	100
1987	0	73	7	78
1986	0	82	21	78
1985	0	86	12	86
1984	5	96	15	81
1983	5	90	6	95
1982	5	80	5	82
1981	20	71	27	94

2 Lindy (Mrs. Hale) Boggs (D)

Of New Orleans — Elected 1973

Born: March 13, 1916, Brunswick Plantation, La.
Education: Tulane U., B.A. 1935.
Occupation: High school teacher.
Family: Widow of Rep. Hale Boggs; three children.
Religion: Roman Catholic.
Political Career: No previous office.
Capitol Office: 2353 Rayburn Bldg. 20515; 225-6636.

In Washington: The grace and courtly charm that made Lindy Boggs a skilled congressional wife for nearly 30 years have since made her a beloved House member in her own right. It is now almost two decades since she succeeded her late husband, Hale Boggs — the majority leader who disappeared in a plane over Alaska in 1972 — and in that time, she has earned a Capitol Hill reputation all her own.

Boggs keeps a low profile in the House. She is well ensconced on the Appropriations Committee, where she asks for a limited number of things, most of them for her district. Her relationship with congressional chieftains is such that she always gets a hearing, and often gets her language included in legislation before the markup process even begins. When Boggs does take an issue public, she is rarely turned down.

Boggs looks out for her New Orleans district in a variety of ways. In the 100th Congress, she authored a compromise amendment to the energy and water appropriations bill directing the Energy Department to give priority to high-unemployment states (like Louisiana) in approving expenditures of court-ordered refunds from oil companies that overcharged customers. In the 99th Congress, the House accepted her amendment to a housing authorization bill forgiving a $1.6 million debt owed by New Orleans to the federal government under the now-defunct Model Cities program. In the 98th, she won House approval of a $333 million navigation project to deepen the Mississippi River to 55 feet between Baton Rouge and the Gulf of Mexico.

When Boggs is not tending to the immediate needs of her constituents, she is often working to preserve the past. An American history buff, Boggs was a board member of the American Revolution Bicentennial Administration and chaired the joint Senate-House arrangements committee for the 1976 congressional celebrations. In 1987, she was chosen by her colleagues to preside over the special congressional ceremony in Philadelphia honoring the 200th anniversary of the Constitution.

That event occurred in the midst of the Iran-contra hearings. Boggs' involvement in the celebration as well as her reputation for fairness made her the choice to deliver a sensitive Democratic response to President Reagan's weekly national radio message. Her address on the Constitution had a pointed emphasis on the separation of powers between the legislative and executive branches.

Like most accomplished public women of her generation, Boggs' résumé is filled with firsts. Among others, she is the first female Louisianan to serve in the House, and in 1976, became the first woman to chair the Democratic National Convention.

While she opposes abortion, Boggs speaks out on carefully chosen women's issues, notably civil service pay equity, domestic violence and the effort to ease credit access for women. In 1983, she led efforts to shift the emphasis in the Appropriations Committee's $4 billion jobs bill away from construction work and toward jobs women perform. "The longer you stay here," she once remarked, "the more aware of inequities you become."

Still, Boggs is temperamentally uncomfortable with strategies that alienate male colleagues, or anyone for that matter. Once asked by an incredulous reporter whether it was true that she really liked everyone, she said it was. While some of her more hard-boiled colleagues are occasionally put off by her unwavering niceness, it has made her one of the chamber's most popular members.

All of Boggs' children are also public figures. Barbara Sigmund is the mayor of Princeton, N.J.; Thomas Hale Boggs Jr. is a prominent Washington lobbyist; and Cokie Roberts is a correspondent for National Public Radio and ABC News.

At Home: Boggs has never had much trouble holding onto the seat her husband occupied for 27 years. The daughter of a wealthy sugar planter, she is well-known and popular, and has made a point of remaining on good terms with most of the diverse groups that make up her New Orleans district.

But Boggs' tenure is far from a sure thing

Louisiana 2

Jefferson Parish — New Orleans

New Orleans seems slighly exotic to most Americans, but it is a patchwork of ethnic neighborhoods, just like every other large industrial city in the country. Besides the black community that makes up more than half the city's population, there are large numbers of Italians, Irish, Cubans and the largest group of Hondurans outside Central America. These groups are not as separate from each other as they would be in other cities; the ethnic communities are scattered throughout the city in "marble cake" fashion.

The Algiers section, which sits on the west bank of the Mississippi River, is a microcosm of the city as a whole, a blend of high- and low-income residents, new condominiums and well-tended historic buildings. On the east bank, between the Mississippi and Lake Pontchartrain, is a fascinating variety of neighborhoods: comfortable Carrolton, an area of middle-class whites on the west side of the city; the wealthy Uptown section, with its professionals and academics clustered around Tulane and Loyola universities; the predominantly black Lower 9th Ward; and fast-growing New Orleans East, reaching into the city's marshland, with its middle-class black and white families.

The district also holds all of the New Orleans that tourists expect to see: the French Quarter, which includes Boggs' home on Bourbon Street; the Garden District and its historic mansions with wrought-iron fences; and downtown New Orleans.

The 75,000-seat Louisiana Superdome — site of the 1988 Republican National Convention — is the centerpiece of the construction boom that has transformed the downtown area. Along nearby Poydras Avenue, most of the major oil companies have built large office towers. Across the Mississippi River is the site of the 1984 World's Fair; it has been turned into a convention center and a food and shopping emporium called Riverwalk.

Still, in spite of the development, New Orleans sometimes seems more like the older cities of the North than the boom towns of the Sun Belt. It has lost population in recent decades, as a steady exodus of whites to the suburbs followed integration in 1960. In recent years, its unemployment rate has been high, as the oil, gas and shipping industries declined and the building boom of previous years slowed down.

Since 1980, the city has had a black majority. Now, so does the 2nd: A 1983 redistricting plan, which by court order had to create a majority-black congressional district, placed the 2nd entirely within New Orleans. With its new shape, the district is 59 percent black, making long tenure an unlikely proposition for any white incumbent.

Population: 525,331. White 205,407 (39%), Black 307,865 (59%), Other 7,697 (2%). Spanish origin 17,732 (3%). 18 and over 370,324 (71%), 65 and over 58,513 (11%). Median age: 28.

these days. Redistricting and the changing politics of race are the sources of her problem. In 1983 the Louisiana Legislature, acting under federal court order, redrew the 2nd District to give it a black majority for the first time.

Over the years, Boggs has built up strong support in the black community by backing civil rights legislation and a variety of social programs. But many in the increasingly powerful New Orleans black community feel it is time to send one of their own to Congress.

That led in 1984 to a challenge from former Appeals Court Judge Israel Augustine Jr., a longtime civil rights activist who was one of the first blacks elected to a citywide post in New Orleans. Avoiding direct attacks on Boggs, Augustine focused his efforts on spurring black turnout. But his challenge failed to win open support from powerful black Mayor Ernest N. Morial. And while Augustine had almost no support from white voters, Boggs retained a substantial base among blacks, particularly the elderly. She won by almost 30,000 votes.

Since then there has been talk of a high-profile challenge to Boggs from within the black community, but no candidate has emerged. Boggs is in her 70s, and potential candidates may simply wait for her to retire from the House.

Lindy Boggs was the only major candidate in the special election that followed her husband's death in 1972. She won the five-way Democratic primary with almost three-quarters of the vote and coasted to an even more one-sided victory over her Republican rival.

The only significant Republican effort against her came in 1980, when the national party provided some financial support to an aggressive young lawyer, Rob Couhig, who criticized the incumbent as a liberal big spender. But with support from much of the civic leadership and strong backing among blacks, Boggs won re-election by a margin of nearly 2-to-1.

Committees

Appropriations (14th of 35 Democrats)
Energy and Water Development; Legislative Branch; VA, HUD and Independent Agencies

Select Children, Youth and Families (4th of 18 Democrats)

Elections

1988 Primary †

Lindy (Mrs. Hale) Boggs (D)	63,762	(89%)
Roger C. "Captain" Johnson (R)	7,505	(11%)

1986 Primary †

Lindy (Mrs. Hale) Boggs (D)	105,661	(91%)
Roger C. "Captain" Johnson (R)	8,474	(7%)
Landi Dyess (I)	2,387	(2%)

† In Louisiana the primary is open to candidates of all parties. If a candidate wins 50 percent or more of the vote in the primary, no general election is held.

Previous Winning Percentages: **1984** (60%) **1982** (77%) **1980** (61%) **1978** (87%) **1976** (93%) **1974** (82%) **1973 *** (80%)

** Special election.*

District Vote For President

	1988	1984	1980	1976
D	111,706 (68%)	116,744 (62%)	102,723 (61%)	98,378 (62%)
R	50,134 (31%)	70,886 (38%)	60,105 (36%)	57,593 (36%)
I			3,653 (2%)	

Campaign Finance

	Receipts	Receipts from PACs	Expend-itures
1988			
Boggs (D)	$266,033	$144,300 (54%)	$252,835
1986			
Boggs (D)	$318,411	$157,150 (49%)	$261,984

Key Votes

1987

Raise speed limit to 65 mph	N
Approve Gephardt "fair trade" amendment	Y
Ban testing of larger nuclear weapons	?
Delay "re-flagging" of Kuwaiti tankers	Y
Approve tax-raising deficit-reduction bill	Y

1988

Approve aid to Nicaraguan contras	N
Enact civil rights restoration bill over Reagan veto	Y
Kill 60-day plant-closing notification measure	N
Pass omnibus trade bill over Reagan veto	Y
Approve death penalty for drug related murders	N
Bar federal funds for abortions in cases of rape and incest	Y
Oppose seven-day waiting period for purchase of handguns	N

Voting Studies

	Presidential Support		Party Unity		Conservative Coalition	
Year	**S**	**O**	**S**	**O**	**S**	**O**
1988	27	69	83	8	39	50
1987	28	67	86	5	49	47
1986	22	72	85	10	48	44
1985	28	68	82	9	38	55
1984	40	47	71	11	32	44
1983	38	60	77	14	51	44
1982	42	52	78	13	52	38
1981	53	45	71	27	59	39

Interest Group Ratings

Year	ADA	ACU	AFL-CIO	CCUS
1988	80	5	100	18
1987	68	5	93	13
1986	80	18	100	25
1985	65	19	88	29
1984	70	29	75	31
1983	70	25	88	21
1982	50	18	70	36
1981	45	7	67	32

3 W.J. "Billy" Tauzin (D)

Of Thibodaux — Elected 1980

Born: June 14, 1943, Chackbay, La.
Education: Nicholls State U., B.A. 1964; Louisiana State U., J.D. 1967.
Occupation: Lawyer.
Family: Wife, Gayle Clement; five children.
Religion: Roman Catholic.
Political Career: La. House, 1971-80.
Capitol Office: 2342 Rayburn Bldg. 20515; 225-4031.

In Washington: Tauzin's Cajun story-telling exterior conceals a shrewd legislative mind and a knowledge of energy policy that allows him to bargain successfully in the fiercely competitive Energy and Commerce Committee.

Tauzin's hopes to move beyond the House were dashed in 1987 when his gubernatorial bid flopped. But he quickly rebounded and plunged back into the familiar bayous of his committee.

Energy and Commerce is a good spot for this truck driver's son, who made his way to Washington with unusual purpose. By the age of 10 his grandfather was referring to him as "the lawyer," even though he had to overcome a rustic naiveté and a lisp before becoming student body president in high school. He went to law school at Lousiana State, where he was a classmate of John B. Breaux, now the state's junior senator. At ease in the recondite world of Louisiana politics, Tauzin is able to think on several planes at once — a valuable asset when operating in the shadow of the vulpine John D. Dingell, chairman of Energy and Commerce.

Tauzin is more than just a player on numerous issues that come before Energy and Commerce. He is a play-maker, building coalitions to win support for his point of view. His involvement with a proposal is usually a clear signal that it has to be taken seriously.

It is a key committee for Louisiana's oil and gas industry, and Tauzin is one of the industry's most knowledgeable allies. But through much of the 1980s, as the industry has been preoccupied with adjusting to softer, post-boom prices, Tauzin has also been involved in other issues — such as broadcasting deregulation, satellite-dish television reception, and an arcane offshoot of railroad deregulation.

In typical Tauzin fashion, his major influence lately has been behind the scenes, on an issue crucial to the state's economy: an effort to rewrite the Clean Air Act. He was a member of the so-called "group of nine" — Energy and Commerce members trying to forge a compromise between Dingell's protection of the automobile industry and Midwestern utilities, and environmentalists led by California's Henry A. Waxman, chairman of the Health and the Environment Subcommittee.

Tauzin's district makes him sensitive both to job and environmental concerns, and he offered a key compromise on toxic air pollutants that won support from both camps. But not enough breakthroughs were made on other aspects of the issue during the 100th Congress, and the debate carried over into the 101st.

In recent years, Tauzin has spent much of his energy trying to fashion the "superfund" hazardous-waste cleanup program in a way favorable to Louisiana industry. For petrochemical companies, the overriding issue in the 99th Congress was how the new program would be funded. Tauzin and other industry supporters were on the losing end of a 220-206 vote in 1985 that would have broadened the base of industry taxes to pay the increased costs of the expanded cleanup program. In the final 1986 legislation, a compromise tax was adopted, and the domestic oil industry won some relief, since higher fees were put on imported oil than on domestic oil.

Tauzin has made partial headway on another longstanding cause: making changes in the 1980 railroad deregulation act to aid "captive shippers" — particularly electric utilities dependent on a single rail line to bring them coal. In the 99th Congress, he won subcommittee approval of an amendment designed to help these shippers get relief from the Interstate Commerce Commission as part of legislation returning government-held Conrail to private ownership. But the amendment was stripped from the bill in full committee on a 22-20 vote, despite support from Dingell.

On non-industry issues that come before the committee, Tauzin is often a crucial swing vote, reluctant to take sides in advance and eager to negotiate.

When he does take a stand, it often has a populist flavor, as with his championing of the cause of satellite-dish owners. For several years he pushed to force cable companies to make unscrambled signals available to dish owners, who often live in rural areas not served by either regular or cable TV. In 1988 he succeeded in getting such a bill approved by an En-

Louisiana 3

South Central — Houma; New Iberia

Just west of New Orleans, Cajun Louisiana begins. The Cajuns — the word is a slurring of "Acadians" — are descendants of 15,000 French settlers who moved south from Acadia (Nova Scotia) in the 18th century. Their territory roughly covers the southern half of Louisiana. This is a predominantly Catholic area, one of the few in the Deep South, and there is a historic antipathy to the hard-shell Protestantism of north Louisiana and neighboring states.

The area is different from most of the state politically as well as culturally. There are relatively few blacks, and race is less of an issue than in other regions. There has been more loyalty to the national Democratic Party than elsewhere in Louisiana.

Most of the people in the 3rd live along a corridor that parallels U.S. 90, the thoroughfare that connects New Orleans and Lafayette. Houma, Morgan City and New Iberia are the major towns along this corridor. Dotted with marshland and bayous, this part of Louisiana has traditionally been valued for its salt, sugar cane and shrimp. But the dominant feature of the economy in recent years has been oil. Deposits are centered in St. Mary and Terrebonne parishes, as well as offshore.

High-paying oil jobs once drew thousands of workers from outside Louisiana to the coastal parishes. But with the oil boom's ebb, the region has had some of its tranquility restored. Because jobs here required few references, the "oil patch" became a haven for fugitives, runaways and illegal aliens; many of the "foreigners" who flocked here in the 1970s and early '80s, however, have moved off in search of jobs elsewhere.

At the eastern end of the district is the low, flat marshland of Plaquemines and St. Bernard parishes. For generations Plaquemines had been a world of its own, ruled with an iron hand by segregationist Leander Perez until his death in 1969. Reflecting Perez' wishes, Plaquemines cast more than 75 percent of its presidential ballots for Dixiecrat Strom Thurmond in 1948, Barry Goldwater in 1964 and George C. Wallace in 1968. But Perez' descendants have not matched his influence; they have played only a minor role in recent campaigns. George Bush carried it with roughly 60 percent of the vote in 1988.

Lying closer to New Orleans, St. Bernard has a growing blue-collar population; many of its residents work in large Kaiser Aluminum and Tenneco plants. The blue-collar element often votes Democratic in closely contested statewide races. But the GOP's presidential vote surpassed 70 percent in 1984 and 60 percent in 1988.

In the 1980s round of redistricting, the district picked up some working-class suburban territory in Jefferson Parish. In these suburbs, oil field service companies and boating and fishing firms line the intracoastal waterway feeding into the Mississippi.

Population: 527,280. White 413,383 (78%), Black 103,379 (20%), Other 8,689 (2%). Spanish origin 17,100 (3%). 18 and over 346,013 (66%), 65 and over 36,606 (7%). Median age: 26.

ergy and Commerce subcommittee on a 13-11 vote. That, and a similar bill approved by Senate Commerce the previous year, helped pressure the industry to accommodate dish owners.

On the broader issue of broadcast deregulation, Tauzin and Iowa Republican Tom Tauke teamed up in the 98th Congress to sponsor a bill favored by broadcasters to cut what they considered excessive red tape. They gathered more than 200 cosponsors, but were stalemated by Colorado's Tim Wirth, then chairman of the Telecommunications Subcommittee, and the issue never got to the floor.

Earlier in the 98th Congress, Tauzin succeeded in helping block a bill to prevent insurance companies from charging higher premiums to women than to men, which they have done on the grounds that women usually live longer. Tauzin's amendment exempted most individual policies, and also required higher premiums for health insurance that covered abortions. Faced with these complications, feminists and civil rights groups decided to drop the whole issue.

At Home: Tauzin won his House seat in 1980 with the help of an influential ally, Edwin W. Edwards, who was then between terms as governor. Seven years later the two ended up as rivals in a hot gubernatorial contest.

Tauzin's decision to run for governor in 1987 came as no great surprise; many expected him to be a strong contender for statewide office someday. But his bid was greatly complicated by the presence of incumbent Edwards, a colorful figure whose political stock had plummeted as a result of well-publicized legal entanglements from which he was eventually acquitted. Even when Edwards insisted he would seek another term, many suspected he would eventually drop out of the race.

But Edwards stayed in, and in a field of five major candidates, that spelled trouble for Tauzin. Both he and Edwards were popular among southern Louisiana Cajuns and blacks. Tauzin also had some difficulty distancing himself from his one-time mentor, though he was very critical of Edwards' candidacy.

In the end there was a surge for Democratic Rep. Buddy Roemer, and Tauzin ran a poor fourth. Edwards finished second, while GOP Rep. Bob Livingston, who competed on the same ballot, was third.

Most of Tauzin's political outings have proven more successful. His victory in a 1980 special election restored control of the 3rd District to French-speaking, Democratic south Louisiana, after nearly a decade under a Republican from suburban New Orleans, David C. Treen.

When Treen vacated the seat after winning the governorship, he tried to pick a successor, James J. Donelon, a Democrat-turned-Republican. Edwards campaigned ardently for Tauzin.

Like Edwards, Tauzin is as comfortable speaking French as English. After practicing law in the bayou towns of Houma and Thibodaux, he won a state legislative seat in 1971. During eight years in the Legislature he emerged as Edwards' protégé, serving as his floor leader in the lower chamber.

With the help of Edwards, Tauzin finished a strong second in the first round of the special election to fill Treen's House vacancy. Donelon led the four-man field, but not by a large enough margin to avoid a runoff.

The second round was bitter and expensive. Tauzin won by more than 7,000 votes, building a big lead in the Cajun parishes that offset Donelon's advantage in his home base, the New Orleans suburbs of Jefferson Parish. The unexpectedly large margin of defeat discouraged GOP leaders from trying again; they have not fielded a candidate against Tauzin since then.

Committees

Energy and Commerce (13th of 26 Democrats)
Energy and Power; Telecommunications and Finance; Transportation and Hazardous Materials

Merchant Marine and Fisheries (6th of 26 Democrats)
Coast Guard and Navigation (chairman); Fisheries and Wildlife Conservation and the Environment

Elections

1988 Primary †

W. J. "Billy" Tauzin (D)	72,110	(89%)
Millard Clement (D)	8,602	(11%)

1986 Primary ‡

W. J. "Billy" Tauzin (D)	Unopposed

† In Louisiana the primary is open to candidates of all parties. If a candidate wins 50 percent or more of the vote in the primary, no general election is held.

‡ In Louisiana a candidate unopposed in the primary and general elections is declared elected. His name does not appear on the ballot in either election.

Previous Winning Percentages: 1984 (100%) **1982** (100%) **1980** (85%) **1980 *** (53%)

** Special election.*

District Vote For President

	1988	1984	1980	1976
D	90,163 (43%)	71,890 (33%)	84,048 (43%)	81,155 (50%)
R	113,371 (55%)	142,625 (66%)	102,882 (53%)	76,767 (47%)
I	3,963 *(2%)		3,604 (2%)	

** David Duke, Independent Populist*

Campaign Finance

	Receipts	Receipts from PACs	Expend-itures
1988			
Tauzin (D)	$347,890	$263,228 (76%)	$707,085
1986			
Tauzin (D)	$378,802	$150,975 (40%)	$329,823

Key Votes

1987	
Raise speed limit to 65 mph	?
Approve Gephardt "fair trade" amendment	Y
Ban testing of larger nuclear weapons	N
Delay "re-flagging" of Kuwaiti tankers	Y
Approve tax-raising deficit-reduction bill	N
1988	
Approve aid to Nicaraguan contras	Y
Enact civil rights restoration bill over Reagan veto	Y
Kill 60-day plant-closing notification measure	N
Pass omnibus trade bill over Reagan veto	Y
Approve death penalty for drug-related murders	Y
Bar federal funds for abortions in cases of rape and incest	Y
Oppose seven-day waiting period for purchase of handguns	Y

Voting Studies

	Presidential Support		Party Unity		Conservative Coalition	
Year	S	O	S	O	S	O
1988	45	54	61	37	97	3
1987	19	24	36	20	37	5
1986	49	51	56	44	98	2
1985	54	43	55	37	91	5
1984	44	53	46	47	83	17
1983	54	45	35	60	90	10
1982	57	36	35	63	82	15
1981	67	28	36	60	91	7

Interest Group Ratings

Year	ADA	ACU	AFL-CIO	CCUS
1988	45	64	86	62
1987	20	53	75	56
1986	20	64	50	72
1985	25	65	53	65
1984	15	67	31	53
1983	25	74	35	70
1982	5	73	20	73
1981	0	71	21	79

4 Jim McCrery (R)

Of Shreveport — Elected 1988

Born: Sept. 18, 1949, Leesville, La.
Education: Louisiana Tech U., B.A. 1971; Louisiana State U., J.D. 1975.
Occupation: Lawyer.
Family: Single.
Religion: Methodist.
Political Career: Candidate for Leesville City Council, 1978.
Capitol Office: 1721 Longworth Bldg. 20515; 225-2777.

In Washington: Because he worked as an aide to Democrat Buddy Roemer, his predecessor in the 4th, McCrery came to Congress with knowledge of the legislative process. But arriving in late April 1988 after a special election, he did not have much time to put his background to use in the 100th Congress.

Both parties proved accommodating in creating a slot for McCrery on the Budget Committee, but while it was a plum that he could tout in Louisiana, it did not give him much real opportunity to legislate. Most of the panel's work was finished.

At the start of the 101st Congress, McCrery kept his spot on Budget, and he added another committee — Armed Services.

McCrery is far more mild-mannered than Roemer, now Louisiana's governor, and he shed the Democratic label that occasionally seemed ill-fitting for the conservative Roemer.

McCrery is a former business lobbyist, an orientation that did not take long to appear in Washington. When the House voted for trade legislation that included provisions requiring certain employers to notify workers in advance of plant closings, McCrery spoke out against "handcuffing" management. "My district needs jobs, not congressional micromanagement which will serve as a disincentive for the creation of jobs."

Many members long for publicity, but McCrery could have done without the attention he got in a 1989 *Roll Call* story. The article detailed his visit to a topless club in South Carolina, where he wore a dancer's bra on his head. "I'm not going to live like a monk while I'm in Congress," said McCrery.

At Home: More than any other candidate competing to succeed Roemer, McCrery was positioned to campaign on the departing incumbent's record. Many others claimed to be like Roemer, but only McCrery had worked as his aide; in a sense, Roemer's record was also his.

McCrery's GOP label, which he acquired in late 1987 before his House bid began, was an important factor in his victory. He is originally from Leesville, in the southern end of the northwest Louisiana district, and he served at one time as assistant city attorney in Shreveport. In recent years he had worked in Baton Rouge, the state capital, as a lobbyist for Georgia-Pacific Corp.

That background, and his work for Roemer, did not make him anything close to a well-known figure in the 4th. In the 10-person field vying for Roemer's seat in the March primary, McCrery stood out largely because he was the only Republican.

McCrery also put together a strong campaign. He was not a scintillating stump speaker, but he impressed many with his knowledge of legislative issues. He had gained a good reputation among legislators in Baton Rouge, where he led a 1987 lobbying effort by the Louisiana Association of Business and Industry to change tort laws. And while linking himself to Roemer, he also associated himself with Republican figures, running ads featuring President Reagan and holding a fund-raiser with former Supreme Court nominee Robert H. Bork. In a district that tends to favor Republicans in national and state elections, McCrery's conservative ties helped him outdistance the large field; Democratic state Sen. Foster Campbell ran second, earning a place in the April runoff.

Campbell was a flamboyant campaigner, particularly popular among blacks and labor, and his base was in the 4th's northern rural parishes. He had trouble in conservative Caddo Parish (Shreveport), where roughly half the vote is cast. A month before the election, Campbell was seriously injured in a car crash while driving on a closed highway. Further, it was public knowledge that Roemer planned to vote for his former aide.

After the special election, McCrery had little time to prepare for November. Fortunately for him, the Democratic effort in the 4th fizzled unexpectedly. Potential challengers stopped in their tracks when Roemer's mother, Adeline, entered the race. The 64-year-old grandmother was a poor campaigner, but no credible Democrat would challenge her name recognition and money-raising potential. Mrs. Roemer, who had once referred to McCrery as "one of the family," ended up losing badly.

Louisiana 4

Northwest — Shreveport

The 4th District is dominated by Shreveport, the conservative stronghold that fought Huey P. Long in the 1930s and became a center of Republican voting in the 1970s. It still offers the economic and social conservatism for which it long has been known.

Shreveport once conducted its battles against the rest of the state from a position of wealth and prominence made possible by the presence of the oil industry. But the oil and gas boom in northwest Louisiana has long since faded, and while Shreveport remains a branch-office town for oil companies, it has relatively few new high-paying jobs to attract people. The population growth in Shreveport and surrounding upcountry parishes has been quite slow.

The city has helped itself some by diversifying. AT&T Consumer Products (formerly Western Electric) is the major employer now, and General Motors has opened a large plant to produce light trucks. Diversification has maintained the influence of non-Southerners that began with the oil boom early this century.

Blacks constitute 41 percent of Shreveport's population and industrialization has given organized labor a toehold, but their influence is far outweighed by conservative sentiments.

Across the Red River from Shreveport is Bossier City (population 57,000), the site of Barksdale Air Force Base, headquarters for a unit of the Strategic Air Command. Many military retirees have settled here, drawn by low taxes and nearby lakes.

Nearly half of the district population lives in Caddo Parish. Another 15 percent resides in Bossier Parish. The rest are in rural parishes to the south and east.

The district's six southern parishes, with nearly one-quarter of the vote, form a transitional area between the Cajun parishes of the south and the Louisiana upcountry. They usually vote Democratic. Timber and cattle are important here, with cotton still grown in the bottomlands of the Red River. Along the Texas border is the 70-mile-long Toledo Bend Reservoir, a source of recreational dollars for Vernon and Sabine parishes.

Population: 525,194. White 352,137 (67%), Black 166,040 (32%), Other 4,030 (1%). Spanish origin 10,682 (2%). 18 and over 363,684 (69%), 65 and over 58,547 (11%). Median age: 28.

Committees

Armed Services (20th of 21 Republicans)
Investigations; Military Personnel and Compensation

Budget (10th of 14 Republicans)
Task Forces: Defense, Foreign Policy and Space; Urgent Fiscal Issues

Elections

1988 Primary †		
Jim McCrery (R)	72,228	(69%)
Adeline Roemer (D)	28,027	(27%)
Robert "Bob" Briggs (D)	5,103	(5%)
1988 Special Election		
Jim McCrery (R)	63,590	(51%)
Foster L. Campbell Jr. (D)	62,214	(49%)
1988 Special Primary †		
Jim McCrery (R)	39,624	(31%)
Foster L. Campbell Jr. (D)	24,220	(19%)
Stan Tiner (D)	19,567	(16%)
June Phillips (D)	16,829	(13%)
Claude "Buddy" Leach (D)	13,646	(11%)

† In Louisiana the primary is open to candidates of all parties. If a candidate wins 50 percent or more of the vote in the primary, no general election is held.

District Vote For President

	1988	1984	1980	1976
D	77,042 (40%)	67,788 (34%)	81,619 (44%)	68,747 (45%)
R	111,878 (59%)	130,400 (65%)	99,476 (54%)	80,311 (53%)

Interest Group Ratings

Year	ADA	ACU	AFL-CIO	CCUS
1988	12	94	20	100

Key Votes

1988	
Pass omnibus trade bill over Reagan veto	N
Approve death penalty for drug-related murders	Y
Bar federal funds for abortions in cases of rape and incest	#
Oppose seven-day waiting period for purchase of handguns	Y

Campaign Finance

	Receipts	Receipts from PACs	Expend-itures
1988			
McCrery (R)	$791,895	$287,341 (36%)	$742,158
Roemer (D)	$176,655	$6,500 (4%)	$175,450
Briggs (D) †	$50	0	$127
1988 Special Election ‡			
McCrery (R)	$284,110	$63,221 (22%)	$235,760
Campbell (D)	$293,930	$56,300 (19%)	$255,865

† Totals based on incomplete data.
‡ Totals based on pre-election data.

Voting Studies

	Presidential Support		Party Unity		Conservative Coalition	
Year	S	O	S	O	S	O
1988	61 †	35 †	80 †	18 †	94 †	0 †

† Not eligible for all recorded votes.

5 Jerry Huckaby (D)

Of Ringgold — Elected 1976

Born: July 19, 1941, Hodge, La.
Education: Louisiana State U., B.S. 1963; Georgia State U., M.B.A. 1968.
Occupation: Farmer; engineer.
Family: Wife, Suzanna Woodard; two children.
Religion: Methodist.
Political Career: No previous office.
Capitol Office: 2421 Rayburn Bldg. 20515; 225-2376.

In Washington: Huckaby was the Boll Weevils' choice in 1989 for a slot informally designated for a Southern Democrat on the Budget Committee. And if the leadership permits committee members a meaningful role in the 101st Congress, Huckaby's disposition and connections suggest he will be among those to play it.

Huckaby takes his political bearings from home — rural Louisiana — but he does not shy from highly technical issues, is not afraid to cut deals and could serve as a bridge to conservatives of both parties. He is also a known quantity to the Budget chairman, Democrat Leon E. Panetta of California; each entered the House in 1977 and each rose to chair subcommittees on the Agriculture Committee.

Huckaby has used the Agriculture and Interior committees to defend his and his state's interests — cotton, sugar, soybeans, timber and oil. In his first try for the Budget Committee in 1985, he argued that no one else was representing farmers' point of view in budget deliberations. He did not get the seat, but has spent the years since speaking loudly for farmers as chairman of the Agriculture Subcommittee on Cotton, Rice and Sugar.

Huckaby left his imprint on most of the 100th Congress' major agriculture measures. During the overhaul of the Farm Credit System, for instance, he played a key role in negotiations, arguing for a broadly powered board to ride herd on bad loans and supervise financial assistance to system banks. Still, parochial interests led him to vote against the bill as it left committee, the lone Democrat to do so. The bill restructured Louisiana's farm credit banks in a manner that made it impolitic to vote yes.

The large growers that Huckaby speaks for on Agriculture are sophisticated players in the legislative process, adept at using lobbying, campaign contributions and honoraria to make sure their voices are heard. Huckaby helps them make decisions about which members need to be courted at which times.

Although cotton and rice growers make up a relatively small group compared with other commodity interests, Huckaby and other members representing Southern states where cotton and rice are grown played a proportionately larger role in the 1985 reauthorization of the farm bill. With a significant amount of help from Southerners in the Senate, Huckaby worked for cotton and rice programs that contained some of the boldest — and possibly most expensive — provisions in the entire farm package.

Those provisions included a new market-oriented price-support mechanism for cotton and rice growers called a "marketing loan." Rather than allow growers to default on their price-support loans if prices failed to rise above the loan rate (as happened under the existing system), the agriculture secretary must allow rice growers, and has the option to allow cotton growers, the chance to repay the loan at the lower rate commodities bring on the market.

"We're going back to the marketplace," Huckaby said of the plan, "and it's clear to me we are going to increase sales. I think the wheat and corn people are going to want to go this approach before long."

After the farm bill had passed, Huckaby continued to look out for his growers, especially the largest ones. In 1986, with concern about the cost of farm programs growing, Massachusetts Republican Silvio O. Conte pushed to amend an appropriations bill to prevent farmers from legally escaping limits on payments to individual recipients.

Some commodity groups would not have been particularly hurt by stricter limits and actually favored the proposal as a way to mollify critics of farm spending, but it would have hurt some cotton producers. Huckaby knew he could not block the reformers, so he joined them to craft a measure better to his liking; it protected many cotton producers.

In 1987, he worked on the compromise in the year-end budget reconciliation bill that capped the farm income payments at $100,000 and further tightened the loopholes.

Huckaby tried unsuccessfully in 1988 to rework the cotton programs. Cotton growers are

Louisiana 5

North — Monroe

The rural 5th is one of the poorest areas of Louisiana. Incomes are less than half the level of those in Louisiana's major urban centers, and the area has been losing population. Forests cover much of the district, and what little industry exists is timber-related. Lumber mills are scattered throughout the 5th.

Small farmers backed the populism embodied by Gov. Huey P. Long, a native of Winn Parish, in the 5th District. But after World War II, the region became a segregationist bulwark. Both Barry Goldwater in 1964 and George C. Wallace in 1968 drew a higher vote in the 5th than in any other Louisiana district. In recent years, most of the parishes here have been reliably Republican in presidential elections. One of them — LaSalle — gave George Bush almost 75 percent of its vote in 1988.

GOP strength is concentrated in the district's only major population center, Ouachita Parish (Monroe), home for about one-quarter of the district's voters. Monroe (population 56,000) is at the center of a large gas field and long has been the trading hub of northeast Louisiana. The opening of Interstate 20 has pumped new life into the city, making it a convention center and overnight stop along the heavily traveled thoroughfare from Atlanta to Dallas. Monroe is nearly one-half black. Ouachita Parish gave Bush more about 69 percent in 1988.

The Democratic areas in the 5th are along the Mississippi and Red rivers; blacks comprise a majority of the population in three of the four parishes adjoining those waterways. Two of them — East Carroll and Madison — were the only parishes in north Louisiana to buck the local Wallace tide and vote for Hubert H. Humphrey for president in 1968. Both voted for Michael S. Dukakis in 1988.

Population: 527,220. White 359,467 (68%), Black 164,664 (31%). Spanish origin 5,361 (1%). 18 and over 360,687 (68%), 65 and over 66,071 (13%). Median age: 28.

subject to a so-called 50-92 provision, which allows them to collect 92 percent of government crop income-subsidy payments if they opt to plant only 50 percent of their acreage. As cotton supplies rose, and prices fell, though, Huckaby tried to bring cotton growers under the 0-92 program (plant no land and get 92 percent) legislated in 1987 for wheat and feed grain producers. Huckaby's bill passed the House but went no farther. A bill to promote extra-long staple cotton did become law.

Huckaby had an important hand in the sugar provisions of the 1985 farm bill. When an attempt was made on the floor to reduce sugar price supports to help consumers and open U.S. markets to sugar-producing nations that needed money to repay debts to U.S. banks, Huckaby and his allies on Agriculture argued that the price supports were protecting U.S. jobs. "This is the first opportunity you are going to have to vote on a trade bill, on a jobs bill," Huckaby said during debate. "There are 100,000 American jobs at stake in this industry.

Although much of Huckaby's focus has been on crop subsidies, agriculture is not his only interest. Huckaby, once a farmer, is also an electrical engineer. And in the 100th Congress, he again showed a penchant for plunging into the work of the Interior Subcommittee on Energy.

Huckaby introduced House-passed legislation in 1988 to require commercial nuclear plants, during any unusual event, to electronically transmit data on pressure, temperature and water levels to the Nuclear Regulatory Commission in Washington so its experts could monitor and advise on the situation.

He continued work begun in the 99th Congress to settle a fight in the Interior Committee over nuclear liability. Huckaby helped negotiate the successor to the Price-Anderson Act, raising the nuclear power industry's liability to $7 billion in an accident. He pressed the industry's position in the debate over how to compensate lawyers in liability suits.

Shell Oil Co. became his cause when it appeared that legislation to sanction South Africa for its apartheid society would prevent Shell, because of the activities in South Africa of its parent corporation, from bidding on new U.S. oil leases in the Gulf of Mexico. Shell is the largest wildcat driller in the gulf and employs thousands in Louisiana. Huckaby led the fight against the measure in Interior and on the floor, joining forces with conservative Republicans in opposing the bill. It is one reason why liberals on the committee are not unhappy to see him take a leave from Interior while he serves on Budget.

In the 99th Congress he was one of many coastal-state representatives fighting to win a greater share of disputed revenues from oil and gas formations straddling the border between state and federal offshore lands. The 1986 budget resolution included a compromise of 27 percent for the states, and Huckaby did his part on the Interior Committee to push for the same percentage of future revenues. During work on budget reconciliation, Interior Chairman Morris K. Udall proposed dividing those royalties by the actual amount of oil or gas drained from the common pool, but Huckaby bested him in a series of close votes.

At Home: While ambitious young politicians waited for veteran Rep. Otto E. Passman to retire, Huckaby took the risk of challenging him in 1976, defeated him in the Democratic primary and won the seat. It was Huckaby's first campaign. But the wealthy dairy farmer mounted an aggressive, well-financed challenge that capitalized on Passman's advanced age (76) and political problems.

The 15-term incumbent had been beset with charges of irregularities in his congressional travel expenses. And he had been criticized for his 1971 vote against a constitutional amendment to permit prayer in public schools.

With Passman's defeat, Republicans had high hopes of capturing the seat. Their candidate, Monroe businessman Frank Spooner, had a large treasury.

But Spooner was unable to document his basic campaign theme — that Huckaby was a liberal Democrat out of step with the conservative district. Huckaby offset the Republican's 7,000-vote plurality in the district's major population center, Ouachita Parish (Monroe), and repeated his strong primary showing in the rural parishes to win the seat by 8,000 votes.

Some Democratic politicians within the district were annoyed that the upstart Huckaby had taken the prize so many of them had been waiting for. One of them, state Sen. James H. Brown Jr., challenged Huckaby in 1978. But Huckaby won easily and has had no trouble since.

Committees

Agriculture (7th of 27 Democrats)
Cotton, Rice and Sugar (chairman); Forests, Family Farms and Energy

Budget (15th of 21 Democrats)
Task Forces: Budget Process, Reconciliation and Enforcement; Community Development and Natural Resources

Elections

1988 Primary †		
Jerry Huckaby (D)	51,113	(71%)
Jack Wright (D)	14,343	(20%)
Bradley Thomason Roark (R)	6,403	(9%)
1986 Primary †		
Jerry Huckaby (D)	96,200	(68%)
Thomas "Bud" Brady (D)	32,284	(23%)
Fred Huenefeld (D)	11,966	(9%)

† In Louisiana the primary is open to candidates of all parties. If a candidate wins 50 percent or more of the vote in the primary, no general election is held.

Previous Winning Percentages: 1984 (100%) **1982** (83%) **1980** (89%) **1978** (52%) **1976** (53%)

District Vote For President

	1988	1984	1980	1976
D	70,477 (36%)	69,254 (32%)	83,040 (42%)	83,034 (48%)
R	122,309 (62%)	140,427 (66%)	110,824 (56%)	85,900 (50%)
I	3,771 *(2%)			

** David Duke, Independent Populist*

Campaign Finance

	Receipts	Receipts from PACs	Expend-itures
1988			
Huckaby (D)	$266,854	$131,650 (49%)	$194,021
Wright (D) †	$9,021	0	$9,007
1986			
Huckaby (D)	$234,409	$113,895 (49%)	$326,332
Brady (D)	$41,294	0	$41,293
Huenefeld (D)	$25,634	0	$25,634

† Totals based on incomplete data.

Key Votes

1987	
Raise speed limit to 65 mph	Y
Approve Gephardt "fair trade" amendment	Y
Ban testing of larger nuclear weapons	Y
Delay "re-flagging" of Kuwaiti tankers	Y
Approve tax-raising deficit-reduction bill	N
1988	
Approve aid to Nicaraguan contras	Y
Enact civil rights restoration bill over Reagan veto	Y
Kill 60-day plant-closing notification measure	N
Pass omnibus trade bill over Reagan veto	Y
Approve death penalty for drug-related murders	Y
Bar federal funds for abortions in cases of rape and incest	Y
Oppose seven-day waiting period for purchase of handguns	Y

Voting Studies

	Presidential Support		Party Unity		Conservative Coalition	
Year	S	O	S	O	S	O
1988	44	45	56	35	84	5
1987	43	55	61	32	91	5
1986	41	49	53	31	80	4
1985	49	49	51	38	89	7
1984	49	46	48	42	80	14
1983	54	45	44	51	85	13
1982	51	38	46	46	75	14
1981	67	25	33	61	83	9

Interest Group Ratings

Year	ADA	ACU	AFL-CIO	CCUS
1988	40	65	57	77
1987	44	35	50	64
1986	20	65	31	73
1985	35	57	41	71
1984	25	57	15	57
1983	35	70	35	65
1982	25	48	32	45
1981	10	93	27	76

6 Richard H. Baker (R)

Of Baton Rouge — Elected 1986

Born: May 22, 1948, New Orleans, La.
Education: Louisiana State U., B.A. 1971.
Occupation: Real-estate broker.
Family: Wife, Kay Carpenter; two children.
Religion: Methodist.
Political Career: La. House, 1973-87; candidate for La. Senate, 1980.
Capitol Office: 404 Cannon Bldg. 20515; 225-3901.

In Washington: Baker spent most of his political career as a labor-oriented Democrat, but all that changed when he switched parties and made his way to the House. In his first term he was as conservative as any Republican in his delegation, voting with the GOP leadership more often than his Louisiana colleagues, and earning an AFL-CIO rating of just 15.

Baker made it to the state House by the time he was 22, but that achievement has not made him a legislative hot dog. In his first House term he proved to be one of the most low-key members of his class.

Some of Baker's low-profile efforts were on high-profile issues. In 1988 he offered an amendment to an omnibus drug bill in the House making the illegal sale of anabolic steroids a felony rather than a misdemeanor. Baker voiced concern that too many had been abusing steroids, particularly athletes. "I think that amateur and professional athletics ought to be measured by one's own self-sacrifice and hard work and not the result of some pharmaceutical achievement," he said.

Baker also was concerned about U.S. embassy security in communist countries in the wake of revelations of security breaches in the Soviet Union. To reduce the potential for embassy guards to be wooed by those countries, he offered an amendment to the State Department authorization to limit Marine guards to six month assignments in communist nations. The House agreed to a substitute changing the limit to 12 months and allowing the secretary of defense to waive it.

Baker was probably more visible in Louisiana. In addition to regular political and constituent work, he chaired George Bush's Louisiana campaign and led the state's delegation at the convention in New Orleans.

Baker, a real-estate developer, spent his first two years on the Interior Committee, but in the 101st Congress will be in a better position to pursue business-oriented interests as a member of the Banking Committee. He also serves on the Small Business Committee.

At Home: After GOP Rep. W. Henson Moore announced plans to run for the Senate in 1986, Baker put together an unusual coalition of country-club Republicans and blue-collar Democrats to defeat a better-financed Democratic opponent, state Senate president pro tempore Thomas Hudson.

It was an odd election. Baker had spent 15 years in the Legislature as a Democrat, switching parties in 1985 at the urging of GOP leaders who saw him as the only candidate capable of stopping Hudson. Representing a blue-collar Baton Rouge district, he had been identified for most of his career as a labor-oriented lawmaker. Hudson, on the other hand, represented a white-collar constituency.

Baker could not compete with Hudson when it came to endorsements from the district's organized political forces. His 1976 stand against right-to-work legislation cost him important business backing, and his party switch cost him support from the previously supportive AFL-CIO. Only in the rural parishes, where he had Farm Bureau backing, did Baker receive help from a significant pressure group.

But Baker did have a core of committed GOP volunteers, many of them affluent suburbanites who had supported Moore. TV ads linked Baker to the popular Republican incumbent and gave him momentum. Baker also had a reputation as a "clean government" reformer, and he expressed his desire to work for revised campaign finance and ethics-in-government measures in Congress.

Baker also developed an effective appeal to diverse religious groups. He had been a Methodist lay preacher, and he expanded his support among fundamentalists with an endorsement from Baton Rouge-based TV evangelist Jimmy Swaggart, then still an influential figure. Many Catholics appreciated Baker's opposition to abortion and his support for state aid to parochial schools.

TV advertisements showing him with his wife and children contrasted Baker with his twice-divorced foe. And Baker made many personal appearances, especially in blue-collar areas where he needed to reinforce his popularity. On Election Day, Baker nearly carried Hudson's Senate district, and did carry Hudson's own precinct. Only in black areas of Baton Rouge was there a uniformly strong Democratic vote.

Louisiana 6

East Central — Baton Rouge

The 6th extends from the state capital and university community of Baton Rouge on the west to Bogalusa, a town on the Mississippi River known for racial turmoil, on the east. The territory in between is primarily rural, with pine forests and small farms providing the base for lumbering and agriculture. But there has been increasing suburbanization, as commuters from Baton Rouge and New Orleans have moved out to get more breathing space.

Baton Rouge now has a population of 241,000 and has surpassed Shreveport as the second-largest city in Louisiana. State government employees and service workers in Baton Rouge provide a large white-collar base that has made Republicans dominant here in state and national elections. But the large academic communities at Louisiana State University (27,000 students) and predominantly black Southern University (9,800 students), the extensive labor presence and the city's 37 percent black population keep Democrats competitive.

About two-thirds of the voters in the 6th reside in the Baton Rouge area. The rest live to the east, in the Florida parishes, so named because they were part of Spanish Florida until 1810. Culturally, this area is more similar to neighboring Mississippi than to the rest of Louisiana. Locally, the Democratic Party remains strong, although suburbanization has brought increased Republican strength in Livingston Parish.

Farther east is Tangipahoa Parish. Its leading town, Hammond (population 20,000), lies at the junction of two Interstate highways and is the trade center for the Florida parishes. The Hammond area, home to a large Italian-American community, is one of the nation's leading suppliers of strawberries. Washington Parish, at the eastern end of the district, is a heavily forested rural backwater bounded on the north and east by Mississippi.

Population: 524,770. White 387,238 (74%), Black 131,746 (25%), Other 3,406 (1%). Spanish origin 8,268 (2%). 18 and over 362,252 (69%), 65 and over 41,937 (8%). Median age: 27.

Committees

Banking, Finance and Urban Affairs (17th of 20 Republicans)
Financial Institutions Supervision, Regulation and Insurance; Housing and Community Development; International Development, Finance, Trade and Monetary Policy

Small Business (10th of 17 Republicans)
Procurement, Tourism and Rural Development; SBA, the General Economy and Minority Enterprise Development

Elections

1988 Primary ‡

Richard H. Baker (R)	Unopposed	

1986 Primary †

Richard H. Baker (R)	76,833	(51%)
Thomas H. Hudson (D)	67,774	(45%)
Willis E. Blackwell (D)	6,120	(4%)

† In Louisiana the primary is open to candidates of all parties. If a candidate wins 50 percent or more of the vote in the primary, no general election is held.

‡ In Louisiana a candidate unopposed in the primary and general elections is declared elected. His name does not appear on the ballot in either election.

District Vote For President

	1988		1984		1980		1976	
D	82,815	(39%)	77,570	(35%)	85,067	(44%)	73,695	(53%)
R	125,710	(60%)	141,115	(64%)	103,932	(53%)	61,253	(44%)
I					4,192	(2%)		

Campaign Finance

	Receipts	Receipts from PACs	Expend-itures
1988			
Baker (R)	$287,230	$124,525 (43%)	$270,899
1986			
Baker (R)	$434,290	$85,467 (20%)	$433,281
Hudson (D)	$714,938	$202,660 (28%)	$712,083

Key Votes

1987	
Raise speed limit to 65 mph	Y
Approve Gephardt "fair trade" amendment	N
Ban testing of larger nuclear weapons	N
Delay "re-flagging" of Kuwaiti tankers	N
Approve tax-raising deficit-reduction bill	?
1988	
Approve aid to Nicaraguan contras	Y
Enact civil rights restoration bill over Reagan veto	N
Kill 60-day plant-closing notification measure	Y
Pass omnibus trade bill over Reagan veto	N
Approve death penalty for drug-related murders	Y
Bar federal funds for abortions in cases of rape and incest	Y
Oppose seven-day waiting period for purchase of handguns	Y

Voting Studies

	Presidential Support		Party Unity		Conservative Coalition	
Year	**S**	**O**	**S**	**O**	**S**	**O**
1988	63	32	80	10	97	3
1987	66	30	76	16	84	5

Interest Group Ratings

Year	ADA	ACU	AFL-CIO	CCUS
1988	5	100	15	100
1987	4	81	6	100

7 Jimmy Hayes (D)

Of Lafayette — Elected 1986

Born: Dec. 21, 1946, Lafayette, La.

Education: U. of Southwestern Louisiana, B.S. 1967; Tulane U., J.D. 1970.

Military Career: Louisiana Air National Guard, 1968-74.

Occupation: Lawyer; real-estate developer.

Family: Wife, Leslie Owen; three children.

Religion: Methodist.

Political Career: No previous office.

Capitol Office: 503 Cannon Bldg. 20515; 225-2031.

In Washington: House Democratic leaders are always looking for alliances with shrewd Southern Democrats, and in Hayes they found their sentiments requited. As a freshman, he made a name for himself by emerging as the party point man in a battle over controversial drug-related amendments pushed by conservative Pennsylvania Republican Robert S. Walker.

The Science Committee is rarely the center of House activity, but that was where Hayes had a chance to shine. His moment came in 1988, when Walker, also on Science, began pushing amendments to authorization bills barring spending for any grant or contract "until the recipient shall certify to the government that they will provide a drug-free work place."

Democrats cried that the amendment could wreak havoc on contracts and create a police-state mentality, but they were clearly in a pinch, wary of seeming weak on drugs in an election year. Hayes volunteered to try to forge a compromise. Working with Walker, he helped hammer out a softer version that was adopted in subcommittee even before it was committed to paper. The compromise included expanded provisions for appeal and gave the government an option not to enforce provisions for withholding funds. Some Democrats still objected, but the revised language was attached to a Science authorization measure.

However, Walker took his "drug-free work place" crusade to the floor, targeting other bills. The Democratic leadership appointed a task force, led by Hayes, to respond. Ultimately it produced a plan based on the compromise from the Science Committee; in attaching it to an omnibus drug bill, Hayes' group won the support of Walker. A key change in the final compromise prevented the government from withholding payments for a single violation.

Hayes' involvement in the complicated and sensitive drug issue established him as an operator in the House; he impressed colleagues with his grasp of substance, amused them with his wit, and showed a knack for rounding up Southern support for the leadership. When it came time to orient new freshmen in 1988, Hayes was called on to help them learn the ropes.

At Home: Hayes had never run for office when he began his 1986 House campaign, and he was not the clear choice of Democratic regulars or activists. But thanks to his steady emphasis on traditional Democratic issues, he was able to benefit from the same coalition of unions, blacks and courthouse politicians that lifted John B. Breaux, his predecessor in the 7th, to victory in Louisiana's 1986 Senate contest.

Hayes, an investor and developer, had the money to court any audience. The son of a prominent independent oilman, he launched his campaign with a flurry of ads stressing his concerns about two issues crucial to troubled south Louisiana: jobs and agriculture.

But Hayes, who resigned his appointed job as state commissioner of financial institutions to campaign, was challenged from the right and left by experienced foes: On the right was state Rep. Margaret Lowenthal, a wealthy pro-business Democrat; on the left was state Rep. James David Cain, a labor-oriented legislator backed by many blacks and blue-collar workers.

Hayes' strong personality initially put off some potential supporters, but he made steady improvements as a campaigner, and built support in business and political circles in his hometown of Lafayette. That, added to his media effort, put him in a runoff with Lowenthal.

Despite the blue-collar tilt of her legislative district, Lowenthal's record was regarded as anti-labor by many Cain supporters. Hayes seized the center, won Cain's backing and made a special effort to woo his labor and rural allies. Lowenthal, known as a maverick in the Legislature, played up her independence and her reformist image: Noting Hayes' state job, she tried to tie him to scandal-tainted Democratic Gov. Edwin W. Edwards.

The Realtors and the American Medical Association made independent expenditures for Lowenthal, but Hayes ran ads with local doctors and Realtors asking why the national groups were directing them. Hayes won with 57 percent.

Louisiana 7

Southwest — Lake Charles; Lafayette

It would be difficult to call the 7th a depressed district, if only because the "bon temps" Cajun ethic is so thoroughly a part of its identity. But, economically at least, the 7th has had a rough time. It suffered after the bust of southern Louisiana's oil boom.

Founded by Acadian refugees, Lafayette is the traditional center of Cajun culture. Many of the street signs are in French, and the radio station at the University of Southwest Louisiana broadcasts in both French and English.

But the city's boom and bust have caused rapid changes. The offshore oil discoveries that drew oil company branch offices transformed Lafayette from a Cajun market town into a mini-Houston during the 1970s. At its peak in the early 1980s, the city was becoming a stronghold of white-collar Republicanism.

With its recent troubles, however, Lafayette's Cajun outline is beginning to reassert itself. Republican candidates still do well in the southern half of the city, home to executives for the corporations that remain. But gone are many of the risk-taking businessmen who helped the the boom get started, and many of the workers lured from other states by oil-related jobs.

In the smaller towns dotting the rest of this part of Acadiana, the Cajun heritage has always remained strong. To the east of Lafayette in St. Martin Parish is St. Martinville, once known as Le Petit Paris because it was a haven for Royalists after the French Revolution. The farm land west of Crowley is one of the nation's leading sources of rice.

Beyond the rice fields lies a much different part of the 7th, a grimy concentration of heavy industry that centers on Lake Charles and extends into Texas. Blue-collar workers are a more dominant influence in this region. With a heavy concentration of petrochemical plants, Lake Charles is one of the most unionized cities in Louisiana, and it is strongly Democratic. Michael S. Dukakis drew more than 53 percent of the vote in 1988 in Lake Charles and surrounding Calcasieu Parish; he got less than 40 percent in Lafayette, and was neck and neck with George Bush in Acadia Parish.

Population: 525,361. White 415,979 (79%), Black 105,508 (20%). Spanish origin 8,920 (2%). 18 and over 355,571 (68%), 65 and over 46,188 (9%). Median age: 27.

Committees

Public Works and Transportation (22nd of 31 Democrats)
Aviation; Water Resources

Science, Space and Technology (25th of 30 Democrats)
Investigations and Oversight; Science, Research and Technology; Space Science and Applications

Elections

1988 Primary ‡

Jimmy Hayes (D)	Unopposed	

1986 General

Jimmy Hayes (D)	109,205	(57%)
Margaret Lowenthal (D)	82,293	(43%)

‡ In Louisiana a candidate unopposed in the primary and general elections is declared elected. His name does not appear on the ballot in either election.

District Vote For President

	1988		1984		1980		1976	
D	105,717	(49%)	91,106	(40%)	96,448	(48%)	95,887	(59%)
R	106,169	(49%)	132,813	(59%)	98,749	(49%)	62,691	(38%)
I					4,097	(2%)		

Campaign Finance

	Receipts	Receipts from PACs	Expend-itures
1988			
Hayes (D)	$304,917	$206,100 (68%)	$268,116
1986			
Hayes (D)	$850,942	$46,550 (5%)	$846,953
Lowenthal (D)	$352,661	$75,282 (21%)	$350,505

Key Votes

1987	
Raise speed limit to 65 mph	Y
Approve Gephardt "fair trade" amendment	Y
Ban testing of larger nuclear weapons	Y
Delay "re-flagging" of Kuwaiti tankers	Y
Approve tax-raising deficit-reduction bill	N
1988	
Approve aid to Nicaraguan contras	Y
Enact civil rights restoration bill over Reagan veto	Y
Kill 60-day plant-closing notification measure	N
Pass omnibus trade bill over Reagan veto	Y
Approve death penalty for drug-related murders	Y
Bar federal funds for abortions in cases of rape and incest	Y
Oppose seven-day waiting period for purchase of handguns	Y

Voting Studies

	Presidential Support		Party Unity		Conservative Coalition	
Year	S	O	S	O	S	O
1988	35	57	70	23	87	13
1987	36	57	72	19	79	19

Interest Group Ratings

Year	ADA	ACU	AFL-CIO	CCUS
1988	55	52	92	62
1987	48	22	69	53

8 Clyde C. Holloway (R)

Of Forest Hill — Elected 1986

Born: Nov. 28, 1943, Lecompte, La.
Education: Attended National School of Aeronautics, Kansas City, Mo., 1966.
Occupation: Nursery owner.
Family: Wife, Cathy Kohlhepp; four children.
Religion: Baptist.
Political Career: Sought GOP nomination for U.S. House, 1980, 1985.
Capitol Office: 1206 Longworth Bldg. 20515; 225-4926.

In Washington: Holloway is no legislative star, but his Republican colleagues have reason to look up to him. At a time when they are deeply frustrated by their inability to win a House majority, Holloway is a reminder that political miracles do happen. He not only wins in a district that is roughly 85 percent Democratic, he does so while siding with his party 76 percent of the time.

Holloway is an affable nurseryman who does not seem to run scared in Washington; he seems to run happy, simply enjoying the opportunity to serve from a district so heavily stacked against his party. Day in and day out, he supported President Reagan and voted with a majority of Republicans just about as often as many members from solidly Republican districts.

But Holloway is not blind to political realities, and on some high-profile issues he departs from the party line. In 1987, he voted to override Reagan's veto of a highway bill that had funding earmarked for Louisiana. And in 1988, he voted to override Reagan's veto of an omnibus trade bill that included plant-closing notification provisions.

"I wouldn't vote for a few of the bills that I vote for if I was in Bob Livingston's district in Louisiana," Holloway said in 1987, "because it is a conservative district, and they don't have the very, very, very hard times that we have in my district."

Like most freshmen on the Agriculture Committee, Holloway made no big impression, but he did generate some favorable publicity at home. During debate on the drought-relief bill, he kept an eye out for Louisiana soybeans.

Holloway got much more attention on the subject of day care, a hot issue in the 100th Congress. Holloway, one of a number of Republicans to offer his own alternative to a Democratic day-care bill, proposed giving a refundable tax credit to all parents with preschool children, not just to parents who pay for day care. The bill, which some felt would encourage home care, never went anywhere, but some conservatives, including Education Secretary William J. Bennett, latched onto it. Some legislators who barely knew the Louisiana freshman were surprised to receive mass mailings from conservatives touting the "Holloway Bill."

At Home: There is such a thing as being in the wrong place at the right time.

In 1986, a crowd of Democrats lined up to succeed retiring Rep. Cathy (Mrs. Gillis) Long, but Holloway was the only Republican on the nonpartisan primary ballot. His narrow political base was firm enough to send him into a November runoff against attorney Faye Williams, a liberal black Democrat whose base was equally narrow. Had any of several white Democrats made it to the runoff against Holloway, the Republican would have had little chance.

He had entered the contest with a reputation as something of a political bumpkin, stemming from two clumsy and ill-fated congressional campaigns — one in 1980 against Democratic Rep. Gillis W. Long, and another in 1985 against Cathy Long, who won the 8th in a special election following her husband's death.

Despite the impression given by those efforts, Holloway's involvement in local issues had left him with a dedicated following and demonstrated that he possessed some degree of political skill. He first appeared on the scene in 1980, when he was point man in a protest against busing to achieve integration in Alexandria and surrounding Rapides Parish. Holloway led efforts to create a private school as an alternative for anti-busing parents in his hometown of Forest Hill, and he became the school's chairman of the board.

There was never any doubt that race would be a crucial factor in a contest between a black woman and a white Republican known for his anti-busing activism. But Holloway did not directly raise the issue, and sought to dispel any impression that he was racist by arguing that he had fought busing, not integration. "I believe it is an evil," he said of busing at one point. "I believe blacks think it is an evil." His campaign brochures pictured him in a schoolroom with several black children.

Holloway tried to put Williams on the

Louisiana 8

Central — Alexandria

In some ways, the 8th is a microcosm of Louisiana. It starts in the piney woods of the north, moves southeast through Cajun country, crosses the Mississippi River and ends up on the outskirts of metropolitan New Orleans.

But the district is poorer, more rural, and more loyally Democratic than the state as a whole. Jimmy Carter carried it in both the 1976 and 1980 presidential elections with a percentage higher than he received in any other district in Louisiana. The 8th went for Reagan in 1984, but Holloway's two election victories still cut against the normal political grain. Democrat Michael S. Dukakis carried the district in 1988.

The 8th is centered on Rapides Parish, including Alexandria (population 51,000), the district's major population center and its biggest outpost of conservative thinking. With neighboring Pineville (population 14,000), Alexandria is the commercial and military center of central Louisiana. Nearby forests fuel lumber mills. Just outside town is England Air Force Base.

Rapides, Avoyelles and Evangeline parishes together cast about 40 percent of the district vote. These three parishes constitute a border between Louisiana's Protestant north and its Cajun Catholic south. Cotton, a leading crop of north Louisiana, is grown along the Red River. Rice and sugar cane are grown nearby.

The 8th takes in the northern tip of Cajun country, which begins just below Rapides Parish and extends south and east toward Baton Rouge. This area is racially more tolerant than the rest of the district, and it is reliably Democratic in most elections.

Farther east are the Mississippi River parishes, the center of Louisiana's productive "sugar bowl." Along the river south of Baton Rouge are a number of old plantations, a reminder of the wealth and power of the antebellum planters. The plantation buildings coexist incongruously with modern petrochemical plants, a source of pollution, jobs and working-class voters.

The combination of organized labor and blacks — about 40 percent of the population in the six river parishes — makes this area one of the most Democratic in the state.

Population: 524,861. White 320,931 (61%), Black 200,966 (38%). Spanish origin 8,254 (2%). 18 and over 349,177 (67%), 65 and over 53,220 (10%). Median age: 27.

defensive by making her ideology and background the issues. Williams' résumé was more than reasonable for a congressional candidate; she was a lawyer and former U.S. House aide who spent several years working with the Michigan Education Association. But in gathering her experience, Williams had spent most of her adult life outside Louisiana. While questioning Williams' roots, Holloway stressed that he was a local nurseryman.

Holloway also ran ads claiming that Williams was "ultra-liberal, pro-abortion, for gay rights, for gun control" — an attempt to create the impression that she was far more unacceptably liberal than he was unacceptably conservative to the average voter. He had some help from Williams, who did little to distance herself from those issues or personally ingratiate herself with many white courthouse Democrats. Holloway won over enough rural and blue-collar Democrats to eke out a narrow victory.

Although some immediately dubbed him "two-year Clyde," Holloway's political stock rose considerably in 1988 when it became clear that local Democrats had not learned from history and were preparing to repeat it. Williams competed with two prominent white Democrats and again made it into the runoff with Holloway.

Williams, blaming some of her 1986 defeat on opposition to her race and sex, hoped to win greater acceptance in her second campaign. But some normally loyal Democrats who had supported her first effort backed away the second time, finding her views too liberal and her personality wearing. Many had learned they could live with Holloway, an approachable man who impressed even some hard-core Democrats with his attention to the district.

It was evident in the primary that Holloway would be tough to oust: He came within several points of winning a majority of the vote. In November he took an amazing 57 percent of the vote. Still, it is unlikely he will ever rest comfortably in this district, given its Democratic complexion.

Committees

Agriculture (16th of 18 Republicans)
Conservation, Credit and Rural Development; Cotton, Rice and Sugar

Select Children, Youth and Families (6th of 12 Republicans)

Small Business (14th of 17 Republicans)
Procurement, Tourism and Rural Development; SBA, the General Economy and Minority Enterprise Development

Elections

1988 General		
Clyde C. Holloway (R)	116,241	(57%)
Faye Williams (D)	88,564	(43%)
1988 Primary †		
Clyde C. Holloway (R)	58,831	(44%)
Faye Williams (D)	46,088	(34%)
Robert L. "Bobby" Freeman (D)	14,814	(11%)
J. E. Jumonville Jr. (D)	14,009	(10%)
1986 General		
Clyde C. Holloway (R)	102,276	(51%)
Faye Williams (D)	96,864	(49%)

† In Louisiana the primary is open to candidates of all parties. If a candidate wins 50 percent or more of the vote in the primary, no general election is held.

District Vote For President

	1988	1984	1980	1976
D	114,647 (53%)	109,857 (49%)	116,443 (56%)	107,574 (59%)
R	97,428 (45%)	113,154 (50%)	86,624 (42%)	69,186 (38%)

Campaign Finance

	Receipts	Receipts from PACs	Expend-itures
1988			
Holloway (R)	$690,080	$315,886 (46%)	$629,950
Williams (D)	$518,494	$182,683 (35%)	$434,854
1986			
Holloway (R)	$452,410	$133,803 (30%)	$454,661
Williams (D)	$402,226	$117,922 (29%)	$397,412

Key Votes

1987	
Raise speed limit to 65 mph	Y
Approve Gephardt "fair trade" amendment	N
Ban testing of larger nuclear weapons	N
Delay "re-flagging" of Kuwaiti tankers	N
Approve tax-raising deficit-reduction bill	N
1988	
Approve aid to Nicaraguan contras	Y
Enact civil rights restoration bill over Reagan veto	N
Kill 60-day plant-closing notification measure	Y
Pass omnibus trade bill over Reagan veto	Y
Approve death penalty for drug-related murders	Y
Bar federal funds for abortions in cases of rape and incest	Y
Oppose seven-day waiting period for purchase of handguns	Y

Voting Studies

	Presidential Support		Party Unity		Conservative Coalition	
Year	**S**	**O**	**S**	**O**	**S**	**O**
1988	65	27	76	11	92	3
1987	66	26	77	15	95	5

Interest Group Ratings

Year	ADA	ACU	AFL-CIO	CCUS
1988	0	96	36	92
1987	0	20	93	82

Maine

U.S. CONGRESS

SENATE 1 D, 1 R
HOUSE 1 D, 1 R

LEGISLATURE

Senate 20 D, 15 R
House 97 D, 54 R

ELECTIONS

1988 Presidential Vote	
Bush	55%
Dukakis	44%
1984 Presidential Vote	
Reagan	61%
Mondale	39%
1980 Presidential Vote	
Reagan	46%
Carter	42%
Anderson	10%
Turnout rate in 1984	65%
Turnout rate in 1986	48%
Turnout rate in 1988	62%

(as percentage of voting age population)

POPULATION AND GROWTH

1980 population	1,124,660
1988 population estimate (38th in the nation)	1,205,000
Percent change 1980-1988	+7%

DEMOGRAPHIC BREAKDOWN

White	99%
Black	0.3%
(Spanish origin)	4%
Urban	47%
Rural	53%
Born in state	73%
Foreign-born	4%

MAJOR CITIES

Portland	62,670
Lewiston	38,980
Bangor	30,160
Auburn	22,870
South Portland	21,620

AREA AND LAND USE

Area	30,995 sq. miles (39th)
Farm	7%
Forest	90%
Federally owned	1%

Gov. John R. McKernan Jr. (R)
Of Cumberland — Elected 1986

Born: May 20, 1948, Bangor, Maine.
Education: Dartmouth College, A.B. 1970; U. of Maine, J.D. 1974.
Military Career: Army National Guard, 1970-73.
Occupation: Lawyer.
Religion: Protestant.
Political Career: Maine House, 1973-77, assistant minority leader, 1975-76; U.S. House, 1983-87.
Next Election: 1990.

WORK

Occupations	
White-collar	46%
Blue-collar	37%
Service workers	13%
Government Workers	
Federal	16,834
State	25,066
Local	46,018

MONEY

Median family income	$ 16,167 (47th)
Tax burden per capita	$ 864 (22nd)

EDUCATION

Spending per pupil through grade 12	$ 3,472 (31st)
Persons with college degrees	14% (34th)

CRIME

Violent crime rate	152 per 100,000 (44th)

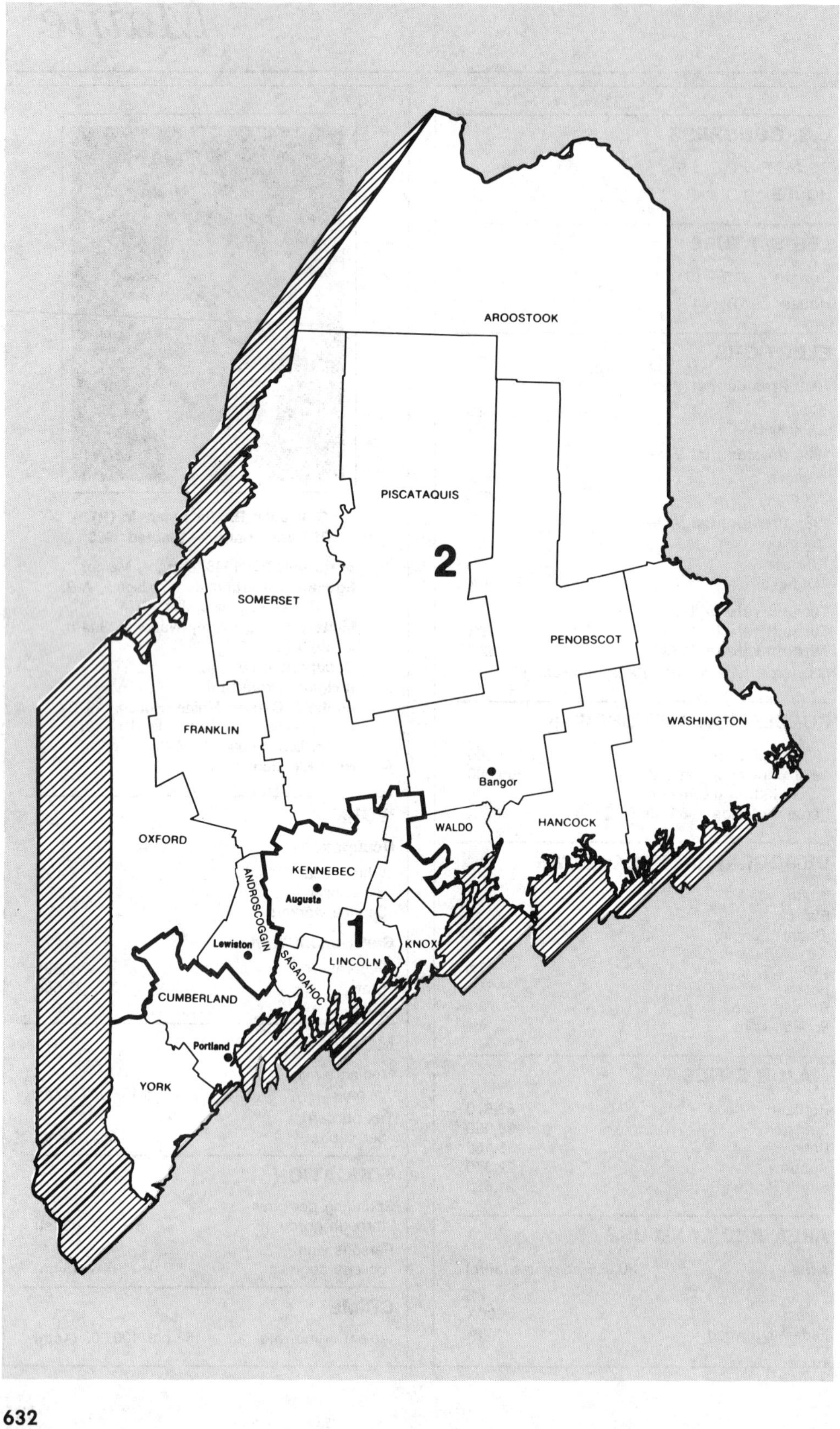
AROOSTOOK
PISCATAQUIS
2
SOMERSET
PENOBSCOT
FRANKLIN
WASHINGTON
Bangor
WALDO
HANCOCK
OXFORD
KENNEBEC
Augusta
ANDROSCOGGIN
1
KNOX
Lewiston
LINCOLN
SAGADAHOC
CUMBERLAND
Portland
YORK

William S. Cohen (R)

Of Bangor — Elected 1978

Born: Aug. 28, 1940, Bangor, Maine.
Education: Bowdoin College, B.A. 1962; Boston U., LL.B. 1965.
Occupation: Lawyer.
Family: Divorced; two children.
Religion: Unitarian.
Political Career: Bangor City Council, 1969-72; mayor of Bangor, 1971-72; U.S. House, 1973-79.
Capitol Office: 322 Hart Bldg. 20510; 224-2523.

In Washington: Cohen's ego is at least as big as anyone's in the Senate; the difference is that his seems almost divorced from his membership in that elite chamber. Cerebral and deservedly self-assured, he exudes a sense that he would be equally fulfilled if he left office tomorrow and returned to Maine to devote full time to his poetry.

He once wrote of his House days, "I wondered why I wanted to participate in this silliness and stupefaction." After a year in the Senate, he published a diary in which he complained that he and his colleagues "careened from ... speech to speech, crisis to crisis, without the time to reflect on whether we have simply doubled our deeds without fixing our destinations."

Congress does not always provoke such serious public soul-searching in Cohen. At times he appears to view it with bemused and fascinated detachment as a living drama, as grist for his writings, even when he is playing a lead role himself. With former Sen. Gary Hart, his friend from the Armed Services Committee, Cohen wrote a spy thriller, "The Double Man," about a moderate senator caught in a web of terrorist intrigue. More recently, he co-authored "Men of Zeal: A Candid Inside Story of the Iran-Contra Hearings" with fellow Mainer George J. Mitchell, now the Senate majority leader.

The impression that Cohen is less than totally absorbed by Congress' daily doings, that he occasionally appears above it all, can grate on some colleagues. So do the self-conscious literary allusions and recitations that so frequently mark his speeches. But no one mistakes Cohen for some dreamy dilettante. Instead, he is widely respected as an artful legislator equally conversant in the most tedious details of bills and the complexities of defense and foreign policy, particularly arms control.

Though conservative by Maine standards, Cohen definitely ranks as a moderate in Congress, celebrated by the media there (if not by die-hard Republicans) for his well-articulated breaks from the party line. As a House freshman, he voted for President Richard M. Nixon's impeachment after careful questioning on the Judiciary Committee. More than a decade later, as minority vice chairman of both the Intelligence Committee and the special Iran-contra investigatory panel, Cohen was the most outspoken Republican detractor of President Reagan and his administration.

He tried to avoid direct blasts at Reagan, but as revelations unfolded about arms sales to Iran and the diversion of profits to the Nicaraguan contras, Cohen became increasingly critical. In January 1987 he not only resisted administration pressure to release an Intelligence staff report exonerating the president of direct knowledge, but he also took to the Senate floor to say that Reagan "should have known." The president "took foreign policy underground," Cohen added.

A month later, he said Reagan's own Tower Commission showed "the president conducted the office as if he were an absentee landlord while the tenants were running around smashing the windows and breaking up the furniture." By July, near the end of the congressional panel's investigation, Cohen noted that the arms sales had continued against the advice of Reagan's top defense and foreign policy advisers. "You can only conclude that that had to be because somebody in the White House wanted it to continue," he said, "that somebody being the president of the United States."

Cohen proved such a tough examiner that GOP Rep. Henry J. Hyde cracked that he was "vying for first place in the vigorous question department." While Hyde and most other Republicans tried to turn the hearings into a promotion for Reagan's pro-contra policy, Cohen spotlighted the contradictions in the president's oft-changing rationale for aiding the rebels. To Lt. Col. Oliver L. North, who unashamedly declared that he violated a ban on contra aid, Cohen lectured, "We have to respect the rule of law until we can change the law itself, because otherwise the rule of law will be reduced to the law of rule."

Cohen ultimately was one of only three

Republicans to sign the majority report that held Reagan responsible for his "cabal of zealots." Cohen also sponsored the only major bill to result, requiring presidents to notify Congress of covert actions within at least 48 hours and closing loopholes that had allowed Reagan to conceal the arms sales.

Conservatives complained the bill would impede the president's authority, and the administration warned of a veto, but Cohen countered, "If we're going to be asked to share the responsibility by appropriating the money, we simply want to know about it." The Senate overwhelmingly approved the measure but House Republicans forced Democratic leaders there to shelve it late in 1988.

The Iran-contra affair was only the most evident example of Cohen's willingness to criticize Reagan. In mid-1988, he and Intelligence Chairman David L. Boren accused the administration of leaking word of a covert plan to undermine Panama strongman Manuel Antonio Noriega to make it appear Congress had let the secret out, and thus discredit the 48-hour notice bill. Cohen condemned it as "a set-up deal.... I am offended by it."

On Armed Services, he has been a key member of a centrist group seeking a middle ground between administration nuclear weapons policies and liberal arms controllers' demands. Though that often puts him at odds with Republican committee colleagues, Cohen may be their leader before too many years. He ranks third behind two much older men — John W. Warner and Strom Thurmond, who opted for the Judiciary Committee's top GOP spot instead.

Given his close working relationship with committee Democrats, Cohen attracted attention in early 1989 for energetically leading the GOP defense of former Armed Services Chairman John Tower, President Bush's unsuccessful nominee for defense secretary. He denounced the panel's recommendation against confirmation, which was based on allegations of drunkenness, womanizing and financial conflicts of interest, as "a political execution."

In earlier years, Cohen did not express much interest in arms control, and he strongly opposed the SALT II treaty. But by the mid-1980s he was urging continued compliance with the unratified pact. He prefers the single-warhead Midgetman missile to the more vulnerable 10-warhead MX. In 1983, he was the first to propose the "build-down" concept: The two superpowers would agree to eliminate one or more existing nuclear weapons for each new one deployed.

Reagan quickly expressed interest, but both administration hard-liners and arms-control groups resisted. Working with Democratic defense expert Sam Nunn and others, Cohen arranged a deal that traded support for the MX for administration backing of the build-down idea. After months of negotiations, the administration accepted it. But Armed Services and the Soviets rejected the concept, and interest in "build-down" faded.

The focus of the arms debate shifted to Reagan's strategic defense initiative (SDI); there, too, Cohen had considerable impact. Although he expressed doubts about the program, Cohen backed Reagan's early funding requests. By 1986, he was more critical. Allied again with Nunn, and splitting with Republicans, Cohen was responsible for an amendment that cut proposed SDI funding and directed the program toward the more limited goal of protecting the U.S. missile force.

The next year, again alone among Armed Services Republicans, Cohen joined Democrats in opposing Reagan's attempt to reinterpret the 1972 anti-ballistic missile (ABM) treaty in a way that would allow space tests of SDI components. In 1988, the ABM question threatened Reagan's own accord with the Soviets, the intermediate-range nuclear-force (INF) treaty, when Democrats insisted on attaching a provision specifying that presidents could not reinterpret treaties. Republicans just as adamantly objected. Cohen drafted compromise language, defusing the only major obstacle to the treaty's ratification.

Cohen also focuses on more prosaic questions, promoting Maine's Bath Iron Works, where the Navy builds many of its ships, and earmarking funds for armored bomb-sweeping cars built in his state. Combining interests on both Armed Services and the Governmental Affairs Committee, he has sponsored proposals for stricter controls on government contracting and procurement, especially for defense, and for tougher federal anti-fraud laws.

As ranking Republican on Governmental Affairs' Oversight Subcommittee, Cohen in 1987 cosponsored legislation that made permanent the Watergate-era law providing for independent counsels to investigate top executive officials. The bill was opposed by the administration, but Cohen's involvement was natural; he had a lead House role in passing the original 1978 law and sponsored a 1982 revision in the Senate. Also in the 100th Congress, Cohen finally won enactment of a law guaranteeing due-process rights to citizens whose benefits are threatened if their names surface when federal agencies swap computerized records on fraud and abuse.

At Home: Over his years in Maine politics, Cohen has built a loyal following that cuts across party lines and forms the core of one of the smoothest-running political organizations anywhere. His office churns out newsletters for almost every constituency group, and carefully tends his relations with both the press and home-state politicians. In his TV advertising, Cohen balances his reputation as a star in Washington with an image of a man still willing to help in the family's Bangor bakery.

In his 1984 re-election, Cohen won nearly three-fourths of the votes cast. The result would have been less lopsided had he faced the candidate Democrats wanted — Gov. Joseph E. Brennan. But Brennan made it clear early in 1984 that he was not interested in taking on Cohen. Into his place stepped state House Majority Leader Elizabeth H. Mitchell.

Mitchell's outspoken liberalism, particularly her support for a nuclear freeze, gave her a dedicated band of volunteer supporters. But her rejection of political action committees' money led much of the Democratic establishment to write off her campaign as hopelessly quixotic.

Cohen all but assured himself of statewide office on the day he spoke out for Nixon's impeachment, carving an image as a Republican of conscience. His good looks, easygoing manner and careful questioning were perfect for TV.

But even if there had been no Watergate, the odds are he would be in the Senate. His Watergate performance merely added to the "rising star" reputation he had enjoyed from his collegiate basketball days to the Bangor City Council and, in 1971, the mayoralty.

He did not hold the mayor's job very long. In 1972, Democratic Rep. William D. Hathaway ran for the Senate, leaving his 2nd District seat open. Cohen won it easily, doing exceptionally well for a Republican in many Democratic areas.

After the 1974 period of Watergate celebrity, Cohen began to think about the proper timing for a Senate effort; he spent nearly a year considering a 1976 campaign against Maine's senior senator, Edmund S. Muskie. But while private polls showed him close, prudence dictated a two-year wait and a campaign against Hathaway, more liberal and less of an institution than Muskie.

Knowing he was in trouble, Hathaway worked hard to save himself in 1978, but Cohen had almost no weaknesses. The personal glamour of 1974 had never really worn off, and state and national media refurbished it for the campaign. Cohen shifted slightly to the right, arguing that Hathaway was too liberal for most of Maine. He also worked for Democratic votes, concentrating his efforts in such places as Portland's Irish-Catholic Munjoy Hill section.

Hathaway had not done anything to offend the voters, but the challenger overwhelmed him. He was held in a three-way contest to 34 percent, one of the lowest figures in modern times for any Senate incumbent.

Committees

Select Intelligence (Vice Chairman)

Armed Services (4th of 9 Republicans)
Projection Forces and Regional Defense (ranking); Conventional Forces and Alliance Defense; Strategic Forces and Nuclear Deterrence

Governmental Affairs (3rd of 6 Republicans)
Oversight of Government Management (ranking); Government Information and Regulation; Permanent Subcommittee on Investigations

Special Aging (2nd of 9 Republicans)

Elections

1984 General

William S. Cohen (R)	404,414	(73%)
Elizabeth H. Mitchell (D)	142,626	(26%)

Previous Winning Percentages: **1978** (57%) **1976 *** (77%) **1974 *** (71%) **1972 *** (54%)

* *House elections.*

Campaign Finance

	Receipts	Receipts from PACs	Expenditures
1984			
Cohen (R)	$1,158,160	$421,451 (36%)	$1,022,134
Mitchell (D)	$437,517	$450 (0.1%)	$428,990

Key Votes

1987

Enact omnibus highway bill over Reagan veto	N
Limit testing of space-based anti-ballistic missiles	Y
Oppose banning tests of larger nuclear weapons	Y
Confirm Robert H. Bork as Supreme Court justice	Y

1988

Allow vote on campaign-finance overhaul	N
Pass civil rights restoration bill over Reagan veto	Y
Enact omnibus trade bill over Reagan veto	Y
Approve death penalty for drug-related murders	?
Oppose "workfare" amendment to welfare overhaul bill	N

Voting Studies

	Presidential Support		Party Unity		Conservative Coalition	
Year	S	O	S	O	S	O
1988	52	43	39	59	41	54
1987	55	42	57	42	63	38
1986	78	22	63	33	74	25
1985	63	27	55	38	55	32
1984	62	30	42	53	53	47
1983	66	29	60	36	73	23
1982	67	31	62	36	47	52
1981	76	19	69	25	59	36

Interest Group Ratings

Year	ADA	ACU	AFL-CIO	CCUS
1988	35	46	57	57
1987	55	58	40	67
1986	50	52	20	63
1985	35	55	45	68
1984	80	45	73	28
1983	45	30	47	33
1982	55	50	27	42
1981	35	47	33	76

George J. Mitchell (D)

Of Portland — Elected 1982

Appointed to the Senate 1980

Born: Aug. 20, 1933, Waterville, Maine.
Education: Bowdoin College, B.A. 1954; Georgetown U., LL.B. 1960.
Military Career: Army, 1954-56.
Occupation: Lawyer; judge.
Family: Divorced; one child.
Religion: Roman Catholic.
Political Career: Maine Democratic Party chairman, 1966-68; Democratic nominee for governor, 1974.
Capitol Office: 176 Russell Bldg. 20510; 224-5344.

In Washington: At the end of the 100th Congress, Mitchell completed a four-year charge from the back benches of the Senate to the forefront of national politics by being elected Senate majority leader.

His election on Nov. 29, 1988, was declared unanimous after he had dominated two rivals on the first ballot. The victory capped a remarkable seven-month campaign in which Mitchell overcame seniority, regional rivalry and reservations about his liberal views and low-key style.

In the end, he won with a certain flair, not just because he got more votes but because he had held his coalition together under intense pressures — both internal and external. His competitors both attempted to declare themselves the winners in advance and create momentum — with one making his pitch in the cloakroom and the other in the news media.

But Mitchell, who probably led the race wire to wire, struck a cautious pose in public while pursuing his votes systematically in private. Not until a few days before the secret ballot did he begin publicizing his own vote tally — which, in the end, proved accurate.

Mitchell's coalition was based on liberals, Easterners, senators elected in the 1980s and senators with strong interest in the environment. But he supplemented these categories with votes from all levels of seniority, every region and most of the Senate Democrats' ideological range. Mitchell divided the spoils of his triumph, both the real positions of power and the more honorific posts, with generosity to the defeated and their supporters.

In the early months of 1989, Mitchell assumed his new power with what might be called due deliberate speed. He ceded often to others, as he had promised to do. He had Sen. Lloyd Bentsen of Texas deliver the Senate Democrats' TV response to President George Bush's first address to Congress. He stepped aside while Sen. Sam Nunn of Georgia led the first battle with Bush, the rejection of former Sen. John Tower, Bush's nominee for secretary of defense.

He seemed intent on rationalizing the Senate floor routine, as he had promised. But the early months of the session were, with the exception of the Tower affair, relatively leisurely. The real test of Mitchell's regime against the clock and the calendar would come later.

Mitchell did have one sharp test in the early months: the proposed 51 percent congressional pay raise. Initially, Mitchell said he would prefer a smaller increase but that some increase was needed. When the moment of truth came, he voted "no" (as did all but five senators).

Meanwhile, in the House, Speaker Jim Wright was alienating colleagues by scheduling a vote when he was supposed to let the raise take effect automatically. Mitchell's matador-style handling of the issue was equally disappointing to some, but it attracted far less attention.

Mitchell did endorse tying the raise to a ban on honoraria, which in the Senate can equal 40 percent of salary. But this proposal stalled when the raise went down.

On the legislative side, Mitchell's newfound power had the potential to affect two major issues with which he had been previously associated. One was the Iran-contra affair, which returned to the news as former Marine Lt. Col. Oliver L. North stood trial in the spring of 1989. Documents introduced at North's trial had not been available, in the same form, to the congressional Iran-contra investigating committee on which Mitchell served. The new leader made it clear he wanted to reopen the inquiry, despite the lack of widespread public interest and despite the potential involvement of President Bush.

The other issue was acid rain. Mitchell had devoted much of the 100th Congress to endless, closed-door negotiations toward a compromise between the regions, between industry and environmentalists and between the House and

Senate. He had coaxed a bill out of the Senate Environment Committee in the first session, only to see it stymied for nearly a year by then-Majority Leader Robert C. Byrd, who had long opposed controls he thought would hurt coal mining in West Virginia. The 1988 negotiations eventually broke down, and in announcing the failure in October, Mitchell bitterly denounced the various parties to the disagreement.

In the 101st Congress, a new bill received fast-track treatment in the House, and a package of bills was expected to be voted on by the Senate in the autumn.

When Mitchell came to town as an appointed senator in 1980, he struck colleagues as a low-key former judge who generally kept partisan rhetoric out of his speeches. Few could have imagined then that he would soon chair the Democratic Senatorial Campaign Committee and lead his party's 1986 charge to retake control of the Senate.

But Mitchell's long public career has been as much politics as it has law — he was a Democratic state chairman years before he was a judge — and it did not take him much time in the Senate to show that there was a vocal and aggressive politician lurking behind the soft-spoken intellectual facade.

During the 1986 campaign, Mitchell's combative side was often in evidence. The son of a janitor and a strong believer in the Democratic Party's working-class roots, he sometimes seemed personally offended by the philosophy and style of the Reagan administration.

Responding to Reagan's 1986 State of the Union speech, Mitchell portrayed Reagan as a man who relied on "rhetoric that refuses to face the real world." After the Iran-contra arms revelations convinced many Americans that Reagan was, at best, absent-minded, Mitchell all but gloated. "Never again will there be the period of the dominant Reagan presidency of the first six years," he said.

Mitchell took the campaign committee job for 1986 knowing that history clearly favored Democratic chances of toppling the GOP's 53-47 Senate majority. Ever since popular Senate elections began in 1914, an administration's sixth-year election had cost the president's party an average of seven Senate seats.

But with the GOP enjoying its typically large financial advantage and Reagan campaigning all-out for vulnerable Republican incumbents, no one expected the Democrats to retake the chamber so decisively, with 55 seats.

To reward Mitchell when they organized the 100th Congress, Senate Democrats gave him the position of deputy president pro tempore, a job that was created for Hubert H. Humphrey in 1977 and had not been occupied since Humphrey's death. Winning such a prestigious post clearly marked Mitchell as a man on the move, but another role lay ahead — one that would add a critical dimension to his drive for majority leader: He became one of six Democrats on the special Senate committee investigating the Iran-contra affair.

In July 1987, Mitchell took over the public questioning of North and walked the former Marine through a series of lawyerly questions. He cut off the show-stealing answers North had given other interrogators on the panel, and delivered one of the most memorable lines of the hearings. "... Recognize that it is possible for an American to disagree with you on aid to the contras and still love God and still love this country just as much as you do," he told North.

Later, when Reagan delivered his national address on the subject in August, Mitchell was chosen to give the Democrats' response. It was a measured, serious performance that made little effort to charm. But it was a hit. Mitchell briefly became a regular on broadcast news shows, and his stock rose sharply.

Mitchell blends his partisanship with a keen memory for detail and an ability to pursue several complicated tasks at once. These traits are evident in his handling of the environmental issues that have been his primary legislative concern. This focus began early in his Senate career, when he plunged into the Environment Committee's markup of the "superfund" bill, requiring chemical companies to finance hazardous-waste cleanup. "This Senate has made the judgment that property is more significant than human beings," he said in protest when the bill reached the Senate floor in a watered-down form. "We are telling the people of this country that under our value system property is worth compensating, but a human life is not."

Mitchell kept up his efforts to win compensation for toxic-waste victims when the superfund program came up for reauthorization. Finally, in 1985, he won Environment Committee approval of an experimental program to compensate victims of toxic incidents at up to 10 sites to be chosen by the Environmental Protection Agency. The price tag was $30 million annually for five years.

During final Senate debate on approving the superfund bill in September 1985, Mitchell's "victims assistance" program stirred a major controversy. Opponents saw it as a risky "foot in the door" that would be politically difficult to restrain if health monitoring and victims' compensation costs began to soar.

Mitchell defended his proposal as "a cautious, limited in scope, limited in time, limited in funding effort to learn whether or not there is indeed a problem.... Those who now say, 'Kill this provision,' are, in effect, saying, 'Do nothing.' " But by a 46-49 vote, Mitchell lost.

In the 99th Congress, Mitchell worked with GOP Sen. John H. Chafee on a bill reauthorizing the Clean Water Act. At the end of 1986, Reagan pocket-vetoed the measure as too costly. But in 1987, Democrats brought the bill back, and with Mitchell as floor manager, the Senate passed the reauthorization a second time and later overrode Reagan's veto, as did the House.

On the Finance Committee, Mitchell did not play a prominent role in shaping tax bills in the 97th and 98th Congresses, but he was active in the tax-code overhaul enacted by the 99th Congress. Mitchell argued that middle-income taxpayers should benefit as much from revision as those in high- and low-income groups, and he sought to ensure that new restrictions on real-estate tax shelters would not eliminate the incentive to build and maintain low-income housing.

The tax bill that came out of Finance also called for a two-tiered rate structure for individuals. On the Senate floor, Mitchell tried to add a third tier, an effort to get more tax revenue from the highest-income taxpayers. In the end, Mitchell's plan lost by 71-29; the decisive margin sent a signal that the Senate would resist all major changes in the tax rates and basic reform elements of the Finance Committee's bill.

Later, Mitchell did get the Senate to approve a tax credit that preserved incentives for investing in low-income housing.

Mitchell has fought in Finance and elsewhere to protect Maine's declining shoe industry from cheap foreign competition. He was a member of the congressional coalition that fought successfully to ensure that the administration's Caribbean Basin Initiative, cleared by Congress in 1983, did not go too far in easing barriers against the importing of shoes and other products from the region.

At Home: Mitchell's feats on the national stage are matched by his political accomplishments in Maine in the 1980s. He started the decade as an appointed senator scrapping to win election on his own; by 1989, he was the holder of the state record for the most lopsided Senate victory. His election to majority leader is a much-discussed point of pride in Maine.

Mitchell was assured an easy re-election campaign in 1988 when GOP Rep. Olympia J. Snowe decided not to challenge him. Instead, he faced Jasper Wyman, a leader in the 1986 anti-pornography state referendum campaign and head of the Christian Civic League. For the Senate contest, Wyman stepped back from his conservative social agenda and focused on taxes and national defense. But he was no match for Mitchell, who campaigned aggressively on the theme "Leadership that works for Maine and the nation." On Election Day, Mitchell won 81 percent of the vote, the widest margin of any 1988 Senate candidate as well as a state record.

As resounding a victory as that was, the thrill was much greater for Mitchell when he won in 1982. A year before that election, appointee Mitchell looked like a sitting duck: He had failed in his only previous attempt to win statewide office, and he trailed by 36 points in a poll released by Republican David F. Emery, a four-term House member with designs on Mitchell's seat.

Yet on Election Day, Mitchell crushed Emery with 61 percent of the vote, a stronger showing than even the invincible Edmund S. Muskie had posted when winning his fourth Senate election in 1976.

A share of the credit for Mitchell's resurgence was due Emery. In the early stages of the campaign, the challenger's passion for tinkering with details contributed to organizational disarray, which in turn led to some well-publicized blunders. One of the worst was a letter Emery sent to veterans in which he boasted that the Veterans of Foreign Wars (VFW) had rated his voting record at 92, and a zero for Mitchell.

The VFW statistics were compiled in June 1980, just a month after Mitchell took office. They contained no votes in which the senator could have participated. That incident prompted newspaper editorials criticizing Emery for practicing the "politics of distortion," an especially unkind cut in Maine, where voters expect better.

In July, Emery reshuffled his campaign organization, bringing in two top aides of GOP Sen. William S. Cohen. But during the months that Emery was struggling, Mitchell was working his way into the good graces of voters. In his frequent visits home, he impressed many as an articulate defender of Maine's interests who possessed the intellectual potential to influence national policy. He made an issue of the fact that he had left a lifetime judicial appointment to go to Congress; he portrayed Emery as a detail-minded errand boy for his House constituents who would be in over his head in the Senate.

Mitchell succeeded in winning strong support from blue-collar millworkers, a voting bloc Emery had courted effectively in his House campaigns. Many working-class voters were laid off or fearing for their jobs in 1982, and they were not consoled by Emery's strong support for Reaganomics. Much more soothing to them was Mitchell's promise that Democrats would not accept high unemployment. In the end, he won all but one county.

Mitchell's move into national politics in 1980 came out of his longstanding relationship with Muskie. The two had been allies since the early 1960s, when Mitchell worked as Muskie's administrative assistant. After Muskie moved to the State Department in 1980, he suggested that Mitchell be named to succeed him in the Senate. Democratic Gov. Joseph E. Brennan agreed.

It was a broadly acceptable choice. Mitchell had few enemies and seemed the perfect compromise, allowing Brennan to bypass the more prominent but more controversial contenders, former Sen. William D. Hathaway and former Gov. Kenneth M. Curtis. Mitchell had defeated Brennan in the 1974 gubernatorial primary, but that contest had left no ill feelings. Curtis, by contrast, had not had good relations with the governor, while Hathaway had the liability of a disastrously unsuccessful campaign for re-election to the Senate in 1978.

The campaign for governor in 1974 had been Mitchell's one statewide effort, and it had been an embarrassing defeat. Widely considered the favorite that fall, he underestimated the independent candidacy of James Longley, a Lewiston businessman running on a platform of reduced state spending. Longley drew thousands of blue-collar votes that Mitchell took for granted, and he won by 15,000 votes.

Mitchell has had an extensive career in government and politics. From working-class roots, he worked his way through law school as an insurance adjuster and spent two years in the Justice Department's antitrust division before joining Muskie's staff.

After returning to Maine to practice law in 1965, Mitchell served as Democratic state chairman and national committeeman. In the wake of the 1972 McGovern defeat, he staged an unsuccessful drive to become chairman of the Democratic National Committee. As the choice of the party's liberal faction, he lost to Robert S. Strauss of Texas.

On Muskie's recommendation, President Jimmy Carter named Mitchell U.S. attorney for Maine in 1977. Two years later the same connection won Mitchell the federal judgeship he gave up after only a few months to accept the Senate appointment.

Committees

Majority Leader

Environment and Public Works (3rd of 9 Democrats)
Environmental Protection; Superfund, Ocean and Water Protection; Water Resources, Transportation and Infrastructure

Finance (7th of 11 Democrats)
Health for Families and the Uninsured; International Trade; Medicare and Long-Term Care

Veterans' Affairs (4th of 6 Democrats)

Elections

1988 General

George J. Mitchell (D)	452,590	(81%)
Jasper Wyman (R)	104,758	(19%)

Previous Winning Percentage: **1982** (61%)

Campaign Finance

	Receipts	Receipts from PACs	Expend-itures
1988			
Mitchell (D)	$1,810,602	$724,547 (40%)	$1,340,157
Wyman (R)	$147,981	$2,599 (2%)	$147,760

Key Votes

1987

Enact omnibus highway bill over Reagan veto	Y
Limit testing of space-based anti-ballistic missiles	Y
Oppose banning tests of larger nuclear weapons	N
Confirm Robert H. Bork as Supreme Court justice	N
1988	
Allow vote on campaign-finance overhaul	Y
Pass civil rights restoration bill over Reagan veto	Y
Enact omnibus trade bill over Reagan veto	Y
Approve death penalty for drug-related murders	N
Oppose "workfare" amendment to welfare overhaul bill	Y

Voting Studies

	Presidential Support		Party Unity		Conservative Coalition	
Year	**S**	**O**	**S**	**O**	**S**	**O**
1988	43	57	95	4	5	95
1987	36	64	90	10	31	69
1986	31	66	84	14	25	74
1985	33	67	87	13	30	70
1984	36	61	84	15	15	85
1983	40	60	84	15	30	70
1982	35	63	89	11	16	84
1981	45	51	88	10	24	75

Interest Group Ratings

Year	ADA	ACU	AFL-CIO	CCUS
1988	95	0	100	21
1987	95	8	90	28
1986	85	14	87	32
1985	65	17	86	31
1984	90	9	73	37
1983	80	12	76	42
1982	95	40	88	30
1981	90	7	95	35

1 Joseph E. Brennan (D)

Of Portland — Elected 1986

Born: Nov. 2, 1934, Portland, Maine.
Education: Boston College, B.S. 1956, M.A. 1958; U. of Maine Law School, LL.B. 1963.
Military Career: Army, 1953-55.
Occupation: Lawyer.
Family: Divorced; two children.
Religion: Roman Catholic.
Political Career: Maine House, 1965-71; Cumberland County district attorney, 1970-72; Maine Senate, 1973-75; Maine attorney general, 1975-79; governor, 1979-87; sought Democratic gubernatorial nomination, 1974.
Capitol Office: 1428 Longworth Bldg. 20515; 225-6116.

In Washington: The first governor elected to the House since 1960, Brennan benefited from the great expectations attending his arrival in the 100th Congress. For his first term, he won assignment to Armed Services and was named by the Democratic Caucus as an at-large whip.

Yet in making the difficult transition from state leader to one of 435 legislators, Brennan may have disappointed some Hill veterans who were expecting a dynamic figure. With his cautious, low-key manner, Brennan did not make a stunning impression as a freshman.

Social policy was Brennan's long suit as governor, but as a House member, he exercised his interest in U.S. foreign policy, especially his deeply felt opposition to President Reagan's policies in Latin America.

Even before his first House session, Brennan visited Nicaragua and Honduras; he later made a privately funded trip to Cuba. Also, in July 1987, he was one of a dozen Armed Services members who visited the Middle East to examine Reagan's Persian Gulf policy following the Iraqi bombing of the USS *Stark*.

Brennan met with some criticism at home for his foreign focus, but he responded effectively. He said his overseas trips were vital to his ability to legislate on defense issues, pointing to his trip to the Persian Gulf as a learning experience: Though he had been skeptical of the U.S. Navy acting as policeman in the war-torn region, he came home supportive of the policy after meeting with Arab leaders.

Brennan also worked to counter any impression he was ignoring state interests. He took credit for making certain that Maine's Bath Iron Works would retain its large share of the Navy's contracts for building the Aegis cruiser, by working to block inclusion of a Louisiana shipyard on the list of potential contractors.

At Home: Governors often run for the Senate, but few try for the House. The move, however, made sense for Brennan, who has served in one office or another virtually his entire adult life. Maine law barred him from a third term as governor, and with no Senate election in 1986, his best chance for staying in public life was to try for the 1st, which Republican John R. McKernan Jr. was vacating to run for governor.

Though Brennan was rated a sure bet in 1986, he drew an aggressive GOP challenger in H. Rollin Ives, a clinical psychologist and political newcomer. Ives got attention for saying Brennan's low-key bid "should be ticketed for loitering." Brennan scored a comfortable 20,000-vote victory, but against the unheralded Ives, it was seen as only an average showing for a man of stature.

Brennan's focus on Central America and other foreign policy matters got Republicans grumbling that he was neglecting local concerns and constituent service. In 1988, two sought the GOP nomination: moderate party activist Ted O'Meara (a former aide to GOP Sen. William S. Cohen), and Linda Bean-Jones, heiress to the L. L. Bean mail-order house fortune and a prominent conservative. O'Meara's centrist philosophy and his popularity among GOP regulars allowed him to score an upset in a poorly attended primary.

But Republicans sorely underestimated the importance of Brennan's financial advantage and his ability to convey a sense of compassion for the average Maine wage-earner. O'Meara scarcely laid a glove on the incumbent.

While Brennan is not an exciting speaker, his affinity for the working class comes naturally. He grew up in the blue-collar Munjoy Hill area of Portland, where he was one of eight children of an Irish immigrant longshoreman. In 1964, just one year after graduating from law school, he won a seat in the state House. After six years there, he served two years as Cumberland County (Portland) district attorney, two as a state senator and four as state attorney gen-

Maine 1

South — Portland; Augusta

Maine's industrial Democratic core follows Interstate 95 from Biddeford in the south to Waterville in the north, right through the heart of the 1st. With the exception of Androscoggin County (Lewiston), all the state's most populous and Democratic counties lie in the district. The 1st is made competitive for Republicans by the small coastal towns that stretch northeast from Portland.

Powered by the waters of Maine's rivers, industries here have made shoes, ships, textiles, lumber and paper throughout the 20th century. Low wages and high unemployment in the area in the postwar years made southern Maine a fertile recruiting ground for Edmund S. Muskie and other Democratic leaders in the 1950s.

Portland is Maine's largest city with 63,000 people, and its Irish and Franco-American community, combined with a large environmentalist white-collar vote, has kept surrounding Cumberland County in the Democratic column in most contests. The spread of high-technology industry up the coast from Boston has brought a modest boom to Portland in recent years; unemployment is low and its downtown streets are home to trendy boutiques and restaurants. A steep increase in prices for upscale housing is displacing many native Mainers and even jolting the yuppies who are moving into the Portland area from out of state.

Biddeford and Saco, heavily Franco-American factory towns south of Portland, and Waterville, a textile city at the northern edge of Kennebec County, are other Democratic strongholds. Nearby Augusta, the state capital, has a smaller Franco-American population than any of the others and is more evenly split between factory workers and white-collar government workers.

The district's Republican heartland lies along the coast. Lincoln, Knox, and Waldo counties consist mainly of coastal Republican towns that help make Maine the No. 1 lobster state, as well as the "Vacation State."

In 1988, George Bush was considered something of a native son — his family has long owned a vacation compound in Kennebunkport — which helped him win every county in the state.

Population: 563,073. White 557,507 (99%), Black 1,636 (0.3%), Other 2,667 (1%). Spanish origin 2,683 (1%). 18 and over 405,831 (72%), 65 and over 72,456 (13%). Median age: 31.

eral (a post elected by the Legislature) before winning the governorship in 1978.

Brennan has failed only once in his political career: He lost his first bid for governor in 1974, when he was unable to surmount an image as the "Portland" candidate. But he won the office four years later, capitalizing on publicity he received by taking a hard-line position as attorney general against a controversial Indian lands claim.

Brennan earned high marks as governor for charting a steady fiscal course. In his successful 1982 re-election bid, he could boast that the state's bond rating had gone up, that unemployment had come down, and that he had kept his 1978 promise not to raise taxes.

His second term, however, featured sparring with an old ally — organized labor. To enhance the state's business climate, Brennan pushed through changes in the state's worker-compensation law in 1985 that scaled down benefits. His action irked labor leaders, and in 1986 the state AFL-CIO refused to endorse him. After two years in the House, Brennan had patched up his differences with labor and won their backing in 1988.

Committees

Armed Services (25th of 31 Democrats)
Investigations; Seapower and Strategic and Critical Materials

Merchant Marine and Fisheries (19th of 26 Democrats)
Coast Guard and Navigation; Merchant Marine; Oceanography

Select Narcotics Abuse and Control (17th of 18 Democrats)

Elections

1988 General

Joseph E. Brennan (D)	190,989	(63%)
Edward S. O'Meara Jr. (R)	111,125	(37%)

1986 General

Joseph E. Brennan (D)	121,848	(53%)
H. Rollin Ives (R)	100,260	(44%)

District Vote For President

	1988	1984	1980	1976
D	131,078 (43%)	120,708 (40%)	114,661 (42%)	120,645 (48%)
R	169,292 (56%)	180,808 (60%)	122,193 (45%)	123,020 (49%)
I			30,118 (11%)	

Campaign Finance

	Receipts	Receipts from PACs	Expend-itures
1988			
Brennan (D)	$496,668	$280,229 (56%)	$464,541
O'Meara (R)	$294,632	$46,582 (16%)	$286,699
1986			
Brennan (D)	$287,821	$130,410 (45%)	$287,691
Ives (R)	$258,714	$25,850 (10%)	$261,403

Key Votes

1987

Raise speed limit to 65 mph	N
Approve Gephardt "fair trade" amendment	Y
Ban testing of larger nuclear weapons	Y
Delay "re-flagging" of Kuwaiti tankers	N
Approve tax-raising deficit-reduction bill	Y

1988

Approve aid to Nicaraguan contras	N
Enact civil rights restoration bill over Reagan veto	Y
Kill 60-day plant-closing notification measure	N
Pass omnibus trade bill over Reagan veto	Y
Approve death penalty for drug-related murders	N
Bar federal funds for abortions in cases of rape and incest	N
Oppose seven-day waiting period for purchase of handguns	Y

Voting Studies

	Presidential Support		Party Unity		Conservative Coalition	
Year	**S**	**O**	**S**	**O**	**S**	**O**
1988	22	78	91	8	29	71
1987	17 †	83 †	92 †	5 †	23 †	74 †

† Not eligible for all recorded votes.

Interest Group Ratings

Year	ADA	ACU	AFL-CIO	CCUS
1988	90	12	100	29
1987	100	0	94	7

2 Olympia J. Snowe (R)

Of Auburn — Elected 1978

Born: Feb. 21, 1947, Augusta, Maine.

Education: U. of Maine, B.A. 1969.

Occupation: Concrete company executive; public official.

Family: Husband, John R. McKernan Jr.

Religion: Greek Orthodox.

Political Career: Maine House, 1973-77; Maine Senate, 1977-79.

Capitol Office: 2464 Rayburn Bldg. 20515; 225-6306.

In Washington: As the 1980s drew to a close, Snowe found herself with no shortage of friends in high places. She was an early enrollee in the 1988 presidential campaign of George Bush, whose Kennebunkport retreat is in Snowe's native Maine. She had an "in" with new GOP Whip Newt Gingrich, having made a seconding speech for his nomination to the post. And she was newly married to Maine's Republican governor, John R. McKernan Jr., a former House colleague.

It will be interesting to see what Snowe makes of all these connections in the post-Reagan era. The White House tenure of the California conservative was not a particularly comfortable time for Snowe, who is one of Congress' most moderate Republicans. In 1987 and 1988, she supported the president's positions on House votes less than 40 percent of the time.

Trade issues in particular have separated Snowe from her party mainstream. Because the 2nd District's textile, shoe and timber industries as well as its farm economy are affected by foreign competition, Snowe is more favorable to trade protection than many Republicans. She was one of only 10 GOP members to vote against the U.S.-Canada free-trade agreement in August 1988. She said the pact did little to offset competition from government-subsidized businesses in Canada, and pointed to "government-modernized sawmills located right across the border in Canada," and Canadian subsidies to that nation's fishermen.

Snowe is also known as an outspoken proponent of legislation to aid women. In the early 1980s, Snowe was co-chair of the Congressional Caucus for Women's Issues with liberal Democrat Patricia Schroeder of Colorado. "I think it's important for women in Congress to ensure equity for women," she said in 1983. "If we don't, who will?"

Frustrated in the mid-1980s with the direction of the GOP and its "permanent" minority status in the House, Snowe helped establish the '92 Group — a caucus of GOP moderates dedicated to developing programs and strategies to gain the Republicans a House majority by 1992. At about the same time, Gingrich was building his Conservative Opportunity Society. In 1989, the moderates and conservatives — both dissatisfied with the status quo — united against establishment "Old Bull" Republicans to elect Gingrich as whip.

Snowe's high-profile support for the conservative Southerner was somewhat out of character for her; even moderate allies say she is prone to over-caution and seems unusually focused on constituent feedback for someone who always wins re-election with ease.

Prior to the whip election, Snowe had been most visible during the 100th Congress in the foreign policy arena, where she found some common ground with Reagan. She supported the administration's February 1988 request for $36 million in military and non-military aid to the Nicaraguan contras, and she opposed a South Africa sanctions bill later that year.

Snowe's top committee position is as senior Republican on the Foreign Affairs Subcommittee on International Operations. It was in this capacity that she took the lead in calling for demolition of the "bug"-riddled U.S. Embassy being built in Moscow.

Early in 1987, U.S. officials revealed that the unfinished embassy had been seeded with listening devices by Soviet operatives. Snowe traveled to the embassy site with then-subcommittee Chairman Daniel A. Mica, and soon became adamant that the building was unsalvageable and should be torn down.

Snowe, Mica and others also took steps to retaliate against the Soviets, attaching an amendment to a State Department authorization bill calling on the president to bar the Soviets from occupying their new embassy in Washington — built under a 1969 treaty — unless he certified to Congress that the move was vital to national security. The measure also called on the president to counteract possible Soviet spying from the new embassy, which is located on a high spot in Washington.

The Reagan administration initially opposed the provisions, both as encumbrances on

Maine 2

North — Lewiston; Auburn; Bangor

America's largest congressional district east of the Mississippi, the 2nd accounts for the vast bulk of Maine's territory. Across its northern reaches stretch the pine forests that have fueled the northwoods economy since the 18th century. Its people are clustered at the southern end, closer to the state's industrial core.

The one portion of the district actually within Maine's industrial belt is Androscoggin County, anchored by the twin cities of Lewiston (population 39,000) and Auburn (population 23,000). Ancient factory towns — Auburn claims to be the birthplace of the shoe industry in Maine — the cities traditionally anchor the Democratic vote in the district. Lewiston, the state's second-largest city, is the more Democratic of the two — it went narrowly for Walter F. Mondale in 1984 and gave Michael S. Dukakis 56 percent in 1988. Auburn — which voted for Jimmy Carter in 1976 — has gone Republican for president ever since. Both cities, however, tend to abandon any Democratic tradition to vote for Snowe and Republican Sen. William S. Cohen.

The only other city of any size in the 2nd is Bangor (Penobscot County), the third-largest in the state. Bangor's heyday as a ship-making center is over, as are the days when woodsmen from the north would come to squander their paychecks in the neighborhood known as the "Devil's Half-Acre." But its wood-products industry and modest port remain in operation.

Though still Democratic in local elections, Bangor is a more dependable Republican vote at the national level than the two cities farther south. Like Reagan in 1980 and 1984, George Bush narrowly carried Bangor. But when Democrats put up a strong candidate, Bangor will show its Democratic stripes; in 1982, Democratic Sen. George J. Mitchell won 63 percent in Penobscot County.

The rest of the district is rural, much of it covered with the forests that supply trees for huge lumber and paper mills. The land that is left raises apples, blueberries, corn, chickens and Maine's biggest cash crop, potatoes. The potatoes are grown largely in Aroostook County, the huge northern tract that is bigger than four states.

Yankee Republican farmers form a solid majority outside the industrial cities, and their votes keep the district Republican in most elections. Still, the chronic poverty that afflicts the area is gradually bringing some of its residents into the Democratic column as they turn to the government for assistance. Pockets of severe poverty are found in the woodlands in Aroostook County and in coastal Washington County, which lacks the tourist attraction of the more accessible coastal regions. With the large Franco-American population, Democrats often prevail in Washington County, though Bush carried it with 56 percent in 1988.

Population: 561,587. White 552,343 (98%), Black 1,492 (0.3%), Other 4,367 (1%). Spanish origin 2,322 (0.4%). 18 and over 397,442 (71%), 65 and over 68,462 (12%). Median age: 30.

presidential flexibility and as a threat to U.S.-Soviet rapprochement. The measure was nonetheless adopted as part of the fiscal 1988 State Department appropriations bill. Though the law barred any action against the Soviet Embassy in fiscal years 1988 and 1989, it left open the possibility of abrogating the embassy treaty if the problem of the U.S. Embassy in Moscow was not solved by October 1989.

At Home: No one in Washington is likely to confuse the fashionable Snowe with Margaret Chase Smith, the flinty Republican who represented the same part of Maine a generation ago. But she has all of Smith's ambition and talent for winning votes.

An orphan at age 9, Snowe was raised by her aunt, a textile mill worker, and her uncle, a barber. Like most working-class Auburn families, they voted Democratic. But after working as an intern for Democratic Gov. Kenneth M. Curtis, Olympia Bouchles met Peter Snowe, a young Auburn businessman involved in GOP politics. She married him in 1969, taking his name and partisan allegiance.

In 1973, four months after she began working in the district office of GOP Rep. William S. Cohen, Snowe's husband was killed in an automobile accident while returning from Augusta, where he was serving his second term in the state House. A month later she was elected to fill his seat. After winning another term on her own, she was elected to the state Senate in 1976. At that point, Snowe began contemplating a run for the U.S. House amid rumors that Cohen was eyeing the Senate.

Republicans at the state and national levels felt she was the ideal replacement for Cohen, and they arranged for her to be the only GOP candidate in 1978. Her Democratic foe, Maine Secretary of State Markham L. Gartley, had attracted some attention with his 1974 campaign against Cohen — in which he won only 29 percent — and because he was the first prisoner of war released by the North Vietnamese.

To broaden her exposure and help soften her "Fifth Avenue" image, Snowe traded her designer clothes for a wool shirt and hiking boots and walked across the district — a tactic Cohen had used successfully. Opposing the construction of the Dickey-Lincoln Dam and favoring "some kind" of national health insurance, Snowe appealed to many Democrats who were put off by Gartley's conservative stance. She ran far ahead of the GOP ticket in Democratic Androscoggin County, her home base, and picked up the usual Republican vote in the rest of the district to defeat Gartley handily. Since then, Democrats have found no effective counter to Snowe's popularity.

Snowe has twice passed up the chance to run for Senate against Democrat George J. Mitchell. In 1982 — when Mitchell looked vulnerable — she deferred to the ambitions of her GOP House colleague, David F. Emery, who had served in Congress longer. Snowe said her outlook was so similar to Emery's that a primary contest between them would focus mainly on personalities and might divide the party. Looking back on 1982, some Republicans may wish that Snowe had been their Senate nominee. Emery's campaign faltered, and in the end he lost to Mitchell by a wide margin.

Six years later, the GOP again looked to Snowe as their strongest potential challenger to Mitchell. But by 1988, the Democrat's popularity in the state was at an all-time high, and Snowe was unwilling to give up her safe House seat for an iffy Senate bid.

Republican officials were able to recruit Snowe for one new role in 1988 — deputy permanent chairman of the GOP national convention, a job that frequently put her in front of the TV cameras in New Orleans. As a woman of Greek extraction, Snowe was an ideal choice to give the party a more inclusive image and counter Michael S. Dukakis' ethnic appeal.

Committees

Foreign Affairs (6th of 18 Republicans)
International Operations (ranking); Arms Control, International Security and Science

Select Aging (5th of 27 Republicans)
Human Services (ranking)

Joint Economic
Economic Goals and Intergovernmental Policy; Education and Health; International Economic Policy

Elections

1988 General

Olympia J. Snowe (R)	167,229	(66%)
Kenneth P. Hayes (D)	85,346	(34%)

1986 General

Olympia J. Snowe (R)	148,770	(77%)
Richard A. Charette (D)	43,614	(23%)

Previous Winning Percentages: 1984 (76%) **1982** (67%) **1980** (79%) **1978** (51%)

District Vote For President

	1988	1984	1980	1976
D	112,491 (45%)	93,807 (37%)	106,383 (42%)	111,634 (48%)
R	137,839 (55%)	155,692 (62%)	116,329 (46%)	113,300 (49%)
I			23,209 (9%)	

Campaign Finance

	Receipts	Receipts from PACs	Expend- itures
1988			
Snowe (R)	$229,929	$72,300 (31%)	$202,317
Hayes (D)	$69,218	$26,772 (39%)	$68,857
1986			
Snowe (R)	$216,402	$79,075 (37%)	$215,659
Charette (D)	$28,780	$1,000 (3%)	$23,779

Key Votes

1987	
Raise speed limit to 65 mph	N
Approve Gephardt "fair trade" amendment	Y
Ban testing of larger nuclear weapons	Y
Delay "re-flagging" of Kuwaiti tankers	N
Approve tax-raising deficit-reduction bill	N
1988	
Approve aid to Nicaraguan contras	Y
Enact civil rights restoration bill over Reagan veto	Y
Kill 60-day plant-closing notification measure	N
Pass omnibus trade bill over Reagan veto	Y
Approve death penalty for drug-related murders	Y
Bar federal funds for abortions in cases of rape and incest	N
Oppose seven-day waiting period for purchase of handguns	Y

Voting Studies

	Presidential Support		Party Unity		Conservative Coalition	
Year	**S**	**O**	**S**	**O**	**S**	**O**
1988	37	63	54	46	82	18
1987	38	58	48	50	65	35
1986	44	54	53	47	64	36
1985	48	52	56	43	69	31
1984	49	51	47	53	64	36
1983	50	50	46	53	49	49
1982	47	52	53	46	58	40
1981	67	33	68	32	69	31

Interest Group Ratings

Year	ADA	ACU	AFL-CIO	CCUS
1988	60	40	86	50
1987	56	22	44	73
1986	50	48	64	61
1985	35	48	53	59
1984	55	25	38	38
1983	35	43	29	75
1982	50	36	35	57
1981	45	87	40	89

Maryland

U.S. CONGRESS

SENATE 2 D

HOUSE 6 D, 2 R

LEGISLATURE

Senate 40 D, 7 R

House 125 D, 16 R

ELECTIONS

1988 Presidential Vote	
Bush	51%
Dukakis	48%
1984 Presidential Vote	
Reagan	53%
Mondale	47%
1980 Presidential Vote	
Reagan	44%
Carter	47%
Anderson	8%
Turnout rate in 1984	51%
Turnout rate in 1986	32%
Turnout rate in 1988	49%

(as percentage of voting age population)

POPULATION AND GROWTH

1980 population	4,216,975
1988 population estimate (19th in the nation)	4,622,000
Percent change 1980-1988	+10%

DEMOGRAPHIC BREAKDOWN

White	75%
Black	23%
Other	2%
(Spanish origin)	2%
Urban	80%
Rural	20%
Born in state	54%
Foreign-born	5%

MAJOR CITIES

Baltimore	752,800
Rockville	46,900
Bowie	35,740
Fredrick	33,800
Hagerstown	33,670

AREA AND LAND USE

Area 9,837 sq. miles (42nd)

Farm	41%
Forest	42%
Federally owned	3%

Gov. William Donald Schaefer (D)
Of Baltimore — Elected 1986

Born: Nov. 2, 1921, West Baltimore, Md.

Education: Baltimore City College, B.A. 1939; U. of Baltimore, LL.B. 1942, LL.M. 1951.

Military Career: Army, 1942-45; Army Reserve, 1945-79.

Occupation: Lawyer.

Religion: Episcopalian.

Political Career: Baltimore City Council, 1955-71, president, 1967-71; Baltimore mayor, 1971-87.

Next Election: 1990.

WORK

Occupations	
White-collar	61%
Blue-collar	25%
Service workers	13%
Government Workers	
Federal	129,177
State	90,062
Local	163,251

MONEY

Median family income	$ 23,112	(3rd)
Tax burden per capita	$ 984	(16th)

EDUCATION

Spending per pupil through grade 12	$ 4,450	(9th)
Persons with college degrees	20%	(4th)

CRIME

Violent crime rate	768 per 100,000 (6th)

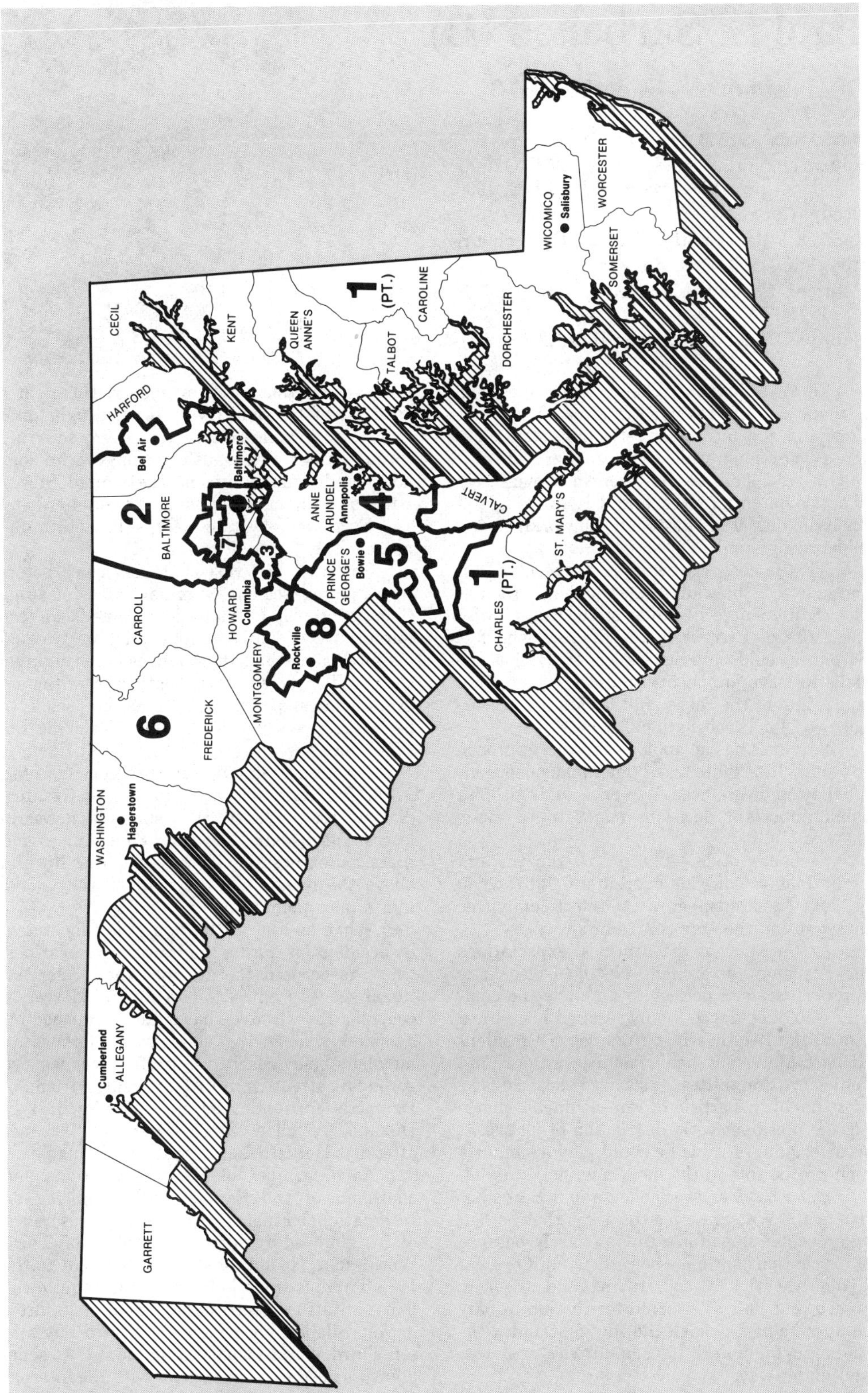
GARRETT
ALLEGANY
Cumberland
WASHINGTON
Hagerstown
6
FREDERICK
CARROLL
MONTGOMERY
Rockville
8
HOWARD
Columbia
3
7
BALTIMORE
2
Bel Air
HARFORD
Baltimore
CECIL
KENT
QUEEN ANNE'S
ANNE ARUNDEL
Annapolis
4
PRINCE GEORGE'S
Bowie
5
1 (PT.)
CHARLES
CALVERT
ST. MARY'S
TALBOT
CAROLINE
1 (PT.)
DORCHESTER
WICOMICO
Salisbury
SOMERSET
WORCESTER

Paul S. Sarbanes (D)

Of Baltimore — Elected 1976

Born: Feb. 3, 1933, Salisbury, Md.

Education: Princeton U., A.B. 1954; Oxford U., England, B.A. 1957; Harvard U., LL.B. 1960.

Occupation: Lawyer.

Family: Wife, Christine Dunbar; three children.

Religion: Greek Orthodox.

Political Career: Md. House, 1967-71; U.S. House, 1971-77.

Capitol Office: 332 Dirksen Bldg. 20510; 224-4524.

In Washington: When asked a question, Sarbanes is apt to fold his arms, furrow his brow and slip into quiet reflection, sometimes for a very long while. His answer, when it comes, will likely be delivered in a measured, almost deferential voice, and it is apt to reflect his basic liberal instincts and the workings of a penetrating mind.

To the core, Sarbanes is deliberate. It is the source of the wide respect he has earned as one of the Senate's leading intellects, and also the cause of frustration to admirers who feel Sarbanes could be a Senate leader. He has the skills to leave opponents sputtering, but often comes late to the cause and focuses his fire too narrowly for broad national debate.

Sarbanes has no apologies for his approach to issues. "It is quite true I don't make decisions off the top of my head," he once said. "I don't think important decisions ought to be made that way."

Sarbanes' style — both its strengths and limitations — got wide exposure in 1987, when he served as a member of the select committee investigating the Iran-contra affair.

At the start of the hearings, expectations for Sarbanes were high. His cool, legalistic approach seemed perfect to untangle the complex web of evidence. Many recalled his critical role in the 1974 hearings to impeach President Richard M. Nixon; then a member of the House Judiciary Committee, Sarbanes drafted the most important article of impeachment, charging the president with obstruction of justice. It seemed quite possible he could play a similarly high-profile role in the new, emerging scandal.

But what was overlooked about Sarbanes' role in the Watergate hearings was that he had taken center stage for a time precisely because of his cautious nature. The case he built against Nixon was tightly constructed and cogently argued, but he was selected for the job in part because he had avoided the spotlight and withheld an opinion until the committee's work was well under way.

During the Iran-contra hearings, Sarbanes was a methodical and detailed questioner, but he never became a central player. He spent a good bit of his time trying to shed light on a scheme to generate funds for covert activities through a complex transfer of high-technology items and weapons among the United States, Israel and China. The plan never got anywhere, and Secretary of State George P. Shultz dismissed it as "nutty."

Sarbanes had vexed his colleagues before by targeting seemingly minor issues, leading them to conclude that his judgment on the importance of subjects does not always equal his intelligence and thoroughness in examining them. When he spars at length with witnesses over technical questions, he sometimes seems to be missing the big picture for nit-picking the small ones.

For a man who has made politics his life's work, Sarbanes has a curious, if refreshing, distaste for publicity. He issues few news releases and disdains television appearances and press conferences. While these qualities lift him above the headline-hungry rabble, they make him a poor point man.

When he draws attention, it is almost as if by accident, as during the Iran-contra hearings, when he accused the attorney for former national security adviser John M. Poindexter of coaching the witness. His comment touched off a hostile exchange that ended with references to members being coached by staff. Sarbanes also got media attention in 1988 for being a friend of Democratic presidential nominee Michael S. Dukakis. A fellow Greek-American, Sarbanes attended Harvard Law School with Dukakis.

As a member of Foreign Relations and chairman of the Banking Subcommittee on International Finance, Sarbanes spends much of his time addressing the problem of Third World debt. He authored an amendment to the 1988 omnibus trade bill that would require the United States to seek establishment of an international debt-management facility to buy and sell Third World loans at a discount. "At some point we need to come to grips with the international debt problem," he said.

Maryland is a strong labor state with a

major shipping port, and Sarbanes reflected these priorities throughout the debate on the trade bill. He authored an amendment to require countries that get U.S. economic aid in cash to use an equivalent amount to buy American products and ship them on U.S. vessels.

In 1989, when the Foreign Relations Committee debated a resolution to block a joint U.S.-Japanese deal to build the FS-X fighter, Sarbanes was a tough critic. "How do you propose we bring down this trade imbalance?" he demanded of three administration officials. "Here was an opportunity ... for Japan to make a major contribution toward remedying that trade deficit," by buying F-16s right off the U.S. production line.

Sarbanes' interests were even more directly parochial when the Senate debated a 1986 bill to transfer control of two major Washington, D.C., area airports from the federal government to a regional authority. Marylanders saw the bill as an economic threat to their state's one major airport, Baltimore-Washington International.

Backed by the Reagan administration, the bill appeared headed for easy passage, but Sarbanes took to the Senate floor to launch the first filibuster of his career. He talked for five days, with an uncharacteristic enthusiasm that won concessions aimed at providing some protection for Maryland's interests.

Sarbanes also served in the 100th Congress as chairman of the Joint Economic Committee, which in recent years has released two annual economic reports — a majority report featuring a gloomy forecast and a minority report with a rosy view. Sarbanes and the Democrats contended that short-term success "is taking place in the context of long-run trends that ought to be of very deep concern" — the federal deficit and the trade imbalance.

Sarbanes described the 1988 report as aimed neither at Congress nor the White House, but at the public. "This is an effort to forewarn, to say, 'If we don't address this, it's all going to come home to roost on us,' " he said.

In addition to the attention he received during the Watergate hearings, Sarbanes had another high-visibility moment in the 1970s, during the Senate's 1978 debate on the Panama Canal treaties. Characteristically, he did not make up his mind until the eve of committee markup sessions. But once he decided, he was an effective advocate. As floor manager for the bill, he doggedly defended U.S. transfer of the canal against all criticism, and won praise from treaty supporters and foes for the depth of his knowledge.

The one issue that consistently sparks passion in Sarbanes is Greece, his family's homeland. A vehement critic of the 1974 Turkish invasion of Cyprus, he has fought over the years to bar U.S. arms to aid Turkey.

At Home: In winning three terms in the House and three more in the Senate, Sarbanes has yet to break a serious sweat. His 1988 win with 62 percent of the vote over Republican Alan L. Keyes, a former diplomat, was typical.

The son of Greek immigrant parents, Sarbanes grew up on Maryland's Eastern Shore, attended Princeton, won a Rhodes scholarship and graduated from Harvard Law School magna cum laude. He settled into Baltimore's legal community, but soon began to consider a bid for the state Legislature. In 1966 he won a seat in the House of Delegates.

During his four-year tenure there, Sarbanes developed the quiet, meticulous approach to problem-solving that has marked his Washington career. He left the Legislature in 1970 to challenge veteran Democratic Rep. George H. Fallon, the chairman of the House Public Works Committee. Running as an anti-war, anti-machine insurgent, Sarbanes defeated the aging Fallon for the Democratic nomination in Baltimore's multi-ethnic 4th District. With Democrats enjoying nearly a 4-to-1 registration advantage in the 4th, he had no general-election trouble.

Two years later, redistricting threw him together with another old-time Democrat, Rep. Edward Garmatz, but Garmatz retired.

By 1976 Sarbanes was ready to move to the Senate, and one-term Republican J. Glenn Beall Jr. was ready to be taken. Sarbanes first had to dispose of former Sen. Joseph D. Tydings, trying for a comeback in the Democratic primary. He did that easily, deflecting Tydings' charges that he was too liberal. In the fall, Beall called him an inactive legislator, and Sarbanes responded with television spots playing up his Judiciary Committee role during Watergate. Sarbanes beat Beall by nearly a quarter-million votes.

There were early signs that his 1982 reelection campaign might be more difficult. After the Republican success in the 1980 elections, Sarbanes' name was at the top of GOP target lists. The National Conservative Political Action Committee (NCPAC) launched a half-million-dollar advertising attack in 1981.

But by early 1982, Sarbanes' opponents had lost their confidence. Many felt the NCPAC campaign had backfired: The Democrat had stepped up his schedule of personal appearances, lashed out at NCPAC as "an alien force" and raised money aggressively.

Meanwhile, the GOP was having trouble finding a prominent candidate willing to challenge the incumbent. After state party leaders failed in their attempts to enlist several big names, the nomination went to Prince George's County Executive Lawrence J. Hogan — whose criticism when he served in the U.S. House of President Nixon had chilled his relationship with many Maryland Republicans.

Hogan called Sarbanes "the phantom," a do-nothing senator whose complaints about the Reagan administration's economic program were not backed up by alternative proposals. But the charges did not faze Sarbanes. Sweeping all but three counties, he won 64 percent of the vote.

Approaching 1988, state Republicans again talked a good game, describing Sarbanes' liberal politics as out of step in a state that had voted for Ronald Reagan in 1984. The GOP eventually fielded an aggressive candidate in Keyes, who drew additional attention as one of two black Senate contenders in 1988. But Sarbanes still won easily.

Keyes was hindered by a very late start. Not only was he not the first Republican choice for the seat, he was not even in the running when the GOP first picked a nominee. The party's March Senate primary had featured nine little-known contenders. Wealthy businessman Thomas L. Blair spent freely and easily won nomination. But he withdrew in May, citing business obligations.

At a state party convention to replace Blair on the ballot, conservatives lobbied for Keyes, a former State Department official who had served as a top assistant to U.N. Representative Jeane J. Kirkpatrick. Though Keyes had not previously been active in the state party, he gained the nomination.

Keyes, one of a still-small group of black conservative leaders, gained some national media attention at the Republican National Convention and also in the fall. In a basically liberal-voting state with a large urban black population, he denounced "welfare-state" policies that he said promoted dependency, and he opposed anti-apartheid sanctions against South Africa.

But Keyes also exhibited an independent streak that alienated some Republicans. He rejected a draft of a convention speech, suggested by the Bush campaign, as tokenistic, and called on the state GOP chairman to resign after the mailing of a party fund-raising letter linking Dukakis with furloughed rapist Willie Horton.

Meanwhile, Sarbanes raised a large treasury and kept a big lead in the polls. With the incumbent campaigning confidently — he spent nearly as much time plugging for Dukakis as for himself — Keyes could not reverse the impression that the outcome was predetermined. Though his 38 percent was not bad considering his low name recognition, Keyes lagged far behind Bush, who carried the state.

Committees

Banking, Housing and Urban Affairs (3rd of 12 Democrats)
International Finance and Monetary Policy (chairman); Housing and Urban Affairs

Foreign Relations (3rd of 10 Democrats)
International Economic Policy, Trade, Oceans and Environment (chairman); European Affairs; Near Eastern and South Asian Affairs

Joint Economic (Vice Chairman)
International Economic Policy (chairman); Economic Resources and Competitiveness; National Security Economics

Elections

1988 General		
Paul S. Sarbanes (D)	999,166	(62%)
Alan L. Keyes (R)	617,537	(38%)
1988 Primary		
Paul S. Sarbanes (D)	309,923	(86%)
B. Emerson Sweatt (D)	25,932	(7%)
A. Robert Kaufman (D)	25,450	(7%)

Previous Winning Percentages: 1982 (64%) **1976** (57%) **1974 *** (84%) **1972 *** (70%) **1970 *** (70%)

* *House elections.*

Campaign Finance

	Receipts	Receipts from PACs	Expenditures
1988			
Sarbanes (D)	$1,477,516	$604,799 (41%)	$1,466,477
Keyes (R)	$684,383	$63,352 (9%)	$662,651

Key Votes

1987	
Enact omnibus highway bill over Reagan veto	Y
Limit testing of space-based anti-ballistic missiles	Y
Oppose banning tests of larger nuclear weapons	N
Confirm Robert H. Bork as Supreme Court justice	N
1988	
Allow vote on campaign-finance overhaul	Y
Pass civil rights restoration bill over Reagan veto	Y
Enact omnibus trade bill over Reagan veto	Y
Approve death penalty for drug-related murders	Y
Oppose "workfare" amendment to welfare overhaul bill	Y

Voting Studies

	Presidential Support		Party Unity		Conservative Coalition	
Year	**S**	**O**	**S**	**O**	**S**	**O**
1988	40	59	96	4	8	92
1987	31	67	95	4	6	94
1986	18	81	96	3	3	95
1985	22	74	90	5	8	87
1984	30	64	94	2	0	98
1983	41	58	88	9	11	84
1982	25	65	91	3	2	78
1981	38	61	93	6	7	93

Interest Group Ratings

Year	ADA	ACU	AFL-CIO	CCUS
1988	90	4	100	29
1987	100	0	90	28
1986	100	0	100	16
1985	100	0	100	25
1984	100	0	100	21
1983	95	0	100	16
1982	85	28	92	15
1981	95	0	95	11

Barbara A. Mikulski (D)

Of Baltimore — Elected 1986

Born: July 20, 1936, Baltimore, Md.
Education: Mount Saint Agnes College, B.A. 1958; U. of Maryland School of Social Work, M.S.W. 1965.
Occupation: Social worker.
Family: Single.
Religion: Roman Catholic.
Political Career: Baltimore City Council, 1971-77; Democratic nominee for U.S. Senate, 1974; U.S. House, 1977-87.
Capitol Office: 320 Hart Bldg. 20510; 224-4654.

In Washington: Because of her well-known image as a tough-talking liberal advocate of federal social programs and of causes affecting women and minorities, Mikulski earned prominent mention at both the Democratic and Republican presidential nominating conventions in 1988.

Early in a presidential nomination acceptance speech that highlighted his own immigrant heritage, Democrat Michael S. Dukakis portrayed Mikulski — a second-generation Polish-American, former social worker, and the first Democratic woman elected to the Senate without being preceded by her husband — as a symbol of the party's commitment to persons of all races and ethnic background.

"My friends, the dream that carried me to this platform is alive tonight in every part of our country," said Dukakis, highlighting Democrats such as Mikulski, San Antonio Mayor Henry Cisneros, New York Gov. Mario M. Cuomo and the Rev. Jesse Jackson.

Not surprisingly, at the Republican convention, the portrayal of Mikulski was less flattering. In his speech to the GOP delegates, religious broadcaster Pat Robertson portrayed Mikulski as a symbol of big-spending social liberalism and regulatory intrusion. He said Democrats want America to be "one big family," with "Jim Wright as the daddy, Barbara Mikulski as the momma and Teddy Kennedy as Big Brother."

Mikulski clearly has the capacity to stir strong emotions. One of the most liberal members of Congress to emerge from a working-class, urban constituency, Mikulski maintains undying support from women's rights and minority rights activists, and from advocates of federal action on a range of domestic problems. Yet the former House member from Baltimore remains beloved by her blue-collar base, thanks to her attentions to constituents' "pothole" problems and her support for the interests of organized labor.

Conservatives tend to share Robertson's view of Mikulski as a left-wing menace. In her 1986 Senate contest, Mikulski, who is single, faced fierce GOP attacks that included apparent innuendoes about her sexual orientation. But Mikulski won a solid 61 percent of the vote to become Maryland's first female U.S. senator.

During her years in the House, Mikulski was best known for her efforts on social issues. She was an architect of the Child Abuse Act, which passed Congress in 1984, and helped add sections on domestic violence and a computerized child-care information system. She advocated "unisex" insurance legislation that would end the practice of giving women lower life insurance annuity payments than men because they tend to live longer. A member of the Energy and Commerce Committee, she allied herself with the panel's consumerist faction. She also consistently received high ratings from the AFL-CIO.

As a senator, Mikulski has pursued similar interests. But thanks to the Senate's smaller numbers, which allow for a quicker rise to positions of influence, Mikulski pursues her issues from a much higher plane. When she left the House after 10 years, her most senior position was as chairman of the low-profile Merchant Marine Subcommittee on Oceanography. After just two years in the Senate, Mikulski became chairman of the Appropriations subcommittee with jurisdiction over the Department of Housing and Urban Development, the Department of Veterans Affairs, the Environmental Protection Agency, the National Aeronautics and Space Administration (NASA), and other independent agencies.

The position gives Mikulski a leadership role on issues that are central to her political agenda — housing, community development, homeless assistance and pollution control. But her jurisdiction over NASA in the catchall subcommittee has broadened Mikulski's horizons; she is an advocate of enhanced funding for the U.S. space program, including the proposed permanent manned space station.

There is a parochial angle to her pro-space stands. The Goddard Space Flight Center in

Greenbelt, Md., plays a key role in monitoring U.S. space activity, and is coordinating part of the space station program.

The sometimes-clashing priorities of the programs guided by the subcommittee caused Mikulski some difficulty during the 100th Congress, her first in the Senate. A consensus to fund the space station fully had been established on the subcommittee; but in order to do so under the mandate of fiscal restraint, the panel had to shift $600 million from housing and environmental programs. Mikulski and several other Democrats tried on the Senate floor to restore those cuts by taking $600 million from defense, but they failed.

The lesson was not lost on Mikulski. As chairman, she has tried to get the interest groups with a stake in programs funded by her subcommittee to work together for a bigger share of federal funds, rather than fight over a smaller pie. "Let's make sure we have an alliance for the veterans, who fought to save our planet, the homeless, who have a right to live on it with dignity, the environmentalists, who take care of it, and you, who explore it," Mikulski said in a 1989 speech to the American Institute of Aeronautics and Astronautics.

Still, it is the liberal social agenda that drives much of Mikulski's work. A member of the Labor and Human Resources Committee, she is a leading supporter of the Act for Better Child Care bill. Though the measure failed in the 100th Congress, it was reintroduced and passed by the Labor Committee in early 1989.

An early inductee in the feminist movement, Mikulski is a staunch supporter of allowing women to choose abortion. In September 1988, she backed an unsuccessful proposal to reverse a ban on Medicaid funding of abortions in cases of rape or incest. "Abortion is a legal medical procedure that is now available to women who are well off," Mikulski said. "Denying this option to poor women is discrimination, pure and simple." In early 1989, she was one of the leaders of a congressional coalition that filed a brief in *Webster v. Reproductive Health Services,* a Supreme Court case that challenged the validity of the 1973 *Roe v. Wade* decision, which legalized abortion.

Her stance on abortion may not be shared by many of the ethnic, blue-collar Marylanders she has relied on for support. However, Mikulski has persuaded these voters to overlook such differences by projecting a personal concern for issues where they share common ground.

In March 1987, Mikulski, a supporter of long-term health care legislation, testified for a proposal to mitigate rules that required individuals to exhaust virtually all their assets before receiving Medicaid assistance for expensive nursing-home care. In doing so, she reached into her personal experience for illustration: Her father, the longtime owner of a Baltimore grocery, was then confined to a nursing home with Alzheimer's disease (from which he died in 1988).

"We were able to grapple with that because of the resources within my own family," Mikulski said. "But not every family has a daughter who is a United States senator who can help when this crisis occurs." Echoing the frustrations of those who had scrimped for their retirement, only to face penury before receiving federal long-term-care assistance, Mikulski said, "If my father had spent his life savings by going to Atlantic City and gambling his money away, we would be eligible for the same Medicaid."

At Home: When veteran GOP Sen. Charles McC. Mathias Jr. decided to retire in 1986, Mikulski jumped into the fray to succeed him. Many questioned whether the pudgy, 4-foot-11 Mikulski would strike voters as "senatorial"; the appeal of her urban image to suburbanites also was suspect. But Mikulski proved that the political skills that elected her in Baltimore transferred to the statewide level.

Mikulski's vibrant campaign style gave her a big edge in the primary against two prominent Democrats, 8th District Rep. Michael D. Barnes and outgoing Gov. Harry R. Hughes. Barnes was expected to earn some liberal backing with his strong opposition to Reagan's Central America policies, but his colorless campaign was unable to attract much support outside his Montgomery County turf. The taciturn Hughes, undercut by a state savings and loan crisis, was almost invisible. Mikulski outpolled Barnes by 100,000 votes; Hughes was a distant third.

Mikulski then had to overcome a negative campaign by Republican Linda Chavez. A longtime Democrat, Chavez had lived only briefly in Maryland. But she had gained a conservative following during her tenure as staff director of the U.S. Commission on Civil Rights, where she angered some minority activists with her stands against affirmative action and busing.

Chavez was never more than a long shot against Mikulski. But the Republican did not go quietly. After Chavez described Mikulski as a "San Francisco-style" liberal, Mikulski supporters accused her of raising that city's image as a haven for homosexuals as part of a campaign of innuendo against Mikulski.

But Mikulski managed to keep her own legendary temper in check, resisting the bait to engage in battle with an opponent who was no electoral threat. Winning 83 percent of the vote in her home city of Baltimore, and carrying better than 60 percent in Baltimore County and the Washington, D.C., suburbs of Montgomery and Prince George's counties, Mikulski coasted to victory.

Mikulski had already grown used to easy wins. Having made a name for herself as a civic activist and a Baltimore City Council member, she had no trouble winning a 1976 Democratic House primary to succeed Democrat Paul S. Sarbanes, then running in his first Senate election. In five House general elections, she faced no serious Republican opposition.

The granddaughter of Polish immigrants, Mikulski's interest in her ethnic roots first gained her a political following. In 1970, Mikulski, then a social worker, wrote a *New York Times* opinion piece about the "forgotten" ethnic American, whose interests were neglected by urban planners. Mikulski accused government officials of polarizing black and ethnic communities when they should be cooperating on a working-class agenda.

At the time, Mikulski was a community organizer fighting against a highway that would have leveled several Baltimore neighborhoods. Her campaign preserved the communities and saved a tract that later became Harborplace, the hub of Baltimore's downtown revival.

Mikulski's activism propelled her into the City Council in 1971. She also established herself in the feminist movement. She was appointed by Democratic National Committee Chairman Jean Westwood in 1972 to serve on a commission to review the party's delegate selection, and later became commission chairman.

When no prominent Maryland Democrat stepped forward to challenge Mathias in 1974, Mikulski filled the vacuum. She had little money, and Mathias pre-empted much of her natural base by winning the support of the state AFL-CIO. Still, the energetic Mikulski drew a respectable 43 percent of the vote, carrying Baltimore city and Baltimore County.

Committees

Appropriations (12th of 16 Democrats)
HUD-Independent Agencies (chairman); Foreign Operations; Legislative Branch; Transportation and Related Agencies; Treasury, Postal Service and General Government

Labor and Human Resources (9th of 9 Democrats)
Education, Arts and Humanities; Employment and Productivity; Labor

Small Business (9th of 10 Democrats)
Export Expansion (chairman); Urban and Minority-Owned Business Development

Elections

1986 General		
Barbara A. Mikulski (D)	675,225	(61%)
Linda Chavez (R)	437,411	(39%)
1986 Primary		
Barbara A. Mikulski (D)	307,876	(50%)
Michael D. Barnes (D)	195,086	(31%)
Harry Hughes (D)	88,908	(14%)
Debra Hanania Freeman (D)	9,350	(2%)
Edward M. Olszewski (D)	7,877	(1%)
A. Robert Kaufmann (D)	6,505	(1%)
Others (D)	6,322	(1%)

Previous Winning Percentages: **1984** * (68%) **1982** * (74%) **1980** * (76%) **1978** * (100%) **1976** * (75%)

* *House elections.*

Campaign Finance

	Receipts	Receipts from PACs	Expend-itures
1986			
Mikulski (D)	$2,160,812	$660,260 (31%)	$2,057,216
Chavez (R)	$1,716,192	$285,253 (17%)	$1,699,175

Key Votes

1987	
Enact omnibus highway bill over Reagan veto	Y
Limit testing of space-based anti-ballistic missiles	Y
Oppose banning tests of larger nuclear weapons	N
Confirm Robert H. Bork as Supreme Court justice	N
1988	
Allow vote on campaign-finance overhaul	Y
Pass civil rights restoration bill over Reagan veto	Y
Enact omnibus trade bill over Reagan veto	Y
Approve death penalty for drug-related murders	N
Oppose "workfare" amendment to welfare overhaul bill	Y

Voting Studies

	Presidential Support		Party Unity		Conservative Coalition	
Year	**S**	**O**	**S**	**O**	**S**	**O**
1988	40	58	93	3	5	92
1987	28	64	93	4	13	84
House Service						
1986	11	80	75	4	10	64
1985	18	83	89	4	18	82
1984	24	65	84	6	12	75
1983	15	84	90	6	18	76
1982	31	68	90	7	18	79
1981	32	68	84	9	11	87

Interest Group Ratings

Year	ADA	ACU	AFL-CIO	CCUS
1988	95	0	100	29
1987	100	4	100	28
House Service				
1986	90	5	93	20
1985	80	10	100	32
1984	85	0	83	21
1983	90	9	94	11
1982	90	23	100	19
1981	100	7	87	16

1 Roy Dyson (D)

Of Great Mills — Elected 1980

Born: Nov. 15, 1948, Great Mills, Md.
Education: Attended U. of Baltimore, 1970-71; U. of Maryland, 1971-72.
Occupation: Lumber company executive.
Family: Single.
Religion: Roman Catholic.
Political Career: Md. House, 1975-81; Democratic nominee for U.S. House, 1976.
Capitol Office: 326 Cannon Bldg. 20515; 225-5311.

In Washington: After a year of bizarre circumstance that nearly cost him his seat in 1988, Dyson's survival skills will be tested in the 101st Congress. He meets the danger well armed, having gained a place on the Agriculture Committee and a Merchant Marine subcommittee chairmanship to add to his position on Armed Services. But the Pentagon procurement scandal, to which Dyson has been linked in press reports, continues to loom over him.

The 100th Congress brought a host of horrors to Dyson's doorstep. His chief aide killed himself following a newspaper account of his peculiar office management practices. Dyson was obliged to deny that he is a homosexual. Then, he was highlighted as a recipient of campaign funds and honoraria from contractors and consultants tied to Pentagon purchasing fraud. The siege of bad publicity took its toll at the polls; against a dark horse Republican, Dyson survived by only 1,540 votes.

Dyson's problems started in April 1988, with reports alleging that Tom Pappas, Dyson's administrative assistant, failed to report campaign consulting fees on Federal Election Commission and House disclosure forms. Reporters from *The Washington Post* probing the story turned up numerous Dyson staffers who had quit or been fired after protesting Pappas' management style. The Post's sources portrayed Pappas as someone who hired young male aides, then tried to dominate their lives by requiring them to drink and dine with him.

On May 1, the day the article appeared in the Post, Pappas leaped from the New York City hotel where he and Dyson stayed after a meeting with officials of Unisys, a defense contractor. Though shaken by the death of Pappas — who had hired him to his first job at the Democratic National Committee in 1972, then guided his career — Dyson held a news conference a few days later. Since the article had centered on male socializing, Dyson, who is single, seemed prepared for questions about his personal life. When a reporter asked if he was homosexual, Dyson calmly answered "no."

But as discussion of the Pappas incident was fading, questions were raised about Dyson's House efforts on behalf of defense contractors that had given him honoraria or contributed to his campaign. It was reported that Dyson voted to authorize purchase of Army trucks from the Oshkosh Corp., shortly after receiving a $2,000 honorarium for speaking at a company breakfast.

Then, the Justice Department revealed its investigation into bribery and fraud in Pentagon procurement. Though Defense officials, contractors and consultants were the targets, several House members found themselves linked to the probe. One was Dyson, who had provoked suspicion by working to protect a naval electronic-warfare system built by Unisys. In July, Dyson confirmed that during a trip to a company facility the previous year, Unisys Vice President Charles Gardner presented his campaign with 17 $1,000 checks from individuals with Unisys links.

Dyson insistently denied trading his vote for money, and said he worked with contractors only to obtain defense contracts for his district. "I made no bones about the fact that when I went into Congress I was going to attempt to get onto the Armed Services Committee, because the committee would directly benefit the region," Dyson told the Post.

That statement came as no surprise to those who knew Dyson's work on Armed Services, where he is seen as far more interested in pork-barrel bargaining than in global defense issues. When President Reagan summoned several House members to the White House in early 1988 to lobby for military aid to the Nicaraguan contras, Dyson — by his own account — told Reagan he would vote for the contras "right now" if the president would block Pentagon plans to move a squadron from Patuxent Naval Air Station in the 1st District.

Though Dyson has undertaken no concerted public-relations campaign to improve his image, he appears to be getting help from the Democratic leadership. The party gave him a seat on Agriculture, which may help him regain support from the district's many chicken and

Maryland 1

Eastern Shore; Southern Maryland

The remote fishing villages and farm towns of the Chesapeake Bay region long took pride in their semi-isolation. Some of the watermen living on the small islands of the Bay speak with the Elizabethan twang of their ancestors who landed here over three centuries ago.

However, the modern world has been moving in on the area that comprises the 1st. Suburbs from the Washington, D.C., and Baltimore areas have spread into the district, and subdivisions of vacation homes have sprouted near the Bay and the Atlantic Ocean.

Pollution caused by rapid growth in the Philadelphia-Washington megalopolis threatens the Bay's aquatic life. This, combined with an unrelated parasite problem, has reduced oyster harvests, making life even harsher for the watermen who symbolize the region. Environmental concerns have also hit home near the Army's Aberdeen Proving Ground in the northwest part of the 1st; toxic waste and nerve gas disposal issues have embroiled residents there.

Yet while these problems have led district voters to demand environmental consciousness of their officials, their overall tone remains conservative. This is true throughout the 1st, even though it is a discontiguous mass running from the northeastern edge of the state down through the entire Eastern Shore, then west across the Bay to three Southern Maryland counties.

The district, especially the rural Eastern Shore, long held Southern Democratic sympathies: it was a hotbed of support for Alabama Gov. George C. Wallace's presidential campaigns. But a swelling of GOP registration during the Reagan era has given the 1st a more Republican tone. George Bush took 63 percent of the district vote and won every county in 1988. Democratic Sen. Paul S. Sarbanes, a Salisbury native, also won the 1st, though by a lesser margin than in the state's more urban areas.

The once-isolated Eastern Shore has experienced substantial growth in the three decades since the Chesapeake Bay Bridge linked it conveniently to the rest of Maryland. But despite the high-rise growth in the vacation capital of Ocean City, the region on the whole remains farm country; Frank Perdue's chicken business is headquartered here.

The small cities of the Eastern Shore, including Salisbury and Cambridge, contain much of the district's black population, which makes up about 20 percent of the total.

Southern Maryland, on the western side of the Bay, has long had the same rural ambience as the Eastern Shore, but that is fading in the face of urban sprawl and declining use of its mainstay product, tobacco. Shopping centers and subdivisions have sprung up in Charles County, which is becoming an outer suburb of Washington, D.C.

To the north, the 1st takes in a portion of Harford County, which is being absorbed into Baltimore's orbit. Along with Harford's Aberdeen Proving Ground, southern Maryland provides the district with a strong military presence. The Patuxent Naval Air Center and the Indian Head Naval Ordnance Station are both located there.

Population: 526,206. White 422,847 (80%), Black 97,779 (19%), Other 3,911 (1%). Spanish origin 5,170 (1%). 18 and over 369,721 (70%), 65 and over 54,049 (10%). Median age: 30.

crop farmers, who have Southern Democratic roots but recent GOP voting tendencies. And because of his seniority on Merchant Marine, a committee of importance to the Chesapeake Bay area, Dyson is now chairman of the Panama Canal/Outer Continental Shelf Subcommittee.

But Dyson does not have to look far over his shoulder to see the shadow of the Pentagon scandal. In 1989, several Unisys employees, including Gardner, were convicted on bribery or fraud charges. With each case came reports noting Dyson's ties to the scandal figures.

At Home: When Dyson's troubles hit in 1988, he appeared fortunate that his GOP foe was a political unknown, college guidance counselor Wayne T. Gilchrest. But even with a huge fund-raising edge and a reputation for constituent service, Dyson barely won.

Because of Dyson's 2-to-1 victory in 1986, Republicans had no luck recruiting a strong 1988 challenger. Only Gilchrest and John Vance Meyers, the director of Indian housing with the federal Department of Housing and Urban Development, signed up for the primary.

The state party endorsed Meyers, but he did little campaigning. Meanwhile, Gilchrest, with a treasury of about $300, drove around the district in his family car to drum up support. He won a lightly attended primary.

When Dyson's image began to deteriorate after Pappas' suicide, district Republicans considered asking Gilchrest to drop out in lieu of a better-known figure. But Gilchrest refused, and as Dyson's troubles deepened, he began to emerge as a legitimate contender. The former high school teacher exhibited a common-man appeal many found refreshing. He spent part of the year moonlighting as a house painter. By the end of the campaign, he had raised over $100,000, enough to run a radio ad featuring an endorsement from President Reagan.

But with Dyson employing all his resources, Gilchrest's late rush fell short.

Dyson's 1988 dilemma continued an odd tradition in the 1st: Scandal has plagued its recent representatives, including Dyson's predecessor, Republican Robert E. Bauman.

Dyson was serving in the state Legislature — the 10th member of his deeply rooted Maryland family to do so — when he challenged Bauman in 1978. At the time, Bauman was viewed as a brilliant but acerbic conservative and the leading GOP parliamentary strategist in the House. Dyson played up his own legislative record and his previous work in Washington for the DNC and as a congressional aide, but Bauman won with 54 percent.

Dyson was the underdog when he challenged Bauman again in 1980. But that changed drastically in October, when Bauman was charged with soliciting sex from a teenage boy. Dyson surged ahead in the polls overnight, and held on to win by 6,000 votes.

Bauman sought a comeback in 1982, but dropped out of the contest in midsummer after accusing his GOP primary foe, former state Sen. C. A. Porter Hopkins, of resurrecting the homosexuality issue. Dyson went on to beat Hopkins by better than 2-to-1.

With Bauman permanently on the sidelines — he admitted his homosexuality and became a spokesman for gay conservatives — the GOP offered Cecil County farmer and real-estate agent Harlan C. Williams in 1984 and 1986. Williams sought to paint Dyson as a liberal, but lacked campaign experience. Dyson won 58 percent in 1984 and 67 percent in 1986.

The controversies that embroiled Dyson and Bauman made them a part of a 1st District tradition of troubled incumbency. In 1973, GOP Rep. William O. Mills committed suicide after being linked to a Watergate-era campaign contribution. And Democrat Thomas F. Johnson, who served the 1st from 1959-63, was convicted of financial irregularities.

Committees

Agriculture (25th of 27 Democrats)
Wheat, Soybeans and Feed Grains

Armed Services (13th of 31 Democrats)
Procurement and Military Nuclear Systems; Readiness

Merchant Marine and Fisheries (9th of 26 Democrats)
Panama Canal/Outer Continental Shelf (chairman); Fisheries and Wildlife Conservation and the Environment

Elections

1988 General		
Roy Dyson (D)	96,128	(50%)
Wayne T. Gilchrest (R)	94,588	(50%)
1988 Primary		
Roy Dyson (D)	39,207	(86%)
Morris C. Durham (D)	6,379	(14%)
1986 General		
Roy Dyson (D)	88,113	(67%)
Harlan C. Williams (R)	43,764	(33%)

Previous Winning Percentages: **1984** (58%) **1982** (69%) **1980** (52%)

District Vote For President

	1988		1984		1980		1976	
D	75,575	(36%)	64,381	(35%)	75,300	(42%)	76,207	(49%)
R	131,161	(63%)	121,294	(65%)	94,343	(52%)	78,180	(51%)
I					9,912	(6%)		

Campaign Finance

	Receipts	Receipts from PACs	Expend-itures
1988			
Dyson (D)	$691,251	$403,647 (58%)	$684,204
Gilchrest (R)	$119,429	0	$118,568
1986			
Dyson (D)	$356,603	$243,049 (68%)	$354,240
Williams (R)	$172,110	$11,907 (7%)	$166,376

Key Votes

1987	
Raise speed limit to 65 mph	N
Approve Gephardt "fair trade" amendment	Y
Ban testing of larger nuclear weapons	N
Delay "re-flagging" of Kuwaiti tankers	Y
Approve tax-raising deficit-reduction bill	Y
1988	
Approve aid to Nicaraguan contras	N
Enact civil rights restoration bill over Reagan veto	Y
Kill 60-day plant-closing notification measure	N
Pass omnibus trade bill over Reagan veto	Y
Approve death penalty for drug-related murders	Y
Bar federal funds for abortions in cases of rape and incest	Y
Oppose seven-day waiting period for purchase of handguns	Y

Voting Studies

	Presidential Support		Party Unity		Conservative Coalition	
Year	**S**	**O**	**S**	**O**	**S**	**O**
1988	29	57	71	18	63	11
1987	47	49	67	27	72	28
1986	53	47	57	39	88	12
1985	55	44	66	29	71	27
1984	45	54	65	33	71	29
1983	39	60	63	36	75	24
1982	55	43	68	29	62	37
1981	61	39	52	48	92	8

Interest Group Ratings

Year	ADA	ACU	AFL-CIO	CCUS
1988	55	50	92	36
1987	44	32	81	27
1986	30	64	69	50
1985	30	65	59	50
1984	25	46	69	38
1983	50	52	82	30
1982	35	50	70	43
1981	30	60	80	47

2 Helen Delich Bentley (R)

Of Lutherville — Elected 1984

Born: Nov. 28, 1923, Ruth, Nev.
Education: Attended U. of Nevada, 1941-42; George Washington U., 1943; U. of Missouri, B.A. 1944.
Occupation: Journalist; international trade consultant.
Family: Husband, William Roy Bentley.
Religion: Greek Orthodox.
Political Career: Republican nominee for U.S. House, 1980, 1982.
Capitol Office: 1610 Longworth Bldg. 20515; 225-3061.

In Washington: Bentley's effort to look out for American manufacturers and shippers has evolved into an obsession with a place far away from her beloved Port of Baltimore: Japan.

The gruff, raspy voiced former newspaperwoman feels so strongly that America is getting the short end of the trade stick that Japan-bashing has become a staple of her work. During a three-week period in the spring of 1988, for instance, she took to the House floor 11 times to lambaste the Japanese on a variety of trade-related matters.

The summer before, she organized a media event on the steps of the Capitol in which she and several Republican members used sledgehammers to destroy a Toshiba radio. It was intended as a symbolic denouncement of the Japanese firm's sale of sensitive technology to the Soviet Union. While it illustrated congressional frustration over the flood of Japanese imports, it was widely regarded as a silly stunt.

No one questions Bentley's sincerity in trying to protect American workers and level the playing field of trade between the United States and Japan. But the fervor and frequency with which she sees Japanese conspiracies can make colleagues' eyes roll.

Bentley's criticism of Toshiba was consistent with her opposition to transferring strategic technology to U.S. allies. She sponsored an amendment to a 1988 defense authorization bill providing that if a U.S. contractor is required to give the Pentagon technical data for use by a second contractor making the same item, the data can be transferred only to a U.S. firm.

Bentley, now in her third term, was elected on a promise to pry loose funds for dredging the Port of Baltimore. She used her seat on Public Works to lobby for inclusion of the harbor-deepening project in a water resources bill, and then fought to get the funds into a 1986 supplemental appropriation. By year's end, some $17 million had been appropriated, and by February 1987, the contracts were awarded. Bentley was not alone in pushing the project, but her persistence was an important factor. That sort of success has earned her a reputation as a consummate protector of her district's interests.

At times, she approaches the legislative process like a suspicious watchdog who thinks somebody might be stealing something from her district. She pores over bills line by line to see what effect they might have on Baltimore County. She has been known to vote against multibillion-dollar legislation on the grounds that minor provisions in it would cost the district a small amount of money.

Bentley lobbied to include Baltimore as part of the Norfolk Homeport under the Navy's "homeporting" plan for ship repair. That meant the shipyard at Sparrows Point in her district could bid on ship maintenance contracts ranging from $30 million to $50 million. Later, she had the shipyard designated a "Foreign Trade Subzone" so it would not have to pay duties on foreign component parts. As a former chairman of the Federal Maritime Commission, Bentley has valuable contacts in the executive branch and the maritime agency. Even if she does not know a bureaucrat personally, she is not shy about calling to let him know in very clear terms what she wants done for her district.

When Bentley has ventured into broader political terrain, her success has been mixed. She caught flak from environmentalists for an apparent flip-flop on oil drilling in Alaska. In 1986, Bentley supported legislation that would have declared the Arctic National Wildlife Refuge in Alaska off limits for oil and gas production. The next year she cosponsored a bill inviting bids for oil and gas rights in the coastal plains area of the refuge.

The Sierra Club was livid about the switch. Bentley defended it, saying that she supported the 1986 bill only out of respect for its sponsor, Arizona Democrat Morris K. Udall, and that she did not recall Udall's bill including the ban on oil production.

In the 101st Congress, Bentley took a leave of absence from the largely parochial and bipartisan Public Works Committee and moved onto the Budget Committee, a more partisan panel

Maryland 2

Baltimore Suburbs

Baltimore County, which constitutes the bulk of the 2nd, is affluent and Republican as it reaches north, away from the city of Baltimore: In such prosperous towns as Towson, Lutherville and Cockeysville sit the spacious homes of Baltimore's business establishment. To the east of the city (which is not in the district), the 2nd is more blue-collar and traditionally Democratic.

This mix kept Democrats in competition in the 2nd through the early 1980s. In 1980, Ronald Reagan bested President Carter here by only 3 percentage points; Democratic Rep. Clarence D. Long held off two determined challenges by Bentley. However, Bentley's 1984 victory and subsequent success, combined with Reagan's popularity, have made the 2nd more dependably Republican. Reagan scored a 2-to-1 victory in the district in 1984; George Bush took it with 62 percent in 1988.

Residents of northern Baltimore County are careful to point out that their area has nothing to do with the urban Democratic politics of Baltimore city. However, not many today are anxious to hail a figure who was once a local hero: Republican Spiro T. Agnew, who began his political career in Towson and rose to county executive and governor, prior to his ill-fated tenure as vice president.

The southern area of the county inside the Baltimore Beltway is a demographic extension of the city. Dundalk, just east of the city, is heavily Polish. The Bethlehem Steel mill at Sparrows Point has been a fixture there for years, but the industry's hard times have led to decline and layoffs. Bentley's tough-talking image and protectionist trade stance have enabled her to erode the Democratic base there.

The most important change in the district for the 1980s — and the one that helped bring about Long's eventual demise — was the addition of burgeoning western Harford County, northeast of Baltimore. This portion of Harford favors Republicans, especially for president: Bush took 68 percent of its vote.

Western Harford used to be farm land, but people have followed Interstate 95 out of Baltimore and turned the pastures into subdivisions.

Population: 526,354. White 488,860 (93%), Black 28,590 (5%), Other 7,227 (1%). Spanish origin 4,446 (1%). 18 and over 388,788 (74%), 65 and over 46,971 (9%). Median age: 31.

because of its responsibility for setting overall budget priorities. There she introduced a resolution calling for a two-year across-the-board freeze in the federal budget at 1989 levels. It lost in committee.

Still, her passion is most visible as a protectionist. She has been an avid supporter of a range of "Buy American" amendments — requiring government purchase of U.S. goods and monitoring the loss of American jobs as the result of foreign imports.

Sometimes that stance can get awkward. At the 1988 GOP National Convention, Bentley chaired the Maryland delegation and was given a sporty green cap to wear as a designation of her leadership role. She refused to wear it, however, saying, "Damned if I'm going to mess up my hair." But the cap, which had George Bush's name printed on it, posed another problem: It was made in Taiwan. "I'm not too happy about even carrying it," Bentley said.

At Home: Persistence paid big dividends for Bentley. It took her three tries to convince suburban Baltimore voters that veteran Democrat Clarence D. Long had overstayed his welcome. But within two years of her 1984 victory, Bentley was rising to state and national prominence, beating back a $1 million challenge by Democrat Kathleen Kennedy Townsend, a daughter of the late Sen. Robert F. Kennedy.

Bentley, who dubbed herself "the fighting lady," lost to Long in 1980 and 1982, but she improved with each campaign. Her theme was that Long had mishandled Baltimore's harbor economy.

Her cause was aided by the recognition that she had expertise on harbor issues. Bentley worked for 25 years as a maritime reporter and editor for *The Sun* of Baltimore. She also produced a local weekly TV program on the harbor that ran for 15 years. In 1969, Bentley was appointed chairman of the Federal Maritime Commission by President Nixon, becoming the highest-ranking woman in federal government at that time. She was also active in GOP politics.

In her first two campaigns against Long, Bentley contended that his opposition to dredging the Baltimore harbor had cost jobs; she won 43 percent the first time, 47 percent the second. To earn the chance for a third try, she had to weather a 1984 primary challenge from Dave Smick, a former aide to GOP Rep. Jack F. Kemp.

That fall, Bentley did little to alter her previous campaign pitch, even though the 11-term incumbent had backed off his opposition to the harbor-dredging project. Long, meanwhile, ran the most professional campaign of his career. But Bentley was aided by a redistricting change that bolstered the GOP presence in the 2nd and by Reagan's strong showing there. By registering solid margins in GOP strongholds along Baltimore County's central corridor and cutting into Long's strength in such Democratic towns as Dundalk and Essex, Bentley won with 51 percent.

Bentley's first-term emphasis on harbor dredging and trade issues helped secure her base, but they did not earn her respite from a vigorous re-election challenge.

The Democratic candidate was a relative newcomer to the district, but had no name identification problem. Townsend, a 35-year-old attorney, was Robert F. Kennedy's eldest child. She quickly drew media attention, both locally and from national and foreign journalists. Many reports highlighted the "two siblings" angle —Townsend's brother, Joseph P. Kennedy II, was running to succeed retiring House Speaker Thomas P. O'Neill Jr. in Massachusetts.

While Bentley was slowed with a kidney ailment, Townsend campaigned vigorously, literally running from door-to-door. Many observers speculated that Townsend's broad smile and cheerleader-like enthusiasm would contrast well with Bentley's gruff persona.

Townsend, who had recently moved to the district from Boston, campaigned under the name of her husband, a district native and a college teacher in Annapolis. But Bentley, who chafed at the publicity the newcomer was receiving, ran hard on the carpetbagger issue. Despite Townsend's upbringing in the Virginia suburbs of Washington, D.C., Bentley referred to her as "the money machine from Massachusetts." Townsend tried to portray herself as a "new ideas" Democrat, but Bentley saw her as an heir to her family's liberal agenda.

Bentley's strongest card was her record of constituent service; she focused heavily on the largess she had brought to the 2nd. Her incumbency also helped her raise more money than the heavily financed Democrat. Bentley won an impressive 59-41 percent victory.

Though Townsend said she was not done with her political career, she passed on the 1988 election. Bentley's convincing 1986 victory also deterred other prominent Democrats. The job of challenging Bentley fell to state Rep. Joseph Bartenfelder, a well-regarded young legislator who was unable to dent Bentley's growing popularity. She won with 71 percent.

Committees

Budget (14th of 14 Republicans)
Task Forces: Defense, Foreign Policy and Space; Human Resources

Merchant Marine and Fisheries (10th of 17 Republicans)
Coast Guard and Navigation; Merchant Marine; Panama Canal/Outer Continental Shelf

Select Aging (13th of 27 Republicans)
Health and Long-Term Care

Elections

1988 General

Helen Delich Bentley (R)	157,956	(71%)
Joseph Bartenfelder (D)	63,114	(29%)

1986 General

Helen Delich Bentley (R)	96,745	(59%)
Kathleen Kennedy Townsend (D)	68,200	(41%)

Previous Winning Percentage: **1984** (51%)

District Vote For President

	1988	1984	1980	1976
D	85,451 (37%)	74,102 (34%)	98,946 (44%)	87,259 (46%)
R	141,948 (62%)	145,320 (66%)	107,701 (47%)	102,243 (54%)
I			18,513 (8%)	

Campaign Finance

	Receipts	Receipts from PACs	Expend-itures
1988			
Bentley (R)	$850,900	$293,984 (35%)	$782,796
Bartenfelder (D)	$69,042	$17,865 (26%)	$65,023
1986			
Bentley (R)	$1,076,329	$361,985 (34%)	$1,070,161
Townsend (D)	$1,076,161	$185,373 (17%)	$1,071,603

Key Votes

1987	
Raise speed limit to 65 mph	N
Approve Gephardt "fair trade" amendment	Y
Ban testing of larger nuclear weapons	N
Delay "re-flagging" of Kuwaiti tankers	N
Approve tax-raising deficit-reduction bill	N
1988	
Approve aid to Nicaraguan contras	Y
Enact civil rights restoration bill over Reagan veto	N
Kill 60-day plant-closing notification measure	Y
Pass omnibus trade bill over Reagan veto	Y
Approve death penalty for drug-related murders	Y
Bar federal funds for abortions in cases of rape and incest	Y
Oppose seven-day waiting period for purchase of handguns	Y

Voting Studies

	Presidential Support		Party Unity		Conservative Coalition	
Year	**S**	**O**	**S**	**O**	**S**	**O**
1988	46	45	74	16	87	11
1987	49	48	68	25	84	16
1986	57	38	60	30	80	14
1985	64	34	74	19	85	13

Interest Group Ratings

Year	ADA	ACU	AFL-CIO	CCUS
1988	10	86	69	79
1987	32	57	63	73
1986	15	62	67	63
1985	20	76	24	73

3 Benjamin L. Cardin (D)

Of Baltimore — Elected 1986

Born: Oct. 5, 1943, Baltimore, Md.
Education: U. of Pittsburgh, B.A. 1964; U. of Maryland School of Law, LL.B. 1967.
Occupation: Lawyer.
Family: Wife, Myrna Edelman; two children.
Religion: Jewish.
Political Career: Md. House, 1967-87, Speaker, 1979-87.
Capitol Office: 507 Cannon Bldg. 20515; 225-4016.

In Washington: Like most state legislators, Cardin was perceived as having taken a step up when he moved to Congress from the Maryland House. But Cardin gave up considerable power in doing so. He had served as House Speaker in Annapolis for almost a decade, and had grown accustomed to calling the legislative shots.

Cardin's transition to lowly freshman was not glitch-free. But his understanding of the legislative process and his willingness to help the Democratic leadership was noted by senior members, who named him an at-large whip. Cardin's driving ambition to be an insider on a prestige committee is well-known, but in pursuing that goal, he has managed to stay on friendly personal terms with most colleagues.

The Baltimore Democrat arrived in Congress brimming with confidence that his reputation as a legislative deal-maker and budgetary expert would win him a coveted seat on Budget, or maybe even Ways and Means. Though those committees are usually unreachable for a freshman, Cardin lobbied hard — a bit too hard, perhaps — and in the end, he had to settle for Judiciary and Public Works.

But Cardin did not waste time sulking over missing out on a top committee assignment. He dug into the work of his two panels, and carried the water for his party when needed. On Judiciary, he offered an amendment to the 1988 drug bill to strike "user accountability" language. Like many liberals, Cardin maintained that convicted drug users who had gone to jail had paid their debt to society and should not be disqualified from federal benefits, such as education and job training. His amendment was rejected in favor of one requiring drug offenders to complete rehabilitation programs.

Cardin's work has helped him overcome his overly assertive entrance. He still has his eyes on Ways and Means, and it is a fairly good bet that he will eventually reach the committee.

Like many who want to get ahead in the House, Cardin spends a fair amount of time on the floor, listening to the proceedings and talking with members one-on-one. When he did rise to speak during the 100th Congress, it was often about the plight of individual Soviet Jewish "refuseniks," an important concern in his district.

At Home: Cardin's legislative talents helped him acquire a leadership role in the Maryland House at an extraordinarily young age. He was 23 when first elected to the Legislature in 1966. By 1975 he was chairman of the House Ways and Means Committee. Four years later, at 35, Cardin became the youngest Speaker in the history of the Maryland House.

Cardin was generally popular among his colleagues in Annapolis. Those who viewed him as tough but fair far outnumbered critics who complained that he planted pliable allies in chairmanships, and rushed favored bills through without debate. On such difficult issues as pension laws and bank deregulation, Cardin adopted a conciliatory and bipartisan approach. Though he opposed extreme tax-limitation measures, Cardin established a Spending Affordability Committee to restrain the growth in state spending.

Cardin initially hoped that his strong legislative record would earn him his party's nomination in 1986 to succeed outgoing Democratic Gov. Harry Hughes. But William Donald Schaefer, the popular Democratic mayor of Baltimore, also decided to run for governor. Cardin recognized that Schaefer would overshadow him, so he opted to seek the 3rd District House seat that Democrat Barbara A. Mikulski was leaving to run for the Senate.

Cardin's reserved demeanor is in sharp contrast to Mikulski's pugnacity. But the strength of his credentials easily offsets the relative mildness of his personality. His House elections have been non-events: He drew no significant primary opposition in 1986, and he has twice brushed aside perennial GOP candidate Ross Z. Pierpont.

Maryland 3

Baltimore; Northern and Southern Suburbs

Blue-collar neighborhoods in East Baltimore dominate this district and provide most of its Democratic vote. In Little Italy, Greektown, Canton and Hamilton, the "Bawlamer" accent is strong and the attachment to the baseball Orioles deep.

East Baltimore is the state's industrial core. It includes the city's busy port, which handles everything from delicate electronic parts to coal. But the area's most celebrated aspect is Harborplace, a complex of shops and restaurants that replaced a stretch of decaying warehouses and became the hub of Baltimore's vaunted downtown revitalization.

This project has been accompanied by the renewal of the adjacent Otterbein neighborhood. To the south is the district's largest community of blacks, in the Cherry Hill section.

Unlike his predecessor Barbara A. Mikulski, who was a symbol of ethnic Baltimore, Cardin finds his base in the upscale communities in Baltimore's northwest corner, and the suburbs added in the 1980s' redistricting. Pikesville, northwest of the city, absorbed much of the Jewish population that fled northwest Baltimore as the city's black ghetto expanded.

Southwest of the city, the district takes in most of Catonsville, a middle-class ethnic town. When radicals poured blood on the files of the Catonsville draft board during the Vietnam War, the resulting trial brought national attention to the quiet community.

The district also includes the planned community of Columbia, in Howard County. It was designed in the mid-1960s by James W. Rouse — also the developer of Harborplace — whose idealistic social goals for Columbia attracted liberal-minded people to the town. About one-fifth black, Columbia has subsidized housing scattered about to avoid segregation.

While the 3rd is predominately Democratic, its residents are not totally averse to supporting Republican candidates; the 3rd went narrowly to President Reagan in 1984. Michael S. Dukakis brought it back to the Democrats in 1988, winning 54 percent of the vote.

Population: 527,699. White 433,741 (82%), Black 84,523 (16%), Other 6,957 (1%). Spanish origin 5,674 (1%). 18 and over 399,019 (76%), 65 and over 73,372 (14%). Median age: 33.

Committees

Judiciary (20th of 21 Democrats)
Administrative Law and Governmental Relations; Courts, Intellectual Property and the Administration of Justice

Public Works and Transportation (20th of 31 Democrats)
Public Buildings and Grounds; Surface Transportation; Water Resources

Elections

1988 General		
Benjamin L. Cardin (D)	133,779	(73%)
Ross Z. Pierpont (R)	49,733	(27%)
1988 Primary		
Benjamin L. Cardin (D)	52,850	(86%)
Charles Walker (D)	8,451	(14%)
1986 General		
Benjamin L. Cardin (D)	100,161	(79%)
Ross Z. Pierpont (R)	26,452	(21%)

District Vote For President

	1988		1984		1980		1976	
D	113,869	(54%)	108,399	(49%)	105,804	(54%)	108,801	(51%)
R	95,071	(45%)	110,231	(50%)	72,565	(37%)	102,500	(49%)
I					15,537	(8%)		

Campaign Finance

	Receipts	Receipts from PACs	Expend-itures
1988			
Cardin (D)	$405,789	$208,148 (51%)	$354,701
Pierpont (R)	$50,364	0	$48,101
1986			
Cardin (D)	$518,530	$143,977 (28%)	$487,797
Pierpont (R)	$50,855	$200 (0.4%)	$46,542

Key Votes

1987	
Raise speed limit to 65 mph	N
Approve Gephardt "fair trade" amendment	Y
Ban testing of larger nuclear weapons	Y
Delay "re-flagging" of Kuwaiti tankers	Y
Approve tax-raising deficit-reduction bill	Y
1988	
Approve aid to Nicaraguan contras	N
Enact civil rights restoration bill over Reagan veto	Y
Kill 60-day plant-closing notification measure	N
Pass omnibus trade bill over Reagan veto	Y
Approve death penalty for drug-related murders	N
Bar federal funds for abortions in cases of rape and incest	N
Oppose seven-day waiting period for purchase of handguns	N

Voting Studies

	Presidential Support		Party Unity		Conservative Coalition	
Year	**S**	**O**	**S**	**O**	**S**	**O**
1988	22	76	93	4	18	79
1987	22	75	90	3	19	81

Interest Group Ratings

Year	ADA	ACU	AFL-CIO	CCUS
1988	90	4	93	36
1987	88	0	94	13

4 Tom McMillen (D)

Of Crofton — Elected 1986

Born: May 26, 1952, Elmira, N.Y.
Education: U. of Maryland, B.S. 1974; Oxford U., England, M.A. 1978.
Occupation: Professional basketball player; communications equipment distributor.
Family: Single.
Religion: Roman Catholic.
Political Career: No previous office.
Capitol Office: 327 Cannon Bldg. 20515; 225-8090.

In Washington: McMillen spent an energetic first two years in the House, showing he has the aptitude and vigor for pursuing a range of interests and no pressing concern about picking a specialty. This legislative personality would be well suited to the committee McMillen tried for at the start of the 101st Congress — Energy and Commerce, whose broad jurisdiction encourages its members to juggle issues. But a pair of more senior Democrats had claim to Energy openings, leaving McMillen to hope for better luck in the future.

After a razor-thin margin in his first election, McMillen showed with a convincing 1988 victory that he has a future in Congress. Much of his freshman-term effort went to shore up his base in the conservative-leaning 4th. He devoted attention to the Chesapeake Bay cleanup, holding a hearing in Annapolis shortly before Election Day on medical waste and ocean dumping. He raised $50,000 for a biotechnology symposium hosted by the state of Maryland. He won continued funding for a program to develop giant blimps for the Navy; the program's management team works near Baltimore-Washington International Airport. The Navy requested no money for the project, but McMillen sought $40 million and saw $25 million authorized.

Elected president of his party's freshman class, McMillen created Class PAC, which gave campaign funds to freshman Democrats. He also campaigned for some of his freshman colleagues in 1988, capitalizing on his celebrity as a former pro basketball player to draw crowds.

On the Banking Committee, McMillen and Paul E. Kanjorski of Pennsylvania introduced a bill to abolish the Federal Asset Disposition Association, which disposes of real estate from bankrupt thrifts acquired by the Federal Savings and Loan Insurance Corporation. FADA came under criticism for its management and compensation practices, including a lucrative severance contract for its top executives should the agency be abolished. The bill came within five votes of passing on the floor.

McMillen's freshman term was marred by one notable misfire. During 1987 debate on trade legislation, he told the House of seeing a high-level Japanese government memo that said Japanese investment in the United States, including PAC contributions, would be targeted to influence House elections. The memo was bogus, however, and not until *The New York Times* reported that eight months later did McMillen apologize on the floor for his error.

At Home: McMillen proved how quickly incumbency can change a candidate from shaky to secure. In 1986, political rookie McMillen survived by just 428 votes against a GOP state legislator. Two years later, McMillen coasted to re-election over an unknown.

The 6-foot-11 McMillen starred in basketball at the University of Maryland — where he earned a Rhodes scholarship — then played 11 years in the National Basketball Association. Though he spent most of his career with Atlanta, he was traded in 1983 to the Washington Bullets, who play in Landover, Md. After the trade, McMillen ran a communications equipment company, engaged in civic work and prepared to run in the 4th.

McMillen left sports for politics when seven-term GOP Rep. Marjorie S. Holt announced in 1986 she would retire. Holt's success had shown that the 4th, with its many defense-related employers, leaned right despite a Democratic registration edge. So McMillen positioned himself as a moderate, bringing in such prominent Southerners as Georgia Sen. Sam Nunn and former Virginia Gov. Charles S. Robb to campaign for him. He also spent over $650,000 to boost his already high name recognition.

McMillen gained a big lead in polls over Republican Robert Neall, who had not enjoyed wide publicity in his position as leader of the small GOP contingent in the state House. But Neall made a late charge. A lifelong district resident and father of four, he said McMillen, a wealthy bachelor, was not in touch with the average voter's concerns.

McMillen had to wait two weeks — after absentee ballots were counted — to declare victory. Neall had no stomach for a rematch in 1988, and McMillen won two-thirds of the vote.

Maryland 4

Anne Arundel, Southern Prince George's Counties

The 4th begins at the suburbs of Baltimore and ends at the suburbs of Washington, D.C., with Annapolis in the middle. Like most Maryland districts, the 4th has a large Democratic registration advantage. But with its military presence — symbolized by the U.S. Naval Academy in Annapolis — and its defense-related industries, the district also has a conservative bent. Republican Marjorie S. Holt held it for 14 years before McMillen's election; Ronald Reagan and George Bush easily won there in the last two elections.

Anne Arundel County is the core of the district. Annapolis, the county seat and state capital, has an electorate heavy with government workers. It has a black community that dates back three centuries and composes a third of the town.

Just north of Annapolis, suburban Baltimore begins and the Republican vote increases. The GOP is in firm control in Severna Park, where corporate executives live in homes fronting Chesapeake Bay. Closer to Baltimore, the suburbs tend to be less affluent. A band of blue-collar, Democratic-leaning towns occupies the northernmost end of the district.

Back toward Washington, Crofton, a bedroom community founded in the late 1960s, usually tilts Republican, although it is McMillen's home base. Northwest of Crofton is Fort George G. Meade, which faces a phase-out, with the loss of some 500 jobs, under a base realignment plan enacted in 1989.

The suburban-and-exurban Republican vote in Anne Arundel goes a long way toward offsetting the Democratic lean in Annapolis. Bush carried the county with 64 percent of the vote in 1988.

Southern Prince George's County, with a large contingent of federal workers and blacks, is the more liberal part of the 4th. But the military vote near Andrews Air Force Base provides the area with some Republican turf. The district also contains a small chunk of outer-suburban Howard County, which generally goes Republican.

Population: 525,453. White 404,506 (77%), Black 108,571 (21%), Other 9,207 (2%). Spanish origin 7,393 (1%). 18 and over 372,900 (71%), 65 and over 32,775 (6%). Median age: 29.

Committees

Banking, Finance and Urban Affairs (23rd of 31 Democrats)
Financial Institutions Supervision, Regulation and Insurance; International Development, Finance, Trade and Monetary Policy

Science, Space and Technology (22nd of 30 Democrats)
Natural Resources, Agriculture Research and Environment; Space Science and Applications; Transportation, Aviation and Materials

Elections

1988 General		
Tom McMillen (D)	128,624	(68%)
Bradlyn McClanahan (R)	59,688	(32%)
1988 Primary		
Tom McMillen (D)	39,661	(87%)
Edward B. Quirk (D)	3,941	(9%)
1986 General		
Tom McMillen (D)	65,071	(50%)
Robert R. Neall (R)	64,643	(50%)

District Vote For President

	1988		1984		1980		1976	
D	87,650	(42%)	79,144	(40%)	73,667	(41%)	80,239	(50%)
R	120,027	(57%)	115,669	(59%)	89,510	(50%)	80,601	(50%)
I					12,927	(7%)		

Campaign Finance

	Receipts	Receipts from PACs	Expend-itures
1988			
McMillen (D)	$730,652	$392,892 (54%)	$599,881
1986			
McMillen (D)	$796,615	$307,549 (39%)	$796,344
Neall (R)	$632,560	$160,137 (25%)	$630,494

Key Votes

1987	
Raise speed limit to 65 mph	N
Approve Gephardt "fair trade" amendment	Y
Ban testing of larger nuclear weapons	Y
Delay "re-flagging" of Kuwaiti tankers	N
Approve tax-raising deficit-reduction bill	N
1988	
Approve aid to Nicaraguan contras	N
Enact civil rights restoration bill over Reagan veto	Y
Kill 60-day plant-closing notification measure	N
Pass omnibus trade bill over Reagan veto	Y
Approve death penalty for drug-related murders	Y
Bar federal funds for abortions in cases of rape and incest	N
Oppose seven-day waiting period for purchase of handguns	N

Voting Studies

	Presidential Support		Party Unity		Conservative Coalition	
Year	**S**	**O**	**S**	**O**	**S**	**O**
1988	27	73	90	10	58	42
1987	32	68	92	8	60	40

Interest Group Ratings

Year	ADA	ACU	AFL-CIO	CCUS
1988	75	12	100	36
1987	80	4	100	27

5 Steny H. Hoyer (D)

Of Berkshire — Elected 1981

Born: June 14, 1939, New York, N.Y.
Education: U. of Maryland, B.S. 1963; Georgetown U., J.D. 1966.
Occupation: Lawyer.
Family: Wife, Judith Pickett; three children.
Religion: Baptist.
Political Career: Md. Senate, 1967-79, president, 1975-79; sought Democratic nomination for lieutenant governor, 1978.
Capitol Office: 1513 Longworth Bldg. 20515; 225-4131.

In Washington: As a middle-level manager in the House Democratic hierarchy, Hoyer had to spend much of the spring of 1989 defending his party's embattled leadership. But this duty was not without reward. When Speaker Jim Wright and Majority Whip Tony Coelho resigned, Hoyer was in line for promotion.

As House Democrats reconstituted their leadership, Hoyer emerged as chairman of the Democratic Caucus, the fourth-ranking elective position. The caucus chair lacks a long tradition of importance, but it has served as the first leadership rung for each of the party's new top three — Speaker Thomas S. Foley, Majority Leader Richard A. Gephardt and Majority Whip William H. Gray III. Hoyer defeated his one rival for the chairmanship, Barbara B. Kennelly of Connecticut, by a margin of 2-to-1 on June 21. Hoyer had been the vice chairman of the caucus since the beginning of the year, and he was helped by his ties to both the old leadership (especially Coelho) and the new (especially Gephardt).

Hoyer's ascent into the party leadership could have major implications for the House in years to come. While many junior House Democrats want the institution to move further toward democracy, Hoyer would like to see it move the other way. Despite the impeccable grooming and polished charm that mark him as a media-age congressman, Hoyer is at least as comfortable with old-fashioned machine Democrats as he is with activists or reformers. Tough, bright and liberal, he is an inside player who has quickly reached the leadership circle.

Hoyer's party loyalty has stood him in good stead. In 1983, he won a seat on the Appropriations Committee, and in his third term joined the Steering and Policy Committtee, taking a hand in making committee assignments.

A product of the Maryland Legislature, where the House Speaker can maintain iron control, he thinks power in Congress is too fragmented. Early in 1985, when the overwhelming majority of Democrats voted to make the position of party whip elective, Hoyer dissented. He said future Speakers should have the power to name their own lieutenants.

That position seemed ironic two years later when, as a leader among Coelho's supporters, Hoyer hoped to be named chief deputy whip. Instead, Speaker Wright used the chief deputy whip position to appease nervous elements of the party's left, tapping David E. Bonior of Michigan. As a consolation, Hoyer might have taken the chairmanship of the Democratic Congressional Campaign Committee (although some thought he would not relish the travel that job entails). In the end, the DCCC went to Rep. Beryl Anthony Jr. of Arkansas.

After the decisions were made, Hoyer said it was just as well he did not rise higher in the leadership, because he wanted to have more time for his job as chairman of the Helsinki Commission, which monitors human rights policies in Europe and the Soviet Union. In this capacity, Hoyer led delegations to each of the Eastern bloc nations during the 100th Congress. He serves as the commission's co-chairman in the 101st Congress.

Hoyer has not been shy about getting ahead. Defeated in a statewide race at 39, he got back on track when an incumbent's illness vacated a House seat. After just a year in the House, he scratched his way to a seat on Appropriations, succeeding despite the opposition of a senior Maryland colleague already on the panel.

Hoyer takes an interest in the issues before the House, but his interest is often visibly driven by politics. Early in 1985, while most members were considering the MX missile as a question of pure defense policy, Hoyer was preoccupied with the Democratic Party's soft-on-defense image. Hoyer argued that Democrats needed to change this image before they could start winning national elections. He voted for the MX, angering liberals and breaking, uncharacteristically, with party leadership.

More typically, Hoyer serves the leadership. During the 100th Congress, he led leadership task forces on AIDS and on welfare reform.

Maryland 5

Northern Prince George's County

The federal bureaucracy provides a secure, if modest, standard of living for the thousands of white and black residents of "P.G." County. Prince George's County is a few status rungs down from its neighbor, Montgomery County, one of the nation's wealthiest jurisdictions. But Prince George's has a relatively high median income and some comfortable neighborhoods that belie its middle-brow reputation.

This was where Washington's white working class moved after World War II as the city became increasingly black. In the past 15 years there has been a second migration, as middle-class blacks have left D.C. for the suburbs.

The black population of Prince George's County doubled during the 1970s; today, more than a third of the 5th's residents are black. Years of black activism for integration of housing and schools spawned a generation of assertive black politicians who are gaining recognition as powerful members of the reigning Democratic coalition in Prince George's County.

The black vote has remained the solid base for Hoyer's House wins and for Democratic presidential victories; Michael S. Dukakis carried the 5th with 59 percent. Strong black support earlier had enabled the Rev. Jesse Jackson to win the 5th in the 1988 Maryland Democratic primary, as he did in 1984.

However, these gains do not represent an unbroken line of progress for county blacks. While many residents of both races find suburban tranquility in Prince George's County, some lower-income residents have found urban violence following them to the suburbs. An exploding illegal drug trade, centered in the Landover area, sparked a rash of murders beginning in 1988 that coincided with D.C.'s surge of drug-related violence.

There is a core of conservative whites who see black gains as their losses. But this conservative backlash was more evident in an older version of the 5th, which elected a Republican in 1968, 1970 and 1972. By the mid-1970s, the black population was so large that Democratic victory was almost assured.

Despite GOP efforts to appeal to working-class voters in the inner suburbs and to more affluent residents of such eastern Prince George's County towns as Bowie and Laurel, no GOP presidential candidate has received more than 42 percent in the 5th in the 1980s.

The district also includes College Park, site of the University of Maryland's main campus.

Population: 527,469. White 323,052 (61%), Black 183,887 (35%), Other 14,206 (3%). Spanish origin 11,862 (2%). 18 and over 374,737 (71%), 65 and over 29,585 (6%). Median age: 28.

Hoyer's most consistent issue concerns have related to the federal employees who populate his district in the Washington, D.C., suburbs. In the 100th Congress, he bucked the tide on drug testing for federal employees, fighting random testing as unconstitutional. Early in 1989, Hoyer was an outspoken supporter of the 51 percent pay increase for Congress set in motion by a presidential commission; many federal employees expected the raise to ripple through the rank and file.

In the 100th and 101st Congresses, Hoyer was co-chairman of the Federal Government Service Task Force, which seeks to convince other members that more should be spent on federal employee pay and benefits.

But Hoyer has been able to do more for federal workers as a member of Appropriations. His base of operations has been the Subcommittee on Treasury, Postal Service and General Government — a secondary assignment that many members ignore, but for Hoyer a gold mine of constituent service. In the 100th Congress, the subcommittee gave him a platform from which to sponsor increases in federal pay. It enabled him to block controversial new dismissal rules proposed for federal employees in 1983 and 1984 by the Office of Personnel Management.

On the full Appropriations Committee, Hoyer works to protect federal funding for construction of the Washington, D.C., area's Metrorail transit system. He has also supported funding for projects in Baltimore, such as harbor dredging or a new VA hospital.

At Home: From the presidency of his state's Young Democrats to the presidency of the Maryland Senate to his House career, Hoyer has been preoccupied with politics nearly all his adult life. A losing bid for lieutenant governor stalled him in 1978, but after a three-year hiatus, he was back on the road.

Hoyer was barely out of law school when he was first elected to the state Senate in 1966. After two terms he was chosen Senate president with the help of Gov. Marvin Mandel, becoming the youngest person to occupy that post in Maryland history. Hoyer's rise to power coincided with the growing influence of the Prince George's County Democratic organization, which he helped build and lead.

He made no secret of his ambition to be governor and announced as a candidate in 1978. But he decided he lacked the support to win, and agreed to run for lieutenant governor on a ticket headed by Acting Gov. Blair Lee III. Lee was not nominated.

In February 1981, the 5th District House seat held by Democrat Gladys Noon Spellman was declared vacant. Spellman had never regained consciousness after suffering a heart attack the previous October.

The special-election primary to succeed Spellman drew 31 candidates, the largest number in any congressional primary in the nation in 20 years. Hoyer's chief competition came from Spellman's husband, Reuben, who was backed by his wife's loyal supporters. But with the help of most of the coalition of liberals, labor and blacks that had been instrumental in his earlier rise to power, Hoyer emerged on top.

In the general election that May, Hoyer faced the Republican mayor of Bowie, Audrey Scott. The Reagan economic program was the campaign's central issue, and both candidates pulled in substantial help from their national parties. But while Hoyer went into the election with the local party united behind him, the GOP lacked a similar harmony. In the primary, Scott had defeated the son of Prince George's County Executive and former U.S. Rep. Lawrence J. Hogan in the primary, and Hogan refused to endorse her. Hoyer took 55 percent of the vote.

Since then, Hoyer has trounced weak GOP challengers. His bigger political concerns have been within his own party, particularly as his district has become increasingly black. Leaders of the 5th's large and increasingly assertive black constituency were disturbed in both 1984 and 1988 by Hoyer's reluctance to endorse the Rev. Jesse Jackson, who carried the district primary vote in both of his campaigns for the Democratic presidential nomination. But for now, Hoyer's record on issues of importance to black voters and his rising status in the House Democratic hierarchy have forestalled a serious black challenge in the primary.

Committee

Appropriations (27th of 35 Democrats)
District of Columbia; Labor, Health and Human Services, Education and Related Agencies; Treasury, Postal Service and General Government

Elections

1988 General		
Steny H. Hoyer (D)	128,437	(79%)
John Eugene Sellner (R)	34,909	(21%)
1986 General		
Steny H. Hoyer (D)	82,098	(82%)
John Eugene Sellner (R)	18,102	(18%)

Previous Winning Percentages: **1984** (72%) **1982** (80%) **1981 *** (55%)

* *Special election.*

District Vote For President

	1988	1984	1980	1976
D	107,195 (59%)	108,074 (58%)	78,156 (51%)	88,033 (58%)
R	72,873 (40%)	79,134 (42%)	61,644 (40%)	63,897 (42%)
I			12,215 (8%)	

Campaign Finance

	Receipts	Receipts from PACs	Expend-itures
1988			
Hoyer (D)	$490,736	$239,828 (49%)	$416,187
1986			
Hoyer (D)	$382,725	$166,262 (43%)	$368,388

Key Votes

1987	
Raise speed limit to 65 mph	N
Approve Gephardt "fair trade" amendment	Y
Ban testing of larger nuclear weapons	Y
Delay "re-flagging" of Kuwaiti tankers	Y
Approve tax-raising deficit-reduction bill	Y
1988	
Approve aid to Nicaraguan contras	N
Enact civil rights restoration bill over Reagan veto	Y
Kill 60-day plant-closing notification measure	N
Pass omnibus trade bill over Reagan veto	Y
Approve death penalty for drug-related murders	N
Bar federal funds for abortions in cases of rape and incest	N
Oppose seven-day waiting period for purchase of handguns	N

Voting Studies

	Presidential Support		Party Unity		Conservative Coalition	
Year	S	O	S	O	S	O
1988	23	77	98	1	18	82
1987	25	75	93	3	28	72
1986	21	79	95	3	26	72
1985	29	71	93	5	29	71
1984	42	57	89	9	32	63
1983	32	67	91	6	29	70
1982	38	57	69	19	25	71
1981	40 †	55 †	86 †	11 †	32 †	67 †

† *Not eligible for all recorded votes.*

Interest Group Ratings

Year	ADA	ACU	AFL-CIO	CCUS
1988	95	0	100	21
1987	84	0	100	7
1986	95	5	93	22
1985	75	14	94	32
1984	75	8	92	33
1983	80	9	100	25
1982	75	18	85	32
1981	72	0	92	12

6 Beverly B. Byron (D)

Of Frederick — Elected 1978

Born: July 27, 1932, Baltimore, Md.
Education: Attended Hood College, 1963-64.
Occupation: Civic leader.
Family: Husband, Kirk Walsh; three children.
Religion: Episcopalian.
Political Career: No previous office.
Capitol Office: 2430 Rayburn Bldg. 20515; 225-2721.

In Washington: Despite her Democratic label, in Maryland Byron stands apart from the party liberals who dominate state politics. And in the House, she is a pro-defense conservative who plays a hawkish role on the Armed Services Committee — a very different profile from most of the women in the Democratic Caucus.

In fact, there is a seeming role reversal between Byron and her Republican neighbor to the south, 8th District Rep. Constance A. Morella. Despite her GOP affiliation, Morella exhibits the liberal leanings and federal government orientation of the Washington, D.C., suburbs. Byron's district reaches down to the affluent Washington suburb of Potomac, but her voting record clearly reflects the political tenor of the mill towns, mines and mountain communities of rural western Maryland.

In 1988, Byron supported President Reagan on nearly half of the House votes on which the president took a position; she had the fourth-highest pro-Reagan percentage among House Democrats. That same year, Byron joined with Republicans and Southern Democrats on every vote on which the so-called "conservative coalition" arose.

Byron's conservatism is most noticeable in her role on Armed Services. She is a member of the committee's pro-Pentagon "Old Guard," and was a strong supporter of conservative Texas Democrat Marvin Leath in his unsuccessful 1987 effort to oust Armed Services Chairman Les Aspin, a more liberal Wisconsin Democrat.

Byron consistently has supported most of the Defense Department's priority projects, such as the MX missile. She has also worked with panel conservatives to counter the efforts of liberal committee members to advance an arms control agenda thought too extreme by Republican administrations.

In 1986, as House arms control advocates brought to the floor a measure calling for a resumption of U.S.-Soviet negotiations on banning nuclear-weapons tests, she and Republican Henry J. Hyde of Illinois offered a weaker version, one more palatable to the Reagan administration. Byron and Hyde endorsed administration contentions that a test ban should be implemented only after deep reductions have been made in existing nuclear stockpiles. "Why legislate the Soviet position and impose it on our negotiators?" Byron argued. Though her position failed in the House, the test-ban effort died in the Senate.

A similar scenario played out in 1987. Byron's amendment supporting a "prudent and reasonable" program of nuclear-weapons tests was passed by Armed Services. The full House replaced Byron's provision with a test-ban amendment, which again went no further.

While Byron occasionally involves herself in debate on the committee's big issues, she is preoccupied with her position as chairman of the Subcommittee on Military Personnel and Compensation. Though the panel has jurisdiction over more than 40 percent of the Pentagon budget, it is the "unglamorous" work. Her subcommittee deals with issues such as the formulas for determining retirement benefits for the survivors of military veterans, and the maximum amounts that military retirees can be charged under the Defense Department hospitalization plan, known as CHAMPUS.

Byron first tried to gain the subcommittee chairmanship in 1985, when Aspin said he would yield it to concentrate on his new job as full committee chairman. But a turf fight evolved between Byron, who matched the thinking of the committee's conservative Democrats, and liberal Colorado Democrat Patricia Schroeder, who had a seniority advantage. In the end, Aspin decided to keep the Personnel panel himself for the 99th Congress and avoid a civil war on the committee.

In 1987, however, Byron finally got the Personnel chairmanship without controversy. Schroeder, then content with her subcommittee chairmanship at Post Office and Civil Service, decided not to bid for it. Byron thus became the first woman to hold a subcommittee chair on Armed Services.

Byron's pro-Pentagon views are something of an inheritance. Her father, a Navy officer, was a friend and close aide to General Dwight D. Eisenhower during World War II. When she succeeded her late husband, Democratic Rep.

Maryland 6

West — Hagerstown; Cumberland

Democrat Byron is so strong in the 6th that district Republicans rarely bother to put up an effort against her. Her security, however, is due to her conservative leanings and her legendary last name, not her party line. The western 6th, which competes with the eastern 1st District for the title of Maryland's most rural, has a strong conservative flavor.

Aside from Byron, that conservatism is beneficial to Republican candidates, especially at the national level. George Bush took 65 percent of the district's vote in 1988, just below the 69 percent won by President Reagan in 1984. Although the 6th has the smallest black population percentage of any Maryland district, black conservative Republican Alan L. Keyes ran well there in his 1988 challenge to Democratic Sen. Paul S. Sarbanes, losing to Sarbanes by fewer than 1,000 votes out of more than 225,000 cast.

The district stretches from the Baltimore and Washington suburbs over rolling farm land to the Appalachian Mountains. Though it takes in the wealthy Montgomery County suburb of Potomac and some of the county's more rural areas, the 6th rarely gets much attention in the Washington media.

District affairs provoke much more interest in Frederick, an 18th-century museum piece that arrested its earlier economic decline by crafting a new identity as a restaurant and boutique center, and by courting high-technology industry. Now the district's largest city with over 34,000 people, Frederick grew by more than 20 percent between 1980 and 1986. Many residents commute to work in the high-tech corridor that sprouted along Interstates 70 and 270.

Just east of Frederick, Baltimore's suburban sprawl has moved out into Carroll County, bringing a surge of subdivisions to once sleepy towns. The county also saw its population jump by over 15 percent in the early 1980s.

While the economies of these areas thrive, several places in the western part of the district have not done as well. Job losses at a Fairchild Industries aircraft plant and a Mack Trucks factory in the early 1980s caused some problems in the Hagerstown area in Washington County.

But the problems of industrial decline have been most marked in Allegany County, located in the Appalachian foothills. The population in the manufacturing city of Cumberland fell by 10 percent in the early 1980s, as major factories shut their doors. There is slim hope that many of the high-paying, heavy-industry jobs will return; local optimists are staking their hopes on attracting smaller-scale manufacturers and boosting tourism in the scenic area.

At the far western end lies rural Garrett County, whose fealty to the GOP is rivaled only by Allegany. Garrett, home to Deep Creek Lake and Backbone Mountain, Maryland's tallest, has a year-round tourist economy, hosting skiers in winter and boaters in summer. Some visitors are from the Baltimore-Washington area, but more come from around Pittsburgh.

The one common political thread between the district's counties is the Republican bias in presidential voting. Bush swept the five counties totally within the district, all by wide margins. Keyes carried three of those counties, plus the 6th's portion of Howard County.

Population: 528,168. White 502,767 (95%), Black 19,829 (4%), Other 4,138 (1%). Spanish origin 3,983 (1%). 18 and over 376,405 (71%), 65 and over 54,034 (10%). Median age: 31.

Goodloe E. Byron, in 1979, she also took his place on Armed Services. In addition, Byron has a son who is an Air Force captain.

Her personal proclivities also inform her work on the Interior Committee, to which she devotes less time than Armed Services. A physical fitness buff, Byron has lobbied for money to improve hiking trails in Maryland and to make a federal inventory of hiking trails in the United States. In 1988, she wrote a bill encouraging the Interior Department to convert abandoned railroad rights-of-way into recreational trails; a companion Senate bill was signed into law.

Byron has also promoted the concept that physical education programs should be required on a daily basis for all children from kindergarten on through high school. Congress passed a concurrent resolution along those lines in December 1987.

At Home: Family history repeated itself in 1978 when Byron succeeded her late husband in the House. In 1941 Goodloe Byron's father, U.S. Rep. William D. Byron, was killed in an airplane crash. The elder Byron's widow won the election that year to fill out his term.

Goodloe Byron, a physical fitness buff despite his heart condition, collapsed while jogging along the Chesapeake and Ohio Canal near

Washington, and died at the age of 49. District Democratic leaders instantly offered Beverly Byron the nomination and she accepted it within 24 hours.

Mrs. Byron had met her husband while she was in high school. She got into politics when he first ran for the Maryland House of Delegates in 1962 because, she said, "It meant I either stayed at home by myself or joined him." She helped organize Byron's campaigns, and shared his interest in exercise and the national park system.

Winning the 1978 election posed little problem for her. Republican officials had not offered an opponent against her husband, letting a perennial office-seeker, Melvin Perkins, win the GOP line. A self-described pauper, Perkins spent part of the fall campaign in jail in Baltimore County, where he had been charged with assaulting a woman bus driver. Mrs. Byron romped.

Two years later, Byron's constituent work and conservative voting record proved effective in defusing serious opposition. She triumphed easily over a lackluster primary field, and in the general election registered a landslide victory over her conservative Republican challenger, state Rep. Raymond E. Beck.

Byron has coasted to easy re-elections since then. In 1982, her opponent was Roscoe Bartlett, a scientist and farmer from Frederick who sought to outflank her on the right. Byron crushed him.

In 1984, she faced former state Rep. Robin Ficker, a political gadfly who had run for a wide range of Maryland offices over the course of the previous decade. Ficker unnerved Byron with a string of complaints about her attendance record, her foreign travel and her attitudes toward the unemployed. But his success in irking the incumbent made little difference in the result. Byron won going away.

Committees

Armed Services (6th of 31 Democrats)
Military Personnel and Compensation (chairman); Research and Development

Interior and Insular Affairs (9th of 26 Democrats)
National Parks and Public Lands; Water, Power and Offshore Energy Resources

Select Aging (9th of 39 Democrats)
Housing and Consumer Interests

Elections

1988 General		
Beverly B. Byron (D)	166,753	(75%)
Kenneth W. Halsey (R)	54,528	(25%)
1988 Primary		
Beverly B. Byron (D)	38,123	(81%)
Anthony Patrick Puca (D)	9,101	(19%)
1986 General		
Beverly B. Byron (D)	102,975	(72%)
John Vandenberge (R)	39,600	(28%)

Previous Winning Percentages: 1984 (65%) **1982** (74%) **1980** (70%) **1978** (90%)

District Vote For President

	1988	1984	1980	1976
D	82,781 (34%)	66,062 (31%)	64,800 (35%)	71,206 (44%)
R	158,808 (65%)	146,543 (69%)	108,821 (58%)	91,657 (56%)
I			11,896 (6%)	

Campaign Finance

	Receipts	Receipts from PACs	Expend-itures
1988			
Byron (D)	$218,098	$142,722 (65%)	$213,554
1986			
Byron (D)	$213,159	$126,603 (59%)	$206,120
Vandenberge (R)	$137,435	$4,550 (3%)	$137,069

Key Votes

1987	
Raise speed limit to 65 mph	N
Approve Gephardt "fair trade" amendment	Y
Ban testing of larger nuclear weapons	N
Delay "re-flagging" of Kuwaiti tankers	N
Approve tax-raising deficit-reduction bill	N
1988	
Approve aid to Nicaraguan contras	Y
Enact civil rights restoration bill over Reagan veto	Y
Kill 60-day plant-closing notification measure	N
Pass omnibus trade bill over Reagan veto	?
Approve death penalty for drug-related murders	Y
Bar federal funds for abortions in cases of rape and incest	Y
Oppose seven-day waiting period for purchase of handguns	Y

Voting Studies

	Presidential Support		Party Unity		Conservative Coalition	
Year	**S**	**O**	**S**	**O**	**S**	**O**
1988	49	46	61	34	100	0
1987	44	54	58	34	86	12
1986	50	50	55	37	78	18
1985	52	43	63	30	80	13
1984	50	48	47	45	81	17
1983	57	40	43	51	87	10
1982	56	40	44	49	79	15
1981	62	33	38	56	93	4

Interest Group Ratings

Year	ADA	ACU	AFL-CIO	CCUS
1988	30	68	77	69
1987	48	35	63	60
1986	20	71	46	63
1985	10	65	47	59
1984	20	65	46	38
1983	25	74	59	58
1982	30	55	45	52
1981	15	73	50	65

7 Kweisi Mfume (D)

Of Baltimore — Elected 1986

Born: Oct. 24, 1948, Baltimore, Md.
Education: Morgan State University, B.S. 1976; Johns Hopkins U., M.A. 1984.
Occupation: Radio station program director; talk show host.
Family: Divorced; five children.
Religion: Baptist.
Political Career: Baltimore City Council, 1979-87.
Capitol Office: 128 Cannon Bldg. 20515; 225-4741.

In Washington: Mfume, whose adopted Swahili name means "conquering son of kings," came to Congress with a reputation as a confrontational Baltimore city councilman. But if he brought the reputation, he did not bring the style. Mfume has made a widely favorable first impression in Congress as an engaging personality and a collegial institutional player. Holding a safe Democratic district, he may be in a position to play for years to come.

While Mfume does not have to worry much about re-election, he is under more pressure to assist his constituents than are most representatives of Washington-area districts, which tend to be more affluent than the 7th. It has its share of inner-city problems, and Mfume is still regarded by some at home as the man to turn to for solutions to neighborhood problems, since that was his role as a councilman.

Amid the chorus of voices expressing concern over drug abuse and proposing grand plans to combat it, Mfume has tried to make a dent in the problem by focusing on a small corner of the issue. In the 101st Congress, he began pushing to curb sales of electronic beepers to minors, who, he says, use them to arrange drug deals. Mfume said a curb could "turn up the heat and make it a little more difficult" for dealers to do business.

On the Banking Committee, Mfume is in a position to look out for some important urban needs, such as low-income housing. And Mfume, who had a self-described "wild" stage as a high-school dropout, also has pushed a Youth Employment Services Act, intended to encourage partnerships between businesses and local governments to put teenagers to work.

At Home: Prior to his 1986 House election, Mfume was well-known in Baltimore for his careers in broadcasting and on the City Council, and admired for his rise from the streets. But he also had fathered five illegitimate sons during his troubled youth — not a typical congressional credential.

Mfume was born Frizzell Gray in the slums of West Baltimore. After his mother died when he was 16, Gray quit high school, drifted through a series of jobs and, between the ages of 17 and 22, fathered five sons by four different women. But in his early 20s, he adopted a new name and way of life, climbing the career ladder at Morgan State University's radio station. Mfume finished high school, graduated from Morgan State at 27, and earned an advanced degree from Johns Hopkins University.

After achieving popularity as a radio talk show host, Mfume won a seat on the Baltimore City Council, where he promoted the causes of his inner-city constituents and established a maverick image. Criticized early on by some colleagues for his confrontational style, Mfume developed a more temperate approach that helped win some victories, including passage of a law ordering the city to sell investments in companies doing business with South Africa.

Though he was well-known in the 7th District, Mfume entered the Democratic House primary as an underdog. But the favorite, state Sen. Clarence M. Mitchell (the nephew of retiring Rep. Parren J. Mitchell), was damaged by reports focusing on his personal finances and his alleged relationship with a jailed drug dealer.

At first, the Rev. Wendell H. Phillips, a veteran of the civil rights movement, was seen as the beneficiary of Mitchell's problems. But Mitchell hurt Phillips by accusing him of being cozy with the city's white power structure.

Meanwhile, Mfume quietly promoted himself as the compromise candidate and kept his distance from the feud, a strategy that aided him in the primary and later helped him unify the party. Assisted by a group of black clergy, Mfume swept to an easy primary victory.

Though Mfume was seemingly unbeatable in the heavily Democratic 7th, his GOP opponent, Saint George I. B. Crosse III, harassed him by making an issue of his children born out of wedlock. Mfume met the issue head-on, stating that he supported his sons financially and emotionally, and the local press portrayed Mfume's rise from poverty in a positive light. He won with 87 percent of the vote and quickly settled in, meeting no opposition in 1988.

Maryland 7

Baltimore — West and Central

Anchored in inner-city Baltimore, the 7th is overwhelmingly Democratic and overwhelmingly black. Its 73 percent black population is exceeded by only three districts nationwide.

Baltimore has had a significant black population dating back to the early 1800s. But it was not until the 1980 census that a majority of the city's population was shown to be black.

The 7th is not as compact as in past years. To compensate for the stream of people leaving the city during the 1970s, the district had to reach into the western suburbs. Baltimore has continued to lose population, dropping just over 4 percent between 1980 and 1986.

These changes, however, have hardly altered the 7th's Democratic cast. Michael S. Dukakis in 1988 and Walter F. Mondale in 1984 both carried the district with over 80 percent of the vote.

The only problem Democrats have here is getting people to the polls. Although Baltimore now has a black mayor, Kurt Schmoke, many low-income blacks are disenchanted with Baltimore's "power structure," which they see as favoring downtown development over neighborhood revitalization, and with the national Democratic Party, which they regard as taking them for granted. These sentiments manifested themselves in Democratic primary wins for the Rev. Jesse Jackson in 1984 and 1988.

The 7th spreads out from downtown Baltimore, past tenement neighborhoods that were Jewish before World War II, then turned black in the 1950s. Moving west, the tenements give way to neat row houses owned by Baltimore's black middle class.

The district also includes the gentrified areas of Bolton Hill and, a step down the ladder of upward mobility, Druid Hill Park. It takes in Johns Hopkins University and the working-class neighborhoods around Memorial Stadium, home of the baseball Orioles.

Outside the city, the 7th reaches into suburban Woodlawn, taking in the huge Social Security complex. The rest of the district's suburban territory has a handful of Republican loyalists, but their votes are drowned by the urban Democrats.

Population: 527,590. White 134,200 (25%), Black 386,759 (73%), Other 4,396 (1%). Spanish origin 4,556 (1%). 18 and over 376,566 (71%), 65 and over 56,465 (11%). Median age: 29.

Committees

Banking, Finance and Urban Affairs (26th of 31 Democrats)
Financial Institutions Supervision, Regulation and Insurance; Housing and Community Development

Education and Labor (22nd of 22 Democrats)
Employment Opportunities

Select Narcotics Abuse and Control (16th of 18 Democrats)

Small Business (19th of 27 Democrats)
Procurement, Tourism and Rural Development; SBA, the General Economy and Minority Enterprise Development

Elections

1988 General		
Kweisi Mfume (D)	117,650	(100%)
1986 General		
Kweisi Mfume (D)	79,226	(87%)
Saint George I. B. Crosse III (R)	12,170	(13%)

District Vote For President

	1988		1984		1980		1976	
D	123,261	(81%)	151,669	(82%)	127,824	(78%)	120,831	(77%)
R	26,360	(17%)	32,980	(18%)	27,659	(17%)	35,937	(23%)
I					6,768	(4%)		

Campaign Finance

	Receipts	Receipts from PACs	Expend-itures
1988			
Mfume (D)	$130,466	$72,250 (55%)	$110,565
1986			
Mfume (D)	$149,882	$61,523 (41%)	$104,550
Crosse (R)	$53,049	$4,000 (8%)	$52,593

Key Votes

1987	
Raise speed limit to 65 mph	N
Approve Gephardt "fair trade" amendment	Y
Ban testing of larger nuclear weapons	Y
Delay "re-flagging" of Kuwaiti tankers	Y
Approve tax-raising deficit-reduction bill	Y
1988	
Approve aid to Nicaraguan contras	N
Enact civil rights restoration bill over Reagan veto	Y
Kill 60-day plant-closing notification measure	N
Pass omnibus trade bill over Reagan veto	Y
Approve death penalty for drug-related murders	Y
Bar federal funds for abortions in cases of rape and incest	N
Oppose seven-day waiting period for purchase of handguns	N

Voting Studies

	Presidential Support		Party Unity		Conservative Coalition	
Year	S	O	S	O	S	O
1988	23	76	93	4	21	79
1987	13	86	93	3	9	88

Interest Group Ratings

Year	ADA	ACU	AFL-CIO	CCUS
1988	95	4	100	21
1987	100	0	100	7

8 Constance A. Morella (R)

Of Bethesda — Elected 1986

Born: Feb. 12, 1931, Somerville, Mass.
Education: Boston U., B.A. 1954; American U., M.A. 1967.
Occupation: College professor.
Family: Husband, Anthony C. Morella; nine children.
Religion: Roman Catholic.
Political Career: Md. House, 1979-87; sought GOP nomination for U.S. House, 1980.
Capitol Office: 1024 Longworth Bldg. 20515; 225-5341.

In Washington: Republican officials were grateful to Morella in 1986 for recapturing a suburban Washington seat vacated by a Democrat, but they were frustrated by her first-term voting pattern. Despite Morella's pleasing personality, her liberal leanings hardly endeared her to the GOP leadership: In 1988, she led all Republicans in opposition to President Reagan's positions on House votes.

However, this record was deemed satisfactory by her constituents in the 8th, a liberal-leaning district packed with federal bureaucrats and political activists. Facing an aggressive challenge in her first re-election campaign, Morella won by a landslide.

While many House members labor to curry favor with party bigwigs to get on "prestige" committees, Morella's lower-profile assignments suit her just fine. The Post Office and Civil Service Committee handles issues of interest to the 90,000 current and retired federal workers in her district; the Science Committee deals with programs affecting the many research laboratories in Montgomery County.

Morella's outgoing style and her attention to district interests make her a favorite of local TV interviewers in the nation's capital. She was seen frequently in early 1989, during and after the debate over the proposed 51 percent congressional pay raise. Like most House members, she voted against the unpopular proposal. But she then submitted a bill to give up to 20 percent increases to judges and senior officials of federal agencies, whose raises were also killed by the House vote.

Stating that the government was having trouble competing with the private sector for talented managers and scientists, Morella said, "We almost seem to be operating on the premise of the government that governs best, pays least." She also called on President Bush to do better than the 2 percent pay increase he proposed for lower-ranking federal employees.

At Home: In 1986, Morella reawakened the 8th District's proclivity for moderate-to-liberal Republican representation, which had lapsed during the four-term tenure of Democrat Michael D. Barnes. Morella linked herself to the GOP moderates — Charles McC. Mathias Jr., Gilbert Gude and Newton I. Steers Jr. — who held the district for 20 years prior to Barnes' election. (Steers, trying a comeback after his 1978 loss to Barnes, thwarted Morella's first House bid in a 1980 primary.)

Though Morella was not an activist in the Maryland Legislature, she had shown interest in environmental and social issues. The biggest factor in Morella's success was her personality. A vivacious English professor who quoted glibly from Shakespeare, Morella also played up her family's immigrant heritage and her working-class upbringing.

Morella noted as well that she and her husband had raised nine children (including her late sister's six), while her Democratic opponent, state Sen. Stewart Bainum, was a 40-year-old bachelor. That was not the only comparison that worked to Morella's advantage: Bainum possessed a wooden campaign style that contrasted poorly with Morella's manner.

A millionaire businessman, Bainum tried to spend his way past his shortcomings with a costly campaign that emphasized his liberal views and portrayed him as in the Kennedy-Roosevelt tradition of public service. But many voters saw him as trying to buy a House seat. Morella won by more than 10,000 votes.

Highly visible because of the proximity of her district to Washington, Morella reinforced her standing with a record that marked her as an independent, if not maverick, Republican. None of the Democratic Party's big names deigned to challenge her re-election.

The task went to state Rep. Peter Franchot, a hard-charging liberal who accused Morella of flip-flopping on defense issues, and of hiding her GOP allegiance to appeal to Democrats. But Morella emphasized her independence and touted the importance of her committee posts to district interests. She won with 63 percent of the vote.

Maryland 8

Montgomery County

Explosive population growth over the last 25 years has turned the 8th into a compact district encompassing the more densely populated Montgomery County suburbs of Washington, D.C. Though the posh, close-in suburbs give the county one of the nation's highest per capita incomes, it also takes in numerous middle-income town-house communities, and lower-income neighborhoods in Silver Spring, Takoma Park and Rockville.

A coalition of working-class voters and affluent liberals has given Democrats a stranglehold on local political power in Montgomery County. However, the 8th has a tradition of supporting moderate-to-liberal Republicans for the House.

Democratic loyalties are also tenuous at the presidential level. In 1988, Michael S. Dukakis took 53 percent of the 8th District vote, and in 1984 Walter F. Mondale took 51 percent.

Though Ronald Reagan fared well in the 8th (coming within 7,500 votes of twice carrying it), there are many voters here who do not share his anti-big-government sentiment. The federal government is the economic engine for the trade association executives, lawyers, government agency heads — and no small number of congressmen — who contribute to Montgomery County's affluent status. It also provides jobs for the thousands of bureaucrats who commute to Washington or to such local federal facilities as the National Institutes of Health in Bethesda and the National Institute of Standards and Technology in Gaithersburg.

Bethesda and Chevy Chase, with their oriental-carpet stores and gourmet shops, are at the hub of the district's upper-middle-class prosperity. Both of these suburbs, as well as the more upscale areas of Rockville, have sizable Jewish populations. Many of these residents abandoned less-affluent Silver Spring, where they were supplanted mainly by minority-group members.

Rockville, with 47,000 residents, is the largest incorporated city in the 8th. To the north, Gaithersburg (32,000 people) and the unincorporated areas in between have enjoyed a boom, associated with the expansion of the high-tech corridor along Interstate 270.

Population: 528,036. White 448,865 (85%), Black 48,212 (9%), Other 22,257 (4%). Spanish origin 21,662 (4%). 18 and over 391,309 (74%), 65 and over 48,358 (9%). Median age: 32.

Committees

Post Office and Civil Service (6th of 9 Republicans)
Civil Service (ranking); Compensation and Employee Benefits

Science, Space and Technology (15th of 19 Republicans)
Science, Research and Technology; Space Science and Applications

Select Aging (22nd of 27 Republicans)
Human Services

Elections

1988 General		
Constance A. Morella (R)	172,619	(63%)
Peter Franchot (D)	102,478	(37%)
1986 General		
Constance A. Morella (R)	92,917	(53%)
Stewart Bainum Jr. (D)	82,825	(47%)

District Vote For President

	1988		1984		1980		1976	
D	150,522	(53%)	136,104	(51%)	100,363	(40%)	125,996	(52%)
R	129,919	(46%)	128,747	(49%)	116,514	(47%)	116,064	(48%)
I					31,201	(13%)		

Campaign Finance

	Receipts	Receipts from PACs		Expend-itures
1988				
Morella (R)	$829,437	$305,374	(37%)	$821,574
Franchot (D)	$461,350	$190,203	(41%)	$460,847
1986				
Morella (R)	$623,956	$147,240	(24%)	$630,317
Bainum (D)	$1,502,302	$172,690	(11%)	$1,500,531

Key Votes

1987	
Raise speed limit to 65 mph	N
Approve Gephardt "fair trade" amendment	N
Ban testing of larger nuclear weapons	Y
Delay "re-flagging" of Kuwaiti tankers	Y
Approve tax-raising deficit-reduction bill	N
1988	
Approve aid to Nicaraguan contras	N
Enact civil rights restoration bill over Reagan veto	Y
Kill 60-day plant-closing notification measure	N
Pass omnibus trade bill over Reagan veto	Y
Approve death penalty for drug-related murders	N
Bar federal funds for abortions in cases of rape and incest	N
Oppose seven-day waiting period for purchase of handguns	N

Voting Studies

	Presidential Support		Party Unity		Conservative Coalition	
Year	S	O	S	O	S	O
1988	28	68	30	67	32	66
1987	34	65	29	66	40	60

Interest Group Ratings

Year	ADA	ACU	AFL-CIO	CCUS
1988	90	8	79	46
1987	60	22	50	40

Massachusetts

U.S. CONGRESS

SENATE 2 D
HOUSE 10 D, 1 R

LEGISLATURE

Senate 32 D, 8 R
House 128 D, 32 R

ELECTIONS

1988 Presidential Vote

Bush	45%
Dukakis	53%

1984 Presidential Vote

Reagan	51%
Mondale	48%

1980 Presidential Vote

Reagan	42%
Carter	42%
Anderson	15%

Turnout rate in 1984	58%
Turnout rate in 1986	33%
Turnout rate in 1988	58%

(as percentage of voting age population)

POPULATION AND GROWTH

1980 population	5,737,037
1988 population estimate (13th in the nation)	5,889,000
Percent change 1980-1988	+3%

DEMOGRAPHIC BREAKDOWN

White	94%
Black	4%
Other	1%
(Spanish origin)	3%
Urban	84%
Rural	16%
Born in state	72%
Foreign-born	9%

MAJOR CITIES

Boston	573,600
Worcester	157,770
Springfield	149,410
New Bedford	96,450
Brockton	93,870

AREA AND LAND USE

Area 7,825 sq. miles (45th)

Farm	12%
Forest	62%
Federally owned	2%

Gov. Michael S. Dukakis (D)
Of Brookline — Elected 1982
(also served 1975-79)

Born: Nov. 3, 1933, Brookline, Mass.
Education: Swarthmore College, B.A. 1955; Harvard U., LL.B. 1960.
Military Career: Army, 1955-57.
Occupation: Lawyer; television commentator.
Religion: Greek Orthodox.
Political Career: Mass. House, 1963-71; Democratic nominee for lieutenant governor, 1970; defeated for renomination as governor, 1978; Democratic nominee for president, 1988.
Next Election: 1990.

WORK

Occupations

White-collar	58%
Blue-collar	28%
Service workers	13%

Government Workers

Federal	58,872
State	100,587
Local	219,006

MONEY

Median family income	$ 21,166	(14th)
Tax burden per capita	$ 1,137	(7th)

EDUCATION

Spending per pupil through grade 12	$ 4,562	(8th)
Persons with college degrees	20%	(6th)

CRIME

Violent crime rate	565 per 100,000 (14th)

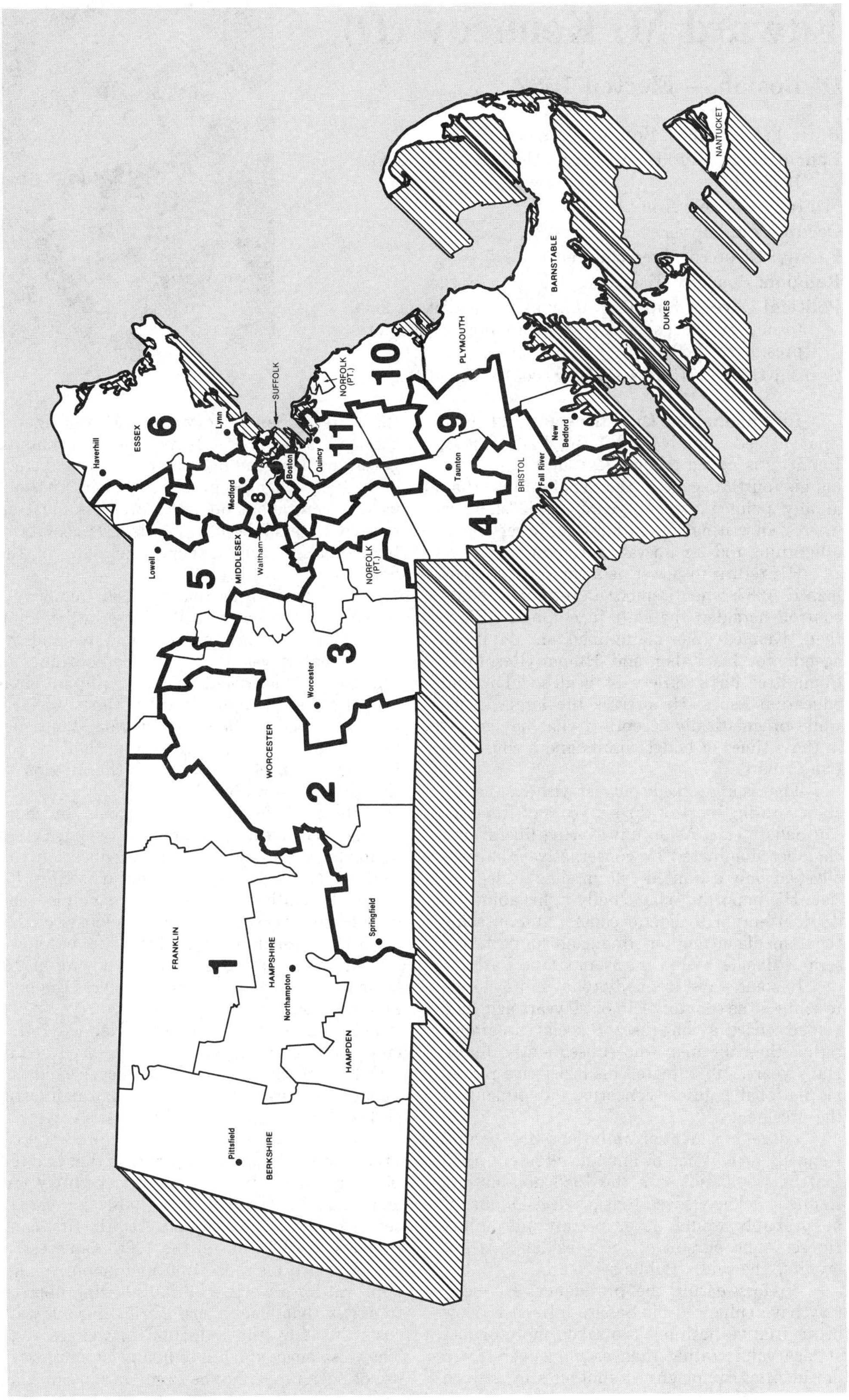
NANTUCKET
BARNSTABLE
DUKES
PLYMOUTH
10
NORFOLK (PT.)
SUFFOLK
9
New Bedford
BRISTOL
Fall River
Taunton
4
11
Quincy
Boston
8
Medford
7
Waltham
6
ESSEX
Lynn
Haverhill
Lowell
5
MIDDLESEX
NORFOLK (PT.)
3
Worcester
WORCESTER
2
Springfield
1
FRANKLIN
HAMPSHIRE
Northampton
HAMPDEN
Pittsfield
BERKSHIRE

Edward M. Kennedy (D)

Of Boston — Elected 1962

Born: Feb. 22, 1932, Boston, Mass.
Education: Harvard U., A.B. 1956; U. of Virginia, LL.B. 1959.
Military Career: Army, 1951-53.
Occupation: Lawyer.
Family: Divorced; three children.
Religion: Roman Catholic.
Political Career: Suffolk County assistant district attorney, 1961-62; sought Democratic nomination for president, 1980.
Capitol Office: 315 Russell Bldg. 20510; 224-4543.

In Washington: Once the youthful heir to what seemed a family deed to the White House, Kennedy is now a graying legislator approaching his fourth decade in the Senate. More than at any point in recent years, he is showing interest in writing laws rather than in serving as a lightning rod for liberal sentiment.

His return to power as a committee chairman in 1987, when Democrats regained Senate control, heralded the shift in emphasis. Since then, Kennedy has maintained an ambitious agenda for his Labor and Human Resources Committee on a variety of health, labor and education issues. He presses the larger goals, while pragmatically accepting what he can get in these times of budget limits and a conservative climate.

That is in marked contrast with Kennedy's stance during most of the six years of Republican Senate rule. As an unwavering liberal in a chamber dominated by conservatives, he usually had only a limited role in shaping legislation. His importance lay chiefly in his ability to draw attention to liberal causes, guaranteeing them media attention, financial support and serious debate within the Democratic Party.

In some ways, Kennedy today more closely resembles the senator of 15 or 20 years ago, who helped enact a long list of social programs, rather than the man who subsequently, for so many years, subordinated his legislative role to his national political concerns and pursuit of the presidency.

Those presidential ambitions are behind Kennedy now. When he announced late in 1985 that he would not seek the 1988 nomination, Kennedy acknowledged that his decision meant he probably would never occupy the White House. "The pursuit of the presidency is not my life," he said. "Public service is."

By forswearing the presidency, Kennedy may have enhanced his Senate influence. Now his legislative positions are taken more or less at face value, rather than as maneuvers for a presidential campaign. In another step toward the center of Senate power, he has reconsidered the traditional liberal commitment to massive government spending programs. Ever since early 1985, when he proclaimed that "those of us who care about domestic progress must do more with less," he has prodded Democrats to temper their social demands in light of the deficit.

Still, true to his rousing 1980 Democratic convention speech, with its liberal affirmation that "Hope lives on, the cause endures and the dream shall never die," Kennedy continues to espouse grandiose plans of his own in anticipation of better fiscal and political times. In early 1988, he called for "a major program of national investment in our children, equivalent to the Marshall Plan of the 1940s, or the mission to the moon of the 1960s."

He has refashioned other goals, by mandating that local governments or businesses assume certain costs for health, education and welfare. Kennedy's quarter-century effort for national health insurance, for example, had evolved so that by 1989 he was no longer calling for a government-sponsored benefit, but for a hybrid requiring private employers to insure their workers while government covers the poor and unemployed.

On less ambitious projects, Kennedy often cultivates potential allies outside his own liberal faction. Even when Republicans held the Senate, he worked with Labor Chairman Orrin G. Hatch and other Republicans on a variety of health bills, including legislation to allow U.S. drug companies to export products that had not been approved for sale in this country. As chairman, he and Hatch — now the panel's senior Republican — cosponsored the first comprehensive AIDS bill in the 100th Congress.

The two men also won unanimous Senate approval for a welfare bill authorizing bonuses to states that place beneficiaries in jobs, with costs offset by the reduction in welfare rolls. They also enacted a bill to ban most employers' use of polygraphs. As the Immigration Subcommittee chairman on the Judiciary Committee, Kennedy has allied with ranking Republican Alan K. Simpson to overhaul the legal immigration system; their bill passed the Senate overwhelmingly in 1988, but died in the House.

On Labor and Judiciary, Kennedy occasionally leaves it to other liberals, notably Ohio Democrat Howard M. Metzenbaum, to lead the partisan charge. That was true during Judiciary's consideration of President Reagan's nomination of William H. Rehnquist to be chief justice. Similarly, Kennedy did not make an all-out effort to kill what became the 1986 law against illegal immigration, despite liberals' concerns that imposing sanctions on employers who hire illegal aliens would lead to discrimination against those who appear foreign.

This is not to suggest that Kennedy is no longer partisan; on occasion he still is reflexively and stridently so. Unlike other Senate Democrats who initially withheld their fire after Reagan nominated controversial conservative Robert H. Bork to the Supreme Court in 1987, Kennedy delivered his blast within an hour of the announcement, saying that Bork "stands for an extremist view of the Constitution and the role of the Supreme Court."

As the 1988 presidential election neared, Kennedy at times seemed to treat Labor's agenda like a party platform, drawing contrasts with Republicans' positions on child care, the minimum wage and civil rights to needle GOP candidate George Bush. Senate Republicans gave as good as they got, successfully filibustering labor-supported bills raising the minimum wage, requiring notice to workers of job-related health risks and mandating unpaid job leaves for new parents. The major labor victory during Kennedy's first term as chairman was a bill requiring that workers receive advance notification of plant closings.

He had a major role in the 100th Congress in steering into law two of the most important civil rights bills since the 1960s. One, the *Grove City* bill, expanded four landmark anti-bias laws that were narrowed by a 1984 Supreme Court ruling. The other strengthened the 1968 fair housing law — "a toothless tiger," Kennedy said — by giving federal regulators authority to crack down on discrimination in the sale or rental of housing.

Though civil rights and domestic programs have been the focus of Kennedy's career, and he is not a particularly active member of the Armed Services Committee, he can be an outspoken liberal voice on defense and foreign policy. However, even with Democrats in the majority, Kennedy's position puts him in the Senate minority on most questions.

On some issues, notably South Africa, Kennedy can play an important role by virtue of his celebrity. His heavily publicized visit to that country in early 1985 helped harden public opinion against its white-minority government, setting in motion the events that led to passage of tough economic sanctions in 1986.

But publicity and power do not always go together. In 1988, reacting to Pretoria's continued repression and to Reagan's laxity in enforcing the law, Kennedy sponsored a near-total trade embargo to "end, once and for all time, American complicity in and support for apartheid." But without key Republicans' support, the bill died.

Not much involved in arms control issues previously, Kennedy adroitly seized the leadership of the growing nuclear freeze movement in 1983. But he could never muster a majority, and the freeze movement soon faltered. More recently, his proposals to ban all but the smallest nuclear arms tests — passed several times by the House — have lost by wide margins in the Senate.

Along with other Senate liberals, Kennedy had little success against Reagan's Central America policy. He lost repeated efforts to cut aid to El Salvador and to block military aid to the Nicaraguan contras, and he could not prod Democrats into forming a common front in opposition. But by 1988, House and Senate Democrats coalesced for a time behind a contra package limited to "humanitarian" aid, which Kennedy supported — like many other Democrats — only because otherwise Reagan's military aid request would pass.

Kennedy started his career without any of the leadership pressures that descended on him later. He was 30 years old, his brothers were running the country, and he voted with them while looking out for his state's interests.

In time, he became an innovative and often successful legislator. Kennedy was largely responsible for creating the Teacher Corps. He helped eliminate draft deferments for college students, saying they were unfair to the poor, and he spoke for Hispanic farm workers and Alaska's Indians.

But Kennedy's strongest legislative period was in the early 1970s, following not only the 1969 Chappaquiddick tragedy but also his most embarrassing Senate defeat, his ouster as majority whip in 1971.

Kennedy had been elected whip in 1969, beating Finance Chairman Russell B. Long, who had performed erratically in the post. The vote was taken only months after Sen. Robert F. Kennedy's assassination, and the youngest Kennedy was seen as the rising liberal star.

But he was too bored with the odd parliamentary jobs on the floor that make an effective Senate leader. Then that summer, his image was shattered for all time when he drove his car off a bridge at Chappaquiddick and his companion in the car, Mary Jo Kopechne, drowned. When Senate Democrats elected their leaders in 1971, they chose Robert C. Byrd for whip, 31-24.

Kennedy went back to the legislative process. He became chairman of Labor's Health Subcommittee and formed a productive partnership with his House counterpart, Florida Democrat Paul G. Rogers. Together they wrote legislation funding research into cancer and heart and lung diseases, family planning and doctor training. Virtually every year brought a greater federal role in health. But Kennedy's most important proposal, for national health insurance, never moved close to enactment.

Meanwhile, Kennedy was chairing Judiciary's Subcommittee on Administrative Practice and Procedure, and using it to investigate a range of subjects, from the Freedom of Information Act to the Food and Drug Administration. Critics said he used the panel for publicity, but Kennedy's hearings sometimes led to major bills, such as a 1979 revision of drug laws.

When Kennedy became chairman of Judiciary in 1979, his tenure seemed likely to last as long as he remained in the Senate. But he did not accomplish much; by fall, he was running for president and the next year's elections brought a Republican takeover.

When Kennedy let his Senate duties lapse, he doomed an artful compromise with Judiciary's senior Republican, Strom Thurmond, on his top-priority bill to rewrite the criminal code. The bill did not reach the floor. After losing the presidential nomination, Kennedy returned to work and tried desperately to rescue an open housing bill that had passed the House. But it fell to conservatives' filibuster threats.

Over the years at Judiciary, Kennedy has worked on bills to admit more refugees and to provide aid to those abroad. He promoted the vote for 18-year-olds in 1970. Outside his committees, Kennedy became an outspoken advocate of tax reform, coordinating the opposition to Finance's tax bills since the committee's liberals were reluctant to challenge Long, their chairman until 1981.

In 1976, when Finance wrote the most complex tax bill in 20 years, Kennedy and allies sought unsuccessfully to raise the minimum tax on the wealthy, restrict corporate tax shelters and provide a credit for retirees. The 1986 tax-overhaul law would do many of the same things.

Kennedy also became identified with the issue of industry deregulation, sometimes in alliance with conservatives. He tried as Judiciary chairman to bring deregulation bills under his jurisdiction, but failed after the Commerce Committee counterattacked; Democrat Ernest F. Hollings of South Carolina complained of "Kennedy hegemony."

Kennedy may not be the most brilliant senator, but he is tenacious. Moreover, he comes to his issues well-grounded by one of Congress' best staffs, a team drawn by Kennedy's name and the higher salaries that he personally supplements.

Similarly, Kennedy is not the most articulate politician, but his speechwriters help greatly; when he is psychologically ready, he can still stir an audience like few others in American politics, as he did at the 1980 convention.

That stirring speech in New York helped restore some of Kennedy's political luster after his embarrassing loss to President Carter for the nomination. It had been a curious, bizarre campaign. Since 1968, people had looked to Kennedy to run for president. In the fall of 1979, apparently deceived by early polls showing him far ahead of Carter, Kennedy launched his campaign without offering any clear idea of why he wanted to be president. He talked of the need for stronger leadership, but so clumsily as to raise the question of whether he could provide it. Meanwhile, Carter was devoting his attention to the American hostages in Iran, in a carefully staged display of his leadership.

Only in the campaign's second half — by which time Kennedy was essentially beaten — did he present the clear liberal argument he took to the convention. After Jan. 28, when he attacked Carter's hard-line anti-Soviet policy as "Cold War II," Kennedy was a different candidate. The changes did not bring him any closer to nomination, but they kept him alive as a liberal leader.

At Home: In Massachusetts, Kennedy usually has had to run against his own track record. To "win," he has to run up a lopsided margin against his modest Republican opposition, preserving his reputation for invincibility at home and his image as a national leader.

It has not always been easy. He set a tough standard for himself in 1964, when he won his first full term less than a year after his brother John's assassination. Bedridden after an airplane crash, he beat Republican Howard Whitmore Jr. by the widest margin in state history: 1,129,244 votes.

That number, rather than GOP candidate Josiah Spaulding, was the real test in 1970. There was no way Kennedy could pass it. The Chappaquiddick accident had occurred the year before, and the national skepticism over his handling of it had its effect even at home. Given that, his 62 percent was comfortable.

Kennedy's stands for Medicaid abortions and busing in Boston seemed to pose problems in 1976, but he had a good year. He brushed aside three anti-busing and right-to-life challengers in the primary, then crushed GOP businessman Michael Robertson by a million votes.

In 1982 Kennedy had the first Republican foe able to draw some attention on his own. Raymond Shamie, a wealthy inventor and engineer, spent over $1 million in a quixotic but imaginative campaign. In an effort to force Kennedy to debate him, Shamie had airplanes circle baseball games, county fairs, national monuments and crowded freeways around the country, towing banners offering a $10,000 reward to whoever could "GET TED KENNEDY

TO DEBATE RAY SHAMIE."

Kennedy fought back with his own attention-getting ploy. Confronting the "character" issue that had plagued his 1980 presidential bid, his campaign aired effective TV ads showing Kennedy intimates talking about his personal side — his stoicism in the face of personal tragedy and his compassion toward other people.

A month before the election, Kennedy accepted Shamie's offer, asking that the reward go to a Catholic school in Hanover, Mass. The debate gave Shamie greater recognition statewide, but did little else to help him or hurt Kennedy. The final result — 61 percent for Kennedy — was the senator's weakest showing since 1962, although one that most of his colleagues would be happy to accept.

In 1988, Kennedy had a trouble-free reelection. Joe Malone, a 33-year-old former state GOP executive director, saw his bid more as a party-building endeavor than a contest with Kennedy. Rather than attack the incumbent, Malone appealed to minorities and working-class voters to take a second look at the beleaguered Bay State GOP. He made scant progress against Kennedy, but by the campaign's end, he was considered someone with a future in politics.

Meanwhile, Massachusetts Gov. Michael S. Dukakis' presidential campaign was getting as much political ink as the state could absorb. Kennedy turned over management of his campaign to two of his children and coasted to a comfortable 65 percent victory.

Kennedy burst into politics in 1962 by winning the election to fill the remaining two years of his brother's Senate term. John F. Kennedy had arranged for family friend Benjamin A. Smith to get the seat when he became president in 1961, and Smith then stepped aside for the younger Kennedy in 1962.

Edward J. McCormack, nephew of House Speaker John W. McCormack, was not as obliging. He derided Kennedy's qualifications, noting his meager experience as an assistant district attorney in Boston, and said in a Democratic primary debate: "If your name were Edward Moore [instead of Edward Moore Kennedy], your candidacy would be a joke." Kennedy did not lose his temper and the attacks created a backlash against McCormack.

Kennedy easily won the primary, carrying every ward in Boston and winning outstate as well. In November he took 55 percent of the vote against Republican George Cabot Lodge.

Committees

Labor and Human Resources (Chairman)

Armed Services (4th of 11 Democrats)
Projection Forces and Regional Defense (chairman); Manpower and Personnel; Strategic Forces and Nuclear Deterrence

Judiciary (2nd of 8 Democrats)
Immigration and Refugee Affairs (chairman); Constitution; Patents, Copyrights and Trademarks

Joint Economic
Fiscal and Monetary Policy (chairman); Economic Goals and Intergovernmental Policy; International Economic Policy

Elections

1988 General

Edward M. Kennedy (D)	1,693,344	(65%)
Joseph D. Malone (R)	884,267	(34%)

Previous Winning Percentages: **1982** (61%) **1976** (69%) **1970** (62%) **1964** (74%) **1962** * (55%)

* *Special election.*

Campaign Finance

	Receipts	Receipts from PACs	Expend-itures
1988			
Kennedy (D)	$3,304,580	$322,972 (10%)	$2,702,865
Malone (R)	$617,806	0	$587,323

Key Votes

1987

Enact omnibus highway bill over Reagan veto	Y
Limit testing of space-based anti-ballistic missiles	Y
Oppose banning tests of larger nuclear weapons	N
Confirm Robert H. Bork as Supreme Court justice	N

1988

Allow vote on campaign-finance overhaul	Y
Pass civil rights restoration bill over Reagan veto	Y
Enact omnibus trade bill over Reagan veto	Y
Approve death penalty for drug-related murders	N
Oppose "workfare" amendment to welfare overhaul bill	Y

Voting Studies

	Presidential Support		Party Unity		Conservative Coalition	
Year	S	O	S	O	S	O
1988	36	55	84	4	3	89
1987	29	62	85	5	6	81
1986	28	69	79	16	24	70
1985	27	69	81	7	17	73
1984	30	58	84	7	6	91
1983	36	54	70	17	11	82
1982	29	64	83	5	2	88
1981	31	60	80	9	4	87

Interest Group Ratings

Year	ADA	ACU	AFL-CIO	CCUS
1988	95	0	100	27
1987	90	0	100	24
1986	80	10	77	47
1985	85	9	90	39
1984	85	5	100	24
1983	85	0	100	22
1982	75	6	96	0
1981	100	0	94	6

John Kerry (D)

Of Boston — Elected 1984

Born: Dec. 22, 1943, Denver, Colo.
Education: Yale U., B.A. 1966; Boston College Law School, J.D. 1976.
Military Career: Navy, 1968-69.
Occupation: Lawyer.
Family: Divorced; two children.
Religion: Roman Catholic.
Political Career: Mass. lieutenant governor, 1982-84; Democratic nominee for U.S. House, 1972.
Capitol Office: 421 Russell Bldg. 20510; 224-2742.

In Washington: Kerry begins the 101st Congress with a lingering image problem: He seems to have done too many things with an eye toward how they would look. To his credit, he seems acutely aware of this reputation. And while he continues to struggle with the dichotomies of appearance and substance, his career seems likely to be long enough to work them out.

The Senate is more tolerant of ambition in freshmen than it once was, but it is still thought poor form to seem to be running for president in one's first term. Though Kerry denies the indictment, he has often seemed overeager to his colleagues.

The impression is enhanced by characteristics Kerry shares with a legendary Massachusetts politician with the same initials. Like John F. Kennedy, Kerry is a product of social privilege (his middle name, Forbes, salutes his mother's blue-blood family). Like Kennedy, Kerry was decorated for his daring as a small-craft commander in the Navy and went quickly into politics in the party of the lower income classes. But Kerry's career has been more anti-establishment than Kennedy's, especially at critical junctures.

He first came to prominence as a veteran protesting the Vietnam War, and at times in his first years in the Senate he still seemed to be carrying a protester's banner. The dutiful study he devoted to complex issues such as anti-satellite weapons testing was appreciated, but his effort to address the issue with amendments on other senators' unrelated bills was not.

But there is another, less headstrong Kerry, a character more visible as his first term draws toward its end. A debater at Yale, he can display both a polished speaking style and an analytical intellect. He has also heightened his standing in the party by guiding the Democratic Senatorial Campaign Committee for the 1988 election cycle.

In the 100th Congress, Kerry gained some national note by taking on Panamanian strongman Manuel Antonio Noriega. As chairman of the Foreign Relations Subcommittee on Terrorism, Narcotics and International Operations, Kerry had investigators probing possible ties between drug smuggling and illegal shipments of weapons to the Nicaraguan contras. Kerry suggested Noriega was being protected by the United States because of what he knew about the connection.

George Bush, then vice president and the 1988 GOP presidential nominee, attacked Kerry by name. Early in the 101st Congress, Kerry sometimes acted in concert with the Bush administration — as when he supported the certification of Mexico's cooperation on drug interdiction and voted for Bush's compromise humanitarian-aid package for the contras. But Kerry opposed certifying the drug interdiction efforts of the Bahamas. And he released a two-volume report on drugs and foreign policy that said such objectives as military support of the contras had interfered with the war on drugs.

Kerry's general approach to Central America has been such that conservative groups use his name for bait in fund-raising appeals. Shortly after being elected, Kerry traveled to Managua with fellow freshman Sen. Tom Harkin of Iowa and returned saying the Sandinista regime was ready to talk about a cease-fire. When, soon after, Nicaraguan President Daniel Ortega went to Moscow to ask for more Soviet aid, many people thought the two senators had allowed themselves to be used.

Worse, in the view of others in the Senate, was his early tendency to charge ahead on the floor with little apparent regard for the chances of success or the costs of defeat.

During debate on the 1985 contra-aid bill, Kerry offered an amendment to bar use of any funds for activities violating international law. Cornered, Republicans offered to accept the amendment by voice vote. But Kerry insisted on a roll call, angering Majority Leader Bob Dole, who was trying to speed action on the bill. Dole was able to block the amendment, forcing Kerry to accept a watered-down version.

Later that year, Kerry picked the immigration bill as a vehicle for an amendment that would delay tests on an anti-satellite weapon. Convinced that the amendment faced certain rejection, arms-control lobbyists implored him not to offer it. But he did offer it and it was defeated.

Since then, however, Kerry has made some headway in getting people to take him more seriously. He has taken the time to master the technical aspects of issues such as the anti-ballistic missile treaty, and has shown a willingness to compromise and work within the system.

Moreover, Kerry has had the satisfaction of seeing other members of Congress come around to his views on controversial foreign policy issues. Early on, he was an outspoken critic of the regime of Philippine President Ferdinand E. Marcos, warning of a communist takeover if change did not occur.

He also opposed White House efforts to aid the contras after Congress cut off military assistance. Throughout 1986, he pressed Foreign Relations Chairman Richard G. Lugar for an investigation of the private network funneling funds to the rebels.

When that was not forthcoming, Kerry launched his own inquiry. In October 1986, he issued a report that outlined possibly illegal administration ties to the contras, as well as alleged contra corruption and human rights abuses. Within a few weeks, the initial revelations about the Iran-contra affair seemed to confirm some of Kerry's charges.

Kerry does not want to appear preoccupied exclusively with foreign affairs. "Nicaragua pushed me more to the forefront on the international scene than in fact I have been," he says. "I would like to be known as a domestic-oriented Massachusetts senator."

That interest began to be more obvious in the 101st Congress, with Kerry's re-election year approaching. Kerry signaled he would take a livelier role in legislation limiting emissions that cause acid rain, and in efforts to provide low-income housing.

Kerry also has a new reputation earned by running the campaign committee for 1988. He had a tough act to follow because in 1986 the Democrats had gained eight seats and taken control of the Senate. The 1988 circumstances were less favorable, but Democrats did manage to win 19 of the 33 Senate races despite Bush's solid presidential victory.

The Kerry-led committee raised $16.3 million, more than any previous Democratic campaign committee, substantially narrowing the gap with its GOP counterpart. This was a personal coup for Kerry, whose fund-raising potential for the committee had been questioned because he himself refuses contributions from political action committees. Kerry also helped recruit a crop of candidates that included several current or former governors and other statewide officeholders. His campaign operation made little news of its own to distract from the efforts of the candidates.

Still, Kerry gets noticed at least as often for the glamor of his persona — his command of European manners, his contacts in the world of entertainment and his photogenic looks enhanced by cosmetic surgery. Since his divorce became final in 1988, he has been officially among the most eligible bachelors in Washington. So he is an ideal subject for tabloid treatment, and his name has been linked with those of various actresses.

None of this may seem overly burdensome, but Kerry obviously wants to be taken seriously in the Senate — whether or not he really wants to be president. So he resists being cast as a lothario and has tried to reduce his public profile somewhat — a difficult turnaround for someone once satirized in Boston as "Senator Liveshot."

At Home: In 1971, Kerry, a leader of Vietnam Veterans Against the War, joined with other demonstrators as they threw their medals over the White House fence. When the incident is recounted, Kerry takes pains to explain that he opposed the returning of medals as a tactic and returned none of his own (three Purple Hearts, a Silver Star and a Bronze Star). He did throw the medals of a veteran from Worcester, Mass., who could not come to Washington, and he also threw several of the ribbons he had received with his own medals.

Kerry's ambivalence about the war protests of his day may be shared by much of his generation. But it also fits the pattern of irony in Kerry's career. He has never fully divested himself of the trappings of his privileged youth or his career as a decorated naval officer. But his political rise has been notable for its anti-establishment tone.

He became a national figure in the 1971 Vietnam protests, gaining front-page coverage by asking the Senate Foreign Relations Committee, "How do you ask a man to be the last man to die for a mistake?" He tried to exploit the publicity by moving to Lowell and running in the open 5th Congressional District in 1972. Kerry won his 10-way primary, but lost in the fall to Republican Paul Cronin.

After that defeat, Kerry went to law school, and worked as assistant district attorney in Middlesex County. In 1980, he bowed out of a House campaign in a second suburban district in favor of fellow liberal Barney Frank.

In 1982, Kerry ran for lieutenant governor in a challenge to the regular Democratic establishment. With help from Ray Flynn, then a member of the Boston City Council and now the mayor, he carried Suffolk County and edged out Evelyn Murphy in the primary.

The anti-establishment theme surfaced again in 1984, in his fight with U.S. Rep. James

M. Shannon for the nomination to replace retiring Sen. Paul E. Tsongas. Kerry contrasted his image as an independent liberal to Shannon's reputation as a House insider.

Shannon argued that his knowledge of Capitol Hill was an asset Kerry could not match. But Kerry called Shannon a "backroom" politician, and cast himself as an outsider who could stand up to the Reagan administration. He won by about 25,000 votes.

In the general election, Kerry faced conservative businessman Ray Shamie, who won the GOP nomination in a stunning upset over longtime national figure Elliot Richardson. Indications that Shamie had picked up primary votes from working-class Democrats, along with Reagan's popularity in lunch-bucket territory, forced Kerry to moderate his image. He played down foreign policy, talked about economics, and muted his anti-war background.

It turned out there was little to worry about. *The Boston Globe* ran articles tying Shamie to the ultra-conservative John Birch Society, and Shamie was not helped when some of his supporters questioned Kerry's loyalty as a U.S. citizen. Kerry took Boston by better than 2-to-1 and devastated Shamie in most other cities, winning with 55 percent overall.

Committees

Banking, Housing and Urban Affairs (11th of 12 Democrats)
Consumer and Regulatory Affairs; Housing and Urban Affairs

Commerce, Science and Transportation (8th of 11 Democrats)
Aviation; Communications; Science, Technology and Space; National Ocean Policy Study

Foreign Relations (6th of 10 Democrats)
Terrorism, Narcotics and International Communications (chairman); International Economic Policy, Trade, Oceans and Environment; Western Hemisphere and Peace Corps Affairs

Small Business (8th of 10 Democrats)
Urban and Minority-Owned Business Development (chairman); Innovation, Technology and Productivity; Rural Economy and Family Farming

Elections

1984 General		
John Kerry (D)	1,393,150	(55%)
Raymond Shamie (R)	1,136,913	(45%)
1984 Primary		
John Kerry (D)	322,470	(41%)
James M. Shannon (D)	297,941	(38%)
David Bartley (D)	85,910	(11%)
Michael Joseph Connolly (D)	82,999	(11%)

Campaign Finance

	Receipts	Receipts from PACs		Expend-itures
1984				
Kerry (D)	$2,162,530	0		$2,070,000
Shamie (R)	$4,196,521	$21,185	(1%)	$4,180,961

Key Votes

1987	
Enact omnibus highway bill over Reagan veto	Y
Limit testing of space-based anti-ballistic missiles	Y
Oppose banning tests of larger nuclear weapons	N
Confirm Robert H. Bork as Supreme Court justice	N
1988	
Allow vote on campaign-finance overhaul	Y
Pass civil rights restoration bill over Reagan veto	Y
Enact omnibus trade bill over Reagan veto	Y
Approve death penalty for drug-related murders	N
Oppose "workfare" amendment to welfare overhaul bill	Y

Voting Studies

	Presidential Support		Party Unity		Conservative Coalition	
Year	**S**	**O**	**S**	**O**	**S**	**O**
1988	40	55	88	4	0	92
1987	38	59	89	8	9	84
1986	22	75	85	12	16	79
1985	26	73	91	7	13	87

Interest Group Ratings

Year	ADA	ACU	AFL-CIO	CCUS
1988	90	0	93	36
1987	85	4	100	25
1986	90	9	93	32
1985	85	5	95	38

1 Silvio O. Conte (R)

Of Pittsfield — Elected 1958

Born: Nov. 9, 1921, Pittsfield, Mass.
Education: Boston College, LL.B. 1949.
Military Career: Navy, 1942-44.
Occupation: Lawyer.
Family: Wife, Corinne Duval; four children.
Religion: Roman Catholic.
Political Career: Mass. Senate, 1951-59.
Capitol Office: 2300 Rayburn Bldg. 20515; 225-5335.

In Washington: The ranking GOP chair on the Appropriations Committee is a precarious position for a Republican as liberal as Conte. His views grate on younger conservatives, and he can be irascible even with allies. But Conte's backslapping joviality has helped him keep a grip on the committee's leadership post.

Active on virtually every Appropriations subcommittee, Conte has more to say about the budget than just about any other House Republican. He operates with a free-wheeling independence that most members cannot afford.

Although he votes against the majority of his party more than two-thirds of the time, he tries to establish his credentials as a fiscal conservative by railing against government waste and pork-barrel spending.

To hear Conte screaming about fiscal injustice on the House floor — in a voice loud enough to penetrate the farthest reaches of the Capitol — one would think he is an angry man.

But Conte fights more in bluster than in anger. His face often breaks into a smile before his harangue is even finished, and as soon as it ends, he is off to joke with his opponent. For Conte, the fight against waste is not only politically helpful, it is lots of fun.

But the fact of the matter is that Conte, a plain-talking, cigar-smoking horse-trader, has as much in common with urban ethnic Democrats as he does with the typical GOP member.

Conte makes no apology for his liberalism. In the 100th Congress, he was one of three Republicans on Appropriations to join Democrats in backing an arms control amendment opposed by the White House. He also ignored veto threats in supporting labor protections for workers hurt by airline mergers. He endorses foreign aid and environmental controls.

As ranking Republican on the Appropriations Subcommittee on Labor, Health and Human Services, and Education, Conte is at least as committed to health and social-service programs as his Democratic chairman, William H. Natcher of Kentucky. Once, when the House passed a bill that included large increases for such Conte favorites as biomedical research, maternal and child health programs and college student aid, he crooned, "I do not think there were any thorns here, just beautiful roses."

Conte's politics have always caused him some trouble on Appropriations; he was muscled onto the panel as a freshman by then-senior Republican Joseph W. Martin of Massachusetts, but was kept off the Labor-Health, Education and Welfare Subcommittee for years while junior members were appointed ahead of him. When he finally got on in 1971, he had to give up seniority on his other subcommittees to do it.

More recently, he has come into conflict with conservative backbenchers who complain that senior Republican appropriators are too cozy with Democrats in the committee's bipartisan ethos of logrolling. Complaints from the right were especially loud in mid-1987, when Conte and other senior Republicans joined committee Democrats in fighting floor amendments to make across-the-board cuts in the committee's bills.

Conte does genuinely believe in the political value of working with the Democratic majority where possible. He gets some credit from conservatives for his sincerity and for trying to explain to his critics why bipartisanship is good for the GOP, not just a way for individual Republicans to cut deals for themselves.

His willingness to deal with committee Democrats has also allowed Conte to play the broker's role on some intractable issues. When the House and Senate first became deadlocked on the abortion issue in 1976 — the House banning all federal funding of abortions, the Senate generally favoring abortion funding — Conte broke an 11-week impasse by writing compromise language to prohibit federal funding of abortions "except where the life of the mother is endangered."

Conte can, however, be a tough Republican partisan, as he was in 1985 during the battle for better GOP committee ratios in the House. Because of their election gains in 1984, Republicans felt entitled to more seats on key committees; some even staged a brief boycott of com-

Massachusetts 1

West — Berkshire Hills; Pioneer Valley

Extending over parts of five counties, the 1st is the closest thing to a rural district remaining in Massachusetts. It is dominated by small manufacturing centers and placid hill towns set amid woodland. The only heavily developed patch is a string of small cities along the winding Connecticut River, running through the Pioneer Valley on Interstate 91.

While it has significant Italian, Irish, Polish and French-Canadian enclaves, the 1st as a whole is not as heavily ethnic as eastern Massachusetts. Residents of the area west of the Connecticut River often feel cut off from Boston's influence, and this is one of the few parts of New England where as many baseball fans cheer for the New York Yankees as for the Boston Red Sox. It is also an area of the state where Republicans often run well.

All of the territory's cities, primarily redbrick mill towns with industry based on textiles, electrical equipment and light manufacturing, lost residents during the 1970s and early '80s.

Holyoke's loss was somewhat greater than that in Northampton, Pittsfield and North Adams.

The one center of population growth has been Hampshire County, which includes the youth-oriented "five-college" area that is home to the University of Massachusetts and Smith, Mount Holyoke, Amherst and Hampshire colleges.

The district's largest employer, the sprawling General Electric installation in Pittsfield, produces plastics and weapons guidance systems.

The plant's reliance on cyclical military contracts and the gradual shift of GE operations to the Sun Belt keep the local economy alternating between periods of stability and decline.

The second-oldest commercial nuclear-power plant in the nation, the Yankee Atomic plant in isolated Monroe Bridge near the Vermont border, has eased the area's dependence on imported oil, but has been the focus of a local controversy over waste disposal.

Outside the cities, dairy farming remains important to the western Massachusetts economy, although the number of farms is comparatively small. Some tobacco is also grown near the Connecticut border.

Population: 522,540. White 505,906 (97%), Black 6,097 (1%), Other 2,844 (1%). Spanish origin 10,665 (2%). 18 and over 391,008 (75%), 65 and over 66,994 (13%). Median age: 31.

mittee meetings to protest Democratic "stacking" of major panels. "It is simple fairness to allow proportional representation on committees in the House," Conte scolded the majority party.

In his campaign against wasteful spending, one of Conte's pet peeves for more than a decade has been federal aid to beekeepers. His decade-long fight is an object lesson in how hard it is to dislodge an entrenched farm program, no matter how small its constituency. In late 1988, he won approval of a provision limiting loans to beekeepers, but it was not as stringent a limit as he originally sought.

One of Conte's favorite targets for cuts close to home is congressional staffing. Ridiculing the size of the Capitol police force — two policemen for every member of Congress — he has said, "We ought to have a workmen's compensation fund, in case they trip over each other and get hurt."

Conte regularly takes aim at omnibus appropriations bills larded with water projects and items he considers pork-barrel spending. In 1983, he called a news conference to denounce a $120 million package of water projects; he was wearing a "Miss Piggy" face mask, with a large round nose and floppy ears.

"I thought it was very descriptive of what's going on here," he said, in between guffaws, "where the congressmen have their nostrils right in the trough and they're slurping it up for their districts at the expense of all the taxpayers."

Yet Conte himself is sometimes accused of parochialism. He was rebuffed in August 1988 when the House rejected a bill he sponsored to write off a federal loan to Boston College for a library in honor of former House Speaker Thomas P. O'Neill Jr.

Conte's parochial interests often help explain his liberal positions. Hailing from a region dependent on foreign oil, he backs more aid to the poor for home heating and opposes an oil-import fee. Conte has supported legislation to ease the effects of plant closings, a problem in some industrial quarters of his district during the early 1980s recession.

With Massachusetts on the receiving end of winds bringing acid rain from the Midwest, Conte has allied with liberal Henry A. Waxman of California on legislation to combat that environmental threat. In late 1987, the two cosponsored a successful amendment to set an anti-air-pollution deadline in mid-1988 in hopes of putting election-year pressure behind a strong clean-air bill. But the 100th Congress ended with the issue unresolved.

At Home: Conte is a man who feels strongly about his ethnic roots. Both his parents were immigrants, and Conte grew up in Pittsfield's Italian neighborhood. When he came home from World War II, the Italian community threw a parade for him. Five years later, after Conte earned a law degree on the GI Bill, the Italian-Americans helped put him in the state Senate.

Since then, Conte has expanded his base of support so broadly that the 1st District is his political preserve, even though most of it is nominally Democratic. After four terms in the state Senate, where he wrote the nation's first law to extend health and accident insurance to all state and municipal employees, Conte ran in 1958 for the House seat of retiring Republican Rep. John W. Heselton. His opponent was historian James MacGregor Burns.

Burns was a close friend of Sen. John F. Kennedy, who was seeking re-election that year, and Burns hoped to ride Kennedy's coattails to the House. Kennedy won 70 percent in the 1st District, but Conte proved a stronger candidate than Burns. Promising to bring federal aid to towns with unemployment, and stressing his legislative record, Conte won 55 percent.

Since then, no one has come close. Part of the reason is Conte's independent, bipartisan image. A visitor to his Capitol Hill office finds as many Democrats as Republicans pictured on the walls.

In 1962, when Conte's campaign brochure included photographs of him with President Kennedy and Democratic House Speaker John W. McCormack, Conte won a higher vote than any Republican representative in the country with Democratic opposition. It was 10 years before another Democrat even filed against him. In all, Conte has run without Democratic opposition in seven of his 16 House contests. After cancer surgery in 1987, there was talk Conte might retire, but he filed for another term and won more than 80 percent of the vote.

Committees

Appropriations (Ranking)
Labor, Health and Human Services, Education and Related Agencies (ranking); Legislative Branch; Transportation and Related Agencies

Small Business (2nd of 17 Republicans)
Procurement, Tourism and Rural Development (ranking)

Elections

1988 General

Silvio O. Conte (R)	186,356	(83%)
John R. Arden (D)	38,907	(17%)

1986 General

Silvio O. Conte (R)	113,653	(78%)
Robert S. Weiner (D)	32,396	(22%)

Previous Winning Percentages: **1984** (73%) **1982** (100%) **1980** (75%) **1978** (100%) **1976** (64%) **1974** (71%) **1972** (100%) **1970** (100%) **1968** (100%) **1966** (100%) **1964** (100%) **1962** (74%) **1960** (69%) **1958** (55%)

District Vote For President

	1988	1984	1980	1976
D	134,252 (58%)	110,691 (49%)	98,141 (43%)	131,832 (56%)
R	96,012 (41%)	115,204 (51%)	92,388 (40%)	94,134 (40%)
I			36,143 (16%)	

Campaign Finance

	Receipts	Receipts from PACs	Expend-itures
1988			
Conte (R)	$142,186	$72,624 (51%)	$131,566
Arden (D)	$772	0	$472
1986			
Conte (R)	$255,921	$130,577 (51%)	$204,921
Weiner (D)	$124,095	$2,275 (2%)	$123,426

Key Votes

1987	
Raise speed limit to 65 mph	N
Approve Gephardt "fair trade" amendment	Y
Ban testing of larger nuclear weapons	Y
Delay "re-flagging" of Kuwaiti tankers	Y
Approve tax-raising deficit-reduction bill	N
1988	
Approve aid to Nicaraguan contras	N
Enact civil rights restoration bill over Reagan veto	Y
Kill 60-day plant-closing notification measure	N
Pass omnibus trade bill over Reagan veto	Y
Approve death penalty for drug-related murders	N
Bar federal funds for abortions in cases of rape and incest	Y
Oppose seven-day waiting period for purchase of handguns	N

Voting Studies

	Presidential Support		Party Unity		Conservative Coalition	
Year	S	O	S	O	S	O
1988	29	66	30	65	29	68
1987	27	71	24	73	42	58
1986	27	72	25	73	22	76
1985	36	60	43	53	31	62
1984	38	56	25	70	20	76
1983	40	56	30	65	31	67
1982	52	45	35	62	40	58
1981	55	42	45	54	44	53

Interest Group Ratings

Year	ADA	ACU	AFL-CIO	CCUS
1988	90	8	93	46
1987	80	9	81	29
1986	75	14	100	22
1985	75	14	100	32
1984	75	13	69	50
1983	55	26	41	55
1982	80	11	60	41
1981	55	67	40	67

2 Richard E. Neal (D)

Of Springfield — Elected 1988

Born: Feb. 14, 1949, Worcester, Mass.
Education: American International College, B.A. 1972; U. of Hartford, M.P.A. 1976.
Occupation: Public official.
Family: Wife, Maureen Conway; four children.
Religion: Roman Catholic.
Political Career: Springfield City Council, 1978-84; Springfield mayor, 1984-89.
Capitol Office: 437 Cannon Bldg. 20515; 225-5601.

The Path to Washington: If the first House race is the toughest, then Neal, who faced no major-party opposition in 1988, is likely to have a very long tenure. And assuming he brings to Washington the same traits that characterized his career in Springfield — polish, patience, seriousness and a willingness to compromise — Neal may become a player in Congress as well.

In the meantime, though, he must adjust to a change in stature from powerful mayor to freshman representative, and he must work to fill the big shoes of Democrat Edward P. Boland, the 36-year veteran he succeeded. Boland was ranking on Appropriations for many years; Neal's first rung on the Hill power ladder is the Banking Committee, where he was assigned for the 101st Congress.

Though Neal was perceived as Boland's likely heir in the 2nd, his success at clearing the field of serious competition was a remarkable feat, particularly in a state known for its abundance of ambitious pols. Neal was expected to draw some opposition from the ranks of local elected officials. But by keeping his retirement plans secret until April, Boland made it tougher for potential candidates to raise money and build an organization.

The April announcement was no problem for Neal. He had begun touring the district's 38 towns and cities more than a year in advance, clearly indicating his desire to succeed Boland, but always maintaining there was "no power on Earth that could have persuaded me to run against him." He even printed campaign paraphernalia that, he said later, "could have been saved for two more years."

Neal also made skillful use of his position as mayor — and his close relationship with Springfield's business community — to amass a $200,000 campaign treasury before Boland stepped down.

This was not the first time Neal had positioned himself to be the only serious contender for an office. In 1983, his preparations to challenge Springfield's Democratic mayor helped persuade the incumbent to retire. Neal then won the office with a landslide margin that he matched in 1985 and 1987. With about 40 percent of the 2nd District's voters living in Springfield and its suburbs, these electoral successes gave Neal a solid base from which to run for the House.

In reaching out to the rest of the district — which tends to be more dependent on light industry, more blue-collar and relatively more conservative — Neal touted the economic revival of Springfield, which has enjoyed the fruits of Massachusetts' high-technology growth. Added to this fiscal message, Neal's opposition to abortion eased concern in some quarters about his liberal reputation on social-policy matters.

Attention to political detail is another hallmark of Neal's career. During the development of Springfield's Monarch Place — a $110 million public-private project Neal negotiated as mayor — he proposed renaming a nearby road Boland Way. Boland demurred and the idea never got off the ground, but it reinforced Neal's relationship with the congressman.

During his tenure as mayor, Neal stirred grumblings from some who thought he took too few risks and paid too much attention to appearances, such as his effort to plant trees and flowers along streets in the city. But public criticism of him was rare, and usually mild — noteworthy because mayors normally get embroiled in nasty local controversies and personality battles. Springfield's one newspaper is very supportive of Neal, and with cultivation of the eastern portion of the district, he should have little electoral trouble in coming years.

Neal began his political career in 1972, as co-chairman of George McGovern's presidential campaign in western Massachusetts. After a five-year stint working as an aide to Springfield Mayor William C. Sullivan, Neal in 1977 was elected to the first of the three terms on the City Council.

Massachusetts 2

West-Central — Springfield

The 2nd takes in a long stretch of central Massachusetts Yankee villages, binding them with industrial Springfield and Chicopee at one end, and the smaller factory towns of Leominster and Fitchburg at the other.

Springfield, western Massachusetts' commercial center, has about 30 percent of the district's population. It is an ethnic city, heavily French-Canadian, Irish and Polish, and 16 percent black. The district as a whole has the fifth-highest percentage of ethnic French residents in the country.

Springfield's largest employers are the Baystate Medical Center and the Massachusetts Mutual Life Insurance offices, but the city has a variety of manufacturing firms — including Smith & Wesson firearms — and commercial enterprises that attract shoppers from the outlying towns. The city diversified its economy after the mid-1970s' recession and survived the economic downturn of the early 1980s in comparatively good shape, although some smaller manufacturing firms are facing stiff competition from imports.

Chicopee, the second-largest city in the district, has begun to climb back after a gloomy decade in the 1970s. Almost a fifth of its population left when several rubber and metals plants closed and the Strategic Air Command closed its Westover Air Force Base bomber field — once the largest on the East Coast. In recent years, however, the city has begun to attract new high-technology industries. Together with Springfield, Chicopee anchors the Democratic vote in the 2nd, outweighing the conservative bent of the rest of the district.

From Springfield and Chicopee, the 2nd reaches north and east past a series of small towns to Fitchburg, near the New Hampshire border. Most of the villages along the way have kept their uncluttered, placid Yankee character, but several are sites for major area employers, such as Milton Bradley games in East Longmeadow and Digital Equipment Corp. in Westminster.

The rural area is fertile ground for Republicans. No town in the district other than Springfield and Chicopee went to Walter F. Mondale in the 1984 presidential contest, and Republican Senate candidate Raymond Shamie carried a comfortable majority of the towns in the 2nd. Gov. Michael S. Dukakis could manage only 52 percent in his 1988 presidential bid.

Population: 521,949. White 479,121 (92%), Black 27,543 (5%). Spanish origin 19,408 (4%). 18 and over 377,798 (72%), 65 and over 66,787 (13%). Median age: 31.

Committees

Banking, Finance and Urban Affairs (31st of 31 Democrats)
Economic Stabilization; General Oversight and Investigations; Housing and Community Development

Small Business (25th of 27 Democrats)
Antitrust, Impact of Deregulation and Privatization; Procurement, Tourism and Rural Development

Campaign Finance

	Receipts	Receipts from PACs	Expend-itures
1988			
Neal (D)	$352,265	$87,000 (25%)	$268,094

Election

1988 General

Richard E. Neal (D)	156,262	(80%)
Louis R. Godena (I)	38,446	(20%)

District Vote For President

	1988	1984	1980	1976
D	113,877 (52%)	100,218 (46%)	100,089 (45%)	135,571 (61%)
R	102,349 (47%)	116,729 (54%)	88,677 (40%)	80,355 (36%)
I			29,764 (14%)	

3 Joseph D. Early (D)

Of Worcester — Elected 1974

Born: Jan. 31, 1933, Worcester, Mass.
Education: College of the Holy Cross, B.S. 1955.
Military Career: Navy, 1955-57.
Occupation: Teacher and basketball coach.
Family: Wife, Marilyn Powers; eight children.
Religion: Roman Catholic.
Political Career: Mass. House, 1963-75.
Capitol Office: 2349 Rayburn Bldg. 20515; 225-6101.

In Washington: By Massachusetts standards, Joe Early is a conservative. He is against abortion and busing and skeptical about foreign aid, like most of his blue-collar constituents. But when it comes to labor and domestic spending, Early is solidly in the New Deal tradition, a strong defender of federal spending for education, health and social services.

A portly, rumpled cigar smoker, Early looks the part of a Massachusetts pol. But he does not really act like one. He is a private person who cares more about his issues than about House politics, and he prides himself on his independence from any Democratic faction. Early's was one Massachusetts vote that Thomas P. O'Neill Jr. could not always count on during his 10 years as House Speaker.

Early rarely speaks out on the House floor, and when he does it is clear he has given some thought to what he is saying. One appearance in the 100th Congress came as the House was debating the impeachment of U.S. District Court Judge Alcee L. Hastings, who had been charged with accepting a bribe and leaking wiretap information, but who had not been convicted in a court of law. There was overwhelming sentiment to impeach, but Early stood up to voice his reservations. "Here we have an individual that was not convicted," he said. "Ethics is not supposed to be a political thing.... The ethics that has happened in the past year in this House is shameful, shameful. It is political totally." The House voted 413-3 to impeach; Early was one of four members voting "present."

Early also stood apart from the majority of his colleagues early in the 101st Congress, when he spoke out for a 51 percent pay raise that was the subject of heated debate around the country. Early lamented the potential loss of judges that would follow the rejection of a federal pay raise, and said that members had to act responsibly rather than bow to public pressure. "You have to look at the intrinsic worth of the job, and you have to show leadership," he said. "A number of years ago in the House we didn't ... and, in the name of public opinion, sent Marines into Beirut. There were 244 Marines killed.... We went with public opinion and were not leaders."

It was O'Neill, then serving as majority leader, who helped Early gain his seat on the Appropriations Committee in 1975. Early devotes almost all of his energies to his work on the committee, and if he is not the most visible member, he is tenacious at lobbying for what he wants, even if it takes some dealing to get it.

On the Labor, Health and Human Services Subcommittee, Early has fought hard against spending cuts in programs ranging from medical school grants to fuel aid for the poor. As tight budgets have put pressure on domestic programs, Early has had to give ground, but he digs in with the persistence of a bulldog if the program cuts affect his district.

Perhaps his most consistent cause has been the National Institutes of Health. Colleagues on Appropriations have said that Early's guardianship is responsible for hundreds of thousands more dollars per year in the NIH budget.

On his other subcommittee, with jurisdiction over the State Department budget, Early is stingier about spending federal money. And on foreign aid issues, outside his subcommittees, he is even more skeptical. He regularly votes to cut U.S. contributions to international organizations and aid to Third World regimes both left and right.

When he was relatively new to the House, Early won a foreign relations dispute in which the odds seemed stacked badly against him. The issue was the U.S. ambassadorship to Ireland. Early favored William Shannon, a *New York Times* columnist who grew up in Worcester. Both Speaker O'Neill and Sen. Edward M. Kennedy had their own candidates. But Early worked through the State-Justice Appropriations Subcommittee, and President Carter eventually named Shannon to the post.

Early also serves on the Democratic Steering and Policy Committee, which makes committee assignments for the Democratic majority. He takes a less active interest in this assignment than he does in Appropriations, rarely lobbying to win a spot for a protégé, the

Massachusetts 3

Central — Worcester

Close to a third of Early's constituents live in Worcester, an old industrial city that belies the faded image commonly held of 19th-century Northeastern manufacturing towns. Worcester started as a textile and wire-making center, but it now has a broadly based economy — focused on the metals and machine-tool industries — that even during the early 1980s recession enabled it to maintain an unemployment figure below the statewide average and far below the national rate.

The Norton Company, the world's largest maker of grinding wheels, is one of Worcester's leading employers. Computer companies have been attracted in recent years to Marlborough and other communities east of Worcester on Interstate 495, the outer highway surrounding Boston. Digital Equipment Company is in Marlborough, Data General in Westborough.

Three major insurance companies are located in Worcester, as are 10 colleges. Clark University's Public Affairs Research Center has emerged as a major political science institute. Holy Cross, a Jesuit school founded in 1843 as the first Catholic college in New England, towers over the city from a scenic hillside.

To the south of Worcester is the historic Blackstone Valley, which holds a chain of old mill towns — classic company towns like Uxbridge, Dudley, Millville and Whitinsville. But the mills that once darkened the valley's air are defunct now; the area is the poorest in the district, and most of the blue-collar residents who have jobs commute to work in Worcester.

Farther north the towns are wealthier. Some of them look toward Worcester as a commercial and cultural center, while the ones farthest to the east are in the Boston orbit. Sherborn and Holliston are home to high-tech professionals who work along Route 128 or I-495, and the area is Republican; both communities went for George Bush in 1988 and GOP Senate candidate Ray Shamie in 1984. The suburbs closest to Worcester tend to be most amenable to voting Democratic; many of them split their votes in 1984, supporting Ronald Reagan but voting Democratic for the Senate.

At the northern end of the 3rd, small New England towns like Berlin and Stow are surrounded by apple orchards and woods. Voters hold to the Yankee Republicanism that has marked their voting habits for decades.

Population: 521,354. White 504,822 (97%), Black 7,685 (2%), Other 3,408 (1%). Spanish origin 10,736 (2%). 18 and over 376,641 (72%), 65 and over 61,279 (12%). Median age: 31.

way most Democrats on the panel do.

But Early made an exception at the start of the 100th Congress, when he went all out to try to win a seat on Energy and Commerce for O'Neill's Massachusetts successor, freshman Democrat Joseph P. Kennedy II. Early's impassioned speech to the steering committee went for naught, though; the prestigious Commerce panel is virtually closed to freshmen.

At Home: Though one would not know it to look at his rounded physique these days, Early first became known to his future constituents in the 1950s as a basketball star at Worcester's College of the Holy Cross. Early was captain of the 1954 Holy Cross team that won the National Invitational Tournament; one of his teammates, Tom Heinsohn, went on to a notable career as a player and coach for the Boston Celtics.

After a brief career as a teacher and basketball coach, Early won a seat in the Massachusetts House. He served there from 1963 to 1975, developing a reputation as a supporter of social programs and organized labor. In his final state House term, he moved up to the vice chairmanship of the Ways and Means Committee, a position that enabled him to play a key role in the passage of legislation providing a minimum income for the elderly.

Well matched to his blue-collar constituency, Early never had much trouble convincing voters to keep him in Boston. But getting to Washington was a slightly more difficult task.

When Democrat Harold Donohue retired in 1974 after 28 less-than-illustrious years in the House, six Democrats scrambled to take his place. Two of Early's opponents had held major office and had ethnic community support. Former Worcester Mayor Paul V. Mullaney was popular among that city's Irish-Americans; Gerard D'Amico, a youthful member of the Worcester school committee, had Italian-American support. But Early's solid reputation as a Democratic regular in the state House helped him stave off the opposition. In August, he received a critical endorsement from the AFL-CIO. Though Early won the Democratic nomination with just 32 percent of the vote, he finished nearly 7 percentage points ahead of Mullaney, his nearest rival.

In the general election against Republican state Rep. David J. Lionett, Early took the role of the conservative. He opposed the state's new public campaign finance law and supported the death penalty. Lionett had developed a reputation as a liberal and reformer in the Legislature.

Running in a Democratic district in an election year dominated by the Watergate scandal, Early defeated Lionett by more than 18,500 votes. But with an independent candidate siphoning off 12 percent of the total vote, Early won with a plurality of just under 50 percent.

As it turned out, that modest score was no harbinger of long-term difficulties. By 1976, his place in the 3rd District had become entrenched. He has faced no serious opposition since. Four of his seven re-election bids have failed to draw a Republican opponent.

Committee

Appropriations (12th of 35 Democrats)
Commerce, Justice and State, the Judiciary and Related Agencies; Labor, Health and Human Services, Education and Related Agencies; Treasury, Postal Service and General Government

Elections

1988 General		
Joseph D. Early (D)	191,005	(100%)
1986 General		
Joseph D. Early (D)	120,222	(100%)

Previous Winning Percentages: **1984** (67%) **1982** (100%) **1980** (72%) **1978** (75%) **1976** (100%) **1974** (50%)

District Vote For President

	1988	1984	1980	1976
D	120,907 (49%)	97,581 (43%)	91,764 (41%)	135,116 (58%)
R	123,471 (50%)	127,551 (57%)	98,707 (44%)	91,022 (39%)
I			32,720 (15%)	

Campaign Finance

	Receipts	Receipts from PACs	Expend-itures
1988			
Early (D)	$222,053	$93,250 (42%)	$205,989
1986			
Early (D)	$243,369	$86,710 (36%)	$186,651

Key Votes

1987	
Raise speed limit to 65 mph	N
Approve Gephardt "fair trade" amendment	Y
Ban testing of larger nuclear weapons	Y
Delay "re-flagging" of Kuwaiti tankers	?
Approve tax-raising deficit-reduction bill	Y
1988	
Approve aid to Nicaraguan contras	N
Enact civil rights restoration bill over Reagan veto	Y
Kill 60-day plant-closing notification measure	N
Pass omnibus trade bill over Reagan veto	Y
Approve death penalty for drug-related murders	Y
Bar federal funds for abortions in cases of rape and incest	Y
Oppose seven-day waiting period for purchase of handguns	N

Voting Studies

	Presidential Support		Party Unity		Conservative Coalition	
Year	S	O	S	O	S	O
1988	21	66	85	7	11	66
1987	13	72	82	6	23	67
1986	13	80	80	6	16	78
1985	28	69	82	6	11	78
1984	23	62	72	11	12	71
1983	6	83	74	10	17	73
1982	36	52	86	5	19	70
1981	25	62	73	13	24	64

Interest Group Ratings

Year	ADA	ACU	AFL-CIO	CCUS
1988	85	8	100	36
1987	92	0	94	8
1986	85	14	93	20
1985	80	10	100	21
1984	75	26	73	38
1983	85	18	87	6
1982	80	6	100	17
1981	85	14	87	0

4 Barney Frank (D)

Of Newton — Elected 1980

Born: March 31, 1940, Bayonne, N.J.
Education: Harvard U., B.A. 1962, J.D. 1977.
Occupation: Lawyer.
Family: Single.
Religion: Jewish.
Political Career: Mass. House, 1973-81.
Capitol Office: 1030 Longworth Bldg. 20515; 225-5931.

In Washington: Frank stands out among House liberals as one of the most sagacious debaters, possessing a keen mind and a stinging rhetorical style that can amuse as well as wound. Early in his House career, he seemed to ricochet from one issue to the next, but in recent years, Frank has added a commitment to coalition-building to his legislative arsenal; this has earned him a reputation as a serious lawmaker and an inside operator.

During the early Reagan years, Frank's liberalism alone stamped him as an outsider, an image he seemed determined to bolster. Almost defiantly unkempt, he was renowned for a 1976 campaign poster that boldly declared, "Neatness isn't everything." That appeal worked well in his campaigns for the state Legislature, but his new House colleagues found it quirky.

At the time, the breadth of Frank's interests also seemed counter-productive. While he can quickly turn from housing policy to weapons systems to agricultural marketing orders, this scattershot approach to legislation resulted early on in more pithy quotes than substantive achievements.

Frank's public evolution began in 1984, when a diet and exercise regime helped him shed 70 pounds. He polished the new look with a fresh hair style and a fashionable wardrobe. Then in 1987, he became the first member of Congress to acknowledge voluntarily that he is homosexual. "I answer every other question I'm asked," he said. "I have nothing to hide, nothing to advertise."

Also in 1987, Frank became chairman of the Judiciary Committee's Administrative Law Subcommittee. In that job, he ushered a handful of bills through the legislative mill, conveying a capacity to focus his efforts. Though he still serves on four committees and speaks out on many issues, Frank seems to realize that results speak louder than words. "I think I was distracting people with being more frenetic," he said in 1989. "And it occurred to me I'd been too acerbic."

Frank may be more focused and less frenetic, but no matter how much he tries to moderate his verbal tone, he still plunges into heated debates with a blend of indignation and humor. His speeches come out in what a colleague once described as a "staccato, rapid-fire Jersey-Bay State accent." His reaction to the 1986 drug bill — "the legislative equivalent of crack" (a potent form of cocaine) — was quintessential Frank. "It yields a short-term high," he said, "but does long-term damage to the system, and is expensive to boot."

And even the new Frank, when piqued, can lift off. In June 1989, on the day new Speaker Thomas S. Foley was being sworn in, a Republican Party memo called Foley "out of the liberal closet," and compared him to Frank and no one else. Widely dubbed a smear, the tactic prompted Frank to tell reporters that he would name prominent gay Republicans in Congress and elsewhere if the GOP doesn't "cut the crap." He said later he believed "that if we did not threaten retaliation, they would continue unilateral shelling."

Frank legislates by matching his liberalism with hard-nosed pragmatism. He will readily revise a bill to broaden its support. In working toward passage of the controversial 1987 independent counsel reauthorization — which reduced the attorney general's discretion in appointing special prosecutors — Frank accepted, and even offered, a variety of amendments, noting, "The bill was deliberately drafted as broadly as possible because it is always easier to cut back than to add on."

The measure ultimately passed by such lopsided margins that President Reagan signed it despite misgivings about its constitutionality. And when former Reagan administration officials challenged the law's legality, the Supreme Court found in favor of the congressional bill.

Frank also played a leading role in passing an ethics bill in 1988. "This is not everybody's favorite piece of legislation," he deadpanned in the midst of tense but eventually successful negotiations to persuade Congress to restrict its own post-government activities, as well as those of administration appointees. In the heat of the election year, the bill won widespread support in Congress, but it was vetoed by Reagan before he left office. In the 101st Congress, Frank

Massachusetts 4

Boston Suburbs; Fall River

The 4th is a study in contrasts. It is a district that binds the genteel Boston suburbs along its northern boundary to the gritty working-class towns at its southern end. Democrats running in districtwide elections are welcomed in both places, but they need to be sure-footed campaigners, as comfortable in the faded neon-lit taverns of Fall River as they are at catered receptions in Brookline.

Fall River, with its excellent harbor and easy access to water power, was one of the first New England towns to emerge as a textile center. Its mills — which already were being called "time-darkened" in the 1930s — drew French and Portuguese workers during the boom decades before the Great Depression; today, a politician campaigning in the city still needs multilingual literature. Job losses in the needle trades have been partially offset by the growth in high-technology fields.

At the opposite end of the district, but with an even firmer Democratic bent, are Brookline and Newton. These two affluent Boston suburbs long have been a domain for white-collar professionals who like their politics liberal as long as it does not threaten their comfortable way of life. Brookline allows no on-street parking overnight, a rule designed to keep streets clean and outsiders out. In 1988, Brookline got national exposure as the home of Democratic presidential nominee Michael S. Dukakis.

The middle section of the district is more conservative territory, a string of poorer suburbs and working-class communities where social liberalism is not received with the kind of enthusiasm usually accorded it at the northern end. The largest town in this part of the district is Attleboro, whose jewelry trade is giving way to high-technology industries.

Population: 521,995. White 507,211 (97%), Black 5,000 (1%), Other 6,678 (1%). Spanish origin 7,357 (1%). 18 and over 386,245 (74%), 65 and over 66,544 (13%). Median age: 32.

renewed his efforts to get ethics legislation enacted into law.

Amending the McCarthy-era McCarran-Walter Act, which establishes grounds for denying visas to foreigners (including some based on political ideology or expression), is a long-term Frank goal. Late in 1987, he won a one-year change in the law; it mandated that aliens be judged by their actions rather than their beliefs. Judiciary approved a measure to make the change permanent in 1988, and though it never made it to the floor, Frank introduced a new measure at the start of the 101st Congress.

The Banking Committee gives Frank a forum for his social liberalism, and he has become a driving force on housing policy. He views housing legislation through the prism of the nation's poorest families, and was the leading advocate of language in the 1987 housing bill prohibiting government development projects from displacing low-income housing. The final measure was much amended and the authorization levels slashed, but it was the first free-standing housing bill to clear Congress during the Reagan years; and Frank's amendment survived. "I've never been so happy to support a bill I think is so inadequate," he quipped.

At Home: Frank is capable of shifting on a moment's notice from the language of the Harvard government department to that of old-fashioned ward politics.

He was studying for a Ph.D. in political science when he left Harvard in 1967 to help Democrat Kevin H. White win his first term as Boston's mayor. He became White's executive assistant, establishing ties to local leaders and learning the ways of Boston politics.

In 1972 he learned that the state representative in his area was retiring, and decided to try for the job. His political contacts helped him in the primary, and that November, with a large presidential-election turnout in the district among Boston University students, Frank won the seat. "I'm one of the few people in the country who can say he benefited from George McGovern's coattails," he later commented. Frank compiled an unabashedly liberal record in the Legislature, scrapping frequently with its entrenched Democratic leadership.

When Democratic Rep. Robert F. Drinan left Congress in 1980, bowing to the papal prohibition against priests running for office, Frank went for his seat. He had to move into the district to run, but his record in the Legislature and high profile in national liberal Democratic circles won him endorsements from Drinan and many liberal organizations.

Frank won the primary by 5 percentage points. But instead of coasting through the general election, he nearly lost under a last-minute flurry of ads by his little-known GOP opponent attacking his liberal stands in the Legislature.

Two years later, Massachusetts had to lose one House seat in redistricting; hostile former colleagues in the Legislature paired him with

GOP Rep. Margaret M. Heckler in a district that drew 70 percent of its vote from Heckler's old territory. "If you asked legislators to draw a map in which Barney Frank would never be a congressman again," he said, "this would be it."

But Frank overcame his initial hesitation. From the beginning of 1982 until Election Day, he pursued Heckler relentlessly, raising money and building steam while she largely rested on her record over eight terms in the House.

Heckler's 1981 votes for President Reagan's economic program gave Frank his issue in the 4th. Hammering at her support for Reagan, appealing to the district's elderly, blue-collar and poor residents, Frank gradually drew former Heckler backers to his side.

Taken aback by his criticism, Heckler kept a low profile most of the year and was highly defensive when she did speak out in public. Her campaign took shape only a month before the election, and consisted largely of attacks on Frank's stands in the Legislature on behalf of homosexuals and the creation of an "adult entertainment" zone in Boston.

But while Frank's 1980 Republican opponent had used that theme with some success, it made little difference in 1982. Frank won by nearly 40,000 votes, surprising even his own managers.

Heckler's departure for Reagan administration appointments as secretary of health and human services and as ambassador to Ireland left district Republicans without a serious threat to Frank. After winning easily in 1984, he ran without Republican opposition in 1986.

If there was any lingering doubt about Frank's popularity in the 4th, his 1988 re-election eliminated it. After he acknowledged publicly in mid-1987 that he is homosexual, Frank prepared for the possibility that his candor about his personal life would generate a political challenge. While his Republican opponent Debra Tucker — a little-known supporter of religious broadcaster Pat Robertson's presidential campaign — tried to make an issue of it, she failed. Frank won with 70 percent.

Committees

Banking, Finance and Urban Affairs (12th of 31 Democrats)
Financial Institutions Supervision, Regulation and Insurance; Housing and Community Development; International Development, Finance, Trade and Monetary Policy

Government Operations (9th of 24 Democrats)
Employment and Housing

Judiciary (10th of 21 Democrats)
Administrative Law and Governmental Relations (chairman); Immigration, Refugees and International Law

Select Aging (14th of 39 Democrats)
Health and Long-Term Care

Elections

1988 General		
Barney Frank (D)	169,729	(70%)
Debra R. Tucker (R)	71,661	(30%)
1986 General		
Barney Frank (D)	134,387	(89%)
Thomas D. DeVisscher (AM)	16,857	(11%)

Previous Winning Percentages: 1984 (74%) **1982** (60%) **1980** (52%)

District Vote For President

	1988	1984	1980	1976
D	141,008 (57%)	122,389 (52%)	101,534 (43%)	130,677 (54%)
R	104,853 (42%)	113,540 (48%)	95,429 (40%)	101,713 (42%)
I			38,947 (16%)	

Campaign Finance

	Receipts	Receipts from PACs	Expend-itures
1988			
Frank (D)	$431,299	$141,635 (33%)	$343,097
Tucker (R)	$34,528	$1,750 (5%)	$34,368
1986			
Frank (D)	$208,533	$68,975 (33%)	$213,909

Key Votes

1987	
Raise speed limit to 65 mph	Y
Approve Gephardt "fair trade" amendment	Y
Ban testing of larger nuclear weapons	Y
Delay "re-flagging" of Kuwaiti tankers	Y
Approve tax-raising deficit-reduction bill	Y
1988	
Approve aid to Nicaraguan contras	N
Enact civil rights restoration bill over Reagan veto	Y
Kill 60-day plant-closing notification measure	N
Pass omnibus trade bill over Reagan veto	Y
Approve death penalty for drug-related murders	N
Bar federal funds for abortions in cases of rape and incest	N
Oppose seven-day waiting period for purchase of handguns	N

Voting Studies

	Presidential Support		Party Unity		Conservative Coalition	
Year	S	O	S	O	S	O
1988	17	79	87	8	0	97
1987	14	79	92	3	12	88
1986	18	81	91	8	12	88
1985	25	74	91	4	5	91
1984	30	66	87	7	8	88
1983	17	82	88	8	9	89
1982	34	62	81	10	15	78
1981	29	64	85	11	9	87

Interest Group Ratings

Year	ADA	ACU	AFL-CIO	CCUS
1988	100	0	93	21
1987	100	0	94	7
1986	100	0	86	17
1985	100	10	94	23
1984	95	0	69	25
1983	95	0	100	20
1982	90	15	100	30
1981	100	7	87	11

5 Chester G. Atkins (D)

Of Concord — Elected 1984

Born: April 14, 1948, Geneva, Switzerland.
Education: Antioch College, B.A. 1970.
Occupation: Public official.
Family: Wife, Corinne Hobbs; two children.
Religion: Unitarian.
Political Career: Mass. House, 1971-73; Mass. Senate, 1973-85.
Capitol Office: 504 Cannon Bldg. 20515; 225-3411.

In Washington: Atkins came to Congress from the Massachusetts Legislature with a reputation as a reserved and serious Yankee who could cut deals with all the skill — and enjoyment — of the canniest Boston ward politician. But it was his third term before he landed a place on the committee best suited for pols with backroom skills.

Atkins won a coveted seat on the Appropriations Committee in the 101st Congress after a bruising battle among New England Democrats. At issue was who would get the seat vacated by the retirement of Democrat Edward P. Boland; the Democratic leadership had promised that it would go to whomever the region's caucus endorsed. Atkins got the region's nod over Joseph P. Kennedy II in a secret-ballot triumph that was as much an expression of anti-Kennedy sentiment as a vote of confidence in Atkins.

A number of members were turned off by the heavy-handed lobbying of Sen. Edward M. Kennedy on his nephew's behalf, and by the suspicion that the young Kennedy would not remain in the House for long. About a year before winning the slot, Atkins renounced his own ambition to run for Massachusetts governor in 1990, reassuring state colleagues who wanted someone on Appropriations who would rise in seniority there.

In the end, Atkins had the support of most of the Massachusetts delegation, while Kennedy tapped the votes of other New England states and of the non-voting delegates who are lumped in with that region for committee-assignment purposes.

Atkins' assignment to Appropriations will put him in a better position to deliver for his constituents and for the Bay State. That is an important form of political life insurance as the delegation girds for post-1990 reapportionment, when Massachusetts is nearly certain to lose a House seat.

Atkins has been regarded as a dependable leadership ally from the day he arrived in the House — so dependable, in fact, that in his second term he was assigned to the House ethics committee.

But he demonstrated his independence in 1989, when, early in the ethics committee's investigation of Speaker Jim Wright, he was one of two Democrats to join panel Republicans in a key vote to pass the most serious charges against the Texan.

As a freshman, Atkins took advantage of then-Speaker O'Neill's patronage to win a place on the Budget Committee. In exchange, he agreed to join Public Works, which had jurisdiction over one of the former Speaker's pet projects, a new harbor tunnel for Boston.

At Home: Atkins knew what he wanted early on. In 1970, the 22-year-old Atkins unseated a Republican state representative. Two years later he defeated a Republican state senator in one of the most expensive legislative campaigns in the state.

As chairman of the state Senate Ethics Committee in 1977, he handled rules changes resulting from the extortion trial of two Senate leaders in a way that convinced the party of his steady hand. He was rewarded in 1979 when Senate President William Bulger named him chairman of the Ways and Means Committee.

Though Atkins had a liberal voting record, his loyalty to Bulger's budget priorities chagrined reform-minded colleagues. But Atkins also promoted real change in the state budget. When tax-slashing Proposition 2½ was passed in 1980, he insisted that state government be cut and savings passed on to municipalities.

As state party chairman since 1977, Atkins was in good position to go for Congress in 1984 when the 5th opened up. But his primary turned out to be harder than expected. His opponent, state Sen. Philip Shea, was a former Golden Gloves boxer whose working-class roots appealed to lunch-bucket Democrats in Lowell and Lawrence. The voting broke down along cultural lines. Atkins' victories in the suburbs and the high-tech town of Framingham enabled him to hold off Shea, who won Lowell, Lawrence and Methuen. In November, Atkins faced Gregory S. Hyatt, who led the fight for Proposition 2½. Hyatt campaigned on his anti-tax record, but Atkins easily won his liberal suburban base and carried Lawrence and Lowell.

Massachusetts 5

North — Lowell; Lawrence

Centered around two gritty mill towns where the American textile industry began in the early 19th century, the 5th has seen economic decline and, lately, modest renewal.

The long-running rivalry of Lowell and Lawrence springs from their different histories as textile centers: Lowell, the model "company town," was carefully watched over by paternalistic Yankee Protestants, while Lawrence's unsafe work places and substandard living quarters gave rise to immigrant workers' resentment of the Boston financiers who owned the community. Soon after mill workers won Lawrence's strike of 1912, textile companies began leaving for cheaper labor in the South.

Twenty years ago, both towns were in sad economic shape. Since the mid-1970s, though, Lowell's economy has been revitalized by the arrival of high-technology firms. Wang, a computer company employing 10,000 people in the Lowell area, is one of the city's largest employers. Raytheon employs over 15,000 people in the area.

The nation's first urban historical park has been established in Lowell around the Merrimack River's system of canals.

Lawrence has been slower to profit from the technology boom, but in the late 1970s new light manufacturing firms began moving into its abandoned mill spaces. Both cities are solidly Democratic.

About half the district's vote is cast in Boston suburbs to the south, including well-to-do communities such as Andover, Concord, Wayland and Sudbury. All gave pluralities to Reagan in 1980 and 1984, but they have strong liberal factions; Concord gave 22.5 percent to John B. Anderson's presidential campaign in 1980.

In 1988, Gov. Michael S. Dukakis carried Concord and Wayland, but lost Andover and Sudbury to George Bush. Lincoln, as affluent as any of the district's suburbs, chose Walter F. Mondale over Reagan in 1984 and Dukakis over Bush in 1988.

Framingham, in the 5th's southwestern corner, blends light manufacturing and middle-class neighborhoods. Carter carried it in 1980, but Reagan took it in 1984. Dukakis won Framingham in 1988.

Population: 518,313. White 494,365 (95%), Black 7,766 (2%), Other 4,944 (1%). Spanish origin 20,255 (4%). 18 and over 368,925 (71%), 65 and over 53,808 (10%). Median age: 30.

Committees

Appropriations (34th of 35 Democrats)
Interior and Related Agencies; VA, HUD and Independent Agencies

Standards of Official Conduct (6th of 6 Democrats)

Elections

1988 General		
Chester G. Atkins (D)	181,860	(84%)
T. David Hudson (LIB)	34,339	(16%)
1986 General		
Chester G. Atkins (D)	113,690	(100%)

Previous Winning Percentage: **1984** (53%)

District Vote For President

	1988	1984	1980	1976
D	112,301 (47%)	97,882 (43%)	89,068 (40%)	126,779 (55%)
R	120,945 (51%)	129,819 (57%)	100,189 (44%)	96,540 (42%)
I			35,942 (16%)	

Campaign Finance

	Receipts	Receipts from PACs	Expend-itures
1988			
Atkins (D)	$359,508	0	$344,978
Hudson (LIB)	$15,434	0	$15,396
1986			
Atkins (D)	$556,364	$5,127 (1%)	$557,531

Key Votes

1987	
Raise speed limit to 65 mph	Y
Approve Gephardt "fair trade" amendment	Y
Ban testing of larger nuclear weapons	Y
Delay "re-flagging" of Kuwaiti tankers	Y
Approve tax-raising deficit-reduction bill	Y
1988	
Approve aid to Nicaraguan contras	N
Enact civil rights restoration bill over Reagan veto	Y
Kill 60-day plant-closing notification measure	N
Pass omnibus trade bill over Reagan veto	Y
Approve death penalty for drug-related murders	N
Bar federal funds for abortions in cases of rape and incest	N
Oppose seven-day waiting period for purchase of handguns	N

Voting Studies

	Presidential Support		Party Unity		Conservative Coalition	
Year	**S**	**O**	**S**	**O**	**S**	**O**
1988	16	81	96	1	3	97
1987	11	87	93	2	14	86
1986	18	77	86	6	10	88
1985	20	79	86	4	13	82

Interest Group Ratings

Year	ADA	ACU	AFL-CIO	CCUS
1988	96	0	94	7
1987	100	0	100	23
1986	90	0	92	25
1985	90	5	81	33

6 Nicholas Mavroules (D)

Of Peabody — Elected 1978

Born: Nov. 1, 1929, Peabody, Mass.
Education: Graduated from Peabody High School, 1947.
Occupation: Personnel supervisor.
Family: Wife, Mary Silva; three children.
Religion: Greek Orthodox.
Political Career: Peabody City Council, 1958-61 and 1964-65; mayor of Peabody, 1968-79; candidate for Peabody City Council, 1955; candidate for mayor of Peabody, 1961.
Capitol Office: 2432 Rayburn Bldg. 20515; 225-8020.

In Washington: Few members of the Armed Services Committee have defied expectations as greatly as Mavroules. After his 1978 election, the panel was not his first choice, but he joined it at the behest of other Massachusetts members who asked him to watch over the state's defense contracting interests. Then, after a few years of quiet, parochial service, Mavroules emerged as one of the committee's more activist members.

Mavroules has been a leader in efforts to reform the Defense Department's purchasing practices. He has also been the point man in Democratic efforts to derail the MX missile.

His activism on the MX issue even led Mavroules into an unsuccessful 1987 campaign against Armed Services Chairman Les Aspin of Wisconsin, whose support for the MX during the 99th Congress had angered many House liberals. However, the mildness of Mavroules' campaign enabled him to quickly mend fences; he has since worked smoothly with Aspin.

Mavroules entered the MX debate with the backing of arms control activists in his district and throughout the Boston area. During consideration of the defense authorization bill in 1984, he offered an amendment blocking production of the MX and forced a House vote. Though his amendment lost by three votes, he declared a limited victory, saying, "We have raised the public awareness of this issue."

In 1985, he shared leadership duties on the anti-MX side with such crusading committee liberals as Les AuCoin of Oregon and Thomas J. Downey of New York. Mavroules lacked their knowledge of overall defense policy. But as a low-key member who cast an occasional pro-Pentagon vote, Mavroules was also less burdened by identification as an unyielding partisan; during much of the debate, he was the one coordinating strategy.

To the chagrin of the anti-MX forces, newly elected Armed Services Chairman Aspin lined up with Reagan in early 1985 and helped tip the scales against Mavroules' side; an amendment to scrap the missile again lost in a 213-219 vote. By mid-1985, both sides wearied of the battle, and settled on a compromise. Mavroules joined the more conservative Democratic Rep. Dave McCurdy of Oklahoma and won a permanent cap of 50 MX missiles.

Though MX opponents declared this a major advance for their cause, they still blamed Aspin for his "betrayal." In a mutinous mood, many were prepared to join anti-Aspin conservatives in support of Texas Democrat Marvin Leath's challenge to the chairman following the 99th Congress. But at the end of 1986, Mavroules ambled into the fray to provide a "liberal alternative" for Democrats uncomfortable with Leath's conservatism.

Mavroules never became a serious contender. He finished fourth on the first ballot, trailing the two main contenders and Florida Democrat Charles E. Bennett, whose seniority claim on the chairmanship was rejected. After Aspin won re-election, Mavroules renewed his ties to the chairman, who had appointed him to head a task force on defense procurement policy.

Mavroules rejoined the MX fight in the 100th Congress. Defense strategists were divided between supporters of the rail-based MX and those favoring the more mobile, truck-mounted Midgetman. Though not thrilled with the Midgetman, Mavroules and other liberals hoped they could use it to vanquish the MX. After Armed Services voted to provide $500 million for both missiles, Mavroules and AuCoin pushed an amendment through the House raising Midgetman funding to $600 million, and cutting the MX to $100 million. Eventually, though, the House and Senate agreed to provide $250 million for each, with $350 million in escrow pending a presidential decision on the missiles in spring 1989. At that time, President Bush proposed to pursue both weapons.

Outside the MX debate, Mavroules has been most active on the Pentagon procurement issue. He joined in the early chorus of criticism

Massachusetts 6

North Shore — Lynn; Peabody

The 6th offers chronically depressed mill towns, workaday factory cities, comfortable suburbs, pockets of aristocratic wealth and scenic ocean-front villages. Its vote-heavy areas are at the southern end of Essex County and are strongly Democratic.

Lynn, historically a shoe-manufacturing center but now the home of a large General Electric Co. aircraft engine plant, is the 6th's largest city. Lynn and nearby Peabody, which was once the largest leather-processing city in the world, are conservative Democratic territory. They supported Edward J. King in his 1978 and 1982 Democratic gubernatorial primary battles against the more liberal Michael S. Dukakis. In 1988, when Dukakis ran for president, Lynn and Peabody supported him, although George Bush gathered a solid 48 percent of the districtwide vote.

East of Peabody is Salem, which resembles it in its Democratic roots and dependence on the electronics industry. Salem's image, however, is inextricably bound up with Colonial New England's history. It was the scene of the famous witch trials of the 1690s and later a prosperous port from which Yankee traders set sail for the Orient and Europe. Its narrow streets were the setting for Nathaniel Hawthorne's dark explorations of the New England psyche.

North of Salem in Essex County, the aristocratic Yankee tradition provides GOP votes, although they have tended to be moderate-to-liberal ones. Bush ran well in this area in 1988, carrying the towns of Ipswich, Wenham, Georgetown and Manchester. In 1980, Wenham was one of only three towns in the state where John B. Anderson outpolled Jimmy Carter.

On the northern coast, maritime interests are central to Gloucester, home of the Fisherman's Memorial landmark, and Rockport, a historic fishing village deluged with tourists and artists in the summer. Newburyport, whose 19th-century clipper ship economy gave way to light manufacturing, is the "Yankee City" singled out for study by sociologists in the 1920s. In recent years it has attracted many urban emigrants. All three went for Dukakis in 1988.

Haverhill, on the New Hampshire border, saw its economic base in the shoe industry disintegrate, but there has been recent growth in the availability of high-technology jobs, and the city's comparatively low living costs have lured some younger professionals who cannot afford to live in Boston.

Population: 518,841. White 508,101 (98%), Black 5,084 (1%). Spanish origin 5,898 (1%). 18 and over 383,191 (74%), 65 and over 68,157 (13%). Median age: 33.

following reports of overpriced spare parts, and worked on efforts, headed by Alabama Democrat Bill Nichols, to fashion the 1985 law aimed at streamlining Pentagon purchasing practices. As an extensive defense contracting scandal unfolded, he then took a leadership role on the issue — first at the head of the informal task force and, in the 101st Congress, as chairman of the Armed Services Subcommittee on Investigations.

After allegations of defense contractor bribery of Defense Department officials hit the headlines in June 1988, Mavroules blistered Robert Costello, a Defense Department under secretary who testified before Armed Services: "Many in Congress and much of the public at large are more than disappointed, they are tired of hearing about a defense acquisition system that cannot seem to iron out its systematic problems," he said. When the official demurred on whether the Pentagon would institute the code of ethics for defense contractors suggested by a special commission, Mavroules retorted, "I think it's time you took the bull by the horns; darn it, do it."

While he takes a hard line on some issues, Mavroules is not reflexively anti-Pentagon. In 1987, he opposed efforts to cancel deployment of 100 B-1B bombers, despite the plane's troubled performance record. Noting the already heavy investment in the B-1B, Mavroules said, "You don't take $20 billion and throw it out the window."

He also still tends the home interests that got him on Armed Services in the first place. He has used his seat to assist his district's largest defense contractor, General Electric Co., whose plant in Lynn makes engines for the Navy's F-18 attack fighters. A directive pushed by Mavroules, ordering the Defense Department to use more renewable energy technologies, has benefited a photovoltaic demonstration project in the city of Beverly in his district.

At Home: It took Mavroules a while to get settled in this seat, but since 1984, when he won 70 percent, he has won with ease.

As a traditional urban ethnic Democrat, Mavroules has little in common with the Yankee elite that populates much of his district. He learned his politics in Peabody's City Hall, where he served 16 years, first on the City Council and later as mayor.

In 1978, Mavroules sensed that Democratic Rep. Michael J. Harrington had lost his rapport with working-class Democrats. There was a feeling he had spent too much of his career on human rights in Chile rather than on unemployment in Lynn. So Mavroules entered the primary.

Harrington, however, decided to retire rather than fight. Mavroules won the Democratic nomination against a state representative from Lynn and an Essex County commissioner who had Harrington's endorsement, but little else.

That November, Mavroules faced William E. Bronson, a conservative airline pilot making a second try after holding Harrington under 55 percent in 1976. With stronger party backing, Bronson posed a real threat to Mavroules, but he wound up winning with 54 percent.

Bronson wanted another chance in 1980, but he lost the GOP primary narrowly to Tom Trimarco, a moderate lawyer with Italian ethnic support.

Viewed as the strongest candidate Republicans had put up in a decade, Trimarco worked hard to tie Mavroules to the Carter administration. He held down Mavroules' margins everywhere outside the old factory towns — Peabody, Salem and Lynn — that were responsible for the Democrat's initial election. Only a 20,000-vote plurality in those three cities allowed Mavroules to win.

Trimarco tried again in 1982, assembling a better-funded and more solidly organized campaign, and gearing his pitch to the blue-collar cities that had helped Mavroules hang on in 1980. Trimarco stressed his working-class origins and tried to put some distance between himself and the Reagan administration.

But Mavroules was stronger. His work in the House against the MX missile had helped him shake his reputation as an old-fashioned party loyalist who initiated little on his own, and gave him appeal along the moderate Republican North Shore. He also used GOP economic policies effectively against Trimarco, winning back Democrats who had defected or sat out in 1980.

Committees

Armed Services (7th of 31 Democrats)
Investigations (chairman); Military Installations and Facilities

Select Intelligence (10th of 12 Democrats)
Oversight and Evaluation

Small Business (6th of 27 Democrats)
SBA, the General Economy and Minority Enterprise Development

Elections

1988 General		
Nicholas Mavroules (D)	177,643	(70%)
Paul McCarthy (R)	77,186	(30%)
1986 General		
Nicholas Mavroules (D)	131,051	(100%)

Previous Winning Percentages: 1984 (70%) **1982** (58%) **1980** (51%) **1978** (54%)

District Vote For President

	1988	1984	1980	1976
D	131,246 (50%)	110,771 (45%)	94,549 (38%)	132,384 (53%)
R	124,871 (48%)	137,258 (55%)	109,933 (44%)	109,094 (44%)
I			41,896 (17%)	

Campaign Finance

	Receipts	Receipts from PACs	Expend-itures
1988			
Mavroules (D)	$349,184	$107,360 (31%)	$337,199
McCarthy (R)	$62,747	$2,865 (5%)	$63,013
1986			
Mavroules (D)	$235,761	$91,250 (39%)	$184,485

Key Votes

1987	
Raise speed limit to 65 mph	N
Approve Gephardt "fair trade" amendment	Y
Ban testing of larger nuclear weapons	Y
Delay "re-flagging" of Kuwaiti tankers	Y
Approve tax-raising deficit-reduction bill	Y
1988	
Approve aid to Nicaraguan contras	N
Enact civil rights restoration bill over Reagan veto	Y
Kill 60-day plant-closing notification measure	N
Pass omnibus trade bill over Reagan veto	Y
Approve death penalty for drug-related murders	Y
Bar federal funds for abortions in cases of rape and incest	Y
Oppose seven-day waiting period for purchase of handguns	N

Voting Studies

	Presidential Support		Party Unity		Conservative Coalition	
Year	**S**	**O**	**S**	**O**	**S**	**O**
1988	24	71	87	4	26	74
1987	21	76	86	3	28	67
1986	19	80	87	5	18	80
1985	20	76	87	6	13	87
1984	33	62	87	8	25	75
1983	21	76	87	7	18	80
1982	40	56	85	7	25	70
1981	36	63	84	14	28	72

Interest Group Ratings

Year	ADA	ACU	AFL-CIO	CCUS
1988	90	8	100	23
1987	76	0	100	7
1986	85	5	93	24
1985	85	10	94	27
1984	75	4	92	38
1983	85	9	100	20
1982	80	9	100	19
1981	80	7	87	16

7 Edward J. Markey (D)

Of Malden — Elected 1976

Born: July 11, 1946, Malden, Mass.
Education: Boston College, B.A. 1968, J.D. 1972.
Military Career: Army Reserve, 1968-73.
Occupation: Lawyer.
Family: Wife, Susan Blumenthal.
Religion: Roman Catholic.
Political Career: Mass. House, 1973-77.
Capitol Office: 2133 Rayburn Bldg. 20515; 225-2836.

In Washington: Most politicians who want to change their image do so by courting the media, but Markey has done just the opposite, shunning the spotlight for the serious legislating that takes place offstage. The transformation of his reputation on Capitol Hill has been remarkable.

Not long ago lampooned as a flake, a liberal gadfly and a camera hound, Markey has emerged as one of Congress' most respected lawmakers. A witty, gregarious sort, he remains quick with an apt one-liner or sound-bite. But he is also conversant in the mind-numbing details of the most complex issues of the day, patient enough for the prolonged wrangling of the legislative process and willing to play the conciliator as often as the crusader.

Now in his second term as chairman of the Energy and Commerce Committee's important Subcommittee on Telecommunications and Finance, Markey oversees those industries at a time of rapidly evolving changes on Wall Street and in the banking, telephone, broadcast and entertainment businesses. Meanwhile, away from the subcommittee, he remains personally committed to the two issues for which he previously was best known, arms control and nuclear power.

Before 1985, Markey was perceived less as a legislator than as a mouthpiece for the outside groups dedicated to his causes; House colleagues complained that he preferred the moral high ground to the lowly work of political compromise. But returning to the House that year after an aborted Senate campaign, Markey seemed a different man.

Colleagues speculated that he simply wanted to dispel the flake image, which the brief Senate race had only enhanced, or that he was resigned to a career in the House. Whatever the reason, Markey immediately impressed his skeptics. First as chairman of the Energy Conservation and Power Subcommittee in the 99th Congress, and then as the Telecommunications and Finance head since the 100th, he has proven adept at building consensus. With his affability, evenhanded attention to substance and, most important, his habit of consulting with members individually on pending matters, Markey has co-opted Democrats and Republicans alike.

The business of the subcommittee since Markey's ascension has been business — corporate mergers and hostile takeovers, insider-trading abuses, banking deregulation and, after the October 1987 stock market crash, the whole question of financial markets' regulation. The controversies pit corporate interests against one another, producing no clear answers about what, if anything, needs to be done and spelling stalemate for Congress.

In the flurry of legislative and executive branch activity, Markey's panel in 1988 produced the only major statute — increasing civil and criminal penalties for insider trading, providing federal bounties and holding firms accountable for their employees. It was approved unanimously in the House, propelled by news of an unprecedented federal complaint against one of Wall Street's largest investment houses, Drexel Burnham Lambert Inc.

Early in the 100th Congress, Markey also cosponsored legislation with full committee Chairman John D. Dingell to curtail the most-criticized tactics of both the raiders who capture firms and the corporate managers who defend against takeovers. His panel worked through 1987, but the effort floundered under pressure from competing lobbies and the states' rights argument that corporate law is the states' preserve. In the Senate, a one-sided bill aimed mostly at raiders moved to the floor and died there.

Meanwhile, after the stock market crash, Markey turned to the question of better regulating what he called a "giant casino." He introduced a bill strengthening the authority of the Securities and Exchange Commission and the Federal Reserve Board, at the expense of the Commodity Futures Trading Commission. He said he was setting the stage for action in the 101st Congress, acknowledging there was too much dissension and too little time to pass a bill in the 100th Congress.

Markey is well placed on Telecommunica-

Massachusetts 7

Northern Suburbs — Medford; Malden

A collection of medium-sized communities on the edge of metropolitan Boston, the 7th strings together some of Massachusetts' wealthiest towns and some of its poorest. It is nearly always Democratic territory. Ronald Reagan edged Walter F. Mondale in the 7th in 1984, though very narrowly; Democratic Senate nominee John Kerry took it easily. Four years later, Massachusetts governor and Democratic presidential nominee Michael S. Dukakis won the 7th.

The same Irish and Italian families have lived for generations in towns like Melrose, Malden, Medford and Everett. All four have seen serious decline over the past generation, as their commercial centers have faded away, but the spread of high-technology and service industries has somewhat improved conditions.

Energetic urban improvement efforts have helped Malden, which is at the end of the MBTA's Orange Line and has seen a spurt of office development. The other cities have tried to copy Malden's growth, but have lagged behind.

To the south are Revere and Chelsea, which have had even more severe troubles. Once a resort community for middle- and working-class Bay Staters, Revere's beach area was devastated by a blizzard in 1978. The most significant influx there has been of Vietnamese immigrants, who are drawn by service-sector jobs in downtown Boston and affordable housing in Revere.

Chelsea is one of Massachusetts' poorest cities. Rebuilt after a fire devastated it in 1908, it saw its downtown burn to the ground again in 1973; recovery this time has been slow, although there has been development at both ends of the housing market — subsidized units as well as condominiums.

Reading, Wilmington and Billerica, in the northern part of the district, are bedroom communities filled with second- and third-generation Irish and Italian families whose roots are in Medford or Revere. Old-timers in these one-time summer resort communities have watched with alarm as the towns have been swallowed up by suburban Boston's growth.

The district's upper crust live in Winchester and Lexington. Winchester is the district's Republican enclave. Lexington, however, is not the stronghold of Yankee Republicanism it once was. It can now be depended upon to back liberal Democrats against most opponents from the more conservative side of the GOP.

Population: 523,982. White 511,209 (98%), Black 5,714 (1%), Other 4,310 (1%). Spanish origin 7,538 (1%). 18 and over 387,217 (74%), 65 and over 65,637 (13%). Median age: 32.

tions and Finance to look after the interests of Massachusetts' many high-tech firms. But he also can use the post to play the consumer advocate. A persistent foe of AT&T and a supporter of competitiveness in the telecommunications industry, he has resisted calls to lift court-imposed antitrust restrictions on the business activities of AT&T's former subsidiaries, the regional Bell Telephone companies, doubting the resolve of the Federal Communications Commission to protect consumers from abuses.

He has vowed to keep pressing for two communications bills President Reagan vetoed in the 100th Congress on First Amendment grounds. One would write into law the long-standing Fairness Doctrine, which requires broadcasters to air both sides of controversial issues. The other would limit advertising on children's TV shows and encourage quality programming by making stations' performance a factor in their license renewal; its veto, Markey said, was "a victory for the toy and cereal hucksters, but a major defeat for our nation's children."

In the 99th Congress, as both the Energy Conservation and Power chairman and a member of the Interior Committee's Energy Subcommittee, Markey led the effort to set national energy efficiency standards for major appliances. Though Reagan vetoed it on free-market grounds, the bill was revived early in the 100th Congress with a minor change, and the president signed it into law.

Markey also successfully resolved a battle between private and public utilities over relicensing of hydropower plants. Those utilities have long competed for access to hydropower, but public utilities years ago were given a preference in the licensing process. Markey brokered a bill removing those preferences, and putting greater emphasis on environmental concerns in the licensing process. It became law in 1986.

The Energy Conservation and Power chair also gave Markey an official platform for his crusade against the nuclear power industry. The climate for Markey's criticisms had improved, particularly in the wake of the Chernobyl nuclear accident in the Soviet Union, and Markey regularly attacked the Nuclear Regulatory Commission, the Energy Department and private companies. He blocked legislation to streamline nuclear plant licensing and reduce public participation in licensing decisions, pointing to Chernobyl as "a glaring example of the dangers of nuclear power if public pressure for safety is stifled."

At the same time, he pushed legislation to renew and strengthen the controversial Price-Anderson Act, which set up a system for compensating victims of nuclear accidents that limited industry liability to $640 million. Markey and other critics wanted to raise the cap at least tenfold, if not lift it altogether. Faced with strong opposition on his subcommittee, Markey kept the bill alive with a 9-7 vote to send it to the full committee without recommendation.

There, Republicans and Southern Democrats argued that the proposed $6.5 billion limit could bankrupt utilities. But Markey pointed out that utilities would pay only if there were an accident, adding with some sarcasm, "I take the nuclear industry at their word — that they are safe, clean, efficient and responsible." The committee ultimately approved the higher level, along with Markey's amendment to tie liability limits to inflation, but the bill went no further. Legislation did become law in the 100th Congress, although Markey, who had moved to the Telecommunications chair, had only a supporting role.

His most visible anti-nuclear effort in the 100th Congress was a locally oriented one. He repeatedly tried and failed to pass an amendment that would bar operating licenses for the Seabrook power plant in New Hampshire and the Shoreham plant on Long Island, which are opposed, respectively, by officials in Massachusetts and New York. Against strong utility opposition, he lost first in Interior, 15-23, then in Energy and Commerce on a tie vote and ultimately on the House floor, 160-261. "The most powerful lobbying group in the country was able to flex its muscles tonight," he said afterward. But, he added, "it would be foolish to say that this is the end of the battle."

As with nuclear power, the debate over arms control often follows hardened lines. Still, Markey has displayed a growing sense of the importance of cooperation, with some results.

He and a small cadre of liberal arms controllers exploited widespread unease with Reagan's arms policies and succeeded for three years running, 1986 through 1988, in winning House approval of a ban on nuclear testing, contingent on Soviet restraint. But in all three years, the test ban was dropped under pressure from the Senate, reflecting members' desire to close ranks behind the president once he finally had begun arms control talks with Soviet leader Mikhail S. Gorbachev.

In 1988, however, conferees accepted an alternative Markey amendment requiring the Energy Department to devise a non-explosive method of testing the nuclear arsenal's reliability. He had lost in the House, 201-220, but at his prodding, Armed Services Committee Chairman Les Aspin pressed for Markey's provision in the conference.

Markey's earlier arms control efforts centered around opposition to the MX missile and support for a nuclear weapons freeze resolution, which he first introduced in 1982. During the freeze debate in the 98th Congress, Markey scornfully referred to defense experts as "that elite group of nuclear theologians who have controlled the fate of this earth." He put the freeze in more blunt terms than some of its supporters would have liked, telling critics, "You want to build the MX, the Trident II and all the first-strike weapons. We don't want to build them."

That rhetoric was ammunition for Reagan's side, which depicted the freeze as a generally anti-defense position. In the end a freeze did pass the House, but with amendments making it conditional upon mutual arms reductions by the United States and Soviet Union.

At Home: Markey has restabilized his political base after a surge of political ambition almost cost him his district in 1984.

When Democratic Sen. Paul E. Tsongas decided against running for re-election, Markey was the first Democrat to announce for his seat. His prominence on the nuclear weapons freeze and on nuclear energy issues had earned him a following of anti-nuclear enthusiasts, and they became the core of his campaign.

But Markey's candidacy did not keep several other prominent contenders from entering the Senate contest, including fellow Rep. James M. Shannon and Lt. Gov. John Kerry. As the campaign heated up, it became clear that despite his high name recognition, Markey was at best an even bet against his chief competitors. Early in May, he decided to drop out of the Senate race and file again for re-election to his House seat.

Markey said he wanted to return to the House to continue working on nuclear arms issues. He told reporters it no longer made sense to him to "go out and scrap for another nine months in the campaign, when I had a chance to advance the freeze in the House." Skeptics pointed out that Markey seemed in danger of losing the state party endorsement to either Shannon or Kerry, who were both staking strong claims to the support of liberal activists.

Markey had to struggle just to win renomination against former state Sen. Samuel Rotondi, a combative campaigner who chose to stay in the House contest, hoping the reaction to Markey's indecision would help his campaign.

"First he was going to be a senator," a Rotondi ad noted, "now he wants to be a congressman some more. It kind of makes you dizzy, doesn't it, seeing Ed Markey twirling around like that." But Markey struck back with charges that Rotondi had received campaign contributions from executives of utility companies and nuclear industries. Rotondi, he said at a debate, "has so much radioactive money in his Federal Election Commission report it glows in the dark."

Markey ended up winning the primary with 54 percent, and a routine victory in the general election. In 1986 and 1988, he was unopposed.

Before 1984, Markey's only difficult congressional campaign was his first, in 1976. When the critically ill Torbert H. MacDonald announced his retirement that year after serving 21 years in the House, virtually every prominent Democratic officeholder with any political base in Boston's northern suburbs thought about trying to replace him.

It was clear that a primary with a dozen aspirants would be decided mostly by simple name identification. Markey already had quite a bit. He had received a fair amount of attention for his arguments in the Legislature with the Democratic leadership, which had once closed his office and banished him to a desk in the hall. "They can tell me where to sit," Markey boasted, "but they can't tell me where to stand."

The notoriety helped him in the primary, as did his endorsement from Michael J. Harrington, who represented the adjoining area in the Congress. Markey lost three of the four largest towns in the district to favorite sons, but won his own hometown, Malden, and six of the remaining 11. That gave him 21 percent of the vote, enough for a comfortable win.

The 22,137 votes Markey received in the primary all but guaranteed his future. His only regular GOP opposition came in 1982, from a Woburn investment counselor who ended up with 22 percent of the general-election vote.

Committees

Energy and Commerce (6th of 26 Democrats)
Telecommunications and Finance (chairman); Energy and Power

Interior and Insular Affairs (4th of 26 Democrats)
Energy and the Environment; General Oversight and Investigations; Water, Power and Offshore Energy

Elections

1988 General

Edward J. Markey (D)	188,647	(100%)

1986 General

Edward J. Markey (D)	124,183	(100%)

Previous Winning Percentages: **1984** (71%) **1982** (78%) **1980** (100%) **1978** (85%) **1976** (77%)

District Vote For President

	1988	1984	1980	1976
D	133,241 (53%)	121,018 (49%)	103,873 (42%)	138,724 (58%)
R	114,124 (45%)	123,559 (50%)	103,704 (42%)	91,541 (38%)
I			36,344 (15%)	

Campaign Finance

	Receipts	Receipts from PACs	Expend-itures
1988			
Markey (D)	$484,319	0	$134,388
1986			
Markey (D)	$411,801	$10,600 (3%)	$314,056

Key Votes

1987

Raise speed limit to 65 mph	N
Approve Gephardt "fair trade" amendment	Y
Ban testing of larger nuclear weapons	Y
Delay "re-flagging" of Kuwaiti tankers	Y
Approve tax-raising deficit-reduction bill	Y

1988

Approve aid to Nicaraguan contras	N
Enact civil rights restoration bill over Reagan veto	Y
Kill 60-day plant-closing notification measure	N
Pass omnibus trade bill over Reagan veto	Y
Approve death penalty for drug-related murders	N
Bar federal funds for abortions in cases of rape and incest	N
Oppose seven-day waiting period for purchase of handguns	N

Voting Studies

	Presidential Support		Party Unity		Conservative Coalition	
Year	**S**	**O**	**S**	**O**	**S**	**O**
1988	17	78	93	3	3	97
1987	13	86	94	1	5	95
1986	11	80	86	5	8	84
1985	23	76	90	4	2	98
1984	17	58	76	3	0	85
1983	21	77	91	6	8	90
1982	32	62	90	3	8	92
1981	34	66	91	8	8	88

Interest Group Ratings

Year	ADA	ACU	AFL-CIO	CCUS
1988	90	0	100	23
1987	96	0	100	0
1986	95	0	85	13
1985	100	10	100	29
1984	90	5	85	23
1983	90	0	94	20
1982	100	0	100	9
1981	90	0	80	5

8 Joseph P. Kennedy II (D)

Of Boston — Elected 1986

Born: Sept. 24, 1952, Boston, Mass.
Education: U. of Massachusetts, B.A. 1976.
Occupation: Energy company executive.
Family: Separated; two children.
Religion: Roman Catholic.
Political Career: No previous office.
Capitol Office: 1208 Longworth Bldg. 20515; 225-5111.

In Washington: By the end of Kennedy's first term, no small number of his colleagues had concluded that he had come to Congress asking not what he could do for the House, but what the House could do for him.

The first of the second-generation Kennedys to win office, he moved quickly as a freshman to promote the cause of the poor and minorities. But at the same time, he also exploited his family's name and political heritage to an astonishing degree to promote himself within the House. Just before the 101st Congress began, a no-holds-barred bid for a coveted seat on Appropriations sealed his budding reputation as grasping and headstrong; the bid divided his own Massachusetts delegation, and ultimately, it failed.

Many members resent newcomers who seem to be serving in the House on their way to something bigger, and in the 100th Congress, Kennedy evidenced enough frustration with legislative life to be regarded in that light. Such members generally are not favored for prize posts such as Appropriations, which traditionally go to those who show signs of making the House their career.

So when Massachusetts Democrats had a chance in late 1988 to fill the Appropriations seat vacated by Massachusetts Rep. Edward P. Boland, who retired after 36 years, they leaned toward a young colleague likely to stay put and build seniority and clout — Chester G. Atkins, also the state Democratic chairman. But then Kennedy announced his candidacy, and a fight was on. Turning up the pressure on members already torn between loyalty to the Kennedy dynasty and empathy for Atkins or a third candidate, Bruce A. Morrison of Connecticut, the scion employed lobbying from his uncle, Sen. Edward M. Kennedy. Both Kennedys thus violated a cardinal commandment: Members of the Senate and House shall not interfere in each other's internal politics.

The choice was to be made by the New England Democratic caucus, which is dominated by Massachusetts but, by a quirk of House party rules, also includes non-voting delegates from the District of Columbia and the Virgin Islands and Puerto Rico's resident commissioner. Sen. Kennedy leaned especially on those three since his nephew did not have much support from the Bay State, and he pressed Barbara B. Kennelly of Connecticut, whose father had been national party chairman thanks to President John F. Kennedy. Joe Kennedy was expected to win by a single vote, but he lost 8-9, prompting a round of finger-pointing for the unknown defector that added a final note of bitterness to the whole affair.

The eldest child of Robert F. Kennedy probably would have benefited from a quiet, workmanlike term or two to convince House skeptics that he is a serious legislator willing to pay his dues. From the start, however, Kennedy drew reviews as impetuous, self-centered and openly impatient with the pace of the House. There were reports of flip and sophomoric behavior at the Harvard orientation for House freshmen. Then he asked House leaders for a seat on the Energy and Commerce Committee, despite advice that it was a top assignment that rarely goes to freshmen. He lost.

The problem with being a Kennedy, of course, is that such incidents might be unnoticed or forgotten if not for the high expectations that attend the famous name. Outside the House, Kennedy gets plenty of publicity, but not all of it is good, and the rest just feeds his colleagues' envy. *Gentlemen's Quarterly* put him on its cover, and in early 1989, *People* magazine reported his split with his wife.

A small press corps accompanied him in 1988 to Protestant Northern Ireland, where the Irish Catholic Kennedy traded insults with a British soldier after his car was stopped at gunpoint. Back home later that year, he was in the news after a car accident with a constituent provoked a shoving match and a lawsuit that was dropped only after Kennedy apologized. In 1987, he drew predictable notice when he rebuked Reagan administration official Elliott Abrams as a liar for deceiving Congress about Central American policy, and then stalked out of the subcommittee hearing to protest Abrams' presence.

Having lost his preferred assignments,

Massachusetts 8

Boston and Suburbs — Cambridge

Ethnic, working-class Cambridge coexists peacefully, if not always sympathetically, with the Harvard-MIT colossus that surrounds it. There is a political cohesiveness that transcends cultural differences — both communities are Democratic and liberal on economic issues.

The cultural divisions, however, are real. Outside the university precincts exists a crowded, grimy city. The proximity of trendy Harvard Square and seedy Central Square makes Cambridge no stranger to town-gown tensions. One city councilman made a career of baiting the Ivy League school, suggesting repeatedly that Harvard Yard be paved over to relieve the city's parking problems.

With a straight-ticket Democratic voting history, Cambridge gave 74 percent of its vote to George McGovern in the 1972 presidential race — his majority statewide was 54 percent — and gave Walter F. Mondale 76 percent in 1984. Massachusetts governor and Democratic presidential nominee Michael S. Dukakis carried the 8th with 66 percent in 1988.

Although Cambridge is the political center of the district, more votes are actually cast within the city of Boston. The inner-city neighborhoods of Allston and Brighton, historically centers for Boston's Jewish community, today have a large transient student population. Harvard Business School, Northeastern University, Harvard Medical School, Boston University and part of Boston College are within its boundaries on the Boston side of the Charles River.

Other areas of Boston included within the district are affluent Back Bay, a symbol of high-income urban gentrification; Beacon Hill, where liberal Democrats live in 18th-century homes built by Federalists; Irish working-class Charlestown; and heavily Italian East Boston.

To the west, the district includes the working-class city of Somerville and middle-class Arlington and Watertown. Suburban Belmont, the home of the John Birch Society's national headquarters, does not have much in common with Birch Society politics; 1984 Republican Senate candidate Ray Shamie, whose past links to the Birch Society won him extensive coverage during the campaign, won only 45 percent there. In 1988 Dukakis took 55 percent in Belmont.

Farther west is the medium-sized city of Waltham, which has its own town-and-gown problems. It has a blue-collar majority, largely Italian, and is also the home of Brandeis University, with an aggressively liberal student and faculty community.

Population: 521,548. White 473,975 (91%), Black 23,901 (5%), Other 15,196 (3%). Spanish origin 15,644 (3%). 18 and over 434,109 (83%), 65 and over 67,920 (13%). Median age: 29.

Kennedy pursued his agenda on the Banking Committee, particularly its Housing Subcommittee, and to a lesser extent on the Veterans' Affairs panel. He amended Banking's 1987 housing bill to include incentives for units affordable to low-income families. Earlier, he had joined about a dozen members for a cold night on a steam grate to draw attention to the homeless. In 1988, he was active in the panel's work to encourage investment in poor communities by tightening the law against banks' "redlining."

Later that year, Kennedy allied with other subcommittee members on the House floor in an unsuccessful effort to shift scarce funds from space programs to earthly needs such as housing. In perhaps his most eloquent moment, Kennedy recalled his late uncle, and said, "Twenty-five years ago an American president challenged this country to open a new frontier in space. But no one, no one who stood for that grand and noble dream ever thought it would be financed at the expense of the very poorest and most vulnerable people here on Earth."

Kennedy has set global sights. As a member of Banking's International Finance Subcommittee, he objected to U.S. funding for the World Bank without assurances that loans to Third World nations, especially in Latin America, would promote development and not simply flow back to U.S. banks to repay the nations' debts. In 1988, the House adopted his amendment to a defense bill barring military contracts to foreign firms that discriminate in employment.

At Home: Once Kennedy won the 1986 Democratic nomination, there was little doubt that he could hold the 8th as long as he wanted. The question then became, how long would he want it? In a December 1987 interview with *The Boston Globe*, Kennedy mused about his political future: "I mean, I know I love the job, but I don't know that it is right for me or my family, and I don't know that I am the most effective person in it, and I am just trying to figure it out."

Throughout his first term, he bristled at suggestions that he might run for governor in

1990, but he could not make the questions go away. Soon after his landslide 1988 re-election to the House, speculation about his intentions became front-page news when Democratic Gov. Michael S. Dukakis announced that he would not seek re-election. In early 1989, Kennedy finally called a halt to speculation about his 1990 political plans, declaring that he would not run for governor. Simultaneously, he announced that he was separating from his wife.

Being the front-runner in his 1986 House race to replace the retiring incumbent, Speaker Thomas P. O'Neill Jr., did not spare Kennedy a tough campaign. In addition to his familial advantages, Kennedy had attained favorable press on his own as founder of the non-profit Citizens Energy Corporation, which buys cheap oil wholesale and provides discounts on heating oil to low-income residents of New England.

But his primary campaign was no coronation. He became the target for a large field of opponents and some journalists, who questioned his political and personal qualifications. Voters were reminded that Kennedy struggled through high school and graduated from college through the aid of correspondence courses. Stories rehashed the 1973 accident that crippled a passenger in the Jeep Kennedy was driving.

Kennedy's opponents also derided him as an inexperienced newcomer. He was labeled as inarticulate after some stumbling campaign performances, with one Boston columnist stating that Kennedy had "vapor lock on the brain."

But Kennedy grew more sure of himself and the issues as the campaign progressed. He espoused liberal positions on such issues as health care and education, but surprised some observers by positioning himself as the moderate in a field of liberals, supporting the death penalty and assailing unwieldy government bureaucracies.

This centrist move defied the 8th District's liberal image, and an activist backlash fueled the campaign of state Sen. George Bachrach, a self-styled maverick who emerged as Kennedy's closest rival. But Kennedy's moderate posture appealed to blue-collar voters — including many elderly and longtime Kennedy loyalists — in such communities as East Boston and Somerville.

Kennedy closed with a kick. He was endorsed by O'Neill, by Boston Mayor Raymond Flynn and by the Boston daily newspapers. Carrying working-class wards by huge margins while running even on Bachrach's home turf of Somerville, Kennedy won the 11-candidate primary with a majority of the vote.

The rigors of the primary were not repeated in the general election against Republican Clark Abt, the founder of a Cambridge social science research firm. Though Abt spent nearly $600,000, the outcome was predestined in a district that has an enormous Democratic advantage and a tradition of electing Kennedy family members. In 1988, he faced scant competition from perennial candidate Glenn Fiscus.

Committees

Banking, Finance and Urban Affairs (24th of 31 Democrats)
Financial Institutions Supervision, Regulation and Insurance; Housing and Community Development; International Development, Finance, Trade and Monetary Policy

Select Aging (31st of 39 Democrats)
Human Services

Veterans' Affairs (12th of 21 Democrats)
Hospitals and Health Care; Oversight and Investigations

Elections

1988 General

Joseph P. Kennedy II (D)	165,745	(80%)
Glenn W. Fiscus (R)	40,316	(20%)

1986 General

Joseph P. Kennedy II (D)	104,651	(72%)
Clark C. Abt (R)	40,259	(28%)

District Vote For President

	1988		1984		1980		1976	
D	141,366	(66%)	144,320	(63%)	106,217	(51%)	134,941	(62%)
R	70,811	(33%)	83,631	(37%)	67,209	(32%)	73,957	(34%)
I					33,656	(16%)		

Campaign Finance

	Receipts	Receipts from PACs		Expend-itures
1988				
Kennedy (D)	$1,678,216	$272,840	(16%)	$1,445,249
1986				
Kennedy (D)	$1,822,025	$77,795	(4%)	$1,800,781
Abt (R)	$594,510	$7,850	(1%)	$591,652

Key Votes

1987	
Raise speed limit to 65 mph	Y
Approve Gephardt "fair trade" amendment	N
Ban testing of larger nuclear weapons	Y
Delay "re-flagging" of Kuwaiti tankers	Y
Approve tax-raising deficit-reduction bill	Y
1988	
Approve aid to Nicaraguan contras	N
Enact civil rights restoration bill over Reagan veto	Y
Kill 60-day plant-closing notification measure	N
Pass omnibus trade bill over Reagan veto	Y
Approve death penalty for drug-related murders	Y
Bar federal funds for abortions in cases of rape and incest	N
Oppose seven-day waiting period for purchase of handguns	N

Voting Studies

	Presidential Support		Party Unity		Conservative Coalition	
Year	S	O	S	O	S	O
1988	18	80	95	3	3	89
1987	14	86	90	5	12	88

Interest Group Ratings

Year	ADA	ACU	AFL-CIO	CCUS
1988	95	4	100	21
1987	96	9	88	13

9 Joe Moakley (D)

Of Boston — Elected 1972

Born: April 27, 1927, Boston, Mass.
Education: Attended U. of Miami; Suffolk U., J.D. 1956.
Military Career: Navy, 1943-46.
Occupation: Lawyer.
Family: Wife, Evelyn Duffy.
Religion: Roman Catholic.
Political Career: Mass. House, 1953-65; Mass. Senate, 1965-69; Boston City Council, 1971-73; sought Democratic nomination for U.S. House, 1970.
Capitol Office: 221 Cannon Bldg. 20515; 225-8273.

In Washington: The last time Moakley faced an election, his opponent assailed him as an "old-style politician, a back-room type person." The critique was on the money, and Moakley no doubt took it as high praise. "I'd like to be a Tip O'Neill-type guy if I could," Moakley said when he came to Congress in 1973. Basically, he has been. Like the former Speaker, he is a party man — genial, reliable and as concerned about politics and personalities as the fine print in the bills.

These traits should serve Moakley well as chairman of the Rules Committee, where process is as important as policy. Moakley ascended to the chairmanship following the May 1989 death of Florida Democrat Claude Pepper.

The Rules post extends Moakley's reach farther than anything he knew as a top lieutenant under O'Neill. For years, he spent much of his time in the Speaker's inner office in the recess of the Capitol's East Front, talking about Massachusetts politics with old O'Neill cronies. At times, when the House had to hold *pro forma* sessions, O'Neill returned home and left Moakley to wield the ceremonial gavel.

O'Neill's successor as Speaker, Jim Wright, took from Moakley the chairmanship of the House Democratic Personnel Committee, which dispenses patronage. Wright handed the plum to Jack Brooks of Texas, insisting that a member from the Speaker's home state should run the committee. Moakley got mad at Wright, but he did not withdraw in anger. Instead, he channeled his energy into party labors, rounding up votes as one of the most active members of the whip organization, where his political judgment is respected.

One of Moakley's most effective weapons is his humor. He uses it to defuse tense situations and make bitter political pills easier to swallow. His ability to read the mood of the House is also respected. The new Speaker, Thomas S. Foley of Washington, is likely to rely on it more than Wright did.

If his past is any guide, Moakley will use his chairmanship to advantage. The committee is often described as the gatekeeper of the House, because it works in concert with the leadership to control the flow of legislation and set the terms of floor debate. This makes the chairman one of Congress' premier horse traders.

Moakley has been selective about the issues he involves himself with. Often they are local, and now that he is dean of New England Democrats, they likely will become more so. In the 100th Congress, he used his post to block legislation offensive to Boston's Logan Airport and ensure the monies for what Beantowners are calling "the big dig": a third tunnel under Boston Harbor and a new downtown expressway built below ground level.

In the 99th Congress, he looked after New England's financial institutions, helping bottle up legislation regulating "non-bank banks" — institutions that escape restrictions on financial services and interstate banking by avoiding legal definition as banks. Boston is headquarters for such non-bank bank giants as Fidelity Management and Research Co. and John Hancock Mutual Life Insurance Co.

Even Moakley's forays into foreign relations hew to the dictum that all politics are local. Making the district rounds in 1983, he met some constituents working through their church with Salvadoran refugees. Since then, he has been a proponent of granting special immigration status to people immigrating illegally to the United States from the civil wars in El Salvador and Nicaragua. Moakley's proposal to suspend temporarily their deportation made it into the 1986 immigration bill, courtesy of Rules, but was dropped in conference.

After Moakley pressured the Reagan administration and the Salvadoran government on the issue, El Salvador, fearing the economic impact of the deportation of hundreds of thousands of immigrants, came over to his side. Moakley suggested that then-President José Napoleón Duarte inform the administration of his shift in position by letter; Duarte did. The

Massachusetts 9

Boston; Southern Suburbs

While the 8th District has most of the fashionable neighborhoods of Boston, Moakley's 9th contains some of its tourist spots and most of its workaday precincts.

But more than 50 percent of the district vote is now cast outside Boston, in towns such as Stoughton, Taunton, and Bridgewater. All but two of the towns outside Boston in the district went for both President Reagan and Republican Senate candidate Ray Shamie in 1984. In his 1988 presidential bid, Gov. Michael S. Dukakis carried Taunton and Stoughton, but lost Bridgewater to George Bush.

The population of Boston itself has dipped below the 600,000 mark, and the ethnic character of the city is changing dramatically. White population dropped by 25 percent during the 1970s; in contrast, the number of blacks in Boston grew. By the 1980 census blacks accounted for 22 percent of the city's population. Blacks and Hispanics together make up about 30 percent of the city.

The inner-city part of the 9th includes the heavily Italian North End; the trendy Waterfront area, where young professionals live; the old West End, where towering high-rises replaced a thriving ethnic community in the 1950s; the Government Center complex; and most of the downtown shopping district. Conversion of the historic Quincy Market into a glittery emporium of upscale merchandise has injected new life into the center city.

Beyond these areas are communities that have experienced serious racial tensions in the past decade. South Boston, still 99 percent white and overwhelmingly Irish, was the center of bitter opposition to school busing in the 1970s. In the 1976 Democratic presidential primary, George C. Wallace had a considerable following in this area.

In recent years, South Boston has seen substantial gentrification around Thomas Park; the condo market for yuppies has made it more difficult for low- and moderate-income families to find affordable housing.

A bit to the west, Roxbury and Mission Hill are predominantly black. Some middle-class blacks have been renovating areas of Roxbury, especially around Dudley Square, but poverty is still widespread.

Neighboring Jamaica Plain, once a predominantly white area, has become an ethnic and racial melting pot with a good number of Central American refugees. It is one of the more politically active sections of the city, with a well-organized network of community and church groups.

Outside Boston, the district is largely middle-class suburban, settled in many places by South Boston emigrants. At its southern end, it takes in towns that have long considered themselves far outside the orbit of the inner city. Taunton, an old industrial city plagued until recently by high unemployment, reaped some benefits from the high-technology boom of the "Massachusetts miracle."

Population: 519,226. White 408,101 (79%), Black 82,873 (16%), Other 8,577 (2%). Spanish origin 26,218 (5%). 18 and over 380,987 (73%), 65 and over 63,703 (12%). Median age: 31.

measure passed the House in 1987 only to be blocked in the Senate. It was reintroduced in both chambers in early 1989.

Moakley can display a liberal ideological streak. He was out of the blocks early with his opposition to space-based weapons. In the early 1980s, his office became a gathering spot for a group of scientists and politicians that met informally each Tuesday to swap information and plot strategy against missiles based in space.

For most of his years on Rules, Moakley's priorities were O'Neill's. But he also showed streaks of independence. Moakley in 1976 backed a move in the House Democratic Caucus to make the whip's position elective, against O'Neill's wishes.

Perhaps the most publicized — and personally painful — demonstration of Moakley's independence came early in 1984 during an ugly exchange between the Speaker and conservative "Young Turk" Republicans. O'Neill, in retribution for GOP attacks on Democrats during after-hours "special order" debates, quietly ordered House TV cameras to start using wide-angle shots of the House — revealing that Republicans were talking to an empty chamber.

The next day, with Moakley in the chair as presiding officer, Georgia Republican Newt Gingrich took to the floor to harangue O'Neill about the unannounced change. The Speaker lumbered up the aisle to respond, and in the shouting match that ensued, denounced Gingrich's tactics as "the lowest thing that I have ever seen in my 32 years in Congress."

Recognizing a breach of the prohibition against personal insults on the floor, Republicans demanded that O'Neill be declared out of order. The House parliamentarian concurred, and Moakley had no choice but to rule against his friend and mentor, telling O'Neill that "that type of characterization should not be used in debate." It was the first time since 1797 that a Speaker had been officially rebuked for his language.

At Home: Moakley is from the same school of party politics as O'Neill, but it took a striking display of independence to elect him to Congress.

A champion boxer in college, he was a state representative by age 25 and knew early in his career that he would like to succeed John W. McCormack in the House. He spent 17 years in the state Legislature, where he specialized in urban affairs and environmental legislation, and waited for McCormack to retire. But when the aged Democratic Speaker finally stepped down in 1970, Moakley found himself overmatched in the primary against the more visible Louise Day Hicks, who had nearly been elected mayor of Boston three years earlier on an anti-busing platform. With 39 percent of the primary vote, Hicks took the nomination over Moakley and a black attorney and won in November.

Then things began to turn Moakley's way. Hicks lost a second try for the mayor's job in 1971, straining her reputation as a political force, and the next year the district was substantially rearranged. Much of Hicks' South Boston base was removed and replaced with a suburban area where she was not as strong. Moakley, meanwhile, regained a political forum by winning a seat on Boston's City Council.

By 1972 Hicks was one of the state's most vulnerable incumbents. In the primary she was held to 37 percent; she won renomination only because five other candidates split the opposition.

Moakley was not one of the primary challengers. In the most successful political gamble of his life, he had decided to run as an independent against Hicks in the general election. Insisting that he was a lifelong Democrat, he worked to stake out a position well to the incumbent's left. Hicks carried the part of Boston remaining in the district, but by only 192 votes, as Moakley cut into her vote in Irish neighborhoods and swept the black areas. He won the seat with over 5,000 votes to spare.

Since then, only once has Moakley's re-election tally fallen below 70 percent. In 1982, Republicans drafted state Rep. Deborah R. Cochran, promising to produce all her media ads. Though Cochran managed to carry several small towns in Bristol and Plymouth counties, Moakley's urban constituents gave him 74 percent of their vote. His 64 percent overall total was convincing enough to ward off GOP opposition in the last three elections.

Committee

Rules (Chairman)
Rules of the House (chairman)

Elections

1988 General		
Joe Moakley (D)	160,799	(100%)
1986 General		
Joe Moakley (D)	110,026	(84%)
Robert W. Horan (I)	21,292	(16%)

Previous Winning Percentages: **1984** (100%) **1982** (64%) **1980** (100%) **1978** (92%) **1976** (70%) **1974** (89%) **1972** (41%)

District Vote For President

	1988	1984	1980	1976
D	115,814 (54%)	110,396 (51%)	89,233 (44%)	118,663 (54%)
R	96,849 (45%)	104,268 (48%)	84,915 (42%)	91,849 (42%)
I			27,255 (13%)	

Campaign Finance

	Receipts	Receipts from PACs	Expend-itures
1988			
Moakley (D)	$385,654	$180,830 (47%)	$273,488
1986			
Moakley (D)	$403,732	$171,485 (42%)	$314,452

Key Votes

1987	
Raise speed limit to 65 mph	N
Approve Gephardt "fair trade" amendment	Y
Ban testing of larger nuclear weapons	Y
Delay "re-flagging" of Kuwaiti tankers	Y
Approve tax-raising deficit-reduction bill	Y
1988	
Approve aid to Nicaraguan contras	N
Enact civil rights restoration bill over Reagan veto	Y
Kill 60-day plant-closing notification measure	N
Pass omnibus trade bill over Reagan veto	Y
Approve death penalty for drug-related murders	Y
Bar federal funds for abortions in cases of rape and incest	Y
Oppose seven-day waiting period for purchase of handguns	N

Voting Studies

	Presidential Support		Party Unity		Conservative Coalition	
Year	S	O	S	O	S	O
1988	21	77	95	3	5	92
1987	19	78	91	1	12	84
1986	16	79	87	3	16	84
1985	23	65	80	4	11	85
1984	29	63	86	5	12	76
1983	22	74	89	5	11	82
1982	39	52	89	5	25	70
1981	36	47	81	8	23	63

Interest Group Ratings

Year	ADA	ACU	AFL-CIO	CCUS
1988	90	8	100	21
1987	84	5	100	7
1986	85	5	100	18
1985	90	5	100	23
1984	85	4	92	33
1983	80	5	94	21
1982	75	9	100	18
1981	55	7	86	6

10 Gerry E. Studds (D)

Of Cohasset — Elected 1972

Born: May 12, 1937, Mineola, N.Y.
Education: Yale U., B.A. 1959, M.A.T. 1961.
Occupation: High school teacher.
Family: Single.
Religion: Episcopalian.
Political Career: Democratic nominee for U.S. House, 1970.
Capitol Office: 237 Cannon Bldg. 20515; 225-3111.

In Washington: Not long ago, Studds' career looked to be all but over; he was censured by the House, temporarily stripped of a subcommittee chairmanship and threatened at the polls. Now he appears to have a lock on his district, and but a short wait before he will be eligible to chair the Merchant Marine and Fisheries Committee.

As a rookie congressman in the mid-1970s, he decried the tendency of senior members to grow so accustomed to Washington that they lost touch with their districts. Over time, Studds has seemed to become even more oriented toward the parochial concerns of his coastal district — perhaps more than he ever imagined when he arrived in the House as a veteran of the civil rights and anti-war movements.

In part, that is because seniority has put Studds in a powerful position on the Merchant Marine Committee, which has jurisdiction over fishing, shipping and boating, ocean and coastal pollution and the Coast Guard — all matters that are crucial to his constituents. But his assiduous attention to their interests also is a matter of political survival; it has allowed him to overcome a scandal that would have toppled many members — his 1983 House censure for sexual misconduct with a young male page.

An experience that would have reshaped the personality of a different member left Studds the same self-confident, argumentative and articulate liberal, just as tough on his opposition as before. "My sexual preference has nothing to do with my ability to do this job well or to do it badly," he said at the height of the controversy. "I'm a good or bad congressman quite apart from my sexual preference."

The censure briefly cost Studds his base of legislative power as chairman of Merchant Marine's Coast Guard and Navigation Subcommittee. But he got that back after he was re-elected in 1984, and, in 1987, he inherited what he calls "the premier subcommittee," the Fisheries and Wildlife panel.

Meanwhile, during the 100th Congress, the second-ranking Democrat on the full committee, Mario Biaggi of New York, left the House rather than face expulsion after his felony corruption conviction, while third-ranking Glenn M. Anderson of California became chairman of the Public Works Committee. That leaves Studds next in line to succeed Merchant Marine's aging and infirm chairman, Walter B. Jones of North Carolina.

For now, Fisheries and Wildlife is the most active legislative panel on Merchant Marine and the best spot for Studds to promote not only his district's interests, but also his broader environmental priorities. His first move there was to introduce a bill providing stiff federal penalties for dumping plastic waste into U.S. ocean waters, where it kills fish and marine mammals. A similar version of that bill became law in the 100th Congress, as part of a larger measure to implement an international treaty prohibiting ships from discarding such garbage.

Also in the 100th Congress, Studds had an active role in enacting measures to prohibit dumping of medical wastes, after syringes and such trash washed up on East Coast beaches; to renew laws protecting endangered species, marine mammals and striped bass; to extend various international fishery agreements; to strengthen enforcement of wildlife conservation laws; and to impose a moratorium on oil drilling leases off Massachusetts' coast.

In 1988, Studds amended a major drug bill to block the Reagan administration's much-publicized "zero tolerance" policy, under which private boats had been seized when even small quantities of drugs were found aboard. Claiming that innocent boat owners had been penalized by an irrational policy, Studds proposed to bar seizures if only "personal use" amounts were found. He also helped steer into law a bill stiffening requirements for safety equipment on commercial vessels, but he had to drop its main provisions limiting owners' liability for accidents, due to fierce opposition from trial lawyers, whose fees are based on damage awards.

On the issue of whether to open Alaska's vast Arctic National Wildlife Refuge to oil exploration, Studds has treaded gingerly between environmentalists and his committee chairman. In deference to Jones, he moved

Massachusetts 10

South Shore; Southeast; Cape Cod

While most of Massachusetts showed little population increase in the early 1980s, the 10th grew by 8 percent. It grew by nearly a quarter in the 1970s as its South Shore suburbs attracted a new generation of Boston commuters, and scenic Cape Cod continued its transformation from summertime retreat to year-round residence.

Some of the area qualifies as a last Republican outpost in a Democratic state. Three of the four Massachusetts counties that Richard M. Nixon carried in 1972 — Barnstable, Nantucket and Dukes (Martha's Vineyard) — are in the 10th. Ronald Reagan's percentage in the 10th outran his statewide showing in 1984, and in 1988, two of the counties in the state carried by George Bush were in the 10th — Barnstable and Plymouth (half of which is in the district).

Lying on Buzzards Bay in Bristol County, New Bedford is the only large city in the district. It became the world's whaling center in the early 19th century and still retains its fishing orientation. The city was a pre-Civil War way station along the "Underground Railroad" that spirited runaway slaves to safety, and now it is home to a large number of illegal immigrants who live amid the city's significant legal migrant population from Portugal and the Cape Verde Islands. New Bedford gave 72 percent of its vote to Democratic Senate nominee John Kerry in 1984, and it has always anchored Studds' re-election campaigns.

Plymouth County has seen a steady influx of new residents over the past several years, many of them ethnic Bostonians who have resettled in its South Shore towns. Northeast Plymouth County towns such as Norwell, Hanover and Hanson were the centers of opposition to Studds in both his 1984 primary and general election contests. These same towns went Republican in the 1988 presidential election as well.

Cape Cod is all in Barnstable County, where every town has seen at least modest growth in recent years, and some have boomed. Overall, the county's population grew by 15 percent to 170,000 people between 1980 and 1986. Along the curve of the Cape lies the sandy National Seashore preserve, a mecca for summer tourists but a lonely winter outpost for seamen in a still vigorous fishing trade. The Cape is heavily Republican; Studds' home base of Provincetown, an artists' retreat and popular tourist attraction at its tip, and the towns directly south, Truro and Wellfleet, were the only towns on Cape Cod to back Mondale in 1984. In 1988, all three went for Gov. Michael S. Dukakis for president.

The 10th also includes the islands of Nantucket and Martha's Vineyard. Nantucket County provided independent presidential candidate John B. Anderson his highest nationwide showing in 1980, 21.7 percent, and Dukes County was his third-highest territory, with 21 percent.

Population: 522,200. White 498,543 (96%), Black 7,221 (1%), Other 2,999 (1%). Spanish origin 7,761 (2%). 18 and over 377,639 (72%), 65 and over 77,422 (15%). Median age: 33.

through his subcommittee in 1988 Jones' bill to permit limited oil leasing, though Studds himself voted against it. Studds supports the argument that whatever oil could be gained in Alaska would be unnecessary if Congress would restore auto fuel-efficiency standards to their pre-Reagan level. The March 1989 oil spill of the *Exxon Valdez* clouded prospects for any expansion of oil exploration in Alaska.

In the 99th Congress, Studds was a strong advocate for renewal of the toxic-waste cleanup "superfund." Years earlier, in his first term, Studds enjoyed perhaps his single most important success when he pushed a bill extending U.S. territorial waters to a 200-mile limit, a change the fishing industry felt was essential to fight foreign competition. Later, when President Carter proposed a new U.S.-Canadian fishing treaty, Studds opposed it because his state's fishermen thought it favored Canada.

The district-oriented work Studds has done on Merchant Marine over the years has given him the political freedom to protest what he sees as U.S. military adventurism from his seat on the Foreign Affairs Committee.

His ability to articulate global policy, in a brashly opinionated style spiced with sarcasm and one-liners, has made Studds a key player on the panel's left flank — and perhaps the least popular member among Republicans and State Department officials. He attacks those who blame regional turmoil in Central America and elsewhere on Soviet expansionism, insisting that poverty and nationalism are the major causes of instability. "We can protect our friends from communists," he once said, "but we cannot protect them from their own people."

He spoke loudly against Reagan administration policies in El Salvador and Nicaragua. In early 1985, he asked Secretary of State

George P. Shultz at a hearing on Nicaragua, "Can't we do better than ... to provide aid to a mixed group of mercenaries, thugs and democrats? Surely a struggle for freedom should be something other than one between their terrorists and our terrorists."

Studds visited El Salvador early in 1989 as the country held elections that brought to power the right-wing ARENA party, which has been linked to death-squad activities. He said afterward he would be watching to see if the new leaders honor human rights; if not, he said he would push to cut off U.S. aid.

In the 100th Congress, Studds was one of the few members who wanted to take a strong stand against President Reagan's policy of giving Navy escorts to Kuwaiti oil tankers in the Persian Gulf. Most lawmakers were critical, but they were reluctant to challenge the president.

Though Studds has worked hard to move beyond the incident, he probably will always be best remembered outside Congress as the member censured in 1983 for having had sex with a 17-year-old page. He publicly acknowledged his homosexuality and admitted an "error in judgment," but he never apologized. "I do not believe," he said in a prepared statement, "that a relationship which was mutual and voluntary; without coercion; [and] without any preferential treatment express or implied ... constitutes 'improper sexual conduct.'"

In contrast, GOP Rep. Daniel B. Crane of Illinois, who was cited at the same time for having sex with a teenage female page, appeared at a press conference in tears to ask for forgiveness. When the two cases came to the floor, the House voted for censure — a more severe penalty than the reprimand recommended by the ethics committee, but milder than expulsion, which several members demanded.

Censure requires that a member appear before the House to hear the reading of punishment. An emotional Crane faced his colleagues as Speaker Thomas P. O'Neill Jr. read the resolution against him. But Studds stood stoically facing O'Neill, his back to his colleagues. Crane left the chamber after the reading; Studds remained. He later issued a statement thanking his constituents for their support, adding, "All members of Congress are in need of humbling experiences from time to time."

At Home: Studds' homosexuality has turned out to have only slightly more relevance to the vote here in the 1980s than his liberalism had in the 1970s.

When he first ran for Congress, many considered Studds much too liberal for a district that had consistently been in the GOP column. By the middle of the decade, that was ancient history. And in 1984, in the midst of the scandal surrounding his censure, Studds again proved his popularity by winning with 56 percent of the vote. In 1986, with the controversy faded, Studds won 65 percent. In 1988, he did even better, winning 67 percent.

The son of a Long Island architect, Studds went through a flurry of Washington jobs in the early 1960s before "retiring" to teach in an exclusive boarding school in New Hampshire.

In 1967, motivated by his opposition to the war in Vietnam, he enlisted in Eugene J. McCarthy's presidential campaign and ended up as one of the coordinators of the senator's New Hampshire primary effort. Then he moved to Massachusetts' old 12th District, sensing that incumbent Republican Hastings Keith was potentially vulnerable for 1970.

A moderate state senator, William D. Weeks, also thought the conservative Keith might be an easy target and challenged him in the Republican primary. While Studds was organizing the local area's anti-war opposition into his congressional campaign force, Weeks was inadvertently helping the cause — telling Republican voters that Keith could not win the general election.

Studds won a four-way Democratic primary with a clear majority of the vote, while Keith had an ominously hard time winning renomination over Weeks. In the general election, Studds' labor support in New Bedford and anti-war loyalists on Cape Cod brought him tantalizingly close. But Keith won back just enough of Weeks' primary vote in the fall to defeat Studds by 1,522 votes out of nearly 200,000 cast.

Over the next two years, redistricting made the district slightly more Democratic. Keith decided to retire, and Weeks was unopposed for the GOP nomination. Studds never stopped campaigning. He learned Portuguese between elections to communicate better with New Bedford's Portuguese fishing community. He began talking less about Vietnam, although he remained a "peace" candidate, and more about unemployment and President Nixon's economic programs. The outcome was even closer than in 1970 — 1,118 votes — but this time Studds won.

By 1976, just four years after he had become the first Democrat to represent the district in more than half a century, Studds was running unopposed. His highly visible attention to constituent needs and overwhelming support in the New Bedford area made him invulnerable. His only significant opposition — until his censure — came in 1982, when wealthy Realtor John E. Conway challenged him. Conway enjoyed widespread name recognition and had the energy for extensive personal campaigning. But Studds had one of the most accomplished and smoothly run organizations in the state, and he carried every town in the district.

When Studds returned to the district after his censure in 1983, he embarked on a round of meetings with constituents. His traditional supporters received him warmly, while smaller groups of critics demonstrated outside. Studds waited until early 1984, after the furor subsided, to announce he would run again.

The censure brought out two primary opponents, but only one posed a threat: Plymouth County Sheriff Peter Y. Flynn, a law-and-order Democrat with close ties to the conservative wing of the party. At first, Flynn played down the censure. But when it became clear he was making no headway, Flynn started denouncing Studds for the incident, accusing him of "seducing a young child." The attacks backfired, stirring up Studds' supporters and alienating many others. Studds carried all but four of the towns in the district on primary day.

The general election looked to be tougher. Studds' opponent was Lewis Crampton, a former official of the Environmental Protection Agency. A boyhood friend of Studds who had once been a community organizer for the Model Cities Program, Crampton scrupulously stayed away from the censure issue except to argue that it had diminished Studds' effectiveness in the House. He cast himself as a fiscal conservative who was moderate on environmental and some foreign policy issues. Like Studds, Crampton supported a nuclear weapons freeze.

Democrats feared that Crampton's moderate approach and freedom from scandal might make him attractive enough to overcome Studds' superior organization and past popularity. But Studds was tireless in reassuring voters that his effectiveness was unimpaired, pointing to recent accomplishments on fishing and foreign policy issues.

Crampton, unable to match that record, ended up with strength in only two areas — the northern part of the 10th District, where an influx of blue-collar ethnic families from Boston had turned voting habits conservative, and parts of Cape Cod, a traditional Republican stronghold. Boosted by his usual massive margins in New Bedford and the coastal communities at the southern end, Studds prevailed.

Committees

Foreign Affairs (5th of 28 Democrats)
Arms Control, International Security and Science; Western Hemisphere Affairs

Merchant Marine and Fisheries (2nd of 26 Democrats)
Fisheries and Wildlife Conservation and the Environment (chairman); Coast Guard and Navigation; Oceanography

Elections

1988 General		
Gerry E. Studds (D)	187,178	(67%)
Jon L. Bryan (R)	93,564	(33%)
1986 General		
Gerry E. Studds (D)	121,578	(65%)
Ricardo M. Barros (R)	49,451	(27%)
Alexander Byron (I)	15,687	(8%)

Previous Winning Percentages: **1984** (56%) **1982** (69%) **1980** (73%) **1978** (100%) **1976** (100%) **1974** (75%) **1972** (50%)

District Vote For President

	1988	1984	1980	1976
D	143,938 (51%)	116,933 (45%)	86,914 (35%)	120,609 (51%)
R	136,345 (48%)	142,887 (55%)	118,065 (48%)	110,035 (46%)
I			40,799 (16%)	

Campaign Finance

	Receipts	Receipts from PACs	Expend-itures
1988			
Studds (D)	$243,095	$83,545 (34%)	$235,946
Bryan (R)	$122,953	0	$121,056
1986			
Studds (D)	$384,646	$83,820 (22%)	$396,216
Barros (R)	$90,610	$4,550 (5%)	$97,191

Key Votes

1987	
Raise speed limit to 65 mph	N
Approve Gephardt "fair trade" amendment	Y
Ban testing of larger nuclear weapons	Y
Delay "re-flagging" of Kuwaiti tankers	Y
Approve tax-raising deficit-reduction bill	Y
1988	
Approve aid to Nicaraguan contras	N
Enact civil rights restoration bill over Reagan veto	Y
Kill 60-day plant-closing notification measure	N
Pass omnibus trade bill over Reagan veto	Y
Approve death penalty for drug-related murders	N
Bar federal funds for abortions in cases of rape and incest	?
Oppose seven-day waiting period for purchase of handguns	N

Voting Studies

	Presidential Support		Party Unity		Conservative Coalition	
Year	**S**	**O**	**S**	**O**	**S**	**O**
1988	16	77	94	4	0	97
1987	12	86	93	2	2	95
1986	16	84	93	3	6	88
1985	21	78	93	3	5	95
1984	23	66	85	5	5	83
1983	18	77	91	5	6	88
1982	32	66	92	8	10	90
1981	33	67	91	9	7	93

Interest Group Ratings

Year	ADA	ACU	AFL-CIO	CCUS
1988	100	0	100	21
1987	100	0	100	0
1986	95	0	86	19
1985	100	10	100	27
1984	90	0	75	29
1983	85	0	88	32
1982	95	14	95	23
1981	100	7	80	11

11 Brian Donnelly (D)

Of Dorchester — Elected 1978

Born: March 2, 1946, Dorchester, Mass.
Education: Boston U., B.S. 1970.
Occupation: High school teacher.
Family: Wife, Virginia Norton; two children.
Religion: Roman Catholic.
Political Career: Mass. House, 1973-79, assistant majority leader, 1977-79.
Capitol Office: 2229 Rayburn Bldg. 20515; 225-3215.

In Washington: After 10 years in the House, Donnelly may not be as well-known as some of his classmates who have risen to subcommittee chairmanships or into the middle ranks of the party leadership, but his name is practically a household word in Ireland.

A 1986 law he sponsored eased immigration restrictions on the Irish and created "Donnelly visas," which have allowed thousands to settle legally in the United States. That has made his name so well-known that a columnist in the *Irish Times* saw fit to quote a U.S. official deflating any notion that Donnelly would be a future candidate for president.

Donnelly's involvement in immigration is not a matter of foreign affairs; it is constituent service for a member whose district includes one of the largest populations of Irish emigrants in the country.

Proud of his roots in the Irish-American neighborhood of Dorchester, Donnelly likes to present himself as a streetwise working-class Democrat who keeps some social distance from the issue-oriented liberal intellectuals who make up most of the junior generation of his party.

He is a solid Democrat and no stranger to the liberal positions generally associated with Massachusetts lawmakers, but Donnelly has a streak of blue-collar conservatism. His voting record in the 100th Congress got one of the lowest ratings of all Massachusetts Democrats from the liberal Americans for Democratic Action. And he has voiced skepticism about the direction the Democratic Party has taken.

"We have become the party of the gays, the abortionists, the far-out feminists, you name it," he said in 1985.

Donnelly is involved with some of the most sensitive and difficult national policy issues as a member of the Ways and Means Committee. Although he generally has good relations with Chairman Dan Rostenkowski of Illinois, Donnelly is an independent operator who can be unpredictable.

He parted ways with the committee and the majority of his party — for iconoclastic more than conservative reasons — during the House's 1987 debate on catastrophic health insurance for Medicare beneficiaries.

He was one of 15 Democrats to vote against the House version of the bill, after having tried unsuccessfully in committee to redirect the bill from capping hospital-related costs to coverage of what many elderly consider a much greater threat to their financial well being: long-term care outside the hospital.

"To call this legislation catastrophic protection is a misnomer," he said. "It was too quickly put together and costs too much for the benefits it offers."

Although Donnelly's fundamental criticisms were not met by the time the bill cleared Congress in 1988, he did vote for adoption of the conference report on the bill.

However, Donnelly was prescient in warning that because the bill makes the elderly bear the cost of the new benefits through higher premiums, Congress would be pressured to revisit the issue. Within a year after the law's enactment, the elderly were up in arms over the higher premiums they faced.

As a member of Ways and Means, Donnelly can be territorial when Dorchester and his district are involved. He showed a willingness to challenge Rostenkowski, a usual ally, during debate on the tax-revision bill in 1985. "I can't walk out on the floor with a bill that puts New England, or my slice of New England, at a competitive disadvantage," Donnelly said. "Everyone is saying in the back of their minds, 'If they get theirs, what do we get?' "

One of Donnelly's efforts during the tax debate was on behalf of the Quincy Shipyard. Rostenkowski and President Reagan proposed eliminating a deduction for funds set aside by shipowners for the construction of commercial ships, but Donnelly pushed successfully for retention of the tax break.

On the Ways and Means Subcommittee on Health in 1987, Donnelly cosponsored an amendment that would channel more Medicare money to industrial states, a version of which was enacted into law despite opposition from subcommittee Chairman Pete Stark of California.

Massachusetts 11

Part of Boston and South Shore Suburbs

The 11th is a forgotten part of Massachusetts. Occupying the southern corner of Boston and the suburbs beyond, it has watched as the economic development that has revitalized other communities has passed around it. The inflow of real-estate capital and investment enjoyed by neighborhoods closer to downtown has yet to reach the four Boston wards of the 11th District, and the high-technology belt that surrounds the city ends just outside the district's border.

At the same time, the district has avoided much of the social dislocation that other areas of the state have undergone. Populated by blue-collar workers and their families, it remains one of the most Irish districts in the country. In the Boston part of the 11th, covering Dorchester, Hyde Park, Neponset and Mattapan, many middle-aged adults live within a few blocks of where they were born and raised. Most of the suburbanites still have family in the city neighborhoods. Boston's recent wave of yuppie gentrification has come to Dorchester.

The South Shore suburb of Quincy is the largest community in Norfolk County. It is heavily ethnic, with Irish, Italian and French-Canadian pockets.

The Quincy shipyards along the Fore River were dealt a severe blow by General Dynamics' decision to close its operations, a move that cost thousands of jobs. President Reagan managed a 900-vote victory in the city in 1984, but generally Democrats have little to worry about in Quincy. Still, Gov. Michael S. Dukakis, his popularity on the wane, managed only 51 percent in Quincy in his 1988 presidential bid.

Brockton, with 95,000 residents, is the largest city in Plymouth County, and was long the shoemaking center of the nation. Then named North Bridgewater, it shod half the Union Army in the Civil War. But the city's footwear industry has been in decline for a generation. Reagan and George Bush carried Brockton in 1984 and 1988.

Population: 525,089. White 471,482 (90%), Black 42,395 (8%), Other 3,731 (1%). Spanish origin 9,563 (2%). 18 and over 382,888 (73%), 65 and over 68,280 (13%). Median age: 31.

In the 99th Congress, Donnelly fought off a proposal by Stark that would have raised $6.4 billion over three years for Medicare by requiring all present and future state and local employees to participate in the program.

A considerable amount of the new taxes would have been paid in Massachusetts. Roughly 70 percent of the state and local employees nationwide participated in the program under existing law, but some states, including Massachusetts, had lower rates of participation.

In the end, Donnelly offered a successful proposal that made Medicare participation mandatory for all newly hired state and local employees. That compromise promised to raise only $500 million over three years.

During his years on Ways and Means, Donnelly has shown interest in regulation of the use of tax-exempt revenue bonds — an interest that dates back to his years as a state legislator at a time when Massachusetts was one of the largest issuers of such bonds.

Since coming to the House in 1979, Donnelly has matured steadily as a legislator. As a freshman, he failed to win a choice committee assignment because he did not ask then-Speaker Thomas P. O'Neill Jr. to give him one. That omission has not been repeated. He made it to the Budget Committee in his second term, then left in 1985 for Ways and Means. Meanwhile, Donnelly won the confidence of Speaker Jim Wright, who appointed him to the influential Steering and Policy Committee, the panel that makes committee assignments, in 1987 and again in 1989.

On the Budget Committee, Donnelly worked closely with the liberal Democratic bloc, questioning the spending cutbacks of the Reagan administration. But his conservative streak showed when it came to federal entitlement programs, which he considers a huge source of waste.

In the 98th Congress, he was chairman of the committee's Entitlements Task Force and sponsored a change in civil service retirement benefits, suggesting an end to cost-of-living increases for those whose salaries exceeded $30,000.

At Home: Donnelly owes his seat in the House largely to support from James A. Burke, his Democratic predecessor, and former state Sen. Joseph Timilty, an influential Dorchester Democrat. Their strong endorsements in the 1978 primary identified Donnelly as the choice of party loyalists determined to keep the district out of the hands of Patrick McCarthy, a liberal maverick. McCarthy had challenged Burke's renomination in 1976, and the aging incumbent wanted to make sure the young "upstart" did not win on his second try.

Among the six Democrats who entered the primary to succeed Burke, Donnelly had the best base of support in the Boston part of the district. For six years, he had represented about a fifth of the Boston section of the district in the Legislature. He was assistant House majority leader for three years.

Donnelly's first endorsement came from Timilty, a locally popular legislator who had run for mayor three years before. When Burke added his public backing, the game was all over for McCarthy, and for the other four candidates as well. Donnelly carried the four Boston wards by a 6-to-1 margin and won 43 percent districtwide, to McCarthy's second-place 20 percent.

Although Donnelly has yet to reach the level of personal popularity that Burke enjoyed, his careful attention to constituents has achieved the same political results. Donnelly faced no opposition whatsoever in the early 1980s, and neither of the Republicans he faced in 1986 and 1988 exceeded 20 percent of the vote.

In 1984, Donnelly let it be known that he was toying with the idea of running for the Senate seat being vacated by Democrat Paul E. Tsongas. Eventually, though, he decided not to make the bid. He felt his centrist record seemed too much of an obstacle in the face of what he called "the machinelike dominance of would-be party bosses" — the liberal Dukakis wing of the state Democratic Party.

At the state Democratic convention that summer, Donnelly challenged party rules requiring Senate candidates to have the support of at least 15 percent of the convention delegates in order to go on to a primary. The move was defeated.

Committee

Ways and Means (18th of 23 Democrats)
Health; Select Revenue Measures

Elections

1988 General		
Brian Donnelly (D)	169,692	(81%)
Michael C. Gilleran (R)	40,277	(19%)
1988 Primary		
Brian Donnelly (D)	40,122	(86%)
David J. Petersen (D)	6,709	(14%)
1986 General		
Brian Donnelly (D)	114,926	(100%)

Previous Winning Percentages: **1984** (100%) **1982** (100%) **1980** (100%) **1978** (92%)

District Vote For President

	1988	1984	1980	1976
D	113,465 (51%)	107,407 (48%)	92,420 (42%)	124,179 (56%)
R	104,005 (47%)	116,490 (52%)	98,415 (44%)	90,036 (40%)
I			29,073 (13%)	

Campaign Finance

	Receipts	Receipts from PACs	Expend-itures
1988			
Donnelly (D)	$264,323	$131,300 (50%)	$167,960
Gilleran (R)	$18,687	$500 (3%)	$18,090
1986			
Donnelly (D)	$253,794	$138,065 (54%)	$46,171

Key Votes

1987	
Raise speed limit to 65 mph	N
Approve Gephardt "fair trade" amendment	Y
Ban testing of larger nuclear weapons	Y
Delay "re-flagging" of Kuwaiti tankers	Y
Approve tax-raising deficit-reduction bill	Y
1988	
Approve aid to Nicaraguan contras	N
Enact civil rights restoration bill over Reagan veto	Y
Kill 60-day plant-closing notification measure	N
Pass omnibus trade bill over Reagan veto	Y
Approve death penalty for drug-related murders	Y
Bar federal funds for abortions in cases of rape and incest	Y
Oppose seven-day waiting period for purchase of handguns	N

Voting Studies

	Presidential Support		Party Unity		Conservative Coalition	
Year	**S**	**O**	**S**	**O**	**S**	**O**
1988	15	69	86	8	18	66
1987	20	74	83	8	35	60
1986	18	79	86	4	18	82
1985	26	74	90	6	24	73
1984	35	56	83	7	24	71
1983	17	80	84	12	22	75
1982	38	60	84	13	33	60
1981	33	55	81	10	25	63

Interest Group Ratings

Year	ADA	ACU	AFL-CIO	CCUS
1988	80	8	100	23
1987	76	5	94	21
1986	75	14	93	29
1985	80	5	100	23
1984	80	8	92	27
1983	80	9	88	20
1982	80	14	95	30
1981	65	14	93	0

Michigan

U.S. CONGRESS

SENATE 2 D

HOUSE 11 D, 7 R

LEGISLATURE

Senate 18 D, 20 R

House 61 D, 49 R

ELECTIONS

1988 Presidential Vote

Bush	54%
Dukakis	46%

1984 Presidential Vote

Reagan	59%
Mondale	40%

1980 Presidential Vote

Reagan	49%
Carter	43%
Anderson	7%

Turnout rate in 1984	58%
Turnout rate in 1986	35%
Turnout rate in 1988	54%

(as percentage of voting age population)

POPULATION AND GROWTH

1980 population	9,262,078
1988 population estimate (8th in the nation)	9,240,000
Percent change 1980-1988	0%

DEMOGRAPHIC BREAKDOWN

White	85%
Black	13%
Other	1%
(Spanish origin)	2%
Urban	71%
Rural	29%
Born in state	72%
Foreign-born	5%

MAJOR CITIES

Detroit	1,086,220
Grand Rapids	186,530
Warren	149,800
Flint	145,590
Lansing	128,980

AREA AND LAND USE

Area 56,954 sq. miles (22nd)

Farm	30%
Forest	50%
Federally owned	10%

Gov. James J. Blanchard (D)
Of Pleasant Ridge — Elected 1982

Born: Aug. 8, 1942, Detroit, Mich.
Education: Michigan State U., B.A. 1964, M.B.A. 1965; U. of Minnesota, J.D. 1968.
Occupation: Lawyer.
Religion: Unitarian.
Political Career: U.S. House, 1975-83.
Next Election: 1990.

WORK

Occupations

White-collar	51%
Blue-collar	34%
Service workers	14%

Government Workers

Federal	56,843
State	158,299
Local	397,059

MONEY

Median family income	$ 22,107	(8th)
Tax burden per capita	$ 956	(18th)

EDUCATION

Spending per pupil through grade 12	$ 4,176	(11th)
Persons with college degrees	14%	(35th)

CRIME

Violent crime rate 780 per 100,000 (5th)

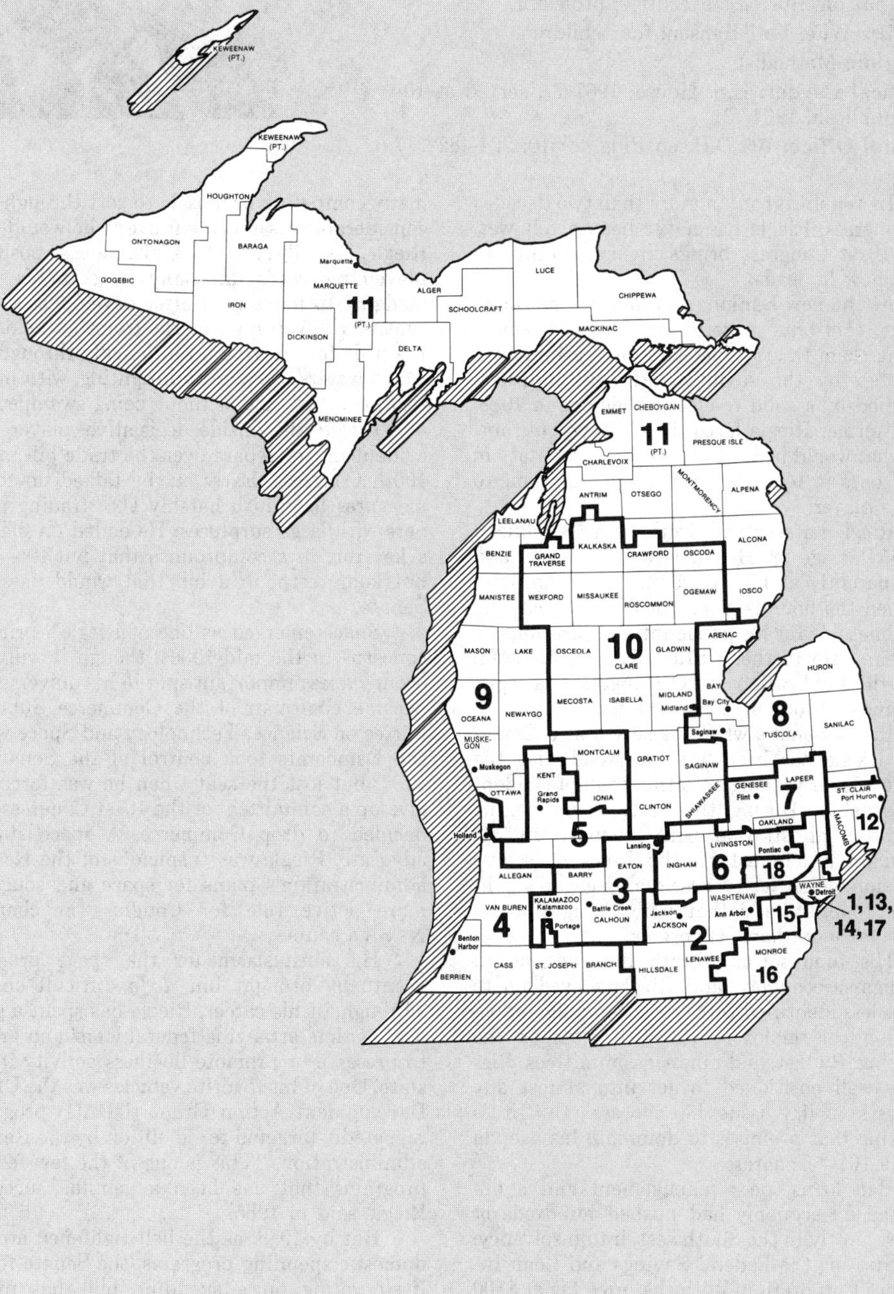
KEWEENAW (PT.)
KEWEENAW (PT.)
HOUGHTON
ONTONAGON
BARAGA
Marquette
GOGEBIC
MARQUETTE
ALGER
LUCE
CHIPPEWA
IRON
11 (PT.)
SCHOOLCRAFT
DICKINSON
DELTA
MACKINAC
MENOMINEE
EMMET
CHEBOYGAN
11 (PT.)
PRESQUE ISLE
CHARLEVOIX
MONTMORENCY
ANTRIM
OTSEGO
ALPENA
LEELANAU
KALKASKA
ALCONA
BENZIE
GRAND TRAVERSE
CRAWFORD
OSCODA
MANISTEE
WEXFORD
MISSAUKEE
ROSCOMMON
OGEMAW
IOSCO
ARENAC
MASON
LAKE
OSCEOLA
10
CLARE
GLADWIN
HURON
9
OCEANA
NEWAYGO
MECOSTA
ISABELLA
MIDLAND
Midland
BAY
Bay City
8
TUSCOLA
SANILAC
MUSKE-GON
Saginaw
Muskegon
MONTCALM
GRATIOT
SAGINAW
KENT
LAPEER
OTTAWA
Grand Rapids
IONIA
CLINTON
SHIAWASSEE
GENESEE
Flint
7
ST. CLAIR
Port Huron
Holland
5
OAKLAND
MACOMB
12
Lansing
LIVINGSTON
Pontiac
ALLEGAN
BARRY
EATON
INGHAM
6
18
3
WAYNE
Detroit
VAN BUREN
KALAMAZOO
Kalamazoo
Battle Creek
WASHTENAW
Ann Arbor
15
1,13,
14,17
4
Portage
CALHOUN
Jackson
JACKSON
Benton Harbor
2
CASS
ST. JOSEPH
BRANCH
HILLSDALE
LENAWEE
MONROE
16
BERRIEN

Donald W. Riegle Jr. (D)

Of Flint — Elected 1976

Born: Feb. 4, 1938, Flint, Mich.

Education: Attended Flint Junior College, 1956-57; Western Michigan U., 1957-58; U. of Michigan, B.A. 1960; Michigan State U., M.B.A. 1961; graduate work, Harvard Business School, 1964-66.

Occupation: Business executive; professor.

Family: Wife, Lori Hansen; four children.

Religion: Methodist.

Political Career: U.S. House, 1967-77; served as Republican, 1967-73.

Capitol Office: 105 Dirksen Bldg. 20510; 224-4822.

In Washington: In more than two decades in Congress, Riegle has never been a follower. The 101st Congress brings an opportunity to show how he leads.

As the new Banking Committee chairman, Riegle confronts a series of tests, foremost among them the troubles laid on Washington's doorstep by the savings and loan industry. Steadied by a solid re-election victory in 1988, third-termer Riegle faces the challenge of forging what would be his third political reputation: from *enfant terrible,* to strident partisan, to inside player.

Riegle entered the House as a Republican in 1967 at age 28. He was seen as a brash and transparently ambitious young man who overstepped the bounds of protocol by announcing the timetable for his presidential aspirations — 15 years. He further ruffled feathers in 1972, with the publication of "O Congress," a legislate-and-tell look at life in the Capitol.

In the Senate, where he serves as a Democrat, Riegle has been less burdened with the image of overweening ambition than of strident partisanship. During the early years of the Reagan administration, with Michigan and its dominant auto industry in the throes of a severe recession, he criticized President Reagan's policies in tones so harsh that many thought he did his cause more harm than good.

His tone softened with the rebound in Michigan's economy, and Riegle moved on to issues less identified with the automobile industry, long his major focus. With seats on the Banking, Budget, and Finance committees, Riegle is well positioned to get into almost any domestic policy issue he chooses. But it is Banking that promises to dominate his agenda in the 101st Congress.

Bad loans, poor management and a depressed oil economy had pushed hundreds of S&Ls, mostly in the Southwest, into insolvency, bankrupting the Federal Savings and Loan Insurance Corporation. With the price tag at $100 billion and climbing, the Congress in 1989 faced many competing proposals to sort through and considerable disagreement over who would pay. Riegle, usually one to stake out a position, played his cards unusually close to his vest, pledging to move only after developing a consensus. He won high marks from both sides of the aisle for steering a bill quickly through the rough waters of industry infighting, with bipartisan courtesy and without being swamped.

Riegle the inside legislative player was evident in the debate over the trade bill in the 100th Congress. Early on, he talked up tough measures to punish harshly U.S. trading partners with large surpluses. He ended up playing a key role in a compromise that put less bite, but kept teeth, in a bill that would pass the Senate.

Space emerged as one of Riegle's primary concerns in the mid-1980s, though it will now occupy a less important spot in his universe. He became chairman of the Commerce Subcommittee on Science, Technology and Space when the Democrats took control of the Senate in 1987, but lost the seat when he was forced to give up a committee for the 101st Congress and decided to drop Commerce. A space station advocate, Riegle was suspicious of the Reagan administration's plans for space and sought a more active role for Congress in charting NASA's course.

His enthusiasm for the space program eventually brought him to a difficult choice. Throughout his career, Riegle has spent a good deal of time arranging federal loans and grants to preserve or promote business activity in his state. One of his favorite vehicles was the Urban Development Action Grant (UDAG) program, repeatedly targeted for abolition by the Reagan administration. "This is one of the few federal programs that has been a genuine success," Riegle said in 1985.

But by 1988, as the belt tightened around domestic spending programs, the Senate found itself voting on a spending bill that pitted NASA's expanding goals against UDAG's very existence. Riegle cast his vote with the space agency, but vowed to bring UDAG back to life in the 101st Congress.

On the Budget Committee, Riegle has been a relentless opponent of cuts in domestic spending programs. In 1985, he strongly resisted efforts to freeze cost-of-living adjustments (COLAs) for Social Security recipients. When the committee endorsed that step as part of a spending plan it approved in March 1985, Riegle denounced the Republicans who drafted it. "You didn't have the courage to run on that basis," he said, noting Reagan's 1984 campaign pledge not to tamper with Social Security.

Riegle and New York's Daniel Patrick Moynihan vowed to try to block the COLA freeze on the Senate floor, and lobbying groups for the elderly swung into high gear, denouncing Reagan for going back on his word and pressuring senators up for re-election in 1986. A preliminary vote revived the COLAs, but they were frozen in a GOP leadership budget approved 50-49 after Vice President George Bush came in to break a tie.

But in the end, Riegle got his way. To the dismay of Senate GOP leaders, Reagan reversed field, abandoned the budget Bush had supported and threw in with a House-drafted budget that preserved Social Security COLAs.

Riegle's long record of devotion to the automobile industry and the United Auto Workers is well-known. Whether fighting auto-emission standards, promoting federal loan guarantees for a beleaguered Chrysler Corp. or demanding curbs on foreign car imports, Riegle has gone all out for Detroit.

A few years ago, when he was grand marshal of a parade in Traverse City, Mich., he refused to ride in the foreign car assigned to him; flustered organizers of the event hastily located a Chevrolet for the senator.

In 1977, when the Clean Air Act was up for renewal, Riegle offered the industry's principal amendment to relax standards for carbon monoxide emissions from automobiles. It was turned aside in favor of a stricter substitute version, whose passage led Riegle to complain, "We just cannot mandate technology that does not exist." But Riegle had won some tangible concessions; the ultimate language was somewhat looser than the version that earlier had passed the Environment and Public Works Committee.

Riegle was crucial in the 1979 passage of the Chrysler bailout, arranging a compromise that averted a filibuster and moving the plan through the full Senate just before the year's recess. The compromise involved more than $500 million in wage concessions on the part of Chrysler employees, in addition to federal protection for the company's future loans.

When auto industry layoffs put thousands out of work in the early 1980s, Riegle, on both Banking and Labor, fought for more federal benefits for the unemployed, usually against strong administration resistance.

That he is often a voice for labor was demonstrated again on the issue of catastrophic health care during the 100th Congress. He authored a small, but important, amendment that required employers to expand benefits in other directions if the new federal coverage for retirees' catastrophic illnesses replaced their own.

At Home: Riegle's first plunge into politics was enough to give anyone visions of grandeur. He was working toward a business degree at Harvard in 1966 when his hometown Republican Party, which had been having trouble finding candidates, recruited him to run against Democratic Rep. John C. Mackie. Riegle's name had some advantage; his father was active as a Republican officeholder in Flint and surrounding Genesee County.

Ignoring the odds in his heavily Democratic district, Riegle campaigned furiously, winding up his handshaking only after the polls had closed on Election Day. Mackie, ignoring the warnings of friends, decided he would have no trouble winning and lapsed into a somnolent campaign. He woke up with an 11,000-vote deficit. Riegle quickly concluded that if he could win a Democratic House seat that easily, there was no reason to restrain his ambitions.

Although he quickly developed a maverick reputation in the House, Riegle managed to stay on good terms with his party leader, Gerald R. Ford. Even after Riegle tried to take the 1970 Michigan Senate nomination away from Lenore Romney, the choice of GOP leaders, Ford seemed to remain an ally.

The Vietnam War, however, gradually turned Riegle from maverick to full-time rebel. He was one of a small group of anti-war Republicans that backed Rep. Paul N. McCloskey Jr. of California against President Nixon during the 1972 Republican primaries. Also that year, Riegle's "O Congress" book about his House experiences criticized the dominance of senior members.

By then he had burned his Republican bridges and was winning re-election by comfortable margins mainly because he was popular among Flint's blue-collar Democratic majority. He became a Democrat in 1973, won a fifth term the next year and began a well-financed effort to win the Senate seat vacated in 1976 by Democrat Philip A. Hart.

In the 1976 Democratic primary, he closed fast to upset the favorite, black Secretary of State Richard H. Austin. Austin was hurt by criticism of alleged irregularities in the collection of his campaign funds and by his refusal to debate his opponents. Riegle, campaigning with his usual vigor, stressed the contrast between his age (38) and Austin's (63).

Sparking a crossover primary vote by liberal Republicans and independents, Riegle won stunning victories in all of the state's Democratic strongholds except Wayne County (Detroit), which he lost by just 2,000 votes.

Riegle's primary win put him on a clear path toward a Senate victory that fall against moderate GOP Rep. Marvin Esch. Despite Esch's attempt to woo suburban Detroit Democrats by attacking busing and abortion, Riegle maintained a comfortable lead.

Then *The Detroit News* published transcripts of taped conversations between Riegle and a staff member with whom he had had an affair in 1969. Riegle acknowledged the affair, calling it a "foolish mistake." He also sought to create a sympathetic backlash in his favor, charging that Esch's campaign had been misrepresenting his policy positions. "I hold Marvin Esch personally responsible for the gutter-level tone of this campaign," Riegle declared. The defense worked, and Riegle withstood a last-minute media flurry by Esch.

In 1982, although few vestiges were left of the earlier "young man in a hurry," Riegle again had to fight off attacks on his character. His opponent, former Republican Rep. Philip E. Ruppe, latched onto a *Washington Post* article in which Republican senators were quoted to the effect that Riegle's confrontational approach cost him legitimacy.

That was Ruppe's only decent weapon against Riegle. With Michigan in the throes of a depression that many voters blamed on GOP policies, the time was anything but auspicious for a Republican. Moreover, Riegle's work on behalf of the auto industry had already preempted some traditional sources of GOP funding in Michigan, including Henry Ford II. Riegle had little trouble, winning even the Upper Peninsula, Ruppe's base, with 55 percent.

Six years later, Michigan's Republican Party was fractured by feuding caused by their complex presidential delegate-selection process. With party regulars — loyalists of George Bush — openly battling supporters of religious broadcaster Pat Robertson, the GOP scarcely had time to think about challenging Riegle. The Republican nomination fell to former Rep. Jim Dunn, an East Lansing developer who had been on the outs with the party hierarchy after a bitter and unsuccessful Senate primary bid in 1984.

While Dunn was never considered a serious threat, Riegle took absolutely no chances. His campaign produced more than 20 TV commercials, including an environmental spot featuring the senator fishing with his 4-year-old daughter, and a testimonial by New Jersey Sen. Bill Bradley likening Riegle's work on the trade bill to that of an athletic star leading his team to a championship. Pumping well over $3 million into his campaign, Riegle outspent Dunn nearly 8-to-1 and won more than 60 percent of the vote.

Committees

Banking, Housing and Urban Affairs (Chairman)

Budget (4th of 13 Democrats)

Finance (9th of 11 Democrats)
Health for Families and the Uninsured (chairman); International Debt; International Trade

Elections

1988 General

Donald W. Riegle Jr. (D)	2,116,865	(60%)
Jim Dunn (R)	1,348,219	(38%)

Previous Winning Percentages: **1982** (58%) **1976** (53%) **1974** * (65%) **1972** * (70%) **1970** * (69%) **1968** * (61%) **1966** * (54%)

* *House elections.*

Campaign Finance

	Receipts	Receipts from PACs		Expend-itures
1988				
Riegle (D)	$3,289,327	$1,281,641	(39%)	$3,383,849
Dunn (R)	$470,976	$8,055	(2%)	$442,693

Key Votes

1987

Enact omnibus highway bill over Reagan veto	Y
Limit testing of space-based anti-ballistic missiles	Y
Oppose banning tests of larger nuclear weapons	N
Confirm Robert H. Bork as Supreme Court justice	N

1988

Allow vote on campaign-finance overhaul	Y
Pass civil rights restoration bill over Reagan veto	Y
Enact omnibus trade bill over Reagan veto	Y
Approve death penalty for drug-related murders	Y
Oppose "workfare" amendment to welfare overhaul bill	Y

Voting Studies

	Presidential Support		Party Unity		Conservative Coalition	
Year	S	O	S	O	S	O
1988	41	57	94	3	24	73
1987	35	64	92	6	19	78
1986	18	82	96	4	5	95
1985	24	74	87	10	22	75
1984	31	68	92	6	2	98
1983	34	64	93	4	14 †	86 †
1982	24	66	89	3	4	86
1981	34	60	88	4	7	87

† *Not eligible for all recorded votes.*

Interest Group Ratings

Year	ADA	ACU	AFL-CIO	CCUS
1988	90	4	93	36
1987	100	4	100	17
1986	95	9	93	26
1985	95	4	90	24
1984	100	5	100	28
1983	85	4	94	28
1982	80	24	92	16
1981	90	14	89	22

Carl Levin (D)

Of Detroit — Elected 1978

Born: June 28, 1934, Detroit, Mich.
Education: Swarthmore College, B.A. 1956; Harvard U., LL.B. 1959.
Occupation: Lawyer.
Family: Wife, Barbara Halpern; three children.
Religion: Jewish.
Political Career: Detroit City Council, 1970-73, president, 1974-77.
Capitol Office: 459 Russell Bldg. 20510; 224-6221.

In Washington: Levin got a chilling "October surprise" in 1988 when President Reagan vetoed the "whistleblower" protection bill Levin had shepherded to passage. The White House had assured the senator that Reagan would sign the bill of rights for federal employees who expose corruption or mismanagement. But after Congress had adjourned for the year, Reagan balked.

This pocket veto seemed to have ruined a session's work for Levin and other sponsors, who had done their job well enough to win a 418-0 vote in the House and voice-vote approval in the Senate. Feeling double-crossed, Levin warned of "hell to pay" in the next Congress — suggesting some of those involved would rue their actions when their reappointments came before the Senate for confirmation.

But as it turned out, the voice behind the veto was that of Attorney General Dick Thornburgh. Replacing Edwin Meese III late in the summer of 1988, Thornburgh had developed questions about the bill in his first few weeks on the job, after Levin had completed his work. Thornburgh was back in 1989, renamed to his post by President Bush. Levin put aside talk of retribution and instead talked publicly of Bush's commitment to protecting whistleblowers. When Levin reintroduced the bill, Thornburgh's approval was part of the prepackaged deal and Levin was pleased to describe the product as new and improved. The bill was among the first to become law in 1989.

The stages of the whistleblower bill showed the lawyerly Levin at his most meticulous, his most combative and ultimately his most accommodating. Overall, it illustrated his effectiveness. He is renowned for his ability to recoup when a situation appears lost, or to sweeten a deal even after it appears to have been closed.

These are the skills Levin has brought to his prime bailiwick: the Armed Services Committee. In the 100th Congress, he continued his emphasis on procurement issues, particularly with respect to consultants. He tried to get the Pentagon to require disclosure of its consultants' other clients, so as to prevent unwitting reliance on those with a hidden agenda. He was rebuffed, but he was back in 1989 when the committee reviewed the nomination of former Sen. John Tower to be secretary of defense.

Unlike most who followed the Tower contretemps, Levin seemed less concerned with allegations about Tower's personal life than with Tower's potential conflicts of interest. Levin asked whether Tower would recuse himself from decisions on programs he had advocated as a paid lobbyist from 1986 through 1988. Tower refused to commit to doing so and said he would consider each case on its own. Levin used this as a basis for his vote against confirmation.

Levin had taken a hard line as a critic of Meese's financial dealings and as a supporter of the independent counsel's office, the Office of Government Ethics, and proposed limitations on lobbying by former members of Congress and their staffs.

Levin also took a lead, and lonely, position on capital punishment, sustaining a major setback on the issue late in 1988. Despite Levin and allies' entreaties, the omnibus anti-drug bill of 1988 included a death penalty for traffickers who intentionally kill in the course of their business. Levin was able to persuade the leadership to accept a package of 17 modifying amendments. It was the first new federal law to include a death penalty since 1974 legislation against airline hijacking.

Although reliably liberal on such issues, Levin likes to take rhetorical aim at old-fashioned liberal assumptions. "We messed up those social programs," he likes to say. "Those of us who believe in them have an obligation to make them work."

But the career of this thoughtful, pragmatic Democrat reflects the elusive nature of the revisionist liberalism that Levin and his allies seem interested in. Except for some moves to rein in "unaccountable bureaucrats" through congressional veto power, it is hard to see many instances where Levin's record differs from a traditional liberal one.

On Armed Services, Levin has been a constructive, well-informed Pentagon critic, but a consistent critic nevertheless. He complained that the Defense Department under Reagan put too much emphasis on buying complicated new weapons systems, especially nuclear ones, while ignoring the maintenance and training that the military would need in the conduct of a conventional war.

One of Levin's strengths is his ability to appropriate the tactics of his adversaries to make his own points. After Reagan warned that the Soviets had far outstripped U.S. military capability, Levin responded with "Chart Wars" — elaborate graphics showing that the United States had the upper hand in a number of important military categories. To back up his claim, he solicited from the chairman of the Joint Chiefs of Staff the admission that "not on your life" would he trade U.S. military forces for those of the Soviet Union.

Levin's interest in Pentagon procurement, which accounts for 80 percent of the goods and services purchased by the federal government, had been longstanding. He often comes across as the Armed Services version of a tough city prosecutor, looking for corruption in defense spending and for ways to weaken what he sees as the too-close connection between the Pentagon and defense contractors.

Over the years, Levin has sponsored a number of bills to do that, by increasing competition among contractors, slowing the "revolving door" through which officials move from the Pentagon to high-paying jobs with contractors, and toughening penalties against illegal kickbacks to Defense Department employees.

Levin's mastery of the subject, together with his credibility among Pentagon critics, also allows him to play a mediating role on procurement issues in the committee. As ranking member of the panel's Procurement Task Force in the 98th Congress, he helped work out a compromise on the touchy subject of warranties — the legislative requirement that Pentagon contractors pay for repairs of weapons that do not meet agreed-upon standards.

On the Governmental Affairs Committee, Levin spent much of his time in the 98th Congress fighting Reagan regulations governing the Social Security disability program.

Governmental Affairs also has been the forum for Levin's most conspicuous anti-government crusade — in favor of the legislative veto, which would allow Congress to revoke federal regulations of all sorts. Levin had some success here, but it was largely overturned by the Supreme Court in 1983. More recently, Levin has questioned the growing power of the Office of Management and Budget over regulations issued by government agencies. Upset that the budget office conducted its reviews behind closed doors, he forced it in 1986 to disclose what regulatory changes it was demanding.

In his approach to domestic policy, though, Levin is an old-fashioned labor Democrat. He wants all the federal help he can get for the struggling industries and workers of Michigan. He worked hard in the first half of the 1980s to preserve unemployment benefits for the many jobless workers in his state. He pushed legislation to extend unemployment benefits in regions of high joblessness, and was the author of an unsuccessful bill to ease penalties on high-unemployment states that fail to repay federal loans for jobless benefits.

At Home: Money and political sophistication brought Levin a second term in 1984 against an opponent who was short of both commodities. The Democrat may need to stock up even further for 1990, when he is likely to face a GOP nominee with more competitive resources — perhaps Rep. Bill Schuette of the north-central 10th District.

Levin had been anticipating a tough re-election in 1984. He pumped up his fund raising early by issuing dire warnings that the national GOP planned to channel millions into Michigan to unseat him. The warnings worked so well that Levin outspent his Republican opponent, former astronaut Jack Lousma, who went heavily into debt in the primary and was strapped for funds in the fall campaign.

But Levin needed more than a monetary advantage to save his job. In the final days of the fall campaign, as Walter F. Mondale's presidential campaign faded, it became apparent that Reagan's coattails could cause Levin real problems. So he unveiled an "October surprise." He aired a film clip of Lousma warming up a Japanese audience in 1983 by telling them about the Toyota he owned. In Michigan, where Japanese cars mean joblessness, Lousma's statement was a major embarrassment. Few were soothed by his weak plea that the Toyota belonged not to him, but to his son.

The Toyota film clip meshed well with the overall theme of the Levin campaign. Realizing that his anti-administration record would be risky in a big Reagan year, Levin had billed himself as "A Proven Fighter for Michigan" and stressed his work to limit auto imports, extend unemployment benefits and help relieve the state unemployment compensation debt.

Lousma, who had flown on Skylab and space shuttle missions in the 1970s and early 1980s, was strongly supported by anti-abortion forces, anti-tax advocates and other conservative Republicans, who helped him win nomination over former U.S. Rep. Jim Dunn. But he suffered from his own unfamiliarity with politics and Michigan issues. He had retired from NASA in Houston and moved to his boyhood home of Grand Rapids just before launching his campaign. In one unfortunate moment during the summer, he told an audience that any Michigan schoolboy could understand the state's problems in a few hours. Many voters were not so sure.

In spite of those handicaps, Lousma might have been able to ride Reagan's coattails to victory had Levin's fund raising been less vigorous and his strategy less well devised. Reagan carried Michigan with 59 percent — one of his strongest showings in a major industrial state — but Levin held on to win with 52 percent.

Levin's older brother, Sander, now in the U.S. House, first spread the family name statewide with gubernatorial campaigns in 1970 and 1974. Carl Levin made his name in politics in the mid-1970s as president of the Detroit City Council, where he teamed with black Mayor Coleman A. Young to provide for demolition of thousands of abandoned buildings. The two men strayed apart at times in the late 1970s, but this probably helped Levin as a statewide candidate — it showed suburban voters that he was not inextricably tied to the city's black majority.

The big break in Levin's successful 1978 Senate challenge was a major misstep by the GOP incumbent, Robert P. Griffin. Disappointed at losing the contest for Senate Republican leader in 1977, Griffin announced he would retire the next year and began skipping votes on the floor. He eventually changed his mind about running, but by that time had missed a third of the Senate votes over an entire year. Levin said Griffin was obviously tired of the job, and the voters agreed that the incumbent deserved a rest.

Committees

Armed Services (3rd of 11 Democrats)
Conventional Forces and Alliance Defense (chairman); Readiness, Sustainability and Support; Strategic Forces and Nuclear Deterrence

Governmental Affairs (3rd of 8 Democrats)
Oversight of Government Management (chairman); Government Information and Regulation; Permanent Subcommittee on Investigations

Small Business (4th of 10 Democrats)
Innovation, Technology and Productivity (chairman); Rural Economy and Family Farming

Elections

1984 General

Carl Levin (D)	1,915,831	(52%)
Jack Lousma (R)	1,745,302	(47%)

Previous Winning Percentage: 1978 (52%)

Campaign Finance

	Receipts	Receipts from PACs	Expend-itures
1984			
Levin (D)	$3,517,444	$707,766 (20%)	$3,504,962
Lousma (R)	$1,772,925	$473,204 (27%)	$1,749,786

Key Votes

1987

Enact omnibus highway bill over Reagan veto	Y
Limit testing of space-based anti-ballistic missiles	Y
Oppose banning tests of larger nuclear weapons	N
Confirm Robert H. Bork as Supreme Court justice	N

1988

Allow vote on campaign-finance overhaul	Y
Pass civil rights restoration bill over Reagan veto	Y
Enact omnibus trade bill over Reagan veto	Y
Approve death penalty for drug-related murders	N
Oppose "workfare" amendment to welfare overhaul bill	?

Voting Studies

	Presidential Support		Party Unity		Conservative Coalition	
Year	**S**	**O**	**S**	**O**	**S**	**O**
1988	42	52	91	6	14	84
1987	32	67	89	8	28	69
1986	23	77	91	9	11	88
1985	25	73	89	6	25	72
1984	34	61	89	8	9	85
1983	33	66	86	12	14	82
1982	34	63	92	6	5	94
1981	35	63	92	5	6	93

Interest Group Ratings

Year	ADA	ACU	AFL-CIO	CCUS
1988	80	0	92	21
1987	90	4	90	17
1986	90	9	87	26
1985	85	4	90	31
1984	100	14	82	35
1983	95	8	94	16
1982	95	20	96	14
1981	100	7	100	0

1 John Conyers Jr. (D)

Of Detroit — Elected 1964

Born: May 16, 1929, Detroit, Mich.
Education: Wayne State U., B.A. 1957, LL.B. 1958.
Military Career: National Guard, 1948-52; Army, 1952-53; Army Reserve, 1953-57.
Occupation: Lawyer.
Family: Single.
Religion: Baptist.
Political Career: No previous office.
Capitol Office: 2313 Rayburn Bldg. 20515; 225-5126.

In Washington: Conyers has always seemed more interested in being a rebel within the House than in becoming a power broker. But in the 101st Congress, after a quarter-century in the institution, seniority brought him a position where he will be expected to be a legislative leader. If Conyers chooses to meet those expectations, he could build a significant power base as chairman of the Government Operations Committee.

One thing that has hurt Conyers in the House is a style that a number of colleagues feel is sarcastic and abrasive. That has made it difficult for him to coordinate alliances needed to pass legislation. But Conyers did make a positive impression in the 100th Congress, demonstrating his ability to lead on a politically difficult issue — the impeachment of U.S. District Judge Alcee L. Hastings.

As chairman of the Judiciary Subcommittee on Criminal Justice, Conyers was in charge of leading the investigation into Hastings, who had been accused of conspiring to solicit a bribe and leaking wiretap information. Impeachment proceedings are never taken lightly, and the Hastings case was particularly sensitive. Conyers, a black veteran of the civil rights movement, was responsible for leading the investigation of a black judge who claimed the charges against him were racially motivated. Further, Hastings had been acquitted by a jury.

When Conyers began the proceedings in 1987, he indicated that he was troubled by the Hastings impeachment inquiry because of what he saw as a pattern of "racially motivated conduct throughout this country for many years." But as the investigation progressed, Conyers reached what he later called the most difficult decision of his House career: that Hastings was guilty and had fabricated his court defense.

"We did not fight the civil rights struggle to replace one sort of judicial corruption with another," Conyers said, recalling the difficulties blacks had had with white judges. He said it would be "disloyal to the essential principles of the civil rights movement and my oath of office to attempt to set up a double standard for those who share my principles and those who oppose them."

Conyers, who held a special briefing on the Hastings case with members of the Black Caucus, worked to move the 17-count resolution of impeachment through the House smoothly. It easily cleared the subcommittee and full committee, and when the case came to the floor, Conyers gave a speech that brought him a standing ovation and helped to deliver a vote of 413-3. With that, the Hastings impeachment moved to the Senate in the 101st Congress.

To colleagues, Conyers' leadership on the Hastings case was a departure from the legislative personality he most often displays. He is near the top of the Judiciary Committee, but the two subcommittees he has chaired moved relatively few pieces of legislation.

In 1986, Conyers embarked on a full-scale campaign to stifle his subcommittee's bill aimed at curtailing use of a federal anti-racketeering law. The law, known as the Racketeer Influenced and Corrupt Organizations Act (RICO), was designed to combat organized crime, but had been used increasingly for civil suits against corporations with no criminal record.

Business and labor lined up behind Virginia Democrat Rick Boucher's bill to restrict the use of the civil RICO suits. Conyers fought the bill throughout the process, forcing Boucher to enlist the help of Judiciary Chairman Peter W. Rodino Jr. in prying the bill out of subcommittee for a vote. When it reached the floor, Conyers tried a parliamentary stall to block its passage. He said the bill would hinder efforts against white-collar crime. It cleared the House, but died in the Senate.

In the 100th Congress the fight continued. While proponents of the effort to restrict RICO suits pressed their case, Conyers introduced a "study bill" that would expand RICO crimes to include terrorist acts and bank fraud, areas where the current law was fuzzy. His bill also blocked use of RICO in trivial cases. No legislation emerged from the Criminal Justice panel.

Michigan 1

Detroit — North Central; Highland Park

Detroit was not all that special at the turn of the century. It brewed beer and turned out carriages and stoves, and its complacent citizens took to calling it "the most beautiful city in America." But Henry Ford's first large factory in Highland Park, built in 1909, was followed by others, plants put up by Buick, R. E. Olds and the Fisher brothers. The north side of Detroit became a sea of single- and two-family houses for the workers who flocked to the assembly lines from rural Michigan, Appalachia and Eastern Europe.

The 1st, now overwhelmingly black (71 percent) and Democratic, is generally better off than its inner-city neighbor, the 13th. More of its homes are owner-occupied, and its residents are better educated. The racially mixed communities north of Seven Mile Road have a high percentage of professionals and white-collar city employees living in well-preserved prewar houses.

East of Southfield Road, the neighborhoods are poorer and more exclusively black. Both skilled and unskilled workers live in Highland Park and in the area north of the University of Detroit.

Highland Park, a city entirely surrounded by Detroit, is the home of the Chrysler Corp. Once a white-ethnic bastion, Highland Park is now 84 percent black. Although the city retained its middle-class character through most of the 1960s and early 1970s, hard times and rising unemployment have hurt its increasingly marginal neighborhoods.

The several white enclaves in the district include Poles living in the northeast corner, north of Hamtramck, and middle-class ethnics around the Southfield Freeway in the southwest. These voters tend to be older and more conservative.

Population: 514,560. White 137,827 (27%), Black 364,021 (71%), Other 3,202 (1%). Spanish origin 10,587 (2%). 18 and over 349,182 (68%), 65 and over 47,777 (9%). Median age: 28.

The subcommittee did produce some legislation under Conyers. In the 99th Congress President Reagan signed into law a bill narrowing the coverage of a 1984 law aimed at curbing bribery in the banking industry. The bill, sponsored by Conyers, addressed complaints of banking officials that the law was making it a crime for them to accept lunches or football tickets from business associates. Conyers' bill made clear that the law was violated only if a gift was given with "corrupt" intent.

Before taking over the Government Operations chairmanship, Conyers was less visible on that panel than on Judiciary. But Texas Democrat Jack Brooks' switch to the Judiciary chairmanship moved Conyers to center stage. Early on he gave indications that his priorities as chairman would be somewhat different from Brooks'. Conyers said one of his goals is to use the chairmanship to channel the government procurement budget toward economically depressed areas and to minority businesses.

Conyers has always seen a role for himself that goes beyond day-to-day legislative politics. He has spent considerable time outside Washington and his district campaigning for other black politicians. In 1988 he claimed to have spent more days campaigning for Jesse Jackson than any other black member of the House.

Conyers' interest in civil rights also blends in with a strong interest in jazz music. "Whites who have had all kinds of trouble with me have never had any trouble embracing Belafonte," he has said, referring to popular singer Harry Belafonte. "Cultural endeavors are a useful area.... We reach a common base from which all America springs." Conyers has a stand-up bass in his office along with jazz posters. In 1987 he sponsored a successful House resolution that said jazz is "a rare and valuable national American treasure."

At Home: The son of an autoworker, Conyers became interested in politics while in law school and worked loyally in the party apparatus. The creation in 1964 of a second black-majority district in Detroit gave him his first opportunity. He ran for Congress on a platform of "Equality, Jobs and Peace," pledging to strengthen the United Nations and to exempt low-income families from paying federal income tax.

Among the qualifications Conyers cited for holding office were three years as a district aide to Rep. John D. Dingell and service on a panel of lawyers picked by President Kennedy to look for ways of easing racial tensions in the South. Conyers won the primary by just 108 votes over Richard H. Austin, a Detroit accountant who has remained a political rival ever since.

Racial troubles in Conyers' district exploded in 1967, when rioting destroyed many blocks in the heart of the district. Conyers was booed when he stood atop a car telling rioters to return to their homes. Later his office was gutted by fire. But those episodes had no lasting political impact, nor did his initial reluctance to support Hubert H. Humphrey in 1968.

Conyers' primary challenges have been infrequent and minor, though he has not always been on the best of terms with Detroit Mayor Coleman A. Young and the United Auto Workers, the major political powers in the city. Some Conyers partisans were worried that he might have trouble in the 1982 redistricting process; his district had lost substantial population, and the state had to give up one seat in the House. But Conyers' territory remained basically intact.

Committees

Government Operations (Chairman)
Legislation and National Security (chairman)

Judiciary (4th of 21 Democrats)
Civil and Constitutional Rights; Crime; Criminal Justice

Small Business (17th of 27 Democrats)
SBA, the General Economy and Minority Enterprise Development

Elections

1988 General

John Conyers Jr. (D)	127,800	(91%)
Bill Ashe (R)	10,979	(8%)

1986 General

John Conyers Jr. (D)	94,307	(89%)
Bill Ashe (R)	10,407	(10%)

Previous Winning Percentages: **1984** (89%) **1982** (97%) **1980** (95%) **1978** (93%) **1976** (92%) **1974** (91%) **1972** (88%) **1970** (88%) **1968** (100%) **1966** (84%) **1964** (84%)

District Vote For President

	1988	1984	1980	1976
D	108,814 (90%)	144,684 (86%)	143,653 (86%)	148,065 (84%)
R	11,376 (9%)	23,737 (14%)	19,341 (12%)	27,136 (15%)
I			3,471 (2%)	

Campaign Finance

	Receipts	Receipts from PACs	Expend-itures
1988			
Conyers (D)	$151,676	$82,614 (54%)	$124,823
1986			
Conyers (D)	$132,208	$66,845 (51%)	$163,360

Key Votes

1987

Raise speed limit to 65 mph	N
Approve Gephardt "fair trade" amendment	Y
Ban testing of larger nuclear weapons	Y
Delay "re-flagging" of Kuwaiti tankers	Y
Approve tax-raising deficit-reduction bill	Y

1988

Approve aid to Nicaraguan contras	N
Enact civil rights restoration bill over Reagan veto	Y
Kill 60-day plant-closing notification measure	N
Pass omnibus trade bill over Reagan veto	Y
Approve death penalty for drug-related murders	N
Bar federal funds for abortions in cases of rape and incest	N
Oppose seven-day waiting period for purchase of handguns	N

Voting Studies

	Presidential Support		Party Unity		Conservative Coalition	
Year	S	O	S	O	S	O
1988	13	74	83	1	3	89
1987	8	81	82	2	5	81
1986	11	73	71	4	4	78
1985	13	68	69	6	7	67
1984	21	73	88	6	5	92
1983	6	73	73	6	4	73
1982	22	60	68	8	8	75
1981	32	59	78	9	9	85

Interest Group Ratings

Year	ADA	ACU	AFL-CIO	CCUS
1988	90	0	100	21
1987	92	0	100	0
1986	85	0	92	9
1985	75	12	92	28
1984	95	4	85	21
1983	100	0	100	11
1982	80	6	88	6
1981	90	9	93	0

2 Carl D. Pursell (R)

Of Plymouth — Elected 1976

Born: Dec. 19, 1932, Imlay City, Mich.
Education: Eastern Michigan U., B.A. 1956, M.A. 1961.
Military Career: Army 1957-59; Army Reserve 1959-65.
Occupation: High school teacher; real-estate salesman; owner of office supply business.
Family: Wife, Peggy Jean Brown; three children.
Religion: Protestant.
Political Career: Wayne County Commission, 1969-70; Mich. Senate, 1971-77; sought Republican nomination for Mich. Senate, 1966.
Capitol Office: 1414 Longworth Bldg. 20515; 225-4401.

In Washington: Watching Carl Pursell now — as he quietly pursues bipartisan compromise from the precincts of the Appropriations Committee — one can almost forget that in 1981 and early 1982, he was something of a liberal renegade among Republicans, challenging Reagan administration budget priorities as leader of the high-profile "Gypsy Moth" faction of Frost Belt Republicans.

Some of Pursell's transformation has to do with Michigan's economic recovery: The early 1980s recession was severe in the state, and widely blamed on Ronald Reagan's policies, so political prudence demanded that Pursell distance himself from the White House.

In addition, redistricting in 1982 gave Pursell a district that was safely Republican and markedly more conservative; he had fallen below 60 percent in 1980, but the new lines pushed him well above that in November 1982. Pursell can now afford to support the GOP leadership on most matters, and he does. In 1988, when he faced a well-financed Democratic challenger, Pursell voted with his party more often than at any time in his career.

Pursell's evolution has enabled him to win the confidence of the GOP hierarchy. In 1979, when he was clearly identified as a liberal, fellow Republicans nearly blackballed him from the Appropriations Committee; only his friendship with soon-to-be Minority Leader Robert H. Michel got him a seat there. Those days are over. In the 100th Congress, Pursell was selected a deputy Republican whip.

But if Pursell is now more of an insider and loyalist, there are still obvious signs that he will never be any kind of conservative ideologue. In the 100th Congress, he voted against the overwhelming majority of Republicans who opposed a seven-day waiting period for handgun purchases and a 60-day plant-closing notification amendment. Also, while he has been generally supportive of aid to the Nicaraguan contras, Pursell authored legislation to establish a bipartisan commission on Central America to develop a national consensus and long-term U.S. policy for the region.

Pursell is also active in the '92 Group, a caucus of mostly moderate Republicans working to create a GOP House majority. Formerly chairman of the group's budget task force, he has played a role in developing budget alternatives entailing more money for social programs and less for defense than other GOP proposals.

On Appropriations, Pursell is well liked and can often bridge the gap between the GOP's conservative and moderate wings. He also has ties to the Democratic side of the aisle, joining with Michigan Democrat Bob Carr to protect home-state interests.

Pursell's position on the Appropriations subcommittee that handles education funding is crucial to him, because there he can lobby for federal help for the University of Michigan, whose 35,000 students make it a dominant industry in the district. When Pursell tells voters about his subcommittee's spending bill, he makes a point to highlight any funds it contains that benefit the university.

He advocates increased funding for the Pell Grant program, as well as numerous research grants. In the 100th Congress, for instance, he spoke out in favor of continuing funding for biomedical research grants, which Reagan had proposed eliminating.

Though Pursell is not an uncritical supporter of federal expenditures in the labor, human resources and education funding bill that his subcommittee handles, his working assumption is that most of the money is justified. "In this particular bill," he once said, "the mandatory and entitlement programs are so high and the relatively small discretionary piece is so critical to the nation that we cannot come back and make budget reductions. . . ."

Pursell has also been a consistent supporter of federal funds for nursing programs, and he is a champion of the National Center for

Michigan 2

Southeast — Ann Arbor; Jackson

The 2nd, which reaches south and west from the Detroit suburbs to the northern edge of the Corn Belt, is home to an uneasy mix of academics, blue-collar workers and conservative farmers.

The GOP dominates the rural townships. The small towns and farms that dot the flat land of Hillsdale, Lenawee, Jackson and Branch counties are a steady source of Republican votes. The last time any of those counties voted for a Democratic presidential candidate was in 1944.

The other block of Republican votes comes from the Detroit suburbs. About a fifth of the district's residents live in a sliver of Wayne County that begins only a mile and a half west of Detroit in the upper-middle-class neighborhoods of Livonia. Professionals and middle-level managers from the area's auto plants give northern Livonia its Republican character, although some blue-collar Democrats live in the older northeast corner of the city.

In Washtenaw County, which holds a third of the district's population, there is a clash of interests. The students and academic community at the University of Michigan in Ann Arbor give that city a bohemian image; that stands in marked contrast to the conservatism found among the vegetable farms to the south and west.

The two poles of the county — the rural west and urban east — have swung Washtenaw from Republican to Democratic in recent presidential elections; it was the only county in the nation to support George McGovern in 1972, then back Gerald R. Ford in 1976. In the 1980s, Washtenaw has gone Republican once (1984) and Democratic twice (1980 and 1988).

Besides Ann Arbor, most of the district's Democratic vote comes from Jackson, an industrial city with nearly 40,000 residents. Jackson's Democrats work in the tool-and-die and auto parts factories scattered throughout the city. Unlike Detroit's autoworkers, however, many of those living here were raised in the surrounding Republican countryside, and they sometimes reflect that background in statewide and national elections.

Population: 514,560. White 478,266 (93%), Black 24,349 (5%), Other 7,767 (2%). Spanish origin 6,677 (1%). 18 and over 375,911 (73%), 65 and over 45,010 (9%). Median age: 29.

Nursing Research, located in Bethesda, Md. When Reagan opposed federal funding for the Center in 1985, Pursell described his stand as "an insult to American nurses."

On the Energy and Water Subcommittee, Pursell has taken an interest in the St. Lawrence Seaway. In the 100th Congress, he backed language to conduct a study of improvements needed to keep the waterway competitive, which would benefit the Great Lakes shipping that contributes to Michigan's economy.

The normally placid Pursell made the biggest splash of his House career with his stand against Reagan's domestic priorities during the 1981-82 budget battles. A group of Southern "Boll Weevil" Democrats positioned themselves as swing votes to win concessions from the GOP on budget issues. Feeling that the Weevils' success came at the expense of the Northeast and Midwest, Pursell's Gypsy Moths organized and used similar tactics. "It's the economic well-being of the region," he explained. "We've just got to express a point of view. Otherwise we get kicked in the teeth."

In 1981, the administration called the Labor-Health and Human Services appropriation too expensive, and called for further cuts. In a display of Republican defiance rare that year, 39 Republicans — 22 of them Gypsy Moths — voted against the administration, and the bill passed. Meanwhile, Pursell was organizing his group into a formal organization, the Steering Committee of Northeast-Midwest Republicans.

At Home: Pursell's record has stood him well during his years representing the starkly diverse 2nd. He is liberal enough on social issues and independent enough from the national GOP to pick off some votes in the Democratic-leaning university community at Ann Arbor, and the rural communities in his district generally prefer any Republican at all to a Democrat.

When he first came to Congress, Pursell took his political cues from Marvin L. Esch, the five-term moderate Republican he succeeded when Esch ran unsuccessfully for the Senate in 1976. Pursell has knit together the different parts of his district as did his predecessor.

Pursell won his first term in 1976 by just 344 votes, due to his strength in Wayne County, which he represented in the state Senate. He won 65 percent there, while losing the rest of the district to Democrat Edward C. Pierce, a much more liberal Ann Arbor doctor.

His first re-election was a breeze, but he slipped almost 10 percentage points in 1980 against Kathleen O'Reilly, whose tenure as director of the Consumer Federation of America had won her enthusiastic liberal support in Washington. But she had trouble uniting feuding factions of local Democrats, and her campaign could not broaden its appeal beyond Ann Arbor.

Redistricting in early 1982 brought the 2nd more in line with the GOP mainstream, shoring up Pursell against the threat of a strong Democratic attack.

After winning routinely in 1982 and 1984, Pursell dropped under 60 percent again in 1986, when he faced Democrat Dean Baker, a University of Michigan graduate student. Baker based his campaign on strong opposition to Reagan's Central American policies. The appeal of that issue in Ann Arbor helped Baker carry Washtenaw County by a 350-vote margin. But Pursell swamped him elsewhere, especially in the Republican's Wayne County base, where he won 70 percent of the vote.

Pursell's 59 percent tally against the unheralded Baker inspired Democratic state Sen. Lana Pollack to launch a challenge in 1988. While her liberal record in the Legislature was considered a liability by most local observers, it helped Pollack win the backing of the auto workers' union, which had never before made a concerted effort to oust Pursell. Pollack also gained credibility when she proved to be a prolific fund-raiser; her total expenditures for the campaign exceeded $750,000.

Pollack claimed that despite Pursell's moderate image, he voted like a conservative in Washington. She got a boost when Environmental Action named him to its "Dirty Dozen" list of House members. But while Pollack had a devoted following in Ann Arbor, she ran into the usual obstacle of a Democratic nominee in the 2nd — wooing independents and moderate Republicans, especially those in rural areas whose votes are essential to victory.

Pursell took the challenge seriously. Spending more than $875,000 and airing the first television advertisements of his political career, the genial incumbent campaigned like a man on the run. His final tally of 55 percent was Pursell's lowest re-election total, but because he held his ground against such an aggressive and well-funded opponent, Pursell may have given pause to other Democrats thinking of challenging him.

Committee

Appropriations (9th of 22 Republicans)
Energy and Water Development; Labor, Health and Human Services, Education and Related Agencies

Elections

1988 General		
Carl D. Pursell (R)	120,070	(55%)
Lana Pollack (D)	98,290	(45%)
1986 General		
Carl D. Pursell (R)	79,567	(59%)
Dean Baker (D)	55,204	(41%)

Previous Winning Percentages: **1984** (69%) **1982** (66%) **1980** (57%) **1978** (68%) **1976** (50%)

District Vote For President

	1988	1984	1980	1976
D	92,837 (43%)	79,684 (36%)	88,499 (37%)	90,250 (41%)
R	122,482 (56%)	142,867 (64%)	125,724 (52%)	126,141 (57%)
I			21,730 (9%)	

Campaign Finance

	Receipts	Receipts from PACs	Expend-itures
1988			
Pursell (R)	$811,384	$264,993 (33%)	$876,779
Pollack (D)	$764,491	$238,912 (31%)	$750,493
1986			
Pursell (R)	$231,209	$67,445 (29%)	$140,396
Baker (D)	$33,003	$3,675 (11%)	$32,181

Key Votes

1987	
Raise speed limit to 65 mph	N
Approve Gephardt "fair trade" amendment	N
Ban testing of larger nuclear weapons	N
Delay "re-flagging" of Kuwaiti tankers	N
Approve tax-raising deficit-reduction bill	N
1988	
Approve aid to Nicaraguan contras	Y
Enact civil rights restoration bill over Reagan veto	N
Kill 60-day plant-closing notification measure	N
Pass omnibus trade bill over Reagan veto	Y
Approve death penalty for drug-related murders	Y
Bar federal funds for abortions in cases of rape and incest	N
Oppose seven-day waiting period for purchase of handguns	N

Voting Studies

	Presidential Support		Party Unity		Conservative Coalition	
Year	S	O	S	O	S	O
1988	47	46	62	35	79	16
1987	52	44	51	38	72	21
1986	51	46	50	46	74	22
1985	56	35	57	32	75	20
1984	50	40	53	32	63	20
1983	63	28	56	33	69	26
1982	42	42	38	40	45	37
1981	49	45	42	50	31	60

Interest Group Ratings

Year	ADA	ACU	AFL-CIO	CCUS
1988	45	46	62	79
1987	20	55	20	71
1986	45	55	43	76
1985	15	71	21	75
1984	45	45	36	79
1983	15	61	18	85
1982	45	21	29	71
1981	65	73	53	76

3 Howard Wolpe (D)

Of Lansing — Elected 1978

Born: Nov. 2, 1939, Los Angeles, Calif.
Education: Reed College, B.A. 1960; Massachusetts Institute of Technology, Ph.D. 1967.
Occupation: Political science professor.
Family: Divorced; one child.
Religion: Jewish.
Political Career: Kalamazoo City Commission, 1969-72; Mich. House, 1973-77; Democratic nominee for U.S. House, 1976.
Capitol Office: 1535 Longworth Bldg. 20515; 225-5011.

In Washington: The chairman of the Foreign Affairs Subcommittee on Africa, Wolpe is a leader among the quite small number of House members who pursue U.S.-African issues with zeal. As head of a panel that divides along ideological lines, the former professor of African studies sometimes can be better at constructing an argument for what should be done than at plotting tactics to make it happen. But when it comes to framing an issue, detailing the facts and holding fast to his convictions, Wolpe is an expert.

The author of two books on Nigeria, Wolpe tries to persuade colleagues to look at the effects of U.S. foreign policy from an African point of view. This perspective has put him at the center of the long-running debate over imposing sanctions on the white-minority government of South Africa.

The issue provided Wolpe with his biggest legislative success: During the 99th Congress, Congress approved a law imposing sanctions against South Africa's apartheid regime. But Wolpe's efforts to tighten the squeeze stalled in the 100th Congress, as the wave of public protest over apartheid subsided.

Wolpe has long been a forceful critic of South Africa's policy of forced racial separation. He argued in 1985 that the only effect of President Reagan's "constructive engagement" approach toward South Africa "has been to increase the violence, because the intransigent [white] elements have been led to believe they can engage in repression without any real cost or American response."

In June 1985, Wolpe and Pennsylvania Democrat William H. Gray III moved a bill through the House that would have imposed immediate economic sanctions on South Africa. Though a compromise bill, negotiated by conferees from the House and the Republican-controlled Senate, was never approved by the full Senate, pressure for its passage played a role in Reagan's September 1985 issuance of an executive order incorporating some of the compromise language.

In 1986, South Africa's bombing raids into neighboring countries helped Wolpe and his allies obtain stronger sanctions. The House passed a Wolpe-Gray bill to impose a trade embargo on South Africa and force all U.S. companies to stop doing business there.

When the Senate approved a milder bill, Wolpe urged his House colleagues to press for a conference. But other Democrats, including Gray, concluded that a hard-line approach could scuttle the legislation. They accepted Senate Foreign Relations Chairman Richard G. Lugar's promise to support an override of Reagan's expected veto, and passed the Senate bill. In the end, both houses overrode Reagan's veto, enacting the sanctions into law.

In 1988, Wolpe tried to strengthen the sanctions, proposing an almost complete ban on U.S. trade with South Africa and a withdrawal of investments from that country within six months. Wolpe, as he had earlier, presented the issue in urgent tones, calling his bill "an effort to avert a blood bath" by pressuring South Africa's whites to negotiate with blacks.

However, the political atmosphere this time was not as conducive to passage. The failure of the original sanctions law to weaken South Africa's resolve created doubt in Congress about the measure's efficacy. Also, the election-year momentum Wolpe hoped for never developed; South Africa did not emerge as a cutting campaign issue. Wolpe's sanctions bill passed the House, but died in the Senate.

Along with the issue of South Africa, Wolpe crossed swords with Reagan and his conservative allies over U.S. support for anti-communist insurgencies in countries such as Angola. Though expressing no sympathy for Marxist governments, Wolpe insisted Africans viewed as "absurd" the U.S.-Soviet competition for their favor. "They know in advance," he said once, "that if they are going to call themselves communists, they get assistance from one side; anti-communist, they get assistance from another side."

Opinions like that have provoked conser-

Michigan 3

South Central — Lansing; Kalamazoo

Although the 3rd is anchored by the medium-sized industrial cities of Kalamazoo and Battle Creek, votes from the surrounding farm land have traditionally defined district politics as Republican.

Because the last redistricting added Democratic territory in downtown and western Lansing to the 3rd, the Republican vote is lower than it was in the 1970s, but still a clear majority.

In Kalamazoo, paper mills and automobile assembly plants provide the base of a powerful union presence and blue-collar Democratic vote, although Checker Motors' last car rolled off the lines there in 1982. The city also has a large academic community: Western Michigan University (23,000), where Wolpe once taught, and Kalamazoo College.

But the pharmaceutical workers at the Upjohn Co., the corporate managers in the southern half of the city and the area's Dutch residents give Kalamazoo County a strong moderate-to-conservative Republican vote. Reagan carried the county as a whole with 64 percent in 1984, and George Bush got 54 percent there in 1988.

Battle Creek, half the size of Kalamazoo, is widely recognized by morning cereal-box readers as the source of both Kellogg's and Post breakfast cereals. Together with Ralston-Purina and several truck manufacturers, those companies provide the bulk of the city's jobs. Their unionized workers provide one of the steadiest sources of Democratic votes.

Between the major cities are large patches of rural and suburban GOP territory. White-collar suburbs such as Delta Township, west of Lansing, and Battle Creek Township, home to Kellogg executives, usually provide Republicans with overwhelming electoral margins. The small towns and rolling fields of Eaton, Kalamazoo and Calhoun counties provide strong conservative reinforcement. Only in southern Barry County, settled over the years by workers from Battle Creek and Kalamazoo, do Democrats find a welcome in the countryside.

Population: 514,560. White 456,405 (89%), Black 45,053 (9%), Other 4,691 (1%). Spanish origin 12,462 (2%). 18 and over 367,512 (71%), 65 and over 49,244 (10%). Median age: 28.

vatives into some very angry criticisms of Wolpe. In 1988, GOP Rep. Toby Roth of Wisconsin implied that Wolpe would be responsible for the deaths of starving Ethiopians unless he moved on Roth's bill calling for sanctions against that nation. (Roth accused the Ethiopian government of withholding food from residents of a rebellious region.) And in 1986, Wolpe's Republican opponent in the 3rd District received a personal endorsement from Jonas Savimbi, leader of insurgent forces fighting the Marxist government of Angola.

Wolpe did agree with Reagan on one African issue in which the president appeared to come around to his way of thinking. In 1987, conservatives accused Reagan, who was working for improved ties with socialist Mozambique, of betraying that nation's anti-government "freedom fighters." But Wolpe said, "I think the administration is right on target."

Wolpe's re-election opponents typically argue that the geopolitics of Africa and other issues under his purview on Foreign Affairs are far from the concerns of the factory workers and farmers of his district. Wolpe counters that foreign relations, especially in the area of trade, greatly affect his constituents. "Ask farmers whether what happens elsewhere has some bearing on their economic future," he told *The Detroit News* in 1988.

Wolpe cushions himself politically by focusing the rest of his time on issues closer to home. He is co-chairman of the Northeast-Midwest Congressional Coalition, a caucus that works to help the region shed its Rust Belt image. As a member of the Budget Committee in the 98th, 99th and 100th Congresses, Wolpe pressed to divert funds from defense to "programs that are most critical to our economic future — education, research and development and retraining."

Wolpe's ultimate security blanket, though, is his reputation for constituent service. In a glowing 1988 endorsement, the *Kalamazoo Gazette* said Wolpe and his staff had "raised empathetic listening to a near art form."

At Home: Wolpe continues to succeed in this GOP-majority district in spite of his liberal voting record, but he has yet to make the seat secure. In six House campaigns, he has only once reached the 60 percent mark — in 1986. The constituent-service skills that Wolpe first honed as a Kalamazoo city councilman and as a state legislator clearly have been crucial to his re-elections.

A narrow loser to GOP Rep. Garry Brown in 1976, Wolpe worked for Sen. Donald W. Riegle Jr. for two years while preparing for a rematch. His goal was to reduce Brown's margin in the Lansing suburbs of Eaton County. Without losing support in Kalamazoo, Wolpe won 46 percent in Eaton County, up from 39 percent on his first try. That boosted him to victory.

In both 1984 and 1986, Wolpe survived noisy contests with conservative Jackie McGregor, a former vice chairman of the state GOP with a clear knack for controversy.

In 1984, McGregor received the endorsement of a National Rifle Association official who called Wolpe a communist sympathizer. She then got 4th District GOP Rep. Mark D. Siljander (who was defeated in 1986) to cosign a letter to ministers urging them to "send another Christian to Congress" by supporting her. After Wolpe, who is Jewish, complained, McGregor said it was he who injected religion into the campaign by enlisting six Jewish congressmen to send a letter supporting him.

Key GOP contributors disliked her style, and she fell far behind in fund raising. But aided by Reagan's strong showing in the 3rd, McGregor held Wolpe to 53 percent, which encouraged her to try again in 1986.

In the rematch, McGregor assailed Wolpe's defense record, claiming that his opposition to Reagan's military priorities cost the district defense-related jobs. The candidates also had another exchange over religion. A McGregor brochure stated that Wolpe and actor Ed Asner sent a fund-raising letter to 500,000 people "of their religion outside the district."

Many in the moderate GOP business community closed their wallets to McGregor, and Wolpe cultivated more business support than before. His efforts to block repeal of certain real-estate deductions during the 1986 tax-revision debate earned him National Association of Realtors support. Wolpe's 60 percent tally was the high-water mark of his congressional electoral career.

In 1988, Wolpe slipped under 60 percent again against political newcomer Cal Allgaier, the owner of several local convenience stores. Considered a long-shot challenger, Allgaier gained legitimacy when Kellogg's corporate political action committee endorsed him. Though Wolpe is popular with the cereal company's unionized work force, Kellogg has facilities in South Africa, and management has long objected to his position on U.S. sanctions.

As in the past, Wolpe met his opponent in several debates, where he persuasively defended his liberal record. But George Bush's strong showing in the 3rd boosted Allgaier well over 40 percent — not a bad showing given that he was outspent nearly 4-to-1.

Committees

Foreign Affairs (6th of 28 Democrats)
Africa (chairman); International Economic Policy and Trade

Science, Space and Technology (8th of 30 Democrats)
Energy Research and Development; Natural Resources, Agriculture Research and Environment; Science, Research and Technology

Elections

1988 General		
Howard Wolpe (D)	112,605	(57%)
Cal Allgaier (R)	83,769	(43%)
1986 General		
Howard Wolpe (D)	78,720	(60%)
Jackie McGregor (R)	51,678	(40%)

Previous Winning Percentages: **1984** (53%) **1982** (56%) **1980** (52%) **1978** (51%)

District Vote For President

	1988	1984	1980	1976
D	91,304 (45%)	75,445 (36%)	79,581 (37%)	77,860 (40%)
R	108,237 (54%)	130,891 (63%)	112,115 (52%)	114,346 (58%)
I			20,803 (10%)	

Campaign Finance

	Receipts	Receipts from PACs	Expend-itures
1988			
Wolpe (D)	$576,393	$263,224 (46%)	$600,940
Allgaier (R)	$165,710	$67,000 (40%)	$164,856
1986			
Wolpe (D)	$878,634	$252,649 (29%)	$852,746
McGregor (R)	$221,727	$77,019 (35%)	$223,082

Key Votes

1987	
Raise speed limit to 65 mph	N
Approve Gephardt "fair trade" amendment	Y
Ban testing of larger nuclear weapons	Y
Delay "re-flagging" of Kuwaiti tankers	Y
Approve tax-raising deficit-reduction bill	Y
1988	
Approve aid to Nicaraguan contras	N
Enact civil rights restoration bill over Reagan veto	Y
Kill 60-day plant-closing notification measure	N
Pass omnibus trade bill over Reagan veto	Y
Approve death penalty for drug-related murders	N
Bar federal funds for abortions in cases of rape and incest	N
Oppose seven-day waiting period for purchase of handguns	N

Voting Studies

	Presidential Support		Party Unity		Conservative Coalition	
Year	S	O	S	O	S	O
1988	17	81	92	6	18	82
1987	14	82	91	2	12	88
1986	16	82	91	7	10	88
1985	21	76	91	6	7	93
1984	23	76	93	6	5	95
1983	16	82	93	4	11	88
1982	34	66	88	11	11	88
1981	26	72	92	8	8	91

Interest Group Ratings

Year	ADA	ACU	AFL-CIO	CCUS
1988	100	0	100	36
1987	92	0	94	7
1986	90	5	93	33
1985	85	10	94	20
1984	95	0	92	38
1983	95	0	94	35
1982	100	0	100	18
1981	95	0	80	11

4 Fred Upton (R)

Of St. Joseph — Elected 1986

Born: April 23, 1953, St. Joseph, Mich.
Education: U. of Michigan, B.A. 1975.
Occupation: Congressional aide; budget analyst.
Family: Wife, Amey Rulon-Miller.
Religion: Congregationalist.
Political Career: No previous office.
Capitol Office: 1713 Longworth Bldg. 20515; 225-3761.

In Washington: Upton's early involvement in the budget debate came as a surprise to no one. The former director of legislative affairs for the Office of Management and Budget (OMB), he entered Congress needing no education on the complexities of federal spending.

As a freshman, he joined with an effort led by Republican Tom Tauke of Iowa and Democrat Timothy J. Penny of Minnesota that aimed to shrink the deficit by making small, across-the-board cuts in appropriations bills. Upton offered floor amendments of this sort to several appropriations bills, but none passed.

Upton's aptitude for management and budget matters led to his most noticed first-term victory — blocking an effort to declare a one-time federal holiday on Sept. 17, 1987, commemorating the bicentennial of the U.S. Constitution. "We all realize that the Constitution is a working document," Upton said. "If this is true, does it really make sense to celebrate a working document by taking a day off work?"

Upton's amendment struck out the federal holiday provisions and instead proposed a "National Day of Recognition." He cited OMB estimates that the federal government would save $330 million by not declaring a holiday, and said that would help lower the deficit. Although holiday proponents said the Congressional Budget Office estimated a cost nearer $3 million, Upton held all but 18 of his fellow Republicans and won over 93 Democrats; his amendment was adopted, 237-162.

A serious, detail-minded man, Upton lobbied hard — some colleagues felt too hard — for a seat on the Budget Committee as a freshman. He did not achieve that goal, ending up on the Public Works and Small Business committees. He did win a seat on the Joint Economic Committee at the start of the 101st Congress, and after Newt Gingrich was elected minority whip in March 1989, Upton got a position in the GOP whip organization.

At Home: In 1986, Upton was the only House Republican to unseat an incumbent in a primary. But his victory over GOP Rep. Mark D. Siljander was something less than a total shock.

Much of the local GOP establishment had long disliked Siljander, an activist in the religious right whose efforts to link religion and politics had often led to controversy. And Upton was unusually well positioned to challenge the vulnerable incumbent.

Upton is a member of one of the district's most prominent families — his grandfather was a founder of the Whirlpool appliance company. And although he had never sought office before, Upton had a strong résumé. He spent 10 years as an aide to David A. Stockman during Stockman's tenures as 4th District House member and as President Reagan's OMB director.

Upton worked in Stockman's first House campaign in 1976, then joined his Washington staff, concentrating on constituent service, which helped him develop local contacts. In 1981, Upton followed Stockman to OMB.

Siljander had emerged on the scene in 1981, winning a special election that followed Stockman's move to OMB. He beat a longtime Stockman ally by mobilizing his fundamentalist backers, and he went on to establish a reputation as a conservative firebrand known to denounce the "perverted" philosophy of "secular humanists." Although his voting record was in line with the majority philosophy of the 4th, Siljander's style alienated GOP regulars. Primary challengers fell short in 1982 and 1984, but Upton decided to make a bid when he returned to the district in 1985 after Stockman resigned his OMB post.

Upton generally avoided challenging Siljander's issue positions; instead, he hoped to convince voters that he was simply a more appealing, less confrontational conservative. He got a break late in the campaign, when Siljander committed an astounding gaffe. He taped an appeal to fundamentalist ministers, implying that the challenge to him was linked to evil forces, and calling on voters to "break the back of Satan." Upton aides claim he would have won anyway, but the tape clinched his victory. Since then, his general elections have been uneventful. In a district that has not sent a Democrat to the House since 1932, that is not likely to change.

Michigan 4

Southwest — Holland; Benton Harbor-St. Joseph

Stretching 100 miles on the eastern shore of Lake Michigan and another 100 miles along the Indiana border, the L-shaped 4th is among the most Republican constituencies in the country.

It is overwhelmingly agricultural; fewer than a fifth of its residents live in its five small cities. Cass, St. Joseph and Branch counties form the northeastern edge of the Corn Belt; GOP majorities in these three counties are only slightly diluted by the conservative Democratic votes of workers in the plants and foundries of Dowagiac, Three Rivers and Coldwater.

The gentle climate produced by the lake has made fruits and berries the chief crops of the four lakeshore counties — Berrien, Van Buren, Ottawa and Allegan. Berrien has a small food-processing industry, and several wineries dot the fields around Paw Paw in Van Buren County. The shoreline is also a retirement and tourist draw. Some of Michigan's strongest Republican precincts are in Allegan and Ottawa counties.

The city of Holland, on the line between Ottawa and Allegan, is a GOP bastion. The westernmost point of the "Dutch Triangle" formed by Holland, Grand Rapids and Kalamazoo, Holland and its environs were settled by immigrants from the Netherlands in the mid-19th century. Holland's Dutch character goes beyond its name and its wooden shoe factory and Tulip Festival to a Calvinist religious style.

The major chunk of Democratic votes in the 4th comes from the Benton Harbor-St. Joseph area. Benton Harbor once offered haven to runaway slaves on the underground railroad; today it is mostly black, and fighting industrial decline. St. Joseph, once a bedroom community for Benton Harbor, now has a significant manufacturing base. The blue-collar workers in St. Joseph and towns to the south like conservative Democrats, as do retirees from industrial Illinois and Indiana who now live in shore cottages in towns such as New Buffalo.

Population: 514,560. White 468,675 (91%), Black 37,396 (7%), Other 3,934 (1%). Spanish origin 8,278 (2%). 18 and over 355,746 (69%), 65 and over 56,287 (11%). Median age: 30.

Committees

Public Works and Transportation (14th of 20 Republicans)
Investigations and Oversight; Surface Transportation; Water Resources

Select Hunger (7th of 12 Republicans)
Task Force: Domestic

Small Business (13th of 17 Republicans)
Environment and Labor; Procurement, Tourism and Rural Development

Joint Economic
Economic Growth, Trade and Taxes; Economic Resources and Competitiveness; Fiscal and Monetary Policy

Elections

1988 General		
Fred Upton (R)	132,270	(71%)
Norman J. Rivers (D)	54,428	(29%)
1986 General		
Fred Upton (R)	70,331	(62%)
Dan Roche (D)	41,624	(37%)

District Vote For President

	1988		1984		1980		1976	
D	72,584	(36%)	61,604	(32%)	66,585	(32%)	72,586	(37%)
R	127,631	(63%)	130,742	(68%)	126,001	(60%)	119,110	(61%)
I					13,095	(6%)		

Campaign Finance

	Receipts	Receipts from PACs	Expend-itures
1988			
Upton (R)	$422,884	$117,465 (28%)	$323,829
Rivers (D)	$8,629	$4,300 (50%)	$8,577
1986			
Upton (R)	$383,071	$42,685 (11%)	$382,663
Roche (D)	$15,348	0	$15,314

Key Votes

1987	
Raise speed limit to 65 mph	Y
Approve Gephardt "fair trade" amendment	N
Ban testing of larger nuclear weapons	N
Delay "re-flagging" of Kuwaiti tankers	N
Approve tax-raising deficit-reduction bill	N
1988	
Approve aid to Nicaraguan contras	Y
Enact civil rights restoration bill over Reagan veto	N
Kill 60-day plant-closing notification measure	Y
Pass omnibus trade bill over Reagan veto	Y
Approve death penalty for drug-related murders	Y
Bar federal funds for abortions in cases of rape and incest	N
Oppose seven-day waiting period for purchase of handguns	Y

Voting Studies

	Presidential Support		Party Unity		Conservative Coalition	
Year	S	O	S	O	S	O
1988	60	40	86	14	87	13
1987	60	40	90	10	91	9

Interest Group Ratings

Year	ADA	ACU	AFL-CIO	CCUS
1988	30	64	50	100
1987	16	70	13	87

5 Paul B. Henry (R)

Of Grand Rapids — Elected 1984

Born: July 9, 1942, Chicago, Ill.
Education: Wheaton College, B.A. 1963; Duke U., M.A. 1968, Ph.D. 1970.
Occupation: Political science professor.
Family: Wife, Karen Anne Borthistle; three children.
Religion: Christian Reformed.
Political Career: Mich. House, 1979-83; Mich. Senate, 1983-85.
Capitol Office: 215 Cannon Bldg. 20515; 225-3831.

In Washington: An evangelical Christian, former Peace Corps volunteer and political scientist, Henry brings the full force of his varied life experience to bear in Congress. He has conservative instincts, an open mind and an intellectual approach to legislating.

While this combination sometimes sets Henry apart from most Republicans on key votes, he works hard to quell doubts about his loyalty. When he agrees with his GOP colleagues, he is a forthright team player; when he goes his own way, he does so in a reserved, low-key manner.

Henry's 1987 vote to cut off all aid to the Nicaraguan contras was a typically dexterous defection. In a detailed floor statement, he spoke of the need to "formulate a coherent, bipartisan, multinational policy in the region." He then stuck with the GOP on a party-line vote against the rule to consider the bill. Only on final passage did he vote against the aid, one of 17 Republicans to do so. In 1989, he returned to the GOP fold to support the bipartisan humanitarian contra-aid package.

Henry's opposition to abortion goes over well in Michigan's resurgent conservative GOP wing, and his maverick votes have become easier for partisans to accept as they have occurred less frequently. In 1988, Henry sided with a majority of Republicans over 80 percent of the time, a step to the right since his first term.

When he first ran for Congress, Henry was suspect on the GOP right because he backed moderate Republican John B. Anderson's presidential campaign in the 1980 Michigan primary. Then, just two months into his first term, Henry broke ranks on a key MX missile vote. Earlier, he had said he was "gravely concerned" about the cost and usefulness of the MX, but with the White House making the vote a loyalty test, Henry feared being seen as a renegade. He had a 20-minute talk with Reagan and promised to give the issue "one last think through." But he voted against the MX.

Henry is best known for his work as ranking member of the Education and Labor Subcommittee on Health and Safety. During debate in the 100th Congress on legislation to require notification of workers who may be exposed to hazardous substances, Henry commended the bill's "very laudable goals," but took a lead in warning of "an avalanche" of new liability problems. A substitute he offered with GOP Rep. James M. Jeffords of Vermont to mandate stricter enforcement of existing laws was rejected on a largely party-line vote.

Henry also rebuffed organized labor on the plant-closing notification issue, but he has bucked his party leadership to support some labor causes. He voted for the Gephardt "fair trade" amendment, and he voted to override Reagan's veto of the 1988 trade bill.

At Home: Though the national GOP was touting Reagan-style conservatism when Henry won the 5th in 1984, he built his political credentials in the party's moderate wing. His introduction to politics was his work an an aide to Illinois Rep. Anderson in the late 1960s.

Henry's centrist outlook was the norm for the state GOP in the 1970s, when moderate William G. Milliken was governor. But after the GOP lost the governorship in 1982, the state party shifted right. In his initial House campaign, Henry tried to keep step while retaining his moderate image. "I'm a fiscal conservative," he said, "but not a scrooge." In the GOP primary, Henry was challenged from the right by Keary W. Sawyer, the son of retiring GOP Rep. Harold S. Sawyer.

But Henry contrasted his record in the state House, where he was assistant floor leader, and in the state Senate, where he chaired the Education and Health Committee, with his foe's lack of experience. Sawyer had never sought public office, and he was not plugged into the local party network because his father never had close ties with the GOP establishment. Henry won the nomination by a decisive margin.

Democrat Gary J. McInerney, a lawyer and businessman, seemed to have appeal beyond his party's normal base. But the political neophyte was no match for Henry, who as a state legislator had served about half the people in the 5th. Henry has won so easily since then that he is mentioned as a potential statewide candidate.

Michigan 5

West Central — Grand Rapids

The 5th, Gerald R. Ford's old constituency, is centered on Grand Rapids, Michigan's second-largest city. During Ford's presidency, Grand Rapids attained an image as clean-cut, all-American, middle-class and Republican. The high-tech and service industries in the area — aircraft instrumentation firms, a Keebler cookie distribution center and, nearby, the national headquarters of the Amway Corp. — have brought in technicians, managers and professionals whose neat houses, manicured lawns and GOP votes reinforce that picture.

But Grand Rapids' heavy industry, including furniture and auto-parts factories, gives it a sizable working-class presence. It has the largest black population in Michigan outside the Detroit-to-Bay City auto corridor, and blue-collar voters in the central and western parts of the city put it in the Democratic column in the early post-Ford House elections.

The local GOP is two-pronged. The conservative community around Calvin College and the small-business people in southeast Grand Rapids are largely descendants of the Dutch craftsmen brought in by the city's once-famous furniture industry; they are the "Dutch Wing." The executives and younger professionals to the northeast and in East Grand Rapids and Kentwood are the more cosmopolitan "Ford Wing." Henry, as a Calvin College professor with a moderate approach, unites the two factions.

Outside the city stretch miles of farm land peppered with small towns. Townships north and south of Grand Rapids have generally attracted blue-collar Democrats who moved from the west side. Conservative Dutch influence is strong in the Allegan County towns near Holland.

Population: 514,560. White 472,168 (92%), Black 31,855 (6%), Other 4,932 (1%). Spanish origin 9,750 (2%). 18 and over 359,611 (70%), 65 and over 52,190 (10%). Median age: 28.

Committees

Education and Labor (10th of 13 Republicans)
Health and Safety (ranking); Employment Opportunities; Postsecondary Education

Science, Space and Technology (10th of 19 Republicans)
Energy Research and Development; Natural Resources, Agriculture Research and Environment; Science, Research and Technology

Select Aging (18th of 27 Republicans)
Retirement, Income and Employment

Elections

1988 General		
Paul B. Henry (R)	166,569	(73%)
James M. Catchick (D)	62,868	(27%)
1986 General		
Paul B. Henry (R)	100,577	(71%)
Teresa S. Decker (D)	40,608	(29%)

Previous Winning Percentage: **1984** (62%)

District Vote For President

	1988	1984	1980	1976
D	83,859 (35%)	73,849 (32%)	80,701 (35%)	66,634 (32%)
R	151,713 (64%)	158,992 (68%)	128,842 (55%)	140,552 (67%)
I			19,541 (8%)	

Campaign Finance

	Receipts	Receipts from PACs	Expend-itures
1988			
Henry (R)	$387,878	$97,425 (25%)	$309,436
Catchick (D)	$53,137	$12,200 (23%)	$50,977
1986			
Henry (R)	$344,221	$102,592 (30%)	$304,765
Decker (D)	$17,700	$8,699 (49%)	$17,074

Key Votes

1987	
Raise speed limit to 65 mph	Y
Approve Gephardt "fair trade" amendment	Y
Ban testing of larger nuclear weapons	Y
Delay "re-flagging" of Kuwaiti tankers	N
Approve tax-raising deficit-reduction bill	N
1988	
Approve aid to Nicaraguan contras	N
Enact civil rights restoration bill over Reagan veto	N
Kill 60-day plant-closing notification measure	Y
Pass omnibus trade bill over Reagan veto	Y
Approve death penalty for drug-related murders	Y
Bar federal funds for abortions in cases of rape and incest	Y
Oppose seven-day waiting period for purchase of handguns	N

Voting Studies

	Presidential Support		Party Unity		Conservative Coalition	
Year	S	O	S	O	S	O
1988	49	48	81	17	84	11
1987	56	42	75	22	77	23
1986	43	57	67	31	66	34
1985	60	40	69	29	65	35

Interest Group Ratings

Year	ADA	ACU	AFL-CIO	CCUS
1988	50	52	57	93
1987	36	45	40	87
1986	40	45	43	89
1985	25	67	24	68

6 Bob Carr (D)

Of East Lansing — Elected 1974

Did not serve 1981-83.

Born: March 27, 1943, Janesville, Wis.
Education: U. of Wisconsin, B.S. 1965, J.D. 1968.
Occupation: Lawyer.
Family: Divorced.
Religion: Baptist.
Political Career: Democratic nominee for U.S. House, 1972, 1980.
Capitol Office: 2439 Rayburn Bldg. 20515; 225-4872.

In Washington: Carr's electoral defeat in 1980 did more than keep him out of public office for two years. It transformed his legislative personality, in ways that work both for and against him.

No longer does Carr offend other members with the brash arrogance he displayed as a junior member in the 1970s. But he also seems to have lost the penchant for crusades and innovation that characterizes many of his class of 1974 colleagues. The 1980s Carr is an assiduous Appropriations Committee member who dwells on bread-and-butter, district-oriented issues that will help him keep his seat, but probably will not involve him in cutting-edge policy-shaping — the role he once seemed eager to play.

First elected in the Watergate landslide, Carr made an instant reputation as a rebel by calling for the resignation of House Speaker Carl Albert and leading his fellow freshmen in a series of assaults on the congressional establishment. He seemed thirsty for the battles he now is careful to avoid. In the 100th Congress, Carr's most visible position was as head of the Congressional Arts Caucus.

What intervened was the 1980 Reagan landslide, which helped oust Carr. He regained his seat two years later, but returned with an entirely different mindset. His attack on Albert he has since called "sheer, naive stupidity," adding that "you cannot go through life being an angry young man." And he is so wary of potential controversies that colleagues often find it difficult to get him to commit on an issue. Carr's focus these days is almost entirely on Michigan and his district.

Appropriations is a good home for the new Carr. The media rarely penetrates its backroom deliberations; it is possible for a panel member to be diligent and practically invisible. Carr concentrates on mundane but politically valuable tasks, such as finding money for local highway improvements.

Where Carr shines most is on the Transportation Subcommittee. A pilot, he has a keen interest in the Federal Aviation Administration (FAA), and when aviation issues are discussed, he can speak eloquently on technically complex matters with no notes to guide him. His recognized expertise helps him influence other members, but leaves some of them wondering why he does not also apply his intellect to other issues.

Among Carr's aviation-related pursuits in the 100th Congress was finding a new jet for FAA officials. They were using a 28-year-old Lockheed Jetstar, and Carr had long advocated funding for a replacement. He also helped find the plane, researching the used-plane market and convincing colleagues to make the purchase.

Carr also led a fight to try to cut off funding for Boston's Logan Airport because the Massachusetts Port Authority was nearly tripling the landing fees for small planes while cutting the charge for larger commercial aircraft. The port authority said the move was needed to ease air-traffic congestion, but Carr said it discriminated against small-plane pilots and allowed the local government, rather than the federal government, to control air commerce. Carr wanted to cut off all federal funding to Logan, but in committee had to settle for a compromise that suspended the transportation funds until the Department of Transportation and the courts issued decisions on the fee plan. That compromise, however, was stripped from the transportation funding bill by the Rules Committee.

Where possible, Carr has tried to develop an image as a foe of wasteful spending. When Democrats pushed through a fiscal 1988 budget resolution that called for $18 billion in new taxes, Carr was one of only 19 members of his party to vote against it.

As a newcomer in the mid-1970s, Carr was an activist in a class of activists, unafraid of ruffling the feathers of the House power structure. In 1975, when President Ford requested new military aid for South Vietnam and Cambodia, Carr sponsored a Democratic Caucus resolution opposing the aid. He won, but the move frightened even some of the party's liber-

Michigan 6

Central — Lansing; Pontiac

The 6th stretches from the state capital of Lansing about 70 miles east to the manufacturing city of Pontiac. It is not easy territory for either party; any candidate trying to win it has to stitch votes together from its disparate communities.

The 52,000 residents of Lansing who live in the district — about two-fifths of the city's population — make up a politically marginal bloc. The upper-level professionals and executives in the northwest or in the Groesbeck section along Lansing's eastern edge turn in solid GOP votes, but state employees and younger professionals south of the Grand River are more independent. Democratic votes come from Eastern European and Hispanic blue-collar neighborhoods in the northeastern and southeastern sections.

East Lansing, with a student population of more than 40,000 at Michigan State University, is an important source of Democratic votes, although the students themselves have grown less liberal in the last decade. State government workers and university faculty in the suburban communities of Meridian Township and Okemos give those areas a Democratic tilt, but the business people and company managers who also live there exert a Republican influence.

The truck farms of eastern Ingham County stretch into neighboring Livingston County. During the 1970s, Livingston was the state's second fastest-growing county, though the population has stabilized in the 1980s. One of Michigan's most conservative areas, Livingston was settled by German Protestant farmers who made it a center of German-American Bund activism in the 1930s and a GOP stronghold; Democratic sympathizers trying for local office still run as nominal Republicans.

But the farm land in eastern Livingston County has been eaten up by development spurred by white flight from Lansing, Detroit, Flint and Pontiac. Townships such as Hartland and Hamburg more than doubled in size in the 1970s, and the newcomers moderated the conservative makeup of the county.

To the east is Oakland County; its major city, Pontiac, is made up of low-income blacks, Hispanics and socially conservative Southern whites — George C. Wallace got 51 percent of the vote here in the 1972 presidential primary. Just to the west of Pontiac is Waterford Township, also with a large community of blue-collar whites. They fluctuate politically: Reagan supporters in 1980, they went back to the Democratic ticket in 1982 as the auto industry slump pushed local unemployment toward 30 percent. Oakland County went Republican in the 1988 presidential election, but Democrat Carr has carried it in his last three elections.

Population: 514,559. White 464,591 (90%), Black 36,837 (7%), Other 5,760 (1%). Spanish origin 12,600 (2%). 18 and over 360,961 (70%), 65 and over 36,341 (7%). Median age: 26.

---

als who advocated a strong caucus, since it bypassed the regular committee system altogether. No legislative action that decisive has emerged from the caucus in the years since.

As one of the minority of "doves" on Armed Services, Carr was a constant critic of high military spending. He fought the B-1 bomber and new nuclear submarines, and again was willing to affront his more traditional colleagues. Carr in 1978 offered a floor amendment to a military procurement bill that would have replaced the entire version reported out by Armed Services. Senior committee members, even some dissatisfied with the bill, called his step an attack on the entire committee system; the amendment was soundly defeated.

At Home: Though Carr was a political newcomer when he first ran for the House in 1972, he performed surprisingly well against veteran GOP Rep. Charles E. Chamberlain, taking advantage of the new 18-year-old vote in the college town of East Lansing to come within 2,500 votes. When Chamberlain retired in 1974, Carr won the election to replace him.

Carr's liberalism seemed out of place in his traditionally GOP district, but his strong constituent service helped him defeat his next two challengers. After pulling in 57 percent in 1978, Carr looked secure.

But in 1980, conservative building contractor Jim Dunn poured money into a hard-hitting campaign. A complacent Carr failed at first to see the threat; when he did, it was too late.

After losing narrowly, there was little question Carr would try again in 1982. He was helped by a Democratic remap that removed several GOP counties from the 6th and added Pontiac, a Democratic stronghold, and its blue-collar suburbs. With the district's economy devastated by recession, Carr tied Dunn to Reaganomics and won back his seat.

Dunn bypassed the 1984 House race for an

unsuccessful GOP Senate primary bid. Carr prepared carefully anyway. He emphasized his work on district concerns, and collected over a half-million dollars.

His efforts paid off against Republican Tom Ritter, though not as richly as expected. Carr carried Oakland County with 57 percent and Ingham County with 53 percent. But Ritter, whose family produce business was a fixture in the 6th's eastern end, did well in Livingston County, and he held Carr to 52 percent. The slim margin emboldened Republicans.

Dunn's negative tone during his 1984 Senate primary against eventual nominee Jack Lousma angered many GOP insiders, but his image as Carr's strongest challenger forced them to shelve their reservations when Dunn decided to tackle Carr again in 1986.

From the outset, there was a bitter edge to Dunn's effort. Republican officials claimed Carr owned an airplane, a horse and a Florida condo, but did not have a district residence because he said he could not afford homes in both Washington and Michigan.

Carr denied each charge. He claimed he did have a district residence — a rented room in a friend's East Lansing home. He also said he had sold his airplane and the Florida home, which was built for his mother; the horse, Carr said, belonged to his estranged wife.

Dunn resurrected a 14-year-old newspaper article in which Carr supported marijuana decriminalization. Carr said he had changed his opinions on many issues and noted that Dunn campaigned as a foe of abortion, but had voted for federal abortion funding in the House.

The campaign moved from bitter to bizarre in its closing days. *The Detroit News* reported that Carr's wife Susan had amended her divorce action to request an annulment, charging that Carr failed to inform her at the time of their 1980 marriage that he had "a highly contagious and incurable social disease" that "would prevent child bearing as well as adversely affecting marital relations." The information came from a caller identifying herself as a member of Susan Carr's family. Carr adamantly denied the charges, and claimed they were timed to affect the election outcome.

Despite Dunn's attacks and the last-minute hint of scandal, Carr won with surprising ease. Republicans blamed Dunn's lopsided defeat on Democratic ticket-leader James J. Blanchard's landslide gubernatorial re-election. But Carr's campaign said there was a public backlash against Dunn's negative campaigning.

In 1988, the local GOP was not up for another vigorous assault. Against little-known stockbrocker Scott Schultz, Carr reached 60 percent for the first time in his House career.

Committees

Appropriations (28th of 35 Democrats)
Commerce, Justice and State, the Judiciary and Related Agencies; District of Columbia; Transportation and Related Agencies

Select Hunger (7th of 18 Democrats)
Task Force: International

Elections

1988 General		
Bob Carr (D)	120,581	(59%)
Scott Schultz (R)	81,079	(40%)
1986 General		
Bob Carr (D)	74,927	(57%)
Jim Dunn (R)	57,283	(43%)

Previous Winning Percentages: **1984** (52%) **1982** (51%) **1978** (57%) **1976** (53%) **1974** (49%)

District Vote For President

	1988	1984	1980	1976
D	89,344 (42%)	72,935 (35%)	85,927 (38%)	80,770 (39%)
R	121,258 (57%)	133,362 (64%)	114,729 (50%)	120,518 (58%)
I			23,452 (10%)	

Campaign Finance

	Receipts	Receipts from PACs	Expend-itures
1988			
Carr (D)	$534,741	$277,823 (52%)	$504,217
Schultz (R)	$82,562	$7,910 (10%)	$81,586
1986			
Carr (D)	$734,919	$448,672 (61%)	$692,787
Dunn (R)	$247,463	$36,600 (15%)	$244,913

Key Votes

1987	
Raise speed limit to 65 mph	Y
Approve Gephardt "fair trade" amendment	Y
Ban testing of larger nuclear weapons	Y
Delay "re-flagging" of Kuwaiti tankers	Y
Approve tax-raising deficit-reduction bill	N
1988	
Approve aid to Nicaraguan contras	N
Enact civil rights restoration bill over Reagan veto	Y
Kill 60-day plant-closing notification measure	N
Pass omnibus trade bill over Reagan veto	Y
Approve death penalty for drug-related murders	Y
Bar federal funds for abortions in cases of rape and incest	?
Oppose seven-day waiting period for purchase of handguns	Y

Voting Studies

	Presidential Support		Party Unity		Conservative Coalition	
Year	S	O	S	O	S	O
1988	31	65	80	10	50	47
1987	21	74	82	11	40	56
1986	21	74	75	21	56	44
1985	29	68	81	14	38	56
1984	26	72	87	11	34	66
1983	12	83	86	10	25	72

Interest Group Ratings

Year	ADA	ACU	AFL-CIO	CCUS
1988	80	21	93	46
1987	88	9	100	31
1986	70	24	86	33
1985	65	15	76	50
1984	80	22	85	38
1983	85	17	88	10

7 Dale E. Kildee (D)

Of Flint — Elected 1976

Born: Sept. 16, 1929, Flint, Mich.
Education: Sacred Heart Seminary, B.A. 1952; U. of Detroit, teaching certificate, 1954; U. of Peshawar, Pakistan, Rotary Fellowship, 1958-59; U. of Michigan, M.A. 1961.
Occupation: Teacher.
Family: Wife, Gayle Heyn; three children.
Religion: Roman Catholic.
Political Career: Mich. House, 1965-75; Mich. Senate, 1975-77.
Capitol Office: 2262 Rayburn Bldg. 20515; 225-3611.

In Washington: When conservatives grumble about liberal do-gooders who find it hard to resist any worthy cause, Kildee is the type they have in mind. A former divinity student who switched to political science, he seems to treat politics as an extension of his former calling. His official biography describes his congressional endeavors as based "on the themes of human dignity and quality of life."

In the House, Kildee champions most all social programs to aid the poor, the elderly and the very young. Back in Michigan, he is known to fill out tax forms for senior citizens and help fix their leaky roofs. He was one of the first members of Congress to install a special telephone in his office so he could communicate with deaf callers.

Kildee spent most of the 1980s doggedly fighting Reagan administration budget cuts. In an era when many philosophical debates boil down to bottom-line budget choices, he is no accountant: He simply tries to help as many people as he can, as much as he can. Early in Reagan's first term, Kildee voted present rather than accept $12 billion in cuts in social programs. "I don't know about minuends and subtrahends," he said. "I'm used to addition and multiplication."

At the start of the 101st Congress, Kildee won a coveted seat on the Budget Committee. He was one of a handful of members backed for a Budget berth by Jim Wright, whom Kildee had endorsed early for Speaker.

While there is little doubt how Kildee will vote on most budget questions — he says he will take "a cautious approach to defense spending and a senstive approach to human need" — the Flint Democrat is unlikely to be a militant liberal on the committee. Though he debates with a degree of philosophical purity, he is more comfortable in coalitions than crusades; bare-knuckles power politicking he leaves to others.

Kildee has devoted most of his energy to his work on the Education and Labor Committee, where he is chairman of the Human Resources Subcommittee. In that role, he was chief sponsor in the 99th Congress of the Older Americans Act, which authorized programs ranging from meals-on-wheels to legal services for senior citizens. He subsequently fought for across-the-board funding increases for those programs, and advocated a new program to provide in-home care for the frail elderly. Kildee described the program as "morally more sound because it really respects their dignity — home is where they want to remain. And fiscally, it's more sound because it's much less expensive than putting them in a home."

Kildee's more ambitious schemes for social welfare rarely made it very far during the Reagan era, but his Act for Better Child Care Services — the ABC bill sponsored by Connecticut Democrat Christopher J. Dodd in the Senate — became a touchstone for Democratic candidates in 1988.

The $2.5 billion bill would have set minimum health and safety standards for child care facilities and provided vouchers for low- and middle-income parents and subsidies for child care providers. While Republicans advocated tax credits instead, the real snag on the ABC bill was whether and how to allow religiously affiliated child care providers to receive federal aid.

Seeking compromise, Kildee suggested requiring that government-funded child care slots be open to children of all religions, and dropping a ban on hiring based on religion. But that brought threats of a lawsuit from the American Civil Liberties Union, contributing to the bill's demise in the 100th Congress.

On another major bill — the omnibus education bill in 1987 — Kildee was a key negotiator on bilingual education, but the deal he helped strike to ensure passage was as much capitulation as compromise. The massive reauthorization was threatened by Republican demands to increase funding for programs that use English-only methods instead of native-

Michigan 7

East Central — Flint

This is the most Democratic district in the state outside the Detroit area. About 80 percent of the vote is cast in Flint and surrounding Genesee County, and while the out-county portions of Genesee are politically mixed, the city itself leaves no doubt about its partisan leanings. It swam against the Reagan tides both in 1980 and 1984, although the outlying GOP vote in Genesee enabled Reagan to win the overall county vote in 1984. Michael S. Dukakis got 60 percent in Genesee County in 1988.

Flint has always made its living from General Motors and its Chevrolet, Buick, AC Spark Plug and Fisher Body plants. The United Auto Workers (UAW) is the most potent political force in the city; if the union's endorsement no longer translates directly into rank-and-file votes, it does guarantee volunteers and financial support. Many of the white UAW members arrived in Flint from the South after World War II. George C. Wallace took 15 percent in Genesee County in 1968, his best performance in any of Michigan's urban areas.

Flint has been harmed by its overwhelming reliance on the auto industry. While the well-to-do professionals have stayed put, the empty houses and broken windows of Flint's north side reflect a gloomy statistic: The city has lost more than 40,000 of its residents in the last two decades. The new Great Lakes Technology Center, an $80 million project housed in a renovated auto plant, will employ more than 4,000 design engineers.

Much of the area encircling Flint consists of Democratic and racially mixed blue-collar communities, particularly in Mount Morris and Genesee townships. The GOP is strongest in the southeast corner of the county around the white-collar suburbs of Atlas and Goodrich and in the wealthy developments of Grand Blanc Township.

The 7th includes nearly all of Genesee County's eastern neighbor, largely agricultural Lapeer County. The farmers in the area used migrant labor until several years ago, and the county has small enclaves of Indochinese and Hispanic residents.

Some of suburban Flint's development has spilled over into western Lapeer, where UAW members from Flint's auto plants give the area a Democratic cast. Farther east in Lapeer, the influence of rural Republicans is strong, often strong enough to tilt the overall county vote to the GOP.

Population: 514,560. White 425,935 (83%), Black 78,880 (15%), Other 4,873 (1%). Spanish origin 8,873 (2%). 18 and over 346,868 (67%), 65 and over 40,344 (8%). Median age: 28.

language instruction. Kildee and GOP Rep. Steve Bartlett of Texas sought a middle ground between the two, but when none could be found, the GOP demands by and large prevailed. Hispanic House members were furious. "It was not a happy compromise," Kildee said. "There would be wounds no matter what we would do. This preserved bilingual education and minimized bloodletting."

In the 99th Congress, Kildee was the floor manager of omnibus legislation reauthorizing a variety of social programs, including the Community Services Block Grant program, the Native Americans Program Act of 1974, and the Low-Income Energy Assistance Act. During debate on this bill, he warned against a proposal to delete $7.5 million in funding for Follow Through, a demonstration program designed to meet the continuing needs of Head Start graduates. "That $7.5 million would not even be a blip on [Defense Secretary] Cap Weinberger's computer," Kildee argued. "Hey, Cap, leave the kids alone. Get your money someplace else."

Kildee is also a strong labor loyalist. In his six terms, he has maintained an average AFL-CIO rating of over 90 percent, scoring perfect 100s in the last three Congresses.

On the Interior Committee, Kildee has been a reliable vote for conservationists. In the 100th Congress, he authored legislation to protect over 91,000 acres of forest land in Michigan. (He is on leave from the committee in the 101st.)

As a freshman congressman in 1977, Kildee launched a crusade against child pornography. Revelations in his hometown of Flint about a growing trade in obscene photos of children set off a flurry of letters to him in Washington. He decided to draft a bill setting heavy criminal penalties for using children in pornographic films and photographs.

Kildee was convinced a bill like that would be impossible to oppose on the House floor. But to get to the floor, it had to go through the Judiciary Committee, where Michigan Democrat John Conyers Jr., chairman of the Criminal Justice Subcommittee, considered it a violation of First Amendment rights. Kildee then rewrote the bill so it could be considered by his Education and Labor Committee. He offered it as an amendment to child-abuse legislation, and it passed. Later Conyers conceded and moved a milder bill through his own panel. By 1981, child pornography penalties had become law.

At Home: As a Democrat from the General Motors town of Flint, Kildee draws his political strength from the labor movement he supports in Washington.

The United Auto Workers and the AFL-CIO have deserted him only once — when he first ran for Congress in 1976. Trying to succeed five-term Rep. Donald W. Riegle Jr., who was running for the Senate, Kildee left a state Senate seat he had won only two years before. Labor, which had worked exceptionally hard to help Kildee oust a 26-year state Senate veteran in 1974, felt he should have served out his four-year term. But Kildee insisted on making his move.

Winning was relatively easy, even with division in the ranks of labor. Kildee beat a local union official with 76 percent in the Democratic primary and went on to trounce his general-election opponent. Since then, he has never won less than 75 percent in an election.

After giving up his plans to be a priest, Kildee spent a year studying in Pakistan, then returned to Michigan to teach Latin. By the time he arrived in the Michigan Legislature, he was a political maverick. During his brief state Senate career, he earned the animosity of some of his colleagues as self-appointed head of the "conscience caucus." He attacked the use of state funds for redecorating senators' offices. Kildee also pushed through a "truth in packaging" bill and an act to guarantee civil rights to the handicapped.

Committees

Budget (13th of 21 Democrats)
Task Forces: Community Development and Natural Resources; Human Resources

Education and Labor (7th of 22 Democrats)
Human Resources (chairman); Elementary, Secondary and Vocational Education; Labor-Management Relations

Elections

1988 General

Dale E. Kildee (D)	150,832	(76%)
Jeff Coad (R)	47,071	(24%)

1986 General

Dale E. Kildee (D)	101,225	(80%)
Trudie Callihan (R)	24,848	(20%)

Previous Winning Percentages: **1984** (93%) **1982** (75%) **1980** (93%) **1978** (77%) **1976** (70%)

District Vote For President

	1988	1984	1980	1976
D	112,101 (56%)	94,715 (46%)	98,309 (47%)	95,588 (50%)
R	88,166 (44%)	111,228 (54%)	94,845 (45%)	91,817 (48%)
I			14,107 (7%)	

Campaign Finance

	Receipts	Receipts from PACs	Expend-itures
1988			
Kildee (D)	$152,246	$103,770 (68%)	$150,594
Coad (R)	$1,310	0	$1,310
1986			
Kildee (D)	$96,112	$80,510 (84%)	$101,545

Key Votes

1987

Raise speed limit to 65 mph	N
Approve Gephardt "fair trade" amendment	Y
Ban testing of larger nuclear weapons	Y
Delay "re-flagging" of Kuwaiti tankers	Y
Approve tax-raising deficit-reduction bill	Y

1988

Approve aid to Nicaraguan contras	N
Enact civil rights restoration bill over Reagan veto	Y
Kill 60-day plant-closing notification measure	N
Pass omnibus trade bill over Reagan veto	Y
Approve death penalty for drug-related murders	N
Bar federal funds for abortions in cases of rape and incest	Y
Oppose seven-day waiting period for purchase of handguns	N

Voting Studies

	Presidential Support		Party Unity		Conservative Coalition	
Year	**S**	**O**	**S**	**O**	**S**	**O**
1988	17	83	95	5	11	89
1987	16	84	98	2	0	100
1986	13	87	97	2	6	94
1985	18	78	94	3	4	96
1984	26	74	94	6	7	93
1983	11	89	92	8	9	91
1982	36	64	92	8	10	90
1981	26	74	90	10	15	85

Interest Group Ratings

Year	ADA	ACU	AFL-CIO	CCUS
1988	95	4	100	14
1987	96	4	100	7
1986	95	0	100	17
1985	85	5	100	25
1984	95	8	100	38
1983	90	13	100	5
1982	95	9	100	23
1981	90	0	80	5

8 Bob Traxler (D)

Of Bay City — Elected 1974

Born: July 21, 1931, Kawkawlin, Mich.
Education: Michigan State U., B.A. 1952; Detroit College of Law, LL.B. 1959.
Military Career: Army, 1953-55.
Occupation: Lawyer.
Family: Divorced; three children.
Religion: Episcopalian.
Political Career: Mich. House, 1963-74.
Capitol Office: 2366 Rayburn Bldg. 20515; 225-2806.

In Washington: Traxler has a boisterous sense of humor that can border on clownishness, but he makes all the appropriate moves on the Appropriations Committee. It is evident on the powerful panel, where he has recently joined the "College of Cardinals" — the 13 subcommittee chairmen — and in his Michigan district, which tends to fare well in the appropriations process.

Traxler has less of a media presence than many members of Congress, but he has accumulated considerable power since his 1974 election, and is in a position to gain even more. He mastered the appropriations process working on subcommittees with two very able legislators, Jamie L. Whitten of Mississippi on Agriculture and Edward P. Boland of Massachusetts on Housing and Urban Development. The latter panel fell to Traxler in 1989 after Boland retired, and he will remain a force on Agriculture, where he ranks second behind the 79-year-old chairman.

On the HUD panel, Traxler always worked well with Boland, not only on housing issues but also on the question of funding for space and science research. He has argued against some of the strictest proposed cutbacks for the National Aeronautics and Space Administration and the National Science Foundation. Boosters of a manned space station see Traxler as a legislator sympathetic to their expensive cause.

On Agriculture, Traxler has learned at the feet of Whitten, a master appropriator and chairman of the full committee. For Whitten, Traxler has been an important bridge to the Agriculture Committee when it comes to formulating agricultural spending plans. When the House sets to work on farm-disaster legislation, as it did in 1987 after frost and flooding, or in 1988 after a drought, it is a sure bet that Traxler will play an important role. In particular he sees to it that "non-program" crops, such as the dry beans grown in Michigan, are covered. The Agriculture Committee tends to be dominated by representatives of crops in federal programs, making a voice like Traxler's important to growers of sugar beets, dry beans and potatoes.

In 1986, Traxler authored a bill to give growers of dry beans, potatoes and other vegetables equal treatment with corn, cotton and rice growers under legislation paying farmers to take land out of production. The bill became law as part of a package of amendments to the 1985 farm bill.

Traxler also takes care to provide funds to special projects in his district. He regularly steers funding to Michigan State University to study such things as blueberry shoestring virus and asparagus-yield decline. Press releases tout his efforts, including delivery of federal grants, funds for a veterans' hospital, and support for farmers.

Traxler has devoted a considerable portion of his attention over the years to the auto industry, which is crucial to the health of Bay City and Saginaw, his district's two population centers. Along with Detroit-area Democrat John D. Dingell, Traxler has helped the industry fight off efforts to force the installation of air bags in new cars.

But Traxler is not insensitive to environmental issues — his district is just downstream from the city of Midland, where dioxin pollution from a Dow Chemical facility has been a focus of controversy. In the 1984 HUD-Independent Agencies funding bill, Traxler tacked on a section requiring the Environmental Protection Agency to add the Saginaw Bay area to its national dioxin monitoring program.

Normally one of the more popular members, Traxler probably lost a few friends in 1982 with his amendment to freeze House pay. He said he agreed members deserved more than the $60,660 they were earning annually, but that with the recession, "the timing is very poor." In a dramatic seesaw vote, Traxler first seemed to lose, then to win, and then finally lost as House leaders prolonged the roll call and twisted the necessary arms to defeat him on a 208-208 tie. House pay was thus increased to $69,000. Since then, it has risen to $89,500.

Early in the 101st Congress, Traxler sided

Michigan 8

East — Bay City; Saginaw

When singer-songwriter Paul Simon took off to look for America in the late 1960s, he began in Saginaw, taking four days to hitchhike east. In more recent, less prosperous days, entire families have been leaving Saginaw, but they have headed south looking for work.

Saginaw and Bay City, centers of Democratic strength in the 8th, each lost 16 percent of their population over the 1970s and another 4 percent in the early 1980s, while the Republican counties of Michigan's rural Thumb were growing. The Bay City-Saginaw corridor now has less than one-third of the 8th's residents.

Along the Saginaw River from Bay City to Saginaw is a gray industrial strip of auto plants, chemical and cement factories, tool-and-die shops and port facilities. White ethnics, blacks and Hispanics in Saginaw gave Jimmy Carter 58 percent of the city's vote in 1980 at the same time that Saginaw County as a whole went for Ronald Reagan. In 1988, Democrat Michael S. Dukakis carried the county by 3,175 votes. Bay City's politically active blue-collar Poles join with steel and chemical workers between there and Midland to anchor Democratic strength in Bay County.

While northern Bay County's generally poor farm land gave rise to a Democratic-leaning impoverished rural sector, the rich soil of the Saginaw Valley south of Saginaw produced a well-off and conservative agricultural community specializing in potatoes, dry beans and soft white winter wheat. German Lutheran influence is strong in the eastern part of the county, particularly around the well-kept town of Frankenmuth, whose prosperous burghers live in neat, brown-trimmed Bavarian-style houses.

Arenac County, north of Bay County, is a small, forested area whose proximity both to I-75 and Lake Huron has made it a popular vacation spot and home for retired autoworkers. The United Auto Workers' influence in Arenac County has put it in the Democratic column in recent contests for U.S. Senate and governor. In 1988, Dukakis took 51 percent in Arenac.

Once heavily timbered, the vast flat reaches of Michigan's Thumb now bear sugar beets and dry beans, corn and wheat. The state's top two dairy counties are Sanilac and Huron; the latter has more than twice as many cows as people. The long Lake Huron coastline stretching around the Thumb is dotted with small fishing villages and lakeside resorts. The only heavy industry is in the huge tool-and-die plants at Sebewaing and Elkton at the western end of Huron County.

Although Traxler has made inroads in the Thumb, most of its voters remain die-hard Republicans. Sanilac County, for example, gave 49 percent of its 1988 House vote to Traxler's long-shot GOP opponent.

Population: 514,560. White 463,068 (90%), Black 37,197 (7%), Other 3,457 (1%). Spanish origin 17,488 (3%). 18 and over 350,577 (68%), 65 and over 53,116 (10%). Median age: 29.

with the overwhelming majority in voting against an increase of 51 percent.

At Home: Traxler came to Washington in 1974 amid as much attention as any House newcomer had received in years. He had turned his special election campaign into a referendum on President Richard M. Nixon in the midst of the unfolding Watergate scandal. Traxler called his Republican opponent, James M. Sparling, a "stand-in for Mr. Nixon," who stumped for Sparling in the district against the advice of some local GOP leaders.

With help from organized labor, the Democrat won just enough votes in the urbanized counties to offset his opponent's strength in the rural Thumb region — the area Nixon visited on his whistle-stop tour. Traxler became the first Democrat in 42 years to represent some parts of the district.

Many thought that with Nixon gone by the next election, voters in the 8th would revert to their traditional GOP habits. But Traxler's combination of populism and gregarious constituent relations gave him a firm lock on the 8th, and re-election never has been a problem.

Traxler wins by 2-to-1 and better in Saginaw and Bay City, and has even brought to his side many of the bean and sugar beet farmers in the Republican Thumb; that affable appeal to rural Thumb voters should cushion Traxler as economic change causes the cities to lose population and voting strength.

During 11 years representing Bay City in the Michigan House, Traxler was rated as one of the more able legislators. One of his most conspicuous crusades was for a bill to allow bingo games in churches, a successful campaign that gave him the nickname "Bingo Bob." (which he still carries in the House). As the chairman of the state Judiciary Committee, he helped to modernize the Michigan district court system.

Committee

Appropriations (11th of 35 Democrats)
VA, HUD and Independent Agencies (chairman); Legislative Branch; Rural Development, Agriculture and Related Agencies

Elections

1988 General

Bob Traxler (D)	139,904	(72%)
Lloyd F. Buhl (R)	54,195	(28%)

1986 General

Bob Traxler (D)	97,406	(73%)
John A. Levi (R)	36,695	(27%)

Previous Winning Percentages: **1984** (64%) **1982** (91%) **1980** (61%) **1978** (67%) **1976** (59%) **1974** (55%) **1974 *** (52%)

** Special election.*

District Vote For President

	1988	1984	1980	1976
D	101,006 (49%)	80,321 (39%)	88,369 (41%)	88,638 (45%)
R	102,608 (50%)	123,682 (60%)	113,128 (52%)	107,682 (54%)
I			13,552 (6%)	

Campaign Finance

	Receipts	Receipts from PACs	Expend-itures
1988			
Traxler (D)	$238,000	$148,987 (63%)	$128,400
Buhl (R) †	$4,847	0	$2,188
1986			
Traxler (D)	$149,142	$90,112 (60%)	$98,670
Levi (R)	$32,047	$1,200 (4%)	$31,955

† Totals based on incomplete data.

Key Votes

1987	
Raise speed limit to 65 mph	?
Approve Gephardt "fair trade" amendment	Y
Ban testing of larger nuclear weapons	Y
Delay "re-flagging" of Kuwaiti tankers	Y
Approve tax-raising deficit-reduction bill	Y
1988	
Approve aid to Nicaraguan contras	N
Enact civil rights restoration bill over Reagan veto	Y
Kill 60-day plant-closing notification measure	N
Pass omnibus trade bill over Reagan veto	Y
Approve death penalty for drug-related murders	N
Bar federal funds for abortions in cases of rape and incest	Y
Oppose seven-day waiting period for purchase of handguns	Y

Voting Studies

	Presidential Support		Party Unity		Conservative Coalition	
Year	**S**	**O**	**S**	**O**	**S**	**O**
1988	19	73	84	7	26	68
1987	23	73	86	5	28	60
1986	19	73	79	7	34	54
1985	26	74	83	5	16	71
1984	28	59	80	8	22	66
1983	6	88	82	8	24	70
1982	27	61	84	7	25	68
1981	39	57	79	14	37	56

Interest Group Ratings

Year	ADA	ACU	AFL-CIO	CCUS
1988	80	14	100	21
1987	80	4	94	14
1986	80	9	100	29
1985	80	5	88	27
1984	70	25	69	46
1983	90	22	100	5
1982	75	21	100	19
1981	65	20	73	17

9 Guy Vander Jagt (R)

Of Luther — Elected 1966

Born: Aug. 26, 1931, Cadillac, Mich.
Education: Hope College, A.B. 1953; Yale U., B.D. 1955; Bonn U., Rotary Fellowship, 1956; U. of Michigan, LL.B. 1960.
Occupation: Lawyer.
Family: Wife, Carol Doorn; one child.
Religion: Presbyterian.
Political Career: Mich. Senate, 1965-66.
Capitol Office: 2409 Rayburn Bldg. 20515; 225-3511.

In Washington: The horizons seemed limitless for Vander Jagt as the 1980s dawned. He was bathing in accolades for his stewardship of the National Republican Congressional Committee (NRCC). The NRCC's huge edge over its Democratic counterpart in fund raising and computer technology was widely noted. The committee's slogan — "Vote Republican, For a Change" — had produced big GOP House gains and reinforced Ronald Reagan's conservative presidential campaign message.

Vander Jagt boasted then that Reagan's leadership would lift the Republicans to a House majority. He even promoted himself as a leader for those surging Republicans, running an aggressive though unsuccessful campaign for minority leader in 1981.

What a difference a decade can make.

A GOP House backslide during the 1982 recession preceded a partisan standoff in Reagan's no-coattails 1984 re-election. In the final House elections of the 1980s, Republicans suffered a three-seat loss even as George Bush swept to the presidency. The total number of GOP House seats in the 101st Congress was 175 — 17 fewer than the party held in 1981.

During the 1980s, a revived Democratic Congressional Campaign Committee made major gains in both fund-raising capacity and campaign technology. By 1989, Republican grumblings about a "dead in the water" NRCC were being widely voiced, accompanied by comments that Vander Jagt's earlier reputation as a political strategist was vastly overblown.

By no means was Vander Jagt held solely responsible for the failure of the GOP to attain a House majority. Factors beyond his control — redistricting and the power of incumbency, for instance — played a large role. Some of his advocates even credited him for helping the GOP avoid the cataclysmic midterm losses (in 1982 and 1986) that had been traditional for the party in the White House.

Vander Jagt was also insulated by the personal chits he had earned in his tireless campaign-year efforts. Using his well-honed skills as an orator and fund-raiser, Vander Jagt has assisted practically every Republican House member elected since 1976.

But while Vander Jagt retains much good will within House GOP ranks, there was an overriding sense among Republicans following the 1988 elections that the NRCC needed reinvigoration. So in January 1989, the national party leadership installed an aggressive new team of political operatives, led by Executive Director Edward J. Rollins, to replace the bureaucratic types who had been running the NRCC machinery.

Vander Jagt remains as the committee's top elected official, its spokesman and emissary to hundreds of Republican House candidates. But he is likely to be overshadowed at the national level by Rollins, a former political adviser to President Reagan who announced plans for a full assault on the majority Democrats in 1990 shortly after his appointment. (Republican defeats in two of the three House special elections in early 1989 made it clear that Rollins' road will be a tough one.)

When Rollins was brought in, Vander Jagt hailed him as a "superstar." The veteran incumbent seemed cognizant of the fact that a continued failure to restore the NRCC's competitive edge could have soured his long-term prospects as chairman — a position to which he has virtually dedicated his House career.

Vander Jagt's congressional efforts appeared to lack focus until 1975, when he took over the NRCC chairmanship. He came on board at a time when the committee was developing the innovative campaign tools — campaign schools for budding candidates, a sophisticated year-round polling operation and commercials on prime-time network television — that were to make it a focus of political attention over the next few years.

The payoff for these efforts was not immediate. It seemed at first that Vander Jagt would spend the rest of his career living down his prediction of a Republican House gain of "76 in '76"; the party lost two seats as Democrat Jimmy Carter won the presidency. However, early restiveness over Carter's leadership en-

Michigan 9

West — Muskegon; Traverse City

The Republican 9th covers 150 miles of Lake Michigan shoreline, but it is dominated politically by its two southernmost lakeshore counties, Muskegon and Ottawa, which together hold more than half its residents.

Ottawa County remains the Republican anchor, even though part of it was transferred to the 4th in 1982 redistricting. Ottawa, one of just three Michigan counties to vote Republican in every presidential election since 1960, gave Reagan his highest percentages in the state in 1980 and 1984. In 1988, it voted for George Bush by better than 3-to-1, and gave 68 percent to the GOP's ill-fated Senate nominee, Jim Dunn. Many of those Republican votes were cast in conservative Dutch towns like white-collar Zeeland, by fruit and grain farmers in the county's northern reaches, and in the fast-growing towns west of the border with Kent County (Grand Rapids).

Democrats' strongest constituency in the 9th is in and around the city of Muskegon. A community of 40,000, Muskegon first rose out of the sawdust of Michigan's lumbering era. More recently, the city has built up one of western Michigan's heaviest manufacturing bases, turning out auto parts, tank engines, cranes and hoists, paper, bowling equipment and office furniture.

Democratic strength is highest in the city's ethnic blue-collar neighborhoods, in the black precincts inland from the shore and in black-majority Muskegon Heights. But the party's vote in the city is generally offset by GOP margins from North Muskegon, upper-middle-class suburbs like Norton Shores and Roosevelt Park and farm areas north of Muskegon.

The rest of the 9th District consists of sparsely populated counties whose chief industries are farming, tourism and food processing. Fremont, in Newaygo County, is international headquarters for Gerber baby foods, while Oceana County's fruits and asparagus are processed in towns such as Pentwater and Shelby. The orchards in Leelanau and Benzie counties produce 40 percent of the country's tart cherries and a quarter of its sweet cherries. Towns all along the shore draw retirees and summertime residents, and the inland lakes and forests pull in hikers and hunters year-round.

Population: 514,560. White 481,640 (94%), Black 23,294 (5%), Other 4,416 (1%). Spanish origin 9,909 (2%). 18 and over 356,896 (69%), 65 and over 58,147 (11%). Median age: 29.

abled the Republicans to post an 11-seat gain in 1978.

Republican plaudits for the NRCC began piling up, and Vander Jagt got much of the credit. He was building the committee into a huge public-relations apparatus, one that promoted Vander Jagt's own ideas and image in a glossy magazine every month. His name was on the checks that the NRCC was donating to GOP House challengers across the country. Vander Jagt was chosen to give the keynote speech at the 1980 Republican National Convention, at which he was briefly mentioned as a vice presidential possibility.

In 1980, as Reagan swept Carter from office, the NRCC not only orchestrated a whopping 33-seat pickup, but also helped set the political agenda with an ad campaign centered on the "Change" slogan. Vander Jagt still insists it was the House Republican campaign that carried Reagan, and not the other way around.

The rave reviews he received after 1980 emboldened Vander Jagt to take on Robert H. Michel of Illinois for the Republican House leadership the next year. The effort challenged a basic principle of House leadership contests: Serious candidates have to prove themselves in the legislative process. Vander Jagt, by his own admission, was no parliamentary strategist; he had rarely appeared on the floor during the preceding four years, except to vote.

Vander Jagt argued that the party needed an eloquent House spokesman rather than a tactician like Michel. "We need someone who can project to the American public," he said. "... Inevitably one winds up on 'Face the Nation' or 'Meet the Press.' I think I would be a more forceful spokesman than Bob Michel." He also said he would supply "aggressive confrontation" with the Democratic majority when it was needed.

That argument might have been stronger had Reagan not been elected president, obviating the need for a new party spokesman. Michel was forced to work hard, but he managed to hold Vander Jagt off by 16 votes.

This close but failed campaign marked the apogee of Vander Jagt's national prominence. An economic downturn, the most serious since the Great Depression, hit prior to the 1982 elections. That year, NRCC officials agreed to the campaign theme of "Stay the Course" urged upon them by the Reagan White House. It was not much of a safety net for GOP candidates in recession-burdened districts. In the face of Vander Jagt's contention that Republicans would make "substantial and significant gains" anyway, the Democrats regained 26 House seats that November.

The national mood had changed drastically by 1984, when Reagan rode a strong economic recovery to re-election. But Reagan's don't-rock-the-boat "Morning in America" theme undercut NRCC efforts to develop a case for the sweeping change needed to upset the "permanent" House Democratic majority. Despite the imminent Reagan landslide, Vander Jagt resisted hyperbole and predicted modest GOP House gains. This time, he was right; the Republicans picked up 14 seats.

By the late 1980s, House politics had faded into the background of the nation's political consciousness. Even Vander Jagt appeared to lose some interest. In 1986, a year in which the Democrats made a minor gain of five seats, Vander Jagt spent much of the campaign on a quixotic effort to repeal the constitutional amendment that barred presidents from pursuing third terms.

The NRCC's strong influence over individual Republican House campaigns also appeared to be waning. Describing the committee's ability to steer campaign money, Vander Jagt once said, "If we smile on a candidate, that candidate's fortunes zoom; if we frown, his fortunes plummet." But in 1988, several GOP challengers complained that the NRCC had failed to communicate effectively with them, and failed to help them raise money from political action committees (PACs) and other sources.

Vander Jagt blamed the problem on business-oriented PACs and their increasing tendency to play it safe and give to Democratic incumbents favored for re-election rather than to conservative Republican challengers. In October 1988, Vander Jagt cosigned a letter with Michel warning PACs that Republicans "find it disturbing to see so many contributions going to members who consistently oppose the interests you and other business leaders advocate."

In December, the Republican Conference — voting for the first time on a position previously appointed by the minority leader — unanimously elected Vander Jagt to an eighth two-year term as NRCC chairman. But the appointment of the hard-charging Rollins as executive director made it clear there was some frustration within the party over recent NRCC efforts.

Vander Jagt's partisan labors have clearly exceeded his legislative achievements during a House career of nearly a quarter-century. Though he has risen to the second-ranking Republican position on the high-profile Ways and Means Committee, Vander Jagt is known as neither a legislative crusader nor a craftsman.

Ways and Means colleagues do credit Vander Jagt with being attentive to the committee's business, which can be challenging for him given his extensive travel schedule on behalf of GOP candidates. He served on the House-Senate conference committees that ironed out the final versions of the trade and welfare-reform bills enacted in the 100th Congress. He also worked on legislation making technical corrections to the 1986 tax-revision law, adding an amendment to extend a provision benefiting companies with employer-funded tuition plans.

Vander Jagt also makes a special effort on behalf of his western Michigan district and other state interests. In 1988, he lobbied successfully for the inclusion of a provision in the U.S.-Canada free-trade agreement, calling for country-of-origin labeling of Michigan apple juice concentrate. His proposal to remedy a Medicare reimbursement problem affecting 51 hospitals nationwide, including 15 in Michigan, was enacted during the 100th Congress.

The big issues that come before Ways and Means usually find other champions, though. In 1985, as the deliberations over the wide-ranging trade bill were coming to a head, Vander Jagt voluntarily gave up the ranking Republican position on the Trade Subcommittee, telling colleagues that it was too time-consuming. He took a less demanding job as ranking member on the Select Revenue Measures Subcommittee.

Vander Jagt was generally known in his first years in the House as a moderate Republican in the tradition of his close friend George W. Romney, then Michigan's governor. Vander Jagt's early work against pollution gave him a reputation as an environmentalist. But when he assumed the NRCC chairmanship, he was moving to the right. The limited work he did on Ways and Means in the late 1970s added to the newer image, enabling him to campaign credibly against Michel in 1980 as the conservative choice.

Vander Jagt maintained this mien during the major legislative battles between the Reagan administration and the House Democratic majority. In the 100th Congress, for instance, Vander Jagt was one of a handful of members of either party to vote to sustain Reagan vetoes of the Clean Water Act and the Civil Rights Restoration Act. He was an outspoken supporter of Reagan's final, and futile, effort to provide $36 million in aid to the Nicaraguan contras in 1988.

But while Vander Jagt's overall voting record placed him as a solid Reagan loyalist, it did not rank him among the hardest-line Republican conservatives. During the 100th Congress, Vander Jagt opposed Reagan's position on House legislation more than one-third of the time.

At Home: Traveling the country as campaign chairman is a job for someone who can afford to let his district take care of itself. Vander Jagt can. Since his first election in 1966, he has won less than 60 percent of the vote only one time, in 1974, the year of Watergate. This security gives Vander Jagt time to stump for other GOP candidates and pursue his other political interests.

The son of a livestock dealer and farmer, Vander Jagt grew up on a 120-acre farm near Cadillac. He originally thought the ministry would be a good place to exercise his oratorical skills, but after earning a divinity degree he decided to be a lawyer. He paid for law school with money he made working part time at various radio stations.

After four years practicing law in Grand Rapids with Harold Sawyer, who represented the 5th District from 1977 to 1985, Vander Jagt returned to Cadillac and easily won a state Senate seat. In 1966, when 9th District Rep. Robert P. Griffin was appointed to a Senate vacancy, Vander Jagt announced for Congress and easily won the special election and the one for the full term — both held the same day. His percentage was the highest of any GOP newcomer elected that year.

Committees

Ways and Means (2nd of 13 Republicans)
Select Revenue Measures (ranking); Trade

Joint Taxation

Elections

1988 General

Guy Vander Jagt (R)	149,748	(70%)
David John Gawron (D)	64,843	(30%)

1986 General

Guy Vander Jagt (R)	89,991	(64%)
Richard J. Anderson (D)	49,702	(36%)

Previous Winning Percentages: **1984** (71%) **1982** (65%) **1980** (97%) **1978** (70%) **1976** (70%) **1974** (57%) **1972** (69%) **1970** (64%) **1968** (68%) **1966** * (67%)

* *Elected to a full term and also to fill an unexpired term in a special election held the same day.*

District Vote For President

	1988	1984	1980	1976
D	84,628 (37%)	69,708 (31%)	77,925 (33%)	78,806 (37%)
R	141,226 (62%)	156,545 (69%)	136,272 (59%)	131,374 (62%)
I			15,481 (7%)	

Campaign Finance

	Receipts	Receipts from PACs	Expend-itures
1988			
Vander Jagt (R)	$456,634	$238,725 (52%)	$450,801
Gawron (D)	$15,540	$8,000 (51%)	$14,948
1986			
Vander Jagt (R)	$428,048	$217,830 (51%)	$398,996
Anderson (D)	$18,629	$7,000 (38%)	$18,006

Key Votes

1987	
Raise speed limit to 65 mph	Y
Approve Gephardt "fair trade" amendment	N
Ban testing of larger nuclear weapons	N
Delay "re-flagging" of Kuwaiti tankers	N
Approve tax-raising deficit-reduction bill	N
1988	
Approve aid to Nicaraguan contras	Y
Enact civil rights restoration bill over Reagan veto	N
Kill 60-day plant-closing notification measure	Y
Pass omnibus trade bill over Reagan veto	N
Approve death penalty for drug-related murders	Y
Bar federal funds for abortions in cases of rape and incest	Y
Oppose seven-day waiting period for purchase of handguns	Y

Voting Studies

	Presidential Support		Party Unity		Conservative Coalition	
Year	**S**	**O**	**S**	**O**	**S**	**O**
1988	58	36	81	9	87	5
1987	61	33	68	20	88	12
1986	62	23	76	15	76	10
1985	65	25	74	18	87	5
1984	56	30	62	19	80	3
1983	66	22	70	19	79	13
1982	53	36	62	28	77	14
1981	64	21	68 †	13 †	76	12

† *Not eligible for all recorded votes.*

Interest Group Ratings

Year	ADA	ACU	AFL-CIO	CCUS
1988	15	91	21	100
1987	0	90	13	93
1986	0	79	14	89
1985	5	79	6	89
1984	0	77	31	81
1983	5	64	6	100
1982	15	68	20	65
1981	10	93	7	100

10 Bill Schuette (R)

Of Sanford — Elected 1984

Born: Oct. 13, 1953, Midland, Mich.
Education: Georgetown U., B.S. 1976; U. of San Francisco School of Law, J.D. 1979.
Occupation: Lawyer.
Family: Single.
Religion: Episcopalian.
Political Career: No previous office.
Capitol Office: 415 Cannon Bldg. 20515; 225-3561.

In Washington: Schuette was tagged as a potential star in Michigan GOP politics soon after he first won election to the House in 1984. In his two terms on the Agriculture Committee, he has applied his political talents toward steering federal money to Michigan farmers, paying particularly close attention to dry-bean growers in the central part of the state. His work has earned him considerable media attention, not only in his own 10th District, but also in parts of the seven other House districts that adjoin the 10th.

Schuette's name recognition in central Michigan and his skill at fund raising would serve him well if he does decide to seek statewide office. And if his legislative image has been rather one-dimensional, Schuette can change that now; at the start of the 101st Congress, he took a seat on the Budget Committee, which gives him a chance to expound on a range of economic issues.

In his first term, Schuette aimed straight for the Agriculture Committee. The man he unseated in 1984, three-term Democrat Don Albosta, had given up his place there, and this had been the Republican's key campaign issue. Schuette spent his first term doing everything he could to wrap himself in the mantle of farm issues. "As long as he is in Congress," one piece of Schuette literature vowed, "he will never ever leave the committee."

Accomplishing something on Agriculture was not quite as easy, thanks in large part to Albosta. Apparently determined to make his successor's life as miserable as possible, Albosta attended committee meetings and urged Democrats not to allow Schuette any opportunities to help himself politically. At one crucial committee meeting on the 1985 farm bill, Albosta went right up to the dais and sat in one of the senior Democratic seats, watching every move Schuette made and looking for ammunition for his 1986 rematch campaign.

But Schuette managed to carve out a useful issue by speaking up for Michigan's growers of dry edible beans. Under the terms of the 1985 farm bill, wheat and feed grain farmers were taking land out of production in order to qualify for federal subsidies. But instead of leaving it fallow, they were planting dry beans, which a loophole in the law allowed them to do. This depressed prices for the beans and hurt those who grew them as their basic crop. Schuette pounced on the issue and helped move a bill through Congress closing the loophole.

Schuette won his 1986 rematch with Albosta, and in the 100th Congress, he broadened his work on Agriculture to include farmers beyond his own district. During 1987 committee consideration of a disaster relief bill, he won approval for an amendment adding $135 million to provide full disaster payments to farmers. On the 1988 drought relief bill, the committee adopted Schuette's amendment ensuring minimum disaster payments for growers of sugar beets and sugar cane, who abound in the neighboring 8th District, as well as in parts of the 10th.

Schuette touted his role in convincing the Agriculture Department in late 1988 to purchase 4.7 million pounds of surplus cherries for the department's school lunch program. Schuette said that 4.1 million of the 4.7 million pounds were bought from Michigan companies. Leelanau County, in the next-door 9th, is the leading cherry-growing county in the country.

Schuette has compiled a moderate-to-conservative voting record in the tradition of Michigan Republican William G. Milliken, who ended 14 years as governor in 1983. He voted to override President Reagan's veto of the Civil Rights Restoration Act, and his rate of support for organized labor's positions on 1988 legislation earned him a 50 percent rating from the AFL-CIO. Still, on some of labor's litmus-test votes in the 100th Congress, Schuette voted against labor. He opposed the Gephardt "fair trade" amendment to the 1987 omnibus trade bill, and he voted against plant-closing notification legislation.

At Home: In his first campaign, Schuette had resources that most challengers just dream of. With a $700,000 budget and a computerized approach to everything from schedules to fund raising, Schuette could brashly declare that

Michigan 10

North Central — Midland

The southern half of the 10th, which casts some 70 percent of the district's vote, has a smattering of small cities surrounded by farm land. Midland, with 36,000 residents, is the largest city in the 10th. Dow Chemical's international headquarters and a Dow Corning plant face each other across Midland Road, dominating the city's economy and setting the tone for its Republican politics. The counties around Midland contribute to the normal districtwide Republican success.

Owosso and Alma are more traditional manufacturing cities, reliant on the auto industry and hospitable ground for Democrats. Some of the blue-collar workers here also work small farms in Shiawassee, Saginaw and Gratiot counties, giving the countryside a more Democratic flavor than is found elsewhere in rural Michigan.

Weekend skiers, hikers and snowmobilers fuel the economy of the hilly counties in the northern part of the district; retirees have arrived in force as year-round residents in this region. Population grew faster in the 10th during the 1970s than in any of Michigan's other districts, and most of the growth was in the northern reaches.

The elderly newcomers are mostly from Michigan's industrial southeast, and they have brought with them political and social concerns they developed as urban dwellers and union members. Their migration has forced a gradual shift in the political tone of this part of the 10th. Counties such as Clare, Gladwin and Roscommon were routinely Republican a decade ago; now no GOP candidate can afford to take them for granted. Even against very weak opposition in 1988, Schuette's campaign spent lavishly, and to good effect, as the Republican won nearly three-fourths of the districtwide vote.

Missaukee County has experienced some spillover development in the area near Houghton Lake, although farther west its hilly terrain is still given over to dairy cattle and bedrock conservatism. The depressed industrial city of Cadillac in Wexford County is the population center and its only traditional source of Democratic votes.

Population: 514,560. White 504,863 (98%), Black 2,668 (1%), Other 3,809 (1%). Spanish origin 6,367 (1%). 18 and over 357,369 (69%), 65 and over 52,523 (10%). Median age: 28.

"amateur night is over in this district."

Though he had never sought office before, Schuette was able to professionalize his campaign because of who he was and where he was running. Dow Chemical Co. is the district's dominant industrial presence, and Schuette is the son of a Dow plant manager and stepson of a retired board chairman. Schuette tapped the ample resources of the Dow community in Midland to build his campaign treasury.

Schuette's research convinced him that the way to beat Albosta — a gruff sugar beet farmer who had won three terms in a largely Republican district by playing up his rural roots — was to make the election a matter of party. He trudged through the district reminding voters that they were Republicans, and telling them that a vote for Schuette was a vote for President Reagan.

Schuette's roots were in the moderate wing of the Michigan GOP; he had angered some conservatives with his support for legalized abortion. But his congressional campaign avoided controversial issues.

Schuette hit hard on only one issue — the Democrat's service on the House Agriculture Committee. Albosta had been on the committee briefly in 1982, but had not applied for a permanent seat. Schuette ran TV ads charging that his departure from the committee was "a betrayal of the farmers of mid-Michigan."

Albosta lashed out at Schuette, ridiculing the wealthy young lawyer for taking farm policy advice from "his gardener." Schuette, who knew he had already stung Albosta badly, made no further effort to personalize the campaign, and waited for the Reagan tide to bring him in. It did, but by a bare margin of 1,314 votes.

Albosta refused to concede for several days, then announced he would run again in 1986. He spent much of the intervening time reinforcing his hold on his loyal supporters and trying to win back others he lost to Schuette in 1984.

Much of Schuette's work as a freshman — gaining a seat on the Agriculture Committee, pushing dry-bean legislation — was aimed at establishing a presence in the district's rural areas. When heavy rains caused flooding in the district during the 1986 campaign, Schuette got Vice President Bush to come in and assure farmers that aid would be forthcoming.

But Albosta persisted in his efforts to re-establish his rural base. He decried the depressed state of the farm economy and criticized Schuette for voting for the 1985 farm bill. Albosta again claimed he was more in touch with rural voters than Schuette.

Schuette, confident that his actions as a House member insulated him on farm issues, ignored Albosta's attacks. Again enjoying a huge financial advantage over the Democrat, Schuette ran an innocuous media campaign, featuring the slogan, "On Duty with Bill Schuette," that showed him greeting constituents and at work in Washington.

But when polls in the final weeks of the campaign showed Albosta closing the gap, Schuette finally responded. In one TV ad, a grim-looking Schuette stated, "Don Albosta, in a sad and desperate attempt, is running negative and inaccurate ads," and urged "Don" not to "sell the people short."

Schuette's Midland base gave him the edge he needed to hold the seat. He carried 64 percent of the Midland County vote; that wide margin and victories in seven other counties were enough to hold off Albosta, who took his base, Saginaw County, and also nine other counties.

Though Albosta's decision to decline another rematch assured Schuette an easy election in 1988, he campaigned as though his career depended on it. Schuette spent almost $800,000 to the $8,000 expended by his Democratic opponent, businessman Mathias Forbes. The incumbent blanketed the district with a TV ad campaign touting the accomplishments of "Michigan's Congressman."

In his short time in office, Schuette has mastered the task of being seen back home. He overcame the lack of a centrally located media market within the 10th with accessibility. He is seen regularly on television stations in several widely scattered markets — Flint-Saginaw-Bay City, Lansing, Traverse City-Cadillac, and occasionally on Detroit and Grand Rapids stations carried by some district cable systems. He has recounted how he readily dropped plans to spend a relaxing evening at home alone when a local TV newsman called to request that he do a live interview on their late newscast.

Schuette's visibility, fund-raising prowess and youth have attracted the attention of Michigan GOP officials, who are on a losing streak in statewide elections. Schuette is widely touted as a 1990 challenger to Democratic Sen. Carl Levin.

Committees

Agriculture (13th of 18 Republicans)
Forests, Family Farms and Energy; Wheat, Soybeans and Feed Grains

Budget (13th of 14 Republicans)
Task Forces: Budget Process, Reconciliation and Enforcement; Urgent Fiscal Issues

Select Aging (19th of 27 Republicans)
Housing and Consumer Interests; Retirement, Income and Employment

Elections

1988 General		
Bill Schuette (R)	152,646	(73%)
Mathias G. Forbes (D)	55,398	(26%)
1986 General		
Bill Schuette (R)	78,475	(51%)
Donald J. Albosta (D)	74,941	(49%)

Previous Winning Percentage: **1984** (50%)

District Vote For President

	1988	1984	1980	1976
D	90,052 (41%)	69,336 (32%)	81,232 (36%)	81,184 (41%)
R	126,547 (58%)	146,060 (67%)	122,741 (55%)	114,855 (58%)
I			17,180 (8%)	

Campaign Finance

	Receipts	Receipts from PACs	Expend-itures
1988			
Schuette (R)	$787,377	$292,987 (37%)	$733,533
Forbes (D) †	$7,810	$5,500 (70%)	$7,809
1986			
Schuette (R)	$891,897	$346,481 (39%)	$897,820
Albosta (D)	$420,009	$231,925 (55%)	$405,971

† Totals based on incomplete data.

Key Votes

1987	
Raise speed limit to 65 mph	N
Approve Gephardt "fair trade" amendment	N
Ban testing of larger nuclear weapons	N
Delay "re-flagging" of Kuwaiti tankers	N
Approve tax-raising deficit-reduction bill	N
1988	
Approve aid to Nicaraguan contras	Y
Enact civil rights restoration bill over Reagan veto	Y
Kill 60-day plant-closing notification measure	Y
Pass omnibus trade bill over Reagan veto	N
Approve death penalty for drug-related murders	Y
Bar federal funds for abortions in cases of rape and incest	Y
Oppose seven-day waiting period for purchase of handguns	Y

Voting Studies

	Presidential Support		Party Unity		Conservative Coalition	
Year	S	O	S	O	S	O
1988	52	42	81	17	84	8
1987	55	45	73	24	86	12
1986	60	39	76	20	82	8
1985	68	33	85	13	93	5

Interest Group Ratings

Year	ADA	ACU	AFL-CIO	CCUS
1988	40	63	50	93
1987	16	65	25	80
1986	10	76	23	73
1985	5	81	6	68

11 Robert W. Davis (R)

Of Gaylord — Elected 1978

Born: July 31, 1932, Marquette, Mich.

Education: Attended Northern Michigan U., 1950-52; Hillsdale College, 1951-52; Wayne State U. College of Mortuary Science, B.S. 1954.

Occupation: Funeral director.

Family: Separated; four children.

Religion: Episcopalian.

Political Career: St. Ignace City Council, 1964-66; Mich. House, 1967-71; Mich. Senate, 1971-79, Senate Republican leader, 1974-79.

Capitol Office: 2417 Rayburn Bldg. 20515; 225-4735.

In Washington: When the Merchant Marine Committee was heaping scorn on a 1987 Reagan administration proposal to increase user fees on boaters, Republican Davis showed no hesitation about joining in the criticism. "Hell yes, I'm being parochial," he said.

That, in a nutshell, is Davis' political credo. Generally a backbencher, he can be feisty where his district is concerned, and he will readily put aside partisan loyalty to cater to the pressing needs of his economically struggling northern Michigan district. Though he is the ranking Republican on Merchant Marine, Davis often finds himself aligned with his colleagues across the aisle.

On the issues handled by his other committee, Armed Services, Davis is a more reliable Republican vote. Of course, on that panel, he can hew to the conservative line — invoking hawkish rhetoric and voting for increased defense spending — and still be looking out for his district: The 11th has two major military facilities and numerous small defense contractors.

Davis did stray from a majority of Republicans on one key defense-policy vote in the 100th Congress: He opposed an amendment aimed at preventing Congress from tampering with the recommendations of a commission identifying unneeded military bases. But when the commission's report was issued, Davis could breathe easy: None of the facilities in his district was recommended for cutbacks.

Davis takes pride in his efforts to help local businesses lure federal contracts. "I spend a lot of time getting defense contracts for our people," he says. "I am a strong supporter of defense and I get a sympathetic ear."

Meetings he coordinates between district businesses and government agencies are touted in press releases, as are any ensuing contracts. He estimates that of the $1.2 billion the federal government spent in the 11th in 1987, some $71 million was for contract work, most of it defense-related.

Protecting his district's foundering industries — forest products, iron and copper mining, and shipbuilding — often requires Davis to distance himself from prevailing GOP sentiment on trade and labor issues. In 1987, he voted for the Gephardt amendment, which mandated retaliatory tariffs, and he voted to override the president's veto of the trade bill. Davis also supported legislation to require plant-closing notification.

In 1984, when Reagan refused to place tariffs and quotas on imported copper, Davis complained that "on the day of the president's announcement, the single remaining copper mine in my district — which used to employ over 3,000 people — shut down all operation." Davis introduced his own bill to impose copper tariffs and quotas, but a veto threat persuaded Congress to pass a bill that merely instructed the administration to negotiate voluntary quotas with foreign suppliers.

Protecting funding for the Coast Guard is another priority for Davis, whose district borders three of the Great Lakes. In the 100th Congress, he argued successfully to include the Great Lakes in legislation aimed at controlling the dumping of medical waste.

At Home: Davis has faced vigorous opposition in two of the last three elections, but with nine district offices and a three-person traveling staff, he has his territory covered so thoroughly that no challenger has ever come close to beating him. At election time, his local work is particularly helpful in normally Democratic areas of the Upper Peninsula (UP).

In 1988, Democratic activists had high hopes for their candidate, youthful state Sen. Mitch Irwin. He had a reputation as an activist legislator and could tout his efforts to help assist the elderly and protect the environment. Democrats felt this image would contrast favorably with Davis, who campaigned primarily on seniority and his efforts to bring defense contracts to the district.

Irwin tried to make political hay out of the

Michigan 11

Upper Peninsula; Northern Lower Peninsula

The vast, empty forests that cover the 470 miles from Ironwood on the Wisconsin border to Tawas City on Lake Huron inhabit a sparsely settled district that, despite an abundance of natural resources, offers its residents a depressed standard of living. The 11th has only one city of over 15,000, Marquette.

The 11th is contiguous only because of the Mackinac Bridge which joins Michigan's Upper and Lower peninsulas. The UP, attached by land to Wisconsin, has roughly 60 percent of the district's residents, the bulk of its Democrats and a rough-hewn pride of place that induces occasional secessionist grumblings among its partisans. People in the western part of the UP root for the Green Bay Packers, not the Detroit Lions.

The UP's once-busy mining industry has basically collapsed. Many of the mines have closed, some are played out, and the ones still operating have been hurt by competition from foreign copper and steel. Calumet, located in the northwestern arm of the UP, once was a booming copper-mining town of 50,000. Now it is a village of just 4,000. Ten of the UP's 15 counties lost population in the early 1980s.

Lumber and wood products are still a factor in mill towns like Escanaba and Manistique, but forestry's future seems brighter in more hospitable climates elsewhere in the country.

K. I. Sawyer Air Force Base, located just south of Marquette in the west-central portion of the UP, is one of the district's largest employers.

The western UP, where the most significant population losses have occurred, traditionally has been the one Democratic stronghold of Michigan north of Saginaw. Eastern European and Scandinavian immigrants brought in to mine copper established a liberal, union-oriented tradition; their descendants and other miners, mill workers, loggers and longshoremen still dominate politics in the UP's western counties. In 1988, Michael S. Dukakis carried nine of the 23 counties wholly contained in the 11th.

The eastern UP is far more Republican and representative of the part of the district below the bridge. The only major city in the eastern part of the UP is Sault Ste. Marie, which sends grain, ores and pulpwood eastward from the port cities of Lake Superior. Thanks to the presence of the Army Corps of Engineers and the Coast Guard, much of Sault Ste. Marie's work force is on the federal payroll. Most of Chippewa County and Mackinac County are heavily dependent on tourism and farming, and lacking in the industry that creates Democratic sympathies farther west.

The migration of former city dwellers that has begun to transform the 10th District is also evident in the 11th below the bridge. Many military retirees from Wurtsmith Air Force Base in Oscada have stayed in the district, and retired autoworkers have settled in Emmet, Presque Isle and Cheboygan counties. Democrats have begun to make inroads in local elections. But the area remains mostly as it has been: The communities are conservative and spread far apart, and the emphasis is on farming and tourism, with a few small industries in such Lake Michigan tourist cities as Charlevoix and Petoskey.

Population: 514,560. White 500,721 (97%), Black 2,875 (1%), Other 9,699 (2%). Spanish origin 1,945 (0.4%). 18 and over 367,779 (72%), 65 and over 70,884 (14%). Median age: 30.

Pentagon procurement scandal, vigorously attacking Davis for accepting $25,000 in honoraria, most of it from defense contractors. But with so many defense-related jobs in the 11th, the message failed to resonate. Irwin spent over $400,000, but Davis matched that and added some $200,000 more. The incumbent won by more than 40,000 votes.

Democrats also had an energetic challenger in 1984: Tom Stewart, a young golf professional with a varied background of volunteer activities, including work with Mother Teresa in India and for a nuclear-freeze initiative in Michigan in 1982.

Stewart raised and spent roughly $250,000, about $40,000 more than Davis, and he blamed Davis for not doing enough to help the district's chronically ailing economy. When asked if his work as a golf pro was suitable training for Congress, Stewart noted that Davis was a mortician, then added, "I think a lot more people are interested in golf than in dying."

Davis said he was doing what he could to help the local economy, citing his efforts to steer military contracts into the 11th. In the end, voters preferred his record to Stewart's promises. Though Reagan got only a modest 53 percent in the district's presidential voting,

Davis reached nearly 60 percent, carrying all but five of the district's 28 counties. Two years later, after a minor heart attack, Davis enjoyed a routine re-election.

Davis first won his House seat in 1978. He replaced GOP Rep. Philip Ruppe, who had stepped down to run for the Senate seat of supposedly retiring Republican Robert P. Griffin. When Griffin changed his mind and decided to run again for the Senate, it was too late for Ruppe to get his old seat back. He could only watch as Davis outran eight candidates for a seat Ruppe could have retained easily.

Davis had been a popular figure in the Michigan Legislature. In his first Senate term he was chosen GOP whip, and later he served as the minority leader. When he first ran for Congress, his major problem was geographic: He was from the Lower Peninsula, while a majority of the 11th's voters were from the UP. He won the GOP primary on the strength of Lower Peninsula support, then temporarily moved to the UP and stressed his boyhood roots there.

Campaigning like an incumbent, Davis contrasted his 12 years of legislative experience with the record of Democrat Keith McLeod, a savings and loan executive and political neophyte. McLeod, from the UP, narrowly won that area, but Davis did well enough there to assure a comfortable districtwide win.

In March 1989, Davis announced he was filing for divorce from his wife Marty. As divorce proceedings grew difficult and public, it was disclosed that Davis was living with a 27-year-old woman. After the two had begun dating, Davis had hired the woman for a staff job on the Merchant Marine Committee, though Davis said he checked with the ethics committee before doing so. Marty Davis told *The Washington Post* that she was forced to collect welfare to support herself and their child.

This was not the first time Davis' wife stirred a bit of scandal. In 1985, she wrote to *Washington Dossier* to complain about a story that had described congressional wives as stodgy. The magazine published the letter and an enclosed photo showing Davis, an attractive fitness buff, in a skimpy swimsuit. In 1987, amid a congressional pay-raise controversy, Davis called the members' salary "pin money," citing the difficulties faced by members who maintain houses and cars in their districts while dealing with the high cost of living in Washington. Her remarks brought a strong response from a number of Davis' constituents, but she did not back down, writing an elaborate defense of her views in *The Washington Post*.

Committees

Merchant Marine and Fisheries (Ranking)
Coast Guard and Navigation (ranking)

Armed Services (6th of 21 Republicans)
Procurement and Military Nuclear Systems; Research and Development

Elections

1988 General

Robert W. Davis (R)	129,085	(60%)
Mitch Irwin (D)	86,526	(40%)

1986 General

Robert W. Davis (R)	91,575	(63%)
Robert C. Anderson (D)	53,180	(37%)

Previous Winning Percentages: **1984** (59%) **1982** (61%) **1980** (66%) **1978** (55%)

District Vote For President

	1988		1984		1980		1976	
D	105,251	(47%)	93,179	(46%)	99,755	(42%)	108,130	(48%)
R	116,722	(52%)	106,092	(53%)	119,100	(50%)	112,569	(50%)
I					15,498	(7%)		

Campaign Finance

	Receipts	Receipts from PACs	Expend-itures
1988			
Davis (R)	$582,616	$310,359 (53%)	$680,819
Irwin (D)	$417,196	$140,034 (34%)	$415,660
1986			
Davis (R)	$396,340	$164,190 (41%)	$207,080
Anderson (D)	$58,943	$27,275 (46%)	$58,826

Key Votes

1987	
Raise speed limit to 65 mph	Y
Approve Gephardt "fair trade" amendment	Y
Ban testing of larger nuclear weapons	N
Delay "re-flagging" of Kuwaiti tankers	N
Approve tax-raising deficit-reduction bill	N
1988	
Approve aid to Nicaraguan contras	Y
Enact civil rights restoration bill over Reagan veto	Y
Kill 60-day plant-closing notification measure	N
Pass omnibus trade bill over Reagan veto	Y
Approve death penalty for drug-related murders	Y
Bar federal funds for abortions in cases of rape and incest	Y
Oppose seven-day waiting period for purchase of handguns	Y

Voting Studies

	Presidential Support		Party Unity		Conservative Coalition	
Year	S	O	S	O	S	O
1988	35	62	43	54	66	29
1987	49 †	48 †	34 †	57 †	72 †	21 †
1986	39	43	36	42	76	14
1985	49	49	55	41	78	18
1984	52	38	48	44	78	17
1983	52	44	53	44	73	24
1982	45	47	37	56	62	29
1981	59	36	69	26	84	12

† Not eligible for all recorded votes.

Interest Group Ratings

Year	ADA	ACU	AFL-CIO	CCUS
1988	60	42	100	29
1987	44	33	81	40
1986	35	60	92	57
1985	35	62	65	55
1984	35	50	42	54
1983	35	57	53	40
1982	35	52	74	40
1981	15	87	40	74

12 David E. Bonior (D)

Of Mount Clemens — Elected 1976

Born: June 6, 1945, Detroit, Mich.
Education: U. of Iowa, B.A., 1967; Chapman College, M.A. 1972.
Military Career: Air Force, 1968-72.
Occupation: Probation officer.
Family: Divorced; two children.
Religion: Roman Catholic.
Political Career: Mich. House, 1973-77.
Capitol Office: 2242 Rayburn Bldg. 20515; 225-2106.

In Washington: It came as something of a surprise when Bonior was chosen chief deputy whip by Jim Wright in 1987. He had not been seen as a close ally of the incoming Speaker, but Wright needed a bridge to liberals and Midwesterners, and Bonior fit that part.

Though Bonior was handpicked by Wright, he kept an identity apart from the Speaker, and so had his own legs to stand on when Wright was driven from office by an ethics scandal in mid-1989. In fact, Bonior's personal following was strong enough to make him a contender for a promotion in the leadership scramble that followed the resignations of Wright and Majority Whip Tony Coelho, who also was dogged by ethics questions.

In seeking to replace Coelho in the No. 3 leadership spot, Bonior faced an uphill fight against William H. Gray III of Pennsylvania. Gray had built support across ideological, regional and racial lines as Budget Committee chairman, and demonstrated his popularity in winning the No. 4 leadership job of Democratic Caucus chairman in late 1988. Bonior, by contrast, had never waged a caucuswide campaign.

Bonior's chances briefly seemed to improve when, shortly before the voting for majority whip, media reports said the FBI was investigating irregular personnel practices in Gray's office. But ultimately Gray was not seriously damaged by the reports, which some Democrats regarded as politically motivated attacks. And Bonior had to contend with attacks himself. Some staunch supporters of Israel objected to Bonior's record on issues important to that country, such as his vote against authorizing the president to withhold funds from the United Nations if the World Health Organization admitted the Palestine Liberation Organization.

Bonior took 97 votes to Gray's 134, and Arkansas Democrat Beryl Anthony Jr. got 30 votes. Bonior retained his appointed position as chief deputy whip.

Bonior's 1987 ascent to a formal leadership position was a clear sign of his progression from his early House years as a restless Vietnam-era veteran searching for a role into a seasoned inside strategist. Passionate yet introverted, he has won praise from liberals for his commitment to their issues and from others for his low-key diligence and keen appreciation of the value of teamwork. After becoming chief deputy whip, he said, "It's sometimes necessary to give up your own personal ambitions and recognition in order to foster a team atmosphere. It's sort of like the Boston Celtics."

He has been playing on the team for some time, having been named to the Rules Committee in 1981 and appointed one of seven deputy Democratic whips in 1985.

Bonior has been most passionate in recent years when fighting military aid to the Nicaraguan contras. On Rules, he has been instrumental in structuring floor debate on Central American issues; outside that panel, beginning in 1983, he headed the Democrats' task force coordinating the party's approach to the region. When President Reagan succeeded in passing a military aid package in 1986, Bonior took some of his passion outside Congress, organizing Priorities PAC, a political action committee that collected over $100,000 to help anti-contra aid congressional candidates.

As chief deputy whip, Bonior often seemed primarily to be chief deputy whip for Central American issues. Though Wright had a deserved reputation for acting alone on many issues, on contra aid he did work fairly closely with Bonior. He was the only other House member present at 1987 meetings where Wright tried to help negotiate a settlement with Nicaraguans.

Bonior worked against administration military aid requests, which were rebuffed by the 100th Congress. But to ward off a persistent GOP, it was clear the Democratic leadership had to offer some contra aid alternative. In that effort Bonior was instrumental. When a non-military aid package passed in 1988, it did so with a number of liberal votes brought on board by Bonior. He played that role again in 1989, when Congress and President Bush agreed on another "humanitarian" aid package.

Bonior's job was not easy. He caught criti-

Michigan 12

Southeast — Macomb County; Port Huron

The heart of the 12th is the six-mile industrial corridor from Detroit north to Fraser, in southern Macomb County. More than 40 percent of the vote is cast there, virtually all by blue-collar ethnics.

Southern Macomb County was built on the increasing prosperity of the Poles, Italians, Belgians, Germans and Slovenes who had first settled on the east side of Detroit early in the 20th century. The neighborhoods nearer the city retain their lower-middle-class character; farther out, in Fraser and the northern parts of Roseville, Warren and St. Clair Shores, the lawns are larger and the houses more expensive.

In the inner suburbs, most of the wage earners are autoworkers and United Auto Workers members. While respect for the union and the Democratic Party continues here, blind allegiance does not. Most of these areas have lost population in the last two decades because of migration outward.

North of Fraser, townships like Clinton, Harrison and Macomb have sprouted new subdivisions in recent years. The population here remains mostly blue-collar, but middle-level managers have moved into the classier developments.

Macomb County was at the center of the 1983 anti-tax revolt following Democratic Gov. James J. Blanchard's 38 percent tax increase. County voters recalled a Democratic state senator and replaced him with a Republican. More recently, supporters of religious broadcaster Pat Robertson have given the local GOP an evangelical flavor. Suburban Macomb has moved closer to the GOP, allowing George Bush to win 60 percent of the district's vote in 1988.

The only sizable city in Macomb outside the immediate Detroit area is safely Democratic Mount Clemens, with its diverse 19,000 residents.

The land stretching from Mount Clemens up to Port Huron at the northern end of St. Clair County is rural and primarily Republican. Only in Port Huron, the seat of St. Clair County, do concentrations of blue-collar workers live.

Population: 514,560. White 496,842 (97%), Black 11,009 (2%), Other 4,218 (1%). Spanish origin 5,842 (1%). 18 and over 362,035 (70%), 65 and over 45,200 (9%). Median age: 29.

cism from the right for not supporting more aid, and some criticism from the left for supporting any aid at all. But many saw Bonior's position as necessary and realistic.

With Gray in the new team of party leaders and providing a link to liberals, Bonior's role as chief deputy whip may change. What is not likely to change is his important role on the Rules Committee as a voice for House liberals.

Bonior was instrumental in forming the Vietnam-era Veterans Congressional Caucus in 1977. In that position he has had differences not only with Republican administrations, but also with more senior members of the Veterans' Affairs Committee.

In 1988, Bonior and others in the caucus finally succeeded in winning veterans the right to challenge the federal government in court over the denial of benefits. Their bill was intended to aid Vietnam-era veterans, who had often been at odds with the Veterans Administration (VA) over the delivery of benefits. Conservatives and some national veterans' organizations said veterans would be better off without the meddling of lawyers and judges. But Bonior and judicial review advocates persisted, at times threatening to hold hostage a bill giving the VA Cabinet status, a pet project of Veterans' Affairs Chairman G. V. "Sonny" Montgomery, who stood in the way of their bill. In the end, both bills became law.

At Home: After a decade of easily deflecting GOP charges that he is too liberal for his blue-collar district, Bonior was held to 54 percent of the vote in 1988, a showing that will keep GOP attention focused on the 12th.

It is unclear whether his slippage (he had won two-thirds of the vote in 1986) was caused mostly by genuine voter displeasure, or by outside factors. In the final month of the campaign, President Reagan visited the Macomb County district twice, and George Bush once. This helped Bush carry the county handily. Macomb also was a battleground in a successful state ballot measure to ban abortion funding.

Bonior's GOP opponent was state Sen. Douglas Carl, whose northern Macomb County district takes in about 20 percent of the 12th. Two years earlier — with the help of activists associated with Pat Robertson's presidential campaign — Carl had upset an incumbent GOP legislator. He immediately began building bridges to party establishment figures, and midway through 1988, won their unanimous backing for his challenge to Bonior.

Short on cash, however, Carl was unable to advertise much. And because most of his complaints about Bonior's liberal record were familiar, Carl drew little media attention. Organizationally, Carl looked to conservative activists motivated by the anti-abortion referendum. But his appeal to them was clouded by Bonior's opposition to abortion.

Overall, Bonior's voting record places him to the left of majority opinion in the working-class 12th, and he has occasionally shown political daring by following the Democratic line. In 1979, he opposed an anti-busing constitutional amendment, though the issue had nearly unseated his Democratic predecessor, James G. O'Hara.

Bonior's 1988 endorsement from Michigan's Right-to-Life organization helped him undercut Carl's base, but Bonior owed his victory to his hefty financial advantage and his campaign apparatus, which persuaded many voters going Republican for president to swing back and return a Democrat to the House.

All of Bonior's re-election campaigns have been supported by organized labor and the Macomb County Democratic organization, but he has not been on the closest of terms with either. In the crowded 1976 contest to find a successor to O'Hara, the unions were split and the Macomb Democratic Party favored Bonior's major primary opponent. Bonior narrowly won the primary and general election with an aggressive personal campaign; he went door to door handing out pine tree seedlings.

At the time, Bonior was a two-term state representative, having been elected to the Legislature only months after completing military duty; he served stateside as an Air Force cook. In all his campaigns, he has sought to make the Vietnam War and its veterans a topic of discussion. "No one even wants to talk about the war," he once complained. "It was a disaster."

Committee

Rules (5th of 9 Democrats)
Rules of the House

Elections

1988 General		
Davis E. Bonior (D)	108,158	(54%)
Douglas Carl (R)	91,780	(45%)
1986 General		
David E. Bonior (D)	87,643	(66%)
Candice S. Miller (R)	44,442	(34%)

Previous Winning Percentages: **1984** (58%) **1982** (66%) **1980** (55%) **1978** (55%) **1976** (52%)

District Vote For President

	1988	1984	1980	1976
D	80,158 (39%)	70,125 (33%)	89,069 (39%)	93,854 (45%)
R	123,989 (60%)	144,403 (67%)	124,419 (54%)	109,186 (53%)
I			14,930 (6%)	

Campaign Finance

	Receipts	Receipts from PACs	Expend-itures
1988			
Bonior (D)	$475,462	$328,317 (69%)	$434,200
Carl (R) †	$154,163	$54,662 (35%)	$143,886
1986			
Bonior (D)	$315,545	$203,455 (64%)	$283,904
Miller (R)	$62,247	$8,800 (14%)	$62,244

† Totals based on incomplete data.

Key Votes

1987	
Raise speed limit to 65 mph	N
Approve Gephardt "fair trade" amendment	Y
Ban testing of larger nuclear weapons	Y
Delay "re-flagging" of Kuwaiti tankers	Y
Approve tax-raising deficit-reduction bill	Y
1988	
Approve aid to Nicaraguan contras	N
Enact civil rights restoration bill over Reagan veto	Y
Kill 60-day plant-closing notification measure	N
Pass omnibus trade bill over Reagan veto	Y
Approve death penalty for drug-related murders	N
Bar federal funds for abortions in cases of rape and incest	Y
Oppose seven-day waiting period for purchase of handguns	N

Voting Studies

	Presidential Support		Party Unity		Conservative Coalition	
Year	**S**	**O**	**S**	**O**	**S**	**O**
1988	19	80	93	2	3	92
1987	11	73	79	1	5	88
1986	16	79	90	1	6	84
1985	19	76	90	3	5	84
1984	25	69	84	4	10	83
1983	21	78	87	6	13	81
1982	26	58	85	5	12	71
1981	25	74	86	8	9	85

Interest Group Ratings

Year	ADA	ACU	AFL-CIO	CCUS
1988	95	4	100	21
1987	88	0	100	8
1986	95	0	100	6
1985	90	5	94	25
1984	75	5	92	33
1983	80	4	94	25
1982	70	11	100	5
1981	90	0	79	5

13 George W. Crockett Jr. (D)

Of Detroit — Elected 1980

Born: Aug. 10, 1909, Jacksonville, Fla.
Education: Morehouse College, A.B. 1931; U. of Michigan, J.D. 1934.
Occupation: Lawyer; judge.
Family: Wife, Harriette Clark; three children, two stepchildren.
Religion: Baptist.
Political Career: Judge, Detroit Recorder's Court, 1966-78.
Capitol Office: 2235 Rayburn Bldg. 20515; 225-2261.

In Washington: His 1987 election as chairman of the Foreign Affairs Subcommittee on Western Hemisphere Affairs seemed an opportunity for Crockett, a fierce opponent of aid to the Nicaraguan contras. Revelations of the Iran-contra affair raised liberals' hopes of ending contra aid, and as a chairman with jurisdiction over the issue, Crockett appeared positioned to play a major role in that effort.

As the 100th Congress evolved, however, the personal benefits of the position for Crockett became increasingly questionable. Earlier in the Reagan administration, then-House Speaker Thomas P. O'Neill Jr. allowed the contra issue to take its course through the legislative process; Crockett's predecessor as Western Hemisphere chairman, Maryland Democrat Michael D. Barnes, was at the center of the debate. But as Crockett took the subcommittee helm, new Speaker Jim Wright made it clear that he intended to steer the issue personally.

By the end of the 100th Congress, the contra-aid pendulum had moved in a direction long desired by Crockett. Military aid had ended, humanitarian aid had been limited, and U.S. policy appeared oriented toward negotiation rather than the overthrow of Nicaragua's Marxist government. However, the Democratic accolades for that shift went to Wright. Crockett was never mentioned as having played a major role in bringing the contra-aid policy to fruition.

Yet Crockett's position at the head of the subcommittee that had been a contra-aid forum bought him some headaches: conservative detractors revived innuendos that Crockett, who as a lawyer had defended accused communists in the 1940s and '50s, was himself a communist.

At the same time, younger black activists in Detroit argued that Crockett, who is pushing 80, was wasting his energies on an ideological agenda, while doing little to offset deep-seated problems in his inner-city district. Though the former judge had long been a dominant local figure, he struggled in 1988 to win his Democratic primary with a plurality.

There is some irony that Crockett stood accused of giving short shrift to the troubles of his constituents. Crockett was a local pioneer in the civil rights movement, and was a labor activist in the blue-collar city. But Crockett, who had taken risks by expressing opposition to use of U.S. clout even during the McCarthy era, has devoted his House career to the ideological battles of Foreign Affairs.

Just after arriving in Congress, Crockett led 28 other members in a federal suit challenging U.S. policies in El Salvador. Crockett argued that President Reagan violated the War Powers Resolution by sending U.S. advisers to El Salvador without properly notifying Congress. During the contra debates, Crockett made his opinions known in the strongest terms. "It is clear," Crockett said, "that the intention of the Reagan administration is nothing short of toppling the Nicaraguan government and replacing it with one more amenable to an imperialistic right-wing philosophy."

Crockett had no use for the contra-aid compromise negotiated in 1989 between the Bush administration and congressional leaders, which extended humanitarian aid for a year pending promised free elections in Nicaragua. "What happens if the situation in Nicaragua is not settled to everyone's satisfaction?..." Crockett asked during House debate. "What do we do then? Continue this program indefinitely? Or do we go back to war and military aid?"

Crockett is also generally opposed to the use of U.S. economic muscle to enforce its will on less powerful nations. In March 1988, he was one of two House members to vote "no" on sanctions aimed at ousting Panamanian strongman Gen. Manuel Antonio Noriega. Crockett makes an exception, though, for economic pressure against South Africa; he is a leading advo-

Michigan 13

Downtown Detroit

After their first settlement burned to the ground in 1805, Detroiters coined the motto, "It shall rise again from the ashes." That is what the city has been trying to do since riots in 1967 desolated its inner core, leaving physical and emotional scars that have proved resistant to quick cure.

In the early 1980s, population in the 13th dropped by nearly 14 percent, more than any other congressional district in the country. The district suffered even greater losses in the 1970s, and reapportionment in the early 1980s reduced the overwhelming black majority somewhat. But blacks remain the dominant force, and the area has been represented by a black Democrat since 1955.

Most of the district is a mix of working-class and poverty-level black neighborhoods, largely clustered south of Ford Freeway. The heart of the ghetto is east of Woodward Avenue, which bisects the city, heading northwest through successively wealthier suburbs until it reaches Pontiac.

Outside the inner-city core are moderate-income areas, black and racially mixed, such as Chandler Park and the community around Wayne State University. Working-class white ethnics live in the northeast end of the 13th, around the Detroit City Airport.

Downtown Detroit stands like a denial of its surroundings. Deserted during the "Murder City" days of the early 1970s, it is more lively today, but within well-fortified glass towers. The 73-story Renaissance Center — which its owners tried to sell in 1982 after losing an estimated $140 million since its opening in 1977 — symbolizes the struggle to revitalize the city's commercial core.

To the southwest, the 13th includes many of Detroit's Hispanic neighborhoods, while farther south is an edge of the Arab section that has spilled over from Dearborn. Standing in sharp contrast to most of the district are Grosse Pointe Park and Grosse Pointe at its far eastern end. Upper-middle-class communities of corporate managers and professionals, they are the sole concentrated source of GOP votes in the 13th.

Population: 514,560. White 133,857 (26%), Black 365,835 (71%), Other 5,068 (1%). Spanish origin 16,073 (3%). 18 and over 360,241 (70%), 65 and over 67,365 (13%). Median age: 29.

cate of sanctions against that nation's apartheid government.

Crockett was one of the first public figures arrested in 1984 for demonstrating outside the South African Embassy in Washington. He took his overnight stay in the D.C. police lockup very much in stride. "After all," he said, "it wasn't my first time going to prison." Crockett was jailed in the 1940s for contempt of court while defending people accused of being communists.

The South Africa issue propelled Crockett into a bitter exchange at a 1987 hearing of the Foreign Affairs Subcommittee on Africa. When Alan Keyes — then-assistant secretary of state for international organizations and the highest-ranking black in the State Department — appeared before the subcommittee to defend the Reagan administration's handling of a 1986 sanctions law, Crockett accused him of being a showhorse for Reagan.

"We've been raising hell about employment practices in the State Department and their failure to employ more blacks," Crockett railed at Keyes (a staunch conservative who went on to be the 1988 GOP Senate candidate in Maryland). "So they want to trot out and demonstrate the one black . . . who has assistant secretary status."

His rhetoric and activist history make Crockett a target for those at the other end of the spectrum, who revived the rumors of his radical past shortly after Crockett gained the Western Hemisphere chair. But Crockett met these implications head-on. Describing the "communist" label as a "false and libelous charge," Crockett wrote in the Detroit *Free Press*, "Conservative extremists in this country have a long and checkered history of trying to discredit those with whom they disagree by calling them communists."

Preoccupied by foreign policy, Crockett is not a visible figure on the Judiciary Committee. But in 1988, Crockett was there to vote on the impeachment of black U.S. District Judge Alcee L. Hastings. After voting in favor of one of the three impeachment resolutions, Crockett said he worried that Hastings had been targeted because he is black, but decided "an honest effort was made to put racism aside."

At Home: After 40 years in Detroit politics, Crockett is a near-legendary figure in his urban district, but in the 1988 Democratic primary he was served warning that the younger generation is getting restless for its turn in power.

Two years earlier, Crockett had trounced his Democratic opponents; as a result, few paid much attention when Detroit City Councilman Barbara-Rose Collins and two other candidates entered the 1988 primary. Collins said she simply was "tired of waiting" for Crockett to retire, and that it was time for the district's representative to pay more attention to local concerns than to Central America. She finished a strong second, taking 40 percent of the vote as Crockett was held under 50 percent. For a man who had won near-unanimous support in his four previous House elections, that was a very poor showing.

Crockett was first elected to the House in 1980. Though he was 71 years old, it came as little surprise when he quickly won Charles C. Diggs' endorsement for the House seat Diggs had vacated by resignation. Nor was it a surprise that Detroit Mayor Coleman A. Young, the United Auto Workers (UAW) and the Shrine of the Black Madonna, a major black church in Detroit, also backed the retired judge to fill Diggs' seat.

Crockett is an elder statesman of Detroit's black community. The white-haired judge has been part of Detroit's "Black Bottom" neighborhood since he arrived in 1943 to open a fair-employment practices office for the UAW. In 1952 he defended Young when the one-time union organizer was called before the House Un-American Activities Committee.

During his 12 years as a Recorder's Court judge and a stint as head of Detroit's legal department, Crockett built a reputation for integrity that was essential for a successor to Diggs, who was convicted in 1978 and censured by the House in 1979 on payroll-padding charges.

Diggs' legal problems and eventual resignation brought 16 potential replacements flooding into the 1980 primary and special election, but Crockett's high-level endorsements gave him a clear advantage. He easily won the Democratic nomination for the general and special elections. The elections were held simultaneously in November; in the heavily Democratic 13th District, his success was guaranteed.

Committees

Foreign Affairs (7th of 28 Democrats)
Western Hemisphere Affairs (chairman); Africa

Judiciary (11th of 21 Democrats)
Civil and Constitutional Rights; Courts, Intellectual Property and the Administration of Justice

Select Aging (17th of 39 Democrats)
Retirement, Income and Employment

Elections

1988 General		
George W. Crockett Jr. (D)	99,751	(87%)
John Wright Savage II (R)	13,196	(12%)
1988 Primary		
George W. Crockett Jr. (D)	18,769	(48%)
Barbara Collins (D)	15,609	(40%)
Michael Hartt (D)	2,588	(7%)
Marlene Kler (D)	1,806	(5%)
1986 General		
George W. Crockett Jr. (D)	76,435	(85%)
Mary Griffin (R)	12,395	(14%)

Previous Winning Percentages: 1984 (87%) **1982** (87%)
1980 * (92%)

* *Elected to a full term and to fill a vacancy at the same time.*

District Vote For President

	1988	1984	1980	1976
D	83,633 (85%)	136,454 (85%)	123,194 (91%)	127,666 (80%)
R	13,673 (14%)	24,188 (15%)	8,190 (6%)	29,140 (18%)
I			2,393 (2%)	

Campaign Finance

	Receipts	Receipts from PACs	Expend-itures
1988			
Crockett (D)	$97,827	$63,822 (65%)	$84,024
1986			
Crockett (D)	$71,784	$38,370 (53%)	$56,271
Griffin (R)	$13,662	$1,616 (12%)	$13,663

Key Votes

1987	
Raise speed limit to 65 mph	Y
Approve Gephardt "fair trade" amendment	Y
Ban testing of larger nuclear weapons	Y
Delay "re-flagging" of Kuwaiti tankers	Y
Approve tax-raising deficit-reduction bill	Y
1988	
Approve aid to Nicaraguan contras	N
Enact civil rights restoration bill over Reagan veto	Y
Kill 60-day plant-closing notification measure	N
Pass omnibus trade bill over Reagan veto	Y
Approve death penalty for drug-related murders	N
Bar federal funds for abortions in cases of rape and incest	N
Oppose seven-day waiting period for purchase of handguns	N

Voting Studies

	Presidential Support		Party Unity		Conservative Coalition	
Year	**S**	**O**	**S**	**O**	**S**	**O**
1988	14	67	82	4	3	66
1987	11	80	81	3	9	79
1986	12	76	77	5	2	80
1985	19	70	78	5	5	80
1984	17	66	76	6	10	69
1983	13	71	77	6	8	82
1982	18	65	68	4	3	75
1981	22	47	67	4	7	65

Interest Group Ratings

Year	ADA	ACU	AFL-CIO	CCUS
1988	85	0	100	33
1987	84	0	94	0
1986	95	0	92	15
1985	80	10	92	18
1984	85	0	83	33
1983	100	5	93	10
1982	80	11	100	20
1981	70	0	91	0

14 Dennis M. Hertel (D)

Of Harper Woods — Elected 1980

Born: Dec. 7, 1948, Detroit, Mich.

Education: Eastern Michigan U., B.A. 1971; Wayne State U., J.D. 1974.

Occupation: Lawyer.

Family: Wife, Cynthia S. Grosscup; four children.

Religion: Roman Catholic.

Political Career: Candidate for Detroit City Council, 1973; Mich. House, 1975-81.

Capitol Office: 2442 Rayburn Bldg. 20515; 225-6276.

In Washington: The serious-looking Hertel would prefer to be recognized by his colleagues for his legislative activities on the Armed Services Committee. During nearly a decade in Congress, Hertel has been an activist on defense procurement issues. As a liberal arms control advocate, the Michigan Democrat has pushed a variety of proposals to limit spending on nuclear weapons systems.

But over the past few years, Hertel has been noticed inside the House less for his legislative agenda than for his lack of success at institutional politics. During a series of contentious battles for the Armed Services chairmanship in the 99th and 100th Congresses, Hertel exhibited an unfortunate knack for supporting the losing candidate. Most House members occasionally back the wrong horse, but Hertel bet wrong on the whole racing card.

In 1985, a group of junior Democrats sought to strip the Armed Services chairmanship from veteran Illinois Democrat Melvin Price, whose various infirmities had weakened his leadership abilities. Hertel decided to come to Price's defense, and delivered a speech on his behalf at a closed-door meeting of the Democratic Caucus. But the 80-year-old Price was overheard to ask a nearby listener who Hertel was. Price was deposed and Wisconsin Democrat Les Aspin installed to replace him.

Two years later, an unusual coalition of liberal and conservative dissident Democrats, led by Marvin Leath of Texas, sought to remove Aspin from the chair. Though Hertel did not seem eager to have Aspin back, he supported him in an initial up-or-down vote; Aspin lost. Hertel then switched loyalties, first backing Nicholas Mavroules of Massachusetts for chairman, then Charles E. Bennett of Florida. But Aspin, making a comeback, eliminated these candidates on early ballots.

On the final Aspin-Leath showdown, Hertel went back to Aspin; in doing so, he finally landed on a winner. But his positioning during the chairmanship fights hardly qualified him for membership in Aspin's "kitchen cabinet" of savvy centrists on Armed Services.

His misfortunes in the leadership arena have not forestalled Hertel from plying his trade on Armed Services. Early in his House career, Hertel took up the issue of the exorbitant costs paid by the Defense Department for spare parts and other equipment. His interest in procurement issues led to his appointment as chairman of a House task force on Pentagon waste and fraud during the 99th Congress. A defense authorization bill included a number of the task force's recommendations, including a Hertel amendment providing for stringent criminal penalties.

In 1987, Hertel introduced a bill calling for the creation of a Defense Acquisition Agency, staffed by civilians and independent of the military leadership, to handle weapons contracting and other purchasing for the Pentagon. The bill received little attention at first. But after the Pentagon procurement scandal broke in mid-1988, Hertel resubmitted his proposal, and attracted several dozen cosponsors. The bill stalled, nonetheless, in the face of strong Defense Department opposition.

Hertel, whose Detroit-area district has been affected by foreign competition to U.S. automakers and troubles in other heavy industries, has also tried to push the Pentagon to "buy American." He was particularly angry when he learned in May 1987 that the Defense Department had placed a $21 million order for compact pickup trucks built by the Japanese automaker Mitsubishi. He later attached an amendment to a defense authorization bill calling on the military, with few exceptions, to purchase only vehicles made in North America.

Local economic problems were not far from Hertel's mind when he expressed skepticism in 1988 about the proposal to close certain obsolete military bases. Recalling the impact of recent layoffs at the Army Tank Plant at Warren in his district, Hertel attached an amendment in committee to the base-closing plan, calling for socioeconomic impact studies prior to the closing of any base.

In the report issued by the presidential base-closing commission, the Warren tank

Michigan 14

Detroit Suburbs — Warren

The 14th is a 15-mile corridor with an ethnic and social diversity that takes in the rumbling auto plants of Warren, the graceful old mansions of the Grosse Pointes, the kielbasa of Hamtramck and the pétanque games of Detroit's Belgian neighborhoods.

At the district's far eastern end, the mansions and estates lining Lake Shore Drive in Grosse Pointe Shores and Grosse Pointe Farms — the Ford family estate is among them — offer the kind of Republicanism associated with corporate board rooms and casual access to political power. Farther inland, in Grosse Pointe Woods and Harper Woods, are three-bedroom ranch houses and middle-level managers whose national and statewide allegiance is usually to the GOP, but who are comfortable splitting their tickets in local contests.

To the west stretches northeast Detroit, an ethnic quilt of solid working-class neighborhoods where a Democrat stumping for votes can spend his time productively at the corner bar. The auto industry attracted Poles, Germans, Italians and Belgians who settled here.

The center of Polish activity is Hamtramck, a city-within-a-city. Its neat seas of two-story frame houses, broken only by the spires of Catholic churches, were once home to 50,000 people. Most worked at the huge Dodge plant at the southern end of town.

Now down to a population of 19,000, Hamtramck is dependent these days on jobs at smaller factories.

North of Detroit the 14th takes in a small part of Oakland County and southwestern Macomb County, and these areas have nearly half the district residents. Middle-class ethnics live in East Detroit, Hazel Park and northern Warren, and lower-middle-class Appalachians reside in the shadow of steel plants and auto parts factories in southern Warren. The combination makes this area the socially conservative heart of Democratic strength in this area.

Population: 514,559. White 478,987 (93%), Black 25,311 (5%), Other 7,037 (1%). Spanish origin 4,993 (1%). 18 and over 372,422 (72%), 65 and over 58,019 (11%). Median age: 31.

plant actually was slated to gain 100 civilian jobs. But there is still concern that new employment will come in the form of administrative positions, and perhaps at the expense of blue-collar production jobs.

On strategic issues, Hertel opposed most of President Reagan's priorities on weapons systems. He was one of the Armed Services liberals who proposed to eliminate funding for the MX missile and sharply reduce spending on the strategic defense initiative (SDI); the deepest of these cutbacks, though, were shot down. For example, Hertel's amendment to the fiscal 1989 defense authorization bill, prohibiting the use of Air Force funds for the MX missile, was defeated in the House, 143-265.

Whatever stumbles Hertel has made in Armed Services' leadership fights, he has progressed on the Merchant Marine and Fisheries Committee, where he serves as chairman of the Oceanography Subcommittee. He says he will work, on that panel and as a member of the Armed Services Research and Development Subcommittee, to coordinate the oceanographic programs of the Navy, the National Oceanic and Atmospheric Administration, the National Science Foundation, and the National Aeronautics and Space Administration.

Hertel's interest in oceanography stems from the proximity of the Great Lakes to his district. During the 100th Congress, he was part of a successful effort to get the Great Lakes included in a law prohibiting ocean dumping of medical wastes. He was also a leader of a coalition of members from Great Lakes states who blocked a 1988 request from Midwestern leaders to divert water from Lake Michigan to the drought-stricken Mississippi River basin; Hertel said the action would lower the lakes' water level and hinder shipping.

At Home: The three Hertel brothers dominate politics on the northeastern side of Detroit. Dennis Hertel spent six years in the state Legislature. His older brother, a former state senator, is a Wayne County commissioner, and his younger brother was elected to Dennis' state House seat in 1980. The success of the Hertel family stems from their moderate, labor-oriented politics.

Running for the seat given up by Democratic Rep. Lucien N. Nedzi in 1980, Dennis Hertel assembled a volunteer force 2,500 strong to counter the money and polish of his Republican opponent, Vic Caputo. A former television news anchorman and host of a morning talk show on Detroit's CBS affiliate, Caputo made up for his lack of political experience with oratorical polish and districtwide prominence. With help from the national GOP, he mounted a high-spending effort that relied largely on the media to push his candidacy across to voters.

Lacking the money and the flair of his

opponent, Hertel concentrated on personal visits with voters, reportedly wearing out four pairs of shoes walking through the precincts. With the support of the Democratic organization, he scored a comfortable win.

Hertel went unchallenged in 1982, but in 1984, he faced John Lauve, who had drawn publicity for launching a drive to recall Gov. James J. Blanchard after he pushed through a huge tax increase. Hertel, however, was hard to label as a high-tax advocate; he pointed out that he had never voted for a tax increase during 10 years in state and federal office. Hertel won easily.

In 1986, GOP officials hoped to influence the district's Polish-American community by recruiting Polish immigrant Stanley T. Grot, a former autoworker and owner of a Hamtramck restaurant. But Hertel's popularity among Polish voters blunted Grot's efforts, which enabled the incumbent to win re-election by a margin of nearly 3-to-1.

The GOP all but ignored Hertel in 1988, nominating little-known classroom instructor Kenneth C. McNealy. The Democrat topped 60 percent for the first time in a presidential-election year, outpolling McNealy by nearly 47,000 votes in his 63-36 percent win.

Committees

Armed Services (14th of 31 Democrats)
Investigations; Military Personnel and Compensation; Research and Development

Merchant Marine and Fisheries (8th of 26 Democrats)
Oceanography (chairman); Merchant Marine

Select Aging (19th of 39 Democrats)
Health and Long-Term Care

Elections

1988 General

Dennis M. Hertel (D)	111,612	(63%)
Kenneth C. McNealy (R)	64,750	(36%)

1986 General

Dennis M. Hertel (D)	92,328	(73%)
Stanley T. Grot (R)	33,831	(27%)

Previous Winning Percentages: 1984 (59%) **1982** (95%) **1980** (53%)

District Vote For President

	1988	1984	1980	1976
D	78,626 (43%)	77,597 (37%)	97,621 (43%)	99,782 (46%)
R	102,373 (56%)	130,491 (62%)	114,356 (50%)	114,792 (53%)
I			13,568 (6%)	

Campaign Finance

	Receipts	Receipts from PACs	Expend-itures
1988			
Hertel (D)	$251,004	$154,565 (62%)	$137,560
McNealy (R)	$3,525	0	$3,537
1986			
Hertel (D)	$199,966	$120,549 (60%)	$172,835
Grot (R)	$73,991	$1,750 (2%)	$73,988

Key Votes

1987	
Raise speed limit to 65 mph	N
Approve Gephardt "fair trade" amendment	Y
Ban testing of larger nuclear weapons	Y
Delay "re-flagging" of Kuwaiti tankers	Y
Approve tax-raising deficit-reduction bill	Y
1988	
Approve aid to Nicaraguan contras	N
Enact civil rights restoration bill over Reagan veto	Y
Kill 60-day plant-closing notification measure	N
Pass omnibus trade bill over Reagan veto	Y
Approve death penalty for drug-related murders	N
Bar federal funds for abortions in cases of rape and incest	Y
Oppose seven-day waiting period for purchase of handguns	N

Voting Studies

	Presidential Support		Party Unity		Conservative Coalition	
Year	**S**	**O**	**S**	**O**	**S**	**O**
1988	22	78	92	6	24	76
1987	20	78	93	5	21	79
1986	14	83	90	8	10	90
1985	29	71	88	12	16	84
1984	27	71	84	13	20	75
1983	20	80	87	11	20	78
1982	32	64	80	9	21	68
1981	25	64	80	12	27	73

Interest Group Ratings

Year	ADA	ACU	AFL-CIO	CCUS
1988	95	4	100	21
1987	88	0	100	13
1986	85	9	93	19
1985	80	14	88	27
1984	75	17	92	44
1983	90	13	100	5
1982	75	26	100	15
1981	80	7	79	6

15 William D. Ford (D)

Of Taylor — Elected 1964

Born: Aug. 6, 1927, Detroit, Mich.

Education: Attended Nebraska State Teachers College, 1946; Wayne State U., 1947-48; U. of Denver, B.S. 1949, LL.B. 1951.

Military Career: Navy, 1944-46; Air Force Reserve, 1950-58.

Occupation: Lawyer.

Family: Divorced; three children.

Religion: United Church of Christ.

Political Career: Taylor Township justice of the peace, 1955-57; Melvindale city attorney, 1957-59; Taylor Township attorney, 1957-64; Mich. Senate, 1963-65.

Capitol Office: 239 Cannon Bldg. 20515; 225-6261.

In Washington: Ford was raised by working-class parents, New Deal disciples who told him, "The Democratic Party cared and the Republican Party didn't." He came to the House in time to champion Johnson's Great Society. For a man so steeped in party dogma, recent years have been trying indeed.

In the 1980s, after years on the winning side, Ford had to confront a Republican administration hostile to the idea of government as social engineer, and now a legacy of budget deficits that will bar any major domestic initiatives for years to come. Moreover, he watched as that administration's hostility to government liberalism caught on among his constituents, the traditional blue-collar Democrats of his own stock who came to typify "the Reagan Democrats."

His rampart against the tide has been the Education and Labor Committee. However, under the control of old-style Democrats like himself, the panel has found itself frequently out of step even within the Democratic House, its influence eroded. In such times, second-ranking Ford is expected to take over before too long from Chairman Augustus F. Hawkins of California, who will be 83 when the 101st Congress ends.

While Hawkins remains active, the more aggressive and crusty Ford is already treated in some quarters as chairman. He is associated more often with Education and Labor than with the committee where he actually has been chairman since 1981, the Post Office and Civil Service Committee. It is Education and Labor that oversees his two top priorities.

For many years, Ford concentrated on education. But in the 100th Congress, he focused instead on labor issues. Though the Congress was generally a disappointing one for labor, Ford had the satisfaction of winning a 14-year battle for legislation requiring 60 days' notice of plant closings to ease workers' adjustment.

In 1985, he had miscalculated and the House rejected his plant-closing notification bill even after it was diluted, first by him and then by Republican foes. But in the 100th Congress, the measure became Democrats' *cause célèbre,* the issue they hoped would prove Republicans' callousness to workers and win back the Reagan Democrats in the 1988 election. Though Ford's proposal had lost much in substance, it had gained in political symbolism and thus momentum.

Over some Southern Democrats' opposition, the proposal was attached to a major trade bill in the House. With typical bluntness, Ford repeatedly warned his party's waverers, many from the oil states, that if his provision were challenged, he would go after the section in the trade bill repealing the windfall-profits tax on oil. After Reagan vetoed the trade bill, citing the plant-closing language, Ford angrily objected to Speaker Jim Wright's counter-strategy of severing the two measures and passing them again separately. "Over my dead body," Ford said, fearful that his pet provision could not become law on its own.

The leaders pressed on, but they did agree to push the plant-closing bill first, effectively holding the trade bill hostage. It passed in both houses by margins that indicated Congress could override Reagan's veto. Ultimately the president signed the trade bill, and, silently conceding defeat, allowed the plant-closing bill to become law without his signature.

Ford also had an active role during the 100th Congress in enactment of another labor-protection law prohibiting most uses of lie detectors by employers. He and other labor allies have had a tougher time winning an increase in the minimum wage. For years, Ford has been an advocate of the earned income tax credit (a tax break for the poor), but he has been forced to oppose it in the past couple of years as Republicans have seized the EITC as an alternative to a

Michigan 15

Southwestern Wayne County

The Industrial Expressway heading west from Detroit is the spine of the 15th District. Lining the ribs that branch from it on its way out toward the airport are automobile and chemical plants, trucking firms and auto parts factories. In the distance squat retreating rows of suburban tract houses, home to more than a quarter of the district's voters.

Wayne County holds more than 80 percent of the population of the 15th; the rest is in Ypsilanti and its neighboring townships and a hook south of Ann Arbor around the small city of Saline. Within the territory are several Ford and General Motors plants; the automakers are the district's prime employers.

Most of the towns along the Industrial Expressway are lower-middle-class communities. Almost entirely white and originally settled by Eastern Europeans and migrants from Kentucky and Tennessee, they are Democratic, socially conservative and not particularly friendly to blacks. The politics practiced here are volatile, sometimes marked by a "throw the bums out" attitude that shortens the careers of local officeholders trying to deal with declining tax bases and poverty-stricken school systems.

Farther out in Wayne County, things are less crowded. Small farms are scattered around suburban townships inhabited by autoworkers who were prosperous enough to move beyond the central suburban ring. Canton Township is the district's only substantially Republican community, a white-collar suburb of split-level ranch houses encroaching into the surrounding farm land.

The district's largest population of blacks is in Ypsilanti, which was devastated by the early 1980s recession, and Ypsilanti Township. Many of the white autoworkers living there moved up from the South, and relations between the two communities have sometimes been tense. But together they give Democrats a grip on the area that far outweighs the small Republican margins turned in by the nearby farms.

Population: 514,560. White 476,107 (93%), Black 28,459 (6%), Other 6,777 (1%). Spanish origin 7,788 (2%). 18 and over 356,253 (69%), 65 and over 30,909 (6%). Median age: 27.

minimum-wage hike.

Hard-working and combative, Ford is especially defensive when he believes Education and Labor has been slighted. During consideration of a welfare-overhaul package in 1988, he unsuccessfully resisted when House negotiators, under Senate pressure, moved to drop his panel's provisions requiring that welfare beneficiaries placed in jobs be paid prevailing wages rather than minimum wage. "Education and Labor is not a very important committee in some people's eyes," he snapped, "but we do have some jurisdiction."

Though the committee and its leaders are often criticized for being politically unrealistic and unbending, in 1987 the panel cleared the way for a major bill renewing all federal elementary- and secondary-school programs, and providing some modest increases for the first time in the Reagan years, by compromising with Republicans on bilingual education. While some Democrats balked at giving schools more flexibility to teach English, fearing a return to controversial immersion methods, Ford called for conciliation. "I see this compromise as a political compromise to get enough votes from opponents of bilingual education to keep bilingual education alive," he said.

College aid has been Ford's specialty over the years. As chairman of the Postsecondary Education Subcommittee from 1977-80, and again in 1985-86, he fought for major expansions of grants and loans programs. He helped ensure that aid goes not only to the poor but also to the middle class, whose support Ford believes is politically crucial to the programs' survival. In the 1980s, he primarily fought just to protect the programs against budget cuts, but as the decade ends, he is watching to see if President Bush is true to his campaign pledge to be "the education president."

In 1984, he had helped stall an effort to reauthorize higher-education policies because Paul Simon of Illinois was the Postsecondary Education chairman that year. In 1985, when Simon had moved to the Senate, Ford secured a special House waiver allowing him to chair both the subcommittee and Post Office. Then he brokered a complex bipartisan bill, packed with enough pork-barrel projects for each panel member to have a vested interest in its fate.

He also had to accommodate Congressional Black Caucus members, including Hawkins, who were protective of aid for historically black colleges. "I have real difficulty," Ford said, with the idea "that a school that was created to keep blacks separate from other people in college should have money on a continuing basis." A compromise funneled funds both to black colleges and, as Ford preferred, to mainstream institutions with minority enrollments.

During that 1985 effort, Ford's frustration with budget constraints was plain. "My hope is, the next time we'll be able to consider what's a rational education policy and then find the dollars to pay for it," he said.

Several years earlier, in drafting the 1978 higher education bill, he had helped expand the program of Basic Education Opportunity Grants, which provides money directly to students, and also broadened eligibility for guaranteed loans to all students, including those from upper-income families. Two years later, the 1980 bill provided even more generous aid for students, young and old, who wanted to continue their schooling. By then, colleges and universities were getting nearly half the federal education budget, thanks in part to Ford.

Those funds were targeted for the deepest cuts when Reagan took office. The 1981 budget did not go as far as the president wanted, but some of the most liberal aspects of the education program were curbed. For example, Congress reimposed an income test for student loans, ending the universal eligibility that many viewed as an unnecessary excess.

Although Ford is less active on education issues outside the college level, he is still a force to be reckoned with. In a public display of disunity among Education and Labor members, he led the opposition to a 1986 committee proposal to increase states' share of the cost of vocational training for the disabled. He saw to it that the proposal was watered down beyond recognition before the bill went to the floor.

As chairman of Post Office and Civil Service, Ford is best known for his role as the undertaker eager to bury any proposals that would block pay raises for lawmakers and federal employees. Here, he can indulge his love for legislative sleight of hand and parliamentary craft. And because he has never had serious political problems at home, Ford can afford to lead the pro-pay-raise side. "I know for a fact that the vast majority of the people I represent think I'm vastly underpaid," he boasted at a 1987 hearing.

In 1977 and again in 1987, he bottled up anti-pay raise resolutions, although in 1987, House leaders had to resort to more complicated machinations when the Senate added a pay-repeal provision to the House's homeless aid bill. Speaker Wright scheduled a final vote on the homeless bill for the day after the 30-day deadline for disapproving the $12,100-a-year pay hike had passed, insisting that this tactic would not render the repeal provision moot. But when the vote came, blunt-talking Ford gleefully acknowledged what all knew to be true: "What we do today is meaningless."

Ford was not smiling in early 1989, when Congress did reject a 51 percent raise to $135,000 annually that Reagan and a presidential commission had proposed. Once again, Ford was prepared to sit on any anti-raise measures, but under tremendous public pressure, Wright relented and scheduled a vote. Ford was furious, and confronted the Speaker about the strategy switch at a closed-door leadership meeting.

In the 101st Congress, Post Office and Civil Service will continue to be at the center of efforts to prepare for the 1990 census. As a representative of a state that stands to lose congressional seats to those with growing populations, Ford opposes recurring proposals to ban the counting of illegal aliens, and he supports measures to allow the Census Bureau to adjust for undercounting, which typically omits urban blacks and Hispanics.

He runs the committee in characteristically partisan style, which enrages some Republicans. For example, he harangued the Reagan administration about Postal Service budget cuts, and blamed it for mail service problems. But there is no question he is in control; Post Office is a second assignment for nearly all its members, and few are active enough there to quarrel successfully with what the chairman wants to do.

On both the Post Office and Education and Labor committees, Ford has always been a favorite of unions. As a member of the Labor-Management Relations Subcommittee throughout the 1970s, he sometimes stepped in to handle controversial labor bills, such as those dealing with common-site picketing and labor law revision, when Chairman Frank Thompson Jr. of New Jersey was absent.

On Post Office, Ford is an advocate for the unions that represent federal employees. He espouses repeal of the Hatch Act, which bars civil servants from partisan political activity. He was labor's negotiator on President Jimmy Carter's civil service revision bill in 1978, expressing the union's fears that merit incentives written into the bill would weaken job protection. Ultimately, he reached a compromise on behalf of the unions with the administration and with the bill's chief sponsor, Arizona Democrat Morris K. Udall.

The one issue that Ford has been politically cautious about over the years is busing to achieve racial balance in schools. He supported the 1960s civil rights bills and all of President Johnson's anti-poverty programs, but he drew the line when federal courts ordered busing in the Detroit area in the early 1970s. He signed congressional petitions, held hearings and voted for measures aimed against busing. But when he balked at an effort in 1972 to pry an anti-busing constitutional amendment out of the Judiciary Committee, demonstrators marched around his Michigan office, chanting, "Sign or Resign." Ford insisted he simply did not like stripping a committee of its jurisdiction, but the groups were not appeased. In 1979 he voted for an anti-busing amendment on the floor.

At Home: An energetic Democrat, Ford has never had much trouble winning election even though his constituents are no longer the Democratic "true believers" they once were.

He put in seven years as a political apprentice in township politics on the western side of Wayne County, then went to the state Senate in 1962. It was an easy move because he had the blessing of the man who was retiring.

Taking a U.S. House seat two years later was not too much harder. The newly created 15th District had no incumbent, and most local party leaders favored Ford for the opening. His only significant primary opposition came from township politician William Faust, who later became majority leader of the state Senate. Ford defeated Faust 45-36 percent, with the rest of the vote split among three others.

Since then, Ford has carefully tended to his district. As a senior legislator on education, he has invited city and school officials from Detroit to come to Washington for conferences on how to get money from the federal government. He has been rewarded with routine elections. In 13 campaigns, he has not fallen below 60 percent.

Ford drew more publicity than most secure incumbents in the early 1980s when he had to contend with Gerald Carlson, a "white rights" advocate who once had ties to the Ku Klux Klan and the American Nazi Party. Carlson ran against Ford as a Republican in 1980 and 1984 and as a Democrat in 1982.

Carlson's 1982 candidacy went nowhere, but in November 1984 he polled 40 percent, a result that shocked and embarrassed local Republican officials, who had disavowed him. Pressed to explain how Carlson had won the GOP nomination over a party-endorsed candidate, one Republican official, noting that Carlson took the lightly attended GOP primary with just over 5,000 votes, said, "There are that many rednecks in the district ... that many voters who believe that a little fascism would not be all bad."

Carlson filed to run again in the 1986 Republican primary, but withdrew, setting the stage for a more routine Ford victory.

Committees

Post Office and Civil Service (Chairman)
Investigations (chairman)

Education and Labor (2nd of 22 Democrats)
Elementary, Secondary and Vocational Education; Health and Safety; Labor-Management Relations; Postsecondary Education

Elections

1988 General		
William D. Ford (D)	104,596	(64%)
Burl C. Adkins (R)	56,963	(35%)
1986 General		
William D. Ford (D)	77,950	(75%)
Glen Kassel (R)	25,078	(24%)

Previous Winning Percentages: **1984** (60%) **1982** (73%) **1980** (68%) **1978** (80%) **1976** (74%) **1974** (78%) **1972** (66%) **1970** (80%) **1968** (71%) **1966** (68%) **1964** (71%)

District Vote For President

	1988	1984	1980	1976
D	79,091 (46%)	71,126 (39%)	89,641 (43%)	95,762 (50%)
R	92,840 (54%)	112,328 (61%)	101,740 (49%)	91,237 (48%)
I			14,289 (7%)	

Campaign Finance

	Receipts	Receipts from PACs	Expend-itures
1988			
Ford (D)	$335,331	$267,901 (80%)	$234,435
Adkins (R) †	$8,022	0	$7,993
1986			
Ford (D)	$331,369	$220,735 (67%)	$306,543

† Totals based on incomplete data.

Key Votes

1987	
Raise speed limit to 65 mph	N
Approve Gephardt "fair trade" amendment	Y
Ban testing of larger nuclear weapons	Y
Delay "re-flagging" of Kuwaiti tankers	Y
Approve tax-raising deficit-reduction bill	Y
1988	
Approve aid to Nicaraguan contras	N
Enact civil rights restoration bill over Reagan veto	Y
Kill 60-day plant-closing notification measure	N
Pass omnibus trade bill over Reagan veto	Y
Approve death penalty for drug-related murders	N
Bar federal funds for abortions in cases of rape and incest	N
Oppose seven-day waiting period for purchase of handguns	N

Voting Studies

	Presidential Support		Party Unity		Conservative Coalition	
Year	**S**	**O**	**S**	**O**	**S**	**O**
1988	13	80	83	2	5	89
1987	11	84	88	3	9	88
1986	18	79	84	4	12	78
1985	16	76	71	2	7	87
1984	23	65	82	5	17	75
1983	12	78	87	2	8	82
1982	30	62	90	1	8	77
1981	26	58	84	3	12	68

Interest Group Ratings

Year	ADA	ACU	AFL-CIO	CCUS
1988	100	0	100	23
1987	92	0	100	0
1986	80	5	93	6
1985	80	5	100	20
1984	85	0	100	38
1983	90	0	100	10
1982	85	5	100	14
1981	70	0	100	6

16 John D. Dingell (D)

Of Trenton — Elected 1955

Born: July 8, 1926, Colorado Springs, Colo.
Education: Georgetown U., B.S. 1949, LL.B. 1952.
Military Career: Army, 1944-46.
Occupation: Lawyer.
Family: Wife, Deborah Insley; four children.
Religion: Roman Catholic.
Political Career: Assistant Wayne County prosecutor, 1953-55.
Capitol Office: 2221 Rayburn Bldg. 20515; 225-4071.

In Washington: Dingell has always seemed to care more about accumulating power and winning legislative battles than about being perceived as a nice guy in the process.

"Occasionally, I'm going to have to do ugly things that hurt me politically," he once said. "But I was sent here to win."

That kind of bravado has given Dingell near-legendary status as a legislative giant-killer. But he sets a standard for himself that has been increasingly difficult for him to meet.

As chairman of the Energy and Commerce Committee, Dingell in recent years has helped pass bills on a staggering array of subjects, from laboratory regulation to toxic waste to insider trading. But there have been precious few major legislative accomplishments, the really big wins that are the stuff of the Dingell mystique.

For years, Dingell has been considered one of the House's most skillful legislators, aggressive turf-fighters and hard-nosed negotiators. His mastery of House rules and procedural minutiae is renowned, as is his maxim about the power that knowledge gives him: "If you let me write procedure and I let you write substance," he told the House Rules Committee in 1982, "I'll screw you every time."

It looked like the 100th Congress would only enhance Dingell's power, because he had forged an early and close alliance with the incoming Speaker, Jim Wright of Texas, a moderate Democrat more in tune with Dingell's views than former Speaker Thomas P. O'Neill Jr.

But Dingell suffered a series of setbacks in the 100th Congress that suggest his blunt use of the tools of legislative power is not all it has been made out to be.

Dingell in 1987 staked his reputation on a battle with the Reagan White House over writing the "fairness doctrine" for broadcasting into law, and lost. He went head-to-head with environmentalists in a House floor vote over air-pollution deadlines and lost by a surprisingly large margin. When several committees submitted to the Rules Committee conflicting provisions for an omnibus trade bill, most of Energy and Commerce's proposals were left on the cutting room floor. And Dingell began the 101st Congress with an embarrassing admission that his famed investigative staff had gone too far; he withdrew an allegation of misconduct against a private detective.

Without question, Dingell still has the clout and the skill to triumph in his patented fashion. During 1987 debate on the farm credit system, Dingell took an issue that had little to do with his committee and made it practically his own. He waged a turf war to kill a provision exempting a new secondary market for farm mortgages from federal and state securities regulation. He won, not only on the immediate question, but also gained a foothold for his committee in overseeing the increasingly popular market of securities issued by quasi-governmental agencies.

Further, Dingell's power to obstruct is not to be underestimated: While he might have lost the 1987 battle over how long to put off air-pollution deadlines, he continued to have the upper hand in a more important battle by blocking legislation to make air-quality standards more stringent.

If only because of the expansive array of issues that pass through his committee, Dingell remains a force that each and every House member, at some point, has to reckon with.

But his legislative imperialism is meeting with increasingly restless natives. One day after his farm credit triumph in October 1987, the House said "no" to another Dingell power play. Capitalizing on widespread resentment of Dingell, Public Works Chairman James J. Howard of New Jersey persuaded the House to kill a provision of a Federal Trade Commission bill that would have transferred oversight of airline advertising from Public Works to Energy and Commerce.

"Has the Energy and Commerce Committee Ever Tried to Steal Your Jurisdiction?" read the headline of a "Dear Colleague" letter circulated by Public Works leaders. A growing number of members have been able to answer "yes."

Michigan 16

Southeast Wayne County; Monroe County

The 16th was once called "the most polluted congressional district in the nation" by *The Detroit News.* Redistricting in 1982 probably cost it that honor, not because great strides had been made in cleaning its air or rivers, but because the boundaries were pushed down the Lake Erie shoreline into the small towns and spread-out farms of southeastern Michigan.

Still, the 16th remains an overwhelmingly industrialized district. At its northern end is Dearborn, home of the Ford Motor Co. and site of Ford's immense Rouge plant. The haze-covered stretch of communities along the Detroit River in Wayne County from River Rouge to Gibraltar is a conglomeration of steel mills, foundries, auto factories, tool-and-die shops and chemical plants that looms over a broken sea of apartments, tract homes on uniform lots and one- and two-family houses.

The Wayne County portion of the district, which now accounts for about two-thirds of its population, is one of the most Democratic areas in Michigan. The eastern end of Dearborn, with its dilapidated prewar housing, is home to the country's largest single community of Arab-Americans. They join other residents of Dearborn in solid support of Democratic candidates.

Similar sentiments hold among the autoworkers and steelworkers, many of them black, who fill the duplexes of River Rouge and Ecorse; the tool-and-die and foundry workers of Melvindale; the transplanted Appalachians living in postwar tract homes in Lincoln Park and Southgate; the Polish auto and chemical workers of Wyandotte; and the Eastern Europeans of Allen Park.

Republicans do well among the white-collar residents of Riverview and the company managers of Lincoln Park, many of them reaching retirement age. The shaded streets of western Dearborn and Grosse Ile border large old homes whose owners — executives and wealthy professionals — cast the most solid Republican votes in the area.

Monroe County, south of Wayne, is home to 132,000 of the 16th District's constituents. It is politically marginal territory. Local factories give the county a firm union presence, but the rural western portions are staunchly conservative. The county's Lake Erie shoreline has attracted a large population of retirees from Detroit and Toledo.

The only substantial blue-collar vote outside Wayne County comes from Adrian, which has a large General Motors plant and several chemical plants. Democrats are well organized in the city, but they have little strength among the farmers growing corn and feed grains in the rest of eastern Lenawee County.

Population: 514,560. White 491,483 (96%), Black 14,133 (3%), Other 3,631 (1%). Spanish origin 12,403 (2%). 18 and over 367,589 (71%), 65 and over 52,476 (10%). Median age: 30.

Dingell is a complex man, stubborn and vindictive on occasion, self-confident to the point of arrogance. And yet one has to wonder whether the Dingell "meanness" is at least in part a façade designed to build a public reputation he believes will be helpful to his causes. He is nearly always friendly and helpful to bright young Democrats who join his committee, and he earns the fierce loyalty of his protégés. Many of the colleagues who know him best seem not only to respect him, but genuinely to like him.

But just about everything Dingell does creates the aura of command. He bullies witnesses and badgers colleagues; he intimidates nearly everyone. He has assembled one of the biggest and best technical staffs on Capitol Hill.

Energy and Commerce is an octopus of a committee, with jurisdiction not only over energy but also health, communications, transportation and numerous regulatory agencies.

This does not endear Dingell to other committee chairmen, particularly Dan Rostenkowski of Ways and Means, perhaps the only current chairman who is Dingell's match when it comes to turf warfare.

Rostenkowski and Dingell made a rare alliance in the 100th Congress, however, when they faced a challenge to their shared jurisdiction over Medicare. Those two legislative giants teamed up to beat an effort by Claude Pepper, the revered chairman of the Rules Committee and advocate of the elderly, to bring to the House floor a long-term health-care bill that had circumvented their committees.

Dingell's reign at Energy and Commerce has restored to the full committee a meaningful legislative role it had surrendered to its subcommittees under his innocuous predecessor, Harley O. Staggers of West Virginia.

But even now, Dingell has few shrinking violets to contend with among his subcommittee chairmen. Because he appreciates and encourages aggressive young talent on his committee, he is often required to protect his own power against junior Democrats eager to strike out on their own. Sometimes the only way for Dingell to maintain control against them is to make common cause with the Republican side.

That is how he formed a majority to ram through the committee a business-backed bill to set federal product-liability standards in 1988. He faced a near revolt among Democrats who did not want to consider the divisive issue in an election year — especially since it was clear the bill would go no further than the committee.

The classic family feud at Energy and Commerce is the longstanding stalemate between Dingell and Health Subcommittee Chairman Henry A. Waxman of California over the Clean Air Act, which Dingell would like to relax and Waxman would like to strengthen in order to combat pollution from acid rain.

As the leading legislative spokesman for the U.S. auto industry, which dominates his district, Dingell entered the 1980s with a seemingly strong hand on the issue. He had as allies not only the Reagan administration but a Republican Senate and nearly all the GOP members of his committee.

But he never had the votes to weaken auto-emission standards. He could, however, block Waxman from imposing stricter controls despite growing public concern about the deterioration of air quality. Dingell shored up his lines of defense at the beginning of the 100th Congress when he engineered the appointment of three new coal-country allies to fill vacancies on Energy and Commerce.

The Dingell-Waxman stalemate reached a new breaking point in late 1987, with the approach of a deadline for cities to comply with air-quality standards or face sanctions. Although both sides agreed the deadline should be postponed, they disagreed on how much. Waxman and his environmentalist forces wanted it postponed only until mid-1988, hoping to bring election-year politics to bear on their drive to broaden the Clean Air Act; Dingell wanted to put off the issue until mid-1989, after the elections.

When the House faced the choice between the two options during debate on an omnibus spending bill in December 1987, Dingell predicted he would prevail by a comfortable margin. In fact, he was defeated, 162-257. However, the 100th Congress ended a year later with the Clean Air Act yet to be rewritten.

In the meantime, both Dingell and Waxman have been in danger of losing control of the issue. A group of nine moderate Democrats from Energy and Commerce began meeting in late 1987 to draft a clean-air compromise to bridge the seemingly irreconcilable differences between Dingell and Waxman. But the most serious, though ultimately unsuccessful, effort to reach a compromise at the end of the 100th Congress came from the Senate, not the House.

While Dingell is a formidable legislative opponent, much of his reputation for ruthlessness comes from his role as the House's most aggressive and merciless investigator. As chairman of the Energy and Commerce Subcommittee on Oversight and Investigations, Dingell probes the propriety and performance of federal agencies with the fervor of a crusader. He can force some sluggish federal regulators into action merely by threatening to call them before his subcommittee.

His admirers say his exposés of such problems as pesticides in food and second-rate prescription drugs make him a 220-pound version of Ralph Nader. His detractors say Dingell's oversight of executive agencies is meddlesome, intrusive and an example of congressional government run amok.

In 1983, Dingell's aggressive oversight of problems with the "superfund" hazardous-waste cleanup program led to an institutional conflict between Congress and the White House. Rita M. Lavelle, the director of superfund, was subpoenaed to testify before Energy and Commerce about wrongdoing in the program, but failed to appear. Dingell brought a contempt of Congress resolution before the House; it passed 413-0 and led to Lavelle's indictment.

Overall, Dingell has been a liberal national Democrat, supporting civil rights, Great Society programs and expansion of the role of the federal government. He was an early consumer advocate, working on truth-in-advertising and Federal Trade Commission laws.

But his liberal profile is blurred by his fealty to the auto industry. And Dingell sometimes seems to be a bundle of frustrating contradictions — especially to environmentalists who have benefited enormously from Dingell's effectiveness when he has been on their side.

The Dingell who attacked the Environmental Protection Agency for lax enforcement of hazardous-waste cleanup is the same one who in the 99th Congress promoted a version of superfund legislation that the environmental side considered too weak.

The Dingell who pushed measures to protect endangered species and establish a National Wildlife System infuriates liberals with his militant pro-gun views and active alliance with the National Rifle Association.

In 1972 Ralph Nader called Dingell the consumer's friend. A profile by Nader's organization said, "His record on consumer protection is excellent." In 1980 Nader had a different view. "Given his position, his power, his drive, his corporate allies and his Machiavellian skills," Nader declared, "Dingell can now be considered the No. 1 enemy of consumers on Capitol Hill."

When Energy and Commerce passed the product-liability bill in 1988, Nader scolded: "You should be ashamed of yourself, Mr. Dingell, for this bullying legislation."

At Home: The Dingell family has represented the Detroit area in Congress since 1932. For 23 years, John D. Dingell Sr., a New Deal champion of national health insurance, served from the city's West Side. When he died suddenly in 1955, while undergoing a routine physical examination, his 29-year-old son stepped in.

John Dingell Jr. grew up on Capitol Hill — not in Detroit. It was only when he received his law degree and went to work as an assistant prosecutor that he learned the intricacies of Detroit politics. But after three years as "my father's ears and eyes," he was ready for the 1955 special election. With backing from organized labor, he trounced a dozen Democratic candidates in the primary and went on to overwhelm his 26-year-old GOP opponent.

Since then, Dingell has had to worry about re-election only once, in 1964, when part of his constituency was combined with a larger part of the district held by Democratic Rep. John Lesinski Jr., who had also succeeded his father in the House. The primary between Dingell and Lesinski received national attention because it was thought to be a measure of "white backlash" over recent civil rights legislation. Dingell, whose old district was about one-third black, had voted for the 1964 Civil Rights Act. Lesinski, whose district was nearly all white, was one of four Northern Democrats who had voted against it.

The issue was not brought up in the campaign, but both sides knew it was the main reason Dingell received such strong help from labor, civil rights groups and the state Democratic Party. Dingell won with 55 percent of the vote and has not had any problems since.

Continuing a family tradition, Dingell is now said to be grooming his son, state Sen. Christopher D. Dingell, to succeed him someday.

Committee

Energy and Commerce (Chairman)
Oversight and Investigations (chairman)

Elections

1988 General		
John D. Dingell (D)	132,775	(97%)
Russell W. Leone (I)	3,561	(3%)
1986 General		
John D. Dingell (D)	101,659	(78%)
Frank W. Grzywacki (R)	28,971	(22%)

Previous Winning Percentages: **1984** (64%) **1982** (74%) **1980** (70%) **1978** (77%) **1976** (76%) **1974** (78%) **1972** (68%) **1970** (79%) **1968** (74%) **1966** (63%) **1964** (73%) **1962** (83%) **1960** (79%) **1958** (79%) **1956** (74%) **1955** * (76%)

* *Special election.*

District Vote For President

	1988	1984	1980	1976
D	90,630 (45%)	90,525 (35%)	95,357 (44%)	114,987 (53%)
R	109,695 (54%)	164,851 (64%)	103,367 (48%)	97,607 (45%)
I			13,913 (7%)	

Campaign Finance

	Receipts	Receipts from PACs	Expend-itures
1988			
Dingell (D)	$619,770	$459,242 (74%)	$468,180
1986			
Dingell (D)	$495,660	$375,177 (76%)	$483,019

Key Votes

1987	
Raise speed limit to 65 mph	N
Approve Gephardt "fair trade" amendment	Y
Ban testing of larger nuclear weapons	Y
Delay "re-flagging" of Kuwaiti tankers	Y
Approve tax-raising deficit-reduction bill	Y
1988	
Approve aid to Nicaraguan contras	N
Enact civil rights restoration bill over Reagan veto	Y
Kill 60-day plant-closing notification measure	N
Pass omnibus trade bill over Reagan veto	Y
Approve death penalty for drug-related murders	Y
Bar federal funds for abortions in cases of rape and incest	N
Oppose seven-day waiting period for purchase of handguns	Y

Voting Studies

	Presidential Support		Party Unity		Conservative Coalition	
Year	S	O	S	O	S	O
1988	22	75	88	3	29	61
1987	16	78	88	1	16	74
1986	24	70	80	5	32	58
1985	23	71	76	5	27	64
1984	30	59	84	7	31	63
1983	23	67	84	6	16	78
1982	44	55	90	7	25	74
1981	36	55	73	11	27	55

Interest Group Ratings

Year	ADA	ACU	AFL-CIO	CCUS
1988	80	13	100	29
1987	92	0	100	7
1986	75	19	92	6
1985	85	14	88	25
1984	75	9	92	33
1983	90	0	100	28
1982	80	14	100	18
1981	70	15	86	21

17 Sander M. Levin (D)

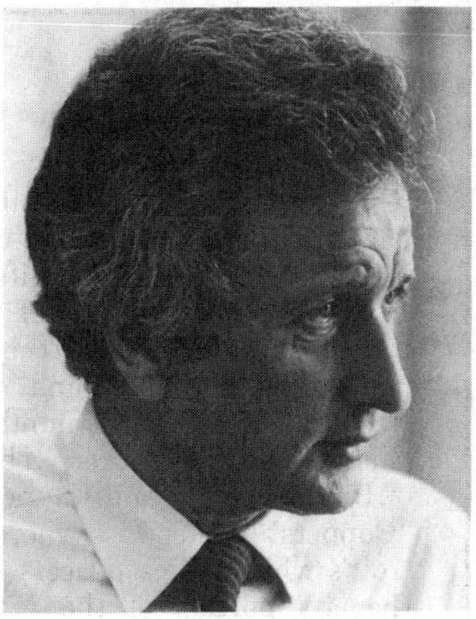

Of Southfield — Elected 1982

Born: Sept. 6, 1931, Detroit, Mich.
Education: U. of Chicago, B.A. 1952; Columbia U., M.A. 1954; Harvard U., LL.B. 1957.
Occupation: Lawyer.
Family: Wife, Victoria Schlafer; four children.
Religion: Jewish.
Political Career: Mich. Senate, 1965-71; Democratic nominee for governor, 1970, 1974.
Capitol Office: 323 Cannon Bldg. 20515; 225-4961.

In Washington: Levin is something of a political hybrid. A junior member, he shares the fiscal concerns of the younger Democrats elected with him in 1982, a year of recession and unprecedented deficits. Yet, as he nears 60, he retains the orthodox liberalism of his first days in politics in the mid-1960s, and thus a zeal to address today's social needs on the scale of the Great Society.

After just three House terms, he has won considerable respect as a thoughtful and judicious legislator determined to find right answers even if they are not simple answers. His standing would be even higher were it not for his penchant for discussing complex issues in all their details and abstractions, a trait that contributed to his losses in two elections for the Michigan governorship in the 1970s.

It could also have cost him a coveted seat on the Ways and Means Committee, but his dogged pursuit of the prize and his support of the panel's 1986 tax-overhaul bill overcame what qualms Chairman Dan Rostenkowski had that Levin would make himself too obtrusive on the tightly controlled panel. Also, Michigan had a geographic claim on the seat. So, in the 100th Congress, Levin joined the committee whose breadth of interests is as wide as his own.

He had something substantive to say on just about every major issue the panel considered. He came equipped with his own legislation overhauling the welfare system, which he had cosponsored in the previous Congress with Democratic Sen. Daniel Patrick Moynihan of New York. It would have required states to establish work, training and education programs for recipients of Aid to Families with Dependent Children and to provide child care, transportation and other services for those trying to become self-sufficient.

Levin filed his bill in early 1987, a day before the House Democratic leadership's version was unveiled at a press conference attended by Rostenkowski and Speaker Jim Wright, among others. In doing so, he staked out the left for the coming debate, and ultimately some of his bill's provisions were reflected in the final product.

In mid-1988, he unsuccessfully opposed a GOP motion instructing House negotiators to settle for the lower price tag on the Senate's welfare-reform package; he knew that any cost-cutting would doom his efforts to raise welfare benefits toward the poverty line. Though the bill was much reduced from the House version, it still contained provisions Levin had long sought, and he voted for it on final passage.

In the 100th Congress, Ways and Means also had the lead House role in passing legislation to revamp trade policy, an area in which Detroiter Levin represented the interests of an auto industry buffeted by foreign imports. He supported the controversial Gephardt "fair trade" amendment, defending it against those who called it protectionist.

Responding to a negative editorial, Levin described himself as a non-isolationist and "a committed internationalist." But, he added, that "doesn't mean allowing others to run roughshod over our home market or lock us out of theirs." He also campaigned vigorously for the amendment's sponsor, Missouri Democratic Rep. Richard A. Gephardt, in the 1988 spring presidential primaries.

Levin again expressed the auto industry's concerns when Ways and Means turned to legislation implementing a U.S.-Canada trade pact phasing out tariffs between the two nations over 10 years. Several industries were worried that Canada would maintain various subsidies and trade barriers to benefit its firms. At one point, Clayton Yeutter and James A. Baker III, then President Reagan's trade representative and Treasury secretary, respectively, testified before Ways and Means to ask members to focus not on individual areas but on the pact's overall benefits. Levin countered, "We don't come from nowhere, or everywhere." In the end, he voted for the bill, which became law.

As a member of Ways and Means' Health Subcommittee, he worked to maintain higher payments to Northeastern and Midwestern hospitals when the panel had to reduce Medi-

Michigan 17

Northwest Detroit; Southeast Oakland County

The 17th combines white-collar suburban territory with a blue-collar presence inside the Detroit city limits.

The Detroit section of the district, at the far western end of the city, includes black neighborhoods and racially mixed Brightmoor, with large numbers of Appalachian blue-collar workers. The civil servants of Rosedale Park and the police families of "Coppers' Corner" — where many of Detroit's white police officers cluster — give the city portion of the 17th a relatively conservative Democratic presence.

The largest of the suburban towns is Southfield, with a population of 73,000. It is one of two centers for corporate headquarters and professional offices in the suburbs northwest of Detroit. Its 40-story high-rises lining the Northwestern Highway house a substantial population of Jewish senior citizens, while many younger, middle-class Jewish people live in the single-family houses away from the expressway. Coupled with the black community in the southern half of Southfield, the Jewish vote helps put the city solidly behind Democratic candidates. There is also a substantial Jewish vote in neighboring Oak Park, where a significant Orthodox community has been growing more conservative politically in recent years.

Black-majority Inkster, an overwhelmingly Democratic blue-collar town, bulges out of the district's southern tip. Nearby Dearborn Heights is politically mixed; the wealthy neighborhoods north and east of Inkster lean Republican while the blue-collar workers in the bungalows north of Ford Road are more sympathetic to Democrats. The liberal young professionals in the eastern tip of Dearborn Heights reinforce the Democratic vote.

There is Republican support here in the Catholic neighborhoods that stand in the shadow of Royal Oak's Shrine of the Little Flower, where Father Charles Coughlin, the right-wing radio commentator, preached in the 1930s. Solid Republican votes also come from the ranch homes of Lathrup Village and Pleasant Ridge and the larger homes of Huntington Woods.

Population: 514,560. White 440,607 (86%), Black 65,691 (13%), Other 5,484 (1%). Spanish origin 5,653 (1%). 18 and over 382,414 (74%), 65 and over 60,307 (12%). Median age: 31.

care during a round of budget-cutting for fiscal 1988 and 1989. He also has focused on legislative efforts to address the AIDS epidemic.

Like his brother Carl in the Senate, Levin was a leader within the House minority that opposed a new federal death penalty included in the 1988 anti-drug package. Unable to block the pre-election wave of support for the provision, opponents could merely pick at it; Levin won adoption of his amendment barring execution of the mentally retarded. Unlike 30 fellow liberals, he voted for the drug bill on final passage despite the capital punishment provision.

While serving on the Banking, Finance and Urban Affairs Committee in his first two terms, he focused on policies for the disadvantaged and unemployed, and on Third World debt. In his first term, Levin worked with Connecticut Democrat Bruce A. Morrison to ensure that jobs funding is targeted to areas with the highest unemployment, such as Michigan.

As a one-time international development official in the Carter administration, he has long taken an interest in economic difficulties faced by other nations, and has been critical of moves to cut funding for the World Bank agency that lends money to the poorest nations.

But Levin's concern for developing countries is tempered by his concern for job losses in this country. In 1986, when the House reauthorized the Export-Import Bank, which makes loans to foreign countries that buy U.S. products and services, he supported an amendment to ban all loans for foreign industries whose products or commodities compete with U.S.-made items. The amendment was watered down before being passed.

On foreign policy, Levin's instincts are generally liberal. He has consistently opposed aid to the Nicaraguan contras, for instance. He has been a frequent critic of the Soviet Union, singling out most often its refusal to grant exit visas for Jews. Levin's district includes a large Jewish community.

Though he was one of the oldest and most politically experienced members of the large 1982 House Democratic class, Levin has been close to his colleagues who are considerably younger, even joining them occasionally on the basketball or squash courts.

He stood with his budget-conscious classmates when, as freshmen, they dramatically signaled their presence to the House. Voting practically as a bloc, they helped defeat an emergency appropriations bill late in 1983, to focus attention on the impasse between Congress and the White House over reducing the federal deficit. When Republicans labeled the move a transparent political gesture, Levin spoke up for the group.

"We had the courage to say something in an excruciatingly difficult situation," he scolded. "You should have the same courage to say to the president, 'You should stop stonewalling on the issue of the deficit.' "

At Home: Levin's 1982 election capped his unexpected return to politics after an eight-year absence from the public eye.

Levin first won office in 1964, taking a state Senate seat in the heavily Jewish Oakland County suburbs north of Detroit. He served as state Democratic Party chairman in the late 1960s and was viewed as one of the party's rising stars in 1970, when he challenged incumbent Republican William G. Milliken for the governorship.

But the low-key, even-tempered manner that had made Levin a successful legislator and party leader was less useful against Milliken. In 1970 and in a 1974 rematch, Levin was unable to develop a knack for fighting Milliken's "nice-guy" image — the more Levin presented voters with detailed factual information about state government programs, the less interested they seemed. One reporter referred to the 1974 campaign as "the bland leading the bland." Levin won almost 49 percent of the vote in 1970, but four years later, he slipped under 47 percent.

After that, Levin's name left the front pages. He ran the technical assistance program for the Agency for International Development under President Jimmy Carter. But when Democratic Rep. William M. Brodhead decided not to seek re-election 12 weeks before the 1982 primary, Levin returned to the area he represented in the state Senate and announced his candidacy.

Levin's name and his support from the party establishment helped him overcome five primary opponents. Critics accused Levin of trying to regain public office on the popularity of his younger brother, Sen. Carl Levin, an accusation that obscured the fact that Sander's statewide races had helped pave the way for Carl's 1978 victory. Sander Levin won the 17th easily in November, and has not been seriously challenged since.

Committees

Select Children, Youth and Families (9th of 18 Democrats)

Ways and Means (21st of 23 Democrats)
Health; Social Security

Elections

1988 General

Sander M. Levin (D)	135,493	(70%)
Dennis M. Flessland (R)	55,197	(29%)

1986 General

Sander M. Levin (D)	105,031	(76%)
Calvin Williams (R)	30,879	(23%)

Previous Winning Percentages: 1984 (100%) **1982** (67%)

District Vote For President

	1988	1984	1980	1976
D	100,638 (53%)	102,650 (46%)	104,307 (48%)	97,333 (45%)
R	87,179 (46%)	119,681 (54%)	94,266 (43%)	114,031 (53%)
I			16,950 (8%)	

Campaign Finance

	Receipts	Receipts from PACs	Expend-itures
1988			
Levin (D)	$300,654	$193,430 (64%)	$233,421
1986			
Levin (D)	$221,609	$121,903 (55%)	$134,327

Key Votes

1987

Raise speed limit to 65 mph	N
Approve Gephardt "fair trade" amendment	Y
Ban testing of larger nuclear weapons	Y
Delay "re-flagging" of Kuwaiti tankers	Y
Approve tax-raising deficit-reduction bill	Y

1988

Approve aid to Nicaraguan contras	N
Enact civil rights restoration bill over Reagan veto	Y
Kill 60-day plant-closing notification measure	N
Pass omnibus trade bill over Reagan veto	Y
Approve death penalty for drug-related murders	N
Bar federal funds for abortions in cases of rape and incest	N
Oppose seven-day waiting period for purchase of handguns	N

Voting Studies

	Presidential Support		Party Unity		Conservative Coalition	
Year	S	O	S	O	S	O
1988	24	73	94	2	11	89
1987	19	80	97	2	19	81
1986	19	81	97	2	12	86
1985	23	78	97	3	13	87
1984	30	70	93 †	7 †	15	85
1983	28	72	94	6	19	81

† Not eligible for all recorded votes.

Interest Group Ratings

Year	ADA	ACU	AFL-CIO	CCUS
1988	100	0	100	31
1987	84	0	100	13
1986	85	0	100	33
1985	85	10	88	32
1984	90	5	85	25
1983	95	0	94	25

18 William S. Broomfield (R)

Of Birmingham — Elected 1956

Born: April 28, 1922, Royal Oak, Mich.
Education: Attended Michigan State U., 1951.
Military Career: Army Air Corps, 1942.
Occupation: Insurance executive.
Family: Wife, Jane Smith Thompson; three children.
Religion: Presbyterian.
Political Career: Mich. House, 1949-55; Mich. Senate, 1955-57.
Capitol Office: 2306 Rayburn Bldg. 20515; 225-6135.

In Washington: While he would not trade away any of his 30-plus years in the House, Broomfield's longevity has given him an undesired place in congressional history. A victim of the "permanent" Democratic dominance of the body, Broomfield shares a record with his 1956 classmate, House Minority Leader Robert H. Michel, for the longest continuous tenure as a member of a minority party.

While Broomfield wishes the situation were otherwise, he long ago adapted himself to the necessity of working with a Democratic majority. The ranking Republican on the House Foreign Affairs Committee since 1975, Broomfield defines his role as that of a "consensus-builder," working to bridge the often wide gap between the Republican White House and Democratic Congress on foreign policy issues.

Broomfield gets along well with the chairman of Foreign Affairs, moderate Florida Democrat Dante B. Fascell. Unlike many of the committee's activist Democrats, Broomfield says, Fascell "doesn't try to pretend he's secretary of state."

Broomfield's conciliatory behavior sets him apart from those younger Republicans who sign up for the committee specifically to crusade for conservative foreign policy positions. "Realizing a consensus involves many activities," Broomfield says. "What it does *not* involve is staking out rigid public positions." During the panel's frequently bitter, ideologically charged debates, Broomfield often fades into the background.

Yet despite Broomfield's mild manner and willingness to deal, he has never been threatened with mutiny within the panel's GOP ranks. This is mainly because he remains, above all else, a party loyalist and a faithful spear-carrier for Republican presidents.

In early 1989, Broomfield waxed effusive about President Reagan, whom he praised for "the finest foreign policy record of any administration" he served under during 32 years in the House. "It is ironic that the candidate who was portrayed . . . as some kind of cowboy who could not understand the subtleties and complexities of international relations would in eight years restore the United States to a position of respect throughout the world," Broomfield said.

During the Reagan years, it was Broomfield who usually packaged and presented the administration's substitutes for Democrat-crafted foreign policy legislation. When the House in December 1987 passed a foreign aid authorization bill that imposed what Reagan said were too many restrictions on his ability to conduct foreign policy, Broomfield proposed a Republican substitute for the entire bill. Though the alternative measure was sweetened with additional funding for fiscal year 1989, it was defeated by a 173-234 House vote.

Broomfield's partisan loyalty came to the fore during the controversy over the Iran-contra affair. While he criticized Reagan for selling arms to the hostile nation of Iran, Broomfield expressed concern that the congressional investigation of the covert policies would become a drawn-out forum for Democratic attacks on Reagan and his policy of aiding the Nicaraguan contras. Broomfield was one of two House members to vote against the resolution establishing the House select committee to investigate Iran-contra.

As senior Republican on Foreign Affairs, Broomfield took a seat on the joint panel anyway, though the ranking position went to Dick Cheney of Wyoming, a higher-profile leadership figure. Broomfield was not one of the committee's dogged inquisitors, joining in mainly to ask lengthy rhetorical questions aimed at eliciting a pro-Reagan response.

In one instance, Broomfield stretched for a metaphor to sum up the need for renewed U.S. support to the contras. In May 1987, he obliquely asked contra leader Adolfo Calero, "Would you say that to the people of Nicaragua yearning for freedom the United States is now viewed more like a lighthouse whose beam is growing dimmer currently or a lighthouse tem-

Michigan 18

Oakland County

This district is the one GOP bastion in metropolitan Detroit. Its Republican core is in the cluster of towns on both sides of Woodward Avenue, the artery running northwest from Detroit and the route along which the city's affluent first escaped to the suburbs. In this area, Republicans and golf courses abound, and GOP presidential candidates prevail by more than 2-to-1.

Bloomfield Hills and Birmingham, like the Grosse Pointes, are dotted with the 1920s mansions and newer ranch houses of top-level auto executives and professionals. Bloomfield Hills was former GOP Gov. George Romney's hometown in his days as an auto executive.

To the west are the only slightly more modest shaded streets of Farmington Hills, a town of lawyers, doctors and business executives. To the east is Troy, a gathering ground for gleaming suburban business headquarters and professionals' offices; off the main roads live upper-middle-class Protestant voters.

The southwestern end of the 18th is a jumble of suburbs whose exploding populations helped make the district the second fastest-growing constituency in the state in the 1970s. Its far western end jabs into two Livingston County townships: the older blue-collar suburbs of Green Oak Township, some of its houses sporting two or three rusting cars in front, and Brighton Township, whose newer subdivisions have attracted a mix of factory workers and professionals from Ann Arbor and Detroit.

The old horse country of western Oakland County has taken on a decidedly blue-collar cast around South Lyon and in more ethnic Commerce Township. Wixom and Walled Lake house factory workers who tend toward conservatism on social issues.

The northern end of the district is less wealthy. Pontiac Township, east of Pontiac, is a melting pot into whose 25-year-old subdivisions the surrounding area's autoworkers, mid-level managers and small-business people have poured. The outlying townships in northeastern Oakland County are strongly Republican and rural, although much of the farm land north of Rochester has been sold off for development.

One of the few Democratic toeholds here is in Shelby Township in Macomb County. Shelby's small, postwar brick houses hold blue-collar workers from Utica and Warren.

Population: 514,560. White 500,199 (97%), Black 4,160 (1%), Other 8,085 (2%). Spanish origin 4,792 (1%). 18 and over 360,726 (70%), 65 and over 36,119 (7%). Median age: 31.

porarily encased in a fog bank of itself by indulgent self-examination?"

One Reagan administration policy that caused some personal difficulty for Broomfield was its "constructive engagement" with the white regime in South Africa. In the 99th Congress, Broomfield voted for a Senate bill invoking mild sanctions against South Africa, stating that "Congress, the administration and the American people deplore the system of apartheid and the human toll that lies in its wake." But he later voted in the minority to uphold Reagan's veto of the bill.

During the 100th Congress, Broomfield was sharply critical of House Democrats who pushed a tougher South Africa sanctions bill to a vote just before the August 1988 Republican National Convention. Broomfield accused the Democrats of trying to "construct the Dukakis-Jackson platform" in an effort to embarrass the Republicans. After the bill passed the House, Broomfield filed an unsuccessful motion to recommit it to Foreign Affairs for the addition of a provision delaying the sanctions until the president certified that they would not damage U.S. national-security interests. The House-passed sanctions bill stalled and died in the Senate, though.

There were rare occasions when Broomfield publicly criticized Reagan. Though he supported Reagan's 1987 policy of using the U.S. Navy to keep shipping lanes open in the war-torn Persian Gulf, he expressed dismay that the administration had ignored Congress in instituting the policy. "One of the lessons of the covert Iran arms sales is that the absence of prior congressional consultation may spell disaster for a high-risk foreign policy," Broomfield said.

But Broomfield's criticisms are mainly reserved for America's foreign adversaries. After the alleged Soviet bugging of the uncompleted U.S. Embassy in Moscow was made public in early 1987, Broomfield worked to make it more difficult for Soviet diplomats to occupy their new Washington embassy, located on a high point overlooking the downtown area. He added an amendment to an intelligence funding bill, requiring the secretary of defense to report to Congress on whether it would be consistent with national security for the Soviets to occupy that embassy. He also joined with a bipartisan group of Foreign Affairs members who attached a package of amendments to the 1987 foreign aid bill to tighten security at U.S. embassies abroad.

At Home: Broomfield's longevity at home has little to do with his work on Foreign Affairs. It is a result of his ability to project himself to his suburban district as a pleasant, service-oriented Republican. Handling constituent requests and flooding the district with newsletters over 30-plus years have made Broomfield all but untouchable.

The few political struggles have come within his own party. But at the two critical junctures in his political career, when he seemed to be up against unfavorable odds, Broomfield managed to be on the popular side.

The first time was 1956, when he challenged a more senior state senator to succeed retiring Republican George A. Dondero, who had served in Congress from suburban Detroit since 1933. The major issue was construction of a toll road through a residential section of Oakland County. Broomfield's opponent, George N. Higgins, supported it. Broomfield, who had fought it in the state Legislature, argued that any new highway should go through a more rural area. Most of the county's voters shared his view, and he narrowly won. The road was never built.

Sixteen years later, Broomfield faced his second political crisis, following the realignment of Oakland County's congressional districts. Since 1964, he had been winning reelection easily in the eastern part of the county. But in 1972, when this area was attached to a blue-collar section of Macomb County, Broomfield decided he would have better luck in western Oakland County, against the GOP incumbent there, Jack H. McDonald.

McDonald was already representing most of the new constituency, but again Broomfield had the paramount issue on his side: busing. His House amendment put him in the forefront of the opposition to federally mandated busing. Even though McDonald was just as firmly opposed to busing, Broomfield had been more vocal. He won the primary with 59 percent.

Committees

Foreign Affairs (Ranking)
Arms Control, International Security and Science (ranking)

Small Business (3rd of 17 Republicans)
Regulation, Business Opportunity and Energy (ranking)

Elections

1988 General

William S. Broomfield (R)	195,579	(76%)
Gary L. Kohut (D)	57,643	(22%)

1986 General

William S. Broomfield (R)	110,099	(74%)
Gary L. Kohut (D)	39,144	(26%)

Previous Winning Percentages: **1984** (79%) **1982** (73%) **1980** (73%) **1978** (71%) **1976** (67%) **1974** (63%) **1972** (70%) **1970** (65%) **1968** (60%) **1966** (68%) **1964** (60%) **1962** (60%) **1960** (56%) **1958** (53%) **1956** (57%)

District Vote For President

	1988	1984	1980	1976
D	80,246 (29%)	65,252 (25%)	67,833 (28%)	76,445 (37%)
R	192,002 (71%)	190,888 (74%)	150,366 (62%)	127,570 (61%)
I			20,583 (9%)	

Campaign Finance

	Receipts	Receipts from PACs	Expend-itures
1988			
Broomfield (R)	$235,699	$57,700 (24%)	$77,103
Kohut (D) †	$9,460	$3,350 (35%)	$9,459
1986			
Broomfield (R)	$179,403	$33,520 (19%)	$68,497
Kohut (D)	$5,929	$1,550 (26%)	$5,929

† Totals based on incomplete data.

Key Votes

1987

Raise speed limit to 65 mph	Y
Approve Gephardt "fair trade" amendment	N
Ban testing of larger nuclear weapons	N
Delay "re-flagging" of Kuwaiti tankers	N
Approve tax-raising deficit-reduction bill	N

1988

Approve aid to Nicaraguan contras	Y
Enact civil rights restoration bill over Reagan veto	N
Kill 60-day plant-closing notification measure	Y
Pass omnibus trade bill over Reagan veto	N
Approve death penalty for drug-related murders	Y
Bar federal funds for abortions in cases of rape and incest	Y
Oppose seven-day waiting period for purchase of handguns	N

Voting Studies

	Presidential Support		Party Unity		Conservative Coalition	
Year	**S**	**O**	**S**	**O**	**S**	**O**
1988	58	35	67	20	84	11
1987	69	30	71	27	84	14
1986	70	29	69	23	72	26
1985	73	24	67	28	84	13
1984	61	31	78	17	90	10
1983	77	18	77	6	80	16
1982	65	26	72	20	82	12
1981	63	26	77	19	73	24

Interest Group Ratings

Year	ADA	ACU	AFL-CIO	CCUS
1988	30	84	36	92
1987	0	96	0	93
1986	5	73	7	100
1985	5	85	13	71
1984	5	71	23	80
1983	5	87	7	95
1982	10	67	16	77
1981	20	80	13	94

Minnesota

U.S. CONGRESS

SENATE 2 R
HOUSE 5 D, 3 R

LEGISLATURE

Senate 45 D, 22 R
House 81 D, 53 R

ELECTIONS

1988 Presidential Vote	
Bush	46%
Dukakis	53%
1984 Presidential Vote	
Reagan	50%
Mondale	50%
1980 Presidential Vote	
Reagan	43%
Carter	47%
Anderson	9%
Turnout rate in 1984	68%
Turnout rate in 1986	45%
Turnout rate in 1988	66%

(as percentage of voting age population)

POPULATION AND GROWTH

1980 population	4,075,970
1988 population estimate (21st in the nation)	4,307,000
Percent change 1980-1988	+6%

DEMOGRAPHIC BREAKDOWN

White	97%
Black	1%
Other	2%
(Spanish origin)	1%
Urban	67%
Rural	33%
Born in state	75%
Foreign-born	3%

MAJOR CITIES

Minneapolis	356,840
St. Paul	263,680
Bloomington	85,740
Duluth	82,380
Rochester	58,130

AREA AND LAND USE

Area	79,548 sq. miles (14th)
Farm	54%
Forest	33%
Federally owned	7%

Gov. Rudy Perpich (D)
Of Hibbing — Elected 1982
(also served 1976-79)

Born: June 27, 1928, Carson Lake, Minn.
Education: Hibbing Junior College, A.A. 1950; Marquette U., D.D.S. 1954.
Military Career: Army, 1946-47.
Occupation: Dentist.
Religion: Roman Catholic.
Political Career: Hibbing Board of Education, 1956-62; Minn. Senate, 1963-71; lieutenant governor, 1971-76.
Next Election: 1990.

WORK

Occupations	
White-collar	53%
Blue-collar	27%
Service workers	14%
Government Workers	
Federal	30,729
State	76,024
Local	180,105

MONEY

Median family income	$ 21,185	(13th)
Tax burden per capita	$ 1,247	(5th)

EDUCATION

Spending per pupil through grade 12	$ 3,941	(17th)
Persons with college degrees	17%	(20th)

CRIME

Violent crime rate	285 per 100,000 (35th)

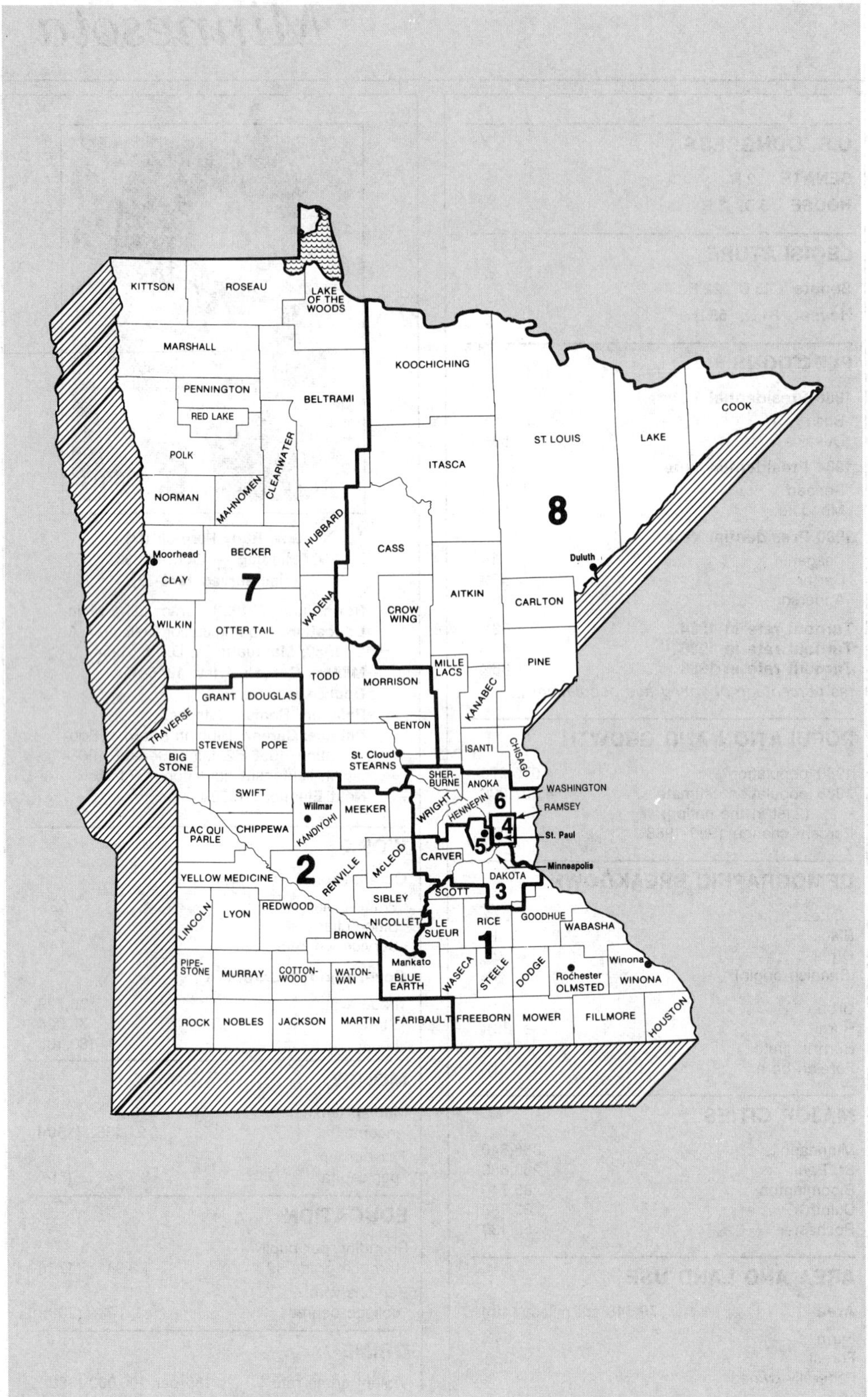
KITTSON
ROSEAU
LAKE OF THE WOODS
MARSHALL
KOOCHICHING
PENNINGTON
RED LAKE
BELTRAMI
COOK
ST. LOUIS
LAKE
POLK
CLEARWATER
ITASCA
NORMAN
MAHNOMEN
8
HUBBARD
CASS
Moorhead
BECKER
Duluth
CLAY
7
AITKIN
CARLTON
CROW WING
WADENA
WILKIN
OTTER TAIL
MILLE LACS
PINE
TODD
MORRISON
KANABEC
GRANT
DOUGLAS
TRAVERSE
BENTON
STEVENS
POPE
ISANTI
CHISAGO
BIG STONE
St. Cloud
STEARNS
SHER-BURNE
ANOKA
WASHINGTON
SWIFT
6
RAMSEY
Willmar
MEEKER
WRIGHT
HENNEPIN
4
LAC QUI PARLE
CHIPPEWA
KANDIYOHI
St. Paul
5
MCLEOD
CARVER
2
Minneapolis
YELLOW MEDICINE
RENVILLE
DAKOTA
3
SIBLEY
SCOTT
REDWOOD
LINCOLN
LYON
NICOLLET
LE SUEUR
RICE
GOODHUE
WABASHA
BROWN
1
PIPE-STONE
MURRAY
COTTON-WOOD
WATON-WAN
Mankato
BLUE EARTH
WASECA
STEELE
DODGE
Rochester
OLMSTED
Winona
WINONA
ROCK
NOBLES
JACKSON
MARTIN
FARIBAULT
FREEBORN
MOWER
FILLMORE
HOUSTON

Dave Durenberger (R)

Of Minneapolis — Elected 1978

Born: Aug. 19, 1934, St. Cloud, Minn.

Education: St. John's U., B.A. 1955; U. of Minnesota, J.D. 1959.

Military Career: Army Reserve, 1956-63.

Occupation: Lawyer; adhesives manufacturing executive.

Family: Wife, Gilda Beth "Penny" Baran; four children.

Religion: Roman Catholic.

Political Career: No previous office.

Capitol Office: 154 Russell Bldg. 20510; 224-3244.

In Washington: The 100th Congress was largely uneventful by the standard Durenberger set in the 99th. That is probably what he wanted, though; few senators stood to gain as much as he by lowering their profile.

But at the outset of the 101st Congress, Durenberger sent a signal that he was looking to reassert his influence over a range of domestic issues, particularly health policy, a legislative arena where he has often been a skilled player. This suggested that after four years of political tumult, and an even longer stretch of upheaval in his private life, Durenberger was aiming to rebuild the reputation for thoughtful legislating that marked his career before he entered, as he once said, his "so-called flake period."

Durenberger's rise to the chairmanship of the Senate Intelligence Committee in 1985 brought repeated confrontations with the Reagan administration and criticism from his colleagues. He had to cope with a series of disturbing revelations about Soviet and Israeli espionage activity in the United States, a public break with the GOP administration over Nicaragua and a nasty feud with William J. Casey, the late CIA director.

Then, just as Durenberger was about to leave the chairmanship at the end of 1986, news of the Iran-contra affair broke. Within days, he was caught in the middle of the most sensitive political inquiry of his career, one topped off by a heated argument with some of his committee colleagues over whether or not to release the results of their investigation.

He incurred the wrath of many of his colleagues after deciding to brief President Reagan on its contents in December 1986. It was the second time in a year that Durenberger was criticized for talking to outsiders about Intelligence Committee business. After a U.S. citizen was caught spying for Israel, Durenberger told a group of American Jews that the United States had once tried to recruit a spy in Israel; he was criticized, but not punished, by the Senate Ethics Committee.

As the 101st Congress began, the committee was also still examining a lucrative book deal in which Durenberger was paid $100,000 to make speeches promoting the book, raising questions about whether he had tried to bypass honoraria limits.

All of this made for a great deal of media exposure and public stress on a man who had always seemed more comfortable immersing himself in the complex details of legislation than attracting attention with symbolic stands on controversial issues. The pressure of events added to the personal difficulties with which Durenberger has been struggling in recent years. He has undergone a particularly trying "mid-life crisis," about which he spoke frankly to newspapers in interviews that detailed his separation from his family and search for happiness.

With seats on the Finance and Environment committees, Durenberger has been able to exercise his legislative skills on an impressive variety of domestic policy over the years. He joined Labor and Human Resources as the 101st Congress began, which with Finance writes most of the law for health and human services legislation.

He served as chairman of the Finance Subcommittee on Health during Republican control of the Senate; he kept the ranking slot with the change in party control in 1987. He was a leading sponsor of the provisions of the 1983 Social Security bill that established the "prospective payment" system for Medicare, perhaps the most significant measure enacted in the legislative drive of the 1980s to cut health-care costs. The plan, originally proposed by the Reagan administration, established the principle that Medicare would pay hospitals fixed amounts for treatment of various types of diseases — replacing the old system under which Medicare paid hospitals their costs to treat patients.

More recently, Durenberger has been active in seeking protection for people who lack adequate health insurance; pushing for tax credits to offset long-term health care costs; seeking new federal payment formulas for rural hospitals; and pressing for preventive health care measures. He sponsored a provision of the 1986 deficit-reduction bill that required employers to continue for a time to provide insurance for laid-off employees, and for the families of workers who died or were divorced.

On Environment, Durenberger has been one of a small group of Republicans who frequently ally with environmental groups in pushing for tighter safeguards. One of Durenberger's projects has been the problem of leaking underground storage tanks, which are a significant threat to drinking-water supplies in Minnesota and elsewhere. His amendment, attached to a hazardous-waste-control bill that cleared in 1984, established the first federal program to prevent gasoline and other hazardous materials stored below ground from entering the water supply. He also has been active in pushing legislation to strengthen federal standards for water and air quality.

Durenberger never really focused attention on Finance's best-known achievement of the decade, the 1986 tax overhaul. He seemed at times to be unable to make up his mind about the measure, backing its central thrust even while worrying that it was "really very silly" to restructure the tax system in the midst of severe budget problems.

He had played a more significant role on the 1981 tax-cut bill, although his chief achievement was not very long-lived. He was a principal author of the amendment to the 1981 tax bill that allowed unprofitable corporations to lease their unused tax breaks to other companies sitting on highly taxable profits. The provision was aimed at aiding needy Frost Belt industries, but had the unintended side effect of allowing many profitable companies to wipe out their tax liabilities. It was an embarrassment that Congress repealed the following year, over Durenberger's resistance.

The 100th Congress marked his return to the domestic policy arena after his preoccupation with intelligence issues in the 99th Congress. Durenberger's service as Intelligence chairman coincided with one of the stormiest periods over aiding the Nicaraguan contras.

The evolution of his thinking on Nicaragua managed to anger just about everyone concerned with the issue: Liberal anti-war protesters were pouring blood on his Minnesota office even as he was being excoriated by conservatives in the Senate and the Reagan administration.

Durenberger's main concern upon taking over the Intelligence panel in 1985 was to put an end to the "covert" U.S. campaign against Nicaragua's leftist government. The strain of running a secret war that was no secret to anyone was destroying CIA morale, he said, and threatening the agency with disintegration. Working with other congressional moderates, he helped draft the 1985 proposal that provided the contras with overt, non-military aid.

By the next year, however, Durenberger had grown disillusioned both with the contras and with the Reagan administration's renewed request for military aid. The contras, he said, were a "second-rate" group more intent on collecting U.S. aid money than in waging what he described as an essentially hopeless military struggle against the government.

Durenberger also expressed an attitude close to contempt for President Reagan's approach to Central America, which he described as "Hollywood oversimplifications." In Durenberger's words, "It's tough to watch Ronald Reagan operate on Nicaragua. It's tough to watch him kill the patient."

At Home: Durenberger's behavior in the 99th Congress seemed to make him a prime target as the 1988 election cycle began. Democrats, frustrated by Durenberger's ability to present himself as a quiet and independent problem-solver in two impressive Senate campaigns, saw an opportunity to present him as an unpredictable "flake." And they had a very well-known candidate to do the job: Hubert H. "Skip" Humphrey III, son of former Vice President Hubert H. Humphrey, the revered Democrat who once held this Senate seat.

But Humphrey's campaign against Durenberger proved to be one of the most disappointing challenges in the country. Throughout his Senate bid, Humphrey, who had built his own popularity as state attorney general, struggled to meet high expectations that came with his famous name. Instead of keeping the focus on Durenberger, Humphrey was fending off unflattering comparisons between himself and his father. Often it was Humphrey's fellow Democrats who were the most critical.

Durenberger, meanwhile, carefully reinforced his old image as a thoughtful legislator. Always a personable campaigner, he spent considerable time traveling the state, holding hearings and forums on health care, rural development and the environment. And Durenberger ignored Humphrey for much of the campaign, much to the frustration of the challenger, who was consistently trailing in the polls and searching for an effective theme.

In one early exchange, Durenberger swatted down a Humphrey ad by effectively drawing the father-and-son comparison that was already plaguing the Democrat. Humphrey's ad sharply criticized Durenberger's record and noted the Ethics Committee rebuke; in response, Durenberger said Humphrey's "late great father would never have started a campaign this way.... Skip Humphrey should know better."

Humphrey's slow organizational start and

inability to meet high fund-raising expectations made it difficult for him to run the sort of media effort many expected at the outset. In the fall, he started throwing some populistic punches. Humphrey accused Durenberger of having misguided priorities, that, among other things, led him to cast votes for the Nicaraguan contras and against Medicare. Humphrey also accused Durenberger of voting for a tax break for corporations that paid for a vacation he took in Puerto Rico.

But by October there was not much evidence that he had done himself any good, and there was some sense that Minnesota voters were tiring of negative media assaults. Durenberger, who had run some ads accusing Humphrey of being soft on crime, halted his negative advertising and challenged the Democrat to do the same. After trying to get Durenberger to drop all ads for the last 10 days of the campaign, Humphrey switched to positive spots. On Election Day, he was swamped, losing 56-41 percent.

Durenberger waged his first two Senate campaigns in a period of four years. His initial race, in 1978, was the easier of the two. He rode a Minnesota Republican tide to a comfortable victory. Four years later he had to buck the economic failures of national and state GOP administrations and the unlimited financial resources of his Democratic rival. Although he won by a narrower margin, his second victory was a more striking personal triumph.

Durenberger's presence in the Senate is the result of an unusual set of events. When the 1978 political year began, he was preparing a gubernatorial challenge that seemed to be going nowhere. When it ended, he was the state's senior senator.

Durenberger had hovered on the periphery of public office for years, as chief aide to GOP Gov. Harold Levander during the late 1960s and as a well-connected Minneapolis lawyer after that. But he was politically untested, and, in spite of a yearlong campaign, he was given little chance to wrest the nomination for governor from popular U.S. Rep. Albert H. Quie.

When interim Sen. Muriel Humphrey announced that she would not run for the remaining four years of her late husband's term, Republican leaders asked Durenberger to switch contests. He was easy to persuade.

Democratic disunity aided Durenberger immensely. The party's endorsed candidate, U.S. Rep. Donald M. Fraser, was defeated in a primary by Bob Short, a blustery conservative whose campaign against environmentalists alienated much of the Democratic left. Some Democrats chose not to vote in the general election, but even more deserted to Durenberger, who had the endorsement of Americans for Democratic Action. As a result, the Republican won a solid victory.

Durenberger's moderate views antagonized some in the Republicans' conservative wing. At the 1980 state Republican convention, a group of conservative activists, mainly from southern Minnesota, warned him to move right if he wanted their backing for re-election in 1982. Durenberger publicly dismissed the Republicans' warning, calling it "minority party mentality."

He cleared a major hurdle in early 1981 when former Vice President Walter F. Mondale, a Minnesota senator from 1964 to 1976, announced that he would not seek the office again. That made Durenberger a heavy favorite for re-election, while opening the Democratic side for Mark Dayton, liberal young heir to a department store empire. Although politically inexperienced, Dayton sank about $7 million of his personal fortune into an intense two-year Senate campaign.

Dayton made no apologies for his spending; he said that unlike Durenberger, he was not dependent on special-interest contributions, and that lavish spending was the only way he could offset the incumbent's perquisites and hefty campaign treasury.

For months Dayton saturated the media with advertising that sought to tie Durenberger to Reaganomics. This expensive blitz pulled Dayton up in the polls, but Durenberger was well positioned for re-election. He contended that while he was an independent voice in Washington, he had the president's respect and could help moderate the Reagan administration's course.

Dayton swept the economically depressed Iron Range and the Democratic Twin Cities, but carried little else. Durenberger built a large lead in the suburbs of Minneapolis-St. Paul and most of rural Minnesota that carried him to a 53 percent victory statewide.

Committees

Environment and Public Works (4th of 7 Republicans)
Superfund, Ocean and Water Protection (ranking); Environmental Protection; Water Resources, Transportation and Infrastructure

Finance (7th of 9 Republicans)
Medicare and Long-Term Care (ranking); Health for Families and the Uninsured; Social Security and Family Policy

Labor and Human Resources (6th of 7 Republicans)
Handicapped (ranking); Aging; Employment and Productivity

Elections

1988 General

Dave Durenberger (R)	1,176,210	(56%)
Hubert H. "Skip" Humphrey III (D)	856,694	(41%)

1988 Primary

Dave Durenberger (R)	112,413	(93%)
Sharon Anderson (R)	5,464	(5%)

Previous Winning Percentages: 1982 (53%) **1978 *** (61%)

* *Special election.*

Campaign Finance

	Receipts	Receipts from PACs	Expend-itures
1988			
Durenberger (R)	$4,969,448	$1,499,382 (30%)	$5,410,783
Humphrey (D)	$2,483,491	$557,234 (22%)	$2,477,068

Key Votes

1987

Enact omnibus highway bill over Reagan veto	Y
Limit testing of space-based anti-ballistic missiles	N
Oppose banning tests of larger nuclear weapons	Y
Confirm Robert H. Bork as Supreme Court justice	Y

1988

Allow vote on campaign-finance overhaul	N
Pass civil rights restoration bill over Reagan veto	Y
Enact omnibus trade bill over Reagan veto	Y
Approve death penalty for drug-related murders	N
Oppose "workfare" amendment to welfare overhaul bill	?

Voting Studies

	Presidential Support		Party Unity		Conservative Coalition	
Year	**S**	**O**	**S**	**O**	**S**	**O**
1988	57	38	43	48	32	59
1987	51	44	54	43	47	50
1986	64	33	65	32	66	34
1985	70	21	59	34	62	25
1984	71	23	68	25	70	21
1983	75	19	60	28	57	36
1982	60	28	45	41	39	48
1981	73	24	68	25	59	33

Interest Group Ratings

Year	ADA	ACU	AFL-CIO	CCUS
1988	60	26	77	43
1987	55	28	90	56
1986	40	43	40	58
1985	30	48	47	54
1984	50	55	25	65
1983	40	38	19	61
1982	70	25	59	28
1981	40	47	26	72

Rudy Boschwitz (R)

Of Plymouth — Elected 1978

Born: Nov. 7, 1930, Berlin, Germany.
Education: Johns Hopkins U., B.S. 1950; New York U., LL.B. 1953.
Military Career: Army, 1954-55.
Occupation: Lawyer; plywood company owner.
Family: Wife, Ellen Lowenstein; four children.
Religion: Jewish.
Political Career: Republican national committeeman from Minnesota, 1971-79.
Capitol Office: 506 Hart Bldg. 20510; 224-5641.

In Washington: The 100th Congress fell far short of expectations for Boschwitz, the New York lawyer-turned Minnesota plywood merchant-turned politician.

The most significant setback may have been the Republicans' failure to pick up Senate seats in the midst of the Electoral College landslide for George Bush. Boschwitz had taken over his party's Senate campaign committee in 1987. It was his first taste of a leadership role, and a chance to concentrate his energies on the political environment in which he has always been most comfortable. Initially, he had been upbeat about gaining seats; he even spoke of recapturing control.

But in the end, the GOP suffered a net loss of one seat, severely diminishing the party's chances of regaining majority status anytime soon. Few seemed to hold Boschwitz responsible. Committee receipts were down 22 percent from the previous cycle, but they still beggared the Democrats' collections by 4-to-1. And Boschwitz himself had traveled tirelessly in pursuit of resources and prospective candidates. Indeed, the party got just the candidates it wanted in several key states, and yet lost.

At the same time, the failure to gain ground in a winning presidential year was hardly a cause for celebration. Like others before him, Boschwitz found it difficult to activate the party's national assets in state elections. And after it was over, he found no new position waiting for him in the party's Senate leadership. The rest of the hierarchy stood pat, so after a single cycle in the leadership he was out, at least temporarily.

In his committee work, Boschwitz continued to emphasize the Agriculture Committee, where in the 100th Congress he became ranking minority member on the Credit Subcommittee and co-authored the 1987 Farm Credit bill with Democratic Sen. David L. Boren of Oklahoma. But now that Democrats are in control of both houses, the credit for the bill was unevenly distributed. Boschwitz was also active on drought-relief measures in 1988.

On some of his other priorities, Boschwitz' success has been even less conspicuous. On Small Business, he pushed the earned-income tax credit as an alternative to the minimum wage increase. In the 101st Congress, he became the ranking GOP member on Small Business, but the tax credit trade-off gathered few supporters, as most attention went toward raising the minimum rate and instituting some kind of subminimum "training wage."

On Foreign Relations, Boschwitz served as a special delegate to the United Nations' 1988 General Assembly and continued his growing interest in the plight of refugees in Southeast Asia. But on the overseas issue most personally important to Boschwitz — Israel's security — he saw an erosion of popular U.S. support for Israel in the face of the Palestinian uprising. Boschwitz, who came to America as a boy from Nazi Germany, is a staunch Israel ally.

He used his previous position as chairman of the Foreign Relations Subcommittee on Near Eastern Affairs to push for increased aid to Israel and to attack U.S. support for its Arab adversaries. Joining with other strong Israel backers on the committee, such as California Democrat Alan Cranston, Boschwitz has argued for more military aid to the Jewish state and against U.S. arms sales to the Arab states.

Boschwitz has also spent more than 10 years on the Budget Committee playing a modest role in the panel's deliberations and pushing ideas such as a spending freeze. Boschwitz was most prominent on budget issues in the 99th Congress when he proposed giving priority to the deficit over tax revision. Early in 1986 he wrote a letter to President Reagan, cosigned by 50 senators, calling for a delay in action on taxes until after an agreement had been reached on ways to meet the deficit-reduction requirements of the Gramm-Rudman law. But Gramm-Rudman was largely invalidated by a federal court, and tax revision became law.

In the 100th Congress, Boschwitz was one more middle-level Budgeteer watching the committee's significance slip away. The new focus was on package deals made at budget summit meetings between the White House and Hill leadership. With the same pattern developing in the 101st Congress, the House and Senate committees' role seemed to be dwindling.

Boschwitz' affable personality has earned him the affection of many colleagues, and he has long had aspirations to climb the ladder of Senate power. But his eccentric style — symbolized by the "happy face" he sometimes adds to his signature on letters — has not struck everyone as the best credential for a legislative leader. Late in 1984, he ran for GOP Conference secretary, but lost by a wide margin to Thad Cochran of Mississippi.

Senate Republicans may also value Boschwitz' taste for partisan combat as they struggle to readjust to minority status. Late in 1986, facing a drive to impose limits on contributions from political action committees (PACs), GOP leaders turned to Boschwitz to devise a tactical response. He came up with an amendment to curb PAC contributions to national parties as well as to candidates — a heavy blow at the financial health of the Democratic Party, which relies on PAC contributions. The amendment allowed Republicans to vote for this reform without any danger it would pass.

When Boschwitz focuses his legislative energy on one subject — such as the federal dairy program so important to Minnesota farmers — he can play an important role. Even then, however, his eccentric inclinations often come out. Arguing that "the real problem with milk is underconsumption, not overproduction," Boschwitz has made a tradition of the banana, root beer and Amaretto flavored milk drinks he hands out on Capitol Hill and in Minnesota.

When most farm programs came up for renewal in 1985, Boschwitz set himself a more ambitious agenda. He seemed to want to establish himself as the leading GOP spokesman on farm issues, but was overshadowed by Cochran and Majority Leader Bob Dole. More important in the long run, however, he did develop ideas for a fundamental change in farm programs.

Boschwitz proposed that the government move toward phasing out the current "target price" system of farm income supports, which he said encouraged farmers to plant crops regardless of market conditions. To help farmers survive the transition to a free-market environment, he suggested that the government give farmers gradually decreasing cash payments regardless of how much they planted.

Boschwitz' ideas generated considerable interest, gaining 42 votes when offered as a floor amendment to the farm bill. But he pushed them in a way that evoked irritation from some of his colleagues, continuing to advocate his proposals well past the point when it became clear they would not be adopted that year.

Still, the concept may influence farm measures later on; a modified version was included in Reagan's fiscal 1988 budget.

At Home: Boschwitz became a statewide figure in Minnesota politics during an era of Republican ascendancy and proceeded to outlast the era. Without ever abandoning the conservatism that brought him into politics, he has effectively emphasized his personal campaigning skills — an orientation he often recommended to others seeking Senate seats in their own states.

Boschwitz is a born campaigner. Each summer he makes the rounds of Minnesota county fairs, greeting voters and handing out samples of flavored milk with an infectious enthusiasm. No nuance of campaign technique, however tiny, escapes his interest. He once distributed a handbook of campaign advice to his colleagues that urged, among other things, that candidates walking in parades stop every hundred yards or so to wipe the sweat from their brows, whether their brows are wet or not.

His zest for campaigning extends to raising money. He has developed a variety of innovative fund-raising techniques, such as the stickers he gives to contributors to ensure that their mailed requests for constituent service receive priority attention from his staff. With his close ties to a large number of wealthy supporters of Israel, Boschwitz has access to a pool of campaign contributions that traditionally has gone to Democrats. "I like that part of the business," he says.

Many Minnesota Democrats thought they would overcome Boschwitz' campaign strengths in 1990 by bringing a political heavyweight out of retirement. But in early 1989 it became clear that they had failed in their effort to woo Walter F. Mondale, former senator, former vice president, and 1984 Democratic nominee for president. Democrats are not without other potential challengers, but Mondale would have been the most formidable.

Boschwitz may breathe a little easier now, but he has never been one to shy from challenges anyway. In fact, he has been on the move much of his life. Born in Berlin, he fled Nazi Germany with his parents when he was 2, moving first to Czechoslovakia, then to Switzerland, the Netherlands, England and the United States. He attended college at Baltimore's prestigious Johns Hopkins University, graduating when he was just 19. He went to law school in New York and practiced law there. But he tired of that, moved to Minnesota and made $5 million with his Plywood Minnesota business, which grew to 67 outlets throughout the upper Midwest.

When a folksy, flannel-shirted Boschwitz began appearing in television ads for his plywood business two decades ago, some Minnesota politicians suspected he might be thinking of selling more than do-it-yourself home furnishings. They were right.

Elected a Republican national committeeman in 1971, he waited patiently for the opportune time to run for office. At the start of each election year he was on everyone's list as a Senate or gubernatorial contender, but until 1978 he always passed up the chance. By then, Boschwitz had a dedicated corps of political allies and a well-known face. He started talking about inflation rather than plywood.

Boschwitz picked the right year, and the right opponent — Sen. Wendell R. Anderson, who as governor had arranged to have himself named to the Senate in late 1976 when Mondale resigned to become Jimmy Carter's vice president. Anderson felt he could perform well enough in the job to overcome the jinx that follows most "self-appointed" senators to Washington. But he could not overcome it.

In the campaign, Boschwitz endorsed standard GOP campaign themes, but said little that was controversial. It was a campaign of personalities rather than issues, and he had the advantage over the more reserved Anderson.

The scenario was not much different in 1984, when Boschwitz was paired against Democrat Joan Growe, the state's feisty but sometimes shrill secretary of state. The liberal Growe was not a widely popular choice even within her own party; she outlasted a field that included Anderson and Rep. James L. Oberstar to win the Democratic endorsement on the 19th ballot at the state convention.

Growe sought to solidify Democratic support by peppering Boschwitz on a wide array of issues, ranging from his strong support of Reagan defense policies to his personal finances. When he refused to release his income-tax returns, Growe charged that he had benefited from some of the Reagan tax cuts he supported.

But Growe was unable to pierce Boschwitz' image as an affable problem-solver and champion of lower taxes. He deflected criticism of his own tax history by using his accountant to disclose highlights of his tax returns. And his "Fair Play" budget, while failing to draw much support in Washington, helped him establish himself at home as an independent thinker willing to challenge a Republican administration.

Growe lacked the finances to press her case, and presidential nominee Mondale, who was originally expected to provide top-of-the-ticket strength, barely won his home state. Taking all but a handful of counties, most on the economically devastated Iron Range, Boschwitz scored another one-sided victory.

Committees

Small Business (Ranking)

Agriculture, Nutrition and Forestry (5th of 9 Republicans)
Nutrition and Investigations (ranking); Agricultural Credit; Agricultural Production and Stabilization of Prices

Budget (3rd of 10 Republicans)

Foreign Relations (4th of 9 Republicans)
Near Eastern and South Asian Affairs (ranking); European Affairs; International Economic Policy, Trade, Oceans and Environment

Elections

1984 General		
Rudy Boschwitz (R)	1,199,926	(58%)
Joan Growe (D)	852,844	(41%)
1984 Primary		
Rudy Boschwitz (R)	162,555	(97%)
Joan Barcelona (R)	3,277	(2%)
Carlan Lesch (R)	2,462	(1%)

Previous Winning Percentage: **1978** (57%)

Campaign Finance

	Receipts	Receipts from PACs	Expenditures
1984			
Boschwitz (R)	$5,983,410	$1,005,187 (17%)	$6,022,365
Growe (D)	$1,611,348	$434,148 (27%)	$1,589,738

Key Votes

1987	
Enact omnibus highway bill over Reagan veto	N
Limit testing of space-based anti-ballistic missiles	N
Oppose banning tests of larger nuclear weapons	Y
Confirm Robert H. Bork as Supreme Court justice	Y
1988	
Allow vote on campaign-finance overhaul	N
Pass civil rights restoration bill over Reagan veto	Y
Enact omnibus trade bill over Reagan veto	N
Approve death penalty for drug-related murders	Y
Oppose "workfare" amendment to welfare overhaul bill	N

Voting Studies

	Presidential Support		Party Unity		Conservative Coalition	
Year	**S**	**O**	**S**	**O**	**S**	**O**
1988	73	23	68	24	76	14
1987	71	26	81	18	81	16
1986	84	16	84	16	84	16
1985	87	13	87	13	92	8
1984	69	31	73	26	66	34
1983	80	15	62	32	66	30
1982	77†	22†	71	28	54†	43†
1981	82	18	78	21	71	29

† Not eligible for all recorded votes.

Interest Group Ratings

Year	ADA	ACU	AFL-CIO	CCUS
1988	20	70	38	69
1987	25	76	40	94
1986	15	57	13	74
1985	5	78	5	79
1984	35	45	27	68
1983	40	36	24	61
1982	30	60	23	60
1981	25	50	5	89

1 Timothy J. Penny (D)

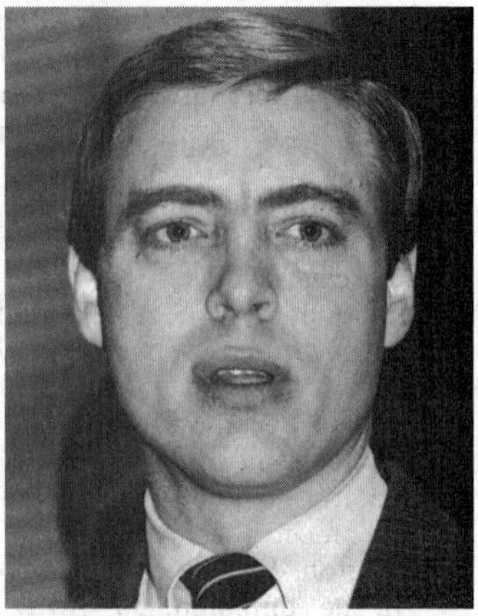

Of New Richland — Elected 1982

Born: Nov. 19, 1951, Albert Lea, Minn.
Education: Winona State U., B.A. 1974; graduate work at U. of Minnesota, 1975.
Military Career: Naval Reserve, 1986-present.
Occupation: Sales representative.
Family: Wife, Barbara Christianson; four children.
Religion: Lutheran.
Political Career: Minn. Senate, 1977-83.
Capitol Office: 436 Cannon Bldg. 20515; 225-2472.

In Washington: Despite his wholesome looks, there is something of the Scandinavian brooder about Penny. He is deeply frustrated with the intractability of federal fiscal problems and the unwillingness of senior members of Congress to strike out in new directions.

Penny has chosen an unenviable role in the House. As a budget watchdog trying to restrain the Democratic Party's inclinations toward generosity in spending, he often jousts with party leaders; in 1987 and 1988, he opposed the Democratic position on partisan votes more often than any other Northern Democrat.

Penny wasted little time in establishing a beachhead from which to wage his war on deficits. Early in 1983, he became chairman of the Freshman Budget Task Force, a group of Democratic first-termers touting an across-the-board budget freeze. Under the leadership of Penny and Florida Rep. Buddy MacKay (and now North Carolina's David E. Price), the task force has evolved into the Budget Study Group, an organization open to all members that discusses deficit-reduction options. The group has grown in both size and acceptance.

In November 1983, Penny and 23 other Democratic freshmen called attention to their deficit dismay by joining with a majority of House Republicans to defeat a stopgap spending measure. The action ultimately proved to be only a temporary delay, but Penny and others hoped it would serve notice that moderates were willing to strike down future spending bills considered excessive. The following year, Penny and Texas Republican Steve Bartlett persuaded the House to hold 1986 spending in a variety of housing programs to 1985 levels.

In 1987, Penny and Iowa Republican Tom Tauke formed the Truth-in-Budgeting Task Force. Recruiting about two dozen other members, they led a drive to reduce the deficit below levels assumed in the congressional budget resolution. "The only way we can meet our deficit reduction is to cut a little more as each opportunity arises," Penny said. Penny, Tauke and other task force members offered amendments to fiscal 1988 appropriations bills making across-the-board cuts in funding levels. They met with limited success; most of the amendments lost, many by sizable margins.

In 1988, Penny and Tauke rolled all their deficit-reduction ideas into one package and proposed their own budget resolution as an alternative to the bipartisan package agreed to at the 1987 White House-congressional budget summit. It was a radical plan that called for replacing the inflation-based Social Security cost-of-living adjustments with a flat-rate COLA increase of $5 per month. The plan would have delayed income tax indexing for a year, trimmed a pay increase for federal and military employees and specified a budget deficit $22 billion below the summit-pact level.

On the floor, Penny struck an ironic tone. By voting against the resolution, he said, "you can be popular, you can say the things folks want to hear and get yourself re-elected. But . . . if you are concerned about next year's deficit being bigger than this year's deficit, you might want to reconsider and vote 'yes.' " Only 27 members did so.

Penny attacks his work with energy and enthusiasm, spinning out ideas and proposals. But erasing the deficit and overhauling farm policy, the two goals that have consumed most of his energy, are tall orders. While Penny has contributed to the dialogue on both issues, his concrete accomplishments have been more modest than if he had pursued less sweeping issues.

On the Agriculture Committee, the assignment most crucial to Penny politically, he is part of a younger generation of lawmakers who contend that farmers are fed up with old subsidy programs and want Congress to try something different. Penny's record makes it clear he is willing to try almost *anything* different. In the 99th Congress, he endorsed two quite dissimilar farm policy overhaul proposals and introduced a third himself.

In 1985, Penny backed Minnesota GOP Rep. Arlan Stangeland's proposal for a "marketing loan" program, which would allow farmers who take out government crop loans to pay

Minnesota 1

Southeast — Rochester; Mankato

It seems odd now, but Penny represents a district that was redrawn in 1982 to be more Republican than the 1st District constituency that had been electing GOP candidates routinely for years.

Farm discontent and Penny's deficit-conscious record have combined to make this the sort of district that explains why Republicans seem stuck in a "permanent minority" in the House.

German Protestants settled southeast Minnesota just north of Iowa before the Civil War. The rolling hills that extend from the Mississippi to the great bend in the Minnesota River offer the corn, grain and hog farmers some of the state's most productive farm land. Except for Rochester and some Mississippi River towns, the population centers in the 1st are devoted to serving the surrounding farms, or, in the case of Austin, processing the primary local product — hogs.

Rochester is the state's fifth-largest city, with 58,000 people. The home not only of the Mayo Clinic but also of a large IBM facility, Rochester has much more of a white-collar orientation than the rest of the district, and its voters are more reliably Republican than many of the district's disgruntled farmers, who have strayed from their GOP traditions. When Ronald Reagan made an election-eve foray into Minnesota in his bid for a 50-state sweep in 1984, he chose Rochester for his campaign stop.

Over the years, the most consistently Democratic area in the district has been Mower County (Austin), where the meatpacking industry is heavily unionized. Since 1932 all Democratic presidential candidates except John F. Kennedy and Adlai E. Stevenson have carried the county. Michael S. Dukakis won it with more than 60 percent of the vote in 1988.

Population: 509,460. White 503,533 (99%), Black 1,007 (0.2%), Other 3,193 (1%). Spanish origin 3,333 (1%). 18 and over 362,626 (71%), 65 and over 66,631 (13%). Median age: 29.

back only as much as their crops earned at the market. Proponents said it would allow prices to fall to natural levels, would guarantee farmers steady income and would protect the government from having to absorb huge quantities of crops, which farmers currently forfeit when they default.

The Agriculture Committee defeated the proposal 22-20, partly because it was such a radical departure from current policy. Said Penny, "We're trying to increase world competition and decrease surpluses. A lot of us thought the marketing loan might be the thing to accomplish both of those objectives. . . . But most of the members weren't ready."

Later, Penny endorsed a farm plan offered by Sen. Tom Harkin and Rep. Richard A. Gephardt that sought to raise crop prices by tightly restricting how much a farmer could produce. But this concept of production controls stirred widespread opposition in Congress.

In search of a politically salable alternative, Penny and Rep. Byron L. Dorgan of North Dakota came forward in 1987 with a plan to target crop subsidies to smaller farmers and close loopholes in current law that allow some large farming operations to collect huge subsidy payments. Penny said the plan would save $24 billion over five years.

Though he is a defender of his home-state dairy farmers, Penny can work with others seeking a middle ground on dairy provisions. The emergency drought-relief bill in 1988 hit a snag over a controversial provision to increase the federal government's price-support payments to dairy farmers by 50 cents per hundredweight. The provision, pushed by dairy-state members and the dairy industry, rankled many members; they felt it violated the spirit of the 1985 farm bill — which called for lowering price supports for commodities — and smacked of favoritism to just one portion of the agriculture community.

The resentment gave rise to a compromise amendment offered by Penny and Wisconsin Republican Steve Gunderson, allowing for a 50-cent increase, but only for the three-month period when dairy farmers would be hardest hit by drought-related feed costs. The House adopted the compromise by a 246-155 vote.

Penny held a "temporary" seat on Education and Labor in his first three terms. Anything but an automatic vote for organized labor's agenda, Penny was out of step with most of the Democrats on the panel.

He was involved during the 99th Congress in reauthorizing the Higher Education Act. His particular concern was seeing that part-time students be made eligible for student aid. In the final reauthorization bill, that group was added to the eligibility list.

In the 100th Congress, he fought to keep a bill increasing the minimum wage from becoming laden with so many special provisions that it could not pass. He and Labor Standards Subcommittee Chairman Austin J. Murphy were the only Democrats opposed to a labor-backed move to add a fourth-year raise, to $5.05 an hour.

At Home: The first Democrat to hold this district in nearly a century, Penny defied GOP predictions that he would be a one-term fluke.

Penny has been running for office virtually his entire adult life. In 1976, barely a year out of graduate school, he ran for the state Senate in south-central Minnesota. Treading in staunchly GOP territory, Penny visited each household in the district three times and drew 52 percent to oust a Republican incumbent.

Redistricting carved up his state Senate district and left him without a familiar place to seek re-election. So he decided to run for Congress in 1982. His chances of making it seemed minimal until a vicious quarrel developed between two GOP incumbents, Tom Hagedorn and Arlen Erdahl, who ended up running against each other after redistricting.

When Hagedorn won the Republican district convention, Penny worked to exploit lingering bitterness, calling himself a moderate in the Erdahl tradition. As the race tightened, Hagedorn unleashed a barrage of charges, including criticism that Penny had never worked in the private sector for a living. Penny responded with ads that showed him with his young family, a contrast with the divorced Hagedorn. Penny prevailed with 51 percent of the vote.

In 1984, Republicans nominated Keith Spicer, a Rochester sales manager with close ties to southern Minnesota's fundamentalist Christian community. Spicer was articulate, but he was a novice campaigner, and he had little appeal to the district's large contingent of moderate Republicans, whom Penny had cultivated. Although Reagan swept the 1st District, Penny carried it by nearly 35,000 votes.

GOP leaders hoped Erdahl would run in 1986, but he bowed out in late 1985, choosing a position in the national office of the Peace Corps. Republicans fielded a weak challenger then, and again in 1988.

Committees

Agriculture (15th of 27 Democrats)
Conservation, Credit and Rural Development; Livestock, Dairy and Poultry; Wheat, Soybeans and Feed Grains

Select Hunger (8th of 18 Democrats)
Task Force: International

Veterans' Affairs (5th of 21 Democrats)
Education, Training and Employment (chairman); Compensation, Pension and Insurance

Elections

1988 General

Timothy J. Penny (D)	161,118	(70%)
Curt Schrimpf (R)	67,709	(29%)

1986 General

Timothy J. Penny (D)	125,115	(72%)
Paul H. Grawe (R)	47,750	(28%)

Previous Winning Percentages: 1984 (57%) **1982** (51%)

District Vote For President

	1988	1984	1980	1976
D	115,800 (48%)	107,763 (44%)	81,000 (36%)	115,365 (48%)
R	121,930 (51%)	134,866 (55%)	120,765 (53%)	117,325 (49%)
I			18,998 (8%)	

Campaign Finance

	Receipts	Receipts from PACs	Expend-itures
1988			
Penny (D)	$284,554	$125,377 (44%)	$165,016
Schrimpf (R)	$86,090	$2,862 (3%)	$85,532
1986			
Penny (D)	$375,626	$151,491 (40%)	$334,484
Grawe (R)	$44,112	$5,309 (12%)	$44,112

Key Votes

1987

Raise speed limit to 65 mph	N
Approve Gephardt "fair trade" amendment	N
Ban testing of larger nuclear weapons	Y
Delay "re-flagging" of Kuwaiti tankers	Y
Approve tax-raising deficit-reduction bill	N

1988

Approve aid to Nicaraguan contras	N
Enact civil rights restoration bill over Reagan veto	Y
Kill 60-day plant-closing notification measure	N
Pass omnibus trade bill over Reagan veto	Y
Approve death penalty for drug-related murders	N
Bar federal funds for abortions in cases of rape and incest	Y
Oppose seven-day waiting period for purchase of handguns	Y

Voting Studies

	Presidential Support		Party Unity		Conservative Coalition	
Year	**S**	**O**	**S**	**O**	**S**	**O**
1988	37	63	59	41	66	34
1987	35	65	59	41	49	51
1986	34	66	61	39	48	52
1985	25	75	53	47	35	65
1984	35	65	69	31	36	64
1983	13	87	84	16	29	69

Interest Group Ratings

Year	ADA	ACU	AFL-CIO	CCUS
1988	60	36	71	64
1987	64	30	50	53
1986	75	18	64	50
1985	60	24	47	50
1984	75	33	38	50
1983	75	17	76	40

2 Vin Weber (R)

Of North Mankato — Elected 1980

Born: July 24, 1952, Slayton, Minn.
Education: Attended U. of Minnesota, 1970-74.
Occupation: Publisher.
Family: Wife, Cheryl Foster.
Religion: Roman Catholic.
Political Career: Republican nominee for Minn. Senate, 1976.
Capitol Office: 106 Cannon Bldg. 20515; 225-2331.

In Washington: Weber has been one of the more creative and independent members of the large class of House Republicans swept into office with Ronald Reagan in 1980. So it was no great surprise in early 1989 when he emerged as a key figure in the intraparty maneuvering over the direction House Republicans should take in the post-Reagan era.

Weber brought an unusual — and sometimes contradictory — perspective to the proceedings. Once a leader of a group of young House conservatives who were ready to make every fight with the Democrats a death struggle, Weber clearly has been tempered by time. "You can't make every battle a scorched-earth battle, because this institution is going to have to confront other issues," he has said.

At the beginning of the 101st Congress, he had the trappings of insider status — a place in the Republican leadership and a seat on the powerful Appropriations Committee.

But while eight years in the House have changed Weber, he has not lost sight of how he wants to change the institution and his party. Even as President Bush was making conciliatory gestures toward the Democratic-controlled Congress in the early months of his administration, Weber preached a more confrontational approach: House Republicans have to highlight, not bridge, their differences with Democrats, Weber said — and they might not take their cues solely from the Bush White House.

"His agenda needs to be fleshed out a bit," Weber said of Bush. "You can lead the White House." For Weber, that fleshing out involves more government activism than most conservatives are used to embracing.

It is no small trick to be an activist conservative working within the House in a confrontational manner while downplaying "scorched-earth" rhetoric. But just a few weeks into the 101st Congress, Weber helped promote an old ally with the same objective in mind: Georgia's Newt Gingrich.

Weber was a key strategist behind Gingrich's March 1989 election as Republican whip, the post second only to minority leader. Gingrich and Weber had been most famously allied in the early 1980s, when they formed the Conservative Opportunity Society (COS), a group of activist young House Republicans that made its name by harassing the Democratic leadership.

When Gingrich decided to run for whip, Weber was his vote-counter. The Georgian's triumph over a more traditional Republican, Edward Madigan of Illinois, signaled the growing impatience of younger Republicans with the conciliatory politics of their senior colleagues.

The same forces had helped Weber win his own place in the lower ranks of the party hierarchy just four months earlier. In a leadership shake-up before the 101st Congress, Weber was elected secretary of the Republican Conference by a 21-vote margin over old-breed Republican Joseph M. McDade of Pennsylvania, a senior member of the Appropriations Committee.

Weber had already begun to make his way from the periphery of the Republican Conference to its inner sanctums of power two years earlier, when he won a seat on the Appropriations Committee at the beginning of the 100th Congress.

Adapting his confrontational style to the clubby, logrolling ethos of that money-wielding committee has been a challenge, and he has not yet been entirely domesticated. Weber and other young members complain that senior GOP appropriators are often more loyal to the committee's products than to party principles. Those complaints peaked in mid-1987, when senior Republicans were joining committee Democrats to fight efforts to cut their spending recommendations.

But Weber is not above crowing about his ability to get federal funds for his district, now that he is so close to the trough. He happily takes credit for securing funding for agriculture research projects in Minnesota, graduate fellowships and other programs overseen by his two Appropriations subcommittees, one on Agriculture and the other on Labor, Health and Human Services and Education.

Minnesota 2

Southwest — Willmar

The landscape of the 2nd District is dotted for mile upon mile with silos and grain elevators, broken up occasionally by small crossroads market centers. The district's largest town, Willmar, has only about 16,000 residents. Bisected by the broad Minnesota River, the sprawling 30-county district includes some of the best farm land in the state, and some that is not so productive.

The well-to-do farmers in the south along the Iowa border enjoy bountiful harvests of corn and soybeans. Worthington, located in Nobles County, claims to be the "Turkey Capital of the World."

Many voters in the southern two tiers of counties are of German ethnic stock. Like those in the adjoining 1st District, they share a strong Republican tradition and an allegiance to the Farm Bureau, the most conservative of the state's three major farm organizations.

As one moves north along the Minnesota River, dairy farms become more common. The flat farm lands yield to a more rolling terrain broken up by lakes. Until one reaches the prairie counties north of the Minnesota River, the political flavor remains largely Republican.

Above the river, north of Renville and Yellow Medicine counties, the land is sandy and rocky and the politics unpredictable. Farmers here have to work harder to scratch out a living, and they display a frequent dissatisfaction with any party in power.

At the turn of the century the Scandinavian settlers in this area battled constantly with railroads, bankers and grain merchants. Disillusioned by Republicans and Democrats alike, they were ripe for third-party alternatives. The Farmer-Labor Party found early support in this region, as did presidential candidate Robert LaFollette in 1924, when his Progressive Party carried the vast majority of the counties north of the Minnesota River that are wholly contained in the district.

Today, with strong support from the National Farmers Union, Democrats often run well in this part of the district. But the vote here is generally not large enough to overcome the more heavily Republican areas to the south and east.

Running a campaign in the 2nd District is an exhausting and expensive exercise. To reach voters via television, a candidate has to buy time not only in the Twin Cities but also in Mankato and Alexandria, Minn., and in Sioux Falls, S.D. Some might prefer to run their campaigns by mail order, in the tradition of one of the district's most famous sons: R. W. Sears, who began shipping watches from Redwood in 1886 with the help of his partner, Alvah Roebuck.

Population: 509,500. White 505,241 (99%), Black 288 (0.1%), Other 2,630 (1%). Spanish origin 2,508 (1%). 18 and over 363,087 (71%), 65 and over 82,298 (16%). Median age: 32.

That pride in parochial accomplishments is the legacy of an important stage in the political education of Weber: a brush with electoral defeat that drove him to spend more time on the day-to-day problems of his troubled farm constituents and less on after-hours speeches with the COS crowd.

He faced a tough re-election contest in 1986, when the farm economy at home was in a tailspin and his opponent was saying Weber was not doing enough to help.

He added office hours in his district, and began soft-pedaling his role as partisan firebrand in the House. He placed plenty of distance between himself and the Reagan administration's farm policies. In early 1985, he wrote Reagan a letter protesting his veto of a farm credit bill. Later, in debate on the 1985 farm bill, Weber was one of a handful of House Republicans to defy the White House and support a "populist" proposal aimed at imposing strict production controls to drive up prices.

As a member of the House Budget Committee, Weber cast the sole Republican vote in 1986 for a Democratic-drafted budget resolution. Among the factors that inclined him favorably to that budget was that then-Chairman William H. Gray III of Pennsylvania had earned Weber's gratitude by holding a hearing on agriculture programs in his Minnesota district.

"I've responded to an ongoing disaster in my district," he said amid the 1986 farm crisis. "I've changed my behavior more than my basic philosophy. But then, it's a misconception that I ever believed in being rigidly ideological."

Indeed, when COS was at its peak as a bomb-throwing force in the early 1980s, Weber always seemed a little miscast as its chief coordinator. In a group given to theatrics and grand ideas, he stood out as a hardheaded pragmatist more concerned with sound strategy than with ideological debating points.

Even as Weber joined his COS colleagues in guerrilla floor tactics, he distinguished himself by reaching out more to other elements of the House GOP. The strident approach often adopted by Gingrich and others alienated many senior Republicans, allowing Weber, who was somewhat less vitriolic, to play a more prominent political role.

While some COS leaders remained in minor committee assignments that left them free to focus on floor confrontation, Weber got a seat on the Budget Committee in his third term, and then won his Appropriations assignment at the start of his fourth term.

At Home: When it comes to campaigning, Weber is a House version of Minnesota's junior U.S. senator, Rudy Boschwitz — a similarity that is not surprising because Weber ran Boschwitz' successful 1978 effort and later worked as his senior aide in Minnesota. Weber votes more conservatively in Congress than Boschwitz, but they use the same high-profile, high-pressure, everywhere-at-once style of running for office.

First elected to the House in 1980, Weber could have won re-election in 1982 and 1984 with something less than the energetic, high-budget campaigns that he mounted. But in 1986, Weber needed to marshal all of his considerable political skills to hold office. He was faced with a double challenge in the form of a depressed agrarian economy and an aggressive Democratic opponent, who pounded away at Weber as a right-wing ideologue who did not understand the depth of the farm crisis.

While the rural 2nd has Republican proclivities, in 1986 it was mired as discouragingly in economic depression as any district in the Farm Belt. Its grain farmers, hard hit by the decline in export markets and plummeting land values, were picketing county courthouses and disrupting farm-foreclosure sales.

Weber sought to insulate himself from the agrarian discontent by distancing himself from the unpopular Reagan administration farm policy — he voted against the 1981 and 1985 farm bills, each of which cut income support to farmers. Before the 1986 election, Weber also held regular office hours in the district to listen to farmers who came to him in search of federal help. In the process, he confessed, he had become "less anti-government, maybe."

But Weber's change of heart was unimpressive to Democratic challenger Dave Johnson, who complained that if the incumbent was really concerned about struggling farmers, he would have taken a seat on the House Agriculture Committee, like Minnesota's other two rural House members.

Johnson maintained that Weber had virtually no influence on agricultural policy. As a third-generation farmer, Johnson claimed a personal understanding of farm problems that he said Weber, whose background is in newspaper publishing, lacked.

Republicans, in turn, sought to depict Johnson as a political opportunist who switched parties on the eve of his congressional bid because his hopes of winning office as a Republican were stymied. Johnson was intensely involved in local GOP politics in the early 1980s, frequently accompanying Weber around the district and even serving as a delegate to the 1984 Republican National Convention in Dallas.

Johnson defended his party switch, saying that he decided to join the Democrats because President Reagan's free-market farm policy was driving prices down and undermining the district's economy.

Making his political debut, Johnson was an unknown quantity to many voters in the large, 31-county district. Despite that, he was able to win a majority of counties in the 2nd; he finished barely 6,000 votes short of Weber.

Johnson might have been able to overcome the deficit if the incumbent had not run a $1 million, state-of-the-art campaign. Weber bombarded voters with an array of appeals ranging from ads on expensive Twin Cities television to direct-mail appeals to individual commodity groups.

By 1988 it was apparent that Weber had shored up his support in the district. He had been more visible tending to district concerns, and had an achievement to tout in 1987 when he took a seat on the Appropriations Subcommittee on Agriculture. Democrats had difficulty coming up with a strong candidate, although Johnson considered another attempt, as did Gene Wenstrom, who had previously mounted three campaigns against Republican Rep. Arlan Stangeland in the 7th District.

The Democratic nomination went to Doug Peterson, a farmer and a party chairman in Lac Qui Parle County. Peterson said that he was a better fit for the predominantly rural district than was Weber, but he had considerable difficulty raising funds to get his message out. With a late start and without much help from the national party, Peterson managed just 42 percent of the vote. Weber won by the second-largest margin of his career.

Lavishly financed campaigns have been a Weber hallmark. When he won the seat of retiring Democratic Rep. Richard Nolan in 1980, Weber put so much money into television ads that to many voters he seemed like an incumbent by November. He rolled to a 14,000-vote victory over former Nolan aide and Farmers Union organizer Archie Baumann.

Two years later, court-ordered redistricting placed Weber and GOP Rep. Tom Hagedorn together in the same rural southwest Minnesota constituency. Rather than challenge Weber, his fellow conservative and one-time press secretary, Hagedorn moved east into the district of GOP Rep. Arlen Erdahl. (That set off a messy game of political musical chairs that ended with both Hagedorn and Erdahl losing in separate districts in November.)

In the 2nd, a sluggish farm economy and a feisty challenger gave Democrats hope of beating Weber. But by building a large lead in the district's eastern counties formerly represented by Hagedorn, Weber offset Democrat Jim Nichols' strength in his home base along the South Dakota border to win by 20,000 votes.

Nichols' decision to become state agriculture commissioner freed Weber to take an active role in national Republican politics in 1984, highlighted by an influential stint on the national convention platform committee. With the Democrats nominating an underfunded political newcomer to oppose him that fall, his own re-election was never in doubt.

For three generations, the Webers have been a conservative voice in southwestern Minnesota, publishing a family-run weekly newspaper. But when Vin Weber first tried to make the leap from journalism to elective office, he failed, drawing only 42 percent in a 1976 campaign for the state Senate. His political career revived when he successfully managed Boschwitz' Senate campaign two years later.

Committee

Appropriations (19th of 22 Republicans)
Labor, Health and Human Services, Education and Related Agencies; Rural Development, Agriculture and Related Agencies

Elections

1988 General		
Vin Weber (R)	131,639	(58%)
Doug Peterson (D)	96,016	(42%)
1986 General		
Vin Weber (R)	100,249	(52%)
Dave Johnson (D)	94,048	(48%)

Previous Winning Percentages: **1984** (63%) **1982** (55%) **1980** (53%)

District Vote For President

	1988	1984	1980	1976
D	112,838 (48%)	105,232 (43%)	101,134 (39%)	128,804 (53%)
R	118,769 (51%)	140,304 (57%)	135,287 (52%)	107,252 (44%)
I			17,000 (7%)	

Campaign Finance

	Receipts	Receipts from PACs	Expend-itures
1988			
Weber (R)	$728,427	$232,704 (32%)	$623,776
Peterson (D)	$154,006	$70,165 (46%)	$152,295
1986			
Weber (R)	$942,499	$283,203 (30%)	$909,607
Johnson (D)	$297,578	$162,170 (54%)	$296,080

Key Votes

1987	
Raise speed limit to 65 mph	Y
Approve Gephardt "fair trade" amendment	N
Ban testing of larger nuclear weapons	N
Delay "re-flagging" of Kuwaiti tankers	N
Approve tax-raising deficit-reduction bill	N
1988	
Approve aid to Nicaraguan contras	Y
Enact civil rights restoration bill over Reagan veto	N
Kill 60-day plant-closing notification measure	Y
Pass omnibus trade bill over Reagan veto	N
Approve death penalty for drug-related murders	N
Bar federal funds for abortions in cases of rape and incest	Y
Oppose seven-day waiting period for purchase of handguns	Y

Voting Studies

	Presidential Support		Party Unity		Conservative Coalition	
Year	**S**	**O**	**S**	**O**	**S**	**O**
1988	61	37	84	11	92	8
1987	62	38	86	14	84	16
1986	69	31	80	17	80	20
1985	64	33	79	12	73	18
1984	60	37	85	11	80	17
1983	63	35	79	16	72	25
1982	61	38	80	18	74	25
1981	55	41	79	20	76	24

Interest Group Ratings

Year	ADA	ACU	AFL-CIO	CCUS
1988	15	96	14	93
1987	20	87	19	80
1986	15	73	21	72
1985	15	85	20	76
1984	15	83	8	69
1983	15	83	6	84
1982	20	77	5	77
1981	30	100	7	74

3 Bill Frenzel (R)

Of Golden Valley — Elected 1970

Born: July 31, 1928, St. Paul, Minn.
Education: Dartmouth College, B.A. 1950, M.B.A. 1951.
Military Career: Naval Reserve, 1951-54.
Profession: Warehouse company executive.
Family: Wife, Ruth Purdy; three children.
Religion: Unspecified.
Political Career: Minn. House, 1963-71.
Capitol Office: 1026 Longworth Bldg. 20515; 225-2871.

In Washington: Frenzel has the intellectual ability, the oratorical skills and the work habits of a superb legislator.

But 16 years in the minority party have taken their toll on him, leading him increasingly often into the role of a naysaying curmudgeon, preoccupied as much with the indignities visited upon Republicans by the majority party as with the legislation at hand.

His frustration with those indignities rose to the surface in early 1989 when Frenzel threw his weight behind an effort by a conservative firebrand to vault into the Republican leadership: He nominated Newt Gingrich of Georgia to be GOP whip.

As a respected senior member of both the Budget and the Ways and Means committees, Frenzel was just the kind of legislatively oriented, older-generation Republican who seemed a natural adversary of Gingrich's confrontational, partisan style.

But support from members such as Frenzel went a long way toward explaining Gingrich's upset victory: Disaffection with Democratic rule was running so deep that even GOP workhorses were getting fed up with their seemingly permanent minority status in the House. "I decided we needed to do something different, we needed to take some risks," Frenzel said.

That was not, however, the first time Frenzel showed sympathy for the impatience and restiveness that was the hallmark of combative young Republicans. Frenzel has been known to add his voice to junior members' complaints that the logrolling ethos of the Appropriations Committee was dulling the partisan edge of the panel's senior Republicans. He has joined young Republicans in challenging the committee's spending recommendations with amendments to impose across-the-board cuts.

Frenzel's affinity with the party's more strident elements seems to have its roots in the experience that embittered Republicans across the spectrum: The seating of a Democrat in a disputed Indiana House election in the 99th Congress. "This is murder," he declared on the House floor. "This is a rape of the system. The issue is the ultimate abuse of representative government." Of the Democratic majority, Frenzel has said, "They think they were born to be kings, and that there's a servant class, and that's the Republicans."

For all his frustrations and outbursts, Frenzel is a truly professional legislator. He is a major figure in tax and trade matters before the Ways and Means Committee, and in the 101st Congress, the Republican Conference elected him ranking minority member of the Budget Committee. His selection over Bill Gradison of Ohio was, in part, a tribute to the in-house political clout Frenzel has accumulated from years on the leadership panel that makes committee assignments.

But it also was a measure of the respect accorded to Frenzel, who is regarded by colleagues as one of the intellectual guardians of GOP economic orthodoxy. Although he backed the massive tax cut enacted at the opening of Reagan's presidency, he never made any secret of his skepticism about supply-side economics.

On Ways and Means, Frenzel is the party's leading voice on trade matters, even though he is not ranking member of the relevant subcommittee. He has argued the merits of free trade; that is good politics in a state whose economy improves with substantial grain sales abroad, but free trade is also a matter of sincere conviction to Frenzel.

But when the 100th Congress enacted a sweeping rewrite of U.S. trade laws, Frenzel backed the final product after controversial import restrictions and a plant-closing notification bill were dropped along the way.

When Ways and Means began writing the bill in early 1987, Frenzel proved willing to negotiate with committee chairman Dan Rostenkowski of Illinois in an effort to keep the bill from straying too far from GOP and White House aims.

He went along with the committee bill in the hope that provisions unpalatable to him would be taken care of later. "I personally had to cough, and spit, and sputter, and swallow hard at the Committee on Ways and Means bill, and finally voted 'aye' not for the product but

Minnesota 3

Southern and Western Twin Cities Suburbs

Once confined only to the inner core of Minneapolis suburbs within Hennepin County, the 3rd now ranges into five counties, extending beyond the western and southern extremities of the metropolitan area. Although the farther reaches of the district still appear largely rural, they are among the fastest growing parts of the state and are feeling the march of suburbanization.

The heart of the district remains the upper-class suburbs just west of Minneapolis, places such as Edina, St. Louis Park and Golden Valley. No fewer than nine golf courses service the white-collar professionals in these three suburbs alone. Many of the weekend golfers spend their weekdays working for such high-technology firms as Control Data and Honeywell, which are headquartered in the Twin Cities area. The Republican vote here and in Minnetonka, just to the west, is overwhelming. In a number of precincts, home-state presidential nominee Walter F. Mondale drew less than one-third of the vote in 1984.

Bloomington, the district's largest suburb and the state's fourth-largest city, is divided between the 3rd and 5th districts. The 3rd District part, west of Interstate 35W, contains about 70 percent of the city's 86,000 residents and is considerably more Republican than the eastern portion.

The 3rd District's quest for voters extends in three directions — everywhere but north. Carver County, on the western side, tends to be the most Republican county in the Twin Cities area. In 1988, it voted about 60 percent for George Bush for president, and it gave GOP Sen. Dave Durenberger two-thirds of its votes in his re-election bid.

More populous but less Republican is Dakota County, which anchors the eastern side of the district. Nearly 150,000 people live in the 3rd District portion of the county in the lower reaches south of St. Paul. This area is the fastest-growing part of the district.

Population: 509,499. White 498,684 (98%), Black 3,280 (1%), Other 5,794 (1%). Spanish origin 2,932 (1%). 18 and over 352,682 (69%), 65 and over 36,066 (7%). Median age: 29.

for the process," he said.

Frenzel's role on the trade bill contrasts with his approach to the 99th Congress' overhaul of the tax code. His opposition to the bill produced by Ways and Means was so intense that he was offered little opportunity to shape it to his liking. He called the tax measure written by the committee "anti-growth, anti-savings, anti-capital accumulation, anti-manufacturing, anti-export, anti-competitiveness, anti-education, anti-housing, anti-charity and lots more."

He warned that Democrats would take away subsidies vital to business investment, and as the subsidies were eliminated, he became more and more upset. Frenzel criticized Ways and Means Democrats for picking tax rates first and writing the code to fit them, rather than developing policies and setting the rates accordingly.

In committee markups, his most visible effort was to try to retain full deductions for business meals and entertainment expenses, which Rostenkowski saw as a symbol of subsidized excess. "Taking someone out to dinner is just as good for some businesses as placing an ad in the newspapers is for others," Frenzel argued. But he lost 17-19 on a key vote after Rostenkowski twisted several arms, and the final bill retained limits on the deductions.

While he serves as ranking minority member on the Budget Committee, Frenzel has had to give up temporarily his post as top Republican on the House Administration Committee — an in-house committee that he has called "sort of my hobby." As a member of that panel, he introduced a bill to create the Federal Election Commission in 1974 and steered it to passage in the House over the acerbic and personal opposition of Ohio Democrat Wayne L. Hays, the House Administration chairman. But by 1978, Frenzel had turned against his own creation. "The FEC is remorseless in trying to stifle politics," he complained. "If it continues to be so picky, it might find itself with a good deal less authority."

Frenzel has taken an interest in congressional ethics. He served on the panel that wrote an ethics code in 1977 and helped generate Republican support for it, though he disagreed with Chairman David R. Obey of Wisconsin on many of the particulars. Frenzel opposed a key provision in the bill giving members an extra $5,000 in office account money in exchange for dropping the customary practice of having unofficial, untraceable private office funds.

At Home: Frenzel made a critical career decision a decade ago when he opted to seek a fifth House term in his safe suburban district, declining to run for either of two open Senate seats he probably could have won. The choice reflected Frenzel's cautious side, not always evident in House politics but part of his makeup nevertheless. Two lesser-known Republicans ran and were elected, pretty much foreclosing Frenzel's statewide ambitions.

He was somewhat bolder in 1970 when he first ran for Congress. An executive in his family's warehousing business, Frenzel had served four terms in the state Legislature. He was part of the "Hennepin County mafia" that sought a moderate image for the state's Republican Party and was an ally of Attorney General Douglas Head, the GOP gubernatorial nominee in 1970.

That year, Frenzel sought the open House seat in suburban Minneapolis, challenging GOP front-runner Robert A. Forsythe, a former state party chairman and 1966 Senate candidate. Forsythe was better known, but Frenzel took advantage of Head's organization to win the party endorsement on the first convention ballot.

In November, Democrats felt they had a good chance to win the district back after 10 years of GOP control. They nominated George Rice, a local commentator on the most widely watched Twin Cities TV station. Again, Frenzel was at a disadvantage in name identification. He stepped up his personal campaign, ringing more than 15,000 doorbells and making numerous late-night visits to bowling alleys, where he claimed he met another 10,000 voters.

But it was Frenzel's August fact-finding trip to the Middle East that seemed to change the situation. It placed his name in the headlines, and when Rice refused Frenzel's challenge to make a similar trip, it created a campaign issue. A larger-than-usual Jewish vote on the Republican side helped Frenzel edge Rice.

Frenzel's moderate brand of Republicanism quickly became popular with his suburban constituents, and they have consistently returned him to office with more than 60 percent of the vote.

Frenzel has not been without critics. To the fundamentalist Christian element within the Minnesota GOP, he is too liberal. To many Democrats within the district, he is still too conservative. But in 1984, when candidates from both camps went against him, Frenzel won with little difficulty.

Committees

Budget (Ranking)

Ways and Means (4th of 13 Republicans)
Trade

Elections

1988 General

Bill Frenzel (R)	215,322	(68%)
Dave Carlson (D)	99,770	(32%)

1986 General

Bill Frenzel (R)	127,434	(70%)
Ray Stock (D)	54,261	(30%)

Previous Winning Percentages: **1984** (73%) **1982** (72%) **1980** (76%) **1978** (66%) **1976** (66%) **1974** (60%) **1972** (63%) **1970** (51%)

District Vote For President

	1988	1984	1980	1976
D	151,187 (45%)	120,859 (41%)	122,756 (41%)	105,384 (45%)
R	183,869 (54%)	174,225 (59%)	141,887 (47%)	122,673 (52%)
I			31,117 (10%)	

Campaign Finance

	Receipts	Receipts from PACs	Expend-itures
1988			
Frenzel (R)	$497,281	$301,578 (61%)	$381,646
Carlson (D)	$21,261	$10,025 (47%)	$20,733
1986			
Frenzel (R)	$493,504	$280,442 (57%)	$323,232
Stock (D)	$57,265	$6,610 (12%)	$52,716

Key Votes

1987	
Raise speed limit to 65 mph	Y
Approve Gephardt "fair trade" amendment	N
Ban testing of larger nuclear weapons	Y
Delay "re-flagging" of Kuwaiti tankers	Y
Approve tax-raising deficit-reduction bill	N
1988	
Approve aid to Nicaraguan contras	Y
Enact civil rights restoration bill over Reagan veto	Y
Kill 60-day plant-closing notification measure	Y
Pass omnibus trade bill over Reagan veto	N
Approve death penalty for drug-related murders	Y
Bar federal funds for abortions in cases of rape and incest	N
Oppose seven-day waiting period for purchase of handguns	N

Voting Studies

	Presidential Support		Party Unity		Conservative Coalition	
Year	S	O	S	O	S	O
1988	64	27	70	22	63	26
1987	64	29	74	15	81	16
1986	66	32	74	22	76	24
1985	63	35	72	19	80	16
1984	73	23	77	17	71	20
1983	68	26	71	21	61	34
1982	74	25	78	18	77	21
1981	64	25	71	17	61	23

Interest Group Ratings

Year	ADA	ACU	AFL-CIO	CCUS
1988	35	57	23	92
1987	16	40	7	87
1986	25	64	0	81
1985	20	67	19	90
1984	30	58	0	75
1983	20	57	12	100
1982	25	68	0	81
1981	30	80	7	100

4 Bruce F. Vento (D)

Of St. Paul — Elected 1976

Born: Oct. 7, 1940, St. Paul, Minn.
Education: U. of Minnesota, A.A. 1961; Wisconsin State U., B.S. 1965; graduate work, U. of Minnesota, 1965-70.
Occupation: Science teacher.
Family: Wife, Mary Jean Moore; three children.
Religion: Roman Catholic.
Political Career: Minn. House, 1971-77.
Capitol Office: 2304 Rayburn Bldg. 20515; 225-6631.

In Washington: Vento is a workhorse. He chairs the Interior Subcommittee on National Parks and Public Lands, a panel with a huge mandate and a massive workload. In the 100th Congress, he held hearings on 110 bills, and though he was up against a White House that fought spending more on national parks, Vento maneuvered around that opposition and got 107 bills enacted.

But even those who admire Vento's legislative diligence acknowledge that he has one problem: He talks and talks and talks. Once he gets started on an issue, he can continue long after those listening have lost the train of thought. And worse, his loquacity has been known to cross into the realm of condescension.

Were he any less conscientious a lawmaker, his verbosity might make it hard for him to build the delicate coalitions needed to pass legislation. Fortunately for his cause, Vento shares the philosophy of the conservationist majority on Interior, and his productivity helps them tolerate his garrulous style.

Vento's subcommittee mandate also allows him to offer colleagues tangible benefits to attract them to his side. In the 100th Congress, the panel approved dozens of new historical sites, designated 2,700 miles of trails, approved wild and scenic designation for rivers in five states, and set aside 2 million acres of wilderness land in six states. In the 99th Congress, Vento also helped guide the creation of Nevada's Great Basin National Park, the first full-scale national park added to the system outside Alaska since 1971.

In 1988, Vento pushed a bill to reorganize the Park Service and give it more independence; he said the Reagan administration had too often overruled Park Service suggestions and favored political appointees over career Park Service personnel. The House approved the reorganization plan by a wide margin, but Republicans derided Vento's proposal as "micromanagement," and it was ultimately derailed in the Senate.

When a mammoth shopping mall was planned near the Manassas National Battlefield Park in Virginia, Civil War buffs found a friend in Vento. His subcommittee approved a bill to annex the proposed mall site as part of a 600-acre parcel that included the site of Gen. Robert E. Lee's headquarters during the second battle of Manassas in 1862. The House cleared the measure over White House objections. It languished in the Senate until a midnight stand by Sen. Dale Bumpers got the House language attached to the technical corrections tax bill.

Vento has also been involved in a range of issues on the Banking Committee. He was one of the first members to urge congressional action to deal with the homeless. In 1982 he attached an amendment to a housing bill to provide $50 million to repair unused buildings to be used as temporary shelters. That bill was never considered by the full House, but Vento has since seen his efforts pay off as many other lawmakers focused on the issue. In the 100th Congress, he was the prime sponsor of the $1.3 million McKinney homeless-aid reauthorization bill, which won widespread support.

Occasionally, Vento conducts direct-action assaults on issues he feels are being ignored. When he launches a crusade, he often does it with a flurry of amendments, public statements and letters. That style has brought him some victories, and valuable publicity at home, but it can generate as much controversy as action.

When the House voted to eliminate the minimum Social Security benefit as part of Reagan's 1981 budget cuts, Vento quickly gathered more than 150 cosponsors on a resolution requiring a conference committee to restore it. House leaders, fearing a showdown that might jeopardize the compromise package of spending cuts already agreed on between the House and Senate, would not allow a vote on the resolution. Vento tried to force one, but was prevented from doing so on a separate roll-call vote. Later, the House voted overwhelmingly to restore the minimum benefit for all recipients, but the Senate decided to limit it to current recipients. Vento did not like the legislation that emerged from conference, but he supported the final compromise on the House floor.

Minnesota 4

St. Paul and Suburbs

St. Paul is a Democratic city with a German- and Irish-Catholic population and a strong labor tradition that grew up in the days when it was a major port and railroading hub. In every aspect except its Democratic loyalties, it differs from its supposed twin, Minneapolis.

The working-class neighborhoods on St. Paul's East Side are drab and solidly Democratic. The precincts here have routinely supported virtually every major statewide Democratic candidate of recent years.

West of Lexington Avenue, where the houses and the spaces between them are larger, Republicans usually do slightly better, but only occasionally do they prevail. Several colleges — Macalester, Hamline, St. Thomas and St. Catherine, and the University of Minnesota's School of Agriculture — give this area a young and culturally vibrant quality that is missing elsewhere in the 4th.

Thirty years ago, when Eugene J. McCarthy represented St. Paul in the U.S. House, nearly 90 percent of the 4th District vote came from the city. But with the growth of the suburbs and a decline in St. Paul's population from its 1960 peak of 313,000 to less than 270,000 in the 1980s, St. Paul makes up just half the current district.

Most of the suburban vote lies north of the city in Ramsey County. There, nearly 190,000 people in postwar suburban housing tracts vote about 10 percent less Democratic than their counterparts in St. Paul itself. While Vento never has difficulty carrying any section of St. Paul, he has sometimes struggled in several of the state legislative districts in suburban Ramsey.

South St. Paul, added to the 4th in 1982 redistricting, is known for its stockyards, which give off an aroma extending as far south into Dakota County as the district itself. This well-worn community of 20,000 is dependent on the meat factory that sits on the west bank of the Mississippi River. West St. Paul is not quite as Democratic as South St. Paul, but still supported Jimmy Carter, Walter F. Mondale and Michael S. Dukakis by convincing margins. In West St. Paul, Dukakis outpolled George Bush 60-39 percent; he carried South St. Paul by 25 percentage points, 62-37 percent.

Mendota Heights, also added in the last remap, votes Republican. Unlike the nearby areas, extensions of the working-class part of St. Paul, Mendota Heights is a new Twin Cities bedroom community.

Population: 509,532. White 476,141 (93%), Black 14,825 (3%), Other 8,694 (2%). Spanish origin 10,151 (2%). 18 and over 375,922 (74%), 65 and over 59,518 (12%). Median age: 29.

In 1988, he helped organize a contingent of House members who rallied on the Capitol steps to urge action on the Clean Air Act. More than 200 House members signed a letter to that effect, but while this action generated some publicity, it did not break the deadlock in negotiations on the bill.

At Home: Vento has the right personal and political background to represent this labor-dominated district.

The son of a Machinists' union official, he was a union steward at a plastics plant, then worked in a brewery and on a refrigerator assembly line before becoming a junior high school teacher and state representative.

During his three terms in the Legislature he echoed the interests of the working-class residents of St. Paul's Phalen Park. A loyal team player, he won the assistant majority leader post under Speaker Martin Olav Sabo, now his Minnesota congressional colleague.

When nine-term House veteran Joseph E. Karth decided to retire in 1976, he endorsed Vento for the seat. Karth's backing and labor support were enough to give him the party endorsement.

Still, Vento faced four foes in the Democratic primary. Two were significant: St. Paul attorney John S. Connolly, running as an even more liberal alternative to Vento, and 27-year-old state auditor Robert W. Mattson, who twice defeated party-endorsed candidates. But Vento had too many factors working in his favor. He won a convincing primary victory with 52 percent. The November election was just as easy for Vento as it usually had been for Karth.

In 1978, Vento met an aggressive, conservative GOP challenger who held the incumbent under 60 percent. But with the same candidate and a much better-financed campaign in 1980, Republicans got no closer. Since then they have offered only token opposition. In 1986 Vento easily turned back a challenge from one of the nation's foremost perennial candidates, Harold E. Stassen, making his first bid for the House after numerous tries for other offices.

Committees

Banking, Finance and Urban Affairs (8th of 31 Democrats)
Economic Stabilization; Financial Institutions Supervision, Regulation and Insurance; Housing and Community Development

Interior and Insular Affairs (7th of 26 Democrats)
National Parks and Public Lands (chairman); Energy and the Environment

Select Aging (13th of 39 Democrats)
Health and Long-Term Care

Elections

1988 General

Bruce F. Vento (D)	181,227	(72%)
Ian Maitland (R)	67,073	(27%)

1988 Primary

Bruce F. Vento (D)	15,117	(93%)
Harold H. Dorland (D)	1,168	(7%)

1986 General

Bruce F. Vento (D)	112,662	(73%)
Harold E. Stassen (R)	41,926	(27%)

Previous Winning Percentages: 1984 (74%) **1982** (73%) **1980** (59%) **1978** (58%) **1976** (66%)

District Vote For President

	1988	1984	1980	1976
D	159,663 (61%)	163,312 (59%)	137,337 (53%)	148,298 (58%)
R	99,668 (38%)	113,641 (41%)	88,633 (34%)	97,026 (38%)
I			25,260 (10%)	

Campaign Finance

	Receipts	Receipts from PACs	Expend-itures
1988			
Vento (D)	$268,237	$189,759 (71%)	$216,172
Maitland (R)	$36,998	0	$35,789
1986			
Vento (D)	$219,213	$145,790 (67%)	$197,906
Stassen (R)	$77,081	$2,706 (4%)	$76,954

Key Votes

1987	
Raise speed limit to 65 mph	?
Approve Gephardt "fair trade" amendment	Y
Ban testing of larger nuclear weapons	Y
Delay "re-flagging" of Kuwaiti tankers	Y
Approve tax-raising deficit-reduction bill	Y
1988	
Approve aid to Nicaraguan contras	N
Enact civil rights restoration bill over Reagan veto	Y
Kill 60-day plant-closing notification measure	N
Pass omnibus trade bill over Reagan veto	Y
Approve death penalty for drug-related murders	N
Bar federal funds for abortions in cases of rape and incest	#
Oppose seven-day waiting period for purchase of handguns	N

Voting Studies

	Presidential Support		Party Unity		Conservative Coalition	
Year	S	O	S	O	S	O
1988	21	77	94	4	11	89
1987	12	85	95	2	5	88
1986	19	81	94	5	6	94
1985	21	78	95	3	4	91
1984	28	67	90	6	3	95
1983	17	82	94	4	4	96
1982	34	65	94	5	5	92
1981	29	61	86	9	9	84

Interest Group Ratings

Year	ADA	ACU	AFL-CIO	CCUS
1988	90	4	100	36
1987	100	0	94	8
1986	90	0	93	28
1985	95	5	100	18
1984	95	0	92	43
1983	90	0	94	20
1982	100	9	100	14
1981	90	0	80	13

5 Martin Olav Sabo (D)

Of Minneapolis — Elected 1978

Born: Feb. 28, 1938, Crosby, N.D.
Education: Augsburg College, B.A. 1959; graduate work, U. of Minnesota, 1960.
Occupation: Public official.
Family: Wife, Sylvia Ann Lee; two children.
Religion: Lutheran.
Political Career: Minn. House, 1961-79, minority leader, 1969-73, Speaker, 1973-79.
Capitol Office: 2201 Rayburn Bldg. 20515; 225-4755.

In Washington: A decade in Congress has not thrust this former Speaker of the Minnesota House into the limelight, but Sabo's quiet and detached manner obscures the fact that he is a busy and thoughtful legislator. His low-key personality is well suited to the Appropriations Committee, where he lends a liberal's perspective to defense and transportation debates. But he clearly has the intellect to play a broader role, and in the 101st Congress, he has that chance, as he takes a seat on the Budget Committee and assumes the chairmanship of the Democratic Study Group.

This full plate of activities may help satisfy Sabo's desire for the kind of leadership role he played in the state Legislature. Sabo once tried for a top leadership job in the House, seeking the Democratic whip post for the 100th Congress (he was already a deputy whip). But he ran an oddly laconic campaign and gave it up in mid-1986 for a seat on the Appropriations Subcommittee on Defense. "I think I know how to count," he said. "My chances of winning are remote."

The Defense Subcommittee seat was a reasonable consolation prize. Sabo has long had an interest in arms control issues, and anti-Pentagon Democrats badly wanted him on the panel. Until the Minnesotan's arrival, Oregon's Les AuCoin was the only subcommittee member with a critical attitude toward the Reagan administration's defense buildup and controversial new weapons systems.

Sabo, who kept his post as deputy whip, was dealt a setback in 1988 when he chaired a task force on the anti-satellite missile (ASAT) test-ban amendment to the defense appropriations bill. The House defeated an amendment to fund ASAT development, but going for a permanent ban proved too ambitious; the House narrowly rejected the idea. Sabo won praise from some quarters for keeping the margin close enough to deny the GOP the momentum to defeat liberals on a host of subsequent arms control votes, but others grumbled that the leadership had been too casual in whipping the vote, lulled by easy victories on past votes to impose temporary ASAT bans.

Some months later, Sabo was tapped to co-chair a whip task force on the vote to delay Reagan administration plans to provide naval escorts for Kuwaiti tankers. This time, the Democratic whips displayed vigor and organizational prowess. In a sharp departure from Congress' usual reluctance to challenge a military commitment by a president, the House voted to delay the re-flagging for three months. The largely party-line vote, however, was symbolic, since Senate Democrats could not cut off a GOP filibuster blocking action there.

Sabo mixes parochial interests and national policy on spending bills through his interest in scientific research. He looks out for the major high-technology firms in his district as well as for the University of Minnesota, while advocating development of a federal policy on supercomputers. He supported amendments to the 1988 and 1989 defense appropriations bill to require the Pentagon to buy only American supercomputers.

On most matters before the Appropriations Committee, Sabo is a reliable liberal vote. In each year since he arrived in Washington, he has offered legislation to provide access to basic health insurance for those who now lack coverage. During the early 1980s, he was furious about Reagan administration budget cuts in social programs and scornful of Democrats who he felt went too far in accommodating the conservative mood.

In 1985, faced with massive deficits and new Reagan administration attempts to wipe out domestic spending programs, Sabo supported the idea of "freezing" federal spending, including most highway and transit projects that pass through the Transportation Subcommittee on which he serves.

Most of the time, though, Sabo uses his place on Transportation to fight for more spending, not less. He plays the money-earmarking game as well as anyone in Congress; when the fiscal 1987 transportation appropriations bill was approved, it contained, among other provisions, $10 million for a "demonstration project" to improve a highway linking

Minnesota 5

Minneapolis and Suburbs

This is one of the few districts in the country where candidates are not afraid to refer to themselves as liberals.

Minneapolis residents account for nearly three-fourths of the district's voters, and except for those on the city's southwest side, they predictably choose liberal candidates over conservatives.

Scandinavians remain the most conspicuous ethnic group; it is no coincidence that Sabo includes his middle name, Olav, on all his official papers. That name eliminates any vestiges of doubt that he is Norwegian, not Italian.

Although many of the flour mills that once lined the Mississippi River at St. Anthony's Falls have moved away, the major milling companies that settled in Minneapolis — Pillsbury and General Mills — have remained and diversified. They are among the major employers in the Twin Cities, along with the new "brain power" firms that find Minneapolis ideally suited for their needs.

Honeywell and Control Data have their worldwide headquarters in the district. The white-collar professionals who have been attracted by these "clean" industries help to give the city a clean-cut image that is reflected in the glistening towers of its downtown area.

But Minneapolis is not only parks, lakes, glass and chrome. Northwest of the downtown office towers are some poor neighborhoods, home to blacks and the city's Chippewa Indian population. East of the Mississippi are older, more traditional blue-collar areas adjoining the main campus of the University of Minnesota.

Even the downtown's aura of prosperity and growth has faded a bit in recent years, with some key stores abandoning Nicollet Mall, the centerpiece of downtown retailing. The city's population, having peaked in 1950 at 522,000, dropped by 29 percent during the 1970s to 371,000 and continues to slide, albeit gradually, in this decade.

To make up for the declining population, the last redistricting expanded the boundaries of the 5th. The southern border, which formerly coincided with the Minneapolis city limits, was extended to include about 60,000 people in Richfield and the eastern portion of Bloomington. Although the southern addition is not as Democratic as Minneapolis, the map was drawn to keep the most Republican parts of Bloomington in the 3rd District.

On the northern side of the 5th, three solidly Democratic suburbs from Anoka County were removed, and three larger communities in Hennepin County added. Again, the area added is not quite as Democratic as the rest of the district, but Robbinsdale, Brooklyn Center and Crystal all have exhibited Democratic preferences.

Population: 509,506. White 458,433 (90%), Black 29,776 (6%), Other 14,993 (3%). Spanish origin 5,544 (1%). 18 and over 401,381 (79%), 65 and over 69,437 (14%). Median age: 30.

downtown Minneapolis and the Twin Cities' airport, and $2.8 million to build a bus transitway on the University of Minnesota campus. Sabo is a strong believer in buses; during his years on the subcommittee, he has lobbied repeatedly for more money for bus service as opposed to more expensive rail mass-transit systems.

On one occasion, Sabo took on his own delegation and another surprised committee chairman. He successfully persuaded the Appropriations Committee to scale down the number of beds in a proposed Veterans Administration hospital at Fort Snelling in Minnesota. Then Veterans' Affairs Chairman Ray Roberts of Texas threatened to "kill the damn project, if that's the way they feel about it." Sabo argued that a new, large hospital would lead to a surplus of beds in the community. In so doing, he riled his Minnesota colleagues; five of the eight members of the state's delegation immediately fired off a "Dear Colleague" letter vowing a fight to restore money for the larger hospital on the House floor. They did, and won.

At Home: Sabo has never been a flashy campaigner, but he has been a significant presence in Minnesota politics virtually all his adult life.

When Democratic Rep. Donald Fraser left the House for his unsuccessful try at the Senate in 1978, nearly a dozen candidates began maneuvering to succeed him. But when Sabo announced he wanted the job, nearly all of them bowed out of the contest. Those who remained lost either at the endorsing convention or in Sabo's 81 percent primary victory.

One of the reasons for Sabo's strength has been his amazing combination of youth and longevity. Elected to the state Legislature at 22, he had been in the public spotlight for 18 years and served as Speaker for six years before running for Congress. He was seen by most voters as the logical liberal successor to Fraser.

Sabo's first Republican opponent, dentist Mike Till, conducted a much more visible campaign than Republicans usually wage in this heavily Democratic district. When businessman Bob Short defeated Fraser in a bitter Senate primary, Till hoped some of the animosity liberals felt toward Short would rub off on Sabo for the general election. But Sabo carefully avoided making any connection between his campaign and Short's, which was a wise move. Short received less than 24 percent in the 5th.

Sabo's winning percentage in 1978 was not quite up to what Fraser had been receiving. But by his second election, he had achieved solid support throughout the area, even in the communities of the district where he was weakest against Till.

Committees

Appropriations (18th of 35 Democrats)
Defense; Transportation and Related Agencies; Treasury, Postal Service and General Government

Budget (16th of 21 Democrats)
Task Forces: Budget Process, Reconciliation and Enforcement; Human Resources

Elections

1988 General		
Martin Olav Sabo (D)	174,416	(72%)
Raymond C. Gilbertson (R)	60,646	(25%)
T. Christopher Wright (I)	6,468	(3%)
1988 Primary		
Martin Olav Sabo (D)	15,240	(92%)
Ole Savior (D)	1,370	(8%)
1986 General		
Martin Olav Sabo (D)	105,410	(73%)
Rick Serra (R)	37,583	(26%)

Previous Winning Percentages: **1984** (70%) **1982** (66%) **1980** (70%) **1978** (62%)

District Vote For President

	1988	1984	1980	1976
D	166,580 (65%)	162,599 (63%)	163,443 (60%)	161,266 (61%)
R	85,100 (33%)	97,062 (37%)	77,062 (28%)	94,618 (36%)
I			29,812 (11%)	

Campaign Finance

	Receipts	Receipts from PACs	Expend-itures
1988			
Sabo (D)	$363,965	$237,550 (65%)	$281,455
Gilbertson (R)	$21,776	$479 (2%)	$16,915
1986			
Sabo (D)	$237,778	$86,681 (36%)	$208,043
Serra (R)	$22,925	$2,665 (12%)	$22,088

Key Votes

1987	
Raise speed limit to 65 mph	N
Approve Gephardt "fair trade" amendment	Y
Ban testing of larger nuclear weapons	Y
Delay "re-flagging" of Kuwaiti tankers	Y
Approve tax-raising deficit-reduction bill	Y
1988	
Approve aid to Nicaraguan contras	N
Enact civil rights restoration bill over Reagan veto	Y
Kill 60-day plant-closing notification measure	N
Pass omnibus trade bill over Reagan veto	Y
Approve death penalty for drug-related murders	N
Bar federal funds for abortions in cases of rape and incest	N
Oppose seven-day waiting period for purchase of handguns	N

Voting Studies

	Presidential Support		Party Unity		Conservative Coalition	
Year	**S**	**O**	**S**	**O**	**S**	**O**
1988	20	80	96	2	8	92
1987	17	80	91	2	12	84
1986	20	80	95	3	12	88
1985	16	84	98	1	5	95
1984	26	70	92	4	12	80
1983	18	80	93	3	9	90
1982	35	64	92	5	10	89
1981	29	70	89	8	7	92

Interest Group Ratings

Year	ADA	ACU	AFL-CIO	CCUS
1988	100	0	100	21
1987	100	0	94	7
1986	95	0	93	11
1985	95	5	94	18
1984	95	4	85	31
1983	100	0	94	30
1982	100	0	95	29
1981	90	0	93	5

6 Gerry Sikorski (D)

Of Stillwater — Elected 1982

Born: April 26, 1948, Breckenridge, Minn.
Education: U. of Minnesota, B.A. 1970, J.D. 1973.
Military Career: Navy Reserve, 1984-present.
Occupation: Lawyer.
Family: Wife, Susan Erkel; one child.
Religion: Roman Catholic.
Political Career: Minn. Senate, 1977-83; Democratic nominee for U.S. House, 1978.
Capitol Office: 414 Cannon Bldg. 20515; 225-2271.

In Washington: The Energy and Commerce Committee has its share of members who regularly play the middle ground, but Sikorski is not one of them. He stands firmly in the environmentalist faction led by California Democrat Henry A. Waxman.

But if his stance seems predictable, that is no sign that he does not think on his own. He is a bright and ambitious lawmaker who makes a contribution on a number of major issues. If there is a limit to his legislative success, it will not be because of a lack of effort or brainpower; it is more likely to result from a quick temper, which rankles some and can undermine his ability to be persuasive.

Sikorski started taking a leading role in promoting acid rain legislation shortly after joining the committee in 1983, and since then, he has built an invaluable alliance with Waxman, one of the most influential members of the House. Along with that, however, has come conflict with committee Chairman John D. Dingell of Michigan, who leads the more industry-oriented faction on clean air issues. There are those who oppose Dingell on clean air, but go out of their way to placate him on other issues. Not Sikorski.

Sikorski began his Energy and Commerce career teaming with Waxman to introduce legislation calling for a 10 million-ton acid rain control program requiring installation of expensive "scrubbers" on the dirtiest utility smokestacks. The authors sought to ease the financial burden on Midwest utility users by spreading the cost nationwide with a tax on non-nuclear power. The measure was popular in the full House, but Dingell and his committee allies managed to kill it by one vote.

Sikorski met with greater success in the 99th Congress as chief sponsor of a somewhat less stringent acid rain bill. Claiming more than 180 sponsors in their second effort, proponents of acid rain legislation were able to win a 16-9 victory in subcommittee after a grueling nine-hour debate. But thanks to Dingell, the bill never made it out of the full committee.

The 100th Congress proved equally frustrating; a Sikorski-backed measure never cleared the subcommittee. But when the 101st Congress began, he was optimistic about breaking the impasse. Some of the old obstacles remained, but environmentalists were encouraged that George Bush had supported acid rain legislation in his presidential campaign, the new majority leader of the Senate was acid rain activist George J. Mitchell of Maine, and the Democratic leadership had labeled the issue a priority.

Sikorski is a force partly because he has considerable energy and the ability to master issues quickly, but sometimes he seems too energetic, and he can anger too quickly for his own good. Opponents who deal with him say the fastest route to victory is often to needle him until he loses his temper, and along with it, his ability to make a sound argument.

His temper and other personal behavior received unfavorable public attention in 1988, when *The Washington Post* ran a story detailing Sikorski's treatment of his staff. The newspaper reported that he often had staff members do personal chores, such as driving his daughter to school or helping his wife's dog-breeding enterprise by bobbing the tails of puppies. It also reported that he could fly into a tirade over seemingly minor incidents, such as preparing the wrong kind of sandwich for his daughter's school lunch. Sikorski claimed that the story was "full of untruths and distortions."

Attention on Sikorski in the 100th Congress was not all negative, however. During work to change the Price-Anderson Act, the law governing compensation for nuclear accident damages, Sikorski got some of the spotlight when he championed a provision to ensure that payments went to accident victims before they went to utility lawyers in cases where damage costs exceed the money in the compensation fund.

The full committee approved Sikorski's plan 24-18, but shortly thereafter, under intense lobbying pressure, the committee reversed itself. With some expressing concern Sikorski's plan could delay insurance claims

Minnesota 6

Northern and Eastern Twin Cities Suburbs

The 6th District surrounds the Twin Cities like a magnet, collecting nearly all the suburban fringe areas on the north, east and west, plus some rural farm land just beyond. It includes many marginally Democratic areas and a few hard-core Democratic strongholds.

Anoka County, which casts nearly 40 percent of the vote, is the real political power base. It is also the strongest Democratic area of the 6th, serving as the cornerstone of Sikorski's congressional victories and remaining loyal to Walter F. Mondale in 1984 and Michael S. Dukakis in 1988. Even in the Democrats' 1978 statewide debacle, in which Republicans took both U.S. Senate seats and the governorship, Democratic Gov. Rudy Perpich and most of his ticket carried Anoka County.

Anoka is a mix of new suburbs, farms and small towns. Lake Wobegon, the mythical sleepy town in Garrison Keillor's one-time weekly radio program "A Prairie Home Companion," is modeled after Keillor's boyhood home in Anoka County. But the Lake Wobegons of this part of Minnesota are quickly disappearing as the Twin Cities metropolitan area expands farther into the surrounding counties.

Changing even more rapidly are Wright and Sherburne counties, the two largest growth areas in the state during the 1970s. Both have been friendly to such moderate Democratic candidates as Perpich, but both went narrowly to George Bush in 1988.

More than a quarter of the vote is cast in Hennepin County, in close-in Minneapolis suburbs, and this is where most of the GOP vote lies. This part of the district includes the affluent area around Lake Minnetonka, which is among the most Republican parts of the state.

Wedged on the eastern side of the district between St. Paul and the St. Croix River is Washington County. It is home for Sikorski and about 20 percent of the district voters. In 1982, the county gave Sikorski a 218-vote margin, but it has since provided him with a more substantial edge.

Population: 509,446. White 499,670 (98%), Black 2,114 (0.4%), Other 5,877 (1%). Spanish origin 3,414 (1%). 18 and over 332,303 (65%), 65 and over 27,040 (5%). Median age: 27.

and jeopardize payments to victims' lawyers, the panel approved an amendment stating that, notwithstanding any part of the bill, a court could authorize payment of legal costs.

"The amendment turns the system of justice and equity and fairness upside down," Sikorski said. "Not women and children first, but attorneys for the industry first." The full House later rejected his amendment, 183-230.

Like many Minnesotans, Sikorski is at odds with his party's official stance on abortion. He opposes abortion, and when Energy and Commerce marked up legislation to set product liability standards in the 100th Congress, he was concerned that new standards would make it easier for manufacturers of contraceptives and abortion-inducing drugs to sell their products. His effort to prevent this from happening was backed not only by anti-abortion groups, but also by a group representing women injured by the Dalkon Shield intrauterine device. Sikorski's wife had been injured by the Dalkon Shield, but had previously settled her claim with the manufacturer.

Sikorski offered a broad amendment in committee that exempted from the new standards products that could threaten a person's ability to generate offspring. Some family-planning advocates said Sikorski's amendment would classify reproduction-related products as more dangerous than others, discouraging research in that area. Many felt the Sikorski language was too broad, and his amendment was rejected 21-21. But the committee did approve an amendment by GOP Rep. Tom Tauke exempting just abortion-inducing drugs and certain contraceptive products. The bill never cleared the House.

While most of Sikorski's attention goes toward Energy and Commerce, he also holds a subcommittee chairmanship on the Post Office and Civil Service Committee.

At Home: Sikorski has been described as a Democratic version of Minnesota Republican Vin Weber — aggressive, smart and well financed. In his affluent suburban constituency, he needs all those attributes.

Republicans view the 6th as favorable terrain, but they have found no way to beat him. Massive redistricting in 1982 created the 6th and enabled Sikorski to unseat GOP Rep. Arlen Erdahl. In 1984, he trounced a well-financed champion of the religious right. And in each of the next two elections, Sikorski won nearly two-thirds of the total vote.

Elected to the state Senate at age 28, Sikorski quickly established a reputation for strong organizational skills and driving ambition. He was just two years into his freshman Senate term in 1978 when he took on Rep. Erdahl in the old 1st District.

That constituency spread north all the way to the border of St. Paul, but most of the vote was cast in nine farming counties. Worse for Sikorski, 1978 was a year in which the GOP took both U.S. Senate seats and the governorship out of Democratic hands.

Sikorski tried to adjust to the Republican year, campaigning for a $50 billion tax cut and stressing his opposition to legalized abortion. But the timing and the district demographics were against him. He was held to 43 percent.

Sikorski returned to the state Senate, becoming majority whip in 1980. But court-ordered redistricting in early 1982 created a new district in the Twin Cities suburbs, and Sikorski was a front-runner from the start. Although he faced opposition from some groups opposed to his stand on abortion, he needed only three ballots to seal his party endorsement over two other state legislators.

Meanwhile, Erdahl was having a complicated year. When the remap placed his home in the solidly Democratic 4th District, Erdahl moved into the redrawn 1st, but lost the nomination to GOP Rep. Tom Hagedorn. Party leaders talked Erdahl into moving to the new 6th, where he drew criticism as a carpetbagger and needed 13 ballots to win the GOP endorsement.

Sikorski seized on the carpetbagging charge, distributing state maps charting Erdahl's tortuous path to the 6th. More important, the circumstances of 1978 were reversed. The new 6th was friendly Democratic territory, and 1982 was almost as good a year for Minnesota Democrats as 1978 had been for Republicans. Sikorski won with 51 percent.

In 1984, the GOP nominated Patrick Trueman, an articulate, energetic campaigner with fervent support from Minnesota's potent anti-abortion movement. He had been a co-founder of its legal arm, Americans United for Life.

Trueman accused Sikorski of being a part of the "Mondale tax increase team," but in a district still reasonably sympathetic to national Democrats, the charge had modest impact. Sikorski drove home his message with a late media blitz, turning what was thought to be a close race into a solid victory.

Committees

Energy and Commerce (19th of 26 Democrats)
Health and the Environment; Oversight and Investigations; Transportation and Hazardous Materials

Post Office and Civil Service (8th of 15 Democrats)
Civil Service (chairman); Human Resources

Select Children, Youth and Families (12th of 18 Democrats)

Elections

1988 General

Gerry Sikorski (D)	169,486	(65%)
Ray Ploetz (R)	89,209	(34%)

1986 General

Gerry Sikorski (D)	110,598	(66%)
Barbara Zwach Sykora (R)	57,460	(34%)

Previous Winning Percentages: 1984 (60%) **1982** (51%)

District Vote For President

	1988	1984	1980	1976
D	148,030 (51%)	124,587 (48%)	73,786 (46%)	85,390 (53%)
R	140,362 (48%)	136,681 (52%)	68,292 (43%)	70,450 (44%)
I			15,258 (10%)	

Campaign Finance

	Receipts	Receipts from PACs	Expend-itures
1988			
Sikorski (D)	$547,198	$358,582 (66%)	$320,437
Ploetz (R)	$103,945	$5,568 (5%)	$100,941
1986			
Sikorski (D)	$506,995	$310,155 (61%)	$492,385
Sykora (R)	$155,275	$27,579 (18%)	$154,337

Key Votes

1987

Raise speed limit to 65 mph	Y
Approve Gephardt "fair trade" amendment	Y
Ban testing of larger nuclear weapons	Y
Delay "re-flagging" of Kuwaiti tankers	Y
Approve tax-raising deficit-reduction bill	Y

1988

Approve aid to Nicaraguan contras	N
Enact civil rights restoration bill over Reagan veto	Y
Kill 60-day plant-closing notification measure	N
Pass omnibus trade bill over Reagan veto	Y
Approve death penalty for drug-related murders	N
Bar federal funds for abortions in cases of rape and incest	Y
Oppose seven-day waiting period for purchase of handguns	Y

Voting Studies

	Presidential Support		Party Unity		Conservative Coalition	
Year	S	O	S	O	S	O
1988	22	77	75	23	16	84
1987	12	88	82	18	14	86
1986	17	81	79	20	22	76
1985	23	78	70 †	28 †	20	78
1984	33	67	85	15	22	78
1983	16	83	89	8	13	87

† Not eligible for all recorded votes.

Interest Group Ratings

Year	ADA	ACU	AFL-CIO	CCUS
1988	90	12	100	36
1987	92	9	94	13
1986	85	5	100	33
1985	75	14	88	27
1984	80	13	92	44
1983	90	4	100	25

7 Arlan Stangeland (R)

Of Barnesville — Elected 1977

Born: Feb. 8, 1930, Fargo, N.D.
Education: Graduated from Moorhead High School, 1948.
Occupation: Farmer.
Family: Wife, Virginia Trowbridge; seven children.
Religion: Lutheran.
Political Career: Minn. House, 1967-75; Barnesville school board, 1976-77.
Capitol Office: 2245 Rayburn Bldg. 20515; 225-2165.

In Washington: Stangeland is a profile in resilience. In an era when the vast majority of House members are easily re-elected, he seems perpetually on the ropes in his marginal northwest Minnesota district. But he keeps coming back, and in doing so has moved to the upper ranks on two major committees, where he is in a position to make a mark for his often struggling district.

The Agriculture Committee is a natural place for Stangeland, and in recent years he has started to break out of his role there as a backbencher. A chain-smoking and occasionally gruff farmer, Stangeland is still not the best spokesman on agricultural issues, but his opinions are given some weight. He is in a good position to voice them as ranking Republican on the Cotton, Rice and Sugar Subcommittee.

The more activist Stangeland began to be apparent during debate on the 1985 farm bill. Although he has spent much of his energy over the years looking out for the sugar beet growers of the Red River Valley, during the farm bill debate he was particularly active on provisions affecting wheat.

Stangeland's increased visibility on the Wheat Subcommittee did not stem from any unusual skill at political maneuvering or from his oratorical gifts. Those have never been his strong suits. Instead, it was his early and firm embrace of a new program of price supports, called "marketing loans," which many others considered too complicated to endorse.

Marketing loans were designed to boost commodity sales by allowing prices to fall, and, at the same time, to avoid having farmers default on the price-support loans. Unlike the existing commodity program, which allows farmers to default, marketing loans would have to be repaid to the government, but only at the price farmers' crops brought at market, which could be significantly below the loan rate.

While Stangeland's proposal won support from many Democrats, it faced considerable opposition from leaders of both parties on the committee, who argued that it was untested and too expensive. Stangeland won approval for the plan in the Wheat Subcommittee, but a few days later the panel reversed itself, giving the secretary of agriculture the discretion to implement or ignore the program and allowing farmers to continue defaulting on loans.

Stangeland tried again in full committee. This time he was criticized by Thomas S. Foley, the Wheat Subcommittee chairman, as a champion of "rural social welfare."

Stangeland challenged that contention. "We have a choice," he argued, "of setting a new course for agriculture that gives some hope to farmers. Is it not now the time to write some innovative new approach that will work? Or shall we procrastinate for four more years?" But the committee rejected the mandatory marketing loan program 20-22.

The effort did not stop there. Stangeland also lost two attempts to revive his plan on the House floor. Instead, the final farm bill included a formula that allowed for the gradual lowering of price supports. Stangeland supported the bill, which he called "the best we could get."

Stangeland's reputation in Washington was enhanced by his work on the farm bill, but he paid a political price at home, where he was the target of many farmers' discontent. Not surprisingly, he is among those who have suggested that the next farm bill be taken up in 1991, an off year, rather than in the 1990 election year.

Although Stangeland did not have to grapple with a giant farm bill in the 100th Congress, he was among those working to fend off a proposal to change the sugar program, which some legislators have attacked for being expensive and keeping prices too high. Stangeland and other supporters said that sugar in the United States is reasonably priced, and that foreign dumping in the world marketplace drives down world prices and gives the incorrect impression that U.S. sugar is overpriced.

"No producer in the world could be expected to successfully compete at prices well below the cost of production," Stangeland said. As it turned out, proposals to change the sugar

Minnesota 7

Northwest — St. Cloud; Moorhead

From the prairie wheat fields along the Red River to the hills, forests and lakes in the middle of the state, this is Minnesota's most marginal district — economically as well as politically.

Farmers struggle each year to meet their high operating costs on land that does not match the quality of the soil farther south. Those living in the chilly central section try to eke out a living any way they can. A few dollars can usually be made from the sportsmen who hunt and fish in the region, and there is some money in the region's lumber business, which once was an economic mainstay but now is in decline. The snowmobile industry, a more recent economic boon to the area, was hurt by the early 1980s recession and several dry winters, and it has been slow to recover.

Politically, the district has been in the marginal category ever since popular Democrat Bob Bergland left in 1977 to become Jimmy Carter's agriculture secretary.

St. Cloud, the seat of Stearns County with 43,000 residents, is the district's largest city. For years a major center for granite quarrying, St. Cloud attracted a diverse ethnic population that German Catholics dominated. Today the descendants of the old stonecutters share their ancestors' support of the Democratic Party on economic issues, but they often stray to the GOP when social issues, especially abortion, become paramount.

Apart from St. Cloud and Moorhead, a sister city to Fargo, N.D., about a half day's drive to the northwest, there are few population centers. But there is a significant Catholic influence in the small towns around St. Cloud, where large Catholic churches loom above the surrounding farm land — giving the area some of the feel of rural France or Germany.

Outside the orbit of St. Cloud, the towns are vintage Americana. Sauk Centre — about 40 miles northwest of St. Cloud — was the birthplace of novelist Sinclair Lewis, who used his hometown as the model for his famous work "Main Street." Street signs along the prime thoroughfare in Sauk Centre, in fact, describe it as the "Original Main Street."

The wheat-growing central sections of the district are slightly more populous than the rest, and also more Republican. Sugar beets are grown around Moorhead in the Red River Valley, which possesses some of the most fertile farm land in the district. In the rolling countryside just to the east are hundreds of lakes — ranging from small ponds to bodies of water several miles wide. The area draws hunters, fishermen and summer tourists.

Farther north, near the Canadian border, the land supports fewer people, and the vote is usually Democratic. The Red Lake and White Earth Indian reservations are in the northern part of the 7th.

Population: 509,521. White 497,050 (98%), Black 660 (0.1%), Other 10,189 (2%). Spanish origin 2,464 (1%). 18 and over 355,632 (70%), 65 and over 68,572 (14%). Median age: 28.

program never got off the ground.

Stangeland was elected with critical help from national New Right organizations, but on the Public Works Committee he is the sort of pork-barrel Republican of whom the ideological right is skeptical. He is bipartisan on that committee, often asking other Republicans to support the position of the Democratic chairman. Stangeland is ranking member of the Water Resources Subcommittee.

Early in the 100th Congress Stangeland was among those voting to override President Reagan's veto of a major highway bill. "The president vetoed [the bill] saying it was a budget buster," Stangeland said. "I just want to tell the people it was not a budget buster."

The bill, which was enacted over Reagan's objections, included funding for a grade-separation project in Moorhead, Minn., allowing a street to run under Burlington Northern railroad tracks. "For those of us who see those projects as very imporant to our constituents and well deserved, we just don't consider that pork," Stangeland said.

The further the issue gets from agriculture or public works, the more likely Stangeland is to sound like an ideological conservative. In 1982, when the House considered a five-year highway bill, Stangeland was one of the more outspoken opponents of the so-called Davis-Bacon requirement that an area's prevailing wage be paid on federally funded highway projects. Davis-Bacon has long been anathema to conservatives, who argue that the prevailing wage usually turns out to be the union wage. Since then, Stangeland has introduced bills to repeal Davis-Bacon.

Although he comes from a Frost Belt district rather than an energy-producing Sun Belt area, he has generally voted on the producer side against consumers and environmentalists. "The idea that every river or stream has to be fishable or swimmable is unrealistic," he once said, criticizing the 1972 Water Pollution Act. Still, Minnesota is known for its numerous lakes, and Stangeland does see a role for the federal government in keeping them clean. He is a strong supporter of the Environmental Protection Agency's clean lakes program.

At Home: If Stangeland has not always stood out in Washington, he usually stands apart from his House colleagues at election time. While most incumbents win with ease, Stangeland is often under siege. But he has always been up to the test. After surviving in 1986 by a scant 121 votes — a margin so slim that his victory was not secure until a recount a month after the voting — Stangeland moved up in 1988 to a more comfortable 55 percent.

That 10-point victory was practically a landslide for Stangeland, who had surpassed 53 percent only once in his previous five re-election efforts.

In winning six full terms, Stangeland has had to struggle against a number of factors. Part of Stangeland's problem has been the politically marginal nature of the district; Democrat Bob Bergland held it for six years before leaving to become President Jimmy Carter's agriculture secretary in 1977. Another problem has been Stangeland's less-than-charismatic persona. Disturbed by his narrow election victories, he paid for a personality analysis after the 1982 election.

But possibly Stangeland's biggest headache has been a perception among many farmers in the rural 7th that his prime constituency is the sugar beet growers around his home base in the fertile Red River Valley. That, and identification with the controversial 1985 farm bill, nearly cost him his seat in 1986.

Stangeland's Democratic challenger, state Sen. Collin C. Peterson, pounded away at the theme that the farm bill was a bad one and that Stangeland's fingerprints were all over it. Peterson blamed the bill for driving down the prices on virtually all farm commodities in northwestern Minnesota, and he noted that Stangeland was on the House-Senate conference committee that drafted the bill. "He is the architect of this farm policy," Peterson declared. "It will all come to roost."

Seeking to put his own stamp on farm policy, Peterson traveled to Washington, D.C., several times in 1985 to lobby for the Democratic farm alternative. He even wrote and recorded a song in support of the legislation.

Meanwhile, Stangeland argued that the version Congress approved in 1985 had not had time to work, and in any case, that it was the best that farmers could get in a Congress that listened to a consumer-oriented Eastern establishment.

The incumbent did not shrink from claiming a leadership role in the House. "A Friend at Home . . . A Leader in Congress" was Stangeland's campaign slogan, and he warned voters not to discard the seniority that had enabled him to become the ranking GOP member on the Cotton, Rice and Sugar Subcommittee.

Still, Stangeland sought to steer debate away from the farm issue as much as possible. He ran ads attacking Peterson as a big spender in the state Senate who was anti-business and out of touch with the district's fairly conservative political mainstream.

But when discussion returned to agricultural policy, Stangeland found himself on the defensive. He did not advertise his GOP affiliation on either his campaign literature or large billboards that dotted the district.

Meanwhile, Peterson conspicuously touted his Democratic affiliation, both on his billboards and in his TV ads that featured "Bessie the talking cow."

A 57-43 percent loser to Stangeland in 1984, Peterson ran virtually neck-and-neck with the incumbent in 1986. The winner in just one of the district's 23 counties in 1984, Peterson carried 14 counties in 1986. But like Democrat Gene Wenstrom, who challenged Stangeland in three straight elections from 1978 through 1982, Peterson fell short.

Two years later Peterson hoped his third-straight bid would put him over the top, but he got a cold reception from many of his fellow Democrats, who felt it was time for a different candidate. The party's endorsement went to former state Sen. Marv Hanson, who was able to defeat Peterson in a September primary.

Hanson was a personally appealing candidate, and many Democratic leaders hoped his background as both a farmer and a lawyer would bring him broad support. But Hanson's home base was in Kittson County, in the far northwest corner of the state, and he faced a challenge just getting his name known around the rest of the large district. The late primary added to his problems; some Democratic funding sources held back until the nomination was settled.

Against Stangeland, Hanson renewed the argument that the 1985 farm bill contained inequities that hurt some farmers. But there seemed to be less resentment toward the bill than existed in 1986, and Stangeland was more practiced at defending it. He won all but six of the 23 counties in the district. Four of the counties Hanson carried were around his home territory in the northwest.

Democrats have been gunning for Stangeland ever since he won an upset victory in the 1977 special election held to replace Bergland. Only four months before, Bergland had won 72 percent, but in replacing him, Democrats gave away a safe seat by running the wrong candidate.

The Democratic nominee in the special election, Mike Sullivan, a former aide to Walter F. Mondale, ran on the slogan, "He's in the

Bergland tradition." But it was clear to the district's Norwegian Lutheran farmers that Sullivan, an Irish Catholic, was not part of their tradition. Stangeland — a farmer whose parents were Norwegian immigrants — was.

After that, the Democrats switched to Wenstrom, who had the right background and ethnicity, and who almost certainly would have held the seat for them had he been nominated in 1977. Wenstrom, a former state legislator, teacher and farmer, held Stangeland to 52 percent of the vote in 1978 and 1980, and ran virtually even with the incumbent in 1982, losing by less than 2,000 votes.

Wenstrom's third campaign offered a change in tactics from his previous efforts. In 1980 he had charged that Stangeland's voting record and list of campaign contributors exposed him as a friend of agribusiness and major oil companies. In 1982 the challenger was relatively gentle to Stangeland — he made Reagan his prime villain. Wenstrom blamed the president for a tight-money policy that he said maintained a depressed farm economy.

Wenstrom carried most of the counties in the 7th, including three counties in the populous St. Cloud area, which had been added by redistricting. But Stangeland ran well ahead around his home base in the central part of the district to eke out a 1,192-vote victory.

After the near-defeat in 1982, Stangeland took an unusual step for an incumbent. Disappointed that he had not managed to secure the district after five years of effort, he underwent a round of personality tests to see if he was relating to constituents effectively on a human level. It was hard to tell whether his comfortable 1984 margin owed more to the testing, to the fact that Reagan carried all but three counties in the district, or to Peterson's lack of name identity and funding in his first challenge to Stangeland.

Committees

Agriculture (5th of 18 Republicans)
Cotton, Rice and Sugar (ranking); Livestock, Dairy and Poultry; Wheat, Soybeans and Feed Grains

Public Works and Transportation (3rd of 20 Republicans)
Water Resources (ranking); Aviation; Surface Transportation

Elections

1988 General		
Arlan Stangeland (R)	121,396	(55%)
Marv Hanson (D)	101,011	(45%)
1986 General		
Arlan Stangeland (R)	94,024	(50%)
Collin C. Peterson (D)	93,903	(50%)

Previous Winning Percentages: 1984 (57%) **1982** (50%) **1980** (52%) **1978** (52%) **1977 *** (58%)

* *Special election.*

District Vote For President

	1988	1984	1980	1976
D	112,654 (48%)	102,205 (43%)	103,081 (42%)	140,207 (54%)
R	119,763 (51%)	135,304 (57%)	123,905 (50%)	109,051 (42%)
I			16,542 (7%)	

Campaign Finance

	Receipts	Receipts from PACs	Expend-itures
1988			
Stangeland (R)	$658,882	$344,281 (52%)	$693,429
Hanson (D)	$287,085	$128,339 (45%)	$286,577
1986			
Stangeland (R)	$578,421	$264,428 (46%)	$547,810
Peterson (D)	$465,585	$217,579 (47%)	$464,246

Key Votes

1987	
Raise speed limit to 65 mph	N
Approve Gephardt "fair trade" amendment	N
Ban testing of larger nuclear weapons	N
Delay "re-flagging" of Kuwaiti tankers	N
Approve tax-raising deficit-reduction bill	N
1988	
Approve aid to Nicaraguan contras	Y
Enact civil rights restoration bill over Reagan veto	N
Kill 60-day plant-closing notification measure	Y
Pass omnibus trade bill over Reagan veto	Y
Approve death penalty for drug-related murders	Y
Bar federal funds for abortions in cases of rape and incest	Y
Oppose seven-day waiting period for purchase of handguns	Y

Voting Studies

	Presidential Support		Party Unity		Conservative Coalition	
Year	**S**	**O**	**S**	**O**	**S**	**O**
1988	62	38	85	11	87	11
1987	58	36	83	12	84	9
1986	68°	29	71	22	84	10
1985	65	33	82	14	89	9
1984	63	36	74	21	90	7
1983	68	28	75	20	75	21
1982	57	31	80	17	85	10
1981	71	28	83	14	93	7

Interest Group Ratings

Year	ADA	ACU	AFL-CIO	CCUS
1988	5	92	29	93
1987	4	83	13	93
1986	10	80	21	59
1985	15	81	0	67
1984	5	75	8	75
1983	5	78	12	89
1982	10	81	5	90
1981	0	93	7	95

8 James L. Oberstar (D)

Of Chisholm — Elected 1974

Born: Sept. 10, 1934, Chisholm, Minn.
Education: College of St. Thomas, B.A. 1956; College of Europe, M.A. 1957.
Occupation: Language teacher; congressional aide.
Family: Wife, Jo Garlick; four children.
Religion: Roman Catholic.
Political Career: No previous office.
Capitol Office: 2209 Rayburn Bldg. 20515; 225-6211.

In Washington: In some ways Oberstar seems miscast for the Public Works and Transportation Committee, despite his quarter-century there as staffer and member. He has the instincts of a scholar and reformer, but Public Works is a place where members like to dig first and ask questions later; policy analysts take a back seat to pork-barrelers.

At the same time, Oberstar is only part scholar. The rest of him is Minnesota Iron Range street-fighter, a self-described bohunk. He is the son of a miner and a shirt-factory worker, and an unrepentant New Deal-style Democrat with deep faith in the job-creating potential of public works and deeper faith yet in his party.

With the 101st Congress, Oberstar assumed his third subcommittee chairmanship on the panel. Having headed the Economic Development and the Investigations and Oversight subcommittees, he now has charge of the one covering aviation. He has made his career and built seniority at Public Works. Even so, not so long ago he was restless enough to want to surrender it for something more. Having failed, it remains to be seen whether he will settle in and make the most of his longtime niche.

Oberstar unsuccessfully sought the Democratic Senate nomination in 1984, and returned to the House in 1985. Then he lost his bid for a seat on the Ways and Means Committee, and it was back to Public Works. Two years later, however, he added a place on the Budget Committee, an assignment that will satisfy that side of Oberstar that seeks a hand in broader policy debate.

He owes the Budget seat to a Public Works connection — former committee member Jim Wright. When Wright became Speaker in 1987, he appointed Oberstar to the Democratic Steering and Policy Committee, the leadership panel that makes committee assignments. In return, Oberstar was among those who spoke up for Wright during the long ethics probe that ultimately forced the Speaker to resign in June 1989.

At the Aviation Subcommittee in 1989, Oberstar the pro-labor partisan quickly jumped into the controversy surrounding a strike against Eastern Airlines that was aimed at its chairman, Frank Lorenzo, a hated symbol of union-busting to organized labor nationwide. When President Bush refused to intervene, Oberstar became Democratic leaders' point man in a strategy designed to paint the president as anti-labor and pro-Lorenzo. He sponsored a bill requiring Bush to set up an emergency panel to forge a settlement.

The subcommittee approved it 21-12, and a week later it passed the House 252-167, both tallies roughly following party lines. "A vote for this legislation is a vote for the continued survival of competition in the airline industry," Oberstar told the House. However, the bill was pronounced dead on arrival in the Senate, where Democratic leaders lacked the votes to choke a threatened GOP filibuster.

Based on the Eastern affair, Oberstar said his Aviation panel would examine broader questions about the effects of airline deregulation after a decade; he believes deregulation prompted concentration in the industry, which in turn has brought higher prices and fewer choices for passengers. Unlike his predecessor as chairman, Norman Y. Mineta of California, he also favors making the Federal Aviation Administration independent of the Transportation Department. Proponents say that would free the FAA of the department's political manipulation, but others fear that a free-standing FAA would have even less clout in battles against the administration and industry.

On the Budget Committee, a late 1987 summit agreement between Congress and President Reagan made 1988 relatively tranquil for budget-writers. But 1987 had been as partisan a time as ever for the committee, with Republicans refusing even to participate. The situation brought out the scrapper in Oberstar. When a panel Republican quipped that Democrats only ask the GOP along on a double date when they do not have enough money or gas themselves, Oberstar said that where he comes from, double-dating with Republicans is unthinkable. Later, when Republicans complained about the final product, he snapped, "At moments of

Minnesota 8

Northeast — Duluth

Based in the barren and remote northern reaches of Minnesota, the 8th District has a long Democratic tradition. Immigrants from Sweden, Finland and Eastern Europe settled here after the turn of the century to work in the iron mines scattered throughout the Mesabi and Vermillion iron ranges in the center of the district. Strongly allied with unions, the workers on the Iron Range today are unswerving in their allegiance to the Democrats.

Life on the Range, as it is called, has not been easy in recent decades. By the end of World War II the high-quality iron ore mines were largely depleted. Singer Bob Dylan, who grew up in Hibbing, bemoaned the fate of his native region in "North Country Blues." Only the discovery of new taconite mining technology saved the local economy from collapse. Taconite, however, is pulled from the earth in huge open-pit mines that require far fewer people to operate than the old underground mines. Today, the prolonged slump of the steel industry has created additional job shortages by chain reaction.

Income from summer and winter tourism is crucial in helping the North Country survive, and Democrats here have little patience with those who want to protect the wilderness areas from recreational development.

The district's only major population center is the port city of Duluth, the state's third-largest city. With 93,000 people, it casts about one-fifth of the district's vote. From Duluth's steep bluffs, 800 feet above Lake Superior, one can look down on the active port where much of the grain from the Plains States is shipped east. Iron ore and other raw materials for heavy industry also pass through the port, although in diminishing amounts.

Duluth and surrounding St. Louis County, which extends to the Canadian border and includes most of the Iron Range population, are firmly Democratic.

Redistricting removed the Twin Cities' suburbs of Anoka County from the district, while adding four more politically marginal rural counties to the north. But this has hardly tempered the Democrats' overwhelming advantage in the 8th.

Population: 509,506. White 497,018 (98%), Black 1,394 (0.3%), Other 10,182 (2%). Spanish origin 1,777 (0.3%). 18 and over 360,529 (71%), 65 and over 70,002 (14%). Median age: 31.

courage, they voted 'present.' At other times, they voted 'no.' "

Oberstar earlier had a voice in budget and tax debates as chairman of the liberal Democratic Study Group (DSG) in the 99th Congress. He was among those urging, unsuccessfully, that the budget include a tougher minimum tax on corporations. And when Ways and Means was drafting its landmark rewrite of the tax code, Oberstar and DSG argued that revenues raised by closing loopholes should be used for deficit reduction, not more tax cuts. "We simply cannot afford to cut taxes at this time," he said.

During his six-year turn on Budget, Oberstar is on leave from the Merchant Marine Committee, where he retains his place among senior members.

As a Public Works subcommittee chairman, Oberstar generally is considered fair and bipartisan by Republicans despite the partisan flashes in House debates. More conservative Democrats consider him someone they can deal with. The full committee is a restive place under new Chairman Glenn M. Anderson of California, who is being watched by Democrats for signs of weakness; at the start of the 101st Congress, Oberstar unsuccessfully proposed that subcommittee chairmen have more power over staff and budgeting decisions. He was opposed by Robert A. Roe of New Jersey, who as chairman-in-waiting would not want to inherit a weakened position, and by other subcommittee heads who feel that under the passive Anderson they already enjoy greater power without changing the committee rules.

A political scientist and amateur linguist, Oberstar can theorize at length about the proper balance for public works policy. In fact, he talks a lot, whether intensively questioning witnesses or explaining a bill. He opened one hearing in early 1989 with a long reading from the prize-winning Thornton Wilder novel, "The Bridge of San Luis Rey." He occasionally beseeches the committee to "rise above" pork-barrel thinking and seek innovative ways to address the nation's problems. For example, an impending Western water shortage demands more planning and fewer projects, he says.

On the other hand, Oberstar has not been known to turn down a new project for northern Minnesota. He spent years learning how to use Public Works to bring Duluth and the Iron Range a share of the pie, as an aide and protégé to John Blatnik, the Minnesota Democrat who chaired Public Works until 1974, when he retired and Oberstar won his seat.

As chairman of the Economic Development Subcommittee prior to 1985, Oberstar was in a key position to help bring jobs to depressed areas like the Iron Range. With ranking Republican William F. Clinger Jr. of Pennsylvania, he helped preserve the Economic Development Administration (EDA), which directs funds to economically troubled communities, against President Reagan's repeated efforts to abolish it.

Early in 1981, Oberstar brought Reagan's budget director David A. Stockman before his subcommittee for a grilling. Oberstar said EDA was one program that created permanent jobs in the private sector, doubling the government's investment through new tax returns. When Stockman insisted EDA was a "shell game" that simply moved jobs around the country, Oberstar disagreed. Duluth had received some $20 million from EDA and its predecessor since 1963. He did propose legislation to streamline the agency, reduce its scope and require areas to show they would use the aid properly. Though Oberstar pushed it through two Congresses, the bill got no farther than House passage.

Along with allies Augustus F. Hawkins of California and Carl D. Perkins of Kentucky, he wrote a jobs bill in 1982 that, with changes, became law the next year. Jobs legislation is another issue that brings out Oberstar's combative side. "I just never cease to be amazed," he said in 1982, "by our colleagues on the other side of the aisle who refuse to do anything to help the unemployed but complain about those who try."

He was even more critical of fellow Democrats in 1985 when the House agreed to end a supplemental compensation program for the long-term unemployed. "We cannot let our party be Reaganized," he declared, adding that Democrats must make clear "we're not backing away" from employment issues.

Oberstar also has defended protectionist efforts to promote domestic employment by limiting imports. He cites his experience as a graduate student during the formation of the European Common Market, which, as Oberstar recalls, promoted economic development by protecting domestic markets.

A couple of issues provide the only exceptions to his traditional liberalism. He opposes gun control bills and supports a constitutional amendment to outlaw abortion. In 1988, he joined other anti-abortion House members in successfully blocking a Senate amendment that would have authorized federal funds for poor women's abortions in cases of rape or incest.

"Taking innocent, unborn life will not ease the abuse of rape," Oberstar said during an emotional House debate. "It will not apprehend the rapist. It will not heal the emotional scars of that violent crime."

He is also against the death penalty. When the House debated a capital punishment provision that became law as part of Congress' 1988 drug bill, Oberstar supported instead an unsuccessful substitute that would have required mandatory life imprisonment for drug-related killers. "Put them in jail," he told the House, "and let 'em think about it for a lifetime."

At Home: After his grueling 1984 Senate campaign ended disappointingly in midsummer, Oberstar had to go back to his Iron Range district and fight hard just to retain his seat.

His Senate candidacy enjoyed the support of much of the state's organized-labor movement, but he could not match the strength of his major rival, Secretary of State Joan Growe; she was the favorite of the liberal party activists who dominated the Democratic endorsement process. She got the party endorsement on the 19th ballot at the state convention in June.

The two contenders actually had agreed two ballots earlier to end the marathon and settle the issue in a primary, but Growe's supporters refused to abide by the agreement and pushed her endorsement through two ballots later.

Oberstar could have continued the fight into a September primary anyway, but decided instead to switch races and run again for his House seat. That was a sensible decision. By the time the angry convention adjourned, it was becoming clear that no Democratic nominee would have much of a chance against the popular Republican incumbent, Rudy Boschwitz.

Oberstar's shift back to the 8th District was made possible by the willingness of the Democrats' endorsed candidate there, state Sen. Ron Dicklich, to step aside. But an old nemesis, former Duluth City Councilman Thomas E. Dougherty, was unwilling to withdraw so Oberstar could return.

Four years earlier, Dougherty had run an aggressive primary challenge that caught Oberstar off guard. Portraying the incumbent as inattentive to his Iron Range constituents and their declining economic status, Dougherty netted 44 percent of the vote. He hammered away on that basic theme in 1984, using as his slogan: "Our District Is His First Choice."

But Oberstar was well prepared for the 1984 rematch. He mended previously frayed ties with the politically powerful Perpich family, and emphasized his work to promote the local iron industry through support of temporary quotas on steel and iron ore imports. He launched one of the most extensive voter identification programs ever seen in northeast Minnesota.

The result was a Democratic primary turnout about 25 percent higher than in 1980, with Oberstar winning by nearly 2-to-1. The general election was anticlimactic, with Oberstar overwhelming his GOP challenger.

Republicans have not cost Oberstar any

sleep since he inherited the 8th District in 1974 from Blatnik, his employer and predecessor. But fighting within the Democratic Party has made his life far from tranquil.

For years there was a feud between the Blatnik wing of the Democratic Party and the faction headed by the three Perpich brothers, whose leader, Rudy, is governor of Minnesota.

The battle between the two sides broke into the open in 1974, and flared up again in 1980. In 1974 Blatnik tried to anoint Oberstar as his successor, but the result was an acrimonious party-endorsing convention lasting 30 ballots. Eventually Blatnik and Oberstar lost, and the party's endorsement went to state Sen. A. J. "Tony" Perpich.

Blatnik then threw all his prestige and political power behind Oberstar in the Democratic primary, and Oberstar won by more than 20,000 votes.

Six years later, Oberstar faced a second Perpich. This time it was Tony's younger brother, George. When Rudy was elected lieutenant governor in 1970, George took his seat in the state Senate and carried on the populist Perpich crusade against the mining companies.

At the 1980 nominating convention, George tried to keep the party endorsement out of the incumbent's hands, arguing for a neutral party stand in the second Oberstar-Perpich match-up. But Oberstar won the endorsement with just one-third of a vote more than the 60 percent needed. Perpich decided not to force a primary, but Dougherty did. Concentrating his campaign in the northern part of the district where unemployment was high, Dougherty picked up votes from Perpich supporters bent on protest. Oberstar was saved by his backing at the southern end of the district, in the Twin Cities media area.

Committees

Budget (9th of 21 Democrats)
Task Forces: Budget Process, Reconciliation and Enforcement; Defense, Foreign Policy and Space

Public Works and Transportation (4th of 31 Democrats)
Aviation (chairman); Investigations and Oversight; Water Resources

Elections

1988 General

James L. Oberstar (D)	165,656	(75%)
Jerry Shuster (R)	56,630	(25%)

1986 General

James L. Oberstar (D)	135,718	(73%)
Dave Rued (R)	51,315	(27%)

Previous Winning Percentages: **1984** (67%) **1982** (77%) **1980** (70%) **1978** (87%) **1976** (100%) **1974** (62%)

District Vote For President

	1988	1984	1980	1976
D	144,668 (60%)	149,807 (59%)	171,636 (54%)	185,726 (63%)
R	92,876 (39%)	100,520 (40%)	117,437 (37%)	101,000 (34%)
I			21,003 (7%)	

Campaign Finance

	Receipts	Receipts from PACs	Expend-itures
1988			
Oberstar (D)	$281,331	$206,320 (73%)	$157,802
Shuster (R) †	$7,744	0	$7,743
1986			
Oberstar (D)	$297,056	$211,347 (71%)	$163,619
Rued (R)	$68,972	$3,396 (5%)	$68,931

† Totals based on incomplete data.

Key Votes

1987

Raise speed limit to 65 mph	N
Approve Gephardt "fair trade" amendment	Y
Ban testing of larger nuclear weapons	Y
Delay "re-flagging" of Kuwaiti tankers	Y
Approve tax-raising deficit-reduction bill	Y

1988

Approve aid to Nicaraguan contras	N
Enact civil rights restoration bill over Reagan veto	Y
Kill 60-day plant-closing notification measure	N
Pass omnibus trade bill over Reagan veto	Y
Approve death penalty for drug-related murders	N
Bar federal funds for abortions in cases of rape and incest	Y
Oppose seven-day waiting period for purchase of handguns	Y

Voting Studies

	Presidential Support		Party Unity		Conservative Coalition	
Year	S	O	S	O	S	O
1988	21	77	93	6	8	92
1987	12	87	93	3	5	95
1986	18	79	92	4	18	82
1985	16	84	91	3	7	93
1984	19	71	88	4	5	83
1983	12	84	90	6	9	89
1982	34	65	95	4	10	89
1981	33	67	89	8	16	81

Interest Group Ratings

Year	ADA	ACU	AFL-CIO	CCUS
1988	90	12	100	21
1987	96	4	94	7
1986	85	5	93	6
1985	95	5	100	18
1984	80	4	89	33
1983	90	9	94	15
1982	100	9	100	14
1981	85	7	87	5

Mississippi

U.S. CONGRESS

SENATE 2 R
HOUSE 4 D, 1 R

LEGISLATURE

Senate 46 D, 6 R
House 113 D, 9 R

ELECTIONS

1988 Presidential Vote	
Bush	60%
Dukakis	39%
1984 Presidential Vote	
Reagan	62%
Mondale	37%
1980 Presidential Vote	
Reagan	49%
Carter	48%
Anderson	1%
Turnout rate in 1984	52%
Turnout rate in 1986	29%
Turnout rate in 1988	50%

(as percentage of voting age population)

POPULATION AND GROWTH

1980 population	2,520,638
1988 population estimate (31st in the nation)	2,620,000
Percent change 1980-1988	+4%

DEMOGRAPHIC BREAKDOWN

White	64%
Black	35%
(Spanish origin)	1%
Urban	47%
Rural	53%
Born in state	79%
Foreign-born	1%

MAJOR CITIES

Jackson	208,420
Biloxi	47,750
Gulfport	43,410
Meridian	42,970
Hattiesburg	40,740

AREA AND LAND USE

Area	47,233 sq. miles (31st)
Farm	41%
Forest	55%
Federally owned	6%

Gov. Ray Mabus (D)
Of Choctaw County — Elected 1987

Born: Oct. 11, 1948, Choctaw County, Miss.
Education: U. of Mississippi, B.A. 1969; Johns Hopkins U., M.A. 1970; Harvard U., J.D. 1976.
Military Career: Navy 1970-73.
Occupation: Lawyer; tree farmer.
Religion: Methodist.
Political Career: Miss. auditor, 1984-88.
Next Election: 1991.

WORK

Occupations	
White-collar	45%
Blue-collar	38%
Service workers	12%
Government Workers	
Federal	24,345
State	48,931
Local	109,960

MONEY

Median family income	$ 14,591	(50th)
Tax burden per capita	$ 693	(45th)

EDUCATION

Spending per pupil through grade 12	$ 2,362	(50th)
Persons with college degrees	12%	(46th)

CRIME

Violent crime rate	270 per 100,000 (37th)

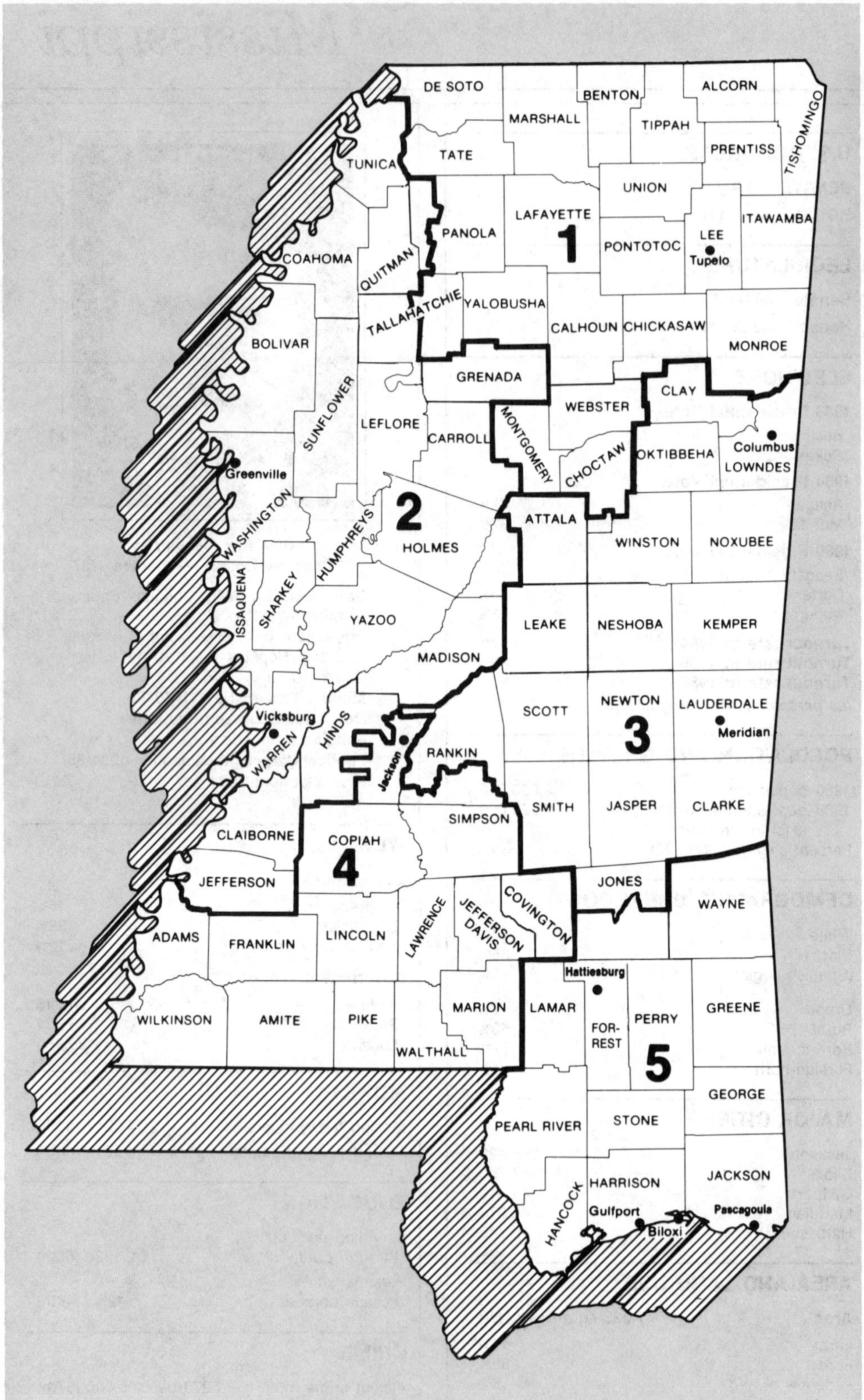
DE SOTO
MARSHALL
BENTON
TIPPAH
ALCORN
PRENTISS
TISHOMINGO
TUNICA
TATE
UNION
PANOLA
LAFAYETTE
1
PONTOTOC
LEE
Tupelo
ITAWAMBA
COAHOMA
QUITMAN
TALLAHATCHIE
YALOBUSHA
CALHOUN
CHICKASAW
MONROE
BOLIVAR
GRENADA
CLAY
SUNFLOWER
LEFLORE
CARROLL
MONTGOMERY
WEBSTER
CHOCTAW
OKTIBBEHA
Columbus
LOWNDES
Greenville
WASHINGTON
HUMPHREYS
2
HOLMES
ATTALA
WINSTON
NOXUBEE
ISSAQUENA
SHARKEY
YAZOO
LEAKE
NESHOBA
KEMPER
MADISON
Vicksburg
WARREN
HINDS
Jackson
RANKIN
SCOTT
NEWTON
LAUDERDALE
Meridian
3
SMITH
JASPER
CLARKE
SIMPSON
CLAIBORNE
COPIAH
4
JEFFERSON
JONES
WAYNE
ADAMS
FRANKLIN
LINCOLN
LAWRENCE
JEFFERSON DAVIS
COVINGTON
Hattiesburg
WILKINSON
AMITE
PIKE
WALTHALL
MARION
LAMAR
FOR-REST
PERRY
GREENE
5
GEORGE
PEARL RIVER
STONE
HANCOCK
HARRISON
JACKSON
Gulfport
Biloxi
Pascagoula

Thad Cochran (R)

Of Byram — Elected 1978

Born: Dec. 7, 1937, Pontotoc, Miss.
Education: U. of Mississippi, B.A. 1959, J.D. 1965.
Military Career: Navy, 1959-61.
Occupation: Lawyer.
Family: Wife, Rose Clayton; two children.
Religion: Baptist.
Political Career: U.S. House, 1973-78.
Capitol Office: 326 Russell Bldg. 20510; 224-5054.

In Washington: Cochran's Senate career started slowly, accelerated rapidly when the GOP seized Senate control in 1981, and then bogged down in the restored Democratic majority in the 100th Congress. Back in the minority, Cochran lost control of the two farm-related subcommittees he had chaired.

Yet Cochran is far from eclipsed. With the 1989 retirement of legendary Democrat John C. Stennis, Cochran is now Mississippi's senior senator (his new colleague is Republican Trent Lott) and a prohibitive favorite for re-election in 1990. Popular among colleagues and staff, and already part of his party's Senate leadership, this is a Southerner who seems destined to be a significant player for many years to come.

Even as a member of the minority party, Cochran still has a fair share of the influence he acquired during the years Republicans ran the Senate. He remains a leading voice for Southern interests on farm issues, and a vital bridge between conservatives and moderates within the GOP itself.

And if Republicans regain control of the Senate in the 1990s, Cochran could scale the pinnacle of Stennis' influence — the chairmanship of the Appropriations Committee — before he is 60 (Stennis got there when he was 85). The four Republicans ahead of Cochran on the committee are all reasonable candidates for retirement in this term or their next. Alternatively, Cochran could find himself chairman of the Agriculture Committee (where only three Republicans outrank him), party leader or part of a national ticket.

Cochran is little inclined to speechmaking, or to blocking legislation through crafty floor maneuvers. He works best when he has the responsibility for getting things done. More than any of his fellow Republicans from the South, he has been able to appeal to a broad spectrum of the GOP by combining a conservative voting record with a moderate image. He rarely can be found in conspicuous opposition to the White House or the party leadership and sometimes helps lead the conservative bloc on the floor — as he did on the bill that sought to limit private employers' use of polygraph tests in March 1988.

Cochran regularly opposes such efforts to dictate to business, and he usually votes for the conservative position on social issues. But he has avoided strong identification with the emotional social issues pushed by other Senate conservatives — "I vote on the social issues because I have to," he once said — and he has been a supporter of programs such as food stamps and rural housing.

In the spring of 1989, Cochran was seen as flexible on issues of the budget, including taxes, and he supported continued federal funding for the Martin Luther King Jr. Federal Holiday Commission. (Lott opposed the money.)

He also has been a member of the moderate GOP Wednesday Group, not only as a senator but as a member of the House earlier in his career. And he has begun to show growing interest in overseas issues, touring several foreign countries with Richard G. Lugar of Indiana and other Republican senators.

Cochran's popularity in the Senate was evident in his campaign to become GOP Conference secretary in the 99th Congress. Running against Rudy Boschwitz of Minnesota, he won the leadership post by a 32-21 vote — the biggest margin of any of the Republican leadership contests held in late 1984. He was re-elected without opposition in 1986 and 1988.

Regardless of whether he moves further up the Senate leadership ladder, Cochran already has had a major influence on Republican farm policy. After just two years in the Senate, he chaired the Appropriations Subcommittee on Agriculture, an important post for his heavily rural state. And he continues to occupy a central position on the Agriculture Committee.

Cochran has played a particularly important behind-the-scenes role in mediating splits within the Agriculture Committee, which is torn by conflicts among commodity interests. His style is well suited to settling disagreements rather than inflaming them.

Precocious in authority, Cochran was already writing key sections of major farm bills in the early 1980s. His influence was even more significant during work on the 1985 farm bill. Allied with Majority Leader Bob Dole, he worked to develop an overall GOP stance on farm issues out of competing regional interests. Moreover, Cochran helped steer the legislation through the Senate without a great deal of guidance from Agriculture Chairman Jesse Helms.

Cochran hardly overlooked the interests of Mississippi and other Southern farmers, though, especially those raising cotton or rice. Making full use of the key tactical position they had during action on the farm bill, Cochran and a few others from the region pushed through a radically new and potentially expensive form of price support for growers of the two crops.

Cochran's work for his Southern planters continued the next year, when he blunted an attack on their government subsidies. Angered by loopholes that allowed many individual cotton and rice growers to receive much more than the $50,000 annual limit on federal farm payments, members from regions dominated by other commodities sought an absolute ceiling. After strenuous efforts, Cochran finally accepted a $250,000 ceiling on total subsidies — but only after adding an exemption big enough to make the limit's impact largely symbolic.

The food stamp issue has forced Cochran to make some difficult choices. A fiscal conservative who would trim the welfare state, he also represents the poorest constituency in the country. Great numbers of Mississippians receive food stamps and other forms of federal food assistance. Cochran has resolved his doubts on the side of the programs, fighting hard to defend them against severe cuts.

Mississippi's poverty and dependence on federal help shape Cochran's point of view on other issues as well. He has been a strong defender of the federal rural housing program, working to turn aside administration attempts to eliminate it. In the 97th Congress, Cochran helped defeat a proposal to convert the program into a block grant to states.

He also successfully sponsored an amendment adding $30 million to the "developing institutions" program, which gives money to traditionally black colleges concentrated in Mississippi and other Southern states.

But Cochran is no liberal. His conservative inclinations have come out most clearly on issues before the Judiciary Committee, where he served during his first two years in the Senate. As soft-spoken as he normally is, he becomes livid at the mention of language in the Voting Rights Act requiring Southern states to get Justice Department approval before making any changes in their election procedures.

"Local officials have to go to Washington, get on their knees, kiss the ring and tug their forelock to all these third-rate bureaucrats," Cochran once complained. He argues that Mississippi officials are now sensitive to the concerns of black voters. But his effort to make all states comply with the same requirements was rejected by the Senate, 16-74.

At Home: Each time Cochran has run for the Senate, he has made history. In 1978, he became the first Republican to win a Mississippi Senate seat in a century. Six years later, he became the first GOP candidate for any major statewide office to capture a majority of the vote since Reconstruction.

Cochran's landslide victory in 1984 over former Democratic Gov. William Winter embellished his credentials as the titular head of the state's Republican Party, which has been divided in recent years into moderate and militantly conservative factions. Cochran, a moderate in home-state politics, has been on the prevailing side much of the time.

In 1976 the Mississippi party was beset by an internal struggle between supporters of Gerald R. Ford and Ronald Reagan for the presidential nomination. Cochran sided with Ford at the national convention in Kansas City, and the delegation voted 30-0 for Ford's position in the critical rules fight that played a large role in ending Reagan's chances. Although there was considerable anger within the delegation at the time, Cochran suffered no lasting damage.

He already had shown a considerable talent for making friends across the political spectrum. Despite his conservative House voting record, Cochran drew significant support in most of his campaigns from blacks, who made up more than 40 percent of his 4th District. After a close first election in 1972, when the presence of a black independent allowed him a narrow victory, he drew over 70 percent of the total vote in both his 1974 and 1976 House campaigns.

His election to the Senate was also made possible in part by an independent black campaign siphoning off votes from the Democratic nominee, ex-Columbia Mayor Maurice Dantin. Democrat James O. Eastland retired in 1978 after 36 years in the Senate and endorsed Dantin to succeed him. But a flamboyant campaign by Fayette Mayor Charles Evers, a veteran black activist, drew more attention than Cochran and Dantin combined.

In a state where Democrats must have the black vote, Evers virtually guaranteed GOP success. Drawing 45 percent statewide, Cochran finished nearly 80,000 votes ahead of Dantin. Cochran swept the Gulf Coast and the Jackson area, and made inroads in the Democratic Hill Country in northern Mississippi, where he was born.

Many Democrats regarded Cochran's election as a fluke, but he proved his vote-getting ability in 1984. Running one-on-one against Winter, Cochran won by a margin of more than 3-to-2 and nearly matched President Reagan's vote total.

Few observers would have predicted the

one-sided outcome. A veteran of more than three decades in state politics, Winter left the governor's chair in early 1984 as a well-respected chief executive. His administration, limited to four years by the state's one-term-and-out law, was highlighted by passage of a landmark education bill designed to improve the quality of public schools in Mississippi and to make the state attractive to new industry.

But Winter dissipated much of the good will when he accepted, then rejected, the University of Mississippi chancellorship in late 1983. By taking more than six weeks after that to decide whether to challenge Cochran, he reinforced an image of indecisiveness. Winter sought to make up ground with an increasingly aggressive campaign. He criticized Cochran as a likable but ineffective "backbencher" whose Senate approach was to "go along to get along."

But with a smooth-running, well-financed operation, Cochran gave Winter few openings. He dominated the airwaves, dismissing Winter's candidacy as Washington-inspired and stressing his own seniority and growing stature in the Senate. Cochran emphasized that he was 15 years younger than Winter and already held two chairmanships of importance to Mississippi, including that of the Appropriations Subcommittee on Agriculture.

To win, Winter needed about one-third of the white vote and a nearly unanimous black vote (roughly 30 percent of the state electorate). Cochran, who had done well among blacks in his House elections, frustrated Winter on both counts. He swept all but a handful of Mississippi's 82 counties, including nearly half of those with majority-black populations.

Lott's election to the Senate in 1988 did little to encourage Democrats hoping to take on Cochran in 1990. The growing Republican strength in Mississippi is obvious. Still, Cochran has been careful to lay the groundwork for another contest. His 1990 campaign was under way before the 1988 elections, and he has continued to reach out to Democrats.

Cochran campaigned for some GOP House candidates in Mississippi in 1988, but he made no visible effort in the Republican campaign against freshman Rep. Mike Espy, the state's first black congressman in a century. That may have just been the result of Cochran's respect for Espy's incumbency, but by not alienating black voters in the Delta district, Cochran probably strengthened his own position.

Committees

Agriculture, Nutrition and Forestry (4th of 9 Republicans)
Domestic and Foreign Marketing and Product Promotion (ranking); Agricultural Production and Stabilization of Prices; Rural Development and Rural Electrification

Appropriations (5th of 13 Republicans)
Agriculture, Rural Development and Related Agencies (ranking); Defense; Energy and Water Development; Interior and Related Agencies; Labor, Health and Human Services, Education and Related Agencies

Labor and Human Resources (7th of 7 Republicans)
Aging (ranking); Education, Arts and Humanities; Labor

Select Indian Affairs (3rd of 3 Republicans)

Elections

1984 General

Thad Cochran (R)	580,314	(61%)
William F. Winter (D)	371,926	(39%)

Previous Winning Percentages: 1978 (45%) **1976 *** (76%) **1974 *** (70%) **1972 *** (48%)

* *House elections.*

Campaign Finance

	Receipts	Receipts from PACs	Expenditures
1984			
Cochran (R)	$2,768,728	$960,361 (35%)	$2,791,749
Winter (D)	$741,534	$340,167 (46%)	$738,739

Key Votes

1987	
Enact omnibus highway bill over Reagan veto	Y
Limit testing of space-based anti-ballistic missiles	N
Oppose banning tests of larger nuclear weapons	Y
Confirm Robert H. Bork as Supreme Court justice	Y
1988	
Allow vote on campaign-finance overhaul	?
Pass civil rights restoration bill over Reagan veto	N
Enact omnibus trade bill over Reagan veto	N
Approve death penalty for drug-related murders	Y
Oppose "workfare" amendment to welfare overhaul bill	N

Voting Studies

	Presidential Support		Party Unity		Conservative Coalition	
Year	**S**	**O**	**S**	**O**	**S**	**O**
1988	70	22	66	22	97	0
1987	68	26	78	19	97	3
1986	88	10	88	10	91	4
1985	80	14	81	14	87	5
1984	87	8	93	5	96	2
1983	71	22	69	28	77	16
1982	77	20	88	9	85	3
1981	82	9	87	11	88	7

Interest Group Ratings

Year	ADA	ACU	AFL-CIO	CCUS
1988	5	96	15	100
1987	20	68	40	78
1986	5	78	0	89
1985	5	74	15	81
1984	10	82	9	74
1983	20	48	18	74
1982	10	72	16	63
1981	10	53	16	94

Trent Lott (R)

Of Pascagoula — Elected 1988

Born: Oct. 9, 1941, Grenada County, Miss.
Education: U. of Mississippi, B.P.A. 1963, J.D. 1967.
Occupation: Lawyer.
Family: Wife, Patricia Elizabeth Thompson; two children.
Religion: Baptist.
Political Career: U.S. House, 1973-89.
Capitol Office: 487 Russell Bldg. 20510; 224-6253.

In Washington: Lott's move to the Senate has required some adjustment for House Republicans, who relied on him as a key strategist both on the Rules Committee and as minority whip.

It has also required an important adjustment for Lott. There is obvious prestige that goes with winning a Senate seat, but unlike many GOP House members who move up, Lott left a position of considerable visibility and influence when he switched chambers. He may still involve himself in formulating party strategy, but he does not have a formal leadership role. So Lott, who was a team planner and legislative generalist in the House, now has the time to carve out a more individual role in policy making.

With his 51-year-old colleague Thad Cochran already giving Mississippi a spot in the GOP leadership, a place for Lott on that ladder is out of the question for the foreseeable future. So he has added incentive to make his mark in the legislative arena. His primary assignments in the 101st Congress are Armed Services and Commerce, Science and Transportation.

Lott in 1981 became the first Deep South Republican to take the position of House minority whip, and he did so more on his friendliness than on legislative achievement. The close contest with Pennsylvania Rep. Bud Shuster went Lott's way partly because he had made many friends and few enemies.

Through his tenure as whip, the list of enemies no doubt grew, particularly among Democrats, but so did his political savvy. Throughout the Reagan years, Lott had a tough balancing act to perform. With a president of his own party trying to set the agenda for a Democratic House, Lott had to win over Democrats while attempting to keep his own unruly troops in line. Neither job was easy.

In his first year as whip, Lott was working in a favorable climate. Ronald Reagan had won easily in 1980, making it easier to sell Reaganomics to a Democratic House. It required careful cultivation of Southern Democratic members, but Lott's dedication to that task in the early months of 1981 paid off handsomely.

He expanded the use of computers to track Democratic voting records and to look for issues offering common ground. He and Minority Leader Robert H. Michel instituted a "buddy system," assigning Republicans to solicit help from Democratic friends one-on-one.

That effort was in part responsible for the 63 Democratic votes for President Reagan's initial budget and the 48 Democratic votes for his tax-cut plan. Reagan's own popularity was the biggest factor ("I've got the best whip organization because Ronald Reagan is in it," Lott said once), but Lott made sure that Democrats considering a vote for the president got plenty of personal encouragement.

A few months later, though, the situation changed. With the economy falling deeper into recession, Lott and Michel had to give up any hope of co-opting Democrats and pay more attention to keeping moderate Republicans loyal. Lott was less adept at this than Michel; a conservative from the Mississippi Gulf Coast, he does not have much in common with his party's Northern urban moderates. But he made it clear he realized different members had different political needs.

The influx of new, partisan-minded Democrats after the 1982 elections made life even more disorderly. It essentially gave the majority the votes to go where it wanted, at least on economic issues. But Lott was careful to keep up his personal ties to moderate and conservative Democrats, and on defense issues in particular he had some success. Throughout the 98th Congress and into the 99th he worked to win Democratic support for the MX missile. On vote after vote, the weapon barely survived.

Lott's work was particularly tough in Reagan's final years in office. Many House Republicans began distancing themselves from unpopular White House policies and searched for a role other than carrying the administration's water.

In 1985, Lott and other GOP leaders brazenly turned their whip organization against Reagan to thwart the progress of his No. 1 domestic priority — tax code overhaul. House Republicans complained bitterly that they were excluded from the production of the bill reported by the Ways and Means Committee, which they said did not live up to Reagan's goals for tax overhaul. Tapping that frustration, Lott masterminded a move to block consideration of the bill by defeating the rule for floor debate. "This isn't a parliamentary government where you go with the party or the prime minister when your convictions tell you otherwise," he said.

There were enough disgruntled Democrats joining with Republicans to defeat the rule, although the action was reversed when Reagan made a personal plea to keep the bill alive.

In early 1987 Lott was among those abandoning Reagan when he vetoed the highway bill. Lott said the veto made sense, because Reagan "has to show consistency, he's got to show toughness." But he said he had to vote for the successful override "for the same reason [as] everyone else — I've got one [demonstration project in his district], I confess."

Lott also had to contend with an increasingly assertive Democratic majority. Democrats who had been on the defensive in 1981 by 1987 did not need a single GOP vote to pass a budget resolution. Republicans did not offer an alternative, and Lott offered this advice to his colleagues: "You do not ever get in trouble for those budgets which you vote against. It is the ones you vote for that you get in trouble on, when you do not know all that is in them."

During one speech in the 100th Congress Lott made pointed reference to the GOP's inability to forge the conservative coalitions that passed much of Reagan's early program. After failing in an effort to trim an Interior spending bill, he asked after the budget-cutting "Boll Weevils" of the early 1980s. "Have all the Boll Weevils turned into cicadas?" Lott said, referring to the insects that emerge only once every 17 years.

In Lott's last years on Rules, the Democratic leadership made increasingly effective use of the committee to limit debate on numerous measures, frustrating Lott and the GOP, outnumbered more than 2-to-1 on the panel. "The Democratic leadership is trying to turn the Rules Committee into the stranglehold on this institution that it was 30 years ago," he said in 1987.

Given the difficulty of playing a constructive role on the committee, Lott spent considerable energy looking for ways to use procedure to frustrate the Democrats. His main function was to try out partisan arguments in committee for presentation later on the House floor.

As whip, Lott had to try to placate both senior traditional Republicans and younger conservatives eager for a more confrontational approach to the majority. While he balanced the needs of the two factions, there has rarely been any doubt about his kinship with the right. During his Senate campaign, Lott sounded themes long used by Democratic candidates, and his support for President Reagan on floor votes dropped to 61 percent (even taking into account votes he missed while campaigning). But over the course of his career, Lott has been a reliable supporter of conservative causes.

In 1981, Lott's intervention persuaded the administration to ask the Internal Revenue Service to grant tax-exempt status for segregated private academies. The resulting outcry from minorities led Reagan to change his mind and seek legislation barring exemptions. "I regret what I did," Lott told a reporter afterward. "I didn't handle it the way I should." Lott described segregation as "a ghost of the past we'd like to put behind us."

At the beginning of his House career, on Judiciary, he took part in the historic impeachment proceedings of 1973 and 1974. Lott was a staunch defender of President Nixon, which was not a liability for him back home. Nixon was still well-liked by many Gulf Coast conservatives when his political support was eroding elsewhere in the country.

At Home: The 1988 presidential election created a favorable atmosphere for Lott to wage a Senate campaign, but he also rose to the occasion. Mississippi, though conservative, is traditional Democratic territory that regularly elected Lott's predecessor, Democratic Sen. John C. Stennis, beginning in 1947. It took a strong campaign for Lott to overcome a skilled opponent, Rep. Wayne Dowdy, with a solid 54 percent of the vote.

While Dowdy depleted his financial resources to win a tough primary campaign, Lott was free to focus on the fall election. And he took the offensive with an early media blitz that Dowdy could not afford to answer for much of the summer. Lott, long identified as a strong supporter of President Reagan's policies, used the airwaves to stress issues that often had been turned against Republicans in the 1980s. To Democrats' dismay, he positioned himself as a champion of Social Security, student loans and public-works spending.

To appeal to rural and blue-collar conservatives who have often sided with Democrats, Lott stressed his background. Though his polished appearance would seem to make him more appealing to the blue-suit conservatives, Lott reminded voters that his father farmed cotton and drove a school bus. He said that Dowdy, whose rumpled appearance and folksy manner belies his family's wealth, was a "millionaire, country-club type."

Dowdy faulted Lott for election-year conversions on issues, and insisted the Republican was out of step with Mississippi. His late-starting ad campaign included a spot criticizing Lott for having a $50,000-per-year "chauffeur," George Awkward. But Lott blasted the ad, which featured a limousine cruising through the countryside, saying that Awkward was a member of the Capitol security force, funded by a bill Dowdy supported. He added that Awkward showed up for work more often than Dowdy, whose House attendance dropped dramatically during the campaign year.

By summer's end, the sophistication of Lott's effort was apparent, and Democrats were complaining that Dowdy, while one of their best candidates on the stump, had not done enough to put together a statewide organization. Michael S. Dukakis' almost non-existent campaign in the state did not boost party spirits.

But while polls showed Lott ahead, many Democrats thought Dowdy's strength might not be apparent until Election Day. Part of that optimism stemmed from Dowdy's apparent appeal in the black community, which accounts for more than a third of Mississippi's population. While Dowdy was first elected as a champion of the Voting Rights Act, Lott had cast several votes that alienated black leaders, including those against renewal of that act and against the Martin Luther King Jr. holiday. Even some Republicans thought Lott would be lucky to get 7 percent of the black vote. In his House district, Dowdy had forged a coalition of blacks, rural whites and organized labor.

But Lott came through on Election Day. In addition to his strong showing among whites, he got a surprising 13 percent of the black vote, according to CBS News-*New York Times* exit polls. Dowdy did win three of the state's five House districts, but even in his home territory his margin was narrow. Lott, meanwhile, got a giant boost from his home district, a GOP bastion.

The 5th has been Republican only since Lott first won it in 1972, and he did not become a Republican until the eve of his first campaign.

As Democratic Rep. William M. Colmer's administrative assistant, he had remained a nominal Democrat. But when the venerable Rules chairman decided to retire in 1972 at age 82, Lott filed in the GOP primary, saying he was "tired of the Muskies and the Kennedys and the Humphreys and the whole lot. . . . I will fight against the ever-increasing efforts of the so-called liberals to concentrate more power in the government in Washington."

The wisdom of Lott's switch was soon confirmed. Running that fall against Democrat Ben Stone, chairman of the state Senate Banking Committee, Lott stayed on the offensive by linking Stone with the national Democratic Party. Aided by the Nixon landslide and an endorsement from Colmer, Lott carried all but two of the district's 12 counties.

Committees

Armed Services (8th of 9 Republicans)
Defense Industry and Technology; Manpower and Personnel; Projection Forces and Regional Defense

Commerce, Science and Transportation (9th of 9 Republicans)
Merchant Marine (ranking); Science, Technology and Space; Surface Transportation; National Ocean Policy Study

Select Ethics (3rd of 3 Republicans)

Small Business (7th of 9 Republicans)
Innovation, Technology and Productivity (ranking); Urban and Minority-Owned Business Development

Elections

1988 General

Trent Lott (R)	510,380	(54%)
Wayne Dowdy (D)	436,339	(46%)

Previous Winning Percentages: **1986 *** (82%) **1984 *** (85%) **1982 *** (79%) **1980 *** (74%) **1978 *** (100%) **1976 *** (68%) **1974 *** (73%) **1972 *** (55%)

* *House elections.*

Campaign Finance

	Receipts	Receipts from PACs	Expend-itures
1988			
Lott (R)	$3,602,481	$1,118,111 (31%)	$3,405,242
Dowdy (D)	$2,195,960	$962,719 (44%)	$2,355,957

Key Votes

House Service

1987

Raise speed limit to 65 mph	Y
Approve Gephardt "fair trade" amendment	N
Ban testing of larger nuclear weapons	N
Delay "re-flagging" of Kuwaiti tankers	N
Approve tax-raising deficit-reduction bill	N

1988

Approve aid to Nicaraguan contras	Y
Enact civil rights restoration bill over Reagan veto	N
Kill 60-day plant-closing notification measure	Y
Pass omnibus trade bill over Reagan veto	N
Approve death penalty for drug-related murders	Y
Bar federal funds for abortions in cases of rape and incest	?
Oppose seven-day waiting period for purchase of handguns	Y

Voting Studies

	Presidential Support		Party Unity		Conservative Coalition	
Year	**S**	**O**	**S**	**O**	**S**	**O**
House Service						
1988	51	33	59	13	84	0
1987	63	24	83	8	88	5
1986	78	18	79	14	84	4
1985	73	24	82	9	89	5
1984	73	25	86	8	97	2
1983	73	22	86	7	97	1
1982	75	17	78	19	88	11
1981	84	16	90	6	95	3

Interest Group Ratings

Year	ADA	ACU	AFL-CIO	CCUS
House Service				
1988	5	95	33	82
1987	4	91	19	77
1986	5	95	23	86
1985	0	90	12	95
1984	0	96	8	80
1983	0	100	6	85
1982	5	85	5	70
1981	0	93	7	95

1 Jamie L. Whitten (D)

Of Charleston — Elected 1941

Born: April 18, 1910, Cascilla, Miss.
Education: Attended U. of Mississippi, 1927-32.
Occupation: Grammar school teacher and principal; lawyer; author.
Family: Wife, Rebecca Thompson; two children.
Religion: Presbyterian.
Political Career: Miss. House, 1931-33; district attorney, 17th District, 1933-41.
Capitol Office: 2314 Rayburn Bldg. 20515; 225-4306.

In Washington: "When you handle money, you're in the strongest position you can be in, in Congress." So says Whitten, chief money-handler of the House, its wily and sometimes infuriating Appropriations Committee chairman.

After more than a decade in the chair, Whitten has a firm grip on the seat that has signified power on Capitol Hill for a century. He is pope to what is irreverently known as the College of Cardinals — Appropriations' 13 subcommittee chairmen. And he is a cardinal himself, having led the Agriculture Subcommittee for the past four decades. That record tenure has earned Whitten another title: permanent secretary of agriculture.

A one-time grammar school principal and county prosecutor, Whitten claims, "I came to Congress by accident; my ambition was to practice law." But after winning a special election the month before Pearl Harbor, he has stayed to become the dean of all House members. He will turn 80 during the 101st Congress, but colleagues expect he will remain at least through 1992, to break the record for continuous House service, or perhaps 1993, when he would celebrate his 50th anniversary on Appropriations. Truth is, most don't expect him to leave at all.

And as long as Whitten is around, so is the spirit of the New Deal. A Depression survivor, he is a true believer in government's pump-priming potential. A shrewd trader in appropriations pork, Whitten sees his role in grander terms than that, in keeping with his theme that the nation's wealth is measured not in money but in its physical assets. He gives that lecture often, stupefying committee colleagues and exasperating senators and administration officials who may have provoked it by challenging him on some spending item.

Whitten, although a power, is hardly omnipotent. At the committee, the cardinals are virtually independent in their spheres. In the House, Whitten is a vassal to Democratic leaders, and answerable to junior activists who have been empowered since the last decade to depose autocratic chairmen. He is the last of a breed — the conservative Southerners who once ruled the Hill — and like the others who survived, he had to adjust.

But while the authority of the chairmanship has been checked, other forces in recent years greatly enhanced Appropriations' collective power. Whitten and his committee have controlled the most important legislation produced by Congress in any given year — the midyear supplemental appropriations bill for programs out of money, and the omnibus "continuing resolution" that finances federal agencies when, as often happens, the 13 regular appropriations bills are not passed by the start of a fiscal year.

Because these money bills are usually considered on an emergency basis, they receive relatively little scrutiny and are all but certain of quick presidential approval. Within their pages, appropriators tuck a variety of items that might not pass muster on their own.

The appropriators' power peaked in 1986 and 1987 when Congress, divided against itself and President Reagan, both years resorted to a continuing resolution in place of all 13 appropriations bills — a single measure worth more than a half-trillion dollars. Reagan, the public and many members were outraged at the evidence of fiscal breakdown, and by subsequent stories of members' hidden provisions.

In fairness, Whitten did not like it either. But he would drawl that his committee had done its work on time; that the president and the Senate had held up the bills. That response illustrates both the limits of Whitten's influence — he does not try to be a force beyond Appropriations — and also the disingenuousness that so frustrates his legislative adversaries.

Prodded by Democratic leaders, in 1988 Congress passed all 13 bills on schedule for the first time since 1976. The commitment remains in effect for the 101st Congress, and perhaps will be eased by President Bush's more conciliatory approach toward Capitol Hill.

If all-encompassing continuing resolutions

Mississippi 1

North — Clarksdale

Whitten's domain for nearly 50 years, the 1st District stretches from the Mississippi River east to the Alabama line, running along the northern border of the state. Not too long ago, this was the state's most reliably Democratic district. Jimmy Carter won 60 percent here in 1976, his best showing in any Mississippi district. Four years later, when he lost statewide, Carter won the area within the 1st with 55 percent.

But there is a limit to the party loyalty of the district's "yellow dog" Democrats. Presidential nominees Walter F. Mondale and Michael S. Dukakis both drew less than 40 percent of the district's vote.

Overwhelmingly rural, the 1st takes in the flat, rich farm land on the edge of the Delta region in northwestern Mississippi and the less fertile plots of the northeastern Hill Country. Although cotton was once the dominant crop in this region, 1st District farmers now also produce soybeans, rice, corn, wheat, livestock and poultry.

The one population center — Tupelo, in Lee County — is an industrial town also famous as the birthplace of Elvis Presley. About 50 miles to the west in Lafayette County is Oxford, the district's cultural center. It was the home base for William Faulkner, and is the site of the University of Mississippi (9,000 students), more popularly known as "Ole Miss."

The district's population grew by nearly 14 percent in the 1970s, with the largest boom occurring in the Memphis, Tenn., suburbs in De Soto County, the second most populous county in the 1st. De Soto's population swelled 50 percent in the 1970s, and another 18 percent in the first half of the 1980s.

As it has grown, De Soto County's politics have been leaning more toward the GOP in races for federal offices. De Soto gave Carter 54 percent of its vote in 1976, but since then, the county has gone with GOP presidential candidates. Republican Trent Lott carried De Soto easily in his successful 1988 Senate race.

There have also been population gains in the eastern and central portions of the district, where the arrival of new industry and construction of the Tennessee-Tombigbee Waterway provided new jobs.

Population: 504,136. White 378,536 (75%), Black 124,179 (25%). Spanish origin 3,701 (1%). 18 and over 345,943 (69%), 65 and over 62,955 (13%). Median age: 29.

do become a thing of the past, a potent instrument is removed from Whitten's control. But he still handles the money, in whatever form. Besides regular appropriations, there are periodic supplemental and disaster-aid bills. And as Whitten once said, according to colleagues' lore, "I've never seen a disaster that wasn't an opportunity."

For years, Whitten blocked administration and Senate attempts to provide open-ended funding for the multibillion-dollar Commodity Credit Corporation (CCC), forcing Reagan to seek more money by midyear so that popular farm programs would not run dry. The president's request then became the engine for a supplemental bill carrying other spending items. To some extent, as Whitten might say with a wink, Reagan had only himself to blame; his budget each year included an unrealistically low request for the CCC, to hold down the deficit, and Whitten devilishly complied. Everyone knew it would not be enough.

In 1987, the Senate tried to outflank Whitten, and added provisions for open-ended CCC funding to three major bills. Whitten countered with a proposal to divide the CCC into various parts, requiring new spending bills when any one of them ran out of funds. The Senate provision became law as part of one measure, while Whitten's was enacted in the agriculture appropriations bill. Whitten won: The Agriculture Department said it was bound by appropriations law.

Whitten does not always prevail. In fact, more notable have been some recent losses.

In 1986, he slipped into the continuing resolution $3.4 billion to resurrect revenue sharing, a popular program of aid to state and local governments that had been eliminated without requiring members to go on record against it. Democrats complained angrily about Whitten's move, and the leadership-controlled Rules Committee forced him to remove the item before it would grant a rule for floor action on the resolution.

The next year, his $11 billion supplemental bill sparked a floor revolt. The House voted by an overwhelming 263-123 for an amendment to slash the bill 21 percent. The sponsor, junior Democrat Buddy MacKay, suggested that the leadership tacitly blessed "guys as dumb as me [who] take on Whitten. Somebody's got to do it."

The result of that eye-opening slap was a pact between Whitten and the leadership: If he complies with the limits of the annual budget resolution, the leaders will shield his bills from meat-ax amendments on the floor.

Such setbacks are rooted in Whitten's disdain for budget law, which he shares with other senior appropriators who opposed creation of the Budget Committee and a centralized budget process in 1974. They also opposed the 1985 Gramm-Rudman-Hollings law, which gave budget resolutions new teeth; in conference, Whitten did everything he could to limit the law's intrusions on Appropriations. "The budget resolution is sound, but only as a target," he said in 1987. "If the target is going to tie the hands of the Congress to meet the need, it is time we begin to look to see whether we should abolish it."

Even as Appropriations faces new restrictions on its spending, it is more involved than ever in the details of programs it funds. Many programs for housing, the environment and aid to the poor — all so sensitive that Congress often cannot agree on bills reauthorizing them — have been kept alive by continuing resolutions from Whitten's committee. In the process, the panel can quietly add language altering the programs.

Through the years, various bills have allowed Whitten to pour money into Mississippi. Often he slips in provisions unnoticed, or explains them in his famous Mississippi mumble that leaves listeners more perplexed than enlightened. He is not apologetic: "Somebody told me, 'Jamie, you're the biggest pork-barreler in Congress.' I said, 'I guess I am, because pork barrel is what you do in the other fella's district, and I've helped more districts than anybody.' "

A 1983 supplemental bill contained a bailout for cotton farmers estimated to cost $100 million, and another included $33 million to widen a highway in Whitten's district. In the 99th Congress, Whitten lost a fight against proposals to increase local beneficiaries' share of the cost of water projects, but he did win an exemption for the Mississippi River basin. With a ceremonial flotilla, in 1985 he viewed the new Tennessee-Tombigbee waterway that cut through his district, financed with federal dollars over two decades. To Whitten it is one of his proudest contributions; to critics, a monument to pork-barrel excess.

Whitten claims he was uninterested in agriculture when he was first elected from his rural district. But except for two years since 1949, his power base has been the Agriculture Subcommittee.

He has fought for crop subsidies, rural electrification and soil conservation programs, and rural home loans. His activism has fed a running turf battle with House Agriculture Committee Chairman E. "Kika" de la Garza. In 1987, de la Garza objected to a Whitten bill during House debate, snapping, "How many days of hearings did you have?" Whitten shot back: "I've been doing this for 39 years!"

At one time, his subcommittee was his virtual fiefdom. From it, as late as the 1960s, he was railing against integration and social programs and dictating crop subsidies without much challenge. In 1971 he got jurisdiction over the Environmental Protection Agency (EPA), the Food and Drug Administration and the Federal Trade Commission, and he soon made clear how he felt about the agencies. He called environmentalists "extremists," and said "those people at EPA have been given more money than they can possibly use."

By 1975, liberals had had enough. Armed with a new rule requiring Appropriations subcommittee chairmen to be elected by the Democratic Caucus, they plotted to oust him. The effort was defused by Appropriations Chairman George H. Mahon, who arranged for Whitten to give up environmental and consumer issues in return for keeping the Agriculture chair.

When Mahon retired four years later, again liberals mobilized to prevent Whitten from inheriting the full committee. They favored instead Edward P. Boland of Massachusetts, longtime roommate of Speaker Thomas P. O'Neill Jr. But O'Neill had always been on good terms with Whitten and he was reluctant to breach seniority. Whitten got the chairmanship.

And O'Neill got a loyal chairman. Whitten, who once voted against civil rights bills, Medicare and anti-poverty programs, now backs party goals even at the risk of political controversy back home. In the 99th Congress, he was the only member from Mississippi to oppose Reagan's request for aid to the Nicaraguan contras. He again opposed contra aid in the 100th Congress.

Once an avowed segregationist, Whitten signed the 1956 Southern Manifesto and said the Supreme Court's 1954 school-desegregation decision had started the nation "on the downhill road to integration and amalgamation and ruin." Today he represents a district that is 26 percent black, a smaller population than in the past but one that votes in significant numbers now. He is as free of racial rhetoric as the younger Southerners who have joined him since the 1970s.

At Home: Whitten has accrued his seniority with barely a scent of opposition in his northern Mississippi district.

Between 1941, when he first won his House seat, and 1978, the year he inherited the Appropriations chairmanship, he faced GOP opposition only once. That challenger did not reach 20 percent of the vote. Nor has there been much challenge inside the Democratic Party; the only real threat was in 1962, when redistricting forced Whitten to battle Rep. Frank Smith for the nomination.

The son of a Tallahatchie County farmer, Whitten has spent his adult life in politics. He was elected to the Mississippi House at 21, and two years later was chosen district attorney. At 31 he was elected to Congress to succeed Wall Doxey, who had moved to the Senate. For the next two decades Whitten ran virtually unopposed. But in 1962, Mississippi lost one House seat in reapportionment. The state Legislature combined the northern Delta region's two districts, forcing a bitter showdown between Whitten and Smith. The two had been on opposite sides during the 1960 presidential election, when Smith backed John F. Kennedy while Whitten supported an unpledged slate of segregationist electors.

The new district's population was more than half black, but virtually none of the blacks voted. Each congressman tried to outdo the other in support of segregation. Smith was a populist, and Whitten claimed that he worked with Northern liberals and the Kennedy administration rather than trying to "preserve the Southern way of life." Smith said Whitten was more of a "prima donna" than an effective champion of Southern rights.

Building a huge lead in the counties of his old constituency, Whitten won easily with 60 percent of the vote. Smith was appointed by President Kennedy to the board of the TVA.

Mississippi's resurgent Republicans have been challenging Whitten in most recent election years, but they have accomplished little. In 1980, while Reagan was carrying Mississippi — although not the 1st District — against Jimmy Carter, GOP challenger T. K. Moffett picked up 37 percent.

That is the closest anyone has come. In 1986, Republican Larry Cobb tried to convince voters that for all Whitten's alleged clout, the area was being shortchanged. Cobb maintained that the Mississippi 1st ranked 391st among the 435 districts in getting federal dollars.

Cobb, a Vietnam fighter pilot, airline pilot and cattleman, covered northeast Mississippi with his placards, while Whitten's campaign was barely visible. But Cobb lacked funds for a media campaign, and he mustered just 34 percent. The GOP's 1988 effort was even weaker.

Committee

Appropriations (Chairman)
Rural Development, Agriculture and Related Agencies (chairman)

Elections

1988 General		
Jamie L. Whitten (D)	137,445	(78%)
Jim Bush (R)	38,381	(22%)
1988 Primary		
Jamie L. Whitten (D)	56,222	(85%)
John Hargett (D)	9,594	(15%)
1986 General		
Jamie L. Whitten (D)	59,870	(66%)
Larry Cobb (R)	30,267	(34%)

Previous Winning Percentages: **1984** (88%) **1982** (71%) **1980** (63%) **1978** (67%) **1976** (100%) **1974** (88%) **1972** (100%) **1970** (87%) **1968** (100%) **1966** (84%) **1964** (100%) **1962** (100%) **1960** (100%) **1958** (100%) **1956** (100%) **1954** (100%) **1952** (100%) **1950** (100%) **1948** (100%) **1946** (100%) **1944** (99%) **1942** (100%) **1941** * (69%)

* *Special election.*

District Vote For President

	1988	1984	1980	1976
D	71,336 (39%)	66,789 (37%)	98,927 (54%)	92,846 (59%)
R	107,290 (59%)	111,841 (62%)	78,095 (43%)	60,313 (38%)
I			3,083 (2%)	

Campaign Finance

	Receipts	Receipts from PACs	Expend-itures
1988			
Whitten (D)	$175,925	$135,400 (77%)	$58,370
1986			
Whitten (D)	$253,863	$187,770 (74%)	$170,878
Cobb (R)	$116,149	$5,500 (5%)	$112,195

Key Votes

1987	
Raise speed limit to 65 mph	N
Approve Gephardt "fair trade" amendment	Y
Ban testing of larger nuclear weapons	N
Delay "re-flagging" of Kuwaiti tankers	Y
Approve tax-raising deficit-reduction bill	Y
1988	
Approve aid to Nicaraguan contras	N
Enact civil rights restoration bill over Reagan veto	Y
Kill 60-day plant-closing notification measure	N
Pass omnibus trade bill over Reagan veto	Y
Approve death penalty for drug-related murders	Y
Bar federal funds for abortions in cases of rape and incest	Y
Oppose seven-day waiting period for purchase of handguns	Y

Voting Studies

	Presidential Support		Party Unity		Conservative Coalition	
Year	**S**	**O**	**S**	**O**	**S**	**O**
1988	28	68	90	8	45	53
1987	33	61	82	10	70	21
1986	30	64	76	16	60	34
1985	33	68	79	13	55	35
1984	39	58	76	18	56	39
1983	30	66	71	22	63	31
1982	40	53	66	27	49	34
1981	50	49	63	36	67	31

Interest Group Ratings

Year	ADA	ACU	AFL-CIO	CCUS
1988	65	20	100	15
1987	68	13	88	13
1986	55	16	69	31
1985	55	26	75	20
1984	50	33	69	60
1983	60	18	88	33
1982	45	52	70	38
1981	30	20	67	22

2 Mike Espy (D)

Of Yazoo City — Elected 1986

Born: Nov. 30, 1953, Yazoo City, Miss.
Education: Howard U., B.A. 1975; U. of Santa Clara School of Law, J.D. 1978.
Occupation: Lawyer; businessman.
Family: Wife, Sheila Bell; two children.
Religion: Baptist.
Political Career: Miss. assistant secretary of state, 1980-84; assistant state attorney general, 1984-85.
Capitol Office: 216 Cannon Bldg. 20515; 225-5876.

In Washington: By ousting a Republican incumbent to become Mississippi's first black representative since Reconstruction, Espy gained national attention even before his first House term began.

But once in Congress, Espy carefully avoided coming across as a man trying to cultivate a national profile; he knew that might put off some constituents at home as well as colleagues in Washington. Instead, he paid assiduous attention to his district and to his committee duties, keeping his eye on one goal — improving on his narrow 1986 victory margin.

Espy is a member of the post-civil rights generation in Mississippi. His electoral success in politically marginal and traditionally polarized territory has depended on his ability to win over white voters, some of them business-oriented Republicans. In 1988, he was one of three members of the Black Caucus who remained neutral in the presidential nominating contest until the national convention; once there, Espy supported the Rev. Jesse Jackson.

Overall, Espy voted against his party only 5 percent of the time in 1988 — less than anyone else in the Mississippi Democratic delegation. But much of his day-to-day emphasis was on economic development issues that can transcend party label.

One effort that brought Espy attention at home in his first term was his support for the Lower Mississippi Delta Development Commission, designed to combat poverty in Mississippi and other Southern states. Working with fellow Mississippi Democrat Jamie L. Whitten, chairman of the House Appropriations Committee, and other members of the affected states, Espy helped pass the bill, which created a commission to study and recommend economic development measures.

"America is a chain of states, and in order to make it strong, you've got to focus on the weak links," Espy said. "Mississippi is a weak link."

Espy also got favorable local notice for his efforts to promote catfish consumption. Most of the nation's catfish farming is done in Espy's district, and he has spent a fair amount of energy trying to persuade people to eat more of the whiskered fish. He pushed successfully to get the Army to increase its purchases of catfish, and helped deliver block grants for two new processing plants for his district. He also made headlines with his successful push for a ceremonial bill establishing a "National Catfish Day."

"A lot of people have an aversion to ceremonial bills," Espy said of the effort. "To the 2nd District, it's more than just a day."

House Democratic leaders did everything they could to boost Espy's re-election chances. They gave him a seat on Agriculture, an obvious plus in the rural and politically marginal Mississippi Delta district. Espy was also the only Democrat in his class to win a spot on the Budget Committee, an attention-getting assignment both at home and in Washington.

Despite his focus on local matters, Espy got more national limelight than a typical House freshman: He was showcased at the Democratic National Convention, where he was asked to introduce the keynote speaker.

At Home: Espy's career in electoral politics is not a very long one, but it has been illustrious. His 1986 House election made Mississippi history; two years later, he was re-elected overwhelmingly, forging the kind of biracial coalition that previously seemed unattainable in this traditionally polarized district.

Espy faced considerable skepticism when he challenged GOP Rep. Webb Franklin in 1986. Espy comes from a prominent Delta family that owns a chain of funeral homes, but he did not begin with a significant political base. Although roughly half the district's voters are black, there had not been evidence that they would turn out in numbers sufficient to produce a congressional-election victory.

In 1982 and 1984, Franklin won as the House vote split essentially along racial lines; each time, black Democratic nominee Robert G. Clark, a state representative and old-line civil rights leader, fell a few thousand votes short.

But Espy effectively combined old-fash-

Mississippi 2

North Central — Mississippi Delta

Ever since swamp-draining technology and cheap black labor transformed the Delta into an agricultural gold mine in the years after the Civil War, the region has had a far larger population of poor rural blacks than comfortable white cotton growers. But throughout the decades, the monied white establishment managed to keep a firm grip on political power; Espy's election marked a passage into a dramatically new political order.

The 2nd was altered substantially by this decade's redistricting, becoming the modern counterpart to the "Delta District" that existed in Mississippi until 1966. The state's first round of redistricting in 1982 balanced the Delta area with counties in the Hill Country, traditionally a poor white region. A court-ordered second round of redistricting in early 1984 increased the black population by removing the Hill Country territory and extending the 2nd southward along the Mississippi River below Vicksburg.

The largest city in the 2nd is Greenville, an old river port and cotton market and the traditional "capital" of the Mississippi Delta. This is one of the few areas in the region that has gained population in recent years. Greenville, the seat of Washington County, is the home of the *Delta Democrat*, the politically moderate newspaper published for a generation by Hodding Carter Jr. and his family. Greenville still has a reputation as one of the more racially tolerant communities in the state.

In the past generation, thousands of Delta blacks have been pushed out of work by farm mechanization and have moved on to Chicago, St. Louis and closer Sun Belt cities such as Little Rock and Memphis. Still, blacks make up 58 percent of the population.

The result is that the 2nd District has displaced the 1st as the Mississippi constituency most favorable to statewide Democratic candidates. Eleven of the 18 Mississippi counties carried by Michael S. Dukakis in 1988 were in the 2nd District.

Vicksburg, seat of Warren County, is the district's second-largest city. Its Catfish Row is considered to be the southern terminus of the Delta region. The major Republican enclave in the 2nd, Warren County gave Franklin a 5,442-vote edge in 1984, but two years later, Espy cut that advantage in half, a major factor in Franklin's downfall. In his 1988 re-election, Espy carried Warren County narrowly.

Population: 503,935. White 207,501 (41%), Black 293,809 (58%), Other 2,599 (1%). Spanish origin 6,109 (1%). 18 and over 323,647 (64%), 65 and over 62,636 (12%). Median age: 26.

ioned inspirational oratory and modern organizational techniques. In his effort to increase the black vote, Espy mounted a skillful turnout drive that, in its attention to detail, exceeded anything the black community had put together in the past.

At the same time, Espy had some success wooing the white Democratic establishment. A well-educated young professional with a low-key, businesslike manner, Espy presented a less threatening front to ingrained white prejudices. He got the backing of several white county sheriffs and of Mississippi's secretary of state and attorney general. He won official neutrality from other white Democratic officials who, rather than put out the word for Franklin as they had in the past, took a wait-and-see attitude. Espy also made a direct play for the support of farmers in the district, many of whom were suffering through hard times and were angered by some of Franklin's laissez-faire rhetoric.

On Election Day, Espy won only about 10 percent of the white vote, but that was enough in a year when white turnout was low and the Delta's black community was mobilized.

It seemed as though Espy could have a big fight on his hands in 1988, when the presidential election would bring out a larger white Republican vote. But Espy worked hard throughout his first term to win over some of the monied establishment that had supported Franklin. It was not long before even some Republicans were heard praising Espy's work.

Republican nominee Jack Coleman, an attorney who had recently worked for a business trade association in Washington, made little secret of his desire for a polarized electorate. Although he touted his own ability to boost economic development, his campaign literature told voters that Espy is "representing the interests of the Radical Left: for unions, for abortions, against jobs, against defense, against America and against Americans." When vandals attacked Espy's home during the campaign and scrawled "nigger" on the door, Coleman suggested that Espy might have staged the whole thing to generate sympathy.

Some GOP leaders found Coleman's effort embarrassing, and most voters found it unconvincing. Espy took roughly 40 percent of the ballots cast by whites, and ended up winning about two-thirds of the overall vote.

Before he ran for Congress, Espy's political experience was essentially administrative, as an assistant secretary of state and then as the director of the attorney general's consumer-protection division.

Committees

Agriculture (22nd of 27 Democrats)
Conservation, Credit and Rural Development; Cotton, Rice and Sugar; Domestic Marketing, Consumer Relations and Nutrition

Budget (12th of 21 Democrats)
Task Forces: Community Development and Natural Resources; Human Resources

Select Hunger (10th of 18 Democrats)
Task Force: Domestic (chairman)

Elections

1988 General		
Mike Espy (D)	112,401	(65%)
Jack Coleman (R)	59,827	(34%)
1988 Primary		
Mike Espy (D)	59,801	(88%)
J. F. "Boja" Clarke (D)	8,250	(12%)
1986 General		
Mike Espy (D)	73,119	(52%)
Webb Franklin (R)	68,292	(48%)

District Vote For President

	1988	1984	1980	1976
D	87,968 (50%)	90,653 (49%)	94,761 (57%)	77,986 (54%)
R	83,997 (48%)	93,213 (50%)	68,715 (41%)	60,798 (42%)

Campaign Finance

	Receipts	Receipts from PACs	Expend-itures
1988			
Espy (D)	$880,227	$480,490 (55%)	$886,540
Coleman (R)	$226,486	$25,377 (11%)	$225,873
1986			
Espy (D)	$600,375	$307,865 (51%)	$591,002
Franklin (R)	$557,673	$195,647 (35%)	$574,120

Key Votes

1987	
Raise speed limit to 65 mph	Y
Approve Gephardt "fair trade" amendment	Y
Ban testing of larger nuclear weapons	Y
Delay "re-flagging" of Kuwaiti tankers	Y
Approve tax-raising deficit-reduction bill	Y
1988	
Approve aid to Nicaraguan contras	N
Enact civil rights restoration bill over Reagan veto	Y
Kill 60-day plant-closing notification measure	N
Pass omnibus trade bill over Reagan veto	Y
Approve death penalty for drug-related murders	Y
Bar federal funds for abortions in cases of rape and incest	N
Oppose seven-day waiting period for purchase of handguns	Y

Voting Studies

	Presidential Support		Party Unity		Conservative Coalition	
Year	S	O	S	O	S	O
1988	20	69	78	5	42	50
1987	20	73	89	4	40	58

Interest Group Ratings

Year	ADA	ACU	AFL-CIO	CCUS
1988	85	12	93	25
1987	84	0	88	7

3 G.V. "Sonny" Montgomery (D)

Of Meridian — Elected 1966

Born: Aug. 5, 1920, Meridian, Miss.
Education: Mississippi State U., B.S. 1943.
Military Career: Army, 1943-46; National Guard, 1946-80, active duty, 1951-52.
Occupation: Insurance executive.
Family: Single.
Religion: Episcopalian.
Political Career: Miss. Senate, 1956-66.
Capitol Office: 2184 Rayburn Bldg. 20515; 225-5031.

In Washington: For most members, the Veterans' Affairs Committee is a backup assignment, mainly valuable for impressing the many veterans who vote back home. But for Chairman Sonny Montgomery, it is a labor of love, the premier spot to pursue the cause to which he has devoted his career.

He spent more than half his life in the military, as a decorated Army veteran of World War II and Korea, and a member of the Mississippi National Guard, from which he retired as a major general only in 1980. He ran for Congress in 1966 pledging to "bring the boys home" from Vietnam in honor, won a seat on Veterans' Affairs in his second term and added a place on the Armed Services Committee two years later.

Given his interests, perhaps the Armed Services chairmanship would be the only better post for Montgomery. But whatever hopes he had for that prize were dashed in 1985 when junior Democrat Les Aspin of Wisconsin ousted enfeebled Chairman Melvin Price. Like the other hawkish conservatives Aspin leapfrogged on his way to the chair, Montgomery was a secondary casualty of the coup. He now is the third-ranking Democrat on Armed Services, but the panel is increasingly dominated by the younger Aspin's centrist coalition.

Montgomery, a bachelor, approaches the military community practically as family. The older veterans, those of retirement age like himself, are brothers from two past wars. The younger ones from the Vietnam era are more like sons, and daughters, too, and in his approach to these veterans and their demands Montgomery has occasionally suffered from the generation gap typical of the divisive Vietnam era.

He partly bridged that gap in the 100th Congress. Among several notable bills he helped pass was one that Vietnam veterans' groups had long favored and Montgomery, allied with older veterans' organizations, repeatedly had buried in his committee despite majority support in both chambers. It would allow veterans to go to federal court to appeal Department of Veterans Affairs decisions denying their benefits claims.

Montgomery had objected that appeal rights would result in excessive litigation and poison relations between the VA and veterans. But backers in the Senate, which had passed the bill four times before, and the measure's sponsor on Veterans' Affairs, Montgomery's liberal friend and tennis partner Don Edwards of California, argued that veterans — of all people — were entitled to constitutional due process.

Then in 1988, when the Senate passed the legislation a fifth time, Montgomery said he "would not be a stumbling block." His softening was attributed to pressure from congressional leaders, and to evidence that the VA claims process was flawed. Weeks before Congress adjourned, he offered a substitute that Veterans' Affairs approved; though too limited to satisfy proponents (it did not allow appeals beyond a special federal court), the bill was the basis for the eventual compromise. The final measure permits certain cases to be appealed as far as the Supreme Court.

The agreement in turn removed potential Senate roadblocks to a pet project of Montgomery's, enactment of a 60-year-old proposal to make the VA a Cabinet department. "Veterans' programs are too important to be left to mid-level decision makers" in the president's budget office, he argued.

Also in the 100th Congress, Montgomery helped steer into law a variety of bills expanding veterans' health, education, housing and survivors' benefits. The GI Bill, similar to the one that has financed veterans' college education since World War II, was made permanent and named for Montgomery.

"Another burst of veteran-o-mania," complained assistant Senate Republican leader Alan K. Simpson, "and there's no money in the budget."

As a critic, Simpson was all but alone given the political appeal of veterans' bills. With

Mississippi 3

South Central — Meridian

The 3rd is mostly agricultural, but it includes a burgeoning timber industry, outlying suburbs of Jackson and a major Air Force base at Columbus.

In the 1970s the district extended west into the Mississippi Delta, but redistricting for the 1980s centered it in the Hill Country at the eastern end of the state. The rural hill counties are still reliably Democratic in local contests, but the 3rd's suburban and small-city vote has been tilting toward the GOP.

Lauderdale County, on the Alabama border, is the largest county wholly within the 3rd. Meridian, population 42,970, the seat of Lauderdale County, is an increasingly Republican industrial town with Lockheed and General Motors facilities. The Meridian Naval Air Station is a training center for naval pilots.

Another small city with growing Republican strength is Laurel, population 22,000. The seat of Jones County on the district's southern edge, Laurel is home to a timber-related industry fueled by its proximity to Mississippi's Piney Woods. Oil and gas drilling in southern Mississippi have spawned oil-related industries in the area, though they have struggled as oil has slumped in recent years. Court-ordered redistricting in early 1984 split the increasingly Republican county, with the northern half, including Laurel, remaining in the 3rd District and the southern half joining the 5th.

Northwest of Jones County is Smith County, the home of the National Tobacco Spitting Contest, which annually attracts curious spectators and serious expectoraters. Neighboring Rankin County is more cosmopolitan; it is home to more than 50,000 suburbanites oriented toward the state capital of Jackson. One of the fastest-growing areas of the state, Rankin went solidly Republican in the 1987 gubernatorial contest, and it gave George Bush nearly 80 percent of its presidential votes in 1988. Like Jones County, it was split by the 1984 redistricting, with the more populous northern portion remaining in the 3rd District and the southern part joining the 4th.

At the far northern end of the district is Columbus, another Republican stronghold in national elections. The seat of Lowndes County, Columbus has a significant population of military-related residents from the North and Midwest. These voters add considerably to the Republican presence in the district. The local Air Force base offers basic training for prospective Air Force pilots. Neighboring Oktibbeha County (Starkville) is home to Mississippi State University and its 11,500 students.

Population: 505,169. White 336,707 (67%), Black 161,833 (32%), Other 5,722 (1%). Spanish origin 4,104 (1%). 18 and over 348,335 (69%), 65 and over 60,228 (12%). Median age: 28.

committee Republicans' assent, Montgomery routinely ignored President Reagan's proposed budget cutbacks. "A lot of them are trial balloons," he once said. "We shoot them down pretty fast."

Still, as his experience through the decade with the GI Bill showed, under budget constraints some measures had to be more modest or took longer to enact than he would have liked, due to administration and Senate resistance. And he complains that VA hospitals are so woefully underfunded to meet increased patient loads that many could close.

On Armed Services, Montgomery has been the spokesman for military reserve units and the National Guard. He is largely responsible, for example, for the new planes the Air National Guard obtains in each year's defense bill. In 1983, as Armed Services was cutting back personnel in other branches, he persuaded the panel to add 35,000 positions for the reserves.

In 1986, it was his amendment to the defense bill that barred governors from ordering state Guard units not to participate in Pentagon-sponsored training exercises, as governors had done in call-ups for Central America. The House adopted the amendment, 261-159.

Long worried about the ability of the all-volunteer Army to fight a protracted war, more recently Montgomery has conceded that the system is working better. He still favors the draft, but his past failure to convince Congress has led him to conclude that his bill would not go far "unless somebody's landing on our shores."

In 1988, he was one of the most vocal opponents of an ultimately successful bill authorizing a commission to recommend closure of obsolete military bases. Unlike some other foes, he made no attempt to drape his stance in national security arguments, and in effect he illustrated the other side's point that many bases were no more than jobs programs: "I don't really need any more people on welfare in my state," he said. "The military bases are a good economic measure for my people."

After the upheaval of recent years on Armed Services — Aspin's 1985 takeover, his own near-ouster two years later and his subsequent restoration of moderates' control — the panel quietly changed further in the 100th Congress. Two deaths and a retirement claimed three senior conservative Democrats, leaving Montgomery virtually alone when just a decade ago he was part of the conservative majority that ran the panel. Typically he votes with Republicans, as he did during committee action on the 1988 defense bill to defeat amendments aimed at Reagan's strategic defense initiative.

What bitterness Montgomery feels toward Aspin and his allies is well hidden beneath his courtly Southern gentleman's exterior. And what alienation he has felt among House Democrats in general has been assuaged by the many friendships he has developed by virtue of his genial personality and time spent on paddleball and tennis courts with the likes of the liberal Edwards. One GOP friend from the courts is President Bush, who came to the House with Montgomery in 1967; Bush considered naming his old classmate as secretary of the Army or of the new Cabinet-level VA.

Like most Mississippi Democrats of the civil rights era, Montgomery came to Washington firmly believing that his party had moved too far left for him to support it very often. He voted with his leadership less than half the time, and was one of only three House Democrats to stick by President Nixon even after the Judiciary Committee voted for impeachment.

House Republicans have called him "one of us," and at times have talked him up as a potential leader for a bipartisan conservative coalition to take control of the House. But he never has talked seriously of bolting the Democratic Party — not as long as it controls the House levers of power.

When Reagan's new economic program moved through the House in 1981, Montgomery was nearly as important a White House ally as then-Rep. Phil Gramm, the Texas Democrat who was stripped of his Budget Committee seat as punishment and decided to join the GOP.

Many of the strategy sessions in which conservative Democrats decided to back Reagan were held in Montgomery's office. During House roll calls, he spent much of his time on the Republican side of the floor, monitoring GOP computers and lobbying for pro-Reagan votes. Yet the only price he paid was a less-than-resounding 179-53 vote in the Democratic Caucus for re-election as Veterans' Affairs chairman for the 98th Congress. "We got the message," he said. "I like being a Democrat."

A few weeks later, he went further. "I think we might have gotten carried away with the White House," he said. "We weren't working enough with the Democratic leadership." Montgomery did oppose the 1983 Democratic budget alternative, complaining that defense outlays were too low, but he supported the party's budgets in subsequent years.

His experience illustrates the improved relations generally between conservative and mainstream Democrats since the early days of Reagan's administration. Today he is recognized by dint of seniority and popularity as the leader of the Boll Weevils, a group whose numbers have dropped by Montgomery's own estimate from about 100 when he came to Congress to a third of that. But he declines a formal leadership role. "Sonny Montgomery could do it," a House leadership aide said during the 100th Congress, "but he just doesn't like a visible role."

"I have loyalty to the Democratic Caucus," he said then. "They gave me a chairmanship. . . . I try to help them where I can." Since 1985, he has voted with his party more than half the time — to a high of nearly two-thirds of the votes in 1988.

That recent record attests to a narrowing of the divide that grew between Montgomery and his party since he arrived in Washington at the height of the Vietnam War. He seemed consumed by the conflict and its soldiers. He began traveling to Vietnam in his first year, initially at Agriculture Committee expense to inspect Food for Peace programs. Later, he went on Veterans' Affairs business. But mostly, Montgomery went because he wanted to see the military and the war firsthand. He spent every Christmas for several years visiting soldiers.

As a result, he became an acknowledged expert on the war, but his support for it drove him further from majority opinion in the House "The time is past when we can discuss whether this is the wrong war," he said in 1967. "Our flag is committed." Three years later, he was still defending the ability of American troops to help the South Vietnamese win the war. "The morale of the American fighting man is quite high," he said then. "The one thing that seems to disturb him most is the continued anti-war demonstrations."

But while the House moved far from Montgomery's hawkish approach in ensuing years, it saw him as the logical man after the war to head a committee to determine whether U.S. servicemen were being held prisoner by the North Vietnamese. His panel, known formally as the Select Committee on U.S. Involvement in Southeast Asia, went to Vietnam and to Europe to meet with representatives from Hanoi and finally concluded, in December 1976, that there were no prisoners.

Montgomery resisted pleas from fellow conservatives to continue pressing Hanoi for more information. He was the bearer of bad news: There was no hard evidence, he said, that any of the missing men were still alive. He relented a bit in 1985, joining North Carolina Republican Bill Hendon in calling for a presidential commission to investigate again. His conviction had not wavered, but, he said, "We do agree that we need to finally put this issue to bed." Reagan instead chose an envoy, who negotiated to bring home remains of dead servicemen, but found no prisoners of war.

At Home: For years Montgomery has had the best of both worlds — personal popularity in Congress and bipartisan support back home. Not since 1968 has he won a primary or general election with less than 89 percent of the vote. Montgomery's 1988 GOP opponent, Columbia contractor Jimmie Ray Bourland, was so frustrated by the lack of attention to his effort that he climbed a TV tower to protest. He soon descended back into obscurity, eventually winning 11 percent of the vote.

Montgomery was a state senator and prominent National Guard officer when he first ran for the House in 1966. The 3rd District had gone Republican on a fluke in 1964, electing little-known chicken farmer Prentiss Walker, the only Republican who had filed for Congress anywhere in the state that year. Barry Goldwater carried Mississippi easily in his 1964 presidential campaign, and he propelled Walker into office. Two years later Walker ran for the Senate — he would have been beaten for re-election to the House anyway — leaving the 3rd open.

There were three other candidates for the Democratic House nomination in 1966, but Montgomery won with little difficulty. He drew 50.1 percent of the primary vote, avoiding a runoff.

His general-election campaign was easier. Describing himself as "a conservative Mississippi Democrat," Montgomery said he opposed the new, big-spending Great Society programs but favored older ones like Social Security and rural electrification. He claimed that his Republican opponent, state Rep. L. L. McAllister Jr., was against all federal programs, and he linked McAllister with the national GOP, which he called the "party of Reconstruction, Depression and 'me-too' liberalism." Montgomery won every county.

He had little trouble in 1968, drawing 85 percent of the primary vote against a black civil rights activist and 70 percent in the fall against Walker, who was trying to regain the seat. The Republican had lost his Senate race to veteran Democrat James O. Eastland by 2-to-1, and carried only one county in his comeback attempt against Montgomery.

That crushing defeat seemed to remove any remaining GOP interest in tackling Montgomery.

Committees

Veterans' Affairs (Chairman)
Hospitals and Health Care (chairman)

Armed Services (3rd of 31 Democrats)
Military Installations and Facilities; Military Personnel and Compensation

Elections

1988 General		
G. V. "Sonny" Montgomery (D)	164,651	(89%)
Jimmy Ray Bourland (R)	20,729	(11%)
1986 General		
G. V. "Sonny" Montgomery (D)	80,575	(100%)

Previous Winning Percentages:				**1984**	(100%)	**1982**	(93%)
1980	(100%)	**1978**	(92%)	**1976**	(94%)	**1974**	(100%)
1972	(100%)	**1970**	(100%)	**1968**	(70%)	**1966**	(65%)

District Vote For President

	1988	1984	1980	1976
D	63,886 (33%)	63,693 (33%)	81,147 (44%)	71,731 (46%)
R	124,666 (65%)	125,745 (66%)	99,130 (54%)	83,145 (53%)

Campaign Finance

	Receipts	Receipts from PACs	Expend- itures
1988			
Montgomery (D)	$148,077	$71,650 (48%)	$116,761
Bourland (R) †	$671	0	$671
1986			
Montgomery (D)	$50,708	$31,799 (63%)	$70,580

† Totals based on incomplete data.

Key Votes

1987	
Raise speed limit to 65 mph	Y
Approve Gephardt "fair trade" amendment	N
Ban testing of larger nuclear weapons	N
Delay "re-flagging" of Kuwaiti tankers	N
Approve tax-raising deficit-reduction bill	Y
1988	
Approve aid to Nicaraguan contras	Y
Enact civil rights restoration bill over Reagan veto	Y
Kill 60-day plant-closing notification measure	Y
Pass omnibus trade bill over Reagan veto	Y
Approve death penalty for drug-related murders	Y
Bar federal funds for abortions in cases of rape and incest	Y
Oppose seven-day waiting period for purchase of handguns	Y

Voting Studies

	Presidential Support		Party Unity		Conservative Coalition	
Year	S	O	S	O	S	O
1988	45	53	64	34	89	8
1987	53	43	56	38	93	5
1986	58	42	53	45	92	8
1985	66	34	53	44	98	0
1984	59	41	34	59	97	3
1983	68	30	28	67	94	3
1982	74	23	29	66	90	5
1981	78	21	26	68	97	3

Interest Group Ratings

Year	ADA	ACU	AFL-CIO	CCUS
1988	25	71	57	71
1987	16	65	19	71
1986	5	86	29	76
1985	15	76	18	82
1984	0	70	31	50
1983	10	96	13	80
1982	5	91	5	73
1981	0	93	13	83

4 Mike Parker (D)

Of Brookhaven — Elected 1988

Born: Oct. 31, 1949, Laurel, Miss.
Education: William Carey College, B.A. 1970.
Occupation: Funeral director.
Family: Wife, Rosemary Prather; three children.
Religion: Presbyterian.
Political Career: No previous office.
Capitol Office: 1725 Longworth Bldg. 20515; 225-5865.

The Path to Washington: Parker was a political novice when he began his 1988 House campaign, but as a funeral home director and one-time drama student, he was no neophyte when it came to presenting himself to the public. Parker's 55 percent showing — which came in the face of a solid George Bush victory in the 4th — was clear evidence that he possesses campaign skills beyond his political years.

An early wave of television advertising helped Parker distinguish himself from more than a dozen contenders, Democrats and Republicans, after Democratic Rep. Wayne Dowdy decided to give up the district for a Senate bid. Drawing on sizable personal loans, Parker raised his profile quickly as he touted his business background (he also owns a livestock farm) and dedication to "family" values.

In the primary, Parker ran second to Jackson attorney Brad Pigott, who had better connections to party activists. But Pigott was denied a majority, and in the runoff, Parker stormed past him, winning endorsements from the third- and fourth-place primary finishers and taking the nomination by a 3-to-2 margin.

That strong showing made Parker the November favorite against GOP nominee Thomas Collins, but in a conservative-minded district that has elected GOP House members in the recent past, Parker had to run a careful general-election campaign.

Collins had plenty of his own problems: Also a newcomer to politics, he was slow to build ties with GOP regulars, he had trouble raising money and assembling an organization, and he was hampered by a wooden speaking style. But Collins, who spent nearly eight years as a POW during the Vietnam War, did have significant patriotic appeal — a real plus against the backdrop of a presidential campaign that focused on flag-waving issues such as the Pledge of Allegiance. And Collins' appeal to the district's veterans was enhanced by his recent service as director of the Mississippi Veterans Farm and Home Board.

As the fall campaign progressed, the rising tide for George Bush seemed to boost Collins' stock. Michael S. Dukakis never made much effort in Mississippi, and the extent to which he was viewed as heavy political baggage became clear when Collins ran television ads touting his support for Bush and Parker's support for the Democratic ticket. Collins' ad was standard fare for GOP candidates around the South; it was Parker's response that was newsworthy. He immediately took to the airwaves with an advertisement rebutting the charge. He was not, he said, endorsing Dukakis.

Parker's blunt denial of his party's national nominee set him apart from most other Democratic candidates around the country, and it temporarily infuriated some local party activists. But if it struck some as disloyal, Parker's move was not a dramatic shift in his campaign, which never had embraced the national Democratic agenda.

Parker, who comes from a Republican-leaning county in the southern half of the district, was actually very close to Collins on a number of national issues. Both men supported the strategic defense initiative and military aid for the Nicaraguan contras. And Parker, son of a Baptist preacher, also spoke in favor of organized prayer in schools. An independent candidate in the contest criticized Parker and Collins as the "Bobbsey twins."

Stressing the need for "business principles" in Washington, Parker was also successful at pursuing business-oriented Republicans in Hinds County (Jackson), home to roughly half of the district's voters. Some Republicans who knew Parker before the campaign actually had hoped he would seek the GOP nomination.

But Parker, who describes himself as a "Mike Parker mainstream Mississippi Democrat," took care to reassure the party faithful. "I support the broad principles of the Democratic Party," he said. "The party that gave us Social Security, Medicaid, Medicare, veterans' benefits ... gave us [Rep.] 'Sonny' Montgomery and [Sen.] John Stennis."

As a freshman, Parker has seats on Public Works and Veterans' Affairs, two committees where partisan distinctions are less obvious and ideological sparring less prevalent than in the House as a whole.

Mississippi 4

Southwest — Jackson

It is Southern districts such as the 4th that amply illustrate the Democratic Party's ability to retain its huge advantage in the U.S. House while falling time and time again in elections for the presidency.

Along with the Gulf Coast 5th District, the Jackson-based 4th is the backbone of the GOP resurgence in Mississippi. Those two districts are the only Mississippi constituencies in modern times to elect two Republican representatives in a row, and the 4th is the home base of Thad Cochran, who in 1979 became the state's first Republican senator in over a century.

Yet through the sheer political skill of its candidates — first Wayne Dowdy and now Mike Parker — the Democratic Party has kept the 4th District House seat in its hands since 1981.

With a population of more than 200,000, Jackson is the state's capital and its largest city — until recent years it was the only place in Mississippi resembling an urbanized area. An increasingly prosperous commercial and financial center, Jackson grew by nearly one-third in the 1970s, helped by the migration of corporate business from the North. Jackson has continued to grow in the 1980s, although at a more moderate pace. With its suburbs, it casts nearly half the district's vote.

Jackson and surrounding Hinds County have given Republicans a strong political base to build on. Jackson is home to many of the state GOP's financial kingpins, and Hinds County has not gone Democratic in a presidential election since 1956. It was one of three counties that backed Republican Thomas Collins in his contest against Parker in 1988. In the 1987 gubernatorial election, though, Democrat Ray Mabus managed to carry Hinds, winning 52 percent of the vote.

During the 1970s, independent black candidates were a strong political force in the district, a factor that helps account for the district's Republican leanings in that decade. Independent black challengers in 1972, 1978 and 1980 siphoned enough votes from the Democratic House nominees to elect Republicans Cochran and Jon Hinson. But the GOP lost its grip on the 4th when Hinson resigned in April 1981 after being charged with attempted oral sodomy in a Capitol Hill men's room.

When they are not acting independently — as they have not since the 1980 campaign — black voters make the district winnable for Democrats. Even though redistricting in 1984 removed the heavily black Mississippi River counties of Claiborne and Jefferson plus the western portion of Hinds County, the 4th still has a black population well in excess of 40 percent. A candidate such as Parker or Dowdy who can link black and rural white votes is always going to be in a good position to prevail.

Population: 503,297. White 290,052 (58%), Black 211,376 (42%). Spanish origin 3,975 (1%). 18 and over 345,335 (69%), 65 and over 57,957 (12%). Median age: 28.

Committees

Public Works and Transportation (28th of 31 Democrats)
Public Buildings and Grounds; Surface Transportation; Water Resources

Veterans' Affairs (19th of 21 Democrats)
Compensation, Pension and Insurance; Housing and Memorial Affairs

Campaign Finance

	Receipts	Receipts from PACs	Expend-itures
1988			
Parker (D)	$844,541	$234,164 (28%)	$843,142
Collins (R)	$406,944	$56,311 (14%)	$394,250

Elections

1988 General		
Mike Parker (D)	110,184	(55%)
Thomas Collins (R)	88,433	(44%)
1988 Primary Runoff		
Mike Parker (D)	34,507	(61%)
Brad Pigott (D)	21,122	(39%)
1988 Primary		
Brad Pigott (D)	23,489	(25%)
Mike Parker (D)	17,303	(19%)
Steve Patterson (D)	16,695	(18%)
Bobby Moak (D)	12,037	(13%)
Clint Watkins (D)	9,127	(10%)
Terrell Stubbs (D)	8,425	(9%)

District Vote For President

	1988	1984	1980	1976
D	88,469 (43%)	85,253 (41%)	90,830 (47%)	73,611 (44%)
R	113,449 (56%)	122,466 (59%)	100,650 (52%)	90,090 (54%)

5 Larkin Smith (R)

Of Gulfport — Elected 1988

Born: June 26, 1944, Poplarville, Miss.
Education: William Carey College, B.A. 1979.
Occupation: Law enforcement official.
Family: Wife, Sheila Lamey; one child.
Religion: Roman Catholic.
Political Career: Harrison County sheriff, 1984-89.
Capitol Office: 516 Cannon Bldg. 20515; 225-5772.

The Path to Washington: Not too many sheriffs make it to Congress, but in more ways than one, Smith is not typical of his occupation.

For one thing, he is a Republican, unlike most local officeholders in the South. What's more, he has the keen instincts of a modern, media-age politician. That acumen made him one of the best-known figures along Mississippi's Gulf Coast, and an early 1988 favorite to succeed Republican Rep. Trent Lott, who gave up the 5th after eight terms to run for the Senate.

Smith, who received his college degree in the year of his 35th birthday, has a reputation along the Gulf Coast for steadily working to expand his expertise and influence. He became a leading figure in Harrison County (the 5th District's most populous) not only through his work in law enforcement, but also because he is a polished speaker who made it a point to be very accessible to the local media.

Smith began to make a name for himself in the late 1970s and early 1980s as the chief of police in Gulfport, where he had a running feud with the Harrison County sheriff, whose tenure was plagued by scandal. In 1984, Smith was elected sheriff himself, and he earned plaudits for his efforts to clean up the office and upgrade professional standards.

Smith also built up a tough law-and-order image with his high-profile efforts to attack illegal drug trafficking, which is a particular concern to voters along the coast. He attracted attention with his work to get the federally funded Blue Lightning drug-interdiction task force stationed in Gulfport. He also served on the White House Conference for a Drug-Free America.

Smith made a broad range of contacts as sheriff, and his potential appeal in a race for higher office did not go unnoticed in GOP circles. When President Reagan visited Harrison County in 1984, local Republican leaders saw to it that Smith was asked to emcee the appearance.

After Lott announced he was leaving the 5th, Smith was the choice of many Republican leaders living in the coastal region, the district's most heavily populated territory. But four other Republicans also sought the GOP nomination, and one, businessman George R. Hall of Hattiesburg (in the northern part of the 5th), was thought to have a chance. But Smith, touting his work as sheriff, carried the southern half of the district and nearly won the primary with an outright majority. He easily defeated Hall in the runoff.

Democrats nominated a potentially strong contender in state Sen. Gene Taylor, who was well-versed on the issues of the day and had a positive "reform" image stemming from some of his activities in the Legislature. But Taylor was slow to build his organization and funding base — a fatal flaw in Mississippi's most Republican district. In Washington, word got around to national Democratic Party funding sources that Taylor's sluggish campaign looked like a chancy investment.

Taylor told voters that Smith lacked the legislative experience to make a difference in Washington, and he tried to call attention to his conservatism by saying that Democratic Party officials in Washington were cool to his candidacy because he would not moderate his positions, such as his support for the Nicaraguan contras.

Taylor hoped to reap some benefit from a negative reaction to Smith's forceful personality: Smith did not make a mark as sheriff without also making a few enemies, and what some viewed as toughness, others saw as arrogance and abrasiveness. When Smith pushed for consolidation of the county's law-enforcement agencies, some viewed it mostly as a benefit for Smith, despite his contention that he would not head the consolidated law-enforcement effort.

In the end, Taylor managed to exceed expectations on Election Day, taking about 45 percent of the vote in spite of George Bush's strong showing in the district. But Smith still emerged with a rather comfortable victory margin.

Taylor's major committee assignment for the 101st Congress is Judiciary; he is that panel's only former sheriff.

Mississippi 5

Southeast — Gulf Coast; Hattiesburg

Mississippi's long-dormant Republican Party made its initial modern-day inroads in the 5th District, a solidly conservative region where Democrats are no longer even competitive in national elections. Ronald Reagan carried Mississippi in 1980 only because of a 30,000-vote edge in the 5th. As George Bush carried the state easily in 1988, the 5th was his strongest district. In his 1988 Senate bid, Trent Lott did not lose a county in the 5th.

The political heart of the 5th is the Mississippi Gulf Coast. The coastal counties of Jackson, Hancock and Harrison cast about three-fifths of its vote, and none gave Bush less than 67 percent in 1988. However, all three counties backed Democrat Ray Mabus for governor in 1987.

This area is home for gulf shrimpers and seafood-processing plants, as well as government and military installations. Shipbuilding is big business, especially in Pascagoula, where a Litton Industries shipyard, the leading private employer in the district, handles major Navy contracts.

The Gulf Coast area has little in common with the rest of Mississippi. Tourism is a major source of dollars; U.S. Route 90 between Bay St. Louis and Biloxi is lined with beaches and dotted with seafood restaurants.

The coastal counties have a far smaller black population than other parts of the state, and racial issues have never been an overriding preoccupation. Biloxi, the largest Gulf Coast city, with a population just under 50,000, was built around its seafood industry. In the past 20 years, however, it has developed a white-collar and service-based economy tied to the military and to Litton. Nearby Gulfport is less ethnic than Biloxi and more Republican.

The tier of counties above the coast are part of the poorer Piney Woods region, where the economy is centered on wood products. The land is not particularly good for agriculture, but there is some dairy and poultry farming.

The sole population center in the northern part of the district is Hattiesburg, the seat of Forrest County. Hattiesburg is a white-collar town whose leading employer is Southern Mississippi University, with more than 10,000 students and 650 faculty. The absence of a big blue-collar population has made it fertile GOP territory for 20 years, though Mabus was able to get 48 percent in Forrest.

Population: 504,101. White 402,394 (80%), Black 96,009 (19%), Other 3,870 (1%). Spanish origin 6,842 (1%). 18 and over 343,181 (68%), 65 and over 45,581 (9%). Median age: 27.

Committees

Government Operations (12th of 15 Republicans)
Human Resources and Intergovernmental Relations (ranking)

Judiciary (12th of 14 Republicans)
Administrative Law and Governmental Relations; Crime; Criminal Justice

Campaign Finance

	Receipts	Receipts from PACs	Expend-itures
1988			
Smith (R)	$588,552	$135,150 (23%)	$569,830
Taylor (D)	$171,453	$73,600 (43%)	$165,041

Elections

1988 General		
Larkin Smith (R)	100,185	(55%)
Gene Taylor (D)	82,034	(45%)
1988 Primary Runoff		
Larkin Smith (R)	25,470	(67%)
George R. Hall (R)	12,553	(33%)
1988 Primary		
Larkin Smith (R)	27,260	(49%)
George R. Hall (R)	17,835	(32%)
Glenn Mitchell (R)	6,870	(12%)
Christopher Roosa (R)	3,506	(6%)

District Vote For President

	1988	1984	1980	1976
D	53,686 (29%)	45,663 (26%)	63,102 (39%)	63,802 (46%)
R	126,873 (69%)	128,148 (73%)	93,868 (58%)	71,690 (51%)
I			2,386 (2%)	

Missouri

U.S. CONGRESS

SENATE 2 R
HOUSE 5 D, 4 R

LEGISLATURE

Senate 22 D, 12 R
House 105 D, 58 R

ELECTIONS

1988 Presidential Vote	
Bush	52%
Dukakis	48%
1984 Presidential Vote	
Reagan	60%
Mondale	40%
1980 Presidential Vote	
Reagan	51%
Carter	44%
Anderson	4%
Turnout rate in 1984	57%
Turnout rate in 1986	38%
Turnout rate in 1988	55%

(as percentage of voting age population)

POPULATION AND GROWTH

1980 population	4,916,686
1988 population estimate (15th in the nation)	5,141,000
Percent change 1980-1988	+5%

DEMOGRAPHIC BREAKDOWN

White	88%
Black	11%
Other	1%
(Spanish origin)	1%
Urban	68%
Rural	32%
Born in state	70%
Foreign-born	2%

MAJOR CITIES

Kansas City	441,170
St. Louis	426,300
Springfield	139,360
Independence	112,950
St. Joseph	74,070

AREA AND LAND USE

Area	68,945 sq. miles (18th)
Farm	66%
Forest	28%
Federally owned	5%

Gov. John Ashcroft (R)
Of Jefferson City — Elected 1984

Born: May 9, 1942, Chicago, Ill.
Education: Yale U., B.A. 1964; U. of Chicago, J.D. 1967.
Occupation: Professor; lawyer.
Religion: Assembly of God.
Political Career: Mo. auditor, 1973-75; Mo. attorney general, 1977-85; GOP nominee for U.S. House, 1972.
Next Election: 1992.

WORK

Occupations	
White-collar	51%
Blue-collar	31%
Service workers	14%
Government Workers	
Federal	66,860
State	77,881
Local	185,857

MONEY

Median family income	$ 18,784	(31st)
Tax burden per capita	$ 667	(46th)

EDUCATION

Spending per pupil through grade 12	$ 3,189	(36th)
Persons with college degrees	14%	(39th)

CRIME

Violent crime rate	545 per 100,000	(16th)

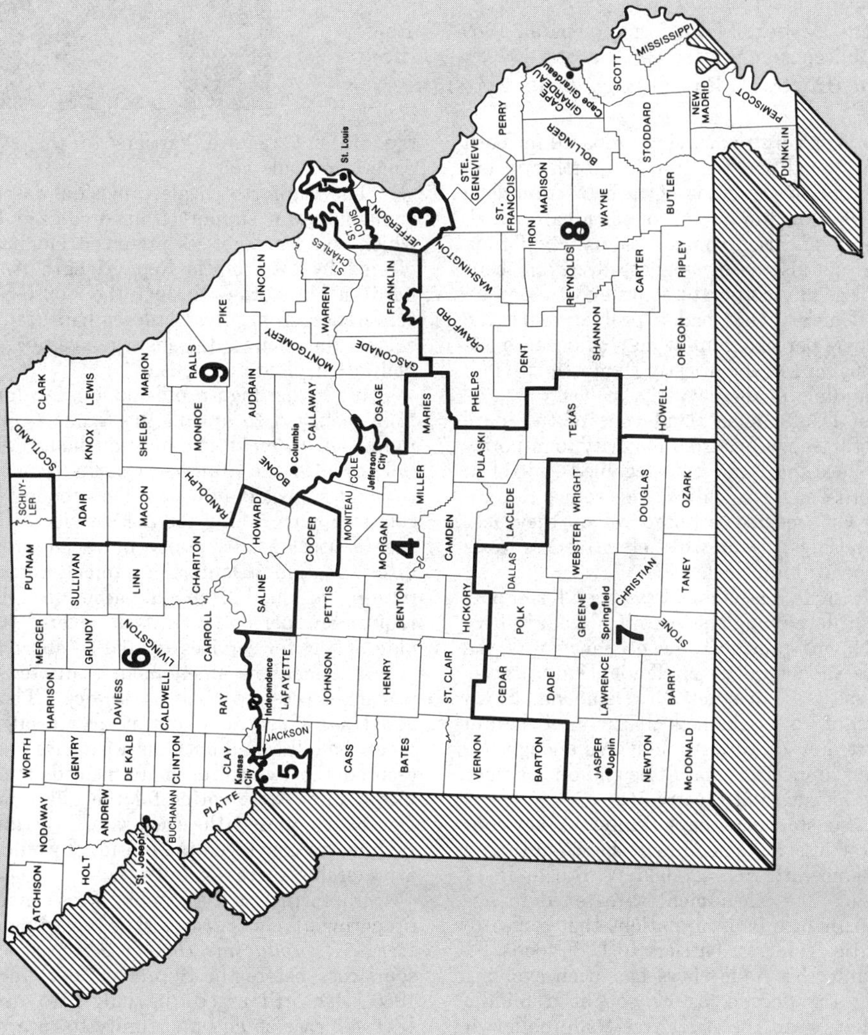
1
2
3
4
5
6
7
8
9
ATCHISON
NODAWAY
WORTH
HARRISON
MERCER
PUTNAM
SCHUY-LER
SCOTLAND
CLARK
HOLT
ANDREW
GENTRY
GRUNDY
SULLIVAN
ADAIR
KNOX
LEWIS
St. Joseph
BUCHANAN
DE KALB
DAVIESS
LIVINGSTON
LINN
MACON
SHELBY
MARION
CLINTON
CALDWELL
CARROLL
CHARITON
RANDOLPH
MONROE
RALLS
PIKE
PLATTE
CLAY
RAY
Kansas City
Independence
LAFAYETTE
SALINE
HOWARD
BOONE
Columbia
AUDRAIN
CALLAWAY
MONTGOMERY
LINCOLN
WARREN
ST. CHARLES
St. Louis
ST. LOUIS
JACKSON
CASS
JOHNSON
PETTIS
COOPER
MONITEAU
COLE
Jefferson City
OSAGE
GASCONADE
FRANKLIN
JEFFERSON
BATES
HENRY
BENTON
MORGAN
MILLER
MARIES
CRAWFORD
WASHINGTON
ST. FRANCOIS
STE. GENEVIEVE
PERRY
VERNON
ST. CLAIR
HICKORY
CAMDEN
PULASKI
PHELPS
DENT
IRON
MADISON
BOLLINGER
CAPE GIRARDEAU
Cape Girardeau
SCOTT
MISSISSIPPI
BARTON
CEDAR
POLK
DALLAS
LACLEDE
TEXAS
SHANNON
REYNOLDS
WAYNE
STODDARD
NEW MADRID
DADE
GREENE
Springfield
WEBSTER
WRIGHT
CARTER
BUTLER
JASPER
Joplin
LAWRENCE
CHRISTIAN
DOUGLAS
HOWELL
OREGON
RIPLEY
NEWTON
BARRY
STONE
TANEY
OZARK
McDONALD
DUNKLIN
PEMISCOT

John C. Danforth (R)

Of Newburg — Elected 1976

Born: Sept. 5, 1936, St. Louis, Mo.
Education: Princeton U., A.B. 1958; Yale U., B.D., LL.B. 1963.
Occupation: Lawyer; clergyman.
Family: Wife, Sally Dobson; five children.
Religion: Episcopalian.
Political Career: Mo. attorney general, 1969-77; Republican nominee for U.S. Senate, 1970.
Capitol Office: 249 Russell Bldg. 20510; 224-6154.

In Washington: Having prepared for both the priesthood and the law, Danforth still exhibits some of the ethos of each. At times, he seems consumed in pursuit of the greater good: famine relief, arms control, safety regulation. But he can also seem as sharp-eyed and contractual as any corporate attorney.

If Danforth has had a problem with the way others perceive him, it may be because the righteous tone of the priestly Danforth is sometimes audible in the lawyerly, as well.

Yet Danforth has made one of the more successful transitions from majority to minority status since the Democrats regained control in the 100th Congress. Unlike some senior Republicans who seemed eclipsed when they lost chairmanships, Danforth's effectiveness does not appear diminished.

The main reason may have been his importance in developing the omnibus trade bill of 1988. Having previously been chairman of the Finance Subcommittee on Trade, Danforth was the ideal GOP partner for Democrat Lloyd Bentsen of Texas, the new chairman of the full committee. And Danforth delivered enough Republican support in committee and on the floor to earn his share of the credit.

On substance, perhaps Danforth's key contribution was an amendment he co-authored with Democratic Sen. Donald W. Riegle Jr. of Michigan. The amendment threatened to impose tariffs or quotas on nations that refuse to dismantle their own barriers to U.S. goods.

Danforth's trade views had been evolving through the decade, as he sought a middle ground between the strict free-trade policy of the Reagan administration and the increasing appeal of protectionism. In the 97th Congress, he and Bentsen pressured the Japanese into voluntary agreements to restrain their car exports. In the 98th, they urged reciprocity without sanctions.

By 1985, though, Danforth was angry enough with the Japanese to call for sterner actions. Bitterly criticizing Japan's restrictive trade policies, he proposed a bill to require restraints on imports from Japan if that country did not remove barriers to the sale of American-made goods.

The Danforth-Riegle provision was tough enough to win support from organized labor, which could not get its preferred language — offered by Democratic Rep. Richard A. Gephardt of Missouri — through the House-Senate conference. Ironically, Danforth had been critical of the Gephardt language, calling it "a bellwether of protectionism."

In another high-profile action, Danforth in 1988 managed to amend the *Grove City* civil rights bill to make it "abortion neutral." The bill reversed the Supreme Court's *Grove City* ruling, which said an institution's federal funds could be cut off only for the activity in which the institution was guilty of racial or other discrimination. Danforth's amendment said nothing in the bill should either prohibit or require any person or entity it covered to provide or pay for services related to abortion.

In effect, the amendment restricted some women's access to abortion services. That angered some sponsors, but it also brought in votes the bill would not otherwise have had and assured the two-thirds margin needed to survive a veto. After voting for the bill, however, Danforth opposed the successful override. He said he was convinced the president would offer a preferable successor bill.

Danforth was also among those members preparing *amicus curiae* briefs regarding *Webster v. Reproductive Health Services,* a Missouri case before the Supreme Court in April 1989. Danforth urged the judges to use the *Webster* case as an opportunity to reverse the 1973 *Roe v. Wade* decision legalizing abortion.

Also in the 100th Congress, Danforth pressed hard for random drug testing of transportation workers. The provision was included in the Senate-passed anti-drug bill, but not in the final version that emerged from the House-Senate conference. Early in 1989, the Supreme Court ruled favorably on drug testing for safety and law-enforcement personnel. Danforth called it "the green light" for his reintroduced legislation.

Danforth supported his president and his party in the first controversy of the Bush administration, the rejection of former Sen. John Tower's nomination as secretary of defense. His primary argument was a defense of the president's right to choose whomever he wished. In 1987, Danforth had been an arch-advocate of ill-fated Supreme Court nominee Robert H. Bork. Danforth had studied under Bork at Yale law school, and he cast the jurist's confirmation as a fundamental moral question of the day.

Also in 1989, Danforth moved from the Budget Committee (which had never ranked high among his priorities) to the Select Committee on Intelligence. There he pledged himself to developing a new bipartisan consensus, a concept he had endorsed in working with the committee's chairman, Democrat David L. Boren of Oklahoma, even before joining the panel.

Overall, Danforth seemed to be bouncing back from the acutely personal disappointment he seemed to have suffered in the final act of the tax-reform drama in 1986. The problem was not that Danforth opposed the conference version of the tax-revision bill. He was one of 23 senators who voted "no," and few others offered as cogent and detailed a critique as Danforth's eloquent, all-afternoon speech before the final vote on the measure.

Nor, for that matter, would many senators necessarily have resented his switch from supporter to critic. In the Finance Committee, he was one of a small group who helped Chairman Bob Packwood put the bill together. But his ire arose after Packwood personally composed the final conference agreement with Rep. Dan Rostenkowski, chairman of the House Ways and Means Committee. Final provisions in the bill affected Missouri interests adversely — notably, a tax accounting change harmful to McDonnell Douglas and other major defense contractors in the state.

It was the manner in which Danforth both supported and opposed the bill that proved disturbing. In both cases, he took a strongly moralistic approach in criticizing anyone who disagreed with his views. Some of his colleagues suspected that Danforth was using a tone of righteous indignation to cover his pique at losing out on his home-state concerns. The essence of his argument was that the measure's combination of business tax increases with personal tax cuts would foster consumption at the expense of long-term investment in the economy.

Danforth has since introduced legislation to restore the credit for low-income housing investments. In this he has allied himself with another Finance Committee member who had misgivings about the 1986 reform, George J. Mitchell of Maine, now the majority leader.

Important as he has been on Finance, Danforth's first committee responsibility has been on Commerce. As chairman of the committee in the 99th Congress, he displayed a more positive attitude toward federal regulation than had Packwood, the previous chairman. Danforth strongly opposed, for example, Packwood's efforts in 1984 to loosen federal broadcasting laws that require radio and television stations to air contrasting views.

Danforth's reluctance to abandon regulation was most apparent on the issue of auto safety. Over the years, he had come into conflict with both the Reagan administration and the auto industry, both of which had tried to reduce federal regulation. He once accused a Reagan-appointed highway safety official of wanting to "search and destroy" auto safety.

Danforth made less progress, however, in his efforts to settle the contentious issue of product liability. After the Commerce panel deadlocked in 1985 over legislation to set federal standards for lawsuits on defective products, he proposed a compromise measure aimed at encouraging out-of-court settlements of liability claims. A key feature of his plan called for a $250,000 limit on awards for pain and suffering in cases in which the plaintiff rejected a pretrial offer from the defendant.

A sharply divided Commerce Committee approved Danforth's bill. But the bill did not reach the floor for months, and when it finally was called up, it fell victim to the threat of a filibuster. Danforth was, however, able to secure final passage of a bill making it easier for small businesses and non-profit institutions to join together to provide their own liability insurance.

Some of Danforth's legislative efforts reflect the humanitarian and moral ideals that led him into the ministry. Deeply concerned about world hunger, he helped win $150 million in emergency food aid for Africa after touring the drought-ravaged continent early in 1984. He also has been active in pushing the Reagan administration to step up the pace of nuclear arms reduction talks with the Soviet Union. "The possibility that a nuclear holocaust could occur has become the most important moral issue in human history," he has said.

At Home: A former Wall Street lawyer and Ralston-Purina heir hardly seems the type to represent a state whose political hero is Harry S. Truman, champion of the common folk. Moreover, Danforth's air of detachment strikes some as a sign of political vulnerability. Prior to his re-election in 1988, there was talk of his being ripe for the taking. But Danforth showed he had learned the lessons of his first re-election (which he won with just 51 percent). He raised millions of dollars early and made manifest to all his intent to fight for his job.

Partly because of Danforth's early effort, the Democrats failed to field a challenger in his weight class. Gephardt decided to run for president and popular six-term Democratic Rep. Ike Skelton decided to stay in the House. The party's top state official, Lt. Gov. Harriett Woods, decided to retire. Woods had given Danforth his scare in 1982, but she had also lost a bruising Senate race in 1986 to the GOP's former governor, Christopher S. Bond.

So the party turned to youthful state Sen. Jay Nixon, a 32-year-old in his first legislative term. Nixon struggled to raise a quarter of the money Danforth had at his disposal. He also struggled to find an effective theme. Danforth never had to run hard. He won all 114 counties, losing only in the city of St. Louis. His share was 68 percent, and he drew over a third of a million votes more than George Bush.

Danforth's patrician pedigree was no hindrance in his early political career; he won his first election in 1968 as an outsider, a young insurgent vowing to rid the state attorney general's office of deadwood that had collected during a succession of Democratic administrations.

But in 1982, after eight years in state office and six more in Washington, Danforth struck many Missouri voters not as a reformer but as a wealthy man distant from their economic concerns. That was why he was nearly ambushed by Woods, a clever liberal Democrat who sold herself as a populist under the slogan "Give 'em hell, Harriett."

Woods' entry had initially brought little cheer to party leaders. She had gained valuable media exposure representing a liberal St. Louis County constituency, but offered a record of questionable appeal to rural and conservative voters and to business interests the Democrats needed to compete with Danforth's fund raising. Woods also supported legalized abortion and the use of busing as a tool to desegregate schools.

But Woods managed to portray herself as an average working person and hit Danforth as an aristocrat who supported cuts in health care, social services and education. As the only female Democratic candidate for the Senate in 1982, her candidacy became a priority for women's groups.

Danforth's fund-raising advantage over Woods was more than 2-to-1. But his money and excellent organization were offset by Woods' most important asset: desire. Voters were impressed with her enthusiastic dawn-to-midnight campaigning, while Danforth gave the impression he was not really hungry to be reelected. More than once, he lamented that the campaign was making it difficult for him to watch the baseball playoffs (the St. Louis Cardinals were on their way to a World Series championship).

But Danforth's strategy changed abruptly Oct. 15, when the *St. Louis Globe-Democrat's* poll showed his comfortable lead of a month earlier had vanished. The incumbent went on the attack. He called Woods a liberal and a throwback to an era of discredited Democratic tax-and-spend practices. He accused her of demagoguery for portraying the Republican Party as a menace to Social Security without offering any constructive suggestions of her own. He brought up abortion and busing, topics he had avoided earlier in the campaign.

The shift to a negative campaign had the desired effect. Some conservative Democrats took a second look at Woods and lost their enthusiasm, and complacent Republicans were jolted into realizing that a high GOP turnout would be necessary to keep the seat.

Woods won where Democrats usually do in Missouri — St. Louis, Kansas City and the majority of rural counties — but in each of those areas, her liberalism cost her just enough votes to enable Danforth to escape.

Despite his 1982 struggle, however, Danforth still enjoys the reputation of being the founder of the modern-day Missouri GOP. Elected state attorney general in 1968 in his political debut, Danforth became the first Republican in 22 years to win statewide office. He lured bright young lawyers to the attorney general's office — among them Bond, who served two non-consecutive terms as governor before his 1986 election to the Senate — and John Ashcroft, who has been governor since Bond left that office in 1985. Danforth also developed a reputation as a protector of consumers and the environment.

In 1970 Danforth was the GOP's only hope to dislodge Democratic Sen. Stuart Symington, who was seeking a fourth term. In an expensive campaign that introduced Missouri to modern media-oriented politics, Danforth won 48 percent of the vote. Two years later, he returned as attorney general by over 450,000 votes, and awaited his next Senate chance.

It came, as expected, when Symington retired in 1976. Democrats appeared to seize the momentum by nominating U.S. Rep. Jerry Litton, described by a state political expert as "one of the most exciting political personalities to come along in years." But Democratic enthusiasm was tragically brief. Litton died in a primary-night plane crash, and Danforth was suddenly the favorite.

The state Democratic committee chose as its replacement former Gov. Warren Hearnes, whose courthouse-style administration had been the focus of Danforth's campaign attacks in 1968. Hearnes had finished a poor second to Litton in the primary. Against Litton, Danforth would have had a difficult contest; against Hearnes, he won easily.

Committees

Commerce, Science and Transportation (Ranking)
National Ocean Policy Study

Finance (4th of 9 Republicans)
International Trade (ranking); Medicare and Long-Term Care; Taxation and Debt Management

Select Intelligence (6th of 7 Republicans)

Elections

1988 General

John C. Danforth (R)	1,407,416	(68%)
Jay Nixon (D)	660,045	(32%)

Previous Winning Percentages: **1982** (51%) **1976** (57%)

Campaign Finance

	Receipts	Receipts from PACs	Expend-itures
1988			
Danforth (R)	$4,077,855	$1,149,207 (28%)	$3,992,995
Nixon (D)	$884,513	$241,231 (27%)	$880,160

Key Votes

1987

Enact omnibus highway bill over Reagan veto	Y
Limit testing of space-based anti-ballistic missiles	N
Oppose banning tests of larger nuclear weapons	N
Confirm Robert H. Bork as Supreme Court justice	Y

1988

Allow vote on campaign-finance overhaul	N
Pass civil rights restoration bill over Reagan veto	N
Enact omnibus trade bill over Reagan veto	Y
Approve death penalty for drug-related murders	N
Oppose "workfare" amendment to welfare overhaul bill	N

Voting Studies

	Presidential Support		Party Unity		Conservative Coalition	
Year	**S**	**O**	**S**	**O**	**S**	**O**
1988	75	23	65	28	76	22
1987	60	37	68	30	75	19
1986	80	20	77	21	82	17
1985	81	17	77	20	70	20
1984	86	13	85	15	83	17
1983	80	16	72	27	64	32
1982	71	19	72	21	76	18
1981	85	13	84	15	83	16

Interest Group Ratings

Year	ADA	ACU	AFL-CIO	CCUS
1988	20	72	42	71
1987	35	54	80	61
1986	30	57	33	61
1985	15	65	19	75
1984	35	68	27	63
1983	40	32	13	53
1982	40	50	23	52
1981	25	73	17	89

Christopher S. Bond (R)

Of Mexico — Elected 1986

Born: March 6, 1939, St. Louis, Mo.
Education: Princeton U., A.B. 1960; U. of Virginia Law School, LL.B. 1963.
Occupation: Lawyer.
Family: Wife, Carolyn Reid; one child.
Religion: Presbyterian.
Political Career: Mo. assistant attorney general, 1969-70; Mo. state auditor, 1971-73; governor, 1973-77, 1981-85; GOP nominee for U.S. House, 1968; GOP nominee for governor, 1976.
Capital Office: 293 Russell Bldg. 20510; 224-5721.

In Washington: Like other former governors, Bond has had a little trouble adjusting to life among the Senate's competing egos. But unlike some others, he has taken a low-key approach to the adjustment. He willingly cut a modest figure in his first Congress, finding his way gradually, choosing his shots with care.

"The senators who have done well here are the ones who've let their ears do the work, rather than their mouths," Bond told the *St. Louis Post-Dispatch.*

Showing no haste, Bond hired a youthful staff (one Missouri newspaper calculated the average age at 28) and set to mastering his down-to-earth committee assignments: Agriculture, Banking, Budget and Small Business.

Having tweaked the Reagan administration in his 1986 campaign for being "too slow to respond" to the farm crisis, Bond found himself on the spot as one of four freshmen — and the only first-term Republican — on the Agriculture Committee. But the committee's influx of aggressive Democrats, all eager to wield their new majority power, kept Bond from making many headlines. He introduced a bill with GOP colleague Rudy Boschwitz of Minnesota to restructure and finance the Farm Credit System. But their efforts were subsumed in those of others. Bond's other early bills tended toward the dull but doable — improving meat and fowl inspection, providing flood relief, reducing farmers' paperwork.

His first moment of high drama came when President Reagan vetoed the highway authorization bill early in 1987. Thirteen Republicans voted to override, but Bond was the only freshman. Reagan had campaigned for Bond three times in 1986 and was presumed to have some leverage. He reportedly made a 30-minute phone call to discuss the vote. Later, he came to the Capitol to meet with the 13 and singled Bond out. Yet the freshman stood firm.

Standing with him was his Missouri GOP colleague, John C. Danforth, who called the highway bill "a grand slam for Missouri" (it included $60 million for projects in the state). Bond also concurred with Danforth on the *Grove City* civil rights restoration bill. Both voted for it, and when Reagan vetoed it, both voted to sustain the veto. But the two do not move in lock step. On the highway bill, they split on the 65 mph speed limit (Bond for, Danforth against).

Although he is generally a chamber of commerce conservative, Bond's vote is not always easy to predict. Most would place him to the right of Danforth, but an ideologue he is not. He supported military aid to the contras, but described the decision as "a close call." On Banking, he supported measures granting faster access to deposited funds and greater disclosure of credit card terms, both of which were resisted by the financial community.

One consistent motivation for Bond is his deference to the states. This often aligns him with other former governors, including Democrats such as David L. Boren of Oklahoma, Bob Graham of Florida and Terry Sanford of North Carolina, who favor regulatory decision making by states. When the Banking Committee mulled banks' right to sell insurance, and when Agriculture debated who would distribute rural development grants, Bond spoke up for letting each state decide. When Banking took up an anti-takeover bill in 1987, Bond sided with the more moderate Republicans who preferred to empower each state to set limits on takeovers.

At Home: Missouri is unique in having two senators who not only attended the same private out-of-state university but studied there at the same time. Like Danforth, Bond is a product of a wealthy family who attended Princeton in the 1950s and then earned a law degree from an exclusive law school. In Bond's case, the family money came from making bricks. At law school, he was class valedictorian.

Through most of Missouri's history, such well-heeled Republicans have stood little chance of statewide office. But the 1960s brought a political sea change in this border state. Danforth was elected attorney general in 1968 and has been in statewide office ever since. Bond went to work for Danforth, and just four years later, at age 33, became governor.

In 1986, Bond was one of the few Republican success stories in a Senate election year fraught with disaster for the GOP. He overcame an aggressive, well-known challenger and the rumblings of farm protest to win the seat vacated by retiring Democrat Thomas F. Eagleton. (He was the only Republican to capture an open Democratic seat in 1986.)

His contest with Lt. Gov. Harriett Woods was a bitter one. Bond offered himself as a budget-conscious conservative, citing his two-term gubernatorial record of avoiding major tax increases. He painted Woods as a liberal with values out of synch with most Missourians.

Woods portrayed herself as a scrappy Truman-style populist, a strategy she had used in nearly upsetting Danforth in 1982. She called Bond a passive governor, an aloof aristocrat and a likely rubber stamp for Reagan.

Woods' campaign foundered, however, when she ran a TV ad depicting a weeping farmer describing how he was foreclosed by a company on whose board Bond served. The ad provoked a firestorm of controversy, as Republicans and editorialists branded it a crass attempt to put farm troubles to political use. The ad damaged Woods' attempts to win conservative rural Democrats.

Bond, too, had past problems with members of his own party. Many conservatives remembered his support of Gerald R. Ford over Ronald Reagan at the 1976 national GOP convention, and never really considered him one of their own. But any lingering doubts they might have had about Bond were drowned out by their antipathy toward Woods. Bond lost in St. Louis and Kansas City, but buoyed by good showings in the suburbs of both cities, and in most rural areas, he won with 53 percent. He had outspent Woods by about $900,000 and campaigned despite physical pain. Early in 1987, he underwent surgery to remove bone spurs in his neck.

Bond broke into politics in 1968, seeking a seat in the U.S. House from northeastern Missouri. Although he lost, it was the year the modern GOP in Missouri was born. Richard M. Nixon carried the state and Danforth was elected attorney general. Bond took a job with Danforth and in 1970 won the office of state auditor. Two years later, he was elected the state's first GOP governor since World War II.

He had a troubled first term. Democrats in the Legislature found him aloof and inaccessible; Republicans chafed at his efforts to abolish patronage jobs. In 1976, he lost to Democrat Joseph P. Teasdale. But he avenged this loss in 1980, riding Reagan's popularity atop the ticket and exploiting Teasdale's image as an incompetent administrator. In his second term, Bond warmed up to the Legislature and generally won points for being more accessible.

Committees

Agriculture, Nutrition and Forestry (7th of 9 Republicans)
Conservation and Forestry (ranking); Agricultural Research and General Legislation; Domestic and Foreign Marketing and Product Promotion

Banking, Housing and Urban Affairs (5th of 9 Republicans)
Consumer and Regulatory Affairs (ranking); International Finance and Monetary Policy

Budget (10th of 10 Republicans)

Small Business (5th of 9 Republicans)
Export Expansion; Rural Economy and Family Farming

Elections

1986 General		
Christopher S. Bond (R)	777,612	(53%)
Harriett Woods (D)	699,624	(47%)
1986 Primary		
Christopher S. Bond (R)	239,961	(89%)
Richard J. Gimpelson (R)	10,471	(4%)
David Andrew Brown (R)	10,407	(4%)
Joyce Padgett Lea (R)	9,022	(3%)

Campaign Finance

	Receipts	Receipts from PACs	Expend-itures
1986			
Bond (R)	$5,464,030	$1,320,353 (24%)	$5,396,255
Woods (D)	$4,380,643	$761,339 (17%)	$4,377,661

Key Votes

1987	
Enact omnibus highway bill over Reagan veto	Y
Limit testing of space-based anti-ballistic missiles	N
Oppose banning tests of larger nuclear weapons	Y
Confirm Robert H. Bork as Supreme Court justice	Y
1988	
Allow vote on campaign-finance overhaul	N
Pass civil rights restoration bill over Reagan veto	N
Enact omnibus trade bill over Reagan veto	Y
Approve death penalty for drug-related murders	Y
Oppose "workfare" amendment to welfare overhaul bill	N

Voting Studies

	Presidential Support		Party Unity		Conservative Coalition	
Year	**S**	**O**	**S**	**O**	**S**	**O**
1988	75	20	73	19	89	8
1987	64	23	86	11	94	0

Interest Group Ratings

Year	ADA	ACU	AFL-CIO	CCUS
1988	0	88	23	86
1987	10	81	25	82

1 William L. Clay (D)

Of St. Louis — Elected 1968

Born: April 30, 1931, St. Louis, Mo.
Education: St. Louis U., B.S. 1953.
Military Career: Army, 1953-55.
Occupation: Real-estate salesman; insurance executive.
Family: Wife, Carol Ann Johnson; three children.
Religion: Roman Catholic.
Political Career: St. Louis Board of Aldermen, 1959-64; St. Louis Democratic committeeman, 1964-67.
Capitol Office: 2470 Rayburn Bldg. 20515; 225-2406.

In Washington: Redistricting after the 1980 census shifted Clay's district from two-thirds black to one where blue-collar whites hold considerable sway. In the years since, Clay has gradually traded in his role as an angry black activist for that of a seasoned labor advocate. And as he enters his third decade in the House, he shares the credit with his labor allies for a number of significant accomplishments.

Clay is the voice of unions both on the Post Office and Civil Service Committee and on Education and Labor, where he serves as chairman of the Labor-Management Relations Subcommittee. Most of his efforts fizzled in the early 1980s, as labor's lobbying effectiveness waned and labor-backed initiatives met with strong opposition from the newly installed Reagan administration. But during the last two Congresses, Clay slowly chipped away at his ambitious agenda, and enacted several major pieces of legislation.

He was a primary House sponsor of the plant-closing notification bill that finally won approval in 1988. Three years earlier, Clay had fallen five votes short of passing a similar bill in the House. Introduced by Clay and Post Office Committee Chairman William D. Ford of Michigan, the original bill required any business planning to close a plant to give employees 90 days' notice of its intentions. It also required companies to consult with workers over their decision. In 1986, Clay and Ford withdrew the bill after the House accepted an amendment eliminating the consultation process.

By 1988, a number of things had changed. With President Reagan's tenure drawing to a close, the political climate was more favorable for pro-labor legislation; the notification idea had gained heavyweight backing in the Senate; and supporters of the measure proved willing to compromise to steer around presidential opposition.

Clay won committee approval of a bill much like the 1985 version, but the Senate was unwilling to go that far. When the measure was finally attached to the trade bill, the notice provision was scaled back to 60 days and the consultation language dropped. Still, the measure provoked a veto from Reagan. But when a separate notification bill then passed both chambers by lopsided margins, Reagan allowed it to become law without his signature.

Protecting workers' pensions is a top priority for Clay. In the 99th Congress, he was co-author, with Republican Sen. John Heinz of Pennsylvania, of the pension law provisions that were included in the Tax Reform Act of 1986. Those provisions were expected to result in new coverage for an estimated 2 million workers, and to shorten the eligibility period (vesting period) for others to five years on the job, rather than 10 under previous law.

The pension revisions were originally proposed in 1985 as separate legislation. Clay did not attempt to get them attached to the tax-overhaul bill being considered that year by the House Ways and Means Committee because he and Heinz were still refining their proposal. But in 1986, Heinz got the pension provisions included in the Senate's version of the new tax bill, and they were retained in conference.

In the 100th Congress, Clay was a leading advocate of legislation that made sweeping changes in the nation's pension protection law, the Employee Retirement Income Security Act (ERISA). Clay's effort was spurred on by the plight of workers in troubled industries that were sidestepping promised pension benefits, and by the soaring deficits of the Pension Benefit Guaranty Corporation (PBGC).

Eventually attached to the 1987 budget reconciliation, the bill required faster funding by employers of currently underfunded pension plans, and it sought to discourage companies from terminating overfunded plans to get at the surplus assets for other purposes.

In each of the last two Congresses, Clay has won House approval of legislation aimed at barring a construction industry strategy to circumvent labor laws, but the measure has never survived in the Senate.

Under the practice, known as "double breasting," unionized construction companies that want to hire non-union labor form non-

Missouri 1

North St. Louis; Northeast St. Louis County

Eero Saarinen's Gateway Arch, despite its modern design, serves as a symbolic reminder of the old St. Louis — a strategically located threshold to the West luring enough steamship, railroad and manufacturing trade to make it one of the nation's leading commercial centers.

But the city's postwar story is one of retreat rather than advance. Blacks and whites alike have fled once-great St. Louis — the well-off to distant suburbia and the less affluent to neighborhoods just outside the borders. Numerous factories and businesses have closed; parts of the downtown area have declined to an extent that shocks even those visitors accustomed to inner-city blight. An ambitious program of renovating historic buildings in the city is under way, but much work remains before St. Louis' image is restored.

Reflecting the exodus from the city, the 1st District lost over one-quarter of its people during the 1970s, more than any other Missouri district. In order to survive for the 1980s, the district had to be stretched south to pick up urban territory, and west and north into the suburbs of St. Louis County. More than half of the district's residents live outside the city limits.

Although suburban communities such as University City are among the most liberal in Missouri, much of the St. Louis County territory is populated with working-class conservatives who find jobs in the auto assembly and aerospace manufacturing facilities ringing the city. In predominantly white communities such as Ferguson, Bellefontaine Neighbors and Jennings, the blue-collar voters are fiercely opposed to abortion and busing. Republicans often win here in statewide elections.

But GOP sentiments are drowned in a tide of Democratic votes from the city portion of the 1st. Most of the district's blacks — who make up 52 percent of the 1st's population — live within the city limits, north of Interstate 44. The poverty of the Near North and Near South sides contrasts with parts of the West End, where some of the city's remaining white-collar professionals live. In 1988, the 1st gave Michael S. Dukakis an overwhelming 72 percent of its presidential vote.

Although St. Louis' manufacturing economy today is overshadowed by the plants outside its limits, the 1st District is not without an industrial presence. Ralston-Purina, the cereal company to which Missouri Republican Sen. John C. Danforth is heir, is headquartered here, and a corridor of light manufacturing is located toward the city's northern end.

Population: 546,208. White 259,259 (48%), Black 281,529 (52%), Other 3,383 (1%). Spanish origin 4,923 (1%). 18 and over 393,146 (72%), 65 and over 74,588 (14%). Median age: 30.

unionized subsidiaries to carry out work. Clay's bill required that multiple construction companies be considered as a single employer if there was evidence of common control. That would make the non-unionized company subject to the collective bargaining agreements affecting the parent company.

"Double-breasting, by freeing one party from its bargaining commitments, distorts the bargaining process and denies workers a voice in the determination of their working conditions," Clay said when the House debated the bill in 1987. Though the proposal won committee approval in the Senate that year, it never reached the floor.

Clay has been similarly frustrated in his efforts to win approval for "family leave" legislation, which would require most employers to allow unpaid, job-protected leave to a worker upon the birth or adoption of a child, or to care for an ailing family member. Clay is one of the original sponsors of the bill, which appeared to gain momentum in 1988, only to fall victim to end-of-the-session politicking in the Senate.

For the third Congress in a row, Clay took up the cause in 1989, saying, "It's not fair to ask a man or woman to choose between their job or caring for a newborn baby."

Another long and frustrating battle for Clay is his effort to revise the Hatch Act, which restricts political activity by government workers. He came close to obtaining the modifications sought by federal employee unions in 1975, when Congress passed his Hatch Act bill but failed to override President Ford's veto. He has introduced legislation to reform the act in each Congress since.

In 1987, again facing the threat of a presidential veto, Clay spent months trying to arrive at an acceptable modification of the Hatch Act. The compromise bill would have allowed federal employees to use their off-duty hours to run for office, manage campaigns and solicit funds. At the same time, the measure would have tightened restrictions on political activities during the day and strengthened protections from coercion by superiors. It was a moment of victory for Clay when the House passed the measure, but the reforms never made it out of the Senate.

Successful or not, these serious legislative endeavors have allowed Clay to move beyond his early bellicose reputation. While he still rarely pulls a punch, the comments of the late 1980s are tame compared with his earlier days in the House. He once referred to President Nixon's vice president as "Zero" Agnew. Early in the Reagan administration, he often implied that racism motivated its efforts to cut the domestic budget, modify civil rights laws and avoid sanctions against the white-minority government of South Africa.

In the 98th Congress, Clay spoke out against Reagan's attempt to establish a subminimum wage for teenagers, saying employers would fire older workers in order to save money with the lower wage. To address the problem of youth unemployment, he said, "the Reagan administration proposes to provide relief for McDonald's and Burger King." In 1983, he said the "War on Poverty" had become the "war on the poverty-stricken," with the rich making out "like fat hogs at a full trough."

Assailing provisions of the 1986 anti-drug bill that applied the death penalty to certain drug crimes, Clay called capital punishment immoral. "Not one rich person has ever gone to the gallows," Clay said. "Only poor whites and minorities are forced to walk the last mile and choose a last supper."

In 1988, his opposition to the death penalty amendment to the drug bill remained, but his rhetoric toned down. "Official violence is not the answer to unofficial violence," he said.

During an earlier period in his House career, Clay's harshest rhetoric was aimed at the House ethics committee. In 1980, when the committee recommended censure of his close friend and Postal Operations Subcommittee ally, Charles H. Wilson of California, he called the panel a "kangaroo court" that was "perverted" and "devoid of fairness, justice and equity."

He spoke equally sharply of the press, referring to reporters as "bloodthirsty scribes ... awaiting the carnage."

Clay himself was the source of some controversy over ethics issues in the 1970s. He was accused at one point of billing the House for trips home he did not take. His administrative assistant went to jail in 1976 for fraudulently placing a sister-in-law on the federal payroll. The Justice Department spent months scrutinizing Clay's tax returns and campaign finances. But no charges were ever filed against him. He settled the House travel account by repaying some of the money, saying there had been a bookkeeping error. When the Justice Department dropped its probe, Clay charged that it had been politically motivated.

At Home: For someone who has spent the better part of the last 20 years in Washington, Clay remains unusually active in local politics. He occasionally uses his congressional mailing privileges to advise constituents of his views on local matters, as he did in a 1987 letter criticizing two tax proposals backed by St. Louis Mayor Vincent C. Schoemehl Jr.

Though both measures passed, Clay won a 1986 round against Schoemehl, when he opposed the mayor's decision to turn control of a city-run health care facility over to a private, non-profit corporation. The dispute prompted Schoemehl to field a slate of candidates to challenge Clay-backed contenders for city offices in the Democratic primary. Clay's slate swept Schoemehl's in the primary.

Clay's career has thrived on confrontation. His own campaign literature once noted that he had been "arrested, convicted of contempt of court [and] served 110 days in jail" for demonstrating at a St. Louis bank.

That incident took place years before his election to the House in 1968. But it was one of a string of such confrontations that gave him a reputation as a civil rights activist and built his political career. In 1954, while going through military training at Fort McClellan in Alabama, Clay found the post swimming pool and barber shop closed to blacks, and the NCO club off limits when there were white women present. He led blacks to swim en masse in the pool, boycott haircuts and picket the club.

After returning to St. Louis, Clay became active in the NAACP and CORE. He was elected to the city's Board of Aldermen in 1959 and became an official in the politically active Pipefitters union in 1966. While keeping his identification as a civil rights militant, he moved closer over the years to the patronage politics of the local Democratic Party.

Redistricting by the Missouri Legislature in 1967 placed most of St. Louis' 257,000 blacks in the 1st District, ending years of fragmentation of the black vote. Democrat Frank M. Karsten, the 1st District representative for 22 years, decided to retire rather than seek reelection in 1968.

With the backing of most local black leaders, Clay emerged from a racially divided four-way primary with a 48 percent plurality. In the general election, he ran on a platform geared to the district's 55 percent black majority. He called for more federal money for jobs, housing, health and education, and for changes in police agencies and the court system to eliminate bias against blacks. The Republican candidate, also black, was Curtis C. Crawford, former director of the local legal aid society. Crawford suggested that Clay's talent was militant protest, not lawmaking. But the district was too strongly Democratic for Crawford to be a serious threat. Clay won 64 percent to become Missouri's first black congressman.

From 1970 through 1980, Clay encountered no strong challengers. Though Republican candidates usually held him even in the predominantly white St. Louis County portion of the district, Clay regularly coasted to re-election by taking 80 percent or more in heavily black North St. Louis.

But as Clay extended his tenure in the House, the population in his district dwindled steadily. The 1st lost one-quarter of its people during the 1970s, and redistricting in 1981 gave Clay nearly 200,000 new constituents, many of them blue-collar workers in largely white sections of St. Louis County. In Clay's old district, two-thirds of the population was black; in the redrawn 1st, blacks barely formed a majority, and more whites than blacks were registered to vote.

A sizable number of Clay's new constituents fiercely objected to his support for abortion and for busing of students to integrate schools. Anti-Clay Democrats coalesced behind a white candidate, state Sen. Al Mueller, an opponent of abortion and busing. Mueller also chided the incumbent for missing roll-call votes, for wasting taxpayers' money on foreign junkets and for billing the government for hotel expenses when he visits St. Louis.

Clay ridiculed his primary opponent as a parochial haggler over trivial matters such as attendance and foreign travel. Saying he could not afford to keep houses in Washington and St. Louis, Clay brushed off the charges about his hotel stays, a practice he continues to this day. Maintaining that his stands on abortion and busing were consonant with current laws and court rulings, Clay also criticized his opponent for ignoring important national problems, such as unemployment and cutbacks in federal aid to the disadvantaged.

In a year when working-class voters of both races were preoccupied with economic troubles, Clay's visible role as a quotable foe of Reaganomics was well received. He won endorsements from union leaders and contributions of money and services from labor groups. To Mueller's dismay, Clay's foreign travel was overlooked by voters as a forgivable peccadillo.

A little more than half the primary vote was cast in the St. Louis County portion of the district. Mueller won there by more than 11,000 votes, not as wide a margin as he had hoped. He was crushed by an overwhelming vote for Clay from the city of St. Louis, where the incumbent took 83 percent of the ballots cast.

Clay has not been threatened seriously since. His 72 percent tally in November 1988 was his biggest since 1970. Clay is reported to have an interest in someday passing the seat along to his son, state Rep. William L. Clay Jr.

Committees

Education and Labor (4th of 22 Democrats)
Labor-Management Relations (chairman); Labor Standards

House Administration (8th of 13 Democrats)
Libraries and Memorials (chairman); Elections

Post Office and Civil Service (2nd of 15 Democrats)
Investigations; Postal Operations and Services

Joint Library

Elections

1988 General		
William L. Clay (D)	140,751	(72%)
Joseph A. Schwan (R)	53,109	(27%)
1986 General		
William L. Clay (D)	91,044	(66%)
Robert J. Wittmann (R)	46,599	(34%)

Previous Winning Percentages:				**1984**	(68%)	**1982**	(66%)
1980	(70%)	**1978**	(67%)	**1976**	(66%)	**1974**	(68%)
1972	(64%)	**1970**	(91%)	**1968**	(64%)		

District Vote For President

	1988		1984		1980		1976	
D	143,802	(72%)	140,858	(65%)	142,545	(65%)	116,330	(56%)
R	54,578	(27%)	74,447	(35%)	68,196	(31%)	82,828	(40%)
I					8,546	(4%)		

Campaign Finance

	Receipts	Receipts from PACs	Expend-itures
1988			
Clay (D)	$204,094	$141,830 (69%)	$159,700
1986			
Clay (D)	$204,437	$141,457 (69%)	$191,113
Wittman (R)	$29,050	$140 (0.4%)	$28,414

Key Votes

1987	
Raise speed limit to 65 mph	N
Approve Gephardt "fair trade" amendment	Y
Ban testing of larger nuclear weapons	Y
Delay "re-flagging" of Kuwaiti tankers	Y
Approve tax-raising deficit-reduction bill	Y
1988	
Approve aid to Nicaraguan contras	N
Enact civil rights restoration bill over Reagan veto	Y
Kill 60-day plant-closing notification measure	?
Pass omnibus trade bill over Reagan veto	Y
Approve death penalty for drug-related murders	N
Bar federal funds for abortions in cases of rape and incest	N
Oppose seven-day waiting period for purchase of handguns	N

Voting Studies

	Presidential Support		Party Unity		Conservative Coalition	
Year	**S**	**O**	**S**	**O**	**S**	**O**
1988	12	67	68	12	0	82
1987	11	74	72	12	2	91
1986	8	78	71	11	2	74
1985	15	80	73	18	4	91
1984	19	65	83	3	2	92
1983	9	80	83	2	2	85
1982	19	43	74	5	3	67
1981	22	68	86	2	4	89

Interest Group Ratings

Year	ADA	ACU	AFL-CIO	CCUS
1988	90	0	100	18
1987	92	0	100	0
1986	75	0	100	15
1985	100	5	100	24
1984	95	5	100	33
1983	90	0	100	17
1982	65	13	100	29
1981	95	0	87	0

2 Jack Buechner (R)

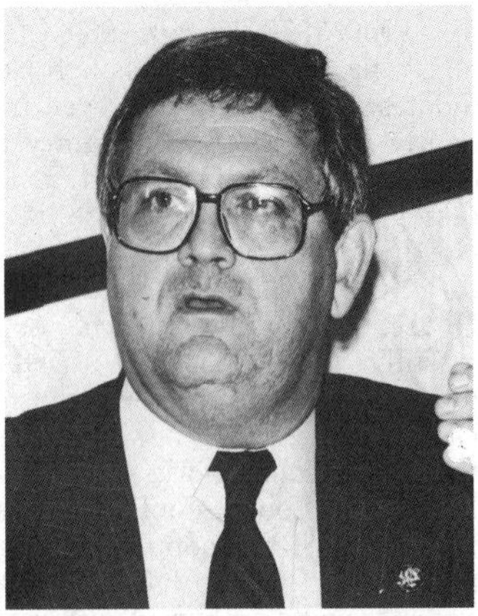

Of Kirkwood — Elected 1986

Born: June 6, 1940, St. Louis, Mo.
Education: Benedictine College, B.A. 1962; St. Louis U., J.D. 1965.
Occupation: Lawyer; real-estate developer.
Family: Wife, Marietta Coon; two children.
Religion: Roman Catholic.
Political Career: Mo. House, 1973-83; Republican nominee for U.S. House, 1984.
Capitol Office: 502 Cannon Bldg. 20515; 225-2561.

In Washington: Buechner spent much of his first term surrounded by quotation marks. Few in his class, or in the entire House, are as skilled at turning a witty phrase, and many Washington journalists have found Buechner an engaging interview. He is not just a joker, however. Many of his quips concern a subject he takes very seriously, the budget deficit.

Most politicians pose as foes of excessive federal spending, but on the Budget Committee, Buechner has delivered his views in uniquely catchy fashion. He predicted the budget process would be "a conspiracy of ostriches" under the 1987 two-year "summit" agreement between congressional leaders and the White House that aimed to reduce the deficit by $76 billion.

At another point he offered a colorful description of deficit politics: "Reducing the deficit is a very broad goal, such as getting into heaven.... Trouble is, everybody wants to get to heaven, but nobody wants to die."

Early in his first term, Buechner sought to live up to his anti-pork campaign promises, supporting presidential vetoes of a highway bill and a clean-water bill, both of which contained money for the St. Louis area. Both votes brought Buechner some criticism at home, but did not cost him significant support in his suburban and mostly Republican constituency.

Science is Buechner's other assignment. There, too, he voices fiscal concerns and speaks when he smells pork. But he also supports spending on space projects, such as a space station.

Buechner sounds like a staunch conservative much of the time, and he voted with his party 82 percent of the time in 1988 — more than the average Republican. But his political history contains streaks of moderation. In the Missouri Legislature, Buechner was known for his efforts to promote legal protection for battered women and for pushing the Equal Rights Amendment. He once engaged in a public debate over the ERA with conservative activist Phyllis Schlafly. He also once opposed as political grandstanding a proposal to recite the Pledge of Allegiance in the legislative chamber. Yet in 1988 he supported a Republican-backed measure to get the U.S. House to recite the pledge.

At Home: Buechner has confounded expectations in each of his three campaigns for Congress.

Challenging Democratic Rep. Robert A. Young amid the 1984 Reagan landslide, Buechner was rated highly. On election night, early returns were so strongly in his favor that two networks declared him the winner. They were wrong.

Two years later, he was expected to have a tougher time. President Reagan was not at the top of the ticket, and Young had heard the warning shot. But Buechner won a solid victory, becoming the only GOP challenger to defeat a Democratic House incumbent in 1986.

Given that distinction, Buechner could count on being targeted in 1988 by the national Democratic strategists. He was, but he turned the race into a runaway.

With typical wit, Buechner said after his 1984 loss that the networks had not been wrong, just premature by two years. He set out to correct some of the deficiencies of his first campaign. "I lost the election last time by $50,000, not 11,000 votes," he told one reporter.

While beefing up his organization and fund raising, Buechner strengthened his appeal among conservative voters, who had been alienated by his reputation in the Legislature. Stressing his fiscal conservatism, he called for a line-item presidential veto and derided Young, a lifetime pipefitters' union member, as a labor lackey. Buechner also hit Young for his "pork-barrel game of bringing home the bacon."

Young shrugged off Buechner's criticism, saying that "it's the political process in action. If that's a fault, I stand guilty." But perhaps the most important element of Buechner's victory was the turnout in the heavily GOP southern half of the 2nd, where voters came to the polls in droves to oppose liberal Lt. Gov. Harriett Woods' Senate bid.

In 1988, Democrats nominated Robert H. Feigenbaum, a 16-year veteran of the Missouri Legislature. But he found no cutting issue against Buechner, who won 2-to-1.

Missouri 2

Western St. Louis County

Anchored in the suburbs west and northwest of St. Louis, the 2nd holds many of the manufacturing and assembly plants that overshadow the remaining industrial activity within the city. McDonnell Douglas, Chrysler, Emerson Electric, Ford and Monsanto are among the district's major employers.

Employees of these companies — and of St. Louis' Lambert International Airport also located here — lend a blue-collar flavor to the eastern half of the 2nd. But more and more, the character of the 2nd is being defined by the white-collar communities in the western part of the district — suburbs such as Ladue and Chesterfield, which are populated by affluent business and banking executives.

Separate from the city of St. Louis since 1876, St. Louis County includes nearly 90 percent of the 2nd's population. The county has steadily filled up with St. Louisans taking refuge from the declining urban center.

Also included in the 2nd is a small chunk of politically marginal eastern St. Charles County. Located just across the Missouri River from St. Louis County is the city of St. Charles, a community of 42,000 that served briefly as Missouri's capital in the 19th century.

From 1951 until he ran for the Senate in 1968, GOP Rep. Thomas B. Curtis held this district. Even during the time that Democrats James Symington and Robert A. Young occupied the 2nd, it favored Republicans in most other contests. Propelled by strong showings in St. Louis County, Republican presidential candidates amassed comfortable margins districtwide in the past four elections. The GOP enjoys similar successes in statewide races.

The 2nd is heavily Catholic territory, and a stand opposing abortion is a valuable asset to politicians seeking to make a favorable impression here. The 2nd also takes in a significant Jewish community.

Population: 546,039. White 509,598 (93%), Black 29,094 (5%), Other 5,631 (1%). Spanish origin 4,646 (1%). 18 and over 386,511 (71%), 65 and over 46,702 (9%). Median age: 31.

Committees

Budget (8th of 14 Republicans)
Task Force: Budget Process, Reconciliation and Enforcement (ranking)

Science, Space and Technology (14th of 19 Republicans)
Science, Research and Technology; Space Science and Applications

Elections

1988 General		
Jack Buechner (R)	186,450	(66%)
Robert H. Feigenbaum (D)	91,645	(33%)
1986 General		
Jack Buechner (R)	101,010	(52%)
Robert A. Young (D)	93,538	(48%)

District Vote For President

	1988	1984	1980	1976
D	111,170 (39%)	87,719 (31%)	93,845 (37%)	97,561 (44%)
R	173,201 (61%)	190,521 (69%)	153,176 (60%)	120,324 (54%)
I			5,216 (2%)	

Campaign Finance

	Receipts	Receipts from PACs	Expend-itures
1988			
Buechner (R)	$721,239	$280,111 (39%)	$693,066
Feigenbaum (D)	$255,142	$106,882 (42%)	$254,492
1986			
Buechner (R)	$326,579	$73,652 (23%)	$326,375
Young (D)	$501,614	$284,160 (57%)	$528,101

Key Votes

1987	
Raise speed limit to 65 mph	Y
Approve Gephardt "fair trade" amendment	N
Ban testing of larger nuclear weapons	Y
Delay "re-flagging" of Kuwaiti tankers	N
Approve tax-raising deficit-reduction bill	N
1988	
Approve aid to Nicaraguan contras	Y
Enact civil rights restoration bill over Reagan veto	N
Kill 60-day plant-closing notification measure	Y
Pass omnibus trade bill over Reagan veto	N
Approve death penalty for drug-related murders	Y
Bar federal funds for abortions in cases of rape and incest	Y
Oppose seven-day waiting period for purchase of handguns	Y

Voting Studies

	Presidential Support		Party Unity		Conservative Coalition	
Year	**S**	**O**	**S**	**O**	**S**	**O**
1988	57	40	82	13	97	0
1987	64	31	83	11	84	14

Interest Group Ratings

Year	ADA	ACU	AFL-CIO	CCUS
1988	15	88	31	79
1987	12	86	6	100

3 Richard A. Gephardt (D)

Of St. Louis — Elected 1976

Born: Jan. 31, 1941, St. Louis, Mo.
Education: Northwestern U., B.S. 1962; U. of Michigan, J.D. 1965.
Military Career: Air National Guard, 1965-71.
Occupation: Lawyer.
Family: Wife, Jane Ann Byrnes; three children.
Religion: Baptist.
Political Career: St. Louis Board of Aldermen, 1971-76; sought Democratic nomination for president, 1988.
Capitol Office: 1432 Longworth Bldg. 20515; 225-2671.

In Washington: Gephardt has shown an intriguing ability to stand apart from the political establishment to which he belongs. Despite his past role as Democratic Caucus chairman and institutional leader, he mounted a 1988 presidential campaign centered on an anti-establishment theme: "It's your fight, too." Rejoining the House leadership track in 1989 and becoming majority leader, he has come full circle — an insider turned outsider, turned inside-out.

Before ethics controversies undermined the careers of Speaker Jim Wright and Democratic Whip Tony Coelho, Gephardt's political purpose seemed a bit fuzzy. He had given up his place on the leadership ladder to seek the White House in 1988, then abandoned that attempt and sought re-election to the House. Many believed he would try to use the House as a platform for another national campaign in 1992. But when his political ally Coelho announced in May 1989 that he was not making an expected race for majority leader and would resign from Congress, Gephardt put presidential ambitions on hold and announced for majority leader.

Immediately Gephardt became an overwhelming favorite over Georgia Democrat Ed Jenkins, whom he ultimately defeated 181-76. That was impressive, but not surprising. Gephardt had built a record inside and outside the House that had strong appeal, particularly in the Democrats' spring of discontent. Gephardt long ago proved his ability to grasp and formulate legislative substance and strategy. And during his 1988 presidential campaign, he proved that he could be an effective public spokesman and withstand intense media scrutiny of his personality.

Gephardt entered the presidential contest with an Eagle Scout reputation and a record as clean as his freshly pressed shirts. He left the campaign with that reputation intact. When presidential aspirants were asked if they had ever tried marijuana, Gephardt grinned and said his college crowd "had trouble getting beer."

The media microscope did hurt Gephardt to some degree by magnifying one key aspect of his House career — his apparent movement on the political spectrum. Many politicians say they do not like political labels, but few are actually as difficult to define as Gephardt. Early in his House career, he was a forceful critic of liberal Democratic thinking, but soon he found himself defending many of the traditional programs from attack by President Reagan. He has fought to control energy prices and to decontrol hospital costs. He has voted for an anti-busing constitutional amendment and a freeze on nuclear weapons. He was long a proponent of an amendment to ban abortions, but has since distanced himself from that position.

In 1984, Gephardt was a founder of the Democratic Leadership Council (DLC), a group hoping to revive the party's national hopes by pulling it toward the center. And he initially envisioned his presidential candidacy as an alternative to traditional liberals, such as Walter F. Mondale or Sen. Edward M. Kennedy. But by the time Gephardt's candidacy was heating up, his campaign was stocked with former Kennedy and Mondale operatives.

Gephardt's White House campaign enjoyed much more success than many initially predicted it would. It is hard for any House member to become a credible national candidate — nobody has gone directly from the House to the presidency since James A. Garfield in 1880. And the conciliatory skills Gephardt honed as caucus chairman seemed ill-suited for a presidential race, where the ability to hammer away at a strong message is vital.

But Gephardt, who ultimately won about 170 delegates, early on out-performed the crowded field in organizing and transformed himself personally. He won the first contest of the season, the Iowa caucuses. Gephardt had been the first Democrat to enter the race in February 1987, and, staking his future on Iowa,

Missouri 3

South St. Louis; Southeast St. Louis County and Jefferson County

Traditionally based in the blue-collar, ethnic neighborhoods of South St. Louis, the 3rd has been forced to change by the city's population decline. Like the 1st District, its companion to the north, the 3rd now reaches into the suburbs of St. Louis County to fill itself out. The city accounts for only a little more than one-third of the district vote.

What remains of St. Louis in the 3rd, however, still has a heavily ethnic cast. Italians are clustered in The Hill, where family-owned taverns, sausage shops and pasta restaurants have survived several generations. Bevo Mill and Carondelat are old-line German communities. The 3rd also includes some signs that South St. Louis is experiencing growth. Lafayette Square, at the northeastern edge of the district, was largely an urban wasteland a decade ago. But it has undergone significant development in recent years.

Once rooted firmly in the New Deal coalition, South St. Louis voters have become increasingly concerned about taxes, government spending, abortion and busing. Nonetheless, they still tend to give Democrats their votes.

Monsanto and Mallinckrodt chemical facilities and barge operations along the Mississippi River are important to the district's economy. But the most prominent enterprise in this part of the city is Anheuser-Busch, the nationally known brewery that employs some 5,000 people in its headquarters and plants located here.

Nearly 40 percent of the 3rd's population lives in suburban St. Louis County, home to more conservative voters who regularly vote for the GOP. The county has been responsible for pushing the 3rd into the GOP column in most recent national and statewide elections; George Bush carried the 3rd with 53 percent in 1988.

Some of the county voters are longtime suburbanites; close-in communities such as Gravois and Lemay are where many of them make their homes. Others grew up on St. Louis' South Side and moved out in the past decade.

The residents of politically marginal Jefferson County constitute the remaining quarter of the district's population. Jefferson has come under the umbrella of metropolitan St. Louis in recent years, and the closer-in places such as Arnold are hard to distinguish from suburban St. Louis County turf. But farther west, Jefferson still is rural. Farmers in the Hillsboro area often truck their produce to markets in downtown St. Louis.

Population: 546,102. White 533,831 (98%), Black 7,442 (1%), Other 3,260 (1%). Spanish origin 5,603 (1%). 18 and over 403,646 (74%), 65 and over 76,186 (14%). Median age: 32.

he spent more time there than any other candidate. He got plenty of help from House colleagues, winning support from 58 by the time of the caucuses. Along the way he became the vehicle for an angry populist message, playing to a "have not" coalition of economically troubled farmers and blue-collar workers concerned with foreign competition.

Gephardt tied his campaign tightly to his top legislative priority, a trade amendment calling for retaliation against countries that maintain large trade surpluses with the United States and have barriers to U.S. exports. The labor-backed Gephardt amendment was one of the most controversial elements of the trade bills put together in the 99th and 100th Congresses. The amendment, which called for mandatory 10 percent annual reductions in targeted surpluses, was weaker than Gephardt originally planned, giving negotiators more time to reach some bilateral accord and allowing the president to ignore the provisions if he determined there would be substantial harm to the United States or the other country.

But the Gephardt amendment was still attacked as a dangerous "protectionist" measure by the administration and a number of House critics. Ways and Means Committee Chairman Dan Rostenkowski said he was supportive of the amendment's goal, but was against the specifics.

Aided by Wright, labor, and colleagues who either liked the amendment or wanted to give his presidential campaign a boost, Gephardt attached his amendment to the trade bill in 1987 by a 218-214 vote. And though House conferees ultimately backed off the amendment after Gephardt's campaign faded, the initial success went over well on the stump, giving credence to his claim that he would take action to improve the country's trade position. Unfortunately for Gephardt, his populistic appeal, which also included a call for aiding farmers with mandatory production controls, did not sell as well outside Iowa. And the media boost he expected from his win there was undercut by headline-grabbing turmoil in the GOP contest, where Vice President George Bush ran third.

Gephardt did manage to finish second in the New Hampshire primary, but that, and a win in South Dakota, was not enough to put his name in lights as he headed into 14 Southern primaries on Super Tuesday. Without the media boost, and without the money to advertise his message and deflect increasing attacks on his record, Gephardt won only his home state on Super Tuesday. A subsequent third-place finish in Michigan brought his campaign to an end.

Gephardt's rise to majority leader seems surprising, considering that he spent much of the 100th Congress as an outsider. But his move into the No. 2 leadership job is consistent with his earlier House career. As a freshman in 1977, Gephardt quickly learned the ways of the House under the tutelage of Richard Bolling, dean of the Missouri delegation and Rules Committee chairman. Bolling helped Gephardt get on Ways and Means in his first term.

At the same time he was learning from his elders, Gephardt was building up friendships with junior members. He has never been the backslapping pol, but he has a style well suited to advancement in the House. The trait he is most noted for is his willingness to listen rather than talk.

Gephardt has also shown a remarkable combination of concern about long-term problems and willingness to hammer out short-term solutions. He does not seem just to tolerate endless meetings on a variety of legislative subjects, he seems to thrive on them. Earnest and well organized, he reminds some colleagues of a grown-up student council president.

Gephardt played a major role in negotiations over the Gramm-Rudman-Hollings anti-deficit law in late 1985, when he was one of the key conferees who nailed down final specifications of the bill. Gephardt subsequently spoke with a proud sense of accomplishment of the 100-plus eye-glazing meetings House Democrats held to forge a party consensus on the bill.

Gephardt was also an early proponent of simplifying the federal tax code with lower individual tax rates. Working with Democratic Sen. Bill Bradley, Gephardt crafted a bill to restructure the tax system, and formed a non-profit group called the Fair Tax Foundation to promote the idea. He predicted that getting the bill enacted "will be the political war to end all wars."

But when the "war" was actually fought and won in the 99th Congress, Gephardt was not a visible player. Partly that was a reflection of other priorities, including trade and Gramm-Rudman. But there were those who suggested that Gephardt was looking for politically popular issues to ride and did not see that quality in the tax overhaul, which for much of the 99th Congress seemed unlikely to become law.

There is no denying, however, that over the years Gephardt has been a heavy lifter on Ways and Means. In 1981 he was among those arguing that the committee should present a clear Democratic alternative to President Reagan's tax plan, regardless of whether anyone thought it would win. When Rostenkowski decided to try to compete with Reagan for conservative votes, Gephardt worked to persuade Southern Democrats to vote with Rostenkowski in exchange for improved tax treatment for the oil industry. He presented the Democratic response to Reagan's televised speech on behalf of his tax plan.

Gephardt also worked on Ways and Means to increase competition in health care as a way of keeping down costs. On this issue he was more in tune with Republicans than with liberal Democrats. Gephardt led the fight in committee against President Carter's hospital cost control program in 1979, working in alliance with then-Rep. David A. Stockman, who was later to become Reagan's budget director.

Gephardt served on the Budget Committee from 1979 through 1984, rotating off at the start of the 99th Congress. He spent his first term there looking for programs to cut, but later joined the panel's liberal Democrats in protesting Reagan reductions in domestic spending. He was a consistent critic of the Republican administration's defense buildup.

All of his efforts helped Gephardt build an image as a rising star, someone destined for success in House politics. And clearly politics in the chamber have been very good to him. He had little trouble winning the position of Democratic Caucus chairman in the 99th Congress — his main opponent, David R. Obey of Wisconsin, dropped out nearly a year before the vote. But by the time Gephardt took over, he had to work hard to defuse an internal leadership controversy.

When he launched his bid for caucus chairman, Gephardt began meeting informally outside Capitol Hill with a group of Democratic allies willing to help in his campaign. Over a period of months, those meetings evolved into gripe sessions in which the shortcomings of Speaker Thomas P. O'Neill Jr. and then-Majority Leader Wright received prominent attention.

At some point, there was talk of alternative choices for those posts, and some Democrats believe that challenges to Wright and O'Neill would have taken place if the 1984 elections had been disastrous for House Democrats. They were not. Gephardt denied ever taking interest in such a scheme, and the issue soon faded.

At Home: The resilience of Gephardt's political base is not difficult to measure. When he was running for president, a large field of Democrats filed to succeed him in Congress. When he folded his presidential campaign in March 1988 and barely met the filing deadline for re-election, the stronger contenders for his seat dropped out. Three remained, but Gephardt took over 80 percent of the primary vote.

In the fall, Gephardt's opponent, 27-year-old attorney Mark F. "Thor" Hearne got only 36 percent of the vote.

Now that Gephardt's devotion to the House is clear, it seems unlikely he will have any problems in this district. Even Missouri's 1981 redistricting, a problem for Gephardt's St. Louis-area House colleagues, posed him no difficulties. The remap gave him over 150,000 new constituents, many of whom vote Republican in most elections. But Gephardt won re-election with 78 percent in 1982. Unopposed in 1984, he was free to stump for his Democratic colleagues and store up credits that proved useful in his presidential campaign.

Gephardt was elected in 1976 on the strength of his reputation as a young activist on the machine-dominated St. Louis Board of Aldermen. While on the board, he had sponsored zoning laws to preserve ethnic neighborhoods, building a constituency among German-American working-class communities on the city's South Side, the core of the 3rd District electorate.

Much of Gephardt's 1976 campaign focused on urban problems. He called for increased federal loans to home buyers and for creation of a national neighborhood commission to recommend federal urban assistance programs. He also announced his support for a constitutional amendment to restrict abortions, a position that he abandoned later in his career.

In the 1976 Democratic primary, Gephardt faced state Sen. Donald J. Gralike, head of an electrical workers' local. Gralike was endorsed by most of the Democratic clubs in the district's suburban townships, but Gephardt was stronger within the city. He also raised money downtown and ran a media campaign Gralike could not match. Benefiting from a 16,000-vote advantage in the city wards, Gephardt won nomination with 56 percent of the vote.

Gephardt's November opponent was Republican Joseph L. Badaracco, who had served eight years as a St. Louis alderman, six of those as board president. Although he had lost a primary race for lieutenant governor in 1972 and a mayoralty bid the next year, Badaracco was a veteran politician with broad name recognition.

Badaracco stressed his reputation for honesty in city politics and tried to convince voters that Gephardt was really a rich downtown lawyer groomed for Congress by the pin-striped establishment. Gephardt promised to emulate the moderate approach of Democratic Rep. Leonor K. Sullivan, who was retiring. Gephardt won 2-to-1 in St. Louis and took nearly 60 percent in St. Louis County to win with ease.

Committees

Majority Leader

Budget (2nd of 21 Democrats)

Elections

1988 General

Richard A. Gephardt (D)	150,205	(63%)
Mark F. "Thor" Hearne (R)	86,763	(36%)

1988 Primary

Richard A. Gephardt (D)	45,784	(82%)
James Vires (D)	4,073	(7%)
James Whitt (D)	3,442	(6%)
Ed Roche (D)	2,747	(5%)

1986 General

Richard A. Gephardt (D)	116,403	(69%)
Roy Amelung (R)	52,382	(31%)

Previous Winning Percentages: **1984** (100%) **1982** (78%) **1980** (78%) **1978** (82%) **1976** (64%)

District Vote For President

	1988		1984		1980		1976	
D	111,956	(47%)	85,385	(35%)	94,314	(40%)	118,403	(50%)
R	126,310	(53%)	156,443	(65%)	127,018	(54%)	114,390	(48%)
I					10,227	(4%)		

Campaign Finance

	Receipts	Receipts from PACs		Expend-itures
1988				
Gephardt (D)	$513,893	$183,196	(36%)	$512,206
Hearne (R)	$209,102	$12,154	(6%)	$202,524
1986				
Gephardt (D)	$830,682	$420,827	(51%)	$881,325

Key Votes

1987	
Raise speed limit to 65 mph	N
Approve Gephardt "fair trade" amendment	Y
Ban testing of larger nuclear weapons	Y
Delay "re-flagging" of Kuwaiti tankers	?
Approve tax-raising deficit-reduction bill	#
1988	
Approve aid to Nicaraguan contras	N
Enact civil rights restoration bill over Reagan veto	?
Kill 60-day plant-closing notification measure	N
Pass omnibus trade bill over Reagan veto	Y
Approve death penalty for drug-related murders	Y
Bar federal funds for abortions in cases of rape and incest	N
Oppose seven-day waiting period for purchase of handguns	N

Voting Studies

	Presidential Support		Party Unity		Conservative Coalition	
Year	**S**	**O**	**S**	**O**	**S**	**O**
1988	18	58	73	4	16	76
1987	5	22	18	0	5	21
1986	16	53	69	1	18	54
1985	26	71	84	6	31	65
1984	33	60	87	7	27	69
1983	26	70	90	6	25	69
1982	44	53	71	24	56	40
1981	54	43	64	33	69	27

Interest Group Ratings

Year	ADA	ACU	AFL-CIO	CCUS
1988	75	10	92	20
1987	20	0	100	0
1986	70	0	100	18
1985	60	19	88	19
1984	75	14	92	38
1983	85	9	94	25
1982	55	33	80	35
1981	45	27	73	11

4 Ike Skelton (D)

Of Lexington — Elected 1976

Born: Dec. 20, 1931, Lexington, Mo.

Education: Attended Wentworth Military Academy, 1949-51; attended U. of Edinburgh, Scotland, 1953; U. of Missouri, B.A. 1953, LL.B. 1956.

Occupation: Lawyer.

Family: Wife, Susan Anding; three children.

Religion: Christian Church.

Political Career: Lafayette County Democratic Committee chairman, 1962-66; Mo. Senate, 1971-77.

Capitol Office: 2134 Rayburn Bldg. 20515; 225-2876.

In Washington: Skelton qualifies as a "pro-defense" Democrat on the Armed Services Committee. But as one of committee Chairman Les Aspin's more conservative allies, Skelton is hardly unskeptical about the military leadership. His particular interest in reforming what he views as inefficiencies in the Defense Department's command structure has made Skelton a leader on esoteric issues that are basic to the Pentagon's operation, if little noticed by the general public.

Skelton was in the forefront of a successful campaign in the 99th Congress for a measure that granted more command authority to the chairman of the Joint Chiefs of Staff at the expense of the individual service branches. Skelton and other Pentagon critics had argued for years that U.S. military strength was being hindered by interservice rivalry, and that power in the military establishment needed to be centralized.

The Pentagon establishment initially opposed the effort, but the resistance wilted when such formidable defense-oriented legislators as Sens. Sam Nunn and Barry Goldwater and Rep. Bill Nichols of Alabama moved to the head of the charge. Though the final bill was entitled the Goldwater-Nichols act, Skelton's early contributions were crucial in bringing the process forward.

Skelton has also criticized the Defense Department for emphasizing management skills over military strategy since the 1960s in its ongoing education programs for the professional officer corps. "An M.B.A. became a prized achievement," Skelton said. "But the management emphasis hasn't reduced cost overruns, while it has reduced the quality of strategic skills."

During the 100th Congress, Skelton served as chairman of an Armed Services task force that studied ways to beef up professional military education. Upon release of the panel's report in November 1988, Skelton said he wanted to "reverse" the shift from military to management skills, noting that "we aren't producing the strategic thinkers of the kind that won World War II."

One of the recommendations in the report was to convert the National War College, based in Washington, D.C., to the National Center for Strategic Studies, which would be attended by military officers from the ranks of colonel/Navy captain to major general/rear admiral, as well as by several civilians involved in the national security sector. Reflecting Skelton's interest in coordinated joint military operations, the task force also recommended that the Armed Forces Staff College in Norfolk, Va., be made the flagship school for officers in "joint specialty" training.

Though committee Chairman Aspin, a Wisconsin Democrat, is substantially more liberal, Skelton has sided with him during debates on several weapons and arms-control issues. In early 1987, Skelton backed Aspin on votes against President Reagan's efforts to reinterpret the anti-ballistic missile and strategic arms limitation treaties signed with the Soviet Union in the 1970s. Skelton is also available for Aspin when the chairman tries to craft middle-of-the-road coalitions on some of the more contentious defense-related issues.

The two members first found common cause during the 99th Congress, when Skelton supported efforts to oust aging and enfeebled Armed Services Chairman Melvin Price of Illinois. Skelton's backing of Aspin boosted his credibility among the Democratic Caucus' more conservative members. Skelton also helped out in 1987 as Aspin fought off a challenge to his chairmanship from Marvin Leath of Texas.

Despite his occasional alliance with members to his left, though, Skelton could never be mistaken for a defense liberal. In the 99th Congress, Skelton led the effort in the House to restore funding for production of lethal chemical weapons for the first time since 1969. The House had fended off administration requests to resume nerve-gas production in 1982, 1983 and 1984. In 1985, Skelton's amendment to include $124 million for binary-weapons pro-

Missouri 4

West — Kansas City Suburbs; Jefferson City

Sprawling across west-central Missouri, the 4th is an amalgam of rural farm land, scenic tourist resorts and blue-collar suburban turf outside Kansas City.

Much of the area is given over to small farming. The 4th's cattle business is focused toward its southern end; corn, soybeans, pork and dairy production are important districtwide. Pockets of rural poverty — especially in parts of Texas County — stand in contrast to the economic climate enjoyed by comfortable landowners living in Lafayette and Pettis counties at the 4th's northern end.

Tourism has supplemented the district's agriculture in recent years. Winding around Camden County's northern border is the Lake of the Ozarks, a stretch of water that draws boaters, swimmers and skiers from around the state and nurtures a growing restaurant and motel trade.

Roughly 40 miles northeast of the lake lies Jefferson City, all but a sliver of which falls within the 4th's boundaries. Missouri's capital since 1826, it has never developed into a city of much size or sophistication. State government is the largest employer.

The district reaches into the Kansas City area to pick up some 80,000 constituents, many of whom commute to work in Kansas City factories. Other population centers in the 4th include Sedalia, a historic rail town and site of the annual Missouri State Fair, and Warrensburg, a grain and livestock center that is home to Central Missouri State University.

Between those two cities is Whiteman Air Force Base, whose Minuteman missiles make civil defense a paramount concern. In addition, the Richards-Gebaur Air Force Base (near Kansas City) and the Army's Fort Leonard Wood (Pulaski County) are located here.

The 4th contains some solidly Democratic areas of Jackson County east of Kansas City. But votes from this region have not been sufficient to overcome the GOP margins districtwide in recent elections for state and national office.

Population: 546,637. White 524,772 (96%), Black 14,950 (3%), Other 4,383 (1%). Spanish origin 5,503 (1%). 18 and over 390,415 (71%), 65 and over 70,341 (13%). Median age: 30.

duction was adopted.

Skelton also consistently supported Reagan's policy of providing aid to the Nicaraguan contras, and was the chief Democratic sponsor in 1986 of the GOP-initiated plan to provide $100 million in military and non-military aid to the contras. However, in a January 1989 article in *Army* magazine, Skelton blamed Reagan for having failed to sell the contra policy effectively to Congress or the public. "The administration's efforts to educate the public on the issues in Central America ... were neither consistent nor sustained," Skelton wrote.

Like nearly all of his Armed Services colleagues, Skelton has no shortage of back-home interests in defense policy. His efforts helped obtain the relocation of the Army Engineering School from Virginia to Fort Leonard Wood, near Waynesville in the 4th District; Whiteman Air Force Base, a Minuteman missile base near Knob Noster, will be receiving an early deployment of the new B-2 "stealth" bomber.

Skelton also looks out for the interests of his heavily rural central Missouri district as chairman of the Congressional Rural Caucus. He has pushed for elimination of differentials, which provide higher Medicare payment rates for urban than rural hospitals; he says that, by percentage, rural hospitals bear a heavier load of providing care for the elderly poor.

Skelton is also a strong supporter of using tourism as an economic development tool in rural areas, an idea he promotes as chairman of the Small Business Subcommittee on Procurement, Tourism and Rural Development. Skelton is regarded as one of a handful of Small Business members who devote serious attention to the agenda of the low-profile panel.

A childhood polio victim who went on to graduate from a military academy, Skelton has worked to add money to boost ROTC scholarships and to require ROTC students to complete their education.

At Home: A small-town lawyer with a sincere and low-key style, Skelton has had only one tough contest since winning election in 1976. In 1982, redistricting threw him together with another incumbent, freshman Republican Rep. Wendell Bailey.

Map makers gave Skelton a head start in the race. When Bailey's old 8th District was dismembered, the largest single block of his constituents was added to Skelton's 4th. So Bailey decided that was the place to seek a second term. But for every one of his old constituents in the new district, there were nearly two of Skelton's.

Numerous political action committees and nationally known politicians came into the 4th and billed the Skelton-Bailey match as a test of the popularity of Reaganomics in the rural heartland. The candidates responded with appropriate rhetoric: Skelton called Bailey a "rubber stamp" because he supported nearly all the president's budget and tax proposals, and Bailey countered that Skelton's mixed record of support for Reaganomics showed him to be a liberal who occasionally waffled to appease conservatives.

Bailey, known as one of Missouri's most effective Republican campaigners, was relying on the gregarious, hard-charging style he developed as a car salesman to help him pull Democrats away from the less-dynamic Skelton.

But in the end, most of the voters chose the man most familiar to them. Of the seven counties that had been part of Bailey's old 8th District, Bailey carried six. But Skelton had represented 13 counties, and managed to carry 12 of them. That brought him in nearly 18,000 votes ahead.

Skelton was a rural state legislator with a narrow political base when he began his 1976 campaign to succeed retiring Democratic Rep. William Randall. Only two counties in his state Senate district were within the borders of the 4th District as it was then drawn. His major rivals for the Democratic nomination were state senators from the Kansas City suburbs, which cast about 40 percent of the district vote.

Skelton chose to emphasize that he was the only major candidate from the rural part of the district, and campaigned actively for farm and small-town support. It was a successful strategy. He ran third in the suburbs, but with the rural vote he won with 40 percent overall.

Independence Mayor Richard A. King was the Republican nominee. A protégé of Republican Gov. (and now Sen.) Christopher S. Bond, King tied his general-election campaign to the GOP ticket of Bond and Senate candidate John C. Danforth, hoping to benefit from their coattails. Skelton emphasized his farm background and fiscal conservatism, voting against a pay raise for state legislators as an example.

King was not greatly helped by the top of the GOP ticket; Danforth carried the 4th, but Bond lost it. Skelton won by 24,350 votes.

Committees

Armed Services (9th of 31 Democrats)
Military Installations and Facilities; Military Personnel and Compensation; Procurement and Military Nuclear Systems

Select Aging (18th of 39 Democrats)
Health and Long-Term Care

Small Business (4th of 27 Democrats)
Procurement, Tourism and Rural Development (chairman)

Elections

1988 General		
Ike Skelton (D)	166,480	(72%)
David Eyerly (R)	65,393	(28%)
1986 General		
Ike Skelton (D)	129,471	(100%)

Previous Winning Percentages: **1984** (67%) **1982** (55%) **1980** (68%) **1978** (73%) **1976** (56%)

District Vote For President

	1988	1984	1980	1976
D	95,131 (40%)	75,862 (33%)	90,030 (40%)	97,502 (48%)
R	139,390 (59%)	155,939 (67%)	125,179 (56%)	103,436 (51%)
I			6,185 (3%)	

Campaign Finance

	Receipts	Receipts from PACs	Expend-itures
1988			
Skelton (D)	$314,323	$195,725 (62%)	$273,316
1986			
Skelton (D)	$300,019	$150,050 (50%)	$183,973

Key Votes

1987	
Raise speed limit to 65 mph	Y
Approve Gephardt "fair trade" amendment	Y
Ban testing of larger nuclear weapons	N
Delay "re-flagging" of Kuwaiti tankers	N
Approve tax-raising deficit-reduction bill	N
1988	
Approve aid to Nicaraguan contras	Y
Enact civil rights restoration bill over Reagan veto	Y
Kill 60-day plant-closing notification measure	N
Pass omnibus trade bill over Reagan veto	Y
Approve death penalty for drug-related murders	Y
Bar federal funds for abortions in cases of rape and incest	Y
Oppose seven-day waiting period for purchase of handguns	Y

Voting Studies

	Presidential Support		Party Unity		Conservative Coalition	
Year	**S**	**O**	**S**	**O**	**S**	**O**
1988	43	52	63	30	92	8
1987	45	48	66	24	81	19
1986	48	47	66	26	76	20
1985	44	46	66	25	85	15
1984	54	38	63	27	76	15
1983	45	50	56	37	74	22
1982	48	34	40	41	73	14
1981	58	39	45	45	91	5

Interest Group Ratings

Year	ADA	ACU	AFL-CIO	CCUS
1988	40	58	83	62
1987	48	38	86	40
1986	35	55	86	47
1985	40	50	63	33
1984	35	36	77	33
1983	50	57	82	30
1982	10	65	50	63
1981	25	43	67	37

5 Alan Wheat (D)

Of Kansas City — Elected 1982

Born: Oct. 16, 1951, San Antonio, Texas.
Education: Grinnell College, B.A. 1972.
Occupation: Government official.
Family: Single.
Religion: Church of Christ.
Political Career: Mo. House, 1977-83.
Capitol Office: 1204 Longworth Bldg. 20515; 225-4535.

In Washington: Wheat was a reserved, deferential apprentice when he first arrived in the House, heeding the advice of his respected predecessor, Richard Bolling. But now he has begun to emerge, and he seems restless to graduate straight into the leadership circle.

He got a ringside seat in his first term, landing on the prestigious Rules Committee thanks to the influence of Bolling, its former chairman. Wheat has used his assignment to win concessions for his urban district, including a multimillion-dollar flood-control project. Other committee leaders are anxious to accommodate members of Rules, given its role as traffic cop for nearly all bills.

Wheat also has the distinction of representing far more white constituents (75 percent) than any other black member. He seeks to appeal to a broad and moderate, but loyally Democratic, base. A trained economist and former state legislator, he personifies the House's younger generation of mainstream-oriented blacks.

Once more of an agitator — as a Grinnell College student, Wheat led a campus protest to demand black-studies courses — in the House he was one of the few blacks who did not start out supporting the Rev. Jesse Jackson's 1988 presidential bid (Wheat's first choice for president was Missouri colleague Richard A. Gephardt). From the start of his House tenure he has declined an active role in the Black Caucus, seeking something more. Wheat considered a race against Steny H. Hoyer of Maryland for Democratic Caucus vice chairman in the 101st Congress, and then unsuccessfully sought a seat on the Budget Committee.

He is a leadership lieutenant in the backroom world of Rules, where the media rarely penetrate. In the 100th Congress, he was visible in pushing for stricter federal regulation of cancer-causing PCBs. He estimated that at one time, 65 percent of the chemicals, once used in electrical equipment, were disposed of by Kansas City-based firms, some perhaps into Missouri waterways.

He rarely introduces legislation of his own but instead sponsors Rules' resolutions for floor debate on issues of interest to him, such as the leadership's top priority homeless-aid bill in early 1987.

At Home: Wheat's election in 1982 breached the custom that candidates of his race win only those districts dominated by liberals and minority voters. Just one-fourth of his district's residents are black and, though the white majority usually votes Democratic, most of the electorate stands to his right.

Wheat attended Grinnell, a prestigious liberal-arts institution in Iowa, then worked in Kansas City for the Department of Housing and Urban Development, and was an aide to the Jackson County executive. Elected at age 25 to the state House, he served three terms and became chairman of its Urban Affairs Committee.

In 1982, Wheat was one of eight Democrats to enter the congressional primary following Bolling's retirement announcement. The only black candidate in the field, Wheat won nomination with 31 percent of the vote.

The bulk of Wheat's support in the primary came from 10 Kansas City wards where the black political organization, Freedom Inc., is an influential force. But he refuted those who said he was the candidate only of blacks by amassing about one-third of his primary vote in mostly white and relatively prosperous neighborhoods in southwest Kansas City.

Republicans nominated state Rep. John A. Sharp, who sought to woo moderate and conservative Democrats who found Wheat too liberal. Though Sharp did not portray the contest in racial terms, he often warned that Wheat would be a tool of Freedom Inc.

But Wheat found a unifying theme, holding up Reaganomics as a threat to the welfare of working-class voters of all races. Armed with Bolling's endorsement, Wheat found support among local business people and union members alike, and he took an impressive 58 percent.

Wheat's liberal leanings and narrow margin of victory in the 1982 primary prompted some conservative white Democrats to seek an alternative candidate for 1984. But no prominent challenger came forward. Wheat solidified his hold on the 5th by winning easily against minor general-election opposition in 1986 and 1988, attaining 70 percent of the vote in his latest victory.

Missouri 5

Kansas City and Eastern Suburbs

Long sensitive about its reputation as an overgrown cow town, Kansas City still offers some support for that point of view — it remains a nationally prominent market for feeder cattle and hard winter wheat.

But that image obscures the diverse economy it has maintained throughout this century. Auto assembly is a major industry; metropolitan Kansas City is the nation's third-largest auto producer. IBM and Hallmark are crucial concerns. Hallmark is a hometown corporation and has spent millions of dollars on commercial redevelopment within the city. The company built Crown Center, which provides an array of restaurants, shops, pricey apartments and a luxury hotel.

The federal government has also been a large employer in recent years; many federal offices have regional branches located in the city. The Reagan administration tried to close some of the local branch offices to streamline the federal bureaucracy and save money, but those efforts were blunted.

Though Kansas City has not suffered the massive flight of people and businesses that has crippled St. Louis, its population has declined to about 425,000 — fewer people than were living in the city 30 years ago. To make up the population deficit, the 5th was extended into the suburbs of Jackson County, but Kansas City still casts about two-thirds of the vote.

The district cuts through the eastern sections of blue-collar Independence and Lee's Summit, leaving most of both towns in the 5th. Partisan allegiances are closely divided in these suburbs, but Kansas City's Democratic vote — bolstered by the black community — usually determines the political outcome districtwide. In 1988, Democratic presidential nominee Michael S. Dukakis won 60 percent of the district's vote — better than either Walter F. Mondale or Jimmy Carter fared in the 5th.

Population: 546,882. White 407,941 (75%), Black 125,181 (23%), Other 5,901 (1%). Spanish origin 15,385 (3%). 18 and over 405,263 (74%), 65 and over 71,266 (13%). Median age: 31.

Committees

District of Columbia (6th of 8 Democrats)
Government Operations and Metropolitan Affairs (chairman); Judiciary and Education

Rules (7th of 9 Democrats)
Legislative Process

Select Children, Youth and Families (13th of 18 Democrats)

Elections

1988 General		
Alan Wheat (D)	149,166	(70%)
Mary Ellen Lobb (R)	60,453	(28%)
1986 General		
Alan Wheat (D)	101,030	(71%)
Greg Fisher (R)	39,340	(28%)

Previous Winning Percentages: **1984** (66%) **1982** (58%)

District Vote For President

	1988		1984		1980		1976	
D	129,421	(60%)	121,869	(54%)	122,645	(55%)	119,296	(57%)
R	83,888	(39%)	105,868	(46%)	89,058	(40%)	84,849	(41%)
I					10,692	(5%)		

Campaign Finance

	Receipts	Receipts from PACs	Expend-itures
1988			
Wheat (D)	$303,515	$205,500 (68%)	$240,623
Lobb (R)	$15,658	$650 (4%)	$14,636
1986			
Wheat (D)	$268,786	$188,627 (70%)	$192,612

Key Votes

1987	
Raise speed limit to 65 mph	N
Approve Gephardt "fair trade" amendment	Y
Ban testing of larger nuclear weapons	Y
Delay "re-flagging" of Kuwaiti tankers	Y
Approve tax-raising deficit-reduction bill	Y
1988	
Approve aid to Nicaraguan contras	N
Enact civil rights restoration bill over Reagan veto	Y
Kill 60-day plant-closing notification measure	N
Pass omnibus trade bill over Reagan veto	Y
Approve death penalty for drug-related murders	N
Bar federal funds for abortions in cases of rape and incest	N
Oppose seven-day waiting period for purchase of handguns	N

Voting Studies

	Presidential Support		Party Unity		Conservative Coalition	
Year	S	O	S	O	S	O
1988	15	83	79	18	5	92
1987	9	91	97	2	5	95
1986	14	86	96	3	12	88
1985	15	84	97	1	5	95
1984	23	77	96	4	3	97
1983	12	87	97	3	10	90

Interest Group Ratings

Year	ADA	ACU	AFL-CIO	CCUS
1988	100	0	93	21
1987	100	0	100	0
1986	95	0	86	22
1985	100	0	100	14
1984	100	0	92	38
1983	95	0	100	15

6 E. Thomas Coleman (R)

Of Kansas City — Elected 1976

Born: May 29, 1943, Kansas City, Mo.
Education: William Jewell College, B.A. 1965; New York U., M.P.A. 1966; Washington U., J.D. 1969.
Occupation: Lawyer.
Family: Wife, Marilyn Anderson; three children.
Religion: Protestant.
Political Career: Assistant attorney general, 1969-72; Mo. House, 1973-77; campaigned for Clay County clerk, 1970.
Capitol Office: 2468 Rayburn Bldg. 20515; 225-7041.

In Washington: A youthful looking Kansas City lawyer with a public administration degree from New York University, Coleman seems an unlikely candidate to be a senior player on rural and agricultural issues. But having come to the House at the young age of 33, he has moved up to become the second-ranking Republican on the Agriculture Committee. Coleman balances his assignment there with his role as the second-ranking Republican on another committee, Education and Labor.

Early in his career on Agriculture, Coleman was most visible as a caustic critic of farm programs sponsored by Democrats. That Coleman is not heard very much anymore. These days, he is often found defending his committee's product, regardless of authorship, against critics in both parties who consider farm subsidies wasteful.

Coleman works to negotiate with Democrats, and as ranking member of the Agriculture Subcommittee on Conservation and Credit he spent much of his time working with one of the most genial Democrats in the House, Chairman Ed Jones. With Jones' retirement at the end of the 100th Congress, Coleman is now adjusting to the leadership style of the new subcommittee chairman, Oklahoma Democrat Glenn English.

In the 100th Congress, Coleman and Jones were leading players on one of the most complicated issues the Agriculture Committee has ever dealt with — the overhaul of the ailing Farm Credit System, the quasi-private lending network for farmers and ranchers. There were a number of contentious issues involved in the farm credit debate, but there was also tremendous pressure for members to act because of the political and economic risks that would coincide with the system's downfall. After some partisan wrangling and marathon legislative sessions the committee voted 41-2 for a bill to bring about the most extensive reorganization of the system since the 1930s.

The Reagan administration had objections to parts of the plan, such as language that Coleman worked on to require the Farmers Home Administration to restructure delinquent loans, if that would be cheaper than foreclosure proceedings. But Reagan never put forward a comprehensive plan of his own. The credit bill became law in 1987.

Coleman also has a strong interest in conservation issues. When the committee wrote a new omnibus farm bill in 1985, Coleman and Jones cooperated on soil conservation provisions, one of the few elements of the legislation with wide bipartisan support. The conservation section included a new "sodbuster" program, designed to conserve soil by denying federal farm benefits to farmers who till highly erodible land.

Despite his work on soil conservation, though, Coleman distanced himself from the farm bill as a whole. He signed and voted for the report produced by House-Senate conferees, but he voted against the report when it reached the floor. He explained later that he voted for the report initially to show support for sections he had helped draft, but did not approve of other provisions, especially those dealing with price supports for wheat and corn.

Coleman continued to distance himself from Reagan administration rural policies in the 100th Congress. Frustrated by efforts to address problems in the agricultural economy, Coleman introduced rural development legislation to target economically distressed areas. The bill, which did not get a warm reception from the administration, would have given priority to rural areas in government contracting and in the building of federal facilities. It also would have given grants for businesses and infrastructure in those areas, and financed career counseling and scholarships for young people.

"The administration has opened its eyes to the crisis in rural America," he said in 1987, "but its response is still out of focus." Coleman renewed his rural-development efforts in the 101st Congress.

When a new administration was elected in

Missouri 6

Northwest — St. Joseph

A vast stretch of northwestern Missouri, the 6th covers 27 whole counties, encompassing some of the most fertile agricultural areas in the state. But half the district's residents live in a three-county patch of urbanized territory in the 6th's southwest corner. In 1988 presidential voting, the 6th was easily the most competitive Missouri district. Out of more than 230,000 ballots cast, George Bush won the 6th by just 200 votes over Michael S. Dukakis.

Although residents of the Kansas City environs in Clay and Platte counties consider themselves "northlanders" and seek an identity distinct from that of the city, many of them find work in its industries and businesses. A Trans World Airlines facility in this area is the district's largest employer, and the Kansas City International Airport is located nearby.

The city of St. Joseph anchors Buchanan County, the third urbanized county in the district. A booming supply depot for prospectors heading to California in search of gold in the 1800s, St. Joseph gained a place in history as the eastern end of the Pony Express. The city today is a flour-milling and agribusiness center.

Partisan preferences in Clay, Platte and Buchanan counties have been somewhat mixed in recent years. All three voted Republican for president both in 1980 and 1984, but in 1988, Clay and Platte backed Bush for president, while Buchanan went for Dukakis.

The rest of the 6th is rural and generally conservative. Parts of the rolling north prairie resemble the Iowa breadbasket; cattle and feed grains dominate the economy.

The closest thing Missouri has to a Yankee influence is found in Putnam, Mercer and a few other 6th District counties on or near the Iowa border. Ohio and Iowa farmers moved into that area long ago, and for years it has rivaled the Ozarks for fidelity to the GOP.

Population: 546,614. White 532,071 (97%), Black 9,571 (2%), Other 2,912 (1%). Spanish origin 5,688 (1%). 18 and over 396,507 (73%), 65 and over 78,169 (14%). Median age: 32.

1988, Coleman's name was floated for the position of agriculture secretary, but it did not float too long before George Bush turned elsewhere.

Coleman also serves as ranking member of the Education and Labor Subcommittee on Postsecondary Education, where he was a leader on efforts to reauthorize the Higher Education Act in the 99th Congress. During work on that legislation, Coleman argued that proposals increasing the cost of student programs should be linked to changes that save money. One way Coleman sought to save money was by pushing provisions to crack down on student-loan defaults by tightening collection procedures.

The default issue continued to receive attention in the 100th Congress, with the Education and Labor Committee approving a measure that required schools to reduce default rates and expanded grants to poor students. Coleman argued against the grant expansion, saying it was too costly and did nothing to address the default problem. But he failed in his effort to strip that from the bill.

One successful Coleman amendment required the secretary of education to publish guidelines to help schools, lenders and loan guarantee agencies carry out provisions in the measure. Coleman also pushed an amendment eliminating consideration of such non-liquid assets as a home when determining eligibility for a loan. While some saw the latter provision as a reversal of administration policy, which had made it more difficult for many students to get loans, Coleman said it was "a refinement of Reagan's policies.... It offers opportunity for people not to be penalized by their assets." Disagreements with the administration over the bill ultimately caused action to be postponed until the 101st Congress.

At Home: Coleman was running what seemed like a hopeless effort in 1976, but he was in the right place at the right time. His opponent's campaign collapsed overnight, and he inherited thousands of Democratic votes.

Morgan Maxfield, a millionaire Texan transplanted to Kansas City, had won the 1976 Democratic primary with the help of an expensive media barrage, and he was outspending Coleman 3-to-1 on the general election.

But less than a month before the voting, the *Kansas City Star* reported that Maxfield had lied about his early life, marital status and educational degrees. His campaign chairman resigned and criticized him. All Coleman had to do was wait for the election, and when it was over, he had swept to a 37,214-vote victory in a district that had not gone Republican in a quarter-century. He entered the House immediately, filling the vacancy caused by the death of Democrat Jerry Litton, who had been killed in an airplane crash in August on the day he was nominated for the Senate.

Democrats in the 6th, kicking themselves for having let Coleman win so easily, mounted vigorous challenges in 1978 and 1982. But in both cases their moderately conservative nominees had trouble finding an issue to use against the resourceful incumbent.

After an easy victory in 1984, Coleman began considering a bid for statewide office. When Democratic Sen. Thomas F. Eagleton announced he would not seek re-election in 1986, Coleman thought seriously about challenging former Gov. Christopher S. Bond for the GOP senatorial nomination. Coleman eventually scuttled his plans, however, citing Bond's widespread support among state party leaders.

His decision did not guarantee him an easy election year, however. A rash of farm foreclosures had ravaged northwestern Missouri in 1986, and Coleman found himself face to face with an angry farmer who held him partly responsible.

The farmer, 35-year-old Vietnam veteran Doug Hughes, had not been active in Democratic politics before. But he proved a charismatic speaker whose pleas for higher farm price supports and mandatory production controls struck an emotional chord among some of the 6th District farmers struggling to cope with the slumping agricultural economy.

Still, Hughes was unable to persuade voters to assign Coleman personal blame for the ailing farm economy. The incumbent took pains to publicize his disagreements with Reagan's agricultural policies, and made regular rounds of farm meetings, urging farmers to experiment with alternative crops and counseling them on coping with stress. Hughes managed to carry seven of the 28 counties wholly or partially in the 6th, but Coleman emerged with a surprisingly strong 57-43 victory.

Hughes was back for a rematch in 1988, but he seemed to have peaked in his first try. Though the appeal of the GOP presidential ticket in rural Missouri was well below what it had been in Ronald Reagan's landslides of 1980 and 1984, Coleman slightly increased his margin over Hughes. The incumbent was not, however, quite able to achieve the 60 percent threshold. He reached that plateau only in the years Reagan led the ticket.

Committees

Agriculture (2nd of 18 Republicans)
Conservation, Credit and Rural Development (ranking); Department Operations, Research and Foreign Agriculture

Education and Labor (2nd of 13 Republicans)
Postsecondary Education (ranking); Elementary, Secondary and Vocational Education; Human Resources

Elections

1988 General		
E. Thomas Coleman (R)	135,883	(59%)
Doug R. Hughes (D)	93,128	(41%)
1988 Primary		
E. Thomas Coleman (R)	28,762	(90%)
Robert L. Buck (R)	3,278	(10%)
1986 General		
E. Thomas Coleman (R)	95,865	(57%)
Doug R. Hughes (D)	73,155	(43%)

Previous Winning Percentages: **1984** (65%) **1982** (55%) **1980** (71%) **1978** (56%) **1976 *** (59%)

** Elected to a full term and to fill a vacancy at the same time.*

District Vote For President

	1988	1984	1980	1976
D	115,470 (50%)	97,920 (40%)	102,849 (42%)	119,405 (52%)
R	115,670 (50%)	145,284 (60%)	122,321 (50%)	107,314 (47%)
I			17,086 (7%)	

Campaign Finance

	Receipts	Receipts from PACs	Expend-itures
1988			
Coleman (R)	$305,961	$175,134 (57%)	$341,344
Hughes (D)	$199,256	$100,250 (50%)	$198,617
1986			
Coleman (R)	$241,448	$126,269 (52%)	$250,606
Hughes (D)	$117,595	$70,999 (60%)	$134,325

Key Votes

1987	
Raise speed limit to 65 mph	Y
Approve Gephardt "fair trade" amendment	N
Ban testing of larger nuclear weapons	N
Delay "re-flagging" of Kuwaiti tankers	N
Approve tax-raising deficit-reduction bill	N
1988	
Approve aid to Nicaraguan contras	Y
Enact civil rights restoration bill over Reagan veto	N
Kill 60-day plant-closing notification measure	Y
Pass omnibus trade bill over Reagan veto	Y
Approve death penalty for drug-related murders	Y
Bar federal funds for abortions in cases of rape and incest	Y
Oppose seven-day waiting period for purchase of handguns	N

Voting Studies

	Presidential Support		Party Unity		Conservative Coalition	
Year	**S**	**O**	**S**	**O**	**S**	**O**
1988	51	46	83	15	95	5
1987	56	40	76	19	95	5
1986	67	28	76	20	82	16
1985	56	40	76	19	89	5
1984	55	43	66	27	80	14
1983	65	33	70	27	83	13
1982	56	32	67	28	75	14
1981	70	28	74	18	85	12

Interest Group Ratings

Year	ADA	ACU	AFL-CIO	CCUS
1988	25	76	64	93
1987	4	62	13	87
1986	5	75	21	75
1985	10	67	29	75
1984	20	70	31	75
1983	15	73	19	74
1982	10	67	25	68
1981	0	100	21	94

7 Mel Hancock (R)

Of Springfield — Elected 1988

Born: Sept. 14, 1929, Cape Fair, Mo.
Education: Southwest Missouri State U., B.S. 1951.
Military Career: Air Force, 1951-52; Air Force Reserve, 1953-65.
Occupation: Businessman.
Family: Wife, Alma "Sug" McDaniel; three children.
Religion: Church of Christ.
Political Career: Sought Republican nomination for U.S. Senate, 1982; Republican nominee for lieutenant governor, 1984.
Capitol Office: 511 Cannon Bldg. 20515; 225-6536.

The Path to Washington: Hancock may strike some as a throwback to the tax rebellions of the late 1970s and early 1980s. Others may see him as a model for conservative populists, a man who likes to say "we've got too darn much government" and "my appeal is to the guy who makes a living with his hands."

At 59, Hancock is the oldest freshman in the 101st Congress, and seven years older than the average House member. But he is more likely to be noticed for his energy, his size (he is almost a head taller than Ronald Reagan in a 1976 photo of the two) and the big bass-baritone voice that he says "tends to carry."

Among his priorities is passage of a constitutional amendment limiting federal spending and taxes. It is modeled on an amendment to Missouri's Constitution that passed in 1980 after a ballot-initiative campaign Hancock led.

That campaign made Hancock a household name in Missouri, though he had never held public office. He subsequently tried to ride the recognition into office, but aimed too high. He lost a Senate primary in 1982 and a bid for the lieutenant governorship in 1984.

But all 17 counties of the 7th District voted for Hancock in 1984. And in 1988, the home folks proved hospitable again as he sought to succeed retiring GOP Rep. Gene Taylor.

Hancock's campaign stressed not only his anti-tax credentials but also his roots in the scenic Ozark hills. Hancock, whose grandfather was a member of the state Legislature, was born in tiny Cape Fair near the Arkansas border. He went to high school and college in the district's center city of Springfield. He eventually took a job at International Harvester, where his father worked. In the late 1960s, he bought orchard land in the area and planted walnut trees. He also took over a franchise security business specializing in bank security.

Hancock was one of the local anti-tax activists who emerged in the 1970s and formed the broad base of the Reagan Revolution. Today, he believes his amendment has kept Missouri's annual budget about $1 billion smaller than it would otherwise be and thus saved every Missourian an average of $200 a year. But he is bitter about court decisions that have weakened it and says state officials, legislators and judges conspire to undermine its effect. At the federal level, Hancock is convinced there are thousands of spending programs that can be canceled.

When Taylor announced he was stepping down, the vacancy created competitive races in both parties. Hancock carried the 7th's dominant Greene County (Springfield) against a well-known state senator from Springfield. But it was triumph in the rural counties that enabled him to hold off Gary Nodler, Taylor's district aide, whose base was in Joplin.

The Democrats nominated their most conservative candidate, a tough judge named Max Bacon. "Maximum Max" was best known for singing gospel duets with GOP Gov. John Ashcroft (also from Springfield). Bacon's down-home style and reputation on the bench immunized him against attacks on political ideology.

Hancock had to counter his one-issue image ("doing something about just one issue is better than just talking about a whole lot of issues"). He also ran into trouble after saying in August he was interested in the idea of a flat tax and did not understand why Social Security payments were partly tax-exempt.

Bacon saw the flat-tax talk as an opening; he said Hancock wanted Social Security payments to be fully taxable. The 7th has many retirees, and it was their sensitivity on Social Security that gave Taylor his closest call in 1982. For the rest of the campaign, Hancock explained that he did not support higher taxes on Social Security and, in fact, believed all Social Security payments should be exempt.

Bacon came within 500 votes in Greene County and fought Hancock to a draw in adjacent Dallas, Polk and Webster counties. But Hancock ran up a 6,000-vote margin in the three counties bordering Kansas and ran away from the Democrat in the 12 outlying counties.

Missouri 7

Southwest — Springfield; Joplin

Long a poor, isolated area resembling Appalachia, the scenic Ozark highlands have been discovered by tourists, retirees and new industry. But while newcomers have streamed into the 7th in the past two decades, they have not greatly altered the district's bedrock Republican character.

The tourist and retiree presence is most obvious in the south-central part of the district around Table Rock Reservoir and Bull Shoals Lake, in Stone and Taney counties.

More than a third of the district's residents live in Springfield and surrounding Greene County, the region's industrial and commercial center. Kraft, Litton, 3M, Rockwell and Zenith are major employers. Springfield also is the home of Southwest Missouri State University, with more than 16,000 students.

The other population center in the district is Joplin, an old lead- and zinc-mining town now also engaged in manufacturing. The GOP preference was cemented in the Joplin area when President Woodrow Wilson lowered tariffs on lead and zinc and crippled the local mining industry.

Despite population growth, the rural and agricultural character of the Ozarks has not yielded completely to development and modernization. There remain many small, isolated communities, the legacy of the region's original settlers — Scotch-Irish mountaineers from eastern Tennessee, western Virginia and Kentucky who generally kept to themselves and coaxed crops from the rocky soil. The international headquarters of the Assemblies of God are in Springfield, reflecting the traditional importance of fundamentalism in the Ozarks.

This area was Republican territory in the Civil War and has been ever since. The Ozark settlers had no use for slavery on their small, hilly farms; most were pro-Union. Today, statewide GOP candidates often take more than 60 percent of the vote in southwest Missouri. In 1984 and 1988, Republican voting was spurred by the presence of gubernatorial nominee John Ashcroft, a Springfield resident, near the top of the ticket. Despite a less-than-impressive victory statewide in 1988, George Bush took all 17 counties in the 7th District.

Population: 545,921. White 535,587 (98%), Black 4,367 (1%), Other 4,881 (1%). Spanish origin 3,392 (1%). 18 and over 399,610 (73%), 65 and over 81,401 (15%). Median age: 32.

Committees

Public Works and Transportation (18th of 20 Republicans)
Aviation; Surface Transportation; Water Resources

Small Business (15th of 17 Republicans)
Regulation, Business Opportunity and Energy; SBA, the General Economy and Minority Enterprise Development

Campaign Finance

	Receipts	Receipts from PACs	Expend-itures
1988			
Hancock (R)	$373,434	$79,913 (21%)	$338,125
Bacon (D)	$219,441	$114,460 (52%)	$215,064

Elections

1988 General		
Mel Hancock (R)	127,939	(53%)
Max E. Bacon (D)	111,244	(46%)
1988 Primary		
Mel Hancock (R)	37,067	(39%)
Gary Nodler (R)	33,940	(36%)
Dennis Smith (R)	20,354	(21%)

District Vote For President

	1988	1984	1980	1976
D	92,861 (38%)	74,275 (31%)	85,364 (36%)	98,916 (47%)
R	148,460 (61%)	164,696 (69%)	141,329 (60%)	110,814 (53%)
I			6,173 (3%)	

8 Bill Emerson (R)

Of Cape Girardeau — Elected 1980

Born: Jan. 1, 1938, St. Louis, Mo.
Education: Westminster College, B.A. 1959; U. of Baltimore, LL.B. 1964.
Military Career: Air Force Reserve, 1964-present.
Occupation: Government relations executive.
Family: Wife, Jo Ann Hermann; four children.
Religion: Presbyterian.
Political Career: No previous office.
Capitol Office: 438 Cannon Bldg. 20515; 225-4404.

In Washington: Emerson began 1988 facing a road to re-election rockier than that of any of his Missouri colleagues, rockier than all but a handful of incumbents in the House. The Democratic challenger who had pushed him hard in 1986 was running again. And, in March, Emerson voluntarily began a 30-day treatment program for alcohol dependency.

Remarkably, however, Emerson's adversities seemed to strengthen him. Reaction to his decision to seek treatment was almost uniformly sympathetic, a testament to his personal standing in the House. By openly seeking help, he seemed to win respect and even admiration from colleagues and constituents alike. And he may have benefited from the contrast with other public figures who have seemed determined to deny their own weaknesses.

Far from crippled, Emerson sailed to re-election with unexpected ease, winning his second-best share of the vote to date.

Emerson has a fondness for conservative rhetoric, and his occasional displays of it on the House floor lead some to consider him an ideologue. But when it comes down to legislating, he is pragmatic.

He first came to the House as a high school student in the 1950s, when he served as a page. Later, he worked as both a House and Senate staffer and as a lobbyist. He cultivates an image as a man who knows how the game is played. He likes to work with Democrats to forge compromises and move bills to passage.

This pragmatism often shows up on the Agriculture Committee's Nutrition Subcommittee, where he is the ranking minority member. The Nutrition panel can be a tough spot for a conservative striving to hold the line on the budget. To do so is sometimes to appear the scrooge. Still, Emerson seems to take a curmudgeonly pride in his ability to cast difficult votes in favor of controlling the cost of the nation's nutrition programs.

In the 99th and 100th Congresses, Emerson worked with subcommittee Chairman Leon E. Panetta of California on a food-stamp bill requiring states to set up employment and training programs for stamp recipients. The language allowed states to tailor their programs to local needs. He was upset when Georgia Republican Newt Gingrich tried to upstage him on the floor by offering a tougher proposal that would have required states to enroll 75 percent of all eligible recipients in some sort of work program. Gingrich's amendment failed 183-227.

Emerson is active on Agriculture outside the Nutrition Subcommittee, and in 1985 introduced the farm bill alternative endorsed by the American Farm Bureau Federation. His major crop interest is the soybean. To aid soybean farmers he has pushed legislation requiring the secretary of agriculture to implement a new marketing loan program. It would allow soybean farmers to repay their price-support loans at the market price, which could be significantly lower than the loan rate.

The more partisan and combative Emerson came out in 1984 during debate over creation of a new House Select Committee on Hunger. He was one of the few members to speak out against the idea. He said creation of a new committee was a vote of no confidence in existing committees working on the issue — including his own Nutrition panel. Emerson predicted that a new select committee "would dispense a great deal of rhetoric ... but little nourishment." Still, when the Select Committee on Hunger was created less than a month later, Emerson accepted appointment to it. By the 101st Congress, he was the committee's vice chairman.

As a member of the committee, Emerson has been a sort of conservative watchdog, willing to challenge the assumptions of the Democratic majority. Like other conservative Republicans, he is concerned about Democrats using hunger in America as a political issue against the Republican administration. But he has taken an interest in the world famine problem; when Chairman Mickey Leland took the panel to observe conditions in Africa early in 1989, Emerson went along.

Emerson uses his post on the Interior Committee mainly as a vehicle for tending to

Missouri 8

Southeast — Cape Girardeau

The state's most sparsely populated district, the 8th extends northwest from the Tennessee border toward central Missouri, covering more than 16,000 square miles.

In the extreme southeastern corner lies the Bootheel, a cluster of counties that looks and votes like the Old South. Predominantly a wheat-growing region until the mid-1920s, the Bootheel underwent a transformation when cotton growers and black sharecroppers, driven north by the boll weevil, settled here amid the rich Mississippi River delta land. The area grows 40 percent of the state's cash crops. Soybeans and corn have since supplanted cotton as the Bootheel's leading crops, but the Southern Democratic habits forged during cotton's heyday have persisted. While three out of the five core counties of the Bootheel voted Republican for president in 1988, they remained firmly in the Democratic column in most down-ballot races.

Above the Bootheel along the Mississippi River, dairy production and beef cattle spark the agricultural economy. The residents of the city of Cape Girardeau work in agribusinesses and a Procter & Gamble Co. paper plant. The names of communities such as Bonne Terre and Beauvais are about all that is left of the area's French heritage.

Offsetting Democratic strength in the Bootheel, Cape Girardeau and neighboring Perry counties are inclined toward the GOP. Both counties typically give Republicans solid margins in contests for statewide offices.

Toward the center of the 8th are Madison and Iron counties, traditional centers for Missouri's lead-mining industry. Farther west, the district moves into the foothills of the Ozark Mountains, some of Missouri's loveliest but poorest territory.

Population: 546,112. White 519,118 (95%), Black 24,050 (4%). Spanish origin 2,970 (1%). 18 and over 387,786 (71%), 65 and over 81,160 (15%). Median age: 31.

local concerns. Although he helped block House passage of a 1982 bill seeking to set aside 17,500 acres of 8th District land as wilderness, Emerson approved of a 1983 version of the bill that reduced to some 15,500 acres the portion of the land, known as the Irish Wilderness, to be protected. That measure passed the House.

At Home: The Washington bug bit Emerson early — when he was a teenage page in the 83rd and 84th Congresses — and he has not strayed far from the city since. Soon after finishing college in Missouri, he was back in Washington working on Capitol Hill.

Emerson held Hill-related jobs throughout the 1960s and 1970s, including lobbying positions with defense and energy-related companies. In 1979 he returned to Missouri to challenge 10th District Democratic Rep. Bill D. Burlison. The incumbent was hurt by charges that he had an affair with a woman, then interceded improperly on her behalf in a dispute involving her performance in a federal job. Burlison denied all charges, but many conservative Democrats deserted him. Aided also by Ronald Reagan's coattails, Emerson became the first Republican in 50 years to take the 10th.

Redistricting in 1981 excluded Jefferson County, forcing Emerson to move from his home there to Cape Girardeau, the 8th's largest city. That gave Democrats an opening to label Emerson a "carpetbagger." Democratic nominee Jerry Ford, a state representative, hoped Democrats who strayed in 1980 would return to the fold in 1982. But Emerson, playing down partisan rhetoric and stressing support from several prominent Democrats and the state Farm Bureau, held on to win with 53 percent.

After winning easily in 1984, Emerson faced a serious 1986 challenge from Democrat Wayne Cryts. A farmer from Puxico, Cryts burst into national prominence in 1981 by leading a band of frustrated cohorts to a bankrupt grain elevator and seizing more than 30,000 bushels of soybeans.

Cryts' actions earned him widespread publicity and made him something of a folk hero to farm activists associated with the American Agriculture Movement. He used this celebrity to launch attacks on Emerson's support for the 1985 farm bill. But Cryts did not command unanimous support in the farm community; the Missouri Farm Bureau and the heads of many state and local farm commodity groups backed Emerson.

Even some farmers sympathetic to Cryts recalled that the incumbent had worked to help spring Cryts from jail following the 1981 soybean raid — and introduced legislation to revise federal bankruptcy laws to allow farmers prompt grain-removal rights.

Cryts carried 15 of the 26 counties wholly or partially contained within the 8th. But that was not enough to overcome Emerson's nearly 5,000-vote margin in Cape Girardeau County. Emerson won with 53 percent.

In 1988, Cryts was back. But the working

boots and blue-denim jackets of his first campaign were gone. This time, Cryts campaigned in a suit and tie. He moved his headquarters from tiny Puxico to Cape Girardeau. He compiled a sizable campaign treasury, raising twice as much as he had in 1986. He aired ads that featured popular neighbor Rep. Richard A. Gephardt, whose bid for the Democratic presidential nomination Cryts had served as farm policy adviser.

Meanwhile, Emerson's alcohol admissions suggested vulnerability. Surveys said voters appreciated the way he was handling his problem, but some observers suspected damage below the waterline.

In August, Cryts won his primary in a rush and seemed to have Emerson in his sights. But the incumbent landed a blow by accusing Cryts of supporting himself on American Agriculture Movement funds while campaigning for Congress. If this was a distraction for Cryts' campaign, a deeper dilemma was the lessened sense of economic crisis among Bootheel farmers. The challenger talked more about trade, education and health care, issues that lit few fires. And as the fall wore on, the stumbling fortunes of Democratic candidates nationally and statewide cost Cryts some of his momentum as well.

Emerson had also redoubled his own fund-raising effort, raising 43 percent more than in 1986 and pushing his spending in this rural, low-cost district to nearly $850,000.

In the end, the outcome recalled Emerson's relatively comfortable wins in the presidential election years of 1984 and 1980. He carried 22 of the 26 counties, including Stoddard, which had once been the base of Cryts' operations. In winning by 34,000 votes, the incumbent added 5 percentage points to the margin by which he had won two years before.

Committees

Select Hunger (Vice Chairman)

Agriculture (7th of 18 Republicans)
Domestic Marketing, Consumer Relations and Nutrition (ranking); Cotton, Rice and Sugar; Wheat, Soybeans and Feed Grains

Public Works and Transportation (15th of 20 Republicans)
Economic Development; Surface Transportation; Water Resources

Elections

1988 General		
Bill Emerson (R)	117,601	(58%)
Wayne Cryts (D)	84,801	(42%)
1986 General		
Bill Emerson (R)	79,142	(53%)
Wayne Cryts (D)	71,532	(47%)

Previous Winning Percentages: 1984 (65%) **1982** (53%) **1980** (55%)

District Vote For President

	1988	1984	1980	1976
D	91,369 (45%)	82,860 (39%)	94,184 (44%)	109,866 (56%)
R	111,605 (55%)	127,137 (61%)	114,559 (54%)	84,280 (43%)
I			4,107 (2%)	

Campaign Finance

	Receipts	Receipts from PACs	Expend-itures
1988			
Emerson (R)	$850,739	$421,852 (50%)	$768,792
Cryts (D)	$662,184	$300,566 (45%)	$650,100
1986			
Emerson (R)	$595,182	$298,571 (50%)	$598,090
Cryts (D)	$310,874	$152,869 (49%)	$309,504

Key Votes

1987	
Raise speed limit to 65 mph	Y
Approve Gephardt "fair trade" amendment	N
Ban testing of larger nuclear weapons	N
Delay "re-flagging" of Kuwaiti tankers	N
Approve tax-raising deficit-reduction bill	N
1988	
Approve aid to Nicaraguan contras	Y
Enact civil rights restoration bill over Reagan veto	N
Kill 60-day plant-closing notification measure	?
Pass omnibus trade bill over Reagan veto	Y
Approve death penalty for drug-related murders	Y
Bar federal funds for abortions in cases of rape and incest	Y
Oppose seven-day waiting period for purchase of handguns	Y

Voting Studies

	Presidential Support		Party Unity		Conservative Coalition	
Year	S	O	S	O	S	O
1988	47	38	75	14	84	3
1987	60	38	86	13	95	2
1986	69	31	82	18	92	8
1985	60	36	78	17	95	2
1984	57	42	78	19	93	5
1983	70	27	85	13	90	9
1982	58	34	88	9	85	10
1981	78	22	90	10	99	1

Interest Group Ratings

Year	ADA	ACU	AFL-CIO	CCUS
1988	10	90	50	83
1987	4	78	25	87
1986	10	77	29	72
1985	10	80	25	81
1984	15	83	31	75
1983	5	87	12	85
1982	10	91	15	86
1981	0	100	20	89

9 Harold L. Volkmer (D)

Of Hannibal — Elected 1976

Born: April 4, 1931, Jefferson City, Mo.
Education: U. of Missouri, LL.B. 1955.
Military Career: Army, 1955-57.
Occupation: Lawyer.
Family: Wife, Shirley Ruth Braskett; three children.
Religion: Roman Catholic.
Political Career: Marion County prosecuting attorney, 1960-66; Mo. House, 1967-77.
Capitol Office: 2411 Rayburn Bldg. 20515; 225-2956.

In Washington: Winning friends has never been Volkmer's strong point in the House. He can be surly when he disagrees with someone, which is not infrequent. But if his social skills do not charm some colleagues, that has not kept him from having an influence on significant legislation.

Volkmer, best known for his opposition to gun-control legislation, is the leading ally of the National Rifle Association (NRA) in the House. The organization's intense lobbying has buoyed Volkmer's anti-gun-control efforts, but lobbyists don't kill bills, legislators do, and Volkmer has shown he can be effective. In the 100th Congress he helped scuttle a portion of a drug bill requiring a seven-day waiting period for the purchase of handguns. Advocates hoped the waiting period would allow background checks on gun buyers; Volkmer said any waiting-period decision should be left to the states.

Volkmer's most notable achievement in this area came in 1986, when he won passage of a bill rolling back gun-control laws that had been on the books nearly 20 years.

Volkmer's crusade against gun control began soon after his arrival in the House. But for years the issue was bottled up in the Judiciary Committee by Chairman Peter W. Rodino Jr. In the 99th Congress, Volkmer did an end run on the committee, gathering 218 signatures on a petition to discharge his bill from Judiciary and bring it to the House floor.

Few members have successfully employed that tactic, but Volkmer has shown an affinity for using it to gain consideration of his proposals. In the 97th Congress he defied Rodino and the Democratic leadership to bring a balanced-budget constitutional amendment to the floor, where it was defeated.

His petition in 1986 was spurred on by Senate passage of a strong anti-gun-control measure, and, inadvertently, by Rodino, who inflamed opponents when he declared the Senate legislation "dead on arrival" in committee. Intensive lobbying by the NRA was also crucial to Volkmer in his quest for signatures.

Unable to block Volkmer's petition, Rodino worked with fellow New Jersey Democrat William J. Hughes to rush a milder bill through the committee and to the floor. But Volkmer's success with the petition gave him considerable clout with the Rules Committee, which sent the issue to the floor under procedures favoring his version instead of Rodino's.

Opponents of Volkmer's proposal, which lifted a ban on the interstate sale of rifles, shotguns and handguns, as well as easing other restrictions, called it "cop killer" legislation. But Volkmer said he was simply protecting the right to bear arms. The House never considered the milder bill, adopting the Volkmer substitute by a 286-136 vote. Opponents managed to retain a ban on interstate sale of handguns, but otherwise the House-passed legislation was very similar to the Senate's.

Volkmer is certain to be involved in more gun-control issues in the 101st Congress, fending off initiatives by gun-control advocates pointing to public concern about shooting incidents, especially drug-related ones.

Volkmer has also shown an aptitude for legislating on the Agriculture Committee, where he chairs the Subcommittee on Forests, Family Farms and Energy. He is an active participant in committee debates, and can be a team player who will sometimes work to whip up support for legislation produced by the committee.

During debate on the 1985 farm bill, Volkmer was an early proponent of imposing mandatory production quotas to raise prices of wheat, corn and other major crops. He pushed the proposal at the Agriculture subcommittee level, but later let others lead. The plan was struck from the bill on the House floor.

When Congress produced disaster-relief legislation for farmers in the 100th Congress, Volkmer pushed a portion that would permit farmers whose crops had been destroyed by floods to receive 92 percent of their deficiency payments without planting fields that are likely to be flooded again.

Volkmer left the Space Subcommittee chairmanship on the Science, Space and Technology Committee to take his Agriculture chair,

Missouri 9

Northeast — Columbia

Among Missouri's earliest settlers were westward-moving Virginians and bluegrass Kentuckians who liked the rich soils in the northeastern part of the state. They planted their Southern roots here, tried to pull Missouri into the Confederacy and have voted Democratic into the modern era.

But latter-day residents of the northeastern Little Dixie area that anchors the 9th have expressed their conservatism by voting Republican in recent national elections. All 22 counties wholly or partially constituting the 9th supported Ronald Reagan in 1984. In 1988, the counties split evenly between the major-party presidential contenders, but George Bush won 54 percent of the vote overall.

The moderate-to-liberal University of Missouri community in Columbia lends uncertainty to Boone County elections. Republicans have carried Boone in the last four gubernatorial contests. Still, Jimmy Carter won the county in his 1976 and 1980 presidential races and Democrat Harriett Woods won it narrowly in her 1986 Senate race; in 1988 Boone County voted Democratic for president and Republican for governor.

East of Boone lies Callaway County, whose residents declared the county a kingdom unto itself in defiance of the Union during the Civil War. Crossing the Missouri River, the 9th includes Osage, Gasconade and Franklin counties. Gasconade is reliably Republican: Its residents gave George Bush 72 percent in 1988, his best showing statewide. The Gasconade town of Hermann displays its German character in its annual Maifest.

Soybeans, corn and cattle drive the economy throughout much of the 9th's remaining territory, and related agribusinesses are found districtwide. Drawing on the clay found around Mexico (Audrain County), the A. P. Green Refractory has fueled the local firebrick business — and enhanced the financial fortunes of Sen. Christopher S. Bond's family for several generations.

Population: 546,171. White 523,344 (96%), Black 18,092 (3%), Other 2,954 (1%). Spanish origin 3,543 (1%). 18 and over 391,319 (72%), 65 and over 68,313 (13%). Median age: 29.

but he still remains active on Science, now ranking seventh among 30 Democrats there. In the 100th Congress, the committee was the forum for a debate on whether to cut off government funds to contractors and grantees found not to have a drug-free work place. When conservative GOP Rep. Robert S. Walker first put forward the idea, Volkmer was skeptical, saying, "I question how much [drug use] this is really going to stop." But a few minutes later he suggested expanding the provision to allow the government to withhold funding if any employee of a contractor or grantee is convicted of drug possession anywhere. Volkmer later was involved with a Democratic task force that produced a much softer compromise.

Volkmer's strength as a legislator, and his weakness in personal relations, stems from his sheer stubbornness. He is a familiar figure in the chamber as he hunches down over a microphone, waiting as long as necessary for a chance to jump into the debate. One day several years ago, Volkmer asked California Democrat John Burton how long he planned to keep talking. If Burton talked much longer, Volkmer said, he would go back to his office. "I think I could probably get unanimous consent," Burton responded, "for the gentleman to go back to his office for the rest of the evening."

But Volkmer is not swayed by criticism of his personality. "I'm not short-tempered," he said in 1986. "Someone's got an erroneous impression. Gruff, possibly. Short shrift sometimes. Sometimes I can cut people off short."

Volkmer supported the Reagan administration more often than most of his fellow Democrats, but at times he was strong in his criticism. In 1987, when the administration was increasing the country's presence in the Persian Gulf, Volkmer was one of those to voice concerns. "Once again this administration is depending on its Rambo-like style of foreign policy to blunder through another ordeal," he said. "Does this bring back memories of Beirut?"

At Home: Though it irks colleagues in the House, Volkmer's tireless, hard-charging style has brought him consistent political success in Missouri. When told that his 1982 opponent called him "abrupt and abrasive," Volkmer replied, "Could be," and went on to take 61 percent of the vote.

A lawyer from the Mississippi River town of Hannibal, Volkmer has always been popular among northeastern Missouri's rural voters.

With the announcement by Democratic Rep. William L. Hungate that he would retire in 1976, Volkmer and 10 other Democrats sought to succeed him. Drawing on his reputation as an influential five-term member of the Missouri House, Volkmer sewed up a comfortable 17,000-vote margin over his closest primary competitor. Although his November opponent, GOP state Sen. J. H. Frappier, was well-known in the area near St. Louis, Volkmer held his own there and mustered enough rural support to capture 56 percent of the vote.

Volkmer faced a tougher test in 1984, squaring off with Republican Carrie Francke, a former state assistant attorney general with close ties to Sen. John C. Danforth and a Boone County (Columbia) base. Francke claimed Volkmer was insufficiently conservative and had waffled on a constitutional amendment to balance the federal budget. She had an impressive array of resources to help her get her message across. Danforth lent his support, and the national GOP helped her establish a healthy treasury.

Despite her advantages, however, Francke had trouble making inroads into the 9th's rural territory. Her support for the Equal Rights Amendment and for legalized abortion did not endear her to conservative Democrats. She did not enhance her image by touring the 9th's corn and cattle country in a pink van.

Francke carried Boone County, and took five more of the 22 counties included in the 9th. But Volkmer's strength in St. Charles County and the rural reaches again pulled him through.

Francke sought a rematch in 1986, but was defeated in the primary by state Sen. Ralph Uthlaut, a conservative farmer whose legislative constituency gave him a base at the 9th's southern end. Against Volkmer, Uthlaut sought to cash in on the farm crisis, touting his farming background and arguing that a gradual withdrawal of government price supports would better aid ailing agriculturists than what he termed Volkmer's "liberal, almost McGovernite" approach to farm policy.

Volkmer took the attacks in stride. He called for higher farm price supports, and argued that he was well positioned to try to help farmers from his post on the Agriculture Committee. Bolstered further in rural Missouri by press reports of his influence in scaling back federal gun controls, Volkmer racked up a comfortable 57-43 percent victory.

Life just got easier for Volkmer thereafter. His 1988 opponent was Mexico Realtor Ken A. Dudley. Volkmer won by more than 2-to-1, his biggest margin of victory in a decade.

Committees

Agriculture (10th of 27 Democrats)
Forests, Family Farms and Energy (chairman); Department Operations, Research and Foreign Agriculture; Livestock, Dairy and Poultry; Wheat, Soybeans and Feed Grains

Science, Space and Technology (7th of 30 Democrats)
Space Science and Applications

Select Aging (25th of 39 Democrats)
Housing and Consumer Interests; Retirement, Income and Employment

Elections

1988 General		
Harold L. Volkmer (D)	160,872	(68%)
Ken Dudley (R)	76,008	(32%)
1986 General		
Harold L. Volkmer (D)	95,939	(57%)
Ralph Uthlaut Jr. (R)	70,972	(43%)

Previous Winning Percentages: **1984** (53%) **1982** (61%) **1980** (57%) **1978** (75%) **1976** (56%)

District Vote For President

	1988		1984		1980		1976	
D	110,436	(45%)	84,495	(36%)	97,269	(42%)	113,745	(50%)
R	131,829	(54%)	150,683	(64%)	126,289	(54%)	112,799	(49%)
I					8,799	(4%)		

Campaign Finance

	Receipts	Receipts from PACs	Expend-itures
1988			
Volkmer (D)	$300,348	$218,185 (73%)	$210,841
Dudley (R) †	$9,561	0	$9,565
1986			
Volkmer (D)	$373,872	$249,736 (67%)	$383,791
Uthlaut (R)	$147,989	$32,420 (22%)	$147,986

† Totals based on incomplete data.

Key Votes

1987	
Raise speed limit to 65 mph	N
Approve Gephardt "fair trade" amendment	Y
Ban testing of larger nuclear weapons	Y
Delay "re-flagging" of Kuwaiti tankers	Y
Approve tax-raising deficit-reduction bill	Y
1988	
Approve aid to Nicaraguan contras	N
Enact civil rights restoration bill over Reagan veto	Y
Kill 60-day plant-closing notification measure	N
Pass omnibus trade bill over Reagan veto	Y
Approve death penalty for drug-related murders	Y
Bar federal funds for abortions in cases of rape and incest	Y
Oppose seven-day waiting period for purchase of handguns	Y

Voting Studies

	Presidential Support		Party Unity		Conservative Coalition	
Year	**S**	**O**	**S**	**O**	**S**	**O**
1988	35	60	72	23	79	13
1987	34	66	77	20	74	26
1986	33	67	79	20	60	40
1985	30	70	77	21	55	44
1984	42	56	72	27	56	44
1983	26	74	71	29	46	54
1982	35	60	66	34	55	41
1981	43	51	65	31	67	29

Interest Group Ratings

Year	ADA	ACU	AFL-CIO	CCUS
1988	60	35	93	50
1987	64	9	88	27
1986	45	32	79	33
1985	40	33	59	36
1984	55	25	69	44
1983	80	17	88	20
1982	45	55	65	52
1981	30	29	67	26

Montana

U.S. CONGRESS

SENATE 1 D, 1 R

HOUSE 1 D, 1 R

LEGISLATURE

Senate 23 D, 27 R

House 52 D, 48 R

ELECTIONS

1988 Presidential Vote	
Bush	52%
Dukakis	46%
1984 Presidential Vote	
Reagan	60%
Mondale	38%
1980 Presidential Vote	
Reagan	57%
Carter	32%
Anderson	8%
Turnout rate in 1984	65%
Turnout rate in 1986	53%
Turnout rate in 1988	62%

(as percentage of voting age population)

POPULATION AND GROWTH

1980 population	786,690
1988 population estimate (44th in the nation)	805,000
Percent change 1980-1988	+2%

DEMOGRAPHIC BREAKDOWN

White	94%
Black	0.2%
Other	5%
(Spanish origin)	1%
Urban	53%
Rural	47%
Born in state	57%
Foreign-born	2%

MAJOR CITIES

Billings	80,310
Great Falls	57,310
Missoula	33,960
Butte-Silver Bow	33,380
Helena	24,670

AREA AND LAND USE

Area	145,388 sq. miles (4th)
Farm	65%
Forest	24%
Federally owned	30%

Gov. Stan Stephens (R)
Of Havre — Elected 1988

Born: Sept. 16, 1929, Calgary, Alberta, Canada.

Education: Graduated West Canada H.S., 1947.

Military Career: U.S. Army, 1951-53.

Occupation: Radio broadcaster; cable television executive.

Religion: Lutheran.

Political Career: Mont. Senate, 1969-1987, Republican floor whip, 1977, majority leader, 1979, 1981, president, 1983, minority leader, 1985.

Next Election: 1992.

WORK

Occupations	
White-collar	50%
Blue-collar	26%
Service workers	15%
Government Workers	
Federal	10,978
State	20,934
Local	35,880

MONEY

Median family income	$ 18,413 (32nd)
Tax burden per capita	$ 776 (36th)

EDUCATION

Spending per pupil through grade 12	$ 4,091 (14th)
Persons with college degrees	18% (18th)

CRIME

Violent crime rate	151 per 100,000 (45th)

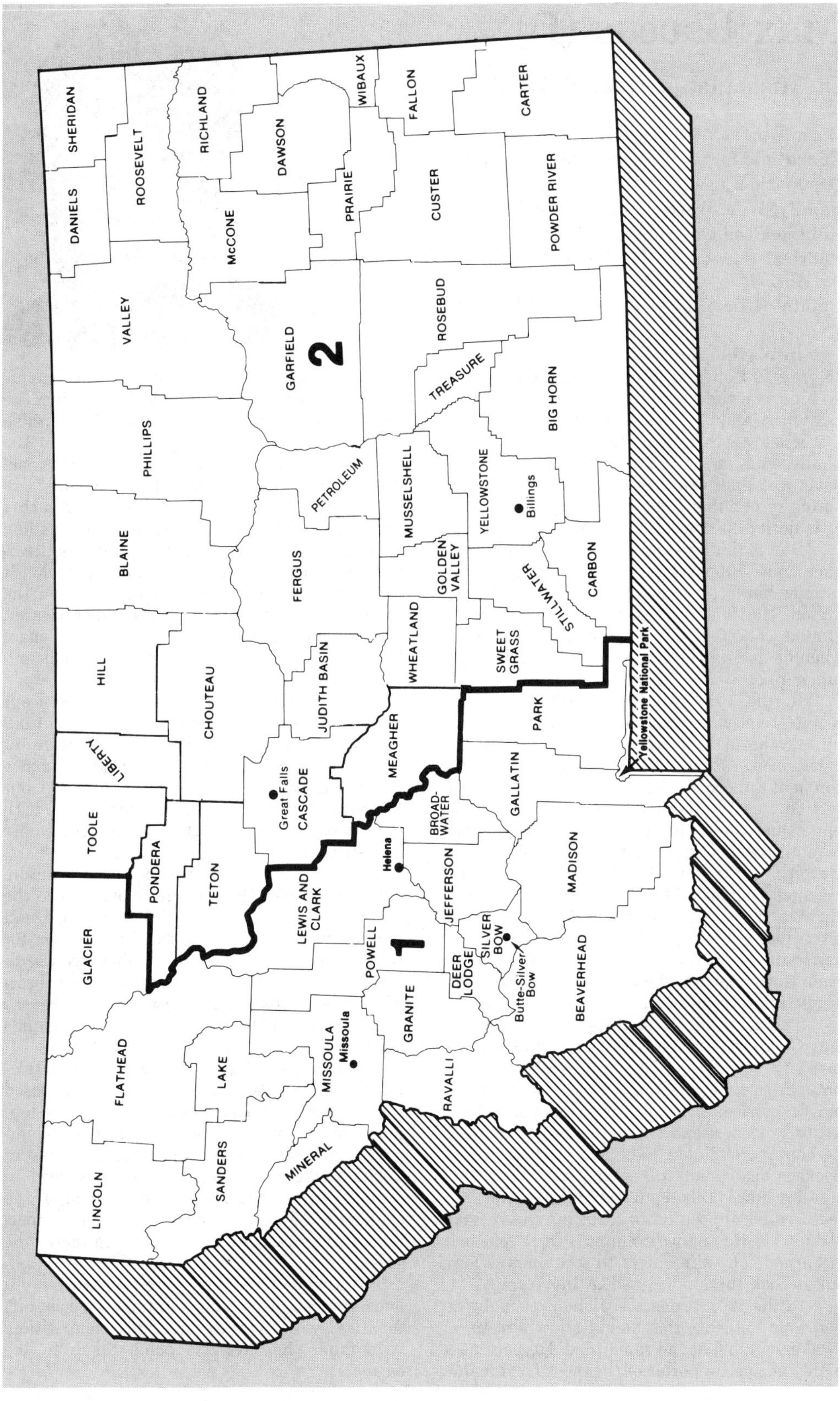
SHERIDAN
DANIELS
ROOSEVELT
RICHLAND
DAWSON
WIBAUX
FALLON
CARTER
McCONE
PRAIRIE
CUSTER
POWDER RIVER
VALLEY
GARFIELD
2
ROSEBUD
TREASURE
BIG HORN
PHILLIPS
PETROLEUM
MUSSELSHELL
YELLOWSTONE
Billings
BLAINE
FERGUS
GOLDEN VALLEY
STILLWATER
CARBON
HILL
CHOUTEAU
JUDITH BASIN
WHEATLAND
SWEET GRASS
Yellowstone National Park
LIBERTY
Great Falls
CASCADE
MEAGHER
PARK
GALLATIN
TOOLE
PONDERA
TETON
BROAD-WATER
Helena
MADISON
GLACIER
LEWIS AND CLARK
JEFFERSON
POWELL
1
SILVER BOW
DEER LODGE
Butte-Silver Bow
BEAVERHEAD
GRANITE
FLATHEAD
LAKE
MISSOULA
Missoula
RAVALLI
MINERAL
SANDERS
LINCOLN

Max Baucus (D)

Of Missoula — Elected 1978

Born: Dec. 11, 1941, Helena, Mont.
Education: Stanford U., B.A. 1964, LL.B. 1967.
Occupation: Lawyer.
Family: Wife, Wanda Minge; one child.
Religion: United Church of Christ.
Political Career: Mont. House, 1973-75; U.S. House, 1975-79.
Capitol Office: 706 Hart Bldg. 20510; 224-2651.

In Washington: Over the course of nearly 15 years in Congress, Baucus has spent considerably more time tending to home-state interests than staking out positions on the controversies of the day. His "Montana First" politics and low profile on most national issues have cushioned him against the effects of a voting record that sometimes strays to the left of majority opinion in Montana.

But if this approach has served him well back home, Baucus has disappointed those who foresaw him achieving greater stature in Washington. He sometimes seems lost in the background, concentrating on parochial matters or, when he does latch onto larger issues, playing a minor role.

In the 101st Congress, with his second Senate re-election campaign looming in 1990, he may have the opportunity to redress that assessment. As the new chairman of the Environment Subcommittee on Environmental Protection, Baucus inherited a choice position at an opportune time. He immediately cosponsored oil-spill liability legislation in the wake of the *Exxon Valdez* calamity in Alaska. He also assumed responsibility for amending the Clean Air Act. That meant tackling the problems of air pollutants, smog and, most ticklish of all, acid rain — which for a decade has divided the regions, the parties, the chambers and the economic interests involved.

The acid-rain job had belonged to Democrat George J. Mitchell of Maine, who became majority leader in late 1988 after having brought an acid rain compromise to the threshold of passage that fall. With a sympathetic majority leader, and with House-side disputes perhaps more soluble, Baucus could preside as a package deal finally takes shape.

Previously, his reputation on the issue had featured his opposition to requiring smokestack "scrubbers" to remove pollutants from coal as it is burned. The alternative to scrubbers is low-sulfur coal, the kind mined in the West.

In the 100th Congress, Baucus thought he had found a cause that would allow him to be local and global at the same time. He became a highly visible supporter of the most fashionable trade concept of the day: America's economic "competitiveness" in the world economy. His crusade for competitiveness found a sizable corps of allies on Capitol Hill. More than 100 members immediately joined the Congressional Caucus on Competitiveness he founded.

But the concept, like the caucus, is such a broad umbrella that it defies quick action; almost everyone favors the idea of competitiveness, but many have their own notion of what it really means. Listening to Baucus discuss the subject does not always make it much clearer. Other members in both the House and Senate had more success in isolating a part of it and winning notice for their efforts.

One opportunity to advance the concept was the omnibus trade bill of 1988. But that bill was bossed primarily by Lloyd Bentsen of Texas, Democratic chairman of the Finance Committee. Baucus had a seat at the table, but his most visible contributions had to do with protecting Montana's cattle, mining and timber industries.

Similarly, Baucus was not a big-picture participant when the committee overhauled the tax code in 1986. But he did press hard and successfully at the end of the 1988 session for passage of a tax-relief bill. His objective was to relieve farmers who, while exempt from diesel fuel taxes, were being forced to pay the tax when they bought fuel and receive refunds later.

Baucus does have a sense of competitiveness on a grander scale. He favors increased support for education, research and development, and capital investment in order to improve the standing of American products in world markets. He thinks Americans need to change their attitudes if they are to fend off the challenge of Japan and other economic competitors. "America has to start hustling more," he says.

But while pursuing answers to those problems, Baucus focuses on Montana's special difficulties with intense foreign competition. "Montana," he says, "is being taken to the cleaners."

More recently, however, elements of the economy both large and small have begun to move past the stage of "Japan bashing." In the spring of 1989, *The Washington Post* reported that a Baucus "get tough" speech in Montana had bombed with much of its audience. It seemed these businessmen had come to view the Japanese as good clients and customers. One state employee was quoted saying Baucus was "about five years behind the curve."

Baucus also has been a vocal critic of the surge in timber imports from Canada, which has contributed to a recession in the logging economy of Montana and other northwestern states in recent years. He has pushed legislation to impose import tariffs to offset alleged subsidization of timber producers by the Canadian government. Baucus was not a fan of the Reagan administration's free-trade agreement with Canada. He voted for it in the Finance Committee only after he and Republican John C. Danforth of Missouri had won a compromise that increased subsidy monitoring.

Baucus' major contribution to economic policy in recent years was his support for a budget "freeze" to combat the federal deficit. Along with Republicans Nancy Landon Kassebaum of Kansas and Charles E. Grassley of Iowa and Democrat Joseph R. Biden Jr. of Delaware, he sponsored a 1984 proposal to fix spending for defense, entitlements and discretionary domestic programs at the previous year's level.

On the Environment Committee, Baucus has usually followed his in-state priorities. Recently, however, he has played a more prominent role on broader issues. He was a prime sponsor of 1986 legislation to strengthen federal standards for drinking-water safety, and fought in committee for tougher controls on pesticides. Chairman of the Hazardous Waste Subcommittee in the 100th Congress, he has expressed particular concern over the threat to the Earth's protective ozone layer posed by chlorofluorocarbons and other gases released into the atmosphere.

At Home: The son of a wealthy Helena ranching family, Baucus used his good looks and personal charm to rise rapidly in Montana politics. After working in Washington as a lawyer for the Securities and Exchange Commission, he returned home to serve as coordinator of the state constitutional convention in 1972. The same year, he won his state legislative seat.

In 1974 Baucus moved up to the U.S. House, dislodging Republican Richard G. Shoup, who was trying for a third term. To gain publicity for the race, Baucus walked 631 miles across his congressional district. He managed to impress the labor-oriented Democrats who dominate the party in western Montana, and he did little to antagonize Republicans. He was a comfortable winner over Shoup in 1974 and an easy winner for re-election in 1976.

Meanwhile, he was focusing on the Senate. His hopes were temporarily frustrated in early 1978 by Democratic Gov. Thomas L. Judge, a political rival. After the death of veteran Democrat Lee Metcalf, the governor bypassed Baucus and appointed Paul Hatfield, chief justice of the Montana Supreme Court, to succeed Metcalf in the Senate.

But Baucus had already begun his 1978 Senate campaign, and he did not step aside for Hatfield. The newly appointed senator could not match Baucus' head start in organizing, and he hurt himself by voting for the Panama Canal treaties. Baucus did not oppose the treaties, but as a member of the House, he did not have to vote on the issue. He easily won the primary.

That fall, he had a hard-nosed Republican competitor in financier Larry Williams, who castigated him as too liberal and ridiculed his periodic awards from the National Taxpayers Union as meaningless. Baucus was hurt by charges of outside liberal influence in his campaign, and Williams seemed on the verge of overtaking him by early October.

Then Baucus' Democratic allies released their "bombshell" — a picture of the "conservative" Williams in shaggy hair and love beads, taken before he moved from California to Montana to launch his campaign. Baucus kept his distance from the issue, but the AFL-CIO made sure the picture was all over Montana in the weeks before the election. The final result was a comfortable Baucus victory.

Heading into 1984, national Republican strategists insisted that Baucus would be one of the nation's most vulnerable senators. They said his voting record was too liberal for a state where Reagan won 57 percent in 1980 and seemed likely to surpass that in 1984.

Baucus prepared for the worst. He organized and raised money at a feverish pace; his campaign phone bank started operating in 1983, reaching into thousands of households to attract new volunteers and contributors before the GOP had even found a candidate. By early 1984, Baucus was well on his way toward raising and spending $1 million, a Montana record.

All this activity by Baucus had a chilling effect on Republican recruiting efforts: No well-known GOP figure stepped forward to take on the incumbent. Three lesser-known conservatives competed in the GOP primary, and former state Rep. Chuck Cozzens emerged as the winner. In the Democratic primary, Baucus brushed aside a challenge from the right.

Cozzens had trouble attracting the attention he needed to be viewed as a credible challenger to Baucus. He tried to solve that problem by airing a series of radio advertisements calling Baucus a "wimp" who "talks out of both sides of his mouth and lives in fear that we'll get wise to his games." But the "wimp" portrayal backfired on Cozzens. Because he had not done much to build up his own image and stress his positive ideas before attacking, many editorial writers and even some Republicans criticized him for running a negative, mudslinging campaign.

With others doing the work of criticizing Cozzens, Baucus was free to ignore his opponent most of the time and concentrate on portraying himself as a moderate pragmatist. He stressed his work for a budget freeze, and he made plain his disagreement with his party's official line in favor of a tax increase. On that issue, "Walter Mondale will speak for himself," Baucus said.

In spite of Reagan's 60 percent showing in Montana, Baucus won 45 of the state's 56 counties, taking 57 percent of the vote.

Committees

Agriculture, Nutrition and Forestry (9th of 10 Democrats)
Agricultural Production and Stabilization of Prices; Conservation and Forestry; Domestic and Foreign Marketing and Product Promotion

Environment and Public Works (4th of 9 Democrats)
Environmental Protection (chairman); Superfund, Ocean and Water Protection; Toxic Substances, Environmental Oversight, Research and Development

Finance (4th of 11 Democrats)
International Trade (chairman); Medicare and Long-Term Care; Taxation and Debt Management

Small Business (3rd of 10 Democrats)
Rural Economy and Family Farming (chairman); Innovation, Technology and Productivity

Elections

1984 General		
Max Baucus (D)	215,704	(57%)
Chuck Cozzens (R)	154,308	(41%)
1984 Primary		
Max Baucus (D)	87,726	(79%)
Bob Ripley (D)	20,979	(21%)

Previous Winning Percentages: 1978 (56%) **1976 *** (66%) **1974 *** (55%)

* *House elections.*

Campaign Finance

	Receipts	Receipts from PACs	Expend-itures
1984			
Baucus (D)	$1,239,892	$653,749 (53%)	$1,224,258
Cozzens (R)	$585,826	$158,630 (27%)	$580,921

Key Votes

1987	
Enact omnibus highway bill over Reagan veto	Y
Limit testing of space-based anti-ballistic missiles	Y
Oppose banning tests of larger nuclear weapons	N
Confirm Robert H. Bork as Supreme Court justice	N
1988	
Allow vote on campaign-finance overhaul	Y
Pass civil rights restoration bill over Reagan veto	Y
Enact omnibus trade bill over Reagan veto	Y
Approve death penalty for drug-related murders	Y
Oppose "workfare" amendment to welfare overhaul bill	Y

Voting Studies

	Presidential Support		Party Unity		Conservative Coalition	
Year	**S**	**O**	**S**	**O**	**S**	**O**
1988	47	51	86	12	51	49
1987	33	65	86	13	44	56
1986	30	66	74	22	37	54
1985	30	68	83	15	47	52
1984	40	58	76	21	34	66
1983	38	60	77	21	45	55
1982	44	53	80	18	31	67
1981	45	50	84	14	29	66

Interest Group Ratings

Year	ADA	ACU	AFL-CIO	CCUS
1988	80	8	86	29
1987	75	8	80	28
1986	80	13	60	37
1985	65	9	75	37
1984	75	14	50	50
1983	75	25	71	32
1982	85	16	85	40
1981	85	13	67	39

Conrad Burns (R)

Of Billings — Elected 1988

Born: Jan. 25, 1935, Gallatin, Mo.
Education: Attended U. of Missouri, 1952-54.
Military Career: Marine Corps, 1955-57.
Occupation: Radio and television broadcaster.
Family: Wife, Phyllis Kuhlmann; two children.
Religion: Lutheran.
Political Career: Yellowstone County commissioner, 1987-89.
Capitol Office: 183 Dirksen Bldg. 20510; 224-2644.

The Path to Washington: When Burns joined the Senate after his 1988 upset of Democratic incumbent John Melcher, the four-member Montana congressional delegation became a 2-2 split in personality as well as partisanship.

Montana's Democrats in Congress, Sen. Max Baucus and Rep. Pat Williams, express an intellectual liberalism most popular in Montana's larger cities. But Burns, along with his Republican colleague, Rep. Ron Marlenee, exude a rugged and rambunctious conservative populism more closely identified with the state's rural traditions.

Burns, who had little political experience before his 1988 Senate campaign, is a self-described cowboy who made his fame as an agricultural broadcaster and a popular speaker on the farm-group dinner circuit. In manner and dress, Burns seldom appears to be far from the ranch. At an orientation session for freshman senators, he was easy to spot among his dark-suited colleagues: He was the one wearing a sports jacket, aged cowboy boots and a leather belt with "Conrad" tooled on the back.

The Eastern press was taken with Burns' folksy style. Two television networks and *The Washington Post* ran friendly profiles of him, as did *USA Today*. (It was in that newspaper that Burns, a tobacco-chewer, promised, "I'll never take a chew under the Capitol dome.") And to his acolytes back home, Burns was an expression of themselves: natural, independent, and unbound by elitist (read: Eastern) pretensions.

But other Montanans felt Burns cut just the kind of image in Washington that the state should avoid. They said efforts to attract high-tech and other growth industries — needed to diversify a flagging state economy that is over-reliant on farming and energy development — are hindered by the perception of Montana as a remote and unsophisticated backwater.

"Burns is making us look like bumpkins," said an editorial in the Bozeman *Chronicle* early in his freshman term. The Billings *Gazette*, which serves Montana's largest city, said, "Thanks, Conrad, thanks for telling the world what hicks we are." The harshest criticism was reserved for Burns' glib remark that "there are awful good folks" in Montana, including some who "can read and write."

But the comment, far from being an attack on his constituents, was typical of the joshing and often self-deprecating humor that made Burns popular on the stump. In his defense, Burns also denied that his cowboy characterization would make him an ineffective spokesman for Montana interests. "I take my job damn serious," Burns told the Post.

Serious is not quite how Burns was taken when he entered the 1988 Senate contest. He had served less than two years in his only elective office, Yellowstone County (Billings) commissioner. He had no broad expertise on national or international issues. And he seemed to be a fall-back candidate, recruited by the National Republican Senatorial Committee (NRSC) for a state party that failed to find a well-known elected official to challenge Melcher.

However, Burns actually had a much stronger political base than most observers, including Melcher, recognized. His broadcasts on the Northern Agricultural Network, which he co-founded, had given him a statewide following and far greater name recognition than any of the state legislators the GOP had tried to recruit. He also had a lifetime of experience in agriculture, a crucial economic sector in Montana.

Melcher, for his part, was a far less formidable incumbent than widely presumed. A veterinarian widely known as "Doc," Melcher had built his popularity with his own folksy charm. But he was a stumbling campaigner, and his Senate voting record, which often earned him 100 percent ratings from the Americans for Democratic Action, left him vulnerable to charges that he was to the left of the state mainstream.

The NRSC spotted this vulnerability early on, and promoted Burns, to a disbelieving political and media establishment, as their "upset special." The campaign committee poured in nearly $200,000, enough to buy plenty of TV ad-time in a state where airtime is inexpensive. Many of the ads blasted Melcher as too liberal and as ineffective in promoting Montana's agenda.

Burns' campaign planted doubt in voters' minds, and Melcher's double-digit lead in the polls slowly began to evaporate. Melcher tried to strike back by portraying Burns as a packaged candidate, bought and controlled by the national Republican political machine. He even reprised a previously successful TV ad concept, "talking" cows who derided the "greenhorn" Republican.

But not even talking cows could save Melcher from an onslaught of untimely news headlines in the last weeks of the campaign. Burns benefited from an article in the Great Falls *Tribune* detailing Melcher's interest in Philippine issues; Burns had labored to draw attention to the fact that the incumbent had visited the Philippines three times in five years. Burns also gained from the publicity attendant a Billings campaign visit by Republican presidential nominee George Bush in late October.

But the event that may have cinched the win for Burns was President Reagan's veto of a wilderness bill, authored by Melcher, just days before the election. The bill, which had long been stalled in Congress, had been an albatross for Melcher, endearing him neither to development interests, who opposed wilderness legislation in general, and environmentalists, who wanted more land protected than the bill provided. Then, when Reagan vetoed the bill, it appeared to reinforce Burns' claim that Melcher lacked the clout to get his proposals enacted.

Burns won by a fairly narrow 52-48 percent margin, but his support was well distributed across the state. In fact, he ran slightly better in the normally Democratic 1st District than in the Republican 2nd, a home base he shared with Melcher.

There was some irony in the committee assignments Burns received after his victory. He supplanted Melcher on the Energy and Natural Resources Committee, and obtained seats on the Commerce and Small Business committees. But while his strong farm base had staked him to victory, Burns was not placed on the Agriculture Committee, where Melcher had been the second-senior Democrat and chairman of the Agricultural Production Subcommittee.

Committees

Commerce, Science and Transportation (7th of 9 Republicans)
Foreign Commerce and Tourism (ranking); Communications; Surface Transportation

Energy and Natural Resources (7th of 9 Republicans)
Water and Power (ranking); Energy Research and Development; Public Lands, National Parks and Forests

Small Business (8th of 9 Republicans)
Urban and Minority-Owned Business Development (ranking); Rural Economy and Family Farming

Campaign Finance

	Receipts	Receipts from PACs	Expend- itures
1988			
Burns (R)	$1,099,488	$315,387 (29%)	$1,076,010
Melcher (D)	$1,237,661	$812,560 (66%)	$1,338,622

Elections

1988 General		
Conrad Burns (R)	189,445	(52%)
John Melcher (D)	175,809	(48%)
1988 Primary		
Conrad Burns (R)	63,330	(85%)
Tom Faranda (R)	11,427	(15%)

1 Pat Williams (D)

Of Missoula — Elected 1978

Born: Oct. 30, 1937, Helena, Mont.

Education: Attended U. of Montana, 1956-57; William Jewell College, 1958; U. of Denver, B.A. 1961; graduate work, Western Montana College, 1962.

Military Career: Army, 1960-61; National Guard, 1962-69.

Occupation: Elementary and secondary school teacher.

Family: Wife, Carol Griffith; three children.

Religion: Roman Catholic.

Political Career: Mont. House, 1967-71; sought Democratic nomination for U.S. House, 1974.

Capitol Office: 2457 Rayburn Bldg. 20515; 225-3211.

In Washington: Undaunted by the conservative politics of the 1980s, Williams remains a traditional New Deal liberal, willing to champion creation of new government programs at a time when most politicians are talking about cutbacks.

This mentality, and the passionate rhetoric that goes with it, leads many conservatives to write him off as a relic of a bygone era. But the Montanan matches his partisanship with healthy doses of pragmatism and patience, and that has earned him some significant legislative accomplishments.

Williams' ties to organized labor helped bring him to Congress a decade ago, and he has been faithful to the union movement. He is a deputy whip designated to watch labor issues in the House, and he serves the same function from his post on the Education and Labor Committee. Indicative of his loyalty, Williams was one of just two committee members to back a 1988 effort to index the minimum wage.

Also in the 100th Congress, Williams was the prime mover of labor-backed legislation to bar most private employers from requiring workers and job applicants to take lie-detector tests. After fighting off a host of weakening amendments, Williams' bill was enacted largely intact; it allowed polygraph tests in only limited cases involving defense and national security work. "Thumbscrews and the rack, even if they are now electronic, should be outlawed," he said.

A former schoolteacher, Williams now chairs the Postsecondary Education Subcommittee, where addressing the problem of student-loan defaults is currently a top priority. While Williams echoes the conservative demand to crack down on "charlatans," his recommendations include expanding the Pell Grant program by increasing the awards and making it an entitlement program, which he says will ensure that students receive the full amount of aid for which they qualify.

This is not an altogether popular proposal, but Williams maintains it will help reduce the default problem. He says defaults have skyrocketed in part because the loan program was intended as a supplement for middle-income students, but instead has become the principal path to college for low-income students, who often are ill-equipped to repay their loans.

Williams' bill cleared the committee in 1988, and the Education Department issued stiff new regulations shortly afterward. Williams ended up negotiating a delay with the administration, in hopes of finding a compromise and avoiding election-year posturing.

For three terms (through 1988), Williams served on the Budget Committee, where he reveled in the fierce partisan rivalry that prevailed early in his tenure, but joined the move toward bipartisanship in recent years.

When he first joined Budget, Williams teamed with a liberal bloc of members who were determined to resist Reagan administration cuts in their priority programs. "Folks believe the nation is not being well governed because the two parties are Tweedledum and Tweedledee," Williams once said. "This time they're going to perceive a real difference between the president's budget and the Democratic budget."

The group managed to work into the 1986 budget resolution some $1.8 billion in spending increases over three years for selected low-income programs, many of them targeted at children. When bipartisanship completely collapsed the following year, Williams nonchalantly commented, "Our system works best when it works with competition."

The committee's mood began to change after the 1987 stock market crash, which prompted a budget summit to craft a deficit-reduction compromise. Williams was named to the House negotiating team, where his role was to protect low- and middle-income programs from Draconian cuts. Early in 1988, as Democrats and Republicans moved toward agree-

Montana 1

Western Mountains — Helena; Missoula

The Continental Divide meanders the length of this district, separating Montana's rugged west from its eastern plains and the labor Democrats of the 1st from the Republican ranchers of the 2nd.

The mountains of western Montana begat lumber mills and mines early in this century. While the prodigious lodes of copper, zinc and lead in Butte's "richest hill on Earth" produced some of the richest mine owners in America, they also spawned strong unions to represent those who labored in them.

Though forestry and mining have not always provided a steady living — a sharp recent decline in demand has forced many miners out of work and caused a population drain near Butte — union-inspired Democratic voting habits have been quite regular at the House level. Only one Republican has represented the 1st since 1942, and he lasted just two terms.

The Democratic loyalties are not nearly as strong in elections for higher office. Ronald Reagan won easily in 1980 and 1984, though George Bush defeated Democrat Michael S. Dukakis by a modest 50-48 percent margin. While western Montana has been a breeding ground for Democratic senators — including former Senate Majority Leader Mike Mansfield and current Sen. Max Baucus — the 1st District in 1988 turned its back on Democratic Sen. John Melcher, an eastern Montanan. Republican Conrad Burns took the 1st with 53 percent on his way to victory statewide.

Nowhere are the district's Democratic ties stronger than in heavily unionized Silver Bow County (Butte) and Deer Lodge County (Anaconda). In 1988, Dukakis took 72 percent of the vote in Silver Bow and 68 percent in Deer Lodge. These counties also supported George McGovern in 1972, Jimmy Carter in 1980 and Walter F. Mondale in 1984.

Dukakis also carried the two counties with sizable urban centers: Missoula and Lewis and Clark (Helena). The district's largest city, Missoula, which lies at the hub of several agricultural valleys, is a lumber processing center and is home to the University of Montana. Dukakis took 54 percent of the county vote in 1988, though Reagan managed an identical margin for the GOP in 1984.

The state capital of Helena is near the eastern edge of the 1st: It got its start when gold was discovered in Last Chance Gulch during the Civil War. Dukakis edged Bush in Lewis and Clark County, though Melcher failed there.

The more rural counties provide the margin for statewide Republicans who carry the 1st. Bush carried Flathead County in the north (where tourists in Glacier National Park provide income for people in Kalispell and Whitefish) and Gallatin County in the south (site of Bozeman and Montana State University) with 57 percent. Republicans tend to be competitive in each of the district's four southernmost counties, which are geared more toward farming and cattle than toward lumber and mining. Tourism in nearby Yellowstone National Park is also an economic source, though the trade was damaged by the forest fires of 1988.

Population: 393,298. White 376,235 (96%), Black 446 (0.1%), Other 14,535 (4%). Spanish origin 3,869 (1%). 18 and over 280,180 (71%), 65 and over 41,811 (11%). Median age: 29.

ment, he reported, "We're serious about giving it the old college try."

Winning appointment to the budget summit was typical of the perquisites that came Williams' way under Jim Wright's tenure as House Speaker. At the start of the 101st Congress, he also won a spot on Steering and Policy, which makes Democratic committee assignments.

Although Williams was appointed a deputy whip by then-Speaker Thomas P. O'Neill Jr. — who shared Williams' New Deal ideology — he was one of the few liberals to strike up a friendship with Wright, a fellow boxing buff. Without stepping back from his liberal agenda, Williams became a strong Wright ally.

When Wright caught flak for the unraveling of the proposed 51 percent congressional pay raise early in 1989, Williams had kinder words for Wright: "It was obvious that this issue was stillborn, and yet people are blaming the midwife," he said. Later, as the Speaker's ethics problems deepened, a rather ominous Williams remark raised eyebrows, given his allegiance to Wright. "The Speaker is in hip-deep water," Williams said after the ethics committee report was released, "and the white rapids are straight ahead."

At Home: While districts all over the mountain West were voting Republican in 1978, Williams was able to win a comfortable victory over a strong Republican opponent, keeping the open 1st District in Democratic hands.

Williams had been active in Montana politics for a decade before coming to Congress. His political career was temporarily derailed in 1974, when he lost the Democratic House nomination to Max Baucus. But when Baucus ran for the Senate in 1978, Williams had another shot at Congress.

He entered a multi-candidate primary, and was blessed with strong labor backing. Williams campaigned on the need for more jobs in the western part of Montana, but also on the need to keep the district's industry clean. He won nomination with 41 percent of the vote.

Williams' Republican opponent was 29-year-old Jim Waltermire, then a Missoula County commissioner. At the time, Waltermire was not well-known outside his home county, and his pro-development views were a liability against Williams, an environmental moderate who stressed the need for protection as well as job development. Williams comfortably defeated Waltermire (who went on to become Montana's secretary of state and a 1988 candidate for governor, but died in a plane crash).

Williams has not been held below 60 percent in any election since, and his strength has led to frequent speculation that he might run for statewide office someday. He may be required to do that in 1992, when congressional reapportionment could drop Montana from two House districts to one at-large seat.

Before 1978, Williams had filled a variety of positions besides serving two terms in the state Legislature. He was Montana director of Hubert H. Humphrey's presidential campaign in 1968 and chairman of the Jimmy Carter campaign in western Montana in 1976. He spent two years on Capitol Hill as an aide to Democrat John Melcher, who was then representing Montana's other district in the House and later served two Senate terms.

Committees

Education and Labor (8th of 22 Democrats)
Postsecondary Education (chairman); Elementary, Secondary and Vocational Education; Employment Opportunities; Labor Standards

Interior and Insular Affairs (8th of 26 Democrats)
National Parks and Public Lands

Elections

1988 General		
Pat Williams (D)	115,278	(61%)
Jim Fenlason (R)	74,405	(39%)
1986 General		
Pat Williams (D)	98,501	(62%)
Don Allen (R)	61,230	(38%)

Previous Winning Percentages: **1984** (66%) **1982** (60%) **1980** (61%) **1978** (57%)

District Vote For President

	1988	1984	1980	1976
D	91,519 (48%)	78,513 (40%)	62,332 (34%)	74,522 (46%)
R	95,054 (50%)	113,967 (58%)	101,743 (55%)	85,786 (53%)
I			15,843 (9%)	

Campaign Finance

	Receipts	Receipts from PACs	Expend-itures
1988			
Williams (D)	$399,066	$185,656 (47%)	$369,486
Fenlason (R)	$106,821	$13,256 (12%)	$106,808
1986			
Williams (D)	$277,611	$168,055 (61%)	$229,170
Allen (R)	$154,994	$22,100 (14%)	$154,551

Key Votes

1987	
Raise speed limit to 65 mph	Y
Approve Gephardt "fair trade" amendment	Y
Ban testing of larger nuclear weapons	Y
Delay "re-flagging" of Kuwaiti tankers	Y
Approve tax-raising deficit-reduction bill	Y
1988	
Approve aid to Nicaraguan contras	N
Enact civil rights restoration bill over Reagan veto	Y
Kill 60-day plant-closing notification measure	N
Pass omnibus trade bill over Reagan veto	Y
Approve death penalty for drug-related murders	N
Bar federal funds for abortions in cases of rape and incest	N
Oppose seven-day waiting period for purchase of handguns	#

Voting Studies

	Presidential Support		Party Unity		Conservative Coalition	
Year	S	O	S	O	S	O
1988	14	77	70	5	13	79
1987	18	79	81	5	21	74
1986	12	82	76	8	18	74
1985	18	80	76	4	7	87
1984	30	65	72	14	17	75
1983	18	72	77	9	18	74
1982	35	61	81	11	16	79
1981	34	62	86	10	21	73

Interest Group Ratings

Year	ADA	ACU	AFL-CIO	CCUS
1988	85	0	100	15
1987	96	0	94	7
1986	85	5	92	20
1985	95	10	94	23
1984	90	13	82	33
1983	90	9	94	37
1982	85	9	100	23
1981	95	20	93	6

2 Ron Marlenee (R)

Of Scobey — Elected 1976

Born: Aug. 8, 1935, Scobey, Mont.
Education: Attended U. of Montana, 1953, 1960; Montana State U., 1960.
Occupation: Rancher.
Family: Wife, Cynthia Tiemann; three children.
Religion: Lutheran.
Political Career: No previous office.
Capitol Office: 2465 Rayburn Bldg. 20515; 225-1555.

In Washington: Like most Mountain state Republicans in the House, Marlenee brings to his work an ornery individualism rooted in resentment of federal control over his state's land. His antipathy toward government involvement in land matters predominates his approach to issues on the Interior Committee; he is equally unyielding toward liberal Democrats on social and foreign policy. But on the Agriculture Committee, Marlenee can be more cooperative as he looks for allies to help him get the best deal for the farmers and ranchers of his vast district.

The best example of Marlenee's ability to tame his fury and work toward a positive goal came during debate on the 1985 farm bill. Marlenee and Wheat Subcommittee Chairman Thomas S. Foley formed an alliance to push through Foley's proposals on the bill. In the crucial voting, Marlenee sided with Foley, even rebuffing Republicans' alternatives to Foley's ideas.

The alliance was logical. Foley was one of Agriculture's most conservative Democrats, an opponent of production controls, and a man whose wheat-growing district in eastern Washington bears some similarities to Marlenee's constituency in eastern Montana.

Marlenee proved his ability to craft deals behind the scenes when Agriculture worked on a bill in the 100th Congress to bail out the Farm Credit System. He teamed with Minnesota Democrat Timothy J. Penny and Missouri Republican E. Thomas Coleman to work out language imposing new loan restructuring and "borrowers' rights" requirements on the Farmers Home Administration (FmHA). Their proposals, opposed by the Reagan administration, required FmHA to restructure delinquent loans, if that would be cheaper than foreclosing.

While Marlenee can cooperate on farm policy, he never seems far from combustion. Such was the case when he launched a one-man crusade against the one section of the 1985 farm bill that had attracted broad bipartisan support. This was the "sodbuster" section, aimed at cutting off crop subsidies to farmers who do not practice soil conservation.

Marlenee had once supported a sodbuster bill himself, but by 1985 he was adamantly against it. He regarded the sodbuster legislation as a step on the road to mandatory crop controls, which he considers pernicious. On the House floor, he referred to a proposal for a farmer referendum on production controls for wheat and feed grains as the "Hollywood-Hayden-Fonda-Willie Nelson-Harkin farm referendum."

Marlenee's deeply rooted resentment of the federal government shows up primarily on Interior, where he is in a good position to fight with environmentalists as ranking member of the National Parks and Public Lands Subcommittee. But Marlenee's inflexibility limits his role as a GOP strategist; he often seems more eager to make his own views known than to solicit others' opinions.

Sheer stubborness, however, did pay off for Marlenee in 1988, as he battled a bill designating more than 1.4 million acres of national forest land in Montana as wilderness. The bill was a compromise worked out among Montana's Senate and House Democrats, including Sen. John Melcher, who was locked in a tough re-election battle. But many environmentalists felt it added too few wilderness acres, and development advocates (including Marlenee) said it added too many. When President Reagan vetoed the bill a week before Election Day, it was a heavy blow to Melcher's prestige, and a factor in his loss to Republican Conrad Burns.

Marlenee may be trying for more such high-visibility victories, because his political agenda could include a statewide race in the near future — either for the Senate in 1990, or for the House in 1992 if, as expected, Montana loses a seat in post-census reapportionment.

One of Marlenee's priorities on Interior is protecting cattlemen whose herds graze on federal lands. One-third of ranch families in Montana have cattle grazing on Forest Service and Bureau of Land Management land, and Marlenee has fought to prevent the government from increasing their grazing fees.

Marlenee's contempt for the central gov-

Montana 2

East

This is flat country — a land of sizzling summer heat and numbing winter cold, given over to wheat growing, cattle raising and, more recently, energy development. Covering three-quarters of the state, the 2nd tends to favor Republicans, but Democrats, especially those with a farm background, can compete there.

One such Democrat was 2nd District resident and two-term Sen. John Melcher. But in 1988, the 2nd abandoned Melcher for an eastern Montana Republican, Yellowstone County (Billings) commissioner and former farm broadcaster Conrad Burns. Melcher, who had taken 35 of the district's 37 counties in 1982, won only 10 against Burns in 1988.

The 2nd was fertile territory for Ronald Reagan, who won it with 63 percent in 1984. His successor, George Bush, had more difficulties in farm areas such as the 2nd; he won it in 1988, but with a modest 54 percent.

Roughly half the district's people live in and around the state's two largest cities, Billings and Great Falls (Cascade County). Billings is the more dependable of the two for Republicans.

From its beginnings as a market center for sugar beets and other farm products, Billings grew in the 1970s to become headquarters for the many energy ventures that sprouted across the plains. Yellowstone County gave Bush 55 percent and Billings resident Burns 52 percent in 1988.

Great Falls is at the western edge of the 2nd. Cheap hydroelectric power drawn from the nearby falls on the Missouri River spurred its industrial development early in the century, as well as a surviving tradition of union activism. Democratic presidential nomineee Michael S. Dukakis barely lost Cascade County in 1988, and Melcher's 53 percent there was one of his better showings in the 2nd.

The district's ranching and wheat-growing counties are sparsely populated, but most of them deliver hefty Republican margins. In huge but almost vacant Garfield County in the center of the district, Bush won by nearly 3-to-1 — and that was down from Reagan's nearly 6-to-1 margin in 1984.

One of the areas transformed by energy development was Rosebud County, east of Billings, where coal discoveries caused a 64 percent population boom during the 1970s, and another 25 percent jump in the first half of the 1980s. The political result has been to render this former GOP bastion into a Democratic-leaning area. Dukakis edged Bush in the county, and Melcher won big there.

Population: 393,392. White 363,913 (93%), Black 1,340 (0.3%), American Indian, Eskimo and Aleut 23,940 (6%). Spanish origin 6,105 (2%). 18 and over 274,615 (70%), 65 and over 42,748 (11%). Median age: 29.

ernment touches even the host city of that government. As reports of violent drug-related crime and municipal corruption in the District of Columbia made national news in 1989, he suggested that the new slogan for the District should be: "D.C., A Work-Free Drug Place." He decried "a city out of control ... with a homicide rate so high its tourist promotion should issue every visitor a handgun."

On most foreign policy matters, Marlenee stands on the conservative wing of his party. He stirred controversy by going to South Africa in 1987 to hunt Cape buffalo, but dismissed critics, saying, "We are not dealing with a banana republic."

At Home: Marlenee's style and opinions are not for everybody: Only once in seven House elections has he won over 60 percent. But only once was his margin really meager — in 1986, when he took 53 percent against Democratic rancher Richard "Buck" O'Brien.

Given O'Brien's background, it was not surprising Marlenee underestimated him. The Democrat had never sought office before; his political experience consisted of work as state party committeeman and as chairman of the Montana Aeronautics Commission. But O'Brien's background as a rancher and farmer lent weight to his complaints that the farm economy was failing because of policies favored by Marlenee and President Reagan.

Seeking shelter from farm-crisis fallout, Marlenee played up his differences with the administration's agricultural policy, and he reminded audiences that his posts on the Agriculture and Interior committees put him in a good position to address farm problems. O'Brien ran close to Marlenee in many of the 2nd's rural counties, but that was not enough to break the incumbent's grip.

Marlenee blamed the close outcome on his own complacency. O'Brien, saying he would have won had his name been better known, set out to overtake Marlenee in a 1988 rematch.

He kept his name in the news during 1987 by issuing a steady stream of press releases, and by piloting his own plane to speaking engagements across the huge district. He blamed Marlenee for continued farm problems and assailed him for visiting South Africa.

But Marlenee applied himself to his reelection. He organized early, spent more than $400,000 (compared with $250,000 in 1986) and ran ads lauding his record and accusing O'Brien of being a liberal in populist's clothing.

Marlenee was bolstered by attention he got for criticizing the National Park Service's "let-burn" policy during the Yellowstone forest fires in mid-1988. Marlenee also got a boost when, as he had suggested, Reagan vetoed Melcher's wilderness bill. Marlenee carried all but three counties, winning 56 percent overall.

Marlenee started farming in 1953 with 320 acres of leased land and built a wheat and Hereford cattle operation known as "Marlenee's Big Sky Ranch." He began working with the Montana Stockgrowers, the Montana Grain Growers and the state political arm of the American Farm Bureau Federation.

These affiliations made him a familiar name in GOP circles, but his 1976 House campaign was his first bid for public office. He started early, announcing before incumbent Democrat Melcher had indicated his intention to run for the Senate. Marlenee had to work against the fact that he came from a rural area remote from most of the district's population, while his chief primary opponent, former state legislator John Cavan, came from Billings, the largest city. But Marlenee overcame Cavan, and went on to win in the fall against Democrat Tom Towe, whose family banking fortune allowed him to run a well-financed campaign, but whose populist approach disturbed conservative Democrats.

In 1982, Democrats nominated a candidate who could compete with Marlenee outside urban areas. He was Howard Lyman, a farmer and rancher with a blunt manner and conservative views. But Lyman ran into trouble when a local newspaper disclosed that he had handed over title to his ranch and feed-lot operation to a creditor to meet $2.5 million in debts. Marlenee took 54 percent of the vote.

Committees

Agriculture (3rd of 18 Republicans)
Wheat, Soybeans and Feed Grains (ranking); Forests, Family Farms and Energy

Interior and Insular Affairs (3rd of 15 Republicans)
National Parks and Public Lands (ranking); Mining and Natural Resources; Water, Power and Offshore Energy Resources

Elections

1988 General		
Ron Marlenee (R)	97,465	(56%)
Richard "Buck" O'Brien (D)	78,069	(44%)
1986 General		
Ron Marlenee (R)	84,548	(53%)
Richard "Buck" O'Brien (D)	73,583	(47%)

Previous Winning Percentages: **1984** (66%) **1982** (54%) **1980** (59%) **1978** (57%) **1976** (55%)

District Vote For President

	1988	1984	1980	1976
D	77,437 (44%)	68,229 (36%)	55,700 (31%)	74,737 (45%)
R	95,358 (54%)	118,483 (63%)	105,071 (59%)	87,917 (53%)
I			13,438 (8%)	

Campaign Finance

	Receipts	Receipts from PACs	Expend-itures
1988			
Marlenee (R)	$416,031	$171,992 (41%)	$380,928
O'Brien (D)	$396,369	$198,284 (50%)	$394,102
1986			
Marlenee (R)	$265,900	$110,725 (42%)	$251,163
O'Brien (D)	$221,142	$45,093 (20%)	$223,231

Key Votes

1987	
Raise speed limit to 65 mph	Y
Approve Gephardt "fair trade" amendment	N
Ban testing of larger nuclear weapons	N
Delay "re-flagging" of Kuwaiti tankers	N
Approve tax-raising deficit-reduction bill	N
1988	
Approve aid to Nicaraguan contras	Y
Enact civil rights restoration bill over Reagan veto	N
Kill 60-day plant-closing notification measure	Y
Pass omnibus trade bill over Reagan veto	X
Approve death penalty for drug-related murders	Y
Bar federal funds for abortions in cases of rape and incest	Y
Oppose seven-day waiting period for purchase of handguns	Y

Voting Studies

	Presidential Support		Party Unity		Conservative Coalition	
Year	**S**	**O**	**S**	**O**	**S**	**O**
1988	68	25	85	8	92	8
1987	69	28	82	10	88	9
1986	74	22	80	9	82	12
1985	61	26	71	16	80	11
1984	54	34	72	15	81	8
1983	63	32	71	17	80	9
1982	55	31	73	17	82	12
1981	66	24	72	21	79	12

Interest Group Ratings

Year	ADA	ACU	AFL-CIO	CCUS
1988	0	96	7	86
1987	8	83	19	93
1986	0	95	7	82
1985	10	95	18	71
1984	5	86	9	87
1983	0	90	13	84
1982	5	74	22	72
1981	20	93	13	79

Nebraska

U.S. CONGRESS

SENATE 2 D

HOUSE 1 D, 2 R

LEGISLATURE

49 nonpartisan senators in unicameral assembly

ELECTIONS

1988 Presidential Vote	
Bush	60%
Dukakis	39%
1984 Presidential Vote	
Reagan	71%
Mondale	29%
1980 Presidential Vote	
Reagan	66%
Carter	26%
Anderson	7%
Turnout rate in 1984	56%
Turnout rate in 1986	47%
Turnout rate in 1988	57%

(as percentage of voting age population)

POPULATION AND GROWTH

1980 population	1,569,825
1988 population estimate (36th in the nation)	1,602,000
Percent change 1980-1988	+2%

DEMOGRAPHIC BREAKDOWN

White	95%
Black	3%
Other	1%
(Spanish origin)	2%
Urban	63%
Rural	37%
Born in state	70%
Foreign-born	2%

MAJOR CITIES

Omaha	349,270
Lincoln	183,050
Grand Island	39,100
Bellevue	32,200
Fremont	23,780

AREA AND LAND USE

Area	76,644 sq. miles (15th)
Farm	92%
Forest	1%
Federally owned	1%

Gov. Kay A. Orr (R)
Of Lincoln — Elected 1986

Born: Jan. 2, 1939, Burlington, Iowa.
Education: Attended U. of Iowa, 1956-57.
Occupation: Homemaker.
Religion: Presbyterian.
Political Career: Neb. treasurer, 1981-87.
Next Election: 1990.

WORK

Occupations	
White-collar	49%
Blue-collar	27%
Service workers	14%
Government Workers	
Federal	15,445
State	34,592
Local	82,664

MONEY

Median family income	$ 19,122	(29th)
Tax burden per capita	$ 648	(47th)

EDUCATION

Spending per pupil through grade 12	$ 3,634	(22nd)
Persons with college degrees	16%	(26th)

CRIME

Violent crime rate	251 per 100,000 (39th)

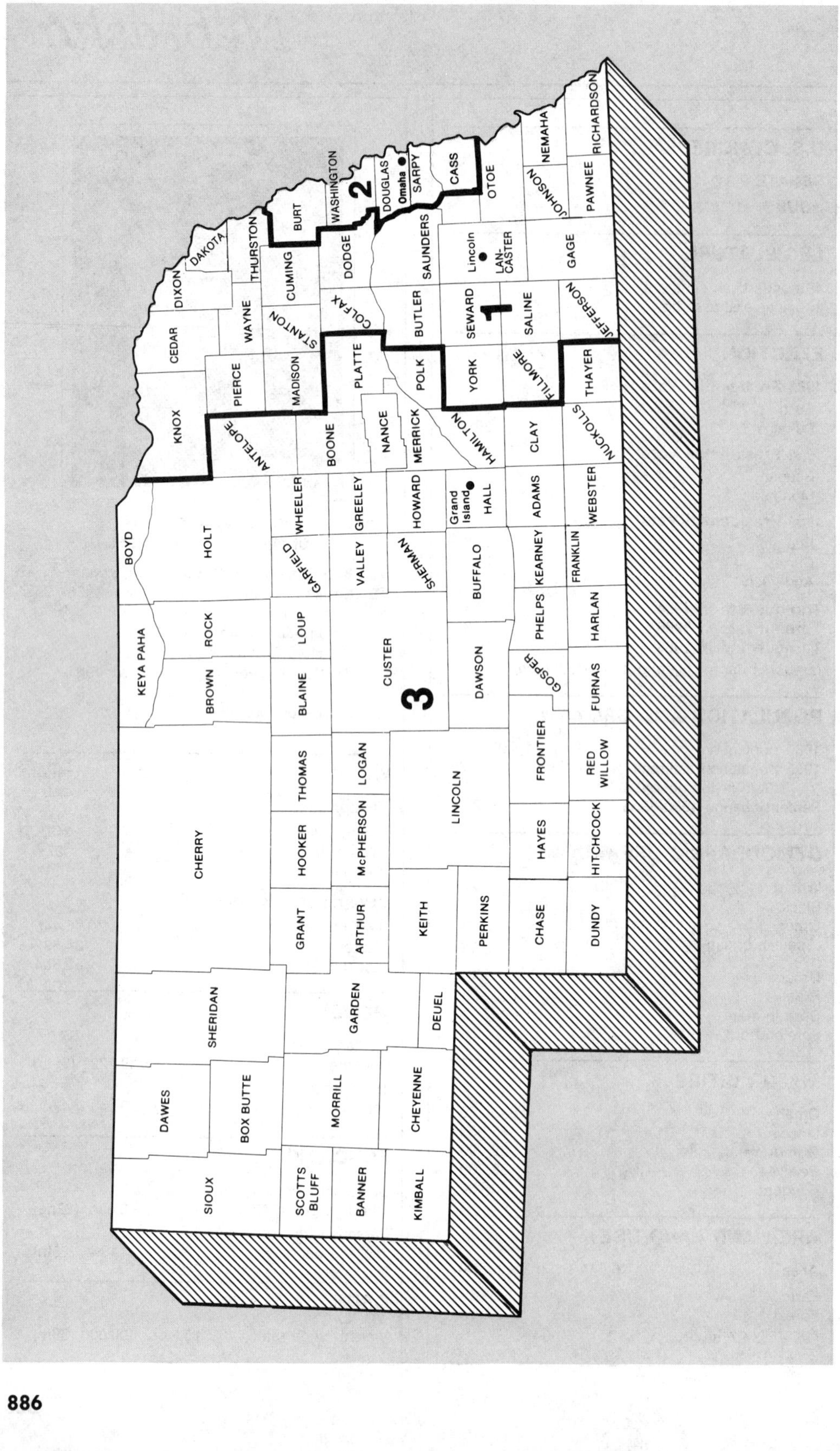
1
2
3
Omaha
Lincoln
Grand Island
DOUGLAS
SARPY
CASS
WASHINGTON
BURT
THURSTON
DAKOTA
DIXON
CEDAR
KNOX
PIERCE
WAYNE
CUMING
DODGE
STANTON
MADISON
PLATTE
COLFAX
SAUNDERS
LAN-CASTER
OTOE
NEMAHA
RICHARDSON
JOHNSON
PAWNEE
GAGE
SALINE
JEFFERSON
SEWARD
BUTLER
POLK
YORK
FILLMORE
THAYER
ANTELOPE
BOONE
NANCE
MERRICK
HAMILTON
CLAY
NUCKOLLS
BOYD
HOLT
WHEELER
GREELEY
HOWARD
HALL
ADAMS
WEBSTER
GARFIELD
VALLEY
SHERMAN
BUFFALO
KEARNEY
FRANKLIN
KEYA PAHA
ROCK
LOUP
CUSTER
PHELPS
HARLAN
BROWN
BLAINE
DAWSON
GOSPER
FURNAS
CHERRY
THOMAS
LOGAN
LINCOLN
FRONTIER
RED WILLOW
HOOKER
McPHERSON
HAYES
HITCHCOCK
GRANT
ARTHUR
KEITH
PERKINS
CHASE
DUNDY
SHERIDAN
GARDEN
DEUEL
DAWES
BOX BUTTE
MORRILL
CHEYENNE
SIOUX
SCOTTS BLUFF
BANNER
KIMBALL

Jim Exon (D)

Of Lincoln — Elected 1978

Born: Aug. 9, 1921, Geddes, S.D.
Education: Attended U. of Omaha, 1939-41.
Military Career: Army, 1941-45; Reserve, 1945-49.
Occupation: Office equipment dealer.
Family: Wife, Patricia Ann Pros; three children.
Religion: Episcopalian.
Political Career: Democratic National Committee member from Nebraska, 1968-71; Neb. governor, 1971-79.
Capitol Office: 330 Hart Bldg. 20510; 224-4224.

In Washington: Exon could not really enjoy his heightened visibility in the early months of the 101st Congress. The issue that thrust him into sudden prominence — the fitness of former Sen. John Tower to be secretary of defense — was far too personal and uncomfortable.

Exon, the second-ranking Democrat on the Armed Services Committee, was the first to announce his conviction that Tower was not up to the job. In the emotional floor debate that ensued, Exon went head to head with Republicans who said Tower's colleagues would have known if he were alcohol dependent. "Just because we did not . . . see anything . . . does not necessarily mean that it did not happen," said Exon.

In the early going, Exon had seemed skeptical of the allegations about Tower. But he said every charge would be explored, noting that "the old-boy network" would not protect the former chairman of Armed Services. A week later, Exon had learned enough to turn thumbs down. "The key test," he said, "is that John Tower most likely would not qualify for duty at Strategic Air Command control center in Omaha."

The Tower flap was the first broad national exposure for the big and plain-spoken ex-governor from the Plains whom friends call "J. J." Exon has not generally been at the center of the action in the Senate. With a few exceptions, he has not been a leader on major legislative issues. But even as a backbencher, he was viewed as an attentive and intelligent contributor and a mirror of public opinion in the heartland. For example, when Exon rebuffed President Reagan's entreaties on behalf of Judge Robert H. Bork, it was clear Bork's 1987 nomination to the Supreme Court was doomed.

In the late 1980s, Exon has begun assuming a larger institutional role. The principal reason is his ascent on Armed Services, where in the 100th Congress he became chairman of the Strategic Forces and Nuclear Deterrence Subcommittee. Few titles bespeak the gravity of their responsibility more clearly. But at the outset of the 101st Congress, the panel was facing a different sort of nuclear challenge: the waste-cleanup crisis at the nation's nuclear-weapons plants. Exon began the year supporting the Department of Energy's management of the plants, but he implied the leash was not long.

As a military policy maker, Exon has been a supporter of the rail-based MX missile and a wary backer of the strategic defense initiative (SDI). But he may have made his most notable mark to date with an amendment he attached to the omnibus trade bill of 1988. It gives the president discretionary power to block a foreign takeover of any U.S. company doing defense work.

In previous years, Exon's most effective forum had been the Budget Committee, where he preached the fiscally conservative gospel that carried him to the governorship and the Senate. He established a reputation for being neither flashy nor creative, but cautious and industrious. And he renewed it regularly with the kind of cracker-barrel skepticism Nebraskans appreciate. Exon regularly returns a substantial portion of his office allowance to the Treasury, and in 1989 he proposed cutting the number of newsletters Congress sends to its constituents by two-thirds.

But he has found the Budget Committee a devalued venue since 1987, when the White House began striking deals with Hill leaders at "budget summit" meetings. Like other committee members, he has had little choice but to grumble and go along. "If anybody thinks Rosemary's baby was ugly, they should take a look at this newly hatched agreement," said Exon after President Bush renewed the summit approach in 1989.

During the Reagan administration, Exon's vote was something of a bellwether of conservative opinion on Reaganomics. In 1981 he supported Reagan's tax and spending cuts, while warning of deficits to come. Two years later, as Reagan's influence on the budget process waned, Exon was siding more regularly with his party on the Budget Committee. But he kept his conservative credentials in order by voting for a balanced-budget constitutional amendment and opposing a congressional pay raise.

Exon developed his own plan for cutting federal deficits. Working with South Carolina Democrat Ernest F. Hollings and North Dakota Republican Mark Andrews, Exon pushed a budget "freeze" proposal barring domestic spending increases and holding the rise in defense spending to the level of inflation.

Even so, Exon had nothing but scorn for the signal effort at deficit reduction in the 99th Congress — the Gramm-Rudman-Hollings balanced-budget amendment. The automatic spending reductions mandated by that 1985 law were a "ruse," he said, aimed at allowing Congress to escape the responsibility of voting on cuts in individual programs. After the Supreme Court struck down the law's key enforcement provisions in 1986, Exon tried without success to force Congress to designate specific savings needed to reach the Gramm-Rudman deficit-reduction goals.

One area in which Exon does not want to see deep cuts is agriculture. Early in 1985, he and Oklahoma Democrat David L. Boren waged a filibuster for emergency credit assistance to help debt-ridden farmers begin spring planting. The two held up Senate business for days, giving new Majority Leader Bob Dole his first test of leadership. The Senate eventually passed a bill giving more credit to farmers, but President Reagan vetoed it. Later that year, Exon and other Farm Belt Democrats fought a lengthy floor battle with Dole over administration efforts to reduce farm price supports.

Exon has been a relative hard-liner on defense, though not an automatic vote for weapons requests. Toward the end of the Reagan administration, he cast himself as a critic of its military spending and arms policies. He joined with the liberal minority on Armed Services to oppose the White House-backed budget levels for the Pentagon, arguing that defense should not be spared from reductions in a period of austerity.

Exon was a strong backer of the Reagan administration's effort to develop anti-satellite missiles. As ranking Democrat on the subcommittee he now chairs, Exon worked with Chairman John W. Warner of Virginia to defend the new weapons, forcing the Senate into secret session to discuss the Soviets' anti-satellite capabilities. Exon helped develop the final compromise that allowed testing of the missiles to go forward during talks with the Soviets to control their deployment.

But he has been less certain about SDI. He accused Reagan of overselling the program and expressed concern that SDI had become "a sponge that sops up far too great a percentage of research and development funds."

Still, Exon has sought a middle approach on SDI funding. During debate on the defense authorization bill in 1986, he supported a level of funding below Reagan's request but above the level sought by many other Democrats. Two years later, with the Senate in Democratic hands, the debate had shifted. Deep cuts of $600 million or more were proposed for the SDI budget. In this atmosphere, Exon voted to protect the program from such cuts.

On the Commerce Committee, Exon has been active in seeking to limit the effects of deregulating various industries. He also has been the committee's chief proponent of new controls on automobile odometer tampering in the used-car market. His bill to require stricter record-keeping requirements on auto mileage cleared Congress in 1986.

At Home: Exon steered toward his 1990 re-election campaign with a clear sense of hazards ahead. His likely opponent, 1st District GOP Rep. Doug Bereuter, backed off. But the GOP continued to target Exon as vulnerable on the basis of his slim re-election margin in 1984.

Exon attributed the closeness of the 1984 contest to his failure to take seriously what he labeled a negative campaign run out of Washington. In gearing up for his 1990 re-election bid, he vowed he would not be caught off guard by that type of campaign again.

For example, Exon fought back immediately in 1988 when the National Rifle Association (NRA) targeted him for a negative mailing. The mailing to gun owners said Exon had opposed their rights by voting to restrict "plastic guns" that do not show up on metal detectors. Exon, a hunter and gun enthusiast, responded by calling the NRA "far off base" and warning that it would provoke "an overreaction by the public and Congress" if it opposed sensible restrictions.

Exon has had a paradoxical political career. A partisan Democratic governor in a Republican state, he bickered continually with the nominally nonpartisan but GOP-controlled Legislature. Yet he achieved a popularity that few Nebraska governors ever have attained, chiefly by keeping a tight hold on state spending and by speaking up for farmers.

Born in South Dakota, Exon went into the office supply business in Lincoln, Neb., in the 1950s and began performing local Democratic Party chores. By the mid-1960s he was one of the better-known Democratic functionaries in a state that has never had an abundance of them. He was state coordinator of Lyndon B. Johnson's 1964 presidential campaign, and in 1968 he became a Democratic National Committee member.

In 1970, public disenchantment over the newly enacted state income and sales taxes gave Exon his big break. The tax issue crippled Republican incumbent Norbert T. Tiemann's bid for a second term. Tiemann was nearly unseated by a primary challenger, and Exon took advantage of the same issues in the fall to oust him.

Exon had no problem turning back GOP state Sen. Richard D. Marvel in 1974. His fiscal austerity produced a state government surplus that year. The 1978 Senate campaign was nearly as easy. Republican Carl T. Curtis chose to retire after four terms, and his former aide, Donald E. Shasteen, was overmatched against Exon from the start. The Democrat drew two-thirds of the vote.

In 1984 it looked as though Exon would again be elected in a walk. But it did not turn out that way. No prominent Republican wanted any part of a campaign against him, and what seemed to be a worthless GOP nomination went to Nancy Hoch, a University of Nebraska regent. Hoch's challenge did not attract much attention in the state initially, but it did arouse the interest of national Republican committees, which were eager to generate publicity for a female candidate.

While Hoch never matched Exon's financial reserves, the GOP backing gave her more visibility than she would have otherwise had, and allowed her to take advantage of the straight-ticket Republican momentum that developed late. Hoch said Exon was an innocuous backbencher with little influence. Exon responded by presenting a long list of bills he had helped enact into law. He also charged that Hoch's campaign was scripted by the GOP Senate campaign committee in Washington.

Boosted by Reagan at the top of the ticket, Hoch came closer to Exon on Election Day than most observers had thought possible. The incumbent won by only 25,000 votes, carrying just over half of the state's counties, mostly in eastern Nebraska.

Committees

Armed Services (2nd of 11 Democrats)
Strategic Forces and Nuclear Deterrence (chairman); Manpower and Personnel; Projection Forces and Regional Defense

Budget (5th of 13 Democrats)

Commerce, Science and Transportation (4th of 11 Democrats)
Surface Transportation (chairman); Aviation; Communications

Elections

1984 General

Jim Exon (D)	332,217	(52%)
Nancy Hoch (R)	307,147	(48%)

Previous Winning Percentage: 1978 (68%)

Campaign Finance

	Receipts	Receipts from PACs	Expend-itures
1984			
Exon (D)	$888,505	$511,613 (58%)	$843,393
Hoch (R)	$585,231	$74,125 (13%)	$583,632

Key Votes

1987

Enact omnibus highway bill over Reagan veto	Y
Limit testing of space-based anti-ballistic missiles	Y
Oppose banning tests of larger nuclear weapons	Y
Confirm Robert H. Bork as Supreme Court justice	N

1988

Allow vote on campaign-finance overhaul	Y
Pass civil rights restoration bill over Reagan veto	Y
Enact omnibus trade bill over Reagan veto	Y
Approve death penalty for drug-related murders	Y
Oppose "workfare" amendment to welfare overhaul bill	N

Voting Studies

	Presidential Support		Party Unity		Conservative Coalition	
Year	**S**	**O**	**S**	**O**	**S**	**O**
1988	65	31	66	30	86	11
1987	44	56	74	23	72	28
1986	34	64	66	31	45	53
1985	43	45	54	30	65	28
1984	58	36	51	45	68	28
1983	54	46	56	43	70	25
1982	55	40	64	33	70	26
1981	56	41	69	27	67	31

Interest Group Ratings

Year	ADA	ACU	AFL-CIO	CCUS
1988	35	48	71	50
1987	65	38	80	50
1986	35	48	53	32
1985	25	59	43	46
1984	55	48	36	65
1983	40	60	44	61
1982	40	74	48	55
1981	45	47	33	50

Bob Kerrey (D)

Of Lincoln — Elected 1988

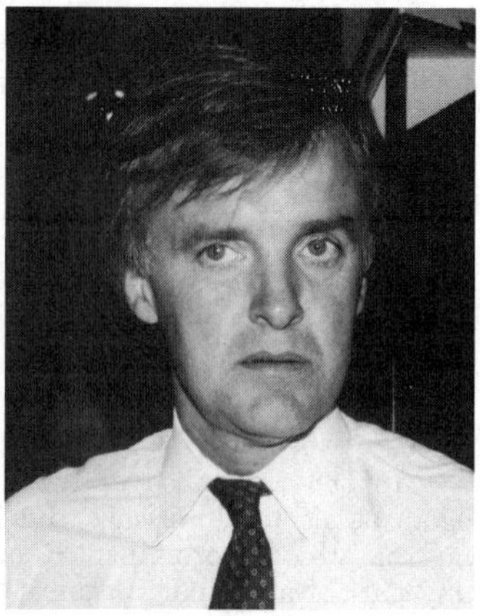

Born: Aug. 27, 1943, Lincoln, Neb.
Education: U. of Nebraska, B.S. 1966.
Military Career: Navy, 1966-69.
Occupation: Restaurateur.
Family: Divorced; two children.
Religion: Congregationalist.
Political Career: Neb. governor, 1983-87.
Capitol Office: 302 Hart Bldg. 20510; 224-6551.

The Path to Washington: In the course of Kerrey's 1988 election campaign, his opponent, appointed Republican Sen. David K. Karnes, accused the former governor of being a liberal who would toe the Democratic Party line. "So what?" Kerrey responded.

An unconventional style and willing disregard for the accepted rules of political behavior vaulted Kerrey from business into the governorship in 1982, and sent him to the Senate six years later. He has a wry, self-deprecating sense of humor that he employs at unlikely moments to disarm foes and win audiences.

Kerrey was a Lincoln restaurateur and political novice when he ousted GOP Gov. Charles Thone in 1982. Thone had a reputation for being bland and indecisive. Kerrey combined an aggressive campaign style with a knack for attracting publicity to score a narrow upset.

As governor, Kerrey was one part politician and one part celebrity. His celebrity status was secured in 1983 when he began dating actress Debra Winger, whom he met while she was making a movie in Lincoln. Their romance and its breakup enhanced Kerrey's reputation as one of the country's more unconventional politicians.

Kerrey's record as a war hero — he lost a leg and earned a Congressional Medal of Honor — helped him thrive in Nebraska despite his criticisms of a president who won more than 70 percent of the state vote in 1984. Kerrey not only attacked President Reagan's economic and farm policies, but also accused the president of taking an approach to foreign affairs that "drapes euphemism and simplistic slogans over the realities of war." His views on war were well-known: After accepting the Medal of Honor, he had protested the Vietnam War as immoral. In 1984, he made two separate speeches to the Democratic National Convention, one on Vietnam veterans.

During his Senate campaign, Kerrey said he favored defense budget increases only to keep up with inflation, and he opposed aid to the Nicaraguan contras. He voiced support for lower but still "robust" spending for research on the strategic defense initiative, and he did not rule out backing development of the Midgetman missile or the rail-based MX missile. Senate Armed Services Chairman Sam Nunn paid Kerrey a campaign visit in October 1988.

Kerrey has a belief in activist government that stems in part from his personal experience. He credits assistance from federal programs in helping him make the transformation from an embittered Vietnam veteran to a wealthy businessman. Kerrey is in a better position than most of his freshman Senate colleagues to translate his beliefs into something tangible: He was the only member of his class to win a seat on the Appropriations Committee for the 101st Congress.

Kerrey's other committee assignment, Agriculture, was promised to him by Chairman Patrick J. Leahy during the campaign. Kerrey takes a middle-of-the-road approach to farming issues. He opposes any "radical departure" from policies set forth in the 1985 farm bill, such as mandatory production controls (favored by many Midwestern Democrats) or "decoupling" government aid from production levels (promoted by Reagan).

In winning seats on Agriculture and Appropriations, Kerrey got his two most-preferred assignments. He sought, but was not awarded, a seat on Intelligence; no freshman won a slot on the committee at the start of the 101st Congress.

During his Senate campaign, Kerrey took the party's position on a number of issues then before the Congress. He supported bills on catastrophic health insurance, parental leave and overhauling the welfare system, among others. Though against a constitutional amendment banning abortions, he opposed using federal money to pay for them. He called for a mix of spending cuts and tax increases to reduce the deficit.

While Kerrey dazzled many Nebraskans with his colorful style, good looks and penchant for speaking his mind as governor, he was not without his detractors. Most of them said that as governor, Kerrey was long on style and short on substance.

Early in his administration, Kerrey acquired an image as an activist chief executive able to resolve issues that had dragged on for years; he pushed deficit-reduction and banking-law-reform measures in his first year in office. By all accounts, that first year was his most productive. Subsequently, his relationship with the unicameral Legislature soured somewhat, partly due to his own glibness. He ridiculed a key committee chairman with whom he was upset by saying that as far as he was concerned, the chairman "doesn't exist." A struggling economy ruled out ambitious government programs.

Still, Kerrey was heavily favored to win a second term. He sealed his reputation for political unpredictability by deciding not to run for re-election. Some tied the decision to distress over the breakup of his romance with Winger. But Kerrey has said since that Winger was just one of many factors, citing business obligations and a desire to spend more time with his two children. When he left office, his job-approval rating was about 70 percent.

It came as no surprise when Kerrey entered the 1988 Senate race. Few Nebraskans expected Kerrey to stay out of politics long when he left the governorship. As soon as he announced, he was the front-runner, even though the Republican nominee had not been determined.

When Democratic Sen. Edward Zorinsky died of a heart attack in March 1987, Republican Gov. Kay A. Orr skipped over prominent GOP political figures to select Karnes, the Omaha chairman of her 1986 campaign, to fill the vacancy. A lawyer and agribusinessman, Karnes was virtually unknown in state GOP circles.

In picking Karnes, Orr snubbed several Republicans angling for the job, including 2nd District Rep. Hal Daub. Daub promptly announced he would challenge Karnes in the primary. Daub was much better known to eastern Nebraska voters — he was first elected to the Omaha-anchored House seat in 1980 — and became the early favorite for the nomination.

But Karnes played his brief incumbency well, noting the work he could do for the state from his seat on the Agriculture Committee. His easygoing style proved more appealing to Nebraska Republicans than Daub's intense persona. Aided by Orr, 3rd District Rep. Virginia Smith and the National Republican Senatorial Committee, Karnes won the nomination handily, 55 percent to 45 percent.

In Kerrey, however, Karnes faced a superior campaigner who would not be outspent, as was Daub. Also, Kerrey was spared any serious primary competition; he launched his media campaign before the May primary, filling the airwaves with "feel-good" biographical ads.

Although Karnes and Kerrey each spent over $3.4 million overall, more than $1 million of Karnes' money went to the primary. By the end of June, his campaign had a debt of nearly $200,000. He could not afford to renew his TV advertising effort until September.

Karnes' sparkling primary campaign gave way to a flawed general-election performance. The most costly misstep came in early September during the one debate of the campaign. In discussing improved agricultural technology, Karnes said, "We need fewer farmers at this point in time," a remark that provoked jeers from the state-fair audience. Karnes immediately retreated, saying he had misspoken, but the damage was done.

Even a flawless campaign might have fallen short of upending the popular Kerrey; one as fraught with errors as Karnes' was doomed. Kerrey won by 15 percentage points, running nearly 20 points ahead of Democratic presidential nominee Michael S. Dukakis.

Committees

Agriculture, Nutrition and Forestry (10th of 10 Democrats)
Agricultural Production and Stabilization of Prices; Agricultural Research and General Legislation; Nutrition and Investigations

Appropriations (16th of 16 Democrats)
Agriculture, Rural Development and Related Agencies; District of Columbia; HUD-Independent Agencies; Treasury, Postal Service and General Government

Campaign Finance

	Receipts	Receipts from PACs	Expend-itures
1988			
Kerrey (D)	$3,485,728	$799,279 (23%)	$3,461,148
Karnes (R)	$3,423,237	$883,895 (26%)	$3,411,361

Elections

1988 General		
Bob Kerrey (D)	378,717	(57%)
David K. Karnes (R)	278,250	(42%)
1988 Primary		
Bob Kerrey (D)	156,498	(91%)
Ken L. Michaelis (D)	14,248	(8%)

1 Doug Bereuter (R)

Of Utica — Elected 1978

Born: Oct. 6, 1939, York, Neb.
Education: U. of Nebraska, B.A. 1961; Harvard U., M.C.P. 1963, M.P.A. 1973.
Military Career: Army, 1963-65.
Occupation: City planner; university professor.
Family: Wife, Louise Anna Meyer; two children.
Religion: Lutheran.
Political Career: Neb. Legislature, 1975-79.
Capitol Office: 2446 Rayburn Bldg. 20515; 225-4806.

In Washington: Bereuter has always sought a more active role in global issues than his home-state House colleagues. And considering that his legislative agenda extends well beyond his district's borders, it was not surprising that he seriously considered running for the Senate against Democrat Jim Exon in 1990. But even though he chose to forgo that race, it is unlikely to limit his broad legislative interests.

Hal Daub, who held the Omaha-based 2nd District from 1981-89, made the intricacies of tax law his specialty, while western Nebraska's Virginia Smith rarely strays from her mission as defender of beef and agricultural interests. But Bereuter is a committed internationalist who spends his time exploring the nuances of American foreign policy and looking for solutions to the crisis in Third World debt — hardly the profile one might expect of a congressman from the largely rural 1st District.

Bereuter is a swing vote on the Foreign Affairs Committee, a moderate Republican who likes to work cooperatively with Democrats but often finds that difficult amid the committee's polarized political situation. He sometimes has found it easier to make common cause with his committee's Democrats than with the hard-line majority on his own side of the aisle. In the 101st Congress, Bereuter took the ranking position on the Human Rights Subcommittee, which has a fairly centrist GOP membership and is chaired by Pennsylvanian Gus Yatron, who is less liberal than a number of other committee Democrats.

In 1986, Bereuter was part of a bare majority of Republicans who sided with almost all House Democrats in overriding President Reagan's veto of a bill imposing economic sanctions against South Africa. But in 1988, when the Foreign Affairs Subcommittee on International Economic Policy worked on a tougher sanctions bill, Bereuter and other Republicans resisted. Bereuter opposed the new sanctions, calling them "irrational" because they were too far-reaching. Lacking the bipartisan support of 1986 and without Senate backing, the bill died.

Although some of Bereuter's work on international affairs might not seem of prime concern to his rural constituents, he does use his position to boost agricultural exports, which are critical to the local economy. On the 1988 South Africa sanctions bill, for example, he sponsored an amendment in the full committee to allow continued exports to South Africa of agricultural commodities and products. The amendment was adopted, but Bereuter still voted against the bill.

Like most farm-state members, Bereuter opposes cargo-preference requirements, which mandate that certain goods be shipped by U.S.-flag vessels. In 1987, he was a leading opponent in committee and on the floor of a cargo-preference amendment attached to a foreign aid bill by New Jersey Democrat Robert G. Torricelli. The amendment required certain countries receiving U.S. economic aid to spend a like amount on U.S. products and to ship at least half their purchases on U.S. vessels. Bereuter said Torricelli's amendment would lead to retaliation against American farmers, and added that there was "no limit to the greed" of the U.S. maritime industry and its affiliated labor unions. The amendment was approved, but later was amended on the floor by Virginia Smith to exempt agricultural commodities.

Bereuter opposed omnibus trade legislation in 1986 because amendments were added that he thought would have a detrimental effect on agricultural exports. He has lobbied Japanese and European leaders to try to insulate the commodities trade from growing protectionist pressure. He proposed that the federal government pay the costs incurred by farmers because of cargo-preference provisions requiring that half of all government-sponsored agricultural exports be shipped on more expensive American vessels. This amendment was defeated by the House.

When Foreign Affairs was debating the Export Administration Act during the 98th Congress, Bereuter was able to attach an amendment that would prevent the president from using food embargoes as a foreign policy tool.

Nebraska 1

East Central — Lincoln

The state capital, Lincoln, gives the 1st District a modest urban flavor, but the city does not dominate the district the way Omaha influences the neighboring 2nd.

Lancaster County, which includes Lincoln and its few suburbs, casts just under 40 percent of the vote. Essentially a white-collar town, Lincoln is dominated by the state government and the University of Nebraska (23,000 students).

Partisan registration in the county is nearly evenly split and Lancaster can go either way in a close statewide election. In 1988, George Bush won Lancaster over Democrat Michael S. Dukakis by 345 votes out of over 90,000 cast. In his successful 1988 Senate bid, Democrat Bob Kerrey carried Lancaster with 64 percent over appointed GOP Sen. David K. Karnes, as Bereuter took 65 percent.

The rest of the district is made up largely of prosperous, predominantly Republican farming areas where corn is the major crop. The few small cities, such as Fremont, Norfolk and Beatrice, are market centers closely tied to farming.

The counties along the Platte River (Colfax, Dodge, Butler and Saunders) provide some Democratic votes, along with Saline County, southwest of Lincoln, and Dakota, a meatpacking area along the Missouri River that is becoming a suburb of Sioux City, Iowa.

The rest of the district's 27 counties, particularly those toward the northern border, are overwhelmingly Republican.

When Nebraska redistricted for the 1980s, there was talk of moving Knox County, on the South Dakota border, from the 1st District to the 3rd. But Bereuter had been active on behalf of the Santee Indians, who have a reservation in that county. He did not want to lose it, and the Legislature accommodated him.

Population: 523,079. White 509,424 (97%), Black 4,026 (1%), Other 7,026 (1%). Spanish origin 4,795 (1%). 18 and over 383,987 (73%), 65 and over 74,959 (14%). Median age: 30.

As a member of the Asian and Pacific Affairs Subcommittee in the 99th Congress, Bereuter generally worked well with Stephen J. Solarz of New York, the Democratic chairman. Like Solarz, he was a critic of the Marcos regime in the Philippines and called for restrictions on U.S. military aid to that government, which fell in 1986. Bereuter also backed Solarz' bill providing aid to the non-communist resistance in Cambodia.

Bereuter lists on his *vita* membership on such international panels as the North Atlantic Assembly's Interparliamentary Committee to Consider the Future of NATO, and the U.S. Congress Interparliamentary Exchange with the European Parliament. While some regard these sorts of groups mainly as vehicles for overseas junkets, Bereuter takes his participation in their activities seriously, arriving at meetings with his notes and thoughts well organized.

Bereuter also serves on the Banking Committee, a logical assignment because it has jurisdiction over urban affairs and he is a city planner by profession. But here, too, Bereuter has spent most of his time on international economics and foreign aid.

At the end of the 97th Congress, a combination of retirements and re-election defeats created a vacancy in the ranking GOP spot on the International Development Institutions and Finance Subcommittee at Banking. In line for it was Californian David Dreier, regarded by many as a conservative isolationist in world finance. Moderate Republicans on the subcommittee, fearing Dreier could destroy the bipartisan internationalist consensus that had existed there, asked Bereuter to join the panel and use his overall seniority to claim the vacancy. J. William Stanton of Ohio, the ranking Republican on the subcommittee as well as the full committee, gave up his seat to Bereuter, who retained the ranking slot through the 100th Congress.

Bereuter took his usual bipartisan approach. During the 98th Congress, he joined the subcommittee's Democratic leadership in supporting money for several international development banks. He said failure by the United States to keep up payments to development banks would hurt the nation's credibility in areas of strategic importance.

In the 100th Congress, he supported subcommittee efforts to approve a six-year infusion of new capital for the World Bank.

As the Bush administration embarked on reducing developing countries' massive debt burden, Bereuter voiced wariness over proposals to force banks to grant debt relief. "If debt relief is mandated, then we have to be concerned about the chilling effect with respect to future lending," he said.

In the 101st Congress, he is ranking Republican on the new Policy Research and Insurance Subcommittee.

Earlier in his career, Bereuter spent most of his time at the Interior Committee, where he took a pro-conservation line on environmental issues, often siding with Democrats. He called on his party to retake the lead in environmental protection.

At Home: Bereuter's background is unusual for a Nebraska politician. He took an early interest in urban affairs, and he held the state's top city-planning post under moderate GOP Gov. Norbert Tiemann from 1969-71.

He served one four-year term in the Nebraska Legislature after that, winning a reputation as one of the more liberal members by sponsoring a land-use planning bill that left much of Nebraska's farming and ranching lobby complaining of government intrusion in private-property decisions. He also operated a private consulting business in which he helped fast-growing energy boom towns cope with the demands of unplanned growth.

Bereuter used conservative rhetoric during his 1978 House campaign, but he was still looked upon as a moderate because of his legislative record and his Tiemann connections. That helped him attract Lincoln voters in the GOP primary, in which he had to defeat a conservative state senator oriented toward the rural areas of the district. Bereuter prevailed only by carrying Lancaster County (Lincoln) overwhelmingly. He did not have a majority in the rest of the district.

In November he had an easier time, drawing united GOP support and a large independent vote to defeat Hess Dyas, the former Democratic state chairman. Bereuter seemed visibly nervous in some of his public appearances with Dyas, but he proved himself a well-informed candidate, and his solid political base in Lincoln brought him home with a 58 percent victory. Since then, he has never won less than 60 percent. He crushed his 1988 Democratic foe, former American Agriculture Movement President Corky Jones, by better than 2-to-1.

Bereuter had been hinting at a 1990 run at Democratic Sen. Exon since early 1988, when he bypassed a primary challenge to appointed GOP Sen. David K. Karnes. But he announced in June 1989 that he would not challenge Exon.

Committees

Banking, Finance and Urban Affairs (7th of 20 Republicans)
Policy Research and Insurance (ranking); Financial Institutions Supervision, Regulation and Insurance; Housing and Community Development; International Development, Finance, Trade and Monetary Policy

Foreign Affairs (8th of 18 Republicans)
Human Rights and International Organizations (ranking); International Economic Policy and Trade

Select Hunger (6th of 12 Republicans)
Task Force: International

Select Intelligence (5th of 7 Republicans)
Oversight and Evaluation

Elections

1988 General

Doug Bereuter (R)	146,231	(67%)
Corky Jones (D)	72,167	(33%)

1986 General

Doug Bereuter (R)	121,772	(64%)
Steve Burns (D)	67,137	(36%)

Previous Winning Percentages: **1984** (74%) **1982** (75%) **1980** (79%) **1978** (58%)

District Vote For President

	1988	1984	1980	1976
D	96,105 (43%)	69,741 (33%)	57,724 (28%)	82,128 (41%)
R	123,621 (56%)	143,356 (67%)	129,333 (62%)	116,065 (57%)
I			17,348 (8%)	

Campaign Finance

	Receipts	Receipts from PACs	Expend-itures
1988			
Bereuter (R)	$215,704	$99,120 (46%)	$221,530
Jones (D)	$97,118	$28,940 (30%)	$96,278
1986			
Bereuter (R)	$200,466	$101,757 (51%)	$227,910
Burns (D)	$93,225	$476 (1%)	$92,746

Key Votes

1987

Raise speed limit to 65 mph	Y
Approve Gephardt "fair trade" amendment	N
Ban testing of larger nuclear weapons	N
Delay "re-flagging" of Kuwaiti tankers	N
Approve tax-raising deficit-reduction bill	N

1988

Approve aid to Nicaraguan contras	Y
Enact civil rights restoration bill over Reagan veto	Y
Kill 60-day plant-closing notification measure	Y
Pass omnibus trade bill over Reagan veto	Y
Approve death penalty for drug-related murders	Y
Bar federal funds for abortions in cases of rape and incest	Y
Oppose seven-day waiting period for purchase of handguns	Y

Voting Studies

	Presidential Support		Party Unity		Conservative Coalition	
Year	S	O	S	O	S	O
1988	56 †	42 †	79 †	20 †	87 †	13 †
1987	59	41	63	35	81	19
1986	58	42	73	26	78	22
1985	58	43	74	22	78	18
1984	54	43	64	35	71	29
1983	61	37	69	26	70	29
1982	75	25	77	23	79	21
1981	68	30	75	23	79	19

† Not eligible for all recorded votes.

Interest Group Ratings

Year	ADA	ACU	AFL-CIO	CCUS
1988	20	76	57	93
1987	24	57	19	80
1986	15	59	21	72
1985	15	67	12	82
1984	35	54	23	63
1983	25	70	6	95
1982	26	68	20	86
1981	20	87	0	89

2 Peter Hoagland (D)

Of Omaha — Elected 1988

Born: Nov. 17, 1941, Omaha, Neb.
Education: Stanford U., A.B. 1963; Yale U., LL.B. 1968.
Military Career: Army, 1963-65.
Occupation: Lawyer.
Family: Wife, Barbara Erickson; four children.
Religion: Episcopalian.
Political Career: Neb. Legislature, 1979-87.
Capitol Office: 1415 Longworth Bldg. 20515; 225-4155.

The Path to Washington: During eight years as a member of Nebraska's unicameral Legislature, Hoagland came to be known as an aggressive, liberal-minded advocate of "open government" who — in the view of GOP critics — was overly mindful of getting his name in the headlines. In his 1988 campaign for the open 2nd, Hoagland needed plenty of headlines — and money, too — to overcome a primary foe with a better-known name and then a heavy-spending Republican.

A fifth-generation Omahan, Hoagland spent most of the time from his late teens until his early 30s away from his native city. The 1960s and early 1970s found him attending Stanford as an undergraduate, serving in Army intelligence in Washington, D.C., earning a law degree at Yale, and then working in Washington as a clerk for a federal judge and as a trial attorney for the District of Columbia public defender service.

Those experiences behind him, he returned to Omaha in 1973, began private practice as a trial attorney and got involved in public affairs.

Hoagland first worked from the outside to spur passage of open-government legislation, helping to push a tough "Sunshine Act" through the Nebraska Legislature in 1976. It created a state ethics commission that regulates campaign finances, monitors legislative lobbying and looks out for potential conflicts of interest by public officials. Hoagland was later elected to the national governing board of Common Cause, the self-styled citizens' lobbying group.

Once elected to the Legislature in 1978, Hoagland teamed with like-minded activists to advocate initiatives on water conservation, hospital care cost containment and education. In his 1988 House campaign, Hoagland heard some charges from former legislative colleagues that he had been too quick to grab the spotlight on issues. He rejected that criticism and produced editorials and testimonials praising his work. Hoagland does say that his alignment with more maverick legislators delayed his rise to the chairmanship of the Judiciary Committee, a post he attained at the end of his sixth year in the Legislature.

With their registration edge in Douglas County (Omaha), Democrats had long viewed the 2nd as winnable. But the four largest counties in the present-day 2nd District had been represented by a Democrat in only six of the last 46 years. The last Democrat to hold the seat was John J. Cavanaugh, a popular young liberal who in 1979 chose to forgo a third term in order to spend more time with his family. Cavanaugh was succeeded by Republican Hal Daub, who decided to try for the GOP Senate nomination in 1988.

Hoagland was a decided underdog in his contest for the Democratic nomination against Cece Zorinsky, widow of Democratic Sen. Edward Zorinsky. She began the race with superior name recognition and a wealth of good will. But Hoagland's television advertising cast doubt on her mastery of important issues. Surging in the last month with endorsements from labor and education groups, he won the nomination by 51 percent to 43 percent.

His Republican opponent, pathologist Jerry Schenken, was not well-known, having toiled behind the scenes on Daub's behalf in past campaigns. But his massive campaign treasury bought him instant credibility. For the entire campaign cycle, Schenken spent more than $1.1 million. Hoagland's spending for the cycle was nearly $860,000.

In the final weeks of the fall contest, Hoagland appeared at several campaign events with popular former Gov. Bob Kerrey, who was on his way to a resounding victory over appointed GOP Sen. David K. Karnes. Hoagland's association with Kerrey, coupled with his greater name recognition, boosted him to a 2,981-vote victory.

Hoagland was awarded a seat on the Banking, Finance and Urban Affairs Committee for the 101st Congress. In addition to giving him an outlet for some of his legislative energies, that panel may enhance Hoagland's appeal in Omaha's business community, a potential source of campaign contributions for any future Republican challenger.

Nebraska 2

East — Omaha

The 2nd is dominated by the Missouri River city of Omaha, Nebraska's largest city and the seat of Douglas County, which casts four-fifths of the district's vote. Omaha's newspapers and television stations are the main source of information not only for the 2nd, but also for many residents of southwest Iowa. Taking into account Omaha's smaller sister-city across the river — Council Bluffs, Iowa — metropolitan Omaha is home to more than 600,000 people.

Omaha is famous for the stockyards that traditionally have served the region's cattle, hog and sheep growers. Although meatpacking, dairy products and food processing are the major industries, the economy is diversified. Omaha is an insurance, medical and educational center and the headquarters of the Union Pacific Railroad.

Omaha's blue-collar electorate, heavily Irish and Slavic, resembles that of ethnic areas in other Midwestern cities, but has somewhat weaker Democratic Party ties. Omaha's 12 percent black population helps boost the Democratic vote.

In presidential elections, Douglas County is reliably, if not overwhelmingly, Republican. It has voted for the GOP White House candidate every time but once in the post-Roosevelt era. In 1988, George Bush won Douglas County with 56 percent of the vote.

But in contests for other offices, Douglas often goes Democratic. In the 1988 Senate race, it gave Democrat Bob Kerrey more than 60 percent of its vote. And it was big news in 1986 when GOP gubernatorial candidate Kay A. Orr managed to carry Douglas, though by just 605 votes.

Although growth in Omaha's suburbs and population decline in the city made Douglas County favorable ground for GOP House candidates during most of the 1980s, Democrat Hoagland carried it narrowly in 1988, sealing his victory districtwide.

After Douglas, the largest county in the 2nd is Sarpy County, just to the south of Omaha. Located there is Offut Air Force Base, which provides jobs for thousands of military and civilian personnel and is headquarters for the Strategic Air Command. Sarpy County nearly always votes Republican; Hoagland managed a decent showing there in 1988, reaching 46 percent of the vote.

Population: 522,919. White 467,490 (89%), Black 43,681 (8%), Other 5,792 (1%). Spanish origin 10,747 (2%). 18 and over 364,998 (70%), 65 and over 50,168 (10%). Median age: 28.

Committees

Banking, Finance and Urban Affairs (30th of 31 Democrats)
Domestic Monetary Policy; Financial Institutions Supervision, Regulation and Insurance; General Oversight and Investigations; Housing and Community Development; International Development, Finance, Trade and Monetary Policy

Small Business (24th of 27 Democrats)
Exports, Tax Policy and Special Problems

Campaign Finance

	Receipts	Receipts from PACs	Expend-itures
1988			
Hoagland (D)	$860,865	$325,900 (38%)	$858,762
Schenken (D)	$1,162,518	$179,672 (15%)	$1,158,294

Elections

1988 General		
Peter Hoagland (D)	112,174	(50%)
Jerry Schenken (R)	109,193	(49%)
1988 Primary		
Peter Hoagland (D)	33,394	(51%)
Cece Zorinsky (D)	28,635	(43%)

District Vote for President

	1988	1984	1980	1976
D	94,100 (42%)	70,050 (33%)	61,075 (30%)	75,218 (39%)
R	130,246 (58%)	144,478 (67%)	123,845 (61%)	114,370 (59%)
I			15,621 (8%)	

3 Virginia Smith (R)

Of Chappell — Elected 1974

Born: June 30, 1911, Randolph, Iowa.
Education: U. of Nebraska, B.A. 1936.
Occupation: Farmer.
Family: Husband, Haven Smith.
Religion: Methodist.
Political Career: No previous office.
Capitol Office: 2202 Rayburn Bldg. 20515; 225-6435.

In Washington: Smith has spent her life tirelessly representing the concerns of Nebraska's ranchers and farmers. Now in her final term, Smith has seen her persistence bring her some degree of sway in Washington. But it is at home where her clout is truly on display.

Hal Daub discovered the scope of Smith's influence in her district when he sought the GOP Senate nomination in 1988 against appointed Sen. David K. Karnes. Although Smith had pledged neutrality in the primary, there was little doubt where her sympathies lay. She and Daub, the Republican who represented the Omaha-based 2nd District, had clashed in 1985 over a Nebraska judgeship, when both recommended candidates to fill a vacancy on the U.S. District Court bench in Omaha. Daub's candidate prevailed.

Smith's 3rd District is the trove of Republican votes in Nebraska, and the keystone of any statewide GOP primary strategy. Karnes forged an alliance in Washington with Smith soon after his 1987 appointment. Later, he appeared with her to announce emergency funding for district farmers whose crops had been damaged. Less than a month before the primary, Smith defended Karnes' record on Nebraska water issues, rebutting a Daub TV ad that criticized Karnes. Headlines proclaimed, "Smith Backs Karnes on Water Issues," and her constituents got the message. In the primary, Karnes carried all but one county in the 3rd, propelling him to a 55-45 percent victory over Daub.

Smith came to Congress in 1975 after 40 years of involvement in farm organizations, and her House career has largely been a continuation of her activities in Nebraska. As the ranking Republican on the Appropriations Subcommittee on Agriculture, she is an incessant spokesman for the beef and grain producers of her district. She speaks for meat whenever she gets a chance, defending the interests of the ranchers who produce it and urging consumers to eat as much of it as possible. She once denounced a federal agriculture appointee as an "avowed vegetarian."

The 3rd's agriculture-driven economy has been buffeted during the past decade, most recently by the drought that has plagued the Farm Belt. The problems have made the grandmotherly Smith an even more aggressive defender of rural interests.

During debate on the 1987 bill that made supplemental appropriations to the Commodity Credit Corporation, New York Democrat Charles E. Schumer offered an amendment to cut $432 million from the $6.6 billion targeted to the CCC. That, Schumer said, was the amount the General Accounting Office said went to farmers who defrauded the government by splitting farm ownership to avoid the $50,000 per-farm limit on price-support payments.

His amendment sparked a strong response from Smith and other farm-state members. She spoke of the problems of farmers who were "trying to hold on to the land, and to have some young people on the farm," and added, "I would like to invite Mr. Schumer to come to Nebraska" to learn firsthand the problems of family farmers. Schumer's amendment was whittled down to a $90 million cut.

Smith's name would not be found at the top of a list of those members most influential in setting broad agricultural policy, but she has consistently used her Appropriations assignment to steer federal money to Nebraska. She prides herself on having secured funding for dozens of agricultural research and water projects.

Smith was at the center of one pitched battle affecting her area in 1988, when fiscal conservatives and environmentalists joined to try to cut funds for construction of the Davis Creek Dam. The dam came under fire from the Office of Management and Budget, which said it would add to the already massive corn surplus and amount to a double subsidy — providing federally subsidized water to increase production of surplus corn.

Smith led the opposition to the assault on the irrigation project. "It does not add to the present temporary corn surplus," she said. "We have a long record of disappearance of surpluses almost overnight." The amendment,

Nebraska 3

Central and West — Grand Island

Covering three-quarters of the state's land area, this rural district runs from the Corn Belt at its eastern end to the wheat and ranching highlands west of the 100th meridian. One can drive for hours along some of its straight, flat roads without passing any community larger than a village. Many of the 62 counties have one market town and little else but pasture.

The 3rd is the most Republican district in the state — it gave more than 70 percent of its vote to Ronald Reagan in 1980 and 1984, and 67 percent to George Bush in 1988. Popular Democrats like Sen. J. James Exon can sometimes carry the region, but the huge GOP registration advantage — exceeding 70 percent in some counties — is more than enough to keep most Republican candidates comfortable. In 1984, even Exon was able to carry just 25 of the district's counties. Forty of the 45 counties won by appointed GOP Sen. David K. Karnes in his luckless 1988 election bid were in the 3rd.

The only city with more than 30,000 people is Grand Island, a retail center for the surrounding farm lands. Grand Island's major industries are farm implements and meatpacking. There is a small group of Southeast Asians in the city, most of whom work at the Montfort meatpacking facility.

The smaller population centers of Kearney, North Platte and Scottsbluff are strung along the Platte River west of Grand Island. In November 1988, IBP Inc. announced plans to open a new meatpacking facility in Lexington, west of Kearney along the Platte, which will provide as many as 1,500 jobs.

North Platte, located in the valley where the North and South Platte rivers meet, was the home of Buffalo Bill, and tries to coax Omaha-to-Denver travelers into staying awhile by putting on Buffalo Bill shows and rodeos. The Union Pacific runs through North Platte and is its biggest employer. Corn and livestock are raised in the valley, with wheat fields to the west and huge cattle ranches to the north.

The Oregon and Mormon trails run through Scottsbluff, which has the only sizable Hispanic population in western Nebraska, a legacy of the migrant labor used to harvest sugar beets over a period of several decades. Great northern beans are a major crop in the farm areas surrounding Scottsbluff. With recent layoffs at the Lockwood Corp., the major employer in town is now the Regional West Medical Center, a health-management organization employing around 850 people.

North of Grand Island are three heavily Democratic counties (Sherman, Greeley and Howard) and two others (Nance and Platte) that have slimmer Democratic registration edges. In many elections, residents of these counties still tend to vote almost as Democratic as their Polish and Irish ancestors did generations ago.

In the 1970s, more than half the counties in the 3rd District lost population. Most were in cattle lands just beyond the Platte River, or in the western panhandle, the state's major wheat-growing area. Since then, the 3rd has been hard hit by debt crisis and drought. Some farmers have drifted to the towns in search of work, but with farm machinery and equipment companies on the decline, there are few jobs to be found.

Population: 523,827. White 513,467 (98%), Black 683 (0.1%), Other 3,379 (1%). Spanish origin 12,483 (2%). 18 and over 373,670 (71%), 65 and over 80,557 (15%). Median age: 31.

which was the single major challenge to projects included in the energy and water funding bill, was rejected 161-243.

Smith also is a staunch opponent of "cargo preference" laws, which require that a percentage of exported commodities be transported on U.S. ships. In 1987, she notched a victory for farm interests by winning adoption of her amendment to exempt agricultural exporters from such requirements. The amendment, adopted 225-192, was added to the foreign aid authorization, which died in the 100th Congress.

On non-agricultural issues, Smith often finds ways to promote a rural angle. Noting that the farm recession had diminished the revenue base of rural communities, Smith opposed the elimination of federal revenue sharing in the 99th Congress.

A conventional Republican on most other issues, Smith regularly submits legislation to prohibit abortion, legalize prayer in public schools, and establish English as the official language of the United States. Her political career owes little to the feminist movement — when she first came to Congress, she wanted to be known as "Mrs. Haven Smith," identifying her with the Nebraska wheat farmer to whom she has now been married for 57 years.

At Home: First elected to Congress in

1974 by an extremely small margin, Smith has become an institution in the 3rd District. After breezing through three re-election bids, Smith in 1982 became the first House member from Nebraska to go unchallenged in a general election since statehood. She won easily again in 1984, when her opponent received less than 17 percent of the vote.

In 1986, Smith faced Scott E. Sidwell, a 35-year-old lawyer and her most persistent opponent in years. Sidwell campaigned across the huge district, attacking Smith's vote for the 1985 farm bill and blaming her and the Reagan administration for the farm crisis. But Smith took 70 percent of the vote. In 1988, she garnered 79 percent. In June 1989, she announced that she would not seek a ninth term.

For the quarter-century before her election to Congress, Smith was an inveterate clubwoman, active not only in Nebraska but in national farm politics and Republican affairs. She spent 20 years on the board of directors of the American Farm Bureau Federation, and was chairman of its leading women's group. She was a county GOP chairman and a delegate to Republican national conventions.

So name recognition was no problem for the 63-year-old Smith when she finally decided to pursue elective office in 1974. Incumbent Republican Rep. Dave Martin's retirement that year sparked a wide-open GOP primary. Eight candidates entered, with Smith's main competition coming from Don Blank, a dentist and former mayor of McCook, and state Sen. Gerald Stromer, former president of the Nebraska Young Republicans. The finish between Smith and Blank was so close that a recount was necessary. Smith won by 141 votes.

Democrats chose former state Sen. Wayne Ziebarth as their nominee. Ziebarth had run a statewide race for the Democratic Senate nomination in 1972 and was well-known throughout the district. And 1974 was a good Democratic year, even in Nebraska. But toward the end of the campaign Ziebarth made a fatal mistake: He said that women do not belong in politics. That worked against him and probably cost him the election. Smith won by only 737 votes. But by 1976, she was solidly entrenched, defeating her Democratic opponent by a nearly 3-to-1 margin.

Committee

Appropriations (8th of 22 Republicans)
Rural Development, Agriculture and Related Agencies (ranking); Energy and Water Development

Elections

1988 General		
Virginia Smith (R)	170,302	(79%)
John D. Racek (D)	45,183	(21%)
1986 General		
Virginia Smith (R)	136,985	(70%)
Scott E. Sidwell (D)	59,182	(30%)

Previous Winning Percentages: **1984** (83%) **1982** (100%) **1980** (84%) **1978** (80%) **1976** (73%) **1974** (50%)

District Vote For President

	1988	1984	1980	1976
D	69,030 (32%)	47,598 (22%)	48,052 (21%)	76,346 (36%)
R	144,087 (67%)	171,000 (78%)	166,759 (72%)	129,270 (61%)
I			12,024 (5%)	

Campaign Finance

	Receipts	Receipts from PACs	Expend-itures
1988			
Smith (R)	$271,730	$138,715 (51%)	$229,109
Racek (D)	$16,590	$5,000 (30%)	$16,588
1986			
Smith (R)	$219,973	$86,475 (39%)	$253,292
Sidwell (D)	$75,177	$14,323 (19%)	$74,227

Key Votes

1987	
Raise speed limit to 65 mph	Y
Approve Gephardt "fair trade" amendment	N
Ban testing of larger nuclear weapons	N
Delay "re-flagging" of Kuwaiti tankers	Y
Approve tax-raising deficit-reduction bill	N
1988	
Approve aid to Nicaraguan contras	Y
Enact civil rights restoration bill over Reagan veto	N
Kill 60-day plant-closing notification measure	Y
Pass omnibus trade bill over Reagan veto	Y
Approve death penalty for drug-related murders	Y
Bar federal funds for abortions in cases of rape and incest	Y
Oppose seven-day waiting period for purchase of handguns	Y

Voting Studies

	Presidential Support		Party Unity		Conservative Coalition	
Year	S	O	S	O	S	O
1988	53	46	64	36	92	8
1987	60	40	67	32	86	12
1986	64	32	62	33	78	16
1985	58	43	65	32	82	18
1984	64	36	73	27	80	20
1983	72	28	74	23	80	20
1982	70	29	82	18	81	19
1981	70	30	84	15	89	11

Interest Group Ratings

Year	ADA	ACU	AFL-CIO	CCUS
1988	25	80	43	93
1987	0	78	6	93
1986	10	71	8	81
1985	10	62	12	73
1984	15	75	15	63
1983	10	78	6	85
1982	25	73	5	86
1981	10	100	7	84

Nevada

U.S. CONGRESS

SENATE 2 D

HOUSE 1 D, 1 R

LEGISLATURE

Senate 8 D, 13 R

House 30 D, 12 R

ELECTIONS

1988 Presidential Vote

Bush	59%
Dukakis	38%

1984 Presidential Vote

Reagan	66%
Mondale	32%

1980 Presidential Vote

Reagan	63%
Carter	27%
Anderson	7%

Turnout rate in 1984	42%
Turnout rate in 1986	36%
Turnout rate in 1988	45%

(as percentage of voting age population)

POPULATION AND GROWTH

1980 population	800,493
1988 population estimate (41st in the nation)	1,054,000
Percent change 1980-1988	+32%

DEMOGRAPHIC BREAKDOWN

White	87%
Black	6%
Other	4%
(Spanish origin)	7%
Urban	85%
Rural	15%
Born in state	22%
Foreign-born	7%

MAJOR CITIES

Las Vegas	191,510
Reno	110,430
Sparks	51,980
North Las Vegas	50,290
Carson City	36,900

AREA AND LAND USE

Area 109,894 sq. miles (7th)

Farm	14%
Forest	13%
Federally owned	85%

Gov. Bob Miller (D)
Of Carson City — Assumed Office 1989

Born: March 30, 1945, Evanston, Ill.
Education: U. of Santa Clara, B.A. 1967; Loyola Law School, Los Angeles, J.D. 1971.
Military Career: Air Force Reserve, 1967-73.
Occupation: Lawyer.
Religion: Roman Catholic.
Political Career: Clark County district attorney, 1979-86; lieutenant governor, 1987-89.
Next Election: 1990.

WORK

Occupations

White-collar	50%
Blue-collar	23%
Service workers	26%

Government Workers

Federal	9,646
State	16,278
Local	36,543

MONEY

Median family income	$ 21,311 (11th)
Tax burden per capita	$ 1,005 (14th)

EDUCATION

Spending per pupil through grade 12	$ 3,440 (32nd)
Persons with college degrees	14% (33rd)

CRIME

Violent crime rate	696 per 100,000 (7th)

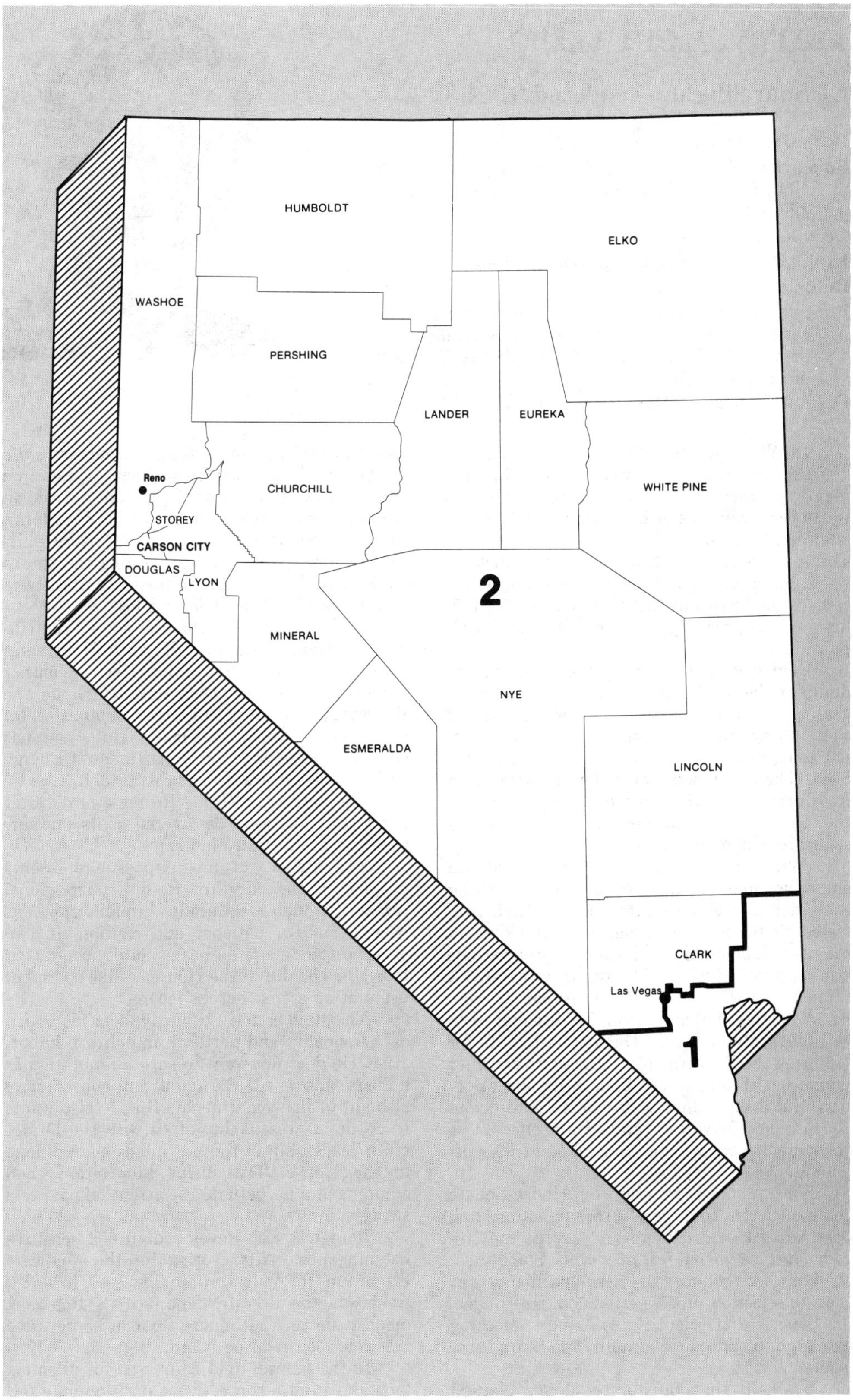
HUMBOLDT
ELKO
WASHOE
PERSHING
LANDER
EUREKA
Reno
CHURCHILL
WHITE PINE
STOREY
CARSON CITY
DOUGLAS
LYON
2
MINERAL
NYE
ESMERALDA
LINCOLN
CLARK
Las Vegas
1

Harry Reid (D)

Of Searchlight — Elected 1986

Born: Dec. 2, 1939, Searchlight, Nev.

Education: Southern Utah State College, A.S. 1959; Utah State U., B.A. 1961; George Washington U., J.D. 1964.

Occupation: Lawyer.

Family: Wife, Landra Gould; five children.

Religion: Mormon.

Political Career: Nev. Assembly, 1969-71; lieutenant governor, 1971-75; U.S. House, 1983-87; Democratic nominee for U.S. Senate, 1974; candidate for mayor of Las Vegas, 1975.

Capitol Office: 324 Hart Bldg. 20510; 224-3542.

In Washington: When Sen. J. Bennett Johnston of Louisiana was campaigning for majority leader in 1988, he knew better than to waste time in Reid's office. Late in 1987, Johnston had been the leading force behind a decision to focus the search for a national nuclear-waste dump on Nevada. That decision, which came to be known as the "Screw Nevada" bill, has cast a spreading shadow over the state's politics.

Reid had been resisting the siting of the dump at Yucca Mountain, Nev., since 1985. At that point, others in the state's establishment were saying the dump might mean jobs. "I'm not going to go chasing jobs for jobs' sake," said Reid. The dump was not a dominant issue in Reid's election in 1986, but Johnston's moves in the Energy and Appropriations committees soon brought it to the fore.

Johnston was able to amass a coalition among members in the House and Senate who were glad to see Nevada picked and their own states off the hook. His plan was embodied in the fiscal 1988 energy and water appropriations bill, against which Reid staged a two-week filibuster on the Senate floor. Aided by Sen. Brock Adams of Washington, Reid managed to get a majority of Senate Democrats to vote for requiring the Department of Energy to consider public health and safety first in its site selection. But even so favorably worded a test vote got him only 37 votes overall. He needed 41 to resist a cloture petition that would close off debate.

Johnston also won in the House-Senate conference on that year's reconciliation bill, persuading House conferees to accept the Nevada site as a virtual *fait accompli.* Since then, Reid has been reduced to a rear-guard action as the site-selection process grinds on. One lingering hope is that scientists will find something wrong with Yucca Mountain and look elsewhere.

To help that possibility along, Nevada asked for $23 million in federal funds for state double-checking of the Department of Energy's site studies. Reid, who had won a seat on Appropriations at the outset of his first term, pressed the state's request. But Johnston whittled it down to $11 million, calling the state's work redundant. Reid took the fight all the way to the floor in June 1988 and lost.

In the fall of 1988, the dump issue contributed to Democratic Gov. Richard H. Bryan's victory over GOP Sen. Chic Hecht. Neither Bryan nor Reid has been able to get on the Energy and Natural Resources Committee (of which Johnston is chairman). But Reid has continued to pepper the Department of Energy with his disapproval from a distance. In 1988 he gave the agency a "Globe Rotter award" after radiation leaks were discovered at its nuclear-weapons production plants.

The intensity of the dump issue represents a spike in the curve of Reid's congressional career. Through two decades in politics, he has been a man of patience and caution. In two years in the Senate he has generally conducted himself as he did in the House — like a climber negotiating a treacherous ledge.

The style is derived partly from his political personality and partly from political imperative. He does not want to earn a reputation as a liberal and so rile the significant conservative element of his constituency. But he also wants to cooperate reasonably often with the Democratic leadership in the Senate, as he had done in the House. That helps him retain good standing and perpetuate the attention paid to a swing voter.

Reid has also developed into a sensitive listening post. After voting for the Medicare expansion for catastrophic illnesses in 1988, Reid was the first to denounce its financing mechanism on the Senate floor after negative reactions began to be heard.

In the House, Reid addressed his dilemma by staking out a conservative position on a few highly publicized issues, then voting with the majority of Democrats much of the rest of the time. Reflecting the cultural values of his state and his own Mormonism, he shared Ronald Reagan's opposition to the Equal Rights Amendment (ERA) and legalized abortion. He has also supported the MX missile program. But on a wide range of other issues — the nuclear-weapons freeze, aid to the Nicaraguan contras, anti-satellite missile testing and funding for several social programs — Reid sided with the more liberal Democratic leadership.

Conventional wisdom holds that a Nevada congressman should serve on committees that relate closely to the state's interest in tourism, mining and public-lands issues. But after a futile effort to win a place on the House Energy and Commerce Committee in the 98th Congress, Reid struck out in a different direction by taking seats on Foreign Affairs and Science and Technology. He was the first Nevadan in a century to take a seat on Foreign Affairs. He cast his work there in a "Nevada First" context. He told constituents that serving on the panel gave him an opportunity to lobby foreign leaders to invest in Nevada. In key votes on the committee, Reid struck a centrist posture, proclaiming himself open to Republican persuasion but ultimately casting his lot with the majority Democrats most of the time.

At every opportunity, Reid has promoted tourism, the lifeblood of Las Vegas. He gave speeches on the House bemoaning what might be called a "tourism gap" — he said the United States' failure to keep pace with other developed nations in promoting tourism from abroad is causing our share of the world market to drop.

Similarly, Reid tried to use the Science assignment to promote Nevada as a site for high-technology industry. He argued that Nevada's economy should diversify into that sector rather than move further into nuclear-related activities, such as the existing nuclear test-site facilities.

At Home: Reid's race with Republican Jim Santini in 1986 was one of the year's most closely watched contests — not only because it seemed so evenly matched, but also because Santini's fortunes reflected on retiring Sen. Paul Laxalt and Republican National Committee Chairman Frank J. Fahrenkopf Jr., a former head of the Nevada GOP. Both were involved in recruiting Santini, a former four-term Democratic House member, to the Republican Party in 1985, and in clearing the way for him to run for the Senate.

But Santini's campaign had headaches from the start. Supporters of GOP Rep. Barbara F. Vucanovich only slowly warmed to Santini, since his entry derailed her Senate ambitions. And many Nevada Democrats were outraged by his candidacy. A number of them were still smoldering over Santini's primary challenge to veteran Democratic Sen. Howard W. Cannon in 1982, which they believe weakened Cannon so much that he lost his seat that fall to Hecht.

Santini sought to depict the 1986 race as "the classic conservative vs. liberal test," but he was stymied a bit by his own Democratic past. Reid responded to Santini's efforts to tag him as a big-spending "Tip O'Neill" liberal by noting that when Santini sought re-election in 1978, Fahrenkopf lambasted him as a big spender and O'Neill came into the state for a Santini fund-raiser.

The heated byplay between the candidates obscured the fact that they held similar positions on many issues. Reid clearly had been more sympathetic to organized labor, but both he and Santini were opposed to abortion, the ERA and gun control. Both supported the death penalty and said they were generally supportive of Reagan's foreign policy.

Reagan helped raise money for Santini, and Laxalt campaigned extensively for him. But Reid minimized their impact by tapping the state's distrust of Washington with an "us vs. them" campaign intimating that Washington power brokers were forcing Santini onto Nevada voters.

When all the votes were counted, Reid had carried only two of the state's 16 counties. But one of them was Clark County (Las Vegas), Reid's political base and home for a majority of Nevada voters. Reid amassed a 32,000-vote lead in the county, enough to offset Santini's 18,000-vote advantage in the rest of the state.

Reid's self-made career has been part skyrocket and part slow, hard climb. He was born in modest circumstances in remote Searchlight. He worked his way through school, including a stint as a policeman in the U.S. Capitol while attending law school in Washington. Within five years he was a successful lawyer in booming Las Vegas, well on his way toward becoming a millionaire and a freshly elected member of the state Legislature — all before he was 30.

In 1970, he ran successfully for lieutenant governor on a ticket with his former high school boxing coach, Mike O'Callaghan, who was elected governor. After one term in the No. 2 job, at the age of 34, Reid came within 625 votes of election to the U.S. Senate. It was 1974, and the Watergate scandal almost lifted Reid past the state's Republican former governor, Laxalt. But Reid's youth and even more boyish appearance did not wear well over the course of the campaign; the firm, articulate and mature Laxalt seemed to fit the part of a senator better. Seeking a quick rebound a year later, Reid lost a bid to be mayor of Las Vegas. Some thought he was through in politics.

Then, in 1977, O'Callaghan appointed him chairman of the Nevada Gaming Commission. While Reid held that job, an FBI investigation uncovered evidence of organized-crime influence in the Nevada gaming industry, and one reputed mobster accused Reid of being on the take.

Reid was cleared of charges that he intervened on behalf of organized-crime figures in cases before the Gaming Commission. When he finally left the commission in 1981, Reid was praised for weathering the earlier difficulties and staying on to help eliminate criminal elements from the gaming industry. Politically, he was alive again.

Redistricting in 1981 created a House seat for Las Vegas separate from the rest of Nevada; it would have been held by Santini, but he decided to run for the Senate in 1982 against Cannon. Reid announced his House campaign early, seeking support from friends and from business leaders he dealt with as Gaming Commission chairman. Reid was able to raise and spend more than $250,000 against inconsequential primary foes.

In November Reid faced an attractive, articulate Republican, former state Rep. Peggy Cavnar. She had run an impressive race in 1980 for the state Senate, losing narrowly in a district where Democrats normally had a clear advantage.

But her House bid was strapped for funds because she had embarrassed the Las Vegas GOP establishment by defeating its handpicked candidate in the primary. And she was unable to cast the contest in liberal-conservative terms, partly because Reid was careful not to criticize Reagan and partly because he concurred with her stands against the ERA and abortion. Reid's superior financial resources and organization resulted in a 58 percent win.

In a 1984 rematch, both Reid and Cavnar were in a stronger position to compete. Reid had the advantages of incumbency, while Cavnar had gained the backing of the state GOP establishment. The new advantages offset each other, and Reid won convincingly, with just a slightly lower percentage than he took in 1982.

Committees

Appropriations (13th of 16 Democrats)
Legislative Branch (chairman); Energy and Water Development; Interior and Related Agencies; Labor, Health and Human Services, Education and Related Agencies; Military Construction

Environment and Public Works (7th of 9 Democrats)
Toxic Substances, Environmental Oversight, Research and Development (chairman); Nuclear Regulation; Water Resources, Transportation and Infrastructure

Special Aging (8th of 10 Democrats)

Elections

1986 General		
Harry Reid (D)	130,955	(50%)
Jim Santini (R)	116,606	(45%)
1986 Primary		
Harry Reid (D)	74,275	(83%)
Manny Beals (D)	7,039	(8%)

Previous Winning Percentages: 1984 * (56%) **1982 *** (58%)

* *House elections.*

Campaign Finance

	Receipts	Receipts from PACs	Expend-itures
1986			
Reid (D)	$2,089,246	$817,377 (39%)	$2,055,756
Santini (R)	$2,696,285	$768,378 (28%)	$2,688,462

Key Votes

1987	
Enact omnibus highway bill over Reagan veto	Y
Limit testing of space-based anti-ballistic missiles	Y
Oppose banning tests of larger nuclear weapons	Y
Confirm Robert H. Bork as Supreme Court justice	N
1988	
Allow vote on campaign-finance overhaul	Y
Pass civil rights restoration bill over Reagan veto	Y
Enact omnibus trade bill over Reagan veto	Y
Approve death penalty for drug-related murders	Y
Oppose "workfare" amendment to welfare overhaul bill	N

Voting Studies

	Presidential Support		Party Unity		Conservative Coalition	
Year	**S**	**O**	**S**	**O**	**S**	**O**
1988	56	40	76	20	54	46
1987	40	58	88	11	44	56
House Service						
1986	26	74	84	16	48	52
1985	44	55	87	13	40	60
1984	42	58	84	16	42	58
1983	29	67	86	13	35	65

Interest Group Ratings

Year	ADA	ACU	AFL-CIO	CCUS
1988	55	28	92	29
1987	80	19	90	22
House Service				
1986	60	32	93	44
1985	55	29	82	32
1984	75	17	100	38
1983	70	35	82	25

Richard H. Bryan (D)

Of Carson City — Elected 1988

Born: July 16, 1937, Washington, D.C.
Education: U. of Nevada, B.A. 1959; U. of California, Hastings College of Law, LL.B. 1963.
Military Career: Army, 1959-60.
Occupation: Lawyer.
Family: Wife, Bonnie Fairchild; three children.
Religion: Episcopalian.
Political Career: Nev. Assembly, 1969-73; Nev. Senate, 1973-79; Nev. attorney general, 1979-83; governor, 1983-89; Democratic nominee for Nev. attorney general, 1974.
Capitol Office: 364 Russell Bldg. 20510; 224-6244.

The Path to Washington: Bryan arrived in the Senate with a mandate from Nevada's voters to defend his state aggressively against federal efforts to put a nuclear-waste dump there. The dump site was a salient issue for Bryan in unseating one-term GOP Sen. Chic Hecht in 1988.

Bryan launched a broadscale attack on Hecht's achievements and competence, but its cutting edge was the dump. Hecht's failure to block the siting decision, or even to oppose it in its formative stage, lent weight to criticism that he was out of his league in the Senate.

However, Bryan was not able to tackle the issue promptly in Washington. He did not get the seat on the Energy and Natural Resources Committee he sought (the two open slots went to more senior Democrats facing re-election in 1990). And the other two committees where he might have a swing at the siting decision — Appropriations and Environment — already had a Democratic member from Nevada in Harry Reid.

Beyond that, the siting issue simply was not before the Senate. Until a specific opportunity in funding or authorizing legislation arises, Bryan will have to content himself with finding a niche in the Senate like any other freshman.

In that regard, the twice-elected governor seems generally in step with Democrats. On the one major controversy to divide the Senate early in 1989, the nomination of former Sen. John Tower as secretary of defense, Bryan voted with the majority of his party (without giving a floor speech). But he is also a fiscal conservative, and as a Westerner he may go his own way on defense and public-lands issues.

The committees he did receive — Banking and Commerce — were somewhat unusual for a Western senator. But they might suit the businesslike Bryan well. Banking, in particular, offered a role in one of the hotter responsibilities of the 101st Congress — rewriting the financial laws in a historic state of flux.

On Commerce, Bryan's first natural interest is tourism, an industry of inestimable importance to Nevada. Bryan is on the Tourism Subcommittee, but he has the chairmanship of the Consumer Subcommittee. This is an unusual opportunity for a senator in his first Congress, and Bryan could be tested early in handling the telephone-marketing fraud issue.

Bryan is also a freshman member of the Democratic Senate Policy Committee and has taken an interest in strategy sessions for the party's campaign committee in 1990.

Bryan ran for the Senate in the middle of his second term as governor. First elected to that job in 1982, he was re-elected in 1986 with 72 percent of the vote. Even then, it was widely assumed he would challenge Hecht in 1988.

Bryan won his reputation as a fiscal conservative when he cut hundreds of state government jobs in a budget-balancing drive in his first term. He was helped by growth in the state's revenues from gambling, which made higher burdens on the state's taxpayers largely unnecessary. In his second term, a health-cost-containment bill, successfully steered through the Legislature, was one of his major projects.

Bryan began his political career as a public defender and prosecutor in Clark County (Las Vegas), which includes slightly more than half the state's population. He had also served a decade in the state Assembly and Senate before winning his first statewide office, state attorney general, in 1978.

By the time Bryan sought the Senate, Hecht offered an irresistible target. He had been elected in 1982 in large part because the Democratic incumbent, Howard W. Cannon, was rendered vulnerable by a tough primary and by the trial of Teamsters union officials charged with trying to bribe him. Despite these circumstances, Hecht won with just 50 percent.

In the interim, Hecht had enjoyed some sunny moments, including passage of his amendment restoring the 65 mph speed limit.

But he had also been battered by the nuclear-waste controversy. When Hecht finally turned against siting the dump in Nevada, the momentum in Congress for choosing the state was unstoppable. For years before, Hecht had viewed the dump as a patriotic duty and as a potential source of federal money and jobs.

Hecht also had to compensate for an unimposing personal presence and a tendency to utter malapropisms (he once said the state should not become a "a nuclear suppository"). After Bryan announced his candidacy early in 1988, he emphasized these perceptions of Hecht. At one point he referred to the state's senior senator as being "unable to find the men's room."

These tactics played into the hands of Hecht's campaign managers, who used some of their $2 million treasury for a TV blitz that defined the early stage of the campaign. The ads portrayed a humble, hard-working Hecht, devoted to helping the little guy. Bryan, by contrast, came off seeming harsh and a touch arrogant.

But Bryan righted his campaign in the summer, moving belatedly to counter Hecht's efforts on the airwaves and shifting his aim to issues. He kept up the heat on the dump, an issue that had helped Reid move up from the House in 1986.

Bryan's other attacks on Hecht also helped contrast the two on domestic issues: He targeted Hecht's votes to eliminate cost-of-living adjustments to Social Security and against restoration of certain Medicare benefits. Bryan found support from labor groups; he backed the bill Congress passed in 1988 to give workers 60 days' notice of plant closings. Hecht opposed it. Bryan's support for contra aid, however, placed him apart from the mainstream of Democrats nationally.

With all his ammunition, and despite a resurgent lead in the summer polls, Bryan could not knock Hecht flat. The plucky incumbent had to deal with a state GOP rife with internal disputes involving new leaders associated with the presidential campaign of Pat Robertson. He was distracted when the Clark County GOP chairman impugned Bryan's marital fidelity on a radio program. Still, Hecht pressed his case, raking Bryan for leaving the governorship in midterm and for being too close to the power elements of the national Democratic Party.

The race was close to the end. At one point on election night, at least one TV network projected Hecht the winner. Bryan ran nearly 43,000 votes ahead of his party's presidential ticket, but still got just over 50 percent.

Committees

Banking, Housing and Urban Affairs (12th of 12 Democrats)
Consumer and Regulatory Affairs; Housing and Urban Affairs

Commerce, Science and Transportation (10th of 11 Democrats)
Consumer (chairman); Foreign Commerce and Tourism; Science, Technology and Space

Joint Economic
Economic Resources and Competitiveness; Investment, Jobs and Prices; National Security Economics

Campaign Finance

	Receipts	Receipts from PACs	Expend-itures
1988			
Bryan (D)	$2,986,727	$802,792 (27%)	$2,957,789
Hecht (R)	$2,907,927	$977,024 (34%)	$3,007,864

Elections

1988 General		
Richard H. Bryan (D)	175,548	(50%)
Chic Hecht (R)	161,336	(46%)
1988 Primary		
Richard H. Byran (D)	62,278	(79%)
Pat M. Fitzpatrick (D)	4,721	(6%)

1 James Bilbray (D)

Of Las Vegas — Elected 1986

Born: May 19, 1938, Las Vegas, Nev.
Education: American U., B.A. 1962; Washington College of Law, J.D. 1964.
Military Career: National Guard, 1955-63; Reserve, 1963-present.
Occupation: Lawyer.
Family: Wife, Michaelene Mercer; three children.
Religion: Roman Catholic.
Political Career: Nev. Senate, 1981-87; Democratic nominee for U.S. House, 1972.
Capitol Office: 319 Cannon Bldg. 20515; 225-5965.

In Washington: Bilbray is not the most adroit legislator in his class, but for the 101st Congress he did manage to get the committee assignment of his choice, Armed Services — after two unsuccessful attempts in the 100th and after newcomers to the House picked off two other vacancies on the committee for the current Congress.

Although Bilbray came to the House in 1987 with legislative experience under his belt, that is not always evident to his colleagues. At times he can be so unconventional as to appear unsophisticated.

When he tried for a spot on the Science Committee in his first term, he thought he could do himself some good by stationing himself outside the room where the Democratic Steering and Policy Committee was meeting, and lobbying the members as they arrived. Shaking their hands as they entered, he said that shaking hands door-to-door worked in Las Vegas and he hoped it would get him a seat on Science and Technology. It did not.

Bilbray did get credit at home for fighting some serious battles for Nevada. Perhaps the most frustrating one was the fight against a decision to place the nation's high-level nuclear waste site in Nevada. When Senate and House negotiators agreed to the plan, Bilbray took to the floor and announced he was sending his colleagues maps of the routes on which waste would be carried to his state.

"Most of you in this room will be receiving trucks in the numbers of thousands per month that will be . . . passing through your communities endangering the lives of your citizens," he said. But there was little a freshman could do to stop the process.

More successful local attention-getters included Bilbray's effort to delay deactivation of the 474th Tactical Fighter Wing at Nellis Air Force Base, and his work to establish a veterans' cemetery and hospital in Nevada.

At Home: When Democrat Harry Reid vacated this House seat to run for the Senate in 1986, Bilbray was a logical replacement. Son of the longtime Clark County assessor, he had close personal ties to the Las Vegas hotel and casino establishments. He had chaired the Taxation Committee in the state Senate. And he was running in a district with a 3-to-2 Democratic advantage. But by Election Day, Bilbray's campaign had run into so many problems that his victory over Republican state Sen. Bob Ryan turned out to be something of a surprise.

Some problems were of Bilbray's own making. At a meeting of the state AFL-CIO in September, he warned of the dangers of a sympathy vote for Ryan because the Republican was blind. "Voters feel sorry for a man who knocks on their door with a white cane," he said. Bilbray made a personal apology to Ryan the next day.

Meanwhile, Bilbray had to fend off questions about his personal ethics. The attacks had begun in the Democratic primary, when his principal opponent asked Bilbray why he acted as legal counsel to companies that stood to benefit from legislation he promoted in the state Senate. Bilbray denied any wrongdoing, but his narrow primary victory encouraged Ryan to keep up the line of attack in the fall.

But Bilbray survived with some hardball of his own. On election eve, he sent out an anti-Ryan mailer that pictured Sirhan Sirhan and Charles Manson on the cover and suggested that Ryan supported measures that would let killers like Sirhan and Manson out of jail. Ryan protested that his positions were being distorted. But the mailer, coupled with Bilbray's superiority in grass-roots organization and fund raising, brought him a 10-percentage-point victory. Two years later, Bilbray won in a romp.

Bilbray's recent successes have softened the memories of a 1972 House effort. Then, as a youthful and more liberal Democrat, he upset 10-term House veteran Walter S. Baring in the Democratic primary. But Baring and many of his supporters remained cool to Bilbray, and a virtually unknown Republican defeated him in the general election.

Nevada 1

South — Las Vegas

Las Vegas has come a long way from its days as a Mormon mission in the mid-1800s. In the 50 years since legalized gambling and the building of Boulder Dam brought a construction boom to the city, it has developed from a dusty town of fewer than 10,000 people to a neon extravaganza with 192,000 full-time residents. Clark County, including Las Vegas and its suburbs, grew by nearly 70 percent in the 1970s. Today, this one corner of Nevada contains almost 60 percent of the state's population. The 1st District itself takes in most of Las Vegas and the southeastern half of Clark County.

The "Strip" of casinos, nightclubs and hotels that gives Las Vegas its vaguely disreputable image is actually outside the city limits. But the Strip is the economic focal point of the area. Most of the 1st District's residents are connected in some way to the gaming, entertainment and tourism industries; whenever recessions strike, Las Vegas quickly feels the pinch, because there are fewer visitors with money to burn; in early 1983, Las Vegas' unemployment rate hit 13 percent.

Most voters in the 1st are registered Democrats, but in general elections party affiliation tends to be less important than ideology. In 1988, for instance, Clark County supported George Bush for president and Democratic Gov. Richard H. Bryan in his successful bid for the Senate. Las Vegas' large Mormon community has long been a potent force for conservatism; government workers employed at nearby Nellis Air Force Base and the Department of Energy's Nevada Test Range also help GOP candidates in Clark County.

But the bulk of the vote comes from the area's service workers, many of whom are unionized. This group includes a sizable black population.

North Las Vegas, whose portion of the 1st is 42 percent black, and Las Vegas' West Side — its poorest area — hold most of the district's 40,000 blacks.

Population: 400,636. White 338,725 (85%), Black 39,797 (10%), Other 10,447 (3%). Spanish origin 30,345 (8%). 18 and over 292,870 (73%), 65 and over 32,739 (8%). Median age: 30.

Committees

Armed Services (29th of 31 Democrats)
Military Installations and Facilities; Readiness

Select Aging (33rd of 39 Democrats)
Housing and Consumer Interests

Small Business (18th of 27 Democrats)
Antitrust, Impact of Deregulation and Privatization; Exports, Tax Policy and Special Problems; Procurement, Tourism and Rural Development

Elections

1988 General		
James Bilbray (D)	101,764	(64%)
Lucille Lusk (R)	53,588	(34%)
1986 General		
James Bilbray (D)	61,830	(54%)
Bob Ryan (R)	50,342	(44%)

District Vote For President

	1988		1984		1980		1976	
D	67,468	(41%)	47,267	(36%)	32,778	(30%)	43,872	(51%)
R	90,671	(56%)	82,023	(63%)	64,073	(59%)	40,483	(47%)
I	4,575 *	(3%)			7,270	(7%)		

* *"None of these candidates"*

Campaign Finance

	Receipts	Receipts from PACs	Expend-itures
1988			
Bilbray (D)	$669,014	$300,116 (45%)	$652,199
Lusk (R)	$148,957	$19,645 (13%)	$147,891
1986			
Bilbray (D)	$391,041	$166,825 (43%)	$387,717
Ryan (R)	$280,820	$95,957 (34%)	$276,138

Key Votes

1987	
Raise speed limit to 65 mph	Y
Approve Gephardt "fair trade" amendment	Y
Ban testing of larger nuclear weapons	N
Delay "re-flagging" of Kuwaiti tankers	Y
Approve tax-raising deficit-reduction bill	N
1988	
Approve aid to Nicaraguan contras	N
Enact civil rights restoration bill over Reagan veto	Y
Kill 60-day plant-closing notification measure	N
Pass omnibus trade bill over Reagan veto	Y
Approve death penalty for drug-related murders	Y
Bar federal funds for abortions in cases of rape and incest	Y
Oppose seven-day waiting period for purchase of handguns	Y

Voting Studies

	Presidential Support		Party Unity		Conservative Coalition	
Year	S	O	S	O	S	O
1988	30	67	79	16	68	29
1987	34	66	79	17	67	30

Interest Group Ratings

Year	ADA	ACU	AFL-CIO	CCUS
1988	60	44	93	43
1987	68	26	94	33

2 Barbara F. Vucanovich (R)

Of Reno — Elected 1982

Born: June 22, 1921, Camp Dix, N.J.
Education: Attended Manhattanville College, 1938-39.
Occupation: Travel agent; congressional aide.
Family: Husband, George F. Vucanovich; five children.
Religion: Roman Catholic.
Political Career: No previous office.
Capitol Office: 206 Cannon Bldg. 20515; 225-6155.

In Washington: The "Nevada connection" was in its heyday as Vucanovich served her freshman term in Congress. Her mentor, GOP Sen. Paul Laxalt, was a close friend of President Reagan, and the national party was being run by a former Nevada state GOP chairman, Frank J. Fahrenkopf Jr. Back then, Vucanovich herself had a reasonably high profile in national conservative circles as the "tough grandmother" from the Silver State.

But now, Laxalt, Reagan and Fahrenkopf are gone, and Vucanovich has settled into more parochial legislative pursuits. Tending to Nevada's needs, however, was a full-time job in the 100th Congress, which enacted a law to put all of the nation's high-level nuclear waste in Yucca Mountain, Nev.

Vucanovich was a bit slow to join opponents of the waste site, but once she did, she became one of their most ardent advocates. From her post on the Interior Committee, she contributed to a bill sponsored by committee Chairman Morris K. Udall that would have established a special commission to study placement of a waste site. Vucanovich offered successful amendments to lengthen the study period and to give federal aid to state and local governments affected by the commission's work.

Unfortunately for Vucanovich, the real action occurred in the Senate, where Democrat J. Bennett Johnston strong-armed passage of an amendment to the 1988 budget-reconciliation bill to accelerate the site-selection process. With no Nevadans on the House-Senate conference committee considering the bill, Johnston struck a deal to name Nevada as the dump site.

Vucanovich condemned the action, saying Congress was trying "to turn our state into a federal colony," and complaining that members were "behaving like a pack of wolves going in for the kill." But she was powerless to stop the juggernaut. The bill became law in 1987.

At the start of the 101st Congress, Vucanovich pledged to hold hearings to locate U.S. nuclear waste on the Marshall Islands in the Pacific, where the U.S. conducted atomic testing between 1946 and 1958. She also made the controversial suggestion that Nevada begin negotiating for federal financial compensation for accepting the dump. Many Nevadans objected, saying this would be tantamount to consent.

In the last two Congresses, the Interior Committee wrestled with legislation to designate wilderness land in Nevada. Vucanovich was among those most strongly opposed to a large designation, and her side had the upper hand for a time. But now, Vucanovich is the only Republican in the state's four-member House and Senate delegation, so the incentive to compromise is greater.

Vucanovich got embroiled in the wilderness issue in the 99th Congress, when she went head-to-head with the state's other House member, Democrat Harry Reid (now a U.S. senator). Reid's proposal, backed by then-Gov. Richard H. Bryan (also now a U.S. senator), was to establish wilderness areas totaling 592,000 acres as well as the first national park in Nevada, Great Basin National Park, with 174,000 acres. Vucanovich's competing proposal, supported by the state's two GOP senators, would have set aside only 137,000 acres.

The House passed Reid's proposal after a party-line vote rejecting Vucanovich's amendment to kill creation of the park. With then-Sens. Laxalt and Chic Hecht stifling action in the Senate, the House finally agreed to a compromise late in 1986 to create a more modest 77,000-acre Great Basin National Park.

When the wilderness issue was revisited in the 100th Congress, Vucanovich proved more accommodating. She did not fight a House bill calling for a 730,000-acre wilderness preserve after Interior Democrats agreed to a few compromises. Among them: Mount Rose was designated a recreation area instead of wilderness, and certain lands on Ruby Mountain were exempted for use as a helicopter ski area. That bill died in the Senate, but it was an issue in Bryan's successful 1988 Senate race against Hecht, and is expected to resurface.

Vucanovich was also involved in congressional debate over legislation to overhaul the

Nevada 2

North — Reno and the Cow Counties

Although 15 percent of its people live in metropolitan Las Vegas, the 2nd is referred to as the "non-Las Vegas" district. It is dominated by Reno, a Republican stronghold containing nearly half the district's voters.

Gambling is an all-important component of the Reno (Washoe County) economy, but Reno and Lake Tahoe take pains to differentiate themselves from Las Vegas. This is "old Nevada," the part of the state that was built on mining in the 19th century and dominated politics until Las Vegas overshadowed it in the 1950s. Republicans have a registration advantage in Washoe County and nearby Douglas County and Carson City. Those three areas have awarded Republican presidential candidates significant margins in the last elections. But while GOP Sen. Chic Hecht won Douglas County in 1988, he lost Washoe on his way to a narrow statewide defeat.

About one-fourth of the district's residents are dispersed through the "Cow Counties," a huge expanse of mountain and desert that occupies most of the state. Cattle and sheep raising are the main economic activities here, but silver and gold mining are mounting a comeback as technological improvements make it profitable to extract and process low-grade ore.

The Cow Counties were populist and Democratic for most of this century, but their voters are gradually turning Republican in frustration over national Democratic liberalism, especially the party's land and water policies. (Nearly all of the land in the 2nd District is federally owned.) Most residents thought President Jimmy Carter's plan to place a mobile-MX missile system in this region would strain the meager water supply, and there was rejoicing when Ronald Reagan decided not to pursue that idea.

Population: 399,857. White 361,620 (90%), Black 11,202 (3%), Other 17,025 (4%). Spanish origin 23,534 (6%). 18 and over 291,824 (73%), 65 and over 33,017 (8%). Median age: 30.

nation's main nuclear-insurance law, the Price-Anderson Act, which limits the nuclear industry's liability in accidents. During Interior Committee debate in 1986, Udall needed support for an amendment sharply raising the industry's liability limit from the subcommittee-approved level of $2.5 billion to $8.2 billion. He gained a key convert in Vucanovich, who had supported the lower amount in subcommittee, in return for Udall's support of her amendment to remove the ceiling on compensation for a single accident involving nuclear waste. Vucanovich's support proved pivotal. Her language passed 20-13, while the liability-limit amendment eked through 21-20.

That bill died in the Senate at the end of the 99th Congress, but moved quickly the next year. Though the House again went along with Vucanovich's amendment, the Senate balked. Under the law passed in 1987, the industry's liability for an accident involving nuclear waste is the same as for any other incident, roughly $7.4 billion.

At Home: Vucanovich entered politics as a protégée of Laxalt, but the veteran Republican leader was no help to her when she was thinking of running for his open Senate seat in 1986. Laxalt encouraged former Democratic Rep. Jim Santini to switch parties, and then — Vucanovich supporters complained — pressured her to drop her Senate ambitions so Santini would have a clear shot for the GOP nomination.

But she landed on her feet. While Santini lost the Senate race to Democrat Reid, Vucanovich easily won a third House term.

Vucanovich's first election to the House rewarded her long involvement in Republican politics. She had worked in presidential campaigns since the Eisenhower era and had been president of several GOP women's groups.

In 1962 she signed on with Laxalt, and for two decades worked behind the scenes for him as a grass-roots organizer and constituent-service specialist. Laxalt returned the favor in 1982 by actively helping her win the newly created 2nd District. Laxalt's backing all but guaranteed Vucanovich the GOP nomination against five other Republicans.

Much of her campaign time was spent boosting her low name recognition. She benefited from TV ads featuring the popular Laxalt. But her grandmotherly image also helped her establish a rapport with voters. She won a solid 43 percent in the large primary field.

In the general-election campaign, Democrat Mary Gojack urged voters not to elect a Laxalt clone. A former state senator and unsuccessful challenger to Laxalt in 1980, Gojack was a stronger personal campaigner than Vucanovich. But she suffered in much of the district from her reputation as a feminist liberal closer to the politics of the East than to those of Nevada. Vucanovich played up her devout conservatism and relied less on Laxalt, and she won 56 percent of the vote. In 1984, she handily won a second term.

Two years later, Vucanovich drew a challenge from Reno Mayor Peter J. Sferrazza, the recent chairman of the Nevada Democratic Party. Sferrazza sought to make an issue of the proposed placement of a nuclear-waste dump in the vast desert reaches of the district, saying he had been against it while Vucanovich was trying to make up her mind. One Sferrazza TV ad featured a campaign volunteer in goggles and an iridescent painter's suit checking a Vucanovich campaign sign with a Geiger counter.

Despite Sferrazza's creativity, he was burdened with a liberal image that hurt his fund raising. A veteran of the Peace Corps whose first job in Nevada was as director of a legal services office for Indians, he was not shy about identifying himself with the underprivileged and minorities. And as a proponent of limited growth in Reno, he was unable to raise much money from the city's gambling operators and other business interests whose support he needed to be competitive.

As a result, Sferrazza had to resort to campaign gimmicks — such as a six-day, 340-mile, cross-district bicycle trip along the shoulder of Interstate 80 in the dog days of August. The well-financed Vucanovich crisscrossed the district in her private plane.

The results were predictable. Vucanovich took 56 percent of the vote in populous Washoe County (Reno), home base for both her and Sferrazza, and won with 58 percent overall.

In 1988, another popular mayor stepped forward to challenge Vucanovich. He was James Spoo, the mayor of Sparks. Spoo raised more than six times the money Sferrazza did, and he projected the kind of moderate-to-conservative image Democrats have found success with in the mountain West. The perfect symbol of this appeal arrived when Sen. Lloyd Bentsen of Texas, the Democratic nominee for vice president, came through the 2nd and campaigned with Spoo.

But Vucanovich should not have been in any trouble in a presidential year, and she was not. The Republican ticket headed by George Bush was far from reaching the heights that the Reagan campaigns here had (70 percent in 1984). But Vucanovich prevailed by 57 percent districtwide.

Committees

House Administration (4th of 8 Republicans)
Accounts (ranking)

Interior and Insular Affairs (7th of 15 Republicans)
General Oversight and Investigations (ranking); Energy and the Environment; Mining and Natural Resources

Select Children, Youth and Families (3rd of 12 Republicans)

Elections

1988 General		
Barbara F. Vucanovich (R)	105,981	(57%)
James Spoo (D)	75,163	(41%)
1986 General		
Barbara F. Vucanovich (R)	83,479	(58%)
Pete Sferrazza (D)	59,433	(42%)

Previous Winning Percentages: 1984 (71%) **1982** (56%)

District Vote For President

	1988	1984	1980	1976
D	65,270 (35%)	44,388 (29%)	32,358 (24%)	46,521 (44%)
R	115,369 (61%)	106,747 (70%)	86,565 (65%)	57,957 (55%)
I	6,813 *(4%)		9,784 (7%)	

* *"None of these candidates"*

Campaign Finance

	Receipts	Receipts from PACs	Expend-itures
1988			
Vucanovich (R)	$608,009	$201,719 (33%)	$614,853
Spoo (D)	$434,976	$176,950 (41%)	$430,155
1986			
Vucanovich (R)	$328,346	$126,534 (39%)	$367,044
Sferrazza (D)	$69,960	$23,300 (33%)	$69,777

Key Votes

1987	
Raise speed limit to 65 mph	Y
Approve Gephardt "fair trade" amendment	N
Ban testing of larger nuclear weapons	N
Delay "re-flagging" of Kuwaiti tankers	N
Approve tax-raising deficit-reduction bill	N
1988	
Approve aid to Nicaraguan contras	Y
Enact civil rights restoration bill over Reagan veto	N
Kill 60-day plant-closing notification measure	Y
Pass omnibus trade bill over Reagan veto	N
Approve death penalty for drug-related murders	Y
Bar federal funds for abortions in cases of rape and incest	Y
Oppose seven-day waiting period for purchase of handguns	Y

Voting Studies

	Presidential Support		Party Unity		Conservative Coalition	
Year	**S**	**O**	**S**	**O**	**S**	**O**
1988	68	32	92	4	92	3
1987	63	31	89	7	91	9
1986	69	24	84	12	90	10
1985	70	29	87	9	91	7
1984	64	31	83	11	90	5
1983	78	16	87	6	90	7

Interest Group Ratings

Year	ADA	ACU	AFL-CIO	CCUS
1988	10	92	14	77
1987	20	74	19	86
1986	0	86	7	89
1985	10	86	13	95
1984	10	96	8	75
1983	0	96	0	90

New Hampshire

U.S. CONGRESS

SENATE 2 R
HOUSE 2 R

LEGISLATURE

Senate 8 D, 16 R
House 119 D, 281 R

ELECTIONS

1988 Presidential Vote

Bush	63%
Dukakis	36%

1984 Presidential Vote

Reagan	69%
Mondale	31%

1980 Presidential Vote

Reagan	58%
Carter	28%
Anderson	13%

Turnout rate in 1984	53%
Turnout rate in 1986	32%
Turnout rate in 1988	55%

(as percentage of voting age population)

POPULATION AND GROWTH

1980 population	920,610
1988 population estimate (40th in the nation)	1,085,000
Percent change 1980-1988	+18%

DEMOGRAPHIC BREAKDOWN

White	99%
Black	0.4%
(Spanish origin)	1%
Urban	52%
Rural	48%
Born in state	49%
Foreign-born	5%

MAJOR CITIES

Manchester	97,280
Nashua	76,510
Concord	32,770
Portsmouth	25,970
Dover	23,770

AREA AND LAND USE

Area 8,993 sq. miles (44th)

Farm	8%
Forest	88%
Federally owned	13%

Gov. Judd Gregg (R)
Of Greenfield — Elected 1988

Born: Feb. 14, 1947, Nashua, N.H.
Education: Columbia U., A.B. 1969; Boston U., J.D. 1972, LL.M. 1975.
Occupation: Lawyer.
Religion: Protestant.
Political Career: N.H. Governor's Executive Council, 1979-81; U.S. House, 1981-89.
Next Election: 1990.

WORK

Occupations

White-collar	52%
Blue-collar	35%
Service workers	12%

Government Workers

Federal	7,328
State	22,017
Local	38,281

MONEY

Median family income	$ 19,723	(25th)
Tax burden per capita	$ 435	(50th)

EDUCATION

Spending per pupil through grade 12	$ 3,542	(25th)
Persons with college degrees	18%	(13th)

CRIME

Violent crime rate	150 per 100,000 (46th)

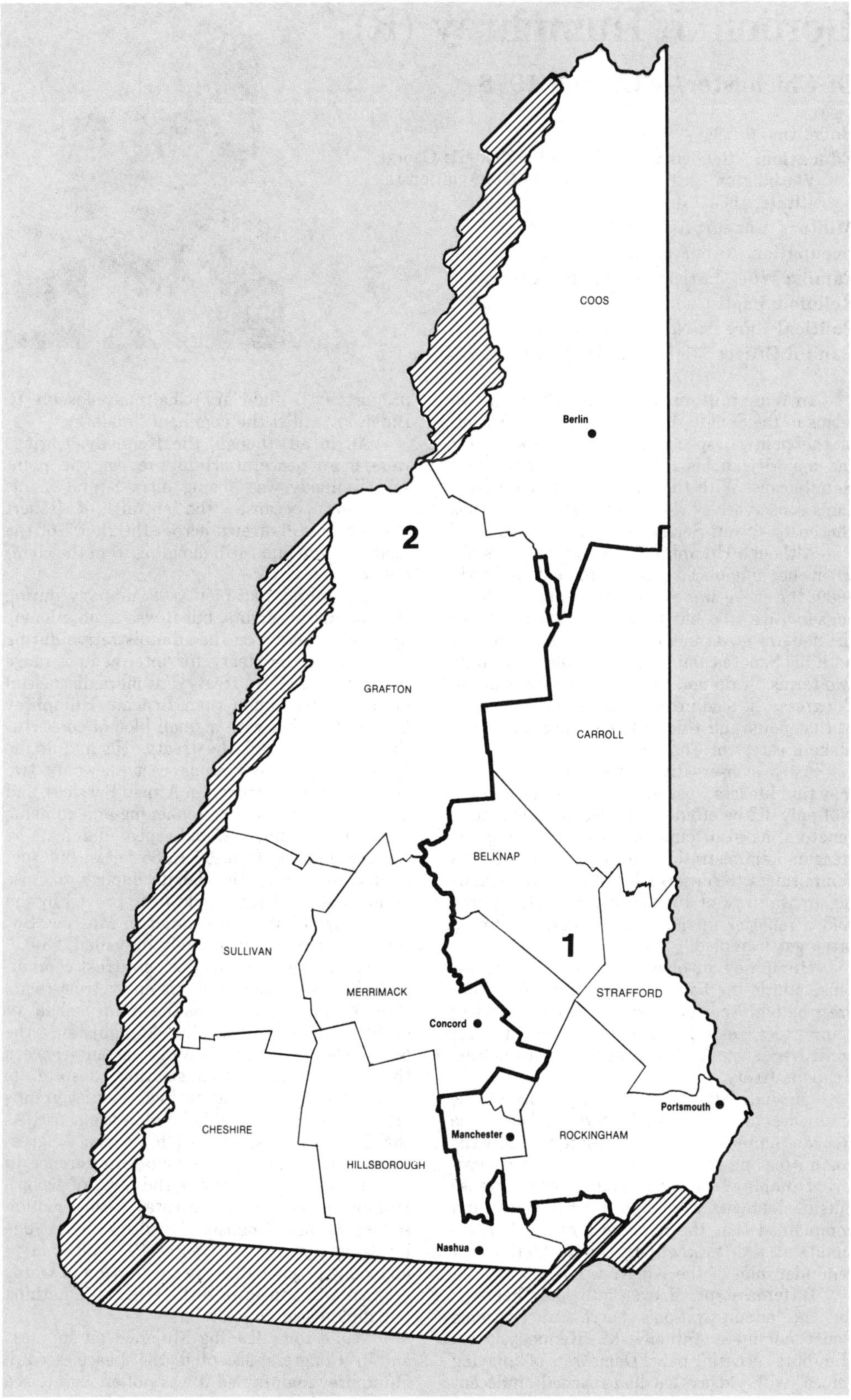
COOS
Berlin
2
GRAFTON
CARROLL
BELKNAP
SULLIVAN
MERRIMACK
1
STRAFFORD
Concord
Portsmouth
Manchester
ROCKINGHAM
CHESHIRE
HILLSBOROUGH
Nashua

Gordon J. Humphrey (R)

Of Chichester — Elected 1978

Born: Oct. 9, 1940, Bristol, Conn.

Education: Attended U. of Maryland, 1960-61; George Washington U., 1962-63; Burnside-Ott Aviation Institute, 1965.

Military Career: Air Force, 1958-62.

Occupation: Airline pilot.

Family: Wife, Patricia Greene; two children.

Religion: Baptist.

Political Career: No previous office.

Capitol Office: 531 Hart Bldg. 20510; 224-2841.

In Washington: Humphrey has spent two terms in the Senate sitting out on the right end of the political spectrum, making trouble for the majority to his left, both Democrats and Republicans. With the passing of Ronald Reagan's conservative "revolution," Humphrey has chosen to sit out Senate politics entirely.

Although Humphrey was only 48 years old when he announced his retirement in early 1989, the move was not a surprising one for a conservative who has never been enamored of the federal government. He had promised in both his Senate campaigns he would serve only two terms. "I do not want to spend 18 years in Congress," he said in 1989. "It becomes a career at that point and I don't believe people should make a career of Congress."

As a conservative crusader, Humphrey may find life less frustrating outside the Senate. Not only did he often go against the tide among senators, he also found himself criticizing the Reagan administration for backsliding in its commitment to conservatism. "I'm often standing in the way of the herd here," Humphrey told a reporter in the 100th Congress. "And I often get trampled."

Humphrey involved himself in some intense and losing battles during the 100th Congress on both the Judiciary and Armed Services committees, as the Senate wrangled over controversial judicial nominees and a nuclear-weapons treaty.

On Judiciary, Humphrey was one of the staunchest defenders of Robert H. Bork, the Reagan Supreme Court nominee rejected by the committee and the full Senate as too conservative. Humphrey seemed offended by the intense outside lobbying campaign against Bork, and complained that the nominee's critics had intimidated pro-Bork witnesses with tactics that reminded him of the Ku Klux Klan.

Bitterness spilled over into later hearings for the administration's successful Supreme Court nominee, Anthony M. Kennedy, with Humphrey accusing panel Democrats of "playing games" with judges that had reached "indecent proportions." Judiciary Chairman Joseph R. Biden Jr. called the comment "malarky."

All in all, though, the Kennedy hearings were more peaceful. Humphrey at one point said Kennedy was "being ultra-careful in his testimony" because "the entrails of Robert Bork were still strewn across the floor" of the hearing room and "still dangling from the chandeliers."

Humphrey had plenty of company during the nomination fights, but it was a more lonely experience taking on the administration during debate over the treaty for intermediate-range nuclear-force (INF) treaty. Far more distrustful of the Soviet Union than Reagan, Humphrey banded together with a small bloc of conservatives to try to kill the treaty. He and Idaho Republican Steve Symms cast the only two votes against the treaty on Armed Services, and then pushed numerous weakening amendments on the floor. They suffered repeated defeats by margins ranging from 67 to 85 votes, but succeeded in slowing the debate enough to raise doubt that the treaty could be approved by the time Reagan left for a summit in Moscow. But treaty proponents ultimately prevailed, 93-5.

Humphrey not only does not trust communists, he does not trust others not to trust them. One of his crusades has been on behalf of anti-Soviet guerrillas in Afghanistan, the Mujahedeen, and he showed constant concern that the Reagan administration, despite its reputation for backing anti-communist groups around the globe, would abandon the cause. As the administration pushed for a peace agreement that would limit outside interference in Afghanistan after Soviet withdrawal of troops, Humphrey said it "constitutes a slow-motion sellout, in plain English." He also said a pledge by Secretary of State George P. Shultz not to abandon the guerrillas "is a collection of words . . . that will vanish into the ether. It's nothing but diplomatic doubletalk."

While some leading Mujahedeen supporters in Congress accepted the peace accord, Humphrey maintained it was not enough to see

Soviet troops withdraw. "Even if the Soviets leave," he said late in 1988, "that's only half the battle from the point of view of the resistance. The other half is getting rid of the puppet government, which is not going to be as easy a mark as the State Department seems to think." On more than one occasion, Humphrey was at odds with the State Department, holding up ambassadorial nominations while waiting for the administration to appoint a special envoy to the Afghan rebels.

Humphrey joined the Foreign Relations Committee in the 101st Congress, allowing him to spend his last two Senate years concentrating on such matters.

Humphrey has shown time and again that he feels deeply about some issues, and he seems unafraid of alienating others in pursuit of his agenda. His willingness to be a loner is partly illustrated by his desire to do much of his work in a small computerized hideaway office, which the former airline pilot has likened to a cockpit — a quiet control room from which he can communicate electronically with his staff.

He also showed his willingness to be a thorn in fellow Republicans' sides during the 1988 presidential campaign, when he got considerable media attention for challenging George Bush's conservative credentials. Hoping to exert pressure on Bush to name a conservative running mate, Humphrey — who worked on Jack F. Kemp's presidential campaign — organized a group called "The Coalition for a Winning Ticket," set up an office at the national convention, and threatened to push the group's own choice for vice president if Bush's pick was deemed unacceptable. He ended up cheering the selection of Dan Quayle.

Humphrey has also been one of the most vocal critics of congressional pay raises, and is particularly angry that they can go into effect unless rejected by Congress. "We run from accountability as cockroaches run from bright light," he said once. His court challenges to the process have failed, but he did come out on the winning end early in the 101st Congress, when he was among those seeking rejection of a proposed 51 percent pay increase.

If there is an area where Humphrey seems less conservative, it is when working on environmental issues. Originally viewed as very rigid on environmental matters, Humphrey made a sharp turn toward the center as his first term drew to a close. Spurred by changes in his own thinking as well as by the dictates of his 1984 re-election campaign, he found himself allied on many issues with the same environmentalists and anti-nuclear activists he was vehemently denouncing a few years before. "I'm man enough and frank enough to admit in public that I've changed my mind," he said at the time.

Humphrey initially thought warnings of the danger of acid rain were "the latest alarmist issue seized upon by more extreme environmentalist groups." But after a lengthy lobbying effort by environmental groups, he began joining them in pushing for curbs on the burning of coal, which is believed to account for much of the acid rain damaging New Hampshire's rivers and lakes.

Humphrey left the Environment Committee in the 100th Congress, but rejoined it for the 101st.

At Home: For most of his early Senate career, Democrats confidently viewed Humphrey as a sure one-term senator. For much of that term, he feuded not only with liberals in his state but also with the arch-conservative Manchester *Union Leader*, which condemned him for opposing its choice in the 1980 GOP Senate primary.

But Humphrey surprised his critics the way he had surprised incumbent Democratic Sen. Thomas J. McIntyre in 1978. Rather than seeking re-election as a doctrinaire supporter of the New Right, Humphrey ran for a second term on a variegated platform that made him difficult to label. He remained the crusty individualist and the self-described Senate "skinflint," but he also talked about his keen interest in protecting New Hampshire's air, wilderness and fragile coastline.

Humphrey maintained that his belated interest in the environment came after long study, not as a result of political pressure. But his Democratic challenger, U.S. Rep. Norman E. D'Amours, saw otherwise, accusing Humphrey of an election-year flip-flop designed to win a large share of the "green" vote that he did not deserve.

The chairman of the House Subcommittee on Oceanography, D'Amours had built much of his congressional record on environmental issues. His Senate candidacy ultimately drew endorsements from both the League of Conservation Voters and the Sierra Club. But he was largely frustrated in his efforts to get voters to believe that the Humphrey of 1984 was little different from the earlier model that had been in lock step with the New Right.

In five terms in the House, D'Amours had cultivated a reputation as a political moderate, becoming virtually invincible in his Manchester-based 1st District. But the Republican had more money, stronger coattails with President Reagan atop the ticket, and the vocal support of the *Union Leader*, which had resolved its differences with Humphrey. Throughout the campaign the paper peppered D'Amours as a liberal ally of House Speaker Thomas P. O'Neill Jr., who it said was out of step with New Hampshire's common-sense values. On Election Day, Humphrey swept nine of New Hampshire's 10 counties, en route to a comfortable 68,000-vote victory. He even carried D'Amours' home base of Manchester, which the Democrat had not lost in five House races.

A co-pilot for Allegheny Airlines, Humphrey moved to New Hampshire in 1974. He had no political involvement before 1977, when he attended a meeting of the state Conservative Caucus and was named coordinator.

That post allowed him to develop connections to national New Right figures, who later helped him raise large sums for his Senate race. Humphrey remained at his airline job for the rest of the year, but he devoted increasing amounts of attention to conservative causes, especially fighting the Panama Canal treaties.

In 1978 Humphrey set his sights on McIntyre, a supporter of the Panama accords who had been in the Senate since 1962. Few New Hampshire politicians took the challenger seriously, but Humphrey fought his way to attention in the Republican primary field with a meticulous organization and carefully timed press releases.

The primary provided the first clue to what a stranger could do in New Hampshire politics if he had ideological loyalists, money and skill. Humphrey drew more than twice as many votes as either of his moderate Republican rivals, a former mayor of Keene and a veteran state senator.

McIntyre saw little reason to panic. In both 1966 and 1972, he had easily defeated conservative Republicans by ridiculing them as tools of the far right. Neither of those challengers, however, had Humphrey's campaign organization, nor the money to buy advertising on Boston television — which reaches the vast majority of New Hampshire voters.

Humphrey attacked McIntyre's canal votes and called for tax reductions, an effective appeal to the voters just across the Massachusetts border who came to New Hampshire to avoid high taxes. The incumbent continued to portray his challenger as a shrill ideologue, even though that notion seemed at variance with his quiet style. The one tactic likely to discredit Humphrey — an all-out attack on him as an opportunist — was not tried because Democrats considered it unnecessary.

On election night they found out otherwise. Humphrey built a surprising lead in early returns, and while McIntyre narrowed it as the night went on, he fell 5,800 votes short.

Committees

Environment and Public Works (7th of 7 Republicans)
Environmental Protection; Water Resources, Transportation and Infrastructure

Foreign Relations (8th of 9 Republicans)
International Economic Policy, Trade, Oceans and Environment (ranking); Terrorism, Narcotics and International Operations

Judiciary (6th of 6 Republicans)
Technology and the Law (ranking); Antitrust, Monopolies and Business Rights

Elections

1984 General

Gordon J. Humphrey (R)	225,828	(59%)
Norman E. D'Amours (D)	157,447	(41%)

Previous Winning Percentage: 1978 (51%)

Campaign Finance

	Receipts	Receipts from PACs	Expenditures
1984			
Humphrey (R)	$1,699,044	$728,608 (43%)	$1,683,536
D'Amours (D)	$1,070,220	$506,570 (47%)	$1,066,485

Key Votes

1987

Enact omnibus highway bill over Reagan veto	N
Limit testing of space-based anti-ballistic missiles	N
Oppose banning tests of larger nuclear weapons	Y
Confirm Robert H. Bork as Supreme Court justice	Y

1988

Allow vote on campaign-finance overhaul	N
Pass civil rights restoration bill over Reagan veto	N
Enact omnibus trade bill over Reagan veto	N
Approve death penalty for drug-related murders	?
Oppose "workfare" amendment to welfare overhaul bill	N

Voting Studies

	Presidential Support		Party Unity		Conservative Coalition	
Year	**S**	**O**	**S**	**O**	**S**	**O**
1988	68	27	80	15	57	35
1987	69	27	92	6	84	16
1986	92	5	83	14	86	9
1985	80	14	87	8	72	22
1984	68	32	76	23	79	17
1983	55	42	70	25	82	11
1982	81	18	84 †	16 †	80 †	20 †
1981	82	16	84	13	85	15

† Not eligible for all recorded votes.

Interest Group Ratings

Year	ADA	ACU	AFL-CIO	CCUS
1988	5	100	8	79
1987	5	96	11	94
1986	0	86	0	89
1985	5	90	17	83
1984	15	86	0	89
1983	15	86	0	78
1982	15	95	8	50
1981	10	93	5	83

Warren B. Rudman (R)

Of Nashua — Elected 1980

Born: May 18, 1930, Boston, Mass.
Education: Syracuse U., B.S. 1952; Boston College, LL.B. 1960.
Military Career: Army, 1952-54.
Occupation: Lawyer.
Family: Wife, Shirley Wahl; three children.
Religion: Jewish.
Political Career: N.H. attorney general, 1970-76 (appointed).
Capitol Office: 530 Hart Bldg. 20510; 224-3324.

In Washington: Rudman seemed all but ready to abandon the capital in 1985. "I don't like this town. I don't like the whole atmosphere. There's too much money, too much influence, too much phoniness. And I just don't like it. Period."

But he discovered that he need not like the press, embassy parties or even his colleagues in order to make a difference. Even as he threatened in 1985 to quit the Senate out of disgust with the federal deficit, Congress approved a radical new procedure aimed at balancing the budget, and thus began Rudman's second life in Washington.

The Gramm-Rudman-Hollings anti-deficit amendment that became law in the fall of 1985 was not only a personal watershed for Rudman. It was a national watershed as well, the catchbasin for a tide of anger that grew from the political system's failure to cut the deficit. The law still drives the budget process.

The achievement could not help but contribute to Rudman's considerable estimate of his own influence. He is a man of unusual intelligence and ability; a man of modesty he is not.

Neither is he a man of modest accomplishment. While he is not well liked, he is respected. The blunt and determined former attorney general has a bulldog's tenacity. He was well suited for his service in the 100th Congress as vice chairman of the select committee that investigated the Iran-contra affair. He formed a working partnership with the chairman, Daniel K. Inouye of Hawaii, and by charting a tough, independent course comported himself well in the eyes of most of his colleagues, save those on his right.

While many Republicans used the Iran-contra hearings to promote a conservative agenda for Central America, Rudman seemed more interested in developing facts. He hammered away at witnesses and scoffed at the notion that Lt. Col. Oliver L. North was any kind of hero. Rudman's only bias seemed to be a determination to show that President Reagan was ill-served by a "whole bunch of imbeciles" around him.

In the end, Rudman signed the majority report, dismissing the minority report as "pathetic." His GOP colleagues, he said, seemed to believe that "somehow Republicans don't want the truth laid out."

Rudman is nothing if not sure of himself, and colleagues can tire of his lecturing manner, especially on his favorite topic, the law. This became obvious during the early 1989 battle over President Bush's nomination of John Tower to be secretary of defense. Rudman became a staunch supporter of Tower, arguing there was "not one iota, one shred" of evidence to support claims that Tower was impaired by alcohol while a senator or arms control negotiator.

When Majority Leader George J. Mitchell of Maine characterized Rudman's conclusion as "opinion, pure opinion," Rudman countered: "One thing I learned in 24 years of practicing law is how to read evidence, and I know how to state it, and I know how not to misstate it."

Replied Mitchell, himself a former federal judge: "I think I know how to do that just as well as you do."

The 100th Congress reworked unconstitutional aspects of the 1985 Gramm-Rudman-Hollings budget-balancing law. But by then the original trio was not playing the leading role it occupied in 1985 when Rudman read that Texas Republican Phil Gramm was planning to amend a bill raising the ceiling on the federal debt with a balanced-budget plan. Since his thoughts ran along similar lines, Rudman quickly joined with Gramm to develop a proposal calling for a series of annually decreasing ceilings on the deficit until it is eliminated. The key was a mechanism that forced Congress either to act or to watch automatic, across-the-board spending cuts accomplish the task for it.

Gramm and Rudman, who were soon joined by South Carolina Democrat Ernest F. Hollings, formed an effective legislative alliance. Rudman helped arrange some of the complex procedural compromises needed to flesh out the idea and added a touch of levity to the bombastic rhetoric employed on both sides of the issue: "This is a bad idea whose time has come," he said on more than one occasion.

As this episode shows, there is little doubt that Rudman is a capable legislator. It took him only a short time to win a reputation in the Senate for hard and thoughtful work, particularly on the Appropriations Committee. If he has irritated some with his healthy sense of his own importance, he has gained the trust of the GOP leadership, as evidenced not only by the Iran-contra assignment but also by the Ethics Committee chairmanship, which he took in the 99th Congress. At the end of the 100th Congress, he was also assigned to play an important leadership role in shaping anti-drug legislation.

In 1988 Rudman also was instrumental in devising legislation, eventually pocket-vetoed by President Reagan, to restrict post-employment lobbying by government officials, including legislators. Rudman worked to strike provisions he considered unconstitutional and to eliminate language he thought would drive top-level officials from the government.

When Republicans held the Senate, Rudman served for several years as de facto chairman of Appropriations' Commerce-Justice-State Subcommittee. The actual chairman, Nevada's Paul Laxalt, was content to let Rudman handle most of the day-to-day work and manage the annual appropriations bill.

Defense of the Legal Services Corporation, which was targeted for extinction by the Reagan administration, has been one of Rudman's most visible causes on the spending panel. Rudman helped work out a compromise proposal in 1984 that pleased both friends and critics of legal aid; it extended restrictions on lobbying and political activities, while also providing recipients of legal services protection against the loss of assistance.

His work for the Legal Services Corporation is not the only example of Rudman's refusal to fall in line behind every conservative cause. He votes against school prayer and for abortion funding, and he has called for new taxes, especially on alcohol and tobacco, if they would pay for programs he favors, such as drug interdiction.

Rudman has been an outspoken supporter of tough federal enforcement of trade and antitrust laws. In 1982 he waged a heated battle against the American Medical Association, which wanted to prevent the Federal Trade Commission from pursuing violations of antitrust and consumer protection laws by professionals. He used his position on Appropriations to push through an amendment allowing the antitrust regulations if the agency did not interfere with state laws governing the subject.

Rudman is also a force on the Appropriations Subcommittee on Defense. Ever since his maiden speech in the Senate, he has been expressing concern over the "fascination" he feels Pentagon strategists have with complicated, expensive, high-technology weaponry.

Instead, Rudman wants the United States to buy cheaper, less complex weapons that are easier to maneuver and maintain. One of his targets was the Viper, a disposable bazooka that had grown far more expensive and complicated than originally planned. After a determined assault by Rudman, the Pentagon eventually canceled its Viper contract.

At Home: Democrats would have been hard-pressed to oust Rudman from the Senate in 1986 even if they had been well organized and well financed. As it turned out, they were neither. Neither of the state's best-known Democrats — former Sen. John Durkin or former Rep. Norman E. D'Amours — expressed much interest in a long-shot challenge to Rudman. Only when the Democratic nomination threatened to go by default to a supporter of Lyndon H. LaRouche Jr. were party leaders able to coax Endicott Peabody, a former governor of Massachusetts (1963-65), into the race.

Peabody had moved to Hollis, N.H., several years earlier to practice law. But while he possessed a familiar name, he had not cut a wide swath in Granite State politics. In 1984, Peabody lost a race for a seat in the 400-member New Hampshire House of Representatives, and he was vulnerable to charges of being a carpetbagger.

For Peabody to have even an outside chance of winning, a conservative independent candidate — retired Navy officer Bruce Valley — needed to carve deeply into Rudman's base. That did not happen. Valley mustered only 5 percent of the vote, while Rudman swamped Peabody by a margin of nearly 2-to-1.

Rudman had come to Washington in 1980 without experience in elective politics, but with a reputation for activism that he built during six years as New Hampshire attorney general.

He overhauled the little-noticed office in the early 1970s by creating a consumer protection division, and he successfully fought the legalization of gambling in New Hampshire. That gave him the statewide recognition he used in his contest for the Senate in 1980.

Rudman's background dovetailed with one of his major campaign themes — the need for clean government. He pledged not to accept any contributions from out-of-state political action committees and recommended a two-term limit for senators.

As a former legal counsel to Gov. Walter Peterson (1969-73), Rudman was clearly viewed as a part of the New Hampshire GOP's moderate wing. But he was not anathema to conservatives. Rudman campaigned on a platform of increased defense spending and opposition to the Equal Rights Amendment.

Although the 1980 Senate race marked his

debut as a candidate — the state attorney general's post was appointive — Rudman proved to be an aggressive campaigner, interspersing political argument with stories of his days as a platoon commander in Korea.

Rudman led the 11-man GOP primary with only 20 percent of the vote, but moved quickly to unite the party by installing the primary runner-up, former state Rep. (later governor, and now White House chief of staff) John H. Sununu as his campaign manager. Former Gov. Wesley Powell, who ran third in the primary, briefly considered running in the fall election as an independent — a move that would have seriously crippled Rudman against Durkin, the Democratic incumbent. But Republican leaders, including Ronald Reagan, persuaded Powell to stay out.

Durkin tried to consolidate his position with New Hampshire's conservative electorate by attacking Soviet expansionism, but Rudman peppered Durkin's generally liberal, pro-labor voting record. Rudman criticized Durkin for representing "big labor" and not New Hampshire.

Reagan's long coattails helped sweep Rudman to victory. Although Durkin ran 70,000 votes ahead of President Jimmy Carter, he fell short of Rudman by 16,000 votes.

It was sweet revenge for Rudman. Bad blood had developed between the two politicians in 1974, when Rudman was a member of the state panel that overturned the certification of Durkin's election in a virtually even contest with Republican Louis C. Wyman. (That forced a 1975 special election that Durkin won.)

Durkin returned the favor shortly afterward. When Rudman was nominated by President Gerald R. Ford to chair the Interstate Commerce Commission, Durkin worked behind the scenes to block the nomination. Rudman subsequently withdrew his name.

Committees

Select Ethics (Vice Chairman)

Appropriations (8th of 13 Republicans)
Commerce, Justice, State, the Judiciary and Related Agencies (ranking); Defense; Foreign Operations; Interior and Related Agencies; Labor, Health and Human Services, Education and Related Agencies

Budget (8th of 10 Republicans)

Governmental Affairs (4th of 6 Republicans)
Government Information and Regulation (ranking); Oversight of Government Management; Permanent Subcommittee on Investigations

Elections

1986 General

Warren B. Rudman (R)	154,090	(63%)
Endicott Peabody (D)	79,222	(32%)
Bruce Valley (I)	11,423	(5%)

Previous Winning Percentage: 1980 (52%)

Campaign Finance

	Receipts	Receipts from PACs		Expend-itures
1986				
Rudman (R)	$852,877	$5,200	(1%)	$831,098
Peabody (D)	$309,968	$46,950	(15%)	$307,760
Valley (I)	$37,410	$955	(3%)	$35,322

Key Votes

1987

Enact omnibus highway bill over Reagan veto	N
Limit testing of space-based anti-ballistic missiles	N
Oppose banning tests of larger nuclear weapons	Y
Confirm Robert H. Bork as Supreme Court justice	Y

1988

Allow vote on campaign-finance overhaul	N
Pass civil rights restoration bill over Reagan veto	Y
Enact omnibus trade bill over Reagan veto	N
Approve death penalty for drug-related murders	Y
Oppose "workfare" amendment to welfare overhaul bill	N

Voting Studies

	Presidential Support		Party Unity		Conservative Coalition	
Year	**S**	**O**	**S**	**O**	**S**	**O**
1988	65	28	58	36	68	32
1987	71	26	79	12	88	6
1986	90	8	89	10	91	8
1985	84	14	80	17	78	20
1984	81	17	79	19	74	26
1983	85	15	82	17	80	20
1982	73	27	79	20	69	31
1981	83	14	82	16	70	25

Interest Group Ratings

Year	ADA	ACU	AFL-CIO	CCUS
1988	15	68	29	93
1987	25	80	30	75
1986	10	83	0	84
1985	10	68	14	86
1984	30	82	0	84
1983	25	40	18	58
1982	35	47	35	52
1981	15	53	21	94

1 Robert C. Smith (R)

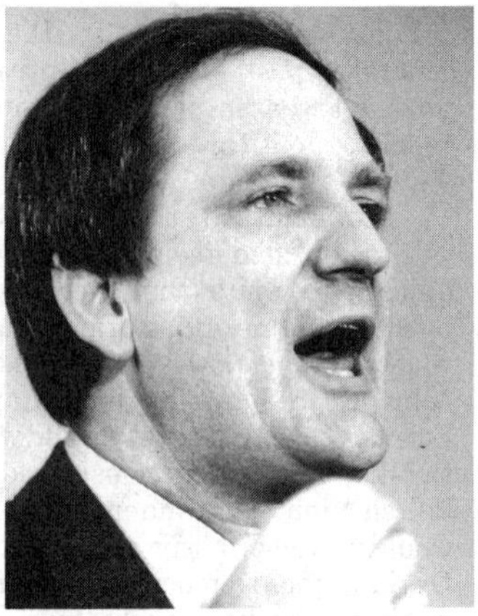

Of Tuftonboro — Elected 1984

Born: March 30, 1941, Trenton, N.J.
Education: Lafayette College, B.A. 1965.
Military Career: Navy, 1965-67.
Occupation: Real-estate broker; teacher.
Family: Wife, Mary Jo Hutchinson; three children.
Religion: Roman Catholic.
Political Career: Gov. Wentworth Regional School Board (Wolfeboro, N.H.), 1978-84; sought GOP nomination for U.S. House, 1980; GOP nominee for U.S. House, 1982.
Capitol Office: 115 Cannon Bldg. 20515; 225-5456.

In Washington: When the House voted in February 1989 to block a proposed 51 percent pay raise for members of Congress, Smith was a big winner, and a big loser.

He was a winner because he — along with Republicans Tom Tauke of Iowa and William E. Dannemeyer of California — had led the fight against a procedure that would have allowed the raise to be enacted without a House vote.

"Would I like to have a $45,000 raise?... You're damned right I would," Smith said in early 1989. "But that's not the way to get it. If we can't convince the American people we should have a raise, then we shouldn't have it."

Smith was a loser, though, because so many House colleagues resented the way in which he helped provoke a public backlash against the raise. Smith is a large man physically, and rhetoric can be a blunt instrument in his hands. While Tauke could oppose the pay raise and retain his reputation in the House as a moderate insider, Smith was derided by many of his colleagues as a hard-right iconoclast at best, and a demagogue at worst.

Smith's manner of expressing his conservatism caused him trouble even before the pay-raise vote was cast. When Republicans made committee assignments for the 101st Congress, Smith's request for a seat on Armed Services was rejected, leaving him with low-profile slots on Science and Veterans' Affairs. Smith attributed this rebuke to his activism on the pay issue, and said the "cold shoulder of the leadership of my own party hurt me the most."

With his House career clearly going nowhere, Smith announced in March 1989 that he would run in 1990 for the Senate seat being vacated by retiring Republican Sen. Gordon J. Humphrey. Whatever his chances in that effort, Smith is unlikely to suffer much in New Hampshire because of his maverick image in the House. Granite State voters traditionally have shown a fondness for obstreperous conservatives, including Humphrey.

Smith's voting record is undoubtedly one of the most conservative in the House. In 1987, he backed President Reagan's position 80 percent of the time on floor votes, tying for the fourth-most supportive record in the House. In 1988, he received a 100 percent rating from the American Conservative Union.

But Smith joins with environmentalists on acid rain, an issue that cuts across party and ideological lines in New Hampshire, whose lakes and streams show signs of damage from the pollution problem. In the 101st Congress, Smith was elected co-chairman of the House Republican Task Force on Acid Rain.

Smith performs more of a tightrope act on the state's most divisive environmental issue, the Seabrook nuclear power plant, located on New Hampshire's small Atlantic coastline. Smith calls the plant "a mistake from the beginning." But he says it should be opened if it can be safely operated, while being kept closed during the summer when crowds at nearby beaches would cause evacuation problems.

A Vietnam veteran, Smith has frequently called for stepped-up efforts to locate the U.S. servicemen who remain missing in action in Southeast Asia. He is one of those House members who believes that Americans are still being held as prisoners of war in Vietnam.

At Home: Smith's 1984 election to the seat vacated by Democrat Norman E. D'Amours capped a four-year quest that included as many setbacks as successes.

On his first try in 1980, Smith lost the GOP primary in the 1st. On his second try in 1982, he won the primary but lost in the fall to D'Amours. Finally, in 1984, when D'Amours ran for the Senate, Smith triumphed with a general-election victory over the highest-ranking Democrat in state government, Executive Councilor Dudley Dudley. His success returned the eastern New Hampshire House seat to the GOP for the first time in a decade.

Unlike D'Amours, whose roots were in ethnic Manchester, Smith reflects small-town Yan-

New Hampshire 1

East — Manchester

New Hampshire's eastern district, extending from the state's 13 miles of coastline to the granite peaks of the White Mountains, is an area of rich geographical and political variation.

The district's southern tier is dominated by ethnic industrial cities, while the rugged northern territory is home to small Yankee Republican towns. While Democrat Norman E. D'Amours represented the district for a decade, the 1st often backs Republicans in national and statewide elections.

The state's largest concentration of voters is in Manchester. Textile mills, attracted there in the 19th century by the hydropower of the Merrimack River, drew large numbers of immigrants, especially French Canadians. But the Depression paralyzed the region's economy. Some of the city's long-abandoned redbrick mills are finding new life as light manufacturing or retail space, but others still stand empty.

The huge Franco-American vote in Manchester is nominally Democratic, but often is influenced by the *Union Leader's* blistering editorials urging voters to abandon Democratic candidates accused of liberalism or worse. Even though Manchester was home base for D'Amours and the 1984 Democratic gubernatorial candidate, each lost the city to his Republican rival. In the 1988 House contest, Manchester voted for Smith over his Manchester-based opponent.

New Hampshire's major coastal town is Portsmouth, home to wealthy sea captains two centuries ago. It has been in decline most of this century, but its architectural grace and proximity to Boston recently have made it a fashionable day-trip tourist center. Although the Portsmouth Naval Shipyard is centered across the river estuary in Kittery, Maine, many shipyard workers live in New Hampshire, where they generally cast Democratic votes. The area took an economic hit in early 1989, when Pease Air Force Base in nearby Newington was ordered closed by a national commission, throwing several hundred civilian employees out of work.

In Strafford County, the University of New Hampshire, with 10,700 students, dominates the town of Durham and leads the area in supporting liberal candidates. Sparsely populated Carroll County to the north is among the most Republican counties in the nation. It has provided overwhelming margins for the GOP in every statewide race since World War II.

Population: 460,863. White 455,399 (99%), Black 2,169 (1%), Other 2,168 (1%). Spanish origin 3,028 (1%). 18 and over 332,498 (72%), 65 and over 51,279 (11%). Median age: 30.

kee New Hampshire. It was there that he wrote his brief political résumé as a member and chairman of the Wolfeboro School Board. In private life, he was a civics and gym teacher at the local junior high school.

Rather than embellish his modest credentials when he ran for the House, Smith presented himself as a citizen-politician who understood New Hampshire's common-sense values. His first campaign in 1980 trumpeted the slogan, "Mr. Smith Goes to Washington." His later races were only slightly more sophisticated — long on coffee klatches and Rotary Club luncheons, short on media advertising. Each campaign played up the affable, down-home manner of the big, burly baseball coach and emphasized his fervent conservatism.

Smith began the 1984 campaign with a lingering debt from his earlier efforts. But with wide name identification and outspoken support from the state's largest newspaper, the conservative Manchester *Union Leader*, he easily outdistanced a crowded GOP primary field. He entered the fall campaign with momentum, running on a strong ticket headed by Reagan in an open district with GOP moorings.

Democrat Dudley, in contrast, struggled through an unexpectedly close primary race, burdened by a reputation as a liberal Democrat that Smith reinforced with references to her as "Dudley Dudley, Liberal Liberal."

Noting her battles within state government for environmentalists and consumers, Dudley portrayed herself as an independent fighter for New Hampshire with valuable political experience that Smith lacked. Her opponent, she contended, was a simplistic conservative beholden to the *Union Leader*.

But the charges hardly hurt Smith. He swamped Dudley by a margin of about 3-to-2, sweeping not only rural portions of the 1st but also blue-collar cities such as Manchester and Rochester.

In 1986, Smith had to put down a Republican primary challenge from Executive Councilor Louis J. Georgopoulos, a Manchester haberdasher whose political post and gregarious nature gave him high name identity. He called Smith, who grew up in New Jersey and boasted close ties to national conservative groups, an "outsider," and he criticized Smith's preoccupation with tracing the whereabouts of missing Vietnam-era servicemen, contrasting it with his own work to keep nuclear waste out of the state. But the genial incumbent had perfected his low-budget, "man of the people" style of campaigning and again enjoyed strong editorial support from the *Union Leader*. When all the ballots were counted, Smith had amassed a 3-to-1 majority.

In the fall, Smith faced an aggressive challenger in former state Rep. James M. Demers, who won the Democratic primary easily after falling 1,100 votes short of nomination two years earlier. Demers offered himself as a centrist Democrat, not saddled with the liberal reputation that hurt Dudley in 1984.

Demers had legislative experience as assistant minority whip in the Democratic state House leadership; he had a French name that sounded similar to that of the district's previous Democratic incumbent; and he had been campaigning virtually non-stop since 1984.

Demers took up Georgopoulos' criticism that Smith was inattentive to district concerns, a charge that Smith disputed by pointing to 80 town meetings and hundreds of senior-citizen forums he had held during his freshman term. Demers carried Democratic coastal cities such as Portsmouth, Rochester and his hometown of Dover, but won little else. In spite of his French name, he lost heavily ethnic Manchester by about 2,000 votes.

In 1988, Democratic nominee Joseph F. Keefe, a Manchester attorney, began and ended his campaign with less of a following than Demers had. Smith won by more than 45,000 votes, surpassing 60 percent for the first time.

Committees

Science, Space and Technology (9th of 19 Republicans)
Natural Resources, Agriculture Research and Environment; Space Science and Applications

Veterans' Affairs (10th of 13 Republicans)
Housing and Memorial Affairs; Oversight and Investigations

Elections

1988 General		
Robert C. Smith (R)	131,824	(60%)
Joseph F. Keefe (D)	86,623	(40%)
1986 General		
Robert C. Smith (R)	70,739	(56%)
James M. Demers (D)	54,787	(44%)

Previous Winning Percentage: **1984** (59%)

District Vote For President

	1988	1984	1980	1976
D	80,604 (35%)	58,709 (30%)	53,617 (27%)	71,632 (43%)
R	145,996 (64%)	137,615 (70%)	115,356 (60%)	93,141 (56%)
I			23,122 (12%)	

Campaign Finance

	Receipts	Receipts from PACs	Expend-itures
1988			
Smith (R)	$454,815	$109,500 (24%)	$424,346
Keefe (D)	$267,618	$97,234 (36%)	$266,617
1986			
Smith (R)	$385,544	$160,518 (42%)	$387,532
Demers (D)	$243,745	$123,745 (51%)	$242,845

Key Votes

1987	
Raise speed limit to 65 mph	Y
Approve Gephardt "fair trade" amendment	N
Ban testing of larger nuclear weapons	N
Delay "re-flagging" of Kuwaiti tankers	N
Approve tax-raising deficit-reduction bill	N
1988	
Approve aid to Nicaraguan contras	Y
Enact civil rights restoration bill over Reagan veto	N
Kill 60-day plant-closing notification measure	Y
Pass omnibus trade bill over Reagan veto	N
Approve death penalty for drug-related murders	Y
Bar federal funds for abortions in cases of rape and incest	Y
Oppose seven-day waiting period for purchase of handguns	Y

Voting Studies

	Presidential Support		Party Unity		Conservative Coalition	
Year	**S**	**O**	**S**	**O**	**S**	**O**
1988	73	26	97	2	95	5
1987	80	20	95	5	81	19
1986	82	18	96	4	94	6
1985	84	16	91	8	82	18

Interest Group Ratings

Year	ADA	ACU	AFL-CIO	CCUS
1988	5	100	14	93
1987	4	96	13	100
1986	0	91	14	100
1985	5	90	18	95

2 Chuck Douglas (R)

Of Concord — Elected 1988

Born: Dec. 2, 1942, Abington, Pa.
Education: Attended Wesleyan U., 1960-62; U. of New Hampshire, B.A. 1965; Boston U., J.D. 1968.
Military Career: Army National Guard, 1968-present.
Occupation: Lawyer; judge.
Family: Wife, Lorenca Rosal; two children, two stepchildren.
Religion: Episcopalian.
Political Career: N.H. Superior Court associate justice, 1974-76; N.H. Supreme Court associate justice, 1977-83; senior justice, 1983-85.
Capitol Office: 1338 Longworth Bldg. 20515; 225-5206.

The Path to Washington: A maverick with his roots in the conservative wing of New Hampshire's conservative Republican Party, Douglas does not shy away from speaking his agile mind. During his 1988 campaign for the House, he made headlines by telling a *Wall Street Journal* reporter at the Republican National Convention that Ronald Reagan had been "a disappointment" who turned government over to "a bunch of squishes" rather than to true conservatives.

It may seem a bit odd, then, that Douglas' Democratic opponent in the 2nd, Nashua Mayor Jim Donchess, tried to make Douglas out to be soft on crime.

At issue for much of the general-election campaign — which began after Douglas won a surprisingly strong victory in a competitive September primary — was Douglas' career as a judge. At age 34, Douglas was appointed to the state Supreme Court by militant conservative Gov. Meldrim Thomson Jr., who had earlier employed him as a legal counsel. On the court, Douglas surprised some by exhibiting a streak of civil libertarianism that brought him down on the side of the individual over the state in some controversial cases.

Donchess, trying to grab the law-and-order mantle that eluded the national Democratic Party in 1988, blasted some of Douglas' past stands, such as his support for a 1985 decision striking down state police roadblocks intended to stop drunk drivers. (Douglas said the roadblocks would stop people not suspected of any wrongdoing.) In speeches, press releases and hard-hitting television ads, Democrat Donchess hammered at Douglas as a criminal-coddler. But Douglas, who called Donchess a "slime artist" and "a press conference crime fighter," had some significant advantages, not the least of which was his party label: The 2nd District last elected a Democrat to Congress in 1912.

And Douglas' conservative support was unshakable. In addition to his ties to Thomson, Douglas had played a leading role in GOP Rep. Jack F. Kemp's 1988 presidential campaign, and he had strong backing from the the conservative Manchester *Union Leader*, which receives statewide attention.

Douglas, whose background also includes service as an assistant to the state House majority leader, stressed that he had experience in all three branches of government and portrayed Donchess as a man to the left of mainstream New Hampshire. While Donchess presented himself as a practical manager who had worked as mayor to balance growth and environmental concerns, Douglas said the well-financed Democrat was beholden to labor groups who had donated to his campaign. Douglas lumped his opponent and Michael S. Dukakis together as liberals enamored of government solutions.

Despite his important presidential primary win in New Hampshire, Dukakis failed to reach 40 percent there on Election Day. Donchess did better, but Douglas still won comfortably.

Douglas has had some run-ins with John H. Sununu, the former governor and now White House chief of staff. In the 2nd District GOP primary, Sununu worked actively for former state Rep. Betty Tamposi, Douglas' leading opponent.

Douglas won a seat on the Judiciary Committee when he came to Washington, and he soon made national headlines by making an issue of another committee member's homosexuality. Speaking to a group of insurance executives, Douglas, explaining "the liberalism of the Judiciary Committee," described Massachusetts Democrat Barney Frank as one of two members "who are only interested in [people] of their own sex.... That gives you a little feel for the committee, so to speak."

Frank wrote a letter to Douglas blasting his "appeals to prejudice" and saying he was "disappointed that you chose to begin your working relationship with your colleagues in this way." Douglas said he had just been trying to give the audience "a flavor" for the committee.

New Hampshire 2

West — Concord; Nashua

New Hampshire's scenic western district is lightly populated outside the fast-growing southern tier that borders Massachusetts.

Nashua, the largest city in the 2nd, has grown to more than 76,000 people. Spurred by the arrival of high-technology firms, Nashua feeds into the belt of electronics-oriented industry that straddles the Bay State border. Area residents tend to be well-educated, upwardly mobile refugees from "Taxachusetts." Nearby Salem has shared in the southern tier's boom.

Despite its growth, Nashua has been slow to break its longtime Democratic voting habit. George Bush did carry Nashua handily in 1988, but in the open House race the city sided with its Democratic mayor, Jim Donchess. Salem favors Republicans most of the time.

State government workers dominate the capital city, Concord, but New Hampshire does not have a large or politically influential bureaucracy, and Concord has not grown very rapidly in the past 20 years. The city's electorate is generally liberal, but independent. It opposed Meldrim Thomson Jr., the state's belligerently conservative three-term governor of the 1970s, but the city supported Ronald Reagan and narrowly went for George Bush in 1988.

Outside the Concord-Nashua corridor, the district is mostly rural Republican territory. Coos County is New Hampshire's "North Country," an isolated woodland. The only town of any size in the North Country is Berlin, a lonely Democratic outpost in a solidly Republican area. In 1976, Carter carried only four communities in Coos County, but his sweep of Berlin provided him his winning county margin. No Democratic presidential candidate — not even Massachusetts Gov. Michael S. Dukakis in 1988 — has carried a county in New Hampshire since then.

Berlin's paper mills on the Androscoggin River attracted many Canadian immigrants; the area remains so heavily ethnic that some radio stations broadcast in French.

Population: 459,747. White 454,700 (99%), Black 1,821 (0.4%), Other 2,113 (1%). Spanish origin 2,559 (1%). 18 and over 330,030 (72%), 65 and over 51,688 (11%). Median age: 30.

Committees

Government Operations (11th of 15 Republicans)
Commerce, Consumer and Monetary Affairs; Environment, Energy and Natural Resources

Judiciary (13th of 14 Republicans)
Administrative Law and Governmental Relations; Economic and Commercial Law

Campaign Finance

	Receipts	Receipts from PACs	Expend-itures
1988			
Douglas (R)	$735,185	$169,555 (23%)	$730,803
Donchess (D)	$532,390	$213,253 (40%)	$519,336

Elections

1988 General		
Chuck Douglas (R)	119,742	(57%)
Jim Donchess (D)	89,677	(43%)
1988 Primary		
Chuck Douglas (R)	22,824	(48%)
Betty Tamposi (R)	19,902	(42%)
Stephen Gregg (R)	2,552	(5%)
Alf E. Jacobson (R)	1,500	(3%)

District Vote For President

	1988	1984	1980	1976
D	83,092 (37%)	61,638 (32%)	70,171 (31%)	76,003 (44%)
R	135,541 (61%)	129,435 (67%)	124,612 (55%)	92,794 (54%)
I			31,629 (14%)	

New Jersey

U.S. CONGRESS

SENATE 2 D
HOUSE 8 D, 6 R

LEGISLATURE

Senate 24 D, 16 R
House 38 D, 41 R, 1 Vacancy

ELECTIONS

1988 Presidential Vote	
Bush	56%
Dukakis	43%
1984 Presidential Vote	
Reagan	60%
Mondale	39%
1980 Presidential Vote	
Reagan	52%
Carter	39%
Anderson	8%
Turnout rate in 1984	56%
Turnout rate in 1986	27%
Turnout rate in 1988	52%

(as percentage of voting age population)

POPULATION AND GROWTH

1980 population	7,364,823
1988 population estimate (9th in the nation)	7,721,000
Percent change 1980-1988	+5%

DEMOGRAPHIC BREAKDOWN

White	83%
Black	13%
Other	1%
(Spanish origin)	7%
Urban	89%
Rural	11%
Born in state	57%
Foreign-born	10%

MAJOR CITIES

Newark	316,240
Jersey City	219,480
Paterson	139,130
Elizabeth	106,540
Trenton	91,160

AREA AND LAND USE

Area 7,468 sq. miles (46th)

Farm	19%
Forest	43%
Federally owned	3%

Gov. Thomas H. Kean (R)
Of Livingston — Elected 1981

Born: April 21, 1935, New York, N.Y.
Education: Princeton U., B.A. 1957; Columbia U., M.A. 1963.
Military Career: National Guard, 1957-58.
Occupation: High school teacher; real estate executive.
Religion: Episcopalian.
Political Career: N.J. Assembly, 1968-77, majority leader, 1971-72, Speaker 1972-74, minority leader, 1974-77; sought GOP nomination for U.S. House, 1974, and for governor, 1977.
Next Election: 1989.

WORK

Occupations	
White-collar	59%
Blue-collar	29%
Service workers	12%
Government Workers	
Federal	74,096
State	109,756
Local	323,035

MONEY

Median family income	$ 22,906	(4th)
Tax burden per capita	$ 1,021	(12th)

EDUCATION

Spending per pupil through grade 12	$ 5,395	(3rd)
Persons with college degrees	18%	(12th)

CRIME

Violent crime rate 541 per 100,000 (17th)

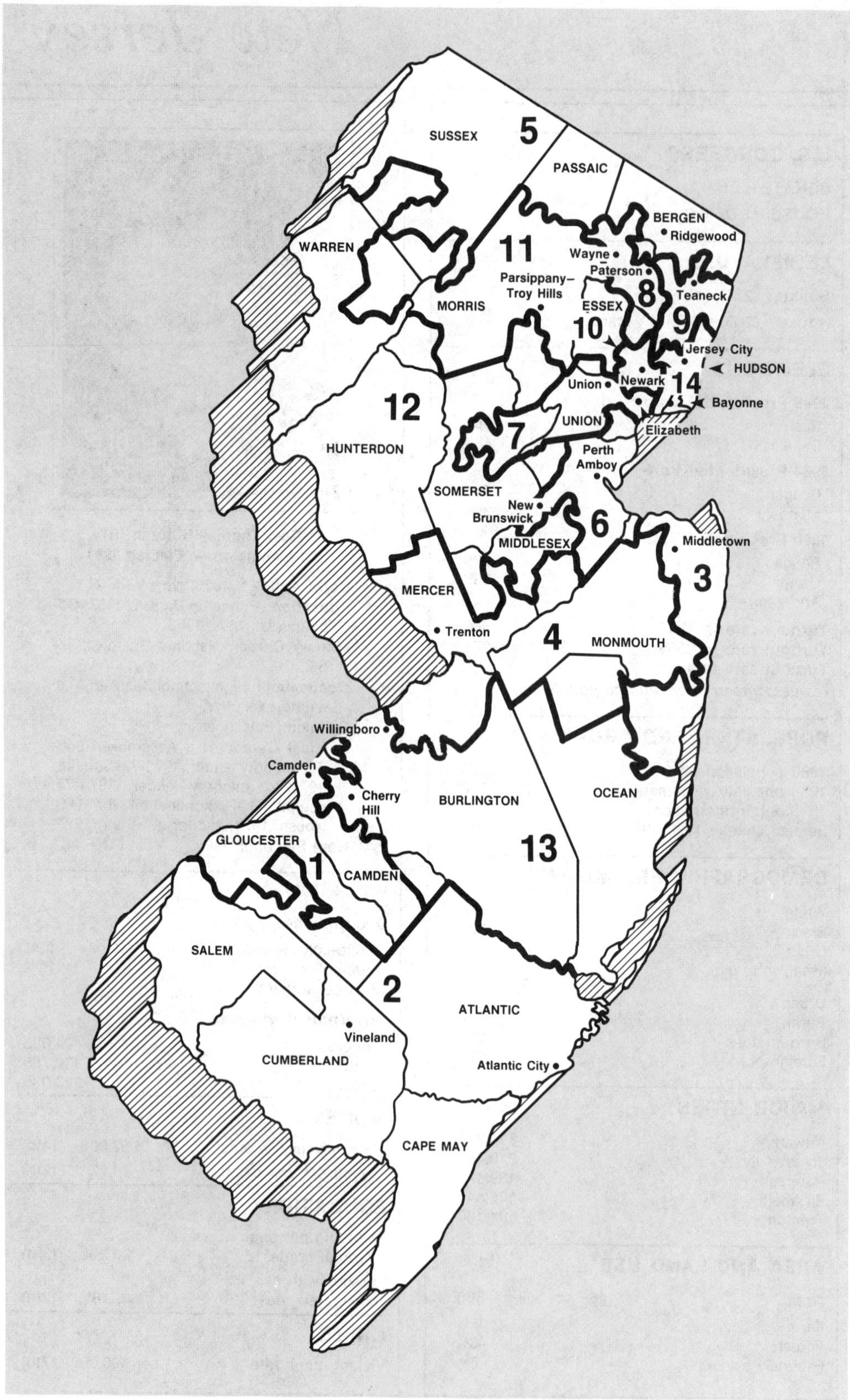
SUSSEX
5
PASSAIC
BERGEN
Ridgewood
WARREN
11
Wayne
Paterson
Parsippany–
Troy Hills
8
Teaneck
MORRIS
ESSEX
9
10
Jersey City
HUDSON
Union
Newark
14
12
Bayonne
UNION
Elizabeth
7
HUNTERDON
Perth
Amboy
SOMERSET
New
Brunswick
6
MIDDLESEX
Middletown
3
MERCER
Trenton
4
MONMOUTH
Willingboro
Camden
Cherry
Hill
BURLINGTON
OCEAN
GLOUCESTER
13
1
CAMDEN
SALEM
2
ATLANTIC
Vineland
CUMBERLAND
Atlantic City
CAPE MAY

Bill Bradley (D)

Of Denville — Elected 1978

Born: July 28, 1943, Crystal City, Mo.
Education: Princeton U., B.A. 1965; Oxford U., England, M.A. 1968.
Military Career: Air Force Reserve, 1967-78.
Occupation: Professional basketball player; author.
Family: Wife, Ernestine Schlant; one child.
Religion: Protestant.
Political Career: No previous office.
Capitol Office: 731 Hart Bldg. 20510; 224-3224.

In Washington: If not for Bradley's height and giraffe-like lope, it might be easy to forget that a basketball court rather than the Senate floor provided his first professional arena. During more than a decade in office, he has shown a zest for the tedious substance of policy making, and little of the back-slapping collegiality and street-smart style expected of sports figures.

Outside Washington, however, Bradley's sports-hero celebrity remains a big electoral attraction; that helps explain why his forthcoming 1990 re-election contest for a third term is all but ignored in the speculation about Bradley's potential for the 1992 presidential sweepstakes. At the same time, Bradley's Senate performance to date raises questions whether this cerebral loner and political maverick has the kind of style and personality that would wear well through a long national campaign.

Celebrity alone would not have put Bradley's name on Democrats' short list of potential presidential candidates. He earned a place there with the kind of hard legislative work that led to enactment of the landmark 1986 tax revision law. Bradley's role in that remarkable legislative history best illustrates and defines this paradoxical man.

On the tax bill, as throughout his public life, he went about his business without taking much notice of the customary rules of politics. His sheer determination and intellectual persistence kept the idea alive for years and, in the end, his seeming indifference to political advantage and to tactical maneuvering was crucial in pushing the bill through Congress. He succeeded where a craftier political operator might well have failed.

Bradley's preference for arcane policy details and abstract arguments are as uncommon in the Senate as his evident distaste for the politics of backscratching. Considering that he has been famous since he was in college, Bradley's character is all the more extraordinary. If there is a stereotype that celebrity politicians are more style than substance, Bradley is evidence against it. With his rumpled suits and tousled hair, he looks more like a professor than the media superstar he was at Princeton and with the New York Knicks. Considered somewhat aloof by his colleagues, he does not frequent the Senate equivalents of a locker-room.

Only an uncommon politician like Bradley would even have conceived in the early 1980s that the tax code was ready for a massive overhaul. Long before President Reagan and others had adopted the idea, Bradley was urging that the accumulated layers of deductions and special-interest provisions be replaced by a simpler system based on lower tax rates.

Certainly the prospects for tax restructuring did not look particularly bright to most experienced political professionals when Bradley finally presented his "Fair Tax" proposal in 1982. The public showed little enthusiasm, lobby groups were intent on preserving the protections they had obtained over the years from Congress, and most lawmakers were focused on a separate economic issue, the deficit. Despite strenuous efforts, Bradley could not persuade Walter F. Mondale to include the idea in his 1984 Democratic presidential campaign.

Gradually, though, Bradley's perseverance began to pay off, as tax-revision proposals similar to his own surfaced. When a reform bill began moving in the House in 1985, Bradley backed up his tireless public advocacy with some private persuasion of the good-old-boy sort that is rare for him — playing basketball with House members.

Bradley's most significant contribution, though, came when the Senate Finance Committee drafted its bill the following spring. There, too, a more savvy political gamesman would have concluded that the cause was hopeless. Certainly most of the Washington community did, as committee members proceeded to load the "reform" bill down with amendments for new tax breaks instead of eliminating old ones. Patiently but to little avail, Bradley kept reminding his colleagues they were reducing the bill's benefits for the middle class every time they approved a costly tax advantage for corporations and the wealthy. "It's getting lonelier and lonelier," he confessed, when he won only three votes in his efforts to limit tax subsidies to a variety of industries.

When committee members realized they had a package that would reduce federal revenues by some $30 billion, the bill seemed doomed. In desperation, Chairman Bob Packwood huddled with Bradley and a few others to produce a radically new proposal that looked a lot like Bradley's original plan. Enthusiasm for its low rates carried the measure through the Senate almost unscathed. Aided by Bradley, who served as a kind of intermediary between Packwood and House Ways and Means Committee Chairman Dan Rostenkowski, conferees soon produced the compromise that led to the most profound change in the tax code in a generation.

Bradley's account of his role would seem like false modesty, or a passage from a high school civics textbook, if it were not so clearly sincere — and true. "If you do your homework," he says, "if you think through an idea, if you figure out how to communicate it and focus on the big picture and what it means to people's lives, you can persuade your colleagues against all odds."

With the passage of the 1986 tax bill, Bradley turned his attention to another idea of limited appeal and great complexity — relief from the huge debt burden carried by Third World nations, particularly those in Latin America. He says the fiscal austerity required of debtor nations to meet their obligations to international lenders threatens explosive social unrest and also forces them to cut back on purchases of U.S. goods, which contributes to the trade deficit and costs jobs.

Bradley opposed Reagan administration policies to increase loans to developing nations, charging that debt was being piled on debt. In 1986, he proposed his own debt relief plan, calling for interest-rate reductions and selective forgiveness of loans, combined with new policies aimed at promoting economic growth within debtor nations. As chairman of Finance's International Debt Subcommittee, Bradley welcomed early signals from the Bush administration that its proposals would look more like his own.

Although he was basically allied with the Reagan administration on tax revision, Bradley was a forceful critic of Reagan's overall economic policies. He was the only member of Finance to vote against the 1981 tax cut, which he opposed as excessive and too generous to the wealthy. When deficits subsequently climbed, he told administration officials, "Basically what you did is give too much away."

But Bradley made sure that, if goodies were being distributed, New Jersey was not left out. With New York Democrat Daniel Patrick Moynihan, he inserted into the bill a "rent-a-bus" provision that allowed big tax breaks to go indirectly to mass transit companies such as the New Jersey Transit Corp.

Bradley also has taken advantage of Finance's responsibility for taxes and federal health policies to become one of the leading and most innovative proponents of aid to the poor. A son of privilege who came of age in the civil rights and Great Society years, and a man grown rich thanks to his physical and intellectual gifts, Bradley exhibits a sense of social obligation to those lacking his advantages.

Teamed with California Rep. Henry A. Waxman, Bradley has worked to expand Medicaid to reach more of the poor, especially mothers and infants, and to stretch Medicare to cover more home-care costs for the elderly. Given budgetary constraints, Bradley and Waxman are content with incremental advances, adding provisions here and there to various bills rather than pushing a major package whose size and price tag would draw fire. Bradley also has long favored enlarging the earned income tax credit, a break for the working poor.

Even the Senate's trade bill drew a Bradley anti-poverty amendment in 1987; it allowed the president to weigh the effect on the poor of price increases before slapping retaliatory quotas or tariffs on foreign goods. The next year, Bradley targeted a miscellaneous tax package, proposing that the nearly $3 billion it would raise should go either to liberalize the tax credit for the poor or to pay for new but unfunded anti-drug programs. But senators were in no mood to cancel dozens of special-interest tax breaks that the new revenues would offset. They rejected Bradley's ideas overwhelmingly. In protest, he voted against the tax bill — the only senator to do so.

It is not unusual for Bradley to act as a sort of Senate conscience or scold, even if it is not a role that endears him to colleagues.

During action on the 1988 welfare-overhaul bill, Bradley embarrassed lawmakers into preserving a tax credit for child care; both the House and Senate bills would have phased out the credit for middle- and upper-income families to offset the cost of new welfare benefits. "We are paying for welfare reform with a tax on child care," Bradley objected. "I am against punishing women for their success." He proposed instead to end the business entertainment deduction for those making more than $360,000 a year. The Senate went along, although another financing measure was substituted in conference. While Bradley succeeded in protecting the child-care credit, his stand may have cost him a place on the conference committee.

He wages other fights that, taken alone, might not cost much. But collectively, they aggravate a good many senators. Bradley espouses higher cigarette taxes and other anti-smoking measures, provoking tobacco-state members. In past years, he proposed a bill to return disputed South Dakota lands to the Sioux, pleasing Indians he met during basketball clinics there in the 1970s but not the state's senators. In the interests of his oil-consuming state, he battles the oil industry and its allies, including Finance Chairman Lloyd Bentsen of Texas. In 1987, Bradley helped convince the Senate to strike from the trade bill Bentsen's provision to limit oil imports, although Bentsen prevailed in a second skirmish to repeal the windfall-profits tax.

Bradley is less influential on the Energy and Natural Resources Committee, where his strong pro-conservation and anti-industry sentiments often put him in a small minority on that industry-oriented panel. In the 100th Congress, for example, he was in the opposition on a 13-2 vote for a uranium industry bailout and on a 17-2 vote for a bill reauthorizing the law limiting nuclear plants' liability for accidents. In the latter case, Bradley objected that the panel, under industry pressure, had softened proposed penalties for negligent federal nuclear contractors.

Bradley also sits on the Intelligence Committee. In a move seen as a sign of his ambition, he considered a maneuver to seize the chairmanship for the 101st Congress from Oklahoma Democrat David L. Boren. The plan was quickly aborted for lack of support, however.

On Intelligence, Bradley received special insight into Reagan administration policies against Nicaragua. As a liberal (or self-described "roaring moderate") and a past opponent of contra aid, Bradley stunned colleagues in 1986 by voting for a $100 million military aid package. He said he did so to keep pressure on Nicaragua's rulers to democratize. But by 1988, Bradley again opposed contra aid, citing Reagan's failure to pursue diplomatic moves. Though the 1986 vote contributed to Bradley's reputation as a maverick, it was a measure of the respect he enjoys that the reversals were perceived not as flip-flops but as the result of serious deliberation.

At Home: The retirement of two-term GOP Gov. Thomas H. Kean after the 1989 election will give Bradley an undisputed position as New Jersey's most popular officeholder. Republicans will have difficulty finding anyone of stature to challenge his re-election bid in 1990. They may also find it hard to explain why they are bothering, after spending the 1988 election year praising Bradley to the skies.

Most of the unexpected accolades came from Pete Dawkins, the 1988 Republican candidate against Democratic Sen. Frank R. Lautenberg. A Wall Street executive, retired Army general and winner of college football's Heisman Trophy, Dawkins projected a "star quality" image in an effort to diminish Lautenberg, who had spent much of his first term laboring on state issues. Dawkins frequently invoked Bradley's name, insisting that he had potential to be a national figure like Bradley.

Bradley was undoubtedly pleased (if not amused) by the plaudits coming his way from a Republican, but he rejected Dawkins' assertions. Bradley strongly endorsed Lautenberg, praised his Senate efforts on behalf of New Jersey's interests, and campaigned for him. Lautenberg prevailed by a comfortable margin.

The similarities between Bradley's background and that of Dawkins were actually striking. Both are former sports stars, Princeton University graduates and Rhodes scholars. Also, both ran for statewide office in New Jersey not long after moving to the state. But unlike Dawkins, who was badly damaged by a "carpetbagger" label applied by Lautenberg, Bradley did not suffer much criticism during his Garden State emergence.

Bradley's advantage was that he was already well-known in New Jersey from his basketball success with Princeton and the New York Knicks. During his 10-year pro career, Bradley was looking ahead to politics. During the off-season, he spoke at Democratic Party gatherings, worked as a reading teacher in Harlem and spent a summer doing administrative work in the federal Office of Economic Opportunity in Washington.

His interest in politics came early, nurtured by his father, a Republican banker in Crystal City, Mo., and by his days at Princeton, where he wrote his senior thesis on Harry S Truman's 1940 Senate campaign.

Bradley considered returning to Missouri to seek office, but marriage to a New Jersey college professor and years of television exposure in the New York metropolitan area convinced him to run in the Garden State. To finance his 1978 Senate bid, he relied on some of his own wealth, then valued at nearly $1.6 million, and on fund-raising events by such prominent friends as singer Paul Simon and actor Robert Redford.

With superior name recognition, Princeton and Oxford degrees and a clean-cut reputation, he scored an easy Democratic primary victory over Gov. Brendan T. Byrne's candidate, former state Treasurer Richard C. Leone.

Bradley drew as his general-election opponent Jeffrey Bell, a former campaign aide to Ronald Reagan. Bell had ousted four-term Sen. Clifford P. Case in the Republican primary, and his campaign had split the GOP badly. Without the liberal Case on the November ballot, labor and minorities felt free to go with Bradley.

Bell spoke enthusiastically of the Kemp-Roth tax-cut plan, but his campaign lacked substance outside the issue of taxes. Though he insisted that the passage of California's Proposition 13 proved there was a market for tax-cutters, New Jersey voters did not seem to agree. Bradley was not much as a personal campaigner, but he made the most of his status as a fresh face in a state dominated by organization politicians. He won with 55 percent.

Bradley's hard work and attention to detail soon made him a rising star in the Senate. But his personal image was just as important to his rise to dominance in New Jersey politics. His first term coincided with efforts, particularly by Kean, to improve the image of a state that had been derided for years as a chemical junkyard and a playground for organized crime. Bradley, with his intellectual bearing and distance from grimy organization politics, was a model for how New Jerseyans preferred their state to be viewed.

By 1984, Bradley was poised for a landslide re-election. Once clearly uncomfortable on the stump, he worked crowds now with more ease. He had learned the nuts and bolts of politics, assembling a talented political organization and showing an impressive ability to raise funds. He had $2 million salted away before the Republicans even came up with an opponent.

The candidate they finally settled on was Mary Mochary, the mayor of Montclair, who hitched her wagon to Reagan's re-election campaign, trying to convince Reagan supporters that the Democrat would stand in the way of the president's goals. It made no difference. Bradley won close to two-thirds of the vote.

Committees

Energy and Natural Resources (5th of 10 Democrats)
Water and Power (chairman); Energy Regulation and Conservation; Public Lands, National Parks and Forests

Finance (6th of 11 Democrats)
International Debt (chairman); Health for Families and the Uninsured; International Trade

Select Intelligence (4th of 8 Democrats)

Special Aging (3rd of 10 Democrats)

Elections

1984 General		
Bill Bradley (D)	1,986,644	(64%)
Mary V. Mochary (R)	1,080,100	(35%)
1984 Primary		
Bill Bradley (D)	404,301	(93%)
Elliot Greenspan (D)	30,680	(7%)

Previous Winning Percentage: 1978 (55%)

Campaign Finance

	Receipts	Receipts from PACs	Expend-itures
1984			
Bradley (D)	$4,317,423	$665,782 (15%)	$4,566,758
Mochary (R)	$965,782	$40,350 (4%)	$956,398

Key Votes

1987	
Enact omnibus highway bill over Reagan veto	Y
Limit testing of space-based anti-ballistic missiles	Y
Oppose banning tests of larger nuclear weapons	Y
Confirm Robert H. Bork as Supreme Court justice	N
1988	
Allow vote on campaign-finance overhaul	Y
Pass civil rights restoration bill over Reagan veto	Y
Enact omnibus trade bill over Reagan veto	Y
Approve death penalty for drug-related murders	Y
Oppose "workfare" amendment to welfare overhaul bill	Y

Voting Studies

	Presidential Support		Party Unity		Conservative Coalition	
Year	S	O	S	O	S	O
1988	48	45	81	9	22	70
1987	32	55	81	12	38	56
1986	51	48	66	24	36	61
1985	33	59	69	23	17	73
1984	42	45	66	25	28	60
1983	42	58	82	18	23	75
1982	37	63	87	13	14	85
1981	44	48	80	10	11	77

Interest Group Ratings

Year	ADA	ACU	AFL-CIO	CCUS
1988	75	9	75	25
1987	80	21	100	28
1986	85	23	87	31
1985	85	9	81	28
1984	85	35	64	29
1983	85	16	82	32
1982	100	15	85	29
1981	90	7	82	13

Frank R. Lautenberg (D)

Of Montclair — Elected 1982

Born: Jan. 23, 1924, Paterson, N.J.
Education: Columbia U., B.S. 1949.
Military Career: Army, 1942-46.
Occupation: Computer firm executive.
Family: Wife, Lois Levinson; four children.
Religion: Jewish.
Political Career: No previous office.
Capitol Office: 717 Hart Bldg. 20510; 224-4744.

In Washington: Lautenberg came to the Senate pledging to put "New Jersey first." He survived one of 1988's meanest and most expensive Senate campaigns in part by demonstrating that he had.

In his first term, he became a key player on transportation and pollution policy, two matters of considerable concern in the Garden State. His position was enhanced when the Democrats took control of the Senate in 1987.

But learning to make the system work should not be confused with liking it. As with many self-made men, Lautenberg has trouble coming to terms with the slow grind of legislation.

This was never clearer than in March 1989 when Lautenberg took the Senate floor to push a resolution calling for a presidential commission to investigate the explosion of Pan Am Flight 103 over Scotland, an act of terrorism that took 270 lives. He sought to short-circuit the legislative process in a manner requiring the consent of every senator.

Lautenberg got ticked when Alan Simpson of Wyoming objected on the GOP's behalf. "This ain't the usual stuff," Lautenberg protested, seeking to distinguish the trauma of terrorism from his usual legislative efforts. He characterized the GOP as telling victims' relatives they would get no answers. "No, no, your government is inactive because the process has not been appropriately observed."

Similar frustration has accompanied Lautenberg throughout his brief career as a lawmaker. The tough, hard-driving entrepreneur elbowed his way into issues where his presence was not always welcome. Nonetheless, he generally has done so without alienating colleagues.

Lautenberg showed he had learned to play the game with skill in 1987. He steered a smoking ban on certain domestic airline flights through the Senate, besting a master obstructionist, Jesse Helms of North Carolina. When the measure came over from the House attached to a spending bill, Lautenberg turned back procedural arguments and on a crucial committee vote produced enough proxies to win. Later, during floor action, he fashioned an overnight compromise that led to passage. The compromise, however, held the ban to two years. He looked to resume the fight in the 101st Congress.

Upon arriving in the Senate, Lautenberg joined the Banking and Commerce committees, but he had shed both by the 100th Congress. Lautenberg is among those who would confer Cabinet status on the Environmental Protection Agency (EPA), and in 1987 he became chairman of the Environment and Public Works subcommittee that has jurisdiction over EPA's "superfund" toxic-waste cleanup program. Thus, he was able to conduct field hearings in New Jersey, home of 100 toxic-waste sites bad enough to make the superfund list.

New Jersey has long resented New York City's sludge washing up on its shores. Lautenberg was instrumental in putting through a measure that will eventually halt this practice. He also pressed for laws to halt ocean dumping of other garbage, including plastics that do not degrade like organic materials.

Lautenberg was deeply involved in the ultimately successful effort to reauthorize the superfund program, a struggle that dragged on through the 98th and 99th Congresses. He allied with environmentalists in calling for a five-year, expanded version of the existing program, and in 1986 worked to keep the program from running out of money while House and Senate conferees dickered over its renewal.

With the EPA running out of superfund money and the conferees far from agreement and close to the deadline, Lautenberg resisted calls for a one-year renewal; he feared President Reagan would veto superfund unless it got to his desk before the 1986 elections. Lautenberg called for the two-month extension approved by Congress that kept pressure on the conferees.

The five-year superfund reauthorization eventually passed, and one section of the bill reflected Lautenberg's oft-expressed concern that people be told more about the chemicals around them. The bill contained new "right-to-know" language requiring chemical companies to tell surrounding communities what they are producing, handling and storing. The law also mandated new mechanisms for emergency response to hazardous-chemical spills and leaks.

Lautenberg's subcommittee broadened its scope in the 101st Congress, enhancing its reach on New Jersey matters. Ocean dumping, drinking water, groundwater and indoor pollution were added to its jurisdiction.

Lautenberg's other subcommittee chairmanship, the Transportation Subcommittee on Appropriations, allowed him to plunge even deeper into issues of rail, air and highway safety. In the 98th Congress, Lautenberg had won legislation aimed at curbing drunken driving by forcing states to raise their minimum drinking age to 21.

To get the bill through the Senate, Lautenberg worked out a "stick-and-carrot" compromise — threatening states that refused to raise their drinking age with the loss of up to $500 million a year in federal highway money, while also offering them incentives to try other measures to reduce drunken driving.

In the 99th Congress, Lautenberg moved to close a loophole in the drinking-age law that would have ended the fiscal sanctions on states within two years: Some states had passed laws raising the drinking age to 21 only until 1988.

After taking over the Transportation Subcommittee, he resisted efforts to eliminate the sanctions, which some states regard as "federal blackmail." He also sought to enlarge the carrot, but failed to enhance highway funding for states that revoke the licenses of drivers failing a sobriety test.

Lautenberg hounded the Reagan administration to rehire air-traffic controllers who were fired after they went on strike in 1981. Contending that the current controllers are so overworked that the Federal Aviation Administration is hard-pressed to keep the skies safe, Lautenberg has tried to get the rehiring ban lifted. The Senate endorsed his proposal in 1986, but backed down when Reagan threatened to veto the transportation funding bill to which it was attached.

With his leverage increased in the 100th Congress, he continued to harass the FAA, saying it could make the system even safer with additional measures. He sought more money for air safety, including air-traffic control.

On the Budget Committee, he was a reliable opponent of Reagan spending priorities. In 1986, when the committee's Democratic and Republican leaders were trying to put together a bipartisan budget, Lautenberg offered one of his own that reduced defense spending $20 billion below the bipartisan plan, increased revenues by about $1 billion and distributed the extra cash among education, health, environmental and other non-defense accounts. His alternative lost, 16-5.

Lautenberg has been a fast friend of Israel and Jewish causes, although he joined with other senators in signing a 1988 letter that expressed displeasure with Israeli Prime Minister Yitzhak Shamir for saying he rejected a negotiating formula that would trade land for peace. He also sponsored legislation to allow the wearing of yarmulkes in the military.

At Home: For the New York City and Philadelphia TV stations that provide most of New Jersey's news coverage, Lautenberg's workmanlike performance on state issues has been pretty dull stuff, especially compared with the activities of senior Democratic Sen. Bill Bradley and GOP Gov. Thomas H. Kean, both players on the national stage in their parties. So when Lautenberg began his 1988 re-election campaign, he had a fairly low public profile.

But by the end of the contest, Lautenberg's name and deeds were widely known, and he had beaten back an aggressive challenge from Republican Pete Dawkins by 250,000 votes.

Dawkins was the national GOP's premier "résumé" candidate for Senate in 1988. His life had been an unbroken string of accomplishments — winner of the Heisman Trophy (while playing for Army in 1958), a Rhodes scholar, the Army's youngest brigadier general, a high-ranking Pentagon official, a Wall Street financial executive. He tried to mold his golden image to political advantage, describing himself as a potential national leader in the Bradley-Kean mold. He denigrated Lautenberg as "the junior senator."

But Dawkins soon found his superstar image challenged. An article in a Manhattan business magazine described him as a failure in a variety of military and business positions, who still was promoted because of the public relations value of his all-American image. It was said that he had shopped for a state in which to seek public office and settled on New Jersey, moving in just before announcing his Senate candidacy.

While Dawkins denied that assertion and dismissed the magazine story, he and his campaign were caught in several instances of résumé padding that had to be retracted. These included statements that Dawkins had played a major combat role in Vietnam, and that he had been an innovator in international finance as an executive for a Wall Street brokerage firm.

Dawkins spent $1 million-plus in the spring to get his name in front of voters, but he entered the fall trailing Lautenberg in the polls. At that point, Lautenberg went on the attack, beginning with an unusual ad showing Dawkins himself making a flowery statement about the glories of New Jersey. "Be Real, Pete" was superimposed on the film clip, conveying Lautenberg's theme that Dawkins was a carpetbagger and a phony. Another ad accused Dawkins of viewing New Jersey as a pit stop on his route to national office.

Dawkins bemoaned Lautenberg's mudslinging, but then got into a tit-for-tat war of negativism that sank to its lowest when Dawkins charged multimillionaire Lautenberg with using his Senate seat for personal profit.

Lautenberg's lead weathered the fierce exchanges, Dawkins' money dried up and the incumbent at the end switched to positive ads extolling his work for the state. In spite of George Bush's solid victory in New Jersey, Lautenberg won 54 percent of the vote.

While Lautenberg had been involved for years as a Democratic activist and fund-raiser — his $90,000 contribution to George McGovern's campaign in 1972 earned him a place on President Nixon's "enemies list" — he had never sought office prior to his 1982 bid for the seat vacated by appointed GOP Sen. Nicholas F. Brady (now Treasury secretary). After winning with a plurality in a Democratic primary, he came from behind to defeat Republican Rep. Millicent Fenwick.

Both candidates were wealthy. But while Fenwick inherited her fortune, Lautenberg, the son of an immigrant silk-mill worker, was a self-made man. The Democrat spent some $4 million of his own money to drive home that contrast. At one campaign stop, he pointed to the gap between his front teeth and said, "If my parents had money I wouldn't have this. I keep it as a badge of my roots."

Irreverent, witty and eccentric, Fenwick was frequently profiled and quoted in the national media, and was a heroine to numerous good-government causes. She started out with a sizable lead over Lautenberg.

But Lautenberg overcame Fenwick's reformist credentials and personal popularity by painting her and the GOP as insensitive to working-class people. He touted himself as an expert on creating jobs, talking about how he had turned his company, Automatic Data Processing, from a three-man business into one of the world leaders in computer services.

To erase organized labor's doubts about him, Lautenberg advocated a minimum tax on corporations and elimination of the third year of Reagan's tax cut for those earning over $40,000 per year. Labor finally went along with him against Fenwick, overlooking the absence of unions at ADP. Lautenberg said no one had tried to organize the firm.

With the endorsements of several major newspapers, the unions and such liberal forces as the National Organization for Women, Lautenberg showed Fenwick's lead was soft. He hammered on her votes for the 1981 Reagan economic package. She could not equal his media effort, as she would not dip as heavily into her wealth and refused donations from political action committees. Lautenberg rejected her request that each side limit spending to $1.6 million. He won with 51 percent of the vote.

Committees

Appropriations (10th of 16 Democrats)
Transportation and Related Agencies (chairman); Commerce, Justice, State, the Judiciary and Related Agencies; Defense; Foreign Operations; HUD-Independent Agencies

Budget (6th of 13 Democrats)

Environment and Public Works (5th of 9 Democrats)
Superfund, Ocean and Water Protection (chairman); Environmental Protection; Water Resources, Transportation and Infrastructure

Elections

1988 General

Frank R. Lautenberg (D)	1,599,905	(54%)
Pete Dawkins (R)	1,349,937	(45%)

1988 Primary

Frank R. Lautenberg (D)	326,072	(78%)
Elnardo J. Webster (D)	51,938	(12%)
Harold J. Young (D)	41,303	(10%)

Previous Winning Percentage: **1982** (51%)

Campaign Finance

	Receipts	Receipts from PACs	Expenditures
1988			
Lautenberg (D)	$7,087,476	$1,410,360 (20%)	$7,289,663
Dawkins (R)	$7,766,535	$855,144 (11%)	$7,616,249

Key Votes

1987

Enact omnibus highway bill over Reagan veto	Y
Limit testing of space-based anti-ballistic missiles	?
Oppose banning tests of larger nuclear weapons	N
Confirm Robert H. Bork as Supreme Court justice	N

1988

Allow vote on campaign-finance overhaul	Y
Pass civil rights restoration bill over Reagan veto	Y
Enact omnibus trade bill over Reagan veto	Y
Approve death penalty for drug-related murders	N
Oppose "workfare" amendment to welfare overhaul bill	Y

Voting Studies

	Presidential Support		Party Unity		Conservative Coalition	
Year	**S**	**O**	**S**	**O**	**S**	**O**
1988	42	53	92	4	0	92
1987	33	63	87	6	19	72
1986	30	69	79	15	12	86
1985	28	69	85	14	7	92
1984	35	61	85	12	6	91
1983	40	56	77	20	14	80

Interest Group Ratings

Year	ADA	ACU	AFL-CIO	CCUS
1988	90	0	100	17
1987	85	8	89	33
1986	85	17	100	22
1985	90	4	95	32
1984	100	0	91	24
1983	85	16	94	26

1 James J. Florio (D)

Of Gloucester Township — Elected 1974

Born: Aug. 29, 1937, Brooklyn, N.Y.

Education: Trenton State College, B.A. 1962; graduate work, Columbia U., 1962-63; Rutgers U. Law School, J.D. 1967.

Military Career: Navy, 1955-58, Naval Reserve, 1958-74.

Occupation: Lawyer.

Family: Wife, Lucinda Coleman; three children.

Religion: Roman Catholic.

Political Career: N.J. Assembly, 1970-74; Democratic nominee for U.S. House, 1972; sought Democratic gubernatorial nomination, 1977; Democratic nominee for governor, 1981.

Capitol Office: 2162 Rayburn Bldg. 20515; 225-6501.

In Washington: Florio has spent a long time in Washington trying to get to the governor's mansion in Trenton, and during those years he has devoted exhaustive attention to national issues like the environment and consumer affairs that also happen to play particularly well in New Jersey. In the 101st Congress he began his eighth term as a House member, and his third as a gubernatorial candidate. Florio won his party's nomination in June 1989, as Republicans tapped 12th District Rep. Jim Courter to meet him in the November election.

Shrewd and well studied, Florio is talented enough to have accomplished a considerable amount, particularly in the area of hazardous-waste cleanup. He has done so without making many of the close political friendships that typically grease Congress' wheels.

Florio can seem aloof and intensely serious; the familiar impression is of an unsmiling man with a corrugated forehead. Especially among colleagues on the Energy and Commerce Committee, the one-time Navy boxer from Brooklyn is considered a scrappy and occasionally ruthless competitor, and one who almost always exits the ring alone. Some members go to the House gym for team sports, mixing exercise and camaraderie. Florio would go to hit a punching bag.

He is typical of the strong-willed subcommittee chairmen at Energy and Commerce, but perhaps no one other than California Democrat Henry A. Waxman has worse relations with the imperious full committee chairman, John D. Dingell of Michigan. As a subcommittee head, Florio likes to control legislative situations closely, consulting few others.

At times, his temperament has had legislative costs. In the 99th Congress, a mutiny on his Commerce, Transportation and Tourism Subcommittee cost him the lead role in renewing the "superfund" toxic-waste law of which he is widely considered the father. The episode scarred relations between Florio and some colleagues, particularly Dingell.

The original 1980 law, though more modest than Florio had proposed, authorized hundreds of millions of dollars for cleanups in a number of states — with New Jersey heading the list. Costs were split between the chemical industry and the federal government. When debate began anew in 1985, there were important areas of agreement. Most subcommittee members favored enlarging the fund, but Florio, who led a faction of environmentalists, faced opposition on several issues from a coalition of Republicans, oil-state Democrats — and Dingell. Still, he was unyielding in his pursuit of more stringent cleanup standards, and of citizens' rights to sue those responsible for waste-related health problems.

As a result, he lost control of the issue. His foes' industry-backed legislation prevailed, and almost all of Florio's last-ditch attempts to amend what he called its "basic flaws" lost on 13-5 votes. He was more successful in full committee, but nevertheless opposed the superfund bill on the panel's final 31-10 vote, complaining that it was too weak.

In the end, environmentalists got much of what they wanted, but the credit and headlines back home went to two other New Jersey Democrats, Public Works Committee leaders James J. Howard and Robert A. Roe; Roe was one of Florio's unsuccessful rivals for the 1981 gubernatorial nomination. Public Works approved a superfund bill more to environmentalists' liking, forcing Energy and Commerce to compromise on the version that went to the House floor.

Though Florio was involved, he was an outsider. He was barred from inter-committee negotiations and was not one of the bill's floor managers. He did vote for the bill when it passed the House 391-33, and helped shape the

New Jersey 1

Southwest — Camden

The 1st is an amalgam of decaying urban areas, older suburbs and a rapidly developing countryside once covered by tomato patches but now sprouting subdivisions. Many of the suburbanites have Philadelphia roots and retain their Democratic loyalties. The Philadelphians were largely responsible for the district's switch in representation in 1974, when it elected Florio after choosing only Republicans for 75 years.

Democrats long have prevailed in the industrial region near the Delaware River — Camden and the other river towns, and the layer of blue-collar suburbs beyond them. But in the 1980s, election outcomes here have revealed a degree of blue-collar disaffection with national Democratic tickets.

Numerous businesses and residents have fled depressed Camden, leaving block after block of boarded-up and burnt-out buildings. Camden lost 17 percent of its population during the 1970s. Its per capita income in 1985 — $5,731 — was the lowest of any major city in the state.

However, an economic upturn across the river in downtown Philadelphia has helped stabilize the economy and population in Camden, which with 83,000 residents remains the district's hub. Campbell Soup Co., RCA and the Camden County government complex are the major indigenous employers. Slightly more than half of Camden's residents are black; the rest are largely Italian and Hispanic.

Pennsauken (population 34,000) is a port city like Camden, filled with factories and oil storage yards. Pennsauken is still essentially Democratic, as are some of the older suburban communities near it on the Black Horse Pike. Italian-Americans have a strong influence.

Farther east, in what was recently farm country, are the newer, fast-developing suburbs such as Winslow Township (population 25,000), which grew by nearly 80 percent in the 1970s, and by another 25 percent in the early 1980s. The political complexion of these newer suburbs is marginal, thanks to the residual Democratic ties of many of the expatriate Philadelphians.

Population: 526,069. White 427,390 (81%), Black 78,545 (15%), Other 4,025 (1%). Spanish origin 21,405 (4%). 18 and over 370,997 (71%), 65 and over 52,874 (10%). Median age: 30.

conference committee product that became law in 1986.

Evidence that the fight also had further soured his relations with Dingell was obvious when Energy and Commerce Democrats met early the next year to reorganize subcommittees for the 100th Congress. The shake-up left Florio with a choice between the chairs of two panels, both with narrower jurisdictions than his previous subcommittee. He declined the one responsible for hazardous waste and took instead the Commerce, Consumer Protection and Competitiveness Subcommittee, overseeing trade, insurance and product safety.

But he stayed involved in the environmental issues so important to his state. Florio provisions were included in legislation aimed at controlling radon in buildings and ocean-dumping of medical wastes. He hounded a reluctant Reagan administration to spend appropriations for removing asbestos from schools. But he failed to toughen a committee bill closing loopholes in the law regulating disposal of toxic chemicals, PCBs; it was approved by voice votes both in committee and on the floor, with Florio dissenting.

Typical of Energy and Commerce's work, Florio spends as much time monitoring federal regulators as he does legislating. In recent years his targets have been certain GOP appointees on the Consumer Product Safety Commission. "Under its current leadership," he said in 1987, "the commission has strayed so far from its mission that it poses a threat to the very consumers it is supposed to protect."

He lambasted what he considered its lax response to deaths and injuries from all-terrain vehicles, disposable lighters and infants' toys. His panel and the full committee approved a bill overhauling the commission and effectively removing its chairman, but like other CPSC reauthorization bills in the Reagan years, it went no farther.

The subcommittee's major bill in the 100th Congress — legislation to establish the first federal product-liability statute — was something of a departure for Florio. It put him in an uneasy and ultimately unworkable alliance with Dingell and business groups while disappointing his allies among consumer groups, who object that the proposal favors manufacturers over victims of unsafe products.

He became part of the so-called "Big Four," along with Dingell, senior committee Republican Norman F. Lent of New York and New Mexico Democrat Bill Richardson, the bill's sponsor, who acted as a group to support the measure. Florio said he decided a uniform law was desirable, and that consumers actually would benefit from proposed arbitration procedures. Unspoken was the fact that Dingell was going to push the legislation anyway, and Florio would be a non-player on his own subcommittee unless he aligned with the chairman.

The subcommittee approved a bill in late 1987, but Dingell had to delay full committee action for months because members did not want to choose between consumers and business supporters over a bill certain to die in the Senate. When the panel finally endorsed an amended measure, 30-12, in mid-1988, Florio was a last-minute defector to the opposition.

After helping to block consumer-backed amendments, Florio announced that adoption of one business amendment had so tipped the scales against consumers that he could no longer support the bill. That amendment, on behalf of chemical companies, would have prevented states from adopting separate environmental product liability laws — as New Jersey had done. The bill never got to the floor.

Florio is one of the most knowledgeable legislators on insurance matters. In 1984, he failed against industry opposition to win committee approval of a "unisex insurance" bill banning gender-based rates or benefits, a priority of women's and civil rights groups. More recently he focused on certain businesses' problems obtaining affordable liability insurance, and on insurance companies' investments in high-risk "junk bonds."

The subcommittee changes in the 100th Congress not coincidentally removed Florio from prominence as a proponent of railroad deregulation, and gave jurisdiction over the issue to Thomas A. Luken, who supports re-regulation as desired by coal producers, utilities, agribusinesses and other shippers seeking lower rates. Luken's panel did approve a bill in 1987 that Florio opposed, but it did not advance.

In 1980, Florio and Illinois Republican Edward Madigan had produced what became the rail deregulation law, designed to encourage competition in the industry. Despite shippers' opposition, Florio steered it to passage with impressive tactical moves, compromising just enough to keep his coalition together. Then in the 99th Congress, he bested Dingell and defeated efforts to reimpose price regulation on certain routes; Dingell initially persuaded Florio's subcommittee to approve some of the changes, but Florio and other foes reversed that decision in full committee.

Coming from an area along the nation's heaviest-traveled train route, Florio fought Reagan's efforts to end funding for Amtrak. He also had a hand in the 98th and 99th Congresses in altering an administration plan to sell the Conrail freight system.

Florio favored a public stock offering instead. In the 99th Congress, a Senate-passed bill to implement a proposed sale to Norfolk Southern met fierce opposition from Florio and other Energy and Commerce members. In 1986 the administration finally backed successful legislation for a $2 billion stock offering. But on the conference committee, Florio ended up rejecting the package, partly due to concerns that it did not sufficiently guard against a merger between Conrail and Norfolk Southern, which would have created a monopoly along some Eastern lines.

Florio also is a member of the Veterans' Affairs Committee. He is less active there, but has backed efforts to compensate Vietnam veterans for illnesses that could be linked to the wartime defoliant Agent Orange.

At Home: Though he has been secure in his South Jersey district since his election in 1974, Florio has been frustrated twice in his overriding goal to become governor of New Jersey. But with GOP Gov. Thomas H. Kean — who inflicted a painfully narrow defeat on Florio in 1981 — barred by law from seeking a third term in 1989, Florio is giving it another try.

The state's odd-year gubernatorial election lessens the risk to Florio and Courter: The loser will return to the House.

In Florio's first try in 1977, he was a long shot in a pack of Democrats unsuccessfully challenging Democratic Gov. Brendan T. Byrne; he finished fourth in the field of 10.

Four years later, Florio became the first Italian-American ever nominated for governor of New Jersey, and entered the general election campaign favored over Kean. But he lost by 1,797 votes, in the closest gubernatorial election in state history.

Florio had won the Democrats' nomination to succeed Byrne by outrunning another large field of contenders. He aired commercials all over the state, stressing the work he had done on toxic waste and transportation. Florio ran well even in some northern counties where Democratic Rep. Roe had expected to score heavily. Florio took 26 percent of the vote, while Roe got 16 percent.

But Florio fell short in the fall campaign. As a product of the working class running against Kean, an old-money millionaire, Florio had the credentials to mobilize blue-collar Democrats. But his mundane speeches and chilly, impersonal style made him seem stiff in contrast to Kean, who escaped the "patrician" label with his engaging campaign style.

Florio also suffered from his distant relations with some Democratic county leaders. He failed to pile up the lopsided margins expected in such old-line Democratic counties as Hudson and Middlesex. Florio's South Jersey base also did not provide the margins he needed to hold off Kean.

The 1981 loss turned Florio cautious for 1982. Though he was the most prominent Democrat in New Jersey, he declined to run for the

Senate against GOP Rep. Millicent Fenwick, who was ultimately beaten by Democrat Frank R. Lautenberg. It was a logical decision since Fenwick had seemed formidable, but it signaled a temporarily reduced role for Florio in state politics. In 1985, he chose not to try again for governor — a decision that was vindicated when Kean won re-election in a landslide.

Florio's statewide setbacks did not affect him in the Camden-based 1st District. He won his House races there with better than 70 percent, and came to dominate a Camden County Democratic organization that in turn controlled county politics and government.

The Camden County GOP has tried, without much success, to tie Florio directly to alleged patronage abuses in the Democrat-dominated county government. The issue was picked up in the 1989 Democratic gubernatorial primary by state Rep. Alan J. Karcher, who alternately described Florio as a machine boss and as a tool for the state's 21 county Democratic chairmen; they had put aside any old difficulties with Florio and endorsed him.

But Florio brushed off the criticism, saying he was too busy in Congress to be involved in the workings of the Camden Democrats, and noting that the county government underwent a housecleaning in 1988. Heavily favored over Karcher and Princeton Mayor Barbara Boggs Sigmund, Florio spent most of the campaign fashioning a warmer image. At his victory rally after breezing to nomination, Florio lavished attention on his family, including his wife, elderly parents, grown children from his first marriage, and infant grandson.

Born in Brooklyn, where his father painted ships at the Navy yard, Florio left high school to join the Navy, won his diploma on an equivalency test and went on to graduate from Trenton State College, winning election as student body president.

After college, he worked as assistant urban renewal director in Glassboro, N.J. He worked his way through Rutgers University law school as night watchman at the Camden County courthouse, a patronage job from a Democratic ward leader who liked him.

Florio moved up in politics by offering free legal help to party regulars, and in 1969 he ran for the state Assembly as a protégé of Camden Mayor Angelo Errichetti. He made it by 400 votes in a year of statewide Republican success.

Florio first ran for Congress in 1972, against GOP Rep. John E. Hunt. He fell about 10,000 votes short, but the margin showed Hunt's weaknesses. In 1974, after Hunt defended President Nixon on the House Judiciary Committee, Florio made it. He soon drifted apart from Errichetti, who was convicted in 1980 on Abscam bribery charges. By then, Florio had built his own political organization.

Committees

Energy and Commerce (5th of 26 Democrats)
Commerce, Consumer Protection and Competitiveness (chairman); Transportation and Hazardous Materials

Select Aging (3rd of 39 Democrats)
Housing and Consumer Interests (chairman); Health and Long-Term Care

Veterans' Affairs (8th of 21 Democrats)
Hospitals and Health Care; Housing and Memorial Affairs; Oversight and Investigations

Elections

1988 General		
James J. Florio (D)	141,988	(70%)
Frank A. Cristaudo (R)	60,037	(30%)
1986 General		
James J. Florio (D)	93,497	(76%)
Fred A. Busch (R)	29,175	(24%)

Previous Winning Percentages: **1984** (72%) **1982** (73%) **1980** (77%) **1978** (79%) **1976** (70%) **1974** (58%)

District Vote For President

	1988		1984		1980		1976	
D	97,534	(48%)	96,877	(45%)	87,763	(47%)	120,345	(57%)
R	107,017	(52%)	118,015	(55%)	91,587	(49%)	85,452	(41%)
I					6,663	(4%)		

Campaign Finance

	Receipts	Receipts from PACs	Expend-itures
1988			
Florio (D)	$790,850	$359,310 (45%)	$924,427
Cristaudo (R)	$55,802	$6,250 (11%)	$55,301
1986			
Florio (D)	$475,582	$265,860 (56%)	$322,534

Key Votes

1987	
Raise speed limit to 65 mph	N
Approve Gephardt "fair trade" amendment	Y
Ban testing of larger nuclear weapons	Y
Delay "re-flagging" of Kuwaiti tankers	Y
Approve tax-raising deficit-reduction bill	Y
1988	
Approve aid to Nicaraguan contras	N
Enact civil rights restoration bill over Reagan veto	Y
Kill 60-day plant-closing notification measure	N
Pass omnibus trade bill over Reagan veto	Y
Approve death penalty for drug-related murders	Y
Bar federal funds for abortions in cases of rape and incest	N
Oppose seven-day waiting period for purchase of handguns	N

Voting Studies

	Presidential Support		Party Unity		Conservative Coalition	
Year	S	O	S	O	S	O
1988	23	71	83	8	24	68
1987	13	86	86	3	14	81
1986	19	80	87	6	28	66
1985	25	73	89	5	22	75
1984	26	70	87	7	19	76
1983	13	80	81	9	26	70
1982	32	66	87	7	18	75
1981	20	37	52	10	16	41

Interest Group Ratings

Year	ADA	ACU	AFL-CIO	CCUS
1988	80	9	100	21
1987	92	4	100	0
1986	70	10	100	15
1985	85	10	100	14
1984	80	21	92	38
1983	85	23	100	17
1982	85	14	100	33
1981	40	23	82	8

2 William J. Hughes (D)

Of Ocean City — Elected 1974

Born: Oct. 17, 1932, Salem, N.J.
Education: Rutgers U., A.B. 1955, J.D. 1958.
Occupation: Lawyer.
Family: Wife, Nancy L. Gibson; four children.
Religion: Episcopalian.
Political Career: Assistant prosecutor, Cape May County, 1960-70; Ocean City solicitor, 1970-74; Democratic nominee for U.S. House, 1970.
Capitol Office: 341 Cannon Bldg. 20515; 225-6572.

In Washington: Public concern about violence, drug trafficking and white-collar crime has given impetus over the last several years to congressional efforts to strengthen the federal criminal code. With widespread voter support for their efforts to "get tough," recent Congresses have fashioned legislative packages aimed at expanding federal law-enforcement powers and increasing criminal penalties.

As chairman of the Judiciary Subcommittee on Crime since 1981, Hughes has been in the middle of the action. His central position in the debate over crime legislation allowed Hughes to play a key role in the passage of the 1986 and 1988 laws against the drug trade, the 1984 overhaul of the federal criminal code, a stronger law against child pornography and a measure to ban "plastic" guns.

But while it is true that Hughes has been deeply involved — supporting many stringent proposals while working with other Democrats to temper the impulses of some of the more conservative House members — he has hardly been able to ride herd over the politically charged debates on such issues as gun control and penalties for drug offenders. While the diligent former prosecutor is respected and liked by most House colleagues, he has suffered his share of frustrations and defeats.

The debate over the 1988 drug bill provides an illustration. When the draft bill came before his subcommittee, Hughes urged members to use restraint in amending it, lest it become a legislative "Christmas tree" (he brought a small decorated tree to the hearing as a prop). The message went unheeded, though, as panel members proposed numerous amendments.

Hughes nonetheless pronounced the bill that advanced from the Judiciary Committee — which created the federal "drug czar" position, increased aid to local police and barred certain federal benefits to repeated drug offenders — as a "dynamite piece of legislation." But some of the more draconian measures added on by the full House and Senate, such as the death penalty for so-called "drug kingpins," made the moderate Hughes uneasy. Though he went on to support the measure, Hughes said just before the September 1988 House vote, "I never thought I would see a bill so butchered that came out of my committee."

By the time the final bill was passed in October 1988, Hughes had secured some victories. Tough Senate amendments against child pornography, similar to those proposed in the House by Hughes and ranking Crime Subcommittee Republican Bill McCollum of Florida, were attached to the bill. At the same time, Hughes fought off efforts by Senate conservatives to expand greatly the reach of federal law on adult pornography.

In a House-Senate conference, Hughes accepted the establishment of a federal crime of intentionally possessing obscene materials for sale, but won the deletion of a provision allowing the government to seize the assets of retailers who inadvertently carried obscene items. "We made it very clear that there were just some threshold areas that there would be no movement on," Hughes said.

Hughes also persuaded Congress to pass his legislation banning firearms made mostly of plastic, which could not be picked up by conventional metal detectors. Hughes had the backing from law-enforcement officials that has become common in recent gun-control debates, but also had the rare, if reluctant, support of the National Rifle Association.

However, NRA opposition helped crush a drug bill amendment, favored by Hughes, to mandate a seven-day waiting period to purchase a handgun. Hughes said the amendment, proposed by Democrat Edward F. Feighan of Ohio, would prove "how tough we are when it comes to bucking the NRA and the gun lobby." But the House dumped the waiting period by a 46-vote margin.

The debate recalled a gun-control battle during the 99th Congress that resulted in Hughes' most discouraging setback. When gun-control opponents introduced a bill relaxing laws against interstate sales of rifles, shotguns and handguns, Hughes and Judiciary Committee Chairman Peter W. Rodino Jr. underesti-

New Jersey 2

South — Atlantic City; Vineland

Atlantic City, the 2nd District's largest population center, is actually two cities. There is the one that local officials prefer outsiders to think of: the home of glitzy gambling casinos and luxury hotels which over the past decade have revived Atlantic City's once-faded image as an adult playground-by-the-sea. To the busloads of working-class elderly hoping to win a fortune and the high-rollers who come to spend some of theirs, Atlantic City has been reborn as a year-round resort.

But those visitors who wander from the seafront hotel strip will find the other Atlantic City: a seedy, blighted town, whose predominately black population has been disappointed in the casinos' failure to bring in the pervasive prosperity promised when New Jersey legalized gambling in the 1970s. The city's population (currently about 36,000) fell by 14 percent in the 1970s, and lost another 11 percent in 1980-86.

This Atlantic City contrasts sharply with the rest of the 2nd District. The story elsewhere is one of growth. The small communities outside Atlantic City, once summer towns, recently have attracted thousands of new year-round residents, many of them refugees from older, urban parts of the state. Retirement communities have sprung up inland.

The Democratic voting tendencies of Atlantic City's minority population are also not duplicated elsewhere. Though Hughes' personal popularity has made him safe — he carried every district county by wide margins in 1988 — the district is far more favorable to Republicans running statewide.

In 1988, George Bush easily carried all four counties — Atlantic, Cape May, Cumberland and Salem — that are completely within the 2nd. In the closely contested Senate race, Democratic incumbent Frank R. Lautenberg held onto Atlantic County and Cumberland County, which has a glass industry centered in the towns of Bridgeton, Millville and Vineland. But his GOP opponent, Pete Dawkins, took Salem and Cape May counties.

Though Cape May is Hughes' home county, the summer-resort area is probably the most Republican in the district. From north to south, the county takes in family-oriented Ocean City, wealthy Avalon and Stone Harbor, then honky-tonk Wildwood, whose amusement parks were celebrated by pop singer Bobby Rydell in "Wildwood Days." The elegant Victorian homes of Cape May city are at the southern tip.

Like Cumberland, Salem County has an industrial presence in the chemical plants that line the Delaware River. But both counties are mainly agricultural.

Population: 526,070. White 435,627 (83%), Black 73,331 (14%), Other 3,825 (1%). Spanish origin 23,022 (4%). 18 and over 381,227 (72%), 65 and over 75,506 (14%). Median age: 32.

mated their determination. They even drafted legislation to strengthen the gun laws.

But while Hughes tried to bottle up the pro-gun bill, Missouri Democrat Harold L. Volkmer staged a petition drive to bypass the Crime Subcommittee and bring the bill to the floor. Hughes belatedly hammered out some concessions, including retention of the existing ban on interstate handgun sales. Still, the episode constituted a defeat for gun-control forces.

Though contentious, high-profile issues like drug crime and gun control occupy much of Hughes' time, he has made a personal cause of cracking down on white-collar crime. With his efforts boosted by publicity about the Pentagon procurement scandal in mid-1988, Hughes pushed through a bill making it a federal crime to commit fraud in government contracts of $1 million or over. Hughes' amendment to the 1986 drug bill created a new crime of "money laundering," by which criminals disguise illegally obtained funds by channeling them through banks and other legitimate businesses.

When not preoccupied with his Judiciary activities, Hughes can usually be found defending the interests of his coastal district on the Merchant Marine and Fisheries Committee. It was in that capacity that Hughes pulled off a major coup, gaining enactment of a ban after 1991 on the ocean dumping of sewage sludge.

For years, New York City and other municipalities, including some in New Jersey, had dumped their sludge at a site 12 miles off the New Jersey shore — in 1988, they moved 106 miles offshore — and resisted efforts by environmentalists to end the practice. However, concerns over effects on the state's shoreline led the New Jersey Legislature to ban ocean dumping. The issue reached a boil in the summer of 1988, when a related problem, beach wash-ups of ocean-dumped garbage and medical waste, damaged the state's tourist industry.

At first, the ocean-dumping issue shaped up as a New Jersey-New York turf battle. But the beach problems, along with the unusual interest in the issue shown by the Republican and Democratic presidential candidates, gave momentum to Hughes' effort. His bill, which orders dumpers to find alternative disposal means by Dec. 31, 1991, sailed through Congress and was signed by President Reagan in November 1988. It also included Hughes' provisions making it a crime to dispose of medical waste in U.S. coastal or navigable waters.

At Home: Though Hughes votes a standard Democratic line on most issues, he occasionally will cast an atypical vote. For instance, he was the only New Jersey Democrat to vote against the retaliatory Gephardt amendment to the trade bill in the 100th Congress. Such actions, combined with his tough-on-crime image, have made Hughes a secure and popular figure in the Republican-leaning 2nd District.

Hughes was Ocean City solicitor in 1974 when he challenged four-term Republican Rep. Charles W. Sandman Jr. He had run against Sandman once before, in 1970, coming within 6,000 votes. The second time he began in a stronger position, because Sandman had hurt himself badly with his slashing attacks on President Nixon's detractors during the 1974 impeachment debate. The result was as much a decision on Sandman as it was a triumph for Hughes, but it was overwhelming — the incumbent drew only 41 percent of the vote.

Hughes worked hard to cultivate this sprawling district. His mobile van constantly toured the area, looking for people in need of help. Hughes was visible on numerous local issues, helping to get military uniform contracts for the ailing garment industry in Cumberland County, pushing for higher gasoline allocations to help seashore tourism during the 1979 energy crunch and fighting against local storage of nuclear waste. These efforts paid off in terms of security; Hughes never received less than 58 percent of the vote for re-election.

In his last two elections, the NRA, angered by Hughes' pro-gun-control efforts, hinted at playing an active role to defeat him. But the NRA lacked a horse to back: Hughes' popularity deterred high-profile Republicans from challenging him, leaving the chore to lesser-known GOP candidates. Hughes won easily each time, taking 68 percent of the vote in 1986 and 66 percent in 1988.

Committees

Judiciary (6th of 21 Democrats)
Crime (chairman); Courts, Intellectual Property and the Administration of Justice

Merchant Marine and Fisheries (4th of 26 Democrats)
Coast Guard and Navigation; Fisheries and Wildlife Conservation and the Environment; Oceanography

Select Aging (5th of 39 Democrats)
Human Services

Select Narcotics Abuse and Control (10th of 18 Democrats)

Elections

1988 General		
William J. Hughes (D)	134,505	(66%)
Kirk W. Conover (R)	67,759	(33%)
1986 General		
William J. Hughes (D)	83,821	(68%)
Alfred J. Bennington Jr. (R)	35,167	(29%)

Previous Winning Percentages: **1984** (63%) **1982** (68%) **1980** (58%) **1978** (66%) **1976** (62%) **1974** (57%)

District Vote For President

	1988	1984	1980	1976
D	89,367 (41%)	84,704 (38%)	80,965 (39%)	109,701 (52%)
R	127,327 (59%)	138,241 (62%)	107,007 (52%)	97,824 (46%)
I			15,271 (7%)	

Campaign Finance

	Receipts	Receipts from PACs	Expend-itures
1988			
Hughes (D)	$283,532	$112,150 (40%)	$235,629
Conover (R)	$45,426	$100 (0.2%)	$47,159
1986			
Hughes (D)	$247,513	$98,915 (40%)	$241,948
Bennington (R)	$142,764	$8,938 (6%)	$138,115

Key Votes

1987	
Raise speed limit to 65 mph	N
Approve Gephardt "fair trade" amendment	N
Ban testing of larger nuclear weapons	Y
Delay "re-flagging" of Kuwaiti tankers	Y
Approve tax-raising deficit-reduction bill	Y
1988	
Approve aid to Nicaraguan contras	N
Enact civil rights restoration bill over Reagan veto	Y
Kill 60-day plant-closing notification measure	N
Pass omnibus trade bill over Reagan veto	Y
Approve death penalty for drug-related murders	Y
Bar federal funds for abortions in cases of rape and incest	N
Oppose seven-day waiting period for purchase of handguns	N

Voting Studies

	Presidential Support		Party Unity		Conservative Coalition	
Year	**S**	**O**	**S**	**O**	**S**	**O**
1988	30	68	85	15	47	50
1987	24	75	79	17	49	51
1986	28	72	78	20	32	68
1985	30	70	76	23	40	60
1984	41	58	71	24	46	47
1983	34	66	74	26	38	62
1982	43	57	80	19	40	59
1981	41	58	64	31	41	59

Interest Group Ratings

Year	ADA	ACU	AFL-CIO	CCUS
1988	70	16	100	43
1987	80	9	81	27
1986	75	9	79	22
1985	75	19	82	41
1984	60	25	46	40
1983	70	17	82	25
1982	80	18	90	27
1981	65	13	71	24

3 Frank Pallone Jr. (D)

Of Long Branch — Elected 1988

Born: Oct. 30, 1951, Long Branch, N.J.
Education: Middlebury College, B.A. 1973; Tufts U., M.A. 1974; Rutgers U., J.D. 1978.
Occupation: Lawyer.
Family: Single.
Religion: Roman Catholic.
Political Career: Long Branch City Council, 1982-88; N.J. Senate, 1984-88.
Capitol Office: 1207 Longworth Bldg. 20515; 225-4671.

The Path to Washington: A political alliance played an important role in Pallone's 1988 election to the House: He was a protégé of Democratic Rep. James J. Howard, whose death during his 12th term in office left the 3rd District open.

But Pallone's own state Senate record on environmental issues affecting the pollution-conscious 3rd made the difference in his campaign against a game Republican opponent, former state legislator Joseph Azzolina.

Pallone inherited his political interest from his father, an activist in local Democratic politics who was involved in Howard's House campaigns. The younger Pallone developed friendships with the veteran incumbent and his family members.

It was Howard who urged Pallone, a maritime lawyer, to run for the Long Branch City Council in 1982. Just one year later, Pallone won a state Senate seat in Monmouth County, upsetting Republican incumbent Brian Kennedy with 51 percent of the vote. (Kennedy went on to lose to Howard in the Democrat's last two House contests.)

Serving a shore district that included a number of resort and retirement communities (as well as working-class Asbury Park), Pallone sponsored laws to limit ocean dumping of garbage and sewage sludge, and he worked to set up a committee on coastal pollution that he later headed. He became chairman of the Senate Aging Committee, politically helpful since his constituency contained a high proportion of elderly residents.

Pallone's legislative efforts paid electoral dividends in 1987, when he won re-election with 60 percent of the vote. The next March, Howard, chairman of the House Public Works Committee, died of a heart attack. Many Democratic insiders, including Howard's widow, lined up behind Pallone, and he won the House nomination without a contest.

Azzolina, who had filed to run against Howard, easily won a primary for the Republican nomination. The owner of a supermarket chain, Azzolina had weathered an up-and-down political career dating to 1965, when he won the first of three terms in the state Assembly. He moved on to the state Senate, but served just two years before losing in 1973. In 1985, he came back to win an Assembly seat, but then lost a 1987 Senate contest in a Monmouth County district.

Though both candidates had name-recognition problems outside their home areas, Pallone enjoyed an advantage because of his work on environmental issues. Coastal pollution dominated the campaign agenda after medical waste and other garbage washed up in the district, discouraging beachgoers and damaging the district's crucial summertime tourist industry.

Azzolina tried to increase his visibility on the issue, releasing a 12-point plan to combat ocean pollution. The Republican also sought to tie Pallone to Democratic presidential nominee Michael S. Dukakis, who was blasted by George Bush during a 3rd District visit for seeking permission for Massachusetts to dump sludge off the New Jersey coast.

But Pallone's activism in Trenton earned him endorsements from leading environmental groups, with whom he was well connected; one of his top aides was a former head of the New Jersey Environmental Lobby.

Pallone's strong showing in his home area — he took 73 percent in Long Branch — helped him carry the Monmouth County part of the district by nearly 14,000 votes. Azzolina won the county's largest community, his home city of Middletown Township, with a modest 53 percent. He carried generally Republican Ocean County by fewer than 3,000 votes.

Also in November, Pallone won a special election to serve out the remaining weeks of Howard's unexpired term in the 100th Congress. He thus gained a slight edge in seniority over the 17 Democratic freshmen in the class of 1988.

When committee assignments for the 101st were handed out, Pallone got two that dovetail with his legislative background — Merchant Marine and Public Works.

New Jersey 3

Central Coast — Asbury Park; Long Branch

Jersey shore towns like Long Branch and Asbury Park were places where 19th-century plutocrats, presidents and gangsters came to bathe, mingle on the boardwalks and play. Ulysses S. Grant, the Guggenheims and Diamond Jim Brady all stayed there. President James A. Garfield was brought to his summer cottage in Long Branch in 1881 after he was shot; he died there a few weeks later.

Today, this area along the coast in Monmouth County is a mixed collection of wealthy shore communities and working-class towns. Although no longer the elitist playground that it once was, the 3rd remains a popular seaside vacation spot as well as a year-round home to some half a million people.

The 13 consecutive Democratic victories in the 3rd belie a politically competitive district; the Monmouth County portion of the 3rd, which casts three-fifths of the overall vote, went solidly for George Bush in 1988, at the same time it was giving Pallone a comfortable margin.

The Democratic heart of the district is in the north, in the chain of communities along the Lower New York Bay shore. The Asbury Park glorified by local hero Bruce Springsteen is on the road to recovery with the recent renovation of the Berkeley-Carteret Hotel. Towns along the coastline are economically diverse: Working-class Asbury Park, Bradley Beach and Belmar have little in common with the more affluent towns farther south.

Spring Lake, locally known as the "Irish Riviera," is home to the transplanted North Jerseyites who abound in the 3rd. Predominantly Republican, a large percentage commute into the city daily. A quick but costly ferry service has started up between Atlantic Highlands and Wall Street, carrying white-collar executives to the financial capital in just 45 minutes.

Other bastions of Republicanism are located in the bordering seaside communities of Deal and Rumson. Inland Monmouth shows the same mix. Towns such as Old Bridge and Manalapan contain New York commuters who hold the usual suburban GOP allegiance.

Middletown Township, the 3rd's second-largest political entity, votes firmly Republican. Across the Navesink River, however, is working-class Red Bank, hometown of jazz musician Count Basie. Democrats have their strongest inland enclave there.

Ocean County turns in a bit over a third of the vote, and is less favorable territory for Democrats than Monmouth. Brick Township is a middle-income suburb that is growing rapidly and proving amenable to Republicans. So are the small beachfront towns that line the Ocean County shore. In Toms River, the voters sometimes reassert their Democratic heritage in local elections, but tend to be Republican in state and national politics.

Population: 526,074. White 474,254 (90%), Black 41,093 (8%), Other 4,921 (1%). Spanish origin 15,009 (3%). 18 and over 379,673 (72%), 65 and over 76,485 (15%). Median age: 33.

Committees

Merchant Marine and Fisheries (23rd of 26 Democrats)
Fisheries and Wildlife Conservation and the Environment; Merchant Marine; Oversight and Investigations

Public Works and Transportation (26th of 31 Democrats)
Surface Transportation; Water Resources

Select Aging (37th of 39 Democrats)

Campaign Finance

	Receipts	Receipts from PACs	Expend-itures
1988			
Pallone (D)	$681,073	$437,739 (64%)	$680,647
Azzolina (R)	$998,854	$137,800 (14%)	$981,865

Elections

1988 General		
Frank Pallone Jr. (D)	117,024	(52%)
Joseph Azzolina (R)	107,479	(47%)
1988 Special Election *		
Frank Pallone Jr. (D)	116,988	(52%)
Joseph Azzolina (R)	106,489	(47%)

** On Election Day, Pallone was elected to a full term and to fill out the remainder of the term of Rep. James J. Howard, who died March 25, 1988.*

District Vote For President

	1988	1984	1980	1976
D	91,035 (37%)	79,811 (33%)	74,361 (34%)	92,176 (43%)
R	151,517 (62%)	161,447 (67%)	128,729 (58%)	117,780 (55%)
I			15,771 (7%)	

4 Christopher H. Smith (R)

Of Hamilton Square — Elected 1980

Born: March 4, 1953, Rahway, N.J.
Education: Trenton State College, B.A. 1975.
Occupation: Sporting goods wholesaler.
Family: Wife, Marie Hahn; four children.
Religion: Roman Catholic.
Political Career: Republican nominee for U.S. House, 1978.
Capitol Office: 2440 Rayburn Bldg. 20515; 225-3765.

In Washington: Smith has established himself as one of the more moderate House Republicans, with a strongly pro-labor voting record, a special zeal for federal spending programs benefiting children and veterans, and an overriding interest in human rights issues. These positions have made Smith politically secure in the largely urban and industrial 4th District — confounding those who recognize him only for his hard-line activism against abortion.

When Smith, then 27, won his House seat in 1980, he was derided by Democrats as a fluke, a New Right crusader swept in on President Reagan's coattails over a scandal-tainted Democratic veteran. But as Smith settled in and made the seat his own, he proved to have much more extensive legislative interests than just the abortion issue that had driven him to politics in the first place.

Smith defines his "pro-life" politics broadly enough to include such issues as immunizing children in the Third World and promoting adoption of babies born to American fathers and Asian mothers. Since the 99th Congress, Smith has carried out his humanitarian agenda as a member of the Foreign Affairs Committee.

Most other Republican members of that panel spend considerable time in ideological debate with liberal Democrats over U.S. aid to anti-communist insurgents. Smith has played a lower-profile role on these hot-button issues, concentrating instead on building a legislative record on causes ranging from child health to human rights.

One of Smith's priorities is the Child Survival Fund, a U.S. program that provides funds for immunization of children in poor countries against serious illnesses. In the 99th Congress, Smith persuaded the Foreign Affairs Committee to authorize $125 million over a two-year period, even though the Reagan administration did not initially recommend any money for the fund. In the 100th Congress, Smith secured an even larger sum, $170 million over two years.

Smith's advocacy for the Peace Corps on Foreign Affairs earned him that agency's "Leadership for Peace" award in 1989. In the 100th Congress, Smith successfully attached his proposal increasing funding for the Peace Corps as an amendment to a foreign aid authorization.

As these measures indicate, Smith has proved skillful at promoting his initiatives as amendments to foreign aid bills, the only real legislative vehicles available to a member of that panel. Smith sees the amendment process as the most efficient way to get legislation moved, even if he has to sacrifice credit for authorship. "It's a faster and more certain way to generate a law," he told a Trenton newspaper in 1988.

Smith has also become an active member of the Foreign Affairs Subcommittee on Human Rights. He serves as a member of the Commission on Security and Cooperation in Europe, a human rights watchdog organization better-known as the Helsinki commission.

Like other Foreign Affairs Republicans, Smith frequently expresses his contempt for the Soviet Union's human rights record, and has called on the Soviets to provide emigration rights to Jewish "refuseniks" and freedom to worship for Christian victims of religious persecution. But he is also critical of rightist regimes he views as violative of human rights, a position that often places him in league with members across the aisle. In both the 99th and 100th Congresses, Smith was one of a handful of GOP members on Foreign Affairs to support legislation invoking economic sanctions against the white-minority government of South Africa.

The South Africa issue is certainly not the only one on which Smith bucked the Reagan administration. In 1987, Smith voted against Reagan's position on House legislation 62 percent of the time, the sixth-highest opposition score among House Republicans. His pro-labor voting record earned Smith a 100 percent rating from the AFL-CIO in 1988.

But his economic liberalism and foreign affairs moderation has had no effect on Smith's staunch opposition to abortion. The co-chairman of the Congressional Pro-Life Caucus, Smith applauded in early 1989 when the U.S. Supreme Court agreed to hear a Missouri case

New Jersey 4

Central — Trenton

"Trenton Makes, the World Takes" is the motto of the city that forms the core of the 4th. While many state-capital cities now boast of their post-industrial economies based on professional employment, Trenton — which produces metal products, pharmaceuticals, auto parts and electrical wiring — still emphasizes its blue-collar heritage.

Trenton is 45 percent black, and blacks have begun to advance in local political offices. But Italian-Americans, clustered in the Chambersburg section of town, have retained a large share of political power.

With just over 90,000 residents, Trenton retains its standing as the district's largest city, but just barely. While Trenton's population has dropped slightly, the suburbs of Hamilton Township have boomed; its population stood at 87,000 in 1986.

Their solid base in industrial Trenton enables Democrats to carry Mercer County in most competitive statewide elections. Democratic presidential candidate Michael S. Dukakis edged out George Bush there in 1988, and Democratic Sen. Frank R. Lautenberg carried the county by more than 30,000 votes in his contest with Republican Pete Dawkins.

However, the suburban growth outside Trenton, combined with the Republican leanings in the exurban areas of Burlington, Middlesex, Monmouth and Ocean counties that make up the balance of the district, have given the 4th an overall GOP tilt in recent elections. Ronald Reagan carried the district twice; Bush won there with 56 percent of the vote.

Population: 526,080. White 442,773 (80%), Black 69,793 (13%), Other 5,627 (1%). Spanish origin 15,153 (3%). 18 and over 379,038 (72%), 65 and over 58,139 (11%). Median age: 32.

that challenged the 1973 *Roe v. Wade* decision legalizing abortion.

"Real progress is being achieved," Smith said. Pointing to 1988 legislation he supported — which threatened the cutoff of federal funds to the District of Columbia if any federal money was used by the city to subsidize abortions — Smith said the nation was viewing "the incremental dismantling of *Roe*."

Smith has also used his position on Foreign Affairs to take the anti-abortion cause worldwide. Criticizing China for stringent population-control policies that he said promoted infanticide, Smith won passage in the 98th Congress of an amendment denying U.S. funds for programs that support population control in China. He also has pushed for a cutoff of all American contributions to international family-planning agencies operating in countries that promote infanticide or forced abortion.

Smith has thus vexed colleagues of both parties at various junctures of his House career: His pro-life activities antagonize liberal Democrats, while his independence from Republican administration policy on other issues draws him sidelong glances from some fellow Republicans. However, in his other major field of legislative endeavor, Smith joins in the bipartisan consensus in favor of veterans' programs.

As ranking Republican on the Veterans' Affairs Subcommittee on Education, Training and Employment, Smith is a strong advocate of the educational programs for veterans under the GI Bill. Also a member of the subcommittee dealing with veterans' hospitals and health care, Smith helped obtain a Veterans Administration outpatient clinic for central New Jersey.

At the start of the 101st Congress, Smith was also active in unsuccessful efforts by the New Jersey delegation to get Congress to reverse the recommendation by the presidential military base-closing commission severely restricting operations at the Army's Fort Dix.

While his colleagues emphasized the economic impact on surrounding communities, Smith underlined the possibility that the shutdown could lead to termination of the Army's contract with New Jersey, which allowed the state to house up to 533 convicts in a base facility. "The confusion over Fort Dix's future ... may result in dumping over 500 inmates on a correctional system already operating beyond its capacity," Smith said.

At Home: There was a widespread belief after Smith's original victory that his win was a temporary happenstance. But Smith became ensconced in the 4th with surprising ease, demolishing Democratic hopes of recapturing a district that was long theirs.

Smith's diligent constituent work and well-run campaigns were important, but the secret of his success was his unexpectedly moderate voting record. Though steadfast in the anti-abortion activism that drew him into politics, his attention to the interests of blue-collar workers and organized labor gave Smith considerable crossover appeal.

Smith had ousted 13-term Democrat Frank Thompson Jr. in 1980 solely because of Thompson's involvement in Abscam. In 1978, as a political novice running almost exclusively on his contacts in the right-to-life movement, Smith had failed to draw even 40 percent against Thompson. On the second try, after Thompson's bribery indictment, Smith won every major town in the 4th except Trenton.

Though he defeated Thompson by a substantial margin, Smith was viewed as certain to fall victim in 1982 to Democrat Joseph P. Merlino, the former president of the New Jersey Senate. As it turned out, Merlino came across in areas outside Trenton as a gruff, horse-trading pol. After one debate, when Smith approached him to exchange pleasantries, Merlino growled, "Beat it, kid." Smith made the most of Merlino's image problem; one of his television spots simply showed a lit cigar in an ashtray.

Two years later, the Democrats tried again with a protégé of Merlino, former Mercer County Freeholder James C. Hedden. Unlike his mentor, Hedden took Smith seriously. He campaigned extensively door-to-door, accusing his opponent of being obsessed with abortion.

But Smith, who picked up new, marginally GOP areas and lost some Democratic territory in a court-ordered remap, had used his second term further to cultivate constituents. He carried Mercer County by double his 1982 margin, and ran ahead everywhere else, winning districtwide with 61 percent of the vote.

The 1986 Democratic nominee was Jeffrey Laurenti, a researcher for a New York City public-affairs foundation. Laurenti, who lost the 1984 primary to Hedden, campaigned persistently, continuing the Democratic theme that Smith was, at heart, a right-winger. But Smith played up his moderate House voting record, dismissed Laurenti as an extreme liberal, and won again with 61 percent.

The 1988 campaign underlined Smith's evolution into the district's dominant political figure. He defeated Betty Holland, the wife of veteran Trenton Mayor Arthur Holland, by a 2-to-1 margin. En route to that re-election, Smith was endorsed by a local of the United Auto Workers, a testament to his liaison with district unions.

Committees

Foreign Affairs (9th of 18 Republicans)
Europe and the Middle East; Human Rights and International Organizations

Select Aging (10th of 27 Republicans)
Health and Long-Term Care

Select Hunger (11th of 12 Republicans)

Veterans' Affairs (5th of 13 Republicans)
Education, Training and Employment (ranking); Hospitals and Health Care

Elections

1988 General

Christopher H. Smith (R)	155,283	(66%)
Betty Holland (D)	79,006	(33%)

1986 General

Christopher H. Smith (R)	78,699	(61%)
Jeffrey Laurenti (D)	49,290	(38%)

Previous Winning Percentages: 1984 (61%) **1982** (53%) **1980** (57%)

District Vote For President

	1988	1984	1980	1976
D	110,261 (44%)	98,386 (41%)	88,317 (41%)	104,217 (50%)
R	139,123 (56%)	141,308 (59%)	105,443 (49%)	99,564 (48%)
I			17,937 (8%)	

Campaign Finance

	Receipts	Receipts from PACs	Expend-itures
1988			
Smith (R)	$329,835	$124,781 (38%)	$252,823
Holland (D)	$55,145	$1,658 (3%)	$53,964
1986			
Smith (R)	$324,732	$98,850 (30%)	$338,244
Laurenti (D)	$333,243	$74,749 (22%)	$304,077

Key Votes

1987	
Raise speed limit to 65 mph	N
Approve Gephardt "fair trade" amendment	Y
Ban testing of larger nuclear weapons	Y
Delay "re-flagging" of Kuwaiti tankers	N
Approve tax-raising deficit-reduction bill	N
1988	
Approve aid to Nicaraguan contras	Y
Enact civil rights restoration bill over Reagan veto	Y
Kill 60-day plant-closing notification measure	N
Pass omnibus trade bill over Reagan veto	Y
Approve death penalty for drug-related murders	N
Bar federal funds for abortions in cases of rape and incest	Y
Oppose seven-day waiting period for purchase of handguns	N

Voting Studies

	Presidential Support		Party Unity		Conservative Coalition	
Year	**S**	**O**	**S**	**O**	**S**	**O**
1988	40	59	44	53	68	32
1987	38	62	39	59	77	23
1986	46	54	32	66	60	40
1985	45	55	43	53	55	44
1984	56	44	45	48	63	37
1983	50	50	44	56	60	39
1982	49	51	41	57	52	47
1981	64	36	65	35	67	33

Interest Group Ratings

Year	ADA	ACU	AFL-CIO	CCUS
1988	60	48	100	43
1987	52	39	81	53
1986	45	45	93	33
1985	65	52	88	41
1984	45	43	69	50
1983	40	48	53	40
1982	50	41	75	57
1981	40	87	40	79

5 Marge Roukema (R)

Of Ridgewood — Elected 1980

Born: Sept. 19, 1929, West Orange, N.J.

Education: Montclair State College, B.A. 1951, graduate work, 1951-53; Rutgers U., 1975.

Occupation: High school government and history teacher.

Family: Husband, Richard Roukema; two children.

Religion: Protestant.

Political Career: Ridgewood Board of Education, 1970-73; Republican nominee for U.S. House, 1978.

Capitol Office: 303 Cannon Bldg. 20515; 225-4465.

In Washington: When labor issues are the topic, the Education and Labor Committee is a cauldron of some of the most entrenched partisanship in the House. There, pro-labor Democrats wage battle with pro-business Republicans over upgrading work-place conditions and employees' benefits. On a panel with little middle ground, Roukema tries to stake out territory as a compromiser.

It is a role that wins her few friends among her conservative GOP colleagues, and precious few legislative victories. More often than not, her efforts at achieving bipartisan consensus on Education and Labor — or on the Labor-Management Relations Subcommittee, where she is ranking Republican — are rebuffed by Democrats and Republicans alike. But Roukema occasionally finds reward for her work at other stages in the legislative process.

One saga of Roukema's tough luck on Education and Labor has come in the committee's perennial debate on parental (or "family") leave, which Roukema calls a "bedrock family issue." In the 100th Congress (after failing in the 99th), Labor-Management Relations Chairman William L. Clay sponsored a parental-leave bill along with Colorado Democrat Patricia Schroeder in the House and Connecticut Democrat Christopher J. Dodd in the Senate. It required employers to grant unpaid leave to new parents, disabled workers and those needed at home to care for a seriously ill child.

The majority sentiment of committee Republicans toward the measure was summed up by Texan Dick Armey, who described himself as "unalterably opposed." Roukema voiced support for the concept of "family leave," but said the Democrats' bill would place an intolerable burden on small companies. She offered a substitute in the Labor-Management Relations Subcommittee that would have decreased the amount of time allowed for parental and disability leave.

Clay said that while he was open to compromise, Roukema's bill went too far. "I hope I'm not going to be bludgeoned from both the left and the right," Roukema said. But the subcommittee rejected her substitute by voice vote, with hers as the only voice in support.

Subsequently, Clay and Schroeder made some compromises that prompted Roukema to support the bill in full committee. But only liberal James M. Jeffords of Vermont broke GOP ranks to vote with her. The measure never reached the House floor. Early in the 101st Congress, Roukema, Clay and Dodd reintroduced the bill.

Roukema has also come up short trying to attain bipartisan harmony on another recurring Education and Labor initiative: enacting legislation aimed at stopping the practice known as "double breasting," whereby unionized construction firms set up separate companies to perform similar work on a non-union basis.

In the 100th Congress, Roukema and Texas Republican Steve Bartlett led the opposition to the Democratic bill, labeling the measure compulsory unionism. Roukema said the bill was too broad, but the subcommittee rejected her substitute by voice vote. The bill passed the House, but died in the Senate, just as it had in the 99th Congress.

On two other matters handled by the committee, polygraph testing and plant-closing notification, Roukema's position ultimately prevailed. On the bill to restrict most private employers from making workers take a lie-detector test as a condition of employment, Roukema's amendments to allow polygraph tests in selected businesses were turned back. But when the bill reached the House floor, her amendment to permit certain security firms to use lie-detector tests was adopted, 210-209; it was one of only two amendments to the bill approved in 11 hours of floor debate.

On the plant-closing bill, Roukema warned committee Democrats that their goals — to require employers to give up to six months' notice of a plant closing or layoff, and consult with employees and local officials — would encounter the same fate it did in the 99th Congress. Then, a business coalition led by the

New Jersey 5

North and West — Ridgewood

In the 98th Congress, Roukema's district was an ungainly flight of cartographic fancy dubbed "the Swan." Her current territory is still extensive, but no longer quite the affront to tidiness it once was.

The 5th runs from river to river along the New York border, from the wealthy Bergen County suburbs fronting the Hudson to the back country of the Delaware Water Gap in Sussex County.

Its political complexion is a matter of shades of Republicanism. In 1988, Roukema's winning percentages ranged from 74 percent in Bergen County to 82 percent in Sussex.

Along the Delaware in Sussex County, one finds rural values, farming and a deep-seated suspicion of government. Close to the New York border, the terrain is mountainous and even less populous, with old vacation homes scattered among small lakes. The Ramapo Mountains extend into upper Passaic County, where a back-country group long known as the "Jackson Whites" lives in cultural isolation. They are descendants of miners, a symbol of the old Ringwood ironworks that made cannonballs for the American Revolutionary War.

Although both Sussex and Passaic bid to become New Jersey's next boom area as commuters move out along Route 80, Bergen County has the district's most important single voting bloc. Two-thirds of the vote is cast there. The Bergen towns are politically well organized and Republican voters are active in helping local candidates. Bergen's reputation as New Jersey's banner Republican county comes from the large turnout its northern section produces. Still, this part of the district is more moderate than either Sussex or Passaic; a candidate cannot move too far to the right without risking a loss of support.

Affluent Upper Bergen communities such as Alpine, Tenafly and Norwood are filled with business executives who commute to New York or to the county's many corporate offices.

Population: 526,076. White 509,409 (97%), Black 4,884 (1%), Other 9,483 (2%). Spanish origin 10,082 (2%). 18 and over 377,765 (72%), 65 and over 52,981 (10%). Median age: 33.

U.S. Chamber of Commerce worked to kill the bill; the House rejected it by 203-208.

In the 100th Congress, Roukema offered a substitute eliminating the consultation requirement — especially troubling to business — and requiring only a 60-day notice. Clay dismissed her substitute as too weak, and the committee rejected it 10-22. But when plant-closing legislation reached the floor nearly a year later as part of the omnibus trade bill, the Senate had agreed to a 60-day notice period without a consultation requirement. Still, Roukema voted to strip the measure from the trade bill; she later voted for the separate plant-closing bill that became law.

Roukema also sits on the Banking Committee; one of her most determined efforts there in the 100th Congress was scrapping some of the federal programs for the homeless and sending the money to state and local governments in the form of block grants. Her plan met resistance on the Housing Subcommittee, where she is ranking Republican; on the full committee, which rejected it 19-30; and on the floor, where it was ultimately quashed, 203-215.

On about two in three floor votes, Roukema sides with the majority of House Republicans. But those on the party's right wing view her askance because of her moderate outlook on certain high-profile issues and her readiness to seek compromise on hard-fought labor-business battles. Also, some of Roukema's recent political choices have not endeared her to the GOP right. She signed on to manage the gubernatorial campaign of former New Jersey Attorney General Cary Edwards, a moderate Republican running against Roukema's conservative House colleague, Jim Courter. And when several moderate Northeastern Republican women were earning publicity for endorsing conservative Newt Gingrich's candidacy for GOP whip in 1989, Roukema backed the more moderate Edward Madigan of Illinois.

Roukema has also devoted time to the Select Committee on Hunger, where she was ranking Republican from its creation in 1984 through the 100th Congress. When the panel was set up, many Republicans feared that Democratic Chairman Mickey Leland of Texas would use it to charge the Reagan administration with ignoring hunger in America. Roukema herself voted against creating the panel, but as a member she worked closely with Leland and sought to protect the committee's funding.

One of the few women in the House who does not belong to the Congressional Caucus for Women's Issues, Roukema nonetheless has been active in women's affairs. She successfully pushed for passage of a bill designed to collect delinquent payments for child support. She gave a passionate speech in 1988 denouncing the successful effort to bar the District of Columbia from financing abortions. The amendment, sponsored by California Republican Robert K. Dornan, made her "irate," Roukema said. "Members of Congress should not tell women what their choice should be" on abortions, she said.

At Home: Roukema struggled to wrest a seat from a Democratic incumbent in 1980. But redistricting gave her a constituency that is content with moderate GOP representation.

The Democratic Legislature's 1981 remap paired her with fellow Republican Jim Courter, but Courter moved to the 12th. Roukema then coasted in 1982 against Democratic lawyer Fritz Cammerzell. In 1984, a second redistricting plan gave her a more compact but equally Republican district. Roukema won 71 percent.

Two years later, Roukema had to work harder in the primary than in the general election. Her GOP opponent, conservative businessman Bill Grant, accused Roukema of being too liberal, especially on defense, and voting too often against Reagan. But Roukema easily dismissed Grant's challenge. She went on to defeat a little-known Democrat by a 3-to-1 margin, a feat she repeated in 1988.

Elections were much more difficult for Roukema in her original House district. The old 7th was less Republican, and she had to run twice there to unseat liberal Democrat Andrew Maguire. In 1978, her first challenge, she lost by only 8,815 votes. A former teacher returning to politics five years after leaving the Ridgewood Board of Education, she attacked Maguire for being "anti-defense."

In 1980, she focused on complaints that Maguire, a critic of big oil companies during the 1979 gasoline shortage, was anti-business. With a strong Reagan showing in northern New Jersey, she won by nearly 10,000 votes.

Committees

Banking, Finance and Urban Affairs (6th of 20 Republicans)
Housing and Community Development (ranking); Economic Stabilization; Financial Institutions Supervision, Regulation and Insurance

Education and Labor (4th of 13 Republicans)
Labor-Management Relations (ranking); Elementary, Secondary and Vocational Education; Postsecondary Education

Select Hunger (2nd of 12 Republicans)
Task Force: Domestic

Elections

1988 General

Marge Roukema (R)	175,562	(76%)
Lee Monaco (D)	54,828	(24%)

1986 General

Marge Roukema (R)	94,253	(75%)
H. Vernon Jolley (D)	32,145	(25%)

Previous Winning Percentages: 1984 (71%) **1982** (65%) **1980** (51%)

District Vote For President

	1988	1984	1980	1976
D	73,330 (33%)	75,000 (29%)	67,719 (27%)	88,261 (35%)
R	146,095 (66%)	182,030 (71%)	150,854 (61%)	163,146 (64%)
I			24,589 (10%)	

Campaign Finance

	Receipts	Receipts from PACs	Expenditures
1988			
Roukema (R)	$406,465	$181,513 (45%)	$400,555
Monaco (D)	$28,134	$1,280 (5%)	$28,137
1986			
Roukema (R)	$357,780	$156,837 (44%)	$304,786
Jolley (D)	$38,941	$3,050 (8%)	$23,139

Key Votes

1987	
Raise speed limit to 65 mph	N
Approve Gephardt "fair trade" amendment	N
Ban testing of larger nuclear weapons	N
Delay "re-flagging" of Kuwaiti tankers	N
Approve tax-raising deficit-reduction bill	N
1988	
Approve aid to Nicaraguan contras	Y
Enact civil rights restoration bill over Reagan veto	Y
Kill 60-day plant-closing notification measure	Y
Pass omnibus trade bill over Reagan veto	Y
Approve death penalty for drug-related murders	Y
Bar federal funds for abortions in cases of rape and incest	N
Oppose seven-day waiting period for purchase of handguns	N

Voting Studies

	Presidential Support		Party Unity		Conservative Coalition	
Year	S	O	S	O	S	O
1988	42	55	68	28	79	21
1987	45	51	61	36	70	28
1986	56	43	62	26	64	36
1985	49	50	56	41	60	40
1984	51	45	57	38	56	42
1983	61	35	49	47	47	51
1982	62	34	57	39	60	37
1981	66	32	70	29	56	41

Interest Group Ratings

Year	ADA	ACU	AFL-CIO	CCUS
1988	40	50	79	69
1987	36	52	38	87
1986	30	36	43	78
1985	45	40	29	68
1984	45	36	15	63
1983	40	30	18	80
1982	50	41	30	68
1981	35	80	27	89

6 Bernard J. Dwyer (D)

Of Edison — Elected 1980

Born: Jan. 24, 1921, Perth Amboy, N.J.
Education: Attended Rutgers U.
Military Career: Navy, 1940-45.
Occupation: Insurance salesman and executive.
Family: Wife, Lilyan Sudzina; one child.
Religion: Roman Catholic.
Political Career: Edison Township Council, 1958-69; mayor of Edison, 1969-73; N.J. Senate, 1974-80, majority leader, 1980.
Capitol Office: 2428 Rayburn Bldg. 20515; 225-6301.

In Washington: Elected to Congress at age 59 after decades of loyal service to the Middlesex County Democratic organization, Dwyer quickly earned the confidence of his party's leadership in the House. But he is so low-key that, after eight years in Congress, his tracks are invisible to all but his closest committee colleagues.

The leadership's confidence is written all over Dwyer's résumé. He has won an array of committee assignments that only a trusted insider could compile — Appropriations, Intelligence, Budget and ethics.

Dwyer decided as a freshman to try for the seat on Appropriations that had been held by his Democratic predecessor, Edward J. Patten. Several first-term members were competing for the single freshman opening on the panel, but Dwyer was the one whose background virtually guaranteed that he would deliver his vote when the leadership asked.

In the years since, the Democratic hierarchy has not been disappointed. Dwyer has supported his party majority at least 90 percent of the time every year since coming to Congress; in 1985, only one Democrat voted with the party more often.

He won another plum in the 99th Congress, when he expressed interest in a seat on the Intelligence Committee. Speaker Thomas P. O'Neill Jr. put him on after being lobbied on Dwyer's behalf by a mutual friend, Joseph D. Early of Massachusetts.

Dwyer sat on the ethics committee when it faced its most politically sensitive task: The 1988-89 investigation of House Speaker Jim Wright, which led to the Speaker's June 1989 resignation. Early in the panel's deliberations, Dwyer put himself in a political crucible when he was one of two Democrats to join committee Republicans in a key vote against Wright.

Throughout his House career, Dwyer's legislative focus has been local. In the 100th Congress, he won $6 million for beach restoration at New Jersey's Sandy Hook. He has gone to bat more than once for Rutgers, the New Jersey state university that is in his district. In 1984, he worked to make sure that the university's medical school would be eligible for funding for a library.

At Home: Dwyer was known in the New Jersey Senate as a legislative tactician who avoided the public spotlight and preferred behind-the-scenes maneuvering.

His most notable individual accomplishments attracted little public attention. Dwyer pushed through a ban on state government purchase of imported cars and a $50 million bond issue to weatherize state buildings. Much of his work was done at the Joint Appropriations Committee, which he chaired at one point during his Senate career.

In his 1980 campaign to succeed Patten, Dwyer ran with a confidence born of solid party support, particularly in Middlesex County with its powerful Democratic organization. Dwyer's work and familiarity as a state legislator also helped him sweep the endorsements of the district's leading newspapers. He finished atop a five-candidate primary field, and won 53 percent of the general-election vote.

Dwyer had little trouble in his first re-election campaign. But in 1984 he came up against a vigorous opponent and new district lines that included several GOP towns in Monmouth County. Republican Dennis Adams charged that Dwyer was a Democratic leadership tool who was betraying his mainly conservative constituents; the incumbent slipped under 60 percent of the vote.

The result, as it turned out, was not a real signal of vulnerability. Dwyer won going away against a less active Republican foe in 1986, and he was still above 60 percent in 1988, against GOP Mayor Peter J. Sica of Carteret.

Dwyer has won easily even though he is something of a holdout from the era of escalating campaign costs. In 1988, he spent just over $120,000 on his campaign, far less than any other active New Jersey incumbent.

New Jersey 6

Central — New Brunswick; Perth Amboy

Exxon's giant Bayway refinery, with its flaring gas and oppressive stench, is responsible for much of New Jersey's image problem. Travelers seeing the refinery from the turnpike wonder why anyone would live near it. But thousands of the 6th's voters do. They are predominantly white ethnics and Hispanics, many of them within sight and smell of the refinery complex.

The 6th extends for miles beyond the refinery and the turnpike. Covering most of industrial Middlesex County, it traditionally has favored Democrats, whose organization is one of the few strong county machines left in the state. In his 1988 reelection bid, Democratic Sen. Frank R. Lautenberg carried the 6th with 56 percent.

The 1988 county results for president indicate that those Democratic tendencies no longer apply at the top of the ticket. George Bush took Middlesex with 57 percent, nearly matching President Reagan's 59 percent four years earlier. But the more exurban sections of Middlesex are in the 4th and 12th districts; the sections in the 6th, closest to New York City, are more industrial, have more minority-group residents, and are more dependably Democratic.

Middlesex is a place where heavy things are made. The closer one gets to the Arthur Kill, separating New Jersey and Staten Island, the heavier and dirtier the industry becomes. Bleak Perth Amboy, over 40 percent Hispanic, illustrates the economic problems troubling this industrial belt. A Canadian company opened a steel plant there in 1977, but ensuing layoffs dashed hopes it would spark a resurgence.

The presence of Rutgers University and a one-quarter black population keep New Brunswick reliably Democratic. Though parts of the city are faded, Johnson & Johnson led an effort to revitalize New Brunswick several years ago by building its new headquarters in the middle of downtown.

Population: 526,075. White 459,480 (87%), Black 44,718 (9%), Other 8,690 (2%). Spanish origin 34,643 (7%). 18 and over 394,413 (75%), 65 and over 51,841 (10%). Median age: 31.

Committees

Appropriations (26th of 35 Democrats)
Commerce, Justice and State, the Judiciary and Related Agencies; Labor, Health and Human Services, Education and Related Agencies

Budget (17th of 21 Democrats)
Task Forces: Budget Process, Reconciliation and Enforcement; Community Development and Natural Resources

Select Intelligence (6th of 12 Democrats)
Oversight and Evaluation; Program and Budget Authorization

Standards of Official Conduct (3rd of 6 Democrats)

Elections

1988 General		
Bernard J. Dwyer (D)	120,125	(61%)
Peter J. Sica (R)	74,824	(38%)
1986 General		
Bernard J. Dwyer (D)	67,460	(69%)
John D. Scalamonti (R)	28,286	(29%)

Previous Winning Percentages: **1984** (56%) **1982** (68%) **1980** (53%)

District Vote For President

	1988		1984		1980		1976	
D	100,931	(47%)	94,024	(41%)	90,536	(42%)	110,702	(52%)
R	115,055	(53%)	135,654	(59%)	105,490	(49%)	97,129	(46%)
I					14,110	(7%)		

Campaign Finance

	Receipts	Receipts from PACs	Expend-itures
1988			
Dwyer (D)	$136,330	$113,000 (83%)	$123,632
Sica (R)	$39,483	0	$38,919
1986			
Dwyer (D)	$144,564	$106,325 (74%)	$115,192
Scalamonti (R)	$18,594	$564 (3%)	$18,461

Key Votes

1987	
Raise speed limit to 65 mph	N
Approve Gephardt "fair trade" amendment	Y
Ban testing of larger nuclear weapons	Y
Delay "re-flagging" of Kuwaiti tankers	?
Approve tax-raising deficit-reduction bill	Y
1988	
Approve aid to Nicaraguan contras	N
Enact civil rights restoration bill over Reagan veto	Y
Kill 60-day plant-closing notification measure	N
Pass omnibus trade bill over Reagan veto	Y
Approve death penalty for drug-related murders	N
Bar federal funds for abortions in cases of rape and incest	N
Oppose seven-day waiting period for purchase of handguns	N

Voting Studies

	Presidential Support		Party Unity		Conservative Coalition	
Year	**S**	**O**	**S**	**O**	**S**	**O**
1988	21	75	92	7	32	66
1987	19	77	90	4	35	60
1986	19	80	95	3	22	78
1985	25	75	97	2	18	82
1984	37	60	91	7	24	75
1983	22	76	93	4	17	82
1982	39	57	94	5	22	78
1981	41	57	93	5	16	83

Interest Group Ratings

Year	ADA	ACU	AFL-CIO	CCUS
1988	85	4	100	31
1987	84	0	100	7
1986	80	9	100	22
1985	80	0	100	23
1984	75	13	92	38
1983	85	9	100	25
1982	90	0	90	27
1981	75	7	93	22

7 Matthew J. Rinaldo (R)

Of Union — Elected 1972

Born: Sept. 1, 1931, Elizabeth, N.J.
Education: Rutgers U., B.S. 1953; Seton Hall U., M.B.A. 1959; New York U., D.P.A. 1979.
Occupation: Industrial relations consultant.
Family: Single.
Religion: Roman Catholic.
Political Career: Union County Board of Freeholders, 1963-64; N.J. Senate, 1968-72.
Capitol Office: 2469 Rayburn Bldg. 20515; 225-5361.

In Washington: Rinaldo is a cautious man. He is wary of straying from his script even in informal settings, and rarely makes an important move without making sure it will play in Union County. But if his solicitous style disqualifies Rinaldo from being regarded as a legislative powerhouse, it has also given him a toehold in areas where Republicans are not often players.

Rinaldo's "New Jersey first" record — which more often than not requires him to vote in opposition to a majority of GOP House members — has helped him build a strong following in his district's urban Democratic areas. And his willingness to work with Democrats has made him a relatively productive member of the Energy and Commerce Committee, where less yielding Republicans are confined to mere nay-saying.

Unlike some other moderate Republicans, Rinaldo has largely been spared criticism within the GOP for his renegade record. His state party embraces moderates, and in Congress, Rinaldo's insistence that he is just "voting New Jersey" gives him cover with most GOP partisans. But Rinaldo's sensitivity to the shifting winds of constituent opinion can prove frustrating to those looking for a commitment. Rinaldo is a hard man to pin down; he likes to keep his options open until the last moment.

When Energy and Commerce debated nuclear-accident liability legislation in 1987, liberals on the committee pushed a controversial amendment to pay victims before utility lawyers if damage from a nuclear disaster exceeded a $7 billion compensation fund. Rinaldo kept silent until the last moment, and then surprised panel members by voting for the amendment, which passed narrowly. But a week later, the committee reconsidered the victims' compensation proposal, and this time, Rinaldo was one of three members to switch his vote, which led to the proposal's defeat.

Rinaldo has done his most significant legislative work at the Commerce Subcommittee on Telecommunications and Finance, where he serves as ranking member. His moderate views on government regulation of the securities industry allow him to work comfortably with Chairman Edward J. Markey on most issues.

In the wake of insider-trading scandals on Wall Street, Rinaldo shared the majority view that stronger enforcement and stiffer penalties were needed to prevent abuses by those with non-public information. He was among the sponsors of legislation to put new demands on firms to police the activities of their employees. Congress enacted this concept as well as language that Rinaldo advocated to commission a special study of federal securities laws to determine what changes could be made to protect stock market investors.

Rinaldo is far more responsive to the interests of organized labor than the average Republican. In 1988 he rated a 100 percent approval score from the AFL-CIO. When the Finance Subcommittee debated legislation to eliminate abuses in corporate takeovers, Rinaldo focused more on protecting workers than stockholders. Together with Norman F. Lent, ranking Republican on the full committee, he crafted a bill that would require purchasers to state the potential impact of a takeover on the firm's employees and location of its plants.

In the 100th Congress he was one of only 29 Republicans to vote against eliminating language on the omnibus trade bill requiring companies to give advance notice of plant closings. He was also one of just 17 Republicans to vote for the Gephardt "fair trade" amendment, which sought to mandate retaliatory tariffs against countries with unfair trade practices. It was ultimately dropped from the trade bill.

Trade issues have helped earn Rinaldo media attention at home. In 1988, he invited a top Japanese diplomat to appear on his cable TV show to discuss trade, and then spent much of the 30-minute broadcast berating the official. This prompted an angry phone call from the Japanese Embassy to Rinaldo's office, but no apology.

During the Telecommunications Subcommittee debate on children's television — which critics say has declined in quality and quantity

New Jersey 7

North and Central — Elizabeth

Anchored by blue-collar Elizabeth and Plainfield, the 7th is a district Democrats have every reason to covet. But votes from the suburbs outside those two grimy industrial cities make it difficult for Democratic candidates to win.

Elizabeth found its place on the 19th-century industrial map as a manufacturing town for Singer Sewing Machines, and it became an ethnic, working-class city. Today, it retains an ethnic diversity reinforced by an infusion of blacks and Hispanics. It casts a fifth of the district vote, and in most elections is heavily Democratic.

The petrochemical industry and heavy manufacturing make Elizabeth a dingy place with a history of toxic-waste problems. The city is run by Democratic Mayor Tom Dunn, whose willingness to deal with GOP politicians, including President Reagan and Rinaldo, has not endeared him to the state's Democratic hierarchy. However, Dunn did back Democrat Michael S. Dukakis in the 1988 presidential election.

In the southwest corner of Union County is predominantly black Plainfield, which was the first of New Jersey's cities to explode in the summer of 1967. The city has recently mounted a major effort to rehabilitate its decaying areas.

Clustered between Elizabeth and Plainfield in northern Union County are mostly Republican, suburban towns such as Summit, Westfield and Cranford. This is an area of bedroom communities for Newark and New York. Liberal young professionals here frequently prefer Democrats for local office, but at the national level, the towns anchor the 7th's GOP vote.

For the most part, the Somerset County portion of the 7th is equally Republican. Nestled against the Watchung Mountains, affluent towns such as Watchung, Warren and Bridgewater Township give Democratic candidates scarcely a glance. The industrial boroughs to the south, however, Bound Brook and Manville, often join Elizabeth and Plainfield in voting Democratic.

Population: 526,076. White 449,916 (86%), Black 58,922 (11%), Other 7,084 (1%). Spanish origin 38,374 (7%). 18 and over 393,910 (75%), 65 and over 64,042 (12%). Median age: 35.

in the 1980s — it was Rinaldo who found the middle ground between those seeking to mandate one hour of children's educational programming per day and those wanting a temporary suspension of antitrust laws to allow broadcasters and advertisers to work out a solution on their own. Rinaldo's compromise plan, which cleared both the House and Senate, capped advertising time during children's programs. The bill was vetoed by President Reagan, but an identical version passed Energy and Commerce in early 1989.

Rinaldo often sides with environmentalist Democrats on Energy and Commerce. He has introduced his own legislation to restrict acid-rain pollution, and has pushed to have acid-rain controls and the "superfund" toxic-waste clean-up program included in the platform of the national Republican Party.

In addition to his duties on Energy and Commerce, Rinaldo serves as ranking Republican on the Select Aging Committee. He has long advocated establishing the Social Security Administration as a separate entity outside the Department of Health and Human Services.

At Home: Rinaldo is a traditional big-city neighborhood politician, and that helps explain his success in Union County's blue-collar bastions such as Elizabeth. Even though the 7th was drawn to be a Democratic district in 1982, he carried it handily against an aggressive, high-spending Democrat. Rinaldo then benefited from another remap before the 1984 election, which favored the GOP.

The ever-watchful Rinaldo seldom fails to make the rounds of weddings and testimonial dinners in his district, stroking the labor leaders who have political influence. He receives quiet help from Elizabeth Mayor Tom Dunn, a sympathetic Democrat who in 1984 backed Ronald Reagan for re-election, and while the Union County GOP organization is more conservative than Rinaldo, it has always been supportive.

Because of his reputation as a Republican who attracts Democrats, Rinaldo used to be mentioned as a possible candidate for governor or senator. But his caution always kept him from taking the plunge.

Rinaldo guaranteed himself a place in the hearts of the state GOP leadership in 1982. A congressional map drawn up by the Democratic Legislature threw his hometown of Union into the 12th District, a much safer Republican constituency than the 7th. Rinaldo agreed to run in the 7th as a favor to two other Republican incumbents, Jim Courter and Marge Roukema. Rinaldo's decision freed the 12th for Courter, and left Roukema alone and secure in the 5th.

By that act of generosity, Rinaldo also

guaranteed himself a tough re-election campaign. Adam K. Levin, former state consumer affairs director, had helped mold the new 7th with himself in mind as its congressman. The son of a multimillionaire shopping center developer, Levin had given copiously from his inherited wealth to the campaigns of Democratic legislators, and they remembered his gifts when drawing the congressional map.

Until 1982, Rinaldo never had won a House contest with less than 60 percent of the vote. In 1974, when Levin had made a first try at age 25, the Republican had crushed him.

It was clear from the beginning, however, that the second challenge was serious. The Democrat threw Rinaldo on the defensive with repeated personal attacks. Television ads lambasted Rinaldo for junketeering and accused him of being an ineffective legislator.

Far behind his challenger in campaign funds (one of the few incumbents in the country who was), Rinaldo did not run any TV spots. He retaliated against Levin by taking full advantage of his incumbency, deluging the new parts of the district with franked mailings, a batch of press releases and a mobile constituent-service van.

Rinaldo also benefited in Elizabeth from the help of Dunn, who disliked Levin. The Republican's longstanding support of union-backed legislation brought him endorsements from groups that normally stick with Democratic candidates, including the New Jersey AFL-CIO. In the end, Levin managed to win only the liberal Mercer County portion of the 7th.

Running within more favorable lines since the court-ordered second redistricting prior to his 1984 contest, Rinaldo has returned to his normal landslide margins. In the presidential years of 1984 and 1988, he won by better than 100,000 votes.

Committees

Select Aging (Ranking)
Health and Long-Term Care

Energy and Commerce (4th of 17 Republicans)
Telecommunications and Finance (ranking); Transportation and Hazardous Materials

Elections

1988 General

Matthew J. Rinaldo (R)	153,350	(75%)
James Hely (D)	52,189	(25%)

1986 General

Matthew J. Rinaldo (R)	92,254	(79%)
June S. Fischer (D)	24,462	(21%)

Previous Winning Percentages: **1984** (74%) **1982** (56%) **1980** (77%) **1978** (73%) **1976** (73%) **1974** (65%) **1972** (64%)

District Vote For President

	1988	1984	1980	1976
D	90,584 (41%)	88,874 (37%)	82,436 (36%)	87,131 (42%)
R	132,211 (59%)	151,973 (63%)	126,362 (55%)	116,182 (56%)
I			18,650 (8%)	

Campaign Finance

	Receipts	Receipts from PACs	Expend-itures
1988			
Rinaldo (R)	$607,728	$271,527 (45%)	$370,387
1986			
Rinaldo (R)	$630,990	$230,823 (37%)	$387,616
Fischer (D)	$12,213	$500 (4%)	$7,644

Key Votes

1987	
Raise speed limit to 65 mph	N
Approve Gephardt "fair trade" amendment	Y
Ban testing of larger nuclear weapons	N
Delay "re-flagging" of Kuwaiti tankers	N
Approve tax-raising deficit-reduction bill	N
1988	
Approve aid to Nicaraguan contras	Y
Enact civil rights restoration bill over Reagan veto	Y
Kill 60-day plant-closing notification measure	N
Pass omnibus trade bill over Reagan veto	Y
Approve death penalty for drug-related murders	Y
Bar federal funds for abortions in cases of rape and incest	Y
Oppose seven-day waiting period for purchase of handguns	N

Voting Studies

	Presidential Support		Party Unity		Conservative Coalition	
Year	**S**	**O**	**S**	**O**	**S**	**O**
1988	48	51	44	54	71	29
1987	41	59	40	57	65	35
1986	40	58	34	63	60	40
1985	50	45	43	51	71	29
1984	50	49	42	54	54	44
1983	46	51	36	61	53	44
1982	45	49	26	71	41	58
1981	63	33	58	39	71	28

Interest Group Ratings

Year	ADA	ACU	AFL-CIO	CCUS
1988	45	54	100	36
1987	56	39	88	47
1986	45	55	100	28
1985	55	52	81	41
1984	45	41	92	64
1983	65	41	82	21
1982	60	36	95	38
1981	20	71	47	84

8 Robert A. Roe (D)

Of Pompton Lakes — Elected 1969

Born: Feb. 28, 1924, Wayne, N.J.
Education: Attended Oregon State U. and Washington State U.
Military Career: Army, 1943-46.
Occupation: Construction company owner; engineer.
Family: Single.
Religion: Roman Catholic.
Political Career: Wayne Township committeeman, 1955-56; mayor of Wayne Township, 1956-61; Passaic County freeholder, 1959-63; sought Democratic nomination for governor, 1977 and 1981.
Capitol Office: 2243 Rayburn Bldg. 20515; 225-5751.

In Washington: After two decades in Congress, Roe is not only chairman of one committee, but also the unofficial leader of another. To both panels he brings an almost religious faith in the national benefits of massive public works, and a crusader's drive to spread them "from the sewers to the stars."

That phrase is how Roe described his ascent at the start of the 100th Congress from subcommittee chairman of the Public Works Committee's Water Resources panel, where he controlled the House spigot for any water projects, to full chairman of the Science and Technology Committee. In one of his first acts, Roe added "Space" to the committee's title to highlight its importance to his future agenda.

Subsequently, in just his second year as chairman, Roe was the subject of speculation among Public Works Democrats who hoped he would leave the Science chair to head Public Works after the death of Chairman James J. Howard, Roe's longtime ally from New Jersey. That would have meant ousting Glenn M. Anderson of California, the one man ahead of Roe in seniority on Public Works; Roe, loyal to Anderson and House tradition, urged his junior colleagues to give the unassertive Anderson a chance. Still, Roe is a dominant member of Public Works, the chairman-in-waiting.

Yet in no way has he treated Science as a waiting room. Though not especially active there before he became chairman, Roe has shown the same zeal and attention to detail that marked his tenure as Water Resources Subcommittee chairman.

He has begun mastering the science agencies' wish lists, and supporting most of the big-ticket items — a manned space station, space shuttles, overhaul of the nation's research labs, and the biggest proposed public works project ever, the superconducting supercollider for physics research. If colleagues have a complaint, it is that Roe is spreading a limited budget too thinly rather than choosing priorities. But just as with water projects, Roe takes an apocalyptic view that the nation cannot afford not to invest in space.

"The greatest threat facing this nation, short of nuclear war," he once said as Water Resources chairman, "is the destruction and poisoning of our water supply." As Science chairman, he believes his panel's work can salvage the nation's economy and its leadership in science and technology. He wants to double the science budget, an ambitious goal that runs counter to a growing space-vs.-butter debate pitting Roe against members who want to take from NASA to pay for earthbound social programs. "Do we have a confrontation in cost and budget? Yes, we do," Roe said in late 1987. "What we're doing is forcing that issue."

A bachelor who has called a motel room his home during two decades in Washington, Roe works long stretches of 16-hour days. He takes an almost pedagogical approach to his panel, referring to himself as "the chairman" or "we," insisting that members and witnesses stick to defined themes, summing up testimony and dismissing what he considers errant points. But he is responsive to his members, accommodating their requests for projects at home. He jealously guards his turf, and his strategy. Roe can be counted on to resist compromise until the last minute, a tactic that has not always been a winning one.

Above all, he does not tolerate the words commonly used to describe his work. "They use the word pork barrel and they use the word boondoggle," he complained in 1987. "The boondoggle is if you do not get it in your own state."

Roe hews to his party's New Deal tradition; he advocates public works as an economic boost and a force for progressive change. Pinched by deficits, Roe has been able to carry on partly due to the changing nature of public works. At Water Resources, the sewers and toxic-waste cleanups he espoused were popu-

New Jersey 8

North — Paterson

To Alexander Hamilton, the Great Falls of the Passaic River was an ideal location for a factory town. Then Treasury secretary, he set up the Society for Establishing Useful Manufactures in 1791 to build Paterson.

In time, the thriving "Silk City" became one of the world's leading textile producers, attracting Irish, Polish, Italian and Russian craftsmen to work the looms; Democratic Sen. Frank R. Lautenberg's father was a Paterson millworker. Paterson also played out a history of labor strife and strong unions whose influence lives on.

During the 1960s and '70s, though, Paterson tumbled into a sharp industrial decline which left a trail of unemployment and poverty, particularly among the blacks and Hispanics who now make up the majority of the city's population. Racial tensions also were palpable, particularly after the controversial 1967 case in which black boxer Rubin "Hurricane" Carter was found guilty for the murders of three white patrons in a local tavern.

During the last several years, Paterson's situation has stabilized somewhat; unemployment rates fell below double digits and population remained steady through the early 1980s. But Paterson continues to present a rough-edged image to the nation: Its best-known personage at present is Joe Clark, the baseball bat-wielding principal whose use of strong-arm tactics to regain control of his ghetto high school have been both praised and vilified.

Paterson still contains 25 percent of the district's electorate, and it is firmly Democratic. The Passaic County suburbs next to Paterson, such as Clifton, Totowa and West Paterson, are where the white ethnics went when they fled the city. They will still vote Democratic in most contests, but are showing signs of giving up their residual ties to the party. Down the Passaic River lies the city of Passaic, a smaller but equally troubled version of Paterson, whose textile employment also has evaporated.

To the north, the district is more Republican. Wayne Township houses the headquarters of American Cyanamid. Its subdivisions usually vote Republican but have made an exception for favorite-son Roe. The affluent Franklin Lakes area is the sole outpost of upper-crust Bergen County in the 8th District, and is rock-solid Republican.

The 8th also reaches south from Passaic into Essex County, where it picks up the politically mixed older suburbs of Montclair and Nutley. Affluent Montclair, with its mansions built as summer places by the 19th-century New York rich, blends quiet, tree-shaded streets and large frame houses with more modest homes and neighborhoods; the ethnic and class mix makes it more competitive politically than some of the other suburban territory in the 8th. Along with the Oranges, Montclair is a center of the Essex Democratic Party's liberal wing.

Population: 526,087. White 415,905 (79%), Black 72,054 (14%), Other 7,900 (2%). Spanish origin 64,546 (12%). 18 and over 390,558 (74%), 65 and over 67,534 (13%). Median age: 33.

larly defensible as environmental programs against foes, including President Reagan, who cried "pork." At Science, projects fit the vogue for high technology and international competitiveness.

In his first Congress as chairman, Roe oversaw NASA's revival of the space shuttle program. In 1986, he had presided over the panel's investigation of the *Challenger* explosion, and cast himself as the tough customer in a company town. "Congress and NASA must begin a new era," he said, "one in which Congress must apply the same strong oversight to NASA that it does to any other government agency."

He is intent on instituting multi-year budgeting for NASA. His insistence, over the objections of Senate counterpart Ernest F. Hollings (chairman of the Commerce, Science and Transportation panel), appeared to doom a bill reauthorizing the space agency. Finally, an 11th-hour compromise on Congress' last day in 1988 authorized $11 billion for fiscal 1989 only. Roe did win a three-year, $6 billion commitment to the space station and agreement that NASA would submit a long-term plan.

Another last-minute compromise cleared a bill Roe favored that limited private launch firms' liability in case of major accidents. It was a victory for the fledgling rocket industry, which Roe wants to promote. But he had held the bill hostage until he was sure the industry would not try to attach a provision blocking a U.S.-China deal to launch three private U.S. satellites on Chinese rockets. Roe supported the deal on diplomatic, economic and scientific grounds. When Sen. Jesse Helms, a China foe, tried to kill the deal with an amendment to a foreign aid bill, Roe worked feverishly to scrap Helms' amendment in the House. It was rejected by an overwhelming 23-234 vote.

He helped derail an administration plan to rent space on a private unmanned shuttle, fearing it would siphon funds from a manned space station. Also, Roe is a key advocate of the superconducting supercollider (SSC). Derided by some as a boondoggle for Texas, Roe says the project "will enable the United States to regain its world leadership in high-energy physics." Yet he does not always cloak his support in such hype. "It is a public works job," he said in 1989. "It's like building a great big dam. Anybody that doesn't understand that the SSC is 90 percent a public works project doesn't understand the process."

In the 100th Congress, Roe's committee was the source of one controversial measure that proved beyond his control. Republican Robert S. Walker amended bills for two science agencies with proposals to cut funding to departments and contractors not free of drugs in the work place. Roe could have killed the proposal outright but, accustomed to bipartisanship on his committees, he delayed debate, thinking Walker could be placated. Instead, the panel was stalemated for weeks, more bills were snagged and two rival committees demanded to review bills Walker amended. Roe redrafted the amendment to escape others' jurisdiction, but House leaders stepped in to engineer a final compromise with Walker, defusing the drug issue without threatening hundreds of federal contractors.

As Water Resources chairman from 1981-87, Roe teamed with Howard to emphasize urban water systems rather than the flood control and irrigation projects that traditionally had priority when rural Southerners and Westerners ran the panel. But both men were more than willing to satisfy farm-state colleagues to build support for their own legislative goals.

Roe presided over some $50 billion in federal largess, playing a lead role in twice extending the Clean Water Act, in 1982 and 1987, and in passing a landmark water-projects bill and a "superfund" hazardous-waste cleanup bill in 1986. The hundreds of projects in those measures probably reached every district. The 1987 Clean Water Act became law over Reagan's veto because Republicans and Democrats alike had a stake in its anti-pollution projects.

The 1986 water bill, the first such legislation in more than a decade, broke a deadlock over how much of the cost local beneficiaries should pay. Roe consistently demanded more projects and lower local costs than either Reagan or the Senate would support. The impasse killed a 1984 House bill for $18 billion; in 1986, Roe led the House to increase that to $20 billion for more than 350 projects. But in the 99th Congress' last hour, the differences were resolved and a $16 billion bill with innovative cost-sharing provisions became law.

Though supportive of environmentalists, Roe often collided with them by his advocacy of various dams and dredging projects. But in the 99th Congress, he emerged as their darling in the effort to renew superfund.

After James J. Florio, his former rival for the New Jersey governorship, failed to win the Energy and Commerce Committee's approval of a measure strong enough for environmentalists to support, Roe and Howard pushed a bill more to their liking through Public Works. Voters in New Jersey were passionate on the issue because the state had more superfund sites than any other. The two committees eventually compromised, but environmentalists got much of what they wanted.

For six years before taking over the water subcommittee, Roe was chairman of Public Works' Economic Development Subcommittee. In 1978, he expanded President Jimmy Carter's proposal for a $1 billion jobs bill aimed at labor-intensive projects for the disadvantaged, adding $2 billion more for traditional capital-intensive works. It died late in the Congress. He pressed his demand for the next two years, ultimately dooming Carter's bill to expand the Economic Development Administration (EDA).

The House passed an EDA bill with the public works funds in 1979, but Carter and the Senate wanted the EDA only. By 1980, Carter gave in but the Senate would not. Roe seemed ready to bargain just as Congress recessed for the 1980 elections. But when Ronald Reagan and a GOP Senate were elected, Republicans no longer wanted to deal. The bill died.

Roe successfully managed his first major public works package in 1975, aimed both at creating 250,000 jobs and stimulating investment. In conference, he added a provision not discussed in either chamber, making smaller cities eligible for a redevelopment program. Roe's district is dominated by declining industrial cities of modest size. The bill was enacted in 1976 over President Ford's veto.

At Home: Pork-barrel politics, by whatever name, endear Roe to his constituents, especially to the labor unions that benefit from the jobs his programs have created.

Thanks to his works, Roe's district has received a large number of new town halls, fire stations and other structures that have generated construction employment. He also has secured grants to rescue a plant and to restore Paterson's historic Great Falls area.

Passaic County was Roe's base for forays into statewide politics, but it was not enough to bring him his goal — the Democratic nomination for governor. New Jersey chooses its governors in off years, so House members can seek the Statehouse without giving up their places in Washington.

Roe tried twice. In 1977 he ran a strong primary race against incumbent Brendan T.

Byrne, coming within 40,000 votes of an upset. That showing made him a front-runner in 1981, when his main competition was fellow Rep. Florio.

But Florio defeated Roe easily. Roe had refused public financing and tried to make an issue of the state's public-financing system. The strategy never caught on, and he was left underfunded. Florio, who accepted public financing and was also better on television than Roe, took the nomination by more than 150,000 votes. (Florio went on to lose to Republican Thomas H. Kean in New Jersey's closest gubernatorial election ever.)

Since that defeat, Roe has avoided statewide politics. Given his new prominence as Science chairman and dean of New Jersey's delegation, he seems content to stay in the House. With Kean retiring in 1989 after two terms, Roe is campaign chairman for his former rival, Florio, who is making his third attempt to become governor.

Roe's dominance in Passaic has never been seriously threatened. He was long known as a peacemaker for various local Democratic factions, presiding over conclaves at Paterson's Brownstone House restaurant. He also gained a foothold in Republican towns, supplementing his usual big margins in blue-collar Democratic bastions. In 1988, Roe ran without GOP opposition for the first time.

Part of the reason for Roe's appeal in the Republican suburbs may be that he is not a product of Paterson, the district's biggest town and a home of organization politics. He is from suburban Wayne Township, which swings between the two parties. Roe boasts that he knows all levels of government, having served at each — city, county, state and federal.

He won his House seat in a tight 1969 special election to replace Democrat Charles S. Joelson, who became a state judge. Since then, he has always won re-election with more than 60 percent of the vote.

Committees

Science, Space and Technology (Chairman)
Investigations and Oversight (chairman)

Public Works and Transportation (2nd of 31 Democrats)
Investigations and Oversight; Surface Transportation; Water Resources

Select Intelligence (4th of 12 Democrats)

Elections

1988 General

Robert A. Roe (D)	96,036	(100%)

1986 General

Robert A. Roe (D)	57,820	(63%)
Thomas P. Zampino (R)	34,268	(37%)

Previous Winning Percentages: **1984** (63%) **1982** (71%) **1980** (67%) **1978** (75%) **1976** (71%) **1974** (74%) **1972** (63%) **1970** (61%) **1969** * (49%)

* *Special election.*

District Vote For President

	1988	1984	1980	1976
D	94,329 (44%)	89,625 (42%)	74,286 (40%)	89,494 (47%)
R	121,172 (56%)	121,422 (58%)	93,766 (51%)	96,428 (50%)
I			13,667 (7%)	

Campaign Finance

	Receipts	Receipts from PACs	Expend-itures
1988			
Roe (D)	$490,884	$273,100 (56%)	$267,609
1986			
Roe (D)	$367,272	$204,483 (56%)	$211,235
Zampino (R)	$14,850	$200 (1%)	$14,848

Key Votes

1987	
Raise speed limit to 65 mph	N
Approve Gephardt "fair trade" amendment	Y
Ban testing of larger nuclear weapons	Y
Delay "re-flagging" of Kuwaiti tankers	Y
Approve tax-raising deficit-reduction bill	Y
1988	
Approve aid to Nicaraguan contras	N
Enact civil rights restoration bill over Reagan veto	Y
Kill 60-day plant-closing notification measure	N
Pass omnibus trade bill over Reagan veto	Y
Approve death penalty for drug-related murders	Y
Bar federal funds for abortions in cases of rape and incest	Y
Oppose seven-day waiting period for purchase of handguns	N

Voting Studies

	Presidential Support		Party Unity		Conservative Coalition	
Year	**S**	**O**	**S**	**O**	**S**	**O**
1988	29	66	84	8	50	47
1987	22	74	83	5	49	44
1986	22	77	89	6	28	68
1985	18	76	89	6	24	73
1984	34	59	86	8	29	61
1983	24	72	87	9	26	71
1982	35	60	83	12	33	66
1981	39	39	70	16	36	51

Interest Group Ratings

Year	ADA	ACU	AFL-CIO	CCUS
1988	70	13	100	21
1987	80	9	93	23
1986	75	10	100	18
1985	75	11	94	29
1984	70	4	85	38
1983	80	13	100	21
1982	75	23	90	55
1981	60	8	100	17

9 Robert G. Torricelli (D)

Of Englewood — Elected 1982

Born: Aug. 26, 1951, Paterson, N.J.
Education: Rutgers U., A.B. 1974, J.D. 1977; Harvard U., M.P.A. 1980.
Occupation: Lawyer.
Family: Wife, Susan Holloway.
Religion: Methodist.
Political Career: No previous office.
Capitol Office: 317 Cannon Bldg. 20515; 225-5061.

In Washington: Torricelli is bright and cocksure, a young man in a hurry who so far has left a trail in the House marked more by the compelling, made-for-TV quote or deed than by legislative substance.

In part, that is because he has chosen to make his mark mainly on the Foreign Affairs Committee, which is less a bill mill than a policy oversight board. Also, as a man with acknowledged ambitions for higher office, Torricelli aims for a larger audience than the House, where his brash and self-assertive style rubs some colleagues the wrong way. Having dropped long-held plans to run for governor in 1989, it remains to be seen whether he will devote more time in the House to the sustained and largely unseen work of legislating.

Even among his media-oriented contemporaries, Torricelli has shown a flare for garnering the kind of news coverage once reserved for senior members. In his first month in office, at 31, national TV followed his trip to El Salvador, where he arranged for the return of the body of a journalist, a New Jersey native, who had been murdered there. He also drew publicity for obtaining a papal audience for a 97-year-old constituent — "Great television," he said.

But Torricelli took his most notable step to date in 1989, when he became a surprise addition to the legal team defending Speaker Jim Wright. Torricelli said he did so after reviewing the ethics committee's report against the Speaker, at Wright's request, and concluding that Wright was getting a raw deal. Still, colleagues had trouble seeing what was in it for Torricelli beyond national publicity.

Torricelli had not been a close associate of Wright before, and he joined the Speaker's defense when Wright's political demise was imminent. For a man with statewide ambitions in New Jersey, he seemingly had nothing to gain by becoming linked to the Texan's ethics case. And he subsequently ruffled other members by his arguments that all lawmakers, like Wright, have friends at home who ingratiate themselves with the local congressman while asking nothing in return, appearances to the contrary.

Torricelli's brief role in the Speaker's behalf was a departure for a man who until then concentrated on Foreign Affairs. Widely traveled since joining the panel, he seems to have formed opinions on just about every area of policy. "I'd like to be more of a deep thinker on national and foreign affairs ... an architect of national policy," he said after his first term. From the start he was an outspoken liberal critic of Reagan's policies, with a sharply cynical view of the president's stewardship.

After his El Salvador trip, Torricelli blasted U.S. support for its government. Also in 1983, he endorsed a nuclear weapons freeze, saying, "I want Ronald Reagan to hear a desperate voice from the American people. No more phony arms control negotiations; no more talk of limited nuclear war or winnable nuclear war."

When the scandal over arms sales to Iran broke in 1986, Torricelli twitted Reagan by recalling the president's frequent accusation that Democrats are weak toward hostile nations: "We now discover that the emperor has no clothes." He supported sanctions against South Africa, contrasting Congress' initiative with Reagan's opposition: "We're not talking about apartheid. We're not studying it. We don't want to have anything to do with it."

In 1987, Torricelli bitingly objected to Reagan's policy of providing Navy escorts for Kuwaiti tankers in the Persian Gulf, and not only because Congress was not consulted. "We cannot assume," he said, "that contingencies have been considered, options have been explored, the military have been consulted — in short, that competent people are making intelligent judgments about the policies."

The next year he was out front again after the United States downed an Iranian civilian airliner, killing 290 people. Torricelli proposed a measure opposing Reagan administration moves to compensate the victims' families, arguing, "It is going to be an American admission of error that will divert attention from the fact that Iran was grossly negligent in its operations." Neither the administration's negotiations with Iran nor

New Jersey 9

North — Fort Lee; Hackensack

The George Washington Bridge, connecting Manhattan's 181st Street and the New Jersey Palisades, is a fitting symbol for the 9th. Opened in 1931, the majestic span spurred the growth of Bergen County.

Today, the bridge's tired roadbed requires frequent commuter-vexing repairs. Similarly, the 9th's close-in suburbs are showing signs of age. Population has slumped slightly, as suburbanites push deep into New Jersey in search of more open spaces.

However, the southern part of Bergen regularly receives a temporary influx of outsiders, who come to attend sports events and concerts at the Meadowlands stadium complex. The jewel of the otherwise homely marshlands along the New Jersey Turnpike, the Meadowlands includes Giant Stadium, a state-of-the-art facility that drew both of New York City's National Football League teams, the Giants and the Jets, to New Jersey. To the chagrin of New Jersey boosters, though, the teams continue to identify themselves as "New York." There is also an indoor arena, named for former Democratic Gov. Brendan T. Byrne, and a horse-racing track.

The complex is surrounded by several working-class towns, where warehouses and truck depots predominate. But the Meadowlands development has had a salutary effect on the city of Secaucus. Once a pig-farming area whose odoriferous atmosphere made it a laughingstock, Secaucus is attracting hotels and other new housing. Hartz Mountain Corp., which is headquartered there, owns the upscale Harmon Cove condominiums, popular with Republican business people.

The area closest to the George Washington Bridge is Democratic and mainly liberal. Apartments in Fort Lee, Cliffside Park and Edgewater line the Hudson River Palisades and house younger professionals who work in New York City. Academics who teach at New Jersey colleges have an enclave in Leonia and also vote Democratic. Englewood, 40 percent black, votes Democratic.

To the west, out Route 4, are largely Democratic towns such as Lodi, Garfield and Lyndhurst. Hackensack is blue-collar and has a large black population, although the western part of the town is more affluent. Rutherford and East Rutherford are generally lower middle class, and conservative on social matters. Teaneck and Fair Lawn are heavily Jewish and Democratic.

Population: 526,066. White 478,193 (91%), Black 29,687 (6%), Other 12,466 (2%). Spanish origin 23,162 (4%). 18 and over 415,175 (79%), 65 and over 73,688 (14%). Median age: 36.

Torricelli's proposal went any further.

During the downfall of Philippine President Ferdinand E. Marcos, he was in the national spotlight supporting Corazon Aquino and strongly opposing Marcos' admission to the United States. With many Jews among his constituents, Torricelli is quick to oppose any suggested cuts in aid to Israel.

He also has used his Foreign Affairs seat to promote the interests of the maritime industry and unions. In 1987, the House adopted his amendment to the foreign aid bill requiring countries that receive cash aid to buy U.S. goods and ship them on U.S. ships. The bill died in the Senate. In 1988, he amended the House defense bill to direct the Navy to encourage U.S. construction of diesel-powered submarines for allies; the Navy had ordered shipyards not to build such subs for Israel, reportedly out of fear that the Navy then would be pressured to buy some diesel models in lieu of nuclear-powered subs.

Torricelli also is an active member of the Science, Space and Technology Committee. As such, he attracted wide attention after the 1986 explosion of the space shuttle *Challenger* for quickly proposing legislation to build a new vehicle and for bluntly criticizing both the National Aeronautics and Space Administration and Congress. "Congress just didn't support NASA, it believed in it," he said. "We still believe in it, but NASA will no longer be left to its own devices."

He subsequently took up the cause of Hercules Inc., an aerospace company that wanted to break Morton Thiokol's monopoly on booster rockets; two years later, his efforts paid off when NASA decided to pursue a new generation of rockets, and threw the competition wide open. From his seat on Science, in 1986 Torricelli was able to include provisions for research and development projects in the law that reauthorized the "superfund" toxic-waste cleanup program.

At Home: Torricelli's political résumé reflects the same drive and intensity that have marked his career in Washington. He began his political apprenticeship as a teenager by working for the Bergen County Democratic organization. In college, he was an active campus politician who ran three successful campaigns for class president using a sound truck to attract voters. He went on to become an aide to Democratic Gov. Brendan T. Byrne.

After a brief stint as executive director of the New Jersey Democratic Party, Torricelli joined the staff of Vice President Walter F. Mondale. That connection got him the important job of running the 1980 Illinois primary for President Carter, whose lopsided victory over Sen. Edward M. Kennedy proved he did well.

In 1982, redistricting made the 9th District attractive to Democrats, so Torricelli moved there from his original home in northern Bergen County and began preparing a campaign against GOP Rep. Harold Hollenbeck. A moderate Republican who enjoyed labor support, Hollenbeck had survived three terms in his blue-collar constituency, but had never before faced strong opposition.

Hollenbeck played down his partisan affiliation, but he had backed President Reagan's economic plan in 1981, something Torricelli emphasized. The incumbent also suffered from his lackadaisical manner, staying in Washington while Torricelli campaigned door-to-door. Hollenbeck returned home during the October recess, but even his own staff sometimes did not know where to find him. Torricelli ended up winning only 12 of the district's 38 towns, but nearly all were among the larger ones; he won 53 percent of the overall vote.

Aided by a redistricting plan that gave him a somewhat more Democratic constituency, Torricelli did not meet much GOP opposition in 1984. In 1986, district Republicans hoped that a hot contest down the ballot, for Bergen County executive, would spur turnout and give county legislator Arthur F. Jones a chance against Torricelli. But the reverse occurred: Torricelli won with 69 percent of the vote, his biggest margin ever. He took two-thirds of the vote in 1988.

Torricelli's big winning margins sparked speculation about his potential as a future statewide candidate, which the Democrat fueled by testing the waters for a 1989 campaign to succeed retiring GOP Gov. Thomas H. Kean. But by early 1989, his Democratic House colleague James J. Florio — the party's gubernatorial nominee and a narrow loser to Kean in 1981 — had established himself as the front-runner. Torricelli took himself out of the competition and strongly endorsed Florio — even writing a letter to other potential Florio foes, suggesting they stay out of the race to avoid a divisive primary.

Committees

Foreign Affairs (12th of 28 Democrats)
Asian and Pacific Affairs; Europe and the Middle East

Science, Space and Technology (14th of 30 Democrats)
International Scientific Cooperation; Space Science and Applications

Elections

1988 General		
Robert G. Torricelli (D)	142,012	(67%)
Roger J. Lane (R)	68,363	(32%)
1986 General		
Robert G. Torricelli (D)	89,634	(69%)
Arthur F. Jones (R)	40,226	(31%)

Previous Winning Percentages: 1984 (63%) **1982** (53%)

District Vote For President

	1988	1984	1980	1976
D	107,910 (46%)	103,831 (41%)	92,979 (38%)	119,853 (48%)
R	125,417 (54%)	150,514 (59%)	127,731 (52%)	127,785 (51%)
I			20,687 (9%)	

Campaign Finance

	Receipts	Receipts from PACs	Expenditures
1988			
Torricelli (D)	$631,151	$177,488 (28%)	$403,059
Lane (R)	$59,127	$250 (0.4%)	$57,260
1986			
Torricelli (D)	$579,688	$170,048 (29%)	$408,779
Jones (R)	$67,325	$1,364 (2%)	$64,091

Key Votes

1987	
Raise speed limit to 65 mph	N
Approve Gephardt "fair trade" amendment	Y
Ban testing of larger nuclear weapons	Y
Delay "re-flagging" of Kuwaiti tankers	Y
Approve tax-raising deficit-reduction bill	Y
1988	
Approve aid to Nicaraguan contras	N
Enact civil rights restoration bill over Reagan veto	Y
Kill 60-day plant-closing notification measure	N
Pass omnibus trade bill over Reagan veto	Y
Approve death penalty for drug-related murders	Y
Bar federal funds for abortions in cases of rape and incest	N
Oppose seven-day waiting period for purchase of handguns	N

Voting Studies

	Presidential Support		Party Unity		Conservative Coalition	
Year	S	O	S	O	S	O
1988	23	71	88	6	39	58
1987	18	78	81	5	33	63
1986	19	74	85	7	20	68
1985	24	71	87	4	18	78
1984	31	61	76	17	31	66
1983	17	78	82	6	16	80

Interest Group Ratings

Year	ADA	ACU	AFL-CIO	CCUS
1988	85	4	100	25
1987	84	5	93	15
1986	70	9	100	13
1985	80	5	100	19
1984	70	13	69	31
1983	85	4	100	15

10 Donald M. Payne (D)

Of Newark — Elected 1988

Born: July 16, 1934, Newark, N.J.
Education: Seton Hall U., B.A. 1957.
Occupation: Community development executive.
Family: Widowed; two children.
Religion: Baptist.
Political Career: Essex County Board of Chosen Freeholders, 1972-78; Newark Municipal Council, 1982-88; sought Democratic nomination for Essex County executive, 1978; sought Democratic nomination for U.S. House, 1980, 1986.
Capitol Office: 417 Cannon Bldg. 20515; 225-3436.

The Path to Washington: Most people would be satisfied with any of the careers in which Payne has had success — local politics, business and education. But for years, Payne cherished another goal — to become New Jersey's first black member of the U.S. House. That goal eluded him until 1988.

There is a good reason why it took Payne three tries to win in the majority-black, Newark-based 10th District: His path was blocked by the legendary Democratic Rep. Peter W. Rodino Jr., who held the seat for 40 years. Rodino, chairman of the Judiciary Committee, achieved national fame during the 1974 Watergate hearings, but it was Rodino's steadfast advocacy of civil rights legislation that earned him the loyalty — and votes — of many black residents in the 10th.

Insisting that the time had come for Newark-area blacks to be represented by one of their own, Payne challenged Rodino in the 1980 Democratic primary, and again in the 1986 primary. While paying tribute to Rodino's years of service, Payne said blacks needed someone with a deeper understanding of their problems, such as education, employment, housing, health care and drug abuse.

However, black good will toward Rodino, combined with his base in Newark's mainly Italian North Ward, enabled the incumbent to win easily. Payne got 23 percent of the vote in 1980 and 36 percent in 1986.

But when Rodino indicated after the 1986 contest that he had waged his last campaign, local Democratic officials moved behind Payne, a longtime party insider who had served on the Essex County Board and was in his second term on the Newark City Council.

In early 1988, Rodino hedged a bit, causing some uneasy moments in the Essex County Democratic organization. But there was some gentle behind-the-scenes pressure, and in March, Rodino confirmed that he would not seek re-election.

Though several state legislators and local elected officials were mentioned as possible candidates for the 10th, Payne's only opposition came from City Council colleague Ralph T. Grant Jr., who asserted that he was the candidate of a "grass-roots" coalition. But Payne's advantages — party support, a sizable campaign treasury and recognition earned in his earlier campaigns — brought him the nomination in a landslide. Payne's November victory over Republican Michael Webb, a teacher, was a formality in the overwhelmingly Democratic district.

For a man so determined to become a black political pioneer, the soft-spoken Payne does not cut a dynamic figure. A high school teacher and football coach after college, he moved into business in 1963 as community affairs director for the Newark-based Prudential Insurance Co. More recently, he was vice president of a computer forms company founded by his brother.

Payne also played a prominent role in several charitable and social organizations. The head of a "storefront YMCA" in inner-city Newark in the late 1950s, Payne was elected in 1970 as the first black president of the National Council of YMCAs, and he later served two four-year terms as chairman of the YMCA's international committee on refugees. While participating in all these activities, the widowed Payne was raising two children and building his political career.

At the start of the 101st Congress, Payne won assignment to the Education and Labor Committee, a liberal-dominated panel that should offer him a good forum to air his concerns about the pressing needs of his constituency. He also serves on the Government Operations Committee, newly chaired in 1989 by veteran black Democratic Rep. John Conyers Jr. of Michigan.

New Jersey 10

Newark

When Peter W. Rodino Jr. won his first House term in 1948, Newark was a city of nearly a half-million people in which Irish and Italians competed for political power. Today, freshman Rep. Payne serves a city with just over 300,000 residents, and there is no dispute over who holds political power. Blacks make up 58 percent of the population, and a black has held the mayoralty since 1970 — first Kenneth Gibson, and now Sharpe James.

"Wherever America's cities are going," Gibson once said, "Newark will get there first." The city did in fact foreshadow many of the urban problems that have spread throughout the Northeast in the past decade. Its Central Ward, devastated by riot in 1967, has not recovered in the years since.

But Newark remains the largest city in the state, and the corporate headquarters of Prudential Insurance and other companies keep the central business area alive by day. Newark Airport and the busy docks provide other economic mainstays.

Newark is an ethnic potpourri. Blacks populate the Central, West and South wards; Hispanics live in the East Ward. Nearly all of the remaining white population is found in the heavily Italian North Ward.

Newark now makes up only about 60 percent of the district; towns such as Hillside and Irvington fill out the 10th's population. They resemble Newark — blue-collar whites living in uneasy coexistence with blacks.

The 10th also includes Orange and East Orange, whose stockbrokerage houses once earned it the nickname "Wall Street of New Jersey." Both have their own problems with poverty; East Orange has a higher share of blacks (83 percent) than Newark.

Political intrigue and corruption are constant issues in Newark and its environs. Gibson's predecessor, Hugh Addonizio, was convicted in 1970 of extorting payments from municipal contractors. Gibson, who defeated Addonizio for mayor that year, had his own problems with the law — a grand jury indicted him in 1981 for giving an ally an alleged "no-show" city job, even though this is common practice in New Jersey and many other states.

Gibson later was cleared, but his vaunted organization lost steam as the 1980s progressed, and Gibson was upset by James in the 1986 mayoral primary. James, who has fashioned himself as something of a spokesman for the interests of blacks all across New Jersey, is popular enough in the city to be an early favorite for re-election in 1990.

Population: 525,886. White 177,814 (34%), Black 304,047 (58%), Other 5,551 (1%). Spanish origin 71,650 (14%). 18 and over 360,309 (69%), 65 and over 52,645 (10%). Median age: 29.

Committees

Education and Labor (14th of 22 Democrats)
Elementary, Secondary and Vocational Education; Labor Standards; Select Education

Foreign Affairs (28th of 28 Democrats)
Africa

Government Operations (22nd of 24 Democrats)
Human Resources and Intergovernmental Relations

Campaign Finance

	Receipts	Receipts from PACs	Expend-itures
1988			
Payne (D)	$545,049	$205,177 (38%)	$413,338

Elections

1988 General		
Donald M. Payne (D)	84,681	(77%)
Michael Webb (R)	13,848	(13%)
Anthony Imperiale (I)	5,422	(5%)
1988 Primary		
Donald M. Payne (D)	40,608	(73%)
Ralph T. Grant Jr. (D)	14,908	(27%)

District Vote For President

	1988	1984	1980	1976
D	91,060 (78%)	110,470 (75%)	90,284 (70%)	97,465 (68%)
R	24,150 (21%)	36,554 (25%)	32,945 (26%)	42,429 (30%)
I			4,469 (4%)	

11 Dean A. Gallo (R)

Of Parsippany — Elected 1984

Born: Nov. 23, 1935, Hackensack, N.J.
Education: Graduated Boonton (N.J.) High School.
Occupation: Real-estate broker.
Family: Divorced; two children.
Religion: Methodist.
Political Career: Parsippany-Troy Hills Township Council, 1968-71; Morris County freeholder, 1971-75; N.J. Assembly, 1976-84, minority leader, 1981-84.
Capitol Office: 1318 Longworth Bldg. 20515; 225-5034.

In Washington: Nobody spends 25 years as a real-estate developer without learning how to make deals, and Gallo pursues them in the House with the same zest he devoted to new shopping centers and subdivisions in Parsippany. In the 101st Congress, he has a chance to cut deals with the best of them, having won seats on the Appropriations and Budget committees.

While some find Gallo's garrulous, glad-handing style a bit abrasive, nearly all agree he is a man who knows how to put a deal across. His enthusiasm for bargaining made him a natural choice to become freshman whip for the GOP leadership in his first term. He likes to spend time on the House floor, trading gossip on who is doing what to whom in House politics.

For an urban Republican from the Northeast, Gallo is relatively loyal to the conservative GOP majority: In 1988, he backed party positions 80 percent of the time. His energy and loyalty were rewarded when he captured the Northeastern seat on Appropriations that had been held by Jack F. Kemp of New York.

But the Northeasterner in Gallo shows on the Public Works Committee, where he tends to vote an environmentalist position. On New Jersey-related issues such as medical-waste disposal and ocean dumping of sewage sludge, which were hot topics in the 100th Congress, and the Clean Water Act, acid rain and the toxic-waste cleanup "superfund," which the committee handled in the 99th Congress, Gallo's voting record is as environmentalist as any. His floor votes on environmental issues mirror New Jersey Democrats James J. Florio and Robert A. Roe.

In the early months of the 100th Congress, Gallo voted to override two presidential vetoes: on the Clean Water reauthorization, which approved home-state sewer projects, and on the highway bill, which contained money for construction on Interstates in his district.

On Small Business, Gallo served on a GOP task force seeking an alternative to a Democratic-sponsored trade bill. He was the only New Jerseyan voting to sustain President Reagan's 1988 veto of the trade bill.

In the 99th Congress, Gallo staked out a portion of the "superfund" legislation as his specialty by proposing a "community right to know" amendment, joining with Bob Wise, a West Virginia Democrat. The idea was to provide federal money for local committees to gather information about dangerous substances and develop plans for dealing with any emergency that might occur. Right-to-know language was included in the superfund bill as enacted.

At Home: Though he does not have a very high public profile, Gallo's support is sought after by statewide GOP candidates: He is well connected in state party circles, and popular among moderates and conservatives alike.

In 1981, Gallo, then the state Assembly Republican leader, joined U.S. Rep. Jim Courter as a co-chairman of Thomas H. Kean's successful gubernatorial campaign. With Kean retiring in 1989, Gallo signed on as chairman of Courter's campaign for the GOP nomination.

Gallo was a beneficiary of New Jersey's redistricting chaos. In 1983, the U.S. Supreme Court struck down the Democratic-drawn district map used for the 1982 elections. The new court-drawn plan gave the 11th a Republican coloration, placing veteran Democratic Rep. Joseph G. Minish at a disadvantage.

Gallo was recognized as Minish's greatest threat. A business-oriented moderate and Kean ally, he had been elected minority leader of the Assembly in 1981, and represented the eastern half of heavily Republican Morris County, added to the 11th by the remap.

Gallo had the 1984 House primary field to himself, giving him an early start on campaigning against Minish. In letters to GOP and independent voters, Gallo hammered at the incumbent, a former union official, for being anti-business and for opposing Reagan's tax and budget policies.

An old-school personal campaigner, Minish reacted slowly to Gallo's targeted mailings and radio ads. Minish eventually went on the offensive, criticizing Gallo for supporting tax increases in the Legislature. But Gallo, helped by Reagan's strong showing, won easily, as he has in two re-election campaigns since.

New Jersey 11

North — Morris County

Before redistricting in 1984, the 11th had enough Democratic territory in Essex County to offset the growing strength of suburban Republicans. The new lines changed that.

The bulk of the votes are now in suburban Republican villages and towns dotting the green Morris County landscape. At its eastern end, the 11th still reaches into Essex County to include West Orange and several other traditionally Democratic towns.

The largest community in the 11th is Parsippany-Troy Hills, a middle-class township in eastern Morris County; after years of fast growth, it has leveled off at about 50,000 people, just bigger than Essex County's Bloomfield Township. Around Parsippany, towns such as Chatham and Florham Park are well-to-do bastions of moderate Republicanism.

Farther west, the district is pastoral, with newer tract developments set among woods and rolling hills. Towns here, such as Randolph and Roxbury, are viscerally Republican. So are the communities at the exurban and rural western end, where the 11th juts into Warren and Sussex counties. There is some Democratic vote from the central Morris towns of Dover and Rockaway, which are blue-collar in character, and from the hamlet of Victory Gardens, which is about 40 percent black and Hispanic.

The remnant of the district in Essex County is the only solid Democratic base. Here, close to Newark, white flight from the city determined the ethnic distribution of the suburbs. Verona was fed by the heavily Italian North Ward of Newark. West Orange is home to Jews who once lived in Newark's South Ward. Farther west are politically marginal suburbs; Livingston, hometown of departing two-term GOP Gov. Thomas H. Kean, is filled with wealthy Republicans and a large Jewish community that often votes Democratic.

Population: 526,078. White 503,714 (96%), Black 9,803 (2%), Other 9,543 (2%). Spanish origin 12,145 (2%). 18 and over 381,844 (73%), 65 and over 51,245 (10%). Median age: 33.

Committees

Appropriations (22nd of 22 Republicans)
District of Columbia (ranking); Foreign Operations

Budget (12th of 14 Republicans)
Task Force: Budget Process, Reconciliation and Enforcement

Elections

1988 General		
Dean A. Gallo (R)	154,654	(70%)
John C. Shaw (D)	64,773	(30%)
1986 General		
Dean A. Gallo (R)	75,037	(68%)
Frank Askin (D)	35,280	(32%)

Previous Winning Percentage: 1984 (56%)

District Vote For President

	1988	1984	1980	1976
D	84,568 (35%)	78,701 (31%)	69,321 (30%)	97,922 (41%)
R	155,998 (65%)	171,632 (69%)	136,120 (59%)	136,658 (57%)
I			23,168 (10%)	

Campaign Finance

	Receipts	Receipts from PACs	Expend-itures
1988			
Gallo (R)	$531,548	$151,245 (28%)	$490,751
1986			
Gallo (R)	$713,273	$178,936 (25%)	$660,059
Askin (D)	$168,255	$27,792 (17%)	$167,857

Key Votes

1987	
Raise speed limit to 65 mph	N
Approve Gephardt "fair trade" amendment	N
Ban testing of larger nuclear weapons	N
Delay "re-flagging" of Kuwaiti tankers	N
Approve tax-raising deficit-reduction bill	N
1988	
Approve aid to Nicaraguan contras	Y
Enact civil rights restoration bill over Reagan veto	Y
Kill 60-day plant-closing notification measure	Y
Pass omnibus trade bill over Reagan veto	N
Approve death penalty for drug-related murders	Y
Bar federal funds for abortions in cases of rape and incest	N
Oppose seven-day waiting period for purchase of handguns	N

Voting Studies

	Presidential Support		Party Unity		Conservative Coalition	
Year	**S**	**O**	**S**	**O**	**S**	**O**
1988	59	40	84	14	87	13
1987	55	44	71	27	88	12
1986	70	29	71	27	86	14
1985	63	38	80	19	82	18

Interest Group Ratings

Year	ADA	ACU	AFL-CIO	CCUS
1988	30	72	31	79
1987	32	57	44	67
1986	35	68	57	61
1985	20	81	29	68

12 Jim Courter (R)

Of Hackettstown — Elected 1978

Born: Oct. 14, 1941, Montclair, N.J.
Education: Colgate U., B.A. 1963; Duke U., J.D. 1966.
Occupation: Lawyer.
Family: Wife, Carmen McCalman; two children.
Religion: Methodist.
Political Career: Allamuchy Township attorney, 1975-78.
Capitol Office: 2422 Rayburn Bldg. 20515; 225-5801.

In Washington: During a decade in Congress, Courter has focused almost exclusively on defense and foreign policy issues — an unusual combination for a man who is aiming to be New Jersey's next governor. But Courter hopes the qualities that enabled him to stand out in House GOP circles will help him appeal to home-state voters in his November 1989 contest against Democratic Rep. James J. Florio.

Aggressive and conservative on most military matters, Courter has impressed many colleagues on the Armed Services Committee with his diligence and expertise. The right appreciates his ardent support for the strategic defense initiative (SDI); the left respects his willingness to confront the defense establishment over its controversial procurement practices.

Courter also has a knack for gaining media attention, though his tireless efforts to promote himself and his opinions often annoy colleagues on both sides of the aisle. A prolific contributor to newspapers ranging from local New Jersey dailies to *The New York Times,* in 1986 he compiled a 256-page book of his speeches and writings entitled "Defending Democracy." Early in 1989, Courter let it be known that the White House had contacted him about becoming defense secretary, but that running for governor was more important to him.

Late in 1988, local issues meshed with Courter's interest in defense, when New Jersey's Fort Dix was slated for near-closure by an independent commission evaluating base needs. The move will cost more than 4,500 jobs in the state, but blocking it was near-impossible because of 1988 legislation, which Courter backed, requiring Congress to accept or reject the commission's proposal intact. Like other members representing bases scheduled for realignment, Courter cited problems in the data on which the commission based its decisions. But he was the lone vote against the proposal in Armed Services in early 1989, and in a small minority of opponents when it came before the full House.

As Courter positioned himself to run for governor, his record on domestic issues became somewhat more moderate in the 100th Congress. As the GOP was drafting its 1988 platform, Courter sought to put the party "in the vanguard of the civil rights movement" with a plank guaranteeing the right of victims of discrimination to sue for damages. One local newspaper called the move "an unusual step to the left for Courter," but favorably compared it to GOP Gov. Thomas H. Kean's efforts to woo minority voters. Other planks proposed by Courter were more in line with conservative orthodoxy: calls for enterprise zones, a subminimum wage and private ownership of housing projects.

Also in 1988, Courter earned a career-high 64 rating from the AFL-CIO. Though a year earlier he had opposed the Gephardt amendment to the trade bill — calling it "protectionist" and "dangerous" — he supported the controversial plant-closing notification amendment in 1988, one of only 29 Republicans to do so. Later, he was one of 60 GOP House members voting to override President Reagan's veto of the omnibus trade bill.

Throughout the Reagan years, Courter generally supported the president's economic agenda. But like other New Jersey Republicans, he is more environmentally conscious than many GOP conservatives. A one-time legal aid attorney, he also fought Reagan's efforts to kill the Legal Services Corporation.

Mostly, however, Courter is known for his outspoken views on defense and foreign policy. A member of the special Iran-contra committee in 1987, Courter leveled some tough criticisms at Reagan. But rather than focusing on the constitutional and criminal aspects of the covert operation, Courter blamed the fiasco on Reagan's reluctance to act firmly and publicly in the face of what he views as "Soviet aggression" in Central America: "The fact is, the Reagan administration's whole foreign policy approach is marked by a kind of camouflage, by a refusal to take America into its confidence, to say what must be done."

During the hearings, Courter also aggressively attacked the panel's Democratic leadership, primarily by challenging the questioning of the two majority counsels. He argued for

New Jersey 12

North and Central — Morristown

On paper, the 12th is an ungainly blotch. It contains only one whole county; the pieces of the other six seem to be leftovers from map-drawing efforts in the rest of northern New Jersey.

On the ground, however, there is little that is ugly about the 12th. Large stretches of rolling countryside and wood-shaded lakes mingle with some of the state's most affluent communities. The entire prospect is especially pleasing to Republicans, who have a tight hold on the loyalties of most voters.

New Jersey's hunt country is in the district, in towns such as Far Hills and Peapack, nestled in northern Somerset County. Quaint Morristown and its surrounding old-line Morris County suburbs are home to commuters who work on Wall Street and elsewhere in the Manhattan business world. Farther west and south the district grows more rural, dotted with middle-class subdivisions.

However, this pastoral and remote area has undergone change in recent years, as the New York City metropolis crept down Route 1 to Princeton and beyond. With its growing high-technology industry, Route 1 is becoming New Jersey's answer to Massachusetts' Route 128. Recently completed Interstate 78, running from Newark into Pennsylvania, has also drawn some corporate headquarters from Manhattan to the rolling greenery of Morris and Somerset counties.

Though farming still dominates in Hunterdon and Warren counties, that far-flung corner of the state is beginning to see the first signs of corporate development as well. Hunterdon was New Jersey's third-fastest growing county in the early 1980s, its population jumping by 10 percent between 1980 and 1986.

The growth in these areas has not changed their Republican leanings. Ronald Reagan and George Bush both dominated in the 12th District. Hunterdon, the only county wholly within the 12th, gave 70 percent of its 1988 presidential vote to Bush, and 79 percent of its House vote to Courter.

There are a few pockets of Democratic strength, however. The portion of Middlesex County in the district includes the blue-collar towns of Piscataway and South Plainfield. Democrats also have small strongholds in Princeton, with a liberal academic segment associated with its Ivy League university; in industrial Raritan and Somerville, with their chemical and pharmaceutical works; and in Courter's home base of Hackettstown, where there is blue-collar employment at an M&M/Mars candy factory.

Population: 526,063. White 485,399 (92%), Black 27,563 (5%), Other 9,946 (2%). Spanish origin 9,117 (2%). 18 and over 380,628 (72%), 65 and over 48,331 (9%). Median age: 32.

letting Lt. Col. Oliver L. North present the slide show he developed for contra fund-raising purposes. The committee allowed North to make the presentation, but without audio-visual aids.

Courter is a leading House proponent of SDI. He offered a floor amendment in 1987 that would have ordered the Pentagon to prepare for deployment of a system that could be used to destroy a nuclear missile launched by accident. He said he hoped that protection against an accidental missile launch would be so appealing that his amendment would sail through. "It would have been the first acknowledgement [by the House] that stopping missiles is a good thing," he said. His amendment lost, 121-297.

Early in his career on Armed Services, Courter was chief spokesman for Reagan's request for chemical weapons production. He offered a compromise to allow production of new binary munitions in exchange for dismantling of older weapons. He lost at first, but his position prevailed in the 99th Congress.

At Home: Despite his defense and foreign policy focus in the House, Courter has not been a stranger to state politics. In 1981 and 1985, he was campaign chairman for Kean's gubernatorial bids, and he came to be considered as Kean's Washington voice.

Still, Courter's biggest hurdle in the June 1989 GOP gubernatorial primary was proving that he was as well versed on state issues as his three main opponents, all state officeholders with strong local bases. They argued that Courter had done little to prepare himself for the issues he would face as governor, such as property tax relief, state budget shortfalls, high auto insurance rates and garbage disposal.

But in a series of candidate forums, Courter proved conversant on state issues. And though he was making his first statewide run and was not well-known outside his 12th District, the bit of extra publicity Courter had received as a House conservative spokesman provided him with a crucial edge.

Each major candidate carried his home base, but Courter's support was broadest: He ran first or second in 18 of 21 counties. His plurality in the Balkanized primary was just 29 percent, but he had a nearly 27,000-vote cushion over the runner-up.

Courter had been mentioned as a potential statewide GOP candidate ever since he first won his House seat in 1978. Running in the old 13th District, he unseated Democratic Rep. Helen Meyner, wife of former Gov. Robert B. Meyner.

Thereafter, the biggest threat to Courter was not from a House opponent, but from the Democratic state legislators who drew New Jersey's first redistricting map for the 1980s. When the remap paired him in 1982 with another GOP incumbent, Marge Roukema, Courter prevented an intraparty battle by moving to the open 12th District. While 85 percent of the voters there were new to him, the district had been drawn as a Republican bastion.

Touting an endorsement from Reagan, Courter easily dismissed Morris County Freeholder Rodney Frelinghuysen in a Republican primary, then breezed to victory that November. In 1984, a second redistricting plan again forced Courter to make some adjustments, giving him still another new district with a 50 percent new constituency. But again, he had no trouble either in the primary or the general election.

With Courter receiving frequent mention as a rising Republican star, Democrats hoped they could hold down his victory margin in 1986 by running David B. Crabiel, a funeral home owner and member of the powerful Middlesex County Democratic machine. However, only part of Middlesex is in the 12th, and Crabiel could not compete with Courter in the exurbs and "hunt country" suburbs that make up the rest of the district. Courter won 63 percent of the vote.

In 1988, Courter had to put up with a primary challenge from Thomas Young, a 24-year-old conservative who accused the incumbent of softening his ideological line in preparation for a run for governor. But Courter swamped the upstart and again won easily in November.

Committees

Armed Services (4th of 21 Republicans)
Procurement and Military Nuclear Systems (ranking); Military Installations and Facilities

Select Aging (7th of 27 Republicans)
Health and Long-Term Care

Elections

1988 General		
Jim Courter (R)	165,918	(69%)
Norman J. Weinstein (D)	71,569	(30%)
1988 Primary		
Jim Courter (R)	25,816	(89%)
Thomas J. Young (R)	3,177	(11%)
1986 General		
Jim Courter (R)	72,966	(63%)
David B. Crabiel (D)	41,967	(37%)

Previous Winning Percentages: 1984 (65%) **1982** (67%) **1980** (72%) **1978** (52%)

District Vote For President

	1988	1984	1980	1976
D	93,339 (36%)	84,541 (35%)	74,811 (34%)	92,672 (43%)
R	162,814 (63%)	160,027 (65%)	122,046 (55%)	117,774 (55%)
I			21,566 (10%)	

Campaign Finance

	Receipts	Receipts from PACs	Expend-itures
1988			
Courter (R)	$1,211,060	$167,173 (14%)	$1,333,882
Weinstein (D)	$17,334	0	$17,334
1986			
Courter (R)	$730,514	$115,888 (16%)	$779,078
Crabiel (D)	$319,667	$22,790 (7%)	$318,869

Key Votes

1987	
Raise speed limit to 65 mph	N
Approve Gephardt "fair trade" amendment	N
Ban testing of larger nuclear weapons	N
Delay "re-flagging" of Kuwaiti tankers	N
Approve tax-raising deficit-reduction bill	X
1988	
Approve aid to Nicaraguan contras	Y
Enact civil rights restoration bill over Reagan veto	Y
Kill 60-day plant-closing notification measure	N
Pass omnibus trade bill over Reagan veto	Y
Approve death penalty for drug-related murders	Y
Bar federal funds for abortions in cases of rape and incest	Y
Oppose seven-day waiting period for purchase of handguns	N

Voting Studies

	Presidential Support		Party Unity		Conservative Coalition	
Year	**S**	**O**	**S**	**O**	**S**	**O**
1988	49	39	70	18	71	13
1987	51	39	65	22	81	12
1986	69	29	75	24	84	14
1985	70	28	76	18	84	13
1984	51	40	66	21	71	12
1983	70	23	74	22	74	20
1982	64	25	65	24	78	14
1981	63	32	77	19	80	13

Interest Group Ratings

Year	ADA	ACU	AFL-CIO	CCUS
1988	25	74	64	62
1987	24	57	40	62
1986	25	64	57	61
1985	15	86	35	57
1984	15	79	22	69
1983	20	83	29	70
1982	10	83	22	75
1981	15	86	7	95

13 H. James Saxton (R)

Of Vincentown — Elected 1984

Born: Jan. 22, 1943, Scranton, Pa.
Education: East Stroudsburg (Pa.) State College, B.A. 1965; Temple U., graduate studies, 1967-68.
Occupation: Owner of realty company.
Family: Wife, Helen Gadomski; two children.
Religion: Methodist.
Political Career: N.J. Assembly, 1976-82; N.J. Senate, 1982-84.
Capitol Office: 324 Cannon Bldg. 20515; 225-4765.

In Washington: For two terms, Saxton has remained a rarely visible backbencher with a record reflecting conservatism and party loyalty. It is not unusual for him to vote with a majority of the GOP 80 percent of the time in a year — much more often than the average Eastern Republican.

Saxton's loyalty, however, did not keep him from receiving a post-Christmas lump of coal in 1988, when the defense secretary's commission charged with drawing up recommendations for closing military bases listed the Army's Fort Dix, which lies partly in the 13th, for near-total closure, eliminating some 4,600 military and civilian jobs.

Saxton and Republican Christopher H. Smith, whose 4th District contains the other part of Fort Dix, objected to the commission's findings. On the House floor in early 1989, Saxton said the commission used inaccurate and incomplete information on Fort Dix; he called the base-closing plan "flawed, seriously flawed," and said it would "wrongly disrupt the lives of thousands of individuals." But an effort to kill the plan failed, 43-381.

The Fort Dix controversy was a rare moment in the spotlight for Saxton; he is not as well-known in the House as Dean A. Gallo, his more gregarious New Jersey colleague in the 1984 GOP class. Saxton spends much of his time in his district, while Gallo is an inside player, with seats on Appropriations and Budget.

Saxton's concern for his district has led him to support some domestic spending programs that conservatives typically question. In the 99th and 100th Congresses, Saxton lobbied for impact aid, the federal education subsidy that grants money to local governments to compensate for federal installations that use their services but pay no taxes. The Reagan administration had made several efforts to cut impact aid. That was a problem for Saxton, since his district has not only Fort Dix, but also a large Air Force base. Impact aid was reauthorized on a 1988 education bill.

Early in 1985, after his elderly constituents bombarded him with complaints about proposed reductions in Social Security, Saxton announced he was forming a "COLA Coalition" to preserve inflation-based cost-of-living increases for Social Security recipients.

After a summer riddled with reports of medical waste washing up on New Jersey beaches, Saxton and New Jersey Democrat William J. Hughes, a fellow Merchant Marine member, sponsored a bill in 1988 to ban the dumping of medical waste in oceans and the Great Lakes.

At Home: Saxton struggled to win the GOP nomination for the seat left open by the March 1984 death of GOP Rep. Edwin B. Forsythe. But after surviving a tough primary, all else has been easy in this heavily Republican district.

Saxton's 1984 primary contest was mostly a matter of geography. A state legislator for eight years, he came in with the backing of the strong GOP organization in Burlington County, which has roughly half of the 13th's people. But the 13th also includes Camden and Ocean counties, and each supplied a candidate.

The stiffest challenge to Saxton came from M. Dean Haines and his Ocean County organization. Assemblyman John A. Rocco of Camden County was also in the primary, but his differences with his county organization resulted in the GOP endorsement of Saxton.

The lesser-known Haines concentrated his efforts on Ocean County, where turnout had traditionally been high. Saxton, with his large state Senate constituency, broadened his base, running Philadelphia TV ads to reach voters in Camden and Burlington County.

The strategy paid off. With Saxton and Haines winning on their home turf, the contest was decided in Camden County. Saxton's second-place showing behind Rocco there allowed him to win the primary by about 1,400 votes.

Saxton won easily over James B. Smith, the Democratic mayor of Mount Holly. Saxton pledged not to raise taxes and proposed a balanced-budget amendment, but he departed from conservative orthodoxy on environmental issues, promising to support the "superfund" program.

New Jersey 13

South and Central

The 13th runs the width of south-central New Jersey, from the Delaware River towns of western Burlington County to the oceanfront strip of Long Beach Island. There is a bit of everything: densely settled suburbs, small villages, beach resorts, patches of industrial development and the Pine Barrens wilderness.

But the diversity does little to dilute the area's Republican cast. Ocean County has long been a GOP stronghold. The portion of Burlington County in the 13th has some pockets of Democrats as well as many independent-minded voters, but the GOP usually commands their loyalty. Only Camden County is competitive, but its most Democratic areas, including the city of Camden, are in the neighboring 1st District.

The population center of Burlington County is at its western end, in Philadelphia suburbs such as Moorestown and Mount Laurel. By design, it is difficult to find apartment buildings or low-income housing in much of this area.

But the traditional residential patterns continue to prevail, and the affluent area remains firmly Republican. There is an exception, though, in Willingboro, the planned town built in the late 1950s as Levittown, which has many black voters.

Eastward toward the Pinelands, the population thins out. Agriculture is a major trade, but the region's small towns have been highly dependent through the years on McGuire Air Force Base and also on Fort Dix, which is now slated for near-shutdown.

The portion of Camden County in the 13th is dominated by Cherry Hill, one of New Jersey's first post-World War II suburbs. The city and its environs have many affluent GOP voters, but there are also young professionals and Jewish voters, and they are prone to vote Democratic.

Southern Ocean County is mostly residential. Manchester Township has huge retirement communities; along the shore are resort towns drawing summer residents from nearby states.

Population: 526,062. White 472,404 (90%), Black 40,734 (8%), Other 7,767 (2%). Spanish origin 10,372 (2%). 18 and over 377,446 (72%), 65 and over 68,455 (13%). Median age: 32.

Committees

Banking, Finance and Urban Affairs (14th of 20 Republicans)
Consumer Affairs and Coinage; Financial Institutions Supervision, Regulation and Insurance; Housing and Community Development; International Development, Finance, Trade and Monetary Policy

Merchant Marine and Fisheries (8th of 17 Republicans)
Fisheries and Wildlife Conservation and the Environment; Oceanography; Oversight and Investigations

Select Aging (12th of 27 Republicans)
Health and Long-Term Care

Elections

1988 General		
H. James Saxton (R)	167,470	(69%)
James B. Smith (D)	73,561	(31%)
1986 General		
H. James Saxton (R)	82,866	(65%)
John Wydra (D)	43,920	(35%)

Previous Winning Percentage: **1984** (61%) †

† Elected to a full term and to fill a vacancy at the same time.

District Vote For President

	1988		1984		1980		1976	
D	97,084	(38%)	86,540	(35%)	73,063	(36%)	89,933	(45%)
R	156,439	(61%)	161,435	(65%)	124,823	(61%)	105,241	(53%)
I					3,862	(2%)		

Campaign Finance

	Receipts	Receipts from PACs	Expend-itures
1988			
Saxton (R)	$491,036	$195,430 (40%)	$411,620
1986			
Saxton (R)	$395,300	$154,238 (39%)	$325,522
Wydra (D)	$70,633	$27,175 (39%)	$60,843

Key Votes

1987	
Raise speed limit to 65 mph	N
Approve Gephardt "fair trade" amendment	N
Ban testing of larger nuclear weapons	N
Delay "re-flagging" of Kuwaiti tankers	N
Approve tax-raising deficit-reduction bill	N
1988	
Approve aid to Nicaraguan contras	Y
Enact civil rights restoration bill over Reagan veto	Y
Kill 60-day plant-closing notification measure	Y
Pass omnibus trade bill over Reagan veto	Y
Approve death penalty for drug-related murders	Y
Bar federal funds for abortions in cases of rape and incest	Y
Oppose seven-day waiting period for purchase of handguns	N

Voting Studies

	Presidential Support		Party Unity		Conservative Coalition	
Year	**S**	**O**	**S**	**O**	**S**	**O**
1988	57	42	80	19	82	16
1987	58	42	73	27	91	9
1986	64	34	67	33	78	22
1985	61	39	81	19	76	24

Interest Group Ratings

Year	ADA	ACU	AFL-CIO	CCUS
1988	30	72	50	79
1987	24	52	38	73
1986	30	64	57	56
1985	15	81	12	82

14 Frank J. Guarini (D)

Of Jersey City — Elected 1978

Born: Aug. 20, 1924, Jersey City, N.J.
Education: Dartmouth College, B.A. 1947; New York U. Law School, J.D. 1950, LL.M. 1955.
Military Career: Navy, 1944-46.
Occupation: Lawyer.
Family: Single.
Religion: Roman Catholic.
Political Career: N.J. Senate 1966-72; sought Democratic nomination for U.S. Senate, 1970.
Capitol Office: 2458 Rayburn Bldg. 20515; 225-2765.

In Washington: While Guarini's authentic Jersey accent and roots in Hudson County politics would seem to make him a natural ally for Ways and Means Chairman Dan Rostenkowski, Guarini is an unpredictable individualist rather than a team player, and he is not part of the committee's powerful inner circle.

Unlike the gritty urban-machine Democrats the chairman prefers, Guarini is at least part Eastern establishment. When he is home, he spends some of his time in a luxury apartment overlooking Central Park in New York's Manhattan, across the river from his district. When he travels abroad on congressional business, he often returns with expensive *objets d'art*, the purchase of which is made possible by his substantial private fortune.

It was Guarini's training as a tax lawyer — coupled with some lobbying by influential home-state colleague Robert A. Roe — that helped him win a seat on Ways and Means early in his career. Guarini has fashioned an image as a spokesman for the small taxpayer, but he also watches out for those in the upper echelon.

His unpredictable voting pattern disappointed committee Democrats who expected him to be a loyal ally, but it is a point of pride for Guarini. Asked about his loyalties on the committee, he once said: "You don't walk a middle ground. You walk to the left, to the right, to the middle. You always have to keep them guessing, so they need you."

Such rhetoric gives Guarini almost a populist appeal in his working-class district, but while he speaks out on a variety of issues on Ways and Means, his interests sometimes turn out to be wider than they are deep. He has a reputation for moving on ideas without rounding up support from other committee members or fully considering all the policy implications of his proposal.

In the 100th Congress, Guarini championed a popular proposal to expand tax breaks for education benefits, but he had not won over Ways and Means members to the idea, and they nearly derailed it.

Under existing law, employees were allowed to deduct up to $5,250 in tuition benefits, but the exclusion was set to expire at the end of 1987. "This could slam the door on many young people in America," he said.

Guarini gathered more than 300 cosponsors for his bill to continue the current exclusion and add one for graduate students who receive tuition waivers for teaching or other services. He hewed to Rostenkowski's decree that any member advocating a tax break on the "technical corrections" bill also propose an offsetting revenue source: Guarini suggested that the exclusion be limited to lower-paid workers.

But when Ways and Means voted on the measure, they accepted only Guarini's revenue-increase language. The committee rejected his expansion for graduate teaching assistants, denied employee benefits for postgraduate work, and ultimately capped undergraduate benefits at $1,500. Fortunately for Guarini's cause, the Senate opted for the higher cap, which was agreed to in conference.

Guarini currently holds one of Ways and Means' seats on the Budget Committee, but he is not regarded as an influential conduit between the two powerful panels. In his first term on Budget, he delivered some hard-line rhetoric on deficit reduction, once complaining about farm subsidies, "In my part of the country, if an industry can't cut the mustard, they close down."

Guarini has sometimes argued that taxes on the wealthy ought to be higher. In the 98th Congress, he was one of the most enthusiastic sponsors of a bill to cap the final year of the Reagan tax cut at $700 per taxpayer. "If there are those in New Jersey who are in the upper 10 percent of our bracket and have to pay," he said, "so be it." The House passed the bill, but it died in the Senate.

But other Guarini efforts have included pushing the controversial "love boat" deduction for expenses incurred while attending a convention on a cruise ship and arguing for a 10 percent investment tax credit on the cost of any

New Jersey 14

North — Jersey City

Heavily ethnic and heavily Democratic, Hudson County long embodied all the color — and meanness — of urban machine politics. From 1917 to the late 1940s, the legendary political boss, Frank "I Am the Law" Hague, ruled the county by sending his opponents to jail or the hospital. Unions were equally rough in Hudson, especially along the docks, which remain central to the county's economy; the 1954 film "On the Waterfront" was set in Hoboken.

As in most urban areas, Hudson County's machine has lost much of its iron-fisted dominance in recent years. Independent-voting young professionals, driven across the river by New York City's high housing prices, have set up pockets of "gentrification" in grimy Jersey City and Hoboken. Communities of Cuban-Americans, now 8 percent of the 14th District population, are mainly staunch anti-communists who idolize Ronald Reagan. Even some of the bedrock blue-collar Democrats have become amenable to national Republican candidates because of their conservative social views.

But while Reagan and Republican Gov. Thomas H. Kean carried Hudson County in the mid-1980s, it is still, in the main, a Democratic county. Guarini has easily rebuffed even highly touted GOP challengers. In 1988, Democratic presidential candidate Michael S. Dukakis took Hudson with 54 percent of the vote.

Jersey City, with 220,000 residents, has nearly two-fifths of Hudson County's population. About 45 percent black and Hispanic, it has its problems with poverty, much of it concentrated in the Paulus Hook section. The city contains Liberty State Park, and local boosters are fond of pointing out that the Statue of Liberty actually stands within their city limits, not New York's. However, the statue has its back to Jersey City's rugged industrial waterfront.

Bayonne — site of huge shipping terminals — has a longstanding political rivalry with equally Democratic Jersey City. Because it is No. 2 in the county in size, with less than a third of Jersey City's population, Bayonne often loses out.

Union City and West New York, located in the northern part of Hudson County, house most of the burgeoning Cuban population. The Cubans, many of them professionals and merchants, have helped stabilize a deteriorating urban area; their shops now crowd Bergenline Avenue. While their conservative foreign policy views lead many of these voters to the Republican line for national office, they are more favorable to Democrats at the local level.

Population: 526,062. White 395,189 (75%), Black 68,892 (13%), Other 15,414 (3%). Spanish origin 143,203 (27%). 18 and over 388,408 (74%), 65 and over 66,005 (13%). Median age: 32.

horse up to $100,000. Before coming to Congress, Guarini was attorney for the Standard Breeders and Owners Association of New Jersey. He has also been a racehorse owner himself.

Guarini was not one of the more important participants when Ways and Means overhauled the tax code in the 99th Congress. He did, however, look after New Jersey interests. One of his efforts was to keep a provision that allowed the New Jersey Sports and Exposition Authority to go ahead with plans to finance construction of a baseball stadium with tax-free bonds.

Guarini was somewhat more active on trade issues in the 99th and 100th Congresses. In 1987, he backed an amendment to help firms seeking to sue foreign manufacturers accused of dumping goods in the United States at prices below production costs. He also pushed for quick action on the U.S.-Canada free-trade agreement, noting that Canada is New Jersey's largest trading partner. In 1989, he was appointed to the House Task Force on Trade and Competitiveness.

Guarini is perhaps most aggressive when he is involved in border disputes between New Jersey and New York. In 1989, he sponsored legislation to bar New York from increasing the income-tax rates on commuters. Earlier in his career, he was one of the leading opponents of the multibillion-dollar Westway highway and land development project on Manhattan.

Guarini is a friend of labor on most issues, an old-fashioned public works Democrat who believes in federally subsidized jobs as part of the answer to economic stagnation. In the 97th and 98th Congresses he introduced legislation to create a Reconstruction Finance Corporation, similar to the Depression-era agency, to back new industrial projects that would provide jobs on a massive basis.

At Home: Guarini developed keen political instincts while navigating his way through Hudson County's Byzantine power struggles. Apart from an unsuccessful primary bid against Democratic Sen. Harrison A. Williams Jr. in

1970, Guarini, a former Hudson County Democratic chairman, has taken no false steps; he has won each of his House elections with at least 64 percent of the vote.

In 1977, Democratic Rep. Joseph A. LeFante backed the loser in a divisive Jersey City mayoral election and chose to retire after one term rather than face a challenge for renomination. Guarini, a former state senator who was on the winning side in the mayoral contest, had the seat all but handed to him.

Another shift in 1981 brought a new set of people into power in Jersey City. But Guarini by then had moved into a protective neutral posture.

After a series of easy elections, Guarini's fine-tuned political radar enabled him to head off a possible threat in 1986. A slackening of the Democratic stranglehold over Hudson County — President Reagan and GOP Gov. Thomas H. Kean carried the county in the early 1980s — emboldened district Republicans to think that Guarini could be weakened. They recruited Albio Sires, a member of the county's small but staunchly conservative Cuban-American community, to run against the incumbent.

Sires, a strong Reagan supporter who decried Guarini's opposition to aid to the Nicaraguan contras, did help Republicans solidify their Cuban base. But the inexperienced candidate, a state official and former teacher, failed to expand his appeal to the other ethnic groups that populate Hudson County.

For his part, Guarini was not about to be blindsided. After coaxing an unusually large turnout for his routine primary win, he campaigned diligently and made good use of his large campaign treasury. Guarini's nearly 3-to-1 victory margin dispelled GOP notions of his vulnerability: His 1988 win was routine.

Committees

Budget (10th of 21 Democrats)
Task Forces: Defense, Foreign Policy and Space; Economic Policy, Projections and Revenues

Select Narcotics Abuse and Control (7th of 18 Democrats)

Ways and Means (10th of 23 Democrats)
Trade

Elections

1988 General		
Frank J. Guarini (D)	104,001	(67%)
Fred J. Theemling Jr. (R)	47,293	(31%)
1988 Primary		
Frank J. Guarini (D)	35,964	(67%)
Robert P. Haney Jr. (D)	10,680	(20%)
Edward A. Allen (D)	7,027	(13%)
1986 General		
Frank J. Guarini (D)	63,057	(71%)
Albio Sires (R)	23,822	(27%)

Previous Winning Percentages: **1984** (66%) **1982** (74%) **1980** (64%) **1978** (64%)

District Vote For President

	1988	1984	1980	1976
D	91,042 (55%)	89,414 (47%)	87,026 (50%)	105,453 (56%)
R	73,382 (44%)	102,475 (53%)	78,796 (45%)	80,607 (43%)
I			7,465 (4%)	

Campaign Finance

	Receipts	Receipts from PACs	Expend-itures
1988			
Guarini (D)	$552,280	$213,835 (39%)	$369,578
1986			
Guarini (D)	$374,304	$293,078 (78%)	$305,003
Sires (R)	$76,264	$8,800 (12%)	$62,073

Key Votes

1987	
Raise speed limit to 65 mph	N
Approve Gephardt "fair trade" amendment	Y
Ban testing of larger nuclear weapons	Y
Delay "re-flagging" of Kuwaiti tankers	Y
Approve tax-raising deficit-reduction bill	Y
1988	
Approve aid to Nicaraguan contras	N
Enact civil rights restoration bill over Reagan veto	Y
Kill 60-day plant-closing notification measure	N
Pass omnibus trade bill over Reagan veto	Y
Approve death penalty for drug-related murders	Y
Bar federal funds for abortions in cases of rape and incest	N
Oppose seven-day waiting period for purchase of handguns	N

Voting Studies

	Presidential Support		Party Unity		Conservative Coalition	
Year	**S**	**O**	**S**	**O**	**S**	**O**
1988	26	65	85	8	37	61
1987	23	76	88	6	35	65
1986	22	76	89	8	28	70
1985	21	79	93	3	15	80
1984	27	60	80	5	15	64
1983	18	76	90	4	15	80
1982	34	60	89	7	23	71
1981	33	57	85	5	16	77

Interest Group Ratings

Year	ADA	ACU	AFL-CIO	CCUS
1988	70	14	100	46
1987	88	0	94	20
1986	80	14	93	17
1985	85	5	94	20
1984	70	14	92	31
1983	90	9	100	21
1982	90	10	90	21
1981	85	7	93	0

New Mexico

U.S. CONGRESS

SENATE 1 D, 1 R
HOUSE 1 D, 2 R

LEGISLATURE

Senate 26 D, 16 R
House 45 D, 25 R

ELECTIONS

1988 Presidential Vote	
Bush	52%
Dukakis	47%
1984 Presidential Vote	
Reagan	60%
Mondale	39%
1980 Presidential Vote	
Reagan	55%
Carter	37%
Anderson	7%
Turnout rate in 1984	52%
Turnout rate in 1986	37%
Turnout rate in 1988	47%

(as percentage of voting age population)

POPULATION AND GROWTH

1980 population	1,302,894
1988 population estimate (37th in the nation)	1,507,000
Percent change 1980-1988	+16%

DEMOGRAPHIC BREAKDOWN

White	75%
Black	2%
American Indian	8%
(Spanish origin)	37%
Urban	72%
Rural	28%
Born in state	52%
Foreign-born	4%

MAJOR CITIES

Albuquerque	366,750
Santa Fe	55,980
Las Cruces	54,090
Roswell	44,110
Farmington	39,050

AREA AND LAND USE

Area	121,335 sq. miles (5th)
Farm	61%
Forest	24%
Federally owned	33%

Gov. Garrey Carruthers (R)
Of Las Cruces — Elected 1986

Born: Aug. 29, 1939, Alamosa, Colo.
Education: New Mexico State U., B.S. 1964, M.S. 1965; Iowa State U., Ph.D. 1968.
Occupation: Business consultant; professor.
Religion: Methodist.
Political Career: Assistant U.S. secretary of interior, 1981-84.
Next Election: 1990.

WORK

Occupations	
White-collar	54%
Blue-collar	29%
Service workers	14%
Government Workers	
Federal	25,584
State	42,172
Local	54,390

MONEY

Median family income	$ 16,928	(42nd)
Tax burden per capita	$ 993	(15th)

EDUCATION

Spending per pupil through grade 12	$ 3,195	(35th)
Persons with college degrees	18%	(16th)

CRIME

Violent crime rate	629 per 100,000 (11th)

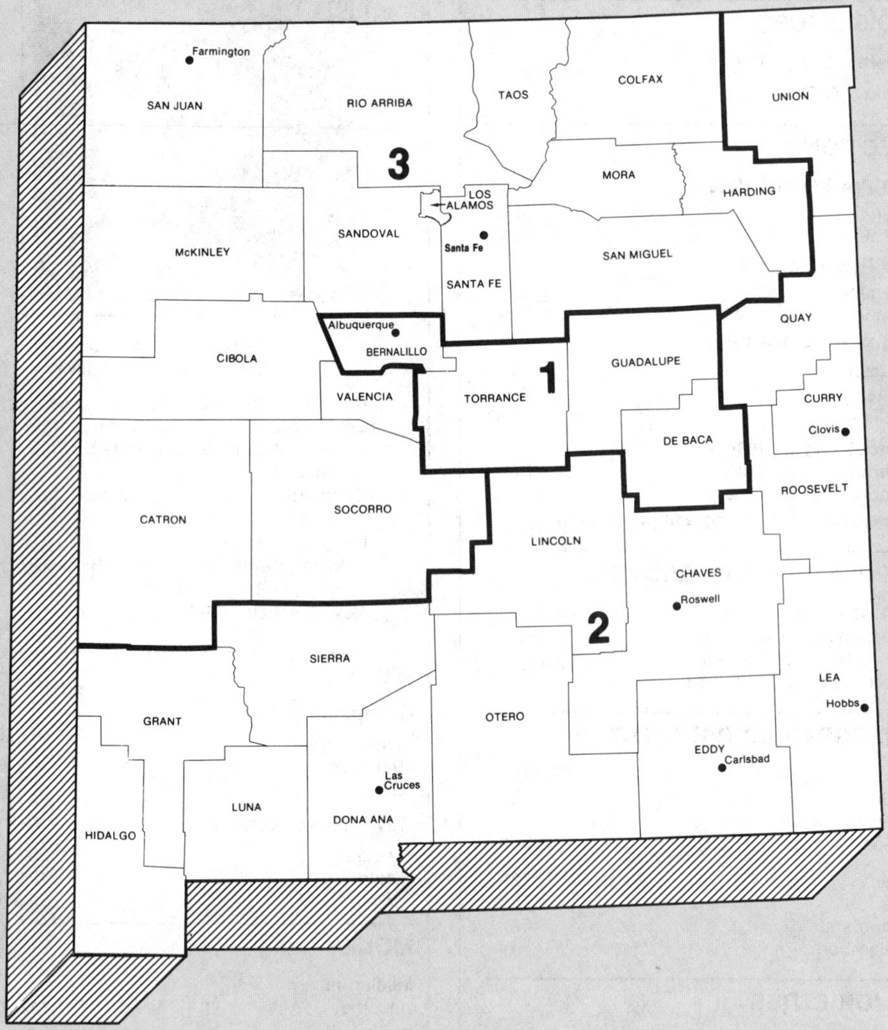
Farmington
SAN JUAN
RIO ARRIBA
TAOS
COLFAX
UNION
3
LOS ALAMOS
MORA
HARDING
McKINLEY
SANDOVAL
Santa Fe
SAN MIGUEL
SANTA FE
Albuquerque
BERNALILLO
QUAY
CIBOLA
1
GUADALUPE
VALENCIA
TORRANCE
CURRY
Clovis
DE BACA
CATRON
SOCORRO
ROOSEVELT
LINCOLN
CHAVES
Roswell
2
SIERRA
LEA
Hobbs
GRANT
OTERO
EDDY
Carlsbad
Las Cruces
LUNA
DONA ANA
HIDALGO

Pete V. Domenici (R)

Of Albuquerque — Elected 1972

Born: May 7, 1932, Albuquerque, N.M.
Education: U. of Albuquerque, 1950-52; U. of New Mexico, B.S. 1954; U. of Denver, LL.B. 1958.
Occupation: Lawyer.
Family: Wife, Nancy Burk; eight children.
Religion: Roman Catholic.
Political Career: Albuquerque City Commission, 1966-70, chairman and ex-officio mayor, 1967-70; Republican nominee for governor, 1970.
Capitol Office: 434 Dirksen Bldg. 20510; 224-6621.

In Washington: Domenici laid down the burden of the Budget Committee chairmanship after the 99th Congress, but he remains his party's best-known budget spokesman on Capitol Hill. As such, he has been a pivotal participant in the "summit meetings" between congressional leaders and the president that have dominated the budget process since late 1987.

Even if the GOP had not lost control of the Senate in the 1986 elections, the new pattern of summitry would have changed Domenici's life. After a summit, it is not necessary for budget committee leaders to spend tortuous months negotiating daily with White House minions, Senate colleagues and emissaries from the House Budget Committee.

The summit mechanism also enables the minority Republicans on the Hill to bring their big gun, the GOP president, to bear at the outset of congressional budget deliberations. So Domenici, who enjoys a certain rapport with President Bush, has not suffered the power loss he might have in losing the Budget chairmanship. He may not spend as much of the year patching together a fragile, centrist consensus, but his word retains authority.

For example, even as the first such budget agreement was being thrashed out, Domenici rushed to the floor to oppose a waiver of budget-related procedural rules on a housing bill. His appeal, no less eloquent for being extemporaneous, was heard by a number of senators arriving to vote. The waiver was defeated.

After the April 1989 budget-summit agreement with the White House, Domenici and Democratic Budget Chairman Jim Sasser of Tennessee were able to sell their end of the deal to their committee on a vote of 16-7. It was clear that few, if any, really difficult decisions had been attempted on the way to meeting the deficit-reduction target for fiscal 1990. The real pain of a tax vs. cut decision had been postponed until deliberations for fiscal 1991. Nevertheless, Sasser and Domenici had prepackaged the deal to appeal to a bipartisan majority of their committee.

This was much the same sort of partnership Domenici had achieved with Sasser's predecessor in the 100th Congress, Lawton Chiles of Florida, who retired rather than seek re-election in 1988. But while he has mastered the art of the possible, Domenici has seemed at times to long for a more decisive offensive against the deficit.

At times during his six years in the Budget chairmanship, the struggle seemed to push Domenici to the brink of despair. "I think we're getting very close to abandoning the notion of ever truly balancing the budget," he said in 1986. The best he could see for the future was an endless succession of painful fights over spending. "Maybe senators are destined to spend our mortal life pushing, shoving, cajoling and fighting this thing called the budget," he added.

Nevertheless, Domenici carried out his duties with energy born of his belief that the congressional budget process was the only way out of the federal government's fiscal predicament. If this duty-driven man was able to make only modest progress in curbing the deficit, he demonstrated a sincere commitment to goals that many of his colleagues seemed satisfied to pursue with nothing more than rhetoric.

Along the way, though, Domenici became less a leader than a manager, a technician focused more on getting *something* passed than on enacting his own conservative views. More than once, he voted for a budget resolution he did not like just to avoid a deadlock.

Domenici worked hard to build unity on his committee, accommodating his colleagues and heeding their wishes on everything from meeting times to spending priorities. He avoided using high-pressure tactics to persuade senators to do things they did not want to do.

But Domenici's earnest temperament sometimes produced irritated outbursts that worked against his consensus-building efforts. He is an intense presence, smoking heavily in committee rooms where he may be the only one smoking. He is a sensitive man who appears genuinely distressed when a colleague is angry at him. He does not suffer criticism lightly, and frequently bristles at reporters and others who question his actions.

Domenici's record as chairman loomed over his campaign to become majority leader at the start of the 99th Congress. His fellow Republicans saw him as hard-working and intelligent, but without the flair for firm direction that an eventual majority saw in winner Bob Dole of Kansas. Domenici received nine votes on the first round of balloting, and was eliminated on the second ballot.

Before the Republican takeover of the Senate in 1981 imposed the Budget chair on Domenici, he had been a legislative dabbler, stubborn and intense about promoting a variety of issues but not widely identified with any. Much of his hardest work had been oriented to New Mexico. The budget job complicated his life in this regard. By nature, it reduces its occupant at times to hectoring. And that can create problems when, on occasion, the chairman needs to look after his own political constituency. It has not always been easy for Domenici to press his concerns with colleagues whose own requests he often must refuse. On one occasion in 1986 he had to ask colleagues to waive the Budget Act with respect to a particular stretch of road in New Mexico that led to a federal facility. The project had been inadvertently left off a list of road projects, and Domenici had to make his pitch for it on the floor. When the waiver was granted, Domenici sent each supporting colleague a personal note of thanks.

Added to the Appropriations Committee in the 98th Congress, Domenici has been a voice for spending restraint — as one would expect — and for the traditional Western concerns of water, power and rangeland agriculture. But he has also been a strong, often impassioned advocate of spending on science and research. He has been among those in the 101st Congress petitioning Bush to appoint, and listen to, a top-level science adviser. Some of his concern stems from the role of Los Alamos' laboratories in New Mexico. But he has also warned that a diminished commitment to pure science, including the National Science Foundation's programs, will diminish the nation's future.

Freed from the constant siege of budget business in the 100th Congress, Domenici could devote more time to other legislative interests. One was the drug bill of 1988, where he supported expedited procedures and tougher penalties for drug users, who could face civil fines of up to $10,000. But he shied from some of the more onerous details of the House plan. "Ours is better than the House provision because it is constitutional," he said at one juncture.

Like many Western senators, Domenici took a close interest in the free-trade pact with Canada, especially in a feature he persuaded the administration to include. It contained the substance of his long-sought bailout for the U.S. uranium industry, including a federal commitment to buy $750 million of U.S. uranium. The bailout also committed the government and the industry to a billion-dollar cleanup of uranium tailings — the radioactive residue produced when uranium ore is mined.

Domenici and other Westerners wanted the deal stuck to the Canadian agreement because that country is a major source of the uranium now used in the United States. But the maneuver aroused the opposition of the Senate Finance Committee and three House committees and was dropped from the administration's final package of legislation implementing the trade pact. Later, the bailout was attached to other energy legislation and passed overwhelmingly by the Senate. But it was not given consideration in the House.

It was the renewal of an old crusade for Domenici. He held up passage of a Nuclear Regulatory Commission bill in the 97th Congress until he could get the Senate to agree to suspend proposed NRC regulations requiring the cleanup of uranium tailings, which have piled up in the West for decades. The industry considered the proposed regulations burdensome. Domenici proposed instead that the Environmental Protection Agency issue health standards; based on those standards, the NRC would issue new regulations, which would have to take costs into consideration. His proposal became law.

On the same measure, Domenici won a limit on uranium imports, despite opposition from the Reagan administration. Domenici's proposal required that at least 80 percent of the uranium used by utilities be produced in the United States. In addition, his plan required a two-year moratorium on new contracts for uranium imports if imports rose above 37.5 percent of U.S. consumption.

Since then, Domenici has continued his efforts on behalf of his state's hard-pressed mining industry. He won Energy Committee approval in 1986 of a bill limiting uranium imports to no more than 50 percent of domestic consumption, and succeeded in adding to the 1985 textile import bill an amendment calling for negotiations to limit world production of copper.

Although he left the Environment Committee at the start of the 100th Congress, Domenici was an active member of the panel for several years. In the 99th Congress, he helped hammer out the compromise in the toxic-waste "superfund" cleanup bill regarding settlement terms for private entities responsible for cleanup costs. He was a vocal proponent of the industry point of view on reauthorization of the Clean Air Act, urging relaxation of some pollution standards.

Domenici was responsible for two major sections of the clean-air bill written in the 97th

Congress. With Colorado Democrat Gary Hart and Washington Republican Slade Gorton, Domenici crafted a compromise on a provision of the law designed to prevent "significant deterioration" in cities with air cleaner than national standards.

Under their plan, states could, under certain circumstances, "opt out" of a requirement that pollution be allowed to increase only up to pre-established levels.

Also with Hart, Domenici successfully sponsored a compromise on emissions in high altitudes. The Domenici-Hart plan called for standards that could be met by retuning existing low-altitude equipment, rather than installing additional equipment.

Still, as Domenici nears the end of his third term, he is remembered best for his six years as Senate budget helmsman. In the historic session of 1981, he led the committee and the full Senate in approving the spending cuts President Reagan wanted. But he was more interested in balancing the federal budget than in providing the fiscal stimulus sought by "supply side" conservatives (Reagan budget director David A. Stockman called him "a Hooverite"). He feared the full tax-cut program of the Reagan administration would deepen the deficit, and he later worked with Dole and then-Majority Leader Howard H. Baker Jr. to pass the $98 billion tax bill of 1982.

Domenici's budget odyssey proved equally difficult in 1985, and even more dramatic. He had to cope not only with a deadlock over spending priorities, but with a dominant new ally in Dole, who had succeeded Baker and whose active involvement threatened to overshadow the Budget chairman. The two partners worked for months to forge a consensus GOP plan, barely getting a budget plan out of committee only to have it begin to unravel on the Senate floor.

Eventually, Domenici and Dole were able to pass a compromise budget by pulling out all the stops. They brought an ailing Pete Wilson of California from the hospital in an ambulance to cast the tying vote, and secured a 50-49 majority with a tie-breaking vote cast by Vice President George Bush. "We have achieved what I'm sure the cynics thought was impossible," Domenici rejoiced.

Domenici was even more assertive during 1986 budget debates. He openly criticized the Reagan administration's tax and spending policies, and forged a bipartisan compromise with Chiles to produce a budget plan. His proposal got through the Senate easily enough, but ran into the same House vs. administration deadlock he had confronted in the past. Domenici could do little more than referee the clash, which eventually produced a budget he confessed to being not particularly proud of. "We just can't do any more than the United States Congress lets us, and the president will support," he said. "That's it."

Late in 1986, as he ended his six-year tenure as head of the Budget Committee, Domenici tried to squelch speculation that he was glad to be rid of the job. "Anyone around here who's saying, 'Isn't it neat that I don't have to worry about being chairman any more,' is just not being truthful," he insisted.

At Home: Seeking a first term in 1972, Domenici had the advantage of speaking Spanish in a state that was 37 percent Hispanic. He also had a Hispanic-sounding surname, even though he was born Pietro Vichi Domenici, the son of an immigrant Italian grocer. He drew more votes in Hispanic northern New Mexico than Republicans normally do.

Domenici's background was in municipal government. After law school, he had made his first political foray by winning a seat on the Albuquerque City Commission, and later became chairman, the equivalent of mayor. As a city official, he prided himself on neighborhood meetings he held to hear residents' complaints.

Counting on his Bernalillo County (Albuquerque) base, which cast a third of the vote in the state, Domenici ran for governor in 1970. He captured the Republican nomination in a six-way race with slightly less than 50 percent of the vote. Domenici was seen as a moderate in that campaign. His closest primary rival was Stephen C. Helbing, the GOP floor leader in the state House, who advocated a crackdown on student demonstrators.

In the fall, Bernalillo County did not come through for Domenici the way he had hoped. He carried it by only 8,909 votes, not enough for him to win statewide against Democrat Bruce King, the state House Speaker. King had the party registration advantage and was better known statewide. Domenici tried to raise doubts about King by criticizing his lack of administrative experience, but with little success.

Undeterred, Domenici came back in 1972, this time running for the Senate seat being vacated by Democrat Clinton P. Anderson. His Democratic opponent was former state Rep. Jack Daniels, who had also run for governor in 1970 but lost to King in the Democratic primary.

Daniels, a wealthy banker, differed little from Domenici on the issues. But Domenici pointed out that Daniels had stood on the same platform as Sen. George McGovern that year and pledged to back him as the Democratic presidential nominee. While Daniels had repudiated McGovern's call for reduced defense spending, the association hurt him. Domenici won with 54 percent of the vote.

Domenici's percentage dropped slightly in 1978. The Democratic candidate, state Attorney General (and later one-term Gov.) Toney Anaya, was Hispanic. Domenici had taken most of the heavily Hispanic counties in 1972, but six years later he lost most of them. In addition, his 1972 plurality of 31,240 votes in Bernalillo shrank to 6,766 in 1978.

Fortunately for Domenici, Anaya did not have a united Democratic Party behind him. As chief state prosecutor, he had secured indictments against several important party figures, arousing resentment among regulars and prompting many of them to stay away.

With a massive campaign treasury and his new national role as chairman of the Budget Committee, Domenici's re-election in 1984 was never much in doubt. He all but locked up the victory when no prominent Democrats chose to challenge him.

Domenici's eventual opponent, liberal state Rep. Judith A. Pratt, attempted to tie him to Reagan budget cuts that she said had hurt the state, but in a Republican year she could not begin to make a dent in Domenici's lead. The incumbent won a third term with more than 70 percent of the vote.

Committees

Budget (Ranking)

Appropriations (10th of 13 Republicans)
Treasury, Postal Service and General Government (ranking); District of Columbia; Energy and Water Development; Interior and Related Agencies; Transportation and Related Agencies

Energy and Natural Resources (3rd of 9 Republicans)
Energy Research and Development (ranking); Energy Regulation and Conservation; Public Lands, National Parks and Forests

Special Aging (6th of 9 Republicans)

Elections

1984 General

Pete V. Domenici (R)	361,371	(72%)
Judith A. Pratt (D)	141,253	(28%)

Previous Winning Percentages: 1978 (53%) **1972** (54%)

Campaign Finance

	Receipts	Receipts from PACs	Expenditures
1984			
Domenici (R)	$2,638,991	$784,295 (30%)	$2,618,105
Pratt (D)	$304,186	$106,073 (35%)	$301,661

Key Votes

1987

Enact omnibus highway bill over Reagan veto	N
Limit testing of space-based anti-ballistic missiles	N
Oppose banning tests of larger nuclear weapons	Y
Confirm Robert H. Bork as Supreme Court justice	Y

1988

Allow vote on campaign-finance overhaul	N
Pass civil rights restoration bill over Reagan veto	Y
Enact omnibus trade bill over Reagan veto	N
Approve death penalty for drug-related murders	Y
Oppose "workfare" amendment to welfare overhaul bill	N

Voting Studies

	Presidential Support		Party Unity		Conservative Coalition	
Year	**S**	**O**	**S**	**O**	**S**	**O**
1988	76	19	77	19	97	0
1987	69	31	78	20	88	13
1986	88	12	89	10	95	5
1985	82	15	90	6	88	8
1984	88	8	86	14	91	9
1983	74	18	72	14	75	9
1982	85	15	90	9	97	3
1981	84	13	86	8	94	4

Interest Group Ratings

Year	ADA	ACU	AFL-CIO	CCUS
1988	15	72	46	79
1987	20	65	30	78
1986	5	83	13	79
1985	5	82	10	83
1984	25	77	36	63
1983	15	44	19	35
1982	15	55	19	80
1981	15	64	11	94

Jeff Bingaman (D)

Of Santa Fe — Elected 1982

Born: Oct. 3, 1943, El Paso, Texas.
Education: Harvard U., B.A. 1965; Stanford U., J.D. 1968.
Military Career: Army Reserve, 1968-74.
Occupation: Lawyer.
Family: Wife, Anne Kovacovich; one child.
Religion: Methodist.
Political Career: N.M. attorney general, 1979-83.
Capitol Office: 524 Hart Bldg. 20510; 224-5521.

In Washington: Bingaman operates much like a mechanic. He lets others drive fast and chase the checkered flag; he is content to keep his head under the hood, where he pursues a genuine interest in the engine that drives the nation's military and economic policy.

A serious, thoughtful man, Bingaman rarely comes up with anything colorful or quotable to say. Once or twice a week, he abandons his Senate office for a quiet corner of the Supreme Court library down the street. He had a similarly secluded cubbyhole in Santa Fe when he was New Mexico attorney general — a place where he could retreat to study and think.

This studious style has served him well on the Armed Services Committee, where he has mastered the details of military management and impressed defense specialists as intelligent and thorough. As his second term unfolds, he appears most likely to make his mark here. His affinity for the nuts and bolts of the military-industrial complex has positioned him to leave the shadow of New Mexico's active senior senator, Republican Pete V. Domenici.

The Defense Industry and Technology Subcommittee he chairs was tailored for him when the Democrats recaptured the Senate majority in 1986. His work there rarely attracts headlines, but his concern for the structural health of the nation's defense-industrial base has begun to influence legislation. He is a leader among the defense centrists who have cautioned against using scorched-earth techniques to overhaul military procurement practices. Although he will vigorously assail what he considers waste in the military, Bingaman wants to make sure contractors capable of building complex weapons systems exist in the 21st century. Thus, he talks up formulas for allocating research and development costs in a manner that will not break contractors' backs.

Bingaman's crusades on defense and foreign policy issues at times reveal liberal instincts, but he is open-minded enough to be regarded as a reflective, not a reflexive, politician.

After Armed Services recommended 3 percent real growth in defense spending for fiscal 1986, Bingaman kept arguing for a no-growth budget. Comparing the aircraft, ships, tanks and personnel that could be afforded under the two spending options, he said the higher figure bought "relatively little additional security." With zero growth, Bingaman claimed, "we would still be able to continue our defense modernization at a rapid pace."

Advocates of the higher figure became less insistent after the Pentagon announced it had a $4 billion surplus because inflation and purchasing costs had been lower than expected. Bingaman later won approval of an amendment requiring the Pentagon to provide additional information in its quarterly reports to Congress on the cost of major weapons programs.

In 1986, Bingaman suggested another cost-cutting move that turned out to be an important test vote on the Navy's strategy of "homeporting" — dispersing ships to a larger number of ports. Although Bingaman's amendment was aimed at eliminating just two of the proposed new ports, it prompted a full-blown debate on the policy. Bingaman got support from Armed Services Chairman Barry Goldwater, who called homeporting a "terrific waste of money," but their view lost, 34-65.

Still, Bingaman does not hesitate to protect New Mexico's defense industry, which with research facilities such as the Los Alamos National Laboratory depends heavily on the government for weapons-research monies.

Bingaman was a critic of the Reagan administration's foreign aid spending priorities. During 1985 debate on a foreign aid bill, he said the administration had a "shortsighted" policy of boosting military sales overseas while reducing economic-development programs. "We cannot continue to increase security assistance," he said, "while droughts in Africa continue and 40,000 children die each day."

But Bingaman lost, 56-39, when he proposed cutting $100 million earmarked for loans to countries buying U.S. weapons. The next year, the Senate also rejected Bingaman's call to forbid the government from converting arms-export loans to grants. He said that conversions could cost the United States almost $7 billion in forgone interest income.

Bingaman's domestic agenda often aligns him with the "competitiveness" camp — the group that assesses government spending on programs in education, worker training, basic research and even defense in light of its contribution to the nation's ability to compete in the worldwide marketplace. And his willingness to tackle difficult subjects is not limited to national security: He introduced legislation in 1988 to overhaul the way the federal work force is paid.

Overall, Bingaman's voting record developed a less liberal cast over the course of his first six years in the Senate. Early in his first term, he once chalked up a 100 score from the liberal Americans for Democratic Action; now he is more likely to post a 65 or 70. Whether coincidentally or not, that trend in Bingaman's record was simultaneous with the plummeting popularity of the liberal Democratic movement in New Mexico, a decline brought on by controversies and scandals plaguing Gov. Toney Anaya (1983-87), who was succeeded in the governorship by Republican Garrey Carruthers.

At Home: When he launched his 1982 Senate campaign, Bingaman was in his third year as New Mexico's attorney general, little-known outside the legal and political communities. His main asset was being politically unscarred.

Lucky or shrewd, he stayed that way through his successful primary campaign against former Democratic Gov. Jerry Apodaca and then against GOP Sen. Harrison Schmitt.

In the primary, he capitalized on Apodaca's political baggage. The ex-governor was hamstrung by reports that he had ties to underworld figures. Bingaman did not directly mention Apodaca's problems, but he gave voters a not-so-subtle reminder with his slogan — "a senator we can proudly call our own."

Bingaman steadily gained strength against his controversial rival. He was endorsed by the state AFL-CIO, and then he narrowly won the support of the party convention. In the primary, he swept to nomination by a margin of nearly 3-to-2.

Incumbent Schmitt, a former Apollo astronaut, lacked Apodaca's political scars. But he was vulnerable, because many voters had the impression he was more interested in pet subjects such as 21st-century technology than in the state's struggling economy.

Labor backing, a voter-targeting program by the Democratic National Committee and a heavy Hispanic turnout for gubernatorial candidate Anaya all contributed to Bingaman's victory. He also owed a literal debt of thanks to his wife, a successful Santa Fe lawyer. Together, she and Bingaman lent his campaign more than $600,000, keeping it financially competitive with Schmitt's.

Bingaman spent much of the fall lambasting Schmitt for supporting supply-side economics, sharp increases in defense spending and cuts in Social Security payments. With statewide unemployment at 10 percent, Schmitt's connection with President Reagan was a campaign liability.

Schmitt hurt himself with a set of poorly researched advertisements that accused Bingaman, as attorney general, of condoning the release of a convicted murderer and failing to prosecute the instigators of a deadly prison riot. The charges backfired when the head of the state Supreme Court and an archbishop of the Catholic Church in New Mexico defended Bingaman. Bingaman went on to win with 54 percent of the vote.

Long before the calendar turned to 1988, national Republican Party operatives were portraying Bingaman as one of their top targets in the nation. His low-profile manner had left him with a fairly undefined image after one term in the Senate, and the GOP planned to fill in the blanks, claiming that Bingaman lacked the stature of colleague Domenici and had achieved little in Congress.

But the Republican line lost credibility when the party decided on a nominee who had stature problems of his own, and who could be less compelling on the stump even than Bingaman.

The GOP got in this predicament because the state's most prominent Republicans opted not to challenge Bingaman. There was a four-way primary won by state Sen. Bill Valentine. He worked hard to put Bingaman on the defensive, arguing that the Democrat canceled out Domenici's vote in the Senate. But Bingaman and Domenici are not known for having many confrontations with one another, and Bingaman deftly reminded voters that the Constitution calls for each state to have two senators, "not a senator and an assistant."

Valentine had considerable trouble whipping up enthusiasm, or money, for his campaign. Bingaman's low-key style may have left him with an somewhat undefined image, but it also helped him avoid offending any significant bloc of voters. There was simply no significant animosity toward Bingaman that Valentine could capitalize on. And with plenty of money to run waves of advertising that began early in the year, Bingaman was able to raise his profile and remind voters of his efforts in the Senate. On Election Day, Valentine did not even reach 40 percent of the vote.

Bingaman grew up in the isolated New Mexico mining town of Silver City, the son of a professor and nephew of John Bingaman, a confidant of Democratic Sen. Clinton Anderson. At Stanford Law School, Bingaman worked for Robert F. Kennedy's 1968 presidential campaign.

Returning to New Mexico, he served as counsel to the 1969 state constitutional convention. Although the new constitution was defeated at the polls, Bingaman's work caught the eye of the legal community. In 1972 he became a partner in the law firm of former Democratic Gov. Jack M. Campbell.

Bingaman ran for attorney general six years later. During the primary against another Santa Fe lawyer, Richard C. Bosson, Bingaman emphasized his concept of the office as a public law firm.

Criticizing Bingaman's lucrative private practice, Bosson contended that he was the true populist. But Bingaman drew the support of much of the legal community and won nomination handily. When his Republican opponent withdrew, Bingaman was guaranteed election.

Committees

Armed Services (5th of 11 Democrats)
Defense Industry and Technology (chairman); Readiness, Sustainability and Support; Strategic Forces and Nuclear Deterrence

Energy and Natural Resources (6th of 10 Democrats)
Mineral Resources Development and Production (chairman); Energy Regulation and Conservation; Public Lands, National Parks and Forests

Governmental Affairs (6th of 8 Democrats)
Government Information and Regulation (chairman); General Services, Federalism and the District of Columbia; Oversight of Government Management

Joint Economic
National Security Economics (chairman); Economic Resources and Competitiveness; Education and Health

Elections

1988 General

Jeff Bingaman (D)	321,983	(63%)
Bill Valentine (R)	186,579	(37%)

Previous Winning Percentage: **1982** (54%)

Campaign Finance

	Receipts	Receipts from PACs	Expend-itures
1988			
Bingaman (D)	$3,176,793	$1,100,451 (35%)	$3,164,973
Valentine (R)	$661,825	$91,363 (14%)	$659,624

Key Votes

1987

Enact omnibus highway bill over Reagan veto	Y
Limit testing of space-based anti-ballistic missiles	Y
Oppose banning tests of larger nuclear weapons	Y
Confirm Robert H. Bork as Supreme Court justice	N

1988

Allow vote on campaign-finance overhaul	Y
Pass civil rights restoration bill over Reagan veto	Y
Enact omnibus trade bill over Reagan veto	Y
Approve death penalty for drug-related murders	Y
Oppose "workfare" amendment to welfare overhaul bill	Y

Voting Studies

	Presidential Support		Party Unity		Conservative Coalition	
Year	**S**	**O**	**S**	**O**	**S**	**O**
1988	52	47	71	22	68	30
1987	32	60	74	21	53	38
1986	41	58	70	29	41	59
1985	33	66	75	24	37	60
1984	40	56	79	19	28	72
1983	45	54	81	15	25	73

Interest Group Ratings

Year	ADA	ACU	AFL-CIO	CCUS
1988	70	20	77	43
1987	65	13	90	40
1986	65	35	73	26
1985	70	13	81	34
1984	100	9	91	42
1983	90	4	94	42

1 Steven H. Schiff (R)

Of Albuquerque — Elected 1988

Born: March 18, 1947, Chicago, Ill.

Education: U. of Illinois, Chicago, B.A. 1968; U. of New Mexico, J.D. 1972.

Military Career: N.M. Air National Guard, 1969-present.

Occupation: Lawyer.

Family: Wife, Marcia Lewis; two children.

Religion: Jewish.

Political Career: Bernalillo County district attorney, 1981-89; candidate for district judge, 1978.

Capitol Office: 1520 Longworth Bldg. 20515; 225-6316.

The Path to Washington: Schiff won election to Congress in 1988 on a pledge to deliver constituent service, a rather modest agenda for a Republican who toppled two family dynasties to win in a politically competitive district.

But constituent service had been the hallmark of the Republican Schiff succeeded, Manuel Lujan Jr., and it may have been a sign of Schiff's shrewdness that he based his campaign on a promise that even a freshman can keep. (Lujan will be able to look over his successor's shoulder if he chooses, since he stayed on in Washington as President Bush's interior secretary.)

When Lujan announced his plans to leave the House after 20 years, a dozen candidates jockeyed to succeed him, including his brother, former state GOP Chairman Edward Lujan, and Democrat Tom Udall, the son of former Interior Secretary Stewart Udall and nephew of Arizona Rep. Morris K. Udall.

Schiff, a popular two-term Bernalillo County district attorney, had been contemplating a Senate bid, but quickly shifted his sights to the open House seat. Nearly all of the 1st District vote comes out of Bernalillo County (Albuquerque), where Schiff ousted a Democratic district attorney in 1980 and easily won re-election in 1984. In eight years on the job, Schiff became a familiar face in the media as he directed the prosecution of numerous high-profile criminal cases — including the brutal, random murder of a woman in 1986 that engrossed the city and helped transform its self-image from that of a small town to a major Sun Belt metropolis.

In spite of his high public profile, Schiff was an underdog in the primary against Edward Lujan, who seemed capable of sustaining his brother's coalition of business-oriented Republicans and Hispanic Democrats.

Outspent nearly 2-to-1, Schiff came under fire for his willingness to plea bargain. But the criticism just grazed Schiff, whose image as a studious, law-and-order prosecutor was deeply ingrained. Schiff successfully attacked Lujan for trying to inherit public office, a line he revisited in the general election.

In Democrat Udall, a 40-year-old attorney and environmental activist, Schiff faced a well-funded and well-organized foe whose name had helped him win a 10-way primary that included several prominent Hispanics.

The November campaign was personal and negative. While Schiff boasted that his office had won the most death-penalty cases in state history, he was again accused of letting criminals off easy. In addition, he came under fire for his lack of legislative experience.

Schiff countered by noting he was chief lobbyist for the state prosecutors' association, and he added that he understood military matters thanks to his 19 years in the Air National Guard — a plus in a district where the Sandia National Laboratories and Kirtland Air Force Base are major employers.

Schiff's counterattack on Udall included an accusation that the Democrat had failed to repay a student loan until he became a House candidate. In fact, Udall had repaid the loan six years earlier, well ahead of schedule, but he *was* a candidate at the time — in New Mexico's 3rd District, which covers the northern and western portions of the state. That exchange raised the carpetbagging issue, which was ultimately more damaging to Udall than any other. Schiff himself had moved from Chicago to New Mexico in 1969 to attend law school, but he made much of the fact that he and his wife had lived in the same house for the previous 16 years.

Though Schiff says he thinks of himself as a "lousy politician," he nevertheless brags that he made the news 2,000 times during his tenure as district attorney, and he is clearly a dogged political competitor. After losing his first bid for elective office — a judgeship race in 1978 — he invested his $20,000 life savings in a last-minute television ad blitz in his 1980 district attorney race.

New Mexico 1

Central — Albuquerque

Originally a health resort and trade center, Albuquerque had fewer than 40,000 residents in 1940. Its postwar emergence as a Republican stronghold was fueled by the development of a prosperous military-aerospace industry. By 1960 the population exceeded 200,000, and now it is almost twice that.

During the past two decades a diversified economy has sustained the boom. The city's population grew 36 percent in the 1970s and another 10 percent in the 1980s, enhancing Albuquerque's position as New Mexico's commercial hub and major population center. Including the Bernalillo County suburbs, the Albuquerque area is home for one-quarter of New Mexico's 1.5 million residents.

Electronics firms have provided the impetus for Albuquerque's latest round of population growth. Young engineers and scientists, attracted by jobs, and retirees, attracted by the weather, have helped in recent years to preserve the county's Republican tilt. Albuquerque and surrounding Bernalillo County have voted Republican in all but one presidential election since 1952.

But Albuquerque is not as militantly conservative as some of the other Sun Belt population centers. Though it was strong territory for George Bush in 1988, at the same time it went Democratic for U.S. Senate.

The county's large minority population provides a good Democratic base vote. Hispanics comprise 37 percent of the county's population. In addition, the newest generation of white-collar migrants exhibits some liberal tendencies. Independent John B. Anderson drew 10 percent of the county vote in his 1980 presidential bid, well above his statewide mark of 6 percent.

Three sparsely populated counties east of Albuquerque are also included in the 1st. Together, the three — De Baca, Guadalupe and Torrance counties — hold only 3 percent of the district's population. Ranching is the mainstay of the economy in De Baca and Guadalupe counties.

Population: 434,141. White 345,939 (80%), Black 9,816 (2%), Other 14,937 (3%). Spanish origin 162,171 (37%). 18 and over 307,647 (71%), 65 and over 35,961 (8%). Median age: 28.

Committees

Government Operations (10th of 15 Republicans)
Commerce, Consumer and Monetary Affairs; Government Information, Justice and Agriculture

Science, Space and Technology (18th of 19 Republicans)
Energy Research and Development; Space Science and Applications

Campaign Finance

	Receipts	Receipts from PACs	Expend-itures
1988			
Schiff (R)	$563,429	$158,911 (28%)	$559,134
Udall (D)	$580,819	$226,631 (39%)	$576,677

Elections

1988 General		
Steven H. Schiff (R)	89,985	(51%)
Tom Udall (D)	84,138	(47%)
1988 Primary		
Steven H. Schiff (R)	14,028	(41%)
Edward L. Lujan (R)	12,801	(37%)
John A. Budagher (R)	7,393	(22%)

District Vote For President

	1988	1984	1980	1976
D	81,687 (45%)	70,395 (39%)	57,566 (35%)	67,451 (45%)
R	96,586 (54%)	108,766 (60%)	87,583 (54%)	79,679 (54%)
I			15,291 (9%)	

2 Joe Skeen (R)

Of Picacho — Elected 1980

Born: June 30, 1927, Roswell, N.M.
Education: Texas A&M U., B.S. 1950.
Military Career: Navy, 1945-46; Air Force Reserve, 1949-52.
Occupation: Rancher.
Family: Wife, Mary Jones; two children.
Religion: Roman Catholic.
Political Career: Republican state chairman, 1962-65; N.M. Senate, 1961-71, minority leader, 1965-71; GOP nominee for lieutenant governor, 1970; GOP nominee for governor, 1974, 1978.
Capitol Office: 1007 Longworth Bldg. 20515; 225-2365.

In Washington: Skeen is a Western Republican of the old-school legislative style. Elected as a write-in candidate the year Ronald Reagan first swept to the presidency, Skeen shares the conservative ideology that prevails in his 1980 GOP class. But unlike some of his more rabble-rousing classmates, Skeen melds well with the establishment figures who have traditionally guided GOP politics in the House.

The difference between Skeen and his generation of House Republicans was evident during the 1989 GOP contest for minority whip. The race between Newt Gingrich and Edward Madigan was cast as one between change and the status quo, with Madigan representing the latter. While Gingrich's conservatism might have appealed to Skeen, he was not part of the group of younger Republicans credited with engineering the Georgian's victory; Skeen sided with Madigan.

That vote was consistent with Skeen's pattern of loyalty to House Minority Leader Robert H. Michel. During Reagan's two terms, Skeen was strongly supportive of his legislative agenda, but when GOP leaders decided to buck the president, Skeen generally went along. When Michel voted not to take up the Reagan-supported tax bill in late 1985, Skeen did, too. "My commitment to the leadership goes to Bob Michel," he said. "We've only got one leader on the Republican side, and that's Bob." When Reagan's lobbying efforts persuaded Michel to switch his vote on a second roll call, Skeen switched along with him.

Skeen's best-known legislative cause is his perennial effort with Indiana Democrat Andrew Jacobs Jr. to reduce the allowances and pensions for former presidents. The usual routine is for Jacobs to propose a draconian cut, and then for Skeen, the ranking Republican on Appropriations' Treasury Subcommittee, to offer a more modest reduction. In 1988, the full House approved Skeen's amendment to reduce the proposed $1.3 million allotment by $200,000. In 1986, they accepted Skeen's substitute to cut $58,000 from the budget item.

Prior to joining Appropriations in the 99th Congress, Skeen was noted for using his tough debating style to slug it out with Democrats on the Agriculture Committee. But since moving to Appropriations, he has adopted the mellower approach typical of that committee, where members with liberal and conservative attitudes toward federal spending try to develop a bipartisan consensus, and watch out for their constituents in the meantime.

Like his committee colleagues, Skeen looks for ways to bring federal dollars to his district. In his first term on the committee, he attached an amendment to the omnibus drug bill to provide $350,000 for the Los Alamos National Laboratory's research on a low-level radar detection system that could aid efforts to interdict drug smugglers.

A member of the Appropriations Subcommittee on Agriculture, Skeen is a dogged supporter of his district's sheep and cattle ranchers. A former rancher himself, he opposed efforts by senior Appropriations Democrat Sidney R. Yates in 1985 to triple fees charged to ranchers for the use of federal grazing lands. Yates managed to get his proposal through Appropriations, but when it came to the floor, Skeen complained that it constituted a tax provision in what was supposed to be a spending bill. Yates decided to withdraw the provision.

Skeen is one of the few House members willing to entertain the idea of locating a nuclear-waste site in his district. The Waste Isolation Pilot Project is proposed for the salt beds below ground near the 2nd District city of Carlsbad. The controversial plan would make Carlsbad the first permanent facility to store defense-generated low-level waste. But discovery of water leaking into the caves abruptly halted progress on authorizing legislation during the 100th Congress. Skeen intends to revisit

New Mexico 2

South and East — Las Cruces; Roswell

Southern New Mexico was once firmly Democratic, but traditional party ties have eroded there. During the 1970s, the area developed a strong habit of voting Republican in statewide contests, as ranchers and other Southern-style Democrats came to resent their party's national program.

The centerpiece of the 2nd District is "Little Texas," the southeastern corner of New Mexico. Settled by Texans early in the 20th century, the region is economically, culturally and politically similar to the adjoining Texas plains. Most of the land here is devoted to grazing cattle or sheep. But oil and military projects have reshaped voting habits in a Republican direction.

Nearly half the vote in the 14-county district is concentrated in four counties of "Little Texas." The oil- and gas-producing centers of Chaves County and Lea County are bastions of conservatism. Equally conservative Curry County is the site of a large Air Force base.

Near Carlsbad in Eddy County are the nation's most productive potash mines, and the area's unionized miners occasionally give Democrats enough votes to carry the county. George Bush won it in 1988, but it has twice supported Democratic Sen. Jeff Bingaman.

To the west are Otero and Dona Ana counties, which account for nearly one-third of the district population. Otero County favors the GOP. Dona Ana, which contains Las Cruces, has a Hispanic majority, giving the Democrats a substantial base, but Republicans generally carry it. Parts of Dona Ana, Otero and Sierra counties hold the sprawling White Sands Missile Range.

The district's lone Democratic strongholds are in the Mexican Highlands, along the Arizona border, where copper and lead mines have attracted union labor. But they have less than 10 percent of the vote.

Population: 436,261. White 359,531 (82%), Black 12,144 (3%), Other 6,438 (2%). Spanish origin 146,474 (34%). 18 and over 297,158 (68%), 65 and over 45,900 (11%). Median age: 28.

the issue in the 101st Congress, and says he will work "to ease the fears of individuals who are misinformed about the hazards of nuclear waste and its disposal."

Skeen favors government action when it comes to bolstering the flagging mining and energy industries that are crucial to New Mexico's economy. A staunch opponent of the windfall-profits tax on oil and natural gas, he offered an amendment to the 1987 supplemental appropriations bill to abolish the tax for certain types of oil. The amendment was rejected.

In late 1986, he cosponsored a package of measures that he said would provide incentives to domestic oil and gas companies to increase production. The proposals included repealing the windfall-profits tax and the Fuel Use Act (an energy crisis-era law that barred new electric power plants from using natural gas or oil), requiring that 50 percent of the oil purchased for the Strategic Petroleum Reserve be from domestic producers, and analyzing the economic impact of an oil import tax.

Skeen has called on Congress to find ways to revive the nearly dormant domestic uranium mining industry. "Because this industry is extremely important to this nation's national security and its energy security, it is time Congress takes the appropriate steps to ensure the viability of the uranium industry in the United States," he says.

Skeen once proposed that the Reagan administration negotiate with trading partners to set up voluntary restraints on copper imports. In the 97th Congress, worried that copper stockpiles in the strategic minerals reserve were far below target levels, Skeen supported a measure requiring the government to purchase copper. That bill was defeated when critics said the government's limited resources should buy metals not produced domestically.

At Home: After narrowly losing two carefully planned bids for governor, Skeen won a House seat without even being on the ballot. He is one of the few write-in candidates ever elected to the House.

Skeen's unusual victory came after Democratic Rep. Harold E. Runnels, who was unopposed for re-election, died on Aug. 5, 1980. Runnels' death set off three months of complex maneuvering, with Skeen and Runnels' widow, Dorothy, mounting unsuccessful court challenges to win a spot on the ballot against the substitute Democratic nominee, David King.

Skeen and Mrs. Runnels pursued separate write-in campaigns, aided by negative publicity that hit King. A former state finance commissioner, King had moved to the district only after Harold Runnels' death, and there were complaints that his choice was arranged by his uncle, Democratic Gov. Bruce King.

Skeen based his campaign on the contention that no one should be appointed to Congress. His write-ins totaled 38 percent of the vote, enough to win the three-way contest.

He has had little trouble since then. In

1982, Skeen easily dispatched his underfunded Democratic challenger, a state senator and deputy police chief from Clovis. Two years later, the Republican pulled down nearly 75 percent of the vote.

For a time, it appeared as though Skeen might face a serious challenge in 1986. His Democratic foe was Mike Runnels, son of Skeen's predecessor and a successful politician in his own right. Mike Runnels had four years as lieutenant governor under his belt when he launched his bid against Skeen.

Despite the advantage of solid name recognition, however, Runnels' bid never really got off the ground. The Democrat was slow to assemble an organization and had trouble generating enthusiasm for his campaign. Runnels' problems were complicated further by his connections to Democratic Gov. Toney Anaya, whose administration had been plagued by legislative deadlock and reports of scandal. Skeen, whose careful cultivation of the district had earned him even some Democrats' praise, went on to post a 63-37 percent victory. Two years later, Skeen ran unopposed.

Before his election in 1980, Skeen showed more interest in the New Mexico governor's mansion than he did in a U.S. House seat. In 1974 and 1978, he was the Republican candidate for governor, offering an aggressive conservative campaign that emphasized his support for right-to-work legislation. He lost each time by less than 3,800 votes, but was a substantial winner in the counties that now make up his district. Skeen was mentioned as a possible 1990 gubernatorial candidate, but in March 1989, he said he wanted to stay in the House.

Committee

Appropriations (16th of 22 Republicans)
Treasury, Postal Service and General Government (ranking); Rural Development, Agriculture and Related Agencies

Elections

1988 General		
Joe Skeen (R)	100,324	(100%)
1986 General		
Joe Skeen (R)	77,787	(63%)
Mike Runnels (D)	45,924	(37%)

Previous Winning Percentages: 1984 (74%) **1982** (58%) **1980** (38%)

District Vote For President

	1988	1984	1980	1976
D	67,307 (41%)	53,600 (33%)	50,472 (35%)	60,392 (46%)
R	96,142 (58%)	108,723 (66%)	86,337 (60%)	68,581 (53%)
I			4,843 (3%)	

Campaign Finance

	Receipts	Receipts from PACs	Expend-itures
1988			
Skeen (R)	$143,944	$87,050 (60%)	$67,727
1986			
Skeen (R)	$287,216	$119,602 (42%)	$293,428
Runnels (D)	$96,828	$34,000 (35%)	$83,866

Key Votes

1987	
Raise speed limit to 65 mph	Y
Approve Gephardt "fair trade" amendment	N
Ban testing of larger nuclear weapons	N
Delay "re-flagging" of Kuwaiti tankers	N
Approve tax-raising deficit-reduction bill	N
1988	
Approve aid to Nicaraguan contras	Y
Enact civil rights restoration bill over Reagan veto	N
Kill 60-day plant-closing notification measure	Y
Pass omnibus trade bill over Reagan veto	N
Approve death penalty for drug-related murders	Y
Bar federal funds for abortions in cases of rape and incest	Y
Oppose seven-day waiting period for purchase of handguns	Y

Voting Studies

	Presidential Support		Party Unity		Conservative Coalition	
Year	**S**	**O**	**S**	**O**	**S**	**O**
1988	56	43	80	19	89	11
1987	63	34	76	24	93	7
1986	68	30	79	20	94	6
1985	68	31	81	17	93	4
1984	62	38	84	15	93	7
1983	82	17	89	8	94	4
1982	82	16	90	10	100	0
1981	75	24	83	15	96	4

Interest Group Ratings

Year	ADA	ACU	AFL-CIO	CCUS
1988	5	100	29	93
1987	12	83	25	80
1986	10	82	7	67
1985	0	76	6	86
1984	15	75	15	69
1983	5	91	0	90
1982	5	82	5	82
1981	0	100	20	89

3 Bill Richardson (D)

Of Santa Fe — Elected 1982

Born: Nov. 15, 1947, Pasadena, Calif.
Education: Tufts U., B.A. 1970, M.A. 1971.
Occupation: Business consultant.
Family: Wife, Barbara Flavin.
Religion: Roman Catholic.
Political Career: Executive director, New Mexico Democratic Party, 1978-80; Democratic nominee for U.S. House, 1980.
Capitol Office: 332 Cannon Bldg. 20515; 225-6190.

In Washington: Congress has a few legislative octopuses, members whose legislative reach goes in a variety of directions. On paper, Richardson could qualify; he has an uncommon number of major committee assignments. But the fact is, while he is tenacious and ambitious enough, he has developed a widespread reputation for lacking the consistent follow-through essential to successful lawmaking.

He is a member of the Energy and Commerce, Interior, and Intelligence committees, and he also served in the 100th Congress on a fourth panel, Education and Labor. Meanwhile, Richardson has assumed a prominent role in Democratic Party affairs, particularly as a national spokesman for fellow Hispanics. He keeps a high profile in New Mexico, where he is expected to seek statewide office someday.

All of this could make for a broad power base, but instead Richardson seems to be spread too thin. A smart and likable man, he nonetheless rankles some colleagues with his habit of offering numerous amendments to bills, and arguing for them in a way that appears designed not to win votes, but to score political points with constituents or some business interest.

In his first term, he told an interviewer, "You got to be aggressive, and recognize your credibility is the most important thing you have here." But even those who work closely with Richardson say he can be more aggressive about seeking credit than reliable in doing the legislative heavy lifting.

Richardson's reputation on this count was not enhanced by his performance in the 100th Congress as chief sponsor of an industry-backed bill to pre-empt state laws and establish the first federal product-liability law governing claims against manufacturers of unsafe products. Though the bill included concessions to consumer groups and trial lawyers, who earn their fees from damage awards, opponents said it still favored businesses over plaintiffs.

On Energy and Commerce's first day of work on the bill, Richardson did not show up. He was absent other times throughout the deliberations, although the fight had been taken over by Chairman John D. Dingell of Michigan, a strong proponent of product-liability limits on behalf of Detroit's auto industry. After many delays and much contentiousness, the committee approved the bill in mid-1988, 30-12. But it died when Congress adjourned several months later.

Widely identified as a liberal Democrat on most issues, Richardson is regarded as a centrist, business-oriented vote on Energy and Commerce. He is a voice both there and at Interior for the oil, gas and uranium industries of the Southwest.

When an Energy and Commerce subcommittee began considering legislation to reauthorize the "superfund" hazardous-waste cleanup program, Richardson resisted a proposal to add petroleum leaks, including 261 in his home state, to the list of targeted sites. New Mexican oil companies worried that they could be held partly liable for supplying fuel to service stations with leaking tanks. But when the full committee approved a superfund bill in late 1985, Richardson joined nine other Democrats in rejecting it as too weak.

Although he bears an Anglo name, Richardson is the son of a Mexican mother and has been a leader on Hispanic issues. At the end of his first term, he was chosen to chair the Hispanic Caucus, but he later stepped down, saying he wanted to spend more time on state issues. His decision came at a time of controversy over his support for an immigration bill that a majority of the caucus opposed.

The bill combined legalization of many illegal aliens with new sanctions against employers of undocumented workers. Most Hispanic members objected that the sanctions would lead to discrimination against anyone who looked or sounded foreign. Richardson had voted against immigration reform himself in 1984, but in 1986 he said, "There's going to be an immigration bill anyway. I hate to fall on my sword." He voted for the bill that became law, calling it "the last gasp for legalization to take place in a humane way."

New Mexico 3

North and West — Farmington; Santa Fe

With three-fifths of its voters either Hispanic or Indian, the 3rd is decidedly more liberal and more Democratic than either of the state's other constituencies.

The population is divided between the Hispanic counties of northern New Mexico and the energy-rich Indian lands along the Arizona border.

Of the two regions, the Hispanic north is the most loyally Democratic. It contains eight of the 10 New Mexico counties carried by Michael S. Dukakis in 1988.

The centerpiece of the region is Santa Fe, the second-largest city in the state, and a pleasant mix of Spanish and Indian cultures has attracted a steady influx of young Anglos.

The rest of the Hispanic north is primarily mountainous, semi-arid grazing land that supports some subsistence farming. Unemployment has been high in the area; the Mora County jobless rate was well above 30 percent for much of this decade.

An economic oasis is the Anglo community of Los Alamos, where the atomic bomb was developed during World War II. One of the most prosperous counties in the country, its unemployment rate has been negligible in the 1980s. Its voters — well educated and scientifically inclined — are largely Republicans. But there is a strong moderate streak in some of those Republicans; John B. Anderson's presidential bid drew 15 percent in Los Alamos County in 1980.

The Indian country divides more closely at the polls. The Indians, most of them Navaho, usually vote Democratic. But they turn out in small numbers and occasionally bolt to the Republicans.

The largest county in the region is San Juan County, where a conservative Anglo population settled around Farmington to tap the vast supply of oil, gas and coal in the Four Corners area. San Juan County went solidly for George Bush in 1988.

Population: 432,492. White 272,117 (63%), Black 2,060 (1%), American Indian, Eskimo and Aleut 90,403 (21%). Spanish origin 168,577 (39%). 18 and over 280,182 (65%), 65 and over 34,045 (8%). Median age: 26.

During his one term on Education and Labor, Richardson and Matthew G. Martinez of California unsuccessfully fought to keep nearly all bilingual education funds earmarked for schools that offer English classes combined with other classes taught in students' native languages. Other Democrats compromised with Republicans to approve a GOP amendment permitting schools to spend more of their funds on alternative instruction, including the "English-only" immersion method that many Hispanics oppose. Richardson threatened to challenge the compromise on the House floor but did not; the provision was approved as part of a major education package that became law.

He also pays particular attention to the needs of American Indians, a significant presence in his district. His proposals addressing alcohol and drug abuse among Indians, health, education and job training have made their way into various pieces of legislation, although some, like Indian health bills, were stymied by disagreements between the House on one side and President Reagan and the Senate on the other.

Richardson's background is in foreign policy, and in 1987 he joined the Intelligence Committee after several years of activity on the most contentious issue of the decade, Reagan's policy of aid to the Nicaraguan contras. His position on contra aid evolved over time. In his first term, he staunchly opposed the contras. But after a 1985 visit with the leftist Sandinista leaders, he warned that the rulers needed to "clean up their act." Months later he supported non-military aid for the rebels, saying, "I am willing to give the president of the United States a chance and the benefit of the doubt."

The House subsequently adopted his amendment requiring the president to ensure that aid did not buy weapons. In 1986, he opposed Reagan's bid for military aid, joining with Indiana Democrat Lee H. Hamilton to offer an unsuccessful substitute providing $27 million in humanitarian aid and funding for regional peace talks.

At Home: A former staff member of the Senate Foreign Relations Committee, Richardson made his entry into politics in 1978, when he moved to New Mexico to become executive director of the Democratic State Committee. Within months he was planning a 1980 congressional campaign against GOP Rep. Manuel Lujan Jr. He was criticized as a carpetbagger, but he responded that his ethnic heritage — he was raised in Mexico City by a Mexican mother and an American father — made heavily Hispanic New Mexico a logical home.

By coming within 5,200 votes of the seemingly entrenched Lujan, Richardson became a star in his state party overnight. When the northern New Mexico 3rd District was created the next year, he was the early favorite to win.

His campaign survived some serious problems. He had to retract a statement in his literature that identified him as a "top" foreign policy adviser to the late Sen. Hubert H. Humphrey. Questions about a $100,000 campaign loan produced a probe by the Federal Election Commission. Although he was eventually cleared of any wrongdoing, the probe did bring his campaign unwanted negative publicity.

Richardson countered the bad press by campaigning dawn to dusk through the small towns and pueblos, reaching the Hispanic and Indian voters who together cast a majority of the ballots. With his 1980 organization still in place and a substantial campaign treasury, Richardson won the four-way primary with 36 percent. In the most loyally Democratic House constituency in the state, his win was tantamount to election.

Richardson has not had any problems since then, although at least one of his campaigns attracted attention. In 1986, he was challenged for re-election by former GOP Gov. David F. Cargo, a whimsical man who was seeking a political comeback 15 years after leaving office, following a long absence from the state.

Cargo managed to land some blows. When Richardson accepted an honorarium for touring a southwest Virginia coal mine, the Republican branded him "Peso Bill" — a move that generated home-state pressure and eventually helped encourage Richardson to donate the money to charity.

Unfortunately for Cargo, his organization and vote-getting abilities did not match his capacity for one-liners. Richardson, capitalizing on publicity he received for his work on a bill to grant a national historic designation to the Santa Fe Trail, blew Cargo away with over 70 percent of the vote.

Richardson almost passed up politics for a career in professional baseball. Following his boyhood in Mexico City, he moved to the United States to attend school. At age 18, he was drafted by the Kansas City (now Oakland) Athletics. But an elbow injury ended his sports career.

After graduating from Tufts University, Richardson moved to Washington and found work in the State Department's congressional relations office. He subsequently worked for three years as a Senate Foreign Relations Committee staffer before moving to New Mexico.

Committees

Energy and Commerce (17th of 26 Democrats)
Energy and Power; Health and the Environment; Telecommunications and Finance

Interior and Insular Affairs (14th of 26 Democrats)
Energy and the Environment; National Parks and Public Lands

Select Aging (24th of 39 Democrats)
Health and Long-Term Care; Housing and Consumer Interests

Select Intelligence (11th of 12 Democrats)
Legislation; Program and Budget Authorization

Elections

1988 General		
Bill Richardson (D)	124,938	(73%)
Cecilia M. Salazar (R)	45,954	(27%)
1986 General		
Bill Richardson (D)	95,760	(71%)
David F. Cargo (R)	38,552	(29%)

Previous Winning Percentages: **1984** (61%) **1982** (65%)

District Vote For President

	1988	1984	1980	1976
D	95,503 (54%)	77,774 (46%)	59,788 (40%)	73,305 (53%)
R	77,613 (44%)	89,612 (53%)	76,859 (52%)	63,159 (46%)
I			9,325 (6%)	

Campaign Finance

	Receipts	Receipts from PACs	Expend-itures
1988			
Richardson (D)	$456,787	$297,898 (65%)	$267,633
Salazar (R)	$41,848	$2,750 (7%)	$41,669
1986			
Richardson (D)	$370,329	$244,188 (66%)	$354,849
Cargo (R)	$88,365	$24,092 (27%)	$86,865

Key Votes

1987	
Raise speed limit to 65 mph	Y
Approve Gephardt "fair trade" amendment	Y
Ban testing of larger nuclear weapons	Y
Delay "re-flagging" of Kuwaiti tankers	N
Approve tax-raising deficit-reduction bill	N
1988	
Approve aid to Nicaraguan contras	N
Enact civil rights restoration bill over Reagan veto	Y
Kill 60-day plant-closing notification measure	N
Pass omnibus trade bill over Reagan veto	Y
Approve death penalty for drug-related murders	Y
Bar federal funds for abortions in cases of rape and incest	Y
Oppose seven-day waiting period for purchase of handguns	Y

Voting Studies

	Presidential Support		Party Unity		Conservative Coalition	
Year	S	O	S	O	S	O
1988	28	66	83	12	55	34
1987	26	71	88	9	58	42
1986	24	76	90	9	52	44
1985	25	71	89	6	33	65
1984	31	66	89	9	19	80
1983	16	82	87	9	29	71

Interest Group Ratings

Year	ADA	ACU	AFL-CIO	CCUS
1988	75	21	93	42
1987	80	9	88	29
1986	75	18	100	41
1985	70	14	76	32
1984	85	17	100	43
1983	95	13	88	20

New York

U.S. CONGRESS

SENATE 1 D, 1 R

HOUSE 21 D, 13 R

LEGISLATURE

Senate 27 D, 34 R

House 92 D, 58 R

ELECTIONS

1988 Presidential Vote	
Bush	48%
Dukakis	52%
1984 Presidential Vote	
Reagan	54%
Mondale	46%
1980 Presidential Vote	
Reagan	47%
Carter	44%
Anderson	8%
Turnout rate in 1984	51%
Turnout rate in 1986	29%
Turnout rate in 1988	48%

(as percentage of voting age population)

POPULATION AND GROWTH

1980 population	17,558,072
1988 population estimate (2nd in the nation)	17,909,000
Percent change 1980-1988	+2%

DEMOGRAPHIC BREAKDOWN

White	80%
Black	14%
Other	2%
(Spanish origin)	10%
Urban	85%
Rural	15%
Born in state	69%
Foreign-born	14%

MAJOR CITIES

New York	7,262,750
Buffalo	324,820
Rochester	235,970
Yonkers	186,080
Syracuse	160,750

AREA AND LAND USE

Area	47,377 sq. miles (30th)
Farm	30%
Forest	62%
Federally owned	5%

Gov. Mario M. Cuomo (D)
Of Holliswood — Elected 1982

Born: June 15, 1932, Queens, N.Y.
Education: St. John's U., B.A. 1953, LL.B. 1956.
Occupation: Lawyer.
Religion: Roman Catholic.
Political Career: N.Y. secretary of state, 1975-79; lieutenant governor, 1979-83; sought Democratic nomination for lieutenant governor, 1974; sought Democratic nomination for New York City mayor, 1977; Liberal Party nominee for New York City mayor, 1977.
Next Election: 1990.

WORK

Occupations	
White-collar	59%
Blue-collar	26%
Service workers	14%
Government Workers	
Federal	156,437
State	292,930
Local	918,499

MONEY

Median family income	$ 20,180	(19th)
Tax burden per capita	$ 1,164	(6th)

EDUCATION

Spending per pupil through grade 12	$ 6,011	(2nd)
Persons with college degrees	18%	(14th)

CRIME

Violent crime rate	1,008 per 100,000 (2nd)

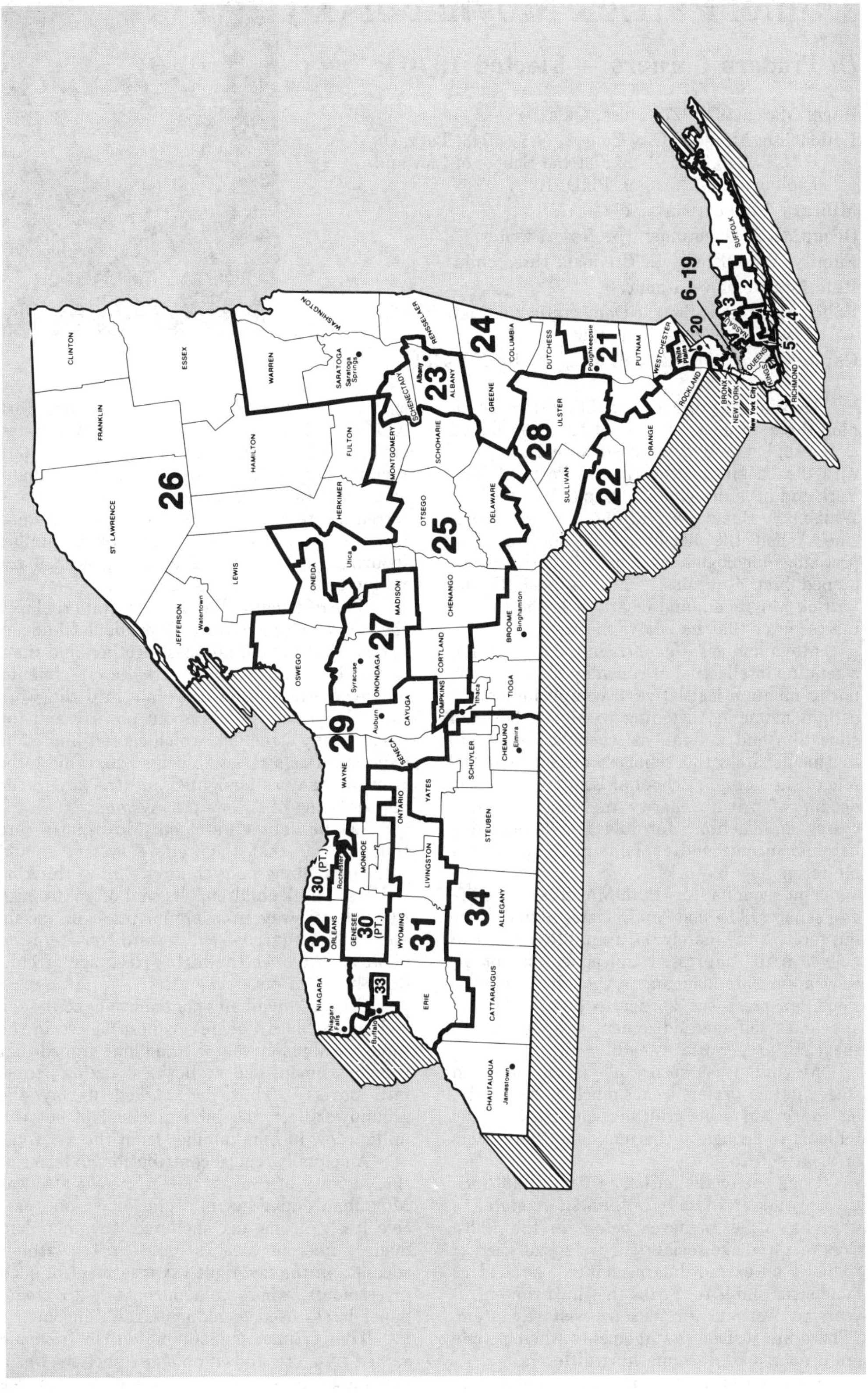
CLINTON
ESSEX
FRANKLIN
ST. LAWRENCE
26
HAMILTON
WARREN
WASHINGTON
SARATOGA
Saratoga Springs
FULTON
HERKIMER
LEWIS
JEFFERSON
Watertown
ONEIDA
Utica
OSWEGO
ONONDAGA
Syracuse
MADISON
27
CAYUGA
Auburn
29
WAYNE
SENECA
ONTARIO
YATES
MONROE
Rochester
30 (PT.)
ORLEANS
32
GENESEE
WYOMING
31
LIVINGSTON
NIAGARA
Niagara Falls
33
Buffalo
ERIE
CHAUTAUQUA
Jamestown
CATTARAUGUS
ALLEGANY
34
STEUBEN
SCHUYLER
CHEMUNG
Elmira
TOMPKINS
Ithaca
TIOGA
CORTLAND
BROOME
Binghamton
CHENANGO
OTSEGO
25
DELAWARE
MONTGOMERY
SCHOHARIE
SCHENECTADY
Albany
23
ALBANY
RENSSELAER
24
COLUMBIA
GREENE
ULSTER
28
SULLIVAN
22
ORANGE
DUTCHESS
Poughkeepsie
21
PUTNAM
WESTCHESTER
White Plains
20
ROCKLAND
BRONX
NEW YORK
New York City
KINGS
QUEENS
RICHMOND
NASSAU
6-19
1
2
3
4
5
SUFFOLK

Daniel Patrick Moynihan (D)

Of Pindars Corners — Elected 1976

Born: March 16, 1927, Tulsa, Okla.
Education: Attended City College, N.Y., 1943; Tufts U., B.N.S. 1946, B.A. 1948; Fletcher School of Law and Diplomacy, M.A. 1949, Ph.D. 1961.
Military Career: Navy, 1944-47.
Occupation: Government professor; writer.
Family: Wife, Elizabeth Brennan; three children.
Religion: Roman Catholic.
Political Career: Sought Democratic nomination, N.Y. City Council president, 1965.
Capitol Office: 464 Russell Bldg. 20510; 224-4451.

In Washington: In a public career spanning three decades, Moynihan has been hailed as a prophet and denounced as a racist, run with the backing of the Liberal Party of New York and been designated "man of the year" by William F. Buckley's *National Review* magazine. When the height of fashion required prefixing ideologies as "neo-," both camps pinned him. But mostly he has been Daniel Patrick Moynihan, and clearly it is the title of U.S. senator that he enjoys most.

Moynihan is *sui generis* in today's Senate, a genuine intellectual of considerable scholarly, not to mention legislative, accomplishment. At certain moments, listening to him is both an education and a treat, as when he interrupts routine debate with a scholarly discourse on the role of the London School of Economics, or the decline of private charity in Europe, or discusses an algebraic formula for determining national income and explains in comprehensible terms how it works.

Few seem happier than Moynihan with life as a senator. The body appreciates high oratory but forgives the merely partisan. Moynihan can deliver both. Impressed colleagues do not always appreciate his manner, though; his digressions can cross the border to pomposity and appear as self-aggrandizement wrapped in disheveled, professorial tweed.

Moynihan has been a player on the world stage, and he prefers to act much as he speaks, on the grand scale. But he can frustrate by refusing to engage in the mundane that others must attend to.

Long one of the nation's foremost authorities on work and family in the welfare state, he was challenged as never before in the 100th Congress to make social policy of social science. "This is an extraordinary chance," he said as momentum built to try for the third time in 20 years to overhaul the nation's welfare system. "There are just so few moments when people are prepared to do something different."

He rose to the occasion as the chief Senate sponsor of welfare legislation. He did homework and legwork along with brain work writing an entitlement program designed to move welfare recipients into the work force. It was in many ways vindication, but one he would have preferred not to have collected, for experience had come to support his theory that black families in urban ghettoes would break up even if the nation as a whole prospered.

The restructured welfare program replaced the Aid to Families with Dependent Children. It aims first to hold families together, and then, if they break apart, to move welfare recipients, mostly mothers, from the dole into the work force. Moynihan's ideas about poverty and the black family structure, which caused him to be denounced as a racist 25 years ago, came to be seen by many as farsighted and the key to the restructuring of the welfare system.

As the debate unfolded, Moynihan's core thought was that the welfare system should focus on helping poor children. "Stop thinking welfare. Think children," he said often, to push the debate away from arguments over racism and "welfare queens" and toward consideration of ways to reduce the high percentage of children living in poverty.

One of Moynihan's contributions to the tax code in the 99th Congress is best viewed in the same social policy vein. He had long argued that the government had no business taxing people into poverty. Thus, he worked to lay the groundwork for the bill's removal of some 6 million low-income families from the tax rolls.

An equally crucial contribution, in terms of the viability of the tax bill in the Senate, was Moynihan's advocacy of a crackdown on "passive loss" income-tax shelters. Moynihan had made numerous attacks in the past, without success, on the favorable tax treatment of such investments, whose sole purpose is to create paper losses used to reduce taxable income.

The estimated $50 billion in revenue gained by a crackdown on those shelters was a key factor in saving the Finance Committee from the tax-bill deadlock into which it had fallen in the spring of 1986. Joining the small group of members who drafted the legislation along with committee Chairman Bob Packwood, Moynihan won inclusion of restrictive passive-loss provisions. They helped finance the low individual rates that gave the measure the momentum needed to become law. It was not the first time Moynihan had attacked unproductive measures in the tax code; he had complicated investment strategies called tax straddles clipped as part of the 1981 Kemp-Roth tax cuts.

On many other domestic issues, though, Moynihan has been less intent on rethinking fundamental questions than on lining up emotionally with liberal Democrats in support of preserving the New Deal and Great Society. His ringing declarations of support for traditional Democratic Party ideas strike some colleagues as cynical political rhetoric, since they remember when he was identified as a critic of those ideas.

But Moynihan has made the transition back from neo-conservative to bread-and-butter liberal with great success in New York, and without terrible cost in the Senate. In his choice of a committee assignment at the very start, Moynihan made clear his intention to bring home the goods to New York. At first he eschewed the Foreign Relations Committee, a natural post given his service as United Nations ambassador. He took aim at the Finance Committee, on which no New Yorker had sat for half a century.

An abiding theme in Moynihan's career is that New York has been shortchanged in the distribution of federal funds for a variety of programs. One area in which he has fought to correct that imbalance is water policy, a subject he has been involved in both as ranking Democrat and now chairman on the Environment Subcommittee on Water Resources and Transportation.

Arguing that water projects have been disproportionately concentrated in Southern and Western states, he has pushed to give states more authority in determining where projects will be located. New York state has a deteriorating water distribution system that needs billions of dollars for repairs.

Early in 1987, he managed the $88 billion highway bill on the Senate floor — and did an impressive job, considering that he had not even been a member of the Transportation Subcommittee until the previous month.

Before tax and welfare reform became the subjects of major legislation, Moynihan's most prominent Finance Committee issue was Social Security. He was the most outspoken Democratic opponent of the Reagan administration's proposals to cut back Social Security in 1981, and was instrumental in working out the compromise that led to the Social Security reform legislation of 1983.

In leading the 1981 fight against Social Security changes, Moynihan argued that the system was basically solvent and could meet any short-term problems through relatively minor adjustments. By the next year, however, he had changed his mind. Working with Finance Committee Chairman Bob Dole, he developed the last-minute agreement that allowed the National Commission on Social Security Reform to issue a set of recommendations for saving the system with a combination of tax increases and benefit restraints.

Foreign policy questions no longer preoccupy Moynihan the way they did when, as U.N. ambassador, he was a staunch anti-communist and the scourge of radical Third World regimes. In the Senate, Moynihan has figured prominently as an arms control supporter and critic of support for the Nicaraguan contras.

Moynihan's much-publicized change of mind on Nicaragua reflected his flair for the dramatic gesture as well as his new political stance. As vice chairman of the Senate Intelligence Committee in the 98th Congress, Moynihan initially backed the administration's program of covert aid to the contras. Gradually, however, he began to have doubts, pressing President Reagan for assurances that the aid was directed at halting alleged Nicaraguan arms shipments to leftists in El Salvador, rather than at overthrowing the Nicaraguan regime.

But the disclosure in early 1984 that the CIA had been involved in mining Nicaraguan harbors was too much for Moynihan. Bitterly attacking the CIA for failing to inform the Intelligence Committee of the operation, he announced his resignation as panel vice chairman. Eventually, after CIA Director William J. Casey apologized, Moynihan withdrew his resignation. But he continued to oppose aid to the contras.

Known at the United Nations for his outspoken defense of Israel, Moynihan has been equally militant in the Senate. He sponsored a resolution, unanimously adopted by the Senate, threatening to pull the United States out of the United Nations if Israel was expelled. He also has been a leading advocate of the controversial proposal to move the U.S. Embassy in Israel from Tel Aviv to Jerusalem.

Moynihan has often been involved with nuclear arms control. He is knowledgeable about the subject, but hard to pin down. For example, he tried to find a midpoint between Reagan's position and that of backers of a nuclear freeze and the SALT II treaty.

In 1979 Moynihan published a lengthy article in the *New Yorker* magazine arguing that the United States had been consistently taken advantage of in arms negotiations with the Soviets. But he did not immediately oppose the SALT II treaty. Instead, he used his potential vote as a bargaining point to change what he considered a serious defect — the fact that the treaty allowed both countries to add new strategic weapons, rather than forcing reductions. Moynihan prepared an amendment that would have voided the treaty if U.S. and Soviet negotiators did not agree on real reductions in arms levels by the end of 1981. Later, Moynihan announced that he favored adoption of the SALT II treaty as an interim executive agreement.

At Home: The professorial Moynihan may not have the populist appeal of his earthier colleague, Republican Sen. Alfonse M. D'Amato. But Moynihan's election results powerfully attest to his political popularity. After unseating GOP Sen. James L. Buckley in 1976, Moynihan won his first re-election in 1982 with 65 percent of the vote. In 1988, he defeated Republican attorney Robert R. McMillan with 67 percent — breaking his own state record for Senate vote percentage and setting a national record with his margin (2.2 million votes).

At the outset of the 1988 campaign, a Moynihan landslide was no given: Possible Republican opponents included U.S. Attorney Rudolph W. Giuliani, the high-profile prosecutor of organized-crime figures and corrupt Wall Street financiers, and Rep. Jack F. Kemp, then a candidate for the GOP presidential nomination.

Moynihan prepared as if he would face the fight of his life, raising money early and running TV ads in January. He even took the unusual step of denying a persistent but unsubstantiated rumor that he had a problem with alcohol.

His concerns turned out to be unfounded. Giuliani became embroiled in a public feud with D'Amato concerning his possible successor as U.S. attorney and decided to stay on as prosecutor. Kemp was courted after ending his White House bid, but also declined.

The New York Republicans were left with McMillan. The longtime GOP activist had many friends inside the state party, but was virtually unknown to the voting public. He had run one previous race, a losing campaign for New York City Council in 1964.

McMillan campaigned hard, driving across the state in his personal car, caustically criticizing Moynihan. Running as a "compassionate conservative," McMillan described Moynihan's support for a federal grant for a homosexual "safe sex" program as a vote for "safe sodomy." He portrayed Moynihan as aloof and lazy, with poor management skills that resulted in high turnover on his Senate staff.

But few New Yorkers heard McMillan's attacks. Republican financial backers wrote off the race as a loss; McMillan raised a meager half a million dollars, enough to buy one week of one ad in the expensive New York TV market. Meanwhile, Moynihan was flooding the airwaves with ads lauding his accomplishments, including his September victory on welfare reform. He swept the state, losing just a single rural county in upstate New York.

The landslide was a crowning moment in Moynihan's rise from Manhattan's ethnic, blue-collar precincts to the heights of academia and government. Moynihan's father, a hard-drinking journalist, walked out on the family when the senator was 6; his mother ran a saloon near Times Square. Moynihan walked into the entrance exam for City College with a longshoreman's loading hook sticking out of his back pocket.

After establishing himself as an academic — he taught his personal combination of economics, sociology and urban studies at Harvard and at the Joint Center for Urban Studies — Moynihan turned to government service in the 1960s. He worked in the Labor Department in the Kennedy and Johnson administrations, and as an urban affairs expert for Nixon.

In the latter role, Moynihan was the architect of the ill-fated Nixon "family assistance" welfare proposal, whose history he detailed in a book. He also caused himself great trouble when he counseled "benign neglect" toward minorities. The dispute caused by this advice revived accusations that Moynihan's scholarship was highbrow racism, an issue that first surfaced in 1965, when his book "Beyond the Melting Pot" attributed social problems among blacks to unstable family structure. Though Moynihan insisted he had been misunderstood, his social views created a gulf between him and some minority-group leaders that had to be bridged after he entered elective politics.

But the positive press Moynihan earned in his other roles in GOP administrations — as ambassador to India and to the United Nations under Presidents Nixon and Ford — set him on the road to political success. In his last year in New Delhi, Moynihan drew attention for his articles criticizing a lack of firmness in U.S. foreign policy, especially toward the Third World. His reputation made him a logical choice in 1975 for the U.N. post, whose most recent appointees had been inconspicuous.

Moynihan's service at the United Nations clearly helped his political prospects in New York, although he denied any connection. His staunch defense of Israel earned him support among New York's sizable Jewish constituency, and his televised militance at the United Nations in 1975 allowed him to begin the 1976 campaign as a celebrity, rather than just an articulate Harvard professor. "He spoke up for America," one campaign advertisement said. "He'd speak up for New York."

Given his previous work for GOP presidents and his neo-conservative profile, Moynihan would have had difficulty running in a Democratic primary against a single liberal candidate in 1976. But he found himself challenged not only by Rep. Bella S. Abzug, the flamboyant feminist leader, but also by two other well-known figures of the Democratic left: former U.S. Attorney General Ramsey Clark and New York City Council President Paul O'Dwyer. Moynihan's chief political sponsor, Erie County Democratic Chairman Joseph Crangle, saw to it the liberal vote would remain split by pushing the state Democratic convention to guarantee ballot spots for all three liberal candidates.

Abzug depicted Moynihan as a Buckley in Democratic clothing and emerged as his main rival. But Clark and O'Dwyer took a combined 19 percent, enough to sink her. Moynihan's 36 percent gave him first place, 10,000 votes up on Abzug; he split most of the New York suburbs with her, won the upstate counties and took every city borough except Manhattan.

Buckley had won the seat six years earlier as the Conservative Party candidate, taking advantage of a three-way contest involving liberal Republican incumbent Charles Goodell and liberal Democratic challenger Richard L. Ottinger. He had no such advantage in 1976.

Moynihan started with a strong lead over Buckley in the polls, and he neither said nor did anything in the fall to fracture his tenuous party harmony. He spent much of his time in Massachusetts, teaching at Harvard to protect his tenure. When he did speak out, he called Buckley a right-wing extremist out of step with the state's politics — citing Buckley's initial opposition in 1975 to federal loan guarantees for New York City. Moynihan won all the suburban counties except Suffolk on Long Island and rolled up large margins in the city. Overall, he sailed to victory over Buckley by a half-million votes.

For the first few years of his Senate career, it seemed likely he would be challenged from the left in seeking renomination in 1982. But by the time of the primary, his belligerent and unexpected defense of traditional Democratic policies had had its effect. New York's Democratic left was pacified, and the National Conservative Political Action Committee helped Moynihan by airing TV ads calling him "the most liberal United States senator." Even the Liberal Party, which had been upset by his support of tuition tax credits for non-public schools, backed Moynihan in 1982.

Former U.S. Rep. Bruce F. Caputo wanted the Republican nomination, and he might have made an attractive GOP candidate. But he was forced to withdraw following a disclosure that he had misstated his military background. Caputo claimed he had served as an Army lieutenant.

No other major Republican felt a campaign was worth waging. Conservative state Assemblywoman Florence Sullivan won the nomination; she carried only 16 rural counties in November.

Committees

Environment and Public Works (2nd of 9 Democrats)
Water Resources, Transportation and Infrastructure (chairman); Environmental Protection; Nuclear Regulation

Finance (3rd of 11 Democrats)
Social Security and Family Policy (chairman); International Trade; Private Retirement Plans and Oversight of the Internal Revenue Service

Foreign Relations (9th of 10 Democrats)
Near Eastern and South Asian Affairs (chairman); African Affairs; Terrorism, Narcotics and International Operations

Rules and Administration (7th of 9 Democrats)

Joint Library

Joint Taxation

Elections

1988 General

Daniel Patrick Moynihan (D)	4,048,649	(67%)
Robert R. McMillan (R)	1,875,784	(31%)

Previous Winning Percentages: **1982** (65%) **1976** (54%)

Campaign Finance

	Receipts	Receipts from PACs	Expend-itures
1988			
Moynihan (D)	$4,350,271	$892,773 (21%)	$4,809,810
McMillan (R)	$536,445	$33,495 (6%)	$528,989

Key Votes

1987

Enact omnibus highway bill over Reagan veto	Y
Limit testing of space-based anti-ballistic missiles	Y
Oppose banning tests of larger nuclear weapons	N
Confirm Robert H. Bork as Supreme Court justice	N

1988

Allow vote on campaign-finance overhaul	Y
Pass civil rights restoration bill over Reagan veto	Y
Enact omnibus trade bill over Reagan veto	Y
Approve death penalty for drug-related murders	Y
Oppose "workfare" amendment to welfare overhaul bill	Y

Voting Studies

	Presidential Support		Party Unity		Conservative Coalition	
Year	S	O	S	O	S	O
1988	48	47	91	6	27	70
1987	37	60	93	5	19	78
1986	40	59	72	25	36	63
1985	33	65	81	13	27	67
1984	36	53	68	25	21	66
1983	46	51	74	21	16	80
1982	28	71	86	11	14	84
1981	41	47	71	14	8	87

Interest Group Ratings

Year	ADA	ACU	AFL-CIO	CCUS
1988	90	8	93	31
1987	95	0	100	31
1986	85	13	67	39
1985	90	4	100	33
1984	85	18	80	39
1983	80	8	82	26
1982	95	22	96	22
1981	75	13	94	33

Alfonse M. D'Amato (R)

Of Island Park — Elected 1980

Born: Aug. 1, 1937, Brooklyn, N.Y.
Education: Syracuse U., B.S. 1959, J.D. 1961.
Occupation: Lawyer.
Family: Wife, Penny Collenburg; four children.
Religion: Roman Catholic.
Political Career: Nassau County public administrator, 1965-68; receiver of taxes, town of Hempstead, 1969-71; Hempstead town supervisor, 1971-77; presiding supervisor, 1977-81; Nassau County Board of Supervisors, 1971-80.
Capitol Office: 520 Hart Bldg. 20510; 224-6542.

In Washington: D'Amato has taken a tried and true formula for success in local politics — catering to his constituents' every need — and applied it to one of the largest constituencies imaginable: New York state's 18 million people.

It is physically exhausting, and the nickname he has earned, "Senator Pothole," does not stem from filling the shoes of a statesman. But his parochialism pays off at the polls. Elected in 1980 by 81,000 votes in a three-way race, he won a second term in 1986 by almost 700,000.

Nearly nine years into his Senate career, D'Amato still operates like the town supervisor he once was. His legislative pursuits are guided by voters' concerns, not by any personal philosophical compass. D'Amato can be genial, but when it comes to protecting New York, he is brazen, pushy and persistent — and effective. His style often leaves colleagues fuming, but the anger soon passes; they have come to accept the irrepressible D'Amato's *modus operandi.*

Less than a month before the 1986 election, as the 99th Congress was striving to finish its work and head home, D'Amato brought business to a halt in an effort to protect the jobs of workers at a Long Island aircraft plant.

As the Senate debated an omnibus appropriations bill, essential to keep the government running, it came to an amendment to halt production of the T-46 trainer airplane, built by the Fairchild Republic Co. on Long Island. Cost and quality problems with the T-46 convinced the Air Force to refurbish the 1960s-era T-37 trainer, built by Cessna.

D'Amato vowed to hold up the amendment indefinitely, no matter the cost. "To this product, to this company, this is life or death.... I'm not going to sit by and allow that company to be closed."

Negotiations dragged on through the night and into the next day. At noon Oct. 17, there was still no airplane compromise and thus no catchall spending bill, so non-essential federal functions were shut down and workers sent home.

Later that day, the impasse finally was broken. D'Amato won a temporary reprieve for his plane. But in the end, his work was futile. Both planes ultimately lost out to a third, the T-45, built by McDonnell Douglas.

On occasion, the concerns of D'Amato's constituents coincide with the national interest. Such was the case with the war on illegal drugs he conducted during the 100th Congress. D'Amato berated the U.S. government to get tough with Panama's strongman, Gen. Manuel Antonio Noriega, whom D'Amato and others have accused of being in league with drug traffickers. He advocated placing the Coast Guard and the Customs Service in an agency united under the Treasury Department, with the new Office of Enforcement and Border Affairs to be charged with interdicting drug smugglers.

But it was his advocacy of the death penalty for the "kingpins" of the drug trade that kept D'Amato's name in the news throughout 1988. "Those who traffic in death should pay with their own death," he said. At first he tried to attach his measure — to permit the death penalty for racketeers convicted of murder in the course of drug trafficking — to a defense authorization bill. He feared, rightly so, that free-standing death-penalty legislation would never get out of committee in the House. But he backed off when Democrats promised him an up-or-down vote on the death penalty in the Senate. The death penalty eventually became law as part of omnibus anti-drug legislation.

It was not D'Amato's first time out on the popular anti-drug issue. As chairman of the Banking Subcommittee on Securities, he had won approval of a measure beefing up federal efforts to detect money laundering, a common ploy of drug traffickers. In 1986, D'Amato won Senate approval for shifting $100 million from government furnishings to drug-abuse prevention and rehabilitation programs.

Meanwhile, D'Amato managed to win publicity all over the country — and on nearly every front page in his home state — by dressing in Army fatigues and accompanying police officers as they staged a drug purchase in Manhattan shortly before the 1986 election.

D'Amato campaigned in 1980 as a hard-line suburban conservative, hostile to inner-city liberal causes, and many feared that as a senator he would carry out Long Island's revenge on Manhattan. It has not turned out that way. Though he supported President Reagan most of the time, he defied the administration in defense of his urban constituents' interests, especially on transportation issues.

When the administration proposed huge cuts in mass transit funding in 1982, D'Amato objected fiercely. "There's no way I'm going to be a good ol' boy and roll along with the team," he said. Five years later, when Reagan needed just one more vote to sustain his veto of a highway and mass transit funding bill, D'Amato was not available. The bill Reagan vetoed contained $3 billion in mass transit money for New York City, money D'Amato badly wanted to deliver.

A member of the Appropriations Committee, he is adept at getting goodies for New York into large, catchall spending bills. He often seeks to enhance their prospects of passage by dealing key senators into the funding action. In a 1986 supplemental appropriations measure, for example, he helped earmark $55 million for defense research projects at nine universities.

In November 1985, D'Amato failed to get $32 million extra for the Economic Development Administration to finance four projects to train microelectronic engineers, including one at the Rochester (N.Y.) Institute of Technology. Undeterred, he came back a month later with the same request, but this time he packaged it as part of the Pentagon's research and development budget in an omnibus appropriations bill. The money was approved.

D'Amato's work on the Banking Committee, where he chaired the Securities Subcommittee while the Republicans held the Senate, has led him to form partnerships with one of the Senate's leading liberals, Democrat Alan Cranston of California. Together, they have defended the securities industry in debates over financial services. As the 101st Congress began, they were chief sponsors of legislation to overhaul national housing policy. The soaring cost of owning a home on Long Island has made D'Amato an enthusiastic backer of measures to extend government insurance to larger mortgages.

D'Amato has to do a careful balancing act when banking and securities industry interests intersect. Wall Street has provided a constant source of campaign funds, but New York City is also headquarters for many of the nation's largest banks. D'Amato played a key role in killing legislation to rewrite the Glass-Steagall Act, the firewall erected between banking and securities industries in 1933. When a measure that would have permitted banks to underwrite certain securities neared passage as an amendment to thrift legislation late in the 100th Congress, D'Amato saw to its death. He blocked the bill's route to the floor under the guise that its provisions for a study of the savings and loan crisis were poorly written.

But he has backed the banks on other matters of deregulation. He was the leading critic of one provision opposed by New York City's Citibank and Chase Manhattan. It would have allowed banks in most parts of the country — but not New York — to form regional compacts to prevent banks based outside their region from doing business in their area. He failed to defeat the proposal in committee, then waged a losing weeklong filibuster on the Senate floor.

D'Amato's ability to bring home the bacon for New Yorkers gained a new wrinkle in May 1989 as a scandal unfolded within the Department of Housing and Urban Development. The village of Island Park in the town of Hempstead, over which D'Amato once presided as supervisor, was cited in a 1984 audit uncovered by *The New York Times* for distributing funds in a manner that favored the politically well-connected, including D'Amato's cousin. D'Amato personally lobbied for HUD funds to build a seaside swimming pool for the village at a cost of nearly $1 million.

At Home: New York's ranking GOP officeholder, D'Amato has played a part in moving the state party to the right since the 1979 death of former vice president and longtime Gov. Nelson A. Rockefeller. But D'Amato has had limited success as a home-state power broker. His avid support of Kansas Sen. Bob Dole's 1988 White House bid irritated the Bush supporters who came to dominate the state's delegate-selection process (including state party finance director Jonathan Bush, the vice president's brother).

Also in 1988, D'Amato tried to recruit popular U.S. Attorney Rudolph W. Giuliani to challenge Democratic Sen. Daniel Patrick Moynihan. But Giuliani demanded the right to nominate his successor as U.S. attorney, a prerogative that was D'Amato's as the state's leading GOP official. D'Amato and Giuliani feuded, and Giuliani passed up the Senate bid.

D'Amato is the product of one of the last old-fashioned political organizations, the Nassau County Republican Party, formerly headed by Joseph M. Margiotta Jr. With county and local officials serving the party as fund-raisers and contributors, Margiotta — convicted in 1981 of fraud and extortion — built a wealthy and powerful political machine.

D'Amato's father and brother also have long been part of the machine. D'Amato himself was fresh out of law school when a friend of his father got him a job in the Island Park town attorney's office. He worked up through various local offices until he was elected presiding supervisor of Hempstead Township in 1977.

His political skills and his following in Nassau County placed him in line to be county executive and, possibly, Margiotta's successor. Instead, D'Amato ran for the Senate in 1980 as a conservative challenger to veteran GOP incumbent Jacob K. Javits.

D'Amato aggressively sought nomination from the Conservative and Right-to-Life parties, neither of which liked Javits. He won both, and Margiotta, breaking with tradition, agreed to back him against Javits. D'Amato got enough support from downstate Republicans at the state GOP committee meeting to force a primary.

D'Amato's controversial campaign struck at Javits as too old (76), too ill — he had a progressive motor neuron disease — and too liberal. Javits stressed his years of service and aired endorsements from luminaries such as Gerald R. Ford and Sen. Barry Goldwater. But D'Amato was armed with ample funding and many volunteers. He swept New York City's suburbs and edged Javits in the city and upstate.

The general election was equally volatile, with Javits still in the contest on the Liberal Party line and Rep. Elizabeth Holtzman the Democratic nominee. Holtzman went after D'Amato, bringing up alleged illicit practices of the Nassau GOP organization. D'Amato denied involvement in anything unlawful (later he was the subject of three separate investigations, all of which absolved him of any wrongdoing). Wanting Javits to attract some of Holtzman's liberal support, D'Amato became much kinder to him. He concentrated on Holtzman, calling her "an absolute witch" for attacking him. Holtzman came within 81,000 votes of D'Amato; Javits' liberal backing held her back.

D'Amato's narrow victory and the image as a hard-right zealot he carried from his primary fight against Javits convinced Democrats he would be vulnerable in 1986. But state party leaders had enormous difficulty finding a challenger of stature. His aggressive attention to New York interests had won widespread praise, even from Democrats.

In the end, the Democratic nominee was lawyer and author Mark Green, a former associate of consumer crusader Ralph Nader; he had a base among Manhattan liberals. Green raised questions about D'Amato's activities as chairman of the Banking Subcommittee on Securities (a *Wall Street Journal* article said D'Amato had received generous campaign contributions from Wall Street firms he had aided legislatively), and about D'Amato's ties to the Nassau GOP (D'Amato testified in a summer 1985 trial that charged the organization with coercing financial contributions from county employees seeking raises or promotions).

But the accusations rolled off D'Amato's back. Reminding voters of his avid efforts to funnel federal funds into the state, D'Amato won easily, despite Democratic Gov. Mario M. Cuomo's re-election landslide.

Committees

Appropriations (7th of 13 Republicans)
Transportation and Related Agencies (ranking); Defense; Foreign Operations; HUD-Independent Agencies; Treasury, Postal Service and General Government

Banking, Housing and Urban Affairs (3rd of 9 Republicans)
Housing and Urban Affairs (ranking); Consumer and Regulatory Affairs; Securities

Select Intelligence (7th of 7 Republicans)

Elections

1986 General

Alfonse M. D'Amato (R)	2,378,197	(57%)
Mark Green (D)	1,723,216	(41%)

Previous Winning Percentage: **1980** (45%)

Campaign Finance

	Receipts	Receipts from PACs	Expend-itures
1986			
D'Amato (R)	$6,523,394	$855,518 (13%)	$8,104,587
Green (D)	$1,640,154	0	$1,635,676

Key Votes

1987

Enact omnibus highway bill over Reagan veto	Y
Limit testing of space-based anti-ballistic missiles	N
Oppose banning tests of larger nuclear weapons	Y
Confirm Robert H. Bork as Supreme Court justice	Y

1988

Allow vote on campaign-finance overhaul	N
Pass civil rights restoration bill over Reagan veto	Y
Enact omnibus trade bill over Reagan veto	N
Approve death penalty for drug-related murders	Y
Oppose "workfare" amendment to welfare overhaul bill	N

Voting Studies

	Presidential Support		Party Unity		Conservative Coalition	
Year	**S**	**O**	**S**	**O**	**S**	**O**
1988	68	30	70	28	84	16
1987	58	38	65	33	69	28
1986	77	23	66	32	66	30
1985	71	28	69	28	88	8
1984	68	25	67	25	72	19
1983	67	28	67	30	70	27
1982	71	26	76	22	78	17
1981	82	14	81	13	78	17

Interest Group Ratings

Year	ADA	ACU	AFL-CIO	CCUS
1988	15	80	57	64
1987	30	56	70	44
1986	35	70	53	56
1985	20	70	62	62
1984	25	85	36	78
1983	20	44	33	63
1982	15	50	46	47
1981	10	64	22	94

1 George J. Hochbrueckner (D)

Of Coram — Elected 1986

Born: Sept. 20, 1938, Queens, N.Y.

Education: Attended State U. of New York, 1959-60; Hofstra U., 1960-61; Pierce College, 1961-62; U. of California, Northridge, 1962-63.

Military Career: Navy, 1956-59.

Occupation: Aerospace engineer.

Family: Wife, Carol Ann Joan Seifert; four children.

Religion: Roman Catholic.

Political Career: N.Y. Assembly, 1975-85; Democratic nominee for U.S. House, 1984.

Capitol Office: 124 Cannon Bldg. 20515; 225-3826.

In Washington: All Armed Services Committee members angle to obtain defense contracts for their districts. But none is better grounded than Hochbrueckner when it comes to making technical arguments about the superiority of military aircraft produced in his district. An aerospace engineer, the Long Island Democrat worked for such major local contractors as Grumman prior to his legislative career.

The 1st District's dependence on defense employment made Hochbrueckner's appointment to Armed Services a practical imperative. Given his district's Republican orientation, his work on behalf of district defense interests provided him with cover for his generally liberal views, not only on domestic policy, but on some defense issues as well. An arms control advocate, Hochbrueckner joined Florida Democrat Charles E. Bennett on an unsuccessful April 1988 amendment to reduce funding for the strategic defense initiative.

Hochbrueckner's committee position makes him a point man for 1st District interests fighting to keep their defense contracts as the Pentagon budget is pruned. When Defense Secretary Dick Cheney appeared before Armed Services in April 1989 to outline proposed cutbacks, including cancellation of the Navy's F-14 interceptor built by Grumman, Hochbrueckner railed, "You are putting Grumman out of business!"

Hochbrueckner worked, however, to reorient his district's high-tech industry away from its defense reliance. He helped obtain funding for research on X-ray lithography, a process that may produce smaller, faster computer chips; much of the research is being performed at Long Island's Brookhaven National Laboratory.

Though occupied with Armed Services, Hochbrueckner did not forget the issue that got him to Congress: district opposition to the Shoreham nuclear-power plant. He worked for a House amendment, proposed by Massachusetts Democrat Edward J. Markey, to bar the Nuclear Regulatory Commission from licensing Shoreham and a nuclear plant in Seabrook, N.H., over the objections of state and local officials. But the measure failed, 160-261.

At Home: Hochbrueckner's 1988 win with 51 percent of the vote could be viewed with optimism by both parties. To Democrats, it proved they could hold the GOP-leaning district in a presidential year. To Republicans, it said Hochbrueckner was still vulnerable.

It took Hochbrueckner two tries to win the seat, and he won on an issue that cut across party lines: opposition to Shoreham, which critics viewed as located dangerously in a densely populated area. From his seat in the state Assembly, which he held from 1975-85, Hochbrueckner became one of the leading Shoreham opponents.

In 1984, Hochbrueckner challenged pro-nuclear GOP Rep. William Carney, and came within about 12,000 votes of winning. Two years later, the Democrat was primed for a rematch, but Carney decided to retire. Republicans replaced him with county legislator Gregory J. Blass. But while Blass was also a Shoreham opponent — he had challenged and nearly defeated Carney on the issue in a 1984 primary — Hochbrueckner stood out as the candidate who had opposed Shoreham earliest and loudest. He won by almost 12,000 votes.

In 1988, the Republicans turned to county legislator Edward Romaine, another Shoreham foe. Though he appealed to his GOP base by calling the incumbent a liberal, Romaine profiled himself as a moderate interested in the environment, education and other domestic issues.

Despite his vigorous campaign efforts, Romaine was never able to raise his name recognition to match Hochbrueckner, who had maintained his visibility with a series of town meetings. Romaine did receive a boost from Bush's victory in the 1st. But the well-financed Hochbrueckner, who received a big chunk of defense PAC money, hung on to win.

New York 1

Long Island — Eastern Suffolk County

There has been a full generation of population growth in eastern Suffolk County, the potato fields giving way to housing developments and the commercial fishing fleets yielding the waters to pleasure boats.

The demographic changes in the district have not affected its voting habits, however. The 1st is nearly always reliably Republican turf. Prior to Hochbrueckner's 1986 election, the area within the boundaries of the 1st had voted Democratic in a race for federal office only once since 1976; it has gone Republican for president in every contest since 1964.

Republicans come in three varieties here: the longtime residents who fish and farm; the landed gentry living on inherited wealth; and the middle-income ethnics moving farther and farther from New York City. The fishermen generally work out of Montauk, while the remaining farmers are found mostly around Southold. The rich live in Sag Harbor and Shelter Island. Shirley, Mastic and the Moriches host large numbers of ethnic newcomers.

The district's Republican tendencies have been bolstered over the years by its dependence on defense manufacturing: Grumman maintains major facilities here. Thus, the 1st — which enjoyed the fruits of the Reagan administration's defense buildup in the early 1980s — finds itself vulnerable to defense cuts resulting from President Bush's agreement with Congress to spread the pain of deficit-related budget reductions. Already reeling from the Navy's 1988 decision to cancel its A-6 bomber project, Grumman was rocked in April 1989 by a Bush administration proposal to cancel production of the Long Island-built F-14 fighter.

One project initially touted as a technological plus for the district is literally a non-starter. The Shoreham nuclear plant — controversial because of cost overruns and safety concerns — sits completed but unopened on the North Shore. After years of negotiations, it appeared in early 1989 that New York state would purchase the plant from the Long Island Lighting Co. and close it permanently. But Energy Secretary James D. Watkins warned he would intervene to block any effort to mothball the plant permanently.

Population: 516,407. White 486,111 (94%), Black 20,253 (4%), Other 5,453 (1%). Spanish origin 18,408 (4%). 18 and over 350,987 (68%), 65 and over 55,046 (11%). Median age: 30.

Committees

Armed Services (24th of 31 Democrats)
Military Personnel and Compensation; Research and Development; Seapower and Strategic and Critical Materials

Merchant Marine and Fisheries (20th of 26 Democrats)
Coast Guard and Navigation; Fisheries and Wildlife Conservation and the Environment

Elections

1988 General		
George J. Hochbrueckner (D)	105,624	(51%)
Edward P. Romaine (R)	102,327	(49%)
1986 General		
George J. Hochbrueckner (D)	67,139	(51%)
Gregory J. Blass (R)	55,413	(42%)

District Vote For President

	1988		1984		1980		1976	
D	85,652	(39%)	70,592	(34%)	61,687	(33%)	85,138	(46%)
R	131,180	(60%)	137,855	(66%)	105,748	(57%)	100,390	(54%)
I					15,180	(8%)		

Campaign Finance

	Receipts	Receipts from PACs	Expend-itures
1988			
Hochbrueckner (D)	$738,139	$417,961 (57%)	$734,621
Romaine (R)	$218,458	$42,950 (20%)	$217,971
1986			
Hochbrueckner (D)	$416,038	$245,054 (59%)	$416,332
Blass (R)	$275,599	$63,465 (23%)	$275,329

Key Votes

1987	
Raise speed limit to 65 mph	N
Approve Gephardt "fair trade" amendment	Y
Ban testing of larger nuclear weapons	Y
Delay "re-flagging" of Kuwaiti tankers	Y
Approve tax-raising deficit-reduction bill	Y
1988	
Approve aid to Nicaraguan contras	N
Enact civil rights restoration bill over Reagan veto	Y
Kill 60-day plant-closing notification measure	N
Pass omnibus trade bill over Reagan veto	Y
Approve death penalty for drug-related murders	N
Bar federal funds for abortions in cases of rape and incest	Y
Oppose seven-day waiting period for purchase of handguns	N

Voting Studies

	Presidential Support		Party Unity		Conservative Coalition	
Year	**S**	**O**	**S**	**O**	**S**	**O**
1988	22	78	89	10	37	63
1987	18	81	87	5	19	81

Interest Group Ratings

Year	ADA	ACU	AFL-CIO	CCUS
1988	80	12	93	36
1987	92	4	93	27

2 Thomas J. Downey (D)

Of Amityville — Elected 1974

Born: Jan. 28, 1949, Ozone Park, N.Y.
Education: Cornell U., B.S. 1970; attended St. John's U. Law School, 1972-74; American U., J.D. 1978.
Occupation: Personnel manager.
Family: Wife, D. Chris Milanos; two children.
Religion: Methodist.
Political Career: Suffolk County Legislature, 1972-75.
Capitol Office: 2232 Rayburn Bldg. 20515; 225-3335.

In Washington: The kid congressman finally turned 40 at the start of the 101st Congress, still bearing a youthfulness that belies not only his age but also his standing as an old pro of a legislator.

That reputation was advanced — and probably the aging process also — by Downey's dogged, politically harrowing and ultimately successful effort in the 100th Congress for a major overhaul of the welfare system. Unexpectedly thrust into a lead role early in 1987, he spent the next 18 months shepherding that complex, controversial legislation into law. It was a characteristic performance throughout, with Downey at times brash and bitingly partisan, and yet also patient and conciliatory enough with foes and waverers to overcome some missteps and see the cause to completion.

Now in his eighth term, Downey retains some of the wise-guy reputation of his first, occasionally alienating opponents and even would-be allies with sarcasm and intellectual arrogance that detracts from his recognized debating skills. However, he is respected in both parties as a serious legislator who holds his own in highly technical arguments, whether the subject is welfare, the tax code or arms control. He is an organizer and a leader, from the bipartisan basketball games in the House gym to the caucus of his fellow House liberals that waged a sustained and partly successful assault on President Reagan's arms buildup.

With his work on the welfare bill in the 100th Congress, Downey came to focus most of his attention on the Ways and Means Committee, and less on the defense and foreign policy issues that had been his primary concerns since he sat on the Armed Services Committee a decade ago.

He remains acting chairman of the Ways and Means Subcommittee on Human Resources, the panel charged with handling welfare issues. Downey got the post after Harold E. Ford of Tennessee, the chairman since 1981, had to step down after he was indicted on federal corruption charges in April 1987. Ironically, it was the second chairmanship to fall to Downey for the same reason in the space of a few weeks. He had become head of a Select Aging subcommittee when Mario Biaggi of New York was indicted, and inherited the seat in his own right when Biaggi resigned from the House after his conviction.

Through the long and contentious welfare debate, Downey was a tenacious advocate, expressing confidence that a bill would pass, telling doubters, "You've got Beltway fever." Yet he did not underestimate the difficulty. "Welfare reform is very hard to do," he said before House passage, "because it is so subject to mythologies and prejudices and racism."

The bill aimed to help welfare recipients get off the dole and into jobs, while improving benefits for those, especially single mothers, who depend on assistance. He moved it through Ways and Means on a party-line vote, and fueled some of the partisanship himself. Referring to GOP objections about his bill's proposed cost and expanded benefits, he said, "There's just a very different view of how we treat the poor and how to encourage people to get off welfare. [Republicans] want to reduce benefits. We want to give them training and education."

Next, Downey monitored the work of three other committees with minor parts in the process, and engineered the compromises necessary to fashion a package for the House floor. Getting there, however, was a rocky road.

In late October 1987, he persuaded House leaders to roll the welfare bill into a pending deficit-reduction package of spending cuts and minor tax increases; he hoped the budget-cutting vehicle would carry his bill through the Senate and past Reagan's desk. But it created a politically explosive mix — higher welfare spending and higher taxes — and the tactic backfired. Many Democrats joined Republicans in opposition, forcing the welfare bill to be stripped off. On several occasions, floor debate on the stand-alone bill was postponed as Democrats balked, conservatives offered their own version and everyone worried about the economy after the October stock market crash.

A fellow Democrat suggested Downey himself could be part of the problem: "Tom is

New York 2

Long Island — Western Suffolk County

The 2nd is filled with technicians and executives who work for the defense contractors and other aerospace companies that constitute the district's dominant industry. Fairchild Republic operates a huge aircraft plant in Farmingdale, and spinoff companies abound along the Route 110 industrial corridor. Grumman Aerospace Corp. and Unisys Corp. (formerly Sperry Systems) also operate plants here.

But defense is not the 2nd District's only major industry. As with the 1st, the 2nd's proximity to the water has spawned an important local vacation economy. Many residents have boat slips on the Great South Bay. Each Saturday morning during warm weather, the ferry is full from Bay Shore to Ocean Beach on Fire Island. Cars are banned on Fire Island, where summer people run errands with toy wagons in tow. Bay Shore hosts a commercial fishing industry.

Although Democrat Downey has represented the 2nd for a decade and a half, the district generally votes Republican in statewide contests.

The heavy Republican vote comes from such well-to-do towns as Babylon Village and Sayville, located on Long Island's South Shore. Italian-American Copiague is a bastion of blue-collar Republican voting. North Babylon and Deer Park have high Republican enrollments, although Downey has made inroads there. Another of the district's swing areas is blue-collar Lindenhurst, once a German community.

Pockets of Democratic strength exist in Dix Hills and in North Amityville, which contains a population of low-income blacks whose ancestors moved to Long Island to work as servants in the mansions of South Amityville.

Population: 515,595. White 457,700 (89%), Black 44,364 (9%), Other 4,125 (1%). Spanish origin 34,579 (7%). 18 and over 351,055 (68%), 65 and over 40,282 (8%). Median age: 29.

usually so convinced that he is right that he doesn't have a lot of sympathy for people who hold opposing views," said Ways and Means liberal Don J. Pease of Ohio.

But Downey countered, "I understand that successful politics is the art of compromise." Amid the delays, he tried to show patience toward reluctant Democrats, and credited Republicans for the bill's premise — putting welfare recipients to work. "We have to give the conservatives their due," he said. "They always emphasized the importance of work."

Finally the bill came to the floor in mid-December, and was approved 230-194. But the key vote had come earlier on the rule opening debate, which allowed just two amendments: a GOP substitute sure to fail, and a leadership amendment cutting $500 million from the bill's five-year cost as a gesture to conservatives. With Democratic whips frantically rounding up votes, the rule narrowly passed, 213-206.

After the Senate passed its bill in 1988, a sometimes rancorous conference met over the summer to reconcile the House's $7.1 billion plan and the Senate's $2.8 billion version. Meanwhile, twice the House voted for non-binding GOP resolutions endorsing the Senate's price tag. Finally, the two sides settled on a $3.34 billion compromise. It included a workfare provision sought by conservatives — "the price of passing a welfare bill," Downey told complaining liberals. For liberals, there were guarantees of medical and child care for parents moving from the welfare rolls to jobs.

Even before the welfare debate, Downey had established himself as a significant Democratic force on Ways and Means, despite his attention to defense policy. He now ranks ninth among 23 Democrats, and generally is an ally of Chairman Dan Rostenkowski. However, during the tax-revision debate in the 99th Congress the two split over Rostenkowski's proposed limit on the deduction for state and local taxes.

The outcry in New York and other high-tax states was considerable. "People are telling me, 'No compromise,'" Downey said. "That's going to be my position. It's a matter of political survival."

Becoming a self-described "guerrilla warrior," he made deals with oil- and timber-state members to protect certain deductions, and cast some early votes against Rostenkowski in committee to send a signal. Faced with such intense opposition from Downey and others, and realizing the provision had become a major stumbling block, Rostenkowski had little choice but to retain the state and local tax deduction. Downey in turn supported the chairman's tax bill.

He also played a major role during the 99th Congress in shaping the taxes to pay for an expanded "superfund" hazardous-waste cleanup program. The 1980 superfund law had made oil and chemical companies responsible for most of the financing, and Downey wanted the practice continued. After Ways and Means approved a new broad-based tax on business, he assembled a diverse coalition to win approval of a floor amendment putting the burden back on the oil and chemical industries responsible for the wastes. A House-Senate conference later produced a compromise that included a smaller tax on a broad base of businesses.

Whatever Downey's responsibilities at Ways and Means, it seems unlikely he will ever drop his involvement with defense policy. Since leaving Armed Services, he has continued to seek institutional posts from which to pursue his goals. In 1984 he proposed creation of a special arms control committee to combine the jurisdiction split between Armed Services and the Foreign Affairs Committee; the Democratic Caucus rejected his idea under pressure from members of the two turf-conscious panels.

He did make use of his temporary stint on the Budget Committee, chairing its Defense Task Force in the 99th Congress and thus leading the House fight for a lower defense budget in conferences with the Senate. His term on Budget ended with that Congress, in 1986, but by then he had begun convening weekly meetings of arms control activists in his office. They came to play a major role during Reagan's second term in slowing the president's ambitious arms buildup.

Working with liberal allies Les AuCoin of Oregon, Edward J. Markey of Massachusetts and Patricia Schroeder of Colorado, Downey exploited widespread unease with Reagan's policies and helped convince House leaders and moderate Democrats of the political advantages of attack. He later attributed Democrats' unity and success (after the divisiveness during Reagan's first term) to the fact that Republican defense positions were "increasingly strident and irrelevant."

From 1985 on, it became routine for the House to slash Reagan's defense budget, specifically his requests for the strategic defense initiative (SDI); to mandate compliance with past arms control treaties; and, for three of the four years, to ban most nuclear arms tests. Though the provisions were either dropped or modified in conference with the Senate, they served to push compromises to the left and to pressure Reagan to negotiate arms cuts with the Soviets. Ironically, Reagan's doing so diminished support for the arms controllers' efforts, as members became reluctant to undermine the president during his talks with Soviet leader Mikhail S. Gorbachev.

The activists' biggest victory was in 1985, when Congress capped the number of MX missiles. Downey and his allies had the support of House Democratic leaders to try to kill the missile and they came within a handful of votes of victory, losing to Reagan's all-out lobbying blitz. Even so, the loss set the stage for the ultimate compromise limiting the number of the multi-warhead missiles to 50.

With the arrival of a new administration in 1989, Downey was one of 20 Democrats, including Armed Services Chairman Les Aspin, who wrote President Bush petitioning him to respect that cap in the interests of political consensus, and also to support the smaller, single-warhead Midgetman missile. Bush wants more MXs, and on a mobile rail system instead of the current underground silos, thus renewing debate over the weapon.

In the 100th Congress, Downey traveled with Democrats Jim Moody of Wisconsin and Bob Carr of Michigan deep inside the Soviet Union, where they videotaped the controversial Krasnoyarsk radar project, and determined for House leaders that it was of little military significance. That contradicted the administration, which considered the radar a dangerous breach of U.S.-Soviet accords against anti-ballistic missile systems, proof of Soviet duplicity and reason to proceed with SDI. A Pentagon official charged that Downey's mission had been used for a Soviet "propaganda coup."

In earlier years while a member of Armed Services, Downey was a militant critic of the B-1 bomber, but he supported the neutron bomb, the cruise missile system and fighter planes manufactured on Long Island. (In 1989, he fought Bush's decision to end production of the Navy's F-14, made in his district.)

Soon he became one of the most visible and quotable advocates of strategic arms limitation. "Listen carefully, all you hardware freaks," he once said. "If you want a new MX missile, you'd better see that SALT II is ratified." His bluster proved baseless the next year, however, when Reagan came to power. Without pushing for ratification of the arms treaty, Reagan was able to muster majority support for the MX, forcing Downey to spend several years of hard work organizing congressional and grass-roots opposition before the 1985 compromise to stop production.

He was part of a small liberal minority on Armed Services, at a time when hawkish conservatives still were firmly in control. But in early 1985, after he had left for Ways and Means, Downey was one of the colonels who helped oust enfeebled Chairman Melvin Price and install Aspin in his place. Two years later, though disappointed himself with Aspin's support of the MX and contra aid, Downey helped defend Aspin against a near-successful coup by a coalition of disaffected liberals and vengeful conservatives. He said he advised Aspin to commit to "no more MXs, and a change of heart on contras."

At Home: Downey's election in 1974 at age 25 made him the youngest member of Congress in a decade and brought him front-page attention in *The New York Times*, which ran a picture of an unbelievably young-looking congressman-elect shooting baskets in his back yard.

But Downey had already developed a reputation for precocity. In 1971, as a 22-year-old college student, he was elected to the Suffolk County Legislature. In his three years there, he sponsored legislation to regulate sewer construction, restrict smoking in public places and impose rent control on trailer courts.

He won his congressional seat in a strongly Republican district represented by GOP Rep. James R. Grover. Grover's winning margins had been so large he was thought to be invulnerable, an opinion he shared. Even Downey's surprisingly strong showing in a debate did little to shake GOP confidence. But Downey won by nearly 5,000 votes.

Once Downey took office, he practiced all the new techniques of constituent service and pioneered some of his own. He stayed in his office in the evening telephoning voters personally and held teas for them on Sundays.

His methods worked. Republicans thought they had a winner in 1976 when they nominated Peter F. Cohalan, a popular town supervisor from Islip who later became Suffolk County executive. Cohalan described his campaign as one of "sanity" vs. "extreme liberalism," and complained about Downey's refusal to support an anti-busing constitutional amendment. But Downey dispatched him with surprising ease, and followed with three easy re-election victories.

In the last two presidential election years, district Republicans tried to imitate Downey's own youthful rise by nominating extremely fresh faces to challenge him. The tactic failed.

In 1984, 28-year-old Paul Aniboli, a former Suffolk County prosecutor, attacked Downey's political style and philosophy, branding the incumbent a "radical liberal," "dangerous," and "a wimp." Despite Aniboli's support from national conservative groups and a strong showing by Reagan in Suffolk County, Downey won 55 percent.

After Downey took 64 percent in 1986, Suffolk Republicans in 1988 nominated a 28-year-old attorney, Joseph Cardino Jr. But Downey again coasted to victory, taking 62 percent of the vote.

Committees

Select Aging (2nd of 39 Democrats)
Human Services (chairman); Retirement, Income and Employment

Ways and Means (9th of 23 Democrats)
Human Resources (acting chairman); Trade

Elections

1988 General		
Thomas J. Downey (D)	107,646	(62%)
Joseph Cardino Jr. (R)	66,972	(38%)
1986 General		
Thomas J. Downey (D)	69,771	(64%)
Jeffrey A. Butzke (R)	35,132	(32%)

Previous Winning Percentages: **1984** (55%) **1982** (64%) **1980** (56%) **1978** (55%) **1976** (57%) **1974** (49%)

District Vote For President

	1988	1984	1980	1976
D	70,283 (38%)	62,326 (34%)	61,484 (34%)	78,810 (45%)
R	111,927 (61%)	123,453 (66%)	106,088 (58%)	94,673 (54%)
I			12,226 (7%)	

Campaign Finance

	Receipts	Receipts from PACs	Expenditures
1988			
Downey (D)	$790,000	$333,761 (42%)	$564,732
Cardino (R) †	$52,912	0	$35,057
1986			
Downey (D)	$823,272	$251,005 (30%)	$739,062
Butzke (R)	$30,756	$1,055 (3%)	$30,153

† Totals based on incomplete data.

Key Votes

1987	
Raise speed limit to 65 mph	N
Approve Gephardt "fair trade" amendment	N
Ban testing of larger nuclear weapons	Y
Delay "re-flagging" of Kuwaiti tankers	Y
Approve tax-raising deficit-reduction bill	Y
1988	
Approve aid to Nicaraguan contras	N
Enact civil rights restoration bill over Reagan veto	Y
Kill 60-day plant-closing notification measure	N
Pass omnibus trade bill over Reagan veto	Y
Approve death penalty for drug-related murders	N
Bar federal funds for abortions in cases of rape and incest	N
Oppose seven-day waiting period for purchase of handguns	N

Voting Studies

	Presidential Support		Party Unity		Conservative Coalition	
Year	S	O	S	O	S	O
1988	23	77	93	4	8	92
1987	21	78	93	3	12	86
1986	18	81	91	4	16	80
1985	21	75	91	4	9	87
1984	29	67	92	4	5	93
1983	26	71	90	4	10	84
1982	38	58	92	4	11	88
1981	29	63	84	7	12	81

Interest Group Ratings

Year	ADA	ACU	AFL-CIO	CCUS
1988	100	0	86	36
1987	92	9	87	20
1986	95	5	79	17
1985	85	5	94	26
1984	95	4	77	31
1983	85	5	82	37
1982	100	0	95	18
1981	80	0	85	11

3 Robert J. Mrazek (D)

Of Centerport — Elected 1982

Born: Nov. 6, 1945, Newport, R.I.
Education: Cornell U., B.A. 1967.
Military Career: Navy, 1967-68.
Occupation: Congressional aide.
Family: Wife, Catherine Susan Gurick; two children.
Religion: Methodist.
Political Career: Suffolk County Legislature, 1976-83; sought Democratic nomination for U.S. House, 1972; Democratic nominee for N.Y. Senate, 1978.
Capitol Office: 306 Cannon Bldg. 20515; 225-5956.

In Washington: For a man who arrived in the House as an instant leadership favorite, and was rewarded accordingly, Mrazek is no lackey.

He is not disloyal; with liberal instincts, Mrazek is among the most reliable supporters of the party line, even though he hails from a Republican-minded district. But the same independence and political passion that prompt Mrazek to vote in ways that could be troublesome back home also make him unafraid to buck the Democratic hierarchy. Inevitably, that will vex the colleagues he challenges, and even Mrazek's admirers suggest he might pick his fights more carefully. Generally, however, Mrazek operates with enough fairness, savvy and good humor to remain popular and respected.

Mrazek's independence is all the more notable since he sits on the disciplined and tradition-bound Appropriations Committee. He got the coveted seat as a freshman, because then-Speaker Thomas P. O'Neill Jr. was grateful that Mrazek had ousted Rep. John LeBoutillier, an iconoclastic Republican who had spent much of his single term harassing O'Neill.

Like his friend and fellow member of the Democrats' large 1982 class, Richard J. Durbin, Mrazek has not hesitated to press his case on Appropriations, even if it means opposing the proud subcommittee chairmen who make up the committee's "College of Cardinals." Also, unlike most Appropriations insiders, who concentrate their legislative efforts there, Mrazek has interests that take him far from the committee — and far from Long Island.

He does tend carefully to parochial concerns. Mrazek has used his seat on Appropriations' Transportation Subcommittee to steer funds to his suburban region to help relieve its crowded highways and improve its mass transit; his provisions have earmarked money for the electrification of a section of the Long Island Rail Road and banned smoking on the line — a combination that testifies to appropriators' unique power not only to secure funding but also to legislate non-money matters. Off Appropriations, Mrazek has been part of the fight to prevent Long Island's Shoreham nuclear power plant from operating.

But Mrazek is better known for his involvement in an eclectic range of national policy issues, large and small. He prides himself on being a preservationist — cultural, historical and environmental — and it is to that end that he is at his scrappiest.

In the 100th Congress, he was intent on blocking the colorization of classic black-and-white films, arguing that the old movies are artworks and deserving of protection. But many Appropriations colleagues did not share Mrazek's passion. Nor, as a matter of custom, do they like being drawn into controversies that divide the committee and threaten its spending bills.

Mrazek's proposal pitted Hollywood artists — actors, writers and directors — against movie owners and producers on the industry's business side, including some top Democratic Party contributors who had the support of "Cardinal" Vic Fazio of California. Mrazek had help from such stars as Jimmy Stewart, but his more important ally was Sidney R. Yates, the equally independent chairman of Appropriations' Interior Subcommittee, which has jurisdiction over the arts.

Yates included an anti-colorization proposal in his subcommittee's annual spending bill, and helped Mrazek negotiate with Judiciary Committee members who had First Amendment concerns about limiting forms of expression. But threatened with a point of order that would kill his provision on the floor, Mrazek had to accept a weak compromise. The substitute that became law would not prevent colorization, but instead set up a national film preservation board to identify U.S. film classics and to see that they are labeled to disclose any alteration.

Working largely through the Interior Committee, of which he is not a member, Mrazek has led environmentalists' fight to preserve the Tongass National Forest in Alaska. His bill,

New York 3

Long Island — Parts of Nassau and Suffolk Counties

The 3rd is almost evenly split between Long Island's two giant suburban counties: In the 1988 House race, Nassau cast 53 percent of the district vote, while Suffolk provided 47 percent. Its suburban nature gives the 3rd a Republican tilt, but Democrats can do well there, as Mrazek has proven.

Defense remains the crucial industry. The district hosts the Hazeltine works in Huntington and the Unisys operation in Lake Success. Many of the residents who are not involved in defense commute to jobs in New York City.

The Nassau portion of the district is a partisan patchwork. Northern Oyster Bay houses Republican corporate executives in such prosperous communities as Bayville and Muttontown. Largely Jewish Roslyn turns in a heavy Democratic vote. North Hempstead communities such as Manhasset and New Hyde Park lean to the GOP.

F. Scott Fitzgerald set "The Great Gatsby" on Long Island's North Shore. While affluent people still live in Gatsby's estate country, some of the mansions have been turned into museums. A small garment industry is attracting Hispanic residents to Glen Cove. The Hispanics there vote Democratic, cutting into the GOP vote.

The Suffolk portion of the district displays a more uniformly Republican cast, although Democrats have made inroads in local offices. Huntington is home to many Irish and Italian Republicans. Smithtown, another ethnic area, lies to the east. Huntington and Smithtown, settled earlier than much of burgeoning Suffolk County, have grown minimally in recent years.

Population: 516,610. White 491,113 (95%), Black 14,344 (3%), Other 7,846 (2%). Spanish origin 13,902 (3%). 18 and over 378,027 (73%), 65 and over 53,356 (10%). Median age: 34.

which would repeal federal timber harvesting concessions and logging subsidies, has brought Mrazek in conflict with one of Congress' more volatile members, Alaska Republican Rep. Don Young. Furious about what he regarded as Mrazek's meddling, Young once berated Mrazek on the House floor while clutching his ever-present hunter's knife. A version of Mrazek's bill easily passed the House in 1988 but died in the Senate; the fight resumed in the 101st Congress.

Also working through Interior, Mrazek in 1988 successfully cosponsored a bill expanding Virginia's Manassas National Battlefield Park so a shopping mall could not be built on the land. A Civil War buff whose office is lined with memorabilia of the period, Mrazek asked foes who questioned the purchase, "What is the price of our national historical heritage?"

From Appropriations' Foreign Operations Subcommittee, Mrazek opposed much of the Reagan foreign and defense policy. He once described as his proudest moment in Congress the House's adoption of his 1986 amendment barring U.S. personnel from providing assistance to the contras within 20 miles of Nicaragua's border. Mrazek aimed to avoid provoking a Nicaraguan attack that would provide a "Gulf of Tonkin pretext" for direct U.S. involvement. The amendment passed the House, 215-212, and later was adopted by the Senate. However, a similar amendment failed in 1987, 197-225, in the wake of the furor over Nicaragua's invasion of Honduras to disrupt contra border camps.

A Vietnam-era Navy veteran, Mrazek in 1987 sponsored a law expediting immigration of Amerasians to the United States. He has been a leader in the fight to reduce funding for the proposed strategic defense initiative. And as a representative for a large Jewish constituency, he supports Israel in foreign aid debates. On a trip to Jordan in early 1985, Mrazek refused to join colleagues in a meeting with Palestine Liberation Organization leader Yasir Arafat. In 1987, however, he vocally criticized Israel's handling of the Jonathan Jay Pollard spy case.

A devoted free-trader, Mrazek was one of only two Democrats to oppose the 1988 trade bill, which was a leadership priority, and he cast the only Democratic vote in support of President Reagan's veto of the measure.

Well-known as outspoken, Mrazek still shocked colleagues in early 1989 when he gave *The New York Times* one of the earliest and bluntest on-the-record assessments from a Democrat on Speaker Jim Wright's ethics problems. "There is a recognition by virtually all of the people I would consider professional politicians that he will not survive," Mrazek said.

Mrazek has an appealing, self-deprecating wit, but he can be emotional and sarcastic in debate. He once objected to then-Rep. Phil Gramm's use of Vietnam parallels to defend contra aid, arguing that policy makers did not need advice from "armchair warriors" such as Gramm, who did not serve in Vietnam.

At Home: Mrazek won election in this GOP-leaning district by making LeBoutillier's personality the major campaign issue.

LeBoutillier's abrasive outspokenness had offended both parties. He had described GOP Sen. Charles H. Percy of Illinois as "a wimp," and O'Neill as "big, fat and out of control." For most of 1982, it was thought that his potshots had played better on Long Island than in Washington. But Mrazek convinced voters that the incumbent's "obnoxious behavior" had rendered him ineffective.

Mrazek charged that LeBoutillier was so busy grandstanding that he had neglected the district. Meanwhile, a confident LeBoutillier was campaigning in Massachusetts, heading an independent effort to defeat O'Neill. The Speaker won with 75 percent and LeBoutillier lost by 10,000 votes.

The 1984 GOP hope was Robert Quinn, who, despite a late entrance and a lack of political experience, came within an eyelash of victory. One reason was money. Quinn was a millionaire who had recently retired as a general partner of the investment firm Salomon Brothers. Digging into his own pocket, Quinn filled the airwaves with radio ads that gave him a districtwide identity. Mrazek attacked Quinn as naive and shallow on issues, and reminded voters that the Republican had not voted since 1980. Mrazek won with 51 percent, carrying his Suffolk County base (as he did in 1982), and also winning narrowly in Republican Nassau County, where the GOP organization did not make Quinn a top priority.

In 1986, Republicans put up an organization insider, Joseph Guarino. Guarino said Mrazek was inattentive to local concerns, but the charges would not stick. Mrazek had received regular publicity for his efforts to procure funding for public transit and toxic-waste cleanup. Guarino also was hindered by a fallout with some Nassau machine lieutenants. Mrazek won comfortably.

The 1988 election was further evidence of Mrazek's growing security in the seat. Unlike the previous presidential campaign year, Republicans put little stock in their ability to dislodge Mrazek, and provided meager support for challenger Robert Previdi, a Citicorp national advertising vice president. Mrazek won with a career-high 57 percent.

Mrazek has been in government his entire adult life. After a stint in the Navy, where he lost partial sight in one eye during a training exercise, he worked for Sen. Vance Hartke, an Indiana Democrat. After one failed campaign for the congressional nomination in 1972, he won a seat in the Suffolk County Legislature in 1975. He held it easily even in GOP territory.

Mrazek developed a reputation on Long Island as a reform-minded official with a special interest in environmental issues. He exposed corruption in the Southwest Sewer District and sponsored rules mandating financial disclosure for Suffolk officials. Easygoing in his approach, he brought together the feuding Democratic minority in the Legislature and became the group's leader in 1979.

Committee

Appropriations (29th of 35 Democrats)
Foreign Operations; Transportation and Related Agencies

Elections

1988 General		
Robert J. Mrazek (D)	128,336	(57%)
Robert Previdi (R)	91,122	(41%)
1986 General		
Robert J. Mrazek (D)	83,985	(56%)
Joseph A. Guarino (R)	60,367	(41%)

Previous Winning Percentages: **1984** (51%) **1982** (52%)

District Vote For President

	1988		1984		1980		1976	
D	94,975	(40%)	897,643	(36%)	82,250	(34%)	128,327	(47%)
R	142,108	(59%)	159,039	(64%)	132,779	(55%)	146,614	(53%)
I					20,457	(9%)		

Campaign Finance

	Receipts	Receipts from PACs		Expend-itures
1988				
Mrazek (D)	$447,902	$176,931	(40%)	$364,087
Previdi (R)	$93,063	$3,480	(4%)	$90,892
1986				
Mrazek (D)	$726,814	$239,608	(33%)	$646,610
Guarino (R)	$204,750	$27,664	(14%)	$200,651

Key Votes

1987	
Raise speed limit to 65 mph	N
Approve Gephardt "fair trade" amendment	N
Ban testing of larger nuclear weapons	Y
Delay "re-flagging" of Kuwaiti tankers	Y
Approve tax-raising deficit-reduction bill	Y
1988	
Approve aid to Nicaraguan contras	N
Enact civil rights restoration bill over Reagan veto	Y
Kill 60-day plant-closing notification measure	N
Pass omnibus trade bill over Reagan veto	N
Approve death penalty for drug-related murders	N
Bar federal funds for abortions in cases of rape and incest	N
Oppose seven-day waiting period for purchase of handguns	N

Voting Studies

	Presidential Support		Party Unity		Conservative Coalition	
Year	**S**	**O**	**S**	**O**	**S**	**O**
1988	19	75	91	4	13	84
1987	16	81	91	4	7	93
1986	17	77	86	8	16	80
1985	24	70	87	7	16	80
1984	28	68	88	7	17	83
1983	23	73	85	11	27	73

Interest Group Ratings

Year	ADA	ACU	AFL-CIO	CCUS
1988	95	4	79	31
1987	96	9	88	13
1986	80	5	85	31
1985	90	19	81	43
1984	80	0	92	33
1983	85	22	88	25

4 Norman F. Lent (R)

Of East Rockaway — Elected 1970

Born: March 23, 1931, Oceanside, N.Y.
Education: Hofstra U., B.A. 1952; Cornell U., J.D. 1957.
Military Career: Navy, 1952-54.
Occupation: Lawyer.
Family: Wife, Barbara Morris; three children.
Religion: Methodist.
Political Career: N.Y. Senate, 1963-71.
Capitol Office: 2408 Rayburn Bldg. 20515; 225-7896.

In Washington: A product of the Nassau County Republican machine, Lent seems to enjoy making deals and getting things done. He is not the most eloquent member of the Energy and Commerce Committee, but he has forged good personal relationships with Republicans and Democrats alike, and that has helped make him an effective ranking member of the powerful panel.

Lent filled a vacancy in the committee's No. 1 GOP spot in the midst of the 99th Congress, and the move required some adjustment. He had spent much of his career tending to his Long Island district, not acting as the spokesman for his side of the aisle. That function had been served by Lent's predecessor, James T. Broyhill of North Carolina, and to a degree by Illinois Republican Edward Madigan, the committee's No. 3 Republican and an activist legislator known for his substantive grasp of issues.

But Lent's adjustment into the top spot has generally gone well, with the New Yorker comfortably brokering debates among members of the committee and with Republican administrations. There is, however, one area where some members are not comfortable tipping their hand to Lent: telephone issues. His wife works for Nynex, the New York-based offspring of AT&T.

Lent initially campaigned for the House as a challenger to "dangerous leftists," but he has since proven he is not a partisan ideologue. He is, however, a man who knows what he wants. Lent brings a bluntness to negotiation that one might expect from the product of a political machine. Some complain that his high-pressure style is better suited to salesmanship than to statesmanship, but when he is through negotiating, he usually has gotten much of what he wanted.

Lent's strong will is occasionally a little surprising. At one point in the 100th Congress he fought with a vengeance to defeat an amendment designed to prevent startup of the Shoreham Nuclear Plant on Long Island, and another in New Hampshire. During the debate, Lent attacked fellow New Yorker George J. Hochbrueckner, whose successful House campaign centered on opposition to Shoreham.

"Many of us in this room were elected here on the basis of running against something," Lent said, "but after we get here awhile we calm down a little bit and we try to become statesmen." The amendment failed.

Like many other Republicans representing districts troubled by hazardous chemicals and acid rain, Lent has a strong interest in environmental legislation. In recent years he has been actively involved in crafting "superfund" legislation to clean up toxic-waste sites.

Lent was ranking Republican on the Commerce, Transportation and Tourism Subcommittee during the period it was chaired by New Jersey Democrat James J. Florio. He went along with Florio in pushing the original superfund bill, toward the end of President Jimmy Carter's administration.

But in the fights over superfund reauthorization in the 98th and 99th Congresses, the two were on opposite sides. Both wanted to see the fund increased, but Lent sought to give the Environmental Protection Agency (EPA) more leeway in administering the program than did most environmentalists. He feared that Florio's anti-EPA position would jeopardize passage of any superfund bill.

Congress failed to reauthorize the program in the 98th Congress, but in the 99th a compromise was reached that overwhelmingly passed the House. President Reagan still opposed it, in part because he considered the fivefold increase in funding too high, but he had little chance of blocking it. When he considered not signing the bill and then killing it by pocket veto after Congress adjourned, Lent urged him not to. "A majority are willing to stay for the duration," he said. "I am."

As ranking member, Lent has worked cooperatively with Chairman John D. Dingell on a number of issues. In the 100th Congress he was one of the "Big Four" leading the effort to set a national standard for product liability. Along with Dingell, Florio and New Mexico Democrat Bill Richardson, Lent helped to produce a

New York 4

Long Island — Southeastern Nassau County

In 1947, row after row of inexpensive Cape Cod homes began sprouting on what had been Long Island farm land, and Levittown was under way. Today, the last farm land has long since been developed, and Levittown and the surrounding middle-income suburbs of the 4th have the settled, comfortable look of established suburbia. They also generally vote Republican.

The 4th is an overwhelmingly white, middle-class area. The aerospace and electronics industries are major employers in the district; the Grumman Corp. maintains its headquarters in Bethpage, and many residents of the 4th cross district lines to work in defense plants in the neighboring 2nd. As elsewhere in Nassau, the railroad platforms are filled each morning with commuters clutching their early editions of *Newsday*, the Long Island daily.

While thousands of the 4th's constituents may stream into New York City on weekdays, thousands of city dwellers head for the district on summer weekends — in particular to Jones Beach, a state park on the Atlantic Ocean.

The district is ethnically diverse. Massapequa attracted a combination of Jewish and Italian homeowners following World War II, leading wags to refer to it as "Matzo-Pizza." Massapequa today is largely Italian and increasingly Republican. Plainview, toward the district's northern end, is a middle-income Jewish suburb.

The 4th includes all of Levittown except the western area. Its share of the community shows Republican leanings but occasionally supports Democrats in statewide elections.

Closer to the water, identification with the Republican Party is stronger. Alfonse M. D'Amato, the one-time GOP municipal official and twice-elected U.S. senator, comes from this section of the 4th. The now-faded older suburbs here that boomed in the postwar years — Baldwin, Oceanside and Freeport, a commercial fishing center — are Irish and Italian strongholds. Bellmore, Merrick and Seaford have a more prosperous look and equally firm GOP ties. The same can be said for the half of Long Beach Island in the 4th.

Population: 516,641. White 489,145 (95%), Black 19,186 (4%), Other 4,695 (1%). Spanish origin 15,428 (3%). 18 and over 376,675 (73%), 65 and over 42,004 (8%). Median age: 33.

scheme to replace conflicting state laws used by courts to determine whether a person injured by a defective product recovers damages from a manufacturer. The bill, opposed by consumer groups and plaintiffs' lawyers because it might make it tougher for victims to receive damages, passed the committee 30-12, but later died. It was the first time a product-liability revision had cleared a House committee.

In the 99th Congress, Lent joined with Democrats in writing successful legislation to help small businesses obtain affordable liability insurance by allowing them to pool to form insurance cooperatives. The Liability Risk Retention Act became law in 1986.

Before taking over the ranking spot on the full committee, Lent was senior Republican on the Transportation Subcommittee. There he was a very active supporter of Conrail. When the Reagan administration wanted to break up the railroad and sell it to private enterprise in the 97th Congress, Lent insisted on giving Conrail a little more time to make a profit.

By 1984 it was profitable, and two years later the committee cleared a $2 billion Conrail sale package calling for a stock offering to transfer control of the government's 85 percent share of the railroad. Much of the controversy surrounding the sale had to do with deregulation measures attached to the bill. Fearing that those measures could bring a presidential veto or potentially jeopardize the sale in other ways, Lent worked to strip the deregulation changes from the legislation. He failed at the subcommittee level, but he reversed that decision in the full committee, winning a 22-20 victory for a milder amendment removing most of the major deregulation provisions. The package later cleared Congress.

Lent is also in the top ranks on the Merchant Marine and Fisheries Committee. There he has supported ocean pollution control and coastal management legislation important to Long Island's numerous wetlands, inlets, estuaries and beaches.

In the 100th Congress, that committee involved him in the debate on legislation banning the dumping of sewage sludge in the ocean. New Jersey, whose beaches bear the brunt of ocean pollution, had fought with New York, a major dumper, over the issue for years. Lent complained in committee that the measure, which imposed fees and penalties on municipalities failing to halt dumping by the early 1990s, was designed to "beat up" on New York. The city, he said, is reaching "environmental gridlock. . . . The waste can't be burned because of clean air (requirements), and we can't bury it because of groundwater."

But in the 100th Congress there was no real argument about whether there should be a bill, just about what shape it would take. Lent eventually took some credit for helping to hammer out a compromise. It set a deadline in 1991 for dumping to end, and set a schedule of fees and penalties that would initially go into a trust fund, which could be spent for the development of waste-disposal alternatives.

Lent also worked to add provisions to the bill to help protect the Peconic Bay estuarine system under the national estuary program. The fishing and boating in Peconic Bay could be threatened by an algae problem.

Representing a district with a large Jewish population, and frequently confronting Jewish challengers in general elections, Lent has been one of the most prolific authors of resolutions and speeches supporting the rights of Jews in the Soviet Union. He frequently inserts letters and telegrams in the *Congressional Record* urging the Soviets to release Jews they have detained. A fervent supporter of Israel, Lent opposed Reagan administration efforts to withhold F-16 fighters from Israel and to sell Stinger missiles to Saudi Arabia.

At Home: Lent rose through the ranks as a satrap of the Nassau County Republican organization, during the heyday of organization chief Joseph Margiotta. He started as an associate police justice in East Rockaway, then was elected to the state Senate in 1962. As a candidate Lent, a well-behaved young lawyer, veteran and family man, appealed to Margiotta.

In 1968 the late Democratic activist Allard K. Lowenstein had captured the southernmost Nassau congressional district, much to the displeasure of the GOP organization. So in 1970, when lines were redrawn by the state GOP after a court order, thousands of Democratic votes were taken out of the district and Lent was the organization's handpicked choice to oust Lowenstein. It was a bitter contest in which Republicans implied that Lowenstein was the dupe of radical leftists, and Lowenstein responded with the hordes of volunteers that had become his political trademark. Lent's allies urged the district to "give up Lowenstein for Lent." Though the incumbent's backers tried to portray the slogan as a slap at Jews, Lent won.

He has had a relatively easy time in subsequent elections, winning with at least 60 percent since 1976; he took 70 percent in 1988.

Committees

Energy and Commerce (Ranking)
Oversight and Investigations

Merchant Marine and Fisheries (3rd of 17 Republicans)
Merchant Marine (ranking)

Elections

1988 General		
Norman F. Lent (R)	151,038	(70%)
Francis T. Goban (D)	59,479	(28%)
1986 General		
Norman F. Lent (R)	92,214	(65%)
Patricia Sullivan (D)	43,581	(31%)

Previous Winning Percentages: **1984** (69%) **1982** (60%) **1980** (66%) **1978** (66%) **1976** (56%) **1974** (54%) **1972** (62%) **1970** (51%)

District Vote For President

	1988	1984	1980	1976
D	93,960 (41%)	88,949 (36%)	70,189 (34%)	99,242 (48%)
R	134,425 (58%)	155,948 (64%)	117,359 (57%)	107,420 (52%)
I			15,434 (8%)	

Campaign Finance

	Receipts	Receipts from PACs	Expend-itures
1988			
Lent (R)	$589,323	$358,299 (61%)	$436,310
Goban (D)	$5,427	$3,500 (64%)	$4,715
1986			
Lent (R)	$492,418	$274,092 (56%)	$337,118
Sullivan (D)	$12,685	$500 (4%)	$11,829

Key Votes

1987	
Raise speed limit to 65 mph	N
Approve Gephardt "fair trade" amendment	N
Ban testing of larger nuclear weapons	N
Delay "re-flagging" of Kuwaiti tankers	N
Approve tax-raising deficit-reduction bill	N
1988	
Approve aid to Nicaraguan contras	Y
Enact civil rights restoration bill over Reagan veto	Y
Kill 60-day plant-closing notification measure	Y
Pass omnibus trade bill over Reagan veto	N
Approve death penalty for drug-related murders	Y
Bar federal funds for abortions in cases of rape and incest	Y
Oppose seven-day waiting period for purchase of handguns	N

Voting Studies

	Presidential Support		Party Unity		Conservative Coalition	
Year	S	O	S	O	S	O
1988	48	42	61	33	76	13
1987	58	35	54	36	77	21
1986	61	33	65	27	72	18
1985	65	33	72	25	89	9
1984	55	35	65	24	80	14
1983	68	24	65	29	78	19
1982	66	27	60	32	71	27
1981	68	30	75	23	80	17

Interest Group Ratings

Year	ADA	ACU	AFL-CIO	CCUS
1988	25	68	62	69
1987	12	59	33	79
1986	20	64	46	64
1985	10	75	31	57
1984	10	70	38	79
1983	10	76	19	80
1982	35	50	50	65
1981	10	93	13	95

5 Raymond J. McGrath (R)

Of Valley Stream — Elected 1980

Born: March 27, 1942, Valley Stream, N.Y.
Education: State U. of New York, Brockport, B.S. 1963; New York U., M.A. 1968.
Occupation: Physical education teacher.
Family: Wife, Sheryl Peterson; two children.
Religion: Roman Catholic.
Political Career: N.Y. Assembly, 1977-81.
Capitol Office: 205 Cannon Bldg. 20515; 225-5516.

In Washington: McGrath is pretty much known for three things: his good looks, his district-first approach to lawmaking, and his friendship with Dan Rostenkowski.

McGrath's willingness to deal with powerful Ways and Means Chairman Rostenkowski has yielded benefits for his Long Island district. Both men were products of political "machines," and both are given more toward skillfully winning political fights rather than getting swept up in ideological debates.

But McGrath's relationship with Rostenkowski has spawned criticism from some GOP colleagues that his dealmaking is a sellout.

Shortly after joining the Ways and Means Committee in 1985, McGrath made it clear that he put parochialism above partisanship. During debate on the 1986 tax code overhaul, McGrath focused his attention on trying to save the deductibility of state and local taxes. Both the administration and Rostenkowski wanted to eliminate the deduction; that proposal caused a widespread uproar, especially in New York, a high-tax state that would have been hit particularly hard by the change.

McGrath and many others stood adamant against Rostenkowski over the deduction. After the chairman gave in to their demands, McGrath repaid the favor by supporting Rostenkowski's bill. His support was important, because Rostenkowski was struggling to get Republicans signed on to his proposal so he could bill it as a bipartisan measure.

McGrath's support for Rostenkowski helped him get favorable consideration for "transition rules" beneficial to projects in his district, including a tax break on bonds to build a waste-disposal plant. But it also angered some of his Republican colleagues. McGrath was not the only GOP member of Ways and Means to work with Rostenkowski — four others voted to report out the bill — but he was the only Republican to oppose a GOP alternative offered in committee. McGrath did not like the limits that the alternative would have placed on the state and local deduction.

Responding to Republican criticism at one point, he said, "I'm an old-fashioned guy. When you make a deal, you stick with it."

When Ways and Means Democrats staged an impromptu champagne celebration in the wee hours of the morning after voting to approve the legislation, McGrath, who has a reputation for enjoying Washington's social scene, joined them. His presence was a clear gesture of bipartisanship; it may also have reflected his reluctance to pass up a party at any hour.

McGrath also has been willing to side with Rostenkowski on other matters. When Ways and Means Democrats passed their own version of an outpatient prescription drug benefit plan to be added to the catastrophic health insurance bill in 1987, McGrath was the sole Republican to vote with the Democrats.

McGrath's working relationship with Rostenkowski evolved in part because they are both, in a sense, "old-fashioned." Rostenkowski is a product of the well-known Chicago Democratic political machine, while McGrath has long been involved in Republican machine politics in Nassau County.

At Home: McGrath made it to Congress as the handpicked candidate of Joseph Margiotta, the former Nassau County Republican chairman. There was an opening in the 5th District in 1980 because of the retirement of GOP Rep. John W. Wydler, who had served 18 years in the House.

McGrath had been a loyal Margiotta organization man in the Legislature, working primarily on issues of local interest to suburban Nassau County. He labored to end a state toll on a local parkway, and to require the state to pay for school busing it ordered in a Nassau County town. He helped win state approval for local hospital expansion.

McGrath had no opposition in the 1980 primary. In November, his strong party base helped him defeat Democrat Karen Burstein, a former member of the state Public Service Commission. She waged a spirited campaign, but foundered in the face of the local Republican machine, the conservative trend in 1980, and the effectiveness of McGrath's campaign.

By 1982, many of McGrath's constituents

New York 5

Long Island — Southwestern Nassau County

The horse races here are at Belmont Park, not at the polls. Politics in the home district of former GOP boss Joseph Margiotta has been under control for more than two decades. Republicans have held the 5th since its creation in 1962 — thanks in large part to the effective GOP machine Margiotta built.

The organization has undergone change in the last few years. Margiotta was convicted in 1981 on federal mail fraud and extortion charges, and was forced to give up his post as chairman of the Nassau GOP organization. His successor, Joseph N. Mondello, was initially viewed as a Margiotta puppet, but has been consolidating his own power base. The party apparatus, organized down to the block level in some places, remains perhaps the most potent political machine in the country.

But while the local GOP lock boosts Republican presidential candidates, they tend to win by somewhat less spectacular margins than farther out on Long Island. George Bush won the 5th with 56 percent of the vote, his lowest percentage of any Long Island district. The same was true for President Reagan in 1984, though he took 60 percent of the 5th District vote.

The village of Hempstead is the seat of enormous Hempstead Township, most of whose roughly 750,000 residents vote in the 5th District. Hempstead Township is Margiotta's original political base. Hempstead Village hosts Hofstra University and a mixture of light industries.

Republican totals are padded by the vote from such towns as Elmont and Valley Stream, McGrath's hometown. Residents here are primarily Irish and Italian homeowners a generation removed from Brooklyn or Queens.

Predominantly black North Freeport and the sizable black communities in Roosevelt and Hempstead Village contribute to the district's Democratic vote. Other Democratic pockets are Long Beach, a run-down seaside resort given over to senior-citizen residential hotels, and the wealthy "Five Towns" area in Nassau's southwestern corner. These communities — Woodmere, Cedarhurst, Inwood, Lawrence and Hewlett — have the district's largest concentration of Jews. Jewish voters make up about 30 percent of the 5th's population.

Population: 516,712. White 442,946 (86%), Black 63,361 (12%), Other 5,130 (1%). Spanish origin 18,818 (4%). 18 and over 386,288 (75%), 65 and over 62,806 (12%). Median age: 34.

had gained from President Reagan's defense spending proposals, since higher defense spending meant work for Grumman and other Long Island contractors. Still, voter doubts about Reaganomics and the presence of another respectable Democratic candidate — Arnold Miller, a former Carter White House aide — kept McGrath under 60 percent in his second campaign.

In 1984, McGrath faced Michael D'Innocenzo, a Uniondale history professor who accused the Republican of "putting public relations above the public good." McGrath dispatched him with 62 percent.

McGrath was the subject of some unusual publicity in 1986 — the result of an unorthodox investigation into his private life conducted by his Democratic opponent.

The Democrat, Valley Stream attorney Michael Sullivan, hired female undercover investigators — equipped with hidden tape recorders — to record conversations McGrath had in a Capitol Hill restaurant. Sullivan claimed that on one segment of the tapes, whose poor sound quality made conversation difficult to discern, McGrath was instructing fellow Republican Rep. George C. Wortley on how to get around campaign contribution limits with the help of a prominent Syracuse businessman.

For his actions, Sullivan was roundly criticized by fellow New York Democrats and by the local press. McGrath denied any wrongdoing, launched a counteroffensive blasting his opponent for "Watergate dirty tricks" and looked on as Sullivan's campaign essentially collapsed. McGrath won going away. He had no difficulty in 1988. With 65 percent of the vote, he easily outran George Bush in the 5th.

Committee

Ways and Means (8th of 13 Republicans)
Oversight; Select Revenue Measures

Elections

1988 General

Raymond J. McGrath (R)	134,881	(65%)
William G. Kelly (D)	68,930	(33%)

1986 General

Raymond J. McGrath (R)	93,473	(65%)
Michael T. Sullivan (D)	49,728	(35%)

Previous Winning Percentages: **1984** (62%) **1982** (58%) **1980** (58%)

District Vote For President

	1988	1984	1980	1976
D	97,609 (44%)	95,566 (39%)	76,701 (36%)	111,254 (48%)
R	124,622 (56%)	146,086 (60%)	117,106 (55%)	118,897 (52%)
I			14,561 (7%)	

Campaign Finance

	Receipts	Receipts from PACs	Expend-itures
1988			
McGrath (R)	$502,509	$251,324 (50%)	$337,792
Kelly (D)	$37,167	$4,200 (11%)	$35,627
1986			
McGrath (R)	$439,322	$242,669 (55%)	$294,365
Sullivan (D)	$66,458	0	$66,389

Key Votes

1987	
Raise speed limit to 65 mph	N
Approve Gephardt "fair trade" amendment	N
Ban testing of larger nuclear weapons	N
Delay "re-flagging" of Kuwaiti tankers	N
Approve tax-raising deficit-reduction bill	N
1988	
Approve aid to Nicaraguan contras	Y
Enact civil rights restoration bill over Reagan veto	Y
Kill 60-day plant-closing notification measure	Y
Pass omnibus trade bill over Reagan veto	Y
Approve death penalty for drug-related murders	Y
Bar federal funds for abortions in cases of rape and incest	Y
Oppose seven-day waiting period for purchase of handguns	N

Voting Studies

	Presidential Support		Party Unity		Conservative Coalition	
Year	**S**	**O**	**S**	**O**	**S**	**O**
1988	46	42	62	20	74	18
1987	54	42	61	28	77	19
1986	60	37	61	31	70	26
1985	64	33	62	25	75	20
1984	49	34	60	26	73	17
1983	60	35	69	25	79	20
1982	61	34	66	31	66	29
1981	64	34	78	20	75	23

Interest Group Ratings

Year	ADA	ACU	AFL-CIO	CCUS
1988	25	55	83	82
1987	28	59	44	64
1986	20	55	43	69
1985	20	71	41	52
1984	20	74	30	64
1983	15	83	18	60
1982	35	68	50	73
1981	15	93	7	89

6 Floyd H. Flake (D)

Of Queens — Elected 1986

Born: Jan. 30, 1945, Los Angeles, Calif.

Education: Wilberforce U., B.A. 1967; attended Payne Theological Seminary, 1968-70; Northeastern U., 1974-75; St. John's U., 1982-85.

Occupation: Minister.

Family: Wife, M. Elaine McCollins; four children.

Religion: African Methodist Episcopal.

Political Career: No previous office.

Capitol Office: 1427 Longworth Bldg. 20515; 225-3461.

In Washington: A handsome and elegantly dressed minister who speaks in the captivating cadences of the black church, Flake has inspired comparisons with another black clergyman elected to Congress from New York — the late Rep. Adam Clayton Powell Jr. But Flake endured a rough first term discovering that emulating Powell's flamboyance is not the fastest route up the power ladder in Congress.

Flake is a contemporary of the new generation of black House members who view their role less in racial terms than do some more senior Black Caucus members. Recently elected Democrats Alan Wheat of Missouri, Mike Espy of Mississippi and Kweisi Mfume of Maryland exemplify this new generation; they try to effect change by working through the power structure, rather than by agitating primarily from the outside.

But in style and ideology, Flake does not fit quite so readily with the new generation, as he can be more vociferous and controversial. His failure in a bid for the Budget Committee in the 101st Congress may have been caused as much by the impression Flake made on his colleagues as a freshman as by their knowledge of a difficulty Flake had with a woman in his district.

On the Banking Committee, Flake attached an amendment to the omnibus housing authorization bill in the 100th Congress to provide for timely repair of major equipment systems in public-housing facilities. From his spot on the Small Business Committee, he worked on legislation overhauling the minority set-aside program for federal contracts.

At Home: Flake brought a diverse background to politics. After working in corporate marketing, he spent three years as an associate dean of students at Pennsylvania's Lincoln University. He moved to Boston University, where he spent four years in the mid-1970s as dean of students, chaplain and director of the Martin Luther King Jr. Afro-American Center.

But it was his long tenure as pastor of the Allen African Methodist Episcopal (AME) church, a 4,000-member congregation in southern Queens, that made Flake a public figure. From that post, he arranged construction of a 300-unit senior-citizens' home, developed a church-based home-care agency and encouraged a small-business revival in his Queens neighborhood.

Despite the base these activities provided, Flake endured a rigorous ordeal in winning the 6th. Within a few weeks in 1986, he suffered a special-election defeat and a protracted court battle before clinching the nomination that set him on the path to eventual victory.

Black leaders had targeted the 6th after 1982 redistricting gave it a black majority. An opportunity evolved following the April 1986 death of Democratic Rep. Joseph P. Addabbo; it occurred at a time of chaos within the white-run Queens Democratic machine — chaos brought on by a corruption scandal and the suicide of county Democratic leader Donald M. Manes.

The June special primary was won by black state Assemblyman Alton R. Waldon Jr., whose support from surviving fragments of the Democratic organization was just enough for him to edge out Flake. But Flake, who did not appear on absentee ballots because of a filing technicality, appealed the results in court. He lost that battle, but the case helped Flake rally backers who believed the election was stolen by a corrupt Queens machine.

That sentiment gave Flake momentum going into the September primary to choose a nominee for a full term in the 100th Congress. Fusing his support in the black church with elements of black organized labor, and courting white support with the help of New York City Mayor Edward I. Koch, Flake defeated Waldon and two other black primary candidates.

By 1988, Flake was firmly in charge: He drew no significant opposition. His only difficulty was of a personal nature. In May, Thelma M. Singleton-Scott, a former aide to Flake at his Queens church, appeared before a conference of AME churches to accuse Flake of harassing her to quit after she broke off a sexual affair she said she had with him. Flake denied the accusations; a church panel rejected the woman's claim.

New York 6

Southern Queens — Ozone Park; Jamaica

In some respects, this southern Queens constituency has not changed much since it was settled by New York's burgeoning Catholic middle class a generation ago. Civil servants, teachers and small-business people abound, occupying block upon block of single-family brick homes.

But if the presence of a solid middle class has remained a constant, its composition has changed dramatically. Many of the Irish and Italian families that initially settled here have left; today, most of the middle-class population is black. Blacks are most prevalent in quiet, tree-lined communities such as Springfield Gardens and St. Alban's. In Jamaica, though, the black community is poorer, and urban problems of drugs and crime are more rife.

There is a diverse mixture across Jamaica Bay in the Rockaways, whose beaches attract myriad New Yorkers in the summertime. Far Rockaway has many elderly Jews. Neponsit is home to wealthy Jews and WASPs.

South of Jamaica lies Ozone Park, a white working-class area populated by Italians and Jews. Nearby Howard Beach has a similar makeup but a rougher reputation, due to a notorious racial incident in 1986, in which a group of white youths chased a black man onto a highway, where he was struck and killed by a car.

There have been other instances of racial strife here. White parents in Rosedale staged demonstrations in 1981 over a court order to transfer their children to a mostly black school. White flight from the 6th has taken its toll on the local economy. But the district's demographic changes have only reinforced its Democratic cast. The 6th supported Michael S. Dukakis for president in 1988, and Walter F. Mondale in 1984.

Population: 516,312. White 227,798 (44%), Black 259,693 (50%), Other 7,691 (1%). Spanish origin 48,653 (9%). 18 and over 368,500 (71%), 65 and over 61,547 (12%). Median age: 32.

Committees

Banking, Finance and Urban Affairs (25th of 31 Democrats)
Financial Institutions Supervision, Regulation and Insurance; General Oversight and Investigations; Housing and Community Development; International Development, Finance, Trade and Monetary Policy

Select Hunger (11th of 18 Democrats)

Small Business (20th of 27 Democrats)
SBA, the General Economy and Minority Enterprise Development

Elections

1988 General		
Floyd H. Flake (D)	94,506	(86%)
Robert L. Brandofino (C)	15,547	(14%)
1986 General		
Floyd H. Flake (D)	58,317	(68%)
Richard Dietl (R)	27,773	(32%)

District Vote For President

	1988	1984	1980	1976
D	100,131 (71%)	111,658 (70%)	89,495 (58%)	115,346 (69%)
R	39,160 (28%)	47,665 (30%)	55,064 (36%)	50,369 (30%)
I			7,737 (5%)	

Campaign Finance

	Receipts	Receipts from PACs	Expend-itures
1988			
Flake (D)	$344,391	$150,681 (44%)	$370,236
Brandofino (C) †	$3,139	0	$3,071
1986			
Flake (D)	$401,263	$23,350 (6%)	$359,382
Dietl (R)	$72,952	$8,400 (12%)	$55,318

† Totals based on incomplete data.

Key Votes

1987	
Raise speed limit to 65 mph	N
Approve Gephardt "fair trade" amendment	Y
Ban testing of larger nuclear weapons	Y
Delay "re-flagging" of Kuwaiti tankers	Y
Approve tax-raising deficit-reduction bill	Y
1988	
Approve aid to Nicaraguan contras	N
Enact civil rights restoration bill over Reagan veto	Y
Kill 60-day plant-closing notification measure	N
Pass omnibus trade bill over Reagan veto	Y
Approve death penalty for drug-related murders	N
Bar federal funds for abortions in cases of rape and incest	Y
Oppose seven-day waiting period for purchase of handguns	N

Voting Studies

	Presidential Support		Party Unity		Conservative Coalition	
Year	S	O	S	O	S	O
1988	14	74	82	3	5	82
1987	13	75	79	2	12	70

Interest Group Ratings

Year	ADA	ACU	AFL-CIO	CCUS
1988	95	0	100	30
1987	92	0	100	0

7 Gary L. Ackerman (D)

Of Queens — Elected 1983

Born: Nov. 19, 1942, Brooklyn, N.Y.
Education: Queens College, B.A. 1965.
Occupation: Teacher; publisher and editor; advertising executive.
Family: Wife, Rita Gail Tewel; three children.
Religion: Jewish.
Political Career: N.Y. Senate, 1979-83; sought Democratic nomination for N.Y.C. councilman at large, 1977.
Capitol Office: 238 Cannon Bldg. 20515; 225-2601.

In Washington: Ackerman labored in his early House years to earn regard as a legislator. On Foreign Affairs, he was a human rights crusader and staunch defender of Israel. A subcommittee chairman on Post Office and Civil Service, he opposed extensive drug-testing programs.

But at the start of the 100th Congress, Ackerman, who weighed nearly 300 pounds, was still known more for his girth than his agenda. His hearty laugh, vaguely demonic goatee and ever-present boutonniere gave Ackerman — who lives in a houseboat on the Potomac River — the persona of a Falstaffian eccentric.

Realizing this image was preventing him from being taken seriously, Ackerman set about to change it. He went public with a diet-and-exercise regimen that helped him shed 100 pounds. While serving as New York campaign coordinator for Democratic presidential candidate Michael S. Dukakis, he shaved the goatee.

Ackerman says the makeover changed perceptions. "My colleagues . . . used to pass me by; now they come over and slap me on the back," he told *Roll Call* newspaper. "People called me jolly; now they say I'm witty."

But Ackerman still has not lost his zeal for his native New York cuisine: "kosher deli." Decrying the lack of a decent deli sandwich in Washington, he stages an annual fund-raiser for which he ships down huge amounts of corned beef, pastrami and other delicacies from a restaurant in his Queens district.

The district has a large Jewish population, and Ackerman has pursued their concerns for Israel in the House. In 1988, he rejected a letter sent to the Israeli government by 30 senators, which called on Israel to soften its resistance to Palestinian demands. "We're not talking about a banana republic," Ackerman said. "We're talking about a democratic society that is struggling to maintain normal processes in the face of enormous pressures."

Ackerman's interest in human rights often centers on the oppression he sees Jews facing. He is an outspoken supporter of the right of Soviet Jewish "refuseniks" to emigrate to Israel. In July 1988, he helped arrange the release of 25 Jews from jail in Ethiopia, where they had been held for attempting to emigrate.

A member of the Select Hunger Committee, Ackerman staged a campaign in 1985 for Ethiopian famine relief that raised nearly $200,000 from New York City schoolchildren. His "Children to Children" crusade became the subject of an ABC television documentary.

On Post Office and Civil Service, Ackerman first gained note as a foe of proposals for widespread drug testing of federal workers without probable cause. Later, working with GOP Rep. Frank R. Wolf, Ackerman established a program allowing federal employees to donate annual leave time to co-workers needing extra time due to illness or family emergencies. The "leave-sharing" measure became law in 1988.

At Home: When veteran Democratic Rep. Benjamin S. Rosenthal died in early 1983, Ackerman did not lead the list of likely successors. He had been a frequent antagonist of the Queens Democratic organization, then led by Borough President Donald R. Manes. But with a hard-charging campaign style and his own organization, Ackerman forced Queens Democrats to take him seriously. His prospects improved when a popular state legislator dropped from the race. Ackerman then convinced Democratic leaders he could help shield the party from an independent campaign by Douglas Schoen, a wealthy pollster viewed as an outsider.

Schoen did mount an independent effort, and eclipsed the GOP nominee as Ackerman's most formidable foe. But Ackerman won the special election with 50 percent. He gained a full term in 1984; by 1988, he was unopposed.

A former social studies teacher, Ackerman started in politics in 1977, when, as publisher of a weekly community newspaper in Queens, he editorialized against the Manes-backed incumbent in a City Council race. Challenging the incumbent as an independent, he finished second. He ran for an open state Senate seat in 1978 and defeated several Manes allies.

New York 7

Central Queens — Hollis; Kew Gardens

The 7th District travels from semi-suburban neighborhoods near the Nassau County border to apartment towers in the heart of Queens. Mostly white and largely Jewish, the district is solidly Democratic. It gave 60 percent of its presidential vote to Democrat Michael S. Dukakis in 1988, has voted overwhelmingly for Queens Democrat Mario M. Cuomo for governor.

Besides its territory in eastern Queens, the 7th extends south to take in East Elmhurst, Kew Gardens and part of Jamaica, which contributes much of its black population. Another concentration of minorities is in Corona's massive Lefrak City complex. Middle-income whites have been leaving the 20-building development off the Long Island Expressway, and blacks and Hispanics have been replacing them.

Rego Park, developed in the 1920s, typifies the middle-class Jewish portion of the district that formed the support base of the late Democratic Rep. Benjamin S. Rosenthal. A community of six-story apartment buildings and tightly spaced brick houses, Rego Park has turned more conservative on social issues, but most of its residents remain loyal Democrats.

The most significant Republican enclave in the 7th is near the Queens-Nassau line in tree-shaded Bellerose and Queens Village. The suburban-oriented homeowners there, most of Irish and Italian background, regularly flout their Democratic registration and vote for GOP candidates in state and national elections.

Like much of the rest of Queens, the 7th is almost exclusively bedroom communities, with no major industrial activity. Hospitals such as the Long Island Jewish Hillside Medical Center in New Hyde Park are its largest employers.

Population: 516,544. White 377,844 (73%), Black 61,190 (12%), Asian and Pacific Islander 35,365 (7%). Spanish origin 101,893 (20%). 18 and over 407,309 (79%), 65 and over 81,051 (16%). Median age: 35.

Committees

Foreign Affairs (18th of 28 Democrats)
Asian and Pacific Affairs; Europe and the Middle East; Human Rights and International Organizations

Post Office and Civil Service (10th of 15 Democrats)
Compensation and Employee Benefits (chairman); Postal Operations and Services

Select Hunger (9th of 18 Democrats)
Task Force: Domestic

Elections

1988 General		
Gary L. Ackerman (D)	93,120	(100%)
1986 General		
Gary L. Ackerman (D)	62,836	(77%)
Edward Nelson Rodriguez (R)	18,384	(23%)

Previous Winning Percentages: **1984** (69%) **1983 *** (50%)

* *Special election.*

District Vote For President

	1988	1984	1980	1976
D	87,703 (60%)	89,940 (52%)	75,859 (49%)	110,300 (63%)
R	57,244 (39%)	81,401 (47%)	68,309 (44%)	65,412 (37%)
I			9,734 (6%)	

Campaign Finance

	Receipts	Receipts from PACs	Expend-itures
1988			
Ackerman (D)	$280,467	$196,120 (70%)	$142,041
1986			
Ackerman (D)	$181,226	$87,417 (48%)	$116,950
Rodriguez (R)	$15,586	0	$8,456

Key Votes

1987	
Raise speed limit to 65 mph	N
Approve Gephardt "fair trade" amendment	Y
Ban testing of larger nuclear weapons	Y
Delay "re-flagging" of Kuwaiti tankers	Y
Approve tax-raising deficit-reduction bill	Y
1988	
Approve aid to Nicaraguan contras	N
Enact civil rights restoration bill over Reagan veto	Y
Kill 60-day plant-closing notification measure	N
Pass omnibus trade bill over Reagan veto	Y
Approve death penalty for drug-related murders	N
Bar federal funds for abortions in cases of rape and incest	N
Oppose seven-day waiting period for purchase of handguns	N

Voting Studies

	Presidential Support		Party Unity		Conservative Coalition	
Year	**S**	**O**	**S**	**O**	**S**	**O**
1988	15	74	93	0	3	87
1987	19	74	93	2	7	86
1986	12	79	91	0	4	82
1985	20	74	87	3	4	95
1984	22	66	85	5	5	86
1983	20†	79†	91†	4†	12†	87†

† Not eligible for all recorded votes.

Interest Group Ratings

Year	ADA	ACU	AFL-CIO	CCUS
1988	95	0	100	23
1987	96	0	100	14
1986	85	0	100	13
1985	100	10	100	20
1984	95	9	92	36
1983	85	0	100	22

8 James H. Scheuer (D)

Of Queens — Elected 1964

Did not serve 1973-75.

Born: Feb. 6, 1920, New York, N.Y.
Education: Swarthmore College, A.B. 1942; Harvard Business School, M.A. 1943; Columbia U. Law School, LL.B. 1948.
Military Career: Army, 1943-45.
Occupation: Lawyer.
Family: Wife, Emily Malino; four children.
Religion: Jewish.
Political Career: Sought Democratic nomination for mayor of N.Y.C., 1969; defeated for renomination to U.S. House, 1972; returned to House, 1974.
Capitol Office: 2466 Rayburn Bldg. 20515; 225-5471.

In Washington: In the House, Scheuer is scarred forever by his defeat in battle with John D. Dingell, the autocratic chairman of the Energy and Commerce Committee. At the start of the 97th Congress in 1981, the business-oriented Dingell fended off Scheuer, an irascible liberal, for the committee chair. He proceeded to strip his rival of power: Though second in seniority on Energy and Commerce, Scheuer holds no subcommittee chairmanship.

Scheuer — who electorally has endured some extreme permutations of redistricting — has shown a good deal of resilience. On consumer and environmental issues, the ornery survivor remains a crusader, often acting as a front man for California Democrat Henry A. Waxman, the committee's leading liberal, who prefers to play the inside game. Scheuer has also found a niche in the chairmanship of the lower-profile Science Subcommittee on Natural Resources, Agriculture Research, and Environment.

Scheuer's most notable characteristic, though, remains the gruff and belligerent manner that hindered him in his fights with Dingell. No one ever accused Dingell of disarming opponents with charm, but he expertly charted the deal-cutting route to institutional power. Scheuer, on the other hand, was the angry activist, firing off bromides against injustices done to consumers and the environment. While Scheuer was making caustic statements, Dingell was making political allies.

The chairmanship battle grew out of an animosity that developed between the two men over several years. Dingell's main legislative role on Energy and Commerce had been to protect the automakers based in or near his Detroit-area district; Scheuer was a leading proponent of requiring air bags, a safety device, in cars, an idea Dingell vehemently opposed. Dingell also was irked by Scheuer's persistent calls for stringent anti-pollution standards under the Clean Air Act, and his defense — while serving in the 1970s as chairman of the Energy and Commerce Subcommittee on Consumer Protection — of the Federal Trade Commission, which had become an irritant to many members by seeking to regulate business activity.

For years, the two rarely spoke to each other. And after Dingell defeated Scheuer to take over the full committee in 1981, he "decided" Energy and Commerce had too many subcommittees. There was little doubt which one had to go: Scheuer's cherished Consumer Protection panel.

The deed was done over the furious objections of Scheuer, who said he was being punished for his air-bag crusade. But the 14-7 vote stripping him of his subcommittee also reflected his standing among colleagues. The abrasive Scheuer had not impressed many with his abilities as chairman, and had not made up for that in personal terms.

In the years since, Scheuer has continued in his role as an outspoken activist. But his limited legislative clout is illustrated by the history of the legislation to ban smoking on passenger-airline flights. For years, Scheuer had submitted anti-smoking proposals that went nowhere. But in the 100th Congress, Illinois Democrat Richard J. Durbin, a fast-rising junior member of Appropriations, took up the cause, built a constituency for it, and pushed to passage a smoking ban on flights of two hours or less.

Scheuer has had some success in using his knowledge of House procedures to put obstacles in Dingell's legislative path. In 1987, Dingell was pushing a product-liability bill; it was favored by business interests, who preferred a single federal standard in place of the patchwork of state liability laws, but opposed by consumer advocates, who said injured parties would have a harder time recovering damages. When Dingell tried to force committee markup on the bill that November, Scheuer invoked a

New York 8

Northern Queens; Eastern Bronx; Western Nassau County

The 8th is one of those masterworks of redistricting craftsmanship. It starts in the east Bronx, leaps across the broad East River into Queens, then out of New York City into the Nassau County suburbs.

Northeast Queens, a middle- to upper-middle-class residential area, makes up the heart of the district. Large homes front Little Neck Bay and Long Island Sound.

However, Flushing has more closely packed housing and a more urban feel. This old section of Queens was a Dutch settlement as early as 1645, and its downtown area is a historic district. Flushing was the site of world's fairs in 1939 and 1964 and today contains both Shea Stadium and La Guardia Airport.

In all, the Queens portion of the district has about two-thirds of the population. Roughly 8 percent of the district's residents live across the city line in Nassau County; the Bronx contributes the remainder, a little more than 20 percent.

The Nassau portion of the 8th takes in more than 10,000 constituents in suburban Great Neck, an affluent, largely Jewish community. Jutting into Long Island Sound, Great Neck is the site of the U.S. Merchant Marine Academy at Kings Point.

On the other side of Flushing Bay, in the Bronx, the 8th reaches north from the East River almost up to the Bronx Zoo. Jews, many of them elderly, dominate the quiet neighborhoods of Parkchester, Van Ness and Pelham Parkway. Scheuer represented some of this territory in his original constituency in the 1960s.

South of the Cross Bronx Expressway, the 8th has its main concentration of blacks and Hispanics in Soundview. Their votes help affirm the district's Democratic nature, but their political ties tend to be with the western end of the Bronx, outside the district.

The 8th is strongly, though not monolithically, Democratic. Walter F. Mondale won it narrowly in 1984, but Michael S. Dukakis improved on that showing four years later.

Population: 516,165. White 407,294 (79%), Black 51,618 (10%), Asian and Pacific Islander 25,547 (5%). Spanish origin 71,542 (14%). 18 and over 402,776 (78%), 65 and over 81,916 (16%). Median age: 36.

rule barring committee action while the full House was considering certain business. Though Dingell eventually forged ahead, the bill ultimately stalled in committee.

Earlier, Scheuer lost a legislative battle with Dingell and other pro-auto industry members, but was vindicated by the Supreme Court. In 1982, Congress exercised its "legislative veto" power for the first time, overturning a proposed rule requiring car dealers to disclose defects in used cars that they sold. Scheuer strongly opposed the veto action, calling it "violently and flagrantly anti-consumer, and in my opinion, grossly against the wishes of the American people." In 1983, the Supreme Court issued a sweeping decision that declared most uses of the legislative veto unconstitutional.

The blow of his 1981 chairmanship defeat was cushioned somewhat by the fact that his Science Subcommittee has jurisdiction over the Environmental Protection Agency (EPA). Scheuer went to war with the Reagan administration over what he viewed as its efforts to eviscerate the EPA's regulatory functions, and rushed to the forefront of the investigation into misconduct at that agency in 1982.

It was Scheuer who charged that former EPA official Rita M. Lavelle might have perjured herself in denying that she sought the dismissal of an employee who criticized management of hazardous-waste programs. That charge was one of several that led to Lavelle's dismissal in early 1983; she was later convicted and sentenced to time in federal prison. Scheuer also charged that EPA kept a "hit list" on which staff scientists and scientific advisers were rated for political acceptability during the Reagan transition.

In the 100th Congress, Scheuer promoted his proposal to create an executive branch advisory board on issues affecting biotechnology, the field in which scientists perform genetics research into improved strains of agricultural plants and animals, and cures for diseases such as cancer and AIDS. Scheuer's bill was approved by the Science Committee in August 1988, despite the Reagan administration's opinion that it would create an unnecessary layer of bureaucracy. But the bill was blocked in Energy and Commerce by Dingell.

When Scheuer first came to Congress in 1965, he was a strong advocate of President Lyndon B. Johnson's "War on Poverty," and he remains supportive of those programs that have survived the years. He describes Head Start, the preschool program for children of low-income families, as "the jewel in the crown of the poverty program ... and it has had an unblemished record of success."

At Home: Scheuer has had one of the most

peripatetic political careers of any House member in recent years. He has challenged three incumbent members of his own party for renomination and beaten two of them. He has run in five different districts and won in four.

The son of a wealthy real-estate man, Scheuer had a highly successful career himself in home building and construction, specializing in urban renewal. He entered politics in 1964 as part of the reform wave that swept over the Bronx that year, winning a seat in Congress by defeating Rep. James Healey, a Democrat allied with the traditional party organization.

He mounted a disastrous campaign for mayor of New York City in 1969, finishing last in a field of five candidates despite an expenditure of $550,000.

In 1970, when a new Hispanic district was created in the South Bronx, much of it from Scheuer's territory, he moved into a neighboring district and defeated Rep. Jacob Gilbert, another Democratic organization loyalist, for renomination. Two years later, the Bronx lost a district and Scheuer was thrown in with Democratic Rep. Jonathan B. Bingham. This time he was not successful, and he had to retire from the House.

But Scheuer did not give up on a congressional career. Political developments in Brooklyn opened another opportunity for him. Democratic Rep. Frank J. Brasco of the 11th District got into legal trouble and retired in 1974. Scheuer decided to run in that district and won the primary over the candidate backed by the Brooklyn organization. After that, his electoral career quieted down for the balance of the decade. The organization did not challenge him, and he did not bother the organization.

This peaceful arrangement served Scheuer well in 1982, when the Legislature merged his district with that of Queens Democrat Joseph P. Addabbo. Scheuer moved one more time, to the new 8th, and Queens Borough President Donald Manes, who was also the county Democratic chairman, persuaded local party figures not to run against him. He has not had any trouble since then. In 1988, Scheuer drew no Republican opposition.

Committees

Energy and Commerce (2nd of 26 Democrats)
Commerce, Consumer Protection and Competitiveness; Health and the Environment

Science, Space and Technology (3rd of 30 Democrats)
Natural Resources, Agriculture Research and Environment (chairman); International Scientific Cooperation; Space Science and Applications

Select Narcotics Abuse and Control (4th of 18 Democrats)

Joint Economic
Education and Health (chairman); Investment, Jobs and Prices

Elections

1988 General		
James H. Scheuer (D)	100,240	(100%)
1986 General		
James H. Scheuer (D)	70,605	(90%)
Gustave Reifenkugel (R)	7,679	(10%)

Previous Winning Percentages: **1984** (63%) **1982** (90%) **1980** (74%) **1978** (79%) **1976** (74%) **1974** (72%) **1970** (72%) **1968** (83%) **1966** (84%) **1964** (84%)

District Vote For President

	1988	1984	1980	1976
D	100,779 (58%)	99,844 (52%)	71,229 (45%)	105,219 (59%)
R	69,751 (41%)	91,933 (48%)	73,444 (47%)	72,954 (41%)
I			10,091 (6%)	

Campaign Finance

	Receipts	Receipts from PACs	Expend-itures
1988			
Scheuer (D)	$77,854	$55,600 (71%)	$98,919
1986			
Scheuer (D)	$81,374	$45,300 (56%)	$65,543

Key Votes

1987	
Raise speed limit to 65 mph	N
Approve Gephardt "fair trade" amendment	Y
Ban testing of larger nuclear weapons	Y
Delay "re-flagging" of Kuwaiti tankers	Y
Approve tax-raising deficit-reduction bill	Y
1988	
Approve aid to Nicaraguan contras	N
Enact civil rights restoration bill over Reagan veto	Y
Kill 60-day plant-closing notification measure	N
Pass omnibus trade bill over Reagan veto	Y
Approve death penalty for drug-related murders	N
Bar federal funds for abortions in cases of rape and incest	N
Oppose seven-day waiting period for purchase of handguns	?

Voting Studies

	Presidential Support		Party Unity		Conservative Coalition	
Year	S	O	S	O	S	O
1988	21	70	82	8	13	74
1987	15	78	81	4	14	77
1986	18	79	88	5	8	92
1985	19	73	90	3	7	91
1984	32	64	84	8	15	80
1983	21	77	92	5	10	90
1982	35	60	91	6	14	82
1981	32	61	92	5	13	83

Interest Group Ratings

Year	ADA	ACU	AFL-CIO	CCUS
1988	85	5	86	46
1987	84	5	79	9
1986	95	0	100	18
1985	90	0	100	23
1984	90	4	67	21
1983	85	0	100	20
1982	95	0	95	14
1981	90	0	93	11

9 Thomas J. Manton (D)

Of Queens — Elected 1984

Born: Nov. 3, 1932, New York, N.Y.
Education: St. John's U., B.B.A. 1958, LL.B. 1962.
Military Career: Marine Corps, 1951-53.
Occupation: Lawyer.
Family: Wife, Diane Mason Schley; four children.
Religion: Roman Catholic.
Political Career: New York City Council, 1970-84; sought Democratic nomination for U.S. House, 1972, 1978.
Capitol Office: 331 Cannon Bldg. 20515; 225-3965.

In Washington: Manton brought from Queens to Congress a keen understanding of political machinations. As chairman of the Democratic organization in Queens, he has been deeply involved in the complex politics of his home turf; in Washington, he has worked to find the centers of power and gravitated toward them.

Although much of Manton's political career has concentrated on housing issues, an obvious concern in New York, in the 101st Congress he gave up his seat on the committee with primary jurisdiction in that area, Banking. He won a place on Energy and Commerce, a committee of considerable reputation and legislative reach.

Manton had tried for Energy and Commerce in the 100th Congress, but failed to win the backing of the New York delegation. He laid careful groundwork for his second try, playing an active role in 1987 and 1988 on the Democratic Congressional Campaign Committee, raising money and generating support for party candidates. He was also careful to court committee Chairman John D. Dingell, who has worked hard to add members to his panel who will not undermine his efforts to block tough clean-air legislation that he sees as hostile to industry. Manton was among those in the House who refused to sign a letter to Dingell in the 100th Congress urging him to release clean-air legislation, which has been caught in a committee crossfire for years.

Manton headed to the Banking Subcommittee on Housing when he first got to Congress, but soon learned he could not make things happen there as he had when he led the Housing Committee on the New York City Council. In those days, when Manton decided there should be smoke detectors in over a million New York apartments, he sponsored a bill to require them, and it became law. When he thought landlords deserved a rent increase, they got one. But in Washington, the Banking panel has difficulty getting housing bills enacted, and when action is taken, the group rarely stops to listen to newcomers.

At Home: Whatever Geraldine A. Ferraro's 1984 vice presidential campaign accomplished for the national Democratic Party or the cause of women in politics, it was a boon to Manton, who suddenly found himself with a clear shot at the House seat he had twice sought without success.

In 1972, as a junior member of the New York City Council, Manton unsuccessfully challenged longtime Democratic Rep. James J. Delaney in the primary. He tried again when Delaney retired in 1978, but Ferraro defeated him decisively and quickly entrenched herself.

But when Walter F. Mondale tapped Ferraro as his running mate, Manton quickly became a front-running contender to replace her. Having served 14 years on the council, he had the edge in name recognition in the 1984 campaign. But he still had to overcome strong opposition from a state assemblyman, a prominent lawyer and a Queens election official whose campaign manager was one of Ferraro's cousins. Stressing his Irish-Catholic working-class roots, Manton eked out a narrow primary win.

In November, Manton faced Serphin R. Maltese, then-executive director of New York's Conservative Party. Maltese carried the burden of an almost 3-to-1 Democratic registration edge, plus labor union anger at his role in helping hire replacement teachers during a strike at a parochial school. His support for the gradual elimination of rent control did not endear him to area tenants. Still, Maltese surprised many by holding Manton to 53 percent.

Manton strengthened his grip on the 9th in 1986, racking up 69 percent against Queens attorney Salvatore Calise. He ran without Republican opposition in 1988.

The ease of Manton's re-election campaigns enabled him to devote time to his position as Queens Democratic chairman. Manton won the post in October 1986, after pledging to revive and improve the image of the scandal-plagued Democratic organization. He succeeded an interim replacement to Donald Manes, the Queens borough president and longtime party chairman who committed suicide in April 1986 following his implication in a city corruption scandal.

New York 9

Western Queens — Astoria; Jackson Heights

Queens' melting-pot 9th encompasses old factories, drug-ridden slums, world-class tennis courts and the home of Archie Bunker, of TV's "All in the Family" fame. Bunker's opinions on race, drugs and modern morality are often expressed in the row houses of Astoria and Ridgewood. The neighborhood shown in the program was on Astoria's Steinway Street.

Though the 9th votes consistently Democratic for the House, it has shown GOP tendencies in presidential elections. It gave Ronald Reagan a majority in 1984 even with Ferraro as the Democratic vice presidential nominee. In 1988, a boost from the large community of his fellow Greek-Americans in Astoria helped Michael S. Dukakis carry the 9th, but George Bush still got 48 percent districtwide. Many of the Greeks moved in during the 1960s, when their country was under military rule. Some of the city's best gyros can be bought on Ditmars Boulevard.

Aging industrial loft buildings are clustered in Long Island City and Sunnyside. Former occupants, mostly light manufacturers, have moved to suburban facilities. But Long Island City has taken on a new identity as yuppies restore its old living quarters, and Citicorp recently built Queens' biggest office skyscraper. These events are applauded by city economic development officials, but not always by the area's blue-collar bedrock.

Generally liberal Democratic politics prevail in Forest Hills, where affluent Jews and WASPs live in elegant Tudor-style homes. In the early 1970s Forest Hills displayed its own streak of conservatism, objecting to the construction of public housing within its borders.

Until the 1970s, Jackson Heights was mostly white and middle class. Then low-income minorities moved in, many from South America, and some neighborhoods deteriorated. Among the white residents, Jews and Italians predominate, many of them elderly. There is a large Irish-American population, including numerous illegal aliens who left their homeland in recent years in search of greater economic opportunity.

Population: 516,143. White 433,944 (84%), Black 18,962 (4%), Asian and Pacific Islander 28,615 (6%). Spanish origin 85,780 (17%). 18 and over 407,420 (79%), 65 and over 87,148 (17%). Median age: 37.

Committees

Energy and Commerce (26th of 26 Democrats)
Telecommunications and Finance; Transportation and Hazardous Materials

Merchant Marine and Fisheries (17th of 26 Democrats)
Coast Guard and Navigation; Fisheries and Wildlife Conservation and the Environment; Oceanography

Select Aging (27th of 39 Democrats)
Housing and Consumer Interests; Retirement, Income and Employment

Elections

1988 General		
Thomas J. Manton (D)	72,851	(100%)
1986 General		
Thomas J. Manton (D)	50,738	(69%)
Salvatore J. Calise (R)	18,040	(25%)
Thomas V. Ognibene (C)	4,348	(6%)

Previous Winning Percentage: 1984 (53%)

District Vote For President

	1988		1984		1980		1976	
D	70,764	(51%)	64,860	(42%)	57,779	(40%)	82,228	(51%)
R	66,203	(48%)	87,573	(57%)	76,761	(53%)	79,869	(49%)
I					7,849	(5%)		

Campaign Finance

	Receipts	Receipts from PACs	Expend-itures
1988			
Manton (D)	$424,381	$263,545 (62%)	$256,832
1986			
Manton (D)	$415,865	$246,776 (59%)	$416,151

Key Votes

1987	
Raise speed limit to 65 mph	N
Approve Gephardt "fair trade" amendment	Y
Ban testing of larger nuclear weapons	Y
Delay "re-flagging" of Kuwaiti tankers	Y
Approve tax-raising deficit-reduction bill	Y
1988	
Approve aid to Nicaraguan contras	N
Enact civil rights restoration bill over Reagan veto	Y
Kill 60-day plant-closing notification measure	N
Pass omnibus trade bill over Reagan veto	Y
Approve death penalty for drug-related murders	Y
Bar federal funds for abortions in cases of rape and incest	Y
Oppose seven-day waiting period for purchase of handguns	N

Voting Studies

	Presidential Support		Party Unity		Conservative Coalition	
Year	S	O	S	O	S	O
1988	24	67	89	6	32	63
1987	19	78	92	2	23	77
1986	18	77	88	3	30	60
1985	23	71	88	5	24	69

Interest Group Ratings

Year	ADA	ACU	AFL-CIO	CCUS
1988	60	18	100	23
1987	80	4	100	7
1986	75	9	100	29
1985	70	10	81	27

10 Charles E. Schumer (D)

Of Brooklyn — Elected 1980

Born: Nov. 23, 1950, Brooklyn, N.Y.
Education: Harvard U., B.A. 1971, J.D. 1974.
Occupation: Lawyer.
Family: Wife, Iris Weinshall; two children.
Religion: Jewish.
Political Career: N.Y. Assembly, 1975-81.
Capitol Office: 126 Cannon Bldg. 20515; 225-6616.

In Washington: It is often said that there are no limits to what a politician can accomplish if he doesn't worry about who gets the credit. Schumer's career offers a pointed exception. He does not mind doing the work, but he does want the credit. And this method has in no way limited his accomplishments.

Indeed, he has done more before the age of 40 than many legislators manage in a career. A keen mind and an abundance of energy have enabled him, in just five terms, to put his imprint on housing, trade, immigration, farm and banking policy.

Most New York City liberals tend to be suspect in Democratic leadership circles, but Schumer has made his way in the House as a leadership insider. He has benefited from sharing a house on Capitol Hill with Democrats Marty Russo of Illinois and George Miller and Leon E. Panetta of California, well-placed, more experienced members who have helped channel Schumer and smooth his abrasiveness.

When he needs to build support for a key legislative proposal, he can also call on allies in the Wall Street business community or on the editorial board of *The New York Times.* He makes skillful use of the media, publishing countless opinion pieces in national newspapers and appearing so often on TV news talk shows that it is sometimes hard to tell whether he is a guest or a host.

Schumer thrives not just in the public eye, but in the back-room meetings that are the incubators of legislative accomplishment. He is shrewd and tough, sees the big picture but tends to detail, and can make necessary compromises.

The nicknames he has earned on two continents are instructive of the Schumer style. He is known as "Hurricane Schumer" in some Japanese business circles; his amendment in the 1988 trade bill seeks to force open Japanese securities markets to U.S. companies. On the Banking Committee, admirers of his ability to move on an array of issues simultaneously call him "monsoon."

Schumer was in his element in early 1989 as Congress struggled with legislation to bail out the troubled savings and loan industry. He managed at once to be the Bush administration's biggest helper and hindrance.

He assisted the administration by using his Judiciary and Banking posts to help lead the fight to force a higher standard of financial underpinning on S&Ls. But he also used his assignment as head of the Budget Committee Task Force on Urgent Fiscal Needs to make a case for adding the cost of the bailout directly to the budget, in opposition to the administration.

As the S&L battle went down to the wire, Schumer looked to match his performance in the 99th Congress when, more than anyone in the House, he did the work that led to passage of landmark new U.S. immigration laws.

The legislation was at least five years in the making, and Schumer did not become a major player until the 98th Congress. By then, much of the groundwork had been laid. But Schumer stepped in to play a critical role in resolving a farm labor controversy that was the last major obstacle to enactment in 1986.

After seemingly interminable negotiations with two California Democrats — Panetta, who represented the interests of Western growers, and Howard L. Berman, a close ally of organized labor — Schumer brokered a compromise that would give growers the supply of foreign labor they were demanding to help pick perishable crops. That concession to Panetta's side was linked to a new program Berman wanted to protect foreign workers against exploitation.

Schumer stuck with the issue even after a Republican-led revolt blocked the immigration bill from coming to the floor in late 1986 — largely because Democratic leaders insisted on barring amendments to the delicately crafted farm worker provisions. Although some lawmakers then left the immigration bill for dead, Schumer helped revive it with negotiations that put the bill back on the road to enactment.

Coming from an urban district where con-

New York 10

Central and Southern Brooklyn — Flatbush

The 10th is a loose descendant of the heavily Jewish Flatbush-based district that sent Democrat Emanuel Celler to Congress for 50 years before his primary loss to Elizabeth Holtzman in 1972. The old district changed dramatically in the 1970s, with Jews moving out and blacks coming to constitute a majority.

But the 1982 remap essentially restored the district's earlier ethnic complexion. Map makers shifted black areas in the district's northern half to the two Brooklyn districts designed for black representation.

More than 80 percent of the people in the 10th are white. Jews predominate, although Italians are a significant presence.

The 10th retains its Democratic cast, though the party's victory margins have fluctuated considerably in recent presidential elections. After winning 68 percent of the district's vote in 1976, Jimmy Carter slipped to just 50 percent four years later. Walter F. Mondale barely kept the district Democratic in 1984, but Michael S. Dukakis won the 10th with a more comfortable 57 percent in 1988.

The chief tensions here are between the "reform" and "regular" wings of the Democratic Party. Holtzman's win over Celler in 1972 was a victory for the reform faction. Schumer is considered a reformer, but he has maintained friendly relations with some regulars in the Brooklyn Democratic Party organization.

Flatbush is an amalgam of run-down apartment buildings and single-family homes, such as the one on Marlboro Road where portions of the motion picture "Sophie's Choice" were filmed. The yeshivas and bagel bakeries along Ocean Parkway testify to the area's ethnic character.

Blue-collar Canarsie and Sheepshead Bay contain a mixture of Italians and Jews. Many residents work in small factories, turning out plastics and electrical parts. A different breed of Democrat inhabits Park Slope, where the town houses are elegant and the politics liberal. Park Slope has become increasingly attractive for young professionals with jobs in Manhattan.

Population: 516,471. White 455,541 (88%), Black 26,732 (5%), Other 14,145 (3%). Spanish origin 45,481 (9%). 18 and over 401,703 (78%), 65 and over 86,395 (17%). Median age: 36.

stituents' only contact with perishable crops is at the market, Schumer was an unlikely character to be playing the central role in farm labor negotiations. But it was because of this freedom from special interests that he could be a broker between growers and labor.

The rewards of Schumer's friendships in high places have been tangible. When it came time to fill seven open slots on the Budget Committee for the 99th Congress, Schumer was the personal favorite of those making the assignments. They chose him, then settled down to haggling over the rest of the selections.

From his seat on Budget, Schumer has been able to defend programs that help urban areas — New York City in particular. He also is part of an aggressive faction of liberals, including housemates Russo and Miller, that has become a force to be reckoned with. Of particular concern to Schumer has been to make sure that farm programs suffer the same spending cuts as the social programs that benefit cities.

Much of Schumer's time on the Banking Committee has been spent on housing issues. In the 99th Congress, at a time when few social initiatives were being ventured, Schumer helped win House approval of a new program to help moderate-income families buy their first homes. The so-called "Nehemiah program," named for the Biblical prophet who rebuilt the walls of Jerusalem, passed both chambers in 1987.

In 1983, Schumer managed with Sen. Christopher J. Dodd of Connecticut to gain passage of a proposal to help the low- and middle-income renters who provide the bulk of the demand for housing in New York. Schumer's plan was to replace ordinary rent subsidies with a new approach under which cities would get grants to help developers build or renovate units in areas of housing shortages. The program was enacted as part of a housing authorization despite Reagan administration objections, after Schumer convinced then-Banking Chairman Fernand J. St Germain to fuse it to a measure the administration wanted badly — an increase in the U.S. contribution to the International Monetary Fund.

Schumer also took the lead in the 99th and 100th Congress on legislation providing new consumer protection for credit card users. He became so closely associated with the credit card issue, one trade paper said, that mail addressed to "Credit Cards, Washington, D.C." was delivered to his office.

Schumer originally pushed a bill to impose a cap on credit card interest rates, but it did not get out of subcommittee in the 99th Congress.

In the 100th Congress, though, Schumer managed to get his fallback position through; he won passage of a measure that forces banks to disclose more fully the terms under which a credit card is used.

Another issue on which Schumer will continue to play a role is bank deregulation. Arguing on the side of the New York securities industry — and against the major banks — Schumer has opposed the entry of banks into such fields as securities and insurance.

Schumer does try to speak up for New York banking interests when he can. He has pushed for a form of nationwide branch banking — a development the major Wall Street banking institutions want. With congressmen from other regions trying to keep the powerful New York banks out by allowing interstate banking only within regions, Schumer has declared his opposition to any such measures unless they are a prelude to nationwide banking.

At Home: When Democratic Rep. Elizabeth Holtzman announced her 1980 bid for the Senate, she endorsed Schumer as her successor. Schumer was a liberal along Holtzman's lines. A three-term member of the state Assembly, he previously had served as an Assembly aide to Democrat Stephen J. Solarz, now his colleague in the Brooklyn delegation.

To win his House seat, Schumer had to beat two more conservative candidates in the Democratic primary. Theodore Silverman attracted Orthodox Jewish support with his stand in favor of the death penalty; Susan Alter criticized Schumer for not fighting hard enough against pornography. But Schumer had the best organization, and he won centrist support and an endorsement from Mayor Edward I. Koch. He took almost 60 percent of the vote, and sailed through the general election.

Early in 1982, it seemed redistricting might force Schumer into a primary against Solarz. Schumer raised over $400,000, but map makers gave him a safe district. He has never won less than 72 percent in a general election.

His strength at home and rising prominence in Washington have led some to speculate on Schumer's potential as a statewide candidate. But with Gov. Mario M. Cuomo and Sens. Daniel Patrick Moynihan and Alfonse M. D'Amato still popular, Schumer's options have been limited.

Should Schumer entertain an opportunity to run for higher office at a future date, he may find himself handicapped by the lack of coverage that local television stations give to individual House members in the crowded New York City media market. Comparing New York members with those from broader geographical areas who dominate their media markets, Schumer says, "Local television is a far less important part of our lives."

Schumer adds that New York-area members are lucky to get on local TV twice a year. But unlike most of his metropolitan colleagues, Schumer has made up some of the media deficit by availing himself of frequent opportunities to appear on national television.

Committees

Banking, Finance and Urban Affairs (11th of 31 Democrats)
Consumer Affairs and Coinage; Financial Institutions Supervision, Regulation and Insurance; Housing and Community Development; International Development, Finance, Trade and Monetary Policy

Budget (6th of 21 Democrats)
Task Forces: Urgent Fiscal Issues (chairman); Budget Process, Reconciliation and Enforcement

Judiciary (12th of 21 Democrats)
Criminal Justice (chairman); Immigration, Refugees and International Law

Elections

1988 General

Charles E. Schumer (D)	107,056	(78%)
George S. Popielarski (R)	24,313	(18%)

1986 General

Charles E. Schumer (D)	76,318	(93%)
Alice Gaffney (C)	5,472	(7%)

Previous Winning Percentages: **1984** (72%) **1982** (79%) **1980** (78%)

District Vote For President

	1988	1984	1980	1976
D	88,439 (57%)	90,540 (51%)	64,034 (50%)	105,965 (68%)
R	65,354 (42%)	85,358 (48%)	56,294 (44%)	49,084 (32%)
I			6,588 (5%)	

Campaign Finance

	Receipts	Receipts from PACs	Expend-itures
1988			
Schumer (D)	$437,574	$137,325 (31%)	$87,129
1986			
Schumer (D)	$163,140	$52,025 (32%)	$95,951

Key Votes

1987

Raise speed limit to 65 mph	N
Approve Gephardt "fair trade" amendment	N
Ban testing of larger nuclear weapons	Y
Delay "re-flagging" of Kuwaiti tankers	Y
Approve tax-raising deficit-reduction bill	Y

1988

Approve aid to Nicaraguan contras	N
Enact civil rights restoration bill over Reagan veto	Y
Kill 60-day plant-closing notification measure	N
Pass omnibus trade bill over Reagan veto	Y
Approve death penalty for drug-related murders	N
Bar federal funds for abortions in cases of rape and incest	N
Oppose seven-day waiting period for purchase of handguns	N

Voting Studies

	Presidential Support		Party Unity		Conservative Coalition	
Year	**S**	**O**	**S**	**O**	**S**	**O**
1988	20	77	90	5	5	92
1987	18	76	88	4	9	86
1986	17	78	88	5	14	82
1985	28	64	84	7	7	84
1984	29	68	87	6	3	93
1983	23	73	89	5	13	84
1982	29	64	91	4	7	92
1981	30	67	83	11	12	83

Interest Group Ratings

Year	ADA	ACU	AFL-CIO	CCUS
1988	100	4	86	36
1987	88	9	81	21
1986	85	5	86	29
1985	90	14	93	32
1984	90	4	83	33
1983	85	0	100	25
1982	95	0	100	16
1981	100	0	93	6

11 Ed Towns (D)

Of Brooklyn — Elected 1982

Born: July 21, 1934, Chadbourn, N.C.
Education: North Carolina A&T U., B.S. 1956; Adelphi U., M.S.W. 1973.
Military Career: Army, 1956-58.
Occupation: Social worker; teacher.
Family: Wife, Gwen Forbes; two children.
Religion: Protestant.
Political Career: Deputy Brooklyn borough president, 1977-82 (appointed).
Capitol Office: 1726 Longworth Bldg. 20515; 225-5936.

In Washington: Towns has progressed in politics more because of whom he has aligned himself with than because of what he has done. His ties to New York's regular organization Democrats gave him a solid base to build on in Brooklyn; in Washington, Towns sticks close to his party leaders nearly all the time. In six years in the House, Towns has differed with the majority Democratic position on less than 3 percent of the votes.

Towns' unobtrusive party loyalty is matched by a low-profile legislative agenda. One item on Towns' agenda has drawn more attention than the others: his cosponsorship of the Student-Athlete Right-to-Know Act. During the NCAA basketball tournament in early 1989, Towns joined for the second consecutive Congress with Rep. Tom McMillen and Sen. Bill Bradley, both former pro basketball stars, to offer legislation requiring colleges to provide information about the graduation rates of their scholarship athletes.

As athletics has become a big business for many colleges, sports reporters have focused attention on schools that seem more concerned about drawing paying customers to games than about making sure athletes meet graduation requirements. "Students and their families are entitled to information about the quality of education that an institution provides," said Towns. "The bill supports the efforts of those campuses that are doing a good job of graduating their athletes and it will force those who are not to do a better job. . . ."

On other matters, Towns is a relatively passive member of the Public Works and Government Operations committees. His statements on the House floor have ranged from recognizing the anniversary of Taiwan to supporting the efforts of Jamaican labor leaders to promote their ethanol industry.

At Home: Towns is as liberal as his predecessor in this district, but the similarities end there. A black social worker, Towns succeeded a white millionaire, Democrat Frederick W. Richmond, who resigned from the House in 1982 and later was convicted of income-tax evasion and marijuana possession.

Richmond's political demise was Towns' first piece of luck. The second was redistricting. Although New York's Legislature wanted to make the 11th a largely Hispanic district, black Democrats in Brooklyn objected to the plan, and the Justice Department ultimately threw it out. The final version, creating a constituency almost evenly split between blacks and Hispanics, was much more congenial to Towns.

In the turbulent world of Brooklyn politics, Towns benefited from a lack of enemies. He had the support not only of his own party, then headed by Meade H. Esposito, but of the "reform" faction led by black power broker and then-state Assemblyman Al Vann, plus many of the borough's Hispanic officeholders.

In the end, no established politician challenged Towns for the nomination. John Jack Olivero, a former telephone company executive, and Louis Hernandez, an insurance broker, emerged as his only competitors. Olivero called Towns "the machine candidate"; Hernandez criticized him for concentrating too much on the black community.

As it turned out, Olivero and Hernandez split the Hispanic vote, helping Towns capture the nomination with just under 50 percent in the primary. In the heavily Democratic 11th, Towns' November victory was all but assured.

Towns had to work to win renomination in 1984. Rafael Esparra, a former adviser to New York City Mayor Edward I. Koch, was his lone opponent, and Esparra pushed to unify the Hispanic vote. Armed with Koch's endorsement, Esparra argued that Towns had focused on black issues at Hispanics' expense. But if Hispanics had complaints with Towns, they did not turn to Esparra; Towns won with 65 percent. He has had no difficulty since.

New York 11

Northern Brooklyn — Bedford-Stuyvesant

The desires of both Hispanics and blacks for greater representation came into conflict in New York City in the early 1980s. To satisfy the city's large Hispanic community, which wanted a second House seat to go with the 18th, state legislators created an 11th District that stretched from Brooklyn to the Lower East Side and East Harlem in Manhattan. But Brooklyn blacks said the remap diluted their voting strength, and the Justice Department agreed. State mapmakers removed the Manhattan portion, yielding an 11th nearly half black, almost 40 percent Hispanic and overwhelmingly Democratic.

Bedford-Stuyvesant is the district's oldest black community. Once a fashionable white area, large parts of "Bed-Stuy" now resemble the devastated South Bronx. But some efforts have been made to rejuvenate the area. In the late 1960s Sen. Robert F. Kennedy helped establish a shopping mall and office complex, and International Business Machines opened a typewriter assembly plant. Still, the 11th has little industry of major importance.

East New York has not enjoyed even modest revitalization. Until the 1960s, this was an Italian and Jewish neighborhood. But as low-income blacks and Hispanics have moved there from Bedford-Stuyvesant seeking better housing, whites have fled. A small section of overwhelmingly black Brownsville, long one of the most blighted areas anywhere in the nation, also is in the 11th.

Roughly 40 percent of the 11th was culled from the old 14th, which was a north Brooklyn mix of minorities and upper-middle-class white professionals. But the 11th does not include the latter group; the white population, about 30 percent of the district's total, is largely Italian and working-class, settled in old neighborhoods just outside Williamsburg and Greenpoint.

Population: 516,554. White 151,797 (29%), Black 244,060 (47%), Other 6,763 (1%). Spanish origin 196,603 (38%). 18 and over 331,181 (64%), 65 and over 38,165 (7%). Median age: 26.

Committees

Government Operations (14th of 24 Democrats)
Environment, Energy and Natural Resources; Government Information, Justice and Agriculture

Public Works and Transportation (14th of 31 Democrats)
Aviation; Economic Development; Surface Transportation

Select Narcotics Abuse and Control (14th of 18 Democrats)

Elections

1988 General		
Ed Towns (D)	73,755	(89%)
Riaz B. Hussain (R)	7,418	(9%)
1988 Primary		
Ed Towns (D)	14,570	(76%)
Riaz B. Hussain (D)	4,575	(24%)
1986 General		
Ed Towns (D)	41,689	(89%)
Nathaniel Hendricks (R)	4,053	(9%)

Previous Winning Percentages: **1984** (85%) **1982** (84%)

District Vote For President

	1988	1984	1980	1976
D	85,212 (81%)	94,083 (78%)	71,142 (70%)	88,151 (76%)
R	18,421 (18%)	25,285 (21%)	25,844 (25%)	27,437 (24%)
I			3,664 (4%)	

Campaign Finance

	Receipts	Receipts from PACs	Expend-itures
1988			
Towns (D)	$327,722	$129,291 (39%)	$278,709
Hussain (R)	$253,860	$2,000 (1%)	$265,034
1986			
Towns (D)	$224,253	$116,618 (52%)	$185,565

Key Votes

1987	
Raise speed limit to 65 mph	N
Approve Gephardt "fair trade" amendment	Y
Ban testing of larger nuclear weapons	Y
Delay "re-flagging" of Kuwaiti tankers	Y
Approve tax-raising deficit-reduction bill	Y
1988	
Approve aid to Nicaraguan contras	N
Enact civil rights restoration bill over Reagan veto	Y
Kill 60-day plant-closing notification measure	N
Pass omnibus trade bill over Reagan veto	Y
Approve death penalty for drug-related murders	X
Bar federal funds for abortions in cases of rape and incest	X
Oppose seven-day waiting period for purchase of handguns	?

Voting Studies

	Presidential Support		Party Unity		Conservative Coalition	
Year	S	O	S	O	S	O
1988	13	71	76	2	0	76
1987	14	77	80	1	2	86
1986	14	77	81	4	8	86
1985	11	75	81	3	2	87
1984	18	69	78	4	3	86
1983	12	87	90	2	7	89

Interest Group Ratings

Year	ADA	ACU	AFL-CIO	CCUS
1988	90	0	100	33
1987	92	0	100	0
1986	95	0	100	15
1985	95	5	93	15
1984	85	5	100	36
1983	95	0	100	25

12 Major R. Owens (D)

Of Brooklyn — Elected 1982

Born: June 28, 1936, Memphis, Tenn.
Education: Morehouse College, B.A. 1956; Atlanta U., M.S. 1957.
Occupation: Librarian.
Family: Divorced; three children.
Religion: Baptist.
Political Career: N.Y. Senate, 1975-83.
Capitol Office: 114 Cannon Bldg. 20515; 225-6231.

In Washington: Owens is reserved and sometimes gruff, but he is a diligent legislator capable of impassioned oratory in defense of causes important to his poor, mostly black, district.

Chairman of the Education and Labor Subcommittee on Select Education, Owens worked in the 100th Congress to pass a four-year reauthorization of federal programs to curb family violence and child abuse. President Reagan wanted to cut the programs by 50 percent, a proposal Owens said illustrated a "basic callousness" toward "those with the least amount of power in our society."

Owens' subcommittee initially approved $84 million for 1989, but when Republicans protested, he agreed to reduce funding to $75 million — a modest increase over existing spending — if the bill went to the House under a fast-track procedure barring amendments. It did, and was signed into law in 1988.

Owens also authored the House version of successful legislation to help find homes for babies abandoned in hospitals, particularly babies with AIDS.

The only trained librarian in Congress, Owens regularly emphasizes the importance of libraries in creating a literate society. He also works to protect funding for historically black colleges and aid for poor students. Owens wrote a section of the higher-education bill providing graduate education grants for talented but underprivileged students. "We need more role models who will open new possibilities for those who have been excluded from the dreams that others take for granted."

He is also a watchdog of the political strife in Haiti, frequently updating his colleagues on the situation in the country by putting statements in the *Congressional Record.*

Sometimes Owens brings his library background to bear on issues that go beyond books. During one committee session, he suggested that a variation of the Dewey Decimal System be used on child-welfare program information.

At Home: Owens co-founded the black "reform" faction of the Brooklyn Democratic Party, and his 1982 primary victory over an organization stalwart testified to the movement's progress. With then-state Assemblyman Al Vann, Owens fought the organization for nearly a decade.

Owens began public life as a community organizer in 1964, setting up the Brownsville Community Council, which brought government programs to this devastated area. Under Mayor John V. Lindsay, he headed the city's Community Development Agency. In his first bid for elective office (in 1974), Owens led a slate seeking to oust machine-backed incumbents. He won a state Senate seat, and his allies wrested several other posts from party regulars.

Owens faced a tough task when he set his sights on the House in 1982. His opponent was state Sen. Vander Beatty, whose influence as deputy Democratic leader in the state Senate allowed him to build a patronage empire in the Brooklyn black community. His supporters included Democratic Rep. Shirley Chisholm and Brooklyn Borough President Howard Golden.

But Beatty had a weakness that Owens exploited well — unsavory connections. A longtime Beatty ally, former City Councilman Samuel Wright, was convicted of extortion and conspiracy in 1978. Owens emphasized his own reputation for honesty, noting his scandal-free tenure as community development chief. Armed with an endorsement from *The Amsterdam News*, an important force in the black community, Owens won that election by a narrow margin.

Beatty challenged the result of that election, accusing Owens' forces of forging signatures on voter-registration cards. Although an acting state Supreme Court judge in Brooklyn ordered a second vote, Owens ultimately triumphed in the New York Court of Appeals, which canceled the rerun and cleared his path to Congress.

Since then, Owens has faced only one foe of note. In the 1986 primary, he met Congress of Racial Equality Chairman Roy Innis, who had drawn attention with his brashly conservative stands against crime. But Owens romped to victory with 78 percent of the vote.

Owens is less familiar to most Americans than another member of his family. His son, Geoffrey Owens, is an actor on TV's "The Cosby Show."

New York 12

Central Brooklyn — Crown Heights

The 12th is the most solid minority district in New York City. It is 80 percent black, only 13 percent white, and thoroughly Democratic.

The district would have had an even higher black population had the Justice Department not complained in 1982 that it was being packed with blacks to keep them out of the neighboring 11th, designed initially by the Legislature for Hispanic representation.

Map makers substantially reshaped the 12th at the behest of the Justice Department, moving chunks of Bedford-Stuyvesant and other black neighborhoods into the 11th and pushing the 12th south.

The courts have been the crucible of Brooklyn's black congressional representation. Pressured by the Supreme Court, the Legislature in 1968 made the 12th the city's second black-majority district; the first was the traditional one in Harlem.

Urban blight and poverty characterize most of the 12th, as they do the 11th. In Brownsville, economic survival is the overriding concern. Large public housing projects and a sizable welfare clientele are basic parts of the district.

Most of the district's white vote comes from the northern part of Flatbush, a longstanding middle-class Jewish community in which Brooklyn College is located.

Crown Heights, just north of Flatbush, once was predominantly Jewish. Now it is largely black and Hispanic, although tightly knit communities of orthodox Jews remain. While some of Crown Heights' neighborhoods are declining, others still maintain a middle-class stability. Ebbets Field, home of the Brooklyn Dodgers, was in Crown Heights. After the Dodgers left for Los Angeles in 1958, an apartment complex replaced the ballpark.

Population: 516,983. White 66,870 (13%), Black 413,909 (80%), Other 8,454 (2%). Spanish origin 52,403 (10%). 18 and over 348,549 (67%), 65 and over 37,671 (7%). Median age: 28.

Committees

Education and Labor (10th of 22 Democrats)
Select Education (chairman); Elementary, Secondary and Vocational Education; Labor-Management Relations; Postsecondary Education

Government Operations (13th of 24 Democrats)
Government Activities and Transportation

Elections

1988 General		
Major R. Owens (D)	74,304	(93%)
Owen Augustin (R)	5,582	(7%)
1986 General		
Major R. Owens (D)	42,138	(92%)
Owen Augustin (R)	2,752	(6%)

Previous Winning Percentages: 1984 (91%) **1982** (91%)

District Vote For President

	1988	1984	1980	1976
D	91,590 (87%)	91,492 (86%)	68,133 (60%)	99,093 (73%)
R	12,449 (12%)	14,978 (14%)	39,400 (35%)	36,579 (27%)
I			5,181 (5%)	

Campaign Finance

	Receipts	Receipts from PACs	Expend-itures
1988			
Owens (D)	$154,022	$125,085 (81%)	$193,618
Augustin (R) †	$7,507	0	$7,099
1986			
Owens (D)	$169,403	$92,500 (55%)	$167,617
Augustin (R)	$24,223	0	$23,386

† Totals based on incomplete data.

Key Votes

1987	
Raise speed limit to 65 mph	N
Approve Gephardt "fair trade" amendment	Y
Ban testing of larger nuclear weapons	Y
Delay "re-flagging" of Kuwaiti tankers	Y
Approve tax-raising deficit-reduction bill	Y
1988	
Approve aid to Nicaraguan contras	N
Enact civil rights restoration bill over Reagan veto	Y
Kill 60-day plant-closing notification measure	N
Pass omnibus trade bill over Reagan veto	Y
Approve death penalty for drug-related murders	N
Bar federal funds for abortions in cases of rape and incest	N
Oppose seven-day waiting period for purchase of handguns	N

Voting Studies

	Presidential Support		Party Unity		Conservative Coalition	
Year	**S**	**O**	**S**	**O**	**S**	**O**
1988	13	73	79	3	3	79
1987	9	85	88	3	7	88
1986	11	83	89	2	6	90
1985	16	76	86	1	4	82
1984	18	78	90	4	3	93
1983	12	77	79	2	6	78

Interest Group Ratings

Year	ADA	ACU	AFL-CIO	CCUS
1988	95	0	100	15
1987	100	0	100	0
1986	95	0	93	20
1985	95	0	100	14
1984	90	5	100	44
1983	85	0	100	26

13 Stephen J. Solarz (D)

Of Brooklyn — Elected 1974

Born: Sept. 12, 1940, New York, N.Y.
Education: Brandeis U., A.B. 1962; Columbia U., M.A. 1967.
Occupation: Public official.
Family: Wife, Nina Koldin; two children.
Religion: Jewish.
Political Career: N.Y. Assembly, 1969-75; sought Democratic nomination for Brooklyn borough president, 1973.
Capitol Office: 1536 Longworth Bldg. 20515; 225-2361.

In Washington: The world of House members, from fund raising to public exposure, is largely circumscribed by their committee assignments. And from the day he arrived in the House in 1975, Solarz has acted as if he did not know that the House Foreign Affairs Committee is supposed to play a secondary role in charting foreign policy. He has negotiated with foreign leaders and argued with American presidents while building a reputation at home and abroad as a man whose opinion matters.

Solarz insists that "in Congress, information is the key to influence." And his appetite for information is insatiable, whether he is grilling an administration witness at a committee hearing or prying loose facts from a prime minister in a marathon interview.

His pursuit of the facts takes him to dozens of nations every year. But he is no mere junketeer, and a trip with Solarz is no vacation: Colleagues have learned from experience that staying home is far easier.

There is no question that Solarz has accomplished a lot during his years in the House. He has been involved in U.S. policy toward virtually every continent, and his is a major voice on the Foreign Affairs Committee. No foreign aid bill leaves the committee without his imprint. The one common criticism of Solarz is that, by moving on so many fronts at once, he sometimes spreads himself too thin, or at least strains his political alliances. His face is familiar on the TV news circuit, and his columns can often be found in the nation's major newspapers. Solarz might make secretary of state someday, but for now, not every member is happy to see him speaking out on subjects in which they consider themselves expert — and proving to be more knowledgeable than they are.

As America increasingly looks to the East — to Asia and the Pacific Rim — Solarz is trying to guide what it sees. He has used his position as chairman of the Asian and Pacific Affairs Subcommittee to campaign for democratic reforms throughout the region, particularly the Philippines and South Korea.

Solarz basked in publicity brought by the 1986 downfall of Philippine President Ferdinand E. Marcos — and justifiably so, given his work toward that end. For years a Marcos critic, Solarz did his best to find legislative weapons to force change despite President Reagan's contention that the only available alternative to Marcos was communism.

Solarz persuaded his colleagues in 1984 and 1985 to reduce military aid to the Philippines and bolster economic assistance instead. The message: Marcos could no longer carry on business as usual. Within a year, Marcos was out, and Corazon Aquino, long a Solarz favorite, became president in what Solarz called "one of the few authentic democratic revolutions of our time." He began to push immediately for extra U.S. aid to the Philippines — a battle he is still waging — and persuaded Aquino to address a joint session of Congress in September 1986. An enthusiastic House that same day approved an extra $200 million.

More controversial were hearings Solarz held in January 1986, just before the fraudulent election that ultimately caused Marcos' undoing. The Asian Affairs Subcommittee focused attention on Marcos' accumulation of great wealth, including extensive real-estate holdings in the United States; Solarz said he was investigating possible misuse of U.S. foreign aid. Solarz was also on hand for the event that captured even wider American attention, the discovery of Imelda Marcos' thousands of pairs of shoes — shoes that came to symbolize the Marcoses' greed.

Solarz' work on behalf of the Aquino government continued during the 100th Congress. He played a lead role in pressing for higher levels of U.S. aid to the Philippines, including U.S. participation in the "mini-Marshall plan" with other Asian nations, set to push total U.S. aid to nearly $650 million in fiscal 1990.

The Asian mainland increasingly captured his attention in the late 1980s, especially the

New York 13

Western and Southern Brooklyn — Bensonhurst; Brooklyn Heights

The elongated 13th reaches north from Brooklyn's Atlantic beaches to the East River waterfront. It is overwhelmingly white, and has one of the largest percentages of Jewish residents in the country. Redistricting in 1982 extended the 13th's boundaries to include Williamsburg, center of Hasidic Jewish life in America.

The 13th is usually Democratic territory, even in national Republican years. In each of the last three presidential elections, the district went Democratic.

The heart of the district is in middle-class Bensonhurst. Jewish delicatessens and Italian open-air markets signal its ethnic makeup. The Jews generally live in the apartment buildings in Bensonhurst, while Italians inhabit its row houses. Brighton Beach, south of Bensonhurst, has become a magnet for Soviet Jewish immigrants. Russian is spoken routinely on its business streets, and its restaurants bear such names as "Café Odessa."

Coney Island is the best-known section of the district. At one time New Yorkers of all races and incomes flocked to Coney's beaches, thrill rides and hot dog stands. Now this fun center attracts mostly low-income minorities; the beaches and amusements are run-down. Puerto Ricans, blacks and elderly Jews live in uneasy coexistence.

The 13th also takes in the Brooklyn Navy Yard, an old federal facility now owned by the city. Although some ships are still repaired there, light-manufacturing firms occupy most of the yard. A Norwegian community, descended from merchant seamen, lives on in otherwise Hispanic Sunset Park.

Brooklyn Heights, where expensive co-ops and town houses abound, displays an upper-class liberalism. Celebrities abound there, lured by the elegant brownstones and the spectacular views of the Lower Manhattan skyline.

Farther north up the East River is the nation's largest concentration of Hasidic Jews. The Hasidim in Williamsburg form an insular community not often involved in politics. However, the fundamentalist religious beliefs and austere lifestyles of this community, combined with its tense relations with neighboring minority communities, has made some Hasidic Jews friendly to conservative candidates; Ronald Reagan's ethnic outreach operation made some successful inroads.

Synagogues give way to Catholic parishes in Greenpoint, which lies to the north. Poles and Italians inhabit Greenpoint's neatly kept row houses.

Population: 516,512. White 424,123 (82%), Black 37,376 (7%), Other 11,155 (2%). Spanish origin 82,554 (16%). 18 and over 387,947 (75%), 65 and over 85,695 (17%). Median age: 34.

subcontinent, where India and Pakistan warily eye one another. Solarz has made the case for India in foreign aid battles, often an uphill fight given the country's history of chilly relations with the United States. He also has pushed for restrictions on U.S. aid to Pakistan, linking aid to a disavowal of offensive weapons, including nuclear arms. The now-deceased ruler of Pakistan, Mohammad Zia ul-Haq, in 1987 called Solarz the "voice of India," intended as criticism but taken as a compliment.

The common thread in the Solarz foreign policy is human rights. For much of his career, Africa was the focus of his work. He defended many nationalist movements, including leftist ones, and once prompted Robert E. Bauman, the vitriolic Maryland Republican, to refer to him sarcastically as "the gentleman from Africa." Over the years, he laid much of the groundwork for the sanctions imposed against South Africa in 1986.

Solarz has taken an increasingly centrist view of U.S. policy — positioning himself during the Reagan administration to the left of the president but to the right of those Democrats who rejected activism abroad. In the 99th Congress, this view manifested itself in his unexpected push for U.S. aid to anti-communist guerrillas in Cambodia. Almost entirely on Solarz' recommendation, the House agreed to provide $5 million to Thailand, which would then turn the money over to the non-communist resistance in neighboring Cambodia.

This presented a difficult political tightrope to walk — abroad and at home. While working to lessen Vietnamese influence over Cambodia, Solarz has also sought to prevent the Khmer Rouge from returning to power in the vaccum left by the Vietnamese. Meanwhile, he must answer liberal critics who fear renewed U.S. involvement in Southeast Asia. "We need to learn the lessons of Vietnam," Solarz says, "but it would be a tragic mistake if we were to be paralyzed by them."

Cambodia is not the only example of Solarz' departure from his usual roost on the left in the House Democratic Caucus. He also has opposed a reduction in U.S. ground troops in

Europe, arguing that a troop cut would be seen by the Soviets as well as U.S. allies as a weakening of American commitment, thus increasing the risk of war. Solarz also sided with Republicans in 1987 on the issue of replacing a dozen aging French-made fighter jets in Honduras with F-5E/Fs, but he cautioned against reading anything more into the vote than an endorsement to replace those particular jets.

Year in and year out, one constant for Solarz is Israel. Representing a district that has one of the highest concentrations of Jewish voters in the United States, he has devoted much of his time to the issue. But of late he has not moved in lock step with Israel's staunchest supporters. For instance, he supported the sale of Stinger missles to Bahrain, an important U.S. ally and headquarters for U.S. forces in the Middle East. His relations with the American Israel Public Affairs Committee, the chief pro-Israel voice in Washington, have been better. Further, Solarz does not receive heavy contributions from pro-Israel PACs, as do many other Jewish members of the Foreign Affairs Committee.

His visibility on Asian issues has enabled Solarz to turn a difficult trick for a member of Foreign Affairs: raising money on an issue other than Israel. Since 1985, he has developed an extensive list of supporters who hail from India, the Philippines, Taiwan and South Korea, becoming one of the premier fund-raisers in the House. These contacts led to his interest in the issue of discrimination by the states against foreign medical graduates; he has filed legislation that would prevent the practice.

Solarz admits that his activities sometimes leave Brooklyn voters behind. "To most of the people in my district," Solarz once told a reporter, "Zimbabwe sounds like a new Baskin-Robbins flavor."

But he has also won battles that are not hard to understand in his district. He won legislation to ensure the right of Jewish servicemen to wear yarmulkes in uniform. And he pressed the State Department to reverse its opposition to making public the United Nations war-crime files containing records from Nazi Germany. The department relented.

Solarz made a conspicuous effort on one local issue in 1985, but was not successful. He tried to delete language in an appropriation bill mandating that tolls on New York's Verrazano-Narrows Bridge be collected only on the Brooklyn side, not the Staten Island side. He said it would cost New York City $10 million a year from people who would ride from Staten Island to Brooklyn and then find another means of making the return trip. But after an hour of floor debate, Solarz lost to Staten Island Republican Guy V. Molinari, who complained about air pollution from traffic jams at the toll plaza on his side. Some saw this as a personal vote against Solarz.

Solarz has recently taken some steps in Washington to bolster his position at home. He took a seat on the Merchant Marine and Fisheries Committee, a convenient position from which to look after the Brooklyn waterfront. He has also been more vocal on behalf of the elderly — a category that includes many of his constituents — on the Education and Labor Committee.

At Home: A native Brooklynite, Solarz was quick to join the ranks of reform Democrats when he returned from Brandeis and Columbia universities in the mid-1960s. In 1966 he managed the anti-war campaign of Mel Dubin, who ran for the 13th District congressional seat held by longtime Democratic Rep. Abraham Multer. Dubin lost that contest by fewer than 1,000 votes.

Two years later, Solarz struck out on his own and won a seat in the Assembly. Though close to the reform movement, he maintained cordial relations with party regulars in Albany.

In 1973 Solarz made what seemed to be a quixotic campaign as a reform candidate for Brooklyn borough president. But he did relatively well in the Democratic primary, running only 11 percentage points behind the winner, Sebastian Leone. Solarz carried the 13th District in the boroughwide primary.

The next year, Solarz got his opportunity to come to Congress. Incumbent Democrat Bertram L. Podell had been indicted in 1973 on charges of conspiracy, bribery, perjury and conflict of interest. He protested his innocence and insisted on seeking renomination. The organization backed him, but Solarz put on a strong campaign and ousted the incumbent.

Since then, Solarz has faced no serious challenges. In recent campaigns, his formidable fund-raising ability has bolstered his security.

In 1982 Brooklyn had to give up one of its districts, and Solarz faced the prospect of seeing the 13th merged with a neighboring constituency. So he amassed nearly $700,000, gathering substantial donations from Jewish contributors in cities around the country.

He need not have worried. The Legislature paired Solarz with Democratic Rep. Fred Richmond, who pleaded guilty to income-tax evasion and other federal charges. Richmond first decided to run in another district, then resigned.

Committees

Foreign Affairs (4th of 28 Democrats)
Asian and Pacific Affairs (chairman); Arms Control, International Security and Science; Western Hemisphere Affairs

Merchant Marine and Fisheries (22nd of 26 Democrats)
Fisheries and Wildlife Conservation and the Environment; Merchant Marine

Select Intelligence (12th of 12 Democrats)
Legislation; Program and Budget Authorization

Joint Economic
Economic Growth, Trade and Taxes; Economic Resources and Competitiveness; International Economic Policy; Investment, Jobs and Prices

Elections

1988 General

Stephen J. Solarz (D)	81,305	(75%)
Anthony M. Curci (R)	27,536	(25%)

1986 General

Stephen J. Solarz (D)	61,089	(82%)
Leon Nadrowski (R)	10,941	(15%)

Previous Winning Percentages: 1984 (66%) **1982** (81%) **1980** (79%) **1978** (81%) **1976** (84%) **1974** (82%)

District Vote For President

	1988	1984	1980	1976
D	71,418 (54%)	74,815 (52%)	65,323 (50%)	101,302 (65%)
R	60,376 (45%)	69,193 (48%)	55,585 (43%)	52,759 (34%)
I			6,547 (5%)	

Campaign Finance

	Receipts	Receipts from PACs	Expend-itures
1988			
Solarz (D)	$910,663	$60,605 (7%)	$564,882
1986			
Solarz (D)	$608,701	$40,370 (7%)	$417,975

Key Votes

1987

Raise speed limit to 65 mph	N
Approve Gephardt "fair trade" amendment	Y
Ban testing of larger nuclear weapons	Y
Delay "re-flagging" of Kuwaiti tankers	Y
Approve tax-raising deficit-reduction bill	Y

1988

Approve aid to Nicaraguan contras	N
Enact civil rights restoration bill over Reagan veto	Y
Kill 60-day plant-closing notification measure	N
Pass omnibus trade bill over Reagan veto	Y
Approve death penalty for drug-related murders	N
Bar federal funds for abortions in cases of rape and incest	N
Oppose seven-day waiting period for purchase of handguns	N

Voting Studies

	Presidential Support		Party Unity		Conservative Coalition	
Year	**S**	**O**	**S**	**O**	**S**	**O**
1988	24	73	88	5	11	82
1987	19	76	91	3	14	86
1986	18	76	89	5	16	80
1985	24	69	89	4	11	87
1984	35	59	85	6	15	78
1983	24	55	76	5	16	72
1982	38	58	94	4	11	86
1981	36	58	82 †	6 †	13	77

† Not eligible for all recorded votes.

Interest Group Ratings

Year	ADA	ACU	AFL-CIO	CCUS
1988	95	4	93	33
1987	88	0	94	8
1986	90	5	86	20
1985	90	14	94	20
1984	85	4	69	33
1983	90	0	100	24
1982	95	0	95	10
1981	90	0	80	6

14 Guy V. Molinari (R)

Of Staten Island — Elected 1980

Born: Nov. 23, 1928, New York, N.Y.
Education: Wagner College, B.A. 1949; New York Law School, LL.B. 1951.
Military Career: Marine Corps, 1951-53.
Occupation: Lawyer.
Family: Wife, Marguerite Wing; one child.
Religion: Roman Catholic.
Political Career: N.Y. Assembly, 1975-81.
Capitol Office: 2453 Rayburn Bldg. 20515; 225-3371.

In Washington: Though Molinari has been involved in debate on such significant national issues as aviation safety during his House tenure, the thoughts of this consummate "pothole" politician have never been far from his home base, the New York City borough of Staten Island. Molinari proved that beyond doubt in May 1989, when he announced plans to run that November for Staten Island borough president, a position roughly equivalent to that of a county executive.

Before committing to a return to local politics, Molinari did make a major bid for national prominence, lobbying hard to be named President Bush's secretary of transportation.

Molinari's claim was based on his work on transportation issues as a member of the Public Works Committee, and on his labors for the Bush presidential campaign: Molinari had pulled off something of a coup during the primaries, lining up support for Bush from every New York GOP House member except Jack F. Kemp, who was himself running for president. But Bush bypassed Molinari and selected Samuel K. Skinner, then director of the Chicago regional transit authority, to head the Department of Transportation.

Soon thereafter, Molinari, who had aligned himself with former U.S. Attorney Rudolph W. Giuliani's 1989 challenge to Democratic New York Mayor Edward I. Koch, decided to return to the local fray: He announced he would seek to unseat the incumbent borough president, Democrat Ralph Lamberti.

It will not take long for Molinari to gear up for the contest, since he has never lost his zeal for local issues. In 1988, as his Democratic opponent sought to engage him on his House voting record, Molinari involved himself in a community movement to block plans for a new jail on Staten Island.

In the 100th Congress, Molinari obtained over $3 million to complete a sea wall and build a boat ramp at Staten Island's Great Kills beach. His advocacy of the Navy's "homeporting" program in the 99th Congress helped him obtain a base for Staten Island, which will be one of the few facilities to gain personnel under the 1989 plan to close a number of obsolete bases.

Molinari has also been an activist on local issues with national bearing. With Staten Island burdened with large landfills and the pollution problems attendant its location between Manhattan and industrial New Jersey, Molinari has been more outspoken on environmental issues than many House Republicans.

When the House debated a measure in 1988 to prohibit New York City and other localities from dumping sewage sludge in the ocean by 1992, Molinari moved quickly to make certain that the city did not use his territory as an alternative dumping ground. His amendment, prohibiting sludge dumping in any Staten Island landfill, was approved as part of the larger bill.

Earlier, Molinari had been involved in one of the larger environmental controversies of the Reagan presidency. During his first term, he demanded that the Environmental Protection Agency look into illegal dumping of toxic waste at a Staten Island site. The ensuing inquiry sparked a struggle over access to EPA information that eventually resulted in the resignation of agency head Anne M. Burford.

When not watching over Staten Island's interests in the House, Molinari has generally had his eyes on the skies. He has made a specialty of aviation safety issues, and was one of the toughest critics of airline industry oversight by the Reagan administration.

The aviation issue was one of the few points of contention between Molinari and a Republican administration which he strongly backed on most issues. But Molinari complained that the Federal Aviation Administration (FAA) and the passenger airlines were neglecting serious safety and efficiency problems, and became known for his often-volatile exchanges with Reagan's transportation secretaries, Elizabeth H. Dole and Jim Burnley, over the urgency of his proposed reforms.

Molinari persistently pushed for the rehir-

New York 14

Staten Island; Southwest Brooklyn

Staten Island's physical isolation ended with the 1964 opening of the Verrazano-Narrows Bridge (the longest suspension bridge in the world), connecting it with Brooklyn. But the island remains in many ways a place apart from the rest of New York City.

Despite a major population influx in the decade following the bridge's opening, Staten Island remains the most suburban of New York City's five boroughs. But Staten Island's landfills and its location in the soiled waters of New York harbor make residents not only more environment-conscious than most other New Yorkers, but also sensitive to an image of the island as a city dumping ground.

As a suburban area with a large, upwardly mobile, conservative ethnic population, Staten Island also deviates from the liberal Democratic dominance in the rest of the city. Though the more popular statewide Democrats, such as Sen. Daniel Patrick Moynihan and Gov. Mario M. Cuomo, have done as well there as elsewhere, Republican presidential candidates win easily: George Bush took 62 percent of the vote there in 1988, just below President Reagan's 65 percent four years earlier.

The Irish and the Italians are the most visible ethnic groups on Staten Island. The few minority-group residents (about 10 percent of the total) cluster in low-income housing in such northern shore communities as Stapleton (the site of the Navy homeport Molinari lobbied vigorously for) and Port Richmond. Generally, incomes are higher south of the Staten Island Expressway. Many registered Republicans reside in the large homes of Todt Hill and Emerson Hill. The South Shore and Tottenville areas are middle-income.

Although Staten Island provides nearly 75 percent of the district's vote, its population is too small to constitute an entire district on its own. Linked with liberal Lower Manhattan during the 1970s, the island is now joined with Brooklyn's more conservative Bay Ridge.

With its row houses and brownstones, Bay Ridge displays a more urban character than Staten Island. Overwhelmingly white and largely Italian, this is the community John Travolta danced and swaggered his way through in "Saturday Night Fever." Bay Ridge also has a distinctive Scandinavian presence. There are few minorities.

Population: 516,537. White 464,689 (90%), Black 26,351 (5%), Other 12,722 (2%). Spanish origin 33,961 (7%). 18 and over 379,638 (74%), 65 and over 66,743 (13%). Median age: 33.

ing of some of the air-traffic controllers whom Reagan had fired and permanently barred in 1981 for conducting an illegal strike. Though Molinari at first supported the firings, he became convinced that the replacement work force was too inexperienced and overworked to handle the demands of the job. He used a series of news reports on airport overcrowding and midair "near-misses" to bolster his argument.

But the Reagan administration remained intractably opposed to rehiring any of the fired workers, forestalling Molinari's efforts to get his idea through Congress. His 1986 amendment to call back 1,000 of the most qualified controllers over two years failed in the House, 193-226.

When he tried again in 1988, Molinari went out of his way to assuage fellow Republicans who did not want to cross Reagan on a sensitive issue. "It is not a referendum on the president's [1981] action," he told the House. "It would be malfeasance if we failed to take this action on behalf of public safety." The argument earned him a victory in the House, where the bill passed by a 234-180 vote. However, the proposal then died in the Senate.

Molinari also regularly blamed the FAA for reacting to disasters rather than working to prevent them. Shortly after the 1986 collision of a jetliner and a small plane over Cerritos, Calif., the FAA began a push for the installation of collision-avoidance equipment in passenger jets. Molinari said the FAA should have promoted the technology before the accident happened. "It is the FAA's job to take the lead where safety is involved and it is failing miserably," he said.

Earlier that year, Molinari praised a General Accounting Office report that raised questions about the safety of the air-traffic control system. "FAA has insisted all along that improvements were being made and that the system not only was safe, but was getting safer," he said. "That fiction has now been laid to rest."

Molinari's dogged pursuit of aviation reform earned him some national attention; he was a guest on several network TV news shows. But his harsh questioning of Reagan officials rubbed some of his partisan colleagues the wrong way, and undoubtedly influenced some in the new president's inner circle who viewed him as abrasive and too adversarial to be transportation secretary.

In the 101st Congress, Molinari reclaimed the ranking Republican spot on the Public Works Subcommittee on Investigations and Oversight, a post he had held in the 98th Congress. But in the 99th Congress, the committee's GOP leadership backed the bid by Georgia Republican Newt Gingrich to exercise his seniority and claim that position from Molinari, who was temporarily relegated to the ranking spot on a much lower-profile panel, the Subcommittee on Public Buildings and Grounds.

At Home: The rough edge colleagues often notice in Molinari is a legacy of his rise in New York's urban politics. Taking conservative Republican stands in a liberal Democratic city, and hailing from an area — Staten Island — that often sees itself as ignored or put upon by the rest of the city, Molinari has always seemed to be fighting against the mainstream.

Yet Molinari's path to political success was paved for him by his father, who also served in the state Assembly. And after struggling to win his House seat over a scandal-plagued incumbent, Molinari has had no political worries.

Molinari's opportunity for Congress came in 1980, when Democratic Rep. John Murphy got caught up in the FBI's Abscam investigation. Murphy could not withstand Molinari's personal popularity or his ethnic appeal; Italian-Americans are Staten Island's strongest voting bloc. Still, Molinari won his first contest with only a 48 percent plurality.

Prior to the 1982 elections, the New York state Legislature adjusted the congressional district map to compensate for the loss of five seats. Although Brooklyn Democrat Leo Zeferetti was the New York House delegation's liaison to the Legislature on redistricting, the final plan placed him in a single district with Molinari.

Zeferetti's old 15th District, based in Brooklyn's Bay Ridge, contributed just 30 percent of the reshaped constituency. Meanwhile, Molinari maintained his entire Staten Island base, while shedding some Manhattan territory that was not especially friendly to him. The shape of the remap may have been the decisive factor. Zeferetti carried the Brooklyn section of the district by a modest margin, but Molinari won handily in Staten Island and by more than 15,000 votes overall. He quickly made himself a fixture, winning easily his last three times out.

Committee

Public Works and Transportation (5th of 20 Republicans)
Investigations and Oversight (ranking); Aviation; Water Resources

Elections

1988 General		
Guy V. Molinari (R)	99,179	(63%)
Jerome X. O'Donovan (D)	57,503	(37%)
1986 General		
Guy V. Molinari (R)	64,647	(69%)
Barbara Walla (D)	27,950	(30%)

Previous Winning Percentages: **1984** (70%) **1982** (56%) **1980** (48%)

District Vote For President

	1988	1984	1980	1976
D	75,069 (42%)	61,933 (34%)	55,789 (36%)	72,736 (47%)
R	99,788 (56%)	118,437 (66%)	87,135 (56%)	81,884 (53%)
I			9,286 (6%)	

Campaign Finance

	Receipts	Receipts from PACs	Expend-itures
1988			
Molinari (R)	$234,952	$77,006 (33%)	$228,796
O'Donovan (D)	$221,868	$80,997 (37%)	$229,849
1986			
Molinari (R)	$200,527	$58,020 (29%)	$152,312
Walla (D)	$41,828	$2,250 (5%)	$41,310

Key Votes

1987	
Raise speed limit to 65 mph	N
Approve Gephardt "fair trade" amendment	N
Ban testing of larger nuclear weapons	N
Delay "re-flagging" of Kuwaiti tankers	N
Approve tax-raising deficit-reduction bill	N
1988	
Approve aid to Nicaraguan contras	Y
Enact civil rights restoration bill over Reagan veto	Y
Kill 60-day plant-closing notification measure	?
Pass omnibus trade bill over Reagan veto	Y
Approve death penalty for drug-related murders	Y
Bar federal funds for abortions in cases of rape and incest	Y
Oppose seven-day waiting period for purchase of handguns	N

Voting Studies

	Presidential Support		Party Unity		Conservative Coalition	
Year	S	O	S	O	S	O
1988	53	37	74	14	76	16
1987	53	38	73	21	72	19
1986	69	29	75	24	76	24
1985	64	36	74	26	69	31
1984	60	40	73	27	81	19
1983	65	24	57	24	70	24
1982	52	36	62	33	67	30
1981	68	30	74 †	22 †	72	24

† Not eligible for all recorded votes.

Interest Group Ratings

Year	ADA	ACU	AFL-CIO	CCUS
1988	30	63	73	91
1987	28	74	47	71
1986	15	59	36	72
1985	30	67	35	64
1984	15	75	15	63
1983	5	95	13	67
1982	15	65	17	67
1981	25	92	27	79

15 Bill Green (R)

Of Manhattan — Elected 1978

Born: Oct. 16, 1929, New York, N.Y.
Education: Harvard College, B.A. 1950; Harvard Law School, J.D. 1953.
Military Career: Army, 1953-55.
Occupation: Lawyer.
Family: Wife, Patricia Freiberg; two children.
Religion: Jewish.
Political Career: N.Y. Assembly, 1965-68; sought GOP nomination to U.S. House, 1968.
Capitol Office: 1110 Longworth Bldg. 20515; 225-2436.

In Washington: Bill Green is a remnant of the silk-stocking Republicans who once dominated his Manhattan district. Like his partisan predecessors in the House, his pedigree is aristocratic, but like his constituents today, Green is decidedly liberal on most social-policy issues.

Throughout the 1980s, Green parted company with Ronald Reagan more often than many Democrats, but then Green represents a district swept by Walter F. Mondale in 1984 presidential balloting and by Michael S. Dukakis in 1988. While some Republicans question whether Green is more liberal than even his constituents demand, most find his renegade record an acceptable trade-off for possession of a House seat that should not be theirs.

Green periodically tests the tolerance for his dissident views in public confrontations with his party. In 1988, he unsuccessfully implored the GOP platform-drafting committee to include the Equal Rights Amendment (ERA) and to soften the anti-abortion language. In a subsequent column in *The Washington Post,* Green rooted his rebellion in GOP tradition. "In 1919, it was a Republican Congress that proposed the 19th Amendment giving women the vote," he wrote. "It was the Republican Party that, in 1940, placed the ERA in its platform, four years before the Democrats."

Green has grown slowly into his role as a spokesman for Republican moderates, shedding the reticence that marked his early House years. Now, in the post-Reagan era, he may find a place at the Republican table, but it seems highly unlikely that the socially liberal GOP he envisions will come to pass any time soon.

On Appropriations, Green is ranking Republican on the VA, HUD and Independent Agencies Subcommittee. In recent years, the panel has been the scene of an increasingly tense tug of war between funding for NASA and funding for other domestic social needs. Green, a former Department of Housing and Urban Development (HUD) administrator, generally comes down on the side of urban programs.

He is an advocate of increased funding for housing, and was a leading foe of conservative attempts to eliminate urban development action grants (UDAGs). This comfortably allied him with past subcommittee Chairman Edward P. Boland, a Massachusetts Democrat who shared Green's urban perspective. The new chairman of the panel, Michigan's Bob Traxler, is also a housing advocate, but he is far more supportive of NASA than Green, who has been an outspoken critic of NASA's space policies, which he says place too much emphasis on manned flights at the expense of unmanned scientific research.

In 1988, Green helped the panel arrive at a compromise by finally abandoning UDAGs. When an amendment was offered on the floor to shift funds from NASA to HUD and UDAG programs, he voted against it. Ironically, his acquiescence was won in part because of a 1987 rule change that was expected to widen the base of support for UDAGs by spreading the money more widely. Instead, that move decreased the program's impact in the Northeast and cost the UDAG program its most loyal advocates.

On the full Appropriations Committee, Green's support for feminist causes is often on display. He backs federal funding of abortion, and has opposed the "Hyde amendment" to the health appropriations bill, which bars funding of abortions even in cases of rape and incest. In 1988, he co-authored an amendment to fund an investigation of bombings at clinics that perform abortions.

Green also occasionally joins committee liberals on foreign policy and defense issues. Over Reagan administration objections, he and Democrat Les AuCoin of Oregon sponsored a successful amendment to the 1987 supplemental appropriations bill to bar all but the smallest nuclear weapons tests, provided the Soviet Union obverses a similar moratorium.

Beyond Appropriations, Green's agenda remains reflective of his social liberalism. In both 1987 and 1988, he joined with Minnesota Democrat Bruce F. Vento in presenting the Energy and Commerce Committee with letters

New York 15

Manhattan — East Side

The combination of a soaring cost of living in its affluent neighborhoods and urban collapse in its poorer areas has cost Manhattan most of its middle-class population. Former residents of modest means complain that the island at the heart of New York City has become a province of "the very rich and the very poor."

The chasm between those at the ends of the economic spectrum is amply evident in the 15th, mainly located on Manhattan's East Side. From the midtown business center to the exclusive shops and expensive apartments of the Upper East Side, the district smacks of wealth. The 15th contains most of the elements — the office towers, the fine restaurants and hotels, the cultural attractions — that make New York the nation's most vibrant city. But the 15th also reaches into the meaner streets of the Lower East Side, a heavily Hispanic area plagued by poverty, unemployment, drugs and crime.

Despite the economic gulf between them, the rich and the poor share a common thread politically. The 15th is a liberal-voting place. Low-income minority voters show the expected Democratic tendencies, but so do the affluent; this is, after all, where the phrase "limousine liberal" was born. Michael S. Dukakis' 66 percent here was crucial to his state win; Walter F. Mondale's 61 percent in 1984 was one of his highest percentages anywhere. A liberal Republican voting record has been the key to Green's survival.

This political trend is fairly recent. In the 1930s, the "Silk Stocking District" on Manhattan's East Side was a bastion of aristocratic Republicans who disdained the New Deal. But by 1980, Republican presence in the East Side area making up the 15th had dwindled to less than 20 percent of the district's registered voters. Signs of the area's changing political climate were evident as early as 1968, when Edward I. Koch, now New York City's mayor, became the first Democrat to represent the East Side district.

Many district residents work in the corporate headquarters that loom over midtown Manhattan, threatening to block the sun entirely from some of its streets. One of those buildings is Trump Tower, a mixed office-and-residential skyscraper named for its controversial developer, billionaire Donald Trump. Though there is still plenty of "old money" around, today's Manhattan is more associated with the brash, Trump-style entrepreneurship.

In addition to the Lower East Side, the 15th takes in Chinatown and Little Italy.

Population: 516,409. White 399,014 (77%), Black 27,086 (5%), Asian and Pacific Islander 51,886 (10%). Spanish origin 75,144 (15%). 18 and over 444,395 (86%), 65 and over 78,336 (15%). Median age: 37.

from some 200 House members urging action on clean-air legislation.

He was one of just a few Republicans to cosponsor California Democrat Henry A. Waxman's AIDS legislation, which sought to ensure confidentiality of test records and to protect those who test positive for the virus from discrimination. Green describes himself as "a longtime supporter of the rights of gay men and lesbian women."

In the early 1980s, Green was among the "Gypsy Moth" moderate Republicans who sought to protect Medicaid, mass transit and social programs from the budget-cutting axe. Green and other like-minded Republicans withheld their votes on key appropriations bills in 1981 until mass transit and low-income energy assistance funding was preserved.

At Home: During the early part of Green's House career, local Democrats persisted in believing that Green could be ousted from a district that otherwise had become inhospitable to Republicans. But by practicing his liberal brand of politics and dipping deeply into his family fortune — he is a supermarket heir — Green thwarted all challenges.

He applied a *coup de grâce* to Democratic hopes with his crushing 1984 victory over a well-known opponent, Manhattan Borough President Andrew Stein. Though Stein, the son of a wealthy real-estate developer, spent $1.8 million to Green's $1.1 million (the combined total was a House campaign-spending record at the time), Green won 56 percent of the vote.

In doing so, Green overcame an atypical problem. While scores of House Democrats were struggling in 1984 to escape the effects of President Reagan's coattail power, Green faced a strong pro-Mondale tide.

He also had to contend with Stein, a tough young political veteran. Stein hired consultant David Garth to produce TV ads condemning Green for supporting Reagan budget cuts that Stein claimed had cost New York City federal funds. Green at first responded by accusing Stein of absenteeism in his earlier New York

Assembly career. But Green abandoned that approach midway through the fall campaign, opting to return to his normal low-key methods. Wary of the effects of his party label, he took pains to remind voters that he was on the November ballot on both the GOP and Independent lines.

In the end, Green's chief asset was his ability to cultivate Democrats dissatisfied with Stein, who suffered from a reputation as shallow on issues and who came under fire from some liberals for his ties to midtown Manhattan real-estate interests. The Democratic crossover helped Green to a comfortable victory, even as Mondale won the 15th with 61 percent.

Green's 1986 opponent, magazine publisher George Hirsch, echoed Stein's complaint that the incumbent was too supportive of Reagan's economic program, while presenting himself as a fresh face unfettered by ties to the political establishment. But Green quietly emphasized his significant differences with the administration en route to a 58 percent tally. Though his 1988 opponent, attorney Peter G. Doukas, was active locally in the Dukakis campaign and shared a Greek-American heritage with the Democratic presidential nominee, he drew little attention; Green won with 61 percent, a personal best.

Green's career was in housing and urban finance before 1978. He was chief counsel to the New York Legislative Committee on Housing and Urban Development from 1961 to 1964. He then spent four years in the state Assembly before moving to HUD in 1970.

He burst into congressional politics in February 1978, upsetting a legendary Manhattan politician — Bella S. Abzug. The two met in a special election forced by the resignation of Democratic Rep. Edward I. Koch after his 1977 election as New York City mayor. Abzug, an outspoken liberal and feminist who had represented Manhattan's West Side, moved to the East Side for a comeback after losing bids for Senate and mayor. Green won partly because of an anti-Abzug vote, and partly because he spent a large sum of money on the campaign. Although he was little known to the average voter when he began, he invested $150,000 in radio and television commercials, mass mailings and bus ads that boosted his visibility, enabling him to edge out Abzug.

Committee

Appropriations (12th of 22 Republicans)
VA, HUD and Independent Agencies (ranking); District of Columbia

Elections

1988 General		
Bill Green (R)	107,599	(61%)
Peter G. Doukas (D)	64,425	(37%)
1986 General		
Bill Green (R)	58,214	(58%)
George A. Hirsch (D)	42,147	(42%)

Previous Winning Percentages: **1984** (56%) **1982** (54%) **1980** (57%) **1978** (53%) **1978 *** (50%)

** Special election.*

District Vote For President

	1988	1984	1980	1976
D	130,661 (66%)	122,204 (61%)	94,130 (52%)	118,721 (65%)
R	65,654 (33%)	77,223 (39%)	64,562 (36%)	62,931 (34%)
I			19,429 (11%)	

Campaign Finance

	Receipts	Receipts from PACs	Expend-itures
1988			
Green (R)	$656,289	$154,233 (24%)	$602,942
Doukas (D)	$171,965	$24,700 (14%)	$171,838
1986			
Green (R)	$696,203	$127,630 (18%)	$709,384
Hirsch (D)	$403,626	$41,575 (10%)	$395,185

Key Votes

1987	
Raise speed limit to 65 mph	N
Approve Gephardt "fair trade" amendment	N
Ban testing of larger nuclear weapons	Y
Delay "re-flagging" of Kuwaiti tankers	N
Approve tax-raising deficit-reduction bill	N
1988	
Approve aid to Nicaraguan contras	N
Enact civil rights restoration bill over Reagan veto	Y
Kill 60-day plant-closing notification measure	Y
Pass omnibus trade bill over Reagan veto	N
Approve death penalty for drug-related murders	Y
Bar federal funds for abortions in cases of rape and incest	N
Oppose seven-day waiting period for purchase of handguns	N

Voting Studies

	Presidential Support		Party Unity		Conservative Coalition	
Year	**S**	**O**	**S**	**O**	**S**	**O**
1988	37	63	38	59	29	66
1987	37 †	61 †	28 †	65 †	62 †	38 †
1986	38	62	26	73	36	64
1985	35	61	34	62	33	67
1984	42	56	29	69	29	69
1983	48	50	33	64	35	64
1982	51	42	32	60	30	67
1981	55	39	39	58	35	63

† Not eligible for all recorded votes.

Interest Group Ratings

Year	ADA	ACU	AFL-CIO	CCUS
1988	75	25	50	64
1987	56	13	50	47
1986	70	18	64	39
1985	60	35	65	57
1984	70	25	62	69
1983	50	22	35	55
1982	70	14	60	52
1981	70	60	40	72

16 Charles B. Rangel (D)

Of Manhattan — Elected 1970

Born: June 11, 1930, New York, N.Y.

Education: New York U. School of Commerce, B.S. 1957; St. John's School of Law, LL.B. 1960.

Military Career: Army, 1948-52.

Occupation: Lawyer.

Family: Wife, Alma Carter; two children.

Religion: Roman Catholic.

Political Career: N.Y. Assembly, 1967-71; sought Democratic nomination for N.Y. City Council president, 1969.

Capitol Office: 2252 Rayburn Bldg. 20515; 225-4365.

In Washington: Not so long ago, a taste for cigars and hardy laughter were the kindred qualities of House Democratic leaders. But those days have passed, and so too, it seems, has Rangel's chance for a higher rung on the leadership ladder.

His climb was stalled in part by the same easygoing style that makes him a popular House member. At the start of the 100th Congress, Rangel lost a bid for majority whip after a campaign that came across as halfhearted. He was then denied the chief deputy whip's position, the next spot in the hierarchy. At the same time, Rangel lost his closest leadership ally with the retirement of Speaker Thomas P. O'Neill Jr. in 1986. While he remains a deputy whip, a middle-level leadership post he has held since 1983, the New Yorker now confronts a younger generation of Democrats clamoring for a chance at the top.

But there are other routes to power in the House, and in time, Rangel may ascend to one of the most coveted chairmanships, that of the powerful Ways and Means Committee. He is currently its No. 4 Democrat, behind three members who may leave Congress before he does.

In the meantime, Rangel can take satisfaction in the widespread attention now being paid to the impact of drugs on society. Chairman of the Select Committee on Narcotics since 1983, he was among the first politicians to decry the problem, which is severe in parts of his district.

Rangel played a role in passing both the 1986 and 1988 drug bills, although conservative forces took the 1988 House bill further than Rangel wanted it to go. Tapping election-year fears, the final bill carried a death penalty for major drug dealers and eased exclusionary rules to allow courtroom presentation of evidence seized without a search warrant. Though Rangel supported the bill, it was not entirely to his liking.

Though even the most vigilant legislator would have had trouble halting that juggernaut, that was not the first time Rangel was faulted for a laid-back style. "Charlie doesn't seem to know what it is he wants to be — mayor of New York, chairman of Ways and Means or Speaker of the House," said one New York Democrat.

Rangel's manner placed him at a disadvantage in the whip's race against Tony Coelho of California, who worked virtually non-stop to win the election, building on his success as chairman of the Democratic Congressional Campaign Committee. Rangel's principal argument — that electing a whip from New York would bring regional balance to the leadership — did not carry much weight.

Any chance Rangel might have had to catch up was undercut by the impression that in seeking a job that demands strong buttonholing skills, Rangel was simply not courting support as vigorously as Coelho. Rangel made a final tactical error, when he traveled to Asia with a congressional delegation not long before the vote. In the end, the race was not even close. Coelho got 167 votes to Rangel's 78.

On the heels of that loss, Rangel mounted a last-minute bid to reassert his seniority on Ways and Means and recapture the Health Subcommittee chairmanship, which he had held from 1979-81. But there was an incumbent in the post, Pete Stark of California, who lobbied hard to keep the job. His work paid off; committee Democrats voted 17-4 to retain Stark, leaving Rangel to continue as chairman of the less important Select Revenue Measures Subcommittee.

On the full committee, Rangel can be effective in dealing with the internal workings of the tax system. In the 99th Congress, Rangel's rapport with Chairman Dan Rostenkowski helped him win a prized place on the conference committee wrestling with tax code overhaul; that position enabled Rangel to promote aspects of tax revision helpful to his constituents.

But it is the drug issue for which Rangel is best known. He has warned repeatedly against any move toward legalization of narcotics. In

New York 16

Manhattan — Harlem

A territory once divided among four districts, Harlem today forms the core of just one. With its mainly minority population, that district, the 16th, is bedrock Democratic. Republican presidential candidates can count on little more than 15 percent of the vote here.

Home to wealthy whites in the 19th century, Harlem was transformed after World War I, as Southern blacks drawn by the prospect of jobs flocked to its low-rent housing units. Musicians such as Cab Calloway and Duke Ellington and writers such as James Baldwin and Ralph Ellison made it the center of American black cultural life; the parents of Ronald H. Brown, the current Democratic National Committee chairman, managed a thriving hotel near the famed Apollo Theater.

But Harlem lost this flashy veneer years ago. Modern-day Harlem is plagued by crime, drug problems, deteriorating housing and a lack of job opportunities. Its central business district along 125th Street is seedy. Polo Ground Towers and other low-income projects house many of the residents. Sugar Hill, once the home of black professionals, declined as many prosperous blacks gravitated to less troubled regions of the metropolitan area.

East Harlem, Italian until mid-century, now boasts the largest population of Puerto Ricans outside Puerto Rico. Beneath the elevated railroad tracks on Park Avenue lies La Marqueta, a diverse open retail market.

West of Harlem, across Morningside Park, is Columbia University, where a major student revolt in 1968 was sparked by the school's plans to build a new gymnasium despite the objections of many of the school's low-income black neighbors. Today Columbia is more aloof from the black community.

The 16th's Hispanic areas at the northern end of Manhattan lie east of Broadway in the Washington Heights and Inwood sections. Many of the residents come from South America.

While signs of Harlem's poverty are ubiquitous, there are also signs of change. Young white professionals have refurbished brownstones in areas such as the Mount Morris Park Historic District, and some middle-class blacks have begun to move back in. After years of dormancy, the Apollo Theater has reopened its doors.

Population: 516,405. White 126,438 (25%), Black 250,555 (49%), Other 8,539 (2%). Spanish origin 195,920 (38%). 18 and over 381,724 (74%), 65 and over 66,773 (13%). Median age: 32.

1984, he made an emotional appeal against a proposal to permit the use of heroin as a painkiller for dying patients, saying that to open the door even a bit was dangerous. When the issue of legalizing some narcotics came up in 1988, Rangel accused the idea's promoters of surrendering before the war was fought. He is equally adamant in his opposition to programs that provide intravenous drug users with free needles to combat the spread of AIDS.

Rangel is sometimes criticized for a lack of innovation in his "get tough" approach to drugs, but he fires back that a lack of funding and administrative follow-through are the biggest obstacles to progress. When Senate Republicans proposed financing the 1986 drug bill by allowing taxpayers to check off a box on their tax forms to earmark part of their refunds for anti-drug efforts, Rangel fumed. "I don't think this should be a volunteer effort. I don't see them proposing a tax checkoff for aid to the [Nicaraguan] contras."

Rangel denounced President Reagan when — less than three months after he signed the drug bill into law — his budget proposal called for sharp cuts in anti-drug spending.

Early in 1989, Rangel accompanied a state task force on a raid of New York City pharmacists who improperly billed Medicaid and doctors who over-prescribed amphetamines and barbiturates. Rangel called them "bums."

Rangel also plays an active role in House debates on South Africa. A strong advocate of tougher sanctions against the apartheid regime, Rangel authored a far-reaching provision enacted as part of the 1987 budget reconciliation to end foreign tax credits for income derived from South African holdings.

Rangel is widely regarded as the least ideological of the senior black members of Congress, the one most likely to choose modest but tangible help for his constituents over the opportunity to express outrage. As chairman of the Congressional Black Caucus in its early years, Rangel stressed the possibilities for legislative trading and compromise. "We don't have to walk away from people because we don't agree with them," he said.

At Home: In 1970 Rangel gave the *coup de grâce* to the fading political career of Harlem's flamboyant Rep. Adam Clayton Powell Jr. Accusing Powell of being an absentee, part-time representative and promising to work full time for his constituents, Rangel upset Powell in the Democratic primary.

Rangel had the backing of a coalition of younger black politicians who were tired of Powell's behavior and wanted someone who would work harder for blacks and for New York.

A high school dropout, Rangel joined the Army and fought in the Korean War. He then returned to Manhattan and entered college in his mid-20s. He got his law degree in 1960, and the next year was appointed as assistant U.S. attorney for the Southern District of New York.

In 1966 Rangel won a seat in the New York Assembly. Three years later, he made a quixotic bid for citywide office by running for City Council president in the Democratic primary on a ticket headed by U.S. Rep. James H. Scheuer. Rangel ran last in a field of six, but received publicity in black areas as the only citywide black candidate.

The following year, Rangel went after Powell. The incumbent's old coalition, built around the Abyssinian Baptist Church, of which he was pastor, and the Alfred E. Isaacs Democratic Club, could no longer carry the burden of his political reputation.

The veteran Democrat had been "excluded" from the 90th Congress on charges that he had misused committee funds for parties and travel to the Caribbean. The Supreme Court later ruled the exclusion unconstitutional, and Powell was seen as a martyr by constituents. But when he took a seat in the 91st Congress and then spent most of the following year out of the country, that view changed. Though the anti-Powell vote was split four ways, Rangel's coalition of younger blacks and liberal whites prevailed.

The primary win immediately established Rangel as the dominant political figure in his district. Rangel was endorsed by both the Democratic and Republican parties that November, and in every election since.

In recent years, Rangel has been one of a number of New York City leaders critical of Mayor Edward I. Koch and what they view as his antagonistic approach to minority issues. With his strong base in the black community and the potentially broad appeal of his anti-crime and anti-drug stands, Rangel was mentioned as a possible challenger to Koch in 1989. At first he did not discourage speculation, but he eventually endorsed Manhattan Borough President David Dinkins' prospective mayoral campaign.

Committees

Select Narcotics Abuse and Control (Chairman)

Ways and Means (4th of 23 Democrats)
Select Revenue Measures (chairman); Oversight

Elections

1988 General

Charles B. Rangel (D)	107,620	(97%)

1986 General

Charles B. Rangel (D)	61,262	(96%)

Previous Winning Percentages: **1984** (97%) **1982** (98%) **1980** (96%) **1978** (96%) **1976** (97%) **1974** (97%) **1972** (96%) **1970** (87%)

District Vote For President

	1988		1984		1980		1976	
D	113,324	(86%)	122,516	(83%)	108,892	(75%)	129,187	(82%)
R	16,996	(13%)	23,346	(16%)	24,017	(17%)	26,088	(17%)
I					9,471	(7%)		

Campaign Finance

	Receipts	Receipts from PACs		Expend-itures
1988				
Rangel (D)	$583,012	$358,875	(62%)	$479,427
1986				
Rangel (D)	$480,918	$305,749	(64%)	$375,344

Key Votes

1987

Raise speed limit to 65 mph	N
Approve Gephardt "fair trade" amendment	Y
Ban testing of larger nuclear weapons	Y
Delay "re-flagging" of Kuwaiti tankers	Y
Approve tax-raising deficit-reduction bill	Y

1988

Approve aid to Nicaraguan contras	N
Enact civil rights restoration bill over Reagan veto	Y
Kill 60-day plant-closing notification measure	N
Pass omnibus trade bill over Reagan veto	Y
Approve death penalty for drug-related murders	N
Bar federal funds for abortions in cases of rape and incest	?
Oppose seven-day waiting period for purchase of handguns	N

Voting Studies

	Presidential Support		Party Unity		Conservative Coalition	
Year	S	O	S	O	S	O
1988	14	71	80	2	5	87
1987	9	76	85	2	2	79
1986	17	73	89	2	4	92
1985	16	75	89	1	7	91
1984	23	67	84	4	8	85
1983	20	71	88	4	9	87
1982	31	69	87	5	10	88
1981	33	63	83	6	4	92

Interest Group Ratings

Year	ADA	ACU	AFL-CIO	CCUS
1988	85	0	100	31
1987	88	0	100	0
1986	100	0	93	11
1985	90	0	100	10
1984	90	0	92	27
1983	100	0	94	20
1982	100	0	95	19
1981	95	0	93	6

17 Ted Weiss (D)

Of Manhattan — Elected 1976

Born: Sept. 17, 1927, in Hungary.
Education: Syracuse U., B.A. 1951, LL.B. 1952.
Military Career: Army, 1946-47.
Occupation: Lawyer.
Family: Wife, Sonya Hoover; two children.
Religion: Jewish.
Political Career: N.Y. City Council, 1962-77; sought Democratic nomination for U.S. House, 1966, 1968.
Capitol Office: 2467 Rayburn Bldg. 20515; 225-5635.

In Washington: A House member typically earns the most publicity from working on his highest-profile committee, and Weiss — a sharp critic of U.S. foreign policy during the Reagan years — certainly gets his share of headlines as a member of the Foreign Affairs Committee. But Weiss' primary personal soapbox is his chairmanship of the lower-profile Government Operations Subcommittee on Human Resources and Intergovernmental Relations; it gives the liberal activist Weiss an outlet for his crusades on health-care issues.

Though the panel he chairs has no specific legislative mandate, it has wide berth to oversee and investigate the functions of a number of federal departments, including Health and Human Services. Weiss has held a series of hearings and released a number of reports aimed at exposing what he views as weaknesses in federal health-care funding and regulation. He has also established himself as a watchdog of the Food and Drug Administration (FDA), which, among its other functions, approves and regulates marketing of new therapeutic drugs.

One health issue in which Weiss has a particular interest is combating AIDS; his district on the West Side of Manhattan has large homosexual and minority populations, which have been hard hit by the disease. Weiss has frequently called the federal bureaucracy to task over what he describes as its slow response to the spread of AIDS.

During the 100th Congress, Weiss called for an expedited process for testing experimental drugs used to contain the deadly disease, and lambasted the Reagan administration for not providing enough funding for the National Institute for Allergy and Infectious Diseases (NIAID). It was at a Human Resources Subcommittee hearing in April 1988 that NIAID director Anthony S. Fauci said clinical trials of several AIDS drugs had been delayed because of staff shortages; that led to a congressional move to fund 200 more research positions in fiscal 1989.

Weiss regarded the beefed-up research effort as far preferable to the administration's April 1987 regulation allowing the Office of Management and Budget (OMB) to supersede the FDA by releasing unapproved experimental drugs for use by the critically ill. To Weiss, the rule had more to do with the Reagan administration's urge to deregulate business — in this case, the drug industry — than its response to the urgency of AIDS.

Though gentlemanly in person and well-liked by most colleagues, Weiss can confront adversarial witnesses with accusatory tones. When an official of the Health Resources and Services Administration told Weiss' subcommittee in February 1989 that the agency had not projected the number of health-care workers needed to deal with the growing number of children with AIDS, Weiss responded angrily: "The problem I have with all of you is that all we get back when we ask for action are words. If the Public Health Service does nothing else, the least it can do is project what the needs will be. Is that too much to ask?"

On other health issues, Weiss can be just as hard-line. At a May 1988 hearing, he blamed the FDA for lax supervision that allowed several drug companies to commit possibly "criminal behavior" by allegedly failing to provide required documents on possible severe or fatal reactions caused by medicines for which they sought approval.

The subcommittee's intergovernmental-relations mandate has faded in recent years with the death of the revenue-sharing program. During the early 1980s, Weiss fought off Reagan's efforts to kill the multibillion-dollar program, which funneled federal money to 39,000 local governments with no strings attached. But in 1986, opposition from House leaders and mounting bipartisan concern about federal deficits overpowered the program, which was allowed to expire.

As on Government Operations, Weiss on Foreign Affairs found plenty to dislike in Reagan administration policy. When Reagan sent U.S. troops to occupy the Caribbean island nation of Grenada in 1983, Weiss and seven other liberal members called for his impeach-

New York 17

West Side Manhattan — Part of the Bronx

The West Side is a citadel of unalloyed liberalism. Some of the most active members of its aging Jewish community have lifelong roots in left-wing politics, and the more than one-quarter of the district that is black or Hispanic reinforces that tradition. Despite their national difficulties in recent years, Democratic presidential candidates regularly take over 70 percent of the 17th District vote.

Much of the West Side has been upgraded from the slum conditions prevalent a generation ago. In recent years, its roomy apartments have attracted those tired of the more cramped conditions closer to the East River. The elderly Jewish people who line its park benches observe a passing parade that includes chic young professionals as well as street people.

Other West Side neighborhoods never deteriorated at all. Central Park West still contains some of the most graceful apartment buildings in the city. The century-old Dakota is popular among celebrities; former Beatle John Lennon resided there until his 1980 assassination at its front door.

Many more unknown performers and artists live in the district, waiting tables and hoping for a break. Although the Broadway theaters and most of the city's cultural institutions are in the 15th District, the 17th includes the Lincoln Center for the Performing Arts. Above the Upper West Side, the district threads along the Hudson and includes the parts of Inwood and Washington Heights west of Broadway. Many elderly Jews live here, and many Puerto Ricans as well. The 17th extends north and east to take in the Bronx community of Williamsbridge, a middle-class black section.

The district also covers Greenwich Village and the Wall Street area to the south. The Village's bohemian culture has not been much diluted by the upper-income people who have moved in and made it fashionable during the past two decades. The Village was once an Italian political stronghold. Today, homosexuals are a more important political faction, though gay-rights activism, on the upswing until the mid-1980s, has been overshadowed by the priority of dealing with the AIDS crisis.

Rapid growth over the past 10 years has turned lofts in the former industrial districts of Soho and Tribeca into residences for artists and upscale Manhattanites. Few people live around Wall Street, though that is changing with the development of Battery Park City, a large residential-office complex on landfill in the Hudson.

Population: 516,239. White 377,091 (73%), Black 81,675 (16%), Other 17,676 (3%). Spanish origin 80,203 (16%). 18 and over 442,060 (86%), 65 and over 79,933 (15%). Median age: 35.

ment. Weiss was also persistent in his scathing rejection of aid to the Nicaraguan contras, saying the policy had "taken us closer and closer to direct military involvement.'"

Though military aid to the contras ended during the 100th Congress, Weiss was no more supportive of the 1989 compromise agreement between the Bush administration and congressional leaders, which extended humanitarian aid to the contras for another year. "If the intention of the administration is to keep them alive as a military presence or threat, then they're going to have a lot of trouble and lose a lot of support," said Weiss, who voted against the compromise.

Weiss' anti-militarist tone carries over to his stands on defense issues. In each of the past few years, Weiss submitted an amendment on the House floor calling for a ban on deployment of the submarine-based Trident II missile. He is part of a cadre of arms control advocates who say the missile's extreme accuracy — it is designed to score direct hits on Soviet ballistic missile silos — could provoke the Soviets to launch a first strike in a crisis. However, this is a minority position in the House: Weiss' 1988 amendment to kill the Trident II was defeated by a 79-307 vote.

Another of Weiss' pet ideas is his proposed Defense Economic Adjustment Act. The bill would create a Cabinet-level Defense Economic Adjustment Council to draw up plans for converting military facilities and defense plants to civilian uses, and would set up Alternative Use Committees at large defense facilities. Conservatives deride the measure as part of a typical liberal effort to eliminate defense programs and convert military funding to domestic purposes. But Weiss insists that "in a new era of superpower relations and zero or negative growth in defense budgets, economic conversion has become a virtual necessity."

At Home: Weiss has never been as flamboyant as his predecessor, Bella S. Abzug, a liberal Democratic activist and a national feminist leader. But in pursuing liberal political goals, Weiss has been no less determined.

A long-term survivor of the Byzantine Democratic politics of Manhattan's West Side, Weiss lost three competitive primaries before making it to the House on his fourth try.

He was a 38-year-old city councilman, allied with the reform faction of the Democratic Party, when he ran as a peace candidate against machine-backed Rep. Leonard Farbstein in the 1966 Democratic primary. Weiss appeared to have fallen 151 votes short that June, but he got another chance in a special primary in September after the state Supreme Court found 1,153 invalid ballots and ordered a new election. He lost that one, however, by more than 1,000 votes, and when he tried again in 1968, the organization brought Farbstein a 3,000-vote victory.

After that, it was eight years before Weiss saw an opening. When Farbstein finally lost in 1970, it was to Abzug, and only when she ran for the Senate in 1976 did Weiss re-enter the picture. By then, his dues were more than paid. In an unusual show of unity for West Side politics, he won nomination without opposition. When Abzug lost her Senate primary, some party figures suggested that Weiss accept a judgeship and let her reclaim the district. But after 10 years of waiting, he was not about to withdraw.

Weiss cruised to victory that November, riding the district's overwhelming Democratic tide. He has had no trouble since; his 84 percent showing in 1988 continued his unbroken string of winning general elections with better than 80 percent of the vote.

Weiss was hospitalized for chest pain in the fall of 1986, and underwent coronary bypass surgery in early October. He recovered without incident.

Weiss' unswerving liberal principles are popular among the majority of his constituents. His list of organization memberships reads like a litany of liberal causes: the New Democratic Coalition; Americans for Democratic Action; American Civil Liberties Union; National Association for the Advancement of Colored People; and Amnesty International, U.S.A.

Committees

Foreign Affairs (17th of 28 Democrats)
Human Rights and International Organizations; International Operations; Western Hemisphere Affairs

Government Operations (5th of 24 Democrats)
Human Resources and Intergovernmental Relations (chairman); Employment and Housing

Select Children, Youth and Families (6th of 18 Democrats)

Elections

1988 General		
Ted Weiss (D)	157,339	(84%)
Myrna C. Albert (R)	29,156	(16%)
1988 Primary		
Ted Weiss (D)	29,064	(88%)
Harry C. Fotopoulos (D)	4,043	(12%)
1986 General		
Ted Weiss (D)	95,094	(86%)
Thomas A. Chorba (R)	15,587	(14%)

Previous Winning Percentages: **1984** (82%) **1982** (85%) **1980** (82%) **1978** (85%) **1976** (83%)

District Vote For President

	1988	1984	1980	1976
D	168,115 (78%)	165,064 (74%)	104,832 (62%)	131,226 (72%)
R	44,841 (21%)	55,903 (25%)	47,241 (28%)	48,786 (27%)
I			12,630 (8%)	

Campaign Finance

	Receipts	Receipts from PACs	Expend-itures
1988			
Weiss (D)	$171,815	$64,890 (38%)	$170,567
Albert (R)	$3,685	0	$2,851
1986			
Weiss (D)	$277,935	$95,927 (35%)	$242,860
Chorba (R)	$19,790	0	$13,305

Key Votes

1987	
Raise speed limit to 65 mph	X
Approve Gephardt "fair trade" amendment	Y
Ban testing of larger nuclear weapons	Y
Delay "re-flagging" of Kuwaiti tankers	Y
Approve tax-raising deficit-reduction bill	Y
1988	
Approve aid to Nicaraguan contras	N
Enact civil rights restoration bill over Reagan veto	Y
Kill 60-day plant-closing notification measure	N
Pass omnibus trade bill over Reagan veto	#
Approve death penalty for drug-related murders	N
Bar federal funds for abortions in cases of rape and incest	N
Oppose seven-day waiting period for purchase of handguns	N

Voting Studies

	Presidential Support		Party Unity		Conservative Coalition	
Year	**S**	**O**	**S**	**O**	**S**	**O**
1988	15	72	80	5	5	84
1987	13	85	88	4	0	95
1986	12	79	81	4	4	76
1985	23	76	93	3	5	95
1984	21	74	88	7	2	93
1983	15	78	87	6	9	87
1982	18	56	74	4	7	79
1981	36	64	89	10	4	96

Interest Group Ratings

Year	ADA	ACU	AFL-CIO	CCUS
1988	75	0	100	21
1987	92	0	100	14
1986	95	0	79	25
1985	100	5	100	18
1984	100	8	77	31
1983	100	0	100	20
1982	90	0	95	24
1981	100	0	87	5

18 Robert Garcia (D)

Of the Bronx — Elected 1978

Born: Jan. 9, 1933, New York, N.Y.

Education: Attended City College of New York; Community College of New York; RCA Institute, E.E. 1957.

Military Career: Army, 1950-53.

Occupation: Computer engineer.

Family: Wife, Jane Lee; two children, four stepchildren.

Religion: Pentecostal.

Political Career: N.Y. Assembly, 1965-67; N.Y. Senate, 1967-78.

Capitol Office: 2338 Rayburn Bldg. 20515; 225-4361.

In Washington: The dark cloud of the Wedtech scandal moved over Garcia during the 100th Congress, ruining what should have been his crowning moment as a House member. After a long struggle, Garcia saw his "enterprise zone" plan for inner-city development become law in February 1988. But by that time, Garcia had been implicated in the wide-ranging influence-peddling scheme; in November, just after his election to a sixth term, he and his wife were indicted on bribery charges.

The indictment had a tangible impact on Garcia's House status: At the start of the 101st Congress, he was forced to yield his position as a subcommittee chairman on the Banking Committee. But as he awaited his federal trial, scheduled to begin in September 1989, Garcia had much more to worry about than his immediate political future. If convicted on bribery, extortion and other felony charges, Garcia could be sentenced to more than 20 years in prison.

Though Garcia had not faced ethical problems before, he was an early target for the Wedtech probe. Wedtech, a small machine shop that grew into a major defense contractor, was based in Garcia's South Bronx district. And Garcia, the only member of Puerto Rican ancestry in Congress, was an advocate of the minority set-aside contracts that built Hispanic-run Wedtech into a multimillion-dollar concern.

After failing to meet deadlines on a contract for military engines, Wedtech unraveled. The Justice Department uncovered a massive bribery-and-extortion network reaching into the executive branch and Congress. In a bleak omen for Garcia, his Bronx colleague, 19th District Democrat Mario Biaggi, was convicted in August 1988 on Wedtech bribery charges and was forced to resign from the House.

It was during Biaggi's trial that Garcia's name was first publicly mentioned in connection with Wedtech; a company executive said he had paid Garcia for his help in lobbying for contracts. Though Garcia denied this, Wedtech was an issue in his 1988 primary, his toughest-ever as an incumbent. Two weeks after a routine November re-election in his solidly Democratic district, Garcia was indicted.

Federal prosecutors charged that Garcia and his wife had received over $80,000 from Wedtech between 1984 and 1986; the money was allegedly laundered by attorney Ralph Vallone Jr., who was also indicted. Garcia and his wife were also charged with accepting other payments, loans and gifts from Wedtech officials.

Following the indictment, Garcia emotionally stated he would fight to clear himself. "I maintain my innocence and that of my wife and pledge to fight this case with all of my God-given strength," he said.

But the criminal charges were clearly a blow to the prestige of Garcia, a two-time Korean War Bronze Star winner, the second mainland Puerto Rican to be elected to Congress, and a leading House advocate of Hispanic issues.

During the 100th Congress, Garcia chaired the Banking Subcommittee on International Finance, Trade and Monetary Policy. For the 101st Congress, that subcommittee was merged with another panel dealing with international finance, and its chair was taken by a Democrat more senior than Garcia. Seniority would have given Garcia the right to lead a newly created Subcommittee on Policy Research and Insurance, which has a mandate to study such urban-related issues as housing and community development. But Garcia's legal problems forced him to stand aside; the acting chairman is Alabama Democrat Ben Erdreich.

Garcia has tried to present a business-as-usual attitude. He has appeared at news conferences praising the public-private partnerships, which he helped to put together, that have built over 1,000 housing units in the South Bronx and other devastated New York City neighborhoods. He has proposed a program providing student aid in exchange for voluntary national

New York 18

South Bronx

The acres of abandoned and vandalized buildings in the South Bronx have made it the nation's symbol of contemporary urban decay. In the most blighted sections, Mott Haven and Melrose, one can sometimes walk for blocks meeting no one but the occasional stray dog.

A quick glance at Census Bureau statistics draws the rough parameters of the region's plight. The 18th has a lower per capita income than any other district in the country, and more people live below the poverty line here than anywhere else.

For more than a dozen years, presidential candidates have made a point of pledging to help the South Bronx, but little has happened to reverse or even contain its decline. Community self-help organizations exercise some political power, but this is limited because of the low voting participation among the Puerto Ricans and other Hispanics who live here.

The scene of a mass exodus during the 1970s, the South Bronx district by 1980 had seen its official census population shrink to less than half its 1970 count. Garcia felt this was because many of its "undocumented" residents, fearing deportation or the authorities in general, avoided the census-takers. The South Bronx was flooded then by illegal aliens from Latin America and the Caribbean. Since the census, there has been a substantial influx of legal newcomers from Cuba, classified as refugees.

In any case, the district had to double in size in redistricting to meet population requirements. Maintaining the ethnic makeup was not difficult — map makers were able to shift substantial numbers of Hispanics from adjoining constituencies. When redrawn in the early 1980s, the district was 51 percent Hispanic.

The additions to the district give it slightly more middle-class territory. Fordham Heights has a considerable Italian population remaining, and Jews still live in East Tremont.

The prevalence of low-income, minority-group residents gives the Democrats an unassailable edge in the 18th. Democratic presidential nominees Michael S. Dukakis in 1988 and Walter F. Mondale in 1984 topped 80 percent there.

Population: 517,278. White 126,174 (24%), Black 226,213 (44%), Other 6,089 (1%). Spanish origin 265,768 (51%). 18 and over 327,637 (63%), 65 and over 35,026 (7%). Median age: 25.

service, a counterpoint to the plan by Sen. Sam Nunn of Georgia and Rep. Dave McCurdy of Oklahoma, which would make such aid contingent on mandatory national service.

Garcia, along with New York Democrat Charles B. Rangel, has also submitted legislation to put more "teeth" in the federal enterprise zone plan passed in the 100th Congress. It is this piece of legislation that Garcia is most closely associated with. Garcia in 1980 first proposed the enterprise zone plan, which would give private firms tax breaks and other incentives to invest in depressed urban areas; his cosponsor was conservative upstate Republican Jack F. Kemp, with whom Garcia agreed on few other issues. President Reagan, who had made a well-publicized visit to the South Bronx in his 1980 presidential campaign, adopted the idea.

During the early 1980s, Reagan's strong support actually was a millstone for Garcia's program. While a number of states and localities adopted their own versions of enterprise zones, the concept floundered in Congress: Though Garcia himself was a strong critic of Reagan's overall urban policy, many urban-program advocates viewed the plan as a Reagan front to cover efforts to slash housing and community development funding. Finally, at the start of the 100th Congress, Garcia found a "fast track" — a long-stalled housing bill that was suddenly moving to passage. The bill, signed by Reagan after nearly a year of discussion, included enterprise zones. But it was not all that Garcia hoped for: The provision authorized the secretary of housing and urban development (HUD) to designate 100 such zones, in which businesses would be provided with tax and regulatory incentives by state and local governments — but it contained no federal tax incentives.

The 1989 Garcia-Rangel bill would provide federal tax benefits to businesses willing to relocate to the enterprise zones. The plan runs up against the hard realities of the deficit; the tax-writing committees are skeptical of any revenue-losing measure.

But Garcia now has a friend in a high place. Kemp, who was appointed HUD secretary by President Bush, has stated his intention to keep enterprise zones at the center of the urban-issues agenda. It is not clear at this point, though, whether Garcia will be able to play a leading role in the debate.

At Home: Garcia followed his friend Herman Badillo — the original mainland Puerto Rican member of Congress — into the House in a 1978 special election. Badillo had resigned to become deputy mayor of New York City, and a district Democratic convention under the control of the Bronx County organization selected state Assemblyman Louis Nine as the Democratic nominee to replace him. But reform Democrats joined in an unusual coalition with the Liberal and Republican parties to back Garcia, then a state senator.

The decisive factor in the contest was Badillo, who walked the streets of the South Bronx with Garcia, investing in him the influence he had built up as Bronx borough president and as a Puerto Rican pioneer in the House. Garcia carried the district with 55 percent of the vote. Although he was elected on the Liberal and GOP lines, Garcia said he would caucus with the Democrats.

Garcia was re-elected that November with 98 percent, and won with ease until 1988. In that year, though, the allusions to Garcia's Wedtech ties during the Biaggi trial gave him an aura of vulnerability that two Democratic primary challengers sought to exploit.

The strongest of the two, community health center director Pedro Espada Jr., described himself as a reform candidate, hoping to energize voters already wearied by a series of Bronx corruption scandals. The 34-year-old Espada drew local media attention with his door-to-door campaign, but Garcia responded with a vigorous effort of his own, and he prevailed by 61-27 percent.

The son of a minister, Garcia was born and raised in the Bronx. He left to serve as an Army infantryman in the Korean War, then returned to New York to go to school. Garcia attended City College and New York Community College before taking training as a computer programmer at the RCA Institute.

Garcia made his first bid for public office in 1964, winning election to the New York Assembly. In 1966, he became the first Puerto Rican elected to the state Senate. He rose through the ranks to become deputy minority leader of the chamber in 1975, and served in that capacity until he ran for Congress in 1978.

Committees

Banking, Finance and Urban Affairs (10th of 31 Democrats)
Economic Stabilization; Housing and Community Development; Policy Research and Insurance

Post Office and Civil Service (4th of 15 Democrats)
Census and Population; Postal Operations and Services

Elections

1988 General

Robert Garcia (D)	75,459	(91%)
Fred Brown (R)	5,764	(7%)

1988 Primary

Robert Garcia (D)	16,868	(61%)
Pedro Espada Jr. (D)	7,531	(27%)
Ismael Betancourt Jr. (D)	3,433	(12%)

1986 General

Robert Garcia (D)	43,343	(94%)
Melanie Chase (R)	2,479	(5%)

Previous Winning Percentages: **1984** (89%) **1982** (99%) **1980** (98%) **1978** (98%) **1978 *** (55%)

* *Special election.*

District Vote for President

	1988	1984	1980	1976
D	92,069 (86%)	94,474 (81%)	79,399 (73%)	104,520 (79%)
R	13,051 (12%)	22,290 (19%)	24,351 (22%)	27,059 (21%)
I			3,572 (3%)	

Campaign Finance

	Receipts	Receipts from PACs	Expend-itures
1988			
Garcia (D)	$306,376	$187,075 (61%)	$448,391
1986			
Garcia (D)	$409,702	$150,900 (37%)	$314,485

Key Votes

1987

Raise speed limit to 65 mph	N
Approve Gephardt "fair trade" amendment	Y
Ban testing of larger nuclear weapons	Y
Delay "re-flagging" of Kuwaiti tankers	+
Approve tax-raising deficit-reduction bill	Y

1988

Approve aid to Nicaraguan contras	N
Enact civil rights restoration bill over Reagan veto	Y
Kill 60-day plant-closing notification measure	N
Pass omnibus trade bill over Reagan veto	Y
Approve death penalty for drug-related murders	N
Bar federal funds for abortions in cases of rape and incest	X
Oppose seven-day waiting period for purchase of handguns	-

Voting Studies

	Presidential Support		Party Unity		Conservative Coalition	
Year	S	O	S	O	S	O
1988	13	69	77	2	5	79
1987	11	76	79	2	9	84
1986	13	81	83	2	2	84
1985	21	75	82	1	4	87
1984	30	62	81	4	7	86
1983	16	68	83	1	9	84
1982	26	58	77	4	10	82
1981	25	50	81	3	3	76

Interest Group Ratings

Year	ADA	ACU	AFL-CIO	CCUS
1988	85	4	100	31
1987	100	0	100	8
1986	95	0	100	17
1985	95	0	100	19
1984	90	0	92	50
1983	80	5	100	26
1982	95	11	95	24
1981	70	7	100	0

19 Eliot L. Engel (D)

Of the Bronx — Elected 1988

Born: Feb. 18, 1947, New York, N.Y.
Education: Hunter-Lehman College, B.A. 1969; Lehman College, M.A. 1973; New York Law School, J.D. 1987.
Occupation: Public official; teacher.
Family: Patricia Ennis; two children.
Religion: Jewish.
Political Career: N.Y. Assembly, 1977-88.
Capitol Office: 1407 Longworth Bldg. 20515; 225-2464.

The Path to Washington: Engel's 1988 election was predicated on an unusual risk.

He announced in June 1988 that he was giving up his state Assembly seat for a primary challenge to Democratic Rep. Mario Biaggi, who was then on trial in federal court for bribery, conspiracy and extortion. Biaggi was still highly popular in the 19th District despite a separate 1987 conviction for accepting illegal gratuities, but Engel ventured that the incumbent eventually would be brought down by his ongoing legal problems.

Engel gambled right. Following his August conviction in the case involving Wedtech Corp., a now-defunct Bronx defense contractor, Biaggi resigned the seat he had held for nearly 20 years. Though Biaggi's name remained on the primary- and general-election ballots due to a legal technicality, Engel easily won both contests to claim the seat.

Ironically, Engel first entered elective politics in much the same manner. In 1977, the public school guidance counselor won a special election to succeed an assemblyman who had resigned after a bribery conviction. Though Engel was a Democratic leader in the huge Co-op City apartment complex, he ran on the Liberal Party line and defeated the Democratic organization candidate.

That campaign enabled Engel to establish his credentials in the "reform" wing of a Bronx Democratic Party that became scandal-plagued over the next decade.

Engel, however, was not always at odds with the party establishment during his political career. During his 1982 effort to fend off a primary challenge from a New York City councilman, Engel received an endorsement from a familiar organization man: Mario Biaggi.

Though he was a low-key figure in Albany, Engel rose to positions that would serve him well in his congressional race. He chaired the Assembly subcommittee on "Mitchell-Lama" programs, which provide subsidies for moderate-income housing. As chairman of a committee on drug and alcohol abuse, Engel promoted rehabilitation funding and tough penalties against drug dealers.

When the 1988 House campaign began, Biaggi seemed nearly as formidable as ever. As he had since his first re-election in 1970, Biaggi received the endorsement not only of the Bronx Democratic Party, but also of the local GOP. Though several Democratic officials sensed that Biaggi might be vulnerable and tested the waters, only Engel and former state Rep. Vincent A. Marchiselli took the leap. Marchiselli had been unseated in a 1984 primary and lost a 1986 comeback attempt.

Biaggi's second conviction and resignation opened the door to Engel, whose unblemished victory record gave him an advantage over Marchiselli. However, Engel had to contend with Biaggi's specter: Because the incumbent had resigned after the candidate-withdrawal deadline, he remained on the Democratic primary ballot and on the GOP line in the general election.

Engel waged a vigorous campaign, with an emphasis on areas in the West Bronx and Yonkers outside his base. He stressed his legislative experience, eschewing harsh criticisms of Biaggi (who did not campaign) in order to avoid antagonizing his loyalists. Despite speculation that there would be a large "tribute" vote for Biaggi, Engel won nearly 50 percent of the primary vote; Marchiselli and Biaggi split the rest.

The fall campaign played much like the primary. Engel won with 56 percent, though Biaggi's 27 percent was not unimpressive for a convicted former member. Engel took nearly two-thirds of the Bronx vote, but got only a plurality in Yonkers, where he was not well-known, and where voter anger over a federal housing desegregation plan helped the Conservative Party candidate garner 15 percent.

In early 1989, Engel was one of only two Democrats in the class of 1988 to win a spot on the Foreign Affairs Committee. Though the panel's subject matter might seem a bit removed from the Bronx, the sizable Jewish population in Co-op City has considerable interest in U.S. policy in the Middle East.

New York 19

South Yonkers; East and Central Bronx

Stretching from the eastern extremes of the Bronx to the Westchester County city of Yonkers, the 19th is a collection of ethnic neighborhoods, most of them with strong community ties and conservative social values.

The district has three arms that reach out for blue-collar Democrats. One goes south to Throgs Neck, a community of Italian- and Irish-Americans that lends its name to a bridge connecting the Bronx with Queens. Another extends west to Belmont, home to Italians and Hispanics. The third runs north to take in much of Yonkers, which in appearance, ethnicity and economic status is closer to the Bronx than to the rest of suburban Westchester.

Included in the district is Co-op City, a huge high-rise project in the East Bronx which is Engel's political base. Its 35 buildings house more than 35,000 residents, many of whom are Jewish; blacks and Hispanics have also moved into Co-op City in large numbers recently.

Minority-group residents make up about 20 percent of Yonkers' total, and are mainly isolated in the western part of the city. In 1986, U.S. District Court Judge Leonard B. Sand decided this was not an accident. He ruled the city had located low-income housing so as to isolate minorities, and ordered the city immediately to construct 200 units of low-income housing in mostly white neighborhoods.

The order spurred a backlash, mainly from blue-collar ethnics who had moved to Yonkers in the "white flight" from New York City. After activists disrupted a series of City Council meetings, their supporters on the council voted to stonewall the judge's order. But when Sand, in 1988, instituted fines that could have bankrupted Yonkers, the council gave in and agreed to build the housing. The final outlines of the desegregation plan remain in dispute.

Population: 516,498. White 399,252 (77%), Black 67,720 (13%), Other 8,218 (2%). Spanish origin 81,422 (16%). 18 and over 398,578 (77%), 65 and over 90,103 (17%). Median age: 36.

Committees

Foreign Affairs (24th of 28 Democrats)
Africa; Arms Control, International Security and Science; International Economic Policy and Trade

Select Hunger (17th of 18 Democrats)

Small Business (27th of 27 Democrats)
Environment and Labor; Regulation, Business Opportunity and Energy

Campaign Finance

	Receipts	Receipts from PACs	Expend-itures
1988			
Engel (D)	$187,088	$99,600 (53%)	$183,145
Biaggi (R)	$152,548	$36,950 (24%)	$468,631

Elections

1988 General		
Eliot L. Engel (D)	77,158	(56%)
Mario Biaggi (R)	37,454	(27%)
Martin J. O'Grady (RTL)	11,271	(8%)
Robert Blumetti (C)	11,182	(8%)
1988 Primary		
Eliot L. Engel (D)	12,181	(48%)
Vincent A. Marchiselli (D)	6,700	(26%)
Mario Biaggi (D)	6,525	(26%)

District Vote For President

	1988	1984	1980	1976
D	84,084 (55%)	86,353 (48%)	64,980 (51%)	86,329 (60%)
R	67,775 (45%)	93,165 (52%)	54,709 (43%)	55,862 (39%)
I			5,859 (5%)	

20 Nita M. Lowey (D)

Of Harrison — Elected 1988

Born: July 5, 1937, Bronx, N.Y.
Education: Mount Holyoke College, B.A. 1959.
Occupation: Public official.
Family: Husband, Stephen Lowey; three children.
Religion: Jewish.
Political Career: N.Y. assistant secretary of state, 1985-87.
Capitol Office: 1313 Longworth Bldg. 20515; 225-6506.

The Path to Washington: A neighborly act in 1974 led Lowey to a career in state government and then a 1988 upset victory over Republican Rep. Joseph J. DioGuardi. It helped a lot that the neighbor she aided 14 years ago was Mario M. Cuomo.

Now a national force as the two-term Democratic governor of New York, Cuomo then was a Queens attorney running in a primary for lieutenant governor. Lowey, who had been active in civic organizations, opened her home for a meeting of his supporters.

Though Cuomo lost the primary, his campaign inspired Lowey, who had a degree in political science but had shelved plans for a professional career to raise a family. When Cuomo was appointed by Democratic Gov. Hugh Carey as New York secretary of state, he hired Lowey to work in his department's anti-poverty division. She also worked in Cuomo's unsuccessful 1977 campaign for New York City mayor, and was appointed in 1978 as deputy director of the department's economic opportunity division.

When Cuomo ran for governor in 1982, Lowey stayed on in the secretary of state's office, specializing in economic development and neighborhood preservation. Her duties included lobbying Congress to fund the New York State Coastal Management Program. In 1985, she was promoted to the job of assistant to Secretary of State Gail S. Shaffer, and also named to the state Child Care Commission.

In the meantime, Lowey and her husband, an attorney, moved to the affluent Westchester County suburb of Rye. Her state job gave her contacts with local officials, and her work with organizations such as the YWCA, Westchester Jewish Community Services and the League of Women Voters earned her friends who helped her build a political base when she set her sights on Congress.

Thanks to her network, Lowey survived a September Democratic primary against Hamilton Fish III, publisher of *The Nation* magazine and son of a House member, and businessman Dennis Mehiel.

DioGuardi, a conservative-leaning Republican, had been aided by the 1984 Reagan landslide when he won the seat long held by liberal Democrat Richard L. Ottinger, who retired that year. DioGuardi's victory in his 1986 re-election had much to do with his success at portraying his foe, former Democratic representative and liberal activist Bella S. Abzug, as an extremist and a carpetbagger. She had moved into the 20th to challenge him.

Against Lowey, DioGuardi again tried the tactic of portraying his opponent as an ideological fringe figure, clashing with her on issues such as abortion and the strategic defense initiative. But Lowey came across as a more mainstream candidate than Abzug had, and her residency was never in question.

With DioGuardi unable to make his challenger the issue, the campaign centered on differing views of his House record. DioGuardi spent more than $1.5 million to portray himself as a leader on such issues as drug abuse, housing and Long Island Sound pollution. Lowey, however, spent $1.3 million overall in making her point that DioGuardi supported Reagan defense spending plans at the expense of local needs. She also claimed that the incumbent — who touted his background as a certified public accountant — spent much of his congressional time on a quixotic effort to have the federal budget run on business principles.

In the end, though, ethical questions doomed DioGuardi. In mid-October, a chain of Westchester newspapers reported that the owner of a large New Rochelle auto dealership — a DioGuardi campaign official — had funnelled $57,000 in corporate contributions to DioGuardi's campaign through his employees. Though he denied any knowledge of the alleged pass-through scheme, the revelations put DioGuardi on the defensive and turned the tide in Lowey's favor.

The combined campaign expenditures of Lowey and DioGuardi amounted to nearly $2.9 million, making this the second most expensive House election in the country.

New York 20

Central and Southern Westchester County

The elitist Westchester County that John Cheever wrote about still exists, replete with fieldstone patios, gin-and-tonics and Republican loyalties. But the county has always been more varied than that picture implies. Westchester's politics are determined at least as much by liberal Jewish suburbanites and more conservative middle-class Italian neighborhoods as by WASP enclaves.

The overall suburban profile of the 20th tends to give Republicans a slight edge in presidential voting and in competitive statewide contests. George Bush edged Michael S. Dukakis in the district with 52 percent of the vote in 1988, extending the GOP winning streak here to four presidential elections.

There are several communities in today's Westchester where mansions, with estate-like grounds, still outnumber the split-levels. Bronxville had a 1985 per capita income of over $34,000; Larchmont and Rye nudged $30,000. These places have traditionally been Republican bastions, and for the most part, they remain so. One exception, though, is Scarsdale, which had a per capita income of $38,000, but whose large Jewish population provides a liberal counterbalance to its upper-class Republicanism.

Though these towns have much of the 20th District's wealth, they are modest in size. Much of the district's population is in the more densely populated and economically mixed cities.

White Plains (population 45,000) is the county seat and its political nexus. The city, which had turned seedy by the 1960s, was revived by urban renewal and is now a thriving corporate and retail center. Its populace is a mix of upper-middle-class suburbanites and lower-income residents, many of whom are black.

The district then travels down crowded Central Avenue (N.Y. 100) to Yonkers, and takes in a chunk made up mainly of middle-class Jewish and Italian-American communities. In between, there are such comfortable suburbs as Hartsdale and Edgemont. But the road itself is lined with a solid phalanx of shopping centers, and a prolific number of Chinese restaurants catering to the suburban clientele.

To the east of Yonkers are the two largest cities contained wholly within the 20th. New Rochelle (69,000) was once a resort town on the Long Island Sound, and was the archetypal suburbia as portrayed on the old "Dick Van Dyke Show." But while it still has its upper reaches, the city has a more working-class feel and a growing minority population.

These demographics are even more prevalent in Mount Vernon (68,400), which has much more in common with the neighboring Bronx than the rest of Westchester. By 1980, blacks had gained an edge over the largely Italian white population; Mount Vernon is currently headed by a black mayor. The city usually provides the Democrats with a strong base vote.

Population: 516,507. White 416,373 (81%), Black 80,822 (16%), Other 9,703 (2%). Spanish origin 28,907 (6%). 18 and over 388,570 (75%), 65 and over 69,213 (13%). Median age: 35.

Committees

Education and Labor (15th of 22 Democrats)
Elementary, Secondary and Vocational Education; Human Resources; Postsecondary Education

Merchant Marine and Fisheries (25th of 26 Democrats)
Coast Guard and Navigation; Oceanography

Select Narcotics Abuse and Control (18th of 18 Democrats)

Campaign Finance

	Receipts	Receipts from PACs	Expenditures
1988			
Lowey (D)	$1,338,147	$164,175 (12%)	$1,309,873
DioGuardi (R)	$1,553,890	$374,079 (24%)	$1,567,129

Elections

1988 General

Nita M. Lowey (D)	102,235	(50%)
Joseph J. DioGuardi (R)	96,465	(47%)

1988 Primary

Nita M. Lowey (D)	10,533	(44%)
Hamilton Fish III (D)	8,578	(36%)
Dennis Mehiel (D)	4,849	(20%)

District Vote For President

	1988	1984	1980	1976
D	94,237 (48%)	99,756 (43%)	65,774 (37%)	89,956 (47%)
R	102,392 (52%)	129,323 (56%)	92,933 (52%)	102,539 (53%)
I			15,010 (9%)	

21 Hamilton Fish Jr. (R)

Of Millbrook — Elected 1968

Born: June 3, 1926, Washington, D.C.
Education: Harvard College, A.B. 1949; New York U., LL.B. 1957.
Military Career: Naval Reserve, 1944-46.
Occupation: Lawyer.
Family: Wife, Mary Ann Knauss; four children.
Religion: Episcopalian.
Political Career: GOP nominee for U.S. House, 1966.
Capitol Office: 2269 Rayburn Bldg. 20515; 225-5441.

In Washington: When Fish joined the Judiciary Committee as a House freshman in 1969, he was in step with the numerous moderate Republicans on the panel who supported civil rights and other liberal social causes. Today, Fish is alone at the top, the committee's senior Republican and its lone defender of the old GOP traditions.

Having weathered this sea change, Fish faces a new Democratic chairman in the 101st Congress, Jack Brooks of Texas. While the previous chairman, Peter W. Rodino Jr., was far more liberal than Fish, his cautious, dignified style suited the New Yorker's patrician sensibilities. Brooks and Fish may be more ideologically compatible, but the Texan is a far more crusty character than the mild-mannered Fish is accustomed to dealing with.

His experience during the early and mid-1980s, however, might gird Fish for coping with Brooks. During those years, Fish presided awkwardly over the aggressively conservative GOP bloc on Judiciary, a group committed to causes such as promoting school prayer and fighting abortion. Though he did not agree with the conservatives on much, Fish won the respect of his fellow Republicans largely on the strength of his good word and decency.

Those traits, however, were not always enough to keep tensions from boiling over. In the 99th Congress, Republicans on Judiciary protested that the Democrats were stacking the subcommittees with more of their number than the makeup of the House dictated. While Fish tried to avoid a confrontation with Rodino, his GOP troops would not budge, and the Judiciary subcommittee assignments were delayed for weeks before a compromise could be reached.

In the late 1980s, with the conservative social agenda stalled in Congress and other issues moving to the fore, Fish has been able to play an important role in legislative bargaining. Democrats have long looked to him to give their proposals at least a veneer of bipartisanship. In the 100th Congress, when several key measures were under consideration, Democratic vote counters considered Fish essential, estimating that his influence might sway the votes of two dozen or so GOP members.

Fish's pivotal role was never more evident than during debate on amending the Fair Housing Act, which had stood at a partisan impasse for nearly a decade. Despite widespread agreement that the Department of Housing and Urban Development (HUD) needed more authority to enforce the law, no consensus could be reached on how to achieve that goal.

In 1988, the Judiciary Committee approved a bill, with Fish's support, to set up a new system of administrative-law judges to hear cases of alleged housing discrimination. But debate over whether this would subject a defendant to fines without benefit of a jury trial was so contentious that the bill appeared doomed.

Fish, however, initiated negotiations between civil rights advocates and Democrats on the left, and Realtors and the Reagan administration on the right. Soon his role became so critical that the bill's chief sponsor, Californian Don Edwards, said he would not bring the measure to the floor without Fish's seal of approval. After more than six weeks of talks, the two sides agreed to allow either HUD or the alleged discriminator to opt for a full jury trial instead of adjudication by the administrative judge. This breakthrough ensured House passage two days later; the bill was signed into law soon afterward.

Fish was long an ardent supporter of legislation to overturn the Supreme Court's *Grove City* ruling, which substantially narrowed the enforcement scope of four key civil rights laws. When Judiciary took up the legislation in 1986, Fish and Hank Brown of Colorado were the only Republicans to vote for it. Two years later — when House leaders bypassed Judiciary and brought a Senate bill directly to the floor — Fish was among those credited with engineering approval of the bill and the subsequent presidential veto override.

Fish finds common ground with his conservative GOP colleagues on issues involving Justice Department operations, as well as on mat-

New York 21

Hudson Valley — Poughkeepsie

Hamilton Fish Sr. used to infuriate Franklin D. Roosevelt all the more because he was FDR's congressman — the Roosevelt family home at Hyde Park was part of the Fish constituency, and Fish won re-election easily every two years.

The last redistricting severed that link with history by removing Hyde Park from the 21st. But the district has changed very little in partisan terms. Most of the communities that returned the elder Fish to Washington are as solidly Republican as they were 40 years ago. The only real difference is in ideology. The current constituency is far closer to the moderate politics of Hamilton Fish Jr. than to those of his conservative father.

The 21st starts in the New York suburbs of upper Westchester County, where moderate GOP politics gets a good response from "Rockefeller Republicans" in Bedford and other comfortable towns. To the north, the subdivisions of Putnam County are also wellsprings of GOP votes; the only county entirely within the 21st, Putnam gave 66 percent of its vote to George Bush in 1988.

The still-rural northern parts of Putnam give way to similar terrain in Dutchess County, a Republican territory stretching from the Hudson River to the Connecticut border that is dotted with country mansions.

Poughkeepsie, with 30,000 residents, is the district's best-known city. An important river port and conduit for Dutchess County farm products in the late 18th and early 19th centuries, Poughkeepsie today relies more heavily on electronics equipment and agricultural machinery. The Dutchess County seat is a blend of ethnic Democrats and academics from Vassar College.

Dutchess County also includes Beacon, whose population has rebounded modestly in recent years after a long-term decline caused by the loss of its hat industry. Directly across the Hudson, in Orange County, is the struggling city of Newburgh, which has also suffered a long-term industrial decline. More picturesque is the campus of the U.S. Military Academy at West Point, located on a series of hills overlooking the Hudson.

Environmental concerns animate the politics of this district on the fringe of a vast New York metropolitan region. The Hudson River gentry united in the early 1970s to stop a planned hydropower project at Storm King. And controversy plagues the nuclear power complex at Indian Point on the Hudson. Often shut down due to technical problems, the plant sits atop a geological fault line 35 miles from New York City.

Population: 516,778. White 471,247 (91%), Black 34,028 (7%), Other 5,336 (1%). Spanish origin 15,971 (3%). 18 and over 365,060 (71%), 65 and over 53,214 (10%). Median age: 31.

ters of copyright and antitrust law. When Judiciary debated price-fixing legislation in 1987, Fish offered an amendment that in effect would have made it more difficult for plaintiffs to press lawsuits alleging illegal price fixing. After Fish's language was defeated on a party line vote, he worked out a compromise with committee Democrats protecting the right of a defendant to get a dismissal early in the litigation process if the evidence shows "no inference of concerted action."

Prior to taking over the senior GOP position on the full committee, Fish held the ranking post on the Immigration Subcommittee, where he worked to allow more Cambodian refugees into the country and to expand various refugee assistance programs. During the major immigration debates of the 1980s, Fish was not the primary GOP strategist, but he lent assistance without upstaging the leading sponsors. Late in 1986, after a decisive House vote appeared to kill the immigration bill, Fish joined in four days of negotiation that led to a critical compromise.

Fish was a strong supporter of the immigration bill's basic approach of granting amnesty to many illegal aliens already in the country while penalizing employers who hired those arriving illegally in the future. In 1986, he co-authored a letter in *The New York Times* defending employer sanctions as the key to immigration reform. The sanctions went into effect late in 1988.

Against the grain of recent Republican orthodoxy, Fish has long been a firm supporter of the Equal Rights Amendment. But when Democrats tried to bring the ERA to the floor in 1983 under a fast-track procedure barring amendments and providing less than an hour of debate, Fish balked. He denounced the move as a political gimmick designed to frustrate legitimate discussion, and he voted against it. That defection was a key setback for ERA advocates, and the measure failed by six votes.

At Home: Fish came to the House with one of the most impressive pedigrees in American politics. His great-grandfather Hamilton Fish was governor of New York, U.S. senator and secretary of state. His grandfather Hamilton Fish was a U.S. representative. And his father, Hamilton Fish Sr., spent 20 years in the House arguing for American business and against President Franklin D. Roosevelt's New Deal.

Hamilton Fish Jr., now the veteran 21st District House member, had been engaged in civic activities in his ancestral Dutchess County for years when his opportunity came to run for the House in 1966. Historically Republican, the district had gone Democratic in 1964, and the GOP was determined to retake it.

Fish engaged in a highly publicized "patrician primary" against Alexander Aldrich, cousin of Gov. Nelson A. Rockefeller. Fish won, but was beaten in November by the Democratic incumbent, Joseph Y. Resnick.

In 1968 Resnick ran for the Senate. Fish again won his primary, this time against a then-little-known lawyer, G. Gordon Liddy. Fish won the seat, and has held it comfortably ever since.

In 1988, Fish's son, Hamilton Fish III, tried to extend the family's political reach by running for the 20th District House seat in southern Westchester County. However, the youngest Fish was of a far more liberal bent — he had been publisher of *The Nation,* a liberal opinion journal — and entered the Democratic primary, aiming for a shot at GOP Rep. Joseph J. DioGuardi.

Fish Jr. greeted his son's decision with equanimity, stating that he was supportive of his personal goals even though he could not campaign for him as a member of the opposition party. But Fish Sr., ever the Republican warrior at age 100, denounced his grandson for his "leftist" views and his betrayal of the family's Republican roots. The family was spared a deepening of the quarrel, though; Fish III finished second in the primary to Nita M. Lowey, who went on to upset DioGuardi.

Committees

Judiciary (Ranking)
Economic and Commercial Law (ranking); Courts, Intellectual Property and the Administration of Justice; Immigration, Refugees and International Law

Joint Economic
Education and Health; Investment, Jobs and Prices; National Security Economics

Elections

1988 General		
Hamilton Fish Jr. (R)	150,443	(75%)
Lawrence W. Grunberger (D)	47,294	(23%)
1986 General		
Hamilton Fish Jr. (R)	102,070	(77%)
Lawrence W. Grunberger (D)	28,339	(21%)

Previous Winning Percentages: **1984** (78%) **1982** (75%) **1980** (81%) **1978** (78%) **1976** (71%) **1974** (65%) **1972** (72%) **1970** (71%) **1968** (48%)

District Vote For President

	1988	1984	1980	1976
D	83,635 (38%)	71,014 (32%)	60,495 (31%)	80,741 (42%)
R	136,078 (62%)	150,345 (68%)	115,998 (59%)	110,434 (57%)
I			17,012 (9%)	

Campaign Finance

	Receipts	Receipts from PACs	Expend-itures
1988			
Fish (R)	$357,841	$196,388 (55%)	$277,680
1986			
Fish (R)	$246,927	$140,224 (57%)	$217,637
Grunberger (D)	$6,341	$250 (4%)	$6,340

Key Votes

1987	
Raise speed limit to 65 mph	N
Approve Gephardt "fair trade" amendment	N
Ban testing of larger nuclear weapons	Y
Delay "re-flagging" of Kuwaiti tankers	N
Approve tax-raising deficit-reduction bill	N
1988	
Approve aid to Nicaraguan contras	Y
Enact civil rights restoration bill over Reagan veto	Y
Kill 60-day plant-closing notification measure	Y
Pass omnibus trade bill over Reagan veto	Y
Approve death penalty for drug-related murders	Y
Bar federal funds for abortions in cases of rape and incest	?
Oppose seven-day waiting period for purchase of handguns	Y

Voting Studies

	Presidential Support		Party Unity		Conservative Coalition	
Year	**S**	**O**	**S**	**O**	**S**	**O**
1988	37	59	37	59	58	42
1987	45	54	40	56	72	28
1986	40	56	33	60	56	38
1985	45	46	42	45	44	44
1984	50	43	38	51	53	37
1983	54	37	45	47	55	40
1982	45	44	41	51	49	44
1981	57	38	48	46	40	56

Interest Group Ratings

Year	ADA	ACU	AFL-CIO	CCUS
1988	60	32	86	71
1987	44	35	44	53
1986	45	32	57	44
1985	35	40	80	55
1984	40	23	42	69
1983	20	43	29	74
1982	45	43	55	33
1981	50	57	27	78

22 Benjamin A. Gilman (R)

Of Middletown — Elected 1972

Born: Dec. 6, 1922, Poughkeepsie, N.Y.
Education: U. of Pennsylvania Wharton School, B.S. 1946; New York Law School, LL.B. 1950.
Military Career: Army Air Corps, 1943-45.
Occupation: Lawyer.
Family: Wife, Rita Gail Kelhoffer; four children, two stepchildren.
Religion: Jewish.
Political Career: N.Y. Assembly, 1967-73.
Capitol Office: 2185 Rayburn Bldg. 20515; 225-3776.

In Washington: Gilman has a wide range of legislative interests and tries to involve himself in all of them. His position as a senior member on two standing committees (Foreign Affairs and Post Office and Civil Service) and two select committees (Hunger and Narcotics Abuse) has enabled Gilman to register his views on foreign aid, U.S.-Israeli relations, terrorism, drugs, famine relief, census overcounts, and sundry other issues.

Though his efforts to cover this vast territory generate a succession of foreign fact-finding trips, news conferences and press releases, Gilman is regarded as much more of a plugger than a policy leader. He rarely rises to speak in debate; when he does, he usually reads at ponderous length from a prepared text. On Foreign Affairs — his major assignment — Gilman's moderate, bipartisan approach excludes him from the ideological combat that engages the committee's most recognized figures.

But as a tenured member, Gilman is not without influence. During the 100th Congress, he was named as ranking Republican on a special task force empaneled to review the U.S. foreign assistance program, which has been criticized for years as unwieldy and inefficient. A task force report, issued in February 1989, has become the basis for debate in the 101st Congress on the proposed revamping of the foreign aid system.

The task force, which was chaired by Indiana Democrat Lee H. Hamilton, described foreign aid as "vital to promoting U.S. foreign policy and domestic interests," and said it "contributes much to U.S. development interests and to U.S. relationships with recipient countries." But the panel also concluded that "the program is hamstrung by too many conflicting objectives, legislative conditions, earmarks and bureaucratic red tape." The task force suggested a fresh start by enacting an International Economic Cooperation Act of 1989 to replace the much-amended Foreign Assistance Act of 1961.

Gilman agreed with most of the report's conclusions, but expressed reservations about a proposal to end completely the practice of congressional "earmarking" of aid to nations of strategic importance. Though he said the practice — which is criticized for limiting presidential flexibility in targeting foreign aid — should be restricted, he stressed the need to maintain earmarks for Greece, Egypt and Israel "to make clear our unequivocal support for the security of those countries."

That Israel is on Gilman's priority list is no surprise. As ranking Republican on the Foreign Affairs Subcommittee on Europe and the Middle East, Gilman is a staunch supporter of aid to Israel, and an opponent of weapons sales that might threaten that nation. He spoke out against the sale of Stinger anti-aircraft missiles to Saudi Arabia in 1986. "A 'moderate' Saudi Arabia has not been active in the Middle East peace process," Gilman said during floor debate. "That same 'moderate,' well-armed Saudi Arabia will probably not be any more active."

Gilman's interest in Israel's security and in the general Middle East situation has made him a maven on the subject of terrorism. Gilman and Republican John Miller of Washington attached an amendment to the 1985 foreign aid bill that allowed the president to ban all trade with a country that supports or advocates terrorism. The amendment, aimed mainly at the Libyan regime of Muammar el-Qaddafi, was used in early 1986 by President Reagan as justification for his cutoff of trade with Libya and his order for all American citizens to leave that nation.

Gilman also uses his Foreign Affairs position to advance his interest in human rights, especially the cause of Jewish "refuseniks" who have been frustrated in their effort to emigrate from the Soviet Union. In 1986, Gilman was involved in American efforts to obtain the freedom of jailed Soviet dissident Anatoly Shcharansky. The New York Republican flew to East Berlin and met with East German lawyer Wolfgang Vogel, who later took part in negotiations that led to Shcharansky's release.

New York 22

Lower Hudson Valley

Starting in a patch of graceful old Westchester County suburbs, the 22nd crosses the Hudson River and moves west through the outer suburbia of Rockland and Orange counties to the Catskill Mountain resorts in lower Sullivan County. A Democratic registration advantage benefits the more popular Democratic statewide officials, including Sen. Daniel Patrick Moynihan and Gov. Mario M. Cuomo. But the suburban/exurban district goes Republican for president and backed GOP Sen. Alfonse M. D'Amato in 1986; it has been most hospitable territory for Gilman.

The Westchester section of the district, a place of tree-lined streets, contains white-collar New York City commuters and ethnic blue-collar families who fled the city and try to avoid its concerns. These suburbs — Hastings, Irvington, Tarrytown — have been densely populated for decades. There is a solid Jewish element here.

Rockland and Orange used to be bucolic, but that changed substantially during the big growth years of the 1970s. Rockland's numerous New York City commuters and a large blue-collar work force help make the county an electoral battleground. But in Orange, where there is still some farming done, GOP tendencies are stronger.

Jewish retirees help keep Democrats competitive in Sullivan County. Along Route 17 in the southern part of the county is the lower end of the Catskill Borscht Belt, which contains the Concord Hotel and other noted resorts.

Population: 516,625. White 464,735 (90%), Black 35,226 (7%), Other 9,216 (2%). Spanish origin 20,961 (4%). 18 and over 363,184 (70%), 65 and over 52,470 (10%). Median age: 32.

Outside of Foreign Affairs, Gilman fills his busy calendar with the business of the Post Office and Civil Service Committee, where he became ranking member in the 101st Congress. On the most contentious issue before that committee in recent years, Gilman expresses skepticism over proposals to adjust the 1990 census to account for the expected omission of millions of people, mainly minority-group urban residents. "No matter how accurate, any adjustment will raise suspicions about tampering and manipulation," Gilman said during a 1988 debate.

Gilman also has been active as ranking Republican on the Select Committee on Narcotics Abuse and Control, a post he relinquished at the start of the 101st Congress. Higher-profile House members may have dominated the scene during the highly charged debates on the 1986 and 1988 omnibus drug bills. But Gilman points out that his position on the select committee gave him a role in the early efforts to crack down on illegal drugs, well before it became a hot political issue.

Gilman also has a strong interest in nutrition issues. In 1984 he and Texas Democrat Mickey Leland sponsored legislation to establish a 17-member Select Committee on Hunger to study and make recommendations on hunger and malnutrition in the United States and other countries. Though other committees held jurisdiction over the issue, Gilman said creating the select panel would help by bringing more visibility to the problem. The measure passed, 309-78, and Gilman took a seat on the committee.

At Home: Gilman quietly worked his way through the ranks of appointive and elective office to reach the House in 1972.

Shortly after receiving his law degree, he was appointed a deputy assistant attorney general of New York, and in two years he became an assistant attorney general. Later, he served as attorney for New York state's Temporary Commission on the Courts and counsel to the Assembly's Committee on Local Finance.

Following reapportionment of the state Legislature in the mid-1960s, Gilman won a newly created Assembly seat from Orange County. After three terms in the Assembly, he decided to challenge Democratic Rep. John G. Dow.

Viewed as a moderate, Gilman had to defeat conservative builder Yale Rapkin for the Republican nomination. Strong support from his home base of Orange County allowed him to beat Rapkin, who was from Rockland County.

Though Dow was the incumbent, Gilman had demographics on his side in the general election. Dow had been elected in a historically Republican district in the 1964 Johnson landslide, and redistricting in 1972 had made the district even more Republican. Gilman won comfortably even though Rapkin siphoned off 13 percent as the Conservative Party candidate.

His re-elections went smoothly for a decade, until his district was combined with that of Democratic Rep. Peter A. Peyser in 1982. In what legislative map makers of both parties billed as a "fair fight," Peyser had the party-registration advantage and Gilman the edge in familiar territory. Territory won out.

It was a far angrier campaign than Gilman

had been used to. Peyser went after the Republican on the war-and-peace issue, criticizing him for opposing a nuclear-weapons freeze and for backing military aid to El Salvador. Gilman put aside his soft-spoken ways and attacked Peyser as an "ultra-liberal Democratic congressman" and the "candidate of Teddy Kennedy and Tip O'Neill." Unions, which had backed Gilman before, now sided with Peyser.

Gilman's close ties to his geographically dominant Rockland-Orange base paid off. Because of his good constituent service and outspoken opposition to rail and utility rate increases, he carried those two counties solidly. The fact that Gilman is Jewish helped him in a normally Democratic portion of Sullivan County that was placed in the district for the first time. Peyser took the Westchester County portion, his home base, but it was not enough.

Having survived the test posed by redistricting, Gilman in 1984 reverted to his practice of winning easily, taking over two-thirds of the vote against Democratic attorney Bruce Levine. He repeated that feat in both 1986 and 1988 against Democrat Eleanor F. Burlingham, an elderly environmental activist.

Committees

Post Office and Civil Service (Ranking)
Investigations

Foreign Affairs (2nd of 18 Republicans)
Europe and the Middle East (ranking); International Operations

Select Hunger (4th of 12 Republicans)
Task Force: International

Select Narcotics Abuse and Control (2nd of 12 Republicans)

Elections

1988 General

Benjamin A. Gilman (R)	144,227	(71%)
Eleanor F. Burlingham (D)	54,312	(27%)

1986 General

Benjamin A. Gilman (R)	94,244	(70%)
Eleanor F. Burlingham (D)	36,852	(27%)

Previous Winning Percentages: **1984** (69%) **1982** (53%) **1980** (74%) **1978** (62%) **1976** (65%) **1974** (54%) **1972** (48%)

District Vote For President

	1988	1984	1980	1976
D	97,516 (43%)	88,142 (40%)	91,403 (34%)	123,237 (46%)
R	129,595 (57%)	132,044 (60%)	147,407 (55%)	142,770 (53%)
I			22,397 (8%)	

Campaign Finance

	Receipts	Receipts from PACs	Expend-itures
1988			
Gilman (R)	$428,176	$166,797 (39%)	$411,056
Burlingham (D)	$10,342	0	$10,427
1986			
Gilman (R)	$345,314	$129,771 (38%)	$305,258
Burlingham (D)	$17,418	0	$16,066

Key Votes

1987

Raise speed limit to 65 mph	N
Approve Gephardt "fair trade" amendment	Y
Ban testing of larger nuclear weapons	N
Delay "re-flagging" of Kuwaiti tankers	N
Approve tax-raising deficit-reduction bill	N

1988

Approve aid to Nicaraguan contras	Y
Enact civil rights restoration bill over Reagan veto	Y
Kill 60-day plant-closing notification measure	N
Pass omnibus trade bill over Reagan veto	Y
Approve death penalty for drug-related murders	Y
Bar federal funds for abortions in cases of rape and incest	N
Oppose seven-day waiting period for purchase of handguns	Y

Voting Studies

	Presidential Support		Party Unity		Conservative Coalition	
Year	**S**	**O**	**S**	**O**	**S**	**O**
1988	41	54	39	58	55	42
1987	38	61	33	60	58	42
1986	43	53	31	67	66	30
1985	44	55	43	53	60	38
1984	45	55	43	57	58	42
1983	57	43	42	56	61	38
1982	53	42	41	56	45	52
1981	51	29	42	48	48	51

Interest Group Ratings

Year	ADA	ACU	AFL-CIO	CCUS
1988	55	42	93	50
1987	68	26	88	21
1986	40	55	92	28
1985	45	43	82	27
1984	40	33	62	44
1983	45	57	65	45
1982	50	38	75	36
1981	45	66	43	72

23 Michael R. McNulty (D)

Of Green Island — Elected 1988

Born: Sept. 16, 1947, Troy, N.Y.
Education: College of the Holy Cross, A.B. 1969.
Occupation: Public official.
Family: Wife, Nancy Ann Lazzaro; four children.
Religion: Roman Catholic.
Political Career: Green Island supervisor, 1970-77; Green Island mayor, 1977-83; N.Y. Assembly, 1983-89; Democratic nominee for N.Y. Assembly, 1976.
Capitol Office: 1431 Longworth Bldg. 20515; 225-5076.

The Path to Washington: Among the freshmen in the 101st Congress, none received his party's nomination as effortlessly as McNulty. New York's July candidate filing deadline had already passed when Democratic Rep. Samuel S. Stratton, a 30-year House member, announced his retirement. Democratic county leaders in the 23rd met within hours of the announcement and selected McNulty, a young political veteran, to replace Stratton on the ballot.

Though some local Democrats groused about the selection procedure, the choice was vindicated in November: McNulty defeated Republican Peter Bakal with 62 percent of the vote.

McNulty says that serving in Congress has been a lifelong goal, but he did not expect to have the chance so soon. Stratton, a member of the House Armed Services Committee and a conservative on defense issues, had seen his name come up in reports on the Pentagon procurement scandal, but he had filed to run for a 16th term and was expected to win. Then, just before the state deadline for candidates to withdraw, Stratton announced he was retiring, citing health reasons. Since the filing deadline had passed, state law authorized party officials to choose his replacement.

Despite the suddenness of these events, there was no real surprise in the Democrats' choice of McNulty, a three-term state legislator and an elected official for nearly 20 years.

Along with his own credentials, McNulty benefited from the large network of contacts developed by his family, which has been influential in Albany County politics — and virtually dynastic in their home base of Green Island — for more than a half-century. McNulty's grandfather was elected town tax collector in 1914, and went on to serve as town supervisor, county board chairman and county sheriff. McNulty's father was supervisor for eight years, mayor for 16 years and county sheriff for six.

McNulty joined his elders in 1969, winning a seat on the town board at age 22. While in this post, he waged his only unsuccessful campaign, a 1976 challenge to a Republican assemblyman. He recouped the next year by winning a contest for Green Island mayor, then won an Assembly seat in 1982 after a remap created a solidly Democratic district.

McNulty did not amass much seniority in his brief tenure in Albany, but he got involved in a number of policy areas, sitting on committees dealing with corrections, state-local relations and government employees, and serving as chairman of the Transportation Capital Improvements panel. McNulty mainly followed his party's leadership on votes, and had the support of the state's Liberal Party. One area of divergence from the party line was abortion, which he opposes.

In his House campaign, McNulty said he would pattern himself after Stratton, a liberal on domestic issues, but a hawk on defense. McNulty said he had no major differences with Stratton on defense, and said his goal was a seat on Armed Services, the committee that had enabled Stratton not only to convey his defense views, but also to oversee the interests of the Watervliet Arsenal and other local defense facilities.

In the November campaign, Republican Bakal said he was closer to Stratton on defense, but McNulty responded with an advertisement featuring an endorsement from Stratton. Attacking on another front, Bakal called for action on acid rain. But McNulty earned the support of environmental groups.

At the beginning of the 101st Congress, McNulty got his committee wish, taking one of only two seats on Armed Services that went to freshmen.

New York 23

Hudson and Mohawk Valleys — Albany; Schenectady

State bureaucrats, blue-collar workers and a strong party organization give Democrats a big edge in Albany County, site of New York state's capital city. The vote there, combined with the Democratic leanings of industrial workers elsewhere in the district, make the 23rd a pleasant place for Democrats up and down the ticket.

Michael S. Dukakis easily carried the district with 57 percent of the vote in 1988; Democratic Sen. Daniel Patrick Moynihan did even better. Despite his delayed start brought about by veteran Rep. Samuel S. Stratton's late retirement announcement, McNulty swept all four district counties by wide margins.

McNulty's base is in Albany County, where his family members have held political office for over 70 years. Though he comes from the small village of Green Island (population 2,600), the former state assemblyman is well-known in Albany, the district's dominant city with 97,000 residents.

Albany's most familiar location is the mammoth state office complex named for longtime Republican Gov. (and later Vice President) Nelson A. Rockefeller (the expensive project was derided at the time of its inception as Rockefeller's monument to himself). The center stands out in an otherwise plain city with a large working-class contingent.

Democratic candidates usually dominate Albany County, which provides about three-fifths of the 23rd District vote. Dukakis won 59 percent there in 1988, and McNulty took 65 percent. Moynihan really cleaned up, winning 74 percent in his landslide Senate win.

The 23rd reaches across the Hudson River to take in a piece of Rensselaer County, including the aging industrial city of Troy (population 54,000). Also the site of Rensselaer Polytechnic Institute, Troy is strongly Democratic. McNulty carried the Rensselaer section of the district by nearly 2-to-1.

From the Albany-Troy area, the district heads north and west along the Mohawk River, picking up another industrial city, Schenectady, along the way. That city maintains its history as a company town: Thousands of its residents work for General Electric, assembling turbines, generators and other products. Democrats again hold the edge in Schenectady, though a tradition of Republican voting among the city's Italian-Americans tempers Democratic margins somewhat. Dukakis took Schenectady County with a modest 52 percent; McNulty won 56 percent.

The district also takes in a small piece of Montgomery County, including the city of Amsterdam (21,000). Rocked by the closing of its Mohawk Carpet plant in the early 1960s, Amsterdam today is sustained by smaller-scale industry.

Population: 516,943. White 482,010 (93%), Black 27,101 (5%), Other 4,688 (1%). Spanish origin 6,432 (1%). 18 and over 389,983 (75%), 65 and over 73,332 (14%). Median age: 32.

Committees

Armed Services (31st of 31 Democrats)
Readiness; Research and Development

Select Hunger (15th of 18 Democrats)
Task Force: International

Small Business (22nd of 27 Democrats)
Exports, Tax Policy and Special Problems; Procurement, Tourism and Rural Development; Regulation, Business Opportunity and Energy

Campaign Finance

	Receipts	Receipts from PACs		Expenditures
1988				
McNulty (D)	$314,940	$141,975	(45%)	$306,072
Bakal (R)	$167,450	$8,625	(5%)	$174,790

Elections

1988 General

Michael R. McNulty (D)	145,040	(62%)
Peter M. Bakal (R)	89,858	(38%)

District Vote For President

	1988	1984	1980	1976
D	140,440 (56%)	120,950 (47%)	120,535 (48%)	121,113 (47%)
R	106,755 (43%)	135,744 (53%)	98,824 (40%)	133,750 (52%)
I			24,591 (10%)	

24 Gerald B.H. Solomon (R)

Of Glens Falls — Elected 1978

Born: Aug. 14, 1930, Okeechobee, Fla.
Education: Attended Siena College, 1949-50; St. Lawrence U., 1952-53.
Military Career: Marine Corps, 1951-52.
Occupation: Insurance salesman.
Family: Wife, Freda Parker; five children.
Religion: Presbyterian.
Political Career: Warren County Legislature, 1968-72; N.Y. Assembly, 1973-79.
Capitol Office: 2265 Rayburn Bldg. 20515; 225-5614.

In Washington: A staunch conservative and a Reagan administration loyalist, Solomon was rewarded by the Republican leadership with an assignment to the House Rules Committee at the start of the 101st Congress. But the move did not come without a cost: Solomon had to give up his seats on the Foreign Affairs Committee, a forum for his anti-communist rhetoric, and Veterans' Affairs, where the strait-laced ex-Marine was one of the most stalwart defenders of veterans' benefit programs.

Coming to Rules at a time of high Republican turnover — of the four GOP members in the 100th Congress, only ranking Republican James H. Quillen of Tennessee remains — Solomon will play a larger role than a new arrival otherwise might. And it is likely that the hard-charging, ultra-serious Solomon will raise his voice when he thinks the nine-member Democratic majority is unfairly stacking the deck against Republican legislative prerogatives.

Now entering his second decade in the House, the upstate New York Republican has exhibited two rather different legislative personalities in the past. He can either be the crusading Solomon of Foreign Affairs, where his fierce denunciation of liberal views often irritated those across the aisle, or the Solomon of Veterans' Affairs, where he showed himself willing and able to work with the equally pro-vet Democrats who inhabit the committee.

Solomon leaves Veterans' Affairs just after his signal achievement, and his most notable show of bipartisan cooperation. In 1987, he submitted a bill embodying one of his long-held goals, the elevation of the Veterans Administration to Cabinet-level status. But when Texas Democrat Jack Brooks — then the chairman of the Government Operations Committee — submitted his own bill, Solomon signed on and worked for its passage.

The enactment of the bill was cinched when President Reagan climbed aboard in November 1987. Solomon and other advocates had gone to the White House for a pre-Veterans Day ceremony, hoping to lobby the president, a longtime opponent of expanding the federal bureaucracy. But Reagan surprised his visitors by expressing strong support for the proposal. "We came here to sell you a bill of goods, and you were already sold," Solomon told Reagan.

Only when Reagan proposed reductions in veterans' programs as part of his overall budget cutbacks did Solomon publicly disagree with his party's leader. Even then, he did so with a muted voice. He described Reagan's fiscal 1988 VA budget proposal as "expected ... in these times of necessary frugality," but added, "If it is too lean, it should be fine-tuned."

A corollary of Solomon's respect for veterans is his disdain for those who shirk military duty. Since 1982, Solomon has successfully sponsored amendments barring men who avoid their draft-registration requirements from receiving federal student aid, job training funds, and contracted defense work. "The rights of citizenship in this country of ours carry with them certain duties," Solomon told an audience in 1986, "among them that of being there when your country needs you. I did it. So did many of you. And I don't want one dime of your money going to those who don't."

Solomon's strongest words, though, were saved for Foreign Affairs, where he regularly excoriated committee Democrats for being too hard on American allies and too soft on anti-American regimes and insurgent movements. One of the staunchest supporters of the Nicaraguan contras, Solomon charged during one of the debates on cutting off U.S. aid to the contras that the committee was "about to sell the United States down the drain and is aiding and abetting the spread of communism in Central America."

A December 1986 appearance by Marine Lt. Col. Oliver L. North before the Foreign

New York 24

Upper Hudson Valley — Saratoga Springs

Anchored in the developing suburbia of the Albany-Schenectady-Troy area, the 24th is one of the most consistently Republican districts in the state.

GOP presidential candidates win easily here: In 1984, President Reagan took 69 percent of the 24th District vote, defeating Democrat Walter F. Mondale by nearly 90,000 votes. George Bush could not match Reagan's numbers in 1988, but still carried the district with 59 percent even as Democrat Michael S. Dukakis won the state. Democratic Sen. Daniel Patrick Moynihan's landslide 1982 and 1988 re-elections against weak Republican opponents marked the only times the 24th has strayed from the GOP column in contests for federal office since 1976.

Growth in the tri-cities area's suburbs made the 24th one of only six New York districts that registered a population increase during the 1970s. Such suburban towns as Greenbush, Half Moon and Clifton Park reliably give comfortable margins to GOP candidates.

Democrats running in the district used to find consolation in the city of Troy, a community of 56,000, packed with blue-collar residents involved in its heavy industry. But 1982 redistricting moved Troy to the neighboring 23rd. Pockets of blue-collar Democratic voting remain in Glens Falls (Warren County), Hudson (Columbia County), and Rensselaer.

The 24th dips south to take in the upper part of Dutchess County, where the landed gentry maintained their estates. Hyde Park, the home of President Franklin D. Roosevelt, overlooks the Hudson River in Dutchess County.

Despite the suburban growth, agricultural pursuits still occupy much of the 24th. Dairy farming is a mainstay of the local economy. Columbia County, in the district's southern arm, specializes in horse breeding. The Catskill Mountains of Greene County and the Adirondacks of Warren County are year-round resort areas. Lake George, in the district's northern end, is popular for boating and fishing.

But Saratoga Springs attracts the most notice from the outside world. Located about 30 miles north of Albany up Interstate 87, the old town is widely known for its mineral spas, elegant architecture and beautiful race track. The resort also has developed into a regional winter-sports center, with speed skating, cross-country skiing and snowshoe competitions luring crowds of sports fans.

Population: 515,614. White 504,100 (98%), Black 7,664 (2%). Spanish origin 4,313 (1%). 18 and over 364,047 (71%), 65 and over 62,425 (12%). Median age: 31.

Affairs Committee during early House deliberations on the Iran-contra affair provided a revealing glimpse of Solomon. Some members criticized North, who at the time was invoking his Fifth Amendment rights to avoid answering committee questions. But Solomon, whose 24th District includes North's hometown, heaped praised on his fellow Marine and ideological soul mate. "You are truly a great American, Colonel, and we back home deeply admire and respect your past history and what you've done for your country," Solomon said.

Early in 1989, Solomon acted in behalf of another ideological ally, fellow Foreign Affairs Republican Henry J. Hyde of Illinois. Solomon sought to nominate Hyde for the open GOP whip post. Hyde demurred, however, saying he would not run as long as his home-state colleague, Edward Madigan, was in the race. Nonetheless, Solomon said he would nominate Hyde for the job. But the morning of the vote, Hyde prevailed upon Solomon and other supporters not to submit his name for whip.

Solomon is as clearly opposed to leftist-oriented insurgent groups as he is supportive of groups like the contras. During 1988 debate on a bill to toughen sanctions against South Africa, Solomon attached an amendment barring the African National Congress, an anti-apartheid rebel group, or the South West Africa People's Organization, based in neighboring Namibia, from administering any part of a $4 million refugee-assistance program. The overall bill, opposed by Solomon, passed the House, but died in the Senate.

During another discussion of South Africa, Solomon displayed his sensitivity to criticisms of Reagan. In 1984, Bishop Desmond Tutu of South Africa, winner of the Nobel Peace Prize, made a half-hour statement to the Foreign Affairs Subcommittee on Africa, which was followed by a highly unusual standing ovation from subcommittee members. Solomon was the only member who refused to stand; he was angered by the bishop's attacks on administration policy.

Solomon is unsparingly critical of the Islamic-fundamentalist regime of Iran. After a

U.S. Navy ship, while patrolling the war-torn Persian Gulf, shot down an Iranian passenger jet, Solomon called on Reagan to reject suggestions that the United States pay reparations to the survivors of the victims.

"Like every American, I consider the loss of innocent lives to be a tragedy, but these particular lives, and hundreds of thousands of others, wouldn't have been lost if the criminal regime in Iran wasn't thumbing its nose at the civilized world with its bloody seven-year war," Solomon said. Declaring that "we don't need to put a phony guilt out on display for the benefit of America-haters," Solomon asked rhetorically where the outcry for reparations had been when Iran-allied Middle East terrorists took American hostages or blew up a Marine barracks in Beirut in 1983.

At Home: Running as an outspoken conservative in a solidly conservative district, Solomon was an easy winner in 1978 over Democratic Rep. Ned Pattison, one of the Watergate winners of 1974. Unlike Pattison's upset win four years earlier — when he became the first Democrat to represent the district in the 20th century — Solomon's victory was not a surprise.

Though Pattison had managed to hold his seat in 1976, he was burdened in his 1978 campaign against Solomon by his own candid interview in *Playboy* magazine, in which he admitted that he had smoked marijuana. Conservatives referred to him derisively as "Pottison."

Solomon had been a popular state legislator who regularly won his Assembly seat by wide margins. His Assembly constituency lay entirely within the old 29th District, so he had a good base from which to launch a congressional bid.

In addition, he was able to reconstruct the Republican-Conservative coalition. The two parties ran separate candidates in 1976, and Pattison captured a second term with less than a majority of the vote. But Solomon was backed by both parties, pretty much guaranteeing him victory. He has had no serious electoral trouble since then, winning two-thirds of the vote or better in each of his re-election campaigns.

Co-founder of an insurance and investment firm, Solomon got his start in politics in 1968, winning election as Queensbury town supervisor. He held that post — and served simultaneously as a member of the Warren County Legislature — until 1972, when he won a seat in the New York Assembly. He served there until his 1978 election to Congress.

Committee

Rules (2nd of 4 Republicans)
Rules of the House (ranking)

Elections

1988 General		
Gerald B. H. Solomon (R)	162,962	(72%)
Fred Baye (D)	62,177	(28%)
1986 General		
Gerald B. H. Solomon (R)	117,285	(70%)
Edward J. Bloch (D)	49,225	(30%)

Previous Winning Percentages: **1984** (73%) **1982** (74%) **1980** (67%) **1978** (54%)

District Vote For President

	1988	1984	1980	1976
D	98,968 (41%)	72,837 (31%)	79,593 (35%)	85,243 (39%)
R	142,159 (59%)	162,234 (69%)	121,819 (54%)	134,171 (61%)
I			19,885 (9%)	

Campaign Finance

	Receipts	Receipts from PACs	Expend-itures
1988			
Solomon (R)	$210,592	$79,150 (38%)	$212,652
Baye (D)	$15,957	$80 (0.5%)	$15,936
1986			
Solomon (R)	$162,192	$63,780 (39%)	$153,651
Bloch (D)	$84,327	$11,915 (14%)	$79,334

Key Votes

1987	
Raise speed limit to 65 mph	Y
Approve Gephardt "fair trade" amendment	N
Ban testing of larger nuclear weapons	N
Delay "re-flagging" of Kuwaiti tankers	N
Approve tax-raising deficit-reduction bill	N
1988	
Approve aid to Nicaraguan contras	Y
Enact civil rights restoration bill over Reagan veto	N
Kill 60-day plant-closing notification measure	Y
Pass omnibus trade bill over Reagan veto	Y
Approve death penalty for drug-related murders	Y
Bar federal funds for abortions in cases of rape and incest	Y
Oppose seven-day waiting period for purchase of handguns	Y

Voting Studies

	Presidential Support		Party Unity		Conservative Coalition	
Year	**S**	**O**	**S**	**O**	**S**	**O**
1988	65	32	90	9	95	5
1987	69	29	92	5	88	7
1986	79	16	84	10	92	4
1985	70	20	86	5	82	13
1984	64	34	85	10	83	14
1983	76	21	92	5	94	4
1982	60	26	85	9	78	10
1981	70	24	92	5	93	4

Interest Group Ratings

Year	ADA	ACU	AFL-CIO	CCUS
1988	15	88	57	86
1987	4	91	20	86
1986	0	81	21	83
1985	15	84	25	86
1984	5	79	31	81
1983	5	96	6	80
1982	5	90	22	76
1981	5	100	7	89

25 Sherwood Boehlert (R)

Of New Hartford — Elected 1982

Born: Sept. 28, 1936, Utica, N.Y.
Education: Utica College, A.B. 1961.
Military Career: Army, 1956-58.
Occupation: Congressional aide.
Family: Wife, Marianne Willey; four children.
Religion: Roman Catholic.
Political Career: Oneida County executive, 1979-82; sought GOP nomination for U.S. House, 1972.
Capitol Office: 1127 Longworth Bldg. 20515; 225-3665.

In Washington: Unlike other progressive House Republicans, "Sherry" Boehlert refuses to concede that Ronald Reagan and his California conservatives redefined the Grand Old Party and pushed old-stock Easterners like Boehlert to the fringe. Though a junior member, he aggressively stakes out his ground on the issues — the environment, the economy, education — and insists that this is where the party *really* stands.

With George Bush, a man of similar political heritage, in the White House, Boehlert could have a new opportunity to help demonstrate that the Reagan years were an aberration. During those years, Boehlert ran into a good deal of bad luck in angling for a seat on a prestige House committee; he tried to win appointment to Ways and Means and Appropriations, but was passed over for members more loyal to the party line.

Other Republicans have scored higher in opposition to Reagan or to the party line, but they tend to be senior members who arrived in a past era, or junior members who are excused because they come from Democratic-leaning districts. As a representative of solid GOP territory, Boehlert gets cut little slack by party leaders in Washington. In Reagan's second term, he opposed the president up to 60 percent of the time.

Perhaps to position himself better for the next round of committee openings, Boehlert backed conservative champion Newt Gingrich in his successful bid for House GOP whip early in the 101st Congress. For now, Boehlert remains a member on two second-line panels, Public Works and Science, which operate in the kind of bipartisan fashion that allows an affable and articulate activist like Boehlert to thrive.

He is also involved in issues off his committees. He has been a leader in the fight against acid rain, reflecting not only his parochial concern for the acidic Adirondack lakes, but also his general worry about his party's image. "A lot of people have the traditional belief that Republicans don't give a damn about the environment," he said in 1989. "Well, a lot of people are wrong."

On Public Works' Aviation Subcommittee, he has been a voice for airline consumer and safety bills. On Science, he has opposed the proposed superconducting supercollider, an atom-smasher that could be the largest public works project in U.S. history, not on the merits but due to the budget-busting cost.

As senior Republican on the Science, Research and Technology Subcommittee, he sponsored a bill to avail small businesses of the fruits of federal scientific research, an idea based on the longstanding agricultural extension service. That reflects his belief that the government has a big role in economic development, a belief that put him at fundamental odds with Reagan. Boehlert joined Democrats, and many Republicans, in blocking Reagan's persistent efforts to kill the Economic Development Administration, which provides seed capital to depressed communities.

At Home: Boehlert's moderate voting record vexed some of the more conservative Republican elements in the 25th. In 1986, they put forward music professor Robert S. Barstow, who was also the Conservative Party candidate, to challenge Boehlert in the GOP primary. But Boehlert prevailed by a 2-to-1 margin, and his subsequent victory in November with nearly 70 percent of the vote must have impressed conservative Republicans and Democrats alike; he ran without primary or general-election opposition in 1988.

This apparent security was hard-won for Boehlert, a longtime congressional aide whose House ambitions were deferred for a decade after an initial defeat in 1972. That year, Boehlert had hoped to succeed his boss, retiring GOP Rep. Alexander Pirnie, but lost to Donald J. Mitchell in a Republican primary.

Boehlert swallowed his disappointment and went to work for Mitchell. In 1977, he left Washington to run Mitchell's Utica office, which put him in the right place when the Oneida County executive position opened up. He held that job from 1979 to 1982.

By 1982, Mitchell was ready to retire.

New York 25

Central — Rome; Utica

The 25th is a Republican patchwork stitched together from several old New York districts that stretched across the central portion of the state. The boundaries reach from the outskirts of Ithaca on the west to the suburbs of Albany on the east, and the district juts north to include part of Oneida County, in the Mohawk Valley.

Oneida County casts a bit over 40 percent of the district's vote. Democrats normally hold their ground in Utica (population 70,000) and Rome (42,000), aging industrial cities undergoing a steady population decline. But outside this Mohawk Valley corridor, Oneida has a reliable Republican majority. George Bush carried the county (part of which is in the 29th District) with 54 percent of the vote in 1988; it last went Democratic for president in 1964.

The rural Republican vote dominant in the rest of the district reinforces that GOP trend. Otsego County also gave Bush 54 percent; he ran even stronger in Chenango and Cortland counties, 59 percent in each.

Otsego, by a slight margin over the others, provides the second-largest number of votes in the district. The college town of Oneonta, home of Hartwick College and a State University of New York campus, has 14,000 residents. But Cooperstown, on Otsego Lake, is far better known. Though the village of 2,300 contributes little vote, it draws much of central New York's tourist trade: It is the site of the Baseball Hall of Fame, as well as a museum dedicated to native son James Fenimore Cooper, author of "The Last of the Mohicans."

During the 1970s, sleepy Schoharie County on the eastern edge of the 25th saw a burst of suburban growth. An influx of suburbanites from the Albany-Schenectady area sent county population soaring 20 percent, to nearly 30,000. This turned out to be just a spurt, though; population remained level through the early 1980s.

Population: 516,201. White 501,968 (97%), Black 9,457 (2%), Other 2,612 (1%). Spanish origin 4,511 (1%). 18 and over 374,606 (73%), 65 and over 68,669 (13%). Median age: 31.

Boehlert was driving along an Interstate highway in Oneida County when he heard the news. He pulled into a rest stop, called a radio station and announced his candidacy.

As county executive he had earned high marks from labor unions, and was one of only two New York state Republicans to win the state AFL-CIO's endorsement in the 1982 elections. Lining up Republican support in each of the 25th's nine counties, he won the primary comfortably.

In November, Boehlert had a huge organizational and financial advantage over his Democratic foe, dairy farmer Anita Maxwell, who had lost badly to Mitchell in 1976. She hewed to a traditional New Deal Democratic line, and attacked Boehlert for proposing a county budget deficit that forced consideration of a sales tax for the first time. Boehlert took a relaxed attitude toward those criticisms, and made no issue of the fact that her residence was outside the district.

Committees

Public Works and Transportation (9th of 20 Republicans)
Aviation; Investigations and Oversight; Surface Transportation

Science, Space and Technology (4th of 19 Republicans)
Science, Research and Technology (ranking); Investigations and Oversight

Select Aging (11th of 27 Republicans)
Health and Long-Term Care

Elections

1988 General

Sherwood Boehlert (R)	130,122	(100%)

1986 General

Sherwood Boehlert (R)	104,216	(69%)
Kevin J. Conway (D)	33,864	(22%)
Robert S. Barstow (C)	12,999	(9%)

Previous Winning Percentages: 1984 (73%) **1982** (56%)

District Vote For President

	1988	1984	1980	1976
D	94,654 (45%)	79,242 (37%)	79,689 (39%)	87,132 (42%)
R	114,280 (54%)	136,248 (63%)	105,701 (51%)	120,009 (58%)
I			17,027 (8%)	

Campaign Finance

	Receipts	Receipts from PACs	Expend-itures
1988			
Boehlert (R)	$235,512	$90,173 (38%)	$145,883
1986			
Boehlert (R)	$293,347	$98,113 (33%)	$268,122
Barstow (C)	$31,567	$1,000 (3%)	$31,567

Key Votes

1987

Raise speed limit to 65 mph	N
Approve Gephardt "fair trade" amendment	Y
Ban testing of larger nuclear weapons	Y
Delay "re-flagging" of Kuwaiti tankers	Y
Approve tax-raising deficit-reduction bill	N

1988

Approve aid to Nicaraguan contras	N
Enact civil rights restoration bill over Reagan veto	Y
Kill 60-day plant-closing notification measure	N
Pass omnibus trade bill over Reagan veto	Y
Approve death penalty for drug-related murders	Y
Bar federal funds for abortions in cases of rape and incest	N
Oppose seven-day waiting period for purchase of handguns	N

Voting Studies

	Presidential Support		Party Unity		Conservative Coalition	
Year	S	O	S	O	S	O
1988	37	59	58	40	58	37
1987	37	60	46	49	65	35
1986	46	54	53	45	66	32
1985	41	59	54	44	56	44
1984	58	39	38	59	61	37
1983	52	43	34	61	49	47

Interest Group Ratings

Year	ADA	ACU	AFL-CIO	CCUS
1988	65	24	86	64
1987	60	9	69	67
1986	50	41	93	56
1985	45	52	65	57
1984	65	25	62	47
1983	45	30	47	55

26 David O'B. Martin (R)

Of Canton — Elected 1980

Born: April 26, 1944, St. Lawrence County, N.Y.
Education: U. of Notre Dame, B.B.A. 1966; Albany Law School, J.D. 1973.
Military Career: Marine Corps, 1966-70.
Occupation: Lawyer.
Family: Wife, DeeAnn Hedlund; three children.
Religion: Roman Catholic.
Political Career: St. Lawrence County Legislature, 1974-77; N.Y. Assembly, 1977-81.
Capitol Office: 442 Cannon Bldg. 20515; 225-4611.

In Washington: Martin served as a Marine Corps officer in Vietnam in the late 1960s, a time of wrenching debate over the U.S. military's role in Southeast Asia. But in Congress, his method and his mission are clear: He keeps his head down, seldom engaging in lofty philosophical exchanges, and he keeps his eye trained on finding ways for his constituency to benefit from Pentagon spending.

Armed Services is an ideal assignment for a member who has to balance a generally conservative outlook with a concern for job opportunities in his economically struggling district. For Martin, being pro-military and pro-jobs go hand-in-glove.

Martin's most determined congressional effort involved convincing the Army to locate a new light infantry division at Fort Drum, in the 26th District city of Watertown. He launched a personal lobbying campaign to land the prize in the fall of 1984, and it paid off early the next year, when the Department of the Army announced the activation of the 10th Mountain Division at Fort Drum. In 1987 alone, the establishment of this unit meant more than $1 billion for the area in government contracts, payrolls and related services. The work force is expected to increase to 13,500 by 1991.

Martin is the ranking GOP member of the Military Installations Subcommittee, and he is nearly always friendly to requests for money to construct new facilities. In 1985, he urged those seeking Pentagon spending cuts to concentrate on major items in the defense budget, and not to express their frustrations on the relatively small issue of military construction.

On the Readiness Subcommittee, Martin places high priority on his work on the Morale, Welfare and Recreation panel, where he focuses on improving the quality of life of military personnel. The panel approves spending of non-appropriated funds (which accrue from surcharges soldiers pay) for building commissaries, recreation centers and the like.

Also active on veterans' issues, Martin was involved in the negotiations over constructing the Vietnam Veterans Memorial, dedicated in Washington, D.C., in 1982. He was one of several members selected to represent the House during a ceremony to inter the remains of the Unknown Soldier of the war in Vietnam.

The St. Lawrence Seaway, headquartered in the 26th District, also occupies Martin. During the 97th Congress, he argued strongly in behalf of a measure aimed at keeping down costs for its users. In 1984, Martin was an outspoken opponent of winter navigation of the seaway. Arguing that an extension of the navigation season into the frozen winter months could lead to nautical disasters, he lobbied successfully to delete a provision from a water-resources bill allowing it.

At Home: Martin follows the orthodox Republicanism of his predecessor, Robert C. McEwen, who retired in 1981 after his eighth term.

After returning from Vietnam and graduating from law school, Martin entered politics in 1973 at the county level. In 1976 he received party backing for the state Legislature and moved on to Albany. A regular Republican who worked closely with the party leadership, Martin had the support of six of the seven county GOP chairmen in his 1980 bid for Congress.

Martin defeated a well-known Democrat for the House seat — former New York Lt. Gov. Mary Anne Krupsak. Krupsak moved into the 26th District to run, but could not break the stronghold the Republican organization has kept there.

During the campaign, Martin proposed adapting fellow New York Republican Jack F. Kemp's proposal for "enterprise zones," designed for high-unemployment urban areas, to his district's economically suffering rural areas and small towns. Martin won handily, and has had no trouble since. He racked up over 70 percent in each of his last four outings.

New York 26

North — Plattsburgh; Watertown

Democrats competing for the 26th must feel a little fatalistic about their task. Residents of this sparsely populated region have not strayed from the Republican column in a single House election in this century. This is also fertile territory for GOP presidential candidates. President Reagan won 67 percent here in 1984; George Bush took 55 percent.

Bounded by Canada to the north and the Adirondacks to the east, the 26th is the state's largest House district. While the district is dotted with such small cities as Watertown, Massena and Plattsburgh, its best-known location is the village of Lake Placid, which hosted the 1932 and 1980 Winter Olympics.

Though the district contains some of the most economically depressed regions in the state outside New York City — location and terrain make it difficult to attract large-scale industry — the rural 26th is solidly Republican.

The 26th's landmark economic event of the 1980s — the basing of an Army light infantry division at huge Fort Drum near Watertown — has given the district an even more conservative tilt. Martin, who lobbied hard to bring the Army division to the district, described the $1.3 billion expansion of Fort Drum as the largest military construction project since World War II. However, the Strategic Air Command base in Plattsburgh is slated for job cuts under the military base-closure plan enacted in 1989.

The St. Lawrence Seaway helps the North Country's economy. Billions of dollars' worth of minerals and manufactured goods move through its locks yearly.

In the 26th's rural counties, Yankee dairy farmers maintain their Republican heritage. Leavening the district's conservative bent is an environmental consciousness brought on by the threat acid rain poses to fish in the Adirondack lakes.

Population: 516,196. White 506,428 (98%), Black 3,665 (1%), Other 4,564 (1%). Spanish origin 3,439 (1%). 18 and over 364,170 (71%), 65 and over 62,928 (12%). Median age: 29.

Committee

Armed Services (8th of 21 Republicans)
Military Installations and Facilities (ranking); Readiness

Elections

1988 General		
David O'B. Martin (R)	131,043	(75%)
Donald R. Ravenscroft (D)	43,585	(25%)
1986 General		
David O'B. Martin (R)	94,840	(100%)

Previous Winning Percentages: **1984** (71%) **1982** (72%) **1980** (64%)

District Vote for President

	1988		1984		1980		1976	
D	87,213	(44%)	67,605	(33%)	79,352	(43%)	62,609	(36%)
R	109,749	(55%)	140,016	(67%)	91,909	(49%)	103,830	(59%)
I					13,212	(7%)		

Campaign Finance

	Receipts	Receipts from PACs	Expend-itures
1988			
Martin (R)	$133,256	$84,316 (63%)	$120,423
Ravenscroft (D)	$11,348	0	$10,635
1986			
Martin (R)	$123,746	$73,656 (60%)	$76,301

Key Votes

1987	
Raise speed limit to 65 mph	Y
Approve Gephardt "fair trade" amendment	N
Ban testing of larger nuclear weapons	N
Delay "re-flagging" of Kuwaiti tankers	N
Approve tax-raising deficit-reduction bill	N
1988	
Approve aid to Nicaraguan contras	Y
Enact civil rights restoration bill over Reagan veto	Y
Kill 60-day plant-closing notification measure	Y
Pass omnibus trade bill over Reagan veto	Y
Approve death penalty for drug-related murders	Y
Bar federal funds for abortions in cases of rape and incest	Y
Oppose seven-day waiting period for purchase of handguns	Y

Voting Studies

	Presidential Support		Party Unity		Conservative Coalition	
Year	S	O	S	O	S	O
1988	45	47	66	28	84	8
1987	54 †	39 †	61 †	30 †	86 †	12 †
1986	53	41	56 †	34 †	86	8
1985	59	40	66	26	75	18
1984	54	38	58	28	81	10
1983	73	23	72	18	88	11
1982	62	27	77	19	88	7
1981	63	25	80	8	75	7

† Not eligible for all recorded votes.

Interest Group Ratings

Year	ADA	ACU	AFL-CIO	CCUS
1988	25	68	64	79
1987	20	64	38	57
1986	15	74	42	79
1985	15	71	47	71
1984	20	57	23	85
1983	0	83	18	75
1982	15	67	22	65
1981	5	100	13	88

27 James T. Walsh (R)

Of Syracuse — Elected 1988

Born: June 19, 1947, Syracuse, N.Y.
Education: St. Bonaventure U., B.A. 1970.
Occupation: Businessman.
Family: Wife, DeDe Ryan; three children.
Religion: Roman Catholic.
Political Career: Syracuse Common Council, 1978-89, president, 1987-89; sought nomination for Onondaga County executive, 1987.
Capitol Office: 1238 Longworth Bldg. 20515; 225-3701.

The Path to Washington: Walsh's comfortable 1988 victory over Democrat Rosemary S. Pooler suggested that incumbents are not always a party's best bet at the polls.

When the election year began, it appeared the 27th would see a repeat of its 1986 pairing, in which Pooler finished just 939 votes behind Rep. George C. Wortley, a Reaganite whom Pooler portrayed as too conservative for the district.

But Wortley decided to retire after four terms, and his replacement by the more moderate Walsh — a longtime local official and the son of a former House member — dramatically changed the campaign's chemistry. Though Pooler again had strong support from labor unions and liberal activists, Walsh established a lead in public-opinion polls, and Pooler never found a way to close the gap.

Though he lacked the benefits of incumbency, Walsh entered the campaign with some clear advantages over the retiring Wortley. An advocate of urban programs and a former Peace Corps volunteer, Walsh had a centrist profile that seemed to fit the Syracuse-based district better than that of Wortley, a steadfast Reagan backer whose support for aid to the Nicaraguan contras caused him difficulty in 1986. But Walsh, an executive with the NYNEX telephone company, was conservative enough to reassure Syracuse's mainly Republican business community.

Democratic success in the 27th hinged on a strong showing in Syracuse, the district's core city; Pooler did well there in 1986. That fact was not lost on the Republicans promoting Walsh to succeed Wortley, a suburban newspaper publisher who never developed a loyal following in Syracuse.

Walsh came in with a solid base built in his campaigns for Syracuse City Council, a 1986 citywide victory for council president, and a narrow 1987 defeat in the GOP primary for Onondaga County executive. He also had one of the city's best-known political names: His father, William F. Walsh, served as mayor prior to his 1973-79 tenure in the House.

During his House campaign, Walsh made his pitch to conservatives by describing Pooler as an extreme liberal and an adversary of business who favored tax increases and deep cuts in military spending. But he also appealed to moderate voters, defending the federal Urban Development Action Grants program and claiming credit for obtaining a state "economic development [enterprise] zone" for Syracuse.

Pooler countered that Walsh was nonchalant about the decline of the region's industrial base. Early in the campaign, Walsh commented that unemployment was "an issue for people who don't have jobs." Pooler insisted Walsh had said unemployment was "only" a problem for the jobless, and she used the statement to back her assertion that Walsh was insensitive to working-class voters.

With "jobs" the central issue, the House campaign became a miniature version of the national economic debate. Pooler said Syracuse's recent economic rebound masked an attrition of blue-collar jobs — a version of Michael S. Dukakis' "Swiss cheese economy" theme. But Walsh, noting the slide in local unemployment to under 5 percent from double-digit levels in the early 1980s, praised the Reagan-Bush administration for fostering prosperity.

The voters apparently favored Walsh's optimistic view. He carried Onondaga County — which Pooler won in 1986 — by some 30,000 votes, taking about 57 percent of the ballots cast. In more rural Madison County, Walsh's winning percentage was even higher.

When Walsh came to Washington and began lobbying for his place in the committee system, he calculated that a good way to broaden his appeal beyond his urban base and protect his district's dairy and other farming interests would be to seek a seat on the Agriculture Committee. Capitalizing on contacts with senior Republicans who served with his father, Walsh got his way, becoming the only freshman to win assignment to Agriculture.

New York 27

Central — Syracuse

Despite its industrial heritage and large blue-collar population, Syracuse was for years a solid Republican bastion. The electorate's GOP leanings, spurred by the typical upstate antipathy toward Democratic New York City, were reinforced by a ward-based Republican organization that mirrored the Democratic machines in other Northern cities.

In recent years, though, events have weakened the Republicans' iron grip. The disappearance of jobs in the chemical, steel and other industries sent Syracuse's population tumbling from 216,000 in 1960 to 161,000 in 1986, and made those left more amenable to Democratic messages on jobs programs and trade protection. The weakening of the old GOP machine also aided city Democrats, who have now controlled the mayor's office for nearly two decades.

Republicans continue to dominate, however, in the Onondaga County suburbs and outlying rural areas, enabling Republican candidates for the House and for president to salvage the 27th District as a whole. Walsh, boosted by his personal strength within Syracuse, swept Onondaga and Madison counties; George Bush prevailed in both counties as well.

In the 1970s, Syracuse was divided between two congressional districts. But with the city's population declining, the Legislature in 1982 reunited the city in one constituency.

Once the nation's leading supplier of salt, Syracuse still has a base in heavy industry and electronics. But the clear skies over the once-sooty downtown area symbolize a conversion to a service economy: The Mutual of New York insurance company has expanded its white-collar operations, and AT&T is building an office tower there.

Syracuse has a diverse ethnicity. Italians, blacks, Poles, Jews, Lithuanians and Irish traditionally have had their own well-defined neighborhoods, although gentrification of sections such as Tipperary Hill, the old Irish enclave, has blurred distinctions somewhat. The eastern part of town, the site of Syracuse University (16,000 students), is white-collar and Republican.

Places such as Baldwinsville and Skaneateles set the Republican tone in the Onondaga County suburbs. Democrats do better in industrial Salina, which was named during salt's 19th-century heyday.

The remaining 10 percent comes from solid Republican, bucolic Madison County, all but a sliver of which lies within the 27th. The only hint of a Democratic vote is in Hamilton, home of Colgate University.

Population: 516,364. White 476,544 (92%), Black 30,457 (6%), Other 6,324 (1%). Spanish origin 5,000 (1%). 18 and over 372,785 (72%), 65 and over 55,655 (11%). Median age: 29.

Committees

Agriculture (17th of 18 Republicans)
Department Operations, Research and Foreign Agriculture; Livestock, Dairy and Poultry

House Administration (8th of 8 Republicans)
Elections; Libraries and Memorials; Office Systems

Select Children, Youth and Families (11th of 12 Republicans)

Joint Library

Campaign Finance

	Receipts	Receipts from PACs	Expend-itures
1988			
Walsh (R)	$610,935	$202,620 (33%)	$594,965
Pooler (D)	$643,565	$313,269 (49%)	$647,959

Elections

1988 General

James T. Walsh (R)	124,928	(57%)
Rosemary S. Pooler (D)	90,854	(42%)

District Vote For President

	1988	1984	1980	1976
D	103,274 (47%)	88,234 (39%)	78,189 (37%)	83,172 (39%)
R	116,123 (53%)	135,976 (60%)	107,128 (51%)	128,045 (60%)
I			20,213 (10%)	

28 Matthew F. McHugh (D)

Of Ithaca — Elected 1974

Born: Dec. 6, 1938, Philadelphia, Pa.

Education: Mount St. Mary's College, B.S. 1960; Villanova U., J.D. 1963.

Occupation: Lawyer.

Family: Wife, Eileen Alanna Higgins; three children.

Religion: Roman Catholic.

Political Career: Tompkins County district attorney, 1969-72.

Capitol Office: 2335 Rayburn Bldg. 20515; 225-6335.

In Washington: McHugh is one of those rare members of whom colleagues like to say, he doesn't have an enemy in the House. He has capitalized on that popularity to carve out an influential role for himself, becoming in effect politically bilingual: His first language is that of a dedicated liberal, but McHugh also can speak as a trusted pragmatist to those of different ideological tongues.

He is quiet, courteous and respected on both sides of the aisle for his intellectual and personal integrity. An unflappable negotiator, he often is singled out to be the Appropriations Committee's emissary when the panel needs to settle jurisdictional or procedural tiffs with other committees or with Republicans. Yet for the reservoir of good will he enjoys, McHugh so far has fallen short of his goal of a formal House leadership post.

He is well established as a central figure on foreign policy questions, as a member of both the Intelligence Committee and the Appropriations Subcommittee on Foreign Operations. McHugh has been eclipsed on that subcommittee in recent years, however, by one of his best friends and longtime allies, David R. Obey of Wisconsin, a forceful Democrat who became Foreign Operations chairman in 1985. Under the previous chairman, the eccentric and unpredictable Clarence D. Long of Maryland, McHugh had helped fill a power vacuum and provided direction for the subcommittee's work; then-Secretary of State George P. Shultz often would breakfast with McHugh to gauge matters on the crucial panel.

Obey turned up the partisan temperature of the subcommittee deliberations, directing cuts in President Reagan's foreign aid requests as if to reciprocate for administration efforts to cut social programs. McHugh, not nearly so aggressive or partisan, has at times seemed uncomfortable with his friend's style.

In 1985, he was one of two Democrats who broke with Obey and voted to fund international development banks; Obey had blocked the money to force Republicans to support the politically sensitive funds, a favorite target of conservatives who charge that U.S. aid to the banks subsidizes communist regimes. The funds were later approved. In 1986, however, Republicans and conservative Democrats were disappointed when McHugh declined to join their coalition for a larger foreign aid budget than Obey wanted. The alternative never materialized.

In general, McHugh is an articulate advocate for a strong congressional role in foreign policy, a proponent of economic and humanitarian foreign aid over military assistance to allies, and an opponent of military intervention in Central America — all stances that usually placed him, along with Obey, at odds with Reagan. He expressed cautious optimism about President Bush's initial overtures toward bipartisanship, although he was skeptical about a compromise plan to maintain the contras with "humanitarian" aid pending elections in Nicaragua; he suggested that Bush's approach might be the "old policy under different rhetoric."

During Reagan's tenure, McHugh used his Appropriations seat to challenge administration policies through the power of the purse. He was among those seeking to tie production money for the strategic defense initiative to progress in arms control talks with the Soviet Union. He backed the cutoff of aid to the contras and, when it passed, he noted that "there is a growing assertion by Congress of its legitimate right to participate in foreign policy."

He ardently supports the 1973 War Powers Resolution, which requires presidents to consult Congress when U.S. forces are committed to hostile areas. Opposed by every administration since its enactment, the law has become a lightning rod for the two branches' longstanding debate over their shared constitutional powers to declare and fight wars. "I really believe that the War Powers act is not just Congress stamping its feet, but that it makes long-term sense," McHugh says. He maintains that presi-

New York 28

Southern Tier — Binghamton; Ithaca

The elongated 28th reaches from high above Cayuga's waters to high above those of the Hudson. Made up mainly of small cities and rural areas, the district maintains a Republican lean. But pockets of industry and academia have helped Democrat McHugh become a fixture; popular statewide Democrats such as Sen. Daniel Patrick Moynihan and Gov. Mario M. Cuomo also win easily here.

Broome County, which includes the "Triple Cities" of Binghamton, Johnson City and Endicott, provides nearly 45 percent of the district vote. Binghamton — by far the 28th's largest city with 53,000 residents — is industrial but politically marginal. This is the area in which Thomas J. Watson located his first IBM plant, and it still reflects some of the corporate paternalism the Watson family practiced for generations.

Conservative working-class voters, many of them Italian, can join with white-collar technicians and professionals to form a potent bloc for the GOP. Binghamton was represented for years by state Senate Majority Leader Warren Anderson, a Republican who retired in 1988. However, Democrats win here on occasion: Michael S. Dukakis edged out George Bush in Broome County in 1988 by a little over 500 votes.

The northwest corner of the 28th takes in a portion of Tompkins County, McHugh's political base and site of Cornell University and Ithaca College. Cornell dominates the picturesque city of Ithaca economically and politically. The Ivy League school, sitting on a hill overlooking Lake Cayuga, keeps the city Democratic and relatively liberal. The heavily Jewish parts of Sullivan County, well-known for Grossinger's and other Catskill resort hotels, also lean to the Democrats.

However, Ulster County, at the district's eastern end, generally provides a powerful Republican counterbalance. The county, which contributes the district's second-largest bloc of votes, went 57 percent for Bush in 1988. There are, however, some Democratic votes in Kingston, a textile city of 24,000 people.

The best-known site in Ulster County is an open field in the village of Bethel. It was here that the famous rock festival, named after the nearby artists' colony in Woodstock, was held in 1969.

Population: 516,402. White 492,630 (95%), Black 14,330 (3%), Other 5,070 (1%). Spanish origin 9,240 (2%). 18 and over 382,338 (74%), 65 and over 63,575 (12%). Median age: 30.

dential policies backed by Congress rest on more secure political footing.

McHugh was a leading critic in the 100th Congress of both the Reagan administration's performance in the Iran-contra scandal and its policy of providing Navy escorts for Kuwaiti oil tankers in the war-torn Persian Gulf.

Though many lawmakers were critical of the Persian Gulf operation when it became public, McHugh was among the few who unsuccessfully argued that Reagan's policy should be canceled. He acknowledged the diplomatic costs of doing so, but insisted "there's a much greater risk to American credibility down the road" if U.S. casualties and public outcry force a retreat. Typically, he insisted his call was not partisan, but intended as "a plea for meaningful consultation so we can develop a bipartisan policy which will effectively advance our interests."

He lamented the limitations of the Intelligence Committee when it was divulged that the administration secretly had sold arms to Iran and that proceeds had gone to the contras, all at a time when U.S. military aid to the rebels was banned. "If you have an administration that is determined to violate the law," he said, "it's difficult to do oversight."

As chairman of the Intelligence Subcommittee on Legislation, McHugh opposed a suggestion that the House and Senate Intelligence panels be combined, an idea that gained adherents after the Iran-contra hearings. He said the existence of two panels with rotating memberships potentially broadens support for the intelligence community; McHugh said he personally had "a deeper appreciation of the importance" of the CIA and other agencies, although a "more cautious" approach to covert actions, as a consequence of his service.

He did take charge of the one bill that resulted from the Iran-contra affair, a measure requiring presidents to inform Congress of all covert operations within 48 hours. The bill passed the Senate by a bipartisan margin, but died in the House after it became the focus of Republican attacks on Speaker Jim Wright for allegedly divulging classified information about the CIA in Nicaragua. Though McHugh had vowed to revive the bill in the 101st Congress, Wright — still fearing GOP attacks — shelved it early in 1989, ostensibly as a bipartisan welcoming gesture to Bush. McHugh publicly endorsed Wright's move.

McHugh has been a prominent foe of aid to Angolan rebels, objecting that it aligned the United States with South Africa's apartheid regime, which also supported the guerrillas. In late 1985, he led liberals' unsuccessful drive to kill further assistance. But in 1988, as U.S.-backed negotiations appeared to make progress, McHugh alone among liberals backed a small amount of aid as a gesture of encouragement to the talks.

He also has stepped out of the crowd lately to voice gentle criticism of Israel, though he represents a significant number of Jews. Long a strong supporter of assistance to that country, he publicly protested when it was discovered that American Jonathan Jay Pollard had spied on the United States for Israel. Then, in early 1989, he urged Israeli leaders to reverse stance and negotiate directly with the Palestine Liberation Organization. McHugh acknowledged the political risk of his statement, but added that even Israel's supporters "don't have to accept every policy position the Israeli government takes."

Though outspoken, McHugh is not as aggressive as some allies might like. Still, beyond his personal reserve lies a reservoir of ambition.

To get on Appropriations in 1978, he had to win the support of his state's New York City-dominated Democratic delegation for a seat that had belonged to Manhattan's former representative (and later mayor), Edward I. Koch. But McHugh campaigned assiduously and defeated a candidate from the city, James H. Scheuer, 14-11, drawing several city votes. New York Democrats backed McHugh again in late 1985, choosing him over Samuel S. Stratton and Gary L. Ackerman for the Steering and Policy Committee, the leadership panel that makes Democrats' committee assignments.

He was less successful in 1980, when he tried to become chairman of the House Democratic Caucus. The other candidates, Gillis W. Long and Charlie Rose, were both Southerners, and McHugh saw an opening for a Northern liberal. But he started late, and in challenging Long, he was up against one of the most popular members. McHugh finished a distant third, with 41 votes, to 146 for Long and 53 for Rose. He considered trying again for the caucus post when the 101st Congress was getting organized, but was dissuaded by the thought of a long campaign and by William H. Gray III's early lead.

In the meantime, however, McHugh did serve in his first important leadership position, as chairman of the Democratic Study Group (DSG), the organization of liberal and moderate Democrats, during the 98th Congress. He won unopposed in late 1982.

The DSG, long influential in House affairs, had been less conspicuous in the early 1980s. McHugh set out to reverse this trend. Under his leadership in 1984, DSG offered an alternative budget to the House Budget Committee's product. It would have reduced the federal deficit by about $260 billion in three years, chiefly by freezing defense spending at the inflation rate and increasing taxes substantially. The draft's appeal beyond liberal Democrats was limited, but it still drew 132 votes on the floor.

In early 1987, McHugh played a bit of uncharacteristic hardball in helping Armed Services Committee Chairman Les Aspin to withstand a near-successful coup by popular conservative Marvin Leath. Aspin's base among liberals had eroded badly due to his support for the MX missile and contra aid, but McHugh joined with Don Edwards of California for a liberal counterattack. The two men circulated a letter documenting Leath's conservative voting record in detail, and concluding that the Texan "has made a career of voting against his party." It broke Leath's momentum, and Aspin was reelected on a third ballot.

At Home: McHugh's victory in the 1974 Democratic sweep made him the first Democrat to represent the Binghamton area in this century. He succeeded a popular Republican, Howard W. Robison, promising to carry on in the retiring Robison's moderate tradition. He was helped in that stance by the hard-line conservative campaign of his Republican opponent, Binghamton Mayor Alfred Libous.

McHugh's security in the former Republican bastion was ensured by the district GOP's habit of putting up flawed challengers against him. In 1978 and 1980, businessman Neil Tyler Wallace demonstrated an abrasive personality that cost him votes. In 1982 lawyer David F. Crowley seemed a bright and formidable challenger until he committed a series of gaffes that doomed his candidacy.

For instance, in an attempt to show how military spending could be cut, Crowley suggested that the military's LAMPS III helicopter be scrapped. It turned out that a plant in the 28th District made parts for the aircraft. McHugh won comfortably.

That track record did not dim Republicans' optimism about their chances against McHugh in 1984. Their candidate, former Cornell University administrator Constance E. Cook, had built up her name recognition as a member of the New York state Assembly for a decade until her retirement in 1976. Cook also benefited from the special interest the national GOP took in female congressional candidates that year.

Unlike Crowley, Cook avoided making any glaring errors. But the 65-year-old Republican still had formidable problems in trying to blaze a comeback trail. She expressed reservations about the Reagan administration's cuts in social welfare programs, and scored McHugh for opposing federal funding for abortions — stands that did not sit well with many of the district's conservatives. Further, Cook negotiated a campaign spending limit with McHugh that wound up impairing her ability to spread her name outside of her Ithaca base.

Cook got a boost in mid-September, when President Reagan spoke in the district on her behalf. But even that did not help her generate sufficient momentum. McHugh, who openly attacked Reagan's economic policies and embraced Walter F. Mondale's call for a tax increase, took 57 percent of the vote.

McHugh has faced absolutely no strain since. He won by 2-to-1 in 1986, and drew no Republican opposition in 1988.

Before running for Congress, McHugh served as district attorney of Tompkins County, at the far western edge of the sprawling 28th District. In that office, he was popular with the Cornell University community in Ithaca. He organized a local drug treatment facility and demanded peaceful handling of student protests.

Committees

Appropriations (16th of 35 Democrats)
Foreign Operations; Rural Development, Agriculture and Related Agencies

Select Children, Youth and Families (5th of 18 Democrats)

Select Intelligence (5th of 12 Democrats)
Legislation (chairman); Oversight and Evaluation

Elections

1988 General		
Matthew F. McHugh (D)	141,976	(93%)
Mary C. Dixon (RTL)	10,395	(7%)
1986 General		
Matthew F. McHugh (D)	103,908	(68%)
Mark R. Masterson (R)	48,213	(32%)

Previous Winning Percentages: **1984** (57%) **1982** (56%) **1980** (55%) **1978** (56%) **1976** (67%) **1974** (53%)

District Vote For President

	1988	1984	1980	1976
D	108,157 (48%)	94,304 (39%)	83,039 (38%)	110,702 (48%)
R	118,542 (52%)	147,818 (61%)	108,287 (49%)	121,263 (52%)
I			24,117 (11%)	

Campaign Finance

	Receipts	Receipts from PACs	Expend-itures
1988			
McHugh (D)	$276,595	$129,633 (47%)	$172,905
1986			
McHugh (D)	$279,235	$85,414 (31%)	$287,080
Masterson (R)	$7,671	$500 (7%)	$7,218

Key Votes

1987	
Raise speed limit to 65 mph	N
Approve Gephardt "fair trade" amendment	N
Ban testing of larger nuclear weapons	Y
Delay "re-flagging" of Kuwaiti tankers	Y
Approve tax-raising deficit-reduction bill	Y
1988	
Approve aid to Nicaraguan contras	N
Enact civil rights restoration bill over Reagan veto	Y
Kill 60-day plant-closing notification measure	N
Pass omnibus trade bill over Reagan veto	Y
Approve death penalty for drug-related murders	N
Bar federal funds for abortions in cases of rape and incest	Y
Oppose seven-day waiting period for purchase of handguns	N

Voting Studies

	Presidential Support		Party Unity		Conservative Coalition	
Year	**S**	**O**	**S**	**O**	**S**	**O**
1988	25	70	91	7	21	76
1987	18	78	93	3	14	86
1986	23	76	91	6	18	82
1985	25	73	92	4	11	87
1984	35	62	89	9	24	75
1983	24	76	92	5	12	87
1982	39	53	89	8	19	81
1981	32	68	89	11	19	80

Interest Group Ratings

Year	ADA	ACU	AFL-CIO	CCUS
1988	95	4	92	46
1987	92	9	88	13
1986	80	9	71	17
1985	85	10	94	18
1984	75	21	38	19
1983	90	9	88	30
1982	100	10	95	23
1981	95	0	73	11

29 Frank Horton (R)

Of Penfield — Elected 1962

Born: Dec. 12, 1919, Cuero, Texas.
Education: Louisiana State U., B.A. 1941; Cornell U., LL.B. 1947.
Military Career: Army, 1941-45.
Occupation: Lawyer.
Family: Wife, Nancy Richmond; two children.
Religion: Presbyterian.
Political Career: Rochester City Council, 1955-61.
Capitol Office: 2108 Rayburn Bldg. 20515; 225-4916.

In Washington: A liberal Republican with few partisan instincts, Horton has devoted his political career to painstaking, often frustrating, reviews of federal governmental processes. During the early 1980s, his task was complicated by his conflicts with a Reagan administration much more conservative than him. Now, as he nears the end of his third decade in the House, Horton may find George Bush's GOP a more comfortable place to do his work.

In seven of President Reagan's eight years in office, Horton voted against a majority of his GOP colleagues on House votes far more often than he voted with them; only in 1981 did his support of Reagan's legislative positions reach 50 percent.

Horton's opposition may have been consistent, but he was no rabble-rouser. The mild-mannered Republican sometimes uses confrontational rhetoric in press releases to his politically marginal Rochester district, but it is rarely heard in the halls of Congress. Some GOP conservatives gripe that he is more liberal than his district demands, but overall, Horton's low-key style protects him from being the target of much criticism from his party's right.

As if to signal a new chapter in his (and his party's) political life, Horton in 1989 helped secure President Bush's signature on the Whistleblowers Protection Act, which Reagan had pocket-vetoed late in 1988.

Horton and Democrat Patricia Schroeder had introduced the bill, which was designed to protect federal workers who expose waste and fraud. Congress had proceeded on the assumption that Reagan supported the bill; many members were taken aback by his veto. Reagan said he feared workers could "manipulate the process to their advantage," to which Horton, the ranking Republican on the Government Operations Committee, responded with uncharacteristic harshness. He called Reagan's veto a "reprehensible act" that was "orchestrated after adjournment of Congress to prevent an override."

In 1989, Horton and Schroeder reintroduced the bill, and although the initial veto had come at the urging of Reagan-appointed Attorney General Dick Thornburgh — who continued in office under Bush — negotiations progressed swiftly, and the bill was approved in April 1989.

But if Horton can expect more cooperation from the White House, the same may not be true for him on Government Operations, where Michigan Democrat John Conyers Jr. took over as chairman in 1989. Conyers is more liberal than the previous chairman, Texan Jack Brooks, and his leadership talents are untested. With Brooks, Horton often played the "good cop" to the chairman's "bad cop." This relationship helped defuse conflicts on the committee, but its success was based on the rapport between the two senior members.

Horton's other major committee assignment is on Post Office and Civil Service, where he is a leading advocate of removing the U.S. Postal Service from the federal budget and thereby insulating it from future budget cuts. The agency had enjoyed that status from 1973 until 1985, when the Reagan administration shifted it. Horton complained that the administration "put up a roadblock" each time Congress prepared to move on the proposal, but the House eventually passed such a bill in the 100th Congress. Though it died, Horton vowed to revisit it in the 101st Congress.

Horton has worked hard over the years to place "inspectors general" in various federal agencies to root out waste. In 1988, he worked on successful legislation to create new inspector general offices in five federal departments and agencies. Four years earlier, he supported moves to add the position to the Treasury and Justice departments. Horton claims these offices, which exist in 18 other federal agencies, have saved $120 billion over the last decade. He first succeeded in securing the appointment of an inspector general to the Pentagon in the 97th Congress, a difficult accomplishment considering fears that classified information might be released.

In his earlier years on Government Operations, Horton was the only Republican to give

New York 29

West — Part of Rochester

The House representation of divided Rochester is something of a paradox. The working-class and minority neighborhoods of east Rochester, which generally lean Democratic, are represented by 29th District Republican Horton. But the more affluent west Rochester communities, which were thought at the time of the last redistricting to reinforce the neighboring 30th District's GOP tilt, have since 1986 favored Democratic Rep. Louise M. Slaughter.

The inclusion of the more Democratic parts of Rochester in Horton's district does not trouble him, since he has one of the most liberal records among House Republicans. In 1988, Rochester and the eastern Monroe County suburbs — which provide about two-fifths of the 29th District vote — gave Horton 68 percent.

The Rochester portion of the 29th includes the black and Puerto Rican neighborhoods in the northeastern part of the city, which contrast with the generally rural and suburban character of the rest of the district. Some of the Eastman Kodak plants that anchor the city's industrial base are in this section.

The district also takes in the affluent Republicans who live along East Avenue, which leads out to the suburbs. The suburbs contain a Xerox facility and other high-tech plants that employ engineers who maintain Republican voting habits.

The remainder of the 29th is rural Republican country that stretches from the Lake Ontario shoreline to the fruit orchards of central New York. Oswego County, which contains a State University of New York campus at Oswego, provides the district's second-largest bloc of votes; the county gave George Bush 58 percent in 1988.

Cayuga and Seneca counties, at the heart of the scenic Finger Lakes area, are tourist magnets. These mainly rural counties are generally Republican, but not overwhelmingly so; Cayuga in particular has some Democratic votes in the working-class city of Auburn (population 31,000).

The 29th contains a slice of Oneida County, but not the most populous part; Utica and Rome are in the neighboring 25th District. Some 29th District residents are military personnel who work at Griffiss Air Force Base, also across the district line in the 25th.

Population: 515,404. White 483,123 (94%), Black 23,683 (5%), Other 3,933 (1%). Spanish origin 7,774 (2%). 18 and over 365,972 (71%), 65 and over 59,666 (12%). Median age: 30.

enthusiastic support to creation of the Department of Education, and one of just a few to support establishing the Department of Energy. In both cases, he avoided philosophical debates, saying he simply wanted to make government more efficient and cost-effective. During the 100th Congress' consideration of legislation to elevate the Veterans Administration to a Cabinet-level position, Horton was part of the GOP majority that backed the proposal. He said high-level representation was needed to ensure that commitments are carried out.

The one long-term crusade of Horton's career has been to analyze and reduce government paperwork. He steered legislation through Congress in 1975 to set up a paperwork study commission, and headed the inquiry himself. After two years, 36 reports and 770 recommendations, the commission issued its findings.

Citing a "profusion of inconsistent and often conflicting laws, policies and practices," the commission recommended that government policy makers, including Congress, consider paperwork costs when writing and implementing laws. It suggested consolidating federal forms, writing regulations in understandable English and creating a new Cabinet agency, a Department of Administration. Horton was able to write some of these recommendations into law later, in the 1980 Paperwork Reduction Act. This legislation set up a central bureau in the Office of Management and Budget to identify unnecessary paperwork.

Horton, now the dean of the New York delegation, has such a low-key style that few regard him as a deal maker in the House. But as New York's spokesman on the Republican committee assignment panel, he pulls off some impressive moves, despite his lack of party fealty. The opening of the 99th Congress was one of his best moments. In a year when there were few vacancies on major committees, he managed to get one home-state colleague on Ways and Means and another on Energy and Commerce.

At Home: While thousands were leaving upstate New York for the Sun Belt after World War II, Horton was moving in the other direction. Born in Texas and educated in Louisiana, he headed north, graduated from Cornell Law School, and settled in Rochester to become a practicing attorney.

Had he remained in Texas in the 1950s, he would have found it difficult to get far in politics as a Republican. In Rochester, he fit right in.

Elected to the Rochester City Council in 1955 to fill an unexpired term, Horton was re-elected in 1957 for a four-year term. During his time on the council he was chairman of its Public Utilities and Special Services Committee. He served until 1961, when he became a casualty of a political sweep by the Democrats. It was the first time the GOP had lost control of the city government in 25 years.

Meanwhile, he had become involved in minor-league baseball. He was president of the Rochester Redwings and executive vice president of the International League from 1959-60.

In 1962 a Rochester-area congressional seat opened up with the illness and retirement of Republican Rep. Jessica Weis, who had been a power in the national Republican Party as New York committeewoman for 20 years. Horton was the consensus choice of the Republican leaders in the district, and became the GOP nominee without a primary.

Horton's comfortable win that November set the pattern for his career. Although a series of redistrictings over the years has taken away some of his Rochester base, his Democratic opposition has been minimal; he regularly gets two-thirds of the vote or better.

In 1976 Horton was arrested for speeding and drunken driving. He pleaded guilty, accepted a punishment of a few days in jail, and weathered the incident without political damage.

Committees

Government Operations (Ranking)
Legislation and National Security (ranking)

Post Office and Civil Service (2nd of 9 Republicans)
Postal Operations and Services (ranking)

Elections

1988 General

Frank Horton (R)	132,608	(69%)
James R. Vogel (D)	51,243	(27%)

1986 General

Frank Horton (R)	99,704	(71%)
James R. Vogel (R)	34,194	(24%)

Previous Winning Percentages: **1984** (70%) **1982** (66%) **1980** (73%) **1978** (87%) **1976** (66%) **1974** (68%) **1972** (72%) **1970** (71%) **1968** (70%) **1966** (67%) **1964** (56%) **1962** (59%)

District Vote For President

	1988	1984	1980	1976
D	99,636 (46%)	82,066 (37%)	83,709 (40%)	77,962 (42%)
R	113,988 (53%)	140,599 (63%)	101,446 (49%)	108,699 (58%)
I			18,552 (9%)	

Campaign Finance

	Receipts	Receipts from PACs	Expend-itures
1988			
Horton (R)	$163,751	$126,560 (77%)	$130,597
Vogel (D)	$7,478	0	$4,514
1986			
Horton (R)	$134,984	$101,850 (76%)	$96,489
Vogel (D)	$22,015	0	$20,893

Key Votes

1987

Raise speed limit to 65 mph	Y
Approve Gephardt "fair trade" amendment	Y
Ban testing of larger nuclear weapons	Y
Delay "re-flagging" of Kuwaiti tankers	Y
Approve tax-raising deficit-reduction bill	N

1988

Approve aid to Nicaraguan contras	N
Enact civil rights restoration bill over Reagan veto	Y
Kill 60-day plant-closing notification measure	N
Pass omnibus trade bill over Reagan veto	Y
Approve death penalty for drug-related murders	Y
Bar federal funds for abortions in cases of rape and incest	N
Oppose seven-day waiting period for purchase of handguns	Y

Voting Studies

	Presidential Support		Party Unity		Conservative Coalition	
Year	S	O	S	O	S	O
1988	30	58	28	62	55	34
1987	35	59	27	64	74	26
1986	27	67	18	74	48	40
1985	31	68	25	66	51	36
1984	48	45	35	59	68	32
1983	39	56	32	61	43	47
1982	39	47	39	50	55	36
1981	50	34	45	37	37	44

Interest Group Ratings

Year	ADA	ACU	AFL-CIO	CCUS
1988	65	22	92	50
1987	52	10	69	43
1986	75	10	100	31
1985	50	30	82	35
1984	60	21	69	56
1983	40	32	44	53
1982	50	18	65	35
1981	35	69	53	82

30 Louise M. Slaughter (D)

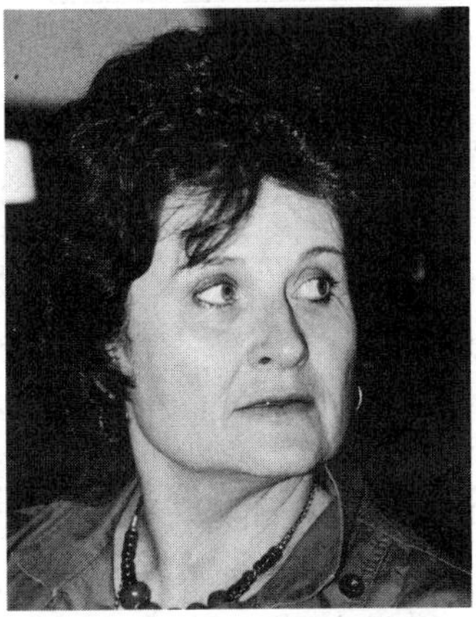

Of Fairport — Elected 1986

Born: Aug. 14, 1929, Harlan County, Ky.
Education: U. of Kentucky, B.S. 1951, M.S. 1953.
Occupation: Market researcher.
Family: Husband, Robert Slaughter; three children.
Religion: Episcopalian.
Political Career: Monroe County legislator, 1975-79; N.Y. Assembly 1983-87.
Capitol Office: 1707 Longworth Bldg. 20515; 225-3615.

In Washington: Slaughter could go far in the House on her personal charm alone. But her ability to win and hold a normally Republican district and her record as a liberal Democratic loyalist have quickly ingratiated Slaughter to the party leadership.

When House Democrats caucused to organize for the 101st Congress, Slaughter's popularity was evident: She was asked to make nominating speeches for four members of the leadership. Speaking in the Kentucky accent that belies her longtime residency in upstate New York, Slaughter stood to praise House Majority Leader Thomas S. Foley, Caucus chairman nominee William H. Gray III, Chief Deputy Whip Steny H. Hoyer, and Budget Committee chairman nominee Leon E. Panetta.

Having friends in such high places was of great benefit to Slaughter, who was named to the high-profile Rules Committee early in her second House term. In June 1989, she was named to a Rules vacancy caused by the death of committee Chairman Claude Pepper of Florida.

Even in her freshman term, Slaughter found little to complain about in her assignment to Public Works. Like most freshmen, she concentrated on bringing federal projects to her district.

Slaughter's seats on the Government Operations and Select Aging committees enabled her to play a broader legislative role. Slaughter, who has a master's degree in public health, authored an amendment to the Older Americans Act to fund a preventive-medicine program for the elderly.

But even much of her policy work seemed to lead Slaughter back home. When she added a provision to the 1988 Railway Safety Act — requiring that Northeast Corridor trains be fitted with automatic controls to keep them from running stop signals — Slaughter reminded constituents that General Railway Signal, a 30th District firm, is one of two U.S. companies producing such equipment.

At Home: Slaughter's engaging personality, grass-roots organization and fund-raising capacity were major factors in her 1986 upset of conservative GOP Rep. Fred J. Eckert. The same qualities enabled her to hold the seat easily in 1988 over a more moderate opponent.

With her liberal views and Southern accent (she moved north from Kentucky in the 1950s), Slaughter is a rather singular figure in western New York politics. In the 1970s, she served in the Monroe County Legislature and worked for Mario M. Cuomo, then New York's secretary of state. In 1982, she won a state Assembly seat, upsetting a GOP incumbent.

Slaughter's arguments with the state's private power companies gave her a populist image that earned her support from liberals and labor activists. These groups provided the base of her 1986 challenge to Eckert.

A former state legislator, Eckert had won in 1984 to succeed popular GOP Rep. Barber B. Conable Jr. But Eckert's staunch conservatism contrasted with Conable's more moderate image, discomfiting even many Republicans in the middle-of-the-road district. With Democratic PACs targeting Eckert for defeat, Slaughter edged him in fund raising with nearly $600,000. She ran a series of TV ads, including one featuring an Eckert imitator slapping the word "NO" on legislation with a huge rubber stamp. Parrying Eckert's efforts to portray her as an ultraliberal, Slaughter won with 51 percent of the vote.

She moved quickly to solidify her popularity, providing access to constituents and the local media. She repeated her fund-raising success, collecting nearly $900,000.

Her 1988 Republican opponent, 33-year-old Monroe County legislator John D. Bouchard, ran a two-pronged campaign, patterning himself after Conable, and portraying Slaughter as a puppet of organized labor. But his campaign never jelled; Slaughter won with 57 percent.

New York 30

West — Part of Rochester; Batavia

Over the years, the Rochester-area districts — including the present 30th — were Republican strongholds. The region's corporate giants — the Eastman Kodak Co. and the Xerox Corp. — spawned a large white-collar managerial class that leaned Republican. The generally moderate GOP leadership seldom antagonized the blue-collar population enough to benefit Democratic candidates. Add in the traditional upstate animosity to Democratic New York City, and the 30th contained the ingredients for Republican dominance.

However, in 1984, conservative hard-liner Fred J. Eckert succeeded Republican Barber B. Conable Jr., a popular centrist. Two years later, voter qualms about Eckert opened the door for Slaughter, who quickly secured the seat for her party.

The rapid shift in voter attitudes was amplified in 1988. In 1986, Slaughter had narrowly won on the strength of the urban and suburban vote in west Rochester and its Monroe County environs; Eckert held on in the more rural areas spread across four counties. By 1988, though, Slaughter was not only winning big in metro Rochester, but also carrying the outlying counties.

There is some irony in the recent Democratic upsurge: The redistricting of the early 1980s seemingly made the district more Republican. Rochester was split, and the district's political tone was seemingly set by the GOP-minded suburbs along Lake Ontario, such as Greece and Parma. Their normal GOP tendencies were fortified by the addition of Irondequoit, also on Lake Ontario, and Perinton, Pittsford and Mendon, Monroe County suburbs southeast of Rochester, which are largely bedroom communities for middle-management employees of Kodak, Xerox and other firms.

Outside Rochester and its immediate environs, the district is mainly dairy and vegetable farm land that is more reliable for Republicans. But Genesee County harbors industrial Batavia. Through the county flows the Genesee River, one of the few in the United States that flows northward.

Population: 516,819. White 481,183 (93%), Black 25,075 (5%), Other 4,741 (1%). Spanish origin 9,174 (2%). 18 and over 371,098 (72%), 65 and over 54,869 (11%). Median age: 30.

Committees

Rules (9th of 9 Democrats)
Rules of the House

Select Aging (32nd of 39 Democrats)
Human Services

Elections

1988 General

Louise M. Slaughter (D)	128,364	(57%)
John D. Bouchard (R)	89,126	(39%)

1986 General

Louise M. Slaughter (D)	86,777	(51%)
Fred J. Eckert (R)	83,402	(49%)

District Vote For President

	1988	1984	1980	1976
D	106,373 (45%)	86,561 (37%)	107,324 (45%)	113,013 (44%)
R	127,468 (54%)	146,976 (63%)	106,460 (44%)	143,933 (56%)
I			21,123 (9%)	

Campaign Finance

	Receipts	Receipts from PACs	Expend-itures
1988			
Slaughter (D)	$882,554	$444,422 (50%)	$953,577
Bouchard (R)	$319,621	$78,448 (25%)	$310,704
1986			
Slaughter (D)	$582,059	$292,984 (50%)	$553,072
Eckert (R)	$564,664	$239,308 (42%)	$565,374

Key Votes

1987	
Raise speed limit to 65 mph	N
Approve Gephardt "fair trade" amendment	Y
Ban testing of larger nuclear weapons	Y
Delay "re-flagging" of Kuwaiti tankers	Y
Approve tax-raising deficit-reduction bill	N
1988	
Approve aid to Nicaraguan contras	N
Enact civil rights restoration bill over Reagan veto	Y
Kill 60-day plant-closing notification measure	N
Pass omnibus trade bill over Reagan veto	Y
Approve death penalty for drug-related murders	N
Bar federal funds for abortions in cases of rape and incest	N
Oppose seven-day waiting period for purchase of handguns	N

Voting Studies

	Presidential Support		Party Unity		Conservative Coalition	
Year	S	O	S	O	S	O
1988	23	73	92	8	37	61
1987	17	78	83	9	35	60

Interest Group Ratings

Year	ADA	ACU	AFL-CIO	CCUS
1988	85	8	100	43
1987	76	10	87	29

31 Bill Paxon (R)

Of East Aurora — Elected 1988

Born: April 29, 1954, Buffalo, N.Y.
Education: Canisius College, B.A. 1977.
Occupation: Public official.
Family: Single.
Religion: Roman Catholic.
Political Career: Erie County Legislature, 1978-82; N.Y. Assembly, 1983-89.
Capitol Office: 1173 Longworth Bldg. 20515; 225-5265.

The Path to Washington: When Republican Rep. Jack F. Kemp made clear his intent to run for the 1988 presidential nomination, Paxon was touted as his heir apparent. In December 1987, Kemp described Paxon, a like-minded conservative, as "our next congressman in the 31st District."

But Paxon's election did not turn out to be quite so predetermined as that: He had to weather a vigorous Democratic challenge from Erie County Clerk David Swarts. In the end, though, Paxon's decade-long career in state and local office as well as the GOP tilt of the suburban and rural district tipped the scales; Paxon won with 54 percent of the vote.

Paxon is the only member of the freshman class who was under age 35 when he took office, yet he is a veteran of politics in western New York. The son of an Erie County family-court judge, Paxon worked while in college as an aide to the Republican minority in the state Assembly, and as an assistant to then-Erie County Executive Edward Regan (the current state comptroller).

Paxon jumped into politics himself right after his 1977 graduation from Buffalo's Canisius College; at age 23, he became the youngest-ever member of the Erie County Legislature. Endorsed by the county GOP organization, he easily won the party primary, then defeated a Democrat with 56 percent of the vote.

Paxon's chairmanship of the county Legislature's Economic Development Committee earned him an appointment to a state development task force. He pushed Kemp's "enterprise zone" concept of providing tax incentives for businesses that locate in economically depressed urban areas.

Paxon twice was re-elected to his county post by huge margins, then easily won an open state Assembly seat in 1982. He cut a conservative profile in Albany, promoting Republican efforts to cut state welfare costs, and often opposing efforts to expand state regulation. Paxon also gained the ranking position on the Assembly corrections committee; his district included the Attica state prison.

An outgoing personality and good constituent service helped keep him popular with voters. He had no Democratic opposition in 1984, when he served as regional chairman of President Reagan's re-election campaign, and none again in 1986.

Since Paxon's district encompassed the Erie County suburbs that form the population core of the 31st District, Republicans were confident about his prospects of succeeding Kemp. They believed that his conservatism fit a district served for 18 years by Kemp, a national conservative spokesman.

But Democrats had long insisted that Kemp's electoral success was based more on his celebrity as a former Buffalo Bills football star than on his ideology. They found a strong spokesman for their view in Swarts, a former teacher. He had honed his campaign skills in a futile 1983 challenge to a popular Republican Erie County executive and in a successful 1986 bid for county clerk.

Swarts described Paxon as an ideologue with a reflexive opposition to business regulation. As evidence of his foe's alleged "extremism," Swarts' literature included lists of Paxon's Assembly votes against bills backed by consumer and environmentalist groups. Paxon accused Swarts of distorting his record, and countered by describing the Democrat as an "off-the-scale" liberal.

Swarts drew the attention of national Democratic Party campaign officials in Washington, who made the 31st a priority contest. The race was close in Erie County, where Paxon prevailed with just 51 percent of the vote. But he had more breathing room elsewhere, including rural Wyoming County, where he won nearly 70 percent.

Paxon's background helped him earn a seat on the Banking, Finance and Urban Affairs Committee for the 101st Congress.

New York 31

West — Buffalo Suburbs; Canandaigua

During the years leading up to longtime 31st District Republican Rep. Jack F. Kemp's presidential bid, it was often said that he would have unusual Republican appeal to industrial workers, since he was from a Buffalo district. But in reality, Kemp always represented the Erie County suburbs, not the heavily unionized and Democratic city of Buffalo. The redistricting of the early 1980s moved the district to the east, making it even more likely that a 31st District voter would be a banker, not a blue-collar worker.

Still, there are a few working-class towns, such as West Seneca and Hamburg, in the Erie County part of the district, making it a place where Democrats can compete; Kemp's protégé Paxon lost narrowly to his Democratic opponent there. But the Republican nature of the more rural counties that make up the rest of the district make the 31st, as a whole, a fairly comfortable place for Paxon and other Republican candidates.

Losing Erie County, though, went a long way toward holding down Paxon's victory margin; 75 percent of the district vote is cast there. It includes Amherst, site of the State University of New York at Buffalo campus and, with 110,000 residents, easily the district's largest city. The 31st's slice of Erie County also takes in Orchard Park, a small town most notable as the site of Rich Stadium, home of the Buffalo Bills football team on which Kemp once starred.

To the south, the 31st takes in a small, working-class strip of Cattaraugus County. The district then ranges east, absorbing all of rural Wyoming County. This is the most solidly Republican turf in the district. Paxon won the county by a better than 2-to-1 margin; George Bush took 64 percent of the vote.

Completing the eastern flank of the district are large portions of Livingston and Ontario counties. In Ontario County, the 31st takes in a portion of the scenic Finger Lakes region. Republicans have the registration advantage over Democrats in both counties.

Population: 516,271. White 501,526 (97%), Black 6,545 (1%), Other 6,386 (1%). Spanish origin 3,943 (1%). 18 and over 369,104 (72%), 65 and over 56,281 (11%). Median age: 31.

Committees

Banking, Finance and Urban Affairs (20th of 20 Republicans)
Economic Stabilization; Housing and Community Development; International Development, Finance, Trade and Monetary Policy; Policy Research and Insurance

Select Narcotics Abuse and Control (11th of 12 Republicans)

Campaign Finance

	Receipts	Receipts from PACs	Expend-itures
1988			
Paxon (R)	$702,136	$242,558 (35%)	$702,038
Swarts (D)	$457,504	$233,314 (51%)	$457,262

Election

1988 General

Bill Paxon (R)	117,710	(53%)
David J. Swarts (D)	102,777	(47%)

District Vote For President

	1988	1984	1980	1976
D	101,948 (44%)	88,266 (38%)	89,161 (40%)	94,307 (43%)
R	130,099 (56%)	145,871 (62%)	112,088 (50%)	123,578 (56%)
I			17,605 (8%)	

32 John J. LaFalce (D)

Of Tonawanda — Elected 1974

Born: Oct. 6, 1939, Buffalo, N.Y.
Education: Canisius College, B.S. 1961; Villanova U., J.D. 1964.
Military Career: Army, 1965-67.
Occupation: Lawyer.
Family: Wife, Patricia Fisher; one child.
Religion: Roman Catholic.
Political Career: N.Y. Senate, 1971-73; N.Y. Assembly, 1973-75.
Capitol Office: 2367 Rayburn Bldg. 20515; 225-3231.

In Washington: An observer of LaFalce's work once said that the blunt, intense New Yorker "has an innate ability to rub people the wrong way." But if LaFalce sometimes comes across as temperamental and overbearing, he is also regarded as highly intelligent and well versed on banking law and small-business issues.

LaFalce's intellect and his will to win were both on display at the start of the 101st Congress, when he mounted a legislative assault on the purview of the Ways and Means Committee, took on its powerful chairman, Dan Rostenkowski, and came out on top.

The battle was over a bill LaFalce had introduced to repeal controversial new language in the tax code that required employers to provide similar benefits to all workers, regardless of pay. LaFalce called the non-discrimination rules "a legal straitjacket," and organized a House-wide revolt to scrap the so-called "Section 89" rules.

Early on, Rostenkowski railed against members urging repeal of Section 89, but LaFalce rounded up enough support to force the issue. "I didn't sit down and talk until I had 218 cosponsors," he said. Once he did, Rostenkowski backed down, introducing a bill that would, in effect, repeal Section 89 and start over.

LaFalce has served on the Banking Committee throughout his House career, and he has never been known to shy from a good fight there. In 1983, when committee Democrats chose a new chairman for the important Economic Stabilization Subcommittee, his aggressiveness and ability brought him the post. Carroll Hubbard Jr. of Kentucky had seniority over LaFalce, but could not match him in legislative skill. Committee members made it clear they wanted LaFalce, and Hubbard decided not to pursue the position.

As chairman of the panel, LaFalce was determined to crystallize the diverse arguments for some sort of "national industrial policy" into practical legislation. That effort yielded some piecemeal success, but in 1987 LaFalce gave up the subcommittee chair to attack from a different direction as chairman of the Small Business Committee.

LaFalce succeeded Parren J. Mitchell, a black Democrat from Maryland who had chaired Small Business for three terms. As the committee's first white chairman in six years, LaFalce was viewed skeptically by some black members, who feared he planned a major shift from Mitchell's focus on minority business programs. LaFalce laid out plans to emphasize a broader array of issues, including liability insurance and economic competitiveness.

Tensions between black committee members and LaFalce had brewed for several months when they finally boiled over at a meeting of Procurement Subcommittee Democrats in the summer of 1987. The panel was working on a bill LaFalce had crafted to overhaul a Small Business Administration (SBA) procurement program aimed at fostering minority-owned businesses. The program, which set aside non-bid contracts for minority-owned firms, had been widely viewed as suffering from abuse and mismanagement.

As LaFalce outlined his plan to the Procurement panel, Gus Savage, a black Democrat from Chicago and one of the House's more combustible members, became upset, in essence calling the bill a disaster. LaFalce and Savage got into a shouting match, with Savage questioning LaFalce's commitment to minority businesses and LaFalce accusing Savage of stirring up opposition among his black constituents.

LaFalce's comments centered on a story in *The Buffalo News* quoting the president of a Mitchell-chaired lobbying firm, who criticized the LaFalce package. LaFalce accused Savage of sending people to his district to attack him; Savage retorted that he did not have to do that — he would go to Buffalo himself. Once tempers cooled, Esteban E. Torres of California, a well-respected Hispanic member of the subcommittee, voiced support for LaFalce's proposal. That helped quiet the storm; the sub-

New York 32

West — Niagara Falls; Part of Rochester

The 32nd, which stretches all the way from the west side of Rochester to the north side of Buffalo, provides one of the more even partisan balances in New York state. It has gone for Republican Sen. Alfonse M. D'Amato; but it has also been dominated by Democratic Sen. Daniel Patrick Moynihan and Gov. Mario M. Cuomo. In presidential races, it tends to be close; in 1988, Democrat Michael S. Dukakis carried the 32nd with 51 percent.

Veteran Democratic House member LaFalce, who has close ties to northwestern New York's sizable Italian-American community, has always won easily in the 32nd. Italian neighborhoods dominate north Buffalo; significant numbers of Italians also live in the Rochester portion of the district, which also is home to many blacks and young professionals. Rochester hosts much of the district's industry: Bausch & Lomb and Eastman Kodak both maintain their corporate headquarters here.

But while the elongated district grabs off chunks of western New York's largest cities, the biggest share of the vote — over 40 percent — comes from Niagara County. Western Niagara County has the Democratic mill cities of North Tonawanda, Lockport and Niagara Falls.

Niagara Falls is, of course, renowned for its natural beauty. But the city of 65,000 developed a sinister ecological reputation a decade ago, when the local chemical industry was held responsible for contaminating the groundwater in the Love Canal residential neighborhood. In recent years, some people have returned to the area, which was evacuated in 1978, but the toxic-waste cleanup continues.

The more rural areas of eastern Niagara County, where fruit trees abound, provide a Republican balance to the blue-collar cities. Dukakis carried the county with 51 percent of the vote. Neighboring Orleans County, which is heavily farmed, is mainly Republican; George Bush took 60 percent there.

Population: 516,387. White 465,285 (90%), Black 43,511 (8%), Other 4,717 (1%). Spanish origin 5,937 (1%). 18 and over 375,165 (73%), 65 and over 60,874 (12%). Median age: 31.

committee approved LaFalce's proposal, sending it to the full committee, which backed it 40-1. President Reagan signed the bill in 1988.

Another LaFalce bill signed by Reagan in the 100th Congress made it easier for women-owned small firms to get commercial bank loans.

A Roman Catholic whose district includes blue-collar, ethnic neighborhoods, LaFalce has pushed to remove mention of abortion from the Democratic Party's national platform, which currently contains a plank supporting abortion rights. "We're just inviting people to vote against us," he told *The Wall Street Journal* in 1989. ". . . We're alienating the ethnics and the Catholics that have built the party." (His own district gave Michael S. Dukakis a narrow 51 percent victory in 1988 presidential voting.)

On Banking in the 100th Congress, LaFalce weighed in on congressional plans to rescue the ailing Federal Savings and Loan Insurance Corporation (FSLIC). After opposing Banking Chairman Fernand J. St Germain in his efforts to pass a bailout bill in 1987 — he favored a higher recapitalization amount than St Germain and the thrift industry wanted — LaFalce teamed with St Germain to introduce a bill in 1988. It extended for a year a moratorium on healthy savings and loan institutions' (S&Ls) switching deposit insurers. The concern was that healthy S&Ls would change their charters to those of banks and join the more robust Federal Deposit Insurance Corporation, putting the ailing FSLIC in even worse shape. LaFalce supported forcing thrifts to make a down payment toward the FSLIC's future. "There has to be a quid pro quo," he insisted. "We demanded it of Chrysler and New York City."

LaFalce pursued his pet "industrial policy" project doggedly through much of the 98th Congress, using his Economic Stabilization panel to hold a series of hearings that featured a long parade of captains of industry.

LaFalce and his subcommittee eventually settled on a proposal to create four new federal mechanisms: a Council on Industrial Competitiveness to design broad industrial development strategies; an Advanced Technology Foundation to commercialize promising technologies; a Bank for Industrial Competitiveness to make $8.5 billion worth of loans over 10 years to rising industries; and a Federal Industrial Mortgage Association to encourage long-term lending to these firms.

But industrial policy faced strong opposition from the Reagan administration, many GOP House members, and even some Democrats who were dubious about the bank. Industrial policy lost some of its luster as a compelling national issue once the recession of the early 1980s receded.

While the campaign for LaFalce's more ambitious plans essentially withered, in the 99th and 100th Congresses, the House passed omnibus trade legislation that included a new Council on Industrial Competitiveness.

LaFalce turned more of his attention to monetary policy as a way to approach the competitiveness issue. In the 99th Congress he worked on provisions in the trade bill that set the attainment of a "competitive" currency exchange rate as an explicit U.S. economic policy goal; the Treasury Department would be required to intervene in foreign currency markets to keep the dollar at the competitive target. LaFalce also played a leading role in crafting the Banking package included in the trade bill in the 100th Congress.

It is LaFalce's fate to represent the Love Canal area near Buffalo. He introduced a bill in 1979 that would have created an industry-financed fund to clean up chemical dump sites like that one, but later switched to lobbying for a similar "superfund" bill in Commerce. He spent much of 1980 working on the issue, testifying on it before virtually every committee that would listen. The superfund was created at the end of that year.

When superfund was reauthorized in the 99th Congress, LaFalce pushed an amendment requiring the Environmental Protection Agency to study potential dangers to those inhabiting contaminated areas around Love Canal. His successful amendment also allowed the EPA to purchase non-residential properties there.

At Home: A Buffalo lawyer, LaFalce burst onto the political scene in 1970 with an upset victory for the state Senate in a suburban district. Determined to cut short his political career, Republicans in the Legislature redrew the Senate district in 1972 to make his re-election hopeless. So he decided to take a step down and run for a seat in the state Assembly. When he won that, he secured a reputation as one of the strongest Democratic candidates western New York had seen in years.

While in the Legislature, LaFalce concentrated on procedural reform. He was a strong critic of Gov. Nelson A. Rockefeller and capitalized in his campaigns on deep-seated resentments against Rockefeller in Buffalo.

In 1974, when GOP Rep. Henry P. Smith retired, LaFalce campaigned in a district that had not been won by a Democrat in 62 years. His aggressive style produced a solid win, and has brought him subsequent easy re-elections. He had no Republican opponent in 1986.

Committees

Small Business (Chairman)
SBA, the General Economy and Minority Enterprise Development (chairman)

Banking, Finance and Urban Affairs (6th of 31 Democrats)
Economic Stabilization; Financial Institutions Supervision, Regulation and Insurance; Housing and Community Development; International Development, Finance, Trade and Monetary Policy

Elections

1988 General		
John J. LaFalce (D)	133,917	(73%)
Emil K. Everett (R)	50,229	(27%)
1986 General		
John J. LaFalce (D)	99,745	(91%)
Dean L. Walker (C)	6,234	(6%)

Previous Winning Percentages: **1984** (69%) **1982** (91%) **1980** (72%) **1978** (74%) **1976** (67%) **1974** (60%)

District Vote For President

	1988		1984		1980		1976	
D	104,507	(51%)	98,894	(45%)	89,401	(46%)	95,793	(46%)
R	98,419	(48%)	119,656	(55%)	87,703	(45%)	111,359	(54%)
I					15,345	(8%)		

Campaign Finance

	Receipts	Receipts from PACs	Expend-itures
1988			
LaFalce (D)	$241,784	$141,022 (58%)	$133,738
Everett (R)	$13,703	0	$13,702
1986			
LaFalce (D)	$151,800	$79,112 (52%)	$108,258

Key Votes

1987	
Raise speed limit to 65 mph	N
Approve Gephardt "fair trade" amendment	Y
Ban testing of larger nuclear weapons	Y
Delay "re-flagging" of Kuwaiti tankers	Y
Approve tax-raising deficit-reduction bill	N
1988	
Approve aid to Nicaraguan contras	N
Enact civil rights restoration bill over Reagan veto	Y
Kill 60-day plant-closing notification measure	N
Pass omnibus trade bill over Reagan veto	Y
Approve death penalty for drug-related murders	N
Bar federal funds for abortions in cases of rape and incest	Y
Oppose seven-day waiting period for purchase of handguns	N

Voting Studies

	Presidential Support		Party Unity		Conservative Coalition	
Year	S	O	S	O	S	O
1988	24	70	85	11	32	61
1987	20	77	83	9	26	74
1986	19	76	80	11	20	64
1985	30	66	77	15	22	73
1984	35	56	78	13	25	68
1983	30	67	84	12	19	75
1982	38	57	80	10	21	73
1981	36	61	78†	15†	27	68

† Not eligible for all recorded votes.

Interest Group Ratings

Year	ADA	ACU	AFL-CIO	CCUS
1988	80	8	93	38
1987	88	5	87	14
1986	85	10	83	25
1985	70	14	94	38
1984	80	24	83	43
1983	80	9	94	35
1982	85	5	94	24
1981	70	7	87	17

33 Henry J. Nowak (D)

Of Buffalo — Elected 1974

Born: Feb. 21, 1935, Buffalo, N.Y.
Education: Canisius College, B.B.A. 1957; U. of Buffalo, J.D. 1961.
Military Career: Army, 1957-62.
Occupation: Lawyer.
Family: Wife, Rose Santa Lucia; two children.
Religion: Roman Catholic.
Political Career: Erie County comptroller, 1966-74.
Capitol Office: 2240 Rayburn Bldg. 20515; 225-3306.

In Washington: Nowak plays politics in the House the way he learned to in the Erie County Democratic organization: He tends to the voters who elect him, listens to his party leaders and leaves lofty speechmaking to members who yearn for recognition beyond their constituencies.

Elected in a class of activist Democrats with wide-ranging agendas, Nowak stands out as one who has kept his politics local. Fortunately for him, he is a senior member of a committee where good personal relations are more important than rhetorical ability in getting things done. Nearly everybody on Public Works is there to bring federal money to his district, and Nowak's reluctance to make speeches has never been a disadvantage in securing federal funds. The Buffalo *News* has described him as "Buffalo's foremost ambassador to Washington in winning federal aid for vital community projects."

Nowak gauges that he has snagged several hundred million federal dollars for public works projects in Buffalo and Erie County. They range from the Buffalo Light Rail Transit Project to a swimming pool at Cazenovia Park.

In the 100th Congress, Nowak gained the chairmanship of the Public Works Subcommittee on Water Resources, which Robert A. Roe of New Jersey gave up after his signal achievement, passage of the 1986 Water Resources Act. Before taking over the chairmanship, Nowak had played no leadership role on the subcommittee, but he had characteristically made sure his district got its share of funds. His profile was not much higher as subcommittee chairman, but he kept the projects flowing home.

The 1986 water resources law authorized several Buffalo-area projects, including $9 million for a Gateway Bridge across the Buffalo River, $3.5 million for improvements in the Buffalo port area, and $1.54 million for Cazenovia Creek flood control. The act also provided for the federal government to fund 50 percent of the operation and maintenance costs of the New York State Barge Canal.

In 1988, the Water Resources Subcommittee produced another water-projects bill, putting the regular cycle of biennial authorizations back on track. (It took a 10-year struggle to enact the 1986 bill.) The 1988 bill authorized a $2 million repair — of which the federal government would pay $1 million — at a Buffalo small-boat harbor.

In the 99th Congress, Nowak served as chairman of the Public Works Subcommittee on Economic Development. In 1985, he tried to protect the Economic Development Administration from the Reagan administration's cutback efforts. His bill, authorizing the EDA for three years, passed the House easily, and though the Senate took no action, the EDA survived.

Nowak was also a member of the Small Business Committee. In 1984, he offered a bill to improve the secondary market for Small Business Administration loans, allowing lenders to pool the loans for sale. Language similar to Nowak's version was signed into law at the end of the 98th Congress.

At Home: Nowak made his way in politics as a solid party loyalist allied with Buffalo Democratic leader Joseph Crangle. He has rarely disappointed the Erie County organization, and it has rarely disappointed him.

After serving for a year as an assistant district attorney, Nowak was plucked from obscurity by Crangle in 1965 at the age of 30 and made the Democratic nominee for Erie County comptroller. His Polish name and background as a basketball star at Canisius College made him a good choice, and a strong Democratic showing in the county that year led to his election. He was re-elected twice, in 1969 and 1973.

In time, Nowak became known as the heir apparent to Democratic Rep. Thaddeus J. Dulski, chairman of the House Post Office Committee. When Dulski decided to retire in 1974, he waited until four days before the filing deadline so nobody could mount a serious campaign against Nowak.

His specialty of tending to district interests has paid off at the polls. In seven re-election campaigns, Nowak has never slipped below 75 percent of the vote.

New York 33

West — Buffalo

Decades of Rust Belt decline had a corrosive effect on Buffalo's morale and national image. Though still one of the nation's 50 largest cities with just under 325,000 people, Buffalo lost over 20 percent of its population in the 1970s, and another 9 percent in the first half of the 1980s. The grimy and economically flagging city became the butt of derogatory jokes, much the way Philadelphia and Cleveland had before.

In the last few years, though, city officials have begun to fight back. They have pointed to their efforts to revive the downtown area, including construction of a light-rail system down one of the main boulevards. A sparkling new ballpark has replaced venerable War Memorial Stadium — where the baseball movie "The Natural" was filmed — and the big crowds attending the AAA-level minor league games there have stoked the city's efforts to obtain a major league baseball team. City leaders have even asked for apologies from TV weathermen who joke about Buffalo's legendary winter weather, insisting that the Lake Erie snow belt is miles to the south.

Located some 400 miles north and west of New York City, Buffalo (the state's second-largest city) has much more in common with the cities of the industrial Midwest.

Blue-collar Poles are the predominant ethnic group in the city and throughout the district. They are concentrated in single-family frame houses on the eastern side of Buffalo and in the grimy town of Lackawanna, just to the south. Lackawanna suffered from the closing of a Bethlehem Steel plant in 1983, though it maintains some steel-finishing facilities.

Though Democratic loyalties have slipped at the presidential level in many ethnic blue-collar cities, they remain strong in Buffalo. Michael S. Dukakis, who carried the state, won the 33rd District with 66 percent of the vote. In 1984, Walter F. Mondale took 63 percent of the district's vote. Democratic strength here is bolstered by a black community that amounts to nearly 30 percent of Buffalo's population.

Population: 516,392. White 406,449 (79%), Black 98,074 (19%), Other 4,334 (1%). Spanish origin 11,024 (2%). 18 and over 383,256 (74%), 65 and over 69,957 (14%). Median age: 31.

Committees

Public Works and Transportation (5th of 31 Democrats)
Water Resources (chairman); Aviation; Public Buildings and Grounds; Surface Transportation

Science, Space and Technology (20th of 30 Democrats)
Natural Resources, Agriculture Research and Environment

Elections

1988 General		
Henry J. Nowak (D)	139,604	(100%)
1988 Primary		
Henry J. Nowak (D)	39,860	(91%)
Charles H. Carman (D)	3,706	(9%)
1986 General		
Henry J. Nowak (D)	109,256	(85%)
Charles A. Walker (R)	19,147	(15%)

Previous Winning Percentages: **1984** (78%) **1982** (84%) **1980** (83%) **1978** (79%) **1976** (78%) **1974** (75%)

District Vote For President

	1988		1984		1980		1976	
D	130,124	(66%)	138,667	(63%)	126,145	(63%)	127,760	(57%)
R	65,217	(33%)	82,638	(37%)	60,282	(30%)	94,722	(42%)
I					11,125	(6%)		

Campaign Finance

	Receipts	Receipts from PACs	Expend-itures
1988			
Nowak (D)	$122,306	$91,225 (75%)	$94,042
1986			
Nowak (D)	$110,284	$34,050 (31%)	$76,902
Walker (R)	$8,002	0	$8,432

Key Votes

1987	
Raise speed limit to 65 mph	N
Approve Gephardt "fair trade" amendment	Y
Ban testing of larger nuclear weapons	Y
Delay "re-flagging" of Kuwaiti tankers	Y
Approve tax-raising deficit-reduction bill	Y
1988	
Approve aid to Nicaraguan contras	N
Enact civil rights restoration bill over Reagan veto	Y
Kill 60-day plant-closing notification measure	N
Pass omnibus trade bill over Reagan veto	Y
Approve death penalty for drug-related murders	N
Bar federal funds for abortions in cases of rape and incest	+
Oppose seven-day waiting period for purchase of handguns	N

Voting Studies

	Presidential Support		Party Unity		Conservative Coalition	
Year	**S**	**O**	**S**	**O**	**S**	**O**
1988	25	70	93	4	16	74
1987	19	78	89	5	30	67
1986	18	82	92	5	16	82
1985	23	76	89	4	11	89
1984	32	64	88	7	19	76
1983	23	74	91	6	12	85
1982	34	65	90	8	14	86
1981	38	61	87	10	17	77

Interest Group Ratings

Year	ADA	ACU	AFL-CIO	CCUS
1988	90	12	100	36
1987	76	4	100	7
1986	95	5	100	28
1985	80	10	100	27
1984	85	17	92	40
1983	85	17	94	30
1982	100	5	100	23
1981	75	0	67	17

34 Amo Houghton (R)

Of Corning — Elected 1986

Born: Aug. 7, 1926, Corning, N.Y.
Education: Harvard U., B.A. 1950, M.B.A. 1952.
Military Career: Marine Corps, 1945-46.
Occupation: Glassworks company executive.
Family: Separated; four children.
Religion: Episcopalian.
Political Career: No previous office.
Capitol Office: 1217 Longworth Bldg. 20515; 225-3161.

In Washington: Not many corporate chief executive officers cap their careers by becoming a member of the minority party in a legislative chamber of 435. But Houghton, former CEO for Corning Glass Works and scion of one of the nation's wealthiest families, has done just that. At age 62 he openly states that he does not plan to stay in Washington long; while here, however, he has a missionary's enthusiasm for making a contribution.

Houghton's business acumen helped him get a seat on the Budget Committee as a freshman. Many Republicans — especially junior ones — feel the Democrats on Budget run roughshod over the GOP minority. But for a man used to giving orders, Houghton has shown little frustration. He is affable, with a sense of humor he can turn on himself, and there is a certain amount of the diplomat in his blood. His father was an ambassador to France; his grandfather, Alanson Bigelow Houghton, was an ambassador and a U.S. representative. In the 101st Congress, Houghton won an assignment befitting the family background — a seat on Foreign Affairs.

Houghton is to the left of many of his GOP colleagues; he supported President Reagan only a little more than half the time in 1988. One major area where Houghton split with Reagan was on the president's support for military aid to the Nicaraguan contras. Houghton found another way to try to make an impact in Central America: In the 100th Congress, he worked to put together private funding for a scholarship program to bring Nicaraguan students to colleges and universities in western New York.

"Here was a way to help a country rather than just posturing," Houghton said of the plan. "Many times when congressmen go down there, they look at what's happened, they fly down on a military plane, they come back and have a press conference and that's all. Here is a way of saying 'we want to help' in a human way."

At Home: The Houghton family tradition can be summed up in these words: Corning Glass and public service. Houghton followed his forebears into the executive suite of Steuben County's Corning Glass Works Co., serving 19 years as chief executive officer. Then, at age 60, he entered the public sector, as had his father and grandfather.

Houghton's political baptism came in 1986, after 34th District Democratic Rep. Stan Lundine was tapped by Gov. Mario M. Cuomo to run for lieutenant governor. The opportunity provided by the open seat appealed to the semi-retired Houghton, who had been working on efforts to provide economic relief for the African nation of Zimbabwe.

Houghton was already popular in his hometown, where Corning Glass is the major employer. In 1972, the company helped finance restoration after a flood devastated the city. So while he had never been particularly active in local Republican affairs, he had little trouble securing the GOP House nomination.

In an effort to build across-the-board appeal, Houghton pointed to his experience at creating jobs. He also touted his service as co-chairman of a labor-industry coalition that lobbied heavily for a Democratic-sponsored trade bill in Congress.

Nonetheless, Houghton's Democratic opponent, Cattaraugus County District Attorney Larry Himelein, tried to portray him as a Brahmin elitist. "Running for Congress isn't going to finishing school, it's not going to the country club," Himelein said during the campaign.

Had he been running against a less able candidate, Himelein might have been able to exploit a satirical front-page profile of Houghton published in *The Wall Street Journal.* The article focused on Houghton's posh campaign style: If he could not get to a political stop in the plush motor home he had stocked with liquor, cigars and homemade cookies, he flew there in his private plane.

But Houghton ably deflected criticism arising from the article with his fine-tuned sense of humor. Staked by a 3-to-1 margin in Steuben County, Houghton won 60 percent of the districtwide vote. He quickly established himself as a popular fixture, running in 1988 without opposition.

New York 34

Southern Tier — Jamestown; Elmira

The long and narrow 34th stretches across the bottom of New York state — the Southern Tier — all the way from Lake Erie on the west to Elmira in the east. Though Democrat Stan Lundine, now lieutenant governor, held the House seat for a decade, he was an exception; these hilly, rural counties favor the GOP.

In 1988, George Bush took Chautauqua County, the district's largest, with 55 percent of the vote, and won 2-to-1 in both Steuben County, the district's second-largest, and in more rural Alleghany County.

Steuben County contains Houghton's home base of Corning, one of America's better-known company towns. Corning Glass produces utilitarian dishes and cookware; its Steuben Glass Works makes more costly decorative crystal pieces. Long a rather seedy industrial town, Corning (population 12,000) suffered severe flood damage from Hurricane Agnes in 1972. Corning Glass financed its rehabilitation, including a new City Hall and an "old town" style downtown area that is now a tourist attraction. The northern part of Steuben County is overtaken by wine vineyards. The state's most widely known wines, Taylor and Great Western, are produced there.

On the western edge of the 34th is Chautauqua County. It contains Chautauqua Lake, a popular tourist spot first developed in 1876 as a center for religious training.

Chautauqua also contains much of the 34th's Democratic vote. The city of Jamestown there is the district's largest (35,000 people); Lundine was its mayor before moving to Congress. Jamestown's Democratic industrial workers are a counterbalance to the GOP dairy farmers elsewhere in the county.

In Chemung County, at the 34th's eastern end, Republican farmers are arrayed against the blue-collar Democrats of Elmira, a city of 32,000. Like Corning, Elmira suffered severe hurricane damage, but it did not bounce back as well.

Population: 516,154. White 502,383 (97%), Black 7,720 (2%), Other 3,564 (1%). Spanish origin 4,212 (1%). 18 and over 368,422 (71%), 65 and over 67,643 (13%). Median age: 31.

Committees

Budget (9th of 14 Republicans)
Task Forces: Budget Process, Reconciliation and Enforcement; Community Development and Natural Resources

Foreign Affairs (17th of 18 Republicans)
Africa; International Economic Policy and Trade

Elections

1988 General		
Amo Houghton (R)	131,078	(96%)
Ian Kelly Woodward (L)	4,797	(4%)
1986 General		
Amo Houghton (R)	85,856	(60%)
Larry M. Himelein (D)	56,898	(40%)

District Vote For President

	1988	1984	1980	1976
D	78,930 (40%)	67,870 (32%)	71,056 (37%)	83,721 (42%)
R	118,087 (60%)	142,401 (68%)	104,050 (54%)	116,622 (58%)
I			15,091 (8%)	

Campaign Finance

	Receipts	Receipts from PACs	Expend-itures
1988			
Houghton (R)	$501,195	$129,950 (26%)	$362,990
1986			
Houghton (R)	$722,833	$149,388 (21%)	$720,843
Himelein (D)	$107,116	$44,330 (41%)	$107,100

Key Votes

1987	
Raise speed limit to 65 mph	Y
Approve Gephardt "fair trade" amendment	N
Ban testing of larger nuclear weapons	N
Delay "re-flagging" of Kuwaiti tankers	N
Approve tax-raising deficit-reduction bill	N
1988	
Approve aid to Nicaraguan contras	N
Enact civil rights restoration bill over Reagan veto	Y
Kill 60-day plant-closing notification measure	Y
Pass omnibus trade bill over Reagan veto	Y
Approve death penalty for drug-related murders	Y
Bar federal funds for abortions in cases of rape and incest	X
Oppose seven-day waiting period for purchase of handguns	Y

Voting Studies

	Presidential Support		Party Unity		Conservative Coalition	
Year	S	O	S	O	S	O
1988	52	45	61	32	92	8
1987	63	35	62	33	84	14

Interest Group Ratings

Year	ADA	ACU	AFL-CIO	CCUS
1988	45	56	57	100
1987	28	39	38	80

North Carolina

U.S. CONGRESS

SENATE 1 D, 1 R

HOUSE 8 D, 3 R

LEGISLATURE

Senate 37 D, 13 R

House 74 D, 46 R

ELECTIONS

1988 Presidential Vote	
Bush	58%
Dukakis	42%
1984 Presidential Vote	
Reagan	62%
Mondale	38%
1980 Presidential Vote	
Reagan	49%
Carter	47%
Anderson	3%
Turnout rate in 1984	47%
Turnout rate in 1986	33%
Turnout rate in 1988	43%

(as percentage of voting age population)

POPULATION AND GROWTH

1980 population	5,881,766
1988 population estimate (10th in the nation)	6,489,000
Percent change 1980-1988	+10%

DEMOGRAPHIC BREAKDOWN

White	76%
Black	22%
Other	1%
(Spanish origin)	1%
Urban	48%
Rural	52%
Born in state	76%
Foreign-born	1%

MAJOR CITIES

Charlotte	352,070
Raleigh	180,430
Greensboro	176,650
Winston-Salem	148,080
Durham	113,890

AREA AND LAND USE

Area	48,844 sq. miles (29th)
Farm	33%
Forest	61%
Federally owned	7%

Gov. James G. Martin (R)
Of Lake Norman — Elected 1984

Born: Dec. 11, 1935, Savannah, Ga.
Education: Davidson College, B.S. 1957; Princeton U., Ph.D. 1960.
Occupation: Professor.
Religion: Presbyterian.
Political Career: U.S. House, 1973-85.
Next Election: 1992.

WORK

Occupations	
White-collar	45%
Blue-collar	41%
Service workers	11%
Government Workers	
Federal	45,179
State	111,376
Local	259,304

MONEY

Median family income	$ 16,792 (43rd)
Tax burden per capita	$ 831 (26th)

EDUCATION

Spending per pupil through grade 12	$ 2,982 (42nd)
Persons with college degrees	13% (43rd)

CRIME

Violent crime rate	484 per 100,000 (20th)

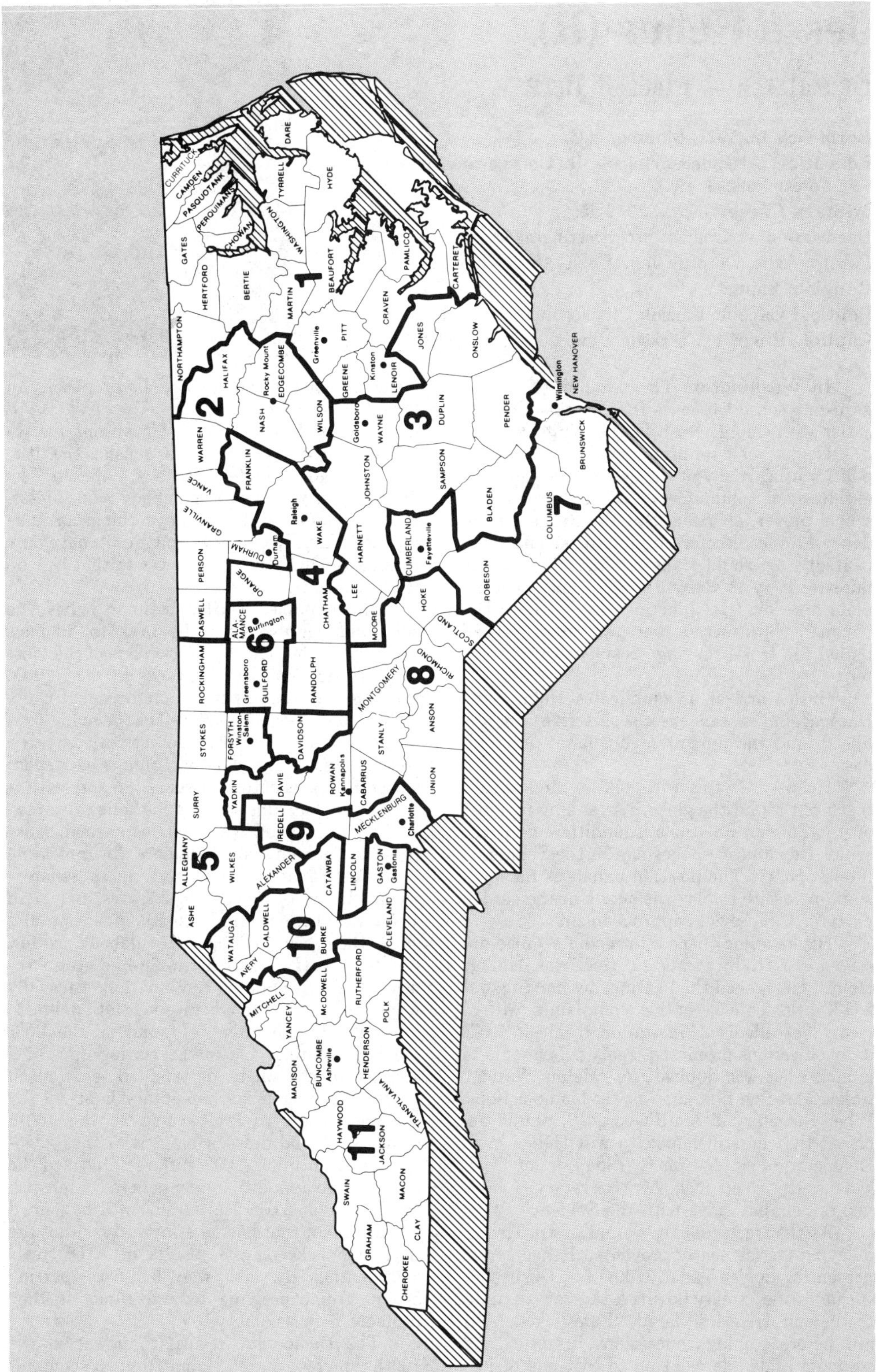
1
2
3
4
5
6
7
8
9
10
11
CURRITUCK
CAMDEN
PASQUOTANK
PERQUIMANS
CHOWAN
GATES
HERTFORD
BERTIE
NORTHAMPTON
HALIFAX
DARE
TYRRELL
HYDE
WASHINGTON
MARTIN
BEAUFORT
PAMLICO
CARTERET
CRAVEN
PITT
Greenville
EDGECOMBE
Rocky Mount
NASH
WILSON
GREENE
Kinston
LENOIR
JONES
ONSLOW
WAYNE
Goldsboro
DUPLIN
PENDER
NEW HANOVER
Wilmington
BRUNSWICK
WARREN
VANCE
FRANKLIN
JOHNSTON
SAMPSON
BLADEN
COLUMBUS
GRANVILLE
WAKE
Raleigh
HARNETT
CUMBERLAND
Fayetteville
ROBESON
DURHAM
Durham
PERSON
ORANGE
CASWELL
ALAMANCE
Burlington
CHATHAM
LEE
MOORE
HOKE
SCOTLAND
ROCKINGHAM
GUILFORD
Greensboro
RANDOLPH
MONTGOMERY
RICHMOND
ANSON
STOKES
FORSYTH
Winston Salem
DAVIDSON
STANLY
UNION
SURRY
YADKIN
DAVIE
ROWAN
Kannapolis
CABARRUS
MECKLENBURG
Charlotte
ALLEGHANY
WILKES
IREDELL
ALEXANDER
CATAWBA
LINCOLN
GASTON
Gastonia
ASHE
WATAUGA
CALDWELL
BURKE
CLEVELAND
AVERY
MITCHELL
YANCEY
McDOWELL
RUTHERFORD
POLK
MADISON
BUNCOMBE
Asheville
HENDERSON
TRANSYLVANIA
HAYWOOD
JACKSON
SWAIN
MACON
GRAHAM
CHEROKEE
CLAY

Jesse Helms (R)

Of Raleigh — Elected 1972

Born: Oct. 18, 1921, Monroe, N.C.
Education: Attended Wingate Jr. College and Wake Forest College, 1941.
Military Career: Navy, 1942-45.
Occupation: Journalist; broadcasting executive.
Family: Wife, Dorothy Jane Coble; three children.
Religion: Baptist.
Political Career: Raleigh City Council, 1957-61.
Capitol Office: 403 Dirksen Bldg. 20510; 224-6342.

In Washington: The paradox of Helms' hard-line conservatism is that he may find life easier with George Bush in the White House.

Helms rose to prominence in American politics using many of the same issues as Ronald Reagan: communism, liberal bureaucrats, school prayer, abortion. But the Reagan presidency proved discomfiting for the senator: Repeatedly, he would stake out the ideologically pure territory to Reagan's right, and then explain how low-level functionaries — State Department bureaucrats were oft-cited — had pulled the true-believing president to the center.

Bush's arrival uncomplicates Helms' life. Once again, he can exercise his right to life, liberty and the pursuit of dogmatic unhappiness.

Helms does this with zeal — and with a reach felt round the globe. As ranking member on the Foreign Relations Committee, he is the senior Republican spokesman in the Senate on foreign policy. The position enhances his longstanding desire to play the skunk at the garden party of U.S.-Soviet rapprochement.

His handling of the intermediate-range nuclear-force (INF) treaty in 1988 was vintage Helms. He opened the hearings by handing out a 180-page catalog of his complaints with a treaty he called an "invitation to cheat." His daily objections prompted treaty proponents to launch what was dubbed the "Helms Watch," to keep tabs on him and answer his objections. When Secretary of State George P. Shultz declared that he still hoped to win Helms over, Democratic Sen. Joseph R. Biden Jr. of Delaware said, "Good luck, Mr. Secretary. I hope you're not that naive with the Soviets."

As the treaty debate wound down, Helms' delaying tactics nearly prevented Reagan from presenting Soviet leader Mikhail S. Gorbachev with a ratified treaty during a Moscow summit. In the end, Helms declared, "I am licked," but not before gaining concessions in return for stepping aside. He went on to cast one of just five "no" votes against the treaty.

Helms has never minded being on the losing end of a lopsided vote. His propensity to cast the solo "no" led the *The News and Observer* of Raleigh, N.C., his ardent foe, to dub him "Senator No." Helms relishes the title.

"You got to understand how I operate," he once told a reporter. "Somebody said, 'Jesse, why do you so often advance things or take positions that you know you don't have any chance to win?' And my answer to that is, I do it on principle."

His amiable, courtly manner belies the skill and aggressiveness he uses to advance these principles. He stands atop one of the most sophisticated political networks in the nation, the North Carolina-based Congressional Club. Helms' lonely stands play well in the mail boxes of tens of thousands of conservatives across the country. Inside the chamber, Helms uses every weapon in a senator's arsenal — and with a frequency that rubs some of his colleagues raw.

Some laughed when Helms earned back-to-back "golden gavel" honors for presiding over the Senate — drudgery most senators would prefer to avoid — after his arrival in 1973. But he mastered Senate arcanery, and since then has wielded the rulebook as few others. Together with his mule-like stubbornness, it is a formidable combination, especially when he seeks not to advance legislation, but to block it. He can often be found on the floor playing just that role in the closing days of a session when a single, determined senator can tie the chamber in parliamentary knots.

The latest example came as the 100th Congress wound down. Helms, who once advocated quarantining AIDS sufferers, blocked the Senate from appointing members to confer with the House on AIDS legislation until he gained an agreement that barred efforts to see that the government keeps the results of AIDS tests confidential. He also won language barring groups from receiving federal funds if they promote homosexuality.

The Democrats' return to power in the 100th Congress spared Helms from any compulsion to develop and pass an agenda, leaving him free to play the obstructionist role. But it also deprived him of "the one job I'd like to have around here," chairman of Foreign Relations.

Helms could have chaired Foreign Relations for two years after 1984, when the previous chairman was defeated for re-election. But he had just survived a difficult campaign of his own in which he had promised North Carolina's tobacco interests that he would maintain his chairmanship at Agriculture in order to work on behalf of tobacco price supports when the farm bill came up for reauthorization in 1985. He held to that promise, allowing GOP Sen. Richard G. Lugar of Indiana to take over at Foreign Relations. "If I can't keep my word, I don't belong here," Helms said.

The passage of tobacco legislation in 1986 freed Helms to challenge Lugar for the ranking Foreign Relations slot on the basis of seniority. There was a rivalry between the two men that gave a bitter tone to their contest. Though Lugar was a conservative who supported most Reagan foreign policy initiatives, he had shown a willingness to negotiate with Democrats that Helms found distasteful.

Their sharpest exchange occurred during debate on mandating economic sanctions against South Africa. Lugar supported the anti-apartheid bill. But Helms — protective of the Pretoria government's role as an anti-communist force in Southern Africa — not only opposed the bill, but set up phone calls to two senators from Pik Botha, South Africa's foreign minister.

Lugar angrily described Botha's intervention as "despicable" and called Helms' assistance "inappropriate." Helms responded by asserting that Lugar and liberal Massachusetts Democrat Edward M. Kennedy would be responsible for the fall of South Africa to militant leftists.

Seniority clinched the post for Helms, who won the ranking position by a 24-17 vote in the Republican Conference; Lugar moved into the ranking Agriculture position Helms vacated.

The 1986 tobacco legislation was a watershed for Helms in another regard, too. He gained permanent authorization for the tobacco program, a political masterstroke that removed his political Achilles' heel. Opponents under a Helms attack often would threaten to repay him in kind on tobacco legislation. That possibility is now remote.

This enhanced Helms' ability to pursue his crusades abroad. They are generally marked by anti-communist fervor. He opposes close ties with the Soviet Union and other communist nations and usually sides with right-wing governments that share his views. Though he insists these alliances are necessary to counter communist imperialism, he has been criticized by those who see the rightist regimes as totalitarian and abusive of human rights, much as the communist governments Helms has opposed.

During debate on the South Africa sanctions measure, Helms said, "Here we go again, kicking a friend in the teeth because they don't do what we want them to do." He is a supporter of the Chilean government headed by Augusto Pinochet. He opposed the efforts to oust Philippines President Ferdinand E. Marcos in 1986, stating that his replacement by Corazon Aquino "happens to be on the agenda of the socialist world right now."

Helms has often been criticized for trying to run foreign policy from the Senate. Much to the State Department's chagrin, in 1985, he dispatched Agriculture Committee aides with a subpoena for Miroslav Medved, a Ukranian sailor who jumped ship into the Mississippi River.

In 1979, he infuriated the Carter administration by inviting Bishop Abel T. Muzorewa, the newly elected prime minister of Zimbabwe, who he once called a "fine black man," to visit the United States against the administration's wishes. Later that year, the two aides he sent to London to observe a conference on Zimbabwe's future drew protests after they urged the white minority to hold out for more concessions.

During a visit to Chile in 1986, Helms sharply criticized the American ambassador and the State Department's attitude toward Pinochet. "A coalition of the media, the Marxists and the State Department is seeking to destabilize the transition to a full-fledged democracy in Chile," Helms said. When *The New York Times* published an article stating that Helms was being investigated for leaking classified information to Pinochet, Helms alleged that State Department officials planted the information, and accused the CIA of spying on him. "They want to silence me and intimidate me, and you know what? It's not going to work," he said.

Helms, who vigorously fought the Panama Canal treaties, was strongly critical of the Reagan administration's support for centrist José Napoleón Duarte in El Salvador's 1984 presidential election. He instead provided vocal backing for the more conservative Roberto d'Aubuisson, despite allegations that the candidate had been involved with "death squad" murders. "You don't have perfect choices in trying to prevent a communist takeover of this world," Helms said.

After the election, Helms presented evidence on the Senate floor to support his claim that Duarte's victory had been the result of covert CIA assistance. Senate leaders criticized him for releasing secret information, but Helms said all his material was from public sources.

Helms has also nettled administrations by using his parliamentary skills to hold up the appointment of diplomatic appointees whose views he questions. From the very outset of the Reagan years — when he cast one of only two votes against confirmation of Caspar W. Weinberger to be secretary of defense — Helms has placed dozens of executive branch appointees through a long and arduous ordeal.

There were ample signs in the 101st Congress that James A. Baker III, the Bush administration secretary of state, was looking to avoid confrontations with Helms and working deals on appointees. In the past, Helms has sent diplomatic candidates lists of as many as 247 questions to be answered prior to their confirmation hearings.

Helms' efforts in foreign affairs, if not consistently successful, have brought him more victories than his initiatives in domestic social policy. He started the first Reagan term with high hopes for enactment of the New Right social agenda. But it soon became evident that the administration placed more importance on economics and foreign policy than on social issues.

Helms made an all-out push for his anti-abortion and school prayer proposals in the summer of 1982, when the Senate took up legislation increasing the ceiling on the federal debt. His anti-abortion amendment stated that the Supreme Court had erred in its 1973 decision legalizing abortion, permanently banned federal funding of abortion and granted a direct appeal to the Supreme Court for challenges to new anti-abortion laws. The school prayer amendment barred the federal courts from handling cases involving "voluntary" school prayer. But Helms, who had staged so many filibusters in the past, could not overcome one by moderate Republicans; his amendments were tabled.

Despite his inability to prohibit what he calls "the crime of abortion," Helms has persisted. He has demanded numerous roll-call votes on this and other emotional issues, and turned his opponents' votes against them, using the direct-mail capability of his national organization to denounce them for ignoring the will of the conservative electorate.

Helms has continued to build a national apparatus of lobby and fund-raising groups unlike anything possessed by other senators. He and his lieutenants have used high finance, modern technology and knowledge of federal laws to erect an interlocking network of political organizations bent on influencing policy.

The cornerstone of Helms' empire is the National Congressional Club, a direct-mail fund-raising group. There also is a variety of think tanks, such as the Institute for American Relations, the Centre for a Free Society and the American Family Institute, and tax-exempt lobby groups. Each is operated in whole or part by close associates or employees of Helms.

Early in 1985, another Helms group, Fairness in Media, staged an unsuccessful effort to persuade conservatives to buy a controlling interest in the CBS television network. Helms and his allies argued that the network's news coverage was tainted by liberal bias.

In his zeal, Helms has made enemies. He is to liberal activists what Kennedy is to conservatives: an ogre whose name is frequently thrown into fund-raising letters to arouse the anger of potential contributors.

Helms can also antagonize his colleagues in pursuit of his domestic policy ends. When he delayed adjournment in December 1982 with a fruitless filibuster on a gasoline tax increase bill, threatening to keep Congress in through Christmas, several senators denounced him openly on the floor. Fellow Republican Alan K. Simpson of Wyoming called Helms "obnoxious."

Helms again found himself isolated from most of his colleagues in 1983, this time over a proposal to make the birthday of the late Rev. Dr. Martin Luther King Jr. a national holiday. Accusing the slain civil rights leader of espousing "action-oriented Marxism," Helms unsuccessfully filibustered against the bill.

One major success was Helms' push for strong drug abuse laws, long before passage of an omnibus drug bill in 1986. He also attached an amendment to that bill banning "dial-a-porn" telephone services, though he accidentally caused himself some embarrassment in doing so. Included in a pile of documents that Helms submitted for the *Congressional Record* was an unaltered transcript of a sexually graphic telephone message. The transcript was duly published in the Record.

Given the primacy of foreign policy and social issues on Helms' agenda, there is irony in the fact that he spent all six years of the Republican majority as chairman of the Agriculture Committee. It was not an active chairmanship. Indeed, with a few signal exceptions, he virtually abdicated control of the committee during his first four years as chairman, allowing a coalition of Republicans, led by Majority Leader Bob Dole of Kansas, to take the lead on farm legislation.

Helms would have gladly given up the Agriculture post in 1985 were it not for his tobacco constituency. He had angered this interest group in 1982 by voting for a Reagan-backed tax increase bill that included a provision doubling the federal excise tax on cigarettes to 16 cents. Needing every vote he could muster in his 1984 re-election campaign, Helms promised to be there for tobacco farmers in the 99th Congress.

Helms did win the enactment of legislation to reduce tobacco surpluses by allowing cigarette manufacturers to buy up large portions of the tobacco crop at substantial discounts. But he prevailed only with difficulty. He ran into a conflict with Democratic Rep. Charlie Rose of North Carolina, who charged that Helms favored cigarette companies over the growers. Rose suggested that 2 cents of the 16-cents-per-pack cigarette tax be earmarked to pay for tobacco subsidies, a proposal Helms described as a tax increase.

Helms worked out a compromise between manufacturers and growers in a meeting from which Rose, chairman of House Agriculture's Tobacco Subcommittee, was specifically excluded.

Concerned that the omnibus farm bill, the committee's major effort in 1985, would be defeated on the floor, Helms removed the tobacco provisions and attached them to a budget reconciliation bill. To do so, he had to agree to a permanent reauthorization of the 16-cent cigarette tax. Helms' strategy almost backfired. While the farm bill passed, the reconciliation measure stalled and appeared in danger of defeat. However, the bill, with its tobacco provisions, eventually passed, giving Helms an important long-term victory. For while the farm bill returns for reauthorization in the 101st Congress, the tobacco program is tucked safely away, thanks to its passage in the budget measure.

On most other farm issues, Helms remained a hands-off chairman. While Dole worked with House Majority Whip Thomas S. Foley of Washington to iron out the controversial 1985 farm legislation, Helms criticized it as a "budget buster" and held to his prediction that he would become the first Agriculture chairman to vote against a farm bill.

Helms' lack of a central role on the farm bill led to some snide comments from other members. The strongest rebuke came from Iowa Democrat Tom Harkin, who referred to Dole as "Mr. Real Chairman" after Helms left a hearing to take a phone call. Helms reacted defensively. During a floor speech shortly thereafter, he said, "As far as I know, I am still the chairman.... I will tell senators on what terms we are going to meet, and they can like it or lump it."

At Home: Whatever the national implications of Helms' 1984 victory, its lessons at home were clear. In the battle for pre-eminence in North Carolina politics, Helms emerged king of the mountain.

When his bid for re-election to a third Senate term began taking shape two years earlier, Helms' future influence in state politics was very much in doubt. His vaunted political organization, the Congressional Club, had suffered severe setbacks in 1982, losing every one of the five congressional contests it had targeted in the state.

Further, Helms was being plagued by negative publicity. His 1982 vote for raising the cigarette tax had drawn fire from North Carolina's crucial tobacco constituency. He was widely vilified for his unsuccessful efforts to block creation of the King holiday. Pollsters tracking the battle between Helms and Democratic Gov. James B. Hunt Jr. found Helms significantly behind through most of 1983.

But Helms battled back, drawing on financial support from conservatives across the country to invest $16.5 million in the race, shattering the record for the most money spent by a Senate candidate in U.S. history. His ads assaulting Hunt and the national Democratic Party not only bolstered his own campaign, they created a climate in which other North Carolina Republicans could prosper. When the dust settled on election night, the GOP had captured the governorship and three new House seats.

In many ways, it was an unusually static Senate campaign. The national media dutifully detailed each tortuous twist and turn, from Hunt's charge that Helms was a supporter of right-wing death squads in El Salvador, to the incumbent's complaint that Hunt had misused state airplanes. But most North Carolinians seemed little affected by the long and vituperative debate. Faced with a choice between a leading apostle of the New Right and an activist Democratic governor, most knew relatively early on how they would vote. Only 4 percentage points separated the two contenders in polls taken in May 1984; in late October, it was still considered a dead heat.

Hunt focused his campaign on his record as governor, tirelessly sounding his commitment to improved education and arguing he was experienced in bringing the state jobs. He cast Helms as a right-wing radical, too extreme in his views to serve the state's interests effectively.

Helms, putting aside his own significant differences with Reagan, embraced the president wholeheartedly, using taped telephone messages in which Reagan endorsed him. Helms also sought to link Hunt to Democratic presidential candidate Walter F. Mondale and his national party. That charge left Hunt hamstrung, as he sought to distance himself from Mondale's proposal for a tax increase without repudiating his party's presidential nominee.

In the end, Hunt won strong support from the extensive network of teachers, unions, party regulars and other activists he had built up during 10 years in state government. He carried the rural northeast, traditional Democratic territory that both men had taken in previous campaigns. Hunt also carried most of the state's major urban areas, thanks in part to the overwhelming allegiance of black voters.

But Hunt's eastern margins were not as decisive as he had hoped, and his black support helped produce a conservative white backlash that benefited Helms. Further aided by Reagan's top-of-the-ticket strength and a strong turnout from newly registered fundamentalists, Helms built his victory in the small towns and crossroads communities of the central and western Piedmont. He finished with a 52 to 48 percent edge.

Although Helms' 1984 victory was decisive, its effects on North Carolina politics apparently were not long lasting. In 1986, key lieutenants of his Congressional Club got involved in the

GOP Senate primary, backing losing candidate David Funderburk. Helms himself campaigned on behalf of Republican Rep. James T. Broyhill — the eventual GOP nominee — during the fall campaign, but Broyhill lost to Democrat Terry Sanford. Further, GOP Rep. Bill Cobey, one of the three House members elected in 1984 with the aid of Helms' coattails, lost re-election.

For most of his adult life, Helms was a Democrat himself, even while he delivered conservative editorials for 12 years over WRAL-TV in Raleigh. He left the Democratic Party in 1970 and two years later ran for the Senate.

He was an underdog in that campaign against U.S. Rep. Nick Galifianakis, who had convincingly defeated aging Sen. B. Everett Jordan in the Democratic primary. Press accounts regularly described Helms as a "right-winger," but that label was far less dangerous to him than the liberal McGovern-Shriver presidential ticket was to Galifianakis.

Helms played down his rhetoric and shifted to a pro-Nixon tone. "President Nixon Needs Jesse Helms," the advertisements read, although Helms was far to the right of Nixon on most issues. A year earlier he had called Nixon's trip to China "appeasement" of the communists. In a Republican sweep, Nixon won nearly 70 percent of the state's presidential vote. Helms defeated Galifianakis with 54 percent of the vote, and the GOP won the governorship for the first time since 1896.

Six years later, a host of Democrats sought to prove Helms' win a coattail fluke. The early favorite for the nomination was Luther H. Hodges Jr., a moderate banker with a well-financed campaign but a "stuffed shirt" image. Another Democrat, state Insurance Commissioner John Ingram, pledged to fight for the common man against insurance companies, banks and other monied interests he accused both Helms and Hodges of defending. Ingram was underfinanced and disorganized, but he forced Hodges into a runoff and won.

Ingram appeared to pose a threat to Helms. His populist themes had some appeal for rural and working-class conservatives who had supported Helms in 1972. But Helms had a reputation and an organization. Many of his constituents were proud that in a single Senate term he had become an articulate and nationally known defender of the right, one who had been promoted as a vice presidential choice by more than 800 national convention delegates in 1976. Helms' Congressional Club had been powerful enough to engineer Ronald Reagan's victory in the 1976 North Carolina primary.

Helms also had plenty of money. As direct-mail solicitations brought contributions from across the nation, Ingram derided the incumbent as "the six million dollar man." Helms eventually collected about $7.5 million, more than any Senate candidate in U.S. history up to that time, and won with 55 percent.

Committees

Foreign Relations (Ranking)

Agriculture, Nutrition and Forestry (3rd of 9 Republicans)
Agricultural Production and Stabilization of Prices (ranking); Domestic and Foreign Marketing and Product Promotion; Nutrition and Investigations

Rules and Administration (4th of 7 Republicans)

Select Ethics (2nd of 3 Republicans)

Elections

1984 General		
Jesse Helms (R)	1,156,768	(52%)
James B. Hunt Jr. (D)	1,070,488	(48%)
1984 Primary		
Jesse Helms (R)	134,675	(91%)
George Wimbish (R)	13,899	(9%)

Previous Winning Percentages: **1978** (55%) **1972** (54%)

Campaign Finance

	Receipts	Receipts from PACs		Expend-itures
1984				
Helms (R)	$16,522,266	$847,337	(5%)	$16,499,387
Hunt (D)	$10,031,502	$834,601	(8%)	$9,429,924

Key Votes

1987	
Enact omnibus highway bill over Reagan veto	N
Limit testing of space-based anti-ballistic missiles	N
Oppose banning tests of larger nuclear weapons	Y
Confirm Robert H. Bork as Supreme Court justice	Y
1988	
Allow vote on campaign-finance overhaul	N
Pass civil rights restoration bill over Reagan veto	N
Enact omnibus trade bill over Reagan veto	N
Approve death penalty for drug-related murders	Y
Oppose "workfare" amendment to welfare overhaul bill	N

Voting Studies

	Presidential Support		Party Unity		Conservative Coalition	
Year	**S**	**O**	**S**	**O**	**S**	**O**
1988	60	26	72	12	81	5
1987	77	22	94	5	94	3
1986	90	10	95	5	95	5
1985	79	21	94	6	97	3
1984	86	10	90	8	100	0
1983	56	41	77	20	95	2
1982	75	25	87	13	99	1
1981	84	16	88	11	94	6

Interest Group Ratings

Year	ADA	ACU	AFL-CIO	CCUS
1988	5	100	23	75
1987	10	100	20	89
1986	0	100	0	95
1985	0	100	5	93
1984	0	100	0	89
1983	0	100	0	89
1982	0	100	8	95
1981	0	100	5	100

Terry Sanford (D)

Of Durham — Elected 1986

Born: Aug. 20, 1917, Laurinburg, N.C.

Education: Presbyterian Junior College; U. of North Carolina, A.B. 1939, J.D. 1946.

Military Career: Army parachute infantry, 1942-46; N.C. National Guard, 1948-60.

Occupation: Lawyer; FBI agent; university president.

Family: Wife, Margaret Rose Knight; two children.

Religion: Methodist.

Political Career: N.C. Senate, 1953-55; governor, 1961-65; sought Democratic nomination for president, 1972, 1976.

Capitol Office: 716 Hart Bldg. 20510; 224-3154.

In Washington: Sanford entered the Senate as an aging major leaguer: The former governor and Duke University president had built a national, if quixotic, reputation in his party. But in his first inning as a senator, a politically rusty Sanford not only booted a ball, he threw to the wrong base.

A highly publicized series of votes he cast in April 1987 that culminated in the override of President Reagan's veto of an $88 billion highway bill earned him the nickname "Turnaround Terry." He spent the rest of the 100th Congress living the episode down.

Sanford had been the only Democrat to vote against the legislation's conference report, arguing it did not adequately provide for North Carolina. He told a number of public officials in Washington and at home that, accordingly, he would support the president's veto.

When the override vote came, Sanford stood for a full five minutes in the well of the Senate, looking agonized as his arm was roundly twisted from all sides. He first voted "present" to buy time, but when Republicans questioned the quality of his word, he switched his vote to "no," siding with the president. Four hours later, after parliamentary maneuvering enabled the Democrats to schedule another vote, Sanford announced he would vote "yes" to override.

The proceedings did not raise questions about Sanford's intelligence, nor his sincerity in trying to determine the right thing for his constituency. But the episode indicated less self-assurance than might be expected from a veteran of politics. And it deprived a man who expects much of himself from the fast Senate start he so badly wanted.

Sanford played a key role in the fight over Reagan's nomination of Robert H. Bork to the Supreme Court. Sanford's reputation for moderation led Democrats to choose him to respond to Reagan's October 1988 speech castigating the campaign against Bork's nomination. In defending the Senate's right to dissent, Sanford said, "We are tired of having our integrity impugned. We are tired of having our sincerity questioned. We are tired of having our intelligence insulted." His speech won high marks for laying down the proper political covering fire for opponents of Bork, especially Southern ones.

On Foreign Relations, Sanford sought entry into one of the most controversial arenas, Central American policy, from his places on the Western Hemisphere Subcommittee and the Central American Observer Group. He considers the region's prime problem to be economic. On his own, he created an international commission, operating under the auspices of an institute at Duke, to develop a long-range economic development strategy for the region.

Sanford came to the Senate as a leading advocate of U.S. backing for the Central American peace proposal of Oscar Arias, the president of Costa Rica. Nonetheless, Sanford voted in March 1987 to release $40 million in military aid for the Nicaraguan contras to honor a campaign pledge "not to pull the rug out from under the president's contra aid program too abruptly." Subsequently, he worked for nonmilitary aid only.

On Banking, Sanford sought to protect insurance operations within his state's burgeoning banking industry. He also pushed legislation to clamp down on corporate takeovers. This became a hot political issue in North Carolina after several major corporations in the state underwent restructurings following merger-and-acquisition activity.

At Home: Despite a four-decade track record in Democratic politics — and the distinction of having been named one of America's 10 best governors of the century by a Harvard University study — Sanford had to struggle to win the confidence of his own party's hierarchy when he ran for the Senate in 1986.

North Carolina Democratic leaders searching for a candidate in late 1985 and early 1986 were not focusing on Sanford's accolades. What they saw was a 68-year-old man who had not won an election in 25 years.

As a result, party leaders resisted when Sanford first offered to run for the seat being vacated by retiring GOP Sen. John P. East. Only after failing to recruit a top-flight alternative did they champion Sanford's bid. But Sanford surprised many of his critics with a strong Democratic primary showing. Running ads stressing moderate-to-conservative stands on issues and portraying his involvement in a wilderness adventure program (to overcome the age question), Sanford coasted past a weak field.

Republicans, meanwhile, staged a more significant primary battle — one from which Sanford would ultimately benefit. Rep. James T. Broyhill, a moderate, chamber-of-commerce style Republican, faced David Funderburk, a political scientist and former U.S. ambassador to Romania backed by hard-right conservatives loyal to GOP Sen. Jesse Helms' political organization, the National Congressional Club. Broyhill won his primary easily, and shortly afterward was appointed to fill out the remaining months left in the term of East, who committed suicide in June. But Broyhill never came to terms with the GOP right, enabling Sanford to capitalize on North Carolina's natural Democratic majority.

Broyhill's efforts to paint Sanford as a tax-loving liberal in league with the Kennedys (Sanford was one of the first Southern gubernatorial candidates to embrace John F. Kennedy's 1960 presidential campaign) met with only a lukewarm response. Sanford won narrowly.

Election to the Senate capped Sanford's long and distinguished career. Born, raised and educated in North Carolina, he served two years as an FBI agent before joining the Army. He was a paratrooper in World War II, and earned a Purple Heart and a Bronze Star.

He won election to the state Senate in 1952, and organized former Democratic Gov. W. Kerr Scott's successful Senate bid two years later. He made his own statewide move in 1960, winning election as governor. He was known for his moderate stance on race relations and his decision to levy a food tax to help fund an ambitious education program.

Barred by law from seeking re-election, Sanford returned to law practice. He considered challenging Democratic Sen. Sam B. Ervin in 1966; in 1970, he became president of Duke University, a position he held for 15 years.

He served as chairman of Hubert H. Humphrey's national presidential campaign in 1968. Four years later, Sanford was ready to test the national waters himself. In his bid for the presidency, he counted heavily on a strong showing in his home state's presidential preference primary to propel him to greater heights. But George C. Wallace handed him an embarrassing defeat in his own back yard.

Sanford announced for the presidency again in 1976, but withdrew after he discovered insufficient support to compete nationwide. In 1985, he unsuccessfully sought the chairmanship of the Democratic National Committee.

Committees

Banking, Housing and Urban Affairs (7th of 12 Democrats)
International Finance and Monetary Policy; Securities

Budget (8th of 13 Democrats)

Foreign Relations (8th of 10 Democrats)
International Economic Policy, Trade, Oceans and Environment; Terrorism, Narcotics and International Operations; Western Hemisphere and Peace Corps Affairs

Select Ethics (3rd of 3 Democrats)

Elections

1986 General		
Terry Sanford (D)	823,662	(52%)
James T. Broyhill (R)	767,668	(48%)
1986 Primary		
Terry Sanford (D)	409,394	(60%)
John Ingram (D)	111,557	(16%)
Fountain Odom (D)	49,689	(7%)
William Irwin Belk (D)	33,821	(5%)
Theodore Kinney (D)	27,228	(4%)
Others (D)	47,798	(7%)

Campaign Finance

	Receipts	Receipts from PACs	Expend-itures
1986			
Sanford (D)	$4,181,701	$571,787 (14%)	$4,168,509
Broyhill (R)	$5,182,187	$1,367,212 (26%)	$5,168,244

Key Votes

1987	
Enact omnibus highway bill over Reagan veto	Y
Limit testing of space-based anti-ballistic missiles	Y
Oppose banning tests of larger nuclear weapons	N
Confirm Robert H. Bork as Supreme Court justice	N
1988	
Allow vote on campaign-finance overhaul	Y
Pass civil rights restoration bill over Reagan veto	Y
Enact omnibus trade bill over Reagan veto	Y
Approve death penalty for drug-related murders	N
Oppose "workfare" amendment to welfare overhaul bill	Y

Voting Studies

	Presidential Support		Party Unity		Conservative Coalition	
Year	**S**	**O**	**S**	**O**	**S**	**O**
1988	41	52	89	4	24	68
1987	32	56	85	9	41	50

Interest Group Ratings

Year	ADA	ACU	AFL-CIO	CCUS
1988	90	4	85	43
1987	85	8	90	28

1 Walter B. Jones (D)

Of Farmville — Elected 1966

Born: Aug. 19, 1913, Fayetteville, N.C.
Education: North Carolina State U., B.S. 1934.
Occupation: Office supply company executive.
Family: Wife, Elizabeth Fisher; two children.
Religion: Baptist.
Political Career: Mayor of Farmville, 1949-53; N.C. House, 1955-59; N.C. Senate, 1965-66; sought Democratic nomination for U.S. House, 1960.
Capitol Office: 241 Cannon Bldg. 20515; 225-3101.

In Washington: When the physically infirm Jones manages a Merchant Marine bill on the House floor these days, it is hard to recall that almost a decade ago, when he first took over the scandal-plagued committee, he was regarded as something of a fresh breeze. Now, Jones stands shakily at the lectern, reading verbatim from a looseleaf script, turning its pages slowly, rarely lifting his head.

Merchant Marine and Fisheries has a potentially broad mandate: Aspects of trade, environmental and foreign policy legislation come under its purview. But the committee is not a major force in House politics, and the frail Jones, now 76, gets some of the blame for that. "He retired years ago and didn't tell anyone about it," complained one Democrat.

Still, if Jones has failed to chart an ambitious course for his committee, he at least has tried to change its reputation as a den of unsavory ethical behavior. Jones is a stark contrast to the panel's three previous chairmen, two of whom were indicted for criminal links to maritime industry figures. In 1987, after Mario Biaggi's indictment cost him the Merchant Marine Subcommittee chairmanship, Jones, with a calming presence and trustworthy reputation, assumed the post.

When Jones took over the full committee in 1981, he cleared out some deadwood in the staff and dismissed several aides to his predecessor, New Yorker John M. Murphy, who was caught up in the Abscam scandal. He has tried to run the committee in a more open and collegial manner. Maritime industry lobbyists, who still contribute generously to committee members, concede there have been fewer backroom deals during Jones' tenure.

But Jones has not been assertive enough to translate these changes into legislative accomplishments, even on his top priority, helping the ailing merchant marine industry. It is swamped by international competition and split by dissension among unions, shipbuilders and ship operators. But the committee's recommendations to assist the industry have been roundly criticized as unaffordable responses to special-interest pleading.

The last notable merchant marine initiative by the committee dates back to the 98th Congress, when Jones was a leading House supporter of legislation to ease antitrust restrictions on ocean-liner cartels. Jones scored another success for the industry in 1985, when he used his seat on the Agriculture Committee to fight a proposal to exempt agricultural products from existing requirements that half of all government-generated exports be carried on U.S.-operated vessels, which charge shippers considerably more.

But the committee still tries its best to protect its clients. Asked to recommend budget savings in 1987, the Senate proposed increased fees for pleasure boaters, but Jones' committee rejected that idea and instead offered the novel suggestion that fees be assessed to oil tankers accepting U.S. military escorts through the Persian Gulf.

On other matters, the sheer scope of the committee's jurisdiction allows Jones to play a minor role on a variety of major bills. In 1988, his committee had a hand in crafting the drug bill, and the omnibus trade bill includes Jones-backed language to increase the volume of U.S. imports and exports carried by U.S. ships.

Environmental matters have consumed a good bit of the committee's time recently. In the 100th Congress, Jones was a prime sponsor of legislation to allow oil drilling in the Arctic National Wildlife Refuge (ANWR). Merchant Marine swiftly approved his measure, defeating all amendments the chairman did not like. But the bill was widely criticized by environmentalists, and the legislation stalled in the Interior Committee. The 1989 *Exxon Valdez* oil spill in Alaska doomed prospects for drilling in ANWR for the foreseeable future; Jones initiated hearings on oil-spill liability.

During 100th Congress debate on military base-closing legislation, Jones got in the middle of a dispute about how to handle environmental impact statements for bases being considered for closure. Jones said it was too costly and time-consuming to require impact statements

North Carolina 1

Northeast — Greenville; Kinston

The 1st begins at the ocean, passes through fishing ports and coastal swamps, and ends in flat fields of soybeans, corn, peanuts and tobacco.

This long has been the poorest and most agricultural region in North Carolina. Through much of the post-World War II era, out-migration was heavy; young people, especially blacks, fled the farms for urban areas. During the last two decades, however, there has been a population upturn in the district, thanks mainly to rapid growth in resort areas along the Atlantic coast.

On the Outer Banks, a thin strand of sand between the Atlantic and the Albemarle and Pamlico sounds, the flood of people into communities such as Nags Head, Hatteras and Kill Devil Hills increased the population of Dare County nearly 50 percent in just the first half of the 1980s. Carteret, the most populous of the 1st District's coastal counties, grew by 24 percent.

Further inland, the growth of population and economic opportunity has been more modest. Industries process tobacco and make paper and clothing; machinery and chemical factories are moving in, but harvests from the farm land still pay most of the bills. In Northampton and Hertford counties, where blacks are a majority, the problem of out-migration persists.

In the southern half of the district are the small cities of Greenville (Pitt County), Kinston (Lenoir County) and New Bern (Craven County). The counties of Pitt, Lenoir and Craven joined Dare, Carteret and Beaufort counties in supporting Ronald Reagan in 1980 and 1984 and George Bush in 1988, indicating that the district's urbanized areas and increasingly affluent coastal counties are fertile ground for the GOP.

Voters in the 15 rural counties usually stay in the Democratic column in local elections. The Democratic habits of conservative rural whites here go back to the Civil War. Many of the rural counties did cross party lines for Reagan in 1984 and Bush in 1988, but in races for statewide office, their traditions shone through. Only one of the 15 counties defected to the GOP in the 1984 Senate race, and GOP Gov. James G. Martin carried only one in his successful 1988 re-election bid.

Population: 536,219. White 343,468 (64%), Black 189,088 (35%). Spanish origin 5,236 (1%). 18 and over 382,422 (71%), 65 and over 58,247 (11%). Median age: 29.

before a closing decision is made. A compromise was worked out that requires impact statements only after a base is cleared for closing.

Prior to taking over Merchant Marine, Jones scarcely showed up at committee hearings, and when he did, he was so passive that many thought he might yield the chairmanship voluntarily if it ever fell to him. By 1981, when it became vacant, a case of gout had reduced Jones' walk to a shuffle (and has since confined him to a wheelchair for long periods). But he surprised colleagues with a methodical campaign for the chairmanship. His effort and the sway of seniority won him the prize.

Earlier in his career, Jones chaired the Agriculture Subcommittee on Tobacco. There he displayed few interests other than maintaining federal price supports for his district's most important crop. In 1977, when an attempt was made on the House floor to take tobacco out of the Food for Peace program, Jones came up with an unusual argument. "If one is against tobacco," he said, "it is far better to export it than to keep it here."

When he took Merchant Marine, Jones turned over the Tobacco Subcommittee to fellow North Carolinian Charlie Rose. In the 99th Congress, however, Jones opposed a Rose plan to fund tobacco support programs with cigarette tax revenues, saying it would "open a Pandora's box" that would allow liberals to increase taxes. Instead, he supported GOP Sen. Jesse Helms' effort to revamp the program by allowing cigarette manufacturers to buy surplus tobacco from the federal government at discount prices.

At Home: The late Herbert Bonner, whose longtime Merchant Marine chairmanship gave Jones an issue in his campaign for the job, would have had a much shorter tenure if Jones had had his way in the first place.

In 1960, five years after Bonner took over the committee, Jones challenged him for renomination. But Bonner won with 58 percent of the vote, and Jones had to wait until after the chairman's death in 1965 to make it to Washington, defeating John P. East, who went on to serve six years in the U.S. Senate before committing suicide in 1986. Jones won 60 percent against East in the special election in February 1966 and defeated him again in November by a similar margin. He has had little trouble in general elections since then.

In the 1984 Democratic primary, though, Jones faced his first credible challenger since his initial election. His opponent was state Rep.

John B. Gillam III, a 37-year-old peanut farmer who staked his challenge to the 70-year-old incumbent on a call for generational change.

Gillam raised questions about Jones' effectiveness, and claimed the incumbent had confused the 1st's priorities by abandoning the chairmanship of the Tobacco Subcommittee to take over Merchant Marine. "It's time for a change," Gillam argued. "We need to look at our old problems in a new way."

Jones' physical appearance did not help him against such complaints. He often appeared drawn and tired in public, and his foot ailment made it difficult for him to walk.

But Jones battled back by playing up his seniority and citing his role in obtaining funds for a construction project at a heavily used North Carolina coastal inlet, popular with the local fishing industry.

Jones also had plenty of chits to call in. In addition to his loyal following among local party leaders and teachers' groups, Jones picked up support from farmers and others in the tobacco trade who remembered his single-minded defense of that crop during his tenure as Tobacco Subcommittee chairman.

Gillam carried his home base of Bertie County as well as Hertford County, Bertie's neighbor to the north. But the rest of the district was Jones country. He clinched renomination with a resounding 61 percent, and cruised to an easy November victory.

Committees

Merchant Marine and Fisheries (Chairman)
Merchant Marine (chairman)

Agriculture (2nd of 27 Democrats)
Cotton, Rice and Sugar; Tobacco and Peanuts

Elections

1988 General		
Walter B. Jones (D)	118,027	(65%)
Howard D. Moye (R)	63,013	(35%)
1986 General		
Walter B. Jones (D)	91,122	(70%)
Howard D. Moye (R)	39,912	(30%)

Previous Winning Percentages: **1984** (67%) **1982** (81%)
1980 (100%) **1978** (80%) **1976** (76%) **1974** (78%)
1972 (69%) **1970** (70%) **1968** (66%) **1966** (61%)
1966 * (60%)

** Special election.*

District Vote For President

	1988	1984	1980	1976
D	83,301 (46%)	82,194 (43%)	84,207 (52%)	82,605 (61%)
R	97,424 (54%)	109,441 (57%)	72,815 (45%)	53,042 (39%)
I			3,337 (2%)	

Campaign Finance

	Receipts	Receipts from PACs	Expend-itures
1988			
Jones (D)	$141,476	$96,550 (68%)	$82,147
Moye (R) †	$16,758	0	$16,758
1986			
Jones (D)	$196,760	$134,650 (68%)	$87,114
Moye (R)	$47,875	$500 (1%)	$47,184

† Totals based on incomplete data.

Key Votes

1987	
Raise speed limit to 65 mph	N
Approve Gephardt "fair trade" amendment	Y
Ban testing of larger nuclear weapons	?
Delay "re-flagging" of Kuwaiti tankers	Y
Approve tax-raising deficit-reduction bill	Y
1988	
Approve aid to Nicaraguan contras	N
Enact civil rights restoration bill over Reagan veto	Y
Kill 60-day plant-closing notification measure	N
Pass omnibus trade bill over Reagan veto	Y
Approve death penalty for drug-related murders	#
Bar federal funds for abortions in cases of rape and incest	?
Oppose seven-day waiting period for purchase of handguns	Y

Voting Studies

	Presidential Support		Party Unity		Conservative Coalition	
Year	S	O	S	O	S	O
1988	19	72	83	6	37	47
1987	15	57	76	5	28	33
1986	27	62	76	11	56	30
1985	20	74	76	7	38	49
1984	30	50	70	12	49	41
1983	38	57	70	19	62	29
1982	39	44	65	22	56	32
1981	37	30	47	20	40	15

Interest Group Ratings

Year	ADA	ACU	AFL-CIO	CCUS
1988	80	13	75	46
1987	56	0	87	21
1986	55	22	77	40
1985	70	5	71	25
1984	55	19	75	43
1983	60	25	67	42
1982	40	47	61	65
1981	25	21	82	36

2 Tim Valentine (D)

Of Nashville — Elected 1982

Born: March 15, 1926, Nash County, N.C.
Education: The Citadel, A.B. 1948; U. of North Carolina, LL.B. 1952.
Military Career: Army Air Force, 1944-46.
Occupation: Lawyer.
Family: Wife, Barbara Reynolds; four children, three stepchildren.
Religion: Baptist.
Political Career: N.C. House, 1955-61; N.C. Democratic Party chairman, 1966-68.
Capitol Office: 1510 Longworth Bldg. 20515; 225-4531.

In Washington: In an institution brimming with ambition-charged legislators, Valentine is clearly of a different mold. A generation older and more conservative than most of the moderate young "New South" Democrats who flocked to Congress in the 1982 election, Valentine is a quiet voice for his district's interests.

On the Science, Space and Technology Committee, Valentine speaks for the scientific community in the Research Triangle (Durham County, one corner of the Triangle, is in the 2nd). In 1988, he introduced a bill to create a national board to coordinate semiconductor research and development. In the 101st Congress, he takes over the Transportation, Aviation and Materials Subcommittee.

Many of his floor speeches pertain to programs affecting the rural interests of his district. He vehemently opposed President Reagan's 1986 proposal to slash federal funding for rural Cooperative Extension Services, saying it was clear the administration felt farmers' "needs are unimportant and can be ignored."

Valentine gravitated to the bloc of Southerners who swap old-time stories in the back of the House chamber every afternoon. On most issues, his votes follow in the tradition of L. H. Fountain, the 30-year veteran he replaced in 1983. In 1988, Valentine sided with the conservative coalition of Republicans and Southern Democrats on 95 percent of House votes, more than anyone in the North Carolina delegation. But he is no party turncoat; in his second and third terms, Valentine voted with a majority of House Democrats better than two-thirds of the time.

One issue on which Valentine clearly separates from the conservative fold is U.S. policy toward Nicaragua. He voted against Reagan's 1988 request for $36 million in military aid to the contras, saying, "The American people have rejected the argument that we can promote democracy and protect our interests in Central America by sending hundreds of millions of the taxpayers' dollars to the contras."

At Home: Capturing and holding the 2nd has involved Valentine in some racially divisive campaigns. Boundary changes in the 2nd wrought by 1982 redistricting go a long way toward explaining the tensions. Fountain's old small-town and rural constituency was merged with urban Durham County, home to a large and politically assertive black community. The resulting district provided blacks their best shot at winning a House seat in the state.

To win nomination in the 2nd in 1982, Valentine had to overcome H. M. "Mickey" Michaux Jr., a black former U.S. attorney and state legislator from Durham County. Valentine finished second to Michaux in the primary, but won the runoff by casting himself as a conservative and Michaux as a labor lackey desirous of raising taxes and cutting defense. Lingering black dissatisfaction was evident in a general election write-in campaign waged on Michaux's behalf, but Valentine won comfortably.

Two years later, black state Rep. Kenneth B. Spaulding challenged Valentine in a Democratic primary with a different approach than Michaux had used. Determined to avoid being labeled a liberal, Spaulding portrayed himself as a fiscal conservative. That helped him cut his losses among white voters, and the Rev. Jesse Jackson helped Spaulding stoke black voters' passions. But Jackson's activity also sparked a backlash among rural whites that benefited Valentine. The incumbent's rural strength helped him clinch renomination with 52 percent.

The son of a state Supreme Court justice, Valentine was elected to the Legislature in 1954 at age 28. He served three terms, then left to spend more time practicing law. In 1965 he became the legislative liaison for Democratic Gov. Dan K. Moore. Valentine returned to his Nash County home when Moore's term ended, devoting his time to the chamber of commerce and the Baptist Church. He probably would have stayed in Nash County but for an auto accident that killed his wife in August 1981. A desire to put that tragedy behind him persuaded Valentine to run for Congress.

North Carolina 2

North Central — Durham; Rocky Mount

The 2nd is an uneasy marriage of different kinds of voters who happen to share the same party label.

In one corner of the district are the urban Democrats in Durham, where blacks, labor unions and white liberals are a political force. Elsewhere, the 2nd is predominantly rural, and conservative white Democrats are uncomfortable with the movement of blacks toward greater political power.

The 2nd has the largest minority population of any North Carolina district. Two counties are majority-black, and several have black populations exceeding 40 percent.

In Durham, the best-known industry is the one that for a century has given the city its strong aroma — cigarette manufacturing. In addition to the gritty, working-class Durham of tobacco factories and textile mills, there is the ivory tower academic world of Duke University.

Durham's blacks traditionally have played a prominent role in commerce and politics. Today, over 40 percent of the city's people are black, and their influence made possible the strong showings by black Democratic House contenders in the 1982 and 1984 primaries.

Tobacco is equally important in the rural, eastern part of the 2nd District, but it is grown there, not processed in factories. Cotton and peanuts also are important crops. The area's two cities, Rocky Mount and Wilson, are marketing centers for the farms — Wilson has the world's largest flue-cured tobacco warehouse. They also make pharmaceuticals, tires and textiles.

Population: 536,210. White 316,200 (59%), Black 214,899 (40%), Other 4,016 (1%). Spanish origin 4,571 (1%). 18 and over 382,220 (71%), 65 and over 58,389 (11%). Median age: 30.

Committees

Public Works and Transportation (13th of 31 Democrats)
Aviation; Surface Transportation

Science, Space and Technology (13th of 30 Democrats)
Transportation, Aviation and Materials (chairman); Energy Research and Development; Natural Resources, Agriculture Research and Environment

Elections

1988 General		
Tim Valentine (D)	128,832	(100%)
1986 General		
Tim Valentine (D)	95,320	(75%)
Bud McElhaney (R)	32,515	(25%)

Previous Winning Percentages: 1984 (68%) **1982** (54%)

District Vote For President

	1988	1984	1980	1976
D	93,727 (50%)	92,146 (47%)	80,350 (53%)	77,733 (57%)
R	92,745 (49%)	103,780 (53%)	65,911 (43%)	57,761 (42%)
I			4,402 (3%)	

Campaign Finance

	Receipts	Receipts from PACs	Expend-itures
1988			
Valentine (D)	$78,527	$58,650 (75%)	$84,671
1986			
Valentine (D)	$178,317	$109,755 (62%)	$164,680
McElhaney (R)	$69,531	$429 (0.6%)	$69,193

Key Votes

1987	
Raise speed limit to 65 mph	N
Approve Gephardt "fair trade" amendment	Y
Ban testing of larger nuclear weapons	N
Delay "re-flagging" of Kuwaiti tankers	N
Approve tax-raising deficit-reduction bill	Y
1988	
Approve aid to Nicaraguan contras	N
Enact civil rights restoration bill over Reagan veto	Y
Kill 60-day plant-closing notification measure	Y
Pass omnibus trade bill over Reagan veto	Y
Approve death penalty for drug-related murders	Y
Bar federal funds for abortions in cases of rape and incest	N
Oppose seven-day waiting period for purchase of handguns	Y

Voting Studies

	Presidential Support		Party Unity		Conservative Coalition	
Year	**S**	**O**	**S**	**O**	**S**	**O**
1988	40	58	70	25	95	5
1987	40	55	67	30	88	9
1986	41	57	67	31	90	8
1985	46	52	71	25	84	13
1984	43	44	51	38	86	7
1983	44	56	54	42	90	8

Interest Group Ratings

Year	ADA	ACU	AFL-CIO	CCUS
1988	45	48	71	62
1987	44	29	50	60
1986	30	55	43	65
1985	35	48	35	59
1984	20	55	46	38
1983	40	57	35	60

3 H. Martin Lancaster (D)

Of Goldsboro — Elected 1986

Born: March 24, 1943, Wayne County, N.C.
Education: U. of North Carolina, B.A. 1965, J.D. 1967.
Military Career: Navy, 1967-70.
Occupation: Lawyer.
Family: Wife, Alice Matheny; two children.
Religion: Presbyterian.
Political Career: N.C. House, 1979-87.
Capitol Office: 1408 Longworth Bldg. 20515; 225-3415.

In Washington: It came as little surprise in early 1989 when, at a House Democratic Caucus retreat, Lancaster received an award for work on behalf of his party. Many Southern Democrats have kept their national party at arm's length in the 1980s, but Lancaster made it clear from day one of his House career that he saw a role for himself in the party hierarchy.

He immediately began lobbying his freshman classmates for a leadership position, and when he got one, as class whip, he did not slow down. That was not lost on the Democratic leadership, which gave him a seat on Armed Services in the middle of his first term.

North Carolina Democrats tend to vote with the party leadership more often than their Southern colleagues, and Lancaster is no exception. But he is much more than just a reliable vote; he is an astute politician, well-connected around his home state and bent on getting connected in Washington. When Democrats were in a quandary over a controversial pay raise in early 1989, some older members sought Lancaster's advice about how they should respond publicly.

Lancaster's committee assignments put him in a good position to look after his district, whose economy is tied to agriculture and military bases. On Armed Services he is interested in some broad issues, such as changing procurement policies, but he also has a very specific interest in the role of the Marine Corps. The corps' training center at Camp Lejeune is located in the coastal city of Jacksonville. Lancaster's hometown, Goldsboro, is home to the Seymour Johnson Air Force Base.

On Agriculture, Lancaster watches out for other important economic interests, including North Carolina tobacco and corn growers. A bright future for corn growers, Lancaster thinks, lies partly in plastics. He has introduced legislation to mandate degradable plastics for consumer products. The idea would be good for the environment, he says, and also good for corn growers, whose product is used to make plastics degradable.

At Home: When Lancaster announced in 1985 that he was leaving the state Legislature to devote more time to his family and law practice, he did not expect to be back campaigning within six months. But Rep. Charles Whitley's surprise retirement announcement caused him to reassess.

Lancaster had left his mark in the state House on a broad range of issues, from licensing for medical practitioners to the creation of grass-roots arts programs. The high point of his legislative career occurred when Democratic Gov. James B. Hunt Jr. asked him to shepherd through the House a controversial measure to toughen the state's drunken-driving laws. Thanks in part to the favorable exposure, a survey of journalists and lobbyists rated Lancaster the House's fifth most effective legislator.

As soon as he announced his candidacy for Whitley's seat in Congress, Lancaster became the Democratic primary favorite. He moved quickly to shore up his one potential weakness — a perception by some that he had associated with the more liberal bloc of North Carolina Democrats in the state House. Lancaster devoted much of his campaign to courting business leaders and establishing conservative credentials; he seemed to take personal offense at any suggestion that he had ever allied himself with liberals.

The only one of his opponents who could hope to match Lancaster's support was Lewis Renn, Whitley's top aide in Washington. But while Renn had access to a quiet network of Whitley backers scattered throughout the district, he had no broad-based name recognition, and he never managed to achieve very much.

Lancaster was able to take most of the black vote, which comprises a significant proportion of the total in the Democratic primary. He benefited from a high turnout in Wayne County prompted by a liquor-by-the-drink referendum on the ballot there. While each of the candidates won his home county, Lancaster finished either first or second in the remaining seven counties. Renn was eligible for a runoff, but finished so far behind Lancaster in the primary that he chose to pass up the opportunity. The well-financed Lancaster then had little trouble defeating GOP state Rep. Gerald Hurst in this Democratic district.

North Carolina 3

Southeast Central — Goldsboro

The 3rd's flat, sandy countryside is broken up by small market towns serving the tobacco fields that make this district the nation's No. 1 producer of flue-cured tobacco. Goldsboro (Wayne County), the largest city in the 3rd, has a thriving tobacco market, and textiles are also important to the economy. Cotton has begun to make a comeback as a major crop, but it lags behind the leaf. There also is a military component to Goldsboro's economy: the Seymour Johnson Air Force Base, just south of the city.

Recent elections suggest the divided sympathies of the 3rd, where Democrats have traditionally dominated, but GOP candidates are having more success. The areas within the 3rd supported Jimmy Carter in 1976 and 1980, and the district went comfortably for Democrat Terry Sanford in his 1986 Senate contest. But the 3rd has given GOP Sen. Jesse Helms solid margins in his three elections, and it backed GOP Gov. James G. Martin in 1988.

The district's three most populous counties — Wayne, Onslow and Johnston — together cast about 45 percent of the vote. Though Democrats still enjoy a large advantage among registered voters in these counties, Republican candidates frequently win them in national and statewide elections. Reagan carried all three in 1980 and 1984, as did George Bush and Gov. Martin in 1988. Still, Lancaster won all three in 1986.

In addition to tobacco and cotton, soybeans and sweet potatoes grow here, and the district's farmers raise poultry and hogs. Duplin County produces more turkeys than any other in the state. Onslow, one of the district's two Atlantic coast counties, draws many visitors, but most are not seaside tourists; they are the "few good men" being whipped into shape at the Camp Lejeune Marine Corps training center near Jacksonville.

Population: 535,906. White 380,813 (71%), Black 146,519 (27%), Other 5,042 (1%). Spanish origin 8,326 (2%). 18 and over 379,853 (71%), 65 and over 48,581 (9%). Median age: 27.

Committees

Agriculture (26th of 27 Democrats)
Tobacco and Peanuts

Armed Services (27th of 31 Democrats)
Military Personnel and Compensation; Readiness

Small Business (21st of 27 Democrats)
Exports, Tax Policy and Special Problems; Procurement, Tourism and Rural Development

Elections

1988 General		
H. Martin Lancaster (D)	95,323	(100%)
1986 General		
H. Martin Lancaster (D)	71,460	(64%)
Gerald B. Hurst (R)	39,408	(36%)

District Vote For President

	1988	1984	1980	1976
D	62,638 (42%)	62,777 (39%)	71,695 (51%)	71,701 (59%)
R	85,233 (58%)	98,610 (61%)	65,996 (47%)	50,107 (41%)
I			2,042 (2%)	

Campaign Finance

	Receipts	Receipts from PACs	Expend-itures
1988			
Lancaster (D)	$195,992	$132,249 (67%)	$98,956
1986			
Lancaster (D)	$439,428	$140,004 (32%)	$439,725
Hurst (R)	$61,958	$6,822 (11%)	$61,265

Key Votes

1987	
Raise speed limit to 65 mph	N
Approve Gephardt "fair trade" amendment	Y
Ban testing of larger nuclear weapons	N
Delay "re-flagging" of Kuwaiti tankers	Y
Approve tax-raising deficit-reduction bill	Y
1988	
Approve aid to Nicaraguan contras	N
Enact civil rights restoration bill over Reagan veto	Y
Kill 60-day plant-closing notification measure	Y
Pass omnibus trade bill over Reagan veto	Y
Approve death penalty for drug-related murders	Y
Bar federal funds for abortions in cases of rape and incest	N
Oppose seven-day waiting period for purchase of handguns	Y

Voting Studies

	Presidential Support		Party Unity		Conservative Coalition	
Year	S	O	S	O	S	O
1988	38	62	78	19	84	16
1987	37	62	71	25	86	12

Interest Group Ratings

Year	ADA	ACU	AFL-CIO	CCUS
1988	60	40	71	64
1987	60	17	75	40

4 David E. Price (D)

Of Chapel Hill — Elected 1986

Born: Aug. 17, 1940, Johnson City, Tenn.
Education: U. of North Carolina, B.A. 1961; Yale U., B.D. 1964, Ph.D. 1969.
Occupation: Political science professor.
Family: Wife, Lisa Kanwit; two children.
Religion: Baptist.
Political Career: N.C. Democratic Party chairman, 1983-84.
Capitol Office: 1224 Longworth Bldg. 20515; 225-1784.

In Washington: Because Price is an academic-turned-politician, some expected that he would bring a unique, professorial detachment to the maelstrom of House politics, providing a sort of laboratory experiment in alternative politics. But Price, a former chairman of the state Democratic Party, is equal parts pol and prof, and in his first term, he displayed the caution one would typically expect of a freshman trying to hold a competitive district.

Price made an impressive legislative debut on the Banking Committee with his bill requiring banks to disclose fully the terms of home-equity loans. He touted the bill, which was signed into law in 1988, in his re-election campaign, appealing to the sizable white-collar suburbanite population in his district.

Even as Price sought publicity for the issues he pursued, though, he had to confront an issue that pursued him: gun control. In 1987, Price added his name to a growing list of cosponsors of a bill establishing a waiting period for the purchase of handguns. When the issue came to the floor in 1988, Price found himself confronted with the dilemma of bucking the powerful National Rifle Association just weeks before the election, or voting against a proposal he had cosponsored. He decided on the latter course, sparking an outcry from gun-control advocates. A week earlier, in what was widely perceived as another issue testing Democrats' political nerve, Price was one of only seven Democrats supporting a GOP effort to require recitation of the Pledge of Allegiance at the start of each day's House proceedings.

At Home: Price laid the groundwork for his move from academia to electioneering with a long career as a party activist at the state and national level. In 1986, he beat GOP Rep. Bill Cobey by 12 points — the largest victory margin of any House challenger that year.

While teaching political science at Duke, Price spent nearly two years as state party chairman, winning generally high marks for his performance. He also made invaluable contacts with local party leaders in the district, and used them to build an early financial and organizational edge over three primary rivals.

In the primary, Price, a somewhat stiff and awkward campaigner, fell short of the 50 percent needed to avoid a runoff. But his strongest opponent declined to force a runoff.

Cobey, who had won the traditionally Democratic 4th in 1984, was considered vulnerable from the outset. His affable nature and constituent service operation helped him win over some voters who disagreed with his conservative ideology, but he was operating with little margin for error. And he committed a serious one in mid-September.

Cobey mailed out a campaign letter addressed to "Dear Christian Friend," in which he said he was "an ambassador for Christ" who needed the support of fundamentalists "so our voice will not be silenced and then replaced by someone who is not willing to take a strong stand for the principles outlined in the word of God." Injecting religion in the campaign might have been a questionable tactic against any candidate, but it seemed particularly inappropriate against Price, an active Southern Baptist who taught Sunday school and has a divinity degree. The letter aided Price's contention that Cobey was "isolated ... from mainstream thinking in both parties."

Price, who had criticized Cobey throughout the year for opposing such diverse proposals as African famine relief and the Clean Water Act, zeroed in with late TV ads hitting Cobey for casting votes against Social Security and emergency farm credit legislation in 1985.

In 1988, Price faced Republican Tom Fetzer, a former operative for GOP Sen. Jesse Helms' political organization, the National Congressional Club. The Club's past campaign tactics and attention to social issues had put off Democrats and even some Republicans, but the organization's resources helped make Fetzer a threat. Price, however, was on guard to deflect charges that he was too liberal for the 4th; his work on the home-equity legislation aimed straight at affluent suburbanites who might be tempted to vote Republican. In the end, Price improved on his 1986 showing.

North Carolina 4

Central — Raleigh; Chapel Hill

Universities are not only cultural centers in this part of the state — they are major sources of jobs. Home to 14 post-secondary schools, the 4th comprises two corners of the Research Triangle area — Wake County (Raleigh) and Orange County (Chapel Hill).

Chapel Hill hosts the University of North Carolina, and North Carolina State is in Raleigh. Drawing upon them, and employing thousands of white-collar professionals, is a collection of laboratories and research facilities run by private firms and government agencies. Additional white-collar jobs are available in government agencies in Raleigh, North Carolina's capital.

The outlying parts of Wake County are more traditional rural Deep South territory. Wake, which casts a little more than 60 percent of the 4th's vote, has usually split its tickets in recent years. In 1988, Wake went Republican in both the presidential and gubernatorial contests, but voted for Democrat Price in the House race.

Orange County, home to about 15 percent of the district's voters, has a more Democratic bent, thanks in large part to the university community of Chapel Hill. In 1988, Orange County gave Price 72 percent in his House contest.

South of Orange lies Chatham County, largely rural territory dotted with textile plants, tobacco fields and dairy farms. Chatham's agrarian complexion is changing somewhat, however, as growth from Chapel Hill spills over into its northern end.

Chatham County is solidly Democratic in state and local elections, and in 1988, Michael S. Dukakis managed to carry it in presidential voting.

Randolph, which lies just south of the Greensboro-High Point metropolis, is the most populous county in the state in which the GOP enjoys a numerical advantage. Price has lost Randolph decisively in both his House races.

At the district's eastern end lies rural Franklin County, dominated by tobacco and farming. Franklin clings to its Democratic traditions in most statewide and local races.

Population: 533,580. White 421,508 (79%), Black 105,942 (20%), Other 4,270 (1%). Spanish origin 4,152 (1%). 18 and over 395,635 (74%), 65 and over 44,974 (8%). Median age: 29.

Committees

Banking, Finance and Urban Affairs (27th of 31 Democrats)
Consumer Affairs and Coinage; Financial Institutions Supervision, Regulation and Insurance; Housing and Community Development

Science, Space and Technology (23rd of 30 Democrats)
Natural Resources, Agriculture Research and Environment; Science, Research and Technology

Elections

1988 General		
David E. Price (D)	131,896	(58%)
Tom Fetzer (R)	95,482	(42%)
1986 General		
David E. Price (D)	92,216	(56%)
Bill Cobey (R)	73,469	(44%)

District Vote For President

	1988		1984		1980		1976	
D	105,357	(44%)	90,622	(40%)	86,907	(47%)	84,276	(53%)
R	132,495	(55%)	137,174	(60%)	87,832	(47%)	74,839	(47%)
I					9,967	(5%)		

Campaign Finance

	Receipts	Receipts from PACs	Expend-itures
1988			
Price (D)	$1,031,004	$489,658 (47%)	$1,006,641
Fetzer (R)	$759,367	$85,051 (11%)	$759,164
1986			
Price (D)	$863,825	$234,118 (27%)	$854,616
Cobey (R)	$787,678	$305,282 (39%)	$789,135

Key Votes

1987	
Raise speed limit to 65 mph	N
Approve Gephardt "fair trade" amendment	Y
Ban testing of larger nuclear weapons	Y
Delay "re-flagging" of Kuwaiti tankers	Y
Approve tax-raising deficit-reduction bill	N
1988	
Approve aid to Nicaraguan contras	N
Enact civil rights restoration bill over Reagan veto	Y
Kill 60-day plant-closing notification measure	N
Pass omnibus trade bill over Reagan veto	Y
Approve death penalty for drug-related murders	Y
Bar federal funds for abortions in cases of rape and incest	N
Oppose seven-day waiting period for purchase of handguns	Y

Voting Studies

	Presidential Support		Party Unity		Conservative Coalition	
Year	**S**	**O**	**S**	**O**	**S**	**O**
1988	28	68	83	14	71	24
1987	29	69	84	13	72	28

Interest Group Ratings

Year	ADA	ACU	AFL-CIO	CCUS
1988	75	24	93	62
1987	80	9	81	33

5 Stephen L. Neal (D)

Of Winston-Salem — Elected 1974

Born: Nov. 7, 1934, Winston-Salem, N.C.
Education: Attended U. of California, Santa Barbara, 1954-56; U. of Hawaii, A.B. 1962.
Occupation: Publisher; mortgage banker.
Family: Wife, Rachel Landis Miller; two children.
Religion: Presbyterian.
Political Career: No previous office.
Capitol Office: 2463 Rayburn Bldg. 20515; 225-2071.

In Washington: Neal's politically cautious style and the seniority that has put him within sight of the Banking Committee chairmanship have combined to help him survive repeated Republican challenges in a district that leans toward more clear-cut conservatism.

He has fostered ties to the state's business community, especially the financial institutions that have become Southern powerhouses under deregulation. With Neal a Banking subcommittee chairman, and fourth among 31 Democrats in line for the full committee chair, local business leaders have shied from opposing him, even when one of their own is the GOP nominee, as was the case in 1988.

Reserved yet personable, Neal fits in well politically with other North Carolina Democrats, a group of moderates who are the most reliable supporters of House Democratic leaders among Southerners. Meanwhile, he keeps enough distance from the national party's more controversial stands to survive at home.

Still, the full-time effort at electoral survival — he has topped 55 percent only once in eight elections — seems to have detracted from Neal's profile in Banking, and in the House in general. A few years ago, he was whispered as an alternative to autocratic Banking Chairman Fernand J. St Germain in the event of a coup. But as the 1980s wore on, Neal was mentioned less frequently in that regard. All such speculation became moot with St Germain's surprise defeat in the 1988 election.

In the 100th Congress, however, Neal did play a leading role in the controversial effort to save the Federal Savings and Loan Insurance Corporation (FSLIC) from insolvency. He sponsored an S&L industry-backed proposal to raise $5 billion over two years for the FSLIC from higher industry fees. The Reagan administration wanted $15 billion over five years. Foes said the FSLIC could not effectively absorb that much money, but many experts maintained that it would take much more than $15 billion to shut down the many bankrupt S&Ls.

Neal's $5 billion proposal had a formidable supporter in Speaker Jim Wright, who worried that a larger bailout would free federal regulators to close the numerous S&Ls in his state wrecked by fraud and Texas' ailing economy. Wright personally lobbied the committee for the $5 billion plan. A day after a Banking subcommittee approved the administration-backed proposal, Democratic vote switches in the full committee reversed the outcome. Neal's amendment passed, 25-24.

Then it was Wright who switched, along with St Germain, after weeks of negative press coverage of his role. The two men endorsed the $15 billion option. But as Neal said afterward, Wright "wasn't very active" in pushing it, while the S&L lobby came out in force against it. By 153-258, the House defeated the $15 billion plan when St Germain proposed it, and adopted Neal's $5 billion package.

In the end, $10.8 billion was authorized, and Neal had little hand in the outcome. It was negotiated between then-Treasury Secretary James A. Baker III and the House and Senate Banking Committee heads to avert Reagan's veto. At an unusual late-night conference called to ratify the agreement, Neal objected: "This is a new definition of compromise. This is a figure most of us had nothing to do with." The next year, when Banking approved another $5 billion infusion, Neal opposed it, citing the cost to industry. That bill went no farther.

Neal also has opposed consumer advocates' proposals to cap interest rates on credit cards, saying it would drive some companies out of business. On the larger question of further deregulating banks to allow them to trade in securities, Neal sponsored legislation more favorable to banks than St Germain pushed. The panel approved its chairman's bill, but with changes that included a Neal amendment to lower existing barriers between parent banks and their securities affiliates. Among other things, his amendment would allow the entities to share offices and employees. But the entire bill got snared in a dispute with another committee and never came to a House vote.

Neal is chairman of the Subcommittee on Domestic Monetary Policy, which oversees the Federal Reserve Board and its regulation of the

North Carolina 5

Northwest — Winston-Salem

The heart of the 5th is Winston-Salem, an old-time tobacco town whose links to the leaf were established over a century ago. The first factory opened in Winston-Salem in 1872; three years later R. J. Reynolds constructed his first processing plant. The city remains a tobacco-processing center, although it produces textiles and communications equipment as well. The population of Winston-Salem is 40 percent black. The city and surrounding Forsyth County cast 46 percent of the district's overall vote.

In national elections, Forsyth has a Republican tilt that has been building for more than a decade. The county gave Democratic presidential nominee Jimmy Carter the barest of margins in 1976, crossed party lines to go narrowly for Ronald Reagan in 1980, and then went comfortably Republican in the 1984 and 1988 White House contests. Its allegiances are divided in elections closer to home. Forsyth went Democratic for the Senate in 1986 (though by only 403 votes), and backed Republican James G. Martin for governor in 1984 and 1988.

Republicans traditionally have been strong in several of the hill counties in the western reaches of the district, between the Blue Ridge and Appalachian mountains. Early settlers of this area set up small farms with dairy cows, poultry, apple trees and tobacco, and developed strong antagonism toward the flatland tobacco planters, who were wealthier, politically powerful and Democratic.

Wilkes County is especially strong for the GOP. In 1988, the county went Republican in the presidential, gubernatorial and House contests.

Hosiery is the critical branch of the textile industry in the outlying areas of the 5th. Mount Airy, a town of some 7,000 people near the Virginia border, hosts several plants involved in the manufacture of stockings, men's briefs and infants' nightwear.

Population: 535,212. White 445,932 (83%), Black 86,748 (16%). Spanish origin 3,667 (1%). 18 and over 388,006 (63%), 65 and over 58,381 (11%). Median age: 31.

money supply. It is a good place for a monetarist like Neal, who shares with conservative Milton Friedman the idea that national economic health depends on a modest and steady growth in the money supply, rather than any combination of federal tax and spending policies.

Certainly, the subcommittee is less of a burden than Neal's previous job, as chairman of the International Finance Subcommittee. That panel is charged with recommending funding for the U.S. contributions to the International Monetary Fund (IMF) and the Export-Import Bank. At times of suspicion about foreign assistance, bills for these international lenders have provoked conservatives to warfare.

Opponents of legislation for the IMF, which is the source of aid to dozens of Third World nations, in 1983 offered more than 60 amendments, and several passed over Neal's objections. As he predicted, they were killed in conference with the Senate, largely because Reagan was among the backers of IMF funding.

Still, Neal took considerable heat, on the House floor and off, for his role. Conservative Republicans who disagreed with Reagan's stand launched ad campaigns in the districts of many Democrats, including Neal, charging that lawmakers had given aid to communist countries.

Meanwhile, the Ex-Im Bank seemed to gain political strength as members came to see it as a way to protect American jobs by stimulating exports. Neal's job was to fend off Reagan's proposed cuts. In the 99th Congress, the administration recommended that the Ex-Im Bank subsidize interest rates on private banks' loans rather than make direct loans itself to foreign buyers of U.S. goods. But with record trade deficits, the plan found a cool reception on Capitol Hill, since it was perceived as an attempt to kill the bank entirely. "If ever we needed the Ex-Im Bank," Neal said at one point, "we need it now."

His subcommittee rejected Reagan's plan 18-1. It passed a bill reauthorizing the bank, although the measure finally approved by Congress in 1986 did include an experimental program of subsidies for private banks. The bill also included a $300 million "war chest" for grants and low-interest loans to boost exports, an idea backed by Neal and the administration.

Another Neal legislative project has been a solar energy bank. His bill to create a $5 billion lender for new solar projects became law with President Carter's support in 1980. But the Reagan administration immediately tried to kill it and, when that failed, refused to spend the money Congress appropriated. Neal sued along with a pro-solar coalition, and a federal judge ordered the administration to carry out the program. Even so, Reagan continued to oppose it. Finally, in 1987, Congress killed the program.

Neal also is a member of the Government Operations Committee, where he has proposed a bill to raise the Environmental Protection Agency to Cabinet level, in an effort to boost its visibility and clout.

Other of his efforts are more closely linked to the interests of his district, which is perched geographically and politically between the Republican-leaning Appalachian foothills and the traditionally Democratic Piedmont. Aside from banking, Neal promotes two longer-established but more troubled industries, tobacco and textiles.

He opposes the increasing number of measures to raise cigarette taxes and limit smoking; in 1986, he dubbed bills to restrict smoking in federal buildings the "Smokers Segregation and Persecution Acts." In the past two Congresses, he has joined fellow Southerners in a feisty but unsuccessful fight to limit textile imports. Reagan vetoed both trade bills.

Earlier in his career, Neal tenaciously fought a local public-works project. A power company wanted to dam the New River, which flows from North Carolina into Virginia, but Neal countered with a bill to block the project by including part of the river in the protected Wild and Scenic Rivers system. He lobbied nearly every member of the House, pleading that this was of critical political and aesthetic importance to him. He won.

Although it has caused him some problems at home, Neal has voted with the Democratic leadership more often than not. For example, he consistently opposed Reagan's policy of military aid to the Nicaraguan contras. Despite a $40,000 offer for campaign help from the National Conservative Political Action Committee, Neal voted against the Reagan-backed tax cut in 1981. He complained to the Justice Department that the offer was a bribe, but officials concluded it "did not go beyond the bounds of traditionally acceptable lobbying."

At Home: A Watergate-spawned Democrat in a district with a demonstrated affection for the GOP, Neal always expects tough elections, and is always prepared for them. But the wave of Republicanism that has swept through the state in recent presidential elections has tested even his best laid plans.

His opponent in 1980 was state Sen. Anne Bagnal, an energetic Republican who stressed her strong opposition to abortion and the Equal Rights Amendment and criticized Neal's support for President Carter. Although Neal voted with Carter no more often than the average House Democrat, he enthusiastically touted the president and invited him to appear in the district during the campaign.

Reagan carried the 5th over Carter by nearly 15,000 votes, laying down coattails for Bagnal that helped her hold Neal to 51 percent, the worst showing he had made since his initial election to the House in 1974.

Neal rebounded in 1982, winning handily over Bagnal in a good Democratic year in North Carolina. But by 1984, he was in trouble again. Reagan's position at the top of the ticket helped spark an outbreak of straight-ticket GOP voting in North Carolina.

The Republican nominee was broadcast executive Stuart Epperson, a political neophyte who entered the race only shortly before the filing deadline. Epperson's appeal was hampered not only by low visibility but also by his quixotic style. Early on, he sought to attract attention to his candidacy by walking the district with a lantern, asking voters if they had seen Neal.

A graduate of fundamentalist Bob Jones University, Epperson began by stressing his conservative stance on school prayer. But local GOP leaders convinced him that an economic emphasis would give him broader appeal. He spent the later stages of the campaign criticizing Neal's support for U.S. involvement in the IMF, arguing that such a stance would encourage foreign competition and thus hurt local textile markets.

Neal defended his record, and dismissed Epperson as an amateur dependent for support upon Reagan's coattails. "He has no record of accomplishment, service or understanding," the incumbent said. Still, Neal needed all his political strength to hold on to his seat. Bolstered by the campaigns of Reagan, GOP gubernatorial candidate James G. Martin and Sen. Jesse Helms, Epperson carried five of the district's eight counties and came within 3,232 votes of an upset.

Epperson returned for a rematch in 1986, and proved more polished than in his first outing. He also offered a more focused message. Hoping to capitalize on discontent over the slumping textile industry, Epperson spent most of the campaign railing against Neal for supporting IMF loans that the Republican claimed were used to help build textile plants in foreign countries — and thus cost the 5th District jobs. He also touted his efforts to encourage radio stations across the country to donate free air time to a buy-American clothing campaign dubbed "Crafted With Pride."

Neal sought to discredit his opposition by arguing that the only people who saw sinister implications in the IMF were Epperson and fringe political figure Lyndon H. LaRouche Jr. But he also was careful to address Epperson's charges, denying that IMF money had been used to finance any foreign textile plants.

In the end, Epperson could not match the momentum of his 1984 campaign. Without the benefit of the top-of-the-ticket presence of a Reagan or a Helms, the Republican managed to carry only two counties — rural Alexander and Wilkes — as Neal posted a 54 percent tally.

Neal again had cause for concern in 1988. Michael S. Dukakis was not expected to run well in North Carolina, and the GOP offered a different style of candidate in Lyons Gray, a wealthy and well-known business-oriented establishment Republican.

Gray, owner of an industrial roofing company, was a member of a very prominent family in Winston-Salem, and he had had some political exposure as well. Gray lost to Epperson in the 1986 Republican House primary.

Unlike previous GOP nominees, Gray did not try to paint Neal as a dangerous liberal. In fact, his ads said Neal was not a bad representative. But the ads continued, "Not bad isn't good enough." He criticized Neal as an ineffective member overly attentive to big banks.

But Neal, experienced at tough campaigns, quickly put Gray on the defensive. He got an opening in late summer when Gray returned a questionnaire to the AFL-CIO stating his opposition to legislation limiting textile imports. That position is not palatable to most in North Carolina, and Gray quickly insisted it was a staff error. But the incident and a few other missteps shifted the focus from Neal.

In the end, Neal did almost as well as he had in 1986, taking 53 percent of the vote. Gray carried three counties, leaving five, including sizable Forsythe (Winston-Salem) to Neal.

Neal had been one of the nation's most surprising winners in 1974, defeating four-term Rep. Wilmer D. Mizell, one of the most popular Republicans in the state. Mizell, a former National League pitcher, flirted with the idea of running for the Senate in 1974, finally deciding to keep what he and everyone else considered a safe House seat.

But it was not a good year to be a Republican in North Carolina. Neal, a publisher of several suburban newspapers, linked Mizell to the Nixon administration and the state's economic troubles and took 52 percent.

Two years later, Mizell came back for a rematch, arguing that Neal was a liberal who had sold his property in Winston-Salem and "gone Washington." Neal's cautious legislative record helped belie that charge, and a strong Democratic ticket helped him win with 54 percent of the vote.

Committees

Banking, Finance and Urban Affairs (4th of 31 Democrats)
Domestic Monetary Policy (chairman); Financial Institutions Supervision, Regulation and Insurance; Housing and Community Development; International Development, Finance, Trade and Monetary Policy

Government Operations (7th of 24 Democrats)
Legislation and National Security

Elections

1988 General		
Stephen L. Neal (D)	110,516	(53%)
Lyons Gray (R)	99,540	(47%)
1986 General		
Stephen L. Neal (D)	86,410	(54%)
Stuart Epperson (R)	73,261	(46%)

Previous Winning Percentages: **1984** (51%) **1982** (60%) **1980** (51%) **1978** (54%) **1976** (54%) **1974** (52%)

District Vote For President

	1988	1984	1980	1976
D	81,340 (40%)	76,012 (36%)	84,718 (45%)	92,851 (52%)
R	123,725 (60%)	136,330 (64%)	99,410 (52%)	84,578 (48%)
I			4,431 (2%)	

Campaign Finance

	Receipts	Receipts from PACs	Expenditures
1988			
Neal (D)	$715,578	$411,180 (57%)	$756,115
Gray (R)	$717,953	$52,887 (7%)	$718,015
1986			
Neal (D)	$493,483	$294,413 (60%)	$494,014
Epperson (R)	$934,850	$33,313 (4%)	$939,342

Key Votes

1987	
Raise speed limit to 65 mph	Y
Approve Gephardt "fair trade" amendment	Y
Ban testing of larger nuclear weapons	Y
Delay "re-flagging" of Kuwaiti tankers	Y
Approve tax-raising deficit-reduction bill	Y
1988	
Approve aid to Nicaraguan contras	N
Enact civil rights restoration bill over Reagan veto	Y
Kill 60-day plant-closing notification measure	N
Pass omnibus trade bill over Reagan veto	Y
Approve death penalty for drug-related murders	Y
Bar federal funds for abortions in cases of rape and incest	N
Oppose seven-day waiting period for purchase of handguns	Y

Voting Studies

	Presidential Support		Party Unity		Conservative Coalition	
Year	S	O	S	O	S	O
1988	24	68	76	12	55	24
1987	32	67	73	21	74	26
1986	28	71	75	18	54	40
1985	36	64	72	17	60	33
1984	39	51	65	22	51	36
1983	38	50	64	20	55	33
1982	42	44	48	32	59	25
1981	42	55	66	27	64	29

Interest Group Ratings

Year	ADA	ACU	AFL-CIO	CCUS
1988	70	21	92	50
1987	68	5	60	60
1986	65	29	71	50
1985	50	33	53	48
1984	65	32	42	31
1983	60	32	73	59
1982	25	50	60	50
1981	55	20	73	17

6 Howard Coble (R)

Of Greensboro — Elected 1984

Born: March 18, 1931, Greensboro, N.C.

Education: Attended Appalachian State U., 1949-50; Guilford College, 1950-52, 1957-58, A.B. 1958; U. of North Carolina, J.D. 1962.

Military Career: Coast Guard, 1952-56; Coast Guard Reserve, 1960-81.

Occupation: Lawyer.

Family: Single.

Religion: Presbyterian.

Political Career: N.C. House, 1969, 1979-83; secretary, N.C. Department of Revenue, 1973-76; Republican nominee for N.C. treasurer, 1976.

Capitol Office: 430 Cannon Bldg. 20515; 225-3065.

In Washington: Over the years, North Carolina has sent Congress more than its share of smart lawyers who choose to present themselves as ignorant country boys. Coble, who has been a federal prosecutor, headed his state's revenue department and practiced in a prestigious Greensboro law firm, is firmly in that tradition.

"I'm sort of provincial," he insisted to a reporter as he was about to start his first term. "What the hell I'm doing up here, I don't know."

Some of Coble's House colleagues seem willing to accept him as a tobacco-chewing rustic. Others know they don't teach the kind of tennis Coble plays down on the farm; they see someone smarter than his act. Whatever the case, the affable, backslapping Coble appears more charming than ambitious.

Coble declined a chance to sit on the powerful Energy and Commerce Committee, which with its wide-ranging jurisdiction offers entree into almost any issue. Popular among his GOP colleagues, Coble was rated an easy favorite to become the first member on Energy from the Carolinas since the departure of James T. Broyhill in 1986. But he opted instead to continue building seniority on Judiciary, a committee perhaps better suited to his background and training; the Energy seat went to another North Carolinian, Republican Alex McMillan of Charlotte.

Coble's decision to stay put was questioned by some of his colleagues. But there is no questioning Coble's ability to make the right political moves for survival in what had been one of the nation's foremost swing districts. His 1986 victory made him the first incumbent to win re-election in the 6th since 1978.

More than 30,000 of Coble's constituents work in the textile industry, and he has been incessant in his demands for protectionist relief for textile companies. "The only place free trade exists," he says, "is in an economics textbook."

Coble's job of pleading for textile protection was made infinitely more difficult by the refusal of President Reagan to consider any. After voting for textile import restrictions in 1985 and 1988, Coble could only watch helplessly as Reagan vetoed the legislation. It was clear both times there was no hope of overriding; Coble's only option was to argue against the veto, and make sure his district knew he had. That he did, over and over again.

A vice chairman of the Textile Caucus, he is constantly searching for ways to boost the industry. He played a role, for example, in a 1988 skirmish to prevent federal prisons from competing more vigorously with his district's furniture and textile makers.

His major legislative accomplishment is in another area, though: a 1986 amendment that increased the penalties and fines for anyone caught interfering with satellite transmissions.

Coble prides himself on being a fiscal conservative, and he has applied his philosophy in ways not all his colleagues appreciate. Like many, he has been vocal in opposing congressional pay raises, but during his first year in the House, he also introduced a bill to cut pensions. One of his North Carolina colleagues called the bill "demagoguery." Coble's news conference to announce the bill played to a nearly empty room. One of his aides, asked about the empty chairs, said they represented all the cosponsors the legislation had been able to attract.

Coble is ready enough to play the federal spending game, though, when the 6th District is the recipient. Federal sewer and construction grants he announced in 1988 did not hurt his re-election bid.

Eager to demonstrate effectiveness, Coble also does not hesitate to take credit for a victory even if his role has been modest. Early in 1986, the Department of Energy announced two po-

North Carolina 6

Central — Greensboro; High Point

Greensboro, the third-largest city in North Carolina, and surrounding Guilford County are comfortably middle class. The economy is a diverse mixture of manufacturing and service industry. Burlington Industries and Cone Mills, two textle giants, employ thousands, in both headquarters operations and mills, as does AT&T Federal Systems, a key defense contractor. The city also has two major state universities and a large insurer.

The managerial personnel in Greensboro industries have given Guilford County an appreciable Republican vote, but one that is far from monolithic. Guilford backed President Reagan's 1984 bid for re-election, while voting Democratic in contests for the U.S. Senate and House. In 1988, though, Republicans won the presidential, gubernatorial and House contests in Guilford County.

South of Greensboro is High Point, which refers to itself as the "furniture capital of the world." Visitors are directed to a building in the center of town that resembles a giant chest of drawers. Nearby Thomasville, in Davidson County, also a furniture-producing center, boasts a giant chair.

East of Greensboro, the 6th takes in Alamance County and its rapidly diversifying economy: Its agricultural and textile base has been steadily supplemented by branch manufacturing, including a plant where Honda builds lawn mowers.

While Democrats enjoy a registration advantage in Alamance County, that jurisdiction gave Reagan comfortable margins in both 1980 and 1984, and George Bush carried it easily in 1988. Republicans claimed a majority on the Alamance County Commission in 1984 for the first time.

In the district's southwest corner is Davidson County, another traditional furniture- and textile-producing area. Davidson has a substantial population of Republicans. The county's commission and its delegation in the North Carolina Legislature is controlled by the GOP.

Population: 529,635. White 415,746 (79%), Black 109,806 (21%), Other 3,106 (1%). Spanish origin 3,607 (1%). 18 and over 386,301 (73%), 65 and over 54,361 (10%). Median age: 31.

tential sites in North Carolina for nuclear-waste storage, but decided against a site in Coble's district. Energy officials said they had made the decision by applying rigid policy guidelines, but Coble came close to suggesting he had personally talked them into it. "Our office worked long hours to see that the 6th District was removed from the list," he said, "and that is exactly what happened."

At Home: Coble started the 1984 election year thinking about running for governor. He had gained some statewide name recognition among Republicans, not only in the Legislature but as an assistant U.S. attorney, and as secretary of the Department of Revenue under GOP Gov. James E. Holshouser Jr. in the mid-1970s. But he passed up a statewide bid to challenge freshman Democratic Rep. Robin Britt in the 6th.

Despite his reputation, it took all of Coble's efforts just to make himself the Republican nominee. Former state Sen. Walter C. Cockerham, a millionaire construction company owner, already had been stumping the district and courting Republican votes for several months before Coble entered the race.

The primary caused a split between local GOP moderates and the party's more militant conservative faction. Coble's roots were on the moderate side, as evidenced by his close ties to Hoshouser, archenemy of the conservative wing. Cockerham devoted much of his time trying to outflank his opponent on the right, branding Coble a "liberal lawyer" and casting himself as a "consistent conservative" in the tradition of North Carolina's GOP Sens. Jesse Helms and John P. East.

Although Helms himself did not make an endorsement, Cockerham had the support of the Helms-affiliated National Congressional Club, a group Coble had publicly criticized.

But Coble found a theme that enabled him to capture ample conservative support of his own. He played up his reputation for fiscal stinginess in monitoring the state budget, earned following his return to the North Carolina House in 1979. Armed with the support of most local GOP leaders, Coble pulled through by a scant 164 votes.

Coble continued to stress his fiscal conservatism against Britt, whom he sought to paint as an extravagant liberal. Coble criticized the incumbent for having gone against President Reagan on two of every three votes cast in 1983, and accused Britt of voting to spend money to pay people to operate automatic elevators.

Britt did everything he could to fight the liberal label. He ran TV ads reminding voters that he was one of 24 House Democratic freshmen who joined Republicans to derail briefly a stopgap spending measure as a sign of their distaste for deficits in 1983. Reaching into Coble's record, Britt accused him of voting in the Legislature for state funding for abortion, then opposing federal funding as a congressional candidate.

But it was not enough to win him a second term. Although Britt's careful cultivation of the Greensboro business community helped him carry Guilford County, he failed to run up sufficient margins to compensate for Coble's strength in the 6th's outlying territory. Tapping into the flow of conservative Democrats who crossed party lines for Reagan, Coble finished with a 2,662-vote edge out of some 203,000 ballots cast.

But Coble could not rest long on his laurels. Britt returned home to Greensboro following his defeat and began plotting his comeback. The 1986 results would be even closer than in their 1984 run-in; only 79 votes separated the winner and the loser on Election Day.

The major thrust of Britt's campaign was directed at workers in the slumping textile industry. He contended that Coble's inability to persuade his House GOP colleagues to override Reagan's veto of the 1985 textile bill was damaging to local industry.

Coble countered that he had more influence with the Reagan administration than any freshman Democrat could have. The incumbent also took pains to emphasize his fiscally conservative credentials at every turn, frequently reminding audiences that he was a strong supporter of Gramm-Rudman-Hollings.

Coble's strategy helped inoculate him from the charges leveled by Britt and the national Democratic Party, whose leaders had targeted the 6th in part because of the troubled textile industry. But the Republican had very few votes to spare. Britt again carried Guilford County, and also eked out a narrow margin in more rural Alamance County. Only by establishing a 555-vote edge in Davidson County — which is especially dependent on textiles — did Coble secure victory. Britt spent the early months of 1987 appealing the election results, but his challenge proved unsuccessful.

When Britt opted not to make another run in 1988, Democrats turned to Tom Gilmore, a well-known and well-funded former state legislator. But while Gilmore had a zest for campaigning, his campaign itself had little zest. He continued with some of Britt's attacks on the textile issue, and criticized Coble's record on the environment, calling attention to the incumbent's presence on Environmental Action's "Dirty Dozen" list.

But Coble had personally endeared himself to many in the 6th, and he was better positioned to point to his success at delivering for the district after two terms. With national trends going his direction, Coble won 62 percent of the vote.

Committees

Judiciary (9th of 14 Republicans)
Courts, Intellectual Property and the Administration of Justice; Criminal Justice

Merchant Marine and Fisheries (11th of 17 Republicans)
Coast Guard and Navigation; Fisheries and Wildlife Conservation and the Environment

Elections

1988 General		
Howard Coble (R)	116,534	(62%)
Tom Gilmore (D)	70,008	(38%)
1986 General		
Howard Coble (R)	72,329	(50%)
Robin Britt (D)	72,250	(50%)

Previous Winning Percentage: **1984** (51%)

District Vote For President

	1988	1984	1980	1976
D	76,208 (39%)	68,726 (35%)	74,137 (42%)	82,056 (51%)
R	118,565 (61%)	129,630 (65%)	94,162 (54%)	76,934 (48%)
I			5,458 (3%)	

Campaign Finance

	Receipts	Receipts from PACs	Expend-itures
1988			
Coble (R)	$736,254	$282,524 (38%)	$738,088
Gilmore (D)	$586,449	$258,082 (44%)	$583,013
1986			
Coble (R)	$594,943	$253,161 (43%)	$585,245
Britt (D)	$558,992	$285,754 (51%)	$562,711

Key Votes

1987	
Raise speed limit to 65 mph	Y
Approve Gephardt "fair trade" amendment	N
Ban testing of larger nuclear weapons	N
Delay "re-flagging" of Kuwaiti tankers	N
Approve tax-raising deficit-reduction bill	N
1988	
Approve aid to Nicaraguan contras	Y
Enact civil rights restoration bill over Reagan veto	N
Kill 60-day plant-closing notification measure	Y
Pass omnibus trade bill over Reagan veto	N
Approve death penalty for drug-related murders	Y
Bar federal funds for abortions in cases of rape and incest	Y
Oppose seven-day waiting period for purchase of handguns	Y

Voting Studies

	Presidential Support		Party Unity		Conservative Coalition	
Year	S	O	S	O	S	O
1988	61	39	90	10	92	8
1987	70	30	92	7	95	5
1986	68	31	84	14	92	8
1985	69	30	87	9	91	9

Interest Group Ratings

Year	ADA	ACU	AFL-CIO	CCUS
1988	10	92	21	93
1987	4	87	6	100
1986	10	81	36	89
1985	0	81	12	91

7 Charlie Rose (D)

Of Fayetteville — Elected 1972

Born: Aug. 10, 1939, Fayetteville, N.C.
Education: Davidson College, B.A. 1961; U. of North Carolina, LL.B. 1964.
Occupation: Lawyer.
Family: Wife, Joan Teague; three children.
Religion: Presbyterian.
Political Career: Chief district court prosecutor, 12th Judicial District, 1967-71; sought Democratic nomination for U.S. House, 1970.
Capitol Office: 2230 Rayburn Bldg. 20515; 225-2731.

In Washington: Two issues — smoking and his own ethics troubles — kept a tether on the usually wide-ranging Charlie Rose in the 100th Congress. Now that his gubernatorial and House leadership ambitions seem behind him, Rose may simply have to bide his time until the inertia of seniority delivers him the chairmanship of the Agriculture Committee. Currently the panel's No. 4 Democrat, Rose is a dozen years younger than anyone above him.

During his House career, Rose has been a jack-of-all-trades, bringing TV and computers to the House floor, monitoring the U.S. intelligence program, leading a foray against patents on genetically altered animals and advocating the rights of Tibetans. On top of that, Rose looks out for his state's interests as chairman of the Agriculture Subcommittee on Tobacco and Peanuts.

That is an important home-state role, but Rose was somewhat distracted from it in the 100th Congress by a more personal concern: defending himself against a complaint that he improperly converted nearly $64,000 in campaign contributions for his own use and also used campaign funds as collateral for a $75,000 personal loan.

Rose maintained that the $64,000 was repayment for loans he and his father had made to his first campaign. He did not deny he used campaign funds as collateral for the $75,000 personal loan, but said that since he had no legal authority to do that, the transaction was invalid and no House rules had been violated.

The House ethics committee found no evidence that the $64,000 had been considered a loan, and said the collateral-and-loan arrangement was a clear use of campaign funds for personal benefit. In early 1988, the committee issued a formal "letter of reproval" for breaking House rules. Noting that Rose had repaid the funds (although after the inquiry began), the panel recommended no formal sanctions. Rose apologized for "inadvertent human errors."

In May 1989 the Justice Department filed a civil lawsuit against Rose for failing to report the loans on his financial-disclosure forms. Rose accused the administration of political retaliation and released a letter from the ethics panel saying that he did not have to amend his disclosure forms.

As chairman of the Tobacco and Peanuts Subcommittee, Rose has spent the 1980s besieged by anti-smoking forces. Rose has held his own, but there have been some losses, both for the tobacco industry in general and for the growers he champions in the internecine tug of war with cigarette manufacturers.

Rose had his biggest successes in 1981, the first year he led the panel. Newly inaugurated President Reagan proposed eliminating federal allotments for peanut farmers, and tobacco was being attacked by a coalition of consumer advocates and urban fiscal conservatives.

As chief strategist and spokesman, Rose came up with an ingenious argument. He told fellow Democrats that the entire North Carolina Democratic delegation might be wiped out at the polls in 1982 if the tobacco subsidy program died on the House floor. By the time of the vote, Speaker Thomas P. O'Neill Jr. sounded as loyal to tobacco as any Tarheel, and the anti-tobacco onslaught was defeated by almost 50 votes on the floor. Even so, Rose was forced to accept an amendment to the program requiring growers to pay the costs of storing surplus tobacco purchased by the government.

Rose had some struggles to maintain peanut allotments — rules allowing only specified farmers to market peanuts commercially — against the Reagan administration's arguments for more competition. As eventually rewritten, the peanut program did not restrict additional farmers from entering the market, but guaranteed higher price supports to those who had been in it before the change.

In 1982, Rose — aiming to defuse criticism of the tobacco program — won enactment of a measure that made changes in the program so it would run at no net cost to taxpayers, except for administrative expenses.

In the 99th Congress, Rose had additional

North Carolina 7

Southeast — Fayetteville; Wilmington

Nearly half the people in the 7th live in Cumberland County, a part of south central North Carolina that has a heavy military cast. Outside Fayetteville, there are some 50,000 full-time military and civilian personnel at Fort Bragg, including the 82nd Airborne Division. Another 4,000 people work nearby at Pope Air Force Base.

Fayetteville and surrounding Cumberland County maintain a diverse economic base. Among the city's leading products are textiles and power hand tools; farms in Cumberland yield tobacco, corn, soybeans and poultry.

Cumberland County has a Democratic flavor in local and statewide campaigns. It went for Democrat James B. Hunt Jr. in his unsuccessful 1984 challenge to GOP Sen. Jesse Helms, and Cumberland has voted Democratic in the last two governors' races, both won statewide by Republican James G. Martin. Cumberland's presidential vote has drifted toward the GOP in recent years, though. Jimmy Carter won it with 63 percent of the vote in 1976, but dropped to a 49 percent plurality in 1980. Ronald Reagan won Cumberland handily in 1984, and George Bush carried the county in 1988.

Outside Fayetteville, the only other major city in the 7th is Wilmington (New Hanover County). The restoration of Wilmington's historic waterfront district has brought tourism and some white-collar prosperity into this old port and fishing center. Republican sentiment is strong; New Hanover County gave a majority to Ronald Reagan in 1980, the only county in the 7th District to do so. It voted Republican in the 1988 gubernatorial and presidential contests.

Of North Carolina's 65,000 American Indians, 55 percent live in Robeson County, a heavily Democratic area where there are some tensions between the white, black and Indian populations. Robeson County is about the same size as New Hanover County and more than compensates for GOP majorities on the coast.

Population: 539,055. White 340,271 (63%), Black 147,378 (27%), American Indian, Eskimo and Aleut 40,737 (8%), Other 4,641 (1%). Spanish origin 11,897 (2%). 18 and over 371,808 (69%), 65 and over 40,425 (8%). Median age: 26.

frustrations coping with growing tension between tobacco farmers and tobacco companies, which were importing more and more foreign tobacco. He found himself sparring not only with tobacco opponents, but also with GOP Sen. Jesse Helms, a longtime home-state rival.

In the Senate, Helms pushed a tobacco plan that sold government-held tobacco surpluses to cigarette makers at a discount and gave them a role in determining future supplies; in exchange, they picked up part of the cost of the program. Rose, who had been purposefully excluded from discussions that led up to Helms' plan, said the approach, which failed to put any limits on tobacco imports, favored manufacturers at the expense of farmers, who accepted lower price supports.

In the House, Rose promoted his own tobacco plan, which involved setting aside 2 cents of a 16-cent federal excise tax on cigarettes to pay for tobacco supports. A modified version was attached to a House reconciliation measure on Ways and Means. But Helms prevailed in conference and Rose reluctantly supported Helms' plan; it conceded to a permanent extension of the 16-cents-per-pack excise tax in exchange for the discount buyout of surplus tobacco and changes in price supports.

At various times, Rose has worked to fend off requirements for new and tougher warning labels on cigarette packages. He succeeded in 1981, but the idea kept coming back, and by 1984, after months of negotiations — and in hopes of staving off even tougher restrictions — major tobacco companies abruptly dropped their opposition and the warning labels were approved in Energy and Commerce by a vote of 22-0. Afterward, asked if he was pleased with the vote, Rose replied wearily, "No, I'm just glad it's over." In 1986, new warning requirements were added for smokeless tobacco products.

In 1987, Rose and other tobacco legislators were powerless to prevent a ban on smoking for short domestic air flights. The proposal arose on the House floor as an amendment to an appropriation bill and sailed to enactment.

Despite these setbacks, Rose has established good ties with the Ways and Means Committee, which has jurisdiction over cigarette taxes. He has solid relationships with Chairman Dan Rostenkowski of Illinois and New York Democrat Charles B. Rangel, who heads the tax subcommittee. Rose was a strong backer of Rangel's 1986 try for majority whip.

Rose had his own flirtation with leadership dashed in 1980 when he ran for chairman of the Democratic Caucus. He was defeated 146-53 by another moderate Southerner, Gillis W. Long of Louisiana, who had all of Rose's personal popularity and fewer controversial alliances.

While defending tobacco and peanuts is Rose's major legislative chore, computers and Congress' technological capacity are his passion. His office is an electronic village, loaded with expensive equipment that allows him to chart legislation at a glance and hold staff meetings in which computer terminals do all the talking. For years, Rose has been trying to move Congress as far into the computer age as he is himself.

The House had a computer system when Rose arrived in 1973, but it was a primitive one used mainly for payrolls and retrieving information on the status of bills. Rose quickly joined the House Administration Committee and got himself appointed to lead a new task force on computers. By lobbying carefully for funds with the leadership, Rose gradually created an ambitious House information bureaucracy before it was scaled back. The new technology has given members not only better legislative data, but also the computerized mailing lists that have brought incumbents political success courting constituents and contributions in recent years.

While computerizing the institution, Rose was also putting it on television for the first time. He was instrumental in setting up the system that currently broadcasts floor proceedings, implementing a 20-year-old idea that nobody else had been able to sell politically. He helped conquer Speaker O'Neill's suspicion by keeping control of the cameras away from commercial networks and by proposing a limited closed-circuit experiment that paved the way for public gavel-to-gavel TV coverage beginning in 1979.

Rose's interest in the cutting edge of technology combined with home-district farm politics in 1988 on the question of whether patents could be granted for genetically altered animals. Controversy was set off when the U.S. Patent Office granted a patent to Harvard University for a breed of mouse that had been genetically engineered to be more useful in cancer experiments.

Rose introduced a bill to impose a two-year moratorium on such patents, which farmers feared would eventually raise the cost of raising animals. Rose's bill was rejected in a Judiciary subcommittee as interest in technological advances overcame fears of genetic experimentation. On the floor, a compromise was worked out that exempted farmers from making royalty payments, and Rose supported the final bill.

Rose's wide-ranging interests circled the globe to embrace Tibet when, in 1987 and 1988, anti-Chinese riots erupted. Rose sponsored a bill to promote Tibetan rights and got attention when China denied him permission to accompany a Senate Agriculture Committee trip to China.

House leaders appointed Rose to the Select Committee on Intelligence in 1977, and by 1981 he was its third-ranking Democrat. The assignment gave him a chance to explore the technology of electronic surveillance, another of his interests, and to look into what he saw as dangerous Soviet experiments in mind control. He left Intelligence in 1983.

At Home: Unwilling to wait for Rep. Alton Lennon to carry out his long-promised retirement, Rose went after him in a 1970 primary and came close enough that Lennon finally did retire two years later.

To run in 1970, Rose had to take a leave from his work as chief prosecutor in the 12th Judicial District (Cumberland and Hoke counties). Before he took that job, he had been an aide to Gov. Terry Sanford (1961-65), and he was supported by many of the moderate Democrats who found Sanford appealing. Running a well-financed, well-organized campaign that called attention to Lennon's 64 years, Rose received a respectable 43 percent of the vote.

Early in 1971, Rose began producing a monthly television program outlining the history of each county in the district. He said the shows were not political, but made it clear he would try again for Congress in 1972. In December, Lennon announced his retirement.

State Sen. Hector McGeachy and Fayetteville lawyer Doran Berry joined Rose in the 1972 Democratic primary. Few issues separated the three; Rose was better known because of his earlier campaign and because his father and grandfather served in the Legislature.

Rose polled 49 percent of the vote in the initial primary, far ahead of McGeachy's 26 percent. Still, McGeachy demanded a runoff, and Rose won it with 56 percent. The general election was no problem. Rose got 60 percent even as Richard M. Nixon carried the 7th overwhelmingly.

In 1974, McGeachy was back again, challenging Rose in the primary with a campaign that courted the black vote. But Rose had used a mobile office during his first term to keep in touch with rural constituents, and he developed close ties with the district's business community. Rose won renomination with 61 percent, and that was his last significant primary challenge. Rose was unopposed in November 1974.

Some Republicans thought Rose's personal life might hamper him in the 1982 election. Shortly after receiving an uncontested divorce from his wife, Rose was married in September 1982 to a staffer on his Tobacco and Peanuts Subcommittee. Voters, however, were apparently not bothered by the divorce and quick remarriage — Rose got 71 percent of the vote.

Rose was mentioned as a possible candidate for governor in 1984, when incumbent Democrat James B. Hunt Jr. left office. But he decided to stay in the House. Battling a GOP tide that diminished the Democrats' ranks in the congressional delegation from nine members to six, he was re-elected with 59 percent.

Rose also suffered a scare in 1986. He appeared headed for routine re-election when a political bomb dropped on him in mid-September. Press reports that Rose had borrowed money from his campaign committee raised questions about the propriety of his actions — and gave a much-needed burst of momentum to GOP challenger Thomas J. Harrelson. But if voters were concerned about Rose's propriety, they did not show it on Election Day. Although Harrelson, a Southport businessman, former state House member and former state Environmental Management official, amassed more money than any Rose challenger in memory, he managed only 36 percent of the vote districtwide.

The ethics issue kept Republicans talking about Rose for part of the next election cycle, but that was about all they did. Rose was re-elected overwhelmingly.

Committees

Agriculture (4th of 27 Democrats)
Tobacco and Peanuts (chairman); Department Operations, Research and Foreign Agriculture; Livestock, Dairy and Poultry

House Administration (3rd of 13 Democrats)
Office Systems (chairman); Elections

Elections

1988 General

Charlie Rose (D)	102,392	(67%)
George "Jerry" Thompson (R)	49,855	(33%)

1986 General

Charlie Rose (D)	70,471	(64%)
Thomas J. Harrelson (R)	39,289	(36%)

Previous Winning Percentages: **1984** (59%) **1982** (71%) **1980** (69%) **1978** (70%) **1976** (81%) **1974** (100%) **1972** (60%)

District Vote For President

	1988	1984	1980	1976
D	73,231 (48%)	65,964 (43%)	70,334 (54%)	78,021 (66%)
R	77,438 (51%)	87,143 (57%)	57,184 (44%)	39,640 (34%)
I			3,119 (2%)	

Campaign Finance

	Receipts	Receipts from PACs	Expend-itures
1988			
Rose (D)	$293,187	$177,500 (61%)	$185,039
1986			
Rose (D)	$403,808	$211,845 (52%)	$302,654
Harrelson (R)	$403,011	$22,944 (6%)	$403,005

Key Votes

1987	
Raise speed limit to 65 mph	Y
Approve Gephardt "fair trade" amendment	Y
Ban testing of larger nuclear weapons	Y
Delay "re-flagging" of Kuwaiti tankers	Y
Approve tax-raising deficit-reduction bill	?
1988	
Approve aid to Nicaraguan contras	N
Enact civil rights restoration bill over Reagan veto	Y
Kill 60-day plant-closing notification measure	N
Pass omnibus trade bill over Reagan veto	Y
Approve death penalty for drug-related murders	Y
Bar federal funds for abortions in cases of rape and incest	N
Oppose seven-day waiting period for purchase of handguns	Y

Voting Studies

	Presidential Support		Party Unity		Conservative Coalition	
Year	S	O	S	O	S	O
1988	19	65	77	7	47	26
1987	30	61	79	10	72	19
1986	29	64	78	12	54	42
1985	28	70	84	10	53	42
1984	35	50	77	13	47	39
1983	26	61	74	12	42	42
1982	32	49	63	19	60	32
1981	49	43	54	22	63	25

Interest Group Ratings

Year	ADA	ACU	AFL-CIO	CCUS
1988	60	11	100	25
1987	76	5	75	43
1986	55	37	67	44
1985	60	17	56	25
1984	60	14	67	42
1983	75	10	75	31
1982	40	35	58	47
1981	50	23	85	29

8 W.G. "Bill" Hefner (D)

Of Concord — Elected 1974

Born: April 11, 1930, Elora, Tenn.
Education: High school graduate.
Occupation: Broadcasting executive.
Family: Wife, Nancy Hill; two children.
Religion: Baptist.
Political Career: No previous office.
Capitol Office: 2161 Rayburn Bldg. 20515; 225-3715.

In Washington: During the peak of Ronald Reagan's popularity, the House Democratic leadership looked to Hefner as a bridge to conservative Southern Democrats skittish about bucking the president. Hefner played that role willingly and well, a loyal partisan with a collegial attitude. His personality helped him speak up for his party, both in Washington and at home; a gospel singer and former radio executive, he is witty and down-to-earth, a popular man who joins constituents for country-western sing-alongs and colleagues for rounds of golf.

While Hefner is still willing to help his party regain its footing in the region, a number of factors have combined recently to lower his profile. A 1985 heart attack slowed Hefner some (though he still tugs on North Carolina-cured cigarettes). As the decade has progressed, he has had to worry more about the growing strength of the GOP in his district; in 1984 and 1988, he nearly lost re-election.

Hefner was also dealt a setback in Washington at the start of the 100th Congress, when he ran a distant third in the contest for majority whip. Hefner drew only 15 votes, compared with 78 for Charles B. Rangel of New York and 167 for the victor, Tony Coelho of California. Hefner's pitch that he would bring a Southern sensitivity to the leadership was plausible, but he seemed uncomfortable asking colleagues for support — a handicap for a would-be whip.

But Hefner is still a key player on the Appropriations Committee, where he is chairman of the Military Construction Subcommittee, the panel that holds the purse strings for military construction and base improvements around the world. He is an accommodating chairman, willing to watch out for programs important to colleagues. However, as the 101st Congress prepared to endorse a bill aimed at distancing Congress from the decision-making process on base closings, Hefner let it be known that his subcommittee would not become the loophole allowing members later to protect individual bases.

Hefner has worked to protect funding levels for base construction. In the 100th Congress, he crafted legislation reducing the Reagan funding request, but warned colleagues he could go no further. He maintains that new facilities are needed "to get our troops out of World War II barracks and quonset huts," and that further construction delays mean added maintenance and repair costs.

From time to time, Hefner also tangles with the Pentagon. In recent years, his subcommittee has scaled back the Navy's "homeporting" plan, and in the 98th Congress he warned Pentagon officials that he was reluctant to go along with a major funding increase for MX missile construction until he was sure that basing plans for the missile were set. Hefner also was one of the earliest proponents of "burden-sharing," a concept that U.S. allies should pay more for their defense.

Elsewhere on the Appropriations Committee, Hefner fought a proposal to ban smoking on airplane flights. When the ban was first attached to the transportation funding bill in 1987, Hefner objected on the grounds that it was legislating on an appropriations bill, a violation of House rules. Later, when a two-year ban was added to the 1988 continuing resolution, Hefner fought the proposal in conference, but without success.

Hefner had a place on the Budget Committee from 1981-87, years filled with heated debate over the budget priorities of the Reagan administration. Hefner was an especially important moderate voice in that debate, often telling the party leadership what conservative Democrats would and would not accept on the House floor.

In 1981, he tried to fend off the Reagan budget alternative on the floor by offering an amendment to add $6.7 billion for defense. That amendment advertised Hefner's anti-Reagan vote at a time when Democrats from the South were drawing intense lobbying pressure from administration forces.

The normally accommodating Hefner fought with North Carolina Sen. Jesse Helms in 1984, when Helms was actively working for Hefner's GOP challenger in the 8th. The two men started out as allies in fighting a proposed

North Carolina 8

South Central — Kannapolis; Salisbury

Politics in the 8th are delineated by geography. The mountain counties in the northern part of the district and the textile towns in the center lean Republican. The farm counties farther south vote for Democrats.

Yadkin and Davie counties anchor the GOP base at the 8th's northern end. They make their party preference clear in nearly every election, supporting GOP statewide candidates even when they are non-contenders; Yadkin and Davie went Republican for governor in 1980, when the nominee got only 37 percent statewide. Yadkin is one of the district's major tobacco-growing counties; Davie residents are more oriented toward dairy products and grains.

The Democratic stronghold in the district is Hoke County, a rural area where the 44 percent black population combines with a significant American Indian minority to deliver an overwhelming Democratic vote. Hoke is often joined in the Democratic column by nearby Scotland, Richmond and Anson counties.

North of Hoke is the part of Moore County in the 8th, which takes in affluent resort communities such as Pinehurst and Whispering Pines. Pinehurst considers itself the golf capital of the world; more than two dozen golf courses are within the town's 10-mile radius.

Moore County used to share Hoke's Democratic proclivities, but a steady stream of retirees has transformed it into a GOP bastion.

In the center of the district, small cities and towns such as Kannapolis, Salisbury and Concord manufacture textiles and textile machinery. Kannapolis is the district's largest population center, with 32,000 residents. Founded by Cannon Mills, the textile manufacturer, Kannapolis remained an unincorporated company town for years; the company paid for the police and fire departments, and owned many of the city's houses. But the climate changed in Kannapolis in 1982, when Cannon Mills was bought out by a Californian. In 1984, the city voted to become an incorporated community.

Population: 535,526. White 420,470 (79%), Black 107,482 (20%), Other 6,871 (1%). Spanish origin 3,730 (1%). 18 and over 381,299 (71%), 65 and over 62,412 (12%). Median age: 31.

85-mile water pipeline from Lake Gaston, N.C., to Virginia Beach, Va., which North Carolinians felt would divert water they needed. But the alliance collapsed, and the two fell into feuding. Helms called Hefner "dumb" and said the Democrat was so politically driven he would "play politics with the first chapter of Genesis." Hefner said he would "turn the other cheek," adding that he was "a little bit shocked that the good Christian senator would accuse me of playing politics with the Holy Scriptures."

At Home: Through the years, Hefner has been able to neutralize much of the natural GOP sentiment that pervades the 8th District. But in the last two presidential election years, he was almost dragged under.

In 1984, Hefner's GOP opponent was Harris D. Blake, a hardware store owner and former member of the Moore County Board of Education who had challenged him two years earlier. In their first meeting, Blake won 42 percent by arguing that Hefner had not voted the interests of the local textile industry. Hefner cast himself as committed to protecting voters from the budget knife of the GOP.

Blake began his second campaign early and took pains to showcase his support for Reagan, whose popularity increased with improvement in the economy. Blake hit Hefner hard for having opposed the administration's 1981 tax and budget cuts. But the challenger also repeated his complaint that Hefner's vote to grant most-favored-nation status to China aided Chinese textiles in competition with those produced at home. Hefner then met with local textile executives and production workers to discuss legislation affecting the industry.

Blake benefited from Reagan's presence at the top of the ticket, and from the financial support of Helms' National Congressional Club; he carried a five-county area in the northern and central parts of the district. Hefner clung to his base among the traditionally Democratic counties at the district's southern end, eking out 51 percent of the vote overall.

Two years later, Hefner climbed back up to 58 percent, but 1988 brought more trouble for him. The GOP touted its challenger, 38-year-old attorney Ted Blanton, but most Democrats did not take his effort too seriously, and even some Republicans said the race was a long shot. But Blanton, who had worked as an aide for three U.S. senators, used Washington ties to generate attention for his campaign. A number of prominent Republicans visited the district on his behalf, including Assistant Secretary of State Elliot Abrams and former Transportation Secretary Elizabeth H. Dole, who was raised in this part of North Carolina. And Blanton aggressively attacked Hefner as a big spender on the Appropriations Committee.

Blanton put himself in a position to ride a wave of GOP presidential votes, and that wave came crashing in on Election Day. The challenger took 49 percent overall, running particularly well in the northern and central parts of the district and carrying seven counties. Hefner again survived because of his strong base in the Democratic counties in the south; he won five counties.

Running for his first term in Congress in 1974 against the backdrop of Watergate, Hefner pledged to revive "Christian morality" in government and spiced his political speeches with renditions of his favorite hymns. That might have been seen as an incautious church-state mixture in some places, but not in the Bible Belt 8th. Hefner's blend of inspiration, entertainment and politicking helped him soundly defeat GOP Rep. Earl B. Ruth.

Early in 1974, Ruth was not thought to be in any great danger. First elected in 1968, he had won more than 60 percent in 1972. But Hefner was an exceptional candidate. As a promoter and singer of gospel music in the Carolinas and Virginia, he had made many local and statewide TV appearances. He started the campaign with excellent name recognition and gradually won back thousands of conservative Democrats who had drifted toward Ruth.

Committee

Appropriations (21st of 35 Democrats)
Military Construction (chairman); Defense

Elections

1988 General

W. G. "Bill" Hefner (D)	99,214	(51%)
Ted Blanton (R)	93,463	(49%)

1986 General

W. G. "Bill" Hefner (D)	80,959	(58%)
William G. Hamby Jr. (R)	58,941	(42%)

Previous Winning Percentages: **1984** (51%) **1982** (57%) **1980** (59%) **1978** (59%) **1976** (66%) **1974** (57%)

District Vote For President

	1988	1984	1980	1976
D	73,080 (38%)	64,505 (35%)	76,466 (46%)	86,180 (55%)
R	118,357 (62%)	121,459 (65%)	86,672 (52%)	68,522 (44%)
I			3,519 (2%)	

Campaign Finance

	Receipts	Receipts from PACs	Expend-itures
1988			
Hefner (D)	$432,432	$272,625 (63%)	$581,888
Blanton (R)	$243,901	$21,280 (9%)	$242,782
1986			
Hefner (D)	$356,337	$224,892 (63%)	$157,576
Hamby (R)	$51,071	$282 (1%)	$50,554

Key Votes

1987

Raise speed limit to 65 mph	N
Approve Gephardt "fair trade" amendment	Y
Ban testing of larger nuclear weapons	Y
Delay "re-flagging" of Kuwaiti tankers	Y
Approve tax-raising deficit-reduction bill	Y

1988

Approve aid to Nicaraguan contras	N
Enact civil rights restoration bill over Reagan veto	Y
Kill 60-day plant-closing notification measure	N
Pass omnibus trade bill over Reagan veto	Y
Approve death penalty for drug-related murders	Y
Bar federal funds for abortions in cases of rape and incest	#
Oppose seven-day waiting period for purchase of handguns	Y

Voting Studies

	Presidential Support		Party Unity		Conservative Coalition	
Year	S	O	S	O	S	O
1988	29	61	76	15	68	16
1987	33	65	81	15	84	16
1986	30	67	80	13	64	26
1985	35	49	63	12	60	7
1984	48	45	64	25	80	17
1983	40	54	66	21	72	22
1982	47	48	57 †	39 †	87 †	10 †
1981	53	41	57	33	76	23

† Not eligible for all recorded votes.

Interest Group Ratings

Year	ADA	ACU	AFL-CIO	CCUS
1988	65	25	92	50
1987	64	4	75	40
1986	50	36	57	40
1985	25	46	53	37
1984	40	33	54	47
1983	45	27	75	56
1982	20	67	50	64
1981	35	33	79	31

9 Alex McMillan (R)

Of Charlotte — Elected 1984

Born: May 9, 1932, Charlotte, N.C.
Education: U. of North Carolina, B.A. 1954; U. of Virginia, M.B.A. 1958.
Military Career: Army, 1954-56.
Occupation: Food store executive.
Family: Wife, Caroline Houston; two children.
Religion: Presbyterian.
Political Career: Mecklenburg County Commission, 1972-74.
Capitol Office: 401 Cannon Bldg. 20515; 225-1976.

In Washington: McMillan fits his district well. He speaks for the bankers, insurance executives and other affluent capitalists of business-minded Charlotte in the same restrained tones they would use if they were in Washington representing themselves.

Through the 100th Congress, McMillan's chief base of operations was the Banking Committee, where he was the only Republican from North Carolina, whose financial institutions are playing an ever-widening role in regional and national banking. At the start of the 101st Congress, McMillan moved to the Energy and Commerce Committee, which has not had a North Carolina member since the 1986 departure of influential ranking Republican James T. Broyhill. (He was appointed to the Senate.) In his new post, McMillan could — if he can work with the powerful panel's assertive Democratic majority — exercise influence over an array of issues affecting banking and business.

He is the model of a conservative civic leader — sensitive to the problems of the underprivileged, but even more sensitive to the weaknesses of government in trying to help. When the welfare overhaul bill reached the floor in 1987, he protested that it operated "on the insulting assumption that people on public assistance don't want to help themselves." He praised the GOP alternative, saying it provided "a framework for people to move from dependency to self-reliance."

When Democrats brought a housing bill to the floor in 1986, McMillan was among those Republicans seeking to scale back the construction of new public housing units and focus on repairing those that already exist. But he opposed some of more drastic GOP efforts to slash the amount of money in the bill.

McMillan also revealed a more moderate streak during 1988 debate on the omnibus drug bill. He was one of five Southern Republicans voting to retain a seven-day waiting period for handgun purchases. Though he had received over $10,000 in campaign contributions from the National Rifle Association since first running for Congress, he voted against the NRA position because he considered the amendment a reasonable way to keep guns away from convicted felons. He said the waiting period "would not infringe on anybody's right to own a weapon."

In recogntion of the important role the textile industry plays in his district and region, McMillan argued against the president's veto of a textile protection bill in the 99th Congress; two days after the House failed to override the veto, he introduced a bill of his own calling for the licensing of imported textiles. In the 100th Congress, while he argued for a "strong, bipartisan" trade bill, he opposed the Gephardt "fair trade" amendment and voted against the first trade package in 1988 for the same reason President Reagan vetoed it: It contained language requiring employers to give employees 60 days' notice of a plant closing or layoff.

McMillan has taken a general interest in reducing the federal deficit. He is part of the Tauke-Penny ad hoc budget-cutting brigade, a bipartisan group of fiscal conservatives who have tried — with limited success — to trim the deficit by making across-the-board spending cuts on appropriations bills. A member of the Joint Economic Committee in the 100th Congress, McMillan believes that if spending is merely restrained, not cut, revenues will grow on their own and eliminate the deficit.

McMillan also supports the notion of burden-sharing — having U.S. allies pay a greater share of mutual defense efforts. His amendment to the 1988 defense authorization bill, expressing the sense of Congress that the administration should begin negotiations to that effect, was adopted 350-0.

Prior to his election to the House, McMillan's experience in public office was limited to two years as a county commissioner in the early 1970s. When it comes to political infighting, he may be a step behind those who arrived as seasoned legislators. He made a bid for a seat on Energy and Commerce in 1987, but lost out to Sonny Callahan of Alabama, a man with

North Carolina 9

West Central — Charlotte

Charlotte is the largest city of the two Carolinas. Its role as the supply, service and distribution center for the North and South Carolina Piedmont area gives it a diversified economy not directly dependent on the textile-and-tobacco base traditional in the region. Large construction and trucking firms are based here, and insurance concerns abound. North Carolina's major banks have built office towers that give the city an impressive skyline. There is also a new indoor coliseum, home of the Hornets, the recently arrived pro basketball franchise.

Many of Charlotte's bankers, lawyers and insurance executives make their homes in the affluent southeastern part of the city; it is here that the old-line GOP establishment has its base. The Democratic vote is strongest in the northwestern section, where the bulk of Charlotte's black population lives. The city elected its first black mayor, Harvey Gantt, in 1983; his successor, Republican Sue Myrick, is the city's first female mayor.

A blend of white-collar economic conservatism, working-class Democratic allegiances and a 27 percent black population makes for close elections in Mecklenburg County. Mecklenburg voted for Reagan in 1980 and 1984, but sided with Democratic candidates for the Senate in those years. In 1988, Mecklenburg went Republican in both the presidential and gubernatorial contests.

Mecklenburg contains three-quarters of the district's population. The rest is split among three counties to the north of Charlotte — Iredell, Lincoln and Yadkin. In the 1980s, Iredell and Lincoln have seen an influx of residents moving into comfortable new homes along the shores of sprawling Lake Norman. The completion of Interstate 77 in the late 1970s brought the lake within reasonable daily commuting distance of downtown Charlotte.

Most of Iredell is still rural territory; apples and cattle are important to the economy. The county also has developed some light industry, such as electronics companies and manufacturing plants.

Iredell split its tickets in 1980, voting Republican for president and the Senate while giving Democratic Gov. James B. Hunt Jr. an easy margin in his re-election bid. But the county abandoned even Hunt in 1984, backing GOP Sen. Jesse Helms against the Democrat in an outbreak of straight-ticket GOP voting. Lincoln County also voted a straight GOP line in 1984. Republicans carried both Iredell and Lincoln in 1988 voting for president and governor.

Voters in Yadkin County, about one-fourth of which is in the 9th, are oriented more toward nearby Winston-Salem than to Charlotte. Longtime solid GOP territory, Yadkin was one of just 13 North Carolina counties to back Republican Barry Goldwater for president in 1964.

Population: 536,325. White 404,831 (75%), Black 125,148 (23%), Other 4,566 (1%). Spanish origin 4,835 (1%). 18 and over 385,849 (72%), 65 and over 48,307 (9%). Median age: 30.

fewer social graces but a better knowledge of how to operate the levers of power in the House. Energy and Commerce was McMillan's second choice in the 101st Congress; he lobbied hard for a seat on Ways and Means.

At Home: McMillan may have a more patrician demeanor than James G. Martin and Charles Raper Jonas, the previous two GOP incumbents in his district. But his fiscal conservatism and his emphasis on economics over social issues put him firmly in the Martin-Jonas mold.

In securing his 1984 victory, McMillan drew heavily on a local GOP network established a generation ago by Jonas and cultivated by Martin, whose bid for governor opened the 9th. That network, anchored in wealthy southeastern Charlotte, helped McMillan get past a strong Democratic foe by a scant 321 votes.

Although he had last served in public office in 1974, McMillan was widely regarded as a top GOP prospect. A Democrat-turned-Republican, he won his one previous election in 1972, capturing the Mecklenburg County (Charlotte) Commission seat left vacant by Martin, who ran successfully that year for the House. McMillan retired from his post after one term, citing a desire to focus on his business career.

He moved up in the ranks in the retail food industry to become president of Harris-Teeter Super Markets Inc., a local chain. He made a name for himself in civic affairs, promoting a performing arts complex downtown and helping establish an authority to raise money for a public television station. McMillan also kept his hand in local GOP activities.

When Martin announced his gubernatorial candidacy in 1983, McMillan began actively seeking the seat. His support among the local GOP establishment and Charlotte business community made him appear a prohibitive favorite to become the party nominee. But he encountered a formidable obstacle in Carl "Buddy" Horn, who served for two years in the Civil Rights Division of the Reagan Justice Department and who had the endorsement of Sen. Jesse Helms' National Congressional Club. Horn's impassioned support for school prayer and a constitutional amendment to ban abortion rallied fundamentalist Christians, and contrasted markedly with McMillan's more moderate politics and more reserved style.

With early spring polls showing Horn ahead, McMillan went on the offensive, running television ads branding the 32-year-old Horn a "rookie," and reminding Republicans that Horn had voted for Democrat George McGovern for president in 1972. The result was a 58-42 percent primary win for McMillan.

McMillan had an even tougher time in the fall. His opponent was D. G. Martin, a lawyer and political neophyte who proved capable of attracting support not only in Democratic areas but also in Southeastern Charlotte's wealthy white communities. Although unrelated to the departing incumbent, Democrat Martin had the added advantage of bearing a familiar name.

McMillan invoked his experience as a retailer to legitimize his call for a freeze on federal spending. He criticized Martin for his willingness to raise taxes to deal with the deficit, and for supporting homosexual rights.

Martin won Mecklenburg County (Charlotte), which dominates the district, but thanks to a financial advantage and top-of-the-ticket GOP strength, McMillan took sufficient margins in three outlying counties to overcome his Mecklenburg loss.

Martin tried again in 1986. He kept up his visibility between elections by writing a column in a weekly newspaper distributed free throughout Mecklenburg County, and by making regular appearances on a local cable television show. But Martin had trouble finding issues to use against the incumbent. He tried casting McMillan as a prisoner of special interests, pointing to the political action committee contributions McMillan had accepted (and Martin refused). But that failed to stir voters.

McMillan, practicing his quiet brand of chamber of commerce conservatism and returning home regularly, left little to chance. His position on Banking helped him court some of the businessmen who had backed Martin in 1984.

Martin deployed an army of volunteers on Election Day, and he again got a narrow lead in Mecklenburg. But McMillan's well-funded advertising blitz helped him stay close in the Charlotte area, and he overcame the deficit in the outlying counties to win with 51 percent. In 1988, he won a third term handily.

Committee

Energy and Commerce (17th of 17 Republicans)
Oversight and Investigations; Transportation and Hazardous Materials

Elections

1988 General		
Alex McMillan (R)	139,014	(66%)
Mark Sholander (D)	71,802	(34%)
1986 General		
Alex McMillan (R)	80,352	(51%)
D. G. Martin (D)	76,240	(49%)

Previous Winning Percentage: **1984** (50%)

District Vote For President

	1988	1984	1980	1976
D	89,307 (39%)	81,750 (35%)	87,144 (46%)	86,436 (52%)
R	140,731 (61%)	150,223 (65%)	93,258 (49%)	80,603 (48%)
I			7,496 (4%)	

Campaign Finance

	Receipts	Receipts from PACs	Expenditures
1988			
McMillan (R)	$515,294	$214,455 (42%)	$445,852
Sholander (D)	$34,124	$6,000 (18%)	$32,949
1986			
McMillan (R)	$892,228	$319,809 (36%)	$877,235
Martin (D)	$471,972	$6,500 (1%)	$469,541

Key Votes

1987	
Raise speed limit to 65 mph	Y
Approve Gephardt "fair trade" amendment	N
Ban testing of larger nuclear weapons	N
Delay "re-flagging" of Kuwaiti tankers	N
Approve tax-raising deficit-reduction bill	N
1988	
Approve aid to Nicaraguan contras	Y
Enact civil rights restoration bill over Reagan veto	N
Kill 60-day plant-closing notification measure	Y
Pass omnibus trade bill over Reagan veto	N
Approve death penalty for drug-related murders	Y
Bar federal funds for abortions in cases of rape and incest	Y
Oppose seven-day waiting period for purchase of handguns	N

Voting Studies

	Presidential Support		Party Unity		Conservative Coalition	
Year	S	O	S	O	S	O
1988	61	38	79	19	89	11
1987	64	36	83	16	98	2
1986	66	32	69	28	94	6
1985	79	20	81	15	98	2

Interest Group Ratings

Year	ADA	ACU	AFL-CIO	CCUS
1988	15	88	21	100
1987	4	83	6	100
1986	10	82	36	100
1985	5	81	6	91

10 Cass Ballenger (R)

Of Hickory — Elected 1986

Born: Dec. 6, 1926, Hickory, N.C.
Education: Attended U. of North Carolina, 1944-45; Amherst College, B.A. 1948.
Military Career: Navy Air Corps, 1944-45.
Occupation: President of plastics packaging company.
Family: Wife, Donna Davis; three children.
Religion: Episcopalian.
Political Career: Catawba County Board of Commissioners, 1966-74, chairman, 1970-74; N.C. House, 1975-77; N.C. Senate, 1977-87.
Capitol Office: 218 Cannon Bldg. 20515; 225-2576.

In Washington: Ballenger brings a conservative small-business man's perspective to Congress, and finds himself frequently at odds with the proposals advanced by the old-line, pro-labor liberals on the Education and Labor Committee.

In his first term, Ballenger fought efforts to raise the minimum wage, arguing that it would hurt small businesses by increasing production costs through higher labor costs. He opposed committee bills requiring businesses to provide unpaid parental leave and to notify workers who may be exposed to hazardous substances.

Ballenger also opposed a bill requiring employers to notify employees before they could close a plant. "Has anyone in this chamber put a pencil to the costs of this bill to the small employer?" he demanded. He said it would cost an average small-business man laying off 50 employees earning $6 an hour about $156,000. "This amount may not bother politicians here in Washington," he said, "but to a small company trying to save the remaining parts of its business, it is absolute disaster."

As members of Congress debated whether to approve military or non-military aid for the Nicaraguan contras, Ballenger took a personal interest in that country's citizens. In October 1987, he and his wife went to Nicaragua to help resume operation of Radio Catolica, the voice of the Catholic Church. It was not the Ballengers' first trip to Central America. In the 1970s, his wife helped build and he furnished with medical equipment a hospital in Guatemala following the 1977 earthquake. Then Ballenger shipped a fire truck to Guatemala City's volunteer fire department.

Two weeks after Radio Catolica resumed broadcasting, the Sandinista government renewed its censorship of the station. Incensed, Ballenger took the House floor to denounce the government and those more sympathetic to it. "And how long do you think it will take witless peaceniks to begin apologizing for this lapse in democratic reforms? ... If you listen closely, you can already hear the liberal public-relations wheels grinding out excuses," he said.

At Home: The 10th was open in 1986 because its veteran incumbent, Republican James T. Broyhill, was campaigning for the Senate. Both Ballenger and George S. Robinson, his chief GOP rival, promised to emulate Broyhill.

Ballenger was a state senator who had founded a plastics company and built it into a 250-employee business. He reminded audiences that he had been on the state advisory budget commission under two GOP governors, and once served on a White House panel on economic affairs. Robinson, a pro-business state representative from Broyhill's hometown of Lenoir, was president of a lumber company.

Robinson's backers pointed out that their candidate, who at age 40 was roughly 20 years younger than Ballenger, would be able to build seniority in the way Broyhill had. But Ballenger enhanced his link with Broyhill by endorsing him in his Senate primary fight, then chastising Robinson for not doing the same. (Robinson subsequently did.)

Ballenger also accused Robinson of having ties to the National Congressional Club, Sen. Jesse Helms' political organization that was backing Broyhill's primary foe. The claim irked some Robinson supporters all the way through November. Robinson had no official links to the Club, and did have ties to Broyhill: He started his political career as his campaign driver.

Ballenger, a former Catawba County commissioner, had a strong base in the district's second-largest county, and he ran harder than Robinson in Gastonia, the largest population center, where both men were outsiders. Thus, he overcame Robinson's legislative base in four other counties of the 10th. The nomination was tantamount to victory in this district, though Democrats had a respectable candidate in Lester D. Roark, former mayor of Shelby.

North Carolina 10

West — Gastonia; Hickory

The 10th starts at the Tennessee line in Watauga and Avery counties, popular Appalachian mountain retreats, and runs south to industrial Gaston County on the border with South Carolina. Included within those boundaries is some of the best Republican territory in the state.

The 10th gave Ronald Reagan and George Bush their best showings anywhere in North Carolina in the 1980s, and not surprisingly, the district voted solidly for its longtime representative, Broyhill, in his 1986 bid to win a full term in the Senate.

Some Democrats have found footholds here in the past. Democrat James B. Hunt Jr. won 61 percent in the 10th en route to victory in his 1976 race for the governorship; winning re-election four years later, Hunt carried the district again. But he failed to carry a single county in the 10th in his 1984 Senate race against Republican Jesse Helms.

Gastonia, the seat of Gaston County, is the district's largest city by far. Home to some 53,000 people, Gastonia is one of the leading textile-manufacturing centers in the South. But the city has diversified its industrial base. Machinery, electronics and plastics are also part of the economy. Surrounding Gaston County contains some choice farm land.

A triangle of cities in the central part of the district — Hickory, Morganton and Lenoir — make furniture and textiles. Morganton also hosts a sizable psychiatric hospital.

Avery and Watauga counties, in the northwest corner of the 10th, vote strongly Republican. The economic fortunes of both counties are increasingly tied to the continued patronage of skiers and the influx of newcomers who own vacation homes in the mountains. Watauga County also is home to Appalachian State University (enrollment 11,000), in Boone.

Population: 532,954. White 474,151 (89%), Black 56,556 (11%). Spanish origin 2,886 (1%). 18 and over 379,876 (71%), 65 and over 53,367 (10%). Median age: 30.

Committees

Education and Labor (12th of 13 Republicans)
Health and Safety; Labor-Management Relations; Select Education

Public Works and Transportation (13th of 20 Republicans)
Aviation; Economic Development; Water Resources

Elections

1988 General		
Cass Ballenger (R)	112,554	(61%)
Jack L. Rhyne (D)	71,865	(39%)
1986 General †		
Cass Ballenger (R)	83,902	(57%)
Lester D. Roark (D)	62,035	(43%)

† Elected to a full term and to fill a vacancy at the same time.

District Vote For President

	1988	1984	1980	1976
D	63,531 (34%)	59,780 (30%)	71,693 (42%)	87,054 (54%)
R	120,337 (65%)	136,129 (69%)	93,520 (55%)	74,185 (46%)
I			3,775 (2%)	

Campaign Finance

	Receipts	Receipts from PACs	Expend-itures
1988			
Ballenger (R)	$322,903	$153,375 (47%)	$302,215
Rhyne (D)	$44,508	$500 (1%)	$44,329
1986			
Ballenger (R)	$467,780	$116,416 (25%)	$462,333
Roark (D)	$199,453	$39,300 (20%)	$196,438

Key Votes

1987	
Raise speed limit to 65 mph	Y
Approve Gephardt "fair trade" amendment	Y
Ban testing of larger nuclear weapons	N
Delay "re-flagging" of Kuwaiti tankers	N
Approve tax-raising deficit-reduction bill	N
1988	
Approve aid to Nicaraguan contras	Y
Enact civil rights restoration bill over Reagan veto	N
Kill 60-day plant-closing notification measure	Y
Pass omnibus trade bill over Reagan veto	N
Approve death penalty for drug-related murders	Y
Bar federal funds for abortions in cases of rape and incest	Y
Oppose seven-day waiting period for purchase of handguns	Y

Voting Studies

	Presidential Support		Party Unity		Conservative Coalition	
Year	**S**	**O**	**S**	**O**	**S**	**O**
1988	63	35	94	5	95	5
1987	71	27	91	7	98	2

Interest Group Ratings

Year	ADA	ACU	AFL-CIO	CCUS
1988	10	92	14	100
1987	8	82	19	93

11 James McClure Clarke (D)

Of Fairview — Elected 1986

Also served 1983-85.

Born: June 12, 1917, Manchester, Vt.
Education: Princeton U., A.B. 1939.
Military Career: Navy, 1942-45.
Occupation: Foundation executive; farmer.
Family: Wife, Elspeth McClure; eight children.
Religion: Presbyterian.
Political Career: N.C. House, 1977-81; N.C. Senate, 1981-83; Democratic nominee for U.S. House, 1984.
Capitol Office: 217 Cannon Bldg. 20515; 225-6401.

In Washington: A quiet and courtly gentleman, Clarke seems an unlikely representative for one of the country's most politically volatile House districts. He is now serving his second consecutive term — the first member from the 11th to do so in a decade — and he will probably need to continue to expend much of his political energy at home.

Fortunately for his cause, Clarke is unusually popular among House Democrats, who understand his precarious political situation and appreciate his loyalty to the party leadership. He voted with a majority of Democrats more than 80 percent of the time in the 100th Congress, and resisted making a show of it when he stepped away from the party line. Coupled with his pleasant personality, this record helps Clarke open Democrats' doors on Capitol Hill.

Clarke leaves grand legislative initiatives to others and makes relatively modest requests, usually on matters important to his district. This strategy led to a handful of successes in the 100th Congress. He pushed language in the 1987 farm disaster-assistance bill to provide federal aid to apple growers, which he estimates benefited some 300 apple-growers in western North Carolina.

Clarke's family runs a farm in the state, which gives him an attachment to the land that is appreciated by conservationists on the Interior Committee. There he successfully pushed a North Carolina wilderness bill that would have declared 90 percent of the Great Smoky Mountain National Park a federal wilderness area, and thus off-limits to development.

Although Clarke's bill was unanimously approved by the House, a dispute with North Carolina's senior senator, Republican Jesse Helms, blocked passage of the legislation. The problem involved whether or not the federal government would build a road to allow Swain County residents to drive to an old family grave site. Under Clarke's bill the government would make a financial settlement; Helms wanted the road built, and filibustered the bill.

At Home: Most politicians do not launch congressional careers when they have passed their 65th birthday, but that is what Clarke did — twice.

Clarke spent the first six years of his House career engaged in a political pas de deux with Republican Bill Hendon. Clarke first ousted freshman Rep. Hendon in the recession-wracked year of 1982. But Hendon battled back in 1984, bolstered by an economic resurgence that left local voters ripe for Hendon's "no more pain on Main Street" theme.

Clarke immediately began planning for a third showdown, ignoring whispered doubts among Democrats about his ability at 69 to bounce back against an incumbent nearly 30 years his junior. He spent the early months of the campaign reminding audiences of his role in pushing legislation setting aside some 68,000 acres of North Carolina land as wilderness. He also criticized Hendon for having an inadequate environmental record and suggested that, contrary to Hendon's claims, the district might be chosen as the site for a nuclear-waste dump. Hendon answered by citing assurances he had received from the Department of Energy that the dump case was closed, but Clarke succeeded in planting doubts in voters' minds.

Hendon was overconfident. Reluctant to engage in give-and-take on many subjects, the incumbent spent most of his time extolling the positive economic conditions he saw in western North Carolina. Even as his campaign workers began to spot trouble, Hendon seemed convinced he was pulling away. Election Day proved his instinct wrong.

By 1988, Hendon had had enough, but that did not free Clarke from another tough campaign. Against former GOP state legislator Charles Taylor, Clarke ended up winning with just 50 percent of the vote.

North Carolina 11

West — Asheville

Democrats lead comfortably in registration here, but Republicans have been a potent minority in the mountains of western North Carolina since the Civil War.

In recent years, a wave of affluent retirees moving into picturesque Henderson and Polk counties has added to traditional GOP strength. About 20 percent of the population in Polk County is 65 or older, the largest concentration of senior citizens in western North Carolina. The median age in the 11th — 33 years — is the highest in the state.

With help from these newcomers and from national trends favorable to the GOP, Hendon was able to win the 11th in 1980 (the first win for the GOP here since 1928), and in 1984. Henderson and Polk counties backed Ronald Reagan and Sen. Jesse Helms in 1984, and both counties went Republican in 1988 presidential and gubernatorial voting. Clarke was able to hold down his losses in the two counties in 1988, helping secure his narrow re-election victory.

The 11th's sole urban center is Asheville, a resort town, home of author Thomas Wolfe and a regional market center whose relatively small population of 60,000 belies its commercial importance. Along with surrounding Buncombe County, Asheville casts almost 30 percent of the district vote.

Democrats usually enjoy an edge in local Buncombe County contests. But in statewide and national races, the county's partisan preferences are mixed. Buncombe went Republican for president in 1988 — as it has in five of the last six presidential elections — even as it supported Democrat Clarke for the House.

Industrial activity in the counties surrounding Asheville focuses on paper, pulp and textiles. Though much of the terrain is steep and rocky, there is cultivation of tobacco, corn, potatoes and oats. Some Democratic labor strength can be found in the factory towns scattered through the valleys, and Democrats have an edge in traditional courthouse-level organizations.

The federal government has jurisdiction over a significant share of the land in the 11th District; the Nantahala and Pisgah national forests, the Great Smoky Mountains National Park and the Cherokee Indian Reservation are included. Around these scenic areas, tourist dollars boost the economy.

Population: 531,144. White 494,117 (93%), Black 29,291 (6%), Other 7,042 (1%). Spanish origin 3,710 (1%). 18 and over 390,762 (74%), 65 and over 75,737 (14%). Median age: 33.

Taylor was easily more aggressive than the low-key incumbent, and he trooped around the district voicing numerous criticisms of Clarke's record. He claimed Clarke had supported congressional pay raises, had not been supportive enough of defense, and got too much of his campaign funding from out-of-state unions.

Clarke was ready for the challenge, and quickly rebutted all of Taylor's charges. His television ads showed the Iwo Jima memorial in Arlington, Va., and mentioned his service in World War II, undercutting Taylor's soft-on-defense criticism.

By the campaign's end, Democrats were confident that Clarke had done everything he could do to secure victory. But it does not take any major misstep to come up short in such marginal territory, and Clarke nearly did, despite his well-run campaign.

Before his House career, Clarke was known in the mountains of western North Carolina for his lifelong record of civic and charity work. He is related to James G. K. McClure, founder of the Farmers Federation and of the McClure Scholarship Fund, responsible for 50 to 100 college scholarships a year. He managed both programs.

His affiliation with the scholarship fund and his work at Warren Wilson College in Swannanoa led to his 1969 election as chairman of the Buncombe County Board of Education. In 1976, he moved up, winning a seat in the North Carolina House.

During his two terms there, Clarke forced a referendum to prevent the composition of his county's board of education from becoming partisan. The battle increased his popularity in a county that voted 2-to-1 for his referendum. In 1980, he stepped up to the state Senate, where he strengthened his friendship with then-Democratic Gov. James B. Hunt Jr. Clarke's state Senate district, centered in Asheville, provided him a good base from which to launch his 1982 House campaign.

Committees

Foreign Affairs (20th of 28 Democrats)
Arms Control, International Security and Science; Asian and Pacific Affairs

Interior and Insular Affairs (19th of 26 Democrats)
Energy and the Environment; Insular and International Affairs; National Parks and Public Lands

Select Aging (30th of 39 Democrats)
Human Services

Elections

1988 General

James McClure Clarke (D)	108,436	(50%)
Charles H. Taylor (R)	106,907	(50%)

1986 General

James McClure Clarke (D)	91,575	(51%)
Bill Hendon (R)	89,069	(49%)

Previous Winning Percentage: **1982** (50%)

District Vote For President

	1988	1984	1980	1976
D	87,755 (40%)	79,098 (37%)	87,984 (46%)	98,452 (54%)
R	128,469 (59%)	135,030 (63%)	98,258 (51%)	81,747 (45%)
I			5,254 (3%)	

Campaign Finance

	Receipts	Receipts from PACs	Expend-itures
1988			
Clarke (D)	$507,787	$278,867 (55%)	$494,092
Taylor (R)	$503,317	$100,081 (20%)	$503,289
1986			
Clarke (D)	$427,321	$125,290 (29%)	$435,435
Hendon (R)	$473,971	$228,261 (48%)	$474,166

Key Votes

1987

Raise speed limit to 65 mph	Y
Approve Gephardt "fair trade" amendment	Y
Ban testing of larger nuclear weapons	Y
Delay "re-flagging" of Kuwaiti tankers	Y
Approve tax-raising deficit-reduction bill	Y

1988

Approve aid to Nicaraguan contras	N
Enact civil rights restoration bill over Reagan veto	Y
Kill 60-day plant-closing notification measure	Y
Pass omnibus trade bill over Reagan veto	Y
Approve death penalty for drug-related murders	Y
Bar federal funds for abortions in cases of rape and incest	Y
Oppose seven-day waiting period for purchase of handguns	Y

Voting Studies

	Presidential Support		Party Unity		Conservative Coalition	
Year	S	O	S	O	S	O
1988	29	64	82	17	71	21
1987	24	70	81	10	65	35
1984	38	57	79	14	47	42
1983	41	55	78	18	54	44

Interest Group Ratings

Year	ADA	ACU	AFL-CIO	CCUS
1988	60	29	86	57
1987	72	0	88	27
1984	65	20	55	36
1983	65	37	71	40

North Dakota

U.S. CONGRESS

SENATE 2 D
HOUSE 1 D

LEGISLATURE

Senate 32 D, 21 R
House 45 D, 61 R

ELECTIONS

1988 Presidential Vote

Bush	56%
Dukakis	43%

1984 Presidential Vote

Reagan	65%
Mondale	34%

1980 Presidential Vote

Reagan	64%
Carter	26%
Anderson	8%
Turnout rate in 1984	63%
Turnout rate in 1986	58%
Turnout rate in 1988	62%

(as percentage of voting age population)

POPULATION AND GROWTH

1980 population	652,717
1988 population estimate (46th in the nation)	667,000
Percent change 1980-1988	+2%

DEMOGRAPHIC BREAKDOWN

White	96%
Black	0.4%
Other	3%
(Spanish origin)	1%
Urban	49%
Rural	51%
Born in state	73%
Foreign-born	2%

MAJOR CITIES

Fargo	68,020
Bismarck	48,040
Grand Forks	45,090
Minot	35,850
Dickinson	17,320

AREA AND LAND USE

Area 69,300 sq. miles (17th)

Farm	91%
Forest	1%
Federally owned	4%

Gov. George Sinner (D)
Of Casselton — Elected 1984

Born: May 29, 1928, Casselton, N.D.
Education: St. John's U., B.A. 1950.
Military Career: Air Force, 1951-52.
Occupation: Sugar beet farmer; businessman.
Religion: Roman Catholic.
Political Career: N.D. Senate, 1963-67; N.D. House, 1983-85; Democratic nominee for U.S. House, 1964.
Next Election: 1992.

WORK

Occupations

White-collar	46%
Blue-collar	24%
Service workers	15%

Government Workers

Federal	7,711
State	19,821
Local	34,722

MONEY

Median family income	$ 18,023	(34th)
Tax burden per capita	$ 1,011	(13th)

EDUCATION

Spending per pupil through grade 12	$ 3,481	(30th)
Persons with college degrees	15%	(31st)

CRIME

Violent crime rate	57 per 100,000 (50th)

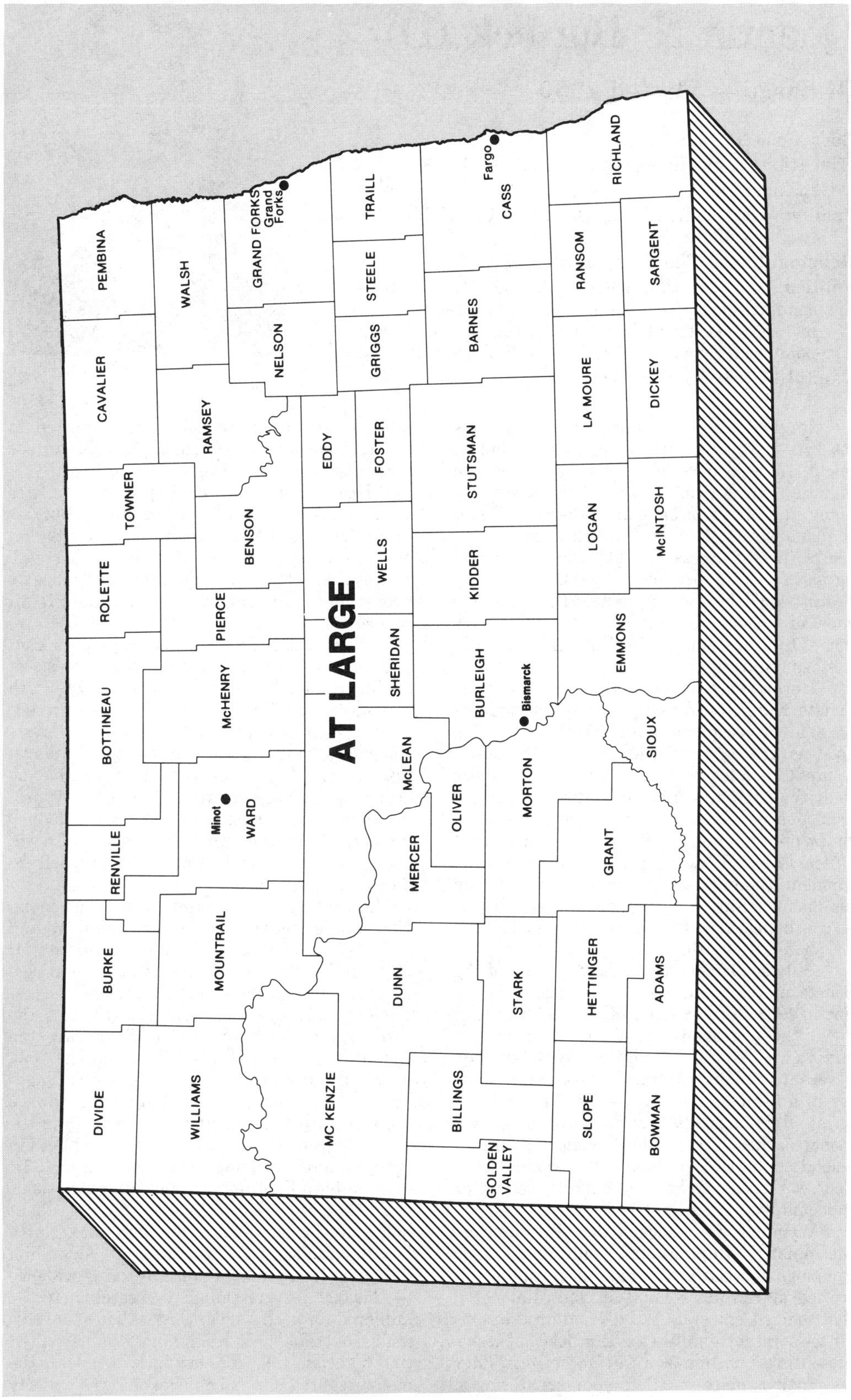
AT LARGE
PEMBINA
WALSH
GRAND FORKS
Grand Forks
TRAILL
CASS
Fargo
RICHLAND
STEELE
RANSOM
SARGENT
NELSON
GRIGGS
BARNES
CAVALIER
RAMSEY
LA MOURE
DICKEY
EDDY
FOSTER
STUTSMAN
TOWNER
BENSON
WELLS
LOGAN
McINTOSH
ROLETTE
PIERCE
KIDDER
EMMONS
SHERIDAN
BURLEIGH
Bismarck
McHENRY
BOTTINEAU
SIOUX
McLEAN
MORTON
OLIVER
Minot
WARD
RENVILLE
MERCER
GRANT
MOUNTRAIL
BURKE
DUNN
STARK
HETTINGER
ADAMS
MC KENZIE
WILLIAMS
DIVIDE
BILLINGS
GOLDEN VALLEY
SLOPE
BOWMAN

Quentin N. Burdick (D)

Of Fargo — Elected 1960

Born: June 19, 1908, Munich, N.D.
Education: U. of Minnesota, B.A. 1931, LL.B. 1932.
Occupation: Lawyer.
Family: Wife, Jocelyn Birch Peterson; four children, two stepchildren.
Religion: United Church of Christ.
Political Career: U.S. House, 1959-60; Republican candidate for N.D. Senate, 1938; Republican nominee for lieutenant governor, 1942; Democratic nominee for governor, 1946, and U.S. Senate, 1956.
Capitol Office: 511 Hart Bldg. 20510; 224-2551.

In Washington: The 100th Congress marked Burdick's 14th as a senator, but it might as well have been his first. Like an ambitious freshman, he worked the press, announced a lengthy agenda and otherwise sought to demonstrate clout. In Burdick's case, it was the politics of necessity. Then 79, he was preparing for a re-election battle in which his health would be the key issue. His counter: a show of Washington muscle to the folks back home. But on Capitol Hill, Burdick's staff did the heavy lifting.

During more than a quarter-century in the Senate, Burdick had never chaired any committee of any consequence until 1987. Self-effacing, good-natured and never one to seek the power or pressure of leadership, it was more Burdick's fault than the system's. He shifted repeatedly from one panel to another, serving at various times on the Interior, Labor, Judiciary, Post Office, Public Works, Appropriations and Environment committees. He voluntarily gave up his membership on several committees just as he was being asked to assume some responsibility for managing them.

But the Democrats regained control of the Senate in 1987, and with his own seat on the line in 1988 Burdick was in no position to turn down the chairmanship of the Environment and Public Works Committee. With an aide never far from his ear, Burdick ran the committee in a somnambulent style, as if following a script. Republican Robert T. Stafford of Vermont coached him on the technical points of amendments and motions. The committee's floor work often fell to the majority leader or subcommittee chairmen.

Wyoming Republican Alan K. Simpson, the minority whip, stumping during the 1988 campaign for Burdick's Republican opponent, scoffed at Burdick's claim of clout and noted that senior Democrats had divvied up the committee's responsibilities in Burdick's absence, presenting it to him as a *fait accompli.* "They just took a piece and left your senator with nothing to do but to call the committee to order," Simpson said. Burdick called Simpson's account "purely political."

Health could continue to present problems for Burdick, who was 80 as the 101st Congress began. Struck by seizures not long after his re-election, he spent several days in the hospital. He cast his vote in the majority leader's race by proxy, and later had difficulty recalling it for reporters.

Burdick has concentrated largely on constituent service and protecting the interests of his home state. "I just want to be a good North Dakota senator," he has said. "I try to represent the people of my state and hope their interests coincide with the national interest." His elevation in the 100th Congress made it possible; he also picked up the chairmanship of the Appropriations subcommittee that doles out money for agriculture and rural development. "I will get everything North Dakota is entitled to now," he proclaimed.

He set about to do just that — and more. His announced agenda for Environment and Public Works was ambitious: legislation on air pollution, hazardous-waste storage, federal pesticide regulation, and maintenance of the nation's highways, sewers and bridges. But the two biggest pieces of legislation to leave the committee were in the works before he took over. The authorization of $88 billion for highway construction and $20 billion for sewage plant construction were leftover items from the 99th Congress. President Reagan vetoed both in 1986; Congress promptly overrode him in 1987.

On both Environment and Appropriations, Burdick largely left others to quarrel about policy as he set about to make sure North Dakota got its share. This strategy enabled him to pepper his campaign literature with evidence — $69,000 for grasshopper research here, $8 million for a weed science center there — of this unabashed ability to bring home the bacon. Of the highway bill, for instance, he said the money snared for North Dakota was "pretty good for an incompetent senator."

Despite Burdick's emergence as a born-again activist, his tenure in the Environment chair has yet to produce major policy shifts. Clean-air legislation, the most thorny issue, remains unresolved. For his part, Burdick was predisposed toward the public works side of the committee's charge to begin with, again a reflection of his homeward orientation. "We don't have any environmental problems out there; we do have highway and road problems," he declared in one newspaper interview.

As a Westerner, Burdick is generally skeptical of Easterners' efforts to mandate nationwide controls on coal emissions in order to curb acid rain. He favors legislation to concentrate coal cleanup efforts on the part of the country that lies east of the Mississippi, and opposes making utility users in the West pay for pollution-control efforts in the Ohio Valley.

Burdick views as his major accomplishment in Congress the 1965 authorization of the Garrison Diversion project in North Dakota, a giant public works program now under fire as unaffordable in this era of high deficits. There have been votes to delete funding for the project, or to scale it back to reduce its cost. But Burdick defends his monument from his Senate Appropriations post; in 1987, he obtained $33 million for the project.

Burdick also has shown an interest in postal issues. Before 1987, the one committee he seemed to want to chair was Post Office and Civil Service; he was in line to head it in 1977, but the Senate decided that year to fold it into the Governmental Affairs Committee as part of a major overhaul of the Senate's committee structure. Piqued by this development, Burdick cast the sole dissenting vote in the Senate on the reform plan.

The North Dakota Democrat has been a fairly consistent liberal throughout his congressional career. He was a staunch supporter of the Kennedy and Johnson administrations, an early critic of the Vietnam War and a strong backer of all major civil rights legislation. He was, however, one of the first Northern Democrats to criticize busing for racial balance and to support anti-busing legislation.

Burdick has long been one of the more absent-minded senators; usually this causes him no particular trouble. In 1983, though, he inserted in the *Congressional Record* not only a statement on the issue of truck-weight regulations, but private instructions he had received on the subject from a lobbyist. Burdick's floor speech that day includes the words, "Greyhound Bus Co. would like you to insert the attached floor statement in today's *Congressional Record.*"

At Home: Burdick's ascent to a committee chairmanship came at a very good time — when he appeared to be facing his most serious electoral challenge in more than 20 years. In the end he used his new position in Washington, and a sophisticated campaign in the state, to win overwhelming approval for another term.

Many North Dakotans assumed that Burdick, who turned 80 in 1988, would retire and make way for popular Democratic Rep. Byron L. Dorgan. When Burdick made it clear he intended to seek another term, it looked as if there might be a primary blood bath. A number of Democrats suggested privately and publicly that Burdick should step aside, and many expected Dorgan to run for the Senate regardless.

But Burdick demonstrated his resolve with his decision to distribute press releases and newspaper clippings citing his newly won importance, and with his decision to run very early media advertising. He touted his new position in Washington and encouraged Dorgan to stay in the House. Seeing that he might have a tough fight on his hands, Dorgan announced late in 1987 that he would not challenge Burdick.

Dorgan's decision was a major boost for Burdick, but it did not signal the end of his vulnerability. In the fall he faced Earl Strinden, the GOP leader in the state House, who repeatedly questioned Burdick's ability to serve in the Senate for another six years.

Burdick worked to dispel doubts about his age, at one point mailing out "The Walking Workout, A Guide to Fitness Walking," a pamphlet describing how he keeps in good condition and how others can as well. But even Democrats were concerned about Burdick's health throughout the election. The subject moved to the headlines a few months before the election, when Burdick underwent surgery to have an 18-inch section of his large intestine removed.

The health issue was not enough to get Strinden past his own problems, however. As a state legislative leader he had developed a reputation as abrasive, a problem exacerbated by his strategy of attacking Burdick. Republicans were frustrated by Burdick's careful campaign, which seemed to keep him either in Washington or in scripted appearances before friendly audiences. The GOP did not get the boost it wanted when the incumbent was finally put on the spot in a candidate debate. Burdick's performance was strong enough to dispel charges that he was incompetent.

Burdick had more than a sophisticated campaign and committee chairmanship going for him. In a state that takes its political history and traditions seriously, his family name has been appearing on North Dakota ballots for most of the 20th century.

Quentin's father, Usher Burdick, served as a state legislator, lieutenant governor and U.S. House member. From 1938 to 1956, Quentin ran unsuccessfully for a string of offices — state senator, lieutenant governor, governor and U.S. senator.

Like his father, Burdick started out as a

Republican. In his early races, he also ran under the banner of the old populist Non-Partisan League. But in 1946, when he tried for governor, he shifted to the Democratic label.

Burdick finally won office in 1958, taking a seat in Congress. In 1960, upon the death of the state's senior GOP senator, William Langer, he upset Republican Gov. John E. Davis in a special election for the unexpired Senate term. The contest turned on farm issues. Burdick owed his narrow victory to his attacks on the unpopular farm policies of the Eisenhower administration.

In 1964, when he ran for a full term, it was Burdick's turn to be on the defensive. Republican businessman Thomas Kleppe, later a House member and U.S. interior secretary, criticized falling farm prices under the Kennedy administration. But Burdick countered by linking Kleppe to GOP presidential nominee Barry Goldwater, who advocated scrapping some farm subsidies altogether.

In a 1970 rematch, Burdick criticized the Nixon administration for refusing to back increased price supports, and benefited from resentment over Kleppe's attempts to link him with "radical liberal" Democrats. He won easily that year and even more easily in 1976, when the GOP essentially gave up and nominated a little-known state legislator.

Republicans tried harder in 1982, but the results were no more satisfying than before. Burdick's opponent was Gene Knorr, a Washington lobbyist, former U.S. Treasury official and member of President Reagan's transition team.

Knorr crisscrossed the state by private plane and van, telling voters that Burdick was simply too liberal for them. Burdick's age and low profile in the Senate seemed to make him a perfect candidate for an upset at the hands of the younger, more energetic Knorr. But the 1980 defeats of several fellow incumbents had alerted Burdick, and he took the challenge seriously, campaigning hard enough to get hospitalized for exhaustion during the summer.

The senator pegged his re-election effort only partly to criticism of Republican economic policies. He also made an issue of Knorr's extended absence from the state. Burdick aired commercials noting that at the time Knorr was nominated in North Dakota, he was still registered to vote in Virginia. The veteran Democrat entertained delegates to a party convention by singing a song entitled, "Carry Gene Back to Ol' Virginny."

Committees

Environment and Public Works (Chairman)

Appropriations (5th of 16 Democrats)
Agriculture, Rural Development and Related Agencies (chairman); Energy and Water Development; Interior and Related Agencies; Labor, Health and Human Services, Education and Related Agencies

Select Indian Affairs (3rd of 5 Democrats)

Special Aging (4th of 10 Democrats)

Elections

1988 General

Quentin N. Burdick (D)	171,899	(59%)
Earl Strinden (R)	112,937	(39%)

Previous Winning Percentages: **1982** (63%) **1976** (62%) **1970** (61%) **1964** (58%) **1960** † (50%) **1958** * (50%)

† Special Senate election.
** House election.*

Campaign Finance

	Receipts	Receipts from PACs	Expend-itures
1988			
Burdick (D)	$1,755,318	$1,059,524 (60%)	$2,026,617
Strinden (R)	$908,607	$254,518 (28%)	$906,807

Key Votes

1987

Enact omnibus highway bill over Reagan veto	Y
Limit testing of space-based anti-ballistic missiles	Y
Oppose banning tests of larger nuclear weapons	N
Confirm Robert H. Bork as Supreme Court justice	N

1988

Allow vote on campaign-finance overhaul	Y
Pass civil rights restoration bill over Reagan veto	Y
Enact omnibus trade bill over Reagan veto	Y
Approve death penalty for drug-related murders	N
Oppose "workfare" amendment to welfare overhaul bill	Y

Voting Studies

	Presidential Support		Party Unity		Conservative Coalition	
Year	S	O	S	O	S	O
1988	43	52	88	10	41	59
1987	33	64	88	10	25	75
1986	18	81	87	13	20	80
1985	25	73	87	10	30	70
1984	31	56	78	11	26	57
1983	46	54	85	14	36	59
1982	50	50	81	17	48	51
1981	52	46	81	17	41	58

Interest Group Ratings

Year	ADA	ACU	AFL-CIO	CCUS
1988	85	16	100	29
1987	95	8	100	24
1986	100	4	93	21
1985	85	9	86	21
1984	100	0	91	33
1983	75	12	82	32
1982	70	25	88	50
1981	75	13	74	44

Kent Conrad (D)

Of Bismarck — Elected 1986

Born: March 12, 1948, Bismarck, N.D.
Education: Stanford U., B.A. 1971; George Washington U., M.B.A. 1975.
Occupation: Management and personnel director.
Family: Wife, Lucy Calautti; two children.
Religion: Unitarian.
Political Career: N.D. tax commissioner, 1981-87; candidate for state auditor, 1976.
Capitol Office: 361 Dirksen Bldg. 20510; 224-2043.

In Washington: North Dakota has long been fertile soil for populists willing to till its natural distrust of powerful outsiders — Eastern bankers, railroad magnates and flour-mill barons. When hard times sweep across the prairie, these attitudes harden, to the benefit of politicians like Conrad. He built his reputation as a tax commissioner willing to take on big business. He spent his first two years in the Senate carrying water for his farmers.

No mere windmill tilter, Conrad earned the sobriquet "Chainsaw" back home because, he once said, "when you are going after big timber you have to use strong tactics." Yet his manner does not suggest a giant-killer: Fresh-faced, earnest, and conservative in style and dress, Conrad looks as if he would fit better with an assembly of junior executives than a crowd of angry farmers. During his first month in office, he shared an elevator with a senator's wife who informed him it was for senators only, and then challenged his claim to the title.

Whether or not Conrad looks his part, he has certainly played it, holding fast by his causes. He cast one of only two votes against the nomination of Alan Greenspan to head the Federal Reserve System, sending a message of protest against the Fed's policy of fighting inflation with tight money. "High real interest rates and an overvalued dollar are literally life or death issues for my area of the country," he said.

Conrad was the least experienced of the 11 Democrats in the Senate class of 1986, all former governors or House members save he. He has taken traditional steps to close this gap — developing expertise in a limited number of areas by doing his homework. This was perhaps even more essential for Conrad than most, for farm policy is one of Capitol Hill's most complex issue areas, politically and substantively.

Seats on the Agriculture and Budget committees position Conrad strategically for defending agriculture as farm programs run headlong into pressures for deficit reduction. In early 1987, during floor action on drought relief for winter-wheat farmers, Conrad bucked Agriculture Committee Chairman Patrick J. Leahy of Vermont — who wanted no amendments on the bill — and managed to amend it to gain treatment for sunflower growers equal to that of soybean producers; the two crops compete in the cooking-oil market. Conrad also pressed the Farmers Home Administration to write down overdue loans instead of foreclosing on them.

While Conrad would tinker with the pricing mechanism for crops, he sees the rural economy in broader terms. He has pushed for a rural development task force in the Senate and is the chief Senate sponsor of the Agricultural Research Commercialization Act. The measure would create a government corporation to help create non-food markets for farm products, such as making plastic from cornstarch.

His other passion is the budget deficit, which he would attack with measures as harsh as a spending freeze, Social Security excepted. He voted against Treasury Secretary Nicholas F. Brady's confirmation after Brady expressed the belief that the nation's economy could simply grow out of the deficit.

Conrad has shown himself a party loyalist in his early going. But he is given more to discussion of policy than politics, and his populism, though no passing fancy, is tempered with pragmatism. "Hard ideological positions carry a danger," he says. "Hiding behind rhetorical barriers doesn't get things done."

Unless things get done quickly, Conrad could end up scrambling to explain away a pledge he made upon coming to Washington: He promised voters he would not seek re-election unless real interest rates fell and the trade and budget deficits came under control (he even specified an 80 percent cut in each). Not surprisingly, he has since backed off the pledge, joking that he wrote it under the influence of a 104-degree fever and saying he might run again even if his goals are not met.

At Home: The troubles besetting North Dakota's farms and small towns gave Conrad a clear opening in 1986 against Republican Sen. Mark Andrews, and his skillful use of the issue propelled him into contention against the favored incumbent. On Election Day, Conrad carried only one of the state's four major population centers; his victory was built in the countryside.

Conrad succeeded Democratic Rep. Byron L. Dorgan as tax commissioner and he won widespread popularity by vigorously auditing out-of-state corporations. He also fought an ongoing battle with the Burlington Northern rail company, challenging its abandonment of rail lines used by farmers within the state.

Conrad's chief Senate campaign issue was the Reagan administration's farm policy, which was wildly unpopular in a state where farms and small-town banks were failing and where rural families were breaking apart as their members headed to the cities to find work. The election, Conrad insisted, was a referendum on Republican farm and economic policies; if voters wanted to send a message to Washington, he told them, he would be the messenger.

He went on the attack early, trying to tie Andrews to the administration's programs. Though the Republican had by and large opposed Reagan agricultural policies, he had voted for the 1985 farm bill, which many farmers believed hurt them. Storming around the state with Dorgan, Conrad relentlessly pressed the point, bringing up Andrews' vote whenever the opportunity arose.

He also set out to undermine Andrews' credibility. When the senator aired a commercial claiming that the price of wheat had risen after the Senate passed an export amendment he had sponsored, Conrad pointed out that the price rise was only a brief interruption in a long-term decline.

Andrews responded in kind. He challenged Conrad's claim to have cut his departmental budget as tax commissioner, and pointed out that Conrad had been endorsed in a *Village Voice* article — a sure sign that he was too liberal for North Dakota.

But the debate between the two may have been secondary to the deeper factors working in Conrad's favor. In addition to the farm situation, there was a growing perception that Andrews had lost touch with his base.

Part of the way into the campaign, Andrews was stung by press stories revealing that a close friend of his had hired private detectives to investigate first Dorgan and then Conrad. Democrats jumped on the matter, trying to tie Andrews directly to the incident; Andrews denied any involvement, but the publicity hurt him all the same.

Possibly as troubling to voters was a multimillion-dollar lawsuit that Andrews and his wife Mary had pursued against family physicians after Mary Andrews was crippled by meningitis. Though early in the case there had been widespread sympathy for the incumbent and his wife, by the time of the election there was evidence that voters had grown uncomfortable with the sight of a wealthy senator demanding large sums of money from family doctors in a state where, as one North Dakota journalist wrote, "not even clergy are more highly thought of."

Andrews was further hurt by the delay in ending Congress' 1986 session. As Conrad's attacks found their mark, Republicans worried that Andrews' continued presence in Washington would only underline the Democrats' contention that he had grown distant from the state's concerns. By the time Andrews did return home, Conrad had taken a slight lead in the polls, and Andrews had to try to make up lost ground. He never succeeded.

Committees

Agriculture, Nutrition and Forestry (6th of 10 Democrats)
Agricultural Credit (chairman); Agricultural Production and Stabilization of Prices; Domestic and Foreign Marketing and Product Promotion

Budget (11th of 13 Democrats)

Energy and Natural Resources (8th of 10 Democrats)
Mineral Resources Development and Production; Public Lands, National Parks and Forests; Water and Power

Select Indian Affairs (5th of 5 Democrats)

Election

1986 General		
Kent Conrad (D)	143,932	(50%)
Mark Andrews (R)	141,797	(49%)

Campaign Finance

	Receipts	Receipts from PACs	Expend-itures
1986			
Conrad (D)	$993,040	$453,440 (46%)	$908,374
Andrews (R)	$2,063,395	$1,019,595 (49%)	$2,270,557

Key Votes

1987	
Enact omnibus highway bill over Reagan veto	Y
Limit testing of space-based anti-ballistic missiles	Y
Oppose banning tests of larger nuclear weapons	N
Confirm Robert H. Bork as Supreme Court justice	N
1988	
Allow vote on campaign-finance overhaul	Y
Pass civil rights restoration bill over Reagan veto	Y
Enact omnibus trade bill over Reagan veto	Y
Approve death penalty for drug-related murders	N
Oppose "workfare" amendment to welfare overhaul bill	Y

Voting Studies

	Presidential Support		Party Unity		Conservative Coalition	
Year	S	O	S	O	S	O
1988	48	50	78	20	35	65
1987	37	63	82	17	47	53

Interest Group Ratings

Year	ADA	ACU	AFL-CIO	CCUS
1988	80	24	93	29
1987	85	8	90	39

AL Byron L. Dorgan (D)

Of Bismarck — Elected 1980

Born: May 14, 1942, Regent, N.D.
Education: U. of North Dakota, B.S. 1965; U. of Denver, M.B.A. 1966.
Occupation: Public official.
Family: Wife, Kimberly Olson; three children.
Religion: Lutheran.
Political Career: N.D. tax commissioner, 1969-80; Democratic nominee for U.S. House, 1974.
Capitol Office: 109 Cannon Bldg. 20515; 225-2611.

In Washington: Dorgan is regarded in the Capitol and in North Dakota as the state's senator-in-waiting. His political caution held him back from challenges to incumbents the last two elections, but he makes no secret of his wish to succeed Democratic Sen. Quentin N. Burdick. It will be a surprise if he does not.

Dorgan is a contemporary echo of the prairie populism that swept North Dakota in the early 1900s. His rhetorical targets are big banks, railroads and grasping corporations. His talk dwells on the struggles of common folk against distant forces over which they have no control. "People feel powerless," he has said, "and they feel powerless because they're preyed upon by bigger interests."

Dorgan's legislative style has little in common with the crude bluster of predecessors like William L. Langer, the North Dakota firebrand who once pounded on a Senate lectern so hard that it broke. Dorgan never shouts or waves his arms, even when denouncing a David Rockefeller or a Paul Volcker. But he denounces them nonetheless.

Dorgan's 11 years as state tax commissioner provided him with expertise and credibility that help make him a force on the Ways and Means Committee. He spends a great deal of time working on schemes to guarantee that the earnings of large corporations are taxed. In the 99th Congress, he was a strong supporter of efforts on Ways and Means to revise the tax code, which he called "a feedlot for the rich, and a straitjacket for the rest."

Dorgan knows how to craft an amendment and round up the support he needs for its passage. During work on the tax bill in 1985, he pushed through an amendment to help farm co-ops by retaining a tax exemption for credit unions. That, in effect, gave them an advantage over competing savings and loans.

On other issues, however, Dorgan argued that achieving an overhaul of the tax code was more important than protecting parochial interests. He opposed some agriculture tax subsidies, such as accelerated write-offs for new hog barns, though some North Dakotans wanted them. "Doing tax reform is like administering medicine," Dorgan said. "They don't like the taste, but they will like the result."

Overall, Dorgan has been careful to put home-state interests first. He was the only "nay" vote in committee against implementing the U.S.-Canada free-trade pact in the 100th Congress, saying it did little to tear down Canadian barriers against imports of U.S. wheat. He astutely voted against the 1985 farm bill; while Dorgan was criticized for not revealing his position until passage was assured, a vote for the bill underpinned the defeat of North Dakota GOP Sen. Mark Andrews in 1986.

Dorgan's populism has made him a skeptic about foreign aid. When the Reagan administration proposed an $8.4 billion increase in the U.S. donation to the International Monetary Fund in 1983, Dorgan joined with colleagues on both the right and the left to block it.

The problem, he said, was that the money was simply being used to help out large banks that had made bad loans to the Third World. "If we could dye those dollar bills purple, within a month after the IMF got the money, the bankers on Wall Street would have deep purple pockets," he said. The measure eventually passed, but Dorgan did amend it on the House floor to prohibit banks from making a profit from the renegotiation of a country's debt.

But Dorgan is not an economic isolationist. He understands how international currency exchanges and interest rates affect the sales of North Dakota grain abroad, and has become one of the Ways and Means members who follow international debt questions closely.

He has been a longtime foe of an unfettered Federal Reserve Board and the high interest rates he says it has caused. In 1981 he introduced a bill he called "The Paul Volcker Retirement Act," which would have let Congress remove the Fed chairman with a 60 percent vote of both chambers. "With a central bank like the Federal Reserve Board," he wrote in a 1983 article on farm problems, "who needs soil erosion, grasshoppers or drought?"

North Dakota — At Large

While North Dakota boasts a strong two-party system, its political character has largely been molded by a third force, the agrarian populist movement. The original vehicle for populism, the Non-Partisan League, has not been a major factor for a generation, but agrarian populism continues to shape the state's politics.

In the 1986 Senate election, incumbent Republican Mark Andrews fell victim to farmers' dissatisfaction caused by the slumping market for wheat, the backbone of the state's economy. Also in 1986, the Democrats won control of the state Senate for the first time in history. They maintained that hold in 1988, while Democratic incumbents were re-elected to the governorship, the Senate and the House. Republicans continue to hold a majority in the state House.

Although the politics of North Dakota have traditionally been the politics of wheat, the state's farm community is more diverse than its political rhetoric would imply. The Red River, which marks the state's eastern border with Minnesota, forms the basis for a rich growing region that produces sugar beets and potatoes. This is the state's most prosperous agricultural area.

Two of the state's largest cities, Grand Forks and Fargo, are in the Red River valley. The combination of large medical facilities, the two major state universities and normally prosperous farmers makes this area Republican in most elections.

Western North Dakota, too dry for a good wheat crop, has developed an economy based on livestock and energy development. The slide in oil prices threw the petroleum industry into decline in the mid-1980s. The coal industry in the southwestern corner of the state, suffering from over-optimistic projections of demand, is stagnating. The Great Plains gasification plant in Beulah, constructed with grand expectations of transforming huge amounts of coal to natural gas, was sold by the federal government in 1988 to the Basin Electric Power Cooperative.

Farmers in the less fertile areas tend to support Democratic candidates because they are viewed as inheritors of the old Non-Partisan League populism. And as more people have relocated from rural areas into the cities, the cities are losing their Republican orientation. This is particularly noticeable in the capital of Bismarck, in the south-central part of the state. In the many small towns, Republican strength persists, although even there the GOP has lost steam because farm problems are affecting Main Street businesses.

Population: 652,717. White 625,557 (96%), Black 2,568 (0.4%), Other 22,137 (3%). Spanish origin 3,902 (1%). 18 and over 461,726 (71%), 65 and over 80,445 (12%). Median age: 28.

One of Dorgan's biggest legislative concerns is the Garrison Diversion water project, an article of faith for most elected officials in North Dakota. The massive project was promised to the state in 1944, but funding for its construction has been a perennial controversy.

Dorgan achieved a major legislative victory in 1983, when he lobbied furiously to help fend off an assault on the project. But work stopped in 1984 while a 12-member commission sought ways to redesign it.

In the ensuing debate over Garrison, Dorgan found himself arguing not only with the project's critics, but also with both of his state's senators, Democrat Burdick and Republican Andrews. Dorgan wanted the Senate to make the first move on a bill to save Garrison; Burdick said he was "incensed" at Dorgan's attitude. In early 1986, a compromise was worked out scaling back the project. But the arguments and delays forced the reallocation of roughly $25 million in appropriations from Garrison to other projects — a loss Burdick claimed Dorgan was partly responsible for.

At Home: Dorgan's revival of the North Dakota populist tradition has made him an odds-on favorite to move to the Senate at some point in the future. What has surprised many is that he is not in the Senate already.

In 1985, some polls suggested he could easily defeat the GOP's Andrews, but he decided not to challenge him. Instead, his one-time protégé and successor as state tax commissioner, Kent Conrad, ran and defeated Andrews.

Heading into the 1988 election, Dorgan got plenty of encouragement from polls and fellow Democrats to run for the Senate seat occupied by Burdick, who was nearing 80 years old. Dorgan backers hoped to pressure the veteran senator into retiring, but it soon became clear there was no budging him. Burdick kicked his campaign into high gear very early, hiring top consultants and running TV ads to boost his standing and discourage Dorgan from challenging his renomination. At the end of 1987

Dorgan said he would seek another House term; Burdick went on to win re-election easily.

It was not the first time Dorgan had been stiff-armed by Burdick. The two went through a similar routine in 1982, with Burdick dismissing retirement rumors and winning re-election. In 1989 Burdick said he would not rule out seeking yet another term in 1994, but by then his health and age may finally be too big an obstacle.

Dorgan's stands are rooted partly in the prairie populism of the state's old Non-Partisan League and partly in the small-town values with which he was raised. His father was active in the Democratic-leaning Farmers' Union in Regent, N.D., where Dorgan grew up and where, he likes to say, he graduated in the top five in his high school class — of nine.

Dorgan was working in the state tax department in 1969 when he caught the eye of Democratic Gov. William Guy; when the incumbent tax commissioner died in 1969, Dorgan was appointed to the post at age 27. It was his ticket to statewide prominence.

As tax commissioner, Dorgan spoke out on local issues such as property tax revision and on global ones such as military spending. He sued out-of-state corporations doing business in North Dakota to force them to pay taxes, sending auditors to ensure that the firms were accurately reporting financial information. The voters loved it.

Dorgan made it clear he had political ambitions by taking on then-Rep. Andrews in 1974. It was an all-uphill battle, but Dorgan held Andrews to 56 percent, the only time he had fallen below 60 percent since 1964.

Dorgan's contest with Andrews laid a foundation for later statewide campaigns, and in 1980 he took advantage of it. Republican Sen. Milton R. Young retired that year, and Andrews was the undisputed Republican choice to succeed him. Dorgan ran for Andrews' House seat.

Although he was the favorite from the start, Dorgan sought to temper his liberal reputation by supporting an anti-abortion constitutional amendment and decrying government waste. That was a successful combination; the state went overwhelmingly for Ronald Reagan, but Dorgan won a comfortable 57 percent of the House vote.

Committees

Select Hunger (6th of 18 Democrats)
Task Force: International

Ways and Means (16th of 23 Democrats)
Oversight; Select Revenue Measures

Elections

1988 General

Byron L. Dorgan (D)	212,583	(71%)
Steve Sydness (R)	84,475	(28%)

1986 General

Byron L. Dorgan (D)	216,258	(76%)
Syver Vinje (R)	66,989	(23%)

Previous Winning Percentages: **1984** (79%) **1982** (72%) **1980** (57%)

District Vote For President

	1988	1984	1980	1976
D	127,739 (43%)	104,429 (34%)	79,189 (26%)	136,078 (46%)
R	166,559 (56%)	200,336 (65%)	193,695 (64%)	153,470 (52%)
I			23,640 (8%)	

Campaign Finance

	Receipts	Receipts from PACs	Expend-itures
1988			
Dorgan (D)	$687,234	$462,346 (67%)	$747,594
Sydness (R)	$261,883	$7,605 (3%)	$260,727
1986			
Dorgan (D)	$458,532	$314,486 (69%)	$391,909
Vinje (R)	$73,995	$900 (1%)	$73,278

Key Votes

1987

Raise speed limit to 65 mph	Y
Approve Gephardt "fair trade" amendment	Y
Ban testing of larger nuclear weapons	Y
Delay "re-flagging" of Kuwaiti tankers	Y
Approve tax-raising deficit-reduction bill	Y

1988

Approve aid to Nicaraguan contras	N
Enact civil rights restoration bill over Reagan veto	Y
Kill 60-day plant-closing notification measure	N
Pass omnibus trade bill over Reagan veto	Y
Approve death penalty for drug-related murders	Y
Bar federal funds for abortions in cases of rape and incest	Y
Oppose seven-day waiting period for purchase of handguns	Y

Voting Studies

	Presidential Support		Party Unity		Conservative Coalition	
Year	**S**	**O**	**S**	**O**	**S**	**O**
1988	28	70	81	16	47	53
1987	13	83	83	12	30	70
1986	26	73	82	15	44	56
1985	23	78	83	15	22	78
1984	33	61	75	22	31	68
1983	18	77	77	18	33	60
1982	36	62	81	17	33	64
1981	37	55	80	18	37	53

Interest Group Ratings

Year	ADA	ACU	AFL-CIO	CCUS
1988	75	17	93	38
1987	92	0	81	14
1986	70	27	71	29
1985	65	10	76	27
1984	75	22	46	33
1983	80	32	67	45
1982	85	5	90	32
1981	65	20	73	16

Ohio

U.S. CONGRESS

SENATE 2 D
HOUSE 11 D, 10 R

LEGISLATURE

Senate 14 D, 19 R
House 59 D, 40 R

ELECTIONS

1988 Presidential Vote	
Bush	55%
Dukakis	44%
1984 Presidential Vote	
Reagan	59%
Mondale	40%
1980 Presidential Vote	
Reagan	52%
Carter	41%
Anderson	6%
Turnout rate in 1984	58%
Turnout rate in 1986	39%
Turnout rate in 1988	55%

(as percentage of voting age population)

POPULATION AND GROWTH

1980 population	10,797,630
1988 population estimate (7th in the nation)	10,855,000
Percent change 1980-1988	+1%

DEMOGRAPHIC BREAKDOWN

White	89%
Black	10%
(Spanish origin)	1%
Urban	73%
Rural	27%
Born in state	73%
Foreign-born	3%

MAJOR CITIES

Columbus	566,030
Cleveland	535,830
Cincinnati	369,750
Toledo	340,680
Akron	222,060

AREA AND LAND USE

Area	41,004 sq. miles (35th)
Farm	59%
Forest	28%
Federally owned	1%

Gov. Richard F. Celeste (D)
Of Columbus — Elected 1982

Born: Nov. 11, 1937, Lakewood, Ohio.
Education: Yale U., B.A. 1959; attended Oxford U., England, 1960-62.
Occupation: Housing company executive.
Religion: Methodist.
Political Career: Ohio House, 1971-75; lieutenant governor, 1975-79; Democratic nominee for governor, 1978.
Next Election: 1990.

WORK

Occupations	
White-collar	50%
Blue-collar	35%
Service workers	13%
Government Workers	
Federal	89,956
State	157,121
Local	435,209

MONEY

Median family income	$ 20,909	(16th)
Tax burden per capita	$ 805	(29th)

EDUCATION

Spending per pupil through grade 12	$ 3,527	(28th)
Persons with college degrees	14%	(40th)

CRIME

Violent crime rate	421 per 100,000	(25th)

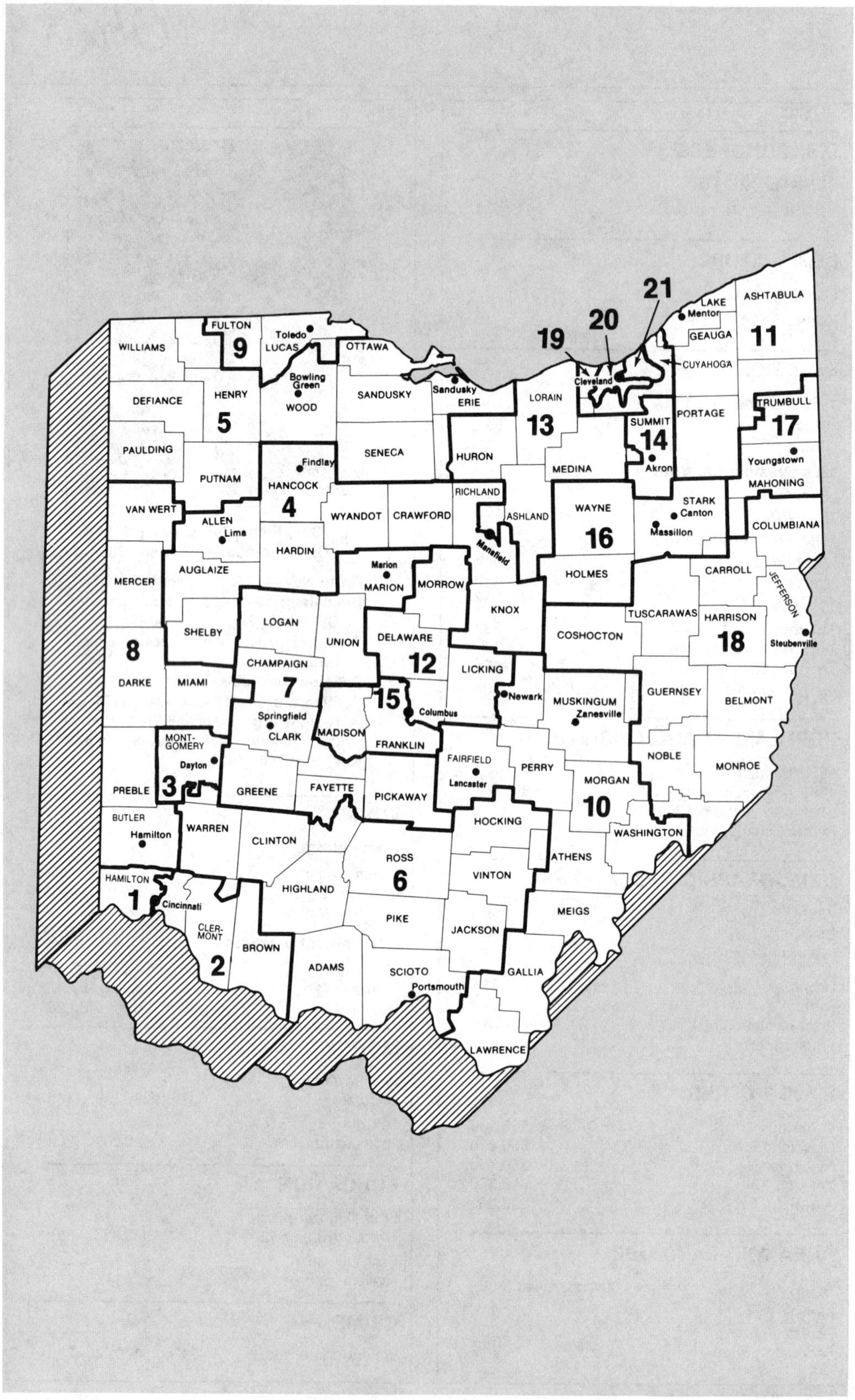
FULTON
9
Toledo
LUCAS
OTTAWA
WILLIAMS
DEFIANCE
HENRY
5
Bowling Green
WOOD
SANDUSKY
Sandusky
ERIE
PAULDING
PUTNAM
Findlay
HANCOCK
4
SENECA
HURON
LORAIN
13
19
20
21
Cleveland
CUYAHOGA
LAKE
Mentor
GEAUGA
ASHTABULA
11
TRUMBULL
17
Youngstown
MAHONING
SUMMIT
14
Akron
PORTAGE
MEDINA
VAN WERT
ALLEN
Lima
WYANDOT
CRAWFORD
RICHLAND
Mansfield
ASHLAND
WAYNE
16
STARK
Canton
Massillon
COLUMBIANA
MERCER
AUGLAIZE
HARDIN
Marion
MARION
MORROW
KNOX
HOLMES
CARROLL
JEFFERSON
SHELBY
LOGAN
UNION
DELAWARE
12
COSHOCTON
TUSCARAWAS
HARRISON
18
Steubenville
8
DARKE
MIAMI
CHAMPAIGN
7
LICKING
Newark
15
Columbus
MUSKINGUM
Zanesville
GUERNSEY
BELMONT
Springfield
CLARK
MADISON
FRANKLIN
MONT-GOMERY
Dayton
FAIRFIELD
Lancaster
PERRY
MORGAN
NOBLE
MONROE
PREBLE
3
GREENE
FAYETTE
PICKAWAY
10
BUTLER
Hamilton
WARREN
CLINTON
HOCKING
WASHINGTON
ROSS
6
ATHENS
VINTON
HAMILTON
1
Cincinnati
HIGHLAND
MEIGS
CLER-MONT
2
BROWN
PIKE
JACKSON
ADAMS
SCIOTO
Portsmouth
GALLIA
LAWRENCE

John Glenn (D)

Of Columbus — Elected 1974

Born: July 18, 1921, Cambridge, Ohio.
Education: Muskingum College, B.S. 1962.
Military Career: Marine Corps, 1942-65.
Occupation: Astronaut; soft drink company executive.
Family: Wife, Anna Margaret Castor; two children.
Religion: Presbyterian.
Political Career: Sought Democratic nomination for U.S. Senate, 1970; sought Democratic nomination for president, 1984.
Capitol Office: 503 Hart Bldg. 20510; 224-3353.

In Washington: Soldier, astronaut, businessman, senator, Glenn is an American icon. Even after his 1984 bid for the presidency had failed miserably, he issued what might be his motto: "You keep climbing." In a career directed ever upward, only in his quest for the nation's highest office has the first American to orbit Earth ever met certain defeat.

Just when Glenn seemed resigned to ending his political career as chairman of the Governmental Affairs Committee, along came Massachusetts Gov. Michael S. Dukakis to tease Glenn's desire to move up one more time. Appearing with Glenn in Ohio less than three weeks before the Democratic National Convention, nominee-presumptive Dukakis asked the crowd of United Auto Workers how they would like to see their favorite son on the ticket. The crowd cheered at the prospect of Glenn as vice president, and pundits began to speculate that Dukakis would try to build a November majority on a Massachusetts-Ohio cornerstone.

But instead, Dukakis turned to Lloyd Bentsen, whom he apparently perceived as a more interesting candidate and who he hoped could put Texas in the Democratic column for president. Ever the good sport, Glenn introduced Bentsen at the convention in what, ironically, was perhaps his best-ever national speech — one that generated more audience response than Bentsen's.

A centrist Democrat with a technocrat's temperament, Glenn is well suited to the nuts-and-bolts matters on the docket of Governmental Affairs. His passion for detail mixes well with the committee's mission to study the government's entrails. This wide jurisdiction has led previous chairmen of this committee to chase headlines by sticking their finger in every pie that passes.

Not Glenn. He is the polar opposite of the typically ambitious legislator; he has spent most of his career focusing on a handful of issues. Chief among these has been preventing the proliferation of nuclear weapons. Unquestionably, it is one of the most important issues of the day, but Glenn has at times pursued it to the exclusion of other matters, both foreign and domestic. Indeed, colleagues who admire Glenn's character and dedication wonder if he might have accomplished more had he not always been so narrowly focused.

To a great extent, Glenn's career has been restricted because that is the way his mind works. He is not a man who takes readily to new concepts, or easily shifts his tactics. Once he gets an idea into his head, he sticks to it tenaciously.

It is a style well suited to the most pressing item on Glenn's agenda in the 101st Congress: cleaning up the nation's nuclear-weapons plants, the cost of which could eventually rival the bailout of the savings and loan industry. Ohio has one of the Department of Energy's dirtiest facilities, a uranium fuel-processing plant near Cincinnati, and Glenn, who also is a member of the Armed Services Committee, is ideally posted to take on the task. He tried and failed to press tough DOE oversight legislation through the 100th Congress, and he seems likely to try again in the 101st. He is also the chief Senate advocate for a bigger cleanup budget.

But Glenn, the master of General Accounting Office detail, does not transfer well into macro politics. This was evident in his 1984 presidential campaign. Advertised for months as the main competitor to Walter F. Mondale for the Democratic nomination, he made weak showings in a succession of primaries and caucuses and quickly dropped out of the race. Poor at public speaking and unable to draw much audience attention, Glenn found himself portrayed increasingly often as the astronaut candidate — a strong image that nonetheless weakened his credibility.

Glenn has been no more exciting on the Senate floor than he was in his presidential campaign. His tendency to read speeches in full — even when no one is listening — can drive his colleagues off the floor.

He played a key role in the passage of legislation to create the Cabinet-level Department of Veterans Affairs. But he unsuccessfully advocated new agencies — created from components of the Commerce Department and the Office of the U.S. Trade Representative — to enhance U.S. competitiveness in trade and industrial policy.

He is no horse-trader. When he is seeking to muster support for an amendment, he merely explains the facts and hopes they will prove persuasive.

Glenn is the acknowledged expert in Congress on the nuclear non-proliferation issue. In 1976, he successfully pushed an amendment prohibiting U.S. aid to countries that exported or imported nuclear reprocessing equipment or materials — technology that can be diverted into nuclear weapons production. He is also the author of the 1978 nuclear non-proliferation act that bars nuclear exports unless the receiving nations agree not to use the material or technology to build nuclear weapons.

Glenn's anti-proliferation efforts brought him into frequent conflict with the Reagan administration. He sought to block foreign aid to nations not complying with international efforts to control the spread of nuclear weapons. In 1981, Glenn persuaded the Senate to approve a provision threatening to cut off aid to India or Pakistan if either detonated a nuclear device. "If we can't draw the line there, then we are incapable of ever drawing the line anywhere," he said.

Glenn kept up his efforts in 1984, winning initial Foreign Relations Committee approval of an amendment barring military aid to Pakistan unless the president certified it was not trying to develop nuclear weapons. Under heavy pressure from the administration, however, the committee later switched and approved a much less stringent substitute — spurring an uncharacteristic outburst from Glenn, who denounced it for "waffling, knuckling under and giving in" to the administration. In 1987, he accused Pakistan of "thumbing its nose" at the United States as he tried again to tie U.S. aid to a Pakistani promise not to develop nuclear weapons.

Glenn took on the administration's proposal to sell nuclear-power materials to China in 1985. Although the resolution approving the sale called for efforts to prevent the Chinese from transferring nuclear weapons technology to other countries, Glenn argued that more protections were needed. In 1988, he opposed a pact between the United States and Japan that waived certain rules for the sale of U.S. nuclear fuels to the Japanese.

At the start of the 99th Congress, Glenn opted to leave the Foreign Relations Committee, where he had spent his whole Senate career, for Armed Services. As chairman of the Manpower and Personnel Subcommittee in the 100th Congress, Glenn pushed the Pentagon to cut the officers corps, whose legions he thought grew too rapidly during the Reagan military buildup.

Over most of his career, Glenn has tilted to the hawkish side on national security matters. "No one has ever accused me of being soft on the Soviets," he says. But his support for the B-1 bomber and binary chemical weapons exaggerates his conservative tilt. His record is that of a centrist who does not hesitate to oppose weapons systems. In 1982, for example, Glenn offered a floor amendment to stop development of the MX missile. And he has reservations about the use of force abroad when it becomes, in his mind, overly adventurist — as in U.S. efforts to protect Kuwaiti tankers.

Glenn's love for detail played an even more important role in the debate over the SALT II treaty. He became the foremost Senate expert on "verification," the procedures for monitoring Soviet compliance with the treaty. While the Carter administration prepared to bring the treaty before the Senate, Glenn was holed up in the archives of the Intelligence Committee, studying the extreme complexities of the verification problem. After the fall of the Shah and the consequent loss of U.S. monitoring stations in Iran, Glenn decided that adequate verification was impossible, and the treaty unacceptable — a position that nearly drove the Carter White House to despair. With the onset of the Reagan administration, however, Glenn warmed to SALT II and to further arms control efforts.

At Home: Not long after he became a national hero as the first American to orbit the Earth, Glenn returned to Ohio to challenge 74-year-old Sen. Stephen M. Young in the 1964 Democratic primary. His space career had brought him into close contact with the Kennedys, and he was influenced by them to make his political career as a Democrat. But he did not get very far in 1964. A bathroom fall injured his inner ear, and he had to drop out.

Following that, Glenn's political energies subsided. Instead of attending party functions, he plunged into business. He served on the boards of Royal Crown Cola and the Questor Corp., oversaw four Holiday Inn franchises he partly owned, lectured and filmed television documentaries.

In 1970, with Young retiring, Glenn decided to run for the seat, competing for the Democratic nomination against Howard M. Metzenbaum, then a millionaire businessman and labor lawyer. Initially a strong favorite, Glenn found that his frequent absences from Ohio over the preceding six years had hurt him politically, giving him the image of an outsider among state Democrats. Metzenbaum had the support of the party establishment and a superb and well-financed campaign organization.

Metzenbaum erased his anonymity

through saturation television advertising. And Glenn, whose celebrity status was bringing out large crowds, was overly confident. On primary day, Glenn carried 75 of the state's 88 counties but was badly beaten in the urban areas. He lost the nomination by 13,442 votes. After this defeat, he did not repeat his previous mistake. He became a regular on the political circuit.

Metzenbaum himself was beaten in the general election by Republican Robert A. Taft Jr. Three years later, however, he made it to the Senate as an appointee, chosen by Democratic Gov. John J. Gilligan to fill a vacancy. Metzenbaum immediately began campaigning for a full term in his own right, and Glenn decided to challenge him for the nomination.

The Metzenbaum appointment outraged Glenn, and gave him an issue during their rematch in the 1974 primary. Glenn rejected Gilligan's offer to be his running mate as lieutenant governor and denounced the governor as a "boss" who practiced "machine politics."

The underdog Glenn of 1974 proved to be much tougher than the favored Glenn of 1970.

This time, he did much better in Metzenbaum's base of Cuyahoga County (Cleveland). Coupled with his customary strength in rural areas, this allowed him to achieve a 91,000-vote primary victory.

In the fall, Glenn crushed a weak Republican opponent, Cleveland Mayor Ralph J. Perk, who was disorganized and underfinanced. Six years later, he had only nominal opposition for a second term.

In 1986, Glenn drew a challenge from GOP Rep. Thomas N. Kindness, a better-financed and more aggressive opponent than the sacrificial lambs the GOP had previously offered. Kindness pounded away at what he saw as Glenn's main weakness — a lingering multimillion-dollar debt from his unsuccessful 1984 presidential campaign.

Glenn had worked hard to mend fences with Ohio voters in the wake of his failed White House bid, making dozens of appearances across the state in 1984 to boost both the Democratic ticket and his own political stock. But he was unable to erase the debt, which included $1.9 million worth of loans from four Ohio banks. (Glenn did not reach an agreement with the Federal Election Commission on paying off the debt until 1987.) Kindness maintained that Glenn received preferential treatment from the banks, which the average Ohioan would not get. But Kindness was unable to drive home the point. Not well-known outside his conservative southwest Ohio district, he lacked the money to mount a statewide media blitz that might have shaken Glenn's image.

Kindness lost in a landslide, although he did have the consolation of carrying nearly a dozen counties. None of Glenn's previous GOP challengers had carried more than one.

While much has been made of the Glenn-Metzenbaum rivalry over the years, there was no public indication of it during Metzenbaum's 1988 re-election campaign against Cleveland Mayor George Voinovich. Many expected Glenn — the state's most popular politician — to give his Senate colleague just token support, but the two were side by side when it counted.

Glenn piloted Metzenbaum around the state the day he formally announced he was seeking a third term. And late in the campaign, after Voinovich accused Metzenbaum of being soft on child pornography, Glenn appeared in a hard-hitting TV ad and accused the Republican of "the lowest gutter politics." While Metzenbaum was already on his way to victory, the Glenn ad was credited with cementing his success.

Committees

Governmental Affairs (Chairman)
Permanent Subcommittee on Investigations (vice chairman)

Armed Services (7th of 11 Democrats)
Manpower and Personnel (chairman); Conventional Forces and Alliance Defense; Strategic Forces and Nuclear Deterrence

Select Intelligence (8th of 8 Democrats)

Special Aging (2nd of 10 Democrats)

Elections

1986 General

John Glenn (D)	1,949,208	(62%)
Thomas N. Kindness (R)	1,171,893	(38%)

1986 Primary

John Glenn (D)	678,171	(88%)
Don Scott (D)	96,309	(12%)

Previous Winning Percentages: 1980 (69%) **1974** (65%)

Campaign Finance

	Receipts	Receipts from PACs	Expend-itures
1986			
Glenn (D)	$2,088,191	$637,186 (31%)	$1,319,026
Kindness (R)	$664,227	$172,648 (26%)	$657,908

Key Votes

1987

Enact omnibus highway bill over Reagan veto	Y
Limit testing of space-based anti-ballistic missiles	Y
Oppose banning tests of larger nuclear weapons	Y
Confirm Robert H. Bork as Supreme Court justice	N

1988

Allow vote on campaign-finance overhaul	Y
Pass civil rights restoration bill over Reagan veto	Y
Enact omnibus trade bill over Reagan veto	Y
Approve death penalty for drug-related murders	N
Oppose "workfare" amendment to welfare overhaul bill	Y

Voting Studies

	Presidential Support		Party Unity		Conservative Coalition	
Year	**S**	**O**	**S**	**O**	**S**	**O**
1988	53	45	86	11	27	73
1987	38	60	82	12	28	66
1986	42	52	74	23	29	70
1985	42	56	79	18	42	57
1984	39	43	55	25	28	51
1983	39	35	57	12	20	52
1982	35	45	67	17	26	51
1981	53	42	74	21	34	66

Interest Group Ratings

Year	ADA	ACU	AFL-CIO	CCUS
1988	80	9	79	31
1987	80	12	100	18
1986	65	30	87	44
1985	75	27	86	34
1984	65	5	67	38
1983	65	16	93	31
1982	70	28	87	55
1981	80	7	68	44

Howard M. Metzenbaum (D)

Of Lyndhurst — Elected 1976

Also served January-December 1974.

Born: June 4, 1917, Cleveland, Ohio.
Education: Ohio State U., B.A. 1939, LL.B. 1941.
Occupation: Lawyer; newspaper publisher; parking lot executive.
Family: Wife, Shirley Turoff; four children.
Religion: Jewish.
Political Career: Ohio House, 1943-47; Ohio Senate, 1947-51; Democratic nominee for U.S. Senate, 1974.
Capitol Office: 140 Russell Bldg. 20510; 224-2315.

In Washington: Metzenbaum has been called many things, and now add to that "lame duck." The term will not faze him any more than the others, nor — as the word implies — is it likely to inhibit his unique effectiveness before he leaves the Senate at the end of 1994.

Metzenbaum's indifference to the often debilitating lame-duck label was clear by his decision to announce his future retirement just as his third six-year term was beginning. The man with a reputation for yielding to no one was deferring to the wishes of his wife, Shirley; in getting Metzenbaum to leave the Senate, she was achieving what Republicans and a variety of special interests had long sought.

But Metzenbaum still has a few years before he bids good-bye, and in that time he will be at the peak of his powers. He is rarely cowed by political pressures, which is why observers were so startled when he set aside his career-long opposition to capital punishment and, in the midst of his 1988 campaign, voted for the death penalty for drug kingpins. Now, liberated from re-election concerns, he can legislate all but free of such pressures.

Most important, he remains as chairman of three subcommittees — one each on the Labor and Human Resources, Judiciary, and Energy and Natural Resources committees.

His productive debut as head of those subcommittees in the 100th Congress, when Democrats regained Senate control, dispelled initial questions about whether Metzenbaum had the necessary skills as a coalition-builder and bill-passer; in the previous decade, he had derived his powers from being the Senate's leading liberal obstructionist and bill-killer.

As Labor Subcommittee chairman, Metzenbaum had a lead role in battling for both a $1 billion worker retraining program and a law mandating advance notice to workers of plant closings, a top Democratic priority in 1988. On Judiciary, where he leads the Antitrust Subcommittee, Metzenbaum and ranking Republican Strom Thurmond enacted antitrust bills, a measure protecting workers' insurance benefits at bankrupt companies, a ban on plastic guns, and a bill, which Reagan vetoed, restricting lobbying by former executive branch officials and members of Congress. Spurred by the defense procurement scandal, Metzenbaum and Judiciary Republican Charles E. Grassley enacted the first penalties aimed at fraud by major contractors.

In legislating, Metzenbaum brings to the table a talent for reading his foes and extracting maximum concessions. "I was a good poker player in my private life," he said in 1987. "I try to put myself in the other person's position. Are they ready to slam down the gate or is it possible to go further?"

He also is more willing to compromise than many give him credit for. On his Labor Subcommittee in 1987, Metzenbaum picked up some industry support by making concessions on a labor-backed bill to require worker notification of job-related health risks. But he kept trying to entice his Republican colleagues, especially ranking member Dan Quayle. "I'm interested in getting to the point," said Metzenbaum, "where Sen. Quayle says, 'Put me on as a cosponsor.' " The subcommittee approved the bill by voice vote, but it died in a Republican filibuster on the floor.

Though his role has changed now that seniority has given Metzenbaum official leadership positions, he has not abandoned the confrontational, independent style that previously forced his influence upon the Senate. He remains the self-appointed scourge of "special interest" legislation on behalf of consumers and the Treasury, regardless of which party controls the Senate.

He defies Senate traditions of quiet, mutual back-scratching, publicly exposing the tax breaks and special provisions that colleagues bury deep within big bills, and opposing federal spending for some members' local projects that typically would get a rubber stamp of approval.

He is a master of Senate rules, and most effective at employing them at the end of each congressional session, when time is short and members are eager to leave town. Just his threat of a filibuster has killed many bills, but he has other tactics. Either Metzenbaum or a member of his staff (considered one of Capitol Hill's best) remains in the chamber, armed with a notebook listing bills he opposes so that nothing slips by unnoticed.

His role is all but institutionalized. Colleagues fret about whether their bills will meet "the Metzenbaum test." Leaders of both parties submit end-of-session legislation to him for a green light; former Democratic leader Robert C. Byrd's staff had a form to clear bills for floor action with checkoff boxes for Byrd, the appropriate committee chairmen — and Metzenbaum.

All this means Metzenbaum is hardly the Senate's most popular member. But like many self-made men, he has a skin grown thick over a long, successful life. Past 70 now, peer approval is not a big thing to him. "I'm not worried about my reputation as a gentleman in opposing legislation of this kind," he said in 1982, after filibustering a bill providing cheap federal water to large farms. "If I'm not the most popular guy in the Senate — well, I can live with that."

But not even Metzenbaum wants to see a Senate with 99 other members behaving as he does; that would be a formula for anarchy. Though he has used the rules to his ends, he says, "That does not mean I approve the procedures that allowed me to succeed." During the 1986 debate on televising the Senate, Metzenbaum spoke in favor of proposals to curb filibusters and other dilatory tactics.

This was the same man who brought the art of the filibuster to a new level back in 1977, his first full year in the Senate. Metzenbaum and South Dakota Democrat James Abourezk filibustered for two weeks against a bill to lift price controls on natural gas. When debate on the bill was formally cut off, the two resorted to a new technique: filibuster by amendment.

Armed with some 500 amendments, the two men sought roll-call votes on each one, sending the Senate into round-the-clock sessions. They might have succeeded, had Byrd not forced a cutoff with the parliamentary aid of Vice President Walter F. Mondale, who was presiding. The incident generated hard feelings all around — particularly toward Metzenbaum, who lacked Abourezk's joviality. But even critics were impressed. "I never saw a man come in here and become an ace filibusterer so fast," said Russell B. Long of Louisiana.

Metzenbaum's tactics were useful to Democrats for the six years after 1980, when Republicans controlled both the Senate and the White House. Generally Republicans accept Metzenbaum, having a few obstructionists of their own. However, his outspoken opposition to some of Reagan's nominees has engendered considerable hostility.

Largely due to Metzenbaum's objections, Senate confirmation of Edwin Meese III to be attorney general became a yearlong battle. His criticisms of Meese's receipt of financial assistance from people who later got government jobs helped force an independent investigation. Finally, after a special prosecutor concluded Meese had committed no crime, the Senate confirmed him in early 1985.

Metzenbaum not only failed to stop Meese, but also he drew unwanted attention to his own financial dealings. During this time, it was disclosed that Metzenbaum had received a $250,000 "finder's fee" for his role in the sale of a Washington hotel. He denied any impropriety, but returned the money.

In 1987, Metzenbaum was especially critical of Supreme Court nominee Robert H. Bork. During Judiciary's hearings, he angered the judge when he told Bork in a memorable exchange, "You're not a frightening man, but you're a man with frightening views.... To you, the Constitution is not a living document ... and if you can't find protection for the individual in the fine print, then the people of this country are out of luck."

Corporate tax advantages have long been among Metzenbaum's prime targets. During floor action on the 1986 tax-overhaul bill, he knocked out several dozen exemptions for favored interests that the Finance Committee had added; he even won praise from Republican Chairman Bob Packwood for wearing a "hair shirt" and taking on members' pet provisions. Though Metzenbaum could do little when the bill came back from conference with nearly 700 such provisions, he did force a public disclosure of the beneficiaries, embarrassing some colleagues who were the sponsors.

The oil and gas industry, in particular, gets Metzenbaum's attention. A proponent of the 1980 windfall-profits tax, he finally lost the fight against its repeal in the 100th Congress. "What is it about the oil companies that always makes us want to feel so sorry for them?" he asked in 1987. "They do not pay their taxes. They get away with an unfair advantage."

What success Metzenbaum has against the industry usually comes on the floor, not in the Energy Committee. There, he is one of just a few consumer- and environment-oriented members. In 1989, he threatened to repeat a past exploit and filibuster a gas-decontrol bill. But when Energy passed it, he put up scant resistance. "I couldn't pass an amendment in that committee if I stood on my head," he said.

At Home: An early and overwhelming success in business, Metzenbaum had to struggle through years of trial and failure in Ohio politics to reach the Senate. But the experience made him a wily, independent politician, adept at gut-level tactics, fund raising and quasi-populist oratory. These traits may not lend much to Senate comity, but they enabled the veteran Democrat to dismiss a well-funded Republican challenger in 1988.

Early on, national GOP officials made Metzenbaum a top priority; they saw Cleveland Mayor George Voinovich as a formidable nominee. Popular in the state's most Democratic territory, Voinovich also had solid business backing. His support was so strong that Rep. Bob McEwen, a conservative from southern Ohio, dropped a long-planned Senate bid.

While the GOP ballyhooed its strategy — Voinovich could win in Republican dominated southern and western Ohio and cut into the Democratic base in Cleveland's Cuyahoga County — Metzenbaum took control of the debate.

Brandishing the national GOP game plan, he convinced even those Democrats with reservations about his style that anyone with such determined Republican enemies must be worth re-electing. With the party united, he raised enough early money to ensure a campaign treasury sufficient for any need.

Metzenbaum also served warning that he would meet every challenge with a sledgehammer. When a national GOP document labeling him a communist sympathizer was leaked to the press in July 1987, Democrats (and some Republicans) took to the Senate floor within hours to defend Metzenbaum and condemn such campaign tactics. Voinovich's repudiation of the document was lost in the well-orchestrated fury.

That episode established the pace and intensity of the campaign. Voinovich sought to portray the Democrat as a cranky liberal gadfly, while Metzenbaum took care to behave in a senatorial fashion. As the Republican struggled to make himself known downstate, Metzenbaum championed his efforts to help the elderly and his leadership on the plant-closing notification bill. And while Voinovich ultimately raised almost as much money as Metzenbaum, the Democrat had enough cash on hand to run almost non-stop TV advertising from mid-summer through Election Day.

In late September, Voinovich ran tough TV ads portraying Metzenbaum as soft on child pornography. The Democrat countered with a testimonial TV ad by Sen. John Glenn condemning Voinovich's "gutter politics." Coming from the well-regarded Glenn — who twice clashed with Metzenbaum in bitter Senate primaries — the ad hit home. Editorialists characterized Voinovich's ad as a desperation tactic.

The flap effectively ended the Republican's campaign. Metzenbaum won Cuyahoga County by 2-to-1 and showed surprising strength downstate. He won a decisive 57 percent overall.

Even before Metzenbaum suggested he would not seek a fourth term, he was promoting his son-in-law, Joel Hyatt, as a future Democratic leader. The founder of Hyatt Legal Services, the younger man frequently appeared at campaign events with Metzenbaum and is said to harbor his own ambitions for elective office.

Glenn's role in Metzenbaum's win seemed to put an end to years of talk about the cool relationship between the two. They first clashed in the 1970 primary to succeed Democratic Sen. Stephen M. Young, who was retiring. At the time Glenn was a national hero and a household name, and Metzenbaum was an obscure figure even in much of Cleveland.

Metzenbaum had worked his way through college selling magazines and Fuller brushes, but soon struck it rich in the parking-lot business, winning franchises for the operation of parking lots at airports.

For a while, Metzenbaum pursued business and politics simultaneously. In 1942, the year after he graduated from law school, he bucked the Cuyahoga County Democratic organization and won a race for the state House. Later, he moved up to the state Senate. His major achievement in the Legislature came in 1949, when he won passage of a bill regulating consumer credit.

Metzenbaum left public office in 1951 to run his parking lots and practice law. His record as a labor lawyer was to help him build a political base in the 1970s.

Over the years, Metzenbaum served as a board member and financial angel for such groups as Karamu, a black cultural institution in Cleveland, and the National Council on Hunger and Malnutrition. He fought to integrate a number of exclusive Cleveland clubs.

Before he sought to go to Washington himself, Metzenbaum worked for other Democrats in Ohio and nationally. He was campaign manager for Young in his 1958 and 1964 Senate bids; he backed both John and Robert Kennedy for president; and supported George McGovern for the White House in 1972.

In the 1970 primary, the aggressive millionaire put Glenn on the defensive by arguing that money should be diverted from the space program to domestic concerns. Glenn had to play down his astronaut days. To counter Glenn's celebrity, Metzenbaum aired a barrage of TV ads presenting himself as an independent-minded businessman driven to run for office by the declining state of government.

Metzenbaum, with years of party work behind him, had the endorsement of most party leaders. He fielded a superior campaign organization and won the nomination by 13,442 votes.

That fall, Metzenbaum faced another famous name, Robert A. Taft Jr., son of Ohio's most dominant political figure of modern times. Taft won narrowly, taking a hard line against campus protesters and labeling the Democrat "an ultra-liberal."

Three years later, Metzenbaum suddenly found himself occupying the office he could not win in 1970. GOP Sen. William B. Saxbe resigned to become President Nixon's attorney general. Democratic Gov. John J. Gilligan, looking for support from organized labor, named Metzenbaum to the vacancy, giving him a full year in the Senate before Saxbe's term was set to expire.

But incumbency was no advantage in his 1974 rematch with Glenn. Metzenbaum's wealth backfired on him in ways he had managed to avoid in 1970. Under pressure from Glenn, he made public his tax returns — thus uncovering the politically damaging fact that he had paid no federal taxes in 1969. Metzenbaum also revealed that he had deposited $110,000 with the Internal Revenue Service to cover a back-tax claim, an action that did not imply any wrongdoing but was politically touchy in the Watergate climate.

So Metzenbaum had to run as a challenger again in 1976 to realize his ambitions for a full Senate term. With the aggressiveness he had displayed all his adult life, he plunged ahead with still another primary campaign. This time he had an advantage in money, name recognition and party support, and the wealth and tax issues were behind him. He easily took the nomination from Rep. James V. Stanton.

In the fall, Metzenbaum launched a new attack on Taft's effectiveness. He claimed he had accomplished more in one year in the Senate than Taft had in six, and focused on the energy issue, blaming much of America's economic problem on the oil companies. He campaigned in alliance with Jimmy Carter in 1976, taking advantage of Carter's spring and summer popularity in Ohio. By November, his winning margin was 117,000 votes — more than 10 times as great as Carter's margin in Ohio.

Metzenbaum's 1982 re-election campaign was never close. His comfortable position was one of the ironies of the staggered six-year Senate term. Had Metzenbaum succeeded in winning re-election in 1974, he might have been drowned in the Reagan tide of 1980. But the decline in the auto and steel industries severely affected Ohio, creating a favorable forum in 1982 for Metzenbaum's feisty brand of economic populism.

The sudden death in April of the front-running GOP challenger, Rep. John M. Ashbrook, was a shock to Republicans. The controversial conservative was in an uphill fight against Metzenbaum, but he was well-known and reasonably well financed. When party leaders were unable to coax a big-name figure into mounting a late challenge, they coalesced behind one of the remaining candidates on the primary ballot, state Sen. Paul E. Pfeifer.

Pfeifer was viewed as more of a mainstream Republican than Ashbrook, but he lacked name identification and money. Metzenbaum, with a large campaign treasury and an assist from Ohio's beleaguered economy, could afford to ignore his rival. Overwhelming Pfeifer in the industrial centers of northern Ohio, he coasted to victory with 57 percent of the vote.

Committees

Energy and Natural Resources (4th of 10 Democrats)
Energy Regulation and Conservation (chairman); Energy Research and Development; Water and Power

Judiciary (3rd of 8 Democrats)
Antitrust, Monopolies and Business Rights (chairman); Constitution; Courts and Administrative Practice

Labor and Human Resources (3rd of 9 Democrats)
Labor (chairman); Aging; Education, Arts and Humanities; Handicapped

Select Intelligence (7th of 8 Democrats)

Elections

1988 General		
Howard M. Metzenbaum (D)	2,480,038	(57%)
George Voinovich (R)	1,872,716	(43%)
1988 Primary		
Howard M. Metzenbaum (D)	1,070,934	(84%)
Ralph A. Applegate (D)	210,508	(16%)

Previous Winning Percentages: **1982** (57%) **1976** (50%)

Campaign Finance

	Receipts	Receipts from PACs	Expend-itures
1988			
Metzenbaum (D)	$7,312,533	$1,028,183 (14%)	$8,547,545
Voinovich (R)	$7,828,764	$1,326,627 (17%)	$8,236,432

Key Votes

1987	
Enact omnibus highway bill over Reagan veto	Y
Limit testing of space-based anti-ballistic missiles	Y
Oppose banning tests of larger nuclear weapons	N
Confirm Robert H. Bork as Supreme Court justice	N
1988	
Allow vote on campaign-finance overhaul	Y
Pass civil rights restoration bill over Reagan veto	Y
Enact omnibus trade bill over Reagan veto	Y
Approve death penalty for drug-related murders	Y
Oppose "workfare" amendment to welfare overhaul bill	Y

Voting Studies

	Presidential Support		Party Unity		Conservative Coalition	
Year	S	O	S	O	S	O
1988	36	55	87	6	24	68
1987	32	65	88	9	3	91
1986	24	76	86	13	5	93
1985	26	72	87	10	17	83
1984	26	69	79	16	4	91
1983	36	60	80	19	11	86
1982	32	64	88	5	4	85
1981	30	59	82	5	7	81

Interest Group Ratings

Year	ADA	ACU	AFL-CIO	CCUS
1988	80	4	100	15
1987	100	4	100	22
1986	100	4	93	21
1985	100	0	100	29
1984	100	5	91	22
1983	100	12	100	11
1982	100	28	92	11
1981	85	0	94	7

1 Thomas A. Luken (D)

Of Cincinnati — Elected 1976

Also served March 1974-January 1975.

Born: July 9, 1925, Cincinnati, Ohio.

Education: Attended Bowling Green State U., 1943-44; Xavier U., A.B. 1947; Chase Law School, LL.B. 1950.

Military Career: Marine Corps, 1943-45.

Occupation: Lawyer.

Family: Wife, Shirley Ast; eight children.

Religion: Roman Catholic.

Political Career: Cincinnati City Council, 1965-67, 1969-71, 1973; mayor of Cincinnati, 1971-72; elected to U.S. House in special election, March 1974; defeated for re-election, 1974.

Capitol Office: 2368 Rayburn Bldg. 20515; 225-2216.

In Washington: Early in his House career, Luken was known as a reformist and labor ally. But a few terms on Energy and Commerce changed his reputation to that of a loyal supporter of committee Chairman John D. Dingell of Michigan — a relationship that often put Luken at odds with his former allies.

When he became chairman of the Subcommittee on Transportation, Tourism and Hazardous Materials in 1987, Luken got a hefty slice of legislative authority and another chance to define himself. The early going suggests that the old activist is now quite comfortable working with industry, and that for a veteran House member, Luken faces an unusual amount of criticism for lacking legislative focus and political savvy.

During the 100th Congress, colleagues from both parties grumbled that Luken's subcommittee needed clearer direction and a better-defined agenda, noting that the panel sometimes held hearings without adequate advance preparation. Some of the blame is directed at Luken's committee staff, but at the start of the 101st Congress, gripes about shoddy staff work were eclipsed by complaints about shabby employee relations.

A former subcommittee counsel so resented Luken that he admonished him in a letter to Dingell, complaining that the Ohioan was prone to "personal tirades and temper tantrums," and that "anything can trigger his screaming sessions." He later added that Luken had "very little grasp of the issues." The story created a stir, prompting reports suggesting that Luken suffered from an unusually rapid staff turnover.

Luken denied the charges, though he acknowledged occasionally losing his temper. "Sure I yell. I'm a yeller sometimes," he told The Associated Press. "Do I yell regularly? No."

Whatever the cause, it took Luken some time to grasp the political impact of the most visible issue that came before his panel in the 100th Congress: drug testing for rail workers. Though adamantly opposed by Dingell and organized labor, the issue gathered steam after the engineer responsible for a 1987 train accident admitted having smoked marijuana shortly before the wreck, in which 16 people died.

Luken's subcommittee had jurisdiction over drug-testing legislation for rail workers, and he initially seemed to ignore mounting public pressure to require random testing.

The father of a victim in the 1987 wreck then paid a personal visit to Luken's district to blast him for what he viewed as the Democrat's intransigence on random testing. He appeared with Luken's 1988 Republican opponent, and got headlines and editorial support in Cincinnati's two leading newspapers urging Luken to push for tough testing requirements.

Shortly thereafter, Luken unveiled a proposal for random testing of rail workers, saying that he had not had a chance to focus on the matter earlier. He eventually became a leading champion of the issue, and succeeded in pushing his bill through the House late in 1988. In the end, however, supporters could not get it attached to the drug bill or other legislation scheduled for floor action in the closing weeks, and the bill died. Luken reintroduced a similar bill at the start of the 101st Congress.

Late in the 100th Congress, Luken was handed another issue when evidence emerged that the government's uranium fuel-processing plant at Fernald in his district had rained some 300,000 pounds of uranium dust over neighboring homes and farms during its 35 years of operation. This time, he ran with the issue, getting considerable media coverage for chairing investigative hearings and advocating legislation to improve regulation of government waste disposal.

Ohio 1

Hamilton County — Western Cincinnati and Suburbs

Nestled snugly in the southwestern corner of the state, the 1st stretches westward from the skyscrapers of downtown Cincinnati to the rolling farm land along the Indiana border.

GOP domination in the suburbs north and west of the city made the district a faithful Republican bastion during the 1970s. But the black population within Cincinnati has helped Luken build a majority here.

The western half of Cincinnati casts nearly 40 percent of the district's vote. Most of the other voters live in middle-class suburbs nearby.

Democrats can count on about 95 percent support from a few solidly black wards in Cincinnati, but the dominant political bloc is the German Catholic group that has defined the city's cautious, conservative personality for more than 100 years.

Once clustered in the West Side section of the city known as "Over-the-Rhine," the German-Americans gradually moved to suburbs like Cheviot and Green Township.

As a Catholic Democrat with a fairly conservative voting record, Luken has been able to retain the support of this crucial bloc in recent congressional races. But in state and national contests, the German Catholics often join with the area's sizable number of Appalachian whites — drawn from the rural hills to work in Cincinnati's industries — in voting Republican.

Cincinnati's diverse economy prevented it from suffering the degree of hardship that hit other industrial cities in the state in the early 1980s' recession. A major Ohio River port and a regional center of commerce, the city is headquarters for the giant Procter & Gamble Co. and Cincinnati Milacron, a world leader in the production of machine tools.

The 1980s defense buildup boosted the revenues of numerous area defense contractors, the largest being General Electric Co. Like several other major Cincinnati employers, G.E. is located in the 2nd District, but it provides jobs for blue-collar workers in the western section of the city.

Population: 514,190. White 426,908 (83%), Black 82,897 (16%), Other 3,133 (1%). Spanish origin 3,106 (1%). 18 and over 364,014 (71%), 65 and over 57,362 (11%). Median age: 29.

No legislation came of the hearings, but at the start of the 101st Congress, Luken took up a related matter when he announced his intention to push for a comprehensive reauthorization of major hazardous waste disposal legislation, the Resource Conservation and Recovery Act (RCRA).

Luken's consumer advocacy is still evident in his initiatives on a variety of matters: He has sponsored legislation aimed at combating scams against consumers who buy products over the phone; requiring manufacturers of products containing asbestos to notify the government; and permitting those who are harmed as a result of smoking to sue the cigarette manufacturers.

However, on clean-air legislation, one of the most complex and important matters to come before the Energy and Commerce Committee in recent years, Luken has consistently sided with industry.

Power plants in the Ohio Valley produce large amounts of sulfur dioxide, which environmentalists blame for causing acid rain that damages fish and forests hundreds of miles to the east. Fearing the economic impact of restricting those emissions, Luken works to prevent acid rain legislation from making its way out of committee. This has put him at odds with some Democrats, but in league with Dingell, who has similar concerns about the impact on auto workers in his district.

Luken was most visible in the debate during the 97th Congress, when he sponsored a business-backed proposal for revising and loosening the Clean Air Act. The bill would have delayed deadlines for meeting clean-air standards, required no controls on acid rain or toxic pollutants, and doubled allowable auto emissions. This last provision was the basis of his alliance with Dingell.

Luken's measure sparked acrimonious debate, drawing support from a bloc of Republicans and Southern Democrats. Though it got through subcommittee, the bill met with harsh criticism in full committee, and after environmentalists won a few crucial test votes, Dingell adjourned for the year. That move killed any chance for industry relief that year, and set up a stalemate that continued into the 100th Congress.

In early 1987, when Energy and Commerce reorganized its subcommittees and the Ohioan was in line for a chairmanship, it appeared that Dingell was rewarding Luken's loyalty by trying to give him a new panel with jurisdiction over trade issues. Dingell strongly denied that he created the choice slot for Luken, and New Jersey Rep. James J. Florio surprised his colleagues when he switched over to take the new panel, leaving the Transportation Subcommittee for Luken.

In recent years, Luken has emerged as a close ally of professional groups worried that changes in federal law would cause them economic harm. He worked with trial lawyers in 1978 against no-fault auto insurance legislation. In 1982, working with the American Medical Association, he led the House fight to exempt professional groups — including doctors — from regulation by the Federal Trade Commission (FTC).

Sounding like a free-market Republican, Luken said, "I don't want the FTC to practice its brand of quackery in regulating these professions." His amendment passed the House, but the Senate would not go along.

The Cincinnati Democrat hews to a conservative line on most social policy issues. He has strongly opposed abortion, and aggressively supported tax credits for private school tuition, both sensitive issues in his district.

At Home: To win this district in 1976, Luken traded in the liberal stripes he had earned in local politics for a more moderate image. His transformation chagrined liberals, but it has been a formula for success in this Republican-leaning district. Luken's background as a civil rights activist helps him retain the loyalty of blacks in Cincinnati, while his conservative economic message and anti-abortion stance play well among Republicans in the Hamilton County portion of the 1st and among conservative German Catholics in the city.

Luken first won a House seat in a special election in Cincinnati's other congressional district in 1974. A reform-minded mayor and city councilman who had marched for civil rights in Alabama in 1965, Luken said his victory was a "a signal to Washington" about middle America's attitude toward the Nixon administration. Playing the role of messenger, Luken attracted help from labor and national liberal groups against Republican Bill Gradison.

Eight months later, running against Gradison again, Luken discovered his survival was no longer that important to many who helped him in March. He was one of four Democratic incumbents in the country who lost in 1974.

Determined to come back, Luken promptly moved into the 2nd District just to the west. The incumbent there in 1976 was Republican Donald D. Clancy. Two years earlier, an unknown Democrat named Edward Wolterman had nearly defeated him in a campaign that criticized Clancy's travels and prolonged absences from the district. Luken shed what was left of his liberal image, and used the same issues against the incumbent. Clancy outspent him, but the Democrat's strength in the urban portion of the district was enough to restore him to office by fewer than 5,000 votes.

Luken had a difficult time in 1978, when he was again outspent, and he was attacked for his shifting political stance. But the Republicans had a divisive primary, and Luken again won by a slim margin. In 1980, for the first time in five elections, he won easily, with 65 percent in Cincinnati and 56 percent in the suburbs.

Republicans caused Luken a few moments of concern in 1982 by placing Hamilton County Recorder John "Jake" Held on the ballot, substituting him for a little-known building superintendent who had won the GOP primary. A colorful, wisecracking politician, Held had been dubbed by some as the "clown prince of Cincinnati politics." But he had never lost an election for office in Hamilton County.

A July 1982 article on Luken in *The Wall Street Journal* appeared to provide grist for Held's campaign. The story reported that Luken received nearly $275,000 from political action committees in his 1980 and 1982 campaigns while fighting for the auto industry and the American Medical Association in some of their key congressional battles.

Luken denied his vote was for sale, and the article had little impact. With a well-financed campaign that Held was unable to match, Luken swept to re-election with his largest-ever majority.

Things were only a little tougher for Luken in 1984, despite more unfavorable publicity. Citing Luken's ties to business interests and alleged cruelty to his staff, *Washington Monthly* named him one of the "10 worst" members of Congress shortly before the general election. The article was front-page news in Cincinnati.

But Luken's Republican opponent, Hamilton County Commissioner Norman A. Murdock, could do little to exploit the opening. The winner of a hard-fought primary over a black city councilman, Murdock was a longtime GOP stalwart with limited appeal outside party ranks. Overriding a strong Reagan vote in the district, Luken won easily.

After being forced to advertise for a candidate in 1986, the Republican party had an eager challenger in 1988: three-term Cincinnati City Councilman Steve Chabot. He ran a door-to-door campaign, hoping to hold a share of the vote in Democratic-leaning Cincinnati and stir enthusiastic support among Republicans in western Hamilton County.

Luken took Chabot's challenge seriously. Outspending his opponent by more than 3-to-1, he ran TV ads featuring voters saying that although they were Republicans, they were also longtime Luken loyalists. The incumbent's political position in the city was also strengthened thanks to the popularity of his son, Mayor Charlie Luken.

In spite of these advantages, Luken appeared to be hurt by Chabot's shoe-leather campaign and by a TV ad that featured a marionette of Luken controlled by political action committee strings.

But Chabot was stopped cold in October when it was disclosed that a Department of Energy uranium fuel-processing facility in Fernald — in the Hamilton County portion of the 1st — was releasing radioactive and chemically toxic waste. Publicity from a congressional inquiry that revealed the government was aware of the danger and took no action gave Luken all the help he needed to wrap up a respectable win.

Committees

Energy and Commerce (7th of 26 Democrats)
Transportation and Hazardous Materials (chairman); Commerce, Consumer Protection and Competitiveness

Select Aging (8th of 39 Democrats)
Health and Long-Term Care

Small Business (3rd of 27 Democrats)
Antitrust, Impact of Deregulation and Privatization

Elections

1988 General		
Thomas A. Luken (D)	117,682	(56%)
Steve Chabot (R)	90,738	(44%)
1986 General		
Thomas A. Luken (D)	90,477	(62%)
Fred E. Morr (R)	56,100	(38%)

Previous Winning Percentages: 1984 (55%) **1982** (64%) **1980** (59%) **1978** (52%) **1976** (51%) **1974** * (52%)

* *Special election.*

District Vote For President

	1988	1984	1980	1976
D	76,661 (37%)	79,193 (35%)	72,697 (36%)	74,367 (38%)
R	131,747 (63%)	146,217 (65%)	116,565 (58%)	115,736 (60%)
I			9,583 (5%)	

Campaign Finance

	Receipts	Receipts from PACs	Expend-itures
1988			
Luken (D)	$774,952	$468,685 (60%)	$908,765
Chabot (R)	$262,325	$38,913 (15%)	$262,162
1986			
Luken (D)	$392,054	$203,261 (52%)	$261,455
Morr (R)	$130,117	$1,585 (1%)	$127,653

Key Votes

1987	
Raise speed limit to 65 mph	N
Approve Gephardt "fair trade" amendment	Y
Ban testing of larger nuclear weapons	Y
Delay "re-flagging" of Kuwaiti tankers	?
Approve tax-raising deficit-reduction bill	N
1988	
Approve aid to Nicaraguan contras	N
Enact civil rights restoration bill over Reagan veto	Y
Kill 60-day plant-closing notification measure	N
Pass omnibus trade bill over Reagan veto	Y
Approve death penalty for drug-related murders	X
Bar federal funds for abortions in cases of rape and incest	Y
Oppose seven-day waiting period for purchase of handguns	N

Voting Studies

	Presidential Support		Party Unity		Conservative Coalition	
Year	**S**	**O**	**S**	**O**	**S**	**O**
1988	32	63	76	21	58	32
1987	29	66	79	11	47	47
1986	21	77	84	9	34	50
1985	33	58	74	17	24	60
1984	35	58	74	21	37	58
1983	29	68	82	12	27	67
1982	34	58	77	14	36	56
1981	55	42	58	33	64	29

Interest Group Ratings

Year	ADA	ACU	AFL-CIO	CCUS
1988	70	14	100	46
1987	56	14	75	29
1986	80	19	86	25
1985	65	32	71	41
1984	65	25	54	31
1983	80	13	94	39
1982	65	25	83	40
1981	40	43	73	32

2 Bill Gradison (R)

Of Cincinnati — Elected 1974

Born: Dec. 28, 1928, Cincinnati, Ohio.
Education: Yale U., B.A. 1948; Harvard U., M.B.A. 1951, D.C.S. 1954.
Occupation: Investment broker.
Family: Wife, Heather Jane Stirton; eight children.
Religion: Jewish.
Political Career: Cincinnati City Council, 1961-74; mayor of Cincinnati, 1971.
Capitol Office: 2311 Rayburn Bldg. 20515; 225-3164.

In Washington: Gradison is better known for his intellect than for his horse-trading skills, but he is the kind of problem-solving pragmatist who would rather make a deal than a speech.

One of his party's most thoughtful legislators, Gradison wants not only to bring some intellectual coherence to conservative economic ideas, but also to put them into action. In the process of trying to do that, he has earned respect that translates into significant influence over tax, budget and health policy.

At the beginning of the 101st Congress, House GOP leaders ratified Gradison's stature on economic matters by naming him the leadership's representative to the Budget Committee, the party's No. 2 post on the panel.

Around the same time, President Bush, a Yale classmate of Gradison, considered naming him to the post of health and human services secretary. But Gradison is probably too liberal and insufficiently orthodox in his opposition to abortion to be acceptable to the party's right wing.

While he never got the nod for the Bush Cabinet, Gradison remains one of the House's most influential Republicans on health policy, as ranking minority member of the Ways and Means Subcommittee on Health.

On Ways and Means, Gradison is among the Republicans most likely to work with committee Democrats. He enjoys a good relationship with Chairman Dan Rostenkowski of Illinois, a fellow Midwesterner who, like Gradison, has the taste for getting the job done that is the hallmark of urban machine politics.

More surprising is Gradison's close relationship with liberal California Democrat Pete Stark, chairman of Ways and Means' Health Subcommittee.

The two teamed up in the 100th Congress to draft the catastrophic health insurance program for Medicare beneficiaries — one of the few social-welfare expansions of the Reagan years. Their plan provided more coverage than an administration proposal and differed in its financing. The administration favored increasing premiums paid by all beneficiaries, while the Stark-Gradison plan set up a two-tiered financing system that hits harder at wealthy beneficiaries and protects the 65 percent of the elderly who do not pay income taxes because their incomes are too low.

While he shared the credit for the law, Gradison also had to share the heat of the political backfire when the elderly began complaining about the higher premiums they had to pay for the new benefit.

"This is an honest disagreement about whether the benefits are worth the cost," said Gradison.

In other health-related matters, Gradison has been a key advocate of federal support for hospice services for dying patients. In 1982 he and California Democrat Leon E. Panetta sponsored a successful bill that made such services eligible for Medicare reimbursement, and in 1984 he won a rate increase for hospice services.

As budget-cutting pressures intensified through the Reagan era, Gradison shared Stark's distaste for repeatedly taking cuts from Medicare and allowing fiscal exigencies to dictate health policy. "We gave at the office," he said when the White House came back for more Medicare economies in early 1988.

Gradison has also been one of Ways and Means' most influential Republicans on tax policy. When the committee overhauled the Internal Revenue Code in the 99th Congress, Gradison was as committed as anyone to the idea of tax reform. He neither denounced the Democrats' control of the tax bill nor scrambled behind the scenes for breaks for parochial interests, as many of his colleagues did. Instead, he stuck to broad concepts, arguing that it was a rare opportunity for a major overhaul, even if most voters were not very interested in the issue.

Gradison decided that in order to make productive changes, it would be necessary to challenge some traditional GOP bastions of support, and he was willing to do so. He endorsed repeal of investment tax credits, for instance, despite their allure for heavy indus-

Ohio 2

Hamilton County — Eastern Cincinnati and Suburbs

The 2nd is a district of political extremes. It includes the most Democratic part of Cincinnati and the most Republican suburbs around it. With the bulk of the voters outside the city, Republican candidates usually win.

The eastern half of Cincinnati houses about one-third of the district's residents. Blacks make up about a third of the total population of Cincinnati, and most live in Avondale and Walnut Hill, within the boundaries of the 2nd.

At the bottom of Walnut Hill, in the flat Ohio River basin, is downtown Cincinnati. The wharves for old stern-wheelers like the *Delta Queen*, the headquarters of Procter & Gamble, and the Taft Museum are mainstays. But the area has undergone a face-lift. Construction of Riverfront Stadium and Coliseum symbolized a downtown renewal project designed to lure suburban dollars back to the city.

Cincinnati's wealthy Republican establishment — including the Taft family — has exercised a great deal of influence over the years. But that influence is now concentrated more in the suburbs than in the city. Unlike suburban Cleveland, suburban Cincinnati is solidly in Republican hands.

The Cincinnati area lacks the heavy industry of the urban centers of northeastern Ohio. But manufacturing plants dot the Mill Creek Valley, which extends north from downtown into the suburbs. While the valley weaves back and forth between the 1st and 2nd districts, the 2nd includes a large Procter & Gamble plant at St. Bernard and a General Electric plant at Evendale, which specializes in aircraft engine production.

In the last redistricting, the 2nd moved eastward, beyond the Cincinnati suburbs and into the rural Ohio River Valley. More than 140,000 of Gradison's constituents are now in fast-growing Clermont County, which grew 35 percent in the 1970s, and another 9 percent in the 1980s. As Clermont moves closer to the Cincinnati metropolitan orbit, it is increasingly Republican.

Population: 514,168. White 425,752 (83%), Black 84,316 (16%), Other 2,972 (1%). Spanish origin 3,092 (1%). 18 and over 370,100 (72%), 65 and over 59,533 (12%). Median age: 30.

tries, including many in Ohio.

In previous Congresses, Gradison's major effort at Ways and Means was for indexing the federal tax system — gradually adjusting tax rates to inflation so that people would not be forced into higher brackets. He won a stunning victory when indexing was included in the Republican substitute to the 1981 tax bill, which the House approved. The administration initially wanted to leave indexing out of the bill; Gradison was largely responsible for persuading them to put it back.

In 1983, with key Democrats seeking to repeal the indexing provisions in order to increase long-term revenues, Gradison won a seat on the Budget Committee to defend the concept. It survived, and the principle, by now firmly entrenched, was included in the 1986 tax code overhaul bill.

On economic policy, Gradison differs sharply from the supply-side theories that came into vogue with the advent of the Reagan administration. He has argued that it is necessary to hold the line on spending and even raise taxes to keep the deficit in line. This set up a confrontation with the most enthusiastic of the supply-siders in Congress, New York's Jack F. Kemp. In 1985, Gradison took on Kemp, then the second-ranking Republican on the Budget panel, in a public exchange of letters that pointed up deep divisions within the ranks of Republicans. Gradison derided Kemp's suggestion that tax cuts could let the economy grow its way out of deficits without making painful budget cuts.

Early in the 100th Congress, Gradison struck out in a different direction from other Budget Committee Republicans, agreeing with Democratic leaders that it was probably necessary to revise upward the $108 billion deficit target set for fiscal 1988 by the Gramm-Rudman-Hollings deficit-reduction law. He said the only ways to reach the $108 billion target might be to make major cuts in defense spending or generate a recession. Gradison had been an important player in the 1985 House-Senate conference that hammered together the Gramm-Rudman concept of annual deficit ceilings. But his 1987 assessment was not particularly popular with most of his GOP colleagues on the Budget Committee, who wanted to be able to charge Democrats with willful failure to meet the target.

A few months later, Gradison joined other Republicans on the Budget Committee in refusing to participate with Democrats in the panel's budget markup sessions. The GOP bloc insisted the Democrats were operating with faulty economic assumptions and were not providing specific enough information about how much they wanted to spend in individual categories.

Gradison has complained about rosy economic assumptions in the past, and he has turned out to be right. In 1986, the deficit turned out to be almost $50 billion higher than the projected $172 billion because of slower growth.

In another effort to make congressional budget-drafting a more accurate reflection of economic reality, Gradison has long championed the idea of revamping the way credit programs are handled in the federal budget, in order to convey more accurately the cost of the subsidies involved.

He also urged the Bush administration, unsuccessfully, not to try to obscure the cost of its bailout of the savings and loan industry by putting it off budget.

On Social Security, another crucial Ways and Means issue, Gradison was an early and vocal critic of interfund borrowing, the practice of financing the system by transferring money from other trust funds. He withheld his signature from a conference report on a Social Security bill in 1981 until the conferees agreed to put a one-year deadline on interfund borrowing. In 1983 he opposed the Social Security rescue plan in subcommittee because of an interfund borrowing provision, but voted for the plan in full committee, and on the House floor.

Gradison has generally supported a free-trade position. He reluctantly voted for the omnibus trade bill that emerged from Ways and Means in 1987, but when it was amended to include strict limits on imports into the United States, he ended up opposing it on the House floor.

Beyond the economic realm, Gradison has generally taken a moderate stand on social issues. This may have hurt him in 1979, when he tried to become chairman of the Republican Research Committee, a middle-level leadership position. He split the "moderate" vote with Pennsylvania's Lawrence Coughlin, allowing conservative Trent Lott of Mississippi to win easily and position himself to become party whip two years later. In the 100th Congress, Gradison was named chairman of the House Wednesday Group, a caucus of moderate Republicans.

Gradison is one of several GOP members of Congress whose wives received appointments in the Reagan administration. Heather Gradison, a former railway company employee, became a commissioner on the Interstate Commerce Commission in 1982, and later was named its chairman.

At Home: Staying in Congress has been rather easy for Gradison. But getting there was complicated.

A member of Cincinnati's City Council for 14 years and a close friend of the Taft family, Gradison first ran for the House in a 1974 special election. As an investment broker, he had been actively involved in the redevelopment of downtown Cincinnati, and he ran a moderate, urban-oriented campaign, trying to keep his distance from the beleaguered Nixon administration. But Watergate was the central issue, and it resulted in a 4,000-vote victory for Gradison's Democratic colleague from the City Council, Thomas A. Luken.

The two men opposed each other again in the general election that fall. By then President Nixon was out of office, and Gradison had worked to win back some of the votes he had lost earlier for refusing to support a constitutional ban on abortion. A larger Republican turnout and a switch of independents back to the GOP side resulted in a 2,600-vote victory for Gradison.

Two years later Luken recognized Gradison's popularity and decided to run in the other Cincinnati-based district, rather than compete with him a third time. Since then, Gradison has not had even a hint of trouble.

Committees

Budget (2nd of 14 Republicans)

Ways and Means (6th of 13 Republicans)
Health (ranking); Social Security

Elections

1988 General		
Bill Gradison (R)	153,162	(72%)
Chuck R. Stidham (D)	58,637	(28%)
1986 General		
Bill Gradison (R)	105,061	(71%)
William F. Stineman (D)	43,448	(29%)

Previous Winning Percentages: **1984** (69%) **1982** (63%) **1980** (75%) **1978** (65%) **1976** (65%) **1974** (51%)

District Vote For President

	1988	1984	1980	1976
D	83,471 (37%)	75,603 (35%)	67,068 (36%)	99,150 (40%)
R	138,729 (62%)	141,544 (65%)	108,486 (58%)	108,668 (58%)
I			8,790 (5%)	

Campaign Finance

	Receipts	Receipts from PACs	Expend-itures
1988			
Gradison (R)	$197,743	0	$125,682
Stidham (D) †	$13,962	$9,700 (69%)	$13,961
1986			
Gradison (R)	$197,857	0	$68,473

† Totals based on incomplete data.

Key Votes

1987	
Raise speed limit to 65 mph	Y
Approve Gephardt "fair trade" amendment	N
Ban testing of larger nuclear weapons	N
Delay "re-flagging" of Kuwaiti tankers	N
Approve tax-raising deficit-reduction bill	N
1988	
Approve aid to Nicaraguan contras	Y
Enact civil rights restoration bill over Reagan veto	Y
Kill 60-day plant-closing notification measure	Y
Pass omnibus trade bill over Reagan veto	N
Approve death penalty for drug-related murders	Y
Bar federal funds for abortions in cases of rape and incest	Y
Oppose seven-day waiting period for purchase of handguns	N

Voting Studies

	Presidential Support		Party Unity		Conservative Coalition	
Year	**S**	**O**	**S**	**O**	**S**	**O**
1988	61	34	62	33	66	24
1987	63	32	65	29	77	14
1986	61	34	59	38	60	34
1985	65	30	63	31	75	22
1984	65	32	68	30	69	31
1983	72	27	72	23	73	26
1982	75	22	76	20	81	18
1981	68	29	67	27	64	33

Interest Group Ratings

Year	ADA	ACU	AFL-CIO	CCUS
1988	35	62	21	83
1987	20	65	6	100
1986	15	59	7	94
1985	20	60	8	85
1984	35	48	0	71
1983	30	74	6	90
1982	20	73	15	73
1981	35	80	7	89

3 Tony P. Hall (D)

Of Dayton — Elected 1978

Born: Jan. 16, 1942, Dayton, Ohio.
Education: Denison U., A.B. 1964.
Occupation: Real-estate salesman.
Family: Wife, Janet Dick; two children.
Religion: Christian.
Political Career: Ohio House, 1969-73; Ohio Senate, 1973-79; Democratic nominee for Ohio secretary of state, 1974.
Capitol Office: 2448 Rayburn Bldg. 20515; 225-6465.

In Washington: A decade in Congress has done little to dampen the sincerity and enthusiasm that Hall brings to his personal crusades against hunger and for human rights. Once a college football star and later a Peace Corps volunteer, he is a dedicated legislator whose agenda flows from his own deeply held religious beliefs.

Hall has earned respect for his pursuit of issues that otherwise might get lost in the legislative shuffle, but he is a very unlikely member of the Rules Committee. He won a seat there in his second term, though Hall has never been inclined toward the stratagems and backroom maneuvering that characterizes most of the committee's work. If he is the least active member of Rules, however, he is well liked by committee colleagues, and generally regarded as a team player by his fellow Democrats.

Hall comes alive on Rules primarily on issues affecting his district, on hunger, and — in the 100th Congress — on the "dial-a-porn" debate. The Senate attached language to the 1988 omnibus education bill to ban the sexually explicit services, but conferees, citing constitutional questions, scaled back the ban and restricted access instead. When the bill arrived at the House Rules Committee, however, Hall was one of two Democrats to buck the leadership and block consideration until a floor vote on an outright ban was secured.

Playing the high-profile obstructionist was an unusual role for Hall, who devotes more time and energy to his work on the Select Committee on Hunger, a panel he helped create. There Hall delves with equal vigor into the problems of mass famine abroad and food shortages at home, and he has demonstrated skill at drawing attention to his concerns. Earlier in his career, he and other House members organized a media-savvy gourmet luncheon serving only food that had been culled from Capitol Hill trash cans.

Consistent with this effort is Hall's promotion of gleaning programs, which gather the produce left behind after commercial harvests. In 1987, Hall helped initiate a gleaning program in his Dayton district that delivered almost 21 tons of fresh fruit and vegetables to area food banks in its first year. The following year, he successfully advocated language in the hunger-prevention bill to require the federal government to offer assistance to local agencies trying to establish similar programs.

Hall uses his role as chairman of the committee's international task force to draw attention to international hunger and to prod federal development assistance. In the 100th Congress, he traveled to Bangladesh to observe disaster-relief programs, and in the 99th Congress, Hall took part in the first congressional visit to Ethiopia.

Hall once advocated legislation to freeze all U.S. military aid to foreign countries, while increasing food distribution. He has also pushed efforts to increase funding for immunization and basic health-care programs. "Development assistance is the most important thing we can do," he said. "Just shoving food at the problem is not going to solve it."

In the 99th Congress, Hall saw his longtime fight against U.S. support for the Marcos regime in the Philippines blossom into a full-fledged movement. Soon after coming to Congress in 1979, he unsuccessfully offered an amendment to cut off American aid to Marcos. In 1980, he persuaded the House to cut $5 million from funds for the Philippines, but the money was restored in conference. A year after the 1983 assassination of leading Philippine dissident Benigno S. Aquino Jr., Congress shifted $60 million originally for military aid to economic assistance, but Hall wanted the House to cut $25 million outright. "Marcos will be laughing all the way to the bank," he warned, though the House did not listen.

In 1985, Hall finally succeeded with an amendment calling into question further military aid to the Philippines unless the Marcos regime made sufficient political, economic and military reforms. A few months later, Marcos was in exile and Aquino's widow, Corazon, became the Philippines' president.

Closer to home, Hall promotes human

Ohio 3

Southwest — Dayton

With a large blue-collar work force and a population 37 percent black, Dayton is a Democratic island in a sea of rural western Ohio Republicanism. Most of Dayton's suburbs yield GOP majorities, but the urban vote has been large enough to keep the 3rd District Democratic in most elections. Jimmy Carter carried the 3rd in both 1976 and 1980, and no GOP candidate for governor or the U.S. Senate has won here in more than a decade. Still, Ronald Reagan and George Bush had little trouble taking the district in 1984 and 1988.

The Dayton area claims to be the birthplace of aviation, the refrigerator, the cash register and the electrical automobile starter. Much of the high-skill industry in the region is a legacy of these local inventions. The city is the headquarters of the NCR Corp. (formerly National Cash Register Co.). General Motors Corp. is a major employer with several plants in the district. The Wright-Patterson Air Force Base northeast of the city is one of the nation's largest military installations.

In the early 1970s, the Dayton area was the most affluent part of Ohio outside the Cleveland suburbs. But in recent years, there have been severe economic problems. GM's large Frigidaire division, Firestone Tire and Rubber and the McCall Publishing Co. have all left. NCR Corp. remains, but the work force has dropped drastically. Without jobs, many people have left the area. Dayton's population declined 16 percent in the 1970s and another 8 percent in the 1980s, to 179,000 in 1986, its lowest level in a half-century.

South of Dayton are the staunchly Republican white-collar suburbs of Kettering and Oakwood. Together they cast about 15 percent of the district vote, compared with Dayton's 40 percent. The fast-growing townships north of the city are largely blue-collar suburban. This is a swing-voting area.

Population: 514,173. White 415,053 (81%), Black 94,065 (18%), Other 3,193 (1%). Spanish origin 3,737 (1%). 18 and over 370,952 (72%), 65 and over 52,874 (10%). Median age: 30.

rights through his advocacy of teaching ethics in American schools. In both the 100th and 101st Congresses, he introduced legislation to establish a commission to identify what values should be taught and how. "Our nation is in the grips of a moral recession," he wrote in a statement for the *Congressional Record.* "We are raising a generation of children who cannot distinguish between right and wrong. They are not prepared to make tough choices when there are gray areas, or when values seem to conflict."

On the issue where values seem to conflict more dramatically than on any other — abortion — Hall stands on the anti-abortion side. In 1988, he was one of 90 Democrats who joined with 126 Republicans in a 216-166 House vote in favor of allowing federal funding of abortions only when the mother's life would be endangered by the pregnancy — not in cases of rape or incest.

In addition to his activism on hunger and human rights, Hall keeps a keen eye on home-state interests. In 1985, for instance, when the Rules Committee was considering a revenue-raising measure as part of the Gramm-Rudman budget-balancing effort, Hall cast the only vote to kill a provision requiring new public employees to contribute payroll taxes toward Medicare coverage. Hall said Ohio civil servants are covered by a state retirement system and do not need Medicare.

In 1981, he revealed his sensitivity to constituent pressure when he voted with the Republican majority on the House floor in favor of President Reagan's budget. Hall's decision, reached after sampling opinion in his Democratic district, stunned House Democratic leaders. They had expected to lose dozens of conservative Southerners on the budget vote, but they did not expect to lose Hall. In the years since then, however, Hall has cast relatively few such conspicuous renegade votes.

Hall received unusual press attention in late 1986 when his brother Sam was arrested in Nicaragua for trespassing on a military installation. Sam Hall claimed to be gathering intelligence for a private American group aiding the contras, but was soon released by the Nicaraguan government, which expressed doubts about his mental stability. Tony Hall said he was unaware of his brother's activities.

At Home: Hall was the clear choice of organized labor and the Montgomery County Democratic Party when liberal GOP Rep. Charles W. Whalen decided to retire in 1978. Once a Little All-America on the football team at Denison University, Hall was well-known in Dayton as its representative in the Ohio Legislature. He had access to ample campaign funds through his father, who ran a lucrative real-estate business and served as the city's mayor for five years.

Four years before his congressional bid, Hall had gained attention as the Democratic nominee for secretary of state against Republican stalwart Ted W. Brown, who had held that post for 24 years. Hall chastised Brown for not reporting campaign contributions from a chicken dinner fund-raising event, brandishing a rubber chicken during one appearance. He came closer to defeating Brown than anyone had in 16 years, and the campaign placed him in a good position to run for Congress.

To reach Washington, Hall had to defeat Republican Dudley P. Kircher, a former chamber of commerce official who was considerably more conservative than Whalen. Hall emphasized his legislative experience and attacked Kircher as the "voice of big business." Strong support from organized labor helped Hall make up for Kircher's $130,000 spending advantage. The Democrat took 70 percent of the vote in Dayton, allowing him to win narrowly districtwide.

Redistricting gave Hall a safer seat in 1982. Republicans did not field a candidate that year or in 1984. In the last two elections, the Democrat faced Ronald Crutcher, one of a small number of blacks active in Ohio's Republican Party. Crutcher has received attention from the national media and was a delegate to the 1984 and 1988 GOP conventions. But he has met with little electoral success, never holding Hall below 70 percent.

Committees

Rules (6th of 9 Democrats)
Rules of the House

Select Hunger (2nd of 18 Democrats)
Task Force: International (chairman)

Elections

1988 General		
Tony P. Hall (D)	141,953	(77%)
Ron Crutcher (R)	42,664	(23%)
1986 General		
Tony P. Hall (D)	98,311	(74%)
Ron Crutcher (R)	35,167	(26%)

Previous Winning Percentages: **1984** (100%) **1982** (88%) **1980** (57%) **1978** (54%)

District Vote For President

	1988	1984	1980	1976
D	83,142 (45%)	87,950 (43%)	93,420 (51%)	99,150 (53%)
R	98,495 (54%)	115,330 (56%)	78,220 (42%)	85,208 (45%)
I			10,953 (6%)	

Campaign Finance

	Receipts	Receipts from PACs	Expend-itures
1988			
Hall (D)	$216,111	$140,160 (65%)	$182,889
Crutcher (R)	$48,661	$1,750 (4%)	$46,403
1986			
Hall (D)	$181,650	$119,510 (66%)	$76,558
Crutcher (R)	$48,440	$16,950 (35%)	$48,368

Key Votes

1987	
Raise speed limit to 65 mph	Y
Approve Gephardt "fair trade" amendment	Y
Ban testing of larger nuclear weapons	Y
Delay "re-flagging" of Kuwaiti tankers	Y
Approve tax-raising deficit-reduction bill	Y
1988	
Approve aid to Nicaraguan contras	N
Enact civil rights restoration bill over Reagan veto	Y
Kill 60-day plant-closing notification measure	N
Pass omnibus trade bill over Reagan veto	Y
Approve death penalty for drug-related murders	Y
Bar federal funds for abortions in cases of rape and incest	Y
Oppose seven-day waiting period for purchase of handguns	N

Voting Studies

	Presidential Support		Party Unity		Conservative Coalition	
Year	**S**	**O**	**S**	**O**	**S**	**O**
1988	24	66	79	8	37	50
1987	23	68	72	11	40	49
1986	14	83	78	13	20	74
1985	29	68	81	12	33	56
1984	27	63	72	15	25	63
1983	21	74	75	17	26	72
1982	36	57	73	14	30	60
1981	47	46	69	24	51	44

Interest Group Ratings

Year	ADA	ACU	AFL-CIO	CCUS
1988	75	17	93	23
1987	72	9	73	29
1986	65	9	64	44
1985	65	11	88	41
1984	70	22	77	38
1983	85	13	94	10
1982	70	17	76	30
1981	45	33	62	44

4 Michael G. Oxley (R)

Of Findlay — Elected 1981

Born: Feb. 11, 1944, Findlay, Ohio.
Education: Miami U. (Ohio), B.A. 1966; Ohio State U., J.D. 1969.
Occupation: FBI agent; lawyer.
Family: Wife, Patricia Pluguez; one child.
Religion: Lutheran.
Political Career: Ohio House, 1973-81.
Capitol Office: 1131 Longworth Bldg. 20515; 225-2676.

In Washington: Oxley is an affable man with a smile and a handshake for nearly everybody, but he also likes to compete, and the competitive energy he does not work off on the golf course or in the House gym, he invests in blunt talk and partisan sparring on the issues of the day.

A former FBI agent and a member of the Select Committee on Narcotics Abuse and Control, he was involved in the 100th Congress' deliberations on an anti-drug bill. Oxley urged that the national drug director be made a Cabinet member, saying, "I want a stud in there fighting the war on drugs, someone with real clout." He successfully offered an amendment to make it easier for the government to set up "sting" operations against money-launderers.

On the Energy and Commerce Committee, Oxley's normally easygoing nature can make him appear to be open to cooperation with the majority side — especially with Chairman John D. Dingell, who shares his opposition to strict controls on acid rain. But in fact, Oxley is one of the more partisan Republicans on the panel, playing the advocate more often than the negotiator.

He has been a vocal critic of Democratic efforts to reinstate the "fairness doctrine" regulation on the broadcasting industry; it was repealed administratively in 1987. President Reagan vetoed a reinstatement bill passed by the 100th Congress, but the Democratic leadership revived the issue in 1989, at a time when many members felt they were getting an unfair rap in the media over a proposed 51 percent congressional pay raise. Oxley joined in the criticism of the media, complaining that, "We had disc jockeys whose total IQ probably doesn't reach the top number on the FM dial, who earn twice as much as a member of Congress, working up the electorate ... giving them false information." But on the vote to reinstate the fairness regulation, he did not budge from his earlier opposition.

Earlier in his career, Oxley spoke up for Reagan administration efforts to cut federal funds for public broadcasting. Like Reagan and many other conservatives, Oxley wanted to limit the federal subsidy for the Corporation for Public Broadcasting (CPB) and encourage public stations to explore other funding sources, such as commercial advertising.

In 1984, an Oxley amendment to restrain federal funding lost on the House floor. Congress then approved a sharp increase in the CPB budget, but Reagan vetoed that bill, as well as a second CPB budget bill. CPB money later was provided in a continuing resolution at a level near what Oxley and Reagan wanted.

At Home: When Republican Rep. Tennyson Guyer died in April 1981, Oxley, a four-term state House member, quickly assumed the heir-apparent role. But while he was supported by Guyer's widow and others in the district GOP establishment, he had trouble winning.

Running in the first few months of the Reagan presidency, Oxley barely survived a GOP primary in which all the candidates tried to out-Reagan one another. His major rival, Robert J. Huffman, a Reagan backer in the 1976 presidential campaign, branded Oxley a Reagan-come-lately because he had supported George Bush for president in 1980. Oxley won by fewer than 2,500 votes out of more than 40,000 cast.

Taking the GOP nomination traditionally had been tantamount to election in this district, but Democrats fielded a strong candidate in state Rep. Dale Locker, a farmer and chairman of the state House Agriculture and Natural Resources Committee. Oxley spent $275,000 and flooded the media with advertisements, but he had trouble developing the personal rapport with voters that had made Guyer safe. Carrying only half of the district's counties, Oxley struggled to a 341-vote victory. A recount delayed his swearing-in for nearly a month.

Locker contemplated a rematch in 1982, but backed off when the state Legislature fashioned new district boundaries to Oxley's advantage. Against a little-known Democrat, Oxley carried every county. His re-elections since then have been similarly automatic affairs.

Ohio 4

West Central — Lima; Findlay

The 4th arches ominously in west-central Ohio like a giant set of jaws about to devour Columbus. It is an imaginative design. But the strange shape is no accident. The 4th includes some of the most Republican counties in the state, placed within its borders to help Oxley.

Not one of the nine counties in the 4th has supported a Democratic presidential candidate since 1944. Two of the three largest — Allen (Lima) and Hancock (Findlay) — have not deserted the GOP national ticket since the Roosevelt-Landon contest of 1936. Allen was the largest county east of the Mississippi carried by Barry Goldwater in 1964.

Dominated by farms and small towns, the 4th is standard Corn Belt GOP territory. The fertile soil supports large farms that raise livestock, soybeans, corn and wheat. Industry is widely scattered and attracts local craftsmen rather than poor migrants.

Lima (population 46,000) and Findlay (37,000) both emerged as small manufacturing centers at the end of the 19th century when oil and gas were found nearby. Lima was one of the original refinery centers for Standard Oil, then owned by John D. Rockefeller. Although the petroleum boom passed long ago, Findlay, as headquarters of Marathon Oil, is the most prosperous part of the 4th.

Close ties to the automobile industry caused economic hardships in Lima and Mansfield (Richland County) during the 1982 recession, but the picture has brightened considerably since then. Lima's Ford engine plant and Mansfield's Fisher body plant are not working at pre-recession capacity, but smaller auto-related companies have taken up some of the slack. In 1982, General Dynamics located in Lima and became the town's largest single employer.

Population: 514,172. White 492,852 (96%), Black 17,622 (3%). Spanish origin 4,244 (1%). 18 and over 360,450 (70%), 65 and over 58,720 (11%). Median age: 30.

Committees

Energy and Commerce (11th of 17 Republicans)
Energy and Power; Oversight and Investigations; Telecommunications and Finance

Select Narcotics Abuse and Control (3rd of 12 Republicans)

Elections

1988 General		
Michael G. Oxley (R)	160,099	(100%)
1986 General		
Michael G. Oxley (R)	115,751	(75%)
Clem T. Cratty (D)	26,320	(17%)
Raven L. Workman (I)	11,997	(8%)

Previous Winning Percentages: **1984** (78%) **1982** (65%) **1981 *** (50%)

* *Special election.*

District Vote For President

	1988		1984		1980		1976	
D	65,992	(32%)	55,078	(26%)	64,890	(32%)	76,257	(40%)
R	140,667	(68%)	158,577	(74%)	128,382	(63%)	108,916	(57%)
I					9,585	(5%)		

Campaign Finance

	Receipts	Receipts from PACs	Expend-itures
1988			
Oxley (R)	$251,619	$170,850 (68%)	$207,157
1986			
Oxley (R)	$215,276	$155,352 (72%)	$184,379

Key Votes

1987	
Raise speed limit to 65 mph	Y
Approve Gephardt "fair trade" amendment	N
Ban testing of larger nuclear weapons	N
Delay "re-flagging" of Kuwaiti tankers	N
Approve tax-raising deficit-reduction bill	N
1988	
Approve aid to Nicaraguan contras	Y
Enact civil rights restoration bill over Reagan veto	N
Kill 60-day plant-closing notification measure	Y
Pass omnibus trade bill over Reagan veto	N
Approve death penalty for drug-related murders	Y
Bar federal funds for abortions in cases of rape and incest	Y
Oppose seven-day waiting period for purchase of handguns	N

Voting Studies

	Presidential Support		Party Unity		Conservative Coalition	
Year	**S**	**O**	**S**	**O**	**S**	**O**
1988	68	31	81	9	92	5
1987	67	26	80	12	98	2
1986	80	16	85	8	86	14
1985	75	24	88	6	96	4
1984	67	26	86	8	93	5
1983	85	12	87	10	83	16
1982	77	17	81	13	90	10
1981	67†	29†	85†	13†	88†	12†

† Not eligible for all recorded votes.

Interest Group Ratings

Year	ADA	ACU	AFL-CIO	CCUS
1988	20	88	14	100
1987	4	95	0	100
1986	0	95	7	100
1985	10	86	0	91
1984	5	75	0	64
1983	10	91	0	95
1982	10	90	15	82
1981	0	83	20	92

5 Paul E. Gillmor (R)

Of Port Clinton — Elected 1988

Born: Feb. 1, 1939, Tiffin, Ohio.
Education: Ohio Wesleyan U., B.A. 1961; U. of Michigan, J.D. 1964.
Military Career: Air Force, 1965-66.
Occupation: Lawyer.
Family: Wife, Karen Lako; two children.
Religion: Protestant.
Political Career: Ohio Senate, 1967-88, minority leader, 1978-80, 1983-84, president, 1981-82, 1985-88; sought GOP nomination for governor, 1986.
Capitol Office: 1008 Longworth Bldg. 20515; 225-6405.

The Path to Washington: While moving from a state Legislature to the U.S. House is uniformly regarded as a promotion, Gillmor gave up a good bit of power to make the move: As president of the Ohio Senate for six of the last eight years, he was the highest-ranking Republican in state government. Well liked for his informal style, Gillmor earned a reputation in the Legislature as an accessible, consensus-oriented leader who was able to move legislation despite the GOP's narrow majority.

In his campaign for Congress, Gillmor played up his fiscal conservatism — pointing to two tax-cut bills he authored and 11 balanced budgets he supported. But in Columbus during the early 1980s — when control of the state Senate shifted in three successive elections — it was Gillmor's image as a centrist that initially brought him success.

After the GOP captured a one-vote majority in 1980, Gillmor won the Senate presidency over a fiery conservative by stressing the need for negotiation within the GOP and with the Democrats, who still controlled the House and governorship. As Senate leader, Gillmor joined a number of popular bipartisan efforts such as increasing aid to education.

But after the Democrats recaptured the chamber in the 1982 elections, and Gov. Richard F. Celeste pushed a personal income tax increase through the Legislature, Gillmor's bipartisan spirit soured. He gained statewide recognition for attacking Celeste's tax-hike proposal, which became the central issue in the 1984 legislative races. The GOP regained Senate control that year, and Gillmor resumed his more conciliatory leadership style.

Gillmor's power, however, did not pave an easy path to Washington. Instead, it made him the rival of the Republican he eventually succeeded, Delbert L. Latta, who served in the House for 30 years. During Gillmor's 22 years in the state Senate, he represented more than two-thirds of Latta's territory, and the two men's struggle for dominance of the local political scene was widely known.

When Latta announced his retirement in 1988, he made it plain that he wanted to pass the 5th to his son, Robert E. Latta, a 32-year-old attorney. The rivalry between Rep. Latta and Gillmor was such that when Gillmor announced he would oppose the younger Latta, Rep. Latta briefly threatened to seek re-election. While he did not follow through on that threat, it set the tone for a bitter, personal primary that was ultimately decided by just 27 votes — the narrowest win in any 1988 House contest.

While Rep. Latta cashed in every chit he had collected in 30 years to build an organization to elect his son, Gillmor ran a media-oriented campaign, highlighting his legislative experience and electoral record. He had always won his Senate seat easily, and though he lost the 1986 GOP gubernatorial nomination to former Gov. James A. Rhodes, Gillmor carried the 5th District that year. And his statewide showing was good enough to mark him as a serious contender for governor in 1990, an ambition he says he gave up to come to Washington.

The narrow margin between Gillmor and Robert Latta surprised many observers who had underestimated Del Latta's zeal. Gillmor's effort was also hampered by his geographic base in the eastern half of the 5th, which tends to be less conservative than the rest of the district.

But that eastern base put him in a strong position for the general election. Gillmor handily defeated wealthy Democratic attorney Thomas Murray, who had gotten just 35 percent of the vote against Latta in 1986. Too busy with his law practice to campaign actively, Murray spent nearly $850,000 (most of it his own) on television advertisements championing his legal efforts to help working people. But the message paled compared with Gillmor's long legislative career.

Ohio 5

Northwest — Bowling Green; Sandusky

The 5th looks like a big bow tie, with Wood County (Bowling Green) representing the knot.

This solidly Republican district is a mixture of good, flat farm land and small towns. The Lake Erie port of Sandusky (population 30,000) is the largest community. Bowling Green (population 25,000), home of Bowling Green State University, is the district's second most-populous city.

The western counties are almost exclusively devoted to agriculture. Packing plants operated by Heinz and Campbell attest to the quality of the region's tomatoes. But the Mexican-American farm workers who live in migrant camps during harvest season have added a degree of tension to the otherwise tranquil region. The 5th has the greatest concentration of Hispanics in Ohio.

Over the past three decades, the district lines have changed four times, gradually bringing in more territory on the east. The latest redistricting gave the 5th all of lakeside Erie County, all of Seneca County and a portion of rural Huron County.

With more than 75,000 residents, Erie County is the key addition. Located midway between Cleveland and Toledo, it has long been a major recreation area. Sandusky, the county seat, is a fishing market and coal port. In the surrounding countryside, fruit orchards and vineyards abound. German immigrants established wineries in Sandusky a century ago that are still a key feature of the local economy. The sizable blue-collar element occasionally pushes Erie County into the Democratic column. But with just 15 percent of the district vote, Erie creates only a ripple in the large Republican pond.

The district's many small auto parts plants, located here because of the proximity to Toledo, Cleveland and Detroit, were hurt badly by the early 1980s economic downturn, although they have recovered to a perceptible degree. In 1982, nine of the district's 12 counties had unemployment rates that surpassed 15 percent; by 1986, only two counties exceeded 10 percent.

Wood County was spared the economic suffering endured by its neighbors mainly because of its lack of industry. This county, which sprawls from the outskirts of Toledo deep into the Ohio Corn Belt, boomed in the 1970s, fed by expansion of Bowling Green State University.

Wood County accounts for one-sixth of the district's voters. The county is consistently Republican, although the 17,000 university students provide a base for moderate-to-liberal contenders. Independent John B. Anderson drew 10 percent of the Wood County vote in 1980, his best county showing in Ohio.

Population: 514,173. White 493,503 (96%), Black 10,318 (2%). Spanish origin 16,537 (3%). 18 and over 358,616 (70%), 65 and over 53,806 (10%). Median age: 28.

Committees

Banking, Finance and Urban Affairs (19th of 20 Republicans)
Economic Stabilization; Financial Institutions Supervision, Regulation and Insurance; General Oversight and Investigations; Housing and Community Development

House Administration (6th of 8 Republicans)
Libraries and Memorials (ranking); Accounts

Joint Library

Campaign Finance

	Receipts	Receipts from PACs	Expend-itures
1988			
Gillmor (R)	$833,178	$319,120 (38%)	$860,603
Murray (D)	$719,754	$21,700 (3%)	$850,819

Elections

1988 General		
Paul E. Gillmor (R)	123,838	(61%)
Tom Murray (D)	80,292	(39%)
1988 Primary		
Paul E. Gillmor (R)	28,694	(45%)
Robert Latta (R)	28,667	(45%)
Rex Damschroder (R)	5,769	(9%)

District Vote For President

	1988	1984	1980	1976
D	80,083 (38%)	69,036 (32%)	66,593 (33%)	83,017 (44%)
R	128,731 (61%)	145,926 (67%)	116,836 (58%)	102,353 (54%)
I			13,995 (7%)	

6 Bob McEwen (R)

Of Hillsboro — Elected 1980

Born: Jan. 12, 1950, Hillsboro, Ohio.
Education: U. of Miami (Fla.), B.B.A. 1972; graduate work, Ohio State U. College of Law, 1973-74.
Occupation: Real-estate developer.
Family: Wife, Elizabeth Boebinger; four children.
Religion: Protestant.
Political Career: Ohio House, 1975-81.
Capitol Office: 329 Cannon Bldg. 20515; 225-5705.

In Washington: McEwen has a reputation as a man who thinks about politics nearly every waking minute, and he added to that image at the start of the 100th Congress by feeding the Washington press corps a stream of publicity about his plans to run for the Senate in 1988.

McEwen did enter the race for the GOP Senate nomination, and he began lining up southern Ohio support against his opponent, Cleveland Mayor George Voinovich. But two months in, McEwen halted his campaign. In retrospect, it was a wise move: Voinovich was crushed by Democratic Sen. Howard M. Metzenbaum.

When McEwen legislates, he nearly always manages to produce something of tangible benefit to his district and the broader political constituency he is courting. He is an enthusiastic conservative on most significant issues, but uses his two committee assignments — Public Works and Veterans' Affairs — to funnel government money back to Ohio in the form of public-works projects and veterans' benefits.

McEwen headed for Public Works as soon as he got to Washington in 1981, and began practicing the skills he had learned from his predecessor, GOP Rep. William H. Harsha, a gifted pork-barreler. McEwen had worked as an aide to Harsha, who served eight years as ranking Republican on Public Works until retiring.

At a time when budget cutbacks were delaying or eliminating many federally funded projects across the country, McEwen employed his congenial personality to lobby successfully for funding of numerous projects in his district. Bridges, dams, flood walls and navigation locks have been McEwen favorites — the Ohio River forms the southern boundary of the 6th. He has also introduced legislation to revive a limited version of revenue sharing, the program eliminated in 1986 that gave unrestricted aid to state and local governments.

His support for local projects notwithstanding, McEwen opposes raising taxes to balance the federal deficit. "I believe the answer to the deficit shortfall in the United States is not from lack of taxes," he said in 1987. "I believe it is from excessive spending in the Congress."

At Home: The Harsha-McEwen brand of pork-barrel politics is the stuff of which re-elections in southern Ohio are made. The 6th, though conservative, is amenable to almost any plan that will help it fight economic decline.

Real-estate development is McEwen's official profession, but his entire adult life has revolved around politics. He was elected to the state Legislature at age 24, and directed two of Harsha's campaigns. When Harsha retired in 1980, McEwen became the likely successor.

Though Harsha remained publicly neutral in the eight-candidate GOP primary, McEwen was the choice of the local Republican establishment and, as a state legislator, the only proven vote-getter. In the Ohio House, he had gained visibility by working to get the state to dredge a flood-prone creek in his district. He also advocated abolishing the Ohio lottery. On primary day, McEwen swept 10 of the district's 12 counties.

He enjoyed Harsha's backing in the general election and presented himself as the incumbent's conservative protégé. Also, he had a campaign treasury about twice as large as that of Democrat Ted Strickland, a minister with a Ph.D. in psychology and counseling. Democratic leaders tried to get a stronger candidate, but no prominent Democrats were interested.

Coasting to re-election in his next three campaigns, McEwen had plenty of time to contemplate a statewide race. After months of promoting his plans to challenge Metzenbaum, McEwen formally announced in October 1987.

While he gathered considerable conservative backing — including an endorsement from Texas Sen. Phil Gramm — McEwen ran into money troubles. Voinovich, by contrast, had strong financial backing from Republican business interests.

So McEwen backed out, saying party unity was vital to winning the Senate seat. Though several candidates had announced their intention to run in the 6th on the assumption that McEwen was leaving it, none pursued his House ambition. McEwen easily won re-election to a fifth term.

Ohio 6

South Central — Portsmouth; Chillicothe

The 6th is a mixture of suburbia and Appalachia. Republican majorities in the Cincinnati and Dayton suburbs and the countryside nearby enable the GOP to win most elections. But when the Democrats run well in Appalachia, as they occasionally do, the outcome can be close.

Nearly one-third of the voters in the 6th live in a suburban sector between Cincinnati and Dayton, part of which was gained in the last redistricting. The territory, which lies north of Interstate 71, the major Cincinnati-to-Columbus artery, is Republican. It grew rapidly in the 1970s as the result of commercial development, and managed to hold its own even through the 1982 recession.

Immediately east is rural Republican country. Clinton and Highland counties and the southern portion of Fayette County lie on the outer fringe of the Corn Belt.

Farther east the land is poorer and GOP strength begins to diminish. When entering Adams County, one is in Appalachia. Adams, Pike and Vinton counties are among the poorest counties in Ohio.

Nearly one-half the land area of this Appalachian portion of the district is enclosed in the Wayne National Forest. What little industry exists is concentrated in Portsmouth and Chillicothe, with about 23,000 people each.

While steel and bricks have been linchpins of Portsmouth's economy throughout the century, the largest employer in the district is the nearby uranium-enrichment facility owned by the Atomic Energy Commission and operated by Goodyear. In Chillicothe, 44 miles due north of Portsmouth, nearby forests support a large paper plant.

Population: 514,173. White 501,021 (97%), Black 10,506 (2%). Spanish origin 2,524 (1%). 18 and over 359,077 (70%), 65 and over 55,960 (11%). Median age: 30.

Committees

Public Works and Transportation (6th of 20 Republicans)
Economic Development (ranking); Aviation; Surface Transportation

Veterans' Affairs (4th of 13 Republicans)
Compensation, Pension and Insurance (ranking); Hospitals and Health Care

Elections

1988 General		
Bob McEwen (R)	152,235	(74%)
Gordon R. Roberts (D)	52,635	(26%)
1986 General		
Bob McEwen (R)	106,354	(70%)
Gordon R. Roberts (D)	42,155	(28%)

Previous Winning Percentages: **1984** (74%) **1982** (59%) **1980** (55%)

District Vote For President

	1988	1984	1980	1976
D	72,552 (35%)	65,222 (31%)	74,614 (38%)	89,145 (48%)
R	134,828 (64%)	140,525 (68%)	110,714 (57%)	93,080 (50%)
I			7,502 (4%)	

Campaign Finance

	Receipts	Receipts from PACs	Expend-itures
1988			
McEwen (R)	$787,103	$147,066 (19%)	$884,754
Roberts (D)	$43,532	$22,450 (52%)	$43,485
1986			
McEwen (R)	$359,968	$147,897 (41%)	$247,971
Roberts (D)	$21,949	$10,750 (49%)	$21,324

Key Votes

1987	
Raise speed limit to 65 mph	N
Approve Gephardt "fair trade" amendment	N
Ban testing of larger nuclear weapons	N
Delay "re-flagging" of Kuwaiti tankers	N
Approve tax-raising deficit-reduction bill	N
1988	
Approve aid to Nicaraguan contras	Y
Enact civil rights restoration bill over Reagan veto	N
Kill 60-day plant-closing notification measure	Y
Pass omnibus trade bill over Reagan veto	N
Approve death penalty for drug-related murders	Y
Bar federal funds for abortions in cases of rape and incest	Y
Oppose seven-day waiting period for purchase of handguns	Y

Voting Studies

	Presidential Support		Party Unity		Conservative Coalition	
Year	**S**	**O**	**S**	**O**	**S**	**O**
1988	65	29	73	21	92	3
1987	60	28	68	16	81	7
1986	67	22	63	26	84	4
1985	69	26	79	13	87	11
1984	60	29	81	9	88	5
1983	72	28	82	13	87	9
1982	58	34	77	18	77	18
1981	76	24	90	8	91	7

Interest Group Ratings

Year	ADA	ACU	AFL-CIO	CCUS
1988	5	96	14	100
1987	4	86	8	90
1986	5	86	31	79
1985	15	85	6	79
1984	5	80	15	71
1983	15	87	12	85
1982	30	85	30	86
1981	0	100	20	89

7 Mike DeWine (R)

Of Cedarville — Elected 1982

Born: Jan. 5, 1947, Springfield, Ohio.
Education: Miami U. (Ohio), B.S. 1969; Ohio Northern U., J.D. 1972.
Occupation: Lawyer.
Family: Wife, Frances Struewing; seven children.
Religion: Roman Catholic.
Political Career: Greene County prosecuting attorney, 1977-81; Ohio Senate, 1981-83.
Capitol Office: 1705 Longworth Bldg. 20515; 225-4324.

In Washington: With his plans to run for governor of Ohio in 1990 taking shape, DeWine's 1987 appointment to the House Iran-contra investigating committee appeared a grand opportunity for him to showcase his talents before a national television audience. But the assignment turned out to be something of a mixed blessing.

DeWine's questioning of witnesses during the hearings clearly boosted his profile in areas outside his semi-rural southwest Ohio district. And when he runs for governor, DeWine can hope that conservative Republicans will recall his strong defense of President Reagan's contra-aid policy, and his criticisms of Reagan aides who, he believed, failed to protect the interests of the president and the nation during the ill-fated secret initiative to sell arms to Iran and divert the profits to the contras.

However, Ohio Democrats, and potential Republican primary rivals, may invoke a different memory of his service on the joint House-Senate committee — that of DeWine dozing. DeWine nodded off several times during committee hearings; to his misfortune, the naps were captured by TV cameras, and duly reported by the print media.

The youngest member of the select committee, DeWine was chosen in part because of his record as a conservative partisan on the Foreign Affairs Committee. Like many Republicans, DeWine initially worried that the Iran-contra investigation would be used by congressional Democrats to pillory Reagan and damage the Republican Party in general.

But he recognized early on that the televised hearings could instead be a convenient forum to promote the policy of U.S. aid to the contras. "The debate has to be carried on, and this is just as good a place as any," DeWine said. "There's nothing wrong with using this as an opportunity to carry on this national debate."

Throughout the hearings, DeWine accepted Reagan's statements that he was not fully informed about the implementation of the arms sales and had no prior knowledge of the contra diversion. While many committee members gave Secretary of State George P. Shultz credit for warning Reagan that the Iran-contra arrangement was misguided and risky, DeWine accused Shultz of throwing in the towel after he failed to persuade Reagan to block the venture. "In my opinion, you purposely cut yourself out from the facts," DeWine chastised. Shultz reacted with disdain, stating, "I'll just say that's one man's opinion, and I don't share it."

A determined partisanship continues to mark DeWine's work on Foreign Affairs. In 1988, shortly after Reagan's request for $36 million in military and non-military aid to the contras was defeated, DeWine blasted the Democratic Party as "not one for a strong national defense, not one that wants to stand against the threat of communism throughout the world."

The prosecutorial tone DeWine often uses in debate stems from his background: He was a chief prosecutor for Greene County, Ohio, prior to his legislative career. While he is best known in Congress for his work in the foreign policy arena, it is his assignment on the Judiciary Committee for which DeWine's professional history has prepared him.

Early in 1986, DeWine acted as one of nine "managers," or prosecutors, during the Senate's impeachment trial of U.S. District Judge Harry E. Claiborne of Nevada. It was an assignment DeWine worked hard to get, and it displayed his courtroom abilities to advantage. As a member of the Judiciary Subcommittee on Civil and Constitutional Rights during the 100th Congress, he was involved in the early hearings on the impeachment of U.S. District Judge Walter L. Nixon Jr. of Mississippi.

One of DeWine's first achievements as an Ohio state senator was his effort to toughen the state's drunken-driving laws. He has continued this personal crusade in Congress.

In October 1988, he attached an amendment to the omnibus drug bill broadening the penalties that federal judges could apply to drivers convicted of driving under the influence on federal lands, such as national parks and military bases. Previously, the law permitted

Ohio 7

West Central — Springfield; Marion

Situated between Columbus and Dayton, the 7th is bisected by U.S. Route 40. North of the highway are four solidly Republican counties casting one-third of the district vote. Combining agriculture and small industry, they have been GOP strongholds for generations. Champaign, Logan and Union counties backed Alfred M. Landon for president in 1936. Marion County was President Warren G. Harding's home.

Marion claims to be the birthplace of the steam shovel, but it has been mired in economic troubles, partly because the demand for large power shovels has decreased since the strip-mining boom of the 1970s. In 1982, unemployment in Marion County was so high that Democratic Gov. Richard F. Celeste nearly carried it, even though GOP gubernatorial nominee Clarence J. Brown Jr. was the area's congressman. Unemployment still topped 10 percent in 1986.

The economic picture is rosier in neighboring Union County. Just northwest of Columbus, it is an attractive site for industries seeking open land and low taxes. Honda has located its first American auto plant in the western part of the county and runs a motorcycle plant nearby.

South of Route 40, the people are concentrated in Clark County (Springfield) and Greene County, which extends into Dayton's eastern suburbs. Greene has a working-class mixture of blacks and Southern whites. Wright-Patterson Air Force Base is responsible for a substantial amount of military-related employment.

Springfield's site along Route 40, the old National Road, enabled it to develop into the area's leading population center. The city suffered substantially in the recession but got a boost in 1983 when International Harvester consolidated its truckmaking in Springfield.

Population: 514,170. White 482,499 (94%), Black 27,488 (5%), Other 2,800 (1&). Spanish origin 3,092 (1%). 18 and over 362,126 (70%), 65 and over 51,300 (10%). Median age: 30.

federal judges to invoke jail terms and fines, but not to apply other tough sanctions typical of state driving laws, such as driver's-license suspensions and enrollment in drug or alcohol rehabilitation programs. DeWine's amendment allowed federal judges to invoke the full range of penalties available in the state where the crime was committed.

In the 101st Congress, DeWine took a position on the Judiciary Subcommittee on Crime, where he may pursue his hard-line positions on drug crime and capital punishment. In his attempt to move up to statewide office, DeWine clearly is going to emphasize his tough-on-crime posture. His early literature for the gubernatorial campaign cites an incident in which DeWine, while serving as prosecutor, rejected a plea bargain for the suspect in a brutal rape.

"The citizens of this county ... did not elect me to cut deals with criminals," the campaign piece credits DeWine with saying. "This guy is going to jail forever."

At Home: DeWine's tough-guy posturing and liberal-bashing has a wearying effect on some Democrats. His frequent complaints about House Democratic efforts to thwart Reagan's policies led some across the aisle to deride him as "DeWhine." And while DeWine is now in his 40s and is the father of seven, his slight build and youthful, gap-toothed appearance — he looks a bit like a cross between Michael J. Fox and Oliver North — emboldens his critics to dismiss him as an immature ideologue.

But his Republican colleagues instead portray DeWine as bright and tenacious, and the voters of Ohio's 7th District seem to agree. His four House election margins ranged from comfortable to unanimous.

DeWine's political climb began in 1976, when — after three years as assistant prosecuting attorney in Greene County — he challenged and defeated his Democratic boss. Scandal had crippled the incumbent prosecuting attorney, who had placed listening devices in his assistants' offices.

In 1980, DeWine moved on, beating a Democratic state senator. In the Ohio Senate, DeWine sponsored a mandatory-sentencing measure and his bill against drunken driving.

But he remained in the Legislature only two years. There was an opening for Congress in 1982 when Rep. Clarence J. Brown Jr. sought the GOP gubernatorial nomination, thus ending the 44-year grip on the 7th that he and his father had held. The Legislature considered breaking up the district to fill out surrounding underpopulated districts, but DeWine persuaded the Senate to keep it intact.

DeWine's Senate constituency included almost half the 7th, so he had little trouble winning the GOP primary against five opponents. He ran a meticulously organized, carefully executed campaign stressing his law-and-order record.

Democrats offered Roger D. Tackett, a

Marine veteran confined to a wheelchair by injuries he suffered in Vietnam. Tackett waged an active campaign, but neither his organization nor his name recognition matched DeWine's. Only Tackett's war record and depressed local economic conditions prevented a DeWine landslide; the Republican won with 56 percent of the vote. He has coasted since.

Committees

Foreign Affairs (10th of 18 Republicans)
International Economic Policy and Trade; Western Hemisphere Affairs

Judiciary (7th of 14 Republicans)
Crime; Economic and Commercial Law

Elections

1988 General

Mike DeWine (R)	142,597	(74%)
Jack Schira (D)	50,423	(26%)

1986 General

Mike DeWine (R)	119,238	(100%)

Previous Winning Percentages: 1984 (77%) **1982** (56%)

District Vote For President

	1988	1984	1980	1976
D	70,238 (35%)	62,580 (31%)	71,020 (36%)	82,201 (44%)
R	126,632 (64%)	136,042 (68%)	105,772 (54%)	98,272 (53%)
I			10,369 (5%)	

Campaign Finance

	Receipts	Receipts from PACs	Expend-itures
1988			
DeWine (R)	$312,200	$112,860 (36%)	$299,553
Schira (D)	$51,994	$8,640 (17%)	$51,478
1986			
DeWine (R)	$184,305	$90,069 (49%)	$140,405

Key Votes

1987	
Raise speed limit to 65 mph	N
Approve Gephardt "fair trade" amendment	N
Ban testing of larger nuclear weapons	N
Delay "re-flagging" of Kuwaiti tankers	N
Approve tax-raising deficit-reduction bill	N
1988	
Approve aid to Nicaraguan contras	Y
Enact civil rights restoration bill over Reagan veto	N
Kill 60-day plant-closing notification measure	Y
Pass omnibus trade bill over Reagan veto	N
Approve death penalty for drug-related murders	Y
Bar federal funds for abortions in cases of rape and incest	Y
Oppose seven-day waiting period for purchase of handguns	Y

Voting Studies

	Presidential Support		Party Unity		Conservative Coalition	
Year	**S**	**O**	**S**	**O**	**S**	**O**
1988	69	31	92	7	89	11
1987	70	28	82	16	93	7
1986	78	20	85	13	82	18
1985	78	23	87	9	87	11
1984	69	28	86	13	88	12
1983	84	15	88	9	89	10

Interest Group Ratings

Year	ADA	ACU	AFL-CIO	CCUS
1988	5	100	14	93
1987	20	87	13	93
1986	0	91	14	94
1985	10	86	18	64
1984	5	75	15	81
1983	5	91	6	84

8 Donald E. "Buz" Lukens (R)

Of Middletown — Elected 1986

Also served 1967-71.

Born: Feb. 11, 1931, Warren County, Ohio.

Education: Ohio State U., B.A. 1954; attended U. of Maryland, 1955-56.

Military Career: Air Force, 1954-60; Air Force Reserve, 1971-83.

Occupation: Business consultant.

Family: Divorced.

Religion: Lutheran.

Political Career: Ohio Senate, 1971-87; sought Republican nomination for governor, 1970; Republican nominee for state auditor, 1978.

Capitol Office: 117 Cannon Bldg. 20515; 225-6205.

In Washington: In a season of concern over House members' professional ethics, Lukens suffered a most personal humiliation. In May 1989, he was convicted on a charge of having sex with an underage girl at his Columbus, Ohio, apartment. Lukens, insistent of his innocence, vowed to remain in office.

Lukens' legal troubles began in February 1989, after a Columbus TV station broadcast a secretly taped meeting between him and Anna Coffman, who accused Lukens of paying to have sex with her daughter Rosie, then 16, and another woman the previous November. On the tape, Lukens was heard saying, "I didn't really know she was a teenager." Coffman alleged that Lukens tried to buy her silence with a government job offer.

Lukens was then indicted on a misdemeanor charge of contributing to the delinquency of a minor. At his May trial, Lukens did not testify on his own behalf, relying instead on his lawyer to undermine the credibility of his accusers. The strategy failed: The jury took 90 minutes to convict him of the charge.

Though Lukens quickly announced he would appeal, many assumed he would resign from the House, and leading Ohio Republicans encouraged him to do so. Ohio GOP Chairman Robert T. Bennett called on him to quit; Chalmers P. Wylie, Ohio's senior House Republican, said leaving would be the "gentlemanly thing" to do. But on June 3, Lukens said he would not cut short his political career.

That career has included two tours in the House, separated by 16 years. Upon his return in the 100th Congress, Lukens plied the same conservative path that marked his original tenure. As a member of the Foreign Affairs Committee, Lukens supported aid to the Nicaraguan contras, and tried to cut U.S. aid to African countries that also received heavy backing from the Soviet Union.

Conservative Lukens did support a new regulatory mandate — a smoking ban on air flights of two hours or less — but he had strong personal reasons for doing so. Earlier in the 1980s, he survived throat cancer that required repeated surgery. A non-smoker, he said, "I know, and all my surgeons agree, that I caught cancer through other people's smoke."

At Home: Lukens' sex scandal contrasted with the square, conservative image he had presented his western Ohio constituencies over more than two decades. In 1963, he was national chairman of the Young Republicans, and was active in the Goldwater movement. In 1966, Lukens challenged the local GOP regulars in what was then the 24th District, and won a House seat.

During his first four-year stint in the House, Lukens was a colleague of then-Texas Rep. George Bush. But the Ohioan proved early on he was a "Reagan Republican": In 1968, he was the first member of the House publicly to back Ronald Reagan as a presidential candidate.

Lukens ran for governor in 1970, but lost in the primary. He gained appointment in 1971 to a vacancy in the Ohio Senate, where he stayed until returning to Washington. A 1978 campaign for state auditor ended in failure.

Still, when GOP Rep. Thomas N. Kindness left the 8th in 1986 to try for the Senate, Lukens was the logical successor. He avoided a primary challenge by winning support from Kindness and the GOP organization in Butler County, the district's political center. That November, and again in 1988, Lukens won easily.

Ohio 8

Southwest — Middletown; Hamilton

Butler County is the anchor of this southern Ohio district that has changed shape several times in recent redistrictings but always remained solidly Republican.

Butler contains two medium-sized manufacturing centers along the Great Miami River — Hamilton (population 65,000) and Middletown (population 46,000). Steel, paper, automobile bodies, machine tools and a variety of other metal products are made in the two cities.

But both cities have lost population in recent years. Most of Butler County's 271,000 residents live not in Hamilton or Middletown but in suburban communities and small towns such as Oxford, the home of Miami University (16,000 students).

The recent growth in Butler County's suburban territory, just north of the Cincinnati beltway, has escalated a rightward trend in the local GOP. In recent years the county has elected some of the most conservative Republican legislators in the state. Ronald Reagan carried Butler in 1980 with 62 percent of the vote, and increased that to 73 percent in 1984. In 1988, George Bush carried Butler with 67 percent of the vote, well above his statewide average of 55 percent.

Half the residents of the 8th live outside Butler County in a string of fertile Corn Belt counties running north along the Indiana border. The land is flat and the roads are straight. Once a motorist leaves the Miami Valley in northern Butler, he can drive north through the district along Route 127 without more than an occasional slight turn of the steering wheel.

Corn and soybeans are major cash crops in the rural counties. Poultry and livestock also are moneymakers. In recent years, Darke and Mercer counties have been the leading Ohio counties in farm income.

Mercer was settled by German Catholics and is the only county in the 8th with much of a Democratic heritage. But Mercer likes its Democrats conservative. It has not backed the party's presidential candidate since 1968.

Population: 514,171. White 496,757 (97%), Black 14,280 (3%). Spanish origin 3,057 (1%). 18 and over 361,343 (70%), 65 and over 52,071 (10%). Median age: 29.

Committees

Foreign Affairs (14th of 18 Republicans)
Africa; Europe and the Middle East

Government Operations (5th of 15 Republicans)
Employment and Housing (ranking)

Elections

1988 General		
Donald E. "Buz" Lukens (R)	154,164	(76%)
John Griffin (D)	49,084	(24%)
1986 General		
Donald E. "Buz" Lukens (R)	98,475	(68%)
John Griffin (D)	46,195	(32%)

Previous Winning Percentages: 1968 (70%) **1966** (59%)

District Vote for President

	1988	1984	1980	1976
D	65,826 (31%)	55,507 (27%)	67,442 (34%)	76,480 (42%)
R	147,196 (69%)	151,869 (73%)	119,158 (60%)	102,855 (56%)
I			10,727 (5%)	

Campaign Finance

	Receipts	Receipts from PACs	Expend-itures
1988			
Lukens (R)	$151,231	$84,880 (56%)	$147,712
1986			
Lukens (R)	$223,679	$136,608 (61%)	$218,387

Key Votes

1987	
Raise speed limit to 65 mph	Y
Approve Gephardt "fair trade" amendment	N
Ban testing of larger nuclear weapons	N
Delay "re-flagging" of Kuwaiti tankers	N
Approve tax-raising deficit-reduction bill	N
1988	
Approve aid to Nicaraguan contras	Y
Enact civil rights restoration bill over Reagan veto	N
Kill 60-day plant-closing notification measure	Y
Pass omnibus trade bill over Reagan veto	N
Approve death penalty for drug-related murders	Y
Bar federal funds for abortions in cases of rape and incest	Y
Oppose seven-day waiting period for purchase of handguns	Y

Voting Studies

	Presidential Support		Party Unity		Conservative Coalition	
Year	S	O	S	O	S	O
1988	68	25	84	7	84	3
1987	72	23	84	4	88	7

Interest Group Ratings

Year	ADA	ACU	AFL-CIO	CCUS
1988	0	96	14	85
1987	8	100	0	100

9 Marcy Kaptur (D)

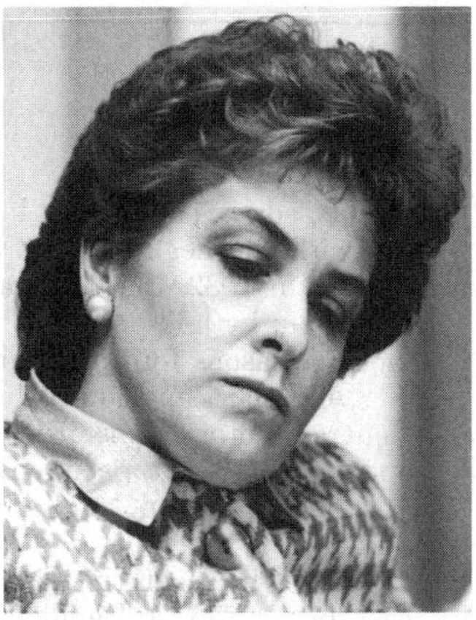

Of Toledo — Elected 1982

Born: June 17, 1946, Toledo, Ohio.
Education: U. of Wisconsin, B.A. 1968; U. of Michigan, M.U.P. 1974.
Occupation: Urban planner.
Family: Single.
Religion: Roman Catholic.
Political Career: No previous office.
Capitol Office: 1228 Longworth Bldg. 20515; 225-4146.

In Washington: Though personable and hard-working, Kaptur came to Congress with less savvy than colleagues in the 1982 Democratic class who — unlike her — had past experience in elective office. But she made up ground quickly by enlisting as a loyalist to Speaker Jim Wright. Loyalty has its rewards.

In the 100th Congress, the new Speaker appointed Kaptur to the panel that makes House Democrats' committee assignments. In the 101st Congress, he put her on his slate for the Budget Committee, a concession prize since she had aspired to Appropriations. He also named her vice chairman of a task force on trade. But when Wright had to relinquish the speakership in June 1989, Kaptur failed in her first solo try for a leadership spot: She ran third in a bid for Democratic Caucus vice chairman.

Kaptur's value to Wright had been evident early in the 100th Congress. In a close vote of a Banking subcommittee, she backed a $15 billion plan to prop up the savings and loan insurance fund. The Speaker supported a lower amount, fearing that federal regulators would use extra funds to close down insolvent S&L's in his home state of Texas. He lobbied Democrats to reverse the decision. The next day in full committee, Kaptur was one of two members to change her vote, opting instead for a $5 billion proposal that won by a single vote.

First swept into office by voter anger over the 1982 recession, Kaptur voices the concerns of industrial Toledo with an emotional commitment bordering on moral outrage. Ronald Reagan's free-trade philosophy particularly set her blood to boiling; "appeasement," she once called it. Kaptur backed the Democratic trade bill that was three years in the making, and, in 1987, strongly supported the Gephardt "fair trade" amendment. She added her own amendment, calling on U.S. trade negotiators to oppose most-favored-nation status for countries not maintaining open markets.

Kaptur has nudged Japan to import more of Toledo's auto parts. She and Democrat Sander M. Levin of Michigan mobilized congressional pressure that led in 1986 to U.S.-Japan talks on transportation equipment. A year earlier in Tokyo, she left the Japanese with souvenirs of Toledo — Champion spark plugs.

Balancing Kaptur's trade stance is her concern for Toledo's port, which has some import traffic. In 1985, she opposed a bill to impose a 25 percent surcharge on certain countries' imports. In 1984 she successfully advocated a three-year suspension of the duty on metal umbrella frames; Toledo has one of the few U.S. umbrella-making firms.

She also has focused on middle-class housing on subcommittees of Banking and Veterans' Affairs; she was chairman of a Veterans' Affairs subcommittee responsible for the VA home-loan program. But in moving to Budget, Kaptur is taking a leave from Veterans.

At Home: Kaptur's victory over GOP Rep. Ed Weber was one of Democrats' surprise successes of 1982. Although a poised and aggressive candidate, she had to overcome a late start and a poorly financed, under-organized campaign with little help from the national party.

Kaptur used Weber's support for Reaganomics as evidence of insensitivity to Toledo's plight. Weber never shifted in his public backing for Reagan's program; that was his undoing in a region with double-digit unemployment.

Overconfident, he failed to exploit one vulnerability in Kaptur's record. Although she was a Toledo native, Kaptur had spent many years away, most recently as the assistant director of urban affairs for President Jimmy Carter. But with Weber ignoring the issue, neither Kaptur's absence nor her Carter connection proved to be any problem.

In 1984, Republicans picked Frank Venner, a longtime TV newscaster, to challenge Kaptur. Although he had no previous political experience, Venner had been a familar figure to a generation of Toledo voters. But Venner had trouble translating his avuncular, non-ideological TV image into a partisan campaign. He had plenty of campaign money, but neither a strong grass-roots organization nor a potent local issue to use against Kaptur. Fortified by labor support and ties to the district's large ethnic population, Kaptur won by 25,000 votes.

Ohio 9

Northwest — Toledo

Toledo is a city whose fortunes rise and fall with the health of the automobile industry. In 1982, the city was in desperate condition; by mid-decade, there were some modest reasons for optimism.

An American Motors Jeep plant and a General Motors transmission factory were operating at full capacity. By 1986, unemployment in Toledo had slipped below 10 percent.

Two-thirds of the vote in the 9th is cast in Toledo, a Democratic outpost in rural Republican northwestern Ohio. But the absence of a large black population keeps Democratic majorities in Toledo lower than those in Dayton or Cleveland. Jimmy Carter carried the city in 1980, but with only 49 percent. Reagan managed to take it in 1984, but four years later it swung back to Democrat Michael S. Dukakis.

Toledo is an ethnic city. There are major concentrations of Germans, Irish, Poles and Hungarians. While traditionally Democratic, most blue-collar ethnics here now vote Republican at least occasionally.

Major glass producers such as Libbey-Owens-Ford, Owens-Illinois and Owens-Corning Fiberglas have headquarters in Toledo. Champion Spark Plug and the Willys-Overland automobile company also were established here in the early 20th century. Willys-Overland went bankrupt during the Depression, but it later converted to the production of Jeeps.

To the east of the city are blue-collar, traditionally Democratic suburbs. Republicans are concentrated in the more affluent suburbs west of Toledo, where Ottawa Hills has one of the highest per capita incomes of any community in Ohio.

The eastern edge of Fulton County was included in the 9th in 1982 redistricting. Fulton is one of the most Republican counties in Ohio, but the portion that joined the 9th is in the orbit of Toledo and includes most of the county's best Democratic precincts.

Population: 514,174. White 438,504 (85%), Black 64,148 (13%), Other 3,454 (1%). Spanish origin 13,253 (3%). 18 and over 364,640 (71%), 65 and over 58,484 (11%). Median age: 29.

Committees

Banking, Finance and Urban Affairs (15th of 31 Democrats)
Consumer Affairs and Coinage; Economic Stabilization; Financial Institutions Supervision, Regulation and Insurance; Housing and Community Development

Budget (20th of 21 Democrats)
Task Forces: Defense, Foreign Policy and Space; Human Resources

Elections

1988 General		
Marcy Kaptur (D)	157,557	(81%)
Al Hawkins (R)	36,183	(19%)
1986 General		
Marcy Kaptur (D)	105,646	(78%)
Mike Shufeldt (R)	30,643	(22%)

Previous Winning Percentages: **1984** (55%) **1982** (58%)

District Vote For President

	1988		1984		1980		1976	
D	107,960	(53%)	103,846	(48%)	91,749	(44%)	112,084	(56%)
R	92,563	(46%)	109,766	(51%)	97,119	(46%)	83,584	(42%)
I					17,998	(9%)		

Campaign Finance

	Receipts	Receipts from PACs	Expend-itures
1988			
Kaptur (D)	$277,724	$201,740 (73%)	$244,030
Hawkins (R)	$47,946	0	$47,945
1986			
Kaptur (D)	$283,989	$185,706 (65%)	$317,798
Shufeldt (R)	$47,626	0	$47,514

Key Votes

1987	
Raise speed limit to 65 mph	N
Approve Gephardt "fair trade" amendment	Y
Ban testing of larger nuclear weapons	Y
Delay "re-flagging" of Kuwaiti tankers	Y
Approve tax-raising deficit-reduction bill	Y
1988	
Approve aid to Nicaraguan contras	N
Enact civil rights restoration bill over Reagan veto	Y
Kill 60-day plant-closing notification measure	N
Pass omnibus trade bill over Reagan veto	Y
Approve death penalty for drug-related murders	Y
Bar federal funds for abortions in cases of rape and incest	Y
Oppose seven-day waiting period for purchase of handguns	N

Voting Studies

	Presidential Support		Party Unity		Conservative Coalition	
Year	S	O	S	O	S	O
1988	21	70	86	8	45	50
1987	19	75	82	6	30	60
1986	17	77	84	4	24	68
1985	26	70	84	9	27	69
1984	26	63	79	12	20	73
1983	12	85	85	10	15	82

Interest Group Ratings

Year	ADA	ACU	AFL-CIO	CCUS
1988	75	13	100	43
1987	80	0	94	21
1986	75	5	93	33
1985	60	14	88	41
1984	75	22	83	33
1983	90	4	94	20

10 Clarence E. Miller (R)

Of Lancaster — Elected 1966

Born: Nov. 1, 1917, Lancaster, Ohio.
Education: Graduated from Lancaster H.S., 1935.
Occupation: Electrical engineer.
Family: Widowed; two children.
Religion: Methodist.
Political Career: Lancaster City Council, 1957-63; mayor of Lancaster, 1963-65.
Capitol Office: 2208 Rayburn Bldg. 20515; 225-5131.

In Washington: Back in the 1970s, Miller made a career out of a simple amendment that earned him the nickname "Five Percent Clarence." Year after year, on bill after bill, he took the floor to propose that appropriations be reduced by 5 percent across the board, or, if that seemed politically impossible, 2 percent.

But as his ideas have taken on an air of legitimacy in the deficit-conscious 1980s, Miller has faded from the debate as younger, more energetic Republicans and fiscally conservative Democrats have become leaders of the across-the-board budget-cut school. In the 100th Congress, not a single Miller-authored budget-cut amendment came up for a recorded vote in the full House.

Miller's courtly manner fits well with the comity of the Appropriations Committee, but he is not a strong force there despite his status as the panel's fourth most senior Republican. In 1985, he gave up his ranking position on the Treasury-Postal Service Subcommittee for a spot on the Defense Subcommittee, where he ranks third in seniority.

Miller picked up his budget-cutting habit initially from Frank T. Bow, the Ohio Republican who was the senior GOP member on Appropriations when Miller came to Congress in 1967. In his first term, he was already standing up to endorse a 5 percent cut proposed by Bow. After Bow retired in 1973, Miller was principal sponsor of the idea.

His first victory came in 1977, when the House agreed to cut foreign aid spending by 5 percent. The next year he modified his strategy, successfully offering an amendment to cut labor, education and welfare spending by a smaller 2 percent. But on foreign aid, he went for too big a slice — 8 percent — and lost by 15 votes. Then his 2 percent cut in agriculture spending, which appeared to have a majority on a roll-call vote, was beaten back with some serious lobbying by the House leadership.

In the next few years, Miller seemed to be on a losing streak; the only Miller amendments that passed were in the 2 percent range. But the enormous deficits of the early 1980s and the difficulty of reducing them any other way brought the Miller method back into fashion, even as he moved into the background. By 1985, automatic or across-the-board budget reductions were being institutionalized as part of the Gramm-Rudman-Hollings deficit-reduction bill.

Beyond his idea of across-the-board cuts, Miller has not been one of the more active legislators. His most noted achievement has been his attendance record, one of the best in the House. He once introduced a resolution providing that members would lose their voting privileges if their participation fell below a certain level. Miller's attendance dropped a bit in 1987, when his wife died, but even then he was on hand for more than 90 percent of House floor votes.

At Home: Miller's election in 1966 over Democratic incumbent Walter H. Moeller was due, in large part, to the long political coattails of James A. Rhodes, the district's native son. Winning re-election as governor in 1966, Rhodes carried the 10th by 34,000 votes — enough to pull Miller into office by 4,401.

Since then, Miller has kept in touch with the voters mostly through newsletters and ceremonial visits to county fairs and other gatherings. Like virtually all Appalachian districts, the 10th is sparsely populated and difficult for challengers to campaign in; Miller's opponents have been frustrated for years by their inability even to make their names known districtwide. Only once in 11 re-election campaigns has Miller lost even one county — and it was removed by redistricting the following year.

In several of his campaigns, Miller has had the easy task of facing professors from Ohio University at Athens. He has been challenged by an economist, a historian and a political scientist, and none has drawn a third of the vote against him. As a countrified ex-mayor with a correspondence degree in engineering, Miller has simply fit the constituency better than they have. Since 1974, Miller's opponents have included an accountant, an auto dealer, a hotel manager and a manufacturing engineer, and they have represented no more of a threat. The manufacturing engineer, John M. Buchanan, has been the Democrats' sacrificial lamb against Miller the last four elections.

Ohio 10

Southeast — Lancaster; Zanesville

Nearly as large as Connecticut, the 10th is a part of Appalachia grafted onto a Midwestern state. While redistricting in 1982 enlarged the industrial blue-collar base, the 10th has not lost its traditional Republican character. It was the only district in the state that failed to elect a Democrat to the House during the New Deal years.

During the 1960s, much of this area was stagnating economically and losing population. In the 1970s, people began moving back, in part because of the increased interest in coal mining. With a 14 percent population increase, the 10th was second in growth among Ohio districts during the decade.

But the economic picture clouded again in the 1980s with the downturn in the coal and petrochemical industries.

Licking County is a pocket of prosperity; the Newark-Granville-Heath metropolitan area is a growing center for manufacturing and research, with Owens-Corning and Diebold electronic securities as major employers. The Newark Air Force station has a large civilian research facility, as does Dow Chemical Co.

Fairfield County has seen more growth in recent years than most any part of the 10th, as bedroom communities blossomed along Route 33, a four-lane highway connecting Lancaster with the thriving city of Columbus, 30 miles to the northwest.

Athens County has a high level of government employment, including Ohio University, with over 15,000 students, and that cushions it somewhat from adverse economic conditions. Athens is the only Democratic-leaning part of the district. It was one of just two Ohio counties to support George McGovern for president in 1972; in 1988, Michael S. Dukakis carried it with 52 percent of the vote.

Many of the poorer voters in other counties along the Ohio River still call themselves Democrats — a remnant of Civil War days — but their conservative outlook leads them toward Republican candidates in most elections.

Population: 514,173. White 499,615 (97%), Black 10,925 (2%). Spanish origin 2,519 (1%). 18 and over 362,509 (71%), 65 and over 57,433 (11%). Median age: 30.

Committee

Appropriations (4th of 22 Republicans)
Defense

Elections

1988 General		
Clarence E. Miller (R)	143,673	(72%)
John M. Buchanan (D)	56,893	(28%)
1988 Primary		
Clarence E. Miller (R)	52,243	(84%)
Ronald E. Shoemaker (R)	9,782	(16%)
1986 General		
Clarence E. Miller (R)	106,870	(70%)
John M. Buchanan (D)	44,847	(30%)

Previous Winning Percentages: **1984** (73%) **1982** (63%) **1980** (74%) **1978** (74%) **1976** (69%) **1974** (70%) **1972** (73%) **1970** (67%) **1968** (69%) **1966** (52%)

District Vote For President

	1988	1984	1980	1976
D	79,268 (38%)	67,532 (33%)	75,455 (39%)	85,428 (47%)
R	125,373 (61%)	136,089 (66%)	108,319 (55%)	92,932 (51%)
I			8,550 (4%)	

Campaign Finance

	Receipts	Receipts from PACs	Expend-itures
1988			
Miller (R)	$129,695	$99,436 (77%)	$99,247
Buchanan (D) †	$9,231	0	$9,429
1986			
Miller (R)	$85,899	$69,349 (81%)	$67,073

† Totals based on incomplete data.

Key Votes

1987	
Raise speed limit to 65 mph	Y
Approve Gephardt "fair trade" amendment	N
Ban testing of larger nuclear weapons	N
Delay "re-flagging" of Kuwaiti tankers	N
Approve tax-raising deficit-reduction bill	N
1988	
Approve aid to Nicaraguan contras	Y
Enact civil rights restoration bill over Reagan veto	N
Kill 60-day plant-closing notification measure	Y
Pass omnibus trade bill over Reagan veto	Y
Approve death penalty for drug-related murders	Y
Bar federal funds for abortions in cases of rape and incest	Y
Oppose seven-day waiting period for purchase of handguns	Y

Voting Studies

	Presidential Support		Party Unity		Conservative Coalition	
Year	S	O	S	O	S	O
1988	62	38	85	13	95	5
1987	60	28	77	15	86	0
1986	77	22	83	14	86	14
1985	70	24	79	11	85	7
1984	60	38	84	16	83	17
1983	68	29	80	18	73	25
1982	70	30	80	18	78	22
1981	72	28	86	14	91	9

Interest Group Ratings

Year	ADA	ACU	AFL-CIO	CCUS
1988	15	92	43	93
1987	8	100	13	71
1986	5	86	14	78
1985	0	89	0	85
1984	5	71	8	75
1983	15	91	6	74
1982	5	96	25	64
1981	5	100	20	84

11 Dennis E. Eckart (D)

Of Mentor — Elected 1980

Born: April 6, 1950, Cleveland, Ohio.
Education: Xavier U., B.S. 1971; Cleveland State U., J.D. 1974.
Occupation: Lawyer.
Family: Wife, Sandra Pestotnik; one child.
Religion: Roman Catholic.
Political Career: Assistant prosecutor, Lake County, 1974; Ohio House, 1975-81.
Capitol Office: 1210 Longworth Bldg. 20515; 225-6331.

In Washington: Unlike many of his younger-generation contemporaries in the House Democratic Caucus, Eckart is as much old-school urban operator as he is reform-minded liberal, perhaps more. Like the reformers, he masters his issues and minds the media. But like the operators, he loves the dealing part of politics, and he does it well.

This combination of traits prompted House leaders to mark Eckart as a comer early in his career, in spite of the youthful brashness that still flares up, even as Eckart nears his 10th anniversary as a congressman.

Eckart, first elected at age 30, won a whip's post in his freshman term, and a seat on Energy and Commerce the next. There he is known as one of Chairman John D. Dingell's favorites. The two have a strong personal relationship, bolstered by time spent pursuing the chairman's favorite sport, hunting. It is an unusual but legislatively useful interest for an urban boy who grew up on the streets of Cleveland.

On Energy and Commerce, Eckart does not always agree with Dingell, but on most major issues, his concerns and those of his suburban Cleveland district have much in common with Dingell's and his Detroit-area voters. When Dingell leaves a hearing, he can trust Eckart to make sure his views are not watered down.

This loyalty is repaid in a variety of ways. In 1987, on the first day of subcommittee hearings on product-liability legislation — which Dingell unsuccessfully pushed during the 100th Congress — the Cleveland *Plain Dealer* ran an article accusing Eckart of cozy connections with business leaders backing the legislation. Dingell later accused a trial lawyer lobbyist of planting the story, and warned him that he would not look kindly on such an act.

Eckart chafes when his liberalism is questioned, but on some key environmental issues, he breaks ranks with the left. Ohio power plants emit more of the pollutants said to cause acid rain than any other state, which causes Eckart to pull back from stringent measures aimed at eliminating acid rain. In 1984, he cast the decisive vote on the Health Subcommittee that doomed acid-rain legislation that year. More recently, he was a member of the committee's moderate "group of nine" that tried to negotiate a compromise acceptable to industry and environmentalists.

When the 100th Congress debated nuclear-accident insurance legislation, however, Eckart was a leader in the environmental-consumer faction. It was not a popular cause with Dingell, but it was appreciated by neighbors of the Perry nuclear plant in Eckart's district.

Eckart teamed up with committee liberals Gerry Sikorski of Minnesota and Edward J. Markey of Massachusetts in an effort to increase safety incentives, victims' compensation and industry accountability. They offered a series of amendments in committee and on the floor, but met with little success. Just a week after Energy and Commerce approved one of their amendments — to pay victims before utility lawyers if damages from an accident exceed the compensation fund — the committee reconvened and reversed itself.

Eckart's pro-nuclear critics said he was trying to gut the law, which was originally drafted in 1957 to help encourage civilian nuclear power by limiting risks that might discourage investors. But Eckart, rarely at a loss for a pithy quote, countered that it was time to "take the training wheels off" the industry. He called the bill a "K-Mart blue-light special for the nuclear-power industry" and a "raw deal for the taxpayers."

By contrast, in the previous Congress, Eckart was at odds with committee environmentalists over the "superfund" hazardous-waste cleanup program. While Eckart, too, wanted to enlarge the fund, the bill's sponsor, James J. Florio of New Jersey, pushed for stricter cleanup standards. Eckart complained that Florio's bill would never win bipartisan support and belonged "in a time capsule" rather than in a practical legislative debate. The Ohioan won a bruising committee fight, but the full House restored much of what Florio wanted.

In that episode, Eckart was credited for his grasp of the issue, but he lost points when he

Ohio 11

Northeast — Cleveland Suburbs

The small industrial cities of northeast Ohio have shared in Cleveland's economic problems, but not in its emerging solutions. Reliant on the steel, chemical and automobile industries for most of their livelihood, the blue-collar communities of the 11th District are among the most depressed parts of the state.

Ashtabula County, on Lake Erie, casts nearly a quarter of the vote. Employment there has recovered only modestly since the early 1980s recession, when the jobless rate hit 20 percent. The steel and chemical plants situated along Lake Erie have been severely hurt by foreign competition, and it is hard to find signs of revival.

Ashtabula is reliably Democratic in most elections; only a strong GOP county organization keeps the party's candidates close.

Southwest of Ashtabula is equally Democratic Portage County, sandwiched between Youngstown on the east and Akron on the west. The population centers of Ravenna and Kent are in the middle of the county.

As migration from Cleveland moved eastward between 1950 and 1970, the population of Lake and Geauga counties more than doubled. The rapid growth has slowed, but the suburbs continue to creep farther east, obliterating the truck gardens and vineyards along Lake Erie.

Lake County's Republican farmers and suburbanites are canceled out politically by ethnic Democrats who have settled in the western part of the county. Geauga, on the other hand, is the GOP mainstay in the 11th. Settled by Yankee Protestants, it was the only county in northeast Ohio to back Republican Alf Landon for president in 1936. It has remained in the GOP column since then, but it casts only 14 percent of the district vote.

Population: 514,173. White 499,454 (97%), Black 10,438 (2%), Other 2,800 (1%). Spanish origin 3,224 (1%). 18 and over 355,787 (69%), 65 and over 43,049 (8%). Median age: 29.

lashed out at environmental groups that claimed his proposals would benefit polluters. He complained of "character besmirchment" by a "few shrill extremists" with an "insatiable appetite" for more concessions.

In the 98th Congress, Eckart tangled with Health Subcommittee Chairman Henry A. Waxman over clean-air legislation. Eckart was considered a key swing vote. Under great pressure from environmental groups and from his district's unions and industries, Eckart worked closely with Waxman to find language that would satisfy both groups of constituents. As the vote approached, they were said to be near agreement. But when a motion was introduced to strip the acid-rain controls from the clean-air bill, Eckart joined several Midwest Democrats in backing it, infuriating Waxman's side. "He brought it all down," Waxman charged.

Eckart did mend some fences later in the 98th Congress, when he took the lead in trying to strengthen clean-water legislation. Working closely with Republican Edward Madigan of Illinois, he helped draft a bill that drew applause from both sides of the aisle. A similar measure became law in 1986.

Eckart also dabbles in national politics. Since 1987, he has been a regional chairman of the Democratic Congressional Campaign Committee, and in 1988, he was an early supporter of Michael S. Dukakis' campaign. Eckart played the role of Dan Quayle during Lloyd Bentsen's vice presidential debate preparations.

At Home: Eckart skillfully navigated the shoals of redistricting in 1982 to take over a brand-new constituency.

The Ohio Legislature gutted his old 22nd District in Cleveland's eastern suburbs, giving Eckart a complicated series of options. He planned at first to follow most of his constituents into the new 19th District, taking a chance on a Democratic primary campaign against the more conservative Ronald M. Mottl, whose residence was also placed in the 19th.

But when GOP Rep. J. William Stanton announced he was retiring, the 11th became more attractive to Eckart, although it contained barely 15 percent of his former constituents. The young Democrat moved his residence from Euclid to a condominium in Concord Township, near Madison, where he grew up.

Eckart portrayed himself as the incumbent, papering the district with franked mail, blaming Reaganomics for the economic troubles in northeast Ohio and talking about his rising stature in Congress. His Democratic primary opponents denounced him as a carpetbagger, but he had an organization, substantial campaign money and a talent for attracting media attention that his two rivals could not match. With endorsements from Cleveland's major newspapers and the help of leading unions in the area, Eckart swept four of the district's five counties, and won easily in the fall.

In the Ohio Legislature, Eckart was a consumer affairs specialist who built much of his name on a bill giving state-subsidized tax credits to the elderly for their energy bills.

Eckart was in line to become chairman of the state House Judiciary Committee in 1980, but when Democratic Rep. Charles A. Vanik announced he would retire, Eckart ran for Congress. His principal primary rival was maverick state Sen. J. Timothy McCormack, who accused him of being "a classic go-along person."

McCormack had antagonized many voters by precipitating the popular Vanik's departure. Vanik loathed fund raising, and when McCormack announced his bid, the 68-year-old incumbent chose retirement. Eckart gained Vanik's support and benefited from a good organization. He won the primary by nearly 12,000 votes.

Republican Joseph Nahra, a former probate judge, offered a well-financed campaign that fall. But he may have been hurt by his identification as an ethnic Lebanese. An estimated 20 percent of the district electorate was Jewish, and Eckart, like Vanik, had been an outspoken supporter of Israel.

After two lopsided victories, Eckart felt secure in 1988 and began dedicating considerable time to the Dukakis campaign. But his little-known GOP foe, 58-year-old social worker Margaret Mueller, began making enough noise to draw Eckart back home by late fall.

Eckart had defeated her decisively in 1986, but this time she came on strong with a vituperative campaign that surprised the Democrat. She poured $500,000 of her own into the campaign, and ran tough TV ads that criticized Eckart as soft on crime and drugs.

Mueller outspent Eckart until late in the campaign, when he fired back. Saying she had "earned a gold medal for sleaze," Eckart ran TV ads that featured a chicken scampering back and forth across a street — symbolizing Mueller changing positions. Eckart also issued a mailing that included a photo of Mueller and the caption, "Good Girls Shouldn't Lie."

On Election Day, Eckart's percentage dropped 10 points from 1986, but he still surpassed 60 percent of the vote.

Committees

Energy and Commerce (16th of 26 Democrats)
Oversight and Investigations; Telecommunications and Finance; Transportation and Hazardous Materials

Small Business (9th of 27 Democrats)
Antitrust, Impact of Deregulation and Privatization (chairman)

Elections

1988 General		
Dennis E. Eckart (D)	124,600	(61%)
Margaret Mueller (R)	78,028	(39%)
1986 General		
Dennis E. Eckart (D)	104,740	(72%)
Margaret Mueller (R)	35,944	(25%)

Previous Winning Percentages: 1984 (67%) **1982** (61%) **1980** (55%)

District Vote For President

	1988	1984	1980	1976
D	93,486 (44%)	84,171 (40%)	66,054 (37%)	89,687 (50%)
R	115,947 (55%)	125,163 (59%)	93,307 (53%)	84,438 (47%)
I			14,025 (8%)	

Campaign Finance

	Receipts	Receipts from PACs	Expend-itures
1988			
Eckart (D)	$569,638	$382,928 (67%)	$561,070
Mueller (R)	$1,006,371	$250 (0%)	$860,766
1986			
Eckart (D)	$403,129	$221,653 (55%)	$348,552
Mueller (R)	$288,097	$925 (0.3%)	$275,584

Key Votes

1987	
Raise speed limit to 65 mph	N
Approve Gephardt "fair trade" amendment	Y
Ban testing of larger nuclear weapons	Y
Delay "re-flagging" of Kuwaiti tankers	Y
Approve tax-raising deficit-reduction bill	N
1988	
Approve aid to Nicaraguan contras	N
Enact civil rights restoration bill over Reagan veto	Y
Kill 60-day plant-closing notification measure	N
Pass omnibus trade bill over Reagan veto	Y
Approve death penalty for drug-related murders	Y
Bar federal funds for abortions in cases of rape and incest	N
Oppose seven-day waiting period for purchase of handguns	N

Voting Studies

	Presidential Support		Party Unity		Conservative Coalition	
Year	**S**	**O**	**S**	**O**	**S**	**O**
1988	21	78	88	12	37	63
1987	19	80	87	11	42	58
1986	21	78	87	13	40	60
1985	24	76	88	10	35	65
1984	31	67	81	16	27	71
1983	18	82	84	14	26	74
1982	31	64	87	10	21	78
1981	33	63	82	17	25	68

Interest Group Ratings

Year	ADA	ACU	AFL-CIO	CCUS
1988	90	8	100	29
1987	88	4	94	29
1986	65	14	86	22
1985	70	19	76	36
1984	75	17	77	25
1983	90	9	94	20
1982	70	36	95	23
1981	80	15	87	11

12 John R. Kasich (R)

Of Westerville — Elected 1982

Born: May 13, 1952, McKees Rocks, Pa.
Education: Ohio State U., B.A. 1974.
Occupation: Legislative aide.
Family: Divorced.
Religion: Roman Catholic.
Political Career: Ohio Senate, 1979-83.
Capitol Office: 1133 Longworth Bldg. 20515; 225-5355.

In Washington: Kasich's rhetorical tirades and cocksure self-promotion drive Democrats to distraction, and even Republican colleagues say they wish this Ohio conservative were not quite so full of himself. But enemy and ally alike say Kasich has some clear goals on the Armed Services Committee, and is willing to work hard to advance them.

Kasich wants to use Armed Services as a forum for debating defense policy with the Democratic majority. Too often, he and his GOP allies feel, members have focused overmuch on the panel's "pork" potential, cooperating to spend defense money in each other's districts and ceding the job of drawing a "big picture" of U.S. military priorities.

A strong supporter of the strategic defense initiative (SDI), Kasich expressed anger at the diversion of money requested by President Reagan for SDI to projects favored by Armed Services members.

When Armed Services in 1988 reduced SDI funding authority to $4.1 billion from the $4.9 billion Reagan requested, Kasich supported adding back money to SDI, and asked the committee to consider whether it had adopted any "parochial add-ons" that could be jettisoned. Committee Chairman Les Aspin responded with mock indignation, "All of the add-ons here are essential to the national defense" — provoking gales of laughter. Kasich did not quite see the humor. "That's what I thought," he shot back.

There is no mistaking Kasich's overall conservative orientation. In 1988, he received a 92 rating from the American Conservative Union. On Armed Services, Kasich joins with Republican members such as Duncan Hunter of California and Jon Kyl of Arizona in forming the committee's right flank. In 1987, he cautioned against cutting Reagan's funding request in the fiscal 1988 defense authorization bill, and did so in partisan terms, warning committee Democrats that voters would get even at the ballot box. "You put those [cutbacks] together and that is not where the American people are at," Kasich said.

Kasich's interest in strategic coherence carries over into the area of military procurement; he has played an active role in efforts to combat waste and fraud in the Pentagon procurement system. His interest in fiscal efficiency also spurred his desire for a seat on the Budget Committee, which he got in the 101st Congress.

Even on defense programs he advocates, Kasich thinks there is harm in haste. In 1987, he opposed an amendment by conservative Republican Jim Courter of New Jersey that called for a deployable SDI system to be developed by 1993. "What I'm afraid you get," Kasich said, "is a system that is not very effective . . . [that would] arm the enemies of SDI to argue that the system is not worth the cost."

The following year, Kasich, an advocate of the proposal by Texas Republican Dick Armey to close obsolete military bases, developed a congressional certification process that became a linchpin of the plan. The base-closing bill, as reported by several committees, called for Congress to have the opportunity to approve the list of potential base closures developed by an independent commission. But Kasich submitted an amendment on the House floor in 1988 allowing Congress to vote only to "disapprove" the entire base-closure list.

The idea seemed like a good one to many members, who saw the need to close some bases but did not want to go on record voting to do the deed. Kasich's plan was approved by a 250-138 vote, and was adopted as part of a "clean bill" later submitted by Armey. In 1989, the House voted overwhelmingly against disapproving the list of base closures that had been recommended by the independent commission.

It was his zeal for Pentagon efficiency that first earned Kasich attention after he arrived in Congress in 1983. Along with Democrat Bill Nichols of Alabama, Kasich led the House inquiry into the high price the Pentagon sometimes pays to get spare parts for weaponry. Arguing that the current system enabled parts makers to limit competition, Kasich proposed legislation generally limiting to seven years the period in which a manufacturer could assert "proprietary" rights over the specifications for

Ohio 12

Northeast Columbus and Suburbs

Columbus has not suffered from the kind of economic collapse that has afflicted most of Ohio's industrial cities in the past few years. It is primarily a white-collar town, one whose diverse industrial base is bolstered by the state government complex, Ohio State University, a major banking center and numerous scientific research firms. For much of the 1980s, Columbus and surrounding Franklin County have had one of the lowest unemployment rates of any metropolitan area in Ohio.

Nearly three-quarters of the 12th District vote is cast in Columbus and its Franklin County suburbs. Democrats have to do extremely well within the city to have a chance districtwide. Blacks comprise 22 percent of Columbus' population, but they are split evenly between the 12th and 15th districts, reducing Democratic prospects in both. As one moves east from the state Capitol building along Broad Street, the black vote goes down and the GOP vote goes up.

About three miles east of the Capitol is affluent Bexley, an independent community of 13,000 surrounded by the city. While normally Republican, Bexley has a large Jewish population and sometimes votes for strong Democratic candidates. Two miles farther east is Whitehall, another independent town. Site of the Defense Construction Supply Center, it has a large blue-collar base with frequent ticket-splitting.

Farther out are newer suburbs. Some of these, such as Reynoldsburg and Gahanna, are predominantly blue-collar. Residents are employed at large plants such as McDonnell Douglas and AT&T. The rest of the 12th is rural and Republican, with a smattering of light industry. The half of Licking County in the district often gives Kasich a 3-to-1 margin, and Delaware and Morrow counties are equally favorable to the GOP.

Population: 514,173. White 430,939 (84%), Black 77,731 (15%), Other 3,233 (1%). Spanish origin 3,534 (1%). 18 and over 366,117 (71%), 65 and over 42,505 (8%). Median age: 29.

a particular part. Kasich won House passage of his proposal. But it was rejected in a House-Senate conference.

Kasich then joined with Democrat Nicholas Mavroules of Massachusetts in shaping the procurement section of the 1986 defense authorization bill. He also continued to work closely with Nichols, the taciturn chairman of the Armed Services Subcommittee on Investigations, who, though a Democrat, acted as something of a mentor to Kasich: He even advised Kasich once that he would get more accomplished if he talked a little less. After Nichols died suddenly just before the beginning of the 101st Congress, Kasich delivered a moving eulogy at his funeral.

A corollary to Kasich's drive against procurement waste is his push for an improved system for the government to collect its debts. Citing a General Accounting Office report he commissioned in 1986 that found the federal government was owed $64 billion in delinquent debts, Kasich called for the creation of a new under secretary at the Treasury Department to act as a "debt czar" who would supervise the collection of the government's bills.

Kasich has also attached a series of amendments to authorization legislation, ordering federal departments to use private-sector collection firms to track down delinquent debts. For instance, an authorization bill passed by the House in April 1989 contained a Kasich amendment requiring the State Department and United States Information Agency to use private collection agencies to handle their delinquent debts. The bill also contained another anti-waste provision authored by Kasich: It limited the number of officials at a U.S. embassy who are entitled to "extraordinarily" spacious housing for purposes of official entertainment.

Though Kasich is widely credited for the vigor of his legislative efforts, he established a propensity early on for getting on people's nerves — a habit many colleagues say he has yet to outgrow. During an Armed Services Committee session following the 1983 bombings that killed 241 Marines in Lebanon, Kasich nettled Marine Corps Commandant Gen. P. X. Kelley by demanding to know why the Marines did not search every vehicle entering the Beirut airport. "Let's use good judgment about this, Mr. Kasich, and not get emotional for the TV cameras," Kelley snarled in reply.

At Home: Elections have been fairly quiet in the 12th since 1984, a stark contrast to the situation early in the decade, when the district twice defied national political trends.

In 1980, while Reagan's presidential campaign was sweeping the country, the 12th was turning out its Republican incumbent for a Democrat, Bob Shamansky. Two years later, Democrats were in good shape virtually everywhere, but in Columbus, voters were ousting

Shamansky in favor of Republican Kasich.

Republicans felt that the 1982 result simply recovered what was rightfully theirs. They considered Shamansky's 1980 victory a fluke, due more to the complacency of GOP Rep. Samuel Devine than to any change in the district's traditional Republican leanings.

Shamansky had the advantage of incumbency in his 1982 campaign against Kasich. But the challenger was well positioned, thanks in large measure to a redistricting plan that had been passed by the Legislature a few months earlier. Some heavily black wards on Columbus' East Side were removed from the district, while a rural, predominantly Republican area was added.

Although Shamansky carried Franklin County (Columbus), his margin was not enough to overcome Kasich's lead in the rural counties.

Kasich's relatively narrow margin that year did not prove to be a harbinger of re-election difficulties. Democrats devoted substantial resources in 1984 to challenger Richard Sloan, a former aide to Sen. Howard M. Metzenbaum, but Sloan could do little to overcome Kasich's superior campaign organization. In 1986 and 1988, Democrats offered only minor opposition.

An energetic grass-roots campaigner, Kasich upset a veteran Democratic state senator in 1978 by visiting every household in his district several times. That was his political debut. His later campaigns have been facsimiles.

Committees

Armed Services (9th of 21 Republicans)
Readiness (ranking); Procurement and Military Nuclear Systems

Budget (11th of 14 Republicans)
Task Forces: Defense, Foreign Policy and Space; Human Resources

Elections

1988 General		
John R. Kasich (R)	154,727	(79%)
Mark P. Brown (D)	41,178	(21%)
1986 General		
John R. Kasich (R)	117,905	(73%)
Timothy C. Jochim (D)	42,727	(27%)

Previous Winning Percentages: 1984 (70%) **1982** (51%)

District Vote For President

	1988	1984	1980	1976
D	83,561 (38%)	72,607 (33%)	79,143 (39%)	79,422 (42%)
R	133,563 (61%)	144,741 (65%)	110,235 (54%)	105,399 (56%)
I			10,361 (5%)	

Campaign Finance

	Receipts	Receipts from PACs	Expend-itures
1988			
Kasich (R)	$370,579	$130,686 (35%)	$351,517
1986			
Kasich (R)	$348,000	$129,817 (37%)	$424,678
Jochim (D)	$22,998	$8,750 (38%)	$22,945

Key Votes

1987	
Raise speed limit to 65 mph	Y
Approve Gephardt "fair trade" amendment	N
Ban testing of larger nuclear weapons	N
Delay "re-flagging" of Kuwaiti tankers	N
Approve tax-raising deficit-reduction bill	N
1988	
Approve aid to Nicaraguan contras	Y
Enact civil rights restoration bill over Reagan veto	N
Kill 60-day plant-closing notification measure	Y
Pass omnibus trade bill over Reagan veto	N
Approve death penalty for drug-related murders	Y
Bar federal funds for abortions in cases of rape and incest	Y
Oppose seven-day waiting period for purchase of handguns	Y

Voting Studies

	Presidential Support		Party Unity		Conservative Coalition	
Year	**S**	**O**	**S**	**O**	**S**	**O**
1988	61	38	76	20	100	0
1987	68	31	74	21	93	5
1986	70	29	75	22	88	12
1985	74	26	90	7	98	2
1984	61	38	82	17	92	8
1983	77	23	90	10	87	13

Interest Group Ratings

Year	ADA	ACU	AFL-CIO	CCUS
1988	15	92	29	93
1987	8	78	0	93
1986	10	82	29	89
1985	5	90	12	86
1984	5	67	23	75
1983	10	91	6	85

13 Don J. Pease (D)

Of Oberlin — Elected 1976

Born: Sept. 26, 1931, Toledo, Ohio.
Education: Ohio U., B.S. 1953, M.A. 1955; attended U. of Durham, England, 1954-55.
Military Career: Army, 1955-57.
Occupation: Newspaper editor.
Family: Wife, Jeanne Wendt; one child.
Religion: Methodist.
Political Career: Oberlin City Council, 1962-64; Ohio Senate, 1965-67 and 1975-77; Ohio House, 1969-75; sought re-election to Ohio Senate, 1966.
Capitol Office: 2410 Rayburn Bldg. 20515; 225-3401.

In Washington: Pease is something of an enigma on the Ways and Means Committee. Soft-spoken and pedantic, he approaches politics as an ethical pursuit and legislation as an intellectual exercise. Yet on a committee known more for its horse-traders than its intellectuals, Pease is a serious player.

His success is largely predicated on an unlikely alliance with Chairman Dan Rostenkowski, the veteran product of Chicago machine politics. Loyalty is the first word in any relationship with the chairman, and Pease abides by it. He also has a personable nature and a shared interest with Rostenkowski in taking care of blue-collar workers. All this has helped give Pease a hand in most major bills that have passed through Ways and Means in recent years.

Representing an economically troubled industrial district, Pease spends much of his time focusing on meat-and-potato labor issues. A member of the Trade Subcommittee and the 1987 conference committee on the omnibus trade bill, Pease substantively leaned toward the protectionist side of the debate, but argued for compromise and a cooling in the rhetorical war.

Fearing the Gephardt "fair trade" amendment could become a "killer" clause that would pull down the trade bill, Pease warned in a 1987 opinion article in *The Christian Science Monitor,* "If the Gephardt amendment passes, many Republicans will no doubt oppose the bill itself. If it fails to pass, some Democrats will feel it is too wimpy to be worth passing." In the end, Pease voted for the Gephardt amendment when it was successfully offered on the floor. But Republican resistance to the amendment resulted in a watered-down version becoming law in 1988.

The bill included a handful of Pease-inspired amendments, including a proposal that combined his labor interest with an interest in human rights abroad — an interest he had previously pursued on the Foreign Affairs Committee. Arguing that American workers cannot compete with imports produced by exploited workers in foreign countries, Pease successfully pushed for language on international labor standards, and he has lobbied for those standards to be included in the international General Agreement on Tariffs and Trade.

Closer to home, Pease argued that the federal government's fiscal policies, particularly the budget deficit, are a major cause of the nation's trade deficit. He authored a successful trade amendment requiring "trade impact statements" in the president's and the Congress' budgets. With these, legislators can "take into account the impact of the budget on our trade accounts and international competitiveness while they draft the budget," he said, "not after it has been passed and the damage is done."

Pease was also active in the 1988 debate on the welfare reform bill. He co-authored successful language with Henry A. Waxman of California to require states to provide coverage to families that move off public assistance for six months, and then to extend certain coverage for an additional 18 months if the family's income does not exceed 185 percent of the federal poverty level.

The committee debate on welfare reform was at times sharply partisan. While Pease generally held traditional Democratic views on the subject, he broke with Ways and Means Democrats on a vote to close a key markup meeting. He was the only Democrat to side with the unanimous but unsuccessful GOP bloc on the matter.

A former newspaper editor, Pease has long supported "sunshine" open government rules, but he is also an experienced legislator. "I hate to say it, but members are more willing to make tough decisions on controversial bills in closed meetings," he once said. "In a closed meeting, you can come out and say, 'I fought like a tiger for you in there, but I lost.' "

During the many closed conference mark-

Ohio 13

North — Lorain

Lying squarely in the midst of industrial northern Ohio, the 13th has all the problems of a declining Frost Belt economy. Heavily dependent on the automobile and steel industries, populous Lorain County approached Depression-era conditions in the early 1980s. In 1986, the county's unemployment rate still stood at 10 percent.

The most serious trouble spot is the once-booming port city of Lorain. But while the local economy there has been battered, the old New Deal coalition is alive and well. Blue-collar ethnics, blacks and Hispanics in Lorain combine with those in nearby Elyria and academics in the college town of Oberlin to produce Democratic majorities. Walter F. Mondale and Pease each won the city of Lorain with 80 percent in 1984, although President Reagan carried Lorain County. Four years later, even the countywide vote was Democratic; Michael S. Dukakis eked out a 51 percent victory there.

As one of the traditional immigration centers on the Great Lakes, the city of Lorain has an ethnic diversity that matches the West Side of Cleveland. Fifty-six different ethnic groups have been counted within its borders. Today, Hispanics alone comprise 14 percent of Lorain's population, a far higher share than in any city in Ohio.

About 10 miles due south of Lorain is Oberlin, which roughly divides urban, Catholic Democrats in the northern part of the district from rural, Protestant Republicans in the southern part. Founded in 1833, Oberlin College was the first coeducational institution of higher learning in the country and among the first to admit black students. The Yankees who founded Oberlin and other towns in this part of Ohio took strong anti-slavery stands in the 19th century, and their descendants (such as Pease) have continued to show an affinity for social reforms and causes of various kinds, including civil rights and the anti-war movement.

South and west is rural Republican territory. Some farms in this area raise grains and livestock, but the emphasis is on dairy products, fruits and vegetables. Democrats can normally count on support in Richland County, especially from the industrial city of Mansfield. But Ashland County usually rewards statewide Republican candidates with 60 percent or more of the vote.

Population: 514,176. White 477,543 (93%), Black 26,559 (5%). Spanish origin 14,618 (3%). 18 and over 350,858 (68%), 65 and over 44,544 (9%). Median age: 28.

ups on the 1986 tax overhaul, Pease was a reliable source for reporters. But when Rostenkowski instructed members to stop leaking news, Pease complied. Given that he had been handpicked by Rostenkowski for the conference committee — over eight more senior members — that was an astute move.

Pease had waited a long time for a chance to overhaul the tax system, and he was not going to deal himself out of the process just to help his former colleagues in the media. Pease began promoting tax reform shortly after his arrival in Washington — long before many other members were interested in talking about it.

But in the 99th Congress, both tax revision and Pease were at the center of Ways and Means' activity. He made himself the chairman's ally during markup of the House bill, helping Rostenkowski fight off unwanted amendments and refraining from offering amendments of his own. The final House bill was consistent with Pease's longstanding desire for a simpler tax code with lower rates for poor and middle-class people and fewer subsidies for corporations and wealthy individuals.

Early in his career, Pease served two terms on the Foreign Affairs Committee, where he argued for a strong commitment to human rights in U.S. foreign policy. Recently he has combined his interest in Third World politics with his new finance-oriented assignment by proposing a sweeping debt-relief plan for developing nations.

At Home: After a string of easy victories against weak Republican opposition, Pease got a chance to flex his political muscles in 1986, when he encountered a well-funded Republican challenger, business executive William D. Nielsen.

Nielsen blanketed the district with billboards, direct-mail appeals and postcards in an aggressive campaign that sought to discredit Pease as a big-spending liberal who had not looked out for the area's troubled manufacturing interests.

But Pease proved to be less vulnerable than Nielsen hoped. The soft-spoken legislator had a place in the Washington spotlight during the summer of 1986 as a House conferee on the tax-revision bill. This meant favorable publicity back home, and contributed to the largest campaign treasury of his career. On Election Day, Pease swept every county in the district. In 1988, the GOP did not offer a tough challenge.

In spite of his sustained success in House elections, Pease had some trouble getting his political career off the ground. After one term in the state Senate, he was defeated for re-election in 1966. He switched to the Ohio House, spent three terms there, then made it back to the state Senate by defeating a GOP incumbent in 1974.

During his legislative career, Pease was a close ally of Ohio's teachers, who joined with other labor organizations to help him easily win the seat of retiring GOP Rep. Charles A. Mosher, a longtime friend whom Pease had succeeded as editor of the *Oberlin News-Tribune.*

Committee

Ways and Means (12th of 23 Democrats)
Human Resources; Trade

Elections

1988 General		
Don J. Pease (D)	137,074	(70%)
Dwight Brown (R)	59,287	(30%)
1988 Primary		
Don J. Pease (D)	52,388	(83%)
John M. Ryan (D)	11,037	(17%)
1986 General		
Don J. Pease (D)	88,612	(63%)
William D. Nielsen Jr. (R)	52,452	(37%)

Previous Winning Percentages: 1984 (66%) **1982** (61%) **1980** (64%) **1978** (65%) **1976** (66%)

District Vote For President

	1988	1984	1980	1976
D	93,620 (46%)	84,403 (40%)	67,998 (37%)	86,395 (51%)
R	109,701 (54%)	121,317 (58%)	98,859 (53%)	77,579 (46%)
I			12,439 (7%)	

Campaign Finance

	Receipts	Receipts from PACs	Expend-itures
1988			
Pease (D)	$292,904	$189,677 (65%)	$157,632
Brown (R)	$16,681	0	$16,682
1986			
Pease (D)	$438,277	$252,800 (58%)	$415,486
Nielsen (R)	$273,490	$11,988 (4%)	$256,604

Key Votes

1987	
Raise speed limit to 65 mph	N
Approve Gephardt "fair trade" amendment	Y
Ban testing of larger nuclear weapons	Y
Delay "re-flagging" of Kuwaiti tankers	Y
Approve tax-raising deficit-reduction bill	Y
1988	
Approve aid to Nicaraguan contras	N
Enact civil rights restoration bill over Reagan veto	Y
Kill 60-day plant-closing notification measure	N
Pass omnibus trade bill over Reagan veto	Y
Approve death penalty for drug-related murders	Y
Bar federal funds for abortions in cases of rape and incest	N
Oppose seven-day waiting period for purchase of handguns	N

Voting Studies

	Presidential Support		Party Unity		Conservative Coalition	
Year	S	O	S	O	S	O
1988	29	69	88	9	24	71
1987	25	74	90	8	30	65
1986	26	74	92	8	32	68
1985	28	71	93	7	20	80
1984	40	59	85	15	22	78
1983	20	80	91	9	18	82
1982	38	61	87	11	16	81
1981	32	64	83	9	16	77

Interest Group Ratings

Year	ADA	ACU	AFL-CIO	CCUS
1988	90	8	86	50
1987	88	0	88	7
1986	75	18	79	17
1985	70	14	82	38
1984	80	8	62	25
1983	90	4	88	35
1982	90	5	100	23
1981	95	0	93	6

14 Thomas C. Sawyer (D)

Of Akron — Elected 1986

Born: Aug. 15, 1945, Akron, Ohio.
Education: U. of Akron, B.A. 1968, M.A. 1970.
Occupation: Teacher.
Family: Wife, Joyce Handler; one child.
Religion: Presbyterian.
Political Career: Ohio House, 1977-83; Akron mayor, 1983-87.
Capitol Office: 1518 Longworth Bldg. 20515; 225-5231.

In Washington: Sawyer is more introverted than many politicians, but he stood out from the crowd in 1989, when he began chairing a subcommittee — a rare responsibility for a second-term member. His subcommittee, on the Post Office Committee, is not high-profile, but it oversees an area very important to House members: the census. The count will dictate the apportionment of House districts for the 1990s.

Sawyer's ascent to a chairmanship was equal parts skillful politicking and good timing. At the start of the 101st Congress, there were two Post Office subcommittee chairs open, and every other Democratic committee member already headed a panel at Post Office or elsewhere. Sawyer gathered enough support to make it onto the full committee, and then competed with another new member, Pennsylvania Democrat Paul E. Kanjorski, for the Census chairmanship.

One key to Sawyer's winning the subcommittee chair was his stand on the counting procedure for the next census. He, along with most House Democratic leaders, wanted to continue the policy of counting undocumented aliens. Kanjorski opposed counting illegal aliens.

Sawyer had also proven himself loyal to the leadership on a range of issues, voting with his party 94 percent of the time in 1988. When there was controversy over a proposed 51 percent congressional pay raise early in 1989, Sawyer was in the minority in saying he would support an alternative 30 percent raise suggested by Speaker Jim Wright.

Sawyer, a former teacher who chaired the Education Committee in the Ohio House, also serves on the Education and Labor Committee. Despite his experience in the field, he seems unusually modest about making a mark quickly on educational policy. "You've got to be patient," he said in 1987. "You get into a position where you're trusted by sufficient numbers of others in those areas where you hope to make a difference."

At Home: Sawyer won his seat by portraying himself as a symbol of the place his district is struggling to become — not the old Rust Belt Akron of rubber and smokestacks, but the new Akron that sees itself as a budding Midwest version of the Silicon Valley.

The battle between old and new was played out in the 1986 Democratic primary. On one side was Sawyer — the young mayor of Akron and an apostle of high technology; on the other was state Sen. Oliver Ocasek — a 60-year-old Humphrey-style, pro-labor war horse.

Some years ago, when Akron was the "rubber capital of the world," Ocasek probably would have won; but as the rubber industry and many of its blue-collar jobs have fled to the Sun Belt, the influence of labor here diminished.

Besides the changing demographics of the area, Sawyer had another key asset: When veteran Democratic Rep. John F. Seiberling announced his retirement, he threw his support to Sawyer.

Sawyer had long been viewed as a rising star in northeast Ohio politics. The son of a prominent Akron businessman, he was a high school teacher before he won a seat in the Ohio House. His election to the Akron mayoralty in 1983 ended nearly 20 years of GOP rule.

But Sawyer's congressional campaign did not meet with universal acceptance. When elected mayor, Sawyer had promised to serve at least one full four-year term; his decision to leave after only three years led the city's dominant newspaper to criticize his untimely political ambition.

But Sawyer proved to be the consummate media-age politician. While Ocasek was garrulous and emotional and boasted ties to old-time labor leaders, Sawyer was reserved, methodical and adept at the task of nuts-and-bolts organization. He emerged from the primary with a comfortable 49-39 percent victory.

Though the GOP had never mounted a serious campaign against Seiberling, they nominated their most prominent local officeholder, Summit County Prosecutor Lynn Slaby, in 1986. He ran a serious, well-funded campaign, emphasizing his blue-collar roots and GOP label.

But he was not as skillful or well organized as Sawyer. When Slaby called his foe a tax-and-spend liberal, Sawyer noted that Akron had not raised taxes during his mayoralty. He won 54 percent, and soared to 75 percent in 1988.

Ohio 14

Northeast — Akron

The 14th District is in a part of Ohio built out of rubber — tires in particular. Located within the district's confines are the corporate headquarters of the Goodyear, Goodrich, Firestone and General Tire companies. The 14th became one of the most Democratic districts in the state on the strength of votes from the blue-collar workers who kept the rubber factories humming.

But the economy of the district is changing. While the major rubber companies are still important employers, the jobs with a future are white-collar, not blue-collar. The last quarter-century has seen a steady transfer of manufacturing from the old, high-wage factories in Akron to new plants in low-wage areas of the Sun Belt. Many Akron residents have left. The city's population dropped precipitously in the 1970s; its 1986 population of 222,000 was less than it was a half-century earlier. Many downtown storefronts are vacant, and the streets can be eerily quiet, especially at night.

Sawyer and other Akron leaders have fought to forge a new high-tech future for the city, and they have had enough success that Akron's unemployment rate has been lower in recent years than in some other industrial centers in northern Ohio.

In the boom years of the rubber industry before World War II, Akron was a mecca for job-seeking Appalachians. The annual West Virginia Day was one of the city's most popular events, and it was said that more West Virginians lived in Akron than in Charleston.

These days, the Appalachian descendants combine with blacks, ethnics and the academic community at the University of Akron to keep the city reliably Democratic. North of Akron, suburbs and farm land in northern Summit County provide Republican votes. Usually, they are too few to overcome the Democratic advantage in Akron and swing the 14th to the GOP. Both Jimmy Carter in 1980 and Michael S. Dukakis in 1988 won Akron by a wide enough margin to narrowly carry Summit County.

Population: 514,172. White 453,372 (88%), Black 56,277 (11%), Other 2,885 (1%). Spanish origin 2,692 (1%). 18 and over 373,433 (73%), 65 and over 57,938 (11%). Median age: 31.

Committees

Education and Labor (13th of 22 Democrats)
Elementary, Secondary and Vocational Education; Human Resources; Labor-Management Relations

Post Office and Civil Service (12th of 15 Democrats)
Census and Population (chairman); Postal Personnel and Modernization

Elections

1988 General		
Thomas C. Sawyer (D)	148,951	(75%)
Loretta A. Lang (R)	50,356	(25%)
1986 General		
Thomas C. Sawyer (D)	83,257	(54%)
Lynn Slaby (R)	71,713	(46%)

District Vote For President

	1988		1984		1980		1976	
D	110,669	(52%)	107,405	(49%)	100,313	(48%)	121,174	(59%)
R	98,478	(47%)	112,288	(51%)	89,588	(43%)	78,215	(38%)
I					14,578	(7%)		

Campaign Finance

	Receipts	Receipts from PACs	Expenditures
1988			
Sawyer (D)	$447,420	$314,754 (70%)	$419,005
Lang (R)	$13,816	0	$13,815
1986			
Sawyer (D)	$500,102	$233,445 (47%)	$480,813
Slaby (R)	$405,113	$79,869 (20%)	$404,236

Key Votes

1987	
Raise speed limit to 65 mph	N
Approve Gephardt "fair trade" amendment	Y
Ban testing of larger nuclear weapons	Y
Delay "re-flagging" of Kuwaiti tankers	Y
Approve tax-raising deficit-reduction bill	Y
1988	
Approve aid to Nicaraguan contras	N
Enact civil rights restoration bill over Reagan veto	Y
Kill 60-day plant-closing notification measure	N
Pass omnibus trade bill over Reagan veto	Y
Approve death penalty for drug-related murders	Y
Bar federal funds for abortions in cases of rape and incest	N
Oppose seven-day waiting period for purchase of handguns	N

Voting Studies

	Presidential Support		Party Unity		Conservative Coalition	
Year	S	O	S	O	S	O
1988	24	75	94	5	18	82
1987	21	79	93	4	30	70

Interest Group Ratings

Year	ADA	ACU	AFL-CIO	CCUS
1988	95	4	93	36
1987	88	0	88	20

15 Chalmers P. Wylie (R)

Of Worthington — Elected 1966

Born: Nov. 23, 1920, Norwich, Ohio.
Education: Attended Otterbein College, 1939-40; Ohio State U., 1940-43; Harvard U., J.D. 1948.
Military Career: Army, 1943-45; Army Reserve, 1945-53; National Guard, 1958-78.
Occupation: Lawyer.
Family: Wife, Marjorie Siebold; two children.
Religion: Methodist.
Political Career: Columbus city attorney, 1954-57; Ohio House, 1961-67.
Capitol Office: 2310 Rayburn Bldg. 20515; 225-2015.

In Washington: The departure of an autocratic committee chairman often presents an opportunity for a strong ranking member to exert more authority in committee business. But the 1988 election defeat of Banking Committee Chairman Fernand J. St Germain is unlikely to bring on a partisan power grab by Wylie, the senior Republican on the committee. He is given more to cooperation than to bare-knuckles confrontation.

Wylie's position involves him in a wide range of banking issues, and his name appears on most of the major pieces of legislation handled by the committee. During the Reagan years, he usually was willing to speak for the administration's point of view. But some of the Republicans under Wylie on Banking have a more activist bent; second-ranking Republican Jim Leach of Iowa could be moving toward a role of greater prominence as a voice for those younger Republicans.

Wylie is at least well prepared for dealing with the new Banking chairman, Henry B. Gonzalez of Texas — a sensitive undertaking given Gonzalez' propensity for pugnacity. Wylie serves on Gonzalez' Housing Subcommittee, where he has steadily pushed for less costly housing bills than those sought by the chairman.

The House passed a housing bill in 1986, but the legislation eventually died due to Senate inaction. The matter was taken up again in the 100th Congress, and while Wylie did not get his way on several points, he ultimately could claim a share of victory, as Congress cleared (and President Reagan signed) the first federal housing bill since 1980.

In the early going, Wylie tried to reduce funding levels in the two-year bill, conveying White House warnings that the proposed $15.9 billion annual authorization would provoke a veto. His amendments to cut almost $2 billion from the bill failed in committee and on the floor. He also failed with an amendment to cut $2.8 billion from Section 8 rental subsidies and add $1.4 billion for administration-backed housing "vouchers." Gonzalez dismissed Wylie's plan as "the son of David Stockman."

But White House objections to the bill's size and provisions nearly killed it. During the House-Senate conference, Wylie pledged that if Democratic majorities on both sides of the conference were willing to go down to $15 billion, conference committee Republicans and the House GOP leadership would support a veto override. The conferees agreed, and the House approved the $15 billion compromise on a 391-1 vote. It nearly expired in the Senate, but a last-minute accord saved the package.

Wylie generally shared St Germain's suspicions of extended banking deregulation, and joined with the chairman in 1984 in sponsoring legislation to block expansion of banks into real estate, insurance and securities. He and St Germain offered a draft deregulation bill in 1988 to grant banks limited new authority to affiliate with securities firms, but it prompted so many complaints from banks that St Germain drew up another bill. That draft lost the support of Wylie and Republicans, and it died at the end of the 100th Congress.

Wylie has, however, supported efforts to remove the longstanding ban on interstate banking. With New York Democrat John J. LaFalce he proposed the main provision of a bill in the 99th Congress sanctioning regional banking laws and paving the way for nationwide banking. The Financial Institutions Subcommittee approved that bill, which included another Wylie provision, offered for the Federal Reserve Board, limiting the size of interstate mergers and acquisitions to guard against overconcentration in the industry. But the interstate bill never made it to the floor.

On the whole, Wylie supported many of the economic policies put forth during Reagan's presidency. He backed a balanced-budget constitutional amendment and a line-item veto.

In 1988, Wylie and other GOP members of the Joint Economic Committee urged Reagan

Ohio 15

Central — Western Columbus and Suburbs

Of the two districts that divide Columbus, the 15th traditionally has been the more Republican. Although it includes most of the academic community at Ohio State University, the Democratic vote there is offset by the solid Republican areas in northern Columbus and the rock-ribbed GOP suburbs west of the Olentangy and Scioto rivers. In Upper Arlington and similar affluent suburbs, it is not unusual for Republican presidential candidates to draw well over two-thirds of the vote.

Apart from the large university vote — Ohio State has 53,000 students — the major pocket of Democratic strength in the district is on the near west side of Columbus. Sandwiched between the Scioto River and the Ohio State Hospital for the Insane are neighborhoods of lower-income Appalachian whites.

The 15th includes some portions of the heavily black East Side of Columbus and blue-collar communities in the southeast portion of Franklin County, which swell the Democratic vote a bit. But these are low-turnout areas.

In 1982 redistricting, the 15th gave up the heart of downtown Columbus, with the state Capitol and the offices of Ohio's major banking and commercial institutions. But with three-quarters of the land area of Franklin County, the district still contains most of the region's expanding service base, which includes three large high-technology research centers.

Columbus is no tourist attraction. Swarms of visitors descend on the city only at Ohio State Fair time in August and on the half-dozen Saturdays in the fall when the Buckeyes are playing football at home. But the area has gained a reputation as a good place to raise a family. During the 1970s, it was the only major urban center in Ohio to gain population, and in the 1980s recession years, the suffering of service-oriented Columbus did not compare to that felt in many other Ohio cities.

Population: 514,176. White 449,644 (87%), Black 56,641 (11%), Other 5,066 (1%). Spanish origin 3,767 (1%). 18 and over 377,458 (73%), 65 and over 46,640 (9%). Median age: 28.

to veto selected items in fiscal 1989 appropriations bills, testing a theory advanced by a conservative constitutional scholar that the president already holds line-item veto authority. The administration remained unconvinced of that interpretation of the Constitution, however, and declined to try.

When the Joint Economic Committee issued a report in 1988 assessing Reagan's eight-year-old economic "experiment," Wylie, as the panel's ranking House Republican, gave lavish praise. "Most Americans feel like they're better off than they were 10 years ago, and I agree with them," he said.

Most of the time, Wylie represents Ohio business on the Banking Committee pretty much as it wishes to be represented. But he has a liberal streak that surfaces now and then. He broke with Reagan, for example, in defending the National Consumer Cooperative Bank, which he helped create in the 1970s and which he has always regarded as a pet project.

Wylie's work on behalf of the consumer cooperatives is one of several facets of his record that makes it difficult to treat him as predictably conservative. In his early years on Banking, he fought to strengthen federal regulation of large one-bank holding companies. Later, he worked for an equal credit opportunity act, banning discrimination in the granting of loans, and a truth-in-leasing bill. In the 100th Congress, Wylie voiced strong support for a bill requiring issuers of credit cards to disclose interest rates and other information to potential card holders.

Those activities tend to counter the conservative reputation Wylie has gained outside the Banking Committee for his work on tough anti-obscenity laws and a constitutional amendment to return prayer to the public schools. He drew national attention in 1971 when he gathered 218 signatures on a discharge petition to pry his school prayer amendment out of House Judiciary. The amendment came to a vote on the floor, but the 240-162 margin in its favor fell short of the two-thirds needed.

He received some attention in the 99th Congress when he added an amendment to an appropriations bill cutting $103,000 from the Library of Congress for Braille reproduction of magazines for the blind. His target was *Playboy* magazine; he said a publication that promoted "wanton and illicit sex" had no place in such a program. Some laughed when Wylie brought a copy of *Playboy* to the floor, and others noted that there would be no pictures in a Braille edition. But Wylie carried the day.

At Home: Bland and affable, Wylie is neither a controversial nor a celebrated figure in the area he has represented in the Legislature and in Congress for nearly 30 years. But he is well liked by GOP voters and Columbus' business community, and he always wins by large margins.

Democrats did not even seriously try to unseat Wylie until 1986, when they enlisted one of the stars in the administration of Democratic Gov. Richard F. Celeste to make the challenge. David L. Jackson was a political neophyte, but he had won high marks as state health director.

Wylie, who had not needed to campaign seriously in years, was nonetheless ready for the test. He returned regularly to Columbus, where he had a weekly radio show; ran ads that detailed the federal funding he had procured for central Ohio projects; and even formed a group called "Physicians for Wylie" to counter Jackson's appeal in the medical community. Meanwhile, Jackson, who was a prominent Cleveland-area neurologist before joining the Celeste administration, faced criticism that he was a carpetbagger.

Jackson pounded away at Wylie for a wide range of "sins" — from flip-flopping on aid to the Nicaraguan contras to being a captive of "rich and powerful" interests in Washington. But with Wylie fitting "his district like a comfortable old shoe" (as one newspaper said), Jackson made no headway. Wylie took 64 percent. In 1988, he won by a 3-to-1 margin.

Wylie's landslide re-election victories are a significant chapter in a long political career that has proceeded rather uneventfully. Once he finished law school in 1948, Wylie began climbing carefully up the political ladder. He started as assistant state attorney general, became city attorney, then moved to the Legislature and eventually to Congress, rarely offending anyone and always making sure of his support before stepping up.

In 1964 Wylie had the good fortune to be on the legislative committee that redrew congressional district lines for the 1966 elections. The plan that emerged included a new district in Columbus that had no incumbent but included most of Wylie's legislative district. With the blessing of the county Republican chairman, Wylie ran and was easily elected.

Committees

Banking, Finance and Urban Affairs (Ranking)
Financial Institutions Supervision, Regulation and Insurance (ranking); Consumer Affairs and Coinage; Housing and Community Development

Veterans' Affairs (3rd of 13 Republicans)
Compensation, Pension and Insurance; Education, Training and Employment

Joint Economic
Economic Goals and Intergovernmental Policy; Economic Growth, Trade and Taxes; International Economic Policy

Elections

1988 General

Chalmers P. Wylie (R)	146,854	(75%)
Mark S. Froehlich (D)	49,441	(25%)

1986 General

Chalmers P. Wylie (R)	97,745	(64%)
David L. Jackson (D)	55,750	(36%)

Previous Winning Percentages: **1984** (72%) **1982** (66%) **1980** (73%) **1978** (71%) **1976** (66%) **1974** (62%) **1972** (66%) **1970** (71%) **1968** (73%) **1966** (60%)

District Vote For President

	1988	1984	1980	1976
D	75,999 (37%)	68,366 (32%)	82,909 (36%)	79,511 (41%)
R	126,613 (62%)	139,407 (66%)	128,975 (56%)	107,607 (56%)
I			13,908 (6%)	

Campaign Finance

	Receipts	Receipts from PACs	Expend-itures
1988			
Wylie (R)	$231,063	$158,415 (69%)	$211,963
Froehlich (D)	$9,910	$7,000 (71%)	$6,682
1986			
Wylie (R)	$305,756	$185,352 (61%)	$338,230
Jackson (D)	$332,078	$94,850 (29%)	$319,640

Key Votes

1987	
Raise speed limit to 65 mph	N
Approve Gephardt "fair trade" amendment	N
Ban testing of larger nuclear weapons	N
Delay "re-flagging" of Kuwaiti tankers	N
Approve tax-raising deficit-reduction bill	?
1988	
Approve aid to Nicaraguan contras	Y
Enact civil rights restoration bill over Reagan veto	N
Kill 60-day plant-closing notification measure	Y
Pass omnibus trade bill over Reagan veto	N
Approve death penalty for drug-related murders	Y
Bar federal funds for abortions in cases of rape and incest	?
Oppose seven-day waiting period for purchase of handguns	N

Voting Studies

	Presidential Support		Party Unity		Conservative Coalition	
Year	**S**	**O**	**S**	**O**	**S**	**O**
1988	54	37	61	30	84	3
1987	66	30	65	24	84	7
1986	63	31	58	36	76	22
1985	68	31	61	32	85	9
1984	53	42	65	24	92	5
1983	79	17	73	20	72	20
1982	56	35	63	29	60	26
1981	64	29	68	22	79	20

Interest Group Ratings

Year	ADA	ACU	AFL-CIO	CCUS
1988	30	80	36	92
1987	4	73	0	100
1986	15	64	31	71
1985	10	76	29	73
1984	20	52	23	67
1983	5	67	13	89
1982	15	65	30	73
1981	20	86	15	94

16 Ralph Regula (R)

Of Navarre — Elected 1972

Born: Dec. 3, 1924, Beach City, Ohio.
Education: Mount Union College, B.A. 1948; William McKinley School of Law, LL.B. 1952.
Military Career: Navy, 1944-46.
Occupation: Lawyer.
Family: Wife, Mary Rogusky; three children.
Religion: Episcopalian.
Political Career: Ohio House, 1965-67; Ohio Senate, 1967-73.
Capitol Office: 2207 Rayburn Bldg. 20515; 225-3876.

In Washington: Regula is well suited to the collegial atmosphere of the Appropriations Committee, where he has served for nearly two decades. A serious man, he is an entrenched establishment Republican who generally works well with Democrats. This has made him a key player on the committee, but his moderate politics and conciliatory disposition can rankle more confrontational right-of-center Republicans.

The ranking GOP member of Appropriations' Interior Subcommittee, Regula is viewed as more sympathetic than many Republicans to environmental concerns. Throughout the Reagan years, he had a hand in crafting legislation to fund the nation's parks, forests and energy conservation programs; the White House often deemed the funding in these bills excessive, and threatened vetoes.

When it comes to energy development, however, Regula sharply disagrees with many Appropriations Democrats. He is ardent in his belief that the United States should aggressively tap its domestic energy resources. While this position places him firmly in his party's pro-development mainstream, Regula has won few friends with his criticism of the administration and Congress for failing to develop a comprehensive energy policy — a lapse he says could lead to a return of gasoline lines in the 1990s.

Though relatively little coal is actually mined in his district, coal is vital to Ohio's economy, and Regula is one of its champions. A leading advocate of the clean-coal technology program, he helped draft compromise language in the 99th Congress that allocated funds to private companies researching cleaner ways of burning coal. When budget pressures appeared to threaten the program in the 100th Congress, he successfully pressed for efforts to fund demonstration of the new technologies in commercial operation.

Regula's pro-energy development views extend far beyond his landlocked district to include fervent support of oil drilling on the Outer Continental Shelf of the United States. He generally gets along well with Interior Subcommittee Chairman Sidney R. Yates, but the two clash annually over this issue, with Yates usually winning. In the 100th Congress, the full Appropriations Committee rebuffed Regula's challenges to the one-year extension of moratoriums on drilling in the Gulf of Mexico off southern Florida and in Georges Bank off the Massachusetts coast.

In the previous Congress, Regula had unusually sharp words for the California activists who fought oil development off their state's coast, charging that their concerns were less for the environment than for the scenic views from their "beautiful houses." He lined up with members from oil states on the full committee, and the proposed four-year ban lost by a single vote.

Knowing that his chances of success on the floor were slim, Regula then tried to strike a compromise between the interior secretary, who shared his pro-development views, and the California delegation, which did not. When these negotiations failed, the House approved a two-year moratorium. Regula did not fight the one-year extension approved in 1988.

While Regula describes himself as a "tree-hugger," he does not embrace the agenda of most environmental groups on acid-rain legislation. This was plain in late 1987, as the deadline for air quality to pass federal health standards approached; scores of cities were certain to fail, which would cause them to lose federal construction funds. Congress debated whether to extend the deadline for eight months or 19 months.

The briefer extension was backed by most environmental groups and sponsored by senior Appropriations Republican Silvio O. Conte, with the support of California Democrat Henry A. Waxman. Regula supported the longer deadline, which was sponsored by John P. Murtha, a close ally of John D. Dingell, both Democrats.

Regula said he supported the Murtha amendment in part because it would allow the

Ohio 16

Northeast — Canton

Although it has undergone a variety of changes over the years, the 16th District is still centered on Stark County and the city of Canton, just as it was when William McKinley represented it a century ago.

While it is a working-class city like Akron and Youngstown and often votes Democratic in local elections, Canton does not share in the solidly Democratic tradition of the rest of northeastern Ohio. That is partly a result of the conservative mentality brought to the community by the family-run Timken Co. — a large steel and roller-bearing firm that is the district's largest employer.

With sizable black and ethnic populations, Canton proper goes Democratic on occasion. But the suburbs in surrounding Stark County are solidly Republican. Since 1920, the only Democratic presidential candidates to carry the county — which accounts for nearly three-quarters of the district's population — have been Franklin D. Roosevelt and Lyndon B. Johnson.

Besides Timken, Canton is the national headquarters of the Hoover Co., the vacuum-cleaner manufacturer, and Diebold Inc., a producer of bank safes and office equipment. But it is more famous as the home of the Pro Football Hall of Fame and for the front porch from which McKinley ran his 1896 presidential campaign. The slain president is buried in a park on the west end of Canton in a large memorial that roughly resembles the Taj Mahal. The Hall of Fame is at the other end of the park.

The portion of the 16th outside Stark County is primarily rural and Republican. Wooster, the Wayne County seat, claims to be the site of America's first Christmas tree. Rubbermaid has its corporate headquarters there. Nearby Orrville is the home base of the Smucker family, which markets jams and peanut butter.

The 16th was extended south in 1982 by redistricting to annex Holmes County from the old 17th District. Many of Holmes' 30,000 residents are Amish, and motorists driving through the county have to be careful not to plow into the back of a horse-drawn buggy. Houses without electricity are common in the county, and the income level is the lowest in the state outside the Appalachian portion of the 6th District. Although leather and noodle factories have brought new employment to the agricultural area, most business is conducted in small Amish family-owned shops that sell buggies and other necessities.

Population: 514,171. White 485,489 (94%), Black 25,465 (5%). Spanish origin 4,047 (1%). 18 and over 363,139 (71%), 65 and over 55,348 (11%). Median age: 30.

Environmental Protection Agency to impose sanctions against states failing to make good-faith efforts to meet air-quality standards, while the Conte amendment barred all sanctions during the extension period. But that was not an argument that moved many environmentalists, and the Murtha amendment went down to a surprisingly lopsided defeat.

Regula also serves on the Appropriations Subcommittee on Commerce, Justice and State, where he gently pushes his minority views. In the 100th Congress, the subcommittee approved his language to cut $3 million from $41.6 million that had been allocated for the Organization of American States (OAS). He said he "had a hard time trying to figure out what the OAS does outside of giving receptions."

Regula also has a firm grasp of the subcommittee's arcanum, which he has used to protect the State Department budget. He worked to get agencies with personnel stationed at U.S. embassies — such as the CIA and the Marines — to fund the administrative costs of maintaining their forces, which had been entirely borne by the State Department. He now hopes to get his cost-sharing plan extended to include security and capital costs.

Representing an industrial district, Regula has taken a number of stands to please union organizers back home. In the 100th Congress, he was one of just 17 Republicans to support the Gephardt amendment to the trade bill. The measure would have mandated retaliatory tariffs against countries with unfair trade practices, but was so controversial most of its provisions were eventually dropped from the bill. Though he backed an unsuccessful effort to strike language requiring plant-closing notification from the trade bill, Regula voted to override the president's veto of the measure.

In 1986, Regula pushed to amend an emergency funding bill with language requiring oil companies to use at least 50 percent American materials and labor when constructing offshore drilling rigs. The amendment passed the House, but not the Senate. When President Reagan threatened to veto the whole bill if it contained the "Buy American" requirement, the amendment was pulled, although it was one of the last of the provisions to be dropped by the House.

One of Regula's minor but more consistent crusades is for federal recognition of President William McKinley, his hometown's most famous native. A graduate of McKinley School of Law, Regula observes the former president's birthday in January by passing out red carnations to his colleagues; he once persuaded the Interior Subcommittee to adopt an amendment making it illegal to rename Mount McKinley in Alaska.

At Home: Regula's re-election is as sure a thing as there is in Ohio politics. He rarely dips much below 70 percent of the vote even in weak Republican years. Double-digit unemployment was a serious political issue in his home base of Stark County (Canton) in 1982, but Regula still defeated an underfinanced political scientist by a margin of nearly 2-to-1. In 1984 he was back up to 72 percent.

Regula came to the House after eight years in the state Legislature, where he specialized in writing conservation bills. His state Senate constituency included a large part of Stark County, the heart of the 16th District, and when Republican Rep. Frank T. Bow retired in 1972 after 22 years in Congress, Regula won Bow's endorsement.

Redistricting that year removed part of Democratic Mahoning County from the district, making it more Republican. Regula defeated Democrat Virgil Musser, who was Bow's last opponent, with 57 percent of the vote.

Committees

Appropriations (7th of 22 Republicans)
Interior and Related Agencies (ranking); Commerce, Justice and State, the Judiciary and Related Agencies; District of Columbia

Select Aging (3rd of 27 Republicans)
Health and Long-Term Care (ranking)

Elections

1988 General

Ralph Regula (R)	158,824	(79%)
Melvin J. Gravely (D)	43,356	(21%)

1986 General

Ralph Regula (R)	118,206	(76%)
William J. Kennick (D)	36,639	(24%)

Previous Winning Percentages: **1984** (72%) **1982** (66%) **1980** (79%) **1978** (78%) **1976** (67%) **1974** (66%) **1972** (57%)

District Vote For President

	1988	1984	1980	1976
D	87,090 (42%)	79,525 (38%)	74,357 (37%)	87,184 (47%)
R	116,518 (57%)	130,136 (62%)	112,060 (56%)	94,013 (51%)
I			10,825 (5%)	

Campaign Finance

	Receipts	Receipts from PACs	Expend-itures
1988			
Regula (R)	$108,672	0	$94,492
1986			
Regula (R)	$128,324	0	$103,471

Key Votes

1987

Raise speed limit to 65 mph	N
Approve Gephardt "fair trade" amendment	Y
Ban testing of larger nuclear weapons	N
Delay "re-flagging" of Kuwaiti tankers	Y
Approve tax-raising deficit-reduction bill	N

1988

Approve aid to Nicaraguan contras	Y
Enact civil rights restoration bill over Reagan veto	N
Kill 60-day plant-closing notification measure	Y
Pass omnibus trade bill over Reagan veto	Y
Approve death penalty for drug-related murders	Y
Bar federal funds for abortions in cases of rape and incest	?
Oppose seven-day waiting period for purchase of handguns	N

Voting Studies

	Presidential Support		Party Unity		Conservative Coalition	
Year	S	O	S	O	S	O
1988	56	43	67	30	87	13
1987	52	48	56	43	81	19
1986	56	44	56	43	80	20
1985	60	40	57	42	82	18
1984	58	41	63	35	78	19
1983	66	32	68	31	80	20
1982	64	35	65	34	75	23
1981	72	28	75	25	79	21

Interest Group Ratings

Year	ADA	ACU	AFL-CIO	CCUS
1988	30	76	64	93
1987	28	52	38	67
1986	15	45	71	61
1985	25	52	35	59
1984	35	33	46	75
1983	25	61	35	75
1982	25	59	35	59
1981	15	87	27	89

17 James A. Traficant Jr. (D)

Of Poland — Elected 1984

Born: May 8, 1941, Youngstown, Ohio.
Education: U. of Pittsburgh, B.S. 1963; Youngstown State U., M.S. (administration) 1973, M.S. (counseling) 1976.
Occupation: Law enforcement official.
Family: Wife, Patricia Choppa; two children.
Religion: Roman Catholic.
Political Career: Mahoning County sheriff, 1981-85.
Capitol Office: 312 Cannon Bldg. 20515; 225-5261.

In Washington: Traficant serves as the self-styled spokesman for the angry blue-collar workers of the "Rust Belt." He does so in a forceful and often crude way that sets him far apart from most other House members.

With his fist pounding and his hair askew, Traficant shouts the frustrations of factory workers whose jobs in heavy industry have disappeared. His approach is usually bombastic and often vulgar: He is probably the only House member for whom the phrase "shit or get off the pot" is common coin in public discourse.

But if there is a madness to Traficant's manner, it certainly is not without its method. His tough talk about industrial decline and foreign competition resonates in the working-class wards of Youngstown and the other aging mill towns of his district. His "raging populist" image has made him a local folk hero, enabling him to thrive even in the face of questions about his personal ethics.

Nor is Traficant's rage unfocused. He has channeled his desire to bolster U.S. industry into a series of legislative amendments, and has had some success in getting them enacted. The core of his effort is "Buy American" legislation aimed at gaining preference for American-made products in federal contracting. Though the idea is not new, early versions of it were often "buy only American" proposals; Congress rejected them as too extreme. Traficant hit on a formula he has attached to a number of spending bills: It calls for an agency to give preference to a bid from an American company if its finished product is made domestically, the "domestic content" is at least half American parts, and the bid is within 6 percent of the lowest foreign bid.

"Giving U.S. firms a fighting chance to compete with foreign firms when bidding on U.S. government contracts is the right thing to do," Traficant said after passage of a National Aeronautics and Space Administration authorization bill containing his language. "Congress is beginning to see the light."

To Traficant, unfair foreign competition is the source of America's industrial slide, and he is unapologetic about his support for tough trade sanctions. "The problem is, most of the people [in Washington] are protecting the interests of foreign workers and foreign companies," Traficant said in 1988. "I want to protect the interests of American workers."

In 1987, Traficant also won approval of a $30 million program to provide counseling for persons faced with mortgage foreclosure because of circumstances beyond their control, such as job layoffs. The measure harked back to the incident that first made him a local legend: In 1982, during his tenure as Mahoning County (Youngstown) sheriff, Traficant went to jail for three days rather than serve several laid-off factory workers with foreclosure orders.

That act helped give Traficant such a loyal following that he has survived legal problems to which other politicians would have succumbed. In 1987, a federal Tax Court ruled that Traficant had accepted $108,000 in bribes from organized-crime figures while serving as sheriff, and held him liable for back taxes, interest and civil penalties. But Traficant — who was acquitted in 1983 on federal criminal charges involving the same allegations — brushed off questions of corruption and portrayed himself as a victim of the Internal Revenue Service (IRS). Traficant vowed to appeal the ruling, adding that he would go over to the IRS and "punch their lights out."

He was even more pugnacious in early 1987, when Miami Beach industrialist Victor Posner took Sharon Steel, the nation's 12th largest steel producer and a major local employer, into bankruptcy. "I think Posner now has to think of someone other than himself," Traficant said. "And if he doesn't, I'm going to go to Florida and assault him.... If he rips off the last industrial facility in the Shenango Valley ... someone should grab him by the throat and stretch him...."

Traficant also gets passionate on the sub-

Ohio 17

Northeast — Youngstown; Warren

Once called America's "Little Ruhr" as a symbol of its industrial productivity, the Youngstown-Warren area now is a symbol of the nation's industrial decline. Many of the giant steel furnaces that once lighted the eastern Ohio sky are dark for good. Most of the workers who have not retired or left the area are scrounging for other jobs.

Located on the state's eastern border with Pennsylvania, the region was long a steel center serving both Cleveland and Pittsburgh. Only a decade ago the large steel plants in the Mahoning River Valley employed more than 50,000 workers. Now the work force is a fraction of that.

The 17th has begun to diversify its economy, but the process is slow and painful. Youngstown lost nearly one-fifth of its population in the last decade, and for those who stayed, an unemployment rate upwards of 20 percent has not been uncommon. In 1986, unemployment still exceeded 13 percent.

With its remaining blue-collar base, the 17th is one of Ohio's solidly Democratic areas in most elections. About 56 percent of the voters live in Mahoning County (Youngstown); 42 percent reside in Trumbull County (Warren). Mahoning and Trumbull were among the 10 Ohio counties that voted for Jimmy Carter in 1980; in 1984 they divided slightly: Walter F. Mondale ran up nearly 60 percent in Mahoning, but Reagan held him to 55 percent in Trumbull. Both were in the Democratic column in 1988.

Most Democratic candidates build comfortable majorities in the string of declining ethnic communities along the Mahoning River. Italians dominate in Niles and Lowellville. Eastern Europeans and Greeks are the most important groups in Campbell. In the two largest cities — Youngstown and Warren — blacks are part of the ethnic mixture.

As one moves south, beyond the steel mills that line the Mahoning Valley, the Republican vote increases. Homes in these suburbs are too expensive for most blue-collar workers. Typical is Boardman Township, due south of Youngstown. One of the most affluent parts of Mahoning County, it is a swing area.

Population: 514,172. White 453,689 (88%), Black 55,177 (11%). Spanish origin 6,694 (1%). 18 and over 372,108 (72%), 65 and over 59,249 (12%). Median age: 32.

ject of the death penalty, which he wants to extend to all 50 states. At the start of the 101st Congress, he resubmitted a bill to cut off federal law-enforcement funds for any state that does not have a death penalty or life imprisonment without parole for first-degree murder or for the killing of a police officer. "I am repulsed by the fact that cold-blooded, vicious murderers are housed, fed, clothed and protected for the rest of their lives at the expense of honest taxpayers," Traficant said.

Even with his mercurial nature and his sense for the dramatic, Traficant startled his colleagues by announcing plans to run in the 1988 Democratic presidential primaries (while seeking House re-election) in order to promote the economic interests of the Rust Belt. Traficant ended up on the ballot only in a handful of House districts in Ohio and Pennsylvania. Still, he did top 30,000 votes in the Ohio primary (just over 2 percent of the total) and earned a delegate to the Democratic National Convention.

At Home: Traficant's forceful personality, combined with voter unrest over local economic conditions, helped make him the only Democratic challenger in the nation in 1984 to defeat a GOP incumbent untouched by scandal.

His 18,000-vote victory was even more remarkable because it came against Lyle Williams, a Republican with a proven record of survival in a Democratic district. A genial ex-barber with a knack for reaching the working-class majority, Williams had comfortably won a third term in 1982 despite severe unemployment in Youngstown and the other decaying industrial towns in the 17th. Few thought he would have much trouble in the Reagan re-election year.

But few incumbents have faced a local legend such as Traficant, who made his mark in the district long before running for Congress. A former football star at the University of Pittsburgh, Traficant ran an anti-drug-abuse program in Mahoning County before being elected sheriff in 1980. He continued his anti-drug campaign in office, claiming credit for record drug busts through undercover operations.

Traficant quickly became a hero to the district's hard-hit factory workers, but he also made some enemies. Within two years, he had alienated virtually every government official in the area, claiming that most were controlled by organized crime. He feuded with the FBI, the local Democratic Party, the Internal Revenue Service, the mayor of Youngstown and even some of his own deputies.

All that paled, however, in comparison with the uproar generated by Traficant's bribery trial. It seemed certain he would be convicted — the FBI had tape recordings of Traficant accepting $163,000 from underworld figures. Despite a lack of legal training, Traficant elected to defend himself in court.

In a tour de force against some of the federal government's best lawyers, Traficant said he took the money only to get evidence against the mobsters. After a seven-week trial, he was acquitted, touching off an ecstatic celebration by his fans in Youngstown and generating national media attention, including a front-page profile in *The Wall Street Journal.*

So Traficant began his House campaign with near-universal name identification. But before he could take on Williams, he had to overcome opposition from the region's regular Democratic organizations. Stung by his attacks on the local establishment, party leaders viewed Traficant with hostility — one official had sought to get him committed to a mental institution. But Traficant crushed primary opponents picked by the Mahoning and Trumbull County organizations.

Traficant brought little of the apparatus of a modern campaign into the general-election contest. Although he had support from some local unions, his conflicts with regular Democrats limited his access to campaign contributions. He ended up spending less than one-fourth of Williams' amount.

But Traficant was an unusually effective personal campaigner, drawing large crowds with his attacks on banks, big business and the IRS. He advocated limits on imported steel, a commission to monitor IRS abuses and the death penalty for illegal-drug sellers.

Saying, "I fight with dignity," Williams warned that Traficant would embarrass the district. But the 17th's continuing high unemployment became an insurmountable problem for one originally elected to bring more jobs.

Traficant's unexpected victory hardly mollified district Democratic leaders. Rather than line up behind him in 1986, they threw their support in the 1986 primary to Austintown Township Trustee Michael R. Antonoff. But he proved incapable of derailing Traficant. Largely ignoring his challenger, Traficant relied on his personal popularity and support from organized labor to win renomination by nearly 4-to-1.

Committees

Public Works and Transportation (17th of 31 Democrats)
Aviation; Surface Transportation; Water Resources

Science, Space and Technology (18th of 30 Democrats)
Energy Research and Development; Investigations and Oversight; Space Science and Applications

Select Narcotics Abuse and Control (15th of 18 Democrats)

Elections

1988 General		
James A. Traficant Jr. (D)	162,526	(77%)
Frederick W. Lenz (R)	47,929	(23%)
1988 Primary		
James A. Traficant Jr. (D)	98,341	(86%)
Van Williams (D)	16,130	(14%)
1986 General		
James A. Traficant Jr. (D)	112,855	(72%)
James H. Fulks (R)	43,334	(28%)

Previous Winning Percentage: **1984** (53%)

District Vote For President

	1988	1984	1980	1976
D	131,232 (62%)	129,520 (57%)	132,461 (62%)	126,759 (60%)
R	80,437 (38%)	95,528 (42%)	64,375 (30%)	80,635 (38%)
I			15,367 (7%)	

Campaign Finance

	Receipts	Receipts from PACs	Expend-itures
1988			
Traficant (D)	$100,063	$54,500 (54%)	$96,003
Lenz (R)	$2,406	0	$2,391
1986			
Traficant (D)	$139,761	$76,780 (55%)	$91,338
Fulks (R)	$91,312	0	$91,035

Key Votes

1987	
Raise speed limit to 65 mph	N
Approve Gephardt "fair trade" amendment	Y
Ban testing of larger nuclear weapons	Y
Delay "re-flagging" of Kuwaiti tankers	Y
Approve tax-raising deficit-reduction bill	#
1988	
Approve aid to Nicaraguan contras	N
Enact civil rights restoration bill over Reagan veto	Y
Kill 60-day plant-closing notification measure	N
Pass omnibus trade bill over Reagan veto	Y
Approve death penalty for drug-related murders	Y
Bar federal funds for abortions in cases of rape and incest	N
Oppose seven-day waiting period for purchase of handguns	N

Voting Studies

	Presidential Support		Party Unity		Conservative Coalition	
Year	**S**	**O**	**S**	**O**	**S**	**O**
1988	17	83	89	10	37	63
1987	17	82	89	7	28	72
1986	10	90	87	13	24	76
1985	13	85	87	7	11	89

Interest Group Ratings

Year	ADA	ACU	AFL-CIO	CCUS
1988	95	8	100	21
1987	88	5	100	0
1986	95	9	100	28
1985	95	0	100	27

18 Doug Applegate (D)

Of Steubenville — Elected 1976

Born: March 27, 1928, Steubenville, Ohio.
Education: Graduated from Steubenville H.S., 1947.
Occupation: Real-estate salesman.
Family: Wife, Betty Engstrom; two children.
Religion: Presbyterian.
Political Career: Ohio House, 1961-69; Ohio Senate, 1969-77.
Capitol Office: 2183 Rayburn Bldg. 20515; 225-6265.

In Washington: Applegate operates rather unobtrusively in Congress, following a moderate Democratic line that is consistent with the thinking of his constituents in hilly southeast Ohio. Though well into his second decade in the House, he seldom draws attention to himself.

There are a couple of policy areas on which Applegate will raise his voice. One is veterans' benefits, an issue on which Applegate has a major say as chairman of the Veterans' Affairs Subcommittee on Compensation, Pension and Insurance.

A strong supporter of efforts during the 100th Congress to establish the Veterans Administration as a Cabinet post, Applegate generally mans the barricades against efforts to reduce veterans' benefits. In 1985, he proposed a 3.4 percent cost-of-living adjustment (COLA) to recipients of veterans' retirement benefits; that was a middle ground between a higher House-passed increase and a lower Senate figure; the Senate prevailed.

Applegate is not inflexible about budget savings, however. In 1988, the full committee was urging a 4.5 percent COLA for disabled veterans, based on an inflation estimate from the Congressional Budget Office. But Applegate went along with the Reagan administration request of 4.2 percent.

The other issue that drives Applegate is economic hardship in his district, whose vital manufacturing industries have been wounded by foreign competition. Applegate has emblazoned his House stationery with the slogan "Buy American! Save American Jobs!" When President Reagan came out against a trade bill in the 99th Congress, Applegate said he "completely fails to recognize the human and monetary loss that has resulted because of the failure to either act or react."

In early 1989, Applegate called on the Customs Service to investigate a "blatantly outrageous" solicitation by a Taiwanese flagmaker, who enticed American companies to save on labor costs by having their U.S. flags made by his company, then switching the labels from "Made in Taiwan" to "Made in the U.S.A." after delivery.

At Home: When he first ran for the House in 1976, Applegate's bland manner helped distance him from the scandal that had felled his flamboyant predecessor, Democrat Wayne Hays. The tyrannical chairman of the House Administration Committee, Hays quit his campaign for a 15th term that year after allegations were published that he had kept a woman, Elizabeth Ray, on his committee payroll solely to provide him with sex.

Though Hays' downfall was unexpected, Applegate was prepared to step in; during much of his career in the state Legislature, he was quietly planning a campaign to succeed Hays when the incumbent retired. Since Hays quit three months before the election, long after the primary, the Democratic nominee was selected by local party leaders. Applegate represented about half the district in the state Senate, so he was a logical choice.

Applegate had little trouble defeating both the Republican candidate and William Crabbe, the Democratic mayor of Steubenville, who earlier had launched an independent campaign aimed directly at Hays.

The first opportunity other Democrats had at this district came in the 1978 primary. But by then Applegate had a firm hold. He took 82 percent of the primary vote.

By 1980 Applegate had silenced any significant primary opposition, including Hays, who openly considered running for the House again. Since then, Applegate has had no serious GOP opposition either.

In 1988, Democratic Rep. James A. Traficant Jr. from the neighboring 17th District entered the Ohio presidential primary as a favorite-son candidate. Applegate followed suit, and wound up winning a delegate to the Democratic National Convention. Like Traficant, Applegate said his main goal was to draw attention to the plight of the region's Rust Belt cities. But he was also trying to blunt the publicity edge held by Traficant, whose district might be combined with Applegate's in the 1990s, when Ohio is likely to lose House seats.

Ohio 18

East — Steubenville

Coal and steel have given the 18th its polluted air, its dirty rivers, its economic livelihood and its Democratic vote.

Cramped along the steep banks of the Ohio River, Steubenville — the district's largest city (population 24,000) — long has had some of the nation's foulest air pollution. But jobs in the smoke-belching plants along a 50-mile stretch of the Ohio take priority over clean air, a fact that successful politicians quickly learn.

Locals boast that there has not been an air pollution alert in Steubenville in the 1980s. But the clearing skies are not a good sign for the local economy. The unemployment rate in Steubenville and surrounding Jefferson County was in the teens for much of the early 1980s, though by 1986 it had dipped to 9 percent.

West of Jefferson is economically depressed Harrison County. The closing in 1985 of a pottery plant that employed about 1,000 people pushed up the already high unemployment rate there. The same dismal conditions exist in Monroe County, on the West Virginia border, where an aluminum plant has taken substantial layoffs. In 1986, unemployment in both counties exceeded 18 percent.

This part of Ohio resembles West Virginia and eastern Kentucky. Some cattle are raised, but the hilly terrain makes farming generally unprofitable. Under the hills, however, there are extensive coal deposits. Although the steelworking and coal-mining Democrats of the district show strong party allegiance, they tend to shy away from liberals.

About half the voters in the 18th live within a few miles of the industrialized Ohio River Valley. As one moves west, the district becomes less Democratic, and the tractors of Republican farmers replace the giant shovels of Democratic coal miners.

Population: 514,173. White 501,793 (98%), Black 10,250 (2%). Spanish origin 1,924 (0.4%). 18 and over 367,705 (72%), 65 and over 66,832 (13%). Median age: 32.

Committees

Public Works and Transportation (7th of 31 Democrats)
Economic Development; Investigations and Oversight; Surface Transportation

Veterans' Affairs (3rd of 21 Democrats)
Compensation, Pension and Insurance (chairman); Oversight and Investigations

Elections

1988 General		
Doug Applegate (D)	151,306	(77%)
William C. Abraham (R)	46,130	(23%)
1986 General		
Doug Applegate (D)	126,526	(100%)

Previous Winning Percentages: **1984** (76%) **1982** (100%) **1980** (76%) **1978** (60%) **1976** (63%)

District Vote For President

	1988		1984		1980		1976	
D	102,997	(52%)	98,096	(46%)	84,479	(44%)	112,109	(54%)
R	93,955	(47%)	114,896	(54%)	97,509	(50%)	92,379	(44%)
I					9,619	(5%)		

Campaign Finance

	Receipts	Receipts from PACs	Expend-itures
1988			
Applegate (D)	$120,435	$66,751 (55%)	$86,061
Abraham (R)	$7,233	$760 (11%)	$7,095
1986			
Applegate (D)	$104,752	$57,825 (55%)	$83,591

Key Votes

1987	
Raise speed limit to 65 mph	N
Approve Gephardt "fair trade" amendment	Y
Ban testing of larger nuclear weapons	Y
Delay "re-flagging" of Kuwaiti tankers	Y
Approve tax-raising deficit-reduction bill	N
1988	
Approve aid to Nicaraguan contras	N
Enact civil rights restoration bill over Reagan veto	Y
Kill 60-day plant-closing notification measure	N
Pass omnibus trade bill over Reagan veto	Y
Approve death penalty for drug-related murders	Y
Bar federal funds for abortions in cases of rape and incest	Y
Oppose seven-day waiting period for purchase of handguns	Y

Voting Studies

	Presidential Support		Party Unity		Conservative Coalition	
Year	S	O	S	O	S	O
1988	28	65	71	24	63	29
1987	31	68	73	23	60	40
1986	24	74	75	20	50	50
1985	29	69	63	23	45	51
1984	39	60	65	32	54	44
1983	27	72	69	27	48	49
1982	39	57	64	31	56	41
1981	45	53	45	50	72	25

Interest Group Ratings

Year	ADA	ACU	AFL-CIO	CCUS
1988	70	24	100	29
1987	64	13	75	27
1986	65	23	93	35
1985	55	19	59	50
1984	50	33	69	44
1983	70	30	88	35
1982	45	46	84	41
1981	35	27	60	21

19 Edward F. Feighan (D)

Of Lakewood — Elected 1982

Born: Oct. 22, 1947, Lakewood, Ohio.

Education: Attended Borromeo College of Ohio, 1965-66; Loyola University (La.), B.A. 1969; Cleveland-Marshall College of Law, J.D. 1978.

Occupation: Lawyer.

Family: Wife, Nadine Hopwood; four children.

Religion: Roman Catholic.

Political Career: Ohio House, 1973-79; Cuyahoga County Commission, 1979-83; candidate for mayor of Cleveland, 1977.

Capitol Office: 1124 Longworth Bldg. 20515; 225-5731.

In Washington: Low-key and bookish-looking, Feighan hardly projects the image of an activist firebrand. Yet his House career revolves around his concerted efforts to push gun-control legislation, and the issue has made him a leading House adversary of one of Washington's most muscular interest groups: the National Rifle Association (NRA).

A member of the Judiciary Committee, Feighan applied much of his effort over the past several years to legislation mandating a waiting period prior to the purchase of a handgun, and to measures barring the sale of certain rapid-fire or easily concealable weapons. So far, his efforts have been largely thwarted. Through the end of the 100th Congress, the NRA had wielded its clout to defeat most of the gun-control proposals.

In the 99th Congress, Feighan proposed instituting a 15-day waiting period on handgun purchases. The purpose of the delay would be to allow law-enforcement officials to identify those potential buyers, especially convicted felons, who were prohibited from owning guns. The measure would also have banned or limited ownership of certain semiautomatic, automatic or "plastic" firearms.

But an opposing House faction marshaled its forces to deal gun-control advocates an embarrassing setback. The pro-gun members pushed through an NRA-backed alternative that not only eliminated many of the gun-control proposals, but even weakened some provisions of the landmark 1968 gun-control law.

Undaunted, Feighan came back in the 100th Congress with a measure calling for a seven-day waiting period. Again, he went head-to-head against the NRA. In an opinion article in *The New York Times* in 1987, Feighan wrote, "Who would argue against legislation that could keep criminals and crazies from buying a handgun? ... Not surprisingly, the National Rifle Association is preparing to fight such legislation with all the high-powered political ammunition it can muster."

For a while, it seemed Feighan's measure might prevail: He succeeded in attaching it to the 1988 omnibus drug bill during Judiciary Committee deliberations. The provision became known as the "Brady amendment," for presidential press secretary James S. Brady, who was seriously wounded in the 1981 assassination attempt on President Reagan, and for his wife, Sarah, a gun-control activist.

However, during House floor debate, Feighan's measure was replaced by a substitute proposed by Republican Bill McCollum of Florida. Rather than a waiting period, the McCollum amendment required the Justice Department to develop a system to enable gun dealers to identify immediately a felon trying to buy a firearm.

But the 100th Congress did bring a more limited success, with the passage of a Feighan-supported bill barring production and sale of guns made mostly of plastic, which could foil conventional metal detectors.

And at the start of the 101st Congress, there was an apparent revival of public interest in gun-control measures, spurred by a proliferation of rapid-fire weapons, an onslaught of drug-related murders, and such incidents as the January 1989 schoolyard massacre in Stockton, Calif.

Aside from provoking the NRA, Feighan's gun-control efforts present other political risks. The issue has traditionally been seen as a liberal standard, and Feighan's district is packed with socially conservative, blue-collar ethnics. However, Feighan has gained some political cover from police organizations that have expressed support for gun limits.

Feighan bolsters his standing with his more conservative constituents with a tough anti-drug stand. A co-chairman on the House Task Force on International Narcotics Control, Feighan also uses his position on the Foreign Affairs Committee to push for tougher economic pressures against nations that are the

Ohio 19

Cleveland Suburbs

The 19th is the "ring around the county" district — a "U-shaped" monstrosity that merges the bulk of Cleveland's two old suburban districts into one. Critics complain that the quickest way from one end of the district to the other is by boat across Lake Erie.

A drive around the "U" takes one through a string of politically diverse suburbs — some dominated by ethnic Democrats, others by white-collar Republicans. There are, however, some common threads. Nearly all these communities are monolithically white and socially conservative.

Along the lake are wealthy GOP towns such as Bay Village and Rocky River. Inland, Democratic bowling alleys replace Republican golf clubs as social centers.

Children and grandchildren of European immigrants have moved out of Cleveland to inner suburbs like Parma, due south of the city. In recent years they have moved again. Parma's population declined in the 1970s and '80s, as residents left their ranch homes of the 1950s for the open spaces of outer suburbs such as Strongsville. But even with the population loss, Parma (population 89,000) is still the ninth-largest city in Ohio and the largest city in the 19th. Nearby steel mills and automobile plants give this section of the district a strong union presence.

Much of the Cleveland financial elite lives in outlying suburbs along Cuyahoga County's eastern boundary. This is solid Republican territory. Two of these affluent communities — Hunting Valley and Chagrin Falls Township — even voted for James E. Betts in his "sacrificial lamb" Senate candidacy against Democrat John Glenn in 1980.

Moving north toward the lake, one reenters the world of ethnic politics. The blue-collar workers of Polish and Slovenian descent who fled the city for suburbs such as Euclid and Mayfield have retained their Democratic allegiance, although it has a conservative cast nowadays.

Population: 514,174. White 499,960 (97%), Black 7,918 (2%), Other 4,785 (1%). Spanish origin 2,946 (1%). 18 and over 386,888 (75%), 65 and over 66,615 (13%). Median age: 35.

source of illegal drug exports to the United States.

His other major role on Foreign Affairs has been as a human rights activist. In 1985, he was roughed up at the Seoul airport while accompanying dissident Kim Dae Jung on his return from exile to South Korea. But his human rights activities also have a local impact: A member of the "Helsinki commission," he has aided several Jewish and Lithuanian families in the Cleveland area in obtaining emigration rights for their relatives in the Soviet Union.

And while he pursues broader national and international issues, Feighan finds time for the sort of local grantsmanship that assures political safety. In the 100th Congress, he helped obtain a $1 million, three-year grant for the Cancer Research Center at Cleveland's Case Western Reserve University, and secured over $3 million for a senior citizens' housing project in the suburb of Fairview Park.

At Home: Though Feighan is no more liberal than other members of the Cleveland-area House delegation, the conservative ethnic nature of his district earned him close Republican scrutiny in three elections. But he exhibited resiliency in the face of all GOP challenges.

Feighan's supposed vulnerability was rooted in the intraparty rift caused by his 1982 primary ouster of a Democratic incumbent. The victim of the Feighan insurgency was conservative Democrat Ronald M. Mottl. A favorite among many of the district's working-class and ethnic voters, Mottl had nonetheless infuriated the local Democratic establishment by supporting President Reagan's 1981 tax and spending cuts. Feighan, a veteran state and county legislator with strong family ties to the Cuyahoga County organization, lined up the offended party loyalists and upset Mottl by 1,113 votes.

The general election was relatively routine for Feighan. Fairview Park Mayor Richard G. Anter, the GOP nominee, never managed to connect with the Mottl constituency. Feighan carried not only the affluent areas but also the blue-collar communities, taking 59 percent.

With Reagan en route to a landslide reelection two years later, Republicans thought they had a good chance of activating the conservative Mottl vote with former Cuyahoga County Auditor Matthew J. Hatchadorian. But Feighan's re-election in 1984 was a case study in the way clever House Democrats managed to avoid Reagan's coattails.

An experienced and aggressive campaigner, Hatchadorian based his challenge on the charge that Feighan was too oriented to the inner city. He criticized Feighan for not supporting Reagan on economic and defense issues and argued that his moderate Republicanism would be better suited to suburban needs.

Feighan refused to back down, but he did

make some efforts to reassure centrist voters, stressing his support for a balanced budget and his work against illegal drugs. In the closing days of the campaign, he unleashed some harsh TV ads, blunting the challenger's momentum and carrying Feighan to a 55 percent victory.

His challenger in 1986 was state Sen. Gary C. Suhadolnik, who in many respects was a GOP version of Mottl. Young and personable, Suhadolnik lived in the ethnic suburbs south of Cleveland that were Mottl's political base. And like Mottl, whose political career was identified with the anti-busing movement, Suhadolnik was associated with high-voltage issues. He was a leader in the 1983 drive to roll back a state income-tax increase and was a high-profile opponent of abortion.

But Suhadolnik's hallmark was grass-roots campaigning. He pounded away at Feighan as a liberal globe-trotter, more concerned with human rights in South Korea than with struggling industrial workers in Cleveland.

Feighan countered by pointing to his formation of the Cuyahoga Partnership Project to mobilize Cleveland-area congressmen to develop ways to assist the local business community. But the incumbent's ace in the hole was experience in tough campaigns and a willingness to use hardball campaign tactics. On separate occasions he accused Suhadolnik of distributing anti-Semitic campaign literature and of playing to "racial fears."

Feighan's well-stocked campaign bought choice TV time in the campaign's closing days and filmed several hard-hitting ads to be aired if the race got extremely tight. The ads were not needed, as he again emerged with 55 percent. With three expensive, futile efforts behind them, the Republicans finally gave Feighan a pass in 1988; he won against a little-known opponent with 71 percent of the vote.

Rather than enjoy the quiet, Feighan decided to clean up some unfinished business from the 1986 campaign. In 1988, he filed charges with the Federal Election Commission against three people he said were involved in distributing anti-Semitic literature in 1986. This led to accusations and finger-pointing within the GOP and a handful of headlines for the Democrat.

Committees

Foreign Affairs (16th of 28 Democrats)
Europe and the Middle East; Human Rights and International Organizations; International Economic Policy and Trade

Judiciary (14th of 21 Democrats)
Crime; Economic and Commercial Law

Elections

1988 General		
Edward F. Feighan (D)	168,065	(71%)
Noel F. Roberts (R)	70,359	(29%)
1986 General		
Edward F. Feighan (D)	97,814	(55%)
Gary C. Suhadolnik (R)	80,743	(45%)

Previous Winning Percentages: 1984 (55%) **1982** (59%)

District Vote For President

	1988	1984	1980	1976
D	114,751 (45%)	94,595 (41%)	81,481 (36%)	90,411 (42%)
R	139,652 (55%)	137,021 (59%)	124,246 (56%)	120,799 (56%)
I			16,943 (8%)	

Campaign Finance

	Receipts	Receipts from PACs	Expend- itures
1988			
Feighan (D)	$391,199	$205,414 (53%)	$226,086
Roberts (R) †	$522	$95 (18%)	$522
1986			
Feighan (D)	$659,975	$345,029 (52%)	$630,326
Suhadolnik (R)	$518,282	$105,903 (20%)	$520,207

† Totals based on incomplete data.

Key Votes

1987	
Raise speed limit to 65 mph	N
Approve Gephardt "fair trade" amendment	Y
Ban testing of larger nuclear weapons	Y
Delay "re-flagging" of Kuwaiti tankers	Y
Approve tax-raising deficit-reduction bill	Y
1988	
Approve aid to Nicaraguan contras	N
Enact civil rights restoration bill over Reagan veto	Y
Kill 60-day plant-closing notification measure	N
Pass omnibus trade bill over Reagan veto	Y
Approve death penalty for drug-related murders	N
Bar federal funds for abortions in cases of rape and incest	N
Oppose seven-day waiting period for purchase of handguns	N

Voting Studies

	Presidential Support		Party Unity		Conservative Coalition	
Year	S	O	S	O	S	O
1988	17	80	86	4	18	79
1987	16	81	88	6	35	63
1986	17	81	90	5	14	86
1985	29	71	88	9	24	76
1984	26	71	81	17	17	81
1983	20	78	86	11	22	75

Interest Group Ratings

Year	ADA	ACU	AFL-CIO	CCUS
1988	95	0	100	38
1987	92	0	100	29
1986	95	0	100	33
1985	70	10	82	32
1984	85	13	77	31
1983	90	4	94	20

20 Mary Rose Oakar (D)

Of Cleveland — Elected 1976

Born: March 5, 1940, Cleveland, Ohio.
Education: Ursuline College, B.A. 1962; John Carroll U., M.A. 1966.
Occupation: High school English and speech teacher.
Family: Single.
Religion: Roman Catholic.
Political Career: Cleveland City Council, 1973-77.
Capitol Office: 2231 Rayburn Bldg. 20515; 225-5871.

In Washington: Oakar has spent much of her House career working faithfully for the Democratic leadership with the aim of someday being a part of it. But when she tried to transform the dues she had paid into the chairmanship of the Democratic Caucus in 1988, her colleagues threw a switch that kept her on the legislative track.

Oakar, who was trained as an actress, often seems to have an emotional approach to issues, but in leadership politics, she carefully calculated her moves. Early in her career, she joined the Democratic whip organization and showed party leaders a capacity for hard work on routine leadership tasks. She joined the House Administration Committee in 1983 to protect leadership interests. Safe for re-election in Cleveland, she traveled to other states to help colleagues under serious challenge. When Geraldine A. Ferraro left the House to run for vice president in 1984, Oakar took her place as secretary (later changed to vice chairman) of the Democratic Caucus.

But in 1988, when Oakar sought to convince her colleagues that she was heir apparent to Caucus Chairman Richard A. Gephardt, she faced serious obstacles. The most obvious was the candidacy of then-Budget Committee Chairman William H. Gray III, the most prominent black member of the House. As Budget chairman, Gray had won praise for his skill at coalition building and his abilities as a public spokesman. And Oakar was certainly not helped by a third candidate, Oklahoma Rep. Mike Synar, whose following was not large, but did include Gephardt.

Oakar also faced obstacles of her own making. In early 1987 the Cleveland *Plain Dealer* had disclosed questionable dealings between Oakar and two aides. In one case, Oakar was found to have kept a former aide and housemate on salary for two years after the woman had moved to New York City; in another, Oakar had given a $10,000 salary increase to an aide the same month she and Oakar bought a house together. The House ethics committee conducted an investigation and found she had broken House rules and federal laws that require a staffer to work in a member's district or Washington office. The committee did not recommend any punishment, and Oakar repaid the money, but the affair clearly did not help her image.

Democrats also took notice in early 1988 when Oakar was one of 45 in her party to vote against a leadership-backed package of non-military aid for the Nicaraguan contras. Some suspected she was afraid of taking political heat for the vote at home, something members of the leadership are often expected to do.

Oakar's supporters portrayed her as the front-runner, and she herself claimed to have almost enough commitments to win. At the same time, her boosters criticized Gray for trying to buy the position by making numerous campaign contributions to colleagues and would-be colleagues. In contrast to Gray's modern-style leadership bid, Oakar made use of traditional campaign tools, including buttons, posters, and newspaper ads. She got 80 votes, while Gray won with 146 votes. Synar drained off 33 votes, a bloc too small to be decisive.

Oakar invests much energy and feeling into legislating. She received training at the Royal Academy of Dramatic Arts in London, and she still seems to be on stage sometimes as she speaks of the plight of women, the elderly, or her beleaguered hometown. There is no questioning her sincerity; there is also no doubt she knows how to invest an issue with emotional appeal. Her critics on the Republican side think her style amounts to demagoguery.

As chairman of the Banking Subcommittee on Economic Stabilization, Oakar is in a good position to look out for economic development issues important to Cleveland and the industrial Midwest. She has a strong interest in enterprise zones, urban development grants and the Economic Development Administration, all of which fall under her jurisdiction. She did fail, however, in an effort to have jurisdiction over the Export-Import Bank moved to her panel in the 101st Congress. Blocked from doing so by freshman Rep. Jim McDermott at an early organizational meeting, Oakar became very upset.

Ohio 20

Cleveland — Central, West Suburbs

The line between the 20th and 21st districts generally divides Cleveland's white and black populations. The 20th is the white district, containing the state's largest concentration of ethnic voters. Poles, Czechs, Italians and Germans are the largest groups, but there are dozens of other ethnic communities represented by at least a restaurant or two on the West Side.

The city's steel industry fueled the ethnic influx around the turn of the century, with immigrants settling near the West Side mills. Steel, automobile and aluminum plants are combined with smaller businesses to make up the employment base today.

But many of the younger people who work there have bought homes in the suburbs. The West Side district suffered a 19 percent population loss in the 1970s, a rate of decline exceeded in Ohio only by the neighboring 21st. A large proportion of those who remain on the West Side are elderly.

As a result of this population loss, almost half the electorate now lies outside the Cleveland city limits. With Berea, Middleburg Heights and part of Strongsville joining the 20th, the district now pushes past the Ohio Turnpike, about 12 miles from downtown Cleveland. It is still a heavily ethnic district, however, and solidly Democratic.

The downtown area remains totally within the 20th. The city's economic problems of the 1970s, notably its near-bankruptcy under then-Mayor Dennis Kucinich, made it a national symbol of urban decay. But Cleveland today is stronger than many industrial cities of the Frost Belt, mainly because it is making the successful transition to a service economy. The new $200 million headquarters of Standard Oil of Ohio (Sohio) is spearheading a downtown construction boom that has taken some of the sting out of the auto and steel slumps.

Condominiums are being constructed near the Sohio headquarters, and old drygoods warehouses are being converted to homes — the first downtown housing to go up in a generation. To help keep suburbanites in the city after dark, several art deco theaters have been restored, and there are plans to give Cleveland's Lake Erie waterfront a facelift in the style of Baltimore's "Inner Harbor."

Population: 514,164. White 486,329 (95%), Black 12,918 (3%), Other 5,254 (1%). Spanish origin 16,217 (3%). 18 and over 383,041 (75%), 65 and over 66,146 (13%). Median age: 32.

Oakar misses few opportunities to promote Cleveland. She conditioned her support for the 1979 Chrysler loan guarantee on assurances that Chrysler would not relocate any plants in the South. In 1983, when the House was considering ways of retaliating against the Soviet Union for the downing of KAL Flight 007, she proposed a ban on Soviet ferroalloy imports — products that compete with those made in Ohio. She is also a booster of space programs, in part because some of the funds trickle to the National Aeronautics and Space Administration's Lewis Research Center in Cleveland.

Oakar is also active on two other committees, House Administration and Post Office and Civil Service. On House Administration, Oakar chairs the Subcommittee on Personnel and Police, where she has pushed to give House employees some benefits already enjoyed by other federal employees. In the 101st Congress she began touting an amendment to the Family and Medical Leave Act giving House employees the same family leave as other federal workers.

The Post Office Committee gives Oakar a forum to pursue the controversial "comparable worth" issue. In recent Congresses she has pushed for a study of federal pay scales to determine whether women are paid less than men not only for the same work, but for work of equivalent responsibility that tends to attract females rather than males. She also wanted guidelines for eliminating any inequities that were uncovered. President Reagan's appointees on the U.S. Civil Rights Commission denounced the idea of government-enforced pay equity as "looney tunes" and "socialism without a plan." While Oakar and her allies have managed to get the study plan through the House, it has never cleared the Senate.

Although Oakar is a strong supporter of women's rights, she opposes federal funding of abortions, like most in her ethnic, heavily Catholic constituency. She prefers that the government encourage family planning and provide counseling to pregnant women.

At Home: Oakar's efforts to help Cleveland may not always bring her legislative success, but they have helped her win elections.

She has always used her communicating ability to make her achievements well-known to constituents. During the four years she represented a largely Irish and Puerto Rican ward on

Cleveland's City Council, she got considerable media attention for her plan to make "creative use" of vacant lots and for working to outlaw the sale of airplane glue to minors.

In 1976, when Democratic Rep. James V. Stanton left the district for an unsuccessful run at the Senate, Oakar and 11 others entered the Democratic primary. Oakar's campaign focused on the fact that she was the only woman running and, among the major candidates, the only one without a law degree. Although she did not mention it as much, she was also the only one who had been a telephone operator or a high school English and speech teacher.

The power blocs in Cleveland divided their support among Oakar and three other candidates. Oakar's most significant endorsements were from a United Auto Workers local and from the Fire Fighters Union. State Sen. Anthony J. Celebrezze Jr. was endorsed by the Cleveland *Plain Dealer*. Former City Councilman Michael L. Climaco had the backing of the Cuyahoga County Democratic organization. City Councilman Basil Russo was supported by GOP Mayor Ralph Perk, whom Democrat Russo had endorsed the previous year. Oakar won the primary with 24 percent; Celebrezze, her nearest rival, won 18 percent.

After the 1980 census Oakar became concerned about the effect of redistricting on her political future. She suggested enlarging the size of the House — "There's nothing magic about 435 members," she said — to protect urban representation. She also offered a job to the daughter of the Speaker of Ohio's General Assembly, which would draw the new districts.

The Legislature made sure Ohio's only female House member would have a safe district, drawing the lines so she retained virtually all her old constituents and gained new Democrats.

Oakar demonstrated her strength in the 20th in 1988. The previous year, the ethics committee inquiry into her payroll practices received prominent coverage in the local media, but not for a moment was Oakar's re-election threatened. Colorful and controversial former Cleveland Mayor Dennis J. Kucinich entered the 1988 Democratic primary. He ran an underfunded and quiet — by Kucinich standards — campaign, scarcely mentioning the ethics issue. Oakar, meanwhile, stumped the district in her usual fashion. She won the primary by a 3-to-1 margin, and had no trouble in November.

Committees

Banking, Finance and Urban Affairs (7th of 31 Democrats)
Economic Stabilization (chairman); Financial Institutions Supervision, Regulation and Insurance; Housing and Community Development

House Administration (6th of 13 Democrats)
Personnel and Police (chairman); Accounts

Post Office and Civil Service (7th of 15 Democrats)
Compensation and Employee Benefits

Select Aging (7th of 39 Democrats)
Health and Long-Term Care; Retirement, Income and Employment

Joint Library

Elections

1988 General		
Mary Rose Oakar (D)	146,715	(83%)
Michael Sajna (R)	30,944	(17%)
1988 Primary		
Mary Rose Oakar (D)	64,417	(77%)
Dennis J. Kucinich (D)	19,530	(23%)
1986 General		
Mary Rose Oakar (D)	110,976	(85%)
Bill Smith (R)	19,794	(15%)

Previous Winning Percentages: **1984** (100%) **1982** (86%) **1980** (100%) **1978** (100%) **1976** (81%)

District Vote For President

	1988		1984		1980		1976	
D	103,933	(57%)	95,297	(51%)	80,701	(55%)	99,119	(61%)
R	77,551	(42%)	88,691	(48%)	57,398	(39%)	59,483	(36%)
I					8,934	(6%)		

Campaign Finance

	Receipts	Receipts from PACs	Expend-itures
1988			
Oakar (D)	$691,256	$392,918 (57%)	$783,180
1986			
Oakar (D)	$409,025	$231,759 (57%)	$378,170

Key Votes

1987	
Raise speed limit to 65 mph	N
Approve Gephardt "fair trade" amendment	Y
Ban testing of larger nuclear weapons	Y
Delay "re-flagging" of Kuwaiti tankers	Y
Approve tax-raising deficit-reduction bill	Y
1988	
Approve aid to Nicaraguan contras	N
Enact civil rights restoration bill over Reagan veto	Y
Kill 60-day plant-closing notification measure	N
Pass omnibus trade bill over Reagan veto	Y
Approve death penalty for drug-related murders	Y
Bar federal funds for abortions in cases of rape and incest	Y
Oppose seven-day waiting period for purchase of handguns	N

Voting Studies

	Presidential Support		Party Unity		Conservative Coalition	
Year	S	O	S	O	S	O
1988	19	65	88	5	8	63
1987	17	77	87	4	19	74
1986	16	80	92	2	8	88
1985	18	79	94	3	11	89
1984	25	73	94	5	8	90
1983	26	73	86	13	22	75
1982	31	61	83	11	22	70
1981	34	59	80	11	23	65

Interest Group Ratings

Year	ADA	ACU	AFL-CIO	CCUS
1988	90	8	100	17
1987	96	5	100	0
1986	95	5	93	12
1985	80	5	94	23
1984	95	4	83	31
1983	80	4	100	20
1982	70	21	100	33
1981	55	7	93	0

21 Louis Stokes (D)

Of Warrensville Heights — Elected 1968

Born: Feb. 23, 1925, Cleveland, Ohio.
Education: Attended Western Reserve U., 1946-48; Cleveland Marshall Law School, J.D. 1953.
Military Career: Army, 1943-46.
Occupation: Lawyer.
Family: Wife, Jeanette Francis; four children.
Religion: African Methodist Episcopal.
Political Career: No previous office.
Capitol Office: 2365 Rayburn Bldg. 20515; 225-7032.

In Washington: With two decades in the House behind him, Stokes has had something of a two-track career. His main line has been his ongoing tenure on the Appropriations Committee, where he works quietly on minority issues and urban policy. But he has frequently been tapped by the Democratic leadership to serve on select committees dealing with some of the most controversial issues to come before the House.

The most recent example of Stokes' higher-profile activities was his tenure, between 1983 and 1989, on the Intelligence Committee. His rise to the chairmanship of that panel during the 100th Congress also earned Stokes a seat on the special committee probing the Reagan administration's secret arms sales to Iran and the diversion of profits from those sales to the Nicaraguan contras.

A strong critic of the administration's actions in the Iran-contra affair, Stokes gained the spotlight with his dogged questioning of committee witnesses. He stood out when he expressed doubts about the truthfulness of Rear Adm. John M. Poindexter, the former national security adviser who insisted he had authorized the contra-aid scheme without ever involving President Reagan.

Stokes also lectured then-Marine Lt. Col. Oliver L. North, whose dramatic professions of patriotic duty had earned him a national constituency. North — who wore his medal-bedecked uniform to the hearings — criticized Congress for failing to back Reagan's policies, and insisted he had been driven to participate in questionable activities, including lying to Congress, by the need to sustain the contras as a force against communism.

But Stokes, who served in the Army during World War II, reminded North that many Americans, including military veterans, opposed aid to the contras. "I hope . . . that you will never forget that others, too, love America just as much as you do and that others, too, will die for America, just as quick as you will," Stokes told North.

Blaming the devolution of the Iran-contra policy on Reagan's failure to consult with Congress, Stokes proposed legislation requiring the president to report to congressional leaders within 48 hours of any covert action. Stokes said the measure was aimed at ensuring that the president would seek congressional advice and did not constitute a "legislative veto" of foreign policy decisions.

However, the bill ran into opposition from Reagan and House Republicans, who said the requirement would tie the president's hands. While a similar bill passed the Senate, Stokes' measure died in the House; he resubmitted it at the start of the 101st Congress.

Though his tenure on Intelligence ended in January 1989, Stokes was soon picked by the leadership to deal with another troublesome issue: House ethics. He was appointed to the House Task Force on Ethics Review, a panel established in the wake of the House investigation of Speaker Jim Wright of Texas.

Stokes' participation on the task force echoes his tenure from 1981 to 1985 as chairman of the ethics committee. Stokes — who first developed his image as a troubleshooter in 1977 while chairing the committee investigating the assassinations of John F. Kennedy and the Rev. Dr. Martin Luther King Jr. — took on the ethics post at the direct request of then-Speaker Thomas P. O'Neill Jr.

He succeeded Florida Democrat Charles E. Bennett, a man who saw ethics as a personal crusade, but was viewed by O'Neill as too rigid. Stokes, in contrast, had often expressed concern for the accused in House ethics cases, and was tabbed by O'Neill largely because he eschewed Bennett's hard-line attitude.

Stokes' flexibility was illustrated in 1983, when the committee brought charges against two members, Democrat Gerry E. Studds of Massachusetts and Republican Daniel B. Crane of Illinois, for engaging in sex with teenage House pages. The committee recommended a reprimand (the lowest level of punishment) in both cases; Stokes called that a stern decision, because, he said, "the member must live with this condemnation forever." After an outcry

Ohio 21

Cleveland — East; Cleveland Heights

One of the axioms of Ohio politics is that to win statewide, a Democratic candidate must build a 100,000-vote edge in Cuyahoga County. Most of that lead has to be built in the 21st, which is anchored in Cleveland's heavily black East Side.

The district includes poor inner-city areas as well as middle-class territory farther from the downtown area. Devastated by the riots of the 1960s, inner-city neighborhoods Hough and Glenville still bear the scars of poverty but can claim some new residential and commercial development. Farther east toward the lake are the middle-class, white ethnic neighborhoods of Collinwood, inhabited by Italians, and St. Clare, dominated by Poles, Yugoslavs and other Eastern Europeans.

The 21st is 62 percent black and heavily Democratic. During the last decade, it has been the most Democratic district in the state. In 11 East Side wards in 1980, Jimmy Carter outpolled Ronald Reagan by margins of at least 20-to-1. In 1984, 10 of these wards gave Walter F. Mondale a 14-to-1 margin over Reagan. In 1988, Michael S. Dukakis carried eight of these wards by 14-to-1 or better over George Bush.

The 21st's major suburbs are Cleveland Heights, Shaker Heights and the western half of University Heights. With a large proportion of Jews and young professionals, these are among Ohio's most liberal communities. North of Shaker Heights is Cleveland Heights, many of whose integrated neighborhoods are a short walk from University Circle, home of Case Western Reserve University and Cleveland's cultural hub.

From the circle area, commuters drive along historic Euclid Avenue to their jobs downtown. While the avenue now bears the marks of poverty, it was known as "Millionaires' Row" at the turn of the century. Few of the old mansions are left today. The one belonging to John D. Rockefeller, founder of Standard Oil, was razed to make way for a gas station.

Population: 514,169. White 186,814 (36%), Black 320,809 (62%), Other 3,314 (1%). Spanish origin 5,059 (1%). 18 and over 372,949 (73%), 65 and over 63,051 (12%). Median age: 31.

from many members that the punishment was too weak, the House increased the penalties to censure.

But while they reversed his position, Stokes' House colleagues praised his leadership on a committee assigned to the onerous job of casting judgment on fellow House members. Republican leader Robert H. Michel called the ethics chairmanship "the most distasteful job in the House," and when Stokes finished his final remarks on the Studds-Crane cases, he received a standing ovation.

The only negative publicity Stokes received in his years as ethics chairman involved his 1983 arrest on a drunken-driving charge. Stokes said he was tired after working late, and pleaded not guilty. He was convicted on a lesser charge and fined $250.

Though Stokes came to Congress in an era of black activism — he was first elected the year King was assassinated — he has not been known for stridency in his advocacy of minority causes. "I think most blacks are still willing to work within the system," he said in 1985.

However, Stokes fumed during the Reagan administration over what he viewed as the president's antipathy toward minority interests, and occasionally his anger boiled over. "Ronald Reagan has made racism respectable ...," Stokes said in a 1987 speech, adding that Reagan had "never uttered a word in six years on behalf of civil rights."

Much of Stokes' legislative activity is informed by the black experience. In making his point to North about respecting even those laws he opposed, Stokes reminisced about being a black soldier in the segregated Army of World War II. "I wore [the uniform] as proudly as you do, even though our government required black and white soldiers in the same Army to live, sleep, eat and travel separate and apart, while fighting and dying for our country," Stokes said.

On the HUD and Labor-HHS subcommittees at Appropriations, Stokes is a consistent spokesman for minority concerns, supporting funds for black colleges and housing programs and backing affirmative action in the work place. In recent years, Stokes has pushed a variety of amendments in Appropriations that illustrate his priorities. One added $140 million for Pell Grants for college tuition, another restored $100 million for grants to elementary schools in poor communities. A third added $25 million in operating subsidies for public housing programs.

In February 1989, Stokes called for an investigation into why the bulk of special federal funds for modernizing Cleveland-area public housing had gone to the mostly white and heavily middle-class 20th District, rather than to the impoverished areas of his mostly black

21st. He accused the federal Department of Housing and Urban Development, as well as the local housing authority, of demonstrating "a total disregard for the responsibility they have been given of providing subsidized housing to poor people. . . ."

At Home: The Stokes family has been the dominant force in Cleveland's black politics since Louis Stokes' younger brother, Carl, first ran for mayor in the mid-1960s. Carl left politics for television after two terms in City Hall (1967-71), but Louis has remained active. Politically secure, he has been free to help friends and quarrel with enemies over city issues.

Louis Stokes' first victory was won as much in court as on Cleveland's East Side. Representing a black Republican, he charged in a 1967 suit that the Ohio Legislature had gerrymandered the state's congressional districts, dividing the minority vote and preventing the election of a black. Stokes won an appeal before the U.S. Supreme Court, forcing the lines to be redrawn.

The new 21st District, represented by white Democrat Charles A. Vanik, was about 60 percent black. Vanik decided to run elsewhere, leaving the 21st vacant.

Fourteen candidates ran in the Democratic primary there in 1968, but the outcome was little in doubt. Stokes' ties to his brother and his reputation as a civil rights lawyer won him 41 percent of the primary vote. That November, he became the first black congressman from Ohio by defeating the Republican he had represented in court the previous year.

Over the last decade, Stokes has consolidated his power through his organization, the 21st District Congressional Caucus. Some black politicians have accused him of turning the caucus into a personal political tool, but he is as popular as he ever was among rank-and-file voters.

Committee

Appropriations (7th of 35 Democrats)
District of Columbia; Labor, Health and Human Services, Education and Related Agencies; VA, HUD and Independent Agencies

Elections

1988 General		
Louis Stokes (D)	148,388	(86%)
Franklin H. Roski (R)	24,804	(14%)
1986 General		
Louis Stokes (D)	99,878	(82%)
Franklin H. Roski (R)	22,594	(18%)

Previous Winning Percentages: **1984** (82%) **1982** (86%) **1980** (88%) **1978** (86%) **1976** (84%) **1974** (82%) **1972** (81%) **1970** (78%) **1968** (75%)

District Vote For President

	1988	1984	1980	1976
D	144,023 (80%)	159,536 (78%)	154,021 (61%)	159,656 (66%)
R	33,866 (19%)	41,967 (21%)	81,587 (32%)	75,312 (31%)
I			16,092 (6%)	

Campaign Finance

	Receipts	Receipts from PACs	Expend-itures
1988			
Stokes (D)	$241,646	$147,800 (61%)	$173,534
1986			
Stokes (D)	$215,960	$103,440 (48%)	$154,321

Key Votes

1987	
Raise speed limit to 65 mph	N
Approve Gephardt "fair trade" amendment	Y
Ban testing of larger nuclear weapons	Y
Delay "re-flagging" of Kuwaiti tankers	Y
Approve tax-raising deficit-reduction bill	Y
1988	
Approve aid to Nicaraguan contras	N
Enact civil rights restoration bill over Reagan veto	Y
Kill 60-day plant-closing notification measure	N
Pass omnibus trade bill over Reagan veto	Y
Approve death penalty for drug-related murders	N
Bar federal funds for abortions in cases of rape and incest	N
Oppose seven-day waiting period for purchase of handguns	N

Voting Studies

	Presidential Support		Party Unity		Conservative Coalition	
Year	S	O	S	O	S	O
1988	16	59	81	1	0	66
1987	13	77	91	1	9	77
1986	11	82	87	2	2	80
1985	15	83	93	1	5	93
1984	22	68	88	3	0	93
1983	11	80	86	3	6	85
1982	27	65	91	4	10	86
1981	29	66	93	4	5	91

Interest Group Ratings

Year	ADA	ACU	AFL-CIO	CCUS
1988	70	0	100	25
1987	88	0	100	7
1986	100	0	93	12
1985	95	0	100	24
1984	95	0	85	33
1983	80	0	94	18
1982	85	10	100	24
1981	90	0	93	11

Oklahoma

U.S. CONGRESS

SENATE 1 D, 1 R
HOUSE 4 D, 2 R

LEGISLATURE

Senate 33 D, 15 R
House 69 D, 32 R

ELECTIONS

1988 Presidential Vote	
Bush	58%
Dukakis	41%
1984 Presidential Vote	
Reagan	69%
Mondale	31%
1980 Presidential Vote	
Reagan	61%
Carter	35%
Anderson	3%
Turnout rate in 1984	52%
Turnout rate in 1986	30%
Turnout rate in 1988	49%

(as percentage of voting age population)

POPULATION AND GROWTH

1980 population	3,025,290
1988 population estimate (27th in the nation)	3,242,000
Percent change 1980-1988	+7

DEMOGRAPHIC BREAKDOWN

White	86%
Black	7%
Other	7%
(Spanish origin)	2%
Urban	67%
Rural	33%
Born in state	63%
Foreign-born	2%

MAJOR CITIES

Oklahoma City	446,120
Tulsa	373,750
Lawton	82,830
Norman	78,390
Midwest City	53,470

AREA AND LAND USE

Area	68,655 sq. miles (19th)
Farm	74%
Forest	17%
Federally owned	2%

Gov. Henry Bellmon (R)
Of Billings — Elected 1986
(also served 1963-67)

Born: Sept. 3, 1921, Tonkawa, Okla.
Education: Oklahoma State U., B.S. 1942.
Military Career: Marine Corps, 1942-46.
Occupation: Farmer; rancher.
Religion: Presbyterian.
Political Career: Okla. House, 1947-49; U.S. Senate, 1969-81; defeated for re-election to Okla. House, 1948.
Next Election: 1990.

WORK

Occupations	
White-collar	51%
Blue-collar	33%
Service workers	13%
Government Workers	
Federal	48,446
State	71,519
Local	124,277

MONEY

Median family income	$ 17,688	(35th)
Tax burden per capita	$ 903	(20th)

EDUCATION

Spending per pupil through grade 12	$ 3,146	(38th)
Persons with college degrees	15%	(28th)

CRIME

Violent crime rate	418 per 100,000 (27th)

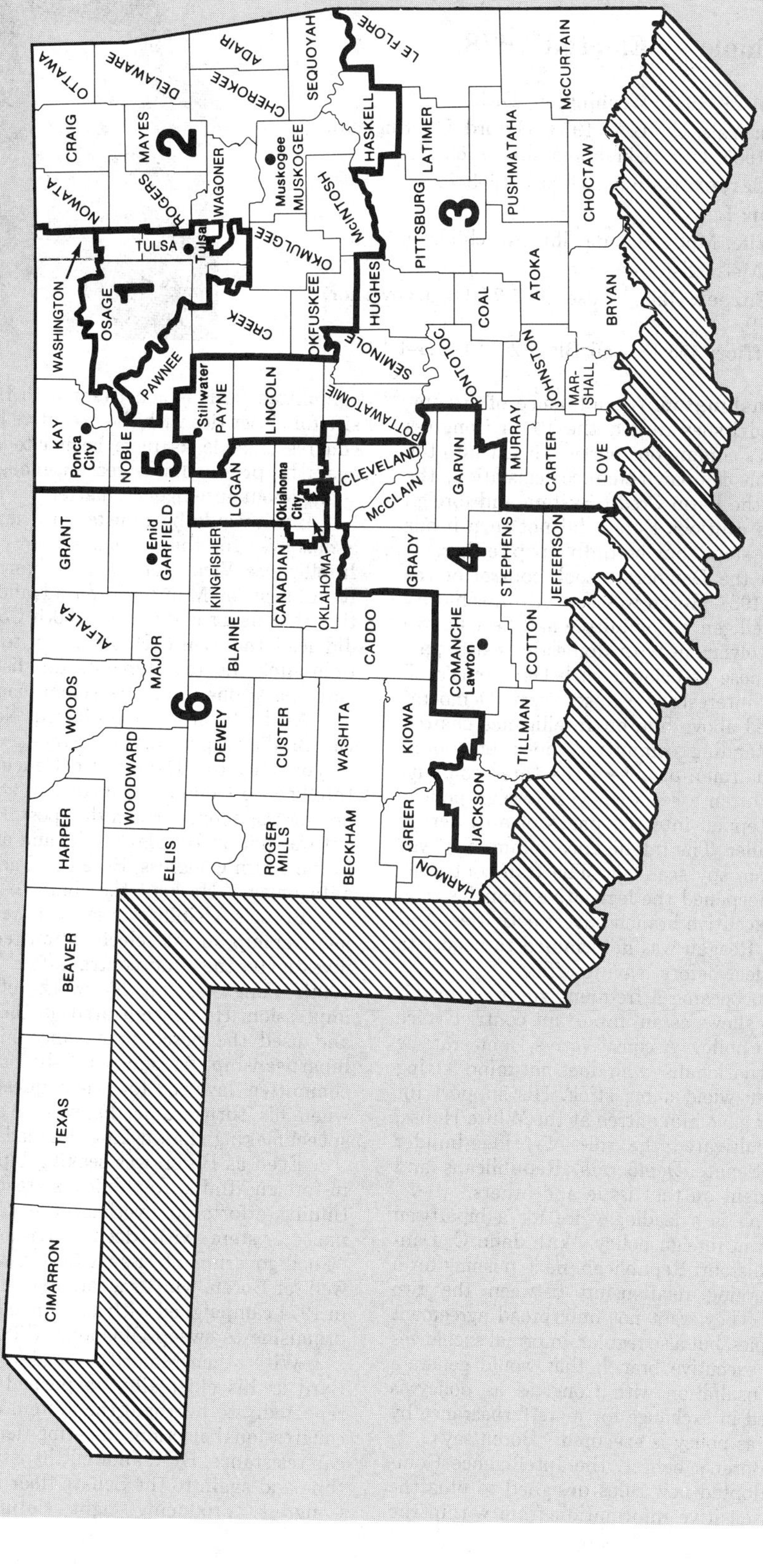

1
2
3
4
5
6
OTTAWA
DELAWARE
ADAIR
CHEROKEE
SEQUOYAH
LE FLORE
McCURTAIN
CRAIG
MAYES
NOWATA
ROGERS
WAGONER
Muskogee
MUSKOGEE
HASKELL
LATIMER
PUSHMATAHA
CHOCTAW
TULSA
Tulsa
OKMULGEE
McINTOSH
PITTSBURG
WASHINGTON
OSAGE
CREEK
OKFUSKEE
HUGHES
COAL
ATOKA
BRYAN
PAWNEE
SEMINOLE
PONTOTOC
JOHNSTON
MAR-SHALL
KAY
Ponca City
NOBLE
Stillwater
PAYNE
LINCOLN
POTTAWATOMIE
MURRAY
CARTER
LOVE
GARVIN
CLEVELAND
McCLAIN
LOGAN
Oklahoma City
GRANT
Enid
GARFIELD
KINGFISHER
CANADIAN
OKLAHOMA
GRADY
STEPHENS
JEFFERSON
ALFALFA
MAJOR
BLAINE
CADDO
COMANCHE
Lawton
COTTON
WOODS
DEWEY
CUSTER
WASHITA
KIOWA
TILLMAN
WOODWARD
HARPER
ELLIS
ROGER MILLS
BECKHAM
GREER
JACKSON
HARMON
BEAVER
TEXAS
CIMARRON

David L. Boren (D)

Of Seminole — Elected 1978

Born: April 21, 1941, Washington, D.C.
Education: Yale U., B.A. 1963; Oxford U., England, M.A. 1965; U. of Oklahoma, J.D. 1968.
Military Career: National Guard, 1968-75.
Occupation: Lawyer.
Family: Wife, Molly Wanda Shi; two children.
Religion: Methodist.
Political Career: Okla. House, 1967-75; Okla. governor, 1975-79.
Capitol Office: 453 Russell Bldg. 20510; 224-4721.

In Washington: A confluence of circumstances and issues turned the 100th Congress into Boren's coming-out party. Thrust into the spotlight on campaign-finance legislation, the bailout of the Farm Credit System and foreign affairs, the cautious Boren did not turn heads with fancy steps, but he didn't trip, either.

When the Democrats took control of the Senate in 1987, Boren was seventh in seniority on the Intelligence Committee and best known for his involvement with domestic issues, particularly those associated with Oklahoma's oil and farm interests. Because every Democrat that ranked above him on Intelligence chaired another standing committee, however, Boren became chairman of one of the three committees most often associated with foreign policy.

He stepped into the pages of an international thriller. The intelligence community was reeling from spy scandals. The Iran-contra affair had deepened the legislative branch's mistrust of executive branch covert activities. And President Reagan was determined to negotiate an arms deal before leaving office.

Boren became a frequent guest on television news shows as an important centrist voice on foreign policy. A conservative Democrat, he is an internationalist who does not mind letting Uncle Sam wield a big stick. His support for contra aid gave him entree at the White House, and he cultivated the role of bridge-builder between Senate Democrats, Republicans and the president on that issue and others.

Boren's is a leading voice for a bipartisan consensus in foreign policy. With John C. Danforth, a Missouri Republican, he is pushing for a closer working relationship between the two branches. They want not only broad agreement on principles, but also regular, informal exchanges with the executive branch that would generate "more consultation with Congress as policy is formulated in exchange for more forbearance by Congress as policy is executed," Boren says.

At Boren's behest, the Intelligence Committee adopted new rules designed to plug the leaks of sensitive information from within the committee. This is consistent with Boren's desire for closer ties with the executive branch, for congressional leaks have been cited time and again by presidents as reason enough to keep silent about intelligence matters.

But it would be a mistake to view Boren as a pushover for the commander in chief. With Intelligence Vice Chairman William S. Cohen, Republican of Maine, Boren advanced legislation that never cleared the 100th Congress but did lead the White House to write new rules tightening the requirements for disclosing covert operations to congressional leaders.

As the 101st Congress began, New Jersey's Bill Bradley reportedly undertook a quiet effort to convince the Democratic Caucus that the Intelligence Committee chairman should serve no more than one term in that post. But precedent was not on Bradley's side, and as chairman in the 100th Congress, Boren had generated no antagonisms. He kept the chair.

Boren's visibility rose as a result of his membership on the select committee named to investigate the Iran-contra affair during the 100th Congress, but his work left no clear impression. He concentrated on the CIA's role and used the perch to advance his views on bipartisanship. At one point, he criticized the committee lawyers for their questions. Still, when his turns came, he was given more to speechmaking than asking detailed questions.

Even as Boren was seeking bipartisanship in foreign affairs, Republicans greeted his continuing efforts to overhaul the campaign finance system with deep partisan suspicion. "Good government" issues have always worked well for Boren, who as a candidate for governor in 1974 campaigned with a broom close to hand, promising to sweep Oklahoma City clean.

With then-Majority Leader Robert C. Byrd as his chief ally, he pushed the Senate repeatedly to overhaul the system of financing congressional elections, meeting fierce Republican resistance. Byrd allowed the issue to return time and again to the Senate floor in the 100th Congress, producing eight cloture votes, a record for a single issue.

Boren's crusade for limits on political action committees and on campaign spending has attracted widespread attention and made him into something of a hero for those who worry about the effects of the current campaign finance system on American politics. He refuses contributions from PACs, though he does accept a substantial share of his own campaign funding from wealthy individual oil producers, and has consistently sought to protect federal support for the oil and gas industry.

Only a politician of Boren's considerable grace could pull off such a deft maneuver. He has a knack for staying close to the shifting tides of political opinion without giving the appearance of being a captive of them. His intelligence and affable good nature allow him to shift stances and defend awkward combinations of positions that might prove difficult for others.

Boren stood out after the 1980 elections as a leading Democratic proponent of cooperation with the new Reagan administration and the GOP leadership in the Senate. Soon after, though, he was back in the Democratic mainstream, helping the party develop economic policy alternatives to Reaganomics and fighting to expand federal help for debt-ridden farmers.

By 1985, Boren was ready to take on the PACs. The explosive growth of PAC funding over the previous decade, he said, was perverting the political system and sapping Congress' ability to make independent judgments. "You begin to ask yourself whether we're going to have any grass-roots democracy left," he worried.

He has worked since to limit the PAC contributions a candidate can accept. The various versions of the legislation have called for spending limits and public financing, bitter pills for many Republicans to swallow, practically or philosophically.

Boren pushed the bill relentlessly even when there were only a handful of other senators who agreed with him. After an initial floor skirmish in 1985 — when an overwhelming majority voted to avoid having to make a decision on the issue — the bill reached an important moment shortly before the 1986 elections. A strong majority actually voted for Boren's plan, 69-30, but this was deceptive. Amendments that drew Republican votes made House passage politically impossible. In 1987 and 1988, Boren and Byrd were unable to muster the 60 votes needed to shut debate, despite reworking the bill several times.

Cynics see Boren's commitment as a reflection not only of his beliefs but of his own special campaign fund-raising situation. Boren can afford to reject PAC money because the independent oil producers and royalty holders so important to Oklahoma's economy generally do not operate through PACs, preferring to give money to candidates on their own.

In his 1984 campaign, he outspent a weak GOP opponent by more than 30-to-1. One-fourth of his contributions came from executives and employees of energy and financial companies.

Meanwhile, Boren has been one of the most effective supporters of the oil and gas industries, working on matters such as the 1988 repeal of the windfall-profits tax on oil. Boren is well suited for this role because he knows how to fight for Oklahoma interests without alienating his party's Northern majority in the Senate. He is a hard man to dislike, even for those who disagree with him.

Boren does not look on first glance to be a power broker or even a politician. Oklahoma political cartoonists used to draw him as the Pillsbury Doughboy. But he knows the system and how to operate within it.

"The appearance of having influence develops rapidly," Boren once said, "and so can the appearance of not having influence." From his first days in the Senate, when he got Finance Committee Chairman Russell B. Long to find him a seat on the tax-writing panel, he has worked to develop that influence for the benefit of his state's oilmen.

Throughout the 1986 debate that produced major tax reform, Boren had little to say about the general philosophy of tax revision, or about most of the issues contained in the legislation. But he played a key role in developing a coalition for it on Finance, providing oil-state support for the bill's attacks on many business tax breaks in exchange for preservation of the depletion allowance and other tax support for the oil and gas industries.

Boren also wants to help oil producers survive the difficult times they are experiencing as a result of the collapse of oil prices by protecting them from foreign competition. He is a prominent supporter of legislation to impose a fee on imported oil.

The 100th Congress was not the first sharp turn in the course of Boren's career. In 1981, he was one of Reagan's most ardent Democratic backers. He helped save the administration from a budget assault led by one of its own, Republican John H. Chafee of Rhode Island, who wanted to restore nearly a billion dollars for urban programs.

Vice President George Bush phoned him seeking help, worrying that GOP senators backing Chafee would tip the GOP's precarious Senate balance away from Reagan. Just before the vote, Bush called again to make certain Boren and fellow conservative Democrats would vote with Reagan. They did. Some 17 Democrats voted with 42 Republicans to beat Chafee handily, even though 11 Republicans defected.

Several days later, Boren announced formation of a 12-member conservative Democratic group to pursue budget-cutting and other issues on which the group's members might feel closer to Republicans than Democrats. His support for the president was rewarded; the successful Reagan-backed version of the 1981 tax cut included two of Boren's pet ideas — easing the terms of the oil windfall-profits tax and ending the inheritance tax for spouses.

But interest in the conservative group soon declined, and Boren drifted away from close support of the administration. Early in 1982 he helped draft a letter to Reagan outlining Democratic alternatives. The letter stressed deferral of the scheduled 1983 tax cut and Pentagon cuts.

Boren was unable to muster majority Democratic support for one of his favorite economic solutions — a constitutional amendment to balance the budget. But he did play an important role in the balanced-budget law that Congress passed in 1985. Boren refers to the measure as the "Gramm-Rudman-Hollings-Boren" amendment, but few others indulge him there.

By 1985, a new, more militant Boren had emerged, most visibly as a spokesman for farmers suffering from the devastated agricultural economy. In tandem with Nebraska Democrat Jim Exon, Boren led Farm Belt Democrats into a confrontation with the Reagan administration and the Senate leadership over emergency help for debt-ridden farmers.

As chairman of the Agriculture Committee's Farm Credit Subcommittee, Boren played a major role in the $4 billion bailout and overhaul of the Farm Credit System. In early 1987, he announced his intention to move quickly. "We're not going to play ring around the rosy around here," he said, adding, "This train is going to move." But it took most of the year for the subcommittee and then the full committee to produce a bill. A major reason was that Boren pushed hard to produce a consensus, requiring dozens and dozens of hours of markups.

A strong critic of the increasing use of the filibuster in the Senate, Boren nevertheless used that and other dilatory tactics to pressure Senate leaders to act on farm credit aid. He and his allies for a time blocked approval of the nomination of Edwin Meese III as attorney general, giving new Majority Leader Bob Dole his first test of strength and leading the White House to denounce the strategy as "blackmail." Eventually, Congress cleared legislation to provide farmers with extra loan money to finance spring plantings. But Reagan vetoed the measure.

Boren's most original contribution to the farm policy debate was a plan he developed in 1985 with Minnesota Republican Rudy Boschwitz. The two Agriculture Committee members proposed that the federal government move toward abolishing the whole system of price supports for farmers. To help ease the transition to a free-market economy, they suggested providing farmers with direct income support for a period of time. The proposal was rejected as an amendment to the 1985 farm bill, but has continued to attract attention. It was included in modified form in the administration's fiscal 1988 budget, although Boren considered that language inadequate and opposed it.

Boren has become increasingly outspoken in criticism of the Senate's procedures, which he sees as leading the institution into paralysis and decline. He believes individual senators have too much power to frustrate the majority.

To solve those problems, Boren has proposed setting up an Emergency Joint Committee for Congressional Reform. He argues that such a committee should consider major changes in Senate rules, especially those that allow senators to propose amendments unrelated to the bill being considered on the floor. "To preserve Congress," Boren had said, "we must reform it."

At Home: Boren advanced very quickly in politics by knowing how to promote the right issue at the right time.

Few Oklahoma Democrats took him seriously in 1974, when, as a four-term state legislator, he decided to run for governor. A Rhodes scholar and political science professor, he had been neither influential nor popular among insiders in the Oklahoma House. But he had a reputation as a reformer, which he exploited at a time of scandal not only in Washington but in Oklahoma City, where Democratic Gov. David Hall was under investigation on corruption charges that later sent him to prison.

Boren campaigned with a broom, promising to sweep out corruption in the state capital, supporting financial disclosure and open government. He edged into a spot in the primary runoff and won big in November.

As governor, Boren changed focus, drawing national attention as a spokesman for his state's oil producers. When he chose to run for the Senate in 1978, he was in a perfect position to seek votes and campaign support as an oil industry loyalist, and he was the favorite throughout the year. He led a seven-man primary field and went on to defeat former U.S. Rep. Ed Edmondson in a runoff.

The primary took a bizarre turn when, after a minor candidate accused the governor of being a homosexual, Boren swore on a Bible that it was not true. The accuser was discredited, and Boren suffered no lasting damage.

Boren's gubernatorial record brought him far more business support than most Democrats can expect in Oklahoma, and he had no trouble against his 1978 Republican opponent.

By 1984, Boren's stock had soared so high that state Republican leaders seemed reluctant even to talk about their chances against him. When no Republicans of stature challenged him for re-election, they shifted attention toward their 1986 chances of capturing the governorship.

Will E. Crozier, a former state Transportation Department worker who became the eventual Republican nominee, voiced concern that Boren had moved too far left on some issues. Boren blew him away, carrying every county in the state in amassing 76 percent of the vote. That is the highest percentage achieved by a U.S. Senate candidate in the history of popular elections in Oklahoma.

Committees

Select Intelligence (Chairman)

Agriculture, Nutrition and Forestry (3rd of 10 Democrats)
Domestic and Foreign Marketing and Product Promotion (chairman); Agricultural Credit; Agricultural Production and Stabilization of Prices

Finance (5th of 11 Democrats)
Energy and Agricultural Taxation (chairman); International Trade; Taxation and Debt Management

Small Business (6th of 10 Democrats)
Government Contracting and Paperwork Reduction; Rural Economy and Family Farming

Elections

1984 General

David L. Boren (D)	906,131	(76%)
Will E. Crozier (R)	280,638	(24%)

1984 Primary

David L. Boren (D)	432,534	(90%)
Marshall Luse (D)	48,761	(10%)

Previous Winning Percentage: **1978** (66%)

Campaign Finance

	Receipts	Receipts from PACs	Expend-itures
1984			
Boren (D)	$983,553	0	$1,080,008
Crozier (R)	$31,380	0	$31,360

Key Votes

1987	
Enact omnibus highway bill over Reagan veto	Y
Limit testing of space-based anti-ballistic missiles	?
Oppose banning tests of larger nuclear weapons	Y
Confirm Robert H. Bork as Supreme Court justice	Y
1988	
Allow vote on campaign-finance overhaul	Y
Pass civil rights restoration bill over Reagan veto	Y
Enact omnibus trade bill over Reagan veto	Y
Approve death penalty for drug-related murders	Y
Oppose "workfare" amendment to welfare overhaul bill	N

Voting Studies

	Presidential Support		Party Unity		Conservative Coalition	
Year	S	O	S	O	S	O
1988	63	31	59	30	81	11
1987	46	46	60	32	91	3
1986	67	30	42	54	92	4
1985	47	45	52	39	75	18
1984	62	29	41	53	91	0
1983	41	56	60	35	73	25
1982	60	38	52	42	87	10
1981	60	35	54	40	86	10

Interest Group Ratings

Year	ADA	ACU	AFL-CIO	CCUS
1988	25	48	62	58
1987	35	63	56	50
1986	40	65	27	65
1985	45	55	47	54
1984	35	71	30	79
1983	55	54	53	56
1982	45	84	50	65
1981	30	60	32	71

Don Nickles (R)

Of Ponca City — Elected 1980

Born: Dec. 6, 1948, Ponca City, Okla.
Education: Oklahoma State U., B.B.A. 1971.
Military Career: Army National Guard, 1970-76.
Occupation: Machine company executive.
Family: Wife, Linda Lou Morrison; four children.
Religion: Roman Catholic.
Political Career: Okla. Senate, 1979-81.
Capitol Office: 713 Hart Bldg. 20510; 224-5754.

In Washington: Nickles may be one of the emerging success stories of the Senate. A long-shot winner in 1980, he was the youngest senator in the 97th Congress. Generally regarded as too young, too ideological and too insubstantial, he seemed an unlikely survivor.

But that assessment has been altered over time. The change came gradually at first, as Nickles adapted to the Senate and distanced himself from Reagan administration energy and farm policies as those sectors suffered in the mid-1980s. The real turnaround came in 1986, when Nickles easily turned back a strong challenge from Democrat James R. Jones, chairman of the House Budget Committee.

Since then, Nickles has been a new man. He traded in three committee assignments — Labor and Human Resources, Small Business, and Select Aging — for more powerful and prestigious seats on Budget and Appropriations. He also began campaigning for the leadership, and his systematic work was rewarded late in 1988 when he was elected chairman of the National Republican Senatorial Committee. He defeated Sen. John McCain of Arizona, who had not spent as much time campaigning and who, after just two years in the Senate, may have been seen as overreaching.

Nickles becomes the first member of the class of 1980 — the first Reagan coattails class — to serve as campaign committee chairman. The job has been held by more senior, and usually more moderate, members. The job has also become something of a hot seat as the number of GOP senators has dwindled.

The presidential party usually struggles in off-year elections, and in 1990, Nickles has 18 seats to defend to the Democrats' 16. At the same time, the slate of GOP incumbents includes few soft spots; and the Democrats' list of safe seats looks short. Nickles' main problem may be persuading some of his senior colleagues to stay in the Senate. Early in 1989, two of his incumbents announced they would not run in 1990 (William L. Armstrong of Colorado and Gordon J. Humphrey of New Hampshire), and half a dozen others were reported to be considering retirement. Most of the prospective retirees, however, were from strong GOP states. Nickles may not need to narrow the Democrats' 55-45 advantage to be judged a success in 1990, but he cannot afford to let it grow.

Meanwhile, Nickles has enjoyed a higher profile in the 100th and 101st Congresses. He has remained a hard-liner, with a career average score from the American Conservative Union of nearly 95. But he softens his impression with his boyish good looks and deferential charm. He also enjoys a reputation for hiring and keeping good staff. In 1989, he assigned Doyce Boesch, who ran his campaigns in 1980 and 1986, to boss the campaign committee staff.

In his second term, Nickles has also had some heightened success as a legislator. In the 100th Congress he finally saw an end to the windfall-profits oil tax. A holdover from the energy crisis of the 1970s, the tax had largely been moot in the lower-price 1980s. But Nickles had argued that it discouraged long-term investment in oil, and he finally saw it repealed by an amendment to the omnibus trade bill that cleared in 1988.

Similarly, Nickles was cosponsor of a bill in early 1989 that would decontrol natural gas prices by 1993. Such decontrol had been a political holy grail in the energy-producing Southwest for more than a decade, but early in the 101st Congress a scenario for passage appeared to have developed. Here again, lowered price levels had made compromise possible with consumer-oriented forces in the House.

Nickles has shown years of patience on the Energy and Natural Resources Committee, where he has served for nearly a decade without gaining much seniority. In part, this was luck of the draw. When he was assigned to the committee in 1981 there were eight Republicans ahead of him. Remarkably, all eight were still in the Senate in 1988. Even in the 101st Congress, Nickles is only sixth on the panel. Still, if he remains popular at home, his sheer youth means he could be Energy's chairman or ranking member someday.

Abortion funding has been another Nickles target. Since joining Appropriations, he has served on the District of Columbia Subcommittee, striving to cut off funding for abortion (including abortion of pregnancies caused by rape or incest). He attached an amendment to the D.C. appropriation in 1988 cutting off funds unless the local government dropped its law requiring insurance companies to insure persons who test positive for AIDS. Nickles has also been a critic of foreign aid appropriations, questioning why the United States should aid potential economic rivals abroad.

Such positions are consistent with the Nickles who arrived in the Senate in 1981 as a conservative "true believer," determined to dismantle the Great Society and enact the New Right's social and economic agenda.

His first term, however, provided ample evidence that an ideologically pure stance would offer only limited assistance in a tough re-election contest. After the near-collapse of Oklahoma's energy and farm economies in the mid-1980s, Nickles shifted his emphasis to aggressive defense of Oklahoma's economic interests.

Early in 1985, Nickles cast the only vote in Oklahoma's congressional delegation against an emergency farm credit bill. Any benefits to farmers in the bill, he argued, were not worth the additional deficit spending. But later that year, he was one of six farm-state Republicans to vote against an administration-backed proposal by Majority Leader Bob Dole to trim the cost of federal farm programs.

Nickles had labor lobbyists quaking in 1981 when he took over the Labor Subcommittee chairmanship on Labor and Human Resources and announced an agenda that was anathema to unions. But he made almost no progress during six years as chairman on his favorite causes, which included establishing a subminimum wage for youth and repealing the Davis-Bacon Act, which increases wage rates on federal construction projects.

Nickles was still making war on Davis-Bacon in 1989. When minimum-wage legislation reached the Senate floor, Nickles tried unsuccessfully to attach amendments restricting application of Davis-Bacon. The Senate showed little interest in joining him.

Nickles, who once said that "before my election, I made an honest living," has been a leading opponent of congressional pay raises and a supporter of limits on service in Congress. Working with Republican Jake Garn of Utah, he pushed legislation to block an automatic 3.5 percent pay raise received by members in early 1984. He was also an outspoken opponent of the 51 percent pay increase proposed for Congress in 1988 and rejected by both houses in 1989.

At Home: When the 1986 campaign began, Nickles was regarded as one of the most vulnerable Republicans facing re-election. He had been aided in 1980 by President Reagan's coattails. And unlike his first contest, in which he defeated former Oklahoma City District Attorney Andy Coats, this one presented him with a formidable Democratic opponent: 1st District Rep. Jones.

Nickles' re-election contest was thus expected to be pivotal in the partisan battle for control of the Senate. But while the Democrats did achieve a Senate majority, the Oklahoma contest did not contribute to it. Convincing voters that Jones was a liberal, Nickles won handily, with 55 percent of the vote.

Nickles' easy win surprised those who regarded Jones as a master politician. In 1972, the Democrat had captured Tulsa's GOP-held House seat, running counter to the Nixon landslide, and his savvy enabled him to hold off a series of aggressive Republican challenges. His efforts on behalf of Tulsa's oil interests gave him access to normally Republican campaign financing sources, and he also earned prominence as Budget Committee chairman.

Jones assailed Nickles for lacking leadership skills needed in a state hard-hit by the energy and farm recessions. He decried the soaring federal deficits and blamed Republican policies for Oklahoma's economic problems. But his campaign was slow in starting; he did not declare his Senate candidacy until May.

The first sign that Jones had problems came in the August Democratic Senate primary. His opponent, George Gentry, a farmer and supporter of political extremist Lyndon H. LaRouche Jr., did not run an active campaign, but still received one of every three votes.

Shortly after the primary, Nickles began his media campaign. Though some of his efforts aimed to reinforce his conservative, clean-cut image, the core of Nickles' campaign was a series of ads portraying Jones as a liberal and accusing him of persistently voting for congressional pay raises. One ad ended with a roughhewn man informing "Jim" that "if you talk like a liberal and act like a liberal and vote like a liberal, you're a liberal."

Jones did not respond immediately to Nickles. Instead, he ran a homespun spot about his working-class childhood in Muskogee during the Great Depression. Another ad showed the balding Jones holding a hair dryer and stating that he would not have to waste much of his valuable time using it.

Finally, with polls indicating that the liberal label was sticking, Jones attempted to refute Nickles' claims. He cited House vote studies that placed him as a Democratic moderate, and quoted Washington sources who said Nickles was distorting Jones' record. But Jones' delayed reaction to Nickles' attacks placed him on the defensive during the crucial late weeks of the campaign.

Nickles carried Jones' heavily Republican Tulsa County base by nearly 17,000 votes. The senator dominated Oklahoma County (Oklahoma City) by a 2-to-1 margin. Despite the farm depression, Nickles also swept the wheat-growing counties in Oklahoma's northwest quarter.

Six years earlier, Nickles had risen from the state Legislature to become the Senate's youngest member. The journey took place almost overnight. Although he had been active in Republican politics for several years, Nickles waited until 1978 to run for public office, winning election to the state Senate. His first-term status there did not deter him from entering the 1980 Republican primary to replace retiring GOP Sen. (and now departing Gov.) Henry Bellmon.

Nickles' calls for a return to traditional family values drew a favorable response from Oklahoma's large evangelical community. Boosted by organizational support from fundamentalist Christian groups, Nickles startled political observers by topping a five-man field in the GOP primary, then winning the runoff by a nearly 2-to-1 margin.

The general election pitted Nickles against Coats, whose role in the prosecution of a famous Oklahoma City murder case made his name a household word in central Oklahoma. But Coats was on the defensive much of the time, seeking to convince voters that he was not a closet liberal, as Nickles alleged. Nickles also charged that the Senate was overrun with lawyers and Coats would add to the surplus.

Nickles' organization mounted successful voter registration drives to shore up Republican strength and helped spread his conservative themes to sympathetic Democrats. Aided by Reagan's strong showing in the state, Nickles won with 54 percent of the vote.

Committees

Appropriations (12th of 13 Republicans)
Legislative Branch (ranking); Foreign Operations; HUD-Independent Agencies; Interior and Related Agencies

Budget (7th of 10 Republicans)

Energy and Natural Resources (6th of 9 Republicans)
Energy Regulation and Conservation (ranking); Energy Research and Development; Mineral Resources Development and Production

Elections

1986 General

Don Nickles (R)	493,436	(55%)
James R. Jones (D)	400,230	(45%)

Previous Winning Percentage: 1980 (54%)

Campaign Finance

	Receipts	Receipts from PACs	Expend-itures
1986			
Nickles (R)	$2,955,708	$886,841 (30%)	$3,252,964
Jones (D)	$2,529,160	$994,491 (39%)	$2,564,983

Key Votes

1987

Enact omnibus highway bill over Reagan veto	N
Limit testing of space-based anti-ballistic missiles	N
Oppose banning tests of larger nuclear weapons	Y
Confirm Robert H. Bork as Supreme Court justice	Y

1988

Allow vote on campaign-finance overhaul	N
Pass civil rights restoration bill over Reagan veto	N
Enact omnibus trade bill over Reagan veto	Y
Approve death penalty for drug-related murders	Y
Oppose "workfare" amendment to welfare overhaul bill	N

Voting Studies

	Presidential Support		Party Unity		Conservative Coalition	
Year	**S**	**O**	**S**	**O**	**S**	**O**
1988	80	20	92	6	100	0
1987	73	22	91	6	91	9
1986	86	14	82	18	99	1
1985	82	18	79	20	87	12
1984	83	14	85	13	96	2
1983	66	34	83	16	91	5
1982	81	19	85	15	95	5
1981	85	13	87	11	89	10

Interest Group Ratings

Year	ADA	ACU	AFL-CIO	CCUS
1988	0	92	7	86
1987	5	100	10	94
1986	0	91	0	79
1985	0	87	0	90
1984	0	91	0	95
1983	10	96	7	78
1982	10	100	4	75
1981	5	100	5	94

1 James M. Inhofe (R)

Of Tulsa — Elected 1986

Born: Nov. 11, 1934, Des Moines, Iowa.
Education: U. of Tulsa, B.A. 1959.
Military Career: Army, 1954-56.
Occupation: Real-estate developer; insurance company executive.
Family: Wife, Kay Kirkpatrick; four children.
Religion: Presbyterian.
Political Career: Okla. House, 1967-69; Okla. Senate, 1969-77; Tulsa mayor, 1978-84; GOP nominee for governor, 1974; GOP nominee for U.S. House, 1976; sought re-election as mayor, 1984.
Capitol Office: 408 Cannon Bldg. 20515; 225-2211.

In Washington: A mainstay on the right wing of Oklahoma politics since the mid-1960s, Inhofe in Congress is following the same unbending conservative course that was his trademark as a state legislator, mayor and gubernatorial aspirant.

The unique thing about Inhofe is not his voting record; there are plenty of down-the-line conservatives like him in the House Republican Conference. What is unusual about Inhofe is his affinity for unbridled personal criticism of House members with whom he does not agree.

Few members, for example, would publicly opine that there are "a bunch" of communists in Congress, as Inhofe told a town meeting in 1987. "It is not five or 10," he said. "It is a very serious problem." He named Michigan Democrat George W. Crockett Jr. as a House member who "has been a member of the Communist Party and has been sympathizing with all of them." (Crockett says he was never in the Communist Party.)

"You have to wonder whose side they [House members] are on sometimes," Inhofe said in 1988. He has also said that Massachusetts Democrat Barney Frank tells his constituents "the reason to keep him in office is that he is a practicing homosexual."

Inhofe says his priorities in Congress are promoting business development in Tulsa and looking for ways to help Oklahoma's struggling energy and agricultural sectors. He can cite some successes: He was involved, for instance, in persuading State Farm Insurance to locate its regional headquarters in Tulsa.

But Inhofe is probably best known for his belief that liberalism is a threat to "family values" and for his strong anti-communist views. Unimpressed with recent events in the Soviet Union and China, he says both countries remain "committed ... to world communist domination."

In his freshman term on the Public Works Committee, Inhofe did something few junior members would dare — confront committee chairman James J. Howard (who died in March 1988). He publicly feuded with the autocratic Howard, who took exception to Inhofe's 1987 votes to sustain vetoes of the Clean Water Act and an omnibus highway reauthorization. Other Republicans on the committee worried that Inhofe was hurting his chances of winning funding for public works projects in his district, but Inhofe was unconcerned. "I wasn't sent here to be a puppet of any chairman of any committee," he said.

Inhofe does not see himself as unschooled in the customs of House comity. In a 1987 interview with the *Tulsa World*, Inhofe said, "I know how coalitions are built. If you ask anyone in the freshman delegation who they have most communication with, who they feel most comfortable talking about issues with, who they seek advice from, I suspect you'd probably find that I was on the top of that list."

At Home: Inhofe was one of the comeback stories of 1986. Two years after being unseated as Tulsa's mayor, he won election to Congress in a district that Tulsa dominates.

But that is the sort of up-and-down career Inhofe has had over two decades in politics. Few officeholders have endured as many setbacks as he has and still remained viable as candidates.

Inhofe won his first elective contest, for a seat in the state House, in 1966. After one term, he moved up to the state Senate, where he opposed the Equal Rights Amendment and sponsored a resolution calling for a constitutional amendment to balance the federal budget. He was an early supporter of Ronald Reagan for president.

Inhofe also established a reputation for being outspoken. In 1972, he said Sen. George S. McGovern should "be hanged with Jane Fonda" after the Democratic presidential nominee implied American soldiers were guilty of atrocities in Vietnam. "There are no gray areas

Oklahoma 1

Tulsa; Parts of Osage, Creek and Washington Counties

In its white-collar Republican leanings and its antagonism to rural Democratic power, Tulsa was a forerunner of other Sun Belt cities now catching up with it. Tulsa County has gone Republican in all but two presidential elections since 1920. The city comprises 67 percent of the district's population.

Once a post office along the trail of the Pony Express, Tulsa was transformed by the discovery of oil in a nearby field in 1906 — and oil has sparked Tulsa's economic development throughout most of this century. Tulsa today calls itself "The Oil Capital of the World," a label justified by the myriad petroleum companies that maintain their corporate headquarters there. Even in this slack time for the oil industry, chief executives and senior engineers regularly gather to discuss business and politics in downtown Tulsa's Petroleum Club.

Tulsa's economy has diversified considerably in recent years. With the opening of the Arkansas River Navigation System in 1971, Tulsa became a deep-water port accessible to the Gulf of Mexico. The city also maintains a thriving aeronautics industry; McDonnell Douglas and Rockwell International are among its leading companies, and American Airlines has moved its national headquarters for flight reservations to Tulsa as well. Tulsa also has a major tourist attraction in Oral Roberts University (4,500 students), which anchors a large fundamentalist community. Visitors flock from around the country to view the "City of Faith," the huge medical complex that offers itself as a nexus of science and prayer.

Tulsa's fundamentalists are concentrated in the eastern part of the city; affluent business executives populate the southeast, and the central section is a mixture of blue-collar whites and young professionals. North Tulsa hosts a sizable black community that provides Democrats with their best Tulsa turf.

Southeast of Tulsa, the 1st takes in most of Broken Arrow, home to many Tulsa workers who commute via the Broken Arrow Expressway. It also contains parts of Osage and Creek counties, which include some growing Tulsa suburbs. In Osage, which has most of the district's land area, cattle ranching supplements the oil and gas trade. Rounding out the northeast side, the 1st District covers southern Washington County.

Population: 503,739. White 423,755 (84%), Black 47,433 (9%), American Indian, Eskimo and Aleut 25,146 (5%), Other 2,976 (1%). Spanish origin 7,894 (2%). 18 and over 365,006 (73%), 65 and over 52,774 (11%). Median age: 30.

in my views," Inhofe has said.

Democratic efforts to portray Inhofe as an extremist contributed to his first defeats. As the GOP nominee for governor in 1974, he suffered a humiliating loss at the hands of then-state Rep. David L. Boren, attracting barely one-third of the vote. Two years later, Inhofe left the state Senate to challenge Democratic Rep. James R. Jones; he lost by almost 9 percentage points.

But Tulsa's conservative communities, including important energy interests and many religious fundamentalists, remained supportive of Inhofe. He built on this base for his first comeback, winning the Tulsa mayoralty in 1978.

As mayor, Inhofe was strongly opposed to federal budget expansion and frequently avoided seeking the kinds of urban assistance from Washington that other cities depended on. While most big-city mayors decried President Reagan's domestic budget cuts, Inhofe defended them.

Having served three terms, Inhofe was a strong favorite for re-election in 1984. But a heavy black turnout in north Tulsa helped Democrat Terry Young win a stunning upset. After the loss, Inhofe said, "I will never run for any office in Oklahoma City or Washington."

Two years later, the 1st District came open with Jones' decision to run for the Senate. Inhofe did not leap into the congressional opportunity; energy company executive D. W. "Bill" Calvert announced early, and lined up many of Inhofe's campaign financiers. Besides, Inhofe had personal financial problems, stemming from the failure of some of his investments in Oklahoma's oil-based recession.

After struggling with the decision for several months, Inhofe finally announced his candidacy in May, describing himself as "a little bit on the hard right." He quickly activated his grass-roots network, and with a significant name-recognition advantage over Calvert, he easily won nomination.

Although Jones had kept the 1st Democratic for seven terms, Democrats failed to recruit a well-known candidate to succeed him. Their nominee, law professor Gary Allison, ran a vigorous campaign, but Inhofe blasted him for supporting legalized abortion and opposing aid to the Nicaraguan contras. Allison accused Inhofe of playing on religion when he brought in TV evangelist Pat Robertson for a fund-raiser. Outspent more than 3-to-1, Allison managed to keep Inhofe's winning tally down to 55 percent.

Inhofe weathered a turbulent 1988. He stirred considerable local publicity by suing his brother over the sale of stock in the family insurance business; his brother countersued. Also, Inhofe's district chief of staff quit, castigating Inhofe for not providing enough staff for adequate constituent service. Inhofe dismissed the incident as office politics.

Fortunately for Inhofe, Democrats offered a candidate with no name recognition and little political experience — 33-year-old Kurt Glassco, who was an assistant district attorney in Tulsa before becoming legal counsel to Democratic Gov. George Nigh. He was more moderate than Inhofe's 1986 foe: Glassco supported some contra aid and favored research on the strategic defense initiative.

Inhofe again had a substantial financial advantage; he outspent Glassco nearly 2-to-1. In spite of that, the incumbent was re-elected with only 53 percent of the vote — a margin that raised eyebrows in Oklahoma and Washington, especially since George Bush won the 1st comfortably.

Committees

Merchant Marine and Fisheries (16th of 17 Republicans)
Coast Guard and Navigation; Merchant Marine

Public Works and Transportation (12th of 20 Republicans)
Aviation; Investigations and Oversight; Water Resources

Select Narcotics Abuse and Control (8th of 12 Republicans)

Elections

1988 General		
James M. Inhofe (R)	103,458	(53%)
Kurt Glassco (D)	93,101	(47%)
1986 General		
James M. Inhofe (R)	78,919	(55%)
Gary D. Allison (D)	61,663	(43%)

District Vote For President

	1988	1984	1980	1976
D	76,540 (39%)	65,241 (29%)	54,809 (31%)	64,514 (38%)
R	120,950 (61%)	158,304 (71%)	114,517 (64%)	101,276 (60%)
I			7,216 (4%)	

Campaign Finance

	Receipts	Receipts from PACs	Expend-itures
1988			
Inhofe (R)	$482,552	$263,222 (55%)	$484,585
Glassco (D)	$255,822	$112,700 (44%)	$256,220
1986			
Inhofe (R)	$415,771	$142,731 (34%)	$410,286
Allison (D)	$120,063	$47,567 (40%)	$119,550

Key Votes

1987	
Raise speed limit to 65 mph	Y
Approve Gephardt "fair trade" amendment	N
Ban testing of larger nuclear weapons	N
Delay "re-flagging" of Kuwaiti tankers	N
Approve tax-raising deficit-reduction bill	N
1988	
Approve aid to Nicaraguan contras	Y
Enact civil rights restoration bill over Reagan veto	N
Kill 60-day plant-closing notification measure	Y
Pass omnibus trade bill over Reagan veto	Y
Approve death penalty for drug-related murders	Y
Bar federal funds for abortions in cases of rape and incest	Y
Oppose seven-day waiting period for purchase of handguns	Y

Voting Studies

	Presidential Support		Party Unity		Conservative Coalition	
Year	S	O	S	O	S	O
1988	64	34	88	6	95	3
1987	73	23	91	2	95	5

Interest Group Ratings

Year	ADA	ACU	AFL-CIO	CCUS
1988	10	92	38	92
1987	4	100	0	100

2 Mike Synar (D)

Of Muskogee — Elected 1978

Born: Oct. 17, 1950, Vinita, Okla.
Education: U. of Oklahoma, B.B.A. 1972, LL.B. 1977; Northwestern U., M.S. 1973; attended U. of Edinburgh, Scotland, 1974.
Occupation: Rancher; real-estate broker; lawyer.
Family: Single.
Religion: Episcopalian.
Political Career: No previous office.
Capitol Office: 2441 Rayburn Bldg. 20515; 225-2701.

In Washington: Synar possesses a brashness that might turn off many of his colleagues if it were not for one thing: He seems genuinely concerned about making what he sees as good public policy, and he has a knack for doing it. There is a macho quality to his style and an affection for winning attention, but at the core, he is a serious pursuer of issues.

Synar seems very anxious to become a leader in the House, and there are those who believe he may indeed build a broad power base in the institution. But he seems a bit too eager: In the 100th Congress he threw his hat in the ring for chairman of the Democratic Caucus, but won just 33 votes. That put him a poor third to Mary Rose Oakar (80 votes) and the winner, William H. Gray III (146).

Synar, who took the unusual step of making a speech on his own behalf before the caucus vote, presented himself as the activist with the most legislative experience. But he had gotten into the race much later than his opponents and had less experience in conducting an institutionwide campaign. Synar's showy nature was also not what some members wanted in a caucus chairman.

Synar has enjoyed much more success with his committee work. While it is sometimes difficult to find a member's fingerprints on legislation, Synar, with an enthusiasm for jumping into major issues, leaves the trail of a child who has dipped his hands in an inkwell. He is among the most active members on the Energy and Commerce Committee, and also contributes to Judiciary and Government Operations, where he chairs the Environment, Energy and Natural Resources Subcommittee.

On Energy and Commerce, Synar freely involves himself in politically difficult issues, and freely reminds others that he does so. "If you don't like fighting fires, don't be a fireman ... and if you don't like voting, don't be a congressman," he said while working on product liability legislation that split business and consumer groups and made some members queasy.

Business groups had long sought federal legislation to pre-empt sometimes conflicting state liability standards (which are used by courts to determine when manufacturers should be held accountable for damages caused by their products). But consumer groups and trial lawyers feared that new legislation would make it more difficult for consumers to claim damages. Energy and Commerce Chairman John D. Dingell wanted Synar to alter a plan then before the committee to make it more palatable to consumer leaders and moderate Democrats.

Synar did produce changes that many Democrats considered more favorable to consumers than the original bill, but many still complained it was worse than existing law. The panel voted to pass it, but acrimony was dulled by the fact that few expected the legislation to become law. It did not.

Synar also worked hard behind the scenes on a relatively thankless task, trying to reauthorize the Clean Air Act. Legislation to address smog and acid rain has for years been trapped in the committee because of a standoff between Dingell and an industry-oriented faction and Democratic Rep. Henry A. Waxman, leader of the panel's staunchest environmentalists. In the 100th Congress the stall continued, but Synar helped make some headway, working with the "group of nine," an informal caucus of moderate Democrats who sought to hammer out the compromise that had eluded the two leading factions. Ultimately the group produced a detailed plan to address urban smog, finding middle ground that generally imposed less stringest pollution controls and stretched out timetables for numerous cities to meet federal air quality standards.

Synar's belief that members should have the courage of their convictions has led him to take some risks and win some glory. He took a heavily publicized gamble in the 99th Congress. While most members rushed to embrace the Gramm-Rudman-Hollings deficit-reduction plan, which was portrayed as a test of congressional will to cut the budget, Synar led the charge against it, splitting with the rest of the Oklahoma delegation on final passage and launching

Oklahoma 2

Northeast — Tulsa; Muskogee

This northeastern Oklahoma territory has had some good fortune. Sheltered somewhat by the low-lying Ozark Mountains, it was spared the worst of the Dust Bowl winds that ravaged much of the state during the 1930s and 1940s. Equally important, it has attracted numerous state and federal water projects over the years — projects that have bolstered agriculture, drawn vacationers and prompted some local chambers of commerce to bill the area as "Green Country."

The growing tourism industry is crowding the area's traditional enterprises, cattle ranching and the oil and gas business. Recent oil and gas activity has been confined largely to recovery from older wells.

With a 27 percent population increase, the 2nd was Oklahoma's fastest-growing district during the 1970s. Much of the growth occurred in the eastern Tulsa suburbs in Rogers and Wagoner counties, home to a substantial number of GOP voters. Muskogee, with 42,000 people the largest city wholly contained in the 2nd, dredges sand from the Arkansas River beds for use in its glass industry; it is Democratic.

The largest Indian population in Oklahoma is concentrated within the 2nd's boundaries, in the area settled by the Five Civilized Tribes in the 19th century. The Cherokee Nation has its headquarters in Tahlequah, the seat of Cherokee County, and members of other tribes are scattered through surrounding counties.

Although the 2nd has had a suburban Tulsa component for some time, 1982 redistricting moved the district into the city limits for the first time. The southeastern Tulsa portion of the 2nd is a GOP haven populated by middle-rung and top-level executives from the city's corporate offices.

The 2nd as a whole retains a basically Democratic cast. Only Haskell County supported Walter F. Mondale for president in 1984, but in 1988, Michael S. Dukakis fared considerably better, carrying 10 counties in the 2nd and winning 47 percent of the districtwide vote. Mostly the district has voted Democratic in other recent statewide and local elections.

Population: 505,149. White 420,537 (83%), Black 22,965 (5%), American Indian, Eskimo and Aleut 58,472 (12%). Spanish origin 4,528 (1%). 18 and over 353,938 (70%), 65 and over 67,761 (13%). Median age: 32.

the legal challenge that succeeded in having the pivotal section of the new law declared unconstitutional. He was blasted by editorial writers and some House critics for standing in the way of fiscal restraint, but the move ultimately enhanced his reputation.

Synar, who was joined by 11 other members in his lawsuit, challenged the provision in the law calling for automatic budget cuts to meet deficit targets. He said that provision "tramples the Constitution" by delegating congressional responsibility for fiscal policy.

"If this delegation is allowed, Congress could put the entire government on automatic pilot," Synar and his allies warned in their legal brief. And he was critical of members abdicating that responsibility. "If members can't make hard choices, they ought to seek other employment," he said at one point.

Synar scored his first victory in early 1986 when a three-judge federal panel ruled that the automatic cuts, intended to enforce discipline in spending, did violate the separation of powers by giving executive power to the comptroller general. His final victory came a few months later when the Supreme Court upheld that ruling in a 7-2 decision.

The best evidence that Synar means what he says about legislating in the national interest is the tenuous connection between many of his crusades and his own political interests in Oklahoma. One of his goals is to pass legislation that would ban all tobacco company advertising and promotions. He sees that as a step that could lead to a tobacco-free society. Not surprisingly, his bill has prompted attacks from advertisers and tobacco companies. But they are not alone. The American Civil Liberties Union has also attacked the plan, claiming it would violate the constitutional right to free speech, a charge Synar disputes.

But Synar also has legislative interests that are strongly connected to the interests of his constituents. In the 100th Congress he joined with Iowa Republican Tom Tauke to chair a Rural Health Care Coalition. The group, which sought to improve medical care in rural areas, was initially dismissed by some as a mere publicity vehicle. But by the end of 1988, it had made some tangible achievements, including the establishment of a separate office on rural health within the Department of Health and Human Services. The group also succeeded in passing a measure giving rural hospitals Medicare inflation increases that are larger than those going to urban centers.

At Home: A clean-cut son of a prominent ranching family, Synar jumped into a House campaign in 1978, just one year after returning home from school to practice law.

Although he was inexperienced at politics, he was the right sort of challenger to Democratic Rep. Ted Risenhoover, who had become controversial because of a divorce and a reputation as a Washington playboy. The incumbent spent much of the primary campaign trying to refute charges that he slept in a heart-shaped water bed in his Washington apartment. Synar campaigned intensively throughout the district and won an 8,000-vote upset. Compared with Risenhoover, Synar appeared fresh, polished and seemly.

Synar was helped by his name. His father and five uncles have been prominent in the Muskogee area for decades. In 1971, they were selected the "Outstanding Family" in the United States by the All-American Family Institute.

After his 1978 election, Synar set up an intensive constituent-service operation. He announced that a majority of his staff members would remain in Oklahoma. These steps helped protect him in 1980 when GOP nominee Gary Richardson attacked him for having a liberal voting record. Synar's percentage was down slightly from 1978, but he still held off Richardson with 54 percent of the vote.

In 1982 Republican Lou Striegel, a lawyer from Broken Arrow, tried his hand against Synar. Striegel ran TV ads pointing out that the incumbent was slipping in his ratings from the U.S. Chamber of Commerce and the National Federation of Independent Business.

But Synar drew more than 70 percent, and scored two similarly easy victories over Republican real estate developer Gary K. Rice.

Conservative Democrats who feel Synar maintains too high a profile on national issues and is too liberal had their chance to gripe in the 1988 Democratic primary, in which controversial state Sen. Frank Shurden challenged Synar from the right. But Synar dismissed him with 70 percent of the vote and won easily again in November.

Committees

Energy and Commerce (12th of 26 Democrats)
Energy and Power; Health and the Environment; Telecommunications and Finance

Government Operations (6th of 24 Democrats)
Environment, Energy and Natural Resources (chairman)

Judiciary (7th of 21 Democrats)
Courts, Intellectual Property and the Administration of Justice; Economic and Commercial Law

Select Aging (11th of 39 Democrats)
Health and Long-Term Care; Retirement, Income and Employment

Elections

1988 General		
Mike Synar (D)	136,009	(65%)
Ira Phillips (R)	73,659	(35%)
1988 Primary		
Mike Synar (D)	62,936	(70%)
Frank Shurden (D)	27,604	(30%)
1986 General		
Mike Synar (D)	114,543	(73%)
Gary K. Rice (R)	41,795	(27%)

Previous Winning Percentages: **1984** (74%) **1982** (73%) **1980** (54%) **1978** (55%)

District Vote For President

	1988		1984		1980		1976	
D	97,030	(47%)	77,923	(36%)	82,689	(42%)	99,467	(54%)
R	110,189	(53%)	139,721	(64%)	108,520	(55%)	82,469	(45%)
I					4,654	(2%)		

Campaign Finance

	Receipts	Receipts from PACs		Expend-itures
1988				
Synar (D)	$310,865	0		$358,705
Phillips (R)	$84,777	$5,447	(6%)	$81,634
1986				
Synar (D)	$270,998	0		$286,491
Rice (R)	$10,956	$1,775	(16%)	$11,276

Key Votes

1987	
Raise speed limit to 65 mph	N
Approve Gephardt "fair trade" amendment	N
Ban testing of larger nuclear weapons	Y
Delay "re-flagging" of Kuwaiti tankers	Y
Approve tax-raising deficit-reduction bill	Y
1988	
Approve aid to Nicaraguan contras	N
Enact civil rights restoration bill over Reagan veto	Y
Kill 60-day plant-closing notification measure	N
Pass omnibus trade bill over Reagan veto	Y
Approve death penalty for drug-related murders	N
Bar federal funds for abortions in cases of rape and incest	N
Oppose seven-day waiting period for purchase of handguns	N

Voting Studies

	Presidential Support		Party Unity		Conservative Coalition	
Year	**S**	**O**	**S**	**O**	**S**	**O**
1988	26	73	93	5	13	87
1987	21	76	90	7	23	74
1986	24	71	83	11	24	70
1985	25	75	88	10	33	65
1984	44	51	80	13	36	53
1983	33	66	85	12	43	55
1982	43	55	79	17	44	52
1981	37	61	90	10	27	72

Interest Group Ratings

Year	ADA	ACU	AFL-CIO	CCUS
1988	100	0	86	38
1987	84	13	75	13
1986	70	15	57	22
1985	75	14	53	36
1984	80	17	38	31
1983	75	17	71	50
1982	55	26	70	50
1981	80	13	73	16

3 Wes Watkins (D)

Of Ada — Elected 1976

Born: Dec. 15, 1938, DeQueen, Ark.
Education: Oklahoma State U., B.S. 1960, M.S. 1961.
Military Career: Okla. Air National Guard, 1961-67.
Occupation: Real-estate salesman; home builder.
Family: Wife, Elizabeth Lou Rogers; three children.
Religion: Presbyterian.
Political Career: Okla. Senate, 1975-77.
Capitol Office: 2348 Rayburn Bldg. 20515; 225-4565.

In Washington: To Watkins, federally funded public works projects are the key to rural prosperity, and his guiding mission in the House is to secure more money for them. When he walks into the Appropriations Committee room, members prepare for a homily on the rigors of life in rural America. And though his set speech can get a bit old to colleagues who have often heard it, none denies his skill at padding bills large and small with funds for rural programs — particularly those in Oklahoma's 3rd District.

Watkins is known for amassing set-asides for projects ranging from roads and dams to innovation fairs and trade studies, each time asking colleagues for just a little money for a small project. Add it all up, however, and he takes home a very sizable piece of the pie. A wall in his House office bears a map of his district marked with yellow and green dots. The yellow dots stand for unfinished projects; the green dots symbolize completed ones.

While some view this as the very definition of pork-barrel politics, Watkins speaks from the heart about the economic plight of rural America. "Some of my first memories were the days around World War II when my family went to California looking for a job," he said in a 1988 newspaper interview. "We went there three times before I was 10 years old."

This experience imbued Watkins with some traditional conservative values, but also with an abiding faith in government assistance. The Reagan era was not an expansionary time for public works spending, but Watkins kept busy laying the groundwork for future endeavors. "My way of getting projects done," he once said, "is to get the feasibility studies completed, so that when they become politically feasible and the money is available, then they are ready to go."

As the regional recession in the oil and farm sectors deepened in the 1980s, Watkins reacted viscerally against President Reagan's economic policies, just as many other Southern Democrats were aligning themselves with them. "The quickest way to destroy a family is for a father not to have a job and to lose his self-esteem with his wife and children," he said. "I saw that happen. It made a burning imprint on my heart."

After voting with a majority of Democrats less than one-third of the time during the Carter administration, Watkins sided with his party on nearly three-quarters of all House votes in Reagan's second term. But despite his increased party fealty, when Democratic colleagues try to line up his vote in advance, Watkins is apt to be noncommittal. This cautiousness is one of the factors that restricts him from being a key player in House politics.

Watkins suffered a setback at the start of the 101st Congress, when he was one of Appropriations Chairman Jamie L. Whitten's two candidates for the Budget Committee. Perhaps because Watkins holds a seat on Steering and Policy — which makes committee assignments — he seemed to take his selection for granted and campaigned little for the job. When the votes were counted, Watkins had lost.

Watkins' nonchalance also hurt him in 1988, when a project of his was shelved by the Rules Committee in its attempt to mediate a feud between the Public Works Committee and the Transportation Subcommittee of Appropriations. Watkins and a number of other members had tacked funds for unauthorized programs onto a transportation spending bill, and Public Works objected. According to Rules Committee members, Watkins' project was one of three knocked off the bill, because he had failed to do his homework. "Sometimes people don't check with Rules," said a senior member. "We imagine they're not that interested."

But for all this, Watkins remains a master appropriator. During markup sessions — whether before the full committee or on the Agriculture or the Energy and Water Subcommittee — Watkins rarely shows up without a long list of projects he wants for his district and other rural constituencies like it. During the six-year period that the GOP held the Senate majority, Watkins' refusal to give up on his arguments led to some tension in House-Senate conferences. On one occasion, he brought a jar

Oklahoma 3

Southeast — "Little Dixie"

The most reliably Democratic district in Oklahoma, the sprawling southeastern 3rd has not elected a Republican to the House in the 82 years since statehood.

The area was settled largely from Texas and Arkansas, and most of its voters are conservative. But the "Little Dixie" region in which the 3rd is based has largely missed out on the oil discoveries that brought wealth — and burgeoning Republicanism — to central and western Oklahoma.

Wracked by rural depression in the 1920s, this region is the least prosperous area of Oklahoma today. The cotton crop that once dominated the local economy has been superseded by livestock production, but the region lacks the expansive ranches that are more common to the west. The Ouachita Mountain pines help fuel the timber trade in the district's southeastern corner; the Weyerhaeuser Co. has a plant in McCurtain County. The relatively small amount of oil exploration here, currently focused on the district's eastern side, picked up as Standard Oil of Ohio began drilling on lands leased from Weyerhaeuser.

The area's poor agricultural base was one reason for the steady exodus of its population between 1920 and 1970; many counties here lost roughly half their people during that time. But the 3rd — which encompasses 19 whole counties and part of another — reversed the trend between 1970 and 1980, showing a 20 percent population increase.

In the two presidential elections when Ronald Reagan was on the Republican ballot, the 3rd broke loose of its Democratic moorings. Before that, though, the district gave Jimmy Carter a big victory in his 1976 White House bid. And in 1988, Democrat Michael S. Dukakis carried 14 counties in the 3rd, falling only 459 votes short of winning the district outright against George Bush. In elections for other offices, the voters of the 3rd harbor little sympathy for the GOP.

Population: 504,268. White 438,897 (87%), Black 22,133 (4%), American Indian, Eskimo and Aleut 38,321 (8%). Spanish origin 5,341 (1%). 18 and over 365,865 (73%), 65 and over 77,856 (15%). Median age: 31.

of ticks into a conference to portray the foul conditions in a southeast Oklahoma swamp that he said could be revitalized by an irrigation project he wanted the panel to approve.

In 1986, Watkins pushed for the speeding up of deficiency payments to wheat farmers. Under the 1985 farm bill, the payment schedule for wheat coincided with that for other grains. But wheat growers complained that, because they had an earlier planting season, they would receive their payments too late. Though some House members from districts that specialized in other grains complained that wheat growers were seeking special treatment, Watkins helped work out a compromise, and the accelerated payments were approved.

In the 99th Congress, a Watkins proposal to set up a grant program that would create "institutes of rural technology development" in depressed rural areas passed the House by voice vote, and was later signed into law. Watkins has also introduced legislation to change the name of the Department of Agriculture to the Department of Agriculture and Rural Development, and proposed to establish a new Rural Development Administration to manage soil conservation and housing programs.

In his district in recent years, his efforts have reaped federal funds to help develop an agricultural research center, an industrial innovation and finance center, a 25,000-acre reservoir, a National Wildlife Refuge, and an industrial park, to name a few. Many of his efforts to develop tourism, agriculture and industry in southeastern Oklahoma have been managed by a state public trust, RedArk, that he helped found in 1981. "I don't know how much we've funneled that way," he said in a newspaper interview, "but I've tried to get it $300,000 to $400,000 each year to carry out the program."

Watkins idolizes the late Robert Kerr, the powerful Democratic senator from Oklahoma who was known during his tenure (1949-63) as the Senate's master dam-builder. Watkins seems to have inherited his zeal for water projects from Kerr, who came from Watkins' district and spent much of his time in Washington seeing that it got irrigated. He likes to point out that Kerr never stopped pushing the Arkansas River Navigation System in Oklahoma, even though he was blocked for years by the Eisenhower administration. Eventually, the massive project was built.

At Home: Watkins reached the House over the opposition of his famous predecessor, House Speaker Carl Albert, who retired in 1976 after 30 years representing the district.

As his successor, Albert favored his longtime chief aide, Charles Ward, and he endorsed

Ward in the Democratic primary. But Watkins, who had been elected to the state Senate in 1974, had been planning a House campaign for several years. He developed the best organization among the six Democrats who entered the primary, and he capitalized on the fact that his wife had served as Democratic congressional district co-chairman. Watkins ran 10,000 votes ahead of Ward in the initial primary, then trounced him in a runoff, taking 63 percent of the vote.

That was Watkins' last competitive election. He breezed to victory that November, and has won routinely since. In 1982, 1984 and 1986, Watkins easily dispatched the same Republican nominee: Patrick Miller, a little-known farmer and electrical engineer from the town of Snow.

In 1988, amid widespread talk of Watkins' gubernatorial ambitions, Republicans failed to recruit a candidate to oppose him. It was his third unopposed re-election.

Watkins originally went into education, completing the course work for a doctorate degree in higher education at Oklahoma State University. After working in the admissions office there, he became a real-estate developer.

Committee

Appropriations (24th of 35 Democrats)
Energy and Water Development; Rural Development, Agriculture and Related Agencies

Elections

1988 General		
Wes Watkins (D)	Unopposed	
1986 General		
Wes Watkins (D)	114,008	(78%)
Patrick K. Miller (R)	31,913	(22%)

Previous Winning Percentages: 1984 (78%) **1982** (82%) **1980** (100%) **1978** (100%) **1976** (82%)

District Vote For President

	1988	1984	1980	1976
D	94,164 (50%)	75,671 (38%)	86,781 (46%)	110,972 (60%)
R	94,623 (50%)	124,798 (62%)	95,640 (51%)	71,260 (39%)
I			4,884 (3%)	

Campaign Finance

	Receipts	Receipts from PACs	Expend-itures
1988			
Watkins (D)	$241,418	$73,900 (31%)	$174,437
1986			
Watkins (D)	$209,653	$79,430 (38%)	$210,936

Key Votes

1987	
Raise speed limit to 65 mph	Y
Approve Gephardt "fair trade" amendment	Y
Ban testing of larger nuclear weapons	N
Delay "re-flagging" of Kuwaiti tankers	Y
Approve tax-raising deficit-reduction bill	Y
1988	
Approve aid to Nicaraguan contras	Y
Enact civil rights restoration bill over Reagan veto	Y
Kill 60-day plant-closing notification measure	Y
Pass omnibus trade bill over Reagan veto	#
Approve death penalty for drug-related murders	Y
Bar federal funds for abortions in cases of rape and incest	Y
Oppose seven-day waiting period for purchase of handguns	Y

Voting Studies

	Presidential Support		Party Unity		Conservative Coalition	
Year	**S**	**O**	**S**	**O**	**S**	**O**
1988	35	64	75	23	87	13
1987	35	63	73	20	67	33
1986	32	67	75	22	66	32
1985	43	56	73	22	67	29
1984	45	48	63	31	78	12
1983	34	63	65	32	79	21
1982	49	45	60	33	74	19
1981	57	43	57	43	89	11

Interest Group Ratings

Year	ADA	ACU	AFL-CIO	CCUS
1988	50	46	79	57
1987	60	17	73	21
1986	40	41	64	29
1985	50	48	47	45
1984	30	45	46	44
1983	70	35	71	40
1982	35	45	60	45
1981	30	27	67	26

4 Dave McCurdy (D)

Of Norman — Elected 1980

Born: March 30, 1950, Canadian, Texas.
Education: U. of Oklahoma, B.A. 1972, J.D. 1975.
Military Career: Air Force Reserve, 1969-72.
Occupation: Lawyer.
Family: Wife, Pamela Plumb; three children.
Religion: Lutheran.
Political Career: Okla. assistant attorney general, 1975-77.
Capitol Office: 2344 Rayburn Bldg. 20515; 225-6165.

In Washington: When House Democrats sit down these days to hammer out a consensus on major defense or foreign policy issues, odds are strong that McCurdy will be in the thick of the debate. A leading voice among "New South" Democratic moderates and a supreme pragmatist, McCurdy is not shy about commending his thoughts to his colleagues.

McCurdy's soft-spoken manner provides a degree of cover for his aggressive pursuit of influence. His maneuver to obtain an unprecedented reappointment to the House Select Committee on Intelligence in the 101st Congress provides a case in point.

Members of the committee, which oversees U.S. intelligence operations, are limited to six consecutive years. McCurdy, who joined the committee in January 1983, had risen to second in seniority in the 100th Congress. But he was due to leave the panel at the end of the 1988 session.

However, McCurdy was determined to extend his involvement in intelligence policy. So he took the unusual step of resigning from the Intelligence Committee in November 1987. By not completing his six-year stretch, he would be eligible for reappointment to a full six-year term on the panel.

In 1989, House Speaker Jim Wright fulfilled McCurdy's desire, and then some. He not only reappointed him to Intelligence — making him the first member to rejoin the committee — but also reinstalled him as second-ranking member, behind new Chairman Anthony C. Beilenson. Since Beilenson's committee tenure was due to expire at the end of 1989, McCurdy appeared certain to become chairman.

But McCurdy's bold stroke became the first victim of Wright's downfall as House Speaker. That July, new Speaker Thomas S. Foley backed a move by members sympathetic to Beilenson to grant the Californian an extra year on Intelligence so he could serve a full term as chairman. Though McCurdy remains second-ranking, his ascension in the 102nd Congress is not automatic: Chairmen of select committees are appointed by the Speaker.

Still, McCurdy is generally held in high regard. He is an associate of Wisconsin Democrat Les Aspin, chairman of the Armed Services Committee, on which McCurdy serves. In 1985, another audacious move by McCurdy toppled the Armed Services seniority system and elevated Aspin to the chairmanship.

With less than two House terms under his belt, McCurdy engineered the ouster of longtime committee Chairman Melvin Price of Illinois, a frail octogenarian. In late 1984, McCurdy sent a letter to other Armed Services members calling for a meeting to discuss Price's waning leadership abilities and the possibility of replacing him with a more forceful figure.

Despite his infirmity, Price made a serious effort to hold his chairmanship, and drew the support of Speaker Thomas P. O'Neill Jr. But their seniority-based pleas before the Democratic Caucus fell short; Price was removed by a 121-118 vote in January 1985.

By that point, McCurdy and others had staged a lobbying campaign on behalf of Aspin, the seventh-ranking Democrat on the committee. Aspin, who had a reputation as a liberal Pentagon critic, actually had not been McCurdy's first choice. But when Bill Nichols of Alabama, a more senior and more conservative member, declined to buck the seniority system, McCurdy turned to Aspin and promoted him as a forceful leader.

That image gave Aspin an advantage over his opponent, Charles E. Bennett of Florida, who, though next in line behind Price, was penalized for having shown no obvious impatience with Price's inability to lead. The caucus opted for Aspin on a 125-103 vote.

On legislative matters, McCurdy brings a centrist Democratic perspective to Aspin's "kitchen cabinet." An Air Force Reserve veteran from a military-oriented district, McCurdy lacks the zeal of more liberal Democrats for slashing the Pentagon budget. However, he also has little in common with the dwindling "Old Guard" of Democratic conservatives who have traditionally been agreeable to Defense Department wishes.

After initially supporting the MX missile,

Oklahoma 4

Southwest — Part of Oklahoma City

This slice of southwestern Oklahoma maintains a military presence that no politician can afford to forget for very long. In addition to Altus Air Force Base and the Army's Fort Sill, near the Texas border, the district stretches northeast to take in Tinker Air Force Base, just east of Oklahoma City. With a combined civilian and military staff averaging 24,000, Tinker is Oklahoma's largest single-site employer. It will house the maintenance center for the new B-2 "stealth" bomber. Fort Sill, the site of the Army's principal artillery training school, employs nearly as many.

Despite the military orientation, most Democratic candidates usually carry the 4th. Sen. David L. Boren polled 72 percent of its vote — his best showing statewide — in his 1978 Senate bid, and carried every county in the 4th in 1984. Michael S. Dukakis carried four counties here in 1988.

But Ronald Reagan took the district easily twice, and in 1980 his coattails helped Republican Senate nominee Don Nickles win it by a narrow margin. The GOP is strongest at the northern end of the 4th, in the Oklahoma City suburbs of Moore and Midwest City.

McCurdy's district is still largely agricultural — it ranks fifth in the nation in cotton production — but over the past decade, it has become increasingly dependent on the energy industry. In the 1970s, Oklahoma's energy boom brought new oil and gas businesses to many of the district's southwestern counties. But declining demand has weakened the economy considerably since.

With 83,000 people, Lawton (Comanche County) is the 4th's largest city and a commercial center of southwest Oklahoma. The Goodyear tire and rubber plant nearby is the third-largest factory in the state.

The city of Norman is home to the University of Oklahoma (21,000 students) and the district's most liberal voters. The economy here is stronger than in most of the other counties; the university and such government-sponsored research programs as the National Severe Storm Laboratory are attracting high-technology industries.

Population: 505,869. White 441,346 (87%), Black 31,953 (6%), Other 20,859 (4%). Spanish origin 16,368 (3%). 18 and over 356,658 (71%), 65 and over 47,534 (9%). Median age: 27.

---

for example, McCurdy joined with committee liberals in 1985 on a compromise that limited the MX without killing it completely. He then joined with Aspin in an unsuccessful 1987 committee effort to scrap the MX and replace it with the more mobile Midgetman.

McCurdy's interest in both defense and intelligence issues has made him a player on the issue of aid to the Nicaraguan contras. While the ideologically charged debate of the mid-1980s swirled around him, McCurdy staked out a middle-ground position, stating that the United States should encourage diplomatic efforts to end the Nicaraguan civil war, while not completely abandoning the contra forces.

McCurdy gained credit for his knowledge on the issue, and was regarded as the bellwether for moderate and conservative Democratic support for contra-aid proposals. Yet McCurdy's efforts to press his own solutions were not markedly successful. In 1985, he gained attention for the "McCurdy compromise," a measure that contained $100 million for the contras but would have required a second, later vote to release the funds. However, President Reagan pushed through his own plan calling for $100 million with no strings attached.

A founder of the congressional Army caucus, McCurdy often complained about the Reagan administration's emphasis on nuclear weapons systems. In 1987, McCurdy said Reagan's defense budget proposal would have "cut America's conventional forces off at the knees."

His interest in bolstering the conventional military also contributed to his proposals in 1987 and 1989 for a national service program for high school graduates. The later proposal, co-authored by Senate Armed Services Chairman Sam Nunn of Georgia, would require prospective college students desiring federal financial aid to serve either two years in the military, or one to two years in community service.

Not all of McCurdy's interests are of such sweeping consequence. He has pushed for legislation to contain the proliferation of commemorative bills introduced each year. Decrying the waste of time over proposals to create such events as National Dairy Goat Awareness Week, McCurdy has proposed a commission to cull commemorative resolutions. He refused to preside over a 1987 House discussion of a resolution, proposed by California Republican Rep. Carlos J. Moorhead, to designate "Snow White Week," marking the 50th anniversary of the Disney animated movie.

McCurdy has his share of parochial interests. From his position on the Science Committee — where he chaired the Transportation, Aviation and Materials Subcommittee in the 100th Congress — McCurdy got funds for weather research and other scientific projects at the University of Oklahoma.

He is also protective of his large military constituency. In November 1987, he fired off an angry letter to an Oklahoma colleague, Republican James M. Inhofe, who had signed onto a GOP petition calling for the budget-saving closure of 42 small military facilities, including one in McCurdy's 4th District.

At Home: A former assistant attorney general with a law practice in Norman, McCurdy had not been active in politics when he began his 1980 campaign. But what McCurdy lacked in political experience he made up for in hustle. With help from several key backers of retiring Democratic Rep. Tom Steed, he built his own organization. That network and his appeal as a "fresh face" enabled McCurdy to get within 5,000 votes of veteran state Rep. James B. Townsend in the primary, and overtake him in the runoff.

The general-election race was just as tight. Republicans nominated Howard Rutledge, a retired Navy captain and former prisoner of war in Vietnam whose calls for strengthening defense capability endeared him to the district's sizable community of military employees and retirees. But McCurdy held on, winning enough support for his conservative economic themes to prevail by 2,906 votes.

Rutledge returned in 1982, seeking conservative Democrats who might be persuaded to cross party lines. Rutledge commercials painted McCurdy as a profligate liberal. But McCurdy carried all 12 counties in the 4th, amassing 65 percent of the vote. He won just as easily in 1984, a good Republican year.

Though some urged McCurdy to make a 1986 Senate bid, he deferred to 1st District Rep. James R. Jones, the state's senior House Democrat. Jones lost to GOP Sen. Don Nickles while McCurdy enjoyed a routine, overwhelming victory.

Committees

Armed Services (11th of 31 Democrats)
Military Installations and Facilities; Research and Development

Science, Space and Technology (11th of 30 Democrats)
Natural Resources, Agriculture Research and Environment; Transportation, Aviation and Materials

Select Intelligence (2nd of 12 Democrats)
Oversight and Evaluation (chairman); Program and Budget Authorization

Elections

1988 General		
Dave McCurdy (D)	Unopposed	
1988 Primary		
Dave McCurdy (D)	52,366	(83%)
Howard Bell (D)	10,728	(17%)
1986 General		
Dave McCurdy (D)	94,984	(76%)
Larry Humphreys (R)	29,697	(24%)

Previous Winning Percentages: **1984** (64%) **1982** (65%) **1980** (51%)

District Vote For President

	1988	1984	1980	1976
D	74,914 (41%)	57,118 (30%)	58,544 (36%)	82,330 (54%)
R	105,870 (58%)	131,690 (69%)	95,129 (59%)	67,060 (44%)
I			6,778 (4%)	

Campaign Finance

	Receipts	Receipts from PACs	Expend-itures
1988			
McCurdy (D)	$273,015	$142,272 (52%)	$251,956
1986			
McCurdy (D)	$247,408	$130,725 (53%)	$176,096

Key Votes

1987	
Raise speed limit to 65 mph	Y
Approve Gephardt "fair trade" amendment	N
Ban testing of larger nuclear weapons	N
Delay "re-flagging" of Kuwaiti tankers	?
Approve tax-raising deficit-reduction bill	Y
1988	
Approve aid to Nicaraguan contras	N
Enact civil rights restoration bill over Reagan veto	Y
Kill 60-day plant-closing notification measure	Y
Pass omnibus trade bill over Reagan veto	Y
Approve death penalty for drug-related murders	?
Bar federal funds for abortions in cases of rape and incest	N
Oppose seven-day waiting period for purchase of handguns	Y

Voting Studies

	Presidential Support		Party Unity		Conservative Coalition	
Year	**S**	**O**	**S**	**O**	**S**	**O**
1988	33	58	73	22	79	13
1987	36	57	74	20	70	21
1986	31	62	70	21	72	24
1985	44	56	68	27	85	15
1984	46	45	56	29	71	12
1983	41	51	55	37	79	13
1982	58	36	48	43	79	19
1981	57	42	55	43	88	12

Interest Group Ratings

Year	ADA	ACU	AFL-CIO	CCUS
1988	60	30	71	64
1987	44	27	36	40
1986	35	38	42	80
1985	30	52	35	64
1984	35	30	33	33
1983	50	50	53	47
1982	25	67	28	62
1981	35	40	60	37

5 Mickey Edwards (R)

Of Oklahoma City — Elected 1976

Born: July 12, 1937, Cleveland, Ohio.
Education: U. of Oklahoma, B.S. 1958; Oklahoma City U. Law School, J.D. 1969.
Occupation: Lawyer; journalist.
Family: Wife, Lisa Reagan; three children.
Religion: Episcopalian.
Political Career: GOP nominee for U.S. House, 1974.
Capitol Office: 2330 Rayburn Bldg. 20515; 225-2132.

In Washington: Edwards has a reputation as something of a conservative heretic, taking high-profile stands now and then that put him at odds with his fellow conservatives. He also is known as a political bridge-builder, particularly on the Appropriations Committee, where he works closely with Democrats to produce legislative results.

There is no doubt Edwards is a part of the Republican right, but as a self-described 19th-century liberal, his outlook is somewhat different from theirs. For instance, while most House Republicans have spent considerable energy in the 1980s touting a line-item veto for the president, Edwards has been very critical of the idea.

"Political conservatism, at its root, is a philosophy of diffusion," Edwards says, arguing that the line-item veto would mean more concentrated power in the presidency. "Unfortunately," he wrote in 1989, "many modern conservatives have become new-age monarchists, advocating ever greater concentrations of power in a new king-like president." Edwards' outlook also leads him to see more of a role for Congress in foreign policy than many House Republicans, who, seeking a free hand for their man in the White House, repeatedly cry foul as House Democrats demand a say in matters overseas.

Edwards also got some attention earlier in the 1980s, by challenging House Republicans over their confrontational approach to the majority. He criticized some of his old-time allies for engaging in "guerrilla warfare" in the name of ideological purity. Instead of "finger-wagging" and "camera-hogging," Edwards said Republicans should rally behind their party leaders and work with Democrats, the Senate and the White House.

Edwards' pragmatic approach may be partly a reflection of his service on Appropriations, a panel where members usually put aside ideological purity in pursuit of money for their districts. Edwards is ranking member on the Appropriations Subcommittee on Foreign Operations, which produces foreign aid legislation that traditionally has been a lightning rod for partisan rancor. But an impressive thing happened in 1988: The subcommittee, and ultimately Congress, passed the first free-standing foreign aid bill since 1981, and did so with remarkably little ideological wrangling.

Edwards has strong views on foreign aid — he is skeptical of it — and subcommittee Chairman David R. Obey is also a man of firm opinions, but the two worked quietly together to produce a $14.3 billion foreign aid bill that nearly matched the request submitted by the Reagan administration. When the subcommittee brought its product before the full committee, it took only 12 minutes to win approval; the full House passed the bill 328-90, with the strongest Republican support for such a bill in at least 23 years.

A fair amount of the credit for the bill goes to the circumstances under which it was produced. A budget-summit agreement had settled the question of how much overall spending there would be; also, members were eager to avoid rolling funding into a giant continuing resolution, so they had to work to build broad support for the bill. But Edwards said the chief contributor to success was "the majority and the minority working together to craft a bill."

During the 99th Congress Edwards was ranking Republican on the Military Construction Appropriations Subcommittee, where he worked amicably with Chairman W. G. "Bill" Hefner of North Carolina. Edwards showed real concern about monitoring costs of construction projects and did his homework on the subcommittee, which attracts interest from few other members.

But Military Construction also drew Edwards into some very visible partisan battles. As the panel's top Republican, Edwards was dealt the role of offering Reagan's successful request for $100 million in aid to the Nicaraguan contras in 1986.

For contra supporters, however, the 100th Congress proved frustrating; support dwindled for administration requests for contra military funding, and the Democratic leadership became more assertive on the issue. When a cease-fire began in 1988, Edwards acknowledged that there was not much argument for military aid if

Oklahoma 5

North Central — Part of Oklahoma City; Bartlesville

Stretching 175 miles from the affluent northern reaches of Oklahoma City at one end to the historic oil town of Bartlesville on the other, the 5th gathers in GOP-minded voters all along the way.

Registered Democrats actually outnumber Republicans in most of the district's counties, but Democratic candidates have trouble winning their votes.

Oklahoma City accounts for nearly half of the 5th's population. The district takes in the northern portion of the city and the well-to-do suburbs of Nichols Hills and The Village. Some of Oklahoma City's wealthiest oil executives make their homes here. This area also includes the corporate headquarters of Kerr-McGee, one of Oklahoma's two big native-born petroleum companies.

Since the discovery of a large oil pool underneath Oklahoma City in the 1930s, much of the economy has revolved about the oil industry. The capital also has important meatpacking, trucking and aviation industries. Along with state government, the military has a significant presence, with Tinker Air Force Base located on the outskirts of the city.

For decades Oklahoma County was a Democratic center, balancing Tulsa's Republicanism. Between 1920 and 1948, the county supported a Republican presidential nominee only once — Herbert Hoover in 1928. But the county has gradually switched its allegiance in the postwar years and now is almost as reliable in its national GOP voting habits as its rival to the northeast. Since 1952, only Lyndon B. Johnson has carried it for the Democrats in a presidential election.

Oil has been of paramount importance to the local economy of Bartlesville (Washington County) since 1897, when production began on a well found here. A town of 30,000 people, Bartlesville is the home of Phillips Petroleum. Across Osage County from Bartlesville lies Ponca City, which hosts a Conoco refinery.

Population: 502,974. White 446,198 (89%), Black 30,826 (6%), Other 19,133 (4%). Spanish origin 9,915 (2%). 18 and over 367,630 (73%), 65 and over 60,357 (12%). Median age: 31.

the contras stopped fighting. "You can't be more contra than the contras," he said. But before long, he was eager to resume military aid, saying that negotiations "aren't going anywhere" without the threat of such aid. The administration opted not to pursue that route, and a bid by House Republicans to do so was rebuffed.

Edwards has taken on an increasingly visible role outside the Appropriations Committee in recent years. He added the Budget Committee to his list of assignments for the 100th Congress, and also won a three-way contest to head the House Republican Research Committee. When he wanted to move up the leadership ladder in the 101st Congress, he was unopposed for the chairmanship of the Republican Policy Committee. One of Edwards' goals is to make sure Republicans are in on every policy debate.

"We will take more positions and publicize them," Edwards said upon taking his new position. "When a bill comes to the floor, the public will be exposed in advance to the Republican position, and we can have a more legitimate debate."

He had worked to see that was the case during the debate on omnibus drug legislation in the 100th Congress. Complaining that the Democratic leadership was not pursuing a bipartisan course, Edwards worked to put together a Republican task force on the issue, and helped craft a bill that imposed stiffer penalties for drug-related crime than did the Democratic plan. By 293-115, the House approved one Edwards amendment to assess civil fines for individuals caught with "personal use" amounts of drugs.

"Weekend cocaine snorters and joint smokers might think they have little in common with back alley heroin and LSD addicts, but both create a demand for illegal drugs," Edwards said.

At Home: After a career in journalism, public relations and teaching, Edwards challenged Democratic Rep. John Jarman for Oklahoma City's congressional seat in 1974 and came within 3,402 votes of winning. That achievement in a national Democratic year made Edwards the logical choice for 1976. Jarman switched to the Republican Party himself in 1975, but did not run again.

Edwards had been unopposed for the 1974 Republican nomination. But in 1976, with the seat open and the Republican chances obviously good, he received a primary challenge from former state Attorney General G. T. Blankenship. It was a close race, but Edwards' non-stop campaign won him the nomination by 1,087 votes.

Edwards also had a harder time in November than had been expected, with stiff competition from Democrat Tom Dunlap, a young hospital administrator and son of the popular state chancellor of higher education. Edwards won by 3,899 votes and quickly set about establishing himself as a popular figure in his district. He has had no trouble winning since then.

In addition to developing close ties with Oklahoma City's blue-collar workers, Edwards has pursued black support more effectively than other area Republicans. In 1979 he asked the U.S. Justice Department to investigate Ku Klux Klan activity in Oklahoma and complained about "foot-dragging" when there was no prompt response.

The state Legislature made the 5th's boundaries more awkward in 1981, stretching the district north to the Kansas border, thus obligating candidates to advertise in the Oklahoma City, Tulsa and Wichita, Kan., media markets. But this has posed no problem for Edwards. The current 5th is more Republican than the old one, and it has given Edwards at least two-thirds of the vote in his last four elections.

Before running for Congress, Edwards was a reporter and editor for the *Oklahoma City Times*, director of public relations for an advertising agency and editor of *Private Practice* magazine, writing editorials in defense of private medicine. He was the author of "Hazardous to Your Health," a treatise against national health insurance.

Committee

Appropriations (10th of 22 Republicans)
Foreign Operations (ranking); Military Construction

Elections

1988 General		
Mickey Edwards (R)	139,182	(72%)
Terry J. Montgomery (D)	53,668	(28%)
1988 Primary		
Mickey Edwards (R)	25,311	(83%)
Bill Maguire (R)	5,142	(17%)
1986 General		
Mickey Edwards (R)	108,774	(71%)
Donna Compton (D)	45,256	(29%)

Previous Winning Percentages: **1984** (76%) **1982** (67%) **1980** (68%) **1978** (80%) **1976** (50%)

District Vote For President

	1988	1984	1980	1976
D	68,503 (32%)	50,701 (23%)	55,490 (25%)	87,988 (42%)
R	145,413 (67%)	170,703 (76%)	150,272 (69%)	117,924 (56%)
I			8,774 (4%)	

Campaign Finance

	Receipts	Receipts from PACs	Expend-itures
1988			
Edwards (R)	$362,570	$122,430 (34%)	$341,250
Montgomery (D) †	$460	0	$302
1986			
Edwards (R)	$303,661	$87,195 (29%)	$284,473
Compton (D)	$16,243	$3,950 (24%)	$16,217

† Totals based on incomplete data.

Key Votes

1987	
Raise speed limit to 65 mph	Y
Approve Gephardt "fair trade" amendment	N
Ban testing of larger nuclear weapons	N
Delay "re-flagging" of Kuwaiti tankers	N
Approve tax-raising deficit-reduction bill	N
1988	
Approve aid to Nicaraguan contras	Y
Enact civil rights restoration bill over Reagan veto	N
Kill 60-day plant-closing notification measure	Y
Pass omnibus trade bill over Reagan veto	Y
Approve death penalty for drug-related murders	Y
Bar federal funds for abortions in cases of rape and incest	Y
Oppose seven-day waiting period for purchase of handguns	Y

Voting Studies

	Presidential Support		Party Unity		Conservative Coalition	
Year	**S**	**O**	**S**	**O**	**S**	**O**
1988	59	39	84	9	95	5
1987	64	30	82	8	84	9
1986	71	23	72	20	82	10
1985	71	25	79	10	91	5
1984	58	36	78	15	80	12
1983	68	27	79 †	14 †	90	7
1982	68	23	78	13	81	12
1981	75	24	84	15	88	11

† Not eligible for all recorded votes.

Interest Group Ratings

Year	ADA	ACU	AFL-CIO	CCUS
1988	10	92	36	93
1987	12	90	7	100
1986	5	85	14	81
1985	5	90	0	85
1984	10	96	23	88
1983	10	95	6	83
1982	5	100	0	81
1981	5	100	7	79

6 Glenn English (D)

Of Cordell — Elected 1974

Born: Nov. 30, 1940, Cordell, Okla.
Education: Southwestern State College, B.A. 1964.
Military Career: Army Reserve, 1965-71.
Occupation: Petroleum landman.
Family: Wife, Jan Pangle; two children.
Religion: Methodist.
Political Career: No previous office.
Capitol Office: 2206 Rayburn Bldg. 20515; 225-5565.

In Washington: When English came to Washington in the Watergate election of 1974, he was viewed as a moderate national Democrat. Instead, he has turned out to be one of the most conservative of Southern members, a man who pays much closer attention to the wishes of his prairie district than to the views of the House Democratic leadership. In 1988, as in the past, he supported President Reagan and broke with his own party more often on House floor votes than any other Democrat in the Oklahoma delegation.

But if English's independence does not win him any awards for party loyalty, he has been able to bring himself a measure of attention and influence on some of the higher-profile issues before Congress.

In the 99th and 100th Congresses, he used his subcommittee chairmanship on Government Operations to help write sweeping anti-drug bills. For the 101st Congress, English gave up that chairmanship to take over the Agriculture Subcommittee on Conservation, Credit and Rural Development, ensuring himself a central role in the 1990 farm bill and in the ongoing federal investigation of fraud in the commodity futures trading markets.

As chairman of Conservation and Credit, which oversees farm credit programs, English is expected to be more combative than the man he replaced, Ed Jones, the mild-mannered Tennessean who retired at the end of the 100th Congress.

Through the years, English has been an unceasing advocate of high price-support levels for wheat and other Oklahoma commodities; some colleagues find that he keeps pressing his rhetoric even in private meetings with other members, where a more conciliatory manner is expected. During work on the farm bill in the 99th Congress, English failed in his attempts to raise or maintain the existing price supports for wheat. He favored a plan to allow farmers to vote for mandatory production controls as a way to raise prices. "It's a decision that's going to affect the destinies of farmers for at least the next 10 years, and I think they ought to have some say in the matter," he said.

Frustrated in those efforts, English ultimately voted against the entire four-year farm bill, arguing that it would drive down market prices and increase surpluses. "It is designed to use the American family farmer as cannon fodder in a war against competition," he said later.

English got an opportunity in the 100th Congress to help disaster-affected wheat growers. His 1987 bill, signed into law that spring, authorized payments to certain winter wheat producers — mainly in Oklahoma, Kansas and Missouri — who could not plant their 1987 crop due to heavy floods.

But instead of giving outright disaster-relief payments, the bill created a separate one-time program that essentially paid farmers not to plant. English's bill gave 92 percent of expected income subsidies to wheat farmers who were unable to plant their crops — and who agreed not to plant another crop in 1987. The so-called "0-92" plan was endorsed by Reagan administration officials as a test case of their "decoupling" strategy, which aimed to eliminate overproduction by encouraging farmers to plant only as much of a crop as they believe will sell on the open market.

On Government Operations, English used his subcommittee chairmanship on Government Information, Justice and Agriculture to crusade for personal privacy and against Reagan administration attempts to soften the Freedom of Information Act (FOIA).

His efforts won him plaudits from civil libertarians, as well as praise from consumer advocate Ralph Nader. They also brought him some criticism from the Reagan administration; one Justice Department official called English's subcommittee the "black hole of Freedom of Information reform." But English remained resolute in his defense of FOIA, even after the Senate passed sweeping changes in the act in the 98th Congress.

English also made drug enforcement a top priority of his subcommittee, pushing successfully to get the military to lend aircraft and radar to the Customs Service to intercept smug-

Oklahoma 6

West and Panhandle; Part of Oklahoma City

The 6th unites rural western Oklahoma and downtown Oklahoma City, an odd combination that creates a constituency with little common politics or sense of identity.

Just over a quarter of the district's population lives in Oklahoma City, the site of the most famous symbols of the state's oil wealth: working wells on the grounds of the state Capitol and the lawn of the governor's residence. Four of the six wells on the Capitol grounds have been restored and are again pumping oil (the ones on the governor's lawn are idle).

The now-slumping petroleum industry has been a major force in the local economy since the discovery of a large oil pool beneath the city in the 1930s. The capital also has important meatpacking, trucking and aviation industries. Tourists are drawn to the city to visit the National Cowboy Hall of Fame.

A Democratic center for decades, Oklahoma City as a whole has begun to shift its allegiance to national Republican candidates in recent years. The 6th's portion of the city has some residual Democratic strength, however; it includes most of Oklahoma City's 60,000 blacks, who bring the black share of the 6th's population to 10 percent.

Beyond Oklahoma City, the 6th sweeps west 300 miles across the dusty plains to the New Mexico border. Part of the Dust Bowl, western Oklahoma was devastated by droughts and soil erosion in the 1930s and '40s. It made great strides toward prosperity in the two postwar decades, becoming a region of massive wheat farms and cattle ranches. But it has begun to slip again amid the farm credit crisis of the 1980s. Water is still a chronic problem in this region; attempts to transport water from the greener eastern section of the state are a periodic issue in Oklahoma politics.

Western Oklahoma is traditionally the state's most conservative region. Residents of this area share a general aversion to most governmental activity other than military expenditures and agricultural subsidies. Democrats such as Sen. David L. Boren have enjoyed strong support here, but the 6th has given healthy margins to recent GOP presidential candidates. In 1988, George Bush won the 6th by 17 percentage points.

Population: 503,291. White 427,058 (85%), Black 49,364 (10%), Other 19,173 (4%). Spanish origin 13,373 (3%). 18 and over 361,309 (72%), 65 and over 69,844 (14%). Median age: 31.

glers. When drugs suddenly became a prominent national issue shortly before the 1986 elections, members racing to familiarize themselves with the subject looked to English. Five of the 12 committees reporting legislation for an omnibus anti-drug package based their recommendations at least in part on proposals by English.

There was a particular legislative plum for Oklahomans in the 99th Congress' drug package: a $20 million National Command and Control Center in Oklahoma City, intended to be the hub for law enforcement, intelligence and planning in the war on drugs.

When the 100th Congress began work on another omnibus anti-drug bill, English was one of the authors of the original package, along with Sens. Alfonse M. D'Amato of New York and Dennis DeConcini of Arizona. English questioned the Reagan administration's commitment to the war on drugs, issuing a report through his subcommittee in 1987 criticizing an administration oversight board for inactivity.

At Home: English started his career as a petroleum landman — someone who arranges oil and gas leases. But politics soon attracted him. In the 1960s he went to California to be chief assistant to the Democrats in the California Legislature, at a time when dictatorial Assembly Speaker Jesse Unruh held sway. English then returned to Oklahoma and served as executive director of the Oklahoma Democratic Party from 1969 to 1973.

In 1974 English entered the Democratic primary in the 6th District, held for the previous three terms by Republican John Newbold Happy Camp, a genial and innocuous small-town banker. English was forced into a runoff against insurance agent David Hutchens, but defeated him by 9,435 votes.

In November, English conducted a town-to-town campaign across the district, contrasting his youth and energy with the barely visible effort conducted by Camp. He beat Camp by 9 percentage points.

English's closest election — and it was not very close — came in 1984. He faced Enid attorney Craig Dodd, who spent most of the campaign trying to get the incumbent to agree to debate. President Reagan's overwhelming victory in western Oklahoma bolstered Dodd, but English still won comfortably, taking almost 60 percent of the vote districtwide.

In 1988, even as George Bush was carrying all but four counties in the 6th, English glided to a 73-27 percent win over Republican Mike

Brown, a young attorney. Earlier in 1988, English faced his first primary opponent since 1974, liberal activist "Batch" Batchelder. He took 84 percent of the vote.

Committees

Agriculture (5th of 27 Democrats)
Conservation, Credit and Rural Development (chairman); Tobacco and Peanuts; Wheat, Soybeans and Feed Grains

Government Operations (3rd of 24 Democrats)
Government Information, Justice and Agriculture; Legislation and National Security

Elections

1988 General		
Glenn English (D)	122,887	(73%)
Mike Brown (R)	45,239	(27%)
1988 Primary		
Glenn English (D)	51,733	(84%)
"Batch" Batchelder (D)	9,490	(16%)
1986 General		
Glenn English (D)		Unopposed

Previous Winning Percentages: **1984** (59%) **1982** (75%) **1980** (65%) **1978** (74%) **1976** (71%) **1974** (53%)

District Vote For President

	1988	1984	1980	1976
D	72,272 (41%)	58,426 (30%)	60,622 (32%)	83,601 (46%)
R	101,322 (58%)	136,314 (69%)	120,834 (64%)	97,052 (53%)
I			5,221 (3%)	

Campaign Finance

	Receipts	Receipts from PACs	Expend-itures
1988			
English (D)	$385,373	$183,408 (48%)	$306,600
Brown (R)	$86,210	$3,190 (4%)	$86,209
1986			
English (D)	$248,458	$132,558 (53%)	$149,998

Key Votes

1987	
Raise speed limit to 65 mph	Y
Approve Gephardt "fair trade" amendment	N
Ban testing of larger nuclear weapons	N
Delay "re-flagging" of Kuwaiti tankers	Y
Approve tax-raising deficit-reduction bill	N
1988	
Approve aid to Nicaraguan contras	Y
Enact civil rights restoration bill over Reagan veto	N
Kill 60-day plant-closing notification measure	Y
Pass omnibus trade bill over Reagan veto	Y
Approve death penalty for drug-related murders	Y
Bar federal funds for abortions in cases of rape and incest	Y
Oppose seven-day waiting period for purchase of handguns	Y

Voting Studies

	Presidential Support		Party Unity		Conservative Coalition	
Year	**S**	**O**	**S**	**O**	**S**	**O**
1988	47	52	65	33	95	5
1987	52	48	62	35	81	16
1986	43	51	63	34	82	18
1985	58	43	53	44	95	4
1984	52	44	43	50	75	12
1983	46	51	53	46	85	15
1982	65	35	43	57	82	16
1981	55	43	54	46	80	20

Interest Group Ratings

Year	ADA	ACU	AFL-CIO	CCUS
1988	40	60	64	71
1987	44	39	38	73
1986	35	48	50	61
1985	15	76	24	82
1984	15	78	23	63
1983	45	61	47	60
1982	20	64	30	77
1981	25	47	47	53

Oregon

U.S. CONGRESS

SENATE 2 R
HOUSE 3 D, 2 R

LEGISLATURE

Senate 19 D, 11 R
House 32 D, 28 R

ELECTIONS

1988 Presidential Vote	
Bush	47%
Dukakis	51%
1984 Presidential Vote	
Reagan	56%
Mondale	44%
1980 Presidential Vote	
Reagan	48%
Carter	39%
Anderson	10%
Turnout rate in 1984	62%
Turnout rate in 1986	51%
Turnout rate in 1988	59%

(as percentage of voting age population)

POPULATION AND GROWTH

1980 population	2,633,105
1988 population estimate (30th in the nation)	2,767,000
Percent change 1980-1988	+5

DEMOGRAPHIC BREAKDOWN

White	95%
Black	1%
Other	2%
(Spanish origin)	3%
Urban	68%
Rural	32%
Born in state	44%
Foreign-born	4%

MAJOR CITIES

Portland	387,870
Eugene	105,410
Salem	93,920
Medford	43,580
Corvallis	39,880

AREA AND LAND USE

Area	96,184 sq. miles (10th)
Farm	29%
Forest	46%
Federally owned	49%

Gov. Neil Goldschmidt (D)
Of Salem — Elected 1986

Born: June 16, 1940, Eugene, Ore.
Education: U. of Oregon, B.A. 1963; U. of California, Berkeley, LL.B. 1967.
Occupation: Business executive.
Religion: Jewish.
Political Career: Portland City Council, 1971-73; mayor of Portland, 1973-79; U.S. secretary of transportation, 1979-81.
Next Election: 1990.

WORK

Occupations	
White-collar	53%
Blue-collar	29%
Service workers	14%
Government Workers	
Federal	27,296
State	57,476
Local	115,121

MONEY

Median family income	$ 20,027	(21st)
Tax burden per capita	$ 738	(39th)

EDUCATION

Spending per pupil through grade 12	$ 4,141	(13th)
Persons with college degrees	18%	(15th)

CRIME

Violent crime rate	540 per 100,000	(18th)

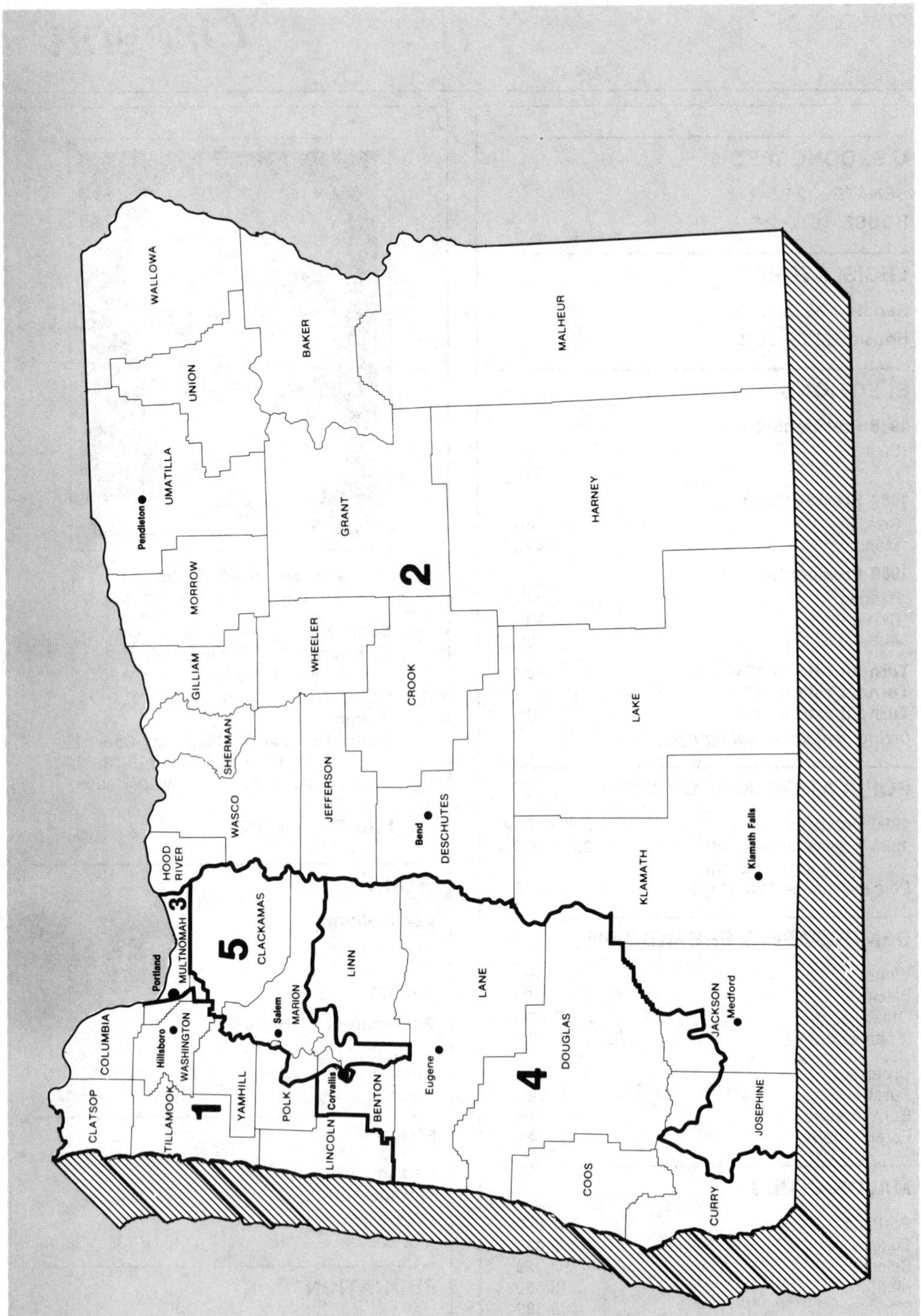

WALLOWA
UNION
BAKER
MALHEUR
UMATILLA
Pendleton
GRANT
HARNEY
MORROW
2
WHEELER
GILLIAM
CROOK
SHERMAN
LAKE
WASCO
JEFFERSON
Bend
DESCHUTES
HOOD RIVER
Klamath Falls
KLAMATH
3
5
CLACKAMAS
Portland
MULTNOMAH
LINN
LANE
Salem
MARION
COLUMBIA
Hillsboro
WASHINGTON
DOUGLAS
JACKSON
Medford
YAMHILL
Eugene
4
CLATSOP
TILLAMOOK
1
POLK
Corvallis
BENTON
JOSEPHINE
LINCOLN
COOS
CURRY

Mark O. Hatfield (R)

Of Tigard — Elected 1966

Born: July 12, 1922, Dallas, Ore.
Education: Willamette U., B.A. 1943; Stanford U., M.A. 1948.
Military Career: Navy, 1943-46.
Occupation: Political science professor.
Family: Wife, Antoinette Kuzmanich; four children.
Religion: Baptist.
Political Career: Ore. House, 1951-55; Ore. Senate, 1955-57; Ore. secretary of state, 1957-59; Ore. governor, 1959-67.
Capitol Office: 711 Hart Bldg. 20510; 224-3753.

In Washington: Perhaps more than anyone else, Hatfield has had an ambivalent relationship with the fortunes of his own party in the Senate of the 1980s. That ambivalence still seems to cling to the idiosyncratic Westerner as he contemplates running for a fifth term in 1990. Another term would take him into his mid-70s and might well be served out in the minority.

When the GOP controlled the Senate from 1981 to 1987, Hatfield held the storied position of Appropriations chairman. Proud as he was of the job, it forced upon him responsibility for a rightward march he himself did not wholly support.

President Reagan's military buildup violated Hatfield's personal philosophy, which is deeply averse to weaponry and war. The tax cuts, he believed, were regressive. The spending cuts, he often said, went too far.

As chairman, Hatfield sometimes seemed little more than an overworked "traffic cop" sorting through the conflicting demands of autonomous subcommittee chairmen. Much of his work consisted of shepherding annual continuing resolutions — massive "emergency" funding bills — through an unruly Senate. That was an arduous undertaking that required endless hours at the end of each session. Yet it yielded only a modest amount of control over spending decisions for Hatfield or his committee.

Moreover, Reagan and his congressional allies pressed repeatedly for procedural changes of which Hatfield disapproved. These included a balanced-budget amendment to the Constitution and a presidential license to veto individual items in appropriations bills. Given his steadfast opposition to both, Hatfield was often cast as an apostate within his own party.

With the return of the Democratic majority in 1987, Hatfield was in some respects liberated. As ranking minority member on Appropriations, he was free to practice his unorthodox combination of moral indignation and pork-barrel politics without the burdens or restraints of the chairmanship.

Yet at times, Hatfield seemed disengaged, as if finding the supporting role unexciting. In the 100th Congress the Democratic chairman was John C. Stennis, with whom Hatfield had worked closely for years. Aged and infirm, Stennis was clearly in need of Hatfield's help. But the authority this may have conferred on the Republican was largely lost to the maneuverings of the panel's other senior Democrats, especially J. Bennett Johnston of Louisiana.

In the 101st Congress, Hatfield has a new chairman on Appropriations in Robert C. Byrd of West Virginia, the former majority leader. The two set a course of cordiality and cooperation in the early, relatively easy, going. But Byrd plainly had accepted this job as part of an arrangement by which he ceded the leadership. Hatfield can hardly expect to find this new chairman eager to share his attenuated power generously with the minority.

Hatfield is now second in Republican seniority only to Strom Thurmond, the octogenarian from South Carolina. But Hatfield's significance in the chamber has always rested less on his formal position than on his ability to impress those with whom he disagrees that he is a man of courtesy and honor. Few senators have achieved Hatfield's popularity while clinging so tenaciously to views that fly in the face of common opinion.

He is a near-pacifist on defense issues and an automatic vote against any military spending bill. Almost alone in the Senate, he argues outspokenly that U.S. policy in the Middle East is tilted too far toward Israel. He moralizes about the importance of human rights as an emphasis in American foreign policy.

In the 100th Congress, Hatfield pressed legislation to grant foreign aid, in the form of disaster relief, to the communist government of Vietnam (he had been elected as an opponent of U.S. involvement in the Vietnam War a generation earlier). He was also willing to stand against the drug bill in the waning days of the 1988 session because it contained a death penalty. "It is not responsible for this body to have an eye-for-eye mentality," he said. Hatfield introduced multiple amendments before casting one of just three votes in the Senate against the politically popular bill.

Yet when the Republicans stormed to Senate control in 1980, Hatfield ascended easily to the Appropriations chairmanship, a job that carries a long tradition of collegiality and accommodation. The reason is that he has always been careful to place personal friendship above ideological combat. While outsiders sometimes listen to Hatfield's speeches and decide he must be sanctimonious, senators find him amiable and unpretentious. He is good at making friends with people whose opinions he would never endorse.

A classic case was his relationship with the hawkish Stennis, who retired from the Senate in 1989. Starting with a mutual interest in waterways and public power, the two men formed a close friendship that survived numerous jousts on defense issues. After Stennis was shot by a burglar in 1973, Hatfield rushed to the hospital and, without identifying himself, took command of a telephone switchboard jammed with calls.

That kind of relationship stood Hatfield in good stead during the 1984 investigation that could have become the greatest ethical crisis of his Senate career. Like the voters of Oregon, Hatfield's colleagues refused to credit charges that might have presented serious problems to a politician with a less sterling reputation. The incident involved his relationship with Greek financier Basil A. Tsakos. Hatfield had supported a trans-African oil pipeline promoted by Tsakos at the same time the senator's wife was being paid $55,000 by the financier for "real-estate services."

The Senate Ethics Committee and the FBI investigated, looking for an improper link between the payment and Hatfield's legislative efforts. The Hatfields insisted there was no wrongdoing, but apologized for making an error in judgment and donated the money to charity. The investigation was dropped.

Hatfield's standing among his fellow Republicans may be an even more remarkable reflection of his ability to generate affection and respect. While some other liberal Republicans were stripped of party influence for straying from the dominant conservative ideology, Hatfield avoided a great deal of criticism despite holding views that many Democrats would find too radical.

It cannot happen very often, for example, that a chairman castigates members of the opposition party for failing to provide strong enough criticism of his own party's president. But it happened in 1986, when Hatfield essentially wrote off the GOP as a source of resistance to the strategic defense initiative and other aspects of President Reagan's defense buildup. "Face up to the facts," he told the Democrats during debate on that year's continuing resolution. "There are only a handful of Republicans ... who will challenge this madness. You are the loyal opposition. Take a stand."

Even while he was denouncing Reagan, Hatfield was working behind the scenes to find a compromise with the president's views on spending. In the first year of the Reagan administration, Hatfield's voting did drift slightly toward the right. He went along with the outlines of Reaganomics — budget and tax cuts — and while he continued to vote against new weapons systems, did not try to use his chairmanship to sabotage the military buildup.

But by 1982, the loosening of Reagan's grip on Congress made it easier for Hatfield to reassert his independent streak. He signed on as co-leader of the nuclear-weapons freeze campaign and championed more spending for job-creation programs.

For the next two years, Hatfield was part of a small group of moderate Republicans who attempted to make their own mark on the budget. They relied on a mixture of confrontation and negotiations with the administration to produce budgets that cut defense spending requests and moderated the assault on social spending.

By the 99th Congress, Hatfield had adopted a more unyielding stance, particularly when the administration tried to change the budget and appropriations process itself. He led the 1985 filibuster that killed Reagan's request for "line-item veto" authority over individual spending programs. He also has been the most vocal critic of what he describes as administration abuse of its deferral powers to kill programs Congress intended to fund.

Even so, Hatfield concluded that accommodations with the administration sometimes were necessary if critical funding bills were to be approved. He frequently urged his colleagues not to approve amendments to spending bills that might incite a presidential veto. During long hours of floor and conference work on continuing resolutions, he usually stayed in close contact with White House officials to see what would be acceptable to the president.

Despite the many frustrations, being chairman of Appropriations was not without its compensations. The position allowed Hatfield to practice the lessons of constituent service he learned at the knees of Pacific Northwest cohort and longtime Appropriations powerhouse Warren G. Magnuson of Washington. The ports along the Oregon coast and the funding for federal lands thus have profited handsomely.

Hatfield once explained that he would like to cut the federal budget substantially, but since that was impossible he was determined to steer as much of it as possible to his home state. He has never been bashful about doing that.

Over the years, his Appropriations assignment has brought him not only political benefits at home (jurisdiction over public forests and range lands, hydroelectric power and harbors) but also leverage in Congress. As a member of Appropriations, he quickly became adept at the senatorial art of quid pro quo.

Most of Hatfield's efforts on Appropriations are quiet, however; he is best known to the public for his sallies on foreign policy and defense issues.

In recent years, he has spoken for Palestinian refugees and advocated limits on military aid to Israel. He has led the opposition to the MX missile and SDI, pressed for human rights concessions from authoritarian foreign regimes, and filibustered against reinstatement of the draft.

He was equally unyielding in opposition to Reagan's policies in Central America. Early in 1984, he led the Appropriations Committee in rejecting an administration attempt to add military aid for the Nicaraguan contras to a home heating assistance bill.

While serving on Appropriations, Hatfield has remained on the Energy and Natural Resources Committee. He ranks second behind Idaho Republican James A. McClure, whose vote he often cancels on matters of concern to the Northwest or on issues of national moment. Hatfield was one of the most active Senate opponents of the nuclear breeder reactor. His feeling was partially explained by the fact that, as a young naval officer, Hatfield was a member of the first American military team to enter Hiroshima, one month after the atom bomb demolished the city.

Hatfield's politics are shaped by a born-again religious conviction. Not to be confused with the fundamentalism of the evangelical right, Hatfield's religious views emphasize help for the poor and separation of church and state.

An opponent of abortion, Hatfield also opposes a constitutional amendment to permit prayer in the public schools. But he does believe that student religious organizations should have access to public educational facilities.

Though he does not flaunt his faith in Senate debate, Hatfield courts a religious constituency with speeches and newsletters. He participates regularly in Capitol prayer meetings and has written three books for religious publishing houses describing the tribulations of a Christian in politics.

Over the years he has developed many bills to encourage neighborhood-based social programs, and he often tells churches that if each of them would take charge of a few poor families, the government welfare burden could be virtually eliminated.

At Home: Hatfield's popularity on Capitol Hill is more than matched in his home state, where he has enjoyed uninterrupted political success — moving undefeated from state legislator to secretary of state, governor and U.S. senator.

Even the 1984 Tsakos controversy did nothing to shake his reputation among constituents. Hatfield spent extra time touring the state after the scandal erupted, and polls soon showed that he had emerged virtually unscathed, having barely tapped the reservoir of good will built up during more than three decades in Oregon politics. Democratic strategists, attracted to the contest by Hatfield's predicament, quickly drew back, discouraged by his continued strength and the campaign being waged by his challenger, state Sen. Margie Hendriksen. Hatfield won 67 percent of the vote, the largest margin of victory of his Senate career.

The result was one more testament to Hatfield's remarkable ability to attract support across partisan and ideological lines. Earlier in his Oregon career, Hatfield won the gratitude of liberals with his opposition to loyalty oaths for teachers; later he cemented that support as a critic of the Vietnam War.

Organized labor, when it has not been able to back him against a Democratic competitor, usually has remained neutral. Hatfield sometimes likes to play up his labor connections; his father, a blacksmith, belonged to the railroad brotherhood.

A political science professor and university dean, Hatfield acquired Republicanism from his mother, who had been raised in the staunchly GOP territory of East Tennessee. In 1958, as secretary of state in Oregon, he blended an effective campaign style with youthful good looks to unseat Democratic Gov. Robert D. Holmes.

As governor, Hatfield ran an administration that kept state spending down and did not raise taxes. He launched an aggressive "Sell Oregon" drive that helped spur exports. And in 1962 he withstood a strong re-election challenge from Democrat Robert Y. Thornton, the state attorney general, who was unable to mobilize the labor support he needed to defeat a popular governor.

Constitutionally forbidden to run for a third term as governor in 1966, Hatfield took aim at the Senate seat being vacated by Democrat Maurine Neuberger.

In that race, the central issue was the Vietnam War, which Hatfield opposed and his Democratic rival, Rep. Robert B. Duncan, favored. As Duncan saw it, the conflict concerned whether "Americans will die in the buffalo grass of Vietnam or the rye grass of Oregon."

Hatfield had been the lone dissenting vote on a National Governors' Conference resolution supporting the war. Afterward, in his Senate campaign, he put up billboards with the word "Courage" in large letters. He blamed the war for the state's lagging lumber industry, reasoning that the conflict had brought a downturn in home construction. Fearful of being painted as unpatriotic, however, Hatfield criticized the "inexcusable excesses of some anti-war demonstrations." Hatfield defeated Duncan, but with a slim 52 percent majority.

Running for re-election six years later, however, he did considerably better against an even more militant Vietnam dove, former Sen. Wayne Morse, who was seeking a comeback as the Democratic nominee. Despite Hatfield's anti-war activities, the Nixon White House cooperated with his re-election that year, and this helped defuse conservative resentment that had built up toward him in Oregon. Morse had difficulty finding an issue to use against Hatfield; in 1966, Morse had announced that he would vote for Hatfield over Duncan because of the war issue.

In 1978, Hatfield finally got an easy Senate re-election. Running against state Sen. Vern Cook, a Democrat who had a loser's reputation after two unsuccessful campaigns for the House, Hatfield won a third term with 62 percent of the vote.

Whether Hatfield will seek a fifth term in 1990 was a matter of much speculation in Oregon as the campaign year approached. Many of the state's leading politicians are eagerly preparing to seek an open Senate seat. But they could well be disappointed. Hatfield may want another term, and if so, he is unlikely to be denied.

Committees

Appropriations (Ranking)
Energy and Water Development (ranking); Commerce, Justice, State, the Judiciary and Related Agencies; Foreign Operations; Labor, Health and Human Services, Education and Related Agencies; Legislative Branch

Energy and Natural Resources (2nd of 9 Republicans)
Public Lands, National Parks and Forests; Water and Power

Rules and Administration (2nd of 7 Republicans)

Joint Library

Joint Printing

Elections

1984 General		
Mark O. Hatfield (R)	808,152	(67%)
Margie Hendriksen (D)	406,122	(33%)
1984 Primary		
Mark O. Hatfield (R)	214,114	(79%)
John T. Schiess (R)	26,848	(10%)
Sherry Reynolds (R)	18,590	(7%)
Ralph H. Preston (R)	12,662	(5%)

Previous Winning Percentages: 1978 (62%) **1972** (54%) **1966** (52%)

Campaign Finance

	Receipts	Receipts from PACs	Expend-itures
1984			
Hatfield (R)	$822,875	$376,693 (46%)	$605,557
Hendriksen (D)	$255,897	$127,551 (50%)	$255,244

Key Votes

1987	
Enact omnibus highway bill over Reagan veto	N
Limit testing of space-based anti-ballistic missiles	Y
Oppose banning tests of larger nuclear weapons	N
Confirm Robert H. Bork as Supreme Court justice	Y
1988	
Allow vote on campaign-finance overhaul	N
Pass civil rights restoration bill over Reagan veto	Y
Enact omnibus trade bill over Reagan veto	N
Approve death penalty for drug-related murders	N
Oppose "workfare" amendment to welfare overhaul bill	N

Voting Studies

	Presidential Support		Party Unity		Conservative Coalition	
Year	**S**	**O**	**S**	**O**	**S**	**O**
1988	55	38	39	51	30	70
1987	41	46	47	48	41	56
1986	42	57	54	43	50	47
1985	45	40	49	35	32	42
1984	43	45	48	48	45	51
1983	64	29	56	33	45	45
1982	61	29	57	27	45	45
1981	76	19	71	26	58	39

Interest Group Ratings

Year	ADA	ACU	AFL-CIO	CCUS
1988	70	30	62	57
1987	65	28	60	61
1986	75	30	47	39
1985	45	18	39	70
1984	75	24	40	72
1983	60	13	29	50
1982	60	30	47	50
1981	55	29	22	88

Bob Packwood (R)

Of Portland — Elected 1968

Born: Sept. 11, 1932, Portland, Ore.
Education: Willamette U., B.A. 1954; New York U. School of Law, LL.B. 1957.
Occupation: Lawyer.
Family: Wife, Georgie Oberteuffer; two children.
Religion: Unitarian.
Political Career: Ore. House, 1963-69.
Capitol Office: 259 Russell Bldg. 20510; 224-5244.

In Washington: The moderate label frequently assigned Packwood is somewhat deceptive. It describes the mean of his extremes rather than the position he occupies on the political spectrum.

Blunt and independent, he is a crusader for abortion rights, Israel and free enterprise. And for the better part of two decades he has taken stances contrary to his party and president. This may diminish now that George Bush is president, but it only adds to the irony that accompanied the pivotal role he played in the 1986 passage of sweeping tax-reform legislation.

This role was one of the the great riddles of recent congressional history. It may never be possible to unravel the tangled threads of sincere conversion and opportunism, of tactical weakness and strategic insight, that marked his performance on the issue that thoroughly preoccupied his tenure as chairman of the Finance Committee.

Packwood had spent a good portion of Ronald Reagan's first term opposing the president on arms sales, civil rights, abortion and other issues. But he sent word to the White House that he wanted to join the team during the second term. To his chagrin, he got his wish in his role as the Senate's chief tax-writer.

Packwood took the Finance chair when Bob Dole of Kansas became majority leader in 1985. It was widely assumed that his chairmanship would follow a predictable course. As he said soon after taking over the committee in 1985, "I kind of like the present tax code."

Certainly there was no question about how Packwood felt toward the network of subsidies, deductions and incentives that filled the old tax system: He was for it. He had always been philosophically indisposed to the very idea of "reform" through elimination of tax subsidies. He believed the tax code should be more than a revenue producer — it should be a tool through which government could enact a social and economic agenda. For more than 15 years in the Senate, Packwood fought for tax cuts targeted to specific ends. He pushed tax breaks for parents who send their children to private schools, for various energy conservation schemes, and for businesses that offer employees health-care coverage.

So Packwood found himself in an uneasy position in 1985 when Reagan proposed eliminating most tax subsidies in order to reduce rates for individual taxpayers. Packwood backed away from his wholesale defense of the existing tax code, but made clear there were two points on which he was immovable: the tax-free status of employee fringe benefits, such as employer-paid health insurance, and the favorable tax treatment granted to the timber industry, an important component of Oregon's economy. He insisted that those be kept.

Packwood anxiously followed televised coverage of House action on tax revision in the hope that the bill would be rejected there, thus sparing him further headaches. But the House passed the bill in late 1985 and sent it on to Packwood's Finance Committee.

Packwood opened committee work on the overhaul with a "reform" proposal that reflected his longtime interests. His bill would have retained many existing tax breaks for business and recovered the cost of reducing individual rates by removing the deduction for state and local taxes and increasing excise taxes on tobacco, liquor and gasoline.

That plan reflected Packwood's basic strategy: gain consensus by doling out a few tax breaks of special importance to each committee member's constituency. But the weight of these items was more than enough to sink the bill.

The Finance markup quickly threatened to become a fiasco. Members kept voting to add new breaks, rejecting efforts to cut back. Within a few weeks, the panel had written legislation adding an estimated $30 billion to the federal deficit. "There are some things that make us look foolish," Packwood said plaintively of an amendment, "and there are some things that *really* make us look foolish."

Packwood faced genuine embarrassment, if not ridicule — one national magazine was calling him "Senator Hackwood." Desperate, he canceled further markups. It was then, over a long liquid lunch with an aide at a Capitol Hill bar, that the Oregon Republican had his key insight. Concluding that his current approach was hopeless, he settled on a drastic tack: Set the top individual tax rate at 25 percent and eliminate virtually all deductions to pay for it. He described it as nothing less than the end of engineering social and economic change through the tax code.

The plan proved too radical — it lacked even a mortgage-interest deduction — but it broke the deadlock. Working with a small core group of allies, Packwood developed a modified plan with a 27 percent top rate that sailed through the committee and even managed to clear the Senate without major amendments.

His role in conference with the House was more controversial. Unable to resolve key differences on the bill, conferees asked Packwood and House Ways and Means Chairman Dan Rostenkowski to work out things in private. They did, but in a way that left a number of Senate Republicans upset at the loss of tax incentives for business. Still, by the end of the year the bill was law, and a good portion of the credit was due to Packwood.

Although Packwood turned 180 degrees — to the point of saying publicly that the tax code should be used to fund the government, not engineer change — he nonetheless left the impression that his true feelings remained masked. Many of the closest observers of the process remained convinced that Packwood fought for tax reform less because he believed in it than because there was no politically safe way to avoid it.

Predictions abounded that the committee under Packwood would return to business as usual in the 100th Congress. But Democratic success in the 1986 Senate elections deprived him of the chair. And it was trade, not taxation, that defined his work as ranking member. With industries that export natural resources and import components, Oregon is especially sensitive to trade matters. So it is not surprising that Packwood is one of the Senate's most active free-traders. He played a major role opposing quotas to restrict textile and shoe imports and he worked for the U.S.-Canada free-trade accord.

His vote for omnibus trade legislation, enacted over a presidential veto in 1988, was crucial. He voted for it only after protecting Israel's interests by specifically exempting its trade agreement with the United States from any damage, and after mitigating the harshest sanctions in the bill for trading partners.

Packwood's most publicized moment in the 100th Congress stemmed from his opposition to campaign-finance legislation pushed by the Democratic leadership. Republicans were dodging quorum calls as a tactic for stalling debate. Packwood had retreated into his office, where he had bolted one door and blocked another with a heavy chair. On orders from the majority leader, the sergeant-at-arms of the Senate arrested Packwood to force his attendance at a quorum call, a tactic not used in the Senate since 1942. Packwood forced the sergeant's deputies to carry him into the chamber. During the fracas he reinjured a broken finger, which he proudly displayed at a press conference the next day.

President Bush may assist Packwood back to his familiar territory of enacting the Republican social agenda under the auspices of the Internal Revenue Service. Bush, like Packwood, supports using tax credits, not direct federal spending, to fund day-care programs.

If the two Republican moderates do get on, it would be a change of pace for Packwood's presidential relations. Much of Washington was startled in early 1982 when Packwood publicly accused Reagan of alienating blacks, Jews, women and blue-collar workers from the Republican Party. He was not only a senior GOP senator; he was chairman of the National Republican Senatorial Committee. Campaign officials do not usually talk that way.

Packwood, however, does. He has always been an active and skilled Republican partisan, but he has never been an acquiescent one. In the Reagan era, he managed to vote with the president almost as often as the average Senate Republican and still become one of the administration's most visible antagonists.

When Reagan promised in 1981 to sell advanced radar aircraft to Saudi Arabia, Packwood, long a devout supporter of Israel, served as the inside orchestrator in a fierce lobbying campaign to prevent Senate approval of the deal. He argued that the Saudis had never repaid earlier U.S. military aid by contributing to the cause of peace in the Mideast. It took an aggressive White House war of attrition to eke out a close victory in what became a major test of presidential prestige.

Three years later, Packwood was so successful in organizing Senate opposition to the proposed sale of Stinger anti-aircraft missiles to Jordan that Reagan dropped the idea. In the 100th Congress, he led the Senate opposition to the sale of 1,600 Maverick anti-tank missles to Saudi Arabia.

Meanwhile, Packwood was reinforcing his reputation as the Senate's foremost advocate of legalized abortion. He helped filibuster to death a 1982 anti-abortion bill that had Reagan's blessing, and led the opposition to a related constitutional amendment that fell well short of the required two-thirds Senate majority in 1983. "More and more," he complained, "my party is certain that it knows what's morally good for you and me."

Packwood got into an equally sharp confrontation with his more conservative colleagues in 1984, this time over a bill to reverse the Supreme Court's *Grove City* ruling limiting the effect of sex-discrimination and other civil rights laws. Working with Massachusetts Democrat Edward M. Kennedy, Packwood led a bipartisan coalition seeking to ensure that educational institutions receiving any federal aid would have to comply with anti-bias laws.

Frustrated in the Labor and Human Resources Committee by the chairman, Utah Republican Orrin G. Hatch, Packwood and his allies sought to attach their proposal to a year-end omnibus spending bill. But after four days of complex parliamentary maneuvering, Packwood gave up his efforts, lest further moves result in bad precedents for Senate rules. It was not until 1988 that legislation overturning the *Grove City* ruling became law, over Reagan's veto.

Packwood's positions have taken their toll on his standing among other Republicans. Once Packwood's negative remarks about Reagan were published in 1982, it was clear he would have to struggle to hold his job as chairman of the campaign committee. Within a few weeks, conservative brewer Joseph Coors was working to organize a boycott of the committee. A mailing that pictured Packwood with the president was destroyed on White House orders. The senator was spared more severe reprisals only because of his friendship with Majority Leader Howard H. Baker Jr. of Tennessee, whom Packwood had helped in the 1977 leadership election.

While Packwood was credited with an effective performance on the campaign committee, he paid the price for his earlier indiscretion after the 1982 elections. Senate Republicans refused him re-election to the committee post, opting instead for Richard G. Lugar of Indiana, who campaigned as a friend of the president. The vote was Lugar 29, Packwood 25. "Being a maverick is great," said Sen. Paul Laxalt, a Reagan ally who nominated Lugar, "but it's a luxury you can't afford in leadership."

Packwood, it seems, relishes his reputation as a maverick. It arrived with him in 1969, when at 36 he was the youngest senator. He was fresh from a stunning upset of veteran Democrat Wayne Morse, and he was heralded by *Newsweek* as one of the "bright new stars" of the Senate. He promptly demonstrated his independent-mindedness by helping Democrats defeat two of President Nixon's Supreme Court nominees and by a series of speeches chiding the Senate as irresponsible, especially in its practice of awarding chairmanships purely by seniority.

Scattershot interests, youthful impatience and a perennially high staff turnover later contributed to an impression that Packwood had not settled into a legislative niche. But in the 96th Congress, when the Commerce Committee began cutting back federal regulation, he demonstrated a tenacious interest. His political skills were instrumental in passing a controversial and complex trucking-deregulation bill over Teamsters' opposition. He helped round up support for passage of a plan to defederalize airports.

Republican control of the Senate elevated Packwood to the Commerce chairmanship, and the deregulating continued. One bill relaxed federal controls on the telecommunications industry (it was ultimately rendered moot by a federal court) and another eased regulation of intercity bus companies. "There's no reason why we should be controlling capitalistic acts by consenting adults," Packwood said.

His efforts in the 98th Congress to advance that philosophy into the field of broadcasting were unsuccessful, however. Arguing that federal oversight of television and radio was no longer necessary, now that new technology had vastly expanded the opportunities for electronic communication, he fought for bills chipping away at the decades-old structure of federal regulation. His bill to weaken federal licensing and competition requirements for broadcasters passed the Senate in 1983, but saw no action in the House. A measure to end the mandate that radio stations air opposing views and give equal time to political candidates was rejected by his own committee in 1984.

Still, Packwood has made a mark on broadcast issues. He helped push through a bill to set up a national policy for cable television, as well as a non-binding resolution urging networks to refrain from early projections of election results. When the Federal Communications Commission (FCC) abolished the fairness doctrine in 1987, he led the forces seeking to keep it in the grave. He considers the measure, which requires broadcasters to cover issues of public importance and to present all sides of an issue, as an unwarranted restriction on freedom of speech.

Another Packwood campaign on Commerce was directed against alleged sex discrimination in insurance. Backed by women's groups, he sponsored a bill to require equal insurance rates and benefits for women and men. The measure languished, however, after House Energy and Commerce approved industry-backed amendments to its companion bill.

Some of Packwood's moves have required unorthodox parliamentary maneuvering that he seemed delighted to try. In the 97th Congress, members of the Senate Budget Committee came up with a new word — "Packwooding" — to describe his efforts to slip a favorite legislative project into an omnibus bill in which it would not be widely noticed.

The 1982 budget resolution, for example, carried Packwood's proposal to reduce the size of the FCC and the Interstate Commerce Commission. The 1982 tax bill included a full reauthorization for the federal airport development program. That move, bypassing Packwood's Commerce Committee, provoked outright hostility from Commerce members who felt they were being dealt out of the process. "That doesn't bother me," Packwood responded. "... All I did was take the budget process and achieve what I wanted."

At Home: The success of his tax-reform efforts, his huge campaign treasury and some chaos on the Democratic side helped Packwood win re-election easily in 1986. It was a first for Packwood, whose Senate career had been shadowed by a cloud of vulnerability.

Packwood's political posture fits in well with Oregon's tradition of electing moderate Republicans. But unlike his mentor, the revered senior Sen. Mark O. Hatfield, Packwood had difficulty obtaining voter allegiance.

Burdened by conservative animosity to his stand on abortion and by his image as a slick political operator, Packwood won less-than-robust margins against modest Democratic opposition in 1974 and 1980. He even faced an unexpectedly strong primary challenge from a young fundamentalist minister in 1986. But a convergence of fortuitous events enabled Packwood to glide comfortably through that year's general election.

Campaigning, organizing and fund raising are in Packwood's blood. His great-grandfather was a member of the 1857 Oregon constitutional convention and held a variety of political appointments; his father was a business lobbyist before the state Legislature.

As an undergraduate at Willamette University, Packwood studied political science under Hatfield, his Senate colleague since 1969. That experience may have colored their future relationship, which was for a long time the cordial but cool cooperation of an established senior statesman and an ambitious rival for public recognition.

As a young politician, Packwood had a reputation for outspokenness and boat-rocking. In 1962, he startled the party establishment by announcing that Sig Unander, that year's GOP Senate nominee against Morse, stood no chance of winning. But however critical Packwood has been of the GOP, he has always seen himself as a force for revitalizing it.

The Morse whom Packwood encountered in 1968 was a weaker political figure than the one who beat Unander. He had narrowly survived a rough primary with former Rep. Robert Duncan, whereas Packwood had negligible party opposition.

Packwood was to the right of Morse on several issues, including the most salient issue of the day, the Vietnam War. While Packwood was critical of the South Vietnamese government, he castigated Morse for voting to cut off funds for the war.

But ideology was not the focal point of the campaign. The main issue was Morse himself. Packwood labeled Morse as ineffective, saying that the state had been harmed by the Democrat's contentious style. Other senators were reluctant to help Morse get federal projects for Oregon, he charged. Morse was 68 years old in 1968; he was feisty and vigorous, but Packwood still managed to win support on the issue of youth vs. age. Starting out far behind but building a splendid campaign organization, Packwood edged Morse by 3,293 votes out of nearly 815,000 cast.

The 1974 contest began as a rematch between Packwood and Morse. But Morse died suddenly in midsummer, and the Democrats replaced him with state Sen. Betty Roberts, who had just lost the 1974 gubernatorial primary. Roberts benefited from statewide name recognition and a good campaign organization, but she also had a large debt from her bid for governor. Packwood worked hard to insulate himself from Watergate in the year of Nixon's resignation. He was sharply critical of the departed president and objected to the pardon he received from President Ford. Packwood's 55 percent of the vote was respectable in a terrible Republican year.

In 1980, abortion rights advocate Packwood found himself targeted by anti-abortion groups. There was talk of a $200,000 "right-to-life" drive to unseat him in the primary. The immediate effect of this rumor was to mobilize support for Packwood in the women's movement. Feminist Gloria Steinem raised $170,000 for him with a fund-raising letter warning that he was "in danger of drowning in a virtual sea of 'right-to-life' money and zealots."

But a strong primary challenger failed to materialize as two conservative Republican opponents, Brenda Jose and Rosalie Huss, spent most of their time fighting each other. Packwood won renomination handily.

In the general election, Packwood's campaign finances became a central issue. Democrat Ted Kulongoski, a state senator, charged that Packwood was trying to buy the election and was also profiting handsomely from speaking engagement fees. But many Democratic voters found Packwood acceptable. Labor had trouble making up its mind, with the state AFL-CIO backing Kulongoski against the wishes of its executive council, which recommended no endorsement. Packwood drew the support of the building trades unions in Portland.

With a nearly 8-to-1 financial advantage and a strong Republican tide building nationwide, Packwood was an overwhelming favorite. He won, but the fact that Kulongoski and one minor candidate held him to 52 percent of the vote seemed to signal that the 1986 campaign could be a challenge.

Packwood responded to his mediocre 1980 finish by embarking on a fund-raising effort that turned out to be awesomely successful. His campaign fund benefited from an extensive national direct-mail strategy targeted at feminists, pro-Israel voters and other activists who supported his policy stands. Adding in a healthy dose of business-related PAC money, Packwood raised over $6 million by the beginning of the 1986 campaign year.

Though his opponents attempted to make an issue of his fund-raising efforts, describing him as a tool of "special interest" campaign contributors, Packwood's tax-reform efforts in 1986 helped blunt these claims. Packwood responded to his critics by noting that the historic bill eliminated numerous tax benefits enjoyed by business interests that had earlier given to his campaign.

But while Packwood was hammering out the landmark law in Washington, his primary opponent, Joe Lutz, was hammering away at Packwood in Oregon. Despite his small campaign budget, the Portland preacher galvanized a grass-roots movement of religious and political conservatives. Though Lutz said he was not a one-issue candidate and spoke fluently on economic issues, the active anti-abortion constituency again provided the fuel for the anti-Packwood Republican movement.

Packwood returned to Oregon and blitzed the airwaves with an expensive media campaign that Lutz could not match. He played up the tax-reform bill as evidence of his experience and clout in Washington, and criticized some of Lutz' statements on economics. But while Packwood prevailed, his below-60 percent tally again raised the specter of vulnerability.

The Democratic primary winner, 4th District Rep. James Weaver, was an aggressive populist and a caustic critic of Packwood's support of Reagan defense policies and his alleged ties to special interests.

But a campaign-finance problem cut short his effort. In August, he was called to testify before the House ethics committee concerning his investment and loss of $89,000 in funds from earlier House campaigns. Though Weaver denied any wrongdoing — he stated that he invested the money to enhance his campaign treasury and not for personal gain — he unexpectedly announced on the eve of his testimony that he was withdrawing from the Senate race.

Scrambling to choose a replacement for Weaver, state Democrats settled on state Rep. Rick Bauman, who earlier in the year had finished last in the three-man Senate primary. Though Bauman, a personable liberal, was respected by his state House colleagues, he lacked name recognition and money.

The last obstacle to Packwood's re-election evaporated when Lutz decided not to run a threatened write-in campaign. Packwood coasted to victory.

Committees

Finance (Ranking)
International Trade; Medicare and Long-Term Care

Commerce, Science and Transportation (2nd of 9 Republicans)
Communications (ranking); Foreign Commerce and Tourism; Surface Transportation; National Ocean Policy Study

Joint Taxation

Elections

1986 General		
Bob Packwood (R)	656,317	(63%)
Rick Bauman (D)	375,735	(36%)
1986 Primary		
Bob Packwood (R)	171,985	(58%)
Joe P. Lutz Sr. (R)	126,315	(42%)

Previous Winning Percentages: **1980** (52%) **1974** (55%) **1968** (50%)

Campaign Finance

	Receipts	Receipts from PACs	Expend-itures
1986			
Packwood (R)	$6,725,027	$974,367 (14%)	$6,523,492
Bauman (D)	$63,394	$16,260 (26%)	$64,139

Key Votes

1987	
Enact omnibus highway bill over Reagan veto	N
Limit testing of space-based anti-ballistic missiles	Y
Oppose banning tests of larger nuclear weapons	Y
Confirm Robert H. Bork as Supreme Court justice	N
1988	
Allow vote on campaign-finance overhaul	N
Pass civil rights restoration bill over Reagan veto	Y
Enact omnibus trade bill over Reagan veto	Y
Approve death penalty for drug-related murders	Y
Oppose "workfare" amendment to welfare overhaul bill	N

Voting Studies

	Presidential Support		Party Unity		Conservative Coalition	
Year	S	O	S	O	S	O
1988	58	40	41	56	54	46
1987	53	45	56	40	38	50
1986	49	45	58	36	63	30
1985	72	25	67	26	63	28
1984	65	27	58	36	62	32
1983	66	24	56	35	50	41
1982	75	24	67	32	59	40
1981	86	13	80	16	71	25

Interest Group Ratings

Year	ADA	ACU	AFL-CIO	CCUS
1988	55	40	64	57
1987	60	31	80	61
1986	60	33	40	58
1985	35	40	43	66
1984	60	33	40	56
1983	30	30	31	47
1982	55	30	58	52
1981	35	47	21	94

1 Les AuCoin (D)

Of Portland — Elected 1974

Born: Oct. 21, 1942, Redmond, Ore.
Education: Pacific U., B.A. 1969.
Military Career: Army, 1961-64.
Occupation: Journalist; public-relations executive.
Family: Wife, Susan Swearingen; two children.
Religion: Protestant.
Political Career: Ore. House, 1971-75, majority leader, 1973-75.
Capitol Office: 2159 Rayburn Bldg. 20515; 225-0855.

In Washington: Most members on the Appropriations Committee operate deep in the shadowy subtotals of their spending bills. AuCoin, however, has seized the limelight as a leading liberal sentinel on arms control. At the same time, he has used his position to protect Northwestern interests in timber and shipbuilding.

The resulting visibility helped AuCoin put down three vigorous re-election challenges during the Reagan era. By 1988, he was back where he began the 1980s — winning two-thirds of the vote — and his name was appearing on lists of House members with aspirations for the Senate.

AuCoin is careful in the issues he chooses, but when he joins a battle he is well prepared, well-spoken, perseverant and confrontational. Unlike many of his Appropriations colleagues of both parties, he relishes floor fights. He enjoyed taking on the Reagan administration, and at the beginning of the 101st Congress he complained that congressional agreements with the Bush administration on contra aid and the budget were responsibility-ducking deals that let liberal values be "smothered in bipartisan summitry."

AuCoin's chief outpost has been the Defense Subcommittee at Appropriations, even though he and other arms control advocates have been consistently outnumbered there. AuCoin developed working relationships with chairmen who did not want to push causes, and took his arms control issues to the House floor, where the argument between the two sides has been closer and where more media attention is available. He pushed wary Democratic leaders to go face to face with the Reagan administration.

"We can't bargain with Reagan," AuCoin declared in 1984. "All the evidence tells us that under his administration there will be no arms control. Period. It's wishful thinking to pretend otherwise."

Repeated floor victories and public-opinion polls finally convinced leaders that strong arms control policies would not hurt them at election time, and pragmatists such as Armed Services Chairman Les Aspin of Wisconsin were swept along in the tide.

Although he has at times been at odds with Aspin, AuCoin has a technological mind-set that gives him more in common with Aspin than with some of the reflexive arms-controllers on the Democratic left. AuCoin is interested not only in persuading the Soviet Union to reduce nuclear weaponry, but also in developing a strategy for reducing the probability of nuclear war. To keep himself abreast of the latest in technology and strategy, AuCoin joined with fellow Democrats Bob Carr of Michigan and Thomas J. Downey of New York to pay the salary of Robert W. Sherman, a leading liberal expert on arms control.

AuCoin served as point man in early struggles against the MX missile, arguing that its basing in Minuteman silos would make it extremely vulnerable to attack. "That's not deterrence at all," he warned in 1983. "That's saying to the Soviets, 'Come on; take 'em out before we use them against you.' "

When a 1985 showdown took place and proponents of the missile won out, AuCoin was bitter that liberals were not joined by Aspin, who had taken over as Armed Services chairman a few weeks earlier. AuCoin and other liberal Democrats had voted for Aspin for chairman on the assumption he would oppose the MX, but he continued to support it.

AuCoin, however, hesitated when others tried to unseat Aspin as chairman at the start of the 100th Congress. After detailed conversations with the Wisconsin Democrat, AuCoin ended up endorsing Aspin in a seconding speech that praised his leadership and intelligence.

Liberal Democrats, with AuCoin as a key player, did win outright victories in the House in the 99th Congress, including a restriction on testing of anti-satellite weapons (ASAT) and a rejection of President Reagan's plan to renew production of chemical weapons. AuCoin in 1985 drafted an ASAT amendment to the committee's appropriations bill that eventually became law. The compromise wording prevented

Oregon 1

Western Portland and Suburbs

Decisions shaping Oregon and the entire Northwest are made by the banks, businesses and law firms of downtown Portland. Many of the important decision makers live in AuCoin's district, in the fashionable West Hills area of the city or the suburbs beyond the western city limits.

Much of this affluent professional community identifies with the Republican Party, but Democrats such as AuCoin have considerable strength there, and independent voters wield decisive influence. In 1980, independent presidential candidate John B. Anderson won nearly 14 percent in western Multnomah County, leaving Jimmy Carter and Ronald Reagan virtually tied.

As one moves farther west into Washington County, GOP strength increases. Republicans outnumbered Democrats in the county in 1980 for the first time, reflecting the enormous demographic changes of the preceding decade, in which population grew 55 percent. The county grew another 10 percent in the first half of the 1980s. Bedroom communities such as Beaverton, Tigard and Hillsboro, once modest in size, have blossomed into economic satellites of Portland, with electronics and computer firms such as Mentor Graphics, Intel and Tektronix providing more than 15,000 high-tech jobs.

The strongest Democratic areas of the district are along the Columbia River and Pacific coast in the fishing and logging counties of Columbia, Clatsop, Tillamook and Lincoln. Columbia has voted for every Democratic presidential candidate since 1932; Clatsop went for Adlai E. Stevenson in 1956 and has stayed Democratic since. Even Walter F. Mondale managed to carry the county in 1984 — by three votes. Michael S. Dukakis carried it more comfortably in 1988.

Some areas of the district were particularly hard hit by the poor economic conditions in the early 1980s. Astoria (Clatsop County), plagued by 20 percent unemployment in 1982, found economic salvation by improving its harbor facilities to handle large shipments of coal from Western states to new markets in Japan, South Korea and Taiwan. Sharply curbed logging activities in the Siuslaw National Forest pushed the jobless rate in Tillamook County above 20 percent in the early 1980s, though the jobless rate now has dipped below 10 percent. Tourism props up the local economy in some coastal areas.

Population: 526,840. White 503,854 (96%), Black 2,717 (1%), Other 11,900 (2%). Spanish origin 11,485 (2%). 18 and over 387,395 (74%), 65 and over 59,440 (11%). Median age: 31.

testing of an ASAT missile as long as the Soviet Union continued its ASAT test moratorium.

In 1987, arms control amendments to a supplemental appropriations bill — with AuCoin as a major sponsor — served early notice that his camp had the votes. The amendments were dropped from that bill, but made it onto the defense authorization bill, with (sometimes reluctant) support from moderate and conservative Democrats.

In 1988, AuCoin joined with Massachusetts Democrat Nicholas Mavroules on an amendment reducing funding for the multiple-warhead MX missile and boosting support for the smaller, single-warhead Midgetman missile.

Overall, the Reagan-era efforts of AuCoin and other staunch arms control advocates served as a counterweight to more centrist Senate positions and thus put pressure on Reagan to negotiate arms cuts with the Soviets. Once Reagan did begin serious talks with Soviet leader Mikhail S. Gorbachev in the late stages of his presidency, many members were reluctant to cast votes that could undermine his position.

When AuCoin joined the Defense Subcommittee in 1983, he said he wanted to combat rampant "pork-barreling" in defense contracts. But he has not been above using his post to protect home-state interests. He has had partial success, for instance, in forcing changes in Navy procedures to help Oregon shipyards get business, even though Portland is not a Navy "homeport."

AuCoin has played a less flashy role on the Interior Subcommittee at Appropriations, but has found it a useful seat for watching over Oregon's coastline and its vast stretches of federally owned land — a practice he began as a member of the Merchant Marine and Fisheries Committee in his first three terms. AuCoin is considered an environmentalist, but a politically sensitive one. He has voted for additional wilderness designations in Oregon, but supports the forest industry's moves for multiple-use management of non-wilderness areas. He and Washington Democrat Norm Dicks worked out a 1988 compromise requiring a study of cutting "old-growth" timber that environmentalists wanted to preserve.

At Appropriations, AuCoin has pushed through programs specific to Oregon, such as a new lock at the federally built Bonneville Dam and money to study how Oregon might be affected by plans (later shelved) for a national nuclear-waste disposal site in nearby Hanford, Wash. In 1987 he joined a suit to keep a Hanford reactor that made weapons-grade plutonium shut down for safety reasons, and he has helped add money to the Energy Department's budget for cleaning up the Hanford site.

Oregon's interests are also behind AuCoin's work against restrictions on imports; he believes other countries would retaliate and keep out the lumber, wheat, electronic instruments and other high-technology products Oregon successfully exports.

AuCoin is mindful of a predecessor whose name has become synonymous with ill-advised protectionism. "There once was another congressman from the 1st District of Oregon named Hawley. He joined a fellow named Smoot," says AuCoin. "I'm not going to be a part of causing history to repeat itself." He was one of only six Democrats to vote against the omnibus trade protection bill that passed the House in 1987.

He supported Delaware Sen. Joseph R. Biden Jr. over Missouri Rep. Richard A. Gephardt in early jockeying for the 1988 Democratic presidential nomination; Gephardt's trade rhetoric, he said, would make him "dead meat in export-sensitive areas."

On another national issue with local implications, AuCoin has closely followed implementation of the 1986 immigration law because of its provisions allowing foreign "guest workers" to come in temporarily to help harvest crops. AuCoin accused the Immigration and Naturalization Service of attempting to inhibit the program, at a time when Oregon strawberries were rotting in the fields for lack of pickers; he won an extension of rules that liberalized the program.

Elsewhere on Appropriations, and on Banking before that, AuCoin has specialized in housing, an issue economically crucial to a state dependent on the timber industry. In 1982 he sponsored a bill allowing low- and middle-income families to receive reduced-rate mortgages on new homes. The bill passed Congress but was vetoed by Reagan.

In the 98th Congress, AuCoin sponsored a timber bill designed to enable small- and medium-sized companies to buy their way out of high-cost federal timber contracts signed in the late 1970s, just before the housing and wood-products market collapsed. The Reagan administration opposed this bill as special-interest relief legislation, but it was not vetoed.

At the same time, AuCoin helped draft an Oregon wilderness bill with fellow Democratic Rep. James Weaver and GOP Sen. Mark O. Hatfield. Out of almost 3 million acres of eligible land, the bill set 1 million acres aside as wilderness. The breadth of its support smoothed the bill to passage over the pro-development objections of Oregon Republican Reps. Denny Smith and Bob Smith, who complained that it would cost forestry jobs in their districts.

At Home: After spending most of this decade as a top target of the Republican Party, AuCoin got a chance to breathe easy in 1988. Redistricting and well-financed opponents forced him to struggle to hold the seat in 1982 and in the following two elections, but as the decade came to a close the GOP barely made an effort. AuCoin clearly has solidified his hold on the district — just as the next round of redistricting approaches.

AuCoin in 1974 became the first Democrat to represent the 1st, but he had no problem deflecting GOP claims that he was too liberal for his constituency in his first re-election efforts. That changed after 1980, when a number of Republican voters were added to the district. His modest victory margins in 1982 and 1984 spurred GOP claims that the district had become permanently "marginal" and would eventually be taken from AuCoin. It was not until 1986 that AuCoin burst the GOP's bubble of optimism by scoring a surprisingly one-sided victory over Tony Meeker, the well-regarded state Senate minority leader.

In both 1982 and 1984, AuCoin was challenged by Bill Moshofsky, a former executive with the forest products firm of Georgia-Pacific and former board member of the Business-Industry Political Action Committee.

The first time, Moshofsky was running in a recession year that was tough on Republicans nationally. He told voters that Oregon's economic problems were not the fault of Reagan policies, but of environmental regulations that diverted capital to compliance and away from job creation. This pitch impressed some in the district's lumber and wood-products industries, but the fishing and logging counties, wary of the former corporate executive, still went for AuCoin, albeit by smaller margins.

Moshofsky came into his second bid with a better organization and an improved campaign style. Between contests he had managed to keep his name in the news through the Coalition for Responsible Spending, an organization he formed to lobby for tighter state budgets.

But this time around, AuCoin was better prepared. He canvassed the district a year before the election, outspent Moshofsky, and also stepped up his overtures to the high-tech business community, strengthening his position in populous Washington County, west of Portland. AuCoin actually won by a slightly smaller margin than in 1982, but considering the strong Reagan tide, AuCoin's 53 percent tally was quite an achievement.

Moshofsky moved on to the state Republican Party chairmanship, but Republicans had high hopes for Meeker in 1986. The 46-year-old state senator had the political base that Moshofsky lacked. He stressed his Senate leadership position and his legislative record, emphasizing juvenile justice and child pornography.

Meeker also approached moderate Republicans and independents by talking about his support for the state ban on no-return bottles, and for efforts to protect women from employment discrimination. But Meeker's appeal to these vital voters was limited by his sponsorship of an anti-abortion initiative on the general-election ballot.

Another major factor in AuCoin's victory was money. The Democrat's aggressive fund-raising efforts gave him one of the largest House campaign treasuries in the nation in 1986, with more than $950,000 available to spend. Meeker's fund-raising was more than respectable, but he still trailed AuCoin by $450,000. The financial disparity enabled AuCoin to dominate the media, and his strong finish gave him a 62 percent win.

A journalist by training, AuCoin had drifted off into public-relations work by 1968, when the Vietnam War motivated him to become active in politics. He campaigned for Sen. Eugene J. McCarthy, who won the Democratic presidential primary in Oregon.

Two years later AuCoin won a seat in the Legislature from Washington County. By 1974, when Republican Wendell Wyatt decided to retire from Congress after five terms, AuCoin had risen to majority leader in the Oregon House. He was an obvious choice for the Democratic nomination from the 1st District.

With that support and a forceful primary campaign leveling most of its criticism at the Nixon administration, AuCoin had little trouble winning over four lesser-known candidates.

His Republican opponent, the former director of the state Department of Environmental Quality, was equally articulate and had Wyatt's strong endorsement. But labor and education groups helped provide AuCoin with a better organization than the GOP could put together in the year of Watergate resentment. AuCoin stressed his legislative record, pointing specifically to pension reform, energy policy and tax relief measures that came out of committees he chaired. He carried every county in the district that year.

Although AuCoin is beginning to gain more visibility on the national scene, he has always been careful to keep his name before a statewide public in Oregon, and he has long been considered a likely future statewide candidate. But AuCoin has played it safe so far, opting not to challenge GOP Sens. Hatfield or Bob Packwood.

Committees

Appropriations (22nd of 35 Democrats)
Defense; District of Columbia; Interior and Related Agencies

Select Hunger (18th of 18 Democrats)
Task Force: Domestic

Elections

1988 General		
Les AuCoin (D)	179,915	(70%)
Earl Molander (R)	78,626	(30%)
1986 General		
Les AuCoin (D)	141,585	(62%)
Tony Meeker (R)	87,874	(38%)

Previous Winning Percentages: **1984** (53%) **1982** (54%) **1980** (66%) **1978** (63%) **1976** (59%) **1974** (56%)

District Vote For President

	1988		1984		1980		1976	
D	137,972	(51%)	112,950	(42%)	96,633	(38%)	92,985	(44%)
R	126,763	(47%)	148,057	(55%)	119,438	(47%)	112,179	(53%)
I					28,388	(11%)		

Campaign Finance

	Receipts	Receipts from PACs		Expend-itures
1988				
AuCoin (D)	$724,149	$340,550	(47%)	$542,224
Molander (R)	$9,825	$100	(1%)	$11,741
1986				
AuCoin (D)	$958,023	$438,377	(46%)	$946,767
Meeker (R)	$498,257	$96,674	(19%)	$492,655

Key Votes

1987	
Raise speed limit to 65 mph	N
Approve Gephardt "fair trade" amendment	N
Ban testing of larger nuclear weapons	Y
Delay "re-flagging" of Kuwaiti tankers	Y
Approve tax-raising deficit-reduction bill	Y
1988	
Approve aid to Nicaraguan contras	N
Enact civil rights restoration bill over Reagan veto	Y
Kill 60-day plant-closing notification measure	N
Pass omnibus trade bill over Reagan veto	Y
Approve death penalty for drug-related murders	N
Bar federal funds for abortions in cases of rape and incest	N
Oppose seven-day waiting period for purchase of handguns	Y

Voting Studies

	Presidential Support		Party Unity		Conservative Coalition	
Year	S	O	S	O	S	O
1988	22	68	81	8	21	76
1987	21	77	82	9	19	81
1986	29	67	82	11	36	64
1985	24	69	71	19	31	64
1984	29	68	72	18	22	71
1983	20	76	75	16	19	75
1982	30	61	76	7	15	71
1981	29	55	67	11	15	67

Interest Group Ratings

Year	ADA	ACU	AFL-CIO	CCUS
1988	95	8	86	43
1987	88	14	81	20
1986	90	9	86	33
1985	65	29	71	64
1984	90	8	77	50
1983	70	18	69	50
1982	85	26	94	26
1981	70	15	79	13

2 Bob Smith (R)

Of Burns — Elected 1982

Born: June 16, 1931, Portland, Ore.
Education: Willamette U., B.A. 1953.
Occupation: Cattle rancher.
Family: Wife, Kaye Tomlinson; three children.
Religion: Presbyterian.
Political Career: Ore. House, 1961-73, Speaker, 1969-73; Ore. Senate, 1973-82, minority leader, 1977-82.
Capitol Office: 118 Cannon Bldg. 20515; 225-6730.

In Washington: Having shown his capacity to make a mark on agriculture policy, Smith broadened his interests by joining the Interior Committee in 1989, after winning party permission to serve on both panels.

A veteran legislative leader in Oregon who was already past age 50 when he came to Congress, Smith started his House career knowing he would never be the power in Washington that he was in Salem. But he soon began looking to escape the status of middle-aged minority backbencher.

The route he found was his relationship with Edward Madigan of Illinois, the shrewd senior Republican on the Agriculture Committee. As the panel began writing the 1985 farm bill, Smith began going to Madigan with strategy ideas — and Madigan realized there was a good deal to be learned from a man with 25 years of legislative experience. Eventually, Smith joined Madigan at agriculture conferences with Bob Dole, the Senate's key farm-policy voice.

Founder and co-chairman of the House beef caucus, Smith often serves as a liaison with Western cattle producers. During work on the farm bill he was upset with a proposal to reduce dairy surpluses by slaughtering dairy cows and adding them to the beef supply. Fearing that the plan would drive down meat prices, Smith pushed for language that required the government to buy up surplus meat for schools and for the military.

On the 1988 emergency drought-aid bill, Smith quashed a move to expand emergency livestock feed assistance programs to livestock producers who do not grow their own feed. (Most cattle ranchers do grow their own feed.) Smith said the new aid would cost the government $2 billion more, and though hog, poultry and dairy interests protested, the Agriculture Committee agreed with Smith, 15-12. Despite pressure on the floor and in House-Senate conference, Smith's position prevailed.

Smith, a rancher himself, believes government should give free enterprise wide latitude. But when he argued that point in the wilderness lands debate in the 98th Congress, he was dismissed by a coalition of environmentalists who felt differently about government's role.

Smith seemed astonished the House would approve 1.1 million acres of new wilderness — most of it in his district — though he and most of his constituents opposed it. He warned of the adverse economic impact of taking national forest lands out of commercial timber production, and expressed exasperation with the federal appeals process that enables environmentalists to delay timberland sales.

This antipathy toward federal involvement will likely define Smith's role on Interior, as he balances his concern for the outdoors with his attention to Oregon's vital timber industry.

In 1988, Smith was the only Oregon member to oppose a landmark river-protection bill for his state. His objections were not eased until the House tacked on a section authorizing construction of Oregon's Umatilla Basin water project.

At Home: Redistricting in 1981 gave Smith an opening to move to Congress. When GOP Rep. Denny Smith chose to run in the newly created 5th, eastern Oregon's rural, sprawling, conservative 2nd was left without an incumbent.

Stressing his legislative experience as Republican leader of the state Senate and Speaker of the Oregon House, Smith easily won his primary. The surprise Democratic primary winner was Larryann Willis, a rancher and Democratic National Committee member.

Trusting in opinion polls that showed him leading, Smith stayed clear of Willis. She tried to provoke Smith; when he refused to debate, she challenged him to a steer-roping contest, but he refused that, too.

Accustomed to easy campaigns in his safe legislative district, Smith had some difficulty adjusting to a hotly contested election. His organization was embarrassed when a poorly planned fund-raiser featuring Bob Hope drew a sparse crowd and actually lost money.

But Smith reassured rural voters with his opposition to designating more wilderness in Oregon, and he convinced others that Willis was a liberal because she advocated deferring the third phase of the Reagan income-tax cut. Smith took 56 percent, beat Willis in a 1984 rematch and has won handily since then.

Oregon 2

East and Southwest — Bend; Medford

There are more jack rabbits than voters here, so any candidate has to focus on a few widely scattered population centers.

In the southwest, Jackson County (Medford) and Josephine County (Grants Pass) together cast one-third of the district vote. Both counties prefer Republicans; in the 1986 gubernatorial contest, GOP nominee Norma Paulus comfortably carried Jackson and Josephine while losing statewide. Josephine was the fastest growing county in the state in the 1980s.

Medford is surrounded by pear, peach and apple orchards of the fruit-growing Rogue River Valley. Lumbering is the main work in Grants Pass, although visitors to the nearby Siskiyou National Forest also contribute to the economy. The only other sizable town in southwest Oregon is Klamath Falls, 75 miles east of Medford. Though the lush forests become drier and thinner on the way east to Klamath Falls, lumbering is still important there. Crater Lake National Park, in the northwestern corner of Klamath County, is a major tourist lure.

The fastest-growing county in Oregon during the 1970s was Deschutes; the county's population center is Bend, in the west central part of the 2nd. Population in Deschutes soared 104 percent during the decade as nearby skiing areas lured people to build summer homes and vacation condominiums.

Many of the newcomers are young and liberal; they helped Democrat Larryann Willis run well in Deschutes County in 1982 and 1984. Wasco County (The Dalles) is the population center in the district's northwest corner. It usually votes Republican, although Michael S. Dukakis won it in 1988.

Most of eastern Oregon is a sparsely populated plateau dusted with sagebrush and dry grasses. In the northern part, most people live along or near the irrigated Columbia River Valley, where wheat ripens on steep golden hillsides. The largest town is Pendleton (Umatilla County). Like most counties here, Umatilla is solidly Republican.

Population: 526,968. White 502,232 (95%), Black 1,082 (0.2%), Other 12,784 (2%). Spanish origin 17,934 (3%). 18 and over 374,066 (71%), 65 and over 64,403 (12%). Median age: 31.

Committees

Agriculture (11th of 18 Republicans)
Forests, Family Farms and Energy; Livestock, Dairy and Poultry; Wheat, Soybeans and Feed Grains

Interior and Insular Affairs (12th of 15 Republicans)
National Parks and Public Lands; Water, Power and Offshore Energy Resources

Select Hunger (5th of 12 Republicans)
Task Force: International (ranking)

Elections

1988 General		
Bob Smith (R)	125,366	(63%)
Larry Tuttle (D)	74,700	(37%)
1986 General		
Bob Smith (R)	113,566	(60%)
Larry Tuttle (D)	75,124	(40%)

Previous Winning Percentages: **1984** (57%) **1982** (56%)

District Vote For President

	1988		1984		1980		1976	
D	98,318	(43%)	85,796	(35%)	59,546	(32%)	87,938	(46%)
R	122,996	(54%)	155,524	(63%)	108,856	(58%)	96,543	(50%)
I					12,765	(7%)		

Campaign Finance

	Receipts	Receipts from PACs	Expend-itures
1988			
Smith (R)	$381,363	$153,366 (40%)	$340,643
Tuttle (D)	$207,190	$94,600 (46%)	$208,513
1986			
Smith (R)	$333,973	$120,154 (36%)	$323,210
Tuttle (D)	$105,658	$48,842 (46%)	$104,266

Key Votes

1987	
Raise speed limit to 65 mph	Y
Approve Gephardt "fair trade" amendment	N
Ban testing of larger nuclear weapons	N
Delay "re-flagging" of Kuwaiti tankers	N
Approve tax-raising deficit-reduction bill	?
1988	
Approve aid to Nicaraguan contras	Y
Enact civil rights restoration bill over Reagan veto	N
Kill 60-day plant-closing notification measure	Y
Pass omnibus trade bill over Reagan veto	N
Approve death penalty for drug-related murders	Y
Bar federal funds for abortions in cases of rape and incest	Y
Oppose seven-day waiting period for purchase of handguns	Y

Voting Studies

	Presidential Support		Party Unity		Conservative Coalition	
Year	**S**	**O**	**S**	**O**	**S**	**O**
1988	66	33	91	8	92	8
1987	57	40	77	15	84	14
1986	66	31	82	13	86	12
1985	63	33	82	14	84	11
1984	53	38	70	20	83	14
1983	71	21	74	8	90	7

Interest Group Ratings

Year	ADA	ACU	AFL-CIO	CCUS
1988	5	92	21	86
1987	24	64	19	86
1986	5	82	14	100
1985	20	75	12	90
1984	10	71	8	75
1983	0	85	12	82

3 Ron Wyden (D)

Of Portland — Elected 1980

Born: May 3, 1949, Wichita, Kan.
Education: Stanford U., A.B. 1971; U. of Oregon, J.D. 1974.
Occupation: Lawyer.
Family: Wife, Laurie Oseran; two children.
Religion: Jewish.
Political Career: No previous office.
Capitol Office: 1406 Longworth Bldg. 20515; 225-4811.

In Washington: A committed liberal, Wyden arrived in Washington in 1981, the start of an era of federal retrenchment. But while blockbuster liberal solutions to pressing social problems are passé these days, Wyden has found a 1980s way to act on his belief in an activist federal government: His strategy is to identify obscure or unnoticed evils, then attack them with a barrage of hearings, press releases and amendments.

He is tireless and imaginative, and by couching his arguments in language that makes him sound more a pragmatist than a crusader, Wyden has been able to pass laws in several areas, including health care, the environment and crime. He succeeds by thinking incrementally, advancing modest legislation with obvious political appeal.

Wyden markets his endeavors aggressively. He is accessible to the media, understands its deadlines and caters to its love of the quotable line. Critics say he is too eager for headlines and — considering his safe Democratic district — too shy about tackling tough issues, choosing instead ones that are almost sure to get favorable play in the press.

But Wyden may have more on his mind than marking notches on his legislative belt. He has been in the House now for almost a decade, and the high-visibility route he is pursuing seems to be leading him toward a bid for higher office.

The near-limitless jurisdiction of the Energy and Commerce Committee suits Wyden well, and his close ties to Chairman John D. Dingell have allowed him to play a role in some high-profile issues. As ranking Democrat on Dingell's Investigations Subcommittee in the previous two Congresses, Wyden participated in hearings on the Pentagon procurement scandal as well as those on Wall Street's insider-trading scandal.

However, the less-noticed Small Business Committee gives perhaps the best quick glimpse of Wyden's legislative style. In 1987, he assumed the chairmanship of a new Small Business Subcommittee on Regulation and Business Opportunities. With limited legislative authority and a small staff, the panel could well have escaped notice under a less ambitious chairman. But Wyden pledged "to use it as a very aggressive tool," and that he does.

Under Wyden, the panel created news with hearings on cosmetics labeling, cosmetic surgery and fertility clinics. It found a niche in many major national stories, including medical waste, child care and computer crime. The subcommittee also gives Wyden a forum for airing Northwest concerns. In 1988, his hearings on Canadian plywood tariffs led to a written assurance from the Reagan administration that the federal government would fight this trade barrier.

As legislators wrestled with the AIDS dilemma in the 100th Congress, Wyden's subcommittee held hearings exposing quality control problems in labs testing for the deadly disease.

This prompted Dingell to bring the issue before his Investigations Subcommittee. As the debate expanded to problems at unregulated physician-run labs conducting Pap tests for cervical cancer — recommended annually for all women — the hearings gained widespread publicity and became a springboard for successful legislation offered by Dingell and Wyden to crack down on the labs.

The two do not always agree like this, but Wyden gives the chairman as many votes as he can. As Wyden tells it, when he first joined Energy and Commerce in 1981, he went straight to Dingell to tell him he could not support his efforts to weaken the Clean Air Act, but would try to help whenever he could. This candor formed the basis of a productive relationship.

At the same time, Wyden is often in philosophical agreement with Dingell rival Henry A. Waxman of California, the powerful chairman of the Health Subcommittee, where Wyden has a seat. Their relationship dates back to the 1982 clean-air debate, when Wyden became a key figure in an alliance of liberals opposed to a Dingell-backed effort to relax pollution controls. The environmentalist faction scored a major victory with Wyden's amendment to keep tight controls in areas that met air quality standards.

Oregon 3

Eastern Portland and Suburbs

Sitting along the Willamette River, Oregon's largest city (population 388,000) has a reputation for being a pleasant, livable place. As the only major metropolitan area between San Francisco and Seattle, Portland has attracted large banks, law firms, headquarters of giant lumber firms and an important shipping trade.

Socially and politically, Portland is two cities. East of the Willamette River, in the 3rd, live most of Portland's working-class people; the area west of the river, in the 1st, is generally more affluent and elegant. Democrats take comfortable margins in the 3rd, thanks to blacks in the Albina section, blue-collar whites in the North End and the East Side's many elderly residents.

The 3rd takes in nearly 90 percent of the population of Multnomah County, which includes Portland and some suburbs. In 1984, Walter F. Mondale carried Multnomah as a whole by nearly 24,000 votes — by far his best showing in the state. He did even better within the 3rd District portion of the county. Michael S. Dukakis took Multnomah by more than 60,000 votes in 1988.

As one moves farther east from the Willamette, light-manufacturing districts give way to comfortable middle-income neighborhoods such as Parkrose, with a blend of business and professional people.

Over the last decade there has been growth in the east side suburbs, a few of which are as sumptuous as the in-town residential areas west of the Willamette. The largest of the suburban cities in the 3rd District is Gresham, which tripled in size during the 1970s and has grown in this decade to a population of almost 40,000. Troutdale, to the north, is smaller than Gresham (about 7,000 residents), but also fast growing, having expanded by more than 20 percent in the first half of the 1980s.

Beyond suburbia, Multnomah County's population quickly thins out. There are a few farms along the Columbia River, the northern boundary of the 3rd, but Mount Hood National Forest occupies most of the eastern part of the county.

Population: 526,715. White 471,726 (90%), Black 28,858 (6%), Other 17,563 (3%). Spanish origin 10,458 (2%). 18 and over 394,345 (75%), 65 and over 68,230 (13%). Median age: 31.

Dingell postponed further action, and the entire Clean Air Act rewrite still languishes.

Wyden first won his House seat as the candidate of environmentalists and the elderly, and many of his efforts in the House are directly linked to the interests of those groups. But if he should ever run for the Senate, he would need to appeal to a more conservative statewide constituency. Each year, his record contains some highly conspicuous votes that would appeal to this broader voting bloc: In 1988, Wyden voted for two controversial amendments to the drug bill: one imposing the death penalty for certain drug-related crimes, and the other eliminating a seven-day waiting period for handgun purchases.

Also on the drug bill, Wyden was a leading advocate of successful language to beef up the power of Forest Service law-enforcement agents, who confront a serious problem of marijuana harvesting on public land. Wyden also backed successful language requiring the federal government to establish guidelines for the safe cleanup of illegal drug labs.

Earlier in his career, concern about the vulnerability of older people to crime prompted Wyden to sponsor a "career criminal" bill allowing the federal government to prosecute certain repeat offenders and punish them with a mandatory 15-year sentence. The 98th Congress approved Wyden's bill, and in 1986, its scope was expanded to include drug traffickers.

Wyden has also been at the forefront of efforts to crack down on incompetent doctors. As part of the larger medical malpractice debate, he proposed a successful measure encouraging doctors to report suspected cases of malpractice by their colleagues. In 1988, a page-one story in *The New York Times* was a press secretary's dream; it discussed the resulting nationwide data bank of malpractitioners and quoted Wyden explaining its benefits. "In the past, incompetents have been able to slip through the cracks in the system, inflicting bad medical care on the American consumer," he said. "The data bank will help us hold down medical costs because hospitals will be able to weed out the incompetents."

At Home: Before Wyden announced his 1980 bid for Congress, he already had a high profile in Portland as executive director of the state's Gray Panthers, an organization promoting senior citizens' interests.

In his primary challenge to incumbent Democrat Robert Duncan, Wyden relied on a sizable volunteer force made up of senior citizens, environmentalists and other young urban liberals like himself. He charged that Duncan's record on mass transit, housing and heating cost issues revealed insufficient sensitivity to urban needs in the 1980s.

Duncan, a more traditional labor Democrat, had loyal supporters in the district's working-class neighborhoods. But Wyden cut into that voting bloc by winning some union endorsements that had routinely gone to Duncan in earlier elections.

While Wyden campaigned full time for several months, Duncan tended to his work in Washington and mostly ignored his opponent. Wyden won the primary comfortably.

He was an easy November winner and has continued in that pattern ever since. Wyden's electoral appeal in the 3rd prompted some Democrats to suggest that he test his popularity before a statewide audience by challenging Republican Sen. Bob Packwood in 1986. Wyden chose not to trade a safe House district for such an expensive gamble, but there is little doubt he is interested in the Senate, particularly if GOP Sen. Mark O. Hatfield retires in 1990.

Committees

Energy and Commerce (14th of 26 Democrats)
Health and the Environment; Oversight and Investigations; Telecommunications and Finance

Select Aging (16th of 39 Democrats)
Health and Long-Term Care

Small Business (8th of 27 Democrats)
Regulation, Business Opportunity and Energy (chairman)

Elections

1988 General		
Ron Wyden (D)	190,684	(99%)
1988 Primary		
Ron Wyden (D)	84,978	(95%)
Sam Kahl Jr. (D)	4,790	(5%)
1986 General		
Ron Wyden (D)	180,067	(86%)
Thomas H. Phelan (R)	29,321	(14%)

Previous Winning Percentages: 1984 (72%) **1982** (78%) **1980** (72%)

District Vote For President

	1988	1984	1980	1976
D	143,542 (60%)	127,701 (54%)	110,009 (47%)	119,325 (53%)
R	89,744 (38%)	111,211 (46%)	93,356 (40%)	98,753 (44%)
I			23,697 (10%)	

Campaign Finance

	Receipts	Receipts from PACs	Expend-itures
1988			
Wyden (D)	$596,224	$316,772 (53%)	$287,996
1986			
Wyden (D)	$269,263	$152,004 (56%)	$242,600

Key Votes

1987	
Raise speed limit to 65 mph	Y
Approve Gephardt "fair trade" amendment	N
Ban testing of larger nuclear weapons	Y
Delay "re-flagging" of Kuwaiti tankers	Y
Approve tax-raising deficit-reduction bill	Y
1988	
Approve aid to Nicaraguan contras	N
Enact civil rights restoration bill over Reagan veto	Y
Kill 60-day plant-closing notification measure	N
Pass omnibus trade bill over Reagan veto	Y
Approve death penalty for drug-related murders	Y
Bar federal funds for abortions in cases of rape and incest	N
Oppose seven-day waiting period for purchase of handguns	Y

Voting Studies

	Presidential Support		Party Unity		Conservative Coalition	
Year	**S**	**O**	**S**	**O**	**S**	**O**
1988	29	70	87	13	34	66
1987	18	79	89	8	23	77
1986	23	76	89	11	38	62
1985	26	74	84	14	36	64
1984	25	75	88	12	20	80
1983	13	85	91	8	15	84
1982	30	69	92	7	8	90
1981	26	68	83	10	12	85

Interest Group Ratings

Year	ADA	ACU	AFL-CIO	CCUS
1988	90	16	86	43
1987	84	9	81	14
1986	80	14	79	28
1985	60	29	71	59
1984	95	8	62	31
1983	90	9	82	35
1982	95	18	95	18
1981	100	13	87	6

4 Peter A. DeFazio (D)

Of Springfield — Elected 1986

Born: May 27, 1947, Needham, Mass.
Education: Tufts U., B.A. 1969; U. of Oregon, M.S. 1977.
Military Career: Air Force, 1967-71.
Occupation: Congressional aide.
Family: Wife, Myrnie L. Daut.
Religion: Roman Catholic.
Political Career: Lane County commissioner, 1983-87.
Capitol Office: 1729 Longworth Bldg. 20515; 225-6416.

In Washington: DeFazio's grasp of legislative detail in his first term came as no surprise to those who knew he had spent several years as a congressional aide. His political positioning was no surprise, either, to those who knew that the representative he had served was aggressive populist Jim Weaver, his predecessor in the 4th.

DeFazio is not Weaver, whose stubbornness and stridency helped him build a reservoir of ill will in the House. But he does share some of Weaver's independent populism, voting against foreign aid and not taking all his cues from the Democratic leadership. He did vote with his party 86 percent of the time in 1988, but differed on some key issues. In the 100th Congress he was one of 48 Democrats to vote against a deficit-reduction package calling for a $12 billion tax increase.

"I think the bill's a turkey," he said. "It was presented as a test of faith in leadership. I am a strong supporter of leadership in the House, but they made a mistake on this bill."

Like most freshmen, DeFazio tended to his district, but he also raised his voice on broader policy matters, opposing President Reagan's efforts to provide naval escorts to Kuwaiti oil tankers in the Persian Gulf.

"It's like Lebanon all over again," DeFazio said. "The president is putting American lives and prestige on the line without any clearly defined goals or objectives."

DeFazio was among the most active in pushing for a showdown with Reagan over the War Powers Resolution, which requires congressional approval for the continued deployment of U.S. forces when hostilities are under way. While the Reagan administration questioned the constitutionality of the law and maintained that U.S. forces were not involved in hostilities, DeFazio introduced legislation to declare that the resolution had been triggered. After the courts dismissed a lawsuit intended to force the president to initiate War Powers procedures, DeFazio introduced a bill tightening the existing law and requiring courts to adjudicate such suits.

Like Oregon's other two Democrats in the House, DeFazio is a legislative activist, and he found opportunity to act, serving on the Public Works and Interior committees. Thanks in part to his background as a staffer, he is already one of the more knowledgeable members on timber and energy issues. Also, he was actively involved in a successful effort to expand the Wild and Scenic Rivers Act to protect 1,400 miles of Oregon's rivers.

Other DeFazio efforts have included pushing a bill to allow states to ban the export of unprocessed logs from state lands. The bill, which is intended to save jobs in Oregon mills, has been opposed by the major timber companies and has not moved. Even with that effort, DeFazio has established a reputation as more open to discussions with timber interests than was Weaver, who frequently butted heads with the major employers in the 4th.

At Home: DeFazio's strength and his weakness as a congressional candidate were the same — his identification with Weaver. In the end, the Weaver connection was more help than hindrance. DeFazio portrayed himself as heir to Weaver's populist appeal, but kept his distance from the incumbent's personal quarrels and financial entanglements.

DeFazio first went to work for Weaver in 1977, fresh from a graduate program in gerontology at the University of Oregon. He handled senior citizens' issues in Weaver's Eugene office, spent two years in Washington as his legislative aide, then returned to Eugene as Weaver's constituent services director. After that, DeFazio won election to the Lane County (Eugene) commission in 1982.

As an elected official, DeFazio proved to be a somewhat more ingratiating personality than the often abrasive Weaver, but he was equally aggressive. He sued to nullify contracts between Oregon utilities and the Washington Public Power Supply System, whose failed nuclear projects had resulted in utility rate increases. He also led the fight against a 1983 proposal for a Eugene city income tax.

When Weaver announced he would not run for re-election in 1986, DeFazio was an instant

Oregon 4

Southwest — Eugene

The 4th starts at the Pacific, crosses the Coastal Range and ends at the Cascade Range, taking in all or part of nine counties in southwestern Oregon. More than half the vote is cast in Lane County, the location of Oregon's second-largest city, Eugene.

Home to the University of Oregon (enrollment 17,000), Eugene earned a reputation in the 1960s and 1970s as a capital of the back-to-nature counterculture. Many of the students stayed in Eugene after graduation, enthralled by the beauty of the surrounding mountains. As they moved into workaday society, they learned how to influence local politics and elect their own candidates — usually liberal Democrats.

Often matched against this environmentalist faction are the people whose paychecks come from the large segment of Eugene's economy that is linked to timber processing. For many millworkers and managers in the lumber industry, jobs and growth are more important than environmental preservation. Industrial employment has been unsteady in Eugene and timber-dominated Springfield, its suburb. The downturn in housing construction during the last recession brought layoffs and plant shutdowns, and though the industry is now healthier, increasing mechanization in the mills means they will never employ as many people as in the past.

As concern over the long-term economic health of the Eugene area has grown, there has been more cooperation between environmentalists and development advocates in Lane County. But there is still a good measure of the conflict that has produced some strongly competitive races in Lane County over the years. Richard M. Nixon carried Lane in 1968 and 1972, but Jimmy Carter won it in 1976; Ronald Reagan was the victor in 1980, but it went for Walter F. Mondale in 1984 and for Michael S. Dukakis in 1988. In contests for Congress, Democrats usually prevail. DeFazio won 59 percent of the Lane County vote in his first House bid in 1986, and more than 70 percent in his 1988 re-election.

Two counties south of Lane together make up about 30 percent of the 4th's vote — Douglas County (Roseburg) and Coos County (Coos Bay). Douglas, given over mostly to farming and sheep raising, is the district's most significant conservative area. It was the base for Bruce Long, the GOP House nominee in 1984 and 1986.

Coastal Coos County suffered in the last recession, with unemployment reaching as high as 20 percent. Dozens of mills went idle, putting thousands out of work. Reopenings have helped matters, but a number of the mills are closed for good. Also, the traditional salmon fishermen have been losing ground to corporate aquaculture facilities that produce higher yields. Coos County narrowly backed Reagan in 1984, but gave DeFazio 58 percent in 1986, and went for Dukakis in 1988.

Population: 526,462. White 509,012 (97%), Black 1,932 (0.4%), Other 10,055 (2%). Spanish origin 9,972 (2%). 18 and over 378,675 (72%), 65 and over 56,042 (11%). Median age: 30.

contender. He had ties to environmentalists and liberals in Eugene's university community, a residence in the timber-oriented suburb of Springfield, and name familiarity throughout Lane County. DeFazio had primary opposition from state Sen. Bill Bradbury, who was popular in the coastal areas, and state Sen. Margie Hendriksen, who had labor and feminist support. But thanks to a big plurality in Lane, DeFazio edged Bradbury by just under 1,000 votes; Hendriksen finished a close third.

Republicans nominated Bruce Long, who had taken 42 percent of the vote against Weaver in 1984. Long's strategy was to cultivate the many voters Weaver had alienated over the years; in speech after speech, he described DeFazio as "Jim Weaver Jr." Allegations that Weaver had used campaign funds to play the commodities market made DeFazio's ties to the incumbent seem even more undesirable.

But DeFazio had no connection with Weaver's financial troubles, and he deflected the "clone" criticisms by insisting that he was an independent thinker who had picked up valuable experience in Weaver's office. DeFazio called Long a dogmatic conservative lacking in sympathy for district voters.

Long was better financed than in 1984, but his media efforts could not undo DeFazio's Lane County base and strong grass-roots organization. DeFazio carried Lane by almost 18,000 votes, won with similar ease in Coos County and held down Long's margin in Douglas County. DeFazio ran poorly only in a few rural areas of the district.

Two years later he defeated Republican Jim Howard, a Pleasant Hill school administrator, with roughly 72 percent of the vote — a showing that far surpassed any of Weaver's election numbers.

Committees

Interior and Insular Affairs (23rd of 26 Democrats)
Mining and Natural Resources; National Parks and Public Lands; Water, Power and Offshore Energy Resources

Public Works and Transportation (19th of 31 Democrats)
Aviation; Water Resources

Elections

1988 General

Peter A. DeFazio (D)	108,483	(72%)
Jim Howard (R)	42,220	(28%)

1986 General

Peter A. DeFazio (D)	105,697	(54%)
Bruce Long (R)	89,795	(46%)

District Vote For President

	1988	1984	1980	1976
D	120,021 (54%)	109,587 (46%)	107,296 (38%)	102,060 (52%)
R	99,106 (44%)	126,453 (53%)	138,645 (49%)	88,526 (45%)
I			23,305 (8%)	

Campaign Finance

	Receipts	Receipts from PACs	Expend-itures
1988			
DeFazio (D)	$330,899	$235,589 (71%)	$283,068
Howard (R)	$60,048	$5,250 (9%)	$58,563
1986			
DeFazio (D)	$303,328	$179,857 (59%)	$295,654
Long (R)	$336,238	$145,543 (43%)	$333,647

Key Votes

1987

Raise speed limit to 65 mph	Y
Approve Gephardt "fair trade" amendment	Y
Ban testing of larger nuclear weapons	Y
Delay "re-flagging" of Kuwaiti tankers	Y
Approve tax-raising deficit-reduction bill	N

1988

Approve aid to Nicaraguan contras	N
Enact civil rights restoration bill over Reagan veto	Y
Kill 60-day plant-closing notification measure	N
Pass omnibus trade bill over Reagan veto	Y
Approve death penalty for drug-related murders	Y
Bar federal funds for abortions in cases of rape and incest	N
Oppose seven-day waiting period for purchase of handguns	Y

Voting Studies

	Presidential Support		Party Unity		Conservative Coalition	
Year	**S**	**O**	**S**	**O**	**S**	**O**
1988	20	71	86	10	24	61
1987	12	87	87	10	19	81

Interest Group Ratings

Year	ADA	ACU	AFL-CIO	CCUS
1988	80	13	86	25
1987	100	4	93	20

5 Denny Smith (R)

Of Salem — Elected 1980

Born: Jan. 19, 1938, Ontario, Ore.
Education: Willamette U., B.A. 1961.
Military Career: Air Force, 1958-60, 1962-67.
Occupation: Newspaper publisher; airline pilot.
Family: Divorced; six children.
Religion: Protestant.
Political Career: No previous office.
Capitol Office: 1213 Longworth Bldg. 20515; 225-5711.

In Washington: Smith's image in Washington has transformed completely since his arrival in 1981, when he was viewed as a man more committed to unyielding conservatism than to legislating. Now he gets rave reviews as a prominent critic of wasteful defense spending on questionable weapons systems. But when Smith was running for re-election in 1988, it was clear that the praise he wins in Washington has not obscured the fact that in Oregon, he is still viewed as a rigid conservative who stands to the right of many of his constituents. Against an underfinanced opponent, Smith very nearly saw his House career come to an end.

Though there are many congressional critics of Pentagon waste, Smith has earned more credibility than most. That is partly due to his military background — he flew missions in Vietnam — and partly because his overall outlook is hawkish. Liberal Pentagon critics must suffer questions about their dedication to defense spending; Smith does not. Smith also has an edge on some self-styled military reformers because, unlike many of them, he has gone beyond politically easy targets such as overpriced toilet seats and coffee makers. He has immersed himself in technical data to uncover major weapons systems whose performance has fallen far short of expectations.

Taking a bipartisan stance that he extends to few other issues, Smith has worked with Democrats for increased competition on defense contracts and improved testing of weapons before full-scale production begins.

Smith's reputation soared in August 1985, when Defense Secretary Caspar W. Weinberger canceled production of the expensive and seriously flawed DIVAD (Division Air Defense) anti-aircraft cannon, known as the "Sergeant York." The DIVAD, a major target of Smith's scrutiny, was the first Pentagon weapons program canceled in mid-production in 20 years.

Smith had persistently lobbied Weinberger, insisting that the Army was squelching discussion of the fact that the radar-guided gun had failed numerous tests. After the Army claimed the gun had shot down several drone planes in a test, Smith obtained evidence that the planes had been destroyed by remote-control detonation. The Pentagon had already spent $1.8 billion for production of the guns, but Smith was able to claim more than $4 billion in savings with its cancellation.

In 1988, Smith was in the news after the USS *Vincennes* accidentally shot down an Iranian airliner. The *Vincennes* was equipped with the Aegis combat system, a system Smith began questioning in 1984, when the Navy touted plans to use it on a new fleet of cruisers and destroyers. Smith said then the system did not perform well in tests; after the jet was downed, he said, "The siutation is predictable given the history of Aegis' tests."

While Smith's efforts have brought him much favorable publicity, they have not brought him a seat on the Armed Services Committee, whose GOP members tend to be less critical of the defense establishment. Smith has indicated interest in that panel, but because he is not on it — and because Oregon receives relatively little in the way of defense spending — he has considerable political freedom to speak out against waste and fraud.

Smith's questioning attitude toward the Pentagon sets him apart from many staunch conservatives, but his overall House record clearly puts him in that ideological camp. His rating from the American Conservative Union has never fallen below 90, and he continues to push highly controversial fiscal ideas.

Smith, who serves on the Budget Committee, was one of the earliest to advocate an across-the-board budget freeze, and he is one of the very few who want a freeze to include Social Security cost-of-living adjustments (COLAs). Those COLAs, he said in 1988, "have bankrupt the Social Security System three times in the last dozen years. I don't think that's the way we want to run this system." That sort of rhetoric is what causes Smith trouble at election time.

Smith has often shown his conservative stripes on the Interior Committee, where he defends his district's mining and timber interests. However, he did get credit at home during the 100th Congress for working with Democrats

Oregon 5

Willamette Valley — Salem; Corvallis

Created in 1981 from parts of three other districts, the 5th contains no entire county, covering instead parts of five counties that lie on either side of the Willamette River south of Portland.

With its mix of blue-collar and white-collar workers, logging towns and affluent suburbs, farming areas and college towns, the 5th reflects much of the state's diversity. Politically, most of it is GOP territory, but the Republicans tend to be moderate, especially on social questions.

Marion County, nearly all of which is in the 5th, casts about 40 percent of the vote and is usually a good Republican base; Smith's paltry 1,500-vote margin there in 1988 set the tone for his near-loss districtwide. Marion includes Salem, which, with over 90,000 people, is the third-largest city in the state. Salem is Oregon's capital, so many of the residents are on the state payroll; the city is also a market town for the Willamette Valley's abundant agricultural produce.

Clackamas County has about as much clout in the 5th as Marion does, casting just over 35 percent of the district's vote. The county's population has expanded with the expansion of Portland's suburbs into the northwest section of the county. Democrats have a considerable edge over Republicans among registered voters in Clackamas, but some who label themselves Democrats frequently cross party lines. Smith carried the county easily in 1984 and 1986, but got only 52 percent there in 1988. Conservatism is strong in affluent white-collar suburbs such as Lake Oswego, which is partially in the district, and in blue-collar towns such as Oregon City and West Linn.

The 5th contains only a small corner of Benton County, but that includes the city of Corvallis, the district's only major city outside Salem. The home of Oregon State University's 15,000 students and numerous political activists, Corvallis is the most liberal area in the district. Benton County has stubbornly gone against Smith, giving his 1988 Democratic foe nearly 60 percent of the vote.

The district also includes the western portion of Linn County, which is dominated by Albany, a conservative blue-collar logging and metal-producing town. Because of its dependence on those troubled industries, Linn has been one of the more economically depressed counties in the state.

Population: 526,120. White 503,786 (96%), Black 2,471 (1%), Other 9,787 (2%). Spanish origin 15,998 (3%). 18 and over 375,567 (71%), 65 and over 55,221 (10%). Median age: 29.

to pass a bill expanding the federal network of wild and scenic rivers in Oregon.

Smith also spent a lot of his energy in the last Congress working on state, rather than federal, policy making. He earned many home-state headlines by championing a successful "anti-crime" ballot initiative, which was designed to prohibit parole or probation for repeat violent felons. A number of politicians criticized the plan, saying that it did not address how the government would pay for such a policy change. But more than a few were also jealous that Smith had so successfully grabbed hold of the crime-fighting image.

At Home: Smith had two tough re-election campaigns before an impressive victory in 1986 seemed to remove his aura of vulnerability. But appearances were deceiving. Confident of victory in 1988, Smith spent much of his energy outside his district, promoting his "anti-crime" ballot initiative and boosting his statewide visibility. On Election Day, he nearly earned visibility as one of just a handful of defeated House incumbents. Not until absentee ballots were counted did he pull ahead of Democratic state Rep. Mike Kopetski.

Until November, 1988 looked like a great year for Smith. He had received plaudits for his defense-waste crusade, and won considerable attention for leading the ballot initiative campaign. Even those who criticized the initiative saw it as a smart political move that would help make Smith a strong contender in a future Senate or gubernatorial contest.

At the same time, Kopetski was viewed by a number of Democrats as a candidate simply building for the future. But while Smith seemed to take his race for granted, Kopetski took limited resources and built a crack organization. He lacked the money for a TV ad campaign, but effectively disseminated his message with free media. Kopetski called Smith a hypocrite for touting his crime-fighting initiative in Oregon, but voting against crime-fighting legislation in the House. He also capitalized on Smith's proposal to freeze Social Security COLAs.

Smith also was the target of an independent cable-TV advertising campaign financed by a wealthy Oregon family unhappy with Smith's conservative record.

Late in the campaign, Smith started to worry, and began running TV ads criticizing

Kopetski as a tax-and-spend liberal. That last-minute offensive may have made the difference. While the ballot initiative passed overwhelmingly, Smith won by just 707 votes. After the voting, Smith was one of the few GOP candidates anywhere to blame his showing on Michael S. Dukakis' coattails. The Democrat narrowly lost the 5th District's presidential vote.

Smith originally was elected in the more rural and conservative 2nd District, but he chose to run in the newly created 5th in 1982 after his hometown of Salem was placed there by redistricting. In his first election there, Democratic state Sen. Ruth J. McFarland launched an outspokenly liberal challenge that pulled together feminists, environmentalists, nuclear-freeze advocates and union members.

In the crucial voting bloc of suburban, white-collar moderate Republicans, many felt uncomfortable with Smith's ideological style, but McFarland was too liberal an alternative. Smith survived by fewer than 5,000 votes.

McFarland was back in 1984 with a better-organized, better-funded campaign, but her image was unchanged, and she shared the ballot with tax-increase advocate Walter F. Mondale. Smith crept up to 54 percent. Two years later, boosted by publicity from his defense-waste activism, he had his first easy campaign.

The son of a former Oregon governor and cousin to Idaho GOP Sen. Steve Symms, Smith has been near politics most of his life. But until his 1980 challenge to Democratic Rep. Al Ullman, chairman of the House Ways and Means Committee, his direct political involvement was limited.

Even as the owner of 16 eastern Oregon newspapers he inherited from his father, Smith's interest was on the business side rather than in editorial content. Most of his professional life had been spent flying jets — in Vietnam and later for Pan American Airways.

Smith's 1980 campaign was largely anti-Ullman. Spending about $700,000, he guaranteed near-saturation publicity for his charge that after 24 years in Washington, Ullman had lost touch with the district. Smith noted that Ullman no longer owned a home in Oregon and had pushed for a nationwide value-added tax most Oregonians opposed. Ullman backed off from the tax proposal in mid-1980, too late to repair its political damage.

Committees

Budget (4th of 14 Republicans)
Task Forces: Defense, Foreign Policy and Space (ranking); Community Development and Natural Resources; Economic Policy, Projections and Revenues

Interior and Insular Affairs (5th of 15 Republicans)
Water, Power and Offshore Energy Resources (ranking); Energy and the Environment

Elections

1988 General		
Denny Smith (R)	111,489	(50%)
Mike Kopetski (D)	110,782	(50%)
1986 General		
Denny Smith (R)	125,906	(60%)
Barbara Ross (D)	82,290	(40%)

Previous Winning Percentages: **1984** (54%) **1982** (51%) **1980** (49%)

District Vote For President

	1988		1984		1980		1976	
D	116,353	(48%)	100,445	(41%)	83,406	(37%)	88,099	(46%)
R	121,517	(50%)	144,455	(59%)	110,749	(49%)	96,119	(50%)
I					24,234	(11%)		

Campaign Finance

	Receipts	Receipts from PACs	Expend-itures
1988			
Smith (R)	$476,246	$211,227 (44%)	$559,616
Kopetski (D) †	$352,829	$174,274 (49%)	$351,806
1986			
Smith (R)	$416,407	$163,026 (39%)	$312,236
Ross (D)	$89,146	$25,902 (29%)	$87,129

† Totals based on incomplete data.

Key Votes

1987	
Raise speed limit to 65 mph	Y
Approve Gephardt "fair trade" amendment	N
Ban testing of larger nuclear weapons	N
Delay "re-flagging" of Kuwaiti tankers	N
Approve tax-raising deficit-reduction bill	N
1988	
Approve aid to Nicaraguan contras	Y
Enact civil rights restoration bill over Reagan veto	N
Kill 60-day plant-closing notification measure	Y
Pass omnibus trade bill over Reagan veto	N
Approve death penalty for drug-related murders	Y
Bar federal funds for abortions in cases of rape and incest	Y
Oppose seven-day waiting period for purchase of handguns	Y

Voting Studies

	Presidential Support		Party Unity		Conservative Coalition	
Year	**S**	**O**	**S**	**O**	**S**	**O**
1988	65	24	89	5	79	0
1987	71	27	91	5	86	14
1986	74	21	86	7	90	10
1985	76	18	87	7	85	7
1984	73	21	85	5	88	7
1983	78	16	83	3	85	6
1982	74	16	94	3	88	4
1981	71	25	92	7	93	4

Interest Group Ratings

Year	ADA	ACU	AFL-CIO	CCUS
1988	5	96	14	92
1987	4	95	6	100
1986	0	95	15	88
1985	10	95	18	95
1984	0	100	8	79
1983	5	100	0	84
1982	5	90	5	86
1981	10	100	0	88

Pennsylvania

U.S. CONGRESS

SENATE 2 R
HOUSE 12 D, 11 R

LEGISLATURE

Senate 23 D, 27 R
House 104 D, 99 R

ELECTIONS

1988 Presidential Vote	
Bush	51%
Dukakis	48%
1984 Presidential Vote	
Reagan	53%
Mondale	46%
1980 Presidential Vote	
Reagan	50%
Carter	43%
Anderson	6%
Turnout rate in 1984	54%
Turnout rate in 1986	37%
Turnout rate in 1988	50%

(as percentage of voting age population)

POPULATION AND GROWTH

1980 population	11,863,895
1988 population estimate (5th in the nation)	12,001,000
Percent change 1980-1988	+1%

DEMOGRAPHIC BREAKDOWN

White	90%
Black	9%
Other	1%
(Spanish origin)	1%
Urban	69%
Rural	31%
Born in state	82%
Foreign-born	3%

MAJOR CITIES

Philadelphia	1,642,900
Pittsburgh	387,490
Erie	115,270
Allentown	104,360
Scranton	82,260

AREA AND LAND USE

Area	44,888 sq. miles (32nd)
Farm	29%
Forest	59%
Federally owned	2%

Gov. Robert P. Casey (D)
Of Scranton — Elected 1986

Born: Jan. 9, 1932, Jackson Heights, N.Y.
Education: College of the Holy Cross, B.A. 1953; George Washington U., LL.B. 1956.
Occupation: Lawyer.
Religion: Roman Catholic.
Political Career: Pa. Senate, 1963-67; Pa. auditor general, 1969-77; sought Democratic nomination for governor in 1966, 1970 and 1978.
Next Election: 1990.

WORK

Occupations	
White-collar	50%
Blue-collar	36%
Service workers	13%
Government Workers	
Federal	131,413
State	143,260
Local	392,908

MONEY

Median family income	$ 19,995 (24th)
Tax burden per capita	$ 857 (24th)

EDUCATION

Spending per pupil through grade 12	$ 4,416 (10th)
Persons with college degrees	14% (41st)

CRIME

Violent crime rate	369 per 100,000 (29th)

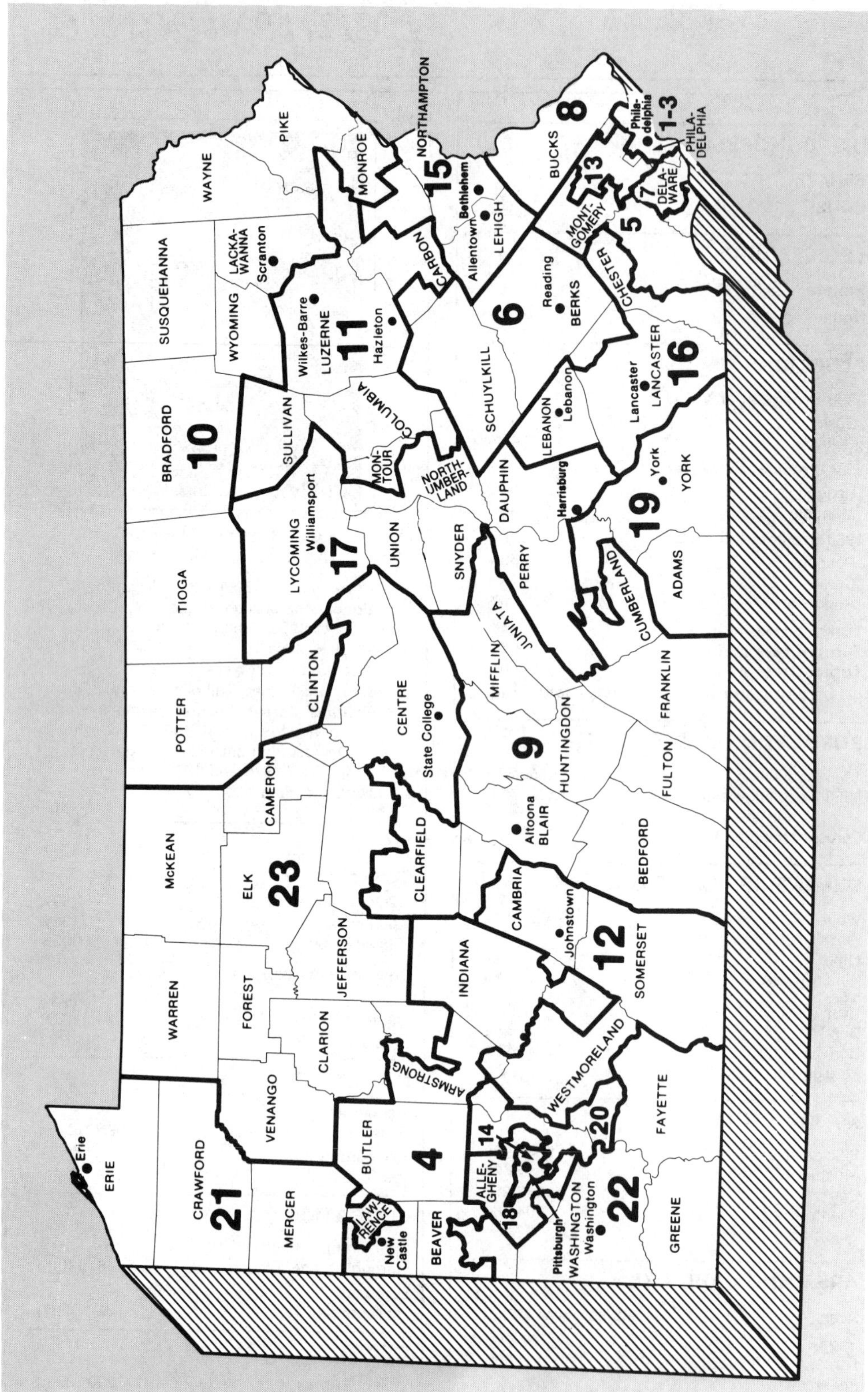
ERIE
Erie
CRAWFORD
21
MERCER
LAWRENCE
New Castle
BEAVER
VENANGO
BUTLER
4
WARREN
FOREST
CLARION
ARMSTRONG
McKEAN
ELK
23
JEFFERSON
CAMERON
POTTER
CLINTON
CLEARFIELD
TIOGA
LYCOMING
Williamsport
17
BRADFORD
10
SULLIVAN
SUSQUEHANNA
WYOMING
LACKAWANNA
Scranton
WAYNE
PIKE
MONROE
NORTHAMPTON
15
Bethlehem
Allentown
LEHIGH
CARBON
LUZERNE
Wilkes-Barre
11
Hazleton
COLUMBIA
MONTOUR
NORTHUMBERLAND
UNION
SNYDER
SCHUYLKILL
6
Reading
BERKS
BUCKS
8
MONTGOMERY
13
Philadelphia
1-3
PHILADELPHIA
DELAWARE
7
5
CHESTER
16
LANCASTER
Lancaster
LEBANON
Lebanon
DAUPHIN
Harrisburg
19
York
YORK
PERRY
JUNIATA
CUMBERLAND
ADAMS
MIFFLIN
CENTRE
State College
9
HUNTINGDON
FRANKLIN
FULTON
BLAIR
Altoona
BEDFORD
CAMBRIA
Johnstown
12
SOMERSET
INDIANA
WESTMORELAND
20
FAYETTE
14
ALLEGHENY
18
Pittsburgh
WASHINGTON
Washington
22
GREENE

John Heinz (R)

Of Pittsburgh — Elected 1976

Born: Oct. 23, 1938, Pittsburgh, Pa.
Education: Yale U., B.A. 1960; Harvard U., M.B.A. 1963.
Military Career: Air Force, 1963-69.
Occupation: Food industry executive.
Family: Wife, Teresa Simoes-Ferreira; three children.
Religion: Episcopalian.
Political Career: U.S. House, 1971-77.
Capitol Office: 277 Russell Bldg. 20510; 224-6324.

In Washington: Heinz may serve long and honorably in the Senate, but one of its beloved figures he will likely never be. His record is a clear demonstration of the way personality sets the bounds of a Senate career. He has gone about as far as a man could go in the chamber by being intelligent, articulate and not very popular.

After a dozen years in the Senate, Heinz has established himself as a capable legislator with a solid record on such complex subjects as health and trade policy, pensions and Social Security. But he has never acquired the knack for being collegial.

Unlike a number of other wealthy senators, Heinz has not developed a plain-folks style. He is a stubborn man who has an intense desire to have his way, and he can be quarrelsome if he does not get it. Nonetheless, Heinz played an instrumental role on major trade and health legislation produced by the Finance Committee in the 100th Congress.

Heinz does not like to think of himself as a protectionist, but as his state's aging industrial economy has fallen victim to competition from other countries, he has emerged as a leading spokesman for a mercantilist U.S. trade policy.

While Heinz does not advocate erecting high tariff barriers, he does think the United States has consistently been taken advantage of in international trade by Japan and other nations. He uses his positions on the Finance and Banking committees to try to reverse that disadvantage, both by promoting exports and applying some curbs on imports.

The return of Senate control to Democrats, along with partisan positioning for the presidential election, helped produce the 1988 omnibus trade bill, which Heinz had a hand in shaping. As the 100th Congress opened, he filed dozens of pieces of trade legislation; his imprint was on the final bill.

Heinz believes free trade is a myth and that reliance on the falling dollar to correct the nation's trade deficit is a foolish proposition. He sees a world in which key U.S. trading partners rely on classic mercantilism to steal away American business. They subsidize key industries so they can cut prices abroad, contributing to overcapacity and inefficiency in markets.

Heinz had long favored a broad revision of the whole structure of U.S. trade laws to help domestic producers compete in world markets. In 1985 he introduced an omnibus trade bill, developed by a coalition of labor unions and major corporations, that called for stronger action against unfair trading practices by other countries and greater protections for troubled U.S. industries.

Heinz has directed some of his efforts toward specific protections for import-threatened industries in Pennsylvania, notably steel. Heinz wants to bar foreign countries from "dumping" steel in the United States at prices below the cost of production. As chairman of the Senate's informal steel caucus, he has argued that the voluntary import restraint program adopted by the administration should be replaced by strict import quotas.

The trade bill is only one half of the equation Heinz sees. He wants to reorient the economy so it is driven to export. As chairman of the International Finance Subcommittee, Heinz sponsored a successful bill in 1983 to push the Export-Import Bank into a more aggressive course, offering cheap loans to compete with the subsidies other countries provide at government expense. In the 99th Congress he was a prime sponsor of legislation, backed by the Reagan administration, to establish a $300 million "war chest" to be used to counter foreign government subsidies.

Heinz also wants to improve the market for U.S. goods abroad by discouraging the use of boycotts and embargoes as foreign policy tools. That was one of his chief goals during work in the 98th Congress on reauthorization of the Export Administration Act.

In the six years of Republican Senate control, Heinz chaired the Special Aging Committee, and he is still its senior Republican. While the panel cannot report legislation, the position was especially important for Heinz because it helped him get a seat on the National Commission on Social Security Reform. Heinz' role on that commission, and in pushing through Congress the legislation that emerged from it, earned him high marks from his colleagues.

The Pennsylvania Republican was influential in the Finance Committee's work to solve the long-range financial problems of the Social Security system. He proposed a successful amendment in committee to begin raising the retirement age and to cut benefits slightly, in the year 2000.

The amendment also touched on a subject dear to Heinz' heart: removing employment barriers for the elderly. A strong backer of eliminating mandatory retirement, Heinz persuaded the Finance Committee to agree to end the financial penalty imposed on Social Security recipients who work after age 65. He followed up on that achievement in 1986, when he was the chief advocate of a successful bill to bar mandatory retirement policies by most employers.

Heinz' seat on Finance lets him play a significant role on other issues involving the elderly; of late, health insurance has been his focus. He was a key player on legislation passed in 1987 to cover catastrophic illness; he was at the center of negotiations with the White House over its final provisions and price tag. He was the leader of Senate efforts to extend catastrophic Medicare insurance to cover 80 percent of drug bills that exceed $600 annually.

Heinz also was on the point rewriting and toughening rules for nursing homes that take Medicare and Medicaid patients. The rules seek to correct deficiences in care, including improper staffing.

In 1986, Heinz advocated the major revision of tax laws governing private pension plans, part of the 1986 tax code overhaul. His proposal sought to encourage firms to provide more retirement protection to their lower- and middle-level workers, instead of concentrating just on their top management. The bill also required firms to provide full pension coverage to workers after only five years of service.

Heinz was deeply skeptical, however, of the main thrust of the tax overhaul. Pennsylvania's industrial base was one of the sectors of the economy most threatened by the tax changes, leaving Heinz much more interested in preserving favorable treatment of particular interests than in the broad outlines of the bill. When Finance was on the verge of killing the bill by loading it down with special protections, Heinz seemed to push the process even closer to disintegration by offering an amendment to aid tuxedo manufacturers.

Heinz became more supportive of the bill, however, after Finance Chairman Bob Packwood and a handful of other committee members designed a new version that included a bailout for the steel industry. Heinz arranged more than $400 million in tax breaks by allowing the companies to apply unused investment tax credits, which were otherwise repealed, to taxes paid in previous years when the companies had made a profit.

The irritation that many senators feel toward Heinz on a personal basis was a problem for him in his efforts to climb the Senate leadership ladder. It was an important issue in 1980, when Republicans rejected him for GOP Conference chairman, the third-ranking leadership position. The defeat was particularly surprising because Heinz had performed brilliantly as chief campaign fund-raiser that year, bringing in more than $20 million and helping the party gain control of the Senate.

Heinz partially avenged that loss in 1984. Running for his old post of campaign committee chairman, he won by a one-vote margin over Malcolm Wallop of Wyoming. Still, it was hardly a ringing endorsement, considering the holdover loyalty Heinz should have enjoyed from senators he helped elect in 1980, and the reluctance of many in the GOP Conference to have two senators from Wyoming — Wallop and Assistant Majority Leader Alan K. Simpson — in the leadership.

It would be unfair to tag Heinz with prime responsibility for the GOP losing Senate control in 1986. Republicans were saddled with some mediocre incumbents and challengers in a year of voter restlessness toward the Reagan administration.

Heinz did make things worse for himself, though. He made the victory predictions customarily expected of a campaign chairman in a harsh tone that sometimes seemed to cross the line between optimism and arrogance. After the election, he authorized payment of large bonuses to campaign committee staffers. Coming on the heels of defeat — and even as the party was making emergency fund-raising appeals — the move embarrassed other national GOP officials.

At Home: Pennsylvania's 1976 Senate contest matched a 38-year-old Democrat with good looks and campaign skill against a Republican of the same age who had similar qualities *and* a personal fortune. The Republican won.

As attractive a candidate as Heinz was, it probably required most of the $2.4 million he spent to guarantee nomination against a strong GOP opponent and election against the Democrat, Rep. William J. Green III.

Heinz spent nearly $600,000 to win the 1976 primary against Arlen Specter, the former Philadelphia district attorney and now Heinz' Senate colleague. Early in the year, Heinz disclosed he had accepted $6,000 in illegal corporate campaign money from Gulf Oil while serving in the House. He returned the donations, but it cast a shadow over the primary campaign. It took extensive TV advertising to offset the negative publicity.

By fall, the issue had faded somewhat, but Heinz had a tough opponent in Green, whose base in Philadelphia matched his own in Pittsburgh. Green said Heinz had been a tool of President Richard M. Nixon; Heinz painted his opponent as a Democratic machine politician and warned that Philadelphia was trying to take over the state.

Heinz cut into the labor support that Democratic statewide candidates generally receive. During five years in the House, representing a suburban Pittsburgh district with a significant blue-collar constituency, he had frequently supported union positions. The United Mine Workers gave him important support against Green, and he carried several normally Democratic mining counties.

Money, labor support and his strong western Pennsylvania base combined to ensure Heinz an easy time in 1982. Front-line Democratic opposition stayed away and he approached 60 percent in a year when the bad economy held Republican Gov. Dick Thornburgh to 51 percent.

After Green (who had become Philadelphia mayor) and other prominent Democrats backed away from challenging Heinz, the task fell to Allegheny County Commissioner Cyril H. Wecht, a forensic pathologist who had offered well-publicized details of celebrity deaths such as those of John and Robert Kennedy.

The garrulous Wecht tried to shake Heinz' composure in a TV debate, but with no success. In the end, Heinz captured Allegheny (Pittsburgh) and every other county in the state except the Democratic bastions of Greene and Fayette and the city of Philadelphia.

Heinz' 1988 re-election was even easier. Having spent 12 years nurturing his political base in western Pennsylvania and much of the last six padding his campaign treasury, Heinz was in position to face the toughest of challengers. Instead, his Democratic opponent, Joe Vignola, was underfinanced and utterly unknown outside his native Philadelphia, where he had won two terms as the city controller.

Heinz enjoyed a big lead in the polls throughout the year — even during the summer months when Democratic presidential nominee Michael S. Dukakis held a double-digit lead over George Bush in Pennsylvania. To avoid the risk of any trickle-down damage to his campaign, Heinz began his TV and radio advertising in June and kept it up through November. He lost only Philadelphia, taking two-thirds of the statewide vote.

Committees

Special Aging (Ranking)

Banking, Housing and Urban Affairs (2nd of 9 Republicans)
Securities (ranking); International Finance and Monetary Policy

Finance (6th of 9 Republicans)
Private Retirement Plans and Oversight of the Internal Revenue Service (ranking); International Trade; Medicare and Long-Term Care

Governmental Affairs (5th of 6 Republicans)
General Services, Federalism and the District of Columbia (ranking); Government Information and Regulation; Oversight of Government Management

Elections

1988 General		
John Heinz (R)	2,901,715	(66%)
Joseph C. Vignola (D)	1,416,764	(32%)

Previous Winning Percentages: **1982** (59%) **1976** (52%) **1974 *** (72%) **1972 *** (73%) **1971 †** (67%)

** House elections.*
† Special House election.

Campaign Finance

	Receipts	Receipts from PACs	Expend-itures
1988			
Heinz (R)	$5,280,540	$1,337,813 (25%)	$5,151,512
Vignola (D)	$549,089	$48,805 (9%)	$544,137

Key Votes

1987	
Enact omnibus highway bill over Reagan veto	Y
Limit testing of space-based anti-ballistic missiles	Y
Oppose banning tests of larger nuclear weapons	Y
Confirm Robert H. Bork as Supreme Court justice	Y
1988	
Allow vote on campaign-finance overhaul	N
Pass civil rights restoration bill over Reagan veto	Y
Enact omnibus trade bill over Reagan veto	Y
Approve death penalty for drug-related murders	Y
Oppose "workfare" amendment to welfare overhaul bill	N

Voting Studies

	Presidential Support		Party Unity		Conservative Coalition	
Year	S	O	S	O	S	O
1988	55	40	40	53	59	32
1987	45 †	49 †	47 †	49 †	53 †	41 †
1986	69	31	56	41	59	38
1985	64 †	31 †	54	40	60	33
1984	64 †	30 †	68	29	70	23
1983	76	20	57	38	52	45
1982	55	39	47	43	41	46
1981	74	20	57	33	51	41

† Not eligible for all recorded votes.

Interest Group Ratings

Year	ADA	ACU	AFL-CIO	CCUS
1988	55	41	79	46
1987	70	35	89	50
1986	55	43	60	59
1985	35	55	67	59
1984	50	41	45	56
1983	35	25	44	37
1982	70	17	71	29
1981	35	36	61	71

Arlen Specter (R)

Of Philadelphia — Elected 1980

Born: Feb. 12, 1930, Wichita, Kan.
Education: U. of Pennsylvania, B.A. 1951; Yale U., LL.B. 1956.
Military Career: Air Force, 1951-53.
Occupation: Lawyer; law professor.
Family: Wife, Joan Levy; two children.
Religion: Jewish.
Political Career: Philadelphia district attorney, 1966-74; GOP nominee for mayor of Philadelphia, 1967; defeated for re-election as district attorney, 1973; sought GOP nomination for U.S. Senate, 1976; sought GOP nomination for governor, 1978.
Capitol Office: 303 Hart Bldg. 20510; 224-4254.

In Washington: Specter is an intelligent, intense and abrasive individualist whose zeal for constitutional debate is matched by his zest for klieg lights and headlines. He may be a loner in the Senate — both personally and politically — but on contentious issues, his moderate instincts and proclivity for withholding his opinion until the last moment make his vote a highly sought-after one.

The 1987 debate over Robert H. Bork's nomination to the Supreme Court encompassed everything Specter seems to relish about the Senate. As the only moderate Republican on the Judiciary Committee, he was almost guaranteed a starring role. Also, the confirmation hearings gave him a chance to display his command of constitutional law as well as the talents he honed in his years as a prosecutor.

During the hearings, Specter put on an impressive show. He was one of Bork's most persistent and aggressive interrogators, and came the closest to matching the judicial nominee's expertise on complex legal issues. Intent on pinning down Bork's judicial philosophy and its ramifications, he engaged Bork in intellectual combat, arguing with him on what he believed the court has said and how it differed from Bork's interpretation. The *Philadelphia Inquirer* called the hearings "Arlen Specter's finest hour"; *The New York Times* dubbed his questioning "brilliant."

Often one of the last committee members to announce his vote on controversial matters, Specter has learned to savor his time at center stage. On the Bork vote, he was lobbied by the White House, deluged with mail and prominently featured in news stories. But as the increasingly combative and partisan debate dragged on through the summer and fall, Specter drew criticism for fence-sitting.

Days before the committee vote, he announced "with great reluctance" that he would vote not to confirm Bork to the Supreme Court. Specter said he was troubled by what he perceived to be discrepancies in Bork's writings and his testimony. Citing concern about Bork's interpretation of equal-protection law, judicial review and freedom of speech, Specter said, "I believe there is a substantial doubt as to how he would apply fundamental principles of constitutional law."

The themes of Specter's performance during the Bork debate — a love of constitutional law, a departure from GOP orthodoxy, prolonged and detailed debate and a penchant for publicity — echo throughout his career. Another important trait of his legislative personality is his go-it-alone style, for which he makes no apologies. "They can't say I'm dumb or crooked, so what do they say?" he once asked a reporter. "That I'm calculating or ambitious? I have always thought those were good qualities."

On the Judiciary Committee, Specter is often allied with liberal Democrats on social policy. He has opposed legislative efforts to curb abortion and busing and was a crucial defector from the GOP in several highly publicized votes on presidential appointees opposed by civil rights groups.

Even when the GOP held a majority in the 99th Congress, they lost Specter on votes to endorse William Bradford Reynolds to be associate attorney general; Daniel A. Manion to be a federal appeals judge; and Jefferson B. Sessions III to be a federal district judge.

His support for three other of President Reagan's nominees — William H. Rehnquist to be chief justice of the United States, and Antonin Scalia and Anthony M. Kennedy (who followed the Bork and Douglas H. Ginsburg nominations) to be associate justices of the Supreme Court — did not soothe conservatives' unhappiness over his other controversial votes.

Overall, Specter's Senate record regularly put him at odds with the Reagan administration. In 1986, when he was seeking re-election,

Specter broke with Reagan's position on two out of every three votes — a record of rebellion no other GOP senator came close to matching. By the last year of Reagan's tenure, however, Specter's presidential support score was up to 63 percent, more in line with his record earlier in the decade.

In the mid-1980s, when moderate Senate Republicans organized to defend social programs against sharp budget cutbacks, Specter did not work closely with them. His individualistic style and temperamental personality seemed to dictate that he strike out on his own.

Protracted partisan debate can get on many senators' nerves, but Specter is apt to complain not when debate runs too long, but when it moves too quickly. In early 1989, he said he wanted another subcommittee hearing before sending legislation to the full Judiciary Committee blocking the sale of certain automatic weapons. Earlier, when GOP Rep. Dick Cheney's nomination to become defense secretary was fast-tracked — after the rejection of former Sen. John Tower — Specter cautioned that while Cheney was "very well qualified," he was concerned about the Senate's "rush to judgment."

He made the same complaint about consideration of the contra accord reached between congressional leaders and the Bush administration early in 1989. This issue also gave him a chance to demonstrate his legal prowess. Senate-watchers have noted that if the Constitution is mentioned in debate, Specter likes to be a part of the discussion. When questions were raised during floor debate about the constitutionality of certain provisions in the contra accord, Specter was soon on the scene. "I heard the comments . . . and thought it appropriate to come to the floor to raise for general consideration some issues which I brought up yesterday in the hearings before the Foreign Operations Subcommittee on Appropriations," he said.

A member of the Appropriations Committee, which had jurisdiction over legislation to carry out the accord, he was concerned about language that enabled any one of four committee chairman (two from each chamber), in effect to nullify the agreement. Though Specter repeatedly said his mind was open, he reiterated his view that this provision seemed the equivalent of a legislative veto, which the Supreme Court had struck down. In the end, Specter was one of nine senators voting against the accord, and the only one to base his objection primarily on constitutional grounds.

Occasionally, Specter will beat the partisan drum, as if to remind his Republican colleagues that he is still one of them.

As a member of the Intelligence Committee, Specter has argued vociferously in favor of a broad interpretation of the anti-ballistic missile treaty — a position shared by many conservative advocates of the strategic defense initiative (SDI). In 1987, when the Senate voted 72-27 to prohibit a president from repudiating, without Senate approval, treaty interpretations presented during the ratification process, Specter condemned the prohibition as "a switchblade knife aimed at the security of the United States."

By contrast, in 1985, Specter tangled with the Reagan administration over the MX missile before finally deciding to go along. Originally opposed to the MX, he grew more sympathetic to the weapon as a bargaining chip for arms control negotiations. But shortly before the crucial vote, his incipient change of mind was stalled when White House aides began hinting that Republicans who did not back Reagan on key issues would be denied White House help in campaign fund raising in 1986.

Outraged by the apparent threat, Specter angrily confronted Reagan at a meeting with GOP senators. Finally, Specter did back the missile, but only after publicly vowing not to accept any campaign help from the president.

Representing a state with more registered Democrats than Republicans, Specter routinely calls attention to the plight of struggling Rust Belt cities, and for a Republican, he earns good marks from labor unions. Specter has pressed for legislation aimed at giving U.S. firms more protection from subsidized imports and goods "dumped" below cost in this country by foreign producers. "At the present, there are tens of thousands, if not hundreds of thousands, of jobs lost as a result of unfair foreign trade practices," he says.

When his proposal was offered as an amendment to the omnibus trade bill in 1987, it was soundly rejected, largely on grounds that it would invite retaliation from trading partners.

On Appropriations, Specter voices skepticism about giving U.S. aid to international agencies that lend money to countries whose subsidized industries compete with American manufacturers. "It's very hard to support foreign aid or contributions to the World Bank," he once said, "given the economic climate in western Pennsylvania in the steel mills and coal mines."

The Foreign Operations Subcommittee also gives Specter a platform for his ardent support for Israel. When the Reagan administration defended its 1986 proposal to sell arms to Saudi Arabia by saying the country had worked "quietly" for Middle East peace, Specter retorted, "It's been inaudible as far as this senator is concerned."

In 1988, when Israel stepped back from a U.S. sponsored peace plan, Specter defended the decision. "This is a question for the people and leaders of Israel to decide," he said. "And why should we sitting 3,000 or 5,000 miles away presume to have the wisdom to be telling them what to do?"

On one issue in the 99th Congress, Specter's interest in foreign affairs, his prosecutorial background and his skill for attracting publicity all converged. In 1985, as the nation watched news broadcasts of TWA passengers held hostage in Lebanon, Specter won notice by proposing to give U.S. courts the authority to try anyone who murders or seriously assaults U.S. citizens abroad. He had proposed the measure after the 1983 Marine barracks bombing in Lebanon, and it won Senate approval in 1986.

At Home: Democrats began the 1986 campaign hopeful that they could defeat Specter and end their 24-year drought in Pennsylvania Senate elections. They ended the year buried under the third-largest landslide in the state in the last half-century.

Specter won with money, high name recognition and the type of moderate Republican image that has enabled GOP candidates to monopolize recent Keystone State Senate elections. An unexpectedly weak campaign by his Democratic rival, Rep. Bob Edgar, boosted Specter.

A liberal from the Philadelphia suburbs, Edgar seemed miscast for a statewide race in heavily blue-collar and ethnic Pennsylvania. But from his first House victory in 1974 to his narrow win in the Democratic Senate primary, he was able to combine an ardent grass-roots organization with a thoughtful and non-threatening persona to defeat a string of opponents who underestimated him.

Specter did not make that mistake. An intense campaigner, he amassed a multimillion-dollar campaign treasury that far exceeded Edgar's, and he claimed to have visited each of Pennsylvania's 67 counties at least four times.

Specter had cleared a big hurdle long before he ever faced Edgar. During the fall of 1985, popular GOP Gov. (now U.S. Attorney General) Dick Thornburgh had weighed a primary challenge to Specter, but decided in December not to run.

Edgar sought to portray Specter as a flip-flopper who claimed to be independent but actually supported the Reagan administration on key issues. But with superior financing, Specter was able to emphasize his political moderation and dominate the airwaves with skillfully crafted, locally targeted ads that illustrated how he had steered federal money into the state from his Appropriations Committee post.

Specter blunted Edgar virtually everywhere. He won 61 counties, including all of rural central Pennsylvania, Allegheny County (the centerpiece of western Pennsylvania) and Delaware County (Edgar's base in the Philadelphia suburbs).

For Specter, the impressive victory added luster to a political career that seemed to be on the verge of expiring just six years earlier. When he started his 1980 Senate campaign, Specter looked like a fading politician making a last-gasp try. Once the bright young star of Pennsylvania GOP politics, he had lost much of his appeal following defeats for mayor of Philadelphia in 1967 and for re-election as the city's district attorney in 1973. When he lost two more statewide primaries, in 1976 and 1978, it appeared that his triumphs were behind him.

But he decided to make one more try when Republican Richard S. Schweiker announced he would not seek re-election in 1980.

Although Specter's past campaigns had given him greater statewide exposure than any other GOP candidate, he was thought to be laden with too much baggage even to win the nomination over Bud Haabestad, the state GOP chairman.

But Haabestad, Thornburgh's handpicked state chairman, was disliked by organization Republicans. Thornburgh had abolished much of the traditional GOP patronage system in Pennsylvania, and Haabestad had borne the bad tidings to Republican workers. This issue allowed Specter to win the primary.

In the general election, Specter had the good fortune of running against a Democrat who was also a two-time statewide loser — former Pittsburgh Mayor Pete Flaherty. Immensely popular in the western part of the state, Flaherty had suffered in the past from a tendency to run his statewide campaigns on his own, disdaining modern organization and financing. In 1980, determined not to make the same mistake, he put more effort into building a statewide network.

It was not enough. Thornburgh and GOP Sen. John Heinz agreed to support Specter after the primary, and with their help, he made inroads on Flaherty's territory in western Pennsylvania. At the same time, Flaherty could not overcome the longstanding suspicion of him in the Philadelphia area. Specter carried Philadelphia by 12,000 votes and won immense margins in the Philadelphia suburbs, enough to offset Flaherty's showing in the west.

Specter's roots in Philadelphia politics reach back to the early 1960s, when he was an assistant district attorney making a name for himself among Democrats as a hard-working young reformer. After a stint with the Warren commission, where he was chief author of the theory that a single bullet hit both President Kennedy and Texas Gov. John B. Connally, he returned to conduct an investigation of Philadelphia's judicial system for the state attorney general.

In 1965, he released a report calling the system a "cesspool" of corruption. The same year he challenged his former boss, James Crumlish, for district attorney. When Crumlish was renominated by the Democrats, Specter ran as a Republican and won.

Two years later, Specter took on Mayor James Tate directly. The Democratic Party had been split by feuds between machine regulars and reformers, and the mayor seemed in no shape to fight off a concerted GOP challenge. Specter and his "clean government" campaign were expected to romp.

They did not. Tate, rejected by the organization, nonetheless won the Democratic nomination easily. Then, as riots were breaking out in other cities, he and his new police chief, Frank Rizzo, clamped a "limited emergency" on the city to prevent disturbances. Specter could not stop Tate from riding voters' gratitude to a narrow victory.

By 1973, as he completed his second term in the district attorney's office, Specter was considered the favorite candidate in state GOP circles to wrest the governorship from Democrats the following year. But the speculation ended abruptly when he lost his campaign for a third term as district attorney that fall.

Specter announced he was going into private law practice, and for the first time in over a decade, his name left the front pages. It did not take long to resurface. In 1976 he entered the GOP primary to replace retiring Sen. Hugh Scott. The front-runner in the contest was then-Rep. Heinz, whose tremendous financial resources gave him a clear edge. But Heinz had been hurt by disclosures that he had received illegal contributions from the Gulf Oil Co., an issue Specter kept alive throughout the campaign. At the end of a bitter contest that kept relations between the two delicate for years, Heinz scraped past Specter.

In 1978, with Democrat Milton Shapp retiring as governor, Specter tried for that office. Though he rounded up strong financial and organizational backing in Philadelphia and its suburbs, he split the area's vote with two other candidates. The winner was Thornburgh — a former assistant attorney general in the Ford administration and the only candidate from western Pennsylvania.

Committees

Appropriations (9th of 13 Republicans)
Labor, Health and Human Services, Education and Related Agencies (ranking); Agriculture, Rural Development and Related Agencies; Defense; Energy and Water Development; Foreign Operations

Judiciary (5th of 6 Republicans)
Antitrust, Monopolies and Business Rights; Constitution

Select Intelligence (4th of 7 Republicans)

Veterans' Affairs (4th of 5 Republicans)

Elections

1986 General		
Arlen Specter (R)	1,906,537	(56%)
Bob Edgar (D)	1,448,219	(43%)
1986 Primary		
Arlen Specter (R)	434,623	(76%)
Richard A. Stokes (R)	135,673	(24%)

Previous Winning Percentage: **1980** (51%)

Campaign Finance

	Receipts	Receipts from PACs	Expend-itures
1986			
Specter (R)	$5,450,763	$1,256,626 (23%)	$5,993,230
Edgar (D)	$3,905,186	$793,871 (20%)	$3,872,779

Key Votes

1987	
Enact omnibus highway bill over Reagan veto	Y
Limit testing of space-based anti-ballistic missiles	N
Oppose banning tests of larger nuclear weapons	N
Confirm Robert H. Bork as Supreme Court justice	N
1988	
Allow vote on campaign-finance overhaul	N
Pass civil rights restoration bill over Reagan veto	Y
Enact omnibus trade bill over Reagan veto	?
Approve death penalty for drug-related murders	Y
Oppose "workfare" amendment to welfare overhaul bill	N

Voting Studies

	Presidential Support		Party Unity		Conservative Coalition	
Year	**S**	**O**	**S**	**O**	**S**	**O**
1988	63	35	48	49	59	35
1987	40	60	46	53	41	59
1986	31	65	27	68	29	64
1985	61	34	51	43	58	37
1984	65	35	67	32	55	45
1983	59	41	46	54	45	55
1982	55	44	50	49	40	59
1981	77	22	64	34	51	47

Interest Group Ratings

Year	ADA	ACU	AFL-CIO	CCUS
1988	60	33	83	62
1987	80	15	90	47
1986	75	33	87	44
1985	55	36	71	55
1984	50	36	45	68
1983	80	16	76	37
1982	70	26	56	35
1981	50	40	58	72

1 Thomas M. Foglietta (D)

Of Philadelphia — Elected 1980

Born: Dec. 3, 1928, Philadelphia, Pa.
Education: St. Joseph's College, B.A. 1949; Temple U., J.D. 1952.
Occupation: Lawyer.
Family: Single.
Religion: Roman Catholic.
Political Career: Philadelphia City Council, 1955-75; GOP nominee for mayor of Philadelphia, 1975.
Capitol Office: 231 Cannon Bldg. 20515; 225-4731.

In Washington: Foglietta stands somewhat apart from Pennsylvania's large faction of urban machine Democrats, who live for local politics. Nearing a full decade of service in the House, Foglietta is as comfortable talking about human rights in South Korea or the intricacies of the SDI program as he is about the workaday problems of his Philadelphia district.

"Unemployment, jobs, the environment, defense, the deficit, inflation — those are the most important things we [congressmen] have to do," Foglietta once said. "I think it is a disservice to the hard-working people of the 1st District to suggest that all they are concerned with is potholes."

Yet it would be wrong to say that Foglietta does not pay attention to his political base. When Armed Services Committee colleagues are asked to associate an issue with Foglietta, they respond, "Philadelphia Navy Yard." And in his contact with voters, he still knows how to come across as "Tommy," a street-smart South Philadelphian with an agile, independent mind and a reformist streak.

During the 100th Congress, Foglietta lobbied hard to keep the Philadelphia Naval Shipyard, located in his district, off the list of military bases to be recommended for closure by a presidential commission. Motivated by the inclusion of the shipyard on a 1985 Pentagon list of possible closures, Foglietta marshaled a coalition of legislators from the tri-state (Pennsylvania, New Jersey and Delaware) area to defend the facility, at which battleships and aircraft carriers are maintained.

In November 1988, Foglietta released a six-page report, with two long appendixes, intended "to demonstrate to the commission's attention that the Philadelphia Navy Yard is the Navy's most efficient and most productive shipyard." Though it is not clear that Foglietta's campaign was a major factor, the commission spared the Philadelphia shipyard from cutbacks when it reported to President Reagan the following month.

However, the commission did recommend the shutdown of the Philadelphia Naval Hospital, an aging facility in the southern part of the 1st District. Foglietta then joined with GOP Sen. John Heinz to propose building a replacement hospital nearby. Foglietta noted that the nearest military hospital serving the area's large veteran population is 45 miles away at Fort Dix, N.J., also targeted for closure.

Foglietta also speaks up for local interests on the Merchant Marine and Fisheries Committee. As chairman of the Oversight and Investigations Subcommittee (a position he assumed during the 100th Congress), Foglietta held hearings on the importation of illegal drugs, disguised as consumer goods, through ports such as Philadelphia. In November 1987, he wrote an opinion article in the *Philadelphia Inquirer* assailing an experimental proposal to incinerate toxic wastes at sea, a plan that would have required the shipment of dangerous chemicals past the city on the Delaware River.

His attention to these local issues provides Foglietta with the political leeway to pursue his esoteric interests in defense policy and international affairs. Though careful, because of his role as the Navy Yard's protector, to avoid the image of an anti-defense gadfly, Foglietta criticized the Reagan administration for an "obsession with expensive, complex, high-tech military hardware."

In the 99th Congress, Foglietta challenged the administration's strategic defense initiative (SDI), and suggested that Congress set up a nonpartisan board of scientists and other policy experts to determine the technical feasibility of SDI. That plan never emerged from committee, but the House did endorse his amendment to the defense authorization bill prohibiting any SDI development that would use nuclear explosions in space.

Foglietta also has taken an interest, unusual for the generally insular Pennsylvania delegation, in the restoration of full democratic procedures in South Korea. He and several other Americans attracted international publicity in 1985 when they were roughed up by government police at the Seoul airport while accompanying exiled opposition leader Kim

Pennsylvania 1

South and Central Philadelphia

William Penn's statue atop Philadelphia's City Hall looks out on a city of distinct ethnic neighborhoods, each with the clannishness and occasional suspicion of outsiders more commonly associated with small towns. The diversity is most apparent in the 1st, which takes in the wealthy liberals of Center City, the Italians of South Philadelphia, the Irish and Poles of the "river wards" and the blacks along North Broad Street. While Ronald Reagan did well among the white ethnics in 1980 and 1984, he did not carry the 1st either time. In 1988, the district went comfortably for Democrat Michael S. Dukakis.

Blue-collar South Philadelphia holds most of the city's piers and the Philadelphia Navy Yard, as well as its huge sports complex — the Spectrum and Veterans and JFK stadiums. Italians are the dominant group here, and though most of them now vote Democratic in local elections, the Republican Party is the party of tradition: A generation ago, most Italian-Americans in Philadelphia sided with the GOP because the Irish controlled the Democratic Party. The law-and-order appeal of former Mayor Frank Rizzo, who grew up here and walked its streets as a patrolman, is strong among the dock and factory workers.

The one ward west of the Schuylkill River included in the 1st has most of the liberal academic community of Drexel University and the University of Pennsylvania. Other centers of liberal Democratic activity are Society Hill and Olde City, the sites of many of the city's historic landmarks and now affluent restoration areas. The gentrification of nearby Queen Village and Fairmount is displacing ethnic whites who esteem Rizzo-style politics with young professionals who disdain it.

Running north from Center City, the Frankford El railway binds together the river wards, a grimy part of town where factories and warehouses sit cheek-by-jowl with row houses. The white ethnic voters here are as Democratic as those in South Philly at the local level, and somewhat more likely to support Democrats for federal offices. But they are conservatives; they matched South Philly in backing Rizzo.

Blacks make up about one-third of the 1st. They are clustered in the rundown neighborhoods extending into North Philadelphia on either side of North Broad Street. The academic enclave of Temple University sits along Broad Street as well.

Population: 515,145. White 310,738 (60%), Black 164,862 (32%), Other 10,310 (2%). Spanish origin 50,440 (10%). 18 and over 374,046 (73%), 65 and over 65,470 (13%). Median age: 29.

Dae Jung on his re-entry into South Korea.

At Home: Foglietta's outward-looking interests caused him some political difficulty early in his House career. He was challenged in the 1984 and 1986 primaries by Jimmy Tayoun, who, in the state House and then the Philadelphia City Council, became famous for tending to the personal needs of his constituents. One Tayoun campaign leaflet noted that he "keeps faith with the Bill Barrett tradition of personal evening service." Barrett, who represented the 1st for 29 years following World War II, was a bit player in Washington, but was very popular in Philadelphia because he returned there every night to hold evening office hours.

In addition to their differing attitudes toward a congressman's role, there were other contrasts between Foglietta and Tayoun in the 1984 primary: Foglietta drew strong support from the district's black voters and from young, liberal professionals in the affluent Center City area. Tayoun's most faithful backers were old-line, working-class whites, including many Irish and Poles in the "river wards" along the Delaware River. Tayoun won the endorsement of a majority of the 1st's Democratic ward leaders.

The crucial votes were in the Italian community of South Philadelphia. Tayoun, who lives there, and voiced more conservative views than Foglietta on social issues, hoped Italians would feel they had more in common with him than with Foglietta, a liberal who lives in a fashionable Center City high-rise apartment.

But Foglietta's roots in the Italian community are deep. His father was a Republican city councilman, and Foglietta followed in those footsteps, serving on the City Council for two decades. With Italian ethnic loyalty prevailing in South Philadelphia and the Rev. Jesse Jackson's presidential candidacy pulling out a large primary vote in the district's black wards, Foglietta won renomination.

When Tayoun ran again in 1986, he sought — in part, at least — to oust the incumbent by making the rematch a referendum on Philadelphia's controversial black Mayor W. Wilson Goode. The mayor — a prominent Foglietta supporter in 1984 — saw his popularity sink in the wake of the city's disastrous 1985 ouster of the MOVE cult and a deterioration in the delivery of basic city services.

Tayoun's effort to link the two politicians failed, though, as Foglietta kept Goode at a distance. And in the rematch, the incumbent had much more money than Tayoun and broader support from Democratic ward leaders. The result was a much more substantial victory. Foglietta's tally — a tenuous 52 percent in 1984 — jumped to 60 percent, and he expanded his base from liberals, blacks and Italians to include some non-Italian ethnics in the "river wards."

In 1988, Foglietta finally earned an uncontested primary, and as usual, scant competition in the general election.

Foglietta got his seat in Congress in 1980 by shedding his lifelong GOP label and fighting his way through a complicated political situation. He ran in November as an independent, normally a guarantee of failure. But Democratic incumbent Michael "Ozzie" Myers, indicted in the Abscam bribery scandal, had won renomination, leaving anti-Myers Democrats without a candidate in the general election. Foglietta became that candidate. When Myers was convicted on bribery charges and expelled from the House Oct. 2, Foglietta gained the strength he needed to win. Once elected, he acknowledged his political debt by voting with Democrats to organize the 97th Congress.

To gain a second term as a Democrat in 1982, Foglietta survived a tough primary that pitted him not only against another incumbent but against the organization of former Mayor Frank Rizzo, still a powerful figure in the 1st. As a Republican, Foglietta had unsuccessfully challenged Rizzo for mayor in 1975.

The 1982 redistricting had paired Foglietta with U.S. Rep. Joseph F. Smith, a machine Democrat and Rizzo loyalist. Rizzo's support helped make Smith competitive in South Philadelphia. But it also brought out a large vote for Foglietta from blacks and Center City liberals antagonistic toward Rizzo.

Smith won big majorities in his home "river wards," but overall, Foglietta won 13 wards to Smith's 10 — even though Smith had the backing of most of the ward leaders.

Committees

Armed Services (12th of 31 Democrats)
Military Installations and Facilities; Research and Development; Seapower and Strategic and Critical Materials

Merchant Marine and Fisheries (7th of 26 Democrats)
Oversight and Investigations (chairman); Merchant Marine

Select Hunger (13th of 18 Democrats)

Elections

1988 General

Thomas M. Foglietta (D)	128,076	(76%)
William J. O'Brien (R)	39,749	(24%)

1986 General

Thomas M. Foglietta (D)	88,224	(75%)
Anthony J. Mucciolo (R)	29,811	(25%)

Previous Winning Percentages: 1984 (75%) **1982** (72%) **1980** (38%)

District Vote For President

	1988	1984	1980	1976
D	105,706 (64%)	140,157 (65%)	117,737 (61%)	137,596 (66%)
R	57,788 (35%)	75,202 (35%)	60,347 (31%)	67,057 (32%)
I			11,420 (6%)	

Campaign Finance

	Receipts	Receipts from PACs	Expend-itures
1988			
Foglietta (D)	$337,467	$172,700 (51%)	$238,277
O'Brien (R) †	$4,182	0	$1,643
1986			
Foglietta (D)	$429,075	$204,445 (48%)	$427,561

† Totals based on incomplete data.

Key Votes

1987

Raise speed limit to 65 mph	Y
Approve Gephardt "fair trade" amendment	Y
Ban testing of larger nuclear weapons	?
Delay "re-flagging" of Kuwaiti tankers	Y
Approve tax-raising deficit-reduction bill	Y

1988

Approve aid to Nicaraguan contras	N
Enact civil rights restoration bill over Reagan veto	Y
Kill 60-day plant-closing notification measure	N
Pass omnibus trade bill over Reagan veto	Y
Approve death penalty for drug-related murders	N
Bar federal funds for abortions in cases of rape and incest	N
Oppose seven-day waiting period for purchase of handguns	N

Voting Studies

	Presidential Support		Party Unity		Conservative Coalition	
Year	**S**	**O**	**S**	**O**	**S**	**O**
1988	16	70	83	4	8	79
1987	16	77	81	2	21	72
1986	16	68	79	5	10	82
1985	20	75	90	4	13	80
1984	22	57	80	2	7	83
1983	24	68	87	4	11	85
1982	32	56	81	5	18	77
1981	25	58	80	8	13	73

Interest Group Ratings

Year	ADA	ACU	AFL-CIO	CCUS
1988	90	4	92	42
1987	84	0	93	8
1986	90	5	100	14
1985	90	5	94	14
1984	95	0	100	50
1983	90	4	100	20
1982	85	5	100	20
1981	90	0	87	11

2 William H. Gray III (D)

Of Philadelphia — Elected 1978

Born: Aug. 20, 1941, Baton Rouge, La.
Education: Franklin and Marshall College, B.A. 1963; Drew Theological Seminary, M.Div. 1966; Princeton Theological Seminary, Th.M. 1970.
Occupation: Clergyman.
Family: Wife, Andrea Dash; three children.
Religion: Baptist.
Political Career: Sought Democratic nomination for U.S. House, 1976.
Capitol Office: 2454 Rayburn Bldg. 20515; 225-4001.

In Washington: As the minister of one of Philadelphia's largest black churches, Gray is used to preaching to the choir. As a politician, however, he has risen quickly in the House leadership by making new converts among those of different political denominations, and by breaking with his own liberal dogma.

He has won the favor of Democratic leaders eager to showcase prominent blacks. In one of the House's toughest assignments, the Budget Committee chairmanship, he showed uncommon skills as a coalition-builder and party spokesman. When that four-year stint expired at the end of 1988, colleagues promoted him to chairman of the House Democratic Caucus and, just months later, to the suddenly vacated No. 3 job of House majority whip.

Just as he was about to ascend to that post, however, Gray became the latest House Democratic leader to figure in a potential scandal; the Justice Department confirmed in late May 1989 that it was examining allegations of payroll padding on Gray's staff. Attorney General Dick Thornburgh said Gray himself was not a target of the probe, and Gray's comfortable margin over his two rivals in the whip election suggested that his stock was still strong. But only the unfolding of events will determine whether he indeed has firm footing on a political ladder that could potentially lead to a historic first — the first black Speaker, or the first black nominee on a major party's national ticket.

Gray has been no Democratic token; he has earned his honors. Still, he is increasingly sensitive to suggestions that he is the white man's alternative to the Rev. Jesse Jackson.

From the time he arrived in Congress just a decade ago as a first-time officeholder in a class full of seasoned pros, Gray jumped knowingly into House politics by aligning with those outside his natural base of urban liberals and the Black Caucus. In particular, fellow Pennsylvanian John P. Murtha, a power broker with a small-town, white ethnic constituency, helped Gray win choice seats on Budget and on Steering and Policy as a freshman. Two years later, Gray landed a coveted place on the Appropriations Committee.

By late 1984, overcoming concern that a black liberal could not be a serious budget-cutter, Gray had put together a diverse regional and ideological coalition to win the Budget chairmanship. The coalition mirrored the unity he would help bring to the once-fractured party over the next four years, as Democrats finally assaulted Reagan's fiscal policies.

The testament to Gray's success is the combined Democratic vote for the four budget resolutions he shepherded through the House in Reagan's second term — 919-77. That means hardly more defections over four years than the party suffered in most single years in Reagan's first term. A clever consensus builder, Gray treated the budget process as a political puzzle, not an economic problem; he saw the budget for what it is: a political statement rather than a blueprint for fiscal governance.

That is not to suggest Gray did not make enemies. His natural allies among Budget and Black Caucus liberals groused throughout the 100th Congress that in his drive to cut deals with conservatives, Gray left liberals' interests — and some of his promises to them — on the cutting room floor. Several would later support his rivals for conference chairman. But Gray retained the trust of Southern Boll Weevils such as Texans Marvin Leath and Charles W. Stenholm, who helped him end the Democratic desertions of the early Reagan years. In a speech to the Democratic Caucus supporting Gray's election as its chairman, Stenholm praised the big city Easterner for showing "West Texas tractor-seat common sense."

From mid-1987, when Gray first announced his candidacy to succeed Caucus Chairman Richard A. Gephardt, he was the front-runner in a contest still more than a year away. He seasoned his political claim to the post with money, giving more than $136,000 to House Democrats. The final tally in December 1988 was 146 votes for Gray, 80 for Caucus Vice Chairman Mary Rose Oakar of Ohio and 33 for

Pennsylvania 2

North and West Philadelphia

Generally speaking, the 2nd is black, poor and Democratic. Whites are just one-fifth of the population, and one in every three residents lives below the poverty line. Democrats Jimmy Carter in 1980, Walter F. Mondale in 1984, and Michael S. Dukakis in 1988 all scored huge wins here, while losing statewide.

But there are wide variations in income and neighborhood character. The 2nd includes the poorest, most blighted areas of black North Philadelphia, but also takes in many well-kept working-class black sections of West Philly. The far northern reaches of the 2nd are quasi-suburban, blending into affluent Montgomery County. At the southern end is Center City's Rittenhouse Square area, filled with condo-dwelling yuppies and with banks, insurance companies and other white-collar employers.

North Philly has more of a reputation as a crime zone than West Philly, so it is ironic that one of the city's worst disasters occurred in West Philadelphia — the May 1985 police battle against the cult group MOVE that killed 11 and destroyed five dozen houses in a black neighborhood at the western edge of the 2nd.

Cutting a wide green swath through the central part of the district is vast Fairmount Park, which flanks the Schuylkill River and contains the city's famous art museum, zoo and "boathouse row." Adjoining the park in the northwest part of the 2nd is Germantown. Once home to Philadelphia's upper crust, it and nearby Mt. Airy now are racially mixed and mostly middle class.

The whites in the Rittenhouse Square area are not a large part of the district vote, but they are influential. Along with nearby Society Hill in the 1st District, the Rittenhouse area is the center for the reform movement in Philadelphia politics. As an activist legislator, Gray is popular among the liberal, socially conscious Rittenhouse voters.

Population: 517,215. White 94,623 (18%), Black 413,852 (80%), Other 4,137 (1%). Spanish origin 6,229 (1%). 18 and over 378,182 (73%), 65 and over 68,596 (13%). Median age: 31.

Mike Synar of Oklahoma. The next June, when Majority Whip Tony Coelho resigned rather than face an ethics investigation, Gray was the immediate favorite to replace him. He took 134 votes on the first ballot — four more than the majority he needed — to 97 votes for David E. Bonior of Michigan and 30 for Beryl Anthony Jr. of Arkansas.

Gray's approach to the leadership, like his style as Budget chairman, probably was best described by Gray himself when he was defining his role as chairman of the Democratic Party's 1988 platform committee. "My job is to make sure all your views come out," he told the platform writers, "and to make sure they all come together."

Those who know only that Gray is a clergyman can be surprised to meet him. Engaging, witty, and casually irreverent, he is as natural a politician in the House as he is on the streets of Philadelphia. He moves through the floor as smoothly as he glides through basketball games in the gym — always in motion, using others to block for him, throwing an elbow now and then. He does not like to give up the ball, and he loves to win.

Gray is never at a loss for words, but his words rarely reveal much about his plans. Behind his strutting self-confidence is a large supply of reticence and caution; he was often reluctant even to show his hand to other Democrats on Budget. He let members debate issues for hours, exasperating them but ultimately forcing them into commitments. Meeting perhaps the hardest test of all, he got along better than his predecessors with the territorial chairmen of the authorizing committees and Appropriations, who do not conceal their disdain for Budget and the spending limitations it seeks to impose.

Gray's skills at Budget politics were evident in 1983, when as a relatively junior member (he had left the committee from 1981-83), he broke a logjam in a House-Senate conference by proposing a reserve fund for new spending to be authorized later by Congress. This satisfied liberals seeking an anti-recession initiative, while conservatives concerned about costs knew that few programs would ever be authorized.

The next year, Gray's campaign for the chairmanship showed his behind-the-scenes acumen. Most Democrats concentrated on the rivalry between James R. Jones, who had been Budget chairman for four years, and Leon E. Panetta, who wanted the job. To be eligible for the chairmanship, both needed a change of the rule limiting service on Budget.

Gray sidestepped the Jones-Panetta argument, simply asking members to vote for him if the rule was not changed. In the end, Speaker Thomas P. O'Neill Jr. opposed the change and the Democratic Caucus went along. When Martin Frost of Texas launched a last-minute bid for chairman, he found Gray had the votes sewn up.

O'Neill took another step that aided Gray. The Speaker named to Budget three Democrats — Leath, Jim Slattery of Kansas and Buddy MacKay of Florida — who served as able links to party moderates and conservatives; with all points of view represented on Budget, Gray could be confident of selling his proposals to the entire Democratic House if he had his panel's support. In 1985, the fiscal conservatives failed to sway the committee, but they promised to support Gray's budget in return for a chance to offer their own on the floor. Theirs lost badly; Gray won all but 15 Democrats and even got 24 Republican votes.

That year, Gray played conspicuously little role in negotiations over the Senate bill that became the 1985 Gramm-Rudman balanced budget law. He did not want to offend committee chairmen by appearing to grab more power over the budget process, and also he did not like the law's approach of automatic cuts across the board to reach a balanced budget by 1991.

In 1986, confronted with Gramm-Rudman's requirement that the deficit be less than $144 billion, Gray hung back to force the Republican White House and Senate to go first — then rushed out a budget that purported to beat the Senate version by almost $7 billion. That resolution was built on compromises forged by the Leath-Slattery-MacKay group, matching defense cuts and modest tax increases with a lid on social spending. In the end, however, Congress and the White House agreed to reach the deficit target largely by accounting gimmicks rather than taxes or spending cuts.

After Democrats regained control of the Senate in 1987, Gray took the lead on that year's budget. In committee Democrats' private talks, he first had to smooth over the growing tension between conservatives concerned about defense cuts and liberals unwilling to endure more domestic program cuts. Republicans, meanwhile, decided not to participate at all, either in committee or on the floor. They simply attacked the Democrats' plan, while offering no substitute of their own and even helping vote down Reagan's budget, 27-394. Gray's budget passed the House without a single GOP vote.

But that year and the next, Gray's fellow Democrats in the Senate would prove the bigger obstacle. The 1987 conference, begun amid optimistic predictions of a quick settlement, all but collapsed; Gray negotiated privately with Senate Budget Committee Chairman Lawton Chiles, whose demands reflected his desire to assuage both conservative Democrats and some Republicans, given Senate Democrats' small majority. It was at this time that Gray's former liberal allies began muttering that he was giving too much away. Still the impasse persisted, until unfavorable publicity spurred congressional leaders to compel an agreement.

Meanwhile in 1987, Gray agreed with Republicans to help fix the Gramm-Rudman law that he had done so little to enact; the Supreme Court had declared a key aspect of its automatic-cuts procedures unconstitutional. Gray was convinced that the law's threatened defense cuts would force Reagan finally to compromise about serious deficit reduction. "Although I am institutionally opposed to the automatic approach," he said, "politically I think it is the only way to engage the president in this debate."

Gray's final year as Budget chairman in 1988 was eased by the fact that, in late 1987, Reagan and congressional leaders did reach a modest, two-year budget agreement. Critics said 1988 was the "Year of the Big Wink." Partisanship was minimal. Yet relations between House and Senate Democrats deteriorated, in a clash that was less one of substance than of egos and institutional rivalries.

In conference, Gray and Chiles exchanged insults and charges of bad faith. Allied with his GOP counterpart, Pete V. Domenici, Chiles insisted on more space and science funding while House Democrats held out for education and anti-poverty programs. Finally the two sides agreed to disagree, but meanwhile they had been rendered all but irrelevant as the House and Senate Appropriations committees began work without a final budget resolution.

Gray's surprise election as Budget chairman at the start of the 99th Congress marked him as the most powerful black member of Congress, stirring some resentment among more senior Black Caucus members. But his new prominence boosted the campaign for economic sanctions against South Africa's apartheid government.

It was Gray's bill to ban new investment or loans in South Africa that the House leadership pushed in 1986. But on the floor, the bill's GOP opponents allowed a far tougher bill requiring total U.S. disinvestment to pass by voice vote, reckoning that passage of such a radical measure would doom the push for sanctions altogether.

Instead, coming in an election year, the House action pressured the GOP Senate to pass a tougher bill than it would have otherwise, and that version became law over Reagan's veto. In the meantime, Gray had to take a back seat in publicity to California's Ronald V. Dellums, sponsor of the stronger House measure.

In his first term, as a member of Foreign Affairs, Gray won establishment of a new African development program, an unusual achievement for a freshman. At Appropriations, he has fought hard for Africa aid programs. He has not been active on that panel since becoming Budget chairman and now a leadership official, but Gray works through his staff and allies on

Appropriations to attend to hometown interests, such as mass transit and housing.

At Home: The church, a dominant institution in black North Philadelphia, was Gray's springboard to a political career. Like his father and grandfather before him, Gray is the chief minister of the 4,000-member Bright Hope Baptist Church. Two Sundays every month, he returns home to preach there. On election days, his parishioners are out working for him.

This church support was vital to him in 1978, when he ousted 73-year-old Robert N. C. Nix Jr., whom Gray dubbed "the phantom," charging that he made only infrequent visits to the district.

Nix had the allegiance of ward leaders and organized labor, and had held off Gray by 339 votes in the 1976 Democratic primary. But Gray trounced him in 1978. Gray got endorsements from such national black figures as Atlanta Mayor Maynard Jackson and Coretta Scott King. He also won the backing of the white Philadelphia business community.

A few old-guard Nix allies still view Gray with suspicion, but his main political troubles have come from young militants who say he is too close to the white power structure.

One faction made an attempt to dump him in 1982. The challenge came from Milton Street, a tough-talking black state senator. Street had switched his party allegiance from Democratic to Republican in 1980 as part of a deal that brought the GOP control of the state Senate.

Street tried to find a black to challenge Gray in the Democratic primary, and when none emerged he decided to become a candidate himself in the general election. The Republican filing deadline had passed, however, so he had to go on the November ballot as an independent.

The result was not even close. Gray drew more than three-fourths of the vote, securing his hold on the district.

Committees

Appropriations (25th of 35 Democrats)
Foreign Operations; Transportation and Related Agencies

District of Columbia (4th of 8 Democrats)
Fiscal Affairs and Health; Government Operations and Metropolitan Affairs

Elections

1988 General

William H. Gray III (D)	184,322	(94%)
Richard L. Harsch (R)	12,365	(6%)

1986 General

William H. Gray III (D)	128,399	(98%)

Previous Winning Percentages: **1984** (91%) **1982** (76%) **1980** (96%) **1978** (82%)

District Vote For President

	1988	1984	1980	1976
D	189,477 (91%)	211,740 (89%)	179,978 (86%)	171,872 (82%)
R	17,125 (8%)	24,613 (10%)	19,058 (9%)	32,849 (16%)
I			7,335 (4%)	

Campaign Finance

	Receipts	Receipts from PACs	Expend-itures
1988			
Gray (D)	$656,859	$377,752 (58%)	$660,456
1986			
Gray (D)	$663,653	$460,861 (69%)	$551,836

Key Votes

1987

Raise speed limit to 65 mph	N
Approve Gephardt "fair trade" amendment	Y
Ban testing of larger nuclear weapons	Y
Delay "re-flagging" of Kuwaiti tankers	Y
Approve tax-raising deficit-reduction bill	Y

1988

Approve aid to Nicaraguan contras	N
Enact civil rights restoration bill over Reagan veto	Y
Kill 60-day plant-closing notification measure	N
Pass omnibus trade bill over Reagan veto	Y
Approve death penalty for drug-related murders	N
Bar federal funds for abortions in cases of rape and incest	?
Oppose seven-day waiting period for purchase of handguns	N

Voting Studies

	Presidential Support		Party Unity		Conservative Coalition	
Year	**S**	**O**	**S**	**O**	**S**	**O**
1988	14	70	78	2	11	74
1987	14	78	85	1	12	74
1986	13	77	88	1	8	82
1985	15	78	82	3	13	73
1984	19	73	90	3	7	86
1983	11	78	93	1	2	93
1982	21	65	80	5	8	84
1981	29	59	87	2	4	88

Interest Group Ratings

Year	ADA	ACU	AFL-CIO	CCUS
1988	95	0	100	31
1987	92	0	100	0
1986	80	5	92	33
1985	95	0	93	15
1984	90	0	92	38
1983	85	0	100	21
1982	85	11	100	26
1981	90	0	93	6

3 Robert A. Borski (D)

Of Philadelphia — Elected 1982

Born: Oct. 20, 1948, Philadelphia, Pa.
Education: U. of Baltimore, B.A. 1971.
Occupation: Stockbroker.
Family: Divorced; three children.
Religion: Roman Catholic.
Political Career: Pa. House, 1977-83.
Capitol Office: 314 Cannon Bldg. 20515; 225-8251.

In Washington: Borski came to Congress after three terms as a backbencher in the Pennsylvania Legislature, and nothing in his record over three House terms suggests he is changing his style of representation.

In a House where many crave a role in national policy making, Borski focuses on his committee work, using the Public Works and Merchant Marine panels to attend to his Philadelphia district. Though he is not a power on either committee, Borski monitors activity affecting Philadelphia's port and strives to prevent federal cutbacks in his district. With the help of Philadelphia colleague William H. Gray III, who sits on the Appropriations Transportation Subcommittee, Borski has co-authored proposals for mass-transit projects, including one to reconstruct a local elevated railway line.

Borski rarely speaks on the floor or attracts publicity outside Philadelphia; he is not well-known to many of his colleagues. But he is a reliable vote for his party leadership on most key issues, except abortion. And he has tallied perfect AFL-CIO vote scores in all but one of his six years in the House.

Borski is a sharp contrast to the man he unseated in 1982, Rep. Charles Dougherty, a high-profile moderate Republican who used his Armed Services seat not only to look out for Philadelphia naval installations but also to participate in broader policy debates.

Borski, first elected with the help of Irish-Americans (who make up roughly one-third of his district's population), sparked some controversy as a freshman during a visit to British-ruled Northern Ireland. While on an overseas tour, Borski paid an unofficial visit to the strife-torn region and met with leaders of Sinn Fein, the political wing of the Irish Republican Army, which militantly opposes British rule.

Borski's visit caught British officials by surprise; Sinn Fein notified the media of the meeting, and the publicity ruffled American and British feathers alike. The fuss seemed to puzzle Borski. "I know I've created a stir, and quite frankly, I'm confused by it," he said. "I've gone about normal business."

At Home: Borski may not cut a high profile in Washington, but his concentration on local issues and his assiduous courtship of constituents has given him a firm grip on a seat that Republicans feel could be theirs.

Overwhelmingly white and middle class, the 3rd was the only Philadelphia district to support George Bush in 1988 and is the only one to elect a GOP congressman in the last three decades. But by playing the role of the old-time urban congressman, Borski has rebuffed GOP challenges.

Borski launched himself toward Congress by managing another candidate's disastrous campaign — the losing 1981 special election effort of Democratic City Chairman David Glancey in the old 3rd District. Borski emerged from the effort with greater visibility and a determination to run for Congress himself. In 1982, when redistricting grafted his state legislative base in the blue-collar "river ward" of Bridesburg onto Dougherty's territory in Philadelphia's semi-suburban Northeast, Borski made his move.

He became a consensus choice, partly because more experienced Democrats stayed out, convinced Dougherty was too strong. Despite the recession, several unions sided with the more dynamic and articulate Dougherty. But concerns about reductions in Social Security helped Borski, and Dougherty's disdain for the Irish Republican Army hurt him. With economic discontent strong in blue-collar Philadelphia, the clean-cut Borski seemed a good vehicle for protesting hard times. He won by 2,664 votes.

After Borski won easily in 1984, Dougherty tried a comeback in 1986, only to lose the GOP primary to former state Sen. Robert A. Rovner. But Rovner was dogged by controversy: He had lost his Senate seat in 1974 after being indicted for extortion and income-tax evasion. Although acquitted, he drew criticism after that for hosting bus trips to Atlantic City for Bucks County district judges.

Rovner tried to tie Borski to Philadelphia's controversial black mayor, W. Wilson Goode, but Borski kept the focus on his steadiness and accessibility, and won by over 40,000 votes. In 1988, Borski again topped 60 percent.

Pennsylvania 3

Northeast Philadelphia

In a city of deep-rooted neighborhoods, Philadelphia's 3rd District is somewhat of an anomaly. With the exception of the "river wards" — the Polish and Irish communities that front the Delaware River — most of the 3rd is made up of people who have migrated there in the past generation from other parts of the city. This is particularly true in the Great Northeast (so named because of its geographic expanse). In much of this area, the surroundings are more suburban than urban. In the 1950s, there were still some farms here.

Much of the migration from the inner city came about after the growth of the black population in North and West Philadelphia. This accounts, in part, for the overwhelmingly white population of the 3rd. Concern about crime inspires conservative social attitudes in the neat little houses along the tree-lined streets of this area. Former Mayor Frank Rizzo's tough law-and-order image made him a hero here.

The Great Northeast has a large Jewish population, concentrated west of Roosevelt Boulevard. Farther east, Irish and other Catholic ethnics predominate.

The 3rd is the only Philadelphia district where Republicans have a chance to be competitive. Ronald Reagan won it against Jimmy Carter in 1980, taking all except two wards. And even though 1982 redistricting added some Democratic river wards, Reagan won the 3rd again in 1984, as did George Bush in 1988. The areas added in the remap were Frankford and Bridesburg, both of which have been hit hard by factory layoffs.

On the presidential level, the best ward for Republicans is the 66th, a favorite residence of police officers and firefighters. Prevailing opinion is different in Oak Lane and West Oak Lane, two sections that line the border with suburban Montgomery County. Here, young professional whites and middle-class blacks prefer a more liberal politics.

Population: 516,154. White 470,248 (91%), Black 39,120 (8%), Other 4,128 (1%). Spanish origin 5,683 (1%). 18 and over 391,605 (76%), 65 and over 80,592 (16%). Median age: 35.

Committees

Merchant Marine and Fisheries (11th of 26 Democrats)
Merchant Marine; Oceanography

Public Works and Transportation (11th of 31 Democrats)
Economic Development; Investigations and Oversight; Water Resources

Select Aging (20th of 39 Democrats)
Health and Long-Term Care

Elections

1988 General		
Robert A. Borski (D)	135,590	(63%)
Mark Matthews (R)	78,909	(37%)
1988 Primary		
Robert A. Borski (D)	61,440	(91%)
John J. Hughes (D)	5,801	(9%)
1986 General		
Robert A. Borski (D)	107,804	(62%)
Robert A. Rovner (R)	66,693	(38%)

Previous Winning Percentages: **1984** (64%) **1982** (50%)

District Vote For President

	1988		1984		1980		1976	
D	105,791	(47%)	116,330	(46%)	100,811	(41%)	148,687	(56%)
R	115,404	(52%)	136,340	(54%)	124,484	(50%)	110,829	(42%)
I					19,789	(8%)		

Campaign Finance

	Receipts	Receipts from PACs	Expend-itures
1988			
Borski (D)	$337,723	$189,654 (56%)	$250,480
Matthews (R)	$23,071	0	$23,101
1986			
Borski (D)	$409,799	$269,014 (66%)	$391,980
Rovner (R)	$446,282	$6,450 (1%)	$446,282

Key Votes

1987	
Raise speed limit to 65 mph	N
Approve Gephardt "fair trade" amendment	Y
Ban testing of larger nuclear weapons	Y
Delay "re-flagging" of Kuwaiti tankers	Y
Approve tax-raising deficit-reduction bill	Y
1988	
Approve aid to Nicaraguan contras	N
Enact civil rights restoration bill over Reagan veto	Y
Kill 60-day plant-closing notification measure	N
Pass omnibus trade bill over Reagan veto	Y
Approve death penalty for drug-related murders	Y
Bar federal funds for abortions in cases of rape and incest	Y
Oppose seven-day waiting period for purchase of handguns	N

Voting Studies

	Presidential Support		Party Unity		Conservative Coalition	
Year	**S**	**O**	**S**	**O**	**S**	**O**
1988	26	73	92	6	24	74
1987	19	81	91	3	26	72
1986	20	77	93	6	24	76
1985	24	74	94	4	20	78
1984	30	68	93	6	17	81
1983	21	73	91	6	16	83

Interest Group Ratings

Year	ADA	ACU	AFL-CIO	CCUS
1988	80	12	100	23
1987	80	5	100	13
1986	75	10	100	33
1985	80	5	88	23
1984	75	8	100	38
1983	85	4	100	20

4 Joe Kolter (D)

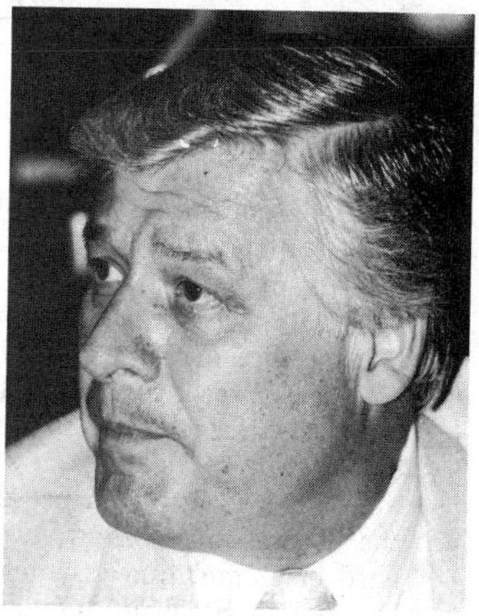

Of New Brighton — Elected 1982

Born: Sept. 3, 1926, McDonald, Ohio.
Education: Geneva College, B.S. and B.A. 1950.
Military Career: Air Force, 1945-46.
Occupation: Accountant.
Family: Wife, Dorothy Gray; four children.
Religion: Roman Catholic.
Political Career: New Brighton City Council, 1962-66; Pa. House, 1968-83; sought Democratic nomination for U.S. House, 1974.
Capitol Office: 212 Cannon Bldg. 20515; 225-2565.

In Washington: After an early 1987 dabble in foreign affairs that brought him both success and some embarrassment, Kolter has resumed the legislative style that marked his first two terms — concentrating on committee work and voicing the concerns of industrial workers in his economically distressed district.

Following revelations that proceeds from U.S. arms sales to Iran had been diverted to the Nicaraguan contras, Kolter proposed in January 1987 that additional contra aid be withheld until all previous aid was accounted for. A modified version of this proposal passed the House in March, but it died in the Senate.

Kolter stirred up trouble for himself, however, with a TV appearance on C-SPAN during which he referred to the U.S.-backed contra forces as "communists" and portrayed UNO, a umbrella contra organization, as an individual rather than a group. Kolter's staff later explained that he meant to call the contras "totalitarian" instead of "communist," and blamed his errors on the fact that he was a last-minute replacement on the show and had misread his notes.

Kolter got into the contra issue partly because many of his constituents are not keen on sending aid abroad when blue-collar workers are struggling to make ends meet. A member of the Public Works Committee, Kolter has persistently demanded that the White House do more to help the import-battered domestic steel industry and the "hungry, cold and desperate" unemployed. In 1988, Kolter lambasted the World Bank for a $400 million loan to help the Mexican steel industry. In response to pressure from Rust Belt congressmen, the Reagan administration voted against the loan.

Kolter uses his post on Public Works to try to funnel federal dollars to the 4th. Sometimes he succeeds; he got a "demonstration project" for his district into the 1987 highway bill. But he has also run into obstacles, including Norman Y. Mineta, who chaired the Aviation Subcommittee in the 100th Congress.

Kolter took the unusual step of inviting committee colleagues to contribute projects to an amendment he planned to offer to the 1987 airport-reauthorization bill. This was a challenge to Mineta, who opposed naming specific programs. One member labeled Kolter's $200 million proposal the "pork amendment of 1987." But Democrat Douglas H. Bosco defended Kolter, saying the only reason to be on Public Works is "to bring home projects.... [It is] certainly not for intellectual stimulation." The amendment was defeated 9-18.

Still, Kolter's political skills on Public Works are much better than his luck in national politics. In the 1988 presidential sweepstakes, he started out backing Gary Hart, switched to Joseph R. Biden Jr. and then to Richard A. Gephardt before settling on Michael S. Dukakis. Kolter quipped that he considered backing George Bush to get him out of the race.

At Home: During 1982 campaign appearances, Kolter repeatedly told the story of a steelworker friend who had been laid off. "His little girl came into the kitchen and asked, 'Why can't my daddy get a job?' " Kolter would recount. Then he would clutch his heart and say, "It kind of gets you right here."

That performance, eventually made into a TV ad, was more effective than anything offered by GOP Rep. Eugene V. Atkinson, a lifelong labor Democrat who had switched parties in 1981.

With saving Atkinson a priority for the national GOP, Kolter was far outspent and could muster the money to run his single TV ad only the week before the election. Still, Kolter's 3-to-2 victory was no surprise, given the towering jobless rate in the 4th. Kolter, who boasted an almost perfect labor record in the Legislature, called Atkinson a traitor to working people, and the Republican's rejoinder — that Reaganomics would benefit the district in the long run — was not well received.

Kolter got special help from the United Steelworkers and appearances from Walter F. Mondale and then-Speaker O'Neill; national Democrats targeted Atkinson to discourage further conversions to the GOP. He lost every county except a wealthy slice of Westmoreland.

Pennsylvania 4

West — New Castle

In redistricting earlier this decade, the GOP-controlled Pennsylvania Legislature tried to make the 4th more Republican, to help its newly converted GOP incumbent hold on in the 1982 election. But Democrat Joe Kolter recaptured the district and has increased his winning percentage in three consecutive re-elections.

But a Republican presence in parts of the 4th is still evident, even through the hard economic times, which tend to boost Democrats. Steel-producing Beaver County is firmly Democratic, though its clout in the 4th was reduced some by the remap; Beaver casts less than one-third of the district's vote, a slightly larger share than neighboring Butler County, which is considerably more Republican.

The northern portion of Beaver is in the 4th, along with Aliquippa and a few other towns in the county. Union influence remains strong in northern Beaver County. Though Republicans often pick up votes from the farms outside Beaver Falls, Democrat Michael S. Dukakis carried the county by nearly 2-to-1 in 1988.

Lawrence County (New Castle), frustrated by steel-plant closings in nearby Youngstown, Ohio, flirted with Ronald Reagan in 1980, almost giving him a majority. But that experiment did not last; Walter F. Mondale won Lawrence in 1984, Dukakis carried it in 1988, and it has voted Democratic in the last two gubernatorial elections.

Butler County is a different matter. It voted Republican for president in 1980, 1984 and 1988. It also went Republican in both the Senate and gubernatorial elections in 1986. Armstrong County is a swing area, though Dukakis won it in 1988. Kittanning, a GOP-leaning commercial center, is the party's best town in Armstrong.

At the eastern end of the 4th is Indiana County, which last went Democratic for president in 1964. A mixture of coal mines and farms, its rural vote is dominant. One small slice of Westmoreland County also is part of the 4th. It is the Ligonier Valley, where the Pittsburgh elite maintain summer homes.

Population: 515,572. White 499,971 (97%), Black 13,506 (3%). Spanish origin 1,876 (0.4%). 18 and over 375,245 (73%), 65 and over 62,104 (12%). Median age: 31.

Committees

Government Operations (16th of 24 Democrats)
Commerce, Consumer and Monetary Affairs; Environment, Energy and Natural Resources

House Administration (10th of 13 Democrats)
Accounts; Office Systems

Public Works and Transportation (12th of 31 Democrats)
Aviation; Economic Development; Water Resources

Elections

1988 General

Joe Kolter (D)	124,041	(70%)
Gordon R. Johnston (R)	52,402	(29%)

1986 General

Joe Kolter (D)	86,133	(60%)
Al Lindsay (R)	55,165	(39%)

Previous Winning Percentages: **1984** (57%) **1982** (60%)

District Vote For President

	1988		1984		1980		1976	
D	97,696	(54%)	106,267	(52%)	82,901	(45%)	92,937	(50%)
R	80,911	(45%)	98,148	(48%)	87,644	(48%)	87,987	(48%)
I					10,289	(6%)		

Campaign Finance

	Receipts	Receipts from PACs	Expend-itures
1988			
Kolter (D)	$175,980	$146,606 (83%)	$90,710
1986			
Kolter (D)	$280,062	$215,132 (77%)	$249,885
Lindsay (R)	$124,003	$5,800 (5%)	$123,800

Key Votes

1987	
Raise speed limit to 65 mph	N
Approve Gephardt "fair trade" amendment	Y
Ban testing of larger nuclear weapons	Y
Delay "re-flagging" of Kuwaiti tankers	Y
Approve tax-raising deficit-reduction bill	?
1988	
Approve aid to Nicaraguan contras	N
Enact civil rights restoration bill over Reagan veto	Y
Kill 60-day plant-closing notification measure	N
Pass omnibus trade bill over Reagan veto	Y
Approve death penalty for drug-related murders	Y
Bar federal funds for abortions in cases of rape and incest	Y
Oppose seven-day waiting period for purchase of handguns	Y

Voting Studies

	Presidential Support		Party Unity		Conservative Coalition	
Year	S	O	S	O	S	O
1988	26	63	78	11	45	37
1987	32	61	78	10	53	44
1986	26	72	83	15	54	44
1985	28	69	80	12	38	60
1984	29	65	80	14	27	64
1983	13	67	77	12	30	62

Interest Group Ratings

Year	ADA	ACU	AFL-CIO	CCUS
1988	60	22	100	17
1987	68	5	100	36
1986	70	14	100	33
1985	65	10	69	23
1984	65	23	92	38
1983	80	14	100	10

5 Richard T. Schulze (R)

Of Berwyn — Elected 1974

Born: Aug. 7, 1929, Philadelphia, Pa.
Education: Attended U. of Houston, 1949-50; Villanova U., 1952; Temple U., 1968.
Military Career: Army, 1951-53.
Occupation: Household-appliance dealer.
Family: Wife, Nancy Lockwood; four children.
Religion: Presbyterian.
Political Career: Pa. House, 1969-75.
Capitol Office: 2369 Rayburn Bldg. 20515; 225-5761.

In Washington: Despite his party label, Schulze found the Reagan years profoundly frustrating, and he may not sleep any better under President Bush. On the issue of utmost importance to Schulze — trade policy — his "fair trade" protectionism has been persistently rebuffed by a GOP White House with a near-dogmatic commitment to free trade. Despite devoting much time and energy calling for punitive sanctions on unfair trade practices, Schulze does not have much to show for his effort.

Schulze promotes the industries of his state just as single-mindedly as his predecessors did in the salad days of the Pennsylvania Manufacturers Association. Economic problems at home have induced some conservative GOP House members to hedge on their fealty to free trade; still, Schulze's protectionist mindset is something of an anachronism.

From his seat on the Ways and Means Trade Subcommittee, Schulze pushes insistently for trade remedies beneficial to Pennsylvania. Such remedies, he has said, are "simply the only way to maintain public support for an open system of trade." Schulze's effectiveness is limited to some extent by his predictability; dug in at the far end of the spectrum in trade debate, he is not often well positioned to cast a decisive vote in the ultimate negotiations. But he does not give up.

Schulze's anger over the U.S. trade deficit has not been limited to the White House. He has scolded his colleagues for failing to recognize the severity of the trade-imbalance problem. As Congress worked on omnibus trade legislation in the 100th Congress, Schulze more than once expressed his "disappointment ... that it took a $170 billion trade deficit to finally remove our rose-tinted glasses."

He has spoken out frequently against foreign "dumping" — the sale of imported goods here at less than fair-market value. In recent years he has been particularly concerned about the dumping of mushrooms by the People's Republic of China, which he says threatens the survival of domestic producers. Many of those domestic producers are in Schulze's district.

When Ways and Means debated a trade bill in 1984, Schulze successfully amended the measure to strike provisions that relaxed the anti-dumping rules applied to communist countries. He added language to the trade bill in the 100th Congress similarly aimed at fending off such dumping.

During the debate on the 1986 trade bill, Schulze was the only Republican member of the Ways and Means Committee to vote for the controversial Gephardt amendment, which threatened action, such as the imposition of tariffs or quotas, to reduce large trade surpluses some countries have with the United States. He altered his course in the 1987 trade debate, and joined most of his Republican colleagues in voting against a similar amendment. Unlike most Republicans, however, Schulze voted for the entire bill even though it contained the Gephardt amendment.

Early in the 99th Congress, Schulze introduced legislation to get tough with foreign competitors by placing a 20 percent across-the-board surcharge on all imports from all countries, to be removed only after each country negotiated a bilateral free-trade agreement with the United States. Surcharge legislation became increasingly popular as the 99th Congress progressed, but Schulze's was considered an extreme version, was anathema to the Reagan administration, and did not come close to enactment.

Schulze supported other trade measures opposed by the administration. "We're viewed around the world as being Mr. Nice Guy," he said at one point. "We talk tough, but we don't usually deliver." In 1986 he backed the unsuccessful attempt to override the president's veto of legislation protecting textile companies from foreign imports.

Not surprisingly, Schulze reserves some of his harshest words on trade for Japan, railing against its "grossly unfair barriers." "It defies common sense," he said in 1987, "how Japan can criticize the protectionist provisions in our trade bill while maintaining some of the most

Pennsylvania 5

Western Philadelphia Suburbs — Chester

Mushrooms, horses and tract houses all grow well in the outer suburbs of Philadelphia. Despite some islands of Democratic industrial territory, this is Republican turf. About half the district's population lives in Chester County, which is the most strongly Republican of the four suburban Philadelphia counties. In 1988, Bush won 67 percent of the vote in Chester, while he tallied 60 percent in Bucks, Delaware and Montgomery counties.

Farmers around the self-designated Mushroom Capital of the World in Kennett Square keep the southern part of Chester County solid for the GOP. Nearby, the Brandywine Creek meanders through estate country, where the du Ponts and other Republican millionaires maintain their mansions.

A housing boom, however, has turned northern Chester County's coloration from rural Republican to suburban Republican. Exton, once a tiny farm town, received a giant shopping mall in the 1970s. Farther north, the 5th covers rural northern Montgomery County — most of whose Mennonite farmers have been voting Republican as a matter of habit for generations.

During the 1970s, the district had Democratic enclaves in Phoenixville and Pottstown. For the 1980s, these have been joined by another small mill town, Coatesville. But a more significant infusion of Democrats comes from the city of Chester, a run-down part of Delaware County with a struggling shipbuilding industry. Democrats in Chester and the other industrial towns in the 5th are consigned to a small minority in the district's electorate.

Population: 515,528. White 449,987 (87%), Black 57,488 (11%), Other 3,666 (1%). Spanish origin 8,294 (2%). 18 and over 370,556 (72%), 65 and over 50,556 (10%). Median age: 31.

stringent import barriers in the world."

Schulze has repeatedly, but unsuccessfully, fought against the granting of most-favored-nation (MFN) trading status to China. As Chinese exports to the United States have expanded, Schulze has complained that this "brutal incursion" into the domestic market not only hurt American producers, but posed potential health hazards for American consumers.

Tax revision was the dominant issue at Ways and Means in the 99th Congress, but Schulze played only a limited role. Bitterly opposed to the tax bill being written largely by the committee's Democrats, he seemed more concerned with sinking it than trying to improve it. He did suggest his own idea, a "business alternative minimum tax" on business receipts, which would have provided revenues for the retention of investment incentives. But this was not seriously considered.

His one departure from predictability in the tax bill debate left most of his colleagues puzzled. He offered an amendment in committee that would have barred the Internal Revenue Service from granting tax-exempt status to religious organizations that promoted "satanism" or "witchcraft." That proposal, which was also pushed by Republican Jesse Helms in the Senate, was not among the priorities set by most committee members.

Schulze did, however, leave some imprint on the committee bill, pushing, among other things, tax breaks for the tuxedo business in Pennsylvania. In 1986, when the House gave final approval to the conference report on the tax bill, Schulze voiced some objections, but voted for it.

The vehicle for tax-law changes in 1988 was the sweeping "technical corrections" bill, which was ostensibly passed to fix typographical errors in the 99th Congress' tax bill, but included a variety of new provisions. Schulze attached a measure to continue an exemption from the Social Security self-employment tax for Amish, Hutterites and Mennonites, who are conscientiously opposed to public insurance. He also was a sponsor of the "Taxpayer Bill of Rights" that was attached to the technical corrections bill.

Schulze was successful in shuttling through the 100th Congress his bill to award a congressional gold medal to American artist Andrew Wyeth, a native of the Delaware County village of Chadds Ford. Reagan signed it into law in 1988.

At Home: A retail appliance dealer, Schulze came up through the ranks of Chester County politics, taking on such chores as chairmanship of Nixon Day festivities in 1968 and county registrar of wills. In November of 1968, he was elected to the state Legislature.

As a dependable party man, he got his chance to run for Congress in 1974 when Republican Rep. John H. Ware III announced his retirement. Schulze received organization backing, but had to face a rough primary fight against four opponents.

Schulze's top competitor was Robin West, a wealthy young former aide in the Nixon White House. West had a host of volunteers and favorable publicity from a laudatory column about him in *Time* magazine.

Using his family money, he outspent Schulze, whom he blasted as "the machine candidate." But Schulze, who reminded voters that "I don't drive a Ferrari," easily outdistanced the field. Since then, he has encountered little trouble.

Schulze's 1984 opponent, lawyer Louis Fanti, complained that his campaign was going nowhere because local Democratic organizations were unenthusiastic about challenging Schulze. "I may well be the last Democratic candidate against Schulze in a long time," he said, receiving 27 percent of the vote.

Fanti's prediction was a bit off the mark. In 1986, Schulze did face an energetic challenger in Tim Ringgold, a West Point graduate and Army captain who left the service to run for office. Despite his military background, Ringgold favored diverting money for weapons into education and other social programs. He mocked the incumbent as "the invisible congressman."

Ringgold drew some good reviews, and the *Philadelphia Inquirer* endorsed Ringgold, saying that it preferred "vigor over seniority."

But in the end, Ringgold fared little better than the incumbent's earlier foes in raising money, and the district demographics were as difficult as ever for a Democratic challenger. Ringgold ran better than any Schulze opponent in a decade, but still managed only 34 percent.

In 1988, Democrats put so little effort into challenging Schulze that a supporter of fringe political figure Lyndon H. LaRouche Jr. got the party's nomination, and Schulze won re-election by the most lopsided margin of his career.

Committee

Ways and Means (5th of 13 Republicans)
Oversight (ranking); Social Security; Trade

Elections

1988 General

Richard T. Schulze (R)	153,453	(78%)
Donald A. Hadley (D)	42,758	(22%)

1986 General

Richard T. Schulze (R)	87,593	(66%)
Tim Ringgold (D)	45,648	(34%)

Previous Winning Percentages: **1984** (73%) **1982** (67%) **1980** (75%) **1978** (75%) **1976** (60%) **1974** (60%)

District Vote For President

	1988	1984	1980	1976
D	70,744 (35%)	66,501 (33%)	57,836 (32%)	73,374 (42%)
R	132,933 (65%)	134,327 (67%)	106,938 (58%)	100,620 (57%)
I			15,678 (9%)	

Campaign Finance

	Receipts	Receipts from PACs	Expend-itures
1988			
Schulze (R)	$428,745	$258,420 (60%)	$444,205
1986			
Schulze (R)	$376,549	$205,038 (55%)	$320,232
Ringgold (D)	$98,629	$35,430 (36%)	$98,121

Key Votes

1987	
Raise speed limit to 65 mph	N
Approve Gephardt "fair trade" amendment	N
Ban testing of larger nuclear weapons	N
Delay "re-flagging" of Kuwaiti tankers	Y
Approve tax-raising deficit-reduction bill	?
1988	
Approve aid to Nicaraguan contras	Y
Enact civil rights restoration bill over Reagan veto	Y
Kill 60-day plant-closing notification measure	Y
Pass omnibus trade bill over Reagan veto	N
Approve death penalty for drug-related murders	Y
Bar federal funds for abortions in cases of rape and incest	Y
Oppose seven-day waiting period for purchase of handguns	Y

Voting Studies

	Presidential Support		Party Unity		Conservative Coalition	
Year	S	O	S	O	S	O
1988	55	40	63	30	84	13
1987	65	28	62	26	84	16
1986	58	37	60	29	60	14
1985	64	33	68	23	82	15
1984	62	27	68	21	85	10
1983	72	23	75	11	83	8
1982	57	31	63	15	73	11
1981	70	14	87	6	93	4

Interest Group Ratings

Year	ADA	ACU	AFL-CIO	CCUS
1988	30	76	46	92
1987	4	77	25	85
1986	15	58	46	81
1985	10	71	29	82
1984	5	60	25	69
1983	10	77	0	80
1982	15	56	31	81
1981	10	100	13	94

6 Gus Yatron (D)

Of Reading — Elected 1968

Born: Oct. 16, 1927, Reading, Pa.
Education: Attended Kutztown State Teachers College, 1950.
Occupation: Professional boxer; ice cream manufacturer.
Family: Wife, Millie Menzies; two children.
Religion: Greek Orthodox.
Political Career: Reading School Board, 1955-61; Pa. House, 1957-61; Pa. Senate, 1961-69.
Capitol Office: 2205 Rayburn Bldg. 20515; 225-5546.

In Washington: A low-key moderate, Yatron lacks the ideological fervor shared by many of his Democratic colleagues on the Foreign Affairs Committee, where suspicion of his zeal for partisan battle even cost him the chairmanship of the Western Hemisphere Affairs Subcommittee in 1981, just as the debate over President Reagan's Central America policies was taking shape.

Yet Yatron has recouped much of his standing in his latest role as chairman of the Foreign Affairs Subcommittee on Human Rights and International Organizations. The non-ideological approach that contributed to that earlier painful rebuke is more appreciated at Human Rights, where he challenges U.S. friends and adversaries alike.

For example, several Yatron-sponsored resolutions protesting human rights violations in the Soviet Union were passed unanimously by the 100th Congress. He has made himself a spokesman for Jews seeking to leave the U.S.S.R. In October 1987, Yatron praised the Soviet decision to provide an exit permit to "refusenik" Ida Nudel, but said the satisfaction was "tempered by the fact that virtually thousands of Soviet Jews are continuing to be denied the right to emigrate."

Yatron applauded President Reagan's efforts to raise human rights issues during his Moscow summit meeting with Soviet leader Mikhail S. Gorbachev in the spring of 1988. He even brushed aside criticism of Reagan's public statement that the Soviet bureaucracy, not government policy, was responsible for emigration problems; Yatron said the president was simply trying to avoid strong criticism of Gorbachev while on Soviet soil.

But while he could be supportive of Reagan, Yatron often criticized the president of a double standard — vigorously assailing violations by communist countries and other U.S. adversaries, while taking a much softer line toward allied nations. In terms of his overall approach to human rights, Yatron has much in common with former President Jimmy Carter, who broadly applied human rights standards in U.S. foreign policy.

An opponent of right-wing "death squads" and strong-arm approaches to dissent in El Salvador, Yatron successfully fought Reagan administration efforts in 1987 to provide $9 million in supplemental aid to that country's national police. He has submitted resolutions calling for an expeditious return to full democratic procedures in South Korea.

Though Reagan's State Department resisted efforts by congressional Democrats to put extreme pressure on U.S. allies, Yatron thought he saw some movement toward his way of thinking. After the State Department submitted a February 1988 report more critical than usual of Chile's rightist military regime, Yatron noted, "The administration is slowly recognizing that a consistent approach in expressing U.S. concerns regarding the human rights records of both totalitarian and authoritarian regimes makes for a more credible and effective foreign policy."

That June, Yatron steered his panel into some politically choppy waters by holding a hearing on alleged Israeli abuses of Palestinian Arabs during unrest on the occupied West Bank. While Yatron assured advocates of Israel — a strong lobbying force in Congress — that U.S. support for that nation had not weakened, he warned that the beating of Palestinians was "unacceptable by any standard."

Yatron's pursuit of his human rights interests was derailed temporarily when he underwent hip-replacement surgery at the start of the 101st Congress. Yatron returned to work in March 1989 after a two-month absence, during which Democrat Wayne Owens of Utah sat in as temporary subcommittee chairman.

Outside the subcommittee, Yatron takes a similarly outspoken approach on U.S. relations with Greece. Working with Maine Republican Olympia J. Snowe, a Foreign Affairs member and a fellow Greek-American, Yatron has worked to advance the interests of Greece, and has persistently lobbied for increased American

Pennsylvania 6

Southeast — Reading

Politics here have changed a bit since the area's two most famous authors wrote novels about their birthplaces.

John Updike's "Rabbit Run" explores the ethnic, working-class life of his home, Berks County (Reading). In Updike's Reading (which he calls Brewer), life has a Democratic flavor. John O'Hara's "Appointment in Samarra" focuses on the wealthy families that rule the fictionalized version of his native Schuylkill County (Pottsville). In Pottsville, which O'Hara calls Gibbsville, Republicans are in charge.

Though the old political patterns are still visible, changing economic conditions have made voting behavior less predictable in both Berks and Schuylkill counties.

Reading, once known for its railroad and heavy industry, now is famous for its discount outlet stores, which lure busloads of bargain hunters from far away. The growth of the outlets and attendant development of a diversified light industrial base around Reading have helped Berks County fare better economically than some other once-mighty industrial centers in Pennsylvania. The power of the local unions has faded somewhat, and with it the Democratic habits of the voters.

In 1982, when GOP Gov. Dick Thornburgh's re-election bid was jeopardized by the recession, Berks voted for Thornburgh. In 1988, George Bush won 62 percent of the Berks vote, aided by strong support from Reading's suburbs and surrounding farming country. Berks also voted Republican in the 1986 governor's race.

At first blush, it seems odd that the GOP should have been the traditional power in Schuylkill County; it is a coal-laden area, and Democrats usually fare well among coal miners. But the Eastern Europeans who toiled in the anthracite pits earlier this century had a reason to be Republican: The O'Hara characters who owned the mines made that a condition of employment.

There is still considerable loyalty to the GOP in Schuylkill, but the decline of employment in the mines has brought hard times to many in the county, and Democrats can occasionally enjoy some success here. In 1986, Schuylkill went narrowly Democratic for governor; in 1988, Michael S. Dukakis won 43 percent of the vote, better than his showing in Berks, but well below his statewide average.

Population: 515,952. White 500,032 (97%), Black 8,055 (2%). Spanish origin 9,653 (2%). 18 and over 384,537 (75%), 65 and over 76,603 (15%). Median age: 34.

pressure on Turkey — a U.S. ally but Greece's traditional enemy — to withdraw its forces from the portion of the island nation of Cyprus it has occupied since 1974.

But even in this area of personal interest, Yatron can take a balanced approach. He has written a number of letters to Greek officials, calling on them to cooperate more fully in U.S. efforts to combat Middle East terrorism.

On other foreign policy issues, Yatron is seldom a major player. The leaders of the revolt that cost him the Western Hemisphere Subcommittee chair have long attributed it to Yatron's perceived lack of interest in the issues over which he had jurisdiction.

The anti-Yatron faction insisted that Yatron had been chairman in name only and that more dynamic members provided the real leadership in the House on Latin American issues. Despite several trips to Latin American nations, he played little role in the argument over the two most controversial Western Hemisphere issues faced by Congress in the late 1970s — the Panama Canal treaties and aid to the newly installed Sandinista government of Nicaragua.

Yatron called the 10-9 vote against him in 1981 a "political power play" on the part of the committee's liberals. But in ensuing years, he made no effort to express his bitterness through his committee votes on the contentious issue of U.S. aid to the Nicaraguan contras. While criticizing the "repressive policies" of the leftist government in Nicaragua, he argued against a Reagan request for $100 million in contra aid in 1986, stating that "realistically the contras do not have the ability to defeat the Sandinistas on the battlefield."

While Yatron's interest in human rights and other foreign policy issues occupies much of his House effort, he hardly ignores the particular interests of the industrial eastern Pennsylvania district that elects him by wide margins every two years. Along with such measures as the "Torture Victim Protection Act of 1988," the list of Yatron's proposed legislation in the 100th Congress included a bill to require the federal government to purchase a three-year supply of anthracite coal "for the national defense stockpile."

Yatron has maintained strong ties to labor unions. He has long supported trade legislation to shield U.S. metal-producing and textile industries — among the major employers in his district — from foreign competition.

In 1984, investigators discovered that a home in Yatron's district recorded the highest reading of carcinogenic radon gas ever found in a private dwelling. Yatron was instrumental in winning approval for funds to allow the Environmental Protection Agency to research the radon problem.

At Home: Old-time Reading residents still remember the night Yatron knocked out Gibraltar Joe Biancone in 1947 — in a bout that touched off a ringside brawl between the two contestants' relatives. But nothing very rough has happened to the amiable ex-boxer since he retired from the ring with a 13-2-1 record.

Through his athletic reputation and the family ice cream-making business, which he ran with his father, Yatron was enough of a local celebrity to launch a highly successful political career. His record in his House elections is 11-0-0.

Yatron may not be smooth and articulate, but he projects a down-to-earth manner that goes over well in a town where people eat pizza at private key clubs. He has a prodigious memory for names and faces, and like many members from areas close to Washington, he returns home on weekends. His son, George, is the Berks County district attorney.

Yatron came up through the ranks of Berks politics, starting on the school board and eventually moving to the state Legislature. When Democrat George M. Rhodes decided to retire in 1968, he anointed Yatron as his successor and served as his campaign chairman.

Yatron won that first House election with just 51 percent; he had some problems in Schuylkill County (Pottsville), where Republicans dominated the electorate and he was not well-known. Since then, Yatron has extended his base by devoting a great deal of time to Schuylkill, where his office specializes in solving black-lung claim problems. Republican strength in Schuylkill County has waned somewhat in the last 20 years, and the county Republican organization no longer exerts itself against Yatron.

Committees

Foreign Affairs (3rd of 28 Democrats)
Human Rights and International Organizations (chairman); International Operations

Post Office and Civil Service (6th of 15 Democrats)
Human Resources; Investigations

Elections

1988 General

Gus Yatron (D)	114,119	(63%)
James R. Erwin (R)	65,278	(36%)

1986 General

Gus Yatron (D)	98,142	(69%)
Norm Bertasavage (R)	43,858	(31%)

Previous Winning Percentages: **1984** (100%) **1982** (72%) **1980** (67%) **1978** (74%) **1976** (74%) **1974** (75%) **1972** (65%) **1970** (65%) **1968** (51%)

District Vote For President

	1988	1984	1980	1976
D	70,916 (38%)	68,281 (36%)	66,156 (36%)	91,016 (49%)
R	112,040 (61%)	121,264 (64%)	104,703 (56%)	93,417 (50%)
I			12,557 (7%)	

Campaign Finance

	Receipts	Receipts from PACs	Expend-itures
1988			
Yatron (D)	$145,914	$109,700 (75%)	$121,435
Erwin (R)	$12,016	$330 (3%)	$12,002
1986			
Yatron (D)	$128,397	$83,380 (65%)	$97,114
Bertasavage (R)	$19,512	$304 (2%)	$18,211

Key Votes

1987	
Raise speed limit to 65 mph	N
Approve Gephardt "fair trade" amendment	Y
Ban testing of larger nuclear weapons	Y
Delay "re-flagging" of Kuwaiti tankers	Y
Approve tax-raising deficit-reduction bill	N
1988	
Approve aid to Nicaraguan contras	N
Enact civil rights restoration bill over Reagan veto	Y
Kill 60-day plant-closing notification measure	N
Pass omnibus trade bill over Reagan veto	Y
Approve death penalty for drug-related murders	Y
Bar federal funds for abortions in cases of rape and incest	Y
Oppose seven-day waiting period for purchase of handguns	Y

Voting Studies

	Presidential Support		Party Unity		Conservative Coalition	
Year	**S**	**O**	**S**	**O**	**S**	**O**
1988	32	66	75	23	76	24
1987	23	73	87	9	44	49
1986	22	76	80	15	48	44
1985	44	54	80	17	49	51
1984	41	53	70	25	58	37
1983	28	70	78	18	42	57
1982	40	56	71	23	52	44
1981	49	50	58	39	72	25

Interest Group Ratings

Year	ADA	ACU	AFL-CIO	CCUS
1988	65	24	100	36
1987	84	13	100	33
1986	65	27	100	38
1985	50	33	69	36
1984	50	35	92	38
1983	60	27	94	26
1982	60	33	85	41
1981	40	47	73	28

7 Curt Weldon (R)

Of Aston — Elected 1986

Born: July 22, 1947, Marcus Hook, Pa.
Education: West Chester State College, B.A. 1969; Delaware County Community College, A.A.S., 1972.
Occupation: Teacher.
Family: Wife, Mary Gallagher; five children.
Religion: Protestant.
Political Career: Marcus Hook mayor, 1977-82; Delaware County Council, 1981-86; GOP nominee for U.S. House, 1984.
Capitol Office: 1233 Longworth Bldg. 20515; 225-2011.

In Washington: A minority-party House freshman often spends his first two years in Congress on the bottom rung of a low-visibility committee, treading carefully through the new territory.

Not Weldon. He got a seat on the high-profile Armed Services panel and had quite a lot to say there; he joined numerous caucuses and served as secretary of the GOP freshman class. His energy was so noticeable that it earned him a reputation in some quarters as overly intense.

Elected from an urban-and-suburban amalgam in and near Philadelphia, Weldon compiled an overall voting record in the 100th Congress that marks him as one of the more moderate House Republicans. In 1988, he voted against President Reagan's position on legislation slightly more often than he voted with him.

This pattern would surprise those who saw Weldon only in Armed Services, where he was a staunch pro-Pentagon conservative. In 1987, he was named the "most effective freshman" by the conservative American Security Council.

Weldon spoke up early in support of Reagan's position that the 1972 U.S.-Soviet anti-ballistic missile (ABM) treaty permitted ABM weapons tests in space. In 1987, he offered an amendment stating the Soviets had violated the treaty by building a large radar facility in western Siberia; it passed 418-0. Weldon's interest in ABM issues led to his appointment to an Armed Services panel studying the strategic defense initiative.

On the Merchant Marine Committee, Weldon's more moderate side comes out, particularly on environmental issues. During committee markup on a 1988 bill to open Alaska's Arctic National Wildlife Refuge to oil drilling, he attached a provision ordering the Interior Department to monitor oil companies' compliance with environmental regulations. He also proposed the creation of a waste-recycling clearinghouse within the Environmental Protection Agency.

While some members try to set the world on fire, Weldon made a splash by helping put one out. In 1988, the former volunteer fireman helped contain a blaze in an office belonging to House Speaker Jim Wright. Having already founded the House Fire and Emergency Services Caucus, Weldon called for creation of a committee to study fire safety on Capitol Hill.

At Home: Weldon's victory in the GOP-leaning 7th ended 12 years of Democratic control. The man who had frustrated Republicans was Bob Edgar, who ran for the Senate in 1986. Weldon was the unanimous choice of local Republicans to succeed Edgar, and he shows no signs of letting Democrats regain the lost territory.

Greeting constituents effusively with the words, "Hey, I'm from Marcus Hook," Weldon leaves no doubt about his roots. The son of a factory worker and the youngest of nine children, Weldon is a former volunteer fireman, schoolteacher and GOP mayor of his hometown. All that makes him a good fit for the 7th's conservative mix of blue- and white-collars.

Weldon rose to prominence as the architect of Marcus Hook's revival. A small working-class city at the southern end of the 7th, it was gripped by economic decline and gang warfare when Weldon became mayor in 1977. Ordering a series of tough police raids, he reduced the Pagan motorcycle gang to insignificance and ended its illicit drug trafficking.

Weldon's accomplishments caught the eye of the powerful Delaware County GOP organization, and in 1981, with machine backing, Weldon won a County Council seat. He was elected chairman by popular ballot in 1984. Styling himself a proponent of economic development, Weldon encouraged county government to lure new businesses to the Delaware River waterfront.

In 1984, Weldon launched a campaign against Edgar, taking on a task that had frustrated five Republicans before him. Weldon came closer than any of them, and his near-miss made him the favorite, when Edgar's 1986 Senate campaign opened the 7th. Nobody even filed against Weldon for the GOP nomination. That November, he won more than 60 percent of the vote, and improved on that showing in 1988.

Pennsylvania 7

Southwest Philadelphia Suburbs

Republican activists breathed a great sigh of relief when Democrat Bob Edgar announced his intention to leave the 7th and run for the Senate in 1986. Edgar's decade of success in the 7th was a tremendous embarrassment to GOP organizers, since it came in the face of a seemingly impregnable 2-to-1 GOP registration advantage.

From the 1920s to the mid-1970s, local politics here were ruled by the "War Board," a secretive group officially called the Delaware County Republican Board of Supervisors. The factional fighting on the board that led to Edgar's election in 1974 later caused its demise. The current Republican organization is a looser confederation, but has been successful enough to give the GOP unanimous control of the County Council and every Delaware County seat in the state Legislature.

Well-off places such as Marple, Newtown and Rose Valley are typical Delaware County bastions of Republicanism. Dependably Republican Springfield, the county's commercial hub, often finds itself a locus of campaign activity, with candidates swarming the shopping centers every Saturday. In adjacent Swarthmore, the academic influence of Swarthmore College makes Democrats competitive in what otherwise would be a business executives' town.

Of the 7th's suburban turf, the Main Line community of Radnor weighs in as the wealthiest, an old-money township where Sun Oil and *TV Guide* have their headquarters. Next door lies Haverford. Since it is not on the Main Line, Haverford is considered a social rung down from Radnor, but it still has its share of large homes.

Closer to Philadelphia are blue-collar, ethnic suburbs such as Upper Darby, Yeadon and Colwyn. But the area's demographics do not translate automatically into Democratic votes. The War Board had potent influence in Upper Darby, and the GOP continues to perform well in these nominally Democratic towns. Along the Delaware River, industrial Tinicum and Eddystone are more reliable for the Democrats.

An amalgam of Irish, Italians and blacks, the part of Southwest Philadelphia in the 7th is a workaday place that holds Philadelphia International Airport, a segment of Interstate 95, many factories and a large expanse of row houses. Encompassing the Eastwick and Elmwood sections, it gives Democrats solid majorities.

Population: 515,766. White 478,934 (93%), Black 30,578 (6%), Other 4,751 (1%). Spanish origin 3,269 (1%). 18 and over 387,309 (75%), 65 and over 68,570 (13%). Median age: 33.

Committees

Armed Services (15th of 21 Republicans)
Research and Development; Seapower and Strategic and Critical Materials

Merchant Marine and Fisheries (12th of 17 Republicans)
Fisheries and Wildlife Conservation and the Environment; Oceanography

Select Children, Youth and Families (8th of 12 Republicans)

Elections

1988 General		
Curt Weldon (R)	155,387	(68%)
David Landau (D)	73,745	(32%)
1986 General		
Curt Weldon (R)	110,118	(61%)
Bill Springler (D)	69,557	(39%)

District Vote For President

	1988		1984		1980		1976	
D	93,469	(40%)	93,850	(38%)	84,935	(35%)	112,341	(43%)
R	141,028	(60%)	155,166	(62%)	136,488	(56%)	141,436	(55%)
I					20,255	(8%)		

Campaign Finance

	Receipts	Receipts from PACs	Expend-itures
1988			
Weldon (R)	$564,109	$215,617 (38%)	$507,360
Landau (D)	$211,213	$27,175 (13%)	$206,591
1986			
Weldon (R)	$641,985	$172,576 (27%)	$617,063
Springler (D)	$166,710	$44,359 (27%)	$166,612

Key Votes

1987	
Raise speed limit to 65 mph	Y
Approve Gephardt "fair trade" amendment	N
Ban testing of larger nuclear weapons	N
Delay "re-flagging" of Kuwaiti tankers	N
Approve tax-raising deficit-reduction bill	N
1988	
Approve aid to Nicaraguan contras	Y
Enact civil rights restoration bill over Reagan veto	Y
Kill 60-day plant-closing notification measure	N
Pass omnibus trade bill over Reagan veto	Y
Approve death penalty for drug-related murders	Y
Bar federal funds for abortions in cases of rape and incest	Y
Oppose seven-day waiting period for purchase of handguns	N

Voting Studies

	Presidential Support		Party Unity		Conservative Coalition	
Year	S	O	S	O	S	O
1988	45	49	66	25	84	16
1987	52	41	69	27	79	16

Interest Group Ratings

Year	ADA	ACU	AFL-CIO	CCUS
1988	30	59	77	71
1987	40	55	40	73

8 Peter H. Kostmayer (D)

Of New Hope — Elected 1976

Did not serve 1981-83.

Born: Sept. 27, 1946, New York, N.Y.
Education: Columbia U., B.A. 1971.
Occupation: Public relations consultant.
Family: Wife, Pamela Jones Rosenberg; two stepchildren.
Religion: Episcopalian.
Political Career: No previous office.
Capitol Office: 123 Cannon Bldg. 20515; 225-4276.

In Washington: Those who had watched Kostmayer since his arrival in Congress in 1977 must have smiled in the early months of 1989. As the House ethics committee pursued a long list of alleged rule violations by Speaker Jim Wright, Kostmayer was among those stepping forward to insist the Speaker be presumed innocent until proven guilty.

"We have to take the heat and say the guy's entitled to fairness," said Kostmayer, who decried "a certain blood lust" in the body politic. Kostmayer was saying just what any deputy whip, elected as a regional member (Pennsylvania) of the whip's organization, would be expected to say. But here was a man first elected — and still, by some, remembered — as a hard-liner on ethics. He was once known primarily for his crusade against the free mailing of wall calendars to constituents.

But that Kostmayer did not survive the election of 1980. Defeated then for re-election, Kostmayer came back two years later determined to change. He wanted to be a House insider, trusted by the Democratic leadership for his work behind the scenes and his disavowal of free-lance headline-grabbing. He loyally took on routine party leadership chores he never would have touched in the old days.

Kostmayer still has his abrasive side, but he is more careful about when to display it. He has a professional background in public relations, and it shows in his masterful handling of constituency groups at home.

But he can also reveal an impolitic strain of candor at times. At the Democratic National Convention in 1988, he offered this description of the party's presidential-election strategy to a Congressional Quarterly reporter: "Just shut up, gays, women, environmentalists. Just shut up. You'll get everything you want after the election. But just for the meantime, shut up so that we can win." The quote was later used in the keynote address to the GOP National Convention by New Jersey's Republican Gov. Thomas H. Kean.

As a member of the Foreign Affairs Committee, he has been known for baiting and challenging administration witnesses, and he is no favorite among the Republican members of the committee. But he no longer works against his own objectives by quarreling with his natural allies.

Early in 1989 he closely questioned James A. Baker III, the nominee to be secretary of state, on President Bush's policy toward El Salvador. He angled for a commitment from the fledgling administration that military aid to that country's new, rightist regime would be cut if human rights abuses were not curtailed. As a member of a leadership task force on Nicaragua, he has been a critic both of Nicaragua's Sandinista government and the contras who oppose it.

Population control has been a Kostmayer priority as a member of Foreign Affairs, and on that subject he fought repeatedly with the Reagan administration. Kostmayer held that rapid population growth deterred economic development in poor countries; many administration officials argued that population growth can help a nation's economy expand. Kostmayer wants the United States to increase funding for international agencies that promote family planning in developing nations, but many conservatives object to those expenditures because some of the money is used for abortions.

Kostmayer is also on the Interior Committee, familiar ground for him because it was his major assignment in his first two terms. In the 101st Congress, it became more of a focus as it provided him with his first chairmanship: the Interior Subcommittee on General Oversight and Investigations. In the intervening years, he had written legislation designating 114 miles of the Delaware River "wild and scenic" in the 95th Congress and setting aside wilderness lands for Pennsylvania in the 98th. In 1987, he wrote a successful bill attaching 35 developable acres to the Gettysburg National Military Park in 1988.

At Home: By bringing together working-class Democrats from lower Bucks County and independent-minded yuppies from upper Bucks, Kostmayer has become the only Demo-

Pennsylvania 8

Northern Philadelphia Suburbs; Bucks County

Known for its winding country lanes and 18th-century stone farmhouses, Bucks County's rural charm helped lure 42,000 new residents in the early 1980s, more than any other Pennsylvania county.

As the county's image of genteel country living suggests, the Republicans have a comfortable registration edge in the 8th, which includes all of Bucks and a small piece of wealthy and very Republican Montgomery County. But most GOP candidates have to show some moderate inclinations to win.

The new suburban voters have an independent streak, and combined with blue-collar workers in Lower Bucks, they can make Democrats competitive here, as Kostmayer has proven.

Lower Bucks tends to be Democratic. Far from the bucolic vistas commonly associated with the rest of the county, lower Bucks offers factories, commercial strips, tract developments and the Keystone Racetrack. Levittown's tightly spaced homes built after World War II attracted thousands of ethnic Democrats moving from inner-city Philadelphia. Lower Bucks has had economic problems in the 1980s, most acutely in Fairless Hills, where there have been layoffs and fluctuations in the remaining work force at the USX Corp. (formerly U.S. Steel) Fairless Works.

The farther north one goes, the more Republican Bucks becomes. But Democrats can hold their own in the county's midsection; they win their share of local elections in communities such as Warminster and Doylestown. Democrats do especially well in and around New Hope, a quaint river town famous for its antique shops and artists' colony. Writer James Michener is one Bucks artist (and liberal Democrat) living near New Hope.

Upper Bucks, with its landed gentry and farmers, usually stays with the Republicans. Towns such as Upper Black Eddy harbor business executives who commute to Manhattan and, when home, vote for Republican candidates.

Population: 516,902. White 497,154 (96%), Black 12,471 (2%), Other 4,508 (1%). Spanish origin 5,923 (1%). 18 and over 364,239 (70%), 65 and over 42,528 (8%). Median age: 30.

crat to succeed in this district in a half-century. His coalition is sometimes shaky: in seven elections since 1976, he has lost once and been held to no more than 51 percent three times.

To survive, Kostmayer must highlight local accomplishments and spend heavily — his last four campaigns cost more than $500,000 apiece, with his 1988 effort topping $1 million. But when it comes to district public relations, Kostmayer has few equals; one of his campaign kickoffs was staged in front of a factory that had reopened because of a federal grant Kostmayer helped secure.

Kostmayer started in 1976 as a long shot even in the Democratic primary, challenging an organization-backed opponent for the seat being vacated by retiring GOP Rep. Edward G. Biester. But Kostmayer, who was regional coordinator for George McGovern's presidential campaign in 1972, had enough support from independents and liberals outside the party apparatus for the nomination. A divisive GOP primary that year had lingering effects that helped Kostmayer win in November. A weak 1978 challenger allowed him a solid re-election margin.

In 1980, however, Republican nominee James K. Coyne criticized Kostmayer as a big spender and, with the help of Reagan's strong showing in the 8th, reclaimed the seat. Kostmayer became a public relations consultant, but immediately began planning for a rematch. He hit on the idea of using campaign volunteers to keep up his constituent service. Coyne was flabbergasted when Kostmayer aides helped local flood victims with lodgings and food.

Although Coyne had deserted Reagan on several important votes, in his 1982 rematch with Kostmayer he refused to back away from his 1981 support for Reaganomics. That did not go over well in Lower Bucks, where unemployment had made many blue-collar workers regret the GOP votes they cast in 1980. Kostmayer reclaimed the seat in a heavy turnout.

In 1984 party leaders drafted David Christian, a highly decorated veteran of the Vietnam War and founder of the United Vietnam Veterans Association. Christian was not as articulate as Coyne, and except for supporting a nuclear freeze, he mainly recited the GOP platform. Yet despite Christian's weaknesses as a candidate and the incumbent's sizable spending advantage, a strong showing by Reagan helped hold Kostmayer's margin under 4,000 votes.

In 1986, Christian shifted strategy and decided to stress his own roots. He recited his military record and upbringing in a blue-collar, Catholic family in Lower Bucks. But Kostmayer kept Christian on the defensive by focusing on one aspect of the challenger's past — his management of a veterans' center. Kostmayer had raised the issue in 1984, accusing Christian of misrepresenting the cost of the center to a state official. In 1986, Kostmayer revived the charge. "If the state of Pennsylvania doesn't trust David Christian, why should we?" intoned one Kostmayer ad.

Christian protested his innocence, accusing Kostmayer of "pure, unmitigated mudslinging." But he was unable to redirect the focus of the campaign. Kostmayer expanded his margin of victory to more than 15,000 votes.

In 1988, the GOP shifted tactics again. Coyne wanted a rematch, but he was knocked off the ballot on a filing technicality, clearing the way for former state Sen. Ed Howard. A supporter of John B. Anderson's 1980 presidential campaign, Howard had a reputation as a liberal maverick on social and environmental issues. This political profile seemed a good fit for the district — where growth and gridlock are now top issues — but Howard proved to be a disappointing campaigner. He also had to spend time defending his attendance record in the state Senate, an issue Kostmayer exploited as effectively as he had gone after Christian's vet center history.

Emphasizing the positive in his own record, Kostmayer touted his efforts to get national historic designation for a portion of the Delaware Canal in the 8th, and he joined with Democratic Gov. Robert P. Casey to announce a federal-state agreement to build a four-lane bypass around burgeoning Newtown. Howard's thrust was more negative; he complained about Kostmayer's campaign donations from developers and his knack for winning publicity.

Howard tried hard to capitalize on Kostmayer's "shut up" quote; his campaign printed "Just Shut Up" T-shirts and hired a plane to fly over a county fair tailing a sign that read, "Peter Kostmayer to Women: Just Shut Up."

But in trying to exploit the quote, Howard did not hone in on the allegation that Kostmayer and the Democratic Party had a "hidden agenda" — perhaps because the moderate Howard's own agenda for the environment and women's rights did not differ much from Kostmayer's. In organizing and fund-raising, Howard lagged the incumbent. Kostmayer advertised heavily on Philadelphia television, while Howard could not afford any TV ads. In the end, Kostmayer won his first comfortable presidential-year election.

Committees

Foreign Affairs (11th of 28 Democrats)
International Economic Policy and Trade; Western Hemisphere Affairs

Interior and Insular Affairs (12th of 26 Democrats)
General Oversight and Investigations (chairman); National Parks and Public Lands; Water, Power and Offshore Energy Resources

Select Hunger (5th of 18 Democrats)
Task Force: International

Elections

1988 General		
Peter H. Kostmayer (D)	128,153	(57%)
Ed Howard (R)	93,648	(42%)
1988 Primary		
Peter H. Kostmayer (D)	34,298	(90%)
Edward T. Czyzyk (D)	3,947	(10%)
1986 General		
Peter H. Kostmayer (D)	85,731	(55%)
David A. Christian (R)	70,047	(45%)

Previous Winning Percentages: **1984** (51%) **1982** (50%) **1978** (61%) **1976** (50%)

District Vote For President

	1988	1984	1980	1976
D	88,334 (38%)	79,185 (36%)	60,414 (32%)	81,782 (47%)
R	139,248 (60%)	142,258 (64%)	105,284 (56%)	90,142 (51%)
I			18,630 (10%)	

Campaign Finance

	Receipts	Receipts from PACs	Expend-itures
1988			
Kostmayer (D)	$1,148,619	$418,821 (36%)	$1,127,812
Howard (R)	$506,241	$49,900 (10%)	$507,682
1986			
Kostmayer (D)	$693,578	$339,213 (49%)	$682,526
Christian (R)	$352,998	$102,763 (29%)	$353,180

Key Votes

1987	
Raise speed limit to 65 mph	N
Approve Gephardt "fair trade" amendment	Y
Ban testing of larger nuclear weapons	Y
Delay "re-flagging" of Kuwaiti tankers	Y
Approve tax-raising deficit-reduction bill	Y
1988	
Approve aid to Nicaraguan contras	N
Enact civil rights restoration bill over Reagan veto	Y
Kill 60-day plant-closing notification measure	N
Pass omnibus trade bill over Reagan veto	Y
Approve death penalty for drug-related murders	N
Bar federal funds for abortions in cases of rape and incest	N
Oppose seven-day waiting period for purchase of handguns	N

Voting Studies

	Presidential Support		Party Unity		Conservative Coalition	
Year	S	O	S	O	S	O
1988	21	76	89	5	16	82
1987	13	87	92	2	7	93
1986	17	81	87	9	24	74
1985	29	70	90	8	20	80
1984	35	63	83	13	20	80
1983	16	77	86	5	8	84

Interest Group Ratings

Year	ADA	ACU	AFL-CIO	CCUS
1988	85	4	100	31
1987	96	0	100	7
1986	90	5	100	39
1985	90	19	76	36
1984	85	4	85	31
1983	90	0	100	25

9 Bud Shuster (R)

Of Everett — Elected 1972

Born: Jan. 23, 1932, Glassport, Pa.

Education: U. of Pittsburgh, B.S. 1954; Duquesne U., M.B.A. 1960; American U., Ph.D. 1967.

Military Career: Army, 1954-56.

Occupation: Computer industry executive.

Family: Wife, Patricia Rommel; five children.

Religion: United Church of Christ.

Political Career: No previous office.

Capitol Office: 2268 Rayburn Bldg. 20515; 225-2431.

In Washington: Those who do great works usually are not memorialized until after they die. But House members who help create public works often have things named after them while they are still very much alive.

Take, for example, the Bud Shuster By-Way. Funding for this brief stretch of four-lane highway, running parallel to the Pennsylvania Turnpike through the town of Everett, was obtained by Shuster, who is now in his prime as the second-ranking Republican on the House Public Works and Transportation Committee and the senior GOP member on the Surface Transportation Subcommittee. Everett also happens to be Shuster's hometown.

Shuster is a prototype of the "Public Works Republican." His overall voting record is quite conservative. Shuster voted in support of Ronald Reagan's position on House legislation over two-thirds of the time in nearly every year of his presidency. This support was not only on defense and foreign policy, but also on many of Reagan's efforts to cut or limit the growth of domestic spending.

However, public works funding, or "infrastructure investment" as it has come to be known, was the one area that was inviolate to Shuster and like-minded committee members. Projects derided by some administration and congressional figures as "pork barrel" were defended by public works advocates as not only worthy, but critical, federal investments in the nation's future economic viability. And some, like Shuster, approached the issue with zeal.

When the Reagan administration attacked congressional proposals for highway "demonstration projects" as wasteful, Shuster was enraged. "It's a congressional prerogative," he said. "We find it absolutely repugnant that an administration can say that it's all right for a faceless bureaucrat to decide where money should be spent, but it's wrong for a congressman to identify crucial, needed projects."

It was on a measure loaded with such demonstration projects — the $88 billion highway bill enacted in the 100th Congress — that Shuster had one of his most notable breaks with Reagan. Working closely, as he had on previous road-funding bills, with then-Public Works Chairman James J. Howard of New Jersey, Shuster helped craft the legislation; when Reagan vetoed the bill, Shuster strongly supported its override. He played a similar role on the Clean Water Act amendments enacted in 1987 over Reagan's veto.

Each of these pieces of legislation contained projects that Shuster had promoted as necessary to economic development and recovery of Pennsylvania's 9th District, a rugged, rural stretch dotted with struggling blue-collar towns like Altoona. Shuster is not shy about the benefits to his district of his senior Public Works position. "I am in a strategic position to ensure that the 9th District gets full consideration for important projects," Shuster wrote in his 1987 year-end newsletter.

The pamphlet listed several such projects that he had gotten into the bill, including a $90 million upgrade for Route 220 from Altoona to Tyrone, a Franklin County exit off Interstate 81, and a $5.5 million Route 36 bypass around the town of Loysburg. Shuster noted that the bill also contained $3.2 million for a bus-testing facility in Altoona, adding that all buses purchased with federal funds after Sept. 30, 1989, would have to be tested there.

Shuster, whose district's industrial areas have an interest in trade protection, also uses his ranking position to promote "Buy American" provisions in public works bills. One "domestic content" provision sponsored by Shuster in the 1987 highway bill increased the minimum amount of American-made parts in transit vehicles from 50 to 60 percent. He also supported the textile trade bill and the omnibus trade act in the 100th Congress, both of which were opposed by Reagan.

Shuster does engage himself in Public Works legislation that is outside the brick-and-mortar (or asphalt-and-concrete) funding arena. He is also second-ranking Republican on the Public Works Aviation Subcommittee. When a decline in the efficiency of passenger airline service became a widely reported subject

Pennsylvania 9

South Central — Altoona

To Pennsylvania Turnpike travelers, this district, which crosses the Allegheny Mountains, is a series of tunnels, long climbs and sharp descents. To Republicans, it is a predictable source of votes.

This central Pennsylvania region long has been a passageway to the West and, other than farming, transportation has been its central focus. Before the coming of the railroad, trade and travel had to take the long way around the mountains, ducking south. The city of Altoona, in Blair County, prospered as a rail center.

With the decline of the rail system, a new travel-related culture sprung up along the turnpike, the nation's first superhighway, which opened in 1940. Its epitome is Breezewood, the celebrated "Town of Motels" — by night, a garish glow of neon signs amid the mysterious mountain darkness.

For the most part, the 9th is a series of small villages scattered among the mountains. It has little industry; its farmers raise cattle for beef and milk. The isolation and agricultural character of the area have bred a strong strain of conservatism. Local Republicans there like to boast that much of the area within the 9th District has gone Republican since 1860.

Altoona, which lost 10 percent of its population in the 1970s and another 7 percent in the early 1980s, used to be a Democratic stronghold. Developed by the Pennsylvania Railroad, it has the giant Samuel Rea Railroad Shops nearby; just to the west of it, the tracks form the famous Horseshoe Curve, an engineering marvel. But many of the railroad workers who voted Democratic lost their jobs and left. Nowadays, Republicans win Blair; George Bush carried it with 62 percent of the vote.

Population: 515,430. White 508,728 (99%), Black 4,727 (1%). Spanish origin 1,841 (0.4%). 18 and over 368,331 (71%), 65 and over 64,934 (13%). Median age: 31.

in 1987, Shuster and other members of the panel called for action.

Describing what he called a "disgraceful deterioration in service," Shuster attached an amendment to an aviation bill during committee markup that dealt with one of the most common and infuriating air passenger grievances: lost luggage. The provision would have required an airline that could not produce a passenger's missing baggage within two hours of arrival to provide the passenger with a one-way standby ticket between the same two cities. A bag missing for more than 24 hours would have cost the airline a round-trip standby ticket.

A series of hot aviation issues, from efficiency to air terrorism to the effects of the 1989 Eastern Airlines strike, has preoccupied the committee in recent months. But there has been something of a lull on Public Works since the passage of the major highway and water bills and the March 1988 death of Shuster's close Democratic ally, committee Chairman Howard.

But while Shuster's working relationship with the new chairman, Glenn M. Anderson of California, has not been tested on major legislation at the full committee level, the two have worked together before. Anderson was chairman and Shuster ranking member on Surface Transportation prior to Howard's death.

Shuster's comfort with his Democratic colleagues on Public Works once sharply contrasted with his highly partisan behavior outside the committee. During his early years in the House, Shuster angled for a Republican leadership position, and tried to earn his stripes by blasting the Democrats from the House floor.

Shuster was president of his 1972 Republican House class; six years later, he outcampaigned front-runner Bill Frenzel of Minnesota for the chairmanship of the Republican Policy Committee. In that position, he gained a reputation as a partisan "hatchet man," firing a verbal barrage at the Democratic majority nearly every day on the floor, launching a brief filibuster to protest changes in the schedule, and bringing a toy duck on the floor to complain about a "lame-duck" session.

However, Shuster's one big thrust at a leadership position, minority whip, was thwarted by Trent Lott of Mississippi in 1981. Starting as a distinct underdog, Shuster campaigned with his typical intensity and closed the gap on the easygoing Southerner. But Lott held on to win by a 96-90 vote of the House Republican Conference.

From then on, Shuster toned down his approach and concentrated on his Public Works duties. However, his appointment to the House Select Intelligence Committee at the start of the 100th Congress did enable him to invoke his more standard Republican conservatism on foreign policy and intelligence issues.

As a member of Intelligence, Shuster traveled to Africa in 1988 and visited the base camp of the Union for the Total Independence of Angola (UNITA), a U.S.-supported insurgent group fighting the Cuban-backed Marxist government of Angola. "I traveled to the African jungle ... to evaluate the communist-inspired charges that Dr. Jonas Savimbi's UNITA freedom fighters had little support among the Angolan people ...," Shuster wrote to his constituents. "What we saw with our own eyes were the dedicated troops that help make up his 65,000-man fighting force." Shuster's mailing including a photo of him holding a military rifle and surrounded by three men described as "Angolan freedom fighters."

At Home: Democrats find Shuster difficult to love, but they also find him impossible to beat. His district has firm Republican loyalties, and his outspoken partisanship on the floor strikes a chord among constituents. While he has had detractors in local political circles, notably in the GOP organization of the 9th's most populous county, Blair (Altoona), he remains untouchable at the polls.

In 1984, he had an interesting, though unsuccessful, Democratic challenger in 62-year-old Nancy Kulp, who played "Miss Jane Hathaway" on "The Beverly Hillbillies" television comedy. Retired from show business and living on a Pennsylvania farm, Kulp decided to challenge Shuster when it looked as if he would win unopposed. She accused Shuster of voting down the line with Reagan and ignoring the needs of farmers, veterans and elderly constituents.

Unaccustomed to aggressive challenges, Shuster counterattacked vigorously, launching a heavy advertising campaign and at one point saying of Kulp, "She's an outstanding comedian. I grew up watching her." The media found Kulp's background and candidacy intriguing, but the district's voters did not seem interested. Shuster won re-election with two-thirds of the vote.

Before entering politics, Shuster had a successful business career with the Radio Corporation of America and as an independent electronics entrepreneur. When Republican Rep. J. Irving Whalley announced his retirement in 1972, Shuster embarked on a self-generated congressional campaign and won the Republican primary over state Sen. D. Elmer Hawbaker. Hawbaker was backed by the party committees of Bedford and Blair counties.

Committees

Public Works and Transportation (2nd of 20 Republicans)
Surface Transportation (ranking); Aviation; Investigations and Oversight

Select Intelligence (3rd of 7 Republicans)
Oversight and Evaluation (ranking); Program and Budget Authorization

Elections

1988 General		
Bud Shuster (R)	158,702	(100%)
1986 General		
Bud Shuster (R)	120,890	(100%)

Previous Winning Percentages: **1984** (67%) **1982** (65%) **1980** (100%) **1978** (75%) **1976** (100%) **1974** (57%) **1972** (62%)

District Vote for President

	1988	1984	1980	1976
D	63,899 (37%)	59,047 (33%)	59,422 (35%)	71,159 (42%)
R	104,396 (61%)	118,500 (67%)	101,766 (60%)	94,421 (56%)
I			7,245 (4%)	

Campaign Finance

	Receipts	Receipts from PACs	Expend-itures
1988			
Shuster (R)	$402,210	$153,665 (38%)	$332,647
1986			
Shuster (R)	$299,910	$152,002 (51%)	$276,463

Key Votes

1987	
Raise speed limit to 65 mph	N
Approve Gephardt "fair trade" amendment	Y
Ban testing of larger nuclear weapons	N
Delay "re-flagging" of Kuwaiti tankers	N
Approve tax-raising deficit-reduction bill	N
1988	
Approve aid to Nicaraguan contras	Y
Enact civil rights restoration bill over Reagan veto	N
Kill 60-day plant-closing notification measure	Y
Pass omnibus trade bill over Reagan veto	N
Approve death penalty for drug-related murders	Y
Bar federal funds for abortions in cases of rape and incest	Y
Oppose seven-day waiting period for purchase of handguns	Y

Voting Studies

	Presidential Support		Party Unity		Conservative Coalition	
Year	S	O	S	O	S	O
1988	68	27	75	21	89	5
1987	66	31	74	23	88	12
1986	77	22	85	11	90	8
1985	66	34	86	10	87	11
1984	63	37	83	15	90	8
1983	71	21	85	5	90	8
1982	56	23	60	13	60	18
1981	76	22	89	11	99	1

Interest Group Ratings

Year	ADA	ACU	AFL-CIO	CCUS
1988	5	100	14	100
1987	20	70	47	80
1986	5	90	29	94
1985	10	81	24	86
1984	0	83	31	56
1983	0	91	0	85
1982	20	80	29	93
1981	0	100	20	89

10 Joseph M. McDade (R)

Of Scranton — Elected 1962

Born: Sept. 29, 1931, Scranton, Pa.
Education: U. of Notre Dame, B.A. 1953; U. of Pennsylvania, LL.B. 1956.
Occupation: Lawyer.
Family: Wife, Sarah Scripture; five children.
Religion: Roman Catholic.
Political Career: No previous office.
Capitol Office: 2370 Rayburn Bldg. 20515; 225-3731.

In Washington: The start of the 101st Congress might have marked the beginning of a comfortable and productive era for McDade. Popular with his colleagues and skilled at the inside give-and-take of the Appropriations Committee, he is beginning his third term as the ranking member of the Defense Subcommittee, where his longtime Pennsylvania colleague John P. Murtha just became chairman.

But looming over McDade's legislative endeavors are media reports that the Federal Bureau of Investigation and a federal grand jury are trying to determine whether the congressman violated bribery or election laws in accepting more than $45,000 in campaign contributions and speaking fees from officials of a now-bankrupt defense firm, United Chem-Con Corp. of Lancaster, Pa.

Reports of the matter first surfaced in a December 1988 *Wall Street Journal* article. At that time, McDade said he helped the minority-owned business obtain Navy contracts in order to help bring jobs to his economically troubled district, but he would not comment further.

Spurring economic development at home is at the heart of McDade's political career, and his committee assignments position him well to pursue that goal. In addition to his place on Defense Appropriations, he is the top Republican on the Small Business Committee. The assignments give him influence with two important sources of federal contracts: the Pentagon and the Small Business Administration. McDade's savvy in using his positions on behalf of his economically struggling constituents has made him secure in what is otherwise considered a politically marginal district.

Shortly after the Journal story appeared, McDade was dealt a setback in the House: He lost a bid to become GOP Conference secretary. For such a senior member to seek such a modest leadership post was unusual, but McDade said he decided to run after Northeastern Republicans caucused and concluded that otherwise they would have no regional representative in the leadership.

Another factor that made the move curious is that McDade's politics do not fit the usual pattern for a party leader. Over the course of his career, he has voted against a majority of House Republicans more often than he has voted with them. McDade, however, has managed to do so without personally alienating party colleagues. He tends to break from the GOP line on labor votes, rather than on the more ideologically divisive social-policy issues. He also has won a few points inside his party recently for carrying the conservatives' water on defense issues.

McDade's strategy for the leadership contest was to call in chits he had collected in years of service on Appropriations. But his timing was off. His strategy served to emphasize his place in the "Old Bull" politics-as-usual wing of the House GOP. This was not what many restive House Republicans wanted in their new leaders, and the Journal story just made matters worse for McDade. Conservative activist Vin Weber of Minnesota was elected instead.

When McDade first took over the ranking spot on Defense Appropriations — after the retirement of Alabama's Jack Edwards in 1985 — many GOP conservatives feared McDade would not be as reliable a party loyalist as his predecessor. McDade had expressed skepticism about spending massive sums on the military, given pressing domestic needs. Shortly before taking over the job, McDade cautioned, "The deficit demands that the defense budget be part of the [spending] reduction process."

But McDade proved to be a dependable foot soldier for Republican views on the panel, though he tended to couch his support for the Reagan administration defense buildup in his own terms. In 1985, he submitted a joint resolution containing President Reagan's request for the production of 21 additional MX missiles. But unlike conservatives who said the weapon was needed to counter the Soviet threat, McDade talked of the missile system's supposed benefits for arms control. The resolution passed by a 217-210 vote.

In the 100th Congress, he warned colleagues against trying to tap the defense budget for domestic programs, saying the Pentagon

Pennsylvania 10

Northeast — Scranton

The city of Scranton dominated the politics of northeastern Pennsylvania in the early part of the century, but as the coal-and-railroad town has declined in population, Scranton and Lackawanna County have had to speak with a quieter political voice.

Generally, they have been a small Democratic voice within an increasingly Republican 10th District. In 1988, Lackawanna gave Democrat Michael S. Dukakis 52 percent while the district went comfortably for George Bush.

Lackawanna County still has half the district's people, despite the prolonged slump in anthracite mining that has led to declines in employment and population. The county's Democratic majority casts its vote in Scranton and in such blue-collar towns as Moosic and Old Forge. The Republicans cluster in affluent suburbs such as Clarks Summit and Dalton (home of former Gov. William W. Scranton). Ethnically, the scramble for political office in this polyglot county has been between the Italians and the Irish.

In contrast to Scranton's shrinkage (its population dropped 14 percent in the 1970s and nearly 7 percent in the early 1980s), there has been spectacular population growth in some of the outlying counties of the 10th. Pike, a Pocono Mountain county east of Scranton, contains many vacation cottages and is home to business executives who commute to New York. Pike's population boomed by 54 percent in the 1970s and another 22 percent in the early 1980s. Republican Monroe County, to the south of Pike, also is home to Pocono resorts such as Buck Hill Falls and Camelback.

West of Scranton are sparsely populated rural counties along the New York border such as Potter and Clinton, which are made up of woods, dairy farms and Republicans.

Population: 515,442. White 510,782 (99%), Black 2,262 (0.4%). Spanish origin 2,214 (0.4%). 18 and over 376,348 (73%), 65 and over 75,215 (15%). Median age: 33.

budget was already as trim as it could get. Further cuts, according to McDade, would mean: "We're in veto country." At the same time, he dismissed a Reagan veto threat over the funding level for the strategic defense initiative (SDI), saying, "We're not going to be able to fund 100 percent of the SDI program. Everybody in town knows that."

The most partisan battles before the subcommittee recently have involved Democratic efforts to include arms control language on the spending bills, which the Reagan administration strongly opposed. Although McDade signed a 1986 letter circulated by other House members urging Reagan not to undercut the SALT II agreement, he was at the forefront of GOP efforts in 1987 to block the Democrats from forcing Reagan to uphold this policy.

During debate on the "no undercut" amendment and one to limit nuclear weapons testing, he argued that such efforts would undermine the position of U.S. arms control negotiators. "The negotiations aren't in this room," he said. "They're in Geneva." While the House Appropriations Committee eventually approved the amendments, the Senate would not go along.

McDade's previous role on Appropriations — ranking member on the Interior Subcommittee — did not require such partisan diligence on his part. For nearly a decade, he and Chairman Sidney R. Yates of Illinois were one of the more successful legislative teams in the House. Rarely did their bills generate much floor opposition on either side of the aisle, even when they exceeded administration budget requests.

Because the panel has control over federal energy research spending, McDade was able to watch out for his coal-producing district. In the early 1980s he was a staunch defender of the Synthetic Fuels Corporation, and later, he became a key backer of the Clean Coal Technology Reserve Fund, a program adopted by some members as an alternative to acid-rain legislation.

McDade has also supported the coal industry outside the Interior Subcommittee. He has developed a reputation as "Mr. Coal" at the Pentagon for his insistence that the Defense Department buy American coal for its facilities overseas. Foreign firms bought 270,000 metric tons of anthracite from Pennsylvania in 1984 for U.S. defense installations in Europe.

At Home: McDade has endeared himself to constituents of both parties with his efforts to promote economic development — vital in this depressed coal-producing region. In 1988, he won a typical landslide re-election.

McDade's Republican label appeals to voters in the outlying, rural portions of the 10th, and his pro-labor voting record pleases the blue-collar Democrats in Lackawanna County (Scranton), the district's focal point. Unions regularly back McDade, and local Democratic organizations stopped endorsing candidates to run against him long ago. As an Irish Catholic, he has unusual appeal for a Republican among the county's large ethnic population.

A lawyer and former municipal solicitor in his home city, McDade succeeded Republican William W. Scranton, after whose ancestors the city is named. Scranton had served one House term and then became governor.

Handpicked by Scranton for the 1962 House nomination, McDade won an unspectacular election victory. In 1964 his winning margin was narrower yet. By 1966, however, he had enlisted the support of organized labor, and his vote tally not has dipped below 60 percent since.

Committees

Small Business (Ranking)
SBA, the General Economy and Minority Enterprise Development (ranking)

Appropriations (2nd of 22 Republicans)
Defense (ranking); Interior and Related Agencies

Elections

1988 General		
Joseph M. McDade (R)	140,096	(73%)
Robert C. Cordaro (D)	51,179	(27%)
1986 General		
Joseph M. McDade (R)	118,603	(75%)
Robert C. Bolus (D)	40,248	(25%)

Previous Winning Percentages: **1984** (77%) **1982** (68%) **1980** (77%) **1978** (77%) **1976** (63%) **1974** (65%) **1972** (74%) **1970** (65%) **1968** (67%) **1966** (67%) **1964** (51%) **1962** (53%)

District Vote For President

	1988	1984	1980	1976
D	80,514 (41%)	75,727 (38%)	79,276 (39%)	101,832 (48%)
R	112,001 (58%)	123,130 (61%)	110,645 (54%)	105,197 (50%)
I			10,128 (5%)	

Campaign Finance

	Receipts	Receipts from PACs	Expend-itures
1988			
McDade (R)	$442,808	$271,620 (61%)	$430,322
Cordaro (D)	$69,674	0	$66,299
1986			
McDade (R)	$394,141	$203,665 (52%)	$291,757
Bolus (D)	$10,195	0	$10,195

Key Votes

1987	
Raise speed limit to 65 mph	N
Approve Gephardt "fair trade" amendment	Y
Ban testing of larger nuclear weapons	N
Delay "re-flagging" of Kuwaiti tankers	?
Approve tax-raising deficit-reduction bill	N
1988	
Approve aid to Nicaraguan contras	Y
Enact civil rights restoration bill over Reagan veto	N
Kill 60-day plant-closing notification measure	N
Pass omnibus trade bill over Reagan veto	Y
Approve death penalty for drug-related murders	Y
Bar federal funds for abortions in cases of rape and incest	Y
Oppose seven-day waiting period for purchase of handguns	Y

Voting Studies

	Presidential Support		Party Unity		Conservative Coalition	
Year	**S**	**O**	**S**	**O**	**S**	**O**
1988	44	51	61	33	71	24
1987	45	47	34	53	72	19
1986	49	42	31	58	66	24
1985	59	38	44	47	67	29
1984	57	35	41	48	63	25
1983	57	30	44	43	60	31
1982	40	45	36	55	53	41
1981	62	30	55	34	63	25

Interest Group Ratings

Year	ADA	ACU	AFL-CIO	CCUS
1988	40	54	86	50
1987	40	37	71	36
1986	45	63	93	35
1985	20	57	75	38
1984	30	41	77	56
1983	30	52	60	60
1982	60	33	75	32
1981	25	93	47	78

11 Paul E. Kanjorski (D)

Of Nanticoke — Elected 1984

Born: April 2, 1937, Nanticoke, Pa.
Education: Attended Temple U. 1957-62; attended Dickinson School of Law, 1962-65.
Military Career: Army, 1960-61.
Occupation: Lawyer.
Family: Wife, Nancy Hickerson; one child.
Religion: Roman Catholic.
Political Career: Sought Democratic nomination for U.S. House, special election 1980, regular primary 1980.
Capitol Office: 424 Cannon Bldg. 20515; 225-6511.

In Washington: Kanjorski's 1989 election to a seat on the Post Office and Civil Service Committee — and his subsequent bid for the Census Subcommittee chairmanship — demonstrated both the extent and the limit of the influence of his Pennsylvania colleague, Democratic power broker John P. Murtha.

At the start of the 101st Congress, Post Office Committee Chairman William D. Ford requested another member for his committee, which had run out of members to fill its subcommittee chairmanships: Every Post Office Democrat chaired a panel either on Post Office or another committee. Murtha backed Kanjorski for the seat. After two ballots, Kanjorski won on a 16-13 vote over Charles A. Hayes of Illinois. The outcome prompted charges of racism from Hayes, a black with a year and a half more seniority than Kanjorski.

Once on Post Office, Kanjorski sought the Census Subcommittee chair. In that job, he would be utile to Murtha in his fight to keep illegal aliens from being counted in the 1990 census. Members from Pennsylvania and other states slated to lose congressional seats had filed a lawsuit to stop the Census Bureau from including illegal aliens.

But the Democratic leadership opposed Murtha's efforts; Speaker Jim Wright of Texas and Whip Tony Coelho of California, who hail from immigrant-rich states, had no incentive to pursue the issue. The leadership supported Ohioan Thomas C. Sawyer for the Census chair. Sawyer, who opposed changing census counts of aliens, won easily. Kanjorski got the Human Resources Subcommittee instead.

This was not the first time Kanjorski had taken his cue from Murtha to move for a position of influence. As a freshman, Kanjorski was Murtha's pick for the one freshman seat on the Steering and Policy Committee, which makes committee assignments for all Democrats. Murtha wanted Kanjorski on that panel to boost Pennsylvania's influence and Murtha's own. Kanjorski asked for the job, the requisite deals were made, and the newcomer found himself at the table as 31 Democrats — nearly all of them senior members — divided the plums of the House committee system.

Representing a district that had rejected three incumbents in four years, Kanjorski spent much of his first term worrying about how sensitive floor votes might affect his popularity at home. Late in 1985, he told Democratic leaders he would back President Reagan's request for contra aid if he noticed any complaints from home that he was soft on defense. In the end, though, Kanjorski joined most Democrats in opposing contra aid.

An easy win over a well-financed opponent in 1986 may have made Kanjorski feel safer. During the 100th Congress, he was a more reliable vote for Democratic partisan positions than he had been in his first two years.

On the Banking Committee, Kanjorski has strongly supported urban-aid programs, especially Urban Development Action Grants (UDAG). He won adoption of a floor amendment adjusting the UDAG formula to benefit aging urban areas, including his own.

Kanjorski was at the forefront of the effort in the 100th Congress to abolish the Federal Asset Disposition Association (FADA). He and Maryland Democrat Tom McMillen introduced a bill to kill the little-known agency that had been created by the Federal Savings and Loan Insurance Corporation to sell off real estate from bankrupt FSLIC-acquired thrifts.

FADA came under fire for spending more than $100 million to dispose of $775 million in property. Its top executives were also provided with a lucrative "golden parachute" severance contract should the agency be abolished. Late in the 100th Congress, the bill to abolish FADA nearly won House passage; Kanjorski picked up the cause in the 101st Congress.

At Home: Kanjorski owes his presence in the House largely to an intestinal parasite and a sunny beach. Those are peculiar agents of change, but the 11th is a district with peculiar

Pennsylvania 11

Northeast — Wilkes-Barre

Nowadays, being the hard-coal center of the world is a dubious honor. The energy crises of the 1970s spurred a modest comeback for anthracite, but mining this coal is very expensive, and no boom is on the horizon. In a town like Wilkes-Barre, unemployment and black lung disease are constant concerns of a legislator's life.

In most years, this is Democratic territory. But Democratic candidates have found some of their fellow partisans to be fickle. The area within the 11th went for Jimmy Carter in 1976, then turned against him four years later. In 1988, George Bush was an easy winner there.

Luzerne County, with two-thirds of the district's population, anchors the district. It is a rich ethnic stew of Eastern Europeans, Italians, Irish and Welsh. The surnames of Wilkes-Barre's many nationalities adorn mailboxes outside white frame homes that betray the town's New England roots.

Wilkes-Barre and Pittston are the county's Democratic vote centers. Another good town for the Democrats is Hazleton, in the southern part of Luzerne County. Republicans predominate in more affluent Kingston and Dallas and in the town of Forty-Fort.

The district also includes a Democratic coal-mining section of Northumberland County and the rural Republican turf of northwestern Monroe County. The Monroe section holds the Tobyhanna Army Depot and resorts such as Mount Pocono.

Rounding out the district are two politically marginal counties that mix farming, mining and light industry (Columbia and Montour) and part of a third (Carbon). Bosky Sullivan County tilts Republican.

Population: 515,729. White 510,659 (99%), Black 2,914 (1%). Spanish origin 2,165 (0.4%). 18 and over 388,822 (75%), 65 and over 83,140 (16%). Median age: 35.

politics. In one five-year span (1980-85), five different people represented it.

The outcome of Kanjorski's 1984 primary challenge to incumbent Democrat Frank Harrison might have been different but for the discovery that water supplies in parts of the 11th were contaminated with the giardiasis parasite. In January, as people boiled their water to make it drinkable, Harrison flew off for his second congressional excursion to Central America.

Kanjorski pounced on Harrison with a largely self-financed blitz of clever ads portraying him as an aloof globe-trotter. One ad showed a picture of a sunny Costa Rican beach and noted Harrison's visit there, then switched to a shot of a tea kettle on a stove and concluded, "It's enough to make you boil."

Harrison tried to ignore Kanjorski and campaigned on a vague, uninspiring "help me continue" line, stressing his experience in Washington. That pitch failed to excite voters, and Kanjorski leaped from long-shot to victor.

Kanjorski was rated the favorite over Republican Robert P. Hudock. But Hudock stirred some life into the race by accusing Kanjorski of charging excessive fees for his private legal work on behalf of local communities seeking federal grants. Hudock also accused Kanjorski of taking payment from citizens and businesses seeking relief money from Washington after Hurricane Agnes hit the area in 1972.

Kanjorski responded that his firm charged competitive fees and said he had helped bring over $50 million in federal aid to the 11th. He noted that during his 18 years of practicing law, he had often provided free legal services, including working without pay as Nanticoke's assistant city solicitor for 14 years.

Kanjorski also cast aspersions on Hudock's fitness to represent the district, noting that Hudock had been living and practicing law in the Virginia suburbs of Washington, D.C. A local reporter who visited Hudock's Pennsylvania office said it seemed little used, and calls to that office were forwarded automatically to Hudock's Virginia office.

An opponent of abortion and gun control and an advocate of prayer in schools and tuition tax credits, Kanjorski was viewed by most voters as reflecting their values, not those of the national Democratic Party. So even though Walter F. Mondale lost the district to Reagan, Kanjorski won with 58 percent of the vote.

In his 1986 re-election bid, Kanjorski was not as much the focus as was his extraordinary GOP challenger, Marc L. Holtzman, who waged one of the country's most novel — and, in the end, most spectacularly unsuccessful — campaigns. In a district that is aging, heavily Catholic and struggling economically, Holtzman was 26 years old, Jewish and wealthy. He counted on White House connections and a treasury well in excess of $1 million to make him competitive.

Kanjorski pointed to things he had already done — such as obtaining federal funds to refurbish the Wilkes-Barre Public Square. And he noted his ties to House leaders through his position on the Steering and Policy Committee.

Holtzman boasted of what he could do if given a chance. Son of the owner of Jewelcor, a Wilkes-Barre-based national catalog sales company, Holtzman had parlayed his role as executive director of Ronald Reagan's 1980 Pennsylvania campaign into contacts with conservative leaders across the country. He said his contacts would help him bring new industry to the 11th. But voters did not buy Holtzman's pitch. He drew a lower share of the vote than any GOP House candidate in the 11th District in a decade — spending approximately $29 per vote in the process.

That victory and Kanjorski's re-election without opposition in 1988 have brought stability to a district that once was a turnstile.

The door began revolving in 1980, after powerful 31-year veteran Daniel J. Flood was forced to resign from the 11th for soliciting illegal campaign contributions. The local Democratic Party fell into squabbling: The Democrat who replaced Flood in an April 1980 special election, Raphael E. Musto, lost to Republican James L. Nelligan that November. Because of the recession, Nelligan lost to Harrison in 1982. In the 1984 Democratic primary, Harrison lost to Kanjorski.

Kanjorski's 1984 campaign was his third try for Congress. In the 1980 special election to replace Flood, Kanjorski finished fourth, trailing Musto, Nelligan and Harrison; shortly afterward, he sought the Democratic nomination for a full two-year term and finished third, behind Musto and Harrison.

Committees

Banking, Finance and Urban Affairs (21st of 31 Democrats)
Economic Stabilization; Financial Institutions Supervision, Regulation and Insurance; Housing and Community Development; Policy Research and Insurance

Post Office and Civil Service (13th of 15 Democrats)
Human Resources (chairman)

Elections

1988 General

Paul E. Kanjorski (D)	120,706	(100%)

1986 General

Paul E. Kanjorski (D)	112,405	(71%)
Marc Holtzman (R)	46,785	(29%)

Previous Winning Percentage: **1984** (59%)

District Vote For President

	1988	1984	1980	1976
D	84,902 (47%)	84,587 (43%)	86,508 (43%)	109,718 (54%)
R	94,100 (52%)	108,063 (56%)	102,980 (51%)	92,193 (45%)
I			8,283 (4%)	

Campaign Finance

	Receipts	Receipts from PACs	Expend-itures
1988			
Kanjorski (D)	$539,603	$286,370 (53%)	$420,305
1986			
Kanjorski (D)	$778,137	$417,690 (54%)	$713,740
Holtzman (R)	$1,256,921	$66,322 (5%)	$1,353,170

Key Votes

1987	
Raise speed limit to 65 mph	N
Approve Gephardt "fair trade" amendment	Y
Ban testing of larger nuclear weapons	Y
Delay "re-flagging" of Kuwaiti tankers	Y
Approve tax-raising deficit-reduction bill	Y
1988	
Approve aid to Nicaraguan contras	N
Enact civil rights restoration bill over Reagan veto	Y
Kill 60-day plant-closing notification measure	N
Pass omnibus trade bill over Reagan veto	Y
Approve death penalty for drug-related murders	Y
Bar federal funds for abortions in cases of rape and incest	Y
Oppose seven-day waiting period for purchase of handguns	Y

Voting Studies

	Presidential Support		Party Unity		Conservative Coalition	
Year	**S**	**O**	**S**	**O**	**S**	**O**
1988	32	68	88	12	50	50
1987	26	74	88	11	56	44
1986	22	78	83	14	54	46
1985	33	63	80	17	47	53

Interest Group Ratings

Year	ADA	ACU	AFL-CIO	CCUS
1988	70	20	100	36
1987	80	4	94	13
1986	65	32	93	28
1985	55	19	76	32

12 John P. Murtha (D)

Of Johnstown — Elected 1974

Born: June 17, 1932, New Martinsville, W.Va.
Education: U. of Pittsburgh, B.A. 1962; graduate work, Indiana U., Pa.
Military Career: Marine Corps, 1952-55, 1966-67.
Occupation: Car wash operator.
Family: Wife, Joyce Bell; three children.
Religion: Roman Catholic.
Political Career: Pa. House, 1969-74.
Capitol Office: 2423 Rayburn Bldg. 20515; 225-2065.

In Washington: Moving noiselessly in a House dominated by media-conscious political free-lancers, Murtha has built a formidable political reputation the old-fashioned way. He is the consummate insider who wields influence in the backrooms of Congress, not before the television cameras.

After years as an omnibus dealmaker-without-portfolio, Murtha acquired an important new power base at the beginning of the 101st Congress. He became chairman of the Defense Appropriations Subcommittee when Bill Chappell Jr. was defeated for re-election in 1988, after the Florida Democrat was battered by press accounts linking him to defense contractors implicated in a procurement scandal.

It is ironic that another member's brush with political scandal should propel Murtha to his most important position of institutional power, because in 1980 it was Murtha's own ethical problems that extinguished his bright hopes for a place in the Democratic leadership.

A special favorite of former Speaker Thomas P. O'Neill Jr. throughout his career, Murtha might well have become majority whip in 1981 — and thus been in line to succeed Jim Wright as Speaker — had it not been for a brush with the Abscam bribery affair the previous year. Although the matter closed in 1981 without any charges being made against him, it effectively ended his leadership ambitions. But Murtha's influence has persisted in other forms.

"John P. Murtha — The 'P' Is for Power." That was the message on Murtha's campaign billboards as he battled for survival in a tough 1982 primary campaign. But there is none of that self-promoting boastfulness in the way Murtha accumulates power and operates in the House. He lets his actions speak for themselves.

Murtha almost never gives a speech on the House floor, but he spends many afternoons there, and is one of the few members who will rarely leave to answer a reporter's question. When he is not plotting strategy with a leadership lieutenant, he is sitting in a remote corner of the chamber, talking politics with some of his "boys" — ethnic machine Democrats from blue-collar districts in Pennsylvania and nearby Ohio and West Virginia.

Unlike most states, Pennsylvania has perhaps half a dozen backbench Democrats who are normally willing to do as they are told by a persuasive and influential home-state colleague. In an era when hardly any member controls even one vote beyond his own, Murtha is one of the last legitimate vote brokers left. On any close roll call, he is an important man to see.

O'Neill's departure was a blow to Murtha because of his close personal rapport with the Massachusetts Democrat. But Murtha makes himself useful to whoever wields power — a knack that leads some to question the depth of Murtha's loyalty. He was an early supporter of Wright's bid to be Speaker, but Murtha has also been closely associated with Dan Rostenkowski of Illinois, a rival of Wright.

Some of Murtha's most dramatic power plays have been to advance Democrats in the Pennsylvania delegation. He engineered the election of William H. Gray III to chair the House Budget Committee in 1985.

He has been particularly masterful during his periodic stints on the Democratic Steering and Policy Committee — an insider's heaven given its responsibility for making committee assignments. In 1985 he won a coveted seat on the Ways and Means Committee for William J. Coyne, helping the Pennsylvania Democrat beat another member backed by then-Majority Leader Wright.

In 1989, Murtha helped Paul E. Kanjorski of Pennsylvania get a seat on Post Office and Civil Service — a vacancy more coveted than usual because its occupant was guaranteed a subcommittee chairmanship.

Murtha was interested in positioning Kanjorski to take over the Census Subcommittee chairmanship, because he was girding for a fight to keep illegal aliens from being counted in the 1990 census. Members from Pennsylvania and some other states slated to lose congressional seats had filed a lawsuit to stop the Census Bureau from including illegal aliens.

Pennsylvania 12

Southwest — Johnstown

In 1984, a Republican official in Johnstown summed up the growing sense of helplessness in that chronically unlucky industrial town. "Four years ago, there was hope," he said. "We were down, but we still labored under the delusion that steel was a necessity, and that the mills would come back. Now, the hope is gone."

Johnstown, the biggest city in the 12th, exemplifies the hard times felt throughout this blue-collar district. A flood, the third in the past century — though not as serious as the first two — devastated Johnstown in 1977. The early 1980s recession devastated the city's coal and steel industries, causing hundreds of workers to lose their jobs. The economic expansion later in the decade did little to help the area.

Spread over the foothills of the Allegheny Mountains, Johnstown's Cambria County and neighboring Westmoreland County are similar in demographics and voting habits, and both are plagued by high unemployment. Their ethnic industrial towns, many of them 95 to 98 percent white, sit in the hollows between the hills, often dependent on one local industry. In Westmoreland County, New Stanton had a Volkswagen assembly plant, but it closed in 1988.

In the past four presidential elections, both Cambria and Westmoreland have gone Democratic. Jimmy Carter won them narrowly in 1980, as some Democrats deserted to Ronald Reagan, hoping he could cure the economic doldrums. In 1984, Walter F. Mondale improved on Carter's showing as voters registered their unhappiness with Reagan's economic policies, including his unwillingness to impose mandatory steel import quotas. And in 1988, Michael S. Dukakis posted comfortable victories in both counties.

The Republican Party might have had a chance to make some inroads in this traditionally Democratic area in the late 1970s, when two top Democratic officials were convicted on charges of extorting payments from highway contractors in Cambria and Somerset counties. But neither that nor Ronald Reagan's national popularity had any impact here.

Population: 515,915. White 507,805 (98%), Black 5,918 (1%). Spanish origin 1,965 (0.4%). 18 and over 374,878 (73%), 65 and over 64,054 (12%). Median age: 32.

But Murtha's influence faltered in the face of Democratic leadership opposition to his efforts: Although Kanjorski got on Post Office, he lost the Census Subcommittee chairmanship to another member backed by the leadership.

In another sign of the limits of Murtha's power and much-vaunted vote-counting abilities, he lost a floor fight over the Clean Air Act by a surprisingly large margin in the 100th Congress.

An enduring source of Murtha's ever-growing wad of political IOUs is his willingness to take on the politically thankless job of increasing his colleagues' salary and benefits. In 1979 he lobbied for three months to pass a 5.5 percent congressional pay raise through the Appropriations Committee and then through the House. On the roll call that finally passed it, 208-203, he patrolled the aisles like the Marine Corps officer he used to be, implying to nervous Democrats that their vote would be regarded as a test of their leadership loyalty, if not their manhood.

In 1981 he came up with another scheme — an increase in the amount of money members could earn each year beyond their regular salaries. This one was a quickie. He brought up the measure on the House floor on the next to last day of the session, then muscled it through in 10 seconds without telling any potential opponents what his resolution was about.

Murtha replayed that scenario in 1986, when he whisked through another increase in the outside earnings limit while almost no one was on the House floor. But that time it did not stick. There was an immediate outpouring of concern from members about the political dangers of such a move, and an embarrassed House reversed itself the next day.

Murtha also has done countless favors for his colleagues from his place on the Appropriations Committee. Now he has risen to a position of responsibility over defense programs that will only enhance his leverage over House politics as well as policy.

He brings to the Defense Subcommittee chairmanship views more hawkish than the mainstream of the Democratic Caucus. He was one of two Democrats to oppose a leadership-backed arms control amendment during 1987 committee debate on a mid-year spending bill. He generally supported the Reagan-era program of military aid to the contras in Nicaragua.

In 1985, while the Democratic leadership was lobbying hard for votes to block deployment of the MX missile, Murtha was siding with the GOP majority in favor of the weapon, one of only 15 Democrats outside the South to do so.

Along with his hawkish views, Murtha brings to the defense portfolio some deeply held convictions about maintaining the maintenance, training, and "quality of life" programs that bear directly on the welfare of military personnel.

A decorated combat veteran, Murtha looks at defense from the foxhole up: He champions the interests of the "grunts" — the young enlisted personnel like those he commanded in 1966-67 as a Marine officer in Vietnam. "I saw their tragedy and suffering," he once said, while members of Congress were "in their air-conditioned offices telling these soldiers what to do."

His place on the Interior Subcommittee at Appropriations gives Murtha an important base for helping home-state concerns. He promotes the interests of those who produce coal, both those who mine it and those who own the mines. On these issues he has worked closely with Joseph M. McDade, the Republican from Scranton, at the eastern end of his state. In the past few years, McDade has been the dominant member of the subcommittee; when the two men work together to obtain something, they usually get it.

On steel, Murtha has advocated measures to protect domestic producers from foreign imports. In 1984 he added $29 million to the U.S. Customs Service budget, to hire more agents to guard against illegal steel imports.

For a time during the 97th Congress, it appeared that Murtha's influence would be permanently limited by his involvement in Abscam.

He was never charged with a crime in the FBI bribery scandal, and he was able to issue a statement in mid-1980 reporting that he had been cleared. But his initial identification as one of those involved in the case hurt his public reputation, and his decision later in the year to testify against two other members raised questions about him in the minds of colleagues.

In February of 1980, Murtha was reported to be one of the targets of the FBI undercover agents who posed as Arab sheiks and offered members of Congress $50,000 to help them get into the United States. Videotapes of the FBI sessions clearly show that Murtha turned down the money. "I'm not interested," he said at one point. "I'm sorry." He explained that he was on the House ethics committee and told the "sheiks" that "if you get into heat with politicians, there's no amount of money that can help."

Murtha said he participated in the meeting only to seek investments by the Arabs in coal mining operations, banks and other businesses in his district. He said pursuing such investments is a normal duty of a conscientious member of Congress, especially one representing an economically depressed area.

The tapes do, however, show Murtha discussing money for Reps. Frank Thompson Jr., D-N.J., and John M. Murphy, D-N.Y. "Let me make it very clear, the other two guys expect to be taken care of," Murtha said at one point.

"I broke no law," he explained later. "I took no money. I was pursuing a policy of trying to attract industry to the district."

In July 1981, after one Abscam defendant had been expelled from Congress, two had resigned and four had been defeated for reelection, Murtha was cleared by the House ethics committee, on which he had served until 1980. The panel said it "found on the basis of the evidence presented no reason to issue a statement of alleged violation."

The committee's special counsel in the case, E. Barrett Prettyman Jr., resigned following the decision not to accept his recommendation of further proceedings against Murtha. But the case was not reopened, and Murtha's career in the House was secure.

At Home: When longtime Republican Rep. John P. Saylor died in 1973, the Cambria County (Johnstown) Democratic organization seized its chance to recapture a nominally Democratic district. They found an attractive candidate in Murtha, a personable state legislator who had won a Bronze Star and two Purple Hearts as a Marine in Vietnam.

Murtha won narrowly over Harry M. Fox, a former Saylor aide, in a 1974 special election focused on the Republican Party's Watergate problems. He handily dispatched Fox the following November and has won easily since.

That includes 1980, when Abscam had become public. Murtha's opponent tried to make the bribery scandal an issue, but he did not succeed. Murtha's plurality was down, but he still drew 59 percent of the vote.

In 1982, Pennsylvania's Republican-controlled Legislature combined Murtha's district with that of fellow-Democrat Don Bailey. The primary paired two excellent campaigners and close friends with similar pro-labor views.

The merged district contained about the same number of former constituents of each candidate, making it a battle between two organizations: Murtha had one in his home, Cambria County, and Bailey had one in his native Westmoreland County. Bailey refused suggestions that he bring up Abscam or a second Murtha liability — his sponsorship of House members' tax breaks and pay increases.

While both Democrats worked hard, Murtha fielded a superior get-out-the-vote operation. In addition, Murtha convinced voters that he could better help the economically depressed steel district through his greater seniority and influence with the House leadership. Murtha won by a comfortable 52-38 percent margin.

The little-known Republican challenger brought up Abscam, but found few voters interested in hearing about it.

Committee

Appropriations (10th of 35 Democrats)
Defense (chairman); Interior and Related Agencies; Legislative Branch

Elections

1988 General

John P. Murtha (D)	133,081	(100%)

1986 General

John P. Murtha (D)	97,135	(67%)
Kathy Holtzman (R)	46,937	(33%)

Previous Winning Percentages: **1984** (69%) **1982** (61%) **1980** (59%) **1978** (69%) **1976** (68%) **1974** (58%) **1974 *** (49%)

** Special election.*

District Vote For President

	1988	1984	1980	1976
D	96,040 (52%)	98,636 (49%)	87,100 (46%)	94,428 (51%)
R	85,953 (47%)	101,854 (51%)	94,584 (49%)	88,982 (48%)
I			7,535 (4%)	

Campaign Finance

	Receipts	Receipts from PACs	Expend-itures
1988			
Murtha (D)	$447,087	$310,815 (70%)	$401,945
1986			
Murtha (D)	$371,308	$244,705 (66%)	$272,436

Key Votes

1987

Raise speed limit to 65 mph	N
Approve Gephardt "fair trade" amendment	Y
Ban testing of larger nuclear weapons	N
Delay "re-flagging" of Kuwaiti tankers	N
Approve tax-raising deficit-reduction bill	Y

1988

Approve aid to Nicaraguan contras	Y
Enact civil rights restoration bill over Reagan veto	Y
Kill 60-day plant-closing notification measure	N
Pass omnibus trade bill over Reagan veto	Y
Approve death penalty for drug-related murders	Y
Bar federal funds for abortions in cases of rape and incest	Y
Oppose seven-day waiting period for purchase of handguns	Y

Voting Studies

	Presidential Support		Party Unity		Conservative Coalition	
Year	**S**	**O**	**S**	**O**	**S**	**O**
1988	35	60	79	16	58	39
1987	43	55	82	12	70	30
1986	42	56	76	15	68	28
1985	52	46	77	20	75	22
1984	52	43	77	18	63	34
1983	54	40	74	22	58	38
1982	53	39	68	21	64	30
1981	45	50	70	27	64	33

Interest Group Ratings

Year	ADA	ACU	AFL-CIO	CCUS
1988	55	46	100	29
1987	60	26	100	13
1986	40	52	93	25
1985	45	50	82	14
1984	40	27	69	38
1983	55	35	88	16
1982	45	37	90	33
1981	45	13	80	22

13 Lawrence Coughlin (R)

Of Plymouth Meeting — Elected 1968

Born: April 11, 1929, Wilkes-Barre, Pa.
Education: Yale U., A.B. 1950; Harvard U., M.B.A. 1954; Temple U., LL.B. 1958.
Military Career: Marine Corps Reserve, 1948-58, active duty, 1951-52.
Occupation: Lawyer.
Family: Wife, Susan MacGregor; four children.
Religion: Episcopalian.
Political Career: Pa. House, 1965-67; Pa. Senate, 1967-69.
Capitol Office: 2309 Rayburn Bldg. 20515; 225-6111.

In Washington: Coughlin's affluent suburban constituents demand little more from him than dignified moderation. This role comes naturally to the patrician Republican, affording him comfortable re-elections and considerable latitude to pursue his legislative interests. For Coughlin, a high-ranking member of the Appropriations Committee, those interests lie chiefly in the realm of urban affairs.

As ranking Republican on Appropriations' Transportation Subcommittee during the Reagan years, Coughlin struggled to balance his support for urban programs with his loyalty to the president's economic policies. More often than not, he wound up endorsing Democratic efforts to restore funds for mass transit, housing subsidies and other programs that are vital to Philadelphia, the city where the bankers and lawyers of his Main Line district spend their workdays.

But if his relative liberalism on these issues puts him at odds with his more conservative GOP House colleagues, Coughlin pleasantly surprised them early in the 101st Congress when he sided with Georgia's Newt Gingrich in his race for House minority whip. Though he might easily have been an ally of more moderate whip hopeful Edward Madigan of Illinois, Coughlin combines his establishment style with activist instincts, and he opted for change.

Increasingly, the most pressing urban problem Congress wrestles with is drugs. In the 101st Congress, Coughlin became the ranking Republican on the Select Committee on Narcotics, which puts him in a position to be a key player on the high-profile issue. Previously, Coughlin had not been intimately involved in drug legislation; his most noticeable initiative on the subject was a proposal to produce drug education videos for use in schools.

Coughlin has a more open-minded attitude toward federal spending than many Republicans, but he has been involved in killing two of the more costly government projects proposed in recent years — Westway, a 4.2-mile highway and land development project on Manhattan's West Side, and the Clinch River breeder reactor in Tennessee. He described them as "wasteful, environmentally questionable boondoggles."

His victory on Westway came in 1985, when Congress cut off federal funds for the controversial multibillion-dollar project. In fighting the program, Coughlin signed on with environmentalists and mass transit advocates, as well New Jersey officials who feared it would depress growth in their state. After his amendments to cut Westway funds were rejected in subcommittee and full committee, Coughlin took his fight to the House floor. There he won a lopsided victory. Eight days later, New York officials announced they would abandon Westway.

Similarly, Coughlin revealed a skepticism about water-project funding in 1987, when Appropriations Chairman Jamie L. Whitten tried to insert language into a supplemental appropriations bill to nullify a cost-sharing agreement requiring local beneficiaries of federal water projects to contribute more to their development. When Coughlin warned that he would challenge it, Whitten elected to drop the one-sentence amendment.

Coughlin has made a crusade of his opposition to the Reagan-advocated anti-satellite weapon (ASAT). He waged an unsuccessful fight against funding ASAT development in 1983. Two years later, he and California Democrat George E. Brown Jr. offered an amendment banning for one year ASAT tests against objects in space, as long as the Soviet Union maintained its existing test moratorium. The House attached the amendment to that year's defense authorization and appropriations bills. In both 1986 and 1987, the ban was extended by a year.

In 1988, however, Coughlin and Brown went for the kill — a permanent ban on the current ASAT weapon so long as the Russians did not test their own ASAT — and they misfired. The amendment went down 197-205.

Pennsylvania 13

Northwest Philadelphia Suburbs — The Main Line

In the last century, the Pennsylvania Railroad developed the rolling countryside along its main line west of Philadelphia. Among the greenery grew the mansions of the city's aristocracy. The Bullitts, Biddles and Cadwaladers still play tennis at the posh Merion Cricket Club and send their children to exclusive private schools such as Episcopal Academy.

The Main Line, which Coughlin calls home, anchors the state's most affluent district. Although only a well-versed socialite knows whether a Bryn Mawr address carries more cachet than a Gladwyne one, even a political novice is aware that both towns and all the others around them turn in a solid Republican vote. Local Republicans show a moderate bent similar to the one Coughlin practices.

Beyond the Main Line, north of the Schuylkill River, old towns like Ambler and Plymouth Meeting add to the big Republican advantage. The far-north end of the district is devoted to farming and occupied by country estates.

Most of the Democrats in the 13th gather by the river. Lined up along the Schuylkill are old mill towns like Conshohocken and Norristown and two blue-collar sections of Philadelphia, Manayunk and Roxborough.

Democratic strength in the 13th was bolstered by 1982 redistricting. Added was another Democratic section of the city — Overbrook — and Philadelphia's wealthiest area, Chestnut Hill, which is nominally Republican but shows an occasional weakness for liberal Democrats. The GOP's districtwide majority among registered voters, however, is still solid.

Population: 514,346. White 472,333 (92%), Black 33,165 (6%), Other 6,941 (1%). Spanish origin 4,156 (1%). 18 and over 392,167 (76%), 65 and over 73,644 (14%). Median age: 35.

After the vote, they speculated that the word "permanent" had made members skittish. Others suggested that earlier successes on temporary bans had spawned overconfidence that stronger language could also pass.

Earlier in his career, Coughlin focused on housing. He was ranking GOP member on the HUD subcommittee at Appropriations before switching to Transportation in 1981, and he remains on the HUD panel. Here, too, he has generally voted with Democrats to fund programs with relative generosity, but he has not always agreed with them about how to distribute the money. In 1980, Coughlin complained that rent subsidies were going to the middle class, and sought to restrict the subsidies to people with incomes below 50 percent of the median, rather than the proposed 80 percent. But members, sensitive to the constituent opposition they would generate by making such a sweeping eligibility change, rejected his idea.

In his private time, Coughlin is a well-known sailor. When two Pennsylvanians were on the crew of the *Stars and Stripes* at the 1987 America's Cup championship, he took to the floor of the House to detail their challenge. He waxed eloquent upon their victory. "Yachting's crown jewel was retrieved in the glittering, sun splashed Indian Ocean off Freemantle, Australia," he said.

At Home: Coughlin looks every bit the Main Line gentleman he is. His bow tie, upper-class accent and prestigious education are the correct trappings for the representative from the state's most affluent district.

Coughlin comes from a prosperous family in upstate Wilkes-Barre. He served in the Marines, then moved to Philadelphia for a business and legal career. A charter member of a group of young professionals that took control of the Montgomery County GOP, he worked to elect Republican William W. Scranton governor in 1962, won election to the Legislature in 1964 and four years later was running for Congress for the seat of GOP Rep. Richard S. Schweiker, who advanced to the Senate.

In most years, Coughlin enjoys effortless re-election. He has faced aggressive opposition only twice, in 1984 and 1986, from Democrat Joe Hoeffel, who left the state House to try for Congress.

In 1984, Hoeffel attacked Coughlin as "a nice guy in a bow tie with a mediocre record and little political courage." The Democrat entered that campaign with experience running in GOP territory; for eight years, he had represented a Montgomery County state House district in which more than 60 percent of the registered voters were Republicans. He charged that Coughlin did not deserve his reputation as a moderate because he had gone along with Reagan in votes on key economic and defense issues.

Hoeffel hoped that years of electoral security had lured Coughlin into complacency, but the incumbent responded with a fair amount of aggressiveness, at one point even calling Hoeffel a "wimp" on defense issues. Coughlin said his Appropriations Committee seniority enabled him to wangle extra money for SEPTA, the

Philadelphia area's regional transit system. He noted his work against the anti-satellite weapon as a sign he supported arms control.

Hoeffel managed to get 44 percent of the vote, enough to encourage him to try again in 1986. In the second campaign, he pursued largely the same themes, mocking the incumbent for spending his career "floating downstream, making no waves." But he met an even more determined Coughlin. The incumbent hired his first full-time press secretary, opened a district office in the Philadelphia portion of the 13th, and accelerated his fund raising.

Coughlin also stepped up his attacks on Hoeffel; one radio ad ridiculed the Democrat as a state legislator "who will tax and spend at every bend, doesn't give a dime about crime, awards himself a big pay raise and then walks off the job for days." Hoeffel slipped to 41 percent, and in 1988, Democrats slipped back into their customary somnambulance in the 13th.

Committees

Select Narcotics Abuse and Control (Ranking)

Appropriations (5th of 22 Republicans)
Transportation and Related Agencies (ranking); VA, HUD and Independent Agencies

Elections

1988 General

Lawrence Coughlin (R)	152,191	(67%)
Bernard Tomkin (D)	76,424	(33%)

1986 General

Lawrence Coughlin (R)	100,701	(59%)
Joseph M. Hoeffel (D)	71,381	(41%)

Previous Winning Percentages: **1984** (56%) **1982** (64%) **1980** (70%) **1978** (71%) **1976** (63%) **1974** (62%) **1972** (67%) **1970** (58%) **1968** (62%)

District Vote For President

	1988	1984	1980	1976
D	101,847 (43%)	97,696 (40%)	83,825 (34%)	109,064 (43%)
R	134,835 (56%)	146,699 (60%)	134,628 (55%)	139,707 (55%)
I			23,544 (10%)	

Campaign Finance

	Receipts	Receipts from PACs	Expend-itures
1988			
Coughlin (R)	$396,262	$150,851 (38%)	$225,412
Tomkin (D)	$62,721	$6,200 (10%)	$60,672
1986			
Coughlin (R)	$705,258	$226,446 (32%)	$702,834
Hoeffel (D)	$460,736	$205,552 (45%)	$455,101

Key Votes

1987

Raise speed limit to 65 mph	N
Approve Gephardt "fair trade" amendment	N
Ban testing of larger nuclear weapons	Y
Delay "re-flagging" of Kuwaiti tankers	N
Approve tax-raising deficit-reduction bill	N

1988

Approve aid to Nicaraguan contras	Y
Enact civil rights restoration bill over Reagan veto	Y
Kill 60-day plant-closing notification measure	N
Pass omnibus trade bill over Reagan veto	Y
Approve death penalty for drug-related murders	Y
Bar federal funds for abortions in cases of rape and incest	N
Oppose seven-day waiting period for purchase of handguns	N

Voting Studies

	Presidential Support		Party Unity		Conservative Coalition	
Year	S	O	S	O	S	O
1988	49	47	70	25	87	8
1987	51	46	56	37	67	28
1986	48	49	51	46	58	40
1985	50	49	63	33	55	45
1984	50	44	49	44	53	46
1983	57	41	56	42	52	45
1982	65	34	65	34	56	42
1981	66	32	62	34	59	39

Interest Group Ratings

Year	ADA	ACU	AFL-CIO	CCUS
1988	50	48	64	79
1987	36	52	38	60
1986	45	41	71	61
1985	50	43	59	57
1984	40	39	38	50
1983	40	45	12	90
1982	45	55	40	59
1981	35	67	33	89

14 William J. Coyne (D)

Of Pittsburgh — Elected 1980

Born: Aug. 24, 1936, Pittsburgh, Pa.
Education: Robert Morris College, B.S. 1965.
Military Career: Army, 1955-57.
Occupation: Accountant.
Family: Single.
Religion: Roman Catholic.
Political Career: Pa. House, 1971-73; Pittsburgh City Council, 1974-81; sought Democratic nomination for Pa. Senate, 1972.
Capitol Office: 2455 Rayburn Bldg. 20515; 225-2301.

In Washington: Coyne has spent his five terms compiling a solid but unremarkable record as a quiet Democratic loyalist. On the Ways and Means Committee, where he was given a seat in 1985, he seldom seeks the spotlight, and spawns few ground-breaking legislative initiatives. He toils unobtrusively behind the scenes, leaving the business of devising grand strategies to the people designated for that job — the party leadership.

Powerful Pennsylvania Democrat John P. Murtha is chiefly responsible for Coyne having a place on the influential tax-writing panel. Coyne did little campaigning in his own behalf, but Murtha made it clear that Coyne was his choice to give the Pennsylvania steel industry some representation on the panel. Coyne had four competitors for one remaining seat, including Michael A. Andrews, a Texan favored by then-Majority Leader Jim Wright. But after some complicated horse-trading that produced an alliance between Murtha and Ways and Means Chairman Dan Rostenkowski, Coyne won by one vote.

Coyne went on to become a strong supporter of tax revision on Ways and Means in the 99th Congress, but he was not noticeably involved in crafting the legislation. Quiet during much of the debate in committee, Coyne spoke out mainly on the subject of industrial development bonds, which are important to Pittsburgh and to the Democratic city government of which he is a loyal ally.

As a member of the Banking Committee in his first two terms, Coyne argued for Pittsburgh's business and financial interests, supporting extension of Clean Air Act compliance dates for the steel industry, backing the Export-Import Bank and supporting money to keep the International Monetary Fund solvent.

One of Coyne's chief concerns has been the plight of urban areas in economic decline. In 1988, he introduced a bill to revive the federal revenue-sharing program and target money to local governments whose communities are suffering high unemployment.

In the 100th and 101st Congresses, he sponsored legislation to require the Bureau of Labor Statistics to collect and report data on so-called discouraged workers. Coyne says that the unemployment rate most widely publicized by the bureau "understates the problem of joblessness in the United States" because it does not include workers who stop looking for work because they no longer believe that they can find a job. Neither of Coyne's proposals has emerged from committee.

Coyne also proposed his own version of the "enterprise zone" concept. He felt the plan advanced during the Reagan administration, offering tax incentives to promote development, would be useful only to big businesses. To help cash-starved small and medium-sized businesses get started, Coyne suggested giving them direct aid through existing programs such as community development block grants.

At Home: Coyne's political career has never forced him to stray very far from his inner-city Pittsburgh roots — he still lives in the house where he was born. Before coming to Congress, he was active in Pittsburgh politics for a decade. He worked closely with the city Democratic organization and always stressed party loyalty.

Coyne was elected to the state House in 1970 but lost a bid for the state Senate two years later. In 1973, he was elected to the City Council. On the council, he served as city chairman of the Pittsburgh Democratic Party.

When the 14th opened up in 1980 with the retirement of longtime Democratic Rep. William S. Moorhead, Coyne had the political connections to claim the seat. He got the backing of the organization and easily defeated Rep. Moorhead's son for the nomination. He went on to an easy victory over the Republican nominee and has never slipped below 75 percent of the vote in his subsequent re-elections.

Pennsylvania 14

Pittsburgh

Downtown Pittsburgh has lost its pollution and griminess over the past generation; the "Golden Triangle" that forms the heart of its business district has been transformed from a train yard into a cluster of office towers, pedestrian plazas and parks. Some local boosters seeking a more cosmopolitan image for Pittsburgh have taken to calling it "the San Francisco of the East," noting the city's hills, funicular railways, ethnic neighborhoods, busy port and large corporate community, which includes Westinghouse, Rockwell, Heinz, Mellon and USAir.

Business and government leaders have made some headway in propelling Pittsburgh beyond its blue-collar "Steeltown" past toward a new economic identity. Along the Monongahela River where steelworks once stood, a high-technology center is being developed, and other projects are under way that will modernize the Pittsburgh airport and promote the city as a center for research in fields such as computers and robotics.

Economic diversification and creeping cosmopolitanism have had little impact on voting habits in the 14th, which encompasses the entire city limits and remains very Democratic. In the city, Democrats enjoy about a 5-to-1 advantage over Republicans among registered voters.

The south side of Pittsburgh gives the city its image as a workingman's "shot-and-beer" town; it is packed with ethnic neighborhoods that revolve around local taverns and Catholic parishes.

In the district's other residential neighborhoods farther north, blacks and ethnics coexist with affluent, Jewish Squirrel Hill and the Oakland academic-medical complex, which includes Carnegie-Mellon University, the University of Pittsburgh and Children's Hospital. Republicans have some strength in the better-off areas, but Democrats still dominate.

Population: 516,629. White 398,072 (77%), Black 112,514 (22%), Other 3,413 (1%). Spanish origin 3,642 (1%). 18 and over 405,532 (78%), 65 and over 82,858 (16%). Median age: 33.

Committee

Ways and Means (19th of 23 Democrats)
Health; Human Resources

Elections

1988 General

William J. Coyne (D)	135,181	(79%)
Richard Edward Caligiuri (R)	36,719	(21%)

1986 General

William J. Coyne (D)	104,726	(90%)
Richard Edward Caligiuri (LIB)	6,058	(5%)

Previous Winning Percentages: **1984** (77%) **1982** (75%) **1980** (69%)

District Vote For President

	1988		1984		1980		1976	
D	140,594	(72%)	157,422	(68%)	123,121	(58%)	132,719	(59%)
R	51,387	(26%)	69,442	(30%)	70,994	(33%)	86,985	(39%)
I					13,337	(6%)		

Campaign Finance

	Receipts	Receipts from PACs	Expend-itures
1988			
Coyne (D)	$168,698	$156,075 (93%)	$80,730
1986			
Coyne (D)	$110,445	$101,100 (92%)	$60,903

Key Votes

1987	
Raise speed limit to 65 mph	N
Approve Gephardt "fair trade" amendment	Y
Ban testing of larger nuclear weapons	Y
Delay "re-flagging" of Kuwaiti tankers	Y
Approve tax-raising deficit-reduction bill	Y
1988	
Approve aid to Nicaraguan contras	N
Enact civil rights restoration bill over Reagan veto	Y
Kill 60-day plant-closing notification measure	N
Pass omnibus trade bill over Reagan veto	Y
Approve death penalty for drug-related murders	N
Bar federal funds for abortions in cases of rape and incest	N
Oppose seven-day waiting period for purchase of handguns	N

Voting Studies

	Presidential Support		Party Unity		Conservative Coalition	
Year	S	O	S	O	S	O
1988	19	76	92	3	11	79
1987	14	86	93	3	19	81
1986	17	81	95	3	6	94
1985	19	79	94	2	9	89
1984	30	68	91	6	17	78
1983	26	67	91	4	12	85
1982	42	57	91	7	26	74
1981	38	62	89	10	16	84

Interest Group Ratings

Year	ADA	ACU	AFL-CIO	CCUS
1988	95	0	100	31
1987	96	0	100	7
1986	100	0	100	22
1985	95	0	100	19
1984	85	5	85	33
1983	90	4	100	20
1982	90	5	95	27
1981	95	0	87	16

15 Don Ritter (R)

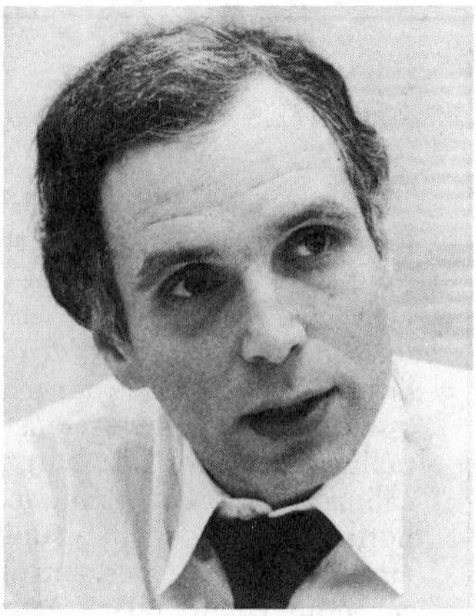

Of Coopersburg — Elected 1978

Born: Oct. 21, 1940, New York, N.Y.
Education: Lehigh U., B.S. 1961; Massachusetts Institute of Technology, M.S. 1963, Sc.D. 1966.
Occupation: Engineering consultant; professor.
Family: Wife, Edith Duerksen; two children.
Religion: Unitarian.
Political Career: No previous office.
Capitol Office: 2447 Rayburn Bldg. 20515; 225-6411.

In Washington: Ritter is a scientist, and he wants you to know it. A former metallurgy professor, he serves on two committees — Energy and Commerce, and Science, Space and Technology — where his expertise is applicable, but not always appreciated. This is because colleagues find that Ritter is prone to holding forth on technical subjects, prefacing his remarks with a reminder that his scientific background gives him special insight. As one observer of Ritter's work noted wryly, "Knowledge can sometimes be more effective when disguised."

An intense and energetic man, Ritter can show impatience with members from lay backgrounds who plunge into complex technical issues. He has made a name for himself as an opponent of scientific pork — or "quark barrell," as he calls it. He is the leading House foe of the superconducting supercollider (SSC). From the outset, Ritter claimed the project amounted to little more than a "triumph of good politics over good science."

In 1987, Ritter sought to amend the SSC authorizing legislation to delay almost all spending on the project until after the site was selected. While his proposal failed, support for the project shrank anyway as the list of potential SSC host states narrowed during 1988. Opponents of the SSC were later instrumental in significantly reducing President Reagan's original request and barring on-site construction.

In November 1988, when Texas was chosen for the SSC, some non-Texans who had been ardent SSC supporters cried "politics." Ritter seemed to take great pleasure in this: "I knew it," he said. "I knew this would happen."

By contrast, Ritter is a vocal supporter of a federal role in developing domestic high-definition television (HDTV), a science the Japanese have pioneered. He is a leading member of the HDTV caucus, which maintains that the semiconductor chip at the heart of HDTV has crucial implications for the future of the American electronics industry.

Ritter's concern for high-tech competitiveness is not surprising; Allentown has a large AT&T facility that manufactures electronic circuitry. But there is another side to Ritter's desire to keep pace with the Japanese, one that reflects the frustrations of the blue-collar workers — particularly steelworkers — in the factories that make up the older industrial foundation of the Lehigh Valley economy.

When Energy and Commerce held a 1989 hearing on allowing an American aerospace company help Japan develop a new fighter plane, the FS-X, Ritter joined the opposition. While some complained that Japan would exploit American technology, Ritter also said that purchase of a U.S.-made jet "would have gone a long way toward demonstrating Japan's sincerity about reducing its $55 billion trade surplus."

Though his overall record is conservative, Ritter frequently strays from the GOP line on labor issues. In the 100th Congress, he was one of just 17 Republicans to favor mandatory retaliation against countries with unfair trade practices, and one of just a handful of Republicans to vote against eliminating a plant-closing notification proposal. Ritter also voted to override Reagan's veto of the trade bill.

In 1987, Ritter joined several House colleagues on the Capitol lawn to sledgehammer Toshiba products. They were protesting the company's selling of restricted high-technology products to the Soviet Union, a country Ritter frequently decries.

A senior Republican member of the Helsinki commission, Ritter matches his eye for detail with rough rhetoric when he reviews Soviet policies. In a May 1989 opinion column in *The Washington Post,* he detailed the Soviet Union's new legal code and condemned the recent reforms, saying that while they are being protrayed as efforts to defend democracy, in fact the reforms are "clearly designed to intimidate would-be critics, dissidents or nationalists into accepting *glasnost* on the state's terms — or else."

Ritter's scientific background and his constituents' concerns also coalesce on clean-air legislation. When the measure was first debated in the 97th Congress, Ritter used his familiarity with the chemical effects of air pollutants to try

Pennsylvania 15

East — Allentown; Bethlehem

The heavy industry, strong unions and large ethnic population (including a sizable Jewish community) of the Lehigh Valley bespeak Democratic sentiments. But disaffection with Democratic candidates, both local and national, has lured voters in the valley to the GOP in recent years. Jimmy Carter carried the area within the 15th in 1976, but Ronald Reagan and George Bush won it in the 1980s.

Lehigh County (Allentown) has the largest population and is politically competitive. Allentown had a Republican mayor until 1981, and in 1988 Lehigh County gave Bush 56 percent. Although singer Billy Joel chose Allentown in 1982 to represent the plight of the new unemployed, the recession did not hit the city quite as hard as some other places because of its diversified economy, which spins out Mack trucks, appliances and clothing.

The showpiece of the "new" Allentown economy is a huge AT&T facility that produces some of the world's most advanced electronic circuitry. Some local factories depend on the high-quality craftsmanship of Pennsylvania Dutch workers, who are attractive to the corporations because they are conservative and resist unionization.

Pennsylvania's fourth-largest city, with a population of more than 100,000, Allentown has an unspectacular downtown, but neat and pleasant residential sections that are a legacy of its Pennsylvania Dutch founders. The prosperous West End is Republican, with blue-collar Democrats spread through the rest of the town.

Neighboring Northampton County has a grittier ambience, thanks to the presence of heavier industry there. The smokestacks of Bethlehem Steel dominate the Bethlehem landscape, and the massive corporation dominates the city, providing its tax base and financing urban-renewal projects. Nearby Easton produces chemicals and paper products.

Outside the Allentown-Bethlehem-Easton corridor, Lehigh and Northampton counties are steady sources of Republican votes. Many of the farmers are of Pennsylvania Dutch heritage. The corridor is becoming a bedroom outpost of New York commuters looking for affordable housing.

Population: 515,259. White 497,609 (97%), Black 8,189 (2%), Other 2,936 (1%). Spanish origin 14,193 (3%). 18 and over 385,814 (75%), 65 and over 65,768 (13%). Median age: 33.

to shoot down the arguments of those who lobbied for tougher standards that would have further burdened industry.

Ritter also took a pro-industry stand during debate over expansion of the "superfund" toxic-waste cleanup program. In the 98th Congress, Ritter and New York Republican Norman F. Lent won adoption of committee amendments limiting the fund to $9 billion and blocking the power of victims to sue polluters in federal court. Ritter ultimately voted for the bill as it passed the House, even though it had been increased to $10.2 billion and did not contain his lawsuit prohibition.

When the bill was taken up again in the 99th Congress, Ritter opposed efforts to require companies to make public an inventory of their chemical emissions known or suspected to cause cancer or birth defects. He argued that there was no scientific evidence of a crisis of hazardous emissions. "Our modern technological society cannot afford to conduct a Salem-type witch hunt on every polysyllabic chemical substance," he said.

At Home: It was Ritter's extraordinary energy, rather than his political program, that brought him victory in 1978 over Democratic Rep. Fred Rooney, chairman of the Commerce Subcommittee on Transportation. Rooney never really made enemies at home; he simply grew less and less visible. By 1978 he was sending telegrams to gatherings he once had attended. Ritter courted Democrats who wondered where Rooney was, and it paid off with a 53 percent victory.

Since then, Ritter has been both a salesman for his philosophy and a spokesman for his district's needs. In an area where steel and other old industries are struggling, he talks fervently about government giving private enterprise free rein so it can generate a new industrial revolution based on high technology.

But Ritter balances his interest in high technology with responsiveness to immediate economic problems. In 1984, his advocacy of import quotas for steel won him valuable publicity at home. Though Reagan did not impose the mandatory quotas sought by Ritter and others, steelworkers in the 15th ended up convinced that Ritter had gone to bat for them.

Local Democratic leaders seem at a loss to find the right kind of candidate to challenge Ritter. Against each of his five re-election opponents, he has won by comfortable, though by no means overwhelming, margins.

The recession brought heavy unemployment to the Lehigh Valley in 1982, but Democrats failed to field a seasoned candidate. They put up Richard J. Orloski, whose lone government experience was as a state deputy attorney general. Four GOP incumbents in Pennsylvania lost that year, but not Ritter.

The 1984 Democratic nominee was not the type one would expect to find seeking office in a working-class district. Jane Wells-Schooley came out of the feminist movement, serving as vice president of the National Organization for Women until 1982.

A number of her positions were controversial; she backed legalized abortion, for example, and supported a nuclear-weapons freeze. She tried to focus voters' attention on economic issues, but the dialogue often strayed onto other topics. At an event kicking off Ritter's campaign, one speaker noted Wells-Schooley's ties to NOW and said that promoting homosexual rights is "the No. 1 goal" of NOW. Most voters saw Wells-Schooley's views as too exotic, and Ritter won easily.

In 1986, Ritter's challenger was Joe Simonetta, a former commander of a NATO missile team in Greece, who focused on the need to slow down the nuclear arms race. Strapped for money, the challenger ran his low-budget, door-to-door effort out of his parents' basement. Ritter was breezing to re-election when he jolted voters with an unexpected issue — his past drug use. The incumbent had initially brought up the topic of drug abuse when he announced that he and his staff would take drug tests. Ritter's admission that he had smoked marijuana a decade or so earlier came only after Simonetta questioned him about past drug use.

While the issue provided Simonetta with an opening he did not previously have, it did not derail Ritter. He won 57 percent of the vote.

In 1988, Democrats made a more concerted effort. Ed Reibman, an attorney active in the local party, won the Democratic nomination on the strength of his strong labor backing and his name, which is familiar because his mother is a well-known state senator from the area (she also was the party's nominee against Ritter in 1980). Reibman chastised Ritter's attendance record and acceptance of honoraria, and criticized his votes on seniors' issues. But outspent nearly 2-to-1, Reibman was no match for Ritter. The Republican portrayed himself as a hard worker, airing TV ads showing him on an airplane, coming home "like clockwork" to the district.

Committees

Energy and Commerce (8th of 17 Republicans)
Commerce, Consumer Protection and Competitiveness (ranking); Telecommunications and Finance

Science, Space and Technology (6th of 19 Republicans)
Investigations and Oversight (ranking); Science, Research and Technology

Elections

1988 General		
Don Ritter (R)	106,951	(57%)
Ed Reibman (D)	79,127	(43%)
1986 General		
Don Ritter (R)	74,829	(57%)
Joe Simonetta (D)	56,972	(43%)

Previous Winning Percentages: **1984** (58%) **1982** (58%) **1980** (60%) **1978** (53%)

District Vote For President

	1988	1984	1980	1976
D	84,618 (44%)	81,072 (42%)	68,570 (39%)	91,229 (52%)
R	103,784 (55%)	110,142 (57%)	89,260 (50%)	81,662 (46%)
I			16,201 (9%)	

Campaign Finance

	Receipts	Receipts from PACs	Expend-itures
1988			
Ritter (R)	$759,713	$293,454 (39%)	$752,332
Reibman (D)	$359,820	$97,650 (27%)	$355,016
1986			
Ritter (R)	$439,700	$153,178 (35%)	$440,370
Simonetta (D)	$51,656	0	$51,639

Key Votes

1987	
Raise speed limit to 65 mph	Y
Approve Gephardt "fair trade" amendment	Y
Ban testing of larger nuclear weapons	?
Delay "re-flagging" of Kuwaiti tankers	N
Approve tax-raising deficit-reduction bill	N
1988	
Approve aid to Nicaraguan contras	Y
Enact civil rights restoration bill over Reagan veto	N
Kill 60-day plant-closing notification measure	N
Pass omnibus trade bill over Reagan veto	Y
Approve death penalty for drug-related murders	Y
Bar federal funds for abortions in cases of rape and incest	Y
Oppose seven-day waiting period for purchase of handguns	Y

Voting Studies

	Presidential Support		Party Unity		Conservative Coalition	
Year	S	O	S	O	S	O
1988	57	39	66	26	84	11
1987	63	33	68	25	81	19
1986	70	29	65	29	88	10
1985	75	23	71	22	76	20
1984	56	42	74	21	73	20
1983	76	22	81	16	82	16
1982	73	26	83	16	78	21
1981	71	24	82	17	76	19

Interest Group Ratings

Year	ADA	ACU	AFL-CIO	CCUS
1988	10	84	62	77
1987	20	64	38	73
1986	10	90	57	94
1985	10	86	38	82
1984	15	52	50	63
1983	10	86	29	79
1982	20	82	30	76
1981	10	100	21	84

16 Robert S. Walker (R)

Of East Petersburg — Elected 1976

Born: Dec. 23, 1942, Bradford, Pa.
Education: Millersville U., B.S. 1964; U. of Delaware, M.A. 1968.
Military Career: Pa. National Guard, 1967-73.
Occupation: High school teacher; congressional aide.
Family: Wife, Sue Albertson.
Religion: Presbyterian.
Political Career: No previous office.
Capitol Office: 2445 Rayburn Bldg. 20515; 225-2411.

In Washington: For Walker, winning appointment as chief deputy whip in March 1989 was an especially personal vindication of the confrontational tactics that he and his allies in the Conservative Opportunity Society (COS) had urged upon a House GOP leadership they viewed as too accepting of minority status.

When the COS first became a force a few years back, its leader, Newt Gingrich, got most of the credit as the spinner of ideas. Walker, on the other hand, was viewed simply as the group's blunt instrument — a strident, repetitious and tiresome obstructionist, the quintessential legislative outsider.

But when Gingrich was elected GOP whip a few weeks into the 101st Congress, he brought Walker into the leadership to help him. Asked afterward whether, like many rebels-turned-insiders, he would become more accommodating to his adversaries, Walker gave no quarter.

"I don't see much evidence that Republicans won great victories when they were not confrontational but passive instead," Walker said. "In 34 years, we were not able to get a majority; there's no victory there."

Walker, Gingrich and others first gained prominence by using C-SPAN — the cable TV system that carries live broadcasts of House proceedings — to sell their conservative message nationwide. In 1984, it was a Walker "special order" speech (at the end of the legislative day) that led to the famous shouting match between Speaker Thomas P. O'Neill Jr. and Gingrich. Two days after Gingrich and Walker used a special order to excoriate Democrats for past foreign policy statements, Walker was giving a special order when O'Neill secretly ordered the TV cameras to pull back and pan the House. For the first time, viewers saw that the chamber was virtually empty. The next day, as Gingrich grilled O'Neill for his unannounced move, O'Neill got so angry at the Georgian that his language overstepped the bounds of House custom; the Speaker was officially rebuked.

While the COS members were often referred to as the Republicans' leading "bomb throwers," their weapons in the early stages were actually more like flash grenades, creating a lot of heat and smoke, but inflicting little injury on their targets. The firebrands crafted and passed few substantive pieces of legislation, and the Democrats expanded their House majority in the 1986 and 1988 elections. The heyday of the COS seemed over.

In fact, the COS leadership had spent a little less time on the House floor railing to an empty chamber, and a lot more time currying favor with a cadre of mainly young, moderate Republican colleagues who were equally frustrated with their "permanent" minority status. The eventual support of such members was crucial to Gingrich's victory for whip over a traditional GOP insider, Edward Madigan of Illinois; one of those moderates, Steve Gunderson of Wisconsin, shares the title of chief deputy whip with Walker.

In the 100th Congress, Walker and his allies also demonstrated a capacity to target their legislative efforts, and even to compromise, to bring a sweeping proposal to fruition. After much wrangling, Walker's "drug-free work place" measure was enacted as part of an omnibus anti-drug abuse bill; it allows the federal government to cut off funding to contractors who fail to make a "good-faith" effort to keep illegal drug use out of their work sites.

Walker's initial version was a draconian concept — allowing a cutoff of federal contracts to a company if an employee was found in possession of a single marijuana cigarette. Democrats treated it as a joke — an example, they said, of COS extremism. When Walker, then the ranking Republican of the Science Subcommittee on Space (and now ranking on the full committee), first submitted his bill in April 1988, committee Democrat Dave McCurdy of Oklahoma laughed out loud. Later, Wisconsin Democrat David R. Obey called it "a laughable piece of garbage."

But Walker laughed last. In his finest confrontational manner, he threatened the bill's opponents with a soft-on-drugs label. "If the opposition thinks it is a good thing to continue to have illegal drug use . . . that is fine with me,"

Pennsylvania 16

Southeast — Lancaster

The image of the 16th District is one of horse-drawn buggies on country lanes and black-clad "plain people" tending crops. But the 16th grew by 15 percent during the 1970s, faster than any district in the state. The district's largest county — Lancaster — grew by nearly 9 percent during the early 1980s, as 31,000 new residents arrived.

One factor helping fuel the growth is the favorable business climate. Companies looking to start new plants are drawn by the strong work ethic of its labor force, a trait of the Pennsylvania Dutch who settled this area and still are an important influence.

The newcomers to the 16th do not wear black as the Amish farmers do, but they share one common outlook — they are conservative Republicans.

Lancaster County does have Democratic pockets in the city of Lancaster, where electrical appliances and other household items are made, and in the Susquehanna River town of Columbia, which has a glass plant. But it is the scenic farm country — with its oddly named hamlets, such as Bird-in-Hand and Intercourse — that sets the tone for the district. And it is a conservative tone indeed.

Three percent of Lancaster County's population is Amish. Some of the sects cling closer to the old ways than others. They range from the Old Order Amish, who in effect live in the mid-19th century, to the "black-bumper Mennonites," who drive cars but paint the chrome bumpers black. The excellent farm land is devoted largely to dairying, although tobacco has a niche in the agricultural economy.

The district also encompasses all of Lebanon County. It is famous for its bologna, much of it produced by a company whose owner is a former Speaker of the Pennsylvania House. Like Lancaster County, Lebanon County is steadfastly Republican; in 1988, both counties voted overwhelmingly for George Bush.

Population: 514,585. White 494,052 (96%), Black 10,641 (2%), Other 3,290 (1%). Spanish origin 11,175 (2%). 18 and over 369,823 (72%), 65 and over 59,793 (12%). Median age: 31.

Walker said portentiously. In an election year in which the increase in drug crime was a major issue, Walker's implied threat was compelling to many Democrats.

Walker attached his proposal to several Science authorization bills, then used his skill at House floor tactics to attach it to a series of appropriations bills. The Democratic leadership, recognizing the political risks of trying to shoot down the measure, developed a strategy to co-opt it. A party task force drew up an alternative that softened the edges of the drug-free work place concept: Contractors would be penalized only for a track record of drug violations, rather than a single instance, and the president could waive the requirement if necessary for the national interest.

Walker at first disclaimed the compromise, calling it a "drugs-in-the-work-place amendment." But by the time the Government Operations Committee attached the revised plan to the omnibus drug bill — virtually guaranteeing its adoption — Walker was on board. Though the final wording made the provision far less stringent than Walker originally planned, he said, "I think we do have a better bill as a result of the compromises that have taken place."

Even with this success, though, it is doubtful that many colleagues outside his circle of allies were waiting with warm congratulations for Walker. He has raised too many hackles and rubbed too many raw nerves to be very popular.

His performance in trying to slow the rush to adjournment at the end of the 100th Congress was vintage Walker. The Democratic leadership was trying to push through a long list of bills, most on relatively minor matters, under "suspension of the rules," which limits debate but requires a two-thirds majority for passage. Walker, stating that he wanted to make a partisan point about the Democrats' rush to pass insignificant legislation while failing to act on such important bills as the Clean Air Act, demanded roll-call votes on each measure.

As a result, a record 40 roll-call votes were held on Oct. 4, 1988, requiring members who were trying to wrap up their year's work to spend their day on the floor, casting votes on less-than-urgent issues. When Walker finally relented, stating he would not request roll calls on all bills the next day, Democrat Leon E. Panetta of California said, "If Walker had continued to do it, his life would have been in jeopardy." The rancor was not limited to Democrats. "It's an asinine series of votes," said Illinois Republican Henry J. Hyde.

With his dilatory floor tactics, Walker has more than once set himself up for accusations that he is insensitive to his colleagues' prerogatives. Just before his roll-call frenzy, Walker had blocked a unanimous-consent request that would have brought to the floor an emergency proposal to extend an expiring program that helped AIDS patients buy life-prolonging drugs. Despite a plea from Georgia Democrat J. Roy Rowland that "it's a matter of life and death for some 200 people in my state," Walker declined to back down, forcing bill supporters to gain Rules Committee approval for floor consideration.

Given Walker's role as a contrarian and his zeal for budget-cutting, some find it ironic that he plays a much more traditional, turf-conscious role as a Republican leader on the Science Committee. He is a strong supporter of the National Aeronautics and Space Administration and other federally funded research agencies.

At Home: Walker's confrontational Republican politics have been successful not only among the new arrivals in burgeoning Lancaster County but also among his more traditionally minded Pennsylvania Dutch constituents. Conservatism sells well here, and Walker is a born salesman.

When he wanted to publicize his campaign against food stamp abuse, he went to work in a grocery store. When he wanted to go after the Department of Energy, he compiled a list of its most questionable-sounding grants — for such things as a solar hot dog cooker — that was then included in Johnny Carson's monologue on the "Tonight" show.

After a short stint working as a teacher, Walker signed on as an aide to his representative, Republican Edwin D. Eshleman, and eventually became his administrative assistant. When Eshleman decided to step down in 1976, he backed his young protégé in an 11-way primary fight for the seat.

Walker stressed his Washington experience and, with the help of Eshleman's endorsement and the top ballot position, he eked out a victory with 20 percent of the vote. Given Lancaster's strong Republican sentiments, he has had no problems since.

Committee

Science, Space and Technology (Ranking)

Elections

1988 General

Robert S. Walker (R)	136,944	(74%)
Ernest Eric Guyll (D)	48,169	(26%)

1986 General

Robert S. Walker (R)	100,784	(75%)
James D. Hagelgans (D)	34,399	(25%)

Previous Winning Percentages: **1984** (78%) **1982** (71%) **1980** (77%) **1978** (77%) **1976** (62%)

District Vote For President

	1988	1984	1980	1976
D	57,122 (30%)	47,806 (26%)	45,062 (26%)	55,703 (36%)
R	132,130 (70%)	137,560 (74%)	115,623 (66%)	97,132 (63%)
I			11,416 (7%)	

Campaign Finance

	Receipts	Receipts from PACs	Expend-itures
1988			
Walker (R)	$106,318	$44,375 (42%)	$91,950
1986			
Walker (R)	$79,700	$31,297 (39%)	$75,730

Key Votes

1987	
Raise speed limit to 65 mph	Y
Approve Gephardt "fair trade" amendment	N
Ban testing of larger nuclear weapons	N
Delay "re-flagging" of Kuwaiti tankers	N
Approve tax-raising deficit-reduction bill	N
1988	
Approve aid to Nicaraguan contras	Y
Enact civil rights restoration bill over Reagan veto	N
Kill 60-day plant-closing notification measure	Y
Pass omnibus trade bill over Reagan veto	N
Approve death penalty for drug-related murders	Y
Bar federal funds for abortions in cases of rape and incest	Y
Oppose seven-day waiting period for purchase of handguns	Y

Voting Studies

	Presidential Support		Party Unity		Conservative Coalition	
Year	**S**	**O**	**S**	**O**	**S**	**O**
1988	78	22	95	3	95	5
1987	83	17	97	3	91	9
1986	82	17	96	4	94	6
1985	80	20	93	5	85	15
1984	66	30	92	6	88	12
1983	80	20	94	6	81	19
1982	68	32	92	8	84	16
1981	72	18	84	12	80	15

Interest Group Ratings

Year	ADA	ACU	AFL-CIO	CCUS
1988	5	100	7	93
1987	4	96	0	87
1986	0	86	14	94
1985	15	86	12	91
1984	10	83	8	60
1983	20	96	6	80
1982	15	96	20	82
1981	10	100	27	89

17 George W. Gekas (R)

Of Harrisburg — Elected 1982

Born: April 14, 1930, Harrisburg, Pa.
Education: Dickinson College, B.A. 1952; Dickinson School of Law, LL.B., J.D. 1958.
Military Career: Army, 1953-55.
Occupation: Lawyer.
Family: Wife, Evangeline Charas.
Religion: Greek Orthodox.
Political Career: Pa. House, 1967-75; Pa. Senate, 1977-83.
Capitol Office: 1519 Longworth Bldg. 20515; 225-4315.

In Washington: Gekas has built his House career around the same issue that brought him prominence in the Pennsylvania Legislature — crime. And sometimes he can be as unyielding toward those who disagree with him on the issue as he is toward the criminals themselves.

Gekas is Congress' leading proponent of capital punishment; he is always on the lookout to attach death-penalty language to bills passing through the Judiciary Committee.

In the last two Congresses, Gekas has brought his conservative doggedness to the debate on anti-drug legislation. In the 99th Congress, he almost single-handedly sidetracked the $1.7 billion drug bill over the death penalty. During House debate, he successfully offered an amendment authorizing the death penalty for certain drug-related crimes. "There can be no ultimate war on drugs," he said, "if we do not cast our ultimate weapon."

The Senate version of the bill passed without the Gekas amendment. Gekas vowed not to permit any bill to become law without his proposal, and when the House received the Senate-passed bill for modifications, it voted to send it back reinstating his language. Gekas' amendment was dropped from the final package, as the drug bill was split into two measures — the compromise bill without a death penalty, and a companion resolution, ignored by the Senate, mandating inclusion of the death penalty.

As work began on the 100th Congress' drug bill, Gekas vowed to use "every parliamentary maneuver known to mankind" to ensure enactment of a death-penalty bill. His amendment, providing the death penalty for individuals convicted of drug-related murders, was adopted 299-111. This time, it remained on the bill and was signed into law.

Other Gekas death-penalty proposals have not fared as well. When Judiciary in 1988 took up a bill implementing a treaty making genocide a crime, Gekas offered an amendment to include the death penalty if a death occurred as a result of a crime defined in the treaty. It was rejected by voice vote. In 1989, he introduced a bill calling for a federal death penalty for espionage, treason and murder.

On Judiciary, Gekas is part of a combative group who chafe at the panel's liberal majority. Since the 99th Congress, he has been ranking Republican on the Criminal Justice Subcommittee. There, he has battled with Democrats over revision of the federal insanity defense. The issue arose after the acquittal on insanity of Ronald Reagan's 1981 assailant, John W. Hinckley Jr. Gekas blasted one Democratic proposal for new insanity language as an "adventurous foray into the unknown" that would grant defendants "new rights." Gekas' proposal to restrict furloughs of criminals acquitted solely by reason of insanity found its way onto the 1988 drug bill.

At Home: A member of Harrisburg's small but influential Greek community, Gekas took the traditional path to political success in central Pennsylvania. He went to a local college and law school, became an assistant district attorney, then moved on to the state Capitol.

Gekas fashioned his state legislative career around the same hard-line stand against crime. He managed capital-punishment legislation, chaired the state Senate Judiciary Committee, and wrote a tough mandatory-sentencing bill.

Gekas encountered remarkably few obstacles on his path to Congress in 1982. He launched his campaign after Democratic Rep. Allen Ertel announced for governor and after the GOP-controlled Legislature approved new district lines favoring election of a Republican.

In the primary, Gekas was endorsed by the GOP in Dauphin County (Harrisburg), and won nomination handily over a candidate backed by the Lycoming County GOP.

Gekas rolled over his November opponent, Dauphin County Commissioner Larry J. Hochendoner, who had lost to Gekas in a 1976 state Senate contest. With a 3-to-1 spending advantage, Gekas ran media ads almost daily, his principal spot showing him at a lunch counter waiting on tables and serving pizza.

Pennsylvania 17

Central — Harrisburg; Williamsport

This elongated district, which follows the Susquehanna River, amply displays the GOP affinities of central Pennsylvania. Democrats held it three terms (until 1982), but that was an aberration. Now back in GOP hands, the 17th seems likely to stay there.

Dauphin County (Harrisburg) has almost half the people in the 17th. To the north, Lycoming County (Williamsport) is second, with slightly more than a fourth.

The large state government complex and manufacturing sector in Harrisburg provide enough Democratic votes to make the party competitive for local and state offices. The state capital, a victim of white flight to the suburbs, now is 40 percent black, enhancing Democratic strength there.

In 1982, Dauphin County went Democratic for governor (the nominee was the 17th's departing incumbent), but in 1986, the county voted Republican in both the gubernatorial and Senate contests. George Bush carried it in the 1988 presidential contest.

The presence of the state government prevents life around Harrisburg from being as placid as it is elsewhere in central Pennsylvania. More serious than the constant political flare-ups was the 1979 accident at the nearby Three Mile Island nuclear plant.

Upriver from Harrisburg, the hills and farms turn out large Republican majorities. Snyder and Union were among the four counties in the state to go for Barry Goldwater in 1964. Democrats can be found in coal-mining Northumberland County and in Williamsport, which manufactures aircraft engines, publishes *Grit* magazine and hosts the Little League World Series.

Population: 515,900. White 476,806 (92%), Black 34,261 (7%), Other 2,399 (1%). Spanish origin 4,637 (1%). 18 and over 376,440 (73%), 65 and over 63,411 (12%). Median age: 31.

Committee

Judiciary (6th of 14 Republicans)
Criminal Justice (ranking); Crime

Elections

1988 General		
George W. Gekas (R)	166,289	(100%)
1986 General		
George W. Gekas (R)	101,027	(74%)
Michael S. Ogden (D)	36,157	(26%)

Previous Winning Percentages: **1984** (73%) **1982** (58%)

District Vote For President

	1988	1984	1980	1976
D	64,516 (36%)	61,212 (33%)	58,724 (32%)	75,275 (40%)
R	112,949 (63%)	123,660 (66%)	110,417 (61%)	108,300 (58%)
I			11,412 (6%)	

Campaign Finance

	Receipts	Receipts from PACs	Expend-itures
1988			
Gekas (R)	$95,878	$46,750 (49%)	$97,611
1986			
Gekas (R)	$149,086	$50,014 (34%)	$90,963

Key Votes

1987	
Raise speed limit to 65 mph	Y
Approve Gephardt "fair trade" amendment	N
Ban testing of larger nuclear weapons	N
Delay "re-flagging" of Kuwaiti tankers	N
Approve tax-raising deficit-reduction bill	N
1988	
Approve aid to Nicaraguan contras	Y
Enact civil rights restoration bill over Reagan veto	N
Kill 60-day plant-closing notification measure	Y
Pass omnibus trade bill over Reagan veto	N
Approve death penalty for drug-related murders	Y
Bar federal funds for abortions in cases of rape and incest	N
Oppose seven-day waiting period for purchase of handguns	Y

Voting Studies

	Presidential Support		Party Unity		Conservative Coalition	
Year	S	O	S	O	S	O
1988	72	27	93	5	97	3
1987	70	29	90	10	84	16
1986	76	23	83	16	92	8
1985	73	28	85	15	87	13
1984	62	35	81	17	88	12
1983	79	20	82	17	76	22

Interest Group Ratings

Year	ADA	ACU	AFL-CIO	CCUS
1988	10	92	21	93
1987	8	83	13	87
1986	10	73	36	83
1985	15	76	29	73
1984	20	67	15	75
1983	20	70	6	95

18 Doug Walgren (D)

Of Mount Lebanon — Elected 1976

Born: Dec. 28, 1940, Rochester, N.Y.
Education: Dartmouth College, B.A. 1963; Stanford U. Law School, LL.B. 1966.
Occupation: Lawyer.
Family: Wife, Carmala Vincent; three children.
Religion: Roman Catholic.
Political Career: Democratic nominee for U.S. House, 1970, 1972 special election, 1972 general election.
Capitol Office: 2241 Rayburn Bldg. 20515; 225-2135.

In Washington: Walgren sometimes seems almost too meek to be a legislative activist. When he speaks up in committee, he sounds apologetic for taking the time of his colleagues. When he argues a point, he notes he is not trying to impose his views on anyone. And when he presides over his subcommittee, he appears uncomfortable employing the gavel.

When it comes to legislation, however, forcefulness is not everything. Quiet persistence coupled with a history of party loyalty can bring some victories. Every two years, Walgren's diligence allows him to compile a respectable legislative record, on issues as diverse as fire prevention and technical training at community colleges.

While Walgren is not one of the key players on Energy and Commerce, he has secured a niche on the Science Committee, where the political wrangling is not as intense. As chairman of the Science, Research and Technology Subcommittee, he has seen a number of initiatives become law. After several years of effort by Walgren, the 99th Congress enacted the Technology Transfer Act, which authorized government-owned laboratories to enter into cooperative research agreements.

Like the full committee chairman, New Jersey's Robert A. Roe, Walgren is a leading advocate of earmarking scientific research funds. Critics dub the practice "scientific pork," saying Congress cannot effectively direct research, but its supporters maintain that earmarking is needed to help emerging schools. The academic research facilities modernization program has been proposed as a way to curb the problems of earmarking, and to help smaller schools develop. Without curbing his appetite for earmarking, Walgren signed on as an advocate. "The new science of tomorrow cannot really be done in the old facilities of today," he says.

Bioethics is another aspect of scientific research where Walgren sees a vital role for Congress. He has expressed concern about the applications of current efforts to map, or sequence, man's genetic code, which could give scientists vast amounts of information about individuals. At a hearing on the subject, Walgren pulled something from his pocket and with a sincere look of puzzlement said to a panel of experts, "I have a toothbrush here. Could you sequence me from this?"

Though the panel could not answer whether science will be able to map genetic codes from traces of saliva, Walgren said the implications of that possibility warrant congressional observation.

On many controversial subjects handled by Energy and Commerce, Walgren tries to balance his personal background of liberal social concern — he was a legal services lawyer in the 1960s — with the more conservative middle-class interests of his suburban Pittsburgh constituency.

His competing allegiances are most clearly tested by deliberations on the Clean Air Act and acid-rain control. While trying to ensure relief for the steel industry, which feels pinched by environmental regulation, Walgren generally sides with the enviromental faction. In 1987, when the House voted to postpone economic sanctions against areas failing to meet air quality standards, Walgren favored the eight-month extension rather than the longer extension sought by industry and Commerce Committee Chairman John D. Dingell.

Earlier in his career, Walgren's backing of environmentalist views alienated U.S. Steel (now USX Corp.) officials, who constitute a significant force in the 18th. But their concerns quieted after Walgren offered his own acid-rain proposal in the 98th Congress requiring the Environmental Protection Agency to review acid-rain research every two years, and issue regulations if federal action was necessary.

Walgren also pushed legislation in the 98th Congress to create a five-year coal science and engineering development program to study ways to reduce sulfur emissions. Ultimately, Congress passed some provisions of the legislation, providing $750 million for coal research. For Walgren the proposal was good politics. The federal government's largest coal research

Pennsylvania 18

Pittsburgh Suburbs

The 18th is a suburban doughnut surrounding Pittsburgh, with a bite taken out of the eastern part of the ring. The Democratic Party has a significantly smaller registration advantage in the 18th than it once did, because the last round of redistricting transferred out western Pittsburgh and some Democratic suburbs. The 18th now can be counted on to vote solidly GOP in presidential elections, but its affluent, highly educated electorate — second in the state in income and schooling only to the suburban Philadelphia 13th — knows how to split tickets, as Walgren's sustained success has shown.

The Democrat has proven his strength in the past in such prosperous Republican suburbs as Mount Lebanon (his home) and Sewickley. Still wealthier Fox Chapel, where zoning in some areas requires a minimum of three acres for building a residence, has generally opposed him.

In addition to this nominal Republican territory, the 18th has several communities where Democrats have a slight registration lead — Jefferson, South Park and Bethel Park. It also includes the steelworker suburbs clustered around the Greater Pittsburgh Airport — North Fayette, Findlay, Moon and Robinson.

North of the Ohio River are more well-off suburbs on the order of Sewickley. The upper part of Allegheny County contains Pine, Richland, McCandless and other newly developing towns that lean Republican. South of the Allegheny River is Penn Hills, a sprawling and diverse township that is marginally Democratic.

Population: 516,050. White 499,453 (97%), Black 12,110 (2%), Other 3,487 (1%). Spanish origin 2,359 (1%). 18 and over 382,408 (74%), 65 and over 59,090 (11%). Median age: 34.

center is located in his district.

Walgren has taken a hand at trying to counter 1980s GOP boasting that Republicans will take a majority by becoming the party of prosperity and growth. Speaking to college students in 1984, Walgren said that Democrats are "going to do very well among young urban types, because statistics show that for every young person who's upwardly mobile, there's two who are downwardly mobile. Any party that exhibits a sympathy for the downwardly mobile will come out with the majority, because the majority are downwardly mobile."

At Home: It took four tries for Walgren to win his House seat, but since his victory in 1976, he has fared quite well in a district where the GOP is locked in a pattern of squandering chances to recapture control. In 1980, 1984 and 1988, when presidential coattails might have helped a credible GOP nominee in the 18th, Republicans offered weak challengers.

Walgren's current success contrasts with the initial stage of his political career, which was studded with setbacks. In his early races for the House, Walgren ran as a Vietnam dove and lost to three different Republicans, including John Heinz in the 1972 general election.

After his third defeat, Walgren settled down to practice law until Heinz ran for the Senate in 1976. By that time, Walgren was more than willing to run in alliance with the regular Allegheny County Democratic organization. He won the nomination in a crowded primary field. In the 1976 general election, Walgren sounded fewer liberal themes as he faced Robert J. Casey, a public relations consultant and one of the founders of the conservative Committee for the Survival of a Free Congress. Casey dismayed many moderate Republicans and angered organized labor with his advocacy of right-to-work laws. Walgren finally won a House seat.

After two uneventful re-elections, Walgren's winning margin narrowed in 1982, after the GOP Legislature lopped off the dependably Democratic inner-city part of his district and added Republican suburbs.

The Republican challenger was Ted Jacob, the same hard-charging, abrasive opponent Walgren had defeated in 1978. Jacob spent freely from his personal wealth, running television ads in midsummer, unusually early for a House race. National Republicans were optimistic that Walgren could be unseated.

But the incumbent responded effectively. He stressed his conservative side, joining Jacob in backing a constitutional amendment to outlaw busing. That appealed to a newly added section of the district that had been involved in a busing controversy.

Heading into 1984, Walgren enhanced his moderate image by being the first Pennsylvania congressman to endorse the Democratic presidential candidacy of Ohio Sen. John Glenn.

More important, though, was the squabbling and consequent disarray in the Allegheny County GOP organization, which hindered the party's effort to recruit a strong candidate. The nomination went to lawyer John Maxwell, a two-time loser in bids for local offices, and Walgren cruised to re-election.

In 1986, the GOP regrouped and fielded a

well-financed challenger, wealthy GOP businessman Ernie Buckman. He spent roughly $1 million that year, but struggled throughout the campaign to find an effective theme.

In spite of voting routinely against most of President Reagan's initiatives, Walgren projected an air of bipartisanship. He often appeared with GOP Sen. Heinz on Pittsburgh-area news shows to report on congressional matters, and his final pre-election congressional newsletter featured photos with Vice President George Bush and Heinz.

Republicans had long complained that Walgren was too liberal, but Buckman tried to argue that he was ineffective as well. In one ad, the challenger maintained that Walgren had introduced 69 bills and gotten only one passed — an alleged "batting average" of .014 for his decade in Congress.

But Walgren dismissed Buckman's statistics as nonsense and derided the challenger for not understanding that legislative goals could be achieved through amendments. Walgren noted that in the previous year alone, 15 of his bills had become law, including one that he pushed from his position as chairman of a Science and Technology subcommittee to make Pittsburgh a "supercomputer" center.

With a hefty half-million-dollar treasury, Walgren easily deflected Buckman's challenge.

Committees

Energy and Commerce (8th of 26 Democrats)
Energy and Power; Health and the Environment; Oversight and Investigations

Science, Space and Technology (5th of 30 Democrats)
Science, Research and Technology (chairman); Energy Research and Development

Elections

1988 General

Doug Walgren (D)	136,924	(63%)
John A. Newman (R)	80,975	(37%)

1986 General

Doug Walgren (D)	104,164	(63%)
Ernie Buckman (R)	61,164	(37%)

Previous Winning Percentages: **1984** (63%) **1982** (54%) **1980** (68%) **1978** (57%) **1976** (60%)

District Vote For President

	1988	1984	1980	1976
D	106,636 (46%)	103,883 (42%)	83,343 (35%)	92,265 (39%)
R	123,482 (53%)	144,352 (58%)	131,462 (56%)	141,049 (59%)
I			15,849 (7%)	

Campaign Finance

	Receipts	Receipts from PACs	Expend-itures
1988			
Walgren (D)	$389,537	$232,214 (60%)	$321,074
Newman (R)	$18,928	0	$16,587
1986			
Walgren (D)	$576,915	$293,409 (51%)	$557,031
Buckman (R)	$992,803	$56,372 (6%)	$983,798

Key Votes

1987

Raise speed limit to 65 mph	N
Approve Gephardt "fair trade" amendment	Y
Ban testing of larger nuclear weapons	Y
Delay "re-flagging" of Kuwaiti tankers	Y
Approve tax-raising deficit-reduction bill	Y

1988

Approve aid to Nicaraguan contras	N
Enact civil rights restoration bill over Reagan veto	Y
Kill 60-day plant-closing notification measure	N
Pass omnibus trade bill over Reagan veto	Y
Approve death penalty for drug-related murders	Y
Bar federal funds for abortions in cases of rape and incest	N
Oppose seven-day waiting period for purchase of handguns	N

Voting Studies

	Presidential Support		Party Unity		Conservative Coalition	
Year	**S**	**O**	**S**	**O**	**S**	**O**
1988	20	75	86	8	37	58
1987	12	83	89	6	28	72
1986	13	81	83	10	24	74
1985	25	74	89	5	16	75
1984	27	72	81	15	19	80
1983	11	83	82	14	17	80
1982	34	61	80	16	23	73
1981	41	57	77	21	28	71

Interest Group Ratings

Year	ADA	ACU	AFL-CIO	CCUS
1988	90	4	100	25
1987	92	0	100	13
1986	85	14	86	41
1985	70	10	88	29
1984	80	9	67	31
1983	95	9	88	15
1982	80	29	95	32
1981	80	13	67	22

19 Bill Goodling (R)

Of Jacobus — Elected 1974

Born: Dec. 5, 1927, Loganville, Pa.
Education: U. of Maryland, B.S. 1953; Western Maryland College, M.Ed. 1956; graduate work, Penn. State U., 1960-62.
Military Career: Army, 1946-48.
Occupation: Public school superintendent.
Family: Wife, Hilda Wright; two children.
Religion: Methodist.
Political Career: Dallastown School Board president, 1964-67.
Capitol Office: 2263 Rayburn Bldg. 20515; 225-5836.

In Washington: If George Bush fleshes out his campaign pledge to be the "education president," he will find no stronger ally among GOP House members than Goodling, the senior Republican on the Education and Labor Committee.

Goodling has focused on education issues since he came to Congress in 1975, leaving behind a career as a teacher and school administrator in his home area of south-central Pennsylvania. He is a devoted supporter of the current array of school-aid programs, many of which he helped craft in recent years. This attitude sometimes puts him at odds with conservatives in his own party. But on the other side of his committee's agenda — labor issues — Goodling's views are much more conventionally Republican.

Goodling is certainly no reflexive big-spender on education. In committee negotiations on such measures as the education reauthorization amendments enacted in 1988, he has acted as a counterbalance to liberal Democrats who wanted more than the modest increases proposed for many programs. But Goodling has worked comfortably through the years with the current Democratic chairman, Augustus F. Hawkins of California, and his long-tenured predecessor, the late Carl D. Perkins of Kentucky.

At the start of the 101st Congress, Goodling became Hawkins' Republican peer, moving into the ranking slot to replace liberal Vermont Republican James M. Jeffords, a fellow school-aid supporter who had won a 1988 Senate contest. But even earlier, Jeffords' overriding interest in labor issues and Goodling's position as senior Republican on the Elementary, Secondary and Vocational Education Subcommittee enabled the Pennsylvanian to play a major role in education policy.

Along with Jeffords, Goodling worked with Hawkins during the 100th Congress to mold the education reauthorization bill. The result was a compromise document aimed at protecting the programs dear to committee Democrats while restraining funding to levels acceptable to President Reagan and his allies on the committee.

The delicate balance was nearly upset, though, by the issue of bilingual education. A pair of Reagan-backed provisions to increase funding for "English-only" instructional programs were strongly opposed by panel Democrats, including the Hispanic members, who favored "native-language" teaching. However, Goodling, who supported the administration position, warned that a failure to compromise on the issue could result in the reopening of discussion on other provisions in the school-aid package. The Reagan position eventually prevailed.

The final bill contained a new anti-illiteracy program, called Even Start, that had been proposed by Goodling. The program may have an influential defender at budget-cutting time, given first lady Barbara Bush's personal interest in the issue of illiteracy.

While he gets along well with most committee Democrats, Goodling has had fierce fights with some of the committee's more conservative Republicans over their efforts, during the Reagan era, to make deep cuts in programs such as school-lunch assistance.

In the 99th Congress, Goodling joined House Democrats in opposing floor amendments offered from his own side of the aisle to cut funding for child-nutrition programs. "This would destroy the National School Lunch Program," Goodling said of one proposal offered by Texas Republican Steve Bartlett, a fellow Education and Labor member. "That's how devastating it is." The Bartlett amendment was defeated.

Goodling's fight to defend nutrition programs dates back to the earliest days of the Reagan administration. When budget director David A. Stockman said that budget cuts in 1981 had not hurt needy children, Goodling labeled the claim "sheer hogwash," and argued that close to 1 million of the 3.5 million children

Pennsylvania 19

South Central — York

This placid farm country has seen little to upset it since 1863, when Robert E. Lee's army met defeat at Gettysburg. Democrats do about as well in many of these counties as Lee did. The 19th used to change hands between the parties occasionally, but it has been solidly Republican since 1974.

The biggest concentration of Democrats lies in the industrial city of York (population 44,000), where turbines, hosiery and barbells are manufactured. Surrounding York County has an even split in terms of partisan registration.

Apart from the outlying Democratic enclave of Hanover, where cans, shoes and potato chips are made, the rest of York County is rural Republican — with a smattering of Pennsylvania Dutch influence to deepen the conservatism. The county's most popular newspaper is not the flashy and liberal *York Daily Record*, but the gray and conservative *York Dispatch*.

In fruit-growing Adams County (peaches, apricots and apples), Republicans hold sway from Gettysburg — the largest town, with 8,200 people — to the farming villages farther north. The Democrats, in the minority, are concentrated in the southeastern part of Adams. Many of them work in Hanover.

Republicans have the upper hand as well in the part of Cumberland County in the 19th, which includes the western suburbs of Harrisburg, Pennsylvania's capital; the city itself lies across the Susquehanna River in the 17th District. State employees and blue-collar workers who spend their days in Harrisburg live in Lemoyne and New Cumberland on the West Shore. Affluent West Shore Republicans reside in Camp Hill. Moving west from the West Shore area, the Cumberland County terrain becomes more rural and Republican.

Population: 516,605. White 499,717 (97%), Black 11,905 (2%), Other 2,879 (1%). Spanish origin 4,051 (1%). 18 and over 376,801 (73%), 65 and over 59,117 (11%). Median age: 32.

disqualified in 1981 were poor.

Yet in pursuing the nutrition issue, Goodling guards himself from being perceived as a crusading liberal. He works closely with food producers and suppliers, for whom nutrition is a business as well as a humanitarian issue. The business support provides a conservative element to Goodling's coalition that broadens the appeal of the programs.

Given his moderate leanings on education and nutrition issues, Goodling's role on the committee's labor agenda is something of a paradox. On labor legislation, Goodling is a dependable vote for the Republican leadership, and can even be harsh on GOP colleagues who bolt the party line.

In March 1989, the House appeared headed for a battle between advocates of a minimum-wage increase who wanted a hike to $4.65 per hour and no subminimum "training wage," and forces led by Goodling who supported President Bush's call for a $4.25 hourly minimum with a six-month training wage. Moderate Pennsylvania Republican Tom Ridge, working with a pair of Democrats, then stepped in with a compromise plan to raise the minimum to $4.55, with a two-month subminimum.

While the Ridge plan passed the House, it angered some Republicans, none more so than Goodling, who saw it as subverting Bush's hard-line stand on the minimum wage. When Goodling was asked if Ridge had any Republican friends left, he fired back, "On our side of the aisle, he would have none."

As a member of the Budget Committee, Goodling also plays a partisan, if limited, role. During the Reagan administration, he often expressed his frustration with the refusal of the committee's Democratic majority to allow Republicans to play a substantive role in responding to President Reagan's annual budget proposals and crafting the yearly congressional budget resolutions.

But Goodling, the ranking Republican on the Human Resources Task Force, has shown that he will come to the defense of his Budget Committee colleagues when they get embroiled in turf fights with their Senate counterparts. When Senate Budget Committee Chairman Lawton Chiles of Florida and ranking Republican Pete V. Domenici of New Mexico angrily attempted to assert Senate primacy in the 1988 budget process, Goodling described them as "two mean, bitter old people" who had "a terrible attitude."

Goodling had sought the Budget seat after a discouraging term on the Select Intelligence Committee, where he took a seat at the urging of Minority Leader Robert H. Michel. Joining Intelligence just as the issue of covert U.S. activity in Nicaragua was coming to the forefront, Goodling found the experience so distasteful that he gave up the position at the end of the 98th Congress. He told colleagues that there were some aspects of foreign policy he would rather not know about.

At Home: Goodling has made this district more securely Republican in his House tenure than his father, who won six times between 1960 and 1972, was ever able to do. George A. Goodling lived with the possibility of defeat each election year and actually lost once, in 1964; his son has won over 70 percent seven consecutive times — even in 1982, when the GOP was in serious trouble all over the state.

They are two different men. The elder Goodling was an indifferent speaker who disdained public appearances. His son is much more outgoing and remains highly visible. Close to the local Republican organizations and active on community issues, Goodling benefits from the proximity of his southern Pennsylvania district, a direct two-hour drive north from Washington.

Until his first run for Congress in 1974, the younger Goodling was a high school principal and had held just one elective office — on the Dallastown School Board. He was the surprise winner in a seven-way congressional primary, outdistancing the favored John W. Eden, who had once challenged Goodling's father. Waging his first general-election campaign in the Watergate year of 1974, the younger Goodling won by barely 5,000 votes.

Committees

Education and Labor (Ranking)
Elementary, Secondary and Vocational Education (ranking); Postsecondary Education

Budget (3rd of 14 Republicans)
Task Forces: Human Resources (ranking); Community Development and Natural Resources

Elections

1988 General		
Bill Goodling (R)	145,381	(77%)
Paul E. Ritchey (D)	42,819	(23%)
1986 General		
Bill Goodling (R)	100,055	(73%)
Richard F. Thorton (D)	37,223	(27%)

Previous Winning Percentages: **1984** (76%) **1982** (71%) **1980** (76%) **1978** (79%) **1976** (71%) **1974** (51%)

District Vote For President

	1988	1984	1980	1976
D	65,536 (34%)	57,956 (30%)	56,017 (31%)	67,964 (39%)
R	127,824 (66%)	131,202 (69%)	108,392 (61%)	101,854 (59%)
I			11,384 (6%)	

Campaign Finance

	Receipts	Receipts from PACs	Expend-itures
1988			
Goodling (R)	$54,123	0	$57,091
Ritchey (D)	$5,304	0	$5,303
1986			
Goodling (R)	$49,648	0	$46,813
Thornton (D)	$19,805	$3,820 (19%)	$19,535

Key Votes

1987	
Raise speed limit to 65 mph	N
Approve Gephardt "fair trade" amendment	N
Ban testing of larger nuclear weapons	Y
Delay "re-flagging" of Kuwaiti tankers	N
Approve tax-raising deficit-reduction bill	N
1988	
Approve aid to Nicaraguan contras	Y
Enact civil rights restoration bill over Reagan veto	Y
Kill 60-day plant-closing notification measure	Y
Pass omnibus trade bill over Reagan veto	N
Approve death penalty for drug-related murders	N
Bar federal funds for abortions in cases of rape and incest	+
Oppose seven-day waiting period for purchase of handguns	Y

Voting Studies

	Presidential Support		Party Unity		Conservative Coalition	
Year	S	O	S	O	S	O
1988	50	47	77	19	84	13
1987	57	39	72	24	79	21
1986	60	37	69	28	76	24
1985	61	38	74	19	69	24
1984	50	44	66	28	71	29
1983	54	40	71	26	61	38
1982	61	36	74	24	66	30
1981	59	36	74	17	65	21

Interest Group Ratings

Year	ADA	ACU	AFL-CIO	CCUS
1988	30	63	50	93
1987	28	48	19	80
1986	25	55	43	88
1985	25	57	18	77
1984	35	48	31	63
1983	35	61	24	65
1982	25	62	25	64
1981	30	93	20	74

20 Joseph M. Gaydos (D)

Of McKeesport — Elected 1968

Born: July 3, 1926, Braddock, Pa.
Education: Attended Duquesne U., 1945-47; U. of Notre Dame, LL.B. 1951.
Military Career: Naval Reserve, 1944-46.
Occupation: Lawyer.
Family: Wife, Alice Gray; five children.
Religion: Roman Catholic.
Political Career: Pa. Senate, 1967-68.
Capitol Office: 2186 Rayburn Bldg. 20515; 225-4631.

In Washington: Gaydos, like his ailing steel-town district, is one of a dying breed in American politics: He comes from one of the last bastions of old-school ethnic politics and industrial union power.

The United Steelworkers of America is the dominant political influence in Gaydos' district, and he focuses his career on the union's interests: occupational safety, pension rights and protection against imports.

As chairman of the Education and Labor Subcommittee on Health and Safety, Gaydos has stood guard over the Occupational Safety and Health Administration (OSHA), an agency reviled from its inception by small businesses that find its regulations onerous. But the end of the Reagan era may present Gaydos with more opportunities for legislative initiative — if he chooses to take them.

Gaydos has always seen his job primarily as a defensive one: fighting efforts to reduce OSHA's scope. The Reagan era was a particularly inopportune time for pushing labor legislation to broaden worker protections.

He sometimes has had to defend himself against demands from his own labor allies that he move aggressively to make OSHA stronger, rather than just protecting the status quo. He has never been what one would call an ambitious legislator.

But as anti-regulation zeal began to wane toward the end of the Reagan administration, Gaydos did take advantage of the new climate and in 1987 shepherded through the House the first important OSHA bill in years. The House passed legislation that required notification of workers who might be exposed to hazardous chemicals or materials on the job.

Along the way, Gaydos accepted changes designed to win some business support. But other business groups remained implacably opposed, saying that risk notification would cause them financial and legal hardship. Those forces prevailed in the Senate, where the bill died in the 100th Congress.

Whatever Gaydos says that does not pertain to job safety usually relates to the trade problems faced by American manufacturers, particularly those in his district's crucial steel industry. Gaydos serves as chairman of the steel caucus, the House group seeking restrictions on steel imports into the United States.

Statements by Gaydos on trade issues have a caustic and sometimes strident tone. In 1982 he introduced legislation that would have allowed the president unilaterally to impose new duties on nations that do not practice "reciprocity" in trade. "People are tired of New Testament trade based on meekness and turning the other cheek," Gaydos said. "They are ready for some Old Testament justice."

During the Reagan presidency, Gaydos sometimes would aim his anger at the administration's efforts to negotiate voluntary import restrictions with foreign countries. "I know President Reagan likes to speak of the free market; unfortunately, there is no such thing . . . ," Gaydos said. "Someone has to pay, and unfortunately, with our open doors and unrestrictive trade system, we are the ones who are paying ... in the form of lost companies, lost jobs, lost manufacturing capability."

The other side of Gaydos the labor advocate is Gaydos the House insider.

In the 100th Congress, he was assigned to the House ethics committee, a less-than-desirable post, but one that usually goes to dependable leadership loyalists. In April 1989, when the ethics committee was conducting its preliminary inquiry into whether Speaker Jim Wright had violated House rules, Gaydos and West Virginia Democrat Alan B. Mollohan voted consistently to drop charges that the committee majority chose to press.

Gaydos' other committee assignment is on House Administration, the panel that handles members' staff budgets and other housekeeping matters that are valuable sources of internal political leverage.

It is likely just a matter of time before Gaydos is chairman of the full House Administration Committee. He is now ranking Democrat under the chairmanship of Frank Annunzio of Illinois, who is more than a decade older than

Pennsylvania 20

Pittsburgh Suburbs — McKeesport

Its banks lined by old steel mills, its waters crowded with barges, the Monongahela River forms the spine of this blue-collar district.

The "Mon Valley" city of Clairton was the setting for the movie "The Deer Hunter," in which young Slavic steelworkers went off to the Vietnam War. The film depicted the ethnic celebrations and bluff male camaraderie that also animate the political life of the 20th. The wise politician here cultivates the Sons of Italy, the Polish Falcons, the Greek Catholic Union, the American Croatian Club and countless other ethnic societies. Although blacks make up a substantial portion of some towns — Clairton is one-quarter black — they are not concentrated enough to be a major political force.

Organized labor is crucial to local politics and has been for a long time. The Steelworkers' locals in the Mon Valley are some of the union's most militant in demanding that the domestic steel industry not be allowed to wither away. Thousands who used to work in the Mon Valley's steel mills now have no prospect for comparable employment because corporate officials have closed the mills for good, declaring that local wage costs are too high, the old mills too inefficient and foreign steel too cheap to make continued operation economically feasible.

It was in the 20th that steel union officials and some church leaders in unemployment-riddled communities stirred a furor in the mid-1980s by staging protests at churches in affluent communities where corporate executives worship. The protesters demanded that local investors put money into revitalizing steel in the Mon Valley.

Pittsburgh's effort to move to a service-oriented economy holds no hope for the typical unemployed steelworker in the 20th, who has no training to handle the high-tech jobs available in the skyscrapers downtown.

Not surprisingly, the 20th is firmly Democratic. Jimmy Carter carried it in both his presidential races, and the district's view of the White House occupant in 1984 was best described by a local steelworkers official, who said, "In this area, if Ronald Reagan bought a cemetery, people would quit dying." In 1988, George Bush barely got above one-third of the vote in the 20th.

Population: 516,028. White 484,336 (94%), Black 28,639 (6%). Spanish origin 2,560 (1%). 18 and over 390,171 (76%), 65 and over 71,817 (14%). Median age: 35.

Gaydos.

Gaydos already is chairman of the Accounts Subcommittee, which oversees most House committees' budgets. That means some of the House's most powerful committee chairmen have to rely on Gaydos' good will to keep their own fiefdoms well staffed.

Although Gaydos seems to relish that role, he has not built it into the kind of institutional power base it was for some of his predecessors in the 1970s. Part of the difference is that it is not so easy to throw money around these days.

Indeed, Gaydos takes public pride in the fact that committee budgets are now tighter than they once were. He says that the average growth rate in committees' authorizations from 1985 to 1988 was less than 2 percent a year.

But in July 1986, he spoke out against an amendment by Republican Bill Frenzel of Minnesota to institute a 3.5 percent across-the-board cut of the legislative branch budget.

"We were pretty tightfisted last year, and we cut things down substantially," Gaydos said. "We were accused of being unreasonable, and I as a chairman . . . am repeatedly turning down many chairmen's requests for additional funds." The Frenzel amendment was defeated, 199-209.

At Home: Gaydos' roots in organized labor and his stalwart defense of the steel industry have been the basis of his career in Pittsburgh. Gaydos' father was a factory worker, and when he himself was a student, he held factory jobs and belonged to three unions (the Glass Workers, the Steelworkers and the United Auto Workers). He later served as a United Mine Workers attorney.

In the 1968 Democratic primary, in which he first ran for the seat, Gaydos used his background to counter the formal labor support claimed by his chief opponent, a Steelworkers' local president.

A first-term state legislator at that time, Gaydos had been tapped by the Allegheny County Democratic organization to replace U.S. Rep. Elmer Holland, whom it considered too old at 74. Holland agreed to retire, then died before his term ended.

Since his initial primary, which he won handily, Gaydos has had a virtual free ride. He has slipped below 70 percent only once. In 1986 and 1988, he faced no Republican opposition.

Committees

Education and Labor (3rd of 22 Democrats)
Health and Safety (chairman); Postsecondary Education

House Administration (2nd of 13 Democrats)
Accounts (chairman); Personnel and Police

Standards of Official Conduct (5th of 6 Democrats)

Joint Printing

Elections

1988 General

Joseph M. Gaydos (D)	137,472	(98%)
Richard W. Wilson (POP)	2,144	(2%)

1986 General

Joseph M. Gaydos (D)	136,638	(99%)

Previous Winning Percentages: **1984** (76%) **1982** (76%) **1980** (73%) **1978** (72%) **1976** (75%) **1974** (82%) **1972** (62%) **1970** (77%) **1968** * (70%)

* *Elected to fill an unexpired term in a special election held the same day as the general election.*

District Vote For President

	1988	1984	1980	1976
D	125,880 (65%)	136,992 (62%)	111,625 (54%)	126,788 (58%)
R	67,120 (34%)	83,148 (37%)	81,023 (39%)	86,535 (40%)
I			10,643 (5%)	

Campaign Finance

	Receipts	Receipts from PACs	Expend-itures
1988			
Gaydos (D)	$184,634	$143,850 (78%)	$137,023
1986			
Gaydos (D)	$159,109	$109,175 (69%)	$119,321

Key Votes

1987

Raise speed limit to 65 mph	Y
Approve Gephardt "fair trade" amendment	Y
Ban testing of larger nuclear weapons	N
Delay "re-flagging" of Kuwaiti tankers	Y
Approve tax-raising deficit-reduction bill	Y

1988

Approve aid to Nicaraguan contras	N
Enact civil rights restoration bill over Reagan veto	Y
Kill 60-day plant-closing notification measure	N
Pass omnibus trade bill over Reagan veto	Y
Approve death penalty for drug-related murders	Y
Bar federal funds for abortions in cases of rape and incest	Y
Oppose seven-day waiting period for purchase of handguns	Y

Voting Studies

	Presidential Support		Party Unity		Conservative Coalition	
Year	**S**	**O**	**S**	**O**	**S**	**O**
1988	26	66	80	13	63	29
1987	31	67	80	11	63	35
1986	33	59	73	17	62	26
1985	28	65	78	14	47	44
1984	37	60	77	18	47	53
1983	40	59	76	17	35	58
1982	38	61	77	17	42	55
1981	43	45	65	25	61	29

Interest Group Ratings

Year	ADA	ACU	AFL-CIO	CCUS
1988	65	24	100	25
1987	64	9	94	27
1986	55	44	100	31
1985	70	15	71	32
1984	45	39	92	38
1983	60	35	94	32
1982	55	41	95	19
1981	40	21	85	12

21 Tom Ridge (R)

Of Erie — Elected 1982

Born: Aug. 26, 1945, Munhall, Pa.
Education: Harvard College, B.A. 1967; Dickinson School of Law, J.D. 1972.
Military Career: Army, 1968-70.
Occupation: Lawyer.
Family: Wife, Michele Moore; two children.
Religion: Roman Catholic.
Political Career: No previous office.
Capitol Office: 1714 Longworth Bldg. 20515; 225-5406.

In Washington: This affable lawyer with a Harvard degree and a chamber-of-commerce appearance generally moves easily within the House Republican Conference, casting frequent left-of-center votes but keeping his image just this side of "maverick."

Republican leaders realize that Ridge needs some flexibility to stray from the party line, since only a moderate could hold the 21st District for the GOP. It is a mainly blue-collar corner of northwest Pennsylvania, centered on the industrial city of Erie. Ridge's working-class, ethnic background — like many Erie men of his generation, he enlisted in the Army and served in Vietnam — and his pro-labor voting record have helped make him overwhelmingly popular at home.

Still, there are times when Ridge breaks with the GOP leadership position in a rather public manner, leaving his more conservative colleagues exasperated. His split with President Bush on the minimum wage in early 1989 was such an incident.

Democratic-led efforts to boost the minimum wage well above the present rate of $3.35 an hour led to the first major legislative confrontation of the Bush administration. President Bush proposed raising the minimum to $4.25, with a six-month subminimum "training wage" for newly hired employees, and he made it clear he would use his veto if he did not get his way. But the House Education and Labor Committee reported a bill containing a hike to $4.65, with no training wage.

At that point, Ridge, joined by Democrats Austin J. Murphy of Pennsylvania and Tommy F. Robinson of Arkansas, stepped in with a compromise. Their bill called for an increase to $4.55 an hour, with a two-month training wage for new hires with minimal work experience.

Urging his fellow Republicans to join him, Ridge described his plan as "a step toward the administration proposal." But while the compromise bill passed 248-171, only 19 of the "ayes" were Republicans. Moreover, many of Ridge's GOP colleagues were angry at him for going against the president. Ridge's fellow Pennsylvanian Bill Goodling, the senior Republican on Education and Labor, was asked after the vote if Ridge had any friends left. "On our side of the aisle, he would have none," Goodling responded icily.

The minimum-wage battle was not the first time Ridge had broken ranks on a priority issue for the GOP leadership.

Ridge, for example, was the only House Republican to make a floor speech in 1987 favoring the tough trade-sanctions amendment proposed by Missouri Democrat Richard A. Gephardt. Most Republicans criticized the Gephardt amendment as a protectionist measure that could start a trade war. But Ridge said the United States needed a substantive threat in order to persuade other nations to end unfair trading practices. "Negotiation with intractable opposition will, by definition, be ineffective," he said.

Positions such as that make Ridge one of organized labor's favorite Republicans. In 1988, he received an 86 percent rating from the AFL-CIO. But rather than shun him for this voting behavior, Republican officials have tended to recognize and showcase Ridge's appeal to the union constituency. In 1988, he was appointed by then-Republican National Chairman Frank J. Fahrenkopf Jr. to serve as chairman of the Republican Labor Council.

A legislative activist with wide-ranging interests, Ridge has made some ventures into defense policy. A skeptic of the strategic defense initiative (SDI), he has teamed with Charles E. Bennett, a senior Florida Democrat and an arms control liberal, in yearly attempts to limit SDI spending. In May 1987, for instance, House Armed Services had already reduced President Reagan's SDI request from $5.7 billion to $3.8 billion. Bennett and Ridge then attached an amendment on the House floor to limit funding to $3.1 billion. The proposal passed, 219-199; the 20 GOP votes rounded up by Ridge were crucial to the outcome.

Ridge has also offered some ideas about reforming the Defense Department's purchas-

Pennsylvania 21

Northwest — Erie

Muscled out by Buffalo to the north and Cleveland to the south, the city of Erie never developed into a Great Lakes metropolis on par with its neighbors. But it is the dominant influence in the 21st. Erie Democrats still hold a wide advantage in voter registration, but changes in the city's ethnic groups are reshaping district politics.

Until the last decade or so, the Italians on Erie's West Side and the Poles on the East Side both were blue-collar communities, tied to assembly-line jobs at General Electric Co. and in heavy industries such as paper, metals and chemicals. But then a trend toward greater mobility among Italians began gaining steam. More Italians than Poles took white-collar jobs, and more of them moved to the suburbs, where their Democratic traditions weakened. By and large, Poles remained in the city and retained their strong Democratic allegiance.

When a Pole defeated an Italian for the 1982 Democratic House nomination, many disappointed Italians supported Ridge in November, helping him win. The results of recent presidential contests reveal what a swing-voting area Erie County has become. Jimmy Carter carried it narrowly in 1976, Ronald Reagan eked out victories here in 1980 and 1984, then Michael S. Dukakis won with a comfortable 58 percent in 1988.

South of Erie in the center of the 21st is Crawford County, kept Republican by dairy farmers and retirees around Conneaut Lake. In Titusville, to the east, Edwin L. Drake drilled the first oil well in 1859.

Below Crawford is Mercer County, where the steel industry in the Shenango Valley sets a Democratic tone. As thoroughly unionized as Erie, the mill towns of Sharon, Wheatland and Sharpsville outvote eastern Mercer's rural Republicans. Mercer was one of just two Pennsylvania counties that supported Reagan in 1980, then switched to Mondale in 1984, mostly because people felt Reagan had not done enough to save the steel industry. Despite the Democratic trend at the top of the ticket in Mercer, Republican Ridge carried the county by almost 2-to-1 in 1984. Again in 1988, Mercer went Democratic for president and Republican for Ridge in the House contest.

Population: 516,645. White 494,271 (96%), Black 18,997 (4%). Spanish origin 2,836 (1%). 18 and over 370,614 (72%), 65 and over 60,943 (12%). Median age: 30.

ing practices. When a Pentagon bribery scandal broke in June 1988, Ridge, along with Michigan Democrat Dennis M. Hertel, proposed a civilian procurement agency to handle defense purchasing. He has served as the GOP chairman of the congressional Military Reform Caucus.

Ridge has been a member of the Banking, Finance and Urban Affairs Committee since his freshman term, reflecting his interest in the problems of cities such as Erie. In 1988, Ridge joined with New Jersey Republican Marge Roukema in an amendment to a new federal program to aid the homeless. They proposed merging three shelter-grant programs into a single "block grant" that would give localities more flexibility in managing funds. The amendment failed, 203-215.

In the 101st Congress, Ridge took a seat on the Post Office and Civil Service Committee and got the ranking GOP slot on its Census and Population Subcommittee. Previously, he and 42 other plaintiffs had filed suit in federal court to block the inclusion of illegal aliens in the decennial U.S. census. Ridge said such an inclusion, which he described as inherently inaccurate, penalized areas (like his home base) that receive few immigrants.

Ridge and his allies appeared to make progress on this issue in 1988, when Indiana Republican Dan Burton attached an amendment barring an illegal-alien count to a bill aimed at correcting the supposed census undercount of minorities. However, the bill's Democratic sponsors let it die in the Post Office Committee rather than send it to the floor with the illegal-alien provision included. Then, in May 1989, a U.S. district judge threw out Ridge's lawsuit on procedural grounds.

On the Veterans' Affairs Committee, Ridge — who suffered partial hearing loss from an injury in Vietnam — works within the panel's consensus in favor of veterans' benefits.

Even here, though, he occasionally finds an issue that stirs some controversy. In 1988, he joined with GOP Sen. John McCain (a former prisoner of war in Vietnam) in calling for informal diplomatic links between the United States and Vietnam through the establishment of unofficial embassies, known as "interest sections," in their respective capitals. The purpose of the move was to increase contacts in hopes of clarifying the status of American servicemen still classified as missing in action from the Vietnam War.

Though many conservatives resisted any move toward détente with the longtime U.S. foe, Ridge said the proposal was nothing "remotely resembling diplomatic relations" with Vietnam. But just as the idea was gaining momentum in Congress, relations between the two countries went chilly as the Hanoi government decried what it saw as a "hostile" attitude in the Reagan administration.

At Home: Blue-collar voters in many parts of the country returned to their Democratic roots in 1982, but not the ones in northwestern Pennsylvania. They elected Ridge over a labor-oriented Democrat in a district that had been expected to return to Democratic control with GOP Rep. Marc L. Marks' retirement.

Ridge capitalized on a good organization and exhaustive personal effort to defeat Democratic state Sen. Buzz Andrezeski by 729 votes. He benefited from Democratic disunity and from his departure from the Reagan line on social program cuts and military spending increases.

Ridge's start in local politics came as chief of George Bush's Erie County 1980 presidential campaign. He won the GOP House nomination after other prominent Republicans decided that Democrats would handily recapture the 21st, which they had held before Marks' 1976 victory.

At first, Ridge had trouble raising money from local business interests, which had written off the race. But Ridge impressed national GOP leaders and key Washington business groups, who sent him the money he needed.

Andrezeski, confident that his labor support would pull him through, campaigned with less vigor than Ridge, who was knocking on doors long before Labor Day. Ridge worked the Italian-dominated West Side of Erie, where the Polish-American Andrezeski was unpopular because he had defeated an Italian in the Democratic primary. Ridge came within 8,000 votes in Erie; votes from suburbs and rural areas elected him.

Ridge has worked hard to bring his district under control, and he has succeeded in scaring away strong Democratic competition.

Located in the extreme northwest corner of Pennsylvania, the 21st is rather isolated from the rest of the state, but Ridge's success with its Democratic voters has added his name to many lists of potential statewide candidates.

Committees

Banking, Finance and Urban Affairs (10th of 20 Republicans)
Consumer Affairs and Coinage; Financial Institutions Supervision, Regulation and Insurance; Housing and Community Development

Post Office and Civil Service (7th of 9 Republicans)
Census and Population (ranking); Civil Service

Select Aging (9th of 27 Republicans)
Health and Long-Term Care; Housing and Consumer Interests

Veterans' Affairs (8th of 13 Republicans)
Education, Training and Employment; Hospitals and Health Care

Elections

1988 General		
Tom Ridge (R)	141,832	(79%)
George R. H. Elder (D)	38,288	(21%)
1986 General		
Tom Ridge (R)	111,148	(81%)
Joylyn Blackwell (D)	26,324	(19%)

Previous Winning Percentages: 1984 (65%) **1982** (50%)

District Vote For President

	1988	1984	1980	1976
D	94,345 (50%)	92,936 (47%)	81,616 (43%)	100,021 (51%)
R	91,544 (49%)	105,501 (53%)	92,732 (49%)	92,089 (47%)
I			12,121 (6%)	

Campaign Finance

	Receipts	Receipts from PACs	Expend-itures
1988			
Ridge (R)	$419,770	$211,711 (50%)	$370,619
1986			
Ridge (R)	$298,273	$138,235 (46%)	$267,525

Key Votes

1987	
Raise speed limit to 65 mph	N
Approve Gephardt "fair trade" amendment	Y
Ban testing of larger nuclear weapons	Y
Delay "re-flagging" of Kuwaiti tankers	Y
Approve tax-raising deficit-reduction bill	N
1988	
Approve aid to Nicaraguan contras	Y
Enact civil rights restoration bill over Reagan veto	Y
Kill 60-day plant-closing notification measure	N
Pass omnibus trade bill over Reagan veto	Y
Approve death penalty for drug-related murders	Y
Bar federal funds for abortions in cases of rape and incest	N
Oppose seven-day waiting period for purchase of handguns	Y

Voting Studies

	Presidential Support		Party Unity		Conservative Coalition	
Year	S	O	S	O	S	O
1988	40	56	66	28	74	26
1987	40	56	59	34	56	42
1986	47	53	59	37	68	32
1985	44	54	60	35	58	36
1984	42	50	45	49	53	44
1983	51	46	56	40	66	31

Interest Group Ratings

Year	ADA	ACU	AFL-CIO	CCUS
1988	50	36	86	71
1987	48	19	60	64
1986	35	41	64	61
1985	30	48	47	73
1984	50	36	38	60
1983	35	39	47	80

22 Austin J. Murphy (D)

Of Monongahela — Elected 1976

Born: June 17, 1927, North Charleroi, Pa.
Education: Duquesne U., B.A. 1949; U. of Pittsburgh, LL.B. 1952.
Military Career: Marine Corps, 1944-46; Marine Corps Reserve, 1948-50.
Occupation: Lawyer.
Family: Wife, Ramona McNamara; six children.
Religion: Roman Catholic.
Political Career: Pa. House, 1959-71; Pa. Senate, 1971-77.
Capitol Office: 2210 Rayburn Bldg. 20515; 225-4665.

In Washington: When 324 of Murphy's colleagues voted in December 1987 to reprimand him for misconduct, he could have been excused for feeling in some ways a victim of bad timing. His punishment came at a time when GOP activists were complaining that alleged improprieties by senior Democrats — including Speaker Jim Wright — were being ignored.

The House ethics committee had voted 11-0 to assess Murphy its mildest punishment — a reprimand — for diverting government resources to his former law firm, for allowing another member to vote for him on the House floor, and for keeping a "ghost employee" on his payroll.

Murphy and a few others said the ethics committee was singling him out for punishment to quiet criticism that the panel was lax. But some who denounced the committee did not exactly heap praise on the six-term Pennsylvanian. Georgia Republican Newt Gingrich blasted the ethics panel, saying, "You do not have the courage at this moment to raise the charges against those with power, but just before Christmas you found a member without power. It is sort of shameful." (Gingrich still voted to reprimand Murphy.)

For Murphy, the reprimand marked the low point of a disappointing 100th Congress. His two most prominent legislative battles culminated in defeat, and his belated move to take an Interior subcommittee chairmanship for the 101st Congress was rebuffed as well.

But in the early months of the 101st Congress, Murphy was able to earn headlines as a player in the battle between Democrats and President Bush over raising the minimum wage, a party goal that had failed under President Reagan.

Murphy represents a steel and coal district, and he is well situated to vote its interests on Education and Labor, which handles pay and safety issues, and Interior, which has jurisdiction over coal issues from slurry pipelines to strip mining.

As chairman of the Education and Labor Subcommittee on Labor Standards, Murphy conducted hearings in the 100th Congress on increasing the minimum wage. On the first day of the 101st Congress, he and full committee Chairman Augustus F. Hawkins together introduced minimum-wage legislation.

The playing field on the issue clearly had shifted in 1989. Unlike Reagan, Bush expressed a willingness to consider a minimum-wage bill — but only if it did not raise the wage above $4.25 an hour, and only if it included a six-month subminimum "training wage." The subminimum wage was anathema to many Democrats and their organized-labor allies in 1988, but with the live prospect of an increase in the wage — which had been at $3.35 an hour since 1981 — labor and Democrats showed signs of flexibility on the issue in 1989.

Murphy forged a winning compromise in March 1989. Murphy, Arkansas Democrat Tommy F. Robinson and Pennsylvania Republican Tom Ridge hastily hammered out a bipartisan package after sponsors realized that the measure reported by Education and Labor — hiking the wage to $4.65 an hour and barring any training wage — would fail. The Murphy-Ridge-Robinson substitute, adopted by 240-179, lowered the increase to $4.55 an hour and created a two-month training wage, equal to 85 percent of the minimum, for first-time workers.

Even in the 100th Congress, Murphy had been more willing than labor and most committee Democrats to compromise on certain aspects of the minimum-wage bill. He questioned whether an increase as large as that sought by committee Democrats could clear Congress, and he backed a move to strip from the bill a controversial, labor-backed "indexing" provision that would have guaranteed future annual increases without congressional action. But the full committee weighted the bill with a fourth installment to boost the wage to $5.05 per hour in 1992. Sponsors could not round up enough votes in either the House or Senate, and the bill

Pennsylvania 22

Southwest — Washington

This coal-rich corner of the state has fed the blast furnaces of the Steel Belt for most of this century, in boom times and bad. Tales of cave-ins, strikes and cutthroat politics still embroider the talk of the miners as they down schooners of beer in the taverns that nestle among the stark hills. The United Mine Workers is an important force, and it has a rough history. UMW President W. A. "Tony" Boyle was convicted here in the 1969 murder of union rival Joseph A. "Jock" Yablonski. The area's legacy of violence dates back to the Whiskey Rebellion in 1791.

The 22nd is thoroughly Democratic: Jimmy Carter won it in both 1976 and 1980; Walter F. Mondale scored in the high 50s or better in every county of the 22nd in 1984; and Michael S. Dukakis carried the district handily in 1988. In the last redistricting, industrial and Democratic southern Beaver County joined the district. That Beaver County territory includes such Ohio River factory towns as Midland and the aptly named Industry, as well as Shippingport, site of the first commercial atomic reactor.

Washington, Murphy's home county, has almost half the 22nd's population and dominates the district. It has a little coal mining, but its economy depends on heavy industry. Charleroi and other Monongahela River towns make steel, glass and industrial equipment.

The city of Washington, home of the county's old factory-owning families, often goes against the grain and votes Republican — as does Peters Township, a white-collar bedroom community for Pittsburgh commuters on the Allegheny County line. But these votes regularly are drowned by the Democratic tide.

Coal is the mainstay of Fayette and Greene counties. Fayette has been mined much longer than less-populous Greene; many of Fayette's deep mines are played out and strip mining has begun.

These two counties display an even firmer Democratic allegiance than Washington County. In the 1976 Senate contest, which was a regional clash between Pittsburgher John Heinz, the Republican, and Philadelphian William Green, the Democrat, Washington joined the rest of western Pennsylvania in supporting Heinz. But Fayette and Greene cast aside geographical considerations and voted for the Democrat.

Population: 515,122. White 495,229 (96%), Black 17,910 (4%). Spanish origin 2,779 (1%). 18 and over 378,475 (73%), 65 and over 69,425 (13%). Median age: 33.

died with the Congress' adjournment.

On another issue in the 100th Congress, Murphy scored a victory, but it proved to be short-lived. Many members were caught off guard when he succeeded in 1988 in tacking onto the defense authorization bill his measure to revise the Davis-Bacon law, which sets wage standards for federal contracts.

Murphy's bill, which Education and Labor approved in 1987, aimed to modernize the Depression-era law regulating federal contracts by raising the dollar threshold above which workers must be paid the prevailing local wage rate (usually union scale). Conservatives sought to boost the threshold considerably higher than Murphy, but his maneuver blunted their efforts. Murphy's Davis-Bacon amendment was not expected to last long, and, indeed, it was dropped in conference.

Murphy struck out when he tried to claim the Interior Subcommittee on Oversight for his own at the start of the 101st Congress. Fellow Pennsylvanian Peter H. Kostmayer had long since locked up his support; Murphy withdrew his bid.

Murphy looks out for coal interests on the Interior Committee, where he regularly sides with pro-development forces against environmentalists. He is generally a pro-industry vote on nuclear-power issues.

During deliberations in the 99th Congress on the reauthorization of the Price-Anderson nuclear-liability insurance law, Interior Chairman Morris K. Udall of Arizona wanted to raise the liability of a nuclear-plant owner in the event of an accident from $640 million to $8.2 billion; Murphy wanted to hold the ceiling to $2.5 billion. Murphy's amendment prevailed in subcommittee, but the full committee approved a version closer to Udall's. It was not until the 100th Congress, however, that a bill reached the floor. The version that Reagan signed into law in 1987 raised the ceiling to about $7 billion.

At Home: The life of a politician in coal country can be a little like the life of a miner — rough. Murphy, proud of his Marine Corps past, displays a relish for combat that suits the 22nd. In 1973 he got into a fight with motorcycle gang members who were harassing him. In 1979, after Iranians seized American hostages, Murphy declared his willingness to rejoin the

Marines and attack Tehran.

In 1988, following his reprimand by the House, Murphy was ready for a fight, but no heavyweight challengers appeared. After headlines announced Murphy was unopposed, Thomas Fullard, a turnpike equipment operator, made the Democratic primary ballot when no one challenged his request in court for a petition waiver. Murphy beat him nearly 3-to-1.

The incumbent's GOP opponent — William Hodgkiss, an electrical tester — staged a write-in campaign to make the November ballot. But he failed to reach 30 percent of the vote.

Murphy might have come to blows with his 1984 GOP foe but for the fact that the adversary was a woman, Nancy Pryor. Her campaign rhetoric was unusually inflammatory: In a series of radio ads, Pryor accused Murphy of wanting to "homosexualize" children because he accepted the endorsement of the National Education Association, which opposes discrimination against teachers because of sexual orientation. Pryor, a former Army ROTC instructor, at one point said Murphy and the national Democratic Party "endorsed and approved of humans having sex with dogs, sex with sheep, sex with chickens, to name only a few."

Murphy ran ads calling Pryor a liar, and filed a defamation suit against her in a local court. In the final weeks of the campaign, Murphy was guarded by U.S. Capitol police because of threatening calls he had received. The election itself was nowhere near as interesting as the campaign; Murphy won by a 4-to-1 margin.

Murphy served almost two decades as a state legislator, waiting for Democrat Thomas E. Morgan, chairman of the House Foreign Affairs Committee, to retire. In this district, the Democratic nomination usually means the election, so a 12-way primary ensued in 1976.

Murphy defeated, among others, the Fayette County Democratic chairman (whom Morgan backed), a former U.S. Senate aide and a local attorney supported by the party organization in Murphy's own Washington County. In November, Republicans offered a solid candidate in state Rep. Roger Fischer, but Murphy took 55 percent. That was the last time the GOP made a serious effort in the 22nd.

Committees

Education and Labor (6th of 22 Democrats)
Labor Standards (chairman); Labor-Management Relations

Interior and Insular Affairs (5th of 26 Democrats)
Energy and the Environment; Mining and Natural Resources; National Parks and Public Lands

Elections

1988 General		
Austin J. Murphy (D)	123,428	(72%)
William Hodgkiss (R)	47,039	(28%)
1988 Primary		
Austin J. Murphy (D)	64,187	(73%)
Thomas J. Fullard (D)	23,193	(27%)
1986 General		
Austin J. Murphy (D)	131,650	(100%)

Previous Winning Percentages: **1984** (79%) **1982** (79%) **1980** (70%) **1978** (72%) **1976** (55%)

District Vote For President

	1988	1984	1980	1976
D	115,045 (65%)	121,832 (61%)	97,195 (53%)	113,800 (60%)
R	61,988 (35%)	76,002 (38%)	77,892 (42%)	72,769 (38%)
I			7,429 (4%)	

Campaign Finance

	Receipts	Receipts from PACs	Expend-itures
1988			
Murphy (D)	$173,164	$128,218 (74%)	$183,335
Hodgkiss (R)	$4,780	$175 (4%)	$4,676
1986			
Murphy (D)	$134,081	$98,586 (74%)	$118,557

Key Votes

1987	
Raise speed limit to 65 mph	Y
Approve Gephardt "fair trade" amendment	Y
Ban testing of larger nuclear weapons	Y
Delay "re-flagging" of Kuwaiti tankers	Y
Approve tax-raising deficit-reduction bill	?
1988	
Approve aid to Nicaraguan contras	N
Enact civil rights restoration bill over Reagan veto	Y
Kill 60-day plant-closing notification measure	N
Pass omnibus trade bill over Reagan veto	Y
Approve death penalty for drug-related murders	Y
Bar federal funds for abortions in cases of rape and incest	?
Oppose seven-day waiting period for purchase of handguns	Y

Voting Studies

	Presidential Support		Party Unity		Conservative Coalition	
Year	**S**	**O**	**S**	**O**	**S**	**O**
1988	28	59	50	36	47	42
1987	21	69	68	20	56	40
1986	21	77	75	19	50	42
1985	36	63	78	20	49	49
1984	35	63	65	28	46	51
1983	22	77	78	18	38	57
1982	35	57	71	19	41	49
1981	38	53	58	30	52	40

Interest Group Ratings

Year	ADA	ACU	AFL-CIO	CCUS
1988	60	24	100	33
1987	60	5	81	15
1986	70	19	93	33
1985	60	19	76	36
1984	55	42	77	47
1983	80	17	94	25
1982	55	33	89	25
1981	55	20	85	29

23 William F. Clinger Jr. (R)

Of Warren — Elected 1978

Born: April 4, 1929, Warren, Pa.
Education: Johns Hopkins U., B.A. 1951; U. of Virginia, LL.B. 1965.
Military Career: Navy, 1951-55.
Occupation: Lawyer.
Family: Wife, Julia Whitla; four children.
Religion: Presbyterian.
Political Career: No previous office.
Capitol Office: 2160 Rayburn Bldg. 20515; 225-5121.

In Washington: Clinger was one of the Republican moderates who set aside ideological trepidations and voted to elect conservative firebrand Newt Gingrich as GOP minority whip in March 1989. A low-key establishment type on Public Works, Clinger seemed to be just the sort of "Old Bull" Republican who would back the whip candidacy of GOP regular Edward Madigan of Illinois.

But in supporting Gingrich, Clinger showed a willingness to play insider politics. Clinger stood to gain legislative influence with a Gingrich victory: The Georgian promised to take a leave of absence from Public Works if he won, opening his ranking GOP position on the high-profile Aviation Subcommittee for Clinger, who was next in seniority.

With his new post on the Aviation panel, Clinger could be much more visible than in the past: air terrorism, airport overcrowding, the effects of deregulation on the airline industry and the impact of the 1989 Eastern Airlines strike were all headline topics when he took the ranking spot early in the 101st Congress. The leaders of the panel also hear a lot from their fellow members, because the subcommittee originates legislation authorizing federal airport improvement projects.

If Clinger does gain recognition in this role, it will be reward for a decade of mainly behind-the-scenes labor on Public Works. Clinger, an attorney, came to Congress with a public works background — he was general counsel to the federal Economic Development Administration (EDA) under President Gerald R. Ford — and he has dedicated his House career to the field.

Though some critics deride the committee as a funnel for "pork-barrel" spending, Clinger is a steadfast supporter of public works projects and a critic of those "shortsighted" people who scorn them as wasteful. "Congressional efforts to cut back on spending have the unfortunate effect of discouraging public and private investment in our infrastructure . . . ," Clinger said in a 1988 speech. "Without a sound infrastructure, we cannot guarantee future economic growth."

Clinger also advocates repealing the limitations placed on municipal tax-exempt bond financing. Local officials say the limitations make it difficult for them to raise money for public works projects.

Early in the 100th Congress, Clinger crossed swords with a Pennsylvania Republican colleague — conservative activist and Gingrich ally Robert S. Walker — over public works funding. Clinger took the House floor to defend an $88 billion highway bill — which included a road-improvement project in his district — stating, "Every project that is funded under this demonstration area is a vitally needed project." Walker disagreed, saying the bill contained "page after page after page after page after page after page of pork."

Clinger is also one of the leading defenders of the EDA; he played a major role in blocking President Reagan's efforts to eliminate the agency. In 1988, Clinger hailed an EDA grant to an economic development project in his northwest Pennsylvania region, describing the program as the "shining star" of his efforts to create jobs in the area.

Clinger also serves as ranking Republican on the Government Operations Subcommittee on Environment, Energy and Natural Resources, where he has taken a strong interest in environmental issues. In 1989, he took credit for a proposal, sent to Congress by President Bush, that allows U.S. exports of hazardous wastes only to nations with the capacity to handle them in an environmentally safe manner.

In 1988, Clinger and Democrat Mike Synar of Oklahoma fought to change a law that required the Environmental Protection Agency (EPA), rather than manufacturers, to pay for the purchase, storage and disposal of unused stocks of pesticides that EPA had banned as unsafe.

Clinger and Synar tried to attach their proposal to the appropriations bill funding EPA. But they were blocked by Agriculture

Pennsylvania 23

Northwest, Central — State College

Except when Penn State's football team plays at home or Punxsutawney Phil, the groundhog, looks for his shadow, this remote part of the state attracts little attention. One Pennsylvania politician, opposed to building an Interstate highway through it, once declared that "all they have up there is a bunch of bears."

Aside from the Penn State academic complex, coal patches and small manufacturing towns, the 23rd has a rural character. It is also one of the most Republican areas of the state, although the GOP advantage is not so daunting that Democrats cannot be competitive, as the close races between Clinger and Wachob proved.

Centre County, home of Penn State in the town of State College, is the biggest population center, casting nearly one-fourth of the district's vote. The county as a whole usually goes Republican, but Democratic votes in State College itself introduce an element of uncertainty. Democrat Wachob, who worked hard to generate support in the university community, bucked a strong tide for President Reagan to win Centre County by a narrow margin in 1984. But it shifted back to Clinger two years later.

A sleepy college town 25 years ago, State College has grown large enough in recent years to form the nucleus of an emerging metropolitan area. The university has spawned a small high-tech industrial complex outside town that attracts Republican-voting engineers. Many have settled in quaint villages around State College, such as Pine Grove Mills, Pleasant Gap, Lemont and Boalsburg, which claims to be the birthplace of Memorial Day. Local boosters call the whole area "Happy Valley," a label credible enough to attract a growing convention and resort trade.

Centre County is a prosperous oasis in a region that otherwise could be considered part of rural Appalachia. Mountainous and heavily forested, most of the land is better-suited for hunting and fishing than for farming. Schools have traditionally closed on the first day of hunting season in the fall so students could tramp through the woods in search of wildlife.

The strongest Democratic county in the 23rd is Elk County, a paper-mill center and producer of the wood that goes into "Louisville Slugger" baseball bats. Elk, Wachob's home base, is one of two counties that backed him in 1984 and 1986. But Republican Arlen Specter carried it in the 1986 Senate race, as did George Bush in 1988 presidential voting.

There are pockets of Democratic strength in other coal-mining and industrial areas of Armstrong, Clinton, and Clearfield counties. In 1988, Democrat Michael S. Dukakis won Armstrong and Clinton.

The district's northern and western counties — sparsely populated Warren, Venango, McKean and Forest — habitually vote Republican. This part of the district produces motor oil, continuing a small industry descended from the mid-19th-century Drake Well in Titusville, in the 21st.

Population: 515,976. White 509,781 (99%), Black 2,726 (0.5%), Other 2,453 (0.5%). Spanish origin 2,030 (0.4%). 18 and over 378,256 (73%), 65 and over 62,705 (12%). Median age: 30.

Committee Chairman E. "Kika" de la Garza, who said his committee had jurisdiction on insecticide issues. A broader insecticide-regulation bill, drawn up by Agriculture and enacted later that year, contained provisions similar to the Clinger-Synar measure.

Though he usually takes a fairly laid-back approach, Clinger was moved to anger in 1988 when the Senate bottled up his House-passed bill creating stricter monitoring procedures for the toxic chemical PCB. "This bill now inexcusably sits on the shelf over in the Senate," Clinger said, saying the measure was "victimized by legislative shortsightedness."

As one of the more moderate Republicans in the House — he voted against Reagan's legislative position in 1988 as often as he voted with him — Clinger was one who frequently needed courting before key votes. In January 1988, prior to a crucial (and ultimately unsuccessful) vote on military aid for the contras, Clinger was in a small group of House Republicans lobbied personally by Reagan at the White House. Though Clinger later said he already had decided to support the president, he added, "I was flattered to have the full-court press."

At Home: After winning two bruising re-elections in 1984 and 1986, Clinger seems to have restored his secure position in this mountainous Pennsylvania district.

Clinger contributed to his earlier electoral woes by getting a bit too comfortable. After he returned the 23rd District to GOP control in 1978, he won two easy re-elections. Then in 1984, he seemed to relax against Democratic challenger Bill Wachob. Although well financed,

Clinger let his challenger control the debate. And the youthful Wachob pounded away at the wealthy incumbent, contending that the district needed a more active congressman who would fight for programs to create more jobs.

Without Reagan's coattails, Clinger might have been defeated in 1984. As it was, he lost five of the district's 12 counties, including the most populous, Centre County (State College).

In their 1986 rematch, Wachob touted his enhanced name identification and fund-raising ability and said Clinger was in deep trouble without Reagan on the ballot.

Clinger said he had made a strategic mistake in 1984 by taking Wachob too lightly, and he campaigned vigorously in 1986. Pointing to his challenger's record as a state legislator, he said Wachob was a "very liberal Democrat" whose views were "out of synch" with the traditionally Republican district. And Clinger maintained that he was much more effective than Wachob painted him, pointing to a number of projects he had won for the district.

Wachob was supported by an array of teachers, environmentalists and consumer activists. But Clinger effectively portrayed himself as a hard-working, moderate Republican, and he had the money to make his case. He swept 10 counties, including Centre, and pushed his share of the vote up to 55 percent.

The son of a businessman in Warren County, at the district's northwest corner, Clinger worked in advertising for a mail-order house, then became a lawyer. Following his work in the Economic Development Administration, he headed home to challenge Democratic Rep. Joseph Ammerman. In 1976, Ammerman had ousted the district's aging GOP incumbent, Albert Johnson.

Ammerman had compiled a liberal voting record in his freshman term, and that might have been enough of a liability for a Democrat in a traditionally Republican district. But in late August 1978, Ammerman broke his hip in an automobile accident and was hospitalized for six weeks, losing valuable campaign time.

Clinger cited his Washington experience to illustrate his campaign theme that many federal programs did not work and needed revamping. His win over Ammerman was not spectacular, but it discouraged any strong opposition until 1984.

Committees

Government Operations (2nd of 15 Republicans)
Environment, Energy and Natural Resources (ranking)

Public Works and Transportation (4th of 20 Republicans)
Aviation (ranking); Investigations and Oversight; Surface Transportation

Elections

1988 General

William F. Clinger Jr. (R)	105,575	(62%)
Howard Shakespeare (D)	63,476	(37%)

1986 General

William F. Clinger Jr. (R)	79,595	(55%)
Bill Wachob (D)	63,875	(45%)

Previous Winning Percentages: **1984** (52%) **1982** (65%) **1980** (74%) **1978** (54%)

District Vote For President

	1988	1984	1980	1976
D	73,714 (43%)	69,325 (37%)	65,367 (38%)	77,107 (45%)
R	97,493 (56%)	117,316 (63%)	94,528 (55%)	92,392 (53%)
I			10,868 (6%)	

Campaign Finance

	Receipts	Receipts from PACs	Expend-itures
1988			
Clinger (R)	$405,537	$189,036 (47%)	$336,675
Shakespeare (D)	$108,104	0	$106,463
1986			
Clinger (R)	$702,712	$287,361 (41%)	$695,266
Wachob (D)	$578,958	$320,602 (55%)	$577,853

Key Votes

1987	
Raise speed limit to 65 mph	N
Approve Gephardt "fair trade" amendment	N
Ban testing of larger nuclear weapons	N
Delay "re-flagging" of Kuwaiti tankers	N
Approve tax-raising deficit-reduction bill	N
1988	
Approve aid to Nicaraguan contras	Y
Enact civil rights restoration bill over Reagan veto	N
Kill 60-day plant-closing notification measure	Y
Pass omnibus trade bill over Reagan veto	Y
Approve death penalty for drug-related murders	Y
Bar federal funds for abortions in cases of rape and incest	Y
Oppose seven-day waiting period for purchase of handguns	Y

Voting Studies

	Presidential Support		Party Unity		Conservative Coalition	
Year	S	O	S	O	S	O
1988	47	47	67	28	76	24
1987	54	42	59	38	74	23
1986	52	47	48	49	84	14
1985	50	48	54	38	65	31
1984	56	42	54	42	64	34
1983	61	39	62 †	37 †	66	34
1982	65	35	61	38	77	23
1981	63	37	69	31	72	28

† Not eligible for all recorded votes.

Interest Group Ratings

Year	ADA	ACU	AFL-CIO	CCUS
1988	25	63	62	86
1987	24	43	50	73
1986	50	45	86	44
1985	35	48	59	57
1984	40	54	38	67
1983	15	52	18	95
1982	25	36	20	64
1981	30	73	20	89

Rhode Island

U.S. CONGRESS

SENATE 1 D, 1 R
HOUSE 2 R

LEGISLATURE

Senate 41 D, 9 R
House 82 D, 18 R

ELECTIONS

1988 Presidential Vote	
Bush	44%
Dukakis	56%
1984 Presidential Vote	
Reagan	52%
Mondale	48%
1980 Presidential Vote	
Reagan	37%
Carter	48%
Anderson	14%
Turnout rate in 1984	56%
Turnout rate in 1986	41%
Turnout rate in 1988	53%

(as percentage of voting age population)

POPULATION AND GROWTH

1980 population	947,154
1988 population estimate (43rd in the nation)	993,000
Percent change 1980-1988	+5%

DEMOGRAPHIC BREAKDOWN

White	95%
Black	3%
Other	1%
(Spanish origin)	2%
Urban	87%
Rural	13%
Born in state	68%
Foreign-born	9%

MAJOR CITIES

Providence	157,200
Warwick	86,960
Cranston	73,760
Pawtucket	72,640
East Providence	50,440

AREA AND LAND USE

Area	1,055 sq. miles (50th)
Farm	9%
Forest	60%
Federally owned	1%

Gov. Edward D. DiPrete (R)
Of Cranston — Elected 1984

Born: July 8, 1934, Cranston, R.I.
Education: College of the Holy Cross, B.S. 1955.
Military Career: Navy, 1955-59; Naval Reserve, 1959-67.
Occupation: Real-estate executive.
Religion: Roman Catholic.
Political Career: Cranston City Council, 1975-79; Cranston mayor, 1979-85.
Next Election: 1990.

WORK

Occupations	
White-collar	50%
Blue-collar	36%
Service workers	14%
Government Workers	
Federal	10,066
State	25,233
Local	26,621

MONEY

Median family income	$ 16,978	(41st)
Tax burden per capita	$ 816	(27th)

EDUCATION

Spending per pupil through grade 12	$ 4,667	(6th)
Persons with college degrees	15%	(27th)

CRIME

Violent crime rate 360 per 100,000 (31st)

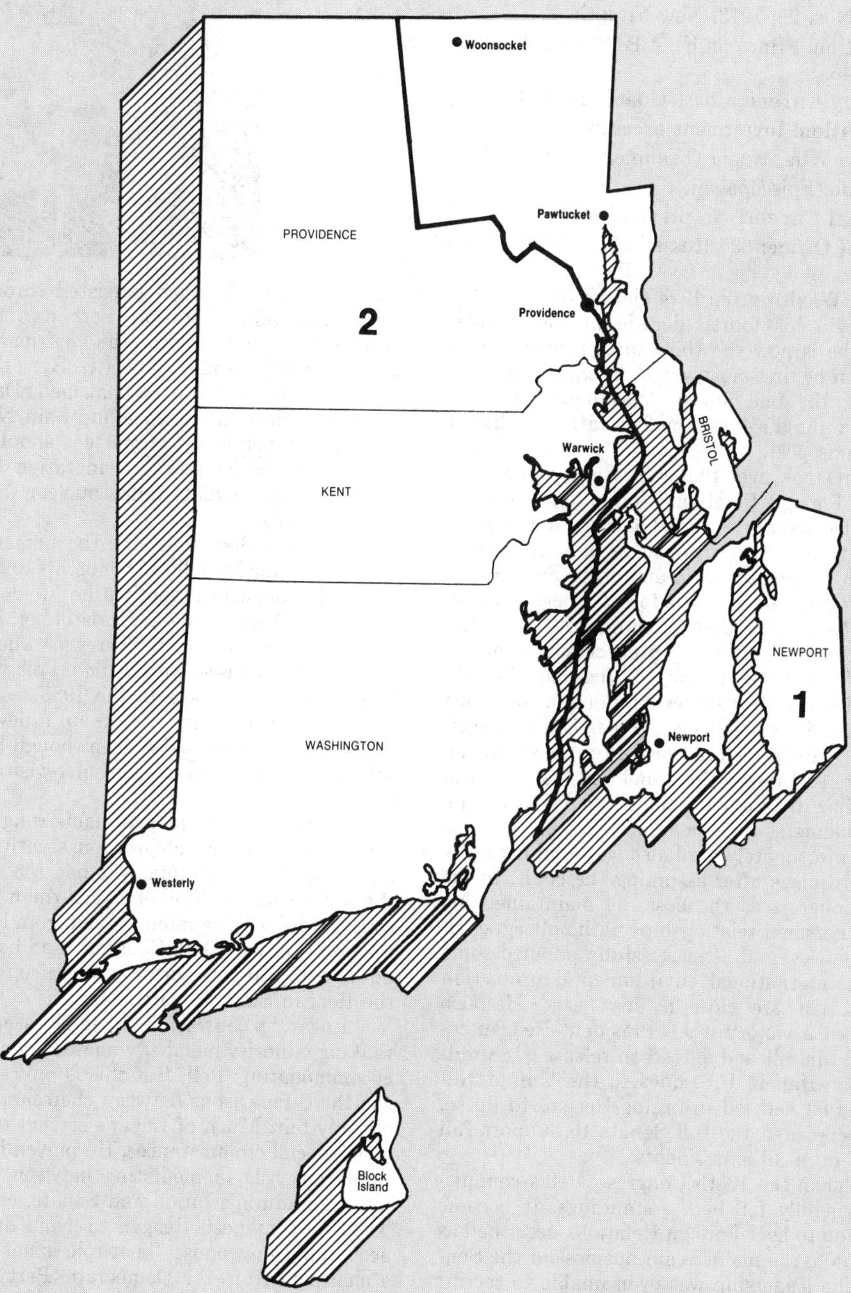
Woonsocket
Pawtucket
PROVIDENCE
2
Providence
BRISTOL
Warwick
KENT
NEWPORT
1
Newport
WASHINGTON
Westerly
Block Island

Claiborne Pell (D)

Of Newport — Elected 1960

Born: Nov. 22, 1918, New York, N.Y.
Education: Princeton U., A.B. 1940; Columbia U., A.M. 1946.
Military Career: Coast Guard, 1941-45.
Occupation: Investment executive.
Family: Wife, Nuala O'Donnell; four children.
Religion: Episcopalian.
Political Career: No previous office.
Capitol Office: 335 Russell Bldg. 20510; 224-4642.

In Washington: If re-elected in 1990, Pell will begin his fourth decade in the Senate, where he is now the third most senior Democrat. But he first must weigh the satisfactions of holding the one job in Washington he has always wanted against the frustrations of life in that same post.

Pell took over that job, the chairmanship of the Foreign Relations Committee, in 1987, when Democrats regained a Senate majority. He had to do so confronting a burden of comparison far heavier than any other new Democratic chairman. Even before he began, many people concluded that he could not match the record established by his predecessor, Republican Richard G. Lugar of Indiana. Widely viewed as the most successful Foreign Relations chairman in recent times, Lugar had managed in two years to restore a significant share of the prestige and power the panel had lost over the preceding decade. Pell seemed unable to escape pre-labeling as a lesser figure.

Unfortunately, Pell also was unable to dispel this image after assuming the chair. In his first Congress as the boss, he maintained his warm personal relationships with colleagues of both parties, and he successfully pursued some of the international environmental protection issues that are close to his heart. He also achieved a victory when President Reagan reversed himself and agreed to release $188 million of withheld U.S. dues to the United Nations. Pell had led in urging Reagan to do so, and persuaded the full Senate to support full payment of all assessments.

Yet in the 100th Congress, Pell's committee generally fell in the standings. It became common to hear Foreign Relations described as oblique to the mainstream business of the Senate. The leadership was even unable to recruit an extra Democrat to keep the roster full during part of the 100th Congress.

Pell also inherited longstanding logjams such as foreign aid appropriations. Unable to pass a free-standing foreign aid bill in 1987, he was able to do so in 1988 after the budget summit at the White House broke the procedural blockade that had persisted throughout the Reagan administration. Perhaps the most disappointing moment for the chairman came when Majority Leader Robert C. Byrd decided that two other committee chairmen, David L. Boren of Select Intelligence and Sam Nunn of the Armed Services Committee, should help Pell quarterback floor consideration of the treaty on intermediate-range nuclear forces in Europe (INF).

Not only does Pell lack the personal authority to bring his fellow Democrats to heel, he has little ideological motivation to do so — aggressive liberals such as Christopher J. Dodd of Connecticut and John Kerry of Massachusetts pursue causes with which Pell is more than comfortable. Late in the 1988 session he allowed the committee to take up a new set of sanctions on South Africa even though he publicly questioned "the wisdom of revisiting this issue."

He was also frequently hamstrung by the aggressive advocacy of archconservative Jesse Helms of North Carolina, who had the will and the staff to act as a kind of co-chairman. He had wrested the ranking minority slot from Lugar at the outset of the 100th Congress, and he used it not only to compete with Pell but also to harass the Reagan State Department.

Lugar, by contrast, had been blessed with a ranking minority member who was gracious and accommodating: Pell. But this is only one reason the comparisons between chairmen are not entirely fair. Much of Lugar's strength derived from special circumstances. He played his most important role in mediating between the Republican administration and Senate, especially when he convinced Reagan to avoid defeat by accepting compromise. That role is not open to a chairman from the Democratic Party.

In normal circumstances, the chairmanship of Foreign Relations simply is not geared to providing its occupant with a lot of power. The committee does not consider a great deal of legislation, and those topics under its jurisdiction — foreign aid, diplomatic nominations and an occasional treaty — do not customarily provide a lot of bargaining clout with other members. The panel attracts young, ambitious senators who are more interested in establishing a name for themselves on controversial issues than in working under the authority of a strong leader. It is no coincidence that the three chairmen before Lugar all found it difficult to maintain much control.

It is also true, though, that many of the doubts about Pell spring from his own personality and image. A diffident socialite, he strikes many as an implausible candidate to become a strong force on controversial matters such as arms control and Central America policy.

Pell has accumulated power mainly through seniority. He possesses no notable flair for internal Senate politics or behind-the-scenes dealing with his colleagues. His aristocratic demeanor can sometimes come across as aloofness or arrogance. Although his voting record on social and economic issues is consistently liberal, he often displays a kind of patrician distance from the concerns of ordinary folk, or even from camaraderie in the Senate. "I have the uncanny facility for making the most exciting matters gray," he cheerfully admits.

Pell did make some efforts early in the 100th Congress to take a more assertive stance. He pressed Byrd to give his committee a role in the investigation into the Iran-contra affair. But the centerpiece of Pell's first months as chairman — ratification of two nuclear test-ban treaties — quickly foundered. Despite Pell's efforts to negotiate a compromise with the Reagan administration, the pacts got bogged down in a dispute over verification.

Arms control is a subject on which Pell may have some credibility problems. His image as an ardent believer in disarmament does not always help his efforts to line up support for his point of view; rightly or wrongly, he makes foreign policy conservatives worry he might support unwise concessions in his eagerness to obtain an arms agreement.

Still, there is no doubt that Pell is a man of conviction in foreign policy. He rarely loses interest in a subject once he decides it is important, and often he gets what he wants in the end. "I am less dynamic than many," he likes to say, "but I have my own course, which I set and try to follow."

Usually, that course brought Pell into sharp conflict with Senate Republicans and the Reagan administration. He tried hard during the 99th Congress, however, to work closely with Lugar. The two men joined in opposing an effort by the Appropriations Committee to reduce their committee's authority over foreign aid programs, and cooperated in 1985 to push the first foreign aid authorization bill to clear Congress in several years.

Pell was one of the most vehement congressional opponents of the 1984 Kissinger commission plan, which called for increased U.S. military and economic aid to Central America. He also fought against the administration's efforts to provide aid to the Nicaraguan contras. His most important step came during work on the 1985 foreign aid authorization, when he won narrow committee approval for an amendment barring the United States from pressuring third countries to help the contras. The Reagan administration strongly opposed the provision, finally using a veto threat to force conferees on the bill to weaken it substantially.

Ocean law is another one of Pell's favorite issues on Foreign Relations. He was involved in the International Law of the Sea Conference, which produced a treaty the United States has refused to sign. He was the author of another treaty, approved by Congress and ratified by numerous countries, that prohibits the placement of weapons on the ocean floor. Still another Pell treaty prohibits the use of environmental modification weapons.

Pell has been interested in the eastern Mediterranean and has repeatedly sponsored increases in aid to Cyprus. A strong partisan of Greece in its conflict with Turkey, he opposed the end of the embargo on arms shipments to Turkey in 1978.

When the final record of Pell's Senate career is written, however, his work in education may outweigh anything he does in foreign affairs. He was the main force behind a change in federal education law that has benefited millions of low- and middle-income college students. In 1972 he pushed through, over the opposition of the House and the indifference of much of the higher education community, legislation establishing the Basic Educational Opportunity Grant (BEOG).

BEOGs quickly became the cornerstone of federal aid to students. The program marked a basic shift in policy, because it provided aid directly to students, instead of channeling it through the institutions, as early aid programs had done. The BEOG program was renamed "Pell Grants" in 1980. While Pell did not push for the change in public, associates say he sought it in private.

The same year the change was made, Reagan was elected president. Soon the grants and other forms of student aid were among the domestic programs targeted for cuts. Pell could do little to block the deep cuts in student aid programs approved by Congress in 1981. In fiscal 1982, the open-ended Pell Grants ended and a specified sum was set for each year.

In subsequent years, however, Pell and his allies generally were able to prevent further deep cuts in student aid. Along with Education Subcommittee Chairman Robert T. Stafford, he helped enact in 1986 a new higher education authorization that increased the limits on individual Pell Grants, while tightening eligibility for guaranteed student loans.

By 1988 the tide had turned enough to

allow legislation that would again expand the program. Both the House and Senate passed bills that included liberalized eligibility rules for Pell Grants. But the administration balked at this and other aspects of the legislation, and in September the issue was postponed into the new year. In 1989, Pell and Massachusetts Sen. Edward M. Kennedy, chairman of the full committee, reintroduced the Senate version of the bill and won passage on the Senate floor in March.

The watershed year of 1980 was also the year of Pell's worst defeat in education legislation. The Senate rejected the conference report on the higher education reauthorization bill he had managed. Critics insisted its estimated $50 billion five-year price tag was too high. Stung by the defeat, Pell was careful to satisfy the objections before he came back with a revised second version. The second conference report, reduced in cost by about $1.4 billion, finally became law.

At Home: Far from resenting Pell's privileged background, his blue-collar constituents have handed him landslide victories four out of five times. Only Republican John H. Chafee, now his Senate colleague, was able to hold him under 60 percent of the vote.

Pell's pro-labor record has kept him in the good graces of the unions, always a potent force in Rhode Island. And while he does not have much personal rapport with the state's ethnic voters, he can talk to them: He speaks Portuguese, Italian and French.

Pell's career not only survived but prospered in the generally Republican election years of 1972, 1978 and 1984. Should he choose to run again in 1990, he should have less to fear from the national tide. But the GOP hopes finally to lure popular five-term Rep. Claudine Schneider into the chase, and she would be expected to give Pell his first real test since Chafee. The state party has been riding high in recent years, twice electing a Republican governor and capturing both the state's congressional seats for the first time since 1940.

Pell will turn 72 in November of 1990, raising the possibility of retirement or a debate over his age. But then Pell's predecessor in this seat, Theodore Green, was about as old as Pell is now when he won the first of four terms. Green became chairman of Foreign Relations and retired in his 90s.

Pell's father, Herbert, was a Democrat who briefly represented Manhattan's Silk Stocking District in the House and served as a foreign envoy for Franklin D. Roosevelt. Claiborne Pell was born in New York, but he spent summers in the exclusive Rhode Island resort of Newport, where the Pells had been going for five generations. The family moved there permanently when he was 9.

Following his graduation from Princeton in 1940, Pell went to Europe to try to help concentration camp inmates. The Nazis arrested him several times. He was a Coast Guard officer during World War II and spent several years in the foreign service, stationed at the United Nations, in Czechoslovakia and Italy. Later, while working as an investment banker and publisher, he dabbled in politics, at one point serving as registration chairman for the Democratic National Committee.

Pell decided to run himself in 1960 and stunned the political community by overwhelming two former governors, Dennis J. Roberts and J. Howard McGrath, to win the Democratic nomination for the Senate. In the fall, he crushed Republican Raoul Archambault, former assistant U.S. budget director, to win his Senate seat. One of Pell's advantages that year was his relationship with John F. Kennedy, who was very popular in Rhode Island. Pell's wife, Nuala, campaigned for Kennedy in West Virginia.

Running for a second term in 1966, Pell had an equally easy time with his GOP opponent — a retired Women's Army Corps officer named Ruth M. Briggs, who insisted upon being called "Colonel." She sought to make an issue out of his dovish line on the Vietnam War and to portray him as a wealthy dilettante, calling Pell "the prize entertainer of the Kennedys." But like Archambault, she failed to draw even a third of the vote.

Chafee, seeking a political comeback in 1972 after serving as Navy secretary in the Nixon administration, provided the only serious Republican opposition Pell has ever had. He linked Pell to a fellow anti-war Democrat, Sen. George McGovern, the Democratic presidential nominee. But Pell, sensitive about the Navy's large influence in Rhode Island, deflected the tactic by repudiating McGovern's call for cutting the defense budget.

And Chafee was still carrying some of the liabilities of his support for a state income tax, an issue that had helped defeat him in his campaign for re-election as governor in 1968. As a moderate Republican, Chafee never managed to come up with a compelling reason for an overwhelmingly Democratic state to turn out an incumbent Democrat. Pell won by 32,000 votes.

Things were back to normal for Pell in 1978, when he buried Republican James G. Reynolds, a little-known bakery executive who complained that Pell was more interested in the arts than in saving jobs for Rhode Island.

Any GOP hopes of ousting Pell in 1984 ended early when Schneider decided to remain in the House rather than challenge the veteran Democrat. The Reagan administration encouraged her to run for the Senate, but she declined despite polls showing her at least even with Pell.

That left the nomination to Barbara Leonard, the president of a screw manufacturing company and widow of a longtime GOP fund-raiser. A political novice, she found it difficult to raise money or even get Pell's attention. Bucking a Republican tide in Rhode Island for the second time in 12 years, Pell was re-elected with 73 percent of the vote, his second-consecutive re-election total over 70 percent.

Committees

Foreign Relations (Chairman)
East Asian and Pacific Affairs; International Economic Policy, Trade, Oceans and Environment; Near Eastern and South Asian Affairs

Labor and Human Resources (2nd of 9 Democrats)
Education, Arts and Humanities (chairman); Aging; Children, Family, Drugs and Alcoholism

Rules and Administration (2nd of 9 Democrats)

Joint Library (Vice Chairman)

Elections

1984 General

Claiborne Pell (D)	286,780	(73%)
Barbara Leonard (R)	108,492	(27%)

Previous Winning Percentages: 1978 (75%) **1972** (54%) **1966** (68%) **1960** (69%)

Campaign Finance

	Receipts	Receipts from PACs	Expend-itures
1984			
Pell (D)	$745,270	$210,592 (28%)	$433,436
Leonard (R)	$164,275	$33,850 (21%)	$162,699

Key Votes

1987

Enact omnibus highway bill over Reagan veto	Y
Limit testing of space-based anti-ballistic missiles	Y
Oppose banning tests of larger nuclear weapons	N
Confirm Robert H. Bork as Supreme Court justice	N

1988

Allow vote on campaign-finance overhaul	Y
Pass civil rights restoration bill over Reagan veto	Y
Enact omnibus trade bill over Reagan veto	Y
Approve death penalty for drug-related murders	N
Oppose "workfare" amendment to welfare overhaul bill	Y

Voting Studies

	Presidential Support		Party Unity		Conservative Coalition	
Year	**S**	**O**	**S**	**O**	**S**	**O**
1988	43	51	89	6	8	92
1987	32	67	92	7	19	81
1986	30	67	75	20	16	80
1985	29	67	82	14	7	92
1984	31	66	82	14	15	81
1983	41	48	81	15	14	82
1982	36	59	75	19	17	78
1981	42	52	82	14	10	82

Interest Group Ratings

Year	ADA	ACU	AFL-CIO	CCUS
1988	100	0	100	36
1987	90	0	90	28
1986	80	17	67	42
1985	95	9	95	29
1984	100	5	100	22
1983	90	0	94	26
1982	95	0	92	37
1981	95	0	95	17

John H. Chafee (R)

Of Warwick — Elected 1976

Born: Oct. 22, 1922, Providence, R.I.
Education: Yale U., B.A. 1947; Harvard U., LL.B. 1950.
Military Career: Marine Corps, 1942-45, 1951-52.
Occupation: Lawyer.
Family: Wife, Virginia Coates; five children.
Religion: Episcopalian.
Political Career: R.I. House, 1957-63, minority leader, 1959-63; governor, 1963-69; defeated for re-election as governor, 1968; U.S. Navy secretary, 1969-72; Republican nominee for U.S. Senate, 1972.
Capitol Office: 567 Dirksen Bldg. 20510; 224-2921.

In Washington: For Chafee, who has seen the good and the bad over three decades in politics, these are neither the best of times nor the worst of times.

His party no longer controls the Senate. But he was not among those who lost a chairmanship or otherwise tumbled when control changed hands in the 100th Congress. Instead, Chafee was re-elected chairman of the Senate Republican Conference, the No. 3 position in the GOP leadership. He has since been elected to a third term in that job.

Moreover, Chafee now serves in a Senate far less driven by or beholden to the New Right politics that had dominated President Reagan's tenure. President Bush's politics seem close to Chafee's own brand of Republicanism. In fact, the two New England-bred Episcopalians studied at Yale at the same time.

Not so long ago, this sort of Northeastern pedigree, and the frequently liberal views that went with it, made Chafee almost as much of an apostate as his neighbor, Lowell P. Weicker Jr. of Connecticut. But Chafee could vote against school prayer, aid to the contras and the balanced-budget amendment without generating animosity among his colleagues or his constituents. He could support campaign-finance reform without seeming to be a showboat about it. And that may partly explain why Chafee was back in the 101st Congress, having defeated a strong Democratic challenger on Election Day. (Weicker was defeated the same day.)

Chafee's election as conference chairman in 1984 was in part a victory for a coalition of moderate senators from the Northeast and Midwest. But his 28-25 win over Jake Garn of Utah also was a product of the Rhode Islander's personal popularity. The same could be said of his 1988 re-election as conference chairman, which was challenged by Sen. Frank H. Murkowski of Alaska. Murkowski said Chafee had opposed the administration too often to be in the leadership. But Chafee prevailed by a vote of 28-17.

These are also promising times for Chafee in that some of his issues, notably environmental protection, seem to be coming to the fore. He is now ranking Republican on Environment and Public Works, a good spot in which to help his state and protect the nature and wildlife that have long occupied his interest.

In 1988 he helped shepherd through a five-year reauthorization of the 1973 Endangered Species Act, working with Western Republicans to allay their concerns. He was the Republican co-author of a bill banning the dumping of sludge in the Atlantic Ocean. And his position on acid rain was tough enough that he joined with environmental groups, and a few other senators, to condemn Maine Sen. George J. Mitchell's proposed compromise on Clean Air Act amendments at the end of the 1988 session. Revisiting that issue early in 1989, he endorsed a package of tougher bills limiting toxic emissions. And he was an early advocate of international cooperation on global warming and the "greenhouse effect."

When Chafee was chairman of the Pollution Subcommittee in the 99th Congress, he was the major mover of a bill reauthorizing the Clean Water Act. The measure was widely popular for its state and local grants for wastewater treatment (including $122 million for Rhode Island). But it also tightened controls on water pollution, increased protection of estuaries and set up a new program to combat contamination of lakes and rivers by runoff from urban areas and farm land. Environmentalists were pleased with the measure, although business interests did win extensions of various unmet cleanup deadlines that had been imposed in the original 1977 act.

It passed overwhelmingly in 1986, but Reagan, denouncing its price tag, killed it with a pocket veto. It was quickly brought up again in the 100th Congress and passed over a second Reagan veto.

Chafee should also find himself far more sympatico with Bush budget priorities, particularly insofar as they follow the "kinder, gentler" paradigm.

Chafee is part of the balanced-budget tradition that never felt comfortable with Reagan's reliance on "supply-side economics" and the deficits that strategy tolerated. This orientation almost caused him to oppose the 1986 tax reform drive. "We've only got so much energy," he said in January 1985, claiming that tax-overhaul efforts might sap resources from reducing the deficit. On the Finance Committee, he was one of the most vocal advocates of a deficit-reducing tax increase, despite Reagan's adamant opposition.

But when Finance Chairman Bob Packwood introduced a revenue-neutral tax-overhaul bill, Chafee adopted the idea and became one of the core group of lawmakers who saw the tax bill through to passage in 1986. In fact, Chafee at times seemed more committed than Packwood to passing a tax bill that reduced special preferences in exchange for lowering rates for individuals and business.

In early 1986, while most other members of the Finance Committee were seeking to preserve or expand their favorite tax preferences, Chafee and New Jersey Democrat Bill Bradley repeatedly stressed that retaining the costly preferences would make it more difficult to afford cuts in individual and corporate tax rates.

When Packwood unveiled a streamlined plan in early May, standing by his side were Chafee and five other committee members who had helped fashion it. Their guiding principle had been to sacrifice tax benefits they wanted in exchange for major rate reductions and simplification of the tax code. The revised plan was approved basically intact by Finance and the Senate. In the House-Senate conference, Chafee objected to the House's emphasis on higher business taxes. But he voted for the final bill.

More recently on Finance, Chafee has been closely associated with tax credits for child care expenses, an idea he continued to push with the Bush administration's support in 1989.

On economic issues, Chafee's chief cause is international trade. He has a reputation as one of the most ardent free-traders in the Senate, and was an early proponent of the free-trade pact with Canada in the 100th Congress. At the same time, increasing concern over the mounting U.S. trade deficit has nudged him into favoring a more active federal role in export promotion. In the trade legislation of 1988, he also joined his Finance colleagues in strengthening retaliatory language against trading partners deemed protectionist. In the previous Congress, Chafee had introduced legislation to bar sales of Japanese communications equipment in America until Japan bought more U.S. gear. "This isn't protectionism," he said. "This is trying to get our products into their markets."

At Home: Chafee's affable personality and moderate record have carried him through three decades of politics in Rhode Island, winning most of the time and recovering from defeat.

His toughness showed in 1988, when he faced a telegenic and talented campaigner, Lt. Gov. Richard A. Licht. The 40-year-old nephew of the man who had ousted Chafee from the governorship in 1968, Licht organized early to assure himself the nomination and the united support of his party. Before being elected statewide, Licht had built a solid record as a legislator on issues of wide voter appeal such as child care and protection of open spaces.

Licht's early fund raising was impressive enough to draw national media attention. He was the only 1988 challenger to begin the year having raised more money than the incumbent. But when Chafee got busy, he was able to turn some of Licht's assets against him. He seized on Licht's campaign treasury to portray himself as the fiscal underdog in the race. And when Licht returned a controversial $250 contribution from Tom Hayden, a leftish California legislator and husband of actress Jane Fonda, Chafee said the Democrat must lack "backbone" if he caved in to pressure "over a measly $250." Such counterthrusts helped Chafee overcome Licht's appeal to youth and his charges that Chafee had larded the 1986 tax reform bill with special breaks for friends.

As expected, Democratic presidential nominee Michael S. Dukakis carried Rhode Island more easily than he did his home state of Massachusetts. But Licht badly lagged the top of his party ticket; Chafee won with a comfortable 55 percent of the vote.

Chafee's survival had been a closer question in 1982, when Democratic challenger Julius C. Michaelson came within 8,200 votes of victory simply by emphasizing that Chafee belonged to the party of Ronald Reagan and that Reagan was no friend of Rhode Island. Michaelson, a liberal former state attorney general, said Chafee had been a "very essential" supporter of the Reagan program.

It was not a bad Democratic strategy. Not only did Reagan fail to carry Rhode Island in 1980, but he drew a smaller share of the vote (37 percent) than he did in any other state.

Chafee fought off Michaelson by reasserting his value to Rhode Island. He boasted of his role in negotiations that persuaded the General Dynamics Electric Boat division to keep its large shipyard in the state.

The position Chafee held on the Finance Committee and his efforts to ease the burden on American businesses abroad helped him build a campaign treasury twice the size of Michaelson's. The challenger, general counsel to the state AFL-CIO, depended heavily on union support.

Michaelson carried Democratic Providence and the industrial Blackstone Valley by nearly

20,000 votes, a margin that Chafee barely offset by sweeping the rest of the state.

The close result was not unusual for Chafee. When he ran for governor in 1962, after serving as state House minority leader, he won by 398 votes over Democrat John A. Notte Jr. The incumbent had damaged himself by advocating a state income tax — the same issue that was to cause Chafee trouble six years later.

As a three-term governor in the 1960s, Chafee pushed for an increase in Rhode Island's social and welfare spending, calling it "a state version of the Great Society." He won re-election easily in 1964 and in 1966.

In 1968, however, running against Democrat Frank Licht, he got caught on the wrong side of a dispute over state taxes. Chafee insisted an income tax was necessary to prevent a boost in the sales tax. Licht disagreed, and upset Chafee by 7,808 votes.

After his defeat, Chafee was appointed Navy secretary in the Nixon administration. That seemed likely to help the 1972 Senate campaign he was planning against Democratic Sen. Claiborne Pell. When he left the Pentagon to begin the campaign, he looked strong.

But it did not turn out that way. Though Pell has always been accused of aloofness, he knew what to do that year, running superb television advertising and speaking a collection of European languages to voters in the ethnic neighborhoods of Providence and the mill towns. And the old tax issue was still a partial liability for Chafee. Even the rare Republican presidential victory in the state that fall did not help him. Pell won 54 percent of the vote.

That might have been the end of Chafee's political career, had Democrats not managed to do everything but throw the state's other Senate seat at him in 1976 by fighting with each other all year.

Gov. Philip W. Noel was the front-runner for the 1976 Democratic nomination, but he crippled himself by making comments in a wire service interview that sounded like racial slurs. He had to resign as the party's national platform chairman, and he went on to lose the Senate primary by 100 votes to Cadillac dealer Richard P. Lorber, who spent lavishly of his own money and accused Noel not only of racial insensitivity but of bossism.

Noel then refused to back Lorber in the general election, allowing Chafee to resurrect his old coalition of the early 1960s — Republicans, independents and dissident Democrats. Lorber tried to paint the well-to-do Chafee as an elitist, but the charge did not stick. Chafee won every town in the state except one.

Committees

Environment and Public Works (Ranking)
Environmental Protection (ranking); Water Resources, Transportation and Infrastructure

Finance (5th of 9 Republicans)
Health for Families and the Uninsured (ranking); International Trade; Medicare and Long-Term Care

Elections

1988 General

John H. Chafee (R)	217,273	(55%)
Richard A. Licht (D)	180,717	(45%)

Previous Winning Percentages: **1982** (51%) **1976** (58%)

Campaign Finance

	Receipts	Receipts from PACs	Expend-itures
1988			
Chafee (R)	$2,455,215	$1,045,319 (43%)	$2,841,985
Licht (D)	$2,838,216	$655,752 (23%)	$2,735,917

Key Votes

1987

Enact omnibus highway bill over Reagan veto	N
Limit testing of space-based anti-ballistic missiles	Y
Oppose banning tests of larger nuclear weapons	N
Confirm Robert H. Bork as Supreme Court justice	N

1988

Allow vote on campaign-finance overhaul	Y
Pass civil rights restoration bill over Reagan veto	Y
Enact omnibus trade bill over Reagan veto	Y
Approve death penalty for drug-related murders	N
Oppose "workfare" amendment to welfare overhaul bill	Y

Voting Studies

	Presidential Support		Party Unity		Conservative Coalition	
Year	S	O	S	O	S	O
1988	45	49	34	63	22	76
1987	50	47	46	54	31	69
1986	67	31	64	34	62	37
1985	72	26	68	30	52	47
1984	71	26	66	28	60	36
1983	80	18	67	33	45	50
1982	54	45	47	50	30	69
1981	75	23	68	29	50	47

Interest Group Ratings

Year	ADA	ACU	AFL-CIO	CCUS
1988	90	4	86	36
1987	80	16	60	56
1986	60	35	33	63
1985	35	39	24	76
1984	60	58	18	56
1983	60	35	29	42
1982	80	14	50	43
1981	45	38	47	61

1 Ronald K. Machtley (R)

Of Portsmouth — Elected 1988

Born: July 13, 1948, Johnstown, Pa.
Education: U.S. Naval Academy, B.S. 1970; Suffolk U., J.D. 1978.
Military Career: Navy, 1970-75; Naval Reserve, 1975-present.
Occupation: Lawyer.
Family: Wife, Kati Croft; two children.
Religion: Presbyterian.
Political Career: No previous office.
Capitol Office: 1123 Longworth Bldg. 20515; 225-4911.

The Path to Washington: Machtley's election was probably the most surprising and most important upset of the 1988 federal elections. It was surprising because Machtley had begun the year as a slightly buffoonish also-ran in a primary many saw as a choice between sacrificial lambs. It was important because Machtley's eventual victim was 28-year veteran Democrat Fernand J. St Germain, the autocratic chairman of the House Banking Committee and a symbol of dubious ethics in Congress.

In a year when the GOP was unable even to field challengers to many key Democrats in the House, taking St Germain's scalp was significant consolation. When Machtley was introduced to the other Republican House freshmen after the election, he reportedly received a round of applause. The GOP freshmen elected him their vice president.

St Germain had been targeted by the National Republican Congressional Committee in 1986 and had been opposed by John A. Holmes Jr., the attractive and articulate former chairman of the Rhode Island GOP. Holmes went after St Germain with hammer and tong, but the incumbent filled the airwaves with ads emphasizing his Woonsocket roots and many works on behalf of consumers. St Germain won with 58 percent.

In 1988, it seemed the worst of St Germain's legal entanglements might be over. Readers of *The Wall Street Journal* were well versed in St Germain's dealings with lobbyists for the savings and loan industry, for which his committee wrote regulatory legislation. But the Justice Department had declined to indict him, and the House ethics committee seemed unlikely to deal harshly with him.

Holmes was back in the chase to challenge St Germain again, but few gave him much chance of improving on his 1986 showing. The district seemed already to have passed its own judgment on its son. And the larger turnout of a presidential year would probably only help him.

Machtley, meanwhile, had burst on the local political scene with a gimmick that seemed sure to overshadow his message. He brought a piglet with him to his candidacy announcement, introducing it as "Lester T. Pork." What we need in Congress, he said, is Ron Machtley and Les Pork. Machtley also organized such conventional stunts as a jog across the district. But he seemed destined to retire from politics remembered only as "the guy with the pig."

Then a series of unforeseen events changed the situation radically. First, Holmes vacated the primary field by inexplicably failing to file his nomination papers on time. Blame fell on a campaign aide, but some muttered that Holmes had simply lost his stomach for another beating. In any event, the nomination was Machtley's by default.

Second, St Germain received a scare in the Democratic primary in September. Scott Wolf, a young but seasoned campaign worker and pollster, collected 45 percent of the primary vote. It was St Germain's worst showing in a primary since he was elected. Suddenly, it became respectable to say St Germain was beatable. And as the fall wore on, quite a few political observers began saying it.

Machtley, having gotten the electorate's attention, knew how to communicate the seriousness of his intentions. He dropped the pig (donating its valuable weight to charity). He produced campaign literature emphasizing his acceptability as an alternative to St Germain, touting his commitment to such nonpartisan subjects as health care, housing, education and clean water.

Machtley had been trained as an engineer at the Naval Academy and served five years on active duty. He had then put himself through law school in Boston while working full time. He had built up a practice and performed community service for such causes as the YMCA and the local hospital. He was an elder in his Presbyterian church.

True, he lacked the roots of most local politicians and had never run for office. But neither was he a flake. He was a respectable Republican attorney with his own firm in New-

Rhode Island 1

East — Part of Providence; Pawtucket

Stretching around scenic Narragansett Bay from the Atlantic Ocean toward the industrial Blackstone River Valley, the 1st offers pristine coastal preserves but also some of the most densely crowded small cities in the nation.

Fishing, shipping and naval operations dominate the coast. The larger towns around the bay tend to vote Democratic; some of the smaller seacoast villages have pockets of wealthy residential areas and tend to favor the GOP. Newport and Tiverton have backed the Democratic nominee in three of the last four presidential elections, voting Republican only in 1984.

The 1st also includes part of the Democratic stronghold of Providence, along with its smaller suburbs. Within the capital city, the 1st includes all of the heavily Italian Fourth Ward and most of the Italian Fifth Ward, both generally Democratic in statewide contests. The WASP-dominated East Side, where liberal voters around the campus of Brown University offset some of the upper-income conservatives, also has communities of newcomers from Portugal and the Cape Verde Islands.

To the north, the 1st includes the industrial corridor in the Blackstone Valley, including the gritty redbrick factory towns of Woonsocket, Central Falls and Pawtucket. Pawtucket was the site of the first factory in the nation, a textile mill founded in 1790 with technology pirated from British firms. The valley's economy now includes metalworking and jewelry firms among much light manufacturing.

The Blackstone Valley is the backbone of Democratic majorities in the state. George McGovern won all three of its major cities in 1972, although Woonsocket broke with Pawtucket and Central Falls by voting for Reagan in 1984. But in 1988, all three went Democratic again.

Population: 474,429. White 452,230 (95%), Black 11,727 (3%), Other 3,657 (1%). Spanish origin: 9,357 (2%). 18 and over 357,096 (75%), 65 and over 66,675 (14%). Median age: 32.

port. He had decided to enter the race as a kind of idealistic statement, yet he seemed to have an idea of what it would take to win.

When his campaign took hold he was still strapped for cash. But he received considerable "free media" coverage, thanks in part to the novelty of a close November race in the district. He hounded St Germain into a debate that Machtley later called the turning point. He was able to establish that investigations of St Germain that had yet to yield an indictment or censure did not constitute total exoneration. And he highlighted the fresh news that the Justice Department had passed along its collection of evidence to the House ethics panel for further review. As the campaign became a true contest, St Germain fought back with the hardy perennial issue of Social Security. But this did not stem the tide.

In reaching almost 56 percent, Machtley ran well in his strongholds (60 percent in Newport, for example) while holding St Germain even in his. And he also managed 57 percent in normally Democratic North Providence.

Committees

Armed Services (21st of 21 Republicans)
Military Personnel and Compensation; Readiness

Select Children, Youth and Families (12th of 12 Republicans)

Small Business (17th of 17 Republicans)

Campaign Finance

	Receipts	Receipts from PACs	Expenditures
1988			
Machtley (R)	$417,449	$81,524 (20%)	$385,402
St Germain (D)	$668,963	$362,556 (54%)	$801,289

Election

1988 General

Ronald K. Machtley (R)	105,506	(56%)
Fernand J. St Germain (D)	84,141	(44%)

District Vote For President

	1988	1984	1980	1976
D	112,131 (57%)	99,348 (49%)	98,522 (48%)	116,362 (57%)
R	82,789 (42%)	101,566 (50%)	74,354 (37%)	86,772 (43%)
I			29,351 (14%)	

2 Claudine Schneider (R)

Of Narragansett — Elected 1980

Born: March 25, 1947, Clairton, Pa.
Education: Windham College, B.A. 1969; graduate work, U. of Rhode Island, 1975.
Occupation: Television producer and moderator.
Family: Divorced.
Religion: Roman Catholic.
Political Career: Republican nominee for U.S. House, 1978.
Capitol Office: 1512 Longworth Bldg. 20515; 225-2735.

In Washington: One of a handful of non-conservatives elected to the House in the sweeping Republican gains of 1980, Schneider quickly established herself as a highly visible GOP antagonist to the Reagan administration.

Because of her readiness to break from party ranks in the House, Schneider is widely perceived as someone who might be more at home in another office — the Senate, perhaps — where she could more freely pursue her individual interpretation of what being a Republican is all about.

Schneider came to Congress insisting that she was not a liberal Republican, but her voting record perennially portrays her as one of the most liberal Republicans in the House.

Shortly after she arrived, she cast one of only three Republican votes against the Reagan-endorsed package of specific budget cuts. She has not strayed far from that path since then. In 1987, she opposed President Reagan's position on House votes three-quarters of the time. That was not only more often than any other Republican, it was even above the opposition average for House Democrats.

Schneider has had a difficult time finding a forum for promoting her legislative goals, which as often as not bring her into conflict with the leadership of her party. She has identified herself with environmental, energy and women's issues, but is not well positioned to have a direct hand in legislation on those matters. While she is innovative in some of her ideas and ambitious in choosing her battles, Schneider still has not earned a seat on one of the more prestigious committees.

As the 101st Congress began, Schneider lost her bid for a seat on the Energy and Commerce Committee, the premier forum for handling the environmental and energy issues on which she has made her name. However, she does remain ranking Republican on the less significant Science, Space and Technology Subcommittee on Natural Resources, Agriculture Research and Environment.

Schneider and South Dakota Republican Sen. Larry Pressler cosponsored a bill in the 100th Congress directing federal agencies involved in exploration of the Earth's crust to cooperate on a continental scientific drilling program. She said the drilling program would help in earthquake and volcano detection. Reagan signed the bill in 1988.

A former television producer and moderator, Schneider has demonstrated an ability to attract attention to her causes. She and California Democrat George E. Brown Jr. chaired a project that set up live, satellite-transmitted television exchanges in 1987 between members of Congress and the Supreme Soviet.

But while Schneider is generally adept at cultivating the media, there have been some clumsy moves. In 1986, a publicity bid backfired when she held a press conference promoting a plan for reducing the deficit by one-third. She drew criticism when it was disclosed that the plan had been drawn up by another House Republican, whom she did not credit, and that she had mistakenly inflated the estimated savings by a multiple of 10.

In the first months of the Bush administration, Schneider got some unflattering notice — especially within her own party — over a story she was telling about Vice President Dan Quayle. Schneider said Quayle told her, "I was recently on a tour of Latin America, and the only regret I have was that I didn't study Latin harder in school so I could converse with those people." Schneider later admitted that Quayle had never made such a statement to her.

Schneider is perhaps best known for her role on the Science Committee in fatally wounding the Clinch River nuclear reactor — a project that enjoyed the support of the president, the nuclear industry and the U.S. Chamber of Commerce, as well as a powerful congressional lobby headed by Senate Majority Leader Howard H. Baker Jr.

Schneider had been in the House only a few months when she and two freshman GOP colleagues notched their first major victory in the Clinch River fight. Schneider had established her reputation in Rhode Island as an environmentalist critic of nuclear power, but

Rhode Island 2

West — Western Providence; Warwick

With about two-thirds of the city of Providence and its vote-heavy southern suburbs, the 2nd is largely a metropolitan district. But the area's geographical diversity — including coastal wildlife refuges, inland Yankee towns and rolling upstate hillsides — belies the image of urban bleakness a traveler sees from the swath of Amtrak rails that slices through downtown Providence.

The capital, a Democratic stronghold whose population has slid from the 1970s to about 157,000, has the largest concentration of votes in the district. The 2nd includes the Providence business district, where pedestrian shopping areas have had some success at reviving the downtown; South Providence, once a mixed Irish and Jewish middle-class neighborhood that is increasingly black; Federal Hill and Silver Lake, where Italian-Americans predominate; and Elmwood, a traditional ethnic enclave now experiencing an influx of young white professionals.

Providence remains a reliable source of Democratic votes. Although Walter F. Mondale lost the state in 1984, he carried Providence by a margin of nearly 2-to-1.

Cranston and Warwick, the capital's largest suburbs, often split their tickets. Michael S. Dukakis won both in 1988, but Republican Sen. John H. Chafee has run well in these towns.

Washington County, with coastal cities and maritime commerce as well as the inland marshes known as the "Great Swamp," was swept by Ronald Reagan in 1984, but in 1988, Michael S. Dukakis won five of Washington's nine towns and carried the county.

A submarine plant is located on the site of the sprawling old Navy installation at Quonset Point, where the mid-1970s phase-out of an air station and construction battalion forced the local economy to diversify.

Westerly is an old shipping center that blends light manufacturing with its fishing trade, although many residents work at the Electric Boat facility in Groton, Conn. Westerly is more frequently found in the Democratic column than most other towns on Rhode Island's western border, many of them old Yankee enclaves.

Population: 472,725. White 444,462 (94%), Black 15,857 (3%), Other 4,544 (1%). Spanish origin 10,350 (2%). 18 and over 347,207 (73%), 65 and over 60,247 (13%). Median age: 31.

she fought Clinch River largely on economic grounds, joining with Vin Weber of Minnesota and Judd Gregg of New Hampshire to charge that it had already cost more than twice the original estimates.

That was an effective strategy with members in a budget-cutting mood; funds were deleted in May of 1981. But it was not until the 98th Congress that opponents dealt Clinch River its fatal blow. Schneider also criticized the high price tag on the superconducting supercollider, a multibillion-dollar atom smasher endorsed by Reagan in 1987.

On other issues, Schneider argues more directly from an environmentalist point of view. Together with Oregon Democrat Ron Wyden, she has unsuccessfully pushed a plan to tax hazardous-waste disposal. Schneider also worked on passing legislation in the 100th Congress to end ocean dumping of sewage sludge.

Schneider played a prominent role in trying to shore up a 1972 law banning sex discrimination in federally funded schools. A 1984 Supreme Court ruling narrowed the scope of that law; after that, Schneider and other women's-rights advocates worked to pass legislation to overturn that decision. Their work paid off in March 1988, when Congress overrode a Reagan veto and restored the broader coverage of the law.

In the 99th Congress, Schneider sponsored legislation that would help older women go to college by expanding financial aid to part-time and other "non-traditional" students. Parts of this were included in a major higher education bill approved in 1986.

At Home: With her feisty brand of independence and liberal voting record, Schneider has become one of the state's strongest political figures. She has come as close as a Republican can to making her district safe for the GOP, and earned mention as a possible contender for statewide office.

In 1984, she was considered a potential challenger to veteran Democratic Sen. Claiborne Pell. Despite encouragement for a Senate race from a host of national and state GOP officials, she opted for the House and an easy re-election campaign against an active but underfunded young Democratic challenger. She took 68 percent of the vote that year. In 1986, her 72 percent share was the highest for a GOP congressional candidate in Rhode Island since 1878; she matched it in 1988.

Schneider's springboard into politics was the environmental movement. She led the fight against construction of a nuclear plant near her home and was immersed in the activities of environmental groups before switching parties and making her political debut in 1978.

Schneider wanted to run for governor of Rhode Island that year after her husband — a federal environmental official — refused to do so. But GOP leaders chose a better-known male to make the race. They offered Schneider the House nomination against Democratic Rep. Edward Beard, an earthy former house painter whose earlier image as a blue-collar hero was gradually giving way to a reputation for being ill-informed and quarrelsome. She took Beard on, and though she was little known and underfinanced, showed a flair for publicity that brought her within 9,000 votes of Beard.

She remained visible after the election by hosting a Sunday morning television talk show in Providence. To broaden her ethnic appeal, she took Italian lessons, augmenting the French and Spanish she already knew. Schneider's 1980 rematch with Beard turned out to be a smashing success for her. Much better funded than she had been in 1978, she defeated him by a margin of 22,000 votes to become the first Republican to win either congressional district in Rhode Island since 1938.

State Rep. James V. Aukerman tried to mount an aggressive challenge to her in 1982. But Schneider had a superior campaign budget, and a variety of endorsements from consumer, education and environmental groups reinforced her image as an outspoken independent. She carried 19 of 21 cities and towns and won easily.

Committees

Merchant Marine and Fisheries (6th of 17 Republicans)
Oversight and Investigations (ranking); Fisheries and Wildlife Conservation and the Environment

Science, Space and Technology (3rd of 19 Republicans)
Natural Resources, Agriculture Research and Environment (ranking); Science, Research and Technology

Select Aging (8th of 27 Republicans)
Health and Long-Term Care

Elections

1988 General

Claudine Schneider (R)	145,218	(72%)
Ruth S. Morgenthau (D)	56,129	(28%)

1986 General

Claudine Schneider (R)	113,603	(72%)
Donald J. Ferry (D)	44,586	(28%)

Previous Winning Percentages: 1984 (68%) **1982** (56%) **1980** (55%)

District Vote For President

	1988	1984	1980	1976
D	111,698 (54%)	97,758 (47%)	98,573 (47%)	110,037 (54%)
R	94,370 (46%)	110,514 (53%)	80,123 (38%)	93,991 (46%)
I			30,015 (14%)	

Campaign Finance

	Receipts	Receipts from PACs	Expend-itures
1988			
Schneider (R)	$419,633	$193,656 (46%)	$443,267
Morgenthau (D)	$332,150	$2,400 (1%)	$328,335
1986			
Schneider (R)	$365,759	$162,999 (45%)	$325,052
Ferry (D)	$67,486	$8,050 (12%)	$67,685

Key Votes

1987	
Raise speed limit to 65 mph	N
Approve Gephardt "fair trade" amendment	N
Ban testing of larger nuclear weapons	Y
Delay "re-flagging" of Kuwaiti tankers	Y
Approve tax-raising deficit-reduction bill	N
1988	
Approve aid to Nicaraguan contras	N
Enact civil rights restoration bill over Reagan veto	Y
Kill 60-day plant-closing notification measure	N
Pass omnibus trade bill over Reagan veto	Y
Approve death penalty for drug-related murders	Y
Bar federal funds for abortions in cases of rape and incest	N
Oppose seven-day waiting period for purchase of handguns	N

Voting Studies

	Presidential Support		Party Unity		Conservative Coalition	
Year	S	O	S	O	S	O
1988	24	65	31	61	50	45
1987	21	75	33	59	33	63
1986	31	66	29	60	34	58
1985	34	61	31	57	25	62
1984	37	57	29	67	27	71
1983	23	71	27	66	24	71
1982	38	56	20	74	22	74
1981	47	50	44	53	33	67

Interest Group Ratings

Year	ADA	ACU	AFL-CIO	CCUS
1988	80	17	100	38
1987	76	26	56	60
1986	80	5	100	47
1985	55	26	63	44
1984	85	18	85	50
1983	75	9	59	35
1982	85	5	82	29
1981	70	53	47	63

South Carolina

U.S. CONGRESS

SENATE 1 D, 1 R
HOUSE 4 D, 2 R

LEGISLATURE

Senate 35 D, 11 R
House 86 D, 37 R

ELECTIONS

1988 Presidential Vote	
Bush	62%
Dukakis	38%
1984 Presidential Vote	
Reagan	64%
Mondale	36%
1980 Presidential Vote	
Reagan	49%
Carter	48%
Anderson	2%
Turnout rate in 1984	41%
Turnout rate in 1986	29%
Turnout rate in 1988	39%

(as percentage of voting age population)

POPULATION AND GROWTH

1980 population	3,121,820
1988 population estimate (25th in the nation)	3,470,000
Percent change 1980-1988	+11%

DEMOGRAPHIC BREAKDOWN

White	69%
Black	30%
(Spanish origin)	1%
Urban	54%
Rural	46%
Born in state	73%
Foreign-born	2%

MAJOR CITIES

Columbia	93,020
Charleston	68,900
North Charleston	61,430
Greenville	58,370
Spartanburg	44,210

AREA AND LAND USE

Area	30,204 sq. miles (40th)
Farm	29%
Forest	64%
Federally owned	6%

Gov. Carroll A. Campbell Jr. (R)
Of Greenville — Elected 1986

Born: July 24, 1940, Greenville, S.C.
Education: Attended U. of South Carolina, 1958 and 1970; American U., M.A. 1985.
Occupation: Real estate broker; farmer.
Religion: Episcopalian.
Political Career: S.C. House, 1971-75; S.C. Senate, 1977-79; U.S. House 1979-87; Republican nominee for lieutenant governor, 1974.
Next Election: 1990.

WORK

Occupations	
White-collar	45%
Blue-collar	41%
Service workers	12%
Government Workers	
Federal	32,354
State	77,825
Local	123,121

MONEY

Median family income	$ 16,978 (41st)
Tax burden per capita	$ 816 (27th)

EDUCATION

Spending per pupil through grade 12	$ 3,058 (40th)
Persons with college degrees	13% (42nd)

CRIME

Violent crime rate	665 per 100,000 (9th)

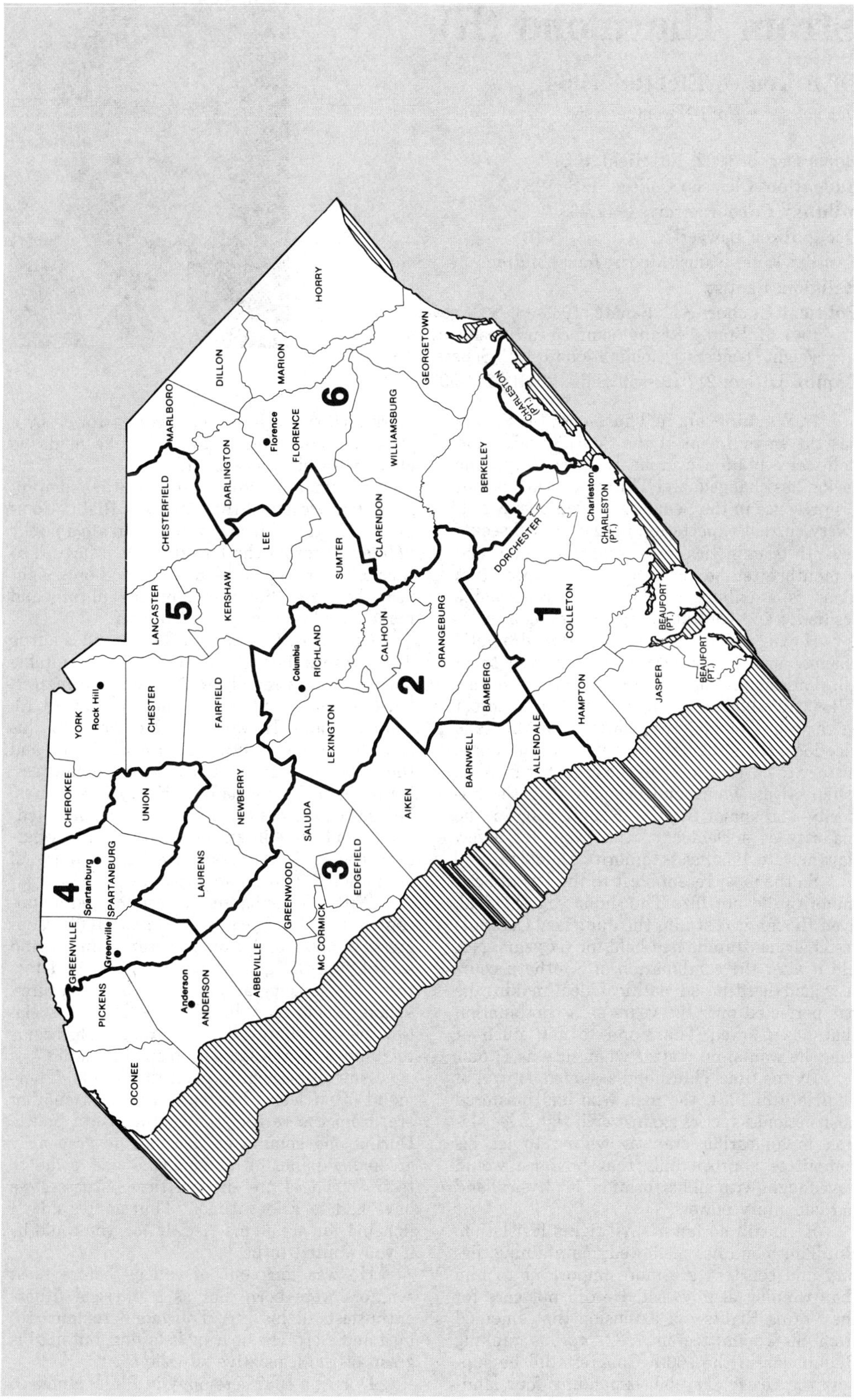
1
2
3
4
5
6
HORRY
GEORGETOWN
MARION
DILLON
MARLBORO
Florence
FLORENCE
WILLIAMSBURG
CHARLESTON (PT.)
BERKELEY
Charleston
CHARLESTON (PT.)
DORCHESTER
CLARENDON
SUMTER
LEE
DARLINGTON
CHESTERFIELD
KERSHAW
LANCASTER
COLLETON
BEAUFORT (PT.)
BEAUFORT (PT.)
ORANGEBURG
CALHOUN
RICHLAND
Columbia
JASPER
HAMPTON
BAMBERG
FAIRFIELD
CHESTER
YORK
Rock Hill
LEXINGTON
ALLENDALE
BARNWELL
AIKEN
NEWBERRY
UNION
CHEROKEE
SALUDA
EDGEFIELD
SPARTANBURG
Spartanburg
LAURENS
GREENWOOD
MC CORMICK
GREENVILLE
Greenville
ABBEVILLE
ANDERSON
Anderson
PICKENS
OCONEE

Strom Thurmond (R)

Of Aiken — Elected 1954

Did not serve April-November 1956.

Born: Dec. 5, 1902, Edgefield, S.C.
Education: Clemson College, B.S. 1923.
Military Career: Army, 1942-46.
Occupation: Lawyer.
Family: Wife, Nancy Moore; four children.
Religion: Baptist.
Political Career: S.C. Senate, 1933-38; S.C. governor, 1947-51; States' Rights nominee for president, 1948; sought Democratic nomination for U.S. Senate, 1950.
Capitol Office: 217 Russell Bldg. 20510; 224-5972.

In Washington: In Thurmond, the Senate has the embodiment of the South's social and political evolution over nearly a century. The region has changed, and Thurmond with it, but his presence in the Senate has been a constant. Every current expectation is that he will seek a seventh term in 1990 — a term that would end a month after he turns 94. That expectation alone is a tribute to the man's remarkable resilience and continued legislative vigor.

Having been through several dramatic changes in his long career and survived them all, Thurmond was the ideal man to console fellow Republicans as they struggled to adjust to their loss of majority power after the 1986 elections. He is the only man in modern Senate history to have seen life in the chamber from all perspectives: Thurmond has served in the minority and majority as a Republican, in the majority as a Democrat, and even, for a few days in late 1954, as a minority Democrat.

So the most recent shift to the Republican minority did not faze Thurmond a great deal, even though it cost him the Judiciary Committee chairmanship he had held for six years. Nor did it alter the combination of Southern courtesy and hard-nosed political deal-making he has perfected over the years — a combination that has allowed Thurmond to get much of what he wants, no matter what side he is on.

By the time Thurmond assumed control of Judiciary in 1981, the man who had mastered obstructionist tactics against civil rights legislation in an earlier era was willing to let his committee approve bills that he once would have fought with all his formidable physical and parliamentary powers.

He is still no fan of civil rights legislation. But Thurmond has mellowed; maintaining dignity and courtesy are more important to him than winning at any cost. He did not care for the Voting Rights Act extension that emerged from his committee in 1982, nor as ranking Republican in the 100th Congress did he support the *Grove City* bill expanding four landmark civil rights laws that were narrowed by a 1984 Supreme Court ruling. But he made no attempt to block either bill.

Thurmond helped produce the compromise that preserved the U.S. Civil Rights Commission in 1983. He also voted to create a public holiday honoring the late Rev. Dr. Martin Luther King Jr., whom he had accused only eight years before of "intentionally and willfully and maliciously" violating federal laws.

On other issues as well, Thurmond is a true conservative, but a pragmatic and adaptable one. He works readily with some of Congress' most liberal members — notably Edward M. Kennedy and Howard M. Metzenbaum, his Democratic colleagues on both Judiciary and the Labor and Human Resources committees. With liberal California Rep. Henry A. Waxman, he has cosponsored legislation to expand Medicaid to alleviate infant mortality. "I take whatever course is necessary to pass a piece of legislation," Thurmond explains.

With Metzenbaum, he cosponsored a gun-control bill that became law in the 100th Congress; it banned the manufacture, import and sale of "plastic" guns that evade security detectors. He is sympathetic to other measures. Where others fear the National Rifle Association, he says simply, "I think the time has come to stand with the law-enforcement people."

Now approaching his 10th decade, Thurmond often seems like an envoy from another era, from the turn-of-the-century rural South. During one committee hearing, he graciously greeted a panel of women who had come to testify. "These are the prettiest witnesses we have had in a long time," Thurmond said. "I imagine you are all married. If not, you could be if you wanted to be."

He was long out of college before most senators were born, but as a physical fitness enthusiast all his life, Thurmond remains robust and alert. His hearing is failing, but not his grasp of the legislative situation.

During a 1987 ceremony in Philadelphia to

commemorate the bicentennial of the compromise that created the bicameral Congress, an aged and befuddled (and now retired) Sen. John C. Stennis was presiding over the Senate's program and mistakenly called on Thurmond to speak. Thurmond, just a year younger than the ailing Stennis, responded with senatorial savoir-faire. Though he had not expected to be called on, he arose and said, "I do not know of any senator who is not ready to respond at any time with any sentiment," then delivered a lucid extemporaneous address on the Constitution — with his characteristic states' rights bent.

That episode also illustrated Thurmond's fondness for ceremony. He relished his role as president pro tempore, which he forfeited to Stennis when Democrats regained control of the Senate, and greatly regretted losing the honor of presiding over the Senate's opening each day. He loves playing host to visiting South Carolinians, taking them to the Senate dining room and introducing them to senators there.

His courtly manner was apparent in his running of Judiciary. He took care that all members had a chance to speak, insisting on silence so they could be heard. Civil rights groups and liberal Democrats always found him polite and fair.

Still, Thurmond is willing to play rough. Indeed, he agreed in 1977 to take the top GOP seat on Judiciary as part of the Senate Republican leadership's effort to keep the chair away from Sen. Charles McC. Mathias Jr. of Maryland, the Republican liberal who ranked next to Thurmond on the panel. In doing so, however, Thurmond had to give up the same post on the Armed Services Committee, where until then he had devoted most of his attention.

When he became Judiciary's chairman in 1981, Thurmond once again acted to deny Mathias a key role. Fearing Mathias would be too active as head of the Antitrust Subcommittee, Thurmond abolished it, and he removed much of the jurisdiction from the Criminal Law panel Mathias did get.

That was a far cry, though, from the drastic tactic he used in an earlier generation against liberal Democrat Ralph Yarborough of Texas. In 1964, Thurmond wrestled Yarborough to the floor outside the committee room to prevent a quorum for action on civil rights legislation. The South Carolinian won the wrestling match, but Yarborough was able to complete the quorum after the committee chairman rescued him.

That brawl, in the year that Thurmond switched to the GOP, reflected the militance with which he once fought anything associated with civil rights. In his early Senate years, Thurmond irritated even fellow Southerners with his intransigence. In 1957, segregationist senators led by Georgia's Richard Russell were willing to let a weak civil rights measure pass, largely to boost the national standing of their Southern colleague and presidential aspirant, Majority Leader Lyndon B. Johnson. Thurmond alone insisted on protesting. His 24-hour, 18-minute filibuster set a record for one man.

Thurmond makes no apologies, and he is proud of his filibuster record. Still, more than 30 years later, he seems like another person — just as much of the South seems a different place.

During his six years as Judiciary chairman, Thurmond racked up a creditable list of legislative successes, although he made little progress in pushing his conservative-backed constitutional amendments. The high-water mark for his proposed balanced-budget amendment — "the only way" to control federal spending, he said — was in 1982, when the measure won the necessary two-thirds Senate vote; it then died in the House. Proposals for prayer in public schools fared even more poorly.

Thurmond's major achievement was a revision of the federal criminal code, which he had promoted for years. Previously, in the 96th Congress, he had forged an alliance with then-Chairman Kennedy, but the legislation never became law. Then in 1982, Thurmond brought another criminal code bill to the floor; confronted with a potential blizzard of controversial amendments from conservatives, he offered a stripped-down measure that cleared Congress. President Reagan vetoed it, however.

Finally, in 1984, the Senate separately passed major components of the legislation. Ultimately the comprehensive package became law as an amendment to the year-end appropriations bill. Included was a change in the exclusionary rule permitting use of illegally obtained evidence in federal trials if police officers could show they acted in the belief their conduct was legal. Thurmond said the exclusionary rule "illustrates much of what is wrong within our present system of criminal justice."

Also in 1984, Thurmond's separate legislation to re-establish the federal death penalty resulted in the first Senate debate on the issue in 10 years. Thurmond asserted that convicted murderers were not people but "more like animals," and "when you have individuals in society more like animals than humans, they have to be dealt with in the most severe manner." The Senate finally passed the bill, but it died in the House. A similar measure got no further than committee approval in 1986. Finally, in 1988, a narrower measure became law as part of an anti-drugs package; it applies to drug traffickers who murder and to those who kill policemen during a drug crime.

A major share of Thurmond's energies in recent years, as Judiciary chairman and then as ranking Republican, was devoted to winning Senate confirmation of Reagan's judicial nominees. Although some nominations, notably of William H. Rehnquist to be chief justice and of

Daniel A. Manion to be a federal district judge, plunged the committee and the Senate into partisan warfare, Thurmond almost always delivered for the president. Only one of nearly 300 judicial nominees was defeated while Thurmond was chairman through 1986.

In 1987, however, Thurmond was all but powerless to save Reagan from an embarrassing chapter of his presidency — the six-month, three-nominee effort to fill a Supreme Court vacancy. Much of that time, the Senate was torn over Reagan's first choice, Robert H. Bork, who was rejected as too ideologically conservative. Thurmond defended Bork against what he and many other Republicans considered Democrats' politicization of the confirmation process; the episode strained his good relationship with Judiciary Chairman Joseph R. Biden Jr.

Thurmond refrained from immediately endorsing Reagan's next choice, Douglas H. Ginsburg — fortunately so, since the nominee quickly withdrew after acknowledging he had smoked marijuana years before. Finally, Anthony M. Kennedy was approved easily.

Besides managing judicial nominations, Thurmond also had to be Reagan's Senate point man in controversies involving the Justice Department, mostly concerning its hostility to civil rights precedents. Then in 1988, as Attorney General Edwin Meese III was embroiled in allegations of financial conflicts of interest, Thurmond was the emissary GOP senators sent to Meese to convey their concerns. Meese eventually resigned; a special prosecutor concluded that he probably had broken the law, but declined to seek an indictment.

Ironically, another administration scandal allowed Thurmond to win the 100th Congress' approval of his legislation to close the "revolving door" between government and lobbying. His effort to bar top executive branch employees from lobbying for several years after they leave government was a reaction to the case of a former Commerce Department official who allegedly disclosed to his clients among Hong Kong textile interests the U.S. strategy in world negotiations on textile-import limits. As a senator from a textile-manufacturing state, Thurmond was outraged.

In the 99th Congress, Thurmond's bill got no further than committee approval. But in the 100th Congress, the effort took momentum from the lobbying controversy surrounding former Reagan aide Michael K. Deaver. With liberals Metzenbaum and Carl Levin, Thurmond easily won Senate approval. "We think people will no more be leaving government to line their own pockets," he said. The final compromise with the House also included the first lobbying controls on former members of Congress and their top staff. But Reagan pocket-vetoed the bill, forcing supporters to start anew in 1989.

Given his senior role on Judiciary, Thurmond is less active on Labor and Human Resources and on Armed Services, where he has served as a pro-Pentagon member since he first came to the Senate. But despite his seniority on Armed Services, he has never been one of its leaders, nor has he specialized in particular defense issues. Thurmond could have returned to the panel's ranking GOP seat in the 100th Congress, but he elected to remain as Judiciary's senior Republican, even though Mathias had retired.

On his committees and off, Thurmond looks out for South Carolina; constituent service is one reason he has survived changing times. He makes sure his state receives a flow of federal largess — even if he votes against the programs that provide the money. And as the Voting Rights Act has made blacks an important political force, they have been conspicuous among the beneficiaries of Thurmond's work. "I'm not a racist," he insists, "and I've done everything I could to help the people of both races throughout my lifetime." In 1971 he became the first Southern senator to hire a black professional staffer; he later sponsored the South's first black federal judge.

In recent years, Thurmond has been especially active in seeking to protect the textile industry against growing foreign competition, defying Reagan's free-trade philosophy. "Free trade will destroy America," Thurmond once said. He and Democratic colleague Ernest F. Hollings won passage of legislation to curb textile imports in each of the past two Congresses, but they lacked the support to override Reagan's vetoes.

At Home: Thurmond has punctuated his long political career with turns and reversals, and always he has managed to carry his constituents with him.

They supported him in 1948 when, as governor, he bolted the Democratic Party to run as the States' Rights candidate for president. In 1964 he announced that he was joining the GOP because the Democrats were "leading the evolution of our nation to a socialistic dictatorship." And despite the state's historic partisan leanings, he easily won re-election two years later.

Since the mid-1960s, black voting strength has grown in South Carolina to 30 percent, and Thurmond has adjusted again, although his efforts to help black communities have never brought much of the black vote; his long record of opposing civil rights is not that easily forgotten. It is unlikely that Thurmond drew even 10 percent of the black vote in 1972 or 1978. But any little bit can help in a close election, and Thurmond tries for it.

For most white South Carolinians, Thurmond's feistiness and physical vigor remain appealing. As a 75-year-old in 1978 competing with a man barely half his age, Thurmond traveled the state with his wife and four young children in a camper called "Strom Trek," passing out family recipes, riding parade elephants and sliding down firehouse poles.

Thurmond learned politics from one of his father's friends, Democratic Sen. Benjamin "Pitchfork Ben" Tillman. Early in his career Thurmond was a populist, representing poor white farmers from the upcountry against the Tidewater establishment. In 1946, after returning from World War II service in Europe, Thurmond was elected governor. He was in his second year in office when the Democratic National Convention decided to adopt a strong civil rights plank, and Thurmond offered himself as a regional candidate for president on the States' Rights Democratic ticket. He carried South Carolina, Alabama, Mississippi and Louisiana.

Thurmond made a first try for the Senate in 1950, but lost the Democratic primary to incumbent Olin D. Johnston. Four years later, however, he won — the first and so far the only senator to be elected as a write-in candidate. Sen. Burnet R. Maybank had died and the 31-member State Democratic Committee froze Thurmond out by choosing state Sen. Edgar A. Brown. Thurmond focused his campaign on whether "31 men" or the voters should make the decision. His write-in campaign defeated Brown by nearly 60,000 votes.

True to a 1954 promise, Thurmond resigned in 1956 and ran for re-election without the benefit of incumbency. No one filed against him — a happy circumstance that repeated itself in 1960, when it was time to run for a full six-year term. In 1966 and 1972 he decimated Democrats Bradley Morrah and Eugene N. Ziegler, respectively.

In 1978 Thurmond encountered a stiff re-election challenge from Charles "Pug" Ravenel, who had won the Democratic primary for governor four years before, but was ruled ineligible for failure to meet residency requirements.

A media-oriented "New South" politician, Ravenel tried to remind blacks of the senator's segregationist past. But Ravenel suffered from a carpetbagger's image. He had left the state to be an investment banker in New York, returning only shortly before his 1974 gubernatorial bid. Thurmond supporters circulated a newspaper column quoting Ravenel as telling New York contributors he would "be a good senator for New York from South Carolina." Thurmond won 56 percent.

The 1984 campaign was no problem for Thurmond. No Democrat of any consequence wanted to challenge him; one of those mentioned as a contender, former U.S. Rep. Kenneth Holland, ended up leading a Democrats-for-Thurmond organization. For a few days in the summer, it appeared the Rev. Jesse Jackson might try an independent campaign, but Jackson quickly reconsidered, and the obscure Democratic nominee, minister Melvin Purvis, failed to reach even a third of the vote.

Committees

Judiciary (Ranking)
Antitrust, Monopolies and Business Rights (ranking); Courts and Administrative Practice

Armed Services (2nd of 9 Republicans)
Strategic Forces and Nuclear Deterrence (ranking); Conventional Forces and Alliance Defense; Readiness, Sustainability and Support

Labor and Human Resources (5th of 7 Republicans)
Employment and Productivity (ranking); Education, Arts and Humanities; Labor

Veterans' Affairs (3rd of 5 Republicans)

Elections

1984 General		
Strom Thurmond (R)	644,815	(67%)
Melvin Purvis Jr. (D)	306,982	(32%)
1984 Primary		
Strom Thurmond (R)	44,662	(94%)
R. H. Cunningham (R)	2,693	(6%)

Previous Winning Percentages: **1978** (56%) **1972** (64%) **1966** (62%) **1960** † (100%) **1956** † * (100%) **1954** † * (63%)

* *Thurmond was elected as a write-in candidate in 1954. He resigned April 4, 1956, and was elected to fill the vacancy caused by his own resignation in a 1956 special election.*
† *Thurmond was elected as a Democrat in 1954-60.*

Campaign Finance

	Receipts	Receipts from PACs	Expend-itures
1984			
Thurmond (R)	$1,921,179	$530,973 (28%)	$1,638,467
Purvis (D)	$11,688	0	$11,760

Key Votes

1987	
Enact omnibus highway bill over Reagan veto	N
Limit testing of space-based anti-ballistic missiles	N
Oppose banning tests of larger nuclear weapons	Y
Confirm Robert H. Bork as Supreme Court justice	Y
1988	
Allow vote on campaign-finance overhaul	N
Pass civil rights restoration bill over Reagan veto	N
Enact omnibus trade bill over Reagan veto	N
Approve death penalty for drug-related murders	Y
Oppose "workfare" amendment to welfare overhaul bill	N

Voting Studies

	Presidential Support		Party Unity		Conservative Coalition	
Year	S	O	S	O	S	O
1988	82	15	80	15	89	0
1987	69	28	88	9	84	16
1986	89	10	91	8	97	0
1985	87	13	92	7	97	3
1984	87	10	95	5	98	0
1983	86	12	92	6	93	7
1982	89	9	92	5	86	4
1981	90	7	91	6	100	0

Interest Group Ratings

Year	ADA	ACU	AFL-CIO	CCUS
1988	0	92	21	93
1987	15	96	30	71
1986	5	91	0	78
1985	0	91	14	97
1984	0	100	9	84
1983	5	70	6	79
1982	5	75	12	86
1981	0	93	5	100

Ernest F. Hollings (D)

Of Charleston — Elected 1966

Born: Jan. 1, 1922, Charleston, S.C.
Education: The Citadel, B.A. 1942; U. of South Carolina, LL.B. 1947.
Military Career: Army, 1942-45.
Occupation: Lawyer.
Family: Wife, Rita Louise Liddy; four children.
Religion: Lutheran.
Political Career: S.C. House, 1949-55; lieutenant governor, 1955-59; governor, 1959-63; sought Democratic nomination for U.S. Senate, 1962; sought Democratic presidential nomination, 1984.
Capitol Office: 125 Russell Bldg. 20510; 224-6121.

In Washington: Hollings has played prominent, if sometimes unpredictable, roles in many of the important policy debates of his era: poverty, civil rights, the budget deficit, arms control. But nimble though his mind may be, his acerbic tongue usually leaves the deeper impression. He fumes and fulminates and quite often infuriates. A stubborn, independent cuss, it is hard to imagine him retreating comfortably into the powerful Commerce Committee barony that is now his.

As the 101st Congress opened, Hollings leaped mouth first into the controversy surrounding John Tower's nomination to become secretary of defense. Republican accusations that Democrats lacked solid facts with which to challenge Tower's credentials angered Hollings. When he took the Senate floor to announce his vote, his summation of the FBI report on Tower's drinking habits demonstrated his ability to crystallize an issue with a few words. "The fact is," he said, "John Tower could not serve in the nuclear Navy. He could not be promoted from corporal to sergeant."

But it was Hollings' description of Tower as "Mr. Alcohol Abuser" that demonstrated his ability to provoke. Minority Leader Bob Dole of Kansas said several days later on television that Hollings had crossed the line to make "vicious personal attacks" on Tower. When Hollings sought vindication on the floor, Dole then recalled, "I have been on this floor when the senator from South Carolina attacked other senators by name."

It is this image of Hollings as impolitic, even mean-spirited, that can isolate him from his colleagues and divert attention from a legislative record lengthy with triumph.

Handsome, graceful and impeccably tailored — even martial in his bearing — Hollings is an impressive presence in committee and on the Senate floor. He speaks in a rich, booming Tidewater patois and has a colorful command of the language. He dismissed the 1983 invasion of Grenada as an "an attack on a golf course." He pronounced U.S. aid to El Salvador, under one regime, as "delivery of lettuce by way of a rabbit."

But his loquaciousness knows no boundaries, and he tends toward bombast; some wonder whether his mind and his mouth simply move too quickly for discretion to keep pace, or whether he just does not care that his judgments fall harshly. Running for president in 1984, he tweaked Democrat John Glenn of Ohio as "Sky King." In 1979, Hollings likened a conference with the House to "feeding the monkeys in the zoo."

During a 1981 debate on his effort to stop the Justice Department from trying to block voluntary school prayer, he described Ohio Democrat Howard M. Metzenbaum as "the senator from B'nai B'rith." "I am the senator from Ohio," responded Metzenbaum, who is Jewish. "I was not throwing off on his religion," Hollings apologized. "I said it only in fun."

The two sides of Hollings' character were apparent during his 1984 presidential campaign. The effort failed early in the year, dragged down in part by several comments he made that enraged various ethnic groups.

At the same time, though, Hollings displayed an integrity that his rivals could not achieve. While many of his competitors were traveling from one interest group to another, pledging their loyalty, Hollings was delivering the same unpleasant message to everyone, exhorting the need to exercise old-fashioned self-restraint to solve the nation's fiscal woes.

He told military officers and Social Security recipients and local government officials that they all had to give up something if the federal budget was ever to be balanced and the economy repaired. He advocated a freeze on domestic and military spending levels that would not spare any of the major beneficiaries, and he advocated a freeze on further tax cuts as well. Whatever the political wisdom of a campaign like that, it was vintage Hollings. He continues to advocate a budget plan that would freeze spending, except for Social Security, Medicare and other entitlements, with cost-of-living increases.

The failure of his presidential bid did not inspire Hollings to rein in his outspoken tendencies. Late in 1986, he was the first prominent politician to go on record essentially accusing President Reagan of lying about his role in the Iran-contra affair. The harshness of the charge unsettled even those who were skeptical of Reagan's claim that he knew nothing of the diversion of funds to the Nicaraguan contras.

Although he sometimes depicts himself as a lonely voice crying out against fiscal weakness, Hollings has scored at least two major budget victories in recent years.

The first came in 1980, when he served briefly as chairman of the Budget Committee. He promoted and moved through the Senate a 1981 budget resolution drawn up to be in balance — the first such achievement in the history of the budget process. While recession eventually forced a deficit of $50 billion, Hollings remains proud of the effort and sensitive to mention of its eventual problems.

Since then, Hollings has focused on pushing his plan for a budget freeze. It was slow going at first; the plan received only 12 votes when he first proposed it in 1982. In 1983 it attracted four more votes. With the massive budget deficit looming large in 1984, though, Hollings and two other senators put forth a three-year budget-freeze package that attracted 38 votes. He garnered 18 votes, though, in a 1989 version.

Hollings also helped develop a radical budget-balancing plan. Although his name does not always get tacked on when the 1985 Gramm-Rudman-Hollings law is mentioned, he can lay claim to a share of the authorship of the proposal.

"Basically this is still a budget freeze spelled out in rhetoric," he said. "We took 158 pages to say 'freeze.' "

Hollings gave up his ranking spot on Budget in 1983 to take the same position on Commerce. He assumed the Commerce chairmanship at the start of the 100th Congress. Because he is also chairman of the Appropriations Subcommittee on Commerce, he is positioned to wield even wider powers than usual; he can control both authorization and spending legislation for programs. The combination is potent when Hollings digs in, and although his reputation is that of a "national senator," he is not above bringing his power to bear on the parochial. He stubbornly held up a Coast Guard authorization bill for more than a year while demanding House acceptance of a new helicopter base in Charleston, S.C.

Home-state concerns were foremost with Hollings in the 100th Congress, when he joined with South Carolina colleague Strom Thurmond in an attempt to curb textile imports. The crush of foreign competition has severely pinched the state's textile industry. The two managed to steer the quota legislation to passage in 1985 and in 1988, both times overcoming entrenched opposition and both times watching it later die by veto. Hollings calls himself a trade hawk, but he sees the need to improve what is protected. He advocates measures to quicken the commercialization of basic research. "The U.S. wins the Nobel prizes and the Japanese win the markets and profits," he says.

Hollings' opinion is often important where the cost of doing business is at issue. A former trial lawyer who retains close ties to the profession, he takes a harsh view of measures that would impose federal limits on a manufacturer's responsibility for harm caused by its products. He blocked the Product Liability Act in 1986 with a filibuster and argues that it would "further injure the injured" by weakening their ability to obtain relief through the courts. He sat on similar legislation in the 100th Congress, but indicated he might let the committee act on its sentiments in the 101st.

He views deregulation skeptically, and with the exception of those for railroads and buses, has vigorously opposed most major deregulation proposals. His opposition stems in part from the loss of flights to South Carolina after airline deregulation.

No issue proved more difficult for Hollings during the 100th Congress than regulation of television broadcasting. He hews strongly to the principle that a broadcasting license is a privilege, and the use of public airwaves comes with strings attached. He called the Reagan-appointed Federal Communications Commission a "runaway animal" and broadcasters the "most greedy group I've ever met in my 40 years of public service."

When the FCC appeared ready in the summer of 1987 to repeal the Fairness Doctrine, he issued a pre-emptive strike. Working with House Energy and Commerce Chairman John D. Dingell of Michigan, he gained passage of legislation to codify the doctrine, only to see Reagan veto it. Lacking the votes to override, the two pulled budget levers and nearly succeeded in gaining passage by attaching the measure to crucial spending legislation.

Hollings also stepped into a controversy regarding publishing magnate Rupert K. Murdoch and Democratic Sen. Edward M. Kennedy of Massachusetts. Under a special waiver from the FCC, Murdoch was permitted to own both a television station and a newspaper in New York City and in Boston. Kennedy, no fan of Murdoch because of unflattering coverage about him in Murdoch's *Boston Herald*, sought Hollings' assistance to block such cross-ownership.

Hollings again used the appropriations process to advantage, preventing Murdoch's cross-ownership in a spending bill. A court later struck down the measure as unconstitutional, but by then Murdoch had sold the *New York Post*.

Hollings moved to the forefront briefly during the debate over campaign financing in 1988. He wants to amend the Constitution to permit laws limiting campaign spending, which is one way to hold down campaign costs without resorting to public financing. The amendment failed to overcome a GOP filibuster, but attracted as much support as any Democratic campaign-finance measure to reach the floor.

Hollings is mistrustful of the Soviets and has long had a reputation as a hawk, despite his attempts to freeze military spending as part of a deficit-reduction package. Although he opposed the MX missile and the B-1 bomber, he has generally backed spending increases for weapons. He is not afraid, though, to cross swords with the Senate's leading conservative Democrat on defense issues, Sam Nunn of Georgia. He trod boldly onto the Armed Services chairman's turf in 1987 by challenging Nunn's reinterpretation of the anti-ballistic missile treaty, perhaps the key issue underlying testing of strategic defense initiative weapons.

Hollings also cast one of the five votes — the only "no" from a Democrat — against the intermediate-range nuclear-force (INF) treaty in 1988. He argued that the treaty went too far by also barring certain non-nuclear missiles. He feared their loss would further tilt the balance of conventional forces in Europe toward the Warsaw Pact.

Hollings has threaded his way carefully through civil rights issues during his long career. As governor, he insisted on the integration of Clemson University and was then associated with President Kennedy. But Hollings voted against some major civil rights legislation as a junior senator during Lyndon B. Johnson's presidency. He opposed the 1968 open-housing bill, but backed an unsuccessful attempt in 1980 to strengthen it. He has consistently supported the 1965 Voting Rights Act and its extensions.

He drew support in civil rights circles in 1969 when he made a tour of rural areas of his state, said he had found hunger and poverty to a degree he had never realized existed, and came out for free food stamps for the neediest. He was active in the Senate on nutrition issues in the years after that. More recently he has talked about abuses in the food stamp program, but he still votes for money to support it.

At Home: Hollings built his political career in South Carolina at a time of emotional argument about racial issues. He succeeded in combining old-time rhetoric with a tangible record of moderation.

As a candidate in the late 1950s, he firmly espoused states' rights and condemned school integration. In his inaugural speech as governor in 1959, Hollings criticized President Eisenhower for commanding a "marching army, this time not against Berlin, but against Little Rock." But as chief executive of the state, he quietly integrated the public schools.

In fact, despite grumblings about his rhetoric, blacks provided Hollings' margin of victory in 1966, when he won his Senate seat against a more conservative Republican opponent. Since then, he never has faced a credible candidate to his left, and blacks have generally supported him.

During the Depression, the Hollings family's paper business went bankrupt, so an uncle had to borrow money to send him to The Citadel, where he received an Army commission. After World War II, Hollings returned for law school, a legal career and eventually politics.

As a young state legislator, he attracted notice with his plan to solve the problem of inferior black schools without integration. He said a special sales tax should be imposed to upgrade the black schools.

Hollings twice won unanimous election to the state House speakership and in 1954 moved up to lieutenant governor. In 1958, Democratic Gov. George B. Timmerman was ineligible to succeed himself. Hollings won a heated three-way race for the nomination, defeating Donald S. Russell, former University of South Carolina president and a protégé of ex-Gov. James F. Byrnes. The primary turned on political alliances and geography. Hollings' base lay in Tidewater and Russell's in Piedmont.

As governor, Hollings worked hard to strengthen his state's educational system, establishing a commission on higher education. In 1960 he campaigned for John F. Kennedy, who carried South Carolina.

Barred from seeking a second gubernatorial term in 1962, he challenged Democratic Sen. Olin D. Johnston. Portraying himself as "a young man on the go," Hollings attacked Johnston's endorsement by the state AFL-CIO and charged that "foreign labor bosses" were seeking to control the state. Hollings failed to draw much more than one-third of the vote.

The senator died in 1965, however, and Donald Russell — by then governor — had himself appointed to the seat. That provided the issue for Hollings' comeback in 1966. He ousted Russell in the special primary to finish Johnston's term.

The 1966 election year was not an ordinary one in South Carolina. The national Democratic Party was unpopular, and GOP state Sen. Marshall Parker seized on Hollings' connections to it in an effort to defeat him. He nearly made it, but Hollings matched his conservative rhetoric and survived by 11,758 votes.

Running for a full term two years later, Hollings had little trouble turning back Parker.

He rolled over weak opponents in 1974 and 1980, but in 1985, Republicans tried to stir up talk that Hollings was dispirited over his failed White House bid and bored with the Senate. The incumbent discredited the rumor early on by stumping all over the state and raising a hefty campaign treasury. Well-known Republicans ducked, leaving the nomination to a little-known former U.S. attorney. He was crushed in the race.

One of the most striking endorsements of the 1988 presidential campaign came from Hollings: In June, he declared he would support the Rev. Jesse Jackson at the Atlanta convention. In 1984, when Hollings' White House bid collapsed early and Jackson went on to dominate the state's Democratic caucuses, Hollings had more than a few unkind words for Jackson, at one point calling his "rainbow coalition" a "blackbow" coalition.

But in 1988, Jackson ran even better in the state's Democratic caucuses. Perhaps with an eye on maintaining a line of communication to black voters — a must-win bloc for any Democrat running statewide — Hollings went along with a majority of the convention delegation in supporting Jackson, who is a native of Greenville, S.C.

Committees

Commerce, Science and Transportation (Chairman)
National Ocean Policy Study (chairman); Communications; Foreign Commerce and Tourism; Surface Transportation

Appropriations (3rd of 16 Democrats)
Commerce, Justice, State, the Judiciary and Related Agencies (chairman); Defense; Energy and Water Development; Interior and Related Agencies; Labor, Health and Human Services, Education and Related Agencies

Budget (2nd of 13 Democrats)

Select Intelligence (3rd of 8 Democrats)

Elections

1986 General

Ernest F. Hollings (D)	465,500	(63%)
Henry D. McMaster (R)	262,886	(36%)

Previous Winning Percentages: 1980 (70%) **1974** (70%) **1968** (62%) **1966** * (51%)

* *Special election.*

Campaign Finance

	Receipts	Receipts from PACs	Expend-itures
1988			
Hollings (D)	$2,395,632	$950,882 (40%)	$2,233,843
McMaster (R)	$584,834	$49,722 (9%)	$584,288

Key Votes

1987	
Enact omnibus highway bill over Reagan veto	Y
Limit testing of space-based anti-ballistic missiles	N
Oppose banning tests of larger nuclear weapons	Y
Confirm Robert H. Bork as Supreme Court justice	Y
1988	
Allow vote on campaign-finance overhaul	Y
Pass civil rights restoration bill over Reagan veto	Y
Enact omnibus trade bill over Reagan veto	Y
Approve death penalty for drug-related murders	Y
Oppose "workfare" amendment to welfare overhaul bill	Y

Voting Studies

	Presidential Support		Party Unity		Conservative Coalition	
Year	**S**	**O**	**S**	**O**	**S**	**O**
1988	49	49	71	25	81	14
1987	47	53	58	42	88	13
1986	70	30	54	46	74	26
1985	52	48	59	41	75	25
1984	32	44	59	22	49	26
1983	8	35	49	8	23	20
1982	44	45	73	20	55	36
1981	54	38	58	35	67	30

Interest Group Ratings

Year	ADA	ACU	AFL-CIO	CCUS
1988	55	48	86	29
1987	40	62	80	17
1986	35	52	73	32
1985	45	52	62	55
1984	60	38	89	40
1983	70	12	90	36
1982	55	50	74	53
1981	55	14	58	35

1 Arthur Ravenel Jr. (R)

Of Mount Pleasant — Elected 1986

Born: March 29, 1927, St. Andrews Parish, S.C.
Education: College of Charleston, B.A. 1950.
Military Career: Marine Corps, 1945-46.
Occupation: Businessman.
Family: Wife, Jean Rickenbaker; six children; four stepchildren.
Religion: French Huguenot.
Political Career: S.C. House, 1953-59; S.C. Senate, 1981-87.
Capitol Office: 508 Cannon Bldg. 20515; 225-3176.

In Washington: At a time when experts are engaged in debate over how to interdict the flow of drugs into the United States, Ravenel has proposed his own version of a "zero tolerance" policy on drug smuggling: When the U.S. military identifies a plane or ship as unquestionably smuggling drugs, "I think those drug planes should be shot down and I think the ships bringing the drugs in should be sunk ... [and] any survivors machine-gunned in the water," he said during his 1988 campaign.

Ravenel's proposal may make civil libertarians cringe, but it clearly does not disturb the majority in his conservative Lowcountry district. He first suggested shooting down drug planes in his successful 1986 campaign; in 1988, he topped 60 percent of the vote.

Ravenel, a man with conservative instincts, also has a penchant for unpredictability. Sometimes it shows itself in unorthodox statements, such as the "shootdown" strategy. Frequently, though, it leads him away from rigid adherence to the GOP line on important issues. In the 100th Congress, he opposed President Reagan's position on House votes more often than any other Southern Republican — in 1988, for instance, nearly half the time.

Ravenel showed this independent streak early in 1987, when the Armed Services Committee was debating a defense authorization bill. Ravenel was the only Republican opposing a Reagan-backed amendment to loosen the interpretation of the 1972 U.S.-Soviet ABM treaty — a change that would have permitted testing of certain anti-missile devices contemplated in the strategic defense initiative (SDI). With Ravenel's opposition, the GOP amendment failed, 24-25. Ravenel said the arguments of South Carolina Democrat John M. Spratt Jr. persuaded him to vote against the proposal. "Spratt has a reputation in South Carolina of being a brilliant individual," Ravenel said. "He has made the ABM treaty and SDI research a particular study."

In his first term, Ravenel gave floor speeches denouncing Japan for their whaling practices. He also urged action on acid rain.

At Home: In South Carolina they call Ravenel "Daddy Rabbit," a nickname that reflects both his colorful personal style and his pioneering role in establishing the Republican Party in the Charleston area.

Entering politics in the 1950s as a Democrat, he represented Charleston in the state House for three terms. He switched to the GOP in 1960 and for the next two decades worked to expand the local party, all the while making a fortune in home building, real estate and cattle raising. In 1980, he unseated a Democratic state senator. Four years later, when reapportionment placed him in another district, he defeated another incumbent Democrat.

Ravenel's personality has enabled him to establish a rapport with blacks and blue-collar workers rarely supportive of conservative GOP businessmen. In the Legislature, his interests included protection of the coastal environment and programs for the mentally retarded.

In 1986, when GOP Rep. Thomas F. Hartnett left the 1st to run for lieutenant governor, Ravenel easily secured the Republican nomination, while Democrats endured a bruising contest eventually won by Jimmy Stuckey, former chairman of the Charleston County Council.

The nominees agreed on most national issues: They supported the Reagan military buildup and opposed any tax increase. Both promised to bring federal funds to the district's military facilities. Their most substantive clashes were on aid to the Nicaraguan contras, which Ravenel favored, and increased federal support for education, which Ravenel opposed.

Ravenel put Stuckey on the defensive by reviving a charge that first had surfaced in the Democratic primary. The charge was that Stuckey as a private attorney had defended drug traffickers. On Election Day, Ravenel won 52 percent, trailing Stuckey in three rural counties, but carrying the city of Charleston, the GOP suburbs in Dorchester and lower Berkeley counties, and the Hilton Head resort area in Beaufort County. In 1988, he padded his margins in all those areas to win with ease.

South Carolina 1

South — Charleston

Henry James, describing the city's listlessness at the turn of the century, disparaged Charleston as "effeminate." No more. While James might still recognize the carefully preserved older streets and quaint houses, the symbol of contemporary Charleston is the defense industry and the enormous postwar growth it has brought this area.

The Charleston Naval Shipyard, Charleston Air Force Base, Parris Island Marine Corps Base and numerous other military facilities place an estimated one-third of the district's payroll in the hands of the Defense Department and draw in military contractors and related businesses.

Most of the people moving into the area have settled in the Charleston suburbs, which have exploded in population. North Charleston, one-third the size of its parent city in 1970, was virtually equal with it in population in the 1980 census. Many of the working-class voters in North Charleston are the type of people who grew up as Southern Democrats but have abandoned the party in droves during the Reagan years. Their growing habit of supporting the GOP supplements the automatic Republican votes that are cast by the residents of more affluent Charleston suburbs.

In Charleston itself and in the poorer rural counties inland, the Democratic presence remains strong. The city, roughly one-half black, still has a Democratic mayor, and blacks in the precincts north of Calhoun Street turn in an overwhelmingly Democratic vote. But the white population, which is beginning to encroach on formerly black areas, tends to vote Republican in national elections.

Emerging as a crucial addition to the GOP column in the 1st is Beaufort County, on the Atlantic coast south of Charleston. The development of the Hilton Head Island resort has brought thousands of well-off residents to a county that was rural and Democratic. In the last two House elections, Ravenel has won well above his districtwide average in Beaufort County — taking 68 percent there in 1988.

Population: 520,338. White 343,616 (66%), Black 168,058 (32%), Other 5,714 (1%). Spanish origin 8,618 (2%). 18 and over 362,866 (70%), 65 and over 38,887 (7%). Median age: 26.

Committee

Armed Services (17th of 21 Republicans)
Military Installations and Facilities; Military Personnel and Compensation

Elections

1988 General		
Arthur Ravenel Jr. (R)	101,572	(64%)
Wheeler Tillman (D)	57,691	(36%)
1986 General		
Arthur Ravenel Jr. (R)	59,969	(52%)
Jimmy Stuckey (D)	55,262	(48%)

District Vote For President

	1988	1984	1980	1976
D	62,437 (38%)	58,199 (35%)	65,690 (44%)	65,254 (53%)
R	99,698 (61%)	105,655 (64%)	78,592 (53%)	56,449 (46%)
I			3,146 (2%)	

Campaign Finance

	Receipts	Receipts from PACs	Expend-itures
1988			
Ravenel (R)	$273,828	$141,080 (52%)	$118,702
Tillman (D)	$82,118	$5,250 (6%)	$82,035
1986			
Ravenel (R)	$272,559	$41,250 (15%)	$265,574
Stuckey (D)	$458,073	$112,578 (25%)	$457,810

Key Votes

1987	
Raise speed limit to 65 mph	Y
Approve Gephardt "fair trade" amendment	N
Ban testing of larger nuclear weapons	N
Delay "re-flagging" of Kuwaiti tankers	N
Approve tax-raising deficit-reduction bill	N
1988	
Approve aid to Nicaraguan contras	Y
Enact civil rights restoration bill over Reagan veto	N
Kill 60-day plant-closing notification measure	Y
Pass omnibus trade bill over Reagan veto	Y
Approve death penalty for drug-related murders	Y
Bar federal funds for abortions in cases of rape and incest	Y
Oppose seven-day waiting period for purchase of handguns	Y

Voting Studies

	Presidential Support		Party Unity		Conservative Coalition	
Year	**S**	**O**	**S**	**O**	**S**	**O**
1988	49	48	55	44	95	5
1987	58	42	61	35	88	12

Interest Group Ratings

Year	ADA	ACU	AFL-CIO	CCUS
1988	25	76	64	86
1987	20	61	31	87

2 Floyd D. Spence (R)

Of Lexington — Elected 1970

Born: April 9, 1928, Columbia, S.C.
Education: U. of South Carolina, A.B. 1952, J.D. 1956.
Military Career: Navy, 1952-54.
Occupation: Lawyer.
Family: Wife, Deborah Williams; four children.
Religion: Lutheran.
Political Career: S.C. House, 1957-63; S.C. Senate, 1967-71, minority leader 1967-71; Republican nominee for U.S. House, 1962.
Capitol Office: 2405 Rayburn Bldg. 20515; 225-2452.

In Washington: The extraordinary double-lung transplant that Spence underwent in May 1988 brought him more publicity than anything he has done legislatively in his House career. During nearly 20 years in Congress, Spence had functioned in a distinctly low-key manner on the Armed Services Committee and, for years, as senior Republican on the ethics committee — tame stuff compared with a transplant that saved his life.

Once a star college athlete, Spence in recent years had required a wheelchair and a portable oxygen supply because of an incurable obstructive lung disease that left him so breathless he could barely speak. After spending part of October 1987 in an intensive-care ward, he was placed on a list of potential lung-transplant recipients.

Six months later, the operation, which replaced both of Spence's damaged lungs with those of a young man who had been killed in a motorcycle accident, was performed in Jackson, Miss. Though the double-transplant procedure is risky and very rare (only about a dozen have been performed in this country), Spence recovered well enough to seek and win a 10th House term in a tough campaign that was dominated by questions about his health.

The change in Spence's appearance is dramatic. "It's just like a new life," he told the Columbia, S.C., *State* in a 1989 interview. "It's more than I could have hoped for."

While he was out of commission in the 100th Congress, Spence resigned from the Committee on Standards of Official Conduct — the ethics committee — where he was the ranking Republican. After more than 15 years on the committee, Spence's departure (in June 1988) came just before deliberations began on the most controversial case ever to come before the committee: The allegations of misconduct against Speaker Jim Wright of Texas, which led to the Speaker's June 1989 resignation.

During his tenure on ethics, Spence enjoyed relating how he came to serve on the committee. Then-Minority Leader Gerald R. Ford told him ethics was a prestigious committee that rarely met and would look good on his record.

Instead, in the changed political climate of the 1970s and '80s, the committee met frequently and handled one difficult assignment after another, including the Korean influence-buying scandals, the Abscam bribery affair, and the punishment of two members for sexual misconduct with teenage congressional pages.

Though the unpleasantness of the committee's tasks led to frequent turnover — many members dropped off after only one term — Spence stayed in his seat there. But even with his seniority, Spence was not a dominant influence. He usually went along with Democratic Chairmen Louis Stokes of Ohio and Julian C. Dixon of California, who generally took a less militant approach toward punishing wrongdoers than had their predecessor as chairman, Florida's Charles E. Bennett.

This cooperative stance caused few problems for Spence, who is well liked by his GOP colleagues. But some Republicans, especially younger conservatives who wanted to use ethics as a political tool against the Democratic House majority, grumbled that the party needed a more aggressive "watchdog" posture on the ethics committee. By the time Spence's health began severely to limit his effectiveness, the ethics committee was moving toward a stricter line, an evolution that culminated in Wright's ouster from the speakership in 1989.

Defense issues have always been Spence's chief legislative interest. He arrived in the House in 1971 determined to serve on Armed Services, largely to look after the military installations scattered over South Carolina by the committee's longtime chairman, L. Mendel Rivers of Charleston. These include the major military installation in Spence's district, Fort Jackson, a large Army basic training center.

Though again not an aggressive force, Spence has risen through seniority to the second-ranking position on Armed Services, behind Alabama Republican Bill Dickinson, and

South Carolina 2

Central — Columbia

The 2nd is a politically polarized district. It lumps together the state capital of Columbia and its fast-growing suburbs with three largely rural, black-majority counties. Republicans in Lexington County and neighboring Richland County, which has Columbia at its western edge, dominate the constituency. The votes from these areas exceed the margins given Democrats in the city of Columbia and in the rural, southern portion of the district.

The greater Columbia area of Richland and Lexington counties is enjoying a strong economic surge; one recent study showed the area registering the nation's third-highest increase in new business growth.

Lexington's new inhabitants are a mix of retirees, white-collar workers who left increasingly black Columbia, and employees of the glass, cement and synthetic-fiber companies that have moved to the county in recent years.

Whatever brought them there, Lexington County residents are overwhelmingly white and Republican. Lexington is one of only three counties in the state with a population less than 10 percent black. Republican Rep. Spence has won roughly 70 percent of Lexington's vote in his last two hotly contested campaigns. George Bush took it with 78 percent in 1988.

Neighboring Richland County has more political and racial diversity. The county has the largest black population in the state, most of it concentrated in Columbia, which is 40 percent black. State employees and the 25,000 students and faculty at the University of South Carolina join with blacks to give much of the city a politically liberal hue and strong Democratic presence. Diluting this influence is the suburban Republican vote, which includes ballots cast by military personnel and retirees settled around Fort Jackson.

The southern portion of the 2nd has its political and geographic center at Orangeburg, where South Carolina State College (4,000 students) is the traditional academic center for the state's blacks. The middle-class black community around the college is potent in local politics, and Orangeburg County and its two rural neighbors — Calhoun and Bamberg — consistently vote Democratic. Whites in the area generally vote Republican.

Population: 522,688. White 335,548 (64%), Black 181,061 (35%), Other 3,897 (1%). Spanish origin 6,623 (1%). 18 and over 372,290 (71%), 65 and over 41,898 (8%). Median age: 27.

he is ranking Republican on the Seapower Subcommittee. He usually eschews weapons controversies, but occasionally speaks out about attempts to pare the defense budget. In 1986, he described a doomed liberal attempt to make deep cuts in the defense budget as an effort to disarm the country unilaterally.

At Home: It is usually to a challenger's advantage to campaign against an incumbent of infirm health. But in 1988, Democrats never could get a handle on the health issue against Spence, even though his illness, transplant surgery and recovery limited his campaigning to just a few weeks in the fall.

Democrats got off to a bad start in the spring, when a national party operative working in South Carolina was quoted as saying of Spence, "If he's out there [campaigning] in a wheelchair, maybe the voters will decide we have to do something else." In the fall, Democratic challenger Jim Leventis had to campaign in the context of flattering media attention of the recovering Spence as a medical marvel who had won a reprieve from death.

Leventis was a strong, well-financed contender. A 50-year-old attorney and banker, he boasted personal or professional contacts with many in the business and political elite of Columbia, the 2nd's largest city. He kept up a vigorous schedule of targeted door-to-door campaigning, and tried to draw Spence into face-to-face exchanges.

But the incumbent refused to oblige, campaigning in his usual low-key manner, turning up the heat just a little at the end by telling voters, "If you like Dukakis, you'll love Leventis." The Democratic presidential nominee lost the 2nd by 20 percentage points; in crucial Lexington County, suburban home of Columbia's professional class, Spence amassed 68 percent of the vote, cushioning himself against Leventis' modest margins in Richland County (Columbia) and majority-black Orangeburg County. Overall, Spence took 53 percent.

After his star athlete days at the University of South Carolina and then practice as a lawyer, Spence launched his political career by winning a state House seat as a Democrat. But he quit the Democratic Party in 1962, complaining it was too liberal, and immediately began campaigning for Congress as a Republican.

Stressing his opposition to the "socialistic" Kennedy administration, Spence was a consensus choice for the 1962 GOP nomination in the open 2nd. But he narrowly lost in the fall to an equally conservative Democrat, state Sen. Albert W. Watson.

Watson himself switched parties in 1965, and in 1970 ran for governor as a Republican. Spence then made his second try for Congress, stressing his opposition to the busing decisions of the U.S. Supreme Court. He defeated Democrat Heyward McDonald by 6,088 votes to keep the seat in GOP hands.

In 1974 he took 56 percent against Matthew Perry, the first black to be nominated for Congress by South Carolina Democrats. Another black Democrat, Ken Mosely, challenged Spence in 1982 and 1984, getting around 40 percent each time. Heading into 1986, dispirited local Democrats were having trouble finding a credible challenger. To prevent the nomination from going to a machine shop owner who was suspected of having ties to Lyndon H. LaRouche Jr., state Democratic Party Executive Director Fred Zeigler filed at the last moment. He ended up laying a good foundation for Leventis' challenge two years later.

Zeigler was late starting and outspent, but not bashful. He issued a steady barrage of attacks on Spence, portraying him as either too tired or too bored to represent the district vigorously. A 39-year-old former University of South Carolina football star, Zeigler accused Spence of dodging him in order to "avoid a side-by-side, live comparison." He said Spence had taken too many taxpayer-financed foreign junkets and had not done enough to help South Carolina's import-pinched textile industry.

Spence did his best to ignore Zeigler's taunts, saying he would not respond to an "obvious campaign tactic of engaging in untrue allegations." He put his faith in the traditional voting patterns of the 2nd, where racial rivalries are strong. Spence got a 70 percent showing out of suburban Lexington County. Zeigler attracted some support among Columbia's young professionals, and their votes added to the 2nd's traditional Democratic base brought him up to 46 percent districtwide.

Committees

Armed Services (2nd of 21 Republicans)
Seapower and Strategic and Critical Materials (ranking); Military Installations and Facilities

Select Aging (20th of 27 Republicans)
Human Services; Retirement, Income and Employment

Elections

1988 General		
Floyd D. Spence (R)	94,960	(53%)
Jim Leventis (D)	83,978	(47%)
1986 General		
Floyd D. Spence (R)	73,455	(54%)
Fred Zeigler (D)	63,592	(46%)

Previous Winning Percentages: **1984** (62%) **1982** (59%) **1980** (56%) **1978** (57%) **1976** (58%) **1974** (56%) **1972** (100%) **1970** (53%)

District Vote For President

	1988	1984	1980	1976
D	67,446 (39%)	61,368 (36%)	52,255 (43%)	70,231 (51%)
R	103,577 (59%)	105,337 (62%)	66,522 (54%)	66,194 (48%)
I			2,261 (2%)	

Campaign Finance

	Receipts	Receipts from PACs	Expend-itures
1988			
Spence (R)	$363,171	$191,268 (53%)	$369,698
Leventis (D)	$389,570	$65,200 (17%)	$378,469
1986			
Spence (R)	$277,527	$144,996 (52%)	$294,665
Zeigler (D)	$180,221	$18,650 (10%)	$179,860

Key Votes

1987	
Raise speed limit to 65 mph	Y
Approve Gephardt "fair trade" amendment	N
Ban testing of larger nuclear weapons	N
Delay "re-flagging" of Kuwaiti tankers	N
Approve tax-raising deficit-reduction bill	X
1988	
Approve aid to Nicaraguan contras	Y
Enact civil rights restoration bill over Reagan veto	N
Kill 60-day plant-closing notification measure	Y
Pass omnibus trade bill over Reagan veto	?
Approve death penalty for drug-related murders	?
Bar federal funds for abortions in cases of rape and incest	?
Oppose seven-day waiting period for purchase of handguns	Y

Voting Studies

	Presidential Support		Party Unity		Conservative Coalition	
Year	**S**	**O**	**S**	**O**	**S**	**O**
1988	37	21	37	14	47	3
1987	61	32	68	20	91	7
1986	69	30	75	23	94	2
1985	61	39	84	13	93	7
1984	59	36	84	13	88	8
1983	74	26	87	10	97	2
1982	74	26	84	15	93	5
1981	74	26	92	8	96	4

Interest Group Ratings

Year	ADA	ACU	AFL-CIO	CCUS
1988	10	85	50	71
1987	4	73	20	93
1986	10	77	43	76
1985	0	81	12	95
1984	5	83	8	63
1983	0	100	6	80
1982	0	91	5	86
1981	0	100	13	89

3 Butler Derrick (D)

Of Edgefield — Elected 1974

Born: Sept. 30, 1936, Springfield, Mass.
Education: Attended U. of South Carolina, 1954-58; U. of Georgia, LL.B. 1965.
Occupation: Lawyer.
Family: Wife, Beverly Grantham; four children.
Religion: Episcopalian.
Political Career: S.C. House, 1969-75.
Capitol Office: 201 Cannon Bldg. 20515; 225-5301.

In Washington: Derrick is without a doubt one of the most impressive Southern legislators in the House, a product of the Democratic class of 1974 who now sits just one place down from the chairmanship of the powerful Rules Committee.

But while he is in an enviable position to deliver for his South Carolina district, he now has to worry about whether his conservative-minded constituency will deliver for him. Derrick's challenge is to be an effective inside player in the House Democratic Caucus while representing a state increasingly enamored of the GOP.

There is some irony in the fact that Derrick had the closest general-election race of his career — against a relatively unheralded candidate — in 1988, just as he was beginning to gain wider recognition for his legislative talents. When Rules Chairman Claude Pepper died in May 1989, Joe Moakley of Massachusetts took over the committee, and Derrick became its No. 2 Democrat. At 52, he is nearly a decade younger than Moakley, and thus seems likely to chair the panel one day, as long as he can keep his political footing at home. For now, Democratic leaders look to Derrick as a key link to the South when it comes to coalition building.

Derrick has been appointed to the Budget Committee two separate times; he served a total of five terms there. During the 100th Congress, his last two years on the committee, he was in charge of managing procedural legislation to implement the budget once it is adopted — a delicate task, since it involved the conflicting jurisdictions and ambitions of numerous House committees.

For a man of the media age, Derrick has a quiet operating style. He is more prone to hammer out a compromise in a corner of the House chamber than to give a speech center stage. His behind-the-scenes pursuits enable him to get much more done in a given Congress than he gets, or takes, credit for. But that is not to say that Derrick shuns high-profile issues. He has been at the center of activity on some issues of national and local concern.

In the 100th Congress Derrick was chairman of the Congressional Textile Caucus, and he took the lead in pushing a major bill to aid the domestic industry, much of which is located in the South. The effort was a popular one at home and among many in Congress, but it pitted Derrick against some powerful opponents: President Reagan, who successfully vetoed the textile bill in the 99th Congress, and key legislators, such as Ways and Means Chairman Dan Rostenkowski, whose committee has jurisdiction over most trade matters.

Derrick and his allies hoped to increase the bill's popularity with some adjustments in the 100th Congress. One major change was the elimination of country-specific import curbs, which had previously been seen as "anti-Asian." The bill also gave the administration some flexibility to decide which countries could increase imports, and to reduce tariffs on other products.

But while Derrick ended up with 244 cosponsors, the administration still blasted the bill as "totally unacceptable and unnecessary." Opponents called the bill protectionism that could not be accommodated under existing trade agreements, and they also said the industry was on sounder economic footing than it had been in the previous Congress. Then-U.S. Trade Representative Clayton Yeutter called the bill "totally unpersuasive on its merits." To that, Derrick responded, "Mr. Yeutter doesn't have any constituents who've lost their jobs."

The House passed the textile bill in 1987 by a vote of 263-156, a substantial margin, but one smaller than the failed veto-override vote in the previous Congress. It came as little surprise in 1988 when Derrick and his allies fell 11 votes short of overriding the president's veto. Some of the shortfall was probably due to the passage of an omnibus trade bill, which had given many members an outlet for their frustration on the issue. Derrick, an at-large Democratic whip, played an important role in delivering votes for that bill.

Derrick is also closely tied to nuclear issues, which can have a major impact on his district, home to the Department of Energy's

South Carolina 3

West — Anderson; Aiken

The 3rd stretches in a band one and two counties wide from the Blue Ridge Mountains in the north to rural Allendale County, only 60 miles from the Atlantic coast beaches. It is a traditionally Democratic-dominated rural and small-town territory where newcomers arriving in a few urbanized areas are measurably enhancing Republican strength.

In the three largest counties of the 3rd — Anderson, Aiken and Pickens — George Bush won a combined 71 percent of the presidential vote in 1988. A more telling sign of changing times — since Democrats still hold most of the local offices throughout the 3rd — is that in 1986, Republican gubernatorial nominee Carroll A. Campbell Jr. managed to carry the 3rd as part of his narrow statewide victory.

Anderson is a traditional textile county that has made a successful transition to diversified manufacturing (more than 140 different industries); its hospital complex is one of the Piedmont's major medical centers, with nearly 600 beds and some 200 doctors.

Pickens County is the site of Clemson University, a mainstay of the economy with nearly 14,000 students and 1,000 faculty. The town of Clemson has a conservative bloc among some faculty and students; spillover growth from Greenville, in the neighboring 4th District, also has increased the GOP base.

The strongest Republican area of the 3rd is Aiken County, GOP Sen. Strom Thurmond's political base. A traditional winter resting place for wealthy Northerners, Aiken was once called "the polo capital of the South." Its county seat of Aiken boasts a public library built by the du Pont family. The bulk of the county's GOP support comes from white-collar suburbs clustered east of Augusta, Ga., and from the executives working at or retired from the Savannah River nuclear complex, which straddles Aiken and Barnwell counties.

There are pockets of Republican votes in other counties, but most of the rural voters consider themselves Democrats except for presidential election purposes. A good share of the farming population remains poor, with the sharecroppers of black-majority Abbeville and McCormick counties in particular scratching meager livings from the soil. Those two counties were the only in the district carried by Michael S. Dukakis in 1988.

Population: 519,280. White 399,161 (77%), Black 117,985 (23%). Spanish origin 3,836 (1%). 18 and over 366,318 (71%), 65 and over 54,173 (10%). Median age: 30.

nuclear reactors at Savannah River. Much of the nation's nuclear weapons production has rested on plutonium and tritium produced at four aging reactors that have been shut down since 1988 because of safety concerns. Derrick has since been in a position of defending the quality of work of thousands of his constituents who have been employed at Savannah River, and trying to see that DOE money continues to come into the state. Along with other South Carolina public officials, Derrick worked in recent years to persuade DOE to build a new reactor for tritium production in his district. In 1988 DOE recommended South Carolina as its preferred site for a new plant.

Although he casts his share of routine votes with the conservative coalition of Republicans and Southern Democrats, Derrick usually comes through when his party needs him. In 1988 he voted with his party 76 percent of the time, more than the average Southern Democrat. He was the only South Carolina House member supporting a ban on U.S. nuclear tests of more than 1 kiloton, contingent on Soviet compliance, and he also voted against the president's request for military aid to the contras in 1988.

But when Democrats were trying to make a major issue of Republican opposition to plant-closing notification legislation in 1988, Derrick was one of 16 House Democrats who voted against the measure — a reflection, perhaps, of his close ties to his district's business establishment.

Derrick is also careful to distance himself from the overall image of the national Democratic Party, whose presidential candidates have been poison in South Carolina. In 1989 Derrick cosponsored a measure banning the importation of American flags manufactured outside the country.

"Some overseas flag makers have no respect for the stars and stripes," he said. "When they look at the red, white and blue, they see only greenbacks. When I pledge allegiance to the flag, I want to know it was made in the U.S.A."

At Home: In November 1988, the Dukakis-Bentsen presidential ticket got just one-third of the vote in the 3rd District, making

Derrick's GOP opponent, surgeon Henry S. Jordan, a bigger obstacle than expected.

Even though Derrick ran more than 34,000 votes ahead of the top of his party's ticket, he finished with a modest 54 percent of the vote. Considering that he spent more than $600,000 and Jordan a good deal less, it was the kind of showing that could entice the national GOP to make a priority of the 3rd in the future.

At the start of the 1988 campaign season, Derrick looked to be in good shape. In the previous presidential year, 1984, he had won comfortably despite a Reagan landslide in the 3rd and opposition from an aggressive young Republican real-estate developer.

Establishment Republicans, pessimistic about their prospects against Derrick in 1988, let a newer wing of the local GOP — evangelical conservatives — take a turn against the incumbent. Jordan, who had been active in Pat Robertson's presidential campaign, had built some name recognition in a failed 1986 bid for the GOP Senate nomination. But he had to spend much of 1988 just trying to prove he had a broader agenda than the social-issues activism associated with Robertson's movement.

Still, on Election Day, Jordan ran well in the areas of the 3rd that are the fastest-growing. He carried Aiken County and stayed close in Anderson and Pickens counties; those three together cast about 60 percent of the district's vote. Derrick ran strongest in the more rural areas of his constituency.

It was a tough fight for a man who had an unusually smooth initial path to Congress, and subsequently uneventful re-elections. The 3rd was up for grabs in 1974 when veteran Democrat W. J. Bryan Dorn retired, and Derrick won it as if he were an incumbent breezing to re-election.

He had been a state representative since 1969 and was a member of the influential Ways and Means Committee of the South Carolina House. He professed fiscal conservatism, right-to-work views and hard-line support for national defense. He also identified himself publicly as a racial moderate, nominating the first black to a South Carolina school board.

Derrick won the Democratic primary with 65 percent of the vote over two political unknowns. In November, he carried all but one county in defeating former state Sen. Marshall J. Parker, twice an unsuccessful GOP Senate candidate, with 62 percent. He won 60 percent in a 1980 rematch with Parker and prevailed with similar ease until 1988.

Committees

Rules (2nd of 9 Democrats)
Legislative Process (chairman)

Select Aging (12th of 39 Democrats)
Health and Long-Term Care

Elections

1988 General		
Butler Derrick (D)	89,071	(54%)
Henry S. Jordan (R)	75,571	(46%)
1986 General		
Butler Derrick (D)	79,109	(68%)
Richard Dickison (R)	36,495	(32%)

Previous Winning Percentages: **1984** (58%) **1982** (90%) **1980** (60%) **1978** (82%) **1976** (100%) **1974** (62%)

District Vote For President

	1988	1984	1980	1976
D	54,507 (33%)	49,116 (32%)	89,433 (51%)	79,979 (60%)
R	108,043 (66%)	102,301 (67%)	82,493 (47%)	53,342 (40%)
I			2,681 (2%)	

Campaign Finance

	Receipts	Receipts from PACs	Expend-itures
1988			
Derrick (D)	$579,468	$370,841 (64%)	$641,429
Jordan (R)	$354,589	$45,511 (13%)	$354,575
1986			
Derrick (D)	$282,849	$167,750 (59%)	$177,714

Key Votes

1987	
Raise speed limit to 65 mph	N
Approve Gephardt "fair trade" amendment	Y
Ban testing of larger nuclear weapons	Y
Delay "re-flagging" of Kuwaiti tankers	N
Approve tax-raising deficit-reduction bill	Y
1988	
Approve aid to Nicaraguan contras	N
Enact civil rights restoration bill over Reagan veto	Y
Kill 60-day plant-closing notification measure	N
Pass omnibus trade bill over Reagan veto	Y
Approve death penalty for drug-related murders	Y
Bar federal funds for abortions in cases of rape and incest	X
Oppose seven-day waiting period for purchase of handguns	Y

Voting Studies

	Presidential Support		Party Unity		Conservative Coalition	
Year	**S**	**O**	**S**	**O**	**S**	**O**
1988	33	60	76	18	66	21
1987	28	68	83	15	56	42
1986	28	68	81	13	52	48
1985	29	69	74	17	60	35
1984	39	54	73	25	61	39
1983	35	57	72	16	42	49
1982	36	52	70	22	56	41
1981	50	45	62	30	55	35

Interest Group Ratings

Year	ADA	ACU	AFL-CIO	CCUS
1988	70	36	71	54
1987	72	17	75	40
1986	55	26	57	44
1985	60	10	53	36
1984	50	35	15	47
1983	75	23	69	53
1982	50	46	55	52
1981	60	40	53	37

4 Liz J. Patterson (D)

Of Spartanburg — Elected 1986

Born: Nov. 18, 1939, Columbia, S.C.

Education: Columbia College, B.A. 1961; attended U. of South Carolina, 1961-62.

Occupation: Legislative aide; recruiting officer, Peace Corps; coordinator, Head Start.

Family: Husband, Dwight Fleming Patterson Jr.; three children.

Religion: United Methodist.

Political Career: Spartanburg County Council, 1975-76; S.C. Senate, 1979-87.

Capitol Office: 1641 Longworth Bldg. 20515; 225-6030.

In Washington: Patterson knew from the day she was first elected to the House in 1986 that November 1988 would be a trial, and her cautious first-term performance reflected that fact of political life.

On partisan matters that came to a vote on the floor, Patterson tended to break with her party more often than the average Southern Democrat. She favored sending military aid to the Nicaraguan contras and opposed a seven-day waiting period for purchasing handguns.

Patterson spent a good deal of her first term back in the 4th District, so a number of her colleagues in Washington got little more than a fleeting impression of her work. On the Veterans' Affairs Committee, she sponsored legislation to authorize child day-care centers at Veterans Administration medical centers. It was attached to a larger veterans' health-care bill and signed into law in 1988.

Patterson calls herself a fiscal conservative, and points to her service on the state Senate Finance Committee, where she says she helped fashion responsible fiscal policy. In the House, she joined a bipartisan group led by Minnesota Democrat Timothy J. Penny and Iowa Republican Tom Tauke dedicated to reducing the federal budget deficit with across-the-board spending-cut amendments to appropriations bills.

While her fiscal conservatism helped her deflect charges of liberalism back home, her vote for Penny's stringent 1988 alternative budget resolution haunted her during her re-election campaign. Among other things, the Penny budget called for replacing the inflation-based Social Security cost-of-living adjustments with a flat-rate COLA increase of $5 per year.

A bold political vote for the most secure of members — it only attracted 27 votes — her support for the Penny budget allowed her GOP opponent to charge that she favored cutting Social Security benefits. After the campaign, Patterson acknowledged that if she could have the vote to take over, she would "probably not" vote for the plan again, "because I found that it's so difficult to explain" such votes to the electorate.

At Home: Patterson is the daughter of a populist, the late U.S. Sen. Olin D. Johnston, and he would have been proud of her campaigns for Congress. Running against a well-financed Republican favorite in 1986, she tied him in knots by portraying him as a tool of corporations and the Greenville country club elite. In 1988, she faced a smooth, well-funded establishment GOP challenger, but her warm, down-to-earth style won out over his cooler approach — even as George Bush rolled up a 2-to-1 margin in the 4th.

Her back-to-back victories make this district one of the Democratic Party's biggest success stories in Southern congressional politics. For eight years, the 4th was solidly Republican, held by Carroll A. Campbell Jr., who left it in 1986 and won election as governor of South Carolina.

Patterson was still a teenager when she started working in Olin Johnston's campaigns, and she continued right up through the last of his four elections to the Senate, in 1962. During the 1970s, she held several posts in the Spartanburg County Democratic Party and served briefly on the Spartanburg County Council. She was elected to the state Senate in 1978.

The eventual Republican nominee in 1986, Greenville Mayor William D. Workman III, was initially thought to have the advantage, given Campbell's string of easy victories in the 4th District.

Patterson had little trouble deflecting Workman's attempts to brand her as a big-spending liberal. Campaigning on the slogan, "I'm one of us," she aired television advertisements that portrayed her as a homemaker steeped in old-fashioned family values. Her down-home style appealed to rank-and-file voters, many of whom saw Workman as something of a stuffed shirt. If they needed further prodding, Patterson gave it to them, seizing on a

South Carolina 4

Northwest — Greenville; Spartanburg

The nucleus of the 4th is Greenville County, the most populous and most industrialized county in the state and a showpiece of the New South. The city of Greenville developed as a center of the textile industry after the Civil War, and it still bustles with mills, clothing manufacturers and textile machinery producers. Reflecting a broader trend, the number of local textile jobs has declined in the 1980s, but unemployment remains low because work is available in the newer industries that business and government leaders have lured to the area.

Since 1960, the city's non-unionized labor force and low wage rate have combined with a favorable tax structure and warm climate to draw investment from the Frost Belt and overseas. Union Carbide, General Electric and Michelin are among the major employers.

Greenville County has a history of conservatism dating to its Tory leanings during the Revolution, and it was one of the first areas in the state to take to Republicanism after World War II. But its tendency to follow the GOP line in national elections masks a more fragmented political life.

The county's Republican Party is an uneasy alliance between mainstream partisans among the corporate business community and an intensely conservative wing made up of evangelical Christians and of fundamentalists who take their cues from Dr. Bob Jones III, president of Greenville-based Bob Jones University (4,100 students).

In the 1986 GOP House primary, the business community won out over the religious establishment, nominating Greenville Mayor William D. Workman III. But hard feelings between the two camps helped hold down Workman's general-election margin in Greenville County; he won it with only 54 percent, dooming his chances against Democrat Patterson. Two years later, Republican House nominee Knox White, also an establishment figure, stayed on better terms with religious conservatives. But he, too, carried Greenville County with just 54 percent. By contrast, George Bush won 71 percent of the Greenville County vote in 1988.

Conservative Democrats are in the majority in Greenville County's outlying parts — the mountainous north and the agricultural southern end. There also is liberal Democratic strength within the city among blacks, organized teachers and textile workers. Patterson mobilizes all those Democratic constituencies.

Greenville's development has spilled over into Spartanburg County, bringing new industries and political change. But older textile mills and huge peach orchards dominate the area; the street signs in downtown Spartanburg have peaches painted on them.

Rank-and-file textile workers and farm laborers give Spartanburg firmer Democratic loyalties than Greenville. In both 1986 and 1988, Patterson carried 60 percent of the vote in Spartanburg County, her home base. She has won even more comfortably in rural, sparsely populated Union County, which rounds out the three-county district.

Population: 520,525. White 416,709 (80%), Black 100,769 (19%). Spanish origin 4,065 (1%). 18 and over 373,015 (72%), 65 and over 52,400 (10%). Median age: 30.

portrayal of the Republican as an instrument of Greenville "fat cats."

Although Patterson was a more deft campaigner than Workman, she probably could not have overcome the 4th's conservative bent had the local GOP been unified. But it was not.

Campbell's departure had provoked competition between two factions of the district GOP that he had held together — the business-oriented mainstream element and the sizable group of religious fundamentalists and evangelicals. Workman was unable to heal the rift by Election Day. Patterson's skillful exploiting of Workman's weaknesses also aroused the antipathy that many rural voters have for Greenville, the district's largest city. Rural votes were crucial to her becoming the first candidate from outside Greenville to win this seat since 1918.

Patterson's 1988 opponent was Knox White, a Greenville city councilman and former congressional aide to Campbell. Even though he beat the same evangelical-backed primary candidate Workman did, he stayed on good terms with the religious community.

White targeted the sizable bloc of Republicans in the city and county of Greenville who were contemplating splitting their ballots to vote for Bush for president and Patterson for Congress. On the stump and in his advertising, he constantly linked his campaign with Bush's, and frequently referred to positions held by "my opponent and Michael Dukakis."

But Patterson had built up a considerable reservoir of good will in her first term. White tried hard to tarnish her image as an independent-thinking, conservative Democrat and portray her as out of the mainstream of the district's social conservatism.

But in the end, more voters preferred the comforting familiarity of Patterson's retail politics to White's rally for conservatism. She stayed close to White in his Greenville County, then rolled up a 12,000-vote victory margin in her Spartanburg County base and padded her advantage by taking two-thirds of the vote in rural Union County. Overall, Patterson took 52 percent of the vote, a slim but decisive victory against the backdrop of Bush's sweep in the 4th.

Committees

Banking, Finance and Urban Affairs (22nd of 31 Democrats)
Economic Stabilization; Financial Institutions Supervision, Regulation and Insurance; Housing and Community Development

Select Hunger (12th of 18 Democrats)
Task Force: Domestic

Veterans' Affairs (13th of 21 Democrats)
Education, Training and Employment; Hospitals and Health Care

Elections

1988 General		
Liz J. Patterson (D)	90,234	(52%)
Knox White (R)	82,793	(48%)
1986 General		
Liz J. Patterson (D)	67,012	(51%)
William D. Workman III (R)	61,648	(47%)

District Vote For President

	1988	1984	1980	1976
D	54,572 (32%)	48,691 (30%)	65,654 (44%)	70,211 (52%)
R	114,191 (67%)	114,650 (70%)	80,298 (54%)	63,018 (47%)
I			2,634 (2%)	

Campaign Finance

	Receipts	Receipts from PACs	Expend-itures
1988			
Patterson (D)	$1,119,822	$412,855 (37%)	$1,143,351
White (R)	$631,287	$86,318 (14%)	$630,913
1986			
Patterson (D)	$619,226	$148,405 (24%)	$594,026
Workman (R)	$643,688	$145,969 (23%)	$639,859

Key Votes

1987	
Raise speed limit to 65 mph	N
Approve Gephardt "fair trade" amendment	Y
Ban testing of larger nuclear weapons	N
Delay "re-flagging" of Kuwaiti tankers	N
Approve tax-raising deficit-reduction bill	N
1988	
Approve aid to Nicaraguan contras	Y
Enact civil rights restoration bill over Reagan veto	Y
Kill 60-day plant-closing notification measure	Y
Pass omnibus trade bill over Reagan veto	Y
Approve death penalty for drug-related murders	Y
Bar federal funds for abortions in cases of rape and incest	N
Oppose seven-day waiting period for purchase of handguns	Y

Voting Studies

	Presidential Support		Party Unity		Conservative Coalition	
Year	**S**	**O**	**S**	**O**	**S**	**O**
1988	37	63	69	29	82	18
1987	36	64	71	25	77	23

Interest Group Ratings

Year	ADA	ACU	AFL-CIO	CCUS
1988	45	48	71	57
1987	68	26	63	60

5 John M. Spratt Jr. (D)

Of York — Elected 1982

Born: Nov. 1, 1942, Charlotte, N.C.
Education: Davidson College, A.B. 1964; Oxford U., England, M.A. 1966; Yale U., LL.B. 1969.
Military Career: Army, 1969-71.
Occupation: Lawyer; insurance executive.
Family: Wife, Jane Stacy; three children.
Religion: Presbyterian.
Political Career: No previous office.
Capitol Office: 1533 Longworth Bldg. 20515; 225-5501.

In Washington: There are members of the House Armed Services Committee with greater oratorical flair, but when committee Chairman Les Aspin has an assignment requiring brainpower, tenacity and a skill for intellectual argument, Spratt is the one to whom he turns.

It is qualities such as these that have made the South Carolina Democrat — an attorney with degrees from Davidson, Oxford and Yale — one of the most influential members of the committee that shapes House policy on national defense. Spratt is one of Aspin's closest allies and advisers. His knowledge of arms control and defense strategy could eventually lead him to a position of influence in the House similar to that enjoyed by Georgia's Sam Nunn in the Senate.

Like Nunn, Spratt is a leader among the centrist Democrats who are regarded as "pro-defense," but who are far more skeptical of Defense Department policies than the Pentagon-allied conservative Democrats who long held sway on the Armed Services Committee. "Our role is to be defense advocates, but not Department of Defense advocates," Spratt has said.

Though he was just starting his third House term at the beginning of the 100th Congress, Spratt had enough expertise on the strategic defense initiative (SDI) that Aspin appointed him to conduct a series of Armed Services hearings on SDI. In 1988, Spratt was chief House negotiator on SDI issues during a House-Senate conference on the fiscal 1989 defense authorization bill. And at the start of the 101st Congress, Aspin named Spratt to head a committee task force studying the difficult-to-solve safety and waste-disposal problems at the nation's nuclear-weapons-production plants.

Respect for Spratt's expertise crosses party lines. When the House was considering a defense authorization bill in early 1987, Spratt led the fight for amendments that were aimed at blocking President Reagan's efforts to reinterpret the 1972 U.S.-Soviet anti-ballistic missile (ABM) treaty in a manner that would allow space-based testing of SDI. One of the House members supporting Spratt's position was a conservative Republican freshman from his home state, Arthur Ravenel Jr.

"Spratt has a reputation in South Carolina of being a brilliant individual," Ravenel said. "He has made the ABM treaty and SDI research a particular study."

Despite such accolades, Spratt and his Republican counterparts are often on opposite sides of hard partisan lines when defense issues such as SDI are debated. He played a key role in one of the most contentious partisan defense battles of the 100th Congress.

During 1988 debate on the defense authorization bill, Reagan and others supporting early deployment of SDI technology argued for accelerated research on "space-based interceptors" (SBIs), small, heat-seeking missiles borne by a network of satellites that would attack Soviet nuclear missiles shortly after launch. Though it was a far more limited concept than Reagan's original SDI "space shield," supporters argued that it was necessary to protect the United States from an accidental Soviet launch or an intentional attack from a smaller nuclear-armed nation.

The supporters of this approach called for its deployment as "phase one" of SDI by the early 1990s. But Spratt, Nunn and others opposed SBIs, describing them as a ploy of SDI backers eager to show a "quick return" on investment in SDI research and thus build support for the entire SDI program. They also said SBIs would violate the 1972 ABM treaty and would divert research dollars from more exotic but promising anti-missile technologies. Their proposal called for a more modest ground-based ABM system, which would be far less expensive and would fall within the bounds of the 1972 treaty.

To enforce this policy direction, Spratt proposed an amendment to the authorization bill limiting "phase one" spending to 40 percent of the total authorized for SDI; the measure passed, 244-174. He also attached an amendment, approved by 239-176, which required any

South Carolina 5

North Central — Rock Hill

Touching on four distinct regions of South Carolina, the 5th extends from the hills of Cherokee County south to the Lowcountry around Sumter. To command a districtwide media presence, a candidate has to buy time in four cities outside the district — Greenville, Columbia, Florence and Charlotte, N.C.

This geographic diversity makes it difficult to pigeonhole the district's personality, but many of the residents are dependent on the textile industry for their livelihood. Springs Mills has a half-dozen plants scattered about the district, including ones in Lancaster, Kershaw and Chester; Du Pont has a huge synthetic fibers plant in Camden. Most of the counties in the central section of the district have at least one town whose name ends in "Mills," with millworkers forming the base of the electorate. The district's southern and eastern counties remain primarily agricultural. Chesterfield and tiny Lee County grow soybeans, corn, cotton and melons.

In nearly all these counties, most voters prefer Democrats for local and state offices. Nine of the district's 11 counties voted Democratic when the GOP won the governorship in 1986. Even Michael S. Dukakis got 40 percent of the 5th's presidential vote in 1988, his second-best district showing in the state. Spratt swept every county in his easy 1988 re-election.

The most populous and dynamic area of the district is at its northern tip, around the city of Rock Hill (York County), a onetime textile town that has become an exurban appendage of flourishing Charlotte, N.C., a half-hour's commute up Interstate 77. While Rock Hill's days as a textile town are fading from memory as more of its residents find work in the Charlotte area's high-tech businesses, York County still has a well-organized Democratic Party that just managed (by 110 votes) to win the county in the 1986 governor's race. But two years later, York went 65 percent for George Bush.

Democrats still dominate in rural western York County; the more affluent and Republican voters are in the suburbanized east. Also in the east, around the town of Fort Mill, is a contingent of fervently religious conservative Republicans who were drawn by the Heritage, U.S.A. recreation complex and religious retreat built by televangelists Jim and Tammy Bakker. After Jim Bakker admitted in 1987 to a sexual encounter with a church secretary, the fate of the complex was cast into doubt. But because of its proximity to Charlotte, it was clear the real estate would not go begging.

The 5th's other GOP pockets are in Sumter and Kershaw counties. Shaw Air Force Base in Sumter has been a major source of federal dollars and conservative votes. In Kershaw, the Du Pont executives and other wealthy business people in Camden back Republican candidates.

Population: 519,716. White 347,770 (67%), Black 168,599 (32%), Other 2,561 (1%). Spanish origin 4,563 (1%). 18 and over 357,907 (69%), 65 and over 51,693 (10%). Median age: 29.

"accidental launch protection system" to comply with the traditional ABM treaty prohibition against space-based weapons.

The bill that emerged from House-Senate conference maintained these provisions. But in the end, a persistent Reagan won out. In August 1988, he vetoed the defense authorization bill, pointing to the limits on SBIs as one of its objectionable features. After weeks of partisan wrangling, a compromise was hammered out that included a removal of the spending cap on SBIs. Spratt called this "a significant concession to the administration," noting, "We had tilted [the] priority in favor of ground-based interceptors."

Until the issue was settled, Democrats argued that Reagan had used his veto politically to portray their party as anti-defense, in keeping with the GOP strategy for winning the White House again in the 1988 election. Democrats' sensitivity on the issue was heightened by the vulnerability of their presidential candidate, Michael S. Dukakis, on defense issues.

Spratt early on counseled Dukakis, who said he supported some SDI research, to spell out specifically what sort of program he favored. In September 1988, Spratt was one of the centrist Democrats who met at Dukakis' home to provide the candidate with advice on defense issues. But their efforts to insulate Dukakis from the "soft-on-defense" label were of limited effect.

Spratt's efforts on Armed Services are more intellectual than parochial: His district contains only one small Army base, and no major defense contractors. He does have a place to pursue his local interests, though, on the Government Operations Committee. A member of the Subcommittee on Commerce, Consumer and Monetary Affairs, he tries to bring attention to the impact of foreign competition on the domestic textile industry, which has numerous outposts in the 5th District.

At Home: With three academic degrees and a background as a lawyer and bank president, Spratt is not the obvious representative for a district where many of the Democratic votes come from poor textile towns and dusty farms. But after emerging from a field of four Democratic hopefuls in 1982, Spratt has had no electoral trouble at all. He won that November with 68 percent of the vote, and then it was six years before the GOP even fielded a candidate against him. He was Bob Carley, a political science professor, and he lost by more than 2-to-1, even as George Bush carried the district handily for president.

In his first campaign, Spratt worked hard to turn his elitist credentials into an asset. "People are glad to see a candidate with these qualifications," he said. "That's my come-on." If his style on the stump remained a bit scholarly, no one seemed to mind.

When Democratic Rep. Ken Holland announced his retirement just before the filing deadline, Spratt jumped for the Democratic nomination, as did former Holland aide John Winburn and state Rep. Ernie Nunnery.

Winburn had Holland's contacts and Nunnery had a base in Chester County, but Spratt's banking interests and his law practice gave him strong connections in political and business circles. Many Democratic leaders quietly backed him.

And when Winburn called Spratt "a millionaire banker, lawyer and hobby farmer" who could not relate to ordinary people, Spratt persuasively argued that his work with small-town clients and depositors had given him an understanding of their circumstances. "I wouldn't have kept my job if I couldn't relate to those people," he said. Spratt finished first in the primary with 38 percent of the vote, then took 55 percent in a runoff against Winburn.

In November, Republican John Wilkerson, a longtime friend and legal client of Spratt, accused the Democrat of being too liberal for the district. But Spratt appealed to the district's partisan loyalties, saying he was "in the mainstream of the Democratic Party."

Spratt had a clear organizational edge. When he visited county courthouses, rural areas and factories, he often had a locally popular political figure close at hand. Wilkerson had fewer contacts; one source described his supporters as "the country club boys — the fellows who put ice in their whiskey."

Unable to rely on a county-by-county apparatus, Wilkerson turned to using negative ads implying that Spratt had tried to buy votes in a previous campaign for Democratic gubernatorial nominee Charles Ravenel in 1974. The commercials galvanized Spratt supporters and sealed Wilkerson's fate.

Committees

Armed Services (18th of 31 Democrats)
Investigations; Procurement and Military Nuclear Systems

Government Operations (15th of 24 Democrats)
Commerce, Consumer and Monetary Affairs; Government Information, Justice and Agriculture

Elections

1988 General		
John M. Spratt Jr. (D)	107,959	(70%)
Bob Carley (R)	46,622	(30%)
1986 General		
John M. Spratt Jr. (D)	95,859	(100%)

Previous Winning Percentages: **1984** (92%) **1982** (68%)

District Vote For President

	1988	1984	1980	1976
D	61,398 (40%)	58,350 (38%)	74,745 (53%)	80,255 (59%)
R	91,385 (60%)	94,269 (62%)	63,496 (45%)	54,153 (40%)

Campaign Finance

	Receipts	Receipts from PACs	Expend-itures
1988			
Spratt (D)	$203,552	$140,970 (69%)	$105,620
Carley (R)	$8,225	0	$8,449
1986			
Spratt (D)	$156,055	$67,226 (43%)	$66,944

Key Votes

1987	
Raise speed limit to 65 mph	N
Approve Gephardt "fair trade" amendment	Y
Ban testing of larger nuclear weapons	Y
Delay "re-flagging" of Kuwaiti tankers	Y
Approve tax-raising deficit-reduction bill	Y
1988	
Approve aid to Nicaraguan contras	N
Enact civil rights restoration bill over Reagan veto	Y
Kill 60-day plant-closing notification measure	Y
Pass omnibus trade bill over Reagan veto	Y
Approve death penalty for drug-related murders	Y
Bar federal funds for abortions in cases of rape and incest	N
Oppose seven-day waiting period for purchase of handguns	Y

Voting Studies

	Presidential Support		Party Unity		Conservative Coalition	
Year	**S**	**O**	**S**	**O**	**S**	**O**
1988	33	63	78	19	82	18
1987	31	66	80	16	81	12
1986	28	71	84	13	54	46
1985	41	58	79	17	73	27
1984	41	58	77	22	56	44
1983	37	61	74	20	60	40

Interest Group Ratings

Year	ADA	ACU	AFL-CIO	CCUS
1988	55	29	79	57
1987	72	9	69	47
1986	60	33	64	59
1985	35	38	38	57
1984	70	21	38	31
1983	65	14	75	50

6 Robin Tallon (D)

Of Florence — Elected 1982

Born: Aug. 8, 1946, Hemingway, S.C.
Education: Attended U. of South Carolina, 1964-65.
Occupation: Clothing store owner.
Family: Wife, Amelia Louise Johns; three children.
Religion: Methodist.
Political Career: S.C. House, 1981-83.
Capitol Office: 432 Cannon Bldg. 20515; 225-3315.

In Washington: Tallon has a three-pronged constituency to satisfy, and he does it in an unassuming, non-confrontational style. He is quite unlike the last Democrat to hold the 6th — the flamboyant John W. Jenrette Jr. of Abscam infamy — but if a few locals still yearn for the entertainment that Jenrette and his *Playboy*-posing wife provided, a large majority endorses Tallon's more conventional manner.

The Pee Dee district is home to rural, traditionally Democratic whites, a good many depending on tobacco for their livelihood; rural, economically disadvantaged blacks with a stake in preserving and expanding government social services; and a growing number of affluent and conservative coastal residents in Myrtle Beach and along the Grand Strand.

Each group exerts pressure on Tallon, often in different directions, but he has managed to satisfy all of the people at least some of the time. His 1988 voting record was fairly typical: He backed President Reagan on 42 percent of House floor votes, got a favorable rating of 79 from the AFL-CIO and earned a Chamber of Commerce rating of 62, the high score among South Carolina's House Democrats.

Tallon is the only South Carolinian on the Agriculture Committee; he tends to his tobacco growers from his seat on the Tobacco and Peanuts Subcommittee. The 6th grows more leaf than any other district in the state, and Tallon vigorously defends the crop. For the most part, he follows the lead on tobacco issues set forth by his neighbor to the north, North Carolina Democrat Charlie Rose, the Tobacco Subcommittee chairman.

In 1988, following a Tobacco Subcommittee oversight hearing, Tallon wrote Attorney General Dick Thornburgh requesting an FBI investigation into tobacco leaf dealers' alleged illicit practice of blending foreign tobacco with domestic and exporting it as 100 percent domestic tobacco under Agriculture Department export-credit programs.

Tallon's Merchant Marine assignment gives him a voice in matters affecting the 6th's booming coastal population, centered on Myrtle Beach. He has earned valuable publicity for his efforts to obtain federal money to study erosion problems there. In 1988, he won House approval of $600,000 for commercialization of the freshwater hybrid striped bass. The agricultural research bill to which the money was attached, however, died in the Senate amid strong veto threats.

At Home: The owner of a chain of men's clothing stores that carries his name, Tallon was elected to Congress with only brief officeholding experience. His first real brush with politics came in 1979, when he attended the White House Conference on Small Business. He returned from it determined to enter politics as a spokesman for small business. In 1980 he easily won an open state House seat.

Tallon soon started talking about running for Congress against GOP Rep. John L. Napier, who had defeated Jenrette in 1980, after his conviction in the Abscam bribery case. When a potentially strong Democratic competitor for 1982 got tangled in a bribery scandal himself, Tallon became the choice of local party leaders and past supporters of Jenrette. He led in first-round voting and won the runoff handily.

Napier, only the second Republican in this century to win the 6th, nevertheless was favored. Tobacco farmers supported him, and he had more money than Tallon.

Tallon focused on personal canvassing, especially among the district's 41 percent black population. Working with church leaders to ensure a high black turnout, he built an extensive get-out-the-vote apparatus. With the sluggish economy making it difficult for Napier to attract white Democratic voters, Tallon won.

Tallon's low legislative profile as a freshman led to speculation that he would be weak in 1984, but nothing came of that gossip. Napier's decision not to seek a rematch enhanced Tallon's position, and then he smashed party activist Mary Demetrious in the primary. The GOP nomination went to state Rep. Lois Eargle, a Democrat-turned-Republican. She tried to ride the Reagan-Thurmond ticket, but fell far short.

Early in 1986 and again in 1988, rumors circulated that Jenrette might seek his old seat. He did not, and his 1989 shoplifting conviction in suburban Washington, D.C., doused whatever political prospects he may have had.

South Carolina 6

East — Florence

Agriculture has traditionally dominated this district, with tobacco the crucial product. Horry County, in the eastern corner of the state, has one of the richest tobacco crops in the country. Broadleaf from Horry's fields is stored in warehouses and bid on at auctions in such towns as Darlington, Marion and Mullins.

But in recent years, industry and tourism have begun to diversify the economy. Industrial parks have cropped up across the 6th as counties work more aggressively to attract manufacturers.

Democrats are still dominant in the rural parts of the 6th. Even Massachusetts' Michael S. Dukakis managed to carry four counties here in 1988, and his 44 percent tally in the 6th was his best in any South Carolina district. The poverty in rural counties such as Williamsburg and Marion keeps them Democratic — they went for Democratic Rep. John W. Jenrette Jr. even in 1980, after his Abscam conviction.

Blacks make up over 40 percent of the 6th's population, the largest proportion in any of South Carolina's districts. Williamsburg, Marion and Clarendon counties have black majorities, and blacks there are better organized than in most of the South.

Coastal Horry County is one of the country's fastest-growing areas, drawing visitors to the surf, hotels and honky-tonk amusements of Myrtle Beach. Military personnel around Myrtle Beach Air Force Base and wealthy retirees who have been moving to the Grand Strand have built GOP strength in Horry and Florence.

Although small factories are scattered throughout the 6th — candies are produced in Marion and Tupperware in Hemingway — Florence is the district's industrial center. A railhead since the Civil War, it has drawn new plants and industries in recent years, accompanied by an influx of managerial people and GOP votes.

Population: 519,273. White 304,420 (59%), Black 212,151 (41%). Spanish origin 5,721 (1%). 18 and over 347,458 (67%), 65 and over 48,277 (9%). Median age: 28.

Committees

Agriculture (12th of 27 Democrats)
Conservation, Credit and Rural Development; Cotton, Rice and Sugar; Tobacco and Peanuts

Merchant Marine and Fisheries (14th of 26 Democrats)
Fisheries and Wildlife Conservation and the Environment; Merchant Marine

Elections

1988 General		
Robin Tallon (D)	120,719	(76%)
Robert Cunningham Sr. (R)	37,958	(24%)
1988 Primary		
Robin Tallon (D)	65,608	(89%)
Luther Lighty (D)	8,448	(11%)
1986 General		
Robin Tallon (D)	92,398	(76%)
Robbie Cunningham (R)	29,922	(24%)

Previous Winning Percentages: **1984** (60%) **1982** (53%)

District Vote For President

	1988		1984		1980		1976	
D	69,938	(44%)	68,572	(42%)	79,783	(53%)	84,895	(61%)
R	88,766	(56%)	92,605	(57%)	69,806	(46%)	52,984	(38%)

Campaign Finance

	Receipts	Receipts from PACs	Expend-itures
1988			
Tallon (D)	$381,464	$203,958 (53%)	$243,559
Cunningham (R)	$10,759	$100 (1%)	$10,604
1986			
Tallon (D)	$344,115	$126,650 (37%)	$269,708
Cunningham (R)	$64,681	$1,144 (2%)	$61,949

Key Votes

1987	
Raise speed limit to 65 mph	Y
Approve Gephardt "fair trade" amendment	Y
Ban testing of larger nuclear weapons	N
Delay "re-flagging" of Kuwaiti tankers	Y
Approve tax-raising deficit-reduction bill	N
1988	
Approve aid to Nicaraguan contras	Y
Enact civil rights restoration bill over Reagan veto	Y
Kill 60-day plant-closing notification measure	N
Pass omnibus trade bill over Reagan veto	Y
Approve death penalty for drug-related murders	Y
Bar federal funds for abortions in cases of rape and incest	Y
Oppose seven-day waiting period for purchase of handguns	Y

Voting Studies

	Presidential Support		Party Unity		Conservative Coalition	
Year	**S**	**O**	**S**	**O**	**S**	**O**
1988	42	56	63	33	82	11
1987	42	56	68	29	81	16
1986	40	56	59	31	86	8
1985	41	56	69	25	84	16
1984	40	54	65	31	63	32
1983	32	66	79	20	55	43

Interest Group Ratings

Year	ADA	ACU	AFL-CIO	CCUS
1988	40	60	79	62
1987	44	39	81	60
1986	40	57	71	44
1985	45	48	53	50
1984	40	46	50	40
1983	75	33	76	33

South Dakota

U.S. CONGRESS

SENATE 1 D, 1 R
HOUSE 1 D

LEGISLATURE

Senate 14 D, 20 R, 1 Independent
House 24 D, 46 R

ELECTIONS

1988 Presidential Vote

Bush	53%
Dukakis	47%

1984 Presidential Vote

Reagan	63%
Mondale	37%

1980 Presidential Vote

Reagan	61%
Carter	32%
Anderson	7%

Turnout rate in 1984	63%
Turnout rate in 1986	57%
Turnout rate in 1988	62%

(as percentage of voting age population)

POPULATION AND GROWTH

1980 population	690,768
1988 population estimate (45th in the nation)	713,000
Percent change 1980-1988	+3

DEMOGRAPHIC BREAKDOWN

White	93%
Black	0.3%
American Indian	7%
(Spanish origin)	1%
Urban	46%
Rural	54%
Born in state	71%
Foreign-born	1%

MAJOR CITIES

Sioux Falls	97,550
Rapid City	52,480
Aberdeen	25,670
Watertown	16,670
Brookings	14,800

AREA AND LAND USE

Area 75,952 sq. miles (16th)

Farm	90%
Forest	3%
Federally owned	6%

Gov. George S. Mickelson (R)
Of Brookings — Elected 1986

Born: Jan. 31, 1941, Mobridge, S.D.
Education: U. of South Dakota, B.S. 1963, J.D. 1965.
Military Career: Army, 1965-69.
Occupation: Lawyer.
Religion: Methodist.
Political Career: Brookings County state's attorney, 1970-74; S.D. House 1975-81, Speaker 1978-79.
Next Election: 1990.

WORK

Occupations

White-collar	45%
Blue-collar	24%
Service workers	15%

Government Workers

Federal	9,098
State	16,661
Local	34,654

MONEY

Median family income	$ 15,993	(48th)
Tax burden per capita	$ 502	(49th)

EDUCATION

Spending per pupil through grade 12	$ 3,051	(41st)
Persons with college degrees	14%	(36th)

CRIME

Violent crime rate 120 per 100,000 (49th)

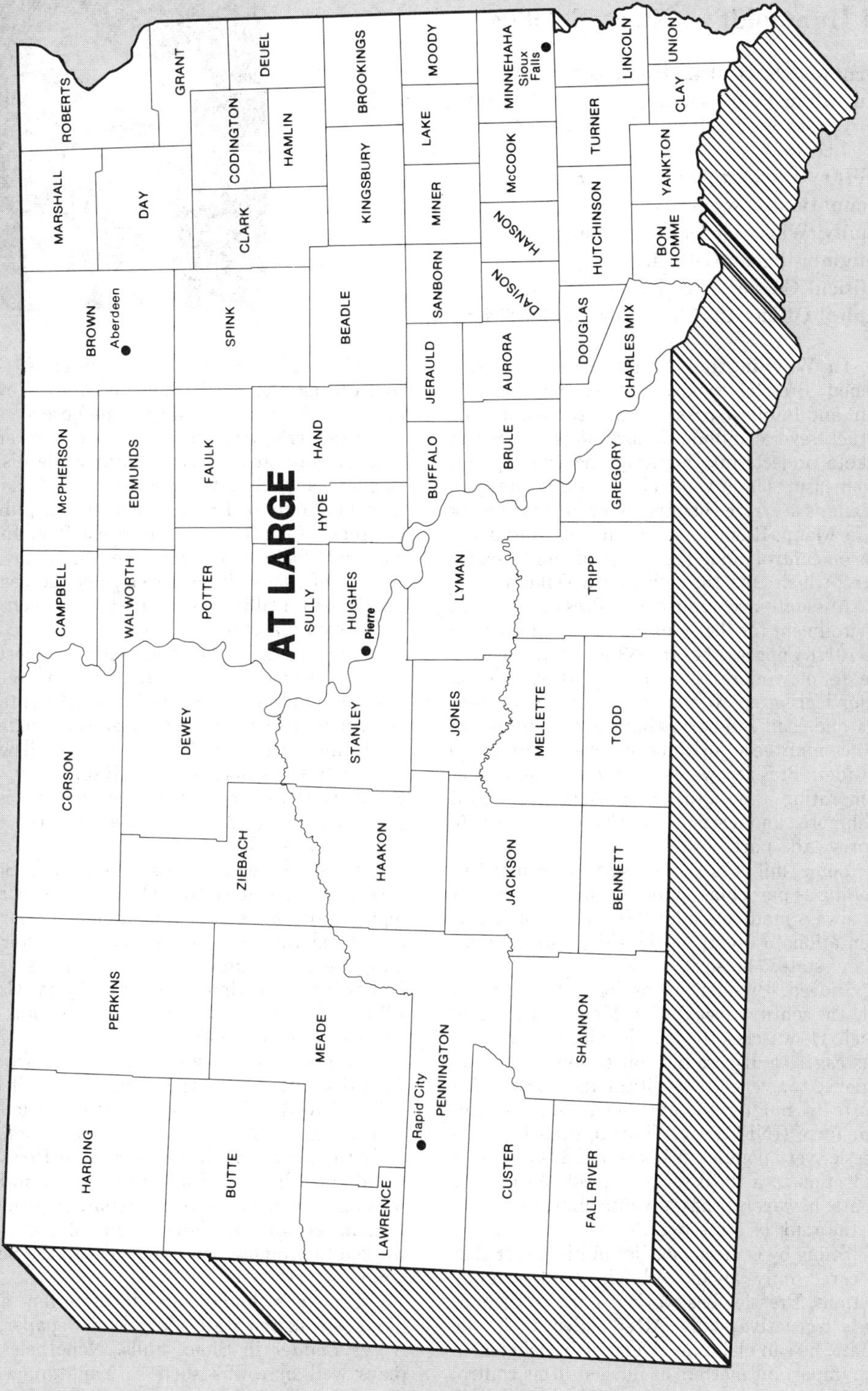
AT LARGE
ROBERTS
GRANT
DEUEL
BROOKINGS
MOODY
MINNEHAHA
Sioux Falls
LINCOLN
UNION
MARSHALL
DAY
CODINGTON
HAMLIN
KINGSBURY
LAKE
McCOOK
TURNER
CLAY
CLARK
MINER
HANSON
HUTCHINSON
YANKTON
BON HOMME
BROWN
Aberdeen
SPINK
BEADLE
SANBORN
DAVISON
DOUGLAS
CHARLES MIX
JERAULD
AURORA
McPHERSON
EDMUNDS
FAULK
HAND
BUFFALO
BRULE
GREGORY
HYDE
CAMPBELL
WALWORTH
POTTER
SULLY
HUGHES
Pierre
LYMAN
TRIPP
CORSON
DEWEY
STANLEY
JONES
MELLETTE
TODD
ZIEBACH
HAAKON
JACKSON
BENNETT
PERKINS
MEADE
PENNINGTON
Rapid City
SHANNON
HARDING
BUTTE
LAWRENCE
CUSTER
FALL RIVER

Larry Pressler (R)

Of Humboldt — Elected 1978

Born: March 29, 1942, Humboldt, S.D.
Education: U. of South Dakota, B.A. 1964; attended Oxford U., England, 1965; Harvard U., M.A. 1971, J.D. 1971.
Military Career: Army, 1966-68.
Occupation: Lawyer.
Family: Wife, Harriet Dent; one stepchild.
Religion: Roman Catholic.
Political Career: U.S. House, 1975-79.
Capitol Office: 133 Hart Bldg. 20510; 224-5842.

In Washington: As the 100th Congress opened, Pressler took a seat on the Environment and Public Works Committee, just in time to tuck several million dollars' worth of South Dakota projects into highway and water pollution measures later vetoed by President Reagan. Pressler's override vote helped ensure road work at the Mount Rushmore National Memorial and erosion control along the banks of the Missouri River, which cuts through South Dakota.

Mission accomplished, Pressler traded Environment for the Banking Committee as the the 101st Congress began. While he arrived too late to play more than a supporting role on major legislation to bail out the troubled savings and loan industry, there is the matter of the committee's jurisdiction over coinage to consider: Pressler wants to mint a coin commemorating the 50th anniversary of Mount Rushmore, and earmark half the proceeds to improve the park.

Some might see this sort of committee hopping as parochial opportunism. But Pressler has always made plain his "South Dakota first" orientation. "I do err on the side of looking out for my state," he says.

Indeed, Pressler seems loath to stray far from the sentiments expressed in the office mail pouch. He watches the mail log like a hawk, and is as eager to discuss his constituent service (a response to every letter within 48 hours) as his efforts to modify the intermediate-range nuclear-force (INF) treaty. This approach makes Pressler very popular at home and a favorite for re-election to a third term in 1990. Within the Senate, however, it has left him short of attaining the rank of statesman.

Stung by criticism earlier in his career that he cared only about publicity and winning elections, Pressler has worked hard to demonstrate legislative skills. After a decade in the Senate, he can claim involvement in debates on such important matters as nuclear arms control and U.S. policy toward South Africa. But in building a case for himself as a serious legislator, Pressler did not help his cause by casting himself as Hamlet for the nightly news — his role during the 1989 drama of John Tower's nomination to be secretary of defense.

Pressler's was one of the few uncertain Republican votes on Tower. But while his colleague Nancy Landon Kassebaum of Kansas kept her counsel, Pressler deliberated publicly whether to confirm or not to confirm. In the days just before the vote, he was a favorite subject of media interviewers, and he seemed unable or unwilling to avoid sharing each step in his soul-searching.

Pressler said he had serious questions about Tower's ability to reform procurement practices and mismanagement at the Pentagon. Of particular concern to Pressler were the faulty electronics in the 34 B-1 bombers at Ellsworth Air Force Base, located near Rapid City, S.D. Before the vote, Pressler received specific assurances from the White House that the B-1s would be fixed. In the end, he voted for Tower.

As a rule, when Pressler is near, a South Dakota angle is never far. One of his legislative high points was a 1980 amendment to bar the use of federal funds to enforce the Carter administration's grain embargo against the Soviet Union. The amendment, opposed by the Carter White House, passed the Senate but was dropped later in conference.

Nonetheless, it was a signal of growing farm discontent with the embargo, and it contributed to the change of attitude that led the Reagan administration to cancel the embargo early the next year. It also enhanced Pressler's standing with South Dakota farmers, who have sent only Democrats to the Senate Agriculture Committee for two decades. Pressler also has worked to promote new grain sales to the Soviet Union.

Pressler's home-state focus often earns him scorn in the state's largest newspaper, the *Argus Leader* in Sioux Falls. Nonetheless, it plays well in towns such as Yankton, where after the local college shut down, Pressler combed the federal bureaucracy until he could find an agency willing to use its campus. The

Bureau of Prisons complied, making plans for a minimum-security prison on the site.

The state's second largest industry is tourism, so it was not surprising that Pressler's first act as the newly installed chairman of the Commerce Subcommittee on Business, Trade and Tourism in 1981 was to move on a tourism promotion bill that had passed the Senate in the previous Congress but was vetoed by President Carter. By the end of January, Pressler had pushed it through the Senate again, taking the Reagan administration by surprise and earning its opposition to the independent agency he proposed. Congress eventually cleared a tourism promotion bill, creating an office within the Commerce Department rather than the independent agency Pressler wanted.

Sensing an opening for the South Dakota School of Mines and Technology, Pressler has worked for several years to develop policy and authorize a program of continental drilling to explore the Earth's crust. He has also used his seat on the Commerce, Science and Transportation Committee to take on other constituent crusades. He has protected a federal satellite data center in his state and advocated for short-line railroads crucial to the farm economy.

For all the credit these activities earn Pressler at home, in Washington he still is prone to come across as unpredictable. In the early 1989 confirmation hearings of Secretary of State James A. Baker III, Pressler asked him about the Middle East and European trade before zeroing in on the diplomatic status of San Marino, a tiny mountain republic in eastern Italy. Though Baker conceded ignorance, the snickers in the audience did not stem from the secretary's geopolitical naiveté.

During an early 1987 hearing on the Nicaraguan contras, Pressler asked whether the contra forces would begin carrying out acts of terrorism. When an administration spokesman demurred, insisting that the contras would hit only military targets, Pressler responded, "I'm not saying that acts of terrorism are all necessarily bad."

Pressler might not have to be working so hard to burnish his reputation had he not launched his Senate career with a brief and implausible campaign for president in 1980. He argued the advantage of his youth (he was 37) and talked about the need to promote rural America. He withdrew after 105 days in which he raised little money, was left out of a key debate in Iowa and failed to carry on long enough to reach the voting in Iowa or New Hampshire. Hardly anyone took his credentials seriously, and when he returned to the chamber early in 1980, he had a reputation for being a little flaky.

But the presidential campaign did lead to his most priceless national attention. Late in 1979, FBI agents posing as Arab sheiks invited him to a Georgetown house to offer him a bribe, knowing that he badly needed money for his presidential effort. Pressler refused to have anything to do with the offer, and stormed out of the meeting. It briefly made him a minor hero. "I turned down an illegal contribution," he said afterward. "Where have we come to if that's considered heroic?"

On the Foreign Relations Committee, Pressler over the years has exhibited a strong streak of independence. He is an important swing vote who often joins with the Democrats.

At first, he opposed the INF treaty ratified in 1988. He voted against it in committee and then tried to amend it on the floor, tying it to a reduction in Warsaw Pact conventional forces. The amendment was defeated and he went on to vote for the treaty, saying his chief objections had been answered in other amendments.

He backed mild economic sanctions against South Africa in 1985, but when a harsher sanctions bill was proposed in 1986, Pressler opposed it. After a visit to South Africa, Pressler said he felt that the government there was moving toward reform, and that harsher sanctions would only hurt those they were intended to help.

Although he and his allies could do little to stop the 1986 sanctions bill, Pressler was able to win a significant change of some importance to South Dakota. The Senate agreed with his proposal to drop a provision authorizing the president to sell U.S. gold stocks in order to reduce the world price of gold. That move was designed to damage South Africa's gold-exporting economy, but it also would have hurt the gold miners of South Dakota's Black Hills.

Pressler has also used his position on Foreign Relations to press for talks with the Soviets on banning weapons from space and to seek greater aid for Greece. He was a prominent opponent of military aid to Turkey in the 98th Congress. Reducing assistance to that country, Pressler argued, would pressure Turkey to make concessions in its dispute with Greece over the island of Cyprus.

Pressler has been a consistent opponent of congressional pay raises and any mechanism that grants them without an up-or-down vote. In 1976, he challenged the constitutionality of federal pay law in court. Through the years he repeatedly sought to block raises or force votes. In early 1989, Pressler's amendment was the vehicle used by the Senate to reject a proposed 51 percent raise.

At Home: Pressler's boyish charm swept a Democrat out of the House in the Democratic year of 1974, and his reputation for being unpretentious and independent-minded has kept him strong ever since.

When a 1977 *Wall Street Journal* article labeled Pressler an image-conscious, do-little legislator, the home-state reaction was overwhelmingly in his favor. Constituents felt the

Eastern press was picking on a local hero who still rode his tractor in county fair parades. The next year, Pressler moved up to the Senate, winning by a 2-to-1 margin. His quixotic 1979 foray into presidential campaigning was forgotten when he sought re-election to the Senate in 1984. He won a second term by a 3-to-1 margin.

From the beginning, Pressler offered his state a political persona that was hard to resist: the good-natured, unassuming farm boy who succeeded early in life on sheer talent. His Rhodes scholarship and his Harvard master's degree combined perfectly with his roots on the Humboldt farm, still his official residence.

Those attributes were more than enough to give Pressler his 1974 victory over Democratic Rep. Frank Denholm. Pressler campaigned as a moderate Republican, noting his membership in Common Cause and criticizing South Dakota's Oahe irrigation project on environmental grounds. He took 55 percent. In 1976, he easily won a second term.

Democratic Sen. James Abourezk chose to retire in 1978, and Pressler began the campaign year as odds-on favorite to succeed him. That never changed, even though Democrats had a competent challenger in former Rapid City Mayor Don Barnett. Pressler had built enormous good will through his faithful attendance at events all over the state, and through conspicuous gestures such as donating a House pay increase to charity.

In 1984, Democrats offered George Cunningham, a longtime aide to former South Dakota Sen. George McGovern. Probably the nation's most colorful Senate loser that year, Cunningham denounced Pressler as a "flash-dancing, Fred Astaire type, blow-dried, cellophane-wrapped representation ... who deals more with public relations than with public policy." Pressler ignored the criticism. Cunningham admitted early in the year that his polling numbers were "in the toilet," and that is where they stayed. Pressler won 74 percent.

Pressler was one of the first senators to support Kansas Sen. Robert Dole's 1988 presidential bid, and some prominent in-state Republicans thought he carried his loyalty to Dole too far when he told the Sioux Falls *Argus Leader* in July 1988 that if he were running in 1988, "I would have serious problems getting re-elected with Bush on the ticket." He added, "If Bush is president when I run for re-election in 1990, I think I would have a tough time. I am not sure I could be re-elected."

Seven leading Republicans in the state Legislature sent Pressler a letter accusing him of the "most selfish, self-serving example of politics at its worst" and charging that Pressler did not care about the GOP's chances in 1988.

Committees

Banking, Housing and Urban Affairs (9th of 9 Republicans)
Housing and Urban Affairs; Securities

Commerce, Science and Transportation (3rd of 9 Republicans)
Science, Technology and Space (ranking); Communications; Surface Transportation; National Ocean Policy Study

Foreign Relations (5th of 9 Republicans)
European Affairs (ranking); Near Eastern and South Asian Affairs

Small Business (3rd of 9 Republicans)
Export Expansion (ranking); Rural Economy and Family Farming

Special Aging (3rd of 9 Republicans)

Elections

1984 General

Larry Pressler (R)	235,176	(74%)
George V. Cunningham (D)	80,537	(26%)

Previous Winning Percentages: **1978** (67%) **1976 *** (80%) **1974 *** (55%)

* *House elections.*

Campaign Finance

	Receipts	Receipts from PACs	Expend-itures
1984			
Pressler (R)	$1,249,604	$522,649 (42%)	$938,709
Cunningham (D)	$174,268	$83,721 (48%)	$166,426

Key Votes

1987	
Enact omnibus highway bill over Reagan veto	Y
Limit testing of space-based anti-ballistic missiles	N
Oppose banning tests of larger nuclear weapons	Y
Confirm Robert H. Bork as Supreme Court justice	Y
1988	
Allow vote on campaign-finance overhaul	N
Pass civil rights restoration bill over Reagan veto	N
Enact omnibus trade bill over Reagan veto	N
Approve death penalty for drug-related murders	Y
Oppose "workfare" amendment to welfare overhaul bill	N

Voting Studies

	Presidential Support		Party Unity		Conservative Coalition	
Year	**S**	**O**	**S**	**O**	**S**	**O**
1988	73	25	88	10	97	3
1987	63	37	75	20	81	13
1986	77	20	72	25	82	16
1985	74	25	72	24	78	15
1984	61	39	50	44	72	23
1983	59	31	64	31	80	16
1982	70	24	67	20	77	13
1981	61	24	58	32	63	27

Interest Group Ratings

Year	ADA	ACU	AFL-CIO	CCUS
1988	0	96	29	79
1987	25	81	50	82
1986	10	86	33	68
1985	10	74	20	71
1984	45	45	55	71
1983	20	57	33	50
1982	10	67	35	70
1981	30	43	41	67

Tom Daschle (D)

Of Aberdeen — Elected 1986

Born: Dec. 9, 1947, Aberdeen, S.D.
Education: South Dakota State U., B.A. 1969.
Military Career: Air Force, 1969-72.
Occupation: Congressional aide.
Family: Wife, Linda Hall; three children.
Religion: Roman Catholic.
Political Career: U.S. House, 1979-87.
Capitol Office: 317 Hart Bldg. 20510; 224-2321.

In Washington: No one would have expected Daschle, an activist House veteran and former Senate aide, to settle for a backbencher's role when he moved to the Senate. Even so, his rise to prominence there has been so rapid as to leave him mindful that a misstep would invite either jealous senators or suspicious South Dakotans to bring him down a peg, or worse.

But the fact that Daschle is conscious of that danger explains why it is unlikely. Over the years, he has assiduously tended to his state, returning there often and stressing farm issues while in Washington, thus tempering any skepticism that he is another liberal "gone national" in the manner of George McGovern, whom voters ousted in 1980. In the Senate, Daschle is known for his ambition and his revolutionary rhetoric about changing its slow, tradition-bound ways: "Simply to come here and work in a museum is not my idea of a modern legislative process," he once said. But those traits are offset by his engaging, almost deferential personality and his recognized ability to work within the system.

He has shown a genius not only for the right political issues, but also for the right mentors. Months before his election, he became the first Democrat in what would be the large and savvy 1986 class to endorse Robert C. Byrd's re-election as majority leader; Byrd in turn engineered Daschle's seating on the most prestigious committee, Finance. When Byrd stepped aside in 1988, Daschle emerged as point man for the ultimate winner of a three-way succession race, George J. Mitchell; Mitchell then named Daschle co-chairman of the Democratic Policy Comittee, a post previously held exclusively by the party leader.

As policy chairman, Daschle drafted Senate Democrats' agenda for the 101st Congress. Characteristically, however, he did so only after careful consultations with others, notably the proud committee chairmen. Daschle puts a premium on collegiality, frequenting a senators-only lunchroom, for example, to pick up intelligence and build the social relationships that grease legislative wheels. He resists the aloof, go-it-alone style typical of the Senate, even objecting that it, unlike the House, assigns floor seating: "Camaraderie develops when you can move around," he said. "The chemistry of intermixing — the collegiality — is very important to the way the House gets its work done."

In the Senate, Daschle has concentrated on the same two causes that dominated his House work, agriculture and veterans. On both Finance and the Agriculture Committee, he has been able to benefit South Dakota's economically depressed farmers. In Finance during the 100th Congress, he helped repeal new taxes on farmers' diesel fuel and heifers, and added amendments to the trade bill that would both encourage U.S. agricultural exports and threaten retaliation against foreign farm-import barriers.

In Agriculture, he led the resistance (as he did in the House) to Reagan administration efforts to cut crop price-support subsidies, and he continued to work for federal assistance to the infant ethanol industry. Daschle became better placed to help that industry, which relies on Midwestern farm crops to manufacture alternative fuel, when he assumed the chairmanship of the Agricultural Research and General Legislation Subcommittee in 1989.

Though not a member of the Veterans' Affairs Committee, as he was in the House, Daschle is a co-chairman of Vietnam-era Veterans in Congress and, from that platform, he persists in his campaign to compensate Vietnam veterans for illnesses believed caused by exposure to the chemical defoliant Agent Orange.

In the 98th Congress, he won House passage of a bill requiring the government to presume that certain illnesses were caused by the chemical; the compromise that became law was a first-step approach directing the Veterans Administration to set guidelines for compensation. But in 1988, the House rejected his Senate amendment for comprehensive Agent Orange benefits. Meanwhile, he lent key Senate support to help pass a House bill providing disability payments to cancer victims among World

War II-era veterans who were exposed to atomic fallout in Japan or at U.S. bombing test sites.

Despite his charm and disarming candor, Daschle was a controversial figure in his earlier years at the House Agriculture Committee. Many of his proposals there went beyond anything likely to become law. They tended to put members of both parties in a spot, skeptical of the sums he wanted for farm subsidies but reluctant to oppose them.

Daschle figured the more ambitious the plan, the more farmers would end up with in the final compromise. But some Republicans condemned his projects, such as a 1981 farm crisis bill, as political demagoguery, and at times Daschle's high-pressure approach even brought conflict with his own party leadership. In 1981, then-Majority Whip Thomas S. Foley, House Democrats' leading agriculture strategist, refused to sponsor the farm crisis bill. It failed in committee on a tie vote.

Generally, however, Daschle was a leadership favorite. He was close to Ways and Means Committee Chairman Dan Rostenkowski, and was an effective insider on Steering and Policy, which makes committee assignments for House Democrats.

Early in 1985, Daschle's shrewd moves were the foundation for his successful Senate bid the next year. He attracted national attention as chief sponsor of a multibillion-dollar effort to advance credit to struggling farmers so they could stay in business another year. President Reagan vetoed the bill, but Daschle succeeded in reinforcing his image as a defender of his state's agriculture while his rival, GOP Sen. James Abdnor, had to struggle against being linked to administration stinginess.

A few months later, Daschle voted against the comprehensive five-year farm bill that passed the House, arguing that its price-support levels were much too low. Abdnor voted for the bill, giving Daschle a valuable campaign issue. In preference to the approach taken in the bill, Daschle supports proposals aimed at raising farm prices by imposing strict production controls on wheat and feed grains. To conservatives, that smacks of Soviet-style central planning.

At Home: When Daschle first began planning his Senate campaign, he was considered one of the Democrats' surest bets in 1986. The farm economy was on the ropes, and incumbent Abdnor had a reputation as bumbling and ineffective.

But Abdnor exceeded expectations, and Daschle needed all the organization and persistence he could muster to eke out a victory.

Abdnor faced a primary challenge from bombastic GOP Gov. William J. Janklow, who hammered at his support for Reagan farm policies and his inability to get things done. But Abdnor's consultants moved aggressively to inoculate the senator against charges of ineffectiveness, starting an extensive TV ad campaign in late 1985. Abdnor, whose amiable and low-key nature had endeared him to voters for nearly three decades, scored a strong primary victory.

Daschle then faced the challenge of framing the November contest as a referendum on Abdnor's politics, not his personality. The challenger showed considerable skill at controlling the campaign debate, and Abdnor handed him an issue shortly after the primary, when he stumbled at a forum by suggesting that farmers might have to "sell below cost" in order to become competitive.

In a long-running TV ad, Daschle showed Abdnor giving his faltering "below cost" explanation and then made his own forceful argument for a fair price for farmers. Abdnor said his remarks were misinterpreted, but his explanation of an explanation of an already complex subject did not erase the original flub.

The contest tightened considerably in the fall, however, with two visits by President Reagan and a bevy of personal attacks on Daschle over the airwaves. In his ads, Abdnor linked Daschle with actress and former anti-war activist Jane Fonda, who had been pictured with Daschle at a fund-raiser. Abdnor hoped to tie Daschle not only to Fonda's liberal reputation, but also to her efforts, in her health books, to discourage the consumption of red meat. Promoting vegetarianism in meat-producing South Dakota is a political felony.

Despite the Fonda connection and a concerted effort by media consultant Roger Ailes to convince the electorate that Abdnor was quietly effective, Daschle prevailed with his contention that Abdnor was instead effectively quiet. Daschle's massive effort to turn out the farm vote, along with his late October charge that Abdnor had voted to cut Social Security, gave him a narrow victory.

Daschle won his House seat originally on sheer energy. In a year, he and his first wife rang more than 40,000 doorbells as they campaigned to win the 1978 Democratic primary over Frank Denholm, the former representative favored to win, and then defeat Republican nominee Leo Thorsness.

The 1st District was vacant in 1978 because incumbent Larry Pressler was running for the Senate. Early in the year, it seemed likely to stay Republican for Thorsness, a former prisoner of war in Vietnam who had drawn 47 percent of the statewide vote in a 1974 challenge to Sen. McGovern.

But Daschle's non-stop campaign brought him even with Thorsness by summer's end, and a few weeks before the election, Daschle looked like an easy winner. At that point, however, Republicans began taking advantage of Daschle's two liabilities — his opposition to an anti-abortion amendment and his promise to vote against right-to-work laws.

By Election Day, the contest was close again; only a final canvass a week later gave Daschle the seat by 139 votes.

Daschle's 1978 campaign had considerable assistance from the remnants of Sen. James Abourezk's Democratic organization, since Abourezk was not seeking re-election. Daschle had become familiar with politics and legislation while working for Abourezk as a legislative assistant. He moved back to South Dakota in late 1976 to become field director for Abourezk and to prepare his own campaign.

It took all of Daschle's ingenuity and public relations skill to win re-election in 1982, when South Dakota's two districts were merged in reapportionment and he met the state's other House incumbent, Republican Clint Roberts.

The contest not only matched the two parties but also the two regions of the state. Daschle represented the Corn Belt territory of eastern South Dakota; Roberts spoke for the western ranching counties. The Republican's homespun conservative style — he wore his cowboy boots on the House floor — reflected western South Dakota's traditional resentment against a liberal Washington establishment.

Roberts tried to pin the Eastern label on Daschle, pointing out that while he had been running a ranch, Daschle had been on a government payroll most of his adult life. But Daschle fought back effectively, telling voters that what the state needed in Congress was not a farmer, but someone who knew how to write farm bills. Daschle had been traveling throughout the state for two years in preparation for the match; he was ahead in name recognition even in some of Roberts' areas. Roberts had the money to compete with Daschle, and his anti-establishment campaign brought him close to an upset. He took virtually every county in his old district, but Daschle managed 59 percent in his eastern territory, for 52 percent overall.

In 1984, challenger Dale Bell had an enormous Republican tide going for him in the state, and sufficient funding from national GOP sources. He also had a talent for attracting media attention — but too much of it was unfavorable. Bell distributed cards to voters with questions and answers critical of the incumbent, but failed to identify his own campaign as the source of them. Daschle called the tactic "sleazy," some of the state's newspapers agreed, and Bell agreed to stop doing it. Daschle bucked the statewide GOP trend with a comfortable 57 percent victory.

Committees

Agriculture, Nutrition and Forestry (8th of 10 Democrats)
Agricultural Research and General Legislation (chairman); Agricultural Credit; Rural Development and Rural Electrification

Finance (11th of 11 Democrats)
International Trade; Medicare and Long-Term Care; Social Security and Family Policy

Select Indian Affairs (4th of 5 Democrats)
Special Committee on Investigations

Elections

1986 General

Tom Daschle (D)	152,657	(52%)
James Abdnor (R)	143,173	(48%)

Previous Winning Percentages: **1984** * (57%) **1982** * (52%) **1980** * (66%) **1978** * (50%)

* *House elections.*

Campaign Finance

	Receipts	Receipts from PACs	Expend-itures
1986			
Daschle (D)	$3,515,482	$1,153,906 (33%)	$3,485,870
Abdnor (R)	$3,306,567	$1,076,326 (33%)	$3,291,101

Key Votes

1987

Enact omnibus highway bill over Reagan veto	Y
Limit testing of space-based anti-ballistic missiles	Y
Oppose banning tests of larger nuclear weapons	N
Confirm Robert H. Bork as Supreme Court justice	N

1988

Allow vote on campaign-finance overhaul	Y
Pass civil rights restoration bill over Reagan veto	Y
Enact omnibus trade bill over Reagan veto	Y
Approve death penalty for drug-related murders	Y
Oppose "workfare" amendment to welfare overhaul bill	Y

Voting Studies

	Presidential Support		Party Unity		Conservative Coalition	
Year	**S**	**O**	**S**	**O**	**S**	**O**
1988	44	52	91	6	30	70
1987	37	62	88	12	44	53
House Service						
1986	20	80	84	15	44	56
1985	16	71	83	9	33	55
1984	32	60	67	17	41	53
1983	16	76	75	12	42	51
1982	31	62	80	14	34	56
1981	42	57	77	17	37	60

Interest Group Ratings

Year	ADA	ACU	AFL-CIO	CCUS
1988	85	13	93	36
1987	85	8	89	33
House Service				
1986	80	18	64	22
1985	70	16	60	38
1984	70	17	46	50
1983	75	17	71	42
1982	80	40	89	35
1981	70	20	71	22

AL Tim Johnson (D)

Of Vermillion — Elected 1986

Born: Dec. 28, 1946, Canton, S.D.
Education: U. of South Dakota, B.A. 1969, M.A. 1970, J.D. 1975.
Occupation: Lawyer.
Family: Wife, Barbara Brooks; three children.
Religion: Lutheran.
Political Career: S.D. House, 1979-83; S.D. Senate, 1983-87.
Capitol Office: 513 Cannon Bldg. 20515; 225-2801.

In Washington: Johnson initially comes across as a more reticent person than the Democrat he replaced in the House — now-Sen. Tom Daschle — but his quiet and thoughtful style earned him solid marks in his freshman term. He spent a good bit of time in his first two years getting to know his constituency better, a big job in his case, since he serves all of South Dakota. In the 101st Congress, with a major new farm reauthorization bill on the horizon, Johnson will be someone to watch on the Agriculture Committee, for he has the tenacity and temperament to be a key player.

Johnson is particularly concerned with oats, a crop South Dakota leads the nation in harvesting. In 1987, he added his Oats Promotion Act to the budget "reconciliation" bill. The measure allowed more oats to be planted in 1988-90, exempting the crop from acreage limitation requirements.

Johnson worked with South Dakota Sens. Daschle and Republican Larry Pressler in 1988 to pass a bill authorizing a $100 million water project for south-central South Dakota. The Mni Wiconi project was needed, Johnson said, because the water in the area contained unsafe levels of chemicals, minerals and other impurities.

During House debate on the 1988 omnibus drug bill, Johnson won approval for his amendment concerning drunken driving. His proposal provided grants to states to implement an anti-drunken-driving enforcement program, but only if the state requires immediate suspension of the driver's license of anyone found driving while drunk.

At Home: A knack for organization and a instinct for knowing how to deal with an opponent who was his own worst enemy propelled Johnson to a resounding first-term victory in 1986. During a political year dominated by militant farm protest on the Dakota plains, Johnson managed to succeed without being a farmer or sounding militant about any subject under discussion.

Johnson's campaign came a long way in a short time. A little-known state senator from the extreme southeast corner of the state, he had not even been the early favorite in his own party to capture the seat left open by Daschle's Senate candidacy.

To win the Democratic nomination, Johnson had to defeat a folksy state senator with longstanding farm credentials; state Sen. Jim Burg had received national publicity when he led a delegation of state legislators on a farm protest mission to Washington in 1985.

The cerebral Johnson, who was one of only two attorneys in the state Senate, sometimes sounded like he was arguing a case when he was socializing with voters. But a strong organization and a sophisticated direct-mail effort lifted him to a narrow primary victory.

The Republican nominee, Dale Bell, began with widespread name recognition stemming from two previous statewide campaigns. But Bell's belligerent ideological conservatism and the contentious nature of his earlier campaigns left him with negative ratings that amounted to a political consultant's nightmare. In a state ripe with resentment of Reagan administration farm policies, 1986 was not a year for a Republican candidate already loaded down with political baggage.

Johnson's strategy was to avoid controversy and make himself the vehicle for Bell's critics in both parties; he presented himself simply as a moderate and experienced alternative to Bell. In the Legislature, Johnson had maintained friendly relations with both sides and worked well with GOP Gov. William J. Janklow. His approach won him backing from the state's major banking interests and the Realtors' association.

Bell tried labeling Johnson a George McGovern liberal and a captive of special interests. At the same time, Bell, whose strength had always been among "movement conservatives," tried to distance himself from Reagan farm policies, developing an opposition-style theme of "Send them a message." The voters sent Bell a message instead, giving Johnson victories in 53 of the state's 66 counties.

In 1988, the state's leading Republicans

South Dakota — At Large

The Missouri River running north to south through the center of South Dakota divides not only the geography and economy of the state, but also its political predilections.

The flat, rich farm land east of the river holds two-thirds of the state's population and nourishes an agricultural economy based on corn. Voters in the east are the most likely to support Democrats in this normally Republican state. "West River" is rolling, arid grassland suited for grazing and ranching. Most voters there are staunch Republicans.

The primacy of corn is symbolized by the Corn Palace in Mitchell, an auditorium whose exterior is festooned with mosaics made from colored corn cobs. Corn feeds cattle and hogs, and it provides the largest share of agricultural income in the state.

Not far from Mitchell is the focal point of eastern South Dakota and the state's largest metropolis, Sioux Falls. A city of 97,000, it is a service center whose banks, insurance companies and farm implement dealers are all tied closely to the agricultural economy.

Efforts to diversify the economy have succeeded in attracting banking credit card operations to the two major cities and light manufacturing to eastern towns such as Watertown and Brookings. Automotive parts and plastics plants have crossed the border from Minnesota, attracted by South Dakota's comparatively low taxes and regulatory costs.

On the western side of the Missouri, the towns are fewer. The land, used for grazing, gradually turns from green to brown. The relatively sedate farms of the east are contrasted with the cowboy and rodeo country of the west. Near the western border of the state is South Dakota's second-largest city, Rapid City, with a population over 52,000. Originally a market for surrounding ranchers and farmers, it grew rapidly in the 1970s and has now settled into a prosperity matched only by Sioux Falls. Tourism has been an important factor in the growth: The Badlands, the Black Hills and Mount Rushmore are nearby. Adding to population growth near Rapid City are retirees who come to live in the Black Hills.

The west-central and southwestern parts of the state are home to many Indians who have returned to the reservations from jobs that disappeared in the Midwestern industrial centers. Of the six counties west of the Missouri won by Democrat Tom Daschle in his close 1986 Senate contest, five were on reservations.

The partisan balance is more even now than in the 1970s, when Democrats controlled the governorship, the Legislature, both Senate seats and one of two House seats through much of the decade. In 1986, Republican George S. Mickelson succeeded William J. Janklow as governor, but farm unrest helped Daschle capture the Senate seat held by Republican James Abdnor, and Johnson took Daschle's place in the House.

Disenchantment with the Reagan administration's farm policy hindered George Bush's 1988 presidential bid, both in the Republican primary and in November against Democratic nominee Michael S. Dukakis. Bush won the state over Dukakis with 53 percent, well below Ronald Reagan's 60 percent-plus showings in 1980 and 1984. Dukakis became only the second Democratic presidential candidate since 1936 to win Minnehaha County (Sioux Falls).

Population: 690,768. White 639,669 (93%), Black 2,144 (0.3%), American Indian, Eskimo and Aleut 44,968 (7%). Spanish origin 4,023 (1%). 18 and over 485,162 (70%), 65 and over 91,019 (13%). Median age: 29.

assessed their chances of unseating Johnson and chose to skip the race. Janklow and former GOP Sen. James Abdnor declined to challenge Johnson, leaving state Treasurer David Volk to lead the GOP charge. Despite having won statewide elections since 1972, Volk was relatively little known by voters, since the treasurer's job is not a high-visibility one.

Unlike in 1986, the GOP united behind their candidate in 1988; prominent Republicans such as Janklow, Abdnor and Gov. George S. Mickelson held fund-raisers for Volk and pledged their support.

Unfortunately for Volk, Johnson's cautious first-term record gave the Republican no compelling ammunition. For that reason, much of Volk's campaign dwelt on a single issue — campaign finance. Volk spent his time criticizing Johnson's acceptance of political action committee money (Volk refused to take PAC contributions).

The PAC attack failed to impress voters. Johnson carried every county in the state on the way to a 72 percent victory, keeping alive a 90-

year streak: South Dakota voters have not unseated a freshman House member in a general election since 1898.

Johnson's victory — the biggest statewide winning margin for a Democrat and the second-largest for any candidate in state history — sparked talk that he might run for higher office. Pressler is up for re-election in 1990, but Johnson is unlikely to make a move that soon.

Committees

Agriculture (19th of 27 Democrats)
Forests, Family Farms and Energy; Livestock, Dairy and Poultry; Wheat, Soybeans and Feed Grains

Veterans' Affairs (14th of 21 Democrats)
Hospitals and Health Care

Elections

1988 General		
Tim Johnson (D)	223,759	(72%)
David Volk (R)	88,157	(28%)
1986 General		
Tim Johnson (D)	171,462	(59%)
Dale Bell (R)	118,261	(41%)

District Vote For President

	1988	1984	1980	1976
D	145,560 (47%)	116,113 (37%)	103,855 (32%)	147,068 (49%)
R	165,415 (53%)	200,267 (63%)	198,343 (61%)	151,505 (50%)
I			21,431 (7%)	

Campaign Finance

	Receipts	Receipts from PACs	Expend-itures
1988			
Johnson (D)	$676,225	$329,446 (49%)	$632,105
Volk (R)	$200,733	0	$199,420
1986			
Johnson (D)	$438,138	$230,864 (53%)	$430,806
Bell (R)	$482,392	$140,919 (29%)	$483,294

Key Votes

1987	
Raise speed limit to 65 mph	Y
Approve Gephardt "fair trade" amendment	Y
Ban testing of larger nuclear weapons	Y
Delay "re-flagging" of Kuwaiti tankers	Y
Approve tax-raising deficit-reduction bill	N
1988	
Approve aid to Nicaraguan contras	N
Enact civil rights restoration bill over Reagan veto	Y
Kill 60-day plant-closing notification measure	N
Pass omnibus trade bill over Reagan veto	Y
Approve death penalty for drug-related murders	Y
Bar federal funds for abortions in cases of rape and incest	Y
Oppose seven-day waiting period for purchase of handguns	Y

Voting Studies

	Presidential Support		Party Unity		Conservative Coalition	
Year	**S**	**O**	**S**	**O**	**S**	**O**
1988	25	75	77	22	66	34
1987	26	74	84	14	56	44

Interest Group Ratings

Year	ADA	ACU	AFL-CIO	CCUS
1988	70	28	93	36
1987	80	13	81	27

Tennessee

U.S. CONGRESS

SENATE 2 D
HOUSE 6 D, 3 R

LEGISLATURE

Senate 22 D, 11 R
House 59 D, 40 R

ELECTIONS

1988 Presidential Vote	
Bush	58%
Dukakis	42%
1984 Presidential Vote	
Reagan	58%
Mondale	42%
1980 Presidential Vote	
Reagan	49%
Carter	48%
Anderson	2%
Turnout rate in 1984	49%
Turnout rate in 1986	31%
Turnout rate in 1988	45%

(as percentage of voting age population)

POPULATION AND GROWTH

1980 population	4,591,120
1988 population estimate (16th in the nation)	4,895,000
Percent change 1980-1988	+7%

DEMOGRAPHIC BREAKDOWN

White	84%
Black	16%
(Spanish origin)	1%
Urban	60%
Rural	40%
Born in state	72%
Foreign-born	1%

MAJOR CITIES

Memphis	652,640
Nashville-Davidson	473,670
Knoxville	173,210
Chattanooga	162,170
Clarksville	60,730

AREA AND LAND USE

Area	41,155 sq. miles (34th)
Farm	47%
Forest	50%
Federally owned	7%

Gov. Ned McWherter (D)
Of Dresden — Elected 1986

Born: Oct. 15, 1930, Palmersville, Tenn.
Education: Graduated Dresden H.S., 1948.
Military Career: Army National Guard, 1948-69.
Occupation: Farmer; businessman.
Religion: Methodist.
Political Career: Tenn. House, 1969-87, Speaker, 1973-87.
Next Election: 1990.

WORK

Occupations	
White-collar	48%
Blue-collar	38%
Service workers	12%
Government Workers	
Federal	57,950
State	81,347
Local	175,160

MONEY

Median family income	$ 16,564	(44th)
Tax burden per capita	$ 630	(48th)

EDUCATION

Spending per pupil through grade 12	$ 2,612	(45th)
Persons with college degrees	13%	(44th)

CRIME

Violent crime rate	534 per 100,000 (19th)

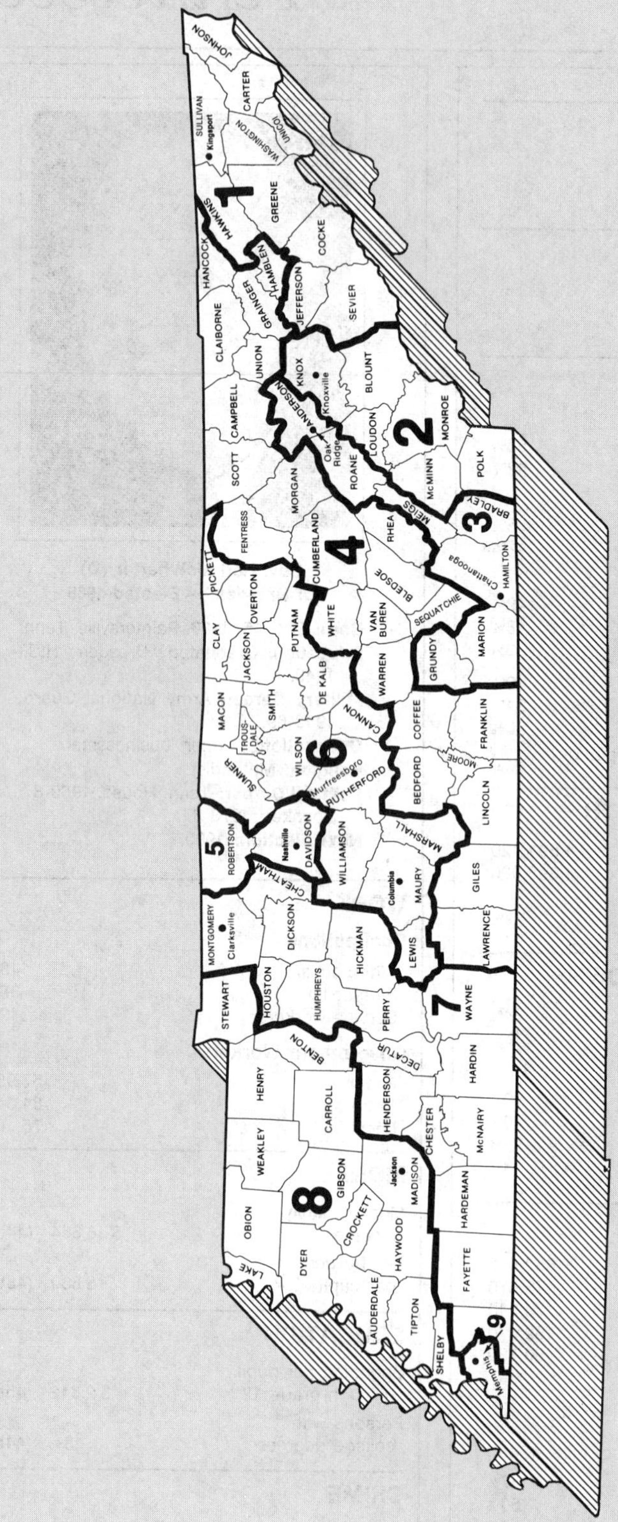
JOHNSON
CARTER
SULLIVAN
Kingsport
UNICOI
WASHINGTON
1
HAWKINS
GREENE
HANCOCK
HAMBLEN
COCKE
GRAINGER
JEFFERSON
CLAIBORNE
UNION
SEVIER
KNOX
Knoxville
BLOUNT
CAMPBELL
ANDERSON
Oak Ridge
LOUDON
2
MONROE
SCOTT
MORGAN
ROANE
McMINN
POLK
MEIGS
BRADLEY
3
FENTRESS
CUMBERLAND
RHEA
4
PICKETT
BLEDSOE
Chattanooga
HAMILTON
OVERTON
CLAY
WHITE
VAN BUREN
SEQUATCHIE
PUTNAM
JACKSON
GRUNDY
MARION
WARREN
DE KALB
SMITH
MACON
CANNON
COFFEE
FRANKLIN
TROUS-DALE
WILSON
6
MOORE
SUMNER
Murfreesboro
RUTHERFORD
BEDFORD
LINCOLN
ROBERTSON
Nashville
DAVIDSON
MARSHALL
5
CHEATHAM
WILLIAMSON
Columbia
MAURY
GILES
MONTGOMERY
Clarksville
DICKSON
HICKMAN
LEWIS
LAWRENCE
HOUSTON
HUMPHREYS
PERRY
7
WAYNE
STEWART
BENTON
DECATUR
HARDIN
HENRY
CARROLL
HENDERSON
CHESTER
McNAIRY
WEAKLEY
GIBSON
Jackson
MADISON
8
CROCKETT
HARDEMAN
OBION
DYER
HAYWOOD
FAYETTE
LAKE
LAUDERDALE
TIPTON
9
SHELBY
Memphis

Jim Sasser (D)

Of Nashville — Elected 1976

Born: Sept. 30, 1936, Memphis, Tenn.
Education: Attended U. of Tennessee, 1954-55; Vanderbilt U., B.A. 1958, J.D. 1961.
Military Career: Marine Corps Reserve, 1957-63.
Occupation: Lawyer.
Family: Wife, Mary Gorman; two children.
Religion: Methodist.
Political Career: No previous office.
Capitol Office: 363 Russell Bldg. 20510; 224-3344.

In Washington: After more than a decade in the Senate without a major focus, Sasser had one forced on him at the start of the 101st Congress, as he became the reluctant heir to the chairmanship of the Budget Committee.

Now Sasser is responsible for the broad fiscal outlines and policy implications of the entire $1 trillion federal budget, where previously he had picked at its million-dollar footnotes and line items to ferret out waste and fraud. Instead of boasting, as he once did, of saving $2 million a year by barring federal funds for watering indoor plants, Sasser must lead the effort to cut a deficit that persists at more than $150 billion annually. Perhaps hardest for this congenial and popular senator, he must be the bearer of bad news to colleagues whose favorite programs need to be cut or taxed.

In a dozen years on Budget, Sasser had rarely been a major participant in its deliberations, and at mid-decade he told a reporter he wanted off. Sasser remained, but even so, he did not seem eager to claim the top seat when Chairman Lawton Chiles announced his impending retirement in 1988. Sasser was third in line, but the more senior Democrats — Ernest F. Hollings and J. Bennett Johnston — already were committee chairmen. Asked in the fall whether he would accept the job, Sasser quipped, "Well, I haven't been able to convince Senators Hollings or Johnston to take it."

By his hesitance and past detachment from budget debates, Sasser could not be more different from his counterpart, new House Budget Committee Chairman Leon E. Panetta, who waited years for the chair and meanwhile built a reputation as Congress' foremost fiscal expert.

Sasser did not distinguish himself in his debut, helping to draft the fiscal 1990 budget. But neither did anyone else. President Bush was intent on setting a more conciliatory tone than existed throughout President Reagan's tenure, and Congress proved willing to accept bipartisanship over serious deficit reduction.

For nine weeks the two sides talked. Panetta moved aggressively, confident House Democrats would back him; Sasser was more cautious, reflecting both his nature and relative inexperience. By April the negotiators had a compromise budget that met the law's $100 billion deficit target, thanks mainly to accounting gimmicks, rosy economic assumptions and unspecified taxes.

Though the pact drew many scoffs, lawmakers were in no mood to fight. With rare speed and bipartisanship, Sasser and Panetta squired the compromise through both houses and a conference by mid-May. "This is the best we can do at this particular time in our history," Sasser told the Senate.

Once Sasser agreed to head Budget, he allowed that the job "offers a significant opportunity to affect some of the major issues of the day." Until then, Sasser had gravitated to the minutiae of policy. He came to Congress at a time when federal waste and fraud were emerging as potent political issues, but he had a difficult time moving beyond them to address complex national problems.

He persuaded the General Accounting Office to install a toll-free hot line for citizens to report government fraud, and claimed to have saved $500 million by attacking federal employees' travel costs. But lacking the flair for self-promotion of other such crusaders, Sasser remained one of the lesser-known, least visible senators.

Sasser had begun assuming a broader role in foreign policy debates. He spoke out against Reagan's policies in Central America aimed at Nicaragua, and tried to develop a consensus Democratic stand on contra aid that would put the party on record in support of a diplomatic solution without seeming to overlook Nicaragua's anti-democratic actions. But even on that issue, Sasser's involvement sprang from his line-by-line approach to policy making.

In the 98th Congress, while others debated overall U.S. strategy in Central America, Sasser was studying federal spending for construction of military facilities in Honduras, Nicaragua's neighbor. As ranking Democrat — and chairman since 1987 — of the Appropriations Subcommittee on Military Construction, he concluded the Reagan administration was preparing for potential armed intervention in the region. Landing strips and facilities for temporary use in training exercises actually were intended to be permanent, Sasser argued.

Sasser had mixed success, however, in his assault on the spending in Honduras. The Senate rejected his amendment to bar conversions of temporary facilities into permanent ones. In 1987, his subcommittee rejected Reagan's request for funds to replace huts for U.S. forces in Honduras with barracks. Sasser noted that a 1987 regional peace plan prohibited outsiders' bases; denial of the funds, he said, would be "a signal of United States support for political solutions to regional problems."

When Reagan made a televised pitch for contra aid in 1986, Democratic leaders picked Sasser to give the party's response. That year, Sasser offered his own proposal tying aid to renewed negotiations; if Nicaragua's rulers refused to negotiate, military aid would be released to the rebels. But that satisfied neither those who favored immediate aid nor those who wanted none at all. Sasser's amendment was rejected by a 2-to-1 margin.

He later adopted a more critical approach. "We're going precisely down the path that this country traveled in Vietnam," he said in August. He did better with a proposal to kill the entire program, losing 54-46.

In the 100th Congress, Sasser had a high-profile role on another issue, after a 1987 Iraqi attack on a U.S. frigate in the Persian Gulf drew critical attention to the Reagan policy of providing Navy escorts for Kuwaiti tankers there. Sasser was part of a Democratic leadership team that reviewed military plans for the escort policy. Also, then-Majority Leader Robert C. Byrd named Sasser one of three senators to go to the Middle East to investigate. Upon his return from the region, Sasser said Reagan should either get Kuwait to withdraw its request for protection or enlist allies' help. "We should not sail in the gulf's troubled waters alone," he said.

Such policy ventures have been real departures from Sasser's past concentration on government economy. When he chaired Appropriations' Legislative Branch Subcommittee, Sasser fought efforts to increase congressional and executive branch pay, and to suspend the limit on senators' outside income — to the occasional irritation of other senators.

On the Governmental Affairs Committee, one of Sasser's early projects was a complex bill to consolidate federal grant programs and increase Congress' control over them. It passed the Senate in 1980, mainly as a courtesy to Sasser since Congress would adjourn before it could become law. Also that year, he pushed a "sunset bill" to terminate federal programs unless they are reauthorized by Congress within a fixed period. The Senate had passed such a bill in 1978, but this time it went no further than the committee.

On the Banking Committee, Sasser is something of a populist in the tradition of Tennessee senators, particularly when the complaint is high interest rates. In 1982 he espoused a resolution calling on the Federal Reserve Board to loosen its monetary policies, and in 1983 he was one of two Banking Democrats to vote against retaining Paul A. Volcker as Fed chairman, arguing that the board's tight-money policies had exacerbated the 1982-83 recession. In 1988, he and fellow Tennessee Sen. Al Gore cast two of only three Senate votes against Fed appointee John P. LaWare, a Boston banker. Sasser has also supported legislation to curb interest rates for credit cards.

Sasser came to the Senate as a loyal supporter of Jimmy Carter. He cooled, however, when the administration opposed some Tennessee federal projects, such as the Tellico Dam that was held up on environmental grounds. Pressed to vote with Carter to transfer the Panama Canal, Sasser did, but not without complaint.

Though Sasser has maintained a liberal-to-moderate record, votes on such issues as the Panama Canal and social controversies do not come easy to a man from a conservative Southern state. One with potentially serious political consequences occurred in 1982, a Sasser re-election year, when he cast the tie-breaking procedural vote to kill Jesse Helms' amendment aimed at restricting abortions. But he consistently supported Helms' bid to restore voluntary prayer in public schools by stripping federal courts of jurisdiction over the issue.

At Home: Sasser's 1976 Senate campaign in behalf of "a government that reflects our decency" bore a pronounced and deliberate similarity to Carter's call for "a government as good as its people." When Carter won the Tennessee presidential primary that year with 78 percent of the vote, Sasser joked that he wanted not only to cling to Carter's coattails, but to get inside the coat.

It was a successful strategy. In November, Carter won Tennessee by nearly 200,000 votes, helping Sasser to a comfortable victory over GOP Sen. William E. Brock III, who a year earlier was considered safe for re-election.

Sasser had used his three-year chairmanship of the state Democratic Party to lay a base of support. His chief Democratic rival was liberal Nashville businessman John J. Hooker, whose unsuccessful tries for the governorship in 1966 and 1970 had given him wide name recognition but a loser's image. Sasser was endorsed by several minority and labor groups who saw him as a fresh face and a possible winner. With support from most of the party leadership, he defeated Hooker convincingly.

Brock displayed the same organizing skill

that later was to make him a successful national GOP chairman. But his background as a candy heir, his upper-crust image and his quiet personal style contrasted unfavorably with Sasser's down-to-earth manner and ready humor.

Sasser portrayed Brock as a country-club Republican, a special-interest senator representing banks and insurance companies. It was a perfect issue in a state always susceptible to populist rhetoric, and doubly so with Carter reinforcing Sasser's themes.

Since Sasser compiled a generally noncontroversial record and avoided political blunders during his first term, he was well positioned for re-election in 1982. Some conservative Republicans thought Sasser's support was soft, and on that supposition GOP Rep. Robin L. Beard gave up a safe House district to try for the Senate.

Beard failed utterly in searching for a theme that would induce voters to desert Sasser. At first, Beard called Sasser a free-spending "Kennedy liberal." In his ads he unveiled a small plastic mouse, dubbed "flipping Jimmy," meant to convince voters that Sasser had shifted from left to center as his re-election neared. In the end, Beard was stressing abortion and school prayer in an attempt to mobilize religious fundamentalists and others with strong feelings on social issues.

Sasser occasionally sparred with Beard, but mostly he stressed his work to improve government accounting practices and reduce bureaucratic costs. He was able to stay on the offensive by blaming economic hard times on Reaganomics. Beard had to contend with Tennesseeans' lukewarm feelings for Reagan — Carter nearly carried the state in 1980 — and with an unemployment rate that was above the national average throughout 1982.

Sasser buried Beard in Middle and West Tennessee, and even carried traditionally Republican East Tennessee; no Democrat had done that since the GOP began seriously contesting statewide elections in the mid-1960s.

Sasser's 1982 showing was still on many minds six years later. GOP leaders again insisted Sasser's support was soft, but they failed to recruit a proven vote-getter, such as former GOP Gov. Lamar Alexander.

Their nominee was little-known Kingsport attorney Bill Andersen, a candidate who had considerable energy, much of which was spent introducing himself to members of his own party.

Andersen criticized Sasser as a man lacking the stature of the state's other leading politicians, including Gore and Alexander. But Andersen had trouble raising money and was not really in a position to talk about stature. Again Sasser romped, taking all but one county in Republican East Tennessee.

Committees

Budget (Chairman)

Appropriations (7th of 16 Democrats)
Military Construction (chairman); Commerce, Justice, State, the Judiciary and Related Agencies; Defense; Energy and Water Development; Transportation and Related Agencies

Banking, Housing and Urban Affairs (6th of 12 Democrats)
Housing and Urban Affairs; Securities

Governmental Affairs (4th of 8 Democrats)
General Services, Federalism and the District of Columbia (chairman); Federal Services, Post Office and Civil Service; Permanent Subcommittee on Investigations

Elections

1988 General

Jim Sasser (D)	1,020,061	(65%)
Bill Andersen (R)	541,033	(35%)

Previous Winning Percentages: **1982** (62%) **1976** (53%)

Campaign Finance

	Receipts	Receipts from PACs	Expenditures
1988			
Sasser (D)	$3,218,986	$1,379,817 (43%)	$3,069,615
Andersen (R)	$612,421	$24,925 (4%)	$613,704

Key Votes

1987

Enact omnibus highway bill over Reagan veto	Y
Limit testing of space-based anti-ballistic missiles	Y
Oppose banning tests of larger nuclear weapons	Y
Confirm Robert H. Bork as Supreme Court justice	N
1988	
Allow vote on campaign-finance overhaul	Y
Pass civil rights restoration bill over Reagan veto	Y
Enact omnibus trade bill over Reagan veto	Y
Approve death penalty for drug-related murders	Y
Oppose "workfare" amendment to welfare overhaul bill	Y

Voting Studies

	Presidential Support		Party Unity		Conservative Coalition	
Year	**S**	**O**	**S**	**O**	**S**	**O**
1988	41	56	87	11	38	59
1987	35	65	94	6	38	63
1986	24	76	87	13	37	63
1985	33	67	87	13	52	48
1984	34	58	88	8	30	62
1983	39	58	85	11	35†	65†
1982	42	55	72	25	62	36
1981	57	40	72	17	57	29

† Not eligible for all recorded votes.

Interest Group Ratings

Year	ADA	ACU	AFL-CIO	CCUS
1988	75	9	86	43
1987	80	12	90	28
1986	70	17	87	32
1985	60	26	86	38
1984	90	18	91	37
1983	75	16	93	32
1982	55	47	84	50
1981	45	31	59	67

Al Gore (D)

Of Carthage — Elected 1984

Born: March 31, 1948, Washington, D.C.
Education: Harvard U., B.A. 1969; attended Vanderbilt School of Religion, 1972; attended Vanderbilt Law School, 1974-76.
Military Career: Army, 1969-71.
Occupation: Journalist; home builder.
Family: Wife, Mary Elizabeth "Tipper" Aitcheson; four children.
Religion: Baptist.
Political Career: U.S. House, 1977-85; sought Democratic nomination for president, 1988.
Capitol Office: 393 Russell Bldg. 20510; 224-4944.

In Washington: Gore's Senate seat is up in 1990, but the campaign his colleagues tend to think of him waging involves higher stakes.

While still in the first half of his first term, Gore launched a campaign for president. He is generally expected to start a second White House bid as soon as he is re-elected.

So Gore is now often viewed as conducting a continuous presidential effort, with his Senate service a means to that end and re-election a pit stop along the way.

Nevertheless, the bright and personable Gore seems comfortable with himself and with the politial trajectory he has chosen. Like other youthful senators before him, such as John F. Kennedy and Gary Hart, he has observed the numbers of potential rivals for the presidency and decided to get a jump on them by taking an early turn at bat. He has been willing to pay the price and take the risks that come with this beat-the-crowd strategy.

That was at least part of the motivation for Gore's plunge into the 1988 presidential contest in the spring of 1987. Another part was Gore's interest in seeing a Southerner in the lists when the nominating process tilted South on Super Tuesday. On that March 8, for the first time, 14 Southern states would hold primaries the same day. This informal regional primary would also come early enough in the year so Gore could skip Iowa's caucus and New Hampshire's primary and retain a plausible scenario for nomination.

Gore, who had been willing to defer to other Southerners had they run, was recruited by a group of prominent, well-heeled Democrats seeking someone more moderate in the field. They wanted someone with a strong labor record who would not offend doctrinaire liberals but who would be pro-defense and appealing to Southerners and younger, more future-oriented voters.

Gore did do well on Super Tuesday. He got a bigger percentage share of the aggregate vote in the 14 Southern states than any Democrat. His delegate take was almost as big as the Rev. Jesse Jackson's. Gore also prevailed in two Western states that held caucuses that day.

But while this generated the most attention Gore had enjoyed to date, he had to share the splash with Jackson, with Massachusetts Gov. Michael S. Dukakis (who won Texas and Florida) and, most of all, with Vice President George Bush — who all but claimed the GOP nomination with a 14-state Southern sweep.

Gore's problem thereafter was finding a breakthrough state above the Mason-Dixon line. He flopped in Illinois, Michigan and then Wisconsin, even though many Democrats had begun actively to seek an alternative to the Jackson-Dukakis choice. Gore shoved his last chips onto New York. He struck a desperate bargain with New York City Mayor Edward I. Koch, who made himself an issue with intemperate remarks about Jews and Jackson. The city wound up voting narrowly for Jackson, Dukakis won nearly everywhere else and Gore got just 10 percent. Two days later, he suspended his campaign.

Still, Gore established himself as a player for 1992 and beyond. No other Southerner can now plot a path to the White House without dealing with the Tennessean first. And Gore has given ample sign he intends to hold his place.

Gore also wants to continue being a legislator, however, and he opened the 101st Congress with a flurry of high-profile activity to underscore that desire. He shifted from the chairmanship of the Consumer Subcommittee on Commerce, Science and Technology to the chairmanship of the subcommittee on Science, Technology and Space. This allows him ample opportunity to explore the futuristic issues that have long captivated him — and on which he would like to build a political movement.

Gore spent most of his pre-congressional career as a reporter, and he brought the skills and interests of a journalist with him to the House in 1977. Few there could match his ability to seize an issue, uncover a pattern of abuses, draw attention in the media and propose a solution.

But since his presidential campaign and change of subcommittee chairs, Gore is less the muckraker than the fact-gathering inspector general. He has traveled to the Antarctic to study the hole in the ozone layer and to Brazil to study the deforestation that may be affecting the global climate. He proposed a new system for warning people of earthquakes. He called for all wrapping materials to be biodegradable. He proposed a bill called the National High Performance Computer Technology Act of 1989 and called on all nations to phase out the use of chlorofluorocarbons (which harm the ozone layer) before 2000.

Gore has always seemed fascinated with the issues of the future, prompting some to comment that the future he cares most about is his own. But beyond the grandstanding, Gore has long seemed genuinely interested in adapting the present to the demands of the future. In his early years in the House, for example, Gore led the campaign for televising the proceedings. When that campaign succeeded, he delivered the chamber's first televised speech in March 1979. Carrying this cause to the Senate, he urged his new neighbors to emulate the House — renewing the fight long pressed by retired GOP leader Howard H. Baker Jr., the Republican who had preceded him in the Senate.

Gore in 1989 also continued to seek a greater voice on the Armed Services Committee (to which he had moved in early 1987 in the best break of his Senate career to date).

In the House, Gore had first become interested in strategic arms in 1980, when he was disturbed to find that an audience of Tennessee teenagers nearly all expected a nuclear war in their lifetime.

In the 1980s, President Reagan pushed hard for deployment of 100 MX missiles in existing silos; MX critics in the House seemed within striking distance of scotching the president's plan entirely. Gore feared this would enable Reagan to brand Democrats as soft on defense and then withdraw from arms negotiations with the Soviets. Gore and a few other Democrats supported limited MX production in return for a promise from the administration of flexibility at the strategic arms talks in Geneva and a commitment to the alternative "Midgetman," a single-warhead missile.

Moving to the Senate early in 1985, Gore and fellow Democrats Sam Nunn, David L. Boren and Robert C. Byrd helped produce an agreement with the administration holding MX deployment to 50 missiles. The White House was not thrilled with that compromise, but by then its attention was shifting to another item on the nuclear arms agenda — the strategic defense initiative (SDI). Gore tried to find a middle ground on this issue as well, but without success.

In 1989, Gore initially seemed enthusiastic about President Bush's nomination of former Sen. John Tower as secretary of defense. He called Tower's performance as an arms negotiator in Geneva "exemplary in every respect" (Gore had been on the Senate's team of observers). But as the nomination soured and Nunn turned against Tower, so did Gore.

Aside from his committee business, Gore was the Senate author of a 1989 bill to aid the working poor by expanding the earned-income tax credit and dependent care credit. With its $34 billion price tag (over five years), the bill would seem to have little chance for passage. But it did serve to hold Bush's feet to the fire regarding some of his campaign pledges.

Gore drew attention in the 99th Congress, when, at the initiative of his wife, "Tipper," he focused congressional attention on rock music lyrics that the Gores felt glorify casual sex, violence and satanic worship. The Commerce Committee held hearings on the subject in 1985, drawing in singing stars to comment on a proposal to put warning labels on music products so parents can monitor what their children are hearing.

At Home: Despite his globe-trotting and his bursting ambition, Gore retains a certain political magic at home. It stems in part from residual support for his father, Albert Gore Sr., a three-term senator in the 1950s and 1960s. But mostly the younger Gore has earned it himself, with 1,000-plus small-town open meetings during his congressional career. Gore clearly has a knack for getting along with Tennesseeans, even if he did grow up in Washington, D.C., and attend exclusive private schools.

Gore's 1984 Senate election bore the mark of inevitability from the moment Baker announced his retirement in 1982. In many past statewide campaigns, Democrats had cut themselves to ribbons in primary competition, paving the way for GOP victory in November. But Gore, with his immense popularity in Middle Tennessee and a name that needed no introduction anywhere in the state, had the Democratic field to himself. It was the Republicans, struggling to hold the seat, who were divided over the nomination.

While they squabbled, Gore campaigned. Starting early in 1983, he worked the grass roots, lining up rural Democratic courthouse networks and urban party organizations.

The eventual winner of the GOP nomination was state Sen. Victor H. Ashe, a wealthy, Yale-educated lawyer from Knoxville whose acerbic manner and habit of needling colleagues in the Legislature had turned off even some Republicans. Ashe toned his manner down in the primary, won an early endorsement from the National Republican Senatorial Committee and easily won nomination. But that endorsement angered New Right activist Ed McAteer, who withdrew from the primary and mounted an independent November campaign, foreclosing any hopes Ashe might have had.

Gore campaigned in the fall as if he were the incumbent. He pointed to his work on such issues as nutritional standards for baby formula, toxic-waste cleanup and the MX, all of which played well to most audiences.

Ashe seemed outmaneuvered at every turn. When he called a press conference to accuse Gore of speaking out against busing but voting for it, Gore ignored him, responding instead by announcing that Reagan had just signed three of his bills — creating a national organ donor program, requiring stronger warning labels on cigarette packages and strengthening penalties against repeat criminal offenders. The election was a rout, with Gore even winning Ashe's home base, heavily Republican Knox County.

Gore's family name did not scare away competition in 1976, when he launched his first campaign for the House. Eight other Democrats entered the contest to succeed retiring Democrat Joe L. Evins. They soon found, however, that they were opposing not only a family tradition but a born campaigner.

Gore's themes had a populist flavor. He called for higher taxation of the rich and tighter strip-mine laws, and criticized "private power trusts" who wanted to dismantle the Tennessee Valley Authority. He favored cuts in defense spending and said the government should create more public jobs.

Gore's chief rival in the crowded field was state House Majority Leader Stanley Rogers. He tried to make an issue of Gore's wealth (net worth $273,000 at the time) and claimed Gore's father was tied to energy monopolies. By stressing his legislative experience, Rogers hoped to cast Gore as a political amateur.

But Rogers' political base was in the southern part of the district, and several other candidates from that area drew votes from him. Gore, who was not seriously challenged in his Smith County base in the district's northern section, finished just ahead of Rogers. House re-elections were no problem for Gore. Only once — in 1980 — was he held below 90 percent.

Committees

Armed Services (8th of 11 Democrats)
Defense Industry and Technology; Projection Forces and Regional Defense; Strategic Forces and Nuclear Deterrence

Commerce, Science and Transportation (5th of 11 Democrats)
Science, Technology and Space (chairman); Communications; Consumer; Surface Transportation; National Ocean Policy Study

Rules and Administration (6th of 9 Democrats)

Joint Economic
Economic Resources and Competitiveness; Education and Health; Investment, Jobs and Prices

Joint Printing

Elections

1984 General

Al Gore (D)	1,000,607	(61%)
Victor Ashe (R)	557,016	(34%)
Ed McAteer (I)	87,234	(5%)

Previous Winning Percentages: 1982 * (100%) **1980 *** (79%) **1978 *** (92%) **1976 *** (94%)

* *House elections.*

Campaign Finance

	Receipts	Receipts from PACs	Expend-itures
1984			
Gore (D)	$3,166,007	$795,581 (25%)	$3,180,975
Ashe (R)	$1,777,975	$241,571 (14%)	$1,777,581
McAteer (I)	$386,997	$11,156 (3%)	$382,364

Key Votes

1987

Enact omnibus highway bill over Reagan veto	Y
Limit testing of space-based anti-ballistic missiles	Y
Oppose banning tests of larger nuclear weapons	-
Confirm Robert H. Bork as Supreme Court justice	N

1988

Allow vote on campaign-finance overhaul	?
Pass civil rights restoration bill over Reagan veto	Y
Enact omnibus trade bill over Reagan veto	Y
Approve death penalty for drug-related murders	N
Oppose "workfare" amendment to welfare overhaul bill	N

Voting Studies

	Presidential Support		Party Unity		Conservative Coalition	
Year	S	O	S	O	S	O
1988	33	30	57	4	11	35
1987	10	41	49	2	9	25
1986	29	71	83	17	33	67
1985	34	66	86	14	50	50
House Service						
1984	46	45	69	22	56	34
1983	29	61	77	13	39	58
1982	45	52	89	11	47	53
1981	39	59	80	17	47	53

Interest Group Ratings

Year	ADA	ACU	AFL-CIO	CCUS
1988	60	9	83	45
1987	60	6	100	10
1986	70	9	87	32
1985	65	17	86	41
House Service				
1984	65	22	62	31
1983	70	20	88	28
1982	70	29	90	18
1981	70	13	93	11

1 James H. Quillen (R)

Of Kingsport — Elected 1962

Born: Jan. 11, 1916, near Gate City, Va.
Education: Graduated from Dobyns-Bennett High School, 1934.
Military Career: Navy, 1942-46.
Occupation: Newspaper publisher; real estate and insurance salesman; banker.
Family: Wife, Cecile Cox.
Religion: Methodist.
Political Career: Tenn. House, 1955-63.
Capitol Office: 102 Cannon Bldg. 20515; 225-6356.

In Washington: After more than a quarter-century in the House, Quillen, the ranking Republican on the Rules Committee, is positioned to be a power broker in Washington. But he has never made that his primary ambition. Instead, he has focused his attention on his district in upper East Tennessee. That effort has paid off handsomely, bringing him the kind of influence on his home turf that few members ever achieve.

Tennessee's statewide GOP candidates would like to assume they have a solid base in Quillen's traditionally Republican territory, but as some have learned, a key element to success in the region is winning over Quillen himself. When former GOP Gov. Winfield Dunn tried to return to the governorship in 1986, his strategists worried that Quillen's network might not mobilize for Dunn because of an old feud between the two men. That is exactly what happened: Dunn's showing in the normally heavily Republican 1st was a factor in his statewide loss to Democrat Ned McWherter.

In 1988, when the GOP was trying to put the best face on its long-shot hopes of upsetting Democratic Sen. Jim Sasser, Quillen's public praise for the senior senator helped render the challenge pointless. Sasser's opponent, Kingsport attorney Bill Andersen, originally had shown some interest in taking Quillen's spot in the House, and Quillen had been miffed by that apparent attempt to nudge him out.

Quillen will be nearly 75 when the 101st Congress ends, and he is often rumored to be weighing retirement. But given Andersen's experience, it seems unlikely any Republican will start jockeying to succeed Quillen until it is very clear he is ready to go.

If Quillen is careful about lending his personal support to candidates in Tennessee, he is even more careful about sharing his massive campaign treasury with GOP candidates around the country. That has frustrated a number of House Republicans, who expect such a senior member to play a party-building role. But Quillen is a self-made man who takes a dim view of handouts, and he has learned to work with the Democratic majority to get what he wants for his district. Not surprisingly, then, Quillen does not make a priority of passing out his money to conservative House candidates who want to topple the Democratic power structure with which Quillen has reached accommodation.

Many of the younger members critical of Quillen come from a very different political school — one that challenges the very role he has found for himself in Washington.

Rules can be a place for partisan strategizing and legislative intrigue, but Quillen is not the person for it. He would rather look after his constituents. The importance of his seniority on Rules would seem to have increased in the 101st Congress, when newcomers took the three GOP committee slots under him. But most expected those newcomers, not Quillen, to take the lead in voicing the GOP position on rules matters that reach the floor.

Quillen does speak out at times, challenging Democratic procedures or policies. In 1987, when the House was voting for $725 million in new aid for the homeless, Quillen was concerned that the money would promote the problem, not redress it. "I don't want the Congress to create more homelessness on our streets," he said. "Instead of solving the problem, we would make it entirely more complicated."

But Quillen is most conspicuous when Tennessee is directly involved in an issue. In 1984, when Rules voted to strip $139 million for water projects from an emergency appropriations bill before sending it to the floor, Quillen, whose district was to get some of the money, cast the only dissenting vote in a 12-1 roll call. He later voted against the committee decision on the floor, helping to defeat it.

Another emergency appropriations bill came to Rules in 1985 packed with controversial water projects — including one worth $5 million in Quillen's district. The committee sent the bill to the floor with a rule that left a number of water projects vulnerable to procedural objec-

Tennessee 1

Northeast — Tri-cities

The Tennessee Valley Authority has freed this district and much of East Tennessee from the pervasive rural poverty of an earlier era. Isolated highland towns, tobacco patches and livestock clearings were once the 1st District norm, but in the past generation small cities have grown up around industries drawn to the area by the availability of TVA power.

But the coming of industry has not changed the district's GOP voting habits. The 10 counties that make up the 1st gave George Bush 68 percent of their presidential vote in 1988; that was just a slight drop from Ronald Reagan's 1984 showing in the district. The 1st is not blindly Republican, however. It will pick Democrats in noncompetitive statewide contests, such as the 1988 Senate race between Democratic incumbent Jim Sasser and Bill Andersen, a little-known attorney from the 1st.

Some 45 percent of the people in the 1st live in Sullivan and Washington counties, which encompass northeast Tennessee's Tri-cities — Johnson City, Kingsport and Bristol. These cities' diverse industries produce an array of items, including textiles, paper, chemicals, electronics and medical equipment.

Because of its industrial work force, the Tri-cities area has a respectable Democratic vote. In 1976 Jimmy Carter took Sullivan and Quillen carried it by only 543 votes; twelve years later, Sasser got his best margins in the district in Sullivan and Washington. But those voters have little use for Democrats of a liberal stripe, such as Michael S. Dukakis.

Even when Democrats do well in the Tri-cities, for the most part they are swamped districtwide. More than half the people in the 1st District still live in rural and small-town counties where the impact of TVA has not shaken natives from their instinctive suspicion of big government. These counties regularly elect GOP candidates by wide margins.

The rural areas raise tobacco, poultry and livestock. Zinc and limestone are mined, and some people commute to factory jobs in Knoxville or the Tri-cities.

At the southern end of the 1st, Sevier County feeds on tourist dollars. It is the gateway to the Great Smoky Mountains National Park, which draws about 10 million visitors yearly. At the park's edge is Gatlinburg, a town of only 3,500 people whose motels sleep tens of thousands. Nearby is Pigeon Forge, which has an even larger extravaganza of tourist offerings, including Dollywood, a huge family amusement area launched recently by country music star Dolly Parton, a Sevier County native.

Population: 512,702. White 500,873 (98%), Black 9,938 (2%). Spanish origin 2,636 (1%). 18 and over 371,177 (72%), 65 and over 57,367 (11%). Median age: 32.

tions — but the projects backed by Quillen and some other Rules members were protected.

The poverty of Quillen's Appalachian district occasionally leads him to break with the party line. For instance, he has backed legislation to restrict textile imports, saying, "The time has come that we must look to the benefit of American workers first and foremost, and keep the textile plants open."

At times, the Tennessean's questions to witnesses before Rules are notable for comic relief, as when he told a committee chairman that a piece of legislation appeared to be "putting the carrot before the cart."

He once broke up a hearing at Rules by putting a goldfish in his water pitcher. The hearing was on a measure softening the Endangered Species Act, which was threatening to block construction of the $119 million Tellico Dam in Tennessee because it would destroy the habitat of a small fish, the snail darter.

Quillen was a booster of the dam. He said he wanted to see how long it would take people to notice the fish in his pitcher, hoping to demonstrate the insignificance of the even-smaller darter.

In 1978 Quillen used his committee position to force a floor vote on a provision to repeal the earned-income limit imposed on members of Congress the previous year. A new ethics code limited outside earned income to 15 percent of salary ($8,625 at that time). Quillen, who was a board member or president of five companies, was making considerably more than that annually in outside earned income and vigorously opposed the limit.

When a financial-disclosure bill came before the committee, Quillen shocked the Democrats by coming up with enough votes to demand floor action on his amendment repealing the limit. House leaders temporarily pulled the entire bill from consideration, then decided to give Quillen his chance. But the effort to repeal the limit lost by better than 2-to-1.

Still, the earned-income limit remained a sore spot for Quillen. In 1981 Majority Leader

Jim Wright of Texas introduced a resolution to repeal it. When Fred Wertheimer of Common Cause came before a Rules subcommittee to oppose repeal, Quillen launched a barrage of questions about Wertheimer's own salary and expenses. He stopped only at the insistence of Gillis W. Long, the Louisiana Democrat who was presiding. Later on, House Democratic leaders quietly succeeded in raising the outside earned-income limit to 30 percent of salary.

Quillen was less successful in 1986, when he backed another move to raise the ceiling on outside income. The day after the House approved a measure lifting the limit, it quickly reversed itself in the face of adverse publicity. Quillen was one of only 68 members voting against a key procedural motion to restore the tighter limits.

At Home: To make it to Congress in 1962, Quillen had to weather the quarrels of a Republican Party cast into disarray by the passing of a political dynasty. GOP Rep. B. Carroll Reece, a former party national chairman, dominated 1st District politics for 40 years until his death in 1961. Reece's widow served out his term, then gave her blessing to Quillen, a four-term state representative.

Quillen called himself a staunch conservative who opposed "wasteful spending overseas to buy friendship when friendship cannot be bought." Though he got only 29 percent of the vote, that topped the five-candidate GOP primary field and gave him the nomination.

The 1st had not elected a Democrat since 1878, yet Quillen was held to 54 percent in the general election. His low total was blamed partly on GOP disunity after the hard-fought primary and partly on a higher-than-usual Democratic turnout. A longstanding patronage arrangement between Reece and local Democrats had collapsed when Reece died.

Once in office, Quillen quickly learned the skills of entrenchment. A prodigious letter-writer, he sent notes of congratulation and condolence and numerous franked mailings. And he made the rounds to county courthouses during his frequent trips home.

By 1964, GOP factional fights had dissipated, and Quillen easily won re-election. Since then, Quillen occasionally has encountered Democratic foes who complain he is little more than a "pen pal" who opposes education, health and welfare measures that his rural constituents need. But none of the foes has made any significant headway.

The most tangible monument to Quillen's work is the Quillen-Dishner College of Medicine at East Tennessee State University in Johnson City. The congressman spent years promoting it, and it is named for him and a generous donor. Dunn's opposition to this school led to the feud between him and Quillen.

Committee

Rules (Ranking)

Elections

1988 General

James H. Quillen (R)	119,526	(80%)
Sidney S. Smith (D)	29,469	(20%)

1986 General

James H. Quillen (R)	80,289	(69%)
John B. Russell (D)	36,278	(31%)

Previous Winning Percentages:

				1984	(100%)	**1982**	(74%)
1980	(86%)	**1978**	(65%)	**1976**	(58%)	**1974**	(64%)
1972	(79%)	**1970**	(68%)	**1968**	(85%)	**1966**	(87%)
1964	(72%)	**1962**	(54%)				

District Vote For President

	1988		1984		1980		1976	
D	54,455	(31%)	51,916	(28%)	62,841	(36%)	72,867	(45%)
R	117,511	(68%)	129,514	(71%)	105,474	(61%)	85,130	(53%)
I					4,623	(3%)		

Campaign Finance

	Receipts	Receipts from PACs	Expend-itures
1988			
Quillen (R)	$617,030	$413,800 (67%)	$227,503
1986			
Quillen (R)	$472,262	$363,400 (77%)	$459,119
Russell (D)	$8,008	$500 (6%)	$8,044

Key Votes

1987	
Raise speed limit to 65 mph	N
Approve Gephardt "fair trade" amendment	N
Ban testing of larger nuclear weapons	N
Delay "re-flagging" of Kuwaiti tankers	N
Approve tax-raising deficit-reduction bill	N
1988	
Approve aid to Nicaraguan contras	Y
Enact civil rights restoration bill over Reagan veto	N
Kill 60-day plant-closing notification measure	Y
Pass omnibus trade bill over Reagan veto	Y
Approve death penalty for drug-related murders	Y
Bar federal funds for abortions in cases of rape and incest	Y
Oppose seven-day waiting period for purchase of handguns	Y

Voting Studies

	Presidential Support		Party Unity		Conservative Coalition	
Year	**S**	**O**	**S**	**O**	**S**	**O**
1988	48	41	59	31	82	5
1987	55	38	55	33	86	5
1986	62	33	49	40	82	8
1985	68	29	56	35	80	11
1984	69	20	60	27	81	12
1983	79	16	70	21	85	10
1982	69	29	68	26	88	11
1981	63	17	70	14	67	3

Interest Group Ratings

Year	ADA	ACU	AFL-CIO	CCUS
1988	15	91	36	100
1987	12	76	31	64
1986	20	77	38	60
1985	15	81	18	67
1984	20	67	42	82
1983	0	83	6	95
1982	10	76	15	76
1981	5	92	21	100

2 John J. "Jimmy" Duncan Jr. (R)

Of Knoxville — Elected 1988

Born: July 21, 1947, Lebanon, Tenn.
Education: U. of Tennessee, B.S. 1969; George Washington U., J.D. 1973.
Military Career: Army National Guard, 1970-87.
Occupation: Lawyer; judge.
Family: Wife, Lynn Hawkins; four children.
Religion: Presbyterian.
Political Career: Knox County criminal court judge, 1980-88.
Capitol Office: 506 Cannon Bldg. 20515; 225-5435.

The Path to Washington: If Duncan's campaign for Congress is any indication, he will not likely play a highly visible role in the House any time soon. He made it abundantly clear that he plans to emulate his father, who made himself a popular congressman in East Tennessee for more than two decades by assiduously tending to local concerns and eschewing the national spotlight.

"I have a firm belief we have too many laws on the books now ...," the younger Duncan said not long before coming to Washington. "I've made it pretty clear I believe constituent service is most important and is where a freshman can be most effective."

After eight years as a criminal court judge in Knox County, the main population center in the 2nd District, Duncan had a reputation and résumé to be a strong candidate in his own right when his ill father decided not to seek another term (the elder Duncan died shortly after making his retirement announcement). But there was little doubt that Duncan, who appeared on the ballot as John J. Duncan Jr., campaigned primarily as his father's son, both in style and substance.

Duncan's strategy proved successful in the end, but it gave Democrats an opening to make a competitive challenge in this Republican bastion. While Duncan waged the sort of old-style door-to-door, barbecue-to-barbecue campaign for which his father was known, Democrat Dudley Taylor waged a hard-hitting media campaign the likes of which had not been seen in this district.

Duncan had reason to believe the election was practically sewn up after the candidate-filing deadline passed. His name and reputation were enough to discourage all but a minor challenger from entering the Republican primary, the contest that counts most in East Tennessee. And before the campaign was even under way, both of Knoxville's major daily newspapers came out with quick endorsements, touting Jimmy Duncan as his father's logical successor.

But as Duncan put together a loose-knit organization run mainly by family and friends, Taylor, who stepped down from his post as state revenue commissioner in order to run, began putting together a strong effort. He had the assistance of influential state Democrats, including his former boss, Democratic Gov. Ned McWherter. Little known to most voters at the outset, Taylor quickly raised his profile by aggressively courting the free press and making use of paid media.

Taylor steadily hammered away at Duncan for running solely on his father's reputation. And the charges got some attention. Duncan was putting considerable energy into his effort, making the rounds at numerous local events, but he also had the aura of incumbency around him. His refusal to debate Taylor even once gave the Democrat an opportunity to score debating points throughout the campaign, as did Duncan's decision to hold only infrequent press conferences.

Duncan also chose to ignore a wave of more negative attacks that came at him. One of Taylor's advertisements played up links between Duncan and financier C. H. Butcher Jr. and a major banking scandal. Federal regulators had sued Duncan and other principals of a failed savings and loan, saying they engaged in a conspiracy in which control of the thrift was given to Butcher in exchange for elimination of debts Duncan's brother owed to Butcher's banks. Taylor also tried to portray Duncan as being soft on crime, criticizing him for having written a letter urging probation for a drug-related felon.

Duncan at first ignored the attacks, but local Republicans began to get worried. They prodded Duncan into taking out ads rebutting Taylor's "vicious and false allegations." He easily won the general election and special election to fill out the remainder of his father's term.

Tennessee 2

East — Knoxville

Since Civil War days, the 2nd has been reliably Republican in nearly every contest for national, congressional and statewide office. The last person to represent the district who was not a Republican was a member of the American, or "Know Nothing," Party. That was more than 100 years ago.

More than 60 percent of Duncan's constituents are Knox Countians; with nearly 175,000 residents, Knoxville is Tennessee's third-largest city. It is headquarters for the Tennessee Valley Authority (3,000 employees) and home of the University of Tennessee's main campus, with 26,000 students and 1,200 faculty. The city grew up on textiles, tobacco marketing and meat-packing, but now has a broader manufacturing base including boats, mobile homes and electronics as well as clothing. In addition, Knoxville is a regional retail and entertainment center: The hordes that throng to games at UT's 91,000-seat football stadium and its 25,000-seat basketball arena enrich merchants, innkeepers and restaurateurs for miles around.

Knoxville underwent a massive overhaul for the 1982 World's Fair, staged on a 70-acre site downtown. The fair stimulated long-needed highway improvements and drew more visitors than expected, but its afterglow was doused by the 1983 collapse of the financial empire of brothers Jake and C. H. Butcher, who were leading fair promoters. Their banks grew dramatically in the 1970s and early 1980s, but folded because sound management was sacrificed for the sake of expansion. Subsequent lawsuits and shakeouts in the local financial community have kept Knoxville's lawyers and bankers busy; civic leaders are still dickering over how to redevelop the fair site.

Federal employees who work for TVA are often Democratic, but the labor vote in private industry is mixed. Though union members are typically Democratic, many blue-collar workers are conservative and vote Republican, shunning unions as an alien influence.

The university also has a conservative orientation, and the outlying sections of Knox County are strongly Republican. Statewide Democratic candidates usually consider 45 percent a good showing in Knox County, although popular Democrats Jim Sasser and Al Gore have won Knox in their recent Senate elections. In 1988, George Bush won well over 60 percent in Knox County.

Blount County, south of Knoxville, has 15 percent of the 2nd's residents. Located there are the sprawling plants of Alcoa Aluminum, a fixture since 1913. Layoffs have cut the work force to about 3,400, but a modernization of Alcoa's rolling facilities should make the remaining jobs secure. In 1988, Blount County gave Bush two-thirds of its vote.

Farther south, toward Georgia, Democratic strength picks up a bit. McMinn and Monroe counties went narrowly for Jimmy Carter in 1976, and Polk County stuck with him even in 1980. Michael S. Dukakis came within a couple of hundred votes of Bush in Polk in 1988, although McMinn and Monroe proved solid Bush territory.

Population: 510,197. White 472,529 (93%), Black 33,945 (7%), Spanish origin 2,971 (1%). 18 and over 375,709 (74%), 65 and over 58,457 (11%). Median age: 31.

Committees

Interior and Insular Affairs (15th of 15 Republicans)
General Oversight and Investigations; National Parks and Public Lands

Public Works and Transportation (17th of 20 Republicans)
Aviation; Investigations and Oversight; Public Buildings and Grounds; Surface Transportation

Select Aging (25th of 27 Republicans)
Housing and Consumer Interests; Human Services

Campaign Finance

	Receipts	Receipts from PACs	Expend-itures
1988			
Duncan (R)	$448,530	$161,675 (36%)	$435,567
Taylor (D)	$396,303	$101,500 (26%)	$381,980

Elections

1988 General		
John J. "Jimmy" Duncan Jr. (R)	99,631	(56%)
Dudley W. Taylor (D)	77,540	(44%)
1988 Special Election *		
John J. "Jimmy" Duncan Jr. (R)	92,929	(56%)
Dudley W. Taylor (D)	70,576	(43%)
1988 Primary		
John J. "Jimmy" Duncan Jr. (R)	33,246	(87%)
Robert D. Proffitt (R)	5,015	(13%)

** On Election Day, Duncan was elected to a full term and to fill out the remainder of the term of Rep. John J. Duncan, who died June 21, 1988.*

District Vote For President

	1988	1984	1980	1976
D	65,552 (36%)	67,339 (35%)	71,287 (38%)	85,485 (49%)
R	117,355 (64%)	123,657 (64%)	106,979 (58%)	88,130 (50%)
I			6,026 (3%)	

3 Marilyn Lloyd (D)

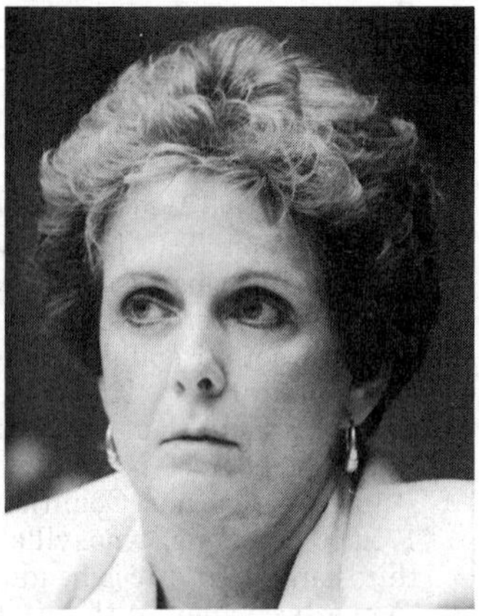

Of Chattanooga — Elected 1974

Born: Jan. 3, 1929, Fort Smith, Ark.
Education: Attended Shorter College, 1958-60 and 1962-63.
Occupation: Radio station owner and manager.
Family: Divorced; four children.
Religion: Church of Christ.
Political Career: No previous office.
Capitol Office: 2266 Rayburn Bldg. 20515; 225-3271.

In Washington: Country music has the Oak Ridge Boys. And in Lloyd, the House has an Oak Ridge congresswoman.

Lloyd's agenda revolves around the Tennessee city and its huge nuclear-research complex. As chairman of the Science Subcommittee on Energy Research and Development and a member of the Armed Services Subcommittee on Procurement, she is well placed to guard the Oak Ridge National Laboratory and the defense- and energy-related contractors working around it.

This devotion plays well at home, but it has earned Lloyd a reputation in Washington as a parochialist working in areas where important national policy is under debate. Her devotion to the legislative process was called further into question when she announced plans to retire at the end of the 100th Congress, then changed her mind several months later.

Lloyd is not without larger responsibilities. Her Science Subcommittee had jurisdiction over the superconducting supercollider project in the 100th Congress; now it is dealing with the waste-cleanup problem at the nation's nuclear-weapons materials plants.

But Oak Ridge is Lloyd's central interest, and she is not shy about saying it. Before passage of the fiscal 1988 energy appropriations bill, she bragged about her role in providing money for the Department of Energy's (DOE) research and development activities in both nuclear and non-nuclear research and development programs. "A great deal of this work is done in Oak Ridge," she said.

Lloyd also does what she can to attract defense contractors to Oak Ridge. When Boeing Corp. expressed interest in building the SRAM II and Sea Lance missiles in Oak Ridge, Lloyd attached a provision to the fiscal 1987 defense authorization bill permitting the transfer of land from DOE to the city. Boeing then bought the land from Oak Ridge for about $1.4 million.

With the many nuclear facilities in her district, Lloyd is well aware of the industry's concerns. When her Science panel debated a revision of the Price-Anderson nuclear-accident liability law, she supported provisions limiting a utility's liability to $7 billion — a figure well above the previous level, but acceptable to the industry.

One project Lloyd opposed was a temporary waste-storage facility proposed for Oak Ridge. In 1986, she said the Monitored Retrievable Storage (MRS) facility would hurt the local economy, since being called a " 'nuclear-waste dump' ... would be a hindrance in promoting the area as a good place to live and do business." In 1987, Lloyd and other MRS opponents won out. Authors of a bill to create a permanent nuclear-waste site in Nevada got support by removing the threat of a dump site from several states, including Tennessee.

Her persistence notwithstanding, Lloyd does not always win on her nuclear priorities. In the early 1980s, she fought without success to keep alive the Clinch River nuclear breeder reactor, which was to be built in her district.

On the broader range of defense issues debated on Armed Services, Lloyd is in the diminishing group of "Old Guard" conservative Democrats. This posture colors her overall record, one of the most conservative among House Democrats. But her pro-Pentagon position is tempered by more typical party stands on social service and economic development programs. She also is a vocal backer of such regional development agencies as the Appalachian Regional Commission and the Tennessee Valley Authority (TVA).

At Home: Early in 1988 it seemed certain Lloyd would not be in the 101st Congress. Following tough re-elections in 1984 and 1986, she said in 1987 she would not seek another term.

But after several months, she surprised those who were vying to succeed her by announcing that she would run again after all. Her change of heart caused a number of local Democrats to put their ambitions on hold, but it was a great relief to state Democratic Party officials; they were were concerned about losing the seat and had urged Lloyd to reconsider.

Two top GOP contenders dropped their candidacies once Lloyd got back in. But one,

Tennessee 3

Southeast — Chattanooga; Oak Ridge

Although the 3rd usually votes GOP in state and national elections, Lloyd has proven that it can accept a conservative, locally oriented Democrat who backs nuclear power. This stance is a must for any legislator representing this area. With nuclear facilities both in Oak Ridge and near Chattanooga, thousands of jobs are tied to atomic energy.

A legislator from here must also pay attention to the coal industry. Anderson County is the largest coal-producing county in the state, and Grundy and Marion counties also have coal activity.

The population center of the 3rd is Chattanooga, a heavily industrialized city producing iron, steel and textiles. Chattanooga and surrounding Hamilton County hold more than half of the 3rd's residents. There has been some racial tension between Chattanooga's working-class whites, many of whom come from rural backgrounds, and blacks, who make up about one-third of the population — a high percentage by East Tennessee standards. But there has also been an ambitious private-public effort in Chattanooga to build and refurbish more than 13,000 homes for low-income residents.

Hamilton County has voted Republican in all but one presidential contest since 1952. That was in 1968, when George C. Wallace finished first and Republican Richard M. Nixon second. George Bush carried Hamilton with more than 60 percent of the vote in 1988. At the same time, Democratic Sen. Jim Sasser won about 55 percent of the vote, a far lower percentage than he received statewide. Lloyd ran even in Hamilton in 1984, then won it narrowly in 1986 and more comfortably in her strong 1988 election.

In many past elections, the district's most Democratic counties have been Anderson and Roane, where the major city is Oak Ridge. Lloyd runs extremely well there. But the presidential political loyalties of the government workers and scientific intelligentsia at Oak Ridge have shifted somewhat as the GOP has taken the leading role in promoting nuclear energy. In 1976, Jimmy Carter won 56 percent in both Anderson and Roane counties, but in 1980 he averaged only 38 percent. Reagan drew over 60 percent in Anderson and Roane in 1984, and the same was true for Bush four years later.

Oak Ridge has had to make some adjustments during the 1980s. The government cut back on funding for some projects, such as a gaseous diffusion plant, causing concern about job losses. But Oak Ridge's work force is attractive to private industry, which has picked up some of the slack. The end of the decade has witnessed the arrival of some new medium-sized firms involved in the nuclear industry, data systems research and other scientific endeavors. And government money does continue to flow, in part because of new defense efforts; a new Boeing missile factory is under way.

Population: 516,692. White 449,455 (87%), Black 63,870 (12%), Other 2,418 (1%). Spanish origin 3,701 (1%). 18 and over 370,457 (72%), 65 and over 55,994 (11%). Median age: 31.

Harold Coker, stayed on and made Lloyd work for another term.

In 1984, Lloyd had failed to pay attention to an aggressive but little-known opponent and nearly lost; two years later, she had a tough campaign against a political neophyte who was initially not considered a serious threat. Coker, unlike those before him, began with a political base and name recognition stemming from his service on the County Commission in Hamilton County, home to roughly half the 3rd's voters. He also owned a chain of tire stores that bore his name.

Coker launched a variety of attacks on Lloyd, saying she had not paid enough attention to the TVA, which had recently laid off a number of workers, and that her 1982 move from the Public Works Committee to Armed Services had boosted her campaign treasury and honoraria totals more than it boosted the district.

But Lloyd, who had obviously learned the dangers of complacency in recent years, was quick to defend herself and strike back at Coker. She was first to issue the challenge for a debate, and she criticized Coker for refusing to release tax returns from his tire business. She also said he was wrong to criticize her for taking honoraria when Republicans appearing in the district on his behalf also took honoraria.

When combined with her conservative voting record and scrupulous attention to her constituents, Lloyd's vigorous campaign effort made it difficult for Coker to make inroads. She ended up with her best showing in three elections, a comfortable 57 percent.

Lloyd's initial victory in 1974 was a surprise. The Democratic nomination had gone to her husband Mort, a well-known Chattanooga newsman. But when he died in a plane crash, the county chairmen chose his widow as the nominee. She had owned and operated a radio station with her husband, but was a political novice and seemed to have little chance against two-term GOP Rep. Lamar Baker.

But Lloyd turned out to be surprisingly aggressive, and she found a winning combination of issues in the Watergate year: opposition to busing, more rights for women and criticism of President Ford's pardon of former President Nixon. She unseated Baker with 51 percent.

In her first term, Lloyd built a following with question-and-answer town hall meetings and covered-dish suppers. Baker tried a comeback in 1976, but lost by a margin of more than 2-to-1. After the 1978 election, Lloyd appeared on voters' ballots as Marilyn Lloyd Bouquard, a result of her marriage to Chattanooga engineer Joseph P. Bouquard. But they divorced in 1983 and she became Marilyn Lloyd once again.

In 1984 she faced John Davis, a political consultant and one-time Republican National Committee aide. Though touted by the national party, Davis had trouble cracking the state GOP establishment, and he started out financially strapped. Lloyd all but ignored him.

As the campaign wore on, however, Davis proved adept at winning media coverage. Outgoing and energetic, he attracted votes in traditionally Republican counties by arguing that Lloyd's "pork-barrel" politics had done less to bring jobs to the 3rd than would his emphasis on wooing new industry. Davis' background in the moderate wing of the GOP also helped him among middle-of-the-road voters who had been turned off by Lloyd's earlier, more conservative opponents. Davis ran virtually even with Lloyd in Hamilton County and won 48 percent districtwide.

Davis was expected back for a rematch in 1986, but he was upset in the primary by Chattanooga attorney Jim Golden, a political outsider with a strong base in the 3rd's sizable evangelical community. Handsome and articulate, Golden broadened his appeal beyond evangelicals by emphasizing economic issues.

But while Golden made a stronger bid than many had expected, establishment Republicans remained wary of his background. Their resistance, combined with Lloyd's renewed attention to her campaign machinery, enabled her to take 54 percent. She narrowly won Hamilton County, and, as in 1984, got much of her margin in Anderson County (Oak Ridge).

Committees

Armed Services (15th of 31 Democrats)
Military Personnel and Compensation; Procurement and Military Nuclear Systems

Science, Space and Technology (4th of 30 Democrats)
Energy Research and Development (chairman); Space Science and Applications

Select Aging (6th of 39 Democrats)
Housing and Consumer Interests; Retirement, Income and Employment

Elections

1988 General		
Marilyn Lloyd (D)	108,264	(57%)
Harold L. Coker (R)	80,372	(43%)
1988 Primary		
Marilyn Lloyd (D)	31,007	(89%)
Walter Ward (D)	2,168	(6%)
Lamar Lasley (D)	1,815	(5%)
1986 General		
Marilyn Lloyd (D)	75,034	(54%)
Jim Golden (R)	64,084	(46%)

Previous Winning Percentages: **1984** (52%) **1982** (62%) **1980** (61%) **1978** (89%) **1976** (68%) **1974** (51%)

District Vote For President

	1988		1984		1980		1976	
D	70,874	(37%)	72,122	(37%)	74,677	(41%)	85,514	(51%)
R	117,220	(62%)	121,921	(63%)	101,094	(56%)	79,510	(48%)
I					4,202	(2%)		

Campaign Finance

	Receipts	Receipts from PACs	Expend-itures
1988			
Lloyd (D)	$621,520	$320,387 (52%)	$618,173
Coker (R)	$628,222	$28,331 (5%)	$626,945
1986			
Lloyd (D)	$636,851	$323,624 (51%)	$637,887
Golden (R)	$455,666	$29,302 (6%)	$455,298

Key Votes

1987	
Raise speed limit to 65 mph	Y
Approve Gephardt "fair trade" amendment	Y
Ban testing of larger nuclear weapons	N
Delay "re-flagging" of Kuwaiti tankers	Y
Approve tax-raising deficit-reduction bill	Y
1988	
Approve aid to Nicaraguan contras	Y
Enact civil rights restoration bill over Reagan veto	Y
Kill 60-day plant-closing notification measure	N
Pass omnibus trade bill over Reagan veto	Y
Approve death penalty for drug-related murders	Y
Bar federal funds for abortions in cases of rape and incest	Y
Oppose seven-day waiting period for purchase of handguns	Y

Voting Studies

	Presidential Support		Party Unity		Conservative Coalition	
Year	**S**	**O**	**S**	**O**	**S**	**O**
1988	47	51	59	37	89	3
1987	40	49	54	27	81	9
1986	53	44	39	55	92	6
1985	52	45	56	39	82	16
1984	52	42	48	47	90	10
1983	54	41	41	50	90	7
1982	47	47	56	38	73	22
1981	57	36	55	41	83	12

Interest Group Ratings

Year	ADA	ACU	AFL-CIO	CCUS
1988	50	54	100	46
1987	28	32	62	42
1986	20	62	50	53
1985	35	48	75	45
1984	35	67	50	50
1983	25	78	47	55
1982	25	55	60	52
1981	30	53	67	37

4 Jim Cooper (D)

Of Shelbyville — Elected 1982

Born: June 19, 1954, Shelbyville, Tenn.
Education: U. of North Carolina, B.A. 1975; Oxford U., B.A., M.A. 1977; Harvard Law School, J.D. 1980.
Occupation: Lawyer.
Family: Wife, Martha Hays.
Religion: Episcopalian.
Political Career: No previous office.
Capitol Office: 125 Cannon Bldg. 20515; 225-6831.

In Washington: Cooper is young, smart and politically secure, but he lacks the brashness one might expect from a member with so many advantages. While he certainly does not shun publicity and headlines, Cooper seems most comfortable working quietly behind the scenes, weighing the issues and studying the personal relationships that often determine whether legislation moves or stalls.

Urbane and soft-spoken, Cooper is almost the antithesis of the backslapping Southern pol, but he is nonetheless adept at building social relationships in the House. For a number of younger members, sweaty games of basketball in the House gym are a primary networking tool. But Cooper decided that the way to get to know some of his more senior colleagues was to meet them on their own ground, so he took up playing golf.

The contacts he made on the links with leadership figures helped him win a seat on Energy and Commerce at the start of the 100th Congress. He outpolled all other hopefuls in his bid for the powerful panel; he had a crucial ally in Chairman John D. Dingell of Michigan, who helped Cooper and two other members from coal-producing states get on the committee. Dingell for years has worked to head off controls on acid rain, which is said to be caused by coal-burning heavy industry, particularly in the Midwest.

In his first term on Energy and Commerce, Cooper threw himself into one of the toughest issues before the committee — the effort to write clean-air legislation to deal with urban smog and acid rain. Renewal of the Clean Air Act had been a political migraine for several years before Cooper got to the committee, because of a standoff between an environmentalist faction, led by California Democrat Henry A. Waxman, and a more industry-oriented faction led by Dingell. To break the deadlock, Cooper teamed with the so-called "group of nine," a caucus of moderate-to-conservative committee Democrats determined to find the acceptable middle ground that had eluded Dingell and Waxman.

"If we don't do anything this year," Cooper said in 1988, "we face a twin danger: the danger of no bill passing for years and the chance of a bill passing that's too tough and too expensive."

Cooper was a diligent player in all aspects of the group's behind-closed-doors effort, even though some of the issues being discussed, such as urban smog, are of little concern to his rural Tennessee constituency. The group was able to produce a detailed proposal for addressing only one of the problems, smog, and talks over those provisions eventually stalled in both houses of Congress. But the group's proposal helped lay the groundwork for debate in the 101st Congress. And Cooper's contributions earned him credibility with other members, perhaps making them more receptive to his views in the coal/acid-rain debate, where he has a more direct interest.

In the 100th Congress, Cooper's effort to find a middle ground on that matter involved a plan setting timetables and standards for reduction of emissions from utilities that are the primary cause of acid rain. To pay for that reduction, Cooper proposed a tax on utilities based on how cleanly they burn coal. His plan also allowed utilities to choose the means of meeting the reduction requirements.

The proposal won some support from utility lobbyists and from Western states, many of which had cleaner-burning plants and did not want to pay for cleanup of Eastern plants. Another player smiling on the effort was Dingell. But as Congress edged toward adjournment, no agreement had been reached in the Senate, and Clean Air Act efforts in both houses ultimately ground to a halt.

Cooper often echoes Dingell's sentiments on Energy and Commerce, but not always. Cooper seems to be one of the committee's strongest supporters of legislation granting banks new powers. In 1988, when Dingell offered a bill with sharper limits on some activities by banks than were included in a Banking Committee bill, Cooper complained it was "a giant step backward."

Evidence that Cooper is no lap dog for his elders also came earlier, in the 99th Congress,

Tennessee 4

Northeast and South Central

The unwieldy 4th sprawls across eastern and Middle Tennessee for nearly 300 miles. One end of it is not far from Mississippi; the other touches the Virginia border. About the only thing these 23 counties have in common is their rural nature.

People here form their political opinions by talking with neighbors in feed stores and roadside cafés and in small-town shops that surround the courthouse squares. There is only one daily newspaper in the district, and while television is available from several cities outside the district, no station pays much attention to the rural counties. The district's largest city is Morristown (Hamblen County), with 20,000 people.

The roots of political preference in this part of Tennessee go back many generations. In the mountainous northern counties, the GOP has been the dominant party since the Civil War. Even in Cooper's sweeping 1982 victory, the north's Hancock County went Republican.

Tobacco grows in the valleys of the northern counties, and beef and dairy cattle graze on hillsides too steep for plowing. Coal long has been an economic staple, but underground activity has mostly given way to surface mining.

As one drives south through the 4th, the terrain levels out and an Appalachian twang gives way to a Southern drawl. Rural Democratic populism has prevailed in the district's southern counties since secession. In Bedford County, Cooper's home and one of the most heavily Democratic counties in the 4th, cotton has been supplanted by soybeans and corn. Sour mash whiskey is made by the Jack Daniel Distillery in Lynchburg (Moore County) and consumed to excess at the annual Tennessee Walking Horse Celebration in Shelbyville (Bedford County).

Population: 510,732. White 489,861 (96%), Black 19,148 (4%). Spanish origin 3,448 (1%). 18 and over 359,160 (70%), 65 and over 61,644 (12%). Median age: 31.

when he was so dissatisfied with life on the Banking Committee that he publicly criticized panel Chairman Fernand J. St Germain. Others were saying privately that Banking was adrift because the autocratic St Germain was preoccupied with an ethics investigation and a tough re-election campaign, but it caused a stir when the normally cautious Cooper aired his frustrations in public.

Not all of Cooper's issues are global in nature. In fact, he said in 1988 that the most important issue he has faced in Congress — in terms of the impact on his district — concerned regulations imposed on the walking-horse industry.

Through shows and horse sales, the industry brings in a reported $37 million annually to Cooper's district, so he was agitated when the Agriculture Department, in response to a lawsuit, banned use of the padded horse shoes and bracelet-like chains that enhance the horses' famous high step. The American Horse Protection Association, which brought the suit, argued that the devices hurt the horses. But Cooper and other members of the Tennessee delegation worked to find a compromise with Agriculture Department officials that would keep the walking-horse industry in business.

Cooper can look beyond the parochial position, even on issues involving his district. There are many tobacco farmers in the 4th, and Cooper has surprised colleagues in Washington with his criticism of cigarette smoking. But Cooper says, "I'm not anti-tobacco, I'm anti-cancer," and points out that he is "anxious to keep [his constituents] alive as long as possible." Of tobacco growers, he says, "They're not dumb. They know what's going on. They know they don't want their children and grandchildren to smoke."

At Home: Though he is a Rhodes scholar who spent his formative years at prestigious schools far from Tennessee, Cooper has an easy rapport with his overwhelmingly rural constituency. He can demonstrate his intelligence without talking down to people, and his middle Tennessee accent survived Groton, Chapel Hill, Oxford and Harvard. Cooper's three-syllable hometown comes out of his mouth as "Shelbvul," just as residents pronounce it.

Most voters in the 4th are as comfortable with Cooper's background as one front-porch philosopher, who, told in 1982 that Cooper was a Rhodes scholar, said, "That's good to hear. It's about time somebody did something about the roads around here."

Several prominent Democrats considered running in the newly created 4th in 1982, but none entered; they were dissuaded by Cooper's full-time campaigning and his family's financial resources. None could match the pedigree that gave Cooper "star quality." His father, Prentice Cooper, was Tennessee's governor from 1939-45, and many older people in the 4th remember voting for or hearing about Prentice.

After an easy primary he faced Republican

Cissy Baker, the 26-year-old daughter of Senate Majority Leader Howard H. Baker Jr.

The general election, pitting two scions of famous political families, drew media from across the nation. This free coverage helped Cooper offset Baker's money advantage; she spent just over $1 million.

Cooper was rated the front-runner because of the district's Democratic leanings and because Baker had struggled in the primary, winning 55 percent against two weak opponents. But few expected Cooper to win as lopsidedly as he did, carrying all but one of 23 counties. Cooper benefited greatly from concern over unemployment, always a chronic problem here and particularly severe in 1982.

Committees

Energy and Commerce (23rd of 26 Democrats)
Energy and Power; Telecommunications and Finance

Small Business (13th of 27 Democrats)
Antitrust, Impact of Deregulation and Privatization; Environment and Labor; SBA, the General Economy and Minority Enterprise Development

Elections

1988 General		
Jim Cooper (D)	94,129	(100%)
1986 General		
Jim Cooper (D)	86,997	(100%)

Previous Winning Percentages: **1984** (75%) **1982** (66%)

District Vote For President

	1988	1984	1980	1976
D	66,656 (42%)	69,685 (42%)	80,216 (48%)	92,374 (60%)
R	91,186 (57%)	95,172 (57%)	81,664 (49%)	59,365 (39%)
I			2,566 (2%)	

Campaign Finance

	Receipts	Receipts from PACs	Expend-itures
1988			
Cooper (D)	$292,770	$244,977 (84%)	$234,375
1986			
Cooper (D)	$146,714	$90,754 (62%)	$127,108

Key Votes

1987	
Raise speed limit to 65 mph	N
Approve Gephardt "fair trade" amendment	Y
Ban testing of larger nuclear weapons	Y
Delay "re-flagging" of Kuwaiti tankers	N
Approve tax-raising deficit-reduction bill	Y
1988	
Approve aid to Nicaraguan contras	N
Enact civil rights restoration bill over Reagan veto	Y
Kill 60-day plant-closing notification measure	Y
Pass omnibus trade bill over Reagan veto	Y
Approve death penalty for drug-related murders	Y
Bar federal funds for abortions in cases of rape and incest	N
Oppose seven-day waiting period for purchase of handguns	N

Voting Studies

	Presidential Support		Party Unity		Conservative Coalition	
Year	S	O	S	O	S	O
1988	34	65	84	15	66	32
1987	25	66	77	14	53	35
1986	31	68	80	14	52	40
1985	43	55	85	13	40	60
1984	42	52	74	20	49	51
1983	32	59	69	24	56	35

Interest Group Ratings

Year	ADA	ACU	AFL-CIO	CCUS
1988	70	28	79	69
1987	68	9	73	43
1986	70	14	64	53
1985	55	24	71	45
1984	80	26	67	53
1983	45	43	59	50

5 Bob Clement (D)

Of Nashville — Elected 1988

Born: Sept. 23, 1943, Nashville, Tenn.

Education: U. of Tennessee, B.S. 1967; Memphis State U., M.B.A. 1968.

Military Career: Army, 1969-71; Tenn. Army National Guard, 1971-present.

Occupation: Former college president.

Family: Wife, Mary Carson; four children.

Religion: Methodist.

Political Career: Tenn. Public Service Commission, 1973-79; sought Democratic nomination for governor, 1978; Democratic nominee for U.S. House, 1982.

Capitol Office: 325 Cannon Bldg. 20515; 225-4311.

In Washington: Nearly 20 years ago, Clement was a fast-rising star in Tennessee Democratic politics. Son of a three-term governor, he was elected statewide at age 29 to an office often used as a steppingstone to higher posts. But several twists of political fate seem to have brought changes in Clement: Once a fiery populist with a driving personal ambition, he is quieter in the House, a loyal party man and junior member of the Public Works Committee.

The senior member of the class of 1988 — he was elected in a January 1988 special election — Clement was named the class representative on the Democratic Steering and Policy Committee, which makes committee assignments.

In his first year in Congress, Clement voted with the Democrats on partisan votes more often than the average Southern Democrat. Two-thirds of the time he opposed President Reagan's position. One of his earliest votes was to reject Reagan's request for $36 million for military and non-military aid to the Nicaraguan contras. Later, he supported "humanitarian" contra aid. Clement was one of only 20 Southern Democrats to vote against killing a seven-day waiting period for purchasing handguns.

Clement had a brush with heart trouble in 1988. In June, he was admitted to a Nashville hospital, where he had an angioplasty to dilate a narrowed artery.

At Home: With his resounding triumph in the 1988 special election in the 5th, Clement resurrected a moribund political career.

By winning the race to succeed former Democratic Rep. Bill Boner, now Nashville's mayor, Clement set aside bitter memories from two previous defeats — including a 1982 House bid he was favored to win — and stepped out of the shadow cast by his father, the late Frank G. Clement, who was Tennessee's governor for three terms in the 1950s and 1960s.

In 1972, Bob Clement became a political "boy wonder" by winning East Tennessee's seat on the state Public Service Commission (PSC). Then 29, he was the youngest candidate ever elected statewide in Tennessee. In six years on the PSC, Clement built up the already formidable visibility of the Clement name. But when he sought nomination for governor in 1978, he lost to wealthy businessman Jake Butcher.

In 1979, President Jimmy Carter appointed Clement to the Tennessee Valley Authority board, where, as he had on the PSC, he drew headlines for his efforts to hold down utility rates. In 1982, Clement lowered his political sights, seeking the open 7th District, which ran from his family's traditional base west of Nashville all the way to Memphis. The 7th leaned Democratic, and the GOP nominee — Memphis businessman Don Sundquist — had a fraction of Clement's name recognition. But a huge Sundquist vote from Memphis' suburbs overcame Clement's rural backing.

Tagged as an itinerant loser, Clement recused himself from politics and became president of Cumberland College. The school's location — in Lebanon, east of Nashville — helped Clement remain visible in the capital.

After Boner was elected mayor in 1987, the special Democratic primary for his House seat boiled down to Clement, who needed a heavy vote from working-class whites who were Boner's strength, and wealthy businessman Phil Bredesen, who narrowly lost the mayoralty to Boner and ran a media-dominated House campaign targeted at more affluent Democrats and GOP-leaning voters. Clement won 40-36 percent.

In the traditionally Democratic 5th, only a flawless campaign by Republican Terry Holcomb would have made inroads, and Holcomb's bid was far from that. Though he raised over $300,000, he ran out of money without airing a single TV ad. Even absent the funding problems, Holcomb faced daunting odds: The home turf of such House members as Andrew Jackson and Sam Houston, Davidson County (Nashville) has not chosen a GOP House member since Reconstruction.

Tennessee 5

Nashville

More than 90 percent of the 5th District vote comes from Nashville and surrounding Davidson County, where Democrats normally prevail. George Bush managed to carry the county (and the district) in 1988, but that did not spark any wave of straight-ticket voting; Democratic Sen. Jim Sasser won Davidson overwhelmingly.

Country music may be Nashville's most famous industry, but state government is its leading employer. Davidson County is home to 17 colleges and universities, and its factories manufacture aircraft parts, glass, clothing and tires. Also, it is headquarters for several publishers of religious materials.

In recent years, Nashville has been gaining a reputation as the next great Sun Belt boom town. As governor from 1979-87, Republican Lamar Alexander successfully touted Tennessee's work force and business climate, particularly to Japanese investors. Nissan built a huge plant south of Nashville, and other Japanese companies have followed, many locating around the city. In addition, General Motors chose a site near Nashville for its massive new Saturn facility. Economic forecasters predict that many other jobs will spin off from these major investments, so the personality of the electorate could be in for some big changes.

But for now, the Democratic inclinations of government workers, the academic communities and labor unions uphold Nashville's traditional position as the focal point of Middle Tennessee Democratic populism. That brand of politics took hold in Nashville early in this century as a reaction to the conservative Democratic machine in Memphis that controlled Tennessee politics until after World War II.

Nashville's population is 23 percent black, a relatively low figure for a large Southern city. Nashville politics has not polarized along racial lines to the degree seen in Memphis and Chattanooga, where blacks make up a higher percentage of the population and whites have drifted from Democratic loyalties. Most white voters here are still Democrats.

Population: 514,832. White 398,418 (77%), Black 111,329 (22%), Other 2,932 (1%). Spanish origin 3,961 (1%). 18 and over 384,057 (75%), 65 and over 57,539 (11%). Median age: 30.

Committees

Merchant Marine and Fisheries (21st of 26 Democrats)
Coast Guard and Navigation; Oceanography

Public Works and Transportation (23rd of 31 Democrats)
Aviation; Surface Transportation; Water Resources

Campaign Finance

	Receipts	Receipts from PACs	Expend-itures
1988			
Clement (D)	$1,267,477	$360,500 (28%)	$1,230,310
1988 Special Election			
Clement (D) †	$396,668	$12,950 (3%)	$352,832
Holcomb (R)	$322,519	$51,550 (16%)	$316,887

† Totals based on pre-election data only.

Voting Studies

	Presidential Support		Party Unity		Conservative Coalition	
Year	**S**	**O**	**S**	**O**	**S**	**O**
1988	31	66	79	14	63	32

Interest Group Ratings

Year	ADA	ACU	AFL-CIO	CCUS
1988	75	20	93	36

Key Votes

1988

Approve aid to Nicaraguan contras	N
Enact civil rights restoration bill over Reagan veto	Y
Kill 60-day plant-closing notification measure	N
Pass omnibus trade bill over Reagan veto	Y
Approve death penalty for drug-related murders	Y
Bar federal funds for abortions in cases of rape and incest	Y
Oppose seven-day waiting period for purchase of handguns	N

Elections

1988 General		
Bob Clement (D)	155,068	(100%)
1988 Special Election		
Bob Clement (D)	56,323	(62%)
Terry Holcomb (R)	32,847	(36%)
1987 Special Primary		
Bob Clement (D)	43,868	(40%)
Phil Bredesen (D)	39,745	(36%)
Jane Eskind (D)	16,128	(15%)
Walter Searcy (D)	9,746	(9%)

District Vote For President

	1988	1984	1980	1976
D	95,154 (47%)	95,254 (48%)	111,122 (60%)	106,554 (62%)
R	104,313 (52%)	103,600 (52%)	69,332 (37%)	63,167 (37%)
I			4,961 (3%)	

6 Bart Gordon (D)

Of Murfreesboro — Elected 1984

Born: Jan. 24, 1949, Murfreesboro, Tenn.
Education: Middle Tennessee State U., B.S. 1971; U. of Tennessee Law School, J.D. 1973.
Occupation: Lawyer.
Family: Single.
Religion: Methodist.
Political Career: Tenn. Democratic chairman, 1981-83.
Capitol Office: 103 Cannon Bldg. 20515; 225-4231.

In Washington: Few junior House members had more cause than Gordon to fret over the ethics investigation of Speaker Jim Wright. Though the amiable Tennesseean is well liked and is recognized as a steady performer on the Rules Committee, he remains best known as the premier Wright protégé from the class of 1984.

Gordon caught Wright's eye early on; a former chairman of the Tennessee Democratic Party, he had clear potential as a team player and leadership loyalist. In late 1986, Wright urged Gordon to run for the Democratic Steering and Policy Committee. He lost to a more senior member, but Wright paved his way onto Rules, which Gordon has called the "Speaker's Cabinet." He also serves as a deputy Democratic whip.

Gordon has rarely disappointed the leadership. In 1988, he voted with the majority of his party 84 percent of the time on the floor. Though he rejects the liberal label thrust at him by his 6th District Republican opponents, Gordon received an 80 percent rating that year from the Americans for Democratic Action, second in Tennessee only to liberal black Democrat Harold E. Ford of Memphis.

In 1987, Gordon was a leader of the whip operation on a controversial amendment to delay President Reagan's order to provide U.S. protection to Kuwaiti oil tankers in the Persian Gulf. Gordon earned the assignment because of his position on Rules; the leadership feared Reagan supporters would try to scuttle the amendment by defeating the rule that made it germane to the Coast Guard authorization bill to which it was attached. Republicans called the amendment a dangerous limitation on the president's decision-making powers; it passed the House, but died in the Senate.

Preoccupied by his partisan role and the nuts-and-bolts activities of Rules, Gordon has left few fingerprints on major bills. Most of his legislative pursuits have had to do with 6th District interests. In the 100th Congress, he lobbied successfully for a bill authorizing a federal land purchase to expand the Civil War battlefield park at Stones River.

At Home: Gordon was still in college when he worked on the unsuccessful 1968 House campaign of a state representative from his hometown. Sixteen years later, the Senate candidacy of Democratic Rep. Al Gore enabled Gordon to wage his own campaign.

Gordon built his political credentials within the state party structure. Fresh out of law school, he won a seat on the state Democratic Executive Committee, and in 1979 he parlayed his contacts into a position as the party's executive director. Two years later, he won the party chairmanship. In that position he computerized the party mailing list and set up a direct-mail program — experience that proved crucial to his House campaign.

Gordon's chief rivals in the 1984 House contest were state Rep. Lincoln Davis, who represented a cluster of counties in the Upper Cumberland region of the 6th, and Bryant Millsaps, the state House chief clerk, who shared Gordon's home base of Murfreesboro.

Gordon set himself apart from his primary opponents by developing a sophisticated phone bank and direct-mail operation. In the final weeks, while Millsaps focused on television advertising and Davis on pulling out his Upper Cumberland vote, Gordon's forces repeatedly wrote and telephoned undecided voters across the district. The effort enabled Gordon to win the six-way contest with 28 percent of the vote.

During the campaign, Gordon had to deal with the potentially explosive issue of a paternity suit that had been brought against him and was later dismissed. Gordon denied fathering the child, and none of his primary opponents raised the issue. But his GOP opponent, Williamson County construction executive Joe Simkins, accused him of a "cover-up," after the *Nashville Banner* alleged that Gordon had paid the woman to drop the suit.

Simkins, whose brother was publisher of the Banner, set a "countdown deadline" for Gordon to explain the settlement. Gordon simply ignored the challenge, as did most voters. He won all but two counties on Election Day.

Tennessee 6

North Central — Murfreesboro

This slice of Middle Tennessee spills out of the hills along the Kentucky border and runs through the lawns of suburban Nashville into the farm country beyond. It has always been Democratic, with old courthouse networks controlling politics and people living at an unhurried pace. But with the expansion of the suburbs and the introduction of two gargantuan vehicle-assembly plants, much is changing.

Republicans have made significant inroads in the metropolitan Nashville part of the 6th. These areas, filling with commuters, have no link to the rural and small-town Democratic traditions of the past. Williamson County, south of Nashville, gave George Bush more than 72 percent of the vote in 1988. In 1984 Williamson went against Gordon.

Outside Williamson, industrial expansion in once-sleepy towns is increasing the 6th's blue-collar work force. For now at least, the labor vote seems inclined to stay Democratic. In Smyrna, southeast of Nashville in Rutherford County, Japan's Nissan Motor Co. makes cars and light trucks at a facility that is the largest Japanese investment in the United States, employing some 3,000 people.

Just south of Williamson County in the tiny Maury County town of Spring Hill, General Motors chose a site for a multibillion-dollar complex to build its Saturn car. The high-tech facility, the largest single industrial investment in U.S. history, is to start production by 1990 and employ 20,000.

By comparison, the "Upper Cumberland" region that makes up the eastern side of the 6th is lagging economically. Farming is in hard times, and the textile trades that hold many of the small towns together are even weaker.

Population: 511,805. White 471,838 (92%), Black 37,301 (7%). Spanish origin 3,377 (1%). 18 and over 362,322 (71%), 65 and over 55,363 (11%). Median age: 30.

Committees

Rules (8th of 9 Democrats)
Legislative Process

Select Aging (26th of 39 Democrats)
Housing and Consumer Interests

Elections

1988 General

Bart Gordon (D)	123,652	(76%)
Wallace Embry (R)	38,033	(24%)

1986 General

Bart Gordon (D)	102,180	(77%)
Fred Vail (R)	30,823	(23%)

Previous Winning Percentage: 1984 (63%)

District Vote For President

	1988	1984	1980	1976
D	72,992 (39%)	75,667 (41%)	92,485 (55%)	93,751 (64%)
R	111,548 (60%)	108,626 (59%)	72,526 (43%)	49,892 (34%)
I			3,209 (2%)	

Campaign Finance

	Receipts	Receipts from PACs	Expend-itures
1988			
Gordon (D)	$587,878	$256,095 (44%)	$454,346
Embry (R)	$12,635	$500 (4%)	$12,635
1986			
Gordon (D)	$399,027	$191,237 (48%)	$253,689
Vail (R)	$3,215	0	$2,006

Key Votes

1987	
Raise speed limit to 65 mph	Y
Approve Gephardt "fair trade" amendment	Y
Ban testing of larger nuclear weapons	Y
Delay "re-flagging" of Kuwaiti tankers	Y
Approve tax-raising deficit-reduction bill	Y
1988	
Approve aid to Nicaraguan contras	N
Enact civil rights restoration bill over Reagan veto	Y
Kill 60-day plant-closing notification measure	N
Pass omnibus trade bill over Reagan veto	Y
Approve death penalty for drug-related murders	N
Bar federal funds for abortions in cases of rape and incest	N
Oppose seven-day waiting period for purchase of handguns	Y

Voting Studies

	Presidential Support		Party Unity		Conservative Coalition	
Year	**S**	**O**	**S**	**O**	**S**	**O**
1988	23	73	84	8	53	45
1987	27	69	82	10	63	37
1986	27	72	83	12	56	40
1985	33	66	79	13	42	56

Interest Group Ratings

Year	ADA	ACU	AFL-CIO	CCUS
1988	80	12	93	36
1987	64	0	87	29
1986	75	9	86	39
1985	55	20	63	45

7 Don Sundquist (R)

Of Memphis — Elected 1982

Born: March 15, 1936, Moline, Ill.
Education: Augustana College (Ill.), B.A. 1957.
Military Career: Navy, 1957-59.
Occupation: Owner of printing, advertising and marketing firm.
Family: Wife, Martha Swanson; three children.
Religion: Lutheran.
Political Career: No previous office.
Capitol Office: 230 Cannon Bldg. 20515; 225-2811.

In Washington: An advertising executive by profession, Sundquist made it to the House in 1983 after years of loyal party work that won him the confidence of influential Republicans in West Tennessee. In Washington, he has shown the same political acumen, quietly working his way into the hearts and minds of his colleagues and party leaders. The payoff in the 101st Congress was a coveted seat on the Ways and Means Committee.

Though Sundquist has been involved in issues strategizing for the GOP, the Ways and Means assignment came to him mostly because of his political sensibilities, not any particular legislative achievement. He has worked hard to get to know his colleagues, and more than a few of them seek his political advice before a difficult vote. In the 99th Congress, he was named regional whip for Southern and border states. Two years later, he was rewarded with a seat on the Budget Committee.

Sundquist's years of service to the GOP have also brought him an important ally outside the House. When he was national chairman of the Young Republicans in the 1970s, Sundquist became acquainted with then-Republican National Committee Chairman George Bush; in the 1988 presidential contest, Sundquist was a chief House organizer for Bush's primary and general-election campaigns.

Sundquist's personal style is not confrontational, but he is a strong believer in party-building, and in the House he wants Republicans to do more to see that the federal government does less. He is the archetypal New South conservative businessman — a man who bemoans bureaucratic inefficiencies and believes that most things the federal government does can be done better by local government or the private sector.

As part of his push for governmental efficiency, Sundquist has called for a revival of federal revenue sharing, as a replacement for a variety of economic-development programs. He has complained that grant formulas developed in years past discriminate against rural areas — such as those in his district — and that administrative costs are excessive and unnecessary. Localities are better suited to make spending decisions, he maintains.

Sundquist is not dead-set against federal spending, however. Until the 101st Congress he served on the Public Works and Transportation Committee, where colleagues noted with grudging admiration how many Memphis projects found their way into legislation. On Public Works, Sundquist targeted his crusade for efficiency at the Tennessee Valley Authority, which he views as a bloated bureaucracy. He has supported cost-cutting measures put into effect by Reagan-appointed TVA officials in recent years.

The Ways and Means assignment gives Sundquist an opportunity to involve himself in a variety of issues. He has already shown interest in trade legislation, serving for several years as chairman of the House Republican Task Force on Trade and Competitiveness. Sundquist has constituents employed in shoe factories, and in the 99th Congress he pushed for footwear-protection provisions in a bill limiting textile imports. While he voted to override a presidential veto of the bill in 1986, he did not support such a move when a textile bill came up in the 100th Congress because he felt the shoe industry's situation had already improved.

In the 100th Congress Sundquist had to pay some attention to a legal problem that ultimately caught the attention of the whole House. Sundquist was the target of a libel lawsuit after he wrote an official letter and held a news conference alleging irregularities and possible legal violations by a Memphis Legal Services office and attorney.

The courts have historically held that members are protected from civil liability for acts they take as public officials, but after a federal district court dismissed the suit against Sundquist, an appeals court ruled that he could be sued. Sundquist tried to take the case to the Supreme Court, and the House — its members fearing increased exposure to litigation — unanimously passed a resolution urging the court to review the case. The justices refused,

Tennessee 7

West Central — Clarksville; Part of Shelby County

If the East Side of Memphis and its adjoining suburbs were not included in this district, Democrats would win it routinely. Most of the 7th is farm land and small towns with names like Dull, Needmore, Spot and Only. A few manufacturing plants are sprinkled through the countryside.

But the Memphis portion of the district, within Shelby County, is home to a coterie of staunchly Republican voters. Much of this area has a nouveau riche feel, with showy homes, shopping malls and office parks that draw commerce away from center-city Memphis. Voter turnout is high, and Republican margins are phenomenal. When Democratic Sen. Jim Sasser won an overwhelming statewide victory in 1988, he barely managed a majority in this part of Shelby.

Although a couple of counties have sizable black populations, most of the voters in the non-Shelby portion of the 7th are white, conservative-populist and traditionally Democratic. Five counties in this area have not voted for a Republican in a major statewide contest since 1974.

Outside Shelby, there is only one city, Clarksville (Montgomery County), near the Kentucky border. Once a marketing center for fire-cured tobacco, today it depends on its factory payroll and the military population at Fort Campbell. Though Sundquist carried Montgomery County in his easy 1986 re-election, it went solidly Democratic in the governor's contest.

There is one pocket of rural Republican strength — a handful of counties along the Highland Rim, in the hilly south-central part of the district. There the terrain and voting behavior resemble Republican East Tennessee. Many farmers in the area opposed secession and have been loyal to the GOP ever since.

Population: 503,611. White 438,768 (87%), Black 60,217 (12%), Other 3,000 (1%). Spanish origin 5,224 (1%). 18 and over 351,201 (70%), 65 and over 46,053 (9%). Median age: 29.

enabling the plaintiff to go forward.

At Home: A winner of three easy reelections in a House district that stretches from Memphis to Nashville, Sundquist is now being mentioned as a possible solution to the Tennessee GOP's dearth of appealing talent for statewide office.

That is remarkable progress for a man who had little public profile just eight years ago, when he launched his first bid for Congress. That race was an impressive debut: He parlayed expertise gained in 12 years of GOP trenchwork into an upset over the scion of a well-known Tennessee political family.

Sundquist began his campaign in late 1981, when GOP Rep. Robin Beard was preparing his Senate bid. Many of the Republican activists Sundquist contacted knew him from his stints as Shelby County (Memphis) party chairman and his work for Beard, former Gov. Winfield Dunn, and former Sens. William E. Brock III and Howard H. Baker Jr.

The district's GOP establishment and crucial business leaders supported Sundquist, keeping other Republicans out of the primary. That sent Sundquist into a tough November contest with Bob Clement, a rural populist and son of the late Gov. Frank G. Clement (Bob Clement was later elected to the House from the 5th District).

The outcome hinged on the "Shelby factor." About 40 percent of the 7th's voters live in eastern Shelby County, a heavily Republican area containing affluent residential sections of Memphis and its suburbs. The 7th's other 15 counties are predominantly rural, and most of the voters there are conservative Democrats. In 1982, unemployment was high in all the rural counties, making them even less receptive to entreaties from a well-off suburban GOP businessman.

To compensate for his problems outside the Memphis area, Sundquist concentrated on mobilizing Shelby County's GOP suburbanites, who found little to like in Clement's political message, an arm-waving populism he inherited from his father.

Sundquist took three-fourths of the Shelby vote, exceeding his most optimistic projections. The combined vote in the district's other 15 counties went 65-35 percent for Clement, but that was not enough to offset the Democrat's dismal showing in Shelby.

For a while, it looked as if Sundquist might face a 1984 battle with former state Rep. Harold Byrd, who had lost to Clement in the 1982 Democratic primary, but that challenge never materialized, nor has any other of significance.

Committee

Ways and Means (12th of 13 Republicans)
Human Resources; Select Revenue Measures

Elections

1988 General		
Don Sundquist (R)	142,025	(80%)
Kenneth Bloodworth (D)	35,237	(20%)
1986 General		
Don Sundquist (R)	93,902	(72%)
M. Lloyd Hiler (D)	35,966	(28%)

Previous Winning Percentages: 1984 (100%) **1982** (51%)

District Vote For President

	1988	1984	1980	1976
D	67,200 (33%)	67,173 (34%)	73,984 (41%)	74,622 (51%)
R	138,246 (67%)	130,862 (66%)	100,694 (56%)	69,443 (48%)
I			3,789 (2%)	

Campaign Finance

	Receipts	Receipts from PACs	Expend-itures
1988			
Sundquist (R)	$393,171	$182,103 (46%)	$307,656
Bloodworth (D) †	$1,130	0	$1,110
1986			
Sundquist (R)	$409,651	$139,739 (34%)	$281,817

† Totals based on incomplete data.

Key Votes

1987	
Raise speed limit to 65 mph	Y
Approve Gephardt "fair trade" amendment	N
Ban testing of larger nuclear weapons	N
Delay "re-flagging" of Kuwaiti tankers	Y
Approve tax-raising deficit-reduction bill	N
1988	
Approve aid to Nicaraguan contras	Y
Enact civil rights restoration bill over Reagan veto	N
Kill 60-day plant-closing notification measure	Y
Pass omnibus trade bill over Reagan veto	N
Approve death penalty for drug-related murders	Y
Bar federal funds for abortions in cases of rape and incest	Y
Oppose seven-day waiting period for purchase of handguns	Y

Voting Studies

	Presidential Support		Party Unity		Conservative Coalition	
Year	**S**	**O**	**S**	**O**	**S**	**O**
1988	64	28	86	5	89	5
1987	60	34	86	10	91	9
1986	74	24	86	13	92	6
1985	75	23	87	10	91	7
1984	73	26	76	20	90	7
1983	70	29	83	14	91	6

Interest Group Ratings

Year	ADA	ACU	AFL-CIO	CCUS
1988	10	96	17	100
1987	8	82	25	80
1986	5	82	14	72
1985	15	81	18	91
1984	5	79	17	69
1983	0	87	18	74

8 John Tanner (D)

Of Union City — Elected 1988

Born: Sept. 22, 1944, Halls, Tenn.
Education: U. of Tennessee, B.S. 1965, J.D. 1968.
Military Career: Navy, 1968-72.
Occupation: Lawyer; banker.
Family: Wife, Betty Ann Portis; two children.
Religion: First Christian Church.
Political Career: Tenn. House, 1977-89.
Capitol Office: 512 Cannon Bldg. 20515; 225-4714.

The Path to Washington: Like his predecessor, longtime Democratic Rep. Ed Jones, Tanner has an easy "country" demeanor and sophisticated political sense that brought him electoral success in 1988 and could well make him a player in the House.

But unlike Jones, a dairy farmer and onetime agriculture official who was primarily a force on farm issues, Tanner has a varied background that would position him to pursue any number of legislative paths. At the outset of his freshman term, Tanner's course was set when he won a prize committee assignment, Armed Services. Only a handful of states have more than one Democratic seat on the committee; with Tanner's appointment, Tennessee joins that elite list.

Jones' retirement after nearly two decades of service brought the rare prospect of a competitive election in the West Tennessee 8th. But Tanner came out of the blocks practically before the contest could begin. A longtime ally of the incumbent — Tanner's grandfather was a friend of Jones — Tanner had been laying the groundwork for an eventual House campaign before the district actually opened up.

When Jones' retirement announcement came, Tanner quickly put together an enviable organization and financial base, boosted by his connections to Jones and to Gov. Ned McWherter, whose home base is in the 8th. Before becoming governor, McWherter was Speaker of the state House, and Tanner served with him in the chamber.

Tanner, a 12-year veteran of the Legislature when he began his congressional campaign, also had some natural appeal to business interests: In Union City he is a member of a local law firm and senior vice president of a local savings and loan association; in the state House he served as chairman of the Commerce Committee.

But Tanner, who went to the University of Tennessee on a basketball scholarship, appeals to more than just the buttoned-down set. His relaxed, "good ol' boy" style helped him win over rural voters, who hold considerable sway in the 8th District. During the primary season, Tanner traveled the district on a 230-stop listening tour, mixing easily with voters at country stores and other local gathering spots. He made a similar tour for the general election.

The election was not a cakewalk, however. Though Tanner's legislative service had made him a familiar figure in part of the sprawling district, many voters had not heard much about him before the campaign. And while his impressive fund raising, organization and connections caused him to be regarded in most political circles as Jones' heir presumptive, there were a few other candidates who saw things differently.

The best-known contenders in the five-way Democratic primary were Jackson Mayor Bob Conger, whose base is one of the 8th's major population centers, and former Democratic Gov. Ray Blanton, who was notorious for a gubernatorial term so scandal-plagued that it eventually landed him in prison.

But none of the Democrats even came close to making a dent in Tanner's armor. On primary day, he garnered 66 percent of the vote.

Tanner's primary margin served to squash any real hopes that the GOP had to take the district, which has a sizable number of conservative-minded voters. The Republican nominee, Jackson attorney Ed Bryant, had organized the district for Pat Robertson's presidential campaign. Bryant made an active effort and tried to convince voters that Tanner would be controlled by a liberal national Democratic Party leadership in Washington. "Bull," said Tanner. "Ed Jones has been his own man and John Tanner will be his own man."

Tanner's support for the death penalty and the presidential line-item veto and his opposition to national health insurance proposals made it difficult for anyone to portray him as a liberal. He won over 60 percent of the vote.

Tennessee 8

West — Jackson; Part of Shelby County

This is a region of soybeans, corn, wheat and cotton. It has neither grown nor changed very much in recent years; 13 rural counties account for two-thirds of the vote, and are nearly always Democratic. Jimmy Carter took all but one of them in 1980; even Walter F. Mondale and Michael S. Dukakis — hardly the type of candidates to engender much enthusiasm in rural West Tennessee — each managed to carry five counties in the 8th when they ran for president.

The fact that politics in this part of Tennessee has not changed much through the years enables some of its elected officials to acquire enough seniority to gain considerable influence. Rep. Ed Jones, who retired in 1989, is one example; another is Ned McWherter, a native of the 7th District town of Dresden who served seven terms as Speaker of the state House before winning the governorship in 1986.

The 8th includes the Frayser area of Memphis and a significant part of northern Shelby County, where suburbia and GOP dominance give way to farms and Democratic leanings. The Memphis Naval Air Station is in north Shelby, near the town of Millington. About 20 percent of the people in the 8th live in Shelby County; that figure was higher in the 1970s, but to keep the 8th securely Democratic, the last round of redistricting excised 75,000 mostly Republican voters in suburban Memphis from the district.

Madison County (Jackson) has another 15 percent of the vote. Republicans are gaining ground there, thanks in part to an influx of managerial personnel to Jackson's increasingly diversified industries, a Procter & Gamble Co. facility that makes Pringles potato chips, Porter Cable (formerly a Rockwell hand tool factory), and Allied Astermarket, once a Bendix auto parts plant.

The surrounding farm counties look to Jackson, the district's largest city, as a source of retail goods and services. Republican statewide candidates can usually hold their own in Madison County; McWherter carried it only narrowly in his 1986 gubernatorial victory, and George Bush won it with nearly 60 percent in 1988.

Population: 504,957. White 400,579 (79%), Black 101,042 (20%). Spanish origin 4,595 (1%). 18 and over 358,805 (71%), 65 and over 65,163 (13%). Median age: 30.

Committees

Armed Services (30th of 31 Democrats)
Investigations; Readiness

Science, Space and Technology (29th of 30 Democrats)
Investigations and Oversight; Natural Resources, Agriculture Research and Environment; Space Science and Applications

Campaign Finance

	Receipts	Receipts from PACs	Expend-itures
1988			
Tanner (D)	$931,539	$283,961 (30%)	$863,425
Bryant (R)	$106,318	$3,800 (4%)	$106,028

Elections

1988 General		
John Tanner (D)	94,571	(62%)
Ed Bryant (R)	56,893	(38%)
1988 Primary		
John Tanner (D)	45,271	(66%)
Bob Conger (D)	10,468	(15%)
Ray Blanton (D)	7,202	(11%)
Ivy Scarborough (D)	5,311	(8%)

District Vote For President

	1988	1984	1980	1976
D	69,420 (43%)	74,732 (43%)	87,477 (51%)	92,833 (60%)
R	89,899 (56%)	98,966 (57%)	80,238 (47%)	59,608 (39%)

9 Harold E. Ford (D)

Of Memphis — Elected 1974

Born: May 20, 1945, Memphis, Tenn.
Education: Tennessee State U., B.S. 1967; John Gupton Mortuary, L.F.D., L.E.D. 1969; Howard U., M.B.A. 1982.
Occupation: Mortician.
Family: Wife, Dorothy Bowles; three children.
Religion: Baptist.
Political Career: Tenn. House, 1971-75.
Capitol Office: 2305 Rayburn Bldg. 20515; 225-3265.

In Washington: Ford had scarcely begun work in the 100th Congress before he found his legislative interests overshadowed by an indictment on bribery charges. His legal problems began just as he had attained a position of real influence as chairman of the subcommittee rewriting national welfare policy.

Two years after the indictment, Ford's trial still had not begun. The venue of the case was changed from Knoxville, where Ford was indicted, to his hometown of Memphis. Several defense motions had stalled proceedings. The judge's caseload was backlogged. Heading into mid-1989, no one was predicting when the case would come to trial, only that a long wait was still in store.

When discussions of overhauling the welfare system picked up steam in early 1987, Ford, as chairman of the Public Assistance Subcommittee at Ways and Means, had the support of the House Democratic leadership for his bill. Although he soon had to cut the measure's cost in half, he moved it through his subcommittee in March 1987. But less than a month later, he had to relinquish the chairmanship when he was indicted on fraud charges, based on allegations that he traded his influence for large loans from Tennessee financiers Jake and C. H. Butcher Jr.

Under Democratic Caucus rules, Thomas J. Downey of New York became acting Public Assistance chairman, a role he maintained in the 101st Congress. Ford was re-elected chairman in the 101st, but cannot serve in that post until his legal problems are resolved. The House ethics committee has not acted on the charges against Ford; the panel typically takes no action involving individuals who are facing trial until court proceedings run their course.

Ford brings a minority-rights perspective to discussions of welfare policy, complementing the viewpoint of his Senate counterpart, New York's Daniel Patrick Moynihan, who is chairman of the Social Security and Family Policy Subcommittee.

Ford did not wait for Moynihan to act before launching his own welfare-overhaul bill, which expanded benefits but required states to make work, education or training mandatory for welfare recipients.

In the opening rounds of the welfare debate, Ford insisted that any bill would have to focus on expanding benefits as well as moving recipients off the welfare rolls whenever possible. The centerpiece of his bill was a program aimed at training welfare recipients so they can move into the work force. Under the plan, welfare mothers with children over age 3 could be required to participate in work or training activities. Major portions of Ford's program were incorporated into the final welfare package that became law in 1988.

One of Ford's more controversial goals was to require states to make two-parent households eligible for support if the principal wage earner is unemployed; under existing law, about half the states help only if one parent is gone. For years, the Black Caucus has complained that this system encourages the breakup of poor families. Unless the federal government mandates change, Ford said, "some of the Southern states will never adopt it."

Ford came close to getting a similar change made twice in 1986, but both times he lost in showdowns with the administration. In 1988, the House-Senate conference snagged over the requirement. White House officials had reluctantly supported adding the language to the Senate version of the bill, but only in concert with a "workfare" provision requiring one parent in such households to perform at least 16 hours of unpaid work each week. House conferees strongly opposed the workfare requirement.

After three months of wrangling, key House, Senate and White House negotiators held a two-and-a-half-hour meeting and emerged with a compromise containing both changes. President Reagan signed the final package into law.

Ford took over the Public Assistance Subcommittee in 1981, and through the decade he got generally good marks for his handling of the panel. He was an especially effective ally of labor unions. In past Congresses, Ford fought

Tennessee 9

Memphis

Thanks to the one-party allegiance of blacks, who make up well over half the population of the 9th, Ford's district has been reliably Democratic in good years and bad. Jimmy Carter won 63 percent of the vote there in 1980, considerably more than in any other Tennessee district; Walter F. Mondale and Michael S. Dukakis also did similarly well. Democrat Al Gore drew 70 percent in the 9th in his successful 1984 Senate campaign; Democratic Sen. Jim Sasser won even bigger in 1988.

But the fact that this district has had black representation for a dozen years should not obscure the significance of the white electorate. Though blacks are a majority of the population, blacks and whites are about even among registered voters. Because of "white flight" from inner-city Memphis in the 1970s, 1982 redistricting added about 80,000 people to the 9th, many of them white working-class people — the same ones who had fled downtown a few years earlier. It is a political challenge keeping both blacks and whites happy, because in Memphis, elections as well as neighborhoods often polarize along racial lines.

The Memphis economy is a mixture of old and new. Cotton marketing and processing of cottonseed into oil continue, as they have for more than a century and a half. But now the emphasis has shifted to employers that deliver goods, people and services. Memphis is headquarters for the air fleet of Federal Express and for the Holiday Inn empire, and the Memphis airport has become a major hub for the mid-South. Memphis has long been the stop of significance on the Mississippi River between St. Louis and New Orleans, but after years in the doldrums, the city seems to be recapturing a sense of itself as a regional capital. Its media look as much to northern Mississippi and to eastern Arkansas as they do to Nashville and the rest of Tennessee.

For years, Memphis seemed uninterested in preserving its character and traditions. But that has changed as well. The historic Peabody Hotel, whose lobby used to be described as the northern outpost of the Mississippi Delta, reopened in 1981, complete with the ducks that ride the elevator down from their rooftop pool to swim in the lobby fountain. Nearby Beale Street, where W. C. Handy and other jazz composers flourished early in this century, is emerging from blight to play host to a new generation of clubs and restaurants. And an entertainment complex on an island in the Mississippi draws attention to the city's river heritage.

Population: 505,592. White 213,131 (42%), Black 289,152 (57%). Spanish origin 4,164 (1%). 18 and over 359,672 (71%), 65 and over 60,008 (12%). Median age: 28.

hard to get the federal government to help jobless workers who had exhausted state unemployment benefits. A 10-week supplemental benefits program was enacted as part of tax legislation in 1982.

In the 99th Congress, Ford struggled to keep the supplemental benefits alive, but Ways and Means refused to go along. The best that Ford and his labor allies could do was provide for a gradual phase-out of the benefits, rather than the immediate cutoff sought by Reagan.

Ford was not one of the more active participants in the debate over tax revision in the 99th Congress. He voted for amendments backed by labor and fought to retain full deduction for charitable contributions.

At Home: Politicians slapped with indictments often fall prey to electoral trouble, but Ford has a strong base to support him. His is the dominant political family in the Memphis black community. His brother John, a former city councilman, serves in the state Senate; his brother James is on the City Council. Shortly after Rep. Ford was indicted, he arrived to a cheering crowd at the Memphis airport and claimed that the federal prosecutor "wants to destroy the black political power in Tennessee." Ford's faithful supporters helped him win another House term easily in 1988.

The Ford organization is extensive, reaching down to the block level in many neighborhoods. In addition to mobilizing that network on their own behalf, the Ford brothers often endorse candidates in Democratic primaries for local and statewide offices.

Harold Ford began his political career in 1970, winning election to the Tennessee House at age 25. In his first term, he was majority whip and chaired a committee that investigated the rates and practices of utilities in the state.

Redistricting in 1972 increased the black population in the Memphis congressional district to 48 percent. That caused trouble for Republican Rep. Dan H. Kuykendall.

Kuykendall had won three House elections with increasing ease by taking virtually all the votes of the district's whites. But in 1972, running within the new borders for the first time, he was held to 55 percent by a black Democrat who made little attempt to attract white support.

Ford challenged Kuykendall in 1974. After winning a six-way Democratic primary, Ford ran a broader and more active campaign than did the 1972 Democratic nominee. Ford reached out to white voters, stressing economic issues and promising to listen to whites as well as blacks if he were elected.

One sensitive issue in the campaign was John Ford's reputation as a political firebrand. Then on the City Council, John had expressed a militance in local issues that had alienated some of the district's white electorate. Though Harold had demonstrated his own brand of populist rhetoric, he went to great lengths to ensure that he was not confused with his brother.

Reaping political benefit from Kuykendall's longstanding personal friendship with Richard M. Nixon, Ford edged past the incumbent by 744 votes, becoming Tennessee's first black congressman.

Before the 1976 election, a court-ordered readjustment of district lines removed 12,000 white suburban voters from Ford's district and put them in the adjoining 6th. The readjustment gave Ford a black majority, and in the next three elections he won handily.

Although 1981 redistricting reduced the share of blacks in the district's voting population to just above 50 percent, Ford won easily in the 1982 primary and general election, demonstrating again his ability to draw votes from both whites and blacks.

Ford's success spawned speculation that he would be a candidate for mayor of Memphis in 1983, but instead he decided to let his brother John run.

Harold Ford took a prominent role in his brother's campaign, but a rather heavy-handed attempt to persuade two other black candidates to drop out of the contest angered some black voters. Whites, worried by John Ford's militant reputation, turned out in enough force on Election Day to give a majority of the vote to incumbent Mayor Dick Hatchett.

Committees

Select Aging (4th of 39 Democrats)
Health and Long-Term Care

Ways and Means (7th of 23 Democrats)
Human Resources; Oversight

Elections

1988 General		
Harold E. Ford (D)	126,280	(82%)
Isaac Richmond (I)	28,522	(18%)
1988 Primary		
Harold E. Ford (D)	35,589	(80%)
Mark Flanagan (D)	8,720	(20%)
1986 General		
Harold E. Ford (D)	83,006	(83%)
Isaac Richmond (I)	16,221	(16%)

Previous Winning Percentages: **1984** (72%) **1982** (72%)
1980 (100%) **1978** (70%) **1976** (61%) **1974** (50%)

District Vote For President

	1988	1984	1980	1976
D	117,491 (66%)	137,826 (64%)	128,962 (63%)	121,879 (60%)
R	59,955 (34%)	77,894 (36%)	69,760 (34%)	79,724 (39%)
I			4,278 (2%)	

Campaign Finance

	Receipts	Receipts from PACs	Expend-itures
1988			
Ford (D)	$298,096	$211,500 (71%)	$364,330
1986			
Ford (D)	$326,829	$225,275 (69%)	$320,227

Key Votes

1987	
Raise speed limit to 65 mph	N
Approve Gephardt "fair trade" amendment	Y
Ban testing of larger nuclear weapons	?
Delay "re-flagging" of Kuwaiti tankers	?
Approve tax-raising deficit-reduction bill	Y
1988	
Approve aid to Nicaraguan contras	N
Enact civil rights restoration bill over Reagan veto	Y
Kill 60-day plant-closing notification measure	N
Pass omnibus trade bill over Reagan veto	Y
Approve death penalty for drug-related murders	N
Bar federal funds for abortions in cases of rape and incest	N
Oppose seven-day waiting period for purchase of handguns	N

Voting Studies

	Presidential Support		Party Unity		Conservative Coalition	
Year	**S**	**O**	**S**	**O**	**S**	**O**
1988	12	57	61	2	5	66
1987	9	48	63	1	9	40
1986	16	73	71	4	12	70
1985	18	78	87	2	7	85
1984	29	57	81	4	15	76
1983	20	65	78	3	10	74
1982	27	56	81	6	19	64
1981	34	59	89	4	9	85

Interest Group Ratings

Year	ADA	ACU	AFL-CIO	CCUS
1988	85	0	100	36
1987	68	0	93	0
1986	100	0	91	8
1985	90	0	94	14
1984	80	0	83	31
1983	75	0	93	35
1982	80	0	100	30
1981	85	0	100	11

Texas

U.S. CONGRESS

SENATE 1 D, 1 R

HOUSE 18 D, 8 R, 1 vacancy

LEGISLATURE

Senate 23 D, 8 R

House 93 D, 57 R

ELECTIONS

1988 Presidential Vote	
Bush	56%
Dukakis	43%
1984 Presidential Vote	
Reagan	64%
Mondale	36%
1980 Presidential Vote	
Reagan	55%
Carter	41%
Anderson	3%
Turnout rate in 1984	47%
Turnout rate in 1986	25%
Turnout rate in 1988	44%

(as percentage of voting age population)

POPULATION AND GROWTH

1980 population	14,229,191
1988 population estimate (3rd in the nation)	16,841,000
Percent change 1980-1988	+18%

DEMOGRAPHIC BREAKDOWN

White	79%
Black	12%
Other	1%
(Spanish origin)	21%
Urban	80%
Rural	20%
Born in state	68%
Foreign-born	6%

MAJOR CITIES

Houston	1,728,910
Dallas	1,003,520
San Antonio	914,350
El Paso	491,800
Austin	466,550

AREA AND LAND USE

Area 262,017 sq. miles (2nd)

Farm	78%
Forest	8%
Federally owned	2%

Gov. William P. Clements Jr. (R)
Of Dallas — Elected 1986
(also served 1979-83)

Born: April 13, 1917, Dallas, Texas.
Education: Attended Southern Methodist U., 1935-36.
Occupation: Businessman.
Religion: Episcopalian.
Political Career: Deputy secretary of defense, 1973-77; GOP nominee for governor, 1982.
Next Election: 1990.

WORK

Occupations	
White-collar	53%
Blue-collar	32%
Service workers	12%
Government Workers	
Federal	172,490
State	225,050
Local	692,915

MONEY

Median family income	$ 19,618	(27th)
Tax burden per capita	$ 705	(43rd)

EDUCATION

Spending per pupil through grade 12	$ 3,298	(33rd)
Persons with college degrees	17%	(23rd)

CRIME

Violent crime rate 631 per 100,000 (10th)

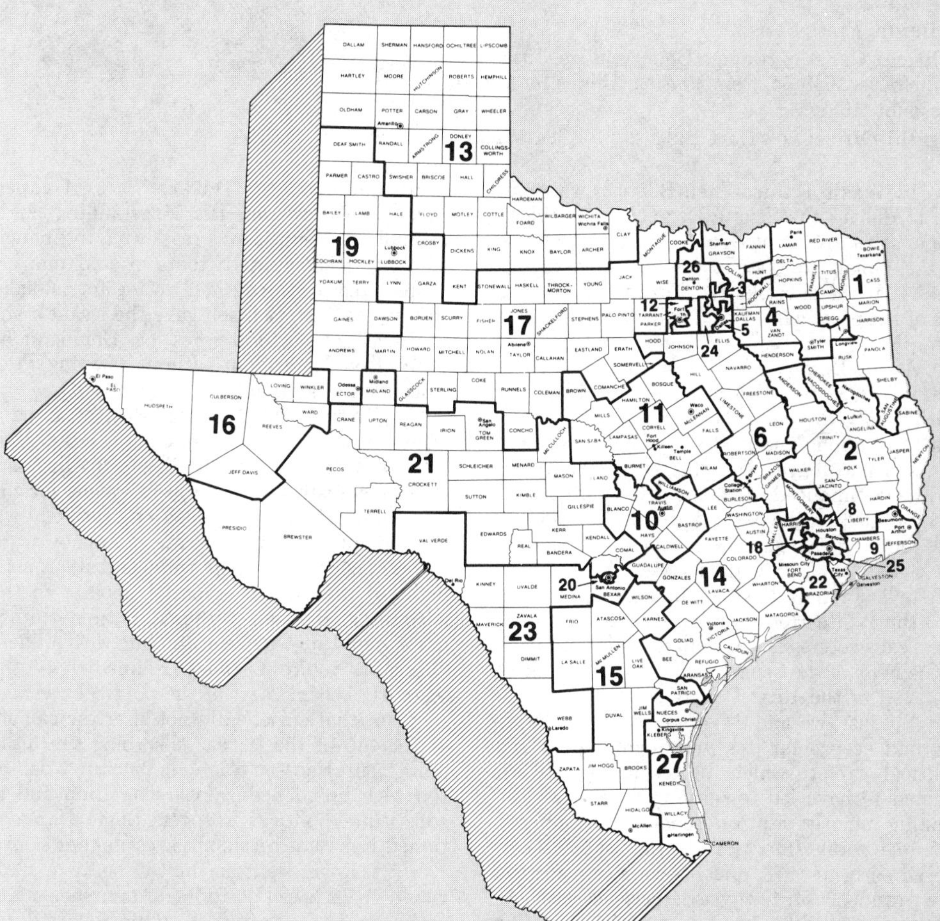

DALLAM
SHERMAN
HANSFORD
OCHILTREE
LIPSCOMB
HARTLEY
MOORE
HUTCHINSON
ROBERTS
HEMPHILL
OLDHAM
POTTER
CARSON
GRAY
WHEELER
Amarillo
DEAF SMITH
RANDALL
ARMSTRONG
DONLEY
13
COLLINGS-WORTH
PARMER
CASTRO
SWISHER
BRISCOE
HALL
CHILDRESS
HARDEMAN
BAILEY
LAMB
HALE
FLOYD
MOTLEY
COTTLE
FOARD
WILBARGER
WICHITA
Wichita Falls
CLAY
19
Lubbock
LUBBOCK
COCHRAN
HOCKLEY
CROSBY
DICKENS
KING
KNOX
BAYLOR
ARCHER
YOAKUM
TERRY
LYNN
GARZA
KENT
STONEWALL
HASKELL
THROCK-MORTON
YOUNG
JACK
WISE
MONTAGUE
COOKE
GAINES
DAWSON
BORDEN
SCURRY
FISHER
JONES
17
SHACKELFORD
STEPHENS
PALO PINTO
Abilene
TAYLOR
CALLAHAN
EASTLAND
ERATH
ANDREWS
MARTIN
HOWARD
MITCHELL
NOLAN
El Paso
HUDSPETH
CULBERSON
LOVING
WINKLER
Odessa
ECTOR
Midland
MIDLAND
GLASSCOCK
STERLING
COKE
RUNNELS
COLEMAN
BROWN
COMANCHE
16
REEVES
WARD
CRANE
UPTON
REAGAN
IRION
San Angelo
TOM GREEN
CONCHO
McCULLOCH
MILLS
HAMILTON
JEFF DAVIS
PECOS
21
CROCKETT
SCHLEICHER
MENARD
MASON
LLANO
SAN SABA
LAMPASAS
CORYELL
Fort Hood
Killeen
Temple
BELL
SUTTON
KIMBLE
GILLESPIE
BLANCO
BURNET
PRESIDIO
BREWSTER
TERRELL
VAL VERDE
EDWARDS
REAL
KERR
KENDALL
BANDERA
COMAL
Del Rio
KINNEY
UVALDE
20
MEDINA
San Antonio
BEXAR
GUADALUPE
WILSON
MAVERICK
ZAVALA
23
DIMMIT
FRIO
ATASCOSA
KARNES
LA SALLE
McMULLEN
15
LIVE OAK
BEE
WEBB
Laredo
DUVAL
JIM WELLS
ZAPATA
JIM HOGG
BROOKS
27
KENEDY
STARR
HIDALGO
McAllen
WILLACY
Harlingen
CAMERON
Sherman
GRAYSON
FANNIN
LAMAR
RED RIVER
BOWIE
Texarkana
Paris
26
Denton
DENTON
COLLIN
3
HUNT
DELTA
HOPKINS
FRANKLIN
TITUS
MORRIS
CASS
1
CAMP
12
TARRANT
Fort Worth
PARKER
HOOD
JOHNSON
24
ROCKWALL
KAUFMAN
DALLAS
5
4
RAINS
WOOD
UPSHUR
MARION
GREGG
HARRISON
VAN ZANDT
Tyler
SMITH
Longview
ELLIS
HENDERSON
RUSK
PANOLA
SOMERVELL
BOSQUE
HILL
NAVARRO
11
Waco
McLENNAN
LIMESTONE
FREESTONE
ANDERSON
CHEROKEE
NACOGDOCHES
SHELBY
FALLS
6
LEON
HOUSTON
Lufkin
ANGELINA
SABINE
ROBERTSON
MADISON
TRINITY
2
POLK
TYLER
JASPER
NEWTON
MILAM
College Station
BRAZOS
GRIMES
WALKER
SAN JACINTO
WILLIAMSON
BURLESON
MONTGOMERY
HARDIN
TRAVIS
Austin
10
HAYS
BASTROP
LEE
WASHINGTON
8
LIBERTY
Beaumont
ORANGE
Port Arthur
CALDWELL
FAYETTE
AUSTIN
18
WALLER
HARRIS
7
Houston
Baytown
CHAMBERS
9
JEFFERSON
GONZALES
COLORADO
Pasadena
25
14
Missouri City
FORT BEND
Texas City
GALVESTON
Galveston
LAVACA
WHARTON
22
BRAZORIA
DE WITT
JACKSON
MATAGORDA
Victoria
VICTORIA
GOLIAD
CALHOUN
REFUGIO
ARANSAS
SAN PATRICIO
NUECES
Corpus Christi
Kingsville
KLEBERG

Lloyd Bentsen (D)

Of Houston — Elected 1970

Born: Feb. 11, 1921, Mission, Texas.
Education: U. of Texas, LL.B. 1942.
Military Career: Army Air Corps, 1942-45; Air Force Reserve, 1950-59.
Occupation: Lawyer; financial executive.
Family: Wife, Beryl Ann "B. A." Longino; three children.
Religion: Presbyterian.
Political Career: Hidalgo County judge, 1946-48; U.S. House, 1948-55; Democratic nominee for vice president, 1988.
Capitol Office: 703 Hart Bldg. 20510; 224-5922.

In Washington: When Bentsen was chosen to deliver the Senate Democrats' televised response to President George Bush's first State of the Union address, it was an acknowledgment that the silver-haired Texan had become one of the party's foremost symbols and spokesmen.

As the Democratic vice presidential nominee in 1988, Bentsen was on a ticket that carried only 10 states, Texas not among them. But after a long and nasty presidential season, Bentsen may have been the least besmirched and most enhanced of all the personalities that had paraded on the national stage. He also had the simultaneous satisfaction of re-election to the Senate in 1988 with his biggest vote ever. Whatever their feelings about Bentsen moving into the White House under Michael S. Dukakis, Texas voters clearly wanted their man back at the helm of the Senate Finance Committee at the start of the 101st Congress.

Yet just two-and-a-half years earlier, Bentsen had been a far less prominent figure. His political career, which began in the 1940s, seemed to have led to nothing more than the ranking minority seat on Senate Environment. His one foray into presidential politics collapsed early in 1976, and his courtship for the vice presidency in 1984 was largely for show. As Bentsen entered his late 60s, even his standing in Texas seemed to have peaked.

A series of events reversed the apparent denouement of Bentsen's career and led on to new heights. The Democrats recaptured control of the Senate in the 1986 elections, and Sen. Russell B. Long of Louisiana, the longtime Democratic dean on Finance, retired. Bentsen took his place. The Finance seat proved warm immediately, as a procession of major bills moved through the committee in the 100th Congress. Bentsen handled them all with aplomb.

A successful season in the Finance chair was the least of Bentsen's contributions to the presidential ticket. A consummate insider, his credentials balanced Dukakis' lack of experience in Washington. His longstanding championship of business was reassuring to financial markets. His Southern roots offered many in Dixie a reason to consider voting for Dukakis. But most of all, Bentsen gave the ticket a shot at Texas' 29 electoral votes. No Democrat has been elected president without carrying Texas since Texas became a state.

As it turned out, George Bush's campaign went straight to Texas to debut some of its attacks on Dukakis on the Pledge of Allegiance, defense spending and prison furloughs for convicted murderers. Bentsen performed well throughout the campaign, but he was only able to distract the spotlight from Dukakis on the night of the vice presidential debate. In that encounter, Bentsen withered Bush's running mate, Sen. Dan Quayle of Indiana with a line — "Senator, you're no Jack Kennedy" — that instantly became part of the political parlance.

But that episode did not alter the calculus at the top of the ticket. Absorbing the disappointment, Bentsen was soon back in Washington with broadened name recognition and reconstituted political prospects. Some even mentioned him as a presidential contender.

A younger Bentsen (he will be 71 in 1992), would be very well positioned to pursue such an ambition. But he returned to his Senate duties with little apparent attention to such concerns. He had enough to occupy his time without them: Much of the legislation passed in the busy 100th Congress was going to require additional action in the 101st.

Chief among these was the monitoring of the omnibus trade bill of 1988. Although its effectiveness has yet to be proven, the bill bespoke a fresh resolve to force reciprocity with trading partners. The first list of "unfair traders" had to be prepared early in 1989. Those on it would face a forced round of bilateral talks that would have to produce a lowering of barriers or otherwise compensate the United States for lost exports. If unsatisfied, the U.S. trade representative would be able to impose new tariffs, quotas or other sanctions.

The bill had included the one element of all the trade activity in the 100th Congress that captured the most attention — a requirement that owners give workers 60 days' notice of plant closings or mass layoffs.

Reagan vetoed the entire trade bill because of the 60-day notice provision. Later he signed the trade bill, which Congress resubmitted without the notice provision. But just before the fall election, a somewhat altered version of the notice requirement, submitted as a free-standing bill, became law without Reagan's signature.

Bentsen had been in the vanguard of tough trade sentiment in 1985, joining with key House Democrats to sponsor a bill threatening a 25 percent surcharge on imports from Japan and other key trading partners. When support for that idea faded, he helped develop a Senate Democratic trade proposal that stressed strengthening of the procedures for setting trade policy. In the early 1980s, he joined with GOP Sen. John C. Danforth of Missouri to pressure Japan into voluntary restraints on their auto exports to the United States.

On the other hand, Bentsen's work in the 100th Congress included passage of the U.S.-Canada free trade agreement.

Finance in the 100th also took part in a major reform of the welfare system, emphasizing education and jobs for welfare recipients, and produced a Taxpayer Bill of Rights authored by Democratic Sen. David Pryor of Arkansas. And the committee also expanded Medicare to give catastrophic-illness protection to all older or disabled citizens.

The catastrophic health insurance bill began to produce an outcry early in 1989, as more affluent senior citizens began to notice the supplemental premium they were paying for the coverage. Bentsen was among the first to support reducing the premium.

Also in the 101st Congress, Finance began seeking means to raise the $5.3 billion in new revenues required by the fiscal 1990 budget-summit compromise between the White House and congressional leaders. Bush wanted a cut in the capital gains tax, which he said would spark enough asset sales to produce more revenue (even at lower rates). Although Bentsen had been friendly to such notions before, he pronounced the case weak in the spring of 1989.

Bentsen may strike some observers as resembling a senior corporate executive more than a politician. Though he is not a dour or cheerless man, he strikes many as aloof and rather formal. He seems happiest working within a structured environment similar to that of a corporation, where written memos are preferred to informal communications and lines of authority are clear. One would not pick him out of a crowd as a Texan, or a man who has spent more than 25 years in public office.

He is a Texan, though, and that fact shone through in March 1989 when he cast one of just three Democratic votes in favor of John Tower's nomination as secretary of defense. Bentsen seemed loath to oppose Armed Services Chairman Sam Nunn on the matter. But Tower had been Bentsen's colleague in the Senate for 14 years, and Bentsen said the FBI reports about Tower's personal behavior did not describe the man he knew. He said there was not enough basis to deny the president his choice for the job. Nevertheless, it was widely believed in the Senate that Bentsen might have voted differently had Nunn not had votes to spare.

Bentsen has devoted much of his career in the Senate to promoting American business. While he has made intense efforts in recent years to aid the hard-pressed domestic oil and gas industries, they are hardly his only interests; he is reliably responsive to the needs of a wide range of businesses on tax and trade issues.

Bentsen laid out a long-term business agenda well over a decade ago, in his 1976 presidential campaign. Running on a platform of economic revival through tax cuts and reductions in the tax on capital gains, he put together a smooth campaign operation that functioned like an efficient medium-sized company. He attracted little public support, but his ideas caught on; within five years, the basics of his proposals had become law, albeit under a Republican president.

Bentsen also combined business and politics successfully in 1984, when he headed the Senate Democrats' campaign committee. Using his business contacts and fund-raising ability, he presided over an operation that raised more than $9 million during the two-year cycle and gave twice as much to the party's Senate candidates as the committee had ever given before. Despite President Reagan's landslide re-election, the party scored a net gain of two seats, paving the way for takeover in 1986.

Such close business ties can have their downside, especially for a leader of the Democratic Party. Some liberals in Washington like to watch Bentsen for signs he is carrying his business loyalties too far. Sometimes he makes their job easy. Soon after taking over the Finance chairmanship, Bentsen informed lobbyists in the capital that they could purchase the right to have breakfast with him once a month for $10,000. Even though his predecessor, Oregon Republican Bob Packwood, had done a similar thing on a smaller scale, the amount sought by Bentsen was so large — and the sale of access seemingly so blatant — that the idea provoked a flurry of criticism. Bentsen soon withdrew the idea, calling it "a doozy" of a mistake.

During the landmark overhaul of the tax code in 1986, Bentsen fought hard to aid certain industries. Along with Oklahoma Democrat David L. Boren, he worked successfully to preserve benefits for the oil and gas industry. He had less success in protecting real-estate investors from the bill's crackdown on "passive loss" tax shelters. Even then, however, he did not give up easily; he was still trying to soften the anti-tax shelter provisions during the conference on the bill.

When he took the Finance chair, Bentsen moved off the Environment and Public Works Committee, where he had been a low-key ranking member. Bentsen did play a major role in creating the expanded "superfund" hazardous-waste cleanup program approved by Congress in 1986. His chief goal was to protect the oil industry from having to bear the brunt of the new taxes needed to finance the enlarged program. He succeeded to a great extent by winning passage of a broad-based tax on corporate earnings as the main revenue source.

At Home: Bentsen began the 1988 election cycle as one of the Senate's best bets for re-election. Even without the $10,000 breakfast club, the Finance chairmanship had made Bentsen the leading collector of political action committee money in Congress. He was without visible political weaknesses other than his age, an issue Bentsen neatly dismissed by noting how active his father still was at 94.

Some Republicans preferred to leave Bentsen unchallenged for re-election in 1988, lest he mobilize his considerable resources in Texas and help other Democrats. But the National Republican Senatorial Committee was loath to have Bentsen distributing his treasury to colleagues' campaigns, so it encouraged a challenge by Rep. Beau Boulter, a two-term conservative from Amarillo. But Boulter allocated little money to the primary and ran second to Wes Gilbreath, a Houston multimillionaire who spent a fortune on TV ads. Boulter dispatched Gilbreath in the runoff, but never mounted much momentum thereafter.

Boulter produced entertaining campaign literature satirizing the $10,000 breakfast incident. And he tried hard to make Bentsen's dual candidacy the issue. But Texans did not seem offended by the so-called "LBJ Law," passed in 1960 to allow Lyndon B. Johnson to run simultaneously for re-election and for vice president. At least, they had no problem applying it to Bentsen, who won more than two-thirds of the counties on his way to a victory margin of more than a million votes.

Historically, Bentsen is part of the Texas Democratic establishment that included Johnson and John B. Connally, but his route into it was unique.

The Bentsen family, which is of Danish stock, has been among the conservative gentry of the lower Rio Grande Valley for most of this century. The senator's father, Lloyd Sr., was known as "Big Lloyd" around their hometown of McAllen, where he became a millionaire landowner and gave his son a lift into local politics. (Lloyd Sr. died in an auto accident in early 1989.)

Returning home from World War II, in which he had flown bombers over Europe, the younger Bentsen was elected judge in Hidalgo County at age 25. In 1948, taking advantage of family money and connections among the small group of Anglo Democrats that controlled politics in his heavily Hispanic South Texas district, he became the youngest member of the U.S. House.

As a representative, Bentsen pleased Texas conservatives with his hard-line anti-communism. He represented a one-party district and was politically secure; after his first primary, he faced no opposition at all.

But by 1954, the House did not seem as attractive to Bentsen as a career in the upper echelons of the Houston business community. He retired from Congress at the age of 33 and became president of Lincoln Consolidated, a holding company. By the time Bentsen was ready for politics again in 1970, he was a millionaire.

Bentsen ran on the Democratic right in 1970 as primary challenger to veteran Sen. Ralph Yarborough, the East Texas populist who had long been an enemy of party conservatives.

Bentsen ran against both Yarborough and the national Democratic Party. When Democratic Sens. Edmund S. Muskie of Maine and Harold Hughes of Iowa came to Texas for Yarborough, Bentsen labeled them "ultraliberal" outsiders. He ran TV ads linking Yarborough to violent anti-war protests and said the senator's vote against Supreme Court nominee G. Harrold Carswell showed he was anti-Southern.

Yarborough punched back by attacking Bentsen and his allies as "fat cats" and "reactionaries." It was not enough to stop Bentsen, who won with almost 100,000 votes to spare.

After the primary, Bentsen moved to the center against GOP nominee George Bush, then a Houston representative. The Bush-Bentsen campaign, a battle between a Houston insurance millionaire and a Houston oil millionaire, was gentle by comparison with the primary. There was little to argue about.

In the end, that helped Bentsen. He continued to promote the conservative image he had fostered in the spring, but recruited Yarborough supporters and campaigned against President Nixon's economic policies. Texas was still unquestionably a Democratic state in 1970 and, given a choice between two conservatives, a majority of voters preferred the Democrat.

In his first term, Bentsen sought to moderate his image, looking toward a presidential campaign in 1976. This angered his more conservative 1970 supporters and brought a primary challenge in 1976 from Texas A&M economist Phil Gramm. Gramm accused Bentsen of abandoning his conservative heritage in a vain bid for national office. Bentsen retained the loyalty of the party establishment and beat Gramm by more than 2-to-1, but the challenger drew over 400,000 votes (Gramm later won election to the House, switched to the GOP and then moved up to the Senate in the 1984 election).

In seeking the Democratic presidential nomination in 1976, Bentsen called himself a "Harry Truman Democrat" and hoped to do well in an early Southern primary. But Southern voters also had Jimmy Carter and George C. Wallace to choose from, and Bentsen got just six delegates in his own home state. He quickly dropped out of national politics to concentrate on his fall campaign against GOP Rep. Alan Steelman.

Steelman reversed Gramm's strategy, hoping to woo Yarborough liberals by calling Bentsen the captive of special interests. But Steelman had neither a firm base in his own party nor a funding base to compete with Bentsen's. Bentsen had a mailing list of 700,000 names and an organization in every county. He won easily.

In 1982 Bentsen brushed aside Republican Rep. James M. Collins, who crusaded across Texas trying to persuade voters to unseat "Liberal Lloyd." Collins had difficulty providing specifics for his case. He faulted the senator's votes to increase the national debt and to approve the Panama Canal treaties, but those examples won Collins few converts. Bentsen paid little attention to Collins. When he did he told voters they were being offered a choice between "effectiveness and incompetence." Bentsen's 1.8 million votes led the statewide ticket to a smashing victory. The party captured the governorship, retained all its U.S. House seats and picked up all three newly created districts.

Committees

Finance (Chairman)
International Trade; Medicare and Long-Term Care; Taxation and Debt Management

Commerce, Science and Transportation (7th of 11 Democrats)
Aviation; Communications; Merchant Marine; Science, Technology and Space; National Ocean Policy Study

Joint Economic
Economic Growth, Trade and Taxes (chairman); Economic Goals and Intergovernmental Policy; Education and Health

Joint Taxation (Vice Chairman)

Elections

1988 General		
Lloyd Bentsen (D)	3,149,806	(59%)
Beau Boulter (R)	2,129,228	(40%)
1988 Primary		
Lloyd Bentsen (D)	1,365,736	(85%)
Joe Sullivan (D)	244,805	(15%)

Previous Winning Percentages: 1982 (59%) **1976** (57%) **1970** (54%) **1952 *** (100%) **1950 *** (100%) **1948 †** (100%)

** House elections.*
† Elected to a full House term and to fill a vacancy at the same time.

Campaign Finance

	Receipts	Receipts from PACs	Expend-itures
1988			
Bentsen (D)	$8,280,013	$2,438,041 (29%)	$8,829,361
Boulter (R)	$1,377,357	$95,021 (7%)	$1,353,345

Key Votes

1987	
Enact omnibus highway bill over Reagan veto	Y
Limit testing of space-based anti-ballistic missiles	Y
Oppose banning tests of larger nuclear weapons	Y
Confirm Robert H. Bork as Supreme Court justice	N
1988	
Allow vote on campaign-finance overhaul	Y
Pass civil rights restoration bill over Reagan veto	Y
Enact omnibus trade bill over Reagan veto	Y
Approve death penalty for drug-related murders	Y
Oppose "workfare" amendment to welfare overhaul bill	N

Voting Studies

	Presidential Support		Party Unity		Conservative Coalition	
Year	S	O	S	O	S	O
1988	61	27	55	20	78	11
1987	44	50	78	19	69	31
1986	60	37	46	50	87	9
1985	50	46	54	40	75	23
1984	52	34	46	28	53	17
1983	51	45	63	31	64	34
1982	61	33	54	41	88	10
1981	70	24	55	42	83	11

Interest Group Ratings

Year	ADA	ACU	AFL-CIO	CCUS
1988	40	42	89	25
1987	60	31	80	44
1986	45	50	33	68
1985	35	62	53	46
1984	55	25	67	46
1983	40	25	71	53
1982	40	74	75	70
1981	25	53	39	71

Phil Gramm (R)

Of College Station — Elected 1984

Born: July 8, 1942, Fort Benning, Ga.
Education: U. of Georgia, B.B.A., 1964, Ph.D. 1967.
Occupation: Economics professor.
Family: Wife, Wendy Lee; two children.
Religion: Episcopalian.
Political Career: U.S. House, 1979-85; sought Democratic nomination for U.S. Senate, 1976.
Capitol Office: 370 Russell Bldg. 20510; 224-2934.

In Washington: Assessments of Gramm's congressional career necessarily begin and end with the same point: results. Regardless of how one feels about him, there can be no doubt that he has accomplished a great deal of what he set out to do, and in a remarkably short time.

It is easy to find people in Washington — his fellow Republicans as well as members of his former party — whose views of Gramm range from disdain to loathing. His critics call him arrogant, transparently ambitious, demagogic and deceitful. If popularity were the barometer of Senate success, he would be a failure.

But the fact remains that in less than a decade Gramm combined politically powerful ideas, good timing and boundless tenacity to enact two landmark laws that have shaped budget debates for the 1980s and beyond. No recent member has had so great an impact in so short a time. In 1981, as a second-term House member, he devised the Gramm-Latta package embodying President Reagan's priority-reordering program of social spending cuts, a defense buildup and tax reductions. In 1985, just a first-year senator who had been kept off the Budget Committee, he was the driving force behind the Gramm-Rudman-Hollings law, a radical overhaul of the budget process imposing a mandated timetable for balancing the books.

Never mind that many colleagues and outside experts grouse that Gramm's first effort set in motion the deficits that his second law is designed to conquer. Or that the second law promised budgetary salvation that it could not deliver as long as a Democratic Congress and Republican administrations remain at odds on tax and spending priorities. The reality is, Congress passed both.

The institution is more accustomed to legislators who mount a sustained siege of several years to push major bills into law; Gramm, a determined ideological crusader, took the place by storm. But time has passed since Gramm-Rudman-Hollings, leaving some colleagues braced for the next attack. If one comes, it will be an inside job; with the 101st Congress, Gramm finally landed seats on both the Budget and Appropriations committees. The question his own party leaders are asking is whether Gramm, as a budget insider, now will be less an independent operator and more a team player.

Senior members of both parties think they have a carrot: Gramm wants funding for the multibillion-dollar superconducting supercollider that is proposed for construction in his economically troubled state. At the same time, they know that this ardent champion of free-market economics does not often bend his principles, even for home-state considerations. He has consistently opposed an oil-import fee, despite attacks like one from a Houston business journal that called Gramm "the third senator from Massachusetts."

Gramm wants to do more than tinker around the edges of the welfare state. He is out to shrink the whole concept of American government on behalf of those he calls "the wagon pullers" — namely, the middle-class "people who do the work, pay the taxes and pull the wagon." For a man given to homespun, self-deprecating humor, Gramm is not modest about his own role in that revolution. "I want to make sure we've changed government forever," he says. "If I don't do it, it may not get done."

His lightning campaign for Gramm-Rudman-Hollings clearly illustrated the keys to Gramm's success. He pressed the issue with an energy and single-minded intensity that was as unstoppable as it was alienating to many of his colleagues. "You don't have to worry about stepping on people's toes," he observes. "They're going to step out of your way." Even more important, perhaps, was Gramm's sense of timing; he is an opportunist, and a good one.

In 1981, Gramm had capitalized on Reagan's honeymoon time, with its consensus that the new president had a mandate for a program that paralleled Gramm's own. By 1985 — a time of pervasive despair over spiraling deficits and Congress' inability to control them through conventional means — Gramm saw that lawmakers and the public were ready for radical steps. He also saw the perfect vehicle to which he could attach his creation — a must-pass resolution extending the government's borrowing authority.

Although Gramm's 1985 proposal was greatly modified during long weeks of negotiations, the core of his concept remained intact. Congress was politically incapable, Gramm believed, of making the decisions needed to eliminate the deficit. The only way to force it to do so was to install a process that threatened a worse alternative — indiscriminate, across-the-board spending cuts.

The appeal of that idea, and fear of the political costs of opposing it, were so great that most members felt they had no choice but to go along, despite strong doubts about the wisdom of approving so fundamental a change with so little study. By the end of 1985, Congress and the president were committed to balancing the budget by 1991.

That initial commitment was short-lived, however. Although one relatively minor round of across-the-board cuts took place in 1986, the Supreme Court soon ruled that a key aspect of the law's automatic-cut procedures was unconstitutional. Gramm and Republican Sen. Warren B. Rudman of New Hampshire tried to fix their proposal to comply with the court, but the House initially refused to go along.

The next year, however, Gramm and a band of House Democrats separately engineered another fiscal crisis — as in 1985, by blocking extension of the federal debt limit — to force a revival of Gramm-Rudman-Hollings. This time, the Reagan administration and many Republicans were opposed, realizing that the law would trigger big defense cuts and tax increases unless its annual deficit targets were relaxed.

The resulting debate was ironic, with Gramm joining the administration in pushing to ease the deficit targets and many Democrats opposing that. The final compromise, besides fixing the law's legally faulty procedures, also moved the deadline for a balanced budget to 1993. Since late 1987, both Reagan and President Bush have reached modest budget agreements with Congress that met the law's targets mainly through accounting gimmickry. The best that is said for the statute is that it has reinforced a consensus on the need for deficit reduction.

Day to day, Gramm's more potent budgetary weapon is his power as a senator to block bills that breach annual spending limits until supporters can muster 60 votes for a budget waiver. In 1987, he single-handedly held up an emergency supplemental appropriations bill for a month, forcing some concessions. Though most of the bill's funds were for farm programs running out of money, Gramm cited the non-emergency add-ons that Appropriations typically includes and called them "part of a process that is little more than piracy."

With his new committee assignments, Gramm himself is now part of that process, and both he and Appropriations are likely to be tested. In landing a place on Budget also, Gramm fulfilled a goal he has had since he was elected to the Senate in 1984. The fact that it took him four years to achieve it is a measure of the institutional response to his brash independence.

Senate GOP leaders, fearing Gramm would prove uncompromising and hard to control, prevented his seating on Budget in the 99th and 100th Congresses by enlisting two more-senior Republicans to serve. But with the 101st Congress, both unwilling recruits got off, and Gramm had the seniority to stake a claim.

He gave up his seat on the Armed Services Committee, where he had been a supporter of Reagan's military buildup best known for two ideological efforts bearing little on defense: an anti-labor push to weaken a law requiring defense contractors to pay union-scale wages, and a fiscal battle against a longstanding mandate that the Pentagon use U.S. coal for its European bases.

Gramm remains on the Banking Committee, a voice for deregulation. During the 100th Congress, amid trouble in the stock and commodity markets, Gramm counseled against government intervention (his wife, Wendy Lee, is chairman of the Commodity Futures Trading Commission). He was one of only two senators to vote against a banking deregulation bill, objecting that it did not go far enough. In the debate over corporate takeovers, Gramm sided with stockholders' groups and raiders such as Texan T. Boone Pickens Jr. in opposing legislation protective of corporate managers.

While other Texans, notably then-House Speaker Jim Wright, were promoting a limited $5 billion bailout for the federal savings and loan insurance fund in 1987 — out of concern that a higher amount would allow regulators to close down many ailing Texas thrifts — Gramm espoused the administration's $15 billion plan. He lost 5-13 in committee, while warning that without a higher amount from S&Ls' premiums, taxpayers eventually would have to finance a bailout. Indeed, the 101st Congress immediately turned to work on a costly package requiring funds from both industry and the Treasury.

Initially at least, Senate Republicans' doubts about Gramm were influenced by his stormy career in the House as a Democrat. Almost as soon as he arrived in 1979, he began fighting with Wright, then the majority leader, and other top Democrats. On the Energy and Commerce Committee, he established a working relationship with senior Democrat John D. Dingell, but he usually voted with Republicans, especially David A. Stockman, soon to be his ally in the Reagan administration. Gramm was a militant critic of President Carter's hospital cost-containment plan on the panel.

When he campaigned for a seat on the

Budget Committee at the start of his second term in 1981, Democratic House leaders sought and received Gramm's written assurance that he would loyally support the party's budget. Just months later, he did the opposite — and in a spectacular way.

Democrats soon discovered that Gramm was secretly collaborating with Republicans on Reagan's budget, while sitting in on Budget Democrats' caucuses and reporting back to the White House, particularly to Reagan's new budget director, Stockman. The alleged spy was barred from Democrats' meetings.

He further alienated Democrats with his success in engineering Reagan's budget victory on the House floor. He led 63 Democrats, mostly Southern Boll Weevils, into a winning coalition with Republicans. Later in 1981, after Budget assembled $37 billion in specific spending cuts to meet the budget's limits, Gramm offered a more stringent package with administration support. The House passed his version rather than Budget's, thanks to the same conservative coalition. Those initiatives were cosponsored by senior Budget Republican Delbert L. Latta, but Gramm played the key role and won the two men's internal contest for top billing.

Gramm said later that his actions should not have surprised anyone. "I have supported the position that I have supported since I came to Congress," he said. But Democrats felt betrayed; at the start of the next Congress, Gramm was evicted from Budget.

He was prepared for that, and had even hired a GOP pollster for some soundings about a party switch. Charging that he had been punished "for practicing in Washington what I preach at home," Gramm left the party, resigned his House seat and won re-election to it as a Republican in 1983. He rejoined Budget, adapting easily to the role of GOP partisan.

While Gramm's special election and 1984 Senate campaign limited his legislative role in the 98th Congress, he did trigger one controversy. During 1983 debate over a bill authorizing U.S. contributions to the International Monetary Fund, Gramm won House passage of an amendment forcing the United States to vote against IMF loans to "communist dictatorships." It was his counterreaction to liberals' efforts to block IMF loans for South Africa.

But the administration objected, because it wanted the IMF bill and feared Gramm's proposal would imperil its passage. Gramm also outraged members of both parties by targeting some 20 Democrats who opposed his proposal with press releases, sent to their home districts, suggesting they had shown a "total disrespect for the freedom we've always fought for." For all the criticism he provoked, Gramm got a partial victory. As passed into law, the compromise included toned-down versions of both the anti-communist and anti-apartheid provisions.

At Home: Whatever the effects of Gramm's 1983 party switch in Washington, the move bolstered his political career back home. His comfortable victory in the 1983 special House election set the stage for his stunning 1984 Senate triumph.

The Democrats' hopes in 1983 rested on forcing Gramm into a runoff. But Gramm won the special election outright, tapping a massive treasury and a superior organization to take 51 percent. His victory gave the 6th District to the GOP for the first time in Texas history.

In building that victory, Gramm invested heavily in media markets encompassing Dallas, Houston and Fort Worth — giving him exposure that proved invaluable in his subsequent Senate campaign. When Republican Sen. John Tower announced he would retire at the end of the 98th Congress, Gramm was already a familiar figure in the state's populous parts.

Bolstered by his superior name recognition, Gramm took a commanding lead for the Republican Senate nomination, and he never looked back. Largely ignoring his intraparty foes, he spent the spring of 1984 canvassing areas not normally hospitable to the GOP.

The Democrats, meanwhile, were conducting a tortuous nominating campaign. State Sen. Lloyd Doggett, a hard-charging liberal, struggled to finish a close second in the grueling primary, then squeezed past conservative U.S. Rep. Kent Hance in a runoff that further polarized the party and ate up Doggett's resources and time.

When Doggett finally emerged for the general-election campaign, Gramm had him fixed firmly in his sights. The Republican launched an aggressive statewide media campaign questioning Doggett's commitment to traditional family values. One ad observed that Doggett had accepted a contribution from a gay group that raised part of the money at an all-male striptease show. Doggett later returned the funds, but the ad kept him on the defensive.

In response, Doggett tried to cast Gramm as a right-wing extremist too radical to represent Texas. He accused Gramm of attempting to cut Social Security and of calling for the eventual elimination of federal education aid.

But Doggett's counteroffensive could not stem the Republican tide. The Democrat ran well among blacks and Hispanics, carried South Texas and his home base of Travis County (Austin). But Gramm's strategy helped him make impressive inroads into conservative, rural East and West Texas, territory that would go Democratic in an ordinary year. Aided by a 3-to-1 spending advantage and fallout from President Reagan's strong campaign, Gramm racked up 59 percent of the vote — the best showing ever achieved by a Republican statewide candidate in Texas.

Since then, Gramm's standing with the voters has probably been enhanced by his high-profile performance in Washington. Several Democrats who might have had the statewide stature to challenge him in 1990 seemed to turn away as the election cycle began, making Gramm a strong early bet to win a second term.

Before he ran for Congress in 1976, Gramm's life was centered around the academic community at Texas A&M, where he taught economics. He wrote extensively on economics and energy and established a consulting firm that did contract research for government and private industry in the United States, Canada and Australia.

Gramm was barely known statewide when he challenged incumbent Lloyd Bentsen in the 1976 Democratic Senate primary. Claiming that Bentsen had moved to the left to mount his ill-fated 1976 presidential campaign, he presented himself as a conservative alternative. Underfinanced, he drew only 29 percent of the vote.

Two years later, with better name recognition and financial support, Gramm sought the Democratic nomination to succeed Olin E. Teague, challenging a Fort Worth television weatherman who was Teague's personal choice.

Gramm survived an expensive primary and runoff by building a campaign treasury of nearly a half-million dollars. In the general election, his national New Right support preempted a successful Republican challenge.

In 1982, Gramm faced a spirited primary challenge from a candidate cheered on by the national Democratic establishment — Jack Teague, son of Gramm's House predecessor. Teague called Gramm a turncoat who had abandoned his party's traditional concern for the disadvantaged and average-income people.

But Gramm cast the election as a referendum on whether he was fulfilling his promises to carry the district's fiscal conservatism to Washington. The incumbent took 62 percent to win the primary. Republicans, who had fielded a candidate in case Gramm lost, showed no interest after his nomination.

Committees

Appropriations (13th of 13 Republicans)
District of Columbia (ranking); Commerce, Justice, State, the Judiciary and Related Agencies; HUD-Independent Agencies; Labor, Health and Human Services, Education and Related Agencies

Banking, Housing and Urban Affairs (4th of 9 Republicans)
International Finance and Monetary Policy (ranking); Consumer and Regulatory Affairs; Housing and Urban Affairs; Securities

Budget (9th of 10 Republicans)

Elections

1984 General		
Phil Gramm (R)	3,111,348	(59%)
Lloyd Doggett (D)	2,202,557	(41%)
1984 Primary		
Phil Gramm (R)	246,716	(73%)
Ron Paul (R)	55,431	(16%)
Rob Mosbacher (R)	26,279	(8%)
Henry C. Grover (R)	8,388	(3%)

Previous Winning Percentages: **1983 †** (55%) **1982 *** (95%) **1980 *** (71%) **1978 *** (65%)

** House elections.*
† Special House election.

Campaign Finance

	Receipts	Receipts from PACs	Expend-itures
1984			
Gramm (R)	$9,863,651	$1,479,851 (15%)	$9,509,724
Doggett (D)	$5,958,005	$804,929 (14%)	$5,880,512

Key Votes

1987	
Enact omnibus highway bill over Reagan veto	N
Limit testing of space-based anti-ballistic missiles	N
Oppose banning tests of larger nuclear weapons	Y
Confirm Robert H. Bork as Supreme Court justice	Y
1988	
Allow vote on campaign-finance overhaul	?
Pass civil rights restoration bill over Reagan veto	N
Enact omnibus trade bill over Reagan veto	N
Approve death penalty for drug-related murders	?
Oppose "workfare" amendment to welfare overhaul bill	N

Voting Studies

	Presidential Support		Party Unity		Conservative Coalition	
Year	**S**	**O**	**S**	**O**	**S**	**O**
1988	78	15	85	4	92	3
1987	87	9	92	5	84	13
1986	99	1	95	4	97	1
1985	87	13	95	5	88	12
House Service						
1984	37	27	58	5	69	8
1983	73	16	79 †	2 †	93	0
1982	84	14	10	87	89	10
1981	75	22	20	77	99	0

† Not eligible for all recorded votes. Gramm resigned from the House Jan. 5, 1983. He had been elected as a Democrat and cast his first three votes of 1983 as a member of that party. His party unity support score as a Democrat was 33 percent; opposition was 67 percent. Gramm was re-elected Feb. 12, 1983, as a Republican and sworn in Feb. 22. The scores for 1983 party unity reflect his votes as a Republican.

Interest Group Ratings

Year	ADA	ACU	AFL-CIO	CCUS
1988	0	95	0	92
1987	5	100	10	89
1986	0	100	0	89
1985	0	95	0	86
House Service				
1984	10	64	22	78
1983	0	100	0	88
1982	10	91	10	73
1981	0	93	13	89

1 Jim Chapman (D)

Of Sulphur Springs — Elected 1985

Born: March 8, 1945, Washington, D.C.

Education: U. of Texas, B.B.A. 1968; Southern Methodist U., J.D. 1970.

Occupation: Lawyer.

Family: Wife, Betty Brice; two children.

Religion: Methodist.

Political Career: District attorney, 8th Judicial District of Texas, 1977-85; sought Democratic nomination for Texas Senate, 1984.

Capitol Office: 429 Cannon Bldg. 20515; 225-3035.

In Washington: Chapman is evidence that while Jim Wright may be gone from the House, his handiwork is still evident in the institution. Wright helped Chapman win a 1985 special election and guided his early House career. At the outset of the 101st Congress, he saw to it that Chapman got a seat on Appropriations.

Only one Democratic seat on the committee — that of retiring Edward P. Boland of Massachusetts — was expected to be open in the 101st, and Wright promised it to New England. However, Florida Democrat Bill Chappell Jr., an Appropriations member, lost his House seat in a 1988 election upset. Hoping to head off a clash between Massachusetts members Chester G. Atkins and Joseph P. Kennedy II — both of whom wanted Appropriations — New England Democrats lobbied Wright for the second seat on the panel as well. But Wright said no: Chapman was his pick for the Chappell vacancy.

Chapman had earned Wright's gratitude in October 1987, when he saved the Speaker from defeat on a controversial budget reconciliation bill. Chapman initially voted against the bill, which contained nearly $12 million in new taxes. But when he got back to his House office, he learned that the roll call was about to close with the bill losing by one vote. As Wright held the vote open past the usual 15-minute limit, Chapman dashed back to change his vote, giving Wright a 206-205 victory amid howls of complaint from the GOP.

Chapman insisted he had done nothing wrong, stating he "could not sit and watch [the bill] go down." But while he got some criticism as a flip-flopper, the incident did more damage to Wright: It fueled sentiment among House Republicans that he was a heavy-handed leader, and it gave further encouragement to those in the GOP who were pressing for an inquiry into Wright's finances.

The vote was the most public event of Chapman's House career. Before moving to Appropriations, he labored quietly on behalf of district and state interests on the Public Works Committee. He claimed credit during the 100th Congress for targeting funds to a variety of local road and water projects, and for obtaining money to construct a new central distribution center at the Red River Army Depot, his district's largest employer.

At Home: In his 1985 special election, Chapman was at the center of a battle the parties saw as crucial to their future in the South.

GOP Sen. Phil Gramm had helped engineer a federal judgeship for Democratic Rep. Sam B. Hall Jr., then helped recruit rancher and engineer Edd Hargett, a former Texas A&M football star, as the GOP candidate to replace Hall. The national GOP threw its weight behind Hargett, seeing a chance for the party to make inroads in traditional Democratic territory.

Chapman was one of six Democrats competing on the same ballot with Hargett. Working to overcome animosity among some Democrats generated by his unsuccessful 1984 challenge to a popular state senator, Chapman managed 30 percent of the vote. That was enough to force a runoff with Hargett, who led with 42 percent.

In the runoff, Chapman presented himself as a traditional conservative Democrat and questioned Hargett's credentials to serve in Congress. He got his biggest boost, however, from a Hargett gaffe. When local newspapers reported the Republican saying, "I don't know what trade policies have to do with bringing jobs to East Texas," Chapman pounced, pointing to layoffs at a local steel plant. Hargett could not overcome the trade issue. With support from courthouse Democrats, labor and trial lawyers, Chapman narrowly won the runoff.

Although national GOP leaders claimed that the party had shown real strength in the South by coming so close, they did not pursue the issue in 1986, allowing Chapman to win a full term unopposed. In 1988, the GOP tried to make an issue of Chapman's vote switch that passed Wright's budget bill. But the only candidate they could line up, farmer-broadcaster Horace McQueen of Troup, got just 38 percent.

Texas 1

Northeast — Texarkana

The 1st District is a collection of farm plots, small towns and county crossroads; to find a big city, one has to travel beyond its boundaries. Texarkana (Bowie County) and Marshall (Harrison County) are the largest population centers (with 33,000 and 24,000 people, respectively). But together, Bowie and Harrison counties account for less than a quarter of the district's population.

Texarkana is the twin city of its namesake across the state line in Arkansas. Although the two are administratively separate, their development has been intertwined. Texarkana is an important regional trading center; it also hosts the Red River Army Depot, a largely civilian facility that services Army vehicles.

Marshall, once the home of an important timber trade, is still known for its scenery and myriad trees, but light industries related to East Texas' oil and natural gas wells are more inportant to the economy now. Defense also contributes to the manufacturing base: The Longhorn Army Ammunitions plant produces rocket fuel and is involved in destroying Pershing missiles covered under the intermediate-range nuclear-force (INF) treaty.

Much of the district's territory not devoted to oil and gas is given to cattle-ranching and the production of dairy goods. Hopkins County, in the western part of the 1st, is one of Texas' largest dairy producers. San Augustine County, at the district's southern end, is an important part of the 1st's lumber industry.

Some of the 1st's key economic underpinnings have been suffering through much of the 1980s — timber because of Canadian imports, cattle-raising due to Mexican competition, and steel making, also because of foreign competition. The sagging fortunes of Lone Star Steel, which has filed for bankruptcy, have done severe damage to the economy in Morris and Upshur counties, near the center of the district.

Population: 527,016. White 417,347 (79%), Black 103,249 (20%). Spanish origin 8,378 (2%). 18 and over 376,964 (72%), 65 and over 85,485 (16%). Median age: 33.

Committee

Appropriations (35th of 35 Democrats)
Energy and Water Development; VA, HUD and Independent Agencies

Elections

1988 General

Jim Chapman (D)	122,566	(62%)
Horace McQueen (R)	74,357	(38%)

1986 General

Jim Chapman (D)	84,445	(100%)

Previous Winning Percentage: **1985 *** (51%)

** Special election runoff.*

District Vote For President

	1988	1984	1980	1976
D	96,668 (47%)	84,954 (41%)	90,448 (50%)	95,599 (59%)
R	107,456 (53%)	120,350 (58%)	89,581 (49%)	65,538 (41%)

Campaign Finance

	Receipts	Receipts from PACs	Expend-itures
1988			
Chapman (D)	$587,159	$270,430 (46%)	$551,611
McQueen (R)	$94,842	$7,514 (8%)	$94,477
1986			
Chapman (D)	$858,143	$197,439 (23%)	$837,817

Key Votes

1987

Raise speed limit to 65 mph	Y
Approve Gephardt "fair trade" amendment	Y
Ban testing of larger nuclear weapons	Y
Delay "re-flagging" of Kuwaiti tankers	N
Approve tax-raising deficit-reduction bill	Y

1988

Approve aid to Nicaraguan contras	Y
Enact civil rights restoration bill over Reagan veto	Y
Kill 60-day plant-closing notification measure	N
Pass omnibus trade bill over Reagan veto	Y
Approve death penalty for drug-related murders	Y
Bar federal funds for abortions in cases of rape and incest	Y
Oppose seven-day waiting period for purchase of handguns	Y

Voting Studies

	Presidential Support		Party Unity		Conservative Coalition	
Year	**S**	**O**	**S**	**O**	**S**	**O**
1988	36	61	70	23	87	3
1987	39	60	71	22	88	9
1986	37	61	69	24	86	10
1985	42 †	56 †	59 †	32 †	94 †	0 †

† Not eligible for all recorded votes.

Interest Group Ratings

Year	ADA	ACU	AFL-CIO	CCUS
1988	50	52	71	64
1987	48	9	63	47
1986	40	38	69	50
1985	—	71	20	92

2 Charles Wilson (D)

Of Lufkin — Elected 1972

Born: June 1, 1933, Trinity, Texas.
Education: Attended Sam Houston State U., 1950-51; U.S. Naval Academy, B.S. 1956.
Military Career: Navy, 1956-60.
Occupation: Lumberyard manager.
Family: Divorced.
Religion: Methodist.
Political Career: Texas House, 1961-67; Texas Senate, 1967-73.
Capitol Office: 2256 Rayburn Bldg. 20515; 225-2401.

In Washington: Wilson went the extra mile in 1989 to defend his close friend, House Speaker Jim Wright. The East Texas Democrat argued strongly and publicly against the ethics charges that eventually toppled Wright, and was among the last of the Speaker's colleagues to give up hope for his political survival.

For many members, taking such an up-front stance in support of the beleaguered Wright was too politically risky. But Wilson, more so than most of his colleagues, is used to living close to the edge.

In the case of his crusade on behalf of the anti-communist rebels battling Soviet forces in Afghanistan, Wilson took chances with his physical safety. A member of the House Appropriations Subcommittee on Foreign Operations, he twice visited rebel forces inside Afghanistan, and has made more than a dozen trips to Pakistan.

But Wilson has also faced some less salutary dangers, ones that might have brought down a member with a less-solid political base than Wilson enjoys in his 2nd District. His taste for high living earned him unwanted attention from the Justice Department, which in 1983 investigated, but did not charge, Wilson during a probe into Capitol Hill drug use (Wilson firmly denied the drug allegations). That same year, Wilson was fined for colliding with a car on a Washington, D.C., bridge, then leaving the scene of the accident; the car he was driving carried his official House license plates.

Wilson even saw one of his Afghanistan adventures tarnished, when it was revealed that he had exacted revenge on the Defense Intelligence Agency (DIA) for denying his girlfriend (now his fiancée) a seat on a U.S. government plane in Pakistan in February 1986. The story came to light nearly two years later, when Wilson slipped a provision into a 1987 year-end omnibus spending bill that cut six planes from the DIA fleet.

None of the negative publicity has seriously damaged the lanky Texan's towering popularity back home. But his "good-time Charlie" reputation has tended to obscure his image on the inside as one of the better lobbyists and vote traders in the House.

Wilson still struts across the House floor with a cocky gait — which, ironically, is less a mannerism that the result of his chronic back problems — and has a quick, wide grin and a handshake ready for whoever is handy. But there is usually a serious purpose lurking behind his roguish friendliness.

For most of the 1980s, Wilson's most serious purpose was the maintenance of U.S. support for the Mujahedeen rebels in Afghanistan. Wilson adopted the cause not long after the Soviet invasion of that central Asian nation in 1979, and persisted in the face of considerable congressional doubt that the loosely organized Afghan guerrillas could survive a military onslaught from the Soviet Red Army.

In promoting the cause of the "Muj," as he called the rebels, Wilson's rhetoric about the Soviet occupiers was clearly from the pre-*glasnost* era. During the 99th Congress, Wilson told a closed meeting of the Appropriations Subcommittee on Defense that he wanted to help the rebels in Afghanistan because "it's the only place in the world where we are killing Russians."

As the war dragged on through the decade, the persistent rebels made gains against the Soviet forces, bolstering the arguments of Wilson and other hard-liners for increased U.S. support for the rebels. Though President Reagan was also a strong supporter of the Afghan cause, it took a concerted effort by Wilson and other members to break down Reagan administration resistance to supplying the Stinger anti-aircraft missiles and other sophisticated weaponry that boosted the military viability of the Mujahedeen forces.

Wilson's high-level efforts on the Afghan issue earned him national attention: CBS' "60 Minutes" television program profiled him as a savior of the rebel cause. Wilson's activism also helped him persuade Wright to find a place for him on the House Select Committee on Intelli-

Texas 2

East — Lufkin; Orange

Traditionally poor, isolated and dependent on timber, the East Texas piney woods 2nd took on a new look in the 1970s with the growth of the oil industry. But oil has proven to be a fickle economic generator. The downturn in oil prices has brought hard times to many here for much of the 1980s.

Lufkin, the district's largest city, once boasted some 275 sawmills, testimony to the importance of the local lumber industry. Now, a prominent employer is Lufkin Industries, which manufactures trailers, shell casings and other metal products. Factories making oil and gas drilling equipment also are prominent.

Orange, located to the southwest, used to draw its revenues from timber, cattle and rice. Today, it is the domain of petrochemical facilities that have been forced to lay off workers. Goodyear, Gulf Oil and Du Pont all maintain plants along Orange's major industrial corridor, known locally as "Chemical Row." The closing of a major shipyard pushed Orange's unemployment to 20 percent in 1987. Defense contract work has helped the city rebound somewhat; current unemployment is about 12 percent. Orange remains the district's only significant concentration of union members.

Independent oil outfits that have sprung up throughout the district in recent years have altered the 2nd's landscape. But the district has not entirely lost its Deep South woodland feel. Four national forests are located in the district; along the fringes, there are places resembling Louisiana's bayous.

Like all of East Texas, the 2nd is conservative territory with strong ties to Dixie. The 2nd's Deep South character was evident in 1968, when it was the only district in the state to back George C. Wallace. Its character is further evident in the slow progress blacks have made in local elections. Although they comprise 15 percent of the district's population, blacks are seldom a significant political force.

Bolstered by a residual populist streak in the rural counties, Jimmy Carter received a favorable reception in the 2nd in 1976; he took nearly 60 percent of the district vote. Even in 1980, when Carter lost the state by a decisive margin, he carried the 2nd.

But in 1984, the national Democratic Party's liberal tilt alienated even some of the most staunchly Democratic voters. Of the 16 counties wholly or partially in the 2nd, only two voted for Walter F. Mondale. In 1988, Michael S. Dukakis — running with Texan Lloyd Bentsen — brought the 2nd back into the Democratic column, although by a margin of just 355 votes over George Bush.

Population: 526,772. White 433,363 (82%), Black 81,820 (16%), Other 2,862 (1%). Spanish origin 16,906 (3%). 18 and over 372,792 (71%), 65 and over 62,165 (12%). Median age: 30.

gence. Wright did so when he became Speaker in the 99th Congress, despite some objections from liberal Democrats; they feared Wilson, the party's self-appointed "head hawk," would too often side with the panel's Republicans.

When the Soviet Union signed a United Nations-crafted agreement in April 1988 to withdraw its troops from Afghanistan over the following 10 months, Wilson declared victory for the rebels and their U.S. supporters. When Soviet leader Mikhail S. Gorbachev called for a negotiated cease-fire during the Soviet pullout late that year, some American conservatives feared he was about to renege. But Wilson counseled not to worry, and did so in his usual brazen style. "It's in their interest to get out," Wilson told his colleagues. "They're getting their butts kicked."

Wilson's affiliation with the Afghan cause also contributed to his stance as one of strongest House supporters of Pakistan, an Afghanistan neighbor and the conduit of much of the U.S. aid to the Mujahedeen. In 1987, he parried efforts by some liberal arms control advocates to condition U.S. aid to Pakistan on that nation's suspension of its efforts to develop a nuclear-weapons capability.

Wilson said supporters of the aid conditions were being "very selective in moral application," and pointed out that Israel, the leading recipient of U.S. foreign aid, was widely believed to have developed a nuclear arsenal. "Are we going to cut off aid to Israel?" Wilson said. "Of course we're not."

Wilson's conservative activism on foreign policy goes back a long way. A member of the House Foreign Affairs Committee in the late 1970s, he was an outspoken opponent of the Nicaraguan leftists who fought, and in 1979 overthrew, Anastasio Somoza in Nicaragua. Through the 1980s, Wilson gave steady support to Reagan's policy of aiding the Nicaraguan contras.

A graduate of the U.S. Naval Academy,

Wilson has also lived up to his reputation as a pro-defense conservative. From his seat on Appropriations' Defense Subcommittee, he has supported weapons systems, such as the MX missile, that have been controversial within the Democratic Caucus.

In 1985, Wilson provided a blunt warning on defense issues to his party's liberal wing. "If the perception persists in this country that the Democratic Party is the party of isolation and ... weakness on defense," he said, "we are flat through in the South and West, and we can forget about winning presidential elections."

But while his hawkish views mesh well with those of his conservative constituency, Wilson's popularity at home is staked more on his attention to local issues. In particular, he has been known throughout his career as the most persistent House defender of independent oil interests.

Wilson developed that reputation during the 1970s, when the rising prices associated with the "energy crisis" had provoked a public reaction against the big oil companies. Striking a populist pose popular in rural Texas, Wilson exploited this anger to the benefit of the smaller independents. At one point, he warned that without federal efforts to protect the independents, "The petroleum industry of the United States will be controlled by the eight men who head the eight major oil companies in the United States."

The rest of Wilson's legislative record on domestic policy is pure East Texas populism. Even with his conservative record on foreign policy and defense issues, Wilson still managed to vote against Reagan's position on House legislation more than half of the time during the 100th Congress. His pro-labor House votes earned him a 93 percent rating from the AFL-CIO in 1987, and an 82 percent mark in 1988.

With his position on Appropriations, Wilson also has been able to obtain funding for the types of projects that earn constituent gratitude. In the 100th Congress, he helped secure money for the relocation of railroad tracks that had become a traffic nuisance in the city of Orange, and for the construction of a Veterans Administration outpatient clinic in Lufkin, his hometown.

At Home: Wilson managed through most of his years in the House to combine his active legislative career with the pursuit of pleasure. He has never seemed embarrassed about being labeled a playboy or a smiling Texas rogue; he seems to enjoy it. "I love what I'm doing," he once told a reporter. "Why should I go around looking like a constipated hound dog? I'm having the time of my life."

In the late 1970s, Wilson was a partner in a downtown Washington discotheque. With his monogrammed cowboy boots and wide-brimmed Western hat, he was a recognized man-about-town, and he always seemed to be escorting a beautiful actress, model or socialite. The divorced Wilson's steadies included a woman whose picture had appeared on the cover of *Playboy*. His 1986 traveling companion, Annelise Ilschenko, was a lobbyist and the 1975 winner of the Miss World USA contest; they became engaged in early 1989.

At one point, Wilson's high-life routine almost wore thin on 2nd District voters. He found himself in political trouble in 1984, a year after his car accident and the federal drug probe in which his name was mentioned. The controversy surrounding these events encouraged primary challenges from four contenders who would never have taken on the popular incumbent in an ordinary year. The candidate best positioned to take advantage of Wilson's troubles was Nacogdoches bank executive Jerry K. Johnson, who was making his first bid for public office. A farm-bred Baptist church deacon and Sunday school teacher, Johnson projected a clean-cut image that contrasted with Wilson's flamboyance.

Like all of Wilson's primary opponents, Johnson avoided overt mention of the drug issue. But he was not shy about painting the incumbent as a man whose taste for glamour had superseded his interest in the concerns of the district. "Unlike the incumbent, I won't go into the Washington real estate and nightclub business and forget where I come from or who I'm working for," Johnson said.

But Wilson was well prepared for the fight. Tapping his close ties to defense contractors and the independent oil industry, he amassed a substantial treasury, using some of his money to run TV ads that showed him talking with laid-off blue-collar workers and trumpeting his support for "domestic content" legislation. He also deployed phone banks for the first time in his political career.

Wilson sought to defuse controversy over the Justice investigation by attacking the department, vehemently denying allegations against him and accusing the Justice Department of prolonging its investigation solely because he was a member of Congress. He told constituents that he was "set up" by an embittered former business partner who had embezzled money from him.

If the investigation hurt Wilson among the district's Democrats, the damage was limited. Johnson, the only challenger to clear 10 percent on primary day, carried his home base of Nacogdoches County. But the rest of the district stayed by Wilson's side. Squelching speculation that he might be forced into a runoff, Wilson captured 55 percent of the districtwide primary vote, and won handily in November.

By 1986, Wilson was back on track. He went unopposed in the primary, and clinched re-election by a comfortable margin. In 1988, no Republican filed to oppose him.

Liberal Democrats in Washington who are

dismayed by the conservative aspects of Wilson's record might be surprised to learn that in 1960, when most Texas Democrats were backing Lyndon B. Johnson for the Democratic presidential nomination, Wilson was for John F. Kennedy. In the Texas Legislature, Wilson was commonly identified as "the liberal from Lufkin"; he crusaded against high utility rates, fought for Medicaid and tax exemptions for the elderly and sponsored bills to remove a ceiling on welfare spending. His career advanced with the help of Arthur Temple, a maverick lumber millionaire who treated Wilson as a protégé and helped with campaign financing.

During his successful congressional race in 1972, Wilson softened his liberalism somewhat, opposing school busing and gun control. But he still drew the support of blacks and labor and easily defeated the wife of Rep. John Dowdy in the Democratic primary. Dowdy's husband had been sentenced to prison earlier in the year for bribery, conspiracy and perjury.

Committees

Appropriations (13th of 35 Democrats)
Defense; Foreign Operations

Select Intelligence (7th of 12 Democrats)
Program and Budget Authorization

Elections

1988 General		
Charles Wilson (D)	145,614	(88%)
Gary W. Nelson (LIB)	20,475	(12%)
1986 General		
Charles Wilson (D)	78,529	(66%)
Julian Gordon (R)	35,986	(30%)

Previous Winning Percentages: **1984** (59%) **1982** (94%) **1980** (69%) **1978** (70%) **1976** (95%) **1974** (100%) **1972** (74%)

District Vote For President

	1988	1984	1980	1976
D	99,075 (50%)	81,989 (42%)	86,056 (50%)	85,850 (59%)
R	98,720 (50%)	114,915 (58%)	81,093 (48%)	59,163 (41%)

Campaign Finance

	Receipts	Receipts from PACs	Expend-itures
1988			
Wilson (D)	$338,839	$254,350 (75%)	$309,355
1986			
Wilson (D)	$367,600	$265,206 (72%)	$339,873
Gordon (R)	$59,138	0	$47,660

Key Votes

1987	
Raise speed limit to 65 mph	Y
Approve Gephardt "fair trade" amendment	Y
Ban testing of larger nuclear weapons	N
Delay "re-flagging" of Kuwaiti tankers	N
Approve tax-raising deficit-reduction bill	Y
1988	
Approve aid to Nicaraguan contras	Y
Enact civil rights restoration bill over Reagan veto	Y
Kill 60-day plant-closing notification measure	N
Pass omnibus trade bill over Reagan veto	Y
Approve death penalty for drug-related murders	Y
Bar federal funds for abortions in cases of rape and incest	N
Oppose seven-day waiting period for purchase of handguns	Y

Voting Studies

	Presidential Support		Party Unity		Conservative Coalition	
Year	S	O	S	O	S	O
1988	36	43	61	20	53	34
1987	39	54	66	17	65	26
1986	38	50	61	18	72	12
1985	40	43	63	15	60	22
1984	36	32	44	21	59	15
1983	45	37	53	28	66	13
1982	47	30	51	30	63	15
1981	57	34	54	36	68	24

Interest Group Ratings

Year	ADA	ACU	AFL-CIO	CCUS
1988	35	55	82	46
1987	56	43	93	8
1986	35	50	92	27
1985	40	55	75	44
1984	35	26	73	38
1983	45	48	75	50
1982	25	47	47	56
1981	20	50	50	58

3 Steve Bartlett (R)

Of Dallas — Elected 1982

Born: Sept. 19, 1947, Los Angeles, Calif.
Education: U. of Texas, B.A. 1971.
Occupation: Owner of tool and plastics company.
Family: Wife, Gail Coke; three children.
Religion: Presbyterian.
Political Career: Dallas City Council, 1977-81.
Capitol Office: 1113 Longworth Bldg. 20515; 225-4201.

In Washington: Quickly after coming to Congress, Bartlett showed an ability to build coalitions and shape legislation with the sureness of a senior member. He is a devout, partisan conservative, but has avoided the stridency that alienates Democrats, and thus has been able to influence an array of bills on subjects as diverse as labor, banking, housing and education.

In the process, however, Bartlett has trodden heavily on his colleagues' toes. Too precocious to be a team player, he has engendered more ill will on his own side of the aisle than he has among Democrats. In 1987 and again in 1988, he ran for the entry-level leadership position of chairman of the GOP Research Committee. Both times he was defeated by more-senior, better-liked members: first by Oklahoma's Mickey Edwards and then by California's Duncan Hunter.

While acknowledging Bartlett's quick grasp of issues, his colleagues also sense his open ambition and quickness to take credit for legislative success. Also, Bartlett sometimes puts other Republicans in an awkward position by pushing conservative alternatives on the House floor that undercut deals senior members have worked hard to put together in committee.

For instance, Bartlett introduced cost-cutting amendments to a 1986 child-nutrition bill that directly challenged Bill Goodling of Pennsylvania, a more senior Republican considered the GOP expert on the programs. The previous year, he led the charge to kill labor-backed legislation to require notification of plant closings, despite the efforts of James M. Jeffords of Vermont, the ranking Education and Labor Republican, to make the bill more acceptable to the GOP.

On Education and Labor, Bartlett has emerged as the committee's most articulate conservative voice. Conservative Republicans generally are loath to serve on Education and Labor, but it was Bartlett's first choice when he came to Congress. He kept that preference quiet, though, winning a seat on the Banking Committee first and then "allowing himself to be persuaded" to join Education and Labor as a gesture of loyalty to party leaders.

Bartlett has been an irrepressible activist on Banking as well as Education and Labor, although on the former he is more influenced by regional interests than by ideology. In both cases, he has assembled some surprisingly broad coalitions in support of his ideas.

He caught many colleagues short during 1986 debate on a housing bill when he won approval of an amendment making a fundamental policy shift by channeling funds into renovation of existing low-income housing rather than into construction of new dwellings. Although the housing bill died at the end of the 99th Congress, key elements of Bartlett's amendment were included in the housing appropriation bill that year. The next year, Bartlett got a less restrictive provision into the only housing reauthorization enacted in the Reagan years. It directed new-construction funds to housing agencies that had brought 85 percent of their units up to standards.

Bartlett's coalition-building skills were best demonstrated on the polarizing issue of bilingual education. In 1984 and again in 1987, he helped coax a compromise when most members thought ethnic tensions would prohibit a satisfactory outcome.

The debate pitted defenders of traditional bilingual education — which offers children academic instruction in their native languages while they learn English — against a Reagan proposal to let schools use other methods. Hispanic groups said that would allow schools to force students to use English at the price of falling behind in academic subjects.

In 1984 Bartlett, sympathetic to the Reagan position, introduced an amendment earmarking a percentage of bilingual funds for new methods. Viewed as a threat by defenders of traditional policy, the proposal was defeated by a vote of 8-10 in subcommittee. But Bartlett sat down with the leading Democratic spokesman for bilingual programs, Dale E. Kildee of Michigan, and hammered out an agreement that provided limited funding for alternatives. The compromise went on to become law. Kildee and

Texas 3

North Dallas; Northern Suburbs

The 3rd is nestled snugly among the affluent neighborhoods and suburbs of North Dallas. The median housing value here is by far the highest in the area and second in the state only to the Houston-based 7th District. Many of Dallas' top corporate executives live here, commuting to work downtown.

But the 3rd also has a sizable business community of its own. High-rise offices and shopping malls have sprung up along the Dallas North Tollway leading into the suburbs, but Texas' economic malaise in recent years has put a damper on growth. Suburban Richardson and Carrollton are populated by young people who arrived during the boom years to take jobs with electronics manufacturers, research firms and corporate branch offices.

Among the wealthiest North Dallas communities are Highland Park and University Park, traditional enclaves of the city's business establishment. University Park hosts Southern Methodist University, a private school with an enrollment of about 9,000 students. Methodist-affiliated SMU has always had an upper-crust air about it — at football games, students have been known to hold up signs that say, "Our maids went to UT" (the University of Texas) — but the school's reputation was besmirched in 1987 when the NCAA canceled its football program because of flagrant rules violations, including payments to players by wealthy alumni. The program is to resume in the fall of 1989.

The GOP is firmly in control throughout the 3rd. In 1988, George Bush won three-quarters of the district's presidential ballots, just a shade below his showing in suburban Houston's 7th District, which Bush represented in the House in the late 1960s. Even GOP Senate candidate Beau Boulter — who lost decisively statewide to Lloyd Bentsen in 1988 — won 55 percent of the vote in the 3rd.

In 1983 redistricting, the 3rd picked up most of the city of Plano, in Collin County. Plano blends in well with the rest of the district; it consists largely of young, upwardly mobile professionals who vote Republican.

Population: 527,023. White 493,748 (94%), Black 17,239 (3%), Other 8,229 (2%). Spanish origin 17,724 (3%). 18 and over 389,627 (74%), 65 and over 37,406 (7%). Median age: 30.

Bartlett cooperated again three years later to give the administration even greater flexibility in distributing funds. The outcome outraged hard-line supporters of bilingual education but cleared the way for a major reauthorization of federal education programs.

On Education and Labor, Bartlett was the prime spokesman for GOP insistence on a subminimum "training wage." He lost in committee on party-line votes in 1988 and 1989, but organized labor finally swallowed a watered-down version of the concept. Nevertheless, Bush vetoed the bill in June 1989 and an override attempt failed in the House.

In Banking action on the savings-and-loan crisis, Bartlett was the voice of business and the voice of Texas thrifts, which in mid-1988 accounted for most of the $7.3 billion in losses. In 1988, Bartlett fought against provisions to require a large amount of equity before failed thrifts could be merged, and voted for the bill in committee after the requirements were cut. The measure never made it to the floor. By the next year, when the focus of the S&L crisis broadened beyond Texas, Bartlett took a lower profile. When the panel supported stricter equity standards, Bartlett philosophically said, "I'd rather have them too tough than too lenient."

As ranking Republican on the Education subcommittee that handles aid for the handicapped, Bartlett in the 99th Congress was the principal ally of school administrators in their fight to limit attorneys' fees in handicapped-education court suits. In the 100th and 101st Congresses, he supported legislation to promote employment of disabled persons, such as allowing recipients of disability insurance to continue their health benefits once they return to work.

Democrats have learned that one way to distract Bartlett is to seize on his activism. In 1987 he had prepared a troublesome amendment paring down the housing and urban development appropriations bill, but he never offered it because he had to fight another battle. That was an amendment offered by a Dallas Democrat with close ties to the leadership, Martin Frost; it would have prevented destruction of 2,600 dilapidated public-housing units in West Dallas. Bartlett said the city would be better off without the crime-ridden housing, but Democrats said the residents had no place to go, and they won a floor vote on the issue.

At Home: Bartlett's 1982 victory in a five-person GOP field all but assured his prolonged tenure in this citadel of affluence and conservatism. But the road to nomination was difficult and confusing.

Bartlett originally had announced for the nearby 5th District, whose Democratic incumbent decided not to seek re-election after redistricting turned the 5th in a GOP direction. But a three-judge federal panel overruled the Legislature's redistricting plan for the Dallas area and redrew both the 3rd and 5th districts, throwing Bartlett's home into the 3rd. Republican Jim Collins, who had been elected seven times in the 3rd, was already running for the Senate, so Bartlett shifted.

Bartlett and Kay Bailey Hutchison, who had represented Houston in the Texas House but had moved to Dallas, became the front-runners for the nomination in the 3rd. Bartlett's district switch initially hurt him, because many of his political allies had committed themselves to Hutchison when they thought the two would be running in different districts, and some refused to break their pledges to her. But he overcame his problems with an outstanding organization and effective media advertising.

Hutchison finished first in the primary, but faced a runoff with Bartlett, who got endorsements from the candidates who lost out. The runoff campaign was a bitter one, with the conservative contestants arguing vigorously over the two issues on which they disagreed — the draft and abortion. Bartlett opposed a military draft in peacetime, preferring to strengthen the volunteer armed services with increased pay and benefits for lower-ranking personnel. Hutchison said she would favor resuming the draft unless studies showed improvement in the quality of volunteer soldiers.

On abortion, Hutchison opposed the proposed Human Life Amendment because it did not provide for abortion in cases of rape, incest or danger to the life of the mother. After waffling for several weeks, Bartlett finally endorsed the proposed constitutional amendment, cementing New Right support.

Helped by an outpouring of money and volunteer support from conservative and anti-abortion groups, Bartlett won the runoff comfortably. That November, Bartlett took 77 percent of the vote, and he has coasted through three subsequent re-elections.

Bartlett — called a "Rising Star of Texas" by *Texas Business* magazine in 1980 — had been an upset winner for an at-large Dallas City Council seat in 1977. After serving a term in city government, he launched his bid for Congress in 1981.

Committees

Banking, Finance and Urban Affairs (11th of 20 Republicans)
Consumer Affairs and Coinage; Financial Institutions Supervision, Regulation and Insurance; General Oversight and Investigations; Housing and Community Development

Education and Labor (6th of 13 Republicans)
Select Education (ranking); Elementary, Secondary and Vocational Education; Labor Standards

Elections

1988 General		
Steve Bartlett (R)	227,882	(82%)
Blake Cowden (D)	50,627	(18%)
1986 General		
Steve Bartlett (R)	143,381	(94%)

Previous Winning Percentages: 1984 (83%) **1982** (77%)

District Vote For President

	1988	1984	1980	1976
D	72,884 (25%)	52,426 (18%)	43,897 (20%)	43,033 (24%)
R	215,154 (75%)	235,644 (82%)	163,106 (75%)	135,688 (75%)
I			7,509 (4%)	

Campaign Finance

	Receipts	Receipts from PACs	Expend-itures
1988			
Bartlett (R)	$769,201	$230,678 (30%)	$1,000,894
Cowden (D)	$17,758	0	$17,757
1986			
Bartlett (R)	$810,359	$169,986 (21%)	$592,304

Key Votes

1987	
Raise speed limit to 65 mph	Y
Approve Gephardt "fair trade" amendment	N
Ban testing of larger nuclear weapons	N
Delay "re-flagging" of Kuwaiti tankers	N
Approve tax-raising deficit-reduction bill	N
1988	
Approve aid to Nicaraguan contras	Y
Enact civil rights restoration bill over Reagan veto	N
Kill 60-day plant-closing notification measure	Y
Pass omnibus trade bill over Reagan veto	N
Approve death penalty for drug-related murders	Y
Bar federal funds for abortions in cases of rape and incest	Y
Oppose seven-day waiting period for purchase of handguns	Y

Voting Studies

	Presidential Support		Party Unity		Conservative Coalition	
Year	S	O	S	O	S	O
1988	72	27	78	20	95	5
1987	78	20	79	16	98	0
1986	77	23	91	7	94	6
1985	89	11	93	4	91	9
1984	81	18	93	6	95	5
1983	87	12	88	9	85	13

Interest Group Ratings

Year	ADA	ACU	AFL-CIO	CCUS
1988	10	96	0	100
1987	4	100	0	100
1986	5	95	7	94
1985	5	95	0	100
1984	5	78	15	92
1983	0	91	0	100

4 Ralph M. Hall (D)

Of Rockwall — Elected 1980

Born: May 3, 1923, Rockwall County, Texas.
Education: Attended Texas Christian U., 1943; U. of Texas, 1946-47; Southern Methodist U., LL.B. 1951.
Military Career: Navy, 1942-45.
Occupation: Lawyer; businessman.
Family: Wife, Mary Ellen Murphy; three children.
Religion: Methodist.
Political Career: Rockwall County judge, 1950-62; Texas Senate, 1963-73; sought Democratic nomination for lieutenant governor, 1972.
Capitol Office: 236 Cannon Bldg. 20515; 225-6673.

In Washington: Hall's conservative voting record is not the kind the Democratic leadership generally appreciates. But on Energy and Commerce, he is a favorite of Chairman John D. Dingell, even though the two do not always see eye-to-eye. Hall's folksy sense of humor and encyclopedic supply of rural Texas stories can defuse tense confrontations, and his political acumen gives him considerable influence when he decides to weigh in on an issue.

That is not to say that Hall is one of the committee's more active members. He makes no pretense of being a workaholic, but when issues important to the energy industry come up, Hall makes his presence felt.

When the committee debated nuclear-accident liability legislation in 1987, Hall offered an amendment to allow utility lawyers to get paid before victims if damage claims exceed the compensation fund. Success required the panel to reverse an earlier decision, but working with industry lobbyists, Hall chalked up a 22-20 win.

Hall also played a role in the committee's 1988 approval of a product liability bill, a longtime industry priority. One of Hall's pro-business amendments — to prohibit states from classifying as "environmental" any injuries that might otherwise fall under product liability — was backed by chemical manufacturers and condemned by consumer activists. Another, more popular, amendment aimed to limit "frivolous" lawsuits by plaintiffs and delaying tactics by defendants. Both proposals passed, though the bill died at the end of the 100th Congress.

Hall's prime interest, however, is oil and gas, and he is known as a shrewd advocate for decontrol. After years of bitter stalemate, Energy and Commerce passed a decontrol bill by voice vote in early 1989. "I wouldn't be more surprised to see my old dog Red sharing his food with the cats," he said of the unanimity, "or the mockingbird not flying down to peck at the squirrels."

On the whole, Hall more often than not is at odds with his party. He tested the limits of his independence in 1985, when he voted "present" rather than support Thomas P. O'Neill Jr. for Speaker. He viewed with equanimity the possibility that the leadership might retaliate by removing him from Energy and Commerce. "I wouldn't blame them if they did," he said cheerfully. "I do what I have to do, and they do what they have to do."

At Home: An early starter in politics, Hall was elected judge in his home county while still in law school. After 12 years, he moved up to the state Senate and spent a decade there, rising to become president pro tem.

In 1972 Hall entered statewide politics, running for lieutenant governor on a conservative platform. But he finished fourth in the Democratic primary, retired from politics and concentrated on business.

When 4th District Democratic Rep. Ray Roberts announced his retirement in 1980, Hall decided to re-enter politics. His opponent in the primary was Jerdy Gary, the son of a former Oklahoma governor. Hall contrasted his Texas upbringing with Gary's Oklahoma roots, and won nomination with 57 percent.

Because of Ronald Reagan's popularity among the 4th's voters, Hall's November contest with Republican John H. Wright turned out to be closer than expected. Though Wright, a Tyler business manager, was well-known only in the eastern part of the district, Reagan's strong showing helped Wright pull 48 percent. But Republicans have not mounted a comparable challenge since. In 1988, he had his best presidential-year showing yet, winning two-thirds of the vote.

One way Hall heads off opposition is to make his feelings about national Democratic politics unmistakably clear; chosen as an uncommitted delegate to the Democratic convention in 1984, he opted not to go, commenting acerbically that he "didn't want to elbow some gay guy out of the way to get to a committee meeting."

Texas 4

Northeast — Tyler; Longview

The 4th is a descendant of the northeast Texas constituency that sent Sam Rayburn to Congress for 48 years; it covers much of the old, rural Rayburn territory.

The Speaker might still recognize some of the northern parts of the district, where slow-growing Fannin and Grayson counties remain oriented toward livestock, grain and peanuts. Sherman, the Grayson County seat, is an old cotton-processing town now turning out meat products, castings, metal pipe and electronics.

The counties in the center of the 4th, however, are caught up in the sprawl of metropolitan Dallas. Population doubled in both Collin and Rockwall counties during the 1970s and nearly doubled again in the first half of the '80s. Many people living here commute to Dallas; others work in the E-Systems facility in Greenville, which develops and modifies aircraft for military and civilian use.

At the eastern end of the 4th, where cotton was dominant a generation ago, are two cities serving as supply and distribution hubs for the East Texas oil fields — Tyler (Smith County) and Longview (Gregg County). Fueled by the expansion of the independent oil industry, those two counties grew rapidly in the 1970s. But oil's downturn took its toll in the '80s; unemployment in Gregg County reached 17 percent in 1986, and has dropped partly because many gave up looking for work and moved away.

Democrats have won the 4th narrowly in most recent statewide contests, but the GOP continues to make strides. Reagan's strong showing in Gregg and Smith counties helped him carry the 4th in 1980, and four years later, he swept nearly 70 percent of the vote in the 4th. George Bush could not match that in 1988, but he still carried the district with ease. In 1986, Gregg, Smith and Fannin counties all voted Republican for governor.

Population: 526,991. White 442,913 (84%), Black 73,672 (14%), Other 2,993 (1%). Spanish origin 14,035 (3%). 18 and over 377,899 (72%), 65 and over 74,813 (14%). Median age: 32.

Committees

Energy and Commerce (15th of 26 Democrats)
Energy and Power; Health and the Environment; Telecommunications and Finance

Science, Space and Technology (10th of 30 Democrats)
International Scientific Cooperation (chairman); Space Science and Applications

Elections

1988 General		
Ralph M. Hall (D)	139,379	(66%)
Randy Sutton (R)	67,337	(32%)
1986 General		
Ralph M. Hall (D)	97,540	(72%)
Thomas Blow (R)	38,578	(28%)

Previous Winning Percentages: **1984** (58%) **1982** (74%) **1980** (52%)

District Vote For President

	1988		1984		1980		1976	
D	82,095	(39%)	65,599	(31%)	73,547	(41%)	79,514	(52%)
R	129,164	(61%)	147,991	(69%)	103,771	(58%)	74,225	(48%)

Campaign Finance

	Receipts	Receipts from PACs		Expend-itures
1988				
Hall (D)	$350,284	$242,743	(69%)	$316,846
Sutton (R) †	$66,711	$1,386	(2%)	$65,068
1986				
Hall (D)	$276,235	$171,616	(62%)	$269,676
Blow (R)	$17,935	0		$20,000

† Totals based on incomplete data.

Key Votes

1987	
Raise speed limit to 65 mph	Y
Approve Gephardt "fair trade" amendment	Y
Ban testing of larger nuclear weapons	N
Delay "re-flagging" of Kuwaiti tankers	N
Approve tax-raising deficit-reduction bill	N
1988	
Approve aid to Nicaraguan contras	Y
Enact civil rights restoration bill over Reagan veto	N
Kill 60-day plant-closing notification measure	Y
Pass omnibus trade bill over Reagan veto	Y
Approve death penalty for drug-related murders	Y
Bar federal funds for abortions in cases of rape and incest	Y
Oppose seven-day waiting period for purchase of handguns	Y

Voting Studies

	Presidential Support		Party Unity		Conservative Coalition	
Year	**S**	**O**	**S**	**O**	**S**	**O**
1988	58	41	47	53	92	8
1987	52	45	44	52	88	9
1986	56	40	38	59	88	10
1985	58	39	45	46	84	5
1984	49	50	44	54	81	17
1983	48	49	38	57	83	11
1982	58	42	40	60	81	19
1981	61	34	40	54	80	15

Interest Group Ratings

Year	ADA	ACU	AFL-CIO	CCUS
1988	15	92	43	86
1987	24	70	44	73
1986	10	80	33	80
1985	15	70	31	67
1984	15	67	46	44
1983	35	62	56	61
1982	5	73	30	64
1981	5	79	27	74

5 John Bryant (D)

Of Dallas — Elected 1982

Born: Feb. 22, 1947, Lake Jackson, Texas.
Education: Southern Methodist U., B.A. 1969, J.D. 1972.
Occupation: Lawyer.
Family: Wife, Janet Elizabeth Watts; three children.
Religion: Methodist.
Political Career: Texas House, 1974-83.
Capitol Office: 208 Cannon Bldg. 20515; 225-2231.

In Washington: Underneath Bryant's low-key nature and hound dog eyes lies a strong-willed populist with driving political ambition. That, combined with a grasp of substantive issues, could have taken him a long way in the House — but he has decided to leave the institution to run for state attorney general.

Bryant was quick to impress some of the more influential members of the House. He won a place on the Energy and Commerce Committee in his first term, and in the 101st Congress, Bryant took a seat on Budget with help from then-Speaker Jim Wright.

Bryant's views seem to put him closer to the national Democratic Party than are many other Texans; only one other member of the state's delegation voted against President Reagan more often in 1988. But his positions are generally cast more as populism than liberalism. One of his most publicized crusades in the 100th Congress was on behalf of an amendment to the omnibus trade bill requiring new disclosures of foreign ownership of U.S. companies' assets.

Bryant's bill imposed reporting requirements in cases where a U.S. business is more than 5 percent foreign-owned; it mandated more extensive ownership disclosure where the foreign stake is 25 percent or more. The measure cleared Energy and Commerce 21-20, and became one of the more contentious issues involved in the debate on trade legislation.

The bill came under strong attack on the floor by opponents who feared it would reduce foreign investment needed to counteract the inflationary effects of the federal deficit. But Bryant said he had altered the plan to meet objections from the securities industry and others who would have to comply with it.

Bryant defeated an attempt to weaken his proposal 190-230, but he faced strong opposition in House-Senate conference. Under threat of a presidential veto, his provisions were dropped from the omnibus trade bill.

That did not end the fight, however, because Bryant pushed the bill separately on the House floor, winning 250-170. It never made it past the Senate, but early in the 101st Congress, Wright infuriated a number of Republicans by indicating he might bring it to the floor directly. Some expected that Wright planned to give Bryant a boost for a statewide campaign, particularly one against GOP Sen. Phil Gramm.

At times, Bryant makes his points with a zeal that critics think borders on demagoguery. When Reagan's Energy Secretary John S. Herrington came before the Energy and Power Subcommittee in 1987 after issuing a report on the oil industry, Bryant, frustrated by the lack of recommendations for aiding the industry, attacked him mercilessly. "I'd like to see an energy secretary that only had one arm," Bryant said, "so he couldn't keep saying 'on the other hand.' " The remark caused Herrington to bristle. "You're not only insulting," he told Bryant, "but you're disrespectful to the process."

Whatever Herrington's view, Bryant's comment probably played well in Texas. And he does more than just speak up for the oil industry. While he has quarreled with various elements of the business community over the years, he has worked with home-state business interests when he can. In the 99th Congress, Bryant led a fight to repeal provisions of the Fuel Use Act of 1978, which prohibited the use of oil and natural gas as boiler fuels for new utility and industrial plants. A repeal measure, strongly desired by the troubled oil industry, passed the House, but did not become law in the 99th. The act was repealed in 1987.

Bryant is generally well liked on the Hill, but he does not shy away from a fight, even with Energy and Commerce Chairman John D. Dingell. A former trial lawyer, Bryant went against Dingell in the 100th Congress when the committee debated legislation to establish a federal product liability standard. Businesses have long pushed for legislation to preempt state laws used by courts to determine the compensation that manufacturers must pay for damages resulting from use of their products. But business has been opposed by trial lawyers and consumer groups, who fear a change would infringe on victims' rights.

Texas 5

Downtown Dallas; Eastern and Southern Suburbs

Few American cities have as controversial a reputation as Dallas. Following the assassination of President Kennedy there in 1963, the city suffered from an image of frontier violence and extremism that was hard to shake. Just as that perception was fading, the television series "Dallas" came along to popularize the image of a metropolis ruled by an oligarchy of oil interests obsessed with money and power.

When Dallas was in the national spotlight during the 1984 Republican National Convention, local boosters were eager for the city to come across as a sophisticated, cosmopolitan place. It succeeded to some degree; visitors were impressed by such amenities as the stunning art museum and the fine restaurants. But many Northerners looking for characteristics that fit their definition of a city did not find them in Dallas. Reflecting on the antiseptic quality of the steel-and-concrete downtown and its rather vacant sidewalks, one joked that "anything that smacks of 'funky' here gets torn down and replaced with a high-rise."

Nonetheless, Dallas and the 5th have some diversity. Just northwest of downtown lies Oaklawn, a fashionable enclave of young professionals with a sizable gay community. East Dallas is a mix of lower-middle- and upper-middle-class residential neighborhoods and more transient young workers. The bulk of the district's black population — which stands at 20 percent — lives in the economically depressed southern part of the city. South Dallas has a sizable Hispanic community.

But while more than 60 percent of the district vote is cast within Dallas, the decisive political areas are blue-collar suburbs such as Mesquite, Sunnyvale, Seagoville and Balch Springs. These are not reliably Democratic areas: In 1980 and 1984, they voted for Ronald Reagan. But in 1988, their support enabled Michael S. Dukakis to win the district by 458 votes.

In suburbs farther south and west, working-class dissatisfaction with Democrats has been less evident, though the voters prefer candidates in the moderate-to-conservative mold. This area includes Hutchins, Wilmer and Lancaster, three towns transferred to the 5th in 1982.

Population: 526,633. White 377,294 (72%), Black 103,339 (20%), Other 6,862 (1%). Spanish origin 64,455 (12%). 18 and over 374,926 (71%), 65 and over 45,962 (9%). Median age: 28.

Bryant was in the latter group, and he offered one successful amendment in committee to make it clear that a manufacturer could be held liable for certain damages. He failed with an amendment that effectively would have allowed states to continue to determine liability for design flaws. But the liability bill, which cleared committee, never cleared the House.

Bryant also has worked on communications issues, and was particularly concerned in the last Congress with the quality of TV programming for children. At a convention of broadcasters in Texas, he bluntly spoke his mind about what he considered to be the sad state of children's TV; in Washington he worked with Democratic Rep. Terry L. Bruce on a bill to protect children from exploitation from commercial broadcasters. Bryant wanted a bill imposing limits on the amount of advertising allowed on children's TV and requiring one hour per day of educational programming for children. A compromise including advertising limits and the consideration of educational programming during license renewal passed the committee and moved through Congress, but was later vetoed.

Bryant is also a player on the Judiciary Committee, where he has been active on immigration issues that are of concern to his Texas constituents. In 1988, he was one of just four Texas House members voting against the wishes of the National Rifle Association in support of a seven-day waiting period for handgun purchases. Bryant had some cover: He is a hunter himself, and he had the support of the Dallas police chief.

At Home: Bryant has established himself as a potentially appealing statewide candidate by balancing the demands of an essentially Democratic district with those of the energy industry — a skill he will need in his 1990 race for state attorney general.

The tortuous course of Texas redistricting worked to Bryant's special advantage in 1982, first throwing the 5th District open and then virtually guaranteeing a Democratic victory.

The Legislature initially altered the Dallas-based 5th to tilt it Republican, and that persuaded incumbent Democrat Jim Mattox to forgo re-election and run for attorney general. A three-judge federal panel restored its Democratic boundaries early in 1982, but by that time, Mattox was committed to his statewide campaign and unwilling to retrace his steps. Bryant was left as the front-runner in a constituency considerably better for Democrats than the one that elected Mattox three times.

The real test for Bryant was the Democratic primary, in which his chief opponent was former Dallas Mayor Pro Tem Bill Blackburn. Although Blackburn had good funding and name recognition, his political ties were to downtown Dallas and its business community, and these were no asset in the blue-collar 5th.

Blackburn sought to link Bryant to liberalism, while Bryant argued that his opponent would be a Boll Weevil and a Reagan sympathizer in the House. The result was surprisingly one-sided, with Bryant taking 66 percent. He had no trouble in the general election, and Republicans did not field a candidate in 1984.

The GOP did show some interest in tackling Bryant in 1986, however. Early on, it appeared the party might attract a top-flight challenger. But when state Sen. Ray Keller, a popular politician well-known in parts of the 5th, decided against making the race, Republican optimism dipped noticeably.

Local GOP leaders ended up fielding an energetic, if inexperienced, candidate. Texas oil and gas lobbyist Tom Carter never had sought public office before, although he had been active in area Republican affairs. He tried to brand Bryant a menace to entrepreneurs. "We need someone who will support the free enterprise system, and vote less taxes on business, not more," Carter argued. The Republican cited the low rating Bryant received from the National Federation of Independent Business to buttress his claim.

But Bryant had established allies in the Dallas business community, including some normally Republican captains of the energy industry; others were wary of working too hard against an influential junior member of the Energy and Commerce Committee. Although Carter managed a strong showing in suburban boom communities such as Garland and Mesquite — part of the district's natural GOP base — he could not excite the kind of enthusiasm necessary to challenge Bryant in the 5th's more politically competitive territory. The incumbent clinched a third term with almost 60 percent. Two years later, he was able to push his victory share back above 60 percent against Dallas attorney Lon Williams.

In the Texas House, Bryant made a name for himself in a battle over taxation of farm land, leading the faction opposing tax advantages for speculators and farming corporations. He was also largely responsible for molding the infant House Study Group into a research body for moderates and liberals — much like the Democratic Study Group of the U.S. House.

By the end of his second term in the Legislature, Bryant had become the leader of a group of liberal Democrats who found themselves frequently at odds with House Speaker Billy Clayton. In 1980, Bryant unsuccessfully challenged Clayton for the Speaker's chair.

Committees

Budget (21st of 21 Democrats)
Task Forces: Defense, Foreign Policy and Space; Urgent Fiscal Issues

Energy and Commerce (20th of 26 Democrats)
Energy and Power; Oversight and Investigations; Telecommunications and Finance

Judiciary (19th of 21 Democrats)
Courts, Intellectual Property and the Administration of Justice; Criminal Justice; Immigration, Refugees and International Law

Elections

1988 General		
John Bryant (D)	95,376	(61%)
Lon Williams (R)	59,877	(38%)
1986 General		
John Bryant (D)	57,410	(59%)
Tom Carter (R)	39,945	(41%)

Previous Winning Percentages: **1984** (100%) **1982** (65%)

District Vote For President

	1988		1984		1980		1976	
D	80,713	(50%)	68,926	(41%)	70,128	(45%)	57,813	(48%)
R	80,255	(50%)	100,261	(59%)	80,636	(51%)	60,885	(51%)
I					4,190	(3%)		

Campaign Finance

	Receipts	Receipts from PACs		Expend-itures
1988				
Bryant (D)	$889,511	$393,057	(44%)	$646,218
Williams (R)	$180,629	$24,676	(14%)	$179,201
1986				
Bryant (D)	$1,016,970	$365,500	(36%)	$994,285
Carter (R)	$353,100	$72,070	(20%)	$349,937

Key Votes

1987	
Raise speed limit to 65 mph	Y
Approve Gephardt "fair trade" amendment	Y
Ban testing of larger nuclear weapons	Y
Delay "re-flagging" of Kuwaiti tankers	Y
Approve tax-raising deficit-reduction bill	Y
1988	
Approve aid to Nicaraguan contras	N
Enact civil rights restoration bill over Reagan veto	Y
Kill 60-day plant-closing notification measure	N
Pass omnibus trade bill over Reagan veto	Y
Approve death penalty for drug-related murders	Y
Bar federal funds for abortions in cases of rape and incest	N
Oppose seven-day waiting period for purchase of handguns	N

Voting Studies

	Presidential Support		Party Unity		Conservative Coalition	
Year	**S**	**O**	**S**	**O**	**S**	**O**
1988	19	74	87	7	42	55
1987	25	71	88	5	49	44
1986	18	80	84	12	54	46
1985	23	78	89	8	31	67
1984	22	62	74	6	17	64
1983	24	76	84	10	36	60

Interest Group Ratings

Year	ADA	ACU	AFL-CIO	CCUS
1988	85	9	100	27
1987	80	4	100	14
1986	65	23	93	44
1985	55	10	88	41
1984	75	0	92	38
1983	80	13	94	20

6 Joe L. Barton (R)

Of Ennis — Elected 1984

Born: Sept. 15, 1949, Waco, Texas.
Education: Texas A&M U., B.S. 1972; Purdue U., M.S. 1973.
Occupation: Engineering consultant.
Family: Wife, Janet Sue Winslow; three children.
Religion: Methodist.
Political Career: No previous office.
Capitol Office: 1225 Longworth Bldg. 20515; 225-2002.

In Washington: Barton is in a good position to look out for Texas' energy interests on the Energy and Commerce Committee, but in his first term on that panel he surprised some with his dogged and methodical work on consumer-protection legislation.

More than many conservatives, Barton has shown an interest in a strong Consumer Product Safety Commission, and in the 100th Congress he pushed a safety issue of his own. An engineer, Barton became concerned about the design of three-wheel all-terrain vehicles (ATVs) after an accident killed an 11-year-old in his district; he got involved in an effort to take ATVs out of circulation. Hounded by controversy about the safety of their product, ATV manufacturers had agreed to halt new sales, but Barton advocated a bill requiring those manufacturers to pay a refund to owners of the estimated 1.5 million ATVs still in use.

In committee, Barton managed to overcome opposition from ATV dealers and the four Japanese ATV manufacturers, who argued that the machines were not inherently unsafe, just misused. But Barton could not get his measure to the House floor.

"The bottom line is that manufacturers are opposed to my [plan] because . . . they've made a lot of money and they want to keep it," said Barton, who had been accused of "Japan-bashing" in going after the manufacturers.

In addition to his consumer-related efforts, Barton also does the work he would be expected to do on the committee — watching out for the energy industry. When pursuing an issue in this area, Barton has shown an ability to work systematically and sound out his colleagues. That approach helped him win passage of legislation repealing a portion of the Natural Gas Policy Act of 1978, which mandated 15-year contracts for gas sales on federal leases on the outer continental shelf. Barton said the gas was not being sold because buyers wanted more flexibility.

Outside his committee work, Barton is known as a more combative Republican partisan. He had barely taken office in 1985 when he became enraged by the refusal of Democratic leaders to seat the Republican claimant in a disputed Indiana election. His frustration drove him to some oddly belligerent tactics — such as organizing a demonstration outside a Fort Worth committee room in which then-Majority Leader Jim Wright was about to speak. Even some of Barton's GOP colleagues thought that approach was a little extreme. And in the 100th Congress, Barton nominated aggressive conservative GOP Rep. William E. Dannemeyer for his long-shot bid to become Republican Conference chairman. In a three-way race, Dannemeyer ran a poor third.

Like most members, Barton has worked to steer federal funds to his district. In part, that meant helping make the case for building the multibillion-dollar superconducting supercollider — a giant atom-smasher — in his state and district. Texas was chosen as the "preferred site" for the SSC in 1988.

At Home: Barton's 1984 victory was a sweet surprise for the Texas GOP, which desperately wanted to make permanent the 6th District's temporary flirtation with Republicanism.

Until 1983, when Democratic Rep. Phil Gramm resigned the seat, switched parties and was re-elected as a Republican, the GOP had never won here. Barton, who held the seat upon Gramm's move to the Senate, represents an important wedge in Texas Republicans' drive for statewide respectability.

An engineering consultant for Atlantic Richfield Co., Barton had never run for office before, and entered the race as the clear underdog. He barely survived a bruising four-way GOP primary.

After primary balloting failed to produce a majority for any candidate, a runoff was held between Barton and Max Hoyt, a former energy-company lobbyist. Although the results of the runoff initially gave Hoyt an 18-vote victory, a recount reversed the outcome, and Barton was certified the winner by just 10 votes. The three losing candidates refused to support Barton in the general election.

Behind the bitterness were accusations

Texas 6

Suburban Dallas-Fort Worth and Houston; Bryan

The 6th District is a long, narrow column of counties that begins near Dallas-Fort Worth and runs southeast to the suburbs of Houston, more than 200 miles away.

In the days of Olin E. "Tiger" Teague, who represented the area from 1946 to 1978, politics in the 6th was dominated by rural conservative Democrats. But changes in the district's demographics and 1983 redistricting helped make it more hospitable for the GOP.

Republicanism is growing fastest in the areas closest to Dallas-Fort Worth and Houston, as GOP-minded white-collar workers flood the suburbs located here.

The 6th contains the two counties that grew faster than any others in Texas during the 1970s. In the northwest corner, spillover from Fort Worth nearly tripled the population of Hood County. Far to the south, Montgomery County grew 160 percent, with affluent professionals commuting to jobs in Houston. In both counties, growth has leveled off during the 1980s.

Hood County and two others in the Dallas-Fort Worth sphere — Johnson and Ellis — have helped boost GOP presidential vote totals in the 1980s, turning away from their 1976 preference for Jimmy Carter. All three counties voted for George Bush in 1988. Montgomery County gave Democrat-turned-Republican Rep. Phil Gramm 69 percent of the vote in the 1983 special election held as a mandate on his party switch. And in 1988, Montgomery voted narrowly for GOP Rep. Beau Boulter in his Senate race against Lloyd Bentsen.

Republican strength in the 6th is further enhanced by Brazos County, the urban exception in the district's mostly rural middle region. Located in Brazos are Bryan and College Station, home of Texas A&M University, which has almost 40,000 students. Lavishly endowed Texas A&M has spent heavily in recent years to recruit academic stars from the Ivy League and other prestigious universities. So far, though, there has been little evidence of an Eastern liberal tilt to the Brazos County vote. In 1984, Brazos voted overwhelmingly for Reagan and Gramm, a former Texas A&M faculty member, and Bush won the county in 1988.

Even in the 6th's traditionally Democratic rural counties, Republican candidates are now running well in contests for state and national office.

Population: 526,765. White 450,732 (86%), Black 57,255 (11%), Other 3,311 (1%). Spanish origin 30,591 (6%). 18 and over 379,330 (72%), 65 and over 65,759 (12%). Median age: 29.

that Barton had misrepresented his experience as a White House fellow, and that he had suggested he had Gramm's support, when in fact Gramm was neutral in the primary competition.

The major controversy involved Barton campaign literature that referred to him as "the proven cost-cutter," claiming he was "a deputy to the secretary of energy" during his one-year fellowship (1981-82), and that he "served on the Grace commission" cost-cutting task force. Critics said he was merely assigned to the Energy Department to help draft suggestions to the Grace commission. Barton dismissed the complaints as semantic and political, but changed the wording.

In the general election, Barton faced Dan Kubiak, a former state representative and rancher with a folksy Texas twang and easygoing style. Kubiak's political reputation had suffered somewhat from two recent defeats, one to Gramm in the 1983 special election, and one in a contest for state land commissioner. But he was a familiar figure after 12 years in the state House, where he served as chairman of the Education Committee.

Barton managed to counter those assets by sticking close to coattails provided by Reagan and Gramm, and by claiming national experience as a White House fellow. He called himself a "committed conservative," while portraying Kubiak as a "convenient conservative." Barton accused Kubiak of supporting Walter F. Mondale's proposals to raise taxes, and hammered away at his sizable contributions from the AFL-CIO (Texas has a "right to work" law).

Barton also made shrewd use of his ties to his alma mater, Texas A&M University in College Station, where he had graduated in engineering. Barton waged an aggressive voter-registration drive on the conservative-leaning campus, and his local radio ads exhorted students to vote for "the Aggie candidate." The effort added an estimated 10,000 new Republican voters to the rolls. That base of support, coupled with the Reagan-Gramm electoral tide and the solid GOP vote in the suburbs of Houston and Fort Worth, were too much for Kubiak to overcome.

Area Democrats were not prepared to concede the 6th, however; they mounted an aggressive challenge to Barton in 1986 behind Fort

Worth attorney Preston M. "Pete" Geren.

Geren had all the assets a Democratic challenger in Texas could ask for: an ample personal fortune, the enthusiastic support of state and national party leaders and close ties to popular Democratic Sen. Lloyd Bentsen. He argued that the two years he spent as director of Bentsen's Texas offices gave him an appreciation of constituent service and an understanding of conservative Democratic philosophy. Geren also claimed Barton had taken conservatism to extremes, placing ideology over the needs of his constituency.

Barton had plenty of weapons to use in his defense. He pointed to meetings he convened to coach local entrepreneurs on how to secure federal contracts, and claimed credit for helping to free offshore oil and gas royalties that had been entangled in state and federal bureaucracy.

Geren performed admirably for a first-time candidate, assembling an organization that helped him carry eight of the 14 counties wholly or partially contained within the 6th's boundaries. But while Geren managed to persuade some rural Democrats to honor their historic partisan ties, he did not build a cushion large enough to compensate for Barton's support in the GOP-minded urban and suburban neighborhoods of Tarrant and Montgomery counties. Barton finished with a solid win.

Three Democrats filed to challenge Barton in 1988, leading to a runoff election that was won narrowly by N. P. "Pat" Kendrick, a 67-year-old business consultant from Joshua. Kendrick was not able to mount a daunting challenge to the incumbent, who collected 68 percent of the vote.

Committee

Energy and Commerce (15th of 17 Republicans)
Commerce, Consumer Protection and Competitiveness; Energy and Power

Elections

1988 General		
Joe L. Barton (R)	164,692	(68%)
N. P. "Pat" Kendrick (D)	78,786	(32%)
1986 General		
Joe L. Barton (R)	86,190	(56%)
Pete Geren (D)	68,270	(44%)

Previous Winning Percentage: **1984** (57%)

District Vote For President

	1988	1984	1980	1976
D	88,308 (38%)	69,508 (30%)	72,477 (42%)	78,207 (52%)
R	141,337 (62%)	158,310 (69%)	95,171 (55%)	70,113 (47%)
I			3,566 (2%)	

Campaign Finance

	Receipts	Receipts from PACs	Expenditures
1988			
Barton (R)	$750,559	$288,083 (38%)	$654,260
Kendrick (D) †	$29,851	0	$17,414
1986			
Barton (R)	$1,024,246	$344,210 (34%)	$1,034,515
Geren (D)	$897,174	$76,948 (9%)	$895,746

† Totals based on incomplete data.

Key Votes

1987	
Raise speed limit to 65 mph	Y
Approve Gephardt "fair trade" amendment	N
Ban testing of larger nuclear weapons	N
Delay "re-flagging" of Kuwaiti tankers	N
Approve tax-raising deficit-reduction bill	N
1988	
Approve aid to Nicaraguan contras	Y
Enact civil rights restoration bill over Reagan veto	N
Kill 60-day plant-closing notification measure	Y
Pass omnibus trade bill over Reagan veto	N
Approve death penalty for drug-related murders	Y
Bar federal funds for abortions in cases of rape and incest	Y
Oppose seven-day waiting period for purchase of handguns	Y

Voting Studies

	Presidential Support		Party Unity		Conservative Coalition	
Year	**S**	**O**	**S**	**O**	**S**	**O**
1988	70	18	89	4	82	0
1987	77	21	90	5	88	7
1986	76	22	93	4	92	4
1985	85	15	94	3	91	5

Interest Group Ratings

Year	ADA	ACU	AFL-CIO	CCUS
1988	5	96	0	100
1987	4	100	6	93
1986	0	95	7	94
1985	5	100	0	95

7 Bill Archer (R)

Of Houston — Elected 1970

Born: March 22, 1928, Houston, Texas.

Education: Attended Rice U., 1945-46; U. of Texas, B.B.A. 1949, LL.B. 1951.

Military Career: Air Force, 1951-53.

Occupation: Lawyer; feed company executive.

Family: Wife, Sharon Sawyer; five children, two stepchildren.

Religion: Roman Catholic.

Political Career: Hunters Creek Village Council, 1955-62; Texas House, 1967-71.

Capitol Office: 1135 Longworth Bldg. 20515; 225-2571.

In Washington: When he vaulted prematurely to the top GOP slot on the Ways and Means Committee in mid-1988, Archer was regarded as a predictable voice for the oil industry. But in his first months in that key position, he surprised observers with his flexibility and potential for effective leadership in one of the trickiest Republican posts on the Hill.

For years Archer had acted as a doctrinaire conservative on most tax issues, but when his senior colleague John J. Duncan of Tennessee announced his retirement and then died in June 1988, Archer seemed to shift. He traded his independence for consultation with senior colleagues, checked staff shifts with others, and set to work on the committee's major product, a "technical corrections" tax bill. While designed chiefly to fix glitches in the 1986 tax overhaul — which Archer had led the charge against — the bill also extended important tax credits and included plums for individual companies.

Ways and Means Chairman Dan Rostenkowski of Illinois had let it be known that grandstanding opponents would be cut out of the locker-room action on issues important to their districts, and Archer did not bother to see if Rostenkowski would carry through with that threat. The Republican voted for the bill on the floor and in conference, while working to hone some features he deplored. When the size of the bill was an issue, he joined with Rostenkowski to pare the House bill from $7.5 billion to $4.5 billion when the Senate insisted it would go no higher than $2.5 billion; the total ended up close to $4 billion.

Archer, however, has hardly become a Rostenkowski crony. Early in the 101st Congress he led a crusade to delay implementation of one of the chairman's proudest projects of the previous year, the program to protect the elderly against catastrophic health costs. Archer and his allies were responding to an outcry from the senior citizens who were having to pay for the program.

The man who took over George Bush's House seat will be in the position of chief lip-reader on the president's tax pledges. While Archer can be counted on to bark at any revenue increase Bush wants to denounce as a tax, he is in a different position with regard to another Bush priority: lowering the tax rate on capital gains to 15 percent. For years, Archer has been the chief advocate of a different approach to capital gains.

In Ways and Means action on the 1978 tax cut, Archer offered an amendment to require indexing of capital gains taxes — adjusting them each year for inflation so that the effective rate would go up only with real income growth. Archer got this idea through the committee, with some liberal Democratic support, and it passed the House, 249-167. The provision was dropped in conference with the Senate, but the concept of indexing all income tax rates finally became law in 1981 as part of that year's Reagan tax cut.

Indexing of capital gains would still offer benefits for investors who had held assets for long periods, and there is Democratic support for Archer's idea. It holds little benefit for venture capitalists, however, since they are more interested in quick gains. And fears that changing the taxation of capital gains would give tax breaks to the rich and increase the federal deficit make it an uphill battle.

In past years, the focus of Archer's work has been taxation of the oil industry, the subject of endless argument at Ways and Means. His expertise on the industry is unquestioned, as is his willingness to explain its workings to colleagues. But for most of the 1980s, when the committee sat down to write an oil tax bill, Archer often was confronted by a Democratic majority that cared less about the intricacies of tertiary recovery than about satisfying current political concerns.

When the so-called windfall-profits tax returned to the House floor after conference in 1980, it was Archer who offered the basic Re-

Texas 7

Western Houston and Suburbs

As Houston has grown into America's fourth-largest city and the commercial center of the Southwest, the 7th has grown dense with the homes of the prosperous corporate community. More than 400,000 people moved into the district during the 1970s, giving the 7th an 86 percent growth rate — higher than any other district in the state.

The 1980s have been a different story, however, as a downturn in the oil economy dried up jobs and left many new office buildings and apartment complexes empty.

The 7th runs west from the northwest part of Houston to the Harris County line. It has the highest property values in Texas. In River Oaks, where much of the oil elite has lived for years, imitation Spanish villas stand proudly next to imitation Tudor mansions and imitation French chateaux.

Although most of Houston's myriad corporate headquarters lie beyond the 7th's boundaries to the east, the district has its own mini-downtowns at the numerous freeway interchanges. Office buildings line the east-west Katy Freeway, and small oil-related companies are scattered throughout the district.

Once-rural areas surrounding Houston have seen rapid development in recent years, as the city's environs have spread farther and farther from its heart. Apartment complexes are burgeoning in residential communities such as Spring Branch. F/M Road 1960, part of the Texas roads system originally set up as a farm-to-market route, is a multi-lane artery today.

Along with the 3rd District in Dallas, the 7th gives Republicans their highest margins in the state. In 1976, Gerald R. Ford swept the presidential vote in the district by nearly 3-to-1. Ronald Reagan improved on that in 1980, scoring his best Texas showing with 78 percent of the vote. He did even better in 1984, and George Bush's best showing in Texas in 1988 also came in the 7th, his old House district.

Population: 527,083. White 482,555 (92%), Black 16,615 (3%), Other 15,149 (3%). Spanish origin 37,320 (7%). 18 and over 375,483 (71%), 65 and over 24,749 (5%). Median age: 29.

publican proposal — to exempt independents producing fewer than 1,000 barrels per day. It drew nearly all Republicans and most Southern Democrats, failing on a close 207-185 vote.

The real sop for the oil industry, however, had been worked out earlier when the bill was softened before clearing the House the first time. While Archer had supported that effort, he was not its architect. In the 100th Congress, with oil prices bottoming out, the windfall-profits tax was repealed as part of the omnibus trade bill.

Archer's other area of expertise is Social Security. He has complained that Social Security benefits are too easily embroiled in partisan politics. In the 99th Congress he supported legislation to make the Social Security Administration a separate agency outside the Department of Health and Human Services. He also advocated restricting the administration's ability to borrow money from the Social Security trust funds to see the government through debt crises.

Earlier, as a member of President Reagan's National Commission on Social Security Reform, Archer consistently sounded the argument that the Social Security system should be made solvent by reducing the growth of benefits, not by increasing the payroll tax rate for the younger people paying in.

In 1983, when the bipartisan group issued its report recommending a combination of modest benefit reductions and significant tax increases, Archer cast one of the dissenting votes in a 12-3 decision. "Any package that closes the gap with only $40 billion of restraint in cash outflow and $125 billion in new taxes," he said, "is not in the best interests of the country in the long term." The package later was amended in Archer's direction on the House floor, with the retirement age increased gradually to 67 to save money. Archer did not consider that to be enough of an improvement, however, and he voted against the legislation.

In the major tax action of recent years, the 1986 overhaul of the tax code, Archer led the battle against it in the House. But he found himself fighting not only against the Democratic House majority, but also against the president and, in the end, his own GOP House leaders.

Archer argued strenuously that the Ways and Means tax bill, and later the compromise worked out in conference, would hurt business and the economy. But his objections were not echoed by those who supported the conference report. That left Archer, second in seniority, to lead the GOP fight against the bill on the floor.

"What's fair about a tax bill that will allow deductions for interest on a second home but not on a first car?" Archer asked during debate on the conference report. But he talked more about economics than about fairness, and dismissed projections by some economists that tax revision, though economically disruptive in the short run, would have a positive impact in the long run. "There will be no long term under this bill," Archer said. "It is not going to last 10 years. So the short term is what we must consider."

Archer managed to win 160 votes for a motion to kill the tax bill by sending it back to conference. But 268 members voted against him, including the Republican leader, Illinois Rep. Robert H. Michel. Archer then voted against the conference report itself, but fewer than half of those in his own party voted on his side.

In 1982 and 1983 Archer argued to the right of President Reagan on budget and tax issues, saying that Reagan had given in too easily to defenders of federal domestic spending. But his proposals to freeze federal spending and block revenue increases fell short on the floor.

At Home: Unlike his predecessor in this House district, New England-born George Bush, Archer is a native Houstonian. Born and raised in the city, he graduated from Rice University and the University of Texas before launching his political career in 1955 as a member of the Hunters Creek Village Council.

Archer made his mark as a conservative Democrat, winning a seat in the Texas Legislature in 1966. But in 1968 he switched parties and won re-election as a Republican. Since the territory of his state legislative district closely coincided with the 7th District, Archer was the early favorite for the House seat two years later when Bush ran for the U.S. Senate.

He easily won the GOP primary, and went on to defeat a young law partner of John B. Connally in November. He has had no electoral problems since then.

Committees

Ways and Means (Ranking)

Joint Taxation

Elections

1988 General

Bill Archer (R)	185,203	(79%)
Dianne Richards (D)	48,824	(21%)

1986 General

Bill Archer (R)	129,673	(87%)
Harry Kniffen (D)	17,635	(12%)

Previous Winning Percentages: **1984** (87%) **1982** (85%) **1980** (82%) **1978** (85%) **1976** (100%) **1974** (79%) **1972** (82%) **1970** (65%)

District Vote For President

	1988	1984	1980	1976
D	53,380 (25%)	40,307 (18%)	34,478 (18%)	51,398 (28%)
R	163,767 (75%)	187,935 (82%)	147,638 (78%)	131,831 (71%)
I			5,193 (3%)	

Campaign Finance

	Receipts	Receipts from PACs	Expend-itures
1988			
Archer (R)	$269,695	0	$180,255
Richards (D)	$10,650	$1,250 (12%)	$11,090
1986			
Archer (R)	$281,736	0	$152,779

Key Votes

1987

Raise speed limit to 65 mph	Y
Approve Gephardt "fair trade" amendment	N
Ban testing of larger nuclear weapons	N
Delay "re-flagging" of Kuwaiti tankers	N
Approve tax-raising deficit-reduction bill	N

1988

Approve aid to Nicaraguan contras	Y
Enact civil rights restoration bill over Reagan veto	N
Kill 60-day plant-closing notification measure	Y
Pass omnibus trade bill over Reagan veto	N
Approve death penalty for drug-related murders	Y
Bar federal funds for abortions in cases of rape and incest	Y
Oppose seven-day waiting period for purchase of handguns	Y

Voting Studies

	Presidential Support		Party Unity		Conservative Coalition	
Year	S	O	S	O	S	O
1988	79	18	80	19	92	3
1987	82	18	84	13	91	7
1986	82	17	81	15	98	2
1985	88	11	80	15	87	7
1984	70	30	94	6	88	12
1983	77	22	92 †	5 †	96	4
1982	82	18	90	8	89	10
1981	67	30	93	5	92	7

† Not eligible for all recorded votes.

Interest Group Ratings

Year	ADA	ACU	AFL-CIO	CCUS
1988	0	100	0	100
1987	0	95	0	100
1986	0	95	0	94
1985	5	100	0	100
1984	0	100	15	94
1983	5	100	0	85
1982	0	100	0	86
1981	5	100	0	89

8 Jack Fields (R)

Of Humble — Elected 1980

Born: Feb. 3, 1952, Humble, Texas.
Education: Baylor U., B.A. 1974, J.D. 1977.
Occupation: Lawyer; cemetery executive.
Family: Wife, Lynn Hughes.
Religion: Baptist.
Political Career: No previous office.
Capitol Office: 108 Cannon Bldg. 20515; 225-4901.

In Washington: Elected in 1980 at age 28, with no political experience but much conservative zeal, Fields was one of the "Reagan robots" in his early House years. But of late, he has been involved in some substantive legislative issues on the Energy and Commerce Committee, where he speaks up for Texas interests, particularly Houston's oil and gas industry.

During the 100th Congress, Fields was visible in working the Texas angle on a pair of difficult environment-related issues: the Clean Air Act extension and the permanent location of a national nuclear-waste dump site.

Houston is known as one of the nation's smoggiest cities, and local officials are sensitive about this. But they are also sensitive to business' needs: Industrial operations run by the oil industry are a cornerstone of the local economy. The oil industry also is ever wary of pollution controls that might restrict auto driving.

City and county officials joined with industry executives in Houston to draft a clean-air proposal calling for increased pollution monitoring, but providing local governments with flexibility to address pollution problems. Fields submitted a version of this proposal as an amendment to the clean-air bill favored by Health and the Environment Subcommittee Chairman Henry A. Waxman of California; he wanted a stronger federal role in pollution control.

The Texas proposal attracted some attention in mid-1988, but it was subsumed by the negotiations between Waxman and his longtime pro-industry nemesis, full committee Chairman John D. Dingell of Michigan. Dingell and Waxman once again failed to reconcile their differences, and the bill remained stalled.

On the matter of siting a nuclear-waste dump, Fields and his four Lone Star colleagues on Energy and Commerce met with success, keeping the dump out of Texas. Federal energy officials had picked three states — Nevada, Washington and Texas — as possible repository sites. But after the Senate passed a bill making the designation of Nevada virtually inevitable, Fields and the other committee Texans went to work in the House. Their proposal barred the designation of a dump site below an aquifer, a criterion that applied to Texas and Washington, but not Nevada. The Texans' amendment prevailed as part of the legislation that designated Nevada for the repository.

At Home: A fifth-generation Houstonian, Fields started out as a campus politician, winning two terms as president of the Baylor student body, something no one had done before. After law school, he joined the family cemetery business as a vice president.

He was a novice at public office when he announced his 1980 candidacy against Democratic Rep. Bob Eckhardt. But Fields showed unusual campaign skill for a newcomer; he drew the interest of New Right activists, national Republicans and corporate contributors, all of whom were eager to defeat Eckhardt, the most liberal member of the Texas delegation and a staunch anti-corporate populist. Potentially strong GOP primary opponents were scared off by Fields' prodigious organizing.

Eckhardt had been losing ground in his changing constituency; in 1978 and 1980, he was challenged in the primary by conservative Democrats who won more than 40 percent. Labor and consumer groups worked hard for him in 1980, but many blue-collar workers abandoned their Democratic voting habits to support Fields and Ronald Reagan. The challenger unseated Eckhardt by under 5,000 votes.

Redistricting strengthened Fields' position for 1982, and he did not draw top-quality Democratic opposition. But he won less than 60 percent, and Democrats waged a more vigorous campaign two years later. Their 1984 nominee, former congressional aide Don Buford, questioned Fields' integrity. Buford argued that a Fields mailing to the district announcing town hall meetings had violated rules governing use of the congressional frank.

But early in October, the House ethics committee cleared Fields of any abuse of the frank. Fields cast Buford as a "suitcase politician" — referring to the Democrat's relatively recent arrival in the district. Bolstered by the district's big Reagan vote, he took 65 percent, and has coasted since.

Texas 8

Houston Suburbs; Eastern Harris County

The 8th is part of metropolitan Houston's suburban sprawl, populated by the thousands of middle-income and upper-middle-income families that have moved into the outer reaches of Harris County in recent years.

Growth here has bolstered the fortunes of the GOP. Republicans thrive in affluent communities such as Humble, Fields' home base, and Kingwood, located toward the district's northeastern end. Outside of these communities, however, support for Republican candidates is not always certain. Fields runs stronger in the 8th than most Republicans at any level.

But the 8th is not as monolithically white-collar and Republican as the 7th, its neighbor to the west. Although the 8th lost many of its petrochemical plants in the last redistricting, a large number of the plants' blue-collar employees maintain their homes in an area stretching west along the Houston Ship Channel from Baytown to the 610 Loop.

Blue-collar Baytown is the site of a huge Exxon refinery as well as other chemical- and petroleum-related businesses.

The 8th also has a significant population in minority areas on Houston's perimeter; 30 percent of the people in the 8th are either black or Hispanic. Lakewood, in the southwestern part of the district, has a sizable minority population, as do nearby North Forest and Aldine.

Population: 527,531. White 396,727 (75%), Black 88,299 (17%), Other 7,310 (1%). Spanish origin 66,032 (13%). 18 and over 347,798 (66%), 65 and over 24,703 (5%). Median age: 26.

Committees

Energy and Commerce (10th of 17 Republicans)
Energy and Power; Health and the Environment; Telecommunications and Finance

Merchant Marine and Fisheries (5th of 17 Republicans)
Panama Canal/Outer Continental Shelf (ranking); Merchant Marine

Elections

1988 General		
Jack Fields (R)	90,503	(100%)
1986 General		
Jack Fields (R)	66,280	(68%)
Blaine Mann (D)	30,617	(32%)

Previous Winning Percentages: **1984** (65%) **1982** (57%) **1980** (52%)

District Vote For President

	1988	1984	1980	1976
D	67,322 (47%)	66,720 (40%)	64,072 (41%)	70,107 (59%)
R	74,907 (53%)	98,706 (60%)	89,301 (57%)	47,856 (40%)
I			3,445 (2%)	

Campaign Finance

	Receipts	Receipts from PACs	Expend-itures
1988			
Fields (R)	$510,950	$271,825 (53%)	$483,544
1986			
Fields (R)	$590,309	$265,683 (45%)	$574,657
Mann (D)	$19,691	0	$19,666

Key Votes

1987	
Raise speed limit to 65 mph	Y
Approve Gephardt "fair trade" amendment	N
Ban testing of larger nuclear weapons	N
Delay "re-flagging" of Kuwaiti tankers	N
Approve tax-raising deficit-reduction bill	N
1988	
Approve aid to Nicaraguan contras	Y
Enact civil rights restoration bill over Reagan veto	N
Kill 60-day plant-closing notification measure	Y
Pass omnibus trade bill over Reagan veto	N
Approve death penalty for drug-related murders	Y
Bar federal funds for abortions in cases of rape and incest	Y
Oppose seven-day waiting period for purchase of handguns	Y

Voting Studies

	Presidential Support		Party Unity		Conservative Coalition	
Year	S	O	S	O	S	O
1988	70	23	92	1	84	3
1987	73	25	94	2	95	5
1986	79	20	95	4	98	2
1985	74	21	89	4	91	9
1984	58	37	84	12	80	15
1983	83	17	91	6	92	4
1982	84	14	89	9	92	8
1981	76	18	88	8	96	1

Interest Group Ratings

Year	ADA	ACU	AFL-CIO	CCUS
1988	0	100	0	100
1987	4	86	13	93
1986	5	95	0	94
1985	10	90	6	91
1984	5	88	23	81
1983	5	96	6	80
1982	5	100	0	86
1981	0	100	7	95

9 Jack Brooks (D)

Of Beaumont — Elected 1952

Born: Dec. 18, 1922, Crowley, La.
Education: Attended Lamar College, 1939-41; U. of Texas, B.J. 1943, J.D. 1949.
Military Career: Marine Corps, 1942-45; Marine Corps Reserve, 1945-72.
Occupation: Lawyer.
Family: Wife, Charlotte Collins; three children.
Religion: Methodist.
Political Career: Texas House, 1947-51.
Capitol Office: 2449 Rayburn Bldg. 20515; 225-6565.

In Washington: Whatever pacifying spirit Speaker Jim Wright might have unleashed by his resignation, and by his valedictory appeal to end partisan "cannibalism," was quickly dispelled on that historic May day in 1989. Next up to the House microphone was Brooks, Wright's biggest supporter, railing about "an evil wind blowing in the halls of Congress ... replacing comity and compassion with hatred and malice."

This from the man who is perhaps Congress' most partisan Democrat, a junkyard dog of a fighter who simply by his crusty presence can rile Republicans, and even some conservatives in his own party. This from a Democrat who thinks the G in GOP is an expletive. And this from a man who believes in getting mad and getting even; Brooks had one word for two junior Democrats on the House ethics committee who joined Republicans in voting against Wright on a key charge: "Pray."

Yet for all those who consider Brooks the meanest, most foul-mouthed character they have served with, there are others who consider him as loyal a friend and ally as there is in politics. His image as an irascible, tough-talking Texan, a man of strong loyalties and fierce independence, is one that Brooks has carefully nurtured; once when *The Washington Post* ran a photograph of Brooks with a snarling expression, he proudly showed it to all around.

No matter how they feel about him, most colleagues like to have Brooks on their side, if only because they do not want him on the other side. "I have never thought being a congressman was supposed to be an easy job," he has said, "and it doesn't bother me a bit to be in a good fight."

Brooks' scrappiness during 14 years as chairman of the Government Operations Committee turned that backwater panel into an aggressive investigatory arm that touched a number of federal agencies. But with the 101st Congress, after nearly four decades in office, Brooks assumed an entirely new challenge as chairman of the Judiciary Committee. Younger Democrats there welcomed his ascension, eager for Brooks' brand of activism and strong leadership after years of passivity under his respected but aging predecessor, Peter W. Rodino Jr.

Meanwhile, this man who arrived in the House in 1953 as a slightly awed 30-year-old protégé of the legendary Speaker Sam Rayburn must adjust to the loss of another Speaker from Texas. Brooks was one of Wright's most important allies, although in 1976 he had backed Californian Phillip Burton over Wright in the majority leadership race that Wright won by a single vote. The two like-minded, strong-willed Texans were born four days apart, suffered Depression-era hardship, served together in the Statehouse and entered Congress two years apart.

As Wright's career sank under the weight of ethics controversies, Brooks to the end was the most combative and outspoken among the Speaker's notably few public defenders. For Brooks, defense was a less familiar role; he is best known as one of the House's most unrelenting inquisitors — a reputation that got national exposure during investigations of scandals involving two Republican presidents.

Brooks had been an early critic of what he perceived as President Richard M. Nixon's abuses of office, and his subcommittee investigated federal spending on Nixon's private homes. When Watergate broke, Brooks was a ready prosecutor during Judiciary's impeachment proceedings. "He didn't even need to hear the evidence," an aide said later. "He was ready to impeach."

Thirteen years later, Wright named Brooks to the Iran-contra investigation committee and, to no one's surprise, the cigar-chomping Brooks was the most vocally partisan critic of the Reagan administration's failures. When GOP member Henry J. Hyde noted approvingly that only one of the House Democrats on the committee "would understand how to throw a hand grenade," it was understood that his exception was Brooks.

Talking to reporters, Brooks called both

Texas 9

Southeast — Beaumont; Galveston

The 9th District's industrial climate is symbolized by its three largest cities: Beaumont and Port Arthur, near the Louisiana border in Jefferson County, and Galveston, farther south along the Gulf of Mexico in Galveston County.

The discovery of oil in the Spindletop Oil Field in January 1901 triggered Beaumont's modern industrial development. Oil is still being pumped at Spindletop within sight of a monument and a museum commemorating the field's contribution to Texas' economy.

Republicans enjoy support in Beaumont's western end, home of middle-management refinery employees and some of the district's oldest oil families.

Port Arthur serves as a shipping center for the district's oil and petrochemical products. The city of Galveston, located on Pelican Island, is also a major port of entry. Looking out to sea from Galveston Bay, the horizon is dotted with offshore oil rigs. Local merchants have made a business of servicing area offshore facilities, shipping out food and laundry to the laborers, who often work a 12-day-on, 12-day-off schedule. Texas City, in Galveston County, is a major petrochemical center.

There are other economic mainstays tied to the 9th's coastal setting. Commercial fishing operations harvest shrimp and a number of finfish. The beaches of Galveston County are a big tourist lure.

The district also hosts a community of people who earn their living in high technology. Reaching into southeastern Harris County, the 9th contains part of Clear Lake City, home to an enclave of Republican engineers who work at the Johnson Space Center.

The 9th is one of the most ethnically diverse regions in the state. Nearly 30 percent of its residents are either black or Hispanic, and a significant portion of the blue-collar work force is of German, Czech or Polish descent. Port Arthur hosts a Cajun community, and Kemah, a Galveston County town, has a growing population of French-speaking Southeast Asians.

One of organized labor's few Texas strongholds, the 9th generally votes Democratic. Jimmy Carter won the district in 1976 and 1980, and after a brief fling with Ronald Reagan in 1984, voters went back to the Democratic side in 1988, giving the Michael S. Dukakis-Lloyd Bentsen ticket 54 percent of the vote.

Population: 526,443. White 390,211 (74%), Black 112,560 (21%), Other 8,694 (2%). Spanish origin 40,073 (8%). 18 and over 370,362 (70%), 65 and over 48,638 (9%). Median age: 29.

former national security adviser John M. Poindexter and former State Department official Elliott Abrams "a lying son of a bitch." Reflecting Government Operations' interests, Brooks charged that Poindexter broke the law protecting presidential records by shredding a key Reagan document.

Brooks was in the minority in opposing limited immunity for Lt. Col. Oliver L. North, calling it "a rotten precedent" since government officials should be accountable for their acts. Ex-Marine Brooks was unintimidated by the brash, uniformed North, and almost alone on the panel he kept up his aggressive questioning despite a wave of public support for North. "I guess the public likes a guy who says, 'Yeah, I lied and I'm glad I did,' " Brooks said.

Before the hearings, Brooks had called Poindexter before a Government Operations subcommittee to testify about an administration policy restricting release of sensitive information in its computers. But Poindexter refused to answer questions about even that limited subject; his lawyer said Brooks' panel probably would stray into the Iran-contra affair, and that it was conducting "a public spectacle."

"I want you to understand that your testimony is not a matter of right. It is a matter of indulgence of the subcommittee, and you're kind of crowding it," Brooks told the lawyer. When he tried to respond, Brooks snapped, "I think I've heard enough from you."

That hearing illustrated Brooks' ability to inject Government Operations — traditionally limited to the minutiae of federal spending — at least to the edges of major national debates, and to bedevil GOP administrations in the process. In the 100th Congress, it was his amendment that led to the creation of a federal drug czar, long opposed by Reagan. With the president's support, Brooks and other proponents also realized a longtime goal of giving the Veterans Administration Cabinet status.

Brooks was frustrated for years in his battle against revenue sharing, the popular program funneling funds to state and local governments. It was finally phased out in 1985 because of budget pressures, though in 1986 Brooks had to help squelch a strong push to revive it. Brooks also opposed the 1985 Gramm-Rudman-Hollings law. Both revenue sharing and Gramm-Rudman violated his basic belief in government accountability — revenue sharing because Brooks feels the government unit that raises money should spend it, and Gramm-Rudman because he believes Congress and the president should not cede their responsibility for deficit reduction to some automatic budget-cutting procedure.

Brooks jealously guarded his turf at Government Operations, and grabbed what more he could; Judiciary colleagues are hoping he will do the same there. Until he became chairman, Brooks had not been active on Judiciary, choosing to focus on Government Operations and bide time waiting for Rodino to retire.

His differences with Rodino are chiefly ones of style; Brooks is expected to be a more aggressive overseer of the Justice Department, for example. On most questions before Judiciary, notably those involving civil and constitutional law, Brooks has voted with the committee's liberal majority. Unlike Rodino, however, Brooks is for the death penalty and opposed to strict gun control. He also is friendlier toward business, an important note since he is also chairman of the Economic and Commercial Law Subcommittee.

In the past, Brooks supported a bill to allow beer distributors to carve up geographic regions without fear of antitrust prosecution. In the 100th Congress, he forced modifications in Rodino's bill to repeal the insurance industry's federal antitrust exemption, and then argued successfully against full committee action, since Congress' time was running out.

When Brooks first arrived in Washington, the youngest Democrat in the 1952 class, he went straight to Speaker Rayburn. He had worked hard against the Democrats-for-Eisenhower movement that swept Texas in 1952, and his party loyalty impressed the equally partisan Speaker. More than three decades later, when some Texas Democrats suggested the state's 10 GOP House members might join the traditional Wednesday delegation luncheons, Brooks — the delegation chairman — thundered against it. The two parties could meet any time, he said, but the lunches were sacred — Rayburn himself had banned Republicans.

Republicans are not the only ones who have to be on guard against Brooks; any rival is wise to be wary. In 1987, Brooks easily got the House's voice vote approval for an amendment adding $2.8 million for the Texas Accelerator Center to an appropriations bill. The victory went largely unnoticed. Later that day, lawmakers from California and Illinois, states competing with Texas to be the site of the multi-billion-dollar superconducting supercollider project, figured that Brooks might have won some advantage for his state. "Not knowing exactly what Jack has in mind, we worry," said one. After midnight, Brooks took the floor to claim his amendment merely paid for ongoing engineering work. His colleagues were not buying. They voted 97-288 to strip it.

In his early House years, Brooks voted like most other Texas congressmen — in favor of the oil industry and against many of the early civil rights bills. He did refuse to sign the segregationist "Southern Manifesto" in 1956. But when his friend and fellow Texan Lyndon B. Johnson became president, Brooks moved significantly to the left. In 1964, he was one of only 11 Southern Democrats to support that year's Civil Rights Act. He voted for every subsequent civil rights bill, and for all of LBJ's Great Society legislation.

At Home: "I'm just like old man Rayburn," Brooks likes to say. "Just a Democrat, no prefix or suffix." That simple label has kept Brooks in business for more than 30 years, although critics have always portrayed him as too liberal for his Gulf Coast district. Brooks had no GOP foe at all in 1988, largely because strong support from the district's sizable union and minority populations has enabled him to withstand repeated conservative challenges.

The most discomfiting of these came from within Brooks' own party in the 1980 Democratic primary. Lightly regarded Wilbur L. "Bubba" Pate, a politically inexperienced bus terminal manager, challenged Brooks from the right and nearly forced him into a runoff.

In addition to faulting Brooks as philosophically out of step with the voters in the 9th, Pate also questioned the incumbent's bank connections and the fact that he had amassed a personal fortune while serving most of his adult life in Congress. Brooks has earned more than $50,000 in salary and director fees from Texas banks in recent years.

Brooks won just over 50 percent in the primary, Pate took 43 percent and seven percent went to a third candidate who had withdrawn too late for his name to be taken off the ballot. Brooks avoided a runoff only because heavily unionized Galveston gave him a hefty majority; he lost two of the three other district counties, including his home base of Jefferson County (Beaumont and Port Arthur).

In November, Jimmy Carter nearly lost the 9th to Ronald Reagan, but Brooks was spared trouble because the GOP offered no House candidate.

Pate tried again in the 1982 Democratic primary, and he was joined by three other right-of-Brooks Democrats who believed the incumbent's 1980 stumble portended a 1982 fall. But 1980 had stirred Brooks' fighting instincts; he had been moving vigorously since then to regain his political footing.

By assuming a higher profile in the district, Brooks countered sentiment that he had grown distant from local concerns. He reminded voters of the federal plums he had brought to the 9th during his long career, including money for improvement of local port facilities and for research at area universities.

Most important, the conservative mood that swept over Texas' blue-collar workers in 1980 had evaporated by 1982; Brooks was on the offensive, criticizing Reaganomics as dangerous to the working-class citizens of the 9th.

With the challengers quibbling among themselves for pre-eminence in a conservative electorate shrunken since 1980, Brooks rolled to victory in every county of the district and won renomination with 53 percent of the vote.

Republicans were hopeful about their chances of retiring Brooks in 1984. They argued that President Reagan's presence at the top of the ticket could encourage the kind of widespread defections among conservative Democrats necessary to capture the 9th.

It did not work out that way. Reagan carried the 9th in presidential voting with 52 percent, but Brooks, stressing his seniority and attacking Reaganomics as a cause of the high unemployment still plaguing parts of the district, turned back Galveston attorney Jim Mahan with 59 percent of the vote. The GOP took its only comfort from the fact that Mahan held Brooks below 60 percent for the first time since the veteran Democrat came to Congress. Brooks climbed back over that barrier, however, in 1986. His 1988 re-election was his seventh in which he faced no Republican challenger.

A child of the Depression, Brooks was born across the state border in Crowley, La., but moved with his family to Beaumont at age 5. He worked his way through the University of Texas, served in the Marine Corps in World War II and won a seat in the state House in 1946. During his four years there, Brooks earned a law degree at the University of Texas.

Promoting himself as a lawyer and small farmer, Brooks ran for Congress in 1952, when Democratic Rep. Jesse M. Combs retired. He won, surviving a 12-way primary and a runoff.

At first, Brooks' district stretched north from his home base of Jefferson County into the rural woodland of eastern Texas. But in the mid-1960s the district was changed significantly. Though Jefferson County remained, the rest of Brooks' district was redrawn to stretch southwestward along the Gulf Coast to Galveston. Subsequent remappings have not significantly altered that configuration.

Committees

Judiciary (Chairman)
Economic and Commercial Law (chairman)

Select Narcotics Abuse and Control (2nd of 18 Democrats)

Elections

1988 General		
Jack Brooks (D)	137,270	(100%)
1986 General		
Jack Brooks (D)	73,285	(62%)
Lisa D. Duperier (R)	45,834	(38%)

Previous Winning Percentages: **1984** (59%) **1982** (68%) **1980** (100%) **1978** (63%) **1976** (100%) **1974** (62%) **1972** (66%) **1970** (65%) **1968** (61%) **1966** (100%) **1964** (63%) **1962** (69%) **1960** (70%) **1958** (100%) **1956** (100%) **1954** (100%) **1952** (79%)

District Vote For President

	1988	1984	1980	1976
D	104,909 (54%)	99,585 (48%)	84,259 (49%)	97,831 (58%)
R	90,891 (46%)	108,937 (52%)	81,669 (47%)	68,490 (41%)
I			4,494 (3%)	

Campaign Finance

	Receipts	Receipts from PACs	Expend-itures
1988			
Brooks (D)	$424,773	$276,562 (65%)	$226,581
1986			
Brooks (D)	$447,111	$242,809 (54%)	$400,038
Duperier (R)	$245,816	$200 (0.1%)	$244,095

Key Votes

1987	
Raise speed limit to 65 mph	Y
Approve Gephardt "fair trade" amendment	Y
Ban testing of larger nuclear weapons	Y
Delay "re-flagging" of Kuwaiti tankers	Y
Approve tax-raising deficit-reduction bill	Y
1988	
Approve aid to Nicaraguan contras	N
Enact civil rights restoration bill over Reagan veto	Y
Kill 60-day plant-closing notification measure	N
Pass omnibus trade bill over Reagan veto	Y
Approve death penalty for drug-related murders	Y
Bar federal funds for abortions in cases of rape and incest	N
Oppose seven-day waiting period for purchase of handguns	Y

Voting Studies

	Presidential Support		Party Unity		Conservative Coalition	
Year	S	O	S	O	S	O
1988	24	70	82	5	26	61
1987	20	75	87	5	40	60
1986	21	69	76	7	50	34
1985	24	74	87	5	35	56
1984	30	58	77	14	46	46
1983	32	63	81	14	47	51
1982	44	44	70	16	55	38
1981	42	33	55	23	57	35

Interest Group Ratings

Year	ADA	ACU	AFL-CIO	CCUS
1988	75	9	100	23
1987	88	0	94	13
1986	70	9	100	33
1985	70	11	94	28
1984	55	11	77	43
1983	75	17	76	32
1982	50	20	74	40
1981	45	21	64	33

10 J.J. "Jake" Pickle (D)

Of Austin — Elected 1963

Born: Oct. 11, 1913, Roscoe, Texas.
Education: U. of Texas, B.A. 1938.
Military Career: Navy, 1942-45.
Occupation: Public relations and advertising executive.
Family: Wife, Beryl Bolton McCarroll; three children.
Religion: Methodist.
Political Career: No previous office.
Capitol Office: 242 Cannon Bldg. 20515; 225-4865.

In Washington: Pickle's Texas hill country twang is an instant reminder of Lyndon B. Johnson, who represented the same congressional district for a decade. And Pickle's legislative career suggests its own echoes of Johnson, for whom he campaigned as a young man and whose name he nearly always pronounces in reverent tones.

Like LBJ, Pickle is a man of rural populist roots who has made his accommodations with the corporate interests crucial to Texas politics. But he seems more comfortable with his role of small-business protector and specialist in the problems of the Social Security system.

Whatever the issue, he is dogged and often successful in getting what he wants. After more than a quarter-century in the House, Pickle has risen to the No. 3 spot on the Ways and Means Committee, where he has been involved in a variety of major issues, including Social Security, trade and revision of the tax code.

On Ways and Means, Pickle is not one of the Democrats who has pledged complete loyalty to Chairman Dan Rostenkowski, but he is the type of senior member who has great respect for the chairmanship. As such, Pickle is unlikely to rear up in a public challenge to Rostenkowski, though he may well find a subtle way to communicate his disagreements when he has them.

Pickle was not the most active player when it came to overhauling the tax code in the 99th Congress, and he cautioned from the start that revising tax laws could aggravate the federal deficit. "While it's exciting to woo the fair maiden of tax reform," he said in 1985, "it's important to make sure the house doesn't fall down while we're wooing the lady." But whatever his reservations, he was generally supportive of the bill, which was near and dear to Rostenkowski's heart. That loyalty enabled him to leave his imprint on the legislation and make it onto the conference committee.

One of Pickle's main goals was to preserve tax breaks for the oil industry and other economic interests in his home state. He was able to attach one amendment to the bill extending a 20 percent tax credit for business research and development. That was of particular importance to high-tech firms, many of which have flocked to Pickle's district in recent years.

Later, when Democratic House conferees offered a compromise that shifted $141.7 billion in taxes from individuals to businesses, he was among those objecting, because he feared it would hurt energy, real-estate and banking industries in Texas. But he did support the panel's final product.

In the 100th Congress, Pickle had some of the same priorities as the committee worked on technical corrections to the tax bill. He had over 270 members sign onto his plan to extend further the research and development tax credit for business and a basic research credit for universities.

"Vigorous research and development is the key to achieving the technological advances that will create and improve on products we can sell here and abroad," he argued. The expiring provisions were all modified to some degree because of revenue concerns, but Pickle took some satisfaction from seeing them extended.

As chairman of Ways and Means' Oversight Subcommittee, Pickle exercises a broad mandate. In the 100th Congress, issues the subcommittee investigated included tax breaks for televangelists and lobbying and election-related activity by tax-exempt public charities. Early in the 101st Congress, Pickle was among those expressing concern about debt-laden corporate takeovers. He warned that companies heavily burdened by debt would have trouble surviving a recession, and could end up dragging down others.

"When the crash comes, everyone is going to turn to Congress and ask, 'Why didn't you do something to protect us against this?' " he said.

Whatever work he does on Oversight, Pickle will have difficulty matching an earlier achievement as head of the Social Security Subcommittee in the 98th Congress.

As chairman of that subcommittee, he was convinced that the way to save the Social Security system was to raise the retirement age. Democratic leaders, including Speaker Thomas

Texas 10

Central — Austin

Though the 10th takes in five counties and most of a sixth, the state capital of Austin and surrounding Travis County dominate its political life. Eighty percent of the district's vote is cast there.

With a large state government work force and a huge academic community affiliated with the University of Texas (48,000 students), Austin traditionally has been one of Texas' most liberal cities.

In 1986, Travis County gave Democrat Mark White 56 percent in his unsuccessful gubernatorial re-election bid. In 1988, support for Michael S. Dukakis in the county helped the Democratic presidential nominee to a 54 percent showing districtwide. More presidential votes were cast in the 10th — nearly 290,000 — than in any other Texas district in 1988, a clear sign of the area's brisk population growth since the last redistricting.

The Austin economy has diversified beyond reliance on state government and the university. Electronics and computer companies have come to the area in recent years, luring upwardly mobile middle-class employees. In 1983, Austin won a bidding war against 56 other cities for the right to host the headquarters of Microelectronics & Computer Technology Corp., a widely publicized research consortium. In 1988, the city won a similar competition to host Semitech, a research and applied technology organization.

The influx of other such firms helped boost Travis County's population by 42 percent in the 1970s, and by 31 percent this decade, both times producing the fastest growth rate among the state's six largest urban counties.

Recently, though, expansion has not been the story in Austin. Savings and loan institutions played a major role in fueling the city's growth, and trouble in the state and national S&L industry has made money for business development hard to come by. The commercial real-estate market has gone soft.

The slowdown in development is not perceived negatively by everyone in Austin; anti-growth forces had for years condemned random, unplanned growth for causing traffic congestion, water problems and overtaxed city services. They see the current slowdown as an opportunity to keep Austin from being "Houstonized."

Beyond the Travis County borders, the 10th extends south and west into largely rural Democratic territory. Blanco County has attracted Republican retirees, but, with a small population, it has a limited electoral impact.

Population: 527,181. White 414,934 (79%), Black 54,566 (10%), Other 5,932 (1%). Spanish origin 97,295 (19%). 18 and over 390,909 (74%), 65 and over 45,569 (9%). Median age: 27.

P. O'Neill Jr. and senior citizens' spokesman Claude Pepper of Florida, wanted to solve long-term financing problems with eventual increases in the payroll tax. Few expected Pickle would prevail on the floor, but he did, in what was the most impressive and significant victory of his career.

Through months of argument over what to do about Social Security, Pickle and Pepper were the spokesmen for two diametrically opposite points of view. When the Florida Democrat said he could not support an increase in the retirement age or any other benefit change, Pickle replied, "There are other possibilities we have to consider. I can take just as intractable a position as you."

In March 1983, Ways and Means approved a compromise package of tax increases and modest benefit cuts, with the understanding that Pickle and Pepper would offer their respective alternatives on the floor.

Pepper wanted to cover Social Security deficits in future years with a payroll tax boost starting in 2010; Pickle proposed a gradual increase in the retirement age from 65 to 67 over the first quarter of the next century.

During the heated debate, Pickle defended his plan by citing the increase in life expectancy. Raising the age, he said, "is not harsh. That is just in keeping with the times."

In the end, the House voted 228-202 for Pickle's plan, with support from most Republicans and a majority of Ways and Means. Pickle said he felt "bruised as a rodeo mule," but added, "I think we've done the right thing and I think history will prove that." Pickle's approach later became law, and he gave up his Social Security chairmanship, explaining that his main task had been accomplished.

Pickle's victory represented the culmination of a long personal struggle to put the system on a sound financial footing. In 1981, recognizing the imminent crisis, he offered a massive reform proposal, only to see it shoved aside because of partisan wrangling.

Partly in response to Pickle's proposal, President Reagan proposed massive benefit cuts in May of that year. That brought a storm of protest from Democrats, and the administration eventually backed down. Pickle was left alone to defend a proposal that both parties had decided was politically too costly.

Reagan then appointed a bipartisan commission to come up with a long-term solution to the problem. The agreement formed the basis of the plan eventually passed by Ways and Means, but it left unsolved an anticipated deficit after the turn of the century. Pickle's retirement-age proposal was designed to address that deficit.

The Social Security Subcommittee also handles the federal disability payment system, and Pickle has been controversial in this area as well. In 1980, convinced that thousands of people were collecting too much money on disability — some making considerably more than they had at work — Pickle's panel wrote a bill limiting any disabled worker's benefits to 80 percent of previous earnings.

The bill brought a storm of protest from recipient groups, especially the organized elderly. Former Health, Education and Welfare Secretary Wilbur J. Cohen, who served under Johnson, went to Pickle's district to attack the idea. A majority of Northern Democrats voted against it. Pepper accused Pickle of "turning to the cripple as the source of saving revenue." But it passed the House easily in early 1980, thanks mostly to overwhelming GOP support.

In 1982, after the Reagan administration began efforts to crack down on disability recipients it thought might be cheating, Pickle introduced legislation ensuring that benefits would flow while such cases were being reviewed. That provoked little opposition. But he also added language making it more difficult for recipients to present new evidence about their condition. That offended groups representing the disabled, and nearly prevented the entire measure from becoming law in the 97th Congress.

In the 98th Congress Pickle worked more closely with those groups, introducing another bill to bolster the rights of disability recipients whose aid had been challenged. Pickle originally worked with the administration as well on this issue, and was furious when Social Security officials testified in the Senate that disability reforms "were not needed."

The tension between Pickle and the administration rose the day before his bill was set for a floor vote. News leaked out that Reagan planned to quell the controversy with an 18-month moratorium on disability reviews. Pickle called the proposal a "cruel hoax" for those on the rolls. Despite the Reagan plan, the House still passed the bill by an overwhelming 410-1. "Sometimes," Pickle said, "you have to slug 'em to get their attention."

Much of Pickle's earlier House career consisted of balancing his own New Deal instincts and LBJ's national goals against his constituents' increasing skepticism about liberal programs. He arrived in the House in December 1963 — less than a month after Johnson's accession — and in his first two years backed both the Civil Rights Act of 1964 and the Voting Rights Act. "I caught hell in my district," he noted later. Pickle also was a strong backer of the Office of Economic Opportunity, especially its jobs programs, ones he saw as similar to those of the National Youth Administration, for which he worked in the 1930s.

But he opposed civil rights legislation in 1966 and 1968, both times on grounds that its open housing provisions were too strong. Since the end of the Johnson administration he has, like most Texas Democrats, gradually moved closer to the voting patterns of Democrats from other Southern states.

At Home: Pickle belongs to a dwindling generation of Texas politicians who were political protégés of LBJ. He solidified his grip on his central Texas district during the Johnson White House years, and it looks safe for him as long as he runs. But if he retires before the next redistricting takes effect (he would turn 79 the month before the 1992 elections), the 10th may well be reshaped.

Pickle was a campaign manager and a congressional aide to Johnson before World War II. After the war, as a partner in a public-relations agency, he was a political adviser and helped in LBJ's 1948 Senate campaign.

But he did not seek office himself until 1963, when he resigned from the Texas Employment Commission to run in a special election. A vacancy had been created when Democratic Rep. Homer Thornberry, Johnson's first successor, retired to accept a federal judgeship.

Long before Pickle made his political debut, however, he had become controversial in Texas politics. He had gained the disfavor of liberal Democrats in 1954, when he worked for the re-election of Gov. Allan Shivers against the liberal favorite, Ralph Yarborough. Pickle was accused of producing a campaign film for Shivers, entitled "The Port Arthur Story," which depicted the strike-ridden city as a victim of organized labor.

Liberals supported their own candidate in the 1963 House race. But Pickle's ties to political and business interests in the 10th, as well as the clever marketing of his name — he handed out pickle-shaped campaign pins and recipe books — made him a formidable candidate.

Pickle ran narrowly ahead of the three-man field in the first round of voting in early November, but fell well short of the majority required. With liberals uneasy about his candidacy, he was expected to have problems winning the December runoff election against a conservative Republican opponent.

But the complexion of the campaign was changed by the Nov. 22 assassination of President John F. Kennedy. Pickle's House race suddenly was transformed into the first test of voter support for the district's most famous citizen, President Johnson. Benefiting from a surge of party harmony, Pickle won easily.

During the height of the Johnson presidency, Pickle had no primary or GOP opposition. In 1968 he had an aggressive Republican challenger, Ray Gabler, who accused him of profiting from land condemnation for a federally aided reservoir project. Pickle denied any breach of ethics but was held to 62 percent.

Pickle had no other serious challenge until 1980, when the Reagan tide in Texas and voter dissatisfaction with a court-ordered busing plan in Austin held him to 59 percent. Pickle had been reluctant to support a constitutional amendment to ban busing, although he did vote for one on the House floor in 1979.

As in earlier races, Pickle ran better in the rural areas than in populous Austin. But he was still able to carry every county, and did not face another Republican opponent until 1986. In that year, the GOP was initially optimistic about its prospects in the 10th. Former Austin Mayor Carole Rylander, a lifelong Democrat, switched parties late in 1985, and decided to run as a Republican against Pickle. Rylander's widespread visibility — she accepted an appointment to the state Board of Insurance following her two terms as mayor — and high-energy campaign style attracted considerable attention from the national GOP, and prompted speculation that Pickle could be in serious trouble.

But Pickle not only rose to the challenge posed by Rylander, he annihilated her. Aided by early fund raising, laser-printed direct-mail technology and the first professional campaign manager he had hired in a half-dozen years, Pickle amassed a stunning 72 percent. Rylander's tally of 28 percent barely kept pace with the 10th's base GOP vote.

That seems to have been enough to convince whatever doubters remained; the GOP once again left Pickle alone in 1988.

Committees

Ways and Means (3rd of 23 Democrats)
Oversight (chairman); Health

Joint Taxation

Elections

1988 General		
J. J. "Jake" Pickle (D)	232,213	(93%)
Vincent J. May (LIB)	16,281	(7%)
1986 General		
J. J. "Jake" Pickle (D)	135,863	(72%)
Carole Keeton Rylander (R)	52,000	(28%)

Previous Winning Percentages: **1984** (100%) **1982** (90%) **1980** (59%) **1978** (76%) **1976** (77%) **1974** (80%) **1972** (91%) **1970** (100%) **1968** (62%) **1966** (74%) **1964** (76%) **1963** * (63%)

** Special runoff election. Under Texas special election law, a majority was required to win the House seat. Since no candidate had a majority in the initial special election, a runoff special election was held between the top two finishers.*

District Vote For President

	1988	1984	1980	1976
D	155,270 (54%)	111,685 (42%)	91,779 (47%)	97,200 (53%)
R	131,918 (46%)	154,300 (58%)	89,926 (46%)	83,817 (46%)
I			10,823 (6%)	

Campaign Finance

	Receipts	Receipts from PACs	Expend-itures
1988			
Pickle (D)	$172,746	$46,463 (27%)	$172,921
1986			
Pickle (D)	$1,151,264	$424,667 (37%)	$1,369,912
Rylander (R)	$302,620	$26,390 (9%)	$302,618

Key Votes

1987	
Raise speed limit to 65 mph	Y
Approve Gephardt "fair trade" amendment	N
Ban testing of larger nuclear weapons	Y
Delay "re-flagging" of Kuwaiti tankers	N
Approve tax-raising deficit-reduction bill	Y
1988	
Approve aid to Nicaraguan contras	N
Enact civil rights restoration bill over Reagan veto	Y
Kill 60-day plant-closing notification measure	N
Pass omnibus trade bill over Reagan veto	Y
Approve death penalty for drug-related murders	Y
Bar federal funds for abortions in cases of rape and incest	N
Oppose seven-day waiting period for purchase of handguns	Y

Voting Studies

	Presidential Support		Party Unity		Conservative Coalition	
Year	S	O	S	O	S	O
1988	32	60	80	12	53	42
1987	34	62	82	16	77	23
1986	39	57	63	25	80	18
1985	40	59	82	15	64	29
1984	47	47	70	22	69	27
1983	44	49	68	25	72	21
1982	53	43	57	36	74	19
1981	61	36	58	39	75	24

Interest Group Ratings

Year	ADA	ACU	AFL-CIO	CCUS
1988	80	16	100	38
1987	60	22	63	43
1986	40	38	43	44
1985	50	38	65	43
1984	65	25	62	40
1983	60	30	56	40
1982	30	43	42	58
1981	40	20	60	58

11 Marvin Leath (D)

Of Waco — Elected 1978

Born: May 6, 1931, Henderson, Texas.
Education: Attended Kilgore Jr. College, 1949-50; U. of Texas, B.B.A. 1954.
Military Career: Army, 1954-56.
Occupation: Banker.
Family: Wife, Alta Ruth Neill; one child.
Religion: Presbyterian.
Political Career: No previous office.
Capitol Office: 336 Cannon Bldg. 20515; 225-6105.

In Washington: To understand Leath's strength in the House, it helps to remember that he arrived after a career as a small-town banker. He is personally and fiscally conservative, but he is willing to cut deals with anyone, knows his customers, bargains in good faith and considers a person's word his bond.

One of Congress' more remarkable stories of recent years was Leath's transformation after he joined the Budget Committee in 1985 from an amiable Boll Weevil backbencher into a major House figure in budget negotiations. The respect and affection he inspired put him within reach by 1987 of the chairmanships of the Armed Services and Budget committees. But those hopes were dashed, and Leath also was frustrated with the failure of Missouri Rep. Richard A. Gephardt's presidential campaign. Leath had campaigned hard for Gephardt, seeing his bid as a vehicle for pulling the Democratic Party toward the center.

Leath still has one term left on Budget in the 101st Congress, but the work there — or, more to the point, the lack of it — just feeds his frustration. Since late 1987, budgets have amounted to cease-fire compromises between GOP administrations and Congress' Democratic leaders; the process has done little to cut the deficits Leath abhors and offers few openings to deal-makers like himself outside the inner circle.

Even so, as long as Leath is in the House, he is likely to be a valued channel for party leaders trying to reach conservative Democrats on budget and defense questions.

As his near-successful 1987 coup against Armed Services Chairman Les Aspin showed, however, Leath's influence transcends ideological lines. His supporters comprised a group that Texas colleague Jim Wright called "the damndest conglomeration of people I've ever seen." They included not only Leath's fellow Southern conservatives, but also all the Armed Services subcommittee chairmen except Florida's Charles E. Bennett (who was also competing), Leath's left-leaning Budget colleagues, other liberals disaffected with Aspin, and Black Caucus members, including Californian Ronald V. Dellums, who nominated Leath with a speech that, in the words of one member, "made grown men cry."

Leath based his candidacy on his straightforwardness and ability to forge consensus. Meanwhile, he exploited Aspin's reputation as untrustworthy among liberals who felt Aspin had reneged on promises to oppose the MX missile and contra aid — promises he made to win their support for his 1985 ouster of enfeebled Armed Services Chairman Melvin Price. Leath had broken with his party on those issues as well, but he alienated few in doing so because no one had expected him to vote any differently.

At first, many Democrats discounted Leath's bid because he was 14th in seniority on the committee and had been a party renegade for so long. But when they caucused six months later, in January 1987, Aspin was unseated on a no-confidence vote. Leath expected an immediate second vote to fill the chair, and he felt he could win it. The leadership delayed the decision two weeks, however, allowing a shaken Aspin to recover. After Bennett and Armed Services liberal Nicholas Mavroules were eliminated on early ballots, Leath fell short, 133-116, in a head-to-head showdown with Aspin.

In the end, Leath lost because most Democrats were unwilling to give power to such an unabashed conservative, no matter how much they liked and trusted him. A particularly damaging letter, circulated by liberals Don Edwards and Matthew F. McHugh, documented his voting record and concluded that Leath "has made a career of voting against his party."

By midyear, Leath had joined the early jockeying to succeed William H. Gray III as Budget chairman. However, he could not rebuild his confounding coalition because key liberal lieutenants, such as Charles E. Schumer and Marty Russo, were allies of contender Leon E. Panetta. Also, Leath refused to run again without Wright's endorsement, but the Speaker insisted on neutrality. Soon Leath left the race, throwing his support to the ultimate winner,

Texas 11

Central — Waco

Most voters here are like Leath — Democratic in name, but more loyal to a philosophy than a party label. When the Democratic nominee meets local conservative standards, he can carry the 11th. But if the Democrat is tainted with liberalism, the electorate here can cross over about as easily as Leath does on the House floor.

The areas most prone to flirt with Republicanism are the district's urbanized counties — McLennan County (Waco) and Bell County (Killeen and Temple). In 1976, Jimmy Carter carried both counties comfortably, but since then, they have voted Republican for president.

Waco, with slightly more than 105,000 people, is sometimes called the "Baptist Rome." It is the home of the largest Baptist-affiliated university in the world, Baylor University (enrollment 11,600). Waco's economy has ridden through recessionary times fairly well because of university-related employment and the city's diversified manufacturing base — products range from candy bars to military aircraft, produced by a recently opened Chrysler plant.

Southwest of Waco, in Bell County, are Temple and Killeen; during the 1970s, the two matured from oversized towns into small cities pushing toward 50,000 in population. Kileen is now approaching 60,000. The federal government's contribution to the Bell County economy is immense because Fort Hood, the second-largest Army base in the country, is located there. The base covers 339 square miles in Bell and Coryell counties and has a combined military and civilian staff of about 70,000 people.

Traditional conservative Democrats hold sway in most of the district's 11 rural counties, where 40 percent of the vote is cast. The rural counties backed George Bush in the 1988 presidential contest, but they usually show their Democratic roots in elections closer to home.

At the eastern end of the 11th, the fertile Blackland Prairie soil grows feed grains, cotton, hay and other crops. Livestock-raising — beef cattle, sheep and hogs — is a major income-producer, especially in the hillier western sections of the district.

Population: 527,382. White 417,065 (79%), Black 74,581 (14%), Other 7,001 (1%). Spanish origin 49,181 (9%). 18 and over 381,013 (72%), 65 and over 65,385 (12%). Median age: 28.

Panetta.

Leath won his place on Budget as part of former Speaker Thomas P. O'Neill Jr.'s reconciliation with conservatives in early 1985. The peacemaking came after Texan Charles W. Stenholm — urged on by Leath — had moved to unseat O'Neill to protest the leadership's disregard of conservative Democrats. Some regular Democrats feared that Leath on the Budget Committee would be another Phil Gramm, the widely unpopular Texan who, before switching to the GOP and then the Senate, used his seat on Budget to lead the Boll Weevils' (and Leath's) 1981 defection to Reaganomics.

Instead, Leath effectively reunited the party. In 1985, he joined other conservative Democrats on the panel to offer a budget-reduction package based on a Social Security freeze, defense and domestic spending cuts and some new taxes. When it was defeated by a wide margin on the floor, after an impassioned speech by Leath that colleagues still recall, he dutifully supported the leadership's plan.

Later that year he helped negotiate what became the Gramm-Rudman anti-deficit law, settling with liberal Rep. Henry A. Waxman on a list of health programs to be shielded from the law's threatened automatic cuts. In 1986, Leath was central to Budget's drafting efforts, impressing liberals with his willingness to support defense cuts in return for their restraint on domestic spending. The panel's budget carried all but 19 Democratic votes as it passed the House easily.

Occasionally, strains still surface. During Budget's 1987 deliberations, Leath espoused a freeze that only Republicans supported. "I'm going to get much closer to where I want to get as a conservative Democrat" by working with Republicans, he said, "than if I'm closeted with my more liberal Democratic colleagues." But he ultimately backed the committee bill, after further domestic cuts were made. On the floor, Leath won warm Democratic applause when he declared that while he did not like the bill, such a compromise was preferable to Republicans' failure to act.

Leath has been less active at Armed Services. True to his word, he moved quickly to cover the breach with Aspin. In 1988, he was named to head the committee's informal Morale, Welfare and Recreation panel. Meanwhile, however, Aspin has solidified his control with a centrist coalition, leaving Leath on the Democratic fringe, often in league with Republicans.

Leath's main interest is protecting Fort

Hood, his district's huge Army base, although he did lead a failed attempt in 1983 to resume production of chemical weapons. Leath remains a hawk on defense, but he argues that the military is paying now for having deceived Congress in its past estimates.

Earlier in his career, Leath served on the Veterans' Affairs Committee. As chairman of its Education and Training Subcommittee, in the 98th Congress he moved through the House a bill providing vocational education and on-the-job training for disabled or unemployed Vietnam and Korean War veterans.

At Home: When Democratic Rep. W. R. Poage retired in 1978 after 21 terms in the House, Republicans thought they had a good chance of winning his district. But Leath's conservative campaign neutralized the GOP offensive in this traditionally Democratic constituency. He won narrowly in 1978 and has been re-elected five times since without significant primary opposition or any GOP challenges.

Leath displays the conservatism of a self-made man. Born into a poor East Texas family during the Depression, he went to work at age 12, washing dishes, driving mules and working on pipelines in the nearby oil fields. Later he won a football scholarship to the University of Texas. After graduation he became a banker, serving the financial needs of the farmers and ranchers of central Texas.

After the death of a young son to leukemia, Leath came to Washington in 1972 to work in Poage's office. He concentrated on constituent problems and managed Poage's last three campaigns. When Poage decided to retire, Leath jumped into the crowded Democratic field. Spending heavily out of his own pocket, he ran second in the primary to make the runoff.

Consolidating the right, he won the runoff over ex-state Rep. Lane Denton, carrying all but two of 19 counties in the district.

In the general election, Leath faced Jack Burgess, who two years earlier had surprised Poage by drawing 43 percent of the vote. Leath's candidacy deprived Republicans of an effective strategy. The GOP had hoped that Denton would be the Democratic nominee, permitting Burgess to attack his liberalism.

Instead, Burgess tried to undermine Leath's Democratic support by accenting the Democrat's 1964 vote for Barry Goldwater over Texan Lyndon B. Johnson. Leath acknowledged that he voted for Goldwater, but said he returned to the Democratic Party immediately afterward. The election was close. Burgess carried McLennan County (Waco) by nearly 5,000 votes, but Leath swept virtually all of the district's smaller counties and won with 52 percent. Altogether, his campaign cost nearly $600,000, one of the most expensive congressional efforts in 1978.

Committees

Armed Services (10th of 31 Democrats)
Procurement and Military Nuclear Systems; Readiness

Budget (5th of 21 Democrats)
Task Force: Defense, Foreign Policy and Space (chairman)

Elections

1988 General

Marvin Leath (D)	134,207	(95%)
Frederick M. King (LIB)	6,533	(5%)

1986 General

Marvin Leath (D)	84,201	(100%)

Previous Winning Percentages: **1984** (100%) **1982** (96%) **1980** (100%) **1978** (52%)

District Vote For President

	1988		1984		1980		1976	
D	75,684	(42%)	59,647	(34%)	71,042	(45%)	83,552	(56%)
R	105,713	(58%)	117,058	(66%)	84,251	(53%)	63,788	(43%)
I					2,872	(2%)		

Campaign Finance

	Receipts	Receipts from PACs	Expend-itures
1988			
Leath (D)	$178,312	$95,150 (53%)	$87,626
1986			
Leath (D)	$157,069	$89,035 (57%)	$84,296

Key Votes

1987

Raise speed limit to 65 mph	Y
Approve Gephardt "fair trade" amendment	Y
Ban testing of larger nuclear weapons	Y
Delay "re-flagging" of Kuwaiti tankers	?
Approve tax-raising deficit-reduction bill	Y

1988

Approve aid to Nicaraguan contras	Y
Enact civil rights restoration bill over Reagan veto	N
Kill 60-day plant-closing notification measure	N
Pass omnibus trade bill over Reagan veto	Y
Approve death penalty for drug-related murders	Y
Bar federal funds for abortions in cases of rape and incest	?
Oppose seven-day waiting period for purchase of handguns	Y

Voting Studies

	Presidential Support		Party Unity		Conservative Coalition	
Year	S	O	S	O	S	O
1988	50	38	50	31	82	8
1987	47	46	50	38	81	9
1986	53	43	55	33	82	16
1985	52	45	46	49	91	4
1984	50	38	36	50	83	3
1983	61	32	29	60	92	1
1982	66	30	31	64	88	4
1981	68	28	30	65	91	7

Interest Group Ratings

Year	ADA	ACU	AFL-CIO	CCUS
1988	15	71	54	77
1987	24	41	40	50
1986	45	57	50	50
1985	10	76	18	77
1984	10	64	31	47
1983	10	100	38	68
1982	10	71	16	67
1981	0	93	21	78

12 No Incumbent

Jim Wright
House Service: 1955-89

Wright's career as House Speaker had barely begun in 1987 when people began touting him as one of the strongest leaders of the postwar Congress.

From that vertiginous height Wright fell after only one full term, ending his 34-year career in Congress as the first Speaker in history to be forced by scandal to leave the office midterm.

"Let me give you back this job you gave me as a propitiation for all of this season of bad will that has grown up among us," Wright said, in his May 31, 1989, speech announcing he would resign rather than continue fighting allegations that he violated House gift and income rules.

Throughout the yearlong ethics committee investigation of his finances that led to his downfall, Wright portrayed himself as a victim — of a partisan vendetta, of an overzealous investigator, of an ethics inquisition that amounted to "mindless cannibalism," as he put it in his resignation speech.

The allegations about Wright's conduct were serious and relentless enough that even a politician more popular than Wright might have had a hard time holding on to the Speaker's office. But Wright's personal and political style made him especially vulnerable.

A loner, an enigma to his colleagues, a man more respected than liked, Wright had reached the pinnacle of congressional power on his own steam. When the going got rough, he was on his own still.

It became more difficult for House Democrats to dismiss the Wright affair as an idiosyncratic personal drama when, around the same time as Wright's resignation, a second member of the Democratic leadership — Majority Whip Tony Coelho of California — resigned rather than face an ethics investigation of his personal finances.

The two resignations gave new impetus to proposals to overhaul House ethics standards regarding money and its influence on the legislative process. Many political obstacles to such changes remained, but rescuing Congress from a crisis of public confidence was one of the first jobs facing Wright's successor as Speaker, Thomas S. Foley of Washington.

If any one man could claim credit for toppling Wright, it was Newt Gingrich, the Georgia Republican who filed a formal complaint against Wright with the ethics committee. But if it had only been a crusade by Gingrich, who until then had been a backbench gadfly, Wright probably would still be Speaker today.

The partisan edge was dulled when the government-watchdog group Common Cause in May 1988 joined the call for an investigation of Wright. He then bowed to the growing pressure and invited the ethics committee to look into his financial affairs — a review Wright thought would be a matter of weeks, not months, let alone a full year.

The inquiry began in June 1988, when the ethics committee announced it would look into six areas of Wright's personal and political affairs, including the circumstances surrounding the publication of Wright's book, "Reflections of a Public Man," and Wright's use of a Fort Worth condominium owned by the family of George Mallick, a Texas developer and long-time friend of Wright.

The ethics panel hired an outside attorney to head the inquiry — an aggressive Chicago trial lawyer, Richard J. Phelan, who worked in secrecy with little word of his findings leaking out.

As the 101st Congress began in 1989, hardly anyone believed Wright's hold on the Speaker's office was at risk, even though the inquiry had dragged on far longer than was initially expected.

The bombshell dropped in April, when the ethics committee announced it had found reason to believe that Wright violated House rules in 69 instances. The panel's report detailed allegations that Wright received $145,000 over ten years in improper gifts from Mallick — including the condominium, the use of a car and an $18,000 annual salary paid to Wright's wife. The committee also alleged that bulk sales of Wright's book were intended as a "scheme" to circumvent House rules limiting all outside income except book royalties.

While Wright awaited a formal hearing on those charges, he continued to be pummeled in the press with new allegations of questionable

Texas 12

Fort Worth; Northwest Tarrant County

Less than half the size of neighboring Dallas, Fort Worth projects a blue-collar and Western roughneck image that contrasts with its more sophisticated neighbor.

But that image of the city — which comprises nearly 60 percent of the 12th's population — is not entirely accurate. Celebrations such as the Southwestern Exposition Fat Stock Show and Rodeo may recall Fort Worth's heyday as a cattle marketing center, but since World War II the city has been a major manufacturer of military and aerospace equipment, and electronics is increasingly prominent. General Dynamics and Bell Helicopter, which lies just beyond the 12th's eastern boundary, are among the area's leading employers.

As many middle- and upper-income Fort Worth residents have fled the city, once-rural territory in surrounding Tarrant County has sprouted shopping malls and suburbs. Old residential neighborhoods on the city's Near South Side are now largely black; the Near North Side hosts a sizable Hispanic community.

Efforts have been made to upgrade urban Fort Worth. A northern portion of the city once given over to stockyards now hosts Billy Bob's, a huge Western-style complex where urban cowboys drink, shop and watch live rodeo.

The affluent western and southwestern sections of the city and its suburbs give the 12th a Republican vote of some significance. The northeastern Mid-Cities area in the corridor between Fort Worth and Dallas is a pocket of affluent, GOP-minded voters. The 12th narrowly favored Ronald Reagan in the 1980 presidential race, and Reagan won it easily in 1984. With Texan Lloyd Bentsen running with him on the Democratic ticket in 1988, Michael S. Dukakis managed 47 percent of the vote in the 12th.

In non-presidential contests, the combined forces of labor, liberals, low-income whites and minorities generally lift Democrats to victory here.

Following Wright's June 30 resignation, GOP Gov. William P. Clements Jr. set a special election for Aug. 12. Four Democrats, three Republicans and a Libertarian ran together on one ballot. To avoid a runoff, one candidate had to receive a majority of the vote.

Population: 527,715. White 400,376 (76%), Black 90,980 (17%), Other 4,695 (1%). Spanish origin 54,851 (10%). 18 and over 374,842 (71%), 65 and over 53,052 (10%). Median age: 29.

business dealings.

The revelation that was the most politically damaging was the one furthest removed from the Speaker's personal finances. In the midst of Wright's troubles, his top aide resigned in the wake of new publicity about a brutal assault the aide had committed as a teenager. The story of that assault provoked a far more emotional reaction among members and the American public than any of the more arcane questions about Wright's finances.

From that point on, it was no longer a question of whether Wright would lose his speakership, but when.

He finally gave up his last hope when, in a public hearing before the ethics committee, it became clear the panel would not grant his lawyers' motion to dismiss the major charges against Wright.

Pressure on Wright to resign intensified when Coelho announced his decision to step down as whip and resign from the House to avoid an ethics committee inquiry.

Wright announced his plans to resign — from the Speaker's office June 9 and from Congress by the end of the month — in an hour-long speech before the House. He summoned the oratorical skill that was his hallmark, but that also marked him as a politician of another era: He was florid, theatrical; his voice broke in sadness and rose in rage.

He portrayed himself as a casualty of a partisan war being fought through attacks on the personal ethics of politicians, and he urged a truce. His parting wish: "All of us, in both political parties, must resolve to bring this period of mindless cannibalism to an end."

But Wright's speakership was remarkable not only for the unprecedented ethics controversy that overwhelmed it. He also presided over a term that was one the most legislatively productive in a generation.

From the outset, Wright made it clear he wanted to be a strong Speaker. He wanted to leave his stamp on national policy, not on the minutiae of procedures. He wanted to produce not just legislation, but an entire Democratic program.

A man of obvious ability, Wright was a forceful leader, not one to be paralyzed by the complexity of problems. He brought to the job a sharp mind and willingness to do the kind of homework that his predecessor, Thomas P. O'Neill Jr., often left to others. The Massachusetts Democrat cared little for legislative detail; Wright's involvement verged on micromanagement.

He spelled out his legislative agenda for the House early in 1987 with a precision and scope unthinkable under O'Neill. He took whatever political risks necessary to get it passed.

Wright began his speakership calling for higher taxes to cut the deficit, and by year's end he seemed vindicated when President Reagan altered his position and signed a modest tax increase into law.

The course of U.S. policy in Nicaragua was altered by Wright's personal involvement in late 1987. But his efforts to foster a regional peace process were criticized by the Reagan administration as an unwarranted intrusion into executive branch powers.

Wright got much of the credit for other major accomplishments of the 100th Congress, which enacted landmark welfare, health and trade laws and passed all 13 annual appropriations bills on time in 1988.

Wright's Democratic colleagues took pride in the legislative record of his speakership, but many resented being excluded from the process of compiling it. Sometimes called the "Lone Ranger," Wright had a record of springing major decisions — on matters from tax policy to Central America to the ill-fated congressional pay raise of early 1989 — without consulting key colleagues.

If Democrats sometimes felt excluded, Republicans often felt mistreated by Wright's hardball pursuit of his legislative goals.

The red-letter date in the Republican history of Wright trespasses was Oct. 29, 1987 — the day Wright mounted an extraordinary effort to win passage of a controversial budget bill. In the final roll call, preserved on videotape by bitter Republicans, a Democrat's decisive vote was switched after a 10-minute delay and after Wright had declared time for voting had expired.

Incidents like that tapped into longstanding GOP suspicions of Wright's partisanship. Even while Wright was majority leader, critics charged that the more statesmanlike he sounded on the House floor, the less statesmanlike he intended to be.

"You watch him and you know when he's going to get partisan," a member of the House GOP leadership once said. "The eyebrows start to rise. The voice begins to stretch out. And the Republicans say, 'Snake oil is at it again.' "

Wright's personal style did little to allay the uneasiness of Democrats and mistrust of Republicans. A remote man who seemed to have few close friends, Wright had a reputation for having a hair-trigger temper. He was as private as O'Neill was affable and open. He never commanded the same affection and reverence from his colleagues as O'Neill did.

All that left Wright with a shallow reservoir of support in his hour of political need — even though he had faced no opposition to his selection as Speaker by the Democratic Caucus in December 1986.

Wright had campaigned for Speaker throughout his 10 years as majority leader. He devoted months of precious time to public appearances and fund-raising missions in districts represented by the junior Democrats whose votes would control the speakership election.

By January 1985, two full years before the speakership vote, Wright was ready to make what he hoped would be a pre-emptive announcement. He declared that he had commitments from 184 House Democrats — far more than the majority he would need to win.

To get to that position of strength, Wright had worked hard in his latter years as majority leader to put behind him some of the issues on which he was vulnerable.

Sensitive to complaints that he was too beholden to Texas oil interests, Wright kept a low profile on issues of parochial interest as his elevation to Speaker neared. He was a longstanding, ardent supporter of the Synthetic Fuels Corporation, but he did not sacrifice any of his credibility as a national leader by trying to block the 1985 drive to kill it.

Wright opposed the tax-code overhaul enacted in 1986, as did many members from energy-producing states who objected to its treatment of the oil industry. But Wright, a proponent of raising taxes to reduce the deficit, insisted he objected to the bill not on parochial grounds but because it would worsen the deficit problem. With the rest of the leadership behind the bill, Wright limited his offensive against it largely to a speech in a closed caucus meeting.

He also took steps to quell suspicions that he was too conservative to lead the predominantly liberal House Democratic Caucus. Throughout his career as majority leader, he was suspect among some of the younger liberal Democrats chosen in 1974 and later. Wright's foreign policy views always seemed a shade too hawkish for those Democrats nurtured in the anti-war politics of the early 1970s.

He created a real problem for himself in April 1983 by voting to support President Reagan's request for funds to deploy the MX missile. Wright was joined in this vote by Foley, who was then majority whip, and several other key Democrats. But in Wright's case, it sent a politically damaging signal — it left some colleagues asking why their leader was helping to enact the Reagan defense program.

Two months after the vote, at the insistence of freshman Rep. Jim Bates of California, House Democrats met in caucus to discuss the issue. After that caucus, neither Wright nor Foley voted for the MX. Wright insisted there was no connection — "I'm just re-examining my priorities," he said in late 1983 — but there was no question his switch defused a potentially significant liability.

On economic issues, Wright never needed to prove himself to his party — he was a mainstream Democrat. Responding to the Reagan economic initiatives of the early 1980s, he was if anything more vocal in his indignation than most junior members.

Few Democrats thought of Wright as a likely winner in 1976 when he announced for majority leader, offering himself as an alternative to the bitterly antagonistic front-runners, Richard Bolling of Missouri and Phillip Burton of California. But he eliminated Bolling by three votes on the second ballot and Burton by one vote on the third.

The Texan had one enormous advantage. Unlike his two rivals, he had few enemies. And having served two decades on the Public Works Committee, Wright had done countless small favors, making sure there was a water project here or a federal building there. He reminded New Yorkers that he had voted for federal aid to their city. He noted that one-third of the House Democrats came from Southern and Southwestern states and said they deserved a spot in the leadership. It was a successful strategy.

Wright's years on Public Works left their unmistakable stamp on his politics. He was a bread-and-butter Democrat who spoke in proud terms about the roads, dams and other forms of tangible government largess in which his old committee specializes.

His days on the Public Works Committee in the expansionist 1950s and 1960s were clearly reflected in the maxim Wright often repeated in his 34 years in Congress: "I believe we make a bigger mistake when we think too small than when we think too big." No one would ever fault Wright, in his short-lived speakership, of ever thinking too small.

Throughout Wright's political ordeal in Washington, he never lost the support of his constituents in the Fort Worth-based 12th. Although the National Republican Congressional Committee threatened to make Wright its No. 1 target in the 1990 House elections, he had heard that sort of bold talk in years past. In fact, the GOP had never devised a consistent electoral strategy for dealing with Wright.

Sometimes, the GOP felt compelled to challenge him, hoping to sell the line that his position in the House leadership had led him to support national Democratic policies too liberal for his constituency. Almost as often, however, GOP strategists despaired of defeating Wright, and left him alone in hopes that his organization would not arise and deliver voters who would hamper other GOP candidates.

Such was the case in 1988, when Texas Republicans were hesitant to mount major drives against senior congressional Democrats, beginning with Sen. Lloyd Bentsen, whose organization hurt them in 1982. In the House, 11 of the 17 Texas House Democrats got a pass. Wright was a beneficiary of this apparent strategy, despite the intense unhappiness his performance had inspired among Republicans nationally.

State party leaders had also followed the "hands-off" course through most of the 1970s. Wright was so secure at home during that period that he was able to devote most of his campaigning time to other Democrats across the country. This field work augmented Wright's influence in the House; candidates elected with his help often became allies.

In 1980, however, the national GOP decided to take a serious shot at Wright, partly just to keep him occupied at home, but also to see whether he had lost touch with Tarrant County, which was being lured rightward by the candidacy of Ronald Reagan.

The Republican nominee was Jim Bradshaw, a former mayor pro tempore of Fort Worth who denounced Wright as beholden to liberals and the Washington establishment. Bradshaw — young, well-known and articulate — convinced conservative money-givers that Wright could be beaten; the Republican collected more than $600,000 from local and national sources.

But Wright would not be outdone. He raised and spent more than $1.1 million, using the money to tout his congressional influence and his ability to draw military contracts and other federal plums to Fort Worth. He even sent a letter to local businessmen, telling them to back Bradshaw if they wished, but reminding them he would still be around and would remember it. Wright retained his seat with ease, winning 60 percent of the vote even though Reagan carried the 12th over Jimmy Carter in presidential voting.

Coming on the heels of such a costly defeat, GOP leaders decided to offer minimal resistance to Wright in 1982. Only carpenter Jim Ryan entered the GOP primary; outspent by more than 10-to-1, he won fewer than one-third of the November ballots. Republicans did not even bother to field a candidate in 1984.

By 1986, however, some area Republicans were ready again to do battle with Wright. Their standard-bearer was Fort Worth business executive Don McNiel, a Democrat-turned-Republican and self-made millionaire.

McNiel's efforts were engineered by Southern Political Consultants (SPC), a group of Houston-based analysts who earned a reputation as upset-makers when they helped create surprise GOP victories in the 13th and 26th districts in 1984.

This time, however, SPC chose too tough a giant to slay. McNiel tried to suggest that Wright was soft on crime, but Wright was receiving a flood of publicity at the time for his role in pushing through the House an omnibus drug bill. Wright racked up nearly 70 percent.

For virtually his entire adult life, Wright was immersed in politics. In 1946, shortly after returning from combat in the South Pacific, he won a seat in the Texas Legislature. He lost a re-election bid two years later, but in 1950 began a four-year tenure as mayor of Weatherford, a small town about 20 miles west of Fort Worth. In 1953, he served as president of the League of Texas Municipalities.

Wright was known in those years as a liberal crusader, thanks to his support for anti-lynching legislation and for federal school aid. In 1954 he challenged the conservative House incumbent, Rep. Wingate Lucas, in the Democratic primary. Wright was opposed by much of the Fort Worth business establishment, but he turned that to his advantage by portraying himself as the candidate of the average man. He went on to defeat Lucas by a margin of about 3-to-2.

Once established in the House, and recognized as a young man of talent and ambition, Wright had to decide whether to stay there. "You reach the point," he complained, "where you're not expanding your influence." The Senate beckoned, and in April 1961 he ran in a special election for the seat vacated by Vice President Johnson. The field of more than 70 candidates badly split the Democratic vote, and Texas elected John G. Tower, its first Republican senator since Reconstruction. Wright placed third, narrowly missing a runoff he probably would have won.

Wright next considered running for governor, but gave it up and began to aim for a 1966 Senate campaign. His vote the year before to repeal state "right-to-work" laws increased his following in organized labor, but it chilled his support in the Texas business community and made it difficult for him to raise money. Low on funds, he made an emotional statewide telecast appealing for $10 contributions to the half-million-dollar fund he said he would need for the race. Only $48,000 flowed in, mostly from his district, and Wright was forced to abandon his candidacy.

District Vote For President

	1988	1984	1980	1976
D	66,906 (47%)	69,159 (41%)	77,202 (48%)	74,846 (53%)
R	75,808 (53%)	97,951 (59%)	79,254 (49%)	63,612 (45%)
I			3,272 (2%)	

13 Bill Sarpalius (D)

Of Amarillo — Elected 1988

Born: Jan. 10, 1948, Los Angeles, Calif.
Education: Texas Tech U., B.A. 1972; West Texas State U., M.A. 1978.
Occupation: Agriculture consultant.
Family: Divorced; one child.
Religion: Methodist.
Political Career: Texas Senate, 1981-89.
Capitol Office: 1223 Longworth Bldg. 20515; 225-3706.

The Path to Washington: By the time Sarpalius ran for the House, the odds makers had given up betting against him. He was a long shot when he first ran for office in 1980, and despite the poor climate for Democrats that year, he managed to upset an incumbent Republican state senator in a decidedly conservative district. Eight years later, when two-term GOP Rep. Beau Boulter ran for the Senate, leaving the 13th open, Sarpalius became the logical choice to recapture the district, which the Democrats had controlled for a decade up to 1985.

Being the favorite, however, was an altogether unfamiliar position for Sarpalius: His compelling — sometimes disturbing — personal saga, well-known to Panhandle voters, is an integral part of his political persona. Struck with polio as a child, Sarpalius was abandoned by his father at age 10. Two years later, his mother, an alcoholic, decided she could not handle Sarpalius and his two younger brothers, and they were sent from their Houston home to Cal Farley's Boys Ranch, a home for wayward boys 40 miles northwest of Amarillo.

In his last year of high school there, Sarpalius became Texas president of the Future Farmers of America. After college, he taught ag-tech at Boys Ranch and earned a master's degree in agriculture. He joined a private agribusiness concern and then won his state Senate seat in 1980. He won re-election in 1984.

Nicknamed "Applecheeks" in Austin, the Democrat served as the Agriculture Committee chairman in his last term. Although he was not considered a legislative heavyweight in the capital, Sarpalius had his greatest success when legislation intersected with his life experience.

A leading advocate of measures to impose stricter penalties on drunk drivers and to prohibit open containers of alcohol in cars, Sarpalius considers the establishment of the Texas Commission on Alcohol and Drug Abuse his most significant accomplishment. Among other things, the program was designed to help substance abusers who cannot afford expensive treatment centers. Sarpalius said he understood this need after having hitchhiked across Texas with his mother in a fruitless search for a center that would help her.

Sarpalius also backed legislation to improve rural ambulance service, which proved lifesaving to him when he broke his back in a 1986 accident on an all-terrain vehicle (ATV). Afterwards, he advocated legislation mandating helmets for ATV riders. Sarpalius figures he would have been killed in the accident had he not been wearing headgear.

But while these legislative actions earned Sarpalius mostly positive headlines, his image was tarnished by an after-midnight incident at Amarillo's Caravan Club in January 1988. Shortly after announcing his candidacy, the recently divorced Sarpalius had gone to celebrate his birthday at the club, where he wound up with his jaw broken in what he claimed from the outset was a setup. A blood-alcohol test that he requested revealed he had not been drinking; subsequent investigations indicated that his assailant was paid by the bar owner to attack him.

Sarpalius' jaw was wired shut for six weeks after the bar incident. The dissonance between this and his Boy Scout image caused concern among some voters. But Sarpalius' sophisticated campaign operation and his wide name-recognition enabled him to win a majority in a three-way primary.

In the general election, these assets were augmented by the relative weakness of his Republican opponent, Larry Milner. A former chamber of commerce director and utility lobbyist, Milner remained financially competitive in part because of the hope that George Bush's and Boulter's coattails would pull him along.

But his campaign never seriously threatened Sarpalius, who had already represented the most conservative two-thirds of the district in the Legislature and who easily garnered the votes of the district's Democrats.

Once in Washington, Sarpalius got off to a good early start. He was elected vice president of the freshman Democratic class, and was the only first-term Democrat to win assignment to the Agriculture Committee.

Texas 13

The Panhandle — Amarillo; Wichita Falls

The 13th is one of the more competitive two-party districts in Texas. Republicans generally rule in the Panhandle and Democrats typically hold sway in the Red River Valley to the south. But the voters are uniformly conservative. Of the 37 counties now in the 13th, 34 voted for Ronald Reagan in 1984, and 31 went for George Bush in 1988.

Because of its scant rainfall, most of this region traditionally was used only for cattle grazing. But discovery of underground water supplies in the 1940s sparked cultivation of wheat, cotton and sorghum grains on huge, highly mechanized farms. The agricultural revolution has been extensive enough to concern public officials about the condition of the Ogallala aquifer. It is slowly receding, and officials estimate that it will dry up within 40 years. Investigation has begun into alternative hydrogeneration projects.

In the farm-boom years of the 1970s, some of the wheat farmers and cattle ranchers went heavily into debt to finance expansion — a strategy that clobbered them when interest rates rose and prices dropped. As long ago as 1979, before the 1980s spate of hard-times-on-the-farm demonstrations, the 13th was well represented when the American Agriculture Movement brought its tractors to Washington to protest low farm prices.

Amarillo (Potter and Randall counties) is a city of nearly 166,000 that serves as the focal point of the Panhandle's farm lands. Its factories pack meat, mill flour and handle oil and natural gas drilled locally. Like the rural areas surrounding it, Amarillo is Republican. Potter County gave GOP Senate candidate — and 13th District incumbent — Beau Boulter a slight advantage in his 1988 Senate challenge to Lloyd Bentsen. It also gave George Bush 62 percent in the presidential contest. Randall County is more solidly Republican territory. Boulter received 61 percent in Randall, while Bush cleared 75 percent. In 1984, Potter gave GOP Senate nominee Phil Gramm 66 percent; Randall gave Gramm 78 percent.

More than 200 miles to the southeast is Wichita Falls (Wichita County), an area whose Democratic affections are the cornerstone of any successful Democratic campaign in the 13th. Wichita voted Democratic in contests for the Senate and the governorship in 1982, but four years later it went narrowly for Republican William P. Clements Jr. in his gubernatorial comeback.

In 1988, Wichita County voted for Democrats Bentsen and Sarpalius, giving each more than 55 percent. However, the county went Republican for president, giving Bush 56 percent of its vote. Wichita Falls has a large industrial sector that makes fiberglass products, wearing apparel and mechanical parts. North of the city is Sheppard Air Force Base, one of the Air Force's largest training facilities and headquarters to the NATO Jet Training Center.

Population: 526,840. White 470,444 (89%), Black 27,091 (5%), Other 5,948 (1%). Spanish origin 46,875 (9%). 18 and over 376,878 (72%), 65 and over 66,383 (13%). Median age: 30.

Committees

Agriculture (23rd of 27 Democrats)
Conservation, Credit and Rural Development; Cotton, Rice and Sugar; Domestic Marketing, Consumer Relations and Nutrition; Wheat, Soybeans and Feed Grains

Select Children, Youth and Families (18th of 18 Democrats)

Small Business (23rd of 27 Democrats)
Procurement, Tourism and Rural Development

Campaign Finance

	Receipts	Receipts from PACs	Expend-itures
1988			
Sarpalius (D)	$387,092	$233,950 (60%)	$384,738
Milner (R)	$483,932	$143,422 (30%)	$476,220

Elections

1988 General		
Bill Sarpalius (D)	98,345	(52%)
Larry S. Milner (R)	89,105	(48%)
1988 Primary		
Bill Sarpalius (D)	37,745	(55%)
Ed Lehman (D)	19,629	(29%)
Randy Hollums (D)	10,755	(16%)

District Vote For President

	1988	1984	1980	1976
D	68,739 (36%)	50,436 (25%)	68,648 (36%)	90,518 (50%)
R	121,121 (64%)	152,448 (75%)	117,716 (62%)	90,173 (50%)
I			3,076 (2%)	

14 Greg Laughlin (D)

Of West Columbia — Elected 1988

Born: Jan. 21, 1942, Bay City, Texas.
Education: Texas A&M U., B.A. 1964; U. of Texas, LL.B. 1967.
Military Career: Army, 1968-70; Army Reserve, 1964-67, 1970-present.
Occupation: Lawyer.
Family: Wife, Ginger Jones; two children.
Religion: Methodist.
Political Career: Democratic nominee for U.S. House, 1986.
Capitol Office: 1022 Longworth Bldg. 20515; 225-2831.

The Path to Washington: Laughlin began his legal career in the metropolis of Houston, which looms just outside this sprawling, primarily rural district. But he does not cotton to being called an outsider. He can point to six generations of ancestors who came to this part of Texas as long ago as 1818 — "a generation before the Texas Revolution."

Laughlin grew up in a small town in Brazoria County, between Houston and the Gulf of Mexico. He went away to college and law school, then served as an intelligence officer in the Army and as an assistant district attorney in Houston. He later entered private practice there. But he wants it understood that he "did move family, home and business back to the district before [he] ran for anything."

Laughlin has handled personal injury cases. But he bristled when, late in the 1988 campaign, GOP Rep. Mac Sweeney sent out campaign literature portraying him as an ambulance chaser. The ad featured a mock advertisement for Laughlin's legal services, and it included a heavy-handed appeal to Hispanics, prompting some to denounce the mailing as subtly racist. The mailing was also criticized by lawyers' organizations and may have helped lift Laughlin to his solid 53 percent majority.

Laughlin had been interested in the 14th ever since its Democratic occupant, Bill Patman (son of the legendary Rep. Wright Patman), lost in 1984. Sweeney, then a 29-year-old administrative aide in the White House, was swept in on President Reagan's re-election tide. Laughlin got the nomination to challenge the young Republican incumbent in 1986. But it was Laughlin's first run for office and he was not well-known. He could only raise and spend less than half Sweeney's funds. And yet, the novice candidate got 48 percent of the vote.

In 1988, more than a dozen unsuccessful challengers from 1986 were back for rematches against incumbents. Laughlin was one of just two who succeeded. He was also one of only three Democrats to defeat a GOP incumbent.

He began by turning aside a Democratic rival in the March primary. He proceeded to raise more than $600,000 — enough to put him on competitive footing financially.

Just as important, Laughlin went beyond the attacks on Sweeney's office problems that had been the staple of his 1986 campaign. Laughlin presented himself as a conservative Democrat in the old school, a man who had prosecuted criminals and who still served as a lieutenant colonel in the Army Reserve.

When drug testing became an issue late in the campaign, Laughlin volunteered to be tested. Sweeney, who had voted for bills requiring the testing of some federal employees, hesitated before agreeing to be tested.

Laughlin's conservative self-portrait was highlighted in campaign appearances by the likes of Sen. Al Gore of Tennessee and Rep. Charles W. Stenholm, a fellow Texan and one of the most conservative Democrats in Congress. Perhaps most important of all was the presence on the ballot of Sen. Lloyd Bentsen, enduring symbol of Texas' Tory Democrats. In November, Texan George Bush carried the district; but Bentsen cut the coattails by taking the 14th with more than 60 percent.

Laughlin's final assist came from the incumbent himself. Sweeney had the second-worst voting attendance record among Texas' 27 House members in 1988. He was also said to have missed numerous opportunities to meet with constituents and address their problems, both in Washington and at home. And he generated bad publicity with his handling of a local toxic-dump issue late in the campaign.

Laughlin, winning 18 of the district's 22 counties, pledged a new devotion to close-to-home issues. While he said he would enjoy a seat on the Armed Services Committee (where Sweeney sat), instead he asked for — and received — Public Works and Transportation (which had just lost its lone Texas Democrat) and Merchant Marine and Fisheries, where the district has more immediate business.

Texas 14

Southeast; Gulf Coast

The 14th sprawls from suburban Austin to the Gulf Coast, but its core is small-town East Texas, where social life revolves around a few local cafés, and the barbershop is still a vital conduit for community news.

Victoria, with 57,000 people, is the district's only sizable city. Once dominated by its cattle and cotton trade, Victoria today has an economy driven by petrochemicals, oil-field equipment and steel products.

Although the economy has lost some of its drive in recent years due to the decline in the oil industry, it is starting to pick up due to the new emphasis on petrochemical development.

The areas within the 14th that rely on oil production, primarily in the north, are stagnating. However, the refining sector of the industry is booming, with an influx of petrochemical concerns to the coastal counties. The $3 billion Formosa Plastics Plant is located in Point Comfort, across Lavaca Bay from Port Lavaca. Up the coast in the portion of Brazoria County in the 14th is the Phillips Petroleum refining complex in Sweeny. The company recently announced that the facility would undergo a $300 million expansion.

Both Victoria and surrounding Victoria County grew by more than 10 percent in the 1980s. The prevailing political climate is conservative, but not necessarily Republican. On the state level, there is considerable support for Democrats. But in races for federal office, the district's conservatism places it more often in the Republican column. In 1988, Laughlin won Victoria County by 22 votes. In the presidential race, the county gave George Bush 62 percent of its vote.

While much of the rural territory outside Victoria traditionally has had a more Democratic cast, conservatism is more important than party label. Burleson County, at the district's northern end, followed Victoria County's example, voting for Laughlin and Bush.

North of Victoria, Jackson and Wharton counties anchor a major southeast Texas rice belt. This part of the district has another, recently publicized claim to fame: LaGrange, the seat of Fayette County, was the site of a brothel made famous in the musical "The Best Little Whorehouse in Texas."

At the district's northern end, the demise of the oil industry has created a new emphasis on agriculture, with grain sorghums among the leading crops. Cattle ranching also plays an important role in the area's economy. The Brenham area of Washington County is home to a number of thoroughbred horse farms, products of a recent Texas law permitting betting on horse racing. Along the coast, in the southern end of the district, aquaculture — farming fish in ponds for commercial use — is a growing industry.

Minorities make up about one-third of the 14th's population. Most of the Hispanics are grouped in the district's southwestern counties; blacks are concentrated in the northeastern part of the district. The district also has more people of German ancestry than any other in the state.

Population: 526,920. White 421,921 (80%), Black 60,531 (12%), Other 3,131 (1%). Spanish origin 105,659 (20%). 18 and over 368,619 (70%), 65 and over 70,506 (13%). Median age: 30.

Committees

Merchant Marine and Fisheries (24th of 26 Democrats)
Coast Guard and Navigation; Merchant Marine; Panama Canal/Outer Continental Shelf

Public Works and Transportation (29th of 31 Democrats)
Aviation; Surface Transportation; Water Resources

Campaign Finance

	Receipts	Receipts from PACs	Expend-itures
1988			
Laughlin (D)	$623,491	$240,699 (39%)	$600,114
Sweeney (R)	$637,167	$240,154 (38%)	$645,988

Elections

1988 General

Greg Laughlin (D)	111,395	(53%)
Mac Sweeney (R)	96,042	(46%)

1988 Primary

Greg Laughlin (D)	59,213	(72%)
Michael L. Herzik (D)	22,770	(28%)

District Vote For President

	1988	1984	1980	1976
D	89,840 (43%)	66,718 (32%)	67,989 (41%)	71,983 (53%)
R	121,148 (57%)	138,615 (67%)	95,107 (57%)	64,145 (47%)
I			2,928 (2%)	

15 E. "Kika" de la Garza (D)

Of Mission — Elected 1964

Born: Sept. 22, 1927, Mercedes, Texas.
Education: St. Mary's U., LL.B. 1952.
Military Career: Navy, 1945-46; Army, 1950-52.
Occupation: Lawyer.
Family: Wife, Lucille Alamia; three children.
Religion: Roman Catholic.
Political Career: Texas House, 1953-65.
Capitol Office: 1401 Longworth Bldg. 20515; 225-2531.

In Washington: Like a good host, de la Garza works hard to see that the members of his Agriculture Committee are happy. As chairman, he goes out of his way to cultivate them, establish a climate of good will and facilitate the passage of some of the most complex and difficult legislation before the House.

De la Garza frequently travels to the districts of junior colleagues to help with their campaigns, and steers political action funds their way. When the time comes to pick members of a conference committee on a bill, he tries to include at least one freshman. His press releases routinely credit the accomplishments of other members of the panel, including Republicans, many of whom play a major role on what is one of the least partisan committees in the institution.

That is not to say that everything goes smoothly in committee. During work on a bill to save the financially ailing Farm Credit System in 1987, there was an unusual amount of partisan bickering. Unable to work out a compromise with leading members of the committee, de la Garza, under pressure from the House leadership and System banks to move a bill, introduced his own legislation weighted toward Texas banks. The bill prompted ranking Republican Edward Madigan, widely known as a cooperative legislator, to resort to obstructionist tactics — for the first time in committee staffers' memories.

But from that point, a measure began to take shape as de la Garza pursued his normal Democratic approach to legislating. He tends to control his committee by not controlling it too much; to put the wrangling to rest on the Farm Credit bill, de la Garza set up committee task forces to hammer out compromises on the most contentious issues. One of those was the establishment of a secondary market for agricultural loans, a provision sought by banks and insurance companies as part of the overall rescue package. Proponents said the plan, allowing lenders to diversify risk by pooling loans and selling them to others, would allow small banks and insurance companies to make more farm loans. Critics felt it would permit commercial lenders to take away much of the land-loan market from the Farm Credit System, undermining its recovery.

Under de la Garza's watch, the panel produced a sweeping reorganization of the Farm Credit System, which passed 41-2.

"No one is entirely happy," he said. "But then no one's saying it's a no-good communist bill. It's somewhere in the middle, which is what good legislation should be."

More compromise was required on the floor, as some aspects of the bill caused disputes with other committee chairman, such as Energy and Commerce Chairman John D. Dingell. But de la Garza worked on alterations to win them over, producing a bill that passed the full House 365-18.

After spending most of this decade perfecting his role as chairman, de la Garza has a good sense of how to pass cumbersome legislation. When Congress began work on the 1985 farm reauthorization, he made it clear he was opposed to President Reagan's call for drastic cuts in agricultural spending. But he saw himself as the coordinator of the massive farm bill, rather than the craftsman of its individual parts. Stressing his role as facilitator, he gave his Agriculture subcommittees considerable freedom to draw up the various sections of the legislation.

De la Garza's approach enabled him to keep the unwieldy farm bill together, and it helped him maintain an effective working arrangement with his predecessor as chairman, Thomas S. Foley of Washington, despite tensions that had existed between the two in previous Congresses. When he first took the chairmanship, de la Garza had been reluctant to consult Foley on much of the committee's business. But in the 99th Congress he deferred willingly to Foley on wheat and feed grains, a major portion of the bill.

Trying to guide his legislation through the House, de la Garza worked steadily with com-

Texas 15

South — McAllen

The 15th is the most heavily Hispanic district in Texas (more than 70 percent of the population), and one of the most faithfully Democratic non-inner city constituencies in the South. In 1988 presidential voting, the 15th was Michael S. Dukakis' best district in Texas outside the all-urban 18th (Houston) and 20th (San Antonio). The Democratic nominee won 63 percent in the 15th.

The economic boom that transformed much of the Southwest in the 1970s and early 1980s touched the Rio Grande Valley, significantly boosting the population in the district's three southernmost counties. But the growth has not brought economic stability.

The 15th District's economy was buffeted by a series of shocks earlier this decade from which it is only now beginning to rebound. The border economy, quite dependent on retail sales, was crippled by the devaluation of the Mexican peso in the early 1980s; Mexicans who flocked across the border to shop in McAllen and other towns in the 15th could no longer afford the goods offered there, and numerous businesses closed.

Even the agriculture industry, the valley's traditional economic base, has suffered in recent years. Traditionally immune to freezes, the area usually enjoys a year-round growing season that produces an abundance of grapefruit and other citrus, vegetables, cotton and grain. But the valley did see freezes in the mid-1980s, and there was considerable crop damage.

Lately, though, the economic outlook has been brightening. Citrus production has rebounded, as have retail sales; McAllen businesses tailored their marketing campaigns to appeal as much to American consumers as to Mexican ones.

There has been a resurgence of jobs on both sides of the border with the blossoming of "maquiladoras," or twin plants. Under this system, Mexican assembly plants receive parts and assemble them into finished products using low-cost labor. The products then are transferred to facilities just across the border in the U.S. that handle distribution.

Tourism remains a reliable revenue producer, with visitors drawn by the sun and the chance to shop and sightsee in Mexico.

North of the valley, beef cattle and other livestock roam the ranches, and feed grains grow well there. When oil and gas prices are strong, their extraction augments the local agrarian economy.

Hidalgo County, home to some 366,000 people, is the district's largest population center. Located on the Texas-Mexico border, it is anchored by McAllen, a major port of entry into Mexico and an important foreign trade center.

Outside of Hidalgo, the most populous county is San Patricio, with just under 62,000 people. San Patricio is closely linked economically to the port city of Corpus Christi, which lies just across the bay in the 27th District.

Republicans have made inroads in San Patricio, and in the rural counties located at the district's northern end. But farther south, Hidalgo County is solidly Democratic, as are such heavily Hispanic rural counties as Duval, Brooks and Jim Hogg.

Population: 527,203. White 450,853 (86%), Black 2,486 (1%). Spanish origin 378,195 (72%). 18 and over 329,023 (62%), 65 and over 52,916 (10%). Median age: 25.

mittee members to avoid having it ambushed on the floor by those who opposed it. He was careful to keep members of his committee apprised of events as they developed. Later, in conference with the Senate, he continued the facilitator's role, allowing Foley to do much of the negotiating on key points.

De la Garza's efforts did not produce a farm bill that clearly bore his imprint, but they did produce a bill that passed the House, and by a lopsided vote, in contrast to the two-vote margin by which the previous bill had cleared Congress in 1981. While the 1985 bill did not wholly satisfy all the agricultural factions involved, it left few strongly dissatisfied. It did not promise the high price levels sought by many farm-state members, but it also did not reflect the deep cuts sought by the Reagan administration. Equally important for de la Garza, who has been watchful of challenges within the committee since he was narrowly elected chairman in 1981, his efforts left the overwhelming majority on the panel satisfied with his stewardship.

In the deficit-conscious climate that has prevailed for much of the 1980s (and seems likely to persist into the 1990s), de la Garza must worry about attacks on farm spending from urban and suburban members. When working on a multibillion-dollar drought-relief measure in 1988 — the broadest relief measure to date — de la Garza first had to work hard to fight off special-interest add-ons. "Even Santa Claus doesn't give you everything you want," he said. Then, presenting the bill to his colleagues, he sought to assure them it was not a federal giveaway. He said it allowed farmers to pay "the feedman, the fertilizer man, the hardware man, the implement dealer, the tax collector. That's where the money goes." The bill passed 368-29.

De la Garza's cooperative style is a benefit within his committee, but he is forced into a more confrontational role when waging turf fights with other panels. During work on a supplemental appropriations bill in 1987, Appropriations Chairman Jamie L. Whitten included $10 million for Agriculture Department studies on mandatory production controls. De la Garza complained that the policy was unrealistic and the maneuver an encroachment on his jurisdiction.

"How many days of hearings did you have?" he demanded. Whitten shot back, "I've been doing this for 39 years!" After some discussion, de la Garza agreed not to move against the studies, and an effort by a third party to do so failed by a wide margin.

De la Garza is a man capable of considerable personal charm, an amateur linguist and gourmet cook who converses with foreign dignitaries in their own languages. But as a descendant of Spanish land-grantees who came to South Texas in the 18th century, he has sometimes displayed an arrogance that made personal relations difficult.

In his earlier years on the Agriculture Committee, de la Garza was known to ridicule the idiosyncrasies of colleagues in a manner that was meant to be funny but was often taken as an insult. Outside the committee, his voting record sometimes frustrated liberal Democrats who found him reluctant to identify with liberal Hispanics of less impressive background. Both these tendencies were factors in his unexpectedly narrow 110-92 election to the Agriculture chairmanship in 1981.

"The thing about all this Chicano and Mexican-American and so forth," he once told a reporter, "is that the Spanish-speaking are members of the white race. Period. Finis."

On Agriculture, he has always paid close attention to the crops of South Texas — sugar and cotton — and to the area's water problems. During his first decade in the House, he worked hardest to obtain a federal sugar allotment for his growers and a project to control the level of salt in the Rio Grande on the Mexican border. Salt in the river's water was making it difficult to irrigate the district's farms.

As he moved toward a senior position on Agriculture, de la Garza continued to be a spokesman for sugar growers. In 1977, when major farm legislation became law, he successfully amended it to set up a sugar price support program similar to the ones for other crops. The next year, arguing that the newly enacted price supports had not been sufficient to keep the industry prosperous, he sponsored a bill to return to a system of strict quotas and fees that would limit the amount of foreign sugar entering the United States. A plan similar to this was later implemented.

De la Garza supports his South Texas growers in their demand for an ample supply of farm workers to help harvest perishable crops. When the House debated immigration policy in 1984, he argued for an Agriculture Committee amendment that established a new "guest worker" program for foreign labor. Agribusiness interests from all over the country backed that effort; Hispanics opposed it. De la Garza was the only member of the Congressional Hispanic Caucus who voted for the amendment, which passed the House. But de la Garza disagreed with other parts of the immigration package and voted against it in 1984 and in 1986. It finally became law in the 99th Congress.

At Home: The election of de la Garza in 1964 was a milestone of sorts for South Texas Hispanics, who had always been the dominant population group in the 15th District but had never elected one of their own.

It was not, however, a political revolution. The new congressman was backed by the same "Anglo" business interests that had sent Democrats Lloyd Bentsen and Joe Kilgore to Congress in the 1950s. In six terms in the Texas Legislature, de la Garza had maintained a conservative voting record and had opposed passage of a state civil rights bill.

With Kilgore's retirement in 1964, the Democratic primary ended in a runoff between de la Garza and state Rep. Lindsey Rodriguez, an ardent supporter of the Johnson administration and the liberal 1964 Democratic platform. De la Garza featured a photograph of Johnson in his campaign literature, but hedged in his commitment to the platform or the Democratic administration.

Rodriguez had the support of PASO (Political Association of Spanish-speaking Organizations), which had succeeded in electing Hispanic slates in several Texas localities. He accused de la Garza, as a descendant of Spanish land-grantees, of being aloof from the problems that faced the large mass of poor Hispanics in the district. De la Garza, he complained, was no more than a puppet for the wealthy "Anglo" business establishment.

While de la Garza's business supporters were controversial, they did provide him a campaign budget that dwarfed Rodriguez', and gave him the courthouse machine backing that traditionally has won elections here. De la Garza coasted to victory by a margin of nearly 2-to-1. That fall he won the seat over nominal GOP opposition by an even wider margin.

Since the 15th is one of Texas' Democratic strongholds, de la Garza has had no trouble in general elections. In his 12 re-elections since 1964, the GOP has offered opposition only four times, and in each instance de la Garza drew at least 65 percent of the vote. Only two times has he had primary opposition, and on both occasions he won handily.

Committee

Agriculture (Chairman)

Elections

1988 General

E. "Kika" de la Garza (D)	93,672	(94%)
Gloria Joyce Hendrix (LIB)	6,133	(6%)

1986 General

E. "Kika" de la Garza (D)	70,777	(100%)

Previous Winning Percentages: **1984** (100%) **1982** (96%) **1980** (70%) **1978** (66%) **1976** (74%) **1974** (100%) **1972** (100%) **1970** (76%) **1968** (100%) **1966** (100%) **1964** (69%)

District Vote For President

	1988	1984	1980	1976
D	109,732 (63%)	89,836 (54%)	79,071 (56%)	84,143 (67%)
R	64,204 (37%)	77,440 (46%)	58,582 (42%)	40,776 (33%)

Campaign Finance

	Receipts	Receipts from PACs	Expend-itures
1988			
de la Garza (D)	$263,843	$127,452 (48%)	$219,469
1986			
de la Garza (D)	$169,003	$134,500 (80%)	$141,973

Key Votes

1987	
Raise speed limit to 65 mph	Y
Approve Gephardt "fair trade" amendment	Y
Ban testing of larger nuclear weapons	Y
Delay "re-flagging" of Kuwaiti tankers	N
Approve tax-raising deficit-reduction bill	Y
1988	
Approve aid to Nicaraguan contras	N
Enact civil rights restoration bill over Reagan veto	Y
Kill 60-day plant-closing notification measure	?
Pass omnibus trade bill over Reagan veto	Y
Approve death penalty for drug-related murders	Y
Bar federal funds for abortions in cases of rape and incest	?
Oppose seven-day waiting period for purchase of handguns	?

Voting Studies

	Presidential Support		Party Unity		Conservative Coalition	
Year	S	O	S	O	S	O
1988	21	57	73	6	32	37
1987	33	59	76	14	65	21
1986	27	64	72	16	64	32
1985	34	59	75	14	60	36
1984	44	46	66	21	59	25
1983	41	50	70	17	61	27
1982	49	32	67	25	67	19
1981	57	39	62	31	68	27

Interest Group Ratings

Year	ADA	ACU	AFL-CIO	CCUS
1988	50	20	73	50
1987	60	5	73	27
1986	55	27	85	39
1985	60	24	76	20
1984	40	43	85	53
1983	50	24	75	42
1982	25	60	61	42
1981	45	40	80	32

16 Ronald D. Coleman (D)

Of El Paso — Elected 1982

Born: Nov. 29, 1941, El Paso, Texas.
Education: U. of Texas, El Paso, B.A. 1963; U. of Texas, Austin, J.D. 1967.
Military Career: Army, 1967-69.
Occupation: Lawyer.
Family: Divorced; two children.
Religion: Presbyterian.
Political Career: Texas House, 1973-83.
Capitol Office: 416 Cannon Bldg. 20515; 225-4831.

In Washington: A hint of partisan arrogance about Coleman, together with his swaggering walk and ever-present thin cigar, prompts comparisons with his senior Texas colleague Jack Brooks, now in his fourth decade as one of Congress' orneriest members. Coleman is not encumbered by Brooks' sort of nasty temperament, but he does have the same legislative skills and instinct for making his way in House politics.

In his previous political life, Coleman was one of the Texas Legislature's most effective members, even though he was an outsider there as the guerrilla leader of a progressive "Gang of Four" (with current House colleague John Bryant) that defied the entrenched conservative leadership.

In Washington, Coleman is squarely in the Democratic mainstream, and also a valued lieutenant to Democratic leaders. Initially he benefited from the patronage of Brooks and then-Majority Leader Jim Wright, but Coleman has steadily established himself as a player in his own right.

Since his second term Coleman has had a coveted seat on the Appropriations Committee, where his savvy and good-humored collegiality allow him to thrive. Since his first term, he has been an at-large whip; as such, he has proven to be good at intelligence-gathering, adept at working the floor and politically gutsy, sticking by the leadership on issues that do not always play so well in conservative West Texas.

For the most part, Coleman has concentrated on parochial matters while cementing his political foundations. As a member of Appropriations' Military Construction Subcommittee, he channels funds to El Paso's Fort Bliss Army base. He also has been a leader, often a lonely one, in addressing the unique problems along the U.S.-Mexico border.

In 1988, Coleman's bid for aid to the "colonias" — squalid border communities lacking basic utilities — reflected both his interest and his legislative technique. When his bill for comprehensive assistance seemed likely to die in at least one of four committees that claimed jurisdiction over its parts, Coleman took the housing portion that the Banking Committee had approved and reintroduced it as a separate bill; with Speaker Wright's help, he took the measure to the House and won unanimous approval in the 100th Congress' last days. Time ran out in the Senate, however.

Early in the 101st Congress, apparently feeling politically secure after his opposition-free 1988 election, Coleman signaled that he intends to broaden his horizons beyond West Texas. To the surprise of Appropriations colleagues, he left the Treasury, Postal Service and General Government Subcommittee to join the one for Foreign Operations.

He already had shown some interest in foreign policy. As a member of House Democrats' whip task force on Nicaragua, he helped mobilize opposition to administration requests for aid to the Nicaraguan contras, not an easy stand to take for a man with border constituents, many of them military retirees.

Well before the Iran-contra scandal broke in November 1986, Coleman was suspicious that Lt. Col. Oliver L. North was covertly financing the contras through a private funding network designed to circumvent a congressional ban on aid. Earlier that year, Coleman had introduced a resolution directing President Reagan to provide the House with information on actions taken by North and other National Security Council personnel in support of the contras. His measure did not reach the floor.

Coleman also has been a champion of improved relations with Mexico. As one of the few "debt hawks" in Congress who follow the issue of Third World debt closely, he agitates in particular for the United States and international bankers to soften Mexico's debt burden to avoid economic and political upheaval there. He also favors bilateral U.S.-Mexico trade negotiations, and sponsored legislation to ease provisions of a 1984 law that limited Mexican

Texas 16

West — El Paso

Although the 16th covers much of far West Texas, eight of every 10 votes in the district are cast in El Paso and the surrounding county of the same name. The 1980 census showed growing El Paso to be Texas' fourth-largest city; today, its population stands just short of one-half million.

El Paso and Ciudad Juarez — its sister city across the Rio Grande — constitute the largest urban concentration on the Mexican-American border. Like many Texas cities hugging the border, El Paso was forced into a difficult economic readjustment by the devaluation of the peso, which has made U.S. goods more expensive for Mexicans used to shopping on the American side of the border.

A key commercial center since the mid-1800s, El Paso has a diversified base of businesses, many of which interact with companies across the border. For instance, there are a number of "twin plant" textile ventures, in which cloth is manufactured on the U.S. side, sent to Mexico (where wages are lower) for assembly into clothing, then sent back to the American side for sale. Copper and oil refining, electronics and food processing plants, and the federal government all provide jobs. The military presence is formidable. The U.S. Army's Fort Bliss is located in El Paso, and many district residents work across the New Mexico state line at the White Sands Missile Range.

The 16th voted Republican for president in 1980 and 1984, but changed course in 1988 and gave the Democratic ticket of Michael S. Dukakis and Texan Lloyd Bentsen 52 percent of its vote. There are a good many Republican votes cast here these days in statewide and local elections, but in most such contests the 16th's traditional conservative Democratic outlook still prevails.

Hispanics make up 60 percent of the population in the 16th and are an important segment of the electorate, although their voter turnout rate is not proportionate to their presence in the population.

Population: 527,401. White 317,443 (60%), Black 19,226 (4%), Other 5,738 (1%). Spanish origin 317,592 (60%). 18 and over 341,560 (65%), 65 and over 35,953 (7%). Median age: 25.

truckers' access to U.S. border markets.

Coleman has voted against the MX missile, and has joined Democrats and moderate Republicans in seeking to trim funding for the strategic defense initiative (SDI). In his first term, he supported a nuclear weapons freeze, along with another liberal cause, the Equal Rights Amendment.

Notwithstanding his support of the Democratic line on such touchy issues, Coleman cannot be deemed an unalloyed liberal. He has voted to ease federal gun control laws and to allow production of chemical weapons. When the administration lobbied Appropriations in October 1985 to leave SDI funding intact in order not to undercut Reagan's position at his November summit with Soviet leader Mikhail S. Gorbachev, Coleman departed from the anti-SDI group to back Reagan. "The reality is that we're heading for a summit," he said. "The timing couldn't be worse" to cut SDI.

At Home: Coleman enjoyed the ultimate luxury in 1988 as Republicans allowed him to win a fourth term without opposition. That effortless victory must have sweetened the satisfaction he first felt in 1982, when his victory in the 16th proved wrong all those Democrats who proclaimed for years that he was too liberal ever to win a congressional election in West Texas.

That year, without noticeably trimming the pro-labor populism he had practiced in Austin, Coleman moved with surprising ease through a five-way Democratic primary, a runoff and a general election that Republicans felt confident they could win.

Democratic Rep. Richard C. White's retirement announcement in October 1981 was a surprise in El Paso, but Coleman reacted quickly. He mobilized his base among labor and teachers, and by early 1982 he had as sophisticated a campaign apparatus as the district had seen. Still, while that support was sufficient to allow Coleman to lead in the first round, doubts remained that it would be enough against his runoff opponent, popular El Paso County Judge T. Udell Moore Jr., who drew on White's conservative following and business ties.

The runoff was a test of strength between business and labor. A few years before, when Mexican-American clothing workers struck El Paso's Farah Manufacturing Co., Coleman was their attorney. Moore made it clear at the time that, if it came to a tie-breaking vote on the county commission, he would vote to deny them food stamps. The greater-than-expected Hispanic vote decided the runoff; with support from the barrios of South El Paso, Coleman won with nearly 55 percent.

For the general-election campaign, the National Republican Congressional Committee designed a candidacy from scratch for El Paso Councilman Pat Haggerty, an ex-seminarian and former Democrat. With the national GOP's promise of the maximum financial help, Haggerty joined the party and aimed to take thousands of White's conservative Democratic supporters with him.

Despite a relatively liberal background, Haggerty campaigned as a Ronald Reagan Republican, denouncing Coleman as a "labor liberal" and charging that the city had become too dependent on federal help. The strategy probably would have worked in 1980, when Reagan swamped Jimmy Carter in El Paso, but in 1982, conservative Democrats seemed more concerned about the local economy. White swallowed his differences and supported the Democratic nominee, while Coleman continued to enjoy active support in the Hispanic community. He scored a 54-44 percent victory.

Republicans had good reason to suspect they might be able to topple Coleman in 1984. Unlike 1982, Sen. Lloyd Bentsen, a magnet for Democratic votes, was not on the ticket, while President Reagan, who would pull in GOP and conservative votes statewide, was. Moreover, GOP leaders felt they had a savvy nominee in Jack Hammond, a former bank executive and Republican activist from El Paso. Recognizing that Coleman's 1982 victory rested on his ability to hold conservative Democrats while picking up most of the Hispanic vote, Hammond chipped away at both pillars of support.

He stressed his business credentials and voiced a pro-Reagan, anti-tax line, but also pointed to his past work with the League of United Latin American Citizens. But Coleman survived it all, both bases intact. He called himself an independent-minded lawmaker, played up his efforts to bolster the local economy, and in the end won with 57 percent while Reagan swept all eight counties within the 16th.

The GOP threw Coleman a curve in 1986, challenging him with retired Mexican-American accountant Roy Gillia. Party leaders figured that Gillia and Roy R. Barrera Jr., the GOP nominee for attorney general, together could produce a Hispanic Republican turnout capable of toppling Coleman. It was not to be. The 16th's Hispanic community showed almost no interest in voting Republican, and Coleman walked away with two-thirds of the vote.

Committee

Appropriations (31st of 35 Democrats)
Foreign Operations; Military Construction

Elections

1988 General		
Ronald D. Coleman (D)	104,514	(100%)
1986 General		
Ronald D. Coleman (D)	50,590	(66%)
Roy Gillia (R)	26,421	(34%)

Previous Winning Percentages: **1984** (57%) **1982** (54%)

District Vote For President

	1988	1984	1980	1976
D	69,550 (52%)	57,337 (43%)	45,471 (40%)	52,104 (51%)
R	63,062 (48%)	75,906 (57%)	61,651 (54%)	49,117 (48%)
I			5,255 (5%)	

Campaign Finance

	Receipts	Receipts from PACs	Expend-itures
1988			
Coleman (D)	$322,822	$175,670 (54%)	$317,444
1986			
Coleman (D)	$518,723	$257,367 (50%)	$511,094
Gillia (R)	$539,056	$41,696 (8%)	$538,622

Key Votes

1987	
Raise speed limit to 65 mph	Y
Approve Gephardt "fair trade" amendment	Y
Ban testing of larger nuclear weapons	Y
Delay "re-flagging" of Kuwaiti tankers	Y
Approve tax-raising deficit-reduction bill	Y
1988	
Approve aid to Nicaraguan contras	N
Enact civil rights restoration bill over Reagan veto	Y
Kill 60-day plant-closing notification measure	N
Pass omnibus trade bill over Reagan veto	Y
Approve death penalty for drug-related murders	Y
Bar federal funds for abortions in cases of rape and incest	N
Oppose seven-day waiting period for purchase of handguns	#

Voting Studies

	Presidential Support		Party Unity		Conservative Coalition	
Year	**S**	**O**	**S**	**O**	**S**	**O**
1988	27	69	89	6	37	58
1987	30	68	92	6	51	49
1986	29	69	81	16	64	36
1985	31	68	89	9	51	47
1984	42	55	76	21	61	37
1983	37	61	81	16	48	49

Interest Group Ratings

Year	ADA	ACU	AFL-CIO	CCUS
1988	80	17	93	29
1987	84	4	100	13
1986	70	35	86	56
1985	60	19	71	33
1984	65	35	92	38
1983	75	4	88	40

17 Charles W. Stenholm (D)

Of Stamford — Elected 1978

Born: Oct. 26, 1938, Stamford, Texas.
Education: Attended Tarleton State Jr. College, 1957-59; Texas Tech U., B.S. 1961, M.S. 1962.
Occupation: Cotton grower.
Family: Wife, Cynthia Ann Watson; three children.
Religion: Lutheran.
Political Career: No previous office.
Capitol Office: 1226 Longworth Bldg. 20515; 225-6605.

In Washington: Stenholm is widely respected as a man of principle and substance, qualities that have helped him make a difference on the Agriculture Committee and a dent on the shape of the Democratic Party. He is a genuine Boll Weevil, and despite his courteous, soft-spoken style, he has scrapped with his party's leadership on a number of occasions.

Stenholm puts most of his energy into the Agriculture Committee, where he is chairman of the Dairy Subcommittee. His influence on agricultural issues stems in part from a willingness to master highly technical legislative matters. In the 100th Congress, Stenholm was a major player on one of the most complex issues ever to come before the committee — the reorganization of the ailing Farm Credit System.

In committee, Stenholm successfully pushed the most radical reorganization of the system since 1971. By a 22-12 vote, the panel approved his plan to trim the 37-bank network down to no more than seven institutions. Provisions pushed by Stenholm also stripped most banking powers from regional money centers, giving loan-making and rate-setting powers to nearly 400 local lending associations run by farmer stockholders. Those provisions were modified before the bill cleared the House, and in conference there were further compromises to accommodate objections from system officials. The final bill called for bank mergers within 12 bank districts, but farmer stockholders were to vote on further mergers.

On the Agriculture Committee, Stenholm also benefits from ideological positioning. His reputation for independence leads to solicitations for his support from all sides when an issue is debated. When Stenholm himself is attempting to round up support for an idea, Republicans tend to look favorably upon it, with an eye to winning him over on another issue later.

Stenholm has generally spoken out in favor of helping farmers cut back on production rather than increasing direct subsidies. But in 1985 he was an adamant opponent of an unsuccessful plan to allow farmers to vote for mandatory production controls as a way of raising prices. He argued that it had not been thoroughly examined, could pose compliance problems and might lead to higher unemployment and foreign production.

Stenholm has earned some degree of prominence in the 1980s for his efforts to nudge his party to the right. Prior to 1981, he had no record of leadership experience, but he emerged as the head of a Boll Weevil group that used its leverage to get conservative Democrats prime committee assignments, and to help shape and pass the 1981 Reagan economic program.

The group, which evolved into the Conservative Democratic Forum (CDF), became less strategically crucial after the 1982 elections, when Democrats added 26 seats to their majority, giving Speaker Thomas P. O'Neill Jr. enough loyalist votes to work his will. The CDF, however, still meets, and now has more than 40 regular members, according to Stenholm.

In 1985, Stenholm considered challenging O'Neill for Speaker. He knew as well as anyone that he could not win, but he wanted to dramatize discontent in the Democratic Party's right wing. In the end, the challenge never came off. Pressured by fellow Texan Jim Wright, O'Neill's heir apparent, and by some of his own loyalists, Stenholm abandoned the challenge a few days before the voting.

Despite his criticism of the Democratic Party, Stenholm has made it clear that he does not plan to leave it. "I'm a Democrat, period," he said in 1986. "Philosophically, I am what I am, and that's a conservative Democrat. I believe that philosophy, tempered with the liberal and moderate viewpoints, is best for the country."

But that cooperative tone does not mean Stenholm has slowed his effort to move the party. Even after Wright became Speaker in the 100th Congress, Stenholm had his share of differences with the leadership.

One of the more dramatic moments came during floor consideration of a leadership-

Texas 17

West Central — Abilene

The 17th stretches across more than 300 miles of rolling West Texas prairie. Its life revolves around cattle, cotton, oil and gas. It is predominantly Democratic territory, but its conservative tilt has brought Republicans some success: It voted for Ronald Reagan in 1980 and 1984 and George Bush in 1988. For years there was no steady habit of GOP voting in state and local races — Republican William P. Clements Jr. carried just a handful of the 17th's counties in his 1982 gubernatorial re-election campaign. But four years later Clements practically swept the district.

Despite Clements' 1986 success, which came about because the oil industry's downturn left voters disgruntled with incumbent Democrat Mark White, Stenholm felt no pressure. As usual, he did not even have a Republican opponent; the GOP has offered a congressional candidate in the 17th only twice in the past quarter-century.

Republicans do best in Taylor County (Abilene), which stands almost in the middle of the 17th and casts about one-fifth of the vote. Bush won Taylor by a 2-to-1 margin.

Abilene sprang to life when the railroad came through in 1881 and cattlemen started driving herds there for shipment. Today the city has nearly 112,000 people, but it still touts its cowhand flavor; one of the biggest annual events is the West Texas Fair.

During the early 1980s, the oil downturn brought considerable unemployment to Abilene, a plight unaccustomed there because the economy is fairly diversified. The city processes cottonseed, meats and dairy products; it makes aircraft parts, trailers and electronic items. Another dependable provider of jobs is Dyess Air Force Base.

Other than Taylor, only six counties in the 17th have more than 20,000 people. Five of them are at the far eastern edge of the district, either in or near the metropolitan sphere of Fort Worth. Population growth there has been brisk, with Parker and Wise counties leading the way. Republicans are gaining strength in the east — Clements got nearly 60 percent in Parker and Wise in 1986.

Settlement is generally sparse among the oil and gas wells, range land and cotton fields in the western half of the 17th. Several counties have just one or two crossroads that rate a dot on the map. While nearly all these western counties backed Clements in 1986, only a few of them traditionally vote Republican.

Population: 526,913. White 470,931 (89%), Black 16,940 (3%), Other 3,194 (1%). Spanish origin 59,274 (11%). 18 and over 380,499 (72%), 65 and over 82,648 (16%). Median age: 32.

backed plan to deliver "humanitarian" aid to the Nicaraguan contras. After Stenholm expressed concern that some of the funding would be taken by the "Ortega brothers" (a reference to Nicaragua's president and defense minister), Wright angrily moved to the microphone and, interrupting Stenholm, said his fellow Texan "is just lying or doesn't understand it." Stenholm did not back down, saying, "I am not lying."

Stenholm was also a major conservative voice on a number of other issues in the 100th Congress, staunchly opposing plant-closing notification and trying to minimize a boost in the minimum wage. When the Democratic leadership pushed a budget reconciliation bill calling for nearly $12 billion in new taxes, Stenholm complained that it was "a tax-and-spend bill" that revived the worst Democratic stereotype. He was also actively involved in conservative efforts to trim appropriations bills as they came to the floor. Many of the budget-cutting amendments were rebuffed, but the efforts did have some impact on appropriators as they prepared their legislation for the floor.

Concerned about a welfare "reform" package expected to cost more than $5 billion, Stenholm worked with Delaware Democrat Thomas R. Carper to fashion a $2.5 billion alternative. After the Rules Committee refused to allow them to offer their plan as a substitute, the two helped whip up opposition to the main bill, and on several occasions forced the leadership to put off consideration of the bill. It ultimately did pass.

Stenholm's concerns about the federal deficit have led him to push a measure that is not very popular with other members: To cut back "pork-barreling," Stenholm has suggested a "truth-in-legislation" plan. It would require bill reports to single out provisions with 10 or fewer beneficiaries, identify the author and those who would benefit. When he suggested his proposal to the Democratic Caucus, it was tabled on a vote of 137-32.

At Home: Stenholm is a third-generation West Texan, descended from a family of Swedish immigrants who settled near Stamford, where he was born. Agriculture has been the focus of his life and the basis of his political career.

He moved into politics in 1966, when the U.S. Agriculture Department made a ruling unfavorable to the cotton-growing plains section of Texas. As executive vice president of the Rolling Plains Cotton Growers Association, Stenholm made several trips to Washington to lobby against the ruling, and was partially successful in changing it.

In 1977, President Jimmy Carter appointed Stenholm to a panel that advises the U.S. Agricultural and Conservation Service. He resigned that position to run for the House in 1978, when veteran Democrat Omar Burleson retired.

Stenholm had a much smaller campaign treasury than his major rival for the Democratic nomination, wealthy Abilene lawyer and businessman A. L. "Dusty" Rhodes. But as a farmer and former member of the state Democratic executive committee, Stenholm had extensive agricultural and party ties.

Although Rhodes spent over $600,000 in an effort to win the nomination, Stenholm ran ahead of the crowded primary field and defeated Rhodes by a 2-to-1 margin in a runoff. An easy winner in the fall, he has not faced a major-party foe since then.

Committees

Agriculture (9th of 27 Democrats)
Livestock, Dairy and Poultry (chairman); Cotton, Rice and Sugar; Department Operations, Research and Foreign Agriculture; Tobacco and Peanuts

Veterans' Affairs (10th of 21 Democrats)
Hospitals and Health Care

Elections

1988 General

Charles W. Stenholm (D)	149,064	(100%)

1986 General

Charles W. Stenholm (D)	97,791	(100%)

Previous Winning Percentages: **1984** (100%) **1982** (97%) **1980** (100%) **1978** (68%)

District Vote For President

	1988	1984	1980	1976
D	84,899 (42%)	65,480 (32%)	79,143 (46%)	99,077 (57%)
R	117,349 (58%)	140,748 (68%)	87,449 (51%)	73,789 (43%)
I			2,988 (2%)	

Campaign Finance

	Receipts	Receipts from PACs	Expend-itures
1988			
Stenholm (D)	$289,551	$111,716 (39%)	$342,766
1986			
Stenholm (D)	$225,411	$91,840 (41%)	$217,744

Key Votes

1987

Raise speed limit to 65 mph	Y
Approve Gephardt "fair trade" amendment	N
Ban testing of larger nuclear weapons	N
Delay "re-flagging" of Kuwaiti tankers	N
Approve tax-raising deficit-reduction bill	N

1988

Approve aid to Nicaraguan contras	Y
Enact civil rights restoration bill over Reagan veto	N
Kill 60-day plant-closing notification measure	N
Pass omnibus trade bill over Reagan veto	Y
Approve death penalty for drug-related murders	Y
Bar federal funds for abortions in cases of rape and incest	Y
Oppose seven-day waiting period for purchase of handguns	N

Voting Studies

	Presidential Support		Party Unity		Conservative Coalition	
Year	S	O	S	O	S	O
1988	57	39	45	50	87	8
1987	64	34	39	57	93	2
1986	66	34	32	67	88	12
1985	66	31	35	64	96	2
1984	58	37	23	70	85	8
1983	63	35	21	77	92	7
1982	74	26	17	78	93	4
1981	75	24	28	67	91	5

Interest Group Ratings

Year	ADA	ACU	AFL-CIO	CCUS
1988	20	78	46	77
1987	12	74	25	80
1986	5	81	21	78
1985	20	90	24	86
1984	10	79	15	56
1983	15	91	13	85
1982	5	91	5	86
1981	0	93	20	84

18 Mickey Leland (D)

Of Houston — Elected 1978

Born: Nov. 27, 1944, Lubbock, Texas.
Education: Texas Southern U., B.S. 1970.
Occupation: Pharmacist.
Family: Wife, Alison Walton; one child.
Religion: Roman Catholic.
Political Career: Texas House, 1973-79.
Capitol Office: 2236 Rayburn Bldg. 20515; 225-3816.

In Washington: Leland has traveled far in the decade since he came to Congress from the Texas House. Though he is still best known for his efforts to help minorities, Leland long ago shed the dashikis that once underlined his differences with the establishment. He has become a player in the legislative process, and now seems as comfortable in conventional politics as he does in his three-piece suits.

The Texas Democrat alternates his rhetoric between hard-nosed and eloquent, but behind closed doors, he will lay aside his more ambitious plans and bargain. At the same time, Leland's seniority has brought him some important assignments. He chairs the Select Committee on Hunger and the Post Office Subcommittee on Postal Operations, and he holds a strategic position on Energy and Commerce.

Like most members who have a flair for winning publicity, Leland sometimes finds his propriety questioned, but none doubts his skill at drawing attention to the causes he cares about. In 1987, he helped organize the "Grate American Sleep-Out" to spotlight a major homeless aid bill pending in Congress. The effort drew colleagues, cameras and movie stars; and while critics derided it as "more hype than help," the House passed the aid bill two days later.

From his post on the Hunger Committee, Leland has become something of a roving congressional ambassador; he travels to hunger trouble-spots around the world and then returns home to fight for increased food and humanitarian aid. "I am now an activist on behalf of humanity everywhere," he said rather immodestly in 1985, "whether it is in Ethiopia . . . South Africa . . . Chile . . . in any part of the world where people are desperate and hungry for the freedoms and rights they deserve."

Early that year, Leland joined with Democrats Ted Weiss of New York and Howard Wolpe of Michigan to sponsor a $1 billion African famine relief package. When they agreed to make adjustments for aid already sent, Congress approved $785 million worth of assistance.

Fresh off that victory, Leland proposed a $1 billion domestic food bill, calling it "a small step toward redressing the structural injustices in our society which allow hunger to endure." That raised the tension level between the Hunger panel and the GOP, which had long worried that Leland would use the forum to make a political statement on hunger in America.

As often happens with Leland's original plans, his domestic hunger bill was too ambitious to be enacted whole. But language to provide homeless people with easier access to food stamps, veterans' pensions and job training was incorporated into another bill. In 1988, Leland sought to provide $1.5 billion for permanent housing for the homeless, but shelved his idea in favor of a more modest plan.

A one-time chairman of the Congressional Black Caucus, Leland resolutely backs South Africa sanctions legislation, and has proposed a humanitarian aid plan for the black "frontline" countries neighboring South Africa. While he differs with some caucus members in his strong support for Israel, he joined with Howard L. Berman of California in co-authoring a 1987 letter condemning Israel's weapons sales to the Pretoria government.

On the whole, Leland seems to move with ease between his role as a national black spokesman and a House insider. He played the former during the 1988 presidential primaries, when he was a leading congressional supporter of the Rev. Jesse Jackson. When an establishment-driven "stop Jackson" movement was rumored after his strong showing in Super Tuesday balloting, Leland leapt to blast would-be participants as part of a "racist, bigoted breed of people in the Democratic Party."

But at the Democratic National Convention, when more militant black leaders complained about Michael S. Dukakis not naming Jackson as his running mate, Leland came to Dukakis' aid. He delivered an important seconding speech for the man who got the No. 2 spot, Texas Sen. Lloyd Bentsen.

Speaking for a fellow Texan in an effort to unite his party was a natural political move for Leland, and one that also served his own ambition. The Houston Democrat is widely known to

Texas 18

Central Houston

The 18th District is at the core of sprawling Houston, a city whose economy has seen incredible boom, debilitating bust and modest recovery over the past two decades. But whether times are good, bad or in between, this minority-dominated area has struggled.

In the 1970s, the district actually lost population in spite of greater Houston's phenomenal oil-fed growth. When the oil market plummeted in the early 1980s, the vacant office towers in the 18th became the symbol of the city's grossly overbuilt commercial real-estate sector.

Now, as many in the Houston area begin to get back on their feet and look to rebuild the economy on high technology and other modern-age ventures requiring skilled workers, the undereducated residents of the 18th fight the despair of continuing economic frustration.

After redistricting following the 1980 census, the 18th was the only Texas district in which whites were not a majority of the population. At the start of the decade, it was about 40 percent white, and, with nearly half of Houston's black population, over 40 percent black.

Since then, there has been considerable movement of whites to outlying suburbs in Harris and Fort Bend counties. Within the city, the Hispanic community has expanded rapidly in the Denver Harbor area. There is also a growing Asian population along the fringes of central Houston.

The 18th does have some residents at the upper end of the economic spectrum. River Oaks, partially contained within the district, is home to some of the district's most affluent — and most conservative — constituents. The Heights area is predominantly middle-income and blue-collar.

This ethnic and economic blend generally produces the largest Democratic margins in the state. In 1988, Michael S. Dukakis won 77 percent in the 18th, his best showing in any Texas district. Although blacks, whites and Hispanics are roughly equal in numbers in the district, the 18th has sent a black Democrat to Congress since its creation in 1971.

Population: 527,393. White 216,421 (41%), Black 215,230 (41%), Other 7,343 (1%). Spanish origin 164,616 (31%). 18 and over 366,424 (70%), 65 and over 50,691 (10%). Median age: 27.

have statewide aspirations, and to be frustrated by the improbability of a black winning such a contest in Texas. Had Bentsen moved up to the vice presidency from the Senate, a multi-candidate, splintered-vote election to succeed him might have given Leland an opening.

On Energy and Commerce, Leland seems to want to broaden his agenda, but he appears constrained by his unofficial role as the Black Caucus representative. He eloquently defends minority set-asides on many bills. While his efforts give him clout — Democrats are reluctant to cross him for fear of offending others in the caucus, and they at times go out of their way to win him over — his role does limit his flexibility.

As chairman of the Postal Operations Subcommittee, Leland has a chance to spread his wings. Early in his chairmanship, he helped secure passage of a bill giving the Postal Service greater power to investigate mail fraud. And having investigated the effectiveness of the 1970 Postal Service reorganization, Leland is now a strong supporter of taking the Postal Service "off budget," thereby protecting it from budget cuts.

Legislation to that effect passed the House overwhelmingly in the 100th Congress, and at the time, Leland accused the Reagan administration of bad-faith bargaining. He said the administration intentionally pushed for budget cuts that would reduce customer service, undermine public confidence in the Postal Service and thus spur pressure for privatizing mail delivery.

When the "old Leland" surfaces these days, he does not stay out very long. A few days after he signed the resolution to impeach Reagan for invading Grenada, he abruptly withdrew as a sponsor. "It was a terribly politically inept thing to do, and I admit it," he said. "I should have expressed my dissent in another way. I should not be messing around with the Constitution like that."

One of Leland's more controversial friendships is with Cuban President Fidel Castro. He has visited Castro on numerous occasions, and in 1983 played a pivotal role in getting two Texans out of Cuban jails. Explaining the longstanding friendship, Leland says: "While I disagree with his fundamental ideology ... I respect him for his intellect."

At Home: Leland has been safe in his Houston district since he claimed it in 1978, but lately he has shown signs of restlessness. He has been mentioned as a potential candidate for governor or senator in 1990, even though he would be hard-pressed to survive a Democratic runoff, much less win in November. Such a race could, however, strengthen his credentials as a candidate for mayor or for a federal appointive position.

Leland came to Congress upon the retirement of Democrat Barbara C. Jordan, who had served three terms and probably could have held the seat indefinitely. Her decision to leave was a surprise, since she had won national prominence on the Judiciary Committee during the Nixon impeachment debate and as a keynote speaker at the 1976 Democratic National Convention.

Leland grew up in a poor, black section of Houston and attended Texas Southern University after, he believes, he was denied entrance to the University of Houston because of his race. He became an active and often strident spokesman for civil rights and the anti-war movement. As a pharmacy student, he also took an interest in health-care issues, helping to establish a free neighborhood health clinic.

When several predominantly black state legislative districts were created in Houston in 1972, Leland easily won one of them. In the Legislature, he sought to be a spokesman for a wide spectrum of black interests.

Muting the militance of his student years, he won a seat on the Democratic National Committee in 1976. But he continued to draw support from left-leaning elements among white and Mexican-American groups and from poorer blacks. When Leland decided to run for Congress in 1978, these groups gave him a near-majority in the seven-way Democratic primary. In the runoff, he won comfortably over state Rep. Anthony Hall.

Leland has had no serious opposition since then, although some members of downtown Houston's business establishment yearn for a congressman more receptive to their point of view. In 1982 a group of businessmen encouraged former municipal Judge Harrell Tillman to challenge Leland in the primary. Tillman failed to receive even one-fifth of the vote. Since 1984, Leland has not had a GOP opponent.

Committees

Select Hunger (Chairman)

Energy and Commerce (10th of 26 Democrats)
Energy and Power; Health and the Environment; Telecommunications and Finance

Post Office and Civil Service (5th of 15 Democrats)
Postal Operations and Services (chairman); Compensation and Employee Benefits

Elections

1988 General		
Mickey Leland (D)	94,408	(93%)
J. Alejandro Snead (LIB)	7,235	(7%)
1988 Primary		
Mickey Leland (D)	38,963	(82%)
Elizabeth Spates (D)	8,321	(18%)
1986 General		
Mickey Leland (D)	63,335	(90%)
Joanne Kuniansky (I)	6,884	(10%)

Previous Winning Percentages: 1984 (79%) **1982** (83%) **1980** (80%) **1978** (97%)

District Vote For President

	1988	1984	1980	1976
D	81,611 (77%)	99,232 (73%)	79,143 (69%)	91,624 (71%)
R	24,291 (23%)	35,601 (26%)	31,836 (28%)	36,665 (28%)
I			2,988 (3%)	

Campaign Finance

	Receipts	Receipts from PACs	Expend-itures
1988			
Leland (D)	$532,832	$347,025 (65%)	$534,732
1986			
Leland (D)	$217,214	$161,506 (74%)	$207,419

Key Votes

1987	
Raise speed limit to 65 mph	N
Approve Gephardt "fair trade" amendment	Y
Ban testing of larger nuclear weapons	Y
Delay "re-flagging" of Kuwaiti tankers	Y
Approve tax-raising deficit-reduction bill	Y
1988	
Approve aid to Nicaraguan contras	N
Enact civil rights restoration bill over Reagan veto	Y
Kill 60-day plant-closing notification measure	N
Pass omnibus trade bill over Reagan veto	Y
Approve death penalty for drug-related murders	N
Bar federal funds for abortions in cases of rape and incest	X
Oppose seven-day waiting period for purchase of handguns	N

Voting Studies

	Presidential Support		Party Unity		Conservative Coalition	
Year	**S**	**O**	**S**	**O**	**S**	**O**
1988	15	71	77	2	5	79
1987	13	80	86	1	5	93
1986	9	83	88	2	2	90
1985	20	80	90	2	7	89
1984	19	65	74	4	2	86
1983	10	83	86	3	4	84
1982	26	68	84	5	8	86
1981	30	53	80	5	8	79

Interest Group Ratings

Year	ADA	ACU	AFL-CIO	CCUS
1988	100	0	100	27
1987	96	0	100	0
1986	100	0	93	12
1985	100	0	94	10
1984	90	6	100	36
1983	85	0	94	24
1982	90	0	100	19
1981	95	0	93	6

19 Larry Combest (R)

Of Lubbock — Elected 1984

Born: March 20, 1945, Memphis, Texas.
Education: West Texas State U., B.A. 1969.
Occupation: Congressional aide; electronics wholesaler.
Family: Wife, Sharon McCurry; two children.
Religion: Methodist.
Political Career: No previous office.
Capitol Office: 1527 Longworth Bldg. 20515; 225-4005.

In Washington: As a protégé of John Tower and a supporter of Edward Madigan for House minority whip, Combest probably did not count early 1989 as a high point in his political career. Tower's nomination to be defense secretary was rejected — in part because of Combest's revelations about the nominee's past drinking — and Madigan lost the whip's race to Newt Gingrich, a man as brash and high-profile as Combest is pragmatic and behind-the-scenes.

Despite the setbacks, Combest has the knowledge, desire and electoral security to become a significant figure in House GOP circles. Gingrich and his combative allies will get more attention, but there will still be plenty of opportunities for legislative deal-making, and that is Combest's forte.

Six months into his first term, Combest warned some of his fellow freshmen against "the illusion of changing things overnight." He said the goal of legislative bargaining is not to stake out an ideological position, but "to get the best you can get." Many "Old Bull" GOP insiders concur, and they felt comfortable enough with Combest to see that he got an added committee assignment in 1989 — Intelligence.

In 1985, Combest was quietly attentive as the Agriculture Committee wrote the five-year farm bill. On farm subsidies, he generally supported the anti-spending views of President Reagan — and many conservative West Texas ranchers — but his fiscal austerity faded some on cotton, the 19th's key crop. He worked well with Charles W. Stenholm, the influential Agriculture Democrat who represents the adjoining 17th. During committee work on the 1988 drought-relief bill, Combest got an amendment passed to compensate cotton producers with crops damaged by hail. In 1988, President Reagan signed Combest's bill authorizing a $27 million research facility for plant stress and water conservation at Texas Tech University in Lubbock. Researchers will try to develop hybrid seeds better able to withstand harsh weather.

The one outspoken crusade Combest has pursued was against the federal program of legal services to the poor. Ranchers and businessmen in Combest's district have attacked the Texas Rural Legal Aid office for organizing unions, promoting strikes, and representing illegal aliens. In 1986, Combest offered a floor amendment to eliminate funding for the entire Legal Services Corporation. His amendment was drowned, 103-278. His 1987 proposal to cut the agency's funding by $25.5 million lost 198-212.

Combest probably was horrified to see his account of Tower's drinking featured in a February 1989 front-page story in *The Washington Post.* According to the Post, Combest told Senate Armed Services Committee Chairman Sam Nunn and ranking Republican John W. Warner that Tower (Combest's boss for seven years) had ended his previous excessive use of alcohol, which in the 1970s included as much as a full bottle of Scotch two to three times a week. Combest later said it was Tower and a group of friends who drank a full bottle in an evening.

At Home: After a stint with the U.S. Agricultural Stabilization Service, Combest went to work for Tower in 1971 as a specialist in agricultural affairs. He later became director of Tower's Texas offices, and served as treasurer for his 1978 re-election campaign. Combest then returned to West Texas to sell electronic equipment, but he remained active in GOP affairs. When Democratic Rep. Kent Hance announced for the Senate in 1984, Combest jumped for the 19th. It had not elected a Republican in its 50-year history, but voted regularly for GOP candidates for state and national office, and was ripe to switch.

Combest was forced into a runoff by a hard-right conservative, but with support from many old-line GOP leaders, he won the runoff easily.

In November, Combest met Don Richards, a former Hance aide. Both stressed their farm roots and their conservatism. Combest portrayed Richards as part of a party that had strayed too far left. Richards distanced himself from the national Democratic line on tax increases and gay rights, and cast himself as a conservative in Hance's mold. Combest carried the most populous counties — Ector and Lubbock — to overcome Richards' rural strength and take 58 percent. He has won easily since then.

Texas 19

Northwest — Lubbock; Odessa

The stubborn, slow-talking farmers and ranchers of the West Texas plains do not change their minds easily about candidates or political parties. They sent George Mahon to the House in 1934, and kept him there for 44 years. They maintained their Democratic voting habits in Texas long after the national party had moved far beyond their generic distrust of government.

But change finally has come. The 19th has given GOP presidential candidates big margins since 1976. And Combest has brought the partisan change down to the House level.

Lubbock County casts 40 percent of the overall vote and now turns in regular GOP majorities for statewide and national office. Irrigation has enabled the agricultural region around Lubbock to replace East Texas as the state's predominant cotton-growing area. Lubbock, a city of about 186,000, calls itself the world's largest cottonseed processing center. Texas Tech U. and Reese Air Force Base are important employers.

More than 100 miles south of Lubbock is Odessa, with 101,000 residents. It primarily refines petroleum and provides equipment and supplies to surrounding oil fields, and has been among the Texas cities hardest-hit by the oil industry slump. Unemployment reached nearly 20 percent in 1986 and has dropped only because many have left to work elsewhere. Odessa and surrounding Ector County are the blue-collar stronghold of the Midland-Odessa population center, but the area is firmly Republican.

Sparsely populated farming and ranching counties fill out the 19th. Though rural residents prefer conservative Democrats, even those voters have been tilting to the GOP.

Population: 527,805. White 432,867 (82%), Black 28,361 (5%), Other 4,072 (1%). Spanish origin 131,919 (25%). 18 and over 360,942 (68%), 65 and over 45,903 (9%). Median age: 26.

Committees

Agriculture (12th of 18 Republicans)
Conservation, Credit and Rural Development; Cotton, Rice and Sugar; Tobacco and Peanuts

District of Columbia (3rd of 4 Republicans)
Government Operations and Metropolitan Affairs (ranking); Fiscal Affairs and Health

Select Intelligence (4th of 7 Republicans)
Oversight and Evaluation; Program and Budget Authorization

Small Business (9th of 17 Republicans)
Environment and Labor; SBA, the General Economy and Minority Enterprise Development

Elections

1988 General		
Larry Combest (R)	113,068	(68%)
Gerald McCathern (D)	53,932	(32%)
1986 General		
Larry Combest (R)	68,695	(62%)
Gerald McCathern (D)	42,129	(38%)

Previous Winning Percentage: 1984 (58%)

District Vote For President

	1988		1984		1980		1976	
D	54,551	(33%)	44,562	(25%)	46,373	(29%)	67,123	(44%)
R	110,148	(67%)	133,422	(75%)	108,936	(68%)	85,190	(56%)
I					3,154	(2%)		

Campaign Finance

	Receipts	Receipts from PACs	Expend-itures
1988			
Combest (R)	$272,401	$119,800 (44%)	$244,821
McCathern (D) †	$44,173	0	$44,082
1986			
Combest (R)	$318,347	$139,266 (44%)	$317,265
McCathern (D)	$114,331	$2,334 (2%)	$112,732

† Totals based on incomplete data.

Key Votes

1987	
Raise speed limit to 65 mph	Y
Approve Gephardt "fair trade" amendment	N
Ban testing of larger nuclear weapons	N
Delay "re-flagging" of Kuwaiti tankers	N
Approve tax-raising deficit-reduction bill	N
1988	
Approve aid to Nicaraguan contras	Y
Enact civil rights restoration bill over Reagan veto	N
Kill 60-day plant-closing notification measure	Y
Pass omnibus trade bill over Reagan veto	Y
Approve death penalty for drug-related murders	Y
Bar federal funds for abortions in cases of rape and incest	Y
Oppose seven-day waiting period for purchase of handguns	Y

Voting Studies

	Presidential Support		Party Unity		Conservative Coalition	
Year	S	O	S	O	S	O
1988	68	29	75	23	97	0
1987	64	25	75	19	86	7
1986	78	22	82	18	100	0
1985	75	25	89	11	96	4

Interest Group Ratings

Year	ADA	ACU	AFL-CIO	CCUS
1988	0	92	21	93
1987	0	89	13	93
1986	5	91	21	94
1985	5	100	0	91

20 Henry B. Gonzalez (D)

Of San Antonio — Elected 1961

Born: May 3, 1916, San Antonio, Texas.

Education: Graduated from San Antonio Junior College, 1937; attended U. of Texas at Austin, 1937-39; St. Mary's U. School of Law, LL.B. 1943.

Occupation: Lawyer; business consultant; translator.

Family: Wife, Bertha Cuellar; eight children.

Religion: Roman Catholic.

Political Career: San Antonio City Council, 1953-56; San Antonio mayor pro tem, 1955-56; Texas Senate, 1957-61; sought Democratic nomination for governor, 1958; candidate for U.S. Senate, special election, 1961.

Capitol Office: 2413 Rayburn Bldg. 20515; 225-3236.

In Washington: Few members of Congress have had a reputation on Capitol Hill so contrary to their image back home as Gonzalez, long revered in San Antonio while all but dismissed in the House as a flake. Yet in his new role as chairman of the House Banking, Finance and Urban Affairs Committee, Gonzalez quickly impressed the Washington critics and began narrowing the gulf between their view of him and that held by his constituents.

Gonzalez has been a fighter from the beginning of his career, whether pressing lonely crusades of principle or personal quarrels. He is a passionate populist, and a sincere if long-winded one. But he can be stubborn and short-tempered, and prone to eruptions of anger that over the years helped earn him the reputation in Washington as a high-strung eccentric.

As a consequence, it seemed Gonzalez might never inherit Banking's top chair if the panel's junior Democrats could prevent it. One reason they had never tried to oust the tyrannical former chairman, Fernand J. St Germain, was the fact that other senior Democrats, led by No. 2 Gonzalez, were no more desirable substitutes. But in 1988, when St Germain lost reelection, Democratic leaders quashed any talk of a block-Gonzalez movement.

Gonzalez benefited from being a Texan and a Hispanic, facts of particular importance to then-Speaker Jim Wright of Texas and of general importance to a party that aggressively courts the Hispanic vote. However, after the Democratic Caucus endorsed Gonzalez for the chair at the outset of the 101st Congress, he alone took the steps that solidified his hold.

For a man attended by such low expectations, Gonzalez assumed power at a time of great demands on Banking policy makers. In addition to the longstanding pressures for banking deregulation and housing initiatives, a crisis in the savings and loan industry threatened to bankrupt the Federal Savings and Loan Insurance Corporation (FSLIC) and ignite a nationwide panic.

By April 1989, Gonzalez had steered through the committee the Bush administration's complex bill tightening S&L regulation and restocking the insurance fund through higher S&L premiums and a taxpayer bailout. For both the liberal crusader and the Republican administration, the alliance was an unusual one. But the White House came to rely heavily on Gonzalez as GOP lawmakers defected under intense lobbying by an industry long favored by the committee. Though the bill had a long way to go, and other controversies lay ahead for Gonzalez, it was his performance during the committee's work on the S&L bill that began to rehabilitate his reputation.

Like most on the committee, Gonzalez traditionally has been an S&L industry supporter. But in late 1988, he signaled a heightened skepticism. "The Congress has given thrifts everything they have asked for the last two decades, and look where we are."

When President Bush's bailout bill first was taken up in the Subcommittee on Financial Institutions Supervision, chaired by Gonzalez' rival Frank Annunzio, Gonzalez quietly bided his time while Annunzio helped weaken the measure with industry amendments. After one especially controversial vote, to roll back stiffer capital requirements for S&Ls, Gonzalez objected, "This is back to the old way of doing things. I won't be a party to it."

He came out charging in the full committee. The panel approved a modified version of Gonzalez' amendment restoring the capital requirement. Also, it adopted a second amendment on which Gonzalez had staked his prestige, this one requiring the federal S&L board to help subsidize low-cost mortgages.

By his manner of presiding in an open and gentlemanly way, Gonzalez proved a welcome change to committee members used to the

Texas 20

Central San Antonio

With a population of almost 915,000, San Antonio is Texas' third-largest city and the 9th-largest in the country. In 1981, it became the first major American city to elect a Mexican-American mayor, Henry Cisneros, who served until 1989.

The 20th District as a whole is 62 percent Hispanic, with the Mexican-American majority concentrated on San Antonio's West Side, one of the poorest areas anywhere in Texas. Blacks, who comprise 9 percent of the district, are most numerous across town on the east side. Northwestern San Antonio is predominantly white, and hosts a mix of business and military people and upper-middle-class professionals. There is an academic community associated with the University of Texas at San Antonio, located across the line in the 21st District.

Despite San Antonio's Hispanic majority and background — it was founded in the early 18th century by the Spanish — its economy has been controlled by Anglos since its early days as a cattle center. Today, federal payrolls are the key economic component. There are more than a half-dozen major military installations in or near San Antonio, including five Air Force bases. Kelly Air Force Base alone employs more than 22,000 people; Fort Sam Houston, a national center for Army medical care and research, employs more than 15,000.

Because of San Antonio's historic past (the Alamo is downtown) and its stint as host for the 1968 HemisFair, the city is an active center for tourism and conventions (the convention center is named for Rep. Gonzalez). Among the sites toured by visitors is the Paseo del Rio, with its myriad small shops, bars and restaurants lining the San Antonio River on its winding course through town.

The district's politics remain solidly Democratic. In 1984, Ronald Reagan won 41 percent of the presidential vote in the 20th, a high-water GOP showing. Michael S. Dukakis' 1988 tally was a more typical Democratic performance; he won 68 percent, his second-best score in all of Texas' districts.

Population: 526,333. White 397,577 (76%), Black 46,167 (9%), Other 4,146 (1%). Spanish origin 324,910 (62%). 18 and over 358,798 (68%), 65 and over 55,129 (10%). Median age: 26.

autocratic St Germain. Moreover, from the outset he satisfied some subcommittee chairmen by allowing them wider berth in their respective fiefdoms.

Gonzalez also did not follow St Germain's practice of chairing Banking's most important subcommittee, Financial Institutions, which has broad jurisdiction and just four fewer members than the full committee. While that left Annunzio, a man long ambitious for the full committee chairmanship, to head the competing power center, Gonzalez preferred to keep the Housing Subcommittee he has chaired since 1981 because that panel reflects his top priority.

As Housing chairman, Gonzalez was a harsh critic of President Reagan's efforts to dismantle many housing programs. But not until the end of his administration was Congress able to enact a free-standing housing authorization. Not only were Congress and the president split, but also Congress was divided until 1987 between House Democrats and Senate Republicans. However, at times Gonzalez displayed an impracticality that exacerbated the stalemate.

He worked hard for a housing bill in the 97th Congress, but the legislation was so far out of step with the national political mood that it never reached the House floor in 1982. His subcommittee and the full committee approved a $29 billion package, more than $12 billion above budget limits.

When a housing bill finally did clear two years later, the credit went to St Germain. Gonzalez helped push it through the House, offering an amendment to cut the bill by one-third to secure a majority's support. Still the bill seemed fated to die in the Senate, until St Germain insisted he would not support an administration bill funding the International Monetary Fund unless Reagan and Republicans accepted the housing measure. A deal was cut and a combined IMF-housing bill became law. But Gonzalez voted against it; he not only opposed the IMF bill, but also he was uneasy with such blatant horse-trading.

In the 99th Congress, Gonzalez agreed to scale back a $22 billion proposal, acknowledging in 1985, "There's no question that we have a housing crisis but we also have the reality of a budget crisis." The House attached a less costly housing bill to a high-priority budget-cutting package, attempting to force Senate approval. But the gambit failed.

The next year, however, Gonzalez took a big step toward breaking the logjam. He backed another scaled-down housing bill, supported by key Republicans, which dropped most of the proposed program expansions Democrats had sought. The House passed the bill, but with the major addition of a GOP amendment shifting the focus of public housing programs from new construction to renovation. Although the Senate did not act before the Congress ended, the housing compromise formed the basis of legislation that finally became law in 1987.

As the 100th Congress opened that year with both chambers in Democrats' control for the first time since 1980, the outlook for a housing bill was bright. The Senate and House quickly passed measures in early 1987, though once again Gonzalez and his liberal House allies had to cut back their more expansive version. That was not enough for senators, and a conference took months to reach an agreement. Conservative Republicans blocked it in the Senate, however, and only a last-hour compromise allowed a $30 billion, two-year measure to clear before Congress went home.

As the 101st Congress turns to the next housing bill, Gonzalez and his liberal Senate counterpart, Housing Subcommittee Chairman Alan Cranston, should be natural allies in drafting the first post-Reagan legislative statement. But instead, they are divided by a basic difference. Cranston wants innovative new programs and modest funding increases, while Gonzalez favors existing programs and big increases. He does have one major new idea, a $2 billion-a-year National Housing Trust to subsidize first-time mortgages for low- and middle-class home buyers.

Gonzalez is motivated by a view of the housing situation nothing short of apocalyptic. "This nation," he said in 1988, "is confronted with a potential social disturbance the like of which is going to shatter it to its foundations."

Through the Reagan years, Gonzalez directed much of his wrath at Housing Secretary Samuel R. Pierce Jr. In 1982, he called Pierce, who is black, "Step'n Fetchit." Days later at a subcommittee hearing, Pierce lashed back at Gonzalez for his "vile, abusive and racist language." He told a HUD audience Gonzalez was "ready for the funny farm." Gonzalez, in turn, said Pierce "has kept his job despite malfeasance and misfeasance and because he is the only black member of the Cabinet."

In 1985, when Pierce came to testify about further housing cuts, Gonzalez submitted his questions in writing, lest a verbal confrontation erupt. That marked a rare appearance for Pierce before either chamber's housing subcommittee, and by 1988 the House panel had to threaten him with a subpoena to compel his attendance. In 1989, with Pierce out of office, Gonzalez was feeling vindicated as his subcommittee began investigating allegations that HUD had routinely awarded housing contracts to administration cronies. "It is indeed ironic that a program the Reagan administration had sought to terminate for six years was misused to feather the financial nest of ... administration favorites," he said.

Gonzalez engaged in another well-publicized feud in 1977 during his brief chairmanship of the House Assassinations Committee — a panel he had suggested to investigate the murders of President Kennedy and the Rev. Dr. Martin Luther King Jr. Within weeks, Gonzalez had fired the panel's prosecutor for allegedly misusing committee funds. With the committee in an uproar, Gonzalez, too, quit a week later, saying the investigation could never succeed because "vast and powerful forces, including the country's most sophisticated crime element, won't stand for it."

Gonzalez' reputation also suffered from his quarrels that have not been merely verbal. In 1963, he threatened to "pistol whip" and then struck a House Republican who claimed Gonzalez' "left-wing voting record" served the socialist-communist cause. Twenty-three years later in a San Antonio restaurant, Gonzalez struck a man who had called him a communist; prosecutors later dropped misdemeanor charges, but not before Gonzalez claimed the administration was seeking revenge because he had called for Reagan's impeachment and had exposed a CIA link to a plane that had crashed near San Antonio.

Gonzalez' passion usually finds more constructive outlets. A longtime civil rights advocate in Texas, he arrived on the House floor for his 1962 swearing-in ceremony already carrying a bill to repeal the poll tax. He also began a drive for a world's fair in San Antonio, and finally HemisFair was held there in 1968. In his first term he opposed creation of a privately operated communications satellite system and, unlike the few other opponents, he never gave up the issue, referring to himself for years as "the man that fought the Telstar giveaway." Gonzalez waged an unceasing battle against the "Bracero" program for immigrant Mexican workers, calling it "slave labor."

In the 96th Congress, he took to the House floor every few weeks to fan interest in the 1979 murder of federal Judge John W. Wood in San Antonio and to warn that organized crime might be involved. Colleagues began to see Gonzalez as a man obsessed. But in 1982, after a grand jury handed down five indictments in the case, FBI Director William H. Webster personally thanked Gonzalez for keeping the issue alive.

In his early years as Housing chairman, Gonzalez gathered documentation on the homeless — an issue that Democratic congressional leaders seized for early action in 1987. Perhaps Gonzalez' most lonely and unsuccessful crusade was his push for Reagan's impeachment. His first call went out in 1983 after the invasion of Grenada. "Nixon is an Eagle Scout compared with this guy," Gonzalez said. But few House members cosponsored his impeachment resolution. He introduced another one in early 1987 amid the Iran-contra scandal, but it went largely unnoticed.

At Home: Gonzalez does not campaign in San Antonio as a voice for Hispanics. "I have never sought public office on an ethnic basis," he says, "and I never will.... I have never palmed myself off as some sort of ethnic leader." But he is a hero to many in his city's Mexican-American neighborhoods, and their votes have helped give him the impregnable House seat he holds today.

Since his original victory in a 1961 special election, Gonzalez has had no electoral problems of any sort. He has never had primary opposition, and the closest the Republicans have come was in 1964, when Gonzalez still won nearly two-thirds of the vote.

But it was different in the beginning for Gonzalez, the son of a Mexican father and a Mexican-American mother, who began climbing the local political ladder after World War II. He ran for office while helping his father, the managing editor of a Spanish-language newspaper, operate a translation service.

Gonzalez made it to the state Senate in 1956, and quickly drew attention by filibustering against Democratic Gov. Price Daniel's bill to allow the state to close schools threatened by disturbances surrounding integration.

In 1958 Gonzalez ran as the liberal alternative to Daniel in the Democratic gubernatorial primary. He was beaten by a margin of more than 3-to-1, but the defeat only encouraged his ambition. Three years later, he sought the Senate seat vacated by Lyndon B. Johnson. While Gonzalez carried his home base, Bexar County, his statewide appeal as a candidate with a Hispanic name was limited. He ran sixth with 9 percent of the vote.

But he soon had another chance. Later in 1961, Democrat Paul Kilday resigned from the House to accept a judgeship, and Gonzalez became the consensus Democratic candidate for the seat.

The special election was a clear liberal-conservative choice. Gonzalez was warmly endorsed by the Kennedy administration. Republican John Goode, a former GOP county chairman, had the active assistance of Arizona Sen. Barry Goldwater and Texas' newly elected GOP senator, John Tower. With strong support in Hispanic areas, Gonzalez won with 55 percent. He became the first person of Mexican-American extraction to be elected to the House from Texas.

Committee

Banking, Finance and Urban Affairs (Chairman)
Housing and Community Development (chairman); Consumer Affairs and Coinage; Domestic Monetary Policy; Financial Institutions Supervision, Regulation and Insurance; General Oversight and Investigations

Elections

1988 General		
Henry B. Gonzalez (D)	94,527	(71%)
Lee Trevino (R)	36,801	(28%)
1986 General		
Henry B. Gonzalez (D)	55,363	(100%)

Previous Winning Percentages: **1984** (100%) **1982** (92%) **1980** (82%) **1978** (100%) **1976** (100%) **1974** (100%) **1972** (97%) **1970** (100%) **1968** (82%) **1966** (87%) **1964** (65%) **1962** (100%) **1961 *** (55%)

* *Special election.*

District Vote For President

	1988	1984	1980	1976
D	92,584 (68%)	82,253 (58%)	82,513 (64%)	84,087 (67%)
R	44,444 (32%)	59,014 (41%)	43,427 (33%)	39,739 (32%)
I			3,373 (3%)	

Campaign Finance

	Receipts	Receipts from PACs	Expend-itures
1988			
Gonzalez (D)	$225,721	$100,387 (44%)	$228,907
Trevino (R)	$58,325	$13,330 (23%)	$58,217
1986			
Gonzalez (D)	$142,694	$28,750 (20%)	$133,055

Key Votes

1987	
Raise speed limit to 65 mph	Y
Approve Gephardt "fair trade" amendment	N
Ban testing of larger nuclear weapons	Y
Delay "re-flagging" of Kuwaiti tankers	Y
Approve tax-raising deficit-reduction bill	Y
1988	
Approve aid to Nicaraguan contras	N
Enact civil rights restoration bill over Reagan veto	Y
Kill 60-day plant-closing notification measure	N
Pass omnibus trade bill over Reagan veto	Y
Approve death penalty for drug-related murders	N
Bar federal funds for abortions in cases of rape and incest	N
Oppose seven-day waiting period for purchase of handguns	N

Voting Studies

	Presidential Support		Party Unity		Conservative Coalition	
Year	**S**	**O**	**S**	**O**	**S**	**O**
1988	16	82	96	3	13	84
1987	15	85	93	6	21	77
1986	17	82	90	7	10	88
1985	21	74	94	3	15	78
1984	26	72	89	10	20	75
1983	11	88	88	10	31	63
1982	45	53	84	14	34	60
1981	34	64	81	15	31	63

Interest Group Ratings

Year	ADA	ACU	AFL-CIO	CCUS
1988	100	0	100	15
1987	96	9	88	7
1986	95	0	93	17
1985	85	0	88	14
1984	95	13	100	38
1983	90	17	88	10
1982	60	27	80	27
1981	70	7	93	0

21 Lamar Smith (R)

Of San Antonio — Elected 1986

Born: Nov. 19, 1947, San Antonio, Texas.
Education: Yale U., B.A. 1969; Southern Methodist U., J.D. 1975.
Occupation: Lawyer; rancher.
Family: Wife, Jane Shoults; two children.
Religion: Christian Scientist.
Political Career: Bexar County Republican chairman, 1978-81; Texas House, 1981-82; Bexar County commissioner, 1983-85.
Capitol Office: 422 Cannon Bldg. 20515; 225-4236.

In Washington: Smith represents a solidly conservative suburban-and-rural constituency that does not put a lot of pressure on him to make new laws. But he does put that pressure on himself. He is probably in a position to hold the 21st for a long time, and he has made it clear he wants to produce more than just a voting record during his stay in the House.

Smith came to Washington in 1987 voicing concerns about ethical standards in Congress, and he set to work on the Judiciary Committee to pass legislation applying a new code of ethics to the legislative branch. In particular, he wanted to restrict the lobbying activities of former members of Congress, and he cosponsored legislation with Democratic Rep. Barney Frank of Massachusetts to bring that about. The bill cleared Congress, but was later killed by President Reagan.

Smith continued his work on ethics in the 101st Congress, but also turned his attention to other matters. Like many Texans, he has an interest in immigration, but he is in a better position than most to look into such issues as ranking Republican on the Immigration Subcommittee. Smith's conservatism came out during one early markup of legislation revising the McCarran-Walter Act, a McCarthy-era law that set the criteria for denying aliens visas to enter the country, including some based on ideology or political expression. The panel voted to soften the restrictions, rejecting by 3-7 a Smith amendment to exclude any foreigner who advocates the overthrow of the U.S. government by violence, or who is, or has been, a member of the Communist Party.

"I, too, am a supporter of free speech," he said. "However, our country's national security interest should never be jeopardized for free speech."

Smith takes pride in having passed a bill of his own in his first term, and while it was not a major deed, it did signal his desire to move legislation. The bill authorized the Park Service to accept the donation of a 67,000-acre ranch next to Texas' Big Bend National Park.

At Home: If Smith's Yale background and polished manner are not the first things you would expect from a West Texas pol, he has made them work for him. When the 21st was open in 1986, he aggressively courted rural voters; two years later, he drew no opposition at all.

Smith spent a year in the Texas House and two years on the Bexar County Commission, representing San Antonio suburbs. In 1985, when GOP Rep. Tom Loeffler announced plans to leave the 21st for a gubernatorial campaign, Smith announced his candidacy immediately.

Smith was the moderate in the GOP House runoff against Van Archer, a San Antonio city councilman known as an outspoken ideologue of the right. Smith finished first by a modest margin in the initial GOP primary and took 53 percent of the runoff vote against Archer.

In the primary and runoff, Smith had to overcome questions about his support of legal abortion (Archer opposed it) and his affiliation with Christian Science. Critics said his religion would prevent him from voting for medical care appropriations — a problem in a district where a medical equipment company is the largest private employer.

But Smith dealt successfully with these problems, and benefited from contacts he made in three years as Bexar County Republican chairman. He had the active support of U.S. Sen. Phil Gramm, for whom he had organized Bexar County in the 1984 campaign.

His Democratic opponent was former state Sen. Pete Snelson, whose political base in Midland, at the western end of the district, positioned him to play to lingering rural perceptions of Smith as an elitist lawyer from the big city.

But Snelson was plagued by debt from previous campaigns. Smith seized the initiative, casting himself as fiscally more conservative and signing a no-tax-increase pledge. He also focused his efforts on Snelson's home turf, Midland. Smith won San Antonio and Midland, overcoming Snelson's rural support.

Texas 21

San Antonio Suburbs; San Angelo; Midland

Spanning 26 whole counties and part of another, the 21st extends from the suburbs of San Antonio 500 miles west across Texas ranch land to the Mexican border. Republicans are not the majority party by registration, but strong Republican candidates run well nearly everywhere in the district.

More than a quarter of the vote is cast in Bexar County, much of that in a predominantly white-collar portion of northern San Antonio that is the 21st's largest population center. These strongly Republican, upper-income suburbanites are the sort of people who gave Lamar Smith his start in local politics.

Most of the way across the district from San Antonio lies another Republican redoubt — Midland County. The city of Midland is the white-collar administrative center for the vast oil fields of the Permian Basin in West Texas; scores of oil companies maintain offices in this city of more than 110,000. Despite the oil industry's troubles, Midland County's faith in the GOP has not wavered; Republican Rep. Beau Boulter captured 63 percent of Midland's vote in his 1988 Senate challenge to Lloyd Bentsen.

Slightly larger and somewhat less Republican than Midland is San Angelo (Tom Green County), also in the northern part of the 21st. The city bills itself "the sheep and wool capital" of the nation and is a center for cattle, goat and sheep raising and wool processing.

There are few other population centers; the dry range land of the rural counties is best suited to grazing and oil drilling. Unlike most other rural parts of the old Confederacy, this area has a long tradition of supporting Republicans that stems from the anti-slavery Germans who settled it in the mid-1800s.

Hispanics are nearly 25 percent of the district's population. Most favor Democrats, but as a group, their turnout rate is low.

Population: 526,846. White 469,790 (89%), Black 15,213 (3%), Other 4,132 (1%). Spanish origin 100,455 (19%). 18 and over 381,130 (72%), 65 and over 63,596 (12%). Median age: 31.

Committees

Judiciary (11th of 14 Republicans)
Immigration, Refugees and International Law (ranking); Administrative Law and Governmental Relations

Science, Space and Technology (13th of 19 Republicans)
Energy Research and Development; Natural Resources, Agriculture Research and Environment; Space Science and Applications

Select Children, Youth and Families (9th of 12 Republicans)

Elections

1988 General		
Lamar Smith (R)	203,989	(93%)
James A. Robinson (LIB)	14,801	(7%)
1986 General		
Lamar Smith (R)	100,346	(61%)
Pete Snelson (D)	63,779	(39%)

District Vote For President

	1988	1984	1980	1976
D	78,971 (29%)	56,785 (22%)	53,079 (28%)	60,148 (37%)
R	192,335 (71%)	200,152 (78%)	131,809 (69%)	99,127 (62%)
I			4,644 (2%)	

Campaign Finance

	Receipts	Receipts from PACs	Expend-itures
1988			
Smith (R)	$567,737	$97,832 (17%)	$418,989
1986			
Smith (R)	$1,047,706	$122,076 (12%)	$1,043,325
Snelson (D)	$346,456	$107,363 (31%)	$345,117

Key Votes

1987	
Raise speed limit to 65 mph	Y
Approve Gephardt "fair trade" amendment	N
Ban testing of larger nuclear weapons	N
Delay "re-flagging" of Kuwaiti tankers	N
Approve tax-raising deficit-reduction bill	N
1988	
Approve aid to Nicaraguan contras	Y
Enact civil rights restoration bill over Reagan veto	N
Kill 60-day plant-closing notification measure	?
Pass omnibus trade bill over Reagan veto	N
Approve death penalty for drug-related murders	Y
Bar federal funds for abortions in cases of rape and incest	Y
Oppose seven-day waiting period for purchase of handguns	Y

Voting Studies

	Presidential Support		Party Unity		Conservative Coalition	
Year	S	O	S	O	S	O
1988	66	32	91	7	97	0
1987	74	25	81	14	95	2

Interest Group Ratings

Year	ADA	ACU	AFL-CIO	CCUS
1988	5	100	23	92
1987	0	96	6	93

22 Tom DeLay (R)

Of Sugar Land — Elected 1984

Born: April 8, 1947, Laredo, Texas.
Education: Baylor U., 1965-67; U. of Houston, B.S. 1970.
Occupation: Pest control company owner.
Family: Wife, Christine Ann Furrh; one child.
Religion: Baptist.
Political Career: Texas House, 1979-85.
Capitol Office: 308 Cannon Bldg. 20515; 225-5951.

In Washington: A classic Texas wheeler-dealer, DeLay toned down the anti-government zealotry he brought to Congress in 1985 as he positioned himself for continued advancement in a more establishment-minded House GOP leadership. But early in the 101st Congress, DeLay gambled and lost on a horse that might have carried him to the job of chief deputy whip. Now, as a younger generation of conservative House Republicans enjoys newfound influence, DeLay has no place in their pecking order.

In his first term, DeLay set his sights on making the GOP panel that determines committee assignments. He lined up the votes he needed and passed the word to a competing colleague that the contest was over. In the 100th Congress, DeLay was named an assistant regional whip, and he impressed many Republicans with his political skill and accurate vote counts. He earned a deputy whip slot at the start of the 101st Congress.

But then, DeLay became chief lieutenant for Illinois' Edward Madigan in his March 1989 campaign against Georgia's Newt Gingrich for the vacant post of minority whip. DeLay's conservatism, age and status as a Southerner suggested he could back Gingrich. But Madigan was the favorite of the establishment leaders DeLay had courted since his freshman term, and the chances were good that if Madigan moved up, so would DeLay. When Madigan lost, Gingrich's new guard pushed DeLay off the leadership ladder.

Fortunately for his cause, DeLay had used his committee assignment role to win membership on Appropriations in 1987. That gives him a base from which to begin rebuilding.

On the Appropriations Subcommittee on Transportation, DeLay generally advocates allowing the private sector to supply mass transit services, but he also works to bring Houston what he considers its "fair return" on tax payments. In the 100th Congress, he claimed credit for earmarking $50 million for the Houston metro rail-connector project.

DeLay developed a strong anti-regulatory streak when he was in the pest control business in Texas. He has issued detailed position papers calling for new deregulation of trucking, airlines, railroads, energy companies and banks, relaxation of environmental, health and safety laws, and scaling back of antitrust provisions. Declaring regulation anti-competitive, DeLay founded a grass-roots organization to fight "red tape."

At Home: When Republican Rep. Ron Paul announced his candidacy for the Senate in 1984, DeLay quickly became the front-runner to fill the 22nd District seat. A six-year veteran of the Texas House, DeLay had already represented parts of the 22nd's constituency, and his efforts to scale back the size of government during his days in the Legislature stood him in good stead in a district whose residents demand an adherence to conservative orthodoxy.

But DeLay did not capture the GOP nomination easily. The 11th-hour entrance of J. C. Helms, a wealthy real-estate developer from Bellaire, gave DeLay a serious scare. Helms had had some success in the neighboring 25th two years earlier, finishing first in the GOP primary but failing to convert on his momentum in the runoff. His alliance with hard-right conservatives in the Harris County (Houston) Republican Party further heightened the impression that he might manage to force a runoff with DeLay.

Helms sought to outflank DeLay on the right, casting himself as the natural philosophical heir to the libertarian Paul. DeLay offered a more mainstream conservative approach. He cited his experience as owner of a pest control company to demonstrate knowledge of small business, and called for a balanced budget.

Helms created a stir late in the campaign by running radio ads accusing DeLay of being late in paying payroll taxes from his business — a charge DeLay acknowledged while reminding Helms that the taxes were eventually paid. Visiting up to 60 homes a day, DeLay held his own in Harris County and won easily in his home base of Fort Bend. He clinched the GOP nomination with 54 percent. Since then, it has been all downhill. In 1986 and 1988, he won reelection with more than two-thirds of the vote.

Texas 22

Southwest Houston and Suburbs; Fort Bend and Brazoria Counties

The 22nd District is a testament to suburban Houston's phenomenal growth over the past two decades. During the 1970s, the district was focused within the city, and the area DeLay now represents was a sparsely populated corner of it. Today that same territory has enough people to be a constituency itself, and DeLay represents more people outside the city limits than within them.

The 22nd's communities are highly transient and bound together by few ties of tradition. What unites them is a universally conservative outlook and a GOP preference.

The part of Houston that remains in the district is largely affluent and white-collar; it casts roughly 40 percent of the vote. Some of the district's most affluent homes lie at its northern border, near the exclusive Galleria shopping mall.

Houston's sprawl has engulfed established residential towns such as Bellaire and West University Place, once considered outlying suburbs, and they are included in the 22nd. Farther out, it also includes Missouri City, a burgeoning community divided between Harris and Fort Bend counties.

Moving south, the district encompasses all of Fort Bend County. Parts of the county are still rural and small-town in character and have little to do with Houston; here rice, cotton and oil spark the local economy, along with some cattle ranching. But high-priced residential subdivisions are becoming the norm. The influx of Houston professionals more than doubled Fort Bend's population in the 1970s, and has nearly doubled it again in the 1980s.

Fort Bend County occasionally backs a moderate Democrat running statewide, but it has not gone Democratic for president since 1964. In 1988, the county voted for Lloyd Bentsen for Senate and George Bush for president.

The 22nd also takes in northeast Brazoria County, where towns such as Alvin have a conservative, blue-collar Democratic bent.

Population: 526,602. White 427,161 (81%), Black 50,585 (10%), Other 15,203 (3%). Spanish origin 71,439 (14%). 18 and over 381,492 (72%), 65 and over 29,577 (6%). Median age: 28.

Committee

Appropriations (20th of 22 Republicans)
Military Construction; Transportation and Related Agencies

Elections

1988 General		
Tom DeLay (R)	125,733	(67%)
Wayne Walker (D)	58,471	(31%)
1986 General		
Tom DeLay (R)	76,459	(72%)
Susan Director (D)	30,079	(28%)

Previous Winning Percentage: **1984** (65%)

District Vote For President

	1988	1984	1980	1976
D	68,391 (38%)	55,587 (30%)	48,188 (30%)	50,146 (37%)
R	112,088 (62%)	128,971 (70%)	104,147 (65%)	83,150 (62%)
I			5,927 (4%)	

Campaign Finance

	Receipts	Receipts from PACs	Expend-itures
1988			
DeLay (R)	$364,837	$171,650 (47%)	$361,255
Walker (D) †	$112,649	$1,500 (1%)	$109,004
1986			
DeLay (R)	$316,191	$157,949 (50%)	$294,850

† Totals based on incomplete data.

Key Votes

1987	
Raise speed limit to 65 mph	Y
Approve Gephardt "fair trade" amendment	N
Ban testing of larger nuclear weapons	N
Delay "re-flagging" of Kuwaiti tankers	N
Approve tax-raising deficit-reduction bill	N
1988	
Approve aid to Nicaraguan contras	Y
Enact civil rights restoration bill over Reagan veto	N
Kill 60-day plant-closing notification measure	Y
Pass omnibus trade bill over Reagan veto	N
Approve death penalty for drug-related murders	Y
Bar federal funds for abortions in cases of rape and incest	Y
Oppose seven-day waiting period for purchase of handguns	Y

Voting Studies

	Presidential Support		Party Unity		Conservative Coalition	
Year	**S**	**O**	**S**	**O**	**S**	**O**
1988	78	18	88	7	97	0
1987	78	19	91	5	100	0
1986	83	14	91	4	100	0
1985	85	13	87	7	96	4

Interest Group Ratings

Year	ADA	ACU	AFL-CIO	CCUS
1988	0	100	0	92
1987	0	100	0	93
1986	0	100	7	94
1985	5	100	0	95

23 Albert G. Bustamante (D)

Of San Antonio — Elected 1984

Born: April 8, 1935, Asherton, Texas.
Education: Sul Ross State College, B.A. 1961.
Military Career: Army, 1954-56.
Occupation: Teacher.
Family: Wife, Rebecca Pounders; three children.
Religion: Roman Catholic.
Political Career: Bexar County commissioner, 1972-78; Bexar County judge, 1978-83.
Capitol Office: 1116 Longworth Bldg. 20515; 225-4511.

In Washington: With his generally liberal views and judicious manner, Armed Services member Bustamante is equipped to participate in the difficult debates on defense policy. But the orientation of his district — it has five Air Force bases and a huge population of military retirees — creates a sizable constituency for a simple "more is better" defense outlook. Bustamante is thus constrained from emerging as an activist in high-profile defense policy debates, many of which involve tough choices about what can be afforded.

So Bustamante has worked since 1985 to make a mark in the lower-visibility detail work of Armed Services. Both on that committee and on Government Operations, he is a member of subcommittees dealing with military nuclear materials, and he spoke out on environmental and safety problems in the nation's nuclear production plants early in 1988, months before the problems showed up in the daily headlines.

Citing safety concerns, Bustamante submitted an amendment to delay funding for the proposed Special Isotope Separation project in Idaho. The $2 billion project was later put on hold.

Bustamante was also involved in pushing the Defense Department to demand in 1987 that Japan abide by patent secrecy contracts relating to joint research on the strategic defense initiative (SDI). Bustamante felt the participation of Japan and other countries in SDI could enable foreign defense contractors to market SDI spinoff products in unfair competition against American industry.

On major defense issues, Bustamante is normally a dependable vote for the Democratic leadership. In the 100th Congress, he supported the nuclear test ban amendments proposed by liberal Democrats in both 1987 and 1988.

However, Bustamante has faced some trying decisions on the issue of U.S. aid to the contras. Because the 23rd is on the nation's southern border, a number of its constituents feel a security threat from events in Central America. But Bustamante, like many fellow Hispanics, has mixed feelings about American support of a military force in that region.

At the start of 1986 he worked with moderate Democrats to find an alternative to President Reagan's pro-contra policy, then surprised them by voting with Reagan to authorize $100 million for the contras. But Bustamante became disenchanted after the Iran-contra revelations and reports that the White House had worked with a conservative lobby group on TV ads questioning the patriotism of anti-contra Democrats.

In 1987, he voted against sending the $40 million remaining from the contra aid approved the year before, saying, "We have no accountability for what has already been spent." He also voted against Reagan's $36 million aid request in 1988, but he did support the bipartisan "humanitarian" aid package worked out by President Bush and Congress in 1989.

At Home: Bustamante's election, assured when he ousted veteran Democratic Rep. Abraham Kazen Jr. in a 1984 primary, was another step in southwest Texas Hispanics' drive to wrest key offices from "Anglo" control.

Bustamante grew up as a migrant laborer, picking fruit and grain crops. Kazen, of Lebanese descent, came from a family associated with the Anglo establishment that has long dominated many of Texas' border towns.

Ethnicity was not an overt issue in their primary. Bustamante tried to paint Kazen as inaccessible and ineffective; Kazen stressed his seniority and influence. But Bustamante clearly needed to rally Hispanics. "Help me on Cinco de Mayo [May 5, a Mexican national holiday as well as Texas' primary date] to declare our independence from an old political family who has controlled the destiny of this area," he told a predominantly Mexican-American audience.

Bustamante got an impressive 59 percent of the primary vote in the 23rd, where 1983 redistricting changes had boosted the Mexican-American population to some 56 percent. Once past the primary, he was home free. He has faced GOP opposition only once, and crushed it.

Texas 23

Southwest — San Antonio Suburbs; Laredo

A diverse patch of southwestern Texas, the 23rd stretches from the white-collar suburbs of San Antonio in Bexar County to the rural, overwhelmingly Hispanic terrain near the Mexican border.

That mixture generally yields Democratic victories. But the 23rd has been competitive in recent statewide races. In 1988 presidential balloting, five of the nine counties in the 23rd went Republican.

The San Antonio-area portion of the 23rd includes communities such as Windcrest, a haven for military retirees with a conservative bias. This area also includes five military installations, including Brooks and Randolph Air Force bases, which are crucial economic and political forces. The suburbs of San Antonio roll west to the fringes of Medina County.

But the last redistricting removed 35,000 GOP-minded residents of northern Bexar County and added Val Verde County, a 63 percent Hispanic area on the Mexican border. That change pushed the 23rd's Hispanic population to 56 percent.

Val Verde and the other Hispanic counties help ensure the district's Democratic cast. Webb County, where nine out of every 10 residents are Hispanic, gave Democrat Lloyd Bentsen 85 percent in his 1988 Senate re-election and gave the Democratic presidential ticket 70 percent.

Webb County's Laredo, with 117,000 people, is the population center in the southern part of the 23rd. A gateway for trade and tourism with Mexico, Laredo has seen its economy hit hard by the devaluation of the Mexican peso. Conditions have improved in Laredo since the end of 1982, when unemployment hit 25 percent. But Mexicans still are not flocking to Laredo merchants in the numbers they once did.

Surrounding Laredo are vegetable-growing farm lands irrigated with water from the Rio Grande. Cattle ranching, oil and gas exploration are in the dry areas north and east.

Population: 526,746. White 440,544 (84%), Black 21,633 (4%), Other 4,814 (1%). Spanish origin 296,148 (56%). 18 and over 332,851 (63%), 65 and over 36,920 (7%). Median age: 25.

Committees

Armed Services (23rd of 31 Democrats)
Military Personnel and Compensation; Procurement and Military Nuclear Systems

Government Operations (19th of 24 Democrats)
Commerce, Consumer and Monetary Affairs; Environment, Energy and Natural Resources; Legislation and National Security

Select Hunger (14th of 18 Democrats)
Task Force: Domestic

Elections

1988 General		
Albert G. Bustamante (D)	116,423	(65%)
Jerry Gonzales (R)	60,559	(34%)
1986 General		
Albert G. Bustamante (D)	68,131	(91%)
Ken Hendrix (LIB)	7,001	(9%)

Previous Winning Percentage: **1984** (100%)

District Vote For President

	1988	1984	1980	1976
D	93,074 (50%)	66,148 (41%)	54,983 (48%)	52,708 (59%)
R	94,826 (50%)	95,732 (59%)	55,483 (49%)	36,020 (40%)
I			2,504 (2%)	

Campaign Finance

	Receipts	Receipts from PACs	Expend-itures
1988			
Bustamante (D)	$280,485	$155,786 (56%)	$187,302
Gonzales (R)	$6,573	0	$6,365
1986			
Bustamante (D)	$253,798	$89,500 (35%)	$190,891

Key Votes

1987	
Raise speed limit to 65 mph	Y
Approve Gephardt "fair trade" amendment	Y
Ban testing of larger nuclear weapons	Y
Delay "re-flagging" of Kuwaiti tankers	Y
Approve tax-raising deficit-reduction bill	Y
1988	
Approve aid to Nicaraguan contras	N
Enact civil rights restoration bill over Reagan veto	Y
Kill 60-day plant-closing notification measure	N
Pass omnibus trade bill over Reagan veto	Y
Approve death penalty for drug-related murders	Y
Bar federal funds for abortions in cases of rape and incest	N
Oppose seven-day waiting period for purchase of handguns	Y

Voting Studies

	Presidential Support		Party Unity		Conservative Coalition	
Year	**S**	**O**	**S**	**O**	**S**	**O**
1988	25	66	88	4	45	47
1987	29	67	84	7	67	26
1986	32	63	82	9	58	30
1985	34	64	85	10	51	44

Interest Group Ratings

Year	ADA	ACU	AFL-CIO	CCUS
1988	70	8	100	21
1987	76	0	93	14
1986	50	33	100	20
1985	65	19	88	24

24 Martin Frost (D)

Of Dallas — Elected 1978

Born: Jan. 1, 1942, Glendale, Calif.
Education: U. of Missouri, B.A. and B.J. 1964; Georgetown U. Law Center, J.D. 1970.
Military Career: Army Reserve, 1966-72.
Occupation: Lawyer.
Family: Wife, Valerie Hall; three children.
Religion: Jewish.
Political Career: Sought Democratic nomination for U.S. House, 1974.
Capitol Office: 2459 Rayburn Bldg. 20515; 225-3605.

In Washington: Frost has played many angles to make his way in the House, but the one he played the most was his close association with Jim Wright, his Fort Worth neighbor. When Frost came to Congress in 1979, Wright was in the early years of his tenure as majority leader. When Wright became Speaker in the 100th Congress, it was almost a dream come true for Frost. But he enjoyed the Speaker's ear for just two short years; Wright's forced departure in 1989 made Frost an ordinary mortal.

Not completely ordinary, to be sure. A shrewd institutional player, Frost still holds seats on Rules and House Administration, where he can have an impact in his own right. But it is also true that Frost worked hard to be seen as Wright's man on those panels. When Frost was arguing for something, many members assumed, whether correctly or not, that he was speaking for Wright as well. A desire by the Democratic Caucus to be done with the Wright era may have factored into Frost's failure in June 1989 to win the post of caucus vice chairman, one of several leadership jobs that came open in the wake of Wright's departure. Frost ran second in the four-way race, but finished far behind Californian Vic Fazio.

Not surprisingly, Frost was one of Wright's most visible and outspoken defenders when he started sinking under the weight of ethics questions. At one point in early 1989, Frost sought to reassure other Democrats Wright was still popular by distributing press clippings touting his strong support in Texas. But by May 1989, even Frost acknowledged the damage. "Really it does interfere with the operation of the House, you can't deny that," he said.

Frost volunteered to clear his own agenda to work for Wright's when he became Speaker. When Wright turned to the Rules Committee for restrictive rules that would make it easier for him to pass his ambitious legislative agenda, he had an ally in Frost.

"The Speaker has correctly been trying to force the House to follow a schedule in the first year to show he means business," Frost said in 1987. "The Rules Committee has been a major factor in making that happen."

Frost does have his own interests, though. While he participates in many grand strategy sessions, he watches out closely for his district. In the 100th Congress, one of his efforts was to try to protect low-income housing in the 24th. Working with fellow Texan Mickey Leland, he offered a successful amendment to the HUD appropriations bill barring use of agency funds to demolish 2,600 units of public housing in West Dallas and 1,000 in Houston.

In 1988 Frost also worked on legislation to prevent LTV, a major corporation in his district, from terminating health and life insurance for retirees after filing for bankruptcy under Chapter 11. The bill, which he worked on with Ohio Rep. Louis Stokes and Judiciary Chairman Peter W. Rodino Jr., required companies to go before a bankruptcy court hearing before altering such benefits.

And like most members of Texas' delegation, Frost also spent part of his time in the 100th Congress helping make the case that his home state should be chosen for the multibillion-dollar superconducting supercollider. Toward the end of the Congress, the Department of Energy chose Texas for the giant atom-smasher.

Frost's soft voice and shy smile suggest a self-effacing personality. But he is a man of calculating ambition and no small amount of self-esteem. Even some who admire his political instincts consider him at times too strong-willed, and wanting in finesse.

As ingratiating as he was with Wright, Frost has crossed swords with some other powerful members. In 1983, Frost was a militant defender of industrial development bonds, a revenue source heavily used by Dallas and other Texas cities, when their unrestricted use was threatened by a Ways and Means tax bill brought before Rules.

Frost's opposition was an important reason why no tax bill went to the floor during that year. Restrictions on the use of the bonds did

Texas 24

South Dallas and Western Suburbs

The 24th contains the largest concentration of black and Hispanic voters anywhere in the Dallas area.

The black population — comprising about one-third of the district total — is mostly at the eastern end of the 24th, south of the Trinity River in Dallas. Hispanics, who account for roughly 15 percent, are more numerous in the central part of the district. The suburbs on the western edge of the 24th, such as Irving and Grand Prairie, are mostly white.

Predominantly blue-collar Grand Prairie hosts two subsidiaries of the LTV Corp., the aerospace giant currently in Chapter 11 bankruptcy proceedings. While the parent company's fate has yet to be determined, Grand Prairie's two plants — one makes aircraft products and the other produces missiles and electronics — are thriving and are unlikely to suffer. Some of the district's most affluent — and most Republican — residents make their homes in northern Irving. The home field of football's Dallas Cowboys — Texas Stadium — is here, benefiting the community.

Both suburbs contain many factory workers and laborers in the construction trades. Another important employer is the sprawling Dallas-Fort Worth Airport, part of which is located in the district's northwestern corner.

The 1983 round of redistricting made minor adjustments in the 24th's boundaries. Map makers removed the district's share of Arlington, uniting it with the rest of the city in the neighboring 26th. In turn, a section of southwest Dallas County was brought into Frost's constituency from the 6th. This added territory includes communities such as DeSoto and Cedar Hill, areas with a substantial blue-collar presence that are caught up in southwest Dallas' urban sprawl.

The heavy minority influence helps make the southwestern Dallas portions of the district predictably Democratic; Grand Prairie and Irving also favor Democrats most of the time. Many of the district's white precincts gave George Bush solid majorities in 1988, but typically, these precincts tend to divide about evenly between the parties in statewide contests. In 1988, Michael S. Dukakis won the 24th with 53 percent, getting a boost from the minority-dominated areas of Dallas.

Population: 527,267. White 309,349 (59%), Black 167,099 (32%), Other 6,164 (1%). Spanish origin 69,340 (13%). 18 and over 352,993 (67%), 65 and over 36,962 (7%). Median age: 27.

become law as part of broader tax legislation the following year, but only after some exemptions were carved out that satisfied many of the members who objected. Frost's effort did not do much to endear him to Ways and Means Chairman Dan Rostenkowski, and the episode still colors their relationship.

For the 101st Congress, when the Democratic Caucus created a spot on House Administration for a representative of exclusive committees, Frost went up against Rostenkowski, who wanted to put Alabama's Ronnie G. Flippo on the panel that oversees committee budgets. A compromise was struck that put both Frost and Flippo on House Administration.

In 1983, Frost took advantage of his place on Rules to win one of that panel's two allotted seats on Budget. The next year he was at the center of a complicated debate over the House Budget chairmanship that kept half the Democratic Caucus guessing his true intentions.

As head of a Rules Committee task force on internal House procedure, Frost recommended that the party retain a rule effectively eliminating the top two contenders for the Budget post. James R. Jones of Oklahoma, the incumbent chairman, and Leon E. Panetta of California, his main challenger, both had exhausted their allotted tenure on Budget and wanted a rules change to stay on longer.

The decision of Frost's task force not to change the rule was made even more controversial by the fact that Frost was interested in heading Budget himself. He said his task force considered the rules change on its merits, without regard to his ambitions. Many colleagues wondered whether that was true, but the Democratic Caucus agreed with Frost's position, thanks in part to lobbying by Wright and Speaker Thomas P. O'Neill Jr.

Shortly after the caucus vote, Frost formally entered the Budget contest, saying he was "someone from the center of the party who can unite all factions within the House." But it soon was evident that William H. Gray III of Pennsylvania already had united all the factions he needed; Frost withdrew, admitting that "the votes simply are not there."

At Home: Frost got to Congress in 1978 by defeating incumbent Dale Milford in a primary, something he had failed to do four years earlier. Milford, a former television weatherman, won the seat in 1972. But Frost was encouraged to mount a challenge in 1974 after redistricting pared away conservative suburban areas while adding black sections of Dallas much less favorable to the incumbent.

Frost complained that Milford was too supportive of the Nixon administration. But the incumbent withstood the challenge to win the 1974 Democratic primary with 58 percent of the vote. Frost bypassed a rematch in 1976 to run Jimmy Carter's campaign in north Texas.

But two years later, he tried again, reviving complaints that Milford was too conservative. Moving beyond personal door-to-door campaigning, Frost built an effective precinct organization. He also got the support of the state AFL-CIO and two of the largest newspapers in the Dallas-Fort Worth area. Drawing 55 percent, he beat Milford.

Frost's Republican rival that November tried to turn the tables, claiming that Frost was a tool of organized labor and too liberal for the district. The Democrat trailed in returns from Tarrant County, but offset the deficit in his home base of Dallas County to win 54 percent.

For a moment in 1982, it seemed Frost might be in some political trouble. The Legislature had redrawn his district to be 64 percent black and Hispanic, and professor Lucy Patterson, the first black woman elected to the Dallas City Council, planned a primary challenge to him, hoping minority voters would unite behind her.

Frost reacted quickly. He gathered early endorsements from many leaders in the black and Hispanic communities. And then, the district's boundaries were changed again before the Democratic primary. A three-judge federal panel undid the Legislature's work, making the 24th a white-majority district, with a combined black and Hispanic population just under 50 percent.

Under the court-drawn lines, there were not enough minority voters in the 24th to sustain Patterson's primary challenge. She ultimately switched parties and ran as a Republican. Frost swamped her, taking more than 70 percent of the vote.

That experience bolstered Frost's confidence for 1984. He spent much of his time early in the year organizing the Texas presidential primary campaign of Colorado Sen. Gary Hart, then signed on as a state coordinator for Walter F. Mondale after Hart was beaten. In the fall, Frost won re-election with 60 percent while the district was going to President Reagan. In 1986, he topped 67 percent; in 1988, the Republicans left him alone entirely.

Committees

House Administration (12th of 13 Democrats)
Elections; Libraries and Memorials; Office Systems; Procurement and Printing

Rules (4th of 9 Democrats)
Legislative Process

Elections

1988 General		
Martin Frost (D)	135,794	(93%)
Leo Sadovy (LIB)	10,841	(7%)
1986 General		
Martin Frost (D)	69,368	(67%)
Bob Burk (R)	33,819	(33%)

Previous Winning Percentages: **1984** (59%) **1982** (73%) **1980** (61%) **1978** (54%)

District Vote For President

	1988		1984		1980		1976	
D	97,339	(53%)	85,078	(47%)	74,070	(50%)	73,589	(56%)
R	87,596	(47%)	96,596	(53%)	70,634	(47%)	56,237	(43%)
I					2,843	(2%)		

Campaign Finance

	Receipts	Receipts from PACs		Expend-itures
1988				
Frost (D)	$590,973	$298,373	(50%)	$438,949
1986				
Frost (D)	$775,479	$336,099	(43%)	$709,864
Burk (R)	$21,231	0		$23,676

Key Votes

1987	
Raise speed limit to 65 mph	N
Approve Gephardt "fair trade" amendment	Y
Ban testing of larger nuclear weapons	Y
Delay "re-flagging" of Kuwaiti tankers	Y
Approve tax-raising deficit-reduction bill	Y
1988	
Approve aid to Nicaraguan contras	N
Enact civil rights restoration bill over Reagan veto	Y
Kill 60-day plant-closing notification measure	N
Pass omnibus trade bill over Reagan veto	Y
Approve death penalty for drug-related murders	Y
Bar federal funds for abortions in cases of rape and incest	N
Oppose seven-day waiting period for purchase of handguns	X

Voting Studies

	Presidential Support		Party Unity		Conservative Coalition	
Year	**S**	**O**	**S**	**O**	**S**	**O**
1988	21	66	84	5	37	42
1987	31	67	83	9	60	30
1986	23	66	74	11	52	38
1985	26	69	83	9	47	47
1984	33	48	63	14	42	47
1983	34	59	79	13	48	47
1982	34	58	82	12	40	59
1981	34	38	70	17	52	41

Interest Group Ratings

Year	ADA	ACU	AFL-CIO	CCUS
1988	70	9	92	23
1987	88	0	93	29
1986	45	26	73	43
1985	55	24	82	35
1984	65	25	100	36
1983	75	22	82	20
1982	70	10	85	23
1981	50	14	77	24

25 Michael A. Andrews (D)

Of Houston — Elected 1982

Born: Feb. 7, 1944, Houston, Texas.

Education: U. of Texas, B.A. 1967; Southern Methodist U., J.D. 1970.

Occupation: Lawyer.

Family: Wife, Ann Bowman; two children.

Religion: Episcopalian.

Political Career: Democratic nominee for U.S. House, 1980.

Capitol Office: 322 Cannon Bldg. 20515; 225-7508.

In Washington: By twice walking the plank in the 100th Congress for Ways and Means Chairman Dan Rostenkowski, Andrews proved his loyalty to the powerful Illinois Democrat who had initially kept him off the committee. Long regarded as an ambitious man with the looks and the yen to run for statewide office, Andrews took on a couple of decidedly unattractive and politically risky assignments: circumventing Southern opposition to a welfare bill and rounding up votes to defeat seniors superhero Claude Pepper's crusade on behalf of long-term home health care.

The first mission came in late 1987, a year after Andrews made it onto Ways and Means. The committee was having trouble with its welfare-overhaul initiative. Southerners rebelled at Rostenkowski's attempt to wrap the welfare bill into a broad-ranging budget "reconciliation" measure. They feared that a bill including both welfare and taxes would be fodder for vicious television ads by election opponents, and they joined Republicans in a vote that kept the welfare bill off the floor.

For seven weeks, Democratic leaders tried to find a way to bring the bill up on its own. They were determined not to allow the bill to be rewritten piecemeal on the floor, and were also intent on sidetracking an alternative welfare bill developed by conservative Democrats Charles W. Stenholm of Texas and Thomas R. Carper of Delaware that would cost less than half the $6.2 billion version pushed by Ways and Means.

To the rescue came Andrews, with an amendment that would slice $500 million from the committee bill in ways that would ease the burden on states and limit welfare expansion. It mollified just enough Democrats. A rule allowing Andrews a floor vote (but denying Carper and Stenholm an opportunity) squeaked by, 213-206. It got no Republican votes, but 15 Southern Democrats switched their votes from the previous confrontation. Andrews' amendment was approved overwhelmingly and the welfare measure passed with a margin of 36 votes.

The next year, Rostenkowski appointed Andrews head of a task force to defeat Pepper's initiative to provide long-term care at home to disabled and elderly people. Rostenkowski was furious that the Florida Democrat had used his Rules Committee chairmanship to bypass Ways and Means over the proposal to pay for the program by raising the Medicare tax some $28 billion over five years. Senior citizens deluged the Capitol with bags of green peppers to symbolize their support for the measure; Andrews said he felt "like cannon fodder" mobilizing opposition. In the end, however, enough members gulped at the cost to keep the bill off the floor by a vote of 169-243.

These tasks marked quite a turnaround in Rostenkowski's view of Andrews. In 1985, then-Majority Leader Jim Wright, eager to place another Texan on Ways and Means, sponsored Andrews for a place there. But Rostenkowski had his own candidate, Pennsylvania's William J. Coyne, and he maintained that Coyne was more of a party loyalist than Andrews, who had shown a tendency in his first term to pay more attention to the wishes of the Houston business community than to Democratic leaders. Coyne got the job.

Wright maintained his commitment to Andrews, however, and there was little question that the incoming Speaker would get his man on Ways and Means before very long. When a committee vacancy developed in mid-1986, Andrews applied for it, and nobody ran against him.

Passing his loyalty tests has not required Andrews to abandon his Houston interests. On Ways and Means, he helped win a change in 1988 in a provision of the 1986 tax-overhaul bill that would have increased tax collections on diesel fuel. Also, he joined with other oil-state members to overcome Rostenkowski's reluctance to repeal the windfall-profits tax on oil as part of the 1988 omnibus trade bill.

In his previous assignment on Science and Technology, Andrews had been a protector of the Johnson Space Center, located in Houston. In 1986, he helped to ferret out and block a plan

Texas 25

South Houston and Southeast Suburbs

The 25th contains all of Harris County south of the Houston Ship Channel, a waterway lined with heavy industry. The cities of Pasadena and Deer Park are filled with blue-collar workers employed at numerous local petrochemical facilities.

These working-class people are nearly all nominal Democrats, but they are not always automatic partisan voters. Ronald Reagan's conservative themes played well enough among blue-collar workers for him to carry the 25th narrowly in 1980 and 1984. He was also boosted by support from the more affluent parts of Pasadena, Deer Park and South Houston. But in 1988, George Bush could not quite match Reagan's appeal, and the district tipped Democratic for president.

Farther west in the district is a concentration of minority voters. Sunnyside, a predominantly black community, is one of Houston's most impoverished areas. The Brentwood neighborhood hosts a large number of middle-class black professionals. This part of the district is also home to the Houston Astrodome, Rice University and a large concentration of Jewish voters in Meyerland.

Blacks and Hispanics make up 39 percent of the district's population; among all the Houston-area districts, only central Houston's 18th has a higher minority percentage. The minority vote helps push the 25th into the Democratic column in most non-presidential contests.

Living in the southeastern corner of the 25th are many employees of NASA's Manned Spacecraft Center, which is across the district boundary in the 9th. But the district's largest single employer is the Texas Medical Center. Described as the largest medical complex in the world, the complex includes schools, research facilities and hospitals. The center's extensive facilities bring to nearly 30 the number of hospitals located within the 25th.

Population: 526,801. White 352,345 (67%), Black 131,660 (25%), Other 8,703 (2%). Spanish origin 72,400 (14%). 18 and over 366,175 (70%), 65 and over 31,561 (6%). Median age: 27.

by NASA to move key work on the space station project from Houston to the space center in Huntsville, Ala. NASA's plan imperiled nearly 2,000 potential jobs as well as $1.5 billion in lost revenue for Houston, already wracked by depressed oil prices.

As chairman of the Congressional Sunbelt Caucus in the 100th Congress, Andrews pushed the group into a newly confrontational stance toward its more established regional rival, the Northeast-Midwest Congressional Coalition.

On a decidedly non-local front, Andrews was one of two sponsors of a bill in the 100th Congress to keep a private developer from building a shopping mall next to the Manassas Civil War battleground in Northern Virginia. His interest came from a tour of the battlefield with a former history professor shortly before the builder announced his plans.

The bill, which in its final form purchased the land to add to the battlefield park, passed the House by a 3-to-1 margin and became law over the administration's objections as part of the 1988 tax code technical-corrections measure.

At Home: Andrews is a political consultant's dream. Handsome and articulate, he was born and educated in Texas and worked as an assistant district attorney in Houston before joining a private law firm. But he did not come by his House seat easily.

Andrews' quest for Congress began in the 1980 Democratic primary in the old 22nd District, held by GOP Rep. Ron Paul. Former Democratic Rep. Bob Gammage, seeking to reclaim the seat he lost to Paul in 1978, was viewed as stale by Democratic financiers, which benefited Andrews. He ran a close second in the primary, and beat Gammage in the runoff.

If there had been no presidential contest, Andrews probably would have won in 1980. He impressed businessmen with his claim to fiscal conservatism, and won labor unionists who preferred him to a libertarian ideologue like Paul. But Ronald Reagan's strong showing in the 22nd gave Paul a narrow 51 percent victory.

In 1981, however, redistricting created a golden opportunity for Andrews — the new 25th was carved from four existing districts in the Houston area, the largest portion coming from Paul's 22nd. It was drawn to be a reliable Democratic district. Andrews, the front-runner from the start, found himself in a runoff with state District Judge John Ray Harrison.

Harrison, whose base was among blue-collar whites in Pasadena, argued that Andrews had shifted to the left to appeal to the district's sizable minority population. Andrews did make an appeal for black votes, appearing arm-in-arm in ads with Democratic Rep. Mickey Leland, the black liberal from central Houston. Harrison passed out copies of the ad in white areas.

But Andrews took 58 percent in the runoff, winning near-unanimous support from minorities and affluent white voters, although faring less well among poorer whites. He won the general election with surprising ease over Mike Faubion, an aggressive Republican who tried to duplicate Reagan's working-class appeal. Andrews has since been re-elected without a difficult test. In 1988, he crushed his GOP challenger by better than 2-to-1.

Committee

Ways and Means (20th of 23 Democrats)
Human Resources; Select Revenue Measures

Elections

1988 General		
Michael A. Andrews (D)	113,499	(71%)
George H. Loefflor Jr. (R)	44,043	(28%)
1986 General		
Michael A. Andrews (D)	67,435	(100%)

Previous Winning Percentages: 1984 (64%) **1982** (60%)

District Vote For President

	1988	1984	1980	1976
D	76,165 (53%)	82,485 (48%)	68,689 (47%)	76,849 (52%)
R	66,767 (47%)	88,412 (52%)	72,831 (49%)	68,959 (47%)
I			4,603 (3%)	

Campaign Finance

	Receipts	Receipts from PACs	Expend-itures
1988			
Andrews (D)	$638,035	$403,635 (63%)	$318,970
1986			
Andrews (D)	$300,074	$134,054 (45%)	$133,817

Key Votes

1987	
Raise speed limit to 65 mph	N
Approve Gephardt "fair trade" amendment	Y
Ban testing of larger nuclear weapons	Y
Delay "re-flagging" of Kuwaiti tankers	N
Approve tax-raising deficit-reduction bill	Y
1988	
Approve aid to Nicaraguan contras	N
Enact civil rights restoration bill over Reagan veto	Y
Kill 60-day plant-closing notification measure	N
Pass omnibus trade bill over Reagan veto	Y
Approve death penalty for drug-related murders	Y
Bar federal funds for abortions in cases of rape and incest	N
Oppose seven-day waiting period for purchase of handguns	Y

Voting Studies

	Presidential Support		Party Unity		Conservative Coalition	
Year	**S**	**O**	**S**	**O**	**S**	**O**
1988	37	62	75	21	87	11
1987	39	60	75	23	81	19
1986	37	61	72	24	96	4
1985	39	59	77	21	84	16
1984	48	50	64	33	81	17
1983	45	54	61	37	78	21

Interest Group Ratings

Year	ADA	ACU	AFL-CIO	CCUS
1988	75	29	86	62
1987	68	0	69	47
1986	50	45	64	61
1985	30	57	50	71
1984	45	29	69	38
1983	60	36	59	65

26 Dick Armey (R)

Of Copper Canyon — Elected 1984

Born: July 7, 1940, Cando, N.D.
Education: Jamestown College, B.A. 1963; U. of North Dakota, M.A. 1964; U. of Oklahoma, Ph.D. 1969.
Occupation: Economist.
Family: Wife, Susan K. Byrd; five children.
Religion: Presbyterian.
Political Career: No previous office.
Capitol Office: 130 Cannon Bldg. 20515; 225-7772.

In Washington: Passage of the measure Armey championed in the 100th Congress — a landmark bill governing the closing of military bases — dramatically altered this conservative Texan's reputation as a legislator. As a freshman in the 99th Congress, he had often come across as an ideologue, someone more interested in lecturing on free-market economics than in building consensus. But by channeling his energies into the base-closing bill and lobbying colleagues one by one to support it, Armey proved that he could listen and persuade, not just lecture.

Seeking support from both Democrats and Republicans was a departure from the confrontational approach Armey used as a freshman, when he was a self-described "budget commando" arguing — mostly unsuccessfully — for federal spending reductions. This change was a conscious strategy by Armey. In June 1988, he told *The Wall Street Journal* that he had "risked being labeled a bomb-thrower, a loose cannon." He added that "you can be so ideologically hidebound you can cut yourself out of the process."

Still, the base-closing bill was a peculiar venture for Armey. He was a junior member of the minority party crusading on the turf of a powerful committee — Armed Services — to which he did not belong. And his mission seemed to carry great potential for failure. In response to a 1976 effort by President Gerald R. Ford to shut dozens of bases, Congress moved to protect members' parochial interests by setting up an obstacle course of environmental regulations to be met before a base could be closed.

To insulate base-closing decisions from politics, Armey proposed giving all base-closing responsibility to an independent commission that would review military needs and develop a list of bases it found unnecessary. His bill also waived many restrictions that had tied up base closings for more than a decade.

In 1987, Armey tried to attach his proposal to the fiscal 1988 defense authorization bill. Though he had lobbied only briefly for the measure, it fell just short, losing 192-199. Convinced he had struck a nerve, Armey tried the same tactic on the next year's defense authorization bill. However, the Armed Services, Government Operations and Merchant Marine committees claimed jurisdiction, taking the bill off its fast track.

When a bill finally emerged from the Rules Committee, it was substantially changed: Congress would have to approve the commission's list, and a variety of environmental and economic issues would have to be addressed. Armey said these changes would make it difficult to close any bases. In July 1988, he submitted a "clean bill" as an amendment on the House floor. The measure removed most of the criteria that had been added to his proposal; in its major concession, it allowed Congress to kill the base-closing plan, but only by passage in both Houses of a resolution disapproving the entire list. Armey's amendment passed 223-186, and became law in October.

At year's end, the blue-ribbon panel released a list of targeted bases that was somewhat more modest than expected. Estimated savings were less than $700 million a year, rather than the originally touted $2 billion-plus. But that modesty ensured the plan's success: Only a few dozen members' districts were affected.

Armey easily parried complaints about job losses in New Jersey, California, Illinois and other states with bases to be closed. "I know it's painful to the communities involved," he said during the April 1989 debate on the resolution to disapprove the commission's recommendations. "But defense dollars are for defense, not for community development." The resolution of disapproval went down 43-381, in effect ratifying the base-closure list.

Armey got a seat on the Budget Committee at the start of his second term in 1987, and surprised colleagues with his willingness to work with ideological opposites. In 1988, he joined with liberal California Democrat Barbara Boxer on an amendment to that year's budget resolution, adding $220 million for Coast Guard drug-interdiction efforts; then-committee

Texas 26

Fort Worth Suburbs — Arlington; Denton

Much of this territory was open country 20 years ago. But the area has been transformed by the influx of migrants to the Sun Belt that brought Texas three new congressional seats for the 1980s. Although the northern part of the 26th is still predominantly rural, more than half the district's land has been engulfed by suburban spread.

About 55 percent of the vote comes from the Fort Worth environs in Tarrant County, although Fort Worth itself is not in the district. Living in the Tarrant suburbs south of the city are doctors, lawyers and other upper-middle-class professionals with a hard-core conservative outlook. Southeastern Tarrant towns such as Mansfield appeal to white-collar city workers seeking a more rural setting still close enough to allow them to commute to work.

Redistricting in 1983 removed the southwestern corner of Tarrant County from the 26th, and also cut out most of the Collin County city of Plano. In exchange, the district expanded to take in all of the city of Arlington, one-third of which was previously outside its boundaries. Those changes, drawn up by the Democratic Legislature, were made in an unsuccessful attempt to bolster Democratic Rep. Tom Vandergriff in 1984.

Arlington, the district's largest population center, sits astride the "mid-cities" corridor between Dallas and Fort Worth, and that location has fueled its phenomenal growth. After growing 78 percent during the 1970s and more than 50 percent in this decade, Arlington is now up to 250,000 people.

Arlington contains a wide array of industries, and tourism and the hotel/motel business are critical to the local economy. The city hosts "Six Flags Over Texas," a giant amusement park, and baseball's Texas Rangers. Boosted by its white-collar population, Republicans generally carry the 26th in election contests.

North of Tarrant lies Denton County, wholly contained within the 26th. Once a rural Democratic bastion, Denton's booming growth has helped make it solidly Republican. There are some residual Democratic votes in older sections of the city of Denton and in the northern areas still devoted to farming and ranching.

Portions of politically conservative Collin and Cooke counties flank the district to the east and north sides, respectively.

Population: 526,598. White 485,990 (92%), Black 19,335 (4%), Other 7,996 (2%). Spanish origin 26,041 (5%). 18 and over 372,244 (71%), 65 and over 32,184 (6%). Median age: 28.

Chairman William H. Gray III kiddingly referred to their alliance as "historic."

On the Education and Labor Committee, where the Democratic majority has a very strong liberal bent, Armey finds it harder to eschew partisanship. He is a staunch opponent of labor-oriented measures that would increase costs or regulatory mandates for business. In this venue, the free-market theories Armey taught as a college professor come into play.

Armey, for instance, has described so-called comparable worth legislation as "sexist socialism." And he has aggressively opposed legislation requiring businesses to provide unpaid "family leave" to workers who need to care for a newborn child or ill family member. In the 100th Congress, he referred to the proposal as regulatory "repression and intrusion." Later, he took a populist tack, maintaining that because only affluent workers could afford unpaid leave, more work would fall to lower-paid employees. Armey called the family leave idea "yuppie welfare . . . a perverse redistribution of income."

At Home: A conservative economics professor with a penchant for making controversial statements, Armey invites comparison with another Texas Republican: Sen. Phil Gramm.

Like Gramm, Armey cites a belief in the free enterprise system as the genesis of his political career. He was popular on the Dallas-area conservative lecture circuit, praising the philosophy of economist George Gilder and extolling "the miracle of the market."

But beyond working as a volunteer for Jim Bradshaw, the GOP nominee in the 26th in 1982, Armey had no previous political experience when he challenged freshman Democratic Rep. Tom Vandergriff in 1984.

Although the district had been voting routinely Republican for most major offices, Vandergriff began with a solid political base in Arlington, the Tarrant County city where he had been mayor for a quarter-century before winning election to the House in 1982. Vandergriff's successful efforts to lure industry and tourist attractions to Arlington helped spur its rapid growth.

But Armey managed to overcome Vandergriff's initial advantage by allying himself firmly with President Reagan and branding

Vandergriff a lackey for House Speaker Thomas P. O'Neill Jr. Taking advantage of an unusual outbreak of straight-ticket GOP voting, Armey emerged with a 51-49 percent win, handing Vandergriff the first defeat of his political career.

Armey's road to victory was not a smooth one, however. At first, he was hampered by a professorial dryness. Later, he seemed to trade that problem for the more serious one of saying things that worked against him.

Following a meeting with the editorial board of the *Fort Worth Star-Telegram*, he was quoted as saying he favored a gradual phase-out of the Social Security system. Although Armey argued that this would not endanger the checks to current beneficiaries, the statement drew negative publicity. Then Armey said he was "embarrassed" to have been a professor, calling some college classes "pure junk," citing black studies courses as an example.

Still, it was Armey's conservative economic notions that dominated the campaign. He endorsed the Grace commission's recommendations for federal spending reductions, and said he could find ways to make further cuts. He also took Vandergriff to task for voting to limit the final installment of President Reagan's three-year tax-cut plan — a notion pushed by O'Neill. Armey forces circulated a comic book depicting Vandergriff tucked in O'Neill's pocket.

Vandergriff, who had won in 1982 by only 344 votes, relied heavily on his reputation and personal appearances to get his message across. He avoided radio and TV advertising altogether, and took out newspaper ads only in the closing two weeks of the campaign. Meanwhile, Armey was conducting a media blitz, aided by a television endorsement spot from Reagan and other GOP assistance. He won by 6,190 votes.

Vandergriff decided against a comeback in 1986, sparing Armey a rematch with one of the few Democrats who could be competitive in this increasingly Republican constituency. Despite some odd publicity — Armey abandoned his Washington apartment and began bedding down in the House gym until he was effectively barred from that practice by his colleagues — the incumbent easily defeated former state Rep. George "Skeet" Richardson in 1986 and Jo Ann Reyes, an Arlington attorney, in 1988.

Committees

Budget (7th of 14 Republicans)
Task Forces: Urgent Fiscal Issues (ranking); Budget Process, Reconciliation and Enforcement; Economic Policy, Projections and Revenues

Education and Labor (8th of 13 Republicans)
Labor-Management Relations; Labor Standards

Elections

1988 General		
Dick Armey (R)	194,944	(69%)
Jo Ann Reyes (D)	86,490	(31%)
1986 General		
Dick Armey (R)	101,735	(68%)
George Richardson (D)	47,651	(32%)

Previous Winning Percentage: 1984 (51%)

District Vote For President

	1988	1984	1980	1976
D	78,818 (31%)	54,062 (23%)	50,731 (32%)	51,362 (42%)
R	174,262 (69%)	182,192 (77%)	102,758 (64%)	69,342 (57%)
I			5,618 (4%)	

Campaign Finance

	Receipts	Receipts from PACs	Expend-itures
1988			
Armey (R)	$419,632	$150,800 (36%)	$314,903
Reyes (D)	$201,183	$44,800 (22%)	$189,780
1986			
Armey (R)	$547,732	$192,410 (35%)	$558,559
Richardson (D)	$148,008	$60,950 (41%)	$147,532

Key Votes

1987	
Raise speed limit to 65 mph	Y
Approve Gephardt "fair trade" amendment	N
Ban testing of larger nuclear weapons	N
Delay "re-flagging" of Kuwaiti tankers	N
Approve tax-raising deficit-reduction bill	N
1988	
Approve aid to Nicaraguan contras	Y
Enact civil rights restoration bill over Reagan veto	N
Kill 60-day plant-closing notification measure	Y
Pass omnibus trade bill over Reagan veto	N
Approve death penalty for drug-related murders	Y
Bar federal funds for abortions in cases of rape and incest	Y
Oppose seven-day waiting period for purchase of handguns	Y

Voting Studies

	Presidential Support		Party Unity		Conservative Coalition	
Year	**S**	**O**	**S**	**O**	**S**	**O**
1988	82	15	94	3	92	8
1987	81	17	95	2	98	2
1986	82	17	97	2	100	0
1985	88	11	94	4	93	5

Interest Group Ratings

Year	ADA	ACU	AFL-CIO	CCUS
1988	0	100	0	100
1987	0	96	0	100
1986	0	100	7	100
1985	15	95	0	95

27 Solomon P. Ortiz (D)

Of Corpus Christi — Elected 1982

Born: June 3, 1937, Robstown, Texas.
Education: Attended Del Mar College, 1966-67.
Military Career: Army, 1960-62.
Occupation: Law-enforcement official.
Family: Divorced; two children.
Religion: Methodist.
Political Career: Nueces County constable, 1965-68; commissioner, 1969-76; sheriff, 1977-82.
Capitol Office: 1524 Longworth Bldg. 20515; 225-7742.

In Washington: On the Armed Services Committee, Ortiz acts as a sentry for the military bases in his Gulf Coast district. Though he looks out for the 27th's two naval air stations and angles to get more Navy ships based at Corpus Christi, he has yet to take a major role in shaping broader defense policy.

Ortiz did play a prominent role, though, on an issue that had a heavy impact on his south Texas district. In early 1989, he was a leader in efforts to get the federal government to take responsibility for dealing with an influx of Central American immigrants.

Mainly from Nicaragua and El Salvador, thousands of newcomers had crossed the Rio Grande into south Texas seeking political asylum. A federal court order restricted the hopeful refugees to the Brownsville area, and encampments of immigrants sprouted up, overtaxing the abilities of local government to provide them with services.

Ortiz' initial reaction to the newcomers was quite sympathetic: "When my children are starving to death ... we are going to try to come to the United States, which is the beacon of light," he said.

But when local officials warned that they could not cope with the influx, Ortiz said the federal government should slow the flow. Noting that most of the newcomers had come for economic reasons, Ortiz said, "That doesn't mean they qualify for political asylum.... We have to draw the line somewhere."

When the Immigration and Naturalization Service established an expedited review process for the Central Americans and set up tent cities to house them, Ortiz was pleased. "They are going to have three meals a day and shelter, and it will remove the burden of the city and county," he said.

Ortiz' concern about maintaining order reflects his background as a former county sheriff. In general, he follows a less liberal line than other Hispanic House members. In 1988, he voted against the Civil Rights Restoration Act, though he later voted to overturn President Reagan's veto of the bill.

In any case, Ortiz' agenda is driven by the local economy, not ideology. In the 100th Congress, he obtained a delay in federal regulations ordering gulf shrimp fishermen to install "turtle excluder devices." Local shrimpers who sought the delay said the cumbersome devices, which keep sea turtles from getting entangled in fishing nets, could sharply reduce their shrimp yields.

At Home: Since his 1964 election as constable, Ortiz has been a ground-breaker for Hispanics in south Texas politics, holding a succession of offices previously closed to Mexican-Americans. He became Nueces County's first Hispanic commissioner in 1968, and its first Hispanic sheriff in 1976.

Redistricting in 1982 gave Ortiz the opening he needed to get to Congress. As adjusted by a three-judge federal panel, the 27th is good territory for a Mexican-American Democrat; its Hispanic population exceeds 60 percent.

Four of the five candidates who filed for the Democratic nomination in 1982 were Hispanic. Although Jorge Rangel was the favorite in the Washington business-money community, Ortiz had the loyal backing of the poorer Hispanics in Corpus Christi who had sustained his long political career. That gave him a first-place primary finish and a spot in the June runoff.

Ortiz' runoff foe was the one non-Hispanic, Joseph Salem, a Corpus Christi jeweler and former state representative. Salem had strong labor ties, but many of the oil and other business interests who had backed Rangel turned to Ortiz, leery that Salem was too liberal.

The decisive runoff votes were cast in Brownsville. Although Salem had some initial appeal to the Hispanic majority there, Ortiz scored a coup by gaining the support of state Pardon and Parole Chairman Ruben M. Torres, who had been Brownsville's choice in the first round of primary voting. With Torres' support, Ortiz won about 60 percent of the Cameron County (Brownsville) runoff vote, allowing him to draw 52 percent districtwide.

That was Ortiz' last competitive contest. In the last two elections, Republicans have not even bothered to run a candidate against him.

Texas 27

Gulf Coast — Corpus Christi; Brownsville

The 27th looks tidy and compact: Four whole counties and the bulk of a fifth are lined up along the Gulf Coast in far southern Texas. The region's two largest cities — Brownsville and Corpus Christi — are placed symmetrically at either end.

But when the boundaries of the 27th were set for the 1980s, there were grumblings in Brownsville, a Mexican-border city in the Rio Grande Valley that has never had a great deal of contact with Corpus Christi, its much larger competitor for tourists and seaport trade. Since about 55 percent of the district's population lives in the Corpus Christi area, some Brownsvillians worry that their interests may be overshadowed.

Among Texas ports, Corpus Christi is second only to Houston in tonnage handled yearly. The city has large petrochemical and aluminum plants and seafood-processing facilities. Manufacturers of clothing and oil-drilling equipment are also important employers. Tourists are drawn to Corpus Christi by its mild climate and direct access to the Padre Island National Seashore.

By comparison, Brownsville offers more of a south-of-the-border flavor. Corpus Christi's Nueces County is not quite half Hispanic, but in Brownsville and Cameron County, more than 80 percent of the residents are Hispanic. Export-import trade with Mexico is vital to the Brownsville economy, and the bounteous harvests of the Rio Grande Valley keep many workers employed processing fruits and vegetables. Brownsville's location on the border makes illegal immigration a big problem, and cross-border trafficking in illegal drugs has increased, partly because of stepped-up enforcement in Florida.

Nueces and Cameron often behave similarly at the polls, as in the 1982 and 1986 gubernatorial results. Both counties backed Democrat Mark White in both elections. Democrats generally win districtwide; the Democratic presidential ticket of Michael S. Dukakis and Lloyd Bentsen carried the 27th comfortably in 1988.

Population: 526,988. White 417,540 (79%), Black 14,443 (3%), Other 3,252 (1%). Spanish origin 324,120 (62%). 18 and over 341,512 (65%), 65 and over 46,546 (9%). Median age: 26.

Committees

Armed Services (20th of 31 Democrats)
Military Installations and Facilities; Readiness; Seapower and Strategic and Critical Materials

Merchant Marine and Fisheries (15th of 26 Democrats)
Coast Guard and Navigation; Fisheries and Wildlife Conservation and the Environment

Select Narcotics Abuse and Control (12th of 18 Democrats)

Elections

1988 General

Solomon P. Ortiz (D)	105,085	(100%)

1986 General

Solomon P. Ortiz (D)	64,165	(100%)

Previous Winning Percentages: **1984** (64%) **1982** (64%)

District Vote For President

	1988	1984	1980	1976
D	79,302 (55%)	76,717 (48%)	72,902 (51%)	86,991 (61%)
R	65,419 (45%)	83,587 (52%)	69,306 (47%)	54,623 (38%)
I			3,117 (2%)	

Campaign Finance

	Receipts	Receipts from PACs	Expend-itures
1988			
Ortiz (D)	$198,217	$100,383 (51%)	$142,651
1986			
Ortiz (D)	$180,246	$105,296 (58%)	$127,793

Key Votes

1987	
Raise speed limit to 65 mph	Y
Approve Gephardt "fair trade" amendment	Y
Ban testing of larger nuclear weapons	Y
Delay "re-flagging" of Kuwaiti tankers	Y
Approve tax-raising deficit-reduction bill	Y
1988	
Approve aid to Nicaraguan contras	Y
Enact civil rights restoration bill over Reagan veto	Y
Kill 60-day plant-closing notification measure	N
Pass omnibus trade bill over Reagan veto	Y
Approve death penalty for drug-related murders	Y
Bar federal funds for abortions in cases of rape and incest	Y
Oppose seven-day waiting period for purchase of handguns	#

Voting Studies

	Presidential Support		Party Unity		Conservative Coalition	
Year	S	O	S	O	S	O
1988	29	61	78	10	53	34
1987	37	55	79	12	81	16
1986	36	59	78	14	70	22
1985	36	61	76	14	64	33
1984	41	51	77	17	53	41
1983	44	52	75	21	66	29

Interest Group Ratings

Year	ADA	ACU	AFL-CIO	CCUS
1988	55	26	100	29
1987	56	17	80	33
1986	45	40	85	29
1985	60	33	88	16
1984	60	29	92	44
1983	65	32	82	32

Utah

U.S. CONGRESS

SENATE 2 R
HOUSE 1 D, 2 R

LEGISLATURE

Senate 7 D, 22 R
House 28 D, 47 R

ELECTIONS

1988 Presidential Vote

Bush	66%
Dukakis	32%

1984 Presidential Vote

Reagan	75%
Mondale	25%

1980 Presidential Vote

Reagan	73%
Carter	21%
Anderson	5%

Turnout rate in 1984	62%
Turnout rate in 1986	41%
Turnout rate in 1988	60%

(as percentage of voting age population)

POPULATION AND GROWTH

1980 population	1,461,037
1988 population estimate (35th in the nation)	1,690,000
Percent change 1980-1988	+16%

DEMOGRAPHIC BREAKDOWN

White	95%
Black	1%
Other	2%
(Spanish origin)	4%
Urban	84%
Rural	16%
Born in state	66%
Foreign-born	4%

MAJOR CITIES

Salt Lake City	158,440
Provo	77,480
Ogden	67,490
Sandy City	67,430
Orem	61,590

AREA AND LAND USE

Area 82,073 sq. miles (12th)

Farm	19%
Forest	31%
Federally owned	64%

Gov. Norman H. Bangerter (R)
Of West Valley City — Elected 1984

Born: Jan. 4, 1933, Granger, Utah.
Education: Attended Brigham Young U., 1951-55; attended U. of Utah, 1956-57.
Military Career: Army, 1951-53.
Occupation: Building contractor.
Religion: Mormon.
Political Career: Utah House, 1975-85, assistant majority whip, 1977-79, majority leader, 1979-81, Speaker, 1981-85.
Next Election: 1992.

WORK

Occupations

White-collar	54%
Blue-collar	31%
Service workers	12%

Government Workers

Federal	35,867
State	38,656
Local	61,272

MONEY

Median family income	$ 20,024	(22nd)
Tax burden per capita	$ 805	(30th)

EDUCATION

Spending per pupil through grade 12	$ 2,390	(49th)
Persons with college degrees	20%	(7th)

CRIME

Violent crime rate	230 per 100,000	(42nd)

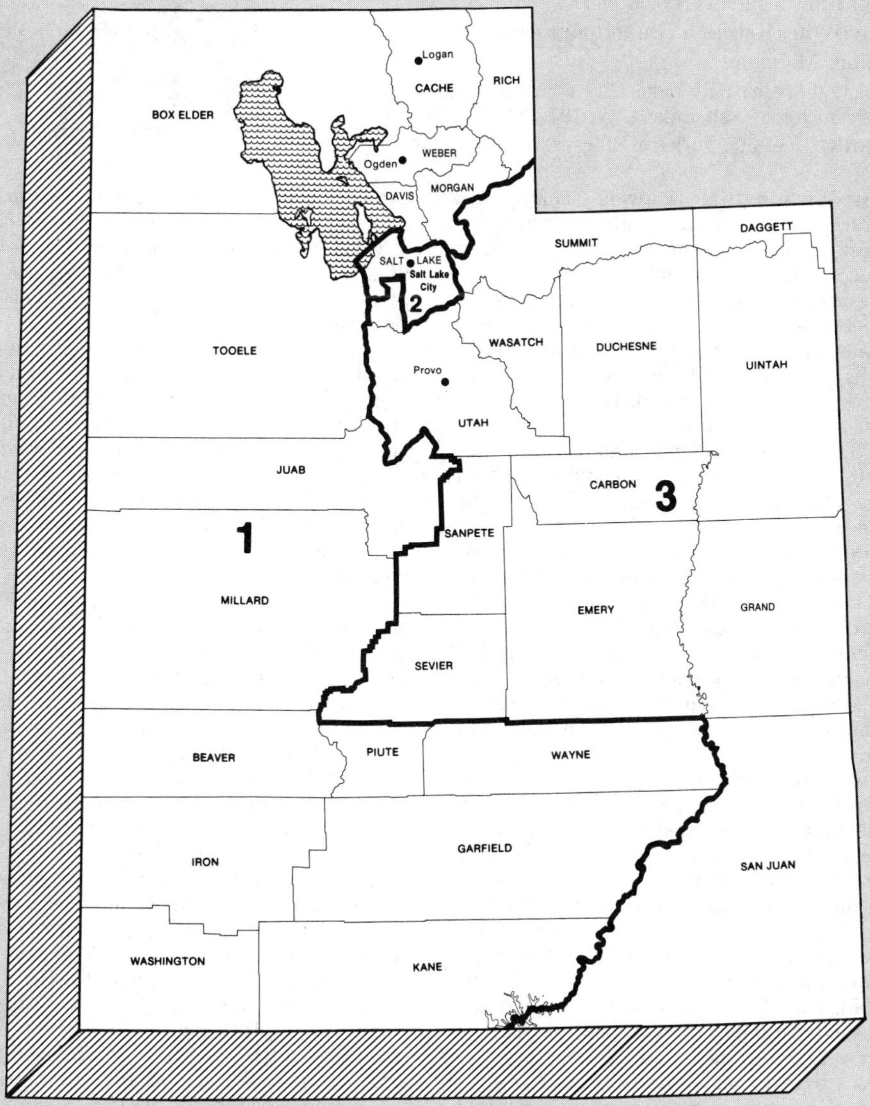

Logan
CACHE
RICH
BOX ELDER
Ogden
WEBER
MORGAN
DAVIS
DAGGETT
SUMMIT
SALT LAKE
Salt Lake City
2
TOOELE
WASATCH
DUCHESNE
UINTAH
Provo
UTAH
JUAB
CARBON
3
1
SANPETE
MILLARD
EMERY
GRAND
SEVIER
BEAVER
PIUTE
WAYNE
GARFIELD
IRON
SAN JUAN
WASHINGTON
KANE

Jake Garn (R)

Of Salt Lake City — Elected 1974

Born: Oct. 12, 1932, Richfield, Utah.
Education: U. of Utah, B.S. 1955.
Military Career: Navy, 1956-60; Air National Guard 1960-69.
Occupation: Insurance executive.
Family: Wife, Kathleen Brewerton; seven children.
Religion: Mormon.
Political Career: Salt Lake City commissioner, 1968-72; mayor of Salt Lake City, 1972-74.
Capitol Office: 505 Dirksen Bldg. 20510; 224-5444.

In Washington: Many a senator has grown frustrated with the manner in which the chamber invites obstruction and delay. Garn gets angry. If, as George Washington said, the Senate is the saucer where legislative passions are cooled, at times it seems that Garn would just as soon smash it against the nearest wall.

His distaste for life and work in the nation's capital is thinly veiled: He boils over at lobbyists and colleagues alike. He sought a third Senate term in 1986 largely because of pleas from GOP leaders, who could not afford to lose Utah and retain hope of keeping the Senate majority.

Garn won easily, but the Senate went Democratic, and he is unlikely to be open to party entreaties in 1992. He moved his family back to Utah in 1986, sold his suburban Virginia home in 1987 and now leads a severe life in Washington. He sleeps in a small apartment after working late into weekday evenings to clear his desk in preparation for each weekend's trip to Salt Lake City.

"This senator's patience is getting very, very thin," Garn told the lobbyists, reporters and bureaucrats assembled at a Banking Committee hearing in 1987. "I'm getting to the point where I don't care what is done as long as we do something.... Frankly, ladies and gentlemen, I'm getting sick of all of you, just really sick."

Garn's attitude might take a newcomer by surprise, for one on one, he is an affable, easygoing man. But he came to Washington disliking the federal government, and the years in Congress have not mellowed him one iota.

As a first-termer in the 1970s, Garn joined other conservatives in battles against the Equal Rights Amendment, the SALT II treaty and the Panama Canal treaties. But he found little to enjoy when he moved into the Senate majority following the 1980 election. His record as chairman of Banking was a series of personal vexations and legislative defeats that sometimes seemed to drive him to the brink of abandoning the Senate in disgust.

It is easy to imagine Garn completing a career of distinction as a military officer, business executive or local government official, all of which he has been in the past. But he seems ill-suited temperamentally to the legislative life; he lacks tolerance for the compromises and slow pace of work in Congress.

Garn's acerbic public personality can alienate those with whom he needs to work. "I am angry," he admitted during one budget debate, appearing in the chamber unexpectedly but holding the floor for nearly an hour, waving his arms and pacing up and down the aisle. "I am angry at this body. I am angry at Congress — I do not care which party, Republican or Democrat — because there are weak-kneed, gutless politicians on both sides."

For a veteran senator, Garn appears to have an unusual conception of the legislative process. That was particularly evident during his long but futile effort while chairman to pass legislation restructuring the nation's banking laws. Faced with the conflicting ambitions of a variety of financial interest groups, Garn alternatively denounced them for their greed and implored them to settle their differences before asking him to move any legislation.

Focusing solely on Garn's legislative abilities, however, omits notice of the personal qualities he exhibited in three experiences that are certain to be highlighted in any retrospective of Garn's Senate career.

In April 1985, Garn became the first incumbent member of Congress to travel in space when he completed an orbital mission aboard the space shuttle *Challenger*. He pressed for the test ride as chairman of the Appropriations subcommittee with jurisdiction over NASA's budget — part of his continuing effort to kick the tires of federal spending, or at least enjoy the toys that come with the job. (He once piloted a protoype B-1 bomber and drove a tank.) He threw himself into training for the *Challenger* mission, and came back transformed by the experience of seeing the Earth from space. "I'd stay up there forever if I could," he said.

Those exhilarating memories turned to

grief when the *Challenger* exploded the following year. Garn knew most of the seven crew members who died, and he made a moving statement on the Senate floor on the afternoon of the tragedy. "It's difficult to lose so many friends all at once," he said in a voice choked with emotion.

The courage Garn had shown on his space flight was overshadowed, however, by his personal sacrifice later that year. He underwent a major operation to donate one of his kidneys to his diabetic daughter.

The frustration Garn has faced as a legislator can be best seen in his efforts to deregulate the banking industry. For six years as chairman of the Banking Committee, he tried and failed to move major deregulation legislation. Even when he was able to get what he wanted from the Senate, he foundered on irreconcilable differences with leading House members.

When he moved into the minority in 1987, he then watched as the Democratic chairman moved legislation to the brink of passage, only to be thwarted by a single senator at the last minute.

Some of his conflicts were philosophical. When Garn was chairman, his House counterpart, Banking Chairman Fernand J. St Germain of Rhode Island, had a basic disagreement over the need for regulation of the banking industry. It is hard to see how Garn could ever have moved his proposals further deregulating the industry past St Germain's adamant opposition.

Garn did have some success with the 1982 Depository Institutions Act, which loosened some Depression-era laws regulating the banking and financial industries. He was able to secure approval of a limited package providing help for troubled institutions, give S&Ls new investment and lending authority and pre-empt state laws banning "due-on-sale" clauses in home mortgages.

Garn in 1983 renewed his campaign to let banks expand into other markets, such as real estate, insurance and municipal bonds. It was unfair to block banks from offering other services, he argued, while security companies were competing with them in the banking business.

The bill made little progress, but picked up momentum the following year because it included popular provisions aimed at curbing the spread of "non-bank banks" — financial subsidiaries formed for the purpose of evading federal restrictions on interstate banking. Garn guided the bill through the Senate intact. But it died when St Germain refused to act on it.

The story was a little different, but the outcome the same, in the 99th Congress. With many farm- and energy-state banks in trouble, there was broad support for legislation to extend Garn's 1982 law giving the government special powers to aid financially weak institutions. Garn sought to combine that with his deregulation bill, but soon gave up when it became clear there was no hope of passage.

Garn has scored victories with his work on export controls. Arguing that U.S. companies were allowing security-related products and technology to become available to the Soviet Union and its allies, he pushed a proposal to revise the Export Administration Act to tighten restrictions on potentially sensitive exports. Garn's bill stirred concern among trade-conscious senators, who worried that it would make it even harder for U.S. businesses to compete abroad. The measure got bogged down and died at the end of the 98th Congress, but was revived and cleared early in 1985.

In the 100th Congress, he led efforts to maintain controls on exports to Soviet-bloc nations. And he doggedly pressed a measure in the omnibus trade bill of 1988 that punished the Toshiba Corp. of Japan because one of its subsidiaries sold sophisticated metal-milling machinery to the Soviet Union that could be used to make quiet propellers for submarines, an advance that makes them harder to track.

Garn's space flight has made him one of the chief advocates of NASA funding. He criticized the Reagan administration for paying little more than "lip service" to the agency's budget.

Garn has been known to become furious at criticism of congressional pay and perquisites. He is not a rich man, and he has a large family to support. "I feel like going home and making as much money as I can before I drop dead," he once said.

Until the Senate voted to limit the amount of honoraria each senator could keep, Garn was among the more active participants on the lucrative speechmaking circuit. He was the most outspoken opponent of 1982 efforts to restore a cap on senators' outside income, denouncing "coupon-clipping" senators who he said could afford to be self-righteous about the issue. He said little, however, during the pay raise debate that accompanied the opening days of the 101st Congress, and voted not to accept the proposed 51 percent raise.

At Home: Garn's longstanding war with things governmental is the basis of his political success. His attitude toward bureaucracy and his affable campaign style brought him a narrow Senate victory in 1974, a bad GOP year, and lifted him to landslide re-election victories in 1980 and 1986.

The son of Utah's first state director of aeronautics, Garn abandoned his career as a Navy pilot after the Korean War. From flying anti-submarine patrols in the Sea of Japan, he moved to the quiet life of an insurance agent in Salt Lake City.

Before long, however, he ran afoul of the municipal government. As a Utah Air National Guard officer, he had a tough time negotiating a lease at the city airport. At one juncture, a city commissioner snapped at him: "If you don't like the way the city is run, why don't you run for election?"

He did that in 1967, winning a term on the City Commission, where he oversaw the sewer and water systems. By 1972 he was mayor. Both were non-partisan posts.

During his tenure as mayor, Garn launched Salt Lake's downtown "beautification" project, which involved adding trees and fountains and widening streets. Although controversial at the time among local business people, who claimed all the construction work was driving off customers, the final result was widely praised.

But Garn gained the most notice as mayor for his strident denunciations of the federal regulations he felt were weakening local government. He often referred to Washington's "dictatorship" and "police-state tactics."

Garn's record as mayor benefited him immeasurably in his 1974 Senate campaign against Democratic Rep. Wayne Owens. Garn projected a much more mature image than the 37-year-old Owens, who looked considerably younger than his age. Owens also was a bit liberal for many Utah voters.

Initially, Garn was far behind Owens in the polls. But on Election Day, he broke even with the Democrat in Salt Lake County and won the mainly Republican rural areas. He defeated Owens by 25,000 votes statewide.

In 1980 Garn triumphed by the greatest percentage any Senate candidate has drawn in Utah history. The hapless loser was Dan Berman, a wealthy lawyer and former executive director of the state Democratic Party.

Berman lashed out at Garn as the puppet of special interests, noting that Garn, then ranking Republican on the Banking Committee, had received thousands of dollars in honoraria from the banking industry. Garn dismissed the attacks with good humor, stressing his conservative record and conducting his customary door-knocking campaign.

In 1986, no prominent Democrat stepped forward to challenge Garn, and the party leadership made little effort to find someone. In a low-turnout Democratic primary, a virtual unknown by the name of Craig Oliver beat Terry Williams, the lone black in the state Senate.

Oliver pounded away at Garn for violating his own stated aversion to congressional careerism, and complained that the incumbent's staunch support of NASA "smells of a political payoff." A loser in previous races for the state Legislature and mayor of Murray, Oliver made no headway against Garn. As in 1980, Garn drew more than 70 percent of the vote.

Committees

Banking, Housing and Urban Affairs (Ranking)

Appropriations (4th of 13 Republicans)
HUD-Independent Agencies (ranking); Defense; Energy and Water Development; Interior and Related Agencies; Military Construction

Energy and Natural Resources (8th of 9 Republicans)
Energy Research and Development; Public Lands, National Parks and Forests; Water and Power

Rules and Administration (6th of 7 Republicans)

Elections

1986 General		
Jake Garn (R)	314,608	(72%)
Craig Oliver (D)	115,523	(27%)

Previous Winning Percentages: **1980** (74%) **1974** (50%)

Campaign Finance

	Receipts	Receipts from PACs	Expend-itures
1986			
Garn (R)	$1,014,148	$576,114 (57%)	$741,645
Oliver (D)	$24,508	0	$24,508

Key Votes

1987	
Enact omnibus highway bill over Reagan veto	N
Limit testing of space-based anti-ballistic missiles	N
Oppose banning tests of larger nuclear weapons	Y
Confirm Robert H. Bork as Supreme Court justice	Y
1988	
Allow vote on campaign-finance overhaul	N
Pass civil rights restoration bill over Reagan veto	N
Enact omnibus trade bill over Reagan veto	N
Approve death penalty for drug-related murders	Y
Oppose "workfare" amendment to welfare overhaul bill	N

Voting Studies

	Presidential Support		Party Unity		Conservative Coalition	
Year	**S**	**O**	**S**	**O**	**S**	**O**
1988	77	14	88	3	73	0
1987	69	21	89	7	91	3
1986	80	5	73	4	75	3
1985	73	11	83	7	72	13
1984	83	14	95	5	98	2
1983	72	28	91	6	100	0
1982	83	16	93	7	93	6
1981	88	9	92	4	89	6

Interest Group Ratings

Year	ADA	ACU	AFL-CIO	CCUS
1988	0	96	7	92
1987	5	96	10	94
1986	0	94	7	100
1985	0	100	21	96
1984	0	100	0	95
1983	5	84	12	95
1982	5	75	4	67
1981	0	93	11	94

Orrin G. Hatch (R)

Of Midvale — Elected 1976

Born: March 22, 1934, Pittsburgh, Pa.
Education: Brigham Young U., B.S. 1959; U. of Pittsburgh, LL.B. 1962.
Occupation: Lawyer.
Family: Wife, Elaine Hansen; six children.
Religion: Mormon.
Political Career: No previous office.
Capitol Office: 135 Russell Bldg. 20510; 224-5251.

In Washington: It often seems that two politicians, one confrontational, the other accommodating, coexist somewhat incongruously underneath Hatch's smooth exterior.

The confrontational Hatch advances a New Right agenda on legal and constitutional issues from his seat on the Judiciary Committee. He is essentially the same conservative militant who came to the Senate in 1977 with a virtual declaration of war on the liberal Washington establishment and its "soft-headed inheritors of wealth." Whether pushing constitutional amendments on school prayer, abortion and a balanced budget, or excoriating Democrats for partisan opposition to judicial nominations favored by conservatives, he displays an unbending zeal that does not often lead to compromise.

The accommodating Hatch chaired the Labor and Human Resources Committee during the six years of GOP Senate control. As chairman and now as ranking member, Hatch has been willing to reach out to his ideological opposites, even finding common ground with a man many conservatives love to hate, liberal Massachusetts Democrat Edward M. Kennedy. Faced with the choice of making major concessions or passing no legislation, he has often opted for compromise even at the expense of conservative purity.

A formidable foe, Hatch is not one to mince words in a backroom negotiation. But in public, he is ever articulate and unruffled in appearance.

Hatch had ample opportunity to confront the majority in the 100th Congress. After being named a member of the select Senate committee investigating the Iran-contra affair, he noted, "Some people no doubt gleefully hope for another Watergate." Determined to prevent this occurrence, he became one of President Reagan's fiercest supporters.

Hatch criticized the scope and duration of the Iran-contra investigation. In hearings, he would often answer his own rapid-fire inquiries before a witness could jump in, or invite witnesses to tout the administration's policy toward Central America. He acknowledged that some key administration decisions were flawed: trading arms for hostages and the apparent effort to divert funds to the Nicaraguan contras. But he also asserted that it was critical for members to understand the "really worthy foreign policy objectives" underlying the initiative with Iran and the support for contras fighting a pro-Soviet regime in a strategically located country.

This was just one example of Hatch working to protect Reagan's conservative legacy. Nowhere was his loyalty to this cause more evident than in his effort to put through one last Reagan appointment to the Supreme Court. It was a task for which Hatch was well prepared and suited; he had won more times than not in his previous efforts on behalf of Reagan's judicial nominees, including Chief Justice William H. Rehnquist.

Hatch is the master of the carefully constructed question that casts a nominee's credentials or positions in the best possible light. Conversely, he can use his lawyer's skills to bore in on an opposing witness. And his anger toward Democrats for their attacks on Reagan nominees had in the past produced some harsh exchanges with Democratic liberals; once he accused Ohio Democrat Howard M. Metzenbaum of conducting a "star chamber" investigation.

Hatch fought to the bitter end for the 1987 nominations of Robert H. Bork and Douglas H. Ginsburg, and then ended up bitter himself about the administration's handling of the nominations. After Bork was beaten, Ginsburg was forced to withdraw once it became known he had smoked marijuana while a law professor. Hatch said the administration aides who approved Ginsburg should resign, and he heaped further criticism on the White House after it severed his access to Reagan during the Ginsburg fight.

"We shouldn't be in this position," he said. "Bork should have been confirmed, and Ginsburg could have been confirmed if the White House hadn't wimped out."

Hatch's name routinely turned up on the

administration's list of nominees. And he might have been named to the court were it not for the constitutional bar against any lawmaker, during the time for which he was elected, assuming any office whose pay was increased during that period. Such was the case with Hatch and pay raises for federal judges.

Hatch's support for Reagan judicial appointees is only one area where he has clashed with civil rights forces, a struggle that he has waged since before the GOP won the Senate. Hatch won a notable 1980 victory on Judiciary in blocking legislation to strengthen federal enforcement of open housing laws.

In the 1983 battle over extending the 1965 Voting Rights Act, Hatch focused on the "intent" concept in the law. Civil rights groups wanted the law to allow the discriminatory results of an election, whether intentional or not, to suffice as proof of a violation. Hatch fought to retain the standard in the law at the time, which required proof that there had been an intent to discriminate in setting up election laws. The "results" test, he warned, would lead to proportional representation of minorities in Congress and state legislatures. Judiciary approved a compromise version essentially retaining the "results" test, and the bill cleared Congress soon after.

Hatch fought civil rights groups for four years over legislation overturning a Supreme Court decision restricting enforcement of the sex-discrimination prohibitions of Title IX of the 1972 education amendments. Reversing past practice, the court had ruled that the anti-bias laws covered only specific programs that received federal funds, not entire institutions.

As a result of the ruling, a broad bipartisan coalition formed to push legislation making clear that any institution receiving federal aid would be covered by anti-bias laws in all its programs. Hatch seemed to have some sympathy with the basic thrust of the proposal, but argued that the measure raised "important constitutional issues" and took civil rights enforcement into wholly new areas. He led but lost the battle to preserve the president's 1988 veto of legislation eventually passed to rewrite the law.

Hatch's conciliatory policies on Labor have been in large part due to the special circumstances of that panel. Even under GOP rule, the committee had a moderate-to-liberal majority, with Democrats and several Republicans combining to frustrate any strict conservative initiatives Hatch undertook as chairman. "The chairman can't just snap his fingers and expect things to happen," Hatch said, and his experience bore him out.

The course pursued by Hatch as chairman was a relatively successful one — at least in terms of the volume of legislation, particularly in the area of health policy, that became law. But his eagerness to compromise left some of his fellow Republicans wondering whether he had abandoned his principles in an unseemly rush to get *something* enacted.

Some House Republicans also faulted Hatch for his performance in conference, particularly when he went up against the Health Subcommittee chairman, Henry A. Waxman. They argued that Hatch allowed himself to be outmaneuvered by the wily Californian.

Hatch's stance on day care illustrates his willingness to reach beyond the conservative agenda for solutions. He underwent an "education" by his staff and constituents to develop day care proposals offered in early 1987, before the issue caught fire politically. Some of his ideas were incorporated into the bill offered by committee Democrats, with his cosponsorship, as the 101st Congress opened.

That Hatch is not afraid to take on his own wing of the GOP, especially on health issues, became even clearer during the 100th Congress' struggle to authorize progams to combat AIDS. Hatch had won some cooperation from Republican Jesse Helms of North Carolina on aspects of anti-AIDS legislation, but disagreement on one point prompted Hatch to chastise Helms for crusading against homosexuality while AIDS victims died. "Let us quit judging and let us start doing what is right," he pleaded.

Hatch has not always displayed a willingness to work with Democrats. "Borin' Orrin," critics called him, after he used a slow monotone to occupy the Senate for weeks as he mounted a successful filibuster against the 1978 labor law revision bill. That was partly sour grapes from backers of the bill, but it reflected a widespread perception even on his own side of the aisle. In 1979, when he ran for the chairmanship of the Senate GOP campaign committee, Hatch thought he had enough support to win. But John Heinz of Pennsylvania beat him. Some senators said afterward that Hatch's reputation as a strident conservative ideologue had cost him votes.

The perception had begun to change by the time Hatch took over the Labor Committee in 1981. It evolved further as he worked to resolve the deep disagreements on the panel over Reagan's proposed budget cuts.

The Reagan administration proposed ending many existing programs and replacing them with "block grants" to the states, at a lower level of funding. But there was no majority for that approach. Hatch sought a compromise that could win a committee majority without losing administration support. Ultimately, he agreed to a compromise turning some programs into block grants, but leaving many intact.

Many labor loyalists were sure Hatch's chairmanship would guarantee angry confrontations between him and the unions. Ever since he led the 1978 labor law filibuster, Hatch had been viewed by labor as its archenemy. The reality was far less cataclysmic.

As chairman, Hatch won committee approval for a few relatively minor bills fighting labor corruption. But more controversial proposals, such as establishment of a subminimum wage for young people, went nowhere. "It is next to impossible to do anything on that committee without the approval of labor union leaders in Washington," he complained.

Hatch continues to favor a subminimum wage. When the Bush administration advanced the idea early in the 101st Congress in a package that also increased the minimum wage, Hatch carried his new general's argument in debate.

Hatch was able to reach agreement on a number of health-related bills in the 98th and 99th Congresses. In 1984, he and Waxman worked out legislation to encourage the production of low-cost generic drugs, ease logistical problems associated with human organ transplant surgery, and require tough new health warnings on cigarettes. They also arranged an omnibus health bill in 1986 that included provisions allowing U.S. drug companies to export their products even if they had not been cleared for sale in this country.

As chairman of the Constitution Subcommittee at Judiciary while Republicans controlled the Senate, Hatch presided over the panel during one of the greatest rushes to amend the Constitution in the nation's history. He became repeatedly enmeshed in controversies over conservative-backed constitutional amendments, many of them proposed by him. He made only intermittent progress in moving the proposals, however, and on occasion found himself at odds with his conservative allies over strategy for getting them through Congress.

Hatch was a leading sponsor of an amendment requiring a balanced federal budget. The high point of his drive for that measure came in 1982, when the Senate gave it the two-thirds majority needed for approval. But the House defeated the amendment, and the idea did not make it that far again in the ensuing years.

In the 99th Congress, Hatch helped arrange a compromise between two versions of the balanced-budget amendment, over the issue of whether tax increases would be allowed to eliminate a deficit. But the revised amendment fell one vote short in the full Senate.

The debate over the balanced-budget proposal was mild, however, compared with the storm of controversy Hatch encountered on the abortion issue. Hatch ended up thoroughly angering many anti-abortionists, but not making much progress on his own anti-abortion proposal.

Hatch argued that only a constitutional amendment would be sufficient to overturn the Supreme Court's decision permitting abortion — a crucial difference with groups wanting simply to ban abortion by statute and avoid the constitutional process. Moreover, Hatch's amendment in effect turned the issue over to the states, allowing them to make their own decision, while some anti-abortion groups sought a national prohibition. Despite his efforts, the amendment was defeated in 1983.

A similar fate befell Hatch's bid to gain approval for a constitutional amendment to allow prayer in public schools. There, too, Hatch pushed a more limited proposal than that sought by some conservative groups, urging that only silent meditation be allowed instead of organized, vocal prayer. But Hatch made little headway on the issue despite repeated attempts.

At Home: While Hatch has grown wise in the ways of Washington, he was a political neophyte when he launched his first Senate campaign in 1976. It was as pure an example of anti-Washington politics as had been seen in recent years.

Hatch's lack of government experience at any level almost certainly helped him. In his private legal practice, he had represented clients fighting federal regulations.

Hatch was recruited for a Senate race against incumbent Democrat Frank E. Moss by conservative leader Ernest Wilkerson, who had challenged Moss in 1964. Hatch's competitor for the GOP nomination was Jack W. Carlson, who had a long résumé in the federal government punctuated by service as assistant secretary of the interior. Carlson, seen as the front-runner, underscored his Washington experience.

That was the wrong record for Utah in 1976. Hatch, sensing that the state was fed up with federal rules, took the opposite approach. The party convention gave him nearly half the vote, and the day before the primary balloting, Hatch reinforced his conservative credentials by running newspaper ads trumpeting an endorsement from Reagan. He won by almost 2-to-1.

The primary gave Hatch a publicity bonus that helped him catch up to Moss, who faced no party competitors. Moss, seen as a liberal by Utah standards, had helped himself at home by investigating Medicaid abuses and fighting to ban cigarette ads from television. He stressed his seniority and the tangible benefits it had brought the state. But Hatch argued successfully that the real issue was limiting government and taxes, and that he would be more likely to do that than Moss.

Bidding for a second term in 1982, Hatch came under strong challenge for being rigid both in his conservative views and his personal style.

Ted Wilson, his affable Democratic opponent, was a well-known figure throughout the state, having served two terms as mayor of Salt Lake City. He carefully began building his challenge to Hatch a year in advance.

Wilson was not the only one with designs on the incumbent. After Hatch blocked the labor law revision in 1978, AFL-CIO President

George Meany had vowed, "We'll defeat you no matter what it takes." But unions are not the most useful allies in conservative Utah. Being a labor target almost certainly did Hatch more good than harm.

Meanwhile, he worked hard to meet complaints about his demeanor. Funding a television campaign with a treasury nearly three times the size of his opponent's, Hatch ran ads that showed him playing with children and dogs.

Wilson, hoping to maintain his early momentum, spent much of the campaign sifting through various strategies searching for a way to undo the incumbent. He branded Hatch's politics as extremist, indicted his style as "strident and contentious," accused him of caring more about national conservative causes than about Utah, and, finally, criticized the Reagan economic philosophy that Hatch vowed he would continue to fight for if re-elected.

The latter approach probably did not help. Utah gave Reagan 73 percent in 1980 — his best showing in the country — and the president's popularity remained high there in late 1982. Buoyed by two Reagan visits to the state during the campaign, Hatch won a solid 58 percent of the vote.

In 1988, Democrats had trouble finding an opponent for Hatch. Popular former Gov. Scott M. Matheson was probably the only Democrat with a chance of beating the incumbent, and he announced in 1987 he would not run. Almost by default the Democratic nomination went to Brian Moss, a businessman and son of the former senator whom Hatch had ousted.

Moss boasted of his family's roots in Utah and took up the complaint that the Pittsburgh-born Hatch was pursuing a national conservative agenda rather than focusing on ways to retool Utah's struggling economy. But Moss had little going for him besides his famous name; he was outspent by a margin of nearly 25-to-1.

As in 1982, Hatch spent much of his money on media advertising that highlighted his caring side. Ads focused on his negotiating role in keeping open the Geneva Steel plant in Orem, and on his legislative proposal to provide home-based health-care services for the elderly and handicapped.

As it turned out, the only campaign problem Hatch encountered was self-inflicted. Speaking in Republican southern Utah in early September, he launched into an assault on the Democratic Party, labeling it "the party of homosexuals ... the party of abortion ... the party that has basically, I think, denigrated a lot of the values that have made this country the greatest country in the world."

Hatch's remarks drew national attention. And in a closer election, they might have seriously hurt his chances. But the underfunded Moss was not in position to take advantage, and Hatch coasted to victory with 67 percent of the vote, the third-highest percentage for any Senate winner in Utah history.

Committees

Labor and Human Resources (Ranking)
Children, Family, Drugs and Alcoholism; Education, Arts and Humanities; Handicapped

Judiciary (2nd of 6 Republicans)
Patents, Copyrights and Trademarks (ranking); Antitrust, Monopolies and Business Rights; Constitution

Select Intelligence (2nd of 7 Republicans)

Elections

1988 General

Orrin G. Hatch (R)	430,089	(67%)
Brian H. Moss (D)	203,364	(32%)

Previous Winning Percentages: **1982** (58%) **1976** (54%)

Campaign Finance

	Receipts	Receipts from PACs	Expend-itures
1988			
Hatch (R)	$4,138,756	$1,173,764 (28%)	$4,005,182
Moss (D)	$153,159	$71,800 (47%)	$153,475

Key Votes

1987

Enact omnibus highway bill over Reagan veto	N
Limit testing of space-based anti-ballistic missiles	N
Oppose banning tests of larger nuclear weapons	Y
Confirm Robert H. Bork as Supreme Court justice	Y

1988

Allow vote on campaign-finance overhaul	N
Pass civil rights restoration bill over Reagan veto	N
Enact omnibus trade bill over Reagan veto	N
Approve death penalty for drug-related murders	Y
Oppose "workfare" amendment to welfare overhaul bill	N

Voting Studies

	Presidential Support		Party Unity		Conservative Coalition	
Year	**S**	**O**	**S**	**O**	**S**	**O**
1988	78	17	82	16	100	0
1987	71	24	88	8	91	6
1986	92	8	92	8	95	5
1985	82	16	85	12	85	15
1984	78	19	91	9	98	2
1983	72	28	90	9	93	7
1982	79	13	80	12	90	6
1981	87	11	89	8	91	7

Interest Group Ratings

Year	ADA	ACU	AFL-CIO	CCUS
1988	5	96	36	86
1987	5	92	11	100
1986	5	96	13	95
1985	10	91	19	86
1984	10	95	18	83
1983	0	80	6	100
1982	5	79	5	70
1981	0	93	11	100

1 James V. Hansen (R)

Of Farmington — Elected 1980

Born: Aug. 14, 1932, Salt Lake City, Utah.
Education: U. of Utah, B.S. 1960.
Military Career: Navy, 1952-54.
Occupation: Insurance executive; land developer.
Family: Wife, Ann Burgoyne; five children.
Religion: Mormon.
Political Career: Farmington City Council, 1963-72; Utah House, 1973-81, Speaker, 1979-81.
Capitol Office: 2421 Rayburn Bldg. 20515; 225-0453.

In Washington: The values of the "Sagebrush Rebellion" live on through Hansen, who joins with other Mountain states conservatives on the Interior Committee to push for loosening the federal hold on Western lands and resources. "We simply don't believe," he has said, "that the bureaucrats on the Potomac know best when it comes to creating a park, expanding a town, drilling for oil or grazing a cow."

But Hansen is no right-wing rabble-rouser. On each of his committee assignments — Interior, Armed Services and ethics — he comes across as a steady, thoughtful legislator who can be flexible when the situation warrants.

Working on wilderness legislation, for example, is seldom a comfortable thing for a conservative Republican. A sizable segment of Mountain states opinion regards such environmentalist bills with deep suspicion. Yet Hansen was willing to play a mediator's role in drawing Utah wilderness boundaries during the 98th Congress.

Hansen initially offered a bill to set aside more than 700,000 acres of U.S. Forest Service land in the state as wilderness, but to release 3 million other acres for development. Soon afterward, oil and gas were discovered in the wilderness area, and Hansen had to negotiate to get the mineral-rich acres out of the protected category. He managed to do that amicably by adding 40,000 more acres of wilderness outside the oil and gas area.

Like most House members from the mountain West, Hansen was outspoken in his support for raising the speed limit on Interstate highways. He took center stage on the issue in the 99th and 100th Congresses, teaming with Oklahoma Democrat Dave McCurdy to boost the speed limit on rural Interstates to 65 mph.

"There's not a law around that's violated as much as this one," Hansen said in 1987. "We call it 'modern-day Prohibition.' " He argued that raising the speed limit would save motorists nearly a half-billion hours in driving time per year, and played down talk that a higher speed limit would cause more fatal accidents. "If safety were the only consideration, reduce the speed limit to 45," Hansen said. "How about 35? How about barricading the highways altogether?"

Hansen tried to change the rule for House consideration of the highway bill in 1987 to allow a speed-limit repeal amendment. But support for that move evaporated once McCurdy, who had led efforts to amend the rule, retreated, having secured leadership assurances that the speed-limit measure would have "a fair shot" on separate legislation. The highway bill later passed, accompanied by the speed-limit increase.

Hansen took his seat on Armed Services in the 100th Congress. There, he looks out for Hill Air Force Base, which is Utah's largest employer. During his 1988 re-election campaign, Hansen pointed to his efforts to block a threatened 12-day furlough of 13,000 workers at Hill.

In 1989, Hansen called for Congress to approve the recommendations of an independent commission on closing unneeded military bases, even though Fort Douglas, in Salt Lake City, was among those targeted for closure. Fort Douglas is in the neighboring 2nd District.

In his first term on Armed Services, Hansen pushed for the Reagan administration's request for more MX missiles and more rapid deployment. But earlier in his House career, he had defended Utah against the federal government on the MX. After the Mormon Church publicly opposed installing the MX in Nevada and Utah, Hansen had to balance his stand favoring the missile with constituent opposition to the "race-track" basing mode planned for his state. After Reagan decided against the race-track basing proposal, the issue slipped from the headlines in Utah.

At Home: Hansen's political fortunes have been closely linked to two individuals — Ronald Reagan and former Democratic Rep. Gunn McKay. Hansen ousted McKay to win the seat in 1980 and beat back his challenges in 1986 and 1988 to hold it. In the first two races, Hansen tied himself closely to Reagan, capitalizing on the fact that the 1st was one of the strongest Reagan districts in the nation.

Utah 1

Ogden and Rural Utah

The railroad center of Ogden and surrounding Weber County comprise the district's Democratic core. It was at Promontory, just north of Ogden, that the golden spike was driven in 1869, creating the nation's first transcontinental rail link. The Church of Jesus Christ of Latter-day Saints (Mormon Church) is an important influence in Weber County, as everywhere in Utah, but the railroads brought a higher number of non-Mormons than in other parts of the state.

Weber was the only one of the district's 16 counties that voted for Democrat Gunn McKay over Hansen in 1988. The county has a large population of blue-collar workers and union members, a legacy of the railroad era. It also has a sizable number of federal employees who work at Hill Air Force Base and nearby defense installations. Hill, the state's largest employer, prospered under the Reagan administration's defense buildup.

But there were difficult periods. Roughly 13,000 workers faced the threat of a 12-day furlough from their base jobs early in 1988. Hansen worked with other congressmen to block the furloughs, and since then, Hill Air Force Base has been awarded a lucrative C-130 maintenance contract.

Rapidly developing Davis County sits in the corridor between Ogden and Salt Lake City. It is a fast-growing county in which Republicans have a decided edge. In recent years, some of Ogden's population has shifted south to work in Salt Lake City and to live in Davis' bedroom communities. For years, Davis trailed Weber County in population, but in 1980, Davis' population finally surpassed Weber's, and by 1986 it had over 20,000 more residents.

Davis' northern part, around Clearfield and Sunset, follows the lead of adjacent Weber and sometimes votes Democratic. In southern Davis, towns such as Bountiful are part of suburban Salt Lake City and go Republican.

The remainder of the district has an almost uniformly Republican coloration — anchored by Cache County (Logan) — the home of Utah State University — in the northeast corner and verdant Washington County in the southwest corner. The population of Washington County has nearly tripled since 1970 as retirees and the wintering wealthy find its semitropical climate attractive. But it is no population center; it has barely a fifth the population of Davis.

Population: 487,833. White 462,032 (95%), Black 4,888 (1%), Other 9,026 (2%). Spanish origin 19,430 (4%). 18 and over 303,406 (62%), 65 and over 38,009 (8%). Median age: 24.

Hansen needed the element of surprise to unseat McKay in 1980. Accustomed to being vulnerable and still winning, McKay was slow in preparing for the campaign.

It was a costly mistake. Hansen was Speaker of the Utah House and had already logged nearly two decades in state and local politics. In the Utah Legislature, he had developed a reputation as a pragmatic conservative adept at conciliation.

While Hansen's own proposals combined fiscal conservatism with opposition to gun control, the Equal Rights Amendment and abortion, he cast McKay as a member of the national Democratic leadership responsible for economic troubles and a weakened defense.

But Hansen probably would not have won without Reagan's coattails. Drawing out GOP voters, Reagan polled more than three-quarters of the vote in the 1st, helping Hansen offset McKay's strength in the Ogden area and enabling the GOP challenger to register a narrow 52-48 percent victory. Against less formidable opposition, Hansen pushed his tally to 63 percent in 1982 and to 71 percent in 1984.

In 1986, McKay was ready for a rematch. But he was hampered by a late start and a district map that was substantially different from when he last ran in 1980. Then, the 1st had extended from northern Utah down the eastern side of the state. In 1986, the 1st covered the western half.

To McKay's advantage, viscerally Republican Utah County (Provo) had been pared out of the 1st; McKay's 13,000-vote deficit there in 1980 accounted for his defeat. But GOP terrain in southwest Utah had been added, and he had never run there.

McKay did possess several significant assets. His slow-talking, "country boy" manner still had great appeal to voters in the vast rural reaches of the 1st. And his impeccable Mormon credentials — a relative, the late David McKay, was a much-revered president of the church — were polished by a stint as president of a Mormon mission in Scotland.

Reagan's absence from the ballot was also considered an asset for McKay's comeback bid, but Hansen still sought to tap the president's popularity by framing the election as a referendum on the administration. He ran separate TV ads that featured Reagan and Utah Sen. Jake Garn. "Do we change direction?" Hansen asked, citing the economic successes and conservative tenor of the Reagan years.

In a district where only one out of every six voters was a Democrat, McKay did not dare take on Reagan. But he had no qualms about criticizing Hansen, whom he dismissed as a rubber stamp for the national GOP and an inadequate spokesman for the district's troubled mining, manufacturing and agricultural interests. McKay pointed to his earlier congressional career as a model of effectiveness and claimed that as a member of the House majority, he could get more done than Hansen could.

McKay's comeback bid fell just short. While the Democrat ran narrowly ahead in the populous northern part of the district that he had represented before, Hansen carried southwest Utah for another 52-48 percent victory.

The close result encouraged McKay to try again in 1988. Both candidates trotted out similar campaign themes, but their tactics changed.

Certain that he had lost narrowly because he had started late, McKay began early to organize and raise money; he also made several visits to the southwest corner of the state.

Certain that his skimpy margin of victory in 1986 was due to a passive campaign, Hansen promised to challenge McKay more aggressively as a liberal in conservative's clothing.

With George Bush running almost as strongly as Reagan had atop the Republican ticket, Hansen was finally able to beat his old rival easily. He swept 15 of the district's 16 counties, taking 60 percent of the overall vote.

Committees

Armed Services (13th of 21 Republicans)
Military Installations and Facilities; Procurement and Military Nuclear Systems

Interior and Insular Affairs (6th of 15 Republicans)
Energy and the Environment (ranking); National Parks and Public Lands; Water, Power and Offshore Energy Resources

Standards of Official Conduct (2nd of 6 Republicans)

Elections

1988 General		
James V. Hansen (R)	130,893	(60%)
Gunn McKay (D)	87,976	(40%)
1986 General		
James V. Hansen (R)	82,151	(52%)
Gunn McKay (D)	77,180	(48%)

Previous Winning Percentages: 1984 (71%) **1982** (63%) **1980** (52%)

District Vote For President

	1988	1984	1980	1976
D	60,188 (27%)	47,259 (22%)	39,968 (19%)	65,603 (35%)
R	162,713 (72%)	170,660 (78%)	158,837 (76%)	117,288 (62%)
I			7,723 (4%)	

Campaign Finance

	Receipts	Receipts from PACs	Expend-itures
1988			
Hansen (R)	$411,486	$258,859 (63%)	$426,902
McKay (D)	$392,478	$264,850 (67%)	$391,928
1986			
Hansen (R)	$405,790	$214,610 (53%)	$419,959
McKay (D)	$244,262	$157,477 (64%)	$244,261

Key Votes

1987	
Raise speed limit to 65 mph	Y
Approve Gephardt "fair trade" amendment	N
Ban testing of larger nuclear weapons	N
Delay "re-flagging" of Kuwaiti tankers	N
Approve tax-raising deficit-reduction bill	N
1988	
Approve aid to Nicaraguan contras	Y
Enact civil rights restoration bill over Reagan veto	N
Kill 60-day plant-closing notification measure	Y
Pass omnibus trade bill over Reagan veto	N
Approve death penalty for drug-related murders	Y
Bar federal funds for abortions in cases of rape and incest	Y
Oppose seven-day waiting period for purchase of handguns	Y

Voting Studies

	Presidential Support		Party Unity		Conservative Coalition	
Year	**S**	**O**	**S**	**O**	**S**	**O**
1988	66	22	78	8	84	0
1987	73	23	86	8	91	9
1986	79	16	80	8	84	8
1985	81	15	85	9	96	2
1984	74	16	88	5	85	5
1983	77	13	83	3	89	2
1982	77	12	77	8	85	5
1981	71	16	80	4	83	4

Interest Group Ratings

Year	ADA	ACU	AFL-CIO	CCUS
1988	0	100	0	100
1987	4	95	0	100
1986	0	91	0	93
1985	5	95	0	86
1984	0	88	15	81
1983	0	100	0	89
1982	0	100	6	81
1981	0	100	8	94

2 Wayne Owens (D)

Of Salt Lake City — Elected 1986

Also served 1973-75.

Born: May 2, 1937, Panguitch, Utah.
Education: Attended U. of Utah, 1958-61; U. of Utah Law School, J.D. 1964.
Occupation: Lawyer.
Family: Wife, Marlene Wessel; five children.
Religion: Mormon.
Political Career: Democratic nominee for U.S. Senate, 1974; Democratic nominee for governor, 1984.
Capitol Office: 1728 Longworth Bldg. 20515; 225-3011.

In Washington: Owens is the prodigal son of the Utah delegation. First elected to the House in 1972 at age 35, he almost immediately took off for greener pastures. In 1974, he ran unsuccessfully for the Senate. Ten years later, he lost a bid for the governorship. Finally, in 1986, as he approached his 50th birthday, Owens won his old House seat back, vowing that his days of political wanderlust were over.

House Democrats celebrated the election of one of their own in conservative Utah, but the leadership balked when Owens spread the word that his victory would be rewarded with a seat on Energy and Commerce. No such promise had been made, it seemed, and Owens' talk of it did not go over well. He settled for seats on Interior and Foreign Affairs.

But if this hard-charging style can seem impolitic at times, it has enabled him to sell his conservative constituents on a voting record that is quite loyal to the Democratic line. Owens voted with a majority of Democrats more than 80 percent of the time in the 100th Congress. That makes it easy for the Democratic leadership to forgive Owens' occasional stray votes. One came in 1987, when Owens was one of just 19 Democrats voting against a Democratic budget resolution that called for higher taxes; it was unanimously opposed by the GOP.

On Foreign Affairs, Owens is particularly interested in the Middle East, but his urgings that Israel open direct negotiations with the Palestine Liberation Organization (PLO) have provoked controversy. After meeting with PLO Chairman Yasir Arafat in early 1989, Owens came away impressed that Arafat was "committed to no violence."

This opinion met with uncharitable skepticism from many in Congress. Republican Sen. Warren B. Rudman of New Hampshire said, "I think to some extent — with all due respect to my colleague from the House, who I don't know — that he was a bit taken in."

Owens fired back at the two-term senator, saying, "With all due respect for my colleague in the other body, who I don't know, I don't think he's looked at the other side of the issue anything akin to what I've done."

Owens' other area of legislative interest is on Interior, where he is lobbying for a 5.1 million-acre wilderness set-aside in Utah, compared with the 1.4 million acres proposed by Utah's Republican governor. In the 100th Congress, Owens was a leading advocate of reestablishing the gray wolf in Yellowstone National Park. Opponents said the wolf was a threat to livestock, but Owens maintained that the wolf had gotten "a bum rap ... very bad press."

At Home: Owens' 1986 House victory marked a political redemption not only for him but also for the Utah Democratic Party, which had not scored a congressional win since 1978. In a way, Owens was an unlikely person to end the drought. Although articulate and well-versed on issues, he has constantly faced charges that he is a liberal in one of the most conservative states in the country.

The liberal connections are part of the record. After a stint as aide to Utah's Democratic Sen. Frank E. Moss, Owens worked as Rocky Mountain states coordinator for Robert F. Kennedy's 1968 presidential campaign. When Edward M. Kennedy was Senate majority whip, Owens was his administrative assistant, and when Owens ran for the House in 1972, Kennedy came to Utah to campaign for him.

While Owens makes no effort to hide the Kennedy connection, he bristles at GOP charges that he is still to the left of Utah's mainstream. Early in the 1986 campaign, Owens undertook an "inoculation" strategy, pointing to his votes during his first stint in Congress to cut President Nixon's budget by $14 billion.

Utah Republicans responded with an ad that featured a man breaking into peals of laughter when he heard Owens described as a fiscal conservative. But the GOP had no aggressive candidate to drive home the point.

Their nominee, Salt Lake County Commissioner Tom Shimizu, did have some advantages

Utah 2

Salt Lake City

There is no mistaking the influence of the Mormon Church in Salt Lake City; Temple Square dominates downtown, relegating the city's two other major institutions located nearby — the seat of state government and the University of Utah — to secondary status on a tour guide's agenda. But even though Mormonism and Republicanism go hand in hand in Utah, the city that is the spiritual capital of the Church of Jesus Christ of Latter-day Saints has enough Democratic blue-collar workers and liberal yuppies to tilt the 2nd Democratic in many elections, as Owens' recent victories have demonstrated.

The portion of Salt Lake County in the 2nd, which includes all of the city proper, favored Democrat Scott M. Matheson in his 1976 and 1980 gubernatorial victories. And countywide returns in 1988 showed Democratic gubernatorial hopeful Ted Wilson (a one-time Salt Lake City mayor) an easy winner.

When Owens left the 2nd in 1974 for his first statewide bid, Democrat Allan T. Howe replaced him. But Howe lost two years later after being convicted of soliciting sex from a policewoman posing as a prostitute. The 2nd may be more tolerant than Utah's other districts, but it has its limits.

Salt Lake City's working-class West Side, traditional home for many copper miners, generally goes Democratic, as does the central-city section. In the northern hills, called The Avenues, professionals in their 20s and 30s sometimes vote Democratic as well. But in the wealthy Wasatch foothills section, called the East Bench, Republicans usually dominate. More 2nd District voters actually live in the Salt Lake suburbs than in the city itself. Voters in such suburban communities as Cottonwood and Murray habitually side with the GOP.

In addition to its role as a center for religion, government and education, Salt Lake City — located about a third of the way between Denver and the West Coast — is a funnel for goods and people. Its airport has become a busy hub for Portland, San Francisco and Los Angeles flights, and Interstate highways heading to each of those cities fan out from the Salt Lake City area. High-technology firms such as Sperry and Litton manufacture items ranging from missiles to communications equipment, and ski slopes east of the city help generate tourism.

Population: 487,475. White 458,410 (94%), Black 3,555 (1%), Other 10,405 (2%). Spanish origin 24,004 (5%). 18 and over 325,863 (67%), 65 and over 43,307 (9%). Median age: 26.

over retiring GOP Rep. David S. Monson, who was weighed down by questionable business relationships and lackluster appeal to voters. Shimizu — who was a relocated Japanese-American internee during World War II — possessed a pleasant manner, a clean-government image and a record of two easy victories in Salt Lake County, which covers the entire district.

But Shimizu did not have the aggressiveness needed to discredit Owens' comeback campaign. Except for one brief flurry where he uncharacteristically referred to Owens as "a crybaby and a boob," Shimizu spent his time seeking to tie himself to President Reagan.

Owens emphasized the need for Utah to have Democratic representation in the Democratic-controlled House. He made inroads in Utah's normally Republican business community, built a $700,000 campaign treasury and won with 55 percent of the vote.

In 1988, Republicans nominated a younger, more aggressive candidate than they did in 1986, picking Richard Snelgrove, the chairman of the Salt Lake County GOP and the manager of his family's large ice cream company.

Snelgrove derided Owens as "Washington Wayne" and highlighted a variety of issues, from taxes to the Pledge of Allegiance, on which he claimed a more conservative position than the incumbent. He contended that Owens was being bankrolled in large part by organized labor, a small and not-too-popular force in Utah.

But Owens proved just as adept at deflecting Snelgrove's charges as he had Shimizu's. Owens continued to draw money from the Salt Lake City business community by wooing small-business men with his opposition to Democratic proposals for an increase in the minimum wage and mandatory parental leave. For good measure, Owens trumpeted his support of a balanced-budget constitutional amendment and a variation of the line-item veto.

Utah Republicans sought to pierce Owens' defenses by requesting a House ethics probe. The GOP state party chairman complained that Owens had paid a lobbyist to help draft legislation, thus violating a House rule prohibiting private donations or in-kind services to support the activities of a congressional office. Owens dismissed the complaint as "an act of total political desperation" and it was dismissed before the election because it was improperly filed.

With a campaign treasury barely one-third the size of Owens', Snelgrove was forced to look for free publicity wherever he could. One way was to conduct daily "honk and waves," where the candidate stood on a soapbox at busy intersections around the Salt Lake City area, waving at motorists and talking to anyone who would stop.

Not enough people did. On Election Day, Owens improved on his 1986 showing, taking 57 percent of the vote.

When Owens made his first congressional race back in 1972, it was he — not his opponent — who wore out the shoe leather. Owens walked more than 1,000 miles across the district, which then covered almost the entire western half of Utah, presenting himself as a fresh face who would vote unconditionally to end the Vietnam War. In a less conservative era of Utah politics, he ousted GOP Rep. Sherman P. Lloyd.

Owens likely could have won re-election in 1974, but he sought the Senate seat of retiring Republican Wallace F. Bennett. Early polls showed Owens ahead of GOP nominee Jake Garn. Garn, however, projected a more mature image than Owens, who looked considerably younger than his age. And Owens, a member of the House Judiciary Committee, was hurt by a lackluster performance in the televised impeachment proceedings of Richard M. Nixon. He lost to Garn, 50-44 percent.

That was the closest Owens came to winning higher office. Seeking the governorship in the more conservative climate of 1984, he was beaten by Republican Norman H. Bangerter by 12 percentage points.

Nowadays, Owens makes it clear his political ambitions have leveled off. "It's not only my intention but my commitment to stay in the House," he has said. "I'm now purged of that need to seek statewide office."

Committees

Foreign Affairs (22nd of 28 Democrats)
Europe and the Middle East; Human Rights and International Organizations

Interior and Insular Affairs (20th of 26 Democrats)
General Oversight and Investigations; National Parks and Public Lands; Water, Power and Offshore Energy Resources

Elections

1988 General

Wayne Owens (D)	112,129	(57%)
Richard Snelgrove (R)	80,212	(41%)

1986 General

Wayne Owens (D)	76,921	(55%)
Tom Shimizu (R)	60,967	(44%)

Previous Winning Percentage: 1972 (55%)

District Vote For President

	1988	1984	1980	1976
D	86,241 (40%)	64,712 (31%)	48,612 (23%)	72,856 (36%)
R	125,619 (58%)	144,966 (68%)	137,579 (66%)	125,057 (61%)
I			17,580 (8%)	

Campaign Finance

	Receipts	Receipts from PACs	Expend-itures
1988			
Owens (D)	$736,198	$455,310 (62%)	$676,472
Snelgrove (R)	$278,426	$60,544 (22%)	$289,305
1986			
Owens (D)	$699,328	$389,113 (56%)	$704,609
Shimizu (R)	$373,778	$107,148 (29%)	$373,077

Key Votes

1987	
Raise speed limit to 65 mph	Y
Approve Gephardt "fair trade" amendment	Y
Ban testing of larger nuclear weapons	Y
Delay "re-flagging" of Kuwaiti tankers	Y
Approve tax-raising deficit-reduction bill	Y
1988	
Approve aid to Nicaraguan contras	N
Enact civil rights restoration bill over Reagan veto	Y
Kill 60-day plant-closing notification measure	N
Pass omnibus trade bill over Reagan veto	Y
Approve death penalty for drug-related murders	N
Bar federal funds for abortions in cases of rape and incest	N
Oppose seven-day waiting period for purchase of handguns	Y

Voting Studies

	Presidential Support		Party Unity		Conservative Coalition	
Year	**S**	**O**	**S**	**O**	**S**	**O**
1988	22	72	84	12	47	50
1987	21	69	83	7	26	56

Interest Group Ratings

Year	ADA	ACU	AFL-CIO	CCUS
1988	75	16	93	36
1987	76	0	93	31

3 Howard C. Nielson (R)

Of Provo — Elected 1982

Born: Sept. 12, 1924, Richfield, Utah.
Education: U. of Utah, B.S. 1947; U. of Oregon, M.S. 1949; Stanford U., M.B.A. 1956, Ph.D. 1958.
Military Career: Air Force, 1943-46.
Occupation: Professor of statistics.
Family: Wife, Julia Adams; seven children.
Religion: Mormon.
Political Career: Utah House, 1967-75, Speaker, 1973-75.
Capitol Office: 1122 Longworth Bldg. 20515; 225-7751.

In Washington: Nielson's limited-government, business-oriented perspective is mirrored by many of his GOP colleagues on Energy and Commerce, where the Democratic majority has an activist, consumerist bent.

He normally espouses an anti-regulatory line in committee, veering off only on the subject of Utah's struggling copper and steel industries, which he feels need protection.

In the 99th Congress, Nielson was unsuccessful in attempts to restrain federal action to protect groundwater, but he did persuade the committee to freeze spending for Indian health programs. During the 100th Congress, he objected to another Indian health programs bill, one that included creation of nine new diabetes clinics. Though one of the clinics would have been in Utah, Nielson said new clinics could not be justified in a time of budget stringency. But by voice vote, the committee rejected his proposal to eliminate funds for the clinics.

Nielson maintains a Western conservative's skepticism toward a large federal bureaucracy, even going so far as to risk alienating powerful constituencies. When the bill giving the Veterans Administration Cabinet rank came to Government Operations in 1987, he told committee Chairman Jack Brooks he was unconvinced the new status was warranted. "I fail to see the need for a Cabinet post," he said. "I don't believe veterans have ever suffered. We always give them what they need." The bill sailed through, however; Nielson's was one of only 17 House votes against it.

A statistician by profession, Nielson is known for carefully poring over the details of legislation and testimony. He is not a spinner of grand legislative schemes. Often he focuses his attention on isolated technical provisions of bills, looking for ways to mimimize federal intervention or improve efficiency.

On Energy and Commerce in the 100th Congress, Nielson toiled on telecommunications issues. During consideration of a bill aimed at curtailing telemarketing fraud, he offered an amendment to instruct the Federal Trade Commission to consider restrictions on the time of day that product-sellers could call potential consumers. It was adopted, but the bill died in the Senate.

Early in the 101st Congress, he introduced legislation to require the Federal Communications Commission to set up standards to allow all public-safety radio equipment to be able to communicate with each other.

At Home: For a while, the 1982 contest in Utah's newly drawn 3rd looked like a faculty meeting at Brigham Young University. Four of the Republicans running in this safe GOP district taught there. Nielson was in the statistics department; Raymond E. Beckham, his leading rival, was a communications professor.

Outside the BYU community, Nielson played down his academic ties. Instead, he portrayed himself to conservative GOP voters as a businessman. While on the BYU faculty, he also was an economic consultant for local businesses and for the Army-run Dugway Proving Ground.

More important, though, Nielson was a seasoned Republican pol. He was a district GOP committeeman in Provo as early as 1960, and when a state House seat opened up in 1966, he was in line for it. He was no orator in the Legislature, but earned a reputation as a man who could read the fine print at the bottom of the bills. Two years after he arrived he was majority leader; in 1973 he became Speaker.

In the 1982 primary, Nielson was the favorite of the GOP rank and file. Beckham had a different base altogether. A professional publicist for BYU and senior lay official in the Mormon Church, he had a myriad of contacts, and a clear edge in personality. But in the closing week, it was revealed that Beckham had given some of his BYU students class credit to work in his campaign. The university president accused him of a lack of sensitivity to "the apparent conflict of interest" and Beckham had to apologize. Nielson won with 54 percent. The general election was routine, and his re-elections have been similarly uneventful.

Utah 3

Provo and Rural Utah

Provo and surrounding Utah County are home to the most intense Mormon community in the state. That is in large part because Provo is the location of Brigham Young University, founded in 1875 to prepare Mormon youth for teaching and religious proselytizing.

Because of the religious connection, Provo is a college town like few others in the country. BYU's sprawling modern campus (with more than 27,000 students and 1,700 faculty) is the focal point of the city's life, and the school's consistently successful sports teams provide an extra element of social cohesion. The Mormon influence makes Utah County one of the nation's most impregnable Republican strongholds. In presidential contests, the GOP margins are awesome. Ronald Reagan drew 83 percent of the county's vote in 1984; George Bush carried it with an only slightly more modest 77 percent in 1988.

The northern section of the county contains Lehi and American Fork — towns whose blue-collar workers have been employed at the Geneva Steelworks plant, which USX Corp. closed in 1987 but has subsequently been reopened under independent management. Even in these communities, however, Mormon values are crucial and Democrats can rarely count on a heavy vote to help them.

Democrats are stronger in the southwest part of Salt Lake County, although voters there differ little from those elsewhere in the district when it comes to national elections. Many of the people there, living in towns such as South Jordan and West Valley City, have worked in the Kennecott copper pit in Kearns. Kennecott severely cut back its Utah operations in 1985 due to losses tied to the depressed world price of copper. But the pit has since been sold to a subsidiary of British Petroleum, and it is operating again with modernized facilities and a work force that exceeds 2,000 at both the pit in Kearns and the refinery in Magna.

The rest of the district is rural and sparsely populated. Much of it contains mountains and desert. Cattle ranching and mining are the leading industries, and Republicans are by far the dominant political party.

Population: 485,729. White 462,108 (95%), Black 782 (0.2%), Other 14,901 (3%). Spanish origin 16,868 (4%). 18 and over 291,663 (60%), 65 and over 27,904 (6%). Median age: 22.

Committees

Energy and Commerce (12th of 17 Republicans)
Commerce, Consumer Protection and Competitiveness; Energy and Power; Health and the Environment

Government Operations (4th of 15 Republicans)
Government Activities and Transportation (ranking)

Elections

1988 General		
Howard C. Nielson (R)	129,951	(67%)
Robert W. Stringham (D)	60,018	(31%)
1986 General		
Howard C. Nielson (R)	86,599	(67%)
Dale F. Gardiner (D)	42,582	(33%)

Previous Winning Percentages: **1984** (75%) **1982** (77%)

District Vote For President

	1988		1984		1980		1976	
D	60,127	(30%)	43,398	(22%)	35,686	(19%)	43,651	(30%)
R	140,110	(69%)	153,479	(77%)	143,271	(77%)	95,563	(65%)
I					4,981	(3%)		

Campaign Finance

	Receipts	Receipts from PACs	Expend-itures
1988			
Nielson (R)	$132,528	$112,800 (85%)	$102,055
Stringham (D)	$20,301	$14,000 (69%)	$20,092
1986			
Nielson (R)	$118,151	$93,990 (80%)	$104,844
Gardiner (D)	$37,961	0	$37,961

Key Votes

1987	
Raise speed limit to 65 mph	Y
Approve Gephardt "fair trade" amendment	N
Ban testing of larger nuclear weapons	N
Delay "re-flagging" of Kuwaiti tankers	N
Approve tax-raising deficit-reduction bill	N
1988	
Approve aid to Nicaraguan contras	Y
Enact civil rights restoration bill over Reagan veto	N
Kill 60-day plant-closing notification measure	Y
Pass omnibus trade bill over Reagan veto	Y
Approve death penalty for drug-related murders	Y
Bar federal funds for abortions in cases of rape and incest	Y
Oppose seven-day waiting period for purchase of handguns	Y

Voting Studies

	Presidential Support		Party Unity		Conservative Coalition	
Year	**S**	**O**	**S**	**O**	**S**	**O**
1988	74	23	83	15	95	5
1987	75	25	86	13	86	14
1986	74	23	84	15	84	14
1985	84	16	89	10	89	9
1984	80	19	90	9	90	10
1983	80	13	88	5	92	7

Interest Group Ratings

Year	ADA	ACU	AFL-CIO	CCUS
1988	5	92	21	100
1987	8	87	13	87
1986	5	95	14	89
1985	5	90	0	100
1984	0	96	15	81
1983	0	95	0	89

Vermont

U.S. CONGRESS

SENATE 1 D, 1 R
HOUSE 1 R

LEGISLATURE

Senate 16 D, 14 R
House 74 D, 76 R

ELECTIONS

1988 Presidential Vote	
Bush	51%
Dukakis	48%
1984 Presidential Vote	
Reagan	58%
Mondale	41%
1980 Presidential Vote	
Reagan	44%
Carter	38%
Anderson	15%
Turnout rate in 1984	60%
Turnout rate in 1986	47%
Turnout rate in 1988	59%

(as percentage of voting age population)

POPULATION AND GROWTH

1980 population	511,456
1988 population estimate (48th in the nation)	557,000
Percent change 1980-1988	+9%

DEMOGRAPHIC BREAKDOWN

White	99%
Black	0.2%
(Spanish origin)	1%
Urban	34%
Rural	66%
Born in state	62%
Foreign-born	4%

MAJOR CITIES

Burlington	38,310
Rutland	18,080
South Burlington	11,420
Barre	10,070
Montpelier	8,120

AREA AND LAND USE

Area	9,273 sq. miles (43rd)
Farm	27%
Forest	76%
Federally owned	5%

Gov. Madeleine M. Kunin (D)
Of Burlington — Elected 1984

Born: Sept. 28, 1933, Zurich, Switzerland.
Education: U. of Massachusetts, B.A. 1956; Columbia U., M.S. 1957; U. of Vermont, M.A. 1967.
Occupation: Journalist; professor.
Religion: Jewish.
Political Career: Vt. House, 1973-79; lieutenant governor, 1979-83; Democratic nominee for governor, 1982.
Next Election: 1990.

WORK

Occupations	
White-collar	51%
Blue-collar	31%
Service workers	13%
Government Workers	
Federal	4,705
State	12,999
Local	19,175

MONEY

Median family income	$ 17,205	(40th)
Tax burden per capita	$ 857	(25th)

EDUCATION

Spending per pupil through grade 12	$ 4,031	(15th)
Persons with college degrees	19%	(10th)

CRIME

Violent crime rate	137 per 100,000 (47th)

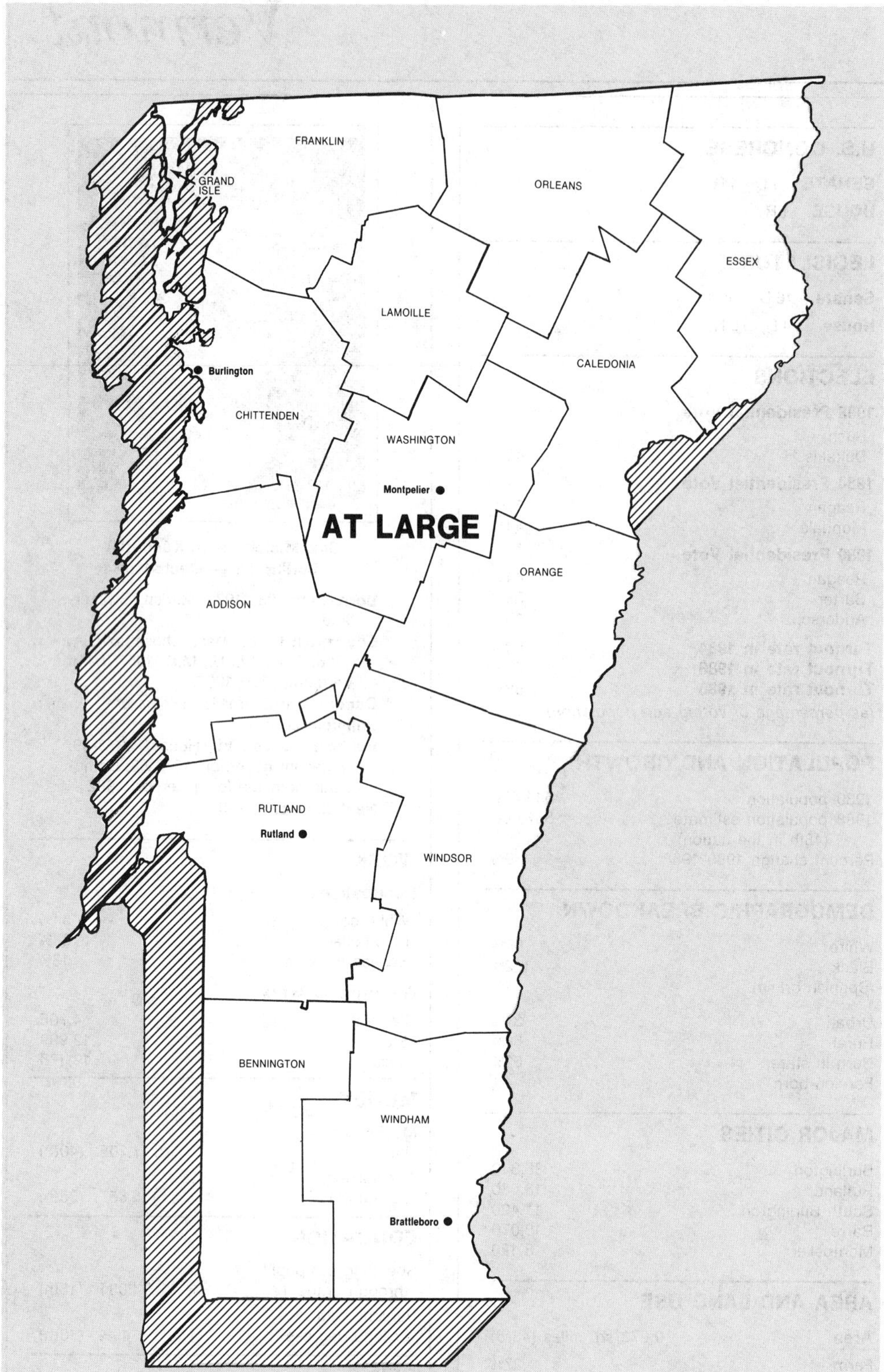

FRANKLIN
GRAND ISLE
ORLEANS
ESSEX
LAMOILLE
CALEDONIA
Burlington
CHITTENDEN
WASHINGTON
Montpelier
AT LARGE
ORANGE
ADDISON
RUTLAND
Rutland
WINDSOR
BENNINGTON
WINDHAM
Brattleboro

Patrick J. Leahy (D)

Of Middlesex — Elected 1974

Born: March 31, 1940, Montpelier, Vt.

Education: St. Michael's College, B.A. 1961; Georgetown U., J.D. 1964.

Occupation: Lawyer.

Family: Wife, Marcelle Pomerleau; three children.

Religion: Roman Catholic.

Political Career: Chittenden County state's attorney, 1967-75.

Capitol Office: 433 Russell Bldg. 20510; 224-4242.

In Washington: Leahy is not your conventional Agriculture Committee chairman, that much is certain. What is not certain is where exactly he wants to move the insular committee, and whether his members will follow.

In contrast with past chairmen, and most current members, Leahy shows relatively little interest in the multibillion-dollar programs subsidizing America's major farm commodities. He is not an opponent, nor a reformer. He simply has other priorities within Agriculture's bailiwick, and they happen to be the issues that most past chairmen treated as secondary interests, or not at all — nutrition programs, the environment and rural development.

He is a big defender of dairy programs important to Vermont and, working alongside senators from the various farm belts, Leahy likes to drop lines about his own rural roots. But no one would mistake Leahy for a rustic; he is more like a gentleman farmer, or like the liberal-leaning hobby farmers who have moved to his bucolic state in recent years to escape big-city anxieties, helping transform Vermont from a Republican state to a Democratic one.

Leahy is a fair and congenial chairman, and both his colleagues and the commodities groups that traditionally have held sway at Agriculture might be content to let him go his way while they go theirs — if not for the fact that everyone competes for the same scarce funds. The $300 million Leahy sought in the 101st Congress for rural development — school subsidies, health care and business seed money — would be a fraction of the farm budget, but that is too much for many commodities interests when their own programs face cutbacks.

Until he became chairman in 1987, Leahy did not devote much attention to farm policy; foreign policy was his main pursuit. But as he took over Agriculture, Leahy had to forfeit the post he had parlayed into prominence on foreign affairs — vice chairman of the Intelligence Committee — after he admitted leaking information to a reporter. With the 101st Congress, he assumed a new role that could restore some of his former influence: chairman of Appropriations' Foreign Operations Subcommittee.

Leahy's early departure from Intelligence, months before his eight-year stint was to expire, was a public embarrassment, and it also reinforced some colleagues' private view of him as a spotlight seeker. That view partly explains Leahy's late 1988 loss when he tried to become secretary of the Senate Democratic Conference; also important was the fact that the winner, moderate David Pryor of Arkansas, offered regional and ideological balance to a liberal leadership circle lacking a Southerner.

The object of Leahy's leak was not classified information, but a draft Intelligence Committee report about the just-revealed Iran-contra affair. It was compiled in the last days of GOP control of the panel, and Democrats voted not to release the report when they took over for the 100th Congress. The Reagan administration, meanwhile, claimed the report cleared the president. Leahy, in a statement, said he let a reporter see the document "to show that it was being held up because there were major gaps and other problems with it, and not because of a desire to embarrass the president."

Leahy served on the committee at a time of intense controversy over intelligence issues, including a string of spy scandals and covert actions in Central America, all of which made the articulate, witty and outspoken administration critic one of the media's most sought-after politicians.

He visited Central America in 1983, hinting afterward that the administration was illegally trying to overthrow the Nicaraguan regime. Leahy found few allies until the 1984 revelation of the CIA's role in the mining of Nicaraguan harbors. By year's end, Congress voted to cut off contra aid; thereafter, Leahy pressed for information about any administration or CIA role in circumventing the ban. In September 1985, national security adviser Robert C. McFarlane assured Leahy and Republican Intelligence Chairman Dave Durenberger that no one in the White House was violating the ban — a line the Iran-contra hearings proved false. Congress resumed open military aid in 1986; Leahy's amendment to bar the CIA from involvement was killed 57-42.

In 1988, no longer on Intelligence, Leahy was one of just four Democrats to oppose a leadership package of "humanitarian" contra aid, offered as an alternative to President Reagan's proposed military aid. But in 1989, Leahy not only backed a humanitarian aid deal between Congress and President Bush, but also, as the new Foreign Operations chairman, managed it on the floor — reflecting his new leadership duties as Foreign Operations chairman.

While on Intelligence, Leahy pushed against State Department resistance to limit the number of Soviet diplomats in this country to the number of U.S. diplomats in the Soviet Union, based on his belief that many Soviet spies were in the United States under diplomatic cover.

After his heady work with covert actions and foreign policy, it was expected that Leahy might find Agriculture a bit boring; in that regard, he resembled the committee's senior Republican, Richard G. Lugar, who had been a celebrated Foreign Relations Committee chairman when Republicans controlled the Senate. Often working together, both men performed creditably on Agriculture in the 100th Congress.

They steered a disaster-aid bill through the Senate in 1987, and emergency drought aid the next year, staving off most amendments that would have expanded the bills' reach and cost. The 1987 action was especially important since it effectively killed any move to rewrite basic farm policy; that had seemed inevitable at the Congress' start, given the dissatisfaction with the big five-year 1985 farm law.

Despite the relative restraint of these two measures, however, Agriculture still engages in its long-held tradition of logrolling, with members from different farming regions trading support for provisions benefiting each others' home-state commodities. As the committee wrote the 1987 disaster bill, Leahy was a reluctant Scrooge while his colleagues began to turn the measure, meant to help wheat farmers, into the proverbial legislative Christmas tree, full of extras for other crop farmers. He pleaded, "You don't want me to start singing Jingle Bells up here, do you?"

Under Leahy, the committee also produced a complex package to bail out and overhaul the Farm Credit System in 1987; Leahy drafted a consensus bill, though Lugar's version actually formed the core of the final bill. A compromise with the House became law the next year.

Long a proponent of tougher pesticide regulations, Leahy helped engineer passage of a limited compromise in 1988 after years of stalemate. It disappointed environmentalists who had higher hopes when Leahy took over the committee, but Agriculture is more responsive to agribusiness owners and farmers, who fear the expense of environmental regulations.

Earlier in the decade, Leahy was best known at Agriculture for his work on dairy programs and for his attacks on Reagan's farm policies. In 1981, he strongly opposed the new president's proposed cancellation of a scheduled increase in dairy prices. In 1983, he backed a controversial bill to pay dairymen for reducing production, which Reagan reluctantly signed. Also, Leahy helped draft the part of the 1985 farm bill that created the "whole herd buy-out" program, which paid milk producers to send their entire herds to slaughter so that milk production would be cut — and with it the government's purchases of dairy surpluses.

Leahy also has led efforts to block severe cuts in the food stamp program, which is among the nutrition programs under Agriculture's jurisdiction. Working closely with Republican Bob Dole, he proposed some moderate reductions that headed off a more draconian package by then-Chairman Jesse Helms of North Carolina.

At the Judiciary Committee, Leahy is chairman of the Technology Subcommittee. As such, in the 100th Congress, he helped win ratification after more than a century of the Berne Convention, which set minimum international copyright standards for artists' works.

He was more visible in his role as head of an informal panel of Democrats that reviewed judicial selections; as Reagan's final term ended, Leahy took the heat from GOP senators complaining about a backlog. He was among the most vocal critics of Reagan for naming too few women and minorities to the bench.

In 1987, he helped defeat conservative Supreme Court nominee Robert H. Bork, in the process coining the much-repeated phrase "confirmation conversion" to suggest that Bork had moderated his views to win approval.

At Home: Though polls throughout Leahy's second term showed him to be popular in Vermont, Republican officials looked forward to taking him on in 1986. Since he had won narrowly in 1980 over an upstart GOP challenger, Leahy was viewed as the most vulnerable Democratic incumbent running in 1986. Republican morale was boosted when former Gov. Richard A. Snelling, who retired in 1985 after four terms, agreed to tackle Leahy.

The expected "battle of the titans" failed to develop. Well prepared and well financed, Leahy won a landslide 63 percent of the vote.

Having been criticized for the low profile of his first term, Leahy had made certain that his constituents knew about his activities through press releases and newsletters. As the senior Democrat on Intelligence, he was often visible on national TV. Leahy also had a strong organizational edge. By fall 1985, he had a grass-roots network and $250,000 that signaled this would be Vermont's most expensive race.

Meanwhile, Snelling spent much of 1985 on an Atlantic sailing excursion. Key Republicans, including Reagan, finally convinced him his candidacy was crucial to maintaining a GOP Senate majority. But a late start was not Snelling's only problem. He was bucking Vermont's pro-incumbent tradition. This bias helped Leahy to large leads in early polls, which in turn hurt Snelling's fund raising.

Snelling's biggest handicap was the lack of political distance between himself and Leahy. Snelling, a moderate, held similar positions to Leahy on many issues. His efforts to run as a Reaganite did not ring true; as governor, he was a sharp critic of Reagan's budget priorities. Snelling resorted to attacking Leahy's attendance record and labeling him one of the Senate's "biggest spenders." The strategy was ineffective, and it enabled Leahy to accuse Snelling of negative campaigning.

Leahy's victory was sweeping. He carried his home base, populous Chittenden County (Burlington), by 2-to-1, and won 59 percent in Shelburne, Snelling's hometown. Leahy also won 10 of the other 12 counties.

When he first won office more than two decades ago, Leahy was in the vanguard of Democratic gains in traditionally Republican Vermont. At 26, he was elected Chittenden County state's attorney in 1967. He revamped the office and headed a national task force of district attorneys probing the 1973-74 energy crisis.

In 1974, Leahy decided to run for the Senate seat being vacated by Republican George D. Aiken. Leahy was just 34, presenting a contrast with the 82-year-old political institution he hoped to replace. But he was already balding and graying, and looked older than he was.

Leahy was an underdog against GOP Rep. Richard W. Mallary. But Mallary turned out to be a rather awkward campaigner, and Watergate made Vermont more receptive to a Democrat than it had been, enabling Leahy to win narrowly.

Leahy survived in 1980 by emphasizing his roots in the state rather than his ties to the Democratic Party. Campaigning against the national GOP tide, he fought off New York-born challenger Stewart Ledbetter with the slogan: "Pat Leahy: Of Vermont, For Vermont."

It took all of Leahy's ingenuity to overcome Ledbetter, former state banking and insurance commissioner. With money from national GOP groups, he argued that Leahy was a free-spender and weak on defense. Reagan's coattails almost elected him; Leahy held on by just 2,755 votes. Six years later, a more senior Leahy won by more than 56,000 votes.

Committees

Agriculture, Nutrition and Forestry (Chairman)

Appropriations (6th of 16 Democrats)
Foreign Operations (chairman); Defense; HUD-Independent Agencies; Interior and Related Agencies

Judiciary (5th of 8 Democrats)
Technology and the Law (chairman); Patents, Copyrights and Trademarks

Elections

1986 General

Patrick J. Leahy (D)	124,123	(63%)
Richard A. Snelling (R)	67,798	(35%)

Previous Winning Percentages: **1980** (50%) **1974** (50%)

Campaign Finance

	Receipts	Receipts from PACs	Expend-itures
1986			
Leahy (D)	$1,919,740	$822,931 (43%)	$1,705,099
Snelling (R)	$1,495,491	$258,377 (17%)	$1,502,304

Key Votes

1987	
Enact omnibus highway bill over Reagan veto	Y
Limit testing of space-based anti-ballistic missiles	Y
Oppose banning tests of larger nuclear weapons	N
Confirm Robert H. Bork as Supreme Court justice	N
1988	
Allow vote on campaign-finance overhaul	Y
Pass civil rights restoration bill over Reagan veto	Y
Enact omnibus trade bill over Reagan veto	Y
Approve death penalty for drug-related murders	N
Oppose "workfare" amendment to welfare overhaul bill	Y

Voting Studies

	Presidential Support		Party Unity		Conservative Coalition	
Year	**S**	**O**	**S**	**O**	**S**	**O**
1988	34	58	93	5	8	92
1987	33	62	85	9	9	84
1986	24	70	83	11	21	75
1985	29	68	83	16	27	73
1984	30	62	85	11	15	77
1983	41	58	89	10	18	82
1982	37	62	91	9	12	88
1981	34	60	76	8	4	84

Interest Group Ratings

Year	ADA	ACU	AFL-CIO	CCUS
1988	100	0	86	36
1987	90	4	89	31
1986	85	9	87	29
1985	70	13	86	41
1984	95	10	91	35
1983	85	4	88	32
1982	90	20	92	45
1981	95	0	89	6

James M. Jeffords (R)

Of Shrewsbury — Elected 1988

Born: May 11, 1934, Rutland, Vt.
Education: Yale U., B.S.I.A. 1956; Harvard U., LL.B. 1962.
Military Career: Navy, 1956-59, Naval Reserve, 1959-present.
Occupation: Lawyer.
Family: Wife, Elizabeth Daley; two children.
Religion: Congregationalist.
Political Career: Vt. Senate, 1967-69; Vt. attorney general, 1969-73; U.S. House 1975-89; sought Republican gubernatorial nomination, 1972.
Capitol Office: 530 Dirksen Bldg. 20510; 224-5141.

In Washington: Jeffords' moderate-to-liberal profile during his 14-year House career earned him a maverick image in the Republican Conference. It also made him a singular target for grumblings from his more conservative colleagues.

But with his graduation to the Senate in the 101st Congress, Jeffords is likely to find he fits in more comfortably. The Senate has a sizable bloc of GOP moderates who, while by no means dominant, tend to have more clout over Republican policy making than their centrist counterparts in the House. Also, individualism, a trait often identified with Jeffords, is better accepted in the Senate than in the discipline-oriented House.

Jeffords came to the Senate with a voting history that has stood out within his party, especially over the past decade. He was one of the leading GOP opponents of President Reagan's policies; in only one year of Reagan's tenure did Jeffords support the president's positions on legislation more often than he opposed them. Often, on the Education and Labor Committee and on the House floor, Jeffords was the only Republican to buck the party line.

In September 1987, for example, House Republicans put up a fierce resistance to efforts by the Democratic leadership to push through a deficit-reduction bill that included $12 billion in new taxes. But Jeffords joined the Democrats in voting for the bill, the only Republican to do so. The bill passed, 206-205.

But if such behavior placed him to the left in the House Republican Conference, Jeffords was never out of the mainstream in Vermont. He is cut from the same cloth as previous moderates — including Sens. George D. Aiken, Winston L. Prouty and Jeffords' predecessor, Robert T. Stafford — who have dominated the state party for a half-century.

And while Jeffords is willing to accept the GOP maverick label, he bridles at the characterization of "gadfly" that has been applied to him. Rejecting the implication that he has simply been a nuisance to fellow Republicans, Jeffords has produced a legislative résumé of his House years that runs over 100 pages, single-spaced. The report is probably unique among members in its detail, explaining nearly every bill, major amendment, and key issue debate in which Jeffords was involved during seven House terms.

Much of that legislative activity took place in the Education and Labor Committee, where he served as ranking Republican during his final two House terms. He will be working the same turf in the Senate, having obtained a seat on the Labor and Human Resources Committee. And thanks to the Senate's smaller membership — and the lack of Republican zeal for service on that liberal-dominated committee — Jeffords starts out as the third-ranking Republican on the full panel, and the ranking Republican on its Labor Subcommittee.

That assignment is appropriate, since Jeffords tended to emphasize labor issues in the House. His support for much of organized labor's legislative agenda usually earned him high ratings from the AFL-CIO, including a 92 percent mark in 1988.

Jeffords showed early in his Senate career that his pro-labor tendencies had not changed. In March 1989, he was one of two Republicans on Labor and Human Resources to vote for a minimum-wage increase that President Bush vowed to veto as excessive. The next month, he was the only committee Republican to favor a bill requiring employers to provide unpaid leave to workers who need time off to care for a new child or because of medical problems.

Both of these issues are carry-overs from the 100th Congress. In 1987, Jeffords joined with Marge Roukema of New Jersey as the only Republicans on House Education and Labor to support a parental-leave bill. Countering arguments that the bill would put U.S. business at a disadvantage with competitors in other nations,

Jeffords said, "Even Japan has a leave policy — and a partially paid leave policy."

But Jeffords did not always vote in support of organized labor's position. In 1987, he tried to soften proposed legislation requiring businesses to notify workers of potential exposure to hazardous chemicals and other substances. His amendment, cosponsored by Michigan Republican Paul B. Henry, would have required stronger enforcement of existing safety laws and a two-year study to determine the need for a risk-notification system. The amendment was defeated, 191-234, but the stronger bill, though passed by the House, later died in the Senate.

Jeffords' most lasting House legacy in the labor arena is in the area of job training. He was particularly active in working with Democrats in 1982 to design a new job training program to replace the expiring Comprehensive Employment and Training Act (CETA). Jeffords introduced his own proposal in the Employment Opportunities Subcommittee.

After changes on the House floor and in conference, the final version signed by the president contained several key elements of Jeffords' original bill. The major change he pushed for was a new focus on job training, as opposed to make-work jobs. On the floor, he added language requiring that at least 70 percent of the program's costs go toward training. Protecting his constituency, Jeffords also included a "small state minimum," which guaranteed Vermont some funds.

In his time as ranking member, the moderate Jeffords worked comfortably with Education and Labor's liberal chairman, California Democrat Augustus F. Hawkins. Along with Hawkins and Pennsylvania Republican Bill Goodling (Jeffords' successor as senior committee Republican), Jeffords crafted a compromise bill in the 100th Congress that reauthorized federal programs for elementary and secondary education. With Hawkins restraining the zeal of Democratic liberals for new programs, and Jeffords and Goodling holding off GOP efforts to cut the budget, the bill breezed to passage.

As a senator, Jeffords may not be as intimately involved in an area that was one of his House concentrations: agriculture. With the Senate Agriculture Committee being chaired by senior Vermont Senator Patrick J. Leahy, the state's dairy farmers are already amply protected.

It is safe to predict, though, that when major agriculture legislation, including the 1990 farm bill, is debated, Jeffords will be on the Senate floor arguing for Vermont's dairy interests. He was one of the staunchest House defenders of federal milk-price supports, to the extent that he often irked members with other farm constituencies, who thought Jeffords was trying to gain an edge for dairy over other agriculture programs.

During House Agriculture Committee markup of a drought-relief bill in 1988, Jeffords attached an amendment providing a 50-cent-per-hundredweight increase in federal milk-price supports. When the bill reached the floor, backers of other farm programs argued that the increase gave dairy farmers a boost not provided to other farmers. But Jeffords and his opponents compromised on a short-term 50-cent increase, which would cover a three-month period in 1989 when dairy farmers were expected to be hit with higher feed costs resulting from drought-related crop losses.

It was during his tenure on House Agriculture that Jeffords faced what appeared to be a reaction by his conservative GOP colleagues to his liberal leanings. After the 1982 election, Jeffords was in line to be ranking minority member on Agriculture. But the panel's conservative Republicans persuaded Edward Madigan of Illinois, who was on leave of absence from the committee but had more seniority than Jeffords, to return and become the ranking Republican.

Jeffords has two other Senate committee assignments: On Environment and Public Works, he carries an environmentalist perspective that reflects the widespread voter interest in maintaining Vermont's pastoral heritage in the face of recent growth pressures. His membership on Veterans' Affairs has a personal angle; Jeffords served a three-year stint in the Navy during the 1950s.

At Home: With his liberal Republican image, Jeffords is well-suited to politics in modern-day Vermont. The traditional bastion of Yankee Republicanism has moved sharply to the left over the last two decades, with the arrival of thousands of liberal urbanites seeking the state's greener pastures. With Democrats gaining viability in the state, only moderate Republicans like Jeffords have had a chance to win statewide.

Jeffords, with his broad appeal, has in fact tended to face stronger opposition from conservatives in own party than he has in general elections. In the 1988 Senate primary, Jeffords received 61 percent of the vote against a conservative neophyte, Michael Griffes. Jeffords then breezed to victory over a Democrat, former U.S. attorney William Gray, with 68 percent of the vote.

Jeffords' only political defeat came early in his career, in a Republican primary. Jeffords served in the state Senate before becoming Vermont's attorney general in 1969. After two terms there, he ran for governor. But the state GOP hierarchy viewed him as too liberal; he narrowly lost the primary to conservative Luther Hackett.

But Jeffords brushed off this setback in 1974, winning a three-way primary for Vermont's open House seat. He went on to defeat Burlington's Democratic Mayor Francis Cain with 53 percent of the vote. Jeffords quickly became indomitable in his House seat. In six re-election contests, he never received less than 65 percent of the vote. In 1986, his last House election, he ran without Democratic opposition.

During his House tenure, Jeffords was often mentioned as a possible candidate for higher office. In 1980, he passed up a challenge to Leahy. In 1982, he was regarded as a likely Republican successor to GOP Gov. Richard A. Snelling, who was thought to be retiring; but conservatives persuaded Snelling to run for another two-year term. In 1984, when Snelling did give up the office, Jeffords bypassed a tough race with former Democratic Lt. Gov. Madeleine M. Kunin.

But as 1988 approached and Stafford's retirement became imminent, Jeffords gained regard as his heir apparent. No Democratic officeholder came forward to contest him, and the honor fell without opposition to Gray, who had never before sought elective office.

Before getting to Gray, Jeffords had to contend with Griffes, a 35-year-old Navy veteran who returned to Vermont from a job with the Washington, D.C., office of Grumman Corp., a defense contractor. Griffes ran an ideological campaign, describing Jeffords as "not a Republican."

But Jeffords responded by pointing out Griffes' lack of Vermont roots: His family moved to the state when he was 17, and he had spent most years since out of state. Citing Griffes' residence in the Arlington suburbs of Washington, D.C., Jeffords said the contest was between a "Vermont Republican" and a "Virginia Republican." He won easily.

Jeffords then entered the general election contest an overwhelming favorite, and was never threatened. Gray's main thrust was to make a connection between a contribution Jeffords received from the Teamsters Union's PAC, and his opposition to federal efforts to take over the corruption-plagued union. But Jeffords quashed the issue, denying any connection between his fund raising and his House voting behavior; he said his position on the Teamsters' takeover was based solely on his opposition to federal intervention in union operations. The Election Day result showed that the issue did Jeffords no serious harm.

Committees

Environment and Public Works (6th of 7 Republicans)
Environmental Protection; Toxic Substances, Environmental Oversight, Research and Development; Water Resources, Transportation and Infrastructure

Labor and Human Resources (3rd of 7 Republicans)
Labor (ranking); Education, Arts and Humanities; Handicapped

Veterans' Affairs (5th of 5 Republicans)

Elections

1988 General		
James M. Jeffords (R)	163,183	(68%)
William Gray (D)	71,460	(30%)
1988 Primary		
James M. Jeffords (R)	30,555	(61%)
Mike Griffes (R)	19,593	(39%)

Previous Winning Percentages: **1986 *** (89%) **1984 *** (65%) **1982 *** (69%) **1980 *** (79%) **1978 *** (75%) **1976 *** (67%) **1974 *** (53%)

* *House elections.*

Campaign Finance

	Receipts	Receipts from PACs	Expend-itures
1988			
Jeffords (R)	$976,451	$650,393 (67%)	$876,877
Gray (D)	$551,423	$109,950 (20%)	$549,908

Key Votes

House Service	
1987	
Raise speed limit to 65 mph	Y
Approve Gephardt "fair trade" amendment	N
Ban testing of larger nuclear weapons	Y
Delay "re-flagging" of Kuwaiti tankers	Y
Approve tax-raising deficit-reduction bill	Y
1988	
Approve aid to Nicaraguan contras	N
Enact civil rights restoration bill over Reagan veto	Y
Kill 60-day plant-closing notification measure	N
Pass omnibus trade bill over Reagan veto	Y
Approve death penalty for drug-related murders	Y
Bar federal funds for abortions in cases of rape and incest	X
Oppose seven-day waiting period for purchase of handguns	Y

Voting Studies

	Presidential Support		Party Unity		Conservative Coalition	
Year	**S**	**O**	**S**	**O**	**S**	**O**
House Service						
1988	26	64	29	61	45	47
1987	25	71	32	60	47	51
1986	41	58	29	69	44	56
1985	30	56	37	53	33	55
1984	47	42	31	52	32	49
1983	41	51	31	60	27	67
1982	44	47	35	58	38	55
1981	41	55	35 †	55 †	24	68

† *Not eligible for all recorded votes.*

Interest Group Ratings

Year	ADA	ACU	AFL-CIO	CCUS
House Service				
1988	70	21	92	54
1987	68	26	50	67
1986	60	14	71	56
1985	55	16	65	59
1984	60	29	18	50
1983	65	27	50	55
1982	65	10	45	53
1981	60	57	40	53

AL Peter Smith (R)

Of Middlesex — Elected 1988

Born: Oct. 31, 1945, Boston, Mass.

Education: Princeton U., B.A. 1968; Harvard U., M.A. 1970, Ed.D. 1984.

Occupation: Educator.

Family: Wife, Sarah Giddings; three children.

Religion: Protestant.

Political Career: Vt. Senate, 1981-83; lieutenant governor, 1983-87; Republican nominee for governor, 1986.

Capitol Office: 1020 Longworth Bldg. 20515; 225-4115.

The Path to Washington: At one point in Vermont's three-way 1988 House campaign, Democratic candidate Paul N. Poirier said that Smith's 40 percent showing in public-opinion polls was evidence that 60 percent of the voters did not want him to serve in Congress. Smith responded that against two competitors — Poirier and independent Bernard Sanders, Burlington's socialist mayor — 40 percent was nothing shabby.

The results bore out Smith's perspective. Though Poirier's campaign faded in the stretch, Sanders' surged, and together the two of them pulled in 56 percent of the vote. Smith's 41 percent was just enough to keep Vermont's at-large seat where it has nearly always been — in the hands of the GOP.

The victory ended a dry spell in Smith's political career. In 1986, after serving four years as lieutenant governor, he received 38 percent of the vote in a failed challenge to Democratic Gov. Madeleine M. Kunin. Prior to that defeat, Smith had been a rising star in Vermont public life.

Just out of graduate school in 1970, Smith received state backing to establish The Community College of Vermont. He served as president of the college — a "community-as-classroom" concept relying on local schools and businesses to provide training — until his 1980 election to the state Senate. Two years later, he won the first of two elections for lieutenant governor.

In terms of ideology, Smith seems to fit the mold of the popular, moderate-to-liberal Republican officials, including James M. Jeffords, whose 1988 bid to move from the House to the Senate opened the at-large seat.

Smith's style, not his substance, may explain why he has hovered around 40 percent in his last two electoral contests. An Ivy Leaguer, Smith has been labeled by detractors as "Peter Preppy." He is no master of common-man gladhand campaigning, nor of the television soundbite. An educator, Smith on the stump sometimes veered off into theoretical discussions of public-private partnerships and other means for dealing with social problems. The media confronted Smith about his abstract approach, and Sanders accused him of being purposefully vague.

From the outset of his fall campaign, Smith seemed likely to benefit from having two opponents to his left. But liberal voters did not end up splitting in the way that was expected. Poirier, the state House majority leader who had narrowly won a four-way Democratic primary, struggled with a name-recognition problem. He also undercut himself by suggesting that the deficit be addressed by ending dairy price supports — a risky position in a state with powerful dairy interests.

Meanwhile, Sanders — who took 14 percent of the vote as a 1986 candidate for governor — ran strongly, melding rhetoric about the dangers of concentrated wealth with claims of his success as Burlington mayor. By the end of October, Smith recognized Sanders as a threat and began portraying him as a gadfly who would be ineffective if elected.

The election was decided in southern Vermont, where Smith was better known because of his statewide experience; he carried Bennington, Windsor and Windham counties by nearly 8,500 votes. Sanders won Burlington with 51 percent, and took a plurality in Rutland. Though Poirier won his home city of Barre with 46 percent, he took less than 20 percent in most towns.

Given his sometimes contentious relationship with the media, Smith's first official act after the election was a surprise: He hired David Karvelas, a political writer for the Burlington *Free Press*, as his chief of staff. Smith's choice of Montgomery Fischer, a leading state environmentalist, to be his legislative director may provide Smith better entree to activist groups.

Vermont — At Large

Some things about Vermont remain immutable. The least-populous state in the Northeast and third smallest in the nation, it has a scenic beauty that remains largely unsullied. The dairy cow remains the dominant symbol of the Green Mountain State.

However, a growth spurt of more than 35 percent since 1960 has driven Vermont's population to about 550,000. This growth has had outsized impacts on the demographics and politics of the state.

Much of the population increase was caused by an influx of young urbanites who left behind the hassles of the Boston-New York megalopolis, but brought their liberal politics with them. Congregating in Burlington in the northwest, in the southern counties of Windham and Bennington, and in the White River Junction area of Windsor County, these émigrés have drawn the state to the left while the rest of the nation appeared to be moving right.

This trend has shattered Vermont's reputation as the sturdiest bastion of Yankee Republicanism. It is now one of the more politically competitive states. Democrat Madeleine M. Kunin was elected in 1988 to her third two-year term; Democratic Sen. Patrick J. Leahy is now in his third term, having swamped Republican Richard A. Snelling (himself a popular former governor) in 1986.

The liberal swing has also reinforced the dominance of moderate-to-liberal leaders in the state Republican Party. Moderate Republican Rep. James M. Jeffords won to succeed like-minded GOP Sen. Robert T. Stafford; Jeffords was succeeded in the House by Smith, who also fits the moderate profile.

One of the more interesting phenomena of Vermont's political shift has been the rise to prominence of Burlington's Mayor Bernard Sanders, who retired in 1989 after eight years as mayor. A populist message has been the font of Sanders' political base. But he was not hurt by the fact that he shepherded the state's largest city through a period of unprecedented prosperity. Though its manufacturing heritage has faded, Burlington (population 38,000) is thriving, thanks in great part to the growth of its electronics industry and the success of its downtown retail mall; unemployment slipped under 2 percent in 1988.

Burlington and surrounding Chittenden County cast one-quarter of the state's vote; with its liberal core, winning there is vital to statewide Democratic candidates. Voters in the Burlington suburbs, home to a growing high-tech industry, tend to be more mainstream than those in the city. However, fear about suburban sprawl works there to the benefit of Democrats (and environmentally conscious Republicans).

Other small urban centers, such as Rutland and the state capital of Montpelier, used to tilt Republican, but are starting to lean Democratic. There have been some Democratic inroads in Bennington, Brattleboro and other southern Vermont towns, but there is more loyalty there to the GOP.

At the village level and in most rural areas — most of the state's people still live in communities of 2,500 or fewer — Yankee Vermonters mainly vote Republican, keeping GOP candidates competitive. One area stands out as an exception: Franklin and Grand Isle counties, in northwest Vermont, have a large French Canadian population that gives them a Democratic complexion.

Population: 511,456. White 506,736 (99%), Black 1,135 (0.2%), Other 2,339 (1%). Spanish origin 3,304 (1%). 18 and over 366,138 (72%), 65 and over 58,166 (11%). Median age: 29.

Committees

Education and Labor (13th of 13 Republicans)
Elementary, Secondary and Vocational Education; Employment Opportunities; Select Education

Government Operations (9th of 15 Republicans)
Human Resources and Intergovernmental Relations; Legislation and National Security

Select Children, Youth and Families (10th of 12 Republicans)

Campaign Finance

	Receipts	Receipts from PACs	Expend-itures
1988			
Smith (R)	$457,737	$159,111 (35%)	$450,162
Sanders (I)	$332,845	0	$331,284
Poirier (D)	$260,771	$128,588 (49%)	$260,535

Elections

1988 General		
Peter Smith (R)	98,937	(41%)
Bernard Sanders (I)	90,026	(37%)
Paul N. Poirier (D)	45,330	(19%)
1988 Primary		
Peter Smith (R)	37,211	(78%)
David Gates (R)	9,954	(21%)

District Vote For President

	1988		1984		1980		1976	
D	115,755	(48%)	95,730	(41%)	81,952	(38%)	80,954	(43%)
R	124,331	(51%)	135,865	(58%)	94,628	(44%)	102,085	(54%)
I					31,761	(15%)		

Virginia

U.S. CONGRESS

SENATE 1 D, 1 R
HOUSE 5 D, 5 R

LEGISLATURE

Senate 30 D, 9 R, 1 vacancy
House 64 D, 34 R, 1 Independent, 1 vacancy

ELECTIONS

1988 Presidential Vote	
Bush	60%
Dukakis	39%
1984 Presidential Vote	
Reagan	62%
Mondale	37%
1980 Presidential Vote	
Reagan	53%
Carter	40%
Anderson	5%
Turnout rate in 1984	51%
Turnout rate in 1986	24%
Turnout rate in 1988	48%

(as percentage of voting age population)

POPULATION AND GROWTH

1980 population	5,346,818
1988 population estimate (12th in the nation)	6,015,000
Percent change 1980-1988	+12%

DEMOGRAPHIC BREAKDOWN

White	79%
Black	19%
Other	1%
(Spanish origin)	2%
Urban	66%
Rural	34%
Born in state	60%
Foreign-born	3%

MAJOR CITIES

Virginia Beach	333,400
Norfolk	274,800
Richmond	217,700
Newport News	161,700
Chesapeake	134,400

AREA AND LAND USE

Area 39,704 sq. miles (36th)

Farm	37%
Forest	63%
Federally owned	10%

Gov. Gerald L. Baliles (D)
Of Richmond — Elected 1985

Born: July 8, 1940, Stuart, Va.
Education: Wesleyan U., B.A. 1963; U. of Virginia, J.D. 1967.
Occupation: Lawyer.
Religion: Episcopalian.
Political Career: Va. House, 1976-82; Va. attorney general, 1982-86.
Next Election: 1989.

WORK

Occupations	
White-collar	55%
Blue-collar	31%
Service workers	12%
Government Workers	
Federal	155,760
State	123,266
Local	217,539

MONEY

Median family income	$ 20,018	(23rd)
Tax burden per capita	$ 783	(34th)

EDUCATION

Spending per pupil through grade 12	$ 3,520	(29th)
Persons with college degrees	19%	(9th)

CRIME

Violent crime rate 295 per 100,000 (34th)

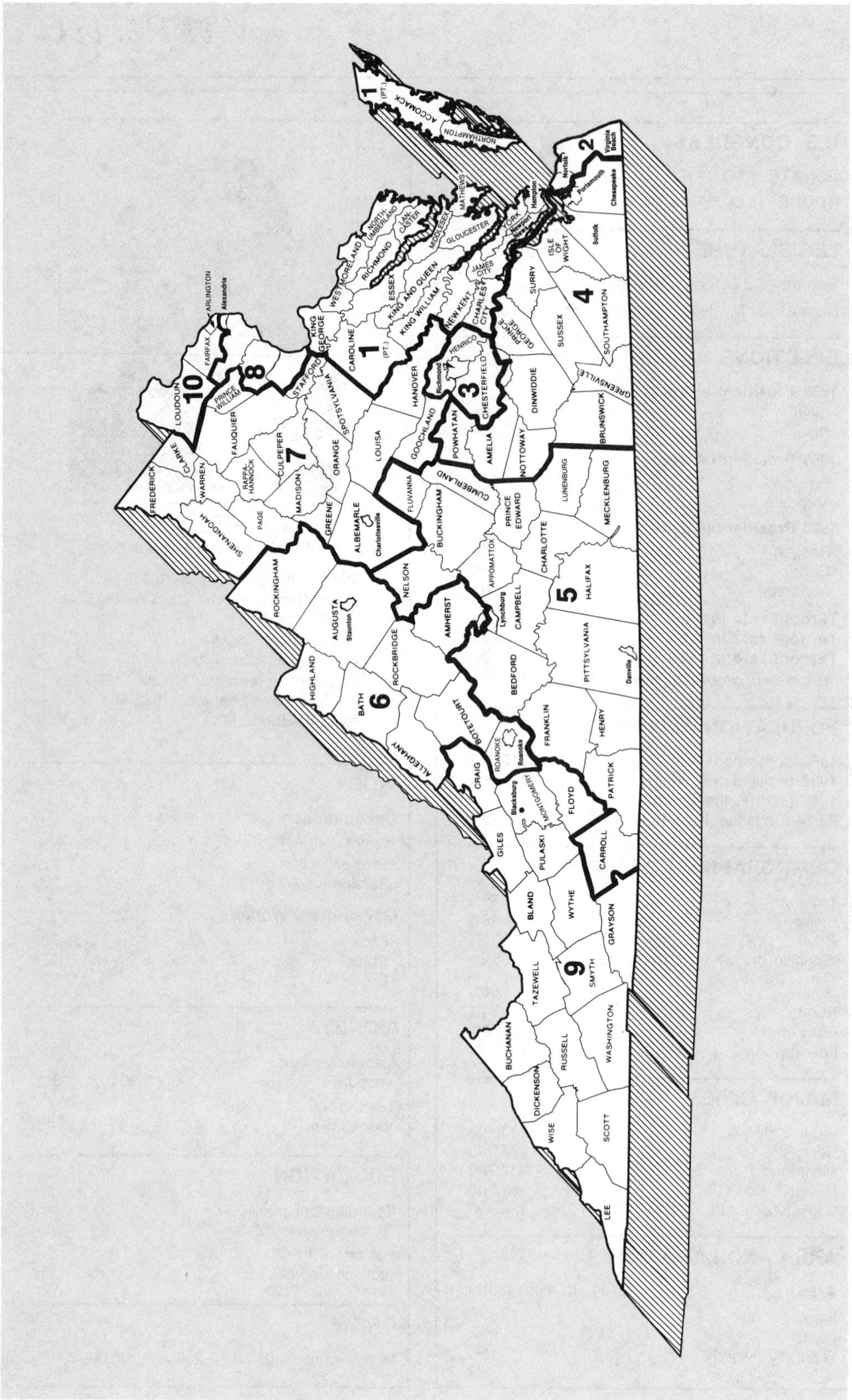
1
(PT.)
ACCOMACK
NORTHAMPTON
2
Virginia Beach
Norfolk
Portsmouth
Chesapeake
Hampton
Newport News
YORK
MATHEWS
GLOUCESTER
MIDDLESEX
LANCASTER
NORTHUMBERLAND
RICHMOND
WESTMORELAND
ESSEX
KING AND QUEEN
KING WILLIAM
JAMES CITY
NEW KENT
CHARLES CITY
ISLE OF WIGHT
Suffolk
SURRY
4
SUSSEX
SOUTHAMPTON
PRINCE GEORGE
HENRICO
Richmond
3
CHESTERFIELD
DINWIDDIE
GREENSVILLE
BRUNSWICK
KING GEORGE
CAROLINE
1
(PT.)
HANOVER
ARLINGTON
Alexandria
FAIRFAX
8
10
LOUDOUN
PRINCE WILLIAM
STAFFORD
SPOTSYLVANIA
LOUISA
GOOCHLAND
POWHATAN
AMELIA
NOTTOWAY
LUNENBURG
MECKLENBURG
CLARKE
FREDERICK
WARREN
FAUQUIER
RAPPAHANNOCK
CULPEPER
7
ORANGE
MADISON
PAGE
GREENE
SHENANDOAH
ALBEMARLE
Charlottesville
FLUVANNA
CUMBERLAND
BUCKINGHAM
PRINCE EDWARD
CHARLOTTE
APPOMATTOX
ROCKINGHAM
AUGUSTA
Staunton
NELSON
AMHERST
Lynchburg
CAMPBELL
5
HALIFAX
PITTSYLVANIA
Danville
ROCKBRIDGE
HIGHLAND
BATH
6
ALLEGHANY
BOTETOURT
BEDFORD
FRANKLIN
HENRY
ROANOKE
Roanoke
CRAIG
Blacksburg
MONTGOMERY
FLOYD
PATRICK
GILES
PULASKI
CARROLL
BLAND
WYTHE
GRAYSON
TAZEWELL
9
SMYTH
BUCHANAN
RUSSELL
WASHINGTON
DICKENSON
WISE
SCOTT
LEE

John W. Warner (R)

Of Middleburg — Elected 1978

Born: Feb. 18, 1927, Washington, D.C.
Education: Washington and Lee U., B.S. 1949; U. of Virginia, LL.B. 1953.
Military Career: Navy, 1944-46; Marine Corps, 1950-52.
Occupation: Lawyer; farmer.
Family: Divorced; three children.
Religion: Episcopalian.
Political Career: No previous office.
Capitol Office: 225 Russell Bldg. 20510; 224-2023.

In Washington: Warner is a man of intense loyalties, and the 101st Congress could not have begun with a more distasteful dilemma for him than the struggle over former Sen. John Tower's nomination as secretary of defense.

Warner had served his first six years on the Armed Services Committee with Tower, who was chairman for four of those years. Warner was loyal to Tower, just as he was to President Reagan and his efforts to strengthen the military. Warner also wanted to be loyal to his new commander in chief, George Bush, who had chosen Tower to head the Pentagon.

But Warner's backing of Tower's nomination did not turn out to be easy, as more and more questions were raised about Tower's personal life and his extensive business relationships with defense contractors. Soon it became clear that Armed Services Chairman Sam Nunn was turning against the nomination. Warner had worked well with Nunn, whom he obviously respected, since joining the committee.

Together, the two had co-authored the Nuclear Risk Reduction Center bill, improving communications between the United States and the Soviet Union in a crisis. They had set out guidelines for selling AWACS planes to foreign governments. They had favored concentrating military pay increases on the career service rather than new recruits. They had worked toward ratification of the intermediate-range nuclear-force (INF) treaty and toward a bipartisan approach to modernizing weapons. Even as the spring of 1989 went on, the two would agree on, for example, the need to tie rail-based MX missile development to parallel approval for the truck-borne Midgetman missile.

Warner strove for a bipartisan resolution of the Tower problem. He and Nunn met Bush together and released a joint statement promising a vote at the earliest possible time. But when the vote came in committee 13 days later, Nunn led a party-line vote to reject the nominee, 11-9.

Later, at the White House, Warner defended Nunn, saying he believed Nunn liked Tower personally and was not trying to run the Pentagon from Capitol Hill. "It's not a power grab," said Warner. "That much I can tell you." Senate GOP leader Bob Dole immediately said some of his colleagues disagreed. When the nomination was pressed to the floor, with Nunn leading the opposition, the administration's forces were spearheaded by the counterattacking Dole, not the anguishing Warner. But the nomination lost, 47-53.

Warner had been on the other side of another nasty nomination fight in October 1987, when he opposed Robert H. Bork's appointment to the Supreme Court. Warner was easily the most surprising of the six Republican "no" votes, and he left some Virginia supporters in shock. He denied political motivations, although some observers noted the importance of the vote to blacks and moderates. Warner, who faces re-election in 1990, announced that he had found Bork lacking "that record of compassion, of sensitivity ... to enable him to sit on the highest court in the land."

Warner is no longer married to Elizabeth Taylor, and the notoriety that accompanied his marriage to the famous actress has faded. Yet his personal image retains something of the theatrical. With his carefully coiffed hair, impeccable tailoring, sonorous voice and purposeful stride, Warner reminds people of an actor portraying a senator.

Warner's style occasionally inclines to the sanctimonious. Once during a television debate, he declared, "When I receive a tough question in the Senate, I reach for either of two things: the Bible or the Constitution."

Beneath Warner's rather self-important exterior, however, there is considerable substance. He was a lawyer and a farmer before becoming secretary of the Navy under President Nixon. But he has made a career of the military in the Senate. He works hard and takes an interest in the voluminous technical detail behind defense issues.

And for all his collegiality and respect for

Nunn, Warner has shown he is willing to be an aggressive partisan opponent to the Georgia Democrat. In the spring of 1987, Warner led GOP forces in a bruising filibuster battle against Nunn's defense bill. Warner argued that a provision in the bill giving Congress veto power over moves to abandon the traditional interpretation of the 1972 anti-ballistic missile treaty would hamstring President Reagan's efforts to develop a nationwide anti-missile defense.

Warner stuck by Reagan defense policies even when that stance cost him politically. That was illustrated by his role in the 1986 debate over the Navy's plan to expand the number of ports around the country where its ships had their home bases.

Coming from the state with the largest existing naval base, at Norfolk, Warner was naturally inclined to oppose the plan. He initially voted against it, but was unaccountably absent when the issue came to a crucial vote in committee. That left the panel deadlocked. When next the subject arose, Warner supported the administration with the crucial vote needed to put the plan over the top.

Warner argued that dispersing the ships was a necessary security move to guard against a devastating surprise attack, and insisted that the move would not hurt Norfolk. Within a few months, however, a major carrier group had been transferred, costing the state jobs and adding to the political sensitivity of Warner's stand.

Before the Democratic takeover of the Senate in 1987, Warner's most important role on Armed Services was as chairman of the Strategic Nuclear Forces Subcommittee. That position put him in a central position on controversial issues such as the MX, arms control, nerve gas and the strategic defense initiative. Warner was credited with a technically skilled and politically astute performance as subcommittee chairman.

Warner initially was skeptical of the MX missile, and especially of the Reagan administration's plan to base it in "superhardened" Minuteman silos. He voted with the president on key Senate tests, including one early in the 99th Congress. But he has remained noncommittal about future production of the missile, joining his subcommittee in 1985 in cutting the request for 48 more missiles to 21.

Warner's non-defense concerns mostly revolve around aiding Virginia's economy. In the mid-1980s he served on the commission that recommended transferring two of metropolitan Washington's airports (both of which are in suburban Virginia) to local control and inserted an enacting amendment in an appropriations bill for 1987. He also supported an amendment authorizing the dredging of the Hampton Roads channel in 1987 legislation, helping Virginia's ports.

At Home: After two terms, some senators will be secure, some will be in trouble and some will look shaky only in the presence of a specific challenger. Warner falls in the third category. His party standing is sure. Despite the incumbent's vote against Bork and his ambivalence in the Tower affair, Republicans know they have nowhere else to go. Warner's one worry would appear to be Democratic Gov. Gerald L. Baliles.

Baliles came to the governorship in 1985, succeeding Democrat Charles S. Robb, who is now Virginia's junior senator. Baliles lacks Robb's glamour, but many credit him with accomplishing more in office. Forbidden by state law from succeeding himself, Baliles will be a private citizen in 1990. But he may let the Senate opportunity pass. If he does, Warner is virtually guaranteed a third term.

Such longevity seemed improbable in 1978, when Warner's political career looked to be stalled. His campaign for the Senate had impressed Virginia Republicans at the state GOP convention in June, but the nomination went to Richard Obenshain.

Then the state's politics and Warner's future were reordered by an airplane accident. Obenshain's light plane crashed Aug. 2 and he was killed instantly. Virginia Republicans needed a nominee, and Warner, the runner-up in June, was the obvious choice.

He had courted the convention delegates with a lavish campaign costing nearly $500,000, and attracted enough votes to force six ballots before being defeated. He had also been a good loser and backed Obenshain afterward.

Warner brought to the fall campaign the same assets he had in June: personal wealth and a statewide reputation, achieved not only as Navy secretary under Nixon and chief bicentennial planner under President Ford, but as Elizabeth Taylor's husband.

He also had liabilities. Despite his Virginia education, he was looked upon as an outsider who arrived late on the state's political scene. Some voters also saw him as a socialite and fortune hunter. Before he married Taylor, he was married to heiress Catherine Mellon and received a reported $7 million from her in their divorce settlement.

But Warner's celebrity wife turned out to be a help to him. Taylor's presence on the campaign trail guaranteed large crowds, and when she proved willing to voice her enthusiasm for conservative causes, Virginia Republicans cheered her on.

The Democratic nominee, former state Attorney General Andrew Miller, was seeking to recover from a defeat in the 1977 gubernatorial primary by the state's best-known liberal Democrat, Henry E. Howell. In 1978 Miller campaigned for the Senate as a fiscal conservative, but Warner tied him to the Democratic Party of Howell, and Miller never managed to extricate himself. Warner won by fewer than 5,000 votes in the closest Senate election in Virginia history.

Six years later, Warner was in a totally different type of contest, winning re-election by more than 805,000 votes in a race that was a mismatch from the beginning.

Gov. Robb led the search for a suitable Democratic challenger, but Warner helped to discourage the effort by raising more than $1 million by the end of 1983. After a host of better-known Democrats turned down the nomination, it went by default to former state Rep. Edythe C. Harrison, who had lost her previous race for the state Legislature.

Harrison peppered Warner with a variety of charges, including conflict-of-interest for investing in defense stocks while serving on the Armed Services Committee. She also made barbed personal attacks. Referring to Warner's celebrated marriages, she declared: "Women took him up, and a woman is going to bring him down."

But even leading Democrats doubted that the woman would be Harrison. A longtime ally of the liberal Howell, she was given lukewarm support by much of her own party.

With money, incumbency, strong ticket mates and a grip on Virginia's conservative political mainstream, Warner swept all but two of the state's 95 counties and all 41 independent cities. According to NBC News exit polls, he also captured nearly one-quarter of the black vote, more than twice the share won in Virginia by Reagan.

Committees

Armed Services (Ranking)

Environment and Public Works (5th of 7 Republicans)
Toxic Substances, Environmental Oversight, Research and Development (ranking); Environmental Protection; Water Resources, Transportation and Infrastructure

Select Intelligence (5th of 7 Republicans)

Special Aging (8th of 9 Republicans)

Elections

1984 General

John W. Warner (R)	1,406,194	(70%)
Edythe C. Harrison (D)	601,142	(30%)

Previous Winning Percentage: 1978 (50%)

Campaign Finance

	Receipts	Receipts from PACs	Expend-itures
1984			
Warner (R)	$2,630,558	$694,588 (26%)	$2,786,140
Harrison (D)	$496,124	$82,817 (17%)	$492,201

Key Votes

1987

Enact omnibus highway bill over Reagan veto	N
Limit testing of space-based anti-ballistic missiles	N
Oppose banning tests of larger nuclear weapons	Y
Confirm Robert H. Bork as Supreme Court justice	N

1988

Allow vote on campaign-finance overhaul	N
Pass civil rights restoration bill over Reagan veto	N
Enact omnibus trade bill over Reagan veto	N
Approve death penalty for drug-related murders	Y
Oppose "workfare" amendment to welfare overhaul bill	N

Voting Studies

	Presidential Support		Party Unity		Conservative Coalition	
Year	**S**	**O**	**S**	**O**	**S**	**O**
1988	74	23	71	26	95	3
1987	60	36	75	16	88	9
1986	87	13	86	13	87	12
1985	82	18	82	18	92	8
1984	86	13	87	12	91	6
1983	82	16	84	14	89	11
1982	83	17	87	13	96	2
1981	87	13	88	8	97	2

Interest Group Ratings

Year	ADA	ACU	AFL-CIO	CCUS
1988	5	87	36	86
1987	25	60	50	94
1986	5	73	7	79
1985	5	74	19	79
1984	10	90	0	89
1983	20	56	18	53
1982	5	86	19	81
1981	5	74	5	100

Charles S. Robb (D)

Of McLean — Elected 1988

Born: June 26, 1939, Phoenix, Ariz.

Education: Attended Cornell U., 1957-58; U. of Wisconsin, B.B.A. 1961; U. of Virginia, J.D. 1973.

Military Career: Marine Corps, 1961-70.

Occupation: Lawyer.

Family: Wife, Lynda Bird Johnson; three children.

Religion: Episcopalian.

Political Career: Va. lieutenant governor, 1978-82; governor, 1982-86.

Capitol Office: 493 Russell Bldg. 20510; 224-4024.

The Path to Washington: Few politicians have found the road to the Senate as smoothly paved as Robb did. Indeed, the handsome ex-Marine and former governor has been seen as a politician of national potential almost since his first bid for public office in 1977. The Senate seat was simply the next logical step.

So popular was Robb after his governorship that he was all but conceded the seat even before he announced he wanted it. The mere belief that he would run was widely believed to have influenced Republican Paul S. Trible Jr.'s decision not to seek re-election in 1988.

But one bump in the 1988 campaign road left Robb with a bruise. A series of newspaper stories during the early fall reported that Robb, while he was governor, socialized at beachfront parties with businessmen under investigation by various law-enforcement agencies on suspicion of cocaine trafficking.

No one suggested that Robb used drugs himself, and he has denied any knowledge of drug use by others at the parties. The election results suggested the stories had done little or no damage to Robb's home-state reputation. But a whiff of impropriety lingered, along with a question about Robb's judgment, casting a cloud over an otherwise limitless future. The issue may resurface should Robb be part of the party's presidential ticket in the future.

Robb maintains this episode is behind him. He arrived in Washington with a full head of steam. He let his colleagues know he would like to serve on several "A" list committees (of which he was assigned to just one). Early reactions to him seemed colored by preconceptions about his political plans.

At the same time, Robb seemed to navigate his first months in the Senate with an eye to refurbishing his reputation for good judgment and judicious conduct. In one of the first hot votes to confront him on the Foreign Relations Committee, he voted with the Bush administration and the panel leadership in favor of developing a new jet fighter plane (the FS-X) with the Japanese — a plan opposed by partisans of the left and right.

When the Senate was debating President Bush's nomination of former Sen. John Tower as secretary of defense, Robb was among the last to declare his intentions. Eventually, he delivered an exegesis on the arguments pro and con before siding with the majority led by Sen. Sam Nunn of Georgia, the man Robb has for years pushed for national party leadership. Noting first "a very substantial deference" to the president's wishes, he said he was torn by the "very firmly held conviction" of Nunn. Concluded Robb: "I must cast my vote with my longtime friend."

Robb's speech was a showcase for his serious, lawyerly side and his devotion to finding the middle. It also showed the kind of elaborate balancing and caution that had marked his successful career in state politics.

It is difficult to overstate the importance of that career to Democrats in Virginia. The collapse of the old Harry Byrd organization in the 1960s had brought an era of Republican dominance at the statewide level. Party-switching was common. Before Robb, the state had elected three GOP governors in succession.

But then came Robb, a decorated Vietnam War hero and former White House guard whose wife was the daughter of former President Lyndon B. Johnson. Robb had left the Marines and gone to law school. After practicing law for four years, he was elected lieutenant governor. Four years later, Robb won the governorship.

In Richmond, Robb carefully built a reputation for fiscal conservatism with a human face. He appointed minorities and women to judgeships and other state posts. But such moves were made with a kind of square-jawed respectability. Robb seemed immune to the taint of liberalism.

State law barred a successive term, but Robb's popularity was talismanic enough in 1985 to help elect a slate of other Democrats — including the first black and the first woman elected statewide in Virginia history.

In the next few years, Robb became a

partner in one of the most prominent law firms in Washington, D.C. But his political energy and profile remained high. He campaigned for a mainstream chairman of the Democratic National Committee (DNC). He helped found the Democratic Leadership Council (DLC), a largely Southern group of officeholders dedicated to moving the party to the center. And he encouraged Southern states to hold their presidential primaries on a single date. He sold this Super Tuesday concept as a means to increase Southern leverage, and conservative influence, in the selection of the party's nominee.

In retrospect, none of these enterprises has been blessed with much success. Robb's candidate to lead the DNC lost in 1985 and again in 1989. The DLC faded somewhat when three of its founders became rival contenders for the 1988 presidential nomination. And the Super Tuesday idea proved counterproductive. After it, two liberals swiftly reduced the rest of the primary season to a duel.

Despite these reversals, Robb's mystique in Virginia only seemed to grow. Virginia had not elected a Democrat to the Senate since 1966, yet polls in 1987 showed Robb running ahead of Trible — who otherwise would have been considered a good bet for re-election in 1988. When Trible stepped aside, the Virginia GOP had no clear replacement — and the prospect of facing Robb attracted no one of note.

Robb raised $1 million almost effortlessly and formally began his campaign in April by warning his supporters not to be complacent. But he himself was confident enough to talk about balancing the federal budget with unpopular cuts and the possibility of revenue increases.

The Republicans scrambled through a long list of celebrity prospects, including Pat Robertson (who was running for president), former Secretary of State Alexander M. Haig Jr. and Lt. Col. Oliver L. North, the linchpin of the Iran-contra controversy. But in the end, they chose a candidate who seemed more of a political novelty than a serious contender.

The Rev. Maurice A. Dawkins had been a civil rights activist, a Baptist minister and, more recently, a Washington lobbyist. He was also a spellbinding speaker. Wielding a baseball bat, he so enthused delegates at the Virginia GOP's convention that they nominated him by acclamation. He became the Virginia GOP's first black candidate for statewide office, and one of only two blacks nominated for the Senate by either party in 1988.

But Dawkins' campaign was erratic from the start, running into controversy over details of his personal business. He was unable to raise money in meaningful amounts, and he was unable to identify issues of concern to Virginians on which his positions were clearly preferable to Robb's. The state party took over management of the campaign, and soon Dawkins was adapting the stories about Robb's Virginia Beach friends for use on the stump.

Robb tried at first to ignore the matter, then to dismiss it out of hand. Although the issue was not affecting the polls, Robb's campaign clearly wanted to bury it. The candidate volunteered for a drug test, which proved negative, and, before joint appearances, confronted Dawkins about Republican use of the issue. Dawkins publicly accepted Robb's account of the facts, but the issue was clearly his only weapon.

The final result was unmercifully lopsided. Robb carried every congressional district and virtually every county and city. His support among blacks was scarcely diminished from what he had received in his earlier races.

If the party's presidential nominee in 1992 is not a Southerner and wants one as a running mate, Robb's name is sure to be on the short list. Robb could be on that ticket without affecting his re-election options in 1994.

Committees

Budget (13th of 13 Democrats)

Commerce, Science and Transportation (11th of 11 Democrats)
Consumer; Science, Technology and Space; Surface Transportation; National Ocean Policy Study

Foreign Relations (10th of 10 Democrats)
Near Eastern and South Asian Affairs; Terrorism, Narcotics and International Operations; Western Hemisphere and Peace Corps Affairs

Election

1988 General

Charles S. Robb (D)	1,474,086	(71%)
Maurice A. Dawkins (R)	593,652	(29%)

Campaign Finance

	Receipts	Receipts from PACs		Expend-itures
1988				
Robb (D)	$3,198,630	$914,763	(29%)	$2,881,666
Dawkins (R)	$283,095	$23,148	(8%)	$282,229

1 Herbert H. Bateman (R)

Of Newport News — Elected 1982

Born: Aug. 7, 1928, Elizabeth City, N.C.
Education: College of William and Mary, B.A. 1949; Georgetown U., J.D. 1956.
Military Career: Air Force, 1951-53.
Occupation: Lawyer.
Family: Wife, Laura Yacobi; two children.
Religion: Presbyterian.
Political Career: Va. Senate, 1968-82; sought GOP nomination for lieutenant governor, 1981.
Capitol Office: 1230 Longworth Bldg. 20515; 225-4261.

In Washington: Though Bateman — a conservative Republican and an Air Force veteran — comes to his pro-defense viewpoint naturally, it also serves him well politically. A member of the Armed Services Committee, Bateman serves a Tidewater Virginia district with a strong military orientation. While the stolid Bateman generally keeps a low profile, he can surely be found in the well of the House when issues affecting his district's defense interests are being debated.

Such was the case in early 1987, when Bateman fought to preserve a provision in a defense authorization bill providing funds for two new nuclear-powered aircraft carriers, which would be built at the huge Newport News Shipbuilding and Drydock Co. in his district.

Advocates of the carriers said they would be needed to replace two aging conventional carriers that are to be decommissioned in the 1990s; they noted that maintaining a fleet of 15 carriers was fundamental to President Reagan's plans for a 600-ship Navy. But opponents countered that, at a time of limited fiscal resources, the amounts targeted for the project — $644 million in fiscal 1988 and $797 million in 1989 — were too high.

When Illinois Republican Lynn Martin and Oklahoma Democrat Dave McCurdy submitted separate floor amendments to cut carrier funding, Bateman rose to defend the project. His main line of argument was on national security grounds. "Why wreck our national maritime strategy?" Bateman asked. "Why cripple our conventional capability and readiness into the 21st century?"

But Bateman also stressed the economic benefits of the carrier program. "This is the most critical vote of this session for our faltering shipbuilding and steel industries," he said. As it turned out, Bateman was preaching to the converted: The House defeated both of the cutback amendments by wide margins.

A longtime state senator before coming to Washington, Bateman is acknowledged as a master of legislative detail. He exhibited his skill at drafting technical amendments in 1988, during debate on a bill that laid ground rules for a commission that was to recommend military bases that should be closed to save money.

During the Armed Services markup, Bateman attached an amendment to the bill ordering the commission to consider the environmental restoration and historic preservation costs of closing a base. That amendment would have pertained to a number of facilities around the country; as it happened, one was Fort Monroe, an ancient Army training base in Bateman's district that had been suggested for closure by the Carter administration.

The moat-encircled fort was built as an artillery base just after the War of 1812; it also contains refuse — ranging from toxic waste to unexploded Confederate shells — that would be difficult and expensive to dispose of if the base were closed.

Proponents of the base-closing plan were wary of efforts to modify the bill with provisions they regarded as parochial. Republican Constance A. Morella of Maryland gently chided Bateman on the House floor, suggesting that Fort Monroe would produce more revenue for local communities if it was converted to a "theme park."

But Bateman was resolute; in response to a critical editorial in *The New York Times*, Bateman called the fort "a well-functioning, well-located headquarters for the Army's Training and Doctrine Command."

The final bill enacted in October 1988 did not contain Bateman's preservation clause, and it had different language on environmental costs. But ultimately, Fort Monroe was exempted from the commission's list of suggested closures. A provision in the charter of the base-closing commission required that the total costs for a base shutdown be offset by budget savings within six years; Pentagon officials suggested it could take 25 years to offset the costs of disposing of Fort Monroe's troublesome wastes.

Though Bateman was one of the most consistent supporters of President Reagan's de-

Virginia 1

East — Newport News; Hampton

Now that Republicans have won the 1st in seven consecutive House elections, it seems safe to say that this Tidewater constituency has come loose from its traditional Democratic moorings. But it is still not automatic for the GOP; because of its black and working-class populations, it can still be a swing district in close statewide elections. In the hotly contested 1985 election for lieutenant governor, for instance, the 1st gave a majority to black Democratic nominee L. Douglas Wilder.

Half the people in the 1st live in two cities at the district's southern end — Hampton and Newport News, both ports of the Hampton Roads harbor. Both are about one-third black, and both economies are tied to extensive military and shipbuilding facilities that Bateman has worked hard in Congress to promote; the Newport News Shipbuilding and Drydock Co. alone employs about 28,000 people and is the largest private employer in the state.

The balance of the district's population is scattered among rural inland counties and along the Chesapeake Bay. Colonial Virginia and its plantation economy were centered in this area; fishing, oystering, crabbing and the growing of corn, soybeans and wheat are important today. So is tourism. Along the southern flank of the district are some of colonial Virginia's leading tourist attractions — Williamsburg, Jamestown and Yorktown.

This basically conservative rural territory is where Republicans first began making significant inroads into the district's traditional Democratic strength. In 1984 and 1988 the GOP presidential contender won all but two counties in the district — Caroline and Charles City.

Population: 535,092. White 358,702 (67%), Black 167,559 (31%), Other 6,072 (1%). Spanish origin 6,920 (1%). 18 and over 384,328 (72%), 65 and over 53,578 (10%). Median age: 30.

fense policies, he questioned the probity of Reagan's decision to re-flag Kuwaiti oil tankers in June 1987 and to provide them with U.S. Navy escorts in the war-torn Persian Gulf. But unlike some liberal Democrats, who rued the foreign policy implications of the president's action, Bateman cited his concern about the impact of re-flagging on the struggling domestic merchant marine industry.

"There are nearly 40 U.S. tankers now laid up, and there is some concern that those vessels should have been given first right of refusal on routes which are to be protected by American naval vessels," said Bateman, a member of the Merchant Marine and Fisheries Committee. He said that the Kuwaiti ships should be held to American safety requirements, and that those that fell short should be upgraded "whenever feasible in U.S. shipyards."

Though not known as an environmental crusader, Bateman has been protective of the ecologically sensitive Chesapeake Bay, the waterway that separates the two parts of his district. In the 100th Congress, he led a successful fight to restrict use of a tin-based pesticide, used to keep barnacles off ships, that had been found to be toxic to fish and crustaceans. He also joined with Maryland Democrat Roy Dyson to block Navy plans to place a powerful electromagnetic generator in the bay to test the effects of pulses caused by nuclear blasts on shipboard electronic gear.

At Home: Bateman has been near the center of Newport News' civic and political life since he set up his legal practice three decades ago. He ran for the state Senate in 1967 as a Democrat and won. He was re-elected three times, twice as a Democrat and once as a Republican.

But until 1982, Bateman was blunted in his tries for higher office; his strong support from Virginia's conservative political establishment was neutralized by a poor sense of timing.

In early 1976, he switched parties with an eye on the Tidewater House seat of retiring Democratic Rep. Thomas N. Downing. But a hard-working young county prosecutor named Paul S. Trible Jr. had the GOP nomination locked up. In 1981 he was encouraged by GOP leaders to run for lieutenant governor. But he was challenged aggressively by a religious fundamentalist and a young state legislator and he finished second at the GOP state convention.

The two rebuffs, coupled with his narrow re-election to the state Senate in 1979, seemed to turn Bateman a little cautious on competing strenuously for higher office. When GOP officials sought a House successor for Trible, who was running for the Senate in 1982, Bateman bluntly told them: "I'm a candidate, if I'm the nominee." Bateman was an easy winner at the district convention.

His Democratic opponent was John McGlennon, a political science professor at William and Mary who stepped in after the original nominee withdrew when the campaign placed him under severe emotional stress. The switch probably doomed any Democratic hopes, but it also seemed to make Bateman somewhat overconfident. He waged a haphazard campaign that brought him victory with a surprisingly low 54 percent.

That result encouraged McGlennon to try again in 1984, when he could take advantage of an earlier start. The Democrat went after Bateman aggressively the second time, calling him a lazy legislator and attempting to prove it with a TV commercial that showed the incumbent apparently asleep at a conference table. But with President Reagan and GOP Sen. John W. Warner both carrying the 1st by more than 50,000 votes, Bateman won with nearly 60 percent.

Democrats figured they still had a good chance to beat Bateman in 1986, when he would not have popular top-of-the-ticket help from Trible or Reagan. But a challenger was slow to emerge. State Sen. Robert C. Scott was encouraged to run only after Democrat L. Douglas Wilder showed in the fall of 1985 that a black could win a major contest in Virginia. (Wilder was elected lieutenant governor.)

Scott was bidding to become the state's first black congressman since the late 19th century. A Harvard-educated lawyer, he had demonstrated biracial appeal in Bateman's home base of Newport News, representing a Senate district roughly two-thirds white, a racial composition similar to the 1st District.

But the incumbent gave Scott few openings to exploit. Scott tried to pound away at Bateman as a captive of Tidewater business interests. But he was playing "catch-up" throughout. While Scott was deciding in the spring whether to run, Bateman was already running television ads. He followed that up by stressing his success at bringing jobs to the district, highlighted by Defense Secretary Caspar W. Weinberger's election-eve appearance with Bateman at the Newport News Shipbuilding and Drydock Co. to help dedicate a nuclear-powered aircraft carrier.

Scott could not match such visual images. Although regarded as a "team player" in the moderately conservative Democratic legislative majority, he had been most active on issues such as teenage pregnancy, prenatal care and urban enterprise zones. While those concerns helped him establish a base in the populous Newport News area, they were little help in his effort to broaden his appeal to the farmers and watermen in the rural Tidewater.

Lack of support there doomed his candidacy. Scott ran virtually even with Bateman in the urban Tidewater, even carrying the city of Hampton. But Bateman rolled up 60 percent of the vote in the rural portion of the 1st to win a third term. In 1988, with the Democrats virtually conceding him a fourth term, Bateman pushed his vote share above 70 percent.

Committees

Armed Services (10th of 21 Republicans)
Military Personnel and Compensation (ranking); Seapower and Strategic and Critical Materials

Merchant Marine and Fisheries (7th of 17 Republicans)
Coast Guard and Navigation; Fisheries and Wildlife Conservation and the Environment; Merchant Marine

Elections

1988 General		
Herbert H. Bateman (R)	135,937	(73%)
James S. Ellenson (D)	49,614	(27%)
1986 General		
Herbert H. Bateman (R)	80,713	(56%)
Robert C. Scott (D)	63,364	(44%)

Previous Winning Percentages: **1984** (59%) **1982** (54%)

District Vote For President

	1988	1984	1980	1976
D	83,291 (38%)	79,051 (37%)	80,434 (45%)	83,549 (51%)
R	131,341 (60%)	132,393 (62%)	90,093 (50%)	77,249 (47%)
I			7,440 (4%)	

Campaign Finance

	Receipts	Receipts from PACs	Expend-itures
1988			
Bateman (R)	$293,109	$162,640 (55%)	$284,702
Ellenson (D)	$40,393	0	$40,392
1986			
Bateman (R)	$621,599	$222,709 (36%)	$602,251
Scott (D)	$349,635	$99,415 (28%)	$348,485

Key Votes

1987	
Raise speed limit to 65 mph	Y
Approve Gephardt "fair trade" amendment	N
Ban testing of larger nuclear weapons	N
Delay "re-flagging" of Kuwaiti tankers	N
Approve tax-raising deficit-reduction bill	N
1988	
Approve aid to Nicaraguan contras	Y
Enact civil rights restoration bill over Reagan veto	N
Kill 60-day plant-closing notification measure	Y
Pass omnibus trade bill over Reagan veto	N
Approve death penalty for drug-related murders	Y
Bar federal funds for abortions in cases of rape and incest	Y
Oppose seven-day waiting period for purchase of handguns	N

Voting Studies

	Presidential Support		Party Unity		Conservative Coalition	
Year	**S**	**O**	**S**	**O**	**S**	**O**
1988	64	35	68	29	92	5
1987	64 †	34 †	63 †	34 †	91 †	9 †
1986	69	29	64	35	88	12
1985	69	31	67	30	89	11
1984	71	27	71	26	90	3
1983	87	10	81	17	85	13

† Not eligible for all recorded votes.

Interest Group Ratings

Year	ADA	ACU	AFL-CIO	CCUS
1988	20	84	14	85
1987	12	74	25	79
1986	0	68	7	78
1985	10	71	6	77
1984	0	76	8	64
1983	0	91	0	100

2 Owen B. Pickett (D)

Of Virginia Beach — Elected 1986

Born: Aug. 31, 1930, Richmond, Va.
Education: Virginia Polytechnic Institute and State U., B.S. 1952; U. of Richmond Law School, LL.B. 1955.
Occupation: Lawyer; accountant.
Family: Wife, Sybil Catherine Kelly; three children.
Religion: Baptist.
Political Career: Va. House, 1973-87; withdrew from campaign for Democratic nomination for U.S. Senate, 1982.
Capitol Office: 1429 Longworth Bldg. 20515; 225-4215.

In Washington: With the Norfolk Naval Base and five other major military facilities in the 2nd District, it is practically an imperative for the district's House member to obtain a seat on the Armed Services Committee. Thus, Pickett received what could have been a political setback at the start of his House tenure in 1987, when he finished fourth in a contest for three open seats on Armed Services.

However, then-Speaker Jim Wright came to the rescue of Pickett, who had won a hard-fought election to succeed a retiring Republican in the 2nd. Wright arranged with the GOP leadership to expand the committee's size, creating a Democratic vacancy that Pickett got.

Operating in a low-key manner during his first term, Pickett voted the mainly pro-Pentagon line that the nature of his constituency would suggest. In both 1987 and 1988, he opposed measures offered by liberal Democrats to institute a mutual U.S.-Soviet nuclear weapons test ban. After intense lobbying by both sides of the contra issue, Pickett went with President Reagan in February 1988, supporting $36 million in aid to the Nicaraguan rebels.

The pro-defense votes satisfied his district's conservative elements, and provided him with cover for his more standard Democratic positions on domestic issues. His votes for civil rights, fair housing and homeless-aid legislation cemented his support in Norfolk's large black community; Pickett was endorsed in 1988 by the Norfolk *Journal & Guide,* a black-oriented newspaper, over his Republican opponent, a black retired Army general.

At Home: Few people know Virginia politics as well as Pickett. By the time he won the congressional seat vacated by retiring Republican G. William Whitehurst in 1986, Pickett had already served as chairman of the state party, launched and then abandoned a Senate bid, headed a Democratic presidential campaign in Virginia and served long enough in the state House of Delegates to be a senior member of the Appropriations Committee.

Neither an orator nor a gregarious backslapper, the wealthy Virginia Beach lawyer-accountant prefers to work studiously behind the scenes. But when state Democrats had important decisions to make, Pickett was nearly always in on them. He played a major role, for example, in fashioning the state's budget and retirement system. In 1980, he was chosen Democratic state chairman at the behest of his mentor, Virginia Beach power broker Sidney Kellam, and of Charles S. Robb, then running for governor. With Virginia Democrats seeking to shuck the liberal image that had dogged the party in the 1970s, Pickett's reputation as a fiscal conservative was an asset.

Pickett chaired the party through Robb's successful gubernatorial campaign in 1981, then left early the following year to launch his own ill-starred U.S. Senate bid. Robb and other Democratic leaders saw Pickett as their favorite, but he quickly drew fire as a lackluster campaigner and poor fund-raiser. Liberals attacked the closed selection process and blacks complained about a lack of attention to their legislative interests. State Sen. L. Douglas Wilder — the top black officeholder in the state — threatened to launch an independent candidacy that would have ripped apart the Democratic coalition and diverted votes from Pickett.

After trying unsuccessfully to defuse the opposition, Pickett finally decided in May to drop his candidacy. The next day, Wilder abandoned his proposed independent campaign and the Democratic Senate nomination eventually went to Lt. Gov. Richard J. Davis.

Two years later, Pickett chaired Walter F. Mondale's campaign in Virginia. That placed him at odds with Robb, Davis and other former allies in the moderate wing of the party who preferred Ohio Sen. John Glenn. But it helped Pickett build bridges to liberals and blacks in Norfolk, the Democratic core of the 2nd. When Pickett launched his House bid, he had the backing of Wilder (by then the lieutenant governor) and Bishop L. E. Willis of Norfolk, head of the Rev. Jesse Jackson's 1984 presidential campaign in Virginia.

Virginia 2

Norfolk; Virginia Beach

The 2nd is composed of adjacent coastal cities: the fast-growing residential and resort municipality of Virginia Beach and the unionized port city of Norfolk, which has been striving to polish its image.

The two cities present a stark political contrast. For years, Norfolk has been one of the few bastions of liberalism within Virginia. It is the home of former Lt. Gov. Henry Howell, an outspoken populist, and Edythe C. Harrison, the party's unsuccessful candidate for senator in 1984. Norfolk, which is 35 percent black, gave Harrison 47 percent of its vote (she won only 30 percent statewide), and it went for Michael S. Dukakis for president in 1988.

Virginia Beach, on the other hand, is one of the state's prime strongholds of conservatism. It is home to the religious broadcasting empire of Pat Robertson, who sought the GOP presidential nomination in 1988. Like the southern portion of the 1st District, the 2nd is heavily dependent on the massive concentration of naval installations, shipbuilders and shipping firms in the Hampton Roads harbor area, which ranks first in export tonnage among the nation's Atlantic ports and is the biggest coal shipper in the world.

Recently, Norfolk has been cultivating a more cosmopolitan image. The builder of Baltimore's Inner Harbor area renovated Norfolk's waterfront, creating an area of offices and shops called "Waterside."

An influx of military families, business people and retirees during recent years has changed Virginia Beach's earlier identity as a summer tourist center. The city's retail and service trade has boomed, and its population reached 262,000 residents in the 1980 census. Estimates of its growth since then indicate that Virginia Beach has supplanted Norfolk as Virginia's largest city.

Population: 529,178. White 389,088 (74%), Black 120,278 (23%), Other 15,237 (3%). Spanish origin 11,234 (2%). 18 and over 383,036 (72%), 65 and over 36,388 (7%). Median age: 26.

From the start, the demographics of the district looked good for Pickett. The support of black leaders left little doubt that he would easily carry Norfolk, which is one-third black and highly unionized, while his roots in more Republican Virginia Beach were expected to help him cut his losses there.

Pickett's GOP opponent, state Sen. A. J. "Joe" Canada, was generally regarded as the more appealing campaigner, and retiring incumbent Whitehurst supported him actively. But Canada was jolted early in the campaign by newspaper stories detailing his involvement with a bankrupt Virginia Beach mortgage company and business deals he had made with a Richmond stockbroker who had been accused of embezzlement. While no one linked Canada to criminal wrongdoing, Pickett said Canada's poor judgment was a legitimate issue. "If you have someone who can't deal with the local yokels and come out on top," declared Pickett, "how is he going to deal with the big-time operators in Washington?"

Canada responded by questioning the relationship of Pickett's law firm to the same bankrupt mortgage company. But Pickett got the better of the exchange, helped by a late media blitz that kept the Republican on the defensive.

Canada narrowly carried Virginia Beach, but Pickett won by nearly 2-to-1 in Norfolk en route to a 49-42 percent victory districtwide. In 1988, Pickett surpassed 60 percent against retired Army general and minister Jerry Curry.

Committees

Armed Services (26th of 31 Democrats)
Military Personnel and Compensation; Research and Development; Seapower and Strategic and Critical Materials

Merchant Marine and Fisheries (18th of 26 Democrats)
Coast Guard and Navigation; Merchant Marine; Oversight and Investigations

Elections

1988 General

Owen B. Pickett (D)	106,666	(61%)
Jerry R. Curry (R)	62,564	(36%)

1986 General

Owen B. Pickett (D)	54,491	(49%)
A. J. "Joe" Canada Jr. (R)	46,137	(42%)
Stephen P. Shao (I)	9,492	(9%)

District Vote For President

	1988	1984	1980	1976
D	71,558 (40%)	63,616 (37%)	60,013 (41%)	65,119 (49%)
R	107,019 (60%)	108,931 (63%)	75,443 (52%)	62,692 (47%)
I			8,163 (6%)	

Campaign Finance

	Receipts	Receipts from PACs	Expend-itures
1988			
Pickett (D)	$437,439	$215,810 (49%)	$414,011
Curry (R)	$194,004	$15,406 (8%)	$189,391
1986			
Pickett (D)	$612,684	$163,949 (27%)	$607,558
Canada (R)	$714,052	$139,477 (20%)	$660,355

Key Votes

1987

Raise speed limit to 65 mph	Y
Approve Gephardt "fair trade" amendment	N
Ban testing of larger nuclear weapons	N
Delay "re-flagging" of Kuwaiti tankers	N
Approve tax-raising deficit-reduction bill	Y

1988

Approve aid to Nicaraguan contras	Y
Enact civil rights restoration bill over Reagan veto	Y
Kill 60-day plant-closing notification measure	N
Pass omnibus trade bill over Reagan veto	Y
Approve death penalty for drug-related murders	Y
Bar federal funds for abortions in cases of rape and incest	N
Oppose seven-day waiting period for purchase of handguns	Y

Voting Studies

	Presidential Support		Party Unity		Conservative Coalition	
Year	**S**	**O**	**S**	**O**	**S**	**O**
1988	34	65	80	16	82	16
1987	39	61	78	19	70	30

Interest Group Ratings

Year	ADA	ACU	AFL-CIO	CCUS
1988	50	40	86	50
1987	72	22	81	40

3 Thomas J. Bliley Jr. (R)

Of Richmond — Elected 1980

Born: Jan. 28, 1932, Chesterfield County, Va.
Education: Georgetown U., B.A. 1952.
Military Career: Navy, 1952-55.
Occupation: Funeral director.
Family: Wife, Mary Virginia Kelley; two children.
Religion: Roman Catholic.
Political Career: Richmond City Council, 1968-77; mayor, 1970-77.
Capitol Office: 213 Cannon Bldg. 20515; 225-2815.

In Washington: A cordial and good-humored former mayor, Bliley has built relationships with members of the Energy and Commerce Committee that have helped make him one of the more active Republican players on a panel dominated by activist Democrats.

But if he is usually regarded as an open-minded person to work with, he can at times be an unyielding spokesman for the conservative point of view. Also, his defense of the increasingly unpopular tobacco industry — a parochial imperative for Richmond's congressman — has put him on the losing end of several battles in recent years.

As a former mayor of Richmond, Bliley has had a long association with his district's conservative business interests. Prominent among them is cigarette manufacturer Philip Morris. Bliley tries to involve himself in a variety of legislative areas, but much of his House career has been spent challenging bills hostile to the cigarette industry. Though he seems sometimes to embrace the role as much with resignation as with enthusiasm, Bliley is identified as the tobacco industry's sentry on the Health Subcommittee at Energy and Commerce.

Relentless anti-smoking campaigns by vocal lobby groups have helped create the impression that the tobacco lobby is fighting a losing battle in Congress. Already barred from advertising on the airwaves, the industry now is fending off demands that it be banned from advertising altogether. Bliley's search for friends for tobacco is becoming more taxing. "The circle is getting smaller and smaller all the time," he said in 1985.

That year, Bliley tried to block an initiative by Health Subcommittee Chairman Henry A. Waxman aimed at snuff and chewing tobacco. Waxman wanted to require health warnings on labels and in ads for these products, and he sought to mandate a label design that incorporated circles and arrows to draw attention to the warning. Bliley, fearing the design requirement would be extended to cigarettes, temporarily managed to block Waxman. But within a few months, the producers, facing the prospect of conflicting labeling requirements in several states, consented to federal regulation — while denying any link between their products and health problems. Waxman also prevailed in an effort to ban radio and TV advertising of chewing tobacco and snuff.

In the 100th Congress, the tobacco industry's biggest loss came when Congress banned smoking on certain domestic airline flights. Bliley was not at the center of that battle, which took place outside Energy and Commerce, but he did speak against the legislation, saying it would cause administrative problems for airlines and airports and could be a fire hazard by causing surreptitious smoking on airplanes. "The bottom line," he said, "is that there is no significant scientific evidence to support the assertion that environmental tobacco smoke is harmful to non-smokers."

While defending tobacco is a necessary focus for Bliley, in the 100th Congress he won much more attention for taking the offensive to ban so-called "dial-a-porn" services. In the teleporn fight in 1988, Bliley joined with conservative GOP Sen. Jesse Helms to change the Communications Act of 1934 in order to prohibit the use of the telephone for "any obscure or indecent communication for commercial purposes," whether directly or by recording. The language had been added to an education bill by Helms; the unrelated rider ended up delaying the bill for several weeks as conferees grappled with the issue.

The House instructed conferees to accept the Senate language, but critics of the ban felt it violated First Amendment rights. In place of the ban, they worked to forge a compromise that would require local phone companies to block access to the pornographic lines unless a customer subscribed to the services.

But Bliley, a conferee, and other proponents of a full ban stood their ground. They wanted a floor vote on the education bill with the "teleporn" ban language. When Democratic leaders pushed a rule that made way for a separate vote on the ban before the education bill vote, Bliley and others objected, fearing the

Virginia 3

Richmond and Suburbs

The 3rd District has two distinct parts: the black-majority, traditionally Democratic city of Richmond, and the surrounding suburbs in Chesterfield and Henrico counties, which are overwhelmingly white and predominantly Republican.

Because the population has grown in the suburbs and shrunk in the city, the 3rd in recent years has emerged as a GOP stronghold. With redistricting in 1981, Bliley saw his constituency become even more of a Republican bastion. To make up for Richmond's 12 percent population decline in the 1970s, the 3rd picked up 33,000 western Chesterfield voters from the 5th.

Although Richmond is probably best-known as the capital of the Confederacy, the city's black majority has made it one of the most loyally Democratic population centers in the South. It has backed the Democratic presidential ticket in five of the last six elections, balking only at supporting George McGovern in 1972. But in the 3rd, Richmond is outvoted by Chesterfield and Henrico, which have never given the Democratic presidential nominee more than one-third of the vote in the same period.

The political split between Richmond and its suburbs was obvious in 1988. George Bush took 69 percent in Henrico County and 83 percent in the Chesterfield County portion of the 3rd. Michael S. Dukakis carried Richmond with 56 percent.

The third-largest city in the state, Richmond has long been the center of Virginia government and commerce. From wood-paneled corporate offices along the Main Street corridor, Richmond's business elite exercises considerable influence over politics in the district and in the state.

The city was also one of the South's early manufacturing centers, concentrating on tobacco processing. Richmond still boasts the country's largest cigarette plant, but manufacturing has diversified into chemicals, textiles, paper and processed foods, and downtown redevelopment has freshened the center city's once-gray image.

Population: 533,668. White 376,664 (71%), Black 150,852 (28%), Other 4,554 (1%). Spanish origin 4,560 (1%). 18 and over 394,810 (74%), 65 and over 54,731 (10%). Median age: 30.

ban would die in the Senate unless it was attached to the education bill. They portrayed support for the rule as the equivalent of supporting pornography, and the rule lost 131-272. The compromise proposal was defeated by voice vote, and a new bill was created that included the education portions of the conference agreement and the teleporn ban. It was approved 397-1. In early 1989 the law's constitutionality was challenged before the Supreme Court.

Bliley is conversant on a variety of health issues, especially preventive medicine. Arguing that increased federal spending for maternity and pediatric care could prevent more expensive medical problems later in life, Bliley joined with liberals on Energy and Commerce in 1983 to back a Child Health Assurance Program, designed to expand Medicaid coverage for mothers and children. He wrote a successful amendment permitting states to make pregnant teenagers eligible for Medicaid regardless of parents' income.

Though he is a fierce critic of abortion, his strong feelings on the issue lead him down a different path than many conservatives follow. He wants to do more than discourage abortion. He wants to encourage federal spending for infant health care. "In order to be fair," he says, "we are under some moral obligation to take care of the living."

Other Bliley pursuits are more in the vein of traditional conservatism. In 1985, he sought to block federal funding for family planning clinics located in or near facilities that perform abortions. The next year, he introduced a bill to prohibit the inclusion of abortion-related expenses as deductible medical care.

The sizable black population in the 3rd District has played a role in shaping Bliley's positions. He praised some of President Reagan's budget in 1987, but also said the cuts in education were "simply not acceptable." "The most disturbing cut," he said, "and one that strongly impacts the Richmond area, is that aid to historically black colleges would be cut by two-thirds. This proposal is clearly out of the question."

Bliley's attitude toward South Africa also differed from some conservatives'. In 1985 and 1986, he went against President Reagan and voted to impose sanctions on South Africa.

At Home: A pleasant, soft-spoken Richmond mortician, Bliley was coaxed into politics in 1968 by civic leaders who sought him out to run for City Council. He left city government in 1977 after nearly a decade of service — including a stint as mayor — to devote more time to his funeral home. But he enthusiastically re-entered politics shortly after Democrat David E. Satterfield announced his retirement from

Congress in 1980.

A Democrat himself when he was involved in Richmond government, Bliley announced his conversion to the GOP only when he launched his House campaign in early 1980. Critics claimed the switch was motivated by the district's GOP voting pattern; Bliley said it was prompted by a leftward swing in the state Democratic leadership.

Bliley's support from the Richmond business community virtually assured his election. With a well-funded campaign, he overwhelmed his little-known Democratic opponent and two independent candidates.

In 1982, Bliley faced a more aggressive challenger in Henrico County Supervisor John Waldrop. The Democrat criticized Bliley for backing deep cuts in social and educational programs, a charge that played well in mostly black Richmond. Bliley lost the city, but won easily in the white suburbs, which deliver most of the votes.

The Democrats did not even bother to field a candidate in 1984, but they ran an ambitious young tax attorney against Bliley two years later. The challenger, Kenneth E. Powell, mounted an extensive grass-roots campaign and sought to discredit Bliley by labeling him a tool of political action committees (PACs). But the incumbent flicked aside the criticism, saying that "PACs don't contribute to losers."

Bliley touted his congressional work in defense of the tobacco industry, and with a large advantage in money, name identification and big-name support, he swept every jurisdiction, including Democratic Richmond.

In 1988, the Democrats again left him alone.

Committees

Select Children, Youth and Families (Ranking)

District of Columbia (2nd of 4 Republicans)
Fiscal Affairs and Health (ranking); Judiciary and Education

Energy and Commerce (9th of 17 Republicans)
Oversight and Investigations (ranking); Health and the Environment; Telecommunications and Finance

Elections

1988 General		
Thomas J. Bliley Jr. (R)	187,354	(100%)
1986 General		
Thomas J. Bliley Jr. (R)	74,525	(67%)
Kenneth E. Powell (D)	32,961	(30%)

Previous Winning Percentages: 1984 (86%) **1982** (59%) **1980** (52%)

District Vote For President

	1988	1984	1980	1976
D	86,678 (36%)	83,310 (35%)	80,943 (38%)	79,505 (41%)
R	151,033 (63%)	155,612 (65%)	121,797 (57%)	109,653 (57%)
I			8,596 (4%)	

Campaign Finance

	Receipts	Receipts from PACs	Expend-itures
1988			
Bliley (R)	$467,449	$270,550 (58%)	$366,816
1986			
Bliley (R)	$779,700	$288,468 (37%)	$816,159
Powell (D)	$229,524	$39,946 (17%)	$225,349

Key Votes

1987	
Raise speed limit to 65 mph	Y
Approve Gephardt "fair trade" amendment	N
Ban testing of larger nuclear weapons	N
Delay "re-flagging" of Kuwaiti tankers	N
Approve tax-raising deficit-reduction bill	N
1988	
Approve aid to Nicaraguan contras	Y
Enact civil rights restoration bill over Reagan veto	N
Kill 60-day plant-closing notification measure	Y
Pass omnibus trade bill over Reagan veto	N
Approve death penalty for drug-related murders	Y
Bar federal funds for abortions in cases of rape and incest	Y
Oppose seven-day waiting period for purchase of handguns	Y

Voting Studies

	Presidential Support		Party Unity		Conservative Coalition	
Year	**S**	**O**	**S**	**O**	**S**	**O**
1988	61	38	86	11	89	8
1987	70	29	86	12	91	7
1986	69	30	82	16	94	6
1985	74	26	83	15	87	13
1984	74	25	82	14	88	8
1983	85	12	87	10	96	3
1982	86	13	92	5	97	3
1981	75	25	88	11	89	9

Interest Group Ratings

Year	ADA	ACU	AFL-CIO	CCUS
1988	10	96	21	93
1987	4	96	6	100
1986	5	73	14	88
1985	5	81	24	82
1984	5	83	15	94
1983	5	96	0	84
1982	0	96	5	91
1981	0	93	13	100

4 Norman Sisisky (D)

Of Petersburg — Elected 1982

Born: June 9, 1927, Baltimore, Md.
Education: Virginia Commonwealth U., B.S. 1949.
Military Career: Navy, 1945-46.
Occupation: Beer and soft drink distributor.
Family: Wife, Rhoda Brown; four children.
Religion: Jewish.
Political Career: Va. House, 1974-82.
Capitol Office: 426 Cannon Bldg. 20515; 225-6365.

In Washington: Sisisky is part of a Virginia delegation on the Armed Services Committee that could be called the "Tidewater Trio." With Sisisky, fellow Democrat Owen B. Pickett and Republican Herbert H. Bateman to look out for the interests of the Norfolk-area naval bases and other southeastern Virginia military facilities, few defense-oriented regions are as well defended on Armed Services.

Sisisky plays an insider's role on the committee, as one of the centrist Democrats whose vote Chairman Les Aspin can count on in his efforts to craft compromise solutions to contentious defense issues. Sisisky is tough-minded and unfailingly self-confident, and at times his genial manner turns curmudgeonly — all qualities one would expect of a rich self-made businessman accustomed to having his way. Sisisky has translated his background into a no-nonsense approach to doing business in the House that many colleagues find refreshing. He uses his booming voice to condemn wasteful Pentagon procurement practices and call for the Defense Department to be run like a business.

It was on a defense purchasing issue that Sisisky made an early mark after coming to Congress in 1983. After learning of a Pentagon request to build schools for military dependents in Western Europe at a price of $8,500 per pupil, Sisisky headed for a hall telephone and called a contact in Virginia's Department of Education to find out how much schools cost. The figure he came back with was roughly half the requested amount. Sisisky later claimed credit for saving some $143 million in the defense budget.

As a member of the Procurement Subcommittee — as well as the Investigations Subcommittee that has looked into purchasing problems — Sisisky searches his business background for ways to evaluate defense procurement. He once opposed an inflation allowance for military contracts, citing his experiences in supplying Pepsi-Cola to military bases.

But while he has broader interests, Sisisky most often speaks up on issues involving the defense interests of his home area. He is a staunch opponent of the Navy's plan to base its fleet in "homeports" in widely dispersed coastal cities; the strategy is seen as a threat to the major basing facility at Newport News, in the neighboring 1st District. During the 100th Congress, he worked to secure military construction funds for Fort Pickett and Fort Lee in his district, as well as for the Newport News shipyard.

Sisisky did support the effort during that period to draw up a list of obsolete military bases to close in order to save money, even though the forts in his district were rumored as possible targets. He approved the process by which Congress would hold a single up-or-down vote on a list of bases to be closed, stating, "This is one way to take it out of the field of politics.... I think it's the only way we are going to do it."

In the end, Sisisky's own parochial interests were not only unharmed — they were enhanced. The presidential commission that developed the base-closing list preserved Sisisky's forts, and even added military and civilian positions at Fort Lee as part of a personnel realignment.

Outside Armed Services, Sisisky showed he would go to some length to promote Virginia interests. In March 1987, he was the only Democrat to vote to uphold President Reagan's veto of an $88 billion highway-funding bill. Sisisky explained he had done this not for Reagan, but for Virginia's Democratic Gov. Gerald L. Baliles, who believed the bill's funding formulas shortchanged the state. The bill also had omitted an improvement project for a hazardous road in Sisisky's district.

Sisisky also applies his business acumen as a member of the Small Business Committee, where he chairs the Subcommittee on Exports, Tax Policy and Special Problems. He proposed a bill in the 100th Congress to promote export opportunities for small businesses.

At Home: After a decade of intraparty friction and underfinanced campaigns, Democrats united behind the wealthy Sisisky in 1982. He combined a large campaign treasury and an affable campaign style to oust veteran GOP Rep. Robert W. Daniel Jr. Since then, he has

Virginia 4

Southeast — Chesapeake; Portsmouth

With Portsmouth's large black population and blue-collar work force joining die-hard rural Democrats, the 4th is a solid Democratic district in most elections. When Democrat Charles S. Robb won election to the Senate in 1988, the 4th gave him a larger share of the vote than any other district in the state. Even Michael S. Dukakis managed a respectable 44 percent here in 1988.

Portsmouth is 45 percent black and casts about one-fifth of the district's vote. The city is oriented toward the naval and shipbuilding economy of Norfolk, Hampton and Newport News. The neighboring city of Chesapeake, slightly larger than Portsmouth, is less black and less industrial. It is home to many who work in Portsmouth's shipyards and factories. In 1988, George Bush won Chesapeake, while Dukakis carried Portsmouth.

There is some industry in the smaller cities of the 4th, which together make up another one-quarter of the district's population. Suffolk processes peanuts, Petersburg makes tobacco products and is home to the Fort Lee military installation, and Hopewell calls itself the chemical capital of the South. Black-majority Petersburg was the only one of the group to go for Dukakis.

Peanuts and tobacco are the important crops in the farm lands of the 4th, where roughly one-third of the district's residents live. Democratic ties are still strong there, particularly in a swath of counties that stretch southwestward from the James River to the North Carolina border.

Population: 535,703. White 317,266 (59%), Black 212,598 (40%), Other 3,927 (1%). Spanish origin 5,735 (1%). 18 and over 377,071 (70%), 65 and over 53,225 (10%). Median age: 30.

been re-elected three times without a Republican opponent.

The son of Lithuanian immigrants, Sisisky was born in Baltimore. But his family moved during the Depression to Richmond, where his father found work in a delicatessen. Sisisky was raised in the Virginia capital and attended a local college.

During the 1982 campaign, Sisisky described himself as a self-made businessman. Critics said he simply married into a wealthy Petersburg family and took over its soft-drink company. But regardless of how he got his start, Sisisky is a natural salesman who turned the operation into one of the most successful Pepsi-Cola distributorships in the country.

After years as a pillar of the business community, Sisisky won a seat in the state House in 1973. With Virginia politics then in a state of flux, he ran as an independent, but caucused with the Democrats and in 1975 ran for re-election as a Democrat. In the Legislature he was known as a master compromiser; he often served as an intermediary between conservative Southside legislators and their more liberal Northern Virginia counterparts.

Sisisky was widely recognized as his party's strongest potential challenger against Daniel in 1982. But his candidacy was almost blunted. When a black activist announced in early 1982 that he might run as an independent, Sisisky threatened to pull out of the race. Only when the threat of an independent candidacy subsided did Sisisky resume his campaign.

Sisisky charged that Daniel's pro-Reagan record did not represent blacks (who make up 40 percent of the population), farmers or the blue-collar workers of industrial Tidewater. Daniel countered by branding Sisisky a liberal and claiming he was trying to buy the election. In the end, Sisisky carried 15 out of 20 jurisdictions, winning overwhelmingly in Petersburg and the blue-collar city of Portsmouth.

When the early list of possible 1989 candidates to succeed Gov. Baliles was drawn up, Sisisky, with his strong southern Virginia base, was mentioned. But Lt. Gov. L. Douglas Wilder declared dibs, and Sisisky showed no interest in thwarting Wilder's effort to become the first elected black governor in American history.

Committees

Armed Services (16th of 31 Democrats)
Investigations; Military Installations and Facilities; Procurement and Military Nuclear Systems; Seapower and Strategic and Critical Materials

Select Aging (22nd of 39 Democrats)
Health and Long-Term Care

Small Business (11th of 27 Democrats)
Exports, Tax Policy and Special Problems (chairman); Regulation, Business Opportunity and Energy

Elections

1988 General

Norman Sisisky (D)	134,786	(100%)

1986 General

Norman Sisisky (D)	64,699	(100%)

Previous Winning Percentages: **1984** (100%) **1982** (54%)

District Vote For President

	1988	1984	1980	1976
D	89,094 (44%)	91,107 (43%)	91,716 (50%)	96,396 (56%)
R	110,155 (55%)	117,579 (56%)	83,955 (46%)	69,501 (41%)
I			4,589 (3%)	

Campaign Finance

	Receipts	Receipts from PACs	Expend-itures
1988			
Sisisky (D)	$185,555	$102,636 (55%)	$93,232
1986			
Sisisky (D)	$164,585	$90,910 (55%)	$53,807

Key Votes

1987

Raise speed limit to 65 mph	Y
Approve Gephardt "fair trade" amendment	N
Ban testing of larger nuclear weapons	N
Delay "re-flagging" of Kuwaiti tankers	N
Approve tax-raising deficit-reduction bill	Y

1988

Approve aid to Nicaraguan contras	Y
Enact civil rights restoration bill over Reagan veto	Y
Kill 60-day plant-closing notification measure	N
Pass omnibus trade bill over Reagan veto	Y
Approve death penalty for drug-related murders	Y
Bar federal funds for abortions in cases of rape and incest	N
Oppose seven-day waiting period for purchase of handguns	Y

Voting Studies

	Presidential Support		Party Unity		Conservative Coalition	
Year	**S**	**O**	**S**	**O**	**S**	**O**
1988	38	61	77	20	76	21
1987	45	54	74	24	86	9
1986	39	60	75	21	70	30
1985	39 †	58 †	76	22	78	20
1984	54	42	66	32	73	24
1983	43	56	61	32	75	21

† Not eligible for all recorded votes.

Interest Group Ratings

Year	ADA	ACU	AFL-CIO	CCUS
1988	55	40	86	50
1987	52	39	63	60
1986	45	48	57	56
1985	40	38	47	36
1984	40	38	46	33
1983	65	43	88	30

5 Lewis F. Payne Jr. (D)

Of Wintergreen — Elected 1988

Born: July 9, 1945, Amherst, Va.
Education: Virginia Military Institute, B.S. 1967; U. of Virginia, M.B.A. 1973.
Military Career: Army, 1968-70.
Occupation: Developer; businessman.
Religion: Presbyterian.
Family: Wife, Susan King; four children.
Political Career: No previous office.
Capitol Office: 1118 Longworth Bldg. 20515; 225-4711.

In Washington: Calling himself a "progressive conservative," Payne managed to symbolize both a fresh start and the traditional values of Southside Virginia in winning two elections for this House seat within five months.

Payne was an engineer and businessman who had spent 15 years building the Wintergreen resort in Nelson County and had never run for office before. So his success in this conservative enclave was as gratifying to Democrats as it was frustrating to the GOP, which had hoped to prevail here for the first time in a century.

Payne first won the 5th in a June 1988 special election to fill the unexpired term of 19-year veteran Dan Daniel, who had died in January. Payne then had to face another Republican opponent in November.

In between, Payne was around for only a few months of the 100th Congress. He did little to attract attention in Washington, concentrating instead on acquainting the district with its new representative. He was assigned first to the Public Works Committee and then to Veterans' Affairs, both solid opportunities to help constituents and both panels on which Virginia had not been represented.

On the floor, Payne generally voted with Virginia's four other Democrats, supporting President Reagan less than half the time. He received a 1988 rating of 83 from the AFL-CIO (more than triple Daniel's average). He opposed efforts to weaken enforcement of the fair housing bill, and he supported a bill to increase sanctions against South Africa.

But his 1988 voting also received approval scores of 56 from the U.S. Chamber of Commerce and 50 from the American Conservative Union. He voted to require at least one parent in a welfare family to work at least 16 hours a week in an unpaid service or subsidized job. He supported the death penalty for drug-related murders and opposed a seven-day waiting period for handgun purchases.

At Home: Republicans targeted the 5th when Daniel announced his retirement Jan. 19. (He died four days later.) Daniel was a product of the old Harry Byrd machine and a one-time advocate of "massive resistance" to desegregation. Although still a Democrat, he usually voted with Republicans in the House.

The leading Republican candidate was Linda Arey, a 43-year-old attorney who had been a public liaison aide in the Reagan White House. Arey successfully organized local and county caucuses leading to the district convention, where she defeated a more traditional Virginia Republican, a state senator from Danville.

Payne, meanwhile, got a late start but quietly organized key Democrats. The son of a state trooper and a schoolteacher, he had become wealthy enough in his development business to finance 40 percent of his special-election campaign's $500,000 cost out of pocket.

At the Democrats' district meeting in March he was declared the nominee by acclamation. He was not an accomplished public speaker. But as a self-made success, Army veteran and family man, he seemed to embody many of the virtues Southside Virginians value. He patterned his pitch on the fiscally conservative models of former Gov. (now Sen.) Charles S. Robb and Gov. Gerald L. Baliles. He managed to alienate neither the blacks who constitute a quarter of the district nor the bedrock Dixiecrats whose votes decide elections in the 5th.

In June, Arey broadcast a radio endorsement from Reagan and got a campaign visit from Vice President George Bush. But her advertising reach was foreshortened by dwindling campaign funds. Payne prevailed with 59 percent, and Arey decided not to run again in November.

In her place, the GOP nominated state Rep. Charles Hawkins, a 44-year-old haberdasher from Chatham. He did not become the party's official nominee until September and could not raise much money. Yet he benefited from the 5th's strong preference for GOP presidential nominee Bush and held Payne to 54 percent of the vote.

Virginia 5

South — Danville

The 5th is in the heart of Virginia's rural "Southside," a largely agricultural region that resembles the Deep South more closely than any other part of the state does. It is relatively poor and has a substantial black population. Tobacco and soybeans are major crops, but this region lacks the rich soil of the Tidewater.

In nominating Payne to succeed Dan Daniel in the House, Democrats chose someone who could continue the party's tradition of success in holding the seat. But the 5th has long refused to swallow more liberal Democratic candidates at the state and national levels. Barry Goldwater carried it with 51 percent in 1964; it was one of only two House districts in Virginia to back George C. Wallace in 1968; and it was the only Virginia district in 1988 where every county and independent city supported George Bush for president.

The district's most famous landmark is Appomattox Court House, where Robert E. Lee surrendered to Ulysses S. Grant to end the Civil War. About 60 miles to the south is the district's largest city, Danville, a tobacco market and textile center on the North Carolina border that has nearly 45,000 residents. The residents of the city and those of surrounding Pittsylvania County make up one-fifth of the district's population.

Just to the west is Henry County, which surrounds the textile-mill town of Martinsville. With nearly 57,000 residents, Henry County is the second most populous in the district after Pittsylvania. Traditionally, Henry County has been the best area in the 5th District for Democratic candidates; Michael S. Dukakis managed 41 percent there in 1988, an improvement over Walter F. Mondale's showing four years earlier.

The rest of the people are scattered through farming areas and a few factory towns. Most of these areas normally vote Republican at the statewide level.

Blacks comprise about one-quarter of the district population and are found in greatest numbers in the eastern counties. In the western portion, the terrain becomes more rugged as the Piedmont Plateau gives way to the foothills of the Blue Ridge Mountains. The Blue Ridge Parkway runs along the district's western flank, roughly separating Southside Virginia from the state's mountainous western Panhandle.

Population: 531,308. White 398,091 (75%), Black 131,482 (25%). Spanish origin 3,753 (1%). 18 and over 382,312 (72%), 65 and over 63,859 (12%). Median age: 32.

Committees

Public Works and Transportation (24th of 31 Democrats)
Aviation; Economic Development; Surface Transportation

Veterans' Affairs (16th of 21 Democrats)
Hospitals and Health Care; Housing and Memorial Affairs

Elections

1988 General		
Lewis F. Payne Jr. (D)	97,242	(54%)
Charles Hawkins (R)	78,396	(44%)
1988 Special Election		
Lewis F. Payne Jr. (D)	55,469	(59%)
Linda L. Arey (R)	38,063	(41%)

District Vote For President

	1988		1984		1980		1976	
D	71,107	(37%)	67,480	(34%)	73,569	(42%)	77,138	(48%)
R	119,560	(62%)	131,912	(66%)	97,203	(55%)	78,306	(49%)
I					3,660	(2%)		

Key Votes

1988	
Approve death penalty for drug-related murders	Y
Bar federal funds for abortions in cases of rape and incest	Y
Oppose seven-day waiting period for purchase of handguns	Y

Campaign Finance

	Receipts	Receipts from PACs	Expend-itures
1988			
Payne (D)	$846,908	$199,500 (24%)	$837,864
Hawkins (R)	$105,871	$5,500 (5%)	$105,872
1988 Special Election			
Payne (D)	$298,985	$36,300 (12%)	$256,481
Arey (R)	$405,046	$167,066 (41%)	$404,468

Voting Studies

	Presidential Support		Party Unity		Conservative Coalition	
Year	**S**	**O**	**S**	**O**	**S**	**O**
1988	41 †	59 †	77 †	21 †	93 †	7 †

† Not eligible for all recorded votes.

Interest Group Ratings

Year	ADA	ACU	AFL-CIO	CCUS
1988	—	50	83	56

6 Jim Olin (D)

Of Roanoke — Elected 1982

Born: Feb. 28, 1920, Chicago, Ill.
Education: Attended Deep Springs College (Calif.), 1941; Cornell U., B.E.E. 1943.
Military Career: Army, 1943-46.
Occupation: Retired electronics executive.
Family: Wife, Phyllis Avery; five children.
Religion: Unitarian.
Political Career: Rotterdam (N.Y.) town supervisor, Schenectady County supervisor, 1953-55.
Capitol Office: 1314 Longworth Bldg. 20515; 225-5431.

In Washington: A moderate Democrat representing a Republican-leaning district, Olin is careful not to make waves at home. The same cannot always be said of his tactics in Washington, where he has shown that the courage of his convictions can be more important than the approval of his colleagues.

Representing a district that contains Virginia's two largest dairy counties, Olin has focused on dairy issues since his arrival in Washington. In the 99th Congress, he led an uphill fight against a bipartisan compromise on the dairy section of the 1985 farm bill.

Olin was the most active opponent of a controversial proposal to authorize "diversion" payments, partially financed by dairy farmers, to those who cut back on milk production. There was some political advantage to his position — farmers in his district were not producing a surplus, and were not enthusiastic about paying for the program.

The leading diversion advocate was Dairy Subcommittee Chairman Tony Coelho of California, who had backing from much of the dairy industry. As a member of that Agriculture subcommittee, Olin frustrated Coelho's efforts to forge a compromise and label the proposal a "dairy unity" bill.

Olin made a lonely attempt to kill the diversion program in subcommittee, which did little to slow it down and much to annoy Coelho. When the bill came to the House floor, Olin joined forces with Minority Leader Robert H. Michel in another attempt to block it. Backed by the Reagan administration and consumer groups, they offered an amendment to tie production more closely to the marketplace by killing the diversion program and steadily reducing price supports. The program was too costly, Olin argued, and high price supports were simply encouraging the surplus that the payments were intended to reduce.

The amendment failed 166-244, but the diversion program was later stripped from the farm bill in conference. The final bill substituted a new program to reduce milk surpluses by requiring the government to buy up entire herds of dairy cows. Olin was critical of that program as well, but voted for the farm package.

Olin again incurred the ire of members from other dairy states in 1987 with an amendment to the omnibus trade bill. His amendment killed a provision, added in the Agriculture Committee, that in effect forestalled a scheduled drop in dairy price supports of 50 cents per hundred pounds of milk. Olin cited Congressional Budget Office figures gauging the cost of the language in the bill at a quarter-billion dollars. While dairy-state members rose to defend the provision, the expected floor fight never materialized; Olin's amendment was agreed to by voice vote.

In 1983, Olin and Virginia Democrat Rick Boucher co-authored a bill that designated as wilderness 56,000 acres of Virginia forests and streams. Olin and Boucher teamed again in the 100th Congress to win passage of a bill preserving some 25,000 more acres from development.

Olin is eager to show that he is a fiscal conservative; he once introduced legislation to repeal a congressional pay raise. But he is no Boll Weevil. In 1987 and 1988, he supported party positions on roll-call votes more often than the average Southern Democrat. He has voted for the Equal Rights Amendment and for a nuclear-weapons freeze; after supporting the MX missile in 1983, he changed his view, and has since opposed it consistently. He has opposed aid to the Nicaraguan contras.

In 1988, he voted against an amendment to prevent the District of Columbia from using its own money to pay for abortions. He later opposed an amendment to block Medicaid funds from being used for abortions in cases of rape and incest. He also backed restoration of broad coverage of four civil rights laws, a proposal strongly denounced by one of Olin's most famous constituents, evangelist Jerry Falwell.

At Home: There are probably few Democratic congressmen who frustrate Republican campaign strategists more than Olin. Not only

Virginia 6

West — Roanoke; Lynchburg

Long before Republicanism was acceptable in other parts of Virginia, it was the preferred political stance in the broad Shenandoah Valley, which runs most of the length of the 6th District. The descendants of the area's 18th-century English, German and Scotch-Irish settlers fought the Tidewater plantation aristocracy and became Republican mavericks in state politics.

But as the Republican Party in Virginia has come to be dominated by suburbanites outside Washington, D.C., and Richmond, and by staunch conservatives who have bailed out of the Democratic Party, the GOP has lost its grip on many voters in the 6th. The brand of Republicanism in the rural valley traditionally has been a moderate one, but there was no moderate on the GOP's statewide ticket in 1985, when Democrats won the three top state offices; all three carried the 6th.

Roanoke, the major population center in the 6th, has an array of industries that produce textiles, furniture and electrical products. Its sizable black and union elements make it the base of Democratic strength in the district. Michael S. Dukakis' best 1988 margin in the district was from the city.

Democrats also can succeed in towns to the north, such as Covington and Clifton Forge and the counties surrounding them, Bath and Alleghany. There are chemical plants and pulpwood and paper mills in that area.

In national elections, Democratic support in the city of Roanoke is usually surpassed by the Republican vote in Roanoke's suburbs, in Lynchburg and in most of the rural areas. In 1988, George Bush narrowly carried Roanoke, but he did much better in suburban Roanoke County, Lynchburg and the rural counties. The nuclear energy firm of Babcock & Wilcox is one of Lynchburg's major employers, but the city is most famous as the home base of evangelist Jerry Falwell, his huge Thomas Road Baptist Church and Falwell-founded Liberty University (7,500 students).

Outside metropolitan Roanoke and Lynchburg, the district depends primarily on dairy farming, livestock and poultry. Republican Rockingham County is a prime supplier of turkeys for Thanksgiving dinners.

Population: 538,360. White 477,114 (89%), Black 58,277 (11%). Spanish origin 3,368 (1%). 18 and over 401,356 (75%), 65 and over 67,927 (13%). Median age: 32.

does he occupy a historically Republican district in the mountains of western Virginia, but he has gone a long way toward putting his personal stamp on it.

Politically unknown when he launched his first congressional campaign in 1982, Olin drew on his civic ties and business background to put together a winning coalition.

With the support of labor, teachers, black leaders and much of the financial community in the district's population center, Roanoke, Olin edged GOP state Rep. Kevin Miller by 1,655 votes. His victory ended a 30-year Republican grip on the Shenandoah Valley House seat, which was left open by the retirement of M. Caldwell Butler in 1982.

Miller, hampered by a bitterly contested nomination fight, tried to recover by painting Olin as a liberal. But although Olin was a mainstream Democrat on social issues, it was hard to tag a former General Electric vice president as a liberal big spender. On Election Day, Olin's 10,000-vote majority in the Roanoke area barely offset Miller's edge in his home base, the rural northern part of the district.

Republicans were confident they could oust Olin in 1984 with a challenger from the Roanoke area. They selected Ray Garland, a former state senator who was noted for his soaring rhetoric and his identification with the moderate wing of the state GOP.

But Garland was bedeviled by controversy. He created a firestorm of criticism when he called the Democratic Party "a busted-out $2 whore sucking the lifeblood out of this country." And many of Garland's longtime moderate supporters were chagrined by his emergence as a born-again conservative. Olin kept his distance from the national ticket and used his seat on Agriculture to gain an entree to rural Republicans in the Shenandoah Valley.

While Reagan swept all nine counties and 10 independent cities in the district, Garland could carry only two of each. Olin won the pivotal Roanoke area by 15,000 votes.

In 1986, Republicans had trouble finding a candidate. Many felt that if they could not oust Olin in 1984, when Reagan pulled two-thirds of the district vote, 1986 was a lost cause. After numerous potential candidates declined to run, the GOP nomination finally went to Republican national committeewoman Flo Traywick, whose only previous campaign was a losing bid for the state House of Delegates.

Traywick used her party connections to bring in GOP celebrities, including Vice President George Bush. She said the outside help demonstrated her ability to open doors in the White House that Olin could not. And while she sought to depict herself as the true conservative in the race, she also made a pitch for the district's relatively small black vote. She brought in Roy Innis, national chairman of the Congress of Racial Equality, to talk on black capitalism, and former University of Virginia basketball star Ralph Sampson (a Harrisonburg native) to help her deliver an anti-drug message.

But with little money or name identification, the grandmotherly Traywick completely failed in denting either Olin's base in the populous Roanoke area or the ties he had forged to rural Republican voters in the valley. Olin won 70 percent, sweeping every county in the 6th and every city except Staunton.

In 1988, the strong showing of the Republican presidential ticket in the 6th did not impede Olin's progress. He won 64 percent of the vote, slightly better than George Bush's tally in the district.

Olin's decision to run for Congress in 1982 followed a long sabbatical from politics. He made his first try for public office during the 1950s when he was elected town supervisor of Rotterdam, N.Y. But his boss at General Electric was upset about the amount of time the job was taking, and he told Olin to choose between the company and politics. Olin chose the company, and went on to complete 35 years before retiring in January 1982.

Committees

Agriculture (14th of 27 Democrats)
Department Operations, Research and Foreign Agriculture; Forests, Family Farms and Energy; Livestock, Dairy and Poultry

Small Business (14th of 27 Democrats)
Regulation, Business Opportunity and Energy; SBA, the General Economy and Minority Enterprise Development

Elections

1988 General

Jim Olin (D)	118,369	(64%)
Charles E. Judd (R)	66,935	(36%)

1986 General

Jim Olin (D)	88,230	(70%)
Flo Neher Traywick (R)	38,051	(30%)

Previous Winning Percentages: 1984 (54%) **1982** (50%)

District Vote For President

	1988	1984	1980	1976
D	74,602 (38%)	68,311 (34%)	82,299 (43%)	82,111 (46%)
R	121,107 (61%)	134,466 (66%)	97,549 (51%)	90,573 (51%)
I			7,368 (4%)	

Campaign Finance

	Receipts	Receipts from PACs	Expend-itures
1988			
Olin (D)	$321,705	$140,400 (44%)	$322,160
Judd (R)	$112,076	$4,150 (4%)	$110,756
1986			
Olin (D)	$363,604	$128,807 (35%)	$356,857
Traywick (R)	$199,912	$13,700 (7%)	$199,880

Key Votes

1987

Raise speed limit to 65 mph	N
Approve Gephardt "fair trade" amendment	N
Ban testing of larger nuclear weapons	Y
Delay "re-flagging" of Kuwaiti tankers	Y
Approve tax-raising deficit-reduction bill	Y

1988

Approve aid to Nicaraguan contras	N
Enact civil rights restoration bill over Reagan veto	Y
Kill 60-day plant-closing notification measure	N
Pass omnibus trade bill over Reagan veto	Y
Approve death penalty for drug-related murders	Y
Bar federal funds for abortions in cases of rape and incest	N
Oppose seven-day waiting period for purchase of handguns	Y

Voting Studies

	Presidential Support		Party Unity		Conservative Coalition	
Year	**S**	**O**	**S**	**O**	**S**	**O**
1988	38	63	82	17	58	42
1987	33	65	77	21	63	37
1986	36	64	71	25	66	30
1985	41	58	72	25	70	36
1984	43	55	65	31	53	42
1983	41	57	64	33	65	34

Interest Group Ratings

Year	ADA	ACU	AFL-CIO	CCUS
1988	70	28	71	64
1987	64	26	63	47
1986	55	14	57	56
1985	50	38	41	67
1984	55	45	58	46
1983	65	30	53	60

7 D. French Slaughter Jr. (R)

Of Culpeper — Elected 1984

Born: May 20, 1925, Culpeper County, Va.
Education: Attended Virginia Military Institute, 1942-43; U. of Virginia, B.A., LL.B. 1953.
Military Career: U.S. Army, 1943-47.
Occupation: Lawyer.
Family: Widowed; two children.
Religion: Episcopalian.
Political Career: Va. House, 1958-78.
Capitol Office: 1404 Longworth Bldg. 20515; 225-6561.

In Washington: A cautious conservative with the reserved style of an old-fashioned Virginia gentleman, Slaughter has carved a quiet niche for himself in the House. He represents a district whose rural character is being squeezed by growth from metropolitan Washington and Richmond, but Slaughter has seemed reticent to plunge into some of the more contentious political issues accompanying urbanization.

When developers announced plans in early 1988 to build a shopping mall next to the historic Manassas National Battlefield Park in Slaughter's district, the publicity soon drew the attention of many members of Congress. Battle lines were drawn, with local development advocates arrayed against preservationists from Virginia and around the country. But Slaughter stayed away from the sound and fury, ceding the headlines to more aggressive Virginia colleagues such as Republican Frank R. Wolf of the neighboring 10th District. Though Slaughter eventually sided with anti-mall forces who pushed through a "legislative taking" of the proposed development site by the federal government, he was conspicuous in his absence from the political fray.

But if Slaughter steers clear of public debate and seems slow to commit himself to a course of action, he is an experienced student of the legislative process, having served two decades in the Virginia House before coming to Congress. He is known to spend time in the House chamber observing floor debate, then offering insights to more harried colleagues who arrive on the floor needing an update on the matter under consideration.

Though he does not raise his voice on many issues, Slaughter has taken serious interest in health care legislation, particularly as it relates to federal workers.

In particular, Slaughter would have the federal government offer group long-term care insurance on a voluntary basis to some of its workers. He has also offered legislation that would create a new Health Care Savings Account and allow people to invest in it rather than in Medicare. His support for this scheme reflects both his fiscal conservatism and his deep-seated distrust of federal welfare programs.

At Home: Over a long career, Slaughter slowly gravitated from the Democratic Party to the GOP, always maintaining the fiscal conservatism that is the hallmark of Virginia politics.

His father served in the state Legislature and was an ally of Democratic Sen. Harry F. Byrd Sr., the dominant force for generations in state government. Elected to the Virginia House in 1957, the younger Slaughter won seats on Appropriations and on Privileges and Elections (which oversees legislative redistricting).

Though not an impressive orator or a high-profile politician, Slaughter was a power in the House by the early 1970s, and a serious contender for the Democratic nomination for lieutenant governor in 1971. He seemed destined to hold a major House committee chairmanship.

But in 1973, he followed the lead of Sen. Harry F. Byrd Jr. and ran for re-election as an independent. It was a calculated gamble. With political upheaval in Virginia, many thought that a coalition of Republicans, independents and conservative Democrats could forge a new majority. But loyalist Democrats prevailed, and Slaughter was relegated to a backbench role.

Like other Byrd allies, Slaughter began a courtship with Virginia's budding Republican Party, and after supporting several GOP candidates in the mid-1970s, he switched parties. When GOP Rep. J. Kenneth Robinson retired in 1984, Slaughter was one of the first to enter the race; he easily won the party's nomination.

The 7th's Republican complexion made Slaughter the front-runner. He denounced foe Lewis M. Costello as a "Mondale-O'Neill" Democrat. But even Slaughter's supporters criticized his wooden campaign manner, and Costello scored points by highlighting Slaughter's one-time support for the "massive resistance" plan to defy federal court desegregation rulings. But with the GOP sweeping the 7th for president and Senate, Slaughter won easily. He drew no challengers in 1986 or 1988.

Virginia 7

North — Charlottesville; Winchester

The 7th runs from Richmond's northern suburbs across the Blue Ridge Mountains to Winchester, the center of the state's apple-growing industry and home of Virginia's political dynasty, the Byrd family.

For generations, the district has been rural and conservative. But like former Sen. Harry F. Byrd Jr., who took over his father's Senate seat in 1965 and later became an independent, the 7th has abandoned its Democratic roots. It has emerged as the state's foremost GOP stronghold. In 1988, George Bush carried every Virginia district, but none more decisively than the 7th, where he took two-thirds of the vote.

In counties along the Blue Ridge Mountains, the agricultural economy is keyed to dairying, livestock and fruit, and there is some manufacturing. In 1988, Bush won 66 percent in the "apple capital" of Winchester, and he did even better in surrounding Frederick County.

Bush's margins were also solid in Spotsylvania and Stafford counties on the eastern flank of the 7th. Those are longtime farming areas that are being taken over by people who drive cars or ride long-distance commuter buses to jobs in metropolitan Washington. Spotsylvania has been one of Virginia's three fastest-growing counties for the past 15 years.

The few Democratic footholds are in the southern part of the district. Charlottesville, the district's largest city and home of the University of Virginia (17,500 students), was the only jurisdiction in the 7th to vote Democratic in the 1988 presidential race.

Like the areas around Washington and Richmond, Charlottesville, too, has seen much growth in recent years, with a commercial strip spreading ever-northward from town along U.S. 29. But such changes in the district have not erased elements of its old, decidedly Southern, personality. One restaurant owner in the small town of Marshall ran afoul of the law in 1984 for refusing to serve meals to blacks.

Population: 535,147. White 465,497 (87%), Black 65,329 (12%), Other 3,012 (1%). Spanish origin 4,185 (1%). 18 and over 383,878 (72%), 65 and over 53,204 (10%). Median age: 30.

Committees

Judiciary (10th of 14 Republicans)
Courts, Intellectual Property and the Administration of Justice; Immigration, Refugees and International Law

Science, Space and Technology (12th of 19 Republicans)
Science, Research and Technology; Space Science and Applications

Small Business (7th of 17 Republicans)
Antitrust, Impact of Deregulation and Privatization; Exports, Tax Policy and Special Problems

Elections

1988 General		
D. French Slaughter Jr. (R)	136,988	(100%)
1986 General		
D. French Slaughter Jr. (R)	58,927	(98%)

Previous Winning Percentage: **1984** (57%)

District Vote For President

	1988	1984	1980	1976
D	76,202 (33%)	64,593 (31%)	59,092 (32%)	71,046 (44%)
R	149,725 (66%)	142,598 (69%)	112,099 (61%)	86,160 (54%)
I			3,660 (2%)	

Campaign Finance

	Receipts	Receipts from PACs	Expend-itures
1988			
Slaughter (R)	$219,559	$94,496 (43%)	$87,195
1986			
Slaughter (R)	$249,223	$78,916 (32%)	$208,448

Key Votes

1987	
Raise speed limit to 65 mph	N
Approve Gephardt "fair trade" amendment	N
Ban testing of larger nuclear weapons	N
Delay "re-flagging" of Kuwaiti tankers	N
Approve tax-raising deficit-reduction bill	N
1988	
Approve aid to Nicaraguan contras	Y
Enact civil rights restoration bill over Reagan veto	N
Kill 60-day plant-closing notification measure	Y
Pass omnibus trade bill over Reagan veto	N
Approve death penalty for drug-related murders	Y
Bar federal funds for abortions in cases of rape and incest	Y
Oppose seven-day waiting period for purchase of handguns	Y

Voting Studies

	Presidential Support		Party Unity		Conservative Coalition	
Year	S	O	S	O	S	O
1988	63	36	86	13	97	3
1987	69	29	86	14	95	5
1986	80	17	86	11	86	12
1985	74	25	90	9	95	5

Interest Group Ratings

Year	ADA	ACU	AFL-CIO	CCUS
1988	10	92	14	93
1987	4	91	13	93
1986	0	91	21	94
1985	0	86	12	95

8 Stan Parris (R)

Of Alexandria — Elected 1980

Also served 1973-75.

Born: Sept. 9, 1929, Champaign, Ill.

Education: U. of Illinois, B.S. 1950; George Washington U., J.D. 1958.

Military Career: Air Force, 1950-54.

Occupation: Lawyer; automobile dealer; commercial pilot; banker.

Family: Wife, Martie Merriam; three children.

Religion: Episcopalian.

Political Career: Fairfax County Board of Supervisors, 1964-67; Va. House, 1969-73; U.S. House, 1973-75; Republican nominee for U.S. House, 1974; sought Republican nomination for governor, 1985, 1989.

Capitol Office: 2434 Rayburn Bldg. 20515; 225-4376.

In Washington: Parris' regular venting of enmity toward the District of Columbia government, Democrats and liberal policies in general finds a receptive audience in the suburban Virginia 8th. But he keeps coming up short in his efforts to advance to a broader forum. His third-place finish in the June 1989 GOP gubernatorial primary was his second failed attempt to win nomination for that office.

Parris has been in a perpetual campaign mode since the start of the 1983-84 campaign cycle. After winning re-election to the House in 1984, he fixed his sights on his party's 1985 gubernatorial nomination, but was denied. Not long after winning another House term in 1986, he simultaneously announced plans to run for the House in 1988 and for governor in 1989.

Any member who spends this much time vote-seeking is going to have trouble being an insider in the legislative process. Combine Parris' constant campaigning with his reputation for outspokenness, and it is not hard to see why he is regarded as a man skilled at calling attention to problems, but not at working behind the scenes to solve them.

But if Parris is better known for his sound and fury, some of his pronouncements have proven prescient. He was haranguing the D.C. government for mismanagement long before the recent spate of media reports on corruption and loose personnel practices in city government. Parris also was one of the earlier voices in Congress to warn of an impending crisis in the savings and loan industry, speaking out in the fall of 1985.

The feud between Parris and the District is one of the longest-running media sideshows on Capitol Hill. He is now ranking Republican on the District of Columbia Committee, a post he gained in May 1987 following the death of Connecticut Rep. Stewart B. McKinney.

The change in leadership could not have been more drastic. McKinney was among the most liberal Republicans in the House; outspoken in his support for civil rights, he was a strong backer of "home rule" for the District and a defender of the city government.

Parris, a conservative who thrives on confrontation, has become the leading congressional irritant to Mayor Marion S. Barry Jr.'s administration. In the 100th Congress, he worked to bar the D.C. government from enforcing a controversial residency requirement for city employees (a number of whom live in Parris' district). His amendment was adopted 246-163 in 1988.

Parris has long advocated incorporating changes in D.C. appropriations bills to modify District government policies. In 1988, his wishes were fulfilled, as the bill Congress cleared contained several riders pushed by conservative members, including one prohibiting the D.C. government from financing abortions.

In 1984, Parris infuriated District home rule advocates by opposing an anti-apartheid measure passed by the D.C. City Council. It barred the District from investing in firms doing business with South Africa. Parris said that basing investment decisions on political considerations might harm the District's pension fund, which is important to retired District employees in Parris' constituency.

Earlier, when he learned the District planned to ship sludge from its sewage treatment plant to Fairfax County — already the site of the D.C. prison and trash dump — Parris went on a tirade: "We get their criminals, we get their garbage, but we are not going to get their sewage.... I don't care what they do with it — they can spread it on the parking lot at RFK stadium — but they are not going to send it to my district." They did not send it.

The criminals referred to are at the District's Lorton Reformatory, located in the 8th.

Virginia 8

D.C. Suburbs — Alexandria; Southern Fairfax County

The 8th includes most of the southern portion of Virginia's Washington-area suburbs. Growth there, originally spurred by the rapid expansion of the federal government, now is fueled by the influx of an array of white-collar and service-industry employers.

The district's close-in suburb is Alexandria. This old colonial seaport casts about one-fifth of the district vote, but it is not typical of the other suburbs. It is reliable Democratic territory. The revitalized "Old Town" part of the city is an affluent competitor to the Georgetown section of Washington, and thousands of Democratic-voting young professionals live there. On the fringe of Old Town is a black community that comprises 22 percent of the Alexandria population and adds to Democratic strength. In 1988, the city was the only jurisdiction within the 8th to vote for Michael S. Dukakis for president and against Parris in the House contest.

Beyond Alexandria to the south and southwest, the suburbs are newer, whiter and more Republican. Population in these outlying areas is booming: Fairfax, Prince William and Stafford counties each grew by about 20 percent from 1980 to 1986, on the heels of similarly rapid growth in the 1970s.

Once-pastoral Fairfax County is now a suburban colossus with over 700,000 people. More than twice as populous as any other jurisdiction in Virginia, Fairfax County is divided nearly evenly between the 8th and 10th districts. Fairfax residents account for a majority of the population in the 8th. In 1988, Parris took 66 percent of the Fairfax County vote.

Outside Alexandria and Fairfax, most of the vote is cast in suburban communities near heavily traveled Interstate 95. Prince William County, whose residents make up another one-fifth of the district's population, has been trending Republican in recent years. It voted for Democratic Rep. Herbert E. Harris II in 1980, but by 1988 was giving Parris 58 percent of its vote and George Bush 66 percent.

Farther south along the Interstate 95 corridor is Republican Stafford County, which is split between the 8th and the 7th districts.

Population: 534,366. White 457,482 (86%), Black 54,114 (10%), Other 15,731 (3%). Spanish origin 15,495 (3%). 18 and over 376,074 (70%), 65 and over 23,284 (4%). Median age: 29.

After a 1982 gun battle between police and a Lorton escapee, Parris declared the penal facility a hazard to his constituents and called for a study to explore moving it into the District. Later, when bullets from a firing range at Lorton strayed into a nearby neighborhood, Parris fumed, "We are mad as hell and aren't going to take it anymore." Periodic inmate disruptions at Lorton draw cameras and headlines and keep Parris and his constituents agitated about the prison.

Parris sometimes expresses a fear that the District will get statehood, making the odds poor for ever getting Lorton out of his territory. He also complains that a "state of D.C." would impose a commuter tax on his constituents driving to work in the city.

Parris pursues more generous salaries and benefits for federal employees and military retirees, both powerful groups in the 8th. And he involves himself in transportation, a politically vital question in the traffic-clogged 8th. Early in 1987, he won approval of an amendment blocking the state of Virginia from extending rush-hour restrictions limiting access to an Interstate highway running through the city of Alexandria and Fairfax County.

Though older than most of the new generation of confrontationalist House Republicans, Parris can attack the Democratic leadership as fervently as anyone. As far back as his 1980 election, he was threatening that the GOP would "rape, ravage and destroy the system" if the majority party did not give Republicans fair representation on House committees.

At Home: Parris has tried twice to use his base in Northern Virginia as a springboard to statewide prominence. In 1989, he drew a respectable 28 percent in a three-way primary. But that put him behind former Sen. Paul S. Trible Jr. (35 percent) and former state attorney general Marshall Coleman, who won the GOP gubernatorial nomination with 37 percent.

In the primary, Parris carried his own 8th District with a hefty 58 percent, and he can probably settle back into it now. Since reclaiming the House seat in a very close 1980 contest, he has gained a secure footing, topping 60 percent in the last two elections.

In 1988, Parris' Democratic foe was state Rep. David G. Brickley, who at age 44 had a dozen years' experience in the Legislature. Brickley ran hard against the highway congestion caused by the combination of untrammeled growth and local anti-tax sentiment. The popularity of that issue, together with his name recognition, was expected to help Brickley. But Parris did just as well as he had two years earlier against a far less formidable foe.

In 1986, Democrats were left without a candidate when their nominee, former Alexandria Mayor Charles E. Beatley, quit the race, citing heart problems. Local party officials had to turn to a man who called himself "Mr. Mumbles" — James H. Boren, a political satirist and cousin of Oklahoma Sen. David L. Boren. In the past, Boren's humor had been aimed at the federal bureaucracy. During the campaign, he focused it on Parris, referring to him as "Sideline Stan," a congressman who was "doing nothing, but doing it with style."

Parris studiously ignored Boren, saying he was too busy with congressional matters. With Parris' huge advantage in campaign money and name familiarity, it was a sound strategy. He swept every jurisdiction in the district, including Democratic Alexandria.

Parris' early congressional career was marked by close and bitter contests with Democrat Herbert E. Harris II. Before their last face-off in 1982, Parris said, "I would be content with the epitaph saying I'm the guy that permanently retired Herb Harris from office."

The Harris-Parris rivalry dated to the 1960s, when they quarreled as members of the Fairfax County Board of Supervisors. Parris was a criminal attorney then, and Harris the president of a civic association.

Parris' political career was interrupted in 1967 when he lost his bid for the county board chairmanship. But in 1969, he won a seat in the state House, where he developed a friendship with future GOP Gov. John Dalton.

When GOP Rep. William Scott ran for the Senate in 1972, Parris returned to Northern Virginia to seek his House seat. With a split in Democratic ranks, he won with 44 percent. But two years later, Parris was not so lucky. He was held to 42 percent as Harris rode the 1974 Watergate tide to an easy victory.

The loss gave Parris, an antique airplane buff, more time to devote to his hobby and various business ventures. He kept active in politics, serving as Virginia's secretary of the commonwealth and its Washington lobbyist.

Parris twice passed up chances to try and avenge his defeat by Harris. But in 1980, he made his move. It was good timing, and Parris made the most of it. He went on the offensive, lambasting Harris as a big-spending supporter of Jimmy Carter. With a hefty media campaign and Reagan's coattails, Parris eked out a 1,094-vote victory. In 1982, he survived another Harris challenge by 1,549 votes. In 1984 against Democratic state Sen. Richard L. Saslaw, Parris won with a relatively comfortable 56 percent.

Committees

District of Columbia (Ranking)
Fiscal Affairs and Health; Government Operations and Metropolitan Affairs; Judiciary and Education

Banking, Finance and Urban Affairs (4th of 20 Republicans)
General Oversight and Investigations (ranking); Financial Institutions Supervision, Regulation and Insurance; Housing and Community Development

Interior and Insular Affairs (11th of 15 Republicans)
Energy and the Environment; National Parks and Public Lands

Select Narcotics Abuse and Control (4th of 12 Republicans)

Elections

1988 General		
Stan Parris (R)	154,761	(62%)
David G. Brickley (D)	93,561	(38%)
1986 General		
Stan Parris (R)	72,670	(62%)
James H. Boren (D)	44,965	(38%)

Previous Winning Percentages: **1984** (56%) **1982** (50%) **1980** (49%) **1972** (44%)

District Vote For President

	1988		1984		1980		1976	
D	102,516	(39%)	89,349	(38%)	63,214	(33%)	75,717	(47%)
R	157,228	(60%)	141,992	(61%)	104,891	(55%)	80,978	(51%)
I					18,128	(10%)		

Campaign Finance

	Receipts	Receipts from PACs		Expend-itures
1988				
Parris (R)	$632,755	$184,452	(29%)	$689,035
Brickley (D)	$276,578	$93,415	(34%)	$273,203
1986				
Parris (R)	$628,266	$177,392	(28%)	$428,788
Boren (D)	$78,538	$2,000	(3%)	$73,981

Key Votes

1987	
Raise speed limit to 65 mph	Y
Approve Gephardt "fair trade" amendment	N
Ban testing of larger nuclear weapons	N
Delay "re-flagging" of Kuwaiti tankers	N
Approve tax-raising deficit-reduction bill	N
1988	
Approve aid to Nicaraguan contras	Y
Enact civil rights restoration bill over Reagan veto	N
Kill 60-day plant-closing notification measure	Y
Pass omnibus trade bill over Reagan veto	N
Approve death penalty for drug-related murders	Y
Bar federal funds for abortions in cases of rape and incest	Y
Oppose seven-day waiting period for purchase of handguns	Y

Voting Studies

	Presidential Support		Party Unity		Conservative Coalition	
Year	**S**	**O**	**S**	**O**	**S**	**O**
1988	57	38	78	16	87	5
1987	67	29	73	20	84	12
1986	70	27	71	22	76	20
1985	64	33	69	25	76	20
1984	61	37	72	23	88	10
1983	70	27	74	19	79	11
1982	58	38	66	31	74 †	24 †
1981	74	21	83	14	83	13

† Not eligible for all recorded votes.

Interest Group Ratings

Year	ADA	ACU	AFL-CIO	CCUS
1988	15	96	29	93
1987	12	82	25	73
1986	5	83	25	71
1985	15	67	35	76
1984	15	79	25	63
1983	15	80	18	83
1982	16	73	21	67
1981	5	100	29	94

9 Rick Boucher (D)

Of Abingdon — Elected 1982

Born: Aug. 1, 1946, Abingdon, Va.
Education: Roanoke College, B.A. 1968; U. of Virginia, J.D. 1971.
Occupation: Lawyer.
Family: Single.
Religion: Methodist.
Political Career: Va. Senate, 1975-82.
Capitol Office: 428 Cannon Bldg. 20515; 225-3861.

In Washington: A slight and bespectacled former Wall Street lawyer, Boucher does not seem a likely representative from hard-scrabble, coal-mining southwest Virginia. But he has made his way in the 9th and in Congress thanks to a reputation for being articulate, diligent and easy to get along with.

Those qualities helped him win a coveted spot on the Energy and Commerce Committee for the 100th Congress. Also in the equation was his stand on the Clean Air Act. Chairman John D. Dingell has long opposed tougher clean-air standards that could hurt his constituents in industrial Michigan, and he handpicked three new members for his committee who would not make trouble for him on that issue. Boucher was one; coming from coal country, he also had reason to be wary of clean-air legislation.

When the committee worked on the long-stalled reauthorization of the Clean Air Act in the 100th Congress, Boucher joined with the so-called "group of nine," a caucus of moderate-to-conservative Democrats who tried to end a stalemate between Dingell and the pro-industry faction and the committee's staunch environmentalists.

Each member saw the complicated issue through the eyes of his constituency, but Boucher was more parochial than had been expected. When the group discussed matters not directly relevant to Virginia, Boucher's attention often was elsewhere. He did not play a major role in hammering out the group's detailed, and ultimately unsuccessful, proposal to deal with urban smog. Most suspected he was waiting to weigh in on the issue of acid rain, which is caused by the burning of coal.

Boucher, one of the most liberal members of his state's delegation, received a perfect score from the AFL-CIO in 1988. But he has also done some work that has enhanced his appeal to the business community.

In the 99th Congress he began pushing legislation limiting the applicability of the Racketeer Influenced and Corrupt Organizations Act (RICO). The 1970 law was originally designed for fighting organized crime, but increasingly it has been used for civil suits against corporations — in part because plaintiffs have the chance to collect triple damages. Business groups saw it as an intrusion on free enterprise, and Boucher agreed. He said the RICO act had been meant solely to help the government seize assets of organized-crime figures and drug dealers, and that it was being abused by greedy litigants.

But Boucher faced a major obstacle. Law enforcement and consumer groups — and more importantly, Criminal Justice Subcommittee Chairman John Conyers Jr. — feared a change could make it more difficult to attack white-collar crime. Conyers launched a campaign to stifle the bill, and forced Boucher to seek the aid of the full committee chairman to move it out of subcommittee. Ultimately the House passed Boucher's legislation eliminating triple-damage awards in most civil cases, but in the Senate, a companion effort by Ohio Democrat Howard M. Metzenbaum was tabled just before Congress adjourned in 1986.

In the 100th Congress, Boucher was back with a modified plan cosponsored by five of the eight subcommitee members. But Conyers complained that the bill favored insurers, accountants and brokers, while hindering the fight against crime. Metzenbaum's companion Senate bill never reached the floor, dashing any hopes Boucher had for a compromise. The outlook, however, seemed brighter early in the 101st Congress, when jurisdiction over RICO moved to the Crime Subcommittee, chaired by William J. Hughes.

Boucher is also a likely participant in future work on product liability legislation on both Judiciary and Energy and Commerce. For years businesses have sought new federal product liability standards, used by the courts to determine damages manufacturers must pay for injuries caused by their products. But trial lawyers and consumer groups have feared that a new standard could impinge on victims' rights. When Chairman Dingell tried to find a compromise on liability legislation before the committee in 1988, Boucher was one member he turned to. He worked up an amendment that essentially weakened manufacturers' protections

Virginia 9

Southwest — Blacksburg; Bristol

The "Fighting Ninth" earned that name not only because of its tradition of fiercely competitive two-party politics but also because of its ornery isolation from the Virginia political establishment in Richmond.

Southwestern Virginia was settled by Scotch-Irish and German immigrants who had little in common with the English settlers in the Tidewater and Piedmont regions. The Civil War divided the anti-secession mountaineers from slaveholding Confederates elsewhere in the state. In the postwar era, when Democrats routinely dominated Virginia politics, the 9th was the only district in which Republicans were consistently strong.

But as the state GOP has moved into alliance with Richmond's business establishment and Northern Virginia's affluent suburbanites, the party has lost ground in the 9th. Some of the region's burley tobacco growers and other small-scale farmers now are teaming with the traditionally Democratic coal miners.

Democrats are strongest in coal-mining counties along the Kentucky and West Virginia borders. In the 1988 presidential contest, Michael S. Dukakis carried five of the eight border counties. Dickenson, Russell and Tazewell counties have suffered recently. A strike by miners against Pittston Coal Group Inc. began in early 1989, making life more difficult for a number of residents already troubled by a weak economy.

Republicans normally have an edge in the corridor of counties roughly traced by Interstate 81 as it runs north from Bristol past Blacksburg. Boucher's 1988 GOP challenger carried Bristol, though he managed only 37 percent overall.

Montgomery County, which contains the district's largest city, Blacksburg, is economically atypical of the 9th. Home to Virginia Tech, the state's largest university (nearly 23,000 students), Blacksburg is a tidy and prosperous-looking city quite unlike the dreary factory and coal towns common throughout the district. Fed by a Tech enrollment boom, Blacksburg's population grew more than 200 percent during the 1970s and has now leveled off at around 30,000.

Population: 538,871. White 523,299 (97%), Black 12,920 (2%). Spanish origin 3,045 (1%). 18 and over 388,333 (72%), 65 and over 58,900 (11%). Median age: 29.

against liability for design defects, and nearly won endorsements by major consumer groups. But that support did not come through, and Boucher never offered his amendment. The committee passed a different plan, but it did not reach the House floor.

At Home: The hard work and careful organization that have helped Boucher in the House have also been the secret of his success in the 9th, where voters no longer seem to mind that he lacks a rough-and-tumble air.

Boucher needed all his assets to weather bruising elections in 1982 and 1984, but in 1986, he became the district's first House candidate since 1853 to run unopposed.

Boucher's 1982 victory over veteran GOP Rep. William C. Wampler was the closest the typically competitive "Fighting Ninth" had seen in nearly three decades, as Boucher won by just 1,123 votes out of more than 150,000 cast. Two years later he expanded his margin of victory to about 8,000 votes, but he still had the closest House race in Virginia.

After Republicans gave the 9th a pass in 1986, the best they could do for 1988 was John C. Brown, a 36-year-old high school teacher; Boucher surpassed 60 percent of the vote.

Despite his scholarly look, Boucher came naturally to politics. Both his grandfather and great-grandfather served in the Virginia state House. His father was commonwealth's attorney in Washington County (Abingdon).

After graduating from the University of Virginia Law School, Boucher joined the Wall Street firm of Milbank, Tweed, Hadley and McCloy. He took time out to work as an advance man for George McGovern's 1972 presidential campaign. The following year he returned to Abingdon to practice law, ultimately joining his family's firm in 1978. Until he was elected to Congress, he and his mother operated the firm, with his mother specializing in real estate and Boucher handling trial work.

He also began laying the groundwork for his political debut, which he made in a 1975 bid for state Senate. Energetically buttonholing district convention delegates, Boucher defeated a veteran incumbent for the Democratic nomination, then coasted to election.

Democratic Gov. Charles S. Robb and other state party leaders urged Boucher to challenge Wampler in 1982. Viewing the high unemployment in the district's coal fields and the politically marginal nature of the 9th, Boucher was not hard to convince. By mid-March he had begun full-time campaigning, interspersing his travels across the 200-mile-long rural district with fund-raising trips to Washington.

Boucher raised $241,000, less than Wampler, but enough to finance billboards and media advertising on the three TV stations that together cover the district. As Boucher's name identification increased, Wampler began to react. He sought to dismiss Boucher as "a Henry Howell with an Ivy League look," a reference to the controversial Tidewater populist who lost decisively in his last gubernatorial race in 1977.

But Boucher jabbed back, describing the affable Wampler — known to constituents as the "bald eagle of the Cumberland" — as a nice man but ineffective legislator. Boucher termed himself the true fiscal conservative, citing Wampler's support for Reaganomics and its ensuing budget deficits.

The economy was a powerful issue. In some of the coal counties, unemployment neared 20 percent in the fall of 1982. Turnout there approached the level of the 1980 presidential election, and Boucher, drawing on the active support of the United Mine Workers, ran exceptionally well. Boucher also neutralized Wampler in his home base, the Bristol area just north of Tennessee. Bristol was also part of Boucher's state Senate district; Wampler won it only narrowly.

When Wampler decided against a rematch in 1984, Boucher became a clear favorite for re-election. But he did not have an easy race against his well-financed GOP challenger, state Rep. Jefferson Stafford.

One of the Legislature's most conservative members, Stafford had been an ardent proponent of reinstituting the death penalty and a zealous foe of financial aid to college students who did not register for the draft. He charged that Boucher was too liberal, tying him to Walter F. Mondale, whose presidential campaign Boucher helped to lead in Virginia.

The incumbent gave Stafford plenty of chances to make his case — they held about a dozen debates across the district. But Stafford could not put his rival on the defensive. Brandishing endorsements from the National Rifle Association and the Veterans of Foreign Wars, Boucher said he was no flaming liberal. His voting record, he added, was dictated by the needs of his low-income constituents, many of them elderly. Boucher emphasized his work for the coal industry and his constituent service, claiming to be an ombudsman for coal miners, farmers and senior citizens in their battles with the federal bureaucracy.

Although Stafford carried most of the 17 counties in the 9th, Boucher survived by taking large majorities in the coal-producing areas.

Committees

Energy and Commerce (22nd of 26 Democrats)
Oversight and Investigations; Telecommunications and Finance; Transportation and Hazardous Materials

Judiciary (17th of 21 Democrats)
Courts, Intellectual Property and the Administration of Justice; Crime

Science, Space and Technology (15th of 30 Democrats)
Energy Research and Development

Elections

1988 General		
Rick Boucher (D)	113,309	(63%)
John C. Brown (R)	65,410	(37%)
1986 General		
Rick Boucher (D)	59,864	(99%)

Previous Winning Percentages: 1984 (52%) **1982** (50%)

District Vote For President

	1988	1984	1980	1976
D	82,873 (45%)	82,522 (41%)	84,218 (47%)	87,783 (52%)
R	98,738 (54%)	117,088 (58%)	86,251 (48%)	76,627 (45%)
I			4,573 (3%)	

Campaign Finance

	Receipts	Receipts from PACs	Expend-itures
1988			
Boucher (D)	$616,821	$367,600 (60%)	$606,420
Brown (R)	$155,094	$3,427 (2%)	$154,515
1986			
Boucher (D)	$348,320	$179,037 (51%)	$262,606

Key Votes

1987	
Raise speed limit to 65 mph	Y
Approve Gephardt "fair trade" amendment	Y
Ban testing of larger nuclear weapons	Y
Delay "re-flagging" of Kuwaiti tankers	?
Approve tax-raising deficit-reduction bill	Y
1988	
Approve aid to Nicaraguan contras	N
Enact civil rights restoration bill over Reagan veto	Y
Kill 60-day plant-closing notification measure	N
Pass omnibus trade bill over Reagan veto	Y
Approve death penalty for drug-related murders	N
Bar federal funds for abortions in cases of rape and incest	N
Oppose seven-day waiting period for purchase of handguns	Y

Voting Studies

	Presidential Support		Party Unity		Conservative Coalition	
Year	S	O	S	O	S	O
1988	19	74	87	5	29	66
1987	22	68	86	7	42	51
1986	23	72	83	6	36	50
1985	29	68	87	7	35	64
1984	35	56	78	12	44	47
1983	22	74	88	7	29	64

Interest Group Ratings

Year	ADA	ACU	AFL-CIO	CCUS
1988	75	9	100	29
1987	76	0	94	7
1986	70	6	86	20
1985	60	19	65	48
1984	70	29	62	33
1983	80	13	88	35

10 Frank R. Wolf (R)

Of Vienna — Elected 1980

Born: Jan. 30, 1939, Philadelphia, Pa.

Education: Pennsylvania State U., B.A. 1961; Georgetown U., LL.B. 1965.

Military Career: Army, 1962-63, Reserve, 1963-67.

Occupation: Lawyer.

Family: Wife, Carolyn Stover; five children.

Religion: Presbyterian.

Political Career: Sought Republican nomination for U.S. House, 1976; Republican nominee for U.S. House, 1978.

Capitol Office: 104 Cannon Bldg. 20515; 225-5136.

In Washington: Wolf, whose district is just across the Potomac from Washington, D.C., represents one of the nation's most affluent, highly educated and politically sophisticated constituencies. But as voters, residents of the 10th are no different from suburbanites anywhere else in the country. National affairs come second to gridlock, and as long as Wolf delivers what they want — highway and mass-transit funds — his constituents do not seem to mind the strong parochial orientation of his congressional record.

A model practitioner of local politics, Wolf is perfectly positioned as a member of the Appropriations Subcommittee on Transportation. He meticulously tends to the auto, rail and air traffic problems of concern to his district; on national policy matters, he generally casts quiet conservative votes on the House floor.

After nearly a decade in the House, Wolf has begun to broaden his activities a bit. In the 101st Congress, he was named to the Helsinki human rights commission; and as a new member of the Select Committee on Hunger, he was among the first House members to travel to rebel territory in southern Sudan, where the civil war is exacerbating famine conditions. In an earlier foreign affairs initiative, Wolf traveled to Ethiopia to study the famine problems there.

In the 100th Congress, Wolf decried human rights conditions in Romania, a cause of national conservative groups, but not one that drew much support from the Reagan administration. Wolf authored an amendment to the trade bill to deny Romania most-favored-nation trading status, and he took to the House floor to criticize the Reagan administration for its indifference to conditions in the country. "The Romanian government is bulldozing churches," he said. "They are bulldozing synagogues, they beat a Catholic priest and are persecuting different religious groups."

Mostly, however, Wolf is interested in streets. Every member tries to obtain highway funding for his district, but none plays a more personal role in trying to unravel traffic tie-ups than Wolf. He promotes himself as sort of an ombudsman for Northern Virginia. In 1987, he wrote to the commissioner of the Virginia Department of Transportation asking him to look for ways to ease backups at the tollgates on a highway in northern Fairfax County. He also helped secure $5 million to improve the George Washington Parkway and add a new inbound lane on the Roosevelt bridge, which connects his district to Washington.

Wolf shows little taste for partisan confrontation, and generally works well with Democrats. On the Transportation Subcommittee, he regularly teams up with Maryland Democrat Steny H. Hoyer to secure funds for Washington's Metro subway system.

During the Reagan era, Wolf was sometimes criticized for his willingness to support most of the president's domestic budget-cutting efforts, except those that would affect federal workers. In 1985 budget deliberations, Wolf said he could support cuts in a number of program areas, but not proposals to freeze pensions for federal employees and veterans.

In the 100th Congress, when the administration objected to labor protection provisions (LPPs) in the 1988 transportation spending bill, Wolf again departed from the GOP line. Rarely a supporter of organized labor, he backed a controversial amendment that would have required airlines to pay benefits to workers hurt by mergers. Wolf's constituents include the many aviation workers based at two large airports — National and Dulles International. The LPPs were ultimately dropped from the bill.

When legislation to reform the Hatch Act came before the House in 1987, however, Wolf not only returned to the GOP fold, he led the charge. The bill, which sought to roll back the limits on political activity by federal workers, had the strong support of unions representing federal employees. Wolf, who represents some

Virginia 10

D.C. Suburbs; Arlington County

The 10th is one of the most affluent districts in any Southern state, but it is hardly fair to identify it with the South. It is basically a set of bedroom communities for civil servants, people who work in the Pentagon, and others whose livelihoods are connected with the federal government. It is one of the most transient areas of the country, with an estimated 20 percent of the registered voters new each year.

Arlington County, just outside Washington, D.C., grew rapidly over the last several decades as the work force of the federal government expanded. Home for more than one out of every four residents in the district, Arlington is the prime source of Democratic votes in the 10th. Ronald Reagan won the county in 1980, but Walter F. Mondale and Michael S. Dukakis took it back for the Democrats.

Although suburban sprawl has peaked in Arlington, there has been some movement of younger, affluent professionals into condominiums and rental housing. These people tend to be more liberal than the average Virginian, but they are transient and hard to rely on politically.

There are relatively few blacks in Arlington, but the county is becoming a melting pot for other minorities. Asians, Hispanics and other minority groups together make up roughly one-quarter of the population. Arlington has the second-highest concentration of Vietnamese in the country, and its "Little Saigon" area is a magnet for Vietnamese-owned businesses.

Moving west from Arlington into the northern part of Fairfax County, the GOP vote increases. Like southern Fairfax, which is in the 8th District, this part of the county is filling up rapidly with new white-collar industries and expensive new housing developments to accommodate their employees. Soaring property assessments and traffic congestion are the top concerns of many Fairfax residents; local government bodies frequently are the stage for pitched battles between pro-growth and slow-growth forces. Getting around by car is such a hassle nowadays that some businesses are turning sour on the county. The American Automobile Association, for instance, decided recently to move its headquarters from Fairfax County to Florida.

George Bush won 60 percent in the Fairfax County portion of the 10th in 1988.

Farther northwest is Loudoun County, home base of long-distance commuters, but also part of Northern Virginia's "hunt" country, a rolling landscape dotted with sprawling country houses, horse farms and an occasional vineyard. Wolf and Bush received solid margins here in 1988.

Population: 535,125. White 466,595 (87%), Black 35,259 (7%), Other 21,974 (4%). Spanish origin 21,573 (4%). 18 and over 401,286 (75%), 65 and over 40,208 (8%). Median age: 31.

70,000 government workers, agreed that the Hatch Act needed revision, but he said the House bill was flawed. The reforms passed the House in 1987, but died in the Senate.

In 1986, Wolf was a leader in the effort to turn over control of Dulles and National airports from federal to local authorities. Working with Democrat Norman Y. Mineta, then-chairman of the Public Works Subcommittee on Aviation, Wolf helped craft the law authorizing the creation of a regional panel that will hold long-term leases on the airports.

At Home: Democrats have derisively referred to Wolf as a "pothole" politician. But wearing the label of localist as a badge of honor, he has built an increasingly secure political base in the Northern Virginia suburbs.

Democratic hopes of ousting Wolf were high in 1986, when the party ran John G. Milliken, a member and past chairman of the Arlington County Board of Supervisors.

Unlike previous challengers, who had to fend off either a liberal reputation or a carpetbagger stigma, Milliken had long experience in local government and a reputation as a moderate Democrat in the mold of the state's former governor (and now senator), Charles S. Robb.

As chairman of the Washington Metropolitan Area Transit Authority and the Northern Virginia Transportation Commission, Milliken had been involved in many of the same transportation questions that Wolf had. As a result, Milliken argued, he could match Wolf's expertise on suburban issues while providing a more forceful voice on national issues.

But while Milliken seemed to have the political image, the local roots and the money — nearly $750,000 — needed to challenge Wolf, he had trouble framing an argument as to why the hard-working, if undynamic, incumbent should be replaced. Viewed widely as a diligent plodder rather than a conservative ideologue, Wolf had never been a lightning rod for controversy.

Milliken tried to make him one, running TV ads that criticized Wolf's 1984 vote to cut federal aid to schools that barred voluntary prayers, spoken or silent. In the ad, Milliken remarked that he would rather fight to place good teachers in the schools than "to spin my wheels pushing a government-written prayer."

Wolf angrily responded that while he supported voluntary school prayers, he opposed mandatory government-written prayers. Wolf ran his own ad featuring GOP Sen. John W. Warner saying that he had never seen a "worse distortion of the truth" than the Milliken ad.

The episode seemed to slow any momentum that Milliken might have had. On Election Day, Wolf swamped Milliken in the populous outer suburbs of Fairfax and Loudoun counties, while running virtually even with his challenger in Democratic Arlington, where Milliken had won re-election to the county board in 1984 with 70 percent of the vote.

Wolf's impressive victory chilled Democrats' spirits in this district. His challenger in 1988 was Bob Weinberg, a prominent Washington attorney with a long history of public service in Arlington. Weinberg ran a heady but woefully underfinanced campaign, and Wolf got his biggest share of the vote to date, 68 percent.

From its beginning, Wolf's career has been a testament to persistence. Barely a year after Democrat Joseph L. Fisher first won this House seat in 1974, Wolf began campaigning to defeat him. His 1976 effort had the backing of local Reagan activists, but did not survive the primary.

Two years later, with more name recognition and better financing, he won the GOP nomination, but lost to Fisher by almost 9,000 votes. His reward came in 1980. Backed by a huge budget, Wolf ended five years of effort with a narrow victory.

Wolf is neither eloquent nor colorful, although he is occasionally accompanied by an aide dressed in a wolf's suit. But he has raised more than $3.5 million since 1979 and run meticulously organized campaigns. In recognition of the multinational nature of some of his district's less affluent neighborhoods, his direct-mail appeals are written in Spanish and Vietnamese as well as English.

In the early campaigns, Fisher chided Wolf for his lack of government experience. But having been a lobbyist, an aide to Republican Rep. Edward G. Biester of Pennsylvania, and deputy assistant secretary of the interior, Wolf could claim he knew his way around the Capitol.

Committees

Appropriations (17th of 22 Republicans)
Transportation and Related Agencies; Treasury, Postal Service and General Government

Select Children, Youth and Families (2nd of 12 Republicans)

Select Hunger (10th of 12 Republicans)

Elections

1988 General

Frank R. Wolf (R)	188,550	(68%)
Robert L. Weinberg (D)	88,284	(32%)

1986 General

Frank R. Wolf (R)	95,724	(60%)
John G. Milliken (D)	63,292	(40%)

Previous Winning Percentages: **1984** (63%) **1982** (53%) **1980** (51%)

District Vote For President

	1988	1984	1980	1976
D	121,878 (42%)	106,911 (41%)	76,676 (34%)	95,532 (47%)
R	163,211 (57%)	154,507 (59%)	120,328 (53%)	104,815 (51%)
I			23,999 (11%)	

Campaign Finance

	Receipts	Receipts from PACs	Expend-itures
1988			
Wolf (R)	$803,080	$237,490 (30%)	$758,365
Weinberg (D)	$242,787	$34,783 (14%)	$241,445
1986			
Wolf (R)	$1,097,358	$310,833 (28%)	$1,124,866
Milliken (D)	$746,532	$200,666 (27%)	$748,918

Key Votes

1987	
Raise speed limit to 65 mph	N
Approve Gephardt "fair trade" amendment	N
Ban testing of larger nuclear weapons	N
Delay "re-flagging" of Kuwaiti tankers	N
Approve tax-raising deficit-reduction bill	N
1988	
Approve aid to Nicaraguan contras	Y
Enact civil rights restoration bill over Reagan veto	N
Kill 60-day plant-closing notification measure	Y
Pass omnibus trade bill over Reagan veto	N
Approve death penalty for drug-related murders	Y
Bar federal funds for abortions in cases of rape and incest	Y
Oppose seven-day waiting period for purchase of handguns	N

Voting Studies

	Presidential Support		Party Unity		Conservative Coalition	
Year	**S**	**O**	**S**	**O**	**S**	**O**
1988	59	40	82	17	87	13
1987	65	35	76	23	79	21
1986	67	33	74	25	78	22
1985	70	30	72	25	75	24
1984	64	33	71	27	86	12
1983	77	23	79	19	87	13
1982	56	39	69	28	78	15
1981	76 †	24 †	83	17	88 †	12 †

† Not eligible for all recorded votes.

Interest Group Ratings

Year	ADA	ACU	AFL-CIO	CCUS
1988	25	88	43	86
1987	16	87	13	73
1986	5	86	21	67
1985	15	71	24	73
1984	10	63	25	63
1983	5	96	6	75
1982	10	67	20	82
1981	10	93	0	100

Washington

U.S. CONGRESS

SENATE 1 D, 1 R
HOUSE 5 D, 3 R

LEGISLATURE

Senate 24 D, 25 R
House 64 D, 34 R

ELECTIONS

1988 Presidential Vote	
Bush	49%
Dukakis	50%
1984 Presidential Vote	
Reagan	56%
Mondale	43%
1980 Presidential Vote	
Reagan	50%
Carter	37%
Anderson	11%
Turnout rate in 1984	58%
Turnout rate in 1986	39%
Turnout rate in 1988	55%

(as percentage of voting age population)

POPULATION AND GROWTH

1980 population	4,132,156
1988 population estimate (18th in the nation)	4,648,000
Percent change 1980-1988	+12%

DEMOGRAPHIC BREAKDOWN

White	92%
Black	3%
Other	5%
(Spanish origin)	3%
Urban	74%
Rural	26%
Born in state	48%
Foreign-born	6%

MAJOR CITIES

Seattle	486,200
Spokane	172,890
Tacoma	158,950
Bellevue	80,940
Everett	60,380

AREA AND LAND USE

Area 66,511 sq. miles (20th)

Farm	39%
Forest	51%
Federally owned	29%

Gov. Booth Gardner (D)
Of Tacoma — Elected 1984

Born: Aug. 21, 1936, Tacoma, Wash.
Education: U. of Washington, B.A. 1958; Harvard U., M.B.A. 1963.
Occupation: Businessman.
Religion: Protestant.
Political Career: Wash. Senate, 1970-73; Pierce County executive, 1981-85.
Next Election: 1992.

WORK

Occupations	
White-collar	55%
Blue-collar	29%
Service workers	13%
Government Workers	
Federal	63,352
State	103,335
Local	166,343

MONEY

Median family income	$ 21,696	(9th)
Tax burden per capita	$ 1,040	(11th)

EDUCATION

Spending per pupil through grade 12	$ 3,881	(18th)
Persons with college degrees	19%	(11th)

CRIME

Violent crime rate 440 per 100,000 (23rd)

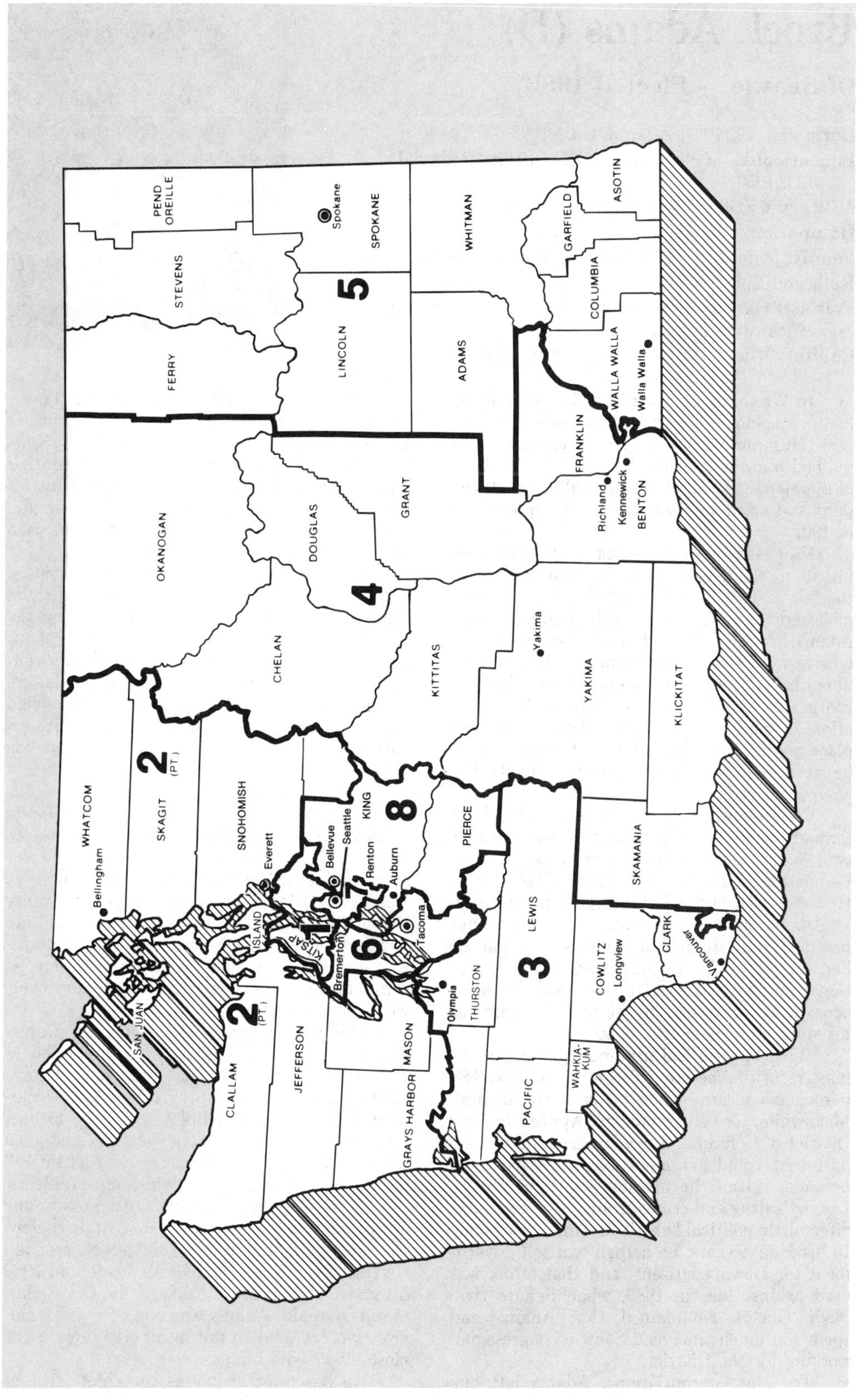
PEND OREILLE
STEVENS
FERRY
Spokane
SPOKANE
5
LINCOLN
WHITMAN
ASOTIN
GARFIELD
COLUMBIA
ADAMS
WALLA WALLA
Walla Walla
FRANKLIN
OKANOGAN
DOUGLAS
GRANT
4
Richland
Kennewick
BENTON
CHELAN
KITTITAS
Yakima
YAKIMA
KLICKITAT
WHATCOM
Bellingham
SKAGIT
2
(PT.)
SNOHOMISH
Everett
KING
Seattle
Bellevue
Renton
Auburn
8
7
1
6
ISLAND
KITSAP
Bremerton
Tacoma
PIERCE
SKAMANIA
LEWIS
3
COWLITZ
Longview
CLARK
Vancouver
SAN JUAN
2
(PT.)
Olympia
THURSTON
JEFFERSON
MASON
CLALLAM
GRAYS HARBOR
PACIFIC
WAHKIA-
KUM

Brock Adams (D)

Of Seattle — Elected 1986

Born: Jan. 13, 1927, Atlanta, Ga.
Education: U. of Washington, B.A. 1949; Harvard U., J.D. 1952.
Military Career: Navy, 1944-46.
Occupation: Lawyer.
Family: Wife, Mary Elizabeth Scott; four children.
Religion: Episcopalian.
Political Career: U.S. House, 1965-77; U.S. secretary of transportation, 1977-79.
Capitol Office: 513 Hart Bldg. 20510; 224-2621.

In Washington: As a liberal with an ebullient, loquacious style, Adams so resembles Hubert Humphrey that a local reporter once dubbed him the "Yappy Warrior." In the wake of a major sex scandal, Adams will need all the fight and spirit he possesses to win re-election in 1992.

He has given every indication that he does intend to fight, ever since the first reports in the fall of 1988 that he had allegedly sexually molested the daughter of family friends. In fact, Adams broke the news himself, taking the offensive with a press conference to deny a still-unpublished magazine account of the woman's charges. In 1989, he won a seat on the Appropriations Committee, which put Adams in the best place possible to take home the federal bounty he needs to offset the negative publicity the charges stirred.

Consequently, the remaining years of his term are likely to be far different from the first two. As one of the older and most experienced Democrats in the impressive 1986 class — with House service and a Cabinet post behind him — Adams enjoyed a reservoir of respect that has inevitably dissipated some. Also, while he had set out to be an influential voice on national and international affairs, now he must concentrate his efforts on the two Washingtons: his state and the capital city.

With his political life endangered, Adams must return home often and tend to his state's parochial concerns when he is in the capital. Meanwhile, as chairman of Appropriations' District of Columbia Subcommittee, he holds a post that could get more exposure than ever before — given the national spotlight on the District's drug and crime problems — though it offers little political benefit for Adams at home. In his House years, he helped win self-government for District citizens, and that effort was used against him in 1986, when Senate rival Slade Gorton complained that Adams had spent too much time as a Seattle congressman working for the District.

To join Appropriations, Adams left one committee — Commerce, Science and Transportation — that played to his expertise both as a House veteran and as President Jimmy Carter's first transportation secretary, and another panel, Foreign Relations, that reflected his interests abroad. He remains on the Labor and Human Resources Committee, where he is a reliable liberal, pro-labor vote.

Adams' skepticism about transportation deregulation, which had led Carter to dismiss him, was back in vogue at Commerce by the time he arrived there, thanks to concerns about airline safety, shoddy service and industry concentration after a decade of relaxed regulation. At the Transportation Department, Adams had not only fought with Carter, but also with an auto industry that resisted his calls for air-bag and mileage requirements.

In the 100th Congress, he helped pass bills tightening safety regulations on the rail and trucking industries. Arguing for the measure to strengthen trucking standards, which he cosponsored with Commerce Republican John C. Danforth, Adams attributed industry safety lapses in part to the 1980 trucking deregulation law that passed after he had quit as transportation secretary. He said the law had prompted companies to skimp on maintenance and overwork their drivers.

The Senate approved a consumer-protection bill for airline passengers, but it died in 1988 due to House objections, which Adams shared, to an unrelated provision requiring random drug testing of employees in the airline, rail, truck and bus industries. Adams said such tests would be an "administrative nightmare" that would not remedy overall safety problems.

In the foreign policy arena, Adams was one of the most staunch Senate foes of President Reagan's program of aid for the Nicaraguan contras. Even when Democratic leaders in 1988 offered an alternative package limited to humanitarian aid, Adams was one of four Democrats who refused to fall into party line on the close 49-47 vote for passage.

He was most visible as the chief critic of

Reagan's 1987-88 policy of providing Navy escorts to protect Kuwaiti tankers in the Persian Gulf. While members of both parties agreed that the policy was ill-conceived and that Reagan should have sought congressional authorization in keeping with the 1973 War Powers Resolution, most of them were loath to do more than criticize an ongoing operation. Adams' repeated attempts to stop the deployment were either rejected or blocked by GOP filibusters.

Still, Adams showed a doggedness that was impressive — if quixotic and aggravating to senators who did not want to vote on the delicate issue — and a savvy grasp of Senate rules. In late 1987, he won a parliamentarian's ruling that effectively protected his anti-escorts resolutions from further filibusters, which in turn led to a complex compromise that assured him of full debate and a vote in 1988.

At stake, he said, was "the power of the Congress of the United States to determine under the Constitution whether or not a war situation exists and whether or not the nation should be mobilized." Nevertheless, in May 1988 the Senate rebuffed his amendment ending the military escorts, 83-12, and a month later voted 54-31 to block another Adams resolution.

Adams also was a high-profile scrapper on the issue of disposing of high-level nuclear waste, in keeping with his potent 1986 campaign charge that Gorton had done little to prevent the Hanford, Wash., federal nuclear reservation from being the nation's first dump site.

In late 1987, he helped Nevada Sen. Harry Reid filibuster a plan that seemed to single out Nevada, contending, "I know and the people of my state know that Washington is a potential site." But other Northwesterners supported the plan, convinced that Hanford was effectively exempted; among them was Washington's other senator, Republican Daniel J. Evans, who called the filibuster "pure blather." Finally Adams abandoned Reid when a year-end deal clearly left Hanford off the hook.

Adams' earlier congressional career was a successful one. He was chairman of the House Budget Committee from 1975-77, during its first two years implementing the new congressional fiscal process, and he led efforts to assert congressional authority over the budget. Adams also was a prime mover behind a 1973 bill creating the Conrail freight system.

At Home: The scandal that swirled about Adams in 1988 involved an allegation by Kari Tupper that the senator seduced her at his home in March 1987 while his wife was away. When Adams was informed in September 1988 that a magazine planned to publish an article on the alleged incident, he held a news conference to strongly refute the charges in advance.

The only thing Adams and Tupper agree on is that the woman, then 24, visited his Washington, D.C., home and stayed overnight. Adams, who had helped Tupper obtain a job as a House aide, said he let her sleep on a couch after she complained of illness while seeking job advice. But Tupper, who said she visited Adams to complain about his alleged sexual advances, insisted she passed out after Adams gave her a doctored drink, and later woke up in his bed.

Though hospital tests taken the next day found no signs of assault, Tupper decided in July 1987 to press charges. However, the U.S. Attorney's office turned up no evidence of Tupper's allegations and declined to prosecute. The incident stayed out of the public eye — until Adams got wind months later that *Washingtonian* magazine was writing a story on Tupper's version of the incident.

Adams held a news conference and described Tupper's charges as "lies." He accused her of seeking a $400,000 "blackmail" payment.

Adams' denial set off a furor back home; in the middle of the presidential and senatorial races, the Seattle *Times* assigned its entire political staff to the story. Tupper, backed by her parents, responded that her story was true. She also said the payment came up after Adams' lawyer raised the issue of a settlement, and that she would have kept only what was needed to cover her medical and legal expenses, donating the rest to a rape-crisis center.

The *Washingtonian* article, published in November, not only took Tupper's word as fact, but also presented a picture of Adams as an aging Casanova. A letter in the following month's magazine, from a woman who identified herself as a former Adams aide, may have hurt the senator more than it helped: While defending him against Tupper's charges, the letter indicated that Adams had pursued extramarital affairs.

The damaging contretemps began for Adams just months after the crowning achievement of his political career. In November 1986, he had unseated Gorton in an upset that helped the Democrats regain control of the Senate.

The contest marked Adams' return from self-imposed exile. After more than a decade (1965-77) as a popular House member from Seattle, Adams was considered a likely successor to one of the state's veteran Democratic senators, Warren G. Magnuson and Henry M. Jackson. But Adams left Congress to join Carter's Cabinet, and after leaving that job in 1979, he remained in Washington, D.C., for several years as a lawyer. In the meantime, Gorton defeated Magnuson in 1980, and former Gov. Evans captured the other seat following Jackson's 1983 death.

By the time he returned for his 1986 challenge to Gorton, Adams had no significant political base remaining. He also was slow to organize his campaign, leaving on a trip to the Far East shortly after announcing his candidacy.

But the situation began to change in mid-summer, after Gorton voted to confirm Daniel A. Manion, a controversial conservative, as a federal appeals court judge. Gorton's vote was intended as a tradeoff for the approval of Washington state lawyer William L. Dwyer to a separate judgeship, but it sparked an uproar. Gorton caught flak from the right for promoting Dwyer, a liberal Democrat, and from the left for favoring Manion. At the same time, Adams and the media attacked him for making a blatant horse trade that politicized judge selection.

Even with the Manion flap, Adams was not taken seriously until September, when he made a strong showing in the state's open primary, which places candidates of both parties together on the ballot and is thus a "dry run" for the November election. Adams ran virtually even with Gorton.

That showing brought Adams the money and media attention he had sorely lacked, and it forced Gorton, who had ignored Adams' attacks during the primary season, to change strategies.

Gorton found the change difficult to accomplish. Though widely acknowledged as a competent senator, his cerebral and aloof manner did not generate as warm a response from voters as Adams' more outgoing nature.

Adams took advantage of the Manion vote to harp on Gorton's image as a cold and calculating politician. He also made headway with his criticism of Gorton for allowing the Department of Energy to choose the Hanford Reservation in southeast Washington as one of three possible locations for a high-level nuclear-waste site. Both candidates tried to tie themselves to a referendum on the November ballot opposing the Hanford choice, but Adams compared Gorton with Jackson and Magnuson, who he said would have fought the waste site more effectively.

Meanwhile, Gorton had trouble finding much ammunition in Adams' legislative record, which was more than a decade old. Gorton tried to tie Adams to Carter and the economic problems the state experienced in the late 1970s.

Near the campaign's end, it appeared that Gorton still held an edge. But in the last week he was victimized by an event designed to seal his victory — a visit from President Reagan.

In advance of Reagan's visit, it was widely rumored that the president would make an important announcement about Hanford to blunt Adams' efforts on the issue. But when the president made his appearance, he barely referred to the waste site. The absence of any major new policy put Gorton back on the defensive, as his influence with Reagan was called into question. The momentum shifted to Adams, who won with 51 percent of the vote.

Committees

Appropriations (14th of 16 Democrats)
District of Columbia (chairman); Agriculture, Rural Development and Related Agencies; Commerce, Justice, State, the Judiciary and Related Agencies; Labor, Health and Human Services, Education and Related Agencies; Legislative Branch

Labor and Human Resources (8th of 9 Democrats)
Children, Family, Drugs and Alcoholism; Employment and Productivity; Handicapped

Rules and Administration (9th of 9 Democrats)

Elections

1986 General		
Brock Adams (D)	677,471	(51%)
Slade Gorton (R)	650,931	(49%)
1986 Primary †		
Slade Gorton (R)	291,735	(46%)
Brock Adams (D)	287,258	(46%)

† In Washington's "jungle primary," candidates of both parties are listed on one ballot.

Previous Winning Percentages: **1976 *** (73%) **1974 *** (71%) **1972 *** (85%) **1970 *** (67%) **1968 *** (66%) **1966 *** (63%) **1964 *** (56%)

** House elections.*

Campaign Finance

	Receipts	Receipts from PACs	Expend-itures
1986			
Adams (D)	$1,973,142	$635,361 (32%)	$1,912,307
Gorton (R)	$3,316,123	$1,192,293 (36%)	$3,290,072

Key Votes

1987	
Enact omnibus highway bill over Reagan veto	Y
Limit testing of space-based anti-ballistic missiles	Y
Oppose banning tests of larger nuclear weapons	N
Confirm Robert H. Bork as Supreme Court justice	N
1988	
Allow vote on campaign-finance overhaul	Y
Pass civil rights restoration bill over Reagan veto	Y
Enact omnibus trade bill over Reagan veto	Y
Approve death penalty for drug-related murders	?
Oppose "workfare" amendment to welfare overhaul bill	Y

Voting Studies

	Presidential Support		Party Unity		Conservative Coalition	
Year	**S**	**O**	**S**	**O**	**S**	**O**
1988	38	56	82	11	16	73
1987	33	65	88	4	6	81

Interest Group Ratings

Year	ADA	ACU	AFL-CIO	CCUS
1988	90	0	77	36
1987	95	4	90	38

Slade Gorton (R)

Of Seattle — Elected 1988

Also served 1981-87.

Born: Jan. 8, 1928, Chicago, Ill.
Education: Dartmouth College, A.B. 1950; Columbia U., LL.B. 1953.
Military Career: Army, 1945-46; Air Force, 1953-56.
Occupation: Lawyer.
Family: Wife, Sally Jean Clark; three children.
Religion: Episcopalian.
Political Career: Wash. House, 1959-69, majority leader, 1967-69; Wash. attorney general, 1969-81.
Capitol Office: 730 Hart Bldg. 20510; 224-3441.

The Path to Washington: The 1988 victory that returned Gorton to the Senate capped a most unusual political journey through the 1980s.

Gorton was not among the most ideologically conservative GOP Senate candidates in 1980, but he rode in with the Reagan revolution that gave Republicans Senate control. Six years later, when Republicans of his centrist ilk were winning new Senate terms, Gorton was tossed out. His political career, said then to be finished, was not. The 1988 retirement of GOP Sen. Daniel J. Evans gave him the chance for a comeback.

Gorton made the most of it, edging Democratic Rep. Mike Lowry to become only the 11th senator in history to be popularly elected, defeated, then returned to the Senate. The last to manage the feat before Gorton was Kentucky Republican John Sherman Cooper, in the 1950s; Ohio Democrat Howard M. Metzenbaum also rebounded in 1976 from a 1974 defeat, but he was an appointed incumbent, not an elected one, when he lost.

In his Senate reprise, Gorton finds himself in a less influential position, a result of his party's loss of Senate control and his own loss of seniority. Before the 1986 election, Gorton served as chairman of subcommittees on three panels — Commerce, Banking, and Small Business; on the Budget Committee, he played an influential role in efforts to give the Republican Senate the lead in reducing the federal deficit. Upon his return, Gorton had to settle for the ranking minority positions on three subcommittees — on the Commerce, Armed Services and Agriculture committees.

Still, Gorton has few complaints, since his rebound was as unexpected as it was rare. Much of the state media had written him off after his 1986 defeat by Democrat Brock Adams. Even Gorton himself was wary about returning to the fray after Evans' retirement announcement. "I was afraid I was going to run the flag up and see that no one wanted to salute it," Gorton told *The Wall Street Journal.*

Gorton had good reason for trepidation. Adams' negative campaign in 1986 left Washington voters with deep concerns about the Republican's stands on key state issues. He also had to overcome the sour public perception of his personal manner; his image as an icy intellectual contributed to his defeat.

On paper, Gorton does not have the type of track record that should cause political problems in the Pacific Northwest. Born to a wealthy Chicago family (whose Yankee ancestors included the founders of the Gorton's of Gloucester fish-processing company), Gorton says he chose to settle in Washington state because of its progressive political legacy. During three terms as state attorney general, he crafted a pro-consumer record that placed him in the moderate mold of the state's most popular Republicans, including Evans, a former governor.

This profile aided Gorton in his 1980 bid against Democratic Sen. Warren G. Magnuson, whose legendary efforts to obtain public works projects for Washington state had earned him six terms in the Senate. Outperforming Ronald Reagan in the state, Gorton ousted Magnuson with 54 percent of the vote.

During his early years in the Senate, Gorton's record provided few surprises. He was generally supportive of President Reagan's policies, backing his first-term attempts at cutting federal programs and taxes. In supporting Reagan's efforts to increase defense spending, Gorton stood with his Senate colleague, Democratic "hawk" Henry M. Jackson (whose 1983 death was followed by Evans' special-election victory over Rep. Lowry). But Gorton maintained his consumerist direction, and was a staunch supporter of federal programs for community development and for the homeless.

Many of Gorton's constituents, however, were never very comfortable with him. Even before 1980, Gorton was a target for political epithets: His image as a political dealmaker earned him the label of "Slippery Slade," and Democrats angered by his harsh partisan behavior called him "Slade the Blade."

These personal "negatives" only worsened during his Senate term. Averse to the hail-fellow world of personal politics, the brusque, cerebral Gorton was also known to cut off political associates and inquisitive constituents in mid-sentence. It was thus easy for state Democrats to convince voters in 1986 that Gorton was "aloof" and "arrogant."

Also, while Gorton did not deliberately seek controversy — he spent much of his time on such un-sexy issues as product liability reform — he did become embroiled in a trio of contentious debates in the last third of his Senate term. Each issue worked to his disadvantage.

In the spring of 1985, Gorton was a leader among Republicans on the Budget Committee who, under the guidance of then-Majority Leader Bob Dole of Kansas, drafted a plan for a federal budget freeze that included a controversial provision eliminating cost-of-living allowances (COLAs) for Social Security recipients. But Reagan, who initially adopted the proposal, later reached an agreement with the Democratic House leadership that rejected the Social Security freeze.

Gorton, attempting to seize the political high ground, lambasted the president's decision, stating, "We have lost the last best chance we had of seriously approaching a balanced budget in the foreseeable future." But Gorton's vote for the freeze was remembered in Washington state; Adams accused him in 1986 of trying to "cut" Social Security.

Then came the Manion affair. Reagan had tapped Daniel A. Manion, an Indiana lawyer with strong ties to the conservative movement, to be a federal judge. At the same time, the White House held up the nomination of Seattle lawyer and Gorton ally William L. Dwyer, whose liberal views alienated key Republican conservatives.

Gorton let it be known he might line up with Senate Democrats opposing Manion; the Democrats, in fact, thought they had Gorton's crucial vote in the bag, and forced a floor vote in June 1986. But in the midst of the roll call, a White House official called Gorton to tell him that Reagan agreed to proceed with the Dwyer nomination; Gorton then voted for Manion, who was narrowly confirmed. In the aftermath, Gorton claimed he dealt with the White House to protect a home-state interest, but Democrats angrily portrayed him as a craven vote-trader.

Perhaps the most damaging issue for Gorton was the future of the Hanford nuclear reservation. During the 99th Congress, Hanford, in south-central Washington, was named as one of three possible sites for a permanent high-level nuclear waste dump, and Adams argued that Gorton had not done enough to block that eventuality. Also, Adams blasted Gorton for supporting continued plutonium production at Hanford's aging "N Reactor," and for promoting a plan to convert an abandoned nuclear power plant there to produce tritium, another component of nuclear weapons.

Adams — who had given up his 7th District House seat to serve as President Carter's transportation secretary in 1977 and had not run for elective office since — started out as a long shot. But he waged an aggressive campaign that played up Gorton's negatives, to which the confident incumbent was slow to respond.

Then, in the final week of the campaign, what was expected to be a triumphant moment turned to disaster for Gorton. Reagan flew to Spokane to appear at a Gorton rally. But when pressed on the Hanford issue by reporters, Reagan showed a lack of familiarity, thus creating an impression that Gorton had little access to the president.

Adams — who highlighted Hanford with a late ad savaging Gorton's support for the N Reactor, which he called a "bomb factory" — sent Gorton packing, winning with 51 percent of the vote. Gorton returned to legal practice in Seattle. In 1987, he worked as a Department of Energy consultant on options for keeping the nuclear industry at Hanford alive, an act that appeared to seal his political fate.

But late that year, Evans, who had voiced distress at the Senate's lack of legislative productivity, announced he would retire. With Democrats holding the governorship, the only Republican figures approaching Gorton's stature were House members Sid Morrison and Rod Chandler. When they demurred, the party leadership turned to Gorton. Though hard-line conservatives complained about Gorton's centrist image and his willingness to publicly air his disagreements with Reagan, they could produce only two weak primary challengers. Gorton breezed into the general election.

He then faced Lowry, who held off House colleague Don Bonker in a more grueling primary. Lowry had succeeded Adams in the 7th District, and had developed a strong liberal activist following with his outspoken support for federal social programs and his opposition to Reagan's defense buildup. But with his scraggly beard, rumpled clothes and penchant for arm-waving harangues, Lowry was vulnerable outside Seattle to GOP charges that he was an extremist. During the 1983 Senate special election, Evans, who went on to win with 55 percent, had made mincemeat of Lowry's stand against the U.S. invasion of Grenada. Even Bonker, who had a liberal record, portrayed Lowry as a gadfly.

The 1988 contest was thus a contest between the losers of the last two Washington Senate races, and both set out to soften the negatives that had previously defeated them. Gorton spent over $1 million during the primary on ads in which he apologized for being arrogant during his previous tenure. Lowry shaved his beard, adopted a neatly pressed appearance, and restrained his rhetoric and his notable temper.

But in its home stretch, the campaign centered on negative messages. Gorton, pointing to the state's "strong defense" tradition — shared even by Democrats such as the late Jackson — portrayed Lowry as far out of the mainstream. With drug trafficking a major national concern, Gorton attacked Lowry's House votes against the 1986 and 1988 omnibus drug bills (Lowry, like many liberals, had reservations about the effect on civil liberties of some of the crackdown measures). In turn, Lowry tried to revive the Social Security and Hanford issues that had stoked Adams' campaign.

This already unusual campaign was overshadowed by a pair of strange events. In late September, the Washington state media turned its attentions to bizarre, unproven allegations that Sen. Adams had drugged and seduced a young woman at his Washington, D.C., home. Then, in early October, Lowry collapsed in Chicago while en route to Seattle, and was hospitalized for several days with a bleeding ulcer.

Lowry returned to the campaign trail, though, and Gorton again faced a contest that entered its last week too close to call. In another similarity to 1986, an exchange on Hanford may have been decisive.

But this time, the breaks went Gorton's way. Hanford was already less of an issue than in 1986: The waste dump was designated for Nevada during the 100th Congress, and the N Reactor was closed for safety reasons. Still, Lowry lashed Gorton in a TV ad for supporting a tritium "bomb factory," and for receiving $60,000 in consulting fees from the Department of Energy. Unlike 1986, though, Gorton quickly responded with a big gun, the popular incumbent Evans. In an ad run in the campaign's final days, Evans described Lowry's charges as "lies, distortion and garbage."

By getting in the last word, Gorton may have tipped the scales. He won with 51 percent, even as Democrat Michael S. Dukakis carried the state in presidential voting.

Gorton's win placed him in the unusual position of being the junior senator to his recent foe Adams. By the end of November, though, Gorton had visited with Adams. "I believe political races should be hotly contested," Gorton said. "I believe with equal firmness that when the election is over, the members of Congress should work together."

Committees

Agriculture, Nutrition and Forestry (9th of 9 Republicans)
Agricultural Credit (ranking); Conservation and Forestry; Domestic and Foreign Marketing and Product Promotion

Armed Services (7th of 9 Republicans)
Readiness, Sustainability and Support (ranking); Projection Forces and Regional Defense; Strategic Forces and Nuclear Deterrence

Commerce, Science and Transportation (8th of 9 Republicans)
Consumer (ranking); Communications; Surface Transportation; National Ocean Policy Study

Elections

1988 General		
Slade Gorton (R)	944,359	(51%)
Mike Lowry (D)	904,183	(49%)
1988 Primary †		
Slade Gorton (R)	335,846	(36%)
Mike Lowry (D)	297,399	(32%)
Don Bonker (D)	241,170	(26%)
Doug Smith (R)	31,512	(3%)
William Goodloe (R)	26,224	(3%)

† In Washington's "jungle primary," candidates of both parties are listed on one ballot.

Previous Winning Percentage: 1980 (54%)

Campaign Finance

	Receipts	Receipts from PACs	Expend-itures
1988			
Gorton (R)	$2,736,101	$939,406 (34%)	$2,851,591
Lowry (D)	$2,202,177	$618,074 (28%)	$2,191,187

Voting Studies

	Presidential Support		Party Unity		Conservative Coalition	
Year	**S**	**O**	**S**	**O**	**S**	**O**
1986	73	25	74	25	72	26
1985	77	19	79	17	70	27
1984	83	17	83	16	81	19
1983	85	15	76	23	70	30
1982	76	24	78	22	76	24
1981	87	13	86	13	77	21

Interest Group Ratings

Year	ADA	ACU	AFL-CIO	CCUS
1986	25	19	69	65
1985	35	47	50	41
1984	35	83	18	78
1983	35	65	24	58
1982	45	43	35	62
1981	10	67	6	94

1 John Miller (R)

Of Seattle — Elected 1984

Born: May 23, 1938, New York, N.Y.

Education: Bucknell U., B.A. 1959; Yale U., M.A., LL.B. 1964.

Military Career: Army, 1960-61; Army Reserve, 1961-69.

Occupation: Lawyer.

Family: Wife, June Marion Makar; one child.

Religion: Jewish.

Political Career: Seattle City Council, 1972-80, president, 1978-80; candidate for Seattle mayor, 1977; independent candidate for Wash. attorney general, 1980.

Capitol Office: 1406 Longworth Bldg. 20515; 225-6311.

In Washington: Miller's agenda is now balanced between his personal interest in U.S. foreign policy and the more mundane concerns of his 1st District residents. But it was not always so. It took a brush with defeat in 1986 to inform Miller of the necessity of constituent contact.

During Miller's first term in the House, he had the air of an intellectual with a zest for debating the big issues, but he did not demonstrate much interest in the everyday concerns of his district. His 1986 Democratic opponent, Reese Lindquist, clubbed Miller with this aloof image, and he came close to scoring an upset.

The scare served as a great awakening for Miller. He moved his main local office from downtown Seattle (in the 7th District) to a suburban site on his own turf. He expanded his staff of constituent caseworkers, whom he gave the title of "community advocates." An attorney and former television commentator, Miller also embarked on a routine of blue-collar "workdays." The new attitude — plus a 1988 campaign budget of $1.3 million — helped Miller win a rematch with Lindquist by a more comfortable margin.

One thing Miller did not do to get re-elected was eschew his interest in U.S. foreign relations. At the start of the 100th Congress, he obtained a seat on the Foreign Affairs Committee. Nor did Miller back off his staunch anti-communist views — including his support for the Nicaraguan contras — that had caused him difficulty in his home district, where there is considerable suspicion of U.S. adventurism abroad.

However, Miller benefited from waning voter interest in the Nicaragua issue following the congressional hearings on the Iran-contra affair in mid-1987. In his second House campaign, Lindquist hammered less on the contras and more on the question of who would do more to aid the elderly or fight the war on drugs. With the coming of the Bush administration, Miller lined up behind efforts to forge a compromise between the Republican White House and the Democratic-controlled Congress on the contras. In March 1989, he voted for a measure that would continue humanitarian aid to the contras while sustaining pressure on the Sandinista government to provide democratic freedoms.

Miller's anti-communist views are evident in his work on the Foreign Affairs Subcommittee on Human Rights, where he is an advocate for Jewish "refuseniks" seeking to emigrate from the Soviet Union and for the natives of the so-called "captive nations" in the Soviet Baltic region. However, he is also critical of rightist regimes he sees as violative of human rights: He was a co-founder of the Ad Hoc Group in Support of Democracy in Chile.

From his seat on the Foreign Affairs Subcommittee on International Economic Policy and Trade, Miller is able to play a role in an area of vital interest to his district. The port of Seattle does a lot of import-export business, and that is reflected in Miller's anti-protectionist stance. In the 100th Congress, he supported President Reagan's veto of a textile trade bill; Washington state is a leading conduit of textile and clothing imports from Asia.

Miller's free-trade views put him in conflict during the 100th Congress with a Washington state colleague, 3rd District Democrat Don Bonker, who was then chairman of the Trade Subcommittee. The 3rd is a major timber producer, and Bonker proposed a ban on the export of whole logs from state-owned lands; his aim was to have the logs processed in local sawmills. Miller and other port-area members opposed the measure, which eventually stalled.

While Miller's anti-Soviet and anti-protectionist stands often put him in league with doctrinaire conservatives, his overall voting record marks him as one of the more moderate

Washington 1

Northern Seattle and Suburbs

The typical 1st District voter pays very little attention to party label in selecting candidates. Miller has kept the House seat in GOP hands, following in the footsteps of former Republican Rep. Joel Pritchard (now Washington state's lieutenant governor). But in 1988, Democrat Michael S. Dukakis carried the 1st, albeit just barely. He received just over 50 percent of the 1st District vote, beating George Bush by about 5,000 votes.

As in many districts in the Pacific Northwest, there are strong environmentalist tendencies. There is also a devoted corps of peace activists in Seattle's large liberal community. The mix in the 1st includes an active Christian fundamentalist community; religious broadcaster Pat Robertson swept the district's delegates in the 1988 Washington state presidential caucuses. But the majority of voters are middle-of-the-road and not partisan-minded.

Shaped like a butterfly hovering over Seattle, the 1st encompasses most of the city's northern suburbs, a collection of largely middle-class communities stretching from northern King County up into Snohomish County, almost to Everett.

Extremes of wealth and poverty are not characteristic of the 1st, but there is some variation. Seattle's northeastern and northwestern corners are part of the 1st, and a few of the neighborhoods there are lower-middle class. The district's ritziest section is the "Gold Coast" — an area on the eastern shore of Lake Washington that includes Hunts Point, Yarrow Point and Medina. Most workers, blue- and white-collar alike, commute to nearby factories or to downtown Seattle offices.

King and Snohomish together account for over 85 percent of the 1st's population. The remainder live across Puget Sound in northern Kitsap County, where several military bases boost the economy. The Navy's Underseas Warfare Engineering Station in Keyport is in the 1st, and just south is Bremerton's Bangor submarine base, home to Trident submarines.

Population: 516,378. White 486,447 (94%), Black 4,632 (1%), Other 19,372 (4%). Spanish origin 8,934 (2%). 18 and over 378,407 (73%), 65 and over 47,894 (9%). Median age: 31.

House Republicans. In 1988, he opposed Reagan's position on House legislation just over 50 percent of the time. During his years as a local official, Miller was known more for his positions on the environment than on foreign policy.

In 1988, Miller, along with Delaware Democrat Thomas R. Carper, drafted a compromise bill on the controversial proposal to open Alaska's ecologically sensitive Arctic National Wildlife Refuge (ANWR) to oil drilling. The bill provided for an up-or-down vote on ANWR drilling in 1991, after the National Academy of Sciences had prepared a national energy plan that would help Congress determine U.S. energy needs. But the compromise fell victim to oil company suspicion that it was a stalling tactic, and to environmentalist fears that it would pave the way for drilling.

At Home: Miller's heightened visibility and state-record fund raising enabled him to fend off Lindquist, a former state teachers' union president, in the 1988 replay of their close 1986 contest. The two tough matches contrasted with Miller's comfortable win in 1984 to succeed retiring GOP Rep. Joel Pritchard.

When he launched his first House campaign, Miller was already well-known from his tenure in the 1970s on the Seattle City Council and his unsuccessful runs for Seattle mayor and state attorney general. The New York-born lawyer had kept his profile up as a Seattle TV and radio commentator.

In his 1984 House bid, Miller's anti-communist views appealed to conservative Republicans, while his reputation for support of environmental causes offset the efforts of his Democratic opponent, environmental activist Brock Evans. Miller won with 56 percent of the vote.

That comfortable victory and the 1st District's Republican leanings may have contributed to Miller's complacency about his 1986 election. For whatever reason, Miller was caught off balance by the aggressive campaign of Lindquist, a teacher and former head of the Washington Education Association.

Lindquist launched his House bid late, but raised roughly $400,000. The contra-aid issue was the centerpiece of his campaign: Lindquist said a majority of district voters opposed the policy, and he used that as evidence that Miller was aloof and indifferent to his constituents' views. Miller just barely hung on, taking 51 percent of the vote.

Democrats had high hopes for Lindquist's second try. He campaigned practically nonstop, and had the whole off year to organize. But Miller was not to be blindsided again. He sought media attention for his "workdays" and beefed-up outreach programs.

Lindquist again ran an energetic campaign, assailing Miller's approach to voters as a ploy, and describing him as opposed to increased funding for education and seniors' programs. Miller responded by portraying Lindquist as a radical who was responsible for a Seattle teachers' strike in 1978.

The campaign evolved into a nasty exchange of TV ads. Lindquist said Miller lacked devotion to the drug war and ran an ad showing a body being wheeled into a morgue; Miller responded by accusing Lindquist of tolerating drug and alcohol abuse on the high-school football team he coached in the 1970s.

District news coverage of the campaign focused on misleading claims in both candidates' ads. But it was Miller's ability to pay for campaign advertising, both positive and negative in nature, that was likely the deciding factor in the contest. Of the $1.3 million Miller spent, nearly $750,000 went for TV commercials. Lindquist raised less than half Miller's total, and spent a little over $200,000 for ads — an amount approximating the size of the loan Miller made to himself from his own bank account for a late blitz. Miller won the rematch by a comfortable 55-45 percent margin.

Committees

Foreign Affairs (13th of 18 Republicans)
Human Rights and International Organizations; International Economic Policy and Trade

Merchant Marine and Fisheries (9th of 17 Republicans)
Fisheries and Wildlife Conservation and the Environment; Merchant Marine

Elections

1988 General		
John Miller (R)	152,265	(55%)
Reese Lindquist (D)	122,646	(45%)
1988 Primary †		
John Miller (R)	69,516	(51%)
Reese Lindquist (D)	62,941	(46%)
Kerman Kermoade (R)	3,005	(2%)
1986 General		
John Miller (R)	97,969	(51%)
Reese Lindquist (D)	92,697	(49%)

† In Washington's "jungle primary," candidates of both parties are listed on one ballot.

Previous Winning Percentage: **1984** (56%)

District Vote For President

	1988	1984
D	134,311 (50%)	100,102 (42%)
R	129,280 (49%)	134,199 (57%)

Campaign Finance

	Receipts	Receipts from PACs	Expend- itures
1988			
Miller (R)	$1,328,979	$333,860 (25%)	$1,321,021
Lindquist (D)	$625,238	$279,275 (45%)	$625,926
1986			
Miller (R)	$594,170	$156,174 (26%)	$592,313
Lindquist (D)	$402,611	$131,605 (33%)	$397,226

Key Votes

1987	
Raise speed limit to 65 mph	N
Approve Gephardt "fair trade" amendment	N
Ban testing of larger nuclear weapons	N
Delay "re-flagging" of Kuwaiti tankers	N
Approve tax-raising deficit-reduction bill	N
1988	
Approve aid to Nicaraguan contras	Y
Enact civil rights restoration bill over Reagan veto	Y
Kill 60-day plant-closing notification measure	Y
Pass omnibus trade bill over Reagan veto	Y
Approve death penalty for drug-related murders	N
Bar federal funds for abortions in cases of rape and incest	N
Oppose seven-day waiting period for purchase of handguns	N

Voting Studies

	Presidential Support		Party Unity		Conservative Coalition	
Year	**S**	**O**	**S**	**O**	**S**	**O**
1988	44	51	50	45	66	26
1987	52	48	57	38	63	33
1986	56	43	60	36	58	40
1985	64	36	65	32	62	36

Interest Group Ratings

Year	ADA	ACU	AFL-CIO	CCUS
1988	60	38	64	79
1987	48	41	44	73
1986	40	55	36	67
1985	25	67	24	86

2 Al Swift (D)

Of Bellingham — Elected 1978

Born: Sept. 12, 1935, Tacoma, Wash.
Education: Attended Whitman College, 1953-55; Central Washington College, B.A. 1957.
Occupation: Broadcaster.
Family: Wife, Paula Jean Jackson; two children.
Religion: Unitarian.
Political Career: No previous office.
Capitol Office: 1502 Longworth Bldg. 20515; 225-2605.

In Washington: Swift's resonant voice is an instant reminder of his days delivering the 11 o'clock news in Bellingham, but it is hard to imagine anyone doing more than Swift to dispel the stereotype of the local TV anchorman as a prisoner of style over substance.

A patient and diligent legislator who often toils outside the spotlight, Swift has thrown himself into some of the more challenging issues before Congress. Most recently, he has plunged into the protracted standoff over crafting clean-air legislation.

As ninth-ranking Democrat on Energy and Commerce, Swift does not have enough seniority to chair a subcommittee, but he has still earned respect for his legislative activity on the panel. That respect, as well as the personal relationships he has forged, helped Swift become de facto chairman of a caucus of nine moderate-to-conservative committee Democrats, who organized in the 100th Congress to try to break a six-year deadlock on reauthorizing the Clean Air Act. Their work on the intractable issue was regarded as impressive, and though no bill passed in 1988, the issue was rejoined in the 101st Congress.

Clean-air legislation has been stalled by a dispute on Energy and Commerce between an environmentalist faction, led by California Democrat Henry A. Waxman, that seeks tougher anti-smog and anti-acid rain measures, and a more industry-oriented faction led by powerful committee Chairman John D. Dingell. Swift's frustration with the stalemate was evident in 1986 when he voted for a Waxman bill he opposed simply to get some vehicle out of committee.

In the 100th Congress, Swift began working behind the scenes with the so-called "group of nine" to find common ground that had eluded Dingell and Waxman. "We didn't see where anything was going to happen if there wasn't a third force," Swift said at the time.

The group hammered out a detailed, 77-page, single-spaced proposal for addressing urban smog, but not acid rain. More than 100 cities were facing federal penalties for noncompliance with air quality standards, and the "group of nine" proposal generally stretched out the timetable for them to meet the standards and imposed somewhat less stringent controls.

Dingell and Waxman both had some disagreements with the proposal, but for a time the group's plan seemed to have a chance. Toward the end of the Congress, however, clean-air talks stalled in both the House and the Senate.

One of Swift's favorite legislative subjects is broadcast deregulation, which emerged as an issue in 1984 after the Federal Communications Commission repealed federal guidelines for TV commercials and public-affairs programming. In general, the battle lines on broadcast deregulation have been drawn between "public interest" forces and those more sympathetic to the broadcast industry. The public-interest side has insisted on strict requirements for news and public-affairs programs, along with a competitive broadcast license-renewal process. The industry has resisted this. Swift has favored a middle-ground approach that would require the FCC to set broad categories of public-interest standards but would drop competitive license renewals.

Swift is involved in numerous communications issues. Since the court-imposed AT&T breakup, he has worked to see that Congress, not the courts, sets telecommunications policy. In recent Congresses he has joined with Republican Tom Tauke of Iowa on legislation to try to decrease local phone rates by allowing regional phone companies to engage in new businesses and expand their revenue bases.

Swift's position on Energy and Commerce also gives him an opportunity to get involved in nuclear-waste issues. That is a hot topic in Washington state, which was one of three possible locations for a high-level nuclear-waste site. In the 100th Congress, though, Swift was active in the effort to make Nevada the designated waste site.

Although Energy and Commerce is involved in enough issues to fill any legislator's schedule, Swift is also an active participant on

Washington 2

Northwest — Everett; Part of Olympic Peninsula

The geographic and political focal point of the 2nd is blue-collar Everett, a city of 60,000 that was built by the timber and shipping industries. Labor conflict plagued those industries between the two world wars, and unions became the basis of the local Democratic strength.

But the blue-collar tendency to vote Democratic is tempered by the reliance on defense-related industry, which has prospered under Republican White House rule. Everett is the site of a new Navy "home-port," and since the 1960s, the city has been closely linked with Boeing's aircraft plants. Electronics and high-technology industries round out Everett's newly diversified economic base.

Everett and surrounding Snohomish County cast about one-third of the district's vote (the populous Seattle suburbs in the southern part of Snohomish are in the neighboring 1st District). The whole county tends to be Republican-leaning, but competitive, in statewide contests. George Bush carried the county with 51 percent in 1988, while GOP Senate winner Slade Gorton took 52 percent.

The second-largest block of 2nd District votes comes from Whatcom County, at the northern edge of the district along the Canadian border. Bellingham (population 45,000), Swift's home base, is dependent on timber, though it also is home to shipping and canning industries. Like most of the northern coast area, it has a large population of Scandinavian descent, especially Norwegian. Michael S. Dukakis took 52 percent of the presidential vote in Whatcom County, breaking a three-election GOP winning streak. Between Snohomish and Whatcom is Skagit County, a more rural and regularly Republican area.

The Olympic Peninsula portion of the 2nd is a lightly populated place of mountains, forests and coastal communities in Clallam, Jefferson and Mason counties. Most of Grays Harbor County is also in the 2nd.

Island County, located between Juan de Fuca Strait and Puget Sound, is still largely a rain-soaked preserve of vegetable farms and forested land. But its position at the edge of the Seattle metropolis has brought it some of that area's rapid growth; population jumped there by 13 percent, to nearly 50,000, between 1980 and 1986. Bush took 60 percent there in 1988.

San Juan County, made up of a chain of islands, has also seen some growth. But it remains mostly rural and lightly populated.

Population: 516,568. White 490,840 (95%), Black 2,501 (1%), Other 17,453 (3%). Spanish origin 9,511 (2%). 18 and over 373,304 (72%), 65 and over 62,626 (12%). Median age: 30.

the House Administration Committee, where he chairs the Elections Subcommittee.

Swift has been at the center of efforts to prevent the TV networks from projecting presidential election outcomes while polling places are still open. He won pledges from the three major networks in 1985 that they would not forecast results for any state while its polls are open. Since then, he has lobbied persistently for a bill that would close all polls in the continental United States simultaneously at 9 p.m. EST in presidential election years.

Critics have derided the so-called "uniform poll closing" measure as "social tinkering" to satisfy "a few people on the West Coast." But the measure satisfied enough members from other regions to pass the House in the 99th and 100th Congresses. Both times it died in the Senate, but Swift renewed his effort in 1989 and won House passage again early in the year.

Swift is also a player in the effort to overhaul campaign-finance laws. While some have pushed to reduce the cost of campaigns through a public-financing mechanism, Swift in the 100th Congress introduced legislation to grant discount mailing and broadcast advertising rates to candidates who accept spending limits.

Swift started in Congress as a protégé of Sen. Warren G. Magnuson, who pulled levers on the opposite side of the Capitol to help him get on Commerce as a freshman.

Swift was the only legislator from his state on the panel in the 96th Congress as it took up the Northwest power bill. The legislation, designed to allocate scarce power resources in Washington and Oregon, was very controversial in those states, but attracted little attention elsewhere. The committee largely left it to Swift to build a regional consensus behind some sort of bill. The compromise Swift finally got through committee was backed by public and private utilities, but many environmentalists and consumer advocates said it gave too great a role to nuclear power and was too generous to private power companies.

At Home: Starting out as a disc jockey after graduating from college, Swift spent more than a decade learning the broadcast trade at KVOS-TV in Bellingham, interspersing his progress there with two separate stints as administrative assistant to the local Democratic congressman, Lloyd Meeds.

By the time he decided to try for Congress in 1978, upon Meeds' retirement, Swift had a decade as a TV news director to his credit, and was familiar to viewers along Puget Sound.

But he was considered a long shot, because the Democratic field also included Brian Corcoran, longtime press secretary to Sen. Henry M. Jackson. Corcoran had Jackson's good will and tapped the senator's contributors. He had a weakness, though, in his tepid personal manner and inarticulate speaking style.

Swift, armed with the self-confidence generated by years in front of the camera, was the perfect challenger to take advantage of the problem. Starting from far behind, Swift defeated Corcoran by 3,881 votes.

Swift's next hurdle was Republican John Nance Garner, a namesake and distant relative of Franklin D. Roosevelt's vice president. Garner had nearly ousted Meeds in 1976, mainly because fishermen in the 2nd felt Meeds had not fought hard enough for them against Indian fishing claims. Garner spent lavishly against Swift in 1978, but no longer had the fishing-rights issue; Swift took a position similar to his. Swift attacked Garner's heavy spending, turning a supposed advantage into a liability. The outcome was a 51 percent victory for Swift.

In the five elections since then, Swift has never dipped below 59 percent of the vote. After GOP Sen. Daniel J. Evans announced plans to retire in 1988, Swift considered running for his seat, but demurred when two Democratic House colleagues, Mike Lowry and Don Bonker, jumped into the primary.

Committees

Energy and Commerce (9th of 26 Democrats)
Energy and Power; Telecommunications and Finance; Transportation and Hazardous Materials

House Administration (5th of 13 Democrats)
Elections (chairman); Accounts

Elections

1988 General		
Al Swift (D)	175,191	(100%)
1986 General		
Al Swift (D)	124,840	(72%)
Thomas S. Talman (R)	48,077	(28%)

Previous Winning Percentages: 1984 (59%) **1982** (60%) **1980** (64%) **1978** (51%)

District Vote For President

	1988	1984
D	120,129 (50%)	104,670 (44%)
R	118,711 (50%)	130,640 (55%)

Campaign Finance

	Receipts	Receipts from PACs	Expend-itures
1988			
Swift (D)	$376,189	$286,312 (76%)	$301,229
1986			
Swift (D)	$264,928	$167,575 (63%)	$239,341
Talman (R)	$5,926	$81 (1%)	$5,926

Key Votes

1987	
Raise speed limit to 65 mph	Y
Approve Gephardt "fair trade" amendment	N
Ban testing of larger nuclear weapons	Y
Delay "re-flagging" of Kuwaiti tankers	Y
Approve tax-raising deficit-reduction bill	Y
1988	
Approve aid to Nicaraguan contras	N
Enact civil rights restoration bill over Reagan veto	Y
Kill 60-day plant-closing notification measure	N
Pass omnibus trade bill over Reagan veto	Y
Approve death penalty for drug-related murders	?
Bar federal funds for abortions in cases of rape and incest	N
Oppose seven-day waiting period for purchase of handguns	N

Voting Studies

	Presidential Support		Party Unity		Conservative Coalition	
Year	**S**	**O**	**S**	**O**	**S**	**O**
1988	23	72	92	4	16	76
1987	21	78	92	4	21	77
1986	19	78	93	4	22	76
1985	26	73	93	5	29	69
1984	33	65	91†	7†	22	78
1983	18	80	91	4	11	89
1982	42	56	90	7	26	73
1981	43	55	86	14	31	69

† Not eligible for all recorded votes.

Interest Group Ratings

Year	ADA	ACU	AFL-CIO	CCUS
1988	90	0	85	36
1987	92	9	88	23
1986	90	9	79	18
1985	75	14	76	27
1984	80	4	77	33
1983	90	0	100	25
1982	85	14	100	23
1981	85	13	80	21

3 Jolene Unsoeld (D)

Of Olympia — Elected 1988

Born: Dec. 3, 1931, Corvallis, Ore.
Education: Attended Oregon State U., 1950-51.
Occupation: Public official.
Family: Widowed; three children.
Religion: Theist.
Political Career: Democratic National Committee member, 1983-88; Wash. House, 1985-89.
Capitol Office: 1508 Longworth Bldg. 20515; 225-3536.

The Path to Washington: The 1988 election was a resounding success for Unsoeld the environmentalist. Initiative 97 — a measure she wrote that would create a state toxic-waste cleanup program — passed easily despite corporate opposition.

But for Unsoeld the House candidate, the 1988 election was considerably more trying. Favored to succeed Democratic Rep. Don Bonker, who ran for the Senate, Unsoeld barely held off a charge by Republican Bill Wight. Her 618-vote victory was not confirmed until a recount was completed more than five weeks after the election.

Unsoeld was not expected to have such difficulty in the reliably Democratic 3rd. But Bonker, a low-key specialist in trade issues, was regarded as a moderate, while Unsoeld, with her ties to environmental and feminist groups, was seen mainly as a liberal activist. Wight's portrayal of Unsoeld as an ideologue apparently struck a nerve with many conservative, blue-collar Democrats.

Unsoeld entered public life as an independent lobbyist in the state capital of Olympia on "good government" issues. She first earned media attention as an advocate of campaign-finance reform. In the 1970s, she published lists of interest-group contributions to state legislators. Unsoeld also was involved in environmental causes, an interest stemming in part from her love of the outdoors. She is the widow of Willi Unsoeld, who was among the first Americans to climb Mount Everest, and Unsoeld herself was an avid mountain climber.

Unsoeld's lobbying earned her a following among liberal activists, and a state position on the Democratic National Committee. She entered elective politics in 1984, winning an open state House seat from Olympia.

Though active on such issues as child care and education, Unsoeld was best known for her legislative work on the environment. In 1987, she proposed a bill requiring polluters to clean up toxic-waste sites and creating a cleanup fund by levying a tax on the sale of hazardous substances. When the Legislature opted for what she regarded as a weaker bill, Unsoeld staged a campaign to get her proposal on the 1988 ballot as Initiative 97.

Unsoeld also entered the contest for Bonker's open seat. Though her primary opponent, Clark County Commissioner John McKibbin, portrayed her as confrontational and antagonistic to business, Unsoeld's base of liberal activists in the Democratic Party carried her through to the nomination.

However, Wight used the same tactic to greater effect. While portraying Unsoeld as an extremist, Wight came off as thoughtful and more moderate than previous GOP nominees in the 3rd, who were hard-line conservatives. A native of the district who returned in 1988, Wight was a West Point graduate, a retired Army lieutenant colonel, a Pentagon congressional liaison on the strategic defense initiative and an adviser to GOP Sen. John W. Warner of Virginia. But Wight did not highlight defense in his campaign, emphasizing instead his ideas for economic development and prevention of drug-related crime.

Unsoeld noted that Wight had not lived in the district since high school and described him as "the hometown boy from the Pentagon." But Wight's determination earned him attention from the local media, and an infusion of money from national GOP campaign officials in Washington, D.C.

Unsoeld held an election night lead of over 1,800 votes, but absentee ballots sliced into that advantage. Unsoeld won 53 percent of the vote in Thurston County (Olympia), and won the Democratic coastal counties. However, Wight won narrowly in Clark County (Vancouver) and nearly pulled off the upset by dominating Lewis County, carrying his base by a 2-to-1 margin.

As a freshman, Unsoeld will be working from the Merchant Marine and Fisheries Committee (on which Bonker had served) as well as the Education and Labor Committee to shore up her support at home.

Washington 3

Southwest — Olympia; Vancouver

The 3rd, stretching from Puget Sound west to the Pacific and south to the Columbia River border with Oregon, is heavy with maritime and timber interests. With its large number of blue-collar voters, it contains some of the most Democratic territory in the state.

In 1988, Democrat Michael S. Dukakis won in all but one of the eight counties that make up the 3rd. The three counties in the southwest corner — Cowlitz, Pacific and Wahkiakum — voted for Walter F. Mondale for president in 1984.

About two-thirds of the district vote comes from two counties: Thurston (Olympia) in the northern end, and Clark (Vancouver) in the south. Dukakis won each, but with narrow majorities.

Olympia, the state capital, is the largest city in Thurston County, but with only 30,000 people, it has a small-town atmosphere. Olympia's communities of environmental and "good government" activists — from which Unsoeld emerged — give Democrats a leg up in the county.

Clark County has seen its population surge with the growth of its Portland, Ore., suburbs. The aluminum industry is strong along the Columbia River. Vancouver, the district's largest city with 44,000 residents, is an industrial center.

The 3rd has vast stretches of woodland, including the scenic Coastal Range and much of the Cascade Mountains, with Mount Rainier just outside the eastern border. Timber thus dominates the economy of the interior, and in recent years, there have been more downs than ups. The area's mills produce paper, timber and cardboard under the state's strict water-pollution standards. Logging is the central activity of Cowlitz County, which includes the cities of Longview and Kelso. Along the coast, fishing and dockwork are predominant, and labor unions are well entrenched among longshoremen.

Rural Lewis County provides the only dependable GOP majorities in the 3rd. George Bush took 62 percent there in 1988.

Population: 516,473. White 495,809 (96%), Black 3,070 (1%), Other 12,496 (2%). Spanish origin 8,264 (2%). 18 and over 360,673 (70%), 65 and over 55,166 (11%). Median age: 30.

Committees

Education and Labor (17th of 22 Democrats)
Elementary, Secondary and Vocational Education; Health and Safety; Human Resources

Merchant Marine and Fisheries (26th of 26 Democrats)
Fisheries and Wildlife Conservation and the Environment; Merchant Marine

Select Aging (38th of 39 Democrats)
Housing and Consumer Interests

Campaign Finance

	Receipts	Receipts from PACs	Expend-itures
1988			
Unsoeld (D)	$690,711	$282,082 (41%)	$687,117
Wight (R)	$354,499	$161,379 (46%)	$354,142

Elections

1988 General		
Jolene Unsoeld (D)	109,412	(50%)
Bill Wight (R)	108,794	(50%)
1988 Primary †		
Jolene Unsoeld (D)	44,838	(40%)
John McKibbin (D)	30,112	(27%)
Bill Wight (R)	21,509	(19%)
Bill Hughes (R)	12,532	(11%)
John Libby Sr. (D)	4,112	(4%)

† In Washington's "jungle primary," candidates of both parties are listed on one ballot.

District Vote For President

	1988	1984
D	109,731 (52%)	96,470 (45%)
R	108,290 (47%)	113,754 (53%)

4 Sid Morrison (R)

Of Zillah — Elected 1980

Born: May 13, 1933, Yakima, Wash.
Education: Attended Yakima Valley College, 1951; Washington State U., B.S. 1954.
Military Career: Army, 1954-56.
Occupation: Fruit grower; nurseryman.
Family: Wife, Marcella Britton; four children.
Religion: Methodist.
Political Career: Wash. House, 1967-75; Wash. Senate, 1975-81.
Capitol Office: 1434 Longworth Bldg. 20515; 225-5816.

In Washington: Morrison's sprawling district forces him to focus his attention in two very different directions. Many 4th District residents are, like Morrison, fruit growers, and he must watch out for their interests on the Agriculture Committee. But many of his constituents also depend on nuclear-related jobs for their livelihood, putting pressure on Morrison to be one of the industry's big boosters. Working for both of those constituencies is not easy, but it has made him an important player in two national issues.

The 1980s were rough for many in the nuclear industry, and that was particularly true at the Hanford Nuclear Reservation in the Tri-Cities area of the 4th. Concerns about safety and about job losses have made Hanford a hot political issue in both Washington and Oregon.

The Tri-Cities received a major blow in 1988, when the Department of Energy (DOE) decided to mothball the "N Reactor," which is the centerpiece of the plutonium-production complex. Morrison, who is ranking Republican on the Science Subcommittee on Energy Research and Development, has advocated restarting the reactor, but switching its product from plutonium to tritium, which is crucial to hydrogen bombs. But he has had to settle for DOE's decision to maintain the reactor for possible future use.

Morrison has also worked to convince DOE that its plan for a new tritium-producing reactor would best be served by converting a mothballed civilian reactor in his district. Morrison says the converted reactor could be on-line two to three times faster than a new project. But he has had to wage his battle on two fronts — not only trying to convince DOE, but also trying to win over some congressional colleagues from his state and from neighboring Oregon. South Carolina, which is also lobbying for the tritium reactor, has been able to put up a solid front of support.

"I'm not willing to hand over the new production reactor to any other state which may offer a unified front," Morrison said in the 100th Congress. But in 1988 DOE made an initial recommendation that South Carolina and Idaho would be superior locations for new facilities.

While continuing his efforts to bring in tritium-production facilities, Morrison is also in pursuit of money to clean up the Hanford Reservation, and on the lookout for new missions for the area, which has now lost thousands of jobs. One idea he pushed in 1988 was for a pilot project to test the possibility of destroying plutonium from dismantled warheads in a Hanford reactor. The idea, which came in the wake of arms control advances, even won praise from some of the anti-nuclear groups that are usually at odds with Morrison.

In 1982, Morrison surprised many of his colleagues when he authored an amendment to ensure that Hanford would be considered as a possible site for the nation's first high-level nuclear-waste facility. Most members at the time were working to keep any of that waste from coming their direction, and had little objection to the amendment, which expedited "site characterization" work at Hanford.

"We don't want to be the nuclear dump for the world, but we are comfortable with nuclear energy," Morrison said, while also stressing that Hanford should not be the only waste site.

By 1986, however, Morrison was displaying considerably more discomfort with Hanford's selection as one of three possible sites for the proposed nuclear dump. Although the plan remained popular with some constituents who saw it as a source of jobs, there was growing controversy in other parts of central Washington over the handling of nuclear waste at Hanford. Morrison eventually turned against the plan, and was relieved in the 100th Congress when legislators agreed to put the waste site in Nevada.

One of Morrison's most significant legislative accomplishments stemmed from his interest in agriculture, but it did not directly involve farm policy. Morrison took a keen interest in immigration legislation that threatened grow-

Washington 4

Central — Yakima; Tri-Cities

For nearly four decades, the Hanford Nuclear Reservation — site of much of the nation's nuclear weapons-materials production — was the healthy heart of a booming local economy in the Tri-Cities of Pasco, Kennewick and Richland. But these cities, located in the southeastern part of the 4th District, have been rocked in recent years by news that this economic heart, suffering from severe environment-related problems, needs surgery, if not a transplant.

In 1988, the federal government shut down Hanford's "N Reactor," a plutonium plant likened in design to the reactor in the Soviet city of Chernobyl, site of the world's worst nuclear accident. The shutdown resulted in the loss of 5,000 jobs, a huge setback in a two-county (Benton and Franklin) area of about 150,000 residents.

The Department of Energy then estimated that the cleanup of radioactive and other hazardous wastes that had accumulated at Hanford over the years would cost more than $57 billion to clean up. In February 1989, the state and federal governments reached agreement on a cleanup plan, which would return 2,000 jobs to the Hanford area. The project is expected to take at least 30 years to complete.

Earlier, Hanford was a key issue in the 1986 Senate race. The federal reservation was then being mentioned as a possible site for a permanent nuclear-waste depository, and Republican Sen. Slade Gorton took some blame from state voters for its inclusion on the list. Gorton was defeated that year by Democrat Brock Adams. By the time of Gorton's comeback victory in 1988, though, Hanford had been eliminated as a waste-dump site.

Though Gorton — who, while out of office, acted as a consultant to Hanford on efforts to keep its nuclear industry alive — may have some problems elsewhere in the state, he has solid support in the Tri-Cities. In 1988, he carried Benton and Franklin counties, where Republican tendencies are strong to begin with, with a combined 79 percent of the vote. George Bush won the counties with 64 percent.

The GOP also dominates Yakima County, one of the nation's premier apple-growing areas. The county, which includes the district's largest city, Yakima (population 49,000), gave Bush 56 percent.

The district contains a famous example of man's effort to control nature, and another of his limited ability to do so. On the Columbia River in Grant County is the Grand Coulee Dam, one of the largest construction projects in human history. But in the southwest corner of the district is Mount St. Helens, site of the explosive 1980 volcanic eruption that killed dozens of people and felled thousands of acres of timber.

Population: 516,426. White 463,119 (90%), Black 4,721 (1%), Other 16,897 (3%). Spanish origin 44,562 (9%). 18 and over 359,287 (70%), 65 and over 54,379 (11%). Median age: 29.

ers' ability to use foreign laborers to harvest crops. To maintain growers' ready access to "undocumented workers," Morrison joined forces with California Democrat Leon E. Panetta.

Rather than opposing the immigration bill outright — a stand many growers endorsed — Panetta and Morrison expressed support for the twin goals of reform advocates — gaining control of U.S. borders and preventing the exploitation of illegal aliens. But they pleaded that it was unfair to deprive growers of their source of labor.

They argued for a "guest worker" program more flexible than what architects of immigration reform wanted. Morrison and Panetta were strongly opposed by labor, which wanted to protect the jobs of American citizens, and by Hispanics, who saw the guest worker system as perpetuating the bad pay and working conditions that field workers have endured.

But the lobbying combination of grower Morrison, a reasonable, moderate-to-conservative Republican, and lawyer Panetta, a Democrat with a reputation for integrity and compassion, was a persuasive one. They got their plan through to the conference, where the bill died because of a separate controversy.

Morrison's efforts were successful at moving debate on the issue to a new point, making it a certainty that foreign worker provisions would be a part of the immigration bill debate in the 99th Congress. Having accomplished that, Morrison took less of a leadership role on the bill that passed in 1986, but he did participate in some key negotiations on the legislation.

Morrison has been less visible on most issues before the Agriculture Committee. Representing mostly growers of unsubsidized commodities, Morrison has more leeway to defend free-market principles than some of his Republican colleagues from wheat- and corn-growing districts. But he also has worked well with Washington Democratic colleague Thomas

S. Foley, who is from a neighboring district and is a major player on agricultural issues.

Morrison does make some conspicuous departures from the free-market approach. One of his main concerns on the committee has been to maintain marketing orders, which were unpopular with the Reagan administration. Those marketing orders, which may be imposed by a vote of growers of some commodities, essentially result in limits on production and on the number of producers.

At Home: Morrison's 1980 victory ended the 10-year reign of Democratic Rep. Mike McCormack, whose survival in the GOP-leaning 4th rested largely on the federal aid he funneled to the area's nuclear industry.

Nuclear power was not at issue in 1980, since both candidates advocated it. Morrison instead chastised McCormack for being too frugal on defense spending. With help from a $400,000 treasury and a GOP surge that brought Washington Republicans the governorship and a U.S. Senate seat, Morrison won 57 percent. He scored 70 percent or better in his next three re-elections.

In late 1987, Republican Sen. Daniel J. Evans announced he would not seek re-election the following year. With former GOP Sen. Slade Gorton, who was unseated by Democrat Brock Adams in 1986, apparently in eclipse, Morrison was urged by party allies to run for the seat.

But Morrison, with his base in Washington's "Eastside," recognized that he was not well-known in the important Seattle media market, and conceded that his close identification with Hanford would likely make his a controversial candidacy. He declined to enter the Senate race, opting instead for another easy House campaign. Meanwhile, Gorton re-emerged in the Senate contest and staged a successful comeback, defeating Democratic Rep. Mike Lowry.

Morrison's 14 years in the Washington Legislature prepared him for a House career. He forged a reputation in Olympia as an articulate centrist. As chairman of the state Senate Labor Committee, he sought to restrain unemployment compensation costs, but backed state housing subsidies for migrant laborers.

Committees

Agriculture (8th of 18 Republicans)
Forests, Family Farms and Energy (ranking); Conservation, Credit and Rural Development; Department Operations, Research and Foreign Agriculture

Science, Space and Technology (7th of 19 Republicans)
Energy Research and Development (ranking); Natural Resources, Agriculture Research and Environment

Select Hunger (3rd of 12 Republicans)
Task Forces: Domestic; International

Elections

1988 General		
Sid Morrison (R)	142,938	(75%)
J. Richard Golob (D)	48,850	(25%)
1988 Primary †		
Sid Morrison (R)	72,633	(73%)
J. Richard Golob (D)	26,638	(27%)
1986 General		
Sid Morrison (R)	107,593	(72%)
Robert Goedecke (D)	41,709	(28%)

† In Washington's "jungle primary," candidates of both parties are listed on one ballot.

Previous Winning Percentages: **1984** (76%) **1982** (70%) **1980** (57%)

District Vote For President

	1988	1984
D	78,620 (42%)	74,423 (35%)
R	108,969 (58%)	134,302 (63%)

Campaign Finance

	Receipts	Receipts from PACs	Expenditures
1988			
Morrison (R)	$202,637	$82,558 (41%)	$194,505
Golob (D)	$58,608	$5,750 (10%)	$58,574
1986			
Morrison (R)	$179,274	$70,244 (39%)	$105,513
Goedecke (D)	$5,246	0	$5,142

Key Votes

1987	
Raise speed limit to 65 mph	Y
Approve Gephardt "fair trade" amendment	N
Ban testing of larger nuclear weapons	N
Delay "re-flagging" of Kuwaiti tankers	N
Approve tax-raising deficit-reduction bill	N
1988	
Approve aid to Nicaraguan contras	Y
Enact civil rights restoration bill over Reagan veto	Y
Kill 60-day plant-closing notification measure	Y
Pass omnibus trade bill over Reagan veto	N
Approve death penalty for drug-related murders	Y
Bar federal funds for abortions in cases of rape and incest	N
Oppose seven-day waiting period for purchase of handguns	Y

Voting Studies

	Presidential Support		Party Unity		Conservative Coalition	
Year	S	O	S	O	S	O
1988	47	52	59	40	87	13
1987	52	46	52	43	86	12
1986	59	41	56	42	80	18
1985	59	40	72	25	84	15
1984	60	38	63	35	85	14
1983	68	28	67	26	79	19
1982	70	29	78	22	89	11
1981	74	26	83	17	92	8

Interest Group Ratings

Year	ADA	ACU	AFL-CIO	CCUS
1988	55	64	36	93
1987	40	52	25	67
1986	25	73	38	67
1985	25	71	29	82
1984	40	46	38	75
1983	20	57	13	80
1982	10	62	25	73
1981	5	93	7	100

5 Thomas S. Foley (D)

Of Spokane — Elected 1964

Born: March 6, 1929, Spokane, Wash.
Education: U. of Washington, B.A. 1951, LL.B. 1957.
Occupation: Lawyer.
Family: Wife, Heather Strachan.
Religion: Roman Catholic.
Political Career: No previous office.
Capitol Office: 1201 Longworth Bldg. 20515; 225-2006.

In Washington: If in politics it is better to be lucky than good, Foley must be said to have been extraordinarily both. For years, his admirers — Democratic and Republican, academic and journalistic — have called him uniquely qualified to be Speaker of the House. A cerebral man with a sense of detachment rare among politicians, Foley is perfectly matched to a job meant to be above partisanship. Yet it was fortune, finally, that elevated him to the pinnacle of power in Congress.

Foley became Speaker on June 6, 1989, following the resignation of Jim Wright of Texas, who decided to leave Congress rather than continue fighting charges he had violated House ethics rules. Most observers had expected Wright to serve multiple terms as Speaker, leaving little if any time for Foley to hold the job. Instead, the Texan became the first Speaker ever forced from office in disgrace. His departure left the House boiling with the bitterest interparty resentments in many years.

This was the cauldron Foley inherited. The majority leader since 1987, he was in line to succeed Wright and was the unanimous choice of his party. The gavel came to him on a party-line vote of 251-164.

Foley had been following Wright in the Democrats' batting order since 1981, when former Speaker Thomas P. O'Neill Jr. chose him as majority whip (with Wright's assent). There is no evidence that Foley actively sought the whip job at that time. Nor has he been perceived as pursuing any of the other posts he has won before or since.

It may be the supreme irony of Foley's career that he has risen to be second in line to the presidency (after the vice president) without having once displayed the kind of vaunting ambition usually associated with such success. Even his first candidacy for Congress in 1964 was reluctantly undertaken at the urging of others.

Since then, Foley has generally enjoyed lopsided re-election victories in his basically Republican district. He became a subcommittee chairman on the Agriculture Committee, then chairman of the Democratic Study Group, chairman of the full Agriculture Committee and chairman of the House Democratic Caucus before becoming whip.

Throughout his rise, Foley has been on good terms with nearly all Democrats and a remarkable number of Republicans, who typically refer to him as their party's favorite Democrat. But even this was not enough to keep Foley's elevation to Speaker from being a troubled event for the House.

Foley's apotheosis was preceded not only by Wright's spectacular fall but also by that of Tony Coelho of California, who had succeeded Foley as whip. Coelho, a hard-driven fund-raiser who had propelled the party's congressional electoral successes, announced in May 1989 that he would resign rather than face a lengthy inquiry into his personal financial dealings by the House ethics committee.

Foley appeared to offer battered Democrats the hope of healing. To Republicans, he offered his reputation for rising above partisanship. In his first remarks as Speaker, he called for debate "with reason and without rancor."

But even in the first hours of his speakership he was confronted with a partisan assault. A memo circulated by the Republican National Committee's (RNC) press office referred to Foley as "coming out of the liberal closet." It also compared him to Barney Frank of Massachusetts, a liberal who has publicly declared himself a homosexual.

President Bush pronounced the memo "disgusting" and its author promptly resigned. But Bush exonerated RNC Chairman Lee Atwater, and that kept many Democrats in the House fuming, threatening to exact revenge on Bush's legislative agenda.

Foley, in a characteristic response, calmly denied the memo's implication and accepted the apologies of embarrassed Republicans. "A very cheap smear," he said. "I think the issue is closed."

It may be that the personal attack, and the ensuing outrage and shame, released some of the pressure that had built in the House during Wright's yearlong ethics trauma. Foley himself had survived these months of limbo with both

Washington 5

East — Spokane

The dominance of Democrat Foley in heavily rural eastern Washington is a bit of an anomaly. Though Democrats running for higher office can compete here, the 5th has a definite Republican tilt in contests for president and senator.

In 1984, President Reagan took the 5th District with 60 percent of the vote. Democrat Michael S. Dukakis put up a battle four years later, but George Bush held the district with 51 percent. That year's Republican Senate victor, Slade Gorton, did even better, taking the 5th with 53 percent. Democratic Gov. Booth Gardner won here, as he did throughout the state, but with a margin that fell short of his landslide advantages elsewhere.

The candidate who wins Spokane is almost certain to carry the district. The city of 173,000 is Washington's second largest. Spokane County, one of 11 counties in the district, contributes two-thirds of the district vote. Bush won the county in 1988, but just barely: His margin was 267 votes out of over 137,000 cast.

Spokane is the banking and marketing center of the "Inland Empire," which encompasses wheat- and vegetable-farming counties in Washington, Oregon, Idaho and Montana. The city's sizable aluminum industry takes advantage of the low-cost hydroelectric power that comes from New Deal dams along the Columbia River. Comparatively isolated and marked by a stable, non-transient population, Spokane is one of the most conservative of America's large cities.

Walla Walla County, dominated for generations by a small group of farming families, bolsters Republican chances in the district. Bush got 57 percent in the county in 1988; Reagan took 65 percent in 1984. The district's third-largest county, Whitman, is the site of Washington State University (16,000 students) in Pullman. Republicans usually win Whitman, but do not necessarily dominate; Bush carried the county with 51 percent.

The rest of the district is mainly rural, sparsely populated and generally Republican. But Ferry County, in the district's northwest corner, could not have been more evenly split in 1988; Bush and Dukakis each received 972 votes.

Population: 516,719. White 489,609 (95%), Black 5,705 (1%), Other 13,486 (3%). Spanish origin 11,700 (2%). 18 and over 373,789 (72%), 65 and over 59,889 (12%). Median age: 29.

his loyalty to Wright and his personal integrity intact. And if anyone in the House is capable of transcending such a bizarre beginning and returning matters to normal, Foley should be.

As a parliamentarian and negotiator, he ranks as high as any member of Congress in recent years. He grew up wanting to be a judge, and sometimes it seems he still wants to be one, even in a political setting. He does not like to commit himself early on controversial issues, and he can be as skillful at making the case for the opposing side as for his own. "I think I am a little cursed," he once said, "with seeing the other point of view and trying to understand it."

Such caution can be frustrating to colleagues, but was also a valuable counterweight to the impulsive and aggressive style to which Wright and Coelho were often prone. If Wright was a legislative activist who could be rash, Foley is a gradualist, skeptical of grand schemes and inclined at times to ask whether difficult problems can be solved legislatively at all. As he said of the 1985 farm bill he helped craft: "There is only so much that government policy can do. An agriculture bill can't turn around world economic decisions."

Foley recalls O'Neill in his imposing physical size (he is more than 6 foot 3 inches and well over 200 pounds) and disarming affability. But he contrasts with the man who started him on the leadership ladder in that he hails from the Far West (the first Speaker from west of the Rocky Mountains). His district thrives on water power and wheat, and his voting patterns have long reflected his constituents' disdain for gun control and other forms of federal intervention.

But if he is a Westerner by birth and bidding, Foley's guiding philosophy has always been consensus politics. "Heightening tension is just another technique," Foley says, "and it is not one I find particularly congenial."

Foley is admired not only for his temperament but for the superior quality of his mind. Staff members say he can leave a meeting and repeat almost verbatim what each participant said. Even rarer than such intelligence, in the House, is Foley's intellectuality. He has an interest in ideas and a taste for the arts. His conversation is rich with select words and historical allusions. An audiophile, his expensive equipment is primarily devoted to classical fare.

He is not comfortable with the backslapping and small talk of political discourse. He generally campaigns in a suit and wing-tip shoes, even in the rural stretches of his mammoth district. He has never been one for news releases or self promotion; when he became Agriculture chairman in 1975 he called reporters into his office one by one to avoid having to hold a press conference.

Foley has risen slowly and cautiously in Democratic ranks, taking advantage of his reputation as a good legislative manager. In 1974 he chaired the Democratic Study Group, the strategy and research arm of liberal and moderate Democrats. In 1977 the chairmanship of the Democratic Caucus was open, and as a veteran of numerous reform battles against secrecy and seniority in the committee system, he was a logical choice. He defeated Shirley Chisholm of New York by a vote of 194-96. His four years as chairman were not particularly lively; few important decisions were made and Foley chose not to be an activist.

In 1981 the defeat of John Brademas of Indiana forced Speaker O'Neill to choose a new whip. Chief Deputy Whip Dan Rostenkowski of Illinois, first in line for promotion, decided instead to take over the Ways and Means Committee. Some Democrats urged O'Neill to select a whip from among the 1970s Democratic generation, but O'Neill was looking for parliamentary skill in the coming arguments with House Republicans. Foley was a parliamentary expert, and he got the job.

Once firmly established on the leadership ladder, he solidified his support with deft handling of several major legislative issues in the 99th Congress. He played a crucial role in drafting the 1985 farm bill and was active in House Democrats' fight against providing military aid to the Nicaraguan contras.

His consensus-building skills proved essential to the House leadership's strategy for handling the Gramm-Rudman-Hollings budget-cutting measure after it was passed by the Senate. Some House Democrats wished simply to oppose the measure and wanted no part of making it more palatable. But Foley's head counts showed Gramm-Rudman could not be defeated outright.

As chairman of a task force to devise a Democratic alternative, Foley tried to make the best of what he saw as a bad deal. He coaxed a consensus out of liberal and conservative Democrats about what changes should be made in the law — such as protections for certain anti-poverty programs — and the House alternative won the support of all but two Democrats.

When Speaker O'Neill first announced his plan to retire at the end of the 99th Congress, Foley did not seem to be guaranteed the No. 2 job in the ensuing leadership shake-up. Some members initially expressed a desire for a more partisan figure. But no challenger ever emerged and Foley was elected majority leader by acclamation.

As the 100th Congress began, Foley sometimes seemed uncomfortable as he sought to define a role for himself alongside Wright, who appeared reluctant to give up all the duties of majority leader upon his accession to the speakership. At times, Foley seemed to be trying out a more confrontational style, as when he concluded debate on aid to the Nicaraguan contras with a speech delivered at a decibel level unusual for him.

Sometimes, as floor leader, Foley appeared to be carrying out a strategy he personally questioned. He himself allows that the notorious "overtime" vote on the reconciliation bill of 1987 (which included a tax increase) had been a mistake. The leadership kept open the vote long enough for one Democrat to switch his "no" vote and pass the bill. Republicans cried foul, but Wright was not about to be denied passage of legislation he considered critical.

Foley is not renowned as a stirring orator, but in the past few years he has had his impressive moments of rhetoric, moments that have called for exactly the skills and style that he has to offer.

In 1982, President Reagan had been persuaded to support $98 billion worth of tax increases over a three-year period as a means of bringing down the federal deficit. Speaker O'Neill favored the plan and asked Foley to make the case for it on national television, hoping to create a climate in which wavering Democrats might go along with the legislation.

Foley responded with a masterful television speech, quietly urging members of both parties to summon up "political courage" and cast a vote in favor of "economic reality." He seemed far more comfortable delivering that speech than he had seemed offering more partisan rhetoric in other settings. Afterward, other Democrats speculated that he might have influenced 60 votes on their side of the aisle. Said O'Neill at the time: "A star is born."

As Speaker, Foley will have to abandon the agriculture issues that preoccupied him for much of his career. Foley was Agriculture Committee chairman from 1975 until 1981, when he gave up the chair to become Democratic whip. But he continued to be chairman of the Subcommittee on Wheat, Soybeans and Feed Grains until the 100th Congress, and still managed to have decisive influence on two major rewrites of federal farm programs in 1981 and 1985.

In 1985, Agriculture Chairman E. "Kika" de la Garza of Texas willingly deferred to Foley on the wheat section of the bill, one of the most delicate parts. Foley was at odds with younger Midwestern Democrats who, seeking dramatic changes in the farm programs, backed massive controls on grain production as a means of raising the market price for farmers. Foley did not fight the issue on the House floor, but in the end his work was done for him. A Republican-led coalition killed the production-control proposal during floor debate.

Foley was unable to attend many sessions of the House-Senate farm bill conference because Gramm-Rudman negotiations were going on at the same time. But when he and GOP Sen. Bob Dole of Kansas finally got together, they hammered out a compromise on key sections of the bill within hours.

Foley won the Agriculture chairmanship in 1975 in unusual circumstances that prefigured those that would make him Speaker 14 years later. The huge bloc of "Watergate baby" Democrats that year was determined to unseat some of the aging, conservative House chairmen. One of these was W. R. Poage of Texas, who, while popular within his Agriculture Committee, was 75 years old and highly conservative. The caucus unseated Poage by a vote of 152-133. Foley opposed the move and stood by the incumbent. He even gave Poage's nominating speech. But when Poage was beaten, the insurgents promoted Foley over several more senior members of the panel.

As chairman, Foley kept major farm bills under his control at the full committee level, rather than parceling them out to subcommittees as most chairmen now do. He was openly bipartisan, usually working out arrangements in advance with ranking Republican William C. Wampler of Virginia.

Foley was a strong Agriculture chairman — one of his best arguments against critics who said he would be indecisive in the leadership — but he operated almost entirely through conciliation. When circumstances seemed to require confrontation, he was less effective. Chairing a committee meeting, he was sometimes reluctant to bang the gavel even against a member who seemed to be asking for it.

For 10 years, Foley also sat on the Interior Committee. There he worked on enlarging the nation's largest power plant, the Grand Coulee Dam, and protecting Northwest water from raids by California and Arizona.

In 1980 Foley was a major sponsor of the Northwest Power bill, which was aimed at allocating scarce energy resources in the Pacific Northwest over the rest of this century. Foley was no longer on Interior, but much of the strategy was worked out in his office. A mini-filibuster delayed passage for a month, but Foley and others ultimately moved it through on a 284-77 vote.

Foley's most controversial moments in recent years involved his position on the MX missile. Along with Wright, he cast a vote for the weapon in May 1983, helping President Reagan win congressional permission to start conducting MX test flights. That angered much of the liberal element of the House Democratic Caucus, and first-term member Jim Bates of California demanded a caucus meeting to determine why party leaders were helping enact the Reagan defense program.

In the first vote after the caucus, Foley opposed the MX, and he has continued to do so ever since. He and Wright (who also changed his mind) insisted they were reacting to new arguments about the merits of the weapon, but it was also agreed that Foley and Wright were making the right political move as they prepared to run for leadership posts in a predominantly dovish House Democratic Party.

At Home: In the course of little more than a decade, Foley took over a Republican district, made himself invincible in it and then almost let it slip out of his hands. It took years of political repair work for him to get it under control again.

Foley wanted to be a judge, as was his father. He spent two years as deputy prosecutor in Spokane County and a year as assistant state attorney general. In 1961 he moved to Washington, D.C., to work for Sen. Henry M. Jackson as counsel to the Senate Interior Committee.

Three years later he was a reluctant congressional candidate, persuaded to run by the favorable political climate for Democrats, by Jackson's encouragement and by a Spokane politico who taunted him about the race on the day before the filing deadline. Foley managed to file with minutes to spare. He had no primary competition because no other Democrats wanted to challenge Republican Walt Horan, who had held the seat since 1942. But Horan was ailing at 66, and Foley had fund-raising help from Jackson and Sen. Warren Magnuson, as well as the advantage of the Johnson presidential landslide. He upset the incumbent in November by 12,000 votes.

After 1964, Foley worked hard to keep his district, and by 1970 Republicans had stopped running strong candidates against him.

But in 1976 he made a political mistake. Republican nominee Charles Kimball was killed in an airplane crash the month before the election, and Foley essentially stopped campaigning. That allowed Duane Alton, a politically unknown tire dealer from Spokane, to hold him under 60 percent of the vote.

The 1976 result convinced Republicans Foley was vulnerable, and Alton ran again in 1978. As Agriculture chairman, Foley had become a target for resentment over farm issues among his wheat-growing constituents, and his low profile in the district gave Alton another issue. Even worse for the incumbent, Indian tribal official Mel Tonasket ran as an independent and took away Democratic votes.

Alton was an inarticulate candidate, reluctant even to debate the man he was challenging, and his militant conservatism was too much for many moderate Republican voters. Yet Foley scraped by with just 48 percent to 43 percent for Alton.

Again in 1980, Republicans had high hopes. Foley's opponent this time was John

Sonneland, a Spokane surgeon who had once served as state co-chairman of Common Cause. Sonneland moved to the right, calling Foley a fiscally irresponsible liberal and airing television ads accusing the incumbent of having voted to allow experimentation on fetuses.

The incumbent campaigned hard, stressing his more conservative ideas, such as a tax cut and congressional veto of federal regulations produced by the executive branch. Foley recaptured most of the vote he had lost to Tonasket in 1978, but the GOP tide left him with the smallest margin of his career, scarcely 7,000 votes.

Sonneland was back in 1982, replacing the more strident personal attacks with attempts to convince voters that Foley had placed national interests above local concerns. "Do voters want to push someone who is ascending the political ladder," Sonneland asked during a debate, "or someone who will go to the mat?"

Such charges might have succeeded a few years earlier. But Sonneland's 1980 failure in a statewide Republican sweep marked him as a loser to national Republicans, hurting him financially. Meanwhile, Foley, chastened by a pair of close calls, paid renewed attention to the district. He not only trounced Sonneland by nearly 2-to-1 in their mutual home base of Spokane County, but also carried most of the 5th District's rural counties for the first time in several elections.

Thereafter, the respect Foley accrued, both nationally and locally, as an honest and temperate Democratic leader became his political armor. By 1984 he was up to 70 percent of the vote against Spokane City Councilman Jack Hebner. Foley won three-quarters of the vote in both 1986 and 1988.

Despite his rising prominence, Foley exhibited no more interest in running for statewide office than he did in suggestions from some quarters in 1988 that he would be an ideal vice presidential choice for Michael S. Dukakis. That same year, the retirement of GOP Sen. Daniel J. Evans left open the Senate seat once held by Foley's mentor Jackson. But early on, Foley made it abundantly clear he would not be a candidate in the Senate contest, which eventually was won by Republican Slade Gorton.

Speaker of the House

Elections

1988 General		
Thomas S. Foley (D)	160,654	(76%)
Marlyn A. Derby (R)	49,657	(24%)
1988 Primary †		
Thomas S. Foley (D)	81,223	(76%)
Marlyn A. Derby (R)	25,300	(24%)
1986 General		
Thomas S. Foley (D)	121,732	(75%)
Floyd L. Wakefield (R)	41,179	(25%)

† In Washington's "jungle primary," candidates of both parties are listed on one ballot.

Previous Winning Percentages: **1984** (70%) **1982** (64%) **1980** (52%) **1978** (48%) **1976** (58%) **1974** (64%) **1972** (81%) **1970** (67%) **1968** (57%) **1966** (57%) **1964** (53%)

District Vote For President

	1988	1984
D	98,331 (48%)	85,833 (39%)
R	103,841 (51%)	133,109 (60%)

Campaign Finance

	Receipts	Receipts from PACs	Expend-itures
1988			
Foley (D)	$968,013	$555,140 (57%)	$663,278
Derby (R)	$13,833	0	$13,534
1986			
Foley (D)	$539,651	$392,701 (73%)	$421,477
Wakefield (R)	$56,516	$2,289 (4%)	$56,502

Key Votes

1987	
Raise speed limit to 65 mph	N
Approve Gephardt "fair trade" amendment	N
Ban testing of larger nuclear weapons	Y
Delay "re-flagging" of Kuwaiti tankers	Y
Approve tax-raising deficit-reduction bill	Y
1988	
Approve aid to Nicaraguan contras	N
Enact civil rights restoration bill over Reagan veto	Y
Kill 60-day plant-closing notification measure	N
Pass omnibus trade bill over Reagan veto	Y
Approve death penalty for drug-related murders	N
Bar federal funds for abortions in cases of rape and incest	N
Oppose seven-day waiting period for purchase of handguns	Y

Voting Studies

	Presidential Support		Party Unity		Conservative Coalition	
Year	S	O	S	O	S	O
1988	23	67	91	4	21	76
1987	25	71	90	4	30	58
1986	23	73	91	4	40	54
1985	29	71	90	3	29	69
1984	38	57	81	12	32	56
1983	29	59	83	8	25	55
1982	39	51	83	12	40	55
1981	54	45	80	17	51	45

Interest Group Ratings

Year	ADA	ACU	AFL-CIO	CCUS
1988	85	4	86	38
1987	80	9	87	27
1986	75	14	86	33
1985	75	10	76	27
1984	80	26	54	56
1983	85	13	81	32
1982	65	27	79	33
1981	55	13	73	32

6 Norm Dicks (D)

Of Bremerton — Elected 1976

Born: Dec. 16, 1940, Bremerton, Wash.
Education: U. of Washington, B.A. 1963, J.D. 1968.
Occupation: Lawyer; congressional aide.
Family: Wife, Suzanne Callison; two children.
Religion: Lutheran.
Political Career: No previous office.
Capitol Office: 2429 Rayburn Bldg. 20515; 225-5916.

In Washington: Dicks rushes into congressional action like the Rose Bowl linebacker he once was, aggressive and confident — or, some say, overaggressive and overconfident. He brought to the House habits he had learned in the Senate as an aide to Warren G. Magnuson, the veteran Appropriations power, and he acts like a junior Magnuson, wheeling and dealing in the Appropriations Committee and on the House floor. With handshakes, pats on the back and even bear hugs, Dicks makes his case bluntly and repeatedly, annoying his opponents but frequently wearing them down nonetheless.

What Dicks relishes is the game itself. His field is defense policy, and he has been involved in nearly every major contest in recent years. It is not always easy to predict what side he will be on; he has argued on the side of liberal Democrats against White House defense priorities, and he has argued in alliance with the administration against the majority in his own party. But whatever he is arguing about, he makes himself heard: Dicks is not a subtle man.

His intensity pays off. In 1987 and 1988, his amendments forced the Reagan administration to back down from plans to exceed weapons limits of the unratified SALT II treaty. This was something of an about-face for him, since early in the Reagan years he had fought against his party's left to preserve the MX missile as a bargaining chip. Eventually he concluded that Reagan was not willing to negotiate the weapons system away, and Dicks' sense of betrayal was a symbol of the tenuous accord on defense policy forged by the Democrats' leading defense strategists, Les Aspin and Sam Nunn. In September 1988, Dicks was among a small group of Democrats invited to a weekend retreat called to reorient Michael S. Dukakis' faltering campaign against its perceived weakness on defense. Dukakis emerged to deliver what Dicks called "a faithful translation" of the defensocrats' views, but his speech could not overcome the damage done by Dukakis' ill-fated photo opportunity riding in a tank with an ill-fitting helmet.

Dicks is not a publicity hound; he aspires more to those inside moves that form part of the appropriations netherworld. And he cracked an important inner circle in 1985 when he complained that junior members were being unfairly left out of House-Senate appropriations conferences. The so-called "College of Cardinals," the 13 Appropriations subcommittee chairmen, gave new slots at the conferences to Dicks and others. In the 101st Congress, Dicks will be working with the quintessential inside player on defense issues, John P. Murtha of Pennsylvania, the new chairman of the Appropriations Defense Subcommittee. Dicks, the No. 2 Democrat on that subcommittee, will provide an important link to the left for hawkish ex-Marine Murtha.

Early in the Reagan years, when the issue was a nuclear weapons freeze, Dicks acted as a conciliator. He was not among the early activists. But by the time the House finally endorsed the concept in May 1983, after more than 40 hours of debate, Dicks had made himself a force in the negotiations. By offering an amendment that allowed the freeze to lapse if no actual progress was made in reducing nuclear weapons, Dicks cleared the way for a final vote on the proposal.

On the MX issue, Dicks' effort to find a middle ground was less successful, and for a time at least, it alienated him from some of his normal liberal allies on defense policy.

When President Reagan said he needed the MX in order to negotiate with the Soviet Union from a position of strength, Dicks chose to accept the premise that the administration would negotiate seriously. He wrote a letter to Reagan in 1983 asking for assurances that MX development would be part of an arms control negotiating strategy, not an alternative to it. Reagan's "Dear Norm" letter giving those assurances led the Defense Appropriations Subcommittee to approve the MX by a 9-3 vote.

Then, forming an alliance with Democrats Les Aspin of Wisconsin and Al Gore of Tennessee, Dicks helped fend off anti-MX amendments on the floor in the remaining months of the 98th Congress and in early 1985, when money for 21 missiles finally cleared.

Dicks traveled to Geneva in March 1985,

Washington 6

Puget Sound — Bremerton; Tacoma

Maritime interests dominate the 6th, which surrounds the sinuous waterways of the Puget Sound and the Hood Canal. Docks, naval installations and shipbuilding centers maintain the peninsula's historic links with the sea.

With 160,000 residents, industrial Tacoma (Washington's third-largest city) is the district's population center. Tacoma is overshadowed by its nearby rival, Seattle, and is sensitive about it. However, the area's major airfield — Seattle-Tacoma International Airport, known as "Sea-Tac" — is named for both cities.

Like much of the Seattle region, Tacoma's fortunes tend to follow the cycles of Boeing's aircraft business. But the city is less dependent on the huge aerospace firm than is Seattle. Commerce at the dockyards of Tacoma's deepwater port has enjoyed brisk growth. The wood-products and metal-smelting industries are also vital elements in the city's economy.

Tacoma's blue-collar, heavily unionized electorate generally tilts Pierce County to Democrats with moderate profiles. Dicks has dominated here, as has Democratic Gov. Booth Gardner, who served as county executive before his first election as governor in 1984. When he won re-election in 1988, Gardner carried Pierce County with 63 percent of the vote.

But for liberal candidates, the county can be dicey. Michael S. Dukakis hung on there with 51 percent in 1988, but the Democratic Senate candidate, Rep. Mike Lowry from Seattle's 7th District, lost by a narrow margin.

Much of the Republican strength in the district has to do with its large military contingent. With its numerous defense facilities, the area was under the microscope when a federal commission studied possible closures and realignments of military bases in late 1988. In the end, though, the 6th wound up a gainer. McChord Air Force Base and the Army's Fort Lewis, both in Tacoma, gained 900 military and civilian positions under the plan.

Bremerton (population 34,000), on the Kitsap Peninsula, has a strong labor vote. But surrounding Kitsap County (much of which is in the 1st District) leans Republican; George Bush carried Kitsap in 1988 by just under 1,000 votes.

Population: 516,561. White 451,581 (87%), Black 31,675 (6%), Other 23,224 (5%). Spanish origin 14,660 (3%). 18 and over 374,063 (72%), 65 and over 50,932 (10%). Median age: 28.

ready to watch Reagan's negotiators follow through on his promise to try harder for an agreement with the Soviets. But the Geneva sessions yielded little. In June, the House again faced the MX question, and this time Dicks joined a coalition of MX opponents who won a permanent limit on the number of missiles deployed.

"We put him in a posture where he could have succeeded [at Geneva], but he just doesn't appear willing to make the ultimate deal," Dicks said. "I suppose it's better to have tried than not to have tried."

In the years since the MX controversy, Dicks has generally voted with Democratic critics against the most important Reagan defense priorities. He has offered key amendments to reduce funding for Reagan's strategic defense initiative (SDI).

On all three of his Appropriations subcommittees — Defense, Military Construction and Interior — Dicks is a parochial congressman as well as a policy player.

He is careful to keep an eye on the interests of Boeing Co., a crucial employer in Washington state, and on funds for naval installations on Puget Sound. When the Navy wanted to build a new "homeport" at Everett suitable for basing an aircraft carrier, Dicks argued loudly for the project, which was approved late in 1986.

Earlier in his career, Dicks maneuvered his way through several major controversies affecting his state's aircraft industry. In 1981, he engineered a reversal of a House vote, winning back money for the Export-Import Bank, which channels business to Boeing. The next year Dicks argued unsuccessfully but vehemently for use by the military of Boeing 747 planes, instead of Lockheed's C-5, for transport purposes.

From his seat on the Interior Subcommittee, Dicks has monitored the Department of Energy's share of SDI funding. Because of his assignments, he is in a fulcrum position on the emerging issue of how to clean up the waste that has accumulated for decades at the nation's nuclear-weapons plants. A near neighbor of the nation's largest facility at Hanford, Wash., he has strong environmental concerns about the waste, while his fellow defense-oriented members seem more concerned about keeping the weapons plants open.

Forestry questions come before the Interior Subcommittee, and Dicks tends to side with industry forces seeking more rather than less development. In the 99th Congress, he persuaded the subcommittee not to halve the Reagan administration's request for construction of logging roads in the national forests.

At Home: After three years as administrative assistant to Magnuson, Dicks decided to go home in 1976 and run for Congress. He had been planning a campaign in the 6th District whenever incumbent Democrat Floyd Hicks chose to retire, and when Hicks was named to the state Supreme Court in 1976, Dicks began running with his usual intensity.

He had to compete with three major candidates for the nomination: a young activist state representative, a former president of Pacific Lutheran University and the mayor of Tacoma. But Dicks' ability to tap the resources of labor and other interest groups helped him put together a winning coalition. He won the primary with 36 percent of the vote.

Dicks had no trouble against a weak Republican that fall, but he went on a slide in the next two elections, pestered by Republican James Beaver, a conservative law professor from Tacoma. Dicks managed to clear 60 percent in 1978, but in 1980, Beaver was buoyed by financial support from the New Right, and held Dicks to 54 percent.

After that narrow escape, Dicks took steps to ensure that his 1982 race would not be so close. He took out full-page newspaper ads to tell voters that "Stormin' Norman" was as effective in the House as he had been on the college gridiron. "I've been back here in the district every other weekend since the '80 election," he claimed during the campaign.

While Beaver had attacked the incumbent from the right, Dicks' 1982 challenger, GOP state Sen. Ted Haley, was more liberal. Haley painted the incumbent as a profligate spender too friendly with military contractors.

But that charge just gave Dicks an excuse to talk about the pork he had brought home. He claimed credit for the completion of the Tacoma Spur Highway and numerous Navy ship overhauls at Bremerton. Dicks' 63 percent tally indicated he was moving toward security, and he has since won overwhelming re-election victories.

Republican Sen. Daniel J. Evans' decision to retire in 1988 at first piqued Dicks' interest. But two of his Democratic House colleagues, Mike Lowry and Don Bonker, jumped into the Senate contest, and Dicks recognized he faced an uncertain future as the most conservative candidate in a primary dominated by liberal voters. He stayed put in the 6th.

Committee

Appropriations (15th of 35 Democrats)
Defense; Interior and Related Agencies; Military Construction

Elections

1988 General		
Norm Dicks (D)	125,904	(68%)
Kevin P. Cook (R)	60,346	(32%)
1988 Primary †		
Norm Dicks (D)	62,833	(69%)
Kevin P. Cook (R)	28,640	(31%)
1986 General		
Norm Dicks (D)	90,063	(71%)
Kenneth W. Braaten (R)	36,410	(29%)

† In Washington's "jungle primary," candidates of both parties are listed on one ballot.

Previous Winning Percentages: **1984** (66%) **1982** (63%) **1980** (54%) **1978** (61%) **1976** (74%)

District Vote For President

	1988	1984
D	98,904 (51%)	82,214 (42%)
R	93,952 (48%)	111,116 (57%)

Campaign Finance

	Receipts	Receipts from PACs	Expend-itures
1988			
Dicks (D)	$366,934	$213,239 (58%)	$288,168
Cook (R)	$38,551	$1,922 (5%)	$35,445
1986			
Dicks (D)	$301,848	$179,660 (60%)	$229,634
Braaten (R)	$57,161	0	$57,166

Key Votes

1987	
Raise speed limit to 65 mph	N
Approve Gephardt "fair trade" amendment	N
Ban testing of larger nuclear weapons	Y
Delay "re-flagging" of Kuwaiti tankers	Y
Approve tax-raising deficit-reduction bill	Y
1988	
Approve aid to Nicaraguan contras	N
Enact civil rights restoration bill over Reagan veto	Y
Kill 60-day plant-closing notification measure	N
Pass omnibus trade bill over Reagan veto	Y
Approve death penalty for drug-related murders	Y
Bar federal funds for abortions in cases of rape and incest	N
Oppose seven-day waiting period for purchase of handguns	N

Voting Studies

	Presidential Support		Party Unity		Conservative Coalition	
Year	S	O	S	O	S	O
1988	29	68	90	7	53	47
1987	28	71	87	5	42	51
1986	27	73	90	7	46	54
1985	35	61	85	9	44	53
1984	43	49	79	15	54	42
1983	38	61	83	11	34	60
1982	40	53	89	8	36	63
1981	50	42	68	24	60	35

Interest Group Ratings

Year	ADA	ACU	AFL-CIO	CCUS
1988	85	9	86	36
1987	76	9	88	13
1986	70	23	79	28
1985	70	24	88	38
1984	70	13	62	38
1983	75	13	94	32
1982	65	10	90	23
1981	50	27	80	42

7 Jim McDermott (D)

Of Seattle — Elected 1988

Born: Dec. 28, 1936, Chicago, Ill.

Education: Wheaton College, B.S. 1958; U. of Illinois, M.D. 1963.

Military Career: Navy, 1968-70.

Occupation: Psychiatrist.

Family: Wife, Virginia Beattie; two children.

Religion: Episcopalian.

Political Career: Wash. House, 1971-72; Wash. Senate, 1975-87; Democratic nominee for governor, 1980; sought Democratic nomination for governor, 1972, 1984.

Capitol Office: 1107 Longworth Bldg. 20515; 225-3106.

The Path to Washington: Political comebacks are not especially rare, so retired state Sen. McDermott's entry into the 1988 contest for the 7th District was not at all startling. What made his candidacy unusual, though, was where it began: He made his intentions known from his job in Kinshasa, Zaire.

McDermott had quit the state Senate in June 1987 to take an assignment as a U.S. Foreign Service psychiatrist. With a three-year commitment to his African post, McDermott appeared to be closing out a political career that included more than 14 years in the state Legislature and three unsuccessful campaigns for governor.

However, in October 1987, Republican Sen. Daniel J. Evans announced he was retiring, and 7th District Democratic Rep. Mike Lowry jumped into the Senate contest. Lowry's departure after five terms drew McDermott's interest. After some preliminary soundings, he announced in February that he had obtained a release from his Foreign Service commitment, and would return home to run.

McDermott's homecoming angered Seattle City Councilman Norm Rice and King County Assessor Ruthe Ridder, who had earlier entered the contest for the Democratic nomination. But McDermott, with his record as a legislative leader on health-care issues and the visibility he had earned in his statewide campaigns, established himself as the front-runner.

Rice, who is black, had a minority base as well as contacts in the business community he developed as chairman of the City Council's Finance Committee. Ridder, a former state senator, had backing from feminist groups. But McDermott got endorsements from the state labor council and from most of the local party organizations. He also had more money, and saved $80,000 for a media blitz that cinched his victory. In the strongly Democratic 7th, McDermott's November victory was a given.

The plunge back into politics was not the first bag-packing event of McDermott's career. The Chicago native first moved to Seattle in 1966 to set up a practice, then left for a stint as a U.S. Navy psychiatrist in Long Beach, Calif.

But in 1970, he came back, entered a state House race, and won in a major upset. Less than two years later, McDermott, who had drawn an activist following with his liberal views, ran a long-shot Democratic primary campaign for governor, finishing third.

After winning state Senate elections in 1974 and 1978, McDermott challenged Democratic Gov. Dixy Lee Ray in a 1980 primary. The contest turned out to be his biggest statewide success: Ray's conservatism and support for nuclear power turned off liberals, whose support enabled McDermott to win nomination with 56 percent of the vote. However, the rough campaign left the Democratic Party split, and Republican John Spellman won the general election by a wide margin.

McDermott flopped in his third try for governor, losing by nearly 2-to-1 in a 1984 primary against Booth Gardner (who went on to unseat Spellman).

But through the years, McDermott had considerable success in the state Senate. While serving as either chairman or vice chairman of the Ways and Means Committee and the joint Legislative Budget Committee during most of the 1980s, McDermott sponsored legislation creating revolving funds for public works and water-pollution control projects.

The area of health care was McDermott's particular bailiwick. In 1980, he led efforts to rewrite the state's nursing-home regulations. In 1987, the Legislature enacted his bill providing state health coverage for the unemployed and uninsured working poor.

At the opening of the 101st Congress, McDermott fared as well in the committee-assignment process as any freshman, getting a seat on Interior (he is the only first-term member there) and also one on Banking.

Washington 7

Seattle and Suburbs

Clear-blue Puget Sound, Mount Rainier looming to the east — these images identify Seattle to most people. The city's pleasant aura, combined with its thriving economy rooted in the aerospace industry and Pacific trade, drew thousands of people to live in the Seattle area.

However, the downside of that growth — gridlocked streets, a skyline crowded with office towers — has sparked widespread concern that Seattle is becoming a less livable place. A burgeoning slow-growth movement scored a big victory in May 1989, with the passage of an initiative placing strict limits on downtown Seattle development.

The downtown growth in recent years has been commercial only; the residential boom is in the suburbs. Seattle's population (about 486,000) actually slipped slightly in the early 1980s.

The core of that population is in South Seattle, which has a working-class profile. It is one of the few sizable ethnic enclaves in the Northwest; its varied blue-collar population includes well-defined Scandinavian and Italian communities.

In geographic and economic terms, the Boeing aircraft company is at the center of the 7th. Interstate 5 heading into Seattle parallels the runway of Boeing Field. Since the district's health depends greatly on that of Boeing, the late 1980s present a mostly positive picture. As the defense boom of the Reagan years evolves into the more austere Bush era, Boeing's aerospace workers watch warily. But a growing concern over the aging of the nation's passenger airliner fleet has spurred an upswing in orders for Boeing commercial aircraft.

The strength of organized labor in this industrial area, a minority population that is the largest among Washington House districts, and a substantial bloc of liberal urbanites make the 7th the most dependably Democratic district in the state. In 1988, Michael S. Dukakis' 67 percent showing here was crucial to his statewide victory.

Population: 516,531. White 412,772 (80%), Black 48,051 (9%), Asian and Pacific Islander 36,744 (7%), Other 7,003 (1%). Spanish origin 13,669 (3%). 18 and over 414,472 (80%), 65 and over 68,925 (13%). Median age: 31.

Committees

Banking, Finance and Urban Affairs (29th of 31 Democrats)
Financial Institutions Supervision, Regulation and Insurance; Housing and Community Development; International Development, Finance, Trade and Monetary Policy

Interior and Insular Affairs (25th of 26 Democrats)
National Parks and Public Lands; Water, Power and Offshore Energy Resources

Campaign Finance

	Receipts	Receipts from PACs	Expend- itures
1988			
McDermott (D)	$373,258	$233,226 (62%)	$354,530
Edwards (R)	$5,921	0	$5,265

Elections

1988 General		
Jim McDermott (D)	173,809	(76%)
Robert Edwards (R)	53,902	(24%)
1988 Primary †		
Jim McDermott (D)	47,026	(38%)
Norm Rice (D)	35,046	(29%)
Ruthe Ridder (D)	23,149	(19%)
Robert Edwards (R)	7,815	(6%)
Robert Blake (R)	7,675	(6%)

† In Washington's "jungle primary," candidates of both parties are listed on one ballot.

District Vote For President

	1988	1984
D	144,221 (67%)	132,482 (60%)
R	67,318 (31%)	86,754 (39%)

8 Rod Chandler (R)

Of Bellevue — Elected 1982

Born: July 13, 1942, La Grande, Ore.
Education: Attended Eastern Oregon State College, 1961-62; Oregon State U., B.S. 1968.
Military Career: Oregon National Guard, 1959-64.
Occupation: Public relations consultant; newscaster.
Family: Wife, Joyce Elaine Laremore; two children.
Religion: Protestant.
Political Career: Wash. House, 1975-83.
Capitol Office: 223 Cannon Bldg. 20515; 225-7761.

In Washington: Many set their sights on the Ways and Means Committee when they come to Congress, but Chandler had special cause: His chairmanship of the Ways and Means panel in the Washington state House gave him valuable expertise in pension and tax-policy matters.

In 1987, at the start of his third term, Chandler got his wish. Geographic considerations aided his bid; at the time, there was no Northwesterner on the committee.

In his first two years on Ways and Means, Chandler put in a quiet, workmanlike performance. He spent time developing proposals to overhaul private pension and retiree health care plans. At the start of the 101st Congress, he introduced an updated version of his retiree health care proposal with Ways and Means Democrat Ronnie G. Flippo of Alabama.

While Chandler has moved in a low-key manner on Ways and Means, he has begun playing a more visible role outside the committee, perhaps looking to a 1992 Senate bid.

In 1987, Chandler teamed with a bipartisan group of moderates demanding more attention to the deficit. They worked successfully to deny a large debt-ceiling increase sought by White House and congressional leaders; Congress passed an unusual short-term increase. That pressured members to "fix" the automatic-cut mechanism of the Gramm-Rudman law invalidated by the Supreme Court in 1986. But it took the October 1987 stock market crash to induce budget-summit talks that focused more seriously on the deficit.

Chandler has shown an increasingly whetted appetite for spending cuts. Throughout the 100th Congress, he participated in efforts to make across-the-board reductions on a variety of appropriations bills, though there was some risk of cutting federal spending in his district. "When I get up in front of the Rotary Club and say, 'I'm against deficits,' I want to have something on the record to show I mean it," Chandler told a local newspaper.

In 1988, Chandler joined with Florida Democratic Rep. Buddy MacKay to offer a compromise plan on aid to the contras. It was displaced by a cease-fire agreement that spring, but Chandler's efforts were in line with his long struggle to find a centrist approach to the polarizing issue. In 1989, Chandler voted for a "humanitarian" contra-aid package worked out by President Bush and congressional leaders.

Chandler gets somewhat higher ratings from conservative and business groups than his GOP colleagues Sid Morrison and John Miller, but on the whole, he shares their moderate instincts. Like them, he opposes restricting access to abortion and voted against the Reagan administration on key civil rights issues.

At Home: Chandler's most serious obstacle in his 1982 House campaign was getting past a primary in which the GOP electorate was more conservative than he was. Though Chandler endorsed a balanced-budget constitutional amendment, his Republican opponents charged that he was a liberal, citing his opposition to a school prayer amendment and his support for a nuclear freeze and legalized abortion.

The early favorite was state Rep. Bob Eberle, who had persuaded legislative colleagues during redistricting to shape the newly created 8th to his liking. Eberle's association with the national New Right movement gave him a spending advantage, but his support base was sapped by King County Councilman Paul Barden, a born-again Christian stressing social issues. Conservatives split between Eberle and Barden, and Chandler won nomination.

In November, Democrats offered Mercer Island Mayor Beth Bland. Though intelligent and capable, Bland had a strident manner that contrasted unfavorably with Chandler's "nice guy" image. He won by a solid margin, and has scored comfortable re-election victories.

When Chandler made his first bid for the state Legislature in 1974, he sought treatment for a drinking problem. "I started to realize that I had a serious problem," he said in a recent interview, "and that I'd better solve it before taking this big political step." Chandler has talked openly about his recovery and has volunteered to help others with drinking difficulties.

Washington 8

Seattle Suburbs — Bellevue

The 8th includes some of Seattle's most prosperous suburbs as well as the landmark that helps give the city its unique allure — snow-capped, 14,410 foot Mount Ranier.

Encompassing the mainly affluent suburbs and exurbs east, south and west of Seattle, the 8th was drawn to be Republican. Though George Bush lost the state in 1988, he won comfortably here, taking 55 percent of the vote.

For the past 20 years, the suburban area covered by the 8th enjoyed its position as a beneficiary of Seattle's economic boom. But while the boom has brought benefits, it has also brought the traffic jams and rising housing costs that are the downside of growth. While not as obvious as the "no-growth" movement in Seattle — where an initiative to restrict downtown development won approval in 1989 — there is a "slow-down" constituency in the 8th. In 1988, the city of Bellevue instituted a moratorium on high-rise development.

With more than 80,000 residents, Bellevue is the population center of the King County suburbs that make up the bulk of the 8th. Separating Seattle and Bellevue is Lake Washington, and in the middle of the lake is the exclusive community of Mercer Island. The other notable island in the 8th is Vashon Island, at the district's western end. Though accessible only by Puget Sound ferry or aircraft, its rural character is giving way to housing tracts and light manufacturing.

On the mainland, the 8th takes in such burgeoning suburbs as Des Moines and affluent Normandy Park. South on Interstate 5 is Federal Way, site of the Weyerhaeuser Co.'s headquarters. Also to the south are Auburn and Kent, middle-class suburbs where many residents work for the Boeing Co.

Population: 516,500. White 488,993 (95%), Black 5,219 (1%), Other 16,666 (3%). Spanish origin 8,716 (2%). 18 and over 358,801 (70%), 65 and over 31,751 (6%). Median age: 29.

Committees

Post Office and Civil Service (8th of 9 Republicans)
Investigations (ranking); Census and Population

Ways and Means (10th of 13 Republicans)
Health; Oversight

Elections

1988 General		
Rod Chandler (R)	174,942	(71%)
Jim Kean (D)	71,920	(29%)
1988 Primary †		
Rod Chandler (R)	76,861	(70%)
Jim Kean (D)	16,418	(15%)
Pat Kennedy (D)	12,625	(11%)
DeMilt Morse (D)	3,972	(4%)
1986 General		
Rod Chandler (R)	107,824	(65%)
David E. Giles (D)	57,545	(35%)

† In Washington's "jungle primary," candidates of both parties are listed on one ballot.

Previous Winning Percentages: **1984** (62%) **1982** (57%)

District Vote For President

	1988	1984
D	99,728 (44%)	79,915 (36%)
R	125,807 (55%)	138,778 (63%)

Campaign Finance

	Receipts	Receipts from PACs	Expend-itures
1988			
Chandler (R)	$333,019	$191,478 (57%)	$300,048
Kean (D)	$14,822	$5,550 (37%)	$14,820
1986			
Chandler (R)	$259,317	$120,581 (46%)	$210,373
Giles (D)	$109,412	$18,395 (17%)	$109,411

Key Votes

1987	
Raise speed limit to 65 mph	Y
Approve Gephardt "fair trade" amendment	N
Ban testing of larger nuclear weapons	N
Delay "re-flagging" of Kuwaiti tankers	N
Approve tax-raising deficit-reduction bill	N
1988	
Approve aid to Nicaraguan contras	Y
Enact civil rights restoration bill over Reagan veto	Y
Kill 60-day plant-closing notification measure	Y
Pass omnibus trade bill over Reagan veto	N
Approve death penalty for drug-related murders	Y
Bar federal funds for abortions in cases of rape and incest	N
Oppose seven-day waiting period for purchase of handguns	N

Voting Studies

	Presidential Support		Party Unity		Conservative Coalition	
Year	S	O	S	O	S	O
1988	52	47	72	24	82	16
1987	57	42	77	19	88	9
1986	56	37	66	25	74	26
1985	61	35	72	22	76	22
1984	62	36	63	32	80	17
1983	66	33	67	28	78	22

Interest Group Ratings

Year	ADA	ACU	AFL-CIO	CCUS
1988	45	56	29	93
1987	36	61	13	93
1986	20	71	21	71
1985	15	67	18	95
1984	45	42	31	88
1983	25	43	6	95

West Virginia

U.S. CONGRESS

SENATE 2 D
HOUSE 4 D

LEGISLATURE

Senate 30 D, 4 R
House 79 D, 21 R

ELECTIONS

1988 Presidential Vote

Bush	48%
Dukakis	52%

1984 Presidential Vote

Reagan	55%
Mondale	45%

1980 Presidential Vote

Reagan	45%
Carter	50%
Anderson	4%

Turnout rate in 1984	51%
Turnout rate in 1986	28%
Turnout rate in 1988	47%

(as percentage of voting age population)

POPULATION AND GROWTH

1980 population	1,949,644
1988 population estimate (34th in the nation)	1,876,000
Percent change 1980-1988	−4%

DEMOGRAPHIC BREAKDOWN

White	96%
Black	3%
(Spanish origin)	1%
Urban	36%
Rural	64%
Born in state	79%
Foreign-born	1%

MAJOR CITIES

Huntington	59,310
Charleston	57,920
Wheeling	39,980
Parkersburg	38,540
Morgantown	26,840

AREA AND LAND USE

Area 24,119 sq. miles (41st)

Farm	23%
Forest	78%
Federally owned	8%

Gov. Gaston Caperton (D)
Of Charleston — Elected 1988

Born: Feb. 21, 1940, Charleston, W.Va.
Education: U. of North Carolina, B.A. 1963.
Occupation: Insurance executive.
Religion: Episcopalian.
Political Career: No previous office.
Next Election: 1992.

WORK

Occupations

White-collar	45%
Blue-collar	41%
Service workers	13%

Government Workers

Federal	14,971
State	40,339
Local	66,884

MONEY

Median family income	$ 17,308	(38th)
Tax burden per capita	$ 958	(17th)

EDUCATION

Spending per pupil through grade 12	$ 3,528	(27th)
Persons with college degrees	10%	(50th)

CRIME

Violent crime rate 137 per 100,000 (47th)

1
2
3
4
HANCOCK
BROOKE
OHIO
Wheeling
MARSHALL
WETZEL
TYLER
PLEASANTS
MONONGALIA
Morgantown
MARION
PRESTON
TAYLOR
HARRISON
DODDRIDGE
RITCHIE
Parkersburg
WOOD
WIRT
JACKSON
MASON
CABELL
Huntington
WAYNE
LINCOLN
PUTNAM
KANAWHA
Charleston
ROANE
CALHOUN
GILMER
LEWIS
UPSHUR
BARBOUR
TUCKER
GRANT
MINERAL
HAMPSHIRE
MORGAN
BERKELEY
JEFFERSON
HARDY
PENDLETON
RANDOLPH
POCAHONTAS
WEBSTER
BRAXTON
CLAY
NICHOLAS
GREENBRIER
MONROE
SUMMERS
FAYETTE
RALEIGH
MERCER
BOONE
LOGAN
MINGO
WYOMING
McDOWELL

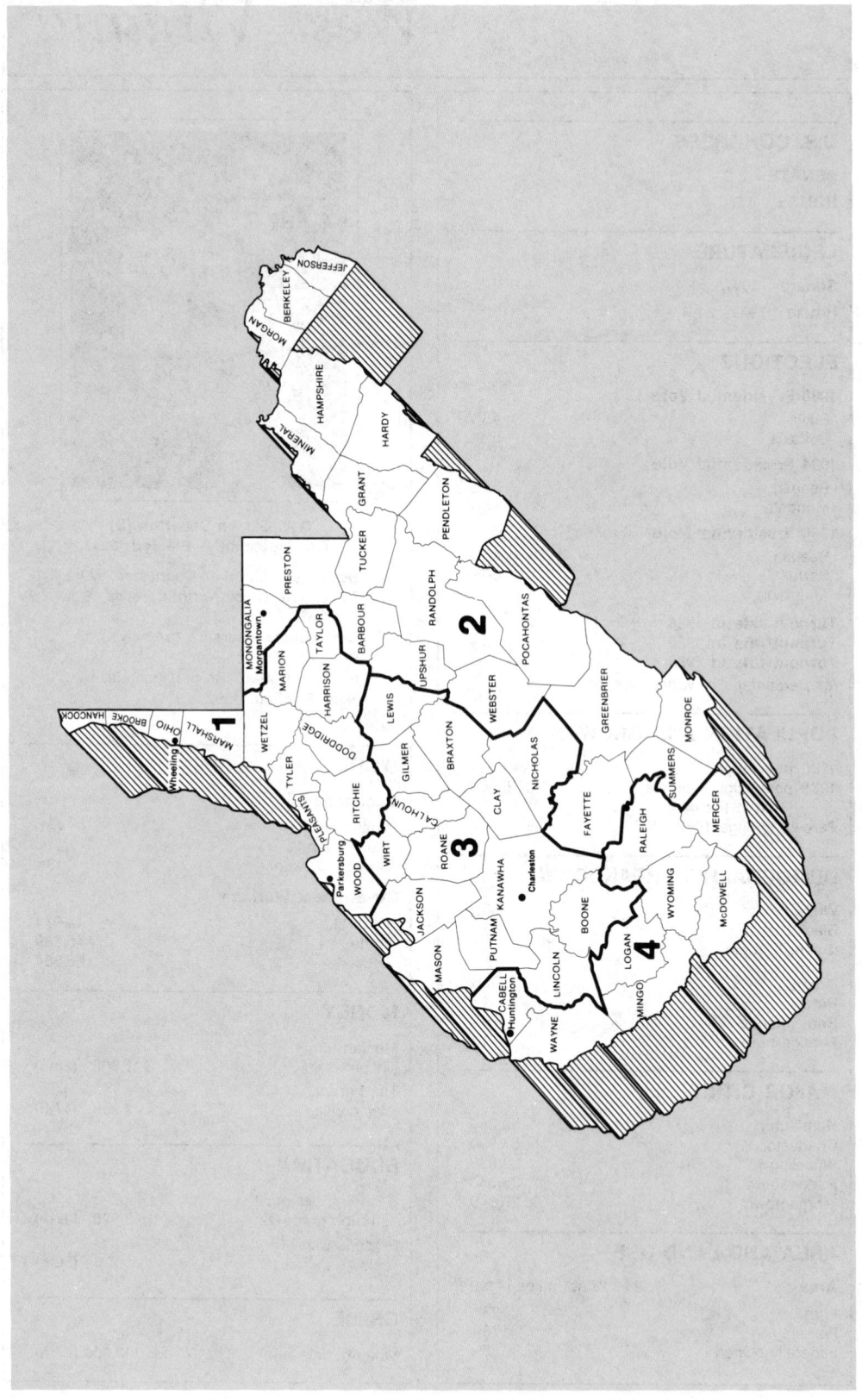

Robert C. Byrd (D)

Of Sophia — Elected 1958

Born: Nov. 20, 1917, North Wilkesboro, N.C.
Education: Attended Beckley College, Concord College, Morris Harvey College, 1950-51; Marshall College, 1951-52; American U., J.D. 1963.
Occupation: Lawyer.
Family: Wife, Erma Ora James; two children.
Religion: Baptist.
Political Career: W.Va. House, 1947-51; W.Va. Senate, 1951-53; U.S. House, 1953-59.
Capitol Office: 311 Hart Bldg. 20510; 224-3954.

In Washington: On the last day that he would preside in the Senate as majority leader, Byrd appeared before reporters in his trademark end-of-session red vest and broke into a jaunty jig. It was an uncharacteristic bit of frivolity for this stuffy man of senatorial ceremony, and one that belied the deep regret he must have felt at giving up the most powerful job in the institution that has been his home for three decades.

Months before, in the spring of 1988, Byrd had told his fellow Democrats he would retire after a dozen years as their leader, at the end of the 100th Congress. Twice in those years he was challenged from within the ranks, and throughout he was criticized as too stilted and old-fashioned for the television age. Though colleagues insisted Byrd would have been re-elected had he run again, the proud man apparently had had enough.

He had a powerful position to fall back on. With the 101st Congress, Byrd inherited the chairmanship of the Appropriations Committee, which he unabashedly vowed to use to get all the federal largess he can for West Virginia. Also, as the senior member of the majority party, Byrd became Senate president pro tempore, a largely ritualistic job that suits his love of traditional formality and one that he is expected to parlay into something more.

At Appropriations, it quickly became evident by his stewardship of a supplemental fiscal 1989 spending bill that Byrd was providing a focus and unity the committee had lacked under its aged and now retired former chairman, John C. Stennis. Byrd also began to make good on his pork-barrel pledge: The final bill included $75 million to rebuild a radio telescope at a West Virginia observatory, among other provisions beneficial to his state.

Though Byrd's adjustment to his change of status has appeared smooth, occasionally on the floor he rises to make a point in a way that suggests he has not totally let go of the leadership. Similarly, during the six years of Republican control until 1987, Byrd never seemed to reconcile himself to being a minority leader. He was a majority-leader-in-exile.

The reason is, no matter what his official status, Byrd long ago assumed the self-appointed role as guardian of the institution's arcane rules and historic traditions. More than any of his colleagues, Byrd has made the Senate his life — not only in terms of length of service, but in the reverence he holds for it as a 200-year-old democratic body. He seems to have found in it the sense of family that was denied him by his chaotic early life.

At the same time, Byrd has never had close bonds to the members of that family. He is a private, withdrawn man. Colleagues respect him, but many consider him peculiar; critics say he is insecure and vindictive. Byrd offered a revealing glimpse of himself in 1987, when he noted from the Senate floor that he had never played golf and did not go to movies, but had read all of Shakespeare's plays in the past year, just completed the Old Testament, and was currently reading the dictionary a second time. The drive for self-improvement that had carried the orphan from the coal patch to the height of U.S. politics still was strong as he neared 70.

Another telling, darker moment had occurred earlier that year. Angered at his own Democrats because he had lost a key budget vote due to absenteeism, Byrd lashed out. Amid the tirade, he said, "I do not expect to get kudos from anybody. I understand that I am not very well liked around here anyhow. I did not get elected to be liked here. I got elected because I thought I could do a job. This is a challenge, and I do not back off from a challenge."

Though such signs of intraparty strains drew attention, more often Byrd was scrapping with Republicans and the Reagan administration. Once restored to his majority leadership in the 100th Congress, Byrd played the partisan spokesman that his Democratic followers seemed to want, while rallying them behind an ambitious agenda designed to prove Democrats could govern. Working closely with Speaker Jim

Wright, Byrd helped make the Congress one of the most productive in more than 20 years.

Republicans met Byrd's return to power with some dread. During his first stint as majority leader in the 1970s, and again in the 100th Congress, they complained that he used his parliamentary skills to override their legitimate minority rights. In 1987, GOP leader Bob Dole hired a former Senate parliamentarian, whom Byrd had fired, to equalize his battle against the undisputed master of the rules.

The minority did kill some major Democratic initiatives by filibuster, including bills for campaign-finance changes, a higher minimum wage and guaranteed job leaves for new parents. Byrd groused that the tactic was being used "promiscuously," but often he was powerless against it; with 54 Democrats, he was six short of the number needed to end filibusters.

Whatever Republicans' complaints, Byrd was no ruthlessly partisan manipulator of the rules. The protection of minority rights is the heart of Senate tradition, for which Byrd has a profound respect. Indeed, his feeling that Dole had ignored that tradition as majority leader in 1985-86 was responsible for much of the hostility between them in the 99th Congress.

Their feud broke into the open once in 1986, during negotiations for floor action on the controversial issues of sanctions against South Africa and contra aid. When Dole accused Byrd of trying to "sneak" a South Africa amendment onto a bill, Byrd exploded. "I have had enough of this business of having the majority leader stand here and act as a traffic cop on this floor," he said. "While a senator today may be in a position to choke off the rights of another senator, the time will come when the worm will turn."

For most senators, Senate rules are useful tools, but clearly secondary to matters of substance. The opposite is true of Byrd; he sometimes seems less concerned with what the Senate does than with how it does it. Even in taking a stand on major issues, for Byrd the decisive factor is often the impact on Senate prerogatives.

Jealous of the Senate's role in approving treaties, he successfully fought throughout the 100th Congress to block Reagan's effort at reinterpreting the 1972 ABM treaty to allow space tests of the strategic defense initiative. When Democrats sought to add a provision to that end to Reagan's intermediate-range nuclear-force (INF) treaty in 1988, Byrd warned Republicans that he would delay ratification of the INF treaty until they agreed to the addition.

He dismissed arguments that the accord should be approved before Reagan's impending summit in Moscow. "Preserving the institutional role of the Senate in the making of treaties is more important than this treaty," he countered. Democrats' stand sent "a clear signal," he added, "that this Senate will not roll over and play dead on any treaty for any president." Republicans were not about to call Byrd's bluff when he saw Senate prerogatives at stake; they compromised and the treaty was ratified in time for Reagan's trip.

When the Judiciary Committee considered Reagan's Supreme Court nominee Robert H. Bork, Democratic foes knew how to ensure Byrd's opposition: They brought to his attention the conservative federal judge's opinions supporting the executive branch over the legislative in balance-of-power cases.

Byrd's emphasis on procedure and prerogatives over policy goes a long way toward explaining the ease with which he has evolved during his career from his party's right toward its left.

Few would have forecast a leadership role for Byrd when he arrived in the Senate in 1959. He was parochial and far to the right of most Democrats. He filibustered the 1964 Civil Rights Act, at one point holding the floor with a 14-hour speech that is among the longest on Senate record. As chairman of Appropriations' District of Columbia Subcommittee, he ordered inspections to see whether female welfare recipients were harboring unreported men.

But by 1967, he had a toehold on the Senate leadership ladder, after defeating veteran liberal Joseph Clark of Pennsylvania to become secretary of the Democratic Conference. Byrd catered to his colleagues, scheduling routine business for their convenience and tending to countless mundane details.

Four years later he ousted a stunned Edward M. Kennedy from the No. 2 leadership job, majority whip. Shaken by the 1969 Chappaquiddick tragedy, Kennedy had been neither an active nor effective whip. Yet he went into the 1971 party caucus full of confidence. Byrd, however, had a pocketful of cashed chits and a deathbed proxy from his mentor, Richard B. Russell of Georgia. He did not need it; he won 31-24.

For six years Byrd was a loyal lieutenant to Majority Leader Mike Mansfield, sitting through long days of floor work while deferring to Mansfield as party spokesman and political leader. When Mansfield retired, some liberals wanted Hubert H. Humphrey to succeed him, believing he would be a more eloquent spokesman than Byrd, who was viewed as a technician. But Byrd once again had a long column of accounts receivable. Humphrey, already seriously ill, withdrew. Byrd was elected by acclamation.

By that time, Byrd had moved leftward enough that ideology was not a question. The hard-liner who broke with a party majority in 1969 to support an anti-ballistic missile system was strongly committed a decade later to the SALT II treaty with the Soviet Union. The one-time critic of self-government for the District of

Columbia won Senate approval for a constitutional amendment giving the District voting representation in Congress. And the senator who once dismissed the Rev. Dr. Martin Luther King Jr. as a "self-serving rabble-rouser" fought the Reagan administration to enact civil rights bills more important than any since the one he had filibustered in 1964.

Through the years, as Byrd went "national," his defense of West Virginia interests, especially coal, never ceased. Almost single-handedly he has killed efforts since 1982 to strengthen the Clean Air Act against urban smog and acid rain. Much of his state's coal is high in sulfur, a key ingredient in acid rain, and Byrd is concerned that new environmental regulations will further depress West Virginia's economy and cost miners' jobs.

In 1988, he and Maine's George J. Mitchell, the Senate's leading proponent of a stronger law, reached a tentative compromise, but it fell under the weight of opposition from industries, environmentalists and Western producers of low-sulfur coal. No longer majority leader, Byrd cannot so easily keep a Clean Air bill off the floor, while Mitchell, as his successor, has new power to push his legislation. No one, however, doubts Byrd's ability to frustrate any effort he has not agreed to.

Byrd became majority leader as Jimmy Carter became president, and the two had an uneasy relationship. Byrd seemed to regard Carter as an amateur at the exercise of power, and made sure the president knew where the credit belonged when Byrd rescued the administration's legislation. He was instrumental in passing Carter's energy program and, most dramatically, saved the Panama Canal treaties through non-stop negotiations with wavering senators and Panamanian officials in 1978.

Many Democrats' lingering unease about Byrd as their leader crystallized after the 1980 elections cost the party the White House and plunged Senate Democrats into the minority. Byrd's caretaker style seemed less appropriate for a party out of power. Ultimately, however, he solidified his position by rebuilding his party ties and helping form a cohesive opposition to the Reagan administration.

Byrd's resistance to the administration was not a sure thing at the start. He voted for Reagan's 1981 tax and budget-cut bills. Soon, however, he became a strong foe, particularly after the administration proposed cuts in Social Security.

To reunite the Democrats, Byrd scheduled weekly luncheons of the Democratic Caucus, which had met rarely when the party had a majority, and weekend retreats in West Virginia. But the feeling that the party needed a more aggressive, telegenic public symbol never went away, and led to an open campaign against Byrd after the 1984 elections.

Challenger Lawton Chiles of Florida began campaigning only four days before Democrats were to vote, when Byrd already had commitments from more than half his colleagues. But the 36-11 vote indicated Byrd was vulnerable to future attack, particularly if the Democrats failed to regain a majority in 1986.

Byrd moved to shore up his strength in the 99th Congress. Despite a reluctance to push himself out front, he became more aggressive, giving the Democratic response to some of Reagan's televised speeches and working to put more verve into his formal oratory.

The unexpectedly large Democratic gains in 1986 ensured that Byrd would remain secure for at least another two years. J. Bennett Johnston of Louisiana had spent much of the year preparing a face-off with Byrd, but he dropped his bid when it became clear the new Democratic majority was in no mood to dump its leader in the midst of triumph.

At Home: Since Byrd was elected to the Senate in 1958, he has held the seat with ease — a tribute both to the respect he has engendered at home and the long-running impotence of the state's Republican Party. In five reelections, Byrd's lowest vote share was 65 percent.

That came in 1988, against freshman GOP state Sen. M. Jay Wolfe. Wolfe campaigned gamely on a conservative platform that combined right-to-work with right-to-life, and enlisted religious broadcaster Pat Robertson to visit West Virginia on his behalf. But he was outspent nearly 10-to-1, and he could not refute Byrd's argument that as Appropriations chairman, he could steer federal money West Virginia's way.

Wolfe had no trouble getting the GOP nomination to meet Byrd, largely because the memory of the incumbent's decisive 1982 victory was vivid in Republicans' minds. A year before that election, the GOP had talked boldly of waging a modern media campaign that would overcome Byrd's 1940s-style stumping.

Taking advantage of a beleaguered economy and a badly mismanaged GOP effort that wasted most of its money, Byrd drew nearly 70 percent of the vote, humiliating the Republican who had left his House seat to run.

That Republican, Cleve Benedict, was an heir to the Procter & Gamble fortune and was able to finance a yearlong media presence. Both he and the National Conservative Political Action Committee (NCPAC) peppered Byrd with negative ads, attacking Byrd's support of the Panama Canal treaties and his failure to maintain a West Virginia residence.

To the surprise of many in the press, the Benedict campaign engaged in a series of controversial pranks. At one stop, a Benedict worker tried to give Byrd a Ku Klux Klan hood, a not-so-subtle reminder of Byrd's past membership. But Byrd had put that issue to rest 30 years earlier; Benedict's attempt to revive it struck many as character assassination.

The attacks ruffled the proud and prickly senator, but he neither overreacted verbally nor campaigned lethargically, as Benedict had hoped he would. Stunned by the huge Democratic Senate losses in 1980, Byrd had prepared well for the challenge. He solidified labor and party support and collected a campaign treasury twice as large as Benedict's. Byrd swept all but one of the state's 55 counties.

The senator was born Cornelius Calvin Sale Jr. When he was 10, his mother died and his father abandoned him, and he spent his childhood with an aunt and uncle, Vlurma and Titus Byrd, in the hard-scrabble coal country of southern West Virginia.

Byrd graduated first in his high school class, but it took him 12 more years before he could afford to start college. He worked as a gas station attendant, grocery store clerk, shipyard welder and butcher before his talents as a fiddle player helped win him a seat in the state Legislature in 1946.

Friends drove Byrd around the hills and hollows, where he brought the voters out by playing "Cripple Creek" and "Rye Whiskey." From then on, he never lost an election. As he himself once put it, "There are four things people believe in in West Virginia — God Almighty, Sears Roebuck, Carters Little Liver Pills and Robert C. Byrd."

When Democrat Erland Hedrick retired from the old 6th District in 1952, Byrd was an obvious contender. But he had to surmount his past membership in the Ku Klux Klan. He had joined the Klan at age 24 and as late as 1946 wrote a letter to the imperial grand wizard urging a Klan rebirth "in every state of the Union."

When this came up publicly in 1952, his opponents and Democratic Gov. Okey L. Patteson called on him to drop out. He refused, explaining his Klan membership as a youthful indiscretion committed because of his alarm over communism. He won the election.

After three House terms, he ran for the Senate in 1958 with AFL-CIO and United Mine Workers support. He crushed his primary opposition and unseated Republican Chapman Revercomb, a veteran who had been in and out of the Senate in the 1940s and won a two-year term in a 1956 comeback. Revercomb was a weak incumbent before the campaign even began, and the 1958 recession hurt the state badly, driving voters closer to New Deal Democratic roots.

For the next two decades, West Virginians returned Byrd to the Senate without fuss. In 1964, he trounced Cooper Benedict, a former deputy assistant secretary of defense and the father of Cleve Benedict. In 1970, the GOP victim was Charleston Mayor Elmer H. Dodson. In 1976, no one at all filed against Byrd.

Committees

Appropriations (Chairman)
Interior and Related Agencies (chairman); Defense; Energy and Water Development; Labor, Health and Human Services, Education and Related Agencies; Transportation and Related Agencies

Armed Services (11th of 11 Democrats)
Conventional Forces and Alliance Defense; Defense Industry and Technology; Manpower and Personnel

Rules and Administration (3rd of 9 Democrats)

Elections

1988 General

Robert C. Byrd (D)	410,983	(65%)
M. Jay Wolfe (R)	223,564	(35%)

1988 Primary

Robert C. Byrd (D)	252,767	(81%)
Bobbie E. Myers (D)	60,186	(19%)

Previous Winning Percentages: **1982** (69%) **1976** (100%) **1970** (78%) **1964** (68%) **1958** (59%) **1956** * (57%) **1954** * (63%) **1952** * (56%)

* *House elections.*

Campaign Finance

	Receipts	Receipts from PACs	Expend-itures
1988			
Byrd (D)	$1,407,167	$938,720 (67%)	$1,099,709
Wolfe (R)	$115,314	$2,103 (2%)	$115,284

Key Votes

1987

Enact omnibus highway bill over Reagan veto	Y
Limit testing of space-based anti-ballistic missiles	Y
Oppose banning tests of larger nuclear weapons	Y
Confirm Robert H. Bork as Supreme Court justice	N

1988

Allow vote on campaign-finance overhaul	Y
Pass civil rights restoration bill over Reagan veto	Y
Enact omnibus trade bill over Reagan veto	N
Approve death penalty for drug-related murders	Y
Oppose "workfare" amendment to welfare overhaul bill	N

Voting Studies

	Presidential Support		Party Unity		Conservative Coalition	
Year	**S**	**O**	**S**	**O**	**S**	**O**
1988	56	44	81	19	49	51
1987	40	60	85	15	44	56
1986	36	64	84	16	30	70
1985	37	63	81	19	55	45
1984	53	45	77	22	45	55
1983	48	51	81	19	36	61
1982	40	60	81	19	56	44
1981	47	48	78	14	43	53

Interest Group Ratings

Year	ADA	ACU	AFL-CIO	CCUS
1988	55	36	86	29
1987	70	23	100	28
1986	75	26	93	16
1985	65	43	90	21
1984	75	50	73	37
1983	65	16	94	37
1982	60	55	92	48
1981	70	86	89	39

John D. Rockefeller IV (D)

Of Charleston — Elected 1984

Born: June 18, 1937, New York, N.Y.

Education: Attended International Christian U., Toyko, Japan, 1957-60; Harvard U., A.B., 1961.

Occupation: Public official.

Family: Wife, Sharon Percy; four children.

Religion: Presbyterian.

Political Career: W.Va. House, 1967-69; W.Va. secretary of state, 1969-73; governor, 1977-85; Democratic nominee for governor, 1972.

Capitol Office: 724 Hart Bldg. 20510; 224-6472.

In Washington: Rockefeller is an old hand at winning over those who think a man born into wealth and power must be spoiled and aloof. More than 20 years ago, he impressed the people of Emmons, W.Va., as a sincere, idealistic VISTA volunteer. He has now reassured the U.S. Senate.

Rockefeller often impresses observers as personable and unpretentious, according courteous treatment to staff and witnesses at hearings. In his early years in the Senate he was often found writing quietly in the chamber, his six-foot-six-inch frame folded into one of the spartan desks. His behavior is the perfect antidote to the expectation of arrogance.

Generally expected to address international issues, his one-time academic specialty, Rockefeller so far has focused on West Virginia concerns — the cost of shipping coal by rail, the job prospects of miners, steel makers and other workers in Rust Belt industries.

Political necessity shapes that agenda. A senator elected with a disappointing 52 percent of the vote after two terms as governor and a $12 million campaign cannot afford to range too far afield — especially not when he faces reelection in 1990. But Rockefeller also seems to delight in disappointing professional Congress-watchers who expect him to grab headlines in preparation for a leap onto the national stage. "I've done my homework," Rockefeller told a West Virginia newspaper in 1989. "I've started out in a low-profile way but I've gained the respect of my colleagues."

Rockefeller did weigh in on the great trade debate of the 100th Congress, and he was among those with the most to say. He had spent several years living in Japan and speaks the language. Yet his state had been badly hurt by competition from Japanese manufacturing. In the end, while supporting the aggressive pursuit of reciprocity in trade, Rockefeller also noted that hard-line protectionism carried risks for West Virginia, which has an export rate far above the national average. Erecting barriers to protect West Virginia steel makers could provoke foreign competitors to stop buying coal from West Virginia mines.

Like several of his Democratic colleagues elected in the 1980s, Rockefeller speaks often of the future. But for him, the future issues often turn out to be the availability of child care in working-class neighborhoods and the survival of rural hospitals with increasing populations of elderly patients. He worked the elderly-care cost issue hard as a member of Finance in the 100th Congress. And in the 101st he was named chairman of a new Finance Subcommittee on Medicare and Long-Term Care.

The thankless nature of this task was soon evident in the storm over higher Medicare premiums (imposed to finance the catastrophic coverage added to Medicare in 1988). But Rockefeller wanted the job, given his state's large population of elderly and of black-lung disease victims.

When Rockefeller does reach for a more glamorous subject, he comes up with something such as government encouragement of alternative fuels. Methanol use would cut pollution and reduce the threat to the ozone layer. It can be made from, among other things, coal. That would give West Virginia a new market for its historic resource. Rockefeller's Alternative Motor Fuels Act was signed into law in 1988, prompting him to announce "the beginning of the end of oil in our transportation sector over the next 30 or 40 years."

That statement might be overlooked if made by the average senator. But Rockefeller is the heir of the man who did for oil what Henry Ford did for cars. He has inherited one of the most recognizable names in American history and a piece of perhaps the greatest fortune. Although he has spent his adult life, in various ways, working for the agenda of the working class and the poor, Rockefeller remains a man who can spend whatever his political campaigns demand out of pocket and still buy a Washington, D.C., estate at a cost of several million dollars.

If Finance was a busy assignment in the

100th, Commerce was Rockefeller's prime focus in the 99th Congress. That panel has responsibility for the Interstate Commerce Commission, which oversees the rates that railroads charge their customers. Rockefeller has repeatedly complained that the ICC allows railroads to charge artificially high rates to West Virginia coal companies with no practical alternative to a single rail line for shipping their goods.

Rockefeller and others sought to revise rail deregulation laws to make it easier for "captive shippers" to win rate reductions from the ICC. But the railroads and the White House balked, and the shippers' controversial cause was set aside late in the 99th Congress as members rushed to complete a much more politically popular rail issue — the sale of government-owned Conrail to private investors. Heading into 1987, Rockefeller was still promising to "crack down on excessive rail rates" in order to make West Virginia coal more competitive in the world market.

The captive shippers issue was not a victory for Rockefeller in the next Congress, however. The last session ended in 1988 with a House bill having been approved. But Rockefeller's Senate companion bill lay dead in committee. Daunted by the threat of a Reagan veto, the committee refused to send the legislation to the floor. Rockefeller promised to be back on the issue in the 101st Congress.

Rockefeller added a new committee in 1989, Energy and Natual Resources. He also has a seat on Veterans' Affairs, often a good place for a member to spend time prior to a re-election campaign. Rockefeller was the sponsor of an amendment shifting $230 million to benefit veterans' programs in the budget resolution for fiscal 1990 passed in May 1989. It was one of very few amendments accepted by the Senate Budget Committee leaders, who had the votes to say no when they needed to.

At Home: As the scion of one of the nation's wealthiest families, Rockefeller seems an odd leader for one of the poorest states.

But in a state where money often talks and Democrats nearly always win, he has been a successful politician. His wealth and celebrity are an automatic turnoff for many voters: Only once in four major statewide races has he drawn more than 55 percent of the vote. But Rockefeller has won many friends by patiently working his way up the political ladder over two decades, serving in low-visibility offices before twice winning the governorship and capturing the Senate seat of retiring Democrat Jennings Randolph in 1984.

Rockefeller moved to West Virginia in 1964 as a VISTA volunteer in the Action for Appalachia Youth program, then decided to stay and enter politics. To avoid the appearance of only using the state as a springboard for his political ambition, Rockefeller started near the bottom, running for a seat in the state's lower house in 1966. After winning that, he captured the statewide office of secretary of state in 1968.

His political ascent was interrupted in 1972 when he lost the governor's race to Republican Arch A. Moore Jr. Rockefeller was hurt by carpetbagger charges and an environmental platform that opposed strip mining. After the election, he recanted some of his environmental positions and strengthened his ties to the state by serving as president of West Virginia Wesleyan College. Running for governor again in 1976, he won by nearly 2-to-1 over former GOP Gov. Cecil H. Underwood (1957-61). Moore was ineligible to seek re-election.

Despite their differing backgrounds, Rockefeller and the Legislature generally got along well in his first term. Rockefeller, the amateur classical pianist with the Harvard degree, and the pols from West Virginia's grimy courthouses reached an understanding, enabling Rockefeller to enjoy some major legislative successes. He won increased funding for reconstruction of the state's secondary roads and removed the sales tax on food.

Still, Rockefeller left nothing to chance in 1980, winning re-election after a campaign that bombarded households with direct-mail appeals and TV commercials. To reach all West Virginia viewers, Rockefeller put ads on Pittsburgh and Washington, D.C., stations.

When it was reported he was spending almost $12 million in his re-election campaign against Moore, who was seeking a comeback, bumper stickers appeared with the slogan, "Make Him Spend It All, Arch." Moore had the satisfaction neither of driving Rockefeller broke, nor driving him out of office. Rockefeller won by 9 points.

In terms of his ability to govern, though, Rockefeller was a big loser in 1980. He boasted during the campaign of his "clout" in Washington, pointing to his close ties to President Jimmy Carter and the state's powerful Democratic senators. But Carter was defeated and the GOP's Senate takeover pushed Robert C. Byrd out of his post as majority leader and Randolph from the chairmanship of Public Works. A once-steady stream of federal funds to West Virginia slowed to a trickle.

Rockefeller's second term was further stymied by the state's economic problems. Heavily dependent on the battered coal industry, West Virginia was staggered by high unemployment and sinking revenues. To Rockefeller's advantage, the West Virginia governorship is an institutionally strong position, especially when it comes to molding the budget. To his disadvantage, that institutional power made him the prime target of criticism when taxes were raised, salaries frozen and state spending cut.

With West Virginia's governors restricted to two consecutive terms, it was long apparent that Rockefeller would run for the Senate in 1984. It was less clear who his opposition would be. Randolph eased the path for him on the Democratic side by announcing his retirement plans in early 1983. About a year later, Moore, his strongest potential GOP rival, decided against a third contest with Rockefeller, and joined the governor's race.

But Rockefeller was not home free. He was near the nadir of his popularity when he entered the Senate race. Even many supporters admitted that he had fallen short of meeting the high expectations he had raised as governor. Instead of creating 50,000 new jobs as he had promised at the beginning of his administration, the state had lost more than 50,000. And instead of fulfilling his pledge to free the coal industry from boom-or-bust cycles, West Virginia struggled toward the end of his second term with the country's highest unemployment rate.

Rockefeller blamed the economic problems on ties to fading industries — steel and glass as well as coal — a global oil glut, and Reagan administration policies. He touted the integrity of his administration and its scattered successes, such as efforts to bolster tourism. "Tough Leadership for Tough Times" became the tag line for his campaign.

But polls showed a large portion of the electorate remained unconvinced. About 20 percent said they would vote for anyone running against Rockefeller; another 20 percent said they would support virtually anyone else.

Republicans nominated a wealthy young political neophyte, John Raese, who promised to match Rockefeller's spending dollar for dollar. But with Rockefeller mounting another $12 million campaign, that was a pipe dream.

Raese was hindered further by his own gaffes. He got into an altercation with a reporter for the *Charleston Gazette* while attending the GOP convention in Dallas. Shortly afterward, he bragged that he had heckled Rockefeller at a Labor Day rally in West Virginia, interrupting Rockefeller's speech and referring sarcastically to him as "big boy."

Raese's tactics enabled Rockefeller to point to his rival as immature and inexperienced. He criticized Raese for treating the Senate race as a "game" and the seat as a "plaything."

But then, rather than returning to more positive themes, Rockefeller made Raese the target of his late media barrage — a tactic widely considered to be a mistake. The attacks gave Raese publicity he could not afford himself. Aided by Reagan's surge atop the ticket, Raese pulled virtually even with Rockefeller in election-eve polls. But Rockefeller survived, building large majorities in the industrial northern Panhandle and in the southern coal fields.

Committees

Commerce, Science and Transportation (6th of 11 Democrats)
Foreign Commerce and Tourism (chairman); Science, Technology and Space; Surface Transportation

Energy and Natural Resources (10th of 10 Democrats)
Energy Research and Development; Public Lands, National Parks and Forests

Finance (10th of 11 Democrats)
Medicare and Long-Term Care (chairman); Health for Families and the Uninsured; International Trade

Veterans' Affairs (5th of 6 Democrats)

Elections

1984 General		
John D. Rockefeller IV (D)	374,233	(52%)
John R. Raese (R)	344,680	(48%)
1984 Primary		
John D. Rockefeller IV (D)	240,559	(66%)
Lacy Wright (D)	51,591	(14%)
Ken Auvil (D)	41,408	(11%)
Homer L. Harris (D)	29,138	(8%)

Campaign Finance

	Receipts	Receipts from PACs		Expend-itures
1984				
Rockefeller (D)	$12,093,549	$533,322	(4%)	$12,057,039
Raese (R)	$1,161,862	$178,310	(15%)	$1,151,621

Key Votes

1987	
Enact omnibus highway bill over Reagan veto	Y
Limit testing of space-based anti-ballistic missiles	Y
Oppose banning tests of larger nuclear weapons	N
Confirm Robert H. Bork as Supreme Court justice	N
1988	
Allow vote on campaign-finance overhaul	Y
Pass civil rights restoration bill over Reagan veto	Y
Enact omnibus trade bill over Reagan veto	Y
Approve death penalty for drug-related murders	Y
Oppose "workfare" amendment to welfare overhaul bill	N

Voting Studies

	Presidential Support		Party Unity		Conservative Coalition	
Year	**S**	**O**	**S**	**O**	**S**	**O**
1988	49	50	88	9	30	68
1987	36	60	92	6	28	72
1986	31	69	79	19	18	80
1985	31	61	83	12	47	47

Interest Group Ratings

Year	ADA	ACU	AFL-CIO	CCUS
1988	70	16	86	36
1987	90	8	100	24
1986	75	13	93	32
1985	60	14	90	36

1 Alan B. Mollohan (D)

Of Fairmont — Elected 1982

Born: May 14, 1943, Fairmont, W.Va.
Education: College of William and Mary, A.B. 1966; West Virginia U. School of Law, J.D. 1970.
Military Service: Army Reserve, 1970-82.
Occupation: Lawyer.
Family: Wife, Barbara Whiting; five children.
Religion: Baptist.
Political Career: No previous office.
Capitol Office: 229 Cannon Bldg. 20515; 225-4172.

In Washington: With his district battered by the decline of its coal and steel industries, Mollohan spends much of his time on the Appropriations Committee soliciting funds for projects aimed at diversifying the local economy. His efforts are not hurt by the fact that West Virginia's other voice in the funding process is Senate Appropriations Chairman (and former Majority Leader) Robert C. Byrd.

During the 100th Congress, his first full term on Appropriations, Mollohan was able to claim some successes on behalf of the 1st District. He pressed for a $200,000 grant to set up a computer software center at Wheeling Jesuit College, and helped obtain a $576,000 grant for a Wheeling business park.

Still, coal and steel remain foremost to Mollohan. He assails trade practices that he says cost jobs in these industries. He also supports "Buy American" legislation that gives preference to domestic materials in U.S. construction projects.

A sure vote for the Democratic leadership on labor and trade, Mollohan breaks with more liberal party colleagues on environmental issues. As he did on the Interior Committee prior to his move to Appropriations, Mollohan counters those who blame acid-rain pollution on coal-burning power plants; he argues that the economic and social costs of curbing acid rain outweigh the environmental benefits.

Mollohan differs from most House Democrats in his opposition to abortion: He is co-chairman of the Congressional Pro-Life Caucus. Mollohan also takes a rather conservative posture on defense. But here, he follows a pattern set by Pennsylvania Democrat John P. Murtha, his regional mentor and the chairman of the Appropriations Defense Subcommittee.

As a Murtha ally, Mollohan was the type of non-wavemaker the leadership likes to see on the ethics committee, to which he was appointed in the 99th Congress. In early 1989, Mollohan and the committee were placed in the position of having to judge House Speaker Jim Wright. Though Wright was cited by the panel for numerous violations, Mollohan and Pennsylvania Democrat Joseph M. Gaydos, another Murtha ally, voted against most of the charges. Mollohan said his contacts with Murtha did not influence his decisions. "No one told me how to vote," he said. "I vote 'em the way I see 'em."

At Home: Mollohan followed in the footsteps of his father, Robert Mollohan, who held the 1st District seat for 18 years prior to his 1982 retirement. That year, the father worked hard to transfer political loyalties to his son.

But it was not an easy campaign. Alan Mollohan was born in Fairmont, but for a decade he had been a Washington, D.C., lawyer who counted Pittsburgh-based Consolidation Coal Co. as a major client. Rank-and-file mine workers were leery about a corporate lawyer representing them; many lined up behind Mollohan's pro-labor primary opponent, state Sen. Dan Tonkovich.

The elder Mollohan, however, had close ties to party officials, business and labor leaders in the 1st. Their support proved crucial to his son, who won the primary by 3,137 votes.

In the fall, GOP state Rep. John F. McCuskey also tried to turn Mollohan's corporate law background into a negative, and nearly blocked a United Mine Workers endorsement of the Democrat. But it was a Democratic year, and Mollohan won with 53 percent.

In 1984, Mollohan had to buck a Republican tide and fend off a GOP challenge from Jim Altmeyer. The well-funded Republican had strong credentials: He was a West Point graduate, a Vietnam veteran, a Catholic in an area with a large ethnic Catholic population, and a civic leader in Wheeling, the district's largest city. But Mollohan mounted a late media barrage focusing on Altmeyer's spotty attendance in the Legislature. With large majorities in the northern Panhandle and the coal-mining areas, Mollohan won easily. He has coasted since.

West Virginia 1

Northern Panhandle — Wheeling

The 1st is iron and steel in the north and coal farther south, with a largely rural midsection.

The iron and steel area is the Panhandle, a narrow strip between the Pennsylvania border and the Ohio River. Brooke and Hancock counties, steel producers at the Panhandle's northern tip, are the most reliably Democratic counties in the 1st. The Panhandle city of Weirton (Hancock County) is home to Weirton Steel, the country's largest employee-owned company.

Ohio County (Wheeling) is the Panhandle's commercial center, with a significant white-collar population that often produces GOP majorities. Ohio County has voted Republican in the last five presidential elections. The Wheeling-Pittsburgh Steel Corp. moved its corporate headquarters from Pittsburgh to Wheeling in late 1987.

To the southeast, coal is mined in Marion and Harrison counties and shipped up to Pittsburgh along the Monongahela River. Like the Panhandle, the coal region is heavily unionized and populated largely by southern and Eastern European ethnics, descendants of immigrants who were drawn by work in the mines. Together with the Panhandle's millworkers, they usually deliver large enough majorities for a statewide Democratic candidate to carry the 1st.

The other important population center is Wood County (Parkersburg), at the southwestern corner of the district, midway between Wheeling and Huntington on the Ohio River. Like the rural counties that separate it from the district's steel and coal regions, Wood County frequently votes Republican. In 1988, George Bush won Wood decisively, but the county shunned incumbent Republican Arch A. Moore Jr. in the gubernatorial contest.

Population: 488,568. White 478,672 (98%), Black 7,906 (2%). Spanish origin 3,238 (1%). 18 and over 353,283 (72%), 65 and over 64,928 (13%). Median age: 32.

Committees

Appropriations (32nd of 35 Democrats)
Commerce, Justice and State, the Judiciary and Related Agencies; VA, HUD and Independent Agencies

Standards of Official Conduct (4th of 6 Democrats)

Elections

1988 General		
Alan B. Mollohan (D)	119,256	(75%)
Howard Tuck (R)	40,732	(25%)
1986 General		
Alan B. Mollohan (D)	90,715	(100%)

Previous Winning Percentages: **1984** (54%) **1982** (53%)

District Vote For President

	1988	1984	1980	1976
D	89,128 (51%)	84,836 (43%)	93,363 (48%)	111,273 (55%)
R	84,142 (49%)	111,290 (57%)	91,307 (47%)	90,173 (45%)
I			8,711 (5%)	

Campaign Finance

	Receipts	Receipts from PACs	Expend-itures
1988			
Mollohan (D)	$168,219	$112,893 (67%)	$103,154
Tuck (R)	$15,350	0	$15,220
1986			
Mollohan (D)	$243,825	$135,583 (56%)	$216,378

Key Votes

1987	
Raise speed limit to 65 mph	N
Approve Gephardt "fair trade" amendment	Y
Ban testing of larger nuclear weapons	N
Delay "re-flagging" of Kuwaiti tankers	Y
Approve tax-raising deficit-reduction bill	Y
1988	
Approve aid to Nicaraguan contras	Y
Enact civil rights restoration bill over Reagan veto	Y
Kill 60-day plant-closing notification measure	N
Pass omnibus trade bill over Reagan veto	Y
Approve death penalty for drug-related murders	N
Bar federal funds for abortions in cases of rape and incest	Y
Oppose seven-day waiting period for purchase of handguns	Y

Voting Studies

	Presidential Support		Party Unity		Conservative Coalition	
Year	S	O	S	O	S	O
1988	36	59	74	19	61	24
1987	40	56	83	12	67	33
1986	36	61	79	15	70	28
1985	40	60	82	17	69	31
1984	49	50	76	22	63	36
1983	34	66	78	21	54	46

Interest Group Ratings

Year	ADA	ACU	AFL-CIO	CCUS
1988	50	48	100	23
1987	68	17	100	13
1986	50	35	100	24
1985	55	38	82	23
1984	55	33	85	44
1983	65	30	94	20

2 Harley O. Staggers Jr. (D)

Of Keyser — Elected 1982

Born: Feb. 22, 1951, Washington, D.C.
Education: Harvard U., B.A. 1974; West Virginia U. School of Law, J.D. 1977.
Occupation: Lawyer.
Family: Wife, Leslie Sergy.
Religion: Roman Catholic.
Political Career: W.Va. Senate, 1981-83; sought Democratic nomination to U.S. House, 1980.
Capitol Office: 1504 Longworth Bldg. 20515; 225-4331.

In Washington: Staggers appears to have inherited the modest style of his father, who spent 32 years in the House and chaired the Commerce Committee for over a decade without wielding much clout. The younger Staggers moves in the same quiet, unaggressive fashion.

In the 101st Congress, he got a platform to call his own: the chairmanship of the Housing and Memorial Affairs Subcommittee on Veterans' Affairs. The panel has jurisdiction over veterans' housing programs.

Staggers has taken an active role in fighting the federal Health Care Financing Administration over denied Medicare home-care benefits. He was a plaintiff in a lawsuit that produced a court ruling in 1988 that HCFA illegally denied Medicare benefits for home health care to many elderly patients. After the ruling, Staggers and Democratic Reps. Barney Frank of Massachusetts and Austin J. Murphy of Pennsylvania called for the resignation of the head of HCFA.

Staggers also called for hearings in Frank's Judiciary Subcommittee on Administrative Law on HCFA's proposal to alter the administrative appeals process for Medicare claims. At the 1987 hearing, he called HCFA's plan to bypass the administrative law judges — who had been overturning denials at a 70 percent clip — and hold hearings by telephone "outside the realm of the absurd." Language barring telephone hearings was attached to the 1987 catchall deficit-reduction bill.

In 1986, when the House reauthorized the Economic Development Administration and the Appalachian Regional Commission — which the Reagan administration tried to eliminate — Staggers praised the programs for maintaining the viability of towns in his district. "I want the people of the 2nd District of West Virginia to be able to remain in the communities they so love," he said.

Likable and low-key, Staggers is a frequent participant in the regular congressional basketball games. He generally tends to issues with a local slant, spending much time on constituent services and local projects.

He does occasionally speak on broader issues he feels strongly about. In 1986, he blasted an amendment to the omnibus drug bill to enforce capital punishment for certain illegal drug offenses. "It is ironic," Staggers said, "that the House is attempting to attach a death penalty to a bill that's ultimate purpose is to save lives.... In a civilized society, there is just no place for capital punishment, just as there is no place in a civilized society for abortion. The taking of a life is morally wrong — in every respect."

At Home: The Staggers family wanted an uninterrupted succession in the 2nd District, but West Virginia voters rejected the idea in 1980. The elder Harley announced his departure that year and anointed his son, but the politically inexperienced Harley Jr. did not make it out of the primary.

State party leaders made sure that Staggers had a strong base from which to mount his second House campaign. After his 1980 primary loss, he was appointed to a vacancy in the state Senate. Staggers kept a low profile, but began touching base for his 1982 House effort and was nominated without opposition.

The fall campaign was name identification against money. The GOP nominee was millionaire former state Sen. J. D. Hinkle Jr., who overwhelmingly outspent Staggers. But Hinkle was hurt by rumors of a drinking problem, and Staggers was more accessible than in 1980. Portraying himself as a mainstream Democrat, he spent much time talking about his love of West Virginia and his deep roots there. Behind the scenes, the elder Staggers worked to revive his political network. His son swept every county.

In 1984, Staggers faced a potentially more formidable foe in Republican Cleve Benedict. He had won the seat in 1980, then gave it up in 1982 for a highly negative campaign against Democratic Sen. Robert C. Byrd. Humiliated by Byrd, he ran for his old House seat in 1984, apologizing to voters for abandoning the House after one term. But Staggers won 56 percent.

West Virginia 2

East — Morgantown; Eastern Panhandle

It does not take long for an incumbent to make himself invulnerable in the 2nd, because challengers find it difficult to reach the voters hidden in its hills and hollows. One of the larger districts east of the Mississippi, the 2nd has no real media markets. Its population growth outstripped the state's other districts in the 1970s, and was greatest in the eastern Panhandle, home to many retirees and commuters from the Baltimore and Washington, D.C., areas. The focal point of the growth has been Jefferson County, at the Panhandle's tip; it has been West Virginia's fastest-growing county since 1970, with a population increase of roughly 50 percent.

Most of the 2nd District is in the Allegheny Mountains, where the standard of living is the lowest in the state. Many mountaineers turn to the large tourist trade to supplement their meager incomes.

Politically, the 2nd is marginal. Republican George Bush carried it narrowly in the 1988 presidential election; it was the only district in West Virginia that he won.

Democratic strength is greatest in the few mining and industrial areas along the western fringe. Monongalia County, one of the state's leading coal-producing counties, combines a sizable number of blue-collar voters with the academic community at West Virginia University in Morgantown. Fayette County is the other major Democratic stronghold. It lies at one end of the industrialized Kanawha Valley.

GOP candidates usually run best in the eastern Panhandle, which includes the fertile farm land of the northern Shenandoah Valley. Pastoral Grant County regularly turns in the highest Republican percentages in the state. It went for Bush by a margin of nearly 4-to-1 in 1988.

Population: 487,438. White 469,213 (96%), Black 15,235 (3%). Spanish origin 3,439 (1%). 18 and over 350,168 (72%), 65 and over 60,621 (12%). Median age: 30.

Committees

Agriculture (13th of 27 Democrats)
Conservation, Credit and Rural Development; Domestic Marketing, Consumer Relations and Nutrition

Judiciary (18th of 21 Democrats)
Administrative Law and Governmental Relations; Economic and Commercial Law

Veterans' Affairs (6th of 21 Democrats)
Housing and Memorial Affairs (chairman)

Select Aging (36th of 39 Democrats)
Human Services

Elections

1988 General

Harley O. Staggers Jr. (D)	118,356	(100%)

1986 General

Harley O. Staggers Jr. (D)	76,355	(69%)
Michele Golden (R)	33,554	(31%)

Previous Winning Percentages: **1984** (56%) **1982** (64%)

District Vote For President

	1988		1984		1980		1976	
D	81,178	(48%)	77,702	(42%)	87,423	(48%)	105,527	(57%)
R	86,633	(52%)	107,719	(58%)	86,471	(47%)	79,607	(43%)
I					8,721	(5%)		

Campaign Finance

	Receipts	Receipts from PACs	Expend-itures
1988			
Staggers (D)	$146,928	$131,953 (90%)	$90,537
1986			
Staggers (D)	$158,284	$133,695 (84%)	$136,766
Golden (R)	$69,919	0	$67,232

Key Votes

1987	
Raise speed limit to 65 mph	N
Approve Gephardt "fair trade" amendment	Y
Ban testing of larger nuclear weapons	Y
Delay "re-flagging" of Kuwaiti tankers	Y
Approve tax-raising deficit-reduction bill	Y
1988	
Approve aid to Nicaraguan contras	N
Enact civil rights restoration bill over Reagan veto	Y
Kill 60-day plant-closing notification measure	N
Pass omnibus trade bill over Reagan veto	Y
Approve death penalty for drug-related murders	N
Bar federal funds for abortions in cases of rape and incest	Y
Oppose seven-day waiting period for purchase of handguns	Y

Voting Studies

	Presidential Support		Party Unity		Conservative Coalition	
Year	**S**	**O**	**S**	**O**	**S**	**O**
1988	23	77	89	11	47	53
1987	17	81	92	5	28	72
1986	18	82	89	8	32	68
1985	29	70	88	9	33	65
1984	30	70	88	10	29	71
1983	16	84	86	12	30	70

Interest Group Ratings

Year	ADA	ACU	AFL-CIO	CCUS
1988	80	12	100	21
1987	96	4	100	13
1986	80	5	100	28
1985	70	19	82	38
1984	65	13	85	38
1983	85	13	94	5

3 Bob Wise (D)

Of Clendenin — Elected 1982

Born: Jan. 6, 1948, Washington, D.C.
Education: Duke U., A.B. 1970; Tulane U. School of Law, J.D. 1975.
Occupation: Lawyer.
Family: Wife, Sandra Casber.
Religion: Episcopalian.
Political Career: W.Va. Senate, 1981-83.
Capitol Office: 1421 Longworth Bldg. 20515; 225-2711.

In Washington: The beginning of the 101st Congress brought confirmation of Wise's transition from populist maverick to party insider. He was appointed to the Budget Committee — as a reward for his loyal service to the Democratic leadership — and seniority gave him a subcommittee chair on the Government Operations Committee.

All this is a marked change from Wise's profile as a freshman in 1983, when he committed a remarkably rebellious act — taking on his more senior colleagues in the West Virginia delegation by opposing (and temporarily halting) a flood control project they had set in motion for the 3rd District.

Soon after that iconoclastic start, however, Wise began working within the system, applying himself to slicing off pieces of the federal pie for his constituency. The reason was simple: economic necessity. There are so many bad roads, decrepit bridges, unemployed workers and black lung disease victims in the 3rd that Wise decided he had to get along with those in the congressional appropriations process who can provide federal dollars for relief.

And Wise has gotten along well. He has become an enthusiastic participant in the Democratic whip organization; his office issues *The Wise Whip Wrapup*, a newsletter that quickly summarizes House Democratic activity (and also includes doodles by Wise). The loyal service has put Wise in good stead with party leaders; when an Armed Services vacancy occurred during the 100th Congress, he was seriously considered for it. Though he did not get the slot, he was promised a Budget post for the 101st.

In 1989, Wise assumed the chairmanship of the Government Operations Subcommittee on Government Information, Justice and Agriculture, which includes among its jurisdictions oversight of the Freedom of Information Act. The previous chairman, Glenn English of Oklahoma, fought off efforts by the Reagan administration to weaken the FOIA. Wise is pushing legislation to ensure that access to information is not lost as it is transferred from file cabinet to computer disk. His bill would direct the Office of Management and Budget to follow specific policies and establish rules for the dissemination of FOIA information stored electronically.

Wise ventured into foreign policy in the 100th Congress, proposing to deny new U.S. energy and mineral leases to companies doing business in South Africa. While his language made it into the House's South Africa sanctions legislation, it was deleted in the Senate version. The weakened Senate bill failed to reach the floor.

Wise came to Washington as a self-described populist with a penchant for challenging established power, and he lived up to that reputation early in his first term. He had been in office only a few months when he took on his state's congressional delegation by opposing the Stonewall Jackson Dam, a long-planned flood-control project in the 3rd.

Wise had campaigned on a promise to fight the dam, and when the 1983 water development appropriations bill came up, he attached an amendment eliminating any money for it. The project, he said, was a waste of money. "If it's not right, it's not right," he said, "no matter whose district it's in."

His move angered the state's other Democratic congressmen, including Senate Democratic leader Robert C. Byrd. Still, Wise managed to convince a majority of the House to go along with him. Only Senate support for the dam saved it; the House-Senate conference preserved funding.

Before very long, Wise had undergone a remarkable transformation in attitude. By the time he won re-election in 1986, he was extolling the virtues of seniority and comity. "I plan to take a page from Sen. Robert Byrd's book," he said, "by looking to see how I can help colleagues so they will help me."

Wise has learned to play the cooperative game as well as he had played the rebel. His efforts on Public Works contributed to the funding of lock and dam renovation projects on the Ohio, Kanawha and Monongahela rivers. He won a grant to develop a West Virginia

West Virginia 3

Central — Charleston

The 3rd centers on Charleston, the seat of state government and commerce as well as the most diverse economy in the state. But even Charleston is tied to the up-and-down cycle in the coal industry. As coal has struggled in the 1980s so has this area, recording an unemployment rate not far below the state average, which has hovered in or near double digits.

The capital city's large white-collar work force frequently produces GOP majorities. But nearly three out of four voters in Kanawha County live outside Charleston. Many are blue-collar workers employed by the numerous chemical companies that line the Kanawha River. Finding a balance between safety and jobs has been a leading issue in the "Chemical Valley" since late 1984, when poisonous gas leakage from a Union Carbide chemical plant in India killed thousands of people. The Union Carbide factory in Institute, less than 10 miles from Charleston, manufactures the same lethal chemical.

Most of the blue-collar workers employed in the county vote Democratic. The result is that Kanawha often swings back and forth between the two parties. In 1984, it voted Republican for president, governor and senator, while backing Wise. In 1988, Kanawha voted a straight Democratic ticket for president, Senate, governor and House.

With more than 220,000 residents, Kanawha is the most populous county in the state and home for nearly half the 3rd's voters. But in the last three decades, its population has decreased by about 30,000, due to decline in the chemical and glass industries and completion of a highway network that has encouraged many residents to move to bedroom communities outside Kanawha. The temporary revival of the coal industry in the 1970s significantly increased population in the surrounding counties, but not in Kanawha itself.

Democratic candidates usually run ahead in the portion of the district outside Kanawha. But Democratic victories there are not guaranteed. Generally, Republicans can count on a good share of the votes in the terrain north of Interstate 79, the highway that runs northeastward from Charleston toward the Pennsylvania border. Tobacco, corn and livestock provide an agricultural base in these counties in or near the Ohio River Valley.

To the south of the Interstate, the Democrats dominate. There is some coal and natural gas but little industrialization. Although the coal counties have been particularly hard hit in recent years, the economy has been distressed throughout the district. That helps explain why only two of the 3rd's counties went Republican in the 1988 governor's race.

Population: 486,112. White 469,089 (97%), Black 14,500 (3%). Spanish origin 2,595 (1%). 18 and over 347,147 (71%), 65 and over 57,194 (12%). Median age: 31.

Defense Logistics Agency to help state businessmen get defense contracts, and he has secured federal funds for several industrial parks, flood control projects and similar improvements in the 3rd.

"We thought the 3rd District was sending a wild man to Washington." the Charleston *Mail* wrote in 1986. "We were wrong."

All this is not to say that Wise has abandoned his fundamental beliefs or his populist style. He insists that "Nobody calls me 'Congressman' more than once. I came in as Bob, and I'll go out as Bob." A reformist streak is still evident in his behavior. He does not mass-mail newsletters to constituents, and he supports a ban on honoraria. Wise accepts the same salary he received when he first came to Congress; the balance from subsequent raises is donated to scholarship funds at four West Virginia colleges. This does not create much hardship at the Wise household, since his wife Sandra is a longtime Ways and Means staffer whose salary is competitive with her husband's.

At Home: While Wise launched his political career as a maverick, he has nurtured it with unabashed displays of state boosterism. He regularly gives district voters what one newspaper described as "an upbeat, feel-good-about-ourselves pitch that sounds like a cross between Norman Vincent Peale ... and President Reagan." And he has gained wide visibility by projects such as "West Virginia First," a TV program designed to encourage high school students to stay in the state.

Critics complain that Wise's real forte is public relations, but there is no doubt he is a rising star in West Virginia politics.

Wise has long demonstrated populist instincts. Rather than join an established firm after law school, he set up his own practice oriented to low- and moderate-income clients. He then directed a statewide tax reform group that repeatedly took coal companies to court to force them to pay more property tax on their large landholdings.

But legal action had its limits, Wise decided. "Where people lose the battle is when they have to actually go to court," he once said. "It's much better if they win their case in the legislative process."

So in 1980 he capitalized on the resentment of teachers against the small size of a pay raise to upset the conservative state Senate president in the Democratic primary. With that reputation as a giant-killer, he ran for Congress in 1982, benefiting from labor support to swamp a Democratic primary field that included the state House majority leader.

GOP Rep. David Michael Staton had won the seat in 1980 with an extensive grass-roots campaign of his own, but his re-election effort was more aloof. He gave few interviews, relying instead on a heavy media barrage that portrayed him as a religious, family-oriented man who reflected the conservative social values of average West Virginians. If Staton was worried about Wise, he did not show it. "I don't think it will even be close," he said at one point.

It was not close. Wise's small campaign budget and feuds with party leaders masked an effective volunteer network and a knack for drawing enough free media attention to neutralize Staton's ads. Wise ran almost even with Staton in the rural GOP counties north of Charleston, while swamping the incumbent in Kanawha County and the economically distressed coal counties nearby. He won a decisive 58 percent of the vote.

Each election since then, Wise has taken a larger share of the vote. Although the result was not close, his most spirited re-election contest was in 1986, when Charleston newscaster Tim Sharp left his job in early September to fill the vacancy on the GOP ticket.

Sharp enjoyed instant name identification as news anchorman on a TV station in the district's largest city. Pointing to threatened plant shutdowns in the 3rd, he said it was time to break up West Virginia's all-Democratic congressional delegation and elect a Republican who could work with the Reagan administration and with GOP Gov. Arch A. Moore Jr. to bring in jobs. A born-again Christian, Sharp also stressed social issues, including opposition to abortion.

The campaign had its testy moments: Wise and Sharp at one point engaged in a shouting match in front of a factory that was to be closed. Yet while Sharp drew ink, he did not undermine Wise's popularity; the incumbent swept every county in the district and won nearly two-thirds of the vote.

Committees

Budget (19th of 21 Democrats)
Task Forces: Community Development and Natural Resources; Human Resources

Government Operations (11th of 24 Democrats)
Government Information, Justice and Agriculture (chairman); Employment and Housing

Select Aging (23rd of 39 Democrats)
Health and Long-Term Care; Retirement, Income and Employment

Elections

1988 General

Bob Wise (D)	120,192	(74%)
Paul W. Hart (R)	41,478	(26%)

1986 General

Bob Wise (D)	73,669	(65%)
Tim Sharp (R)	39,820	(35%)

Previous Winning Percentages: **1984** (68%) **1982** (58%)

District Vote For President

	1988	1984	1980	1976
D	90,179 (53%)	84,527 (44%)	93,700 (49%)	113,707 (58%)
R	81,235 (47%)	107,004 (56%)	89,359 (46%)	82,475 (42%)
I			8,959 (5%)	

Campaign Finance

	Receipts	Receipts from PACs	Expenditures
1988			
Wise (D)	$173,893	$122,952 (71%)	$165,957
Hart (R)	$2,394	$1,027 (43%)	$4,310
1986			
Wise (D)	$147,260	$94,421 (64%)	$138,732
Sharp (R)	$20,410	$1,150 (6%)	$20,411

Key Votes

1987	
Raise speed limit to 65 mph	N
Approve Gephardt "fair trade" amendment	Y
Ban testing of larger nuclear weapons	Y
Delay "re-flagging" of Kuwaiti tankers	Y
Approve tax-raising deficit-reduction bill	Y
1988	
Approve aid to Nicaraguan contras	N
Enact civil rights restoration bill over Reagan veto	Y
Kill 60-day plant-closing notification measure	N
Pass omnibus trade bill over Reagan veto	Y
Approve death penalty for drug-related murders	N
Bar federal funds for abortions in cases of rape and incest	N
Oppose seven-day waiting period for purchase of handguns	Y

Voting Studies

	Presidential Support		Party Unity		Conservative Coalition	
Year	S	O	S	O	S	O
1988	21	73	87	9	58	39
1987	17	80	86	5	40	60
1986	23	72	88	8	40	60
1985	26	74	84	9	27	71
1984	33	61	76	17	37	61
1983	13	85	84	13	30	67

Interest Group Ratings

Year	ADA	ACU	AFL-CIO	CCUS
1988	75	12	100	36
1987	84	0	100	7
1986	75	5	93	22
1985	70	10	82	32
1984	70	18	92	27
1983	90	13	88	10

4 Nick J. Rahall II (D)

Of Beckley — Elected 1976

Born: May 20, 1949, Beckley, W.Va.
Education: Duke U., A.B. 1971; graduate work, George Washington U., 1972.
Occupation: Broadcasting executive; travel agent.
Family: Divorced; three children.
Religion: Presbyterian.
Political Career: No previous office.
Capitol Office: 343 Cannon Bldg. 20515; 225-3452.

In Washington: Rahall is a special-interest legislator, and he has never tried to hide it. Representing one of the nation's leading coal-producing districts, he always puts coal in the forefront of his congressional concerns.

He has worked himself into several positions of influence over coal-related issues. On Interior, he chairs the Mining Subcommittee. He is a member of a Public Works subcommittee that specializes in coal shipping issues, and he is the leader of a congressional coal caucus.

But for a pro-coal man, Rahall can sometimes surprise those who write him off as resolutely pro-industry. On the Interior Committee in the 100th Congress, he advocated a bill extending national park status to parts of three West Virginia rivers. And on many wilderness or historic preservation bills that go through the committee, Rahall votes with conservationists.

But Rahall's occasional ventures into other issues simply highlight how much time he spends on his chief priority. If an issue has a coal-related angle, Rahall is following it.

While many other members fight to broaden their jurisdiction, Rahall looked to narrow his. One of his first acts in the 99th Congress as Mining Subcommittee chairman was to give up the panel's stewardship over such topics as timber and hydroelectric power, offering them to another subcommittee so he could stick to coal.

In 1987, Rahall engineered a compromise on a bill overhauling the system of leasing federal lands for oil and gas drilling. But even here he managed to include a coal-related provision.

His bill aimed to curb abuses in leasing lands by subjecting all lands first to a market test through competitive bidding. That ended the practice of leasing potentially energy-rich land through a lottery, with the winner paying $1 per acre. Rahall blended provisions from a more drastic revision, sponsored by George Miller of California, with others sought by Western members for independent drillers.

In the version approved by his Mining Subcommittee, the bill included a Rahall-authored proposal to prohibit the Interior Department from issuing federal coal leases to companies importing foreign coal. When it reached the full committee, Westerners complained that Rahall's provision was protectionist and an attack on their coal industry from Easterners. On a 25-15 vote, the panel removed the provision before approving the bill 24-16. The measure was included in the fiscal 1988 budget reconciliation package.

Though Rahall's coal boosterism benefits mine owners, he is also protective of the interests of his district's coal miners, and votes a pro-labor line in the House. In early 1987, Rahall pledged to use his subcommittee chairmanship to block proposed Reagan cutbacks in federal mining health and safety research. He introduced bills in the 100th and 101st Congresses to make it easier for miners suffering from black lung disease to claim benefits.

Rahall wants the federal government to play a larger role in promoting U.S. coal trade, and he calls for the creation of a Federal Coal Export Commission. Those arguments have led him into an overall protectionist stance on trade. In 1986, he offered an amendment to the Export-Import Bank bill to prohibit loans that would tend to increase foreign competition to American products.

He reserves some harsh words for the Canadian government and its efforts to urge U.S. citizens to lobby their government to do more to combat acid rain. Rahall points out that since 1978, coal-burning power plants in the United States have been required to install "scrubbers" that reduce sulfur dioxide emissions (a prime component of acid rain), while no Canadian plants are equipped with scrubbers. When the Canadian government unveiled plans in 1988 to use billboards to convey its message on acid rain, Rahall introduced a bill to require posting of signs at every U.S.-Canada border crossing that would read, "Welcome to the United States, land of 142 power plant smokestack scrubbers. Did you see a single one in Canada?"

Rahall wrote an amendment to the Water

West Virginia 4

South and West — Huntington; Beckley

The Appalachian 4th is the most Democratic district in a Democratic state. It has proved its credentials in the last two presidential elections: Among West Virginia's four districts, only the 4th went for Walter F. Mondale in 1984, and in 1988, it gave Michael S. Dukakis a bigger share of the vote than any of the other districts.

In most years, Republican strength in the 4th is limited to Cabell County (Huntington) and Mercer County (Bluefield) on the fringes of the coal fields at opposite ends of the district. With roughly 20 percent of the district population, Cabell is the most populous county in the 4th. Like other Ohio River counties south of Wheeling, it frequently votes Republican. Huntington grew from a railroad center into the largest city in West Virginia; it was overtaken in population by Charleston during the 1970s, but regained the top spot in the mid-1980s.

Between Cabell and Mercer is coal country. This is a lucrative area for the mining companies — the district ranks with the Wyoming at-large district and the Kentucky 7th as one of the national leaders in coal production.

The revival of the industry in the 1970s helped reverse decades of population decline here. As the miners returned, all but one of the southern coal counties grew by at least 10 percent over the decade.

But even this population surge left some counties below their levels of 50 years ago — Logan County had more voters in 1928 than in 1980. And the recession of the early 1980s wiped out much of the gain of the previous years. At mid-decade, the district featured some of the highest unemployment rates in the country — above 35 percent in McDowell and Wyoming counties.

McDowell County is one of the poorest of the coal counties. Blacks make up 15 percent of the population, a higher share than in any other West Virginia county. In recent years, McDowell is the only county that has regularly elected a black representative to the state Legislature.

Population: 487,526. White 457,777 (94%), Black 27,410 (6%). Spanish origin 3,435 (1%). 18 and over 339,410 (70%), 65 and over 55,125 (11%). Median age: 29.

Quality Act revisions (which became law early in the 100th Congress) benefiting certain coal mining operations. The provision allowed federal or state authorities to permit purchasers of abandoned strip mines to operate under modified water quality standards, so they would not be held responsible for water pollution created by the mine's earlier owners. The amendment also required that the re-mining operation ultimately result in improved water quality.

Rahall's calls for a national coal revival do fade somewhat when regional interests are at stake. He has consistently fought plans to build a coal slurry pipeline in the Western United States, which would make Western coal cheaper to transport and more competitive with Eastern coal, including West Virginia's.

In the 98th Congress, Rahall tried and failed to block a slurry plan in the Interior Committee. But he teamed on the House floor with railroad supporters, who said the slurry would cripple the industry's important coal-hauling business. The bill was defeated decisively. In the 100th Congress, Interior again passed a slurry bill over Rahall's protests. But the bill was also referred to the Public Works Committee, where it died.

Rahall's proselytizing on coal leaves him little time for leadership on other issues. On Public Works, he is a member of the pro-development majority, backing dams and other federal largess for his low-income district.

A dependable vote for the Democratic leadership and a longtime labor loyalist — he received "perfect" scores from the AFL-CIO and the National Education Association in 1987 and 1988 — Rahall won a seat in the 101st Congress on the Education and Labor Committee.

Of Lebanese heritage, Rahall has also been a vigorous critic of Israel and a supporter of ties to Arab states. As part of a congressional delegation that toured Beirut in 1982, he met with Palestine Liberation Organization leader Yasir Arafat.

In 1986, Rahall opposed a joint resolution criticizing the Reagan administration's proposed sale of missiles to Saudi Arabia. In the 100th Congress, he fought efforts to close the PLO's office at the United Nations. He also sponsored a resolution supporting Palestinians' efforts toward self-determination and statehood in the occupied West Bank and Gaza in Israel.

At Home: In recent years, Rahall has gone from being the strongest vote-getter in his state's delegation to its weakest, but he still has a grip on his mountain district.

His winning percentage began slipping in 1984, after a Las Vegas gambling casino filed suit against him to collect more than $60,000 in unpaid gambling debts. The suit, which drew headlines a month before the election, was eventually dropped with apologies to the congressman. But coming on the heels of Rahall's separation from his wife, the episode gave his little-known GOP challenger unexpected fodder.

Rahall still won with two-thirds of the vote, but it was the first time since 1976 that he was not the delegation's top vote-getter.

In 1988, Rahall drew a more visible foe in Mercer County GOP Chairman Marianne Brewster. Rahall outraised her by more than 10-to-1, but he handed her an issue by pleading guilty in May to alcohol-related reckless driving. On Election Day, Rahall got a big vote in the overwhelmingly Democratic coal counties. But he drew less than 55 percent in both Cabell County (Huntington) and his home base of Raleigh County (Beckley), and he lost Mercer County (Bluefield). Rahall still topped 60 percent districtwide, but that was his lowest-ever re-election tally.

Rahall was a little-known travel agent and radio sales manager when he entered politics in 1976. His opportunity grew out of Democratic Rep. Ken Hechler's quixotic campaign for governor. Rahall was far from the best-known contender in the field of Democrats aiming to succeed Hechler, and one of his opponents said he looked like a "25-year-old college boy," an assertion that understated Rahall's true age by only a year. But he also had family money, and he used it to conduct a media campaign none of his opponents could match, evoking the names of Hechler, Franklin D. Roosevelt and Sen. Robert C. Byrd, for whom he had worked briefly. Rahall won the primary with 37 percent.

Then, after the primary was over, Hechler — who did not win the gubernatorial nomination — said he wanted to keep his House seat, and mounted a write-in drive. While Rahall could never have beaten Hechler in a primary, the write-in effort was too difficult for even a popular incumbent to carry off, especially after Rahall received Democratic organization support. Hechler got nearly 60,000 write-in votes, but Rahall prevailed.

Hechler immediately announced he would run again in the 1978 primary. But he found that incumbency gave Rahall the advantages he once enjoyed. Bolstered by endorsements from Byrd, the National Rifle Association and the West Virginia AFL-CIO, Rahall added strong local party support and a late media blitz and won renomination with 56 percent of the vote.

Committees

Education and Labor (18th of 22 Democrats)
Elementary, Secondary and Vocational Education

Interior and Insular Affairs (6th of 26 Democrats)
Mining and Natural Resources (chairman); National Parks and Public Lands

Public Works and Transportation (6th of 31 Democrats)
Economic Development; Surface Transportation

Elections

1988 General		
Nick J. Rahall II (D)	78,812	(61%)
Marianne R. Brewster (R)	49,753	(39%)
1988 Primary		
Nick J. Rahall II (D)	56,996	(73%)
William Sanders (D)	12,920	(16%)
Ted T. Stacy (D)	8,503	(11%)
1986 General		
Nick J. Rahall II (D)	58,217	(71%)
Martin Miller (R)	23,490	(29%)

Previous Winning Percentages: **1984** (67%) **1982** (81%) **1980** (77%) **1978** (100%) **1976** (46%)

District Vote For President

	1988		1984		1980		1976	
D	80,531	(58%)	81,060	(50%)	92,976	(56%)	105,407	(63%)
R	58,055	(42%)	79,470	(49%)	67,069	(40%)	62,505	(37%)
I					5,300	(3%)		

Campaign Finance

	Receipts	Receipts from PACs	Expend-itures
1988			
Rahall (D)	$333,159	$175,442 (53%)	$152,271
Brewster (R) †	$32,041	0	$32,039
1986			
Rahall (D)	$212,148	$124,079 (58%)	$68,970

† Totals based on incomplete data.

Key Votes

1987	
Raise speed limit to 65 mph	N
Approve Gephardt "fair trade" amendment	Y
Ban testing of larger nuclear weapons	Y
Delay "re-flagging" of Kuwaiti tankers	Y
Approve tax-raising deficit-reduction bill	Y
1988	
Approve aid to Nicaraguan contras	N
Enact civil rights restoration bill over Reagan veto	Y
Kill 60-day plant-closing notification measure	N
Pass omnibus trade bill over Reagan veto	Y
Approve death penalty for drug-related murders	N
Bar federal funds for abortions in cases of rape and incest	Y
Oppose seven-day waiting period for purchase of handguns	Y

Voting Studies

	Presidential Support		Party Unity		Conservative Coalition	
Year	**S**	**O**	**S**	**O**	**S**	**O**
1988	25	64	85	11	39	50
1987	24 †	71 †	87 †	10 †	35 †	65 †
1986	21	76	90	6	34	66
1985	20	79	88	6	25	75
1984	32	58	83	9	22	64
1983	15	78	76	16	29	62
1982	29	58	77	10	23	55
1981	37	53	77	17	37	53

† Not eligible for all recorded votes.

Interest Group Ratings

Year	ADA	ACU	AFL-CIO	CCUS
1988	70	22	100	29
1987	76	4	100	7
1986	90	9	93	17
1985	80	5	88	18
1984	70	4	83	29
1983	85	9	100	25
1982	70	5	89	25
1981	75	14	93	11

Wisconsin

U.S. CONGRESS

SENATE 1 D, 1 R
HOUSE 5 D, 4 R

LEGISLATURE

Senate 20 D, 13 R
House 56 D, 43 R

ELECTIONS

1988 Presidential Vote	
Bush	48%
Dukakis	51%
1984 Presidential Vote	
Reagan	54%
Mondale	45%
1980 Presidential Vote	
Reagan	48%
Carter	43%
Anderson	7%
Turnout rate in 1984	64%
Turnout rate in 1986	39%
Turnout rate in 1988	62%

(as percentage of voting age population)

POPULATION AND GROWTH

1980 population	4,705,767
1988 population estimate (17th in the nation)	4,855,000
Percent change 1980-1988	+3%

DEMOGRAPHIC BREAKDOWN

White	94%
Black	4%
Other	1%
(Spanish origin)	1%
Urban	64%
Rural	36%
Born in state	77%
Foreign-born	3%

MAJOR CITIES

Milwaukee	605,090
Madison	175,830
Green Bay	93,470
Racine	82,440
Kenosha	74,960

AREA AND LAND USE

Area	54,426 sq. miles (25th)
Farm	50%
Forest	44%
Federally owned	5%

Gov. Tommy G. Thompson (R)
Of Elroy — Elected 1986

Born: Nov. 19, 1941, Elroy, Wis.
Education: U. of Wisconsin, B.S. 1963, J.D. 1966.
Military Career: Army Reserve and National Guard, 1966-76.
Occupation: Lawyer; real estate broker.
Religion: Roman Catholic.
Political Career: Wis. Assembly, 1967-87, Republican floor leader, 1981-87; sought GOP nomination in U.S. House special election, 1979.
Next Election: 1990.

WORK

Occupations	
White-collar	48%
Blue-collar	33%
Service workers	14%
Government Workers	
Federal	27,072
State	93,331
Local	219,952

MONEY

Median family income	$ 20,915	(15th)
Tax burden per capita	$ 1,061	(10th)

EDUCATION

Spending per pupil through grade 12	$ 4,168	(12th)
Persons with college degrees	15%	(30th)

CRIME

Violent crime rate	250 per 100,000 (40th)

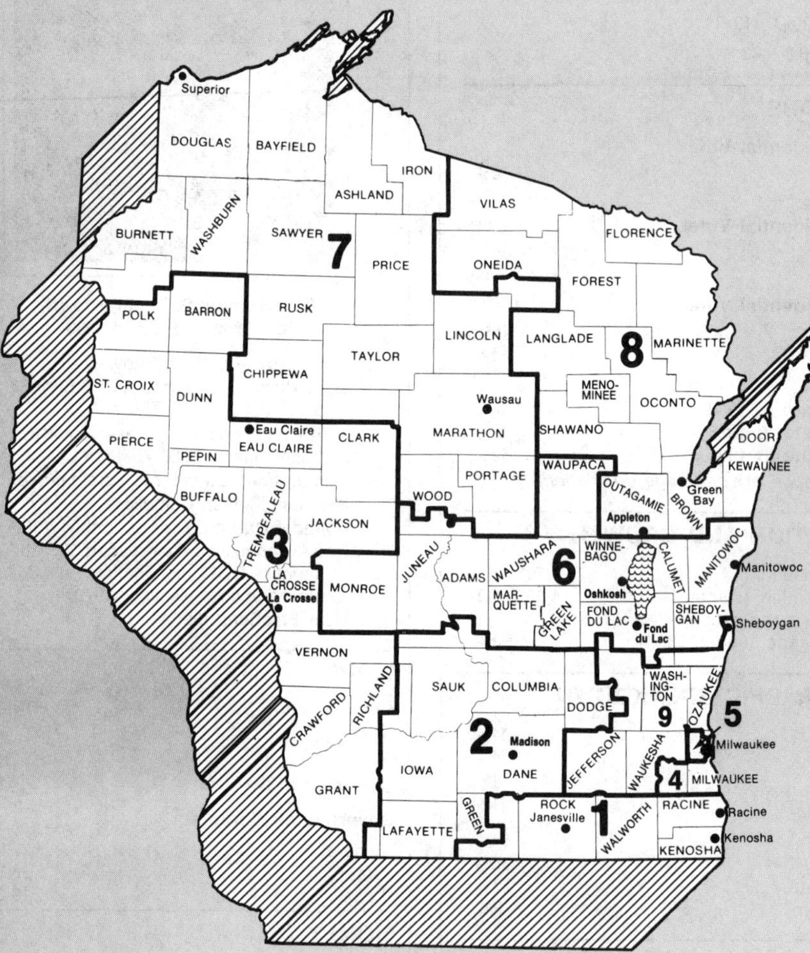
Superior
DOUGLAS
BAYFIELD
IRON
ASHLAND
VILAS
BURNETT
WASHBURN
SAWYER
7
PRICE
ONEIDA
FLORENCE
FOREST
POLK
BARRON
RUSK
LINCOLN
LANGLADE
8
MARINETTE
CHIPPEWA
TAYLOR
ST. CROIX
DUNN
MENO-
MINEE
OCONTO
Wausau
PIERCE
Eau Claire
EAU CLAIRE
CLARK
MARATHON
SHAWANO
DOOR
PEPIN
WAUPACA
KEWAUNEE
BUFFALO
PORTAGE
OUTAGAMIE
Green
Bay
WOOD
BROWN
TREMPEALEAU
JACKSON
Appleton
3
WINNE-
BAGO
CALUMET
MANITOWOC
Manitowoc
JUNEAU
ADAMS
WAUSHARA
6
LA
CROSSE
La Crosse
MONROE
MAR-
QUETTE
Oshkosh
GREEN
LAKE
FOND
DU LAC
Fond
du Lac
SHEBOY-
GAN
Sheboygan
VERNON
WASH-
ING-
TON
OZAUKEE
5
SAUK
COLUMBIA
DODGE
9
RICHLAND
CRAWFORD
2
Madison
Milwaukee
IOWA
DANE
JEFFERSON
WAUKESHA
4
MILWAUKEE
GRANT
ROCK
Janesville
1
RACINE
Racine
GREEN
WALWORTH
LAFAYETTE
KENOSHA
Kenosha

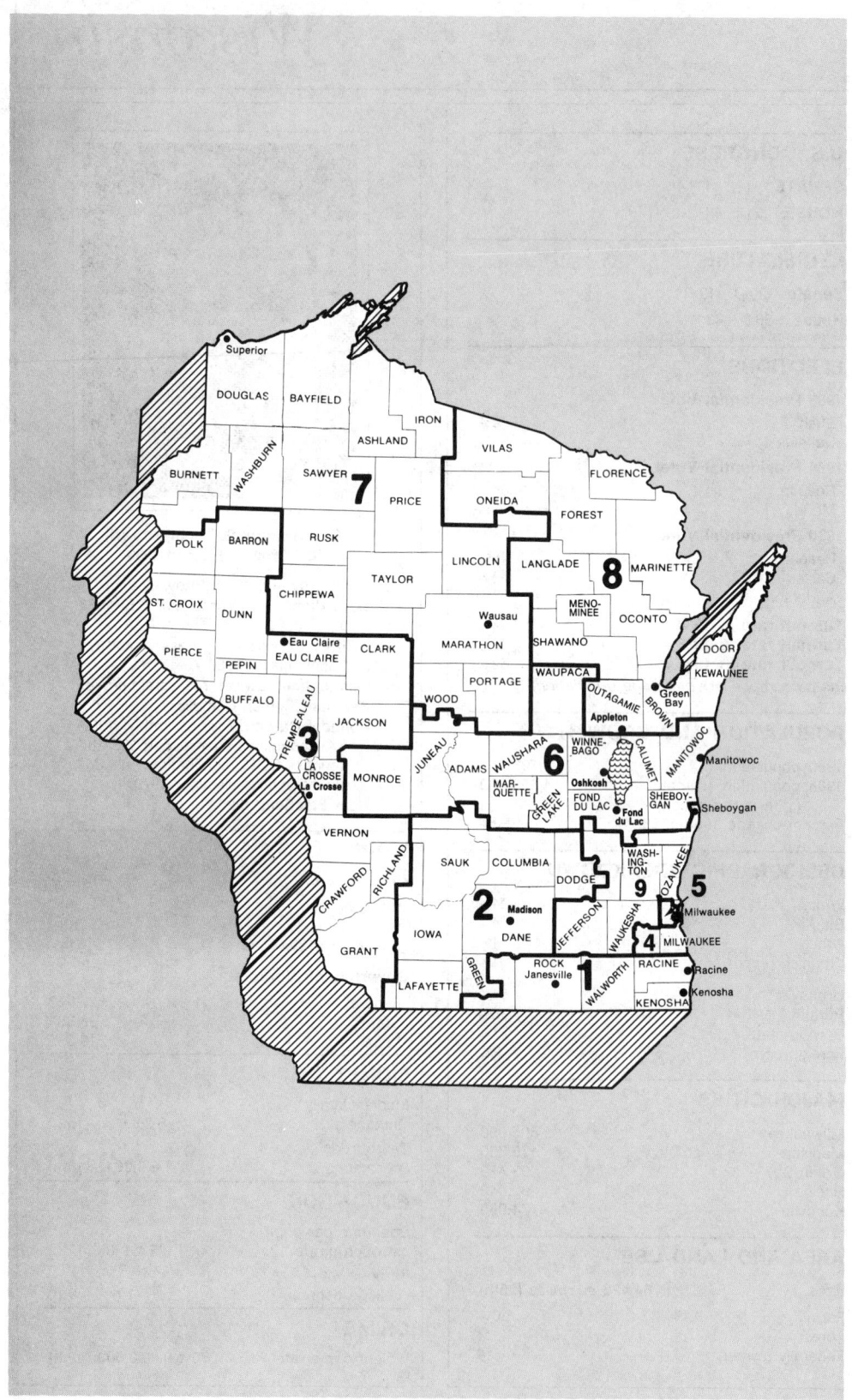

Bob Kasten (R)

Of Milwaukee — Elected 1980

Born: June 19, 1942, Milwaukee, Wis.
Education: U. of Arizona, B.A. 1964; Columbia U., M.B.A. 1966.
Military Career: Wis. Air National Guard, 1967-72.
Occupation: Shoe company executive.
Family: Wife, Eva Jean Nimmons; one child.
Religion: Presbyterian.
Political Career: Wis. Senate, 1973-75; U.S. House, 1975-79; GOP nominee for Wis. Assembly, 1970; sought GOP nomination for governor, 1978.
Capitol Office: 110 Hart Bldg. 20510; 224-5323.

In Washington: For Kasten, the 100th Congress came on the heels of a nasty re-election contest in which his arrest for drunken driving was held up as evidence that his personal qualities were unbefitting a senator.

Kasten won that 1986 campaign with just 51 percent of the vote, and he spent the next two years working to put the unpleasantness behind him. Part of that effort, of course, involved legislative pursuits. But for Kasten, it was even more important to show personal development. That is why, when asked about his most significant recent accomplishments, he pointedly cites his marriage in 1986, and the birth of his daughter in 1987. A "father and legislator," Kasten calls himself.

Throughout his political career, Kasten has had some image problems. He had trouble getting people to take him seriously when he first came to the Senate in 1981. His baby-faced countenance, relatively unremarkable House career and habit of running for higher office made many of his colleagues expect he would not be a major force in writing legislation.

But Kasten has always exceeded expectations. Contrary to the early view, he has made a measurable contribution to the legislative process and to internal GOP affairs.

Kasten has been very active on the Appropriations Subcommittee on Foreign Operations, which he chaired when Republicans controlled the Senate. That panel has responsibility over funding levels for foreign aid programs, which often provoke Senate strife. But Kasten has used the panel to pursue an environmental issue that cuts across partisan lines and has enhanced an image as a legislator with ideas.

One of Kasten's goals on the subcommittee is to get multilateral development banks to put more emphasis on environmental considerations when assessing projects in the Third World. In the 99th Congress, he pressed the World Bank to hold up nearly $500 million in loans for a Brazilian highway that many scientists thought could endanger the Amazon rain forest. The World Bank's leadership promised to alter the system of project approval.

In the 101st Congress, Kasten, as ranking member of the subcommittee, is working with a new chairman, Vermont Democrat Patrick J. Leahy. In the 100th Congress, the Foreign Operations chair was held by Daniel K. Inouye of Hawaii, and he and Kasten helped pass the first free-standing foreign aid bill since 1981. That achievement stemmed partly from the fact that a budget "summit" agreement between the White House and Congress had settled a major issue — how much to spend on foreign aid. With that determined, there was broad support in both chambers for the $14.3 billion bill.

There was still some disagreement, however. For years Kasten, along with Inouye, had pushed to restructure the foreign military aid program, which provides grants and loans to U.S. allies for the purchase of military equipment. Arguing that the loans were adding to the debt burden carried by many poor Third World nations, Kasten has sought to redirect the current program toward outright grants.

But he has had strong opposition from his House counterpart, Wisconsin Democrat David R. Obey, who says converting to an all-grant program would encourage countries to buy weapons they might not need. After some haggling in conference, a compromise was reached that allowed both sides to claim victory. In the latest in a series of steps toward an all-grant program, a plan was approved that reduced the portion of military aid given in loan form.

Kasten also is a staunch supporter of Israel, and has pushed unsuccessfully in the past to ease that country's heavy debt load by reducing the interest on past loans.

Some of Kasten's partisan instincts have shown up in his extracurricular activities, which in 1988 included serving as a co-chairman of the Republican Platform Committee. Also, Kasten has always taken a strong interest in his colleagues' re-election campaigns. His best-known work as a House member was political, not legislative. He was the author of the "Kasten plan," a system of precinct organizing for congressional campaigns. In the 100th Congress he took a leading role in pushing an investigation of Citizen Action, an interest group that he said had illegally given money to Democratic candidates. The National Republican Senatorial Committee in 1988 filed a formal legal complaint with the Internal Revenue Service and the Federal Election Commission.

Given Kasten's interest in campaigns, it is not surprising he has also shown some interest in chairing the campaign committee. He considered running for the position in 1982 and again in 1988, but did not. In 1984 he sought the post of majority whip for the 99th Congress, but he lost by a wide margin to the popular Alan K. Simpson of Wyoming.

Kasten's most visible legislative triumph as a senator came early in his first term. Though he was denounced as a tax cheater's champion, a shill for bankers and a proponent of "government by applause meter," Kasten persevered and won in a 1983 crusade to block tax withholding on income from interest and dividends.

Kasten's chief ally was a massive lobbying effort by the banking industry that induced savers to inundate congressmen with mail calling for repeal of the withholding law, which would have required financial institutions to deduct the tax money starting July 1, 1983.

Senate leaders and the Reagan administration defended withholding, saying it would discourage tax evasion and help reduce the federal deficit. Finance Committee Chairman Bob Dole vowed to filibuster the repeal measure.

But Kasten threatened to attach it to vital legislation providing recession relief and bailing out Social Security, and it became apparent that no one had the votes to stop him. Kasten helped the leadership save face by agreeing to a compromise that kept the withholding law on the books, but made its implementation contingent on later congressional approval, which both sides knew was unlikely.

Kasten has also been a player in the frustrating (and still ongoing) effort to rewrite the nation's product liability laws.

In tackling the product liability system in the 99th Congress, Kasten had a popular issue, at least among many businesses and insurance companies. Reeling from the huge awards sometimes given to consumers injured by faulty products — and struggling to comply with the diverse network of state liability laws — business groups strongly supported his proposal to pre-empt state laws with a federal standard governing liability lawsuits. But Kasten's proposals drew criticism from consumer groups and trial lawyers, who feared they would leave consumers defenseless against negligent or unethical manufacturers.

Kasten and his allies sought to improve their chances by dropping a controversial provision that allowed only one victim of a defective product to win punitive damages from its manufacturer. Still, the bill did not get out of the Commerce Committee, failing on an 8-8 tie.

The following year, Kasten offered one of a number of more modest proposals that aimed at setting some limits on damage awards, without confronting the larger issue of pre-empting state liability laws. The committee approved a bill similar to Kasten's, but it fell victim to filibuster threats on the floor.

Kasten also played a role in the debate on overhauling the tax code in the 99th Congress. He was one of the early advocates of a flat-rate tax structure, offering along with GOP Rep. Jack F. Kemp a "Fair and Simple Tax" plan that entailed a 25 percent rate for individuals and abolished virtually all deductions.

At Home: As the 1986 election year approached, Democrats were eager for the opportunity to prove their contention that Kasten was too far right and too tainted by questions of personal integrity to win again in a state that had not re-elected a Republican in 30 years. They had been spoiling for Kasten ever since he upset Democratic Sen. Gaylord Nelson in 1980.

And Kasten's detractors had reason to be optimistic. Late in 1985, he was arrested for drunken driving in Washington, D.C. Kasten avoided a criminal record by completing a course in alcohol abuse, but he was still subjected to a barrage of negative media coverage and editorials at home.

That incident also served to reignite other concerns that had troubled him earlier in his term. In 1982 his image was tarnished by publicity about his earlier association with a real-estate developer who was accused of theft and fraud and eventually went to jail.

Despite Kasten's potential vulnerability, Democrats failed to pick a candidate strong enough to take advantage of it. Their nominee, former state Deputy Attorney General Ed Garvey, struggled to prove he was not as far to the left of the political consensus as he claimed Kasten was to the right. And in one of the year's most negative contests, Garvey's character became as much of an issue as Kasten's.

Garvey, who was best known for his 13-year tenure outside the state as executive director of the National Football League Players Association, had strong support from organized labor, but he was battered during the primary by an opponent who labeled him a "special-interest puppet."

And though he quickly went on the offensive against Kasten, accusing him of "drinking on the job" and reminding voters that Kasten had once been three years late filing a tax return, Garvey had trouble endearing himself to voters. In September it was reported that a writer hired by Garvey to investigate Kasten had misrepresented himself to gain interviews with several journalists and one Democratic

U.S. representative.

Kasten blasted Garvey for his "Watergate tactics" and ran ads citing a report that $750,000 had disappeared from the players' union during Garvey's tenure. Garvey responded by filing a libel suit against Kasten.

The contest left both candidates splattered with mud and made it difficult for Garvey to sell himself as an attractive alternative for voters disenchanted with the incumbent. And Kasten, in addition to having an enormous campaign treasury, capitalized on his growing stature as a legislator and his well-publicized efforts to bring federal funds into the state. In the end, he won 51-47 percent.

Aggressive and determined, Kasten made it to the Senate in 1981 after a methodical 10-year climb in which he ran for five different offices in six elections and rebounded with surprising agility from his one major defeat.

His early political successes earned him a reputation as the "Golden Boy" of Wisconsin's GOP. He rose quickly from the state Senate in 1973 to Congress in 1975 and became the party's endorsed candidate for governor in 1978.

But his reputation was tarnished that year when he dropped the GOP gubernatorial primary to Lee Sherman Dreyfus, a colorful political novice whose entertaining oratory contrasted with Kasten's more reserved, serious style. In trying to expand his renowned precinct operation to cover the entire state, Kasten spent so much time planning for the general election that he let the primary slip away.

After the unexpected 1978 loss, Kasten knew another failure in 1980 would probably end his political career. But with three unimpressive candidates offering the only opposition for the right to challenge Nelson, he felt it was too good an opportunity to pass up.

Kasten's 1980 campaign showed clearly that he had learned from mistakes made in 1978. Honing his operation for the GOP primary, Kasten focused his efforts in eight key counties — and won all but one. His strength was concentrated in suburban Milwaukee, his old congressional district base.

Still, Kasten entered the 1980 general election as the underdog against Nelson, a two-term governor and three-term senator who had held public office continuously since 1948.

Although Kasten launched his campaign late and trailed significantly in funding, he won narrowly. Many blue-collar Democrats in Milwaukee and the industrial Fox River Valley favored Kasten's calls for less government and lower taxes over Nelson's traditional liberalism.

The nephew of a prominent Milwaukee banker, Kasten worked in a family shoe business before entering politics in the suburbs north and west of the city. After losing a state legislative election at age 28, he defeated a Republican state senator in 1972, then unseated U.S. Rep. Glenn Davis in a 1974 GOP primary.

Committees

Appropriations (6th of 13 Republicans)
Foreign Operations (ranking); Agriculture, Rural Development and Related Agencies; Commerce, Justice, State, the Judiciary and Related Agencies; Defense; Transportation and Related Agencies

Budget (6th of 10 Republicans)

Commerce, Science and Transportation (5th of 9 Republicans)
Surface Transportation (ranking); Aviation; Consumer; Science, Technology and Space; National Ocean Policy Study

Small Business (2nd of 9 Republicans)
Rural Economy and Family Farming (ranking); Government Contracting and Paperwork Reduction

Elections

1986 General

Bob Kasten (R)	754,573	(51%)
Ed Garvey (D)	702,963	(47%)

Previous Winning Percentages: **1980** (50%) **1976 *** (66%) **1974 *** (53%)

** House elections.*

Campaign Finance

	Receipts	Receipts from PACs	Expend-itures
1986			
Kasten (R)	$3,196,093	$1,095,726 (34%)	$3,433,870
Garvey (D)	$1,308,927	$456,082 (35%)	$1,306,702

Key Votes

1987

Enact omnibus highway bill over Reagan veto	N
Limit testing of space-based anti-ballistic missiles	N
Oppose banning tests of larger nuclear weapons	Y
Confirm Robert H. Bork as Supreme Court justice	Y

1988

Allow vote on campaign-finance overhaul	N
Pass civil rights restoration bill over Reagan veto	Y
Enact omnibus trade bill over Reagan veto	N
Approve death penalty for drug-related murders	Y
Oppose "workfare" amendment to welfare overhaul bill	N

Voting Studies

	Presidential Support		Party Unity		Conservative Coalition	
Year	S	O	S	O	S	O
1988	74	19	78	19	84	14
1987	68	31	90	9	91	9
1986	81	19	74	26	87	13
1985	74	26	68	32	75	25
1984	74	21	83	13	87	11
1983	68	32	78	17	93	7
1982	77	22	83	16	88	12
1981	80	20	84	15	88	11

Interest Group Ratings

Year	ADA	ACU	AFL-CIO	CCUS
1988	10	84	43	71
1987	20	92	30	83
1986	15	83	27	74
1985	10	70	38	72
1984	15	95	18	89
1983	10	76	13	79
1982	5	85	16	70
1981	10	80	16	83

Herb Kohl (D)

Of Milwaukee — Elected 1988

Born: Feb. 7, 1935, Milwaukee, Wis.
Education: U. of Wisconsin, B.A. 1956; Harvard U., M.B.A. 1958.
Military Career: Army Reserve, 1958-64.
Occupation: Businessman; professional basketball team owner.
Family: Single.
Religion: Jewish.
Political Career: No previous office.
Capitol Office: 702 Hart Bldg. 20510; 224-5653.

The Path to Washington: Kohl will have to compile a substantial record of achievement in the Senate before people stop talking about how he got there. Making his first try for public office, Kohl announced about six months before the election and yet spent just under $7.5 million, nearly all of it his own. He blew away the best competition in his own party and beat an attractive Republican moderate by 4½ points in November.

But Kohl found it hard to match the pace of his campaign when he came to occupy the office he had won. It took him several months to choose his top aide, and his inexperience in government and politics was often on display. At a meeting of the Wisconsin delegation, he suggested his colleagues had done less than they might have to bring federal spending home. That touchy subject reportedly provoked a rebuke from Wisconsin Democrat David R. Obey, the fifth-ranking Democrat on the House Appropriations Committee.

Kohl's life had been devoted to running his family's enterprises in food, retailing and real estate. So his adjustment may have fit the pattern of executives who arrive in Congress to find they no longer call the tune, not even for themselves. "I'm always subject to a schedule I don't create," Kohl told a reporter in March.

Kohl had shown some rough edges in the campaign as well, on one occasion naming Jimmy Carter's secretary of defense when asked who currently held the job. A multimillionaire who owns Milwaukee's professional basketball team, Kohl made a remark about the employment the team had provided for blacks that some found in poor taste.

But Kohl's errors were swept away in a sea of positive images. Mostly, these were communicated by Kohl's saturation television advertising, which emphasized his private-sector success and commitment to service — beginning with his immigrant parents. It was a campaign on a scale unlike any the state had ever seen. Kohl even bought time on Minnesota stations to reach border counties. His total outlay doubled the previous state record. A Milwaukee columnist suggested that one channel on everyone's TV set simply be rented to Kohl for the duration.

Although his political involvement had been as financier and, briefly, state party chairman, Kohl showed some flair for the give and take of debate. In the primary, facing former Gov. Anthony S. Earl and 1986 Senate nominee Ed Garvey, Kohl deflected their jibes and jabs with affability and a simple message: "Nobody's senator but yours."

Kohl's emphasis on his independence played well against efforts to vilify him as a plutocrat. He found the one political positive he could in being one of the state's richest men. The same theme also enabled him to strike an improbable, but apparently effective, parallel with his predecessor, Democratic Sen. William Proxmire, the legendary pinchpenny.

Proxmire had served three decades without spending much (and sometimes virtually nothing) on his re-election campaigns. He got away with it because he was popular enough to discourage challengers in his weight class. Kohl claimed similar independence based on his ability and willingness to self-finance his campaigns.

Some Wisconsin Democrats had been eager to unleash Kohl's assets in the 1986 election cycle against Republican Sen. Bob Kasten. That was the year after Kohl had personally spent $18.5 million to keep the Milwaukee Bucks franchise from leaving town. Kohl turned down the overtures then; and some of the same Democrats were not happy when Kohl decided the time was right for him two years later.

When Kohl entered the Democratic primary late in the spring, Earl was the front-runner and Rep. Jim Moody of Milwaukee was an apparent second. Moody saw his money and vote base jeopardized by Kohl and decided to stay in his safe House seat. But Earl and Garvey made a bitter fight of it. Earl, underfinanced as ever, spent money on negative ads satirizing Kohl's miscues and lack of political sophistication.

Kohl, meanwhile, could literally afford to stay on the high road and still post an easy plurality in the September primary. His November opponent was Susan S. Engeleiter, GOP leader in the state Senate and perhaps the most successful woman ever in Wisconsin politics. A decade earlier, when just 26, she had come within a few hundred votes of being nominated to a safe Republican seat in the U.S. House. In the meantime she had finished law school, had a family and worked for a GOP governor.

In the GOP primary, Engeleiter had dispatched a much more conservative opponent, former state party Chairman Steve King, who challenged her for the nomination when popular Republican Gov. Tommy G. Thompson demurred. But her margin was smaller than expected, and King's attacks highlighted issues on which she differed from much of her party — including her support for limited abortion rights and for the Equal Rights Amendment. King openly questioned whether Engeleiter, with young children at home, should be in public office at all.

By forcing Engeleiter rightward, King may have given the unabashedly liberal Kohl running room in the center he otherwise would not have had. In the short weeks before the November election, Engeleiter tried to compete with the continuing deluge of Kohl ads on TV by portraying herself as more in tune with ordinary people's problems. She downplayed ideology by labeling herself "A Wisconsin Original."

But her financing had never been in a league with Kohl's, so she tried to break out with a dramatic tactic in a debate between the two candidates. She accused a company Kohl's family had owned of selling coffee cakes to the military at inflated prices. Kohl seemed unperturbed. Newspaper reporters subsequently found the difference in price attributable to a difference in size. The issue fizzled, and Engeleiter never closed the gap. Shortly after the election, President George Bush named her to head the Small Business Administration.

Arriving in Washington to vote for party leaders in November, Kohl announced early for George J. Mitchell of Maine as Senate majority leader. Mitchell went on to win, but it did not seem to help Kohl, who asked for seats on Appropriations (where Proxmire had sat) and on Agriculture and expressed an interest in Budget. He got, instead, seats on Governmental Affairs, Judiciary and the Special Committee on Aging.

In the early going, Kohl generally showed himself to be genial and disinclined to follow Proxmire's idiosyncratic patterns. He quietly followed his party leadership in rejecting the nomination of former Sen. John Tower as secretary of defense and in raising the minimum wage.

But if Kohl promised to be less of a loner than Proxmire, he did seem to have inherited his predecessor's preoccupation with the budget deficit. Kohl's maiden speech was a jeremiad against the deficit, which he said would bring "the economic collapse we all fear." In May, when the budget resolution was brought to the floor for rubber-stamping, Kohl was among those objecting to this *fait accompli* from the White House and top congressional leaders.

Kohl even went so far as to move to recommit the resolution to committee. He wanted the Congressional Budget Office to plug in some real numbers in place of the hedge-and-fudge approach the budget-summit agreement had taken to revenues and spending cuts. The leadership and the Budget Committee chairman and ranking member opposed this, and they brought most of the Senate along.

But Kohl's rebellion attracted an interesting band of supporters. Among the 19 senators voting for his motion to recommit were two highly disparate Republicans: Jesse Helms of North Carolina and Rudy Boschwitz of Minnesota. The 17 Democrats included seven from the classes of 1986 and 1988 and also such senior members as Sam Nunn of Georgia, Bill Bradley of New Jersey and J. Bennett Johnston of Louisiana.

Committees

Governmental Affairs (7th of 8 Democrats)
Federal Services, Post Office and Civil Service; Government Information and Regulation; Oversight of Government Management; Permanent Subcommittee on Investigations

Judiciary (8th of 8 Democrats)
Antitrust, Monopolies and Business Rights; Courts and Administrative Practice; Technology and the Law

Special Aging (10th of 10 Democrats)

Campaign Finance

	Receipts	Receipts from PACs	Expenditures
1988			
Kohl (D)	$7,576,540	0	$7,491,600
Engeleiter (R)	$2,945,328	$993,692 (34%)	$2,908,101

Elections

1988 General		
Herb Kohl (D)	1,128,625	(52%)
Susan Engeleiter (R)	1,030,440	(48%)
1988 Primary		
Herb Kohl (D)	249,226	(47%)
Anthony S. Earl (D)	203,479	(38%)
Ed Garvey (D)	55,225	(10%)

1 Les Aspin (D)

Of East Troy — Elected 1970

Born: July 21, 1938, Milwaukee, Wis.
Education: Yale U., B.A. 1960; Oxford U., England, M.A. 1962; Massachusetts Institute of Technology, Ph.D. 1965.
Military Career: Army, 1966-68.
Occupation: Professor of economics.
Family: Divorced.
Religion: Episcopalian.
Political Career: Sought Democratic nomination for Wis. treasurer, 1968.
Capitol Office: 2336 Rayburn Bldg. 20515; 225-3031.

In Washington: As the House Armed Services Committee chairman in recent years, Aspin has helped restore Democrats' credibility on defense. He still needs to work on his own.

The widespread mistrust that provoked Aspin's former liberal allies to mount a coup in 1987 — just one term after they helped him wrest the chairmanship from enfeebled hawk Melvin Price — lingers on below the surface. At Armed Services, Aspin clearly has solidified his control with a centrist coalition. Yet his relations in the House Democratic Caucus remain fragile, despite his easy re-election there as committee chairman for the 101st Congress.

Aspin's problems with fellow Democrats have always involved issues, notably the MX missile. But at bottom the issue is Aspin's personality. Though publicly extroverted and gregarious, he is a loner no one really knows, not even his closest lieutenants. With academic credentials few can match, Aspin is an intellectual who has always been more comfortable among Washington's defense theorists than among colleagues on the House floor.

There, Democrats came to view him as evasive and misunderstood, at best, or a liar at worst. Even his zest for political wheeling and dealing can arouse suspicion. Aspin gets credit for producing defense bills that, for the first time in years, are supported by a wide majority of House Democrats, but he is criticized for playing his hand too close to the vest, for brokering deals and presenting them as a *fait accompli*, simply ignoring ideas he dislikes.

After 14 years as an independent operator at Armed Services, Aspin had some dramatic adjustments to make when he became chairman. He went a long way to placate the five senior panelists he had leapfrogged; since then, deaths and a retirement among those conservatives have worked further peaceful change at the committee, cementing Aspin's control. Though ever a loner, he benefits from a centrist kitchen cabinet — including junior activists John M. Spratt Jr. of South Carolina and Dave McCurdy of Oklahoma — whose members feel free to talk back and keep him sensitized to other Democrats' feelings.

Aspin was typecast as a "liberal Pentagon critic" in the 1970s, when he led a maverick minority on a very hawkish Armed Services Committee and gained attention for his timely, irreverent press releases. But the current perception of some liberals that Aspin has betrayed beliefs they all once shared has a flaw: A former economist in Robert S. McNamara's Pentagon, he has always been prone to take a harder line than his fellow liberals.

After his first election as chairman in 1985, Aspin said it was "a signal that the Democratic Party ought to be doing some serious looking at defense." He insisted Democrats had to counter voters' image of the party as anti-defense: "If we want to make defense policy in the White House and Pentagon, then we had better stand for something. The voters are not attracted to national-security naysayers."

Even after his near-ouster two years later, a humbled Aspin understood that while his defense policy stands were an issue, his personality was more so. "The message is not that you have to toe the party line on issues," he said after his comeback victory. "What it does say ... is you can't surprise people. You've got to be frank about what you're doing."

At the same time, Aspin's controversial style and his stance on one major issue, the MX, have become inextricably linked. Indeed, liberals' distrust of Aspin flared anew early in the 101st Congress, when they charged that he was collaborating with the Bush administration on a two-missile deal that would permit deployments of both the 10-warhead MX and the smaller Midgetman; until then, House Democrats had appeared to be coalescing around the Midgetman.

Liberals' attacks on Aspin at one meeting were "a reminder," one said, that he should consult with Democrats before negotiating with Republicans. Aspin denied he had made any

Wisconsin 1

Southeast — Racine; Kenosha

Although it is dominated by four industrialized cities, the 1st is far from a Democratic stronghold.

Until Aspin's election in 1970, Democratic candidates had won this district only twice in the 20th century — in 1958 and 1964. Both incumbents were defeated after serving single terms. After Lyndon B. Johnson carried the district for president in 1964, Democrats endured a long dry spell in the 1st. Not until 1988 did it return to the Democratic column, and even then Michael S. Dukakis managed just a slim 51-48 percent victory.

The district's two largest cities are sandwiched between Milwaukee and Chicago on the Lake Michigan shore. Racine, originally settled by Danish immigrants, manufactures a wide range of Johnson's Wax products, from Agree shampoo to Pledge furniture polish.

Ronald Reagan easily defeated both Jimmy Carter and Walter F. Mondale in Racine County, but in 1988, its voters went Democratic in the presidential, Senate and House contests.

Kenosha's economic base is not as diversified as Racine's. The city has a sizable Italian community, a branch of the University of Wisconsin and an assembly plant for Jeeps; Chrysler owns the former American Motors Corp. plant.

In the west-central part of the district are the smaller industrial cities of Janesville and Beloit, both in politically marginal Rock County. Beloit was settled by a group of immigrants from New Hampshire that founded Beloit College in 1847. Janesville's employers include a General Motors plant.

The strongest Republican vote in the 1st comes from Walworth County, between Janesville and Racine-Kenosha. Resort complexes around Lake Geneva and Lake Delavan cater to wealthy vacationers from Milwaukee and Chicago. Soybeans grow so well in the farming sections of Walworth County that the Japanese Kikkoman soy sauce company built a plant in Walworth to brew and bottle its product.

Population: 522,838. White 491,746 (94%), Black 21,956 (4%), Other 3,054 (1%). Spanish origin 13,173 (3%). 18 and over 366,924 (70%), 65 and over 56,852 (11%). Median age: 29.

deal, but Democrats' skepticism was indicative of his ongoing problem.

It is one that predates Aspin's chairmanship. When the liberals in 1983 came close to killing the MX, which they opposed for its cost and vulnerability to a Soviet strike, Aspin and other moderates salvaged it in a deal with the Reagan administration; Aspin had come to defend the missile as a bargaining chip with Moscow, a prod to push President Reagan toward arms control talks, and a chance for Democrats to prove their support for defense.

But, the enraged liberals later claimed, Aspin had led them to believe he would switch and oppose the MX when he enlisted their support for his challenge to Price. Bucking Democratic leaders, who stood by Price and the seniority system, they helped Aspin win the January 1985 vote to dump Price, 121-118, despite an emotional appeal by Speaker Thomas P. O'Neill Jr. The leadership then nominated the committee's ranking Democrat, Charles E. Bennett of Florida, but Aspin beat him 125-103.

Before long, Aspin helped engineer the MX's rescue once again. Then, after enduring bitter personal attacks from fellow Democrats for his role, he negotiated the compromise designed to end the three years of divisive battles. It capped the number of missiles to be deployed in fixed silos at 50; after the measure was approved, Aspin declared it the last word of Congress on the MX: "It's over. It's done."

During that first year of his chairmanship, Aspin also ran into a barrage of criticism that he and his fellow House conferees gave in too easily to the Senate's larger defense budget. Some House members were unhappy, too, with compromises on their amendments to revamp the Pentagon's troubled procurement system.

In 1986, Aspin worked hard to protect his left flank in debate over that year's defense bill. Aligning himself more closely with arms control efforts, he led a rout of Reagan's policies when the defense bill came to the floor. He crafted a procedural strategy for winning passage of five major arms control amendments, including one banning all but the smallest nuclear tests and another requiring U.S. compliance with arms limits in the unratified SALT II treaty. The Senate did not accept those amendments, but the growing pressure from the House was credited with pushing Reagan to deal with the Soviets.

By that time, though, nothing Aspin did could prevent the challenge to him that was already in motion. Moreover, he fanned the opposition with his 1986 vote for military aid to the Nicaraguan contras. At year's end, anti-Aspin sentiment had brought together vengeful conservatives, distrustful moderates and — leading the mutiny — the liberal activists who felt double-crossed by his MX and contra votes.

The rebellion coalesced behind the unlikely candidacy of Marvin Leath, then 14th in line at Armed Services. The conservative Texan seemed an implausible contender to capitalize on the fury of liberals, but his success just proved the extent to which Aspin's character was on trial. Leath's record was far more conservative than Aspin's, but he is well liked and trusted, and had impressed liberals on the Budget Committee with his willingness to deal on defense cutbacks. In the end, however, Aspin supporters were able to exploit Leath's record to deal a decisive blow to his candidacy.

The opposition did unseat Aspin temporarily with a 130-124 no-confidence vote in January 1987, but Aspin turned it around two weeks later on the vote that mattered. He defeated three challengers, beating Leath on the final ballot 133-116.

Subsequently in the 100th Congress, Aspin led Armed Services to take a tough stand on the trouble-plagued B-1 bomber and some other major military programs, in an effort to convince Democratic reformers that the committee could be trusted to oversee the Pentagon.

He continued the final assault on Reagan's defense budget, boasting in 1987 that "it's becoming a much more Democratic defense bill." By 1987, however, the lame-duck president had pared his requests more in line with what Congress and budget limits would allow, and in 1988, spending followed a summit agreement that Reagan and congressional leaders had negotiated earlier. Reagan did veto the defense authorization in August of that year, to dramatize the defense issue for Bush's presidential campaign, but the bill was renegotiated with minor changes.

Despite their differences in style, Aspin has worked closely with Senate Armed Services Committee Chairman Sam Nunn, also a respected defense expert, not only to pass consensus defense bills but also to nudge their party to the political center.

Unlike many Democrats, both Aspin and Nunn were unhappy that Reagan's 1987 intermediate-range nuclear-force (INF) treaty with Soviet leader Mikhail S. Gorbachev banned all such weapons in Europe. Aspin had said that such a deal would erode a NATO doctrine by which the alliance could resort to nuclear weapons against an attack by the Warsaw Pact's larger conventional forces. But he reluctantly supported Senate ratification, assuming that rejection would incite European public opinion and weaken NATO.

With Nunn, Aspin led Democrats' successful fight throughout the 100th Congress to mandate U.S. compliance with the strict traditional reading of the 1972 ABM treaty, thus blocking Reagan's attempt to reinterpret the accord to permit space tests of his strategic defense initiative (SDI). As for SDI, the two chairmen and liberal critics say the Pentagon should stress research on exotica promising an effective anti-missile shield decades from now — not immediate deployment of limited technology as Reagan and conservatives wanted.

Both men also served on the special committee investigating the Iran-contra scandal in the 100th Congress. But Aspin was absent for the initial weeks while he vacationed after House passage of the defense bill, and he attended the hearings only sporadically thereafter.

Aspin has been a member of Armed Services ever since he came to Congress at the height of the Vietnam War. He had to fight for his seat, and thus began his dispute with the committee's pro-war, pro-Pentagon leadership.

Early in 1973, he embarrassed Chairman F. Edward Hebert with a floor amendment reducing the defense budget by about 4 percent. The committee was rarely defeated in the House, but Aspin forged an alliance of liberals and fiscal conservatives to win 242-163. Two years later, he was a ringleader in the coup that ousted Hebert in favor of Price.

Aspin soon won a seat on the Intelligence Committee, but in 1981 O'Neill removed him a year before his six-year stint expired. The Speaker later would say only that he did so at the request of "the highest authorities" and that Aspin "was suspect." Aspin said he left to join Budget, but leadership sources made plain that his social relations with reporters had raised suspicions about leaks.

O'Neill and Aspin irrevocably split later in 1981, when Aspin told constituents in a newsletter that O'Neill was "in a fog." Six years later, O'Neill backed Leath for Armed Services chairman.

At Home: When he launched his 1970 congressional campaign, Aspin was a Marquette University economics professor who had just moved into the district. His academic credentials were impressive, and he had been active in statewide politics, but his ties to local politics were not strong.

Two years earlier he had been signed up by the White House to head President Johnson's re-election effort in Wisconsin. When that effort evaporated just before the state's primary, Aspin switched to Robert F. Kennedy's campaign. That September, Aspin was defeated in his first try at elective office, losing the Democratic primary for state treasurer.

Afterward, he moved into the 1st District and became its Democratic chairman. The 1970 House election looked promising for an eager challenger since the incumbent Republican, Henry C. Schadeberg, had won his last two elections with just 51 percent.

To get at Schadeberg, Aspin first had to defeat former Democratic Rep. Gerald T. Flynn and chemistry professor Douglas LaFollette in the primary. Flynn posed only a slight problem. But LaFollette appealed to the same liberal constituency as Aspin and had a more attractive name — he was a distant relative of the state's legendary governor and U.S. senator, Robert M. LaFollette. Aspin appeared to lose the primary but on a recount, won by 20 votes.

The general election offered a clear philosophical choice. Schadeberg emphasized a "return to America's heritage of order, discipline and hard work." Aspin appealed to peace and ecology groups and, when talking with the larger middle-class segment of the electorate, stressed the need to reduce unemployment. With substantial contributions from organized labor and a well-run campaign, Aspin retired Schadeberg with 61 percent.

The 1978 campaign was Aspin's worst political experience of the decade. Some $27,000 in campaign contributions disappeared, stolen by his campaign chairman, who later confessed he took it. And Republican William Petrie, whom Aspin had beaten easily two years before, waged a surprisingly strenuous campaign, holding Aspin to 55 percent, his lowest-ever tally.

In 1980, Petrie refused to run for a third time without a pre-primary endorsement from the GOP; when he bowed out, the nomination went to surprise primary winner Kathryn H. Canary. For the second consecutive election, Aspin lost the rural areas, but his vote in Racine and Kenosha improved, and he won 56 percent overall.

In 1984, Republicans made one more serious effort behind Pete Jansson, a Racine lawyer armed with a large campaign treasury, backing from the National Republican Congressional Committee and hopes of Reagan coattails. An indication of the seriousness of the challenge was Aspin's acceptance of campaign contributions from the defense contractors he had long criticized. Jansson won conservative Walworth County, but Aspin prevailed in the industrialized areas of Kenosha, Racine and Rock counties, and again won 56 percent.

Committee

Armed Services (Chairman)
Procurement and Military Nuclear Systems (chairman)

Elections

1988 General

Les Aspin (D)	158,552	(76%)
Bernie Weaver (R)	49,620	(24%)

1986 General

Les Aspin (D)	106,288	(74%)
Iris Peterson (R)	34,495	(24%)

Previous Winning Percentages: **1984** (56%) **1982** (61%) **1980** (56%) **1978** (55%) **1976** (65%) **1974** (71%) **1972** (64%) **1970** (61%)

District Vote For President

	1988	1984	1980	1976
D	114,078 (51%)	105,412 (45%)	98,916 (42%)	107,718 (48%)
R	107,375 (48%)	126,758 (54%)	117,710 (50%)	108,964 (49%)
I			16,478 (7%)	

Campaign Finance

	Receipts	Receipts from PACs	Expend-itures
1988			
Aspin (D)	$618,045	$265,249 (43%)	$631,941
Weaver (R)	$18,626	0	$17,760
1986			
Aspin (D)	$503,453	$195,382 (39%)	$497,588
Peterson (R)	$9,833	0	$9,635

Key Votes

1987

Raise speed limit to 65 mph	Y
Approve Gephardt "fair trade" amendment	Y
Ban testing of larger nuclear weapons	Y
Delay "re-flagging" of Kuwaiti tankers	Y
Approve tax-raising deficit-reduction bill	Y

1988

Approve aid to Nicaraguan contras	N
Enact civil rights restoration bill over Reagan veto	Y
Kill 60-day plant-closing notification measure	N
Pass omnibus trade bill over Reagan veto	Y
Approve death penalty for drug-related murders	Y
Bar federal funds for abortions in cases of rape and incest	Y
Oppose seven-day waiting period for purchase of handguns	N

Voting Studies

	Presidential Support		Party Unity		Conservative Coalition	
Year	**S**	**O**	**S**	**O**	**S**	**O**
1988	25	69	78	6	37	50
1987	22	72	81	5	44	51
1986	28	64	83	8	42	48
1985	33	60	82	9	44	49
1984	40	51	73	16	42	54
1983	30	63	84	9	29	67
1982	42	48	77	15	41	53
1981	26	67	80	11	25	68

Interest Group Ratings

Year	ADA	ACU	AFL-CIO	CCUS
1988	75	4	100	27
1987	76	0	94	8
1986	50	24	80	42
1985	65	19	100	10
1984	75	17	85	36
1983	80	14	94	25
1982	85	10	90	24
1981	75	0	86	7

2 Robert W. Kastenmeier (D)

Of Sun Prairie — Elected 1958

Born: Jan. 24, 1924, Beaver Dam, Wis.
Education: U. of Wisconsin, LL.B. 1952.
Military Career: Army, 1943-46.
Occupation: Lawyer.
Family: Wife, Dorothy Chambers; three children.
Religion: Unspecified.
Political Career: Democratic nominee for U.S. House, 1956.
Capitol Office: 2328 Rayburn Bldg. 20515; 225-2906.

In Washington: Kastenmeier has not changed much ideologically during his long House career — he is as solid in his commitment to equal rights and civil liberties as he was when he arrived 30 years ago. But his role has changed enormously. Kastenmeier has evolved from a crusader into a technician.

As conservative in his personal style as he is liberal in outlook, Kastenmeier is a dull speaker with a distaste for flamboyance. He is often overshadowed on Judiciary by members who express their views more militantly.

While other Judiciary Committee Democrats have used their senior positions in recent years to stake out rhetorical opposition to conservatives' priorities, Kastenmeier has said relatively little in public. Instead, during unfavorable times for liberal initiatives, he has busied himself in the complexities of patent law and court administration, using his Subcommittee on Courts, Intellectual Property and the Administration of Justice to push through a variety of technical but important pieces of legislation.

Kastenmeier devoted much of the 1970s to working on the intricacies of copyright law, producing the first comprehensive revision in that field in more than 60 years and guiding it through nearly a decade of debate.

Since then, advances in technology have presented Kastenmeier and his subcommittee with a myriad of new copyright and patent issues to delve into. In 1988, soon after the first patent was issued for a genetically altered animal — a cancer-prone mouse developed by a Harvard University researcher — Kastenmeier sponsored a bill specifically allowing such patents but giving some protection to farmers concerned that their use of genetically altered animals would be restricted. The exemption was broadened as the bill passed the full committee, but the whole issue stalled when Senate action appeared unlikely. In 1989, Kastenmeier reintroduced his bill, warning the biotechnology industry and the agriculture community to settle their differences.

Kastenmeier explores these issues not as fads, but as developments worthy of patience. For six years he pursued ways to improve patent protection for high-technology industries such as electronics, biotechnology and drugs by making liable for patent infringement anyone who imports, sells or uses products made abroad by a process patented in the United States. Carefully working out compromises with the administration, trade groups, House Republicans and the Senate, he got most of what he wanted in the sprawling trade package of 1988.

Kastenmeier's caution and strategy showed in 1988 on a bill to make it easier for businesses to get protection for trademarks. The Senate quickly passed a bill based on the recommendations of a trade association. But Kastenmeier expressed worry about a number of provisions, including one allowing owners of famous trademarks to sue others (including advertisers) who they felt were misusing them. In committee, Kastenmeier inserted a provision giving consumers the right to sue trademark owners for false advertising. Rather than press its case, the Senate decided to drop both Kastenmeier's provision and its own.

Kastenmeier was able to skirt both the administration and Energy and Commerce Chairman John D. Dingell of Michigan in 1988 on a bill to set up a new procedure for satellite companies to re-transmit copyrighted TV programs and to make unscrambled signals available to rural satellite-dish owners. The satellite-dish issue was a significant one in Energy and Commerce, and Dingell fumed about "enthusiastic amateurs" who "know little" about telecommunications when Kastenmeier's subcommittee got first crack at the bill. But no floor fight ensued, and the measure was combined with the more pro-industry trademark bill in order to protect it from a presidential veto. The strategy worked.

Kastenmeier steadfastly avoided contro-

Wisconsin 2

South — Madison

Republicans have most of the land in the 2nd, and Democrats have most of the voters. While the district covers a sizable portion of southern Wisconsin's Republican-voting rural areas, its centerpiece is the traditionally Democratic city of Madison in Dane County.

Madison, the state capital and second largest city in Wisconsin, has its share of industry; meat processor Oscar Mayer, for example, employs nearly 2,500 in its Madison plant. But the city's personality is dominated by its white-collar sector — the bureaucrats who work in local and state government, the 2,300 educators and 43,000 students at the University of Wisconsin, and the large number of insurance company home offices, so many that Madison calls itself a Midwestern Hartford.

Madison boasts a tradition of political liberalism. Since 1924, when Robert M. La Follette carried Dane County as the Progressive Party's presidential candidate, Democrats nearly always have won here. Michael S. Dukakis won the county with 60 percent in 1988, as Democratic Senate candidate Herb Kohl polled 58 percent, compared with 52 percent statewide.

Outside the Madison area, agriculture and tourism sustain the district's economy. Dairying is important, and there is some beef production, although many livestock farmers have switched to raising corn as a cash crop.

In New Glarus (Green County), which was founded by the Swiss, the downtown area has been redone to resemble a village in the mother country. Wisconsin Dells (Columbia County) lures big-city tourists to view the steep ridges and high plateaus along the Wisconsin River.

The majority of farmers and small-town people in the district are conservative, and they chafe at Madison's dominance of district politics. In 1988, Republican House nominee Ann Haney won every county in the 2nd except Dane; Kastenmeier's 64 percent tally in Dane County boosted him to his comfortable overall victory margin of 59 percent to 41 percent.

Population: 523,011. White 509,003 (97%), Black 6,051 (1%), Other 4,986 (1%). Spanish origin 4,233 (1%). 18 and over 383,086 (73%), 65 and over 55,870 (11%). Median age: 29.

versy in the 100th Congress when disagreements arose over how much control artists should have over subsequent use of their works; the dispute threatened to block a bill allowing the United States to join a comprehensive international treaty for copyright protection. Kastenmeier favored making as few changes in U.S. law as possible, and his approach enabled the bill to pass the House 420-0 and become law after a minor compromise with the Senate.

In the 99th Congress, Kastenmeier worked to extend privacy guarantees for telephone conversations to messages transmitted and stored in computers, known as "electronic mail." His legislation drew a broad coalition of support, including business groups and the American Civil Liberties Union; that helped persuade a reluctant Justice Department to come aboard. The bill became law in October 1986.

Kastenmeier's subcommittee also handles the federal courts, and he played a major role in changing the bankruptcy court system, which had been left in limbo by a 1982 Supreme Court decision. He fought a plan, pushed by then-Judiciary Chairman Peter W. Rodino Jr., that would have created a new system of 227 judges with special constitutional standing. The judges would have had life tenure and salaries that could not be reduced by Congress.

Kastenmeier insisted that the new judgeships were not needed, and Congress eventually agreed; bankruptcy judges were made adjuncts to federal district courts.

While he is at the other end of the ideological spectrum from William H. Rehnquist, Kastenmeier responded to the new chief justice's appeals in the 100th Congress and steered two bills into law to help the courts. One gave the Supreme Court greater discretion over which cases to review; the other did the same for lower federal courts and authorized experiments in arbitration to settle disputes. But he opposes appeals for a drastic expansion of federal judgeships, fearing that judges would become specialists with narrow viewpoints. In 1986, Kastenmeier's chairmanship forced him into the public eye during the impeachment and trial of a federal judge. U.S. District Judge Harry E. Claiborne of Nevada was serving a two-year sentence for tax evasion, but refused to resign. Kastenmeier's panel approved four impeachment articles and sent them to the full Judiciary Committee, which approved them 35-0.

Once the committee sent the impeachment resolution to the House, Kastenmeier showed his characteristic distaste for the spotlight by trying — unsuccessfully — to avoid serving as a manager in the Senate trial, which resulted in

Claiborne's removal from office.

One such experience was enough for Kastenmeier. When two more impeachment cases surfaced (concerning U.S. District Judges Alcee L. Hastings of Florida and Walter L. Nixon Jr. of Mississippi) in the 100th Congress, he asked Rodino not to assign them to his subcommittee, even though he had helped draft the 1980 law governing judicial discipline. Rodino complied, although he did not go along with Kastenmeier's suggestion that a special committee panel handle impeachments, instead giving them to other standing subcommittees.

Kastenmeier's subcommittee also has dealt with some of the most sensitive social issues of the 1980s, but he serves his liberal principles on those subjects by taking as little action as possible. He has fought legislation to strip federal courts of jurisdiction over busing, school prayer or abortion. He has held hearings on some of these bills at various times in recent years, but he has never come close to scheduling any action on them.

Kastenmeier came to Congress as one of the small cadre of 1950s peace activists. He complained about the anti-communist "witch hunts" of his state's former GOP senator, Joseph R. McCarthy, and said the "military-industrial complex" was out of control. With two former campaign aides and leftist writers, Marcus Raskin and Arthur Waskow, he set out to produce a manifesto to influence American foreign policy in the 1960s.

They began the Liberal Project and attracted 17 other congressmen who wanted to publish position papers on liberal issues. The 1960 election was not kind to them; 16 of the 18 were defeated. But Kastenmeier continued as head of the redrawn "Liberal Group" and a few years later published the Liberal Papers, calling for disarmament, admission of mainland China to the United Nations and an end to the draft. Republicans labeled them "apostles of appeasement" and most Democrats ignored the work. Since then, Kastenmeier has kept a lower profile both inside the House and out. But many of the ideas were accepted eventually.

His timing has been unusual. His opposition to the Vietnam War was so far ahead of public opinion that by the time the anti-war fervor reached its peak, Kastenmeier had been through it already. He was consistent in his support for the anti-war movement, but he was never a national leader in it.

Early in his career, Kastenmeier and his allies in the Liberal Group — Don Edwards and Phillip Burton of California — worked on efforts to democratize House procedure. But here, too, Kastenmeier did not play a leading role when the changes were actually made a decade later. By then, he had turned his attention to legal work on Judiciary. He supported the procedural reforms but was not publicly associated with them by most members.

Kastenmeier admits that he and other House liberals have modified their approach of days past. "We are less pretentious," he has said. "We don't presume to accomplish as much.... We feel we ought to be the cutting edge of American liberalism in the body politic, yet there is even a limitation to that."

At Home: In an earlier era, it was possible for Kastenmeier to win re-election easily on the mere strength of his opposition to the Vietnam War or his support for the impeachment of President Nixon. Now, he has to take campaigning almost as seriously as he did in the early years of his career. But his seat seems secure for now.

A larger question will arise after 1990, when reapportionment costs Wisconsin a House seat and the remaining districts are redrawn. Kastenmeier's 2nd likely will see the addition of more GOP voters, who predominate in adjoining counties. And the incumbent will be 68 in 1992.

After dropping to 54 percent of the vote in 1980 and losing every county in the district except Dane, home of the University of Wisconsin, Kastenmeier bounced back in his next two elections, taking more than 60 percent. Against a strong candidate in 1986, he slipped back to 56 percent.

Although Kastenmeier never has seemed very comfortable campaigning, he now does the things that careful incumbents have been doing for years. In 1978, he spent a little over $40,000 on his re-election campaign, about half the total of his GOP opponent. Ten years later, Kastenmeier's campaign cost well over $425,000.

The son of an elected minor official from Dodge County, Kastenmeier took only a limited interest in politics until he was nearly 30 years old. Then he became the Democratic chairman of the second-smallest county in the district, and three years later, in 1956, decided to run for the House seat left open by Republican Glenn R. Davis, who was running for the Senate. Kastenmeier lost to GOP nominee Donald E. Tewes by 55-45 percent. But in 1958, with two of Wisconsin's most popular Democrats — William Proxmire and Gaylord Nelson — running on the statewide ticket, many Republicans in the 2nd stayed home, and Kastenmeier won.

Kastenmeier's first three elections were hotly contested affairs that included accusations that the Democrat was sympathetic to communists. In his first successful campaign, in 1958, he was helped by farm discontent with the policies of the Eisenhower administration.

After 1964 redistricting removed Milwaukee's suburban Waukesha County from the district, Kastenmeier's percentages shot up. In 1970, when the old charges were updated to include criticism that Kastenmeier was "soft on radical students," the incumbent won by his highest percentage ever.

Kastenmeier had few problems for a full

decade after that. But in 1980, his refusal to back away from any of his liberal views opened him to Republican assault as being out of step with the new fiscal conservatism. Those attacks, made by his challenger, former yo-yo manufacturer James A. Wright, had particular appeal in the farming communities that surround Madison. Only Kastenmeier's strong support in the Madison university community allowed him to survive the 1980 contest, in which Nelson went down to defeat at the statewide level.

In 1982, Republicans nominated a more moderate candidate, tax consultant Jim Johnson, who tried to appeal to Madison and avoided the Reagan-style rhetoric Wright had used. But the issues were moving back in Kastenmeier's direction. Much of the anti-government feeling of the previous election had subsided, and the issue with the strongest emotional appeal was the nuclear freeze. Wisconsin voted overwhelmingly for the freeze, and Kastenmeier was one of its most vocal supporters.

The GOP did not give Kastenmeier much trouble in 1984, but two years later found an attractive challenger in Ann Haney, a moderate Republican who served in the Cabinet of former GOP Gov. Lee Sherman Dreyfus. A vivacious campaigner, Haney tried to win support in Dane County by challenging Kastenmeier's effectiveness more than his ideology. She argued that Kastenmeier should have spent less time on copyright and patent law and more time on matters important to the district, such as agriculture.

But if Kastenmeier's style and legislative interests did not stir enthusiasm at home, Haney still had difficulty overcoming the loyal following he had built over years in office. She was further hampered shortly before the election when an illness in her family forced her off the campaign trail for more than a week.

Two years later, Haney returned for a rematch in the presidential election year, but there were no GOP coattails here. The state went Democratic and Kastenmeier slightly improved on his 1986 margin, nearly reaching 60 percent.

Committees

Judiciary (2nd of 21 Democrats)
Courts, Intellectual Property and the Administration of Justice (chairman); Civil and Constitutional Rights

Select Intelligence (3rd of 12 Democrats)
Legislation; Program and Budget Authorization

Elections

1988 General		
Robert W. Kastenmeier (D)	151,501	(59%)
Ann Haney (R)	107,457	(41%)
1986 General		
Robert W. Kastenmeier (D)	106,919	(56%)
Ann Haney (R)	85,156	(44%)

Previous Winning Percentages: **1984** (64%) **1982** (61%) **1980** (54%) **1978** (58%) **1976** (66%) **1974** (65%) **1972** (68%) **1970** (69%) **1968** (60%) **1966** (58%) **1964** (64%) **1962** (53%) **1960** (53%) **1958** (52%)

District Vote For President

	1988	1984	1980	1976
D	145,141 (55%)	127,626 (50%)	124,236 (47%)	124,106 (51%)
R	114,114 (44%)	124,014 (49%)	106,003 (40%)	109,405 (45%)
I			25,513 (10%)	

Campaign Finance

	Receipts	Receipts from PACs	Expend-itures
1988			
Kastenmeier (D)	$439,848	$177,484 (40%)	$440,574
Haney (R)	$383,346	$90,992 (24%)	$380,785
1986			
Kastenmeier (D)	$348,293	$106,730 (31%)	$385,947
Haney (R)	$272,390	$74,318 (27%)	$271,077

Key Votes

1987	
Raise speed limit to 65 mph	N
Approve Gephardt "fair trade" amendment	Y
Ban testing of larger nuclear weapons	Y
Delay "re-flagging" of Kuwaiti tankers	Y
Approve tax-raising deficit-reduction bill	Y
1988	
Approve aid to Nicaraguan contras	N
Enact civil rights restoration bill over Reagan veto	Y
Kill 60-day plant-closing notification measure	N
Pass omnibus trade bill over Reagan veto	Y
Approve death penalty for drug-related murders	N
Bar federal funds for abortions in cases of rape and incest	N
Oppose seven-day waiting period for purchase of handguns	N

Voting Studies

	Presidential Support		Party Unity		Conservative Coalition	
Year	S	O	S	O	S	O
1988	20	79	93	6	11	89
1987	13	87	94	5	5	95
1986	16	81	92	5	4	92
1985	16	84	91	4	5	93
1984	25	73	90	6	8	92
1983	11	82	90	6	8	91
1982	26	74	89	10	12	88
1981	22	75	89	11	5	95

Interest Group Ratings

Year	ADA	ACU	AFL-CIO	CCUS
1988	100	4	100	36
1987	100	0	94	0
1986	100	0	86	17
1985	100	5	94	24
1984	95	0	77	25
1983	95	9	100	20
1982	90	0	100	20
1981	95	7	80	5

3 Steve Gunderson (R)

Of Pleasantville — Elected 1980

Born: May 10, 1951, Eau Claire, Wis.
Education: U. of Wisconsin, B.A. 1973.
Occupation: Public official.
Family: Single.
Religion: Lutheran.
Political Career: Wis. House, 1975-79.
Capitol Office: 227 Cannon Bldg. 20515; 225-5506.

In Washington: Gunderson blends a restrained personal manner with an ambitious political agenda, and recently he has started to see one of his most ambitious goals come to fruition. Long identified with the less doctrinaire faction of House Republicans, Gunderson has been eager to build a bridge to his party's aggressive conservative wing. When the leader of those conservatives, Georgian Newt Gingrich, became GOP whip in early 1989 and chose him as one of two chief deputy whips, it was clear Gunderson's work had paid off.

Gunderson showed interest in a leadership position back in 1987, seeking the chairmanship of the House Republican Research Committee. He came in third behind Oklahoma Rep. Mickey Edwards, the winner, and Texas Rep. Steve Bartlett, but that did not discourage him from involvement in party affairs. He served as co-chairman of the '92 Group, which believes the GOP can capture a House majority by 1992 by being, in Gunderson's words, a "diverse, centrist party with positive solutions." Gunderson has also shown an interest in electoral politics outside his district, taking a leading role in party meetings analyzing the 1988 election results.

During all of this, Gunderson worked on building political relationships with conservatives such as Gingrich, who had made a name with an aggressive and confrontational approach to the Democratic majority. When the party whip job opened up in early 1989, Gunderson worked hard for Gingrich in his contest against Illinois' Edward Madigan, whose reputation as a low-key insider might have seemed a better fit for the Wisconsin Republican. "Newt adds an element to the leadership team that doesn't exist today," Gunderson said. "He's a ball of energy. He's a visionary and a strategist."

In his new leadership role, Gunderson aims to push the GOP to put forward positive alternatives to Democratic programs, rather than simply voicing objections. "We need a governing conservatism that responds to real-life problems, but does so in ways that empower people — not bureaucracies — and maximizes choice rather than federal regulation." Working with him as chief deputy whip — and providing a different personal manner and ideological bent — will be bombastic conservative Robert S. Walker of Pennsylvania, a longtime Gingrich ally.

Gunderson has been demonstrating his legislative acumen for some time on the Agriculture Committee, where he is ranking Republican on the subcommittee dealing with the dairy programs crucial to Wisconsin. As he has become more politically secure at home, Gunderson also has branched out into other legislative areas, but he is primarily known as "Mr. Dairy," and is second to none in his understanding of dairy-related matters.

In the 1985 farm bill, Gunderson supported an industry-backed plan to revive a controversial dairy "diversion" program to reduce surpluses by paying farmers not to produce milk — a program supported mostly by Midwestern and New England members. But to ensure support from reluctant lawmakers from the Southeast, where there was no milk surplus, the plan included bonus payments for Southeastern dairy farmers.

Wisconsin dairymen could not go along with that provision; Gunderson led the opposition to it. He complained that the bonuses would in effect prevent the sale of Midwestern milk in the Southeast. But a Gunderson amendment to eliminate the bonus payments was rejected on the House floor.

Gunderson complains that the current dairy pricing system is unfair to the Midwest, because it stimulates local production and denies Midwestern dairy farmers access to a bigger share of the large Sun Belt market. With the writing of the next farm bill around the corner, he has been pushing legislation to restructure the system in such a way as to put dairy producers in the Midwest on a level playing field with producers elsewhere.

During work on a drought-relief bill in the 100th Congress, Gunderson worked on an amendment increasing federal price-support payments to dairy farmers. A number of members of the House felt an increase would violate

Wisconsin 3

West — Eau Claire; La Crosse

In a state famous for its cows, the 3rd stands at the head of the herd; it has more cows than people and is one of the leading milk-producing districts in the nation. The 3rd hugs western Wisconsin's border with Iowa and Minnesota, and most of its people live on farms or in small crossroads market towns.

In presidential voting, these dairy farmers can be a fickle group. Jimmy Carter carried the district narrowly in 1976, but lost it by 5 points in 1980 as independent candidate John B. Anderson polled 7 percent. Ronald Reagan won the 3rd again in 1984, but four years later it was the Democrats' turn once more, as Michael S. Dukakis beat George Bush 52-47 percent.

There are only two sizable cities, roughly equal in size. Democrats traditionally hold sway in Eau Claire and the counties near it in the northern part of the district. Republicans are dominant in La Crosse and counties south of it along the Mississippi.

Eau Claire was once a wild lumber outpost, cutting logs that floated down the Chippewa River from the northern forests. It still has a paper mill producing disposable diapers and napkins, but the largest employer is Uniroyal.

La Crosse is Wisconsin's only major Mississippi River city. Two locally owned *Fortune* 500 companies are its mainstays: the Trane Co., manufacturers of heating and air conditioning equipment, employs about 3,000; G. Heileman Brewing Inc. provides about 1,200 jobs.

The rural areas are still heavily Scandinavian. In Osseo, where Gunderson used to live, dairy farmers habitually greet the day by trading gossip over coffee and cinnamon rolls at the Norske Nook.

Population: 522,909. White 518,219 (99%), Black 798 (0.2%), Other 2,886 (1%). Spanish origin 1,698 (0.3%). 18 and over 374,265 (72%), 65 and over 68,869 (13%). Median age: 29.

the spirit of the farm bill, which generally called for lowering price supports. There were also complaints that such a provision gave an unfair edge to one agricultural group, and could end up boosting consumer costs. But Gunderson, working with Minnesota Democrat Timothy J. Penny, came up with an acceptable compromise that granted a temporary increase during a three-month period when farmers expected to be hardest hit by drought-related feed costs.

Gunderson also serves on Education and Labor, where he is a team player among the moderate Republicans on the panel who try to work with the Democratic majority. In the 100th Congress, though, he did dig his heels in on one partisan issue: When a bill barring most employers from using lie detector tests passed subcommittee, Gunderson cast one of two "nay" votes. Later, the full committee rejected his proposal to allow polygraphs as an investigative tool when a theft or a crime has occurred and an employee is under "reasonable suspicion."

Gunderson tries to steer more federal aid to his rural constituents for education and worker retraining. When the panel authorized federal elementary, secondary and adult education programs in 1987, he worked to change grant formulas so more funding would come to low-income school districts in rural areas.

An active participant in drafting a five-year higher education bill in the 99th Congress, Gunderson focused on expanding aid and services for older, part-time college students — the kind of "non-traditional" students who enroll in large numbers at the many community colleges and technical schools in Gunderson's district. He sponsored, with liberal Democrat Pat Williams of Montana, the overhaul of a near-moribund continuing education program, to focus on such services as mid-career retraining.

He also fought a losing battle on the House floor against what he called the educational pork barrel — special funding for college projects in key members' districts. He offered an amendment to drop such projects from the House higher education bill, but did not push it to a roll-call vote on the floor.

When he objected again in conference, Gunderson initially had the support of Senate conferees, who had no home-state projects in their bill. But the House-Senate differences were resolved by adding an equal sum for senators' projects — a plan accepted by House conferees, 16-4, over Gunderson's objection.

In 1984, Gunderson found himself involved in an intense school prayer debate. As a member of Education and Labor, he was on the floor the day a group of Republicans tried to amend that year's education bill to take away funding from any schools that forbade vocal prayer. Gunderson, who supports silent prayer in schools, drafted a counteramendment that would have guaranteed the "opportunity to participate in moments of organized silent prayer." Then he dropped "organized" to avoid offending school prayer opponents.

Vocal-prayer advocates said his measure would do little to change the existing situation. But Gunderson's alternative passed, and he fought off two attempts to replace his amendment with language similar to the original.

At Home: For a man who insists his real ambition was to become a radio hockey announcer, Gunderson did very well in politics very quickly. He won his broadcasting license at age 23, but was elected to the Legislature the same year.

As a close associate of GOP Gov. Lee Sherman Dreyfus, Gunderson could have obtained a leadership job in the Legislature. But he quit in mid-1979 and went to work in Washington as Rep. Toby Roth's legislative director.

In six months, Gunderson was back in Wisconsin, this time to challenge Democratic Rep. Alvin Baldus. Gunderson's job-hopping stirred some complaints that his ambition exceeded his commitment to public service, but 1980 was an excellent Republican year in Wisconsin, and he beat Baldus by demonstrating the same energy that marked his service in the Legislature. Gunderson personally visited thousands of homes in the rural counties of the district, leaving behind his grandmother's recipe for lefse, a Norwegian potato bread.

Gunderson's 1982 Democratic challenger, state Sen. Paul Offner, hoped to unseat him on the issue of the Reagan connection. An economist with a Ph.D. from Princeton, Offner presented a detailed blueprint for economic recovery, including his own federal budget. But Gunderson's tireless campaigning and artful dairy maneuvers won him 57 percent of the vote.

In 1986, Democrats claimed to have a strong candidate in Leland Mulder, a farmer who hoped to tap into rural resentment toward the Reagan administration. Gunderson, however, had no trouble deflecting that strategy. He won 64 percent and improved on that in 1988, though his district went for Democrat Michael S. Dukakis for president.

Committees

Agriculture (9th of 18 Republicans)
Livestock, Dairy and Poultry (ranking); Conservation, Credit and Rural Development; Tobacco and Peanuts

Education and Labor (5th of 13 Republicans)
Employment Opportunities (ranking); Elementary, Secondary and Vocational Education; Postsecondary Education

Elections

1988 General		
Steve Gunderson (R)	157,513	(68%)
Karl Krueger (D)	72,935	(32%)
1986 General		
Steve Gunderson (R)	104,393	(64%)
Leland E. Mulder (D)	58,445	(36%)

Previous Winning Percentages: 1984 (68%) **1982** (57%) **1980** (51%)

District Vote For President

	1988	1984	1980	1976
D	126,354 (52%)	108,752 (45%)	109,434 (43%)	114,895 (49%)
R	112,830 (47%)	133,386 (55%)	123,312 (48%)	112,422 (48%)
I			18,584 (7%)	

Campaign Finance

	Receipts	Receipts from PACs	Expend-itures
1988			
Gunderson (R)	$404,942	$133,235 (33%)	$359,801
Krueger (D) †	$27,156	$6,000 (22%)	$22,626
1986			
Gunderson (R)	$291,040	$125,847 (43%)	$311,707
Mulder (D)	$62,869	$3,914 (6%)	$62,459

† Totals based on incomplete data.

Key Votes

1987	
Raise speed limit to 65 mph	Y
Approve Gephardt "fair trade" amendment	N
Ban testing of larger nuclear weapons	N
Delay "re-flagging" of Kuwaiti tankers	N
Approve tax-raising deficit-reduction bill	N
1988	
Approve aid to Nicaraguan contras	Y
Enact civil rights restoration bill over Reagan veto	Y
Kill 60-day plant-closing notification measure	N
Pass omnibus trade bill over Reagan veto	Y
Approve death penalty for drug-related murders	Y
Bar federal funds for abortions in cases of rape and incest	Y
Oppose seven-day waiting period for purchase of handguns	Y

Voting Studies

	Presidential Support		Party Unity		Conservative Coalition	
Year	**S**	**O**	**S**	**O**	**S**	**O**
1988	46	52	58	40	84	13
1987	61	38	68	29	84	12
1986	52	44	66	29	78	20
1985	50	50	74	22	73	25
1984	61	39	74	26	75	25
1983	61	39	70	30	65	35
1982	56	44	74	26	68	32
1981	70	30	75	25	75	25

Interest Group Ratings

Year	ADA	ACU	AFL-CIO	CCUS
1988	45	54	79	71
1987	20	65	19	86
1986	40	45	67	72
1985	35	43	29	77
1984	20	50	15	75
1983	20	57	12	85
1982	45	50	21	64
1981	30	100	20	84

4 Gerald D. Kleczka (D)

Of Milwaukee — Elected 1984

Born: Nov. 26, 1943, Milwaukee, Wis.
Education: Attended U. of Wisconsin, 1961-62, 1967, 1970.
Military Career: Wis. Air National Guard, 1963-69.
Occupation: Accountant.
Family: Wife, Bonnie L. Scott.
Religion: Roman Catholic.
Political Career: Wis. Assembly 1969-73; Wis. Senate 1975-84.
Capitol Office: 226 Cannon Bldg. 20515; 225-4572.

In Washington: Kleczka is one of a group of activist, mid-level Democrats on the Banking Committee that includes such sharp-witted liberals as Charles E. Schumer, Barney Frank and Bruce A. Morrison.

As the committee worked on a 1987 bill to bail out the ailing Federal Savings and Loan Insurance Corporation, Kleczka riled the savings and loan industry by sponsoring an amendment to double the bill's proposed "exit fees" on healthy S&Ls that try to bolt the FSLIC system and convert to commercial banks to receive less costly Federal Deposit Insurance Corporation coverage. "We are going to have a stampede of healthy S&Ls to get out of FSLIC," Kleczka warned. But his efforts to amend the bill failed in committee and on the floor.

On the Banking Subcommittee on Housing, Kleczka worked in the 99th and 100th Congresses to crack down on fraud in the Federal Housing Administration's mortgage insurance program. Kleczka said that the FHA program was being cheated by real-estate speculators using false income data and inflated property assessments. He introduced legislation to provide increased penalties for mortgage insurance fraud.

Kleczka has used his Government Operations Committee seat to try to expand the scope of the Freedom of Information Act. He sponsored a bill in 1988 with Oklahoma Democrat Glenn English to do just that. In 1986, he offered a floor amendment to speed up access to government documents.

Kleczka represents a secure Democratic district that kept his predecessor in office for 35 years with little challenge. That security evinces itself in Kleczka's manner. He pursues his work in Congress with the patience of a man who realizes he does not have to get all of it done overnight. He spent 15 years in the Wisconsin Legislature, rising gradually to the chairmanship of the powerful Joint Finance Committee.

In his first two House terms, Kleczka was more interested in learning the customs and making friends than in trying to impress anyone as a legislative phenom. After he arrived in 1984, he spent much time listening quietly to floor speeches, trying to see how the oratorical style differed from that of the Wisconsin Senate. "I don't want to embarrass myself," he said.

Now that he has the measure of the place, though, Kleczka is unlikely to be bashful. He is a street-smart, combative politician who has to keep his temper under control: Early in his state legislative career, he actually came to blows with a lobbyist for a brewery.

Midway through 1988, it looked as though Kleczka was headed toward a seat on Ways and Means in the 101st Congress. Speaker Jim Wright announced that Kleczka would take the Ways and Means slot of fellow Wisconsinite Jim Moody, who was running for the Senate. But Moody changed his mind and decided to stay in the House, keeping Kleczka in place.

At Home: Before coming to Washington, Kleczka spent virtually his entire adult life in the Wisconsin Legislature. His role and reputation there changed considerably over the 15 years following his first election at age 25.

In his early years in Madison, Kleczka was viewed as being like most of the legislators traditionally sent from Milwaukee's South Side — a neighborhood-minded ethnic Democrat concerned more with local politics than abstract issues. He had a reputation for hard-nosed campaigning and occasional quarrels on the Assembly floor.

By the 1980s, however, Kleczka had developed a reputation as an effective budget specialist highly regarded by the Democratic establishment. When Democratic Rep. Clement J. Zablocki, the House Foreign Affairs chairman, died in late 1983, Kleczka quickly became the front-runner for the ensuing special election.

Thanks to his Joint Finance Committee role, Kleczka had no difficulty picking up support from state Senate colleagues and financial help from the economic interests over which his

Wisconsin 4

Southern Milwaukee and Suburbs — Waukesha

Since the turn of the century, Milwaukee's South Side has been the base of the city's huge Polish community. Like many of the Eastern Europeans who migrated to industrial cities, the Poles have been loyal, somewhat conservative Democrats. Their neighborhoods are conspicuously tidy, with immaculate lawns and shrubs.

In the last 20 years, urban flight has influenced a number of Poles, especially younger ones, to leave the South Side and relocate in suburbs such as New Berlin and neighboring Muskego. Some of these migrants have drifted from their political moorings, moving into the Republican column in state and national elections. Waukesha County's strong GOP organization gave Ronald Reagan and George Bush comfortable countywide presidential victories in the 1980s, but districtwide in the 4th, Democrats remain dominant: Michael S. Dukakis carried it easily in 1988 presidential voting.

The departure of some Poles for the suburbs has made room for a greater ethnic mix on the South Side. Though the area remains predominantly Polish, there is a Puerto Rican community on the near South Side, close to Lake Michigan and the downtown business district.

Most residents in the city and the suburbs look to Milwaukee's heavy industries for economic sustenance. Many 4th District constituents make machinery for mining, construction and electronic equipment; the Allis-Chalmers Corp. is headquartered in the 4th, but since its bankruptcy and subsequent purchase by a West German firm, it employs much fewer than it once did. Delco Electronics Corp. and Allen-Bradley Co. are also in the district.

Unemployment is a problem, but the jobless rate is not as high here as in cities dominated by one or two industries, such as Kenosha in the 1st. What worries Milwaukeeans more is the decay of the aging industrial plants, many of which were built in the late 19th and early 20th centuries.

Population: 522,880. White 506,053 (97%), Black 1,509 (0.3%), Other 5,827 (1%). Spanish origin 20,677 (4%). 18 and over 381,822 (73%), 65 and over 57,760 (11%). Median age: 31.

committee held power. He claimed much of Zablocki's backing and was also the choice of the state's Democratic U.S. House delegation.

But while Kleczka's party support was crucial, his advertising stressed a different theme — his roots on the heavily Polish South Side. One TV ad showed an infant in a crib and a grandfather, while a voice-over described Kleczka as "a leader and a neighbor." In another, the camera showed a montage of South Side scenes, while an elderly woman told Kleczka she would vote for him because "you always come back to our neighborhood."

The combination of Kleczka's political status and neighborhood roots brought him 32 percent of the vote — enough to make him the clear winner in a five-way primary that included three other formidable candidates — Milwaukee County District Attorney E. Michael McCann, state Sen. Lynn S. Adelman and Gary Barczak, Milwaukee County circuit court clerk.

By winning big with 44 percent in the city, Kleczka had the votes to overcome his poor showing in affluent suburban precincts and take the nomination decisively over runner-up McCann, who ran respectably everywhere but had no specific base to help him.

Committees

Banking, Finance and Urban Affairs (19th of 31 Democrats)
Financial Institutions Supervision, Regulation and Insurance; Housing and Community Development; International Development, Finance, Trade and Monetary Policy

Government Operations (18th of 24 Democrats)
Government Activities and Transportation; Legislation and National Security

Elections

1988 General		
Gerald D. Kleczka (D)	177,283	(100%)
1986 General		
Gerald D. Kleczka (D)	120,354	(100%)

Previous Winning Percentages: 1984 (67%) **1984 *** (65%)

** Special election.*

District Vote For President

	1988	1984	1980	1976
D	142,074 (56%)	125,624 (52%)	118,444 (48%)	129,927 (54%)
R	111,241 (44%)	112,687 (47%)	108,464 (44%)	101,527 (42%)
I			17,338 (7%)	

Campaign Finance

	Receipts	Receipts from PACs	Expend-itures
1988			
Kleczka (D)	$214,093	$129,383 (60%)	$150,270
1986			
Kleczka (D)	$162,267	$109,983 (68%)	$93,749

Key Votes

1987	
Raise speed limit to 65 mph	N
Approve Gephardt "fair trade" amendment	Y
Ban testing of larger nuclear weapons	Y
Delay "re-flagging" of Kuwaiti tankers	Y
Approve tax-raising deficit-reduction bill	Y
1988	
Approve aid to Nicaraguan contras	N
Enact civil rights restoration bill over Reagan veto	Y
Kill 60-day plant-closing notification measure	N
Pass omnibus trade bill over Reagan veto	Y
Approve death penalty for drug-related murders	N
Bar federal funds for abortions in cases of rape and incest	Y
Oppose seven-day waiting period for purchase of handguns	N

Voting Studies

	Presidential Support		Party Unity		Conservative Coalition	
Year	**S**	**O**	**S**	**O**	**S**	**O**
1988	19	73	90	5	16	79
1987	17	81	89	4	28	70
1986	24	76	85	9	28	70
1985	28	71	87	6	24	75
1984	42 †	56 †	84 †	15 †	28 †	72 †

† Not eligible for all recorded votes.

Interest Group Ratings

Year	ADA	ACU	AFL-CIO	CCUS
1988	95	4	93	36
1987	84	5	88	13
1986	75	9	86	25
1985	75	14	82	23
1984	76	9	67	38

5 Jim Moody (D)

Of Milwaukee — Elected 1982

Born: Sept. 2, 1935, Richlands, Va.
Education: Haverford College, B.A. 1957; Harvard U., M.P.A. 1967; U. of California, Berkeley, Ph.D. 1973.
Occupation: Economist.
Family: Divorced.
Religion: Protestant.
Political Career: Wis. House, 1977-79; Wis. Senate, 1979-83.
Capitol Office: 1019 Longworth Bldg. 20515; 225-3571.

In Washington: His Senate dreams behind him, Moody returns to the task of suppressing his lone-wolf reputation in favor of the inside game played on the House side of the Capitol.

Moody won his seat in Congress with a door-to-door campaign that bypassed all the traditional centers of power, but reality-testing won out over quixotic individualism in his 1988 Senate campaign. He backed out of the Democratic primary contest just before the filing deadline, overwhelmed by the wealth of Herb Kohl, who went on to win nomination and election.

Two years earlier, at the start of the 100th Congress, Moody played the coalition-building game adroitly enough to win a valuable insider's prize: an assignment on the Ways and Means Committee. He won the seat, in part, by using the same canvassing techniques that got him elected to Congress. Campaigning for almost two years to get on Ways and Means, he lobbied more than 80 members who were — or might be — on the leadership panel that makes committee assignments.

Even more important, Moody had the backing of Ways and Means Chairman Dan Rostenkowski of Illinois. He scored points in the 99th Congress as an informal whip helping Rostenkowski line up votes for his prized product, legislation overhauling the tax code. Although he can be unpredictable, Moody struck Rostenkowski as a relatively safe Democrat to place on the committee. As an individualist, he appeared unlikely to mount the sort of coalitions that could threaten the chairman's control on important issues.

Moody did risk Rostenkowski's wrath by cosponsoring Rep. Claude Pepper's expensive home-health-care bill, which circumvented the Ways and Means Committee but ultimately died in the 100th Congress.

Moody went far afield in the 100th Congress in pursuit of arms control. With two other Democrats (Thomas J. Downey of New York and Bob Carr of Michigan) he traveled to the Soviet Union in 1987 to visit a Soviet radar station at Krasnoyarsk that had become a key point of contention in debates over the anti-ballistic missile treaty. The Reagan administration maintained that the station's battle-management capacity flagrantly violated the treaty and showed the need for a space-based missile defense. The congressional delegation — which included its own independent arms control experts — concluded that the station was a long way from completion and could not control an anti-missile network. Defense officials said the members were the victims of "disinformation," but the report strengthened arms control advocates, who ultimately forced the White House to abide by treaty limits.

Even though he has become a team player in the eyes of the Democratic leadership, Moody remains very much the politician he was in his home state — a man comfortable with ideas and skillful at expressing them, but not a joiner or a foot soldier by instinct. The maverick in Moody still has its moments.

During a session of the Public Works Committee in 1986, he startled some colleagues by offering an amendment to a highway bill that would have removed more than $1 billion in funding for special "demonstration" projects in members' districts — a futile challenge to the committee's logrolling principle.

Other members were not pleased. One senior Republican told Moody his amendment was as welcome as "an illegitimate child at a family reunion." Another forced a roll-call vote that Moody did not seek. His amendment was trounced, 48-2.

"The leaders of the committee were trying to embarrass me and intimidate other members," Moody said. "I was trying to confront this baronial style of ladling out money."

In early 1989, Moody was true to form in being the only member of the Wisconsin delegation — and one of only 48 members of the House — voting for a 51 percent pay raise for Congress and top federal officials that was eagerly sought by members but vilified by public opinion. "I owe [constituents] my honest assessment of every single issue — even one so

Wisconsin 5

Northern Milwaukee and Suburbs — Wauwatosa

The Menominee River marks the boundary between Milwaukee's North and South sides, and the 5th is the North Side district, taking in the traditional German neighborhoods and other middle-class territory that has become increasingly black in recent years. The district as a whole is now 28 percent black, and reliably Democratic in virtually any election. In 1988, Michael S. Dukakis won 63 percent in the 5th, easily his best showing in any Wisconsin district.

Nearly all of the black population lives in a concentrated area in the central part of the district. In an effort to promote integrated housing patterns, the centrally located Sherman Park neighborhood has tried to draw blacks west and whites east. That is not an easy task in Milwaukee, where racial tension dates back to violent civil rights demonstrations in the 1960s.

North and west of the black neighborhoods are modest middle-class areas of Milwaukee where many of the names on the mailboxes are still German but there has long since ceased to be much ethnic identification. The farther north and west one goes, the higher the housing values.

On the northeastern side of the district, between the Milwaukee River and Lake Michigan, is an area marked by large, comfortable homes, a gathering of academics who work at the Milwaukee branch of the University of Wisconsin, and white-collar professionals who hold middle- and upper-management positions in downtown offices.

To the west of the city is Wauwatosa, a mostly Republican residential area with older housing stock.

The 5th is the focal point of Milwaukee's best-known industry — brewing. Locally owned Schlitz, Pabst and Miller were once the giants, but the structure of the industry has changed in the past decade. In the early 1970s, Miller was bought out by Philip Morris, a New York-based conglomerate. Beset by financial problems, Schlitz closed its Milwaukee brewery in 1981; no longer is "the beer that made Milwaukee famous" brewed anywhere in the city. Pabst spent millions of dollars to refurbish its Milwaukee headquarters, and appears to be holding on, despite some financial trouble.

Population: 522,854. White 361,847 (69%), Black 147,928 (28%), Other 6,262 (1%). Spanish origin 11,420 (2%). 18 and over 381,248 (73%), 65 and over 67,138 (13%). Median age: 29.

subject to political posturing and pandering as this one has been," Moody said.

Frequently, Moody voices the complaints of someone uncomfortable with a legislative process that does not respond very well to individual initiatives. "The House moves in fits and starts and lurches down the road to some uncertain destination," he said in 1984. "It makes for a lot of time spent . . . not all of which ends up producing results."

At Home: Moody's sense of political timing, and his luck, brought him from academia to the state Legislature to the House in just six years. But both seemed to desert him when he turned his attention to the Senate.

In 1986, he had a strong interest in challenging Republican Sen. Bob Kasten, and Democrats were eager for a candidate with Moody's abilities. But he chose to remain in the House, even after a drunken-driving arrest significantly increased Kasten's vulnerability. That fall, Kasten barely beat a challenger who had never held elective office.

Two years later, Moody seemed to have a second chance. Thirty-year incumbent Sen. William Proxmire retired, and Moody entered the race to succeed him. Polls showed him a strong second in the Democratic field in the spring of 1988. Then multimillionaire Kohl of Milwaukee entered the contest. Kohl not only split Moody's base but also bankrolled the most extensive TV campaign the state had ever seen. Moody recalculated the odds and, in the nick of time, filed for re-election to the House.

This may have been the prudent move, as Kohl swept on to the nomination and won the seat in November. But Moody's change of heart angered candidates who had spent months vying to succeed him in the House (not to mention Milwaukee colleague Rep. Gerald D. Kleczka, who had hoped to replace him on Ways and Means). Other candidates withdrew when Moody got back into the 5th District primary, but former state party Chairman Matthew J. Flynn remained, pressing a bitter fight. In the end, Moody dispatched Flynn rather easily, and in the fall he prevailed over Republican Helen Barnhill, a black businesswoman well connected within Milwaukee's establishment.

Barnhill was the local GOP's first challenger to Moody since his initial election in 1982. Their candidate then had been Rod Johnston, a suburban state senator whose slogan was "Vote the man and not the party." (Despite redistricting, the 5th remained the most Democratic territory in the state.) Moody took nearly

65 percent of the 1982 vote, though he was hard up for money and tired from the ordeal by which he had claimed the Democratic nomination.

Moody had won the 1982 primary with a frenetic door-to-door campaign, a two-year effort that took him to 40,000 households. He presented himself as a compassionate liberal with an impressive background in economics, but issues were clearly secondary. It was Moody's smile, reassuring voice and simple stamina that got him elected.

The Democratic nomination in the 5th was a rare prize. Democrat Henry S. Reuss had held the seat without serious challenge for 28 years, and it was commonly assumed that the next occupant would have a similarly long lease. Ten Democrats filed for the primary.

By spring 1982, however, Moody had become so visible that most of his competitors were copying his door-to-door approach for fear of seeming halfhearted in their pursuit of the nomination. As the campaign entered its closing weeks, Moody had the rest of the field working like a Fuller Brush team. But it was no use; Moody's low-budget campaign, run out of his home with his mother as the manager and financed by the sale of family assets, had become a juggernaut.

Moody has a varied professional background. He was a representative of CARE in Yugoslavia, a Peace Corps official in Pakistan, and a loan officer for the Agency for International Development. He worked for the Department of Transportation, helped in Eugene J. McCarthy's 1968 presidential campaign, and eventually became an economics professor at the University of Wisconsin in Milwaukee. He won a term in the Wisconsin House in 1976, and one in the state Senate in 1978.

Committee

Ways and Means (22nd of 23 Democrats)
Health; Social Security

Elections

1988 General

Jim Moody (D)	140,518	(64%)
Helen I. Barnhill (R)	78,307	(36%)

1988 Primary

Jim Moody (D)	47,789	(59%)
Matthew J. Flynn (D)	19,906	(25%)
Donald Sykes (D)	5,314	(7%)
Terrance L. Pitts (D)	4,966	(6%)

1986 General

Jim Moody (D)	109,506	(99%)

Previous Winning Percentages: 1984 (98%) **1982** (64%)

District Vote For President

	1988	1984	1980	1976
D	146,635 (63%)	139,057 (61%)	136,084 (54%)	135,133 (55%)
R	82,606 (36%)	90,027 (39%)	91,520 (37%)	102,120 (42%)
I			19,114 (8%)	

Campaign Finance

	Receipts	Receipts from PACs	Expend-itures
1988			
Moody (D)	$1,291,564	$524,503 (41%)	$1,278,526
Barnhill (R)	$202,992	$21,932 (11%)	$197,460
1986			
Moody (D)	$279,075	$155,056 (56%)	$302,442

Key Votes

1987	
Raise speed limit to 65 mph	N
Approve Gephardt "fair trade" amendment	Y
Ban testing of larger nuclear weapons	Y
Delay "re-flagging" of Kuwaiti tankers	Y
Approve tax-raising deficit-reduction bill	Y
1988	
Approve aid to Nicaraguan contras	N
Enact civil rights restoration bill over Reagan veto	Y
Kill 60-day plant-closing notification measure	N
Pass omnibus trade bill over Reagan veto	Y
Approve death penalty for drug-related murders	N
Bar federal funds for abortions in cases of rape and incest	N
Oppose seven-day waiting period for purchase of handguns	N

Voting Studies

	Presidential Support		Party Unity		Conservative Coalition	
Year	**S**	**O**	**S**	**O**	**S**	**O**
1988	13	58	70	4	8	50
1987	17	77	82	7	12	81
1986	18	82	87	7	16	80
1985	20	79	89	5	11	85
1984	23	68	82	10	12	75
1983	22	73	84	10	15	82

Interest Group Ratings

Year	ADA	ACU	AFL-CIO	CCUS
1988	80	5	100	23
1987	84	0	93	27
1986	90	5	86	18
1985	80	0	100	18
1984	85	0	83	25
1983	95	0	88	30

6 Thomas E. Petri (R)

Of Fond du Lac — Elected 1979

Born: May 28, 1940, Marinette, Wis.
Education: Harvard U., B.A. 1962, J.D. 1965.
Occupation: Lawyer.
Family: Wife, Anne Neal; one child.
Religion: Lutheran.
Political Career: Wis. Senate, 1973-79; Republican nominee for U.S. Senate, 1974.
Capitol Office: 2443 Rayburn Bldg. 20515; 225-2476.

In Washington: Petri, a moderate Republican who is at home in the Ripon Society and in Wisconsin's reformist tradition, has a taste for innovative ideas and unpopular causes.

His independent streak is evident in his willingness to rile even the House's most powerful members and to crusade against programs nearly sacred to some colleagues.

One of his main targets has been "pork barrel" spending he considers wasteful. He took a seat on the Public Works Committee in 1983 to crusade against such spending — a move roughly comparable to joining Armed Services for the purpose of proposing unilateral disarmament.

In 1988, he led a successful fight to kill legislation writing off a federal loan to build a library in honor of former Speaker Thomas P. O'Neill Jr., putting him at odds with Silvio O. Conte of Massachusetts — a man few want to cross because he is ranking Republican on the Appropriations Committee.

In an accomplishment of broader significance, Petri fought to require local beneficiaries of federal water projects to provide a share of the costs "up front," at the start of construction. Petri maintained that requiring a local commitment early on "should clear away projects that are economic pygmies, but political giants." A version of the cost-sharing scheme was enacted in 1986, when it was added to a water projects authorization bill to make it more acceptable to environmentalists and fiscal conservatives, at a time when budget constraints were threatening approval of new water projects for the foreseeable future. The bill's passage marked the first time in a decade that a new water projects authorization got through Congress.

Petri also has taken on the long-established tobacco price-support system, angering colleagues from tobacco-producing states. He has persisted in this effort despite warnings from some Wisconsin GOP colleagues, who fear that he could bring on a retaliation against dairy programs, which Petri's district and much of Wisconsin need.

Petri's legislative work on the Education and Labor Committee often defies ideological characterization.

During the 1988-89 debate over raising the minimum wage, Petri promoted an alternative that focused on expanding a tax break for the working poor known as the earned income tax credit (EITC). He argued that such a break would target aid to those who needed it, while an across-the-board increase in the minimum wage amounted to "trying to achieve a goal with random bombing when a rapier will do."

House Democrats repeatedly blocked Petri's efforts to offer the idea as an amendment to minimum wage legislation, and he ran into the same resistance that meets any revenue-losing idea in the current deficit-conscious climate. Still, House Democrats showed increasing interest in the idea as a way to help the working poor, and even the chairman of the tax-writing Ways and Means Committee, Dan Rostenkowski, came to express the view that an expanded EITC would make more sense than raising the minimum wage.

Early in his career on Education and Labor, Petri championed the idea of canceling student-loan debts for borrowers who go into the military. He won approval of the concept by taking on senior committee members and beating them on the floor, with the help of members of the Armed Services Committee.

In the 98th Congress, Petri tried to sell the committee on an entirely new student loan program that would not require federal subsidies. Under Petri's plan, the repayment of loans would be based on one's income, with higher interest rates from wealthier individuals subsidizing lower interest rates for other borrowers. The plan did not make much progress. By the 99th Congress, though, Petri had won funding for a demonstration program for income-contingent loans.

Petri prides himself on being a man who keeps his mind open and listens to all sides. And that is a quality the House leadership likes to see in members they appoint to the ethics committee. Petri took that sensitive assignment in the 100th Congress, and sat on the panel through the historic investigation that led to the resignation of Speaker Jim Wright.

Wisconsin 6

Central — Oshkosh; Fond du Lac; Manitowoc

The 6th reaches west from Lake Michigan across 10 largely rural counties of central Wisconsin, ending about 25 miles from the Minnesota border on the west. It has been closely contested in many state and national elections, but it has sent only one Democrat to Washington since 1938.

The farms and market towns are generally Republican, while Democratic strength is in several small industrialized cities in the eastern part of the 6th — Manitowoc and Two Rivers in Manitowoc County, Oshkosh and Neenah-Menasha in Winnebago County and Fond du Lac in Fond du Lac County.

The most Democratic of the bunch is Manitowoc, a prominent Lake Michigan shipbuilding center in the days when wooden vessels plied the seas. More than half the jobs in Manitowoc County today are involved with manufacturing and processing, and unions are an important force. Goods produced include the Mirro Corporation's aluminum pots and pans, and motel ice-making machines. Manitowoc County went solidly for Jimmy Carter in 1976, narrowly for Ronald Reagan in 1980 and 1984, and then swung to Michael S. Dukakis in 1988.

Though nominal Democrats are numerous in Winnebago and Fond du Lac counties, those who vote Democratic usually find themselves in a minority at election time. GOP Sen. Bob Kasten won both counties in his close 1986 re-election, and Bush carried them both in 1988.

Oshkosh is on the western shore of Lake Winnebago, the state's largest lake. Tourism and a state university branch boost the economy, and factories in Winnebago County turn out auto parts and wood and paper products. At the northern end of the lake is Neenah-Menasha, the site of the wood products company of Kimberly Clark, one of the major employers in the district.

At the southern tip of the lake is Fond du Lac County, the home of Mercury outboard motors and Speed Queen laundry equipment. The city of Fond du Lac has strong historical justification for its GOP leanings. Outside the city is Ripon, the 1854 birthplace of the Republican Party.

In nearby Sheboygan County is the Kohler Company, the nation's largest producer of plumbing equipment. Besides the industry in the district, farming has a strong presence. After all-important dairying, output from the district's farms is diverse, including corn, peas, beans and cranberries. The peak of Republican strength in the rural part of the 6th is in Green Lake County, a resort area with large summer homes.

Population: 522,477. White 516,637 (99%), Black 1,205 (0.2%), Other 2,988 (1%). Spanish origin 3,385 (1%). 18 and over 370,486 (71%), 65 and over 69,925 (13%). Median age: 30.

Indeed, Petri is one of the few members who volunteered for the ethics committee assignment, although he did so more out of a sense of duty to the institution than because of active interest. His model was Barber B. Conable Jr., the highly respected New York Republican who served on the ethics committee for a term before the end of his long career in the House.

At Home: Petri built his Wisconsin career out of the moderate Republican politics that worked for his predecessor, William A. Steiger, who died of a heart attack at age 40, one month after winning his seventh House term in 1978.

In the 1979 special election held to choose Steiger's successor, Petri campaigned on the same reformist issues Steiger had used. His campaign literature boasted of the high ratings he had received in the state Senate from the self-styled citizens' lobby, Common Cause. He noted that he had been a Peace Corps volunteer in Somalia and served as executive director of the Ripon Society, a moderate GOP group.

The campaign reinforced the image Petri had created in 1974, when he was the sacrificial Republican Senate nominee against Democrat Gaylord Nelson. He drew only 35 percent of the vote against Nelson in a terrible Republican year, but brought himself some useful attention.

The earlier Senate effort made Petri the logical Republican contender for Steiger's House seat in 1979. But it did not guarantee him victory against Gary Goyke, a fellow state senator with a more forceful campaign style. Goyke made an issue of Petri's generous campaign financing and criticized him for receiving a $5,000 contribution from the political action committee of the American Medical Association. Petri said Goyke had his own source of political funding in organized labor.

Petri won the special election on his strength in the rural areas and his ability to cut into Goyke's vote in blue-collar cities, especially Sheboygan, which Petri narrowly carried.

Eighteen months later there was a rematch. But the 1980 election was a pale shadow of the first contest. Goyke was still in debt from the special election and got a late start. Petri had enhanced his Steiger-like image by hiring some of Steiger's aides and taking his predecessor's place on Education and Labor. With a strong Republican tide at the statewide level, Petri carried every county in the district against Goyke the second time around.

In 1982, despite a strong Democratic trend in statewide politics, Petri romped to another term with 65 percent. He has since received three-fourths of the vote (when he has had an opponent at all).

Committees

Education and Labor (3rd of 13 Republicans)
Labor Standards (ranking); Elementary, Secondary and Vocational Education; Labor-Management Relations

Public Works and Transportation (7th of 20 Republicans)
Public Buildings and Grounds (ranking); Aviation; Water Resources

Standards of Official Conduct (4th of 6 Republicans)

Elections

1988 General		
Thomas E. Petri (R)	165,923	(74%)
Joe Garrett (D)	57,552	(26%)
1986 General		
Thomas E. Petri (R)	124,328	(97%)

Previous Winning Percentages: **1984** (76%) **1982** (65%) **1980** (59%) **1979** * (50%)

** Special election.*

District Vote For President

	1988	1984	1980	1976
D	106,953 (46%)	88,121 (37%)	94,779 (38%)	96,131 (45%)
R	127,820 (53%)	146,167 (62%)	135,709 (54%)	112,146 (53%)
I			14,783 (6%)	

Campaign Finance

	Receipts	Receipts from PACs	Expend-itures
1988			
Petri (R)	$258,876	$120,980 (47%)	$187,714
Garrett (D)	$19,976	$4,750 (24%)	$19,815
1986			
Petri (R)	$204,737	$92,875 (45%)	$106,394

Key Votes

1987	
Raise speed limit to 65 mph	Y
Approve Gephardt "fair trade" amendment	N
Ban testing of larger nuclear weapons	N
Delay "re-flagging" of Kuwaiti tankers	Y
Approve tax-raising deficit-reduction bill	N
1988	
Approve aid to Nicaraguan contras	Y
Enact civil rights restoration bill over Reagan veto	Y
Kill 60-day plant-closing notification measure	N
Pass omnibus trade bill over Reagan veto	N
Approve death penalty for drug-related murders	Y
Bar federal funds for abortions in cases of rape and incest	Y
Oppose seven-day waiting period for purchase of handguns	Y

Voting Studies

	Presidential Support		Party Unity		Conservative Coalition	
Year	S	O	S	O	S	O
1988	62	36	66	32	84	13
1987	55	43	70	28	67	30
1986	73	27	74	25	76	24
1985	61	39	60	35	60	40
1984	54	46	76	24	75	25
1983	60	39	76	23	72	28
1982	53	40	71	28	70	30
1981	57	41	71	23	67	32

Interest Group Ratings

Year	ADA	ACU	AFL-CIO	CCUS
1988	35	75	50	79
1987	16	61	13	80
1986	5	73	0	94
1985	30	62	35	59
1984	20	83	8	63
1983	20	52	24	80
1982	35	64	30	64
1981	40	100	7	83

7 David R. Obey (D)

Of Wausau — Elected 1969

Born: Oct. 3, 1938, Okmulgee, Okla.
Education: U. of Wisconsin, B.S. 1960, M.A. 1962.
Occupation: Real-estate broker.
Family: Wife, Joan Lepinski; two children.
Religion: Roman Catholic.
Political Career: Wis. Assembly, 1963-69.
Capitol Office: 2462 Rayburn Bldg. 20515; 225-3365.

In Washington: Power often tends to change perceptions about a politician more than it changes the politician. For years, colleagues called Obey temperamental, impulsive and bullheaded. He still is and they still do. But now that Obey chairs a key Appropriations subcommittee and is a likely future chairman of the full committee, his personality is seen as central to his effectiveness as a leader who wins through sheer determination and obstinacy.

After an unusually long apprenticeship of 15 years without a subcommittee to run, Obey in 1985 took over Appropriations' Foreign Operations panel and emerged as the House's dominant voice on foreign aid, and on spending priorities overall. In contrast with his long wait to join the "College of Cardinals," as Appropriations' subcommittee chairmen are known, Obey stands to take over the full committee before too many years and at an uncommonly early age. Just past 50, he is fifth in seniority behind three men around 80 and a fourth who will turn 70 in the 101st Congress.

Obey's rise is an example of the seniority system's periodic ability to promote one of the few rebellious sorts on an insular committee that puts a premium on conformity and bipartisan fraternity. He is a loner and a liberal partisan, a complex man of undisputed intelligence and principled independence who suffers neither fools nor phonies well.

Obey seems to divide his colleagues into two types: those who have political "guts" and those who do not. "There is nothing so pitiful as a group of panicked politicians in full flight," he said in a typical remark in 1988, this one lamenting colleagues' support for a Republican's controversial anti-drug provision. But Obey is no fall-on-his-sword liberal, nor does he care for those who are. He is a legislator, and that requires compromise.

Despite his penchant for openly castigating his colleagues, the House as a whole has no stronger defender than Obey, whether the attack comes from the Senate, the executive branch or the media. He shows rare self-awareness about his volatility, and is quick to apologize when his anger is misplaced. And opposite his brooding side is a genial man who picks guitar in a bluegrass band with his sons.

Obey is not widely popular, but respect for his integrity is widespread. That is why Speaker Jim Wright repeatedly invoked his name in 1989 when challenging the ethics committee's interpretation of two House rules the panel had used against Wright.

As the author of the House ethics code, Obey had a stake in its correct interpretation and argued publicly and in an affidavit that a rule covering gifts from associates with a legislative interest had been applied too broadly in Wright's case, and one dealing with book royalties not broadly enough.

Unfortunately for Wright, Obey's influence cut both ways. When it was reported in early May that Obey privately had told some Democrats that, while Wright deserved a chance to defend himself, he was finished politically, the news was one of the clearest signals Wright's fight was lost.

As chairman of the Foreign Operations Subcommittee, Obey has not only filled the power vacuum that existed under his eccentric and unpredictable predecessor, Clarence D. Long of Maryland, but also he has cast the foreign aid debate in such broad political terms that he has become a major figure in the larger budget arena.

First with Ronald Reagan and now with George Bush, Obey has exploited each administration's desire for foreign aid increases to extract budget concessions for domestic programs and to assail the Republican Party's priorities. "Members of the House see we're increasing foreign aid and we're paying for that increase by gutting cancer research, gutting educational opportunities, gutting job training," he once said, in a characteristic argument doubling as Obey's affirmation of Democratic Party priorities.

He wasted no time serving President Bush with notice of potential cuts to come. When Secretary of State James A. Baker III appeared before Obey's subcommittee in early 1989, the chairman was ready with a draft bill cutting the Bush foreign aid budget 10 percent — the po-

Wisconsin 7

Northwest — Wausau; Superior

The 7th reaches from the center of Wisconsin all the way north to Lake Superior. The southern part of the district is devoted largely to dairy farming; in the north, a booming recreation industry has brought new life to old mining and lumbering areas that were exploited and abandoned earlier in this century.

The southern end of the 7th is anchored by Marathon and Wood counties, politically marginal territory that supported Ronald Reagan in 1984, but was of divided mind four years later. Michael S. Dukakis won Marathon County by just 178 votes in 1988, and George Bush carried Wood County by only 475 votes.

Marathon County's major city is Wausau, which has paper mills, prefabricated-home builders and white-collar employment in the insurance industry. In Wood County, Wisconsin Rapids is a paper mill town and Marshfield has a large medical clinic and research facility. The cities are processing centers for the surrounding dairy lands.

The heaviest Democratic vote in the southern part of the 7th comes out of Portage County. The city of Stevens Point there has a large Polish contingent, a branch of the state university and the headquarters of the Sentry Insurance Co. Walter F. Mondale narrowly carried the county in 1984, and Dukakis won it handily in 1988.

A scattering of streams, rivers, lakes, national forests and state parks covers the northern reaches of the 7th, luring tourists and retirees from urban centers.

The northern sections of the 7th share the same solid Democratic traditions found in Minnesota's Iron Range and the nearby western end of Michigan's Upper Peninsula. The major Democratic bastion is the region's only sizable city, Superior, a working-class town.

The port facilities of Superior and its larger neighbor, Duluth, Minn., are a funnel for soybeans, wheat and a wide range of other commodities raised on the farms of the Midwest. Some ore from the Minnesota Iron Range is still handled here.

Population: 522,623. White 514,200 (98%), Black 483 (0.1%), Other 6,924 (1%). Spanish origin 1,784 (0.3%). 18 and over 366,683 (70%), 65 and over 70,537 (14%). Median age: 30.

tential reduction if a budget impasse were to trigger the automatic cuts required by the 1985 Gramm-Rudman-Hollings anti-deficit law.

"The Congress, in my judgment, is not going to raise foreign aid in the context of making some of these other very large reductions on the domestic side of the budget," Obey told Baker. The administration, he added, "must accept the consequences of your own action, which includes cuts in your own pet programs as well as the other guy's."

Soon after, Obey played the foreign aid card to wield influence on another policy front. Reacting to documents released at the 1989 trial of Iran-contra figure Oliver L. North, Obey told Baker his subcommittee would not recommend aid for Central America until the administration acknowledges what Bush had denied: That past aid to Honduras was linked to its support of the Nicaraguan contras.

Obey is not a foe of foreign aid, as his actions at times might suggest, but he is a skeptic. And, not one to bluff, he has determinedly cut administration requests even for programs he enthusiastically supports, in order to force the larger budget debate. In late 1987, describing the foreign aid portion of a governmentwide appropriations bill, Obey noted, "We cut foreign aid more deeply than any other section. . . . I think it was justified." Within the foreign aid budget, meanwhile, Obey blunted Reagan's drive to shift spending toward military aid and away from the economic development programs Obey favors.

Throughout Reagan's second term, Obey emerged from conferences with the Senate with bills making substantial reductions in the president's foreign aid requests, while protecting politically important U.S. allies such as Israel and Egypt at the expense of smaller, less strategic nations. He is an indefatigable, unrelenting negotiator in conference, where his displays of temper have helped him get his way.

Obey also refused to push Reagan's requests for funding for international development banks until the White House rustled up GOP votes on the House floor. In part, he was protecting Democrats from Republican opponents — like Obey's own in 1986 — who would accuse Democrats of aiding communist countries by supporting the banks. "We've carried the Reagan administration's foreign aid bags through the pass while their own buddies are shooting from behind the rocks," he said in 1987.

Owing to a budget-summit agreement between Reagan and Congress in late 1987, foreign aid deliberations in 1988 were marked by rare bipartisanship — from Obey's subcommittee through the entire legislative process. The result was the first stand-alone foreign aid bill since 1981; previous appropriations had been lumped into catchall spending measures.

When Obey arrived at the full committee for action on the compromise, colleagues jokingly yelled, "Sell-out!" and Chairman Jamie L. Whitten, the House's longest-serving member, said, "If you stay here long enough, you'll see everything." More seriously, Obey noted, "It took three years for the administration to see where the center of gravity is."

As an institutionalist committed to House rules, Obey has encouraged the Foreign Affairs Committee to pass foreign aid authorizations, even though its frequent inability to do so — due to inevitable controversies — leaves Obey's subcommittee free to write the funding bill largely to its own specifications. At the same time, Obey is interested in more than just program numbers; he would assume a policy making role whatever Foreign Affairs did.

Obey has been a key House negotiator on the controversial contra aid issue. Obey's instincts were to fight Reagan on the issue, but he realized that Democrats lacked the votes in the Senate to block military aid unless they offered a non-lethal substitute. In 1987 and 1988 he reluctantly joined House Democratic leaders in crafting "humanitarian" aid alternatives.

Some other liberals continued to oppose any sort of aid, however, and Obey's reaction illustrated the limits of his admiration for those who take a stand; his regard does not embrace those Obey perceives to be acting in politically unrealistic or opportunistic ways. In 1988, he said liberal foes of the leadership's humanitarian package were "posing for holy pictures," not facing reality. "Any theology student can tell you that the greatest enemy of morality is moralism," he said.

In early 1989, Obey supported the humanitarian contra-aid pact with Bush. He also welcomed the administration's more conciliatory approach, saying, "It's nice to sit down with somebody and not be considered an enemy of your own country." However, he still expressed doubts about the administration's dedication to a diplomatic settlement with Nicaragua.

On another Appropriations subcommittee — Labor, Health and Human Services — Obey has been a broker between Democrats who favor maximum spending on social welfare programs and the panel's more conservative chairman, Kentucky Democrat William H. Natcher. He has taken particular interest in occupational-health issues, and criticized conservative efforts to ease worker safety regulations.

At the full committee, surrounded by elders who jealously guard Appropriations' authority, Obey is one of the few members to counsel that spending bills must comply with House-passed budget limits or else face fiscal conservatives' attacks on the floor. But outside the committee, he closes ranks against the attackers. Obey and other appropriators see many of the dissidents as opportunists, members who take credit for authorizing popular programs and then later refuse to pay for them on budgetary grounds.

When a bipartisan group targeted spending bills in 1987 with across-the-board cuts, Obey urged Appropriations subcommittees to delete first any provisions requested by those "who then sandbagged you on the floor." Later that year, when conservatives complained that the leadership's summit accord with Reagan did not reduce the deficit enough, he snapped, "Once in a while we need more than good leadership; we also need good follow-ship."

To Obey, passage of Gramm-Rudman in 1985 was political hypocrisy at its worst. But he has done what he could with foreign aid bills to hold the administration and Congress to the law's draconian requirements. "Gramm-Rudman is going to be the shortest-lived government lie in history," he said in 1987. "But when the Washington turkeys make a mistake, as they did in this one, they won't admit it. They'll just look for ways to sneak around it."

Obey's prominence in budget debates is largely a self-made role, but it is grounded in past experience on the Budget Committee that put him within reach of the chairmanship. In late 1980, after four years of a six-year term on Budget, Obey was a logical successor to the retiring chairman, Robert N. Giaimo. But the national sentiment expressed in November 1980 worked to the benefit of Obey's conservative rival, Oklahoma Democrat James R. Jones.

Twice the two men tied. On the third ballot Jones won, 121-116. An angry Obey let it be known he thought Speaker Thomas P. O'Neill Jr. had not worked hard enough for him. Obey also was hurt by some Democrats' lingering resentment about his earlier role in writing a strict ethics code limiting lawmakers' outside income.

As a sort of consolation prize, Obey did chair the Joint Economic Committee in the 99th Congress, which gave him a one-term platform to denounce Reaganomics. In mid-1987, Obey briefly scouted for support to run for Budget chairman again, but he soon dropped out of the race, leaving front-runner Leon E. Panetta unopposed.

Obey's frustrating association with the House ethics code dates to 1977, when he headed a commission to draft new rules. The panel recommended disclosure of personal finances, a limit on gifts, honoraria and outside income, a ban on personal uses of campaign funds, and an end to privately financed office accounts. Obey's doggedness and O'Neill's commitment got the package through, but when Obey returned later with more proposals to restructure the House, he lost, partly due to a backlash.

At Home: Twenty years ago, when *The Wall Street Journal* wanted to write about the advantages of incumbency, it sent a reporter to Obey's district, confident of witnessing an expert. The young Democrat had been in office only a few months at the time, but his techniques were already bearing fruit. He was sending out free government publications, writing columns for local newspapers and flooding the district with newsletters, even though he admitted in one that "there hasn't been that much to talk about yet."

Obey knew that unless he made a strong personal impression with the voters, they would return him to his Wausau real-estate business. Chosen in a 1969 special election to succeed Melvin R. Laird, who was named secretary of defense, Obey was the first Democrat ever to represent the 7th District.

When Laird's seat had opened up, Obey was beginning his fourth term in the state Assembly, where he had been since age 24. The GOP House candidate, state Sen. Walter Chilsen, was a well-known former newscaster who called himself a "Laird Republican." He tried to make student violence a campaign theme. But Obey deflected that issue. He focused on discontent with the Nixon administration's low milk-support prices and on the unpopular fiscal policies of GOP Gov. Warren Knowles. The changed mood in farming areas turned what was a 44,000-vote Laird win in November 1968 into a 4,055-vote margin for Obey five months later. In 1970, he breezed to re-election.

In 1972, redistricting put Obey in the same district with Alvin E. O'Konski, a 30-year House veteran who was twice his age. The new district was marginally Democratic and had more of Obey's old constituents than O'Konski's. The Republican agonized for months over whether he should retire or fight Obey. When he finally decided to retire, it was too late to have his name removed from the ballot. A few months later, Obey finished the job on O'Konski, winning 63 percent of the vote.

Since then, Obey has met little opposition. In 1986 the 7th got some national attention because Obey's opponent, Kevin Hermening, had been one of the 52 American hostages held in Iran. Obey demonstrated his hold on the district by winning 62 percent. In 1988, Hermening was back for more, and he got it, as Obey again won 62 percent.

Committees

Appropriations (5th of 35 Democrats)
Foreign Operations (chairman); Labor, Health and Human Services, Education and Related Agencies; Legislative Branch

Joint Economic
Economic Resources and Competitiveness (chairman); Fiscal and Monetary Policy; National Security Economics

Elections

1988 General

David R. Obey (D)	142,197	(62%)
Kevin Hermening (R)	86,077	(37%)

1986 General

David R. Obey (D)	106,700	(62%)
Kevin Hermening (R)	63,408	(37%)

Previous Winning Percentages: **1984** (61%) **1982** (68%) **1980** (65%) **1978** (62%) **1976** (73%) **1974** (71%) **1972** (63%) **1970** (68%) **1969 *** (52%)

* *Special election.*

District Vote For President

	1988	1984	1980	1976
D	128,849 (54%)	115,125 (46%)	118,482 (46%)	128,419 (55%)
R	108,341 (45%)	133,658 (53%)	116,505 (45%)	99,145 (43%)
I			16,153 (6%)	

Campaign Finance

	Receipts	Receipts from PACs	Expend-itures
1988			
Obey (D)	$530,385	$308,399 (58%)	$450,716
Hermening (R)	$201,293	$11,528 (6%)	$203,969
1986			
Obey (D)	$473,017	$261,906 (55%)	$462,535
Hermening (R)	$127,102	$17,770 (14%)	$124,210

Key Votes

1987	
Raise speed limit to 65 mph	N
Approve Gephardt "fair trade" amendment	Y
Ban testing of larger nuclear weapons	Y
Delay "re-flagging" of Kuwaiti tankers	Y
Approve tax-raising deficit-reduction bill	Y
1988	
Approve aid to Nicaraguan contras	N
Enact civil rights restoration bill over Reagan veto	Y
Kill 60-day plant-closing notification measure	N
Pass omnibus trade bill over Reagan veto	Y
Approve death penalty for drug-related murders	N
Bar federal funds for abortions in cases of rape and incest	N
Oppose seven-day waiting period for purchase of handguns	Y

Voting Studies

	Presidential Support		Party Unity		Conservative Coalition	
Year	S	O	S	O	S	O
1988	20	76	93	4	8	87
1987	13	87	93	3	7	93
1986	19	79	92	5	20	76
1985	15	84	93	4	7	91
1984	31	68	89	9	17	81
1983	22	77	94	5	11	88
1982	38	57	86	11	18	79
1981	29	70	83	11	13	81

Interest Group Ratings

Year	ADA	ACU	AFL-CIO	CCUS
1988	90	4	100	9
1987	100	0	94	0
1986	85	10	93	12
1985	90	5	94	18
1984	85	13	69	25
1983	100	0	94	20
1982	100	5	100	9
1981	85	7	87	11

8 Toby Roth (R)

Of Appleton — Elected 1978

Born: Oct. 10, 1938, Strasburg, N.D.
Education: Marquette U., B.A. 1961.
Military Career: Army Reserve, 1962-69.
Occupation: Real-estate broker.
Family: Wife, Barbara Fischer; three children.
Religion: Roman Catholic.
Political Career: Wis. Assembly, 1973-79.
Capitol Office: 2352 Rayburn Bldg. 20515; 225-5665.

In Washington: "If Reagan weren't president," Roth once told a reporter, "maybe I'd run for president. I see a lot of people here on the Hill; I don't think any of them could do a better job than I could." That may sound like a rather grand self-assessment, but it is not hard to imagine it coming from Roth, a man who takes himself and the world very seriously.

Firmness of purpose is at once Roth's strength and liability: There is no doubt he works hard to advance his conservative agenda on Foreign Affairs and Banking, and he has scored some legislative successes. But in the process, he has earned a reputation as headstrong and prone to bombast.

The length to which Roth will go to gain advantage is evident in what he calls "Project 497" — his aggressive strategy of deriving maximum political advantage from the congressional franked mailing privilege.

Franking regulations prohibit members from sending out a mass mailing 60 days prior to an election; a mass mailing is defined as 500 letters or more. "Project 497" has enabled Roth to send out tens of thousands of letters in batches of 497 during the last two months of the election.

In early 1989, Roth came under fire from some former employees who accused him of using his congressional office and staff for reelection purposes. Roth dismissed the claims as sour grapes from disgruntled former staffers. Subsequently, the Gannett News Service reported that there had been an unusual degree of staff turnover in Roth's Washington office during 1987 and 1988 — a rate much higher than in the offices of other upper Midwestern members.

All this has not distracted Roth from making his presence felt on a number of important questions as senior Republican on the Foreign Affairs subcommittee dealing with trade.

In the 98th and 99th Congresses, he was the Reagan administration's point man in a long battle to enact new high-technology trade rules. During deliberations on reauthorization of the Export Administration Act, Roth set aside his free-trade tendencies and fought for tighter restrictions on the flow of U.S. high technology overseas. "We in this House have a responsibility to business," he said, "but we also have a responsibility to national security."

Although no bill emerged from the 98th Congress, Roth's efforts paid off in 1985, when a compromise version breezed through the House. In a remark consistent with his reputation for overblown rhetoric, Roth noted the culmination of two and a half years of work on the measure thusly: "Children have been born during our deliberations, and some have even begun to walk."

When high-technology products are not involved, Roth is more of a free-trade advocate, concerned about finding markets for Wisconsin milk and cheese and other farm products. He has tried to promote commodity bartering with other countries as a way of reducing domestic surpluses, and he has been enthusiastic about giving grants, not just loans, to foreign purchasers of U.S. products.

Despite this inclination toward generosity, Roth normally has the deficit on his mind when questions of federal spending arise. In 1987, Roth spoke out against increasing aid to the homeless, arguing, "If we spend one-half billion more [for the homeless], we will have one-half billion more in deficits."

Roth is hawkish on most issues that come before the Foreign Affairs Committee. When the Reagan White House refused to provide documents on the Iran-contra arms scandal in late 1986, saying Foreign Affairs did not have adequate facilities to store highly classified material, Roth was one of a few members taking the administration's side. He said members "rushed to the cameras" to disclose what was said in private meetings and that such action "makes a mockery of congressional investigations and shows why the president cannot come to Congress with delicate information."

Among other crusades, Roth wants to keep Ethiopian coffee out of the United States. He has pushed for sanctions against the Marxist government of Ethiopia, which he says has violated human rights by forcing massive resettlement and doing little to combat wide-

Wisconsin 8

Northeast — Green Bay; Appleton

More than half of the 8th District vote is cast in the Fox River Valley counties of Outagamie (Appleton) and Brown (Green Bay). Germans are the most noticeable ethnic group in the industrialized valley. Most of them are Catholic and, even if Democratic, tend to be conservative.

The economy of the valley and the vast wooded area to the north is dependent on trees and paper. The district is an exporter of paper and agricultural products worldwide. Among the economic leaders in Green Bay is the Fort Howard Paper Co. Paper, grain and dairy products go out of Green Bay; fertilizer, cement and coal come in. Green Bay, best known for its football Packers, is the smallest city to host a National Football League club.

Thirty miles southwest is Appleton on the north shore of Lake Winnebago. Here, too, paper manufacturers and paper-making equipment industries are important employers. Appleton also has white-collar jobs at insurance companies and at Lawrence University (1,150 students). It was the hometown of Sen. Joseph R. McCarthy.

Green Bay voted for John F. Kennedy, a Catholic, in the 1960 presidential contest, but it traditionally prefers Republican presidential candidates. Ronald Reagan won Brown County easily in his two White House campaigns, and George Bush edged Michael S. Dukakis there in 1988. Appleton's Outagamie County gave Bush a more comfortable margin, helping him to a 53 percent tally in the district as a whole.

Nature has been generous to the 8th District. The focal points for tourist resorts and vacation homes are Door County, on a peninsula jutting into Lake Michigan, and Vilas County, in a lakes region on the Michigan border. Vilas' population has grown in recent years, as many who had visited there decided to relocate permanently. Both counties are solidly Republican, influenced by the prosperity that has come from serving nature-seekers from all over the Midwest.

The rural counties in the north-central part of the district are mostly Republican, although there are pockets of Democratic strength. Forest County, where lumbering is important, chose Dukakis over Bush in 1988, as did Menominee County, where most of the voters live on the Menominee Indian Reservation.

Population: 523,225. White 509,127 (97%), Black 743 (0.1%), Other 11,938 (2%). Spanish origin 2,302 (0.4%). 18 and over 362,554 (69%), 65 and over 64,184 (12%). Median age: 29.

spread starvation there. His efforts on this issue got a boost in early 1987, when Rep. William H. Gray III, the liberal black Democrat from Philadelphia who has closely monitored African issues, cosponsored Roth's bill.

Roth takes a different stand on the question of sanctions against the apartheid government of South Africa. He has opposed them. Roth tried unsuccessfully in the Foreign Affairs Committee to influence the sanctions bill in the 99th Congress; he wanted to strike a ban on U.S. purchase of gold Krugerrand coins, arguing that a ban would hurt U.S. coin dealers. But colleagues called the Krugerrand the "most obnoxious symbol of South Africa's racial policies," and Roth lost 21-4.

Roth was the only member of Foreign Affairs to oppose sanctions against Iraq in the closing months of the 100th Congress. The committee approved the sanctions to protest the alleged use of chemical weapons on Iraq's Kurdish minority. Roth called the use of chemical weapons "despicable," but said that by applying unilateral sanctions, "we're not doing anything to Iraq; we're shooting our own exporters in the foot."

Roth has also been vocally opposed to increasing U.S. aid to the Philippines, even though this has become a more popular congressional cause since Corazon Aquino took over from the ousted Marcos regime. Roth called a 1988 U.S.-Philippines pact that significantly increased U.S. aid "a disgrace to the country and an insult to the American taxpayer." He said Americans will be "shelling out billions of dollars in benefits to the Philippine government for the privilege of defending that country and allied interests in the Pacific."

At Home: Roth got to the House the same way he has worked to stay there — by assembling a large and efficient volunteer organization and shaking thousands of hands. In his last three re-election years, he has won by margins of better than 2-to-1. And yet, with the state slated to lose a congressional district after 1990, Roth is seen as potentially vulnerable. If Democrats controlled the drawing of the map, Roth might find himself in a district with Republican colleague Rep. Thomas E. Petri or Democratic Rep. David R. Obey.

Roth has made himself secure in terms of the 8th as it is now drawn, but his standing among the other politicians who often decide one's fate in redistricting is not as clear.

In 1978, when Roth decided to challenge vulnerable Democratic Rep. Robert J. Cornell, many GOP leaders were wary. He was not from Green Bay, the political center of the district. And while Roth's eager-beaver campaign style had worked well in Appleton during his campaigns for the Wisconsin Assembly, party veterans thought he might seem overbearing in a broader campaign against Cornell. They were wrong.

Cornell, a Roman Catholic priest, never relished running for office the way Roth does. The incumbent spent his time giving wooden speeches while Roth was out at shopping centers shaking hands. In the last two weeks of the campaign, Roth (by his count) shook 63,000 hands. His volunteer organization and nearly 3-to-1 spending advantage were just as important. Roth won both Brown and Outagamie counties (Green Bay and Appleton) and carried all but four other counties to take 58 percent overall.

Two years later Roth faced former Green Bay Mayor Michael Monfils, used the same approach and won by an even larger margin. His percentage was down significantly in 1982 against Ruth Clusen, former national president of the League of Women Voters, but his 57 percent tally was still comfortable in a year when Democrats were sweeping to victory in statewide contests.

Committees

Banking, Finance and Urban Affairs (12th of 20 Republicans)
Economic Stabilization; Financial Institutions Supervision, Regulation and Insurance; Housing and Community Development; Policy Research and Insurance

Foreign Affairs (5th of 18 Republicans)
International Economic Policy and Trade (ranking); Asian and Pacific Affairs

Elections

1988 General		
Toby Roth (R)	167,275	(70%)
Robert Baron (D)	72,708	(30%)
1986 General		
Toby Roth (R)	118,162	(67%)
Paul Willems (D)	57,265	(33%)

Previous Winning Percentages: **1984** (68%) **1982** (57%) **1980** (68%) **1978** (58%)

District Vote For President

	1988	1984	1980	1976
D	117,217 (47%)	88,922 (36%)	93,714 (37%)	102,935 (46%)
R	132,358 (53%)	154,371 (63%)	139,698 (55%)	115,804 (52%)
I			14,723 (6%)	

Campaign Finance

	Receipts	Receipts from PACs	Expend-itures
1988			
Roth (R)	$339,852	$180,814 (53%)	$227,823
Baron (D)	$14,571	$10,204 (70%)	$14,421
1986			
Roth (R)	$297,407	$140,097 (47%)	$284,287
Willems (D)	$83,003	$35,225 (42%)	$83,853

Key Votes

1987	
Raise speed limit to 65 mph	Y
Approve Gephardt "fair trade" amendment	N
Ban testing of larger nuclear weapons	N
Delay "re-flagging" of Kuwaiti tankers	Y
Approve tax-raising deficit-reduction bill	N
1988	
Approve aid to Nicaraguan contras	Y
Enact civil rights restoration bill over Reagan veto	N
Kill 60-day plant-closing notification measure	Y
Pass omnibus trade bill over Reagan veto	Y
Approve death penalty for drug-related murders	Y
Bar federal funds for abortions in cases of rape and incest	?
Oppose seven-day waiting period for purchase of handguns	Y

Voting Studies

	Presidential Support		Party Unity		Conservative Coalition	
Year	**S**	**O**	**S**	**O**	**S**	**O**
1988	51	39	78	14	87	0
1987	61	37	79	18	84	14
1986	68	27	79	17	88	8
1985	55	36	76	13	73	24
1984	51	44	61	28	83	14
1983	71	27	84	14	82	18
1982	57	38	73	22	78	18
1981	64	33	77	14	80	12

Interest Group Ratings

Year	ADA	ACU	AFL-CIO	CCUS
1988	10	83	36	92
1987	4	91	0	100
1986	0	82	8	81
1985	10	80	13	95
1984	15	65	38	63
1983	5	81	7	72
1982	10	86	16	68
1981	10	100	0	88

9 F. James Sensenbrenner Jr. (R)

Of Menomonee Falls — Elected 1978

Born: June 14, 1943, Chicago, Ill.
Education: Stanford U., A.B. 1965; U. of Wisconsin Law School, J.D. 1968.
Occupation: Lawyer.
Family: Wife, Cheryl Warren; two children.
Religion: Episcopalian.
Political Career: Wis. Assembly, 1969-75; Wis. Senate, 1975-79.
Capitol Office: 2444 Rayburn Bldg. 20515; 225-5101.

In Washington: The adjectives that colleagues use to describe Sensenbrenner's personality — pompous, brusque, nitpicking — make it clear that this conservative Republican would never win a House popularity contest.

But if he is held in icy regard, Sensenbrenner also is recognized as a diligent conservative on the liberal-dominated Judiciary Committee, someone who can go beyond the role of mere objector to package his views into workable legislation.

There is a partisan quotient to the criticisms of Sensenbrenner's personality: Through the years, Judiciary Democrats have been put out by his strongly worded statements against abortion, the Equal Rights Amendment and the Legal Services Corporation, and for capital punishment.

However, even a number of Republican colleagues have found the opinionated Sensenbrenner tough to take. At one meeting of the Judiciary Committee in the 98th Congress, Sensenbrenner became angry because Florida Republican Bill McCollum offered an amendment similar to one he had prepared. His long public outburst bothered McCollum so much that for weeks he refused even to sit next to Sensenbrenner.

But if Sensenbrenner's personality sometimes makes it difficult for him to find allies on either side of the aisle, he clearly is willing to cooperate with anyone, even a Democrat, when he believes strongly in something.

In the 97th Congress, Sensenbrenner played a major role in crafting a compromise with committee Democrats on the extension of the Voting Rights Act. In doing so, he angered Illinois Republican Henry J. Hyde, who had strong objections to the bill and had been trying to stall it. But Sensenbrenner's persistence was vindicated when the Reagan administration, which initially balked at the bill, hailed its passage as one of President Reagan's major civil rights accomplishments.

In another example of his strong-minded independence, Sensenbrenner, who had not been a gun-control advocate, supported a 1988 amendment to the omnibus drug bill mandating a seven-day waiting period prior to the purchase of a handgun. When the National Rifle Association sent a letter into his district criticizing the measure as "back-door registration of American firearms owners," Sensenbrenner turned his fire on the gun lobby, holding a news conference to denounce the mailing as "misleading and inflammatory."

Still, his overall thrust on Judiciary is solidly conservative. The ranking Republican on the Civil and Constitutional Rights Subcommittee, he carried the Republicans' banner in their attempts to modify a pair of civil rights-oriented bills in the 100th Congress.

In 1988, Sensenbrenner led the battle in committee against the provision in a fair-housing bill that would have set up a system of administrative-law judges, empowered to rule on housing discrimination cases and impose financial damages and fines. Taking a position supported by Reagan and the National Association of Realtors, Sensenbrenner argued that the system, under which a violator would be forced to pay fines without the benefit of a jury trial, might be unconstitutional.

His amendment, replacing the administrative law system with an expedited federal court trial procedure, was defeated by a 14-20 Judiciary vote. However, the final bill enacted later that year contained a compromise that met Sensenbrenner's concerns halfway: It set up an administrative-judge process, but gave any party in a discrimination suit the right to request a jury trial.

Sensenbrenner had less success in 1988 when trying to reshape the Civil Rights Restoration Act — a bill so named because it aimed at overriding the Supreme Court's 1984 *Grove City College v. Bell* decision, which said that only the "program or activity" of an institution receiving federal assistance, and not the entire institution, was required to comply with federal

Wisconsin 9

Milwaukee Suburbs; Sheboygan

The 9th is Wisconsin's only full-fledged suburban district. During the 1970s it lured enough people out of Milwaukee's 4th and 5th districts to post a population growth rate of nearly 18 percent, the fastest of any district in the state. Workdays bring a horde of commuters from the 9th to and from Milwaukee's offices and factories.

Not surprisingly, the 9th is also Wisconsin's most staunchly Republican district. In the 1980s, Jimmy Carter, Walter F. Mondale and Michael S. Dukakis all failed to surpass 40 percent of the vote here. The only steady source of Democratic votes comes from heavily unionized, blue-collar Sheboygan.

Republicans generally make their strongest showing in the "Gold Coast" section of the district, a string of exclusive neighborhoods along Lake Michigan north of Milwaukee. In the city's boom days, brewers and other industrial kingpins built mansions on the North Shore; today the property values and the Republican turnouts there are stunning. In some of these affluent communities, such as River Hills, Bush won by margins of more than 2-to-1 in 1988.

The middle-class presence is stronger in the western sections of the 9th. Washington County is a combination of fast-growing bedroom communities and agricultural lands being encroached on by development, with a smattering of industry. The county seat, West Bend, is home to the West Bend Co., whose line of appliances includes the Stir-Crazy Popcorn Popper. Sixty percent of the Washington County vote went for Bush in 1988.

In earlier generations, the lakes of Waukesha County drew Milwaukee's leading families to buy real estate in the county for summer retreats. But in Pewaukee, Hartland and other parts of the county, suburbanization has taken its toll on those large holdings. In 1988, Bush took 65 percent of the county's vote. The areas of Waukesha County where Democrats are most numerous — the city of Waukesha and the southeastern part of the county — were transferred to the 4th District in the last redistricting.

Population: 522,950. White 516,203 (99%), Black 1,919 (0.4%), Other 2,798 (1%). Spanish origin 4,300 (1%). 18 and over 360,879 (69%), 65 and over 53,062 (10%). Median age: 30.

anti-discrimination laws. His alternative to the Democrat-backed bill was defeated by the House on a 146-266 vote.

Though Republicans had many objections to the *Grove City* bill, Sensenbrenner's proposal centered on the "religious tenets" clause, which provided exemptions from the law to "any operation of an entity which is controlled by a religious organization." Sensenbrenner's amendment included a provision to broaden the clause to cover entities controlled by or "closely identified with the tenets" of a religious organization.

But most Democrats and some Republicans, including ranking Judiciary member Hamilton Fish Jr. of New York, objected. Fish denounced the measure as "unwise and unnecessary," and noted that the language was intended to cover seminaries and not colleges with broader enrollments.

Sensenbrenner was not happy with his setback on the bill. When some Science Committee Democrats opposed a bill, written by Pennsylvania Republican Robert S. Walker, mandating sanctions against federal contractors who do not maintain drug-free work places, Sensenbrenner lashed out. "If you object to using the string of federal funds," he said, "then you should not have supported *Grove City*."

At the start of the 101st Congress, Sensenbrenner took over as ranking Republican on the Science Subcommittee on Space. In that spot, he seems likely to be a leader of the panel's bipartisan consensus in favor of U.S. space programs. In a speech supporting the National Aeronautics and Space Administration's budget priorities for fiscal 1990, Sensenbrenner warned those looking for budget savings in those programs that "it's easy to be 'penny-wise' and 'pound-foolish.' "

In the 100th Congress, Sensenbrenner was ranking member on the Science Subcommittee on International Scientific Cooperation, where he argued that the concept of cooperation was not appreciated by America's major trade competitor, Japan. He stated that Japan had taken advantage of the United States by developing and marketing products based on expensive U.S.-financed basic research, and he called on Reagan to be tougher in demanding that the Japanese contribute more to the basic research effort.

Japan's proposal for a limited economic contribution to allied efforts to protect Persian Gulf shipping lanes in 1987 enraged Sensenbrenner. "American servicemen have died far away from home protecting the oil that drives Japanese industry, an industry that takes jobs away from United States workers . . . ," he said in October of that year. "This time the international community should band together to let Japan know its freeloading days are over."

At Home: Sensenbrenner has held public office ever since his graduation from law school. Despite his reputation for pomposity, his personal resources and conservative views have earned him an undefeated record at the polls.

Sensenbrenner is heir to a paper and cellulose manufacturing fortune, much of which stems from his great-grandfather's invention of the sanitary napkin shortly after World War I. Marketing it under the brand name Kotex, Sensenbrenner's ancestor went on to become chairman of the board of Kimberly-Clark.

To reach Congress in 1978, Sensenbrenner had to dip into family wealth to overcome an unexpectedly strong GOP primary challenge. With Republican Bob Kasten leaving the 9th District to run for governor, Sensenbrenner was viewed as the obvious successor. He had been elected to four terms in the state Assembly before moving in 1975 to the state Senate, where he quickly rose to be assistant minority leader. He had a solid political base in the older, more affluent lakeside suburbs, and his conservative stance reminded voters of the popular Kasten.

But his opponent was Susan Shannon Engeleiter, a state legislator who would later become state Senate GOP leader, the party nominee for the U.S. Senate in 1988 and then director of the Small Business Administration. Just 26 when she challenged Sensenbrenner, Engeleiter put on a strong campaign in the western, more middle-class part of the district, which she represented in the state Assembly. More gregarious than Sensenbrenner, she outpolled him by 5,600 votes in the 9th's four western counties. Only Sensenbrenner's familiarity in the areas along Lake Michigan — Ozaukee and the most Republican part of Milwaukee — allowed him to win the primary by 589 votes.

The 1978 Democratic nominee, Milwaukee lawyer Matthew J. Flynn, was also on his way to higher visibility in statewide politics as party chairman and a candidate for the U.S. Senate. But he could not raise enough money to compete with Sensenbrenner on an equal footing. Sensenbrenner campaigned on his support for cutting taxes and defeated Flynn by a solid margin.

Committees

Judiciary (4th of 14 Republicans)
Civil and Constitutional Rights (ranking); Courts, Intellectual Property and the Administration of Justice

Science, Space and Technology (2nd of 19 Republicans)
Space Science and Applications (ranking); International Scientific Cooperation

Select Narcotics Abuse and Control (5th of 12 Republicans)

Elections

1988 General		
F. James Sensenbrenner Jr. (R)	185,093	(75%)
Tom Hickey (D)	62,003	(25%)
1986 General		
F. James Sensenbrenner Jr. (R)	138,766	(78%)
Thomas G. Popp (D)	38,636	(22%)

Previous Winning Percentages: **1984** (73%) **1982** (100%) **1980** (78%) **1978** (61%)

District Vote For President

	1988		1984		1980		1976	
D	99,467	(39%)	97,101	(35%)	87,405	(34%)	100,968	(40%)
R	149,639	(60%)	177,516	(64%)	149,924	(58%)	143,454	(57%)
I					17,971	(7%)		

Campaign Finance

	Receipts	Receipts from PACs	Expend-itures
1988			
Sensenbrenner (R)	$309,612	$109,839 (35%)	$288,505
Hickey (D) †	$14,736	0	$14,686
1986			
Sensenbrenner (R)	$175,697	$60,950 (35%)	$178,698
Popp (D)	$10,753	$2,133 (20%)	$10,753

† Totals based on incomplete data.

Key Votes

1987	
Raise speed limit to 65 mph	Y
Approve Gephardt "fair trade" amendment	N
Ban testing of larger nuclear weapons	N
Delay "re-flagging" of Kuwaiti tankers	Y
Approve tax-raising deficit-reduction bill	?
1988	
Approve aid to Nicaraguan contras	Y
Enact civil rights restoration bill over Reagan veto	N
Kill 60-day plant-closing notification measure	Y
Pass omnibus trade bill over Reagan veto	Y
Approve death penalty for drug-related murders	Y
Bar federal funds for abortions in cases of rape and incest	Y
Oppose seven-day waiting period for purchase of handguns	N

Voting Studies

	Presidential Support		Party Unity		Conservative Coalition	
Year	**S**	**O**	**S**	**O**	**S**	**O**
1988	68	30	92	8	87	13
1987	68	31	92	6	77	21
1986	73	27	89	11	80	20
1985	68	33	87	11	69	31
1984	45	20	56	9	44	12
1983	70	30	85	14	74	25
1982	60	36	84	16	70	30
1981	59	41	77	21	75	24

Interest Group Ratings

Year	ADA	ACU	AFL-CIO	CCUS
1988	15	88	21	100
1987	8	91	0	93
1986	0	77	7	89
1985	20	71	6	86
1984	5	80	11	69
1983	10	83	6	75
1982	25	86	15	73
1981	20	100	13	84

Wyoming

U.S. CONGRESS

SENATE 2 R
HOUSE 1 R

LEGISLATURE

Senate 11 D, 19 R
House 23 D, 41 R

ELECTIONS

1988 Presidential Vote

Bush	61%
Dukakis	38%

1984 Presidential Vote

Reagan	71%
Mondale	28%

1980 Presidential Vote

Reagan	63%
Carter	28%
Anderson	7%

Turnout rate in 1984	53%
Turnout rate in 1986	44%
Turnout rate in 1988	50%

(as percentage of voting age population)

POPULATION AND GROWTH

1980 population	469,557
1988 population estimate (50th in the nation)	479,000
Percent change 1980-1988	+2%

DEMOGRAPHIC BREAKDOWN

White	95%
Black	1%
Other	2%
(Spanish origin)	5%
Urban	63%
Rural	37%
Born in state	39%
Foreign-born	2%

MAJOR CITIES

Cheyenne	53,960
Casper	47,310
Laramie	24,930
Gillette	23,280
Rock Springs	21,970

AREA AND LAND USE

Area 96,989 sq. miles (9th)

Farm	54%
Forest	16%
Federally owned	50%

Gov. Mike Sullivan (D)
Of Casper — Elected 1986

Born: Sept. 22, 1939, Omaha, Neb.
Education: U. of Wyoming, B.S. 1961, J.D. 1964.
Occupation: Lawyer.
Religion: Roman Catholic.
Political Career: No previous office.
Next Election: 1990.

WORK

Occupations

White-collar	47%
Blue-collar	36%
Service workers	13%

Government Workers

Federal	6,301
State	12,625
Local	31,334

MONEY

Median family income	$ 22,430	(7th)
Tax burden per capita	$ 1,584	(2nd)

EDUCATION

Spending per pupil through grade 12	$ 5,114	(4th)
Persons with college degrees	17%	(21st)

CRIME

Violent crime rate 283 per 100,000 (36th)

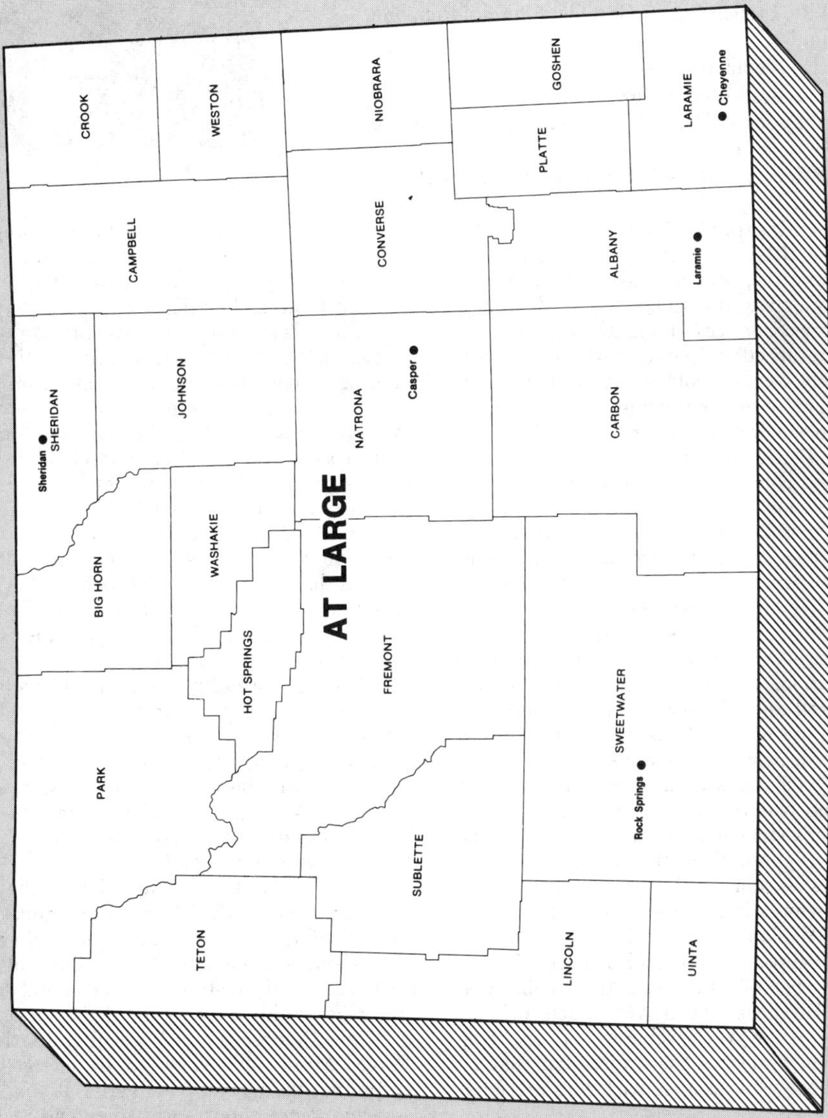
AT LARGE
CROOK
WESTON
NIOBRARA
GOSHEN
PLATTE
LARAMIE
Cheyenne
CAMPBELL
CONVERSE
ALBANY
Laramie
SHERIDAN
Sheridan
JOHNSON
NATRONA
Casper
CARBON
BIG HORN
WASHAKIE
HOT SPRINGS
FREMONT
PARK
SWEETWATER
Rock Springs
SUBLETTE
TETON
LINCOLN
UINTA

Malcolm Wallop (R)

Of Big Horn — Elected 1976

Born: Feb. 27, 1933, New York, N.Y.
Education: Yale U., B.A. 1954.
Military Career: Army, 1955-57.
Occupation: Rancher; meatpacking executive.
Family: Wife, French Carter Gamble; four children, one stepchild.
Religion: Episcopalian.
Political Career: Wyo. House, 1969-73; Wyo. Senate, 1973-77; sought Republican nomination for Wyo. governor, 1974.
Capitol Office: 237 Russell Bldg. 20510; 224-6441.

In Washington: Wallop reported for new duty in the 101st Congress, giving up the Finance Committee, with its wide sway over taxation, entitlement programs and trade, for a seat on Armed Services. It was an odd move for a senator returned in 1988 by fewer than 1,500 votes chiefly because voters felt he had grown distant from Wyoming while plunging ever deeper into the arcane matters of missile throw weights and space defenses.

But the committee switch made sense for Wallop personally, if not politically. He not only sees missiles as a growth industry for Wyoming, he also has put himself forward as an acerbic spokesman for the Republican right on foreign policy and defense issues.

With his party outnumbered in the Senate and conservatives ambivalent about the Bush administration, Wallop's aggressive stance seems suited to a leadership role among his ideological brethren. If he lacks notable skill in oratory or legislative maneuvering, he has a knack for voicing, with an acid sarcasm, the feelings and frustrations of many hard-liners.

Wallop's stridency has not made him one of the more popular members. The rapid rise into leadership ranks of Wyoming's junior senator, GOP whip Alan Simpson, has often overshadowed Wallop's career. He is a man who frequently appears edgy and frustrated with Senate life even when it seems to be going well for him. He does not derive much evident satisfaction from the exchange of opposing views; often, he leaves the impression that he believes those who disagree with him are ignorant.

Sometimes, he seems to suggest that his foes are worse than ignorant. His harsh tone has been most evident toward those on the other side in debates over Central America policy, in which he was one of the Reagan administration's most staunch defenders.

Early in 1987, Wallop told the Senate that consideration of continued aid for the Nicaraguan contras offered a stark choice. To vote to cut off aid, he said, "cannot be interpreted as anything other than a vote in favor of the Sandinista regime.... It is a vote for communism in Central America."

There is an apocalyptic quality to Wallop's foreign policy views. Other conservatives, including Ronald Reagan, voice optimism about restoring American supremacy in the world. Wallop seems to portray the spread of totalitarianism as inexorable, and himself as a lonely voice struggling in vain to fight it. In the 1988 debate over the intermediate-range nuclear-force treaty, Wallop said the United States was "panicking at the knees of the great bear." He warned that the treaty would weaken NATO by removing a keystone of Western nuclear deterrence and could lead to the "collapse of the political order in Europe."

Wallop is well-known as an early advocate of the strategic defense initiative (SDI). Working with a small group of defense scientists, he pushed for construction of laser-armed space satellites long before such ideas were taken seriously. Wallop's isolation ended in 1983, when Reagan announced his support for a space-based defense system.

But Wallop takes a dim view of the direction in which the Reagan administration pushed SDI, calling it "thin gruel." He argues that Pentagon planners have mistakenly pursued the exotic instead of what could be put into place within a few years. He has pressed for a "U.S. Defense Force," coequal to the Air Force, Army and Navy, to be charged with defending the nation from aerial attack of any sort and, more importantly, to defend SDI from interservice rivalry over budgets. Wallop would also scrap the anti-ballistic missile treaty with the Soviet Union and protect MX missiles with anti-missile defenses.

"The drive for anti-missile defense was hijacked by the Reagan administration's incompetent and unfaithful crew," he said on the fourth anniversary of Reagan's SDI speech.

Wallop and a group of conservative allies

favor rapid deployment of a more basic system — one that would not provide a leakproof "umbrella" but would make a Soviet attack too difficult to be attempted. This view was gaining credence in early 1989 within the Bush administration with the so-called "Brilliant Pebbles" defense.

Despite Wallop's preoccupation with foreign policy, one of the most significant roles he has played in the Senate came about because of his shifting views in 1985 and 1986 on overhauling the tax code. A strong advocate of reductions in individual tax rates, Wallop was skeptical of the tax proposal that emerged from the administration in 1985. By the time Finance Committee markups began in spring 1986, he was even more dubious, warning that "none of us are committed to tax reform," and questioning the worth of attacking special-interest tax breaks if marginal rates were still to be above the 25 percent level he favored.

But when committee Chairman Bob Packwood sought to rescue the bill by proposing dramatically lower rates, Wallop became one of his key allies. His backing gave the bill a conservative seal of approval that helped ensure support from others on the right.

Wallop grew disenchanted with the bill as it progressed past Finance. By the conclusion of conference negotiations with the House, he was unhappy enough with the loss of certain business deductions that he voted against it. "I have seen us fritter away the opportunity of a lifetime on the altar of convenience," he complained. But that late criticism did not matter much; the important thing was that he had supported the bill at a critical point.

Along with his conservative crusades, Wallop also has kept a hand in the energy and public-lands issues that dominated the first part of his Senate career. As chairman of the Public Lands and Reserved Water Subcommittee at Energy and Natural Resources, Wallop had a key position defending Wyoming's interests. With nearly half of Wyoming's land federally owned, and with water rights a vital issue, he could monitor every bill affecting those subjects.

Wilderness issues were the focus of Wallop's work on the subcommittee in the 98th Congress. The panel was extremely busy reporting more than a score of bills setting up wilderness areas in most Western states, including Wyoming. Along with Energy Chairman James A. McClure of Idaho, Wallop helped clear the way for passage of the bills by working out a compromise with House Democrats on the fate of areas that might be designated as wilderness.

Wallop also was active in legislation facilitating development of coal-slurry pipelines. The issue was a potentially difficult one for him. Wyoming is a coal state, and coal producers are eager for the pipelines, but they would use large quantities of the state's scarce water, diverting it from farmers and ranchers. Wallop and McClure developed a compromise to the 1983 coal-slurry bill that sought to protect arid Western states from having their water taken for pipelines without their approval. The bill was not enacted.

In 1985, Wallop ran for chairman of the National Republican Senatorial Committee, losing by one vote to John Heinz of Pennsylvania. While he had the support of most of the GOP's conservative wing, Wallop was unable to overcome the reluctance of many senators to have two Wyoming senators in the leadership at the same time.

At Home: Although he has won three elections to the Senate, Wallop has never attained the level of statewide popularity enjoyed by Simpson and former at-large Rep. Dick Cheney (now secretary of defense). As a result, even with Republicans' 3-to-2 edge in voter registration, Wallop's campaigns are always worth watching.

Ironically, in his first statewide campaign, Wallop found himself at odds with the more conservative wing of the Wyoming GOP. Viewed as a moderate in a four-way gubernatorial primary in 1974 — he drew some of his support from voters sympathetic to environmental causes — Wallop came from far behind to finish a close second. When he did not assist the eventual nominee, conservative rancher Dick Jones, many party loyalists were displeased.

But Wallop solved that problem with remarkable ease in 1976, campaigning from the right against three-term Democratic Sen. Gale W. McGee. Although oil companies and other business interests were somewhat leery about backing him, Wallop got valuable help from national conservative organizations. He depicted McGee as supporting big government and criticized him for infrequent visits to the state. He also maintained that no senator should serve more than 12 years.

The challenger's TV ads were especially effective. Wallop saddled up a horse, donned a cowboy hat and urged voters to join the "Wallop Senate drive." He ridiculed environmental regulations by portraying a cowboy forced to hitch a portable toilet to his horse. The ads helped Wallop overcome a personal background that might have been a problem. Although he was a third-generation Wyoming resident and an eight-year veteran of the state Legislature, he was born in New York City, educated at Yale and had a grandfather who once sat in the House of Lords.

By the time of his 1982 election, Wallop found himself under fire from environmentalists, who claimed he had forsaken their cause, and from his Democratic opponent, who accused him of being inaccessible to constituents.

The Democrat was former state Sen. Rodger McDaniel, a 10-year state legislator whose path to nomination was cleared when

Gov. Ed Herschler announced he would seek reelection rather than challenge Wallop. McDaniel painted the incumbent as a servant of big-oil interests and an uncritical defender of Reaganomics. But like Wallop in 1974, McDaniel had to be careful not to alienate more conservative members of his own party — some of whom were hesitant to back a man who had been state coordinator for Edward M. Kennedy's 1980 presidential campaign.

Wallop played up his support for the president and promised to work to protect Wyoming water. McDaniel proved an energetic campaigner and, buoyed by Herschler's strong gubernatorial showing, carried several counties along Wyoming's predominantly Democratic southern tier. But Wallop's $1 million treasury enabled him to nail down a 57 percent victory.

Six years later, Wallop again faced an opponent who accused him of being anti-environment and out of touch with voters. And after six years, Wallop showed he was even more vulnerable to those charges.

The Democratic nominee, state Sen. John Vinich, did not have the profile of a winner in conservative Wyoming. A liberal, pro-labor senator with longish hair and sideburns, Vinich sponsored programs to benefit the elderly and to tighten regulations on business in his 14 years in the Legislature.

Vinich, whose iconoclasm often placed him at odds with state Senate and Democratic leaders, was not the favorite of his party's insiders. After Herschler, who retired in 1987, declined to run, he endorsed Lynn Simons, the state public instruction superintendent, and blasted Vinich as an ineffective legislator.

But Simons' effort was plagued with errors, and Vinich, the first candidate in the race, out-organized and out-campaigned her. He won 14 of Wyoming's 23 counties in the primary; Simons slumped to an embarrassing third-place finish.

Vinich did not try to mask his ideology in the Senate race, but he defied classification as an archetypal liberal. He earned the National Rifle Association's top rating for his anti-gun-control record. And he had been regularly reelected from a county with a solid GOP registration advantage.

Vinich turned on Wallop with both guns blazing. He accused him of concentrating on a national conservative agenda to the detriment of the state's economic interests. He charged Wallop with hypocrisy for criticizing the National Park Service's "let-burn" policy, blamed for prolonging the summer's raging fires in Yellowstone National Park. Vinich said Wallop had ample opportunity to alter the policy when he chaired the subcommittee with jurisdiction over the Park Service.

Wallop had a huge fund-raising advantage, and he maintained a comfortable lead in polls for most of the fall. But Vinich was boosted by an intensive 11th-hour media blitz bankrolled by the national party and labor organizations. He closed a double-digit poll deficit in the last week, but fell 1,322 votes short.

Committees

Armed Services (6th of 9 Republicans)
Defense Industry and Technology (ranking); Readiness, Sustainability and Support; Strategic Forces and Nuclear Deterrence

Energy and Natural Resources (4th of 9 Republicans)
Public Lands, National Parks and Forests (ranking); Mineral Resources Development and Production; Water and Power

Small Business (4th of 9 Republicans)
Export Expansion; Rural Economy and Family Farming

Elections

1988 General		
Malcolm Wallop (R)	91,143	(50%)
John Vinich (D)	89,821	(50%)
1988 Primary		
Malcolm Wallop (R)	55,752	(83%)
Nora Lewis (R)	3,933	(6%)
I. W. Kinney (R)	3,716	(6%)

Previous Winning Percentages: **1982** (57%) **1976** (55%)

Campaign Finance

	Receipts	Receipts from PACs	Expend-itures
1988			
Wallop (R)	$1,492,048	$872,664 (58%)	$1,344,185
Vinich (D)	$491,599	$248,303 (51%)	$490,230

Key Votes

1987	
Enact omnibus highway bill over Reagan veto	N
Limit testing of space-based anti-ballistic missiles	N
Oppose banning tests of larger nuclear weapons	Y
Confirm Robert H. Bork as Supreme Court justice	Y
1988	
Allow vote on campaign-finance overhaul	N
Pass civil rights restoration bill over Reagan veto	N
Enact omnibus trade bill over Reagan veto	N
Approve death penalty for drug-related murders	Y
Oppose "workfare" amendment to welfare overhaul bill	N

Voting Studies

	Presidential Support		Party Unity		Conservative Coalition	
Year	S	O	S	O	S	O
1988	72	16	85	1	89	0
1987	74	15	87	6	88	3
1986	93	5	94	3	95	1
1985	73	14	88	5	83	5
1984	86	4	91	1	94	0
1983	72	22	83	9	82	9
1982	71	18	82	10	86	5
1981	85	9	91	3	93	1

Interest Group Ratings

Year	ADA	ACU	AFL-CIO	CCUS
1988	0	100	11	91
1987	0	96	0	80
1986	0	100	0	95
1985	0	95	5	97
1984	5	91	0	76
1983	5	64	13	83
1982	10	74	8	75
1981	10	71	5	100

Alan K. Simpson (R)

Of Cody — Elected 1978

Born: Sept. 2, 1931, Denver, Colo.
Education: U. of Wyoming, B.S.L. 1954, LL.B. 1958.
Military Career: Army, 1954-56.
Occupation: Lawyer.
Family: Wife, Ann Schroll; three children.
Religion: Episcopalian.
Political Career: Cody City attorney, 1959-69; Wyo. House, 1965-77.
Capitol Office: 261 Dirksen Bldg. 20510; 224-3424.

In Washington: Humor can take a person a long way, and perhaps no one in Congress proves that so well as Simpson. Working in a chamber where ego and vanity have driven more than one balding senator to toupees or hair plugs, Simpson jokes that his own hairless pate makes him "a solar-powered sex machine." In a short time, such wit has helped propel Simpson to Senate Republicans' No. 2 leadership position. It has not, however, made him the unchallenged heir apparent for the top spot.

For a time it appeared Simpson could possibly repeat the success he had in the Wyoming House, where he moved up from committee chairman to party whip and finally to party leader within a dozen years. In the Senate, likewise, Simpson rose from a chairman to whip after just one term and, after a commendable performance in the 100th Congress as acting GOP leader when Bob Dole was busy with his 1988 presidential campaign, Simpson was well placed to bid for the minority leadership had Dole won or been chosen as vice president.

But Simpson would have had to fight more than one ambitious Republican for the leader's job, just as he probably will whenever Dole steps down — a move that does not, in any case, appear imminent.

In Dole and Simpson, Senate Republicans have the funniest leadership team in memory. Simpson, to his credit, more often turns his humor on himself, although both men have a biting side that on occasion has posed a problem for each. Humor alone, however, would not have gotten either man where he is today.

Simpson's six-year campaign for reform of the nation's laws on illegal immigration displayed all the talents that launched him to influence in the Senate. Besides humor, he showed patience, negotiating skill and a bipartisan spirit that were crucial to the ultimate enactment of the 1986 law after it had repeatedly been written off as hopeless.

That patience and bipartisanship were strained in the next two years. Democrats regained control of the Senate for the 100th Congress and flexed their legislative muscles after six years in the minority. Meanwhile, President Reagan was a lame duck weakened by the Iran-contra scandal. Especially in early 1988, with Dole absent, it often fell to Simpson to lead the GOP resistance.

At first, Republicans seemed in disarray, and enough of them joined Democrats in early 1987 to override Reagan's vetoes of bills for highway construction and water projects. But for the rest of the Congress, they repeatedly resorted to filibusters, killing Democratic initiatives on campaign finance and labor benefits, while forcing changes in other measures.

Simpson got along better with Majority Leader Robert C. Byrd than most Republicans, who resented Byrd's hardball mastery of Senate rules. Simpson expressed respect for his adversary. "When you're the leader, you're the leader, and you don't allow the minority to determine what's going to come to the floor," Simpson said in early 1987, even as he was helping orchestrate tactics to do just that.

Yet Simpson's understanding had its limits. When Byrd shelved a spending bill because too few Republicans would support it, Simpson taunted, "We remember the feeling — 'Can you give us a few votes?' " He was enraged later in 1987 when Byrd implied that Republicans' filibuster of a defense bill was unpatriotic in the wake of an Iraqi attack on the U.S.S. *Stark* that killed 37 servicemen.

But what really riles Simpson, and causes his celebrated humor to turn caustic, are attacks on a Republican president and his nominees. Early in 1987, he told reporters that the media was doing a "sadistic little disservice" with its investigation of Reagan's role in the Iran-contra scandal. "You're asking him things because you know he's off balance," he said. "You'd like to stick it in his gazoo."

More often, Simpson is taking on Democrats on the Judiciary Committee in defense of some nominee to the federal courts. When Reagan in 1986 selected William H. Rehnquist to be chief justice, Simpson described Rehnquist's critics as a kind of bird: the "bug-eyed zealot," a species "characterized by ruffled feathers and a pinched bill," that made a "continual thin, whining noise whenever the president pulls one of his appointees out of a bag."

He applied the same term to foes of unsuccessful Supreme Court nominee Robert H. Bork in 1987. With GOP Sen. Orrin G. Hatch, Simpson was Bork's most ardent defender, depicting him as the victim of "tyranny" by opponents who had distorted the judge's words to make him appear hostile to women and blacks.

The 101st Congress began on a similarly sour note for Simpson, when the Senate rejected President Bush's nominee for defense secretary, former Sen. John Tower. Simpson condemned an FBI report on allegations of Tower's womanizing and drunkenness as "absolute garbage," and derided one source as "a screwball."

Simpson's reputation for such bluntness was made late one night in 1982 when he tore into a fellow Republican, Jesse Helms. The North Carolinian was filibustering a gas tax bill while members were eager to adjourn for Christmas. Infuriated, Simpson publicly refused to shake Helms' hand, and said, "Seldom have I seen a more obdurate, more obnoxious performance. I guess it is called hardball. In my neck of the woods we call it stickball. Children play it." He later apologized to Helms.

More often than not, he and Helms are on the same side. Simpson is sometimes portrayed as a moderate — perhaps by journalists who cannot believe that a man of the right could be so likable — but he is in fact one of the most conservative senators. When his humor stings, it often is aimed at those he feels have unfairly attacked his ideological allies.

He has said that he merely represents the orneriness of his constituents. He lopes through life with a half-smile and says he is determined not to take himself or the Senate too seriously. Perhaps that comes easier to the son of a senator (who served with Bush's father). "I'm trying to be the same person I've always been," he says, "and see how it works in the Senate."

Simpson is guided by the conviction, as he once expressed it, that "you can open a door with humor and drive a truck right through." He is not remarkably witty in the mold of the classic British politician or a stand-up comic. But Simpson has a knack for the quick riposte, and for the apt joke that can break a tense legislative moment. His is the voice of an individualistic Westerner, who brings the fresh air of candor to the Senate.

During one long debate on a public works bill, controversial for what some saw as its pork-barrel excesses, Simpson spoke up, "Here's one old cowboy that is just tired of the old crap." He does not hesitate to castigate his colleagues for pushing their own agendas at the expense of broader goals. "Senators bring their own laundry," he says, "and they look at the Senate chamber as a tub to get it laundered."

Simpson likes to call legislation "the driest and dullest form of human behavior," but he shows a zest for his job. "I must be perverse," he once said. "Show me an issue that's filled with guilt, fear and anger, and I want to play with it."

Certainly immigration was that issue. Throughout the long and tortuous history of the legislation that came to be known as Simpson-Mazzoli, Simpson stuck by two ideas that he insisted were crucial to immigration reform. One was that the only effective way to prevent people from coming to America illegally is to deny them the jobs that draw them here by penalizing those who hire them. The other was that many of the millions of illegals who had already been here for years must be offered some way to obtain legal status.

Formidable political obstacles were arrayed against him. Business groups opposed sanctions against employers, and Hispanic leaders warned that the penalties would lead to employment discrimination against Hispanic citizens. Conservatives attacked the notion of amnesty for people who had entered illegally, and state governments worried about the welfare costs of a newly legal population. No group fully backed the bill; each maneuvered and formed new alliances to kill certain sections.

Simpson had some allies, notably Kentucky Democrat Romano L. Mazzoli, chairman of the House Judiciary Committee's Immigration Subcommittee. The Senate's 80-19 passage of the immigration bill in 1982 was a personal triumph for Simpson, but Mazzoli had less success in the House and the bill died there.

In the next Congress, the bill quickly passed the Senate, and even managed to scrape through the House by a five-vote margin. But the conference proved exceedingly difficult. After compromises were reached on amnesty and employer sanctions, and then on less crucial issues, the measure hit a snag in 1984 when the House refused to accept a Reagan-backed provision limiting federal aid to states for services provided to aliens granted amnesty.

Undaunted, Simpson came back in 1985, at the start of the 99th Congress, with a modified proposal that would delay amnesty until employment of illegal aliens had been reduced. Amended in Judiciary to require amnesty within three years, the bill reached the floor in the closing months of 1985 and passed comfortably.

However, over Simpson's vehement objections, the Senate had approved a new "guest worker" program allowing large numbers of seasonal farm workers to enter the country. That provision reflected the most serious unresolved controversy surrounding the issue — Western growers wanted foreign labor for harvest time while labor unions feared exploitation of workers — and it proved to be the bill's major stumbling block in the House.

It bogged down for months in House Judiciary, and did not pass the House until the last two weeks of the Congress. Simpson staged intensive negotiations with House members, especially the core group of liberals who supported protections for guest workers. "Every one of us gave up something as painful as hell," Simpson said of the talks, "but we stayed at the table."

Although he was unhappy with some of the final provisions, Simpson expressed deep satisfaction over the product of his handiwork. The bill was "the very absolute quintessential immigration reform," Simpson said, adding that final passage "really tickled my butt."

In the 100th Congress, he turned to the other half of the immigration issue — laws governing legal entry, which are widely considered outdated. Simpson, the ranking Republican on Judiciary's Immigration Subcommittee, and Chairman Edward M. Kennedy cosponsored legislation to cap annual admissions and to replace the current system's preferences for uniting families with new preferences favoring foreigners with needed skills.

Their bill won the Senate's overwhelming approval, but the House was uninterested. Congress passed only a stripped-down version increasing allowances for the Irish — Kennedy's priority — and for nurses. Simpson and Kennedy revived the effort for a broader legal-immigration overhaul in the 101st Congress, amid more encouraging signs from the House.

Through the decade, the immigration issue illustrated Simpson's ability to deal with Democrats, including Kennedy and the liberals from House Judiciary. Of Kennedy, Simpson said in 1988, "We don't vote together an awful lot, but we legislate together a lot." Similarly, he generally has productive relationships with his Democratic counterparts on two other committees, Veterans' Affairs and Environment.

Simpson chaired Veterans' Affairs for four years before joining the leadership in 1985. The panel produced little legislation, in part because Simpson was trying to carry out Reagan's cost-cutting initiatives, but also because he is skeptical of the generous programs long favored by the panel. A self-described "skunk at the family picnic," Simpson takes literally President Lincoln's words, on a plaque on the Department of Veterans Affairs building, that the nation must "care for him who shall have borne the battle." To Simpson, that means actual combat veterans — a minority of the total veteran population.

Soon after he became chairman, Simpson was on the Senate floor opposing a $330 million increase in Reagan's request for veterans' programs. "I probably shall note the sound of muffled drums somewhere on the parade grounds," he said, "as they prepare a ceremony to strip the chevrons from me after I finish these remarks."

He also resists proposals to compensate Vietnam veterans suffering from illnesses they suspect are related to exposure to Agent Orange, demanding clear evidence of a link between exposure and illness. At a 1988 hearing, Simpson said proponents were in a "continual scab-picking contest to see how long it takes for us to forget Vietnam."

Such stances put Simpson at odds with Alan Cranston, formerly the committee's ranking Democrat and now the chairman, but the two also have worked together on some legislation over the years. Since Cranston also is his party's whip, the working relationship between him and Simpson carried over to other issues as well.

To Simpson's dismay, the 100th Congress was a particularly fruitful one for veterans' groups. He did support a new law giving veterans some rights to appeal VA benefits rulings to federal court, but he was a strong if lonely foe of raising the VA to Cabinet status. Also enacted were bills increasing medical, housing and education benefits; as one such measure was clearing Congress, Simpson groused, "We've had another burst of veteran-o-mania ... and there's no money in the budget" to pay for it.

Simpson focuses much of his effort at Environment on the Clean Air Act. In efforts since 1982 to strengthen that law against urban smog and acid rain, he has been a key player whose assent is essential to any compromise. He represents the views of Western utilities and coal producers. Western coal is lower in sulfur (a key ingredient of acid rain) than much Eastern coal, and Simpson wants legislation that will encourage Eastern and Midwestern utilities to buy cleaner-burning Western coal rather than the high-sulfur Eastern variety.

In the 100th Congress, Environment approved a strong clean-air bill that Simpson unenthusiastically supported, though he predicted correctly that it "would rot at the [Senate] desk" like those in 1982 and 1984. Then in the Congress' final days, the bill's sponsor, Democrat George J. Mitchell, reached a tentative compromise with Byrd, who had blocked previous bills on behalf of West Virginia's high-sulfur coal interests. The compromise was doomed by opposition from environmentalists, utilities and Simpson, who vowed to filibuster. In mid-1989, the Bush administration offered its own comprehensive Clean Air Act proposal in an effort to generate some progress on the issue.

Simpson has also been an active supporter of nuclear power. As chairman of the Environment Subcommittee on Nuclear Regulation, he worked hard in the 99th Congress on legislation raising the longstanding limit on utilities' liability for damage caused by a major nuclear plant accident. The bill never reached the Senate floor, however.

In the 100th Congress, Simpson and the new subcommittee chairman, Democrat John

B. Breaux, cosponsored another bill raising industry liability tenfold, to $7 billion, and providing that further damages could be paid from the Treasury. Taxpayer and environmental groups opposed it, believing utilities should be solely responsible. In the end, a separate House-passed bill became law, with the $7 billion limit but no provision for payments above that amount.

At Home: Like his father Milward, a former governor and U.S. senator, Alan Simpson has developed campaign talents that make him difficult to defeat. He is at his best running an old-fashioned personal campaign, trading ranch talk and old jokes.

His friendliness was an enormous asset during his 1978 Senate campaign, in which more militant conservatives tried to convince voters that Simpson was not really one of them.

He had spent 12 years in the state Legislature, serving at various times as chairman of the House Judiciary Committee, majority whip and majority floor leader. Had he not run for the Senate seat vacated by GOP veteran Clifford P. Hansen, he would have been Speaker of the Wyoming House.

As a state legislator, Simpson had been active in the drafting of a state land-use planning law. His opponent, eccentric oilman Hugh "Bigfoot" Binford, invested in a media campaign charging that Simpson had undermined local control of land decisions. He also said Simpson was shaky in his support of state right-to-work laws.

At first ignoring the assault, Simpson eventually had to take it seriously, calling a news conference to accuse "Bigfoot" of distortion and insist he wanted to preserve local control. In the end, however, his personal acquaintance with thousands of the state's voters was probably enough to guarantee him nomination. He drew 55 percent of the vote in the primary, and coasted in November against liberal Democrat Raymond B. Whitaker.

In 1984, Democrats had a tough time even finding a credible candidate willing to take on Simpson, who had built up a reservoir of support among members of both parties. The outcome of his re-election campaign was certain from the beginning.

The Democrats' eventual nominee, chemistry professor Victor A. Ryan, had never been active in state party affairs, and had never run for public office. Ryan criticized Simpson's stand on immigration, and called for more trained scientists in the country. For his efforts, he received 22 percent of the vote, losing by more than 105,000 votes.

Committees

Environment and Public Works (2nd of 7 Republicans)
Nuclear Regulation (ranking); Environmental Protection; Superfund, Ocean and Water Protection

Judiciary (3rd of 6 Republicans)
Immigration and Refugee Affairs (ranking); Patents, Copyrights and Trademarks

Special Aging (7th of 9 Republicans)

Veterans' Affairs (2nd of 5 Republicans)

Elections

1984 General		
Alan K. Simpson (R)	146,373	(78%)
Victor A. Ryan (D)	40,525	(22%)
1984 Primary		
Alan K. Simpson (R)	66,178	(88%)
Stephen Tarver (R)	9,137	(12%)

Previous Winning Percentages: **1978** (62%)

Campaign Finance

	Receipts	Receipts from PACs	Expend-itures
1984			
Simpson (R)	$906,121	$407,708 (45%)	$702,643

Key Votes

1987	
Enact omnibus highway bill over Reagan veto	N
Limit testing of space-based anti-ballistic missiles	N
Oppose banning tests of larger nuclear weapons	Y
Confirm Robert H. Bork as Supreme Court justice	Y
1988	
Allow vote on campaign-finance overhaul	N
Pass civil rights restoration bill over Reagan veto	N
Enact omnibus trade bill over Reagan veto	N
Approve death penalty for drug-related murders	Y
Oppose "workfare" amendment to welfare overhaul bill	N

Voting Studies

	Presidential Support		Party Unity		Conservative Coalition	
Year	**S**	**O**	**S**	**O**	**S**	**O**
1988	75	25	80	17	86	5
1987	67	24	81	11	78	13
1986	92	8	90	8	92	4
1985	90	10	91	9	85	15
1984	86	9	90	8	89	2
1983	76	20	78	13	75	18
1982	82	14	83	13	91	6
1981	86	11	90	7	89	8

Interest Group Ratings

Year	ADA	ACU	AFL-CIO	CCUS
1988	15	92	21	86
1987	10	79	11	71
1986	10	86	0	76
1985	10	78	10	90
1984	20	68	0	94
1983	25	61	13	59
1982	15	75	16	76
1981	5	80	0	100

AL Craig Thomas (R)

Of Casper — Elected 1989

Born: Feb. 17, 1933, Cody, Wyo.
Education: U. of Wyoming, B.A. 1955; LaSalle U., LL.B. 1963.
Military Career: Marine Corps, 1955-59.
Occupation: Businessman.
Family: Wife, Susan Roberts; four children.
Religion: Methodist.
Political Career: Sought Republican nomination for Wyo. treasurer, 1978, 1982; Wyo. House, 1985-89.
Capitol Office: 1631 Longworth Bldg. 20515; 225-2311.

The Path to Washington: Thomas campaigned for Congress as a pragmatic conservative Republican in the mold of Dick Cheney, who gave up Wyoming's at-large seat in March 1989 to become secretary of defense. But Thomas' closest relationship in Washington probably will be with Republican Sen. Alan K. Simpson.

They have known each other from childhood. Both attended high school in the town of Cody in the ranch country of northwest Wyoming, and both played freshman football at the University of Wyoming. Their paths veered at that point.

Thomas went into the Marines, then launched a career with the Farm Bureau that lasted until he became the general manager of the Wyoming Rural Electric Association in 1975. Yet while Thomas touts his agricultural background, he usually dresses and acts the part of a small-business man. "He is Mr. Mainstream, Mr. Main Street," said one Wyoming reporter.

Thomas had a stumbling start in politics. He twice lost Republican primary contests for state treasurer before winning a seat in the Wyoming House from Natrona County (Casper) in 1984. In the Legislature, he helped promote a reorganization of state government that consolidated dozens of agencies into a Cabinet-style government. And he was the first chairman of the Wyoming House Republican Conference, an arm of the GOP leadership created in 1989 to promote policy discussion and party discipline.

But Thomas was not well-known across Wyoming when the campaign for Cheney's seat began. The GOP state central committee nominated him as much for his party work as for his legislative résumé; Thomas made many contacts as party secretary and Natrona County GOP chairman.

His foe was Democratic state Sen. John Vinich, who came within 1,500 votes of upsetting GOP Sen. Malcolm Wallop in 1988. Thomas not only had to build his name familiarity but also overcome gaffes by the National Republican Congressional Committee (NRCC).

The first came in early April when NRCC co-chairman Edward J. Rollins, embarrassed by special-election defeats in Indiana and Alabama, was quoted as saying he would send two of his top aides to Wyoming to "take charge" of Thomas' campaign. His remarks played poorly in Wyoming, where irritation with out-of-state influence is almost a part of the state psyche.

Rollins' operation provided another headache for Thomas when it was revealed in mid-April that the NRCC had commissioned a poll following a car accident in which Vinich was injured, asking voters if they would be more or less likely to vote for the populist Democrat "if they knew a union boss or politician from the East Coast" was in the car. The accident report did not show there was, leading the state's largest paper, the Casper *Star-Tribune,* to say Thomas should oust the "national GOP bozos" and take charge of his campaign.

Thomas did get significant help from Washington, though. The NRCC raised money for him, House Minority Leader Robert H. Michel promised him Cheney's vacant seat on the Interior Committee, and Senate Minority Leader Bob Dole came to Wyoming on his behalf. (Thomas was co-chairman of Dole's Wyoming presidential campaign in 1988.)

And Vinich helped significantly by making a serious gaffe. Attempting to picture Thomas as soft on crime, Vinich ran an ad denouncing Thomas' vote in the Legislature for a "split-sentencing" law, which allowed less-violent criminals to serve up to a year of their sentence in county jails rather than in the overcrowded state prison.

But it was a measure that Vinich and only two other legislators had voted against. An array of Wyoming Democrats, including popular former Gov. Ed Herschler, disagreed with Vinich's interpretation that support for the bill meant Thomas was a coddler of criminals.

Vinich's misstep tilted many undecided voters toward Thomas. In the April special election, he carried 19 of the state's 23 counties.

Wyoming — At Large

Wyoming has always been fairly easy to explain in terms of partisan politics. Democrats are competitive in the five counties along the state's southern border — Albany, Carbon, Laramie, Sweetwater and Uinta counties. North of these five they rarely win.

Rarely, but sometimes. In the face of a 3-to-2 GOP advantage in party registration, the Democrats in 1986 managed to hold on to the governorship despite the retirement of their three-term incumbent, Ed Herschler, whose personal popularity was always more important than his party label.

Conservative attorney and political neophyte Mike Sullivan won the right to succeed Herschler by capitalizing on Democratic strength in the southern arc and winning in two areas that normally vote Republican — his hometown of Casper and the agricultural counties of eastern Wyoming. Republicans continue to dominate in the state Legislature and in the congressional delegation.

The Democratic voting tradition in southern Wyoming, where two-fifths of the population lives, goes back to the early days of the state. Immigrant laborers, many of them from Italy, were imported to build the Union Pacific rail line through those southern counties. The state's first coal miners followed. Like their counterparts in other states, most of the workingmen were drawn to the Democratic Party. Though their modern-day descendants are conservative on most issues and gave majorities to Ronald Reagan in 1980 and 1984 and George Bush in 1988, their Democratic sentiments are still evident, as Sullivan proved in 1986.

The northern part of the state is the Wyoming of ranch and rock. Its dry plateaus and basins accommodate the cattle ranches that make Wyoming the "Cowboy State." This is conservative country. Ranching interests have traditionally dominated it, although mineral and energy development and the ensuing population growth shook up some county power structures in the 1970s. The people in the north are still widely scattered; Sheridan and Gillette are the region's only towns with more than 15,000 inhabitants.

Wyoming's current economic fortunes are spotty at best. The agriculture market is soft, oil and gas development has slumped, and the uranium extracting industry has been battered by slack demand and low-priced foreign competition.

With ski resorts and Yellowstone National Park as the lures, the tourist economy has held steady, although the toll of the fires at Yellowstone over the summer of 1988 is still being assessed. Steady demand for the low-sulfur coal of the Powder River Basin in northeastern Wyoming has maintained the economy there.

Wyoming's two largest cities have about 50,000 people each. Casper (Natrona County), a 1970s energy boom town, has felt more economic hardship of late than the capital city, Cheyenne (Laramie County), which has a more stable employment base thanks to state government and the Francis E. Warren Air Force Base.

Population: 469,557. White 446,488 (95%), Black 3,364 (1%), Other 9,063 (2%). Spanish origin 24,499 (5%). 18 and over 324,004 (69%), 65 and over 37,175 (8%). Median age: 27.

Committees

Government Operations (14th of 15 Republicans)
Environment, Energy and Natural Resources; Government Information, Justice and Agriculture

Interior and Insular Affairs (14th of 15 Republicans)
National Parks and Public Lands; Water, Power and Offshore Energy Reources

Campaign Finance

	Receipts	Receipts from PACs	Expenditures
1989 Special Election			
Thomas (R)	$564,142	$237,345 (42%)	$527,148
Vinich (D)	$485,494	$266,400 (55%)	$479,705

Elections

1989 Special Election

Craig Thomas (R)	74,384	(52%)
John P. Vinich (D)	60,845	(43%)

District Vote For President

	1988	1984	1980	1976
D	67,113 (38%)	53,370 (28%)	49,427 (28%)	62,239 (40%)
R	106,867 (61%)	133,241 (71%)	110,700 (63%)	92,717 (59%)
I			12,072 (7%)	

Non-Voting Representatives in the House

They are not exactly members of the House, but they are a part of the legislative process. They make speeches, serve on committees, and hold chairmanships, and one of them — Ben Blaz of Guam — was president of the freshman Republican class of 1984. The only thing they are not allowed to do is vote on the House floor.

They are the five people sent to Capitol Hill from Puerto Rico, the District of Columbia, Guam, the Virgin Islands and American Samoa. Four are known officially as "delegates." Puerto Rico sends a "resident commissioner," and unlike the others, he serves a term of four years instead of two.

These positions have existed in some form or other since 1794, when the House received James White as the non-voting delegate from the Territory South of the Ohio River, later to become the state of Tennessee. But most of the current ones are products of the 1970s.

Because the House Interior Committee has jurisdiction over U.S. territorial affairs, the representatives from Puerto Rico, American Samoa, Guam and the Virgin Islands all serve there.

Ron de Lugo of the Virgin Islands chairs the Insular and International Affairs Subcommittee of Interior; Walter E. Fauntroy of the District of Columbia chairs the Banking Subcommittee on International Development, Finance, Trade and Monetary Policy, as well as the District of Columbia Subcommittee on Fiscal Affairs and Health.

Following are capsule profiles of those who serve in the House on a non-voting basis.

Ben Blaz (R)

Of Guam — Elected 1984

Born: Feb. 14, 1928, Agana, Guam.
Education: U. of Notre Dame, B.S. 1951; George Washington U., M.A. 1963; Naval War College, 1971.
Military Career: Marines, 1951-80.
Occupation: Retired brigadier general.
Family: Wife, Ann Evers; two children.
Religion: Roman Catholic.
Political Career: No previous office.
Capitol Office: 1130 Longworth Bldg. 20515; 225-1188.

Ron de Lugo (D)

Of the Virgin Islands — Elected 1972

Did not serve 1979-81.

Born: Aug. 2, 1930, Englewood, N.J.
Education: Attended Colegio San Jose.
Military Career: Army, 1948-50.
Occupation: Radio journalist.
Family: Wife, Sheila Paieworsky; four children.
Religion: Roman Catholic.
Political Career: V.I. Senate, 1956-66; administrator for St. Croix, 1961; Washington representative for the Virgin Islands, 1968; candidate for V.I. governor, 1978.
Capitol Office: 2238 Rayburn Bldg. 20515; 225-1790.

Walter E. Fauntroy (D)

Of Washington, D.C. — Elected 1971

Born: Feb. 6, 1933, Washington, D.C.
Education: Virginia Union U., B.A. 1955; Yale U., B.D. 1958.
Occupation: Pastor.
Family: Wife, Dorothy Simms; one child.
Religion: Baptist.
Political Career: No previous office.
Capitol Office: 2135 Rayburn Bldg. 20515; 225-8050.

Eni F.H. Faleomavaega (D)

Of American Samoa — Elected 1988

Born: Aug. 15, 1943, Vailoatai, American Samoa.
Education: Brigham Young U., B.A. 1966; U. of Houston, J.D. 1972; U. of California, Berkeley, LL.M. 1973.
Military Career: Army, 1966-69; Reserve, 1983-present.
Occupation: Lawyer.
Family: Wife, Hinanui Bambridge Cave; five children.
Religion: Mormon.
Political Career: American Samoa lieutenant governor, 1985-89; Democratic candidate for U.S. House delegate, 1984.
Capitol Office: 413 Cannon Bldg. 20515; 225-8577.

Jaime B. Fuster (Pop. Dem.)

Of Puerto Rico — Elected 1984

Resident Commissioner

Born: Jan. 12, 1941, Guayama, Puerto Rico.
Education: U. of Notre Dame, B.A. 1962; U. of Puerto Rico, J.D. 1965; Columbia U., LL.M. 1966.
Occupation: Law professor; university administrator.
Family: Wife, Mary Jo Zalduondo; two children.
Religion: Roman Catholic.
Political Career: No previous office.
Capitol Office: 427 Cannon Bldg. 20515; 225-2615.

Senate Committees and Subcommittees

The standing and select committees of the U.S. Senate are listed below in alphabetical order. The listing includes telephone number, room number, and party ratio for each full committee. Membership is given in order of seniority on the committee.

Subcommittees are listed alphabetically under each committee. Membership is listed in order of seniority on the subcommittee.

Members of the majority party, Democrats, are shown in Roman type; members of the minority party, Republicans, are shown in italic type.

The word "vacancy" indicates that a committee or subcommittee seat had not been filled at press time. Subcommittee vacancies do not necessarily indicate vacancies on full committees, or vice versa.

Asterisks (*) indicate that chairmen and/or ranking minority members are *ex officio* members of all subcommittees of which they are not regular members.

The partisan committees of the Senate begin on page 1675. Members of these committees are listed in alphabetical order, not by seniority.

The telephone area code for Washington, D.C., is 202. Abbreviations for Senate office buildings are: SD — Dirksen Bldg., SH — Hart Bldg., SR — Russell Bldg. The ZIP code for all Senate offices is 20510.

Agriculture, Nutrition and Forestry

224-2035 SR-328A

Party Ratio: D 10 - R 9

Patrick J. Leahy, D-Vt., chairman *

David Pryor, Ark.	*Richard G. Lugar, Ind.* *
David L. Boren, Okla.	*Bob Dole, Kan.*
Howell Heflin, Ala.	*Jesse Helms, N.C.*
Tom Harkin, Iowa	*Thad Cochran, Miss.*
Kent Conrad, N.D.	*Rudy Boschwitz, Minn.*
Wyche Fowler Jr., Ga.	*Mitch McConnell, Ky.*
Tom Daschle, S.D.	*Christopher S. Bond, Mo.*
Max Baucus, Mont.	*Pete Wilson, Calif.*
Bob Kerrey, Neb.	*Slade Gorton, Wash.*

Agricultural Credit

224-2035 SR-328A

Conrad — chairman

Boren	*Gorton*
Daschle	*Boschwitz*

Agricultural Production and Stabilization of Prices

224-2035 SR-328A

Pryor — chairman

Baucus	*Helms*
Kerrey	*Dole*
Boren	*Cochran*
Heflin	*McConnell*
Harkin	*Boschwitz*
Conrad	*Wilson*

Agricultural Research and General Legislation

224-2035 SR-328A

Daschle — chairman

Kerrey	*Wilson*
	Bond

Conservation and Forestry

224-2035 SR-328A

Fowler — chairman

Heflin	*Bond*
Baucus	*Gorton*

Domestic and Foreign Marketing and Product Promotion

224-2035 SR-328A

Boren — chairman

Pryor	*Cochran*
Fowler	*Helms*
Baucus	*Bond*
Harkin	*Wilson*
Conrad	*Gorton*
	McConnell

Nutrition and Investigations

224-2035 SR-328A

Harkin — chairman

Fowler	*Boschwitz*
Kerrey	*Dole*
Pryor	*Helms*

Rural Development and Rural Electrification

224-2035 SR-328A

Heflin — chairman

Daschle	*McConnell*
Pryor	*Cochran*

Appropriations

224-3471 S-128 Capitol

Party Ratio: D 16 - R 13

Robert C. Byrd, D-W.Va., chairman *

Daniel K. Inouye, Hawaii	*Mark O. Hatfield, Ore.* *
Ernest F. Hollings, S.C.	*Ted Stevens, Alaska*
J. Bennett Johnston, La.	*James A. McClure, Idaho*
Quentin N. Burdick, N.D.	*Jake Garn, Utah*
Patrick J. Leahy, Vt.	*Thad Cochran, Miss.*
Jim Sasser, Tenn.	*Bob Kasten, Wis.*
Dennis DeConcini, Ariz.	*Alfonse M. D'Amato, N.Y.*
Dale Bumpers, Ark.	*Warren B. Rudman, N.H.*
Frank R. Lautenberg, N.J.	*Arlen Specter, Pa.*
Tom Harkin, Iowa	*Pete V. Domenici, N.M.*
Barbara A. Mikulski, Md.	*Charles E. Grassley, Iowa*
Harry Reid, Nev.	*Don Nickles, Okla.*
Brock Adams, Wash.	*Phil Gramm, Texas*
Wyche Fowler Jr., Ga.	
Bob Kerrey, Neb.	

Agriculture, Rural Development and Related Agencies

224-7240 SD-140

Burdick — chairman

Bumpers	*Cochran*
Harkin	*McClure*
Adams	*Kasten*
Fowler	*Specter*
Kerrey	*Grassley*

Commerce, Justice, State, the Judiciary and Related Agencies

224-7277 S-146A Capitol

Hollings — chairman

Inouye	*Rudman*
Bumpers	*Stevens*
Lautenberg	*Hatfield*
Sasser	*Kasten*
Adams	*Gramm*

Defense

224-7255 SD-119

Inouye — chairman

Hollings	*Stevens*
Johnston	*Garn*
Byrd	*McClure*
Leahy	*Kasten*
Sasser	*D'Amato*
DeConcini	*Rudman*
Bumpers	*Cochran*
Lautenburg	*Specter*
Harkin	

District of Columbia

224-2727 S-205 Capitol

Adams — chairman

Fowler	*Gramm*
Kerrey	*Domenici*

Energy and Water Development

224-0335 SD-132

Johnston — chairman

Byrd	*Hatfield*
Hollings	*McClure*
Burdick	*Garn*
Sasser	*Cochran*
DeConcini	*Domenici*
Reid	*Specter*

Foreign Operations

224-7209 SD-137

Leahy — chairman

Inouye	*Kasten*
Johnston	*Hatfield*
DeConcini	*D'Amato*
Lautenberg	*Rudman*
Harkin	*Specter*
Mikulski	*Nickles*

HUD - Independent Agencies

224-7211 SD-142

Mikulski — chairman

Leahy	*Garn*
Johnston	*D'Amato*
Lautenberg	*Grassley*
Fowler	*Nickles*
Kerrey	*Gramm*

Interior and Related Agencies

224-7233 SD-127

Byrd — chairman

Johnston	*McClure*
Leahy	*Stevens*
DeConcini	*Garn*
Burdick	*Cochran*
Bumpers	*Rudman*
Hollings	*Nickles*
Reid	*Domenici*

Labor, Health and Human Services, Education and Related Agencies

224-7283 SD-186

Harkin — chairman

Byrd	*Specter*
Hollings	*Hatfield*
Burdick	*Stevens*
Inouye	*Rudman*
Bumpers	*McClure*
Reid	*Cochran*
Adams	*Gramm*

Legislative Branch

224-7338 SD-132

Reid — chairman

Mikulski	*Nickles*
Adams	*Hatfield*

Military Construction

224-7276 SD-119

Sasser — chairman

Inouye	*Grassley*
Reid	*Garn*
Fowler	*Stevens*

Transportation and Related Agencies

224-7281 SD-156

Lautenberg — chairman

Byrd	*D'Amato*
Harkin	*Kasten*
Sasser	*Domenici*
Mikulski	*Grassley*

Treasury, Postal Service and General Government

224-6280 SD-190

DeConcini — chairman

Mikulski	*Domenici*
Kerrey	*D'Amato*

Armed Services

224-3871 SR-228

Party Ratio: D 11 - R 9

Sam Nunn, D-Ga., chairman *

Jim Exon, Neb.	*John W. Warner, Va. **
Carl Levin, Mich.	*Strom Thurmond, S.C.*
Edward M. Kennedy, Mass.	*William S. Cohen, Maine*
Jeff Bingaman, N.M.	*Pete Wilson, Calif.*
Alan J. Dixon, Ill.	*John McCain, Ariz.*
John Glenn, Ohio	*Malcolm Wallop, Wyo.*
Al Gore, Tenn.	*Slade Gorton, Wash.*
Tim Wirth, Colo.	*Trent Lott, Miss.*
Richard C. Shelby, Ala.	*Daniel R. Coats, Ind.*
Robert C. Byrd, W.Va.	

Conventional Forces and Alliance Defense

224-3871 SR-228

Levin — chairman

Dixon	*Wilson*
Glenn	*Thurmond*
Wirth	*Cohen*
Shelby	*McCain*
Byrd	*Coats*

Defense Industry and Technology

224-3871 SR-228

Bingaman — chairman

Gore	*Wallop*
Wirth	*Lott*
Byrd	*Coats*

Manpower and Personnel

224-3871 SR-228

Glenn — chairman

Exon	*McCain*
Kennedy	*Wilson*
Byrd	*Lott*

Projection Forces and Regional Defense

224-3871 SR-228

Kennedy — chairman

Exon	*Cohen*
Dixon	*McCain*
Gore	*Gorton*
Shelby	*Lott*

Readiness, Sustainability and Support

224-3871 SR-228

Dixon — chairman

Levin	*Gorton*
Bingaman	*Thurmond*
Wirth	*Wallop*
Shelby	*Coats*

Strategic Forces and Nuclear Deterrence

224-3871 SR-228

Exon — chairman

Levin	*Thurmond*
Kennedy	*Cohen*
Bingaman	*Wilson*
Glenn	*Wallop*
Gore	*Gorton*

Banking, Housing and Urban Affairs

224-7391 SD-534

Party Ratio: D 12 - R 9

Donald W. Riegle Jr., D-Mich., chairman *

Alan Cranston, Calif.	*Jake Garn, Utah **
Paul S. Sarbanes, Md.	*John Heinz, Pa.*
Christopher J. Dodd, Conn.	*Alfonse M. D'Amato, N.Y.*
Alan J. Dixon, Ill.	*Phil Gramm, Texas*
Jim Sasser, Tenn.	*Christopher S. Bond, Mo.*
Terry Sanford, N.C.	*Connie Mack, Fla.*
Richard C. Shelby, Ala.	*William V. Roth Jr., Del.*
Bob Graham, Fla.	*Nancy Landon Kassebaum, Kan.*
Tim Wirth, Colo.	*Larry Pressler, S.D.*
John Kerry, Mass.	
Richard H. Bryan, Nev.	

Consumer and Regulatory Affairs

224-1563 SD-537

Dixon — chairman

Graham	*Bond*
Kerry	*D'Amato*
Bryan	*Gramm*

Housing and Urban Affairs

224-6348 SD-535

Cranston — chairman

Sarbanes	*D'Amato*
Dodd	*Mack*
Sasser	*Kassebaum*
Kerry	*Pressler*
Bryan	*Gramm*

International Finance and Monetary Policy

224-1564 SD-537

Sarbanes — chairman

Dixon	*Gramm*
Sanford	*Roth*
Shelby	*Heinz*
Graham	*Bond*
Wirth	*Mack*

Securities

224-9213 SD-541

Dodd — chairman

Cranston	*Heinz*
Sasser	*Kassebaum*
Sanford	*Pressler*
Shelby	*D'Amato*
Wirth	*Gramm*

Budget

224-0642 SD-621

Party Ratio: D 13 - R 10

Jim Sasser, D-Tenn., chairman

Ernest F. Hollings, S.C.	*Pete V. Domenici, N.M.*
J. Bennett Johnston, La.	*William L. Armstrong, Colo.*
Donald W. Riegle Jr., Mich.	*Rudy Boschwitz, Minn.*
Jim Exon, Neb.	*Steve Symms, Idaho*
Frank R. Lautenberg, N.J.	*Charles E. Grassley, Iowa*
Paul Simon, Ill.	*Bob Kasten, Wis.*
Terry Sanford, N.C.	*Don Nickles, Okla.*
Tim Wirth, Colo.	*Warren B. Rudman, N.H.*
Wyche Fowler Jr., Ga.	*Phil Gramm, Texas*
Kent Conrad, N.D.	*Christopher S. Bond, Mo.*
Christopher J. Dodd, Conn.	
Charles S. Robb, Va.	

Commerce, Science and Transportation

224-5115 SD-508

Party Ratio: D 11 - R 9

Ernest F. Hollings, D-S.C., chairman *

Daniel K. Inouye, Hawaii	*John C. Danforth, Mo.* *
Wendell H. Ford, Ky.	*Bob Packwood, Ore.*
Jim Exon, Neb.	*Larry Pressler, S.D.*
Al Gore, Tenn.	*Ted Stevens, Alaska*
John D. Rockefeller IV, W.Va.	*Bob Kasten, Wis.*
Lloyd Bentsen, Texas	*John McCain, Ariz.*
John Kerry, Mass.	*Conrad Burns, Mont.*
John B. Breaux, La.	*Slade Gorton, Wash.*
Richard H. Bryan, Nev.	*Trent Lott, Miss.*
Charles S. Robb, Va.	

Aviation

224-9350 SH-428

Ford — chairman

Exon	*McCain*
Inouye	*Stevens*
Kerry	*Kasten*
Bentsen	

Communications

224-9340 SH-227

Inouye — chairman

Hollings	*Packwood*
Ford	*Pressler*
Gore	*Stevens*
Exon	*McCain*
Kerry	*Burns*
Bentsen	*Gorton*
Breaux	

Consumer

224-0415 SH-227

Bryan — chairman

Gore	*Gorton*
Ford	*McCain*
Robb	*Kasten*

Foreign Commerce and Tourism

224-9325 SH-428

Rockefeller — chairman

Hollings	*Burns*
Bryan	*Packwood*

Merchant Marine

224-4914 SH-425

Breaux — chairman

Inouye	*Lott*
Bentsen	*Stevens*

Science, Technology and Space

224-9360 SH-427

Gore — chairman

Rockefeller	*Pressler*
Bentsen	*Stevens*
Kerry	*Kasten*
Bryan	*Lott*
Robb	

Surface Transportation

224-9350 SH-428

Exon — chairman

Rockefeller	*Kasten*
Hollings	*Packwood*
Inouye	*Pressler*
Gore	*Burns*
Breaux	*Gorton*
Robb	*Lott*

National Ocean Policy Study

224-4912 SH-425

The National Ocean Policy Study is technically not a subcommittee of the Commerce, Science and Transportation Committee; no legislation is referred to it. Numerous *ex officio* members from other Senate committees and from the Senate at large serve on it.

Hollings — chairman

Kerry	*Stevens*
Inouye	*Danforth*
Ford	*Packwood*
Gore	*Kasten*
Bentsen	*Pressler*
Breaux	*Gorton*
Robb	*Lott*

Energy and Natural Resources

224-4971 SD-364

Party Ratio: D 10 - R 9

J. Bennett Johnston, D-La., chairman *

Dale Bumpers, Ark.	*James A. McClure, Idaho* *
Wendell H. Ford, Ky.	*Mark O. Hatfield, Ore.*
Howard M. Metzenbaum, Ohio	*Pete V. Domenici, N.M.*
Bill Bradley, N.J.	*Malcolm Wallop, Wyo.*
Jeff Bingaman, N.M.	*Frank H. Murkowski, Alaska*
Tim Wirth, Colo.	*Don Nickles, Okla.*
Kent Conrad, N.D.	*Conrad Burns, Mont.*
Howell Heflin, Ala.	*Jake Garn, Utah*
John D. Rockefeller IV, W.Va.	*Mitch McConnell, Ky.*

Energy Regulation and Conservation

224-4756 SH-212

Metzenbaum — chairman

Bradley	*Nickles*
Bingaman	*Murkowski*
Wirth	*Domenici*

Energy Research and Development

224-7569 SH-312

Ford — chairman

Rockefeller	*Domenici*
Bumpers	*McConnell*
Metzenbaum	*Nickles*
Wirth	*Burns*
Heflin	*Garn*

Mineral Resources Development and Production

224-7568 SD-362

Bingaman — chairman

Heflin	*Murkowski*
Bumpers	*McConnell*
Ford	*Wallop*
Conrad	*Nickles*

Public Lands, National Parks and Forests

224-7934 SD-308

Bumpers — chairman

Wirth	*Wallop*
Bradley	*Hatfield*
Bingaman	*Burns*
Conrad	*Garn*
Rockefeller	*Domenici*

Water and Power

224-6836 SD-306

Bradley — chairman

Conrad	*Burns*
Ford	*Hatfield*
Metzenbaum	*Garn*
Heflin	*Wallop*

Environment and Public Works

224-6176 SD-458

Party Ratio: D 9 - R 7

Quentin N. Burdick, D-N.D., chairman *

Daniel Patrick Moynihan, N.Y.	*John H. Chafee, R.I.* *
George J. Mitchell, Maine	*Alan K. Simpson, Wyo.*
Max Baucus, Mont.	*Steve Symms, Idaho*
Frank R. Lautenberg, N.J.	*Dave Durenberger, Minn.*
John B. Breaux, La.	*John W. Warner, Va.*
Harry Reid, Nev.	*James M. Jeffords, Vt.*
Bob Graham, Fla.	*Gordon J. Humphrey, N.H.*
Joseph I. Lieberman, Conn.	

Environmental Protection

224-6691 SH-408

Baucus — chairman

Moynihan	*Chafee*
Mitchell	*Simpson*
Lautenberg	*Durenberger*
Breaux	*Warner*
Graham	*Jeffords*
Lieberman	*Humphrey*

Nuclear Regulation

224-5031 SH-415

Breaux — chairman

Moynihan	*Simpson*
Reid	*Symms*

Superfund, Ocean and Water Protection

224-5031 SH-415

Lautenberg — chairman

Mitchell	*Durenberger*
Baucus	*Simpson*
Graham	*Symms*

Toxic Substances, Environmental Oversight, Research and Development

224-3597 SH-505

Reid — chairman

Baucus	*Warner*
Lieberman	*Jeffords*

Water Resources, Transportation and Infrastructure

224-3597 SH-505

Moynihan — chairman

Mitchell	*Symms*
Lautenburg	*Warner*
Breaux	*Jeffords*
Reid	*Humphrey*
Graham	*Durenberger*
Lieberman	*Chafee*

Finance

224-4515 SD-205

Party Ratio: D 11 - R 9

Lloyd Bentsen, D-Texas, chairman *

Spark M. Matsunaga, Hawaii	*Bob Packwood, Ore.* *
Daniel Patrick Moynihan, N.Y.	*Bob Dole, Kan.*
Max Baucus, Mont.	*William V. Roth Jr., Del.*
David L. Boren, Okla.	*John C. Danforth, Mo.*
Bill Bradley, N.J.	*John H. Chafee, R.I.*
George J. Mitchell, Maine	*John Heinz, Pa.*
David Pryor, Ark.	*Dave Durenberger, Minn.*
Donald W. Riegle Jr., Mich.	*William L. Armstrong, Colo.*
John D. Rockefeller IV, W.Va.	*Steve Symms, Idaho*
Tom Daschle, S.D.	

Energy and Agricultural Taxation

224-4515 SD-205

Boren — chairman

Matsunaga	*Armstrong*
	Symms

Health for Families and the Uninsured

224-4515 SD-205

Riegle — chairman

Bradley	*Chafee*
Mitchell	*Roth*
Rockefeller	*Durenberger*

International Debt

224-4515 SD-205

Bradley — chairman

Riegle	*Dole*
	Armstrong

International Trade

224-4515 SD-205

Baucus — chairman

Bentsen	*Danforth*
Matsunaga	*Roth*
Moynihan	*Chafee*
Boren	*Heinz*
Bradley	*Armstrong*
Mitchell	*Packwood*
Riegle	*Symms*
Rockefeller	
Daschle	

Medicare and Long-Term Care

224-4515 SD-205

Rockefeller — chairman

Bentsen	*Durenberger*
Baucus	*Dole*
Mitchell	*Packwood*
Pryor	*Heinz*
Daschle	*Chafee*
	Danforth

Private Retirement Plans and Oversight of the Internal Revenue Service

224-4515 SD-205

Pryor — chairman

Moynihan	*Heinz*

Social Security and Family Policy

224-4515 SD-205

Moynihan — chairman

Daschle	*Dole*
	Durenberger

Taxation and Debt Management

224-4515 SD-205

Matsunaga — chairman

Bentsen	*Roth*
Baucus	*Danforth*
Boren	*Symms*
Pryor	

Foreign Relations

224-4651 SD-446

Party Ratio: D 10 - R 9

Claiborne Pell, D-R.I., chairman *

Joseph R. Biden Jr., Del.	*Jesse Helms, N.C. **
Paul S. Sarbanes, Md.	*Richard G. Lugar, Ind.*
Alan Cranston, Calif.	*Nancy Landon Kassebaum, Kan.*
Christopher J. Dodd, Conn.	*Rudy Boschwitz, Minn.*
John Kerry, Mass.	*Larry Pressler, S.D.*
Paul Simon, Ill.	*Frank H. Murkowski, Alaska*
Terry Sanford, N.C.	*Mitch McConnell, Ky.*
Daniel P. Moynihan, N.Y.	*Gordon J. Humphrey, N.H.*
Charles S. Robb, Va.	*Connie Mack, Fla.*

African Affairs

224-4651 SD-446

Simon — chairman

Cranston	*Kassebaum*
Moynihan	*Mack*

East Asian and Pacific Affairs

224-4651 SD-446

Cranston — chairman

Pell	*Murkowski*
Biden	*Lugar*
Dodd	*McConnell*

European Affairs

224-4651 SD-446

Biden — chairman

Sarbanes	*Pressler*
Simon	*Boschwitz*

International Economic Policy, Trade, Oceans and Environment

224-4651 SD-446

Sarbanes — chairman

Pell	*Humphrey*
Dodd	*Lugar*
Kerry	*Boschwitz*
Sanford	*Murkowski*

Near Eastern and South Asian Affairs

224-4651 SD-446

Moynihan — chairman

Pell	*Boschwitz*
Sarbanes	*Kassebaum*
Robb	*Pressler*

Terrorism, Narcotics and International Operations

224-4651 SD-446

Kerry — chairman

Sanford	*McConnell*
Moynihan	*Murkowski*
Robb	*Humphrey*

Western Hemisphere and Peace Corps Affairs

224-4651 SD-446

Dodd — chairman

Cranston	*Lugar*
Kerry	*Kassebaum*
Sanford	*McConnell*
Robb	*Mack*

Governmental Affairs

224-4751 SD-340

Party Ratio: D 8 - R 6

John Glenn, D-Ohio, chairman *

Sam Nunn, Ga.	*William V. Roth Jr., Del.* *
Carl Levin, Mich.	*Ted Stevens, Alaska*
Jim Sasser, Tenn.	*William S. Cohen, Maine*
David Pryor, Ark.	*Warren B. Rudman, N.H.*
Jeff Bingaman, N.M.	*John Heinz, Pa.*
Herb Kohl, Wis.	*Pete Wilson, Calif.*
Joseph I. Lieberman, Conn.	

Federal Services, Post Office and Civil Service

224-2254 SH-601

Pryor — chairman

Sasser	*Stevens*
Kohl	*Wilson*

General Services, Federalism and the District of Columbia

224-4718 SH-432

Sasser — chairman

Bingaman	*Heinz*
Lieberman	*Stevens*

Government Information and Regulation

224-9000 SH-605

Bingaman — chairman

Nunn	*Rudman*
Levin	*Cohen*
Kohl	*Heinz*

Oversight of Government Management

224-3682 SH-442

Levin — chairman

Pryor	*Cohen*
Bingaman	*Rudman*
Kohl	*Heinz*
Lieberman	*Wilson*

Permanent Subcommittee on Investigations

224-3721 SR-100

Nunn — chairman
Glenn — vice chairman

Levin	*Roth*
Sasser	*Stevens*
Pryor	*Cohen*
Kohl	*Rudman*
Lieberman	*Wilson*

Judiciary

224-5225 SD-224

Party Ratio: D 8 - R 6

Joseph R. Biden Jr., D-Del., chairman *

Edward M. Kennedy, Mass.	*Strom Thurmond, S.C.* *
Howard M. Metzenbaum, Ohio	*Orrin G. Hatch, Utah*
Dennis DeConcini, Ariz.	*Alan K. Simpson, Wyo.*
Patrick J. Leahy, Vt.	*Charles E. Grassley, Iowa*
Howell Heflin, Ala.	*Arlen Specter, Pa.*
Paul Simon, Ill.	*Gordon J. Humphrey, N.H.*
Herb Kohl, Wis.	

Antitrust, Monopolies and Business Rights

224-5701 SH-308

Metzenbaum — chairman

DeConcini	*Thurmond*
Heflin	*Specter*
Simon	*Humphrey*
Kohl	*Hatch*

Constitution

224-5573 SD-524

Simon — chairman

Metzenbaum	*Specter*
DeConcini	*Hatch*
Kennedy	

Courts and Administrative Practice

224-4022 SH-223

Heflin — chairman

Metzenbaum	*Grassley*
Kohl	*Thurmond*

Immigration and Refugee Affairs

224-7878 SD-520

Kennedy — chairman

Simon	*Simpson*

Patents, Copyrights and Trademarks

224-8178 SH-327

DeConcini — chairman

Kennedy	*Hatch*
Leahy	*Simpson*
Heflin	*Grassley*

Technology and the Law

224-3407 SH-815

Leahy — chairman

Kohl	*Humphrey*

Labor and Human Resources

224-5375 SD-428

Party Ratio: D 9 - R 7

Edward M. Kennedy, D-Mass., chairman *

Claiborne Pell, R.I.	*Orrin G. Hatch, Utah* *
Howard M. Metzenbaum, Ohio	*Nancy Landon Kassebaum, Kan.*
Spark M. Matsunaga, Hawaii	*James M. Jeffords, Vt.*
Christopher J. Dodd, Conn.	*Daniel R. Coats, Ind.*
Paul Simon, Ill.	*Strom Thurmond, S.C.*
Tom Harkin, Iowa.	*Dave Durenberger, Minn.*
Brock Adams, Wash.	*Thad Cochran, Miss.*
Barbara A. Mikulski, Md.	

Aging

224-3239 SH-404

Matsunaga — chairman

Pell	*Cochran*
Metzenbaum	*Durenberger*
Dodd	*Coats*

Children, Family, Drugs and Alcoholism

224-5630 SH-639

Dodd — chairman

Pell	*Coats*
Harkin	*Hatch*
Adams	*Kassebaum*

Education, Arts and Humanities

224-7666 SD-648

Pell — chairman

Metzenbaum	*Kassebaum*
Matsunaga	*Cochran*
Dodd	*Hatch*
Simon	*Jeffords*
Mikulski	*Thurmond*

Employment and Productivity

224-5575 SD-644

Simon — chairman

Harkin	*Thurmond*
Adams	*Durenberger*
Mikulski	*Kassebaum*

Handicapped

224-6265 SH-113

Harkin — chairman

Metzenbaum	*Durenberger*
Simon	*Hatch*
Adams	*Jeffords*

Labor

224-5546 SH-608

Metzenbaum — chairman

Matsunaga	*Jeffords*
Harkin	*Cochran*
Mikulski	*Thurmond*

Rules and Administration

224-6352 SR-305

Party Ratio: D 9 - R 7

Wendell H. Ford, D-Ky., chairman

Claiborne Pell, R.I.	*Ted Stevens, Alaska*
Robert C. Byrd, W.Va.	*Mark O. Hatfield, Ore.*
Daniel K. Inouye, Hawaii	*James A. McClure, Idaho*
Dennis DeConcini, Ariz.	*Jesse Helms, N.C.*
Al Gore, Tenn.	*Bob Dole, Kan.*
Daniel Patrick Moynihan, N.Y.	*Jake Garn, Utah*
Christopher J. Dodd, Conn.	*Mitch McConnell, Ky.*
Brock Adams, Wash.	

Small Business

224-5175 SR-428A

Party Ratio: D 10 - R 9

Dale Bumpers, D-Ark., chairman

Sam Nunn, Ga.	*Rudy Boschwitz, Minn.*
Max Baucus, Mont.	*Bob Kasten, Wis.*
Carl Levin, Mich.	*Larry Pressler, S.D.*
Alan J. Dixon, Ill.	*Malcolm Wallop, Wyo.*
David L. Boren, Okla.	*Christopher S. Bond, Mo.*
Tom Harkin, Iowa	*Charles E. Grassley, Iowa*
John Kerry, Mass.	*Trent Lott, Miss.*
Barbara A. Mikulski, Md.	*Conrad Burns, Mont.*
Joseph I. Lieberman, Conn.	*Ted Stevens, Alaska*

Competition and Antitrust Enforcement

224-5175 SR-428A

Harkin — chairman

Lieberman	*Stevens*

Export Expansion

224-5175 SR-428A

Mikulski — chairman

Harkin	*Pressler*
Lieberman	*Wallop*
Bumpers	*Bond*

Government Contracting and Paperwork Reduction

224-5175 SR-428A

Dixon — chairman

Boren	*Grassley*
Lieberman	*Kasten*

Innovation, Technology and Productivity

224-5175 SR-428A

Levin — chairman

Baucus	*Lott*
Kerry	*Stevens*

Rural Economy and Family Farming

224-5175 SR-428A

Baucus — chairman

Nunn	*Kasten*
Levin	*Pressler*
Dixon	*Wallop*
Boren	*Bond*
Kerry	*Grassley*
Bumpers	*Burns*

Urban and Minority-Owned Business Development

224-5175 SR-428A

Kerry — chairman

Nunn	*Burns*
Mikulski	*Lott*

Special Aging

224-5364 SD-G31

Party Ratio: D 10 - R 9

David Pryor, D-Ark., chairman

John Glenn, Ohio	*John Heinz, Pa.*
Bill Bradley, N.J.	*William S. Cohen, Maine*
Quentin N. Burdick, N.D.	*Larry Pressler, S.D.*
J. Bennett Johnston, La.	*Charles E. Grassley, Iowa*
John B. Breaux, La.	*Pete Wilson, Calif.*
Richard C. Shelby, Ala.	*Pete V. Domenici, N.M.*
Harry Reid, Nev.	*Alan K. Simpson, Wyo.*
Bob Graham, Fla.	*John W. Warner, Va.*
Herb Kohl, Wis.	*Nancy Landon Kassebaum, Kan.*

Veterans' Affairs

224-9126 SR-414

Party Ratio: D 6 - R 5

Alan Cranston, D-Calif., chairman

Spark M. Matsunaga, Hawaii	*Frank H. Murkowski, Alaska*
Dennis DeConcini, Ariz.	*Alan K. Simpson, Wyo.*
George J. Mitchell, Maine	*Strom Thurmond, S.C.*
John D. Rockefeller IV, W.Va.	*Arlen Specter, Pa.*
Bob Graham, Fla.	*James M. Jeffords, Vt.*

Select Ethics

224-2981 SH-220

Party Ratio: D 3 - R 3

Howell Heflin, D-Ala., chairman
Warren B. Rudman, R-N.H., vice chairman

David Pryor, Ark.	*Jesse Helms, N.C.*
Terry Sanford, N.C.	*Trent Lott, Miss.*

Select Indian Affairs

224-2251 SH-838

Party Ratio: D 5 - R 3

Daniel K. Inouye, D-Hawaii, chairman
John McCain, R-Ariz., vice chairman

Dennis DeConcini, Ariz.	*Frank H. Murkowski, Alaska*
Quentin N. Burdick, N.D.	*Thad Cochran, Miss.*
Tom Daschle, S.D.	
Kent Conrad, N.D.	

Special Committee on Investigations

224-3701 SH-901

DeConcini — chairman

Daschle	*McCain*

Select Intelligence

224-1700 SH-211

Party Ratio: D 8 - R 7

David L. Boren, D-Okla., chairman
William S. Cohen, R-Maine, vice chairman

Sam Nunn, Ga.	*Orrin G. Hatch, Utah*
Ernest F. Hollings, S.C.	*Frank H. Murkowski, Alaska*
Bill Bradley, N.J.	*Arlen Specter, Pa.*
Alan Cranston, Calif.	*John W. Warner, Va.*
Dennis DeConcini, Ariz.	*Alfonse M. D'Amato, N.Y.*
Howard M. Metzenbaum, Ohio	*John C. Danforth, Mo.*
John Glenn, Ohio	

Partisan Committees

Democratic Leaders

President Pro Tempore —
Robert C. Byrd, W.Va. 224-8160
Majority Leader —
George J. Mitchell, Maine 224-5556
Majority Whip —
Alan Cranston, Calif. 224-2158
Chairman of the Conference —
George J. Mitchell, Maine 224-3735
Secretary of the Conference —
David Pryor, Ark. 224-5551
Chief Deputy Whip —
Alan J. Dixon, Ill. 224-8814

Deputy Whips (listed by region, each with an assistant deputy whip):

East — Patrick J. Leahy, Vt.
Barbara A. Mikulski, Md.

South — Bob Graham, Fla.
Charles S. Robb, Va.

Midwest — Tom Harkin, Iowa
Tom Daschle, S.D.

West — Tim Wirth, Colo.
Brock Adams, Wash.

Policy Committee

224-5551 S-118 Capitol

George J. Mitchell, Maine, chairman

Tom Daschle, S.D., co-chairman

Jeff Bingaman, N.M.	Claiborne Pell, R.I.
Richard H. Bryan, Nev.	David Pryor, Ark. †
Dale Bumpers, Ark.	Charles S. Robb, Va.
Quentin N. Burdick, N.D.	John D. Rockefeller IV, W.Va.
Alan Cranston, Calif. †	Donald W. Riegle Jr., Mich.
John Glenn, Ohio	Terry Sanford, N.C.
Howell Heflin, Ala.	Paul S. Sarbanes, Md.
Ernest F. Hollings, S.C.	Tim Wirth, Colo.
Herb Kohl, Wis.	
Frank R. Lautenberg, N.J.	
Daniel Patrick Moynihan, N.Y.	

† Member *ex officio* from the leadership.

Steering Committee

224-3735 S-309 Capitol

Daniel K. Inouye, Hawaii, chairman

Brock Adams, Wash.
Max Baucus, Mont.
Lloyd Bentsen, Texas
Joseph R. Biden Jr., Del.
Robert C. Byrd, W.Va.
David L. Boren, Okla.
Kent Conrad, N.D.
Alan Cranston, Calif.
Dennis DeConcini, Ariz.
Christopher J. Dodd, Conn.
Jim Exon, Neb.
Wendell H. Ford, Ky.
Wyche Fowler Jr., Ga.
Bob Graham, Fla.
Tom Harkin, Iowa
Edward M. Kennedy, Mass.
John Kerry, Mass
Patrick J. Leahy, Vt.
Carl Levin, Mich.
Howard M. Metzenbaum, Ohio
George J. Mitchell, Maine
Sam Nunn, Ga.
David Pryor, Ark.
Jim Sasser, Tenn.

Democratic Senatorial Campaign Committee

224-2447 430 S. Capitol St. S.E. 20003

John B. Breaux, La., chairman

Alan Cranston, Calif., co-chairman

Lloyd Bensten, Texas
Joseph R. Biden Jr., Del.
Bill Bradley, N.J.
Richard H. Bryan, Nev.
Tom Daschle, S.D.
Christopher J. Dodd, Conn.
Al Gore, Tenn.
Bob Graham, Fla.
J. Bennett Johnston, La.
Bob Kerrey, Neb.
John Kerry, Mass.
Joseph I. Lieberman, Conn.
Howard M. Metzenbaum, Ohio
Barbara A. Mikulski, Md.
George J. Mitchell, Maine †
Sam Nunn, Ga.
David Pryor, Ark. †
Donald W. Riegle Jr., Mich.
Charles S. Robb, Va.
John D. Rockefeller IV, W.Va.
Terry Sanford, N.C.
Jim Sasser, Tenn.
Tim Wirth, Colo.

† Member *ex officio* from the leadership.

Republican Leaders

Minority Leader —
Bob Dole, Kan. 224-3135
Assistant Minority Leader —
Alan K. Simpson, Wyo. 224-2708
Chairman of the Conference —
John H. Chafee, R.I. 224-2764
Secretary of the Conference —
Thad Cochran, Miss. 224-1326

Policy Committee

224-2946 SR-347

William L. Armstrong, Colo., chairman

Christopher S. Bond, Mo.
Thad Cochran, Miss.
William S. Cohen, Maine
John C. Danforth, Mo.
Bob Dole, Kan. †
Pete V. Domenici, N.M.
Jake Garn, Utah
Phil Gramm, Texas
Orrin G. Hatch, Utah
Mark O. Hatfield, Ore.
Jesse Helms, N.C.
Gordon J. Humphrey, N.H.
Richard G. Lugar, Ind.
James A. McClure, Idaho
Frank H. Murkowski, Alaska
Don Nickles, Okla.
Bob Packwood, Ore.
William V. Roth Jr., Del.
Alan K. Simpson, Wyo.
Ted Stevens, Alaska
Strom Thurmond, S.C.
John W. Warner, Va.

† Member *ex officio* from the leadership.

Committee on Committees

224-5842 SR-133

Larry Pressler, S.D., chairman

National Republican Senatorial Committee

675-6000 425 Second St. N.E. 20002

Don Nickles, Okla., chairman

Christopher S. Bond, Mo.
Conrad Burns, Mont.
Alfonse M. D'Amato, N.Y.
John C. Danforth, Mo.
Bob Dole, Kan. †
Dave Durenburger, Minn.
Orrin G. Hatch, Utah
John Heinz, Pa.
James M. Jeffords, Vt.
Bob Kasten, Wis.
Trent Lott, Miss.
Richard G. Lugar, Ind.
Connie Mack, Fla.
John McCain, Ariz.
Bob Packwood, Ore.
Arlen Specter, Pa.
Steve Symms, Idaho
Malcolm Wallop, Wyo.
Pete Wilson, Calif.

† Member *ex officio* from the leadership.

House Committees and Subcommittees

The standing and select committees of the U.S. House are listed below in alphabetical order. The listing includes the telephone number, room number, and party ratio for each full committee. Membership is given in order of seniority on the committee.

If a non-voting delegate or the resident commissioner is a member of a committee, the party ratio reflects that membership. Non-voting representatives, while they cannot vote on the House floor, enjoy equal status as their voting colleagues on committees.

Subcommittees are listed alphabetically under each committee. Membership is listed in order of seniority on subcommittees.

Members of the majority party, Democrats, are shown in Roman type; members of the minority party, Republicans, are shown in italic type.

The word "vacancy" indicates that a committee or subcommittee seat had not been filled at press time. Subcommittee vacancies do not necessarily indicate vacancies on full committees, or vice versa.

Asterisks (*) indicate that chairmen and/or ranking minority members are also *ex officio* members of all subcommittees of which they are not regular members.

The partisan committees of the House are listed on p. 1698. Members of these committees are listed in alphabetical order, not by seniority.

The telephone area code for Washington, D.C., is 202. Abbreviations for House office buildings are: CHOB — Cannon House Office Bldg., LHOB — Longworth House Office Bldg., RHOB — Rayburn House Office Bldg., HOB Annex #1 and #2 — House Office Bldg. Annex #1 and #2, and Capitol. The ZIP code for all House offices is 20515.

Agriculture

225-2171 1301 LHOB

Party Ratio: D 27 - R 18

E. "Kika" de la Garza, D-Texas, chairman *

Walter B. Jones, N.C.	*Edward Madigan, Ill. **
George E. Brown Jr., Calif.	*E. Thomas Coleman, Mo.*
Charlie Rose, N.C.	*Ron Marlenee, Mont.*
Glenn English, Okla.	*Larry J. Hopkins, Ky.*
Leon E. Panetta, Calif.	*Arlan Stangeland, Minn.*
Jerry Huckaby, La.	*Pat Roberts, Kan.*
Dan Glickman, Kan.	*Bill Emerson, Mo.*
Charles W. Stenholm, Texas	*Sid Morrison, Wash.*
Harold L. Volkmer, Mo.	*Steve Gunderson, Wis.*
Charles Hatcher, Ga.	*Tom Lewis, Fla.*
Robin Tallon, S.C.	*Bob Smith, Ore.*
Harley O. Staggers Jr., W.Va.	*Larry Combest, Texas*
Jim Olin, Va.	*Bill Schuette, Mich.*
Timothy J. Penny, Minn.	*Fred Grandy, Iowa*
Richard Stallings, Idaho	*Wally Herger, Calif.*
Dave Nagle, Iowa	*Clyde C. Holloway, La.*
Jim Jontz, Ind.	*James T. Walsh, N.Y.*
Tim Johnson, S.D.	*Bill Grant, Fla.*
Claude Harris, Ala.	
Ben Nighthorse Campbell, Colo.	
Mike Espy, Miss.	
Bill Sarpalius, Texas	
Jill Long, Ind.	
Roy Dyson, Md. ‡	
H. Martin Lancaster, N.C. ‡	
Vacancy	

‡ Member appointed temporarily for the 101st Congress only.

Conservation, Credit and Rural Development

225-0301 1430 LHOB

English – chairman

Tallon	*Coleman*
Penny	*Morrison*
Stallings	*Gunderson*
Nagle	*Combest*
Harris	*Grandy*
Staggers	*Holloway*
Espy	
Sarpalius	
Long	

Cotton, Rice and Sugar

225-1867 1336 LHOB

Huckaby – chairman

Tallon	*Stangeland*
Espy	*Emerson*
Stenholm	*Lewis*
Stallings	*Combest*
Sarpalius	*Herger*
Jones	*Holloway*
Hatcher	
Vacancy	
Vacancy	

Department Operations, Research and Foreign Agriculture

225-0301 1430 LHOB

Brown — chairman

Rose	*Roberts*
Panetta	*Coleman*
Stenholm	*Morrison*
Glickman	*Grandy*
Hatcher	*Walsh*
Olin	
Volkmer	
Jontz	

Domestic Marketing, Consumer Relations and Nutrition

225-1867 1336 LHOB

Hatcher — chairman

Panetta	*Emerson*
Glickman	*Lewis*
Staggers	*Herger*
Espy	
Sarpalius	

Forests, Family Farms and Energy

225-1867 1336 LHOB

Volkmer — chairman

Huckaby	*Morrison*
Olin	*Marlenee*
Stallings	*Smith*
Jontz	*Schuette*
Panetta	*Herger*
Johnson	
Harris	

Livestock, Dairy and Poultry

225-1496 1301A LHOB

Stenholm — chairman

Olin	*Gunderson*
Campbell	*Hopkins*
Johnson	*Stangeland*
Harris	*Lewis*
Rose	*Smith*
Volkmer	*Walsh*
Penny	*Grant*
Nagle	
Long	
Vacancy	

Tobacco and Peanuts

225-8906 1534 LHOB

Rose — chairman

Jones	*Hopkins*
Hatcher	*Combest*
English	*Gunderson*
Tallon	*Grant*
Stenholm	
Lancaster	

Wheat, Soybeans and Feed Grains

225-1494 1301A LHOB

Glickman — chairman

Johnson	*Marlenee*
English	*Stangeland*
Volkmer	*Roberts*
Penny	*Emerson*
Nagle	*Smith*
Sarpalius	*Schuette*
Jontz	*Grandy*
Campbell	
Dyson	
Long	

Appropriations

225-2771 H-218 Capitol

Party Ratio: D 35 - R 22

Jamie L. Whitten, D-Miss., chairman *

William H. Natcher, Ky.	*Silvio O. Conte, Mass.* *
Neal Smith, Iowa	*Joseph M. McDade, Pa.*
Sidney R. Yates, Ill.	*John T. Myers, Ind.*
David R. Obey, Wis.	*Clarence E. Miller, Ohio*
Edward R. Roybal, Calif.	*Lawrence Coughlin, Pa.*
Louis Stokes, Ohio	*C. W. Bill Young, Fla.*
Tom Bevill, Ala.	*Ralph Regula, Ohio*
Bill Alexander, Ark.	*Virginia Smith, Neb.*
John P. Murtha, Pa.	*Carl D. Pursell, Mich.*
Bob Traxler, Mich.	*Mickey Edwards, Okla.*
Joseph D. Early, Mass.	*Bob Livingston, La.*
Charles Wilson, Texas	*Bill Green, N.Y.*
Lindy (Mrs. Hale) Boggs, La.	*Jerry Lewis, Calif.*
	John Porter, Ill.
Norm Dicks, Wash.	*Harold Rogers, Ky.*
Matthew F. McHugh, N.Y.	*Joe Skeen, N.M.*
William Lehman, Fla.	*Frank R. Wolf, Va.*
Martin Olav Sabo, Minn.	*Bill Lowery, Calif.*
Julian C. Dixon, Calif.	*Vin Weber, Minn.*
Vic Fazio, Calif.	*Tom DeLay, Texas*
W. G. "Bill" Hefner, N.C.	*Jim Kolbe, Ariz.*
Les AuCoin, Ore.	*Dean A. Gallo, N.J.*
Daniel K. Akaka, Hawaii	
Wes Watkins, Okla.	
William H. Gray III, Pa.	
Bernard J. Dwyer, N.J.	
Steny H. Hoyer, Md.	
Bob Carr, Mich.	
Robert J. Mrazek, N.Y.	
Richard J. Durbin, Ill.	
Ronald D. Coleman, Texas	
Alan B. Mollohan, W.Va.	
Lindsay Thomas, Ga.	
Chester G. Atkins, Mass.	
Jim Chapman, Texas	

Commerce, Justice and State, the Judiciary and Related Agencies

225-3351 H-309 Capitol

Smith (Iowa) — chairman

Alexander	*Rogers*
Early	*Regula*
Dwyer	*Kolbe*
Carr	
Mollohan	

Defense

225-2847 H-144 Capitol

Murtha — chairman

Dicks	*McDade*
Wilson	*Young*
Hefner	*Miller*
AuCoin	*Livingston*
Sabo	
Dixon	

District of Columbia

225-5338 H-302 Capitol

Dixon — chairman

Natcher	*Gallo*
Stokes	*Green*
AuCoin	*Regula*
Hoyer	
Carr	

Energy and Water Development

225-3421 2362 RHOB

Bevill — chairman

Boggs
Fazio
Watkins
Thomas
Chapman

Myers
Smith (Neb.)
Pursell

Foreign Operations

225-2041 H-307 Capitol

Obey — chairman

Yates
McHugh
Lehman
Wilson
Gray
Mrazek
Coleman

Edwards
Lewis
Porter
Gallo

Interior and Related Agencies

225-3081 B308 RHOB

Yates — chairman

Murtha
Dicks
AuCoin
Bevill
Atkins

Regula
McDade
Lowery

Labor, Health and Human Services, Education and Related Agencies

225-3508 2358 RHOB

Natcher — chairman

Smith (Iowa)
Obey
Roybal
Stokes
Early
Dwyer
Hoyer

Conte
Pursell
Porter
Young
Weber

Legislative Branch

225-5338 H-302 Capitol

Fazio — chairman

Yates
Obey
Murtha
Traxler
Boggs

Lewis
Conte
Myers
Porter

Military Construction

225-3047 B300 RHOB

Hefner — chairman

Alexander
Thomas
Coleman
Bevill
Dicks
Dixon
Fazio

Lowery
Edwards
Kolbe
DeLay

Rural Development, Agriculture and Related Agencies

225-2638 2362 RHOB

Whitten — chairman

Traxler
McHugh
Natcher
Akaka
Watkins
Durbin
Smith (Iowa)

Smith (Neb.)
Myers
Skeen
Weber

Transportation and Related Agencies

225-2141 2358 RHOB

Lehman — chairman

Gray
Carr
Durbin
Mrazek
Sabo

Coughlin
Conte
Wolf
DeLay

Treasury, Postal Service and General Government

225-5834 H-164 Capitol

Roybal — chairman

Akaka
Hoyer
Alexander
Early
Sabo

Skeen
Lowery
Wolf

VA, HUD and Independent Agencies

225-3241 H-143 Capitol

Traxler — chairman

Stokes
Boggs
Mollohan
Chapman
Atkins

Green
Coughlin
Lewis

Armed Services

225-4151 2120 RHOB Party Ratio: D 31 - R 21

Les Aspin, D-Wis., chairman

Charles E. Bennett, Fla.
G. V. "Sonny" Montgomery, Miss.
Ronald V. Dellums, Calif.
Patricia Schroeder, Colo.
Beverly B. Byron, Md.
Nicholas Mavroules, Mass.
Earl Hutto, Fla.
Ike Skelton, Mo.
Marvin Leath, Texas
Dave McCurdy, Okla.
Thomas M. Foglietta, Pa.
Roy Dyson, Md.
Dennis M. Hertel, Mich.
Marilyn Lloyd, Tenn.
Norman Sisisky, Va.
Richard Ray, Ga.
John M. Spratt Jr., S.C.
Frank McCloskey, Ind.
Solomon P. Ortiz, Texas
George "Buddy" Darden, Ga.
Tommy F. Robinson, Ark.
Albert G. Bustamante, Texas
George J. Hochbrueckner, N.Y.
Joseph E. Brennan, Maine
Owen B. Pickett, Va.
H. Martin Lancaster, N.C.
Lane Evans, Ill.
James Bilbray, Nev.
John Tanner, Tenn.
Michael R. McNulty, N.Y.

Bill Dickinson, Ala.
Floyd Spence, S.C.
Bob Stump, Ariz.
Jim Courter, N.J.
Larry J. Hopkins, Ky.
Robert W. Davis, Mich.
Duncan Hunter, Calif.
David O'B. Martin, N.Y.
John R. Kasich, Ohio
Herbert H. Bateman, Va.
Ben Blaz, Guam
Andy Ireland, Fla.
James V. Hansen, Utah
John G. Rowland, Conn.
Curt Weldon, Pa.
Jon Kyl, Ariz.
Arthur Ravenel Jr., S.C.
Robert K. Dornan, Calif.
Joel Hefley, Colo.
Jim McCrery, La.
Ronald K. Machtley, R.I.

Investigations

225-4221 2339 RHOB

Mavroules — chairman

Hertel	*Hopkins*
Sisisky	*Stump*
Spratt	*Kyl*
McCloskey	*Ireland*
Darden	*Hefley*
Brennan	*McCrery*
Evans	
Tanner	
Dellums	

Military Installations and Facilities

225-7120 2120 RHOB

Schroeder — chairman

Montgomery	*Martin*
Skelton	*Dickinson*
McCurdy	*Blaz*
Foglietta	*Spence*
Sisisky	*Ravenel*
Ortiz	*Courter*
Robinson	*Hansen*
Bilbray	*Ireland*
Mavroules	
Hutto	

Military Personnel and Compensation

225-7560 2343 RHOB

Byron — chairman

Montgomery	*Bateman*
Skelton	*Ravenel*
Hertel	*Hefley*
Lloyd	*McCrery*
Robinson	*Machtley*
Bustamante	*Dornan*
Hochbrueckner	
Pickett	
Lancaster	

Procurement and Military Nuclear Systems

225-1240 2343 RHOB

Aspin — chairman

Skelton	*Courter*
Leath	*Davis*
Dyson	*Hopkins*
Lloyd	*Blaz*
Sisisky	*Ireland*
Ray	*Hansen*
Spratt	*Rowland*
McCloskey	*Kasich*
Bustamante	
Evans	

Readiness

225-7991 2340 RHOB

Hutto — chairman

Leath	*Kasich*
Dyson	*Martin*
Ray	*Dornan*
Ortiz	*Hefley*
Lancaster	*Machtley*
Bilbray	
Tanner	
McNulty	

Research and Development

225-6257 2117 RHOB

Dellums — chairman

McCurdy	*Dickinson*
Foglietta	*Davis*
Hertel	*Stump*
Darden	*Hunter*
Hochbrueckner	*Weldon*
Pickett	*Kyl*
McNulty	*Dornan*
Bennett	
Schroeder	
Byron	

Seapower and Strategic and Critical Materials

225-6704 2343 RHOB

Bennett — chairman

Foglietta	*Spence*
Sisisky	*Hunter*
Ortiz	*Bateman*
Robinson	*Weldon*
Hochbrueckner	*Rowland*
Brennan	*Blaz*
Pickett	
Hutto	

Banking, Finance and Urban Affairs

225-4247 2129 RHOB

Party Ratio: D 31 - R 20

Henry B. Gonzalez, D-Texas, chairman

Frank Annunzio, Ill.	*Chalmers P. Wylie, Ohio*
Walter E. Fauntroy, D.C.	*Jim Leach, Iowa*
Stephen L. Neal, N.C.	*Norman D. Shumway, Calif.*
Carroll Hubbard Jr., Ky.	*Stan Parris, Va.*
John J. LaFalce, N.Y.	*Bill McCollum, Fla.*
Mary Rose Oakar, Ohio	*Marge Roukema, N.J.*
Bruce F. Vento, Minn.	*Doug Bereuter, Neb.*
Doug Barnard Jr., Ga.	*David Dreier, Calif.*
Robert Garcia, N.Y.	*John Hiler, Ind.*
Charles E. Schumer, N.Y.	*Tom Ridge, Pa.*
Barney Frank, Mass.	*Steve Bartlett, Texas*
Richard H. Lehman, Calif.	*Toby Roth, Wis.*
Bruce A. Morrison, Conn.	*Al McCandless, Calif.*
Marcy Kaptur, Ohio	*H. James Saxton, N.J.*
Ben Erdreich, Ala.	*Patricia Saiki, Hawaii*
Thomas R. Carper, Del.	*Jim Bunning, Ky.*
Esteban E. Torres, Calif.	*Richard H. Baker, La.*
Gerald D. Kleczka, Wis.	*Cliff Stearns, Fla.*
Bill Nelson, Fla.	*Paul E. Gillmor, Ohio*
Paul E. Kanjorski, Pa.	*Bill Paxon, N.Y.*
Liz J. Patterson, S.C.	
Tom McMillen, Md.	
Joseph P. Kennedy II, Mass.	
Floyd H. Flake, N.Y.	
Kweisi Mfume, Md.	
David E. Price, N.C.	
Nancy Pelosi, Calif.	
Jim McDermott, Wash.	
Peter Hoagland, Neb.	
Richard E. Neal, Mass.	

Consumer Affairs and Coinage

225-8872 604 HOB Annex #1

Lehman — chairman

Gonzalez	*Hiler*
Pelosi	*Wylie*
Hubbard	*Ridge*
Barnard	*Dreier*
Schumer	*Barlett*
Kaptur	*Saxton*
Erdreich	
Price	
Vacancy	
Vacancy	

Domestic Monetary Policy

226-7315 109 HOB Annex #2

Neal (N.C.) — chairman

Barnard	*McCollum*
Gonzalez	*Leach*
Annunzio	*Bunning*
Hoagland	

Economic Stabilization

226-7515 2219 RHOB

Oakar — chairman

LaFalce	*Shumway*
Vento	*Roth*
Kaptur	*Saiki*
Kanjorski	*Roukema*
Garcia	*Gillmor*
Patterson	*Paxon*
Neal (Mass.)	
Vacancy	

Financial Institutions Supervision, Regulation and Insurance

226-3280 212 HOB Annex #1

Annunzio — chairman

Hubbard	*Wylie*
Barnard	*Leach*
LaFalce	*Shumway*
Oakar	*McCollum*
Vento	*Dreier*
Schumer	*Parris*
Frank	*Roukema*
Lehman	*Bereuter*
Kaptur	*Bartlett*
Nelson	*Roth*
Kanjorski	*Hiler*
Gonzalez	*Ridge*
Neal (N.C.)	*McCandless*
Erdreich	*Saxton*
Carper	*Saiki*
Torres	*Bunning*
Kleczka	*Baker*
Patterson	*Stearns*
McMillen	*Gillmor*
Price	
Kennedy	
Fauntroy	
Flake	
Mfume	
Pelosi	
McDermott	
Hoagland	

General Oversight and Investigations

225-2828 B304 RHOB

Hubbard — chairman

Gonzalez	*Parris*
Barnard	*Dreier*
Flake	*Bartlett*
Annunzio	*McCandless*
Hoagland	*Gillmor*
Neal (Mass.)	
Vacancy	

Housing and Community Development

225-7054 2132 RHOB

Gonzalez — chairman

Fauntroy	*Roukema*
Oakar	*Wylie*
Vento	*McCollum*
Garcia	*Bereuter*
Schumer	*Dreier*
Frank	*Hiler*
Lehman	*Ridge*
Morrison	*Bartlett*
Kaptur	*Roth*
Erdreich	*Saxton*
Carper	*Saiki*
Torres	*Bunning*
Kleczka	*Parris*
Kanjorski	*McCandless*
Neal (N.C.)	*Baker*
Hubbard	*Paxon*
Kennedy	*Stearns*
Flake	*Gillmor*
Mfume	
Pelosi	
LaFalce	
Patterson	
Price	
McDermott	
Hoagland	
Neal (Mass.)	

International Development, Finance, Trade and Monetary Policy

226-7511 139 HOB Annex #2

Fauntroy — chairman

Neal (N.C.)	*Leach*
LaFalce	*Bereuter*
Torres	*Shumway*
Morrison	*McCandless*
Schumer	*Saxton*
Kleczka	*Saiki*
Carper	*Bunning*
Kennedy	*Baker*
Pelosi	*Stearns*
Frank	*Paxon*
McMillen	
Flake	
McDermott	
Hoagland	

Policy Research and Insurance

225-1271 140 HOB Annex #2

Erdreich — acting chairman *

Garcia	*Bereuter*
Kanjorski	*Paxon*
Morrison	*Roth*
Vacancy	

* Subcommittee Chairman Garcia was indicted Nov. 21, 1988, on charges of conspiracy, receipt of bribes, extortion and receipt of gratuities. House Democratic Caucus rules require that an indicted member step down from his chairmanship for the duration of the session or until charges are dismissed.

Budget

226-7200 214 HOB Annex #1

Party Ratio: D 21 - R 14

Leon E. Panetta, D-Calif., chairman *

Richard A. Gephardt, Mo. *	*Bill Frenzel, Minn. **
Marty Russo, Ill.	*Bill Gradison, Ohio **
Ed Jenkins, Ga.	*Bill Goodling, Pa.*
Marvin Leath, Texas	*Denny Smith, Ore.*
Charles E. Schumer, N.Y.	*Bill Thomas, Calif.*
Barbara Boxer, Calif.	*Harold Rogers, Ky.*
Jim Slattery, Kan.	*Dick Armey, Texas*
James L. Oberstar, Minn.	*Jack Buechner, Mo.*
Frank J. Guarini, N.J.	*Amo Houghton, N.Y.*
Richard J. Durbin, Ill.	*Jim McCrery, La..*
Mike Espy, Miss.	*John R. Kasich, Ohio*
Dale E. Kildee, Mich.	*Dean A. Gallo, N.J.*
Anthony C. Beilenson, Calif.	*Bill Schuette, Mich.*
	Helen Delich Bentley, Md.
Jerry Huckaby, La.	
Martin Olav Sabo, Minn.	
Bernard J. Dwyer, N.J.	
Howard L. Berman, Calif.	
Bob Wise, W.Va.	
Marcy Kaptur, Ohio	
John Bryant, Texas	

— Task Forces —

Budget Process, Reconciliation and Enforcement

Russo — chairman

Schumer	*Buechner*
Oberstar	*Armey*
Beilenson	*Houghton*
Huckaby	*Gallo*
Sabo	*Schuette*
Dwyer	
Berman	

Community Development and Natural Resources

Jenkins — chairman

Espy	*Rogers*
Kildee	*Goodling*
Huckaby	*Smith*
Dwyer	*Houghton*
Wise	

Defense, Foreign Policy and Space

Leath — chairman

Russo	*Smith*
Oberstar	*McCrery*
Guarini	*Kasich*
Berman	*Bentley*
Kaptur	
Bryant	

Economic Policy, Projections and Revenues

Slattery — chairman

Jenkins	*Thomas*
Guarini	*Smith*
Durbin	*Rogers*
Beilenson	*Armey*

Human Resources

Boxer — chairman

Durbin	*Goodling*
Espy	*Buechner*
Kildee	*Kasich*
Sabo	*Bentley*
Wise	
Kaptur	

Urgent Fiscal Issues

Schumer — chairman

Boxer	*Armey*
Slattery	*Thomas*
Bryant	*McCrery*
	Schuette

District of Columbia

225-4457 1310 LHOB

Party Ratio: D 8 - R 4

Ronald V. Dellums, D-Calif., chairman

Walter E. Fauntroy, D.C.	*Stan Parris, Va.*
Pete Stark, Calif.	*Thomas J. Bliley Jr., Va.*
William H. Gray III, Pa.	*Larry Combest, Texas*
Mervyn M. Dymally, Calif.	*Dana Rohrabacher, Calif.*
Alan Wheat, Mo.	
Bruce A. Morrison, Conn.	
Vacancy	

Fiscal Affairs and Health

225-4457 507 HOB Annex #1

Fauntroy — chairman

Dellums	*Bliley*
Gray	*Parris*
Dymally	*Combest*
Vacancy	

Government Operations and Metropolitan Affairs

225-4457 507 HOB Annex #1

Wheat — chairman

Fauntroy	*Combest*
Stark	*Parris*
Gray	*Rohrabacher*
Vacancy	

Judiciary and Education

225-4457 441 CHOB

Dymally — chairman

Stark	*Rohrabacher*
Dellums	*Bliley*
Wheat	*Parris*
Vacancy	

Education and Labor

225-4527 2181 RHOB

Party Ratio: D 22 - R 13

Augustus F. Hawkins, D-Calif., chairman *

William D. Ford, Mich.	*Bill Goodling, Pa. **
Joseph M. Gaydos, Pa.	*E. Thomas Coleman, Mo.*
William L. Clay, Mo.	*Thomas E. Petri, Wis.*
George Miller, Calif.	*Marge Roukema, N.J.*
Austin J. Murphy, Pa.	*Steve Gunderson, Wis.*
Dale E. Kildee, Mich.	*Steve Bartlett, Texas*
Pat Williams, Mont.	*Tom Tauke, Iowa*
Matthew G. Martinez, Calif.	*Dick Armey, Texas*
Major R. Owens, N.Y.	*Harris W. Fawell, Ill.*
Charles A. Hayes, Ill.	*Paul B. Henry, Mich.*
Carl C. Perkins, Ky.	*Fred Grandy, Iowa*
Thomas C. Sawyer, Ohio	*Cass Ballenger, N.C.*
Donald M. Payne, N.J.	*Peter Smith, Vt.*
Nita M. Lowey, N.Y.	
Glenn Poshard, Ill.	
Jolene Unsoeld, Wash.	
Nick J. Rahall II, W.Va. ‡	
Jaime B. Fuster, Puerto Rico ‡	
Peter J. Visclosky, Ind. ‡	
Jim Jontz, Ind. ‡	
Kweisi Mfume, Md. ‡	

‡ Member appointed temporarily for the 101st Congress only.

Elementary, Secondary and Vocational Education

225-4368 B346-C RHOB

Hawkins — chairman

Ford	*Goodling*
Miller	*Fawell*
Kildee	*Grandy*
Williams	*Smith*
Martinez	*Barlett*
Perkins	*Gunderson*
Hayes	*Petri*
Sawyer	*Roukema*
Owens	*Coleman*
Payne	
Lowey	
Poshard	
Unsoeld	
Rahall	

Employment Opportunities

225-7594 402 CHOB

Martinez — chairman

Williams	*Gunderson*
Fuster	*Henry*
Mfume	*Smith*

Health and Safety

225-6876 B345-A RHOB

Gaydos — chairman

Ford	*Henry*
Unsoeld	*Ballenger*
Vacancy	

Human Resources

225-1850 320 CHOB

Kildee — chairman

Sawyer	*Tauke*
Unsoeld	*Coleman*
Lowey	*Grandy*
Poshard	

Labor-Management Relations

225-5768 2451 RHOB

Clay — chairman

Ford	*Roukema*
Kildee	*Armey*
Miller	*Fawell*
Hayes	*Ballenger*
Owens	*Petri*
Sawyer	*Grandy*
Murphy	
Visclosky	

Labor Standards

225-1927 B346-A RHOB

Murphy — chairman

Williams	*Petri*
Clay	*Bartlett*
Hayes	*Armey*
Perkins	*Fawell*
Payne	

Postsecondary Education

226-3681 616 HOB Annex #1

Williams — chairman

Ford	*Coleman*
Owens	*Goodling*
Hayes	*Roukema*
Perkins	*Tauke*
Gaydos	*Gunderson*
Miller	*Henry*
Lowey	
Poshard	

Select Education

226-7532 518 HOB Annex #1

Owens — chairman

Martinez	*Bartlett*
Payne	*Ballenger*
Jontz	*Smith*

Energy and Commerce

225-2927 2125 RHOB

Party Ratio: D 26 - R 17

John D. Dingell, D-Mich., chairman *

James H. Scheuer, N.Y.	*Norman F. Lent, N.Y. **
Henry A. Waxman, Calif.	*Edward R. Madigan, Ill.*
Philip R. Sharp, Ind.	*Carlos J. Moorhead, Calif.*
James J. Florio, N.J.	*Matthew J. Rinaldo, N.J.*
Edward J. Markey, Mass.	*William E. Dannemeyer, Calif.*
Thomas A. Luken, Ohio	
Doug Walgren, Pa.	*Bob Whittaker, Kan.*
Al Swift, Wash.	*Tom Tauke, Iowa*
Mickey Leland, Texas	*Don Ritter, Pa.*
Cardiss Collins, Ill.	*Thomas J. Bliley Jr., Va.*
Mike Synar, Okla.	*Jack Fields, Texas*
W. J. "Billy" Tauzin, La.	*Michael G. Oxley, Ohio*
Ron Wyden, Ore.	*Howard C. Nielson, Utah*
Ralph M. Hall, Texas	*Michael Bilirakis, Fla.*
Dennis E. Eckart, Ohio	*Dan Schaefer, Colo.*
Bill Richardson, N.M.	*Joe L. Barton, Texas*
Jim Slattery, Kan.	*Sonny Callahan, Ala.*
Gerry Sikorski, Minn.	*Alex McMillan, N.C.*
John Bryant, Texas	
Jim Bates, Calif.	
Rick Boucher, Va.	
Jim Cooper, Tenn.	
Terry L. Bruce, Ill.	
J. Roy Rowland, Ga.	
Thomas J. Manton, N.Y.	

Commerce, Consumer Protection and Competitiveness

226-3160 151 HOB Annex #2

Florio — chairman

Scheuer	*Ritter*
Rowland	*Dannemeyer*
Waxman	*Nielson*
Sharp	*Barton*
Luken	
Slattery	

Energy and Power

226-2500 331 HOB Annex #2

Sharp — chairman

Walgren	*Moorhead*
Swift	*Dannemeyer*
Tauzin	*Fields*
Bates	*Oxley*
Cooper	*Nielson*
Bruce	*Bilirakis*
Markey	*Barton*
Leland	*Callahan*
Synar	
Hall	
Richardson	
Bryant	

Health and the Environment

225-4952 2415 RHOB

Waxman — chairman

Scheuer	*Madigan*
Walgren	*Dannemeyer*
Wyden	*Whittaker*
Sikorski	*Tauke*
Bates	*Bliley*
Bruce	*Fields*
Rowland	*Nielson*
Leland	*Bilirakis*
Collins	
Synar	
Hall	
Richardson	

Oversight and Investigations

225-4441 2323 RHOB

Dingell — chairman

Sikorski	*Bliley*
Bryant	*Lent*
Walgren	*Oxley*
Collins	*Bilirakis*
Wyden	*McMillan*
Eckart	
Boucher	

Telecommunications and Finance

226-2424 316 HOB Annex #2

Markey — chairman

Swift	*Rinaldo*
Leland	*Madigan*
Collins	*Moorhead*
Synar	*Tauke*
Tauzin	*Ritter*
Hall	*Bliley*
Eckart	*Fields*
Richardson	*Oxley*
Slattery	*Schaefer*
Bryant	
Boucher	
Cooper	
Manton	
Wyden	

Transportation and Hazardous Materials

225-9304 324 HOB Annex #2

Luken — chairman

Eckart	*Whittaker*
Slattery	*Rinaldo*
Boucher	*Tauke*
Manton	*Schaefer*
Florio	*Callahan*
Swift	*McMillan*
Tauzin	
Sikorski	
Bates	

Foreign Affairs

225-5021 2170 RHOB

Party Ratio: D 28 - R 18

Dante B. Fascell, D-Fla., chairman

Lee H. Hamilton, Ind.	*William S. Broomfield, Mich.*
Gus Yatron, Pa.	*Benjamin A. Gilman, N.Y.*
Stephen J. Solarz, N.Y.	*Robert J. Lagomarsino, Calif.*
Gerry E. Studds, Mass.	*Jim Leach, Iowa*
Howard Wolpe, Mich.	*Toby Roth, Wis.*
George W. Crockett Jr., Mich.	*Olympia J. Snowe, Maine*
Sam Gejdenson, Conn.	*Henry J. Hyde, Ill.*
Mervyn M. Dymally, Calif.	*Doug Bereuter, Neb.*
Tom Lantos, Calif.	*Christopher H. Smith, N.J.*
Peter H. Kostmayer, Pa.	*Mike DeWine, Ohio*
Robert G. Torricelli, N.J.	*Dan Burton, Ind.*
Lawrence J. Smith, Fla.	*Jan Meyers, Kan.*
Howard L. Berman, Calif.	*John Miller, Wash.*
Mel Levine, Calif.	*Donald E. "Buz" Lukens, Ohio*
Edward F. Feighan, Ohio	*Ben Blaz, Guam*
Ted Weiss, N.Y.	*Elton Gallegly, Calif.*
Gary L. Ackerman, N.Y.	*Amo Houghton, N.Y.*
Morris K. Udall, Ariz.	*Porter J. Goss, Fla.*
James McClure Clarke, N.C.	
Jaime B. Fuster, Puerto Rico	
Wayne Owens, Utah	
Harry A. Johnston, Fla.	
Eliot L. Engel, N.Y.	
Eni F. H. Faleomavaega, American Samoa	
Douglas H. Bosco, Calif. ‡	
Frank McCloskey, Ind. ‡	
Donald M. Payne, N.J. ‡	

‡ Member appointed temporarily for the 101st Congress only.

Africa

226-7807 816 HOB Annex #1

Wolpe — chairman

Crockett	*Burton*
Dymally	*Lukens*
Payne	*Houghton*
Engel	*Blaz*
McCloskey	

Arms Control, International Security and Science

225-8926 2401-A RHOB

Fascell — chairman

Berman	*Broomfield*
Udall	*Gallegly*
Clarke	*Snowe*
Engel	*Hyde*
Studds	*Goss*
Solarz	
Bosco	

Asian and Pacific Affairs

226-7801 707 HOB Annex #1

Solarz — chairman

Faleomavaega	*Leach*
Lantos	*Blaz*
Torricelli	*Lagomarsino*
Ackerman	*Roth*
Clarke	

Europe and the Middle East

225-3345 B359 RHOB

Hamilton — chairman

Lantos	*Gilman*
Torricelli	*Meyers*
Smith (Fla.)	*Lukens*
Levine	*Leach*
Feighan	*Smith (N.J.)*
Ackerman	
Owens	

Human Rights and International Organizations

226-7825 B358 RHOB

Yatron — chairman

Owens	*Bereuter*
Lantos	*Smith (N.J.)*
Feighan	*Meyers*
Weiss	*Miller*
Ackerman	

International Economic Policy and Trade

226-7820 705 HOB Annex #1

Gejdenson — chairman

Wolpe	*Roth*
Kostmayer	*Miller*
Levine	*Houghton*
Feighan	*Bereuter*
Johnston	*DeWine*
Engel	
Faleomavaega	

International Operations

225-3424 709 HOB Annex #1

Dymally — chairman

Yatron	*Snowe*
Smith (Fla.)	*Gilman*
Berman	*Blaz*
Weiss	*Gallegly*
Faleomavaega	

Western Hemisphere Affairs

226-7812 702 HOB Annex #1

Crockett — chairman

Studds	*Lagomarsino*
Kostmayer	*Hyde*
Weiss	*DeWine*
Fuster	*Goss*
Johnston	*Burton*
Solarz	
Gejdenson	

Government Operations

225-5051 2157 RHOB

Party Ratio: D 24 - R 15

John Conyers Jr., D-Mich., chairman *

Cardiss Collins, Ill.	*Frank Horton, N.Y.* *
Glenn English, Okla.	*William F. Clinger Jr., Pa.*
Henry A. Waxman, Calif.	*Al McCandless, Calif.*
Ted Weiss, N.Y.	*Howard C. Nielson, Utah*
Mike Synar, Okla.	*Donald E. "Buz" Lukens, Ohio*
Stephen L. Neal, N.C.	*Dennis Hastert, Ill.*
Doug Barnard Jr., Ga.	*Jon Kyl, Ariz.*
Barney Frank, Mass.	*Christopher Shays, Conn.*
Tom Lantos, Calif.	*Peter Smith, Vt.*
Bob Wise, W.Va.	*Steven H. Schiff, N.M.*
Barbara Boxer, Calif.	*Chuck Douglas, N.H.*
Major R. Owens, N.Y.	*Larkin Smith, Miss.*
Ed Towns, N.Y.	*C. Christopher Cox, Calif.*
John M. Spratt Jr., S.C.	*Craig Thomas, Wyo.*
Joe Kolter, Pa.	*Vacancy*
Ben Erdreich, Ala.	
Gerald D. Kleczka, Wis.	
Albert G. Bustamante, Texas	
Matthew G. Martinez, Calif.	
Nancy Pelosi, Calif.	
Donald M. Payne, N.J.	
Jim Bates, Calif.	
Vacancy	

Commerce, Consumer and Monetary Affairs

225-4407 B377 RHOB

Barnard — chairman

Spratt	*Hastert*
Martinez	*Schiff*
Kolter	*Douglas*
Bustamante	*Cox*
Waxman	

Employment and Housing

225-6751 B349-A RHOB

Lantos — chairman

Frank	*Lukens*
Martinez	*Kyl*
Weiss	*Shays*
Wise	

Environment, Energy and Natural Resources

225-6427 B371-B RHOB

Synar — chairman

Towns	*Clinger*
Bustamante	*Douglas*
Kolter	*Thomas*
Waxman	
Vacancy	

Government Activities and Transportation

225-7920 B350-A RHOB

Collins — chairman

Owens	*Nielson*
Boxer	*Cox*
Kleczka	*Vacancy*
Lantos	

Government Information, Justice and Agriculture

225-3741 B349-C RHOB

Wise — chaiman

Democrats	Republicans
English	*McCandless*
Towns	*Schiff*
Spratt	*Thomas*
Vacancy	
Vacancy	

Human Resources and Intergovernmental Relations

225-2548 B372 RHOB

Weiss — chairman

Democrats	Republicans
Waxman	*Smith (Miss.)*
Pelosi	*Smith (Vt.)*
Payne	*Vacancy*
Vacancy	
Vacancy	

Legislation and National Security

225-5147 B373 RHOB

Conyers — chairman

Democrats	Republicans
Neal	*Horton*
Erdreich	*Kyl*
Kleczka	*Shays*
English	*Smith (Vt.)*
Boxer	
Bustamante	

House Administration

225-2061 H-326 Capitol

Party Ratio: D 13 - R 8

Frank Annunzio, D-Ill., chairman *

Democrats	Republicans
Joseph M. Gaydos, Penn.	*Bill Thomas, Calif.* *
Charlie Rose, N.C.	*Bill Dickinson, Ala.*
Leon E. Panetta, Calif.	*Newt Gingrich, Ga.*
Al Swift, Wash.	*Barbara F. Vucanovich, Nev.*
Mary Rose Oakar, Ohio	*Pat Roberts, Kan.*
Jim Bates, Calif.	*Paul E. Gillmor, Ohio*
William L. Clay, Mo.	*John Hiler, Ind.*
Sam Gejdenson, Conn.	*James T. Walsh, N.Y.*
Joe Kolter, Pa.	
Ronnie G. Flippo, Ala.	
Martin Frost, Texas	
Vacancy	

Accounts

226-7540 611 HOB Annex #1

Gaydos — chairman

Democrats	Republicans
Swift	*Vucanovich*
Oakar	*Thomas*
Gejdenson	*Gillmor*
Kolter	*Hiler*
Flippo	
Vacancy	

Elections

226-7616 802 HOB Annex #1

Swift — chairman

Democrats	Republicans
Rose	*Thomas*
Panetta	*Roberts*
Bates	*Hiler*
Clay	*Walsh*
Frost	
Vacancy	

Libraries and Memorials

226-2307 612 HOB Annex #1

Clay — chairman

Democrats	Republicans
Flippo	*Gillmor*
Frost	*Walsh*

Office Systems

225-1608 722 HOB Annex #1

Rose — chairman

Democrats	Republicans
Kolter	*Walsh*
Frost	*Dickinson*

Personnel and Police

226-7641 720 HOB Annex #1

Oakar — chairman

Democrats	Republicans
Gaydos	*Roberts*
Panetta	*Dickinson*

Procurement and Printing

225-4568 105 CHOB

Bates — chairman

Democrats	Republicans
Flippo	*Roberts*
Frost	*Gingrich*

Interior and Insular Affairs

225-2761 1324 LHOB

Party Ratio: D 26 - R 15

Morris K. Udall, D-Ariz., chairman *

Democrats	Republicans
George Miller, Calif.	*Don Young, Alaska* *
Philip R. Sharp, Ind.	*Robert J. Lagomarsino, Calif.*
Edward J. Markey, Mass.	*Ron Marlenee, Mont.*
Austin J. Murphy, Pa.	*Larry E. Craig, Idaho*
Nick J. Rahall II, W.Va.	*Denny Smith, Ore.*
Bruce F. Vento, Minn.	*James V. Hansen, Utah*
Pat Williams, Mont.	*Barbara F. Vucanovich, Nev.*
Beverly B. Byron, Md.	*Ben Blaz, Guam*
Ron de Lugo, Virgin Islands	*John J. Rhodes III, Ariz.*
Sam Gejdenson, Conn.	*Elton Gallegly, Calif.*
Peter H. Kostmayer, Pa.	*Stan Parris, Va.*
Richard H. Lehman, Calif.	*Bob Smith, Ore.*
Bill Richardson, N.M.	*Jim Ross Lightfoot, Iowa*
George "Buddy" Darden, Ga.	*Craig Thomas, Wyo.*
Peter J. Visclosky, Ind.	*John J. "Jimmy" Duncan Jr., Tenn.*
Jaime B. Fuster, Puerto Rico	
Mel Levine, Calif.	
James McClure Clarke, N.C.	
Wayne Owens, Utah	
John Lewis, Ga.	
Ben Nighthorse Campbell, Colo.	
Peter A. DeFazio, Ore.	
Eni F. H. Faleomavaega, American Samoa	
Jim McDermott, Wash.	
Vacancy	

Energy and the Environment

225-8331   1327 LHOB

Udall — chairman

Miller	*Hansen*
Sharp	*Denny Smith*
Markey	*Vucanovich*
Murphy	*Blaz*
Vento	*Rhodes*
Gejdenson	*Parris*
Richardson	*Lightfoot*
Darden	
Clarke	

General Oversight and Investigations

226-4085   815 HOB Annex #1

Kostmayer — chairman

Markey	*Vucanovich*
Gejdenson	*Rhodes*
Levine	*Duncan*
Owens	
Faleomavaega	

Insular and International Affairs

225-9297   1626 LHOB

de Lugo — chairman

Udall	*Lagomarsino*
Darden	*Blaz*
Fuster	*Gallegly*
Clarke	
Lewis	
Faleomavaega	

Mining and Natural Resources

226-7761   819 HOB Annex #1

Rahall — chairman

Udall	*Craig*
Murphy	*Marlenee*
Campbell	*Vucanovich*
DeFazio	

National Parks and Public Lands

226-7736   812 HOB Annex #1

Vento — chairman

Murphy	*Marlenee*
Rahall	*Lagomarsino*
Williams	*Craig*
Byron	*Hansen*
de Lugo	*Blaz*
Kostmayer	*Rhodes*
Lehman	*Gallegly*
Richardson	*Parris*
Darden	*Bob Smith*
Visclosky	*Lightfoot*
Fuster	*Thomas*
Levine	*Duncan*
Clarke	
Owens	
Lewis	
Campbell	
DeFazio	
McDermott	
Vacancy	

Water, Power and Offshore Energy Resources

225-6042   1522 LHOB

Miller — chairman

Udall	*Denny Smith*
Sharp	*Young*
Markey	*Marlenee*
Byron	*Craig*
Gejdenson	*Hansen*
Kostmayer	*Rhodes*
Lehman	*Bob Smith*
Levine	*Thomas*
Owens	*Vacancy*
Campbell	
DeFazio	
McDermott	
Vacancy	

Judiciary

225-3951   2138 RHOB

Party Ratio: D 21 - R 14

Jack Brooks, D-Texas, chairman *

Robert W. Kastenmeier, Wis.	*Hamilton Fish Jr., N.Y. **
Don Edwards, Calif.	*Carlos J. Moorhead, Calif.*
John Conyers Jr., Mich.	*Henry J. Hyde, Ill.*
Romano L. Mazzoli, Ky.	*F. James Sensenbrenner Jr., Wis.*
William J. Hughes, N.J.	*Bill McCollum, Fla.*
Mike Synar, Okla.	*George W. Gekas, Pa.*
Patricia Schroeder, Colo.	*Mike DeWine, Ohio*
Dan Glickman, Kan.	*William E. Dannemeyer, Calif.*
Barney Frank, Mass.	*Howard Coble, N.C.*
George W. Crockett Jr., Mich.	*D. French Slaughter Jr., Va.*
Charles E. Schumer, N.Y.	*Lamar Smith, Texas*
Bruce A. Morrison, Conn.	*Larkin Smith, Miss.*
Edward F. Feighan, Ohio	*Chuck Douglas, N.H.*
Lawrence J. Smith, Fla.	*Craig T. James, Fla.*
Howard L. Berman, Calif.	
Rick Boucher, Va.	
Harley O. Staggers Jr., W.Va.	
John Bryant, Texas	
Benjamin L. Cardin, Md.	
George E. Sangmeister, Ill.	

Administrative Law and Governmental Relations

225-5741   B351-A RHOB

Frank — chairman

Glickman	*James*
Morrison	*Smith (Texas)*
Staggers	*Douglas*
Cardin	*Smith (Miss.)*
Edwards	

Civil and Constitutional Rights

226-7680 806 HOB Annex #1

Edwards — chairman

Kastenmeier
Conyers
Schroeder
Crockett

Sensenbrenner
Dannemeyer
James

Courts, Intellectual Property and the Administration of Justice

225-3926 2137-B RHOB

Kastenmeier — chairman

Crockett
Berman
Bryant
Cardin
Boucher
Sangmeister
Hughes
Synar

Moorhead
Hyde
Coble
Slaughter
Fish
Sensenbrenner

Crime

225-1695 207 CHOB

Hughes — chairman

Mazzoli
Feighan
Smith (Fla.)
Boucher
Conyers

McCollum
Smith (Miss.)
Gekas
DeWine

Criminal Justice

226-2406 362 HOB Annex #2

Schumer — chairman

Sangmeister
Conyers
Smith (Fla.)
Bryant

Gekas
Coble
Smith (Miss.)

Economic and Commercial Law

225-2825 B353 RHOB

Brooks — chairman

Mazzoli
Glickman
Feighan
Smith (Fla.)
Staggers
Synar
Schroeder
Edwards

Fish
DeWine
Dannemeyer
Douglas
Moorhead
Hyde

Immigration, Refugees and International Law

225-5727 B370B RHOB

Morrison — chairman

Frank
Schumer
Berman
Bryant
Mazzoli

Smith (Texas)
McCollum
Slaughter
Fish

Merchant Marine and Fisheries

225-4047 1334 LHOB

Party Ratio: D 26 - R 17

Walter B. Jones, D-N.C., chairman *

Gerry E. Studds, Mass.
Carroll Hubbard Jr., Ky.
William J. Hughes, N.J.
Earl Hutto, Fla.
W. J. "Billy" Tauzin, La.
Thomas M. Foglietta, Pa.
Dennis M. Hertel, Mich.
Roy Dyson, Md.
William O. Lipinski, Ill.
Robert A. Borski, Pa.
Thomas R. Carper, Del.
Douglas H. Bosco, Calif.
Robin Tallon, S.C.
Solomon P. Ortiz, Texas
Charles E. Bennett, Fla.
Thomas J. Manton, N.Y.
Owen B. Pickett, Va.
Joseph E. Brennan, Maine
George J. Hochbrueckner, N.Y.
Bob Clement, Tenn.
Stephen J. Solarz, N.Y.
Frank Pallone Jr., N.J.
Greg Laughlin, Texas
Nita M. Lowey, N.Y.
Jolene Unsoeld, Wash.

Robert W. Davis, Mich. *
Don Young, Alaska
Norman F. Lent, N.Y.
Norman D. Shumway, Calif.
Jack Fields, Texas
Claudine Schneider, R.I.
Herbert H. Bateman, Va.
H. James Saxton, N.J.
John Miller, Wash.
Helen Delich Bentley, Md.
Howard Coble, N.C.
Curt Weldon, Pa.
Patricia Saiki, Hawaii
Wally Herger, Calif.
Jim Bunning, Ky.
James M. Inhofe, Okla.
Porter J. Goss, Fla.

Coast Guard and Navigation

226-3587 547 HOB Annex #2

Tauzin — chairman

Hutto
Clement
Laughlin
Lowey
Studds
Hughes
Carper
Ortiz
Bennett
Manton
Pickett
Brennan
Hochbrueckner

Davis
Young
Shumway
Bateman
Bentley
Coble
Bunning
Inhofe
Goss

Fisheries and Wildlife Conservation and the Environment

226-3533   543 HOB Annex #2

Studds — chairman

Hughes	*Young*
Carper	*Schneider*
Bosco	*Bateman*
Ortiz	*Saxton*
Manton	*Miller*
Tallon	*Coble*
Hochbrueckner	*Weldon*
Solarz	*Saiki*
Pallone	*Herger*
Unsoeld	
Hutto	
Tauzin	
Dyson	

Merchant Marine

226-3500   531 HOB Annex #2

Jones — chairman

Hubbard	*Lent*
Lipinski	*Young*
Borski	*Shumway*
Bennett	*Fields*
Pickett	*Bateman*
Brennan	*Miller*
Foglietta	*Bentley*
Hertel	*Bunning*
Tallon	*Inhofe*
Solarz	
Pallone	
Laughlin	
Unsoeld	

Oceanography

226-3504   532 HOB Annex #2

Hertel — chairman

Borski	*Shumway*
Clement	*Saxton*
Lowey	*Weldon*
Studds	*Saiki*
Hughes	*Herger*
Bennett	*Goss*
Manton	
Brennan	

Oversight and Investigations

226-3508   541 HOB Annex #2

Foglietta — chairman

Pickett	*Schneider*
Pallone	*Saxton*

Panama Canal/ Outer Continental Shelf

226-3514   579 HOB Annex #2

Dyson — chairman

Lipinski	*Fields*
Laughlin	*Bentley*

Post Office and Civil Service

225-4054   309 CHOB

Party Ratio: D 15 - R 9

William D. Ford, D-Mich., chairman

William L. Clay, Mo.	*Benjamin A. Gilman, N.Y.*
Patricia Schroeder, Colo.	*Frank Horton, N.Y.*
Robert Garcia, N.Y.	*John T. Myers, Ind.*
Mickey Leland, Texas	*Don Young, Alaska*
Gus Yatron, Pa.	*Dan Burton, Ind.*
Mary Rose Oakar, Ohio	*Constance A. Morella, Md.*
Gerry Sikorski, Minn.	*Tom Ridge, Pa.*
Frank McCloskey, Ind.	*Rod Chandler, Wash.*
Gary L. Ackerman, N.Y.	*Vacancy*
Mervyn M. Dymally, Calif.	
Thomas C. Sawyer, Ohio	
Paul E. Kanjorski, Pa.	
Morris K. Udall, Ariz. ‡	
Ron de Lugo, Virgin Islands ‡	

‡ Member appointed temporarily for the 101st Congress only.

Census and Population

226-7523   608 HOB Annex #1

Sawyer — chairman

Garcia	*Ridge*
Dymally	*Chandler*

Civil Service

225-4025   406 CHOB

Sikorski — chairman

Schroeder	*Morella*
McCloskey	*Ridge*

Compensation and Employee Benefits

226-7546   515 HOB Annex #1

Ackerman — chairman

Oakar	*Myers*
Leland	*Morella*

Human Resources

225-2821   603 HOB Annex #1

Kanjorski — chairman

Yatron	*Burton*
Sikorski	*Vacancy*

Investigations

225-6295   219 CHOB

Ford — chairman

Yatron	*Chandler*
Clay	*Gilman*

Postal Operations and Services

225-9124   122 CHOB

Leland — chairman

Clay	*Horton*
Garcia	*Young*
Ackerman	*Vacancy*

Postal Personnel and Modernization

226-7520   209 CHOB

McCloskey — chairman

Sawyer	*Young*
de Lugo	*Myers*

Public Works and Transportation

225-4472 2165 RHOB

Party Ratio: D 31 - R 20

Glenn M. Anderson, D-Calif., chairman *

Robert A. Roe, N.J.	*John Paul Hammerschmidt, Ark.*
Norman Y. Mineta, Calif.	*Bud Shuster, Pa.*
James L. Oberstar, Minn.	*Arlan Stangeland, Minn.*
Henry J. Nowak, N.Y.	*William F. Clinger Jr., Pa.*
Nick J. Rahall II, W.Va.	*Guy V. Molinari, N.Y.*
Doug Applegate, Ohio	*Bob McEwen, Ohio*
Ron de Lugo, Virgin Islands	*Thomas E. Petri, Wis.*
Gus Savage, Ill.	*Ron Packard, Calif.*
Douglas H. Bosco, Calif.	*Sherwood Boehlert, N.Y.*
Robert A. Borski, Pa.	*Jim Ross Lightfoot, Iowa*
Joe Kolter, Pa.	*Dennis Hastert, Ill.*
Tim Valentine, N.C.	*James M. Inhofe, Okla.*
Ed Towns, N.Y.	*Cass Ballenger, N.C.*
William O. Lipinski, Ill.	*Fred Upton, Mich.*
Peter J. Visclosky, Ind.	*Bill Emerson, Mo.*
James A. Traficant Jr., Ohio	*Larry E. Craig, Idaho*
John Lewis, Ga.	*John J. "Jimmy" Duncan Jr., Tenn.*
Peter A. DeFazio, Ore.	*Mel Hancock, Mo.*
Benjamin L. Cardin, Md.	*C. Christopher Cox, Calif.*
David E. Skaggs, Colo.	*Bill Grant, Fla.*
Jimmy Hayes, La.	
Bob Clement, Tenn.	
Lewis F. Payne Jr., Va.	
Jerry F. Costello, Ill.	
Frank Pallone Jr., N.J.	
Ben Jones, Ga.	
Mike Parker, Miss.	
Greg Laughlin, Texas	
Glen Browder, Ala.	
Vacancy	

Aviation

225-9161 2251 RHOB

Oberstar — chairman

Kolter	*Clinger*
de Lugo	*Shuster*
DeFazio	*Stangeland*
Hayes	*Molinari*
Laughlin	*McEwen*
Mineta	*Petri*
Bosco	*Packard*
Valentine	*Boehlert*
Towns	*Lightfoot*
Lipinski	*Inhofe*
Visclosky	*Ballenger*
Traficant	*Duncan*
Skaggs	*Hancock*
Clement	
Payne	
Costello	
Jones	
Nowak	
Lewis	
Vacancy	

Economic Development

225-6151 B376 RHOB

Savage — chairman

Rahall	*McEwen*
Applegate	*Hastert*
Borski	*Ballenger*
Kolter	*Emerson*
Towns	*Craig*
Payne	*Cox*
Vacancy	*Grant*
Vacancy	
Vacancy	
Vacancy	

Investigations and Oversight

225-3274 586 HOB Annex #2

Anderson — chairman

Borski	*Molinari*
Roe	*Clinger*
Mineta	*Shuster*
Oberstar	*Boehlert*
Applegate	*Hastert*
Lipinski	*Inhofe*
Visclosky	*Upton*
Bosco	*Duncan*
Vacancy	*Vacancy*
Vacancy	
Vacancy	
Vacancy	
Vacancy	
Vacancy	

Public Buildings and Grounds

225-9961 B376 RHOB

Bosco — chairman

Lewis	*Petri*
Cardin	*Lightfoot*
Parker	*Duncan*
Nowak	*Cox*
Savage	
Vacancy	

Surface Transportation

225-9989 B376 RHOB

Mineta — chairman

Rahall	*Shuster*
Applegate	*Stangeland*
Valentine	*Clinger*
Towns	*McEwen*
Lipinski	*Packard*
Visclosky	*Boehlert*
Traficant	*Hastert*
Lewis	*Upton*
Cardin	*Emerson*
Skaggs	*Craig*
Clement	*Duncan*
Payne	*Hancock*
Costello	*Cox*
Pallone	*Vacancy*
Jones	
Parker	
Roe	
Nowak	
de Lugo	
Savage	
Laughlin	
Anderson	
Vacancy	

Water Resources

225-0060 B370A RHOB

Nowak — chairman

Roe	*Stangeland*
Oberstar	*Molinari*
Borski	*Petri*
Kolter	*Packard*
DeFazio	*Lightfoot*
Cardin	*Hastert*
Hayes	*Inhofe*
Pallone	*Ballenger*
Parker	*Upton*
Laughlin	*Emerson*
Savage	*Craig*
Clement	*Hancock*
Costello	*Cox*
Jones	
Traficant	
Vacancy	
Vacancy	
Vacancy	
Vacancy	

Rules

225-9486 H-312 Capitol

Party Ratio: D 9 - R 4

Joe Moakley, D-Mass., chairman

Butler Derrick, S.C.	*James H. Quillen, Tenn.*
Anthony C. Beilenson, Calif.	*Gerald B. H. Solomon, N.Y.*
Martin Frost, Texas	*Lynn Martin, Ill.*
David E. Bonior, Mich.	*Charles "Chip" Pashayan Jr., Calif.*
Tony P. Hall, Ohio	
Alan Wheat, Mo.	
Bart Gordon, Tenn.	
Louise M. Slaughter, N.Y.	

Legislative Process

225-1037 1629 LHOB

Derrick — chairman

Frost	*Martin*
Wheat	*Pashayan*
Gordon	
Moakley	

Rules of the House

225-9091 H-152 Capitol

Moakley — chairman

Beilenson	*Solomon*
Bonior	*Pashayan*
Hall	
Slaughter	

Science, Space and Technology

225-6371 2321 RHOB

Party Ratio: D 30 - R 19

Robert A. Roe, D-N.J., chairman *

George E. Brown Jr., Calif.	*Robert S. Walker, Pa.* *
James H. Scheuer, N.Y.	*F. James Sensenbrenner Jr., Wis.*
Marilyn Lloyd, Tenn.	*Claudine Schneider, R.I.*
Doug Walgren, Pa.	*Sherwood Boehlert, N.Y.*
Dan Glickman, Kan.	*Tom Lewis, Fla.*
Harold L. Volkmer, Mo.	*Don Ritter, Pa.*
Howard Wolpe, Mich.	*Sid Morrison, Wash.*
Bill Nelson, Fla.	*Ron Packard, Calif.*
Ralph M. Hall, Texas	*Robert C. Smith, N.H.*
Dave McCurdy, Okla.	*Paul B. Henry, Mich.*
Norman Y. Mineta, Calif.	*Harris W. Fawell, Ill.*
Tim Valentine, N.C.	*D. French Slaughter Jr., Va.*
Robert G. Torricelli, N.J.	*Lamar Smith, Texas*
Rick Boucher, Va.	*Jack Buechner, Mo.*
Terry L. Bruce, Ill.	*Constance A. Morella, Md.*
Richard Stallings, Idaho	*Christopher Shays, Conn.*
James A. Traficant Jr., Ohio	*Dana Rohrabacher, Calif.*
Lee H. Hamilton, Ind.	*Steven H. Schiff, N.M.*
Henry J. Nowak, N.Y	*Tom Campbell, Calif.*
Carl C. Perkins, Ky.	
Tom McMillen, Md.	
David E. Price, N.C.	
Dave Nagle, Iowa	
Jimmy Hayes, La.	
David E. Skaggs, Colo.	
Jerry F. Costello, Ill.	
Harry A. Johnston, Fla.	
John Tanner, Tenn.	
Glen Browder, Ala.	

Energy Research and Development

225-8056 B374 RHOB

Lloyd — chairman

Boucher	*Morrison*
Bruce	*Fawell*
Costello	*Schiff*
Walgren	*Smith (Texas)*
Stallings	*Henry*
Traficant	
Wolpe	
Valentine	

International Scientific Cooperation

225-3636 822 HOB Annex #1

Hall — chairman

Torricelli	*Packard*
Hamilton	*Sensenbrenner*
Brown	*Fawell*
Scheuer	

Investigations and Oversight

225-4494 B374 RHOB

Roe — chairman

Tanner	*Ritter*
Traficant	*Boehlert*
Hayes	
Nagle	

Natural Resources, Agriculture Research and Environment

226-6980 388 HOB Annex #2

Scheuer — chairman

Nowak	*Schneider*
Tanner	*Morrison*
Brown	*Shays*
Wolpe	*Smith (N.H.)*
McCurdy	*Henry*
Valentine	*Smith (Texas)*
McMillen	
Price	
Skaggs	

Science, Research and Technology

225-8844 2319 RHOB

Walgren — chairman

Brown	*Boehlert*
Wolpe	*Schneider*
Hamilton	*Ritter*
Price	*Henry*
Mineta	*Morella*
Bruce	*Campbell*
Nagle	*Slaughter*
Skaggs	*Buechner*
Costello	
Johnston	
Hayes	
Vacancy	

Space Science and Applications

225-7858 2324 RHOB

Nelson — chairman

Volkmer	*Sensenbrenner*
Mineta	*Lewis*
Torricelli	*Packard*
Stallings	*Smith (N.H.)*
Traficant	*Slaughter*
Perkins	*Smith (Texas)*
McMillen	*Buechner*
Nagle	*Rohrabacher*
Hayes	*Morella*
Skaggs	*Schiff*
Johnston	
Scheuer	
Lloyd	
Hall	
Tanner	

Transportation, Aviation and Materials

225-9662 2321 RHOB

Valentine — chairman

Glickman	*Lewis*
McCurdy	*Shays*
Nelson	*Rohrabacher*
McMillen	*Campbell*
Brown	
Vacancy	

Small Business

225-5821 2361 RHOB

Party Ratio: D 27 - R 17

John J. LaFalce, D-N.Y., chairman *

Neal Smith, Iowa	*Joseph M. McDade, Pa.* *
Thomas A. Luken, Ohio	*Silvio O. Conte, Mass.*
Ike Skelton, Mo.	*William S. Broomfield, Mich.*
Romano L. Mazzoli, Ky.	*Andy Ireland, Fla.*
Nicholas Mavroules, Mass.	*John Hiler, Ind.*
Charles Hatcher, Ga.	*David Dreier, Calif.*
Ron Wyden, Ore.	*D. French Slaughter Jr., Va.*
Dennis E. Eckart, Ohio	*Jan Meyers, Kan.*
Gus Savage, Ill.	*Larry Combest, Texas*
Norman Sisisky, Va.	*Richard H. Baker, La.*
Esteban E. Torres, Calif.	*John J. Rhodes III, Ariz.*
Jim Cooper, Tenn.	*Joel Hefley, Colo.*
Jim Olin, Va.	*Fred Upton, Mich.*
Richard Ray, Ga.	*Clyde C. Holloway, La.*
Charles A. Hayes, Ill.	*Mel Hancock, Mo.*
John Conyers Jr., Mich.	*Tom Campbell, Calif.*
James Bilbray, Nev.	*Ronald K. Machtley, R.I.*
Kweisi Mfume, Md.	
Floyd H. Flake, N.Y.	
H. Martin Lancaster, N.C.	
Michael R. McNulty, N.Y.	
Bill Sarpalius, Texas	
Peter Hoagland, Neb.	
Richard E. Neal, Mass.	
Glenn Poshard, Ill.	
Eliot L. Engel, N.Y.	

Antitrust, Impact of Deregulation and Privatization

225-6026 B363 RHOB

Eckart — chairman

Luken	*Dreier*
Cooper	*Campbell*
Bilbray	*Slaughter*
Neal	

Environment and Labor

225-7673 H2-558 HOB Annex #2

Torres — chairman

Poshard	*Hiler*
Engel	*Combest*
Cooper	*Upton*
Vacancy	

Exports, Tax Policy and Special Problems

225-8944 B363 RHOB

Sisisky — chairman

Ray	*Ireland*
Hoagland	*Slaughter*
Mazzoli	*Meyers*
Lancaster	*Rhodes*
McNulty	
Bilbray	

Procurement, Tourism and Rural Development

225-9368 B363 RHOB

Skelton — chairman

Hatcher	*Conte*
Bilbray	*Baker*
Lancaster	*Rhodes*
McNulty	*Hefley*
Sarpalius	*Upton*
Neal	*Holloway*
Poshard	
Torres	
Mfume	

Regulation, Business Opportunity and Energy

225-7797 B363 RHOB

Wyden — chairman

Engel	*Broomfield*
Sisisky	*Hefley*
Olin	*Hancock*
McNulty	

SBA, the General Economy and Minority Enterprise Development

225-5821 2361 RHOB

LaFalce — chairman

Smith	*McDade*
Mazzoli	*Meyers*
Mavroules	*Combest*
Savage	*Baker*
Cooper	*Holloway*
Olin	*Hancock*
Hayes	*Campbell*
Conyers	
Mfume	
Flake	

Standards of Official Conduct

225-7103 HT-2 Capitol

Party Ratio: D 6 - R 6

Julian C. Dixon, D-Calif., chairman

Vic Fazio, Calif.	*John T. Myers, Ind.*
Bernard J. Dwyer, N.J.	*James V. Hansen, Utah*
Alan B. Mollohan, W.Va.	*Charles "Chip" Pashayan Jr., Calif.*
Joseph M. Gaydos, Pa.	*Thomas E. Petri, Wis.*
Chester G. Atkins, Mass.	*Larry E. Craig, Idaho*
	Fred Grandy, Iowa

Veterans' Affairs

225-3527 335 CHOB

Party Ratio: D 21 - R 13

G. V. "Sonny" Montgomery, D-Miss., chairman *

Don Edwards, Calif.	*Bob Stump, Ariz. **
Doug Applegate, Ohio	*John Paul Hammerschmidt, Ark.*
Lane Evans, Ill.	*Chalmers P. Wylie, Ohio*
Timothy J. Penny, Minn.	*Bob McEwen, Ohio*
Harley O. Staggers Jr., W.Va.	*Christopher H. Smith, N.J.*
J. Roy Rowland, Ga.	*Dan Burton, Ind.*
James J. Florio, N.J.	*Michael Bilirakis, Fla.*
Tommy F. Robinson, Ark.	*Tom Ridge, Pa.*
Charles W. Stenholm, Texas	*John G. Rowland, Conn.*
Claude Harris, Ala.	*Robert C. Smith, N.H.*
Joseph P. Kennedy II, Mass.	*Craig T. James, Fla.*
Liz J. Patterson, S.C.	*Cliff Stearns, Fla.*
Tim Johnson, S.D.	*Bill Paxon, N.Y.*
Jim Jontz, Ind.	
Lewis F. Payne Jr., Va.	
Bruce A. Morrison, Conn.	
George E. Sangmeister, Ill.	
Mike Parker, Miss.	
Ben Jones, Ga.	
Jill Long, Ind.	

Compensation, Pension and Insurance

225-3569 337 CHOB

Applegate — chairman

Sangmeister	*McEwen*
Parker	*Wylie*
Evans	*Bilirakis*
Penny	
Jones	

Education, Training and Employment

225-9166 337-A CHOB

Penny — chairman

Robinson	*Smith (N.J.)*
Patterson	*Wylie*
Sangmeister	*Ridge*
Evans	

Hospitals and Health Care

225-9154 338 CHOB

Montgomery — chairman

Rowland (Ga.)	*Hammerschmidt*
Florio	*Stump*
Robinson	*McEwen*
Stenholm	*Smith (N.J.)*
Harris	*Burton*
Kennedy	*Bilirakis*
Patterson	*Ridge*
Johnson	*Rowland (Conn.)*
Jontz	
Payne	
Morrison	

Housing and Memorial Affairs

225-9164 337 CHOB

Staggers — chairman

Jones	*Burton*
Rowland (Ga.)	*Rowland (Conn.)*
Harris	*Smith (N.H.)*
Payne	*Paxon*
Parker	
Florio	

Oversight and Investigations

225-3541 335 CHOB

Evans — chairman

Edwards	*Stump*
Applegate	*Smith (N.H.)*
Florio	*James*
Kennedy	*Stearns*
Long	

Ways and Means

225-3625 1102 LHOB

Party Ratio: D 23 - R 13

Dan Rostenkowski, D-Ill., chairman *

Democrats	Republicans
Sam M. Gibbons, Fla.	*Bill Archer, Texas* *
J. J. "Jake" Pickle, Texas	*Guy Vander Jagt, Mich.*
Charles B. Rangel, N.Y.	*Philip M. Crane, Ill.*
Pete Stark, Calif.	*Bill Frenzel, Minn.*
Andrew Jacobs Jr., Ind.	*Richard T. Schulze, Pa.*
Harold E. Ford, Tenn.	*Bill Gradison, Ohio*
Ed Jenkins, Ga.	*Bill Thomas, Calif.*
Thomas J. Downey, N.Y.	*Raymond J. McGrath, N.Y.*
Frank J. Guarini, N.J.	*Hank Brown, Colo.*
Marty Russo, Ill.	*Rod Chandler, Wash.*
Don J. Pease, Ohio	*E. Clay Shaw Jr., Fla.*
Robert T. Matsui, Calif.	*Don Sundquist, Tenn.*
Beryl Anthony Jr., Ark.	*Nancy L. Johnson, Conn.*
Ronnie G. Flippo, Ala.	
Byron L. Dorgan, N.D.	
Barbara B. Kennelly, Conn.	
Brian Donnelly, Mass.	
William J. Coyne, Pa.	
Michael A. Andrews, Texas	
Sander M. Levin, Mich.	
Jim Moody, Wis.	
Vacancy	

Health

225-7785 1114 LHOB

Stark — chairman

Donnelly	*Gradison*
Coyne	*Chandler*
Pickle	*Crane*
Anthony	*Johnson*
Levin	
Moody	

Oversight

225-2743 1105 LHOB

Pickle — chairman

Anthony	*Schulze*
Flippo	*McGrath*
Dorgan	*Chandler*
Ford	*Shaw*
Rangel	
Jacobs	

Human Resources

225-1025 B317 RHOB

Downey — acting chairman †

Ford	*Shaw*
Pease	*Brown*
Matsui	*Sundquist*
Kennelly	*Johnson*
Andrews	
Coyne	

† Subcommittee Chairman Ford was indicted April 24, 1987, on charges of bank, mail and tax fraud. House Democratic Caucus rules require that an indicted member step down from his chairmanship for the duration of the session or until charges are dismissed.

Select Revenue Measures

225-9710 1111 LHOB

Rangel — chairman

Flippo	*Vander Jagt*
Dorgan	*McGrath*
Kennelly	*Brown*
Andrews	*Sundquist*
Stark	
Donnelly	

Social Security

225-9263 B316 RHOB

Jacobs — chairman

Gibbons	*Brown*
Levin	*Schulze*
Moody	*Gradison*
Vacancy	

Trade

225-3943 1136 LHOB

Gibbons — chairman

Rostenkowski	*Crane*
Jenkins	*Vander Jagt*
Downey	*Frenzel*
Pease	*Schulze*
Russo	*Thomas*
Guarini	
Matsui	
Vacancy	

Select Aging

226-3375 712 HOB Annex #1

Party Ratio: D 39 - R 27

Edward R. Roybal, D-Calif., chairman *

Democrats	Republicans
Thomas J. Downey, N.Y.	*Matthew J. Rinaldo, N.J.* *
James J. Florio, N.J.	*John Paul Hammerschmidt, Ark.*
Harold E. Ford, Tenn.	*Ralph Regula, Ohio*
William J. Hughes, N.J.	*Norman D. Shumway, Calif.*
Marilyn Lloyd, Tenn.	*Olympia J. Snowe, Maine*
Mary Rose Oakar, Ohio	*Tom Tauke, Iowa*
Thomas A. Luken, Ohio	*Jim Courter, N.J.*
Beverly B. Byron, Md.	*Claudine Schneider, R.I.*
Henry A. Waxman, Calif.	*Tom Ridge, Pa.*
Mike Synar, Okla.	*Christopher H. Smith, N.J.*
Butler Derrick, S.C.	*Sherwood Boehlert, N.Y.*
Bruce F. Vento, Minn.	*H. James Saxton, N.J.*
Barney Frank, Mass.	*Helen Delich Bentley, Md.*
Tom Lantos, Calif.	*Jim Ross Lightfoot, Iowa*
Ron Wyden, Ore.	*Harris W. Fawell, Ill.*
George W. Crockett Jr., Mich.	*Jan Meyers, Kan.*
Ike Skelton, Mo.	*Ben Blaz, Guam*
Dennis M. Hertel, Mich.	*Paul B. Henry, Mich.*
Robert A. Borski, Pa.	*Bill Schuette, Mich.*
Ben Erdreich, Ala.	*Floyd D. Spence, S.C.*
Norman Sisisky, Va.	*William F. Clinger Jr., Pa.*
Bob Wise, W.Va.	*Constance A. Morella, Md.*
Bill Richardson, N.M.	*Patricia Saiki, Hawaii*
Harold L. Volkmer, Mo.	*John Porter, Ill.*
Bart Gordon, Tenn.	*John J. "Jimmy" Duncan Jr., Tenn.*
Thomas J. Manton, N.Y.	*Cliff Stearns, Fla.*
Tommy F. Robinson, Ark.	*Craig T. James, Fla.*
Richard Stallings, Idaho	
James McClure Clarke, N.C.	
Joseph P. Kennedy II, Mass.	
Louise M. Slaughter, N.Y.	
James Bilbray, Nev.	
Jim Jontz, Ind.	
Jerry F. Costello, Ill.	
Harley O. Staggers Jr., W.Va.	
Frank Pallone Jr., N.J.	
Jolene Unsoeld, Wash.	
Vacancy	

Health and Long-Term Care

226-3381 377 HOB Annex #2

Vacancy

Florio
Ford
Oakar
Luken
Waxman
Synar
Derrick
Vento
Frank
Wyden
Skelton
Hertel
Borski
Erdreich
Sisisky
Wise
Richardson

Regula
Rinaldo
Schneider
Ridge
Smith
Boehlert
Saxton
Bentley
Lightfoot
Fawell
Henry
Clinger

Housing and Consumer Interests

226-3344 717 HOB Annex #1

Florio — chairman

Lloyd
Byron
Lantos
Volkmer
Gordon
Manton
Bilbray
Pallone
Unsoeld

Courter
Hammerschmidt
Ridge
Fawell
Schuette
Duncan
James

Human Services

226-3348 716 HOB Annex #1

Downey — chairman

Hughes
Lantos
Richardson
Robinson
Clarke
Kennedy
Slaughter
Staggers
Pallone
Vacancy

Snowe
Shumway
Blaz
Spence
Clinger
Morella
Saiki
Duncan

Retirement, Income and Employment

226-3335 714 HOB Annex #1

Roybal — chairman

Downey
Lloyd
Oakar
Synar
Crockett
Wise
Volkmer
Manton
Stallings
Jontz
Costello

Tauke
Shumway
Meyers
Schuette
Spence
Porter
Stearns
James

Select Children, Youth and Families

226-7660 385 HOB Annex #2

Party Ratio: D 18 - R 12

George Miller, D-Calif., chairman *

William Lehman, Fla.
Patricia Schroeder, Colo.
Lindy (Mrs. Hale) Boggs, La.
Matthew F. McHugh, N.Y.
Ted Weiss, N.Y.
Beryl Anthony Jr., Ark.
Barbara Boxer, Calif.
Sander M. Levin, Mich.
Bruce A. Morrison, Conn.
J. Roy Rowland, Ga.
Gerry Sikorski, Minn.
Alan Wheat, Mo.
Matthew G. Martinez, Calif.
Lane Evans, Ill.
Richard J. Durbin, Ill.
David E. Skaggs, Colo.
Bill Sarpalius, Texas

Thomas J. Bliley Jr., Va. *
Frank R. Wolf, Va.
Barbara F. Vucanovich, Nev.
Ron Packard, Calif.
Dennis Hastert, Ill.
Clyde C. Holloway, La.
Fred Grandy, Iowa
Curt Weldon, Pa.
Lamar Smith, Texas
Peter Smith, Vt.
James T. Walsh, N.Y.
Ronald K. Machtley, R.I.

— Task Forces —

Crisis Intervention

226-7660 385 HOB Annex #2

As of press time, task force had not yet been organized.

Economic Security

226-7660 385 HOB Annex #2

As of press time, task force had not yet been organized.

Prevention Strategies

226-7660 385 HOB Annex #2

As of press time, task force had not yet been organized.

Select Hunger

226-5470 507 HOB Annex #2

Party Ratio: D 18 - R 12

Mickey Leland, D-Texas, chairman *
Bill Emerson, R-Mo., vice chairman *

Tony P. Hall, Ohio
Leon E. Panetta, Calif.
Vic Fazio, Calif.
Peter H. Kostmayer, Pa.
Byron L. Dorgan, N.D.
Bob Carr, Mich.
Timothy J. Penny, Minn.
Gary L. Ackerman, N.Y.
Mike Espy, Miss.
Floyd H. Flake, N.Y.
Liz J. Patterson, S.C.
Thomas M. Foglietta, Pa.
Albert G. Bustamante, Texas
Michael R. McNulty, N.Y.
Eni F. H. Faleomavaega, American Samoa
Eliot L. Engel, N.Y.
Les AuCoin, Ore.

Marge Roukema, N.J.
Sid Morrison, Wash.
Benjamin A. Gilman, N.Y.
Bob Smith, Ore.
Doug Bereuter, Neb.
Fred Upton, Mich.
Wally Herger, Calif.
Duncan Hunter, Calif.
Frank R. Wolf, Va.
Christopher H. Smith, N.J.
Vacancy

— Task Forces —

Domestic

226-5470 507 HOB Annex #2

Espy — chairman

Panetta	*Vacancy*
Ackerman	*Roukema*
Flake	*Morrison*
Patterson	*Upton*
Bustamante	
Engel	
AuCoin	

International

226-5470 507 HOB Annex #2

Hall — chairman

Fazio	*Smith (Ore.)*
Kostmayer	*Bereuter*
Dorgan	*Morrison*
Carr	*Gilman*
Penny	*Herger*
Foglietta	
McNulty	
Faleomavaega	

Select Intelligence

225-4121 H-405 Capitol

Party Ratio: D 12 - R 7

Anthony C. Beilenson, D-Calif., chairman

Dave McCurdy, Okla.	*Henry J. Hyde, Ill.*
Robert W. Kastenmeier, Wis.	*Bob Livingston, La.*
Robert A. Roe, N.J.	*Bud Shuster, Pa.*
Matthew F. McHugh, N.Y.	*Larry Combest, Texas*
Bernard J. Dwyer, N.J.	*Doug Bereuter, Neb.*
Charles Wilson, Texas	*John G. Rowland, Conn.*
Barbara B. Kennelly, Conn.	*Robert K. Dornan, Calif.*
Dan Glickman, Kan.	
Nicholas Mavroules, Mass.	
Bill Richardson, N.M.	
Stephen J. Solarz, N.Y.	

Legislation

225-7311 H-405 Capitol

McHugh — chairman

Kastenmeier	*Livingston*
Kennelly	*Rowland*
Glickman	*Dornan*
Richardson	
Solarz	

Oversight and Evaluation

225-5658 H-405 Capitol

McCurdy — chairman

Roe	*Shuster*
Kennelly	*Combest*
Mavroules	*Bereuter*
McHugh	
Dwyer	

Program and Budget Authorization

225-7690 H-405 Capitol

Beilenson — chairman

Kastenmeier	*Hyde*
Dwyer	*Shuster*
Wilson	*Livingston*
Glickman	*Combest*
Richardson	
Solarz	
McCurdy	

Select Narcotics Abuse and Control

226-3040 234 HOB Annex #2

Party Ratio: D 18 - R 12

Charles B. Rangel, D-N.Y., chairman

Jack Brooks, Texas	*Lawrence Coughlin, Pa.*
Pete Stark, Calif.	*Benjamin A. Gilman, N.Y.*
James H. Scheuer, N.Y.	*Michael G. Oxley, Ohio*
Cardiss Collins, Ill.	*Stan Parris, Va.*
Daniel K. Akaka, Hawaii	*F. James Sensenbrenner Jr., Wis.*
Frank J. Guarini, N.J.	*Robert K. Dornan, Calif.*
Dante B. Fascell, Fla.	*Tom Lewis, Fla.*
Walter E. Fauntroy, D.C.	*James M. Inhofe, Okla.*
William J. Hughes, N.J.	*Wally Herger, Calif.*
Mel Levine, Calif.	*Christopher Shays, Conn.*
Solomon P. Ortiz, Texas	*Bill Paxon, N.Y.*
Lawrence J. Smith, Fla.	*Bill Grant, Fla.*
Ed Towns, N.Y.	
James A. Traficant Jr., Ohio	
Kweisi Mfume, Md.	
Joseph E. Brennan, Maine	
Nita M. Lowey, N.Y.	

Partisan Committees

Democratic Leaders

Speaker of the House — Thomas S. Foley, Wash.	225-5604
Majority Leader — Richard A. Gephardt, Mo.	225-0100
Majority Whip — William H. Gray III, Pa.	225-3130
Chairman of the Caucus — Steny H. Hoyer, Md.	226-3210
Vice Chairman of the Caucus — Vic Fazio, Calif.	226-3210
Chief Deputy Whip — David E. Bonior, Mich.	225-0800

Deputy Whips — Tom Bevill, Ala.; Dennis E. Eckart, Ohio; Martin Frost, Texas; W. G. "Bill" Hefner, N.C.; Steny H. Hoyer, Md.; Peter H. Kostmayer, Pa.; Norman Y. Mineta, Calif.; Joe Moakley, Mass.; Charles B. Rangel, N.Y.; Marty Russo, Ill.; Martin Olav Sabo, Minn.; Patricia Schroeder, Colo.; Lawrence J. Smith, Fla.; Pat Williams, Mont.

Whip Task Force Chairmen — Bart Gordon, Tenn.; David R. Obey, Wis.; Leon E. Panetta, Calif.

At-Large Whips — Les Aspin, Wis.; Chester G. Atkins, Mass.; Les AuCoin, Ore.; Howard L. Berman, Calif.; Rick Boucher, Va.; Barbara Boxer, Calif.; Joseph E. Brennan, Maine; Terry L. Bruce, Ill.; Benjamin L. Cardin, Md.; Bob Carr, Mich.; George "Buddy" Darden, Ga.; Butler Derrick, S.C.; Norm Dicks, Wash.; Brian Donnelly, Mass.; Byron L. Dorgan, N.D.; Richard J. Durbin, Ill.; Mike Espy, Miss.; Lane Evans, Ill.; Vic Fazio, Calif.; Ronnie G. Flippo, Ala.; William D. Ford, Mich.; Barney Frank, Mass.; Sam Gejdenson, Conn.; Dan Glickman, Kan.; Frank J. Guarini, N.J.; Ed Jenkins, Ga.; Ben Jones, Ga.; Jim Jontz, Ind.; Barbara B. Kennelly, Conn.; Dale E. Kildee, Mich.; H. Martin Lancaster, N.C.; Richard H. Lehman, Calif.; Mickey Leland, Texas; Mel Levine, Calif.; John Lewis, Ga.; Michael R. McNulty, N.Y.; Dave McCurdy, Okla.; Robert T. Matsui, Calif.; Kweisi Mfume, Md.; George Miller, Calif.; Bruce A. Morrison, Conn.; Robert J. Mrazek, N.Y.; John P. Murtha, Pa.; Dave Nagle, Iowa; Mary Rose Oakar, Ohio; James L. Oberstar, Minn.; Timothy J. Penny, Minn.; Bill Richardson, N.M.; Charlie Rose, N.C.; Dan Rostenkowski, Ill.; Charles E. Schumer, N.Y.; Philip R. Sharp, Ind.; Gerry Sikorski, Minn.; David E. Skaggs, Colo.; Louise M. Slaughter, N.Y.; John M. Spratt Jr., S.C.; Al Swift, Wash.; Mike Synar, Okla.; W. J. "Billy" Tauzin, La.; Robert G. Torricelli, N.J.; Peter J. Visclosky, Ind.; Harold L. Volkmer, Mo.; Bob Wise, W.Va.; Howard Wolpe, Mich.; Ron Wyden, Ore.

Assistant Whips, by zone numbers:

1. Nancy Pelosi, Calif., and Esteban E. Torres, Calif. — California
2. Jim McDermott, Wash. — Arizona, Colorado, Hawaii, Montana, Nevada, New Mexico, Oregon, Utah, Washington, American Samoa
3. Bruce F. Vento, Minn. — Iowa, Minnesota, Nebraska, North Dakota, South Dakota, Wisconsin
4. Sidney R. Yates, Ill. — Illinois, Indiana
5. Tommy F. Robinson, Ark. — Arkansas, Kansas, Missouri, Oklahoma
6. Ronald D. Coleman, Texas, and John Bryant, Texas — Texas
7. Gerry E. Studds, Mass. — Connecticut, Massachusetts, Maine, Virgin Islands, Puerto Rico, District of Columbia
8. Gary L. Ackerman, N.Y., and Thomas J. Downey, N.Y. — New York
9. William J. Hughes, N.J. — New Jersey, Pennsylvania
10. Dennis M. Hertel, Mich., and Thomas A. Luken, Ohio — Michigan, Ohio
11. Carroll Hubbard Jr., Ky. — Delaware, Kentucky, Maryland, Virginia, West Virginia
12. Tim Valentine, N.C. — North Carolina, South Carolina, Tennessee
13. Jimmy Hayes, La. — Alabama, Georgia, Louisiana, Mississippi
14. Harry A. Johnston, Fla. — Florida

The five states not covered — Alaska, New Hampshire, Rhode Island, Vermont and Wyoming — have no Democratic representatives.

Steering and Policy Committee

225-8550 H-324 Capitol

Thomas S. Foley, Wash., chairman
Richard A. Gephardt, Mo., vice chairman
Steny H. Hoyer, Md., 2nd vice chairman

Beryl Anthony Jr., Ark. †	Marcy Kaptur, Ohio *
David E. Bonior, Mich. †	Robert T. Matsui, Calif.
Jim Chapman, Texas *	Frank McCloskey, Ind.
Bob Clement, Tenn. *	Matthew F. McHugh, N.Y.
Butler Derrick, S.C.	Joe Moakley, Mass. †
John D. Dingell, Mich. *	John P. Murtha, Pa.
Brian Donnelly, Mass. *	James L. Oberstar, Minn. *
Vic Fazio, Calif. †	Leon E. Panetta, Calif. †
Ronnie G. Flippo, Ala.	Dan Rostenkowski, Ill. †
Harold E. Ford, Tenn. *	Norman Sisisky, Va.
Martin Frost, Texas	Bob Traxler, Mich.
Sam Gejdenson, Conn.	Wes Watkins, Okla. *
Dan Glickman, Kan.	Pat Williams, Mont.
William H. Gray III, Pa. †	Jamie L. Whitten, Miss. †

† Member *ex officio* from the leadership.
* Member appointed by the Speaker of the House.

Personnel Committee

225-4068 B343 RHOB

Jack Brooks, Texas

Democratic Congressional Campaign Committee

863-1500 430 S. Capitol St. S.E. 20003
Beryl Anthony Jr., Ark., chairman
Dan Rostenkowski, Ill., vice chairman

Co-Chairs: Michael A. Andrews, Texas; Richard J. Durbin, Ill.; Dennis E. Eckart, Ohio *; Mel Levine, Calif.; Thomas J. Manton, N.Y.; Lawrence J. Smith, Fla. *

Oversight Subcommittee: John D. Dingell, Mich; Dave Nagle, Iowa; Mike Synar, Okla.

Gary L. Ackerman, N.Y.	Richard A. Gephardt, Mo. *
Daniel K. Akaka, Hawaii	Bart Gordon, Tenn.
Bill Alexander, Ark.	Lee H. Hamilton, Ind.
Frank Annunzio, Ill.	W. G. "Bill" Hefner, N.C.
Les AuCoin, Ore.	Peter Hoagland, Neb.
Tom Bevill, Ala.	Ed Jenkins, Ga.
James Bilbray, Nev.	Tim Johnson, S.D.
Joseph E. Brennan, Maine	Harry A. Johnston, Fla.
Beverly B. Byron, Md.	Gerald D. Kleczka, Wis.
Thomas R. Carper, Del.	Richard H. Lehman, Calif.
William L. Clay, Mo.	Mickey Leland, Texas
Ron de Lugo, Virgin Islands	Alan B. Mollohan, W.Va.
Norm Dicks, Wash.	John P. Murtha, Pa.
John D. Dingell, Mich.	Dave Nagle, Iowa
Byron L. Dorgan, N.D.	Mary Rose Oakar, Ohio *
Mervyn M. Dymally, Calif. *	James L. Oberstar, Minn.
Joseph D. Early, Mass.	Jim Olin, Va.
Mike Espy, Miss.	Wayne Owens, Utah
Eni F. H. Faleomavaega, American Samoa	Carl C. Perkins, Ky.
Walter E. Fauntroy, D.C.	Bill Richardson, N.M.
Vic Fazio, Calif. *	Patricia Schroeder, Colo.
Edward F. Feighan, Ohio	Jim Slattery, Kan.
James J. Florio, N.J.	John M. Spratt Jr., S.C.
Thomas S. Foley, Wash. †	Richard Stallings, Idaho
Jaime B. Fuster, Puerto Rico	Mike Synar, Okla.
Sam Gejdenson, Conn.	W. J. "Billy" Tauzin, La.
	Morris K. Udall, Ariz.
	Pat Williams, Mont.

† Member *ex officio* from the leadership.
* Member appointed by the Speaker of the House.

Republican Leaders

Minority Leader —
Robert H. Michel, Ill. 225-0600
Minority Whip —
Newt Gingrich, Ga. * 225-0197
Chairman of the Conference —
Jerry Lewis, Calif. 225-5107
Vice Chairman of the Conference —
Bill McCollum, Fla. 225-5107
Secretary of the Conference —
Vin Weber, Minn. 225-5107
Chief Deputy Whips —
Steve Gunderson, Wis.; Robert S. Walker, Pa. 225-0197
Deputy Whips — Joe L. Barton, Texas; Nancy L. Johnson, Conn.; Jon Kyl, Ariz.; Fred Upton, Mich.
Regional Whips — Dean A. Gallo, N.J.; Bill Grant, Fla.; John Hiler, Ind.; Andy Ireland, Fla.; John Miller, Wash.
Strategy Whips — Dick Armey, Texas; Steve Bartlett, Texas; Jack Buechner, Mo.; Rod Chandler, Wash.; Larry E. Craig, Idaho
Freshman Class Whip — Bill Paxon, N.Y.

Committee on Committees

225-0600 H-230 Capitol

Robert H. Michel, Ill., chairman

Bill Archer, Texas
William S. Broomfield, Mich.
Jim Bunning, Ky.
Rod Chandler, Wash.
Jim Courter, N.J.
Bill Dickinson, Ala.
Mickey Edwards, Okla.
Dennis Hastert, Ill.
Frank Horton, N.Y.
Newt Gingrich, Ga.
Jerry Lewis, Calif.
Jim McCrery, La.
Joseph M. McDade, Pa.
Stan Parris, Va.
Ralph Regula, Ohio
Arlan Stangeland, Minn.
Cliff Stearns, Fla.
Bob Stump, Ariz.
Don Young, Alaska
C. W. Bill Young, Fla.

Policy Committee

225-6168 1616 LHOB

Mickey Edwards, Okla., chairman

Bill Archer, Texas
Doug Bereuter, Neb.
Jack Buechner, Mo.
Tom Campbell, Calif.
Silvio O. Conte, Mass.
Tom DeLay, Texas
Mickey Edwards, Okla.
Bill Frenzel, Minn.
Paul E. Gillmor, Ohio
Newt Gingrich, Ga.
Bill Goodling, Pa.
Fred Grandy, Iowa
Bill Green, N.Y.
Steve Gunderson, Wis.
Dennis Hastert, Ill.
Paul B. Henry, Mich.
Duncan Hunter, Calif.
Nancy L. Johnson, Conn.
Jerry Lewis, Calif.
Bill McCollum, Fla.
Robert H. Michel, Ill.
James H. Quillen, Tenn.
John J. Rhodes III, Ariz.
Peter Smith, Vt.
Olympia J. Snowe, Maine
Floyd Spence, S.C.
Don Sundquist, Tenn.
Guy Vander Jagt, Mich.
James T. Walsh, N.Y.
Vin Weber, Minn.
Vacancy

National Republican Congressional Committee

479-7000 320 First St. S.E. 20003

Guy Vander Jagt, Mich., chairman

Michael Bilirakis, Fla.
Ben Blaz, Guam
Jack Buechner, Mo.
Sonny Callahan, Ala.
Howard Coble, N.C.
Silvio O. Conte, Mass.
Lawrence Coughlin, Pa.
C. Christopher Cox, Calif.
Larry E. Craig, Idaho
David Dreier, Calif.
Mickey Edwards, Okla. †
Harris W. Fawell, Ill.
Jack Fields, Texas
Newt Gingrich, Ga. †
John Paul Hammerschmidt, Ark.
James V. Hansen, Utah
John Hiler, Ind.
Larry J. Hopkins, Ky.
Duncan Hunter, Calif. †
James M. Inhofe, Okla.
Jim Kolbe, Ariz.
Jerry Lewis, Calif. †
Jim Ross Lightfoot, Iowa
Bob Livingston, La.
Ron Marlenee, Mont.
David O'B. Martin, N.Y.
Bill McCollum, Fla. †
Robert H. Michel, Ill. †
Constance A. Morella, Md.
Sid Morrison, Wash.
Michael G. Oxley, Ohio
Matthew J. Rinaldo, N.J.
Pat Roberts, Kan.
John G. Rowland, Conn.
Patricia Saiki, Hawaii
Dan Schaefer, Colo.
Claudine Schneider, R.I.
F. James Sensenbrenner Jr., Wis.
Joe Skeen, N.M.
Denny Smith, Ore.
Larkin Smith, Miss.
Peter Smith, Vt.
Robert C. Smith, N.H.
Virginia Smith, Neb.
Olympia J. Snowe, Maine
Floyd D. Spence, S.C.
Don Sundquist, Tenn.
Bill Thomas, Calif.
Craig Thomas, Wyo.
Fred Upton, Mich.
Barbara F. Vucanovich, Nev.
Vin Weber, Minn. †
Frank R. Wolf, Va.
Don Young, Alaska

† Member *ex officio* from the leadership.

Research Committee

225-0871 1622 LHOB

Duncan Hunter, Calif., chairman

Executive Committee

Doug Bereuter, Neb.
Jack Buechner, Mo.
Larry Combest, Texas
Robert K. Dornan, Calif.
Mickey Edwards, Okla.
Newt Gingrich, Ga.
Bill Gradison, Ohio
Bill Grant, Fla.
Steve Gunderson, Wis.
Frank Horton, N.Y.
Henry Hyde, Ill.
Craig T. James, Fla.
Jon Kyl, Ariz.
Jerry Lewis, Calif.
Bill McCollum, Fla.
Robert H. Michel, Ill.
John J. Rhodes III, Ariz.
Pat Roberts, Kan.
Norman D. Shumway, Calif.
Vin Weber, Minn.
C. W. Bill Young, Fla.

Joint Committee Assignments
101st Congress

The joint committees of Congress are listed below in alphabetical order. The listing includes the room number, ZIP code and telephone number. The telephone area code for Washington, D.C., is 202.

Membership is drawn from both chambers and both parties. Membership is given in order of seniority on the committees and subcommittees.

In the listing, Democrats are listed on the left in roman type; Republicans are listed on the right in italics. When a senator serves as chairman, the vice chairman is usually a representative, and vice versa. The chairmanship usually rotates from one chamber to the other at the beginning of each Congress.

Economic

224-5171 SD-G01

Rep. Lee H. Hamilton, D-Ind., chairman

Sen. Paul S. Sarbanes, D-Md., vice chairman

Senate Members

Lloyd Bentsen, Texas	*William V. Roth Jr., Del.*
Edward M. Kennedy, Mass.	*Steve Symms, Idaho*
Jeff Bingaman, N.M.	*Pete Wilson, Calif.*
Al Gore, Tenn.	*Connie Mack, Fla.*
Richard H. Bryan, Nev.	

House Members

Augustus F. Hawkins, Calif.	*Chalmers P. Wylie, Ohio*
David R. Obey, Wis.	*Olympia J. Snowe, Maine*
James H. Scheuer, N.Y.	*Hamilton Fish Jr., N.Y.*
Pete Stark, Calif.	*Fred Upton, Mich.*
Stephen J. Solarz, N.Y.	

Economic Goals and Intergovernmental Policy

224-5171 SD-G01

Rep. Hamilton — chairman

Senate Members

Bentsen	*Roth*
Kennedy	*Wilson*

House Members

Hawkins	*Wylie*
	Snowe

Economic Growth, Trade and Taxes

224-5171 SD-G01

Sen. Bentsen — chairman

Senate Members

	Roth
	Mack

House Members

Hamilton	*Wylie*
Stark	*Upton*
Solarz	

Economic Resources and Competitiveness

224-5171 SD-G01

Rep. Obey — chairman

Senate Members

Sarbanes	*Symms*
Bingaman	
Gore	
Bryan	

House Members

Solarz	*Upton*

Education and Health

224-5171 SD-G01

Rep. Scheuer — chairman

Senate Members

Bentsen	*Wilson*
Bingaman	
Gore	

House Members

Hawkins	*Snowe*
	Fish

Fiscal and Monetary Policy

224-5171 SD-G01

Sen. Kennedy — chairman

Senate Members

	Symms

House Members

Obey	*Upton*
Stark	

International Economic Policy

224-5171 SD-G01

Sen. Sarbanes — chairman

Senate Members

Kennedy	*Roth*
	Mack

House Members

Hamilton	*Wylie*
Solarz	*Snowe*

Investment, Jobs and Prices

224-5171 SD-G01

Rep. Hawkins – chairman

Senate Members

Gore	*Symms*
Bryan	

House Members

Scheuer	*Fish*
Solarz	
Stark	

National Security Economics

224-5171 SD-G01

Sen. Bingaman – chairman

Senate Members

Sarbanes	*Wilson*
Bryan	*Mack*

House Members

Obey	*Fish*
Scheuer	

Library

226-7633 103 HOB Annex #1

Rep. Frank Annunzio, D-Ill., chairman

Sen. Claiborne Pell, D-R.I., vice chairman

Senate Members

Dennis DeConcini, Ariz.	*Mark O. Hatfield, Ore.*
Daniel Patrick Moynihan, N.Y.	*Ted Stevens, Alaska*

House Members

Mary Rose Oakar, Ohio	*Paul E. Gillmor, Ohio*
William L. Clay, Mo.	*James T. Walsh, N.Y.*

Printing

224-5241 SH-818

Sen. Wendell H. Ford, D-Ky., chairman

Rep. Frank Annunzio, D-Ill., vice chairman

Senate Members

Dennis DeConcini, Ariz.	*Ted Stevens, Alaska*
Al Gore, Tenn.	*Mark O. Hatfield, Ore.*

House Members

Joseph M. Gaydos, Pa.	*Pat Roberts, Kan.*
Jim Bates, Calif.	*Newt Gingrich, Ga.*

Taxation

225-3621 1015 LHOB

Rep. Dan Rostenkowski, D-Ill., chairman

Sen. Lloyd Bentsen, D-Texas, vice chairman

Senate Members

Spark M. Matsunaga, Hawaii	*Bob Packwood, Ore.*
Daniel Patrick Moynihan, N.Y.	*Bob Dole, Kan.*

House Members

Sam Gibbons, Fla.	*Bill Archer, Texas*
J. J. "Jake" Pickle, Texas	*Guy Vander Jagt, Mich.*

Seniority in the 101st Congress

Senate Seniority

Senate rank generally is determined according to the official date of the beginning of a member's service, except in the case of new members sworn in at times other than the beginning of a Congress. For those appointed or elected to fill unexpired terms, the date of the appointment, certification or swearing-in determines the senator's rank.

When members are sworn in on the same day, custom decrees that those with prior political experience take precedence. Counted as political experience, in order of importance, is senatorial, House and gubernatorial service. Information on prior experience is given where applicable to seniority ranking. The dates following senators' names refer to the beginning of their present service.

DEMOCRATS

1. Byrd—Jan. 3, 1959
2. Burdick—Aug. 8, 1960
3. Pell—Jan. 3, 1961
4. Kennedy—Nov. 7, 1962
5. Inouye—Jan. 3, 1963
6. Hollings—Nov. 9, 1966
7. Cranston—Jan. 3, 1969
8. Bentsen—Jan. 3, 1971
9. Nunn—Nov. 8, 1972
10. Johnston—Nov. 14, 1972
11. Biden—Jan. 3, 1973
12. Glenn—Dec. 24, 1974
13. Ford—Dec. 28, 1974
14. Bumpers (ex-governor)—Jan. 3, 1975
15. Leahy—Jan. 3, 1975
16. Metzenbaum—Dec. 29, 1976
17. Riegle—Dec. 30, 1976
18. Matsunaga (ex-representative, seven House terms)—Jan. 3, 1977
19. Sarbanes (ex-representative, three House terms)—Jan. 3, 1977
20. DeConcini—Jan. 3, 1977
    Moynihan—Jan. 3, 1977
    Sasser—Jan. 3, 1977
23. Baucus—Dec. 15, 1978
24. Pryor (ex-representative)—Jan. 3, 1979
25. Boren (ex-governor)—Jan. 3, 1979
    Exon (ex-governor)—Jan. 3, 1979
27. Bradley—Jan. 3, 1979
    Heflin—Jan. 3, 1979
    Levin—Jan. 3, 1979
30. Mitchell—May 19, 1980
31. Dodd (ex-representative)—Jan. 3, 1981
32. Dixon—Jan. 3, 1981
33. Lautenberg—Dec. 27, 1982
34. Bingaman—Jan. 3, 1983
35. Kerry—Jan. 2, 1985
36. Harkin (ex-representative, five House terms)—Jan. 3, 1985
    Simon (ex-representative, five House terms)—Jan. 3, 1985
38. Gore (ex-representative, four House terms)—Jan. 3, 1985
39. Rockefeller—Jan. 15, 1985
40. Sanford—Nov. 5, 1986
41. Breaux (ex-representative, seven House terms)—Jan. 6, 1987
42. Adams (ex-representative, six House terms)—Jan. 6, 1987
    Wirth (ex-representative, six House terms)—Jan. 6, 1987
44. Fowler (ex-representative, five House terms)—Jan. 6, 1987
    Mikulski (ex-representative, five House terms)—Jan. 6, 1987
46. Daschle (ex-representative, four House terms)—Jan. 6, 1987
    Shelby (ex-representative, four House terms)—Jan. 6, 1987
48. Reid (ex-representative, two House terms)—Jan. 6, 1987
49. Graham (ex-governor)—Jan. 6, 1987
50. Conrad—Jan. 6, 1987
51. Bryan (ex-governor)—Jan. 3, 1989
    Kerrey (ex-governor)—Jan. 3, 1989
    Robb (ex-governor)—Jan. 3, 1989
54. Kohl—Jan. 3, 1989
    Lieberman—Jan. 3, 1989

REPUBLICANS

1. Thurmond—Nov. 7, 1956 *
2. Hatfield—Jan. 10, 1967
3. Stevens—Dec. 24, 1968
4. Dole (ex-representative)—Jan. 3, 1969
5. Packwood—Jan. 3, 1969
6. Roth—Jan. 1, 1971
7. McClure (ex-representative)—Jan. 3, 1973
8. Helms—Jan. 3, 1973
    Domenici—Jan. 3, 1973
10. Garn—Dec. 21, 1974
11. Danforth—Dec. 27, 1976
12. Chafee—Dec. 29, 1976
13. Heinz (ex-representative)—Jan. 3, 1977
14. Hatch—Jan. 3, 1977
    Lugar—Jan. 3, 1977
    Wallop—Jan. 3, 1977
17. Durenberger—Nov. 8, 1978
18. Kassebaum—Dec. 23, 1978
19. Cochran—Dec. 27, 1978
20. Boschwitz—Dec. 30, 1978
21. Simpson—Jan. 1, 1979
22. Warner—Jan. 2, 1979
23. Armstrong (ex-representative, three House terms)—Jan. 3, 1979
    Cohen (ex-representative, three House terms)—Jan. 3, 1979
25. Pressler (ex-representative, two House terms)—Jan. 3, 1979
26. Humphrey—Jan. 3, 1979

27. Rudman—Dec. 29, 1980
28. Symms (ex-representative, four House terms)—Jan. 3, 1981
29. Grassley (ex-representative, three House terms)—Jan. 3, 1981
30. Kasten (ex-representative, two House terms)—Jan. 3, 1981
31. D'Amato—Jan. 3, 1981
    Murkowski—Jan. 3, 1981
    Nickles—Jan. 3, 1981
    Specter—Jan. 3, 1981
35. Wilson—Jan. 3, 1983
36. Gramm (ex-representative)—Jan. 3, 1985
37. McConnell—Jan. 3, 1985
38. McCain (ex-representative)—Jan. 6, 1987
39. Bond (ex-governor)—Jan. 6, 1987
40. Gorton (ex-senator)—Jan. 3, 1989
41. Lott (ex-representative, eight House terms)—Jan. 3, 1989
42. Jeffords (ex-representative, seven House terms)—Jan. 3, 1989
43. Coats (ex-representative, four House terms)—Jan. 3, 1989
44. Mack (ex-representative, three House terms)—Jan. 3, 1989
45. Burns—Jan. 3, 1989

** Thurmond began his Senate service Nov. 7, 1956, as a Democrat. He became a Republican Sept. 16, 1964. The Republican Conference allowed his seniority to count from his 1956 election to the Senate.*

House Seniority

House rank generally is determined according to the official date of the beginning of a member's service, except in the case of members elected to fill vacancies, in which instance the date of election determines rank.

When members enter the House on the same day, those with prior House experience take precedence, starting with those with the longest consecutive service. Experience as a senator or governor is disregarded. Prior experience is given where applicable to seniority ranking. The dates following members' names refer to the beginning of their present service.

DEMOCRATS

1. Whitten (Miss.)—Nov. 4, 1941
2. Bennett (Fla.)—Jan. 3, 1949
3. Brooks (Texas)—Jan. 3, 1953
4. Natcher (Ky.)—Aug. 1, 1953
5. Fascell (Fla.)—Jan. 3, 1955
6. Dingell (Mich.)—Dec. 13, 1955
7. Kastenmeier (Wis.)—Jan. 3, 1959
    Rostenkowski (Ill.)—Jan. 3, 1959
    Smith (Iowa)—Jan. 3, 1959
10. Udall (Ariz.)—May 2, 1961
11. Gonzalez (Texas)—Nov. 4, 1961
12. Edwards (Calif.)—Jan. 3, 1963
    Gibbons (Fla.)—Jan. 3, 1963
    Hawkins (Calif.)—Jan. 3, 1963
    Roybal (Calif.)—Jan. 3, 1963
16. Pickle (Texas)—Dec. 21, 1963
17. Yates (Ill.) (seven terms previously)—Jan. 3, 1965
18. Annunzio (Ill.)—Jan. 3, 1965
    Conyers (Mich.)—Jan. 3, 1965
    de la Garza (Texas)—Jan. 3, 1965
    Foley (Wash.)—Jan. 3, 1965
    Ford (Mich.)—Jan. 3, 1965
    Hamilton (Ind.)—Jan. 3, 1965
24. Jones (N.C.)—Feb. 5, 1966
25. Bevill (Ala.)—Jan. 3, 1967
    Montgomery (Miss.)—Jan. 3, 1967
27. Gaydos (Pa.)—Nov. 5, 1968
28. Alexander (Ark.)—Jan. 3, 1969
    Anderson (Calif.)—Jan. 3, 1969
    Clay (Mo.)—Jan. 3, 1969
    Stokes (Ohio)—Jan. 3, 1969
    Yatron (Pa.)—Jan. 3, 1969
33. Obey (Wis.)—April 1, 1969
34. Roe (N.J.)—Nov. 4, 1969
35. Aspin (Wis.)—Jan. 3, 1971
    Dellums (Calif.)—Jan. 3, 1971
    Mazzoli (Ky.)—Jan. 3, 1971
    Rangel (N.Y.)—Jan. 3, 1971
39. Brown (Calif.) (four terms previously)—Jan. 3, 1973
40. Lehman (Fla.)—Jan. 3, 1973
    Moakley (Mass.)—Jan. 3, 1973
    Rose (N.C.)—Jan. 3, 1973
    Schroeder (Colo.)—Jan. 3, 1973
    Stark (Calif.)—Jan. 3, 1973
    Studds (Mass.)—Jan. 3, 1973
    Wilson (Texas)—Jan. 3, 1973
47. Boggs (La.)—March 20, 1973
48. Collins (Ill.)—June 5, 1973
49. Murtha (Pa.)—Feb. 5, 1974
50. Traxler (Mich.)—April 16, 1974
51. Jacobs (Ind.) (four terms previously)—Jan. 3, 1975
    Scheuer (N.Y.) (four terms previously)—Jan. 3, 1975
53. AuCoin (Ore.)—Jan. 3, 1975
    Derrick (S.C.)—Jan. 3, 1975
    Downey (N.Y.)—Jan. 3, 1975
    Early (Mass.)—Jan. 3, 1975
    English (Okla.)—Jan. 3, 1975
    Florio (N.J.)—Jan. 3, 1975
    Ford (Tenn.)—Jan. 3, 1975
    Hefner (N.C.)—Jan. 3, 1975
    Hubbard (Ky.)—Jan. 3, 1975
    Hughes (N.J.)—Jan. 3, 1975
    LaFalce (N.Y.)—Jan. 3, 1975
    Lloyd (Tenn.)—Jan. 3, 1975
    McHugh (N.Y.)—Jan. 3, 1975
    Miller (Calif.)—Jan. 3, 1975
    Mineta (Calif.)—Jan. 3, 1975
    Neal (N.C.)—Jan. 3, 1975

Nowak (N.Y.)—Jan. 3, 1975
Oberstar (Minn.)—Jan. 3, 1975
Russo (Ill.)—Jan. 3, 1975
Sharp (Ind.)—Jan. 3, 1975
Solarz (N.Y.)—Jan. 3, 1975
Waxman (Calif.)—Jan. 3, 1975
75. Markey (Mass.)—Nov. 2, 1976
76. Luken (Ohio) (one term previously)—Jan. 3, 1977
77. Akaka (Hawaii)—Jan. 3, 1977
Applegate (Ohio)—Jan. 3, 1977
Barnard (Ga.)—Jan. 3, 1977
Beilenson (Calif.)—Jan. 3, 1977
Bonior (Mich.)—Jan. 3, 1977
Dicks (Wash.)—Jan. 3, 1977
Flippo (Ala.)—Jan. 3, 1977
Gephardt (Mo.)—Jan. 3, 1977
Glickman (Kan.)—Jan. 3, 1977
Huckaby (La.)—Jan. 3, 1977
Jenkins (Ga.)—Jan. 3, 1977
Kildee (Mich.)—Jan. 3, 1977
Murphy (Pa.)—Jan. 3, 1977
Oakar (Ohio)—Jan. 3, 1977
Panetta (Calif.)—Jan. 3, 1977
Pease (Ohio)—Jan. 3, 1977
Rahall (W.Va.)—Jan. 3, 1977
Skelton (Mo.)—Jan. 3, 1977
Vento (Minn.)—Jan. 3, 1977
Volkmer (Mo.)—Jan. 3, 1977
Walgren (Pa.)—Jan. 3, 1977
Watkins (Okla.)—Jan. 3, 1977
Weiss (N.Y.)—Jan. 3, 1977
100. Garcia (N.Y.)—Feb. 14, 1978
101. Anthony (Ark.)—Jan. 3, 1979
Byron (Md.)—Jan. 3, 1979
Dixon (Calif.)—Jan. 3, 1979
Donnelly (Mass.)—Jan. 3, 1979
Fazio (Calif.)—Jan. 3, 1979
Frost (Texas)—Jan. 3, 1979
Gray (Pa.)—Jan. 3, 1979
Guarini (N.J.)—Jan. 3, 1979
Hall (Ohio)—Jan. 3, 1979
Hutto (Fla.)—Jan. 3, 1979
Leath (Texas)—Jan. 3, 1979
Leland (Texas)—Jan. 3, 1979
Matsui (Calif.)—Jan. 3, 1979
Mavroules (Mass.)—Jan. 3, 1979
Nelson (Fla.)—Jan. 3, 1979
Sabo (Minn.)—Jan. 3, 1979
Stenholm (Texas)—Jan. 3, 1979
Swift (Wash.)—Jan. 3, 1979
Synar (Okla.)—Jan. 3, 1979
Williams (Mont.)—Jan. 3, 1979
Wolpe (Mich.)—Jan. 3, 1979
122. Tauzin (La.)—May 17, 1980
123. Crockett (Mich.)—Nov. 4, 1980
124. Coyne (Pa.)—Jan. 3, 1981
Dorgan (N.D.)—Jan. 3, 1981
Dwyer (N.J.)—Jan. 3, 1981
Dymally (Calif.)—Jan. 3, 1981
Dyson (Md.)—Jan. 3, 1981
Eckart (Ohio)—Jan. 3, 1981
Foglietta (Pa.)—Jan. 3, 1981
Frank (Mass.)—Jan. 3, 1981
Gejdenson (Conn.)—Jan. 3, 1981
Hall (Texas)—Jan. 3, 1981
Hatcher (Ga.)—Jan. 3, 1981
Hertel (Mich.)—Jan. 3, 1981
Lantos (Calif.)—Jan. 3, 1981
McCurdy (Okla.)—Jan. 3, 1981
Savage (Ill.)—Jan. 3, 1981
Schumer (N.Y.)—Jan. 3, 1981
Wyden (Ore.)—Jan. 3, 1981
141. Hoyer (Md.)—May 19, 1981
142. Kennelly (Conn.)—Jan. 12, 1982
143. Martinez (Calif.)—July 13, 1982
144. Carr (Mich.) (three terms previously)—Jan. 3, 1983
145. Kostmayer (Pa.) (two terms previously)—Jan. 3, 1983
146. Andrews (Texas)—Jan. 3, 1983
Bates (Calif.)—Jan. 3, 1983
Berman (Calif.)—Jan. 3, 1983
Borski (Pa.)—Jan. 3, 1983
Bosco (Calif.)—Jan. 3, 1983
Boucher (Va.)—Jan. 3, 1983
Boxer (Calif.)—Jan. 3, 1983
Bryant (Texas)—Jan. 3, 1983
Carper (Del.)—Jan. 3, 1983
Coleman (Texas)—Jan. 3, 1983
Cooper (Tenn.)—Jan. 3, 1983
Durbin (Ill.)—Jan. 3, 1983
Erdreich (Ala.)—Jan. 3, 1983
Evans (Ill.)—Jan. 3, 1983
Feighan (Ohio)—Jan. 3, 1983
Kaptur (Ohio)—Jan. 3, 1983
Kolter (Pa.)—Jan. 3, 1983
Lehman (Calif.)—Jan. 3, 1983
Levin (Mich.)—Jan. 3, 1983
Levine (Calif.)—Jan. 3, 1983
Lipinski (Ill.)—Jan. 3, 1983
McCloskey (Ind.)—Jan. 3, 1983
Mollohan (W.Va.)—Jan. 3, 1983
Moody (Wis.)—Jan. 3, 1983
Morrison (Conn.)—Jan. 3, 1983
Mrazek (N.Y.)—Jan. 3, 1983
Olin (Va.)—Jan. 3, 1983
Ortiz (Texas)—Jan. 3, 1983
Owens (N.Y.)—Jan. 3, 1983
Penny (Minn.)—Jan. 3, 1983
Ray (Ga.)—Jan. 3, 1983
Richardson (N.M.)—Jan. 3, 1983
Rowland (Ga.)—Jan. 3, 1983
Sikorski (Minn.)—Jan. 3, 1983
Sisisky (Va.)—Jan. 3, 1983
Slattery (Kan.)—Jan. 3, 1983
Smith (Fla.)—Jan. 3, 1983
Spratt (S.C.)—Jan. 3, 1983
Staggers (W.Va.)—Jan. 3, 1983
Tallon (S.C.)—Jan. 3, 1983
Thomas (Ga.)—Jan. 3, 1983
Torres (Calif.)—Jan. 3, 1983
Torricelli (N.J.)—Jan. 3, 1983
Towns (N.Y.)—Jan. 3, 1983
Valentine (N.C.)—Jan. 3, 1983
Wheat (Mo.)—Jan. 3, 1983
Wise (W.Va.)—Jan. 3, 1983
193. Ackerman (N.Y.)—March 1, 1983

194. Hayes (Ill.)—Aug. 23, 1983
195. Darden (Ga.)—Nov. 8, 1983
196. Kleczka (Wis.)—April 3, 1984
197. Perkins (Ky.)—Nov. 6, 1984
198. Atkins (Mass.)—Jan. 3, 1985
Bruce (Ill.)—Jan. 3, 1985
Bustamante (Texas)—Jan. 3, 1985
Gordon (Tenn.)—Jan. 3, 1985
Kanjorski (Pa.)—Jan. 3, 1985
Manton (N.Y.)—Jan. 3, 1985
Robinson (Ark.)—Jan. 3, 1985
Stallings (Idaho)—Jan. 3, 1985
Traficant (Ohio)—Jan. 3, 1985
Visclosky (Ind.)—Jan. 3, 1985
208. Chapman (Texas)—Aug. 3, 1985
209. Clarke (N.C.) (one term previously)—Jan. 6, 1987
Owens (Utah) (one term previously)—Jan. 6, 1987
211. Bilbray (Nev.)—Jan. 6, 1987
Campbell (Colo.)—Jan. 6, 1987
Cardin (Md.)—Jan. 6, 1987
DeFazio (Ore.)—Jan. 6, 1987
Espy (Miss.)—Jan. 6, 1987
Flake (N.Y.)—Jan. 6, 1987
Harris (Ala.)—Jan. 6, 1987
Hayes (La.)—Jan. 6, 1987
Hochbrueckner (N.Y.)—Jan. 6, 1987
Johnson (S.D.)—Jan. 6, 1987
Jontz (Ind.)—Jan. 6, 1987
Kennedy (Mass.)—Jan. 6, 1987
Lancaster (N.C.)—Jan. 6, 1987
Lewis (Ga.)—Jan. 6, 1987
McMillen (Md.)—Jan. 6, 1987
Mfume (Md.)—Jan. 6, 1987
Nagle (Iowa)—Jan. 6, 1987
Patterson (S.C.)—Jan. 6, 1987
Pickett (Va.)—Jan. 6, 1987
Price (N.C.)—Jan. 6, 1987
Sawyer (Ohio)—Jan. 6, 1987
Skaggs (Colo.)—Jan. 6, 1987
Slaughter (N.Y.)—Jan. 6, 1987
234. Brennan (Maine)—Jan. 8, 1987
235. Pelosi (Calif.)—June 2, 1987
236. Clement (Tenn.)—Jan. 19, 1988
237. Payne (Va.)—June 14, 1988
238. Costello (Ill.)—Aug. 9, 1988
239. Pallone (N.J.)—Nov. 8, 1988
240. Engel (N.Y.)—Jan. 3, 1989
Hoagland (Neb.)—Jan. 3, 1989
Johnston (Fla.)—Jan. 3, 1989
Jones (Ga.)—Jan. 3, 1989
Laughlin (Texas)—Jan. 3, 1989
Lowey (N.Y.)—Jan. 3, 1989
McDermott (Wash.)—Jan. 3, 1989
McNulty (N.Y.)—Jan. 3, 1989
Neal (Mass.)—Jan. 3, 1989
Parker (Miss.)—Jan. 3, 1989
Payne (N.J.)—Jan. 3, 1989
Poshard (Ill.)—Jan. 3, 1989
Sangmeister (Ill.)—Jan. 3, 1989
Sarpalius (Texas)—Jan. 3, 1989
Tanner (Tenn.)—Jan. 3, 1989
Unsoeld (Wash.)—Jan. 3, 1989
256. Long (Ind.)—March 28, 1989
257. Browder (Ala.)—April 4, 1989

REPUBLICANS

1. Broomfield (Mich.)—Jan. 3, 1957
Michel (Ill.)—Jan. 3, 1957
3. Conte (Mass.)—Jan. 3, 1959
4. Horton (N.Y.)—Jan. 3, 1963
McDade (Pa.)—Jan. 3, 1963
Quillen (Tenn.)—Jan. 3, 1963
7. Dickinson (Ala.)—Jan. 3, 1965
8. Vander Jagt (Mich.)—Nov. 8, 1966
9. Hammerschmidt (Ark.)—Jan. 3, 1967
Miller (Ohio)—Jan. 3, 1967
Myers (Ind.)—Jan. 3, 1967
Wylie (Ohio)—Jan. 3, 1967
13. Coughlin (Pa.)—Jan. 3, 1969
Fish (N.Y.)—Jan. 3, 1969
15. Crane (Ill.)—Nov. 25, 1969
16. Archer (Texas)—Jan. 3, 1971
Frenzel (Minn.)—Jan. 3, 1971
Lent (N.Y.)—Jan. 3, 1971
Spence (S.C.)—Jan. 3, 1971
Young (Fla.)—Jan. 3, 1971
21. Gilman (N.Y.)—Jan. 3, 1973
Madigan (Ill.)—Jan. 3, 1973
Moorhead (Calif.)—Jan. 3, 1973
Regula (Ohio)—Jan. 3, 1973
Rinaldo (N.J.)—Jan. 3, 1973
Shuster (Pa.)—Jan. 3, 1973
27. Young (Alaska)—March 6, 1973
28. Lagomarsino (Calif.)—March 5, 1974
29. Goodling (Pa.)—Jan. 3, 1975
Gradison (Ohio)—Jan. 3, 1975
Hyde (Ill.)—Jan. 3, 1975
Schulze (Pa.)—Jan. 3, 1975
Smith (Neb.)—Jan. 3, 1975
34. Coleman (Mo.)—Nov. 2, 1976
35. Edwards (Okla.)—Jan. 3, 1977
Ireland (Fla.)—Jan. 3, 1977 *
Leach (Iowa)—Jan. 3, 1977
Marlenee (Mont.)—Jan. 3, 1977
Pursell (Mich.)—Jan. 3, 1977
Stump (Ariz.)—Jan. 3, 1977 *
Walker (Pa.)—Jan. 3, 1977
42. Stangeland (Minn.)—Feb. 22, 1977
43. Livingston (La.)—Aug. 27, 1977
44. Green (N.Y.)—Feb. 14, 1978
45. Bereuter (Neb.)—Jan. 3, 1979
Clinger (Pa.)—Jan. 3, 1979
Courter (N.J.)—Jan. 3, 1979
Dannemeyer (Calif.)—Jan. 3, 1979
Davis (Mich.)—Jan. 3, 1979
Gingrich (Ga.)—Jan. 3, 1979
Hopkins (Ky.)—Jan. 3, 1979
Lewis (Calif.)—Jan. 3, 1979
Pashayan (Calif.)—Jan. 3, 1979
Ritter (Pa.)—Jan. 3, 1979
Roth (Wis.)—Jan. 3, 1979
Sensenbrenner (Wis.)—Jan. 3, 1979
Shumway (Calif.)—Jan. 3, 1979
Snowe (Maine)—Jan. 3, 1979
Solomon (N.Y.)—Jan. 3, 1979

Tauke (Iowa)—Jan. 3, 1979
Thomas (Calif.)—Jan. 3, 1979
Whittaker (Kan.)—Jan. 3, 1979
63. Petri (Wis.)—April 3, 1979
64. Porter (Ill.)—Jan. 22, 1980
65. Parris (Va.) (one term previously)—Jan. 3, 1981
66. Bliley (Va.)—Jan. 3, 1981
Brown (Colo.)—Jan. 3, 1981
Craig (Idaho)—Jan. 3, 1981
Dreier (Calif.)—Jan. 3, 1981
Emerson (Mo.)—Jan. 3, 1981
Fields (Texas)—Jan. 3, 1981
Gunderson (Wis.)—Jan. 3, 1981
Hansen (Utah)—Jan. 3, 1981
Hiler (Ind.)—Jan. 3, 1981
Hunter (Calif.)—Jan. 3, 1981
Lowery (Calif.)—Jan. 3, 1981
Martin (Ill.)—Jan. 3, 1981
Martin (N.Y.)—Jan. 3, 1981
McCollum (Fla.)—Jan. 3, 1981
McEwen (Ohio)—Jan. 3, 1981
McGrath (N.Y.)—Jan. 3, 1981
Molinari (N.Y.)—Jan. 3, 1981
Morrison (Wash.)—Jan. 3, 1981
Roberts (Kan.)—Jan. 3, 1981
Rogers (Ky.)—Jan. 3, 1981
Roukema (N.J.)—Jan. 3, 1981
Schneider (R.I.)—Jan. 3, 1981
Shaw (Fla.)—Jan. 3, 1981
Skeen (N.M.)—Jan. 3, 1981
Smith (N.J.)—Jan. 3, 1981
Smith, Denny (Ore.)—Jan. 3, 1981
Weber (Minn.)—Jan. 3, 1981
Wolf (Va.)—Jan. 3, 1981
94. Oxley (Ohio)—June 25, 1981
95. Bartlett (Texas)—Jan. 3, 1983
Bateman (Va.)—Jan. 3, 1983
Bilirakis (Fla.)—Jan. 3, 1983
Boehlert (N.Y.)—Jan. 3, 1983
Burton (Ind.)—Jan. 3, 1983
Chandler (Wash.)—Jan. 3, 1983
DeWine (Ohio)—Jan. 3, 1983
Gekas (Pa.)—Jan. 3, 1983
Johnson (Conn.)—Jan. 3, 1983
Kasich (Ohio)—Jan. 3, 1983
Lewis (Fla.)—Jan. 3, 1983
McCandless (Calif.)—Jan. 3, 1983
Nielson (Utah)—Jan. 3, 1983
Packard (Calif.)—Jan. 3, 1983
Ridge (Pa.)—Jan. 3, 1983
Smith, Bob (Ore.)—Jan. 3, 1983
Sundquist (Tenn.)—Jan. 3, 1983
Vucanovich (Nev.)—Jan. 3, 1983
113. Schaefer (Colo.)—March 29, 1983
114. Saxton (N.J.)—Nov. 6, 1984
115. Dornan (Calif.) (three terms previously)—Jan. 3, 1985
116. Armey (Texas)—Jan. 3, 1985
Barton (Texas)—Jan. 3, 1985
Bentley (Md.)—Jan. 3, 1985
Callahan (Ala.)—Jan. 3, 1985
Coble (N.C.)—Jan. 3, 1985
Combest (Texas)—Jan. 3, 1985
DeLay (Texas)—Jan. 3, 1985
Fawell (Ill.)—Jan. 3, 1985
Gallo (N.J.)—Jan. 3, 1985
Henry (Mich.)—Jan. 3, 1985
Kolbe (Ariz.)—Jan. 3, 1985
Lightfoot (Iowa)—Jan. 3, 1985
McMillan (N.C.)—Jan. 3, 1985
Meyers (Kan.)—Jan. 3, 1985
Miller (Wash.)—Jan. 3, 1985
Rowland (Conn.)—Jan. 3, 1985
Schuette (Mich.)—Jan. 3, 1985
Slaughter (Va.)—Jan. 3, 1985
Smith (N.H.)—Jan. 3, 1985
135. Ballenger (N.C.)—Nov. 4, 1986
136. Lukens (Ohio) (two terms previously)—Jan. 6, 1987
137. Baker (La.)—Jan. 6, 1987
Buechner (Mo.)—Jan. 6, 1987
Bunning (Ky.)—Jan. 6, 1987
Gallegly (Calif.)—Jan. 6, 1987
Grandy (Iowa)—Jan. 6, 1987
Grant (Fla.)—Jan. 6, 1987 †
Hastert (Ill.)—Jan. 6, 1987
Hefley (Colo.)—Jan. 6, 1987
Herger (Calif.)—Jan. 6, 1987
Holloway (La.)—Jan. 6, 1987
Houghton (N.Y.)—Jan. 6, 1987
Inhofe (Okla.)—Jan. 6, 1987
Kyl (Ariz.)—Jan. 6, 1987
Morella (Md.)—Jan. 6, 1987
Ravenel (S.C.)—Jan. 6, 1987
Rhodes (Ariz.)—Jan. 6, 1987
Saiki (Hawaii)—Jan. 6, 1987
Smith (Texas)—Jan. 6, 1987
Upton (Mich.)—Jan. 6, 1987
Weldon (Pa.)—Jan. 6, 1987
157. Shays (Conn.)—Aug. 18, 1987
158. McCrery (La.)—April 16, 1988
159. Duncan (Tenn.)—Nov. 8, 1988
160. Campbell (Calif.)—Jan. 3, 1989
Cox (Calif.)—Jan. 3, 1989
Douglas (N.H.)—Jan. 3, 1989
Gillmor (Ohio)—Jan. 3, 1989
Goss (Fla.)—Jan. 3, 1989
Hancock (Mo.)—Jan. 3, 1989
James (Fla.)—Jan. 3, 1989
Machtley (R.I.)—Jan. 3, 1989
Paxon (N.Y.)—Jan. 3, 1989
Rohrabacher (Calif.)—Jan. 3, 1989
Schiff (N.M.)—Jan. 3, 1989
Smith (Miss.)—Jan. 3, 1989
Smith (Vt.)—Jan. 3, 1989
Stearns (Fla.)—Jan. 3, 1989
Walsh (N.Y.)—Jan. 3, 1989
175. Thomas (Wyo.)—April 26, 1989

** Ireland and Stump began their House service Jan. 3, 1977, as Democrats, but later switched parties. The GOP Conference let their seniority count from 1977.*

† Grant began his House service Jan. 6, 1987, as a Democrat, but later switched parties. The GOP Conference let his seniority count from 1987.

Pronunciation Guide for Congress

The following is an informal pronunciation guide for some of the most-often-mispronounced names of members of Congress:

SENATE

Rudy Boschwitz, R-Minn. (BOSH wits)
John B. Breaux, D-La. (BRO)
Alfonse M. D'Amato, R-N.Y. (dah MAH toe)
Tom Daschle, D-S.D. (DASH el)
Dennis DeConcini, D-Ariz. (dee con SEE nee)
Pete V. Domenici, R-N.M. (da MEN ah chee)
Wyche Fowler Jr., D-Ga. (WHYch)
Daniel K. Inouye, D-Hawaii (in NO ay)
Joseph I. Lieberman, D-Conn. (LEE ber mun)

HOUSE

Daniel K. Akaka, D-Hawaii (ah KAH ka)
Les AuCoin, D-Ore. (oh COIN)
Anthony C. Beilenson, D-Calif. (BEE lin son)
Doug Bereuter, R-Neb. (BEE right er)
Michael Bilirakis, R-Fla. (bill a RACK us)
Sherwood Boehlert, R-N.Y. (BO lert)
David E. Bonior, D-Mich. (BON yer)
Rick Boucher, D-Va. (BOUGH cher)
Jack Buechner, R-Mo. (BEEK ner)
Albert G. Bustamante, D-Texas (BOOST uh MAHN tay)
Lawrence Coughlin, R-Pa. (COFF lin)
Peter A. DeFazio, D-Ore. (da FAH zio)
Mervyn M. Dymally, D-Calif. (DIE mal ee)
Ben Erdreich, D-Ala. (ER dritch)
Eni F. H. Faleomavaega, D-Am. Samoa (EN ee FALL eh oh mavah ENGA)
Dante B. Fascell, D-Fla. (DON tay fuh SELL)
Harris W. Fawell, R-Ill. (FAY well)
Vic Fazio, D-Calif. (FAY zee o)
Edward F. Feighan, D-Ohio (FEE an)
Thomas M. Foglietta, D-Pa. (fo lee ET ah)
Jaime B. Fuster, Pop. Dem.-P.R. (HI may foo STAIR)
Elton Gallegly, R-Calif. (GAL uh glee)
Sam Gejdenson, D-Conn. (GAY den son)
Frank J. Guarini, D-N.J. (gwar EE nee)
George J. Hochbrueckner, D-N.Y. (HOCK brewk ner)
Amo Houghton, R-N.Y. (AY mo HO tun)
James M. Inhofe, R-Okla. (IN hoff)
John R. Kasich, R-Ohio (KAY sick)
Barbara B. Kennelly, D-Conn. (ka NEL ly)
Gerald D. Kleczka, D-Wis. (KLETCH ka)
Jim Kolbe, R-Ariz. (COLE bee)
Robert J. Lagomarsino, R-Calif. (LAH go mar SEE no)
Greg Laughlin, D-Texas (LAWF lin)
Richard H. Lehman, D-Calif. (LEE mun)
William Lehman, D-Fla. (LAY mun)
Mel Levine, D-Calif. (la VINE)
Nita M. Lowey, D-N.Y. (LOW ee)
Ronald K. Machtley, R-R.I. (MAKE lee)
Ron Marlenee, R-Mont. (MAR la nay)
Nicholas Mavroules, D-Mass. (mah VROOL iss)
Bob McEwen, R-Ohio (ma KEW in)
Kweisi Mfume, D-Md. (kwy E say mm FU may)
Robert J. Mrazek, D-N.Y. (ma RAH zik)
Frank Pallone Jr., D-N.J. (pa LONE)
Charles "Chip" Pashayan Jr., R-Calif. (pah SHAY an)
Nancy Pelosi, D-Calif. (pel LO see)
Thomas E. Petri, R-Wis. (PEE try)
Glenn Poshard, D-Ill. (pa SHARD)
Arthur Ravenel Jr., R-S.C. (RAV nel)
Ralph Regula, R-Ohio (REG you la)
Dana Rohrabacher, R-Calif. (ROAR ah bach er)
Marge Roukema, R-N.J. (ROCK ah ma)
Patricia Saiki, R-Hawaii (CY kee)
George E. Sangmeister, D-Ill. (SANG my stir)
Bill Sarpalius, D-Texas (sar POLL us)
James H. Scheuer, D-N.Y. (SHOY yur)
Steven H. Schiff, R-N.M. (SHIFF)
Patricia Schroeder, D-Colo. (SHRO dur)
Bill Schuette, R-Mich. (SHOO tee)
Richard T. Schulze, R-Pa. (SHOOLS)
Arlan Stangeland, R-Minn. (STANG land)
Tom Tauke, R-Iowa (TAW kee)
W. J. "Billy" Tauzin, D-La. (TOE zan)
Robert G. Torricelli, D-N.J. (tor ah SELL ee)
Jolene Unsoeld, D-Wash. (UN sold)
Guy Vander Jagt, R-Mich. (VAN der jack)
Peter J. Visclosky, D-Ind. (vis KLOSS key)
Barbara F. Vucanovich, R-Nev. (voo CAN oh vitch)
Gus Yatron, D-Pa. (YA trin)

Few Close Calls in 1988 House Elections

Only 9 percent of House members (38 out of 435) were elected in 1988 with 55 percent or less of their district's total vote, once a bench mark in defining "endangered incumbents," but now just one of several criteria.

In the chart below: House members who were incumbents in 1988 are listed in **boldface** type; challengers who defeated incumbents last November are noted with a dagger (†); the rest were victorious in open-seat contests.

DEMOCRATS

1)	Jolene Unsoeld (Wash. 3)	50.1%
2)	George E. Sangmeister (Ill. 4) †	50.3
	Nita M. Lowey (N.Y. 20) †	50.3
4)	**Roy Dyson (Md. 1)**	**50.4**
	James McClure Clarke (N.C. 11)	**50.4**
6)	Peter Hoagland (Neb. 2)	50.5
7)	**George J. Hochbrueckner (N.Y. 1)**	**50.8**
8)	**W. G. "Bill" Hefner (N.C. 8)**	**51.5**
9)	Frank Pallone Jr. (N.J. 3)	51.6
10)	**Liz J. Patterson (S.C. 4)**	**52.2**
11)	Bill Sarpalius (Texas 13)	52.5
12)	**Jerry F. Costello (Ill. 21)**	**52.6**
	Stephen L. Neal (N.C. 5)	**52.6**
14)	**Philip R. Sharp (Ind. 2)**	**53.2**
	Greg Laughlin (Texas 14) †	53.2
16)	**David E. Bonior (Mich. 12)**	**53.6**
17)	**Butler Derrick (S.C. 3)**	**53.7**
18)	**George E. Brown Jr. (Calif. 36)**	**54.0**
19)	**Lewis F. Payne Jr. (Va. 5)**	**54.2**
20)	Mike Parker (Miss. 4)	54.8
21)	Harry A. Johnston (Fla. 14)	54.9

REPUBLICANS

1)	Peter Smith (Vt. AL)	41.2%
2)	**Denny Smith (Ore. 5)**	**50.1**
3)	**Robert J. Lagomarsino (Calif. 19)**	**50.2**
4)	Craig T. James (Fla. 4) †	50.2
5)	Steven H. Schiff (N.M. 1)	50.6
6)	Tom Campbell (Calif. 12)	51.7
7)	**James M. Inhofe (Okla. 1)**	**52.6**
8)	**Floyd D. Spence (S.C. 2)**	**52.8**
9)	Mel Hancock (Mo. 7)	53.1
10)	Bill Paxon (N.Y. 31)	53.4
11)	Cliff Stearns (Fla. 6)	53.5
12)	**John Hiler (Ind. 3)**	**54.3**
13)	**Arlan Stangeland (Minn. 7)**	**54.6**
14)	**Patricia Saiki (Hawaii 1)**	**54.7**
15)	**Robert H. Michel (Ill. 18)**	**54.7**
16)	**Carl D. Pursell (Mich. 2)**	**54.7**
17)	Larkin Smith (Miss. 5)	55.0

Index

A

B

C

H

I, J

K

L

M

N

O

P

Q, R

S

T

U, V

W

X, Y, Z